TABLE B.2 *(concluded)*   **Percentiles of the *t* Distribution.**

				A			
ν	.98	.985	.99	.9925	.995	.9975	.9995
1	15.895	21.205	31.821	42.434	63.657	127.322	636.590
2	4.849	5.643	6.965	8.073	9.925	14.089	31.598
3	3.482	3.896	4.541	5.047	5.841	7.453	12.924
4	2.999	3.298	3.747	4.088	4.604	5.598	8.610
5	2.757	3.003	3.365	3.634	4.032	4.773	6.869
6	2.612	2.829	3.143	3.372	3.707	4.317	5.959
7	2.517	2.715	2.998	3.203	3.499	4.029	5.408
8	2.449	2.634	2.896	3.085	3.355	3.833	5.041
9	2.398	2.574	2.821	2.998	3.250	3.690	4.781
10	2.359	2.527	2.764	2.932	3.169	3.581	4.587
11	2.328	2.491	2.718	2.879	3.106	3.497	4.437
12	2.303	2.461	2.681	2.836	3.055	3.428	4.318
13	2.282	2.436	2.650	2.801	3.012	3.372	4.221
14	2.264	2.415	2.624	2.771	2.977	3.326	4.140
15	2.249	2.397	2.602	2.746	2.947	3.286	4.073
16	2.235	2.382	2.583	2.724	2.921	3.252	4.015
17	2.224	2.368	2.567	2.706	2.898	3.222	3.965
18	2.214	2.356	2.552	2.689	2.878	3.197	3.922
19	2.205	2.346	2.539	2.674	2.861	3.174	3.883
20	2.197	2.336	2.528	2.661	2.845	3.153	3.849
21	2.189	2.328	2.518	2.649	2.831	3.135	3.819
22	2.183	2.320	2.508	2.639	2.819	3.119	3.792
23	2.177	2.313	2.500	2.629	2.807	3.104	3.768
24	2.172	2.307	2.492	2.620	2.797	3.091	3.745
25	2.167	2.301	2.485	2.612	2.787	3.078	3.725
26	2.162	2.296	2.479	2.605	2.779	3.067	3.707
27	2.158	2.291	2.473	2.598	2.771	3.057	3.690
28	2.154	2.286	2.467	2.592	2.763	3.047	3.674
29	2.150	2.282	2.462	2.586	2.756	3.038	3.659
30	2.147	2.278	2.457	2.581	2.750	3.030	3.646
40	2.123	2.250	2.423	2.542	2.704	2.971	3.551
60	2.099	2.223	2.390	2.504	2.660	2.915	3.460
120	2.076	2.196	2.358	2.468	2.617	2.860	3.373
∞	2.054	2.170	2.326	2.432	2.576	2.807	3.291

Applied Linear Statistical Models

THE IRWIN SERIES IN
PRODUCTION OPERATIONS
MANAGEMENT

Aquilano, Chase, and Davis
Fundamentals of Operations Management
Second Edition

Chase and Aquilano
Production and Operations Management: *Manufacturing and Services*
Seventh Edition

Hill
Manufacturing Strategy: *Text & Cases*
Second Edition

Hopp and Spearman
Factory Physics
First Edition

Lambert and Stock
Strategic Logistics Management
Third Edition

Leenders, Fearon, and England
Purchasing and Materials Management
Ninth Edition

Lotfi and Pegels
Decision Support Systems For Operations and Management Science
Third Edition

Nahmias
Production and Operations Analysis
Second Edition

Niebel
Motion and Time Study
Ninth Edition

Schonberger and Knod
Operations Management: *Continuous Improvement*
Fifth Edition

Stevenson
Production/Operations Management
Fifth Edition

Vollmann, Berry, and Whybark
Manufacturing Planning & Control Systems
Third Edition

Zimmerman
ABC Operations Software
Beta Edition

THE IRWIN SERIES IN
STATISTICS

Aczel
Statistics: *Concepts and Applications*
First Edition

Aczel
Complete Business Statistics
Second Edition

Bryant and Smith
Practical Data Analysis: *Case Studies in Business Statistics, Volumes I and II*
First Edition

Duncan
Quality Control & Industrial Statistics
Fifth Edition

Cooper and Emory
Business Research Methods
Fifth Edition

Gitlow, Oppenheim, and Oppenheim
Quality Management: *Tools and Methods For Improvement*
Second Edition

Hall
Computerized Business Statistics
Fourth Edition

Hanke and Reitsch
Understanding Business Statistics
Second Edition

Lind and Mason
Basic Statistics for Business and Economics
First Edition

Mason and Lind
Statistical Techniques in Business and Economics
Ninth Edition

Neter, Kutner, Nachtsheim, and Wasserman
Applied Linear Statistical Models
Fourth Edition

Neter, Kutner, Nachtsheim, and Wasserman
Applied Linear Regression Models
Third Edition

Shin
The Irwin Statistical Software Series: *Minitab, SAS, SPSS Guides*
First Edition

Siegel
Practical Business Statistics
Second Edition

Webster
Applied Statistics For Business and Economics
Second Edition

Wilson and Keating
Business Forecasting
Second Edition

THE IRWIN SERIES IN
QUANTITATIVE METHODS
AND MANAGEMENT SCIENCE

Bierman, Bonini, and Hausman
Quantitative Analysis For Business Decisions
Eighth Edition

Knowles
Management Science: *Building and Using Models*
First Edition

Lotfi and Pegels
Decision Support Systems For Operations and Management Science
Third Edition

Stevenson
Introduction to Management Science
Second Edition

Turban and Meredith
Fundamentals of Management Science
Sixth Edition

FOURTH EDITION

Applied Linear Statistical Models

John Neter
University of Georgia

Michael H. Kutner
The Cleveland Clinic Foundation

Christopher J. Nachtsheim
University of Minnesota

William Wasserman
Syracuse University

WCB McGraw-Hill

Boston, Massachusetts   Burr Ridge, Illinois   Dubuque, Iowa
Madison, Wisconsin   New York, New York   San Francisco, California   St. Louis, Missouri

To
Dorothy, Ron, David,
Nancy, Michelle, Allison,
Maureen, Abigael, Andrew,
Cathy, Christopher, Timothy, Randall, Erin, Fiona

WCB/McGraw-Hill

*A Division of The **McGraw·Hill** Companies*

Trademark Acknowledgments:
    IBM and IBM PC are registered trademarks of International Business Machines Corporation.

DISCLAIMER

Richard D. Irwin, Inc., makes no warranties, either expressed or implied, regarding the enclosed computer software package, its merchantability or its fitness for any particular purpose. The exclusion of implied warranties is not permitted by some states. The exclusion may not apply to you. This warranty provides you with specific legal rights. There may be other rights that you may have which may vary from state to state.

Irwin Book Team

Publisher: Tom Casson
Senior sponsoring editor: Richard T. Hercher, Jr.
Senior developmental editor: Gail Korosa
Senior Marketing manager: Brian Kibby
Project editor: Lynne Basler
Production supervisor: Laurie Kersch

Designer: Matthew Baldwin
Cover designer: Stuart Paterson
Assistant Manager, Graphics: Charlene R. Perez
Compositor/Art Studio: Graphic Composition, Inc.
Typeface: 10/12 Times Roman
Printer: R. R. Donnelley & Sons Company

Library of Congress Cataloging-in-Publication Data

Applied linear statistical models / John Neter . . . [et al.]. — 3rd ed.
        p. cm.
    Includes index.
    ISBN 0-256-11736-5
    1. Regression analysis. 2. Analysis of variance. 3. Experimental
design. 4 Linear models (Statistics)
QA278.2.A66 1996
519.5′35—dc20   95–37447

Printed in the United States of America
    7 8 9 0 DO 2 1 0

Preface

Linear statistical models for regression, analysis of variance, and experimental designs are widely used today in business administration, economics, engineering, and the social, health, and biological sciences. Successful applications of these models require a sound understanding of both the underlying theory and the practical problems that are encountered in using the models in real-life situations. While *Applied Linear Statistical Models,* Fourth Edition, is basically an applied book, it seeks to blend theory and applications effectively, avoiding the extremes of presenting theory in isolation and of giving elements of applications without the needed understanding of the theoretical foundations.

The fourth edition differs from the third in a number of important respects.

1. In the area of regression analysis, we have reorganized the chapters in order to get to multiple linear regression analysis more quickly. Old Chapter 1 on basic results in probability and statistics has been placed in Appendix A, old Chapter 9 on polynomial regression has been interwoven in the discussion of multiple linear regression, and old Chapter 10 on qualitative predictor variables now comes after a full discussion of multiple regression model building and diagnostics.

We have expanded substantially the discussion of diagnostics and remedial measures. In Chapters 3 and 10, we have added robust tests for constancy of the error variance, smoothing techniques to explore the shape of the regression function, robust regression and nonparametric regression techniques, bootstrapping methods for evaluating the precision of sample estimates for complex situations, and estimation of the variance and standard deviation functions to obtain weights for weighted least squares.

2. We have retained the three chapters on nonlinear regression, logistic regression, and correlation analysis that were dropped from the third edition. Chapter 14 has been extensively revised and expanded to include an introduction to polytomous logistic regression, Poisson regression, and generalized linear models, as well as greater coverage of diagnostic procedures using the model deviance, deviance residuals, and simulated envelopes.

3. In the area of analysis of variance and experimental designs, we have added new Chapters 31 and 32 on fractional factorial designs and response surface method-

ology in view of their importance for total quality improvement programs. Chapter 31 focuses on two-level factorial experimentation and contains discussions of unreplicated factorial experiments, fractional factorial designs, screening experiments, and blocked two-level factorial experiments. An important feature of this chapter is the simple explanation of confounding, the result of carrying forward the standard regression framework emphasized throughout the text. Chapter 32 takes up central composite designs for response surface studies and an introduction to the use of computer-generated optimal designs.

We have also consolidated and expanded in Chapter 24 the discussion of random and mixed ANOVA models. We introduce here interval estimation of variance components, inferences about marginal means for mixed models, as well as maximum likelihood methods for analyzing random and mixed models for unbalanced studies.

4. We have increased the emphasis on diagnostics for the analysis of variance and experimental designs by providing many more diagnostic plots, and by adding discussions of the Box-Cox transformation procedure and weighted least squares as remedial measures. In addition, we have consolidated in Chapter 26 the discussion of power and planning of sample sizes for ANOVA studies. We have also introduced the Holm procedure for improving the power of the Bonferroni simultaneous testing procedure, as well as the analysis of means for identifying important effects.

5. We now include several case studies at strategic places to assist with the integration of the statistical methods discussed.

6. We have given greater emphasis to maximum likelihood methods and have expanded substantially the use of graphic presentation, including the use of scatter plot matrices, three-dimensional rotating plots, three-dimensional response surface and contour plots, and conditional effects plots.

7. Throughout the text, we have made extensive revisions in the exposition on the basis of classroom experience to improve the clarity of the presentation.

The first 15 chapters of the fourth edition of *Applied Linear Statistical Models* have also been published as a separate book under the title *Applied Linear Regression Models,* Third Edition.

A key feature of *Applied Linear Statistical Models,* Fourth Edition, continues to be its unified approach to the application of linear statistical models in regression, analysis of variance, and experimental designs. Instead of treating these areas in isolated fashion, we seek to show the interrelationships between them. Use of a common notation for regression, on the one hand, and analysis of variance and experimental designs, on the other, facilitates a unified view. The notion of a general linear statistical model, which arises naturally in the context of regression models, is carried over to analysis of variance and experimental design models to bring out their relation to regression models. This unified approach also has the advantage of simplified presentation.

We have included in this book not only the more conventional topics in regression, analysis of variance, and basic experimental designs, but also topics that are frequently slighted, though important in practice. We devote three chapters (Chapters 8–10) to the model-building process for regression, including computer-assisted selection procedures for identifying "good" subsets of predictor variables and validation of the chosen regression model. Two chapters (Chapters 11 and 14) are devoted to indicator variables, covering both response and predictor indicator variables. The use of residual analysis and other diagnostics for examining the appropriateness of a statistical model is a recurring theme throughout this book. So is the use of remedial measures that may be helpful when the model is not appropriate. In the analysis of the results of a study, we give greater emphasis to the use of estimation procedures than to significance tests, because estimation is often more meaningful in practice. Also, since practical problems seldom are concerned with a single inference, we stress the use of simultaneous inference procedures.

Theoretical ideas are presented to the degree needed for good understanding in making sound applications. Proofs are given in those instances where we feel they serve to demonstrate an important method of approach. Emphasis is placed on a thorough understanding of the models, particularly the meaning of the model parameters, since such understanding is basic to proper applications. A wide variety of examples and cases is presented to illustrate the use of the theoretical principles, to show the great diversity of applications of linear statistical models, and to demonstrate how analyses are carried out for different problems.

We use "Notes" and "Comments" sections in each chapter to present additional discussion and matters related to the mainstream of development. In this way, the basic ideas in a chapter are presented concisely and without distraction.

Applications of linear statistical models frequently require extensive computations. We take the position that a computer or programmable calculator is available in most applied work and that almost every computer user has access to program packages for regression analysis and analysis of variance of different types. Hence, we explain the basic mathematical steps in fitting a linear statistical model but do not dwell on computational details. This approach permits us to avoid many complex formulas and enables us to focus on basic principles. We make extensive use in this text of computer capabilities for performing computations and preparing graphic plots, and we illustrate a variety of computer printouts and plots and explain how they are used for analysis.

A selection of problems is provided at the end of each chapter. Here readers can reinforce their understanding of the methodology and use the concepts learned to analyze data. We have been careful to supply data-analysis problems that typify genuine applications. In most problems the calculations are best handled on a programmable calculator or computer. To facilitate data entry, a diskette in ASCII format is provided with the text that includes the data sets for all examples, problems, exercises, and projects, as well as the data sets in Appendix C. The README.TXT file on the diskette provides information about the identification of the data sets.

We assume that the reader of *Applied Linear Statistical Models,* Fourth Edition, has had an introductory course in statistical inference, covering the material outlined in Appendix A. Should some gaps in the reader's background exist, the relevant portions of an introductory text can be studied, or the instructor of the class may use supplemental materials for covering the missing segments. Appendix A is primarily intended as a reference of basic statistical results for continuing use as the reader progresses through the book.

Calculus is not required for reading *Applied Linear Statistical Models,* Fourth Edition. In a number of instances, we use calculus to demonstrate how some important results are obtained, but these demonstrations are confined to supplementary comments or notes and can be omitted without any loss of continuity. Readers who do know calculus will find these comments and notes in natural sequence so that the benefits of the mathematical developments are obtained in their immediate context. Some basic elements of matrix algebra are needed for linear models in general and for multiple regression in particular. Chapter 5 introduces these elements of matrix algebra in the context of simple regression for easy learning.

Applied Linear Statistical Models, Fourth Edition, is intended for use in undergraduate and graduate courses in linear statistical models and in second courses in applied statistics. The extent to which material presented in this text is used in a particular course depends upon the amount of time available and the objectives of the course. Some possible courses include:

1. A two-quarter or two-semester course in regression, analysis of variance, and basic experimental designs might be based on the following chapters:

Regression: 1, 2, 3, 4 (Sections 4.1–4.3), 5, 6, 7, 8, 9, 10, 11 (Sections 11.1–11.4).

Analysis of variance: 16, 17, 18, 19, 20, 25.

Experimental designs: 26, 27, 28, 29, 31.

2. A one-quarter or one-semester course in regression analysis might be based on the following chapters: 1, 2, 3, 4 (Sections 4.1–4.3), 5, 6, 7, 8, 9, 10, 11 (Sections 11.1–11.4), 12, 13.

3. A one-quarter or one-semester course in analysis of variance might be based on the following chapters: 16, 17, 18, 19, 20, 21, 22 (selected topics), 23, 24 (selected topics), 25.

4. A one-quarter or one-semester course in regression and analysis of variance might be based on the following chapters:

Regression: 1, 2, 3, 4 (Sections 4.1–4.3), 5, 6, 7, 8, 9, 10, 11 (Sections 11.1–11.4).

Analysis of variance: 16, 17, 18, 19, 20.

5. A one-quarter or one-semester course in basic experimental designs might be based on the following chapters: 26, 27, 28, 29, 30, 31, 32.

As time permits, the instructor can cover additional topics in the text.

This book can also be used for self-study by persons engaged in the fields of business administration, economics, engineering, and the social, health, and biological sciences who desire to obtain competence in the application of linear statistical models.

An *Instructor Solutions Manual,* containing detailed solutions to all numerical problems and analytical exercises, is available from the publisher, Irwin, for use by instructors. To facilitate learning by students, instructors may order from the publisher, Irwin, copies of the *Student Solutions Manual* for use by students. The *Student Solutions Manual* provides intermediate and final numerical results for easy self-checking of solutions for selected problems. We use a check mark ($\sqrt{}$) in front of the problem number to designate the problems for which the solutions appear in the *Student Solutions Manual.*

A book such as this cannot be written without substantial assistance from numerous persons. We are indebted to the many contributors who have developed the theory and practice discussed in this book. We also would like to acknowledge appreciation to our students, who helped us in a variety of ways to fashion the method of presentation contained herein. We are grateful to the many users of *Applied Linear Statistical Models* and *Applied Linear Regression Models* who have provided us with comments and suggestions based on their teaching with these texts. We are also indebted to Professors James E. Holstein, University of Missouri, and David L. Sherry, University of West Florida, for their review of *Applied Linear Statistical Models,* First Edition; to Professors Samuel Kotz, University of Maryland at College Park, Ralph P. Russo, University of Iowa, and Peter F. Thall, The George Washington University, for their review of *Applied Linear Regression Models,* First Edition; to Professors John

S. Y. Chiu, University of Washington, James A. Calvin, University of Iowa, and Michael F. Driscoll, Arizona State University, for their review of *Applied Linear Statistical Models,* Second Edition; to Professor Richard Anderson-Sprecher, University of Wyoming, for his review of *Applied Linear Regression Models,* Second Edition; and to Professors Alexander von Eye, The Pennsylvania State University, Samuel Kotz, University of Maryland at College Park, and John B. Willett, Harvard University, for their review of *Applied Linear Statistical Models,* Third Edition. These reviews provided many important suggestions, for which we are most grateful.

In addition, valuable assistance was provided by Professors Richard K. Burdick, Arizona State University, R. Dennis Cook, University of Minnesota, W. J. Conover, Texas Tech University, and Mark E. Johnson, University of Central Florida, and by Drs. Richard J. Beckman, Los Alamos National Laboratory, and Ronald L. Iman, Sandia National Laboratories. We are most appreciative of their willing help.

We are also indebted to the 88 participants in a survey concerning *Applied Linear Regression Models,* Second Edition, and the 76 participants in a survey concerning *Applied Linear Statistical Models,* Third Edition. Helpful suggestions were received in these surveys, for which we are thankful.

George Cotsonis, A. Pedro Duarte Silva, and Manus Rungtusanatham assisted us diligently in the checking of the manuscript, in preparing computer-generated plots, and in other ways. The initial typing of the manuscript was ably done by Rebecca Brooks, Linda Keith, and Charlyene Harmon. Rebecca Brooks assisted us in outstanding fashion in the many difficult stages of the revision of a complex manuscript, aided by Sheila King. We are most grateful to all of these persons for their invaluable help and assistance.

Finally, our families bore patiently the pressures caused by our commitment to complete this revision. We are appreciative of their understanding.

John Neter
Michael H. Kutner
Christopher J. Nachtsheim
William Wasserman

Contents

PART I

Simple Linear Regression

1 Linear Regression with One Predictor Variable   3

1.1   Relations between Variables   3
1.2   Regression Models and Their Uses   6
1.3   Simple Linear Regression Model with Distribution of Error Terms Unspecified   10
1.4   Data for Regression Analysis   14
1.5   Overview of Steps in Regression Analysis   15
1.6   Estimation of Regression Function   17
1.7   Estimation of Error Terms Variance σ^2 27
1.8   Normal Error Regression Model   29

2 Inferences in Regression Analysis   44

2.1   Inferences concerning β_1 44
2.2   Inferences concerning β_0 53
2.3   Some Considerations on Making Inferences concerning β_0 and β_1 54
2.4   Interval Estimation of $E\{Y_h\}$ 56
2.5   Prediction of New Observation   61
2.6   Confidence Band for Regression Line   67
2.7   Analysis of Variance Approach to Regression Analysis   69
2.8   General Linear Test Approach   78
2.9   Descriptive Measures of Association between X and Y in Regression Model   80
2.10   Considerations in Applying Regression Analysis   84
2.11   Case when X is Random   85

3 Diagnostics and Remedial Measures   95

3.1   Diagnostics for Predictor Variable   95
3.2   Residuals   97
3.3   Diagnostics for Residuals   98
3.4   Overview of Tests Involving Residuals   110
3.5   Correlation Test for Normality   111
3.6   Tests for Constancy of Error Variance   112
3.7 F Test for Lack of Fit   115
3.8   Overview of Remedial Measures   124
3.9   Transformations   126
3.10   Exploration of Shape of Regression Function   135
3.11   Case Example—Plutonium Measurement   138

4 Simultaneous Inferences and Other Topics in Regression Analysis   152

4.1   Joint Estimation of β_0 and β_1 152
4.2   Simultaneous Estimation of Mean Responses   155
4.3   Simultaneous Prediction Intervals for New Observations   158
4.4   Regression through Origin   159
4.5   Effects of Measurement Errors   164
4.6   Inverse Predictions   167
4.7   Choice of X Levels   169

5 Matrix Approach to Simple Linear Regression Analysis   176

5.1   Matrices   176
5.2   Matrix Addition and Subtraction   180

5.3   Matrix Multiplication   182
5.4   Special Types of Matrices   185
5.5   Linear Dependence and Rank of
      Matrix   188
5.6   Inverse of a Matrix   189
5.7   Some Basic Theorems for Matrices   194
5.8   Random Vectors and Matrices   194
5.9   Simple Linear Regression Model in Matrix
      Terms   198
5.10 Least Squares Estimation of Regression
      Parameters   200
5.11 Fitted Values and Residuals   202
5.12 Analysis of Variance Results   205
5.13 Inferences in Regression Analysis   208

PART II

Multiple Linear Regression

6   Multiple Regression—I   217

6.1   Multiple Regression Models   217
6.2   General Linear Regression Model in
      Matrix Terms   225
6.3   Estimation of Regression
      Coefficients   227
6.4   Fitted Values and Residuals   227
6.5   Analysis of Variance Results   228
6.6   Inferences about Regression
      Parameters   231
6.7   Estimation of Mean Response and
      Prediction of New Observation   233
6.8   Diagnostics and Remedial Measures   236
6.9   An Example—Multiple Regression with
      Two Predictor Variables   241

7   Multiple Regression—II   260

7.1   Extra Sums of Squares   260
7.2   Uses of Extra Sums of Squares in Tests for
      Regression Coefficients   268
7.3   Summary of Tests concerning Regression
      Coefficients   271
7.4   Coefficients of Partial Determination   274
7.5   Standardized Multiple Regression
      Model   277
7.6   Multicollinearity and Its Effects   285
7.7   Polynomial Regression Models   296
7.8   Interaction Regression Models   308
7.9   Constrained Regression   315

8   Building the Regression Model I: Selection of Predictor Variables   327

8.1   Overview of Model-Building Process   327

8.2   Surgical Unit Example   334
8.3   All-Possible-Regressions Procedure for
      Variables Reduction   336
8.4   Forward Stepwise Regression and Other
      Automatic Search Procedures for
      Variables Reduction   347
8.5   Some Final Comments on Model Building
      for Exploratory Observational
      Studies   353

9   Building the Regression Model II: Diagnostics   361

9.1   Model Adequacy for a Predictor
      Variable—Partial Regression Plots   361
9.2   Identifying Outlying Y Observations—
      Studentized Deleted Residuals   368
9.3   Identifying Outlying X Observations—
      Hat Matrix Leverage Values   375
9.4   Identifying Influential Cases—*DFFITS*,
      Cook's Distance, and *DFBETAS*
      Measures   378
9.5   Multicollinearity Diagnostics—Variance
      Inflation Factor   385
9.6   Surgical Unit Example—Continued   388

10   Building the Regression Model III: Remedial Measures and Validation   400

10.1 Unequal Error Variances Remedial
      Measures   Weighted Least
      Squares   400
10.2 Multicollinearity Remedial Measures—
      Ridge Regression   410
10.3 Remedial Measures for Influential Cases—
      Robust Regression   416
10.4 Remedial Measures for Unknown
      Response Function—Nonparametric
      Regression   425
10.5 Remedial Measures for Evaluating
      Precision in Nonstandard Situations—
      Bootstrapping   429
10.6 Model Validation   434
10.7 Case Example—Mathematics
      Proficiency   439

11   Qualitative Predictor Variables   455

11.1 One Qualitative Predictor Variable   455
11.2 Model Containing Interaction
      Effects   461
11.3 More Complex Models   464
11.4 Comparison of Two or More Regression
      Functions   468

11.5 Other Uses of Indicator Variables 474
11.6 Some Considerations in Using Indicator Variables 480
11.7 Case Example—MNDOT Traffic Estimation 483

12 Autocorrelation in Time Series Data 497

12.1 Problems of Autocorrelation 497
12.2 First-Order Autoregressive Error Model 501
12.3 Durbin-Watson Test for Autocorrelation 504
12.4 Remedial Measures for Autocorrelation 507
12.5 Forecasting with Autocorrelated Error Terms 517

PART III

Nonlinear Regression

13 Introduction to Nonlinear Regression 531

13.1 Linear and Nonlinear Regression Models 531
13.2 Example 535
13.3 Least Squares Estimation in Nonlinear Regression 536
13.4 Model Building and Diagnostics 547
13.5 Inferences about Nonlinear Regression Parameters 548
13.6 Learning Curve Example 555

14 Logistic Regression, Poisson Regression, and Generalized Linear Models 567

14.1 Regression Models with Binary Response Variable 567
14.2 Simple Logistic Response Function 570
14.3 Simple Logistic Regression 573
14.4 Multiple Logistic Regression 580
14.5 Model Building: Selection of Predictor Variables 585
14.6 Diagnostics 590
14.7 Inferences about Logistic Regression Parameters 599
14.8 Inferences about Mean Response 602
14.9 Prediction of a New Observation 605
14.10 Polytomous Logistic Regression 608
14.11 Poisson Regression 609
14.12 Generalized Linear Models 614

PART IV

Correlation Analysis

15 Normal Correlation Models 631

15.1 Distinction between Regression and Correlation Models 631
15.2 Bivariate Normal Distribution 632
15.3 Conditional Inferences 636
15.4 Inferences on Correlation Coefficients 640
15.5 Multivariate Normal Distribution 645
15.6 Spearman Rank Correlation Coefficient 651

PART V

Analysis of Variance: I

16 Single-Factor ANOVA Model and Tests 663

16.1 Relation between Regression and Analysis of Variance 663
16.2 Experimental and Observational Studies, Factors, and Treatments 666
16.3 Design of Analysis of Variance Studies 668
16.4 Uses of Analysis of Variance Models 670
16.5 Use of Computers 671
16.6 ANOVA Model I—Fixed Factor Levels 671
16.7 Fitting of ANOVA Model 676
16.8 Analysis of Variance 681
16.9 F Test for Equality of Factor Level Means 690
16.10 Alternative Formulation of Model I 693
16.11 Regression Approach to Single-Factor Analysis of Variance 696

17 Analysis of Factor Level Effects 710

17.1 Introduction 710
17.2 Plots of Estimated Factor Level Means 712
17.3 Estimation and Testing of Factor Level Effects 716
17.4 Need for Simultaneous Inference Procedures 724
17.5 Tukey Multiple Comparison Procedure 725
17.6 Scheffé Multiple Comparison Procedure 732
17.7 Bonferroni Multiple Comparison Procedure 736

17.8   Holm Simultaneous Testing
       Procedure   739
17.9   Analysis of Factor Effects when Factor
       Quantitative   742

18   ANOVA Diagnostics and Remedial Measures   756

18.1   Residual Analysis   756
18.2   Tests for Constancy of Error
       Variance   763
18.3   Overview of Remedial Measures   768
18.4   Weighted Least Squares   768
18.5   Transformations of Response
       Variable   772
18.6   Effects of Departures from Model   776
18.7   Nonparametric Rank F Test   777
18.8   Case Example—Heart Transplant   780

PART VI

Analysis of Variance: II

19   Two-Factor Analysis of Variance— Equal Sample Sizes   795

19.1   Multifactor Studies   795
19.2   Meaning of ANOVA Model
       Elements   799
19.3   Model I (Fixed Factor Levels) for
       Two-Factor Studies   812
19.4   Analysis of Variance   817
19.5   Evaluation of Appropriateness of ANOVA
       Model   825
19.6 F Tests   829
19.7   Regression Approach to Two-Factor
       Analysis of Variance   832
19.8   Pooling Sums of Squares in Two-Factor
       Analysis of Variance   837

20   Analysis of Factor Effects in Two-Factor Studies—Equal Sample Sizes   849

20.1   Strategy for Analysis   849
20.2   Analysis of Factor Effects when Factors
       Do Not Interact   851
20.3   Analysis of Factor Effects when
       Interactions Important   859
20.4   Analysis when One or Both Factors
       Quantitative   865

21   Two-Factor Studies—One Case Per Treatment   875

21.1   No-Interaction Model   875
21.2   Tukey Test for Additivity   882

22   Two-Factor Studies—Unequal Sample Sizes and Unequal Treatment Importance   889

22.1   Unequal Sample Sizes   889
22.2   Use of Regression Approach for Testing
       Factor Effects when Sample Sizes are
       Unequal   891
22.3   Inferences about Factor Effects when
       Sample Sizes Are Unequal   897
22.4   Empty Cells in Two-Factor Studies   902
22.5   ANOVA Inferences when Treatment
       Means Are of Unequal Importance   905
22.6   Statistical Computing Packages   915

23   Multifactor Studies   924

23.1   ANOVA Model I for Three-Factor
       Studies   924
23.2   Analysis of Variance   932
23.3   Evaluation of Appropriateness of ANOVA
       Model   938
23.4   Analysis of Factor Effects   938
23.5   Example of Three-Factor Study   942
23.6   Unequal Sample Sizes in Multifactor
       Studies   948

24   Random and Mixed Effects Models   958

24.1   Single-Factor Studies—ANOVA Model
       II   958
24.2   Two-Factor Studies—ANOVA Models II
       and III   976
24.3   Two-Factor Studies—ANOVA Tests for
       Models II and III   981
24.4   Two-Factor Studies—Estimation of Factor
       Effects For Models II and III   984
24.5   Three-Factor-Studies—ANOVA Models II
       and III   989
24.6   ANOVA Models II and III with Unequal
       Sample Sizes   994

25   Analysis of Covariance   1010

25.1   Basic Ideas   1010
25.2   Single-Factor Covariance Model   1014
25.3   Example of Single-Factor Covariance
       Analysis   1019
25.4   Multifactor Covariance Analysis   1028
25.5   Additional Considerations for the Use of
       Covariance Analysis   1032

PART VII

Study Designs

26 Design of Experiments, Randomization, and Sample Size Planning 1045

26.1 Design of Experiments 1045
26.2 Contributions of Statistics to Experimentation 1046
26.3 Randomization Tests 1050
26.4 Planning of Sample Sizes with Power Approach 1052
26.5 Planning of Sample Sizes with Estimation Approach 1060
26.6 Planning of Sample Sizes to Find "Best" Treatment 1063

27 Randomized Block Designs 1072

27.1 Elements of Randomized Block Designs 1072
27.2 Model for Randomized Block Designs 1075
27.3 Analysis of Variance and Tests 1078
27.4 Evaluation of Appropriateness of Randomized Block Model 1081
27.5 Analysis of Treatment Effects 1084
27.6 Factorial Treatments 1086
27.7 Planning Randomized Block Experiments 1088
27.8 Regression Approach to Randomized Block Designs 1091
27.9 Covariance Analysis for Randomized Block Designs 1092
27.10 Nonparametric Rank F Test 1094
27.11 Missing Observations 1097
27.12 Random Block Effects 1100
27.13 Generalized Randomized Block Designs 1106
27.14 Use of More Than One Blocking Variable 1108

28 Nested Designs, Subsampling, and Partially Nested Designs 1121

28.1 Distinction between Nested and Crossed Factors 1121
28.2 Two-Factor Nested Designs 1124
28.3 Analysis of Variance for Two-Factor Nested Designs 1127
28.4 Evaluation of Appropriateness of Nested Design Model 1133
28.5 Analysis of Factor Effects in Two-Factor Nested Designs 1134
28.6 Unbalanced Nested Two-Factor Designs 1138

28.7 Subsampling in Single-Factor Study with Completely Randomized Design 1141
28.8 Pure Subsampling in Three Stages 1148
28.9 Three-Factor Partially Nested Designs 1149

29 Repeated Measures and Related Designs 1164

29.1 Elements of Repeated Measures Designs 1164
29.2 Single-Factor Experiments with Repeated Measures on All Treatments 1166
29.3 Two-Factor Experiments with Repeated Measures on Both Factors 1176
29.4 Two-Factor Experiments with Repeated Measures on One Factor 1184
29.5 Regression Approach to Repeated Measures Designs 1194
29.6 Split-Plot Designs 1194

30 Latin Square and Related Designs 1207

30.1 Basic Elements 1207
30.2 Latin Square Model 1211
30.3 Analysis of Latin Square Experiments 1212
30.4 Planning Latin Square Experiments 1218
30.5 Regression Approach to Latin Square Designs 1220
30.6 Additional Replications with Latin Square Designs 1221
30.7 Replications in Repeated Measures Designs 1225

31 Exploratory Experiments—Two-Level Factorial and Fractional Factorial Designs 1234

31.1 Two-Level Full Factorial Designs 1235
31.2 Analysis of Unreplicated Two-Level Studies 1241
31.3 Two-Level Fractional Factorial Designs 1249
31.4 Screening Experiments 1264
31.5 Incomplete Block Designs for Two-Level Factorial Experiments 1266

32 Response Surface Methodology 1280

32.1 Response Surface Experiments 1280
32.2 Central Composite Response Surface Designs 1281
32.3 Optimal Response Surface Designs 1289
32.4 Analysis of Response Surface Experiments 1297

32.5   Sequential Search for Optimum
          Conditions—Method of Steepest
          Ascent   1303

Appendix A   Some Basic Results in Probability and
                 Statistics   1313
Appendix B   Tables   1333
Appendix C   Data Sets   1365
Appendix D   Rules for Developing ANOVA Models
                 and Tables for Balanced
                 Designs   1373
Appendix E   Selected Bibliography   1391
Index   1400

Simple Linear Regression

Linear Regression with One Predictor Variable

Regression analysis is a statistical methodology that utilizes the relation between two or more quantitative variables so that one variable can be predicted from the other, or others. This methodology is widely used in business, the social and behavioral sciences, the biological sciences, and many other disciplines. A few examples of applications are:

1. Sales of a product can be predicted by utilizing the relationship between sales and amount of advertising expenditures.
2. The performance of an employee on a job can be predicted by utilizing the relationship between performance and a battery of aptitude tests.
3. The size of the vocabulary of a child can be predicted by utilizing the relationship between size of vocabulary and age of the child and amount of education of the parents.

In Part I we take up regression analysis when a single predictor variable is used for predicting the variable of interest. In Parts II and III, we consider regression analysis when two or more variables are used for making predictions. In this chapter, we consider the basic ideas of regression analysis and discuss the estimation of the parameters of regression models containing a single predictor variable.

1.1 Relations between Variables

The concept of a relation between two variables, such as between family income and family expenditures for housing, is a familiar one. We distinguish between a *functional relation* and a *statistical relation*, and consider each of these in turn.

Functional Relation between Two Variables

A functional relation between two variables is expressed by a mathematical formula. If X denotes the *independent variable* and Y the *dependent variable*, a functional relation is of the form:

$$Y = f(X)$$

3

FIGURE 1.1   **Example of Functional Relation.**

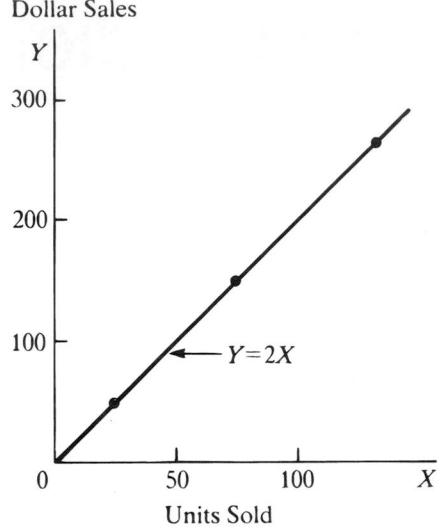

Given a particular value of X, the function f indicates the corresponding value of Y.

Example.   Consider the relation between dollar sales (Y) of a product sold at a fixed price and number of units sold (X). If the selling price is \$2 per unit, the relation is expressed by the equation:

$$Y = 2X$$

This functional relation is shown in Figure 1.1. Number of units sold and dollar sales during three recent periods (while the unit price remained constant at \$2) were as follows:

Period	Number of Units Sold	Dollar Sales
1	75	\$150
2	25	50
3	130	260

These observations are plotted also in Figure 1.1. Note that all fall directly on the line of functional relationship. This is characteristic of all functional relations.

Statistical Relation between Two Variables

A statistical relation, unlike a functional relation, is not a perfect one. In general, the observations for a statistical relation do not fall directly on the curve of relationship.

Example 1.   Performance evaluations for 10 employees were obtained at midyear and at year-end. These data are plotted in Figure 1.2a. Year-end evaluations are taken as the *dependent* or *response variable Y*, and midyear evaluations as the *independent*, *explanatory*,

FIGURE 1.2   **Statistical Relation between Midyear Performance Evaluation and Year-End Evaluation.**

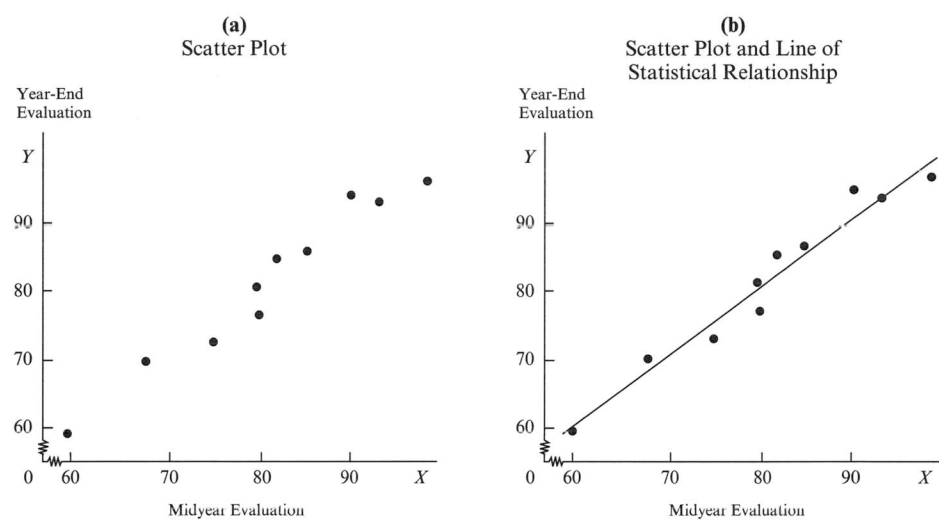

or *predictor variable X*. The plotting is done as before. For instance, the midyear and year-end performance evaluations for the first employee are plotted at $X = 90$, $Y = 94$.

Figure 1.2a clearly suggests that there is a relation between midyear and year-end evaluations, in the sense that the higher the midyear evaluation, the higher tends to be the year-end evaluation. However, the relation is not a perfect one. There is a scattering of points, suggesting that some of the variation in year-end evaluations is not accounted for by midyear performance assessments. For instance, two employees had midyear evaluations of $X = 80$, yet they received somewhat different year-end evaluations. Because of the scattering of points in a statistical relation, Figure 1.2a is called a *scatter diagram* or *scatter plot*. In statistical terminology, each point in the scatter diagram represents a *trial* or a *case*.

In Figure 1.2b, we have plotted a line of relationship that describes the statistical relation between midyear and year-end evaluations. It indicates the general tendency by which year-end evaluations vary with the level of midyear performance evaluation. Note that most of the points do not fall directly on the line of statistical relationship. This scattering of points around the line represents variation in year-end evaluations that is not associated with midyear performance evaluation and that is usually considered to be of a random nature. Statistical relations can be highly useful, even though they do not have the exactitude of a functional relation.

Example 2.   Figure 1.3 presents data on age and level of a steroid in plasma for 17 healthy females between 8 and 25 years old. The data strongly suggest that the statistical relationship is *curvilinear* (not linear). The curve of relationship has also been drawn in Figure 1.3. It implies that, as age increases, steroid level increases up to a point and then begins to decline. Note again the scattering of points around the curve of statistical relationship, typical of all statistical relations.

FIGURE 1.3   **Curvilinear Statistical Relation between Age and Steroid Level in Healthy Females Aged 8 to 25.**

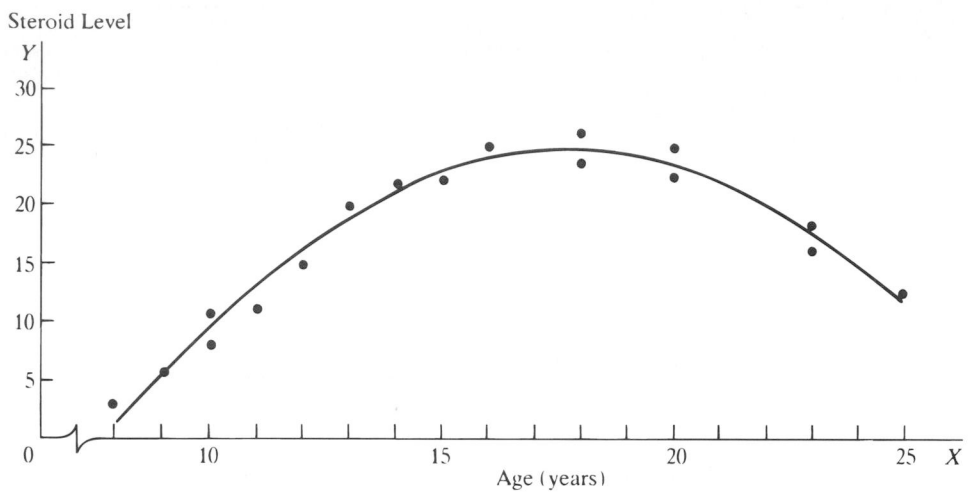

1.2   Regression Models and Their Uses

Historical Origins

Regression analysis was first developed by Sir Francis Galton in the latter part of the 19th century. Galton had studied the relation between heights of parents and children and noted that the heights of children of both tall and short parents appeared to "revert" or "regress" to the mean of the group. He considered this tendency to be a regression to "mediocrity." Galton developed a mathematical description of this regression tendency, the precursor of today's regression models.

The term *regression* persists to this day to describe statistical relations between variables.

Basic Concepts

A regression model is a formal means of expressing the two essential ingredients of a statistical relation:

1. A tendency of the response variable Y to vary with the predictor variable X in a systematic fashion.

2. A scattering of points around the curve of statistical relationship.

These two characteristics are embodied in a regression model by postulating that:

1. There is a probability distribution of Y for each level of X.

2. The means of these probability distributions vary in some systematic fashion with X.

FIGURE 1.4   Pictorial Representation of Regression Model.

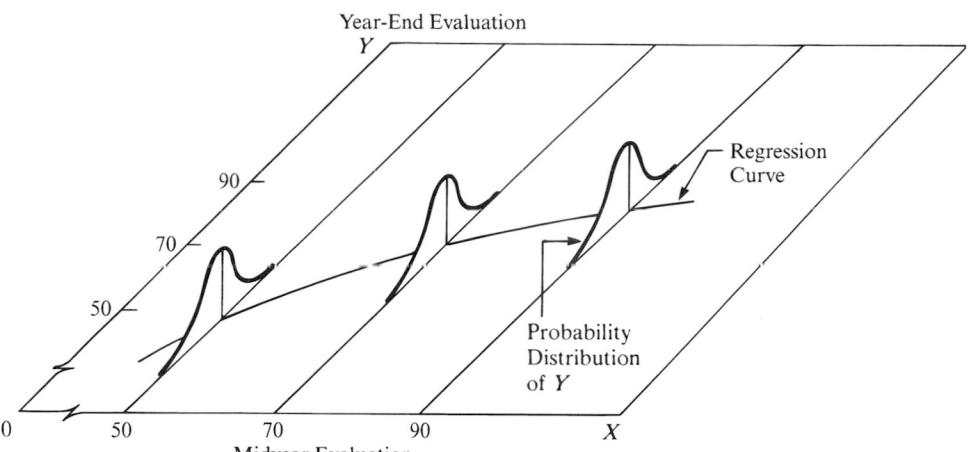

Example.   Consider again the performance evaluation example in Figure 1.2. The year-end evaluation Y is treated in a regression model as a random variable. For each level of midyear performance evaluation, there is postulated a probability distribution of Y. Figure 1.4 shows such a probability distribution for $X = 90$, which is the midyear evaluation for the first employee. The actual year-end evaluation of this employee, $Y = 94$, is then viewed as a random selection from this probability distribution.

Figure 1.4 also shows probability distributions of Y for midyear evaluation levels $X = 50$ and $X = 70$. Note that the means of the probability distributions have a systematic relation to the level of X. This systematic relationship is called the *regression function of Y on X*. The graph of the regression function is called the *regression curve*. Note that in Figure 1.4 the regression function is slightly curvilinear. This would imply for our example that the increase in the expected (mean) year-end evaluation with an increase in midyear performance evaluation is retarded at higher levels of midyear performance.

Regression models may differ in the form of the regression function (linear, curvilinear), in the shape of the probability distributions of Y (symmetrical, skewed), and in other ways. Whatever the variation, the concept of a probability distribution of Y for any given X is the formal counterpart to the empirical scatter in a statistical relation. Similarly, the regression curve, which describes the relation between the means of the probability distributions of Y and the level of X, is the counterpart to the general tendency of Y to vary with X systematically in a statistical relation.

Regression Models with More than One Predictor Variable.   Regression models may contain more than one predictor variable. Three examples follow.

1. In an efficiency study of 67 branch offices of a consumer finance chain, the response variable was direct operating cost for the year just ended. There were four predictor variables: average size of loan outstanding during the year, average number of loans outstanding, total number of new loan applications processed, and index of office salaries.

2. In a tractor purchase study, the response variable was volume (in horsepower) of tractor purchases in a sales territory of a farm equipment firm. There were nine predictor

variables, including average age of tractors on farms in the territory, number of farms in the territory, and a quantity index of crop production in the territory.

3. In a medical study of short children, the response variable was the peak plasma growth hormone level. There were 14 predictor variables, including age, gender, height, weight, and 10 skinfold measurements.

The model features represented in Figure 1.4 must be extended into further dimensions when there is more than one predictor variable. With two predictor variables X_1 and X_2, for instance, a probability distribution of Y for each (X_1, X_2) combination is assumed by the regression model. The systematic relation between the means of these probability distributions and the predictor variables X_1 and X_2 is then given by a regression surface.

Construction of Regression Models

Selection of Predictor Variables.   Since reality must be reduced to manageable proportions whenever we construct models, only a limited number of explanatory or predictor variables can—or should—be included in a regression model for any situation of interest. A central problem in many exploratory studies is therefore that of choosing, for a regression model, a set of predictor variables that is "good" in some sense for the purposes of the analysis. A major consideration in making this choice is the extent to which a chosen variable contributes to reducing the remaining variation in Y after allowance is made for the contributions of other predictor variables that have tentatively been included in the regression model. Other considerations include the importance of the variable as a causal agent in the process under analysis; the degree to which observations on the variable can be obtained more accurately, or quickly, or economically than on competing variables; and the degree to which the variable can be controlled. In Chapter 8, we will discuss procedures and problems in choosing the predictor variables to be included in the regression model.

Functional Form of Regression Relation.   The choice of the functional form of the regression relation is tied to the choice of the predictor variables. Sometimes, relevant theory may indicate the appropriate functional form. Learning theory, for instance, may indicate that the regression function relating unit production cost to the number of previous times the item has been produced should have a specified shape with particular asymptotic properties.

More frequently, however, the functional form of the regression relation is not known in advance and must be decided upon empirically once the data have been collected. Linear or quadratic regression functions are often used as satisfactory first approximations to regression functions of unknown nature. Indeed, these simple types of regression functions may be used even when theory provides the relevant functional form, notably when the known form is highly complex but can be reasonably approximated by a linear or quadratic regression function. Figure 1.5a illustrates a case where the complex regression function may be reasonably approximated by a linear regression function. Figure 1.5b provides an example where two linear regression functions may be used "piecewise" to approximate a complex regression function.

Scope of Model.   In formulating a regression model, we usually need to restrict the coverage of the model to some interval or region of values of the predictor variable(s). The scope is determined either by the design of the investigation or by the range of data at hand. For instance, a company studying the effect of price on sales volume investigated six price levels, ranging from $4.95 to $6.95. Here, the scope of the model is limited to price levels ranging from near $5 to near $7. The shape of the regression function substantially

FIGURE 1.5   **Uses of Linear Regression Functions to Approximate Complex Regression Functions.**

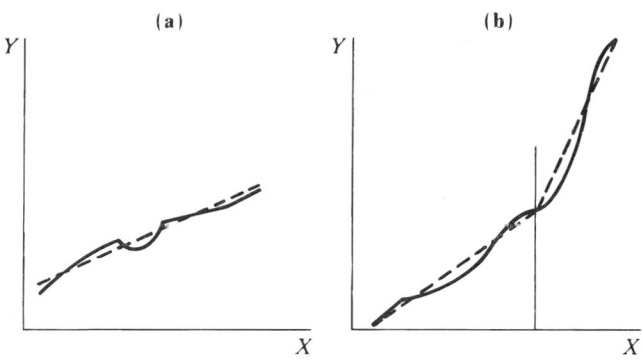

outside this range would be in serious doubt because the investigation provided no evidence as to the nature of the statistical relation below $4.95 or above $6.95.

Uses of Regression Analysis

Regression analysis serves three major purposes: (1) description, (2) control, and (3) prediction. These purposes are illustrated by the three examples cited earlier. The tractor purchase study served a descriptive purpose. In the study of branch office operating costs, the main purpose was administrative control; by developing a usable statistical relation between cost and the predictor variables, management was able to set cost standards for each branch office in the company chain. In the medical study of short children, the purpose was prediction. Clinicians were able to use the statistical relation to predict growth hormone deficiencies in short children by using simple measurements of the children.

The several purposes of regression analysis frequently overlap in practice. The branch office example is a case in point. Knowledge of the relation between operating cost and characteristics of the branch office not only enabled management to set cost standards for each office but management could also predict costs, and at the end of the fiscal year it could compare the actual branch cost against the expected cost.

Regression and Causality

The existence of a statistical relation between the response variable Y and the explanatory or predictor variable X does not imply in any way that Y depends causally on X. No matter how strong is the statistical relation between X and Y, no cause-and-effect pattern is necessarily implied by the regression model. For example, data on size of vocabulary (X) and writing speed (Y) for a sample of young children aged 5–10 will show a positive regression relation. This relation does not imply, however, that an increase in vocabulary causes a faster writing speed. Here, other explanatory variables, such as age of the child and amount of education, affect both the vocabulary (X) and the writing speed (Y). Older children have a larger vocabulary and a faster writing speed.

Even when a strong statistical relationship reflects causal conditions, the causal conditions may act in the opposite direction, from Y to X. Consider, for instance, the calibration of a thermometer. Here, readings of the thermometer are taken at different known temperatures, and the regression relation is studied so that the accuracy of predictions made by using the thermometer readings can be assessed. For this purpose, the thermometer reading is the predictor variable X, and the actual temperature is the response variable Y to be predicted. However, the causal pattern here does not go from X to Y, but in the opposite direction: the actual temperature (Y) affects the thermometer reading (X).

These examples demonstrate the need for care in drawing conclusions about causal relations from regression analysis. Regression analysis by itself provides no information about causal patterns and must be supplemented by additional analyses to obtain insights about causal relations.

Use of Computers

Because regression analysis often entails lengthy and tedious calculations, computers are usually utilized to perform the necessary calculations. Almost every statistics package for computers contains a regression component. While packages differ in many details, their basic regression output tends to be quite similar.

After an initial explanation of required regression calculations, we shall rely on computer calculations for all subsequent examples. We illustrate computer output by presenting output from BMDP (Ref. 1.1), MINITAB (Ref. 1.2), SAS (Ref. 1.3), SPSS-X (Ref. 1.4), SYSTAT (Ref. 1.5), and JMP (Ref. 1.6). We also illustrate computer plots prepared from MINITAB, BMDP, SAS/GRAPH (Ref. 1.7), SYGRAPH (Ref. 1.8), and JMP.

1.3   Simple Linear Regression Model with Distribution of Error Terms Unspecified

Formal Statement of Model

In Part I we consider a basic regression model where there is only one predictor variable and the regression function is linear. The model can be stated as follows:

$$(1.1) \qquad\qquad Y_i = \beta_0 + \beta_1 X_i + \varepsilon_i$$

where:

   Y_i is the value of the response variable in the ith trial

   β_0 and β_1 are parameters

   X_i is a known constant, namely, the value of the predictor variable in the ith trial

   ε_i is a random error term with mean $E\{\varepsilon_i\} = 0$ and variance $\sigma^2\{\varepsilon_i\} = \sigma^2$; ε_i and ε_j are uncorrelated so that their covariance is zero (i.e., $\sigma\{\varepsilon_i, \varepsilon_j\} = 0$ for all $i, j; i \neq j$)

   $i = 1, \ldots, n$

Regression model (1.1) is said to be *simple, linear in the parameters*, and *linear in the predictor variable*. It is "simple" in that there is only one predictor variable, "linear in the parameters" because no parameter appears as an exponent or is multiplied or divided by another parameter, and "linear in the predictor variable" because this variable appears only in the first power. A model that is linear in the parameters and in the predictor variable is also called a *first-order model*.

Important Features of Model

1. The response Y_i in the ith trial is the sum of two components: (1) the constant term $\beta_0 + \beta_1 X_i$ and (2) the random term ε_i. Hence, Y_i is a random variable.

2. Since $E\{\varepsilon_i\} = 0$, it follows from (A.13c) in Appendix A that:

$$E\{Y_i\} = E\{\beta_0 + \beta_1 X_i + \varepsilon_i\} = \beta_0 + \beta_1 X_i + E\{\varepsilon_i\} = \beta_0 + \beta_1 X_i$$

Note that $\beta_0 + \beta_1 X_i$ plays the role of the constant a in theorem (A.13c).

Thus, the response Y_i, when the level of X in the ith trial is X_i, comes from a probability distribution whose mean is:

(1.2) $$E\{Y_i\} = \beta_0 + \beta_1 X_i$$

We therefore know that the regression function for model (1.1) is:

(1.3) $$E\{Y\} = \beta_0 + \beta_1 X$$

since the regression function relates the means of the probability distributions of Y for given X to the level of X.

3. The response Y_i in the ith trial exceeds or falls short of the value of the regression function by the error term amount ε_i.

4. The error terms ε_i are assumed to have constant variance σ^2. It therefore follows that the responses Y_i have the same constant variance:

(1.4) $$\sigma^2\{Y_i\} = \sigma^2$$

since, using theorem (A.16a), we have:

$$\sigma^2\{\beta_0 + \beta_1 X_i + \varepsilon_i\} = \sigma^2\{\varepsilon_i\} = \sigma^2$$

Thus, regression model (1.1) assumes that the probability distributions of Y have the same variance σ^2, regardless of the level of the predictor variable X.

5. The error terms are assumed to be uncorrelated. Hence, the outcome in any one trial has no effect on the error term for any other trial—as to whether it is positive or negative, small or large. Since the error terms ε_i and ε_j are uncorrelated, so are the responses Y_i and Y_j.

6. In summary, regression model (1.1) implies that the responses Y_i come from probability distributions whose means are $E\{Y_i\} = \beta_0 + \beta_1 X_i$ and whose variances are σ^2, the same for all levels of X. Further, any two responses Y_i and Y_j are uncorrelated.

Example

A consultant for an electrical distributor is studying the relationship between the number of bids requested by construction contractors for basic lighting equipment during a week and the time required to prepare the bids. Suppose that regression model (1.1) is applicable and is as follows:

$$Y_i = 9.5 + 2.1X_i + \varepsilon_i$$

FIGURE 1.6   **Illustration of Simple Linear Regression Model (1.1).**

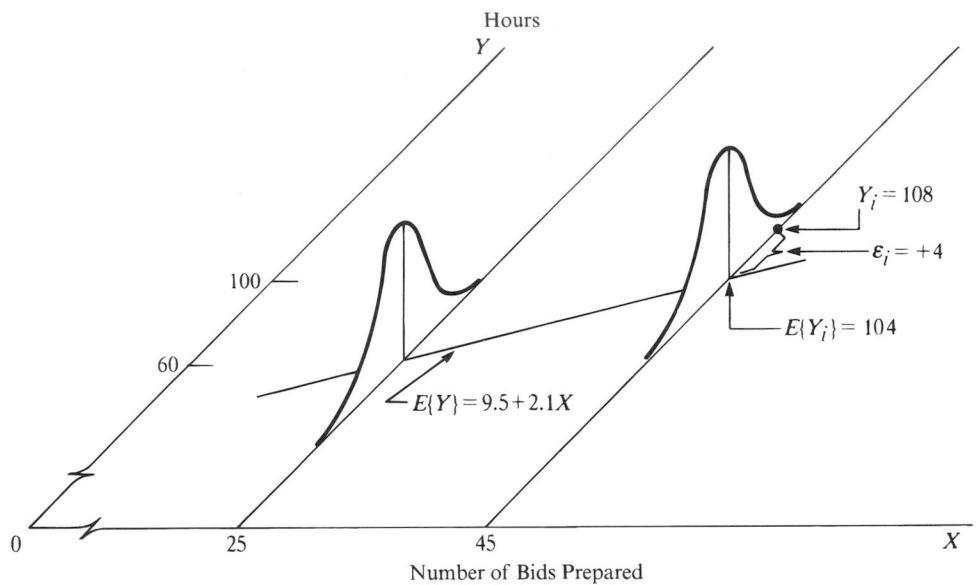

where X is the number of bids prepared in a week and Y is the number of hours required to prepare the bids. Figure 1.6 contains a presentation of the regression function:

$$E\{Y\} = 9.5 + 2.1X$$

Suppose that in the ith week, $X_i = 45$ bids are prepared and the actual number of hours required is $Y_i = 108$. In that case, the error term value is $\varepsilon_i = 4$, for we have:

$$E\{Y_i\} = 9.5 + 2.1(45) = 104$$

and:

$$Y_i = 108 = 104 + 4$$

Figure 1.6 displays the probability distribution of Y when $X = 45$ and indicates from where in this distribution the observation $Y_i = 108$ came. Note again that the error term ε_i is simply the deviation of Y_i from its mean value $E\{Y_i\}$.

Figure 1.6 also shows the probability distribution of Y when $X = 25$. Note that this distribution exhibits the same variability as the probability distribution when $X = 45$, in conformance with the requirements of regression model (1.1).

Meaning of Regression Parameters

The parameters β_0 and β_1 in regression model (1.1) are called *regression coefficients*. β_1 is the slope of the regression line. It indicates the change in the mean of the probability distribution of Y per unit increase in X. The parameter β_0 is the Y intercept of the regression line. When the scope of the model includes $X = 0$, β_0 gives the mean of the probability distribution of Y at $X = 0$. When the scope of the model does not cover $X = 0$, β_0 does not have any particular meaning as a separate term in the regression model.

FIGURE 1.7 **Meaning of Parameters of Simple Linear Regression Model.**

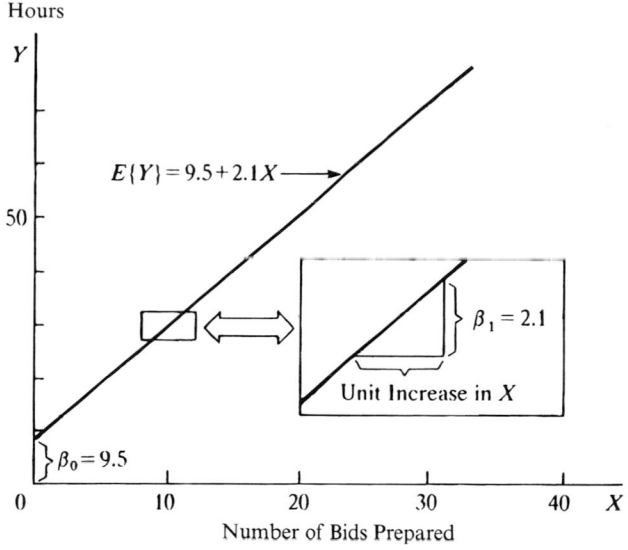

Example. Figure 1.7 shows the regression function:

$$E\{Y\} = 9.5 + 2.1X$$

for the electrical distributor example. The slope $\beta_1 = 2.1$ indicates that the preparation of one additional bid in a week leads to an increase in the mean of the probability distribution of Y of 2.1 hours.

The intercept $\beta_0 = 9.5$ indicates the value of the regression function at $X = 0$. However, since the linear regression model was formulated to apply to weeks where the number of bids prepared ranges from 20 to 80, β_0 does not have any intrinsic meaning of its own here. If the scope of the model were to be extended to X levels near zero, a model with a curvilinear regression function and some value of β_0 different from that for the linear regression function might well be required.

Alternative Versions of Regression Model

Sometimes it is convenient to write the simple linear regression model (1.1) in somewhat different, though equivalent, forms. Let X_0 be a *dummy variable* identically equal to 1. Then, we can write (1.1) as follows:

(1.5) $$Y_i = \beta_0 X_0 + \beta_1 X_i + \varepsilon_i \qquad \text{where } X_0 \equiv 1$$

This version of the model associates an X variable with each regression coefficient.

An alternative modification is to use for the predictor variable the deviation $X_i - \bar{X}$ rather than X_i. To leave model (1.1) unchanged, we need to write:

$$Y_i = \beta_0 + \beta_1(X_i - \bar{X}) + \beta_1 \bar{X} + \varepsilon_i$$
$$= (\beta_0 + \beta_1 \bar{X}) + \beta_1(X_i - \bar{X}) + \varepsilon_i$$
$$= \beta_0^* + \beta_1(X_i - \bar{X}) + \varepsilon_i$$

Thus, this alternative model version is:

$$(1.6) \qquad\qquad Y_i = \beta_0^* + \beta_1(X_i - \bar{X}) + \varepsilon_i$$

where:

$$(1.6a) \qquad\qquad \beta_0^* = \beta_0 + \beta_1 \bar{X}$$

We use models (1.1), (1.5), and (1.6) interchangeably as convenience dictates.

1.4   Data for Regression Analysis

Ordinarily, we do not know the values of the regression parameters β_0 and β_1 in regression model (1.1), and we need to estimate them from relevant data. Indeed, as we noted earlier, we frequently do not have adequate a priori knowledge of the appropriate predictor variables and of the functional form of the regression relation (e.g., linear or curvilinear), and we need to rely on an analysis of the data for developing a suitable regression model.

Data for regression analysis may be obtained from nonexperimental or experimental studies. We consider each of these in turn.

Observational Data

Observational data are data obtained from nonexperimental studies. Such studies do not control the explanatory or predictor variable(s) of interest. For example, company officials wished to study the relation between age of employee (X) and number of days of illness last year (Y). The needed data for use in the regression analysis were obtained from personnel records. Such data are observational data since the explanatory variable, age, is not controlled.

Regression analyses are frequently based on observational data, since often it is not feasible to conduct controlled experimentation. In the company personnel example just mentioned, for instance, it would not be possible to control age by assigning ages to persons.

A major limitation of observational data is that they often do not provide adequate information about cause-and-effect relationships. For example, a positive relation between age of employee and number of days of illness in the company personnel example may not imply that number of days of illness is the direct result of age. It might be that younger employees of the company primarily work indoors while older employees usually work outdoors, and that work location is more directly responsible for the number of days of illness than age.

Whenever a regression analysis is undertaken for purposes of description based on observational data, one should investigate whether explanatory variables other than those considered in the regression model might more directly explain cause-and-effect relationships.

Experimental Data

Frequently, it is possible to conduct a controlled experiment to provide data from which the regression parameters can be estimated. Consider, for instance, an insurance company that wishes to study the relation between productivity of its analysts in processing claims and length of training. Nine analysts are to be used in the study. Three of them will be selected at random and trained for two weeks, three for three weeks, and three for five weeks. The productivity of the analysts during the next 10 weeks will then be observed. The data so obtained will be experimental data because control is exercised over the explanatory variable, length of training.

When control over the explanatory variable(s) is exercised through random assignments, as in the productivity study example, the resulting experimental data provide much stronger information about cause-and-effect relationships than do observational data. The reason is that randomization tends to balance out the effects of any other variables that might affect the response variable, such as the effect of aptitude of the employee on productivity.

In the terminology of experimental design, the length of training assigned to an analyst in the productivity study example is called a *treatment*. The analysts to be included in the study are called the *experimental units*. Control over the explanatory variable(s) then consists of assigning a treatment to each of the experimental units by means of randomization.

Completely Randomized Design

The most basic type of statistical design for making randomized assignments of treatments to experimental units (or vice versa) is the *completely randomized design*. With this design, the assignments are made completely at random. This complete randomization provides that all combinations of experimental units assigned to the different treatments are equally likely, which implies that every experimental unit has an equal chance to receive any one of the treatments.

A completely randomized design is particularly useful when the experimental units are quite homogeneous. This design is very flexible; it accommodates any number of treatments and permits different sample sizes for different treatments. Its chief disadvantage is that, when the experimental units are heterogeneous, this design is not as efficient as some other statistical designs.

1.5   Overview of Steps in Regression Analysis

The regression models considered in this and subsequent chapters can be utilized either for observational data or for experimental data from a completely randomized design. (Regression analysis can also utilize data from other types of experimental designs, but the regression models presented here will need to be modified.) Whether the data are observational or experimental, it is essential that the conditions of the regression model be appropriate for the data at hand for the model to be applicable.

We begin our discussion of regression analysis by considering inferences about the regression parameters for the simple linear regression model (1.1). For the rare occasion where prior knowledge or theory alone enables us to determine the appropriate regression

FIGURE 1.8   **Typical Strategy for Regression Analysis.**

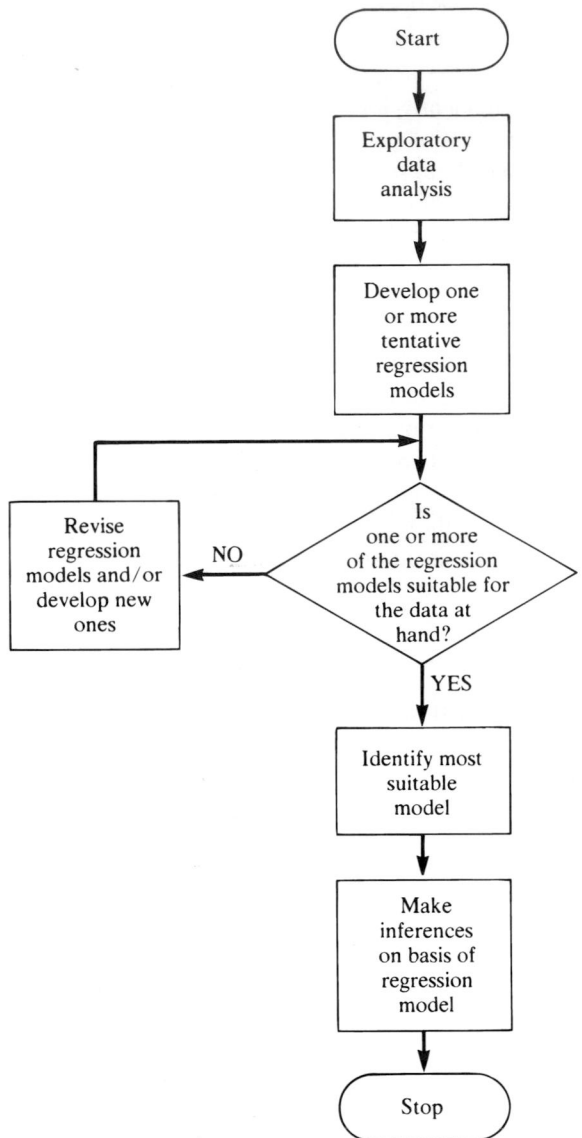

model, inferences based on the regression model are the first step in the regression analysis. In the usual situation, however, where we do not have adequate knowledge to specify the appropriate regression model in advance, the first step is an exploratory study of the data, as shown in the flowchart in Figure 1.8. Based on this initial exploratory analysis, one or more preliminary regression models are developed. These regression models are then examined for their appropriateness for the data at hand and revised, or new models are developed, until the investigator is satisfied with the suitability of a particular regression model. Only then are inferences made on the basis of this regression model, such as inferences about the regression parameters of the model or predictions of new observations.

We begin, for pedagogic reasons, with inferences based on the regression model that is finally considered to be appropriate. One must have an understanding of regression models and how they can be utilized before the issues involved in the development of an appropriate regression model can be fully explained.

1.6   Estimation of Regression Function

The observational or experimental data to be used for estimating the parameters of the regression function consist of observations on the explanatory or predictor variable X and the corresponding observations on the response variable Y. For each trial, there is an X observation and a Y observation. We denote the (X, Y) observations for the first trial as (X_1, Y_1), for the second trial as (X_2, Y_2), and in general for the ith trial as (X_i, Y_i), where $i = 1, \ldots, n$.

Example

In a small-scale study of persistence, an experimenter gave three subjects a very difficult task. Data on the age of the subject (X) and on the number of attempts to accomplish the task before giving up (Y) follow:

Subject i:	1	2	3
Age X_i:	20	55	30
Number of attempts Y_i:	5	12	10

In terms of the notation to be employed, there were $n = 3$ subjects in this study, the observations for the first subject were $(X_1, Y_1) = (20, 5)$, and similarly for the other subjects.

Method of Least Squares

To find "good" estimators of the regression parameters β_0 and β_1, we employ the method of least squares. For the observations (X_i, Y_i) for each case, the method of least squares considers the deviation of Y_i from its expected value:

(1.7)
$$Y_i - (\beta_0 + \beta_1 X_i)$$

In particular, the method of least squares requires that we consider the sum of the n squared deviations. This criterion is denoted by Q:

(1.8)
$$Q = \sum_{i=1}^{n} (Y_i - \beta_0 - \beta_1 X_i)^2$$

According to the method of least squares, the estimators of β_0 and β_1 are those values b_0 and b_1, respectively, that minimize the criterion Q for the given sample observations $(X_1, Y_1), (X_2, Y_2), \ldots, (X_n, Y_n)$.

FIGURE 1.9   **Illustration of Least Squares Criterion Q for Fit of a Regression Line—Persistence Study Example.**

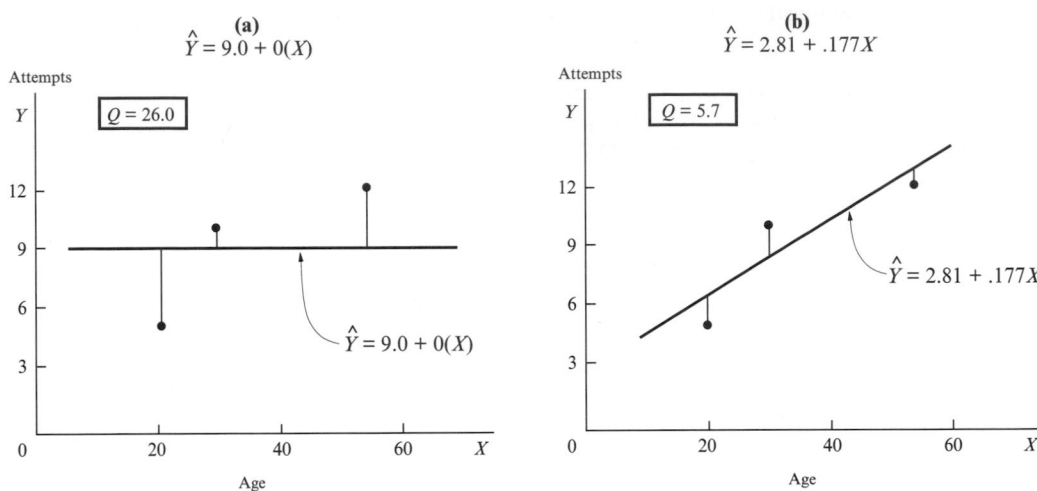

Example.   Figure 1.9a presents the scatter plot of the data for the persistence study example and the arbitrary regression line:

$$\hat{Y} = 9.0 + 0(X)$$

where $\hat{Y}$ denotes the ordinate of the regression line. Note that this arbitrary regression line uses estimates $b_0 = 9.0$ and $b_1 = 0$. Clearly, this regression line is not a good fit, as evidenced by the large vertical deviations of two of the Y observations from the corresponding ordinates $\hat{Y}$ of the regression line. The deviation for the first subject, for which $(X_1, Y_1) = (20, 5)$, is:

$$Y_1 - (b_0 + b_1 X_1) = 5 - [9.0 + 0(20)] = 5 - 9.0 = -4$$

The sum of the squared deviations for the three cases is:

$$Q = (5 - 9.0)^2 + (12 - 9.0)^2 + (10 - 9.0)^2 = 26.0$$

Figure 1.9b shows the same data with the regression line:

$$\hat{Y} = 2.81 + .177X$$

The fit of this regression line is clearly much better. The vertical deviation for the first case now is:

$$Y_1 - (b_0 + b_1 X_1) = 5 - [2.81 + .177(20)] = 5 - 6.35 = -1.35$$

and the criterion Q is much reduced:

$$Q = (5 - 6.35)^2 + (12 - 12.55)^2 + (10 - 8.12)^2 = 5.7$$

Thus, a better fit of the regression line to the data corresponds to a smaller sum Q.

The objective of the method of least squares is to find estimates b_0 and b_1 for β_0 and β_1, respectively, for which Q is a minimum. In a certain sense, to be discussed shortly, these estimates will provide a "good" fit of the linear regression function. The regression line in Figure 1.9b is, in fact, the least squares regression line.

Least Squares Estimators.   The estimators b_0 and b_1 that satisfy the least squares criterion can be found in two basic ways:

1. Numerical search procedures can be used that evaluate in a systematic fashion the least squares criterion Q for different estimates b_0 and b_1 until the ones that minimize Q are found. This approach was illustrated in Figure 1.9 for the persistence study example.

2. Analytical procedures can often be used to find the values of b_0 and b_1 that minimize Q. The analytical approach is feasible when the regression model is not mathematically complex.

Using the analytical approach, it can be shown for regression model (1.1) that the values b_0 and b_1 that minimize Q for any particular set of sample data are given by the following simultaneous equations:

(1.9a)
$$\sum Y_i = nb_0 + b_1 \sum X_i$$

(1.9b)
$$\sum X_i Y_i = b_0 \sum X_i + b_1 \sum X_i^2$$

The equations (1.9a) and (1.9b) are called *normal equations*; b_0 and b_1 are called *point estimators* of β_0 and β_1, respectively.

The normal equations (1.9) can be solved simultaneously for b_0 and b_1:

(1.10a)
$$b_1 = \frac{\Sigma(X_i - \bar{X})(Y_i - \bar{Y})}{\Sigma(X_i - \bar{X})^2}$$

(1.10b)
$$b_0 = \frac{1}{n}\left(\sum Y_i - b_1 \sum X_i\right) = \bar{Y} - b_1 \bar{X}$$

where $\bar{X}$ and $\bar{Y}$ are the means of the X_i and the Y_i observations, respectively. While alternative expressions for the formulas for the least squares estimators b_1 and b_0 are available, formulas (1.10a) and (1.10b) are the appropriate ones to use for computational accuracy. Computer calculations generally are based on many digits to obtain accurate values for b_0 and b_1.

Note

The normal equations (1.9) can be derived by calculus. For given sample observations (X_i, Y_i), the quantity Q in (1.8) is a function of β_0 and β_1. The values of β_0 and β_1 that minimize Q can be derived by differentiating (1.8) with respect to β_0 and β_1. We obtain:

$$\frac{\partial Q}{\partial \beta_0} = -2\sum(Y_i - \beta_0 - \beta_1 X_i)$$

$$\frac{\partial Q}{\partial \beta_1} = -2\sum X_i(Y_i - \beta_0 - \beta_1 X_i)$$

We then set these partial derivatives equal to zero, using b_0 and b_1 to denote the particular values of β_0 and β_1 that minimize Q:

$$-2 \sum (Y_i - b_0 - b_1 X_i) = 0$$

$$-2 \sum X_i (Y_i - b_0 - b_1 X_i) = 0$$

Simplifying, we obtain:

$$\sum_{i=1}^{n} (Y_i - b_0 - b_1 X_i) = 0$$

$$\sum_{i=1}^{n} X_i (Y_i - b_0 - b_1 X_i) = 0$$

Expanding, we have:

$$\sum Y_i - nb_0 - b_1 \sum X_i = 0$$

$$\sum X_i Y_i - b_0 \sum X_i - b_1 \sum X_i^2 = 0$$

from which the normal equations (1.9) are obtained by rearranging terms.

A test of the second partial derivatives will show that a minimum is obtained with the least squares estimators b_0 and b_1. ∎

Properties of Least Squares Estimators. An important theorem, called the *Gauss-Markov theorem*, states:

(1.11)   Under the conditions of regression model (1.1), the least squares estimators b_0 and b_1 in (1.10) are unbiased and have minimum variance among all unbiased linear estimators.

This theorem, proven in the next chapter, states first that b_0 and b_1 are unbiased estimators. Hence:

$$E\{b_0\} = \beta_0 \qquad E\{b_1\} = \beta_1$$

so that neither estimator tends to overestimate or underestimate systematically.

Second, the theorem states that the estimators b_0 and b_1 are more precise (i.e., their sampling distributions are less variable) than any other estimators belonging to the class of unbiased estimators that are linear functions of the observations $Y_1, \ldots, Y_n$. The estimators b_0 and b_1 are such linear functions of the Y_i. Consider, for instance, b_1. We have from (1.10a):

$$b_1 = \frac{\Sigma(X_i - \bar{X})(Y_i - \bar{Y})}{\Sigma(X_i - \bar{X})^2}$$

It will be shown in Chapter 2 that this expression is equal to:

$$b_1 = \frac{\Sigma(X_i - \bar{X})Y_i}{\Sigma(X_i - \bar{X})^2} = \sum k_i Y_i$$

where:

$$k_i = \frac{X_i - \bar{X}}{\Sigma(X_i - \bar{X})^2}$$

TABLE 1.1   **Data on Lot Size and Work Hours and Needed Calculations for Least Squares Estimates—Toluca Company Example.**

	(1) Lot Size	(2) Work Hours	(3)	(4)	(5)	(6)	(7)
Run i	X_i	Y_i	$X_i - \bar{X}$	$Y_i - \bar{Y}$	$(X_i - \bar{X})(Y_i - \bar{Y})$	$(X_i - \bar{X})^2$	$(Y_i - \bar{Y})^2$
1	80	399	10	86.72	867.2	100	7,520.4
2	30	121	−40	−191.28	7,651.2	1,600	36,588.0
3	50	221	−20	−91.28	1,825.6	400	8,332.0
...	...	...	...	...	...	...	...
23	40	244	−30	−68.28	2,048.4	900	4,662.2
24	80	342	10	29.72	297.2	100	883.3
25	70	323	0	10.72	0.0	0	114.9
Total	1,750	7,807	0	0	70,690	19,800	307,203
Mean	70.0	312.28					

Since the k_i are known constants (because the X_i are known constants), b_1 is a linear combination of the Y_i and hence is a linear estimator.

In the same fashion, it can be shown that b_0 is a linear estimator. Among all linear estimators that are unbiased then, b_0 and b_1 have the smallest variability in repeated samples in which the X levels remain unchanged.

Example

The Toluca Company manufactures refrigeration equipment as well as many replacement parts. In the past, one of the replacement parts has been produced periodically in lots of varying sizes. When a cost improvement program was undertaken, company officials wished to determine the optimum lot size for producing this part. The production of this part involves setting up the production process (which must be done no matter what is the lot size) and machining and assembly operations. One key input for the model to ascertain the optimum lot size was the relationship between lot size and labor hours required to produce the lot. To determine this relationship, data on lot size and work hours for 25 recent production runs were utilized. The production conditions were stable during the six-months period in which the 25 runs were made and were expected to continue to be the same during the next three years, the planning period for which the cost improvement program was being conducted.

Table 1.1 contains a portion of the data on lot size and work hours in columns 1 and 2. Note that all lot sizes are multiples of 10, a result of company policy to facilitate the administration of the parts production. Figure 1.10a shows a SYSTAT scatter plot of the data. We see that the lot sizes ranged from 20 to 120 units and that none of the production runs was outlying in the sense of being either unusually small or large. The scatter plot also indicates that the relationship between lot size and work hours is reasonably linear. We also see that no observations on work hours are unusually small or large, with reference to the relationship between lot size and work hours.

FIGURE 1.10 **SYSTAT Scatter Plot and Fitted Regression Line—Toluca Company Example.**

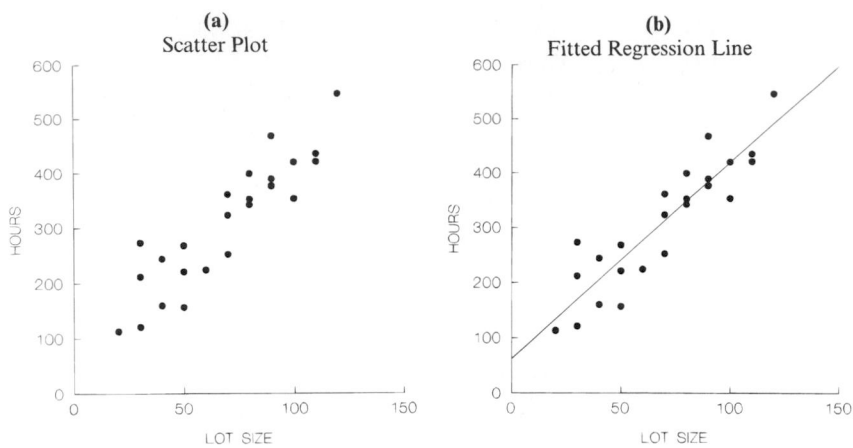

To calculate the least squares estimates b_0 and b_1 in (1.10), we require the deviations $X_i - \bar{X}$ and $Y_i - \bar{Y}$. These are given in columns 3 and 4 of Table 1.1. We also require the cross-product terms $(X_i - \bar{X})(Y_i - \bar{Y})$ and the squared deviations $(X_i - \bar{X})^2$; these are shown in columns 5 and 6. The squared deviations $(Y_i - \bar{Y})^2$ in column 7 are for later use.

We see from Table 1.1 that the basic quantities needed to calculate the least squares estimates are as follows:

$$\sum (X_i - \bar{X})(Y_i - \bar{Y}) = 70{,}690$$

$$\sum (X_i - \bar{X})^2 = 19{,}800$$

$$\bar{X} = 70.0$$

$$\bar{Y} = 312.28$$

Using (1.10) we obtain:

$$b_1 = \frac{\Sigma (X_i - \bar{X})(Y_i - \bar{Y})}{\Sigma (X_i - \bar{X})^2} = \frac{70{,}690}{19{,}800} = 3.5702$$

$$b_0 = \bar{Y} - b_1 \bar{X} = 312.28 - 3.5702(70.0) = 62.37$$

Thus, we estimate that the mean number of work hours increases by 3.57 hours for each additional unit produced in the lot. This estimate applies to the range of lot sizes in the data from which the estimates were derived, namely to lot sizes ranging from about 20 to about 120.

Figure 1.11 contains a portion of the MINITAB regression output for the Toluca Company example. The estimates b_0 and b_1 are shown in the column labeled Coef, corresponding to the lines Constant and X, respectively. The additional information shown in Figure 1.11 will be explained later.

FIGURE 1.11   **Portion of MINITAB Regression Output—Toluca Company Example.**

```
The regression equation is
Y = 62.4 + 3.57 X

Predictor          Coef        Stdev      t-ratio          p
Constant          62.37        26.18         2.38      0.026
X                3.5702       0.3470        10.29      0.000

s = 48.82         R-sq = 82.2%         R-sq(adj) = 81.4%
```

Point Estimation of Mean Response

Estimated Regression Function.   Given sample estimators b_0 and b_1 of the parameters in the regression function (1.3):

$$E\{Y\} = \beta_0 + \beta_1 X$$

we estimate the regression function as follows:

$$(1.12) \qquad\qquad \hat{Y} = b_0 + b_1 X$$

where $\hat{Y}$ (read Y hat) is the value of the estimated regression function at the level X of the predictor variable.

We call a *value* of the response variable a *response* and $E\{Y\}$ the *mean response*. Thus, the mean response stands for the mean of the probability distribution of Y corresponding to the level X of the predictor variable. $\hat{Y}$ then is a point estimator of the mean response when the level of the predictor variable is X. It can be shown as an extension of the Gauss-Markov theorem (1.11) that $\hat{Y}$ is an unbiased estimator of $E\{Y\}$, with minimum variance in the class of unbiased linear estimators.

For the cases in the study, we will call $\hat{Y}_i$:

$$(1.13) \qquad\qquad \hat{Y}_i = b_0 + b_1 X_i \qquad i = 1, \ldots, n$$

the *fitted value* for the ith case. Thus, the fitted value $\hat{Y}_i$ is to be viewed in distinction to the *observed value* Y_i.

Example.   For the Toluca Company example, we found that the least squares estimates of the regression coefficients are:

$$b_0 = 62.37 \qquad b_1 = 3.5702$$

Hence, the estimated regression function is:

$$\hat{Y} = 62.37 + 3.5702X$$

This estimated regression function is plotted in Figure 1.10b. It appears to be a good description of the statistical relationship between lot size and work hours.

TABLE 1.2   **Fitted Values, Residuals, and Squared Residuals—Toluca Company Example.**

Run i	(1) Lot Size X_i	(2) Work Hours Y_i	(3) Estimated Mean Response $\hat{Y}_i$	(4) Residual $Y_i - \hat{Y}_i = e_i$	(5) Squared Residual $(Y_i - \hat{Y}_i)^2 = e_i^2$
1	80	399	347.98	51.02	2,603.0
2	30	121	169.47	−48.47	2,349.3
3	50	221	240.88	−19.88	395.2
...	...	...	...	...	...
23	40	244	205.17	38.83	1,507.8
24	80	342	347.98	−5.98	35.8
25	70	323	312.28	10.72	114.9
Total	1,750	7,807	7,807	0	54,825

To estimate the mean response for any level X of the predictor variable, we simply substitute that value of X in the estimated regression function. Suppose that we are interested in the mean number of work hours required when the lot size is $X = 65$; our point estimate is:

$$\hat{Y} = 62.37 + 3.5702(65) = 294.4$$

Thus, we estimate that the mean number of work hours required for production runs of $X = 65$ units is 294.4 hours. We interpret this to mean that if many lots of 65 units are produced under the conditions of the 25 runs on which the estimated regression function is based, the mean labor time for these lots is about 294 hours. Of course, the labor time for any one lot of size 65 is likely to fall above or below the mean response because of inherent variability in the production system, as represented by the error term in the model.

Fitted values for the sample cases are obtained by substituting the appropriate X values into the estimated regression function. For the first sample case, we have $X_1 = 80$. Hence, the fitted value for the first case is:

$$\hat{Y}_1 = 62.37 + 3.5702(80) = 348.0$$

This compares with the observed work hours of $Y_1 = 399$. Table 1.2 contains the observed and fitted values for a portion of the Toluca Company data in columns 2 and 3, respectively.

Alternative Model (1.6).   When the alternative regression model (1.6):

$$Y_i = \beta_0^* + \beta_1(X_i - \bar{X}) + \varepsilon_i$$

is to be utilized, the least squares estimator b_1 of β_1 remains the same as before. The least squares estimator of $\beta_0^* = \beta_0 + \beta_1 \bar{X}$ becomes, using (1.10b):

(1.14) $$b_0^* = b_0 + b_1 \bar{X} = (\bar{Y} - b_1 \bar{X}) + b_1 \bar{X} = \bar{Y}$$

Hence, the estimated regression function for alternative model (1.6) is:

$$(1.15) \qquad\qquad \hat{Y} = \bar{Y} + b_1(X - \bar{X})$$

In the Toluca Company example, $\bar{Y} = 312.28$ and $\bar{X} = 70.0$ (Table 1.1). Hence, the estimated regression function in alternative form is:

$$\hat{Y} = 312.28 + 3.5702(X - 70.0)$$

For the first lot in our example, $X_1 = 80$; hence, we estimate the mean response to be:

$$\hat{Y}_1 = 312.28 + 3.5702(80 - 70.0) = 348.0$$

which, of course, is identical to our earlier result.

Residuals

The ith *residual* is the difference between the observed value Y_i and the corresponding fitted value $\hat{Y}_i$. This residual is denoted by e_i and is defined in general as follows:

$$(1.16) \qquad\qquad e_i = Y_i - \hat{Y}_i$$

For regression model (1.1), the residual e_i becomes:

$$(1.16a) \qquad\qquad e_i = Y_i \quad (b_0 + b_1 X_i) = Y_i - b_0 - b_1 X_i$$

The calculation of the residuals for the Toluca Company example is shown for a portion of the data in Table 1.2. We see that the residual for the first case is:

$$e_1 = Y_1 - \hat{Y}_1 = 399 - 347.98 = 51.02$$

The residuals for the first two cases are illustrated graphically in Figure 1.12. Note in this figure that the magnitude of a residual is represented by the vertical deviation of the Y_i observation from the corresponding point on the estimated regression function (i.e., from the corresponding fitted value $\hat{Y}_i$).

We need to distinguish between the model error term value $\varepsilon_i = Y_i - E\{Y_i\}$ and the residual $e_i = Y_i - \hat{Y}_i$. The former involves the vertical deviation of Y_i from the unknown true regression line and hence is unknown. On the other hand, the residual is the vertical deviation of Y_i from the fitted value $\hat{Y}_i$ on the estimated regression line, and it is known.

Residuals are highly useful for studying whether a given regression model is appropriate for the data at hand. We discuss this use in Chapter 3.

Properties of Fitted Regression Line

The estimated regression line (1.12) fitted by the method of least squares has a number of properties worth noting. These properties of the least squares estimated regression function do not apply to all regression models, as we shall see in Chapter 4.

1. The sum of the residuals is zero:

$$(1.17) \qquad\qquad \sum_{i=1}^{n} e_i = 0$$

FIGURE 1.12   Illustration of Residuals—Toluca Company Example (not drawn to scale).

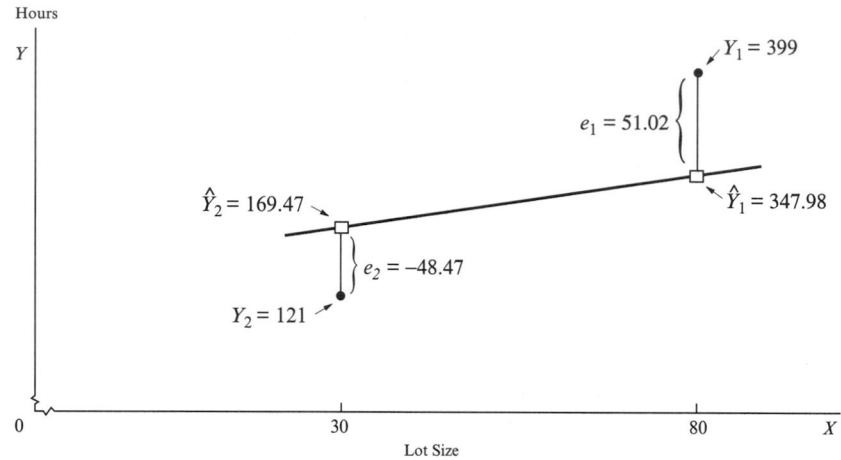

Table 1.2, column 4, illustrates this property for the Toluca Company example. Rounding errors may, of course, be present in any particular case, resulting in a sum of the residuals that does not equal zero exactly.

2. The sum of the squared residuals, Σe_i^2, is a minimum. This was the requirement to be satisfied in deriving the least squares estimators of the regression parameters since the criterion Q in (1.8) to be minimized equals Σe_i^2 when the least squares estimators b_0 and b_1 are used for estimating β_0 and β_1.

3. The sum of the observed values Y_i equals the sum of the fitted values $\hat{Y}_i$:

$$(1.18) \qquad \sum_{i=1}^{n} Y_i = \sum_{i=1}^{n} \hat{Y}_i$$

This property is illustrated in Table 1.2, columns 2 and 3, for the Toluca Company example. It follows that the mean of the fitted values $\hat{Y}_i$ is the same as the mean of the observed values Y_i, namely, $\bar{Y}$.

4. The sum of the weighted residuals is zero when the residual in the ith trial is weighted by the level of the predictor variable in the ith trial:

$$(1.19) \qquad \sum_{i=1}^{n} X_i e_i = 0$$

5. A consequence of properties (1.17) and (1.19) is that the sum of the weighted residuals is zero when the residual in the ith trial is weighted by the fitted value of the response variable for the ith trial:

$$(1.20) \qquad \sum_{i=1}^{n} \hat{Y}_i e_i = 0$$

6. The regression line always goes through the point $(\bar{X}, \bar{Y})$.

Note

The six properties of the fitted regression line follow directly from the least squares normal equations (1.9). For example, property 1 in (1.17) is proven as follows:

$$\sum e_i = \sum(Y_i - b_0 - b_1 X_i) = \sum Y_i - nb_0 - b_1 \sum X_i$$

$$= 0 \qquad \text{by the first normal equation (1.9a)}$$

Property 6, that the regression line always goes through the point $(\bar{X}, \bar{Y})$, can be demonstrated easily from the alternative form (1.15) of the estimated regression line. When $X = \bar{X}$, we have:

$$\hat{Y} = \bar{Y} + b_1(X - \bar{X}) = \bar{Y} + b_1(\bar{X} - \bar{X}) = \bar{Y} \qquad \blacksquare$$

1.7   Estimation of Error Terms Variance σ^2

The variance σ^2 of the error terms ε_i in regression model (1.1) needs to be estimated to obtain an indication of the variability of the probability distributions of Y. In addition, as we shall see in the next chapter, a variety of inferences concerning the regression function and the prediction of Y require an estimate of σ^2.

Point Estimator of σ^2

To lay the basis for developing an estimator of σ^2 for regression model (1.1), we first consider the simpler problem of sampling from a single population.

Single Population.   We know that the variance σ^2 of a single population is estimated by the sample variance s^2. In obtaining the sample variance s^2, we consider the deviation of an observation Y_i from the estimated mean $\bar{Y}$, square it, and then sum all such squared deviations:

$$\sum_{i=1}^{n}(Y_i - \bar{Y})^2$$

Such a sum is called a *sum of squares*. The sum of squares is then divided by the degrees of freedom associated with it. This number is $n - 1$ here, because one degree of freedom is lost by using $\bar{Y}$ as an estimate of the unknown population mean μ. The resulting estimator is the usual sample variance:

$$s^2 = \frac{\sum_{i=1}^{n}(Y_i - \bar{Y})^2}{n - 1}$$

which is an unbiased estimator of the variance σ^2 of an infinite population. The sample variance is often called a *mean square*, because a sum of squares has been divided by the appropriate number of degrees of freedom.

Regression Model.   The logic of developing an estimator of σ^2 for the regression model is the same as when sampling a single population. Recall in this connection from (1.4) that the variance of each observation Y_i for regression model (1.1) is σ^2, the same as that of each error term ε_i. We again need to calculate a sum of squared deviations, but must recognize that the Y_i now come from different probability distributions with different means that depend upon the level X_i. Thus, the deviation of an observation Y_i must be calculated around its own estimated mean $\hat{Y}_i$. Hence, the deviations are the residuals:

$$Y_i - \hat{Y}_i = e_i$$

and the appropriate sum of squares, denoted by *SSE*, is:

$$(1.21) \qquad SSE = \sum_{i=1}^{n}(Y_i - \hat{Y}_i)^2 = \sum_{i=1}^{n} e_i^2$$

where *SSE* stands for *error sum of squares* or *residual sum of squares*.

The sum of squares *SSE* has $n - 2$ degrees of freedom associated with it. Two degrees of freedom are lost because both β_0 and β_1 had to be estimated in obtaining the estimated means $\hat{Y}_i$. Hence, the appropriate mean square, denoted by *MSE*, is:

$$(1.22) \qquad MSE = \frac{SSE}{n-2} = \frac{\Sigma(Y_i - \hat{Y}_i)^2}{n-2} = \frac{\Sigma e_i^2}{n-2}$$

where *MSE* stands for *error mean square* or *residual mean square*.

It can be shown that *MSE* is an unbiased estimator of σ^2 for regression model (1.1):

$$(1.23) \qquad E\{MSE\} = \sigma^2$$

An estimator of the standard deviation σ is simply $\sqrt{MSE}$, the positive square root of *MSE*.

Note

A number of alternative computational formulas for *SSE* are available. However, computational accuracy is best achieved by use of formula (1.21). Computer calculations utilize many digits in making this calculation.   ■

Example

We will calculate *SSE* for the Toluca Company example by (1.21). The residuals were obtained earlier in Table 1.2, column 4. This table also shows the squared residuals in column 5. From these results, we obtain:

$$SSE = 54,825$$

Since $25 - 2 = 23$ degrees of freedom are associated with *SSE*, we find:

$$MSE = \frac{54,825}{23} = 2,384$$

Finally, a point estimate of σ, the standard deviation of the probability distribution of Y for any X, is $\sqrt{2,384} = 48.8$ hours.

Consider again the case where the lot size is $X = 65$ units. We found earlier that the mean of the probability distribution of Y for this lot size is estimated to be 294.4 hours. Now, we have the additional information that the standard deviation of this distribution is estimated to be 48.8 hours. This estimate is shown in the MINITAB output in Figure 1.11, labeled as s. We see that the variation in work hours from lot to lot for lots of 65 units is quite substantial (49 hours) compared to the mean of the distribution (294 hours).

1.8   Normal Error Regression Model

No matter what may be the form of the distribution of the error terms ε_i (and hence of the Y_i), the least squares method provides unbiased point estimators of β_0 and β_1 that have minimum variance among all unbiased linear estimators. To set up interval estimates and make tests, however, we need to make an assumption about the form of the distribution of the ε_i. The standard assumption is that the error terms ε_i are normally distributed, and we will adopt it here. A normal error term greatly simplifies the theory of regression analysis and, as we shall explain shortly, is justifiable in many real-world situations where regression analysis is applied.

Model

The normal error regression model is as follows:

$$(1.24) \qquad\qquad Y_i = \beta_0 + \beta_1 X_i + \varepsilon_i$$

where:

Y_i is the observed response in the ith trial

X_i is a known constant, the level of the predictor variable in the ith trial

β_0 and β_1 are parameters

ε_i are independent $N(0, \sigma^2)$

$i = 1, \ldots, n$

Comments

1. The symbol $N(0, \sigma^2)$ stands for normally distributed, with mean 0 and variance σ^2.

2. The normal error model (1.24) is the same as regression model (1.1) with unspecified error distribution, except that model (1.24) assumes that the errors ε_i are normally distributed.

3. Because regression model (1.24) assumes that the errors are normally distributed, the assumption of uncorrelatedness of the ε_i in regression model (1.1) becomes one of independence in the normal error model.

4. Regression model (1.24) implies that the Y_i are independent normal random variables, with mean $E\{Y_i\} = \beta_0 + \beta_1 X_i$ and variance σ^2. Figure 1.6 pictures this normal error model. Each of the probability distributions of Y in Figure 1.6 is normally distributed, with constant variability, and the regression function is linear.

5. The normality assumption for the error terms is justifiable in many situations because the error terms frequently represent the effects of factors omitted from the model that affect the response to some extent and that vary at random without reference to the variable X. For instance, in the Toluca Company example, the effects of such factors as time lapse since the last

FIGURE 1.13   **Densities for Sample Observations for Two Possible Values of μ—$Y_1 = 250$, $Y_2 = 265$, $Y_3 = 259$.**

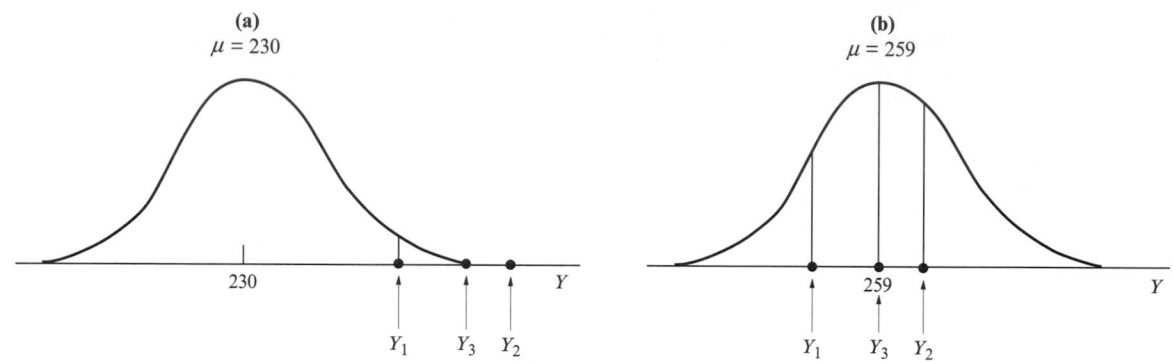

production run, particular machines used, season of the year, and personnel employed, could vary more or less at random from run to run, independent of lot size. Also, there might be random measurement errors in the recording of Y, the hours required. Insofar as these random effects have a degree of mutual independence, the composite error term ε_i representing all these factors would tend to comply with the central limit theorem and the error term distribution would approach normality as the number of factor effects becomes large.

A second reason why the normality assumption of the error terms is frequently justifiable is that the estimation and testing procedures to be discussed in the next chapter are based on the t distribution and are usually only sensitive to large departures from normality. Thus, unless the departures from normality are serious, particularly with respect to skewness, the actual confidence coefficients and risks of errors will be close to the levels for exact normality.   ■

Estimation of Parameters by Method of Maximum Likelihood

When the functional form of the probability distribution of the error terms is specified, estimators of the parameters β_0, β_1, and σ^2 can be obtained by the *method of maximum likelihood*. Essentially, the method of maximum likelihood chooses as estimates those values of the parameters that are most consistent with the sample data. We explain the method of maximum likelihood first for the simple case when a single population with one parameter is sampled. Then we explain this method for regression models.

Single Population.   Consider a normal population whose standard deviation is known to be $\sigma = 10$ and whose mean is unknown. A random sample of $n = 3$ observations is selected from the population and yields the results $Y_1 = 250$, $Y_2 = 265$, $Y_3 = 259$. We now wish to ascertain which value of μ is most consistent with the sample data. Consider $\mu = 230$. Figure 1.13a shows the normal distribution with $\mu = 230$ and $\sigma = 10$; also shown there are the locations of the three sample observations. Note that the sample observations would be in the tail of the distribution if μ were equal to 230. Since these are unlikely occurrences, $\mu = 230$ is not consistent with the sample data.

Figure 1.13b shows the population and the locations of the sample data if μ were equal to 259. Now the observations would be in the center of the distribution and much more likely. Hence, $\mu = 259$ is more consistent with the sample data than $\mu = 230$.

The method of maximum likelihood uses the density of the probability distribution at Y_i (i.e., the height of the curve at Y_i) as a measure of consistency for the observation Y_i. Consider observation Y_1 in our example. If Y_1 is in the tail, as in Figure 1.13a, the height of the curve will be small. If Y_1 is nearer to the center of the distribution, as in Figure 1.13b, the height will be larger. Using the density function for a normal probability distribution in (A.34) in Appendix A, we find the densities for Y_1, denoted by f_1, for the two cases of μ in Figure 1.13 as follows:

$$\mu = 230: \qquad f_1 = \frac{1}{\sqrt{2\pi}(10)} \exp\left[-\frac{1}{2}\left(\frac{250-230}{10}\right)^2\right] = .005399$$

$$\mu = 259: \qquad f_1 = \frac{1}{\sqrt{2\pi}(10)} \exp\left[-\frac{1}{2}\left(\frac{250-259}{10}\right)^2\right] = .026609$$

The densities for all three sample observations for the two cases of μ are as follows:

	$\mu = 230$	$\mu = 259$
f_1	.005399	.026609
f_2	.000087	.033322
f_3	.000595	.039894

The method of maximum likelihood uses the product of the densities (i.e., here, the product of the three heights) as the measure of consistency of the parameter value with the sample data. The product is called the *likelihood value* of the parameter value μ and is denoted by $L(\mu)$. If the value of μ is consistent with the sample data, the densities will be relatively large and so will be the product (i.e., the likelihood value). If the value of μ is not consistent with the data, the densities will be small and the product $L(\mu)$ will be small.

For our simple example, the likelihood values are as follows for the two cases of μ:

$$L(\mu = 230) = .005399(.000087)(.000595) = .279 \times 10^{-9}$$

$$L(\mu = 259) = .026609(.033322)(.039894) = .0000354$$

Since the likelihood value $L(\mu = 230)$ is a very small number, it is shown in scientific notation, which indicates that there are nine zeros after the decimal place before 279. Note that $L(\mu = 230)$ is much smaller than $L(\mu = 259)$, indicating that $\mu = 259$ is much more consistent with the sample data than $\mu = 230$.

The method of maximum likelihood chooses as the maximum likelihood estimate that value of μ for which the likelihood value is largest. Just as for the method of least squares, there are two methods of finding maximum likelihood estimates: by a systematic numerical search and by use of an analytical solution. For some problems, analytical solutions for the maximum likelihood estimators are available. For others, a computerized numerical search must be conducted.

For our example, an analytical solution is available. It can be shown that for a normal population the maximum likelihood estimator of μ is the sample mean $\bar{Y}$. In our example, $\bar{Y} = 258$ and the maximum likelihood estimate of μ therefore is 258. The likelihood value of $\mu = 258$ is $L(\mu = 258) = .0000359$, which is slightly larger than the likelihood value of .0000354 for $\mu = 259$ that we had calculated earlier.

FIGURE 1.14   **Likelihood Function for Estimation of Mean of Normal Population—$Y_1 = 250$, $Y_2 = 265$, $Y_3 = 259$.**

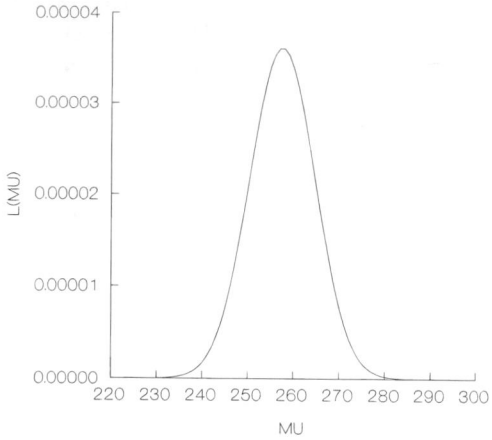

The product of the densities viewed as a function of the unknown parameters is called the *likelihood function*. For our example, where $\sigma = 10$, the likelihood function is:

$$L(\mu) =$$

$$\left[\frac{1}{\sqrt{2\pi}(10)} \right]^3 \exp\left[-\frac{1}{2}\left(\frac{250 - \mu}{10} \right)^2 \right] \exp\left[-\frac{1}{2}\left(\frac{265 - \mu}{10} \right)^2 \right] \exp\left[-\frac{1}{2}\left(\frac{259 - \mu}{10} \right)^2 \right]$$

Figure 1.14 shows a computer plot of the likelihood function for our example. It is based on the calculation of likelihood values $L(\mu)$ for many values of μ. Note that the likelihood values at $\mu = 230$ and $\mu = 259$ correspond to the ones we determined earlier. Also note that the likelihood function reaches a maximum at $\mu = 258$.

The fact that the likelihood function in Figure 1.14 is relatively peaked in the neighborhood of the maximum likelihood estimate $\bar{Y} = 258$ is of particular interest. Note, for instance, that for $\mu = 250$ or $\mu = 266$, the likelihood value is already only a little more than one-half as large as the likelihood value at $\mu = 258$. This indicates that the maximum likelihood estimate here is relatively precise because values of μ not near the maximum likelihood estimate $\bar{Y} = 258$ are much less consistent with the sample data. When the likelihood function is relatively flat in a fairly wide region around the maximum likelihood estimate, many values of the parameter are almost as consistent with the sample data as the maximum likelihood estimate, and the maximum likelihood estimate would therefore be relatively imprecise.

Regression Model.   The concepts just presented for maximum likelihood estimation of a population mean carry over directly to the estimation of the parameters of normal error regression model (1.24). For this model, each Y_i observation is normally distributed with mean $\beta_0 + \beta_1 X_i$ and standard deviation σ. To illustrate the method of maximum likelihood estimation here, consider the earlier persistence study example on page 17. For simplicity, let us suppose that we know $\sigma = 2.5$. We wish to determine the likelihood value for the parameter values $\beta_0 = 0$ and $\beta_1 = .5$. For subject 1, $X_1 = 20$ and hence the mean

FIGURE 1.15 **Densities for Sample Observations if $\beta_0 = 0$ and $\beta_1 = 5$—Persistence Study Example.**

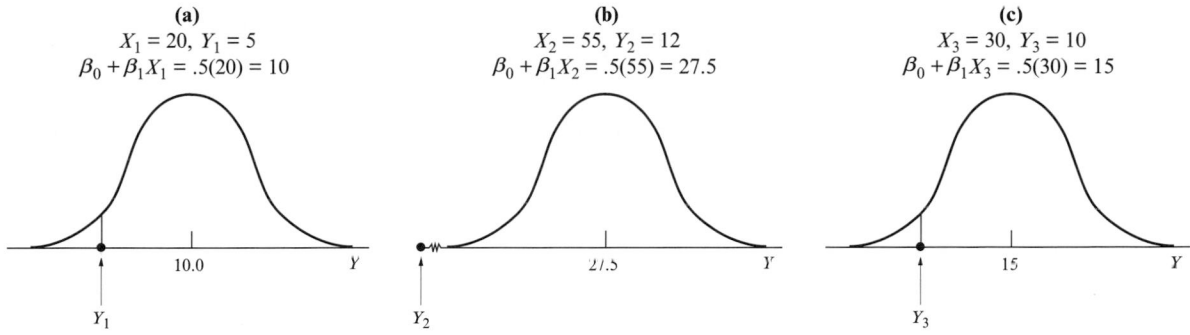

(a)
$X_1 = 20, Y_1 = 5$
$\beta_0 + \beta_1 X_1 = .5(20) = 10$

10.0

Y_1

(b)
$X_2 = 55, Y_2 = 12$
$\beta_0 + \beta_1 X_2 = .5(55) = 27.5$

27.5

Y_2

(c)
$X_3 = 30, Y_3 = 10$
$\beta_0 + \beta_1 X_3 = .5(30) = 15$

15

Y_3

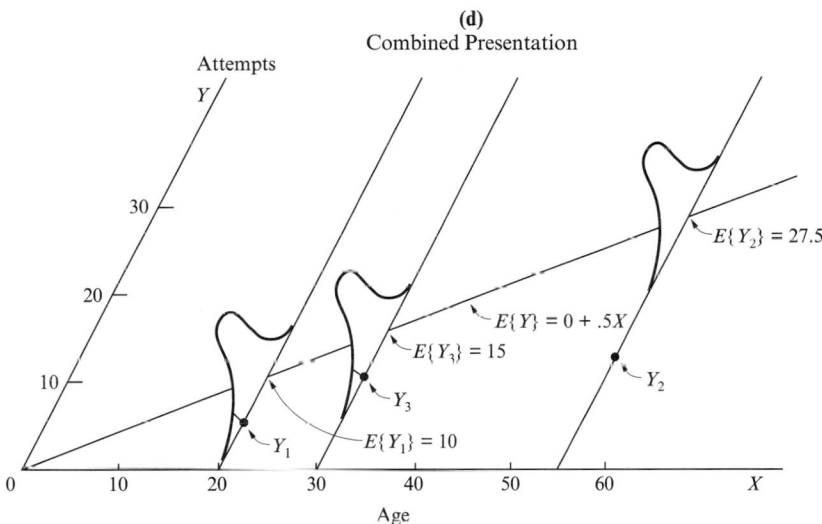

(d)
Combined Presentation

of the probability distribution would be $\beta_0 + \beta_1 X_1 = 0 + .5(20) = 10.0$. Figure 1.15a shows the normal distribution with mean 10.0 and standard deviation 2.5. Note that the observed value $Y_1 = 5$ is in the tail of the distribution and that the density there is relatively small. For the second subject, $X_2 = 55$ and hence $\beta_0 + \beta_1 X_2 = 27.5$. The normal distribution with mean 27.5 is shown in Figure 1.15b. Note that the observed value $Y_2 = 12$ is most unlikely for this case and that the density there is extremely small. Finally, note that the observed value $Y_3 = 10$ is also in the tail of its distribution if $\beta_0 = 0$ and $\beta_1 = .5$, as shown in Figure 1.15c, and that the density there is also relatively small.

Figure 1.15d combines all of this information, showing the regression function $E\{Y\} = 0 + .5X$, the three sample cases, and the three normal distributions. Note how poorly the regression line fits the three sample cases, as was also indicated by the three small density values. Thus, it appears that $\beta_0 = 0$ and $\beta_1 = .5$ are not consistent with the data.

We calculate the densities (i.e., heights of the curve) in the usual way. For $Y_1 = 5$,

$X_1 = 20$, the normal density is as follows when $\beta_0 = 0$ and $\beta_1 = .5$:

$$f_1 = \frac{1}{\sqrt{2\pi}\,(2.5)} \exp\left[-\frac{1}{2}\left(\frac{5 - 10.0}{2.5}\right)^2\right] = .021596$$

The other densities are $f_2 = .7175 \times 10^{-9}$ and $f_3 = .021596$, and the likelihood value of $\beta_0 = 0$ and $\beta_1 = .5$ therefore is:

$$L(\beta_0 = 0, \beta_1 = .5) = .021596(.7175 \times 10^{-9})(.021596) = .3346 \times 10^{-12}$$

In general, the density of an observation Y_i for the normal error regression model (1.24) is as follows, utilizing the fact that $E\{Y_i\} = \beta_0 + \beta_1 X_i$ and $\sigma^2\{Y_i\} = \sigma^2$:

(1.25)
$$f_i = \frac{1}{\sqrt{2\pi}\,\sigma} \exp\left[-\frac{1}{2}\left(\frac{Y_i - \beta_0 - \beta_1 X_i}{\sigma}\right)^2\right]$$

The likelihood function for n observations $Y_1, Y_2, \ldots, Y_n$ is the product of the individual densities in (1.25). Since the variance σ^2 of the error terms is usually unknown, the likelihood function is a function of three parameters, β_0, β_1, and σ^2:

(1.26)
$$L(\beta_0, \beta_1, \sigma^2) = \prod_{i=1}^{n} \frac{1}{(2\pi\sigma^2)^{1/2}} \exp\left[-\frac{1}{2\sigma^2}(Y_i - \beta_0 - \beta_1 X_i)^2\right]$$

$$= \frac{1}{(2\pi\sigma^2)^{n/2}} \exp\left[-\frac{1}{2\sigma^2}\sum_{i=1}^{n}(Y_i - \beta_0 - \beta_1 X_i)^2\right]$$

The values of β_0, β_1, and σ^2 that maximize this likelihood function are the maximum likelihood estimators and are denoted by $\hat{\beta}_0$, $\hat{\beta}_1$, and $\hat{\sigma}^2$, respectively. These estimators can be found analytically, and they are as follows:

Parameter	Maximum Likelihood Estimator	
β_0	$\hat{\beta}_0 = b_0$	same as (1.10b)
β_1	$\hat{\beta}_1 = b_1$	same as (1.10a)
σ^2	$\hat{\sigma}^2 = \dfrac{\Sigma(Y_i - \hat{Y}_i)^2}{n}$	

(1.27)

Thus, the maximum likelihood estimators of β_0 and β_1 are the same estimators as provided by the method of least squares. The maximum likelihood estimator $\hat{\sigma}^2$ is biased, and ordinarily the unbiased estimator *MSE* as given in (1.22) is used. Note that the unbiased estimator *MSE* differs but slightly from the maximum likelihood estimator $\hat{\sigma}^2$, especially if n is not small:

(1.28)
$$MSE = \frac{n}{n-2}\hat{\sigma}^2$$

Example. For the persistence study example, we know now that the maximum likelihood estimates of β_0 and β_1 are $b_0 = 2.81$ and $b_1 = .177$, the same as the least squares estimates in Figure 1.9b.

Comments

1. Since the maximum likelihood estimators $\hat{\beta}_0$ and $\hat{\beta}_1$ are the same as the least squares estimators b_0 and b_1, they have the properties of all least squares estimators:

    a. They are unbiased.

    b. They have minimum variance among all unbiased linear estimators.

In addition, the maximum likelihood estimators b_0 and b_1 for the normal error regression model (1.24) have other desirable properties:

    c. They are consistent, as defined in (A.52).

    d. They are sufficient, as defined in (A.53).

    e. They are minimum variance unbiased; that is, they have minimum variance in the class of all unbiased estimators (linear or otherwise).

Thus, for the normal error model, the estimators b_0 and b_1 have many desirable properties.

2. We find the values of β_0, β_1, and σ^2 that maximize the likelihood function L in (1.26) by taking partial derivatives of L with respect to β_0, β_1, and σ^2, equating each of the partials to zero, and solving the system of equations thus obtained. We can work with $\log_e L$, rather than L, because both L and $\log_e L$ are maximized for the same values of β_0, β_1, and σ^2:

$$(1.29) \qquad \log_e L = -\frac{n}{2}\log_e 2\pi - \frac{n}{2}\log_e \sigma^2 - \frac{1}{2\sigma^2}\sum(Y_i - \beta_0 - \beta_1 X_i)^2$$

Partial differentiation of the logarithm of the likelihood function is much easier; it yields:

$$\frac{\partial(\log_e L)}{\partial\beta_0} = \frac{1}{\sigma^2}\sum(Y_i - \beta_0 - \beta_1 X_i)$$

$$\frac{\partial(\log_e L)}{\partial\beta_1} = \frac{1}{\sigma^2}\sum X_i(Y_i - \beta_0 - \beta_1 X_i)$$

$$\frac{\partial(\log_e L)}{\partial\sigma^2} = -\frac{n}{2\sigma^2} + \frac{1}{2\sigma^4}\sum(Y_i - \beta_0 - \beta_1 X_i)^2$$

We now set these partial derivatives equal to zero, replacing β_0, β_1, and σ^2 by the estimators $\hat{\beta}_0$, $\hat{\beta}_1$, and $\hat{\sigma}^2$. We obtain, after some simplification:

$$(1.30a) \qquad\qquad \sum(Y_i - \hat{\beta}_0 - \hat{\beta}_1 X_i) = 0$$

$$(1.30b) \qquad\qquad \sum X_i(Y_i - \hat{\beta}_0 - \hat{\beta}_1 X_i) = 0$$

$$(1.30c) \qquad\qquad \frac{\sum(Y_i - \hat{\beta}_0 - \hat{\beta}_1 X_i)^2}{n} = \hat{\sigma}^2$$

Formulas (1.30a) and (1.30b) are identical to the earlier least squares normal equations (1.9), and formula (1.30c) is the biased estimator of σ^2 given earlier in (1.27). ∎

Cited References

1.1.   Dixon, W. J., chief editor. *BMDP Statistical Software Manual*. Revised edition. Berkeley, Calif.: University of California Press, 1992.

1.2.   *MINITAB Reference Manual.* PC version, Release 10. State College, Penn.: Minitab Inc., 1994.

1.3.   *SAS/STAT User's Guide.* Release 6.03 edition. Cary, N.C.: SAS Institute, Inc., 1988.

1.4.   *SPSS-X User's Guide.* 3rd ed. Chicago: SPSS Inc., 1988.

1.5.   *SYSTAT for Windows: Statistics.* Version 5 edition. Evanston, Ill.: SYSTAT, Inc., 1992.

1.6.   *JMP IN User's Guide.* Cary, N.C.: SAS Institute, Inc., 1993.

1.7.   *SAS/GRAPH User's Guide.* Release 6.03 edition. Cary, N.C.: SAS Institute, Inc., 1988.

1.8.   *SYSTAT for Windows: Graphics.* Version 5 edition. Evanston, Ill.: SYSTAT, Inc., 1992.

Problems

1.1.   Refer to the sales volume example on page 4. Suppose that the number of units sold is measured accurately, but clerical errors are frequently made in determining the dollar sales. Would the relation between the number of units sold and dollar sales still be a functional one? Discuss.

1.2.   The members of a health spa pay annual membership dues of $300 plus a charge of $2 for each visit to the spa. Let Y denote the dollar cost for the year for a member and X the number of visits by the member during the year. Express the relation between X and Y mathematically. Is it a functional relation or a statistical relation?

1.3.   Experience with a certain type of plastic indicates that a relation exists between the hardness (measured in Brinell units) of items molded from the plastic (Y) and the elapsed time since termination of the molding process (X). It is proposed to study this relation by means of regression analysis. A participant in the discussion objects, pointing out that the hardening of the plastic "is the result of a natural chemical process that doesn't leave anything to chance, so the relation must be mathematical and regression analysis is not appropriate." Evaluate this objection.

1.4.   In Table 1.1, the lot size X is the same in production runs 1 and 24 but the work hours Y differ. What feature of regression model (1.1) is illustrated by this?

1.5.   When asked to state the simple linear regression model, a student wrote it as follows: $E\{Y_i\} = \beta_0 + \beta_1 X_i + \varepsilon_i$. Do you agree?

1.6.   Consider the normal error regression model (1.24). Suppose that the parameter values are $\beta_0 = 200$, $\beta_1 = 5.0$, and $\sigma = 4$.

   a.   Plot this normal error regression model in the fashion of Figure 1.6. Show the distributions of Y for $X = 10, 20$, and 40.

   b.   Explain the meaning of the parameters β_0 and β_1. Assume that the scope of the model includes $X = 0$.

1.7.   In a simulation exercise, regression model (1.1) applies with $\beta_0 = 100$, $\beta_1 = 20$, and $\sigma^2 = 25$. An observation on Y will be made for $X = 5$.

   a.   Can you state the exact probability that Y will fall between 195 and 205? Explain.

b. If the normal error regression model (1.24) is applicable, can you now state the exact probability that Y will fall between 195 and 205? If so, state it.

1.8. In Figure 1.6, suppose another Y observation is obtained at $X = 45$. Would $E\{Y\}$ for this new observation still be 104? Would the Y value for this new case again be 108?

1.9. A student in accounting enthusiastically declared: "Regression is a very powerful tool. We can isolate fixed and variable costs by fitting a linear regression model, even when we have no data for small lots." Discuss.

1.10. An analyst in a large corporation studied the relation between current annual salary (Y) and age (X) for the 46 computer programmers presently employed in the company. The analyst concluded that the relation is curvilinear, reaching a maximum at 47 years. Does this imply that the salary for a programmer increases until age 47 and then decreases? Explain.

1.11. The regression function relating production output by an employee after taking a training program (Y) to the production output before the training program (X) is $E\{Y\} = 20 + .95X$, where X ranges from 40 to 100. An observer concludes that the training program does not raise production output on the average because β_1 is not greater than 1.0. Comment.

1.12. In a study of the relationship for senior citizens between physical activity and frequency of colds, participants were asked to monitor their weekly time spent in exercise over a five-year period and the frequency of colds. The study demonstrated that a negative statistical relation exists between time spent in exercise and frequency of colds. The investigator concluded that increasing the time spent in exercise is an effective strategy for reducing the frequency of colds for senior citizens.

    a. Were the data obtained in the study observational or experimental data?

    b. Comment on the validity of the conclusions reached by the investigator.

    c. Identify two or three other explanatory variables that might affect both the time spent in exercise and the frequency of colds for senior citizens simultaneously.

    d. How might the study be changed so that a valid conclusion about causal relationship between amount of exercise and frequency of colds can be reached?

1.13. Computer programmers employed by a software developer were asked to participate in a month-long training seminar. During the seminar, each employee was asked to record the number of hours spent in class preparation each week. After completing the seminar, the productivity level of each participant was measured. A positive linear statistical relationship between participants' productivity levels and time spent in class preparation was found. The seminar leader concluded that increases in employee productivity are caused by increased class preparation time.

    a. Were the data used by the seminar leader observational or experimental data?

    b. Comment on the validity of the conclusion reached by the seminar leader.

    c. Identify two or three alternative variables that might cause both the employee productivity scores and the employee class participation times to increase (decrease) simultaneously.

    d. How might the study be changed so that a valid conclusion about causal relationship between class preparation time and employee productivity can be reached?

1.14. Refer to Problem 1.3. Four different elapsed times since termination of the molding process (treatments) are to be studied to see how they affect the hardness of a plastic. Sixteen batches (experimental units) are available for the study. Each treatment is to be assigned to four experimental units selected at random. Use a table of random digits or a random number generator to make an appropriate randomization of assignments.

1.15. The effects of five dose levels are to be studied in a completely randomized design, and 20 experimental units are available. Each dose level is to be assigned to four experimental units selected at random. Use a table of random digits or a random number generator to make an appropriate randomization of assignments.

1.16. Evaluate the following statement: "For the least squares method to be fully valid, it is required that the distribution of Y be normal."

1.17. A person states that b_0 and b_1 in the fitted regression function (1.13) can be estimated by the method of least squares. Comment.

1.18. According to (1.17), $\Sigma e_i = 0$ when regression model (1.1) is fitted to a set of n cases by the method of least squares. Is it also true that $\Sigma \varepsilon_i = 0$? Comment.

1.19. **Grade point average**. The director of admissions of a small college administered a newly designed entrance test to 20 students selected at random from the new freshman class in a study to determine whether a student's grade point average (GPA) at the end of the freshman year (Y) can be predicted from the entrance test score (X). The results of the study follow. Assume that first-order regression model (1.1) is appropriate.

i:	1	2	3	. . .	18	19	20
X_i:	5.5	4.8	4.7	. . .	5.9	4.1	4.7
Y_i:	3.1	2.3	3.0	. . .	3.8	2.2	1.5

a. Obtain the least squares estimates of β_0 and β_1, and state the estimated regression function.

b. Plot the estimated regression function and the data. Does the estimated regression function appear to fit the data well?

c. Obtain a point estimate of the mean freshman GPA for students with entrance test score $X = 5.0$.

d. What is the point estimate of the change in the mean response when the entrance test score increases by one point?

√ 1.20. **Calculator maintenance**. The Tri-City Office Equipment Corporation sells an imported desk calculator on a franchise basis and performs preventive maintenance and repair service on this calculator. The data below have been collected from 18 recent calls on users to perform routine preventive maintenance service; for each call, X is the number of machines serviced and Y is the total number of minutes spent by the service person. Assume that first-order regression model (1.1) is appropriate.

i:	1	2	3	. . .	16	17	18
X_i:	7	6	5	. . .	1	4	5
Y_i:	97	86	78	. . .	17	49	68

a. Obtain the estimated regression function.

b. Plot the estimated regression function and the data. How well does the estimated regression function fit the data?

c. Interpret b_0 in your estimated regression function. Does b_0 provide any relevant information here? Explain.

d. Obtain a point estimate of the mean service time when $X = 5$ machines are serviced.

√ 1.21. **Airfreight breakage**. A substance used in biological and medical research is shipped by airfreight to users in cartons of 1,000 ampules. The data below, involving 10 shipments, were collected on the number of times the carton was transferred from one aircraft to another over the shipment route (X) and the number of ampules found to be broken upon arrival (Y). Assume that first-order regression model (1.1) is appropriate.

i:	1	2	3	4	5	6	7	8	9	10
X_i:	1	0	2	0	3	1	0	1	2	0
Y_i:	16	9	17	12	22	13	8	15	19	11

a. Obtain the estimated regression function. Plot the estimated regression function and the data. Does a linear regression function appear to give a good fit here?

b. Obtain a point estimate of the expected number of broken ampules when $X = 1$ transfer is made.

c. Estimate the increase in the expected number of ampules broken when there are 2 transfers as compared to 1 transfer.

d. Verify that your fitted regression line goes through the point $(\bar{X}, \bar{Y})$.

1.22. **Plastic hardness**. Refer to Problems 1.3 and 1.14. Sixteen batches of the plastic were made, and from each batch one test item was molded. Each test item was randomly assigned to one of the four predetermined time levels, and the hardness was measured after the assigned elapsed time. The results are shown below; X is the elapsed time in hours, and Y is hardness in Brinell units. Assume that first-order regression model (1.1) is appropriate.

i:	1	2	3	. . .	14	15	16
X_i:	16	16	16	. . .	40	40	40
Y_i:	199	205	196	. . .	248	253	246

a. Obtain the estimated regression function. Plot the estimated regression function and the data. Does a linear regression function appear to give a good fit here?

b. Obtain a point estimate of the mean hardness when $X = 40$ hours.

c. Obtain a point estimate of the change in mean hardness when X increases by 1 hour.

1.23. Refer to **Grade point average** Problem 1.19.

a. Obtain the residuals e_i. Do they sum to zero in accord with (1.17)?

b. Estimate σ^2 and σ. In what units is σ expressed?

√ 1.24. Refer to **Calculator maintenance** Problem 1.20.

a. Obtain the residuals e_i and the sum of the squared residuals Σe_i^2. What is the relation between the sum of the squared residuals here and the quantity Q in (1.8)?

b. Obtain point estimates of σ^2 and σ. In what units is σ expressed?

√ 1.25. Refer to **Airfreight breakage** Problem 1.21.

a. Obtain the residual for the first case. What is its relation to ε_1?

    b. Compute Σe_i^2 and *MSE*. What is estimated by *MSE*?

1.26. Refer to **Plastic hardness** Problem 1.22.

    a. Obtain the residuals e_i. Do they sum to zero in accord with (1.17)?

    b. Estimate σ^2 and σ. In what units is σ expressed?

√ 1.27. **Muscle mass**. A person's muscle mass is expected to decrease with age. To explore this relationship in women, a nutritionist randomly selected four women from each 10-year age group, beginning with age 40 and ending with age 79. The results follow; X is age, and Y is a measure of muscle mass. Assume that first-order regression model (1.1) is appropriate.

i:	1	2	3	. . .	14	15	16
X_i:	71	64	43	. . .	53	49	78
Y_i:	82	91	100	. . .	100	105	77

    a. Obtain the estimated regression function. Plot the estimated regression function and the data. Does a linear regression function appear to give a good fit here? Does your plot support the anticipation that muscle mass decreases with age?

    b. Obtain the following: (1) a point estimate of the difference in the mean muscle mass for women differing in age by one year, (2) a point estimate of the mean muscle mass for women aged $X = 60$ years, (3) the value of the residual for the eighth case, (4) a point estimate of σ^2.

1.28. **Robbery rate**. A criminologist studying the relationship between population density and robbery rate in medium-sized U.S. cities collected the following data for a random sample of 16 cities; X is the population density of the city (number of people per unit area), and Y is the robbery rate last year (number of robberies per 100,000 people). Assume that first-order regression model (1.1) is appropriate.

i:	1	2	3	. . .	14	15	16
X_i:	59	49	75	. . .	65	89	70
Y_i:	209	180	195	. . .	186	200	204

    a. Obtain the estimated regression function. Plot the estimated regression function and the data. Does the linear regression function appear to give a good fit here? Discuss.

    b. Obtain point estimates of the following: (1) the difference in the mean robbery rate in cities that differ by one unit in population density, (2) the mean robbery rate last year in cities with population density $X = 60$, (3) ε_{10}, (4) σ^2.

Exercises

1.29. Refer to regression model (1.1). Assume that $X = 0$ is within the scope of the model. What is the implication for the regression function if $\beta_0 = 0$ so that the model is $Y_i = \beta_1 X_i + \varepsilon_i$? How would the regression function plot on a graph?

1.30. Refer to regression model (1.1). What is the implication for the regression function if $\beta_1 = 0$ so that the model is $Y_i = \beta_0 + \varepsilon_i$? How would the regression function plot on a graph?

1.31. Refer to **Plastic hardness** Problem 1.22. Suppose one test item was molded from a single batch of plastic and the hardness of this one item was measured at 16 different points in time. Would the error term in the regression model for this case still reflect the same effects as for the experiment initially described? Would you expect the error terms for the different points in time to be uncorrelated? Discuss.

1.32. Derive the expression for b_1 in (1.10a) from the normal equations in (1.9).

1.33. (Calculus needed.) Refer to the regression model $Y_i = \beta_0 + \varepsilon_i$ in Exercise 1.30. Derive the least squares estimator of β_0 for this model.

1.34. Prove that the least squares estimator of β_0 obtained in Exercise 1.33 is unbiased.

1.35. Prove the result in (1.18)—that the sum of the Y observations is the same as the sum of the fitted values.

1.36. Prove the result in (1.20)—that the sum of the residuals weighted by the fitted values is zero.

1.37. Refer to Table 1.1 for the Toluca Company example. When asked to present a point estimate of the expected work hours for lot sizes of 30 pieces, a person gave the estimate 202 because this is the mean number of work hours in the three runs of size 30 in the study. A critic states that this person's approach "throws away" most of the data in the study because cases with lot sizes other than 30 are ignored. Comment.

1.38. In **Airfreight breakage** Problem 1.21, the least squares estimates are $b_0 = 10.20$ and $b_1 = 4.00$, and $\Sigma e_i^2 = 17.60$. Evaluate the least squares criterion Q in (1.8) for the estimates (1) $b_0 = 9$, $b_1 = 3$; (2) $b_0 = 11$, $b_1 = 5$. Is the criterion Q larger for these estimates than for the least squares estimates?

1.39. Two observations on Y were obtained at each of three X levels, namely, at $X = 5$, $X = 10$, and $X = 15$.

   a. Show that the least squares regression line fitted to the *three* points $(5, \bar{Y}_1)$, $(10, \bar{Y}_2)$, and $(15, \bar{Y}_3)$, where $\bar{Y}_1$, $\bar{Y}_2$, and $\bar{Y}_3$ denote the means of the Y observations at the three X levels, is identical to the least squares regression line fitted to the original six cases.

   b. In this study, could the error term variance σ^2 be estimated without fitting a regression line? Explain.

1.40. In fitting regression model (1.1), it was found that observation Y_i fell directly on the fitted regression line (i.e., $Y_i = \hat{Y}_i$). If this case were deleted, would the least squares regression line fitted to the remaining $n - 1$ cases be changed? [*Hint*: What is the contribution of case i to the least squares criterion Q in (1.8)?]

1.41. (Calculus needed.) Refer to the regression model $Y_i = \beta_1 X_i + \varepsilon_i$, $i = 1, \ldots, n$, in Exercise 1.29.

   a. Find the least squares estimator of β_1.

b. Assume that the error terms ε_i are independent $N(0, \sigma^2)$ and that σ^2 is known. State the likelihood function for the n sample observations on Y and obtain the maximum likelihood estimator of β_1. Is it the same as the least squares estimator?

c. Show that the maximum likelihood estimator of β_1 is unbiased.

1.42. **Typographical errors.** Shown below are the number of galleys for a manuscript (X) and the dollar cost of correcting typographical errors (Y) in a random sample of recent orders handled by a firm specializing in technical manuscripts. Assume that the regression model $Y_i = \beta_1 X_i + \varepsilon_i$ is appropriate, with normally distributed independent error terms whose variance is $\sigma^2 = 16$.

i:	1	2	3	4	5	6
X_i:	7	12	4	14	25	30
Y_i:	128	213	75	250	446	540

a. State the likelihood function for the six Y observations, for $\sigma^2 = 16$.

b. Evaluate the likelihood function for $\beta_1 = 17, 18$, and 19. For which of these β_1 values is the likelihood function largest?

c. The maximum likelihood estimator is $b_1 = \Sigma X_i Y_i / \Sigma X_i^2$. Find the maximum likelihood estimate. Are your results in part (b) consistent with this estimate?

d. Using a computer graphics or statistics package, evaluate the likelihood function for values of β_1 between $\beta_1 = 17$ and $\beta_1 = 19$ and plot the function. Does the point at which the likelihood function is maximized correspond to the maximum likelihood estimate found in part (c)?

Projects

1.43. Refer to the **SMSA** data set in Appendix C.2. The number of active physicians in an SMSA (Y) is expected to be related to total population, land area, and total personal income. Assume that first-order regression model (1.1) is appropriate for each of the three predictor variables.

a. Regress the number of active physicians in turn on each of the three predictor variables. State the estimated regression functions.

b. Plot the three estimated regression functions and data on separate graphs. Does a linear regression relation appear to provide a good fit for each of the three predictor variables?

c. Calculate *MSE* for each of the three predictor variables. Which predictor variable leads to the smallest variability around the fitted regression line?

1.44. Refer to the **SMSA** data set in Appendix C.2.

a. For each geographic region, regress total serious crimes in an SMSA (Y) against total population (X). Assume that first-order regression model (1.1) is appropriate for each region. State the estimated regression functions.

b. Are the estimated regression functions similar for the four regions? Discuss.

c. Calculate *MSE* for each region. Is the variability around the fitted regression line approximately the same for the four regions? Discuss.

1.45. Refer to the **SENIC** data set in Appendix C.1. The average length of stay in a hospital (Y) is anticipated to be related to infection risk, available facilities and services, and routine chest X-ray ratio. Assume that first-order regression model (1.1) is appropriate for each of the three predictor variables.

   a. Regress average length of stay on each of the three predictor variables. State the estimated regression functions.

   b. Plot the three estimated regression functions and data on separate graphs. Does a linear relation appear to provide a good fit for each of the three predictor variables?

   c. Calculate *MSE* for each of the three predictor variables. Which predictor variable leads to the smallest variability around the fitted regression line?

1.46. Refer to the **SENIC** data set in Appendix C.1.

   a. For each geographic region, regress average length of stay in hospital (Y) against infection risk (X). Assume that first-order regression model (1.1) is appropriate for each region. State the estimated regression functions.

   b. Are the estimated regression functions similar for the four regions? Discuss.

   c. Calculate *MSE* for each region. Is the variability around the fitted regression line approximately the same for the four regions? Discuss.

1.47. Refer to **Typographical errors** Problem 1.42. Assume that first-order regression model (1.1) is appropriate, with normally distributed independent error terms whose variance is $\sigma^2 = 16$.

   a. State the likelihood function for the six observations, for $\sigma^2 = 16$.

   b. Obtain the maximum likelihood estimates of β_0 and β_1, using (1.27).

   c. Using a computer graphics or statistics package, obtain a three-dimensional plot of the likelihood function for values of β_0 between $\beta_0 = -10$ and $\beta_0 = 10$ and for values of β_1 between $\beta_1 = 17$ and $\beta_1 - 19$. Does the likelihood appear to be maximized by the maximum likelihood estimates found in part (b)?

Inferences in Regression Analysis

In this chapter, we first take up inferences concerning the regression parameters β_0 and β_1, considering both interval estimation of these parameters and tests about them. We then discuss interval estimation of the mean $E\{Y\}$ of the probability distribution of Y, for given X, prediction intervals for a new observation Y, and confidence bands for the regression line. Finally, we take up the analysis of variance approach to regression analysis, the general linear test approach, and descriptive measures of association.

Throughout this chapter, and in the remainder of Part I unless otherwise stated, we assume that the normal error regression model (1.24) is applicable. This model is:

(2.1)
$$Y_i = \beta_0 + \beta_1 X_i + \varepsilon_i$$

where:

> β_0 and β_1 are parameters
> X_i are known constants
> ε_i are independent $N(0, \sigma^2)$

2.1 Inferences Concerning β_1

Frequently, we are interested in drawing inferences about β_1, the slope of the regression line in model (2.1). For instance, a market research analyst studying the relation between sales (Y) and advertising expenditures (X) may wish to obtain an interval estimate of β_1 because it will provide information as to how many additional sales dollars, on the average, are generated by an additional dollar of advertising expenditure.

At times, tests concerning β_1 are of interest, particularly one of the form:

$$H_0: \ \beta_1 = 0$$
$$H_a: \ \beta_1 \neq 0$$

The reason for interest in testing whether or not $\beta_1 = 0$ is that, when $\beta_1 = 0$, there is no linear association between Y and X. Figure 2.1 illustrates the case when $\beta_1 = 0$. Note that

FIGURE 2.1   **Regression Model (2.1) when $\beta_1 = 0$.**

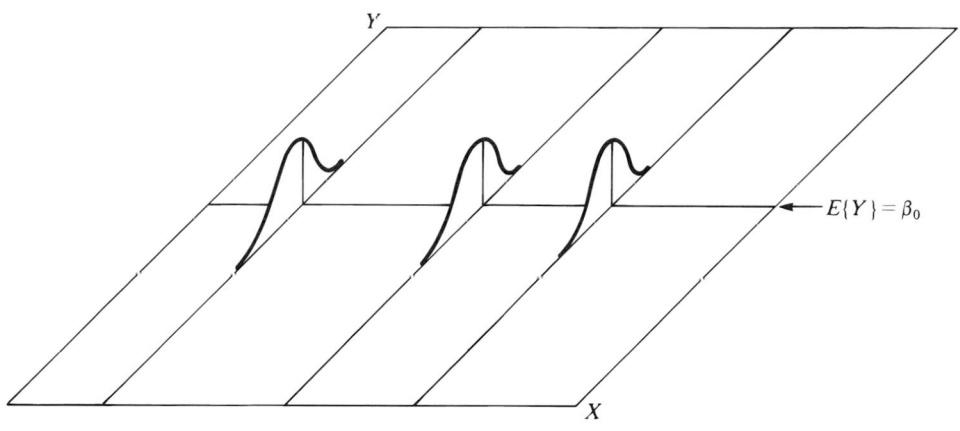

the regression line is horizontal and that the means of the probability distributions of Y are therefore all equal, namely:

$$E\{Y\} = \beta_0 + (0)X = \beta_0$$

For normal error regression model (2.1), the condition $\beta_1 = 0$ implies even more than no linear association between Y and X. Since for this model all probability distributions of Y are normal with constant variance, and since the means are equal when $\beta_1 = 0$, it follows that the probability distributions of Y are identical when $\beta_1 = 0$. This is shown in Figure 2.1. Thus, $\beta_1 = 0$ for the normal error regression model (2.1) implies not only that there is no linear association between Y and X but also that there is no relation of any type between Y and X, since the probability distributions of Y are then identical at all levels of X.

Before discussing inferences concerning β_1 further, we need to consider the sampling distribution of b_1, the point estimator of β_1.

Sampling Distribution of b_1

The point estimator b_1 was given in (1.10a) as follows:

$$(2.2) \qquad b_1 = \frac{\Sigma(X_i - \bar{X})(Y_i - \bar{Y})}{\Sigma(X_i - \bar{X})^2}$$

The sampling distribution of b_1 refers to the different values of b_1 that would be obtained with repeated sampling when the levels of the predictor variable X are held constant from sample to sample.

(2.3)   For normal error regression model (2.1), the sampling distribution of b_1 is normal, with mean and variance:

$$(2.3a) \qquad E\{b_1\} = \beta_1$$

(2.3b)
$$\sigma^2\{b_1\} = \frac{\sigma^2}{\Sigma(X_i - \bar{X})^2}$$

To show this, we need to recognize that b_1 is a linear combination of the observations Y_i.

b_1 as Linear Combination of the Y_i.   It can be shown that b_1, as defined in (2.2), can be expressed as follows:

(2.4)
$$b_1 = \sum k_i Y_i$$

where:

(2.4a)
$$k_i = \frac{X_i - \bar{X}}{\Sigma(X_i - \bar{X})^2}$$

Observe that the k_i are a function of the X_i and therefore are fixed quantities since the X_i are fixed. Hence, b_1 is a linear combination of the Y_i where the coefficients are solely a function of the fixed X_i.

The coefficients k_i have a number of interesting properties that will be used later:

(2.5)
$$\sum k_i = 0$$

(2.6)
$$\sum k_i X_i = 1$$

(2.7)
$$\sum k_i^2 = \frac{1}{\Sigma(X_i - \bar{X})^2}$$

Comments

1. To show that b_1 is a linear combination of the Y_i with coefficients k_i, we first prove:

(2.8)
$$\sum (X_i - \bar{X})(Y_i - \bar{Y}) = \sum (X_i - \bar{X})Y_i$$

This follows since:

$$\sum (X_i - \bar{X})(Y_i - \bar{Y}) = \sum (X_i - \bar{X})Y_i - \sum (X_i - \bar{X})\bar{Y}$$

But $\Sigma(X_i - \bar{X})\bar{Y} = \bar{Y}\Sigma(X_i - \bar{X}) = 0$ since $\Sigma(X_i - \bar{X}) = 0$, Hence, (2.8) holds.

We now express b_1 using (2.8) and (2.4a):

$$b_1 = \frac{\Sigma(X_i - \bar{X})(Y_i - \bar{Y})}{\Sigma(X_i - \bar{X})^2} = \frac{\Sigma(X_i - \bar{X})Y_i}{\Sigma(X_i - \bar{X})^2} = \sum k_i Y_i$$

2. The proofs of the properties of the k_i are direct. For example, property (2.5) follows because:

$$\sum k_i = \sum \left[\frac{X_i - \bar{X}}{\Sigma(X_i - \bar{X})^2} \right] = \frac{1}{\Sigma(X_i - \bar{X})^2} \sum (X_i - \bar{X}) = \frac{0}{\Sigma(X_i - \bar{X})^2} = 0$$

Similarly, property (2.7) follows because:

$$\sum k_i^2 = \sum \left[\frac{X_i - \bar{X}}{\Sigma(X_i - \bar{X})^2} \right]^2 = \frac{1}{\left[\Sigma(X_i - \bar{X})^2 \right]^2} \sum (X_i - \bar{X})^2 = \frac{1}{\Sigma(X_i - \bar{X})^2}$$ ■

Normality.   We return now to the sampling distribution of b_1 for the normal error regression model (2.1). The normality of the sampling distribution of b_1 follows at once from the fact that b_1 is a linear combination of the Y_i. The Y_i are independently, normally distributed according to model (2.1), and theorem (A.40) in Appendix A states that a linear combination of independent normal random variables is normally distributed.

Mean.   The unbiasedness of the point estimator b_1, stated earlier in the Gauss-Markov theorem (1.11), is easy to show:

$$E\{b_1\} = E\left\{ \sum k_i Y_i \right\} = \sum k_i E\{Y_i\} = \sum k_i (\beta_0 + \beta_1 X_i)$$
$$= \beta_0 \sum k_i + \beta_1 \sum k_i X_i$$

By (2.5) and (2.6), we then obtain $E\{b_1\} = \beta_1$.

Variance.   The variance of b_1 can be derived readily. We need only remember that the Y_i are independent random variables, each with variance σ^2, and that the k_i are constants. Hence, we obtain by (A.31):

$$\sigma^2\{b_1\} = \sigma^2\left\{ \sum k_i Y_i \right\} = \sum k_i^2 \sigma^2\{Y_i\}$$
$$= \sum k_i^2 \sigma^2 = \sigma^2 \sum k_i^2$$
$$= \sigma^2 \frac{1}{\Sigma(X_i - \bar{X})^2}$$

The last step follows from (2.7).

Estimated Variance.   We can estimate the variance of the sampling distribution of b_1:

$$\sigma^2\{b_1\} = \frac{\sigma^2}{\Sigma(X_i - \bar{X})^2}$$

by replacing the parameter σ^2 with *MSE*, the unbiased estimator of σ^2:

(2.9)
$$s^2\{b_1\} = \frac{MSE}{\Sigma(X_i - \bar{X})^2}$$

The point estimator $s^2\{b_1\}$ is an unbiased estimator of $\sigma^2\{b_1\}$. Taking the positive square root, we obtain $s\{b_1\}$, the point estimator of $\sigma\{b_1\}$.

Note

We stated in theorem (1.11) that b_1 has minimum variance among all unbiased linear estimators of the form:

$$\hat{\beta}_1 = \sum c_i Y_i$$

where the c_i are arbitrary constants. We now prove this. Since $\hat{\beta}_1$ is required to be unbiased, the following must hold:

$$E\{\hat{\beta}_1\} = E\left\{\sum c_i Y_i\right\} = \sum c_i E\{Y_i\} = \beta_1$$

Now $E\{Y_i\} = \beta_0 + \beta_1 X_i$ by (1.2), so the above condition becomes:

$$E\{\hat{\beta}_1\} = \sum c_i (\beta_0 + \beta_1 X_i) = \beta_0 \sum c_i + \beta_1 \sum c_i X_i = \beta_1$$

For the unbiasedness condition to hold, the c_i must follow the restrictions:

$$\sum c_i = 0 \qquad \sum c_i X_i = 1$$

Now the variance of $\hat{\beta}_1$ is, by (A.31):

$$\sigma^2\{\hat{\beta}_1\} = \sum c_i^2 \sigma^2\{Y_i\} = \sigma^2 \sum c_i^2$$

Let us define $c_i = k_i + d_i$, where the k_i are the least squares constants in (2.4a) and the d_i are arbitrary constants. We can then write:

$$\sigma^2\{\hat{\beta}_1\} = \sigma^2 \sum c_i^2 = \sigma^2 \sum (k_i + d_i)^2 = \sigma^2 \left(\sum k_i^2 + \sum d_i^2 + 2 \sum k_i d_i\right)$$

We know that $\sigma^2 \sum k_i^2 = \sigma^2\{b_1\}$ from our proof above. Further, $\sum k_i d_i = 0$ because of the restrictions on the k_i and c_i above:

$$\sum k_i d_i = \sum k_i (c_i - k_i)$$

$$= \sum c_i k_i - \sum k_i^2$$

$$= \sum c_i \left[\frac{X_i - \bar{X}}{\Sigma(X_i - \bar{X})^2}\right] - \frac{1}{\Sigma(X_i - \bar{X})^2}$$

$$= \frac{\sum c_i X_i - \bar{X} \sum c_i}{\Sigma(X_i - \bar{X})^2} - \frac{1}{\Sigma(X_i - \bar{X})^2} = 0$$

Hence, we have:

$$\sigma^2\{\hat{\beta}_1\} = \sigma^2\{b_1\} + \sigma^2 \sum d_i^2$$

Note that the smallest value of Σd_i^2 is zero. Hence, the variance of $\hat{\beta}_1$ is at a minimum when $\Sigma d_i^2 = 0$. But this can only occur if all $d_i = 0$, which implies $c_i \equiv k_i$. Thus, the least squares estimator b_1 has minimum variance among all unbiased linear estimators. ∎

Sampling Distribution of $(b_1 - \beta_1)/s\{b_1\}$

Since b_1 is normally distributed, we know that the standardized statistic $(b_1 - \beta_1)/\sigma\{b_1\}$ is a standard normal variable. Ordinarily, of course, we need to estimate $\sigma\{b_1\}$ by $s\{b_1\}$, and hence are interested in the distribution of the statistic $(b_1 - \beta_1)/s\{b_1\}$. When a statistic is standardized but the denominator is an estimated standard deviation rather than the true standard deviation, it is called a *studentized statistic*. An important theorem in statistics states the following about the studentized statistic $(b_1 - \beta_1)/s\{b_1\}$:

(2.10) $\qquad \dfrac{b_1 - \beta_1}{s\{b_1\}}$ is distributed as $t(n-2)$ for regression model (2.1)

Intuitively, this result should not be unexpected. We know that if the observations Y_i come from the same normal population, $(\bar{Y} - \mu)/s\{\bar{Y}\}$ follows the t distribution with $n-1$ degrees of freedom. The estimator b_1, like $\bar{Y}$, is a linear combination of the observations Y_i. The reason for the difference in the degrees of freedom is that two parameters (β_0 and β_1) need to be estimated for the regression model; hence, two degrees of freedom are lost here.

Note

We can show that the studentized statistic $(b_1 - \beta_1)/s\{b_1\}$ is distributed as t with $n-2$ degrees of freedom by relying on the following theorem:

(2.11) $\qquad$ For regression model (2.1), SSE/σ^2 is distributed as χ^2 with $n-2$ degrees of freedom and is independent of b_0 and b_1.

First, let us rewrite $(b_1 - \beta_1)/s\{b_1\}$ as follows:

$$\frac{b_1 - \beta_1}{\sigma\{b_1\}} \div \frac{s\{b_1\}}{\sigma\{b_1\}}$$

The numerator is a standard normal variable z. The nature of the denominator can be seen by first considering:

$$\frac{s^2\{b_1\}}{\sigma^2\{b_1\}} = \frac{\dfrac{MSE}{\Sigma(X_i - \bar{X})^2}}{\dfrac{\sigma^2}{\Sigma(X_i - \bar{X})^2}} = \frac{MSE}{\sigma^2} = \frac{\dfrac{SSE}{n-2}}{\sigma^2}$$

$$= \frac{SSE}{\sigma^2(n-2)} \sim \frac{\chi^2(n-2)}{n-2}$$

where the symbol $\sim$ stands for "is distributed as." The last step follows from (2.11). Hence, we have:

$$\frac{b_1 - \beta_1}{s\{b_1\}} \sim \frac{z}{\sqrt{\dfrac{\chi^2(n-2)}{n-2}}}$$

But by theorem (2.11), z and χ^2 are independent since z is a function of b_1 and b_1 is independent of $SSE/\sigma^2 \sim \chi^2$. Hence, by definition (A.44), it follows that:

$$\frac{b_1 - \beta_1}{s\{b_1\}} \sim t(n-2)$$

This result places us in a position to readily make inferences concerning β_1. $\qquad\blacksquare$

TABLE 2.1   **Results for Toluca Company Example Obtained in Chapter 1.**

$$n = 25 \qquad\qquad \bar{X} = 70.00$$
$$b_0 = 62.37 \qquad\qquad b_1 = 3.5702$$
$$\hat{Y} = 62.37 + 3.5702X \qquad SSE = 54{,}825$$
$$\Sigma(X_i - \bar{X})^2 = 19{,}800 \qquad MSE = 2{,}384$$
$$\Sigma(Y_i - \bar{Y})^2 = 307{,}203$$

Confidence Interval for β_1

Since $(b_1 - \beta_1)/s\{b_1\}$ follows a t distribution, we can make the following probability statement:

$$(2.12) \qquad P\{t(\alpha/2; n-2) \le (b_1 - \beta_1)/s\{b_1\} \le t(1 - \alpha/2; n-2)\} = 1 - \alpha$$

Here, $t(\alpha/2; n-2)$ denotes the $(\alpha/2)100$ percentile of the t distribution with $n-2$ degrees of freedom. Because of the symmetry of the t distribution around its mean 0, it follows that:

$$(2.13) \qquad t(\alpha/2; n-2) = -t(1 - \alpha/2; n-2)$$

Rearranging the inequalities in (2.12) and using (2.13), we obtain:

$$(2.14) \qquad P\{b_1 - t(1 - \alpha/2; n-2)s\{b_1\}$$
$$\le \beta_1 \le b_1 + t(1 - \alpha/2; n-2)s\{b_1\}\} = 1 - \alpha$$

Since (2.14) holds for all possible values of β_1, the $1 - \alpha$ confidence limits for β_1 are:

$$(2.15) \qquad b_1 \pm t(1 - \alpha/2; n-2)s\{b_1\}$$

Example.   Consider the Toluca Company example of Chapter 1. Management wishes an estimate of β_1 with 95 percent confidence coefficient. We summarize in Table 2.1 the needed results obtained earlier. First, we need to obtain $s\{b_1\}$:

$$s^2\{b_1\} = \frac{MSE}{\Sigma(X_i - \bar{X})^2} = \frac{2{,}384}{19{,}800} = .12040$$
$$s\{b_1\} = .3470$$

This estimated standard deviation is shown in the MINITAB output in Figure 2.2 in the column labeled Stdev corresponding to the row labeled X. Figure 2.2 repeats the MINITAB output presented earlier in Chapter 1 and contains some additional results that we will utilize shortly.

For a 95 percent confidence coefficient, we require $t(.975; 23)$. From Table B.2 in Appendix B, we find $t(.975; 23) = 2.069$. The 95 percent confidence interval, by (2.15), then is:

$$3.5702 - 2.069(.3470) \le \beta_1 \le 3.5702 + 2.069(.3470)$$

$$2.85 \le \beta_1 \le 4.29$$

Thus, with confidence coefficient .95, we estimate that the mean number of work hours increases by somewhere between 2.85 and 4.29 hours for each additional unit in the lot.

FIGURE 2.2 **Portion of MINITAB Regression Output—Toluca Company Example.**

```
The regression equation is
Y = 62.4 + 3.57 X

Predictor          Coef        Stdev      t-ratio          p
Constant          62.37        26.18         2.38      0.026
X                 3.5702       0.3470        10.29      0.000

s = 48.82       R-sq = 82.2%      R-sq(adj) = 81.4%

Analysis of Variance

SOURCE           DF           SS           MS          F          p
Regression        1       252378       252378     105.88      0.000
Error            23        54825         2384
Total            24       307203
```

Note

In Chapter 1, we noted that the scope of a regression model is restricted ordinarily to some range of values of the predictor variable. This is particularly important to keep in mind when using estimates of the slope β_1. In our Toluca Company example, a linear regression model appeared appropriate for lot sizes between 20 and 120, the range of the predictor variable in the recent past. It may not be reasonable to use the estimate of the slope to infer the effect of lot size on number of work hours far outside this range since the regression relation may not be linear there. ∎

Tests Concerning β_1

Since $(b_1 - \beta_1)/s\{b_1\}$ is distributed as t with $n - 2$ degrees of freedom, tests concerning β_1 can be set up in ordinary fashion using the t distribution.

Example 1: Two-Sided Test. A cost analyst in the Toluca Company is interested in testing, using regression model (2.1), whether or not there is a linear association between work hours and lot size, i.e., whether or not $\beta_1 = 0$. The two alternatives then are:

$$(2.16) \qquad \begin{aligned} H_0\!: \ \beta_1 &= 0 \\ H_a\!: \ \beta_1 &\neq 0 \end{aligned}$$

The analyst wishes to control the risk of a Type I error at $\alpha = .05$. The conclusion H_a could be reached at once by referring to the 95 percent confidence interval for β_1 constructed earlier, since this interval does not include 0.

An explicit test of the alternatives (2.16) is based on the test statistic:

$$(2.17) \qquad t^* = \frac{b_1}{s\{b_1\}}$$

The decision rule with this test statistic when controlling the level of significance at α is:

$$(2.18) \qquad \begin{aligned} &\text{If } |t^*| \leq t(1 - \alpha/2; n - 2), \ \text{conclude } H_0 \\ &\text{If } |t^*| > t(1 - \alpha/2; n - 2), \ \text{conclude } H_a \end{aligned}$$

For the Toluca Company example, where $\alpha = .05$, $b_1 = 3.5702$, and $s\{b_1\} = .3470$, we require $t(.975; 23) = 2.069$. Thus, the decision rule for testing alternatives (2.16) is:

$$\text{If } |t^*| \leq 2.069, \text{ conclude } H_0$$

$$\text{If } |t^*| > 2.069, \text{ conclude } H_a$$

Since $|t^*| = |3.5702/.3470| = 10.29 > 2.069$, we conclude H_a, that $\beta_1 \neq 0$ or that there is a linear association between work hours and lot size. The value of the test statistic, $t^* = 10.29$, is shown in the MINITAB output in Figure 2.2 in the column labeled t-ratio and the row labeled X.

The two-sided P-value for the sample outcome is obtained by first finding the one-sided P-value, $P\{t(23) > t^* = 10.29\}$. We see from Table B.2 that this probability is less than .0005. Many statistical calculators and computer packages will provide the actual probability; it is almost 0, denoted by 0+. Thus, the two-sided P-value is $2(0+) = 0+$. Since the two-sided P-value is less than the specified level of significance $\alpha = .05$, we could conclude H_a directly. The MINITAB output in Figure 2.2 shows the P-value in the column labeled p, corresponding to the row labeled X. It is shown as 0.000.

Note

When the test of whether or not $\beta_1 = 0$ leads to the conclusion that $\beta_1 \neq 0$, the association between Y and X is sometimes described to be a linear statistical association.   ■

Example 2: One-Sided Test.   Suppose the analyst had wished to test whether or not β_1 is positive, controlling the level of significance at $\alpha = .05$. The alternatives then would be:

$$H_0: \ \beta_1 \leq 0$$

$$H_a: \ \beta_1 > 0$$

and the decision rule based on test statistic (2.17) would be:

$$\text{If } t^* \leq t(1 - \alpha; n - 2), \text{ conclude } H_0$$
$$\text{If } t^* > t(1 - \alpha; n - 2), \text{ conclude } H_a$$

For $\alpha = .05$, we require $t(.95; 23) = 1.714$. Since $t^* = 10.29 > 1.714$, we would conclude H_a, that β_1 is positive.

This same conclusion could be reached directly from the one-sided P-value, which was noted in Example 1 to be 0+. Since this P-value is less than .05, we would conclude H_a.

Comments

1. The P-value is sometimes called the observed level of significance.

2. Many scientific publications commonly report the P-value together with the value of the test statistic. In this way, one can conduct a test at any desired level of significance α by comparing the P-value with the specified level α.

3. Users of statistical calculators and computer packages need to be careful to ascertain whether one-sided or two-sided P-values are reported. Many commonly used labels, such as PROB or P, do not reveal whether the P-value is one- or two-sided.

4. Occasionally, it is desired to test whether or not β_1 equals some specified nonzero value β_{10}, which may be a historical norm, the value for a comparable process, or an engineering specification. The alternatives now are:

(2.19)
$$H_0: \beta_1 = \beta_{10}$$
$$H_a: \beta_1 \neq \beta_{10}$$

and the appropriate test statistic is:

(2.20)
$$t^* = \frac{b_1 - \beta_{10}}{s\{b_1\}}$$

The decision rule to be employed here still is (2.18), but it is now based on t^* defined in (2.20).

Note that test statistic (2.20) simplifies to test statistic (2.17) when the test involves $H_0: \beta_1 = \beta_{10} = 0$. ∎

2.2   Inferences Concerning β_0

As noted in Chapter 1, there are only infrequent occasions when we wish to make inferences concerning β_0, the intercept of the regression line. These occur when the scope of the model includes $X = 0$.

Sampling Distribution of b_0

The point estimator b_0 was given in (1.10b) as follows:

(2.21)
$$b_0 = \bar{Y} - b_1 \bar{X}$$

The sampling distribution of b_0 refers to the different values of b_0 that would be obtained with repeated sampling when the levels of the predictor variable X are held constant from sample to sample.

(2.22)   For regression model (2.1), the sampling distribution of b_0 is normal, with mean and variance:

(2.22a)
$$E\{b_0\} = \beta_0$$

(2.22b)
$$\sigma^2\{b_0\} = \sigma^2 \left[\frac{1}{n} + \frac{\bar{X}^2}{\Sigma(X_i - \bar{X})^2} \right]$$

The normality of the sampling distribution of b_0 follows because b_0, like b_1, is a linear combination of the observations Y_i. The results for the mean and variance of the sampling distribution of b_0 can be obtained in similar fashion as those for b_1.

An estimator of $\sigma^2\{b_0\}$ is obtained by replacing σ^2 by its point estimator *MSE*:

(2.23)
$$s^2\{b_0\} = MSE \left[\frac{1}{n} + \frac{\bar{X}^2}{\Sigma(X_i - \bar{X})^2} \right]$$

The positive square root, $s\{b_0\}$, is an estimator of $\sigma\{b_0\}$.

t distribution will provide approximately the specified confidence coefficient or level of significance. Even if the distributions of Y are far from normal, the estimators b_0 and b_1 generally have the property of *asymptotic normality*—their distributions approach normality under very general conditions as the sample size increases. Thus, with sufficiently large samples, the confidence intervals and decision rules given earlier still apply even if the probability distributions of Y depart far from normality. For large samples, the t value is, of course, replaced by the z value for the standard normal distribution.

Interpretation of Confidence Coefficient and Risks of Errors

Since regression model (2.1) assumes that the X_i are known constants, the confidence coefficient and risks of errors are interpreted with respect to taking repeated samples in which the X observations are kept at the same levels as in the observed sample. For instance, we constructed a confidence interval for β_1 with confidence coefficient .95 in the Toluca Company example. This coefficient is interpreted to mean that if many independent samples are taken where the levels of X (the lot sizes) are the same as in the data set and a 95 percent confidence interval is constructed for each sample, 95 percent of the intervals will contain the true value of β_1.

Spacing of the X Levels

Inspection of formulas (2.3b) and (2.22b) for the variances of b_1 and b_0, respectively, indicates that for given n and σ^2 these variances are affected by the spacing of the X levels in the observed data. For example, the greater is the spread in the X levels, the larger is the quantity $\Sigma(X_i - \bar{X})^2$ and the smaller is the variance of b_1. We discuss in Chapter 4 how the X observations should be spaced in experiments where spacing can be controlled.

Power of Tests

The power of tests on β_0 and β_1 can be obtained from Appendix Table B.5. Consider, for example, the general test concerning β_1 in (2.19):

$$H_0: \ \beta_1 = \beta_{10}$$

$$H_a: \ \beta_1 \neq \beta_{10}$$

for which test statistic (2.20) is employed:

$$t^* = \frac{b_1 - \beta_{10}}{s\{b_1\}}$$

and the decision rule for level of significance α is given in (2.18):

If $|t^*| \leq t(1 - \alpha/2; n - 2)$, conclude H_0

If $|t^*| > t(1 - \alpha/2; n - 2)$, conclude H_a

The power of this test is the probability that the decision rule will lead to conclusion H_a when H_a in fact holds. Specifically, the power is given by:

(2.26)   Power $= P\{|t^*| > t(1 - \alpha/2; n - 2) \mid \delta\}$

where δ is the *noncentrality measure*—i.e., a measure of how far the true value of β_1 is from β_{10}:

(2.27)
$$\delta = \frac{|\beta_1 - \beta_{10}|}{\sigma\{b_1\}}$$

Table B.5 presents the power of the two-sided t test for $\alpha = .05$ and $\alpha = .01$, for various degrees of freedom df. To illustrate the use of this table, let us return to the Toluca Company example where we tested:

$$H_0: \beta_1 = \beta_{10} = 0$$

$$H_a: \beta_1 \neq \beta_{10} = 0$$

Suppose we wish to know the power of the test when $\beta_1 = 1.5$. To ascertain this, we need to know σ^2, the variance of the error terms. Assume that $\sigma^2 = 2,500$, so $\sigma^2\{b_1\}$ for our example would be:

$$\sigma^2\{b_1\} = \frac{\sigma^2}{\Sigma(X_i - \bar{X})^2} = \frac{2,500}{19,800} = .1263$$

or $\sigma\{b_1\} = .3553$. Then $\delta = |1.5 - 0| \div .3553 = 4.22$. We enter Table B.5 for $\alpha = .05$ (the level of significance used in the test) and 23 degrees of freedom and interpolate linearly between $\delta = 4.00$ and $\delta = 5.00$. We obtain:

$$.97 + \frac{4.22 - 4.00}{5.00 - 4.00}(1.00 - .97) = .9766$$

Thus, if $\beta_1 = 1.5$, the probability would be about .98 that we would be led to conclude H_a ($\beta_1 \neq 0$). In other words, if $\beta_1 = 1.5$, we would be almost certain to conclude that there is a linear relation between work hours and lot size.

The power of tests concerning β_0 can be obtained from Table B.5 in completely analogous fashion. For one-sided tests, Table B.5 should be entered so that one-half the level of significance shown there is the level of significance of the one-sided test.

2.4   Interval Estimation of $E\{Y_h\}$

A common objective in regression analysis is to estimate the mean for one or more probability distributions of Y. Consider, for example, a study of the relation between level of piecework pay (X) and worker productivity (Y). The mean productivity at high and medium levels of piecework pay may be of particular interest for purposes of analyzing the benefits obtained from an increase in the pay. As another example, the Toluca Company was interested in the mean response (mean number of work hours) for a range of lot sizes for purposes of finding the optimum lot size.

Let X_h denote the level of X for which we wish to estimate the mean response. X_h may be a value which occurred in the sample, or it may be some other value of the predictor variable within the scope of the model. The mean response when $X = X_h$ is denoted by

$E\{Y_h\}$. Formula (1.12) gives us the point estimator $\hat{Y}_h$ of $E\{Y_h\}$:

$$(2.28) \qquad\qquad \hat{Y}_h = b_0 + b_1 X_h$$

We consider now the sampling distribution of $\hat{Y}_h$.

Sampling Distribution of $\hat{Y}_h$

The sampling distribution of $\hat{Y}_h$, like the earlier sampling distributions discussed, refers to the different values of $\hat{Y}_h$ that would be obtained if repeated samples were selected, each holding the levels of the predictor variable X constant, and calculating $\hat{Y}_h$ for each sample.

(2.29)   For normal error regression model (2.1), the sampling distribution of $\hat{Y}_h$ is normal, with mean and variance:

$$(2.29\text{a}) \qquad\qquad E\{\hat{Y}_h\} = E\{Y_h\}$$

$$(2.29\text{b}) \qquad\qquad \sigma^2\{\hat{Y}_h\} = \sigma^2 \left[\frac{1}{n} + \frac{(X_h - \bar{X})^2}{\Sigma(X_i - \bar{X})^2} \right]$$

Normality.   The normality of the sampling distribution of $\hat{Y}_h$ follows directly from the fact that $\hat{Y}_h$, like b_0 and b_1, is a linear combination of the observations Y_i.

Mean.   Note from (2.29a) that $\hat{Y}_h$ is an unbiased estimator of $E\{Y_h\}$. To prove this, we proceed as follows:

$$E\{\hat{Y}_h\} = E\{b_0 + b_1 X_h\} = E\{b_0\} + X_h E\{b_1\} = \beta_0 + \beta_1 X_h$$

by (2.3a) and (2.22a).

Variance.   Note from (2.29b) that the variability of the sampling distribution of $\hat{Y}_h$ is affected by how far X_h is from $\bar{X}$, through the term $(X_h - \bar{X})^2$. The further from $\bar{X}$ is X_h, the greater is the quantity $(X_h - \bar{X})^2$ and the larger is the variance of $\hat{Y}_h$. An intuitive explanation of this effect is found in Figure 2.3. Shown there are two sample regression lines, based on two samples for the same set of X values. The two regression lines are assumed to go through the same $(\bar{X}, \bar{Y})$ point to isolate the effect of interest, namely, the effect of variation in the estimated slope b_1 from sample to sample. Note that at X_1, near $\bar{X}$, the fitted values $\hat{Y}_1$ for the two sample regression lines are close to each other. At X_2, which is far from $\bar{X}$, the situation is different. Here, the fitted values $\hat{Y}_2$ differ substantially. Thus, variation in the slope b_1 from sample to sample has a much more pronounced effect on $\hat{Y}_h$ for X levels far from the mean $\bar{X}$ than for X levels near $\bar{X}$. Hence, the variation in the $\hat{Y}_h$ values from sample to sample will be greater when X_h is far from the mean than when X_h is near the mean.

FIGURE 2.3 **Effect on $\widehat{Y}_h$ of Variation in b_1 from Sample to Sample in Two Samples with Same Means $\overline{Y}$ and $\overline{X}$.**

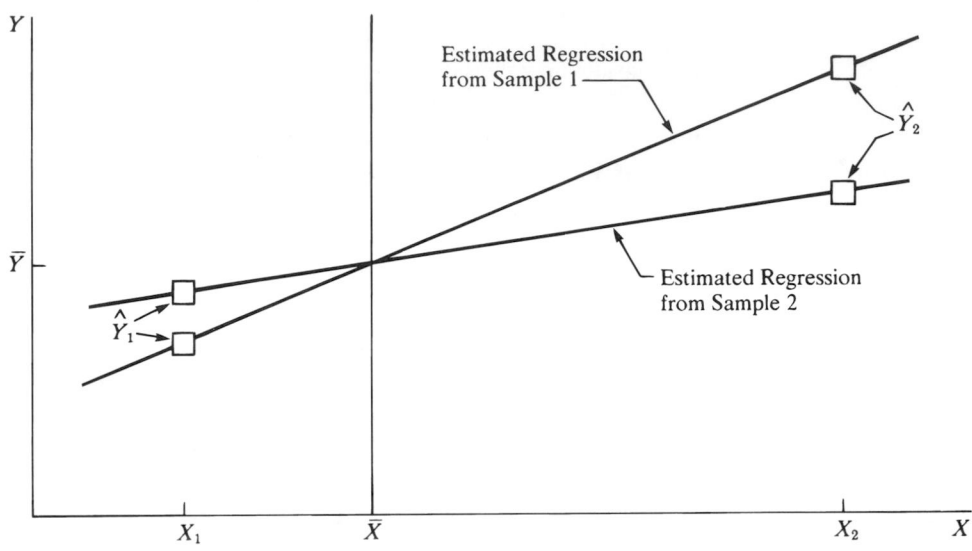

When *MSE* is substituted for σ^2 in (2.29b), we obtain $s^2\{\widehat{Y}_h\}$, the estimated variance of $\widehat{Y}_h$:

$$(2.30) \qquad s^2\{\widehat{Y}_h\} = MSE\left[\frac{1}{n} + \frac{(X_h - \overline{X})^2}{\Sigma(X_i - \overline{X})^2}\right]$$

The estimated standard deviation of $\widehat{Y}_h$ is then $s\{\widehat{Y}_h\}$, the positive square root of $s^2\{\widehat{Y}_h\}$.

Comments

1. When $X_h = 0$, the variance of $\widehat{Y}_h$ in (2.29b) reduces to the variance of b_0 in (2.22b). Similarly, $s^2\{\widehat{Y}_h\}$ in (2.30) reduces to $s^2\{b_0\}$ in (2.23). The reason is that $\widehat{Y}_h = b_0$ when $X_h = 0$ since $\widehat{Y}_h = b_0 + b_1 X_h$.

2. To derive $\sigma^2\{\widehat{Y}_h\}$, we first show that b_1 and $\overline{Y}$ are uncorrelated and, hence, for regression model (2.1), independent:

$$(2.31) \qquad \sigma\{\overline{Y}, b_1\} = 0$$

where $\sigma\{\overline{Y}, b_1\}$ denotes the covariance between $\overline{Y}$ and b_1. We begin with the definitions:

$$\overline{Y} = \Sigma\left(\frac{1}{n}\right)Y_i \qquad b_1 = \Sigma k_i Y_i$$

where k_i is as defined in (2.4a). We now use theorem (A.32), with $a_i = 1/n$ and $c_i = k_i$; remember that the Y_i are independent random variables:

$$\sigma\{\bar{Y}, b_1\} = \sum \left(\frac{1}{n}\right) k_i \sigma^2\{Y_i\} = \frac{\sigma^2}{n} \sum k_i$$

But we know from (2.5) that $\Sigma k_i = 0$. Hence, the covariance is 0.

Now we are ready to find the variance of $\hat{Y}_h$. We shall use the estimator in the alternative form (1.15):

$$\sigma^2\{\hat{Y}_h\} = \sigma^2\{\bar{Y} + b_1(X_h - \bar{X})\}$$

Since $\bar{Y}$ and b_1 are independent and X_h and $\bar{X}$ are constants, we obtain:

$$\sigma^2\{\hat{Y}_h\} = \sigma^2\{\bar{Y}\} + (X_h - \bar{X})^2 \sigma^2\{b_1\}$$

Now $\sigma^2\{b_1\}$ is given in (2.3b), and:

$$\sigma^2\{\bar{Y}\} = \frac{\sigma^2\{Y_i\}}{n} = \frac{\sigma^2}{n}$$

Hence:

$$\sigma^2\{\hat{Y}_h\} = \frac{\sigma^2}{n} + (X_h - \bar{X})^2 \frac{\sigma^2}{\Sigma(X_i - \bar{X})^2}$$

which, upon a slight rearrangement of terms, yields (2.29b). ∎

Sampling Distribution of $(\hat{Y}_h - E\{Y_h\})/s\{\hat{Y}_h\}$

Since we have encountered the t distribution in each type of inference for regression model (2.1) up to this point, it should not be surprising that:

(2.32) $\dfrac{\hat{Y}_h - E\{Y_h\}}{s\{\hat{Y}_h\}}$ is distributed as $t(n - 2)$ for regression model (2.1)

Hence, all inferences concerning $E\{Y_h\}$ are carried out in the usual fashion with the t distribution. We illustrate the construction of confidence intervals, since in practice these are used more frequently than tests.

Confidence Interval for $E\{Y_h\}$

A confidence interval for $E\{Y_h\}$ is constructed in the standard fashion, making use of the t distribution as indicated by theorem (2.32). The $1 - \alpha$ confidence limits are:

(2.33) $$\hat{Y}_h \pm t(1 - \alpha/2; n - 2)s\{\hat{Y}_h\}$$

Example 1.   Returning to the Toluca Company example, let us find a 90 percent confidence interval for $E\{Y_h\}$ when the lot size is $X_h = 65$ units. Using the earlier results in Table 2.1, we find the point estimate $\hat{Y}_h$:

$$\hat{Y}_h = 62.37 + 3.5702(65) = 294.4$$

Next, we need to find the estimated standard deviation $s\{\hat{Y}_h\}$. We obtain, using (2.30):

$$s^2\{\hat{Y}_h\} = 2{,}384 \left[\frac{1}{25} + \frac{(65 - 70.00)^2}{19{,}800} \right] = 98.37$$

$$s\{\hat{Y}_h\} = 9.918$$

For a 90 percent confidence coefficient, we require $t(.95; 23) = 1.714$. Hence, our confidence interval with confidence coefficient .90 is by (2.33):

$$294.4 - 1.714(9.918) \le E\{Y_h\} \le 294.4 + 1.714(9.918)$$

$$277.4 \le E\{Y_h\} \le 311.4$$

We conclude with confidence coefficient .90 that the mean number of work hours required when lots of 65 units are produced is somewhere between 277.4 and 311.4 hours. We see that our estimate of the mean number of work hours is moderately precise.

Example 2.   Suppose the Toluca Company wishes to estimate $E\{Y_h\}$ for lots with $X_h = 100$ units with a 90 percent confidence interval. We require:

$$\hat{Y}_h = 62.37 + 3.5702(100) = 419.4$$

$$s^2\{\hat{Y}_h\} = 2{,}384 \left[\frac{1}{25} + \frac{(100 - 70.00)^2}{19{,}800} \right] = 203.72$$

$$s\{\hat{Y}_h\} = 14.27$$

$$t(.95; 23) = 1.714$$

Hence, the 90 percent confidence interval is:

$$419.4 - 1.714(14.27) \le E\{Y_h\} \le 419.4 + 1.714(14.27)$$

$$394.9 \le E\{Y_h\} \le 443.9$$

Note that this confidence interval is somewhat wider than that for Example 1, since the X_h level here ($X_h = 100$) is substantially farther from the mean $\overline{X} = 70.0$ than the X_h level for Example 1 ($X_h = 65$).

Comments

1. Since the X_i are known constants in regression model (2.1), the interpretation of confidence intervals and risks of errors in inferences on the mean response is in terms of taking repeated samples in which the X observations are at the same levels as in the actual study. We noted this same point in connection with inferences on β_0 and β_1.

2. We see from formula (2.29b) that, for given sample results, the variance of $\hat{Y}_h$ is smallest when $X_h = \overline{X}$. Thus, in an experiment to estimate the mean response at a particular level X_h of the predictor variable, the precision of the estimate will be greatest if (everything else remaining equal) the observations on X are spaced so that $\overline{X} = X_h$.

3. The usual relationship between confidence intervals and tests applies in inferences concerning the mean response. Thus, the two-sided confidence limits (2.33) can be utilized for two-sided tests concerning the mean response at X_h. Alternatively, a regular decision rule can be set up.

4. The confidence limits (2.33) for a mean response $E\{Y_h\}$ are not sensitive to moderate departures from the assumption that the error terms are normally distributed. Indeed, the limits are not sensitive to substantial departures from normality if the sample size is large. This robustness in estimating the mean response is related to the robustness of the confidence limits for β_0 and β_1, noted earlier.

5. Confidence limits (2.33) apply when a single mean response is to be estimated from the study. We discuss in Chapter 4 how to proceed when several mean responses are to be estimated from the same data. ∎

2.5 Prediction of New Observation

We consider now the prediction of a new observation Y corresponding to a given level X of the predictor variable. Three illustrations where prediction of a new observation is needed follow.

1. In the Toluca Company example, the next lot to be produced consists of 100 units and management wishes to predict the number of work hours for this particular lot.

2. An economist has estimated the regression relation between company sales and number of persons 16 or more years old from data for the past 10 years. Based on a reliable demographic projection of the number of persons 16 or more years old for next year, the economist wishes to predict next year's company sales.

3. An admissions officer at a university has estimated the regression relation between the high school grade point average (GPA) of admitted students and the first-year college GPA. The officer wishes to predict the first-year college GPA for an applicant whose high school GPA is 3.5 as part of the information on which an admissions decision will be based.

The new observation on Y to be predicted is viewed as the result of a new trial, independent of the trials on which the regression analysis is based. We denote the level of X for the new trial as X_h and the new observation on Y as $Y_{h(\text{new})}$. Of course, we assume that the underlying regression model applicable for the basic sample data continues to be appropriate for the new observation.

The distinction between estimation of the mean response $E\{Y_h\}$, discussed in the preceding section, and prediction of a new response $Y_{h(\text{new})}$, discussed now, is basic. In the former case, we estimate the *mean* of the distribution of Y. In the present case, we predict an *individual outcome* drawn from the distribution of Y. Of course, the great majority of

FIGURE 2.4   **Prediction of $Y_{h(\text{new})}$ when Parameters Known.**

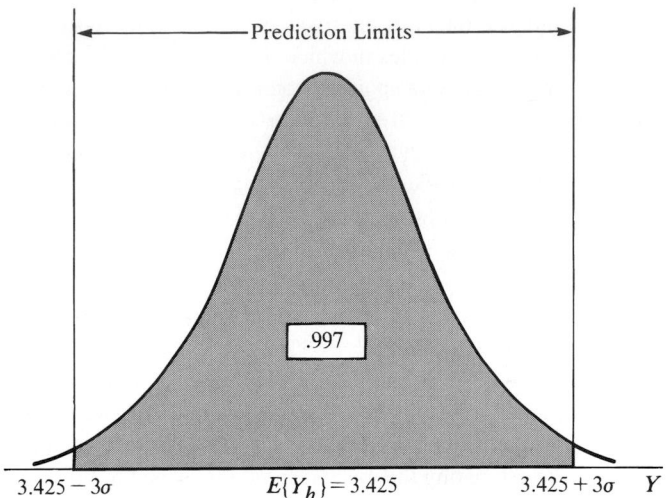

Probability Distribution of Y when $X_h = 3.5$

individual outcomes deviate from the mean response, and this must be taken into account by the procedure for predicting $Y_{h(\text{new})}$.

Prediction Interval when Parameters Known

To illustrate the nature of a *prediction interval* for a new observation $Y_{h(\text{new})}$ in as simple a fashion as possible, we shall first assume that all regression parameters are known. Later we drop this assumption and make appropriate modifications.

Suppose that in the college admissions example the relevant parameters of the regression model are known to be:

$$\beta_0 = .10 \qquad \beta_1 = .95$$

$$E\{Y\} = .10 + .95X$$

$$\sigma = .12$$

The admissions officer is considering an applicant whose high school GPA is $X_h = 3.5$. The mean college GPA for students whose high school average is 3.5 is:

$$E\{Y_h\} = .10 + .95(3.5) = 3.425$$

Figure 2.4 shows the probability distribution of Y for $X_h = 3.5$. Its mean is $E\{Y_h\} = 3.425$, and its standard deviation is $\sigma = .12$. Further, the distribution is normal in accord with regression model (2.1).

Suppose we were to predict that the college GPA of the applicant whose high school GPA is $X_h = 3.5$ will be between:

$$E\{Y_h\} \pm 3\sigma$$

$$3.425 \pm 3(.12)$$

so that the prediction interval would be:

$$3.065 \le Y_{h(\text{new})} \le 3.785$$

Since 99.7 percent of the area in a normal probability distribution falls within three standard deviations from the mean, the probability is .997 that this prediction interval will give a correct prediction for the applicant with high school GPA of 3.5. While the prediction limits here are rather wide, so that the prediction is not too precise, the prediction interval does indicate to the admissions officer that the applicant is expected to attain at least a 3.0 GPA in the first year of college.

The basic idea of a prediction interval is thus to choose a range in the distribution of Y wherein most of the observations will fall, and then to declare that the next observation will fall in this range. The usefulness of the prediction interval depends, as always, on the width of the interval and the needs for precision by the user.

In general, when the regression parameters of normal error regression model (2.1) are known, the $1 - \alpha$ prediction limits for $Y_{h(\text{new})}$ are:

(2.34) $$E\{Y_h\} \pm z(1 - \alpha/2)\sigma$$

In centering the limits around $E\{Y_h\}$, we obtain the narrowest interval consistent with the specified probability of a correct prediction.

Prediction Interval for $Y_{h(\text{new})}$ *when Parameters Unknown*

When the regression parameters are unknown, they must be estimated. The mean of the distribution of Y is estimated by $\hat{Y}_h$, as usual, and the variance of the distribution of Y is estimated by *MSE*. We cannot, however, simply use the prediction limits (2.34) with the parameters replaced by the corresponding point estimators. The reason is illustrated intuitively in Figure 2.5. Shown there are two probability distributions of Y, corresponding to the upper and lower limits of a confidence interval for $E\{Y_h\}$. In other words, the distribution of Y could be located as far left as the one shown, as far right as the other one shown, or anywhere in between. Since we do not know the mean $E\{Y_h\}$ and only estimate it by a confidence interval, we cannot be certain of the location of the distribution of Y.

Figure 2.5 also shows the prediction limits for each of the two probability distributions of Y presented there. Since we cannot be certain of the location of the distribution of Y, prediction limits for $Y_{h(\text{new})}$ clearly must take account of two elements, as shown in Figure 2.5:

1. Variation in possible location of the distribution of Y

2. Variation within the probability distribution of Y

FIGURE 2.5   **Prediction of $Y_{h(\text{new})}$ when Parameters Unknown.**

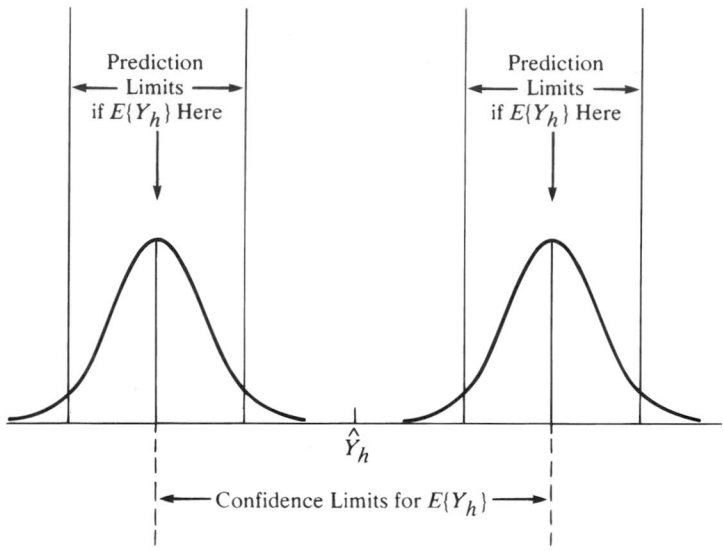

Prediction limits for a new observation $Y_{h(\text{new})}$ at a given level X_h are obtained by means of the following theorem:

$$(2.35) \qquad \frac{Y_{h(\text{new})} - \hat{Y}_h}{s\{\text{pred}\}} \text{ is distributed as } t(n-2) \text{ for normal error regression model (2.1)}$$

Note that the studentized statistic (2.35) uses the point estimator $\hat{Y}_h$ in the numerator rather than the true mean $E\{Y_h\}$ because the true mean is unknown and cannot be used in making a prediction. The estimated standard deviation of the prediction, $s\{\text{pred}\}$, in the denominator of the studentized statistic will be defined shortly.

From theorem (2.35), it follows in the usual fashion that the $1 - \alpha$ prediction limits for a new observation $Y_{h(\text{new})}$ are [for instance, compare (2.35) to (2.10) and relate $\hat{Y}_h$ to b_1 and $Y_{h(\text{new})}$ to β_1]:

$$(2.36) \qquad \hat{Y}_h \pm t(1 - \alpha/2; n-2)s\{\text{pred}\}$$

Note that the numerator of the studentized statistic (2.35) represents how far the new observation $Y_{h(\text{new})}$ will deviate from the estimated mean $\hat{Y}_h$ based on the original n cases in the study. This difference may be viewed as the prediction error, with $\hat{Y}_h$ serving as the best point estimate of the value of the new observation $Y_{h(\text{new})}$. The variance of this prediction error can be readily obtained by utilizing the independence of the new observation $Y_{h(\text{new})}$ and the original n sample cases on which $\hat{Y}_h$ is based. We denote the variance of the prediction error by $\sigma^2\{\text{pred}\}$, and we obtain by (A.31b):

$$(2.37) \qquad \sigma^2\{\text{pred}\} = \sigma^2\{Y_{h(\text{new})} - \hat{Y}_h\} = \sigma^2\{Y_{h(\text{new})}\} + \sigma^2\{\hat{Y}_h\} = \sigma^2 + \sigma^2\{\hat{Y}_h\}$$

Note that $\sigma^2\{\text{pred}\}$ has two components:

1. The variance of the distribution of Y at $X = X_h$, namely σ^2

2. The variance of the sampling distribution of $\hat{Y}_h$, namely $\sigma^2\{\hat{Y}_h\}$

An unbiased estimator of $\sigma^2\{\text{pred}\}$ is:

$$s^2\{\text{pred}\} = MSE + s^2\{\hat{Y}_h\} \tag{2.38}$$

which can be expressed as follows, using (2.30):

$$s^2\{\text{pred}\} = MSE\left[1 + \frac{1}{n} + \frac{(X_h - \bar{X})^2}{\Sigma(X_i - \bar{X})^2}\right] \tag{2.38a}$$

Example. The Toluca Company studied the relationship between lot size and work hours primarily to obtain information on the mean work hours required for different lot sizes for use in determining the optimum lot size. The company was also interested, however, to see whether the regression relationship is useful for predicting the required work hours for individual lots. Suppose that the next lot to be produced consists of $X_h = 100$ units and that a 90 percent prediction interval is desired. We require $t(.95; 23) = 1.714$. From earlier work, we have:

$$\hat{Y}_h = 419.4 \qquad s^2\{\hat{Y}_h\} = 203.72 \qquad MSE = 2{,}384$$

Using (2.38), we obtain:

$$s^2\{\text{pred}\} = 2{,}384 + 203.72 = 2{,}587.72$$

$$s\{\text{pred}\} = 50.87$$

Hence, the 90 percent prediction interval for $Y_{h(\text{new})}$ is by (2.36):

$$419.4 - 1.714(50.87) \le Y_{h(\text{new})} \le 419.4 + 1.714(50.87)$$

$$332.2 \le Y_{h(\text{new})} \le 506.6$$

With confidence coefficient .90, we predict that the number of work hours for the next production run of 100 units will be somewhere between 332 and 507 hours.

This prediction interval is rather wide and may not be too useful for planning worker requirements for the next lot. The interval can still be useful for control purposes, though. For instance, suppose that the actual work hours on the next lot of 100 units were 550 hours. Since the actual work hours fall outside the prediction limits, management would have an indication that a change in the production process may have occurred and would be alerted to the possible need for remedial action.

Note that the primary reason for the wide prediction interval is the large lot-to-lot variability in work hours for any given lot size; $MSE = 2{,}384$ accounts for 92 percent of the estimated prediction variance $s^2\{\text{pred}\} = 2{,}587.72$. It may be that the large lot-to-lot variability reflects other factors that affect the required number of work hours besides lot size, such as the amount of experience of employees assigned to the lot production. If so, a multiple regression model incorporating these other factors might lead to much more precise predictions. Alternatively, a designed experiment could be conducted to determine the main factors leading to the large lot-to-lot variation. A quality improvement program would then use these findings to achieve more uniform performance, for example, by additional training of employees if inadequate training accounted for much of the variability.

Comments

1. The 90 percent prediction interval for $Y_{h(\text{new})}$ obtained in the Toluca Company example is wider than the 90 percent confidence interval for $E\{Y_h\}$ obtained in Example 2 on page 60. The reason is that when predicting the work hours required for a new lot, we encounter both the variability in $\hat{Y}_h$ from sample to sample as well as the lot-to-lot variation within the probability distribution of Y.

2. Formula (2.38a) indicates that the prediction interval is wider the further X_h is from $\bar{X}$. The reason for this is that the estimate of the mean $\hat{Y}_h$, as noted earlier, is less precise as X_h is located further away from $\bar{X}$.

3. The prediction limits (2.36), unlike the confidence limits (2.33) for a mean response $E\{Y_h\}$, are sensitive to departures from normality of the error terms distribution. In Chapter 3, we discuss diagnostic procedures for examining the nature of the probability distribution of the error terms, and we describe remedial measures if the departure from normality is serious.

4. The confidence coefficient for the prediction limits (2.36) refers to the taking of repeated samples based on the same set of X values, and calculating prediction limits for $Y_{h(\text{new})}$ for each sample.

5. Prediction limits (2.36) apply for a single prediction based on the sample data. Next, we discuss how to predict the mean of several new observations at a given X_h, and in Chapter 4 we take up how to make several predictions at different X_h levels.

6. Prediction intervals resemble confidence intervals. However, they differ conceptually. A confidence interval represents an inference on a parameter and is an interval that is intended to cover the value of the parameter. A prediction interval, on the other hand, is a statement about the value to be taken by a random variable, the new observation $Y_{h(\text{new})}$. ∎

Prediction of Mean of m New Observations for Given X_h

Occasionally, one would like to predict the mean of m new observations on Y for a given level of the predictor variable. Suppose the Toluca Company has been asked to bid on a contract that calls for $m = 3$ production runs of $X_h = 100$ units during the next few months. Management would like to predict the mean work hours per lot for these three runs and then convert this into a prediction of the total work hours required to fill the contract.

We denote the mean of the new Y observations to be predicted as $\bar{Y}_{h(\text{new})}$. It can be shown that the appropriate $1 - \alpha$ prediction limits are, assuming that the new Y observations are independent:

(2.39)
$$\hat{Y}_h \pm t(1 - \alpha/2; n - 2)s\{\text{predmean}\}$$

where:

(2.39a)
$$s^2\{\text{predmean}\} = \frac{MSE}{m} + s^2\{\hat{Y}_h\}$$

or equivalently:

(2.39b)
$$s^2\{\text{predmean}\} = MSE\left[\frac{1}{m} + \frac{1}{n} + \frac{(X_h - \bar{X})^2}{\Sigma(X_i - \bar{X})^2}\right]$$

Note from (2.39a) that the variance $s^2\{\text{predmean}\}$ has two components:

1. The variance of the mean of m observations from the probability distribution of Y at $X = X_h$

2. The variance of the sampling distribution of $\hat{Y}_h$

Example.   In the Toluca Company example, let us find the 90 percent prediction interval for the mean number of work hours $\overline{Y}_{h(\text{new})}$ in three new production runs, each for $X_h = 100$ units. From previous work, we have:

$$\hat{Y}_h = 419.4 \qquad s^2\{\hat{Y}_h\} = 203.72$$

$$MSE = 2{,}384 \qquad t(.95; 23) = 1.714$$

Hence, we obtain:

$$s^2\{\text{predmean}\} = \frac{2{,}384}{3} + 203.72 = 998.4$$

$$s\{\text{predmean}\} = 31.60$$

The prediction interval for the mean work hours per lot then is:

$$419.4 - 1.714(31.60) \leq \overline{Y}_{h(\text{new})} \leq 419.4 + 1.714(31.60)$$

$$365.2 \leq \overline{Y}_{h(\text{new})} \leq 473.6$$

Note that these prediction limits are narrower than those for predicting the work hours for a single lot of 100 units because they involve a prediction of the mean work hours for three lots.

We obtain the prediction interval for the total number of work hours for the three lots by multiplying the prediction limits for $\overline{Y}_{h(\text{new})}$ by 3:

$$1{,}095.6 = 3(365.2) \leq \text{ Total work hours } \leq 3(473.6) = 1{,}420.8$$

Thus, it can be predicted with 90 percent confidence that between 1,096 and 1,421 work hours will be needed to fill the contract for three lots of 100 units each.

2.6   Confidence Band for Regression Line

At times we would like to obtain a confidence band for the entire regression line $E\{Y\} = \beta_0 + \beta_1 X$. This band enables us to see the region in which the entire regression line lies. It is particularly useful for determining the appropriateness of a fitted regression function, as we explain in Chapter 3.

The Working-Hotelling $1 - \alpha$ confidence band for the regression line for regression model (2.1) has the following two boundary values at any level X_h:

(2.40) $$\hat{Y}_h \pm W s\{\hat{Y}_h\}$$

where:

(2.40a) $$W^2 = 2F(1 - \alpha; 2, n - 2)$$

and $\hat{Y}_h$ and $s\{\hat{Y}_h\}$ are defined in (2.28) and (2.30), respectively. Note that the formula for the boundary values is of exactly the same form as formula (2.33) for the confidence limits for the mean response at X_h, except that the t multiple has been replaced by the W multiple. Consequently, the boundary points of the confidence band for the regression line are wider apart the further X_h is from the mean $\bar{X}$ of the X observations. The W multiple will be larger than the t multiple in (2.33) because the confidence band must encompass the entire regression line, whereas the confidence limits for $E\{Y_h\}$ at X_h apply only at the single level X_h.

Example

We wish to determine how precisely we have been able to estimate the regression function for the Toluca Company example by obtaining the 90 percent confidence band for the regression line. We illustrate the calculations of the boundary values of the confidence band when $X_h = 100$. We found earlier for this case:

$$\hat{Y}_h = 419.4 \qquad s\{\hat{Y}_h\} = 14.27$$

We now require:

$$W^2 = 2F(1-\alpha; 2, n-2) = 2F(.90; 2, 23) = 2(2.549) = 5.098$$

$$W = 2.258$$

Hence, the boundary values of the confidence band for the regression line at $X_h = 100$ are $419.4 \pm 2.258(14.27)$, and the confidence band there is:

$$387.2 \leq \beta_0 + \beta_1 X_h \leq 451.6 \qquad \text{for } X_h = 100$$

In similar fashion, we can calculate the boundary values for other values of X_h by obtaining $\hat{Y}_h$ and $s\{\hat{Y}_h\}$ for each X_h level from (2.28) and (2.30) and then finding the boundary values by means of (2.40). Figure 2.6 contains a plot of the confidence band for the regression line. Note that at $X_h = 100$, the boundary values are 387.2 and 451.6, as we calculated earlier.

We see from Figure 2.6 that the regression line for the Toluca Company example has been estimated fairly precisely. The slope of the regression line is clearly positive, and the levels of the regression line at different levels of X are estimated fairly precisely except for small and large lot sizes.

Comments

1. The boundary values of the confidence band for the regression line in (2.40) define a hyperbola, as may be seen by replacing $\hat{Y}_h$ and $s\{\hat{Y}_h\}$ by their definitions in (2.28) and (2.30), respectively:

$$(2.41) \qquad b_0 + b_1 X \pm W\sqrt{MSE}\left[\frac{1}{n} + \frac{(X - \bar{X})^2}{\Sigma(X_i - \bar{X})^2}\right]^{1/2}$$

2. The boundary values of the confidence band for the regression line at any value X_h often are not substantially wider than the confidence limits for the mean response at that single

FIGURE 2.6   **Confidence Band for Regression Line—Toluca Company Example.**

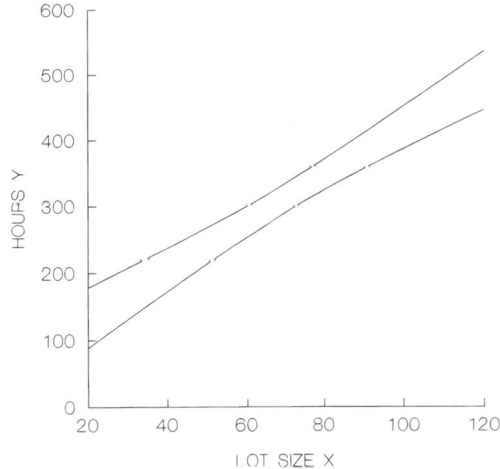

X_h level. In the Toluca Company example, the t multiple for estimating the mean response at $X_h = 100$ with a 90 percent confidence interval was $t(.95; 23) = 1.714$. This compares with the W multiple for the 90 percent confidence band for the entire regression line of $W = 2.258$. With the somewhat wider limits for the entire regression line, one is able to draw conclusions about any and all mean responses for the entire regression line and not just about the mean response at a given X level. Some uses of this broader base for inference will be explained in the next two chapters.

3. The confidence band (2.40) applies to the entire regression line over all real-numbered values of X from $-\infty$ to ∞. The confidence coefficient indicates the proportion of time that the estimating procedure will yield a band that covers the entire line, in a long series of samples in which the X observations are kept at the same level as in the actual study.

In applications, the confidence band is ignored for that part of the regression line which is not of interest in the problem at hand. In the Toluca Company example, for instance, negative lot sizes would be ignored. The confidence coefficient for a limited segment of the band of interest is somewhat higher than $1 - \alpha$, so $1 - \alpha$ serves then as a lower bound to the confidence coefficient.

4. Some alternative procedures for developing confidence bands for the regression line have been developed. The simplicity of the Working-Hotelling confidence band (2.40) arises from the fact that it is a direct extension of the confidence limits for a single mean response in (2.33).   ∎

2.7   Analysis of Variance Approach to Regression Analysis

We now have developed the basic regression model and demonstrated its major uses. At this point, we consider the regression analysis from the perspective of analysis of variance. This new perspective will not enable us to do anything new, but the analysis of variance approach will come into its own when we take up multiple regression models and other types of linear statistical models.

FIGURE 2.7   **Illustration of Partitioning of Total Deviations $Y_i - \bar{Y}$—Toluca Company Example (not drawn to scale; only observations Y_1 and Y_2 are shown).**

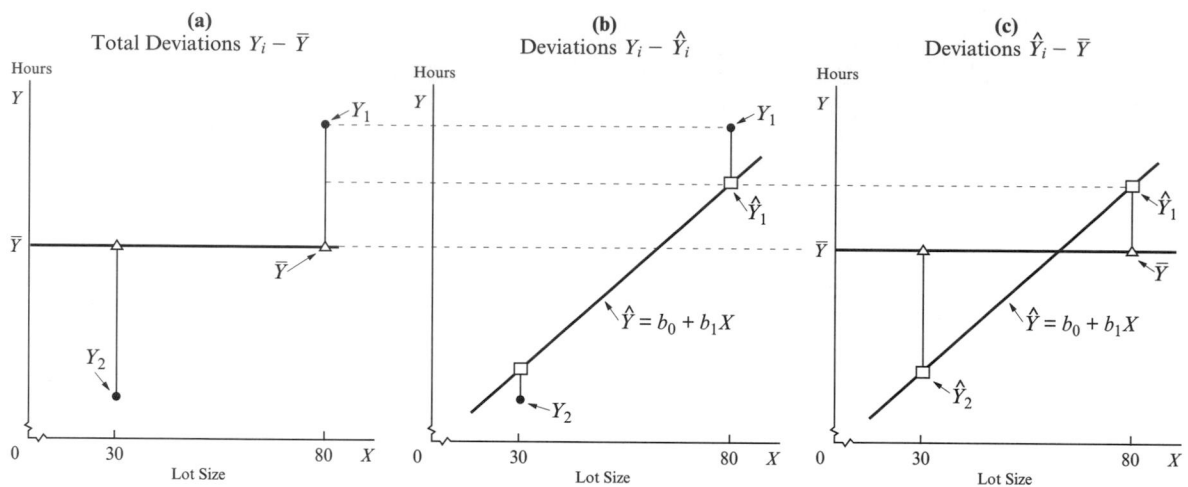

Partitioning of Total Sum of Squares

Basic Notions.   The analysis of variance approach is based on the partitioning of sums of squares and degrees of freedom associated with the response variable Y. To explain the motivation of this approach, consider again the Toluca Company example. Figure 2.7a shows the observations Y_i for the first two production runs presented in Table 1.1. Disregarding the lot sizes, we see that there is variation in the number of work hours Y_i, as in all statistical data. This variation is conventionally measured in terms of the deviations of the Y_i around their mean $\bar{Y}$:

$$(2.42) \qquad Y_i - \bar{Y}$$

These deviations are shown by the vertical lines in Figure 2.7a. The measure of total variation, denoted by *SSTO*, is the sum of the squared deviations (2.42):

$$(2.43) \qquad SSTO = \sum (Y_i - \bar{Y})^2$$

Here *SSTO* stands for *total sum of squares*. If all Y_i observations are the same, $SSTO = 0$. The greater the variation among the Y_i observations, the larger is *SSTO*. Thus, *SSTO* for our example is a measure of the uncertainty pertaining to the work hours required for a lot, when the lot size is not taken into account.

When we utilize the predictor variable X, the variation reflecting the uncertainty concerning the variable Y is that of the Y_i observations around the fitted regression line:

$$(2.44) \qquad Y_i - \hat{Y}_i$$

These deviations are shown by the vertical lines in Figure 2.7b. The measure of variation in the Y_i observations that is present when the predictor variable X is taken into account is

Sampling Distribution of $(b_0 - \beta_0)/s\{b_0\}$

Analogous to theorem (2.10) for b_1, a theorem for b_0 states:

(2.24) $\dfrac{b_0 - \beta_0}{s\{b_0\}}$ is distributed as $t(n-2)$ for regression model (2.1)

Hence, confidence intervals for β_0 and tests concerning β_0 can be set up in ordinary fashion, using the t distribution.

Confidence Interval for β_0

The $1 - \alpha$ confidence limits for β_0 are obtained in the same manner as those for β_1 derived earlier. They are:

(2.25) $$b_0 \pm t(1 - \alpha/2; n - 2)s\{b_0\}$$

Example.   As noted earlier, the scope of the model for the Toluca Company example does not extend to lot sizes of $X = 0$. Hence, the regression parameter β_0 may not have intrinsic meaning here. If, nevertheless, a 90 percent confidence interval for β_0 were desired, we would proceed by finding $t(.95; 23)$ and $s\{b_0\}$. From Table B.2, we find $t(.95; 23) = 1.714$. Using the earlier results summarized in Table 2.1, we obtain by (2.23):

$$s^2\{b_0\} = MSE\left[\frac{1}{n} + \frac{\bar{X}^2}{\Sigma(X_i - \bar{X})^2}\right] = 2{,}384\left[\frac{1}{25} + \frac{(70.00)^2}{19{,}800}\right] = 685.34$$

or:

$$s\{b_0\} = 26.18$$

The MINITAB output in Figure 2.2 shows this estimated standard deviation in the column labeled Stdev and the row labeled Constant.

The 90 percent confidence interval for β_0 is:

$$62.37 - 1.714(26.18) \le \beta_0 \le 62.37 + 1.714(26.18)$$

$$17.5 \le \beta_0 \le 107.2$$

We caution again that this confidence interval does not necessarily provide meaningful information. For instance, it does not necessarily provide information about the "setup" cost (the cost incurred in setting up the production process for the part) since we are not certain whether a linear regression model is appropriate when the scope of the model is extended to $X = 0$.

2.3   Some Considerations on Making Inferences Concerning β_0 and β_1

Effects of Departures from Normality

If the probability distributions of Y are not exactly normal but do not depart seriously, the sampling distributions of b_0 and b_1 will be approximately normal, and the use of the

the sum of the squared deviations (2.44), which is the familiar *SSE* of (1.21):

(2.45)
$$SSE = \sum(Y_i - \hat{Y}_i)^2$$

Again, *SSE* denotes *error sum of squares*. If all Y_i observations fall on the fitted regression line, $SSE = 0$. The greater the variation of the Y_i observations around the fitted regression line, the larger is *SSE*.

For the Toluca Company example, we know from earlier work (Table 2.1) that:

$$SSTO = 307,203 \qquad SSE = 54,825$$

What accounts for the substantial difference between these two sums of squares? The difference, as we show shortly, is another sum of squares:

(2.46)
$$SSR = \sum(\hat{Y}_i - \bar{Y})^2$$

where *SSR* stands for *regression sum of squares*. Note that *SSR* is a sum of squared deviations, the deviations being:

(2.47)
$$\hat{Y}_i - \bar{Y}$$

These deviations are shown by the vertical lines in Figure 2.7c. Each deviation is simply the difference between the fitted value on the regression line and the mean of the fitted values $\bar{Y}$. [Recall from (1.18) that the mean of the fitted values $\hat{Y}_i$ is $\bar{Y}$.] If the regression line is horizontal so that $\hat{Y}_i - \bar{Y} \equiv 0$, then $SSR = 0$. Otherwise, *SSR* is positive.

SSR may be considered a measure of that part of the variability of the Y_i which is associated with the regression line. The larger *SSR* is in relation to *SSTO*, the greater is the effect of the regression relation in accounting for the total variation in the Y_i observations.

For the Toluca Company example, we have:

$$SSR = SSTO - SSE = 307,203 - 54,825 = 252,378$$

which indicates that most of the total variability in work hours is accounted for by the relation between lot size and work hours.

Formal Development of Partitioning. The total deviation $Y_i - \bar{Y}$, used in the measure of the total variation of the observations Y_i without taking the predictor variable into account, can be decomposed into two components:

(2.48)
$$\underbrace{Y_i - \bar{Y}}_{\substack{\text{Total} \\ \text{deviation}}} = \underbrace{\hat{Y}_i - \bar{Y}}_{\substack{\text{Deviation} \\ \text{of fitted} \\ \text{regression} \\ \text{value} \\ \text{around mean}}} + \underbrace{Y_i - \hat{Y}_i}_{\substack{\text{Deviation} \\ \text{around} \\ \text{fitted} \\ \text{regression} \\ \text{line}}}$$

The two components are:

1. The deviation of the fitted value $\hat{Y}_i$ around the mean $\bar{Y}$

2. The deviation of the observation Y_i around the fitted regression line

Figure 2.7 shows this decomposition for observation Y_1 by the broken lines.

It is a remarkable property that the sums of these squared deviations have the same relationship:

$$(2.49) \qquad \sum (Y_i - \bar{Y})^2 = \sum (\hat{Y}_i - \bar{Y})^2 + \sum (Y_i - \hat{Y}_i)^2$$

or, using the notation in (2.43), (2.45), and (2.46):

$$(2.50) \qquad\qquad SSTO = SSR + SSE$$

To prove this basic result in the analysis of variance, we proceed as follows:

$$\sum (Y_i - \bar{Y})^2 = \sum [(\hat{Y}_i - \bar{Y}) + (Y_i - \hat{Y}_i)]^2$$
$$= \sum [(\hat{Y}_i - \bar{Y})^2 + (Y_i - \hat{Y}_i)^2 + 2(\hat{Y}_i - \bar{Y})(Y_i - \hat{Y}_i)]$$
$$= \sum (\hat{Y}_i - \bar{Y})^2 + \sum (Y_i - \hat{Y}_i)^2 + 2 \sum (\hat{Y}_i - \bar{Y})(Y_i - \hat{Y}_i)$$

The last term on the right equals zero, as we can see by expanding it:

$$2 \sum (\hat{Y}_i - \bar{Y})(Y_i - \hat{Y}_i) = 2 \sum \hat{Y}_i (Y_i - \hat{Y}_i) - 2\bar{Y} \sum (Y_i - \hat{Y}_i)$$

The first summation on the right equals zero by (1.20), and the second equals zero by (1.17). Hence, (2.49) follows.

Note

The formulas for $SSTO, SSR$, and SSE given in (2.43), (2.45), and (2.46) are best for computational accuracy. Alternative formulas that are algebraically equivalent are available. One that is useful for deriving analytical results is:

$$(2.51) \qquad\qquad SSR = b_1^2 \sum (X_i - \bar{X})^2 \qquad\qquad\blacksquare$$

Breakdown of Degrees of Freedom

Corresponding to the partitioning of the total sum of squares $SSTO$, there is a partitioning of the associated degrees of freedom (abbreviated df). We have $n - 1$ degrees of freedom associated with $SSTO$. One degree of freedom is lost because the deviations $Y_i - \bar{Y}$ are subject to one constraint: they must sum to zero. Equivalently, one degree of freedom is lost because the sample mean $\bar{Y}$ is used to estimate the population mean.

SSE, as noted earlier, has $n - 2$ degrees of freedom associated with it. Two degrees of freedom are lost because the two parameters β_0 and β_1 are estimated in obtaining the fitted values $\hat{Y}_i$.

SSR has one degree of freedom associated with it. Although there are n deviations $\hat{Y}_i - \bar{Y}$, all fitted values $\hat{Y}_i$ are calculated from the same estimated regression line. Two degrees of freedom are associated with a regression line, corresponding to the intercept and the slope of the line. One of the two degrees of freedom is lost because the deviations $\hat{Y}_i - \bar{Y}$ are subject to a constraint: they must sum to zero.

Note that the degrees of freedom are additive:

$$n - 1 = 1 + (n - 2)$$

For the Toluca Company example, these degrees of freedom are:

$$24 = 1 + 23$$

Mean Squares

A sum of squares divided by its associated degrees of freedom is called a *mean square* (abbreviated *MS*). For instance, an ordinary sample variance is a mean square since a sum of squares, $\Sigma(Y_i - \bar{Y})^2$, is divided by its associated degrees of freedom, $n - 1$. We are interested here in the *regression mean square*, denoted by *MSR*:

(2.52)
$$MSR = \frac{SSR}{1} = SSR$$

and in the *error mean square*, *MSE*, defined earlier in (1.22):

(2.53)
$$MSE = \frac{SSE}{n - 2}$$

For the Toluca Company example, we have $SSR = 252{,}378$ and $SSE = 54{,}825$. Hence:

$$MSR = \frac{252{,}378}{1} = 252{,}378$$

Also, we obtained earlier:

$$MSE = \frac{54{,}825}{23} = 2{,}384$$

Note

The two mean squares *MSR* and *MSE* do not add to $SSTO \div (n - 1) = 307{,}203 \div 24 = 12{,}800$. Thus, mean squares are not additive. ∎

Analysis of Variance Table

Basic Table. The breakdowns of the total sum of squares and associated degrees of freedom are displayed in the form of an analysis of variance table (ANOVA table) in Table 2.2. Mean squares of interest also are shown. In addition, the ANOVA table contains a column of expected mean squares that will be utilized shortly. The ANOVA table for the Toluca Company example is shown in Figure 2.2. The columns for degrees of freedom and sums of squares are reversed in the MINITAB output.

Modified Table. Sometimes an ANOVA table showing one additional element of decomposition is utilized, based on the fact that the total sum of squares can be decomposed into two parts, as follows:

$$SSTO = \sum(Y_i - \bar{Y})^2 = \sum Y_i^2 - n\bar{Y}^2$$

In the modified ANOVA table, the *total uncorrected sum of squares*, denoted by *SSTOU*, is defined as:

(2.54)
$$SSTOU = \sum Y_i^2$$

TABLE 2.2 ANOVA Table for Simple Linear Regression.

Source of Variation	SS	df	MS	E{MS}
Regression	$SSR = \Sigma(\hat{Y}_i - \bar{Y})^2$	1	$MSR = \frac{SSR}{1}$	$\sigma^2 + \beta_1^2 \Sigma(X_i - \bar{X})^2$
Error	$SSE = \Sigma(Y_i - \hat{Y}_i)^2$	$n - 2$	$MSE = \frac{SSE}{n-2}$	σ^2
Total	$SSTO = \Sigma(Y_i - \bar{Y})^2$	$n - 1$		

TABLE 2.3 Modified ANOVA Table for Simple Linear Regression.

Source of Variation	SS	df	MS
Regression	$SSR = \Sigma(\hat{Y}_i - \bar{Y})^2$	1	$MSR = \frac{SSR}{1}$
Error	$SSE = \Sigma(Y_i - \hat{Y}_i)^2$	$n - 2$	$MSE = \frac{SSE}{n-2}$
Total	$SSTO = \Sigma(Y_i - \bar{Y})^2$	$n - 1$	
Correction for mean	$SS(\text{correction for mean}) = n\bar{Y}^2$	1	
Total, uncorrected	$SSTOU = \Sigma Y_i^2$	n	

and the *correction for the mean sum of squares*, denoted by SS(correction for mean), is defined as:

$$(2.55) \qquad SS(\text{correction for mean}) = n\bar{Y}^2$$

Table 2.3 shows the general format of this modified ANOVA table. While both types of ANOVA tables are widely used, we shall usually utilize the basic type of table.

Expected Mean Squares

In order to make inferences based on the analysis of variance approach, we need to know the expected value of each of the mean squares. The expected value of a mean square is the mean of its sampling distribution and tells us what is being estimated by the mean square. Statistical theory provides the following results:

$$(2.56) \qquad E\{MSE\} = \sigma^2$$

$$(2.57) \qquad E\{MSR\} = \sigma^2 + \beta_1^2 \sum(X_i - \bar{X})^2$$

The expected mean squares in (2.56) and (2.57) are shown in the analysis of variance table in Table 2.2. Note that result (2.56) is in accord with our earlier statement that *MSE* is an unbiased estimator of σ^2.

Two important implications of the expected mean squares in (2.56) and (2.57) are the following:

1. The mean of the sampling distribution of *MSE* is σ^2 whether or not X and Y are linearly related, i.e., whether or not $\beta_1 = 0$.

2. The mean of the sampling distribution of *MSR* is also σ^2 when $\beta_1 = 0$. Hence, when $\beta_1 = 0$, the sampling distributions of *MSR* and *MSE* are located identically and *MSR* and *MSE* will tend to be of the same order of magnitude.

On the other hand, when $\beta_1 \neq 0$, the mean of the sampling distribution of *MSR* is greater than σ^2 since the term $\beta_1^2 \Sigma(X_i - \bar{X})^2$ in (2.57) then must be positive. Thus, when $\beta_1 \neq 0$, the mean of the sampling distribution of *MSR* is located to the right of that of *MSE* and, hence, *MSR* will tend to be larger than *MSE*.

This suggests that a comparison of *MSR* and *MSE* is useful for testing whether or not $\beta_1 = 0$. If *MSR* and *MSE* are of the same order of magnitude, this would suggest that $\beta_1 = 0$. On the other hand, if *MSR* is substantially greater than *MSE*, this would suggest that $\beta_1 \neq 0$. This indeed is the basic idea underlying the analysis of variance test to be discussed next.

Note

The derivation of (2.56) follows from theorem (2.11), which states that $SSE/\sigma^2 \sim \chi^2(n - 2)$ for regression model (2.1). Hence, it follows from property (A.42) of the chi-square distribution that:

$$E\left\{ \frac{SSE}{\sigma^2} \right\} = n - 2$$

or that:

$$E\left\{ \frac{SSE}{n - 2} \right\} = E\{MSE\} = \sigma^2$$

To find the expected value of *MSR*, we begin with (2.51):

$$SSR = b_1^2 \sum (X_i - \bar{X})^2$$

Now by (A.15a), we have:

(2.58)
$$\sigma^2\{b_1\} = E\{b_1^2\} - (E\{b_1\})^2$$

We know from (2.3a) that $E\{b_1\} = \beta_1$ and from (2.3b) that:

$$\sigma^2\{b_1\} = \frac{\sigma^2}{\Sigma(X_i - \bar{X})^2}$$

Hence, substituting into (2.58), we obtain:

$$E\{b_1^2\} = \frac{\sigma^2}{\Sigma(X_i - \bar{X})^2} + \beta_1^2$$

It now follows that:

$$E\{SSR\} = E\{b_1^2\} \sum (X_i - \bar{X})^2 = \sigma^2 + \beta_1^2 \sum (X_i - \bar{X})^2$$

Finally, $E\{MSR\}$ is:

$$E\{MSR\} = E\left\{ \frac{SSR}{1} \right\} = \sigma^2 + \beta_1^2 \sum (X_i - \bar{X})^2 \qquad \blacksquare$$

F Test of $\beta_1 = 0$ versus $\beta_1 \neq 0$

The analysis of variance approach provides us with a battery of highly useful tests for regression models (and other linear statistical models). For the simple linear regression case considered here, the analysis of variance provides us with a test for:

(2.59)
$$H_0: \beta_1 = 0$$
$$H_a: \beta_1 \neq 0$$

Test Statistic.   The test statistic for the analysis of variance approach is denoted by F^*. As just mentioned, it compares MSR and MSE in the following fashion:

(2.60)
$$F^* = \frac{MSR}{MSE}$$

The earlier motivation, based on the expected mean squares in Table 2.2, suggests that large values of F^* support H_a and values of F^* near 1 support H_0. In other words, the appropriate test is an upper-tail one.

Sampling Distribution of F^*.   In order to be able to construct a statistical decision rule and examine its properties, we need to know the sampling distribution of F^*. We begin by considering the sampling distribution of F^* when H_0 ($\beta_1 = 0$) holds. *Cochran's theorem* will be most helpful in this connection. For our purposes, this theorem can be stated as follows:

(2.61)   If all n observations Y_i come from the same normal distribution with mean μ and variance σ^2, and $SSTO$ is decomposed into k sums of squares SS_r, each with degrees of freedom df_r, then the SS_r/σ^2 terms are independent χ^2 variables with df_r degrees of freedom if:

$$\sum_{r=1}^{k} df_r = n - 1$$

Note from Table 2.2 that we have decomposed $SSTO$ into the two sums of squares SSR and SSE and that their degrees of freedom are additive. Hence:

If $\beta_1 = 0$ so that all Y_i have the same mean $\mu = \beta_0$ and the same variance σ^2, SSE/σ^2 and SSR/σ^2 are independent χ^2 variables.

Now consider test statistic F^*, which we can write as follows:

$$F^* = \frac{\dfrac{SSR}{\sigma^2}}{1} \div \frac{\dfrac{SSE}{\sigma^2}}{n-2} = \frac{MSR}{MSE}$$

But by Cochran's theorem, we have when H_0 holds:

$$F^* \sim \frac{\chi^2(1)}{1} \div \frac{\chi^2(n-2)}{n-2} \qquad \text{when } H_0 \text{ holds}$$

where the χ^2 variables are independent. Thus, when H_0 holds, F^* is the ratio of two independent χ^2 variables, each divided by its degrees of freedom. But this is the definition of an F random variable in (A.47).

We have thus established that if H_0 holds, F^* follows the F distribution, specifically the $F(1, n-2)$ distribution.

When H_a holds, it can be shown that F^* follows the noncentral F distribution, a complex distribution that we need not consider further at this time.

Note

Even if $\beta_1 \neq 0$, SSR and SSE are independent and $SSE/\sigma^2 \sim \chi^2$. However, the condition that both SSR/σ^2 and SSE/σ^2 are χ^2 random variables requires $\beta_1 = 0$. ∎

Construction of Decision Rule. Since the test is upper-tail and F^* is distributed as $F(1, n-2)$ when H_0 holds, the decision rule is as follows when the risk of a Type I error is to be controlled at α:

(2.62)

$$\text{If } F^* \leq F(1-\alpha; 1, n-2), \text{ conclude } H_0$$

$$\text{If } F^* > F(1-\alpha; 1, n-2), \text{ conclude } H_a$$

where $F(1-\alpha; 1, n-2)$ is the $(1-\alpha)100$ percentile of the appropriate F distribution.

Example. For the Toluca Company example, we shall repeat the earlier test on β_1, this time using the F test. The alternative conclusions are:

$$H_0: \ \beta_1 = 0$$

$$H_a: \ \beta_1 \neq 0$$

As before, let $\alpha = .05$. Since $n = 25$, we require $F(.95; 1, 23) = 4.28$. The decision rule is:

$$\text{If } F^* \leq 4.28, \text{ conclude } H_0$$

$$\text{If } F^* > 4.28, \text{ conclude } H_a$$

We have from earlier that $MSR = 252,378$ and $MSE = 2,384$. Hence, F^* is:

$$F^* = \frac{252,378}{2,384} = 105.9$$

Since $F^* = 105.9 > 4.28$, we conclude H_a, that $\beta_1 \neq 0$, or that there is a linear association between work hours and lot size. This is the same result as when the t test was employed, as it must be according to our discussion below.

The MINITAB output in Figure 2.2 shows the F^* statistic in the column labeled F. Next to it is shown the P-value, $P\{F(1, 23) > 105.9\}$, namely, 0+, indicating that the data are not consistent with $\beta_1 = 0$.

Equivalence of F Test and t Test. For a given α level, the F test of $\beta_1 = 0$ versus $\beta_1 \neq 0$ is equivalent algebraically to the two-tailed t test. To see this, recall from (2.51) that:

$$SSR = b_1^2 \sum (X_i - \bar{X})^2$$

Thus, we can write:

$$F^* = \frac{SSR \div 1}{SSE \div (n-2)} = \frac{b_1^2 \Sigma(X_i - \bar{X})^2}{MSE}$$

But since $s^2\{b_1\} = MSE / \Sigma(X_i - \bar{X})^2$, we obtain:

(2.63)
$$F^* = \frac{b_1^2}{s^2\{b_1\}} = \left(\frac{b_1}{s\{b_1\}}\right)^2 = (t^*)^2$$

The last step follows because the t^* statistic for testing whether or not $\beta_1 = 0$ is by (2.17):

$$t^* = \frac{b_1}{s\{b_1\}}$$

In the Toluca Company example, we just calculated that $F^* = 105.9$. From earlier work, we have $t^* = 10.29$ (see Figure 2.2). We thus see that $(10.29)^2 = 105.9$.

Corresponding to the relation between t^* and F^*, we have the following relation between the required percentiles of the t and F distributions for the tests: $[t(1 - \alpha/2; n - 2)]^2 = F(1 - \alpha; 1, n - 2)$. In our tests on β_1, these percentiles were $[t(.975; 23)]^2 = (2.069)^2 = 4.28 = F(.95; 1, 23)$. Remember that the t test is two-tailed whereas the F test is one-tailed.

Thus, at any given α level, we can use either the t test or the F test for testing $\beta_1 = 0$ versus $\beta_1 \neq 0$. Whenever one test leads to H_0, so will the other, and correspondingly for H_a. The t test, however, is more flexible since it can be used for one-sided alternatives involving $\beta_1(\leq \geq) 0$ versus $\beta_1(> <) 0$, while the F test cannot.

2.8 General Linear Test Approach

The analysis of variance test of $\beta_1 = 0$ versus $\beta_1 \neq 0$ is an example of the general test for a linear statistical model. We now explain this general test approach in terms of the simple linear regression model. We do so at this time because of the generality of the approach and the wide use we shall make of it, and because of the simplicity of understanding the approach in terms of simple linear regression.

The general linear test approach involves three basic steps, which we now describe in turn.

Full Model

We begin with the model considered to be appropriate for the data, which in this context is called the *full* or *unrestricted model*. For the simple linear regression case, the full model is the normal error regression model (2.1):

(2.64)
$$Y_i = \beta_0 + \beta_1 X_i + \varepsilon_i \qquad \text{Full model}$$

We fit this full model, either by the method of least squares or by the method of maximum likelihood, and obtain the error sum of squares. The error sum of squares is the sum of the squared deviations of each observation Y_i around its estimated expected value. In this context, we shall denote this sum of squares by $SSE(F)$ to indicate that it is the error sum of squares for the full model. Here, we have:

$$(2.65) \qquad SSE(F) = \sum[Y_i - (b_0 + b_1 X_i)]^2 = \sum(Y_i - \hat{Y}_i)^2 = SSE$$

Thus, for the full model (2.64), the error sum of squares is simply SSE, which measures the variability of the Y_i observations around the fitted regression line.

Reduced Model

Next, we consider H_0. In this instance, we have:

$$(2.66) \qquad \begin{aligned} H_0 &: \beta_1 = 0 \\ H_a &: \beta_1 \neq 0 \end{aligned}$$

The model when H_0 holds is called the *reduced* or *restricted model*. When $\beta_1 = 0$, model (2.64) reduces to:

$$(2.67) \qquad\qquad Y_i = \beta_0 + \varepsilon_i \qquad\qquad \text{Reduced model}$$

We fit this reduced model, by either the method of least squares or the method of maximum likelihood, and obtain the error sum of squares for this reduced model, denoted by $SSE(R)$. When we fit the particular reduced model (2.67), it can be shown that the least squares and maximum likelihood estimator of β_0 is $\bar{Y}$. Hence, the estimated expected value for each observation is $b_0 = \bar{Y}$, and the error sum of squares for this reduced model is:

$$(2.68) \qquad SSE(R) = \sum(Y_i - b_0)^2 = \sum(Y_i - \bar{Y})^2 = SSTO$$

Test Statistic

The logic now is to compare the two error sums of squares $SSE(F)$ and $SSE(R)$. It can be shown that $SSE(F)$ never is greater than $SSE(R)$:

$$(2.69) \qquad\qquad SSE(F) \leq SSE(R)$$

The reason is that the more parameters are in the model, the better one can fit the data and the smaller are the deviations around the fitted regression function. When $SSE(F)$ is not much less than $SSE(R)$, using the full model does not account for much more of the variability of the Y_i than does the reduced model, in which case the data suggest that the reduced model is adequate (i.e., that H_0 holds). To put this another way, when $SSE(F)$ is close to $SSE(R)$, the variation of the observations around the fitted regression function for the full model is almost as great as the variation around the fitted regression function for the reduced model. In this case, the added parameters in the full model really do not help to reduce the variation in the Y_i about the fitted regression function. Thus, a small difference $SSE(R) - SSE(F)$ suggests that H_0 holds. On the other hand, a large difference suggests that H_a holds because the additional parameters in the model do help to reduce substantially the variation of the observations Y_i around the fitted regression function.

The actual test statistic is a function of $SSE(R) - SSE(F)$, namely:

$$(2.70) \qquad F^* = \frac{SSE(R) - SSE(F)}{df_R - df_F} \div \frac{SSE(F)}{df_F}$$

which follows the F distribution when H_0 holds. The degrees of freedom df_R and df_F are those associated with the reduced and full model error sums of squares, respectively. Large values of F^* lead to H_a because a large difference $SSE(R) - SSE(F)$ suggests that H_a holds. The decision rule therefore is:

$$(2.71) \qquad \begin{aligned} &\text{If } F^* \le F(1 - \alpha; df_R - df_F,\ df_F), \quad \text{conclude } H_0 \\ &\text{If } F^* > F(1 - \alpha; df_R - df_F,\ df_F), \quad \text{conclude } H_a \end{aligned}$$

For testing whether or not $\beta_1 = 0$, we therefore have:

$$SSE(R) = SSTO \qquad SSE(F) = SSE$$

$$df_R = n - 1 \qquad df_F = n - 2$$

so that we obtain when substituting into (2.70):

$$F^* = \frac{SSTO - SSE}{(n - 1) - (n - 2)} \div \frac{SSE}{n - 2} = \frac{SSR}{1} \div \frac{SSE}{n - 2} = \frac{MSR}{MSE}$$

which is identical to the analysis of variance test statistic (2.60).

Summary

The general linear test approach can be used for highly complex tests of linear statistical models, as well as for simple tests. The basic steps in summary form are:

1. Fit the full model and obtain the error sum of squares $SSE(F)$.

2. Fit the reduced model under H_0 and obtain the error sum of squares $SSE(R)$.

3. Use test statistic (2.70) and decision rule (2.71).

2.9 Descriptive Measures of Association between X and Y in Regression Model

We have discussed the major uses of regression analysis—estimation of parameters and means and prediction of new observations—without mentioning the "degree of linear association" between X and Y, or similar terms. The reason is that the usefulness of estimates or predictions depends upon the width of the interval and the user's needs for precision, which vary from one application to another. Hence, no single descriptive measure of the "degree of linear association" can capture the essential information as to whether a given regression relation is useful in any particular application.

Nevertheless, there are times when the degree of linear association is of interest in its own right. We shall now briefly discuss two descriptive measures that are frequently used in practice to describe the degree of linear association between X and Y.

FIGURE 2.8   Scatter Plots when $r^2 = 1$ and $r^2 = 0$.

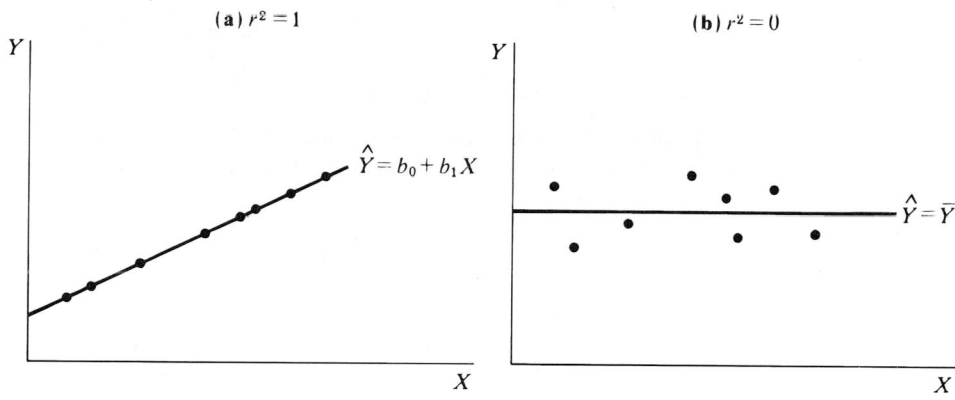

Coefficient of Determination

We saw earlier that *SSTO* measures the variation in the observations Y_i, or the uncertainty in predicting Y, when no account of the predictor variable X is taken. Thus, *SSTO* is a measure of the uncertainty in predicting Y when X is not considered. Similarly, *SSE* measures the variation in the Y_i when a regression model utilizing the predictor variable X is employed. A natural measure of the effect of X in reducing the variation in Y, i.e., in reducing the uncertainty in predicting Y, is to express the reduction in variation ($SSTO - SSE = SSR$) as a proportion of the total variation:

$$(2.72) \qquad r^2 = \frac{SSR}{SSTO} = 1 - \frac{SSE}{SSTO}$$

The measure r^2 is called the *coefficient of determination*. Since $0 \leq SSE \leq SSTO$, it follows that:

$$(2.73) \qquad 0 \leq r^2 \leq 1$$

We may interpret r^2 as the proportionate reduction of total variation associated with the use of the predictor variable X. Thus, the larger r^2 is, the more the total variation of Y is reduced by introducing the predictor variable X. The limiting values of r^2 occur as follows:

1. When all observations fall on the fitted regression line, then $SSE = 0$ and $r^2 = 1$. This case is shown in Figure 2.8a. Here, the predictor variable X accounts for all variation in the observations Y_i.

2. When the fitted regression line is horizontal so that $b_1 = 0$ and $\hat{Y}_i \equiv \bar{Y}$, then $SSE = SSTO$ and $r^2 = 0$. This case is shown in Figure 2.8b. Here, there is no linear association between X and Y in the sample data, and the predictor variable X is of no help in reducing the variation in the observations Y_i with linear regression.

In practice, r^2 is not likely to be 0 or 1 but somewhere between these limits. The closer it is to 1, the greater is said to be the degree of linear association between X and Y.

Coefficient of Correlation

The square root of r^2:

(2.74)
$$r = \pm\sqrt{r^2}$$

is called the *coefficient of correlation*. A plus or minus sign is attached to this measure according to whether the slope of the fitted regression line is positive or negative. Thus, the range of r is:

(2.75)
$$-1 \leq r \leq 1$$

Whereas r^2 indicates the proportionate reduction in the variability of Y attained by the use of information about X, the square root, r, does not have such a clear-cut operational interpretation. Nevertheless, there is a tendency in much applied work to use r instead of r^2.

Since for any r^2 other than 0 or 1, $r^2 < |r|$, use of the coefficient of correlation r may give the impression of a "closer" relationship between X and Y than does the corresponding coefficient of determination r^2. For instance, $r^2 = .10$ indicates that the total variation in Y is reduced by only 10 percent when X is introduced, yet $|r| = .32$ may give an impression of greater linear association between X and Y.

Example

For the Toluca Company example, we obtained $SSTO = 307{,}203$ and $SSR = 252{,}378$. Hence:

$$r^2 = \frac{252{,}378}{307{,}203} = .822$$

Thus, the variation in work hours is reduced by 82.2 percent when lot size is considered.

The correlation coefficient here is:

$$r = +\sqrt{.822} = .907$$

The plus sign is affixed since b_1 is positive.

The MINITAB output in Figure 2.2 shows the coefficient of determination r^2 labeled as R–sq in percent form. The output also shows the coefficent R–sq(adj), which will be explained in Chapter 6.

Limitations of r^2 and r

We noted that no single measure will be adequate for describing the usefulness of a regression model for different applications. Still, the coefficients of determination and correlation are widely used. Unfortunately, they are subject to serious misunderstandings. We consider now three common misunderstandings:

1. *Misunderstanding 1. A high coefficient of correlation indicates that useful predictions can be made.* This is not necessarily correct. In the Toluca Company example, we saw that the coefficient of correlation was high ($r = .91$). Yet the 90 percent prediction interval for the next lot, consisting of 100 units, was wide (332 to 507 hours) and not precise enough to permit management to schedule workers effectively.

FIGURE 2.9   **Illustrations of Two Misunderstandings about Coefficient of Correlation.**

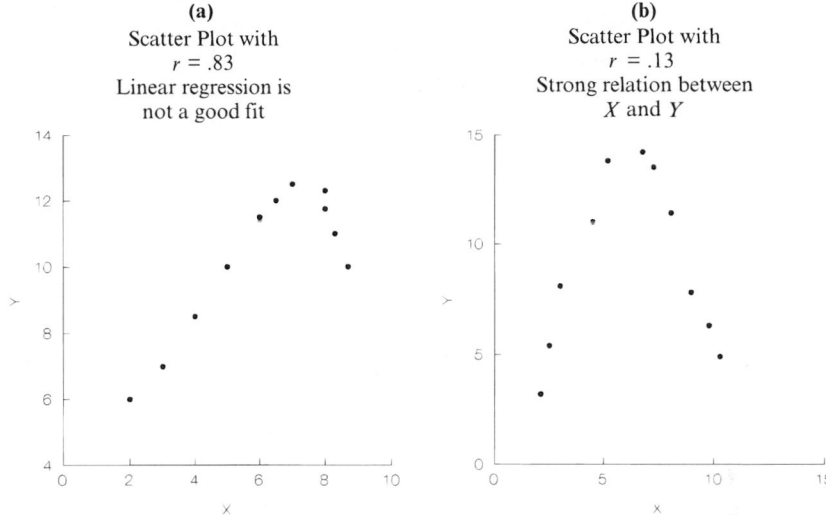

(a)
Scatter Plot with
$r = .83$
Linear regression is
not a good fit

(b)
Scatter Plot with
$r = .13$
Strong relation between
X and Y

2. *Misunderstanding 2. A high coefficient of correlation indicates that the estimated regression line is a good fit.* Again, this is not necessarily correct. Figure 2.9a shows a scatter plot where the coefficient of correlation is high ($r = .83$). Yet a linear regression function would not be a good fit since the regression relation is curvilinear.

3. *Misunderstanding 3. A coefficient of correlation near zero indicates that X and Y are not related.* This also is not necessarily correct. Figure 2.9b shows a scatter plot where the coefficient of correlation between X and Y is $r = .13$. Yet X and Y are strongly related; however, the relationship between the two variables is curvilinear.

Misunderstanding 1 arises because r^2 measures only a relative reduction from *SSTO* and provides no information about absolute precision for estimating a mean response or predicting a new observation. Misunderstandings 2 and 3 arise because r^2 and r measure the degree of *linear* association between X and Y, whereas the actual regression relation may be curvilinear.

Comments

1. A direct computational formula for r, which automatically furnishes the proper sign, is:

(2.76)
$$r = \frac{\Sigma(X_i - \bar{X})(Y_i - \bar{Y})}{\left[\Sigma(X_i - \bar{X})^2 \Sigma(Y_i - \bar{Y})^2\right]^{1/2}}$$

2. The following relation between b_1 and r is worth noting:

(2.77)
$$b_1 = \left[\frac{\Sigma(Y_i - \bar{Y})^2}{\Sigma(X_i - \bar{X})^2}\right]^{1/2} r = \left(\frac{s_Y}{s_X}\right) r$$

where $s_Y = [\Sigma(Y_i - \bar{Y})^2/(n-1)]^{1/2}$ and $s_X = [\Sigma(X_i - \bar{X})^2/(n-1)]^{1/2}$ are the sample standard deviations for the Y and X observations, respectively. Note that $b_1 = 0$ when $r = 0$, and vice versa. Thus, $r = 0$ implies a horizontal fitted regression line, and vice versa.

3. The value taken by r^2 in a given sample tends to be affected by the spacing of the X observations. This is implied in (2.72). SSE is not affected systematically by the spacing of the X_i since, for regression model (2.1), $\sigma^2\{Y_i\} = \sigma^2$ at all X levels. However, the wider the spacing of the X_i in the sample when $b_1 \neq 0$, the greater will tend to be the spread of the observed Y_i around $\bar{Y}$ and hence the greater $SSTO$ will be. Consequently, the wider the X_i are spaced, the higher r^2 will tend to be.

4. The regression sum of squares SSR is often called the "explained variation" in Y, and the residual sum of squares SSE is called the "unexplained variation." The coefficient r^2 then is interpreted in terms of the proportion of the total variation in Y ($SSTO$) which has been "explained" by X. Unfortunately, this terminology frequently is taken literally and, hence, misunderstood. Remember that in a regression model there is no implication that Y necessarily depends on X in a causal or explanatory sense.

5. Regression models do not contain any parameter to be estimated by r or r^2. These coefficients simply are descriptive measures of the degree of linear association between X and Y in the sample observations that may, or may not, be useful in any instance.   ∎

2.10   Considerations in Applying Regression Analysis

We have now discussed the major uses of regression analysis—to make inferences about the regression parameters, to estimate the mean response for a given X, and to predict a new observation Y for a given X. It remains to make a few cautionary remarks about implementing applications of regression analysis.

1. Frequently, regression analysis is used to make inferences for the future. For instance, for planning staffing requirements, a school board may wish to predict future enrollments by using a regression model containing several demographic variables as predictor variables. In applications of this type, it is important to remember that the validity of the regression application depends upon whether basic causal conditions in the period ahead will be similar to those in existence during the period upon which the regression analysis is based. This caution applies whether mean responses are to be estimated, new observations predicted, or regression parameters estimated.

2. In predicting new observations on Y, the predictor variable X itself often has to be predicted. For instance, we mentioned earlier the prediction of company sales for next year from the demographic projection of the number of persons 16 years of age or older next year. A prediction of company sales under these circumstances is a conditional prediction, dependent upon the correctness of the population projection. It is easy to forget the conditional nature of this type of prediction.

3. Another caution deals with inferences pertaining to levels of the predictor variable that fall outside the range of observations. Unfortunately, this situation frequently occurs in practice. A company that predicts its sales from a regression relation of company sales to disposable personal income will often find the level of disposable personal income of interest (e.g., for the year ahead) to fall beyond the range of past data. If the X level does not fall far beyond this range, one may have reasonable confidence in the application of the regression analysis. On the other hand, if the X level falls far beyond the range of past data, extreme caution should be exercised since one cannot be sure that the regression

function which fits the past data is appropriate over the wider range of the predictor variable.

4. A statistical test that leads to the conclusion that $\beta_1 \neq 0$ does not establish a cause-and-effect relation between the predictor and response variables. As we noted in Chapter 1, with nonexperimental data both the X and Y variables may be simultaneously influenced by other variables not in the regression model. On the other hand, the existence of a regression relation in controlled experiments is often good evidence of a cause-and-effect relation.

5. Finally, we should note again that frequently we wish to estimate several mean responses or predict several new observations for different levels of the predictor variable, and that special problems arise in this case. The confidence coefficients for the limits (2.33) for estimating a mean response and for the prediction limits (2.36) for a new observation apply only for a single level of X for a given sample. In Chapter 4, we discuss how to make multiple inferences from a given sample.

2.11   Case when X Is Random

The normal error regression model (2.1), which has been used throughout this chapter and which will continue to be used, assumes that the X values are known constants. As a consequence of this, the confidence coefficients and risks of errors refer to repeated sampling when the X values are kept the same from sample to sample.

Frequently, it may not be appropriate to consider the X values as known constants. For instance, consider regressing daily bathing suit sales by a department store on mean daily temperature. Surely, the department store cannot control daily temperatures, so it would not be meaningful to think of repeated sampling where the temperature levels are the same from sample to sample.

In this type of situation, it may be preferable to consider both Y and X as random variables. Does this mean then that all of our earlier results are not applicable here? Not at all. It can be shown that all results on estimation, testing, and prediction obtained for regression model (2.1) still apply if the following conditions hold:

(2.78)   1. The conditional distributions of the Y_i, given X_i, are normal and independent, with conditional means $\beta_0 + \beta_1 X_i$ and conditional variance σ^2.

   2. The X_i are independent random variables whose probability distribution $g(X_i)$ does not involve the parameters $\beta_0, \beta_1, \sigma^2$.

These conditions require only that regression model (2.1) is appropriate for each *conditional* distribution of Y_i, and that the probability distribution of the X_i does not involve the regression parameters. If these conditions are met, all earlier results on estimation, testing, and prediction still hold even though the X_i are now random variables. The major modification occurs in the interpretation of confidence coefficients and specified risks of error. When X is random, these refer to repeated sampling of pairs of (X_i, Y_i) values, where the X_i values as well as the Y_i values change from sample to sample. Thus, in our bathing suit sales illustration, a confidence coefficient would refer to the proportion of correct interval estimates if repeated samples of n days' sales and temperatures were obtained and the confidence interval calculated for each sample. Another modification occurs in the power of tests, which is different when X is a random variable.

Problems

2.1. A student working on a summer internship in the economic research department of a large corporation studied the relation between sales of a product (Y, in million dollars) and population (X, in million persons) in the firm's 50 marketing districts. The normal error regression model (2.1) was employed. The student first wished to test whether or not a linear association between Y and X existed. The student accessed an interactive simple linear regression program and obtained the following information on the regression coefficients:

Parameter	Estimated Value	95 Percent Confidence Limits	
Intercept	7.43119	−1.18518	16.0476
Slope	.755048	.452886	1.05721

   a. The student concluded from these results that there is a linear association between Y and X. Is the conclusion warranted? What is the implied level of significance?

   b. Someone questioned the negative lower confidence limit for the intercept, pointing out that dollar sales cannot be negative even if the population in a district is zero. Discuss.

2.2. In a test of the alternatives $H_0: \beta_1 \le 0$ versus $H_a: \beta_1 > 0$, an analyst concluded H_0. Does this conclusion imply that there is no linear association between X and Y? Explain.

2.3. A member of a student team playing an interactive marketing game received the following computer output when studying the relation between advertising expenditures (X) and sales (Y) for one of the team's products:

$$\text{Estimated regression equation: } \hat{Y} = 350.7 - .18X$$
$$\text{Two-sided } P\text{-value for estimated slope: .91}$$

The student stated: "The message I get here is that the more we spend on advertising this product, the fewer units we sell!" Comment.

2.4. Refer to **Grade point average** Problem 1.19.

   a. Obtain a 99 percent confidence interval for β_1. Interpret your confidence interval. Does it include zero? Why might the director of admissions be interested in whether the confidence interval includes zero?

   b. Test, using the test statistic t^*, whether or not a linear association exists between student's entrance test score (X) and GPA at the end of the freshman year (Y). Use a level of significance of .01. State the alternatives, decision rule, and conclusion.

   c. What is the P-value of your test in part (b)? How does it support the conclusion reached in part (b)?

√ 2.5. Refer to **Calculator maintenance** Problem 1.20.

   a. Estimate the change in the mean service time when the number of machines serviced increases by one. Use a 90 percent confidence interval. Interpret your confidence interval.

   b. Conduct a t test to determine whether or not there is a linear association between X and Y here; control the α risk at .10. State the alternatives, decision rule, and conclusion. What is the P-value of your test?

c. Are your results in parts (a) and (b) consistent? Explain.

d. The manufacturer has suggested that the mean required time should not increase by more than 14 minutes for each additional machine that is serviced on a service call. Conduct a test to decide whether this standard is being satisfied by Tri-City. Control the risk of a Type I error at .05. State the alternatives, decision rule, and conclusion. What is the P-value of the test?

e. Does b_0 give any relevant information here about the "start-up" time on calls—i.e., about the time required before service work is begun on the machines at a customer location?

√ 2.6. Refer to **Airfreight breakage** Problem 1.21.

a. Estimate β_1 with a 95 percent confidence interval. Interpret your interval estimate.

b. Conduct a t test to decide whether or not there is a linear association between number of times a carton is transferred (X) and number of broken ampules (Y). Use a level of significance of .05. State the alternatives, decision rule, and conclusion. What is the P-value of the test?

c. β_0 represents here the mean number of ampules broken when no transfers of the shipment are made—i.e., when $X = 0$. Obtain a 95 percent confidence interval for β_0 and interpret it.

d. A consultant has suggested, based on previous experience, that the mean number of broken ampules should not exceed 9.0 when no transfers are made. Conduct an appropriate test, using $\alpha = .025$. State the alternatives, decision rule, and conclusion. What is the P-value of the test?

e. Obtain the power of your test in part (b) if actually $\beta_1 = 2.0$. Assume $\sigma\{b_1\} = .50$. Also obtain the power of your test in part (d) if actually $\beta_0 = 11$. Assume $\sigma\{b_0\} = .75$.

2.7. Refer to **Plastic hardness** Problem 1.22.

a. Estimate the change in the mean hardness when the elapsed time increases by one hour. Use a 99 percent confidence interval. Interpret your interval estimate.

b. The plastic manufacturer has stated that the mean hardness should increase by 2 Brinell units per hour. Conduct a two-sided test to decide whether this standard is being satisfied; use $\alpha = .01$. State the alternatives, decision rule, and conclusion. What is the P-value of the test?

c. Obtain the power of your test in part (b) if the standard actually is being exceeded by .3 Brinell unit per hour. Assume $\sigma\{b_1\} = .1$.

2.8. Refer to Figure 2.2 for the Toluca Company example. A consultant has advised that an increase of one unit in lot size should require an increase of 3.0 in the expected number of work hours for the given production item.

a. Conduct a test to decide whether or not the increase in the expected number of work hours in the Toluca Company equals this standard. Use $\alpha = .05$. State the alternatives, decision rule, and conclusion.

b. Obtain the power of your test in part (a) if the consultant's standard actually is being exceeded by .5 hour. Assume $\sigma\{b_1\} = .35$.

c. Why is $F^* = 105.88$, given in the printout, not relevant for the test in part (a)?

2.9. Refer to Figure 2.2. A student, noting that $s\{b_1\}$ is furnished in the printout, asks why $s\{\hat{Y}_h\}$ is not also given. Discuss.

2.10. For each of the following questions, explain whether a confidence interval for a mean response or a prediction interval for a new observation is appropriate.

a. What will be the humidity level in this greenhouse tomorrow when we set the temperature level at 31°C?

b. How much do families whose disposable income is $23,500 spend, on the average, for meals away from home?

c. How many kilowatt-hours of electricity will be consumed next month by commercial and industrial users in the Twin Cities service area, given that the index of business activity for the area remains at its present level?

2.11. A person asks if there is a difference between the "mean response at $X = X_h$" and the "mean of m new observations at $X = X_h$." Reply.

2.12. Can $\sigma^2\{\text{pred}\}$ in (2.37) be brought increasingly close to 0 as n becomes large? Is this also the case for $\sigma^2\{\hat{Y}_h\}$ in (2.29b)? What is the implication of this difference?

2.13. Refer to **Grade point average** Problem 1.19.

a. Obtain a 95 percent interval estimate of the mean freshman GPA for students whose entrance test score is 4.7. Interpret your confidence interval.

b. Mary Jones obtained a score of 4.7 on the entrance test. Predict her freshman GPA using a 95 percent prediction interval. Interpret your prediction interval.

c. Is the prediction interval in part (b) wider than the confidence interval in part (a)? Should it be?

d. Determine the boundary values of the 95 percent confidence band for the regression line when $X_h = 4.7$. Is your confidence band wider at this point than the confidence interval in part (a)? Should it be?

√ 2.14. Refer to **Calculator maintenance** Problem 1.20.

a. Obtain a 90 percent confidence interval for the mean service time on calls in which six machines are serviced. Interpret your confidence interval.

b. Obtain a 90 percent prediction interval for the service time on the next call in which six machines are serviced. Is your prediction interval wider than the corresponding confidence interval in part (a)? Should it be?

c. Management wishes to estimate the expected service time *per machine* on calls in which six machines are serviced. Obtain an appropriate 90 percent confidence interval by converting the interval obtained in part (a). Interpret the converted confidence interval.

d. Determine the boundary values of the 90 percent confidence band for the regression line when $X_h = 6$. Is your confidence band wider at this point than the confidence interval in part (a)? Should it be?

√ 2.15. Refer to **Airfreight breakage** Problem 1.21.

a. Because of changes in airline routes, shipments may have to be transferred more frequently than in the past. Estimate the mean breakage for the following numbers of transfers: $X = 2, 4$. Use separate 99 percent confidence intervals. Interpret your results.

b. The next shipment will entail two transfers. Obtain a 99 percent prediction interval for the number of broken ampules for this shipment. Interpret your prediction interval.

c. In the next several days, three independent shipments will be made, each entailing two transfers. Obtain a 99 percent prediction interval for the mean number of ampules broken in the three shipments. Convert this interval into a 99 percent prediction interval for the total number of ampules broken in the three shipments.

d. Determine the boundary values of the 99 percent confidence band for the regression line when $X_h = 2$ and when $X_h = 4$. Is your confidence band wider at these two points than the corresponding confidence intervals in part (a)? Should it be?

2.16. Refer to **Plastic hardness** Problem 1.22.

a. Obtain a 98 percent confidence interval for the mean hardness of molded items with an elapsed time of 30 hours. Interpret your confidence interval.

b. Obtain a 98 percent prediction interval for the hardness of a newly molded test item with an elapsed time of 30 hours.

c. Obtain a 98 percent prediction interval for the mean hardness of 10 newly molded test items, each with an elapsed time of 30 hours.

d. Is the prediction interval in part (c) narrower than the one in part (b)? Should it be?

e. Determine the boundary values of the 98 percent confidence band for the regression line when $X_h = 30$. Is your confidence band wider at this point than the confidence interval in part (a)? Should it be?

2.17. An analyst fitted normal error regression model (2.1) and conducted an F test of $\beta_1 = 0$ versus $\beta_1 \neq 0$. The P-value of the test was .033, and the analyst concluded H_a: $\beta_1 \neq 0$. Was the α level used by the analyst greater than or smaller than .033? If the α level had been .01, what would have been the appropriate conclusion?

2.18. For conducting statistical tests concerning the parameter β_1, why is the t test more versatile than the F test?

2.19. When testing whether or not $\beta_1 = 0$, why is the F test a one-sided test even though H_a includes both $\beta_1 < 0$ and $\beta_1 > 0$? [*Hint*: Refer to (2.57).]

2.20. A student asks whether r^2 is a point estimator of any parameter in the normal error regression model (2.1). Respond.

2.21. A value of r^2 near 1 is sometimes interpreted to imply that the relation between Y and X is sufficiently close so that suitably precise predictions of Y can be made from knowledge of X. Is this implication a necessary consequence of the definition of r^2?

2.22. Using the normal error regression model (2.1) in an engineering safety experiment, a researcher found for the first 10 cases that r^2 was zero. Is it possible that for the complete set of 30 cases r^2 will not be zero? Could r^2 not be zero for the first 10 cases, yet equal zero for all 30 cases? Explain.

2.23. Refer to **Grade point average** Problem 1.19.

a. Set up the ANOVA table.

b. What is estimated by *MSR* in your ANOVA table? by *MSE*? Under what condition do *MSR* and *MSE* estimate the same quantity?

c. Conduct an F test of whether or not $\beta_1 = 0$. Control the α risk at .01. State the alternatives, decision rule, and conclusion.

   d. What is the absolute magnitude of the reduction in the variation of Y when X is introduced into the regression model? What is the relative reduction? What is the name of the latter measure?

   e. Obtain r and attach the appropriate sign.

   f. Which measure, r^2 or r, has the more clear-cut operational interpretation? Explain.

√ 2.24. Refer to **Calculator maintenance** Problem 1.20.

   a. Set up the basic ANOVA table in the format of Table 2.2. Which elements of your table are additive? Also set up the ANOVA table in the format of Table 2.3. How do the two tables differ?

   b. Conduct an F test to determine whether or not there is a linear association between time spent and number of machines serviced; use $\alpha = .10$. State the alternatives, decision rule, and conclusion.

   c. By how much, relatively, is the total variation in number of minutes spent on a call reduced when the number of machines serviced is introduced into the analysis? Is this a relatively small or large reduction? What is the name of this measure?

   d. Calculate r and attach the appropriate sign.

   e. Which measure, r or r^2, has the more clear-cut operational interpretation?

√ 2.25. Refer to **Airfreight breakage** Problem 1.21.

   a. Set up the ANOVA table. Which elements are additive?

   b. Conduct an F test to decide whether or not there is a linear association between the number of times a carton is transferred and the number of broken ampules; control the α risk at .05. State the alternatives, decision rule, and conclusion.

   c. Obtain the t^* statistic for the test in part (b) and demonstrate numerically its equivalence to the F^* statistic obtained in part (b).

   d. Calculate r^2 and r. What proportion of the variation in Y is accounted for by introducing X into the regression model?

2.26. Refer to **Plastic hardness** Problem 1.22.

   a. Set up the ANOVA table.

   b. Test by means of an F test whether or not there is a linear association between the hardness of the plastic and the elapsed time. Use $\alpha = .01$. State the alternatives, decision rule, and conclusion.

   c. Plot the deviations $Y_i - \hat{Y}_i$ against X_i on a graph. Plot the deviations $\hat{Y}_i - \bar{Y}$ against X_i on another graph, using the same scales as for the first graph. From your two graphs, does SSE or SSR appear to be the larger component of $SSTO$? What does this imply about the magnitude of r^2?

   d. Calculate r^2 and r.

√ 2.27. Refer to **Muscle mass** Problem 1.27.

   a. Conduct a test to decide whether or not there is a negative linear association between amount of muscle mass and age. Control the risk of Type I error at .05. State the alternatives, decision rule, and conclusion. What is the P-value of the test?

   b. The two-sided P-value for the test whether $\beta_0 = 0$ is 0+. Can it now be concluded that b_0 provides relevant information on the amount of muscle mass at birth for a female child?

c. Estimate with a 95 percent confidence interval the difference in expected muscle mass for women whose ages differ by one year. Why is it not necessary to know the specific ages to make this estimate?

√ 2.28. Refer to **Muscle mass** Problem 1.27.

   a. Obtain a 95 percent confidence interval for the mean muscle mass for women of age 60. Interpret your confidence interval.

   b. Obtain a 95 percent prediction interval for the muscle mass of a woman whose age is 60. Is the prediction interval relatively precise?

   c. Determine the boundary values of the 95 percent confidence band for the regression line when $X_h = 60$. Is your confidence band wider at this point than the confidence interval in part (a)? Should it be?

√ 2.29. Refer to **Muscle mass** Problem 1.27.

   a. Plot the deviations $Y_i - \hat{Y}_i$ against X_i on one graph. Plot the deviations $\hat{Y}_i - \bar{Y}$ against X_i on another graph, using the same scales as in the first graph. From your two graphs, does *SSE* or *SSR* appear to be the larger component of *SSTO*? What does this imply about the magnitude of r^2?

   b. Set up the ANOVA table.

   c. Test whether or not $\beta_1 = 0$ using an F test with $\alpha = .10$. State the alternatives, decision rule, and conclusion.

   d. What proportion of the total variation in muscle mass remains "unexplained" when age is introduced into the analysis? Is this proportion relatively small or large?

   e. Obtain r^2 and r.

2.30. Refer to **Robbery rate** Problem 1.28.

   a. Test whether or not there is a linear association between robbery rate and population density, using a t test with $\alpha = .01$. State the alternatives, decision rule, and conclusion. What is the P-value of the test?

   b. Test whether or not $\beta_0 = 0$; control the risk of Type I error at .01. State the alternatives, decision rule, and conclusion. Why might there be interest in testing whether or not $\beta_0 = 0$?

   c. Estimate β_1 with a 99 percent confidence interval. Interpret your interval estimate.

2.31. Refer to **Robbery rate** Problem 1.28.

   a. Set up the ANOVA table.

   b. Carry out the test in Problem 2.30a by means of the F test. Show the numerical equivalence of the two test statistics and decision rules. Is the P-value for the F test the same as that for the t test?

   c. By how much is the total variation in robbery rate reduced when population density is introduced into the analysis? Is this a relatively large or small reduction?

   d. Obtain r.

2.32. Refer to **Robbery rate** Problems 1.28 and 2.30. Suppose that the test in Problem 2.30a is to be carried out by means of a general linear test.

   a. State the full and reduced models.

   b. Obtain (1) $SSE(F)$, (2) $SSE(R)$, (3) df_F, (4) df_R, (5) test statistic F^* for the general linear test, (6) decision rule.

    c. Are the test statistic F^* and the decision rule for the general linear test numerically equivalent to those in Problem 2.30a?

2.33. In developing empirically a cost function from observed data on a complex chemical experiment, an analyst employed normal error regression model (2.1). β_0 was interpreted here as the cost of setting up the experiment. The analyst hypothesized that this cost should be $7.5 thousand and wished to test the hypothesis by means of a general linear test.

    a. Indicate the alternative conclusions for the test.

    b. Specify the full and reduced models.

    c. Without additional information, can you tell what the quantity $df_R - df_F$ in test statistic (2.70) will equal in the analyst's test? Explain.

2.34. Refer to **Grade point average** Problem 1.19.

    a. Would it be more reasonable to consider the X_i as known constants or as random variables here? Explain.

    b. If the X_i were considered to be random variables, would this have any effect on prediction intervals for new applicants? Explain.

2.35. Refer to **Calculator maintenance** Problems 1.20 and 2.5. How would the meaning of the confidence coefficient in Problem 2.5a change if the predictor variable were considered a random variable and the conditions in (2.78) were applicable?

Exercises

2.36. Derive the property in (2.6) for the k_i.

2.37. Show that b_0 as defined in (2.21) is an unbiased estimator of β_0.

2.38. Derive the expression in (2.22b) for the variance of b_0, making use of theorem (2.31). Also explain how variance (2.22b) is a special case of variance (2.29b).

2.39. (Calculus needed.)

    a. Obtain the likelihood function for the sample observations $Y_1, \ldots, Y_n$ given $X_1, \ldots, X_n$, if the conditions in (2.78) apply.

    b. Obtain the maximum likelihood estimators of β_0, β_1, and σ^2. Are the estimators of β_0 and β_1 the same as those in (1.27) when the X_i are fixed?

2.40. Suppose that normal error regression model (2.1) is applicable except that the error variance is not constant; rather the variance is larger, the larger is X. Does $\beta_1 = 0$ still imply that there is no linear association between X and Y? That there is no association between X and Y? Explain.

2.41. Derive the expression for SSR in (2.51).

2.42. In a small-scale regression study, five observations on Y were obtained corresponding to $X = 1, 4, 10, 11$, and 14. Assume that $\sigma = .6$, $\beta_0 = 5$, and $\beta_1 = 3$.

    a. What are the expected values of MSR and MSE here?

b. For determining whether or not a regression relation exists, would it have been better or worse to have made the five observations at $X = 6, 7, 8, 9$, and 10? Why? Would the same answer apply if the principal purpose were to estimate the mean response for $X = 8$? Discuss.

2.43. The normal error regression model (2.1) is assumed to be applicable.

a. When testing H_0: $\beta_1 = 5$ versus H_a: $\beta_1 \neq 5$ by means of a general linear test, what is the reduced model? What are the degrees of freedom df_R?

b. When testing H_0: $\beta_0 = 2$, $\beta_1 = 5$ versus H_a: not both $\beta_0 = 2$ and $\beta_1 = 5$ by means of a general linear test, what is the reduced model? What are the degrees of freedom df_R?

2.44. Derive (2.76) from (2.72), using the result in Exercise 2.41.

Projects

2.45. Refer to the **SMSA** data set and Project 1.43. Using r^2 as the criterion, which predictor variable accounts for the largest reduction in the variability in the number of active physicians?

2.46. Refer to the **SMSA** data set and Project 1.44. Obtain a separate interval estimate of β_1 for each region. Use a 90 percent confidence coefficient in each case. Do the regression lines for the different regions appear to have similar slopes?

2.47. Refer to the **SENIC** data set and Project 1.45. Using r^2 as the criterion, which predictor variable accounts for the largest reduction in the variability of the average length of stay?

2.48. Refer to the **SENIC** data set and Project 1.46. Obtain a separate interval estimate of β_1 for each region. Use a 95 percent confidence coefficient in each case. Do the regression lines for the different regions appear to have similar slopes?

2.49. Five observations on Y are to be taken when $X = 4, 8, 12, 16$, and 20, respectively. The true regression function is $E\{Y\} = 20 + 4X$, and the ε_i are independent $N(0, 25)$.

a. Generate five normal random numbers, with mean 0 and variance 25. Consider these random numbers as the error terms for the five Y observations at $X = 4, 8, 12, 16$, and 20 and calculate Y_1, Y_2, Y_3, Y_4, and Y_5. Obtain the least squares estimates b_0 and b_1 when fitting a straight line to the five cases. Also calculate $\hat{Y}_h$ when $X_h = 10$ and obtain a 95 percent confidence interval for $E\{Y_h\}$ when $X_h = 10$.

b. Repeat part (a) 200 times, generating new random numbers each time.

c. Make a frequency distribution of the 200 estimates b_1. Calculate the mean and standard deviation of the 200 estimates b_1. Are the results consistent with theoretical expectations?

d. What proportion of the 200 confidence intervals for $E\{Y_h\}$ when $X_h = 10$ include $E\{Y_h\}$? Is this result consistent with theoretical expectations?

2.50. Refer to **Grade point average** Problem 1.19.

a. Plot the data, with the least squares regression line for entrance test scores between 3.5 and 6.5 superimposed.

b. On the plot in part (a), superimpose a plot of the 95 percent confidence band for the true regression line for entrance test scores between 3.5 and 6.5. Does the confidence band suggest that the true regression relation has been precisely estimated? Discuss.

2.51. Refer to **Calculator maintenance** Problem 1.20.

a. Plot the data, with the least squares regression line for numbers of machines serviced between 1 and 8 superimposed.

b. On the plot in part (a), superimpose a plot of the 90 percent confidence band for the true regression line for numbers of machines serviced between 1 and 8. Does the confidence band suggest that the true regression relation has been precisely estimated? Discuss.

CHAPTER 3

Diagnostics and Remedial Measures

When a regression model, such as the simple linear regression model (2.1), is considered for an application, we can usually not be certain in advance that the model is appropriate for that application. Any one, or several, of the features of the model, such as linearity of the regression function or normality of the error terms, may not be appropriate for the particular data at hand. Hence, it is important to examine the aptness of the model for the data before inferences based on that model are undertaken. In this chapter, we discuss some simple graphic methods for studying the appropriateness of a model, as well as some formal statistical tests for doing so. We also consider some remedial techniques that can be helpful when the data are not in accordance with the conditions of regression model (2.1). We conclude the chapter with a case example that brings together the concepts and methods presented in this and the earlier chapters.

While the discussion in this chapter is in terms of the appropriateness of the simple linear regression model (2.1), the basic principles apply to all - statistical models discussed in this book. In later chapters, additional methods useful for examining the appropriateness of statistical models and other remedial measures will be presented, as well as methods for validating the statistical model.

3.1 Diagnostics for Predictor Variable

We begin by considering some graphic diagnostics for the predictor variable. We need diagnostic information about the predictor variable to see if there are any outlying X values that could influence the appropriateness of the fitted regression function. We discuss the role of influential cases in detail in Chapter 9. Diagnostic information about the range and concentration of the X levels in the study is also useful for ascertaining the range of validity for the regression analysis.

Figure 3.1a contains a simple *dot plot* for the lot sizes in the Toluca Company example in Figure 1.10. A dot plot is helpful when the number of observations in the data set is not large. The dot plot in Figure 3.1a shows that the minimum and maximum lot sizes are 20 and 120, respectively, that the lot size levels are spread throughout this interval, and that there are no lot sizes that are far outlying. The dot plot also shows that in a number of cases several runs were made for the same lot size.

FIGURE 3.1   **MINITAB and SYGRAPH Diagnostic Plots for Predictor Variable—Toluca Company Example.**

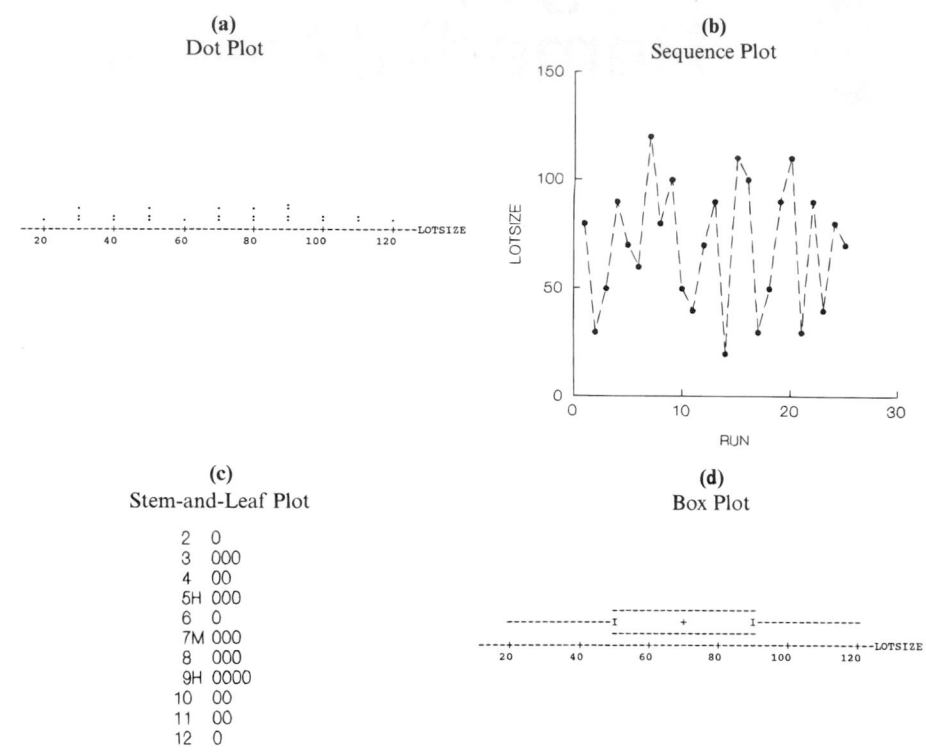

(a)
Dot Plot

(b)
Sequence Plot

(c)
Stem-and-Leaf Plot

```
 2   0
 3   000
 4   00
5H   000
 6   0
7M   000
 8   000
9H   0000
10   00
11   00
12   0
```

(d)
Box Plot

A second useful diagnostic for the predictor variable is a *sequence plot*. Figure 3.1b contains a time sequence plot of the lot sizes for the Toluca Company example. Lot size is here plotted against production run (i.e., against time sequence). The points in the plot are connected to show more effectively the time sequence. Sequence plots should be utilized whenever data are obtained in a sequence, such as over time or for adjacent geographic areas. The sequence plot in Figure 3.1b contains no special pattern. If, say, the plot had shown that smaller lot sizes had been utilized early on and larger lot sizes later on, this information could be very helpful for subsequent diagnostic studies of the aptness of the fitted regression model.

Figures 3.1c and 3.1d contain two other diagnostic plots that present information similar to the dot plot in Figure 3.1a. The *stem-and-leaf plot* in Figure 3.1c provides information similar to a frequency histogram. By displaying the last digits, this plot also indicates here that all lot sizes in the Toluca Company example were multiples of 10. The letter M in the SYGRAPH output denotes the stem where the median is located, and the letter H denotes the stems where the first and third quartiles (hinges) are located.

The *box plot* in Figure 3.1d shows the minimum and maximum lot sizes, the first and third quartiles, and the median lot size. We see that the middle half of the lot sizes range from 50 to 90, and that they are fairly symmetrically distributed because the median is located in the middle of the central box. A box plot is particularly helpful when there are many observations in the data set.

3.2   Residuals

Direct diagnostic plots for the response variable Y are ordinarily not too useful in regression analysis because the values of the observations on the response variable are a function of the level of the predictor variable. Instead, diagnostics for the response variable are usually carried out indirectly through an examination of the residuals.

The residual e_i, as defined in (1.16), is the difference between the observed value Y_i and the fitted value $\hat{Y}_i$:

$$(3.1) \qquad\qquad\qquad e_i = Y_i - \hat{Y}_i$$

The residual may be regarded as the observed error, in distinction to the unknown true error ε_i in the regression model:

$$(3.2) \qquad\qquad\qquad \varepsilon_i = Y_i - E\{Y_i\}$$

For regression model (2.1), the error terms ε_i are assumed to be independent normal random variables, with mean 0 and constant variance σ^2. If the model is appropriate for the data at hand, the observed residuals e_i should then reflect the properties assumed for the ε_i. This is the basic idea underlying *residual analysis*, a highly useful means of examining the aptness of a statistical model.

Properties of Residuals

Mean.   The mean of the n residuals e_i for the simple linear regression model (2.1) is, by (1.17):

$$(3.3) \qquad\qquad\qquad \bar{e} = \frac{\Sigma e_i}{n} = 0$$

where $\bar{e}$ denotes the mean of the residuals. Thus, since $\bar{e}$ is always 0, it provides no information as to whether the true errors ε_i have expected value $E\{\varepsilon_i\} = 0$.

Variance.   The variance of the n residuals e_i is defined as follows for regression model (2.1):

$$(3.4) \qquad\qquad \frac{\Sigma(e_i - \bar{e})^2}{n-2} = \frac{\Sigma e_i^2}{n-2} = \frac{SSE}{n-2} = MSE$$

If the model is appropriate, MSE is, as noted earlier, an unbiased estimator of the variance of the error terms σ^2.

Nonindependence.   The residuals e_i are not independent random variables because they involve the fitted values $\hat{Y}_i$ which are based on the same fitted regression function. As a result, the residuals for regression model (2.1) are subject to two constraints. These are constraint (1.17)—that the sum of the e_i must be 0—and constraint (1.19)—that the products $X_i e_i$ must sum to 0.

When the sample size is large in comparison to the number of parameters in the regression model, the dependency effect among the residuals e_i is relatively unimportant and can be ignored for most purposes.

Semistudentized Residuals

At times, it is helpful to standardize the residuals for residual analysis. Since the standard deviation of the error terms ε_i is σ, which is estimated by $\sqrt{MSE}$, it is natural to consider the following form of standardization:

$$(3.5) \qquad\qquad e_i^* = \frac{e_i - \bar{e}}{\sqrt{MSE}} = \frac{e_i}{\sqrt{MSE}}$$

If $\sqrt{MSE}$ were an estimate of the standard deviation of the residual e_i, we would call e_i^* a studentized residual. However, the standard deviation of e_i is complex and varies for the different residuals e_i, and $\sqrt{MSE}$ is only an approximation of the standard deviation of e_i. Hence, we call the statistic e_i^* in (3.5) a *semistudentized residual*. We shall take up studentized residuals in Chapter 9. Both semistudentized residuals and studentized residuals can be very helpful in identifying outlying observations.

Departures from Model to Be Studied by Residuals

We shall consider the use of residuals for examining six important types of departures from the simple linear regression model (2.1) with normal errors:

1. The regression function is not linear.

2. The error terms do not have constant variance.

3. The error terms are not independent.

4. The model fits all but one or a few outlier observations.

5. The error terms are not normally distributed.

6. One or several important predictor variables have been omitted from the model.

3.3   Diagnostics for Residuals

We take up now some informal diagnostic plots of residuals to provide information on whether any of the six types of departures from the simple linear regression model (2.1) just mentioned are present. The following plots of residuals (or semistudentized residuals) will be utilized here for this purpose:

1. Plot of residuals against predictor variable

2. Plot of absolute or squared residuals against predictor variable

3. Plot of residuals against fitted values

4. Plot of residuals against time or other sequence

5. Plots of residuals against omitted predictor variables

6. Box plot of residuals

7. Normal probability plot of residuals

Figure 3.2 contains, for the Toluca Company example, MINITAB and SYGRAPH plots of the residuals in Table 1.2 against the predictor variable and against time, a box plot, and

FIGURE 3.2   MINITAB and SYGRAPH Diagnostic Residual Plots—Toluca Company Example.

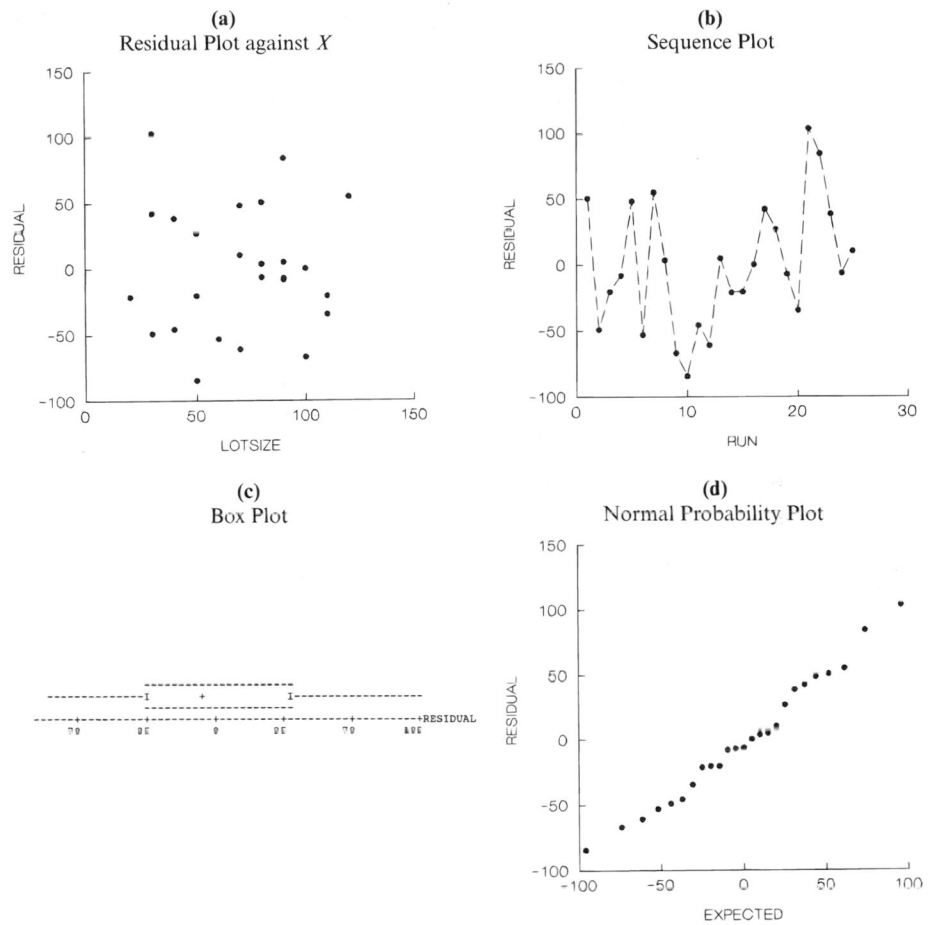

a normal probability plot. All of these plots, as we shall see, support the appropriateness of regression model (2.1) for the data.

We turn now to consider how residual analysis can be helpful in studying each of the six departures from regression model (2.1).

Nonlinearity of Regression Function

Whether a linear regression function is appropriate for the data being analyzed can be studied from a *residual plot against the predictor variable* or, equivalently, from a *residual plot against the fitted values*. Nonlinearity of the regression function can also be studied from a *scatter plot*, but this plot is not always as effective as a residual plot. Figure 3.3a contains a scatter plot of the data and the fitted regression line for a study of the relation between maps distributed and bus ridership in eight test cities. Here, X is the number of bus transit maps distributed free to residents of the city at the beginning of the test period and Y is the increase during the test period in average daily bus rid-

FIGURE 3.3   **Scatter Plot and Residual Plot Illustrating Nonlinear Regression Function—Transit Example.**

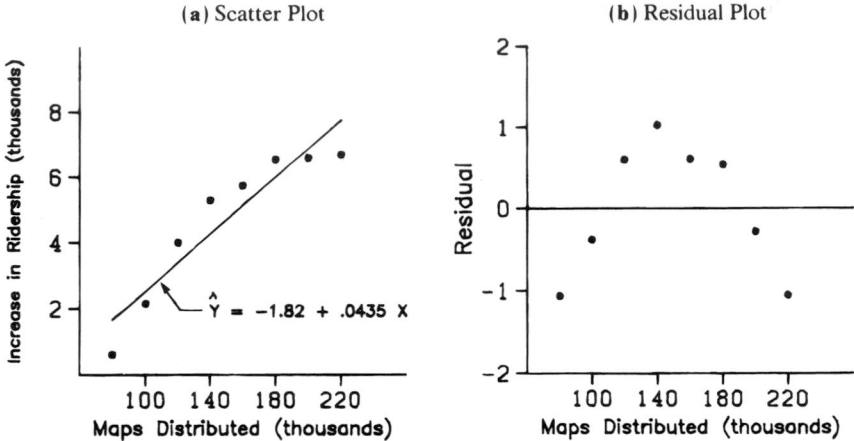

(a) Scatter Plot   (b) Residual Plot

TABLE 3.1   **Number of Maps Distributed and Increase in Ridership—Transit Example.**

City i	(1) Increase in Ridership (thousands) Y_i	(2) Maps Distributed (thousands) X_i	(3) Fitted Value $\hat{Y}_i$	(4) Residual $Y_i - \hat{Y}_i = e_i$
1	.60	80	1.66	−1.06
2	6.70	220	7.75	−1.05
3	5.30	140	4.27	1.03
4	4.00	120	3.40	.60
5	6.55	180	6.01	.54
6	2.15	100	2.53	− .38
7	6.60	200	6.88	− .28
8	5.75	160	5.14	.61

$$\hat{Y} = -1.82 + .0435X$$

ership during nonpeak hours. The original data and fitted values are given in Table 3.1, columns 1, 2, and 3. The plot suggests strongly that a linear regression function is not appropriate.

Figure 3.3b presents a plot of the residuals, shown in Table 3.1, column 4, against the predictor variable X. The lack of fit of the linear regression function is even more strongly suggested by the residual plot against X in Figure 3.3b than by the scatter plot. Note that the residuals depart from 0 in a systematic fashion; they are negative for smaller X values, positive for medium-size X values, and negative again for large X values.

FIGURE 3.4   Prototype Residual Plots.

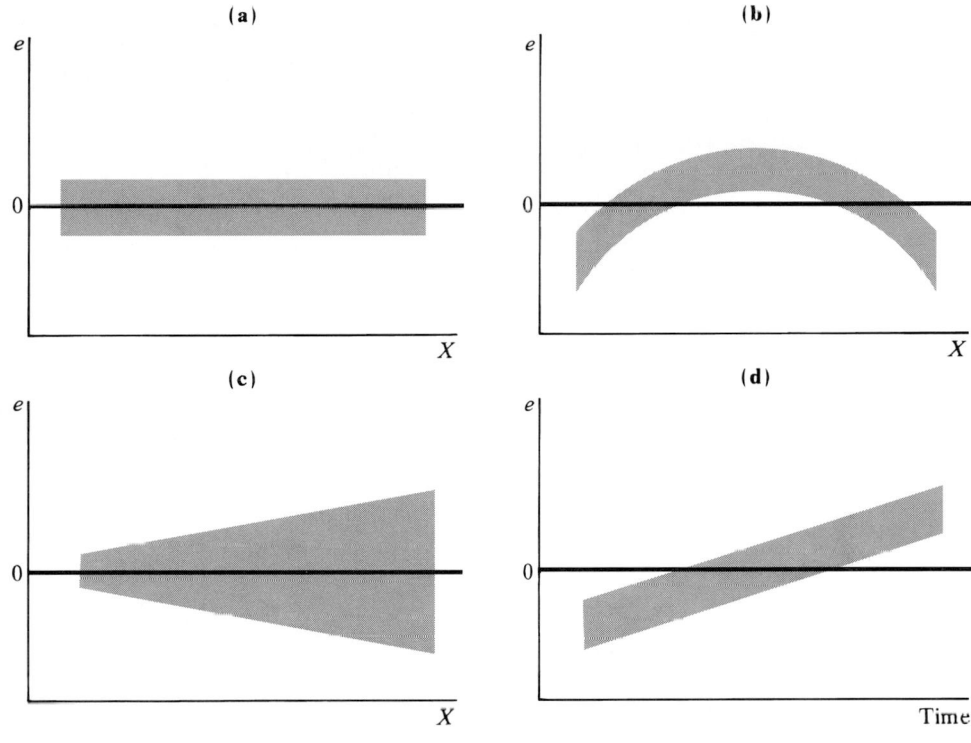

In this case, both Figures 3.3a and 3.3b point out the lack of linearity of the regression function. In general, however, the residual plot is to be preferred, because it has some important advantages over the scatter plot. First, the residual plot can easily be used for examining other facets of the aptness of the model. Second, there are occasions when the scaling of the scatter plot places the Y_i observations close to the fitted values $\hat{Y}_i$, for instance, when there is a steep slope. It then becomes more difficult to study the appropriateness of a linear regression function from the scatter plot. A residual plot, on the other hand, can clearly show any systematic pattern in the deviations around the fitted regression line under these conditions.

Figure 3.4a shows a prototype situation of the residual plot against X when a linear regression model is appropriate. The residuals then fall within a horizontal band centered around 0, displaying no systematic tendencies to be positive and negative. This is the case in Figure 3.2a for the Toluca Company example.

Figure 3.4b shows a prototype situation of a departure from the linear regression model that indicates the need for a curvilinear regression function. Here the residuals tend to vary in a systematic fashion between being positive and negative. This is the case in Figure 3.3b for the transit example. A different type of departure from linearity would, of course, lead to a picture different from the prototype pattern in Figure 3.4b.

Note

A plot of residuals against the fitted values $\hat{Y}$ provides equivalent information as a plot of residuals against X for the simple linear regression model, and thus is not needed in addition

FIGURE 3.5   **BMDP Residual Plots Illustrating Nonconstant Error Variance—Blood Pressure Example.**

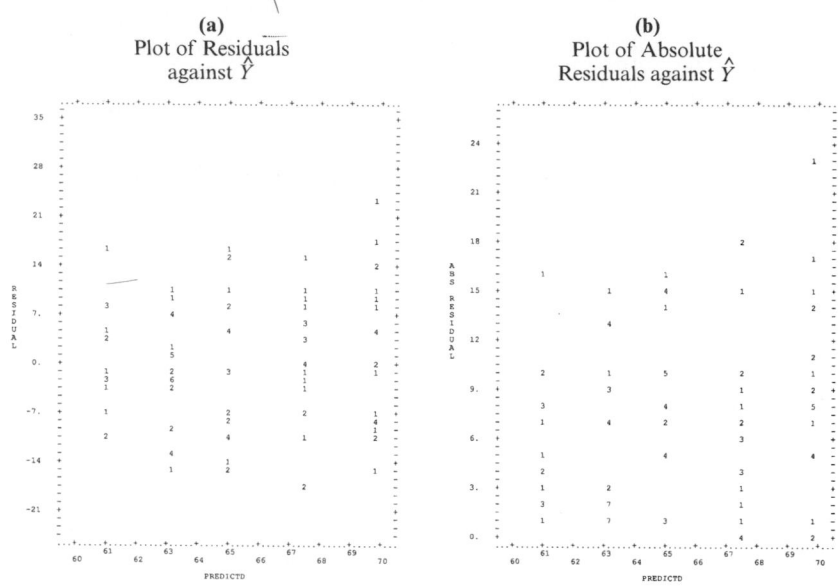

to the residual plot against X. The two plots provide the same information because the fitted values $\hat{Y}_i$ are a linear function of the values X_i for the predictor variable. Thus, only the X scale values, not the basic pattern of the plotted points, are affected by whether the residual plot is against the X_i or the $\hat{Y}_i$. For curvilinear regression and multiple regression, on the other hand, separate plots of the residuals against the fitted values and against the predictor variable(s) are usually helpful.   ∎

Nonconstancy of Error Variance

Plots of the residuals against the predictor variable or against the fitted values are not only helpful to study whether a linear regression function is appropriate but also to examine whether the variance of the error terms is constant. Figure 3.5a shows a BMDP residual plot against the fitted values $\hat{Y}$ for a study of the relation between diastolic blood pressure of female children (Y) and their age (X). Note that the horizontal axis is labeled PREDICTD, which stands for "predicted," an alternative term often used for "fitted" value. The numerical values shown in the graph indicate the number of residuals falling on or near a point. The plot suggests that the larger the fitted value $\hat{Y}$ is, the more spread out the residuals are. Since the relation between blood pressure and age is positive, this suggests that the error variance is larger for older children than for younger ones.

The prototype plot in Figure 3.4a exemplifies residual plots when the error term variance is constant. The residual plot in Figure 3.2a for the Toluca Company example is of this type, suggesting that the error terms have constant variance here.

Figure 3.4c shows a prototype picture of residual plots when the error variance increases with X. In many business, social science, and biological science applications, departures from constancy of the error variance tend to be of the "megaphone" type shown in

Figure 3.4c, as in the blood pressure example in Figure 3.5a. One can also encounter error variances decreasing with increasing levels of the predictor variable and occasionally varying in some more complex fashion.

Plots of the absolute values of the residuals or of the squared residuals against the predictor variable X or against the fitted values $\hat{Y}$ are also useful for diagnosing nonconstancy of the error variance since the signs of the residuals are not meaningful for examining the constancy of the error variance. These plots are especially useful when there are not many cases in the data set because plotting of either the absolute or squared residuals places all of the information on changing magnitudes of the residuals above the horizontal zero line so that one can more readily see whether the magnitude of the residuals (irrespective of sign) is changing with the level of X or $\hat{Y}$.

Figure 3.5b contains a BMDP plot of the absolute residuals against the fitted values for the blood pressure example. This plot shows more clearly that the residuals tend to be larger in absolute magnitude for larger fitted values.

Presence of Outliers

Outliers are extreme observations. Residual outliers can be identified from *residual plots against X or $\hat{Y}$*, as well as from *box plots*, *stem-and-leaf plots*, and *dot plots* of the residuals. Plotting of semistudentized residuals is particularly helpful for distinguishing outlying observations, since it then becomes easy to identify residuals that lie many standard deviations from zero. A rough rule of thumb when the number of cases is large is to consider semistudentized residuals with absolute value of four or more to be outliers. We shall take up more refined procedures for identifying outliers in Chapter 9.

The residual plot in Figure 3.6 presents semistudentized residuals and contains one outlier, which is circled. Note that this residual represents an observation almost six standard deviations from the fitted value.

Outliers can create great difficulty. When we encounter one, our first suspicion is that the observation resulted from a mistake or other extraneous effect, and hence should be discarded. A major reason for discarding it is that under the least squares method, a fitted line may be pulled disproportionately toward an outlying observation because the sum of the *squared* deviations is minimized. This could cause a misleading fit if indeed the outlying observation resulted from a mistake or other extraneous cause. On the other hand, outliers may convey significant information, as when an outlier occurs because of an interaction with another predictor variable omitted from the model. A safe rule frequently suggested is to discard an outlier only if there is direct evidence that it represents an error in recording, a miscalculation, a malfunctioning of equipment, or a similar type of circumstance.

Note

When a linear regression model is fitted to a data set with a small number of cases and an outlier is present, the fitted regression can be so distorted by the outlier that the residual plot may improperly suggest a lack of fit of the linear regression model, in addition to flagging the outlier. Figure 3.7 illustrates this situation. The scatter plot in Figure 3.7a presents a situation where all observations except the outlier fall around a straight-line statistical relationship. When a linear regression function is fitted to these data, the outlier causes such a shift in the fitted regression line as to lead to a systematic pattern of deviations from the fitted line for the other observations, suggesting a lack of fit of the linear regression function. This is shown by the residual plot in Figure 3.7b. ∎

FIGURE 3.6   Residual Plot with Outlier.

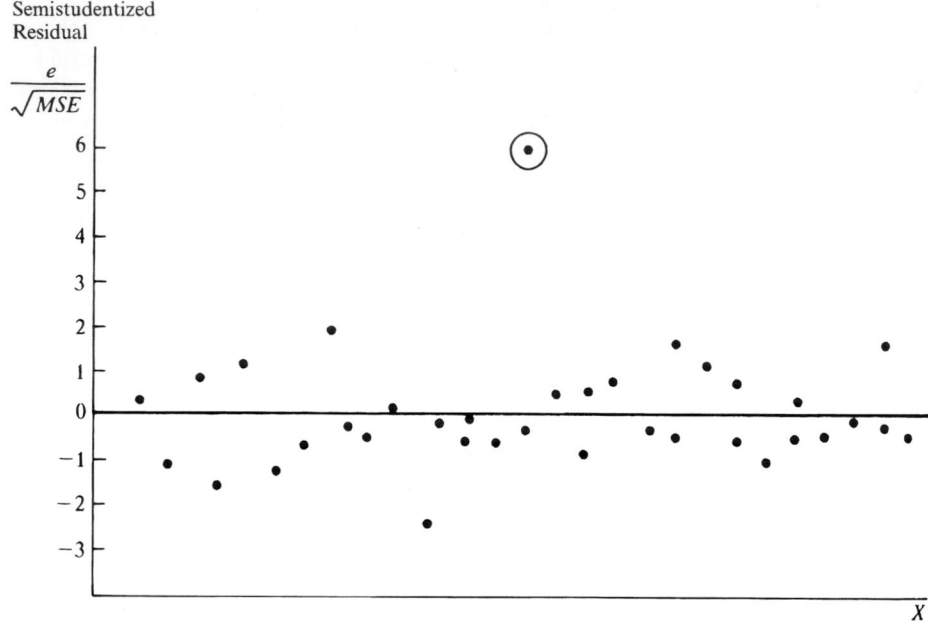

FIGURE 3.7   Distorting Effect on Residuals Caused by an Outlier When Remaining Data Follow Linear Regression.

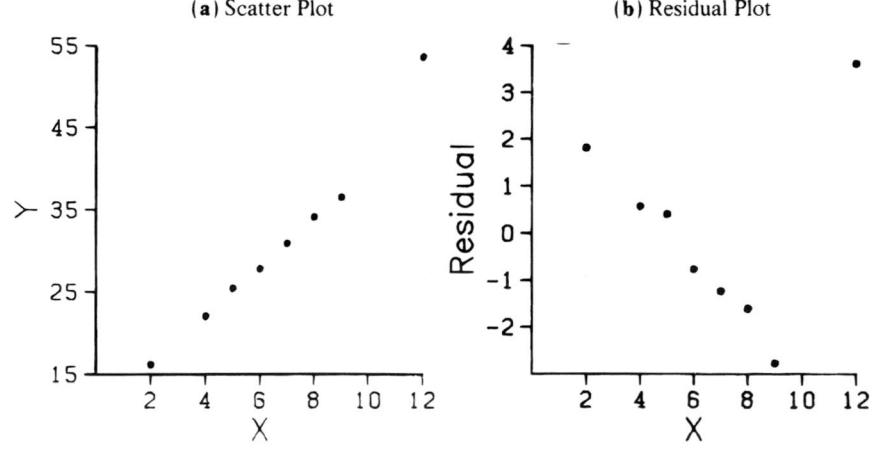

Nonindependence of Error Terms

Whenever data are obtained in a time sequence or some other type of sequence, such as for adjacent geographic areas, it is a good idea to prepare a *sequence plot of the residuals*. The purpose of plotting the residuals against time or in some other type of sequence is to

FIGURE 3.8   **Residual Time Sequence Plots Illustrating Nonindependence of Error Terms.**

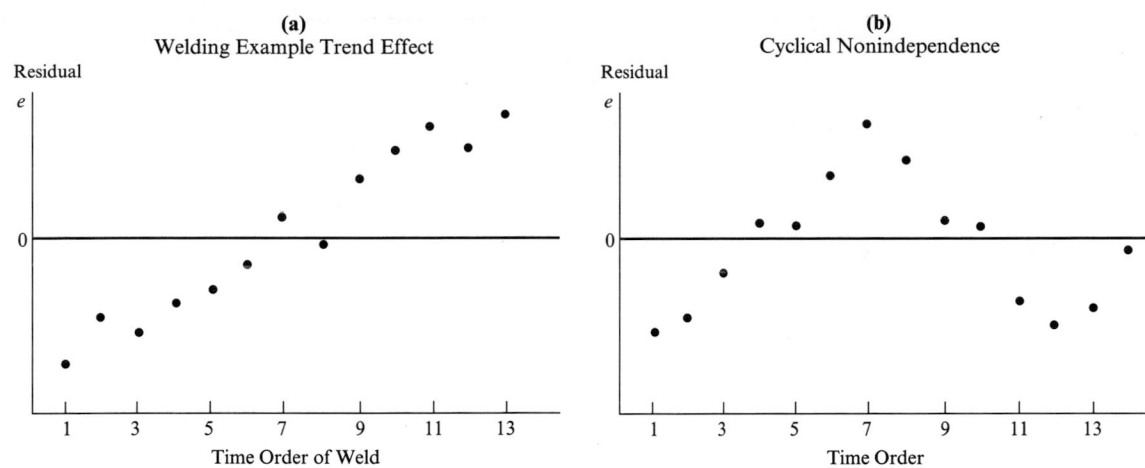

see if there is any correlation between error terms that are near each other in the sequence. Figure 3.8a contains a time sequence plot of the residuals in an experiment to study the relation between the diameter of a weld (X) and the shear strength of the weld (Y). An evident correlation between the error terms stands out. Negative residuals are associated mainly with the early trials, and positive residuals with the later trials. Apparently, some effect connected with time was present, such as learning by the welder or a gradual change in the welding equipment, so the shear strength tended to be greater in the later welds because of this effect.

A prototype residual plot showing a time-related trend effect is presented in Figure 3.4d, which portrays a linear time-related trend effect, as in the welding example. It is sometimes useful to view the problem of nonindependence of the error terms as one in which an important variable (in this case, time) has been omitted from the model. We shall discuss this type of problem shortly.

Another type of nonindependence of the error terms is illustrated in Figure 3.8b. Here the adjacent error terms are also related, but the resulting pattern is a cyclical one with no trend effect present.

When the error terms are independent, we expect the residuals in a sequence plot to fluctuate in a more or less random pattern around the base line 0, such as the scattering shown in Figure 3.2b for the Toluca Company example. Lack of randomness can take the form of too much or too little alternation of points around the zero line. In practice, there is little concern with the former because it does not arise frequently. Too little alternation, in contrast, frequently occurs, as in the welding example in Figure 3.8a.

Note

When the residuals are plotted against X, as in Figure 3.3b for the transit example, the scatter may not appear to be random. For this plot, however, the basic problem is probably not lack of independence of the error terms but a poorly fitting regression function. This, indeed, is the situation portrayed in the scatter plot in Figure 3.3a.   ■

TABLE 3.2   **Residuals and Expected Values under Normality—Toluca Company Example.**

Run	(1) Residual	(2) Rank	(3) Expected Value under
i	e_i	k	Normality
1	51.02	22	51.95
2	−48.47	5	−44.10
3	−19.88	10	−14.76
...	...	...	...
23	38.83	19	31.05
24	−5.98	13	0
25	10.72	17	19.93

Nonnormality of Error Terms

As we noted earlier, small departures from normality do not create any serious problems. Major departures, on the other hand, should be of concern. The normality of the error terms can be studied informally by examining the residuals in a variety of graphic ways.

Distribution Plots.   A *box plot* of the residuals is helpful for obtaining summary information about the symmetry of the residuals and about possible outliers. Figure 3.2c contains a box plot of the residuals in the Toluca Company example. No serious departures from symmetry are suggested by this plot. A *histogram*, *dot plot*, or *stem-and-leaf plot* of the residuals can also be helpful for detecting gross departures from normality. However, the number of cases in the regression study must be reasonably large for any of these plots to convey reliable information about the shape of the distribution of the error terms.

Comparison of Frequencies.   Another possibility when the number of cases is reasonably large is to compare actual frequencies of the residuals against expected frequencies under normality. For example, one can determine whether, say, about 68 percent of the residuals e_i fall between $\pm\sqrt{MSE}$ or about 90 percent fall between $\pm 1.645\sqrt{MSE}$. When the sample size is moderately large, corresponding t values may be used for the comparison.

To illustrate this procedure, we again consider the Toluca Company example of Chapter 1. Table 3.2, column 1, repeats the residuals from Table 1.2. We see from Figure 2.2 that $\sqrt{MSE} = 48.82$. Using the t distribution, we expect under normality about 90 percent of the residuals to fall between $\pm t(.95; 23)\sqrt{MSE} = \pm 1.714(48.82)$, or between -83.68 and 83.68. Actually, 22 residuals, or 88 percent, fall within these limits. Similarly, under normality, we expect about 60 percent of the residuals to fall between -41.89 and 41.89. The actual percentage here is 52 percent. Thus, the actual frequencies here are reasonably consistent with those expected under normality.

Normal Probability Plot.   Still another possibility is to prepare a *normal probability plot of the residuals*. Here each residual is plotted against its expected value under normality. A plot that is nearly linear suggests agreement with normality, whereas a plot that departs substantially from linearity suggests that the error distribution is not normal.

Table 3.2, column 1, contains the residuals for the Toluca Company example. To find the expected values of the ordered residuals under normality, we utilize the facts that (1) the expected value of the error terms for regression model (2.1) is zero, and (2) the standard deviation of the error terms is estimated by $\sqrt{MSE}$. Statistical theory has shown that for a normal random variable with mean 0 and estimated standard deviation $\sqrt{MSE}$, a good approximation of the expected value of the kth smallest observation in a random sample of n is:

$$(3.6) \qquad \sqrt{MSE}\left[z\left(\frac{k - .375}{n + .25} \right) \right]$$

where $z(A)$ as usual denotes the $(A)100$ percentile of the standard normal distribution.

Using this approximation, let us calculate the expected values of the residuals under normality for the Toluca Company example. Column 2 of Table 3.2 shows the ranks of the residuals, with the smallest residual being assigned rank 1. We see that the rank of the residual for run 1, $e_1 = 51.02$, is 22, which indicates that this residual is the 22nd smallest among the 25 residuals. Hence, for this residual $k = 22$. We found earlier (Table 2.1) that $MSE = 2,384$. Hence:

$$\frac{k - .375}{n + .25} = \frac{22 - .375}{25 + .25} = \frac{21.625}{25.25} = .8564$$

so that the expected value of this residual under normality is:

$$\sqrt{2,384}[z(.8564)] = \sqrt{2,384}(1.064) = 51.95$$

Similarly, the expected value of the residual for run 2, $e_2 = -48.47$, is obtained by noting that the rank of this residual is $k = 5$; in other words, this residual is the fifth smallest one among the 25 residuals. Hence, we require $(k - .375)/(n + .25) = (5 - .375)/(25 + .25) = .1832$, so that the expected value of this residual under normality is:

$$\sqrt{2,384}[z(.1832)] = \sqrt{2,384}(-.9032) = -44.10$$

Table 3.2, column 3, contains the expected values under the assumption of normality for a portion of the 25 residuals. Figure 3.2d presents a plot of the residuals against their expected values under normality. Note that the points in Figure 3.2d fall reasonably close to a straight line, suggesting that the distribution of the error terms does not depart substantially from a normal distribution.

Figure 3.9 shows three normal probability plots when the distribution of the error terms departs substantially from normality. Figure 3.9a shows a normal probability plot when the error term distribution is highly skewed to the right. Note the concave-upward shape of the plot. Figure 3.9b shows a normal probability plot when the error term distribution is highly skewed to the left. Here, the pattern is concave downward. Finally, Figure 3.9c shows a normal probability plot when the distribution of the error terms is symmetrical but has heavy tails; in other words, the distribution has higher probabilities in the tails than a normal distribution. Note the concave-downward curvature in the plot at the left end, corresponding to the plot for a left-skewed distribution, and the concave-upward plot at the right end, corresponding to a right-skewed distribution.

FIGURE 3.9   **Normal Probability Plots when Error Term Distribution Is Not Normal.**

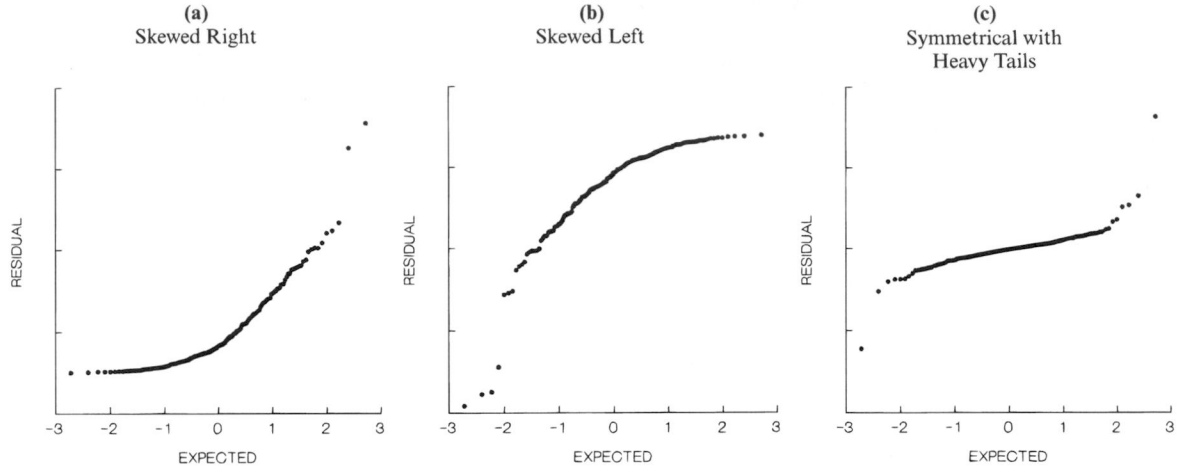

Comments

1. Many computer packages will prepare normal probability plots, either automatically or at the option of the user. Some of these plots utilize semistudentized residuals, others omit the factor $\sqrt{MSE}$ in (3.6), but neither of these variations affect the nature of the plot.

2. For continuous data, ties among the residuals should occur only rarely. If two residuals do have the same value, a simple procedure is to use the average rank for the tied residuals for calculating the corresponding expected values.   ∎

Difficulties in Assessing Normality.   The analysis for model departures with respect to normality is, in many respects, more difficult than that for other types of departures. In the first place, random variation can be particularly mischievous when studying the nature of a probability distribution unless the sample size is quite large. Even worse, other types of departures can and do affect the distribution of the residuals. For instance, residuals may appear to be not normally distributed because an inappropriate regression function is used or because the error variance is not constant. Hence, it is usually a good strategy to investigate these other types of departures first, before concerning oneself with the normality of the error terms.

Omission of Important Predictor Variables

Residuals should also be plotted against variables omitted from the model that might have important effects on the response. The time variable cited earlier in the welding example is an illustration. The purpose of this additional analysis is to determine whether there are any other key variables that could provide important additional descriptive and predictive power to the model.

As another example, in a study to predict output by piece-rate workers in an assembling operation, the relation between output (Y) and age (X) of worker was studied for a sample of employees. The plot of the residuals against X, shown in Figure 3.10a, indicates no ground for suspecting the appropriateness of the linearity of the regression function or the constancy

FIGURE 3.10   **Residual Plots for Possible Omission of Important Predictor Variable—Productivity Example.**

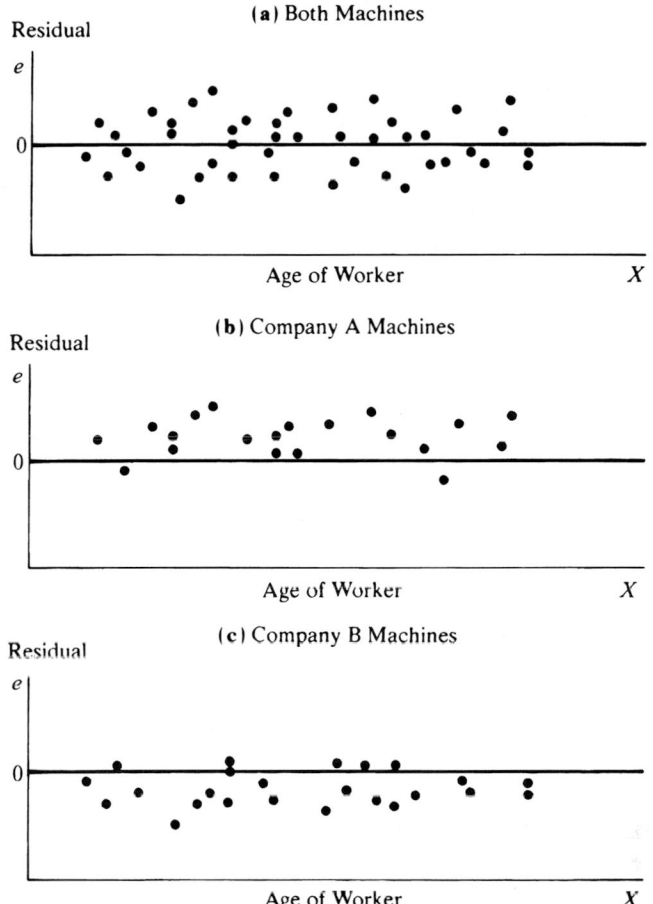

of the error variance. Since machines produced by two companies (A and B) are used in the assembling operation and could have an effect on output, residual plots against X by type of machine were undertaken and are shown in Figures 3.10b and 3.10c. Note that the residuals for Company A machines tend to be positive, while those for Company B machines tend to be negative. Thus, type of machine appears to have a definite effect on productivity, and output predictions may turn out to be far superior when this variable is added to the model.

While this second example dealt with a qualitative variable (type of machine), the residual analysis for an additional quantitative variable is analogous. The residuals are plotted against the additional predictor variable to see whether or not the residuals tend to vary systematically with the level of the additional predictor variable.

Note

We do not say that the original model is "wrong" when it can be improved materially by adding one or more predictor variables. Only a few of the factors operating on any response variable

Y in real-world situations can be included explicitly in a regression model. The chief purpose of residual analysis in identifying other important predictor variables is therefore to test the adequacy of the model and see whether it could be improved materially by adding one or more predictor variables.   ∎

Some Final Comments

1. We discussed model departures one at a time. In actuality, several types of departures may occur together. For instance, a linear regression function may be a poor fit and the variance of the error terms may not be constant. In these cases, the prototype patterns of Figure 3.4 can still be useful, but they would need to be combined into composite patterns.

2. Although graphic analysis of residuals is only an informal method of analysis, in many cases it suffices for examining the aptness of a model.

3. The basic approach to residual analysis explained here applies not only to simple linear regression but also to more complex regression and other types of statistical models.

4. Most of the routine work in residual analysis can be handled on computers. Almost all regression programs supply the fitted values and residuals, and routines are generally available whereby the various types of residual plots can be obtained.   ∎

3.4   Overview of Tests Involving Residuals

Graphic analysis of residuals is inherently subjective. Nevertheless, subjective analysis of a variety of interrelated residual plots will frequently reveal difficulties with the model more clearly than particular formal tests. There are occasions, however, when one wishes to put specific questions to a test. We now briefly review some of the relevant tests.

Most statistical tests require independent observations. As we have seen, however, the residuals are dependent. Fortunately, the dependencies become quite small for large samples, so that one can usually then ignore them.

Tests for Randomness

A runs test is frequently used to test for lack of randomness in the residuals arranged in time order. Another test, specifically designed for lack of randomness in least squares residuals, is the Durbin-Watson test. This test is discussed in Chapter 12.

Tests for Constancy of Variance

When a residual plot gives the impression that the variance may be increasing or decreasing in a systematic manner related to X or $E\{Y\}$, a simple test is based on the rank correlation between the absolute values of the residuals and the corresponding values of the predictor variable. Two other simple tests for constancy of the error variance—the modified Levene test and the Breusch-Pagan test—are discussed in Section 3.6.

Tests for Outliers

A simple test for identifying an outlier observation involves fitting a new regression line to the other $n - 1$ observations. The suspect observation, which was not used in fitting the new line, can now be regarded as a new observation. One can calculate the probability that in n

observations, a deviation from the fitted line as great as that of the outlier will be obtained by chance. If this probability is sufficiently small, the outlier can be rejected as not having come from the same population as the other $n-1$ observations. Otherwise, the outlier is retained. We discuss this approach in detail in Chapter 9.

Many other tests to aid in evaluating outliers have been developed. These are discussed in specialized references, such as Reference 3.1.

Tests for Normality

Goodness of fit tests can be used for examining the normality of the error terms. For instance, the chi-square test or the Kolmogorov-Smirnov test and its modification, the Lilliefors test, can be employed for testing the normality of the error terms by analyzing the residuals. A simple test based on the normal probability plot of the residuals will be taken up in Section 3.5.

Note

The runs test, rank correlation, and goodness of fit tests are commonly used statistical procedures and are discussed in many basic statistics texts.   ∎

3.5   Correlation Test for Normality

In addition to visually assessing the approximate linearity of the points plotted in a normal probability plot, a formal test for normality of the error terms can be conducted by calculating the coefficient of correlation (2.74) between the residuals e_i and their expected values under normality. A high value of the correlation coefficient is indicative of normality. Table B.6, prepared by Looney and Gulledge (Ref. 3.2), contains critical values (percentiles) for various sample sizes for the distribution of the coefficient of correlation between the ordered residuals and their expected values under normality when the error terms are normally distributed. If the observed coefficient of correlation is at least as large as the tabled value, for a given α level, one can conclude that the error terms are reasonably normally distributed.

Example

For the Toluca Company example in Table 3.2, the coefficient of correlation between the ordered residuals and their expected values under normality is .991. Controlling the α risk at .05, we find from Table B.6 that the critical value for $n = 25$ is .959. Since the observed coefficient exceeds this level, we have support for our earlier conclusion that the distribution of the error terms does not depart substantially from a normal distribution.

Note

The correlation test for normality presented here is simpler than the Shapiro-Wilk test (Ref. 3.3), which can be viewed as being based approximately also on the coefficient of correlation between the ordered residuals and their expected values under normality.   ∎

3.6   Tests for Constancy of Error Variance

We present two formal tests for ascertaining whether the error terms have constant variance: the modified Levene test and the Breusch-Pagan test.

Modified Levene Test

The modified Levene test, a modification of the Levene test (Ref. 3.4), does not depend on normality of the error terms. Indeed, this test is robust against serious departures from normality, in the sense that the nominal significance level remains approximately correct when the error terms have equal variances even if the distribution of the error terms is far from normal. Yet the test is still relatively efficient when the error terms are normally distributed. The modified Levene test as described is applicable to simple linear regression when the variance of the error terms either increases or decreases with X, as illustrated in the prototype megaphone plot in Figure 3.4c. The sample size needs to be large enough so that the dependencies among the residuals can be ignored.

The test is based on the variability of the residuals. The larger the error variance, the larger the variability of the residuals will tend to be. To conduct the modified Levene test, we divide the data set into two groups, according to the level of X, so that one group consists of cases where the X level is comparatively low and the other group consists of cases where the X level is comparatively high. If the error variance is either increasing or decreasing with X, the residuals in one group will tend to be more variable than those in the other group. Equivalently, the absolute deviations of the residuals around their group mean will tend to be larger for one group than for the other group. In order to make the test more robust, we utilize the absolute deviations of the residuals around the median for the group (Ref. 3.5). The modified Levene test then consists simply of the two-sample t test based on test statistic (A.67) to determine whether the mean of the absolute deviations for one group differs significantly from the mean absolute deviation for the second group.

Although the distribution of the absolute deviations of the residuals is usually not normal, it has been shown that the t^* test statistic still follows approximately the t distribution when the variance of the error terms is constant and the sample sizes of the two groups are not extremely small.

We shall now use e_{i1} to denote the ith residual for group 1 and e_{i2} to denote the ith residual for group 2. Also we shall use n_1 and n_2 to denote the sample sizes of the two groups, where:

(3.7)
$$n = n_1 + n_2$$

Further, we shall use $\tilde{e}_1$ and $\tilde{e}_2$ to denote the medians of the residuals in the two groups. The modified Levene test uses the absolute deviations of the residuals around their group median, to be denoted by d_{i1} and d_{i2}:

(3.8)
$$d_{i1} = |e_{i1} - \tilde{e}_1| \qquad d_{i2} = |e_{i2} - \tilde{e}_2|$$

With this notation, the two-sample t test statistic (A.67) becomes:

(3.9)
$$t_L^* = \frac{\bar{d}_1 - \bar{d}_2}{s\sqrt{\dfrac{1}{n_1} + \dfrac{1}{n_2}}}$$

where $\bar{d}_1$ and $\bar{d}_2$ are the sample means of the d_{i1} and d_{i2}, respectively, and the pooled variance s^2 in (A.63) becomes:

$$(3.9a) \qquad s^2 = \frac{\Sigma(d_{i1} - \bar{d}_1)^2 + \Sigma(d_{i2} - \bar{d}_2)^2}{n - 2}$$

We denote the test statistic for the modified Levene test by t_L^*.

    If the error terms have constant variance and n_1 and n_2 are not extremely small, t_L^* follows approximately the t distribution with $n - 2$ degrees of freedom. Large absolute values of t_L^* indicate that the error terms do not have constant variance.

Example.   We wish to use the modified Levene test for the Toluca Company example to determine whether or not the error term variance varies with the level of X. Since the X levels are spread fairly uniformly (see Figure 3.1a), we divide the 25 cases into two groups with approximately equal X ranges. The first group consists of the 13 runs with lot sizes from 20 to 70. The second group consists of the 12 runs with lot sizes from 80 to 120. Table 3.3 presents a portion of the data for each group. In columns 1 and 2 are repeated the lot sizes and residuals from Table 1.2. We see from Table 3.3 that the median residual is $\tilde{e}_1 = -19.88$ for group 1 and $\tilde{e}_2 = -2.68$ for group 2. Column 3 contains the absolute deviations of the residuals around their respective group medians. For instance, we obtain:

$$d_{11} = |e_{11} - \tilde{e}_1| = |-20.77 - (-19.88)| = .89$$

$$d_{12} = |e_{12} - \tilde{e}_2| = |51.02 - (-2.68)| = 53.70$$

The means of the absolute deviations are obtained in the usual fashion:

$$\bar{d}_1 = \frac{582.60}{13} = 44.815 \qquad \bar{d}_2 = \frac{341.40}{12} = 28.450$$

Finally, column 4 contains the squares of the deviations of the d_{i1} and d_{i2} around their respective group means. For instance, we have:

$$(d_{11} - \bar{d}_1)^2 = (.89 - 44.815)^2 = 1,929.41$$

$$(d_{12} - \bar{d}_2)^2 = (53.70 - 28.450)^2 = 637.56$$

We are now ready to calculate test statistic (3.9):

$$s^2 = \frac{12,566.6 + 9,610.2}{25 - 2} = 964.21$$

$$s = 31.05$$

$$t_L^* = \frac{44.815 - 28.450}{31.05\sqrt{\frac{1}{13} + \frac{1}{12}}} = 1.32$$

To control the α risk at .05, we require $t(.975; 23) = 2.069$. The decision rule therefore is:

If $|t_L^*| \le 2.069$, conclude the error variance is constant

If $|t_L^*| > 2.069$, conclude the error variance is not constant

TABLE 3.3 **Calculations for Modified Levene Test for Constancy of Error Variance—Toluca Company Example.**

Group 1

i	Run	(1) Lot Size	(2) Residual e_{i1}	(3) d_{i1}	(4) $(d_{i1} - \bar{d}_1)^2$
1	14	20	−20.77	.89	1,929.41
2	2	30	−48.47	28.59	263.25
...	...	...	...	...	...
12	12	70	−60.28	40.40	19.49
13	25	70	10.72	30.60	202.07
	Total			582.60	12,566.6

$$\tilde{e}_1 = -19.88 \qquad \bar{d}_1 = 44.815$$

Group 2

i	Run	(1) Lot Size	(2) Residual e_{i2}	(3) d_{i2}	(4) $(d_{i2} - \bar{d}_2)^2$
1	1	80	51.02	53.70	637.56
2	8	80	4.02	6.70	473.06
...	...	...	...	...	...
11	20	110	−34.09	31.41	8.76
12	7	120	55.21	57.89	866.71
	Total			341.40	9,610.2

$$\tilde{e}_2 = -2.68 \qquad \bar{d}_2 = 28.450$$

Since $|t_L^*| = 1.32 \leq 2.069$, we conclude that the error variance is constant and does not vary with the level of X. The two-sided P-value of this test is .20.

Comments

1. If the data set contains many cases, the two-sample t test for constancy of error variance can be conducted after dividing the cases into three or four groups, according to the level of X, and using the two extreme groups.

2. If the variance of the error terms varies in a more complex fashion than simply increasing or decreasing with the level of X, the data set will need to be divided into more than two groups and the Levene test conducted by means of the analysis of variance F test described in Chapter 16.

3. A robust test for constancy of the error variance is desirable because nonnormality and lack of constant variance often go hand in hand. For example, the distribution of the error terms may become increasingly skewed and hence more variable with increasing levels of X. ∎

Breusch-Pagan Test

A second test for the constancy of the error variance is the Breusch-Pagan test (Ref. 3.6). This test, a large-sample test, assumes that the error terms are independent and normally distributed and that the variance of the error term ε_i, denoted by σ_i^2, is related to the level of X in the following way:

$$(3.10) \qquad\qquad \log_e \sigma_i^2 = \gamma_0 + \gamma_1 X_i$$

Note that (3.10) implies that σ_i^2 either increases or decreases with the level of X, depending on the sign of γ_1. Constancy of error variance corresponds to $\gamma_1 = 0$. The test of H_0: $\gamma_1 = 0$ versus H_a: $\gamma_1 \neq 0$ is carried out by means of regressing the squared residuals e_i^2 against X_i in the usual manner and obtaining the regression sum of squares, to be denoted by SSR^*. The test statistic X_{BP}^2 is as follows:

$$(3.11) \qquad\qquad X_{BP}^2 = \frac{SSR^*}{2} \div \left(\frac{SSE}{n}\right)^2$$

where SSR^* is the regression sum of squares when regressing e^2 on X and SSE is the error sum of squares when regressing Y on X. If H_0: $\gamma_1 = 0$ holds and n is reasonably large, X_{BP}^2 follows approximately the chi-square distribution with one degree of freedom. Large values of X_{BP}^2 lead to conclusion H_a, that the error variance is not constant.

Example.   To conduct the Breusch-Pagan test for the Toluca Company example, we regress the squared residuals in Table 1.2, column 5, against X and obtain $SSR^* = 7,896,128$. We know from Figure 2.2 that $SSE = 54,825$. Hence, test statistic (3.11) is:

$$X_{BP}^2 = \frac{7,896,128}{2} \div \left(\frac{54,825}{25}\right)^2 = .821$$

To control the α risk at .05, we require $\chi^2(.95; 1) = 3.84$. Since $X_{BP}^2 = .821 \leq 3.84$, we conclude H_0, that the error variance is constant. The P-value of this test is .64 so that the data are quite consistent with constancy of the error variance.

Comments

1. The Breusch-Pagan test can be modified to allow for different relationships between the error variance and the level of X than the one in (3.10).

2. Test statistic (3.11) was developed independently by Cook and Weisberg (Ref. 3.7), and the test is sometimes referred to as the Cook-Weisberg test.   ∎

3.7   *F* Test for Lack of Fit

We next take up a formal test for determining whether a specific type of regression function adequately fits the data. We illustrate this test for ascertaining whether a linear regression function is a good fit for the data.

FIGURE 3.11   Scatter Plot and Fitted Regression Line—Bank Example.

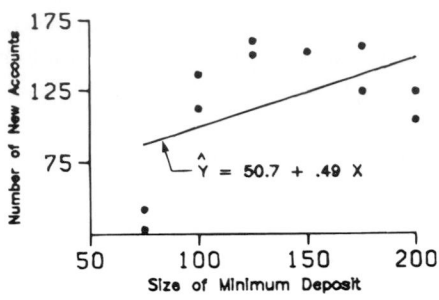

Assumptions

The lack of fit test assumes that the observations Y for given X are (1) independent and (2) normally distributed, and that (3) the distributions of Y have the same variance σ^2.

The lack of fit test requires repeat observations at one or more X levels. In nonexperimental data, these may occur fortuitously, as when in a productivity study relating workers' output and age, several workers of the same age happen to be included in the study. In an experiment, one can assure by design that there are repeat observations. For instance, in an experiment on the effect of size of salesperson bonus on sales, three salespersons can be offered a particular size of bonus, for each of six bonus sizes, and their sales then observed.

Repeat trials for the same level of the predictor variable, of the type described, are called *replications*. The resulting observations are called *replicates*.

Example

In an experiment involving 12 similar but scattered suburban branch offices of a commercial bank, holders of checking accounts at the offices were offered gifts for setting up money market accounts. Minimum initial deposits in the new money market account were specified to qualify for the gift. The value of the gift was directly proportional to the specified minimum deposit. Various levels of minimum deposit and related gift values were used in the experiment in order to ascertain the relation between the specified minimum deposit and gift value, on the one hand, and number of accounts opened at the office, on the other. Altogether, six levels of minimum deposit and proportional gift value were used, with two of the branch offices assigned at random to each level. One branch office had a fire during the period and was dropped from the study. Table 3.4a contains the results, where X is the amount of minimum deposit and Y is the number of new money market accounts that were opened and qualified for the gift during the test period.

A linear regression function was fitted in the usual fashion; it is:

$$\hat{Y} = 50.72251 + .48670X$$

The analysis of variance table also was obtained and is shown in Table 3.4b. A scatter plot, together with the fitted regression line, is shown in Figure 3.11. The indications are strong that a linear regression function is inappropriate. To test this formally, we shall use the general linear test approach described in Section 2.8.

TABLE 3.4   Data and Analysis of Variance Table—Bank Example.

(a) Data

Branch i	Size of Minimum Deposit (dollars) X_i	Number of New Accounts Y_i	Branch i	Size of Minimum Deposit (dollars) X_i	Number of New Accounts Y_i
1	125	160	7	75	42
2	100	112	8	175	124
3	200	124	9	125	150
4	75	28	10	200	104
5	150	152	11	100	136
6	175	156			

(b) ANOVA Table

Source of Variation	SS	df	MS
Regression	5,141.3	1	5,141.3
Error	14,741.6	9	1,638.0
Total	19,882.9	10	

TABLE 3.5   Data Arranged by Replicate Number and Minimum Deposit—Bank Example.

	Size of Minimum Deposit (dollars)					
Replicate	$j = 1$ $X_1 = 75$	$j = 2$ $X_2 = 100$	$j = 3$ $X_3 = 125$	$j = 4$ $X_4 = 150$	$j = 5$ $X_5 = 175$	$j = 6$ $X_6 = 200$
$i = 1$	28	112	160	152	156	124
$i = 2$	42	136	150		124	104
Mean $\bar{Y}_j$	35	124	155	152	140	114

Notation

First, we need to modify our notation to recognize the existence of replications at some levels of X. Table 3.5 presents the same data as Table 3.4a, but in an arrangement that recognizes the replicates. We shall denote the different X levels in the study, whether or not replicated observations are present, as $X_1, \ldots, X_c$. For the bank example, $c = 6$ since there are six minimum deposit size levels in the study, for five of which there are two observations and for one there is a single observation. We shall let $X_1 = 75$ (the smallest minimum deposit level), $X_2 = 100, \ldots, X_6 = 200$. Further, we shall denote the number of replicates for the jth level of X as n_j; for our example, $n_1 = n_2 = n_3 = n_5 = n_6 = 2$ and $n_4 = 1$. Thus, the total number of observations n is given by:

$$(3.12) \qquad\qquad n = \sum_{j=1}^{c} n_j$$

We shall denote the observed value of the response variable for the ith replicate for the jth level of X by Y_{ij}, where $i = 1, \ldots, n_j$, $j = 1, \ldots, c$. For the bank example (Table 3.5), $Y_{11} = 28$, $Y_{21} = 42$, $Y_{12} = 112$, and so on. Finally, we shall denote the mean of the Y observations at the level $X = X_j$ by $\bar{Y}_j$. Thus, $\bar{Y}_1 = (28 + 42)/2 = 35$ and $\bar{Y}_4 = 152/1 = 152$.

Full Model

The general linear test approach begins with the specification of the full model. The full model used for the lack of fit test makes the same assumptions as the simple linear regression model (2.1) except for assuming a linear regression relation, the subject of the test. This full model is:

$$(3.13) \qquad\qquad Y_{ij} = \mu_j + \varepsilon_{ij} \qquad\qquad \text{Full model}$$

where:

μ_j are parameters $\quad j = 1, \ldots, c$

ε_{ij} are independent $N(0, \sigma^2)$

Since the error terms have expectation zero, it follows that:

$$(3.14) \qquad\qquad E\{Y_{ij}\} = \mu_j$$

Thus, the parameter μ_j ($j = 1, \ldots, c$) is the mean response when $X = X_j$.

The full model (3.13) is like the regression model (2.1) in stating that each response Y is made up of two components: the mean response when $X = X_j$ and a random error term. The difference between the two models is that in the full model (3.13) there are no restrictions on the means μ_j, whereas in the regression model (2.1) the mean responses are linearly related to X (i.e., $E\{Y\} = \beta_0 + \beta_1 X$).

To fit the full model to the data, we require the least squares or maximum likelihood estimators for the parameters μ_j. It can be shown that these estimators of μ_j are simply the sample means $\bar{Y}_j$:

$$(3.15) \qquad\qquad \hat{\mu}_j = \bar{Y}_j$$

Thus, the estimated expected value for observation Y_{ij} is $\bar{Y}_j$, and the error sum of squares for the full model therefore is:

$$(3.16) \qquad\qquad SSE(F) = \sum_{j} \sum_{i} (Y_{ij} - \bar{Y}_j)^2 = SSPE$$

In the context of the test for lack of fit, the full model error sum of squares (3.16) is called the *pure error sum of squares* and is denoted by *SSPE*.

Note that *SSPE* is made up of the sums of squared deviations at each X level. At level $X = X_j$, this sum of squared deviations is:

$$(3.17) \qquad \sum_i (Y_{ij} - \bar{Y}_j)^2$$

These sums of squares are then added over all of the X levels ($j = 1, \ldots, c$). For the bank example, we have:

$$SSPE = (28 - 35)^2 + (42 - 35)^2 + (112 - 124)^2 + (136 - 124)^2$$
$$+ (160 - 155)^2 + (150 - 155)^2 + (152 - 152)^2$$
$$+ (156 - 140)^2 + (124 - 140)^2 + (124 - 114)^2$$
$$+ (104 - 114)^2$$
$$= 1,148$$

Note that any X level with no replications makes no contribution to *SSPE* because $\bar{Y}_j = Y_{1j}$ then. Thus, $(152 - 152)^2 = 0$ for $j = 4$ in the bank example.

The degrees of freedom associated with *SSPE* can be obtained by recognizing that the sum of squared deviations (3.17) at a given level of X is like an ordinary total sum of squares based on n observations, which has $n - 1$ degrees of freedom associated with it. Here, there are n_j observations when $X = X_j$; hence the degrees of freedom are $n_j - 1$. Just as *SSPE* is the sum of the sums of squares (3.17), so the number of degrees of freedom associated with *SSPE* is the sum of the component degrees of freedom:

$$(3.18) \qquad df_F = \sum_j (n_j - 1) = \sum_j n_j - c = n - c$$

For the bank example, we have $df_F = 11 - 6 = 5$. Note that any X level with no replications makes no contribution to df_F because $n_j - 1 = 1 - 1 = 0$ then, just as such an X level makes no contribution to *SSPE*.

Reduced Model

The general linear test approach next requires consideration of the reduced model under H_0. For testing the appropriateness of a linear regression relation, the alternatives are:

$$(3.19) \qquad \begin{aligned} H_0&: E\{Y\} = \beta_0 + \beta_1 X \\ H_a&: E\{Y\} \neq \beta_0 + \beta_1 X \end{aligned}$$

Thus, H_0 postulates that μ_j in the full model (3.13) is linearly related to X_j:

$$\mu_j = \beta_0 + \beta_1 X_j$$

The reduced model under H_0 therefore is:

$$(3.20) \qquad Y_{ij} = \beta_0 + \beta_1 X_j + \varepsilon_{ij} \qquad\qquad \text{Reduced model}$$

Note that the reduced model is the ordinary simple linear regression model (2.1), with the subscripts modified to recognize the existence of replications. We know that the estimated expected value for observation Y_{ij} with regression model (2.1) is the fitted value $\hat{Y}_{ij}$:

$$(3.21) \qquad \hat{Y}_{ij} = b_0 + b_1 X_j$$

Hence, the error sum of squares for the reduced model is the usual error sum of squares *SSE*:

$$(3.22) \qquad SSE(R) = \sum\sum[Y_{ij} - (b_0 + b_1 X_j)]^2$$
$$= \sum\sum(Y_{ij} - \hat{Y}_{ij})^2 = SSE$$

We also know that the degrees of freedom associated with $SSE(R)$ are:

$$df_R = n - 2$$

For the bank example, we have from Table 3.4b:

$$SSE(R) = SSE = 14{,}741.6$$
$$df_R = 9$$

Test Statistic

The general linear test statistic (2.70):

$$F^* = \frac{SSE(R) - SSE(F)}{df_R - df_F} \div \frac{SSE(F)}{df_F}$$

here becomes:

$$(3.23) \qquad F^* = \frac{SSE - SSPE}{(n-2) - (n-c)} \div \frac{SSPE}{n-c}$$

The difference between the two error sums of squares is called the *lack of fit sum of squares* here and is denoted by *SSLF*:

$$(3.24) \qquad SSLF = SSE - SSPE$$

We can then express the test statistic as follows:

$$(3.25) \qquad F^* = \frac{SSLF}{c-2} \div \frac{SSPE}{n-c}$$
$$= \frac{MSLF}{MSPE}$$

where *MSLF* denotes the *lack of fit mean square* and *MSPE* denotes the *pure error mean square*.

We know that large values of F^* lead to conclusion H_a in the general linear test. Decision rule (2.71) here becomes:

(3.26)
$$\text{If } F^* \leq F(1 - \alpha; c - 2, n - c), \quad \text{conclude } H_0$$
$$\text{If } F^* > F(1 - \alpha; c - 2, n - c), \quad \text{conclude } H_a$$

For the bank example, the test statistic can be constructed easily from our earlier results:

$$SSPE = 1,148.0 \qquad\qquad n - c = 11 - 6 = 5$$

$$SSE = 14,741.6$$

$$SSLF = 14,741.6 - 1,148.0 = 13,593.6 \qquad c - 2 = 6 - 2 = 4$$

$$F^* = \frac{13,593.6}{4} \div \frac{1,148.0}{5}$$
$$= \frac{3,398.4}{229.6} = 14.80$$

If the level of significance is to be $\alpha = .01$, we require $F(.99; 4, 5) = 11.4$. Since $F^* = 14.80 > 11.4$, we conclude H_a, that the regression function is not linear. This, of course, accords with our visual impression from Figure 3.11. The P-value for the test is .006.

ANOVA Table

The definition of the lack of fit sum of squares $SSLF$ in (3.24) indicates that we have, in fact, decomposed the error sum of squares SSE into two components:

(3.27)
$$SSE = SSPE + SSLF$$

This decomposition follows from the identity:

(3.28)
$$\underbrace{Y_{ij} - \hat{Y}_{ij}}_{\substack{\text{Error} \\ \text{deviation}}} = \underbrace{Y_{ij} - \bar{Y}_j}_{\substack{\text{Pure error} \\ \text{deviation}}} + \underbrace{\bar{Y}_j - \hat{Y}_{ij}}_{\substack{\text{Lack of fit} \\ \text{deviation}}}$$

This identity shows that the error deviations in SSE are made up of a pure error component and a lack of fit component. Figure 3.12 illustrates this partitioning for the case $Y_{13} = 160$, $X_3 = 125$ in the bank example.

When (3.28) is squared and summed over all observations, we obtain (3.27) since the cross-product sum equals zero:

(3.29)
$$\underbrace{\sum\sum(Y_{ij} - \hat{Y}_{ij})^2}_{SSE} = \underbrace{\sum\sum(Y_{ij} - \bar{Y}_j)^2}_{SSPE} + \underbrace{\sum\sum(\bar{Y}_j - \hat{Y}_{ij})^2}_{SSLF}$$

Note from (3.29) that we can define the lack of fit sum of squares directly as follows:

(3.30)
$$SSLF = \sum\sum(\bar{Y}_j - \hat{Y}_{ij})^2$$

FIGURE 3.12   **Illustration of Decomposition of Error Deviation $Y_{ij} - \hat{Y}_{ij}$—Bank Example.**

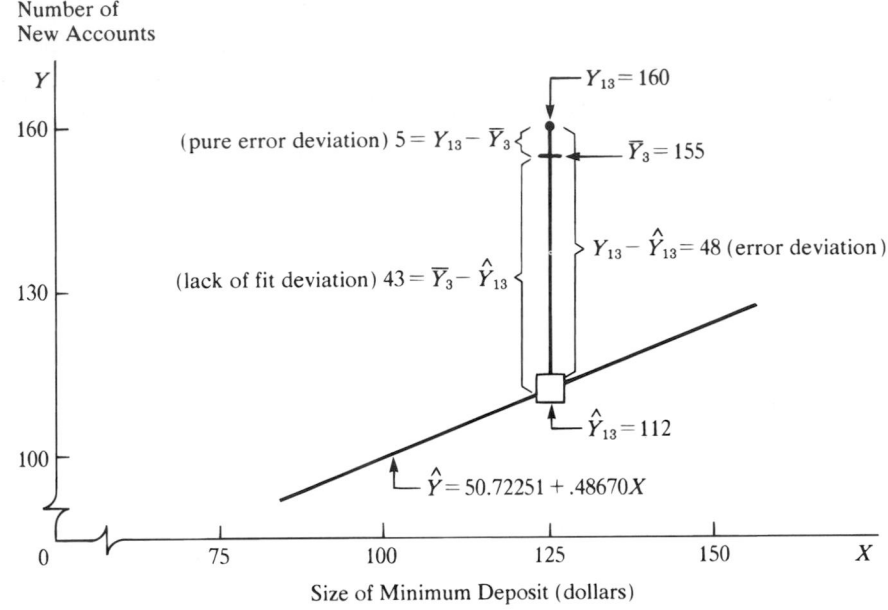

Since all Y_{ij} observations at the level X_j have the same fitted value, which we can denote by $\hat{Y}_j$, we can express (3.30) equivalently as:

$$(3.30a) \qquad SSLF = \sum_j n_j (\bar{Y}_j - \hat{Y}_j)^2$$

Formula (3.30a) indicates clearly why *SSLF* measures lack of fit. If the linear regression function is appropriate, then the means $\bar{Y}_j$ will be near the fitted values $\hat{Y}_j$ calculated from the estimated linear regression function and *SSLF* will be small. On the other hand, if the linear regression function is not appropriate, the means $\bar{Y}_j$ will not be near the fitted values calculated from the estimated linear regression function, as in Figure 3.11 for the bank example, and *SSLF* will be large.

Formula (3.30a) also indicates why $c - 2$ degrees of freedom are associated with *SSLF*. There are c means $\bar{Y}_j$ in the sum of squares, and two degrees of freedom are lost in estimating the parameters β_0 and β_1 of the linear regression function to obtain the fitted values $\hat{Y}_j$.

An ANOVA table can be constructed for the decomposition of *SSE*. Table 3.6a contains the general ANOVA table, including the decomposition of *SSE* just explained and the mean squares of interest, and Table 3.6b contains the ANOVA decomposition for the bank example.

Comments

1. As shown by the bank example, not all levels of X need have repeat observations for the F test for lack of fit to be applicable. Repeat observations at only one or some levels of X are sufficient.

TABLE 3.6   **General ANOVA Table for Testing Lack of Fit of Simple Linear Regression Function and ANOVA Table for Bank Example.**

(a) General

Source of Variation	SS	df	MS
Regression	$SSR = \Sigma\Sigma(\hat{Y}_{ij} - \bar{Y})^2$	1	$MSR = \dfrac{SSR}{1}$
Error	$SSE = \Sigma\Sigma(Y_{ij} - \hat{Y}_{ij})^2$	$n - 2$	$MSE = \dfrac{SSE}{n - 2}$
Lack of fit	$SSLF = \Sigma\Sigma(\bar{Y}_j - \hat{Y}_{ij})^2$	$c - 2$	$MSLF = \dfrac{SSLF}{c - 2}$
Pure error	$SSPE = \Sigma\Sigma(Y_{ij} - \bar{Y}_j)^2$	$n - c$	$MSPE = \dfrac{SSPE}{n - c}$
Total	$SSTO = \Sigma\Sigma(Y_{ij} - \bar{Y})^2$	$n - 1$	

(b) Bank Example

Source of Variation	SS	df	MS
Regression	5,141.3	1	5,141.3
Error	14,741.6	9	1,638.0
Lack of fit	13,593.6	4	3,398.4
Pure error	1,148.0	5	229.6
Total	19,882.9	10	

2. It can be shown that the mean squares *MSPE* and *MSLF* have the following expectations when testing whether the regression function is linear:

$$(3.31) \qquad E\{MSPE\} = \sigma^2$$

$$(3.32) \qquad E\{MSLF\} = \sigma^2 + \frac{\Sigma n_j[\mu_j - (\beta_0 + \beta_1 X_j)]^2}{c - 2}$$

The reason for the term "pure error" is that *MSPE* is always an unbiased estimator of the error term variance σ^2, no matter what is the true regression function. The expected value of *MSLF* also is σ^2 if the regression function is linear, because $\mu_j = \beta_0 + \beta_1 X_j$ then and the second term in (3.32) becomes zero. On the other hand, if the regression function is not linear, $\mu_j \neq \beta_0 + \beta_1 X_j$ and $E\{MSLF\}$ will be greater than σ^2. Hence, a value of F^* near 1 accords with a linear regression function; large values of F^* indicate that the regression function is not linear.

3. The terminology "error sum of squares" and "error mean square" is not precise when the regression function under test in H_0 is not the true function since the error sum of squares and error mean square then reflect the effects of both the lack of fit and the variability of the error terms. We continue to use the terminology for consistency and now use the term "pure error" to identify the variability associated with the error term only.

4. Suppose that prior to any analysis of the appropriateness of the model, we had fitted a linear regression model and wished to test whether or not $\beta_1 = 0$ for the bank example (Table 3.4b). Test statistic (2.60) would be:

$$F^* = \frac{MSR}{MSE} = \frac{5,141.3}{1,638.0} = 3.14$$

For $\alpha = .10$, $F(.90; 1, 9) = 3.36$, and we would conclude H_0, that $\beta_1 = 0$ or that there is no *linear association* between minimum deposit size (and value of gift) and number of new accounts. A conclusion that there is no *relation* between these variables would be improper, however. Such an inference requires that regression model (2.1) be appropriate. Here, there is a definite relationship, but the regression function is not linear. This illustrates the importance of always examining the appropriateness of a model before any inferences are drawn.

5. The general linear test approach just explained can be used to test the appropriateness of other regression functions. Only the degrees of freedom for *SSLF* will need be modified. In general, $c - p$ degrees of freedom are associated with *SSLF*, where p is the number of parameters in the regression function. For the test of a simple linear regression function, $p = 2$ because there are two parameters, β_0 and β_1, in the regression function.

6. The alternative H_a in (3.19) includes all regression functions other than a linear one. For instance, it includes a quadratic regression function or a logarithmic one. If H_a is concluded, a study of residuals can be helpful in identifying an appropriate function.

7. When we conclude that the employed model in H_0 is appropriate, the usual practice is to use the error mean square *MSE* as an estimator of σ^2 in preference to the pure error mean square *MSPE*, since the former contains more degrees of freedom.

8. Observations at the same level of X are genuine repeats only if they involve independent trials with respect to the error term. Suppose that in a regression analysis of the relation between hardness (Y) and amount of carbon (X) in specimens of an alloy, the error term in the model covers, among other things, random errors in the measurement of hardness by the analyst and effects of uncontrolled production factors which vary at random from specimen to specimen and affect hardness. If the analyst takes two readings on the hardness of a specimen, this will not provide a genuine replication because the effects of random variation in the production factors are fixed in any given specimen. For genuine replications, different specimens with the same carbon content (X) would have to be measured by the analyst so that *all* the effects covered in the error term could vary at random from one repeated observation to the next.

9. When no replications are present in a data set, an approximate test for lack of fit can be conducted if there are some cases at adjacent X levels for which the mean responses are quite close to each other. Such adjacent cases are grouped together and treated as pseudoreplicates, and the test for lack of fit is then carried out using these groupings of adjacent cases. A useful summary of this and related procedures for conducting a test for lack of fit when no replicates are present may be found in Reference 3.8. ∎

3.8 Overview of Remedial Measures

If the simple linear regression model (2.1) is not appropriate for a data set, there are two basic choices:

1. Abandon regression model (2.1) and develop and use a more appropriate model.

2. Employ some transformation on the data so that regression model (2.1) is appropriate for the transformed data.

Each approach has advantages and disadvantages. The first approach may entail a more complex model that could yield better insights, but may also lead to more complex procedures for estimating the parameters. Successful use of transformations, on the other hand, leads to relatively simple methods of estimation and may involve fewer parameters than a complex model, an advantage when the sample size is small. Yet transformations may obscure the fundamental interconnections between the variables, though at other times they may illuminate them.

We consider the use of transformations in this chapter and the use of more complex models in later chapters. First, we provide a brief overview of remedial measures.

Nonlinearity of Regression Function

When the regression function is not linear, a direct approach is to modify regression model (2.1) by altering the nature of the regression function. For instance, a quadratic regression function might be used:

$$E\{Y\} = \beta_0 + \beta_1 X + \beta_2 X^2$$

or an exponential regression function:

$$E\{Y\} = \beta_0 \beta_1^X$$

In Chapter 7, we discuss polynomial regression functions, and in Part III we take up nonlinear regression functions, such as an exponential regression function.

The transformation approach employs a transformation to linearize, at least approximately, a nonlinear regression function. We discuss the use of transformations to linearize regression functions in Section 3.9.

When the nature of the regression function is not known, exploratory analysis that does not require specifying a particular type of function is often useful. We discuss exploratory regression analysis in Section 3.10.

Nonconstancy of Error Variance

When the error variance is not constant but varies in a systematic fashion, a direct approach is to modify the model to allow for this and use the method of *weighted least squares* to obtain the estimators of the parameters. We discuss the use of weighted least squares for this purpose in Chapter 10.

Transformations can also be effective in stabilizing the variance. Some of these are discussed in Section 3.9.

Nonindependence of Error Terms

When the error terms are correlated, a direct remedial measure is to work with a model that calls for correlated error terms. We discuss such a model in Chapter 12. A simple remedial transformation that is often helpful is to work with first differences, a topic also discussed in Chapter 12.

If it is desired to express the estimated regression function in the original units of Y, we simply take the antilog of $\hat{Y}'$ and obtain:

$$\hat{Y} = \text{antilog}_{10}(1.135 - .1023X)$$

Comments

1. At times it may be desirable to introduce a constant into a transformation of Y, such as when Y may be negative. For instance, the logarithmic transformation to shift the origin in Y and make all Y observations positive would be $Y' = \log_{10}(Y + k)$, where k is an appropriately chosen constant.

2. When unequal error variances are present but the regression relation is linear, a transformation on Y may not be sufficient. While such a transformation may stabilize the error variance, it will also change the linear relationship to a curvilinear one. A transformation on X may therefore also be required. This case can also be handled by using weighted least squares, a procedure explained in Chapter 10. ∎

Box-Cox Transformations

It is often difficult to determine from diagnostic plots, such as the one in Figure 3.16a for the plasma levels example, which transformation of Y is most appropriate for correcting skewness of the distributions of error terms, unequal error variances, and nonlinearity of the regression function. The Box-Cox procedure (Ref. 3.9) automatically identifies a transformation from the family of power transformations on Y. The family of power transformations is of the form:

(3.33) $$Y' = Y^\lambda$$

where λ is a parameter to be determined from the data. Note that this family encompasses the following simple transformations:

$$\lambda = 2 \qquad Y' = Y^2$$

$$\lambda = .5 \qquad Y' = \sqrt{Y}$$

$$\lambda = 0 \qquad Y' = \log_e Y \qquad \text{(by definition)}$$

$$\lambda = -.5 \qquad Y' = \frac{1}{\sqrt{Y}}$$

$$\lambda = -1.0 \qquad Y' = \frac{1}{Y}$$

The normal error regression model with the response variable a member of the family of power transformations in (3.33) becomes:

(3.34) $$Y_i^\lambda = \beta_0 + \beta_1 X_i + \varepsilon_i$$

Note that regression model (3.34) includes an additional parameter, λ, which needs to be estimated. The Box-Cox procedure uses the method of maximum likelihood to estimate λ, as well as the other parameters β_0, β_1, and σ^2. The likelihood function (1.26) becomes for regression model (3.34):

$$(3.35) \qquad L(\beta_0, \beta_1, \sigma^2, \lambda) = \frac{1}{(2\pi\sigma^2)^{n/2}} \exp\left[-\frac{1}{2\sigma^2} \sum_{i=1}^{n} (Y_i^{\lambda} - \beta_0 - \beta_1 X_i)^2\right]$$

Maximizing this likelihood function with respect to β_0, β_1, σ^2, and λ yields the maximum likelihood estimators of these parameters. In this way, the Box-Cox procedure identifies $\hat{\lambda}$, the maximum likelihood estimate of λ to use in the power transformation.

Since many statistical software packages do not automatically provide the Box-Cox maximum likelihood estimate $\hat{\lambda}$ for the power transformation, a simple procedure for obtaining $\hat{\lambda}$ using standard regression software can be employed instead. This procedure involves a numerical search in a range of potential λ values; for example, $\lambda = -2$, $\lambda = -1.75, \ldots, \lambda = 1.75, \lambda = 2$. For each λ value, the Y_i^{λ} observations are first standardized so that the magnitude of the error sum of squares does not depend on the value of λ:

$$(3.36) \qquad W_i = \begin{array}{ll} K_1(Y_i^{\lambda} - 1) & \lambda \neq 0 \\ K_2(\log_e Y_i) & \lambda = 0 \end{array}$$

where:

$$(3.36a) \qquad K_2 = \left(\prod_{i=1}^{n} Y_i\right)^{1/n}$$

$$(3.36b) \qquad K_1 = \frac{1}{\lambda K_2^{\lambda-1}}$$

Note that K_2 is the geometric mean of the Y_i observations.

Once the standardized observations W_i have been obtained for a given λ value, they are regressed on the predictor variable X and the error sum of squares SSE is obtained. It can be shown that the maximum likelihood estimate $\hat{\lambda}$ is that value of λ for which SSE is a minimum.

If desired, a finer search can be conducted in the neighborhood of the λ value that minimizes SSE. However, the Box-Cox procedure ordinarily is only used to provide a guide for selecting a transformation, so overly precise results are not needed. In any case, scatter and residual plots should be utilized to examine the appropriateness of the transformation identified by the Box-Cox procedure.

Example.   Table 3.9 contains the Box-Cox results for the plasma levels example. Selected values of λ, ranging from -1.0 to 1.0, were chosen, and for each chosen λ the transformation (3.36) was made and the linear regression of W on X was fitted. For instance, for $\lambda = .5$, the transformation $W_i = K_1(\sqrt{Y_i} - 1)$ was made and the linear regression of W on X was fitted. For this fitted linear regression, the error sum of squares is $SSE = 48.4$.

Note from Table 3.9 that the Box-Cox procedure identifies a power value near $\lambda = -.50$ as being appropriate. However, SSE as a function of λ is fairly stable in the range from near 0 to -1.0, so the earlier choice of the logarithmic transformation $Y' = \log_{10} Y$ for the plasma

TABLE 3.9   **Box-Cox Results—Plasma Levels Example.**

λ	SSE	λ	SSE
1.0	78.0	$-.1$	33.1
.9	70.4	$-.3$	31.2
.7	57.8	$-.4$	30.7
.5	48.4	$-.5$	30.6
.3	41.4	$-.6$	30.7
.1	36.4	$-.7$	31.1
0	34.5	$-.9$	32.7
		-1.0	33.9

levels example, corresponding to $\lambda = 0$, is not unreasonable according to the Box-Cox approach. One reason the logarithmic transformation was chosen here is because of the ease of interpreting it. The use of logarithms to base 10 rather than natural logarithms does not, of course, affect the appropriateness of the logarithmic transformation.

Comments

1. At times, theoretical or a priori considerations can be utilized to help in choosing an appropriate transformation. For example, when the shape of the scatter in a study of the relation between price of a commodity (X) and quantity demanded (Y) is that in Figure 3.15b, economists may prefer logarithmic transformations of both Y and X because the slope of the regression line for the transformed variables then measures the price elasticity of demand. The slope is then commonly interpreted as showing the percent change in quantity demanded per 1 percent change in price, where it is understood that the changes are in opposite directions.

Similarly, scientists may prefer logarithmic transformations of both Y and X when studying the relation between radioactive decay (Y) of a substance and time (X) for a curvilinear relation of the type illustrated in Figure 3.15b because the slope of the regression line for the transformed variables then measures the decay rate.

2. After a transformation has been tentatively selected, residual plots and other analyses described earlier need to be employed to ascertain that the simple linear regression model (2.1) is appropriate for the transformed data.

3. When transformed models are employed, the estimators b_0 and b_1 obtained by least squares have the least squares properties with respect to the transformed observations, not the original ones.

4. The maximum likelihood estimate of λ with the Box-Cox procedure is subject to sampling variability. In addition, the error sum of squares SSE is often fairly stable in a neighborhood around the estimate. It is therefore often reasonable to use a nearby λ value for which the power transformation is easy to understand. For example, use of $\lambda = 0$ instead of the maximum likelihood estimate $\hat{\lambda} = .13$ or use of $\lambda = -.5$ instead of $\hat{\lambda} = -.79$ may facilitate understanding without sacrificing much in terms of the effectiveness of the transformation. To determine the reasonableness of using an easier-to-understand value of λ, one should examine the flatness of the likelihood function in the neighborhood of $\hat{\lambda}$, as we did in the plasma levels example. Alternatively, one may construct an approximate confidence interval for λ; the procedure for constructing such an interval is discussed in Reference 3.10.

5. When the Box-Cox procedure leads to a λ value near 1, no transformation of Y may be needed.   ∎

3.10 Exploration of Shape of Regression Function

Scatter plots often indicate readily the nature of the regression function. For instance, Figure 1.3 clearly shows the curvilinear nature of the regression relationship between steroid level and age. At other times, however, the scatter plot is complex and it becomes difficult to see the nature of the regression relationship, if any, from the plot. In these cases, it is helpful to explore the nature of the regression relationship by fitting a smoothed curve without any constraints on the regression function. These smoothed curves are also called *nonparametric regression curves*. They are useful not only for exploring regression relationships but also for confirming the nature of the regression function when the scatter plot visually suggests the nature of the regression relationship.

Many smoothing methods have been developed for obtaining smoothed curves for time series data, where the X_i denote time periods that are equally spaced apart. The *method of moving averages* uses the mean of the Y observations for adjacent time periods to obtain smoothed values. For example, the mean of the Y values for the first three time periods in the times series might constitute the first smoothed value corresponding to the middle of the three time periods, in other words, corresponding to time period 2. Then the mean of the Y values for the second, third, and fourth time periods would constitute the second smoothed value, corresponding to the middle of these three time periods, in other words, corresponding to time period 3, and so on. Special procedures are required for obtaining smoothed values at the two ends of the time series. The larger the successive neighborhoods used for obtaining the smoothed values, the smoother the curve will be.

The *method of running medians* is similar to the method of moving averages, except that the median is used as the average measure in order to reduce the influence of outlying observations. With this method, as well as with the moving average method, successive smoothing of the smoothed values and other refinements may be undertaken to provide a suitable smoothed curve for the time series. Reference 3.11 provides a good introduction to the running median smoothing method.

Many smoothing methods have also been developed for regression data when the X values are not equally spaced apart. A simple smoothing method, *band regression*, divides the data set into a number of groups or "bands" consisting of adjacent cases according to their X levels. For each band, the median X value and the median Y value are calculated, and the points defined by the pairs of these median values are then connected by straight lines. For example, consider the following simple data set divided into three groups:

X	Y	Median X	Median Y
2.0	13.1		
		2.7	14.4
3.4	15.7		
3.7	14.9		
4.5	16.8	4.5	16.8
5.0	17.1		
5.2	16.9		
		5.55	17.35
5.9	17.8		

The three pairs of medians are then plotted on the scatter plot of the data and connected by straight lines as a simple smoothed nonparametric regression curve.

Loess Method

The *loess method*, developed by Cleveland (Ref. 3.12), is a more refined nonparametric method than band regression. It obtains a smoothed curve by fitting successive linear regression functions in local neighborhoods. The name loess stands for *locally weighted regression scatter plot smoothing*. The method is similar to the moving average and running median methods in that it uses a neighborhood around each X value to obtain a smoothed Y value corresponding to that X value. It obtains the smoothed Y value at a given X by fitting a linear regression to the data in the neighborhood of the X value and then using the fitted value at X as the smoothed value. To illustrate this concretely, let (X_1, Y_1) denote the sample case with the smallest X value, (X_2, Y_2) denote the sample case with the second smallest X value, and so on. If neighborhoods of three X values are used with the loess method, then a linear regression would be fitted to the data:

$$(X_1, Y_1) \quad (X_2, Y_2) \quad (X_3, Y_3)$$

The fitted value at X_2 would constitute the smoothed value corresponding to X_2. Another linear regression would be fitted to the data:

$$(X_2, Y_2) \quad (X_3, Y_3) \quad (X_4, Y_4)$$

and the fitted value at X_3 would constitute the smoothed value corresponding to X_3. Smoothed values at each end of the X range are also obtained by the loess procedure.

The loess method uses a number of refinements in obtaining the final smoothed values to improve the smoothing and to make the procedure robust to outlying observations.

1. The linear regression is weighted to give cases further from the middle X level in each neighborhood smaller weights.

2. To make the procedure robust to outlying observations, the linear regression fitting is repeated, with the weights revised so that cases that had large residuals in the first fitting receive smaller weights in the second fitting.

3. To improve the robustness of the procedure further, step 2 is repeated one or more times by revising the weights according to the size of the residuals in the latest fitting.

To implement the loess procedure, one must choose the size of the successive neighborhoods to be used when fitting each linear regression. One must also choose the weight function that gives less weight to neighborhood cases with X values far from each center X level and another weight function that gives less weight to cases with large residuals. Finally, the number of iterations to make the procedure robust must be chosen.

In practice, two iterations appear to be sufficient to provide robustness. Also, the weight functions suggested by Cleveland appear to be adequate for many circumstances. Hence, the primary choice to be made for a particular application is the size of the successive neighborhoods. The larger the size, the smoother the function but the greater the danger that the smoothing will lose essential features of the regression relationship. It may require some experimentation with different neighborhood sizes in order to find the size that best brings out the regression relationship. We explain the loess method in detail in Chapter 10 in the context of multiple regression. Specific choices of weight functions and neighborhood sizes are discussed there.

FIGURE 3.17   **Scatter Plot and Loess Smoothed Curve—Research Laboratories Example.**

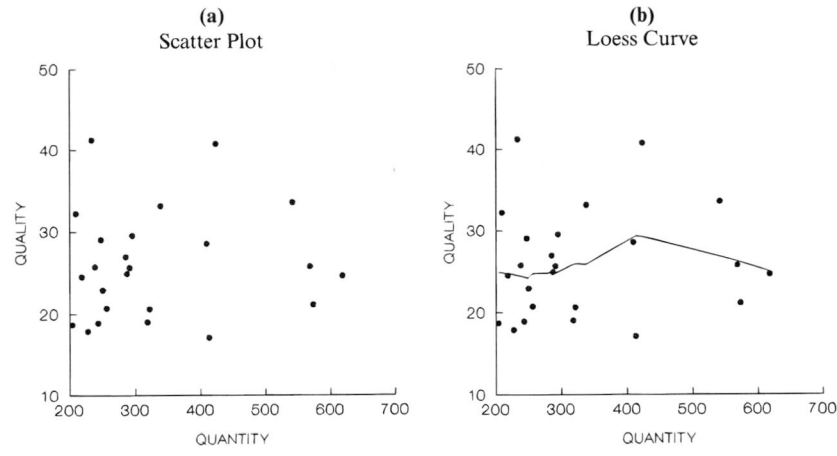

(a)
Scatter Plot

(b)
Loess Curve

Example.   Figure 3.17a contains a scatter plot based on a study of research quality at 24 research laboratories. The response variable is a measure of the quality of the research done at the laboratory, and the explanatory variable is a measure of the volume of research performed at the laboratory. Note that it is very difficult to tell from this scatter plot whether or not a relationship exists between research quality and quantity. Figure 3.17b repeats the scatter plot and also shows the loess smoothed curve. The curve suggests that there might be somewhat higher research quality for medium-sized laboratories. However, the scatter is great so that this suggested relationship should only be considered as a possibility. Also, because any particular measures of research quality and quantity are so limited, other measures should be considered to see if these corroborate the relationship suggested in Figure 3.17b.

Use of Smoothed Curves to Confirm Fitted Regression Function

Smoothed curves are useful not only in the exploratory stages when a regression model is selected but they are also helpful in confirming the regression function chosen. The procedure for confirmation is simple: The smoothed curve is plotted together with the confidence band for the fitted regression function. If the smoothed curve falls within the confidence band, we have supporting evidence of the appropriateness of the fitted regression function.

Example.   Figure 3.18a repeats the scatter plot for the Toluca Company example from Figure 1.10a and shows the loess smoothed curve. It appears that the regression relation is linear or possibly slightly curved. Figure 3.18b repeats the confidence band for the regression line from Figure 2.6 and shows the loess smoothed curve. We see that the smoothed curve falls within the confidence band for the regression line and thereby supports the appropriateness of a linear regression function.

FIGURE 3.18   **Loess Curve and Confidence Band for Regression Line—Toluca Company Example.**

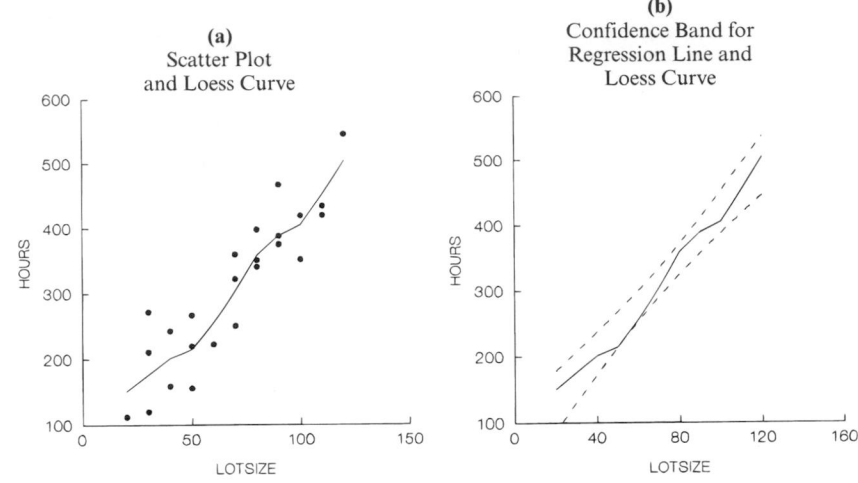

Comments

1. Smoothed curves, such as the loess curve, do not provide an analytical expression for the functional form of the regression relationship. They only suggest the shape of the regression curve.

2. The loess procedure is not restricted to fitting linear regression functions in each neighborhood. Higher-degree polynomials can also be utilized with this method.

3. Smoothed curves are also useful when examining residual plots to ascertain whether the residuals (or the absolute or squared residuals) follow some relationship with X or $\hat{Y}$.

4. References 3.13 and 3.14 provide good introductions to other nonparametric methods in regression analysis.   ■

3.11   Case Example—Plutonium Measurement

Some environmental cleanup work requires that nuclear materials, such as plutonium 238, be located and completely removed from a restoration site. When plutonium has become mixed with other materials in very small amounts, detecting its presence can be a difficult task. Even very small amounts can be traced, however, because plutonium emits subatomic particles—alpha particles—that can be detected. Devices that are used to detect plutonium record the intensity of alpha particle strikes in counts per second (#/sec). The regression relationship between alpha counts per second (the response variable) and plutonium activity (the explanatory variable) is then used to estimate the activity of plutonium in the material under study. This use of a regression relationship involves inverse prediction [i.e., predicting plutonium activity (X) from the observed alpha count (Y)], a procedure discussed in Chapter 4.

The task here is to estimate the regression relationship between alpha counts per second and plutonium activity. This relationship varies for each measurement device and must be established precisely each time a different measurement device is used. It is reasonable to

TABLE 3.10   Basic Data—Plutonium Measurement Example.

Case	Plutonium Activity (pCi/g)	Alpha Count Rate (#/sec)
1	20.000	.150
2	0	.004
3	10.000	.069
. . .	. . .	. . .
22	0	.002
23	5.000	.049
24	0	.106

FIGURE 3.19   Scatter Plot and Loess Smoothed Curve—Plutonium Measurement Example.

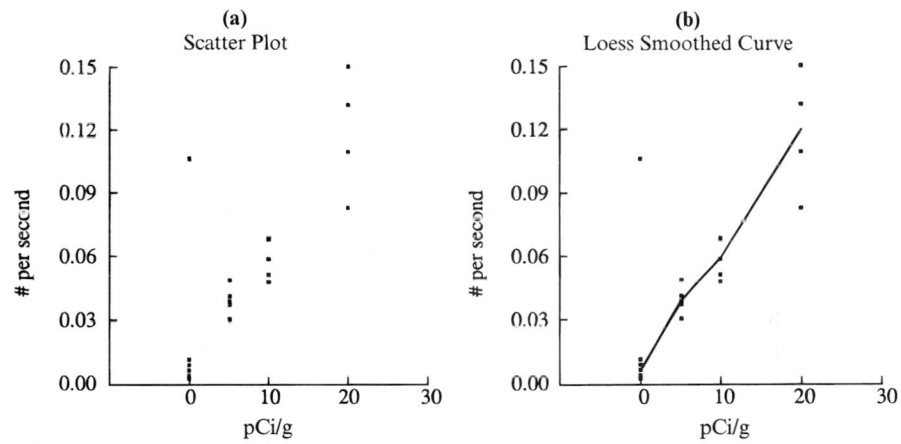

assume here that the level of alpha counts increases with plutonium activity, but the exact nature of the relationship is generally unknown.

In a study to establish the regression relationship for a particular measurement device, four plutonium *standards* were used. These standards are aluminum/plutonium rods containing a fixed, known level of plutonium activity. The levels of plutonium activity in the four standards were 0.0, 5.0, 10.0, and 20.0 picocuries per gram (pCi/g). Each standard was exposed to the detection device from 4 to 10 times, and the rate of alpha strikes, measured as counts per second, was observed for each replication. A portion of the data is shown in Table 3.10, and the data are plotted as a scatter plot in Figure 3.19a. Notice that, as expected, the strike rate tends to increase with the activity level of plutonium. Notice also that nonzero strike rates are recorded for the standard containing no plutonium. This results from background radiation and indicates that a regression model with an intercept term is required here.

FIGURE 3.20   **SAS-JMP Regression Output and Diagnostic Plots for Untransformed Data—Plutonium Measurement Example.**

(a) Regression Output

Term		Estimate	Std Error	t Ratio	Prob>|t|
Intercept		0.0070331	0.0036	1.95	0.0641
Plutonium		0.005537	0.00037	15.13	0.0000

Source	DF	Sum of Squares	Mean Square	F Ratio
Model	1	0.03619042	0.036190	228.9984
Error	21	0.00331880	0.000158	**Prob>F**
C Total	22	0.03950922		0.0000

Source	DF	Sum of Squares	Mean Square	F Ratio
Lack of Fit	2	0.00016811	0.000084	0.5069
Pure Error	19	0.00315069	0.000166	**Prob>F**
Total Error	21	0.00331880		0.6103

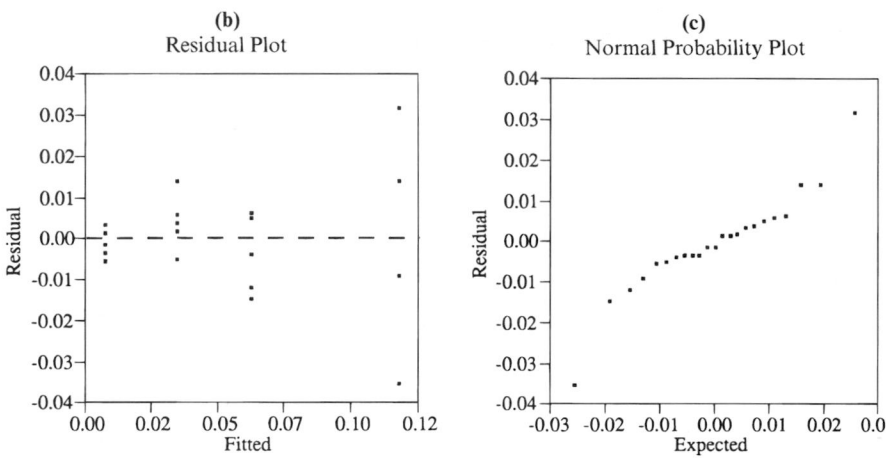

(b) Residual Plot

(c) Normal Probability Plot

As an initial step to examine the nature of the regression relationship, a loess smoothed curve was obtained; this curve is shown in Figure 3.19b. We see that the regression relationship may be linear or slightly curvilinear in the range of the plutonium activity levels included in the study. We also see that one of the readings taken at 0.0 pCi/g (case 24) does not appear to fit with the rest of the observations. An examination of laboratory records revealed that the experimental conditions were not properly maintained for the last case, and it was therefore decided that case 24 should be discarded. Note, incidentally, how robust the loess smoothing process was here by assigning very little weight to the outlying observation.

A linear regression function was fitted next, based on the remaining 23 cases. The SAS-JMP regression output is shown in Figure 3.20a, a plot of the residuals against the fitted values is shown in Figure 3.20b, and a normal probability plot is shown in Figure 3.20c. The JMP output uses the label Model to denote the regression component of the analysis of variance; the label C Total stands for corrected total. We see from the regression output that the slope of the regression line is not zero ($F^* = 228.9984$, P-value $= .0000$) so that a regression relationship exists. We also see from the flared, megaphone shape of the residual plot that the error variance appears to be increasing with the level of plutonium activity.

FIGURE 3.21   **SAS-JMP Regression Output and Diagnostic Plots for Transformed Response Variable—Plutonium Measurement Example.**

(a) Regression Output

Term	Estimate	Std Error	t Ratio	Prob>|t|
Intercept	0.0947596	0.00957	9.91	0.0000
Plutonium	0.0133648	0.00097	13.74	0.0000

Source	DF	Sum of Squares	Mean Square	F Ratio
Model	1	0.21084655	0.210847	188.7960
Error	21	0.02345271	0.001117	Prob>F
C Total	22	0.23429926		0.0000

Source	DF	Sum of Squares	Mean Square	F Ratio
Lack of Fit	2	0.01210640	0.006053	10.1364
Pure Error	19	0.01134631	0.000597	Prob>F
Total Error	21	0.02345271		0.0010

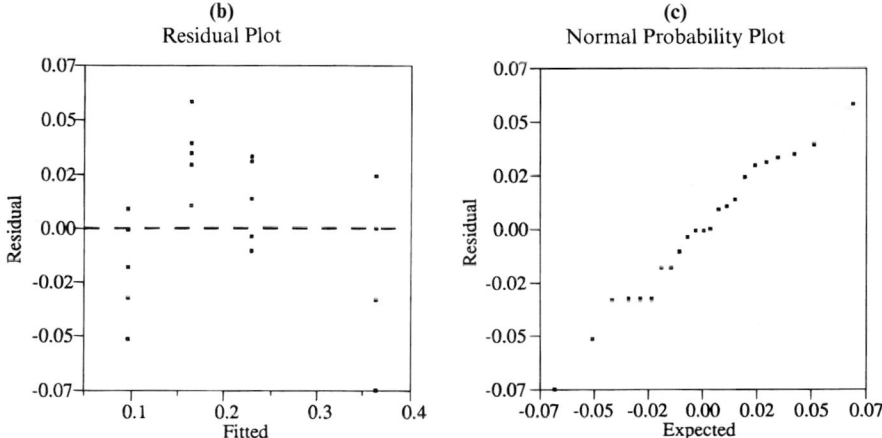

(b) Residual Plot

(c) Normal Probability Plot

The normal probability plot suggests nonnormality (heavy tails), but the nonlinearity of the plot is likely to be related (at least in part) to the unequal error variances. The existence of nonconstant variance is confirmed by the Breusch-Pagan test statistic (3.11):

$$X_{BP}^2 = 23.29 > \chi^2(.95; 1) = 3.84$$

The presence of nonconstant variance clearly requires remediation. A number of approaches could be followed, including the use of weighted least squares discussed in Chapter 10. Often with count data, as discussed in Chapter 18, the error variance can be stabilized through the use of a square root transformation of the response variable. Since this is just one in a range of power transformations that might be useful, we shall use the Box-Cox procedure to suggest an appropriate power transformation. Using the standardized variable (3.36), we find the maximum likelihood estimate of λ to be $\hat{\lambda} = .65$. Because the likelihood function is fairly flat in the neighborhood of $\hat{\lambda} = .65$, the Box-Cox procedure supports the use of the square root transformation (i.e., use of $\lambda = .5$). The results of fitting a linear regression function when the response variable is $Y' = \sqrt{Y}$ are shown in Figure 3.21a.

FIGURE 3.22   **SAS-JMP Regression Output and Diagnostic Plots for Transformed Response and Predictor Variables—Plutonium Measurement Example.**

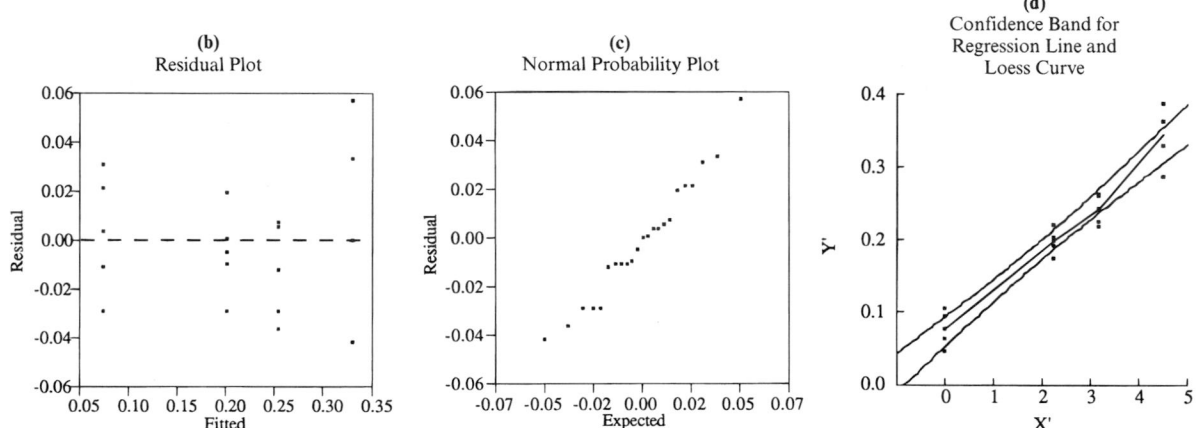

(a) Regression Output

Term		Estimate	Std Error	t Ratio	Prob>|t|
Intercept		0.0730056	0.00783	9.32	0.0000
Sqrt Plutonium		0.0573055	0.00302	19.00	0.0000

Source	DF	Sum of Squares	Mean Square	F Ratio
Model	1	0.22141612	0.221416	360.9166
Error	21	0.01288314	0.000613	**Prob>F**
C Total	22	0.23429926		0.0000

Source	DF	Sum of Squares	Mean Square	F Ratio
Lack of Fit	2	0.00153683	0.000768	1.2868
Pure Error	19	0.01134631	0.000597	**Prob>F**
Total Error	21	0.01288314		0.2992

(b) Residual Plot

(c) Normal Probability Plot

(d) Confidence Band for Regression Line and Loess Curve

At this point a new problem has arisen. Although the residual plot in Figure 3.21b shows that the error variance appears to be more stable and the points in the normal probability plot in Figure 3.21c fall roughly on a straight line, the residual plot now suggests that Y' is nonlinearly related to X. This concern is confirmed by the lack of fit test statistic (3.25) ($F^* = 10.1364$, P-value $= .0010$). Of course, this result is not completely unexpected, since Y was linearly related to X.

To restore a linear relation with the transformed Y variable, we shall see if a square root transformation of X will lead to a satisfactory linear fit. The regression results when regressing $Y' = \sqrt{Y}$ on $X' = \sqrt{X}$ are presented in Figure 3.22. Notice from the residual plot in Figure 3.22b that the square root transformation of the predictor variable has eliminated the lack of fit. Also, the normal probability plot of the residuals in Figure 3.22c appears to be satisfactory, and the correlation test ($r = .986$) supports the assumption of normally distributed error terms (the interpolated critical value in Table B.6 for $\alpha = .05$ and $n = 23$ is .9555). However, the residual plot suggests that some nonconstancy of the error variance may still remain; but if so, it does not appear to be substantial. The Breusch-Pagan test statistic (3.11) is $X_{BP}^2 = 3.85$, which corresponds to a P-value of .05, supporting the conclusion from the residual plot that the nonconstancy of the error variance is not substantial.

Figure 3.22d contains a SYSTAT plot of the confidence band (2.40) for the fitted regression line:

$$\hat{Y}' = .0730 + .0573X'$$

We see that the regression line has been estimated fairly precisely. Also plotted in this figure is the loess smoothed curve. This smoothed curve falls entirely within the confidence band, supporting the reasonableness of a linear regression relation between Y' and X'. The lack of fit test statistic (3.25) now is $F^* = 1.2868$ (P-value $= .2992$), also supporting the linearity of the regression relating $Y' = \sqrt{Y}$ to $X' = \sqrt{X}$.

Cited References

3.1. Barnett, V., and T. Lewis. *Outliers in Statistical Data*. 3rd ed. New York: John Wiley & Sons, 1994.

3.2. Looney, S. W., and T. R. Gulledge, Jr. "Use of the Correlation Coefficient with Normal Probability Plots," *The American Statistician* 39 (1985), pp. 75–79.

3.3. Shapiro, S. S., and M. B. Wilk. "An Analysis of Variance Test for Normality (Complete Samples)," *Biometrika* 52 (1965), pp. 591–611.

3.4. Levene, H. "Robust Tests for Equality of Variances," in *Contributions to Probability and Statistics*, ed. I. Olkin. Palo Alto, Calif.: Stanford University Press, 1960, pp. 278–92.

3.5. Conover, W. J., M. E. Johnson, and M. M. Johnson. "A Comparative Study of Tests for Homogeneity of Variances, with Applications to the Outer Continental Shelf Bidding Data," *Technometrics* 23 (1981), pp. 351–61.

3.6. Breusch, T. S., and A. R. Pagan. "A Simple Test for Heteroscedasticity and Random Coefficient Variation," *Econometrica* 47 (1979), pp. 1287–94.

3.7. Cook, R. D., and S. Weisberg. "Diagnostics for Heteroscedasticity in Regression," *Biometrika* 70 (1983), pp. 1–10.

3.8. Joglekar, G., J. H. Schuenemeyer, and V. LaRiccia. "Lack-of-Fit Testing When Replicates Are Not Available," *The American Statistician* 43 (1989), pp. 135–43.

3.9. Box, G. E. P., and D. R. Cox. "An Analysis of Transformations," *Journal of the Royal Statistical Society B* 26 (1964), pp. 211–43.

3.10. Draper, N. R., and H. Smith. *Applied Regression Analysis*. 2nd ed. New York: John Wiley & Sons, 1981.

3.11. Velleman, P. F., and D. C. Hoaglin. *Applications, Basics, and Computing of Exploratory Data Analysis*. Boston: Duxbury Press, 1981.

3.12. Cleveland, W. S. "Robust Locally Weighted Regression and Smoothing Scatterplots," *Journal of the American Statistical Association* 74 (1979), pp. 829–36.

3.13. Altman, N. S. "An Introduction to Kernel and Nearest Neighbor Nonparametric Regression," *The American Statistician* 46 (1992), pp. 175–85.

3.14. Haerdle, W. *Applied Nonparametric Regression*. Cambridge: Cambridge University Press, 1990.

Problems

3.1. Distinguish between (1) residual and semistudentized residual, (2) $E\{\varepsilon_i\} = 0$ and $\bar{e} = 0$, (3) error term and residual.

3.2. Prepare a prototype residual plot for each of the following cases: (1) error variance decreases with X; (2) true regression function is $\cup$ shaped, but a linear regression function is fitted.

3.3. Refer to **Grade point average** Problem 1.19.

   a. Prepare a box plot for the entrance test scores X_i. Are there any noteworthy features in this plot?

   b. Prepare a dot plot of the residuals. What information does this plot provide?

   c. Plot the residual e_i against the fitted values $\hat{Y}_i$. What departures from regression model (2.1) can be studied from this plot? What are your findings?

   d. Prepare a normal probability plot of the residuals. Also obtain the coefficient of correlation between the ordered residuals and their expected values under normality. Test the reasonableness of the normality assumption here using Table B.6 and $\alpha = .05$. What do you conclude?

   e. Conduct the modified Levene test to determine whether or not the error variance varies with the level of X. Divide the data into the two groups, $X < 4.85$, $X \geq 4.85$, and use $\alpha = .01$. State the decision rule and conclusion. Does your conclusion support your preliminary findings in part (c)?

   f. Information is given below for each student on two variables not included in the model, namely, intelligence test score (X_2) and high school average (X_3). Plot the residuals against X_2 and X_3 on separate graphs to ascertain whether the model can be improved by including either of these variables. What do you conclude?

i:	1	2	3	. . .	18	19	20
X_2:	105	113	118	. . .	109	116	108
X_3:	2.9	2.8	3.1	. . .	3.4	2.6	2.7

√ 3.4. Refer to **Calculator maintenance** Problem 1.20.

   a. Prepare a dot plot for the number of machines serviced X_i. What information is provided by this plot? Are there any outlying cases with respect to this variable?

   b. The cases are given in time order. Prepare a time plot for the number of machines serviced. What does your plot show?

   c. Prepare a stem-and-leaf plot of the residuals. Are there any noteworthy features in this plot?

   d. Prepare residual plots of e_i versus $\hat{Y}_i$ and e_i versus X_i on separate graphs. Do these plots provide the same information? What departures from regression model (2.1) can be studied from these plots? State your findings.

   e. Prepare a normal probability plot of the residuals. Also obtain the coefficient of correlation between the ordered residuals and their expected values under normality. Does the normality assumption appear to be tenable here? Use Table B.6 and $\alpha = .10$.

f. Prepare a time plot of the residuals to ascertain whether the error terms are correlated over time. What is your conclusion?

g. Assume that (3.10) is applicable and conduct the Breusch-Pagan test to determine whether or not the error variance varies with the level of X. Use $\alpha = .05$. State the alternatives, decision rule, and conclusion.

h. Information is given below on two variables not included in the regression model, namely, mean operational age of machines serviced on the call (X_2, in months) and years of experience of the service person making the call (X_3). Plot the residuals against X_2 and X_3 on separate graphs to ascertain whether the model can be improved by including either or both of these variables. What do you conclude?

i:	1	2	3	. . .	16	17	18
X_2:	12	21	38	. . .	29	9	14
X_3:	3	6	2	. . .	5	3	6

√ 3.5. Refer to **Airfreight breakage** Problem 1.21.

a. Prepare a dot plot for the number of transfers X_i. Does the distribution of number of transfers appear to be asymmetrical?

b. The cases are given in time order. Prepare a time plot for the number of transfers. Is any systematic pattern evident in your plot? Discuss.

c. Obtain the residuals e_i and prepare a stem-and-leaf plot of the residuals. What information is provided by your plot?

d. Plot the residuals e_i against X_i to ascertain whether any departures from regression model (2.1) are evident. What is your conclusion?

e. Prepare a normal probability plot of the residuals. Also obtain the coefficient of correlation between the ordered residuals and their expected values under normality to ascertain whether the normality assumption is reasonable here. Use Table B.6 and $\alpha = .01$. What do you conclude?

f. Prepare a time plot of the residuals. What information is provided by your plot?

g. Assume that (3.10) is applicable and conduct the Breusch-Pagan test to determine whether or not the error variance varies with the level of X. Use $\alpha = .10$. State the alternatives, decision rule, and conclusion. Does your conclusion support your preliminary findings in part (d)?

3.6. Refer to **Plastic hardness** Problem 1.22.

a. Obtain the residuals e_i and prepare a box plot of the residuals. What information is provided by your plot?

b. Plot the residuals e_i against the fitted values $\hat{Y}_i$ to ascertain whether any departures from regression model (2.1) are evident. State your findings.

c. Prepare a normal probability plot of the residuals. Also obtain the coefficient of correlation between the ordered residuals and their expected values under normality. Does the normality assumption appear to be reasonable here? Use Table B.6 and $\alpha = .05$.

d. Compare the frequencies of the residuals against the expected frequencies under normality, using the 25th, 50th, and 75th percentiles of the relevant t distribution. Is the information provided by these comparisons consistent with the findings from the normal probability plot in part (c)?

e. Use the modified Levene test to determine whether or not the error variance varies with the level of X. Divide the data into the two groups, $X \leq 24$, $X > 24$, and use $\alpha = .05$. State the decision rule and conclusion. Does your conclusion support your preliminary findings in part (b)?

√ 3.7.   Refer to **Muscle mass** Problem 1.27.

a. Prepare a stem-and-leaf plot for the ages X_i. Is this plot consistent with the random selection of women from each 10-year age group? Explain.

b. Obtain the residuals e_i and prepare a dot plot of the residuals. What does your plot show?

c. Plot the residuals e_i against $\hat{Y}_i$ and also against X_i on separate graphs to ascertain whether any departures from regression model (2.1) are evident. Do the two plots provide the same information? State your conclusions.

d. Prepare a normal probability plot of the residuals. Also obtain the coefficient of correlation between the ordered residuals and their expected values under normality to ascertain whether the normality assumption is tenable here. Use Table B.6 and $\alpha = .10$. What do you conclude?

e. Assume that (3.10) is applicable and conduct the Breusch-Pagan test to determine whether or not the error variance varies with the level of X. Use $\alpha = .01$. State the alternatives, decision rule, and conclusion. Is your conclusion consistent with your preliminary findings in part (c)?

3.8.   Refer to **Robbery rate** Problem 1.28.

a. Prepare a stem-and-leaf plot for the city population densities X_i. What information does your plot provide?

b. Obtain the residuals e_i and prepare a box plot of the residuals. Does the distribution of the residuals appear to be symmetrical?

c. Make a residual plot of e_i versus $\hat{Y}_i$. What does the plot show?

d. Prepare a normal probability plot of the residuals. Also obtain the coefficient of correlation between the ordered residuals and their expected values under normality. Test the reasonableness of the normality assumption using Table B.6 and $\alpha = .05$. What do you conclude?

e. Conduct the modified Levene test to determine whether or not the error variance varies with the level of X. Divide the data into the two groups, $X \leq 69$, $X > 69$, and use $\alpha = .05$. State the decision rule and conclusion. Does your conclusion support your preliminary findings in part (c)?

3.9.   **Electricity consumption.** An economist studying the relation between household electricity consumption (Y) and number of rooms in the home (X) employed linear regression model (2.1) and obtained the following residuals:

i:	1	2	3	4	5	6	7	8	9	10
X_i:	2	3	4	5	6	7	8	9	10	11
e_i:	3.2	2.9	−1.7	−2.0	−2.3	−1.2	−.9	.8	.7	.5

Plot the residuals e_i against X_i. What problem appears to be present here? Might a transformation alleviate this problem?

3.10. **Per capita earnings**. A sociologist employed linear regression model (2.1) to relate per capita earnings (Y) to average number of years of schooling (X) for 12 cities. The fitted values $\hat{Y}_i$ and the semistudentized residuals e_i^* follow.

i:	1	2	3	. . .	10	11	12
$\hat{Y}_i$:	9.9	9.3	10.2	. . .	15.6	11.2	13.1
e_i^*:	−1.12	.81	−.76	. . .	−3.78	.74	.32

    a. Plot the semistudentized residuals against the fitted values. What does the plot suggest?

    b. How many semistudentized residuals are outside ± 1 standard deviation? Approximately how many would you expect to see if the normal error model is appropriate?

3.11. **Drug concentration**. A pharmacologist employed linear regression model (2.1) to study the relation between the concentration of a drug in plasma (Y) and the log-dose of the drug (X). The residuals and log-dose levels follow.

i:	1	2	3	4	5	6	7	8	9
X_i:	−1	0	1	−1	0	1	−1	0	1
e_i:	.5	2.1	−3.4	.3	−1.7	4.2	−.6	2.6	−4.0

    a. Plot the residuals e_i against X_i. What conclusions do you draw from the plot?

    b. Assume that (3.10) is applicable and conduct the Breusch-Pagan test to determine whether or not the error variance varies with log-dose of the drug (X). Use $\alpha = .05$. State the alternatives, decision rule, and conclusion. Does your conclusion support your preliminary findings in part (a)?

3.12. A student does not understand why the sum of squares defined in (3.16) is called a pure error sum of squares "since the formula looks like one for an ordinary sum of squares." Explain.

√ 3.13. Refer to **Calculator maintenance** Problem 1.20.

    a. What are the alternative conclusions when testing for lack of fit of a linear regression function?

    b. Perform the test indicated in part (a). Control the risk of Type I error at .05. State the decision rule and conclusion.

    c. Does your test in part (b) detect other departures from regression model (2.1), such as lack of constant variance or lack of normality in the error terms? Could the results of the test of lack of fit be affected by such departures? Discuss.

3.14. Refer to **Plastic hardness** Problem 1.22.

    a. Perform the F test to determine whether or not there is lack of fit of a linear regression function; use $\alpha = .01$. State the alternatives, decision rule, and conclusion.

    b. Is there any advantage of having an equal number of replications at each of the X levels? Is there any disadvantage?

    c. Does the test in part (a) indicate what regression function is appropriate when it leads to the conclusion that the regression function is not linear? How would you proceed?

3.15. **Solution concentration**. A chemist studied the concentration of a solution (Y) over time (X). Fifteen identical solutions were prepared. The 15 solutions were randomly divided into five sets of three, and the five sets were measured, respectively, after 1, 3, 5, 7, and 9 hours. The results follow.

i:	1	2	3	. . .	13	14	15
X_i:	9	9	9	. . .	1	1	1
Y_i:	.07	.09	.08	. . .	2.84	2.57	3.10

a. Fit a linear regression function.

b. Perform the F test to determine whether or not there is lack of fit of a linear regression function; use $\alpha = .025$. State the alternatives, decision rule, and conclusion.

c. Does the test in part (b) indicate what regression function is appropriate when it leads to the conclusion that lack of fit of a linear regression function exists? Explain.

3.16. Refer to **Solution concentration** Problem 3.15.

a. Prepare a scatter plot of the data. What transformation of Y might you try based on the prototype patterns in Figure 3.15 to achieve constant variance and linearity?

b. Use the Box-Cox procedure and standardization (3.36) to find an appropriate power transformation. Evaluate SSE for $\lambda = -.2, -.1, 0, .1, .2$. What transformation of Y is suggested?

c. Use the transformation $Y' = \log_{10} Y$ and obtain the estimated linear regression function for the transformed data.

d. Plot the estimated regression line and the transformed data. Does the regression line appear to be a good fit to the transformed data?

e. Obtain the residuals and plot them against the fitted values. Also prepare a normal probability plot. What do your plots show?

f. Express the estimated regression function in the original units.

√ 3.17. **Sales growth**. A marketing researcher studied annual sales of a product that had been introduced 10 years ago. The data are as follows, where X is the year (coded) and Y is sales in thousands of units:

i:	1	2	3	4	5	6	7	8	9	10
X_i:	0	1	2	3	4	5	6	7	8	9
Y_i:	98	135	162	178	221	232	283	300	374	395

a. Prepare a scatter plot of the data. Does a linear relation appear adequate here?

b. Use the Box-Cox procedure and standardization (3.36) to find an appropriate power transformation of Y. Evaluate SSE for $\lambda = .3, .4, .5, .6, .7$. What transformation of Y is suggested?

c. Use the transformation $Y' = \sqrt{Y}$ and obtain the estimated linear regression function for the transformed data.

d. Plot the estimated regression line and the transformed data. Does the regression line appear to be a good fit to the transformed data?

e. Obtain the residuals and plot them against the fitted values. Also prepare a normal probability plot. What do your plots show?

f. Express the estimated regression function in the original units.

3.18. **Response errors**. In a small-scale study of response errors in which expenditures incurred during the most recent hunting trip were recalled, the following data on response errors (Y) and number of months since last hunting trip (X) were obtained:

i:	1	2	3	. . .	10	11	12
X_i:	12	5	1	. . .	2	10	4
Y_i:	−94	−68	−41	. . .	−49	−85	−70

a. Prepare a scatter plot of the data. Does a linear relation appear adequate here? Would a transformation on X or Y be more appropriate here? Why?

b. Use the transformation $X' = \sqrt{X}$ and obtain the estimated linear regression function for the transformed data.

c. Plot the estimated regression line and the transformed data. Does the regression line appear to be a good fit to the transformed data?

d. Obtain the residuals and plot them against the fitted values. Also prepare a normal probability plot. What do your plots show?

e. Express the estimated regression function in the original units.

Exercises

3.19. A student fitted a linear regression function for a class assignment. The student plotted the residuals e_i against Y_i and found a positive relation. When the residuals were plotted against the fitted values $\hat{Y}_i$, the student found no relation. How could this difference arise? Which is the more meaningful plot?

3.20. If the error terms in a regression model are independent $N(0, \sigma^2)$, what can be said about the error terms after transformation $X' = 1/X$ is used? Is the situation the same after transformation $Y' = 1/Y$ is used?

3.21. Derive the result in (3.29).

3.22. Using theorems (A.70), (A.41), and (A.42), show that $E\{MSPE\} = \sigma^2$ for normal error regression model (2.1).

3.23. A linear regression model with intercept $\beta_0 = 0$ is under consideration. Data have been obtained which contain replications. State the full and reduced models for testing the appropriateness of the regression function under consideration. What are the degrees of freedom associated with the full and reduced models if $n = 20$ and $c = 10$?

Projects

3.24. **Blood pressure**. The following data were obtained in a study of the relation between diastolic blood pressure (Y) and age (X) for boys 5 to 13 years old.

i:	1	2	3	4	5	6	7	8
X_i:	5	8	11	7	13	12	12	6
Y_i:	63	67	74	64	75	69	90	60

a. Assuming normal error regression model (2.1) is appropriate, obtain the estimated regression function and plot the residuals e_i against X_i. What does your residual plot show?

b. Omit case 7 from the data and obtain the estimated regression function based on the remaining seven cases. Compare this estimated regression function to that obtained in part (a). What can you conclude about the effect of case 7?

c. Using your fitted regression function in part (b), obtain a 99 percent prediction interval for a new Y observation at $X = 12$. Does observation Y_7 fall outside this prediction interval? What is the significance of this?

3.25. Refer to the **SMSA** data set and Project 1.43. For each of the three fitted regression models, obtain the residuals and prepare a residual plot against X and a normal probability plot. Summarize your conclusions. Is linear regression model (2.1) more appropriate in one case than in the others?

3.26. Refer to the **SMSA** data set and Project 1.44. For each geographic region, obtain the residuals and prepare a residual plot against X and a normal probability plot. Do the four regions appear to have similar error variances? What other conclusions do you draw from your plots?

3.27. Refer to the **SENIC** data set and Project 1.45.

a. For each of the three fitted regression models, obtain the residuals and prepare a residual plot against X and a normal probability plot. Summarize your conclusions. Is linear regression model (2.1) more apt in one case than in the others?

b. Obtain the fitted regression function for the relation between length of stay and infection risk after deleting cases 47 ($X_{47} = 6.5$, $Y_{47} = 19.56$) and 112 ($X_{112} = 5.9$, $Y_{112} = 17.94$). From this fitted regression function obtain separate 95 percent prediction intervals for new Y observations at $X = 6.5$ and $X = 5.9$, respectively. Do observations Y_{47} and Y_{112} fall outside these prediction intervals? Discuss the significance of this.

3.28. Refer to the **SENIC** data set and Project 1.46. For each geographic region, obtain the residuals and prepare a residual plot against X and a normal probability plot. Do the four regions appear to have similar error variances? What other conclusions do you draw from your plots?

3.29. Refer to **Calculator maintenance** Problem 1.20.

a. Divide the data into four bands according to the number of machines serviced (X). Band 1 ranges from $X = .5$ to $X = 2.5$; band 2 ranges from $X = 2.5$ to $X = 4.5$; and so forth. Determine the median value of X and the median value of Y in each of the bands and develop the band smooth by connecting the four pairs of medians by straight lines on a scatter plot of the data. Does the band smooth suggest that the regression relation is linear? Discuss.

b. Obtain the 90 percent confidence band for the true regression line and plot it on the scatter plot prepared in part (a). Does the band smooth fall entirely inside the confidence band? What does this tell you about the appropriateness of the linear regression function?

c. Create a series of six overlapping neighborhoods of width 3.0 beginning at $X = .5$. The first neighborhood will range from $X = .5$ to $X = 3.5$; the second neighborhood will range from $X = 1.5$ to $X = 4.5$; and so on. For each of the six overlapping neighborhoods, fit a linear regression function and obtain the fitted value $\hat{Y}_c$ at the center X_c of the neighborhood. Develop a simplified version of the loess smooth by connecting the six $(X_c, \hat{Y}_c)$ pairs by straight lines on a scatter plot of the data. In what ways does your simplified loess smooth differ from the band smooth obtained in part (a)?

3.30. Refer to **Sales growth** Problem 3.17.

a. Divide the range of the predictor variable (coded years) into five bands of width 2.0, as follows: Band 1 ranges from $X = -.5$ to $X = 1.5$; band 2 ranges from $X = 1.5$ to $X = 3.5$; and so on. Determine the median value of X and the median value of Y in each band and develop the band smooth by connecting the five pairs of medians by straight lines on a scatter plot of the data. Does the band smooth suggest that the regression relation is linear? Discuss.

b. Create a series of seven overlapping neighborhoods of width 3.0 beginning at $X = -.5$. The first neighborhood will range from $X = -.5$ to $X = 2.5$; the second neighborhood will range from $X = .5$ to $X = 3.5$; and so on. For each of the seven overlapping neighborhoods, fit a linear regression function and obtain the fitted value $\hat{Y}_c$ at the center X_c of the neighborhood. Develop a simplified version of the loess smooth by connecting the seven $(X_c, \hat{Y}_c)$ pairs by straight lines on a scatter plot of the data.

c. Obtain the 95 percent confidence band for the true regression line and plot it on the plot prepared in part (b). Does the simplified loess smooth fall entirely within the confidence band for the regression line? What does this tell you about the appropriateness of the linear regression function?

Simultaneous Inferences and Other Topics in Regression Analysis

In this chapter, we take up a variety of topics in simple linear regression analysis. Several of the topics pertain to how to make simultaneous inferences from the same set of sample observations.

4.1 Joint Estimation of β_0 and β_1

Need for Joint Estimation

A market research analyst conducted a study of the relation between level of advertising expenditures (X) and sales (Y). The study included six different levels of advertising expenditures, one of which was no advertising $(X = 0)$. The scatter plot suggested a linear relationship in the range of the advertising expenditures levels studied. The analyst now wishes to draw inferences with confidence coefficient .95 about both the intercept β_0 and the slope β_1. The analyst could use the methods of Chapter 2 to construct separate 95 percent confidence intervals for β_0 and β_1. The difficulty is that these would not provide 95 percent confidence that the conclusions for *both* β_0 and β_1 are correct. If the inferences were independent, the probability of both being correct would be $(.95)^2$, or only .9025. The inferences are not, however, independent, coming as they do from the same set of sample data, which makes the determination of the probability of both inferences being correct much more difficult.

Analysis of data frequently requires a series of estimates (or tests) where the analyst would like to have an assurance about the correctness of the entire set of estimates (or tests). We shall call the set of estimates (or tests) of interest the *family* of estimates (or tests). In our illustration, the family consists of two estimates, for β_0 and β_1. We then distinguish between a statement confidence coefficient and a family confidence coefficient. A *statement confidence coefficient* is the familiar type of confidence coefficient discussed earlier, which indicates the proportion of correct estimates that are obtained when repeated samples are selected and the specified confidence interval is calculated for each sample. A *family confidence coefficient*, on the other hand, indicates the proportion of families of estimates that are entirely correct when repeated samples are selected and the specified confidence intervals for the entire family are calculated for each sample. Thus, a family confidence coefficient corresponds to the probability, in advance of sampling, that the entire family of statements will be correct.

To illustrate the meaning of a family confidence coefficient further, consider again the joint estimation of β_0 and β_1. A family confidence coefficient of, say, .95 would indicate here that if repeated samples are selected and interval estimates for both β_0 and β_1 are calculated for each sample by specified procedures, 95 percent of the samples would lead to a family of estimates where *both* confidence intervals are correct. For 5 percent of the samples, either one or both of the interval estimates would be incorrect.

A procedure that provides a family confidence coefficient when estimating both β_0 and β_1 is often highly desirable since it permits the analyst to weave the two separate results together into an integrated set of conclusions, with an assurance that the entire set of estimates is correct. We now discuss one procedure for constructing simultaneous confidence intervals for β_0 and β_1 with a specified family confidence coefficient—the Bonferroni procedure.

Bonferroni Joint Confidence Intervals

The Bonferroni procedure for developing joint confidence intervals for β_0 and β_1 with a specified family confidence coefficient is very simple: each statement confidence coefficient is adjusted to be higher than $1 - \alpha$ so that the family confidence coefficient is at least $1 - \alpha$. The procedure is a general one that can be applied in many cases, as we shall see, not just for the joint estimation of β_0 and β_1.

We start with ordinary confidence limits for β_0 and β_1 with statement confidence coefficients $1 - \alpha$ each. These limits are:

$$b_0 \pm t(1 - \alpha/2; n - 2)s\{b_0\}$$

$$b_1 \pm t(1 - \alpha/2; n - 2)s\{b_1\}$$

We first ask what is the probability that one or both of these intervals are incorrect. Let A_1 denote the event that the first confidence interval does not cover β_0, and let A_2 denote the event that the second confidence interval does not cover β_1. We know:

$$P(A_1) = \alpha \qquad P(A_2) = \alpha$$

Probability theorem (A.6) gives the desired probability:

$$P(A_1 \cup A_2) = P(A_1) + P(A_2) - P(A_1 \cap A_2)$$

Next, we use complementation theorem (A.9) to obtain the probability that both intervals are correct, denoted by $P(\bar{A}_1 \cap \bar{A}_2)$:

(4.1) $$P(\bar{A}_1 \cap \bar{A}_2) = 1 - P(A_1 \cup A_2) = 1 - P(A_1) - P(A_2) + P(A_1 \cap A_2)$$

Note from probability theorems (A.9) and (A.10) that $\bar{A}_1 \cap \bar{A}_2$ and $A_1 \cup A_2$ are complementary events:

$$1 - P(A_1 \cup A_2) = P(\overline{A_1 \cup A_2}) = P(\bar{A}_1 \cap \bar{A}_2)$$

Finally, we use the fact that $P(A_1 \cap A_2) \geq 0$ to obtain from (4.1) the *Bonferroni inequality*:

(4.2) $$P(\bar{A}_1 \cap \bar{A}_2) \geq 1 - P(A_1) - P(A_2)$$

which for our situation is:

$$(4.2a) \qquad P(\bar{A}_1 \cap \bar{A}_2) \geq 1 - \alpha - \alpha = 1 - 2\alpha$$

Thus, if β_0 and β_1 are separately estimated with, say, 95 percent confidence intervals, the Bonferroni inequality guarantees us a family confidence coefficient of at least 90 percent that both intervals based on the same sample are correct.

We can easily use the Bonferroni inequality (4.2a) to obtain a family confidence coefficient of at least $1 - \alpha$ for estimating β_0 and β_1. We do this by estimating β_0 and β_1 separately with statement confidence coefficients of $1 - \alpha/2$ each. This yields the Bonferroni bound $1 - \alpha/2 - \alpha/2 = 1 - \alpha$. Thus, the $1 - \alpha$ family confidence limits for β_0 and β_1 for regression model (2.1) by the Bonferroni procedure are:

$$(4.3) \qquad b_0 \pm Bs\{b_0\} \qquad b_1 \pm Bs\{b_1\}$$

where:

$$(4.3a) \qquad B = t(1 - \alpha/4; n - 2)$$

and b_0, b_1, $s\{b_0\}$, and $s\{b_1\}$ are defined in (1.10), (2.9), and (2.23). Note that a statement confidence coefficient of $1 - \alpha/2$ requires the $(1 - \alpha/4)100$ percentile of the t distribution for a two-sided confidence interval.

Example

For the Toluca Company example, 90 percent family confidence intervals for β_0 and β_1 require $B = t(1 - .10/4; 23) = t(.975; 23) = 2.069$. We have from Chapter 2:

$$b_0 = 62.37 \qquad s\{b_0\} = 26.18$$
$$b_1 = 3.5702 \qquad s\{b_1\} = .3470$$

Hence, the respective confidence limits for β_0 and β_1 are $62.37 \pm 2.069(26.18)$ and $3.5702 \pm 2.069(.3470)$, and the joint confidence intervals are:

$$8.20 \leq \beta_0 \leq 116.5$$
$$2.85 \leq \beta_1 \leq 4.29$$

Thus, we conclude that β_0 is between 8.20 and 116.5 *and* β_1 is between 2.85 and 4.29. The family confidence coefficient is at least .90 that the procedure leads to correct pairs of interval estimates.

Comments

1. We reiterate that the Bonferroni $1 - \alpha$ family confidence coefficient is actually a lower bound on the true (but often unknown) family confidence coefficient. To the extent that incorrect interval estimates of β_0 and β_1 tend to pair up in the family, the families of statements will tend to be correct more than $(1 - \alpha)100$ percent of the time. Because of this conservative nature of the Bonferroni procedure, family confidence coefficients are frequently specified at lower levels (e.g., 90 percent) than when a single estimate is made.

2. The Bonferroni inequality (4.2a) can easily be extended to g simultaneous confidence intervals with family confidence coefficient $1 - \alpha$:

(4.4)
$$P\left(\bigcap_{i=1}^{g} \bar{A}_i\right) \geq 1 - g\alpha$$

Thus, if g interval estimates are desired with family confidence coefficient $1 - \alpha$, constructing each interval estimate with statement confidence coefficient $1 - \alpha/g$ will suffice.

3. For a given family confidence coefficient, the larger the number of confidence intervals in the family, the greater becomes the multiple B, which may make some or all of the confidence intervals too wide to be helpful. The Bonferroni technique is ordinarily most useful when the number of simultaneous estimates is not too large.

4. It is not necessary with the Bonferroni procedure that the confidence intervals have the same statement confidence coefficient. Different statement confidence coefficients, depending on the importance of each estimate, can be used. For instance, in our earlier illustration β_0 might be estimated with a 92 percent confidence interval and β_1 with a 98 percent confidence interval. The family confidence coefficient by (4.2) will still be at least 90 percent.

5. Joint confidence intervals can be used directly for testing. To illustrate this use, an industrial engineer working for the Toluca Company theorized that the regression function should have an intercept of 30.0 and a slope of 2.50. Although 30.0 falls in the confidence interval for β_0, 2.50 does not fall in the confidence interval for β_1. Thus, the engineer's theoretical expectations are not correct at the $\alpha = .10$ family level of significance.

6. The estimators b_0 and b_1 are usually correlated, but the Bonferroni simultaneous confidence limits in (4.3) only recognize this correlation by means of the bound on the family confidence coefficient. It can be shown that the covariance between b_0 and b_1 is:

(4.5)
$$\sigma\{b_0, b_1\} = -\bar{X}\sigma^2\{b_1\}$$

Note that if $\bar{X}$ is positive, b_0 and b_1 are negatively correlated, implying that if the estimate b_1 is too high, the estimate b_0 is likely to be too low, and vice versa.

In the Toluca Company example, $\bar{X} = 70.00$; hence the covariance between b_0 and b_1 is negative. This implies that the estimators b_0 and b_1 here tend to err in opposite directions. We expect this intuitively. Since the observed points (X_i, Y_i) fall in the first quadrant (see Figure 1.10a), we anticipate that if the slope of the fitted regression line is too steep (b_1 overestimates β_1), the intercept is most likely to be too low (b_0 underestimates β_0), and vice versa.

When the independent variable is $X_i - \bar{X}$, as in the alternative model (1.6), b_0^* and b_1 are uncorrelated according to (4.5) because the mean of the $X_i - \bar{X}$ observations is zero. ∎

4.2   Simultaneous Estimation of Mean Responses

Often the mean responses at a number of X levels need to be estimated from the same sample data. The Toluca Company, for instance, needed to estimate the mean number of work hours for lots of 30, 65, and 100 units in its search for the optimum lot size. We already know how to estimate the mean response for any one level of X with given statement confidence coefficient. Now we shall discuss two procedures for simultaneous estimation of a number of different mean responses with a family confidence coefficient, so that there is a known assurance of all of the estimates of mean responses being correct. These are the Working-Hotelling and the Bonferroni procedures.

The reason why a family confidence coefficient is needed when estimating several mean responses even though all estimates are based on the same fitted regression line is that the separate interval estimates of $E\{Y_h\}$ at the different X_h levels need not all be correct or all be incorrect. The combination of sampling errors in b_0 and b_1 may be such that the interval estimates of $E\{Y_h\}$ will be correct over some range of X levels and incorrect elsewhere.

Working-Hotelling Procedure

The Working-Hotelling procedure is based on the confidence band for the regression line discussed in Section 2.6. The confidence band in (2.40) contains the entire regression line and therefore contains the mean responses at all X levels. Hence, we can use the boundary values of the confidence band at selected X levels as simultaneous estimates of the mean responses at these X levels. The family confidence coefficient for these simultaneous estimates will be at least $1 - \alpha$ because the confidence coefficient that the entire confidence band for the regression line is correct is $1 - \alpha$.

The Working-Hotelling procedure for obtaining simultaneous confidence intervals for the mean responses at selected X levels is therefore simply to use the boundary values in (2.40) for the X levels of interest. The simultaneous confidence limits for g mean responses $E\{Y_h\}$ for regression model (2.1) with the Working-Hotelling procedure therefore are:

(4.6)
$$\hat{Y}_h \pm W s\{\hat{Y}_h\}$$

where:

(4.6a)
$$W^2 = 2F(1 - \alpha; 2, n - 2)$$

and $\hat{Y}_h$ and $s\{\hat{Y}_h\}$ are defined in (2.28) and (2.30), respectively.

Example.   For the Toluca Company example, we require a family of estimates of the mean number of work hours at the following lot size levels: $X_h = 30, 65, 100$. The family confidence coefficient is to be .90. In Chapter 2 we obtained $\hat{Y}_h$ and $s\{\hat{Y}_h\}$ for $X_h = 65$ and 100. In similar fashion, we can obtain the needed results for lot size $X_h = 30$. We summarize the results here:

X_h	$\hat{Y}_h$	$s\{\hat{Y}_h\}$
30	169.5	16.97
65	294.4	9.918
100	419.4	14.27

For a family confidence coefficient of .90, we require $F(.90; 2, 23) = 2.549$. Hence:

$$W^2 = 2(2.549) = 5.098 \qquad W = 2.258$$

We can now obtain the confidence intervals for the mean number of work hours at $X_h = 30$, 65, and 100:

$$131.2 = 169.5 - 2.258(16.97) \leq E\{Y_h\} \leq 169.5 + 2.258(16.97) = 207.8$$

$$272.0 = 294.4 - 2.258(9.918) \leq E\{Y_h\} \leq 294.4 + 2.258(9.918) = 316.8$$

$$387.2 = 419.4 - 2.258(14.27) \leq E\{Y_h\} \leq 419.4 + 2.258(14.27) = 451.6$$

With family confidence coefficient .90, we conclude that the mean number of work hours required is between 131.2 and 207.8 for lots of 30 parts, between 272.0 and 316.8 for lots of 65 parts, and between 387.2 and 451.6 for lots of 100 parts. The family confidence coefficient .90 provides assurance that the procedure leads to all correct estimates in the family of estimates.

Bonferroni Procedure

The Bonferroni procedure, discussed earlier for simultaneous estimation of β_0 and β_1, is a completely general procedure. To construct a family of confidence intervals for mean responses at different X levels with this procedure, we calculate in each instance the usual confidence limits for a single mean response $E\{Y_h\}$ in (2.33), adjusting the statement confidence coefficient to yield the specified family confidence coefficient.

When $E\{Y_h\}$ is to be estimated for g levels X_h with family confidence coefficient $1 - \alpha$, the Bonferroni confidence limits for regression model (2.1) are:

(4.7)
$$\hat{Y}_h \pm Bs\{\hat{Y}_h\}$$

where:

(4.7a)
$$B = t(1 - \alpha/2g; n - 2)$$

g is the number of confidence intervals in the family

Example.   For the Toluca Company example, the Bonferroni simultaneous estimates of the mean number of work hours for lot sizes $X_h = 30, 65$, and 100 with family confidence coefficient .90 require the same data as with the Working-Hotelling procedure. In addition, we require $B = t[1 - .10/2(3); 23] = t(.9833; 23) = 2.263$.

We thus obtain the following confidence intervals, with 90 percent family confidence coefficient, for the mean number of work hours for lot sizes $X_h = 30, 65$, and 100:

$$131.1 = 169.5 - 2.263(16.97) \leq E\{Y_h\} \leq 169.5 + 2.263(16.97) = 207.9$$

$$272.0 = 294.4 - 2.263(9.918) \leq E\{Y_h\} \leq 294.4 + 2.263(9.918) = 316.8$$

$$387.1 = 419.4 - 2.263(14.27) \leq E\{Y_h\} \leq 419.4 + 2.263(14.27) = 451.7$$

Comments

1. In this instance the Working-Hotelling confidence limits are slightly tighter than, or the same as, the Bonferroni limits. In other cases where the number of statements is small, the Bonferroni limits may be tighter. For larger families, the Working-Hotelling confidence limits will always be the tighter, since W in (4.6a) stays the same for any number of statements in the family whereas B in (4.7a) becomes larger as the number of statements increases. In practice,

once the family confidence coefficient has been decided upon, one can calculate the W and B multiples to determine which procedure leads to tighter confidence limits.

2. Both the Working-Hotelling and Bonferroni procedures provide lower bounds to the actual family confidence coefficient.

3. The levels of the predictor variable for which the mean response is to be estimated are sometimes not known in advance. Instead, the levels of interest are determined as the analysis proceeds. This was the case in the Toluca Company example, where the lot size levels of interest were determined after analyses relating to other factors affecting the optimum lot size were completed. In such cases, it is better to use the Working-Hotelling procedure because the family for this procedure encompasses all possible levels of X.   ∎

4.3   Simultaneous Prediction Intervals for New Observations

Now we consider the simultaneous predictions of g new observations on Y in g independent trials at g different levels of X. Simultaneous prediction intervals are frequently of interest. For instance, a company may wish to predict sales in each of its sales regions from a regression relation between region sales and population size in the region.

Two procedures for making simultaneous predictions will be considered here: the Scheffé and Bonferroni procedures. Both utilize the same type of limits as those for predicting a single observation in (2.36), and only the multiple of the estimated standard deviation is changed. The Scheffé procedure uses the F distribution, whereas the Bonferroni procedure uses the t distribution. The simultaneous prediction limits for g predictions with the Scheffé procedure with family confidence coefficient $1 - \alpha$ are:

$$(4.8) \qquad \hat{Y}_h \pm Ss\{\text{pred}\}$$

where:

$$(4.8a) \qquad S^2 = gF(1 - \alpha; g, n - 2)$$

and $s\{\text{pred}\}$ is defined in (2.38). With the Bonferroni procedure, the $1 - \alpha$ simultaneous prediction limits are:

$$(4.9) \qquad \hat{Y}_h \pm Bs\{\text{pred}\}$$

where:

$$(4.9a) \qquad B = t(1 - \alpha/2g; n - 2)$$

The S and B multiples can be evaluated in advance to see which procedure provides tighter prediction limits.

Example

The Toluca Company wishes to predict the work hours required for each of the next two lots, which will consist of 80 and 100 units. The family confidence coefficient is to be 95 percent. To determine which procedure will give tighter prediction limits, we obtain the S and B multiples:

$$S^2 = 2F(.95; 2, 23) = 2(3.422) = 6.844 \qquad S = 2.616$$

$$B = t[1 - .05/2(2); 23] = t(.9875; 23) = 2.398$$

We see that the Bonferroni procedure will yield somewhat tighter prediction limits. The needed estimates, based on earlier results, are (calculations not shown):

X_h	$\hat{Y}_h$	$s\{\text{pred}\}$	$Bs\{\text{pred}\}$
80	348.0	49.91	119.7
100	419.4	50.87	122.0

The simultaneous prediction limits for the next two lots, with family confidence coefficient .95, when $X_h = 80$ and 100 then are:

$$228.3 = 348.0 - 119.7 \leq Y_{h(\text{new})} \leq 348.0 + 119.7 = 467.7$$

$$297.4 = 419.4 - 122.0 \leq Y_{h(\text{new})} \leq 419.4 + 122.0 = 541.4$$

With family confidence coefficient at least .95, we can predict that the work hours for the next two production runs will be within the above pair of limits. As we noted in Chapter 2, the prediction limits are very wide and may not be too useful for planning worker requirements.

Comments

1. Simultaneous prediction intervals for g new observations on Y at g different levels of X with a $1 - \alpha$ family confidence coefficient are wider than the corresponding single prediction intervals of (2.36). When the number of simultaneous predictions is not large, however, the difference in the width is only moderate. For instance, a single 95 percent prediction interval for the Toluca Company example would utilize a t multiple of $t(.975; 23) = 2.069$, which is only moderately smaller than the multiple $B = 2.398$ for two simultaneous predictions.

2. Note that both the B and S multiples for simultaneous predictions become larger as g increases. This contrasts with simultaneous estimation of mean responses where the B multiple becomes larger but not the W multiple. When g is large, both the B and S multiples for simultaneous predictions may become so large that the prediction intervals will be too wide to be useful. Other simultaneous estimation techniques might then be considered, as discussed in Reference 4.1. ∎

4.4 Regression through Origin

Sometimes the regression function is known to be linear and to go through the origin at $(0, 0)$. This may occur, for instance, when X is units of output and Y is variable cost, so Y is zero by definition when X is zero. Another example is where X is the number of brands of beer stocked in a supermarket in an experiment (including some supermarkets with no brands stocked) and Y is the volume of beer sales in the supermarket.

Model

The normal error model for these cases is the same as regression model (2.1) except that $\beta_0 = 0$:

$$(4.10) \qquad\qquad Y_i = \beta_1 X_i + \varepsilon_i$$

where:

β_1 is a parameter

X_i are known constants

ε_i are independent $N(0, \sigma^2)$

The regression function for model (4.10) is:

$$(4.11) \qquad\qquad E\{Y\} = \beta_1 X$$

which is a straight line through the origin, with slope β_1.

Inferences

The least squares estimator of β_1 in regression model (4.10) is obtained by minimizing:

$$(4.12) \qquad\qquad Q = \sum (Y_i - \beta_1 X_i)^2$$

with respect to β_1. The resulting normal equation is:

$$(4.13) \qquad\qquad \sum X_i (Y_i - b_1 X_i) = 0$$

leading to the point estimator:

$$(4.14) \qquad\qquad b_1 = \frac{\sum X_i Y_i}{\sum X_i^2}$$

The estimator b_1 in (4.14) is also the maximum likelihood estimator for the normal error regression model (4.10).

The fitted value $\hat{Y}_i$ for the ith case is:

$$(4.15) \qquad\qquad \hat{Y}_i = b_1 X_i$$

and the ith residual is defined, as usual, as the difference between the observed and fitted values:

$$(4.16) \qquad\qquad e_i = Y_i - \hat{Y}_i = Y_i - b_1 X_i$$

An unbiased estimator of the error variance σ^2 for regression model (4.10) is:

$$(4.17) \qquad\qquad MSE = \frac{\sum (Y_i - \hat{Y}_i)^2}{n - 1} = \frac{\sum e_i^2}{n - 1}$$

The reason for the denominator $n - 1$ is that only one degree of freedom is lost in estimating the single parameter in the regression function (4.11).

TABLE 4.1   **Confidence Limits for Regression through Origin.**

Estimate of	Estimated Variance		Confidence Limits
β_1	$s^2\{b_1\} = \dfrac{MSE}{\sum X_i^2}$	(4.18)	$b_1 \pm t s\{b_1\}$
$E\{Y_h\}$	$s^2\{\hat{Y}_h\} = \dfrac{X_h^2 MSE}{\sum X_i^2}$	(4.19)	$\hat{Y}_h \pm t s\{\hat{Y}_h\}$
$Y_{h(\text{new})}$	$s^2\{\text{pred}\} = MSE\left(1 + \dfrac{X_h^2}{\sum X_i^2}\right)$	(4.20)	$\hat{Y}_h \pm t s\{\text{pred}\}$

where: $t = t(1 - \alpha/2; n - 1)$

TABLE 4.2   **Regression through Origin—Warehouse Example.**

	(1) Work Units Performed	(2) Variable Labor Cost (dollars)	(3)	(4)	(5)	(6)
Ware-house i	X_i	Y_i	$X_i Y_i$	X_i^2	$\hat{Y}_i$	e_i
1	20	114	2,280	400	93.71	20.29
2	196	921	180,516	38,416	918.31	2.69
3	115	560	64,400	13,225	538.81	21.19
...	...	...	...	...	...	...
10	147	670	98,490	21,609	688.74	−18.74
11	182	828	150,696	33,124	852.72	−24.72
12	160	762	121,920	25,600	749.64	12.36
Total	1,359	6,390	894,714	190,963	6,367.28	22.72

Confidence limits for β_1, $E\{Y_h\}$, and a new observation $Y_{h(\text{new})}$ for regression model (4.10) are shown in Table 4.1. Note that the t multiple has $n - 1$ degrees of freedom here, the degrees of freedom associated with MSE. The results in Table 4.1 are derived in analogous fashion to the earlier results for regression model (2.1). Whereas for model (2.1) with an intercept we encounter terms $(X_i - \bar{X})^2$ or $(X_h - \bar{X})^2$, here we find X_i^2 and X_h^2 because of the regression through the origin.

Example

The Charles Plumbing Supplies Company operates 12 warehouses. In an attempt to tighten procedures for planning and control, a consultant studied the relation between number of work units performed (X) and total variable labor cost (Y) in the warehouses during a test period. A portion of the data is given in Table 4.2, columns 1 and 2, and the observations are shown as a scatter plot in Figure 4.1.

FIGURE 4.1   **Scatter Plot and Fitted Regression through Origin—Warehouse Example.**

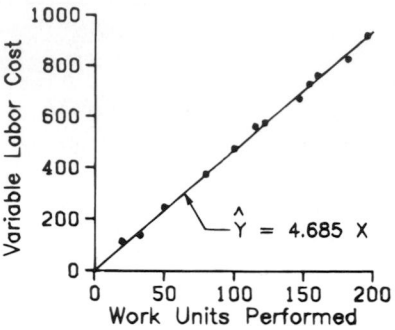

Model (4.10) for regression through the origin was employed since Y involves variable costs only and the other conditions of the model appeared to be satisfied as well. From Table 4.2, columns 3 and 4, we have $\Sigma X_i Y_i = 894{,}714$ and $\Sigma X_i^2 = 190{,}963$. Hence:

$$b_1 = \frac{\Sigma X_i Y_i}{\Sigma X_i^2} = \frac{894{,}714}{190{,}963} = 4.68527$$

and the estimated regression function is:

$$\hat{Y} = 4.68527X$$

In Table 4.2, the fitted values are shown in column 5, the residuals in column 6. The fitted regression line is plotted in Figure 4.1 and it appears to be a good fit.

An interval estimate of β_1 is desired with a 95 percent confidence coefficient. By squaring the residuals in Table 4.2, column 6, and then summing them, we obtain (calculations not shown):

$$MSE = \frac{\Sigma e_i^2}{n-1} = \frac{2{,}457.6}{11} = 223.42$$

From Table 4.2, column 4, we have $\Sigma X_i^2 = 190{,}963$. Hence:

$$s^2\{b_1\} = \frac{MSE}{\Sigma X_i^2} = \frac{223.42}{190{,}963} = .0011700 \qquad s\{b_1\} = .034205$$

For a 95 percent confidence coefficient, we require $t(.975; 11) = 2.201$. The confidence limits, by (4.18) in Table 4.1, are $4.68527 \pm 2.201(.034205)$. The 95 percent confidence interval for β_1 therefore is:

$$4.61 \leq \beta_1 \leq 4.76$$

Thus, with 95 percent confidence, it is estimated that the mean variable labor cost increases by somewhere between \$4.61 and \$4.76 for each additional work unit performed.

Important Cautions when Using Regression through Origin

When using regression-through-the-origin model (4.10), the residuals must be interpreted with care because they do not sum to zero usually, as may be seen in Table 4.2, column 6, for the warehouse example. Note from the normal equation (4.13) that the only constraint on the residuals is of the form $\Sigma X_i e_i = 0$. Thus, in a residual plot the residuals will usually not be balanced around the zero line.

Another important caution for regression through the origin is that the sum of the squared residuals $SSE = \Sigma e_i^2$ for this type of regression may exceed the total sum of squares $SSTO = \Sigma(Y_i - \bar{Y})^2$. This can occur when the data form a curvilinear pattern or a linear pattern with an intercept away from the origin. Hence, the coefficient of determination in (2.72), $r^2 = 1 - SSE/SSTO$, may turn out to be negative. Consequently, the coefficient of determination r^2 has no clear meaning for regression through the origin.

Like any other statistical model, regression-through-the-origin model (4.10) needs to be evaluated for aptness. Even when it is known that the regression function must go through the origin, the function may not be linear or the variance of the error terms may not be constant. In many other cases, one cannot be sure in advance that the regression line goes through the origin. Hence, it is generally a safe practice not to use regression-through-the-origin model (4.10) and instead use the intercept regression model (2.1). If the regression line does go through the origin, b_0 with the intercept model will differ from 0 only by a small sampling error, and unless the sample size is very small use of the intercept regression model (2.1) has no disadvantages of any consequence. If the regression line does not go through the origin, use of the intercept regression model (2.1) will avoid potentially serious difficulties resulting from forcing the regression line through the origin when this is not appropriate.

Comments

1. In interval estimation of $E\{Y_h\}$ or prediction of $Y_{h(new)}$ with regression through the origin, note that the intervals (4.19) and (4.20) in Table 4.1 widen the further X_h is from the origin. The reason is that the value of the true regression function is known precisely at the origin, so the effect of the sampling error in the slope b_1 becomes increasingly important the farther X_h is from the origin.

2. Since with regression through the origin only one parameter, β_1, must be estimated for regression function (4.11), simultaneous estimation methods are not required to make a family of statements about several mean responses. For a given confidence coefficient $1 - \alpha$, formula (4.19) in Table 4.1 can be used repeatedly with the given sample results for different levels of X to generate a family of statements for which the family confidence coefficient is still $1 - \alpha$.

3. Some statistical packages calculate r^2 for regression through the origin according to (2.72) and hence will sometimes show a negative value for r^2. Other statistical packages calculate r^2 using the total uncorrected sum of squares $SSTOU$ in (2.54). This procedure avoids obtaining a negative coefficient but lacks any meaningful interpretation.

4. The ANOVA tables for regression through the origin shown in the output for many statistical packages are based on $SSTOU = \Sigma Y_i^2$, $SSRU = \Sigma \hat{Y}_i^2 = b_1^2 \Sigma X_i^2$, and $SSE = \Sigma(Y_i - b_1 X_i)^2$, where $SSRU$ stands for the uncorrected regression sum of squares. It can be shown that these sums of squares are additive: $SSTOU = SSRU + SSE$.   ■

4.5 Effects of Measurement Errors

In our discussion of regression models up to this point, we have not explicitly considered the presence of measurement errors in the observations on either the response variable Y or the predictor variable X. We now examine briefly the effects of measurement errors in the observations on the response and predictor variables.

Measurement Errors in Y

When random measurement errors are present in the observations on the response variable Y, no new problems are created when these errors are uncorrelated and not biased (positive and negative measurement errors tend to cancel out). Consider, for example, a study of the relation between the time required to complete a task (Y) and the complexity of the task (X). The time to complete the task may not be measured accurately because the person operating the stopwatch may not do so at the precise instants called for. As long as such measurement errors are of a random nature, uncorrelated, and not biased, these measurement errors are simply absorbed in the model error term ε. The model error term always reflects the composite effects of a large number of factors not considered in the model, one of which now would be the random variation due to inaccuracy in the process of measuring Y.

Measurement Errors in X

Unfortunately, a different situation holds when the observations on the predictor variable X are subject to measurement errors. Frequently, to be sure, the observations on X are accurate, with no measurement errors, as when the predictor variable is the price of a product in different stores, the number of variables in different optimization problems, or the wage rate for different classes of employees. At other times, however, measurement errors may enter the value observed for the predictor variable, for instance, when the predictor variable is pressure in a tank, temperature in an oven, speed of a production line, or reported age of a person.

We shall use the latter illustration in our development of the nature of the problem. Suppose we are interested in the relation between employees' piecework earnings and their ages. Let X_i denote the true age of the ith employee and X_i^* the age reported by the employee on the employment record. Needless to say, the two are not always the same. We define the measurement error δ_i as follows:

$$(4.21) \qquad \delta_i = X_i^* - X_i$$

The regression model we would like to study is:

$$(4.22) \qquad Y_i = \beta_0 + \beta_1 X_i + \varepsilon_i$$

However, we only observe X_i^*, so we must replace the true age X_i in (4.22) by the reported age X_i^*, using (4.21):

$$(4.23) \qquad Y_i = \beta_0 + \beta_1 (X_i^* - \delta_i) + \varepsilon_i$$

We can now rewrite (4.23) as follows:

$$(4.24) \qquad Y_i = \beta_0 + \beta_1 X_i^* + (\varepsilon_i - \beta_1 \delta_i)$$

Model (4.24) may appear like an ordinary regression model, with predictor variable X^* and error term $\varepsilon - \beta_1\delta$, but it is not. The predictor variable observation X_i^* is a random variable, which, as we shall see, is correlated with the error term $\varepsilon_i - \beta_1\delta_i$. Theorem (2.78) for the case of random predictor variables requires that the error terms be independent of the predictor variable. Hence, the standard regression results are not applicable for model (4.24).

Intuitively, we know that $\varepsilon_i - \beta_1\delta_i$ is not independent of X_i^* since (4.21) constrains $X_i^* - \delta_i$ to equal X_i. To determine the dependence formally, let us assume the following simple conditions:

(4.25a) $$E\{\delta_i\} = 0$$

(4.25b) $$E\{\varepsilon_i\} = 0$$

(4.25c) $$E\{\delta_i\varepsilon_i\} = 0$$

Note that condition (4.25a) implies that $E\{X_i^*\} = E\{X_i + \delta_i\} = X_i$, so that in our example the reported ages would be unbiased estimates of the true ages. Condition (4.25b) is the usual requirement that the model error terms ε_i have expectation 0, balancing around the regression line. Finally, condition (4.25c) requires that the measurement error δ_i not be correlated with the model error ε_i; this follows because, by (A.21a), $\sigma\{\delta_i, \varepsilon_i\} = E\{\delta_i\varepsilon_i\}$ since $E\{\delta_i\} = E\{\varepsilon_i\} = 0$ by (4.25a) and (4.25b).

We now wish to find the covariance between the observations X_i^* and the random terms $\varepsilon_i - \beta_1\delta_i$ in model (4.24) under the conditions in (4.25), which imply that $E\{X_i^*\} = X_i$ and $E\{\varepsilon_i - \beta_1\delta_i\} = 0$:

$$\sigma\{X_i^*, \varepsilon_i - \beta_1\delta_i\} = E\{[X_i^* - E\{X_i^*\}][(\varepsilon_i - \beta_1\delta_i) - E\{\varepsilon_i - \beta_1\delta_i\}]\}$$
$$= E\{(X_i^* - X_i)(\varepsilon_i - \beta_1\delta_i)\}$$
$$= E\{\delta_i(\varepsilon_i - \beta_1\delta_i)\}$$
$$= E\{\delta_i\varepsilon_i - \beta_1\delta_i^2\}$$

Now $E\{\delta_i\varepsilon_i\} = 0$ by (4.25c), and $E\{\delta_i^2\} = \sigma^2\{\delta_i\}$ by (A.15a) because $E\{\delta_i\} = 0$ by (4.25a). We therefore obtain:

(4.26) $$\sigma\{X_i^*, \varepsilon_i - \beta_1\delta_i\} = -\beta_1\sigma^2\{\delta_i\}$$

This covariance is not zero whenever there is a linear regression relation between X and Y.

If standard regression procedures are applied to model (4.24), the estimators b_0 and b_1 will be biased and lack the property of consistency. Great difficulties are encountered in developing unbiased estimators when there are measurement errors in X. One approach is to impose severe conditions on the problem—for example, to make fairly strong assumptions about the properties of the distribution of the δ_i, the covariance of δ_i and ε_j, and so on. Another approach is to use additional variables that are known to be related to the true value of X but not to the errors of measurement δ. Such variables are called *instrumental variables* because they are used as an instrument in studying the relation between X and Y. Instrumental variables make it possible to obtain consistent estimators of the regression parameters.

Discussion of possible approaches and further references will be found in specialized texts such as Reference 4.2.

Note

It may be asked, what is the distinction between the case when X is a random variable, considered in Chapter 2, and the case when X is subject to random measurement errors, and why are there special problems with the latter? When X is a random variable, the observations on X are not under the control of the analyst and will vary at random from trial to trial, as when X is the number of persons entering a store in a day. If this random variable X is not subject to measurement errors, however, it can be accurately ascertained for a given trial. Thus, if there are no measurement errors in counting the number of persons entering a store in a day, the analyst has accurate information to study the relation between number of persons entering the store and sales, even though the levels of number of persons entering the store that actually occur cannot be controlled. If, on the other hand, measurement errors are present in the observed number of persons entering the store, a distorted picture of the relation between number of persons and sales will occur because the sales observations will frequently be matched against an incorrect number of persons.   ∎

Berkson Model

There is one situation where measurement errors in X are no problem. This case was first noted by Berkson (Ref. 4.3). Frequently, in an experiment the predictor variable is set at a target value. For instance, in an experiment on the effect of room temperature on word processor productivity, the temperature may be set at target levels of 68° F, 70° F, and 72° F, according to the temperature control on the thermostat. The observed temperature X_i^* is fixed here, whereas the actual temperature X_i is a random variable since the thermostat may not be completely accurate. Similar situations exist when water pressure is set according to a gauge, or employees of specified ages according to their employment records are selected for a study.

In all of these cases, the observation X_i^* is a fixed quantity, whereas the unobserved true value X_i is a random variable. The measurement error is, as before:

$$(4.27) \qquad \delta_i = X_i^* - X_i$$

Here, however, there is no constraint on the relation between X_i^* and δ_i, since X_i^* is a fixed quantity. Again, we assume that $E\{\delta_i\} = 0$.

Model (4.24), which we obtained when replacing X_i by $X_i^* - \delta_i$, is still applicable for the Berkson case:

$$(4.28) \qquad Y_i = \beta_0 + \beta_1 X_i^* + (\varepsilon_i - \beta_1 \delta_i)$$

The expected value of the error term, $E\{\varepsilon_i - \beta_1\delta_i\}$, is zero as before under conditions (4.25a) and (4.25b), since $E\{\varepsilon_i\} = 0$ and $E\{\delta_i\} = 0$. However, $\varepsilon_i - \beta_1\delta_i$ is now uncorrelated with X_i^*, since X_i^* is a constant for the Berkson case. Hence, the following conditions of an ordinary regression model are met:

1. The error terms have expectation zero.

2. The predictor variable is a constant, and hence the error terms are not correlated with it.

Thus, least squares procedures can be applied for the Berkson case without modification, and the estimators b_0 and b_1 will be unbiased. If we can make the standard normality and constant variance assumptions for the errors $\varepsilon_i - \beta_1\delta_i$, the usual tests and interval estimates can be utilized.

4.6   Inverse Predictions

At times, a regression model of Y on X is used to make a prediction of the value of X which gave rise to a new observation Y. This is known as an *inverse prediction*. We illustrate inverse predictions by two examples:

1. A trade association analyst has regressed the selling price of a product (Y) on its cost (X) for the 15 member firms of the association. The selling price $Y_{h(\text{new})}$ for another firm not belonging to the trade association is known, and it is desired to estimate the cost $X_{h(\text{new})}$ for this firm.

2. A regression analysis of the amount of decrease in cholesterol level (Y) achieved with a given dosage of a new drug (X) has been conducted, based on observations for 50 patients. A physician is treating a new patient for whom the cholesterol level should decrease by the amount $Y_{h(\text{new})}$. It is desired to estimate the appropriate dosage level $X_{h(\text{new})}$ to be administered to bring about the needed cholesterol decrease $Y_{h(\text{new})}$.

In inverse predictions, regression model (2.1) is assumed as before:

$$(4.29) \qquad Y_i = \beta_0 + \beta_1 X_i + \varepsilon_i$$

The estimated regression function based on n observations is obtained as usual:

$$(4.30) \qquad \hat{Y} = b_0 + b_1 X$$

A new observation $Y_{h(\text{new})}$ becomes available, and it is desired to estimate the level $X_{h(\text{new})}$ that gave rise to this new observation. A natural point estimator is obtained by solving (4.30) for X, given $Y_{h(\text{new})}$:

$$(4.31) \qquad \hat{X}_{h(\text{new})} = \frac{Y_{h(\text{new})} - b_0}{b_1} \qquad b_1 \neq 0$$

where $\hat{X}_{h(\text{new})}$ denotes the point estimator of the new level $X_{h(\text{new})}$. Figure 4.2 contains a representation of this point estimator for an example to be discussed shortly. It can be shown that the estimator $\hat{X}_{h(\text{new})}$ is the maximum likelihood estimator of $X_{h(\text{new})}$ for normal error regression model (2.1).

Approximate $1 - \alpha$ confidence limits for $X_{h(\text{new})}$ are:

$$(4.32) \qquad \hat{X}_{h(\text{new})} \pm t(1 - \alpha/2; n - 2)s\{\text{pred}X\}$$

where:

$$(4.32a) \qquad s^2\{\text{pred}X\} = \frac{MSE}{b_1^2}\left[1 + \frac{1}{n} + \frac{(\hat{X}_{h(\text{new})} - \bar{X})^2}{\Sigma(X_i - \bar{X})^2}\right]$$

FIGURE 4.2   Scatter Plot and Fitted Regression Line—Calibration Example.

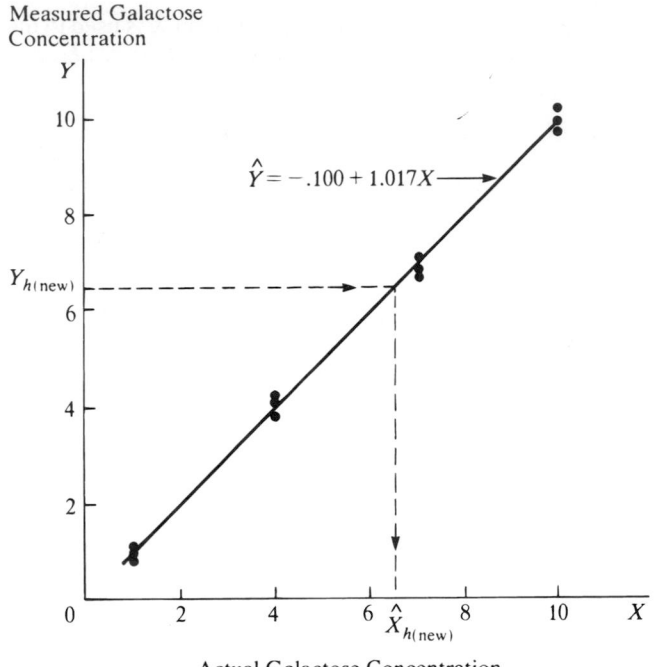

Actual Galactose Concentration

Example

A medical researcher studied a new, quick method for measuring low concentration of galactose (sugar) in the blood. Twelve samples were used in the study containing known concentrations (X), with three samples at each of four different levels. The measured concentration (Y) was then observed for each sample. Linear regression model (2.1) was fitted with the following results:

$$n = 12 \qquad b_0 = -.100 \qquad b_1 = 1.017 \qquad MSE = .0272$$

$$s\{b_1\} = .0142 \qquad \bar{X} = 5.500 \qquad \bar{Y} = 5.492 \qquad \sum(X_i - \bar{X})^2 = 135$$

$$\hat{Y} = -.100 + 1.017X$$

The data and the estimated regression line are plotted in Figure 4.2.

The researcher first wished to make sure that there is a linear association between the two variables. A test of $H_0: \beta_1 = 0$ versus $H_a: \beta_1 \neq 0$, utilizing test statistic $t^* = b_1/s\{b_1\} = 1.017/.0142 = 71.6$, was conducted for $\alpha = .05$. Since $t(.975; 10) = 2.228$ and $|t^*| = 71.6 > 2.228$, it was concluded that $\beta_1 \neq 0$, or that a linear association exists between the measured concentration and the actual concentration.

The researcher now wishes to use the regression relation to ascertain the actual concentration $X_{h(\text{new})}$ for a new patient for whom the quick procedure yielded a measured concentration of $Y_{h(\text{new})} = 6.52$. It is desired to estimate $X_{h(\text{new})}$ by means of a 95 percent confidence interval. Using (4.31) and (4.32a), we obtain:

$$\hat{X}_{h(\text{new})} = \frac{6.52 - (-.100)}{1.017} = 6.509$$

$$s^2\{\text{pred}\,X\} = \frac{.0272}{(1.017)^2}\left[1 + \frac{1}{12} + \frac{(6.509 - 5.500)^2}{135}\right] = .0287$$

so that $s\{\text{pred}\,X\} = .1694$. We require $t(.975; 10) = 2.228$, and using (4.32) we obtain the confidence limits $6.509 \pm 2.228(.1694)$. Hence, the 95 percent confidence interval is:

$$6.13 \le X_{h(\text{new})} \le 6.89$$

Thus, it can be concluded with 95 percent confidence that the actual galactose concentration for the patient is between 6.13 and 6.89. This is approximately a $\pm$ 6 percent error, which is considered reasonable by the researcher.

Comments

1. The inverse prediction problem is also known as a *calibration problem* since it is applicable when inexpensive, quick, and approximate measurements (Y) are related to precise, often expensive, and time-consuming measurements (X) based on n observations. The resulting regression model is then used to estimate the precise measurement $X_{h(\text{new})}$ for a new approximate measurement $Y_{h(\text{new})}$. We illustrated this use in the calibration example.

2. The approximate confidence interval (4.32) is appropriate if the quantity:

(4.33)
$$\frac{[t(1 - \alpha/2; n - 2)]^2 MSE}{b_1^2 \Sigma(X_i - \bar{X})^2}$$

is small, say less than .1. For the calibration example, this quantity is:

$$\frac{(2.228)^2(.0272)}{(1.017)^2(135)} = .00097$$

so that the approximate confidence interval is appropriate here.

3. Simultaneous prediction intervals based on g different new observed measurements $Y_{h(\text{new})}$, with a $1 - \alpha$ family confidence coefficient, are easily obtained using either the Bonferroni or the Scheffé procedures discussed in Section 4.3. The value of $t(1 - \alpha/2; n - 2)$ in (4.32) is replaced by either $B = t(1 - \alpha/2g; n - 2)$ or $S = [gF(1 - \alpha; g, n - 2)]^{1/2}$.

4. The inverse prediction problem has aroused controversy among statisticians. Some statisticians have suggested that inverse predictions should be made in direct fashion by regressing X on Y. This regression is called *inverse regression*. Research in this area is still ongoing.   ∎

4.7   Choice of X Levels

When regression data are obtained by experiment, the levels of X at which observations on Y are to be taken are under the control of the experimenter. Among other things, the experimenter will have to consider:

1. How many levels of X should be investigated?

2. What shall the two extreme levels be?

3. How shall the other levels of X, if any, be spaced?

4. How many observations should be taken at each level of X?

There is no single answer to these questions, since different purposes of the regression analysis lead to different answers. The possible objectives in regression analysis are varied, as we have noted earlier. The main objective may be to estimate the slope of the regression line or, in some cases, to estimate the intercept. In many cases, the main objective is to predict one or more new observations or to estimate one or more mean responses. When the regression function is curvilinear, the main objective may be to locate the maximum or minimum mean response. At still other times, the main purpose is to determine the nature of the regression function.

To illustrate how the purpose affects the design, consider the variances of b_0, b_1, $\hat{Y}_h$, and for predicting $Y_{h(\text{new})}$, which were developed earlier for regression model (2.1):

$$(4.34) \qquad \sigma^2\{b_0\} = \sigma^2 \left[\frac{1}{n} + \frac{\bar{X}^2}{\Sigma(X_i - \bar{X})^2} \right]$$

$$(4.35) \qquad \sigma^2\{b_1\} = \frac{\sigma^2}{\Sigma(X_i - \bar{X})^2}$$

$$(4.36) \qquad \sigma^2\{\hat{Y}_h\} = \sigma^2 \left[\frac{1}{n} + \frac{(X_h - \bar{X})^2}{\Sigma(X_i - \bar{X})^2} \right]$$

$$(4.37) \qquad \sigma^2\{\text{pred}\} = \sigma^2 \left[1 + \frac{1}{n} + \frac{(X_h - \bar{X})^2}{\Sigma(X_i - \bar{X})^2} \right]$$

If the main purpose of the regression analysis is to estimate the slope β_1, the variance of b_1 is minimized if $\Sigma(X_i - \bar{X})^2$ is maximized. This is accomplished by using two levels of X, at the two extremes for the scope of the model, and placing half of the observations at each of the two levels. Of course, if one were not sure of the linearity of the regression function, one would be hesitant to use only two levels since they would provide no information about possible departures from linearity. If the main purpose is to estimate the intercept β_0, the number and placement of levels does not affect the variance of b_0 as long as $\bar{X} = 0$. On the other hand, to estimate the mean response or to predict a new observation at the level X_h, the relevant variance is minimized by using X levels so that $\bar{X} = X_h$.

Although the number and spacing of X levels depends very much on the major purpose of the regression analysis, the general advice given by D. R. Cox is still relevant:

> Use two levels when the object is primarily to examine whether or not . . . (the predictor variable) . . . has an effect and in which direction that effect is. Use three levels whenever a description of the response curve by its slope and curvature is likely to be adequate; this should cover most cases. Use four levels if further examination of the shape of the response curve is important. Use more than four levels when it is required to estimate the detailed shape of the response curve, or when the curve is expected to rise to an asymptotic value, or in general to show features not adequately described by slope and curvature. Except in these last cases it is generally satisfactory to use equally spaced levels with equal numbers of observations per level. (Ref. 4.4)

Cited References

4.1. Miller, R. G., Jr. *Simultaneous Statistical Inference*. New York: Springer-Verlag, 1991.

4.2. Fuller, W. A. *Measurement Error Models*. New York: John Wiley & Sons, 1987.

4.3. Berkson, J. "Are There Two Regressions?" *Journal of the American Statistical Association* 45 (1950), pp. 164–80.

4.4. Cox, D. R. *Planning of Experiments*. New York: John Wiley & Sons, 1958, pp. 141–42.

Problems

4.1. When joint confidence intervals for β_0 and β_1 are developed by the Bonferroni method with a family confidence coefficient of 90 percent, does this imply that 10 percent of the time the confidence interval for β_0 will be incorrect? that 5 percent of the time the confidence interval for β_0 will be incorrect and 5 percent of the time that for β_1 will be incorrect? Discuss.

4.2. Refer to Problem 2.1. Suppose the student combines the two confidence intervals into a confidence set. What can you say about the family confidence coefficient for this set?

√ 4.3. Refer to **Calculator maintenance** Problem 1.20.

   a. Will b_0 and b_1 tend to err in the same direction or in opposite directions here? Explain.

   b. Obtain Bonferroni joint confidence intervals for β_0 and β_1, using a 95 percent family confidence coefficient.

   c. A consultant has suggested that β_0 should be 0 and β_1 should equal 14.0. Do your joint confidence intervals in part (b) support this view?

√ 4.4. Refer to **Airfreight breakage** Problem 1.21.

   a. Will b_0 and b_1 tend to err in the same direction or in opposite directions here? Explain.

   b. Obtain Bonferroni joint confidence intervals for β_0 and β_1, using a 99 percent family confidence coefficient. Interpret your confidence intervals.

4.5. Refer to **Plastic hardness** Problem 1.22.

   a. Obtain Bonferroni joint confidence intervals for β_0 and β_1, using a 90 percent family confidence coefficient. Interpret your confidence intervals.

   b. Are b_0 and b_1 positively or negatively correlated here? Is this reflected in your joint confidence intervals in part (a)?

   c. What is the meaning of the family confidence coefficient in part (a)?

4.6. Refer to **Muscle mass** Problem 1.27.

   a. Obtain Bonferroni joint confidence intervals for β_0 and β_1, using a 99 percent family confidence coefficient. Interpret your confidence intervals.

   b. Will b_0 and b_1 tend to err in the same direction or in opposite directions here? Explain.

   c. A researcher has suggested that β_0 should equal approximately 160 and that β_1 should be between -1.9 and -1.5. Do the joint confidence intervals in part (a) support this expectation?

√ 4.7. Refer to **Calculator maintenance** Problem 1.20.

   a. Estimate the expected number of minutes spent when there are 3, 5, and 7 machines to be serviced, respectively. Use interval estimates with a 90 percent family confidence coefficient based on the Working-Hotelling procedure.

   b. Two service calls for preventive maintenance are scheduled in which the numbers of machines to be serviced are 4 and 7, respectively. A family of prediction intervals for the times to be spent on these calls is desired with a 90 percent family confidence coefficient. Which procedure, Scheffé or Bonferroni, will provide tighter prediction limits here?

   c. Obtain the family of prediction intervals required in part (b), using the more efficient procedure.

√ 4.8. Refer to **Airfreight breakage** Problem 1.21.

   a. It is desired to obtain interval estimates of the mean number of broken ampules when there are 0, 1, and 2 transfers for a shipment, using a 95 percent family confidence coefficient. Obtain the desired confidence intervals, using the Working-Hotelling procedure.

   b. Are the confidence intervals obtained in part (a) more efficient than Bonferroni intervals here? Explain.

   c. The next three shipments will make 0, 1, and 2 transfers, respectively. Obtain prediction intervals for the number of broken ampules for each of these three shipments, using the Scheffé procedure and a 95 percent family confidence coefficient.

   d. Would the Bonferroni procedure have been more efficient in developing the prediction intervals in part (c)? Explain.

4.9. Refer to **Plastic hardness** Problem 1.22.

   a. Management wishes to obtain interval estimates of the mean hardness when the elapsed time is 20, 30, and 40 hours, respectively. Calculate the desired confidence intervals, using the Bonferroni procedure and a 90 percent family confidence coefficient. What is the meaning of the family confidence coefficient here?

   b. Is the Bonferroni procedure employed in part (a) the most efficient one that could be employed here? Explain.

   c. The next two test items will be measured after 30 and 40 hours of elapsed time, respectively. Predict the hardness for each of these two items, using the most efficient procedure and a 90 percent family confidence coefficient.

4.10. Refer to **Muscle mass** Problem 1.27.

   a. The nutritionist is particularly interested in the mean muscle mass for women aged 45, 55, and 65. Obtain joint confidence intervals for the means of interest using the Working-Hotelling procedure and a 95 percent family confidence coefficient.

   b. Is the Working-Hotelling procedure the most efficient one to be employed in part (a)? Explain.

   c. Three additional women aged 48, 59, and 74 have contacted the nutritionist. Predict the muscle mass for each of these three women using the Bonferroni procedure and a 95 percent family confidence coefficient.

d. Subsequently, the nutritionist wishes to predict the muscle mass for a fourth woman aged 64, with a family confidence coefficient of 95 percent for the four predictions. Will the three prediction intervals in part (c) have to be recalculated? Would this also be true if the Scheffé procedure had been used in constructing the prediction intervals?

4.11. A behavioral scientist said, "I am never sure whether the regression line goes through the origin. Hence, I will not use such a model." Comment.

4.12. **Typographical errors**. Shown below are the number of galleys for a manuscript (X) and the total dollar cost of correcting typographical errors (Y) in a random sample of recent orders handled by a firm specializing in technical manuscripts. Since Y involves variable costs only, an analyst wished to determine whether regression-through-the-origin model (4.10) is appropriate for studying the relation between the two variables.

i:	1	2	3	4	5	6	7	8	9	10	11	12
X_i:	7	12	10	10	14	25	30	25	18	10	4	6
Y_i:	128	213	191	178	250	446	540	457	324	177	75	107

a. Fit regression model (4.10) and state the estimated regression function.

b. Plot the estimated regression function and the data. Does a linear regression function through the origin appear to provide a good fit here? Comment.

c. In estimating costs of handling prospective orders, management has used a standard of \$17.50 per galley for the cost of correcting typographical errors. Test whether or not this standard should be revised; use $\alpha = .02$. State the alternatives, decision rule, and conclusion.

d. Obtain a prediction interval for the correction cost on a forthcoming job involving 10 galleys. Use a confidence coefficient of 98 percent.

4.13. Refer to **Typographical errors** Problem 4.12.

a. Obtain the residuals e_i. Do they sum to zero? Plot the residuals against the fitted values $\hat{Y}_i$. What conclusions can be drawn from your plot?

b. Conduct a formal test for lack of fit of linear regression through the origin; use $\alpha = .01$. State the alternatives, decision rule, and conclusion. What is the P-value of the test?

4.14. Refer to **Grade point average** Problem 1.19. Assume that linear regression through the origin model (4.10) is appropriate.

a. Fit regression model (4.10) and state the estimated regression function.

b. Estimate β_1 with a 95 percent confidence interval. Interpret your interval estimate.

c. Estimate the mean freshman GPA for students whose entrance test score is 4.7. Use a 95 percent confidence interval.

4.15. Refer to **Grade point average** Problem 4.14.

a. Plot the fitted regression line and the data. Does the linear regression function through the origin appear to be a good fit here?

b. Obtain the residuals e_i. Do they sum to zero? Plot the residuals against the fitted values $\hat{Y}_i$. What conclusions can be drawn from your plot?

c. Conduct a formal test for lack of fit of linear regression through the origin; use $\alpha = .005$. State the alternatives, decision rule, and conclusion. What is the P-value of the test?

√ 4.16. Refer to **Calculator maintenance** Problem 1.20. Assume that linear regression through the origin model (4.10) is appropriate.

a. Obtain the estimated regression function.

b. Estimate β_1 with a 90 percent confidence interval. Interpret your interval estimate.

c. Predict the service time on a new call in which six machines are to be serviced. Use a 90 percent prediction interval.

√ 4.17. Refer to **Calculator maintenance** Problem 4.16.

a. Plot the fitted regression line and the data. Does the linear regression function through the origin appear to be a good fit here?

b. Obtain the residuals e_i. Do they sum to zero? Plot the residuals against the fitted values $\hat{Y}_i$. What conclusions can be drawn from your plot?

c. Conduct a formal test for lack of fit of linear regression through the origin; use $\alpha = .01$. State the alternatives, decision rule, and conclusion. What is the P-value of the test?

4.18. Refer to **Plastic hardness** Problem 1.22. Suppose that errors arise in X because the laboratory technician is instructed to measure the hardness of the ith specimen (Y_i) at a prerecorded elapsed time (X_i), but the timing is imperfect so the true elapsed time varies at random from the prerecorded elapsed time. Will ordinary least squares estimates be biased here? Discuss.

4.19. Refer to **Grade point average** Problem 1.19. A new student earned a grade point average of 3.4 in the freshman year.

a. Obtain a 90 percent confidence interval for the student's entrance test score. Interpret your confidence interval.

b. Is criterion (4.33) as to the appropriateness of the approximate confidence interval met here?

4.20. Refer to **Plastic hardness** Problem 1.22. The measurement of a new test item showed 238 Brinell units of hardness.

a. Obtain a 99 percent confidence interval for the elapsed time before the hardness was measured. Interpret your confidence interval.

b. Is criterion (4.33) as to the appropriateness of the approximate confidence interval met here?

Exercises

4.21. When the predictor variable is so coded that $\bar{X} = 0$ and the normal error regression model (2.1) applies, arc b_0 and b_1 independent? Are the joint confidence intervals for β_0 and β_1 then independent?

4.22. Derive an extension of the Bonferroni inequality (4.2a) for the case of three statements, each with statement confidence coefficient $1 - \alpha$.

4.23. Show that for the fitted least squares regression line through the origin (4.15), $\Sigma X_i e_i = 0$.

4.24. Show that $\hat{Y}$ as defined in (4.15) for linear regression through the origin is an unbiased estimator of $E\{Y\}$.

4.25. Derive the formula for $s^2\{\hat{Y}_h\}$ given in Table 4.1 for linear regression through the origin.

Projects

4.26. Refer to the **SMSA** data set and Project 1.43. Consider the regression relation of number of active physicians to total population.

    a. Obtain Bonferroni joint confidence intervals for β_0 and β_1, using a 95 percent family confidence coefficient.

    b. An investigator has suggested that β_0 should be -400 and β_1 should be 2.25. Do the joint confidence intervals in part (a) support this view? Discuss.

    c. It is desired to estimate the expected number of active physicians for SMSAs with total population of $X = 500, 1,000, 5,000$ thousands with family confidence coefficient .90. Which procedure, the Working-Hotelling or the Bonferroni, is more efficient here?

    d. Obtain the family of interval estimates required in part (c), using the more efficient procedure. Interpret your confidence intervals.

4.27. Refer to the **SENIC** data set and Project 1.45. Consider the regression relation of average length of stay to infection risk.

    a. Obtain Bonferroni joint confidence intervals for β_0 and β_1, using a 90 percent family confidence coefficient.

    b. A researcher suggested that β_0 should be approximately 7 and β_1 should be approximately 1. Do the joint intervals in part (a) support this expectation? Discuss.

    c. It is desired to estimate the expected hospital stay for persons with infection risks $X = 2, 3, 4, 5$ with family confidence coefficient .95. Which procedure, the Working-Hotelling or the Bonferroni, is more efficient here?

    d. Obtain the family of interval estimates required in part (c), using the more efficient procedure. Interpret your confidence intervals.

Matrix Approach to Simple Linear Regression Analysis

Matrix algebra is widely used for mathematical and statistical analysis. The matrix approach is practically a necessity in multiple regression analysis, since it permits extensive systems of equations and large arrays of data to be denoted compactly and operated upon efficiently.

In this chapter, we first take up a brief introduction to matrix algebra. (A fuller treatment of matrix algebra may be found in specialized texts such as Reference 5.1.) Then we apply matrix methods to the simple linear regression model discussed in previous chapters. Although matrix algebra is not really required for simple linear regression, the application of matrix methods to this case will provide a useful transition to multiple regression, which will be taken up in Parts II and III.

Readers familiar with matrix algebra may wish to scan the introductory parts of this chapter and focus upon the later parts dealing with the use of matrix methods in regression analysis.

5.1 Matrices

Definition of Matrix

A matrix is a rectangular array of elements arranged in rows and columns. An example of a matrix is:

$$
\begin{array}{c}
\\
\\
\text{Row 1} \\
\text{Row 2} \\
\text{Row 3}
\end{array}
\begin{array}{cc}
\text{Column} & \text{Column} \\
1 & 2 \\
\left[\begin{array}{cc}
16{,}000 & 23 \\
33{,}000 & 47 \\
21{,}000 & 35
\end{array}\right]
\end{array}
$$

The *elements* of this particular matrix are numbers representing income (column 1) and age (column 2) of three persons. The elements are arranged by row (person) and column (characteristic of person). Thus, the element in the first row and first column (16,000) represents the income of the first person. The element in the first row and second column (23) represents the age of the first person. The *dimension* of the matrix is 3×2, i.e., 3 rows by 2 columns. If we wanted to present income and age for 1,000 persons in a matrix with the same format as the one earlier, we would require a $1{,}000 \times 2$ matrix.

Other examples of matrices are:

$$\begin{bmatrix} 1 & 0 \\ 5 & 10 \end{bmatrix} \qquad \begin{bmatrix} 4 & 7 & 12 & 16 \\ 3 & 15 & 9 & 8 \end{bmatrix}$$

These two matrices have dimensions of 2×2 and 2×4, respectively. Note that in giving the dimension of a matrix, we always specify the number of rows first and then the number of columns.

As in ordinary algebra, we may use symbols to identify the elements of a matrix:

$$\begin{array}{c} \begin{array}{ccc} j = 1 & j = 2 & j = 3 \end{array} \\ \begin{array}{c} i = 1 \\ i = 2 \end{array} \begin{bmatrix} a_{11} & a_{12} & a_{13} \\ a_{21} & a_{22} & a_{23} \end{bmatrix} \end{array}$$

Note that the first subscript identifies the row number and the second the column number. We shall use the general notation a_{ij} for the element in the ith row and the jth column. In our above example, $i = 1, 2$ and $j = 1, 2, 3$.

A matrix may be denoted by a symbol such as **A**, **X**, or **Z**. The symbol is in **boldface** to identify that it refers to a matrix. Thus, we might define for the above matrix:

$$\mathbf{A} = \begin{bmatrix} a_{11} & a_{12} & a_{13} \\ a_{21} & a_{22} & a_{23} \end{bmatrix}$$

Reference to the matrix **A** then implies reference to the 2×3 array just given.

Another notation for the matrix **A** just given is:

$$\mathbf{A} = [a_{ij}] \qquad i = 1, 2; \ j = 1, 2, 3$$

This notation avoids the need for writing out all elements of the matrix by stating only the general element. It can only be used, of course, when the elements of a matrix are symbols.

To summarize, a matrix with r rows and c columns will be represented either in full:

(5.1)
$$\mathbf{A} = \begin{bmatrix} a_{11} & a_{12} & \cdots & a_{1j} & \cdots & a_{1c} \\ a_{21} & a_{22} & \cdots & a_{2j} & \cdots & a_{2c} \\ \vdots & \vdots & & \vdots & & \vdots \\ a_{i1} & a_{i2} & \cdots & a_{ij} & \cdots & a_{ic} \\ \vdots & \vdots & & \vdots & & \vdots \\ a_{r1} & a_{r2} & \cdots & a_{rj} & \cdots & a_{rc} \end{bmatrix}$$

or in abbreviated form:

$$\mathbf{A} = [a_{ij}] \qquad i = 1, \ldots, r; \ j = 1, \ldots, c$$

or simply by a boldface symbol, such as **A**.

Comments

1. Do not think of a matrix as a number. It is a set of elements arranged in an array. Only when the matrix has dimension 1×1 is there a single number in a matrix, in which case one *can* think of it interchangeably as either a matrix or a number.

2. The following is *not* a matrix:

$$\begin{bmatrix} & 14 & \\ & 8 & \\ 10 & & 15 \\ 9 & & 16 \end{bmatrix}$$

since the numbers are not arranged in columns and rows. ∎

Square Matrix

A matrix is said to be square if the number of rows equals the number of columns. Two examples are:

$$\begin{bmatrix} 4 & 7 \\ 3 & 9 \end{bmatrix} \qquad \begin{bmatrix} a_{11} & a_{12} & a_{13} \\ a_{21} & a_{22} & a_{23} \\ a_{31} & a_{32} & a_{33} \end{bmatrix}$$

Vector

A matrix containing only one column is called a *column vector* or simply a *vector*. Two examples are:

$$\mathbf{A} = \begin{bmatrix} 4 \\ 7 \\ 10 \end{bmatrix} \qquad \mathbf{C} = \begin{bmatrix} c_1 \\ c_2 \\ c_3 \\ c_4 \\ c_5 \end{bmatrix}$$

The vector $\mathbf{A}$ is a 3×1 matrix, and the vector $\mathbf{C}$ is a 5×1 matrix.

A matrix containing only one row is called a *row vector*. Two examples are:

$$\mathbf{B}' = \begin{bmatrix} 15 & 25 & 50 \end{bmatrix} \qquad \mathbf{F}' = \begin{bmatrix} f_1 & f_2 \end{bmatrix}$$

We use the prime symbol for row vectors for reasons to be seen shortly. Note that the row vector $\mathbf{B}'$ is a 1×3 matrix and the row vector $\mathbf{F}'$ is a 1×2 matrix.

A single subscript suffices to identify the elements of a vector.

Transpose

The transpose of a matrix $\mathbf{A}$ is another matrix, denoted by $\mathbf{A}'$, that is obtained by interchanging corresponding columns and rows of the matrix $\mathbf{A}$.

For example, if:

$$\mathbf{A}_{3 \times 2} = \begin{bmatrix} 2 & 5 \\ 7 & 10 \\ 3 & 4 \end{bmatrix}$$

then the transpose $\mathbf{A}'$ is:

$$\mathbf{A}'_{2\times3} = \begin{bmatrix} 2 & 7 & 3 \\ 5 & 10 & 4 \end{bmatrix}$$

Note that the first column of $\mathbf{A}$ is the first row of $\mathbf{A}'$, and similarly the second column of $\mathbf{A}$ is the second row of $\mathbf{A}'$. Correspondingly, the first row of $\mathbf{A}$ has become the first column of $\mathbf{A}'$, and so on. Note that the dimension of $\mathbf{A}$, indicated under the symbol $\mathbf{A}$, becomes reversed for the dimension of $\mathbf{A}'$.

As another example, consider:

$$\mathbf{C}_{3\times1} = \begin{bmatrix} 4 \\ 7 \\ 10 \end{bmatrix} \qquad \mathbf{C}'_{1\times3} = [4 \quad 7 \quad 10]$$

Thus, the transpose of a column vector is a row vector, and vice versa. This is the reason why we used the symbol $\mathbf{B}'$ earlier to identify a row vector, since it may be thought of as the transpose of a column vector $\mathbf{B}$.

In general, we have:

$$\mathbf{A}_{r\times c} = \begin{bmatrix} a_{11} & \cdots & a_{1c} \\ \vdots & & \vdots \\ a_{r1} & \cdots & a_{rc} \end{bmatrix} = \underset{\substack{\nearrow \quad \nwarrow \\ \text{Row} \quad \text{Column} \\ \text{index} \quad \text{index}}}{[a_{ij}]} \qquad i = 1, \ldots, r; \quad j = 1, \ldots, c$$

(5.3)

$$\mathbf{A}'_{c\times r} = \begin{bmatrix} a_{11} & \cdots & a_{r1} \\ \vdots & & \vdots \\ a_{1c} & \cdots & a_{rc} \end{bmatrix} = \underset{\substack{\nearrow \quad \nwarrow \\ \text{Row} \quad \text{Column} \\ \text{index} \quad \text{index}}}{[a_{ji}]} \qquad j = 1, \ldots, c; \quad i = 1, \ldots, r$$

Thus, the element in the ith row and the jth column in $\mathbf{A}$ is found in the jth row and ith column in $\mathbf{A}'$.

Equality of Matrices

Two matrices $\mathbf{A}$ and $\mathbf{B}$ are said to be equal if they have the same dimension and if all corresponding elements are equal. Conversely, if two matrices are equal, their corresponding elements are equal. For example, if:

$$\mathbf{A}_{3\times1} = \begin{bmatrix} a_1 \\ a_2 \\ a_3 \end{bmatrix} \qquad \mathbf{B}_{3\times1} = \begin{bmatrix} 4 \\ 7 \\ 3 \end{bmatrix}$$

then $\mathbf{A} = \mathbf{B}$ implies:

$$a_1 = 4 \qquad a_2 = 7 \qquad a_3 = 3$$

Similarly, if:

$$\mathbf{A}_{3\times2} = \begin{bmatrix} a_{11} & a_{12} \\ a_{21} & a_{22} \\ a_{31} & a_{32} \end{bmatrix} \qquad \mathbf{B}_{3\times2} = \begin{bmatrix} 17 & 2 \\ 14 & 5 \\ 13 & 9 \end{bmatrix}$$

then $\mathbf{A} = \mathbf{B}$ implies:

$$a_{11} = 17 \quad a_{12} = 2$$
$$a_{21} = 14 \quad a_{22} = 5$$
$$a_{31} = 13 \quad a_{32} = 9$$

Regression Examples

In regression analysis, one basic matrix is the vector $\mathbf{Y}$, consisting of the n observations on the response variable:

$$(5.4) \qquad \underset{n \times 1}{\mathbf{Y}} = \begin{bmatrix} Y_1 \\ Y_2 \\ \vdots \\ Y_n \end{bmatrix}$$

Note that the transpose $\mathbf{Y}'$ is the row vector:

$$(5.5) \qquad \underset{1 \times n}{\mathbf{Y}'} = [Y_1 \quad Y_2 \quad \cdots \quad Y_n]$$

Another basic matrix in regression analysis is the $\mathbf{X}$ matrix, which is defined as follows for simple linear regression analysis:

$$(5.6) \qquad \underset{n \times 2}{\mathbf{X}} = \begin{bmatrix} 1 & X_1 \\ 1 & X_2 \\ \vdots & \vdots \\ 1 & X_n \end{bmatrix}$$

The matrix $\mathbf{X}$ consists of a column of 1s and a column containing the n observations on the predictor variable X. Note that the transpose of $\mathbf{X}$ is:

$$(5.7) \qquad \underset{2 \times n}{\mathbf{X}'} = \begin{bmatrix} 1 & 1 & \cdots & 1 \\ X_1 & X_2 & \cdots & X_n \end{bmatrix}$$

5.2   Matrix Addition and Subtraction

Adding or subtracting two matrices requires that they have the same dimension. The sum, or difference, of two matrices is another matrix whose elements each consist of the sum, or difference, of the corresponding elements of the two matrices. Suppose:

$$\underset{3 \times 2}{\mathbf{A}} = \begin{bmatrix} 1 & 4 \\ 2 & 5 \\ 3 & 6 \end{bmatrix} \qquad \underset{3 \times 2}{\mathbf{B}} = \begin{bmatrix} 1 & 2 \\ 2 & 3 \\ 3 & 4 \end{bmatrix}$$

then:

$$\mathbf{A} + \mathbf{B}_{3\times 2} = \begin{bmatrix} 1+1 & 4+2 \\ 2+2 & 5+3 \\ 3+3 & 6+4 \end{bmatrix} = \begin{bmatrix} 2 & 6 \\ 4 & 8 \\ 6 & 10 \end{bmatrix}$$

Similarly:

$$\mathbf{A} - \mathbf{B}_{3\times 2} = \begin{bmatrix} 1-1 & 4-2 \\ 2-2 & 5-3 \\ 3-3 & 6-4 \end{bmatrix} = \begin{bmatrix} 0 & 2 \\ 0 & 2 \\ 0 & 2 \end{bmatrix}$$

In general, if:

$$\mathbf{A}_{r\times c} = [a_{ij}] \qquad \mathbf{B}_{r\times c} = [b_{ij}] \qquad i = 1, \ldots, r; \quad j = 1, \ldots, c$$

then:

(5.8) $$\mathbf{A} + \mathbf{B}_{r\times c} = [a_{ij} + b_{ij}] \quad \text{and} \quad \mathbf{A} - \mathbf{B}_{r\times c} = [a_{ij} - b_{ij}]$$

Formula (5.8) generalizes in an obvious way to addition and subtraction of more than two matrices. Note also that $\mathbf{A} + \mathbf{B} = \mathbf{B} + \mathbf{A}$, as in ordinary algebra.

Regression Example

The regression model:

$$Y_i = E\{Y_i\} + \varepsilon_i \qquad i = 1, \ldots, n$$

can be written compactly in matrix notation. First, let us define the vector of the mean responses:

(5.9) $$\mathbf{E\{Y\}}_{n\times 1} = \begin{bmatrix} E\{Y_1\} \\ E\{Y_2\} \\ \vdots \\ E\{Y_n\} \end{bmatrix}$$

and the vector of the error terms:

(5.10) $$\boldsymbol{\varepsilon}_{n\times 1} = \begin{bmatrix} \varepsilon_1 \\ \varepsilon_2 \\ \vdots \\ \varepsilon_n \end{bmatrix}$$

Recalling the definition of the observations vector $\mathbf{Y}$ in (5.4), we can write the regression model as follows:

$$\mathbf{Y}_{n\times 1} = \mathbf{E\{Y\}}_{n\times 1} + \boldsymbol{\varepsilon}_{n\times 1}$$

because:

$$
\begin{bmatrix} Y_1 \\ Y_2 \\ \vdots \\ Y_n \end{bmatrix} = \begin{bmatrix} E\{Y_1\} \\ E\{Y_2\} \\ \vdots \\ E\{Y_n\} \end{bmatrix} + \begin{bmatrix} \varepsilon_1 \\ \varepsilon_2 \\ \vdots \\ \varepsilon_n \end{bmatrix} = \begin{bmatrix} E\{Y_1\} + \varepsilon_1 \\ E\{Y_2\} + \varepsilon_2 \\ \vdots \\ E\{Y_n\} + \varepsilon_n \end{bmatrix}
$$

Thus, the observations vector $\mathbf{Y}$ equals the sum of two vectors, a vector containing the expected values and another containing the error terms.

5.3   Matrix Multiplication

Multiplication of a Matrix by a Scalar

A *scalar* is an ordinary number or a symbol representing a number. In multiplication of a matrix by a scalar, every element of the matrix is multiplied by the scalar. For example, suppose the matrix $\mathbf{A}$ is given by:

$$
\mathbf{A} = \begin{bmatrix} 2 & 7 \\ 9 & 3 \end{bmatrix}
$$

Then $4\mathbf{A}$, where 4 is the scalar, equals:

$$
4\mathbf{A} = 4\begin{bmatrix} 2 & 7 \\ 9 & 3 \end{bmatrix} = \begin{bmatrix} 8 & 28 \\ 36 & 12 \end{bmatrix}
$$

Similarly, $\lambda\mathbf{A}$ equals:

$$
\lambda\mathbf{A} = \lambda\begin{bmatrix} 2 & 7 \\ 9 & 3 \end{bmatrix} = \begin{bmatrix} 2\lambda & 7\lambda \\ 9\lambda & 3\lambda \end{bmatrix}
$$

where λ denotes a scalar.

If every element of a matrix has a common factor, this factor can be taken outside the matrix and treated as a scalar. For example:

$$
\begin{bmatrix} 9 & 27 \\ 15 & 18 \end{bmatrix} = 3\begin{bmatrix} 3 & 9 \\ 5 & 6 \end{bmatrix}
$$

Similarly:

$$
\begin{bmatrix} \frac{5}{\lambda} & \frac{2}{\lambda} \\ \frac{3}{\lambda} & \frac{8}{\lambda} \end{bmatrix} = \frac{1}{\lambda}\begin{bmatrix} 5 & 2 \\ 3 & 8 \end{bmatrix}
$$

In general, if $\mathbf{A} = [a_{ij}]$ and λ is a scalar, we have:

(5.11)
$$
\lambda\mathbf{A} = \mathbf{A}\lambda = [\lambda a_{ij}]
$$

Multiplication of a Matrix by a Matrix

Multiplication of a matrix by a matrix may appear somewhat complicated at first, but a little practice will make it a routine operation.

Consider the two matrices:

$$\underset{2\times2}{\mathbf{A}} = \begin{bmatrix} 2 & 5 \\ 4 & 1 \end{bmatrix} \qquad \underset{2\times2}{\mathbf{B}} = \begin{bmatrix} 4 & 6 \\ 5 & 8 \end{bmatrix}$$

The product **AB** will be a 2×2 matrix whose elements are obtained by finding the cross products of rows of **A** with columns of **B** and summing the cross products. For instance, to find the element in the first row and the first column of the product **AB**, we work with the first row of **A** and the first column of **B**, as follows:

$$\begin{array}{cc} & \mathbf{A} \\ \text{Row 1} & \begin{bmatrix} \boxed{2 \quad 5} \\ 4 \quad 1 \end{bmatrix} \\ \text{Row 2} & \end{array} \quad \begin{array}{c} \mathbf{B} \\ \begin{bmatrix} \boxed{4} & 6 \\ \boxed{5} & 8 \end{bmatrix} \\ \text{Col. 1 \quad Col. 2} \end{array} \quad \begin{array}{c} \mathbf{AB} \\ \text{Row 1} \begin{bmatrix} 33 & \\ & \end{bmatrix} \\ \text{Col. 1} \end{array}$$

We take the cross products and sum:

$$2(4) + 5(5) = 33$$

The number 33 is the element in the first row and first column of the matrix **AB**.

To find the element in the first row and second column of **AB**, we work with the first row of **A** and the second column of **B**:

$$\begin{array}{cc} & \mathbf{A} \\ \text{Row 1} & \begin{bmatrix} \boxed{2 \quad 5} \\ 4 \quad 1 \end{bmatrix} \\ \text{Row 2} & \end{array} \quad \begin{array}{c} \mathbf{B} \\ \begin{bmatrix} 4 & \boxed{6} \\ 5 & \boxed{8} \end{bmatrix} \\ \text{Col. 1 \quad Col. 2} \end{array} \quad \begin{array}{c} \mathbf{AB} \\ \text{Row 1} \begin{bmatrix} 33 & 52 \end{bmatrix} \\ \text{Col. 1 \quad Col. 2} \end{array}$$

The sum of the cross products is:

$$2(6) + 5(8) = 52$$

Continuing this process, we find the product **AB** to be:

$$\underset{2\times2}{\mathbf{AB}} = \begin{bmatrix} 2 & 5 \\ 4 & 1 \end{bmatrix} \begin{bmatrix} 4 & 6 \\ 5 & 8 \end{bmatrix} = \begin{bmatrix} 33 & 52 \\ 21 & 32 \end{bmatrix}$$

Let us consider another example:

$$\underset{2\times3}{\mathbf{A}} = \begin{bmatrix} 1 & 3 & 4 \\ 0 & 5 & 8 \end{bmatrix} \qquad \underset{3\times1}{\mathbf{B}} = \begin{bmatrix} 3 \\ 5 \\ 2 \end{bmatrix}$$

$$\underset{2\times1}{\mathbf{AB}} = \begin{bmatrix} 1 & 3 & 4 \\ 0 & 5 & 8 \end{bmatrix} \begin{bmatrix} 3 \\ 5 \\ 2 \end{bmatrix} = \begin{bmatrix} 26 \\ 41 \end{bmatrix}$$

When obtaining the product **AB**, we say that **A** is *postmultiplied* by **B** or **B** is *premultiplied* by **A**. The reason for this precise terminology is that multiplication rules for ordinary algebra do not apply to matrix algebra. In ordinary algebra, $xy = yx$. In matrix algebra, $\mathbf{AB} \neq \mathbf{BA}$ usually. In fact, even though the product **AB** may be defined, the product **BA** may not be defined at all.

In general, the product **AB** is only defined when the number of columns in **A** equals the number of rows in **B** so that there will be corresponding terms in the cross products. Thus, in our previous two examples, we had:

$$
\underset{2\times2}{\mathbf{A}} \swarrow \searrow \underset{2\times2}{\mathbf{B}} = \underset{2\times2}{\mathbf{AB}}
\qquad\qquad
\underset{2\times3}{\mathbf{A}} \swarrow \searrow \underset{3\times1}{\mathbf{B}} = \underset{2\times1}{\mathbf{AB}}
$$

Note that the dimension of the product **AB** is given by the number of rows in **A** and the number of columns in **B**. Note also that in the second case the product **BA** would not be defined since the number of columns in **B** is not equal to the number of rows in **A**:

$$
\text{Unequal}
$$
$$
\underset{3\times1}{\mathbf{B}} \swarrow \searrow \underset{2\times3}{\mathbf{A}}
$$

Here is another example of matrix multiplication:

$$
\mathbf{AB} = \begin{bmatrix} a_{11} & a_{12} & a_{13} \\ a_{21} & a_{22} & a_{23} \end{bmatrix} \begin{bmatrix} b_{11} & b_{12} \\ b_{21} & b_{22} \\ b_{31} & b_{32} \end{bmatrix}
$$

$$
= \begin{bmatrix} a_{11}b_{11} + a_{12}b_{21} + a_{13}b_{31} & a_{11}b_{12} + a_{12}b_{22} + a_{13}b_{32} \\ a_{21}b_{11} + a_{22}b_{21} + a_{23}b_{31} & a_{21}b_{12} + a_{22}b_{22} + a_{23}b_{32} \end{bmatrix}
$$

In general, if **A** has dimension $r \times c$ and **B** has dimension $c \times s$, the product **AB** is a matrix of dimension $r \times s$ whose element in the ith row and jth column is:

$$
\sum_{k=1}^{c} a_{ik}b_{kj}
$$

so that:

$$
(5.12) \qquad \underset{r\times s}{\mathbf{AB}} = \left[\sum_{k=1}^{c} a_{ik}b_{kj} \right] \qquad i = 1, \ldots, r; \quad j = 1, \ldots, s
$$

Thus, in the foregoing example, the element in the first row and second column of the product **AB** is:

$$
\sum_{k=1}^{3} a_{1k}b_{k2} = a_{11}b_{12} + a_{12}b_{22} + a_{13}b_{32}
$$

as indeed we found by taking the cross products of the elements in the first row of **A** and second column of **B** and summing.

Additional Examples

1.
$$\begin{bmatrix} 4 & 2 \\ 5 & 8 \end{bmatrix} \begin{bmatrix} a_1 \\ a_2 \end{bmatrix} = \begin{bmatrix} 4a_1 + 2a_2 \\ 5a_1 + 8a_2 \end{bmatrix}$$

2.
$$[2 \quad 3 \quad 5] \begin{bmatrix} 2 \\ 3 \\ 5 \end{bmatrix} = [2^2 + 3^2 + 5^2] = [38]$$

Here, the product is a 1×1 matrix, which is equivalent to a scalar. Thus, the matrix product here equals the number 38.

3.
$$\begin{bmatrix} 1 & X_1 \\ 1 & X_2 \\ 1 & X_3 \end{bmatrix} \begin{bmatrix} \beta_0 \\ \beta_1 \end{bmatrix} = \begin{bmatrix} \beta_0 + \beta_1 X_1 \\ \beta_0 + \beta_1 X_2 \\ \beta_0 + \beta_1 X_3 \end{bmatrix}$$

Regression Examples.   A product frequently needed is $\mathbf{Y'Y}$, where $\mathbf{Y}$ is the vector of observations on the response variable as defined in (5.4):

$$(5.13) \qquad \underset{1 \times 1}{\mathbf{Y'Y}} = [Y_1 \quad Y_2 \quad \cdots \quad Y_n] \begin{bmatrix} Y_1 \\ Y_2 \\ \vdots \\ Y_n \end{bmatrix} = [Y_1^2 + Y_2^2 + \cdots + Y_n^2] = [\Sigma Y_i^2]$$

Note that $\mathbf{Y'Y}$ is a 1×1 matrix, or a scalar. We thus have a compact way of writing a sum of squared terms: $\mathbf{Y'Y} = \Sigma Y_i^2$.

We also will need $\mathbf{X'X}$, which is a 2×2 matrix, where $\mathbf{X}$ is defined in (5.6):

$$(5.14) \qquad \underset{2 \times 2}{\mathbf{X'X}} = \begin{bmatrix} 1 & 1 & \cdots & 1 \\ X_1 & X_2 & \cdots & X_n \end{bmatrix} \begin{bmatrix} 1 & X_1 \\ 1 & X_2 \\ \vdots & \vdots \\ 1 & X_n \end{bmatrix} = \begin{bmatrix} n & \Sigma X_i \\ \Sigma X_i & \Sigma X_i^2 \end{bmatrix}$$

and $\mathbf{X'Y}$, which is a 2×1 matrix:

$$(5.15) \qquad \underset{2 \times 1}{\mathbf{X'Y}} = \begin{bmatrix} 1 & 1 & \cdots & 1 \\ X_1 & X_2 & \cdots & X_n \end{bmatrix} \begin{bmatrix} Y_1 \\ Y_2 \\ \vdots \\ Y_n \end{bmatrix} = \begin{bmatrix} \Sigma Y_i \\ \Sigma X_i Y_i \end{bmatrix}$$

5.4   Special Types of Matrices

Certain special types of matrices arise regularly in regression analysis. We consider the most important of these.

Symmetric Matrix

If $\mathbf{A} = \mathbf{A}'$, $\mathbf{A}$ is said to be symmetric. Thus, $\mathbf{A}$ below is symmetric:

$$
\underset{3\times 3}{\mathbf{A}} = \begin{bmatrix} 1 & 4 & 6 \\ 4 & 2 & 5 \\ 6 & 5 & 3 \end{bmatrix} \qquad \underset{3\times 3}{\mathbf{A}'} = \begin{bmatrix} 1 & 4 & 6 \\ 4 & 2 & 5 \\ 6 & 5 & 3 \end{bmatrix}
$$

A symmetric matrix necessarily is square. Symmetric matrices arise typically in regression analysis when we premultiply a matrix, say, $\mathbf{X}$, by its transpose, $\mathbf{X}'$. The resulting matrix, $\mathbf{X}'\mathbf{X}$, is symmetric, as can readily be seen from (5.14).

Diagonal Matrix

A diagonal matrix is a square matrix whose off-diagonal elements are all zeros, such as:

$$
\underset{3\times 3}{\mathbf{A}} = \begin{bmatrix} a_1 & 0 & 0 \\ 0 & a_2 & 0 \\ 0 & 0 & a_3 \end{bmatrix} \qquad \underset{4\times 4}{\mathbf{B}} = \begin{bmatrix} 4 & 0 & 0 & 0 \\ 0 & 1 & 0 & 0 \\ 0 & 0 & 10 & 0 \\ 0 & 0 & 0 & 5 \end{bmatrix}
$$

We will often not show all zeros for a diagonal matrix, presenting it in the form:

$$
\underset{3\times 3}{\mathbf{A}} = \begin{bmatrix} a_1 & & 0 \\ & a_2 & \\ 0 & & a_3 \end{bmatrix} \qquad \underset{4\times 4}{\mathbf{B}} = \begin{bmatrix} 4 & & & 0 \\ & 1 & & \\ & & 10 & \\ 0 & & & 5 \end{bmatrix}
$$

Two important types of diagonal matrices are the identity matrix and the scalar matrix.

Identity Matrix.   The identity matrix or unit matrix is denoted by $\mathbf{I}$. It is a diagonal matrix whose elements on the main diagonal are all 1s. Premultiplying or postmultiplying any $r \times r$ matrix $\mathbf{A}$ by the $r \times r$ identity matrix $\mathbf{I}$ leaves $\mathbf{A}$ unchanged. For example:

$$
\mathbf{IA} = \begin{bmatrix} 1 & 0 & 0 \\ 0 & 1 & 0 \\ 0 & 0 & 1 \end{bmatrix} \begin{bmatrix} a_{11} & a_{12} & a_{13} \\ a_{21} & a_{22} & a_{23} \\ a_{31} & a_{32} & a_{33} \end{bmatrix} = \begin{bmatrix} a_{11} & a_{12} & a_{13} \\ a_{21} & a_{22} & a_{23} \\ a_{31} & a_{32} & a_{33} \end{bmatrix}
$$

Similarly, we have:

$$
\mathbf{AI} = \begin{bmatrix} a_{11} & a_{12} & a_{13} \\ a_{21} & a_{22} & a_{23} \\ a_{31} & a_{32} & a_{33} \end{bmatrix} \begin{bmatrix} 1 & 0 & 0 \\ 0 & 1 & 0 \\ 0 & 0 & 1 \end{bmatrix} = \begin{bmatrix} a_{11} & a_{12} & a_{13} \\ a_{21} & a_{22} & a_{23} \\ a_{31} & a_{32} & a_{33} \end{bmatrix}
$$

Note that the identity matrix $\mathbf{I}$ therefore corresponds to the number 1 in ordinary algebra, since we have there that $1 \cdot x = x \cdot 1 = x$.

In general, we have for any $r \times r$ matrix $\mathbf{A}$:

(5.16) $$\mathbf{AI} = \mathbf{IA} = \mathbf{A}$$

Thus, the identity matrix can be inserted or dropped from a matrix expression whenever it is convenient to do so.

Scalar Matrix.   A scalar matrix is a diagonal matrix whose main-diagonal elements are the same. Two examples of scalar matrices are:

$$
\begin{bmatrix} 2 & 0 \\ 0 & 2 \end{bmatrix} \qquad \begin{bmatrix} \lambda & 0 & 0 \\ 0 & \lambda & 0 \\ 0 & 0 & \lambda \end{bmatrix}
$$

A scalar matrix can be expressed as $\lambda\mathbf{I}$, where λ is the scalar. For instance:

$$
\begin{bmatrix} 2 & 0 \\ 0 & 2 \end{bmatrix} = 2 \begin{bmatrix} 1 & 0 \\ 0 & 1 \end{bmatrix} = 2\mathbf{I}
$$

$$
\begin{bmatrix} \lambda & 0 & 0 \\ 0 & \lambda & 0 \\ 0 & 0 & \lambda \end{bmatrix} = \lambda \begin{bmatrix} 1 & 0 & 0 \\ 0 & 1 & 0 \\ 0 & 0 & 1 \end{bmatrix} = \lambda\mathbf{I}
$$

Multiplying an $r \times r$ matrix $\mathbf{A}$ by the $r \times r$ scalar matrix $\lambda\mathbf{I}$ is equivalent to multiplying $\mathbf{A}$ by the scalar λ.

Vector and Matrix with All Elements Unity

A column vector with all elements 1 will be denoted by $\mathbf{1}$:

(5.17)
$$
\underset{r\times 1}{\mathbf{1}} = \begin{bmatrix} 1 \\ 1 \\ 1 \\ \vdots \\ 1 \end{bmatrix}
$$

and a square matrix with all elements 1 will be denoted by $\mathbf{J}$:

(5.18)
$$
\underset{r\times r}{\mathbf{J}} = \begin{bmatrix} 1 & \cdots & 1 \\ \vdots & & \vdots \\ 1 & \cdots & 1 \end{bmatrix}
$$

For instance, we have:

$$
\underset{3\times 1}{\mathbf{1}} = \begin{bmatrix} 1 \\ 1 \\ 1 \end{bmatrix} \qquad \underset{3\times 3}{\mathbf{J}} = \begin{bmatrix} 1 & 1 & 1 \\ 1 & 1 & 1 \\ 1 & 1 & 1 \end{bmatrix}
$$

Note that for an $n \times 1$ vector $\mathbf{1}$ we obtain:

$$
\underset{1\times 1}{\mathbf{1'1}} = [1 \quad \cdots \quad 1] \begin{bmatrix} 1 \\ \vdots \\ 1 \end{bmatrix} = [n] = n
$$

and:

$$
\underset{n \times n}{\mathbf{11}'} = \begin{bmatrix} 1 \\ \vdots \\ 1 \end{bmatrix} [1 \quad \cdots \quad 1] = \begin{bmatrix} 1 & \cdots & 1 \\ \vdots & & \vdots \\ 1 & \cdots & 1 \end{bmatrix} = \underset{n \times n}{\mathbf{J}}
$$

Zero Vector

A zero vector is a vector containing only zeros. The zero column vector will be denoted by $\mathbf{0}$:

(5.19)
$$
\underset{r \times 1}{\mathbf{0}} = \begin{bmatrix} 0 \\ 0 \\ \vdots \\ 0 \end{bmatrix}
$$

For example, we have:

$$
\underset{3 \times 1}{\mathbf{0}} = \begin{bmatrix} 0 \\ 0 \\ 0 \end{bmatrix}
$$

5.5 Linear Dependence and Rank of Matrix

Linear Dependence

Consider the following matrix:

$$
\mathbf{A} = \begin{bmatrix} 1 & 2 & 5 & 1 \\ 2 & 2 & 10 & 6 \\ 3 & 4 & 15 & 1 \end{bmatrix}
$$

Let us think now of the columns of this matrix as vectors. Thus, we view $\mathbf{A}$ as being made up of four column vectors. It happens here that the columns are interrelated in a special manner. Note that the third column vector is a multiple of the first column vector:

$$
\begin{bmatrix} 5 \\ 10 \\ 15 \end{bmatrix} = 5 \begin{bmatrix} 1 \\ 2 \\ 3 \end{bmatrix}
$$

We say that the columns of $\mathbf{A}$ are linearly dependent. They contain redundant information, so to speak, since one column can be obtained as a linear combination of the others.

We define the set of c column vectors $\mathbf{C}_1, \ldots, \mathbf{C}_c$ in an $r \times c$ matrix to be linearly dependent if one vector can be expressed as a linear combination of the others. If no vector in the set can be so expressed, we define the set of vectors to be linearly independent. A more general, though equivalent, definition is:

(5.20) When c scalars $\lambda_1, \ldots, \lambda_c$, not all zero, can be found such that:

$$
\lambda_1 \mathbf{C}_1 + \lambda_2 \mathbf{C}_2 + \cdots + \lambda_c \mathbf{C}_c = \mathbf{0}
$$

where **0** denotes the zero column vector, the c column vectors are *linearly dependent*. If the only set of scalars for which the equality holds is $\lambda_1 = 0, \ldots, \lambda_c = 0$, the set of c column vectors is *linearly independent*.

To illustrate for our example, $\lambda_1 = 5, \lambda_2 = 0, \lambda_3 = -1, \lambda_4 = 0$ leads to:

$$
5 \begin{bmatrix} 1 \\ 2 \\ 3 \end{bmatrix} + 0 \begin{bmatrix} 2 \\ 2 \\ 4 \end{bmatrix} - 1 \begin{bmatrix} 5 \\ 10 \\ 15 \end{bmatrix} + 0 \begin{bmatrix} 1 \\ 6 \\ 1 \end{bmatrix} = \begin{bmatrix} 0 \\ 0 \\ 0 \end{bmatrix}
$$

Hence, the column vectors are linearly dependent. Note that some of the λ_j equal zero here. For linear dependence, it is only required that not all λ_j be zero.

Rank of Matrix

The rank of a matrix is defined to be the maximum number of linearly independent columns in the matrix. We know that the rank of **A** in our earlier example cannot be 4, since the four columns are linearly dependent. We can, however, find three columns (1, 2, and 4) which are linearly independent. There are no scalars $\lambda_1, \lambda_2, \lambda_4$ such that $\lambda_1 \mathbf{C}_1 + \lambda_2 \mathbf{C}_2 + \lambda_4 \mathbf{C}_4 = \mathbf{0}$ other than $\lambda_1 = \lambda_2 = \lambda_4 = 0$. Thus, the rank of **A** in our example is 3.

The rank of a matrix is unique and can equivalently be defined as the maximum number of linearly independent rows. It follows that the rank of an $r \times c$ matrix cannot exceed $\min(r, c)$, the minimum of the two values r and c.

When a matrix is the product of two matrices, its rank cannot exceed the smaller of the two ranks for the matrices being multiplied. Thus, if $\mathbf{C} = \mathbf{AB}$, the rank of **C** cannot exceed $\min(\text{rank } \mathbf{A}, \text{rank } \mathbf{B})$.

5.6   Inverse of a Matrix

In ordinary algebra, the inverse of a number is its reciprocal. Thus, the inverse of 6 is $\frac{1}{6}$. A number multiplied by its inverse always equals 1:

$$
6 \cdot \frac{1}{6} = \frac{1}{6} \cdot 6 = 1
$$

$$
x \cdot \frac{1}{x} = x \cdot x^{-1} = x^{-1} \cdot x = 1
$$

In matrix algebra, the inverse of a matrix **A** is another matrix, denoted by $\mathbf{A}^{-1}$, such that:

(5.21)
$$
\mathbf{A}^{-1}\mathbf{A} = \mathbf{A}\mathbf{A}^{-1} = \mathbf{I}
$$

where **I** is the identity matrix. Thus, again, the identity matrix **I** plays the same role as the number 1 in ordinary algebra. An inverse of a matrix is defined only for square matrices. Even so, many square matrices do not have an inverse. If a square matrix does have an inverse, the inverse is unique.

Examples

1. The inverse of the matrix:

$$\underset{2\times 2}{\mathbf{A}} = \begin{bmatrix} 2 & 4 \\ 3 & 1 \end{bmatrix}$$

is:

$$\underset{2\times 2}{\mathbf{A}^{-1}} = \begin{bmatrix} -.1 & .4 \\ .3 & -.2 \end{bmatrix}$$

since:

$$\mathbf{A}^{-1}\mathbf{A} = \begin{bmatrix} -.1 & .4 \\ .3 & -.2 \end{bmatrix}\begin{bmatrix} 2 & 4 \\ 3 & 1 \end{bmatrix} = \begin{bmatrix} 1 & 0 \\ 0 & 1 \end{bmatrix} = \mathbf{I}$$

or:

$$\mathbf{A}\mathbf{A}^{-1} = \begin{bmatrix} 2 & 4 \\ 3 & 1 \end{bmatrix}\begin{bmatrix} -.1 & .4 \\ .3 & -.2 \end{bmatrix} = \begin{bmatrix} 1 & 0 \\ 0 & 1 \end{bmatrix} = \mathbf{I}$$

2. The inverse of the matrix:

$$\underset{3\times 3}{\mathbf{A}} = \begin{bmatrix} 3 & 0 & 0 \\ 0 & 4 & 0 \\ 0 & 0 & 2 \end{bmatrix}$$

is:

$$\underset{3\times 3}{\mathbf{A}^{-1}} = \begin{bmatrix} \frac{1}{3} & 0 & 0 \\ 0 & \frac{1}{4} & 0 \\ 0 & 0 & \frac{1}{2} \end{bmatrix}$$

since:

$$\mathbf{A}^{-1}\mathbf{A} = \begin{bmatrix} \frac{1}{3} & 0 & 0 \\ 0 & \frac{1}{4} & 0 \\ 0 & 0 & \frac{1}{2} \end{bmatrix}\begin{bmatrix} 3 & 0 & 0 \\ 0 & 4 & 0 \\ 0 & 0 & 2 \end{bmatrix} = \begin{bmatrix} 1 & 0 & 0 \\ 0 & 1 & 0 \\ 0 & 0 & 1 \end{bmatrix} = \mathbf{I}$$

Note that the inverse of a diagonal matrix is a diagonal matrix consisting simply of the reciprocals of the elements on the diagonal.

Finding the Inverse

Up to this point, the inverse of a matrix **A** has been given, and we have only checked to make sure it is the inverse by seeing whether or not $\mathbf{A}^{-1}\mathbf{A} = \mathbf{I}$. But how does one find the inverse, and when does it exist?

An inverse of a square $r \times r$ matrix exists if the rank of the matrix is r. Such a matrix is said to be *nonsingular* or of *full rank*. An $r \times r$ matrix with rank less than r is said to be *singular* or *not of full rank*, and does not have an inverse. The inverse of an $r \times r$ matrix of full rank also has rank r.

Finding the inverse of a matrix can often require a large amount of computing. We shall take the approach in this book that the inverse of a 2×2 matrix and a 3×3 matrix can be calculated by hand. For any larger matrix, one ordinarily uses a computer or a programmable calculator to find the inverse, unless the matrix is of a special form such as a diagonal matrix. It can be shown that the inverses for 2×2 and 3×3 matrices are as follows:

1. If:

$$\underset{2\times 2}{\mathbf{A}} = \begin{bmatrix} a & b \\ c & d \end{bmatrix}$$

then:

(5.22)
$$\underset{2\times 2}{\mathbf{A}^{-1}} = \begin{bmatrix} a & b \\ c & d \end{bmatrix}^{-1} = \begin{bmatrix} \dfrac{d}{D} & \dfrac{-b}{D} \\ \dfrac{-c}{D} & \dfrac{a}{D} \end{bmatrix}$$

where:

(5.22a)
$$D = ad - bc$$

D is called the *determinant* of the matrix $\mathbf{A}$. If $\mathbf{A}$ were singular, its determinant would equal zero and no inverse of $\mathbf{A}$ would exist.

2. If:

$$\underset{3\times 3}{\mathbf{B}} = \begin{bmatrix} a & b & c \\ d & e & f \\ g & h & k \end{bmatrix}$$

then:

(5.23)
$$\underset{3\times 3}{\mathbf{B}^{-1}} = \begin{bmatrix} a & b & c \\ d & e & f \\ g & h & k \end{bmatrix}^{-1} = \begin{bmatrix} A & B & C \\ D & E & F \\ G & H & K \end{bmatrix}$$

where:

(5.23a)
$$\begin{array}{lll} A = (ek - fh)/Z & B = -(bk - ch)/Z & C = (bf - ce)/Z \\ D = -(dk - fg)/Z & E = (ak - cg)/Z & F = -(af - cd)/Z \\ G = (dh - eg)/Z & H = -(ah - bg)/Z & K = (ae - bd)/Z \end{array}$$

and:

(5.23b)
$$Z = a(ek - fh) - b(dk - fg) + c(dh - eg)$$

Z is called the determinant of the matrix $\mathbf{B}$.

Let us use (5.22) to find the inverse of:

$$\mathbf{A} = \begin{bmatrix} 2 & 4 \\ 3 & 1 \end{bmatrix}$$

We have:

$$\begin{array}{ll} a = 2 & b = 4 \\ c = 3 & d = 1 \end{array}$$

$$D = ad - bc = 2(1) - 4(3) = -10$$

Hence:

$$\mathbf{A}^{-1} = \begin{bmatrix} \dfrac{1}{-10} & \dfrac{-4}{-10} \\[2ex] \dfrac{-3}{-10} & \dfrac{2}{-10} \end{bmatrix} = \begin{bmatrix} -.1 & .4 \\ .3 & -.2 \end{bmatrix}$$

as was given in an earlier example.

When an inverse $\mathbf{A}^{-1}$ has been obtained by hand calculations or from a computer program for which the accuracy of inverting a matrix is not known, it may be wise to compute $\mathbf{A}^{-1}\mathbf{A}$ to check whether the product equals the identity matrix, allowing for minor rounding departures from 0 and 1.

Regression Example

The principal inverse matrix encountered in regression analysis is the inverse of the matrix $\mathbf{X}'\mathbf{X}$ in (5.14):

$$\underset{2 \times 2}{\mathbf{X}'\mathbf{X}} = \begin{bmatrix} n & \sum X_i \\ \sum X_i & \sum X_i^2 \end{bmatrix}$$

Using rule (5.22), we have:

$$a = n \qquad b = \sum X_i$$
$$c = \sum X_i \qquad d = \sum X_i^2$$

so that:

$$D = n \sum X_i^2 - \left(\sum X_i \right) \left(\sum X_i \right) = n \left[\sum X_i^2 - \frac{(\sum X_i)^2}{n} \right] = n \sum (X_i - \bar{X})^2$$

Hence:

$$(5.24) \qquad \underset{2 \times 2}{(\mathbf{X}'\mathbf{X})^{-1}} = \begin{bmatrix} \dfrac{\sum X_i^2}{n\,\Sigma(X_i - \bar{X})^2} & \dfrac{-\sum X_i}{n\,\Sigma(X_i - \bar{X})^2} \\[3ex] \dfrac{-\sum X_i}{n\,\Sigma(X_i - \bar{X})^2} & \dfrac{n}{n\,\Sigma(X_i - \bar{X})^2} \end{bmatrix}$$

Since $\sum X_i = n\bar{X}$ and $\Sigma(X_i - \bar{X})^2 = \sum X_i^2 - n\bar{X}^2$, we can simplify (5.24):

$$(5.24a) \qquad \underset{2 \times 2}{(\mathbf{X}'\mathbf{X})^{-1}} = \begin{bmatrix} \dfrac{1}{n} + \dfrac{\bar{X}^2}{\Sigma(X_i - \bar{X})^2} & \dfrac{-\bar{X}}{\Sigma(X_i - \bar{X})^2} \\[3ex] \dfrac{-\bar{X}}{\Sigma(X_i - \bar{X})^2} & \dfrac{1}{\Sigma(X_i - \bar{X})^2} \end{bmatrix}$$

Uses of Inverse Matrix

In ordinary algebra, we solve an equation of the type:

$$5y = 20$$

by multiplying both sides of the equation by the inverse of 5, namely:

$$\frac{1}{5}(5y) = \frac{1}{5}(20)$$

and we obtain the solution:

$$y = \frac{1}{5}(20) = 4$$

In matrix algebra, if we have an equation:

$$\mathbf{AY} = \mathbf{C}$$

we correspondingly premultiply both sides by $\mathbf{A}^{-1}$, assuming $\mathbf{A}$ has an inverse:

$$\mathbf{A}^{-1}\mathbf{AY} = \mathbf{A}^{-1}\mathbf{C}$$

Since $\mathbf{A}^{-1}\mathbf{AY} = \mathbf{IY} = \mathbf{Y}$, we obtain the solution:

$$\mathbf{Y} = \mathbf{A}^{-1}\mathbf{C}$$

To illustrate this use, suppose we have two simultaneous equations:

$$2y_1 + 4y_2 = 20$$
$$3y_1 + y_2 = 10$$

which can be written as follows in matrix notation:

$$\begin{bmatrix} 2 & 4 \\ 3 & 1 \end{bmatrix} \begin{bmatrix} y_1 \\ y_2 \end{bmatrix} = \begin{bmatrix} 20 \\ 10 \end{bmatrix}$$

The solution of these equations then is:

$$\begin{bmatrix} y_1 \\ y_2 \end{bmatrix} = \begin{bmatrix} 2 & 4 \\ 3 & 1 \end{bmatrix}^{-1} \begin{bmatrix} 20 \\ 10 \end{bmatrix}$$

Earlier we found the required inverse, so we obtain:

$$\begin{bmatrix} y_1 \\ y_2 \end{bmatrix} = \begin{bmatrix} -.1 & .4 \\ .3 & -.2 \end{bmatrix} \begin{bmatrix} 20 \\ 10 \end{bmatrix} = \begin{bmatrix} 2 \\ 4 \end{bmatrix}$$

Hence, $y_1 = 2$ and $y_2 = 4$ satisfy these two equations.

5.7   Some Basic Theorems for Matrices

We list here, without proof, some basic theorems for matrices which we will utilize in later work.

$$(5.25) \qquad\qquad \mathbf{A} + \mathbf{B} = \mathbf{B} + \mathbf{A}$$

$$(5.26) \qquad\qquad (\mathbf{A} + \mathbf{B}) + \mathbf{C} = \mathbf{A} + (\mathbf{B} + \mathbf{C})$$

$$(5.27) \qquad\qquad (\mathbf{AB})\mathbf{C} = \mathbf{A}(\mathbf{BC})$$

$$(5.28) \qquad\qquad \mathbf{C}(\mathbf{A} + \mathbf{B}) = \mathbf{CA} + \mathbf{CB}$$

$$(5.29) \qquad\qquad \lambda(\mathbf{A} + \mathbf{B}) = \lambda\mathbf{A} + \lambda\mathbf{B}$$

$$(5.30) \qquad\qquad (\mathbf{A}')' = \mathbf{A}$$

$$(5.31) \qquad\qquad (\mathbf{A} + \mathbf{B})' = \mathbf{A}' + \mathbf{B}'$$

$$(5.32) \qquad\qquad (\mathbf{AB})' = \mathbf{B}'\mathbf{A}'$$

$$(5.33) \qquad\qquad (\mathbf{ABC})' = \mathbf{C}'\mathbf{B}'\mathbf{A}'$$

$$(5.34) \qquad\qquad (\mathbf{AB})^{-1} = \mathbf{B}^{-1}\mathbf{A}^{-1}$$

$$(5.35) \qquad\qquad (\mathbf{ABC})^{-1} = \mathbf{C}^{-1}\mathbf{B}^{-1}\mathbf{A}^{-1}$$

$$(5.36) \qquad\qquad (\mathbf{A}^{-1})^{-1} = \mathbf{A}$$

$$(5.37) \qquad\qquad (\mathbf{A}')^{-1} = (\mathbf{A}^{-1})'$$

5.8   Random Vectors and Matrices

A random vector or a random matrix contains elements that are random variables. Thus, the observations vector $\mathbf{Y}$ in (5.4) is a random vector since the Y_i elements are random variables.

Expectation of Random Vector or Matrix

Suppose we have $n = 3$ observations in the observations vector $\mathbf{Y}$:

$$\underset{3 \times 1}{\mathbf{Y}} = \begin{bmatrix} Y_1 \\ Y_2 \\ Y_3 \end{bmatrix}$$

The expected value of $\mathbf{Y}$ is a vector, denoted by $\mathbf{E}\{\mathbf{Y}\}$, that is defined as follows:

$$\underset{3 \times 1}{\mathbf{E}\{\mathbf{Y}\}} = \begin{bmatrix} E\{Y_1\} \\ E\{Y_2\} \\ E\{Y_3\} \end{bmatrix}$$

Thus, the expected value of a random vector is a vector whose elements are the expected values of the random variables that are the elements of the random vector. Similarly, the expectation of a random matrix is a matrix whose elements are the expected values of the corresponding random variables in the original matrix. We encountered a vector of expected values earlier in (5.9).

In general, for a random vector $\mathbf{Y}$ the expectation is:

$$(5.38) \qquad \underset{n \times 1}{\mathbf{E}\{\mathbf{Y}\}} = [E\{Y_i\}] \qquad i = 1, \ldots, n$$

and for a random matrix $\mathbf{Y}$ with dimension $n \times p$, the expectation is:

$$(5.39) \qquad \underset{n \times p}{\mathbf{E}\{\mathbf{Y}\}} = [E\{Y_{ij}\}] \qquad i = 1, \ldots, n; \quad j = 1, \ldots, p$$

Regression Example.   Suppose the number of cases in a regression application is $n = 3$. The three error terms ε_1, ε_2, ε_3 each have expectation zero. For the error terms vector:

$$\underset{3 \times 1}{\boldsymbol{\varepsilon}} = \begin{bmatrix} \varepsilon_1 \\ \varepsilon_2 \\ \varepsilon_3 \end{bmatrix}$$

we have:

$$\underset{3 \times 1}{\mathbf{E}\{\boldsymbol{\varepsilon}\}} = \underset{3 \times 1}{\mathbf{0}}$$

since:

$$\begin{bmatrix} E\{\varepsilon_1\} \\ E\{\varepsilon_2\} \\ E\{\varepsilon_3\} \end{bmatrix} = \begin{bmatrix} 0 \\ 0 \\ 0 \end{bmatrix}$$

Variance-Covariance Matrix of Random Vector

Consider again the random vector $\mathbf{Y}$ consisting of three observations Y_1, Y_2, Y_3. The variances of the three random variables, $\sigma^2\{Y_i\}$, and the covariances between any two of the random variables, $\sigma\{Y_i, Y_j\}$, are assembled in the *variance-covariance matrix of* $\mathbf{Y}$, denoted by $\boldsymbol{\sigma}^2\{\mathbf{Y}\}$, in the following form:

$$(5.40) \qquad \boldsymbol{\sigma}^2\{\mathbf{Y}\} = \begin{bmatrix} \sigma^2\{Y_1\} & \sigma\{Y_1, Y_2\} & \sigma\{Y_1, Y_3\} \\ \sigma\{Y_2, Y_1\} & \sigma^2\{Y_2\} & \sigma\{Y_2, Y_3\} \\ \sigma\{Y_3, Y_1\} & \sigma\{Y_3, Y_2\} & \sigma^2\{Y_3\} \end{bmatrix}$$

Note that the variances are on the main diagonal, and the covariance $\sigma\{Y_i, Y_j\}$ is found in the ith row and jth column of the matrix. Thus, $\sigma\{Y_2, Y_1\}$ is found in the second row, first column, and $\sigma\{Y_1, Y_2\}$ is found in the first row, second column. Remember, of course, that $\sigma\{Y_2, Y_1\} = \sigma\{Y_1, Y_2\}$. Since $\sigma\{Y_i, Y_j\} = \sigma\{Y_j, Y_i\}$ for all $i \neq j$, $\boldsymbol{\sigma}^2\{\mathbf{Y}\}$ is a symmetric matrix.

It follows readily that:

(5.41) $$\boldsymbol{\sigma}^2\{\mathbf{Y}\} = \mathbf{E}\{[\mathbf{Y} - \mathbf{E}\{\mathbf{Y}\}][\mathbf{Y} - \mathbf{E}\{\mathbf{Y}\}]'\}$$

For our illustration, we have:

$$\boldsymbol{\sigma}^2\{\mathbf{Y}\} = \mathbf{E}\left\{\begin{bmatrix} Y_1 - E\{Y_1\} \\ Y_2 - E\{Y_2\} \\ Y_3 - E\{Y_3\} \end{bmatrix} [Y_1 - E\{Y_1\} \quad Y_2 - E\{Y_2\} \quad Y_3 - E\{Y_3\}]\right\}$$

Multiplying the two matrices and then taking expectations, we obtain:

Location in Product	Term	Expected Value
Row 1, column 1	$(Y_1 - E\{Y_1\})^2$	$\sigma^2\{Y_1\}$
Row 1, column 2	$(Y_1 - E\{Y_1\})(Y_2 - E\{Y_2\})$	$\sigma\{Y_1, Y_2\}$
Row 1, column 3	$(Y_1 - E\{Y_1\})(Y_3 - E\{Y_3\})$	$\sigma\{Y_1, Y_3\}$
Row 2, column 1	$(Y_2 - E\{Y_2\})(Y_1 - E\{Y_1\})$	$\sigma\{Y_2, Y_1\}$
etc.	etc.	etc.

This, of course, leads to the variance-covariance matrix in (5.40). Remember the definitions of variance and covariance in (A.15) and (A.21), respectively, when taking expectations.

To generalize, the variance-covariance matrix for an $n \times 1$ random vector $\mathbf{Y}$ is:

(5.42) $$\underset{n \times n}{\boldsymbol{\sigma}^2\{\mathbf{Y}\}} = \begin{bmatrix} \sigma^2\{Y_1\} & \sigma\{Y_1, Y_2\} & \cdots & \sigma\{Y_1, Y_n\} \\ \sigma\{Y_2, Y_1\} & \sigma^2\{Y_2\} & \cdots & \sigma\{Y_2, Y_n\} \\ \vdots & \vdots & & \vdots \\ \sigma\{Y_n, Y_1\} & \sigma\{Y_n, Y_2\} & \cdots & \sigma^2\{Y_n\} \end{bmatrix}$$

Note again that $\boldsymbol{\sigma}^2\{\mathbf{Y}\}$ is a symmetric matrix.

Regression Example. Let us return to the example based on $n = 3$ cases. Suppose that the three error terms have constant variance, $\sigma^2\{\varepsilon_i\} = \sigma^2$, and are uncorrelated so that $\sigma\{\varepsilon_i, \varepsilon_j\} = 0$ for $i \neq j$. The variance-covariance matrix for the random vector $\boldsymbol{\varepsilon}$ of the previous example is therefore as follows:

$$\underset{3 \times 3}{\boldsymbol{\sigma}^2\{\boldsymbol{\varepsilon}\}} = \begin{bmatrix} \sigma^2 & 0 & 0 \\ 0 & \sigma^2 & 0 \\ 0 & 0 & \sigma^2 \end{bmatrix}$$

Note that all variances are σ^2 and all covariances are zero. Note also that this variance-covariance matrix is a scalar matrix, with the common variance σ^2 the scalar. Hence, we can express the variance-covariance matrix in the following simple fashion:

$$\underset{3 \times 3}{\boldsymbol{\sigma}^2\{\boldsymbol{\varepsilon}\}} = \underset{3 \times 3}{\sigma^2\mathbf{I}}$$

since:

$$\sigma^2\mathbf{I} = \sigma^2 \begin{bmatrix} 1 & 0 & 0 \\ 0 & 1 & 0 \\ 0 & 0 & 1 \end{bmatrix} = \begin{bmatrix} \sigma^2 & 0 & 0 \\ 0 & \sigma^2 & 0 \\ 0 & 0 & \sigma^2 \end{bmatrix}$$

Some Basic Theorems

Frequently, we shall encounter a random vector **W** which is obtained by premultiplying the random vector **Y** by a constant matrix **A** (a matrix whose elements are fixed):

(5.43)
$$\mathbf{W} = \mathbf{AY}$$

Some basic theorems for this case are:

(5.44)
$$\mathbf{E}\{\mathbf{A}\} = \mathbf{A}$$

(5.45)
$$\mathbf{E}\{\mathbf{W}\} = \mathbf{E}\{\mathbf{AY}\} = \mathbf{AE}\{\mathbf{Y}\}$$

(5.46)
$$\boldsymbol{\sigma}^2\{\mathbf{W}\} = \boldsymbol{\sigma}^2\{\mathbf{AY}\} = \mathbf{A}\boldsymbol{\sigma}^2\{\mathbf{Y}\}\mathbf{A}'$$

where $\boldsymbol{\sigma}^2\{\mathbf{Y}\}$ is the variance-covariance matrix of **Y**.

Example.   As a simple illustration of the use of these theorems, consider:

$$\underset{\substack{\mathbf{W} \\ 2\times 1}}{\begin{bmatrix} W_1 \\ W_2 \end{bmatrix}} = \underset{\substack{\mathbf{A} \\ 2\times 2}}{\begin{bmatrix} 1 & -1 \\ 1 & 1 \end{bmatrix}} \underset{\substack{\mathbf{Y} \\ 2\times 1}}{\begin{bmatrix} Y_1 \\ Y_2 \end{bmatrix}} = \begin{bmatrix} Y_1 - Y_2 \\ Y_1 + Y_2 \end{bmatrix}$$

We then have by (5.45):

$$\underset{2\times 1}{\mathbf{E}\{\mathbf{W}\}} = \begin{bmatrix} 1 & -1 \\ 1 & 1 \end{bmatrix} \begin{bmatrix} E\{Y_1\} \\ E\{Y_2\} \end{bmatrix} = \begin{bmatrix} E\{Y_1\} - E\{Y_2\} \\ E\{Y_1\} + E\{Y_2\} \end{bmatrix}$$

and by (5.46):

$$\underset{2\times 2}{\boldsymbol{\sigma}^2\{\mathbf{W}\}} = \begin{bmatrix} 1 & -1 \\ 1 & 1 \end{bmatrix} \begin{bmatrix} \sigma^2\{Y_1\} & \sigma\{Y_1, Y_2\} \\ \sigma\{Y_2, Y_1\} & \sigma^2\{Y_2\} \end{bmatrix} \begin{bmatrix} 1 & 1 \\ -1 & 1 \end{bmatrix}$$

$$= \begin{bmatrix} \sigma^2\{Y_1\} + \sigma^2\{Y_2\} - 2\sigma\{Y_1, Y_2\} & \sigma^2\{Y_1\} - \sigma^2\{Y_2\} \\ \sigma^2\{Y_1\} - \sigma^2\{Y_2\} & \sigma^2\{Y_1\} + \sigma^2\{Y_2\} + 2\sigma\{Y_1, Y_2\} \end{bmatrix}$$

Thus:

$$\sigma^2\{W_1\} = \sigma^2\{Y_1 - Y_2\} = \sigma^2\{Y_1\} + \sigma^2\{Y_2\} - 2\sigma\{Y_1, Y_2\}$$

$$\sigma^2\{W_2\} = \sigma^2\{Y_1 + Y_2\} = \sigma^2\{Y_1\} + \sigma^2\{Y_2\} + 2\sigma\{Y_1, Y_2\}$$

$$\sigma\{W_1, W_2\} = \sigma\{Y_1 - Y_2, Y_1 + Y_2\} = \sigma^2\{Y_1\} - \sigma^2\{Y_2\}$$

5.9   Simple Linear Regression Model in Matrix Terms

We are now ready to develop simple linear regression in matrix terms. Remember again that we will not present any new results, but shall only state in matrix terms the results obtained earlier. We begin with the normal error regression model (2.1):

(5.47)
$$Y_i = \beta_0 + \beta_1 X_i + \varepsilon_i \qquad i = 1, \ldots, n$$

This implies:

(5.47a)
$$Y_1 = \beta_0 + \beta_1 X_1 + \varepsilon_1$$
$$Y_2 = \beta_0 + \beta_1 X_2 + \varepsilon_2$$
$$\vdots$$
$$Y_n = \beta_0 + \beta_1 X_n + \varepsilon_n$$

We defined earlier the observations vector $\mathbf{Y}$ in (5.4), the $\mathbf{X}$ matrix in (5.6), and the $\boldsymbol{\varepsilon}$ vector in (5.10). Let us repeat these definitions and also define the $\boldsymbol{\beta}$ vector of the regression coefficients:

(5.48)
$$\underset{n\times 1}{\mathbf{Y}} = \begin{bmatrix} Y_1 \\ Y_2 \\ \vdots \\ Y_n \end{bmatrix} \qquad \underset{n\times 2}{\mathbf{X}} = \begin{bmatrix} 1 & X_1 \\ 1 & X_2 \\ \vdots & \vdots \\ 1 & X_n \end{bmatrix} \qquad \underset{2\times 1}{\boldsymbol{\beta}} = \begin{bmatrix} \beta_0 \\ \beta_1 \end{bmatrix} \qquad \underset{n\times 1}{\boldsymbol{\varepsilon}} = \begin{bmatrix} \varepsilon_1 \\ \varepsilon_2 \\ \vdots \\ \varepsilon_n \end{bmatrix}$$

Now we can write (5.47a) in matrix terms compactly as follows:

(5.49)
$$\underset{n\times 1}{\mathbf{Y}} = \underset{n\times 2}{\mathbf{X}}\underset{2\times 1}{\boldsymbol{\beta}} + \underset{n\times 1}{\boldsymbol{\varepsilon}}$$

since:

$$\begin{bmatrix} Y_1 \\ Y_2 \\ \vdots \\ Y_n \end{bmatrix} = \begin{bmatrix} 1 & X_1 \\ 1 & X_2 \\ \vdots & \vdots \\ 1 & X_n \end{bmatrix} \begin{bmatrix} \beta_0 \\ \beta_1 \end{bmatrix} + \begin{bmatrix} \varepsilon_1 \\ \varepsilon_2 \\ \vdots \\ \varepsilon_n \end{bmatrix}$$

$$= \begin{bmatrix} \beta_0 + \beta_1 X_1 \\ \beta_0 + \beta_1 X_2 \\ \vdots \\ \beta_0 + \beta_1 X_n \end{bmatrix} + \begin{bmatrix} \varepsilon_1 \\ \varepsilon_2 \\ \vdots \\ \varepsilon_n \end{bmatrix} = \begin{bmatrix} \beta_0 + \beta_1 X_1 + \varepsilon_1 \\ \beta_0 + \beta_1 X_2 + \varepsilon_2 \\ \vdots \\ \beta_0 + \beta_1 X_n + \varepsilon_n \end{bmatrix}$$

Note that $\mathbf{X}\boldsymbol{\beta}$ is the vector of the expected values of the Y_i observations since $E\{Y_i\} = \beta_0 + \beta_1 X_i$; hence:

(5.50)
$$\underset{n\times 1}{E\{\mathbf{Y}\}} = \underset{n\times 1}{\mathbf{X}\boldsymbol{\beta}}$$

where $\mathbf{E\{Y\}}$ is defined in (5.9).

The column of 1s in the $\mathbf{X}$ matrix may be viewed as consisting of the dummy variable $X_0 \equiv 1$ in the alternative regression model (1.5):

$$Y_i = \beta_0 X_0 + \beta_1 X_i + \varepsilon_i \qquad \text{where } X_0 \equiv 1$$

Thus, the $\mathbf{X}$ matrix may be considered to contain a column vector of the dummy variable X_0 and another column vector consisting of the predictor variable observations X_i.

With respect to the error terms, regression model (2.1) assumes that $E\{\varepsilon_i\} = 0$, $\sigma^2\{\varepsilon_i\} = \sigma^2$, and that the ε_i are independent normal random variables. The condition $E\{\varepsilon_i\} = 0$ in matrix terms is:

$$(5.51) \qquad\qquad \underset{n \times 1}{\mathbf{E\{\varepsilon\}}} = \underset{n \times 1}{\mathbf{0}}$$

since (5.51) states:

$$\begin{bmatrix} E\{\varepsilon_1\} \\ E\{\varepsilon_2\} \\ \vdots \\ E\{\varepsilon_n\} \end{bmatrix} = \begin{bmatrix} 0 \\ 0 \\ \vdots \\ 0 \end{bmatrix}$$

The condition that the error terms have constant variance σ^2 and that all covariances $\sigma\{\varepsilon_i, \varepsilon_j\}$ for $i \neq j$ are zero (since the ε_i are independent) is expressed in matrix terms through the variance-covariance matrix of the error terms:

$$(5.52) \qquad\qquad \underset{n \times n}{\mathbf{\sigma^2\{\varepsilon\}}} = \begin{bmatrix} \sigma^2 & 0 & 0 & \cdots & 0 \\ 0 & \sigma^2 & 0 & \cdots & 0 \\ \vdots & \vdots & \vdots & & \vdots \\ 0 & 0 & 0 & \cdots & \sigma^2 \end{bmatrix}$$

Since this is a scalar matrix, we know from the earlier example that it can be expressed in the following simple fashion:

$$(5.52a) \qquad\qquad \underset{n \times n}{\mathbf{\sigma^2\{\varepsilon\}}} = \underset{n \times n}{\sigma^2 \mathbf{I}}$$

Thus, the normal error regression model (2.1) in matrix terms is:

$$(5.53) \qquad\qquad \mathbf{Y} = \mathbf{X\beta} + \mathbf{\varepsilon}$$

where:

$\mathbf{\varepsilon}$ is a vector of independent normal random variables with $\mathbf{E\{\varepsilon\}} = \mathbf{0}$ and $\mathbf{\sigma^2\{\varepsilon\}} = \sigma^2 \mathbf{I}$

5.10   Least Squares Estimation of Regression Parameters

Normal Equations

The normal equations (1.9):

(5.54)

$$nb_0 + b_1 \sum X_i = \sum Y_i$$
$$b_0 \sum X_i + b_1 \sum X_i^2 = \sum X_i Y_i$$

in matrix terms are:

(5.55)

$$\underset{2\times2}{\mathbf{X}'\mathbf{X}} \;\; \underset{2\times1}{\mathbf{b}} \;=\; \underset{2\times1}{\mathbf{X}'\mathbf{Y}}$$

where **b** is the vector of the least squares regression coefficients:

(5.55a)

$$\underset{2\times1}{\mathbf{b}} = \begin{bmatrix} b_0 \\ b_1 \end{bmatrix}$$

To see this, recall that we obtained $\mathbf{X}'\mathbf{X}$ in (5.14) and $\mathbf{X}'\mathbf{Y}$ in (5.15). Equation (5.55) thus states:

$$\begin{bmatrix} n & \Sigma X_i \\ \Sigma X_i & \Sigma X_i^2 \end{bmatrix} \begin{bmatrix} b_0 \\ b_1 \end{bmatrix} = \begin{bmatrix} \Sigma Y_i \\ \Sigma X_i Y_i \end{bmatrix}$$

or:

$$\begin{bmatrix} nb_0 + b_1 \Sigma X_i \\ b_0 \Sigma X_i + b_1 \Sigma X_i^2 \end{bmatrix} = \begin{bmatrix} \Sigma Y_i \\ \Sigma X_i Y_i \end{bmatrix}$$

These are precisely the normal equations in (5.54).

Estimated Regression Coefficients

To obtain the estimated regression coefficients from the normal equations (5.55) by matrix methods, we premultiply both sides by the inverse of $\mathbf{X}'\mathbf{X}$ (we assume this exists):

$$(\mathbf{X}'\mathbf{X})^{-1}\mathbf{X}'\mathbf{X}\mathbf{b} = (\mathbf{X}'\mathbf{X})^{-1}\mathbf{X}'\mathbf{Y}$$

We then find, since $(\mathbf{X}'\mathbf{X})^{-1}\mathbf{X}'\mathbf{X} = \mathbf{I}$ and $\mathbf{I}\mathbf{b} = \mathbf{b}$:

(5.56)

$$\underset{2\times1}{\mathbf{b}} = \underset{2\times2}{(\mathbf{X}'\mathbf{X})^{-1}} \underset{2\times1}{\mathbf{X}'\mathbf{Y}}$$

The estimators b_0 and b_1 in **b** are the same as those given earlier in (1.10a) and (1.10b). We shall demonstrate this by an example.

Example. We shall use matrix methods to obtain the estimated regression coefficients for the Toluca Company example. The data on the Y and X variables were given in Table 1.1. Using these data, we define the $\mathbf{Y}$ observations vector and the $\mathbf{X}$ matrix as follows:

$$(5.57) \qquad (a) \quad \mathbf{Y} = \begin{bmatrix} 399 \\ 121 \\ \vdots \\ 323 \end{bmatrix} \qquad (b) \quad \mathbf{X} = \begin{bmatrix} 1 & 80 \\ 1 & 30 \\ \vdots & \vdots \\ 1 & 70 \end{bmatrix}$$

We now require the following matrix products:

$$(5.58) \qquad \mathbf{X'X} = \begin{bmatrix} 1 & 1 & \cdots & 1 \\ 80 & 30 & \cdots & 70 \end{bmatrix} \begin{bmatrix} 1 & 80 \\ 1 & 30 \\ \vdots & \vdots \\ 1 & 70 \end{bmatrix} = \begin{bmatrix} 25 & 1{,}750 \\ 1{,}750 & 142{,}300 \end{bmatrix}$$

$$(5.59) \qquad \mathbf{X'Y} = \begin{bmatrix} 1 & 1 & \cdots & 1 \\ 80 & 30 & \cdots & 70 \end{bmatrix} \begin{bmatrix} 399 \\ 121 \\ \vdots \\ 323 \end{bmatrix} = \begin{bmatrix} 7{,}807 \\ 617{,}180 \end{bmatrix}$$

Using (5.22), we find the inverse of $\mathbf{X'X}$:

$$(5.60) \qquad (\mathbf{X'X})^{-1} = \begin{bmatrix} .287475 & -.003535 \\ -.003535 & .00005051 \end{bmatrix}$$

In subsequent matrix calculations utilizing this inverse matrix and other matrix results, we shall actually utilize more digits for the matrix elements than are shown.

Finally, we employ (5.56) to obtain:

$$(5.61) \qquad \mathbf{b} = \begin{bmatrix} b_0 \\ b_1 \end{bmatrix} = (\mathbf{X'X})^{-1}\mathbf{X'Y} = \begin{bmatrix} .287475 & -.003535 \\ -.003535 & .00005051 \end{bmatrix} \begin{bmatrix} 7{,}807 \\ 617{,}180 \end{bmatrix}$$

$$= \begin{bmatrix} 62.37 \\ 3.5702 \end{bmatrix}$$

or $b_0 = 62.37$ and $b_1 = 3.5702$. These results agree with the ones in Chapter 1. Any differences would have been due to rounding effects.

Comments

1. To derive the normal equations by the method of least squares, we minimize the quantity:

$$Q = \sum [Y_i - (\beta_0 + \beta_1 X_i)]^2$$

In matrix notation:

$$(5.62) \qquad Q = (\mathbf{Y} - \mathbf{X\beta})'(\mathbf{Y} - \mathbf{X\beta})$$

Expanding, we obtain:

$$Q = \mathbf{Y'Y} - \mathbf{\beta'X'Y} - \mathbf{Y'X\beta} + \mathbf{\beta'X'X\beta}$$

since $(\mathbf{X}\boldsymbol{\beta})' = \boldsymbol{\beta}'\mathbf{X}'$ by (5.32). Note now that $\mathbf{Y}'\mathbf{X}\boldsymbol{\beta}$ is 1×1, hence is equal to its transpose, which according to (5.33) is $\boldsymbol{\beta}'\mathbf{X}'\mathbf{Y}$. Thus, we find:

$$(5.63) \qquad Q = \mathbf{Y}'\mathbf{Y} - 2\boldsymbol{\beta}'\mathbf{X}'\mathbf{Y} + \boldsymbol{\beta}'\mathbf{X}'\mathbf{X}\boldsymbol{\beta}$$

To find the value of $\boldsymbol{\beta}$ that minimizes Q, we differentiate with respect to β_0 and β_1. Let:

$$(5.64) \qquad \frac{\partial}{\partial\boldsymbol{\beta}}(Q) = \begin{bmatrix} \dfrac{\partial Q}{\partial \beta_0} \\[2ex] \dfrac{\partial Q}{\partial \beta_1} \end{bmatrix}$$

Then it follows that:

$$(5.65) \qquad \frac{\partial}{\partial\boldsymbol{\beta}}(Q) = -2\mathbf{X}'\mathbf{Y} + 2\mathbf{X}'\mathbf{X}\boldsymbol{\beta}$$

Equating to the zero vector, dividing by 2, and substituting $\mathbf{b}$ for $\boldsymbol{\beta}$ gives the matrix form of the least squares normal equations in (5.55).

2. A comparison of the normal equations and $\mathbf{X}'\mathbf{X}$ shows that whenever the columns of $\mathbf{X}'\mathbf{X}$ are linearly dependent, the normal equations will be linearly dependent also. No unique solutions can then be obtained for b_0 and b_1. Fortunately, in most regression applications, the columns of $\mathbf{X}'\mathbf{X}$ are linearly independent, leading to unique solutions for b_0 and b_1.   ∎

5.11   Fitted Values and Residuals

Fitted Values

Let the vector of the fitted values $\hat{Y}_i$ be denoted by $\hat{\mathbf{Y}}$:

$$(5.66) \qquad \underset{n \times 1}{\hat{\mathbf{Y}}} = \begin{bmatrix} \hat{Y}_1 \\ \hat{Y}_2 \\ \vdots \\ \hat{Y}_n \end{bmatrix}$$

In matrix notation, we then have:

$$(5.67) \qquad \underset{n \times 1}{\hat{\mathbf{Y}}} = \underset{n \times 2}{\mathbf{X}} \; \underset{2 \times 1}{\mathbf{b}}$$

because:

$$\begin{bmatrix} \hat{Y}_1 \\ \hat{Y}_2 \\ \vdots \\ \hat{Y}_n \end{bmatrix} = \begin{bmatrix} 1 & X_1 \\ 1 & X_2 \\ \vdots & \vdots \\ 1 & X_n \end{bmatrix} \begin{bmatrix} b_0 \\ b_1 \end{bmatrix} = \begin{bmatrix} b_0 + b_1 X_1 \\ b_0 + b_1 X_2 \\ \vdots \\ b_0 + b_1 X_n \end{bmatrix}$$

Example.   For the Toluca Company example, we obtain the vector of fitted values using the matrices in (5.57b) and (5.61):

$$(5.68) \qquad \hat{\mathbf{Y}} = \mathbf{Xb} = \begin{bmatrix} 1 & 80 \\ 1 & 30 \\ \vdots & \vdots \\ 1 & 70 \end{bmatrix} \begin{bmatrix} 62.37 \\ 3.5702 \end{bmatrix} = \begin{bmatrix} 347.98 \\ 169.47 \\ \vdots \\ 312.28 \end{bmatrix}$$

The fitted values are the same, of course, as in Table 1.2.

Hat Matrix.   We can express the matrix result for $\hat{\mathbf{Y}}$ in (5.67) as follows by using the expression for **b** in (5.56):

$$\hat{\mathbf{Y}} = \mathbf{X}(\mathbf{X}'\mathbf{X})^{-1}\mathbf{X}'\mathbf{Y}$$

or, equivalently:

$$(5.69) \qquad \underset{n \times 1}{\hat{\mathbf{Y}}} = \underset{n \times n}{\mathbf{H}} \underset{n \times 1}{\mathbf{Y}}$$

where:

$$(5.69a) \qquad \underset{n \times n}{\mathbf{H}} = \mathbf{X}(\mathbf{X}'\mathbf{X})^{-1}\mathbf{X}'$$

We see from (5.69) that the fitted values $\hat{Y}_i$ can be expressed as linear combinations of the response variable observations Y_i, with the coefficients being elements of the matrix **H**. The **H** matrix involves only the observations on the predictor variable X, as is evident from (5.69a).

The square $n \times n$ matrix **H** is called the *hat matrix*. It plays an important role in diagnostics for regression analysis, as we shall see in Chapter 9 when we consider whether regression results are unduly influenced by one or a few observations. The matrix **H** is symmetric and has the special property (called idempotency):

$$(5.70) \qquad \mathbf{HH} = \mathbf{H}$$

In general, a matrix **M** is said to be *idempotent* if $\mathbf{MM} = \mathbf{M}$.

Residuals

Let the vector of the residuals $e_i = Y_i - \hat{Y}_i$ be denoted by **e**:

$$(5.71) \qquad \underset{n \times 1}{\mathbf{e}} = \begin{bmatrix} e_1 \\ e_2 \\ \vdots \\ e_n \end{bmatrix}$$

In matrix notation, we then have:

$$(5.72) \qquad \underset{n \times 1}{\mathbf{e}} = \underset{n \times 1}{\mathbf{Y}} - \underset{n \times 1}{\hat{\mathbf{Y}}} = \underset{n \times 1}{\mathbf{Y}} - \underset{n \times 1}{\mathbf{Xb}}$$

Example.   For the Toluca Company example, we obtain the vector of the residuals by using the results in (5.57a) and (5.68):

$$(5.73) \qquad \mathbf{e} = \begin{bmatrix} 399 \\ 121 \\ \vdots \\ 323 \end{bmatrix} - \begin{bmatrix} 347.98 \\ 169.47 \\ \vdots \\ 312.28 \end{bmatrix} = \begin{bmatrix} 51.02 \\ -48.47 \\ \vdots \\ 10.72 \end{bmatrix}$$

The residuals are the same as in Table 1.2.

Variance-Covariance Matrix of Residuals.   The residuals e_i, like the fitted values $\hat{Y}_i$, can be expressed as linear combinations of the response variable observations Y_i, using the result in (5.69) for $\hat{\mathbf{Y}}$:

$$\mathbf{e} = \mathbf{Y} - \hat{\mathbf{Y}} = \mathbf{Y} - \mathbf{HY} = (\mathbf{I} - \mathbf{H})\mathbf{Y}$$

We thus have the important result:

$$(5.74) \qquad \underset{n \times 1}{\mathbf{e}} = \underset{n \times n}{(\mathbf{I} - \mathbf{H})} \underset{n \times 1}{\mathbf{Y}}$$

where $\mathbf{H}$ is the hat matrix defined in (5.69a). The matrix $\mathbf{I} - \mathbf{H}$, like the matrix $\mathbf{H}$, is symmetric and idempotent.

The variance-covariance matrix of the vector of residuals $\mathbf{e}$ involves the matrix $\mathbf{I} - \mathbf{H}$:

$$(5.75) \qquad \underset{n \times n}{\boldsymbol{\sigma}^2\{\mathbf{e}\}} = \sigma^2(\mathbf{I} - \mathbf{H})$$

and is estimated by:

$$(5.76) \qquad \underset{n \times n}{\mathbf{s}^2\{\mathbf{e}\}} = MSE(\mathbf{I} - \mathbf{H})$$

Note

The variance-covariance matrix of $\mathbf{e}$ in (5.75) can be derived by means of (5.46). Since $\mathbf{e} = (\mathbf{I} - \mathbf{H})\mathbf{Y}$, we obtain:

$$\boldsymbol{\sigma}^2\{\mathbf{e}\} = (\mathbf{I} - \mathbf{H})\boldsymbol{\sigma}^2\{\mathbf{Y}\}(\mathbf{I} - \mathbf{H})'$$

Now $\boldsymbol{\sigma}^2\{\mathbf{Y}\} = \boldsymbol{\sigma}^2\{\boldsymbol{\varepsilon}\} = \sigma^2\mathbf{I}$ for the normal error model according to (5.52a). Also, $(\mathbf{I} - \mathbf{H})' = \mathbf{I} - \mathbf{H}$ because of the symmetry of the matrix. Hence:

$$\boldsymbol{\sigma}^2\{\mathbf{e}\} = \sigma^2(\mathbf{I} - \mathbf{H})\mathbf{I}(\mathbf{I} - \mathbf{H})$$

$$= \sigma^2(\mathbf{I} - \mathbf{H})(\mathbf{I} - \mathbf{H})$$

In view of the fact that the matrix $\mathbf{I} - \mathbf{H}$ is idempotent, we know that $(\mathbf{I} - \mathbf{H})(\mathbf{I} - \mathbf{H}) = \mathbf{I} - \mathbf{H}$ and we obtain formula (5.75).   ∎

5.12   Analysis of Variance Results

Sums of Squares

To see how the sums of squares are expressed in matrix notation, we begin with the total sum of squares *SSTO*, defined in (2.43). It will be convenient to use an algebraically equivalent expression:

$$(5.77) \qquad SSTO = \sum (Y_i - \bar{Y})^2 = \sum Y_i^2 - \frac{(\sum Y_i)^2}{n}$$

We know from (5.13) that:

$$\mathbf{Y}'\mathbf{Y} = \sum Y_i^2$$

The subtraction term $(\sum Y_i)^2 / n$ in matrix form uses $\mathbf{J}$, the matrix of 1s defined in (5.18), as follows:

$$(5.78) \qquad \frac{(\sum Y_i)^2}{n} = \left(\frac{1}{n}\right) \mathbf{Y}'\mathbf{J}\mathbf{Y}$$

For instance, if $n = 2$, we have:

$$\left(\frac{1}{2}\right) [Y_1 \quad Y_2] \begin{bmatrix} 1 & 1 \\ 1 & 1 \end{bmatrix} \begin{bmatrix} Y_1 \\ Y_2 \end{bmatrix} = \frac{(Y_1 + Y_2)(Y_1 + Y_2)}{2}$$

Hence, it follows that:

$$(5.79) \qquad SSTO = \mathbf{Y}'\mathbf{Y} - \left(\frac{1}{n}\right) \mathbf{Y}'\mathbf{J}\mathbf{Y}$$

Just as $\sum Y_i^2$ is represented by $\mathbf{Y}'\mathbf{Y}$ in matrix terms, so $SSE = \sum e_i^2 = \sum (Y_i - \hat{Y}_i)^2$ can be represented as follows:

$$(5.80) \qquad SSE = \mathbf{e}'\mathbf{e} = (\mathbf{Y} - \mathbf{Xb})'(\mathbf{Y} - \mathbf{Xb})$$

which can be shown to equal:

$$(5.80a) \qquad SSE = \mathbf{Y}'\mathbf{Y} - \mathbf{b}'\mathbf{X}'\mathbf{Y}$$

Finally, it can be shown that:

$$(5.81) \qquad SSR = \mathbf{b}'\mathbf{X}'\mathbf{Y} - \left(\frac{1}{n}\right) \mathbf{Y}'\mathbf{J}\mathbf{Y}$$

Example. Let us find *SSE* for the Toluca Company example by matrix methods, using (5.80a). Using (5.57a), we obtain:

$$\mathbf{Y'Y} = [399 \quad 121 \quad \cdots \quad 323] \begin{bmatrix} 399 \\ 121 \\ \vdots \\ 323 \end{bmatrix} = 2{,}745{,}173$$

and using (5.61) and (5.59), we find:

$$\mathbf{b'X'Y} = [62.37 \quad 3.5702] \begin{bmatrix} 7{,}807 \\ 617{,}180 \end{bmatrix} = 2{,}690{,}348$$

Hence:

$$SSE = \mathbf{Y'Y} - \mathbf{b'X'Y} = 2{,}745{,}173 - 2{,}690{,}348 = 54{,}825$$

which is the same result as that obtained in Chapter 1. Any difference would have been due to rounding effects.

Note

To illustrate the derivation of the sums of squares expressions in matrix notation, consider *SSE*:

$$SSE = \mathbf{e'e} = (\mathbf{Y} - \mathbf{Xb})'(\mathbf{Y} - \mathbf{Xb}) = \mathbf{Y'Y} - 2\mathbf{b'X'Y} + \mathbf{b'X'Xb}$$

In substituting for the rightmost **b** we obtain by (5.56):

$$SSE = \mathbf{Y'Y} - 2\mathbf{b'X'Y} + \mathbf{b'X'X(X'X)}^{-1}\mathbf{X'Y}$$

$$= \mathbf{Y'Y} - 2\mathbf{b'X'Y} + \mathbf{b'IX'Y}$$

In dropping **I** and subtracting, we obtain the result in (5.80a).   ∎

Sums of Squares as Quadratic Forms

The ANOVA sums of squares can be shown to be *quadratic forms*. An example of a quadratic form of the observations Y_i when $n = 2$ is:

(5.82) $$5Y_1^2 + 6Y_1Y_2 + 4Y_2^2$$

Note that this expression is a second-degree polynomial containing terms involving the squares of the observations and the cross product. We can express (5.82) in matrix terms as follows:

(5.82a) $$[Y_1 \quad Y_2] \begin{bmatrix} 5 & 3 \\ 3 & 4 \end{bmatrix} \begin{bmatrix} Y_1 \\ Y_2 \end{bmatrix} = \mathbf{Y'AY}$$

where **A** is a symmetric matrix.

In general, a quadratic form is defined as:

$$(5.83) \qquad \underset{1 \times 1}{\mathbf{Y'AY}} = \sum_{i=1}^{n} \sum_{j=1}^{n} a_{ij} Y_i Y_j \qquad \text{where} \quad a_{ij} = a_{ji}$$

$\mathbf{A}$ is a symmetric $n \times n$ matrix and is called the *matrix of the quadratic form.*

The ANOVA sums of squares *SSTO*, *SSE*, and *SSR* are all quadratic forms, as can be seen by reexpressing $\mathbf{b'X'}$. From (5.67), we know, using (5.32), that:

$$\mathbf{b'X'} = (\mathbf{Xb})' = \mathbf{\hat{Y}'}$$

We now use the result in (5.69) to obtain:

$$\mathbf{b'X'} = (\mathbf{HY})'$$

Since $\mathbf{H}$ is a symmetric matrix so that $\mathbf{H'} = \mathbf{H}$, we finally obtain, using (5.32):

$$(5.84) \qquad \mathbf{b'X'} = \mathbf{Y'H}$$

This result enables us to express the ANOVA sums of squares as follows:

$$(5.85a) \qquad SSTO - \mathbf{Y'} \left[\mathbf{I} - \left(\frac{1}{n} \right) \mathbf{J} \right] \mathbf{Y}$$

$$(5.85b) \qquad SSE = \mathbf{Y'} (\mathbf{I} - \mathbf{H}) \mathbf{Y}$$

$$(5.85c) \qquad SSR = \mathbf{Y'} \left[\mathbf{H} - \left(\frac{1}{n} \right) \mathbf{J} \right] \mathbf{Y}$$

Each of these sums of squares can now be seen to be of the form $\mathbf{Y'AY}$, where the three $\mathbf{A}$ matrices are:

$$(5.86a) \qquad \mathbf{I} - \left(\frac{1}{n} \right) \mathbf{J}$$

$$(5.86b) \qquad \mathbf{I} - \mathbf{H}$$

$$(5.86c) \qquad \mathbf{H} - \left(\frac{1}{n} \right) \mathbf{J}$$

Since each of these $\mathbf{A}$ matrices is symmetric, *SSTO*, *SSE*, and *SSR* are quadratic forms, with the matrices of the quadratic forms given in (5.86). Quadratic forms play an important role in statistics because all sums of squares in the analysis of variance for linear statistical models can be expressed as quadratic forms.

5.13   Inferences in Regression Analysis

As we saw in earlier chapters, all interval estimates are of the following form: point estimator plus and minus a certain number of estimated standard deviations of the point estimator. Similarly, all tests require the point estimator and the estimated standard deviation of the point estimator or, in the case of analysis of variance tests, various sums of squares. Matrix algebra is of principal help in inference making when obtaining the estimated standard deviations and sums of squares. We have already given the matrix equivalents of the sums of squares for the analysis of variance. We focus here chiefly on the matrix expressions for the estimated variances of point estimators of interest.

Regression Coefficients

The variance-covariance matrix of $\mathbf{b}$:

$$(5.87) \qquad \underset{2\times 2}{\boldsymbol{\sigma}^2\{\mathbf{b}\}} = \begin{bmatrix} \sigma^2\{b_0\} & \sigma\{b_0, b_1\} \\ \sigma\{b_1, b_0\} & \sigma^2\{b_1\} \end{bmatrix}$$

is:

$$(5.88) \qquad \underset{2\times 2}{\boldsymbol{\sigma}^2\{\mathbf{b}\}} = \sigma^2(\mathbf{X}'\mathbf{X})^{-1}$$

or, using (5.24a):

$$(5.88a) \qquad \underset{2\times 2}{\boldsymbol{\sigma}^2\{\mathbf{b}\}} = \begin{bmatrix} \dfrac{\sigma^2}{n} + \dfrac{\sigma^2\bar{X}^2}{\Sigma(X_i - \bar{X})^2} & \dfrac{-\bar{X}\sigma^2}{\Sigma(X_i - \bar{X})^2} \\ \dfrac{-\bar{X}\sigma^2}{\Sigma(X_i - \bar{X})^2} & \dfrac{\sigma^2}{\Sigma(X_i - \bar{X})^2} \end{bmatrix}$$

When *MSE* is substituted for σ^2 in (5.88a), we obtain the estimated variance-covariance matrix of $\mathbf{b}$, denoted by $\mathbf{s}^2\{\mathbf{b}\}$:

$$(5.89) \qquad \underset{2\times 2}{\mathbf{s}^2\{\mathbf{b}\}} = MSE(\mathbf{X}'\mathbf{X})^{-1} = \begin{bmatrix} \dfrac{MSE}{n} + \dfrac{MSE(\bar{X}^2)}{\Sigma(X_i - \bar{X})^2} & \dfrac{-\bar{X}MSE}{\Sigma(X_i - \bar{X})^2} \\ \dfrac{-\bar{X}MSE}{\Sigma(X_i - \bar{X})^2} & \dfrac{MSE}{\Sigma(X_i - \bar{X})^2} \end{bmatrix}$$

In (5.88a), you will recognize the variances of b_0 in (2.22b) and of b_1 in (2.3b) and the covariance of b_0 and b_1 in (4.5). Likewise, the estimated variances in (5.89) are familiar from earlier chapters.

Example.   We wish to find $s^2\{b_0\}$ and $s^2\{b_1\}$ for the Toluca Company example by matrix methods. Using the results in Figure 2.2 and in (5.60), we obtain:

$$(5.90) \qquad \mathbf{s}^2\{\mathbf{b}\} = MSE(\mathbf{X}'\mathbf{X})^{-1} = 2,384 \begin{bmatrix} .287475 & -.003535 \\ -.003535 & .00005051 \end{bmatrix}$$

$$= \begin{bmatrix} 685.34 & -8.428 \\ -8.428 & .12040 \end{bmatrix}$$

Thus, $s^2\{b_0\} = 685.34$ and $s^2\{b_1\} = .12040$. These are the same as the results obtained in Chapter 2.

Note

To derive the variance-covariance matrix of **b**, recall that:

$$\mathbf{b} = (\mathbf{X'X})^{-1}\mathbf{X'Y} = \mathbf{AY}$$

where **A** is a constant matrix:

$$\mathbf{A} = (\mathbf{X'X})^{-1}\mathbf{X'}$$

Hence, by (5.46) we have:

$$\boldsymbol{\sigma}^2\{\mathbf{b}\} = \mathbf{A}\boldsymbol{\sigma}^2\{\mathbf{Y}\}\mathbf{A'}$$

Now $\boldsymbol{\sigma}^2\{\mathbf{Y}\} = \sigma^2\mathbf{I}$. Further, it follows from (5.32) and the fact that $(\mathbf{X'X})^{-1}$ is symmetric that:

$$\mathbf{A'} = \mathbf{X}(\mathbf{X'X})^{-1}$$

We find therefore:

$$\boldsymbol{\sigma}^2\{\mathbf{b}\} = (\mathbf{X'X})^{-1}\mathbf{X'}\sigma^2\mathbf{IX}(\mathbf{X'X})^{-1}$$

$$= \sigma^2(\mathbf{X'X})^{-1}\mathbf{X'X}(\mathbf{X'X})^{-1}$$

$$= \sigma^2(\mathbf{X'X})^{-1}\mathbf{I}$$

$$= \sigma^2(\mathbf{X'X})^{-1}$$

∎

Mean Response

To estimate the mean response at X_h, let us define the vector:

$$(5.91) \qquad \underset{2\times 1}{\mathbf{X}_h} = \begin{bmatrix} 1 \\ X_h \end{bmatrix} \qquad \text{or} \qquad \underset{1\times 2}{\mathbf{X}_h'} = \begin{bmatrix} 1 & X_h \end{bmatrix}$$

The fitted value in matrix notation then is:

$$(5.92) \qquad \hat{Y}_h = \mathbf{X}_h'\mathbf{b}$$

since:

$$\mathbf{X}_h'\mathbf{b} = \begin{bmatrix} 1 & X_h \end{bmatrix}\begin{bmatrix} b_0 \\ b_1 \end{bmatrix} = [b_0 + b_1 X_h] = [\hat{Y}_h] = \hat{Y}_h$$

Note that $\mathbf{X}_h'\mathbf{b}$ is a 1×1 matrix; hence, we can write the final result as a scalar.

The variance of $\hat{Y}_h$, given earlier in (2.29b), in matrix notation is:

$$(5.93) \qquad \sigma^2\{\hat{Y}_h\} = \sigma^2\mathbf{X}_h'(\mathbf{X'X})^{-1}\mathbf{X}_h$$

The variance of $\hat{Y}_h$ in (5.93) can be expressed as a function of $\boldsymbol{\sigma}^2\{\mathbf{b}\}$, the variance-covariance matrix of the estimated regression coefficients, by making use of the result in (5.88):

$$(5.93a) \qquad \sigma^2\{\hat{Y}_h\} = \mathbf{X}_h'\boldsymbol{\sigma}^2\{\mathbf{b}\}\mathbf{X}_h$$

The estimated variance of $\hat{Y}_h$, given earlier in (2.30), in matrix notation is:

$$(5.94) \qquad s^2\{\hat{Y}_h\} = MSE(\mathbf{X}'_h(\mathbf{X}'\mathbf{X})^{-1}\mathbf{X}_h)$$

Example.   We wish to find $s^2\{\hat{Y}_h\}$ for the Toluca Company example when $X_h = 65$. We define:

$$\mathbf{X}'_h = [1 \quad 65]$$

and use the result in (5.90) to obtain:

$$s^2\{\hat{Y}_h\} = \mathbf{X}'_h s^2\{\mathbf{b}\}\mathbf{X}_h$$

$$= [1 \quad 65]\begin{bmatrix} 685.34 & -8.428 \\ -8.428 & .12040 \end{bmatrix}\begin{bmatrix} 1 \\ 65 \end{bmatrix} = 98.37$$

This is the same result as that obtained in Chapter 2.

Note

The result in (5.93a) can be derived directly by using (5.46), since $\hat{Y}_h = \mathbf{X}'_h\mathbf{b}$:

$$\sigma^2\{\hat{Y}_h\} = \mathbf{X}'_h\sigma^2\{\mathbf{b}\}\mathbf{X}_h$$

Hence:

$$\sigma^2\{\hat{Y}_h\} = [1 \quad X_h]\begin{bmatrix} \sigma^2\{b_0\} & \sigma\{b_0, b_1\} \\ \sigma\{b_1, b_0\} & \sigma^2\{b_1\} \end{bmatrix}\begin{bmatrix} 1 \\ X_h \end{bmatrix}$$

or:

$$(5.95) \qquad \sigma^2\{\hat{Y}_h\} = \sigma^2\{b_0\} + 2X_h\sigma\{b_0, b_1\} + X_h^2\sigma^2\{b_1\}$$

Using the results from (5.88a), we obtain:

$$\sigma^2\{\hat{Y}_h\} = \frac{\sigma^2}{n} + \frac{\sigma^2\overline{X}^2}{\Sigma(X_i - \overline{X})^2} + \frac{2X_h(-\overline{X})\sigma^2}{\Sigma(X_i - \overline{X})^2} + \frac{X_h^2\sigma^2}{\Sigma(X_i - \overline{X})^2}$$

which reduces to the familiar expression:

$$(5.95a) \qquad \sigma^2\{\hat{Y}_h\} = \sigma^2\left[\frac{1}{n} + \frac{(X_h - \overline{X})^2}{\Sigma(X_i - \overline{X})^2}\right]$$

Thus, we see explicitly that the variance expression in (5.95a) contains contributions from $\sigma^2\{b_0\}$, $\sigma^2\{b_1\}$, and $\sigma\{b_0, b_1\}$, which it must according to theorem (A.30b) since $\hat{Y}_h = b_0 + b_1X_h$ is a linear combination of b_0 and b_1. ∎

Prediction of New Observation

The estimated variance $s^2\{\text{pred}\}$, given earlier in (2.38), in matrix notation is:

$$(5.96) \qquad s^2\{\text{pred}\} = MSE(1 + \mathbf{X}'_h(\mathbf{X}'\mathbf{X})^{-1}\mathbf{X}_h)$$

Cited Reference

5.1.   Graybill, F. A. *Matrices with Applications in Statistics*. 2nd ed. Belmont, Calif.: Wadsworth, 1982.

Problems

5.1.   For the matrices below, obtain (1) $\mathbf{A} + \mathbf{B}$, (2) $\mathbf{A} - \mathbf{B}$, (3) $\mathbf{AC}$, (4) $\mathbf{AB'}$, (5) $\mathbf{B'A}$.

$$\mathbf{A} = \begin{bmatrix} 1 & 4 \\ 2 & 6 \\ 3 & 8 \end{bmatrix} \qquad \mathbf{B} = \begin{bmatrix} 1 & 3 \\ 1 & 4 \\ 2 & 5 \end{bmatrix} \qquad \mathbf{C} = \begin{bmatrix} 3 & 8 & 1 \\ 5 & 4 & 0 \end{bmatrix}$$

State the dimension of each resulting matrix.

5.2.   For the matrices below, obtain (1) $\mathbf{A} + \mathbf{C}$, (2) $\mathbf{A} - \mathbf{C}$, (3) $\mathbf{B'A}$, (4) $\mathbf{AC'}$, (5) $\mathbf{C'A}$.

$$\mathbf{A} = \begin{bmatrix} 2 & 1 \\ 3 & 5 \\ 5 & 7 \\ 4 & 8 \end{bmatrix} \qquad \mathbf{B} = \begin{bmatrix} 6 \\ 9 \\ 3 \\ 1 \end{bmatrix} \qquad \mathbf{C} = \begin{bmatrix} 3 & 8 \\ 8 & 6 \\ 5 & 1 \\ 2 & 4 \end{bmatrix}$$

State the dimension of each resulting matrix.

5.3.   Show how the following expressions are written in terms of matrices: (1) $Y_i - \hat{Y}_i = e_i$, (2) $\Sigma X_i e_i = 0$. Assume $i = 1, \ldots, 4$.

√ 5.4.   **Flavor deterioration**. The results shown below were obtained in a small-scale experiment to study the relation between $°F$ of storage temperature (X) and number of weeks before flavor deterioration of a food product begins to occur (Y).

i:	1	2	3	4	5
X_i:	8	4	0	−4	−8
Y_i:	7.8	9.0	10.2	11.0	11.7

Assume that first-order regression model (2.1) is applicable. Using matrix methods, find (1) $\mathbf{Y'Y}$, (2) $\mathbf{X'X}$, (3) $\mathbf{X'Y}$.

5.5.   **Consumer finance**. The data below show, for a consumer finance company operating in six cities, the number of competing loan companies operating in the city (X) and the number per thousand of the company's loans made in that city that are currently delinquent (Y):

i:	1	2	3	4	5	6
X_i:	4	1	2	3	3	4
Y_i:	16	5	10	15	13	22

Assume that first-order regression model (2.1) is applicable. Using matrix methods, find (1) $\mathbf{Y'Y}$, (2) $\mathbf{X'X}$, (3) $\mathbf{X'Y}$.

√ 5.6.   Refer to **Airfreight breakage** Problem 1.21. Using matrix methods, find (1) $\mathbf{Y'Y}$, (2) $\mathbf{X'X}$, (3) $\mathbf{X'Y}$.

5.7.   Refer to **Plastic hardness** Problem 1.22. Using matrix methods, find (1) $\mathbf{Y'Y}$, (2) $\mathbf{X'X}$, (3) $\mathbf{X'Y}$.

5.8.   Let **B** be defined as follows:

$$\mathbf{B} = \begin{bmatrix} 1 & 5 & 0 \\ 1 & 0 & 5 \\ 1 & 0 & 5 \end{bmatrix}$$

a.   Are the column vectors of **B** linearly dependent?

b.   What is the rank of **B**?

c.   What must be the determinant of **B**?

5.9.   Let **A** be defined as follows:

$$\mathbf{A} = \begin{bmatrix} 0 & 1 & 8 \\ 0 & 3 & 1 \\ 0 & 5 & 5 \end{bmatrix}$$

a.   Are the column vectors of **A** linearly dependent?

b.   Restate definition (5.20) in terms of row vectors. Are the row vectors of **A** linearly dependent?

c.   What is the rank of **A**?

d.   Calculate the determinant of **A**.

5.10.   Find the inverse of each of the following matrices:

$$\mathbf{A} = \begin{bmatrix} 2 & 4 \\ 3 & 1 \end{bmatrix} \qquad \mathbf{B} = \begin{bmatrix} 4 & 3 & 2 \\ 6 & 5 & 10 \\ 10 & 1 & 6 \end{bmatrix}$$

Check in each case that the resulting matrix is indeed the inverse.

5.11.   Find the inverse of the following matrix:

$$\mathbf{A} = \begin{bmatrix} 5 & 1 & 3 \\ 4 & 0 & 5 \\ 1 & 9 & 6 \end{bmatrix}$$

Check that the resulting matrix is indeed the inverse.

√ 5.12.   Refer to **Flavor deterioration** Problem 5.4. Find $(\mathbf{X'X})^{-1}$.

5.13.   Refer to **Consumer finance** Problem 5.5. Find $(\mathbf{X'X})^{-1}$.

√ 5.14.   Consider the simultaneous equations:

$$4y_1 + 7y_2 = 25$$
$$2y_1 + 3y_2 = 12$$

a.   Write these equations in matrix notation.

b. Using matrix methods, find the solutions for y_1 and y_2.

5.15. Consider the simultaneous equations:

$$5y_1 + 2y_2 = 8$$
$$23y_1 + 7y_2 = 28$$

a. Write these equations in matrix notation.

b. Using matrix methods, find the solutions for y_1 and y_2.

5.16. Consider the estimated linear regression function in the form of (1.15). Write expressions in this form for the fitted values $\hat{Y}_i$ in matrix terms for $i = 1, \ldots, 5$.

5.17. Consider the following functions of the random variables Y_1, Y_2, and Y_3:

$$W_1 = Y_1 + Y_2 + Y_3$$
$$W_2 = Y_1 - Y_2$$
$$W_3 = Y_1 - Y_2 - Y_3$$

a. State the above in matrix notation.

b. Find the expectation of the random vector **W**.

c. Find the variance-covariance matrix of **W**.

√ 5.18. Consider the following functions of the random variables Y_1, Y_2, Y_3, and Y_4:

$$W_1 = \frac{1}{4}(Y_1 + Y_2 + Y_3 + Y_4)$$
$$W_2 = \frac{1}{2}(Y_1 + Y_2) - \frac{1}{2}(Y_3 + Y_4)$$

a. State the above in matrix notation.

b. Find the expectation of the random vector **W**.

c. Find the variance-covariance matrix of **W**.

√ 5.19. Find the matrix **A** of the quadratic form:

$$3Y_1^2 + 10Y_1Y_2 + 17Y_2^2$$

5.20. Find the matrix **A** of the quadratic form:

$$7Y_1^2 - 8Y_1Y_2 + 8Y_2^2$$

√ 5.21. For the matrix:

$$\mathbf{A} = \begin{bmatrix} 5 & 2 \\ 2 & 1 \end{bmatrix}$$

find the quadratic form of the observations Y_1 and Y_2.

5.22. For the matrix:

$$\mathbf{A} = \begin{bmatrix} 1 & 0 & 4 \\ 0 & 3 & 0 \\ 4 & 0 & 9 \end{bmatrix}$$

find the quadratic form of the observations Y_1, Y_2, and Y_3.

√ 5.23. Refer to **Flavor deterioration** Problems 5.4 and 5.12.

   a. Using matrix methods, obtain the following: (1) vector of estimated regression coefficients, (2) vector of residuals, (3) *SSR*, (4) *SSE*, (5) estimated variance-covariance matrix of **b**, (6) point estimate of $E\{Y_h\}$ when $X_h = -6$, (7) estimated variance of $\hat{Y}_h$ when $X_h = -6$.

   b. What simplifications arose from the spacing of the X levels in the experiment?

   c. Find the hat matrix **H**.

   d. Find $s^2\{e\}$.

5.24. Refer to **Consumer finance** Problems 5.5 and 5.13.

   a. Using matrix methods, obtain the following: (1) vector of estimated regression coefficients, (2) vector of residuals, (3) *SSR*, (4) *SSE*, (5) estimated variance-covariance matrix of **b**, (6) point estimate of $E\{Y_h\}$ when $X_h = 4$, (7) $s^2\{pred\}$ when $X_h = 4$.

   b. From your estimated variance-covariance matrix in part (a5), obtain the following: (1) $s\{b_0, b_1\}$; (2) $s^2\{b_0\}$; (3) $s\{b_1\}$.

   c. Find the hat matrix **H**.

   d. Find $s^2\{e\}$.

√ 5.25. Refer to **Airfreight breakage** Problems 1.21 and 5.6.

   a. Using matrix methods, obtain the following: (1) $(\mathbf{X'X})^{-1}$, (2) **b**, (3) **e**, (4) **H**, (5) *SSE*, (6) $s^2\{\mathbf{b}\}$, (7) $\hat{Y}_h$ when $X_h = 2$, (8) $s^2\{\hat{Y}_h\}$ when $X_h = 2$.

   b. From part (a6), obtain the following: (1) $s^2\{b_1\}$; (2) $s\{b_0, b_1\}$; (3) $s\{b_0\}$.

   c. Find the matrix of the quadratic form for *SSR*.

5.26. Refer to **Plastic hardness** Problems 1.22 and 5.7.

   a. Using matrix methods, obtain the following: (1) $(\mathbf{X'X})^{-1}$, (2) **b**, (3) $\hat{\mathbf{Y}}$, (4) **H**, (5) *SSE*, (6) $s^2\{\mathbf{b}\}$, (7) $s^2\{pred\}$ when $X_h = 30$.

   b. From part (a6), obtain the following: (1) $s^2\{b_0\}$; (2) $s\{b_0, b_1\}$; (3) $s\{b_1\}$.

   c. Obtain the matrix of the quadratic form for *SSE*.

Exercises

5.27. Refer to regression-through-the-origin model (4.10). Set up the expectation vector for **ε**. Assume that $i = 1, \ldots, 4$.

5.28. Consider model (4.10) for regression through the origin and the estimator b_1 given in (4.14). Obtain (4.14) by utilizing (5.56) with **X** suitably defined.

5.29. Consider the least squares estimator **b** given in (5.56). Using matrix methods, show that **b** is an unbiased estimator.

5.30. Show that $\hat{Y}_h$ in (5.92) can be expressed in matrix terms as $\mathbf{b'X}_h$.

5.31. Obtain an expression for the variance-covariance matrix of the fitted values $\hat{Y}_i$, $i = 1, \ldots, n$, in terms of the hat matrix.

Multiple Linear Regression

Multiple Regression—I

Multiple regression analysis is one of the most widely used of all statistical methods. In this chapter, we first discuss a variety of multiple regression models. Then we present the basic statistical results for multiple regression in matrix form. Since the matrix expressions for multiple regression are the same as for simple linear regression, we state the results without much discussion. We conclude the chapter with an example, illustrating a variety of inferences and residual analyses in multiple regression analysis.

6.1 Multiple Regression Models

Need for Several Predictor Variables

When we first introduced regression analysis in Chapter 1, we spoke of regression models containing a number of predictor variables. We mentioned a regression model where the response variable was direct operating cost for a branch office of a consumer finance chain, and four predictor variables were considered, including average number of loans outstanding at the branch and total number of new loan applications processed by the branch. We also mentioned a tractor purchase study where the response variable was volume of tractor purchases in a sales territory, and the nine predictor variables included number of farms in the territory and quantity of crop production in the territory. In addition, we mentioned a study of short children where the response variable was the peak plasma growth hormone level, and the 14 predictor variables included gender, age, and various body measurements. In all these examples, a single predictor variable in the model would have provided an inadequate description since a number of key variables affect the response variable in important and distinctive ways. Furthermore, in situations of this type, we frequently find that predictions of the response variable based on a model containing only a single predictor variable are too imprecise to be useful. We noted the imprecise predictions with a single predictor variable in the Toluca Company example in Chapter 2. A more complex model, containing additional predictor variables, typically is more helpful in providing sufficiently precise predictions of the response variable.

In each of the examples just mentioned, the analysis was based on observational data because the predictor variables were not controlled, usually because they were not suscep-tible to direct control. Multiple regression analysis is also highly useful in experimental situations where the experimenter can control the predictor variables. An experimenter typically will wish to investigate a number of predictor variables simultaneously because almost always more than one key predictor variable influences the response. For example, in a study of productivity of work crews, the experimenter may wish to control both the size of the crew and the level of bonus pay. Similarly, in a study of responsiveness to a drug, the experimenter may wish to control both the dose of the drug and the method of administration.

The multiple regression models which we now describe can be utilized for either observational data or for experimental data from a completely randomized design.

First-Order Model with Two Predictor Variables

When there are two predictor variables X_1 and X_2, the regression model:

$$(6.1) \qquad Y_i = \beta_0 + \beta_1 X_{i1} + \beta_2 X_{i2} + \varepsilon_i$$

is called a first-order model with two predictor variables. A first-order model, as we noted in Chapter 1, is linear in the predictor variables. Y_i denotes as usual the response in the ith trial, and X_{i1} and X_{i2} are the values of the two predictor variables in the ith trial. The parameters of the model are β_0, β_1, and β_2, and the error term is ε_i.

Assuming that $E\{\varepsilon_i\} = 0$, the regression function for model (6.1) is:

$$(6.2) \qquad E\{Y\} = \beta_0 + \beta_1 X_1 + \beta_2 X_2$$

Analogous to simple linear regression, where the regression function $E\{Y\} = \beta_0 + \beta_1 X$ is a line, regression function (6.2) is a plane. Figure 6.1 contains a representation of a portion of the response plane:

$$(6.3) \qquad E\{Y\} = 10 + 2X_1 + 5X_2$$

Note that any point on the response plane (6.3) corresponds to the mean response $E\{Y\}$ at the given combination of levels of X_1 and X_2.

Figure 6.1 also shows an observation Y_i corresponding to the levels (X_{i1}, X_{i2}) of the two predictor variables. Note that the vertical rule in Figure 6.1 between Y_i and the response plane represents the difference between Y_i and the mean $E\{Y_i\}$ of the probability distribution of Y for the given (X_{i1}, X_{i2}) combination. Hence, the vertical distance from Y_i to the response plane represents the error term $\varepsilon_i = Y_i - E\{Y_i\}$.

Frequently the regression function in multiple regression is called a *regression surface* or a *response surface*. In Figure 6.1, the response surface is a plane, but in other cases the response surface may be more complex in nature.

Meaning of Regression Coefficients.   Let us now consider the meaning of the regression coefficients in the multiple regression function (6.3). The parameter $\beta_0 = 10$ is the Y intercept of the regression plane. If the scope of the model includes $X_1 = 0$, $X_2 = 0$, then $\beta_0 = 10$ represents the mean response $E\{Y\}$ at $X_1 = 0$, $X_2 = 0$. Otherwise, β_0 does not have any particular meaning as a separate term in the regression model.

The parameter β_1 indicates the change in the mean response $E\{Y\}$ per unit increase in X_1 when X_2 is held constant. Likewise, β_2 indicates the change in the mean response per

FIGURE 6.1   Response Function is a Plane—Sales Promotion Example.

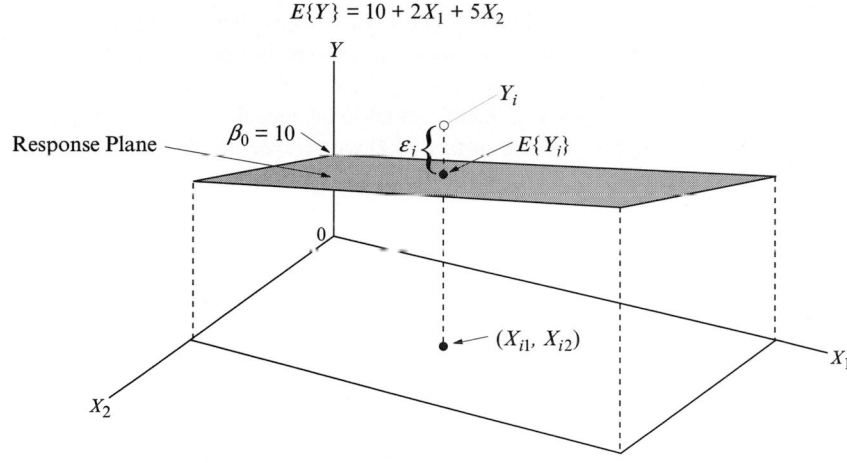

$$E\{Y\} = 10 + 2X_1 + 5X_2$$

unit increase in X_2 when X_1 is held constant. To see this for our example, suppose X_2 is held at the level $X_2 = 2$. The regression function (6.3) now is:

$$(6.4) \qquad E\{Y\} = 10 + 2X_1 + 5(2) = 20 + 2X_1 \qquad X_2 = 2$$

Note that this response function is a straight line with slope $\beta_1 = 2$. The same is true for any other value of X_2; only the intercept of the response function will differ. Hence, $\beta_1 = 2$ indicates that the mean response $E\{Y\}$ increases by 2 with a unit increase in X_1 when X_2 is constant, no matter what the level of X_2. We confirm therefore that β_1 indicates the change in $E\{Y\}$ with a unit increase in X_1 when X_2 is held constant.

Similarly, $\beta_2 = 5$ in regression function (6.3) indicates that the mean response $E\{Y\}$ increases by 5 with a unit increase in X_2 when X_1 is held constant.

When the effect of X_1 on the mean response does not depend on the level of X_2, and correspondingly the effect of X_2 does not depend on the level of X_1, the two predictor variables are said to have *additive effects* or *not to interact*. Thus, the first-order regression model (6.1) is designed for predictor variables whose effects on the mean response are additive or do not interact.

The parameters β_1 and β_2 are sometimes called *partial regression coefficients* because they reflect the partial effect of one predictor variable when the other predictor variable is included in the model and is held constant.

Example.   The response plane (6.3) shown in Figure 6.1 is for a regression model relating test market sales (Y, in 10 thousand dollars) to point-of-sale expenditures (X_1, in thousand dollars) and TV expenditures (X_2, in thousand dollars). Since $\beta_1 = 2$, if point-of-sale expenditures in a locality are increased by one unit (1 thousand dollars) while TV expenditures are held constant, expected sales increase by 2 units (20 thousand dollars). Similarly, since $\beta_2 = 5$, if TV expenditures in a locality are increased by 1 thousand dollars and point-of-sale expenditures are held constant, expected sales increase by 50 thousand dollars.

Comments

1. A regression model for which the response surface is a plane can be used either in its own right when it is appropriate, or as an approximation to a more complex response surface. Many complex response surfaces can be approximated well by a plane for limited ranges of X_1 and X_2.

2. We can readily establish the meaning of β_1 and β_2 by calculus, taking partial derivatives of the response surface (6.2) with respect to X_1 and X_2 in turn:

$$\frac{\partial E\{Y\}}{\partial X_1} = \beta_1 \qquad \frac{\partial E\{Y\}}{\partial X_2} = \beta_2$$

The partial derivatives measure the rate of change in $E\{Y\}$ with respect to one predictor variable when the other is held constant.   ∎

First-Order Model with More than Two Predictor Variables

We consider now the case where there are $p-1$ predictor variables $X_1, \ldots, X_{p-1}$. The regression model:

$$(6.5) \qquad Y_i = \beta_0 + \beta_1 X_{i1} + \beta_2 X_{i2} + \cdots + \beta_{p-1} X_{i,p-1} + \varepsilon_i$$

is called a first-order model with $p-1$ predictor variables. It can also be written:

$$(6.5a) \qquad Y_i = \beta_0 + \sum_{k=1}^{p-1} \beta_k X_{ik} + \varepsilon_i$$

or, if we let $X_{i0} \equiv 1$, it can be written as:

$$(6.5b) \qquad Y_i = \sum_{k=0}^{p-1} \beta_k X_{ik} + \varepsilon_i \qquad \text{where } X_{i0} \equiv 1$$

Assuming that $E\{\varepsilon_i\} = 0$, the response function for regression model (6.5) is:

$$(6.6) \qquad E\{Y\} = \beta_0 + \beta_1 X_1 + \beta_2 X_2 + \cdots + \beta_{p-1} X_{p-1}$$

This response function is a *hyperplane*, which is a plane in more than two dimensions. It is no longer possible to picture this response surface, as we were able to do in Figure 6.1 for the case of two predictor variables. Nevertheless, the meaning of the parameters is analogous to the case of two predictor variables. The parameter β_k indicates the change in the mean response $E\{Y\}$ with a unit increase in the predictor variable X_k, when all other predictor variables in the regression model are held constant. Note again that the effect of any predictor variable on the mean response is the same for regression model (6.5) no matter what are the levels at which the other predictor variables are held. Hence, first-order regression model (6.5) is designed for predictor variables whose effects on the mean response are additive and therefore do not interact.

Note

When $p - 1 = 1$, regression model (6.5) reduces to:

$$Y_i = \beta_0 + \beta_1 X_{i1} + \varepsilon_i$$

which is the simple linear regression model considered in earlier chapters.   ∎

General Linear Regression Model

In general, the variables $X_1, \ldots, X_{p-1}$ in a regression model do not need to represent different predictor variables, as we shall shortly see. We therefore define the general linear regression model, with normal error terms, simply in terms of X variables:

$$(6.7) \qquad Y_i = \beta_0 + \beta_1 X_{i1} + \beta_2 X_{i2} + \cdots + \beta_{p-1} X_{i,p-1} + \varepsilon_i$$

where:

> $\beta_0, \beta_1, \ldots, \beta_{p-1}$ are parameters
>
> $X_{i1}, \ldots, X_{i,p-1}$ are known constants
>
> ε_i are independent $N(0, \sigma^2)$
>
> $i = 1, \ldots, n$

If we let $X_{i0} \equiv 1$, regression model (6.7) can be written as follows:

$$(6.7a) \quad Y_i = \beta_0 X_{i0} + \beta_1 X_{i1} + \beta_2 X_{i2} + \cdots + \beta_{p-1} X_{i,p-1} + \varepsilon_i \qquad \text{where} \quad X_{i0} \equiv 1$$

or:

$$(6.7b) \qquad Y_i = \sum_{k=0}^{p-1} \beta_k X_{ik} + \varepsilon_i \qquad \text{where} \quad X_{i0} \equiv 1$$

The response function for regression model (6.7) is, since $E\{\varepsilon_i\} = 0$:

$$(6.8) \qquad E\{Y\} = \beta_0 + \beta_1 X_1 + \beta_2 X_2 + \cdots + \beta_{p-1} X_{p-1}$$

Thus, the general linear regression model with normal error terms implies that the observations Y_i are independent normal variables, with mean $E\{Y_i\}$ as given by (6.8) and with constant variance σ^2.

This general linear model encompasses a vast variety of situations. We consider a few of these now.

$p - 1$ **Predictor Variables.**   When $X_1, \ldots, X_{p-1}$ represent $p - 1$ different predictor variables, general linear regression model (6.7) is, as we have seen, a first-order model in which there are no interaction effects between the predictor variables. The example in Figure 6.1 involves a first-order model with two predictor variables.

Qualitative Predictor Variables.   The general linear regression model (6.7) encompasses not only quantitative predictor variables but also qualitative ones, such as gender (male, female) or disability status (not disabled, partially disabled, fully disabled). We use indicator variables that take on the values 0 and 1 to identify the classes of a qualitative variable.

Consider a regression analysis to predict the length of hospital stay (Y) based on the age (X_1) and gender (X_2) of the patient. We define X_2 as follows:

$$X_2 = \begin{array}{ll} 1 & \text{if patient female} \\ 0 & \text{if patient male} \end{array}$$

The first-order regression model then is as follows:

$$(6.9) \qquad\qquad Y_i = \beta_0 + \beta_1 X_{i1} + \beta_2 X_{i2} + \varepsilon_i$$

where:

$X_{i1} = $ patient's age

$$X_{i2} = \begin{array}{ll} 1 & \text{if patient female} \\ 0 & \text{if patient male} \end{array}$$

The response function for regression model (6.9) is:

$$(6.10) \qquad\qquad E\{Y\} = \beta_0 + \beta_1 X_1 + \beta_2 X_2$$

For male patients, $X_2 = 0$ and response function (6.10) becomes:

$$(6.10a) \qquad\qquad E\{Y\} = \beta_0 + \beta_1 X_1 \qquad\qquad\qquad \text{Male patients}$$

For female patients, $X_2 = 1$ and response function (6.10) becomes:

$$(6.10b) \qquad\qquad E\{Y\} = (\beta_0 + \beta_2) + \beta_1 X_1 \qquad\qquad \text{Female patients}$$

These two response functions represent parallel straight lines with different intercepts.

In general, we represent a qualitative variable with c classes by means of $c - 1$ indicator variables. For instance, if in the hospital stay example the qualitative variable disability status is to be added as another predictor variable, it can be represented as follows by the two indicator variables X_3 and X_4:

$$X_3 = \begin{array}{ll} 1 & \text{if patient not disabled} \\ 0 & \text{otherwise} \end{array}$$

$$X_4 = \begin{array}{ll} 1 & \text{if patient partially disabled} \\ 0 & \text{otherwise} \end{array}$$

The first-order model with age, gender, and disability status as predictor variables then is:

$$(6.11) \qquad\qquad Y_i = \beta_0 + \beta_1 X_{i1} + \beta_2 X_{i2} + \beta_3 X_{i3} + \beta_4 X_{i4} + \varepsilon_i$$

where:

$X_{i1} = $ patient's age

$$X_{i2} = \begin{array}{ll} 1 & \text{if patient female} \\ 0 & \text{if patient male} \end{array}$$

$$X_{i3} = \begin{cases} 1 & \text{if patient not disabled} \\ 0 & \text{otherwise} \end{cases}$$

$$X_{i4} = \begin{cases} 1 & \text{if patient partially disabled} \\ 0 & \text{otherwise} \end{cases}$$

In Chapter 11 we present a comprehensive discussion of how to model qualitative predictor variables and how to interpret regression models containing qualitative predictor variables.

Polynomial Regression. Polynomial regression models are special cases of the general linear regression model. They contain squared and higher-order terms of the predictor variable(s), making the response function curvilinear. The following is a polynomial regression model with one predictor variable:

$$(6.12) \qquad\qquad Y_i = \beta_0 + \beta_1 X_i + \beta_2 X_i^2 + \varepsilon_i$$

Figure 1.3 shows an example of a polynomial regression function with one predictor variable.

Despite the curvilinear nature of the response function for regression model (6.12), it is a special case of general linear regression model (6.7). If we let $X_{i1} = X_i$ and $X_{i2} = X_i^2$, we can write (6.12) as follows:

$$Y_i = \beta_0 + \beta_1 X_{i1} + \beta_2 X_{i2} + \varepsilon_i$$

which is in the form of general linear regression model (6.7). While (6.12) illustrates a curvilinear regression model where the response function is quadratic, models with higher-degree polynomial response functions are also particular cases of the general linear regression model. We shall discuss polynomial regression models in more detail in Chapter 7.

Transformed Variables. Models with transformed variables involve complex, curvilinear response functions, yet still are special cases of the general linear regression model. Consider the following model with a transformed Y variable:

$$(6.13) \qquad\qquad \log Y_i = \beta_0 + \beta_1 X_{i1} + \beta_2 X_{i2} + \beta_3 X_{i3} + \varepsilon_i$$

Here, the response surface is complex, yet model (6.13) can still be treated as a general linear regression model. If we let $Y_i' = \log Y_i$, we can write regression model (6.13) as follows:

$$Y_i' = \beta_0 + \beta_1 X_{i1} + \beta_2 X_{i2} + \beta_3 X_{i3} + \varepsilon_i$$

which is in the form of general linear regression model (6.7). The response variable just happens to be the logarithm of Y.

Many models can be transformed into the general linear regression model. For instance, the model:

$$(6.14) \qquad\qquad Y_i = \frac{1}{\beta_0 + \beta_1 X_{i1} + \beta_2 X_{i2} + \varepsilon_i}$$

can be transformed to the general linear regression model by letting $Y_i' = 1/Y_i$. We then have:

$$Y_i' = \beta_0 + \beta_1 X_{i1} + \beta_2 X_{i2} + \varepsilon_i$$

Interaction Effects.   When the effects of the predictor variables on the response variable are not additive, the effect of one predictor variable depends on the levels of the other predictor variables. The general linear regression model (6.7) encompasses regression models with nonadditive or interacting effects. An example of a nonadditive regression model with two predictor variables X_1 and X_2 is the following:

$$(6.15) \qquad Y_i = \beta_0 + \beta_1 X_{i1} + \beta_2 X_{i2} + \beta_3 X_{i1} X_{i2} + \varepsilon_i$$

Here, the response function is complex because of the interaction term $\beta_3 X_{i1} X_{i2}$. Yet regression model (6.15) is a special case of the general linear regression model. Let $X_{i3} = X_{i1} X_{i2}$ and then write (6.15) as follows:

$$Y_i = \beta_0 + \beta_1 X_{i1} + \beta_2 X_{i2} + \beta_3 X_{i3} + \varepsilon_i$$

We see that this model is in the form of general linear regression model (6.7). We shall discuss regression models with interaction effects in more detail in Chapter 7.

Combination of Cases.   A regression model may combine several of the elements we have just noted and still be treated as a general linear regression model. Consider the following regression model containing linear and quadratic terms for each of two predictor variables and an interaction term represented by the cross-product term:

$$(6.16) \qquad Y_i = \beta_0 + \beta_1 X_{i1} + \beta_2 X_{i1}^2 + \beta_3 X_{i2} + \beta_4 X_{i2}^2 + \beta_5 X_{i1} X_{i2} + \varepsilon_i$$

Let us define:

$$Z_{i1} = X_{i1} \qquad Z_{i2} = X_{i1}^2 \qquad Z_{i3} = X_{i2} \qquad Z_{i4} = X_{i2}^2 \qquad Z_{i5} = X_{i1} X_{i2}$$

We can then write regression model (6.16) as follows:

$$Y_i = \beta_0 + \beta_1 Z_{i1} + \beta_2 Z_{i2} + \beta_3 Z_{i3} + \beta_4 Z_{i4} + \beta_5 Z_{i5} + \varepsilon_i$$

which is in the form of general linear regression model (6.7).

The general linear regression model (6.7) includes many complex models, some of which may be highly complex. Figure 6.2 illustrates two complex response surfaces when there are two predictor variables, that can be represented by general linear regression model (6.7).

Meaning of Linear in General Linear Regression Model.   It should be clear from the various examples that general linear regression model (6.7) is not restricted to linear response surfaces. The term *linear model* refers to the fact that model (6.7) is linear in the parameters; it does not refer to the shape of the response surface.

We say that a regression model is linear in the parameters when it can be written in the form:

$$(6.17) \qquad Y_i = c_{i0} \beta_0 + c_{i1} \beta_1 + c_{i2} \beta_2 + \cdots + c_{i,p-1} \beta_{p-1} + \varepsilon_i$$

where the terms c_{i0}, c_{i1}, etc., are coefficients involving the predictor variables. For example, first-order model (6.1) in two predictor variables:

$$Y_i = \beta_0 + \beta_1 X_{i1} + \beta_2 X_{i2} + \varepsilon_i$$

FIGURE 6.2   **Additional Examples of Response Functions.**

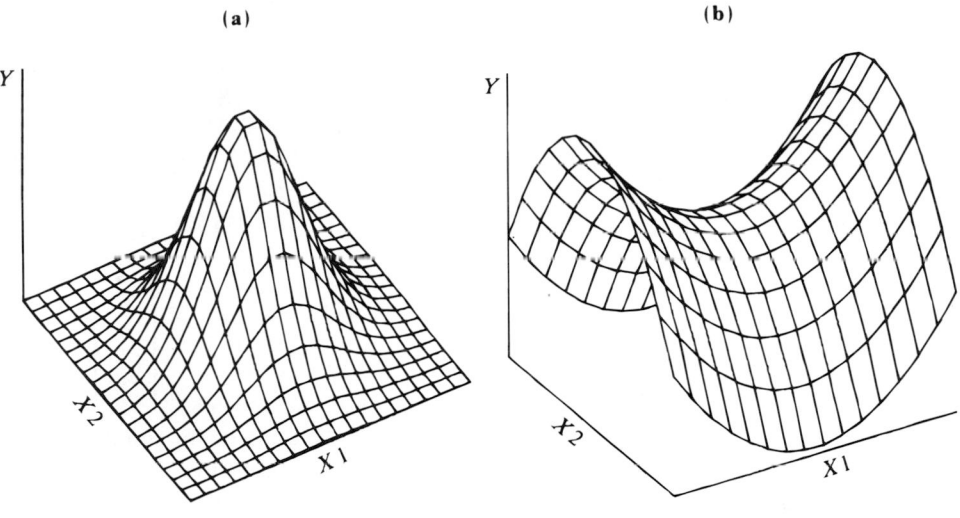

(a)   (b)

is linear in the parameters, with $c_{i0} = 1$, $c_{i1} = X_{i1}$, and $c_{i2} = X_{i2}$.

An example of a nonlinear regression model is the following:

$$Y_i = \beta_0 \exp(\beta_1 X_i) + \varepsilon_i$$

This is a nonlinear regression model because it cannot be expressed in the form of (6.17). We shall discuss nonlinear regression models in Part III.

6.2   General Linear Regression Model in Matrix Terms

We now present the principal results for the general linear regression model (6.7) in matrix terms. This model, as noted, encompasses a wide variety of particular cases. The results to be presented are applicable to all of these.

It is remarkable property of matrix algebra that the results for the general linear regression model (6.7) in matrix notation appear exactly as those for the simple linear regression model (5.53). Only the degrees of freedom and other constants related to the number of X variables and the dimensions of some matrices are different. Hence, we are able to present the results very concisely.

The matrix notation, to be sure, may hide enormous computational complexities. To find the inverse of a 10×10 matrix $\mathbf{A}$ requires a tremendous amount of computation, yet it is simply represented as $\mathbf{A}^{-1}$. Our reason for emphasizing matrix algebra is that it indicates the essential conceptual steps in the solution. The actual computations will, in all but the very simplest cases, be done by programmable calculator or computer. Hence, it does not matter to us whether $(\mathbf{X}'\mathbf{X})^{-1}$ represents finding the inverse of a 2×2 or a 10×10 matrix. The important point is to know what the inverse of the matrix represents.

To express general linear regression model (6.7):

$$Y_i = \beta_0 + \beta_1 X_{i1} + \beta_2 X_{i2} + \cdots + \beta_{p-1} X_{i,p-1} + \varepsilon_i$$

in matrix terms, we need to define the following matrices:

(6.18)

(6.18a)

$$\underset{n \times 1}{\mathbf{Y}} = \begin{bmatrix} Y_1 \\ Y_2 \\ \vdots \\ Y_n \end{bmatrix}$$

(6.18b)

$$\underset{n \times p}{\mathbf{X}} = \begin{bmatrix} 1 & X_{11} & X_{12} & \cdots & X_{1,p-1} \\ 1 & X_{21} & X_{22} & \cdots & X_{2,p-1} \\ \vdots & \vdots & \vdots & & \vdots \\ 1 & X_{n1} & X_{n2} & \cdots & X_{n,p-1} \end{bmatrix}$$

(6.18c)

$$\underset{p \times 1}{\boldsymbol{\beta}} = \begin{bmatrix} \beta_0 \\ \beta_1 \\ \vdots \\ \beta_{p-1} \end{bmatrix}$$

(6.18d)

$$\underset{n \times 1}{\boldsymbol{\varepsilon}} = \begin{bmatrix} \varepsilon_1 \\ \varepsilon_2 \\ \vdots \\ \varepsilon_n \end{bmatrix}$$

Note that the $\mathbf{Y}$ and $\boldsymbol{\varepsilon}$ vectors are the same as for simple linear regression. The $\boldsymbol{\beta}$ vector contains additional regression parameters, and the $\mathbf{X}$ matrix contains a column of 1s as well as a column of the n observations for each of the $p - 1$ X variables in the regression model. The row subscript for each element X_{ik} in the $\mathbf{X}$ matrix identifies the trial or case, and the column subscript identifies the X variable.

In matrix terms, the general linear regression model (6.7) is:

(6.19)

$$\underset{n \times 1}{\mathbf{Y}} = \underset{n \times p}{\mathbf{X}} \ \underset{p \times 1}{\boldsymbol{\beta}} + \underset{n \times 1}{\boldsymbol{\varepsilon}}$$

where:

$\mathbf{Y}$ is a vector of responses

$\boldsymbol{\beta}$ is a vector of parameters

$\mathbf{X}$ is a matrix of constants

$\boldsymbol{\varepsilon}$ is a vector of independent normal random variables with expectation $E\{\boldsymbol{\varepsilon}\} = \mathbf{0}$ and variance-covariance matrix:

$$\underset{n \times n}{\boldsymbol{\sigma}^2\{\boldsymbol{\varepsilon}\}} = \begin{bmatrix} \sigma^2 & 0 & \cdots & 0 \\ 0 & \sigma^2 & \cdots & 0 \\ \vdots & \vdots & & \vdots \\ 0 & 0 & \cdots & \sigma^2 \end{bmatrix} = \sigma^2 \mathbf{I}$$

Consequently, the random vector $\mathbf{Y}$ has expectation:

(6.20)

$$\underset{n \times 1}{E\{\mathbf{Y}\}} = \mathbf{X}\boldsymbol{\beta}$$

and the variance-covariance matrix of $\mathbf{Y}$ is the same as that of $\boldsymbol{\varepsilon}$:

(6.21)

$$\underset{n \times n}{\boldsymbol{\sigma}^2\{\mathbf{Y}\}} = \sigma^2 \mathbf{I}$$

6.3   Estimation of Regression Coefficients

The least squares criterion (1.8) is generalized as follows for general linear regression model (6.7):

$$(6.22) \qquad Q = \sum_{i=1}^{n}(Y_i - \beta_0 - \beta_1 X_{i1} - \cdots - \beta_{p-1}X_{i,p-1})^2$$

The least squares estimators are those values of $\beta_0, \beta_1, \ldots, \beta_{p-1}$ that minimize Q. Let us denote the vector of the least squares estimated regression coefficients $b_0, b_1, \ldots, b_{p-1}$ as **b**:

$$(6.23) \qquad \underset{p \times 1}{\mathbf{b}} = \begin{bmatrix} b_0 \\ b_1 \\ \vdots \\ b_{p-1} \end{bmatrix}$$

The least squares normal equations for the general linear regression model (6.19) are:

$$(6.24) \qquad \mathbf{X'Xb = X'Y}$$

and the least squares estimators are:

$$(6.25) \qquad \underset{p \times 1}{\mathbf{b}} = \underset{p \times p}{(\mathbf{X'X})^{-1}} \underset{p \times 1}{(\mathbf{X'Y})}$$

The method of maximum likelihood leads to the same estimators for normal error regression model (6.19) as those obtained by the method of least squares in (6.25). The likelihood function in (1.26) generalizes directly for multiple regression as follows:

$$(6.26) \quad L(\boldsymbol{\beta}, \sigma^2) = \frac{1}{(2\pi\sigma^2)^{n/2}} \exp\left[-\frac{1}{2\sigma^2} \sum_{i=1}^{n}(Y_i - \beta_0 - \beta_1 X_{i1} - \cdots - \beta_{p-1}X_{i,p-1})^2 \right]$$

Maximizing this likelihood function with respect to $\beta_0, \beta_1, \ldots, \beta_{p-1}$ leads to the estimators in (6.25). These estimators are least squares and maximum likelihood estimators and have all the properties mentioned in Chapter 1: they are minimum variance unbiased, consistent, and sufficient.

6.4   Fitted Values and Residuals

Let the vector of the fitted values $\hat{Y}_i$ be denoted by $\hat{\mathbf{Y}}$ and the vector of the residual terms $e_i = Y_i - \hat{Y}_i$ be denoted by **e**:

$$(6.27) \qquad (6.27a) \quad \underset{n \times 1}{\hat{\mathbf{Y}}} = \begin{bmatrix} \hat{Y}_1 \\ \hat{Y}_2 \\ \vdots \\ \hat{Y}_n \end{bmatrix} \qquad (6.27b) \quad \underset{n \times 1}{\mathbf{e}} = \begin{bmatrix} e_1 \\ e_2 \\ \vdots \\ e_n \end{bmatrix}$$

The fitted values are represented by:

(6.28)
$$\hat{\mathbf{Y}}_{n \times 1} = \mathbf{Xb}$$

and the residual terms by:

(6.29)
$$\mathbf{e}_{n \times 1} = \mathbf{Y} - \hat{\mathbf{Y}} = \mathbf{Y} - \mathbf{Xb}$$

The vector of the fitted values $\hat{\mathbf{Y}}$ can be expressed in terms of the hat matrix $\mathbf{H}$ as follows:

(6.30)
$$\hat{\mathbf{Y}}_{n \times 1} = \mathbf{HY}$$

where:

(6.30a)
$$\mathbf{H}_{n \times n} = \mathbf{X}(\mathbf{X}'\mathbf{X})^{-1}\mathbf{X}'$$

Similarly, the vector of residuals can be expressed as follows:

(6.31)
$$\mathbf{e}_{n \times 1} = (\mathbf{I} - \mathbf{H})\mathbf{Y}$$

The variance-covariance matrix of the residuals is:

(6.32)
$$\boldsymbol{\sigma}^2\{\mathbf{e}\}_{n \times n} = \sigma^2(\mathbf{I} - \mathbf{H})$$

which is estimated by:

(6.33)
$$\mathbf{s}^2\{\mathbf{e}\}_{n \times n} = MSE(\mathbf{I} - \mathbf{H})$$

6.5   Analysis of Variance Results

Sums of Squares and Mean Squares

The sums of squares for the analysis of variance in matrix terms are:

(6.34)
$$SSTO = \mathbf{Y}'\mathbf{Y} - \left(\frac{1}{n}\right)\mathbf{Y}'\mathbf{JY} = \mathbf{Y}'\left[\mathbf{I} - \left(\frac{1}{n}\right)\mathbf{J}\right]\mathbf{Y}$$

TABLE 6.1   ANOVA Table for General Linear Regression Model (6.19).

Source of Variation	SS	df	MS
Regression	$SSR = \mathbf{b'X'Y} - \left(\dfrac{1}{n}\right)\mathbf{Y'JY}$	$p-1$	$MSR = \dfrac{SSR}{p-1}$
Error	$SSE = \mathbf{Y'Y} - \mathbf{b'X'Y}$	$n-p$	$MSE = \dfrac{SSE}{n-p}$
Total	$SSTO = \mathbf{Y'Y} - \left(\dfrac{1}{n}\right)\mathbf{Y'JY}$	$n-1$	

$$(6.35) \qquad SSE = \mathbf{e'e} = (\mathbf{Y} - \mathbf{Xb})'(\mathbf{Y} - \mathbf{Xb}) = \mathbf{Y'Y} - \mathbf{b'X'Y} = \mathbf{Y'(I - H)Y}$$

$$(6.36) \qquad SSR = \mathbf{b'X'Y} - \left(\frac{1}{n}\right)\mathbf{Y'JY} = \mathbf{Y'}\left[\mathbf{H} - \left(\frac{1}{n}\right)\mathbf{J}\right]\mathbf{Y}$$

where $\mathbf{J}$ is an $n \times n$ matrix of 1s defined in (5.18) and $\mathbf{H}$ is the hat matrix defined in (6.30a).

SSTO, as usual, has $n - 1$ degrees of freedom associated with it. *SSE* has $n - p$ degrees of freedom associated with it since p parameters need to be estimated in the regression function for model (6.19). Finally, *SSR* has $p - 1$ degrees of freedom associated with it, representing the number of X variables $X_1, \ldots, X_{p-1}$.

Table 6.1 shows these analysis of variance results, as well as the mean squares *MSR* and *MSE*.

$$(6.37) \qquad MSR = \frac{SSR}{p-1}$$

$$(6.38) \qquad MSE = \frac{SSE}{n-p}$$

The expectation of *MSE* is σ^2, as for simple linear regression. The expectation of *MSR* is σ^2 plus a quantity that is nonnegative. For instance, when $p - 1 = 2$, we have:

$$E\{MSR\} = \sigma^2 + \frac{1}{2}\left[\beta_1^2 \sum (X_{i1} - \bar{X}_1)^2 + \beta_2^2 \sum (X_{i2} - \bar{X}_2)^2 \right.$$
$$\left. + 2\beta_1\beta_2 \sum (X_{i1} - \bar{X}_1)(X_{i2} - \bar{X}_2)\right]$$

Note that if both β_1 and β_2 equal zero, $E\{MSR\} = \sigma^2$. Otherwise $E\{MSR\} > \sigma^2$.

F Test for Regression Relation

To test whether there is a regression relation between the response variable Y and the set of X variables $X_1, \ldots, X_{p-1}$, i.e., to choose between the alternatives:

$$(6.39a) \qquad \begin{array}{l} H_0\colon \beta_1 = \beta_2 = \cdots = \beta_{p-1} = 0 \\ H_a\colon \text{not all } \beta_k \ (k = 1, \ldots, p-1) \text{ equal zero} \end{array}$$

we use the test statistic:

$$(6.39b) \qquad\qquad F^* = \frac{MSR}{MSE}$$

The decision rule to control the Type I error at α is:

$$
(6.39c) \qquad
\begin{aligned}
&\text{If } F^* \le F(1-\alpha; p-1, n-p), \ \text{conclude } H_0 \\
&\text{If } F^* > F(1-\alpha; p-1, n-p), \ \text{conclude } H_a
\end{aligned}
$$

The existence of a regression relation by itself does not, of course, ensure that useful predictions can be made by using it.

Note that when $p - 1 = 1$, this test reduces to the F test in (2.60) for testing in simple linear regression whether or not $\beta_1 = 0$.

Coefficient of Multiple Determination

The coefficient of multiple determination, denoted by R^2, is defined as follows:

$$(6.40) \qquad\qquad R^2 = \frac{SSR}{SSTO} = 1 - \frac{SSE}{SSTO}$$

It measures the proportionate reduction of total variation in Y associated with the use of the set of X variables $X_1, \ldots, X_{p-1}$. The coefficient of multiple determination R^2 reduces to the coefficient of simple determination r^2 in (2.72) for simple linear regression when $p - 1 = 1$, i.e., when one X variable is in regression model (6.19). Just as for r^2, we have:

$$(6.41) \qquad\qquad 0 \le R^2 \le 1$$

where R^2 assumes the value 0 when all $b_k = 0$ ($k = 1, \ldots, p - 1$), and the value 1 when all Y observations fall directly on the fitted regression surface, i.e., when $Y_i = \hat{Y}_i$ for all i.

Comments

1. To distinguish between the coefficients of determination for simple and multiple regression, we shall from now on call r^2 the coefficient of simple determination.

2. It can be shown that the coefficient of multiple determination R^2 can be viewed as a coefficient of simple determination r^2 between the responses Y_i and the fitted values $\hat{Y}_i$.

3. A large value of R^2 does not necessarily imply that the fitted model is a useful one. For instance, observations may have been taken at only a few levels of the predictor variables. Despite a high R^2 in this case, the fitted model may not be useful if most predictions require extrapolations outside the region of observations. Again, even though R^2 is large, MSE may still be too large for inferences to be useful when high precision is required.

4. Adding more X variables to the regression model can only increase R^2 and never reduce it, because SSE can never become larger with more X variables and $SSTO$ is always the same for a given set of responses. Since R^2 usually can be made larger by including a larger number of predictor variables, it is sometimes suggested that a modified measure be used that adjusts for the number of X variables in the model. The *adjusted coefficient of multiple determination*,

denoted by R_a^2, adjusts R^2 by dividing each sum of squares by its associated degrees of freedom:

$$(6.42) \qquad R_a^2 = 1 - \frac{\dfrac{SSE}{n-p}}{\dfrac{SSTO}{n-1}} = 1 - \left(\frac{n-1}{n-p} \right) \frac{SSE}{SSTO}$$

This adjusted coefficient of multiple determination may actually become smaller when another X variable is introduced into the model, because any decrease in SSE may be more than offset by the loss of a degree of freedom in the denominator $n - p$. ∎

Coefficient of Multiple Correlation

The coefficient of multiple correlation R is the positive square root of R^2:

$$(6.43) \qquad R = \sqrt{R^2}$$

When there is one X variable in regression model (6.19), i.e., when $p - 1 = 1$, the coefficient of multiple correlation R equals in absolute value the correlation coefficient r in (2.74) for simple correlation.

Note

From now on, we call r the *coefficient of simple correlation* to distinguish it from the coefficient of multiple correlation. ∎

6.6 Inferences about Regression Parameters

The least squares and maximum likelihood estimators in **b** are unbiased:

$$(6.44) \qquad E\{\mathbf{b}\} = \boldsymbol{\beta}$$

The variance-covariance matrix $\boldsymbol{\sigma}^2\{\mathbf{b}\}$:

$$(6.45) \qquad \underset{p \times p}{\boldsymbol{\sigma}^2\{\mathbf{b}\}} = \begin{bmatrix} \sigma^2\{b_0\} & \sigma\{b_0, b_1\} & \cdots & \sigma\{b_0, b_{p-1}\} \\ \sigma\{b_1, b_0\} & \sigma^2\{b_1\} & \cdots & \sigma\{b_1, b_{p-1}\} \\ \vdots & \vdots & & \vdots \\ \sigma\{b_{p-1}, b_0\} & \sigma\{b_{p-1}, b_1\} & \cdots & \sigma^2\{b_{p-1}\} \end{bmatrix}$$

is given by:

$$(6.46) \qquad \underset{p \times p}{\boldsymbol{\sigma}^2\{\mathbf{b}\}} = \sigma^2 (\mathbf{X}'\mathbf{X})^{-1}$$

The estimated variance-covariance matrix $s^2\{\mathbf{b}\}$:

(6.47)
$$\underset{p \times p}{s^2\{\mathbf{b}\}} = \begin{bmatrix} s^2\{b_0\} & s\{b_0, b_1\} & \cdots & s\{b_0, b_{p-1}\} \\ s\{b_1, b_0\} & s^2\{b_1\} & \cdots & s\{b_1, b_{p-1}\} \\ \vdots & \vdots & & \vdots \\ s\{b_{p-1}, b_0\} & s\{b_{p-1}, b_1\} & \cdots & s^2\{b_{p-1}\} \end{bmatrix}$$

is given by:

(6.48)
$$\underset{p \times p}{s^2\{\mathbf{b}\}} = MSE(\mathbf{X'X})^{-1}$$

From $s^2\{\mathbf{b}\}$, one can obtain $s^2\{b_0\}$, $s^2\{b_1\}$, or whatever other variance is needed, or any needed covariances.

Interval Estimation of β_k

For the normal error regression model (6.19), we have:

(6.49)
$$\frac{b_k - \beta_k}{s\{b_k\}} \sim t(n - p) \qquad k = 0, 1, \ldots, p - 1$$

Hence, the confidence limits for β_k with $1 - \alpha$ confidence coefficient are:

(6.50)
$$b_k \pm t(1 - \alpha/2; n - p)s\{b_k\}$$

Tests for β_k

Tests for β_k are set up in the usual fashion. To test:

(6.51a)
$$H_0: \ \beta_k = 0$$
$$H_a: \ \beta_k \neq 0$$

we may use the test statistic:

(6.51b)
$$t^* = \frac{b_k}{s\{b_k\}}$$

and the decision rule:

(6.51c)
$$\text{If } |t^*| \leq t(1 - \alpha/2; n - p), \ \text{conclude } H_0$$
$$\text{Otherwise conclude } H_a$$

The power of the t test can be obtained as explained in Chapter 2, with the degrees of freedom modified to $n - p$.

As with simple linear regression, an F test can also be conducted to determine whether or not $\beta_k = 0$ in multiple regression models. We discuss this test in Chapter 7.

Joint Inferences

The Bonferroni joint confidence intervals can be used to estimate several regression coefficients simultaneously. If g parameters are to be estimated jointly (where $g \leq p$), the confidence limits with family confidence coefficient $1 - \alpha$ are:

$$b_k \pm Bs\{b_k\} \tag{6.52}$$

where:

$$B = t(1 - \alpha/2g; n - p) \tag{6.52a}$$

In Chapter 7, we discuss tests concerning subsets of the regression parameters.

6.7   Estimation of Mean Response and Prediction of New Observation

Interval Estimation of $E\{Y_h\}$

For given values of $X_1, \ldots, X_{p-1}$, denoted by $X_{h1}, \ldots, X_{h,p-1}$, the mean response is denoted by $E\{Y_h\}$. We define the vector $\mathbf{X}_h$:

$$\mathbf{X}_{h} \atop {p \times 1} - \begin{bmatrix} 1 \\ X_{h1} \\ \vdots \\ X_{h,p-1} \end{bmatrix} \tag{6.53}$$

so that the mean response to be estimated is:

$$E\{Y_h\} = \mathbf{X}'_h \boldsymbol{\beta} \tag{6.54}$$

The estimated mean response corresponding to $\mathbf{X}_h$, denoted by $\hat{Y}_h$, is:

$$\hat{Y}_h = \mathbf{X}'_h \mathbf{b} \tag{6.55}$$

This estimator is unbiased:

$$E\{\hat{Y}_h\} = \mathbf{X}'_h \boldsymbol{\beta} = E\{Y_h\} \tag{6.56}$$

and its variance is:

$$\sigma^2\{\hat{Y}_h\} = \sigma^2 \mathbf{X}'_h (\mathbf{X}'\mathbf{X})^{-1} \mathbf{X}_h \tag{6.57}$$

This variance can be expressed as a function of the variance-covariance matrix of the estimated regression coefficients:

$$\sigma^2\{\hat{Y}_h\} = \mathbf{X}'_h \boldsymbol{\sigma}^2\{\mathbf{b}\} \mathbf{X}_h \tag{6.57a}$$

Note from (6.57a) that the variance $\sigma^2\{\hat{Y}_h\}$ is a function of the variances $\sigma^2\{b_k\}$ of the regression coefficients and of the covariances $\sigma\{b_k, b_{k'}\}$ between pairs of regression coefficients, just as in simple linear regression. The estimated variance $s^2\{\hat{Y}_h\}$ is given by:

$$(6.58) \qquad s^2\{\hat{Y}_h\} = MSE(\mathbf{X}_h'(\mathbf{X}'\mathbf{X})^{-1}\mathbf{X}_h) = \mathbf{X}_h's^2\{\mathbf{b}\}\mathbf{X}_h$$

The $1 - \alpha$ confidence limits for $E\{Y_h\}$ are:

$$(6.59) \qquad \hat{Y}_h \pm t(1 - \alpha/2; n - p)s\{\hat{Y}_h\}$$

Confidence Region for Regression Surface

The $1 - \alpha$ confidence region for the entire regression surface is an extension of the Working-Hotelling confidence band (2.40) for the regression line when there is one predictor variable. Boundary points of the confidence region at $\mathbf{X}_h$ are obtained from:

$$(6.60) \qquad \hat{Y}_h \pm Ws\{\hat{Y}_h\}$$

where:

$$(6.60a) \qquad W^2 = pF(1 - \alpha; p, n - p)$$

The confidence coefficient $1 - \alpha$ provides assurance that the region contains the entire regression surface over all combinations of values of the X variables.

Simultaneous Confidence Intervals for Several Mean Responses

To estimate a number of mean responses $E\{Y_h\}$ corresponding to different $\mathbf{X}_h$ vectors with family confidence coefficient $1 - \alpha$, we can employ two basic approaches:

1. Use the Working-Hotelling confidence region bounds (6.60) for the several $\mathbf{X}_h$ vectors of interest:

$$(6.61) \qquad \hat{Y}_h \pm Ws\{\hat{Y}_h\}$$

where $\hat{Y}_h$, W, and $s\{\hat{Y}_h\}$ are defined in (6.55), (6.60a), and (6.58), respectively. Since the Working-Hotelling confidence region covers the mean responses for all possible $\mathbf{X}_h$ vectors with confidence coefficient $1 - \alpha$, the selected boundary values will cover the mean responses for the $\mathbf{X}_h$ vectors of interest with family confidence coefficient greater than $1 - \alpha$.

2. Use Bonferroni simultaneous confidence intervals. When g interval estimates are to be made, the Bonferroni confidence limits are:

$$(6.62) \qquad \hat{Y}_h \pm Bs\{\hat{Y}_h\}$$

where:

$$(6.62a) \qquad B = t(1 - \alpha/2g; n - p)$$

For any particular application, we can compare the W and B multiples to see which procedure will lead to narrower confidence intervals. If the $\mathbf{X}_h$ levels are not specified in advance but are determined as the analysis proceeds, it is better to use the Working-Hotelling limits (6.61) since the family for this procedure includes all possible $\mathbf{X}_h$ levels.

Prediction of New Observation $Y_{h(new)}$

The $1 - \alpha$ prediction limits for a new observation $Y_{h(new)}$ corresponding to $\mathbf{X}_h$, the specified values of the X variables, are:

$$(6.63) \qquad \hat{Y}_h + t(1 - \alpha/2; n - p)s\{\text{pred}\}$$

where:

$$(6.63a) \qquad s^2\{\text{pred}\} = MSE + s^2\{\hat{Y}_h\} = MSE(1 + \mathbf{X}_h'(\mathbf{X}'\mathbf{X})^{-1}\mathbf{X}_h)$$

and $s^2\{\hat{Y}_h\}$ is given by (6.58).

Prediction of Mean of m New Observations at X_h

When m new observations are to be selected at the same levels $\mathbf{X}_h$ and their mean $\bar{Y}_{h(new)}$ is to be predicted, the $1 - \alpha$ prediction limits are:

$$(6.64) \qquad \hat{Y}_h \pm t(1 - \alpha/2; n - p)s\{\text{predmean}\}$$

where:

$$(6.64a) \qquad s^2\{\text{predmean}\} = \frac{MSE}{m} + s^2\{\hat{Y}_h\} = MSE\left(\frac{1}{m} + \mathbf{X}_h'(\mathbf{X}'\mathbf{X})^{-1}\mathbf{X}_h\right)$$

Predictions of g New Observations

Simultaneous Scheffé prediction limits for g new observations at g different levels $\mathbf{X}_h$ with family confidence coefficient $1 - \alpha$ are given by:

$$(6.65) \qquad \hat{Y}_h \pm Ss\{\text{pred}\}$$

where:

$$(6.65a) \qquad S^2 = gF(1 - \alpha; g, n - p)$$

and $s^2\{\text{pred}\}$ is given by (6.63a).

Alternatively, Bonferroni simultaneous prediction limits can be used. For g predictions with family confidence coefficient $1 - \alpha$, they are:

$$(6.66) \qquad \hat{Y}_h \pm Bs\{\text{pred}\}$$

where:

$$(6.66a) \qquad B = t(1 - \alpha/2g; n - p)$$

A comparison of S and B in advance of any particular use will indicate which procedure will lead to narrower prediction intervals.

FIGURE 6.3   **Region of Observations on X_1 and X_2 Jointly, Compared with Ranges of X_1 and X_2 Individually.**

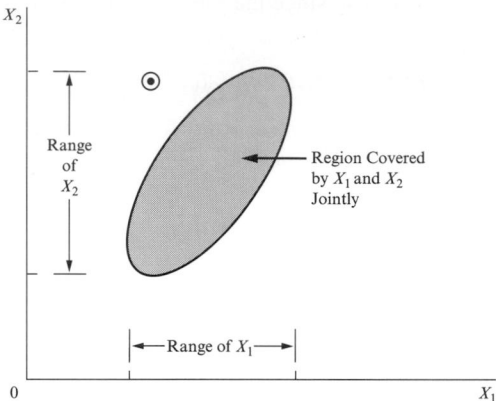

Caution about Hidden Extrapolations

When estimating a mean response or predicting a new observation in multiple regression, one needs to be particularly careful that the estimate or prediction does not fall outside the scope of the model. The danger, of course, is that the model may not be appropriate when it is extended outside the region of the observations. In multiple regression, it is particularly easy to lose track of this region since the levels of $X_1, \ldots, X_{p-1}$ *jointly* define the region. Thus, one cannot merely look at the ranges of each predictor variable. Consider Figure 6.3, where the shaded region is the region of observations for a multiple regression application with two predictor variables and the circled dot represents the values (X_{h1}, X_{h2}) for which a prediction is to be made. The circled dot is within the ranges of the predictor variables X_1 and X_2 individually, yet is well outside the joint region of observations. It is easy to spot this extrapolation when there are only two predictor variables, but it becomes much more difficult when the number of predictor variables is large. We discuss in Chapter 9 a procedure for identifying hidden extrapolations when there are more than two predictor variables.

6.8   Diagnostics and Remedial Measures

Diagnostics play an important role in the development and evaluation of multiple regression models. Most of the diagnostic procedures for simple linear regression that we described in Chapter 3 carry over directly to multiple regression. We review these diagnostic procedures now, as well as the remedial measures for simple linear regression that carry over directly to multiple regression.

Many specialized diagnostics and remedial procedures for multiple regression have also been developed. Some important ones will be discussed in Chapters 9 and 10.

Scatter Plot Matrix

Box plots, sequence plots, stem-and-leaf plots, and dot plots for each of the predictor variables and for the responsevariable can provide helpful, preliminary univariate information

FIGURE 6.4   SYGRAPH Scatter Plot Matrix and Correlation Matrix—Dwaine Studios Example.

(a)
Scatter Plot Matrix

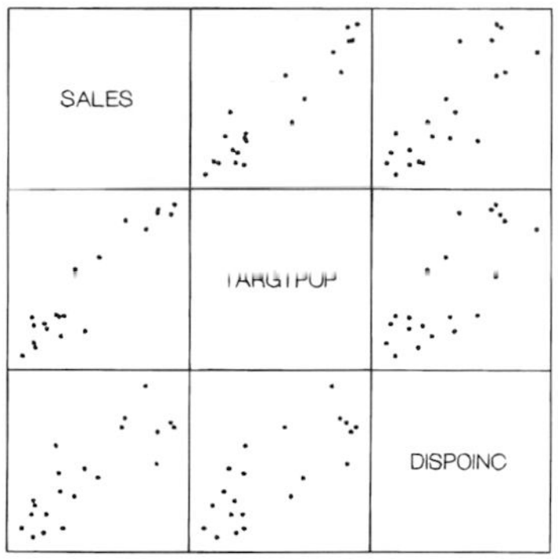

(b)
Correlation Matrix

	SALES	TARGTPOP	DISPOINC
SALES	1.000	.945	.836
TARGTPOP		1.000	.781
DISPOINC			1.000

about these variables. Scatter plots of the response variable against each predictor variable can aid in determining the nature and strength of the bivariate relationships between each of the predictor variables and the response variable and in identifying gaps in the data points as well as outlying data points. Scatter plots of each predictor variable against each of the other predictor variables are helpful for studying the bivariate relationships among the predictor variables and for finding gaps and detecting outliers.

Analysis is facilitated if these scatter plots are assembled in a *scatter plot matrix,* such as in Figure 6.4. In this figure, the Y variable for any one scatter plot is the name found in its row, and the X variable is the name found in its column. Thus, the scatter plot matrix in Figure 6.4 shows in the first row the plots of Y (SALES) against X_1 (TARGETPOP) and X_2 (DISPOINC), of X_1 against Y and X_2 in the second row, and of X_2 against Y and X_1 in the third row. Alternatively, by viewing the first column, one can compare the plots of X_1 and X_2 each against Y, and similarly for the other two columns. A scatter plot matrix facilitates the study of the relationships among the variables by comparing the scatter plots within a row or a column. Examples in this and subsequent chapters will illustrate the usefulness of scatter plot matrices.

A complement to the scatter plot matrix that may be useful at times is the correlation matrix. This matrix contains the coefficients of simple correlation $r_{Y1}, r_{Y2}, \ldots, r_{Y,p-1}$ between Y and each of the predictor variables, as well as all of the coefficients of simple correlation among the predictor variables—r_{12} between X_1 and X_2, r_{13} between X_1 and X_3, etc. The format of the correlation matrix follows that of the scatter plot matrix:

$$(6.67) \qquad \begin{bmatrix} 1 & r_{Y1} & r_{Y2} & \cdots & r_{Y,p-1} \\ r_{Y1} & 1 & r_{12} & \cdots & r_{1,p-1} \\ \vdots & \vdots & \vdots & & \vdots \\ r_{Y,p-1} & r_{1,p-1} & r_{2,p-1} & \cdots & 1 \end{bmatrix}$$

Note that the correlation matrix is symmetric and that its main diagonal contains 1s because the coefficient of correlation between a variable and itself is 1. Many statistics packages provide the correlation matrix as an option. Since this matrix is symmetric, the lower (or upper) triangular block of elements is frequently omitted in the output.

Some interactive statistics packages enable the user to employ *brushing* with scatter plot matrices. When a point in a scatter plot is brushed, it is given a distinctive appearance on the computer screen in each scatter plot in the matrix. The case corresponding to the brushed point may also be identified. Brushing is helpful to see whether a case that is outlying in one scatter plot is also outlying in some or all of the other plots. Brushing may also be applied to a group of points to see, for instance, whether a group of cases that does not fit the relationship for the remaining cases in one scatter plot also follows a distinct pattern in any of the other scatter plots.

Three-Dimensional Scatter Plots

Some interactive statistics packages provide *three-dimensional scatter plots* or *point clouds*, and permit spinning of these plots to enable the viewer to see the point cloud from different perspectives. This can be very helpful for identifying patterns that are only apparent from certain perspectives. Figure 6.6 on page 242 illustrates a three-dimensional scatter plot and the use of spinning.

Residual Plots

A plot of the residuals against the fitted values is useful for assessing the appropriateness of the multiple regression function and the constancy of the variance of the error terms, as well as for providing information about outliers, just as for simple linear regression. Similarly, a plot of the residuals against time or against some other sequence can provide diagnostic information about possible correlations between the error terms in multiple regression. Box plots and normal probability plots of the residuals are useful for examining whether the error terms are reasonably normally distributed.

In addition, residuals should be plotted against each of the predictor variables. Each of these plots can provide further information about the adequacy of the regression function with respect to that predictor variable (*e.g.*, whether a curvature effect is required for that variable) and about possible variation in the magnitude of the error variance in relation to that predictor variable.

Residuals should also be plotted against important predictor variables that were omitted from the model, to see if the omitted variables have substantial additional effects on the response variable that have not yet been recognized in the regression model. Also, residuals should be plotted against interaction terms for potential interaction effects not included in the regression model, such as against X_1X_2, X_1X_3, and X_2X_3, to see whether some or all of these interaction terms are required in the model.

A plot of the absolute residuals or the squared residuals against the fitted values is useful for examining the constancy of the variance of the error terms. If nonconstancy is detected, a plot of the absolute residuals or the squared residuals against each of the predictor variables may identify one or several of the predictor variables to which the magnitude of the error variability is related.

Correlation Test for Normality

The correlation test for normality described in Chapter 3 carries forward directly to multiple regression. The expected values of the ordered residuals under normality are calculated according to (3.6), and the coefficient of correlation between the residuals and the expected values under normality is then obtained. Table B.6 is employed to assess whether or not the magnitude of the correlation coefficient supports the reasonableness of the normality assumption.

Modified Levene Test for Constancy of Error Variance

The modified Levene test statistic (3.9) for assessing the constancy of the error variance can be used readily in multiple regression when the error variance increases or decreases with one of the predictor variables. To conduct the Levene test, we divide the data set into two groups, as for simple linear regression, where one group consists of cases where the level of the predictor variable is relatively low and the other group consists of cases where the level of the predictor variable is relatively high. The Levene test then proceeds as for simple linear regression.

Breusch-Pagan Test for Constancy of Error Variance

The Breusch-Pagan test (3.11) for constancy of the error variance in multiple regression is carried out exactly the same as for simple linear regression when the error variance increases or decreases with one of the predictor variables. The squared residuals are simply regressed against the predictor variable to obtain the regression sum of squares SSR^*, and the test proceeds as before, using the error sum of squares SSE for the full multiple regression model.

When the error variance is a function of more than one predictor variable, a multiple regression of the squared residuals against these predictor variables is conducted and the regression sum of squares SSR^* is obtained. The test statistic again uses SSE for the full multiple regression model, but now the chi-square distribution involves q degrees of freedom, where q is the number of predictor variables against which the squared residuals are regressed.

F Test for Lack of Fit

The lack of fit F test described in Chapter 3 for simple linear regression can be carried over to test whether the multiple regression response function:

$$E\{Y\} = \beta_0 + \beta_1 X_1 + \cdots + \beta_{p-1} X_{p-1}$$

is an appropriate response surface. Repeat observations in multiple regression are replicate observations on Y corresponding to levels of each of the X variables that are constant from trial to trial. Thus, with two predictor variables, repeat observations require that X_1 and X_2 each remain at given levels from trial to trial.

Once the ANOVA table, shown in Table 6.1, has been obtained, SSE is decomposed into pure error and lack of fit components. The pure error sum of squares $SSPE$ is obtained by first calculating for each replicate group the sum of squared deviations of the Y observations around the group mean, where a replicate group has the same values for each of the X variables. Let c denote the number of groups with distinct sets of levels for the X variables, and let the mean of the Y observations for the jth group be denoted by $\bar{Y}_j$. Then the sum of squares for the jth group is given by (3.17), and the pure error sum of squares is the sum of these sums of squares, as given by (3.16). The lack of fit sum of squares $SSLF$ equals the difference $SSE - SSPE$, as indicated by (3.24).

The number of degrees of freedom associated with $SSPE$ is $n - c$, and the number of degrees of freedom associated with $SSLF$ is $(n - p) - (n - c) = c - p$. Thus, for testing the alternatives:

(6.68a)
$$H_0: \quad E\{Y\} = \beta_0 + \beta_1 X_1 + \cdots + \beta_{p-1} X_{p-1}$$
$$H_a: \quad E\{Y\} \neq \beta_0 + \beta_1 X_1 + \cdots + \beta_{p-1} X_{p-1}$$

the appropriate test statistic is:

(6.68b)
$$F^* = \frac{SSLF}{c - p} \div \frac{SSPE}{n - c} = \frac{MSLF}{MSPE}$$

where $SSLF$ and $SSPE$ are given by (3.24) and (3.16), respectively, and the appropriate decision rule is:

(6.68c)
$$\text{If } F^* \leq F(1 - \alpha; c - p, n - c), \quad \text{conclude } H_0$$
$$\text{If } F^* > F(1 - \alpha; c - p, n - c), \quad \text{conclude } H_a$$

> ### Note
>
> When replicate observations are not available, an approximate lack of fit test can be conducted if there are cases that have similar $\mathbf{X}_h$ vectors. These cases are grouped together and treated as pseudoreplicates, and the test for lack of fit is then carried out using these groupings of similar cases.   ∎

Remedial Measures

The remedial measures described in Chapter 3 are also applicable to multiple regression. When a more complex model is required to recognize curvature or interaction effects, the multiple regression model can be expanded to include these effects. For example, X_2^2 might be added as a variable to take into account a curvature effect of X_2, or $X_1 X_3$ might be added as a variable to recognize an interaction effect between X_1 and X_3 on the response variable. Alternatively, transformations on the response and/or the predictor variables can be made, following the principles discussed in Chapter 3, to remedy model deficiencies. Transformations on the response variable Y may be helpful when the distributions of the error terms are quite skewed and the variance of the error terms is not constant. Transformations of some of the predictor variables may be helpful when the effects of these variables are curvilinear. In addition, transformations on Y and/or the predictor variables may be helpful in eliminating or substantially reducing interaction effects.

As with simple linear regression, the usefulness of potential transformations needs to be examined by means of residual plots and other diagnostic tools to determine whether the multiple regression model for the transformed data is appropriate.

Box-Cox Transformations.   The Box-Cox procedure for determining an appropriate power transformation on Y for simple linear regression models described in Chapter 3 is also applicable to multiple regression models. The standardized variable W in (3.36) is again obtained for different values of the parameter λ and is now regressed against the set of X variables in the multiple regression model to find that value of λ that minimizes the error sum of squares SSE.

FIGURE 6.5   **SYSTAT Multiple Regression Output and Basic Data—Dwaine Studios Example.**

(a) Multiple Regression Output

```
DEP VAR:  SALES    N:  21    MULTIPLE R:  0.957    SQUARED MULTIPLE R:
                                                          0.917
ADJUSTED SQUARED MULTIPLE R: .907    STANDARD ERROR OF ESTIMATE:
                                                  11.0074


VARIABLE    COEFFICIENT    STD ERROR    STD COEF    TOLERANCE      T      P(2 TAIL)

CONSTANT     -68.8571       60.0170      0.0000        .        -1.1473    0.2663
TARGTPOP       1.4546        0.2118      0.7484      0.3896      6.8682    0.0000
DISPOINC       9.3655        4.0640      0.2511      0.3896      2.3045    0.0333


                  ANALYSIS OF VARIANCE

SOURCE      SUM-OF-SQUARES    DF    MEAN-SQUARE     F-RATIO       P

REGRESSION     24015.2821      2    12007.6411      99.1035    0.0000
RESIDUAL        2180.9274     18      121.1626


INVERSE (X'X)

                    1            2          3

        1       29.7289
        2        0.0722      0.00037
        3       -1.9926     -0.0056     0.1363
```

(b) Basic Data

CASE	X1	X2	Y	FITTED	RESIDUAL
1	68.5	16.7	174.4	187.184	-12.7841
2	45.2	16.8	164.4	154.229	10.1706
3	91.3	18.2	244.2	234.396	9.8037
4	47.8	16.3	154.6	153.329	1.2715
5	46.9	17.3	181.6	161.385	20.2151
6	66.1	18.2	207.5	197.741	9.7586
7	49.5	15.9	152.8	152.055	0.7449
8	52.0	17.2	163.2	167.867	-4.6666
9	48.9	16.6	145.4	157.738	-12.3382
10	38.4	16.0	137.2	136.846	0.3540
11	87.9	18.3	241.9	230.387	11.5126
12	72.8	17.1	191.1	197.185	-6.0849
13	88.4	17.4	232.0	222.686	9.3143
14	42.9	15.8	145.3	141.518	3.7816
15	52.5	17.8	161.1	174.213	-13.1132
16	85.7	18.4	209.7	228.124	-18.4239
17	41.3	16.5	146.4	145.747	0.6530
18	51.7	16.3	144.0	159.001	-15.0013
19	89.6	18.1	232.6	230.987	1.6130
20	82.7	19.1	224.1	230.316	-6.2160
21	52.3	16.0	166.5	157.064	9.4356

Box and Tidwell (Ref. 6.1) have also developed an iterative approach for ascertaining appropriate power transformations for each predictor variable in a multiple regression model when transformations on the predictor variables may be required.

6.9   An Example—Multiple Regression with Two Predictor Variables

In this section, we shall develop a multiple regression application with two predictor variables. We shall illustrate several diagnostic procedures and several types of inferences that might be made for this application. We shall set up the necessary calculations in matrix format but, for ease of viewing, show fewer significant digits for the elements of the matrices than are used in the actual calculations.

Setting

Dwaine Studios, Inc., operates portrait studios in 21 cities of medium size. These studios specialize in portraits of children. The company is considering an expansion into other cities of medium size and wishes to investigate whether sales (Y) in a community can be predicted from the number of persons aged 16 or younger in the community (X_1) and the per capita disposable personal income in the community (X_2). Data on these variables for the most recent year for the 21 cities in which Dwaine Studios is now operating are shown in Figure 6.5b. Sales are expressed in thousands of dollars and are labeled Y or SALES; the number of persons aged 16 or younger is expressed in thousands of persons and is labeled X_1 or TARGTPOP for target population; and per capita disposable personal income is expressed in thousands of dollars and labeled X_2 or DISPOINC for disposable income.

FIGURE 6.6   **SYGRAPH Plot of Point Cloud before and after Spinning—Dwaine Studios Example.**

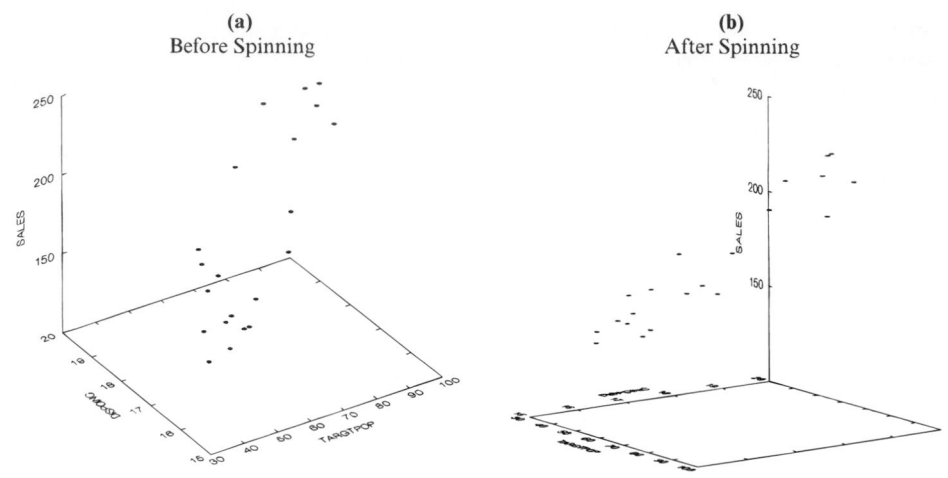

(a)
Before Spinning

(b)
After Spinning

The first-order regression model:

(6.69)
$$Y_i = \beta_0 + \beta_1 X_{i1} + \beta_2 X_{i2} + \varepsilon_i$$

with normal error terms is expected to be appropriate, based on the SYGRAPH scatter plot matrix in Figure 6.4a. Note the linear relation between target population and sales and between disposable income and sales. Also note that there is more scatter in the latter relationship. Finally note that there is also some linear relationship between the two predictor variables. The correlation matrix in Figure 6.4b bears out these visual impressions from the scatter plot matrix.

A SYGRAPH plot of the point cloud is shown in Figure 6.6a. By spinning the axes, we obtain the perspective in Figure 6.6b which supports the tentative conclusion that a response plane may be a reasonable regression function to utilize here.

Basic Calculations

The **X** and **Y** matrices for the Dwaine Studios example are as follows:

(6.70)
$$\mathbf{X} = \begin{bmatrix} 1 & 68.5 & 16.7 \\ 1 & 45.2 & 16.8 \\ \vdots & \vdots & \vdots \\ 1 & 52.3 & 16.0 \end{bmatrix} \qquad \mathbf{Y} = \begin{bmatrix} 174.4 \\ 164.4 \\ \vdots \\ 166.5 \end{bmatrix}$$

We require:

1.

$$\mathbf{X'X} = \begin{bmatrix} 1 & 1 & \cdots & 1 \\ 68.5 & 45.2 & \cdots & 52.3 \\ 16.7 & 16.8 & \cdots & 16.0 \end{bmatrix} \begin{bmatrix} 1 & 68.5 & 16.7 \\ 1 & 45.2 & 16.8 \\ \vdots & \vdots & \vdots \\ 1 & 52.3 & 16.0 \end{bmatrix}$$

which yields:

(6.71)
$$\mathbf{X'X} = \begin{bmatrix} 21.0 & 1,302.4 & 360.0 \\ 1,302.4 & 87,707.9 & 22,609.2 \\ 360.0 & 22,609.2 & 6,190.3 \end{bmatrix}$$

2.

$$\mathbf{X'Y} = \begin{bmatrix} 1 & 1 & \cdots & 1 \\ 68.5 & 45.2 & \cdots & 52.3 \\ 16.7 & 16.8 & \cdots & 16.0 \end{bmatrix} \begin{bmatrix} 174.4 \\ 164.4 \\ \vdots \\ 166.5 \end{bmatrix}$$

which yields:

(6.72)
$$\mathbf{X'Y} = \begin{bmatrix} 3,820 \\ 249,643 \\ 66,073 \end{bmatrix}$$

3.

$$(\mathbf{X'X})^{-1} = \begin{bmatrix} 21.0 & 1,302.4 & 360.0 \\ 1,302.4 & 87,707.9 & 22,609.2 \\ 360.0 & 22,609.2 & 6,190.3 \end{bmatrix}^{-1}$$

Using (5.23), we obtain:

(6.73)
$$(\mathbf{X'X})^{-1} = \begin{bmatrix} 29.7289 & .0722 & -1.9926 \\ .0722 & .00037 & -.0056 \\ -1.9926 & -.0056 & .1363 \end{bmatrix}$$

Algebraic Equivalents.   Note that $\mathbf{X'X}$ for the first-order regression model (6.69) with two predictor variables is:

$$\mathbf{X'X} = \begin{bmatrix} 1 & 1 & \cdots & 1 \\ X_{11} & X_{21} & \cdots & X_{n1} \\ X_{12} & X_{22} & \cdots & X_{n2} \end{bmatrix} \begin{bmatrix} 1 & X_{11} & X_{12} \\ 1 & X_{21} & X_{22} \\ \vdots & \vdots & \vdots \\ 1 & X_{n1} & X_{n2} \end{bmatrix}$$

or:

(6.74)
$$\mathbf{X'X} = \begin{bmatrix} n & \Sigma X_{i1} & \Sigma X_{i2} \\ \Sigma X_{i1} & \Sigma X_{i1}^2 & \Sigma X_{i1}X_{i2} \\ \Sigma X_{i2} & \Sigma X_{i2}X_{i1} & \Sigma X_{i2}^2 \end{bmatrix}$$

For the Dwaine Studios example, we have:

$$n = 21$$

$$\sum X_{i1} = 68.5 + 45.2 + \cdots = 1,302.4$$

$$\sum X_{i1}X_{i2} = 68.5(16.7) + 45.2(16.8) + \cdots = 22,609.2$$

$$\text{etc.}$$

These elements are found in (6.71).

Also note that $\mathbf{X}'\mathbf{Y}$ for the first-order regression model (6.69) with two predictor variables is:

$$(6.75) \qquad \mathbf{X}'\mathbf{Y} = \begin{bmatrix} 1 & 1 & \cdots & 1 \\ X_{11} & X_{21} & \cdots & X_{n1} \\ X_{12} & X_{22} & \cdots & X_{n2} \end{bmatrix} \begin{bmatrix} Y_1 \\ Y_2 \\ \vdots \\ Y_n \end{bmatrix} = \begin{bmatrix} \Sigma Y_i \\ \Sigma X_{i1} Y_i \\ \Sigma X_{i2} Y_i \end{bmatrix}$$

For the Dwaine Studios example, we have:

$$\sum Y_i = 174.4 + 164.4 + \cdots = 3{,}820$$

$$\sum X_{i1} Y_i = 68.5(174.4) + 45.2(164.4) + \cdots = 249{,}643$$

$$\sum X_{i2} Y_i = 16.7(174.4) + 16.8(164.4) + \cdots = 66{,}073$$

These are the elements found in (6.72).

Estimated Regression Function

The least squares estimates $\mathbf{b}$ are readily obtained by (6.25), using our basic calculations in (6.72) and (6.73):

$$\mathbf{b} = (\mathbf{X}'\mathbf{X})^{-1}\mathbf{X}'\mathbf{Y} = \begin{bmatrix} 29.7289 & .0722 & -1.9926 \\ .0722 & .00037 & -.0056 \\ -1.9926 & -.0056 & .1363 \end{bmatrix} \begin{bmatrix} 3{,}820 \\ 249{,}643 \\ 66{,}073 \end{bmatrix}$$

which yields:

$$(6.76) \qquad \mathbf{b} = \begin{bmatrix} b_0 \\ b_1 \\ b_2 \end{bmatrix} = \begin{bmatrix} -68.857 \\ 1.455 \\ 9.366 \end{bmatrix}$$

and the estimated regression function is:

$$\hat{Y} = -68.857 + 1.455 X_1 + 9.366 X_2$$

This estimated regression function indicates that mean sales are expected to increase by 1.455 thousand dollars when the target population increases by 1 thousand persons aged 16 years or younger, holding per capita disposable personal income constant, and that mean sales are expected to increase by 9.366 thousand dollars when per capita income increases by 1 thousand dollars, holding the target population constant.

Figure 6.5a contains SYSTAT multiple regression output for the Dwaine Studios example. The estimated regression coefficients are shown in the column labeled COEFFICIENT; the output shows one more decimal place than we have shown.

The SYSTAT output also contains the inverse of the $\mathbf{X}'\mathbf{X}$ matrix that we calculated earlier; only the lower portion of the symmetric matrix is shown. The results are the same as in (6.73).

Algebraic Version of Normal Equations.   The normal equations in algebraic form for the case of two predictor variables can be obtained readily from (6.74) and (6.75). We have:

$$(\mathbf{X'X})\mathbf{b} = \mathbf{X'Y}$$

$$\begin{bmatrix} n & \sum X_{i1} & \sum X_{i2} \\ \sum X_{i1} & \sum X_{i1}^2 & \sum X_{i1}X_{i2} \\ \sum X_{i2} & \sum X_{i2}X_{i1} & \sum X_{i2}^2 \end{bmatrix} \begin{bmatrix} b_0 \\ b_1 \\ b_2 \end{bmatrix} = \begin{bmatrix} \sum Y_i \\ \sum X_{i1}Y_i \\ \sum X_{i2}Y_i \end{bmatrix}$$

from which we obtain the normal equations:

$$\sum Y_i = nb_0 + b_1 \sum X_{i1} + b_2 \sum X_{i2}$$

(6.77) $$\sum X_{i1}Y_i = b_0 \sum X_{i1} + b_1 \sum X_{i1}^2 + b_2 \sum X_{i1}X_{i2}$$

$$\sum X_{i2}Y_i = b_0 \sum X_{i2} + b_1 \sum X_{i1}X_{i2} + b_2 \sum X_{i2}^2$$

Fitted Values and Residuals

To examine the appropriateness of regression model (6.69) for the data at hand, we require the fitted values $\hat{Y}_i$ and the residuals $e_i = Y_i - \hat{Y}_i$. We obtain by (6.28):

$$\hat{\mathbf{Y}} = \mathbf{Xb}$$

$$\begin{bmatrix} \hat{Y}_1 \\ \hat{Y}_2 \\ \vdots \\ \hat{Y}_{21} \end{bmatrix} = \begin{bmatrix} 1 & 68.5 & 16.7 \\ 1 & 45.2 & 16.8 \\ \vdots & \vdots & \vdots \\ 1 & 52.3 & 16.0 \end{bmatrix} \begin{bmatrix} -68.857 \\ 1.455 \\ 9.366 \end{bmatrix} = \begin{bmatrix} 187.2 \\ 154.2 \\ \vdots \\ 157.1 \end{bmatrix}$$

Further, by (6.29) we find:

$$\mathbf{e} = \mathbf{Y} - \hat{\mathbf{Y}}$$

$$\begin{bmatrix} e_1 \\ e_2 \\ \vdots \\ e_{21} \end{bmatrix} = \begin{bmatrix} 174.4 \\ 164.4 \\ \vdots \\ 166.5 \end{bmatrix} - \begin{bmatrix} 187.2 \\ 154.2 \\ \vdots \\ 157.1 \end{bmatrix} = \begin{bmatrix} -12.8 \\ 10.2 \\ \vdots \\ 9.4 \end{bmatrix}$$

Figure 6.5b shows the computer output for the fitted values and residuals to more decimal places than we have presented.

Analysis of Appropriateness of Model

We begin our analysis of the appropriateness of regression model (6.69) for the Dwaine Studios example by considering the plot of the residuals e against the fitted values $\hat{Y}$ in Figure 6.7a. This plot does not suggest any systematic deviations from the response plane, nor that the variance of the error terms varies with the level of $\hat{Y}$. Plots of the residuals e

FIGURE 6.7 SYGRAPH Diagnostic Plots—Dwaine Studios Example.

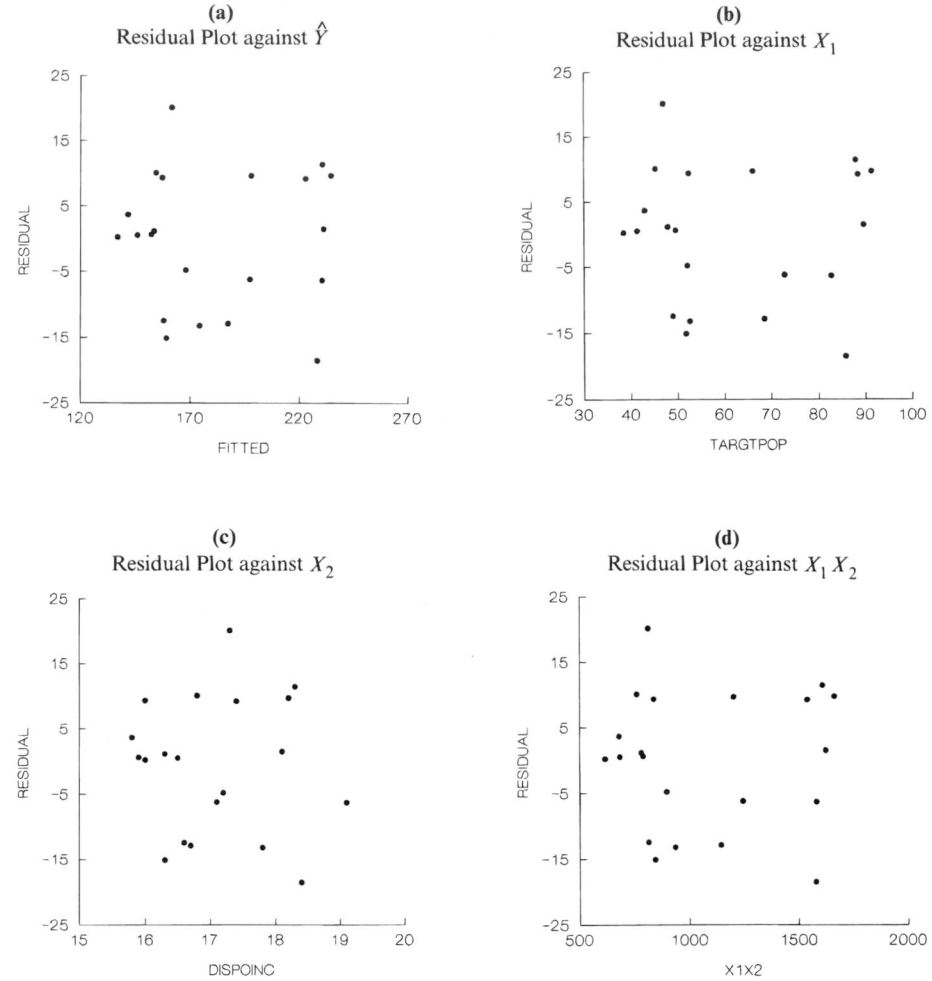

against X_1 and X_2 in Figures 6.7b and 6.7c, respectively, are entirely consistent with the conclusions of good fit by the response function and constant variance of the error terms.

In multiple regression applications, there is frequently the possibility of interaction effects being present. To examine this for the Dwaine Studios example, we plotted the residuals e against the interaction term X_1X_2 in Figure 6.7d. A systematic pattern of this plot would suggest that an interaction effect may be present, so that a response function of the type:

$$E\{Y\} = \beta_0 + \beta_1 X_1 + \beta_2 X_2 + \beta_3 X_1 X_2$$

might be more appropriate. Figure 6.7d does not exhibit any systematic pattern; hence, no interaction effects reflected by the model term $\beta_3 X_1 X_2$ appear to be present.

Figure 6.8 contains two additional diagnostic plots. Figure 6.8a presents a plot of the absolute residuals against the fitted values. There is no indication of nonconstancy of the error variance. Figure 6.8b contains a normal probability plot of the residuals. The pattern

FIGURE 6.8   Additional Diagnostic Plots—Dwaine Studios Example.

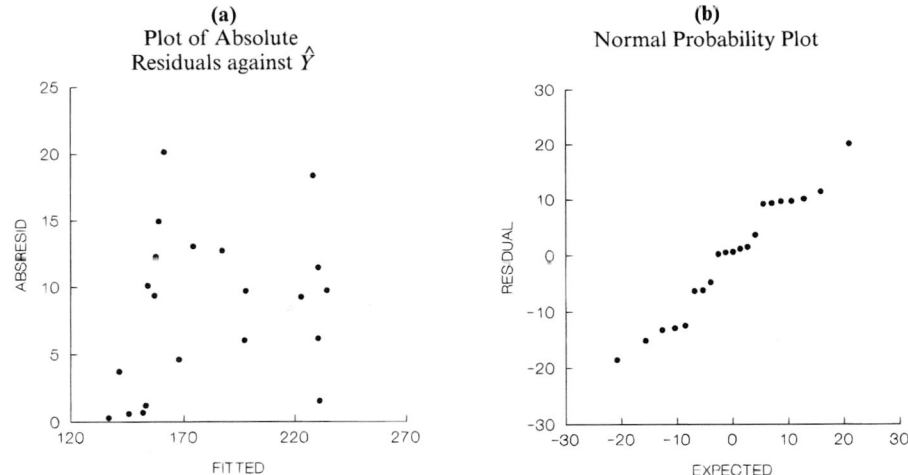

is moderately linear. The coefficient of correlation between the ordered residuals and their expected values under normality is .980. This high value (the interpolated critical value in Table B.6 for $n = 21$ and $\alpha = .05$ is .9525) helps to confirm the reasonableness of the conclusion that the error terms are fairly normally distributed.

Since the Dwaine Studios data are cross-sectional and do not involve a time sequence, a time sequence plot is not relevant here. Thus, all of the diagnostics support the use of regression model (6.69) for the Dwaine Studios example.

Analysis of Variance

To test whether sales are related to target population and per capita disposable income, we require the ANOVA table. The basic quantities needed are:

$$\mathbf{Y}'\mathbf{Y} = [174.4 \quad 164.4 \quad \cdots \quad 166.5] \begin{bmatrix} 174.4 \\ 164.4 \\ \vdots \\ 166.5 \end{bmatrix}$$

$$= 721{,}072.40$$

$$\left(\frac{1}{n}\right)\mathbf{Y}'\mathbf{J}\mathbf{Y} = \frac{1}{21}[174.4 \quad 164.4 \quad \cdots \quad 166.5] \begin{bmatrix} 1 & 1 & \cdots & 1 \\ 1 & 1 & \cdots & 1 \\ \vdots & \vdots & & \vdots \\ 1 & 1 & \cdots & 1 \end{bmatrix} \begin{bmatrix} 174.4 \\ 164.4 \\ \vdots \\ 166.5 \end{bmatrix}$$

$$= \frac{(3{,}820.0)^2}{21} = 694{,}876.19$$

Thus:

$$SSTO = \mathbf{Y}'\mathbf{Y} - \left(\frac{1}{n}\right)\mathbf{Y}'\mathbf{J}\mathbf{Y} = 721{,}072.40 - 694{,}876.19 = 26{,}196.21$$

and, using our results in (6.72) and (6.76):

$$SSE = \mathbf{Y'Y} - \mathbf{b'X'Y}$$

$$= 721{,}072.40 - [-68.857 \quad 1.455 \quad 9.366] \begin{bmatrix} 3{,}820 \\ 249{,}643 \\ 66{,}073 \end{bmatrix}$$

$$= 721{,}072.40 - 718{,}891.47 = 2{,}180.93$$

Finally, we obtain by subtraction:

$$SSR = SSTO - SSE = 26{,}196.21 - 2{,}180.93 = 24{,}015.28$$

These sums of squares are shown in the SYSTAT ANOVA table in Figure 6.5a. Also shown in the ANOVA table are degrees of freedom and mean squares. Note that three regression parameters had to be estimated; hence, $21 - 3 = 18$ degrees of freedom are associated with SSE. Also, the number of degrees of freedom associated with SSR is 2—the number of X variables in the model.

Test of Regression Relation.   To test whether sales are related to target population and per capita disposable income:

$$H_0: \quad \beta_1 = 0 \text{ and } \beta_2 = 0$$

$$H_a: \quad \text{not both } \beta_1 \text{ and } \beta_2 \text{ equal zero}$$

we use test statistic (6.39b):

$$F^* = \frac{MSR}{MSE} = \frac{12{,}007.64}{121.1626} = 99.1$$

This test statistic is labeled F-RATIO in the SYSTAT output. For $\alpha = .05$, we require $F(.95; 2, 18) = 3.55$. Since $F^* = 99.1 > 3.55$, we conclude H_a, that sales are related to target population and per capita disposable income. The P-value for this test is .0000, as shown in the SYSTAT output labeled P.

Whether the regression relation is useful for making predictions of sales or estimates of mean sales still remains to be seen.

Coefficient of Multiple Determination.   For our example, we have by (6.40):

$$R^2 = \frac{SSR}{SSTO} = \frac{24{,}015.28}{26{,}196.21} = .917$$

Thus, when the two predictor variables, target population and per capita disposable income, are considered, the variation in sales is reduced by 91.7 percent. The coefficient of multiple determination is shown in the SYSTAT output labeled SQUARED MULTIPLE R. Also shown in the output is the coefficient of multiple correlation $R = .957$ and the adjusted coefficient of multiple determination (6.42), $R_a^2 = .907$, which is labeled in the output ADJUSTED SQUARED MULTIPLE R. Note that adjusting for the number of predictor variables in the model had only a small effect here on R^2.

Estimation of Regression Parameters

Dwaine Studios is not interested in the parameter β_0 since it falls far outside the scope of the model. It is desired to estimate β_1 and β_2 jointly with family confidence coefficient .90. We shall use the simultaneous Bonferroni confidence limits (6.52).

First, we need the estimated variance-covariance matrix $s^2\{\mathbf{b}\}$:

$$s^2\{\mathbf{b}\} = MSE(\mathbf{X'X})^{-1}$$

MSE is given in Figure 6.5a, and $(\mathbf{X'X})^{-1}$ was obtained in (6.73). Hence:

$$(6.78) \qquad s^2\{\mathbf{b}\} = 121.1626 \begin{bmatrix} 29.7289 & .0722 & -1.9926 \\ .0722 & .00037 & -.0056 \\ -1.9926 & -.0056 & .1363 \end{bmatrix}$$

$$= \begin{bmatrix} 3,602.0 & 8.748 & -241.43 \\ 8.748 & .0448 & -.679 \\ -241.43 & -.679 & 16.514 \end{bmatrix}$$

The two estimated variances we require are:

$$s^2\{b_1\} = .0448 \qquad \text{or} \qquad s\{b_1\} = .212$$

$$s^2\{b_2\} = 16.514 \qquad \text{or} \qquad s\{b_2\} = 4.06$$

These estimated standard deviations are shown in the SYSTAT output in Figure 6.5a, labeled STD ERROR, to four decimal places.

Next, we require for $g = 2$ simultaneous estimates:

$$B = t[1 - .10/2(2); 18] = t(.975; 18) = 2.101$$

The two pairs of simultaneous confidence limits therefore are $1.455 \pm 2.101(.212)$ and $9.366 \pm 2.101(4.06)$, which yield the confidence intervals:

$$1.01 \le \beta_1 \le 1.90$$

$$.84 \le \beta_2 \le 17.9$$

With family confidence coefficient .90, we conclude that β_1 falls between 1.01 and 1.90 and that β_2 falls between .84 and 17.9.

Note that the simultaneous confidence intervals suggest that both β_1 and β_2 are positive, which is in accord with theoretical expectations that sales should increase with higher target population and higher per capita disposable income, the other variable being held constant.

Estimation of Mean Response

Dwaine Studios would like to estimate expected (mean) sales in cities with target population $X_{h1} = 65.4$ thousand persons aged 16 years or younger and per capita disposable income $X_{h2} = 17.6$ thousand dollars with a 95 percent confidence interval. We define:

$$\mathbf{X}_h = \begin{bmatrix} 1 \\ 65.4 \\ 17.6 \end{bmatrix}$$

The point estimate of mean sales is by (6.55):

$$\hat{Y}_h = \mathbf{X}_h'\mathbf{b} = [1 \quad 65.4 \quad 17.6] \begin{bmatrix} -68.857 \\ 1.455 \\ 9.366 \end{bmatrix} = 191.10$$

The estimated variance by (6.58), using the results in (6.78), is:

$$s^2\{\hat{Y}_h\} = \mathbf{X}_h's^2\{\mathbf{b}\}\mathbf{X}_h$$

$$= [1 \quad 65.4 \quad 17.6] \begin{bmatrix} 3{,}602.0 & 8.748 & -241.43 \\ 8.748 & .0448 & -.679 \\ -241.43 & -.679 & 16.514 \end{bmatrix} \begin{bmatrix} 1 \\ 65.4 \\ 17.6 \end{bmatrix}$$

$$= 7.656$$

or:

$$s\{\hat{Y}_h\} = 2.77$$

For confidence coefficient .95, we need $t(.975; 18) = 2.101$, and we obtain by (6.59) the confidence limits $191.10 \pm 2.101(2.77)$. The confidence interval for $E\{Y_h\}$ therefore is:

$$185.3 \leq E\{Y_h\} \leq 196.9$$

Thus, with confidence coefficient .95, we estimate that mean sales in cities with target population of 65.4 thousand persons aged 16 years or younger and per capita disposable income of 17.6 thousand dollars are somewhere between 185.3 and 196.9 thousand dollars. Dwaine Studios considers this confidence interval to provide information about expected (average) sales in communities of this size and income level that is precise enough for planning purposes.

Algebraic Version of Estimated Variance $s^2\{\hat{Y}_h\}$.   Since by (6.58):

$$s^2\{\hat{Y}_h\} = \mathbf{X}_h's^2\{\mathbf{b}\}\mathbf{X}_h$$

it follows for the case of two predictor variables in a first-order model:

(6.79) $s^2\{\hat{Y}_h\} = s^2\{b_0\} + X_{h1}^2 s^2\{b_1\} + X_{h2}^2 s^2\{b_2\} + 2X_{h1}s\{b_0, b_1\}$
$$+ 2X_{h2}s\{b_0, b_2\} + 2X_{h1}X_{h2}s\{b_1, b_2\}$$

Prediction Limits for New Observations

Dwaine Studios as part of a possible expansion program would like to predict sales for two new cities, with the following characteristics:

	City A	City B
X_{h1}	65.4	53.1
X_{h2}	17.6	17.7

Prediction intervals with a 90 percent family confidence coefficient are desired. Note that the two new cities have characteristics that fall well within the pattern of the 21 cities on which the regression analysis is based.

To determine which simultaneous prediction intervals are best here, we find S as given in (6.65a) and B as given in (6.66a) for $g = 2$ and $1 - \alpha = .90$:

$$S^2 = 2F(.90; 2, 18) = 2(2.62) = 5.24 \qquad S = 2.29$$

and:

$$B = t[1 - .10/2(2); 18] = t(.975; 18) = 2.101$$

Hence, the Bonferroni limits are more efficient here.

For city A, we use the results obtained when estimating mean sales, since the levels of the predictor variables are the same here. We have from before.

$$\hat{Y}_h = 191.10 \qquad s^2\{\hat{Y}_h\} = 7.656 \qquad MSE = 121.1626$$

Hence, by (6.63a):

$$s^2\{\text{pred}\} = MSE + s^2\{\hat{Y}_h\} = 121.1626 + 7.656 = 128.82$$

or:

$$s\{\text{pred}\} = 11.35$$

In similar fashion, we obtain for city B (calculations not shown):

$$\hat{Y}_h = 174.15 \qquad s\{\text{pred}\} = 11.93$$

We previously found that the Bonferroni multiple is $B = 2.101$. Hence, by (6.66) the simultaneous Bonferroni prediction limits with family confidence coefficient .90 are $191.10 \pm 2.101(11.35)$ and $174.15 \pm 2.101(11.93)$, leading to the simultaneous prediction intervals:

City A: $167.3 \leq Y_{h(\text{new})} \leq 214.9$

City B: $149.1 \leq Y_{h(\text{new})} \leq 199.2$

With family confidence coefficient .90, we predict that sales in the two cities will be within the indicated limits. Dwaine Studios considers these prediction limits to be somewhat useful for planning purposes, but would prefer tighter intervals for predicting sales for a particular city. A consulting firm has been engaged to see if additional or alternative predictor variables can be found that will lead to tighter prediction intervals.

Note incidentally that even though the coefficient of multiple determination, $R^2 = .917$, is high, the prediction limits here are not fully satisfactory. This serves as another reminder that a high value of R^2 does not necessarily indicate that precise predictions can be made.

Cited Reference

6.1.   Box, G. E. P., and P. W. Tidwell. "Transformations of the Independent Variables," *Technometrics* 4 (1962), pp. 531–50.

Problems

6.1. Set up the **X** matrix and **β** vector for each of the following regression models (assume $i = 1, \ldots, 4$):

a. $Y_i = \beta_0 + \beta_1 X_{i1} + \beta_2 X_{i1} X_{i2} + \varepsilon_i$

b. $\log Y_i = \beta_0 + \beta_1 X_{i1} + \beta_2 X_{i2} + \varepsilon_i$

6.2. Set up the **X** matrix and **β** vector for each of the following regression models (assume $i = 1, \ldots, 5$):

a. $Y_i = \beta_1 X_{i1} + \beta_2 X_{i2} + \beta_3 X_{i1}^2 + \varepsilon_i$

b. $\sqrt{Y_i} = \beta_0 + \beta_1 X_{i1} + \beta_2 \log_{10} X_{i2} + \varepsilon_i$

6.3. A student stated: "Adding predictor variables to a regression model can never reduce R^2, so we should include all available predictor variables in the model." Comment.

6.4. Why is it not meaningful to attach a sign to the coefficient of multiple correlation R, although we do so for the coefficient of simple correlation r?

6.5. **Brand preference**. In a small-scale experimental study of the relation between degree of brand liking (Y) and moisture content (X_1) and sweetness (X_2) of the product, the following results were obtained from the experiment based on a completely randomized design (data are coded):

i:	1	2	3	. . .	14	15	16
X_{i1}:	4	4	4	. . .	10	10	10
X_{i2}:	2	4	2	. . .	4	2	4
Y_i:	64	73	61	. . .	95	94	100

a. Obtain the scatter plot matrix and the correlation matrix. What information do these diagnostic aids provide here?

b. Fit regression model (6.1) to the data. State the estimated regression function. How is b_1 interpreted here?

c. Obtain the residuals and prepare a box plot of the residuals. What information does this plot provide?

d. Plot the residuals against $\hat{Y}$, X_1, X_2, and $X_1 X_2$ on separate graphs. Also prepare a normal probability plot. Interpret the plots and summarize your findings.

e. Conduct the Breusch-Pagan test for constancy of the error variance, assuming $\log \sigma_i^2 = \gamma_0 + \gamma_1 X_{i1} + \gamma_2 X_{i2}$; use $\alpha = .01$. State the alternatives, decision rule, and conclusion.

f. Conduct a formal test for lack of fit of the first-order regression function; use $\alpha = .01$. State the alternatives, decision rule, and conclusion.

6.6. Refer to **Brand preference** Problem 6.5. Assume that regression model (6.1) with independent normal error terms is appropriate.

a. Test whether there is a regression relation, using $\alpha = .01$. State the alternatives, decision rule, and conclusion. What does your test imply about β_1 and β_2?

b. What is the P-value of the test in part (a)?

c. Estimate β_1 and β_2 jointly by the Bonferroni procedure, using a 99 percent family confidence coefficient. Interpret your results.

6.7. Refer to **Brand preference** Problem 6.5.

a. Calculate the coefficient of multiple determination R^2. How is it interpreted here?

b. Calculate the coefficient of simple determination r^2 between Y_i and $\hat{Y}_i$. Does it equal R^2?

6.8. Refer to **Brand preference** Problem 6.5. Assume that regression model (6.1) with independent normal error terms is appropriate.

a. Obtain an interval estimate of $E\{Y_h\}$ when $X_{h1} = 5$ and $X_{h2} = 4$. Use a 99 percent confidence coefficient. Interpret your interval estimate.

b. Obtain a prediction interval for a new observation $Y_{h(new)}$ when $X_{h1} = 5$ and $X_{h2} = 4$. Use a 99 percent confidence coefficient.

√ 6.9. **Chemical shipment**. The data to follow, taken on 20 incoming shipments of chemicals in drums arriving at a warehouse, show number of drums in shipment (X_1), total weight of shipment $(X_2$, in hundred pounds), and number of minutes required to handle shipment (Y).

i:	1	2	3	. . .	18	19	20
X_{i1}:	7	18	5	. . .	21	6	11
X_{i2}:	5.11	16.72	3.20	. . .	15.21	3.64	9.57
Y_i:	58	152	41	. . .	155	39	90

a. Prepare separate stem-and-leaf plots for the numbers of drums in the shipments X_{i1} and the weights of the shipments X_{i2}. Are there any outlying cases present? Are there any gaps in the data?

b. The cases are given in the order that the incoming shipments arrived. Prepare a time plot for each predictor variable. What do the plots show?

c. Obtain the scatter plot matrix and the correlation matrix. What information do these diagnostic aids provide here?

√ 6.10. Refer to **Chemical shipment** Problem 6.9.

a. Fit regression model (6.1) to the data. State the estimated regression function. How are b_1 and b_2 interpreted here?

b. Obtain the residuals and prepare a box plot of the residuals. What information does this plot provide?

c. Plot the residuals against $\hat{Y}$, X_1, X_2, and X_1X_2 on separate graphs. Also prepare a normal probability plot. Interpret the plots and summarize your findings.

d. Prepare a time plot of the residuals. Is there any indication that the error terms are correlated? Discuss.

e. Divide the 20 cases into two groups, placing the 10 cases with the smallest fitted values $\hat{Y}_i$ into group 1 and the other 10 cases into group 2. Conduct the modified Levene test for constancy of the error variance, using $\alpha = .01$. State the decision rule and conclusion.

√ 6.11. Refer to **Chemical shipment** Problem 6.9. Assume that regression model (6.1) with independent normal error terms is appropriate.

a. Test whether there is a regression relation, using level of significance .05. State the alternatives, decision rule, and conclusion. What does your test result imply about β_1 and β_2? What is the P-value of the test?

b. Estimate β_1 and β_2 jointly by the Bonferroni procedure, using a 95 percent family confidence coefficient. Interpret your results.

c. Calculate the coefficient of multiple determination R^2. How is this measure interpreted here?

√ 6.12. Refer to **Chemical shipment** Problem 6.9. Assume that regression model (6.1) with independent normal error terms is appropriate.

a. Management desires simultaneous interval estimates of the mean handling times for the following five typical shipments:

	1	2	3	4	5
X_1:	5	6	10	14	20
X_2:	3.20	4.80	7.00	10.00	18.00

Obtain the family of estimates using a 95 percent family confidence coefficient. Employ the Working-Hotelling or the Bonferroni procedure, whichever is more efficient.

b. For the data in Problem 6.9 on which the regression fit is based, would you consider a shipment of 20 drums with a weight of 5 hundred pounds to be within the scope of the model? What about a shipment of 20 drums with a weight of 19 hundred pounds? Support your answers by preparing a relevant plot.

√ 6.13. Refer to **Chemical shipment** Problem 6.9. Assume that regression model (6.1) with independent normal error terms is appropriate. Four separate shipments with the following characteristics will arrive in the next day or two:

	1	2	3	4
X_1:	9	12	15	18
X_2:	7.20	9.00	12.50	16.50

Management desires predictions of the handling times for these shipments so that the actual handling times can be compared with the predicted times to determine whether any are "out of line." Develop the needed predictions, using the most efficient approach and a family confidence coefficient of 95 percent.

√ 6.14. Refer to **Chemical shipment** Problem 6.9. Assume that regression model (6.1) with independent normal error terms is appropriate. Three new shipments are to be received, each with $X_{h1} = 7$ and $X_{h2} = 6$.

a. Obtain a 95 percent prediction interval for the mean handling time for these shipments.

b. Convert the interval obtained in part (a) into a 95 percent prediction interval for the total handling time for the three shipments.

√ 6.15. **Patient satisfaction**. A hospital administrator wished to study the relation between patient satisfaction (Y) and patient's age (X_1, in years), severity of illness (X_2, an index), and anxiety level (X_3, an index). The administrator randomly selected 23 patients and collected the data presented below, where larger values of Y, X_2, and X_3 are, respectively, associated with more satisfaction, increased severity of illness, and more anxiety.

i:	1	2	3	. . .	21	22	23
X_{i1}:	50	36	40	. . .	29	44	43
X_{i2}:	51	46	48	. . .	52	58	50
X_{i3}:	2.3	2.3	2.2	. . .	2.3	2.9	2.3
Y_i:	48	57	66	. . .	77	52	60

a. Prepare a stem-and-leaf plot for each of the predictor variables. Are any noteworthy features revealed by these plots?

b. Obtain the scatter plot matrix and the correlation matrix. Interpret these and state your principal findings.

c. Fit regression model (6.5) for three predictor variables to the data and state the estimated regression function. How is b_2 interpreted here?

d. Obtain the residuals and prepare a box plot of the residuals. Do there appear to be any outliers?

e. Plot the residuals against $\hat{Y}$, each of the predictor variables, and each two-factor interaction term on separate graphs. Also prepare a normal probability plot. Interpret your plots and summarize your findings.

f. Can you conduct a formal test for lack of fit here?

g. Conduct the Breusch-Pagan test for constancy of the error variance, assuming $\log \sigma_i^2 = \gamma_0 + \gamma_1 X_{i1} + \gamma_2 X_{i2} + \gamma_3 X_{i3}$; use $\alpha = .01$. State the alternatives, decision rule, and conclusion.

√ 6.16. Refer to **Patient satisfaction** Problem 6.15. Assume that regression model (6.5) for three predictor variables with independent normal error terms is appropriate.

a. Test whether there is a regression relation; use $\alpha = .10$. State the alternatives, decision rule, and conclusion. What does your test imply about β_1, β_2, and β_3? What is the P-value of the test?

b. Obtain joint interval estimates of β_1, β_2, and β_3, using a 90 percent family confidence coefficient. Interpret your results.

c. Calculate the coefficient of multiple correlation. What does it indicate here?

√ 6.17. Refer to **Patient satisfaction** Problem 6.15. Assume that regression model (6.5) for three predictor variables with independent normal error terms is appropriate.

a. Obtain an interval estimate of the mean satisfaction when $X_{h1} = 35$, $X_{h2} = 45$, and $X_{h3} = 2.2$. Use a 90 percent confidence coefficient. Interpret your confidence interval.

b. Obtain a prediction interval for a new patient's satisfaction when $X_{h1} = 35$, $X_{h2} = 45$, and $X_{h3} = 2.2$. Use a 90 percent confidence coefficient. Interpret your prediction interval.

6.18. **Mathematicians' salaries.** A researcher in a scientific foundation wished to evaluate the relation between intermediate and senior level annual salaries of bachelor's and master's level mathematicians (Y, in thousand dollars) and an index of work quality (X_1), number of years of experience (X_2), and an index of publication success (X_3). The data for a sample of 24 bachelor's and master's level mathematicians follow:

i:	1	2	3	. . .	22	23	24
X_{i1}:	3.5	5.3	5.1	. . .	5.6	4.8	3.9
X_{i2}:	9	20	18	. . .	27	34	15
X_{i3}:	6.1	6.4	7.4	. . .	4.3	8.0	5.0
Y_i:	33.2	40.3	38.7	. . .	36.8	45.2	35.1

a. Prepare a stem-and-leaf plot for each predictor variable. What information do these plots provide?

b. Obtain the scatter plot matrix and the correlation matrix. Interpret these and state your principal findings.

c. Fit regression model (6.5) for three predictor variables to the data. State the estimated regression function.

d. Obtain the residuals and prepare a box plot of the residuals. Does the distribution appear to be fairly symmetrical?

e. Plot the residuals against $\hat{Y}$, each predictor variable, and each two-factor interaction term on separate graphs. Also prepare a normal probability plot. Analyze your plots and summarize your findings.

f. Can you conduct a formal test for lack of fit here?

g. Divide the 24 cases into two groups, placing the 12 cases with the smallest fitted values $\hat{Y}_i$ into group 1 and the remaining cases into group 2. Conduct the modified Levene test for constancy of the error variance, using $\alpha = .05$. State the decision rule and conclusion.

6.19. Refer to **Mathematicians' salaries** Problem 6.18. Assume that regression model (6.5) for three predictor variables with independent normal error terms is appropriate.

a. Test whether there is a regression relation; use $\alpha = .05$. State the alternatives, decision rule, and conclusion. What does your test imply about β_1, β_2, and β_3? What is the P-value of the test?

b. Estimate β_1, β_2, and β_3 jointly by the Bonferroni procedure, using a 95 percent family confidence coefficient. Interpret your results.

c. Calculate R^2 and interpret this measure.

6.20. Refer to **Mathematicians' salaries** Problem 6.18. Assume that regression model (6.5) for three predictor variables with independent normal error terms is appropriate. The researcher wishes to obtain simultaneous interval estimates of the mean salary level for four typical mathematicians specified as follows:

	1	2	3	4
X_1:	5.0	6.0	4.0	7.0
X_2:	20	30	10	50
X_3:	5.0	6.0	4.0	7.0

Obtain the family of estimates using a 95 percent family confidence coefficient. Employ the most efficient procedure.

6.21. Refer to **Mathematicians' salaries** Problem 6.18. Assume that regression model (6.5) for three predictor variables with independent normal error terms is appropriate. Three mathematicians with the following characteristics did not provide any salary information in the study.

	1	2	3
X_1:	5.4	6.2	6.4
X_2:	17	12	21
X_3:	6.0	5.8	6.1

Develop separate prediction intervals for the annual salaries of these mathematicians, using a 95 percent statement confidence coefficient in each case. Can the salaries of these three mathematicians be predicted fairly precisely? What is the family confidence level for the set of three predictions?

Exercises

6.22. For each of the following regression models, indicate whether it is a general linear regression model. If it is not, state whether it can be expressed in the form of (6.7) by a suitable transformation:

a. $Y_i = \beta_0 + \beta_1 X_{i1} + \beta_2 \log_{10} X_{i2} + \beta_3 X_{i1}^2 + \varepsilon_i$

b. $Y_i = \varepsilon_i \exp(\beta_0 + \beta_1 X_{i1} + \beta_2 X_{i2}^2)$

c. $Y_i = \beta_0 + \log_{10}(\beta_1 X_{i1}) + \beta_2 X_{i2} + \varepsilon_i$

d. $Y_i = \beta_0 \exp(\beta_1 X_{i1}) + \varepsilon_i$

e. $Y_i = [1 + \exp(\beta_0 + \beta_1 X_{i1} + \varepsilon_i)]^{-1}$

6.23. (Calculus needed.) Consider the multiple regression model:

$$Y_i = \beta_1 X_{i1} + \beta_2 X_{i2} + \varepsilon_i \qquad i = 1, \ldots, n$$

where the ε_i are uncorrelated, with $E\{\varepsilon_i\} = 0$ and $\sigma^2\{\varepsilon_i\} = \sigma^2$.

a. State the least squares criterion and derive the least squares estimators of β_1 and β_2.

b. Assuming that the ε_i are independent normal random variables, state the likelihood function and obtain the maximum likelihood estimators of β_1 and β_2. Are these the same as the least squares estimators?

6.24. (Calculus needed.) Consider the multiple regression model:

$$Y_i = \beta_0 + \beta_1 X_{i1} + \beta_2 X_{i1}^2 + \beta_3 X_{i2} + \varepsilon_i \qquad i = 1, \ldots, n$$

where the ε_i are independent $N(0, \sigma^2)$.

a. State the least squares criterion and derive the least squares normal equations.

b. State the likelihood function and explain why the maximum likelihood estimators will be the same as the least squares estimators.

6.25. An analyst wanted to fit the regression model $Y_i = \beta_0 + \beta_1 X_{i1} + \beta_2 X_{i2} + \beta_3 X_{i3} + \varepsilon_i$, $i = 1, \ldots, n$, by the method of least squares when it is known that $\beta_2 = 4$. How can the analyst obtain the desired fit by using a multiple regression computer program?

6.26. For regression model (6.1), show that the coefficient of simple determination r^2 between Y_i and $\hat{Y}_i$ equals the coefficient of multiple determination R^2.

6.27. In a small-scale regression study, the following data were obtained:

i:	1	2	3	4	5	6
X_{i1}:	7	4	16	3	21	8
X_{i2}:	33	41	7	49	5	31
Y_i:	42	33	75	28	91	55

Assume that regression model (6.1) with independent normal error terms is appropriate. Using matrix methods, obtain (a) $\mathbf{b}$; (b) $\mathbf{e}$; (c) $\mathbf{H}$; (d) SSR; (e) $s^2\{\mathbf{b}\}$; (f) $\hat{Y}_h$ when $X_{h1} = 10$, $X_{h2} = 30$; (g) $s^2\{\hat{Y}_h\}$ when $X_{h1} = 10$, $X_{h2} = 30$.

Projects

6.28. Refer to the **SMSA** data set. You have been asked to evaluate two alternative models for predicting the number of active physicians (Y) in an SMSA. Proposed model I includes as predictor variables total population (X_1), land area (X_2), and total personal income (X_3). Proposed model II includes as predictor variables population density (X_1, total population divided by land area), percent of population in central cities (X_2), and total personal income (X_3).

   a. Prepare a stem-and-leaf plot for each of the predictor variables. What noteworthy information is provided by your plots?

   b. Obtain the scatter plot matrix and the correlation matrix for each proposed model. Summarize the information provided.

   c. For each proposed model, fit the first-order regression model (6.5) with three predictor variables.

   d. Calculate R^2 for each model. Is one model clearly preferable in terms of this measure?

   e. For each model, obtain the residuals and plot them against $\hat{Y}$, each of the three predictor variables, and each of the two-factor interaction terms. Also prepare a normal probability plot for each of the two fitted models. Interpret your plots and state your findings. Is one model clearly preferable in terms of appropriateness?

6.29. Refer to the **SMSA** data set.

   a. For each geographic region, regress the number of serious crimes in an SMSA (Y) against population density (X_1, total population divided by land area), total personal income (X_2), and percent high school graduates (X_3). Use first-order regression model (6.5) with three predictor variables. State the estimated regression functions.

   b. Are the estimated regression functions similar for the four regions? Discuss.

   c. Calculate MSE and R^2 for each region. Are these measures similar for the four regions? Discuss.

   d. Obtain the residuals for each fitted model and prepare a box plot of the residuals for each fitted model. Interpret your plots and state your findings.

6.30. Refer to the **SENIC** data set. Two models have been proposed for predicting the average length of patient stay in a hospital (Y). Model I utilizes as predictor variables age (X_1), infection risk (X_2), and available facilities and services (X_3). Model II uses as predictor variables number of beds (X_1), infection risk (X_2), and available facilities and services (X_3).

   a. Prepare a stem-and-leaf plot for each of the predictor variables. What information do these plots provide?

b. Obtain the scatter plot matrix and the correlation matrix for each proposed model. Interpret these and state your principal findings.

c. For each of the two proposed models, fit first-order regression model (6.5) with three predictor variables.

d. Calculate R^2 for each model. Is one model clearly preferable in terms of this measure?

e. For each model, obtain the residuals and plot them against $\hat{Y}$, each of the three predictor variables, and each of the two-factor interaction terms. Also prepare a normal probability plot of the residuals for each of the two fitted models. Interpret your plots and state your findings. Is one model clearly more appropriate than the other?

6.31. Refer to the **SENIC** data set.

a. For each geographic region, regress infection risk (Y) against the predictor variables age (X_1), routine culturing ratio (X_2), average daily census (X_3), and available facilities and services (X_4). Use first-order regression model (6.5) with four predictor variables. State the estimated regression functions.

b. Are the estimated regression functions similar for the four regions? Discuss.

c. Calculate MSE and R^2 for each region. Are these measures similar for the four regions? Discuss.

d. Obtain the residuals for each fitted model and prepare a box plot of the residuals for each fitted model. Interpret the plots and state your findings.

Multiple Regression—II

In this chapter, we take up some specialized topics that are unique to multiple regression. These include extra sums of squares, which are useful for conducting a variety of tests about the regression coefficients, the standardized version of the multiple regression model, and multicollinearity, a condition where the predictor variables are highly correlated. We conclude the chapter by considering two special types of multiple regression models, polynomial and interaction regression models, and regression with constraints on the parameters.

7.1 Extra Sums of Squares

Basic Ideas

An extra sum of squares measures the marginal reduction in the error sum of squares when one or several predictor variables are added to the regression model, given that other predictor variables are already in the model. Equivalently, one can view an extra sum of squares as measuring the marginal increase in the regression sum of squares when one or several predictor variables are added to the regression model.

We first utilize an example to illustrate these ideas, and then we present definitions of extra sums of squares and discuss a variety of uses of extra sums of squares in tests about regression coefficients.

Example.   Table 7.1 contains a portion of the data for a study of the relation of amount of body fat (Y) to several possible predictor variables, based on a sample of 20 healthy females 25–34 years old. The possible predictor variables are triceps skinfold thickness (X_1), thigh circumference (X_2), and midarm circumference (X_3). The amount of body fat in Table 7.1 for each of the 20 persons was obtained by a cumbersome and expensive procedure requiring the immersion of the person in water. It would therefore be very helpful if a regression model with some or all of these predictor variables could provide reliable estimates of the amount of body fat since the measurements needed for the predictor variables are easy to obtain.

Table 7.2 on pages 262 and 263 contains some of the main regression results when body fat (Y) is regressed (1) on triceps skinfold thickness (X_1) alone, (2) on thigh circumference (X_2) alone, (3) on X_1 and X_2 only, and (4) on all three predictor variables. To keep track

TABLE 7.1 **Basic Data—Body Fat Example.**

Subject i	Triceps Skinfold Thickness X_{i1}	Thigh Circumference X_{i2}	Midarm Circumference X_{i3}	Body Fat Y_i
1	19.5	43.1	29.1	11.9
2	24.7	49.8	28.2	22.8
3	30.7	51.9	37.0	18.7
. . .	. . .	. . .	. . .	. . .
18	30.2	58.6	24.6	25.4
19	22.7	48.2	27.1	14.8
20	25.2	51.0	27.5	21.1

of the regression model that is fitted, we shall modify our notation slightly. The regression sum of squares when X_1 only is in the model is, according to Table 7.2a, 352.27. This sum of squares will be denoted by $SSR(X_1)$. The error sum of squares for this model will be denoted by $SSE(X_1)$; according to Table 7.2a it is $SSE(X_1) = 143.12$.

Similarly, Table 7.2c indicates that when X_1 and X_2 are in the regression model, the regression sum of squares is $SSR(X_1, X_2) = 385.44$ and the error sum of squares is $SSE(X_1, X_2) = 109.95$.

Notice that the error sum of squares when X_1 and X_2 are in the model, $SSE(X_1, X_2) = 109.95$, is smaller than when the model contains only X_1, $SSE(X_1) = 143.12$. The difference is called an *extra sum of squares* and will be denoted by $SSR(X_2|X_1)$:

$$SSR(X_2|X_1) = SSE(X_1) - SSE(X_1, X_2)$$

$$= 143.12 - 109.95 = 33.17$$

This reduction in the error sum of squares is the result of adding X_2 to the regression model when X_1 is already included in the model. Thus, the extra sum of squares $SSR(X_2|X_1)$ measures the marginal effect of adding X_2 to the regression model when X_1 is already in the model. The notation $SSR(X_2|X_1)$ reflects this additional or extra reduction in the error sum of squares associated with X_2, given that X_1 is already included in the model.

The extra sum of squares $SSR(X_2|X_1)$ equivalently can be viewed as the marginal increase in the regression sum of squares:

$$SSR(X_2|X_1) = SSR(X_1, X_2) - SSR(X_1)$$

$$= 385.44 - 352.27 = 33.17$$

The reason for the equivalence of the marginal reduction in the error sum of squares and the marginal increase in the regression sum of squares is the basic analysis of variance identity (2.50):

$$SSTO = SSR + SSE$$

Since $SSTO$ measures the variability of the Y_i observations and hence does not depend on the regression model fitted, any reduction in SSE implies an identical increase in SSR.

We can consider other extra sums of squares, such as the marginal effect of adding X_3 to the regression model when X_1 and X_2 are already in the model. We find from Tables 7.2c

---

TABLE 7.2   Regression Results for Several Fitted Models—Body Fat Example.

(a) Regression of Y on X_1

$$\hat{Y} = -1.496 + .8572X_1$$

Source of Variation	SS	df	MS
Regression	352.27	1	352.27
Error	143.12	18	7.95
Total	495.39	19	

Variable	Estimated Regression Coefficient	Estimated Standard Deviation	t^*
X_1	$b_1 = .8572$	$s\{b_1\} = .1288$	6.66

(b) Regression of Y on X_2

$$\hat{Y} = -23.634 + .8565X_2$$

Source of Variation	SS	df	MS
Regression	381.97	1	381.97
Error	113.42	18	6.30
Total	495.39	19	

Variable	Estimated Regression Coefficient	Estimated Standard Deviation	t^*
X_2	$b_2 = .8565$	$s\{b_2\} = .1100$	7.79

---

and 7.2d that:

$$SSR(X_3|X_1, X_2) = SSE(X_1, X_2) - SSE(X_1, X_2, X_3)$$
$$= 109.95 - 98.41 = 11.54$$

or, equivalently:

$$SSR(X_3|X_1, X_2) = SSR(X_1, X_2, X_3) - SSR(X_1, X_2)$$
$$= 396.98 - 385.44 = 11.54$$

We can even consider the marginal effect of adding several variables, such as adding both X_2 and X_3 to the regression model already containing X_1 (see Tables 7.2a and 7.2d):

TABLE 7.2   **(concluded).**

(c) Regression of Y on X_1 and X_2

$$\hat{Y} = -19.174 + .2224X_1 + .6594X_2$$

Source of Variation	SS	df	MS
Regression	385.44	2	192.72
Error	109.95	17	6.47
Total	495.39	19	

Variable	Estimated Regression Coefficient	Estimated Standard Deviation	t^*
X_1	$b_1 = .2224$	$s\{b_1\} = .3034$	.73
X_2	$b_2 = .6594$	$s\{b_2\} = .2912$	2.26

(d) Regression of Y on X_1, X_2, and X_3

$$\hat{Y} = 117.08 + 4.334X_1 - 2.857X_2 - 2.186X_3$$

Source of Variation	SS	df	MS
Regression	396.98	3	132.33
Error	98.41	16	6.15
Total	495.39	19	

Variable	Estimated Regression Coefficient	Estimated Standard Deviation	t^*
X_1	$b_1 = 4.334$	$s\{b_1\} = 3.016$	1.44
X_2	$b_2 = -2.857$	$s\{b_2\} = 2.582$	-1.11
X_3	$b_3 = -2.186$	$s\{b_3\} = 1.596$	-1.37

$$SSR(X_2, X_3|X_1) = SSE(X_1) - SSE(X_1, X_2, X_3)$$
$$= 143.12 - 98.41 = 44.71$$

or, equivalently:

$$SSR(X_2, X_3|X_1) = SSR(X_1, X_2, X_3) - SSR(X_1)$$
$$= 396.98 - 352.27 = 44.71$$

Definitions

We assemble now our earlier definitions of extra sums of squares and provide some additional ones. As we noted earlier, an extra sum of squares always involves the difference between the error sum of squares for the regression model containing the X variable(s) already in the model and the error sum of squares for the regression model containing both the original X variable(s) and the new X variable(s). Equivalently, an extra sum of squares involves the difference between the two corresponding regression sums of squares.

Thus, we define:

$$(7.1a) \qquad SSR(X_1|X_2) = SSE(X_2) - SSE(X_1, X_2)$$

or, equivalently:

$$(7.1b) \qquad SSR(X_1|X_2) = SSR(X_1, X_2) - SSR(X_2)$$

If X_2 is the extra variable, we define:

$$(7.2a) \qquad SSR(X_2|X_1) = SSE(X_1) - SSE(X_1, X_2)$$

or, equivalently:

$$(7.2b) \qquad SSR(X_2|X_1) = SSR(X_1, X_2) - SSR(X_1)$$

Extensions for three or more variables are straightforward. For example, we define:

$$(7.3a) \qquad SSR(X_3|X_1, X_2) = SSE(X_1, X_2) - SSE(X_1, X_2, X_3)$$

or:

$$(7.3b) \qquad SSR(X_3|X_1, X_2) = SSR(X_1, X_2, X_3) - SSR(X_1, X_2)$$

and:

$$(7.4a) \qquad SSR(X_2, X_3|X_1) = SSE(X_1) - SSE(X_1, X_2, X_3)$$

or:

$$(7.4b) \qquad SSR(X_2, X_3|X_1) = SSR(X_1, X_2, X_3) - SSR(X_1)$$

Decomposition of SSR into Extra Sums of Squares

In multiple regression, unlike simple linear regression, we can obtain a variety of decompositions of the regression sum of squares SSR into extra sums of squares. Let us consider the case of two X variables. We begin with the identity (2.50) for variable X_1:

$$(7.5) \qquad SSTO = SSR(X_1) + SSE(X_1)$$

where the notation now shows explicitly that X_1 is the X variable in the model. Replacing $SSE(X_1)$ by its equivalent in (7.2a), we obtain:

$$(7.6) \qquad SSTO = SSR(X_1) + SSR(X_2|X_1) + SSE(X_1, X_2)$$

FIGURE 7.1   **Schematic Representation of Extra Sums of Squares—Body Fat Example.**

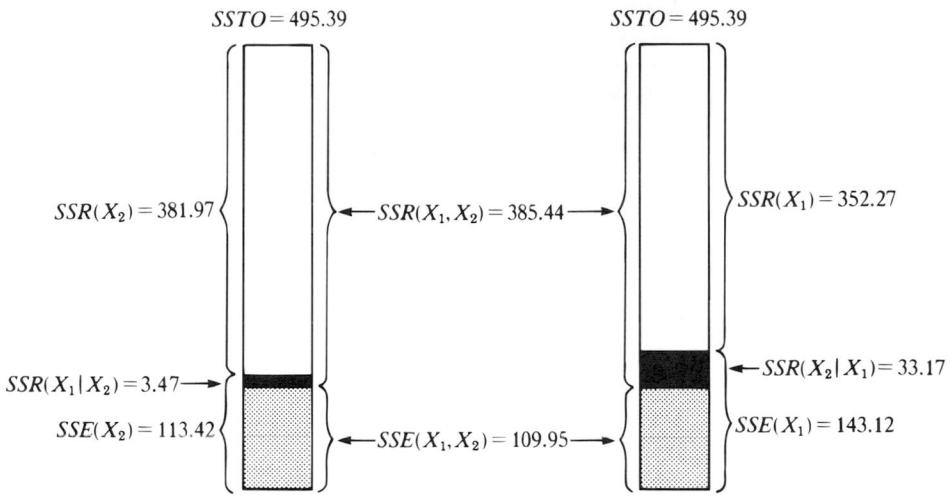

We now make use of the same identity for multiple regression with two X variables as in (7.5) for a single X variable, namely:

$$(7.7) \qquad\qquad SSTO = SSR(X_1, X_2) + SSE(X_1, X_2)$$

Solving (7.7) for $SSE(X_1, X_2)$ and using this expression in (7.6) lead to:

$$(7.8) \qquad\qquad SSR(X_1, X_2) = SSR(X_1) + SSR(X_2|X_1)$$

Thus, we have decomposed the regression sum of squares $SSR(X_1, X_2)$ into two marginal components: (1) $SSR(X_1)$, measuring the contribution by including X_1 alone in the model, and (2) $SSR(X_2|X_1)$, measuring the additional contribution when X_2 is included, given that X_1 is already in the model.

Of course, the order of the X variables is arbitrary. Here, we can also obtain the decomposition:

$$(7.9) \qquad\qquad SSR(X_1, X_2) = SSR(X_2) + SSR(X_1|X_2)$$

We show in Figure 7.1 schematic representations of the two decompositions of $SSR(X_1, X_2)$ for the body fat example. The total bar on the left represents $SSTO$ and presents decomposition (7.9). The unshaded component of this bar is $SSR(X_2)$, and the combined shaded area represents $SSE(X_2)$. The latter area in turn is the combination of the extra sum of squares $SSR(X_1|X_2)$ and the error sum of squares $SSE(X_1, X_2)$ when both X_1 and X_2 are included in the model. Similarly, the bar on the right in Figure 7.1 shows decomposition (7.8). Note in both cases how the extra sum of squares can be viewed either as a reduction in the error sum of squares or as an increase in the regression sum of squares when the second predictor variable is added to the regression model.

TABLE 7.3 Example of ANOVA Table with Decomposition of *SSR* for Three X Variables.

Source of Variation	SS	df	MS
Regression	$SSR(X_1, X_2, X_3)$	3	$MSR(X_1, X_2, X_3)$
X_1	$SSR(X_1)$	1	$MSR(X_1)$
$X_2 \mid X_1$	$SSR(X_2 \mid X_1)$	1	$MSR(X_2 \mid X_1)$
$X_3 \mid X_1, X_2$	$SSR(X_3 \mid X_1, X_2)$	1	$MSR(X_3 \mid X_1, X_2)$
Error	$SSE(X_1, X_2, X_3)$	$n - 4$	$MSE(X_1, X_2, X_3)$
Total	$SSTO$	$n - 1$	

When the regression model contains three X variables, a variety of decompositions of $SSR(X_1, X_2, X_3)$ can be obtained. We illustrate three of these:

$$(7.10a) \qquad SSR(X_1, X_2, X_3) = SSR(X_1) + SSR(X_2 \mid X_1) + SSR(X_3 \mid X_1, X_2)$$

$$(7.10b) \qquad SSR(X_1, X_2, X_3) = SSR(X_2) + SSR(X_3 \mid X_2) + SSR(X_1 \mid X_2, X_3)$$

$$(7.10c) \qquad SSR(X_1, X_2, X_3) = SSR(X_1) + SSR(X_2, X_3 \mid X_1)$$

It is obvious that the number of possible decompositions becomes vast as the number of X variables in the regression model increases.

ANOVA Table Containing Decomposition of SSR

ANOVA tables can be constructed containing decompositions of the regression sum of squares into extra sums of squares. Table 7.3 contains the ANOVA table decomposition for the case of three X variables often used in regression packages, and Table 7.4 contains this same decomposition for the body fat example. The decomposition involves single extra X variables.

Note that each extra sum of squares involving a single extra X variable has associated with it one degree of freedom. The resulting mean squares are constructed as usual. For example, $MSR(X_2 \mid X_1)$ in Table 7.3 is obtained as follows:

$$MSR(X_2 \mid X_1) = \frac{SSR(X_2 \mid X_1)}{1}$$

Extra sums of squares involving two extra X variables, such as $SSR(X_2, X_3 \mid X_1)$, have two degrees of freedom associated with them. This follows because we can express such an extra sum of squares as a sum of two extra sums of squares, each associated with one degree of freedom. For example, by definition of the extra sums of squares, we have:

$$(7.11) \qquad SSR(X_2, X_3 \mid X_1) = SSR(X_2 \mid X_1) + SSR(X_3 \mid X_1, X_2)$$

TABLE 7.4 **ANOVA Table with Decomposition of *SSR*—Body Fat Example with Three Predictor Variables.**

Source of Variation	SS	df	MS
Regression	396.98	3	132.33
X_1	352.27	1	352.27
$X_2\|X_1$	33.17	1	33.17
$X_3\|X_1, X_2$	11.54	1	11.54
Error	98.41	16	6.15
Total	495.39	19	

The mean square $MSR(X_2, X_3|X_1)$ is therefore obtained as follows:

$$MSR(X_2, X_3|X_1) = \frac{SSR(X_2, X_3|X_1)}{2}$$

Many computer regression packages provide decompositions of *SSR* into single-degree-of-freedom extra sums of squares, usually in the order in which the X variables are entered into the model. Thus, if the X variables are entered in the order X_1, X_2, X_3, the extra sums of squares given in the output are:

$$SSR(X_1)$$

$$SSR(X_2|X_1)$$

$$SSR(X_3|X_1, X_2)$$

If an extra sum of squares involving several extra X variables is desired, it can be obtained by summing appropriate single-degree-of-freedom extra sums of squares. For instance, to obtain $SSR(X_2, X_3|X_1)$ in our earlier illustration, we would utilize (7.11) and simply add $SSR(X_2|X_1)$ and $SSR(X_3|X_1, X_2)$.

If the extra sum of squares $SSR(X_1, X_3|X_2)$ were desired with a computer package that provides single-degree-of-freedom extra sums of squares in the order in which the X variables are entered, the X variables would need to be entered in the order X_2, X_1, X_3 or X_2, X_3, X_1. The first ordering would give:

$$SSR(X_2)$$

$$SSR(X_1|X_2)$$

$$SSR(X_3|X_1, X_2)$$

The sum of the last two extra sums of squares will yield $SSR(X_1, X_3|X_2)$.

The reason why extra sums of squares are of interest is that they occur in a variety of tests about regression coefficients where the question of concern is whether certain X variables can be dropped from the regression model. We turn next to this use of extra sums of squares.

7.2 Uses of Extra Sums of Squares in Tests for Regression Coefficients

Test Whether a Single $\beta_k = 0$

When we wish to test whether the term $\beta_k X_k$ can be dropped from a multiple regression model, we are interested in the alternatives:

$$H_0: \ \beta_k = 0$$

$$H_a: \ \beta_k \neq 0$$

We already know that test statistic (6.51b):

$$t^* = \frac{b_k}{s\{b_k\}}$$

is appropriate for this test.

Equivalently, we can use the general linear test approach described in Section 2.8. We now show that this approach involves an extra sum of squares. Let us consider the first-order regression model with three predictor variables:

(7.12) $$Y_i = \beta_0 + \beta_1 X_{i1} + \beta_2 X_{i2} + \beta_3 X_{i3} + \varepsilon_i \qquad \text{Full model}$$

To test the alternatives:

(7.13)
$$H_0: \ \beta_3 = 0$$
$$H_a: \ \beta_3 \neq 0$$

we fit the full model and obtain the error sum of squares $SSE(F)$. We now explicitly show the variables in the full model, as follows:

$$SSE(F) = SSE(X_1, X_2, X_3)$$

The degrees of freedom associated with $SSE(F)$ are $df_F = n - 4$ since there are four parameters in the regression function for the full model (7.12).

The reduced model when H_0 in (7.13) holds is:

(7.14) $$Y_i = \beta_0 + \beta_1 X_{i1} + \beta_2 X_{i2} + \varepsilon_i \qquad \text{Reduced model}$$

We next fit this reduced model and obtain:

$$SSE(R) = SSE(X_1, X_2)$$

There are $df_R = n - 3$ degrees of freedom associated with the reduced model.

The general linear test statistic (2.70):

$$F^* = \frac{SSE(R) - SSE(F)}{df_R - df_F} \div \frac{SSE(F)}{df_F}$$

here becomes:

$$F^* = \frac{SSE(X_1, X_2) - SSE(X_1, X_2, X_3)}{(n-3) - (n-4)} \div \frac{SSE(X_1, X_2, X_3)}{n-4}$$

Note that the difference between the two error sums of squares in the numerator term is the extra sum of squares (7.3a):

$$SSE(X_1, X_2) - SSE(X_1, X_2, X_3) = SSR(X_3 | X_1, X_2)$$

Hence the general linear test statistic here is:

$$(7.15) \qquad F^* = \frac{SSR(X_3 | X_1, X_2)}{1} \div \frac{SSE(X_1, X_2, X_3)}{n-4} = \frac{MSR(X_3 | X_1, X_2)}{MSE(X_1, X_2, X_3)}$$

We thus see that the test whether or not $\beta_3 = 0$ is a marginal test, given that X_1 and X_2 are already in the model. We also note that the extra sum of squares $SSR(X_3 | X_1, X_2)$ has one degree of freedom associated with it, just as we noted earlier.

Test statistic (7.15) shows that we do not need to fit both the full model and the reduced model to use the general linear test approach here. A single computer run can provide a fit of the full model and the appropriate extra sum of squares.

Example.   In the body fat example, we wish to test for the model with all three predictor variables whether midarm circumference (X_3) can be dropped from the model. The test alternatives are those of (7.13). Table 7.4 contains the ANOVA results from a computer fit of the full regression model (7.12), including the extra sums of squares when the predictor variables are entered in the order X_1, X_2, X_3. Hence, test statistic (7.15) here is:

$$F^* = \frac{SSR(X_3 | X_1, X_2)}{1} \div \frac{SSE(X_1, X_2, X_3)}{n-4}$$

$$= \frac{11.54}{1} \div \frac{98.41}{16} = 1.88$$

For $\alpha = .01$, we require $F(.99; 1, 16) = 8.53$. Since $F^* = 1.88 \leq 8.53$, we conclude H_0, that X_3 can be dropped from the regression model that already contains X_1 and X_2.

Note from Table 7.2d that the t^* test statistic here is:

$$t^* = \frac{b_3}{s\{b_3\}} = \frac{-2.186}{1.596} = -1.37$$

Since $(t^*)^2 = (-1.37)^2 = 1.88 = F^*$, we see that the two test statistics are equivalent, just as for simple linear regression.

Note

The F^* test statistic (7.15) to test whether or not $\beta_3 = 0$ is called a *partial F test* statistic to distinguish it from the F^* statistic in (6.39b) for testing whether *all* $\beta_k = 0$, i.e., whether or not there is a regression relation between Y and the set of X variables. The latter test is called the *overall F test*.   ∎

Test Whether Several $\beta_k = 0$

In multiple regression we are frequently interested in whether several terms in the regression model can be dropped. For example, we may wish to know whether both $\beta_2 X_2$ and $\beta_3 X_3$ can be dropped from the full model (7.12). The alternatives here are:

$$(7.16) \qquad \begin{aligned} H_0&: \ \beta_2 = \beta_3 = 0 \\ H_a&: \ \text{not both } \beta_2 \text{ and } \beta_3 \text{ equal zero} \end{aligned}$$

With the general linear test approach, the reduced model under H_0 is:

$$(7.17) \qquad\qquad Y_i = \beta_0 + \beta_1 X_{i1} + \varepsilon_i \qquad\qquad \text{Reduced model}$$

and the error sum of squares for the reduced model is:

$$SSE(R) = SSE(X_1)$$

This error sum of squares has $df_R = n - 2$ degrees of freedom associated with it.

The general linear test statistic (2.70) thus becomes here:

$$F^* = \frac{SSE(X_1) - SSE(X_1, X_2, X_3)}{(n-2) - (n-4)} \div \frac{SSE(X_1, X_2, X_3)}{n-4}$$

Again the difference between the two error sums of squares in the numerator term is an extra sum of squares, namely:

$$SSE(X_1) - SSE(X_1, X_2, X_3) = SSR(X_2, X_3 | X_1)$$

Hence, the test statistic becomes:

$$(7.18) \qquad F^* = \frac{SSR(X_2, X_3 | X_1)}{2} \div \frac{SSE(X_1, X_2, X_3)}{n-4} = \frac{MSR(X_2, X_3 | X_1)}{MSE(X_1, X_2, X_3)}$$

Note that $SSR(X_2, X_3 | X_1)$ has two degrees of freedom associated with it, as we pointed out earlier.

Example.   We wish to test in the body fat example for the model with all three predictor variables whether both thigh circumference (X_2) and midarm circumference (X_3) can be dropped from the full regression model (7.12). The alternatives are those in (7.16). The appropriate extra sum of squares can be obtained from Table 7.4, using (7.11):

$$\begin{aligned} SSR(X_2, X_3 | X_1) &= SSR(X_2 | X_1) + SSR(X_3 | X_1, X_2) \\ &= 33.17 + 11.54 = 44.71 \end{aligned}$$

Test statistic (7.18) therefore is:

$$\begin{aligned} F^* &= \frac{SSR(X_2, X_3 | X_1)}{2} \div MSE(X_1, X_2, X_3) \\ &= \frac{44.71}{2} \div 6.15 = 3.63 \end{aligned}$$

For $\alpha = .05$, we require $F(.95; 2, 16) = 3.63$. Since $F^* = 3.63$ is at the boundary of the decision rule (the P-value of the test statistic is .05), we may wish to make further analyses before deciding whether X_2 and X_3 should be dropped from the regression model that already contains X_1.

Comments

1. For testing whether a single β_k equals zero, two equivalent test statistics are available: the t^* test statistic and the F^* general linear test statistic. When testing whether several β_k equal zero, only the general linear test statistic F^* is available.

2. General linear test statistic (2.70) for testing whether several X variables can be dropped from the general linear regression model (6.7) can be expressed in terms of the coefficients of multiple determination for the full and reduced models. Denoting these by R_F^2 and R_R^2, respectively, we have:

$$(7.19) \qquad F^* = \frac{R_F^2 - R_R^2}{df_R - df_F} \div \frac{1 - R_F^2}{df_F}$$

Specifically for testing the alternatives in (7.16) for the body fat example, test statistic (7.19) becomes:

$$(7.20) \qquad F^* = \frac{R_{Y.123}^2 - R_{Y.1}^2}{(n-2) - (n-4)} \div \frac{1 - R_{Y.123}^2}{n-4}$$

where $R_{Y.123}^2$ denotes the coefficient of multiple determination when Y is regressed on X_1, X_2, and X_3, and $R_{Y.1}^2$ denotes the coefficient when Y is regressed on X_1 alone.

We see from Table 7.4 that $R_{Y.123}^2 = 396.98/495.39 = .80135$ and $R_{Y.1}^2 = 352.27/495.39 = .71110$. Hence, we obtain by substituting in (7.20):

$$F^* = \frac{.80135 - .71110}{(20-2) - (20-4)} \div \frac{1 - .80135}{16} = 3.63$$

This is the same result as before. Note that $R_{Y.1}^2$ corresponds to the coefficient of simple determination r^2 between Y and X_1.

Test statistic (7.19) is not appropriate when the full and reduced regression models do not contain the intercept term β_0. In that case, the general linear test statistic in the form (2.70) must be used.   ∎

7.3   Summary of Tests Concerning Regression Coefficients

We have already discussed how to conduct several types of tests concerning regression coefficients in a multiple regression model. For completeness, we summarize here these tests as well as some additional types of tests.

Test Whether All $\beta_k = 0$

This is the *overall F test* (6.39) of whether or not there is a regression relation between the response variable Y and the set of X variables. The alternatives are:

$$(7.21) \qquad \begin{aligned} &H_0: \beta_1 = \beta_2 = \cdots = \beta_{p-1} = 0 \\ &H_a: \text{ not all } \beta_k \ (k = 1, \ldots, p-1) \text{ equal zero} \end{aligned}$$

and the test statistic is:

$$(7.22) \qquad F^* = \frac{SSR(X_1, \ldots, X_{p-1})}{p-1} \div \frac{SSE(X_1, \ldots, X_{p-1})}{n-p}$$

$$= \frac{MSR}{MSE}$$

If H_0 holds, $F^* \sim F(p-1, n-p)$. Large values of F^* lead to conclusion H_a.

Test Whether a Single $\beta_k = 0$

This is a *partial F test* of whether a particular regression coefficient β_k equals zero. The alternatives are:

$$(7.23) \qquad\qquad H_0: \beta_k = 0$$
$$H_a: \beta_k \neq 0$$

and the test statistic is:

$$(7.24) \qquad F^* = \frac{SSR(X_k | X_1, \ldots, X_{k-1}, X_{k+1}, \ldots, X_{p-1})}{1} \div \frac{SSE(X_1, \ldots, X_{p-1})}{n-p}$$

$$= \frac{MSR(X_k | X_1, \ldots, X_{k-1}, X_{k+1}, \ldots, X_{p-1})}{MSE}$$

If H_0 holds, $F^* \sim F(1, n-p)$. Large values of F^* lead to conclusion H_a. Statistics packages that provide extra sums of squares permit use of this test without having to fit the reduced model.

An equivalent test statistic is (6.51b):

$$(7.25) \qquad\qquad t^* = \frac{b_k}{s\{b_k\}}$$

If H_0 holds, $t^* \sim t(n-p)$. Large values of $|t^*|$ lead to conclusion H_a.

Since the two tests are equivalent, the choice is usually made in terms of available information provided by the regression package output.

Test Whether Some $\beta_k = 0$

This is another *partial F test*. Here, the alternatives are:

$$(7.26) \qquad\qquad H_0: \beta_q = \beta_{q+1} = \cdots = \beta_{p-1} = 0$$
$$H_a: \text{ not all of the } \beta_k \text{ in } H_0 \text{ equal zero}$$

where for convenience, we arrange the model so that the last $p-q$ coefficients are the ones to be tested. The test statistic is:

$$(7.27) \qquad F^* = \frac{SSR(X_q, \ldots, X_{p-1} | X_1, \ldots, X_{q-1})}{p - q} \div \frac{SSE(X_1, \ldots, X_{p-1})}{n - p}$$

$$= \frac{MSR(X_q, \ldots, X_{p-1} | X_1, \ldots, X_{q-1})}{MSE}$$

If H_0 holds, $F^* \sim F(p - q, n - p)$. Large values of F^* lead to conclusion H_a.

Note that test statistic (7.27) actually encompasses the two earlier cases. If $q = 1$, the test is whether all regression coefficients equal zero. If $q = p - 1$, the test is whether a single regression coefficient equals zero. Also note that test statistic (7.27) can be calculated without having to fit the reduced model if the regression package provides the needed extra sums of squares:

$$(7.28) \qquad SSR(X_q, \ldots, X_{p-1} | X_1, \ldots, X_{q-1}) = SSR(X_q | X_1, \ldots, X_{q-1})$$

$$+ \cdots + SSR(X_{p-1} | X_1, \ldots, X_{p-2})$$

Test statistic (7.27) can be stated equivalently in terms of the coefficients of multiple determination for the full and reduced models when these models contain the intercept term β_0, as follows:

$$(7.29) \qquad F^* = \frac{R^2_{Y.1 \cdots p-1} - R^2_{Y.1 \cdots q-1}}{p \quad q} \div \frac{1 - R^2_{Y.1 \cdots p-1}}{n - p}$$

where $R^2_{Y.1 \cdots p-1}$ denotes the coefficient of multiple determination when Y is regressed on all X variables, and $R^2_{Y.1 \cdots q-1}$ denotes the coefficient when Y is regressed on $X_1, \ldots, X_{q-1}$ only.

Other Tests

When tests about regression coefficients are desired that do not involve testing whether one or several β_k equal zero, extra sums of squares cannot be used and the general linear test approach requires separate fittings of the full and reduced models. For instance, for the full model containing three X variables:

$$(7.30) \qquad Y_i = \beta_0 + \beta_1 X_{i1} + \beta_2 X_{i2} + \beta_3 X_{i3} + \varepsilon_i \qquad \text{Full model}$$

we might wish to test:

$$(7.31) \qquad \begin{aligned} H_0&: \beta_1 = \beta_2 \\ H_a&: \beta_1 \neq \beta_2 \end{aligned}$$

The procedure would be to fit the full model (7.30), and then the reduced model:

$$(7.32) \qquad Y_i = \beta_0 + \beta_c (X_{i1} + X_{i2}) + \beta_3 X_{i3} + \varepsilon_i \qquad \text{Reduced model}$$

where β_c denotes the common coefficient for β_1 and β_2 under H_0 and $X_{i1} + X_{i2}$ is the corresponding new X variable. We then use the general F^* test statistic (2.70) with 1 and $n - 4$ degrees of freedom.

Another example where extra sums of squares cannot be used is in the following test for regression model (7.30):

(7.33)
$$H_0: \ \beta_1 = 3, \ \beta_3 = 5$$
$$H_a: \ \text{not both equalities in } H_0 \text{ hold}$$

Here, the reduced model would be:

(7.34)
$$Y_i - 3X_{i1} - 5X_{i3} = \beta_0 + \beta_2 X_{i2} + \varepsilon_i \qquad \text{Reduced model}$$

Note the new response variable $Y - 3X_1 - 5X_3$ in the reduced model, since $\beta_1 X_1$ and $\beta_3 X_3$ are known constants under H_0. We then use the general linear test statistic F^* in (2.70) with 2 and $n - 4$ degrees of freedom.

7.4   Coefficients of Partial Determination

Extra sums of squares are not only useful for tests on the regression coefficients of a multiple regression model, but they are also encountered in descriptive measures of relationship called coefficients of partial determination. Recall that the coefficient of multiple determination, R^2, measures the proportionate reduction in the variation of Y achieved by the introduction of the entire set of X variables considered in the model. A *coefficient of partial determination*, in contrast, measures the marginal contribution of one X variable when all others are already included in the model.

Two Predictor Variables

We first consider a first-order multiple regression model with two predictor variables, as given in (6.1):

$$Y_i = \beta_0 + \beta_1 X_{i1} + \beta_2 X_{i2} + \varepsilon_i$$

$SSE(X_2)$ measures the variation in Y when X_2 is included in the model. $SSE(X_1, X_2)$ measures the variation in Y when both X_1 and X_2 are included in the model. Hence, the relative marginal reduction in the variation in Y associated with X_1 when X_2 is already in the model is:

$$\frac{SSE(X_2) - SSE(X_1, X_2)}{SSE(X_2)} = \frac{SSR(X_1|X_2)}{SSE(X_2)}$$

This measure is the coefficient of partial determination between Y and X_1, given that X_2 is in the model. We denote this measure by $r_{Y1.2}^2$:

(7.35)
$$r_{Y1.2}^2 = \frac{SSE(X_2) - SSE(X_1, X_2)}{SSE(X_2)} = \frac{SSR(X_1|X_2)}{SSE(X_2)}$$

Thus, $r_{Y1.2}^2$ measures the proportionate reduction in the variation in Y remaining after X_2 is included in the model that is gained by also including X_1 in the model.

The coefficient of partial determination between Y and X_2, given that X_1 is in the model, is defined correspondingly:

$$(7.36) \qquad r_{Y2.1}^2 = \frac{SSR(X_2|X_1)}{SSE(X_1)}$$

General Case

The generalization of coefficients of partial determination to three or more X variables in the model is immediate. For instance:

$$(7.37) \qquad r_{Y1.23}^2 = \frac{SSR(X_1|X_2, X_3)}{SSE(X_2, X_3)}$$

$$(7.38) \qquad r_{Y2.13}^2 = \frac{SSR(X_2|X_1, X_3)}{SSE(X_1, X_3)}$$

$$(7.39) \qquad r_{Y3.12}^2 = \frac{SSR(X_3|X_1, X_2)}{SSE(X_1, X_2)}$$

$$(7.40) \qquad r_{Y4.123}^2 = \frac{SSR(X_4|X_1, X_2, X_3)}{SSE(X_1, X_2, X_3)}$$

Note that in the subscripts to r^2, the entries to the left of the dot show in turn the variable taken as the response and the X variable being added. The entries to the right of the dot show the X variables already in the model.

Example

For the body fat example, we can obtain a variety of coefficients of partial determination. Here are three (Tables 7.2 and 7.4):

$$r_{Y2.1}^2 = \frac{SSR(X_2|X_1)}{SSE(X_1)} = \frac{33.17}{143.12} = .232$$

$$r_{Y3.12}^2 = \frac{SSR(X_3|X_1, X_2)}{SSE(X_1, X_2)} = \frac{11.54}{109.95} = .105$$

$$r_{Y1.2}^2 = \frac{SSR(X_1|X_2)}{SSE(X_2)} = \frac{3.47}{113.42} = .031$$

We see that when X_2 is added to the regression model containing X_1 here, the error sum of squares $SSE(X_1)$ is reduced by 23.2 percent. The error sum of squares for the model containing both X_1 and X_2 is only reduced by another 10.5 percent when X_3 is added to the model. Finally, if the regression model already contains X_2, adding X_1 only reduces $SSE(X_2)$ by 3.1 percent.

Comments

1. The coefficients of partial determination can take on values between 0 and 1, as the definitions readily indicate.

2. A coefficient of partial determination can be interpreted as a coefficient of simple determination. Consider a multiple regression model with two X variables. Suppose we regress Y on X_2 and obtain the residuals:

$$Y_i - \hat{Y}_i(X_2)$$

where $\hat{Y}_i(X_2)$ denotes the fitted values of Y when X_2 is in the model. Suppose we further regress X_1 on X_2 and obtain the residuals:

$$X_{i1} - \hat{X}_{i1}(X_2)$$

where $\hat{X}_{i1}(X_2)$ denotes the fitted values of X_1 in the regression of X_1 on X_2. The coefficient of simple determination r^2 between these two sets of residuals equals the coefficient of partial determination $r^2_{Y1.2}$. Thus, this coefficient measures the relation between Y and X_1 when both of these variables have been adjusted for their linear relationships to X_2.   ∎

Coefficients of Partial Correlation

The square root of a coefficient of partial determination is called a *coefficient of partial correlation*. It is given the same sign as that of the corresponding regression coefficient in the fitted regression function. Coefficients of partial correlation are frequently used in practice, although they do not have as clear a meaning as coefficients of partial determination. One use of partial correlation coefficients is in computer routines for finding the best predictor variable to be selected next for inclusion in the regression model. We discuss this use in Chapter 8.

Example.   For the body fat example, we have:

$$r_{Y2.1} = \sqrt{.232} = .482$$

$$r_{Y3.12} = -\sqrt{.105} = -.324$$

$$r_{Y1.2} = \sqrt{.031} = .176$$

Note that the coefficients $r_{Y2.1}$ and $r_{Y1.2}$ are positive because we see from Table 7.2c that $b_2 = .6594$ and $b_1 = .2224$ are positive. Similarly, $r_{Y3.12}$ is negative because we see from Table 7.2d that $b_3 = -2.186$ is negative.

Note

Coefficients of partial determination can be expressed in terms of simple or other partial correlation coefficients. For example:

(7.41)
$$r^2_{Y2.1} = \frac{(r_{Y2} - r_{12}r_{Y1})^2}{(1 - r^2_{12})(1 - r^2_{Y1})}$$

(7.42)
$$r^2_{Y2.13} = \frac{(r_{Y2.3} - r_{12.3}r_{Y1.3})^2}{(1 - r^2_{12.3})(1 - r^2_{Y1.3})}$$

where r_{Y1} denotes the coefficient of simple correlation between Y and X_1, r_{12} denotes the coefficient of simple correlation between X_1 and X_2, and so on. Extensions are straightforward.   ∎

7.5 Standardized Multiple Regression Model

A standardized form of the general multiple regression model (6.7) is employed to control roundoff errors in normal equations calculations and to permit comparisons of the estimated regression coefficients in common units.

Roundoff Errors in Normal Equations Calculations

The results from normal equations calculations can be sensitive to rounding of data in intermediate stages of calculations. When the number of X variables is small—say, three or less—roundoff effects can be controlled by carrying a sufficient number of digits in intermediate calculations. Indeed, most computer regression programs use double-precision arithmetic (e.g., use of 16 digits instead of 8 digits) in all computations to control roundoff effects. Still, with a large number of X variables, serious roundoff effects can arise despite the use of many digits in intermediate calculations.

Roundoff errors tend to enter normal equations calculations primarily when the inverse of $\mathbf{X}'\mathbf{X}$ is taken. Of course, any errors in $(\mathbf{X}'\mathbf{X})^{-1}$ may be magnified when calculating $\mathbf{b}$ and other subsequent statistics. The danger of serious roundoff errors in $(\mathbf{X}'\mathbf{X})^{-1}$ is particularly great when (1) $\mathbf{X}'\mathbf{X}$ has a determinant that is close to zero and/or (2) the elements of $\mathbf{X}'\mathbf{X}$ differ substantially in order of magnitude. The first condition arises when some or all of the X variables are highly intercorrelated. We shall discuss this situation in Section 7.6.

The second condition arises when the X variables have substantially different magnitudes so that the entries in the $\mathbf{X}'\mathbf{X}$ matrix cover a wide range, say, from 15 to 49,000,000. A solution for this condition is to transform the variables and thereby reparameterize the regression model into the standardized regression model.

The transformation to obtain the standardized regression model, called the *correlation transformation*, makes all entries in the $\mathbf{X}'\mathbf{X}$ matrix for the transformed variables fall between -1 and 1 inclusive, so that the calculation of the inverse matrix becomes much less subject to roundoff errors due to dissimilar orders of magnitudes than with the original variables.

Note

In order to avoid the computational difficulties inherent in inverting the $\mathbf{X}'\mathbf{X}$ matrix, many statistical packages use an entirely different computational approach that involves decomposing the $\mathbf{X}$ matrix into a product of several matrices with special properties. The $\mathbf{X}$ matrix is often first modified by centering each of the variables (i.e., using the deviations around the mean) to further improve computational accuracy. Information on decomposition strategies may be found in texts on statistical computing, such as Reference 7.1. ∎

Lack of Comparability in Regression Coefficients

A second difficulty with the nonstandardized multiple regression model (6.7) is that ordinarily regression coefficients cannot be compared because of differences in the units involved. We cite two examples.

1. When considering the fitted response function:

$$\hat{Y} = 200 + 20{,}000X_1 + .2X_2$$

one may be tempted to conclude that X_1 is the only important predictor variable, and that X_2 has little effect on the response variable Y. A little reflection should make one wary of this conclusion. The reason is that we do not know the units involved. Suppose the units are:

Y in dollars

X_1 in thousand dollars

X_2 in cents

In that event, the effect on the mean response of a \$1,000 increase in X_1 (i.e., a 1-unit increase) when X_2 is constant would be an increase of \$20,000. This is exactly the same as the effect of a \$1,000 increase in X_2 (i.e., a 100,000-unit increase) when X_1 is constant, despite the difference in the regression coefficients.

2. In the Dwaine Studios example of Figure 6.5, we cannot make any comparison between b_1 and b_2 because X_1 is in units of thousand persons aged 16 or younger, whereas X_2 is in units of thousand dollars of per capita disposable income.

Correlation Transformation

Use of the correlation transformation helps with controlling roundoff errors and, by expressing the regression coefficients in the same units, may be of help when these coefficients are compared. We shall first describe the correlation transformation and then the resulting standardized regression model.

The correlation transformation is a simple modification of the usual standardization of a variable. Standardizing a variable, as in (A.37), involves centering and scaling the variable. *Centering* involves taking the difference between each observation and the mean of all observations for the variable; *scaling* involves expressing the centered observations in units of the standard deviation of the observations for the variable. Thus, the usual standardizations of the response variable Y and the predictor variables $X_1, \ldots, X_{p-1}$ are as follows:

$$(7.43a) \qquad \frac{Y_i - \bar{Y}}{s_Y}$$

$$(7.43b) \qquad \frac{X_{ik} - \bar{X}_k}{s_k} \qquad (k = 1, \ldots, p - 1)$$

where $\bar{Y}$ and $\bar{X}_k$ are the respective means of the Y and the X_k observations, and s_Y and s_k are the respective standard deviations defined as follows:

$$(7.43c) \qquad s_Y = \sqrt{\frac{\sum_i (Y_i - \bar{Y})^2}{n - 1}}$$

$$(7.43d) \qquad s_k = \sqrt{\frac{\sum_i (X_{ik} - \bar{X}_k)^2}{n - 1}} \qquad (k = 1, \ldots, p - 1)$$

The correlation transformation is a simple function of the standardized variables in (7.43a, b):

$$(7.44a) \qquad Y_i' = \frac{1}{\sqrt{n-1}} \left(\frac{Y_i - \bar{Y}}{s_Y} \right)$$

$$(7.44b) \qquad X_{ik}' = \frac{1}{\sqrt{n-1}} \left(\frac{X_{ik} - \bar{X}_k}{s_k} \right) \qquad (k = 1, \ldots, p-1)$$

Standardized Regression Model

The regression model with the transformed variables Y' and X_k' as defined by the correlation transformation in (7.44) is called a *standardized regression model* and is as follows:

$$(7.45) \qquad Y_i' = \beta_1' X_{i1}' + \cdots + \beta_{p-1}' X_{i,p-1}' + \varepsilon_i'$$

The reason why there is no intercept parameter in the standardized regression model (7.45) is that the least squares or maximum likelihood calculations always would lead to an estimated intercept term of zero if an intercept parameter were present in the model.

It is easy to show that the parameters $\beta_1', \ldots, \beta_{p-1}'$ in the standardized regression model and the original parameters $\beta_0, \beta_1, \ldots, \beta_{p-1}$ in the ordinary multiple regression model (6.7) are related as follows:

$$(7.46a) \qquad \beta_k = \left(\frac{s_Y}{s_k} \right) \beta_k' \qquad (k = 1, \ldots, p-1)$$

$$(7.46b) \qquad \beta_0 = \bar{Y} - \beta_1 \bar{X}_1 - \cdots - \beta_{p-1} \bar{X}_{p-1}$$

We see that the standardized regression coefficients β_k' and the original regression coefficients β_k $(k = 1, \ldots, p-1)$ are related by simple scaling factors involving ratios of standard deviations.

X'X Matrix for Transformed Variables

In order to be able to study the special nature of the $\mathbf{X'X}$ matrix and the least squares normal equations when the variables have been transformed by the correlation transformation, we need to decompose the correlation matrix in (6.67) containing all pairwise correlation coefficients among the response and predictor variables $Y, X_1, X_2, \ldots, X_{p-1}$ into two matrices.

1. The first matrix, denoted by $\mathbf{r}_{XX}$, is called the *correlation matrix of the X variables*. It has as its elements the coefficients of simple correlation between all pairs of the X variables. This matrix is defined as follows:

$$(7.47) \qquad \underset{(p-1)\times(p-1)}{\mathbf{r}_{XX}} = \begin{bmatrix} 1 & r_{12} & \cdots & r_{1,p-1} \\ r_{21} & 1 & \cdots & r_{2,p-1} \\ \vdots & \vdots & & \vdots \\ r_{p-1,1} & r_{p-1,2} & \cdots & 1 \end{bmatrix}$$

Here, r_{12} again denotes the coefficient of simple correlation between X_1 and X_2, and so on. Note that the main diagonal consists of 1s because the coefficient of simple correlation between a variable and itself is 1. The correlation matrix $\mathbf{r}_{XX}$ is symmetric; remember that $r_{kk'} = r_{k'k}$. Because of the symmetry of this matrix, computer printouts frequently omit the lower or upper triangular block of elements.

2. The second matrix, denoted by $\mathbf{r}_{YX}$, is a vector containing the coefficients of simple correlation between the response variable Y and each of the X variables, denoted again by r_{Y1}, r_{Y2}, etc.:

$$(7.48) \qquad \underset{(p-1) \times 1}{\mathbf{r}_{YX}} = \begin{bmatrix} r_{Y1} \\ r_{Y2} \\ \vdots \\ r_{Y,p-1} \end{bmatrix}$$

Now we are ready to consider the $\mathbf{X'X}$ matrix for the transformed variables in the standardized regression model (7.45). The $\mathbf{X}$ matrix here is:

$$(7.49) \qquad \underset{n \times (p-1)}{\mathbf{X}} = \begin{bmatrix} X'_{11} & \cdots & X'_{1,p-1} \\ X'_{21} & \cdots & X'_{2,p-1} \\ \vdots & & \vdots \\ X'_{n1} & \cdots & X'_{n,p-1} \end{bmatrix}$$

Remember that the standardized regression model (7.45) does not contain an intercept term; hence, there is no column of 1s in the $\mathbf{X}$ matrix. It can be shown that the $\mathbf{X'X}$ matrix for the transformed variables is simply the correlation matrix of the X variables defined in (7.47):

$$(7.50) \qquad \underset{(p-1) \times (p-1)}{\mathbf{X'X}} = \mathbf{r}_{XX}$$

Since the $\mathbf{X'X}$ matrix for the transformed variables consists of coefficients of correlation between the X variables, all of its elements are between -1 and 1 and thus are of the same order of magnitude. As we pointed out earlier, this can be of great help in controlling roundoff errors when inverting the $\mathbf{X'X}$ matrix.

Note

We illustrate that the $\mathbf{X'X}$ matrix for the transformed variables is the correlation matrix of the X variables by considering two entries in the matrix:

1. In the upper left corner of $\mathbf{X'X}$ we have:

$$\sum (X'_{i1})^2 = \sum \left(\frac{X_{i1} - \bar{X}_1}{\sqrt{n-1}\, s_1} \right)^2 = \frac{\Sigma (X_{i1} - \bar{X}_1)^2}{n-1} \div s_1^2 = 1$$

2. In the first row, second column of $\mathbf{X'X}$, we have:

$$\sum X'_{i1} X'_{i2} = \sum \left(\frac{X_{i1} - \bar{X}_1}{\sqrt{n-1}\, s_1} \right) \left(\frac{X_{i2} - \bar{X}_2}{\sqrt{n-1}\, s_2} \right)$$

$$= \frac{1}{n-1} \frac{\Sigma(X_{i1} - \bar{X}_1)(X_{i2} - \bar{X}_2)}{s_1 s_2}$$

$$= \frac{\Sigma(X_{i1} - \bar{X}_1)(X_{i2} - \bar{X}_2)}{\left[\Sigma(X_{i1} - \bar{X}_1)^2 \, \Sigma(X_{i2} - \bar{X}_2)^2 \right]^{1/2}}$$

But this equals r_{12}, the coefficient of correlation between X_1 and X_2, by (2.76). ■

Estimated Standardized Regression Coefficients

The least squares normal equations (6.24) for the ordinary multiple regression model:

$$\mathbf{X'Xb} = \mathbf{X'Y}$$

and the least squares estimators (6.25):

$$\mathbf{b} = \mathbf{(X'X)}^{-1}\mathbf{X'Y}$$

can be expressed simply for the transformed variables. It can be shown that for the transformed variables, $\mathbf{X'Y}$ becomes:

$$(7.51) \qquad \underset{(p-1)\times 1}{\mathbf{X'Y}} = \mathbf{r}_{YX}$$

where $\mathbf{r}_{YX}$ is defined in (7.48) as the vector of the coefficients of simple correlation between Y and each X variable. It now follows from (7.50) and (7.51) that the least squares normal equations and estimators of the regression coefficients of the standardized regression model (7.45) are as follows:

$$(7.52a) \qquad \mathbf{r}_{XX}\mathbf{b} = \mathbf{r}_{YX}$$

$$(7.52b) \qquad \mathbf{b} = \mathbf{r}_{XX}^{-1}\mathbf{r}_{YX}$$

where:

$$(7.52c) \qquad \underset{(p-1)\times 1}{\mathbf{b}} = \begin{bmatrix} b'_1 \\ b'_2 \\ \vdots \\ b'_{p-1} \end{bmatrix}$$

The regression coefficients $b'_1, \ldots, b'_{p-1}$ are often called *standardized regression coefficients*.

The return to the estimated regression coefficients for regression model (6.7) in the original variables is accomplished by employing the relations:

$$(7.53a) \qquad b_k = \left(\frac{s_Y}{s_k}\right) b'_k \qquad (k = 1, \ldots, p - 1)$$

$$(7.53b) \qquad b_0 = \bar{Y} - b_1 \bar{X}_1 - \cdots - b_{p-1} \bar{X}_{p-1}$$

Note

When there are two X variables in the regression model, i.e., when $p - 1 = 2$, we can readily see the algebraic form of the standardized regression coefficients. We have:

$$(7.54a) \qquad \mathbf{r}_{XX} = \begin{bmatrix} 1 & r_{12} \\ r_{12} & 1 \end{bmatrix}$$

$$(7.54b) \qquad \mathbf{r}_{YX} = \begin{bmatrix} r_{Y1} \\ r_{Y2} \end{bmatrix}$$

$$(7.54c) \qquad \mathbf{r}_{XX}^{-1} = \frac{1}{1 - r_{12}^2} \begin{bmatrix} 1 & -r_{12} \\ -r_{12} & 1 \end{bmatrix}$$

Hence, by (7.52b) we obtain:

$$(7.55) \qquad \mathbf{b} = \frac{1}{1 - r_{12}^2} \begin{bmatrix} 1 & -r_{12} \\ -r_{12} & 1 \end{bmatrix} \begin{bmatrix} r_{Y1} \\ r_{Y2} \end{bmatrix} = \frac{1}{1 - r_{12}^2} \begin{bmatrix} r_{Y1} - r_{12} r_{Y2} \\ r_{Y2} - r_{12} r_{Y1} \end{bmatrix}$$

Thus:

$$(7.55a) \qquad b'_1 = \frac{r_{Y1} - r_{12} r_{Y2}}{1 - r_{12}^2}$$

$$(7.55b) \qquad b'_2 = \frac{r_{Y2} - r_{12} r_{Y1}}{1 - r_{12}^2} \qquad \blacksquare$$

Example

Table 7.5a repeats a portion of the original data for the Dwaine Studios example in Figure 6.5b, and Table 7.5b contains the data transformed according to the correlation transformation (7.44). We illustrate the calculation of the transformed data for the first case, using the means and standard deviations in Table 7.5a (differences in the last digit of the transformed data are due to rounding effects):

$$Y'_1 = \frac{1}{\sqrt{n-1}} \left(\frac{Y_1 - \bar{Y}}{s_Y}\right) \qquad\qquad X'_{11} = \frac{1}{\sqrt{n-1}} \left(\frac{X_{11} - \bar{X}_1}{s_1}\right)$$

$$= \frac{1}{\sqrt{21-1}} \left(\frac{174.4 - 181.90}{36.191}\right) \qquad = \frac{1}{\sqrt{21-1}} \left(\frac{68.5 - 62.019}{18.620}\right)$$

$$= -.04634 \qquad\qquad\qquad = .07783$$

TABLE 7.5   **Correlation Transformation and Fitted Standardized Regression Model—Dwaine Studios Example.**

(a) Original Data

Case i	Sales Y_i	Target Population X_{i1}	Per Capita Disposable Income X_{i2}
1	174.4	68.5	16.7
2	164.4	45.2	16.8
...	...	...	...
20	224.1	82.7	19.1
21	166.5	52.3	16.0
	$\bar{Y} = 181.90$	$\bar{X}_1 = 62.019$	$\bar{X}_2 = 17.143$
	$s_Y = 36.191$	$s_1 = 18.620$	$s_2 = .97035$

(b) Transformed Data

i	Y_i'	X_{i1}'	X_{i2}'
1	−.04637	.07783	−.10205
2	−.10815	−.20198	−.07901
...	...	...	...
20	.26070	.24835	.45100
21	−.09518	−.11671	−.26336

(c) Fitted Standardized Model

$$\hat{Y}' = .7484 X_1' + .2511 X_2'$$

$$X_{12}' = \frac{1}{\sqrt{n-1}}\left(\frac{X_{12} - \bar{X}_2}{s_2}\right) = \frac{1}{\sqrt{21-1}}\left(\frac{16.7 - 17.143}{.97035}\right) = -.10208$$

When fitting the standardized regression model (7.45) to the transformed data, we obtain the fitted model in Table 7.5c:

$$\hat{Y}' = .7484 X_1' + .2511 X_2'$$

The standardized regression coefficients $b_1' = .7484$ and $b_2' = .2511$ are shown in the SYSTAT regression output in Figure 6.5a, labeled STD COEF. We see from the standardized regression coefficients that an increase of one standard deviation of X_1 (target population) when X_2 (per capita disposable income) is fixed leads to a much larger increase in expected sales (in units of standard deviations of Y) than does an increase of one standard deviation of X_2 when X_1 is fixed.

To shift from the standardized regression coefficients b_1' and b_2' back to the regression coefficients for the model with the original variables, we employ (7.53). Using the data in

Table 7.5, we obtain:

$$b_1 = \left(\frac{s_Y}{s_1}\right)b_1' = \frac{36.191}{18.620}(.7484) = 1.4546$$

$$b_2 = \left(\frac{s_Y}{s_2}\right)b_2' = \frac{36.191}{.97035}(.2511) = 9.3652$$

$$b_0 = \bar{Y} - b_1\bar{X}_1 - b_2\bar{X}_2 = 181.90 - 1.4546(62.019) - 9.3652(17.143) = -68.860$$

The estimated regression function for the multiple regression model in the original variables therefore is:

$$\hat{Y} = -68.860 + 1.455X_1 + 9.365X_2$$

This is the same fitted regression function we obtained in Chapter 6, except for slight rounding effect differences. Here, b_1 and b_2 cannot be compared directly because X_1 is in units of thousands of persons and X_2 is in units of thousands of dollars.

Sometimes the standardized regression coefficients $b_1' = .7484$ and $b_2' = .2511$ are interpreted as showing that target population (X_1) has a much greater impact on sales than per capita disposable income (X_2) because b_1' is much larger than b_2'. However, as we will see in the next section, one must be cautious about interpreting any regression coefficient, whether standardized or not. The reason is that when the predictor variables are correlated among themselves, as here, the regression coefficients are affected by the other predictor variables in the model. For the Dwaine Studios data, the correlation between X_1 and X_2 is $r_{12} = .781$, as shown in the correlation matrix in Figure 6.4.

The magnitudes of the standardized regression coefficients are affected not only by the presence of correlations among the predictor variables but also by the spacings of the observations on each of these variables. Sometimes these spacings may be quite arbitrary. Hence, it is ordinarily not wise to interpret the magnitudes of standardized regression coefficients as reflecting the comparative importance of the predictor variables.

Comments

1. Some computer packages present both the regression coefficients b_k for the model in the original variables as well as the standardized coefficients b_k', as in the SYSTAT output in Figure 6.5a. The standardized coefficients are sometimes labeled *beta coefficients* in printouts.

2. Some computer printouts show the magnitude of the determinant of the correlation matrix of the X variables. A near-zero value for this determinant implies both a high degree of linear association among the X variables and a high potential for roundoff errors. For two X variables, this determinant is seen from (7.54) to be $1 - r_{12}^2$, which approaches 0 as r_{12}^2 approaches 1.

3. It is possible to use the correlation transformation with a computer package that does not permit regression through the origin, because the intercept coefficient b_0' will always be zero for data so transformed. The other regression coefficients will also be correct.

4. Use of the standardized variables (7.43) without the correlation transformation modification in (7.44) will lead to the same standardized regression coefficients as those in (7.52b) for the correlation-transformed variables. However, the elements of the $\mathbf{X'X}$ matrix will not then be bounded between -1 and 1.   ∎

7.6   Multicollinearity and Its Effects

In multiple regression analysis, the nature and significance of the relations between the predictor or explanatory variables and the response variable are often of particular interest. Some questions frequently asked are:

1. What is the relative importance of the effects of the different predictor variables?

2. What is the magnitude of the effect of a given predictor variable on the response variable?

3. Can any predictor variable be dropped from the model because it has little or no effect on the response variable?

4. Should any predictor variables not yet included in the model be considered for possible inclusion?

If the predictor variables included in the model are (1) uncorrelated among themselves and (2) uncorrelated with any other predictor variables that are related to the response variable but are omitted from the model, relatively simple answers can be given to these questions. Unfortunately, in many nonexperimental situations in business, economics, and the social and biological sciences, the predictor or explanatory variables tend to be correlated among themselves and with other variables that are related to the response variable but are not included in the model. For example, in a regression of family food expenditures on the explanatory variables family income, family savings, and age of head of household, the explanatory variables will be correlated among themselves. Further, they will also be correlated with other socioeconomic variables not included in the model that do affect family food expenditures, such as family size.

When the predictor variables are correlated among themselves, *intercorrelation* or *multicollinearity* among them is said to exist. (Sometimes the latter term is reserved for those instances when the correlation among the predictor variables is very high.) We shall explore a variety of interrelated problems created by multicollinearity among the predictor variables. First, however, we examine the situation when the predictor variables are not correlated.

Uncorrelated Predictor Variables

Table 7.6 contains data for a small-scale experiment on the effect of work crew size (X_1) and level of bonus pay (X_2) on crew productivity (Y). The predictor variables X_1 and X_2 are uncorrelated here, i.e., $r_{12}^2 = 0$, where r_{12}^2 denotes the coefficient of simple determination between X_1 and X_2. Table 7.7a contains the fitted regression function and the analysis of variance table when both X_1 and X_2 are included in the model. Table 7.7b contains the same information when only X_1 is included in the model, and Table 7.7c contains this information when only X_2 is in the model.

An important feature to note in Table 7.7 is that the regression coefficient for X_1, $b_1 = 5.375$, is the same whether only X_1 is included in the model or both predictor variables are included. The same holds for $b_2 = 9.250$. This is the result of the two predictor variables being uncorrelated.

Thus, when the predictor variables are uncorrelated, the effects ascribed to them by a first-order regression model are the same no matter which other of these predictor variables are included in the model. This is a strong argument for controlled experiments whenever

TABLE 7.6   **Uncorrelated Predictor Variables—Work Crew Productivity Example.**

Case	Crew Size	Bonus Pay (dollars)	Crew Productivity
i	X_{i1}	X_{i2}	Y_i
1	4	2	42
2	4	2	39
3	4	3	48
4	4	3	51
5	6	2	49
6	6	2	53
7	6	3	61
8	6	3	60

possible, since experimental control permits choosing the levels of the predictor variables so as to make these variables uncorrelated.

Another important feature of Table 7.7 is related to the error sums of squares. Note from Table 7.7 that the extra sum of squares $SSR(X_1|X_2)$ equals the regression sum of squares $SSR(X_1)$ when only X_1 is in the regression model:

$$SSR(X_1|X_2) = SSE(X_2) - SSE(X_1, X_2)$$

$$= 248.750 - 17.625 = 231.125$$

$$SSR(X_1) = 231.125$$

Similarly, the extra sum of squares $SSR(X_2|X_1)$ equals $SSR(X_2)$, the regression sum of squares when only X_2 is in the regression model:

$$SSR(X_2|X_1) = SSE(X_1) - SSE(X_1, X_2)$$

$$= 188.750 - 17.625 = 171.125$$

$$SSR(X_2) = 171.125$$

In general, when two or more predictor variables are uncorrelated, the marginal contribution of one predictor variable in reducing the error sum of squares when the other predictor variables are in the model is exactly the same as when this predictor variable is in the model alone.

Note

To show that the regression coefficient of X_1 is unchanged when X_2 is added to the regression model in the case where X_1 and X_2 are uncorrelated, consider the following algebraic expression for b_1 in the first-order multiple regression model with two predictor variables:

$$(7.56) \qquad b_1 = \frac{\dfrac{\Sigma(X_{i1} - \bar{X}_1)(Y_i - \bar{Y})}{\Sigma(X_{i1} - \bar{X}_1)^2} - \left[\dfrac{\Sigma(Y_i - \bar{Y})^2}{\Sigma(X_{i1} - \bar{X}_1)^2}\right]^{1/2} r_{Y2}r_{12}}{1 - r_{12}^2}$$

TABLE 7.7   Regression Results when Predictor Variables Are Uncorrelated —Work Crew Productivity Example.

(a) Regression of Y on X_1 and X_2

$$\hat{Y} = .375 + 5.375X_1 + 9.250X_2$$

Source of Variation	SS	df	MS
Regression	402.250	2	201.125
Error	17.625	5	3.525
Total	419.875	7	

(b) Regression of Y on X_1

$$\hat{Y} = 23.500 + 5.375X_1$$

Source of Variation	SS	df	MS
Regression	231.125	1	231.125
Error	188.750	6	31.458
Total	419.875	7	

(c) Regression of Y on X_2

$$\hat{Y} = 27.250 + 9.250X_2$$

Source of Variation	SS	df	MS
Regression	171.125	1	171.125
Error	248.750	6	41.458
Total	419.875	7	

where, as before, r_{Y2} denotes the coefficient of simple correlation between Y and X_2, and r_{12} denotes the coefficient of simple correlation between X_1 and X_2.

If X_1 and X_2 are uncorrelated, $r_{12} = 0$, and (7.56) reduces to:

(7.56a)
$$b_1 = \frac{\Sigma(X_{i1} - \bar{X}_1)(Y_i - \bar{Y})}{\Sigma(X_{i1} - \bar{X}_1)^2} \qquad \text{when } r_{12} = 0$$

But (7.56a) is the estimator of the slope for the simple linear regression of Y on X_1, per (1.10a).

Hence, when X_1 and X_2 are uncorrelated, adding X_2 to the regression model does not change the regression coefficient for X_1; correspondingly, adding X_1 to the regression model does not change the regression coefficient for X_2. ∎

TABLE 7.8   **Example of Perfectly Correlated Predictor Variables.**

Case				Fitted Values for Regression Function	
i	X_{i1}	X_{i2}	Y_i	(7.58)	(7.59)
1	2	6	23	23	23
2	8	9	83	83	83
3	6	8	63	63	63
4	10	10	103	103	103

Response Functions:

(7.58) $\hat{Y} = -87 + X_1 + 18X_2$

(7.59) $\hat{Y} = -7 + 9X_1 + 2X_2$

Nature of Problem when Predictor Variables Are Perfectly Correlated

To see the essential nature of the problem of multicollinearity, we shall employ a simple example where the two predictor variables are perfectly correlated. The data in Table 7.8 refer to four sample observations on a response variable and two predictor variables. Mr. A was asked to fit the first-order multiple regression function:

$$(7.57) \qquad E\{Y\} = \beta_0 + \beta_1 X_1 + \beta_2 X_2$$

He returned in a short time with the fitted response function:

$$(7.58) \qquad \hat{Y} = -87 + X_1 + 18X_2$$

He was proud because the response function fits the data perfectly. The fitted values are shown in Table 7.8.

It so happened that Ms. B also was asked to fit the response function (7.57) to the same data, and she proudly obtained:

$$(7.59) \qquad \hat{Y} = -7 + 9X_1 + 2X_2$$

Her response function also fits the data perfectly, as shown in Table 7.8.

Indeed, it can be shown that infinitely many response functions will fit the data in Table 7.8 perfectly. The reason is that the predictor variables X_1 and X_2 are perfectly related, according to the relation:

$$(7.60) \qquad X_2 = 5 + .5X_1$$

Note that the fitted response functions (7.58) and (7.59) are entirely different response surfaces, as may be seen in Figure 7.2. The two response surfaces have the same fitted values only when they intersect. This occurs when X_1 and X_2 follow relation (7.60), i.e., when $X_2 = 5 + .5X_1$.

Thus, when X_1 and X_2 are perfectly related and, as in our example, the data do not contain any random error component, many different response functions will lead to the

FIGURE 7.2   **Two Response Planes That Intersect when $X_2 = 5 + .5X_1$.**

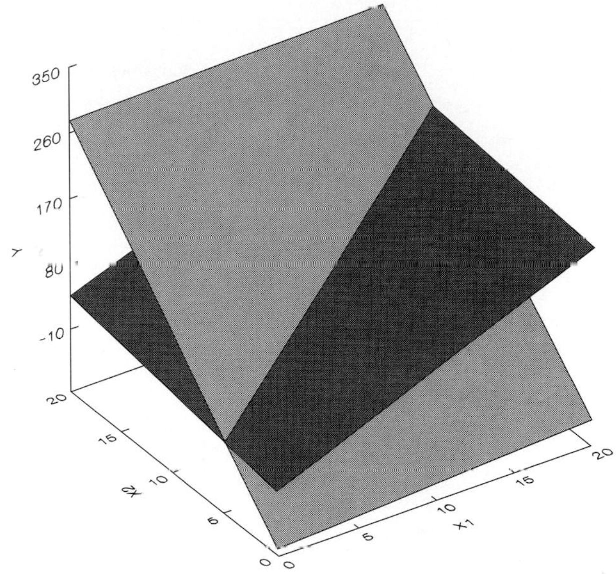

same perfectly fitted values for the observations and to the same fitted values for any other (X_1, X_2) combinations following the relation between X_1 and X_2. Yet these response functions are not the same and will lead to different fitted values for (X_1, X_2) combinations that do not follow the relation between X_1 and X_2.

Two key implications of this example are:

1. The perfect relation between X_1 and X_2 did not inhibit our ability to obtain a good fit to the data.

2. Since many different response functions provide the same good fit, we cannot interpret any one set of regression coefficients as reflecting the effects of the different predictor variables. Thus, in response function (7.58), $b_1 = 1$ and $b_2 = 18$ do not imply that X_2 is the key predictor variable and X_1 plays little role, because response function (7.59) provides an equally good fit and its regression coefficients have opposite comparative magnitudes.

Effects of Multicollinearity

In practice, we seldom find predictor variables that are perfectly related or data that do not contain some random error component. Nevertheless, the implications just noted for our idealized example still have relevance.

1. The fact that some or all predictor variables are correlated among themselves does not, in general, inhibit our ability to obtain a good fit nor does it tend to affect inferences about mean responses or predictions of new observations, provided these inferences are made within the region of observations. (Figure 6.3 on p. 236 illustrates the concept of the region of observations for the case of two predictor variables.)

2. The counterpart in real life to the many different regression functions providing equally good fits to the data in our idealized example is that the estimated regression

FIGURE 7.3   **Scatter Plot Matrix and Correlation Matrix of the Predictor Variables—Body Fat Example.**

(a)
Scatter Plot Matrix of X Variables

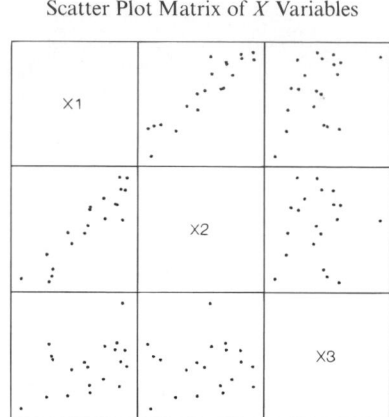

(b)
Correlation Matrix of X Variables

$$\mathbf{r}_{XX} = \begin{bmatrix} 1.0 & .924 & .458 \\ .924 & 1.0 & .085 \\ .458 & .085 & 1.0 \end{bmatrix}$$

coefficients tend to have large sampling variability when the predictor variables are highly correlated. Thus, the estimated regression coefficients tend to vary widely from one sample to the next when the predictor variables are highly correlated. As a result, only imprecise information may be available about the individual true regression coefficients. Indeed, many of the estimated regression coefficients individually may be statistically not significant even though a definite statistical relation exists between the response variable and the set of predictor variables.

3. The common interpretation of a regression coefficient as measuring the change in the expected value of the response variable when the given predictor variable is increased by one unit while all other predictor variables are held constant is not fully applicable when multicollinearity exists. It may be conceptually feasible to think of varying one predictor variable and holding the others constant, but it may not be possible in practice to do so for predictor variables that are highly correlated. For example, in a regression model for predicting crop yield from amount of rainfall and hours of sunshine, the relation between the two predictor variables makes it unrealistic to consider varying one while holding the other constant. Therefore, the simple interpretation of the regression coefficients as measuring marginal effects is often unwarranted with highly correlated predictor variables.

We illustrate these effects of multicollinearity by returning to the body fat example. A portion of the basic data was given in Table 7.1, and regression results for different fitted models were presented in Table 7.2. Figure 7.3 contains the scatter plot matrix and the correlation matrix of the predictor variables. It is evident from the scatter plot matrix that predictor variables X_1 and X_2 are highly correlated; the correlation matrix of the X variables shows that the coefficient of simple correlation is $r_{12} = .924$. On the other hand, X_3 is not so highly related to X_1 and X_2 individually; the correlation matrix shows that the correlation coefficients are $r_{13} = .458$ and $r_{23} = .085$. (But X_3 is highly correlated with X_1 and X_2 together; the coefficient of multiple determination when X_3 is regressed on X_1 and X_2 is .998.)

Effects on Regression Coefficients. Note from Table 7.2 that the regression coefficient for X_1, triceps skinfold thickness, varies markedly depending on which other variables are included in the model:

Variables in Model	b_1	b_2
X_1	.8572	—
X_2	—	.8565
X_1, X_2	.2224	.6594
X_1, X_2, X_3	4.334	−2.857

The story is the same for the regression coefficient for X_2. Indeed, the regression coefficient b_2 even changes sign when X_3 is added to the model that includes X_1 and X_2.

The important conclusion we must draw is: When predictor variables are correlated, the regression coefficient of any one variable depends on which other predictor variables are included in the model and which ones are left out. Thus, a regression coefficient does not reflect any inherent effect of the particular predictor variable on the response variable but only a marginal or partial effect, given whatever other correlated predictor variables are included in the model.

Note

Another illustration of how intercorrelated predictor variables that are omitted from the regression model can influence the regression coefficients in the regression model is provided by an analyst who was perplexed about the sign of a regression coefficient in the fitted regression model. The analyst had found in a regression of territory company sales on territory population size, per capita income, and some other predictor variables that the regression coefficient for population size was negative, and this conclusion was supported by a confidence interval for the regression coefficient. A consultant noted that the analyst did not include the major competitor's market penetration as a predictor variable in the model. The competitor was most active and effective in territories with large populations, thereby keeping company sales down in these territories. The result of the omission of this predictor variable from the model was a negative coefficient for the population size variable. ∎

Effects on Extra Sums of Squares. When predictor variables are correlated, the marginal contribution of any one predictor variable in reducing the error sum of squares varies, depending on which other variables are already in the regression model, just as for regression coefficients. For example, Table 7.2 provides the following extra sums of squares for X_1:

$$SSR(X_1) = 352.27$$

$$SSR(X_1|X_2) = \quad 3.47$$

The reason why $SSR(X_1|X_2)$ is so small compared with $SSR(X_1)$ is that X_1 and X_2 are highly correlated with each other and with the response variable. Thus, when X_2 is already in the regression model, the marginal contribution of X_1 in reducing the error sum of squares is comparatively small because X_2 contains much of the same information as X_1.

The same story is found in Table 7.2 for X_2. Here $SSR(X_2|X_1) = 33.17$, which is much smaller than $SSR(X_2) = 381.97$. The important conclusion is this: When predictor variables are correlated, there is no unique sum of squares that can be ascribed to any one predictor variable as reflecting its effect in reducing the total variation in Y. The reduction in the total variation ascribed to a predictor variable must be viewed in the context of the other correlated predictor variables already included in the model.

Comments

1. Multicollinearity also affects the coefficients of partial determination through its effects on the extra sums of squares. Note from Table 7.2 for the body fat example, for instance, that X_1 is highly correlated with Y:

$$r_{Y1}^2 = \frac{SSR(X_1)}{SSTO} = \frac{352.27}{495.39} = .71$$

However, the coefficient of partial determination between Y and X_1, when X_2 is already in the regression model, is much smaller:

$$r_{Y1.2}^2 = \frac{SSR(X_1|X_2)}{SSE(X_2)} = \frac{3.47}{113.42} = .03$$

The reason for the small coefficient of partial determination here is, as we have seen, that X_1 and X_2 are highly correlated with each other and with the response variable. Hence, X_1 provides only relatively limited additional information beyond that furnished by X_2.

2. The extra sum of squares for a predictor variable after other correlated predictor variables are in the model need not necessarily be smaller than before these other variables are in the model, as we found in the body fat example. In special cases, it can be larger. Consider the following special data set and its correlation matrix:

Y	X_1	X_2
20	5	25
20	10	30
0	5	5
1	10	10

	Y	X_1	X_2
Y	1.0	.026	.976
X_1		1.0	.243
X_2			1.0

Here, Y and X_2 are highly positively correlated, but Y and X_1 are practically uncorrelated. In addition, X_1 and X_2 are moderately positively correlated. The extra sum of squares for X_1 when it is the only variable in the model for this data set is $SSR(X_1) = .25$, but when X_2 already is in the model the extra sum of squares is $SSR(X_1|X_2) = 18.01$. Similarly, we have for these data:

$$SSR(X_2) = 362.49 \qquad SSR(X_2|X_1) = 380.25$$

The increase in the extra sums of squares with the addition of the other predictor variable in the model is related to the special situation here that X_1 is practically uncorrelated with Y but moderately correlated with X_2, which in turn is highly correlated with Y. The general point even here still holds—the extra sum of squares is affected by the other correlated predictor variables already in the model.

When $SSR(X_1|X_2) > SSR(X_1)$, as in the example just cited, the variable X_2 is sometimes called a *suppressor variable*. Since $SSR(X_2|X_1) > SSR(X_2)$ in the example, the variable X_1 would also be called a suppressor variable. ∎

Effects on $s\{b_k\}$.   Note from Table 7.2 for the body fat example how much more imprecise the estimated regression coefficients b_1 and b_2 become as more predictor variables are added to the regression model:

Variables in Model	$s\{b_1\}$	$s\{b_2\}$
X_1	.1288	—
X_2	—	.1100
X_1, X_2	.3034	.2912
X_1, X_2, X_3	3.016	2.582

Again, the high degree of multicollinearity among the predictor variables is responsible for the inflated variability of the estimated regression coefficients.

Effects on Fitted Values and Predictions.   Notice in Table 7.2 for the body fat example that the high multicollinearity among the predictor variables does not prevent the mean square error, measuring the variability of the error terms, from being steadily reduced as additional variables are added to the regression model:

Variables in Model	*MSE*
X_1	7.95
X_1, X_2	6.47
X_1, X_2, X_3	6.15

Furthermore, the precision of fitted values within the range of the observations on the predictor variables is not eroded with the addition of correlated predictor variables into the regression model. Consider the estimation of mean body fat when the only predictor variable in the model is triceps skinfold thickness (X_1) for $X_{h1} = 25.0$. The fitted value and its estimated standard deviation are (calculations not shown):

$$\hat{Y}_h = 19.93 \qquad s\{\hat{Y}_h\} = .632$$

When the highly correlated predictor variable thigh circumference (X_2) is also included in the model, the estimated mean body fat and its estimated standard deviation are as follows for $X_{h1} = 25.0$ and $X_{h2} = 50.0$:

$$\hat{Y}_h = 19.36 \qquad s\{\hat{Y}_h\} = .624$$

Thus, the precision of the estimated mean response is equally good as before, despite the addition of the second predictor variable that is highly correlated with the first one. This stability in the precision of the estimated mean response occurred despite the fact that the estimated standard deviation of b_1 became substantially larger when X_2 was added to the model (Table 7.2). The essential reason for the stability is that the covariance between b_1 and b_2 is negative, which plays a strong counteracting influence to the increase in $s^2\{b_1\}$ in determining the value of $s^2\{\hat{Y}_h\}$ as given in (6.79).

When all three predictor variables are included in the model, the estimated mean body fat and its estimated standard deviation are as follows for $X_{h1} = 25.0$, $X_{h2} = 50.0$, and $X_{h3} = 29.0$:

$$\hat{Y}_h = 19.19 \qquad s\{\hat{Y}_h\} = .621$$

Thus, the addition of the third predictor variable, which is highly correlated with the first two predictor variables together, also does not materially affect the precision of the estimated mean response.

Effects on Simultaneous Tests of β_k.   A not infrequent abuse in the analysis of multiple regression models is to examine the t^* statistic in (6.51b):

$$t^* = \frac{b_k}{s\{b_k\}}$$

for each regression coefficient in turn to decide whether $\beta_k = 0$ for $k = 1, \ldots, p - 1$. Even if a simultaneous inference procedure is used, and often it is not, problems still exist when the predictor variables are highly correlated.

Suppose we wish to test whether $\beta_1 = 0$ and $\beta_2 = 0$ in the body fat example regression model with two predictor variables of Table 7.2c. Controlling the family level of significance at .05, we require with the Bonferroni method that each of the two t tests be conducted with level of significance .025. Hence, we need $t(.9875; 17) = 2.46$. Since both t^* statistics in Table 7.2c have absolute values that do not exceed 2.46, we would conclude from the two separate tests that $\beta_1 = 0$ and that $\beta_2 = 0$. Yet the proper F test for H_0: $\beta_1 = \beta_2 = 0$ would lead to the conclusion H_a, that not both coefficients equal zero. This can be seen from Table 7.2c, where we find $F^* = MSR/MSE = 192.72/6.47 = 29.8$, which far exceeds $F(.95; 2, 17) = 3.59$.

The reason for this apparently paradoxical result is that each t^* test is a marginal test, as we have seen in (7.15) from the perspective of the general linear test approach. Thus, a small $SSR(X_1|X_2)$ here indicates that X_1 does not provide much additional information beyond X_2, which already is in the model; hence, we are led to the conclusion that $\beta_1 = 0$. Similarly, we are led to conclude $\beta_2 = 0$ here because $SSR(X_2|X_1)$ is small, indicating that X_2 does not provide much more additional information when X_1 is already in the model. But the two tests of the marginal effects of X_1 and X_2 together are not equivalent to testing whether there is a regression relation between Y and the two predictor variables. The reason is that the reduced model for each of the separate tests contains the other predictor variable, whereas the reduced model for testing whether both $\beta_1 = 0$ and $\beta_2 = 0$ would contain neither predictor variable. The proper F test shows that there is a definite regression relation here between Y and X_1 and X_2.

The same paradox would be encountered in Table 7.2d for the regression model with three predictor variables if three simultaneous tests on the regression coefficients were conducted at family level of significance .05.

Comments

1. It was noted in Section 7.5 that a near-zero determinant of $\mathbf{X}'\mathbf{X}$ is a potential source of serious roundoff errors in normal equations calculations. Severe multicollinearity has the effect of making this determinant come close to zero. Thus, under severe multicollinearity, the regression coefficients may be subject to large roundoff errors as well as large sampling variances. Hence, it is particularly advisable to employ the correlation transformation (7.44) in normal equations calculations when multicollinearity is present.

2. Just as high intercorrelations among the predictor variables tend to make the estimated regression coefficients imprecise (i.e., erratic from sample to sample), so do the coefficients of partial correlation between the response variable and each predictor variable tend to become erratic from sample to sample when the predictor variables are highly correlated.

3. The effect of intercorrelations among the predictor variables on the standard deviations of the estimated regression coefficients can be seen readily when the variables in the model are transformed by means of the correlation transformation (7.44). Consider the first-order model with two predictor variables:

(7.61)
$$Y_i = \beta_0 + \beta_1 X_{i1} + \beta_2 X_{i2} + \varepsilon_i$$

This model in the variables transformed by (7.44) becomes:

(7.62)
$$Y_i' = \beta_1' X_{i1}' + \beta_2' X_{i2}' + \varepsilon_i'$$

The $(\mathbf{X}'\mathbf{X})^{-1}$ matrix for this standardized model is given by (7.50) and (7.54c):

(7.63)
$$(\mathbf{X}'\mathbf{X})^{-1} = \mathbf{r}_{XX}^{-1} = \frac{1}{1 - r_{12}^2} \begin{bmatrix} 1 & -r_{12} \\ -r_{12} & 1 \end{bmatrix}$$

Hence, the variance-covariance matrix of the estimated regression coefficients is by (6.46) and (7.63):

(7.64)
$$\boldsymbol{\sigma}^2\{\mathbf{b}\} = (\sigma')^2 \mathbf{r}_{XX}^{-1} = (\sigma')^2 \frac{1}{1 - r_{12}^2} \begin{bmatrix} 1 & -r_{12} \\ -r_{12} & 1 \end{bmatrix}$$

where $(\sigma')^2$ is the error term variance for the standardized model (7.62). We see that the estimated regression coefficients b_1' and b_2' have the same variance here:

(7.65)
$$\sigma^2\{b_1'\} = \sigma^2\{b_2'\} = \frac{(\sigma')^2}{1 - r_{12}^2}$$

and that each of these variances become larger as the correlation between X_1 and X_2 increases. Indeed, as X_1 and X_2 approach perfect correlation (i.e., as r_{12}^2 approaches 1), the variances of b_1' and b_2' become larger without limit.

4. We noted in our discussion of simultaneous tests of the regression coefficients that it is possible that a set of predictor variables is related to the response variable, yet all of the individual tests on the regression coefficients will lead to the conclusion that they equal zero because of the multicollinearity among the predictor variables. This apparently paradoxical result is also possible under special circumstances when there is no multicollinearity among the predictor variables. The special circumstances are not likely to be found in practice, however.   ∎

Need for More Powerful Diagnostics for Multicollinearity

As we have seen, multicollinearity among the predictor variables can have important consequences for interpreting and using a fitted regression model. The diagnostic tool considered here for identifying multicollinearity—namely, the pairwise coefficients of simple correlation between the predictor variables—is frequently helpful. Often, however, serious multicollinearity exists without being disclosed by the pairwise correlation coefficients. In Chapter 9, we present a more powerful tool for identifying the existence of serious multicollinearity. Some remedial measures for lessening the effects of multicollinearity will be considered in Chapter 10.

7.7   Polynomial Regression Models

In this section, we consider polynomial regression models for quantitative predictor variables. They are among the most frequently used curvilinear response models in practice because of their ease in handling as a special case of the general linear regression model (6.7). First, we discuss several commonly used polynomial regression models. Then we present a case to illustrate some of the major issues encountered with polynomial regression models.

Uses of Polynomial Models

Polynomial regression models have two basic types of uses:

1. When the true curvilinear response function is indeed a polynomial function.

2. When the true curvilinear response function is unknown (or complex) but a polynomial function is a good approximation to the true function.

The second type of use, where the polynomial function is employed as an approximation when the shape of the true curvilinear response function is unknown, is very common. It may be viewed as a nonparametric approach to obtaining information about the shape of the response function.

A main danger in using polynomial regression models, as we shall see, is that extrapolations may be hazardous with these models, especially those with higher-order terms. Polynomial regression models may provide good fits for the data at hand, but may turn in unexpected directions when extrapolated beyond the range of the data.

One Predictor Variable—Second Order

Polynomial regression models may contain one, two, or more than two predictor variables. Further, each predictor variable may be present in various powers. We begin by considering a polynomial regression model with one predictor variable raised to the first and second powers:

(7.66)
$$Y_i = \beta_0 + \beta_1 x_i + \beta_2 x_i^2 + \varepsilon_i$$

where:

$$x_i = X_i - \bar{X}$$

This polynomial model is called a *second-order model with one predictor variable* because the single predictor variable is expressed in the model to the first and second powers. Note that the predictor variable is centered—in other words, expressed as a deviation around its mean $\bar{X}$—and that the ith centered observation is denoted by x_i. The reason for using a centered predictor variable in the polynomial regression model is that X and X^2 often will be highly correlated. This, as we noted in Section 7.5, can cause serious computational difficulties when the $\mathbf{X'X}$ matrix is inverted for estimating the regression coefficients in the normal equations calculations. Centering the predictor variable often reduces the multicollinearity substantially, as we shall illustrate in an example, and tends to avoid computational difficulties.

FIGURE 7.4   Examples of Second-Order Polynomial Response Functions.

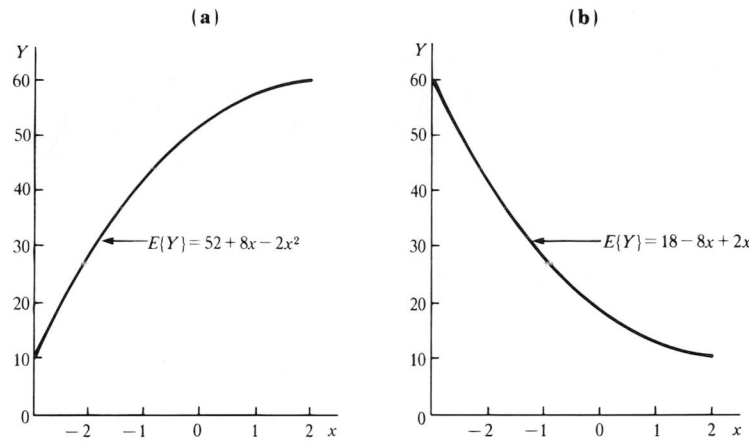

The regression coefficients in polynomial regression are frequently written in a slightly different fashion, to reflect the pattern of the exponents:

(7.66a)
$$Y_i = \beta_0 + \beta_1 x_i + \beta_{11} x_i^2 + \varepsilon_i$$

We shall employ this latter notation in this section.

The response function for regression model (7.66a) is:

(7.67)
$$E\{Y\} = \beta_0 + \beta_1 x + \beta_{11} x^2$$

This response function is a parabola and is frequently called a *quadratic response function*. Figure 7.4 contains two examples of second-order polynomial response functions.

The regression coefficient β_0 represents the mean response of Y when $x = 0$, i.e., when $X = \bar{X}$. The regression coefficient β_1 is often called the *linear effect coefficient*, and β_{11} is called the *quadratic effect coefficient*.

Comments

1. The danger of extrapolating a polynomial response function is illustrated by the response function in Figure 7.4a. If this function is extrapolated beyond $x = 2$, it actually turns downward, which might not be appropriate in a given case.

2. The algebraic version of the least squares normal equations:

$$\mathbf{X'Xb = X'Y}$$

for the second-order polynomial regression model (7.66a) can be readily obtained from (6.77) by replacing X_{i1} by x_i and X_{i2} by x_i^2. Since $\Sigma x_i = 0$, this yields the normal equations:

(7.68)
$$\sum Y_i = nb_0 + b_{11} \sum x_i^2$$
$$\sum x_i Y_i = b_1 \sum x_i^2 + b_{11} \sum x_i^3$$
$$\sum x_i^2 Y_i = b_0 \sum x_i^2 + b_1 \sum x_i^3 + b_{11} \sum x_i^4$$

∎

FIGURE 7.5 **Examples of Third-Order Polynomial Response Functions.**

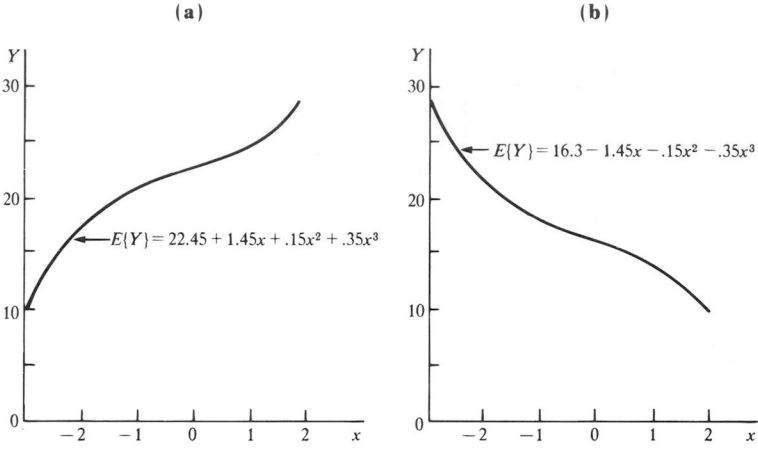

One Predictor Variable—Third Order

The regression model:

$$(7.69) \qquad Y_i = \beta_0 + \beta_1 x_i + \beta_{11} x_i^2 + \beta_{111} x_i^3 + \varepsilon_i$$

where:

$$x_i = X_i - \overline{X}$$

is a *third-order model with one predictor variable*. The response function for regression model (7.69) is:

$$(7.70) \qquad E\{Y\} = \beta_0 + \beta_1 x + \beta_{11} x^2 + \beta_{111} x^3$$

Figure 7.5 contains two examples of third-order polynomial response functions.

One Predictor Variable—Higher Orders

Polynomial models with the predictor variable present in higher powers than the third should be employed with special caution. The interpretation of the coefficients becomes difficult for such models, and the models may be highly erratic for interpolations and even small extrapolations. It must be recognized in this connection that a polynomial model of sufficiently high order can always be found to fit data containing no repeat observations perfectly. For instance, the fitted polynomial regression function for one predictor variable of order $n - 1$ will pass through all n observed Y values. One needs to be wary, therefore, of using high-order polynomials for the sole purpose of obtaining a good fit. Such regression functions may not show clearly the basic elements of the regression relation between X and Y and may lead to erratic interpolations and extrapolations.

FIGURE 7.6   **Example of a Quadratic Response Surface—**
$$E\{Y\} = 1{,}740 - 4x_1^2 - 3x_2^2 - 3x_1x_2.$$

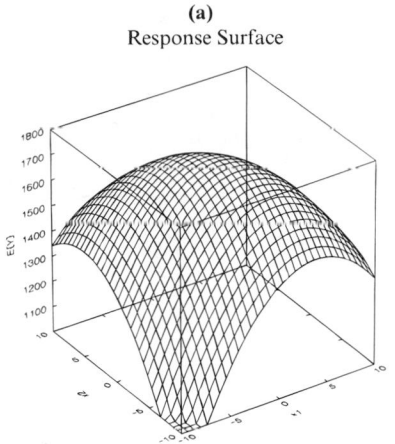

(a)
Response Surface

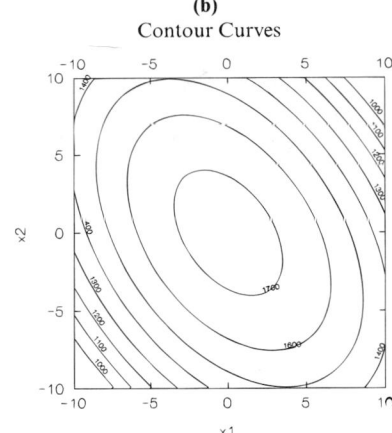

(b)
Contour Curves

Two Predictor Variables—Second Order

The regression model:

$$(7.71) \qquad Y_i = \beta_0 + \beta_1 x_{i1} + \beta_2 x_{i2} + \beta_{11} x_{i1}^2 + \beta_{22} x_{i2}^2 + \beta_{12} x_{i1} x_{i2} + \varepsilon_i$$

where:

$$x_{i1} = X_{i1} - \bar{X}_1$$
$$x_{i2} = X_{i2} - \bar{X}_2$$

is a *second-order model with two predictor variables*. The response function is:

$$(7.72) \qquad E\{Y\} = \beta_0 + \beta_1 x_1 + \beta_2 x_2 + \beta_{11} x_1^2 + \beta_{22} x_2^2 + \beta_{12} x_1 x_2$$

which is the equation of a conic section. Note that regression model (7.71) contains separate linear and quadratic components for each of the two predictor variables and a cross-product term. The latter represents the interaction effect between x_1 and x_2, as we noted in Chapter 6. The coefficient β_{12} is often called the *interaction effect coefficient*.

Figure 7.6 contains a representation of the response surface and the contour curves for a second-order response function with two predictor variables:

$$E\{Y\} = 1{,}740 - 4x_1^2 - 3x_2^2 - 3x_1x_2$$

The contour curves correspond to different response levels and show the various combinations of levels of the two predictor variables that yield the same level of response. Note that the response surface in Figure 7.6a has a maximum at $x_1 = 0$ and $x_2 = 0$. Figure 6.2b presents another type of second-order polynomial response function with two predictor variables, this one containing a saddle point.

Note

The cross-product term $\beta_{12}x_1x_2$ in (7.72) is considered to be a second-order term, the same as $\beta_{11}x_1^2$ or $\beta_{22}x_2^2$. The reason can be seen by writing the latter terms as $\beta_{11}x_1x_1$ and $\beta_{22}x_2x_2$, respectively.   ∎

Three Predictor Variables—Second Order

The *second-order regression model with three predictor variables* is:

$$(7.73) \qquad Y_i = \beta_0 + \beta_1 x_{i1} + \beta_2 x_{i2} + \beta_3 x_{i3} + \beta_{11}x_{i1}^2 + \beta_{22}x_{i2}^2 + \beta_{33}x_{i3}^2$$

$$+ \beta_{12}x_{i1}x_{i2} + \beta_{13}x_{i1}x_{i3} + \beta_{23}x_{i2}x_{i3} + \varepsilon_i$$

where:

$$x_{i1} = X_{i1} - \bar{X}_1$$
$$x_{i2} = X_{i2} - \bar{X}_2$$
$$x_{i3} = X_{i3} - \bar{X}_3$$

The response function for this regression model is:

$$(7.74) \qquad E\{Y\} = \beta_0 + \beta_1 x_1 + \beta_2 x_2 + \beta_3 x_3 + \beta_{11}x_1^2 + \beta_{22}x_2^2 + \beta_{33}x_3^2$$

$$+ \beta_{12}x_1x_2 + \beta_{13}x_1x_3 + \beta_{23}x_2x_3$$

The coefficients β_{12}, β_{13}, and β_{23} are interaction effect coefficients for interactions between pairs of predictor variables.

Implementation of Polynomial Regression Models

Fitting of Polynomial Models.   Fitting of polynomial regression models presents no new problems since, as we have seen in Chapter 6, they are special cases of the general linear regression model (6.7). Hence, all earlier results on fitting apply, as do the earlier results on making inferences.

Hierarchical Approach to Fitting.   When using a polynomial regression model as an approximation to the true regression function, statisticians will often fit a second-order or third-order model and then explore whether a lower-order model is adequate. For instance, with one predictor variable, the model:

$$Y_i = \beta_0 + \beta_1 x_i + \beta_{11}x_i^2 + \beta_{111}x_i^3 + \varepsilon_i$$

may be fitted with the hope that the cubic term and perhaps even the quadratic term can be dropped. Thus, one would wish to test whether or not $\beta_{111} = 0$, or whether or not both $\beta_{11} = 0$ and $\beta_{111} = 0$. The decomposition of *SSR* into extra sums of squares therefore proceeds as follows:

$$SSR(x)$$

$$SSR(x^2|x)$$

$$SSR(x^3|x, x^2)$$

To test whether $\beta_{111} = 0$, the appropriate extra sum of squares is $SSR(x^3|x, x^2)$. If, instead, one wishes to test whether a linear term is adequate, i.e., whether $\beta_{11} = \beta_{111} = 0$, the appropriate extra sum of squares is $SSR(x^2, x^3|x) - SSR(x^2|x) + SSR(x^3|x, x^2)$.

With the hierarchical approach, if a polynomial term of a given order is retained, then all related terms of lower order are also retained in the model. Thus, one would not drop the quadratic term of a predictor variable but retain the cubic term in the model. Since the quadratic term is of lower order, it is viewed as providing more basic information about the shape of the response function; the cubic term is of higher order and is viewed as providing refinements in the specification of the shape of the response function. The hierarchical approach to testing operates similarly for polynomial regression models with two or more predictor variables. Here, for instance, an interaction term (second power) would not be retained without also retaining the terms for the predictor variables to the first power.

Regression Function in Terms of X.   After a polynomial regression model has been developed, we often wish to express the final model in terms of the original variables rather than keeping it in terms of the centered variables. This can be done readily. For example, the fitted second-order model for one predictor variable that is expressed in terms of centered values $x = X - \bar{X}$:

$$(7.75) \qquad \hat{Y} = b_0 + b_1 x + b_{11} x^2$$

becomes in terms of the original X variable:

$$(7.76) \qquad \hat{Y} = b_0' + b_1' X + b_{11}' X^2$$

where:

$$(7.76a) \qquad b_0' = b_0 - b_1 \bar{X} + b_{11} \bar{X}^2$$

$$(7.76b) \qquad b_1' = b_1 - 2b_{11} \bar{X}$$

$$(7.76c) \qquad b_{11}' = b_{11}$$

The fitted values and residuals for the regression function in terms of X are exactly the same as for the regression function in terms of the centered values x. The reason, as we noted earlier, for utilizing a model that is expressed in terms of centered observations is to reduce potential calculational difficulties due to multicollinearity among X, X^2, X^3, etc., inherent in polynomial regression.

Note

The estimated standard deviations of the regression coefficients in terms of the centered variables x in (7.75) do not apply to the regression coefficients in terms of the original variables X in (7.76). If the estimated standard deviations for the regression coefficients in terms of X are desired, they may be obtained by using theorem (5.46), where the transformation matrix **A** is developed from (7.76a–c).   ∎

Case Example

Setting.   A researcher studied the effects of the charge rate and temperature on the life of a new type of power cell in a preliminary small-scale experiment. The charge rate (X_1) was controlled at three levels (.6, 1.0, and 1.4 amperes) and the ambient temperature (X_2) was controlled at three levels (10, 20, 30 °C). Factors pertaining to the discharge of the power cell were held at fixed levels. The life of the power cell (Y) was measured in terms of the number of discharge-charge cycles that a power cell underwent before it failed. The data obtained in the study are contained in Table 7.9, columns 1–3.

The researcher was not sure about the nature of the response function in the range of the factors studied. Hence, the researcher decided to fit the second-order polynomial regression model (7.71):

$$(7.77) \qquad Y_i = \beta_0 + \beta_1 x_{i1} + \beta_2 x_{i2} + \beta_{11} x_{i1}^2 + \beta_{22} x_{i2}^2 + \beta_{12} x_{i1} x_{i2} + \varepsilon_i$$

for which the response function is:

$$(7.78) \qquad E\{Y\} = \beta_0 + \beta_1 x_1 + \beta_2 x_2 + \beta_{11} x_1^2 + \beta_{22} x_2^2 + \beta_{12} x_1 x_2$$

Because of the balanced nature of the X_1 and X_2 levels studied, the researcher not only centered the variables X_1 and X_2 around their respective means but also scaled them in convenient units, as follows:

$$(7.79) \qquad
\begin{aligned}
x_{i1} &= \frac{X_{i1} - \bar{X}_1}{.4} = \frac{X_{i1} - 1.0}{.4} \\[2mm]
x_{i2} &= \frac{X_{i2} - \bar{X}_2}{10} = \frac{X_{i2} - 20}{10}
\end{aligned}$$

Here, the denominator used for each predictor variable is the absolute difference between adjacent levels of the variable. These centered and scaled variables are shown in columns 4 and 5 of Table 7.9. Note that the codings defined in (7.79) lead to simple coded values, $-1, 0$, and 1. The squared and cross-product terms are shown in columns 6–8 of Table 7.9.

Use of the coded variables x_1 and x_2 rather than the original variables X_1 and X_2 reduces the correlations between the first power and second power terms markedly here:

	Correlation between		Correlation between
X_1 and X_1^2:	.991	X_2 and X_2^2:	.986
x_1 and x_1^2:	0.0	x_2 and x_2^2:	0.0

The correlations for the coded variables are zero here because of the balance of the design of the experimental levels of the two explanatory variables. Similarly, the correlations between the cross-product term $x_1 x_2$ and each of the terms x_1, x_1^2, x_2, x_2^2 are reduced to zero here from levels between .60 and .76 for the corresponding terms in the original variables. Low levels of multicollinearity can be helpful in avoiding computational inaccuracies.

The researcher was particularly interested in whether interaction effects and curvature effects are required in the model for the range of the X variables considered.

TABLE 7.9   Data for Power Cells Example.

Cell	(1) Number of Cycles	(2) Charge Rate	(3) Temperature	(4) Coded Values	(5)	(6)	(7)	(8)
i	Y_i	X_{i1}	X_{i2}	x_{i1}	x_{i2}	x_{i1}^2	x_{i2}^2	$x_{i1}x_{i2}$
1	150	.6	10	-1	-1	1	1	1
2	86	1.0	10	0	-1	0	1	0
3	49	1.4	10	1	-1	1	1	-1
4	288	.6	20	-1	0	1	0	0
5	157	1.0	20	0	0	0	0	0
6	131	1.0	20	0	0	0	0	0
7	184	1.0	20	0	0	0	0	0
8	109	1.4	20	1	0	1	0	0
9	279	.6	30	-1	1	1	1	-1
10	235	1.0	30	0	1	0	1	0
11	224	1.4	30	1	1	1	1	1

$$\bar{X}_1 = 1.0 \qquad \bar{X}_2 = 20$$

Setting adapted from: S. M. Sidik, H. F. Leibecki, and J. M. Bozek, *Cycles Till Failure of Silver-Zinc Cells with Competing Failure Modes—Preliminary Data Analysis*, NASA Technical Memorandum 81556, 1980.

Fitting of Model.   Figure 7.7 contains the basic regression results for the fit of model (7.77) with the SAS regression package. Using the estimated regression coefficients (labeled Parameter Estimate), we see that the estimated regression function is as follows:

$$(7.80) \qquad \hat{Y} = 162.84 - 55.83x_1 + 75.50x_2 + 27.39x_1^2 - 10.61x_2^2 + 11.50x_1x_2$$

Residual Plots.   The researcher first investigated the appropriateness of regression model (7.77) for the data at hand. Plots of the residuals against $\hat{Y}$, x_1, and x_2 are shown in Figure 7.8 on page 305, as is also a normal probability plot. None of these plots suggest any gross inadequacies of regression model (7.77). The coefficient of correlation between the ordered residuals and their expected values under normality is .974, which supports the assumption of normality of the error terms (see Table B.6).

Test of Fit.   Since there are three replications at $x_1 = 0$, $x_2 = 0$, another indication of the adequacy of regression model (7.77) can be obtained by the formal test in (6.68) of the goodness of fit of the regression function (7.78). The pure error sum of squares (3.16) is simple to obtain here, because there is only one combination of levels at which replications occur:

$$SSPE = (157 - 157.33)^2 + (131 - 157.33)^2 + (184 - 157.33)^2$$

$$= 1,404.67$$

Since there are $c = 9$ distinct combinations of levels of the X variables here, there are $n - c = 11 - 9 = 2$ degrees of freedom associated with $SSPE$. Further, $SSE = 5,240.44$

FIGURE 7.7   **SAS Regression Output for Second-Order Polynomial Model (7.77)—**
Power Cells Example.

```
Model: MODEL1
Dependent Variable: Y
```

Analysis of Variance

Source	DF	Sum of Squares	Mean Square	F Value	Prob>F
Model	5	55365.56140	11073.11228	10.565	0.0109
Error	5	5240.43860	1048.08772		
C Total	10	60606.00000			

Root MSE	32.37418	R-square	0.9135	
Dep Mean	172.00000	Adj R-sq	0.8271	
C.V.	18.82220			

Parameter Estimates

Variable	DF	Parameter Estimate	Standard Error	T for H0: Parameter=0	Prob > |T|
INTERCEP	1	162.842105	16.60760542	9.805	0.0002
X1	1	-55.833333	13.21670483	-4.224	0.0083
X2	1	75.500000	13.21670483	5.712	0.0023
X1SQ	1	27.394737	20.34007956	1.347	0.2359
X2SQ	1	-10.605263	20.34007956	-0.521	0.6244
X1X2	1	11.500000	16.18709146	0.710	0.5092

Variable	DF	Type I SS
INTERCEP	1	325424
X1	1	18704
X2	1	34202
X1SQ	1	1645.966667
X2SQ	1	284.928070
X1X2	1	529.000000

according to Figure 7.7; hence the lack of fit sum of squares (3.24) is:

$$SSLF = SSE - SSPE = 5{,}240.44 - 1{,}404.67 = 3{,}835.77$$

with which $c - p = 9 - 6 = 3$ degrees of freedom are associated. [Remember that $p = 6$ regression coefficients in model (7.77) had to be estimated.] Hence, test statistic (6.68b) for testing the adequacy of the regression function (7.78) is:

$$F^* = \frac{SSLF}{c - p} \div \frac{SSPE}{n - c} = \frac{3{,}835.77}{3} \div \frac{1{,}404.67}{2} = 1.82$$

For $\alpha = .05$, we require $F(.95; 3, 2) = 19.2$. Since $F^* = 1.82 \le 19.2$, we conclude according to decision rule (6.68c) that the second-order polynomial regression function (7.78) is a good fit.

FIGURE 7.8 **Diagnostic Residual Plots—Power Cells Example.**

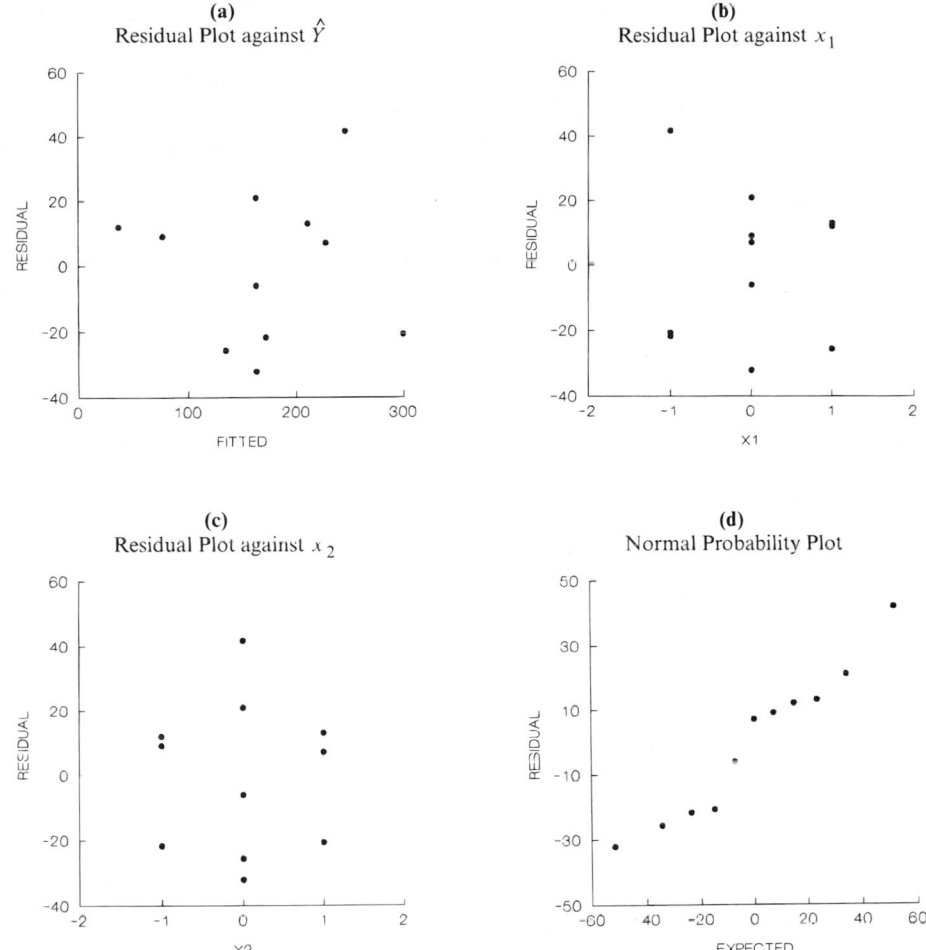

Coefficient of Multiple Determination. Figure 7.7 shows that the coefficient of multiple determination (labeled R-square) is $R^2 = .9135$. Thus, the variation in the lives of the power cells is reduced by about 91 percent when the first-order and second-order relations to the charge rate and ambient temperature are utilized. Note that the adjusted coefficient of multiple correlation (labeled Adj R-sq) is $R_a^2 = .8271$. This coefficient is considerably smaller here than the unadjusted coefficient because of the relatively large number of parameters in the polynomial regression function with two predictor variables.

Partial F-Test. The researcher now turned to consider whether a first-order model would be sufficient. The test alternatives are:

$$H_0: \quad \beta_{11} = \beta_{22} = \beta_{12} = 0$$

$$H_a: \quad \text{not all } \beta s \text{ in } H_0 \text{ equal zero}$$

The partial F test statistic (7.27) here is:

$$F^* = \frac{SSR(x_1^2, x_2^2, x_1 x_2 | x_1, x_2)}{3} \div MSE$$

In anticipation of this test, the researcher entered the X variables in the SAS regression program in the order $x_1, x_2, x_1^2, x_2^2, x_1 x_2$, as may be seen at the bottom of Figure 7.7. The extra sums of squares are labeled Type I SS. The first sum of squares shown is not relevant here. The second one is $SSR(x_1) = 18,704$, the third one is $SSR(x_2 | x_1) = 34,202$, and so on. The required extra sum of squares is therefore obtained as follows:

$$SSR(x_1^2, x_2^2, x_1 x_2 | x_1, x_2) = SSR(x_1^2 | x_1, x_2) + SSR(x_2^2 | x_1, x_2, x_1^2)$$

$$+ SSR(x_1 x_2 | x_1, x_2, x_1^2, x_2^2)$$

$$= 1,646.0 + 284.9 + 529.0 = 2,459.9$$

We also require the error mean square. We find in Figure 7.7 that it is $MSE = 1,048.1$. Hence the test statistic is:

$$F^* = \frac{2,459.9}{3} \div 1,048.1 = .78$$

For level of significance $\alpha = .05$, we require $F(.95; 3, 5) = 5.41$. Since $F^* = .78 \le 5.41$, we conclude H_0, that no curvature and interaction effects are needed, so that a first-order model is adequate for the range of the charge rates and temperatures considered.

First-Order Model. Based on this analysis, the researcher decided to consider the first-order model:

$$(7.81) \qquad Y_i = \beta_0 + \beta_1 x_{i1} + \beta_2 x_{i2} + \varepsilon_i$$

A fit of this model yielded the estimated response function:

$$(7.82) \qquad \hat{Y} = 172.00 - \underset{(12.67)}{55.83 x_1} + \underset{(12.67)}{75.50 x_2}$$

Note that the regression coefficients b_1 and b_2 are the same as in (7.80) for the fitted second-order model. This is a result of the choices of the X_1 and X_2 levels studied. The numbers in parentheses under the estimated regression coefficients are their estimated standard deviations. A variety of residual plots for this first-order model were made and analyzed by the researcher (not shown here), which confirmed the appropriateness of first-order model (7.81).

Fitted First-Order Model in Terms of X. The fitted first-order regression function (7.82) can be transformed back to the original variables by utilizing (7.79). We obtain:

$$(7.83) \qquad \hat{Y} = 160.58 - 139.58 X_1 + 7.55 X_2$$

Figure 7.9 contains a SAS-GRAPH plot of the fitted response plane. The researcher used this fitted response surface for investigating the effects of charge rate and temperature on the life of this new type of power cell.

FIGURE 7.9   **SAS-GRAPH Plot of Fitted Response Plane (7.83)**
            —Power Cells Example.

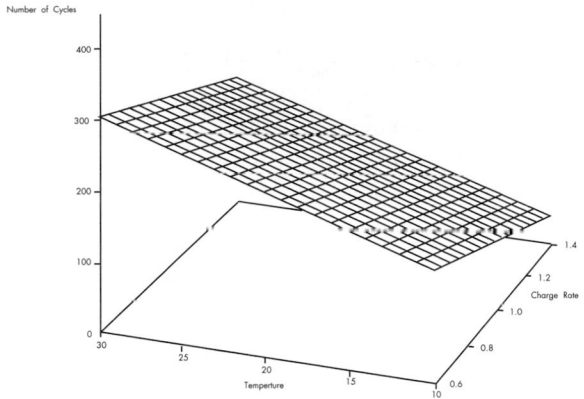

Estimation of Regression Coefficients.   The researcher wished to estimate the linear effects of the two predictor variables in the first-order model, with a 90 percent family confidence coefficient, by means of the Bonferroni method. Here, $g = 2$ statements are desired; hence, by (6.52a), we have:

$$B = t[1 - .10/2(2)] = t(.975; 8) = 2.306$$

The estimated standard deviations of b_1 and b_2 in (7.82) apply to the model in the coded variables. Since only first-order terms are involved in this fitted model, we obtain the estimated standard deviations of b_1' and b_2' for the fitted model (7.83) in the original variables as follows:

$$s\{b_1'\} = \left(\frac{1}{.4}\right)s\{b_1\} = \frac{12.67}{.4} = 31.68$$

$$s\{b_2'\} = \left(\frac{1}{10}\right)s\{b_2\} = \frac{12.67}{10} = 1.267$$

The Bonferroni confidence limits by (6.52) therefore are $-139.58 \pm 2.306(31.68)$ and $7.55 \pm 2.306(1.267)$, yielding the confidence limits:

$$-212.6 \leq \beta_1 \leq -66.5 \qquad 4.6 \leq \beta_2 \leq 10.5$$

With confidence .90, we conclude that the mean number of charge/discharge cycles before failure decreases by 66 to 213 cycles with a unit increase in the charge rate for given ambient temperature, and increases by 5 to 10 cycles with a unit increase of ambient temperature for given charge rate. The researcher was satisfied with the precision of these estimates for this initial small-scale study.

Some Further Comments on Polynomial Regression

1. The use of polynomial models is not without drawbacks. Such models can be more expensive in degrees of freedom than alternative nonlinear models or linear models with

transformed variables. Another potential drawback is that serious multicollinearity may be present even when the predictor variables are centered.

2. An alternative to using centered variables in polynomial regression is to use *orthogonal polynomials*. Orthogonal polynomials are uncorrelated. Some computer packages use orthogonal polynomials in their polynomial regression routines and present the final fitted results in terms of both the orthogonal polynomials and the original polynomials. Orthogonal polynomials are discussed in specialized texts such as Reference 7.2.

3. Sometimes a quadratic response function is fitted for the purpose of establishing the linearity of the response function when repeat observations are not available for directly testing the linearity of the response function. Fitting the quadratic model:

$$(7.84) \qquad Y_i = \beta_0 + \beta_1 x_i + \beta_{11} x_i^2 + \varepsilon_i$$

and testing whether $\beta_{11} = 0$ does not, however, necessarily establish that a linear response function is appropriate. Figure 7.5a provides an example. If sample data were obtained for the response function in Figure 7.5a, model (7.84) fitted, and a test on β_{11} made, it likely would lead to the conclusion that $\beta_{11} = 0$. Yet a linear response function clearly might not be appropriate. Examination of residuals would disclose this lack of fit and should always accompany formal testing of polynomial regression coefficients. ∎

7.8 Interaction Regression Models

We have previously noted that regression models with cross-product interaction effects, such as regression model (6.15), are special cases of general linear regression model (6.7). We also encountered regression models with interaction effects briefly when we considered polynomial regression models, such as model (7.71). Now we consider in some detail regression models with interaction effects, including their interpretation and implementation.

Interaction Effects

A regression model with $p - 1$ predictor variables contains additive effects if the response function can be written in the form:

$$(7.85) \qquad E\{Y\} = f_1(X_1) + f_2(X_2) + \cdots + f_{p-1}(X_{p-1})$$

where $f_1, f_2, \ldots, f_{p-1}$ can be any functions, not necessarily simple ones. For instance, the following response function with two predictor variables can be expressed in the form of (7.85):

$$E\{Y\} = \underbrace{\beta_0 + \beta_1 X_1 + \beta_2 X_1^2}_{f_1(X_1)} + \underbrace{\beta_3 X_2}_{f_2(X_2)}$$

We say here that the effects of X_1 and X_2 on Y are additive.

In contrast, the following regression function:

$$E\{Y\} = \beta_0 + \beta_1 X_1 + \beta_2 X_2 + \beta_3 X_1 X_2$$

cannot be expressed in the form (7.85). Hence, this latter regression model is not additive, or, equivalently, it contains an interaction effect.

A simple and commonly used means of modeling the interaction effect of two predictor variables on the response variable is by a cross-product term, such as $\beta_3 X_1 X_2$ in the above response function. The cross-product term is called an *interaction term*. More specifically, it is sometimes called a *linear-by-linear* or a *bilinear* interaction term. When there are three predictor variables whose effects on the response variable are linear, but the effects on Y of X_1 and X_2 and of X_1 and X_3 are interacting, the response function would be modeled as follows using cross-product terms:

$$E\{Y\} = \beta_0 + \beta_1 X_1 + \beta_2 X_2 + \beta_3 X_3 + \beta_4 X_1 X_2 + \beta_5 X_1 X_3$$

Interpretation of Interaction Regression Models with Linear Effects

We shall explain the influence of interaction effects on the shape of the response function and on the interpretation of the regression coefficients by first considering the simple case of two quantitative predictor variables where each has a linear effect on the response variable.

Interpretation of Regression Coefficients.   The regression model for two quantitative predictor variables with linear effects on Y and interacting effects of X_1 and X_2 on Y represented by a cross-product term is as follows:

(7.86) $$Y_i = \beta_0 + \beta_1 X_{i1} + \beta_2 X_{i2} + \beta_3 X_{i1} X_{i2} + \varepsilon_i$$

The meaning of the regression coefficients β_1 and β_2 here is not the same as that given earlier because of the interaction term $\beta_3 X_{i1} X_{i2}$. The regression coefficients β_1 and β_2 no longer indicate the change in the mean response with a unit increase of the predictor variable, with the other predictor variable held constant at any given level. It can be shown that the change in the mean response with a unit increase in X_1 when X_2 is held constant is:

(7.87) $$\beta_1 + \beta_3 X_2$$

Similarly, the change in the mean response with a unit increase in X_2 when X_1 is held constant is:

(7.88) $$\beta_2 + \beta_3 X_1$$

Hence, in regression model (7.86) both the effect of X_1 for given level of X_2 and the effect of X_2 for given level of X_1 depend on the level of the other predictor variable.

We shall illustrate how the effect of one predictor variable depends on the level of the other predictor variable in regression model (7.86) by returning to the sales promotion example of Chapter 6. The response function (6.3) for this example, relating locality sales (Y) to point-of-sale expenditures (X_1) and TV expenditures (X_2), is additive:

(7.89) $$E\{Y\} = 10 + 2X_1 + 5X_2$$

In Figure 7.10a, we show the response function $E\{Y\}$ as a function of X_1 when $X_2 = 1$ and when $X_2 = 3$. Note that the two response functions are parallel—that is, the mean sales response increases by the same amount $\beta_1 = 2$ with a unit increase of point-of-sale expenditures whether TV expenditures are $X_2 = 1$ or $X_2 = 3$. The plot in Figure 7.10a is

FIGURE 7.10 **Illustration of Reinforcement and Interference Interaction Effects—Sales Promotion Example.**

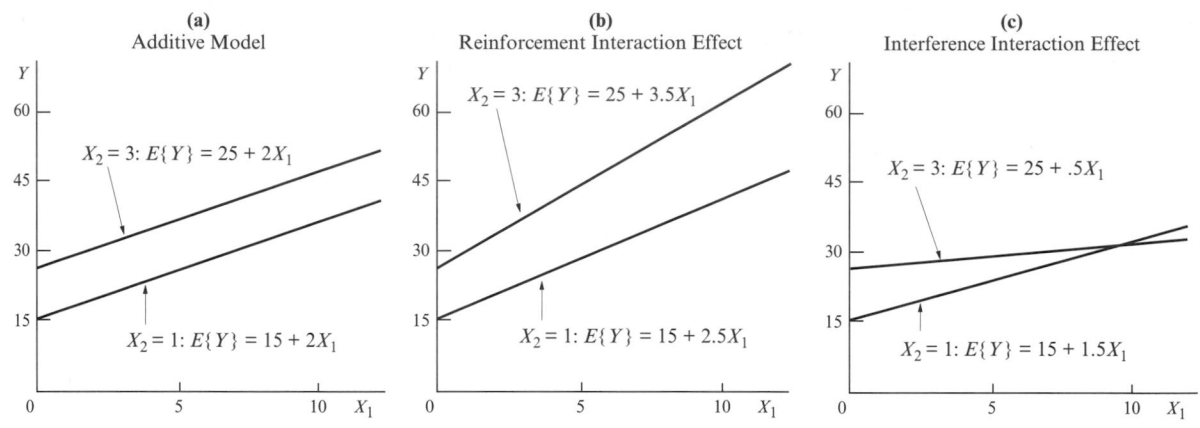

called a *conditional effects plot* because it shows the effects of X_1 on the mean response conditional on different levels of the other predictor variable.

In Figure 7.10b, we consider the same response function but with the cross-product term $.5X_1X_2$ added for interaction effect of the two types of promotional expenditures on sales:

$$(7.90) \qquad E\{Y\} = 10 + 2X_1 + 5X_2 + .5X_1X_2$$

We again use a conditional effects plot to show the response function $E\{Y\}$ as a function of X_1 conditional on $X_2 = 1$ and on $X_2 = 3$. Note that the slopes of the response functions plotted against X_1 now differ for $X_2 = 1$ and $X_2 = 3$. The slope of the response function when $X_2 = 1$ is by (7.87):

$$\beta_1 + \beta_3 X_2 = 2 + .5(1) = 2.5$$

and when $X_2 = 3$, the slope is:

$$\beta_1 + \beta_3 X_2 = 2 + .5(3) = 3.5$$

Thus, a unit increase in point-of-sale expenditures has a larger effect on sales when TV expenditures are at a higher level than when they are at a lower level.

Hence, β_1 in regression model (7.86) containing a cross-product term for interaction effect no longer indicates the change in the mean response for a unit increase in X_1 for any given X_2 level. That effect in this model depends on the level of X_2. Although the mean response in regression model (7.86) when X_2 is constant is still a linear function of X_1, now both the intercept and the slope of the response function change as the level at which X_2 is held constant is varied. The same holds when the mean response is regarded as a function of X_2, with X_1 constant.

Note that as a result of the interaction effect in regression model (7.90), the increase in sales with a unit increase in point-of-sale expenditures is greater, the higher the level of TV expenditures, as shown by the larger slope of the response function when $X_2 = 3$

than when $X_2 = 1$. A similar increase in the slope occurs if the response function against X_2 is considered for higher levels of X_1. When the regression coefficients β_1 and β_2 are positive, we say that the interaction effect between the two quantitative variables is of a *reinforcement* or *synergistic* type when the slope of the response function against one of the predictor variables increases for higher levels of the other predictor variable (i.e., when β_3 is positive).

If the sign of β_3 in regression model (7.90) were negative:

$$(7.91) \qquad\qquad E\{Y\} = 10 + 2X_1 + 5X_2 - .5X_1X_2$$

the result of the interaction effect of the two types of promotional expenditures on sales would be that the increase in sales with a unit increase in point-of-sale expenditures becomes smaller, the higher the level of TV expenditures. This effect is shown in the conditional effects plot in Figure 7.10c. The two response functions for $X_2 = 1$ and $X_2 = 3$ are again nonparallel, but now the slope of the response function is smaller for the higher level of TV expenditures. A similar decrease in the slope would occur if the response function against X_2 is considered for higher levels of X_1. When the regression coefficients β_1 and β_2 are positive, we say that the interaction effect between two quantitative variables is of an *interference* or *antagonistic* type when the slope of the response function against one of the predictor variables decreases for higher levels of the other predictor variable (i.e., when β_3 is negative).

Comments

1. When the signs of β_1 and β_2 in regression model (7.86) are negative, a negative β_3 is usually viewed as a reinforcement type of interaction effect and a positive β_3 as an interference type of effect.

2. To derive (7.87) and (7.88), we differentiate:

$$E\{Y\} = \beta_0 + \beta_1 X_1 + \beta_2 X_2 + \beta_3 X_1 X_2$$

with respect to X_1 and X_2, respectively:

$$\frac{\partial E\{Y\}}{\partial X_1} = \beta_1 + \beta_3 X_2 \qquad \frac{\partial E\{Y\}}{\partial X_2} = \beta_2 + \beta_3 X_1 \qquad\qquad \blacksquare$$

Shape of Response Function. Figure 7.11 shows for the sales promotion example the impact of the interaction effect on the shape of the response function. Figure 7.11a presents the additive response function in (7.89), and Figures 7.11b and 7.11c present the response functions with the reinforcement interaction effect in (7.90) and with the interference interaction effect in (7.91), respectively. Note that the additive response function is a plane, but that the two response functions with interaction effects are not. Also note in Figures 7.11b and 7.11c that the mean response as a function of X_1, for any given level of X_2, is no longer parallel to the same function at a different level of X_2, for either type of interaction effect.

We can also illustrate the difference in the shape of the response function when the two predictor variables do and do not interact by representing the response surface by means of a contour diagram. As we noted previously, such a diagram shows for different response levels the various combinations of levels of the two predictor variables that yield the same level of response. Figure 7.11d shows a contour diagram for the additive response surface in Figure 7.11a when the two predictor variables do not interact. Note that the contour curves are straight lines and that the contour lines are parallel and hence equally spaced.

FIGURE 7.11   **Response Surfaces and Contour Plots for Additive and Interaction Regression Models—Sales Promotion Example.**

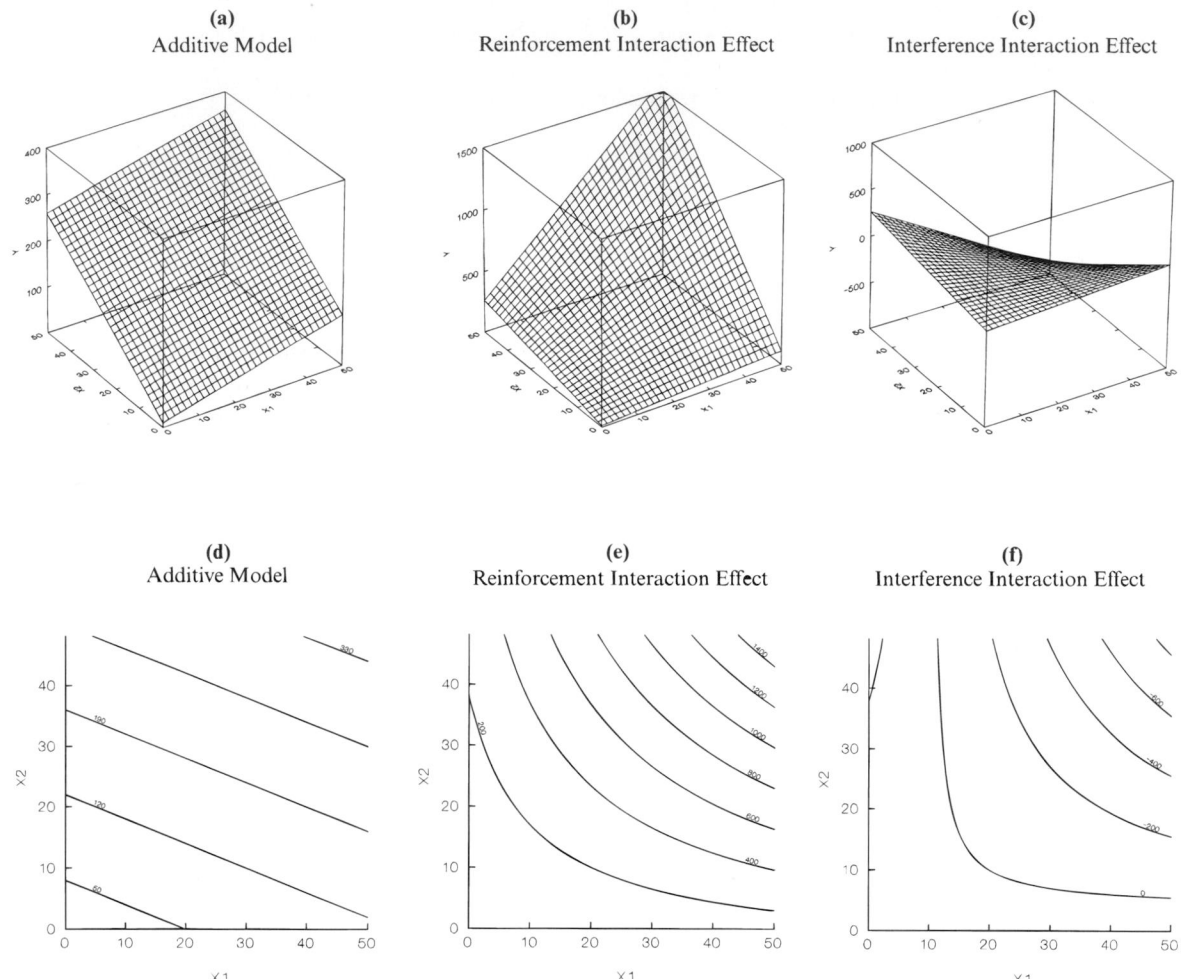

Figures 7.11e and 7.11f show contour diagrams for the response surfaces in Figures 7.11b and 7.11c, respectively, where the two predictor variables interact. Note that the contour curves are no longer straight lines and that the contour curves are not parallel here. For instance, in Figure 7.11e the vertical distance between the contours for $E\{Y\} = 200$ and $E\{Y\} = 400$ at $X_1 = 10$ is much larger than at $X_1 = 50$.

In general, additive or noninteracting predictor variables lead to parallel contour curves, whereas interacting predictor variables lead to nonparallel contour curves.

Interpretation of Interaction Regression Models with Curvilinear Effects

When one or more of the predictor variables in a regression model have curvilinear effects on the response variable, the presence of interaction effects again leads to response functions whose contour curves are not parallel. Figure 7.12a shows the response surface for a study

FIGURE 7.12   **Response Surface and Contour Curves for Curvilinear Regression Model with Interaction Effect.**

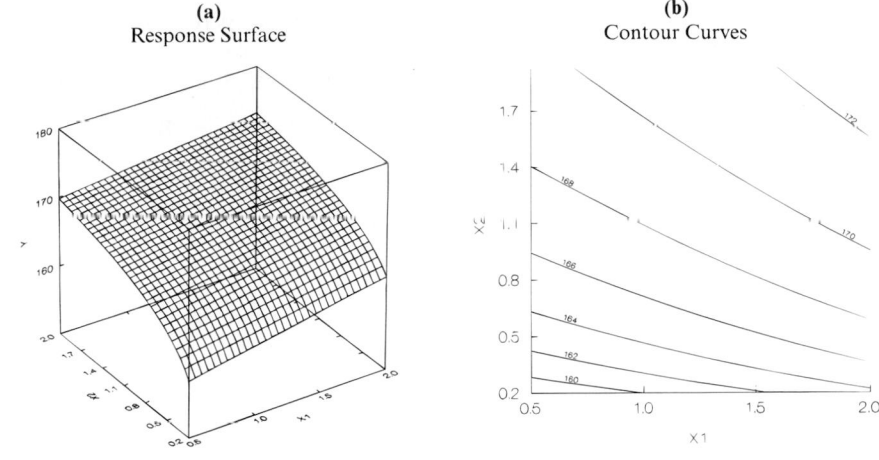

(a)
Response Surface

(b)
Contour Curves

of the yield of a chemical process:

$$E\{Y\} = 165 + 2.6X_1 + 5.3\log_e X_2 - .6X_1\log_e X_2$$

Here, Y is the yield of the chemical process, X_1 is the amount of an enzyme, and X_2 is the duration of the process. Figure 7.12b shows contour curves for this response function. Note the lack of parallelism in the contour curves, reflecting the interaction effect. Figure 7.13 presents a conditional effects plot to show in a simple fashion the nature of the interaction in the relation of process duration (X_2) to the mean yield when enzyme amount (X_1) is held constant at different levels. Note that the difference in yields when the enzyme amount is at low and high levels is substantially smaller when the process duration is high than when it is low.

Implementation of Interaction Regression Models

The fitting of interaction regression models is routine, once the appropriate cross-product terms have been added to the data set. Two considerations need to be kept in mind when developing regression models with interaction effects.

1. When adding interaction terms to a regression model, high multicollinearities may exist between some of the predictor variables and some of the interaction terms, as well as among some of the interaction terms. A partial remedy to improve computational accuracy is to center the predictor variables, i.e., to use $x_{ik} = X_{ik} - \bar{X}_k$.

2. When the number of predictor variables in the regression model is large, the potential number of interaction terms can become very large. For example, if eight predictor variables are present in the regression model in linear terms, there are potentially 28 pairwise interaction terms that could be added to the regression model. The data set would need to be quite large before 36 X variables could be used in the regression model.

It is therefore desirable to identify in advance, whenever possible, those interactions that are most likely to influence the response variable in important ways. In addition to

FIGURE 7.13   **Conditional Effects Plot for Chemical Process Interaction Model.**

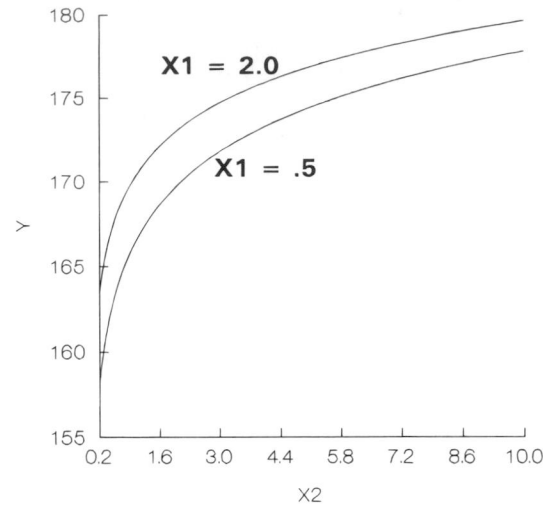

utilizing a priori knowledge, one can plot the residuals for the additive regression model against the different interaction terms to determine which ones appear to be influential in affecting the response variable. When the number of predictor variables is large, these plots may need to be limited to interaction terms involving those predictor variables that appear to be the most important ones based on the initial fit of the additive regression model.

Example

We wish to test formally in the body fat example of Table 7.1 whether interaction terms between the three predictor variables should be included in the regression model. We therefore need to consider the following regression model:

$$(7.92) \quad Y_i = \beta_0 + \beta_1 X_{i1} + \beta_2 X_{i2} + \beta_3 X_{i3} + \beta_4 X_{i1} X_{i2} + \beta_5 X_{i1} X_{i3} + \beta_6 X_{i2} X_{i3} + \varepsilon_i$$

This regression model requires that we obtain the new variables $X_1 X_2$, $X_1 X_3$, and $X_2 X_3$ and add these X variables to the ones in Table 7.1. We find upon examining these X variables that some of the predictor variables are highly correlated with some of the interaction terms, and that there are also some high correlations among the interaction terms. For example, the correlation between X_1 and $X_1 X_2$ is .989 and that between $X_1 X_3$ and $X_2 X_3$ is .998.

We shall therefore use centered variables in the regression model:

$$(7.93) \qquad Y_i = \beta_0 + \beta_1 x_{i1} + \beta_2 x_{i2} + \beta_3 x_{i3} + \beta_4 x_{i1} x_{i2} + \beta_5 x_{i1} x_{i3} + \beta_6 x_{i2} x_{i3} + \varepsilon_i$$

where:

$$x_{i1} = X_{i1} - \bar{X}_1 = X_{i1} - 25.305$$
$$x_{i2} = X_{i2} - \bar{X}_2 = X_{i2} - 51.170$$
$$x_{i3} = X_{i3} - \bar{X}_3 = X_{i3} - 27.620$$

Upon obtaining the cross-product terms using the centered variables, we find that the intercorrelations involving the cross-product terms are now smaller. For example, the largest correlation, which was between X_1X_3 and X_2X_3, is reduced from .998 to .891. Other correlations are reduced in absolute magnitude even more.

Fitting regression model (7.93) yields the following estimated regression function, mean square error, and extra sums of squares:

$$\hat{Y} = 20.53 + 3.438x_1 - 2.095x_2 - 1.616x_3 + .00888x_1x_2 - .08479x_1x_3 + .09042x_2x_3$$
$$MSE = 6.745$$

Variable	Extra Sum of Squares
x_1	$SSR(x_1) = 352.270$
x_2	$SSR(x_2\|x_1) = \ \ 33.169$
x_3	$SSR(x_3\|x_1, x_2) = \ \ 11.546$
x_1x_2	$SSR(x_1x_2\|x_1, x_2, x_3) = \ \ \ \ 1.496$
x_1x_3	$SSR(x_1x_3\|x_1, x_2, x_3, x_1x_2) = \ \ \ \ 2.704$
x_2x_3	$SSR(x_2x_3\|x_1, x_2, x_3, x_1x_2, x_1x_3) = \ \ \ \ 6.515$

We wish to test whether any interaction terms are needed:

$$H_0: \ \beta_4 = \beta_5 = \beta_6 = 0$$

$$H_a: \ \text{not all } \beta s \text{ in } H_0 \text{ equal zero}$$

The partial F test statistic (7.27) requires here the following extra sum of squares:

$$SSR(x_1x_2, x_1x_3, x_2x_3\|x_1, x_2, x_3) = 1.496 + 2.704 + 6.515 = 10.715$$

and the test statistic is:

$$F^* = \frac{SSR(x_1x_2, x_1x_3, x_2x_3\|x_1, x_2, x_3)}{3} \div MSE$$

$$= \frac{10.715}{3} \div 6.745 = .53$$

For level of significance $\alpha = .05$, we require $F(.95; 3, 13) = 3.41$. Since $F^* = .53 \leq 3.41$, we conclude H_0, that the interaction terms are not needed in the regression model. The P-value of this test is .67.

7.9   Constrained Regression

Occasionally, a priori information about one or some of the regression coefficients is available. The a priori information may be of several types. We shall illustrate two principal types of a priori information and how they are incorporated into the fitting process, using for illustration the first-order regression model with two predictor variables:

(7.94) $$Y_i = \beta_0 + \beta_1 X_{i1} + \beta_2 X_{i2} + \varepsilon_i$$

The first type of a priori information involves knowledge of one or several regression coefficients. For instance, we may know that $\beta_1 = 1$. The constrained regression model then is:

$$(7.95) \qquad Y_i = \beta_0 + \beta_1 X_{i1} + \beta_2 X_{i2} + \varepsilon_i \qquad \text{subject to } \beta_1 = 1$$

We can incorporate this constraint directly into the regression model:

$$(7.96) \qquad Y_i - X_{i1} = \beta_0 + \beta_2 X_{i2} + \varepsilon_i$$

Solution of this constrained model in the usual (unconstrained) fashion, using the modified response variable $Y_i - X_{i1}$, leads to the proper estimates of β_0 and β_2.

A second type of a priori information involves knowledge about one or several regression coefficients in the form of inequalities. For instance, in regressing family entertainment expenditures (Y) against family discretionary income (X_1) and age of head of household (X_2), we may know that entertainment expenditures increase with discretionary income and that β_1 cannot be negative. The constrained regression model then is:

$$(7.97) \qquad Y_i = \beta_0 + \beta_1 X_{i1} + \beta_2 X_{i2} + \varepsilon_i \qquad \text{subject to } \beta_1 \geq 0$$

In the case of an inequality constraint for a single regression coefficient, the fitting of the constrained regression model is very simple. We fit the unconstrained model in the usual fashion. If the estimated regression coefficient meets the constraint (in our example, if $b_1 \geq 0$), we are done. If it does not (in our example, if $b_1 < 0$), we use the inequality bound as the estimate (in our example, we use $b_1 = 0$ as the estimate of β_1) and estimate the other regression coefficients (β_2, in our example) by using the bound as an equality constraint ($\beta_1 = 0$, in our example). If there are inequality constraints for several regression coefficients, mathematical programming procedures may be used to find the constrained estimates.

Constrained regression should be used with great caution. In the presence of multicollinearity, placing a constraint on a regression coefficient based on the simple relation of the predictor variable to the response variable may not be appropriate. We saw when discussing multicollinearity, for instance, that the sign of a regression coefficient can be reversed when a correlated predictor variable is added to the model. Also, when constrained regression leads to the use of a boundary value of the constraint, it may well indicate that the regression model has not been specified appropriately.

Cited References

7.1. Kennedy, W. J., Jr., and J. E. Gentle. *Statistical Computing*. New York: Marcel Dekker, 1980.

7.2. Draper, N. R., and H. Smith. *Applied Regression Analysis*. 2nd ed. New York: John Wiley & Sons, 1981.

Problems

7.1. State the number of degrees of freedom that are associated with each of the following extra sums of squares: (1) $SSR(X_1|X_2)$; (2) $SSR(X_2|X_1, X_3)$; (3) $SSR(X_1, X_2|X_3, X_4)$; (4) $SSR(X_1, X_2, X_3|X_4, X_5)$.

7.2. Explain in what sense the regression sum of squares $SSR(X_1)$ is an extra sum of squares.

7.3. Refer to **Brand preference** Problem 6.5.

    a. Obtain the analysis of variance table that decomposes the regression sum of squares into extra sums of squares associated with X_1 and with X_2, given X_1.

    b. Test whether X_2 can be dropped from the regression model given that X_1 is retained. Use the F^* test statistic and level of significance .01. State the alternatives, decision rule, and conclusion. What is the P-value of the test?

√ 7.4. Refer to **Chemical shipment** Problem 6.9.

    a. Obtain the analysis of variance table that decomposes the regression sum of squares into extra sums of squares associated with X_2 and with X_1, given X_2.

    b. Test whether X_1 can be dropped from the regression model given that X_2 is retained. Use the F^* test statistic and $\alpha = .05$. State the alternatives, decision rule, and conclusion. What is the P-value of the test?

    c. Does $SSR(X_1) + SSR(X_2|X_1)$ equal $SSR(X_2) + SSR(X_1|X_2)$ here? Must this always be the case?

√ 7.5. Refer to **Patient satisfaction** Problem 6.15.

    a. Obtain the analysis of variance table that decomposes the regression sum of squares into extra sums of squares associated with X_2; with X_1, given X_2; and with X_3, given X_2 and X_1.

    b. Test whether X_3 can be dropped from the regression model given that X_1 and X_2 are retained. Use the F^* test statistic and level of significance .025. State the alternatives, decision rule, and conclusion. What is the P-value of the test?

√ 7.6. Refer to **Patient satisfaction** Problem 6.15. Test whether both X_2 and X_3 can be dropped from the regression model given that X_1 is retained. Use $\alpha = .025$. State the alternatives, decision rule, and conclusion. What is the P-value of the test?

7.7. Refer to **Mathematicians' salaries** Problem 6.18.

    a. Obtain the analysis of variance table that decomposes the regression sum of squares into extra sums of squares associated with X_2; with X_3, given X_2; and with X_1, given X_2 and X_3.

    b. Test whether X_1 can be dropped from the regression model given that X_2 and X_3 are retained. Use the F^* test statistic and level of significance .01. State the alternatives, decision rule, and conclusion. What is the P-value of the test?

7.8. Refer to **Mathematicians' salaries** Problems 6.18 and 7.7. Test whether both X_1 and X_3 can be dropped from the regression model given that X_2 is retained; use $\alpha = .01$. State the alternatives, decision rule, and conclusion. What is the P-value of the test?

√ 7.9. Refer to **Patient satisfaction** Problem 6.15. Test whether $\beta_1 = -1.0$ and $\beta_2 = 0$; use $\alpha = .025$. State the alternatives, full and reduced models, decision rule, and conclusion.

7.10. Refer to **Mathematicians' salaries** Problem 6.18. Test whether $\beta_1 = \beta_3$; use $\alpha = .01$. State the alternatives, full and reduced models, decision rule, and conclusion.

7.11. Refer to the work crew productivity example in Table 7.6.

a. Calculate r_{Y1}^2, r_{Y2}^2, r_{12}^2, $r_{Y1.2}^2$, $r_{Y2.1}^2$, and R^2. Explain what each coefficient measures and interpret your results.

b. Are any of the results obtained in part (a) special because the two predictor variables are uncorrelated?

7.12. Refer to **Brand preference** Problem 6.5. Calculate r_{Y1}^2, r_{Y2}^2, r_{12}^2, $r_{Y1.2}^2$, $r_{Y2.1}^2$, and R^2. Explain what each coefficient measures and interpret your results.

√ 7.13. Refer to **Chemical shipment** Problem 6.9. Calculate r_{Y1}^2, r_{Y2}^2, r_{12}^2, $r_{Y1.2}^2$, $r_{Y2.1}^2$, and R^2. Explain what each coefficient measures and interpret your results.

√ 7.14. Refer to **Patient satisfaction** Problem 6.15.

a. Calculate r_{Y1}^2, $r_{Y1.2}^2$, and $r_{Y1.23}^2$. How is the degree of marginal linear association between Y and X_1 affected, given additional predictor variables in the model?

b. Make a similar analysis as in part (a) for the degree of marginal linear association between Y and X_2. Are your findings similar to those in part (a) for Y and X_1?

7.15. Refer to **Mathematicians' salaries** Problem 6.18. Calculate r_{Y1}^2, r_{Y3}^2, r_{23}^2, $r_{Y1.2}^2$, $r_{Y1.23}^2$, and R^2. Explain what each coefficient measures and interpret your results. How is the degree of marginal linear association between Y and X_1 affected, given additional predictor variables in the model?

7.16. Refer to **Brand preference** Problem 6.5.

a. Transform the variables by means of the correlation transformation (7.44) and fit the standardized regression model (7.45).

b. Interpret the standardized regression coefficient b_1'.

c. Transform the estimated standardized regression coefficients by means of (7.53) back to the ones for the fitted regression model in the original variables. Verify that they are the same as the ones obtained in Problem 6.5b.

√ 7.17. Refer to **Chemical shipment** Problem 6.9.

a. Transform the variables by means of the correlation transformation (7.44) and fit the standardized regression model (7.45).

b. Calculate the coefficient of determination between the two predictor variables. Is it meaningful here to consider the standardized regression coefficients to reflect the effect of one predictor variable when the other is held constant?

c. Transform the estimated standardized regression coefficients by means of (7.53) back to the ones for the fitted regression model in the original variables. Verify that they are the same as the ones obtained in Problem 6.10a.

√ 7.18. Refer to **Patient satisfaction** Problem 6.15.

a. Transform the variables by means of the correlation transformation (7.44) and fit the standardized regression model (7.45).

b. Calculate the coefficients of determination between all pairs of predictor variables. Do these indicate that it is meaningful here to consider the standardized regression coefficients as indicating the effect of one predictor variable when the others are held constant?

c. Transform the estimated standardized regression coefficients by means of (7.53) back to the ones for the fitted regression model in the original variables. Verify that they are the same as the ones obtained in Problem 6.15c.

7.19. Refer to **Mathematicians' salaries** Problem 6.18.

a. Transform the variables by means of the correlation transformation (7.44) and fit the standardized regression model (7.45).

b. Interpret the standardized regression coefficient b_2'.

c. Transform the estimated standardized regression coefficients by means of (7.53) back to the ones for the fitted regression model in the original variables. Verify that they are the same as the ones obtained in Problem 6.18c.

7.20. A speaker stated in a workshop on applied regression analysis: "In business and the social sciences, some degree of multicollinearity in survey data is practically inevitable." Does this statement apply equally to experimental data?

7.21. Refer to the example of perfectly correlated predictor variables in Table 7.8.

a. Develop another response function, like response functions (7.58) and (7.59), that fits the data perfectly.

b. What is the intersection of the infinitely many response surfaces that fit the data perfectly?

7.22. The progress report of a research analyst to the supervisor stated: "All the estimated regression coefficients in our model with three predictor variables to predict sales are statistically significant. Our new preliminary model with seven predictor variables, which includes the three variables of our smaller model, is less satisfactory because only two of the seven regression coefficients are statistically significant. Yet in some initial trials the expanded model is giving more precise sales predictions than the smaller model. The reasons for this anomaly are now being investigated." Comment.

7.23. Two authors wrote as follows: "Our research utilized a multiple regression model. Two of the predictor variables important in our theory turned out to be highly correlated in our data set. This made it difficult to assess the individual effects of each of these variables separately. We retained both variables in our model, however, because the high coefficient of multiple determination makes this difficulty unimportant." Comment.

7.24. Refer to **Brand preference** Problem 6.5.

a. Fit first-order simple linear regression model (2.1) for relating brand liking (Y) to moisture content (X_1). State the fitted regression function.

b. Compare the estimated regression coefficient for moisture content obtained in part (a) with the corresponding coefficient obtained in Problem 6.5b. What do you find?

c. Does $SSR(X_1)$ equal $SSR(X_1|X_2)$ here? If not, is the difference substantial?

d. Refer to the correlation matrix obtained in Problem 6.5a. What bearing does this have on your findings in parts (b) and (c)?

√ 7.25. Refer to **Chemical shipment** Problem 6.9.

a. Fit first-order simple linear regression model (2.1) for relating number of minutes required to handle shipment (Y) to total weight of shipment (X_2). State the fitted regression function.

b. Compare the estimated regression coefficient for total weight of shipment obtained in part (a) with the corresponding coefficient obtained in Problem 6.10a. What do you find?

c. Does $SSR(X_2)$ equal $SSR(X_2|X_1)$ here? If not, is the difference substantial?

d. Refer to the correlation matrix obtained in Problem 6.9c. What bearing does this have on your findings in parts (b) and (c)?

√ 7.26. Refer to **Patient satisfaction** Problem 6.15.

a. Fit first-order linear regression model (6.1) for relating patient satisfaction (Y) to patient's age (X_1) and severity of illness (X_2). State the fitted regression function.

b. Compare the estimated regression coefficients for patient's age and severity of illness obtained in part (a) with the corresponding coefficients obtained in Problem 6.15c. What do you find?

c. Does $SSR(X_1)$ equal $SSR(X_1|X_3)$ here? Does $SSR(X_2)$ equal $SSR(X_2|X_3)$?

d. Refer to the correlation matrix obtained in Problem 6.15b. What bearing does it have on your findings in parts (b) and (c)?

7.27. Refer to **Mathematicians' salaries** Problem 6.18.

a. Fit first-order linear regression model (6.1) for relating annual salaries (Y) to work quality (X_1) and experience (X_2). State the fitted regression function.

b. Compare the estimated regression coefficients for work quality and experience with the corresponding coefficients obtained in Problem 6.18c. What do you find?

c. Does $SSR(X_2)$ equal $SSR(X_2|X_3)$ here? Does $SSR(X_1)$ equal $SSR(X_1|X_3)$?

d. Refer to the correlation matrix obtained in Problem 6.18b. What bearing does this have on your findings in parts (b) and (c)?

7.28. Prepare a contour plot for the quadratic response surface $E\{Y\} = 140 + 4x_1^2 - 2x_2^2 + 5x_1x_2$. Describe the shape of the response surface.

7.29. Prepare a contour plot for the quadratic response surface $E\{Y\} = 124 - 3x_1^2 - 2x_2^2 - 6x_1x_2$. Describe the shape of the response surface.

7.30. A junior investment analyst used a polynomial regression model of relatively high order in a research seminar on municipal bonds and obtained an R^2 of .991 in the regression of net interest yield of bond (Y) on industrial diversity index of municipality (X) for seven bond issues. A classmate, unimpressed, said: "You overfitted. Your curve follows the random effects in the data."

a. Comment on the criticism.

b. Might R_a^2 defined in (6.42) be more appropriate than R^2 as a descriptive measure here?

√ 7.31. **Mileage study**. The effectiveness of a new experimental overdrive gear in reducing gasoline consumption was studied in 12 trials with a light truck equipped with this gear. In the data that follow, X_i denotes the constant speed (in miles per hour) on the test track in the ith trial and Y_i denotes miles per gallon obtained.

i:	1	2	3	4	5	6	7	8	9	10	11	12
X_i:	35	35	40	40	45	45	50	50	55	55	60	60
Y_i:	22	20	28	31	37	38	41	39	34	37	27	30

Second-order regression model (7.66a) with independent normal error terms is expected to be appropriate.

a. Fit regression model (7.66a). Plot the fitted regression function and the data. Does the quadratic regression function appear to be a good fit here? Find R^2.

b. Test whether or not there is a regression relation; use $\alpha = .05$. State the alternatives, decision rule, and conclusion.

c. Estimate the mean miles per gallon for test runs at a speed of 48 miles per hour; use a 95 percent confidence interval. Interpret your interval.

d. Predict the miles per gallon in the next test run at 48 miles per hour; use a 95 percent prediction interval. Interpret your interval.

e. Test whether the quadratic term can be dropped from the regression model; use $\alpha = .05$. State the alternatives, decision rule, and conclusion.

f. Express the fitted regression function obtained in part (a) in terms of the original variable X.

g. Calculate the coefficient of simple correlation between X and X^2 and between x and x^2. Is the use of a centered variable helpful here?

√ 7.32. Refer to **Mileage study** Problem 7.31.

a. Obtain the residuals and plot them against $\hat{Y}$ and against x on separate graphs. Also prepare a normal probability plot. Interpret your plots.

b. Test formally for lack of fit of the quadratic regression function; use $\alpha = .05$. State the alternatives, decision rule, and conclusion. What assumptions did you implicitly make in this test?

c. Fit third-order model (7.69) and test whether or not $\beta_{111} = 0$; use $\alpha = .05$. State the alternatives, decision rule, and conclusion. Is your conclusion consistent with your finding in part (b)?

7.33. **Piecework operation**. An operations analyst in a multinational electronics firm studied factors affecting production in a piecework operation where earnings are based on the number of pieces produced. Two employees each were selected from various age groups, and data on their productivity last year were obtained (X is age of employee, in years; Y is employee's productivity, coded):

i:	1	2	3	. . .	16	17	18
X_i:	20	20	25	. . .	55	60	60
Y_i:	97	93	99	. . .	109	112	110

The analyst recognized that the relation between age and productivity is complex, in part because earnings targets (which could not be measured) shift in complex ways with age. However, the analyst believed that for purposes of estimating mean responses, the response function can be approximated suitably by a polynomial of third order and that the error terms are independent and approximately normally distributed.

a. Fit regression model (7.69). Plot the fitted regression function and the data. Does the cubic regression function appear to be a good fit here? Find R^2.

b. Test whether or not there is a regression relation; use $\alpha = .01$. State the alternatives, decision rule, and conclusion. What is the P-value of the test?

c. Obtain joint interval estimates for the mean productivity of employees aged 53, 58, and 62, respectively. Use the most efficient simultaneous estimation procedure and a 99 percent family confidence coefficient. Interpret your intervals.

d. Predict the productivity of an employee aged 53 using a 99 percent prediction interval. Interpret your interval.

e. Express the fitted regression function obtained in part (a) in terms of the original variable X.

f. Calculate the coefficient of simple correlation between X and X^3 and between x and x^3. Is the use of a centered variable helpful here? Explain.

7.34. Refer to **Piecework operation** Problem 7.33.

a. Test whether both the quadratic and cubic terms can be dropped from the regression model; use $\alpha = .01$. State the alternatives, decision rule, and conclusion.

b. Test whether the cubic term alone can be dropped from the regression model; use $\alpha = .01$. State the alternatives, decision rule, and conclusion.

7.35. Refer to **Piecework operation** Problem 7.33.

a. Obtain the residuals and plot them against the fitted values and against x on separate graphs. Also prepare a normal probability plot. What do your plots show?

b. Test formally for lack of fit. Control the risk of a Type I error at .01. State the alternatives, decision rule, and conclusion. What assumptions did you implicitly make in this test?

7.36. **Crop yield**. An agronomist studied the effects of moisture (X_1, in inches) and temperature (X_2, in °C) on the yield of a new hybrid tomato (Y). The experimental data follow.

i:	1	2	3	. . .	23	24	25
X_{i1}:	6	6	6	. . .	14	14	14
X_{i2}:	20	21	22	. . .	22	23	24
Y_i:	49.2	48.1	48.0	. . .	42.1	43.9	40.5

The agronomist expects that second-order polynomial regression model (7.71) with independent normal error terms is appropriate here.

a. Fit regression model (7.71). Plot the Y observations against the fitted values. Does the response function provide a good fit?

b. Calculate R^2. What information does this measure provide?

c. Test whether or not there is a regression relation; use $\alpha = .05$. State the alternatives, decision rule, and conclusion. What is the P-value of the test?

d. Estimate the mean yield when $X_1 = 7$ and $X_2 = 22$; use a 95 percent confidence interval. Interpret your interval.

e. Express the fitted response function obtained in part (a) in the original X variables.

7.37. Refer to **Crop yield** Problem 7.36.

a. Test whether or not the interaction term can be dropped from the regression model. Control the α risk at .005. State the alternatives, decision rule, and conclusion.

b. Assuming that the interaction term has been dropped from the regression model, test whether or not the quadratic effect term for temperature can be dropped from the model; control the α risk at .005. State the alternatives, decision rule, and conclusion. What is the combined α risk for both the test here and the one in part (a)?

c. Fit the second-order polynomial regression model omitting the interaction term and the quadratic effect term for temperature. Obtain the residuals and plot them against the fitted values, against x_1, and against x_2 on separate graphs. What do your plots show?

7.38. Consider the response function $E\{Y\} = 25 + 3X_1 + 4X_2 + 1.5X_1X_2$.

   a. Prepare a conditional effects plot of the response function against X_1 when $X_2 = 3$ and when $X_2 = 6$. How is the interaction effect of X_1 and X_2 on Y apparent from this graph? Describe the nature of the interaction effect.

   b. Plot a set of contour curves for the response surface. How is the interaction effect of X_1 and X_2 on Y apparent from this graph?

7.39. Consider the response function $E\{Y\} = 14 + 7X_1 + 5X_2 - 4X_1X_2$.

   a. Prepare a conditional effects plot of the response function against X_2 when $X_1 = 1$ and when $X_1 = 4$. How does the graph indicate that the effects of X_1 and X_2 on Y are not additive? What is the nature of the interaction effect?

   b. Plot a set of contour curves for the response surface. How does the graph indicate that the effects of X_1 and X_2 on Y are not additive?

7.40. Refer to **Brand preference** Problem 6.5.

   a. Fit regression model (7.86).

   b. Test whether or not the interaction term can be dropped from the model; use $\alpha = .05$. State the alternatives, decision rule, and conclusion.

√ 7.41. Refer to **Chemical shipment** Problem 6.9.

   a. Fit regression model (7.86).

   b. Test whether or not the interaction term can be dropped from the model; use $\alpha = .05$. State the alternatives, decision rule, and conclusion.

7.42. Refer to **Brand preference** Problem 6.5. It is known that β_2 in regression model (6.1) cannot be larger than 4.0.

   a. State the constrained regression model.

   b. Based on the fitting of the unconstrained regression model in Problem 6.5b, how do you need to proceed to fit the constrained model?

   c. Fit the constrained regression model. How does the estimated coefficient b_1 compare with the unconstrained estimate obtained in Problem 6.5b?

Exercises

7.43. a. Define each of the following extra sums of squares:
   (1) $SSR(X_5|X_1)$; (2) $SSR(X_3, X_4|X_1)$; (3) $SSR(X_4|X_1, X_2, X_3)$.

   b. For a multiple regression model with five X variables, what is the relevant extra sum of squares for testing whether or not $\beta_5 = 0$? whether or not $\beta_2 = \beta_4 = 0$?

7.44. Show that:

   a. $SSR(X_1, X_2, X_3, X_4) = SSR(X_1) + SSR(X_2, X_3|X_1) + SSR(X_4|X_1, X_2, X_3)$.

   b. $SSR(X_1, X_2, X_3, X_4) = SSR(X_2, X_3) + SSR(X_1|X_2, X_3) + SSR(X_4|X_1, X_2, X_3)$.

7.45. Refer to **Brand preference** Problem 6.5.

   a. Regress Y on X_2 using simple linear regression model (2.1) and obtain the residuals.

   b. Regress X_1 on X_2 using simple linear regression model (2.1) and obtain the residuals.

c. Calculate the coefficient of simple correlation between the two sets of residuals and show that it equals $r_{Y1.2}$.

7.46. The following regression model is being considered in a water resources study:

$$Y_i = \beta_0 + \beta_1 X_{i1} + \beta_2 X_{i2} + \beta_3 X_{i1} X_{i2} + \beta_4 \sqrt{X_{i3}} + \varepsilon_i$$

State the reduced models for testing whether or not: (1) $\beta_3 = \beta_4 = 0$, (2) $\beta_3 = 0$, (3) $\beta_1 = \beta_2 = 5$, (4) $\beta_4 = 7$.

7.47. The following regression model is being considered in a market research study:

$$Y_i = \beta_0 + \beta_1 X_{i1} + \beta_2 X_{i2} + \beta_3 X_{i1}^2 + \varepsilon_i$$

State the reduced models for testing whether or not: (1) $\beta_1 = \beta_3 = 0$, (2) $\beta_0 = 0$, (3) $\beta_3 = 5$, (4) $\beta_0 = 10$, (5) $\beta_1 = \beta_2$.

7.48. Show the equivalence of the expressions in (7.36) and (7.41) for $r_{Y2.1}^2$.

7.49. Refer to the work crew productivity example in Table 7.6.

a. For the variables transformed according to (7.44), obtain: (1) $\mathbf{X'X}$, (2) $\mathbf{X'Y}$, (3) $\mathbf{b}$, (4) $s^2\{\mathbf{b}\}$.

b. Show that the standardized regression coefficients obtained in part (a3) are related to the regression coefficients for the regression model in the original variables according to (7.53).

7.50. Derive the relations between the β_k and β_k' in (7.46a) for $p - 1 = 2$.

7.51. Derive the expression for $\mathbf{X'Y}$ in (7.51) for standardized regression model (7.45) for $p - 1 = 2$.

7.52. Consider the second-order regression model with one predictor variable in (7.66a) and the following two sets of X values:

Set 1:	1.0	1.5	1.1	1.3	1.9	.8	1.2	1.4
Set 2:	12	1	123	17	415	71	283	38

For each set, calculate the coefficient of correlation between X and X^2, then between x and x^2. Also calculate the coefficients of correlation between X and X^3 and between x and x^3. What generalizations are suggested by your results?

7.53. (Calculus needed.) Refer to second-order response function (7.67). Explain precisely the meaning of the linear effect coefficient β_1 and the quadratic effect coefficient β_{11}.

7.54. a. Derive the expressions for b_0', b_1', and b_{11}' in (7.76).

b. Using theorem (5.46), obtain the variance-covariance matrix for the regression coefficients pertaining to the original X variable in terms of the variance-covariance matrix for the regression coefficients pertaining to the transformed x variable.

7.55. How are the normal equations (7.68) simplified if the X values are equally spaced, such as the time series representation $X_1 = 1, X_2 = 2, \ldots, X_n = n$?

Projects

7.56. Refer to the **SMSA** data set. For predicting the number of active physicians (Y) in an SMSA, it has been decided to include total population (X_1) and total personal income (X_2) as predictor variables. The question now is whether an additional predictor variable would be helpful in the model and, if so, which variable would be most helpful. Assume that a first-order multiple regression model is appropriate.

   a. For each of the following variables, calculate the coefficient of partial determination given that X_1 and X_2 are included in the model: land area (X_3), percent of population 65 or older (X_4), number of hospital beds (X_5), and total serious crimes (X_6).

   b. On the basis of the results in part (a), which of the four additional predictor variables is best? Is the extra sum of squares associated with this variable larger than those for the other three variables?

   c. Using the F^* test statistic, test whether or not the variable determined to be best in part (b) is helpful in the regression model when X_1 and X_2 are included in the model; use $\alpha = .01$. State the alternatives, decision rule, and conclusion. Would the F^* test statistics for the other three potential predictor variables be as large as the one here? Discuss.

7.57. Refer to the **SENIC** data set. For predicting the average length of stay of patients in a hospital (Y), it has been decided to include age (X_1) and infection risk (X_2) as predictor variables. The question now is whether an additional predictor variable would be helpful in the model and, if so, which variable would be most helpful. Assume that a first-order multiple regression model is appropriate.

   a. For each of the following variables, calculate the coefficient of partial determination given that X_1 and X_2 are included in the model: routine culturing ratio (X_3), average daily census (X_4), number of nurses (X_5), and available facilities and services (X_6).

   b. On the basis of the results in part (a), which of the four additional predictor variables is best? Is the extra sum of squares associated with this variable larger than those for the other three variables?

   c. Using the F^* test statistic, test whether or not the variable determined to be best in part (b) is helpful in the regression model when X_1 and X_2 are included in the model; use $\alpha = .05$. State the alternatives, decision rule, and conclusion. Would the F^* test statistics for the other three potential predictor variables be as large as the one here? Discuss.

7.58. Refer to the **SMSA** data set. It is desired to fit second-order regression model (7.66a) for relating number of active physicians (Y) to total population (X).

   a. Fit the second-order regression model. Plot the residuals against the fitted values. How well does the second-order model appear to fit the data?

   b. Obtain R^2 for the second-order regression model. Also obtain the coefficient of simple determination r^2 for the first-order regression model. Has the addition of the quadratic term in the regression model substantially increased the coefficient of determination?

   c. Test whether the quadratic term can be dropped from the regression model; use $\alpha = .05$. State the alternatives, decision rule, and conclusion.

   d. Omit case 1 (New York City) from the data set. Fit the second-order regression model (7.66a) based on the remaining 140 SMSAs. Repeat the test in part (c). Has the omission of the outlying case affected your conclusion about whether the quadratic term can be dropped from the model?

7.59. Refer to the **SMSA** data set. A regression model relating serious crime rate (Y, total serious crimes divided by total population) to population density (X_1, total population divided by land area) and percent of population in central cities (X_3) is to be constructed.

   a. Fit second-order regression model (7.71). Plot the residuals against the fitted values. How well does the second-order model appear to fit the data? What is R^2?

   b. Test whether or not all quadratic and interaction terms can be dropped from the regression model; use $\alpha = .01$. State the alternatives, decision rule, and conclusion.

   c. Instead of the predictor variable population density, total population (X_1) and land area (X_2) are to be employed as separate predictor variables, in addition to percent of population in central cities (X_3). The regression model should contain linear and quadratic terms for total population, and linear terms only for land area and percent of population in central cities. (No interaction terms are to be included in this model.) Fit this regression model and obtain R^2. Is this coefficient of multiple determination substantially different from the one for the regression model in part (a)?

7.60. Refer to the **SENIC** data set. Second-order regression model (7.66a) is to be fitted for relating number of nurses (Y) to available facilities and services (X).

   a. Fit the second-order regression model. Plot the residuals against the fitted values. How well does the second-order model appear to fit the data?

   b. Obtain R^2 for the second-order regression model. Also obtain the coefficient of simple determination r^2 for the first-order regression model. Has the addition of the quadratic term in the regression model substantially increased the coefficient of determination?

   c. Test whether the quadratic term can be dropped from the regression model; use $\alpha = .10$. State the alternatives, decision rule, and conclusion.

Building the Regression Model I: Selection of Predictor Variables

In earlier chapters, we considered how to fit simple and multiple regression models and how to make inferences from these models. In this and the next two chapters, we shall discuss how to build a regression model. This includes the selection of the predictor or explanatory variables, diagnostics for examining the appropriateness of a fitted regression model, remedial measures when the model conditions are not met, and validation of the regression model.

In this chapter, we first present an overview of the model-building process. Then we consider in more detail some special issues in the selection of the predictor variables for exploratory observational studies. In the following two chapters, we shall take up diagnostic procedures, remedial measures, and validation. Throughout the three chapters on model building, we shall use the same example to illustrate each of the steps of the model-building process, culminating in a validated regression model.

8.1 Overview of Model-Building Process

At the risk of oversimplifying, we present in Figure 8.1 a strategy for the building of a regression model. This strategy involves three or, sometimes, four phases:

1. Data collection and preparation

2. Reduction of explanatory or predictor variables (for exploratory observational studies)

3. Model refinement and selection

4. Model validation

We consider each of these phases in turn.

Data Collection

The data collection requirements for building a regression model vary with the nature of the study. It is useful to distinguish four types of studies.

FIGURE 8.1 **Strategy for Building a Regression Model.**

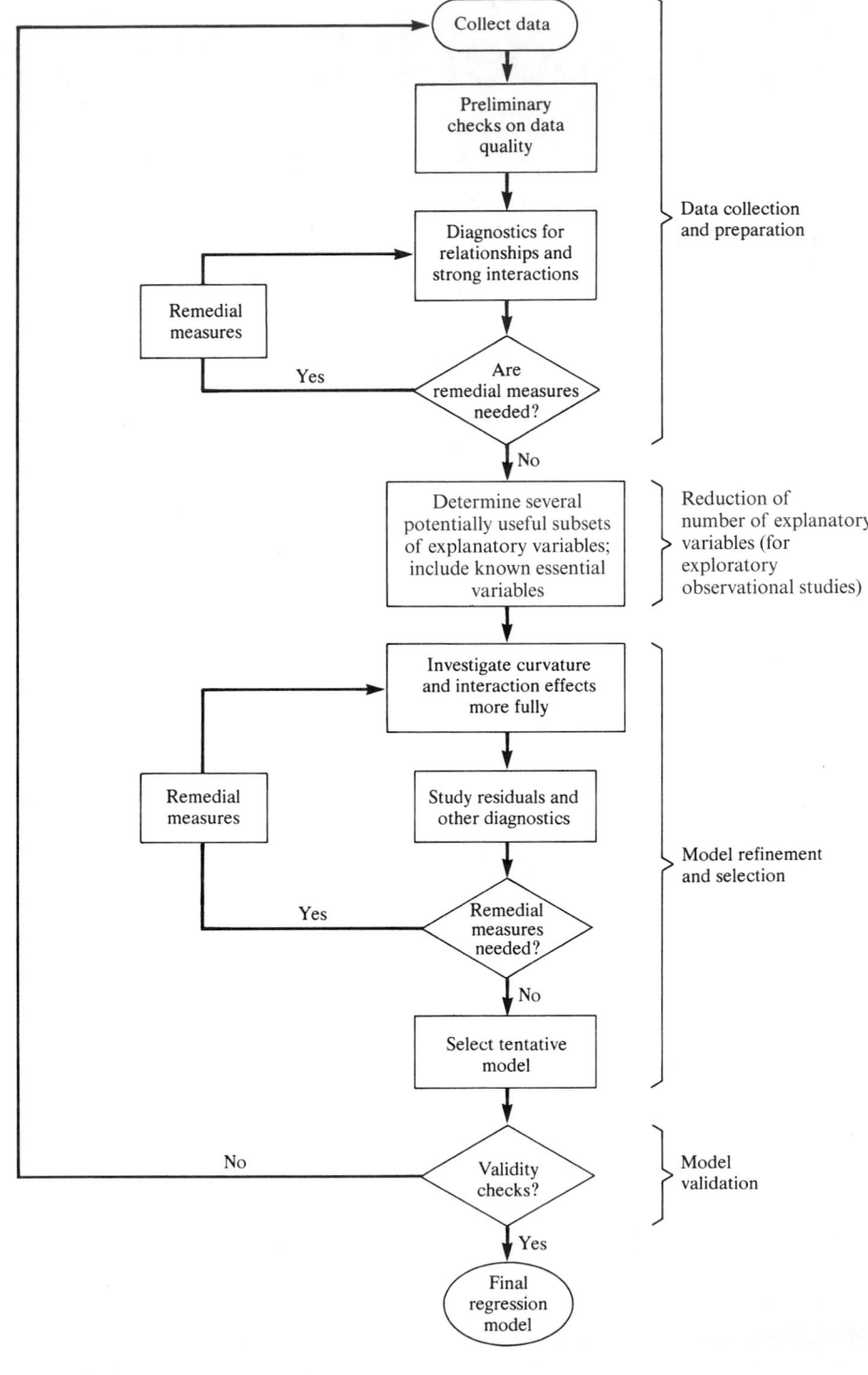

Controlled Experiments.   In a controlled experiment, the experimenter controls the levels of the explanatory variables and assigns a treatment, consisting of a combination of levels of the explanatory variables, to each experimental unit and observes the response. For example, an experimenter studied the effects of the size of a graphic presentation and the time allowed for analysis on the accuracy with which the analysis of the presentation is carried out. Here, the response variable is a measure of the accuracy of the analysis, and the explanatory variables are the size of the graphic presentation and the time allowed. Junior executives were used as the experimental units. A treatment consisted of a particular combination of size of presentation and length of time allowed. In controlled experiments, the explanatory variables are often called *factors* or *control variables*.

The data collection requirements for controlled experiments are straightforward, though not necessarily simple. Observations for each experimental unit are needed on the response variable and on the level of each of the control variables used for that experimental unit. There may be difficult measurement and scaling problems for the response variable that are unique to the area of application.

Controlled Experiments with Supplemental Variables.   Statistical design of experiments, to be discussed in Part VII, uses supplemental information, such as characteristics of the experimental units, in designing the experiment so as to reduce the variance of the experimental error terms in the regression model. Sometimes, however, it is not possible to incorporate this supplemental information into the design of the experiment. Instead, it may be possible for the experimenter to incorporate this information into the regression model and thereby reduce the error variance by including *supplemental* or *uncontrolled variables* in the model.

In our previous example involving the accuracy of analysis of graphic presentations, the experimenter suspected that gender and number of years of education could affect the accuracy responses in important ways. Because of time constraints, the experimenter was able to use only a completely randomized design, which does not incorporate any supplemental information into the design. The experimenter therefore also collected data on two supplemental, uncontrolled variables (gender and number of years of education of the junior executives) in case that use of these supplemental variables in the regression model would make the analysis of the effects of the explanatory variables (size of graphic presentation, time allowed) on the accuracy response more precise.

Confirmatory Observational Studies.   These studies, based on observational, not experimental, data, are intended to test (i.e., to confirm or not to confirm) hypotheses derived from previous studies or from hunches. For these studies, data are collected for explanatory variables that previous studies have shown to affect the response variable, as well as for the new variable or variables involved in the hypothesis. In this context, the explanatory variable(s) involved in the hypothesis are sometimes called the *primary variables*, and the explanatory variables that are included to reflect existing knowledge are called the *control variables* (*known risk factors* in epidemiology). The control variables here are not controlled as in an experimental study, but they are used to account for known influences on the response variable. For example, in an observational study of the effect of vitamin E supplements on the incidence of a certain type of cancer, known risk factors, such as age, gender, and race, would be included as control variables and the amount of vitamin E supplements taken daily would be the primary explanatory variable. The response variable would be the incidence of the particular type of cancer during the period under consideration. (The use of qualitative response variables in a regression model will be considered in Chapter 14.)

Data collection for confirmatory observational studies involves obtaining observations on the response variable, the control variables, and the primary explanatory variable(s). Here, as in controlled experiments, there may be important and complex problems of measurement, such as how to obtain reliable data on the amount of vitamin supplements taken daily.

Exploratory Observational Studies.   In the social, behavioral, and health sciences, management, and other fields, it is often not possible to conduct controlled experiments. Furthermore, adequate knowledge for conducting confirmatory observational studies may be lacking. As a result, many studies in these fields are exploratory observational studies where investigators search for explanatory variables that might be related to the response variable. To complicate matters further, any available theoretical models may involve explanatory variables that are not directly measurable, such as a family's future earnings over the next 10 years. Under these conditions, investigators are often forced to prospect for explanatory variables that could conceivably be related to the response variable under study. Obviously, such a set of potentially useful explanatory variables can be large. For example, a company's sales of portable dishwashers in a district may be affected by population size, per capita income, percent of population in urban areas, percent of population under 50 years of age, percent of families with children at home, etc., etc.!

After a lengthy list of potentially useful explanatory variables has been compiled, some of these variables can be quickly screened out. An explanatory variable (1) may not be fundamental to the problem, (2) may be subject to large measurement errors, and/or (3) may effectively duplicate another explanatory variable in the list. Explanatory variables that cannot be measured may either be deleted or replaced by proxy variables that are highly correlated with them.

The number of cases to be collected for an exploratory observational regression study depends on the size of the pool of potentially useful explanatory variables available at this stage. More cases are required when the pool is large than when it is small. A general rule of thumb states that there should be at least 6 to 10 cases for every variable in the pool. The actual data collection for the pool of potentially useful explanatory variables and for the response variable again may involve important issues of measurement, just as for the other types of studies.

Data Preparation

Once the data have been collected, edit checks should be performed and plots prepared to identify gross data errors as well as extreme outliers. Difficulties with data errors are especially prevalent in large data sets and should be corrected or resolved before the model building begins. Whenever possible, the investigator should carefully monitor and control the data collection process to reduce the likelihood of data errors.

Preliminary Model Investigation

Once the data have been properly edited, the formal modeling process can begin. A variety of diagnostics should be employed to identify (1) the functional forms in which the explanatory variables should enter the regression model and (2) important interactions that should be included in the model. Scatter plots and residual plots are useful for determining relationships and their strengths. Selected explanatory variables can be fitted in regression functions to explore relationships, possible strong interactions, and the need for transformations. Whenever possible, of course, one should also rely on the investigator's prior knowledge and expertise to suggest appropriate transformations and interactions to investigate. This is particularly important when the number of potentially useful explanatory variables is large. In this case, it may be very difficult to investigate all possible pairwise interactions, and prior knowledge should be used to identify the important ones. The diagnostic procedures explained in previous chapters and in Chapter 9 should be used as resources in this phase of model building.

Reduction of Explanatory Variables

Controlled Experiments.   The reduction of explanatory variables in the model-building phase is usually not an important issue for controlled experiments. The experimenter has chosen the explanatory variables for investigation, and a regression model is to be developed that will enable the investigator to study the effects of these variables on the response variable. After the model has been developed, including the use of appropriate functional forms for the variables and the inclusion of important interaction terms, the inferential procedures considered in previous chapters will be used to determine whether the explanatory variables have effects on the response variable and, if so, the nature and magnitude of the effects.

Controlled Experiments with Supplemental Variables.   In studies of controlled experiments with supplemental variables, some reduction of the supplemental variables may take place because investigators often cannot be sure in advance that the selected supplemental variables will be helpful in reducing the error variance. For instance, the investigator in our graphic presentation example may wish to examine at this stage of the model-building process whether gender and number of years of education are related to the accuracy response, as had been anticipated. If not, the investigator would wish to drop them as not being helpful in reducing the model error variance and, therefore, in the analysis of the effects of the explanatory variables on the response variable. The number of supplemental variables considered in controlled experiments is usually small, so no special problems are encountered in determining whether some or all of the supplemental variables should be dropped from the regression model.

Confirmatory Observational Studies.   Generally, no reduction of explanatory variables should take place in confirmatory observational studies. The control variables were chosen based on prior knowledge and should be retained for comparability with earlier studies even if some of the control variables turn out not to lead to any error variance reduction in the study at hand. The primary variables are the ones whose influence on the response variable is to be examined and therefore need to be present in the model.

Exploratory Observational Studies.   In exploratory observational studies, the number of explanatory variables that remain after the initial screening typically is still large. Further, many of these variables frequently will be highly intercorrelated. Hence, the investigator usually will wish to reduce the number of explanatory variables to be used in the final model. There are several reasons for this. A regression model with numerous explanatory variables may be difficult to maintain. Further, regression models with a limited number of explanatory variables are easier to work with and understand. Finally, the presence of many highly intercorrelated explanatory variables may substantially increase the sampling variation of the regression coefficients, detract from the model's descriptive abilities, increase the problem of roundoff errors (as noted in Chapter 7), and not improve, or even worsen, the model's predictive ability. An actual worsening of the model's predictive ability can occur when explanatory variables are kept in the regression model that are not related to the response variable, given the other explanatory variables in the model. In that case, the variances of the fitted values $\sigma^2\{\hat{Y}_i\}$ tend to become larger with the inclusion of the useless additional explanatory variables.

Hence, once the investigator has tentatively decided upon the functional form of the regression relations (whether given variables are to appear in linear form, quadratic form, etc.) and whether any interaction terms are to be included, the next step in many exploratory observational studies is to identify a few "good" subsets of X variables for further intensive study. These subsets should include not only the potential explanatory variables in first-order form but also any needed quadratic and other curvature terms and any necessary interaction terms.

The identification of "good" subsets of potentially useful explanatory variables to be included in the final regression model and the determination of appropriate functional and interaction relations for these variables usually constitute some of the most difficult problems in regression analysis. Since the uses of regression models vary, no one subset of explanatory variables may always be "best." For instance, a descriptive use of a regression model typically will emphasize precise estimation of the regression coefficients, whereas a predictive use will focus on the prediction errors. Often, different subsets of the pool of potential explanatory variables will best serve these varying purposes. Even for a given purpose, it is often found that several subsets are about equally "good" according to a given criterion, and the choice among these "good" subsets needs to be made on the basis of additional considerations.

The choice of a few appropriate subsets of explanatory variables for final consideration in exploratory observational studies needs to be done with great care. Elimination of key explanatory variables can seriously damage the explanatory power of the model and lead to biased estimates of regression coefficients, mean responses, and predictions of new observations, as well as biased estimates of the error variance. The bias in these estimates is related to the fact that with observational data, the error terms in an underfitted regression model may reflect nonrandom effects of the explanatory variables not incorporated in the regression model. Important omitted explanatory variables are sometimes called *latent explanatory variables*.

On the other hand, if too many explanatory variables are included in the subset, then this overfitted model will often result in variances of estimated parameters that are larger than those for simpler models.

Another danger with observational data is that important explanatory variables may be observed only over narrow ranges. As a result, such important explanatory variables may be omitted just because they occur in the sample within a narrow range of values and therefore turn out to be statistically nonsignificant.

Another consideration in identifying subsets of explanatory variables is that these subsets need to be small enough so that maintenance costs are manageable and analysis is facilitated, yet large enough so that adequate description, control, or prediction is possible.

A variety of computerized approaches have been developed to assist the investigator in reducing the number of potential explanatory variables in an exploratory observational study when these variables are correlated among themselves. We present two of these approaches in this chapter. The first, which is practical for pools of explanatory variables that are small or moderate in size, considers all possible subsets of explanatory variables that can be developed from the pool of potential explanatory variables and identifies those subsets that are "good" according to a criterion specified by the investigator. The second approach employs automatic search procedures to arrive at a single subset of the explanatory variables. This approach is recommended primarily for reductions involving large pools of explanatory variables.

Even though computerized approaches can be very helpful in identifying appropriate subsets for detailed, final consideration, the process of developing a useful regression model must be pragmatic and needs to utilize large doses of subjective judgment. Explanatory variables that are considered essential should be included in the regression model before any computerized assistance is sought. Further, computerized approaches that identify only a single subset of explanatory variables as "best" need to be supplemented so that additional subsets are also considered before the final regression model is decided upon.

Comments

1. All too often, unwary investigators will screen a set of explanatory variables by fitting the regression model containing the entire set of potential X variables and then simply dropping those for which the t^* statistic (7.25):

$$t_k^* = \frac{b_k}{s\{b_k\}}$$

has a small absolute value. As we know from Chapter 7, this procedure can lead to the dropping of important intercorrelated explanatory variables. Clearly, a good search procedure must be able to handle important intercorrelated explanatory variables in such a way that not all of them will be dropped.

2. Controlled experiments can usually avoid many of the problems in exploratory observational studies. For example, the effects of latent predictor variables are minimized by using randomization. In addition, adequate ranges of the explanatory variables can be selected and correlations among the explanatory variables can be eliminated by appropriate choices of their levels. ∎

Model Refinement and Selection

At this stage in the model-building process, the tentative regression model, or the several "good" regression models in the case of exploratory observational studies, need to be checked in detail for curvature and interaction effects. Residual plots are helpful in deciding whether one model is to be preferred over another. In addition, the diagnostic checks to be described in Chapter 9 are useful for identifying influential outlying observations, multicollinearity, etc.

The selection of the ultimate regression model often depends greatly upon these diagnostic results. For example, one fitted model may be very much influenced by a single case, whereas another is not. Again, one fitted model may show correlations among the error terms, whereas another does not.

When repeat observations are available, formal tests for lack of fit can be made. In any case, a variety of residual plots and analyses can be employed to identify any lack of fit, outliers, and influential observations. For instance, residual plots against cross-product and/or power terms not included in the regression model can be useful in identifying ways in which the model fit can be improved further.

When an automatic selection procedure is utilized for an exploratory observational study and only a single model is identified as "best," other models should also be explored. One procedure is to use the number of explanatory variables in the model identified as "best" as an estimate of the number of explanatory variables needed in the regression model. Then the investigator explores and identifies other candidate models with approximately the same number of explanatory variables identified by the automatic procedure.

Eventually after thorough checking and various remedial actions, such as transformations, the investigator decides upon the final regression model to be employed. At this point, it is good statistical practice to validate this model.

Model Validation

Model validity refers to the stability and reasonableness of the regression coefficients, the plausibility and usability of the regression function, and the ability to generalize inferences drawn from the regression analysis. Validation is a useful and necessary part of the model-building process. Several methods of assessing model validity will be described in Chapter 10.

Overview of Remainder of Chapter

With the completion of this overview of the model-building process for a regression study, we next present an example that will be used to illustrate all stages of this process as they are taken up in this and the following two chapters. The remainder of this chapter will consider how to reduce the pool of potentially useful explanatory variables in exploratory observational studies.

8.2 Surgical Unit Example

To illustrate the model-building procedures discussed in this and the next two chapters, we use a relatively simple example based on an exploratory observational study in which there were four potential explanatory variables. By limiting the number of potential explanatory variables, we can explain the procedures without overwhelming the reader with masses of computer printouts.

A hospital surgical unit was interested in predicting survival in patients undergoing a particular type of liver operation. A random selection of 54 patients was available for analysis. From each patient record, the following information was extracted from the preoperation evaluation:

X_1 blood clotting score

X_2 prognostic index, which includes the age of patient

X_3 enzyme function test score

X_4 liver function test score

These constitute the pool of potential explanatory or predictor variables for a predictive regression model. The response variable is survival time, which was ascertained in a follow-up study. A portion of the data on the potential predictor variables and the response variable is presented in Table 8.1. These data have already been screened and properly edited for errors.

Since the pool of predictor variables is small, a reasonably full exploration of relationships and of possible strong interaction effects is possible at this stage of data preparation. Stem-and-leaf plots were prepared for each of the predictor variables (not shown). These

TABLE 8.1   **Potential Predictor Variables and Response Variable—Surgical Unit Example.**

Case Number i	Blood-Clotting Score X_{i1}	Prognostic Index X_{i2}	Enzyme Function Test X_{i3}	Liver Function Test X_{i4}	Survival Time Y_i	$Y_i' = \log_{10} Y_i$
1	6.7	62	81	2.59	200	2.3010
2	5.1	59	66	1.70	101	2.0043
3	7.4	57	83	2.16	204	2.3096
4	6.5	73	41	2.01	101	2.0043
...	...	...	...	...	...	...
51	6.6	77	46	1.95	124	2.0934
52	6.4	85	40	1.21	125	2.0969
53	6.4	59	85	2.33	198	2.2967
54	8.8	78	72	3.20	313	2.4955

highlighted several cases as outlying with respect to the explanatory variables. The investigator was thereby alerted to examine later the influence of these cases. A scatter plot matrix and the correlation matrix were also obtained (not shown).

A first-order regression model based on all predictor variables was fitted to serve as a starting point. The normal probability plot of the residuals for this fitted model is shown in Figure 8.2a. It suggests some departure from normality. The coefficient of correlation between the ordered residuals and their expected values under normality is only .826; reference to Table B.6 supports the conclusion of the error terms not being normally distributed.

Various other first-order models were fitted, and many residual plots were prepared. One plot of particular interest was the plot of residuals from the fit of Y on X_2 and X_3 against the interaction term $X_2 X_3$; this plot is shown in Figure 8.2b. Note the suggested strong interaction effects in this plot.

To make the distribution of the error terms more nearly normal and to see if the same transformation would also reduce the $X_2 X_3$ interaction effect, the investigator examined the logarithmic transformation $Y' = \log_{10} Y$. Data for the transformed response variable are also given in Table 8.1. Figure 8.2c shows the normal probability plot of the residuals when Y' is regressed on all predictor variables in a first-order model; the coefficient of correlation between the ordered residuals and their expected values under normality now is .959. It is clear that the transformation was helpful in making the distribution of the error terms more nearly normal. Further, the transformation was also helpful in reducing the interaction effect between X_2 and X_3. Figure 8.2d shows a plot of the residuals against $X_2 X_3$ when Y' is regressed on X_2 and X_3. This residual plot shows much less indication of a strong interaction effect. None of the other residual plots against interaction terms indicated a presence of strong interaction effects either.

The investigator also obtained a scatter plot matrix and the correlation matrix with the transformed Y variable; these are presented in Figure 8.3. In addition, various scatter and residual plots were obtained (not shown here). All of these plots indicate that each of the predictor variables is linearly associated with Y', X_4 showing the highest degree of association and X_1 the lowest. The scatter plot matrix and the correlation matrix further show

FIGURE 8.2   Some Preliminary Residual Plots—Surgical Unit Example.

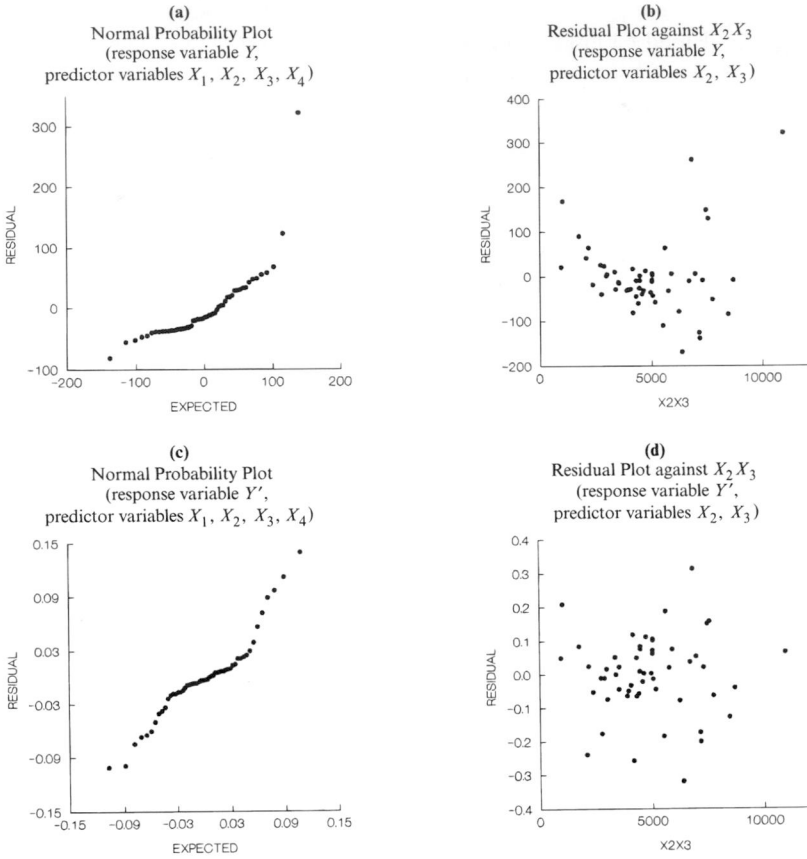

intercorrelations among the potential predictor variables. In particular, X_4 has moderately high pairwise correlations with X_1, X_2, and X_3.

On the basis of these analyses, the investigator concluded to use, at this stage of the model-building process, $Y' = \log_{10} Y$ as the response variable, to represent the predictor variables in linear terms, and not to include any interaction terms. The next stage in the model-building process is to examine whether all of the potential predictor variables are needed or whether a subset of them is adequate. We turn now to some variables reduction procedures for exploratory observational studies.

8.3   All-Possible-Regressions Procedure for Variables Reduction

The *all-possible-regressions procedure* calls for considering all possible subsets of the pool of potential X variables and identifying for detailed examination a few "good" subsets according to some criterion. The different possible subsets that can be formed from a pool of potential X variables are illustrated in Table 8.2 for the surgical unit example. Here, the pool of potential X variables includes four explanatory variables in first-order terms. There

FIGURE 8.3   **Scatter Plot Matrix and Correlation Matrix when Response Variable Is Y'—Surgical Unit Example.**

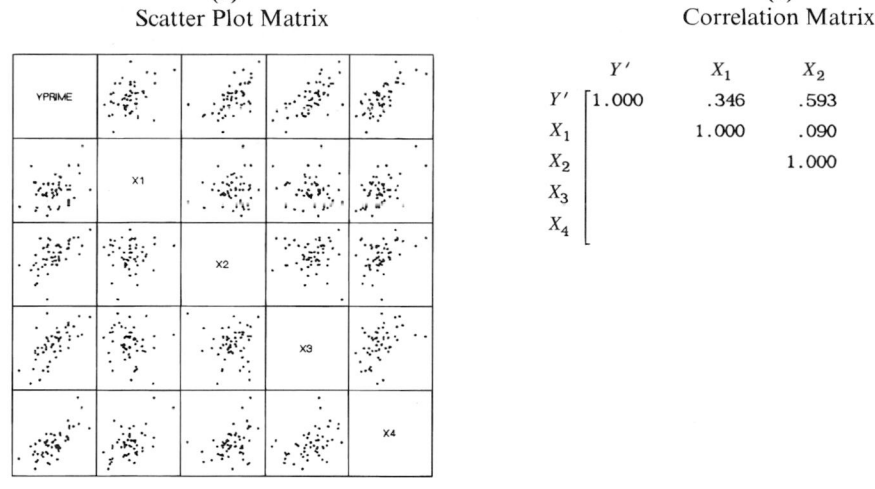

(a)
Scatter Plot Matrix

(b)
Correlation Matrix

	Y'	X_1	X_2	X_3	X_4
Y'	1.000	.346	.593	.665	.726
X_1		1.000	.090	−.150	.502
X_2			1.000	−.024	.369
X_3				1.000	.416
X_4					1.000

are altogether 16 different subset regression models that can be formed here. First, there is the regression model with no X variables, i.e., the model $Y_i = \beta_0 + \varepsilon_i$. Then there are the regression models with one X variable (X_1, X_2, X_3, X_4), with two X variables (X_1 and X_2, X_1 and X_3, X_1 and X_4, X_2 and X_3, X_2 and X_4, X_3 and X_4), and so on.

The purpose of the all-possible-regressions approach is to identify a small group of regression models that are "good" according to a specified criterion so that a detailed examination can be made of these models, leading to the selection of the final regression model to be employed. In most circumstances, it would be impossible for an analyst to make a detailed examination of all possible regression models. For instance, when there are 10 potential X variables in the pool, there would be $2^{10} = 1,024$ possible regression models. (This calculation is based on the fact that each potential X variable either can be included or excluded.) With the availability of high-speed computers and efficient algorithms, running all possible regression models for 10 potential X variables is not time consuming. Still, the sheer volume of 1,024 candidate models to examine carefully would be an overwhelming task for a data analyst.

Hence, unless the pool of potential X variables is very small, the investigator can concentrate on only a few of all of the possible regression models. This limited number might consist of three to six "good" subsets according to the criterion specified, so the investigator can then carefully study these regression models for choosing the final model to be employed.

Different criteria for comparing the regression models may be used with the all-possible-regressions selection procedure. We discuss four: R_p^2, MSE_p, C_p, and $PRESS_p$. Before doing so, we need to develop some notation. We shall denote the number of potential X variables in the pool by $P - 1$. We assume throughout this chapter that all regression models contain an intercept term β_0. Hence, the regression function containing all potential X variables contains P parameters, and the function with no X variables contains one parameter (β_0).

TABLE 8.2 R_p^2, MSE_p, C_p, and $PRESS_p$ Values for all Possible Regression Models—Surgical Unit Example.

X Variables in Model	(1) p	(2) df	(3) SSE_p	(4) R_p^2	(5) MSE_p	(6) C_p	(7) $PRESS_p$
None	1	53	3.9728	0	.0750	1,721.6	4.1241
X_1	2	52	3.4961	.120	.0672	1,510.8	3.8084
X_2	2	52	2.5763	.352	.0495	1,100.1	2.8627
X_3	2	52	2.2153	.442	.0426	939.0	2.4268
X_4	2	52	1.8776	.527	.0361	788.2	2.0292
X_1, X_2	3	51	2.2325	.438	.0438	948.7	2.6388
X_1, X_3	3	51	1.4072	.646	.0276	580.2	1.6095
X_1, X_4	3	51	1.8758	.528	.0368	789.4	2.1203
X_2, X_3	3	51	.7430	.813	.0146	283.7	.8352
X_2, X_4	3	51	1.3922	.650	.0273	573.5	1.5833
X_3, X_4	3	51	1.2453	.687	.0244	507.9	1.4287
X_1, X_2, X_3	4	50	.1099	.972	.00220	3.1	.1405
X_1, X_2, X_4	4	50	1.3905	.650	.0278	574.8	1.6513
X_1, X_3, X_4	4	50	1.1156	.719	.0223	452.0	1.3286
X_2, X_3, X_4	4	50	.4652	.883	.00930	161.7	.5487
X_1, X_2, X_3, X_4	5	49	.1098	.972	.00224	5.0	.1456

The number of X variables in a subset will be denoted by $p - 1$, as always, so that there are p parameters in the regression function for this subset of X variables. Thus, we have:

$$(8.1) \qquad\qquad 1 \leq p \leq P$$

The all-possible-regressions approach assumes that the number of observations exceeds the maximum number of potential parameters:

$$(8.2) \qquad\qquad n > P$$

and, indeed, it is highly desirable that n be substantially larger than P, as we noted earlier, so that sound results can be obtained.

R_p^2 or SSE_p Criterion

The R_p^2 criterion calls for the use of the coefficient of multiple determination R^2, defined in (6.40), in order to identify several "good" subsets of X variables—in other words, subsets for which R_p^2 is high. We show the number of parameters in the regression model as a subscript of R^2. Thus R_p^2 indicates that there are p parameters, or $p - 1$ X variables, in the regression function on which R_p^2 is based.

The R_p^2 criterion is equivalent to using the error sum of squares SSE_p as the criterion (we again show the number of parameters in the regression model as a subscript). With the SSE_p criterion, subsets for which SSE_p is small are considered "good." The equivalence of the R_p^2 and SSE_p criteria follows from (6.40):

$$(8.3) \qquad\qquad R_p^2 = 1 - \frac{SSE_p}{SSTO}$$

Since the denominator $SSTO$ is constant for all possible regression models, R_p^2 varies inversely with SSE_p.

The R_p^2 criterion is not intended to identify the subsets which maximize this criterion. We know that SSE_p can never increase as additional X variables are included in the model. Hence, R_p^2 will be a maximum when all $P - 1$ potential X variables are included in the regression model. The intent in using the R_p^2 criterion is to find the point where adding more X variables is not worthwhile because it leads to a very small increase in R_p^2. Often, this point is reached when only a limited number of X variables is included in the regression model. Clearly, the determination of where diminishing returns set in is a judgmental one.

Example.   Table 8.2 for the surgical unit example shows in columns 1, 2, and 3 the number of parameters in the regression function, the degrees of freedom associated with the error sum of squares, and the error sum of squares for each possible regression model. In column 4 are given the R_p^2 values. The results were obtained from a series of computer runs. For instance, when X_4 is the only X variable in the regression model, we obtain:

$$R_2^2 = 1 - \frac{SSE(X_4)}{SSTO} = 1 - \frac{1.8776}{3.9728} = .527$$

Note that $SSTO = SSE_1 = 3.9728$.

Figure 8.4 contains a plot of the R_p^2 values against p, the number of parameters in the regression model. The maximum R_p^2 value for the possible subsets each consisting of $p - 1$ predictor variables, denoted by $\max(R_p^2)$, appears at the top of the graph for each p. These points are connected by dashed lines to show the impact of adding additional X variables. Figure 8.4 makes it clear that little increase in $\max(R_p^2)$ takes place after three X variables are included in the model. Hence, consideration of the subsets (X_1, X_2, X_3) and (X_2, X_3, X_4) in the regression model appears to be reasonable according to the R_p^2 criterion.

Note that variable X_4, which singly correlates most highly with the response variable, is not in the $\max(R_p^2)$ model for $p = 4$, indicating that X_1, X_2, and X_3 contain much of the information presented by X_4. Note also that the coefficient of multiple determination associated with subset (X_2, X_3, X_4), $R_4^2 = .883$, is somewhat smaller than $R_4^2 = .972$ for subset (X_1, X_2, X_3).

MSE_p or R_a^2 Criterion

Since R_p^2 does not take account of the number of parameters in the regression model and since $\max(R_p^2)$ can never decrease as p increases, the adjusted coefficient of multiple determination R_a^2 in (6.42) has been suggested as an alternative criterion:

$$(8.4) \qquad\qquad R_a^2 = 1 - \left(\frac{n-1}{n-p}\right) \frac{SSE}{SSTO} = 1 - \frac{MSE}{\frac{SSTO}{n-1}}$$

FIGURE 8.4 R_p^2 Plot for Surgical Unit Example.

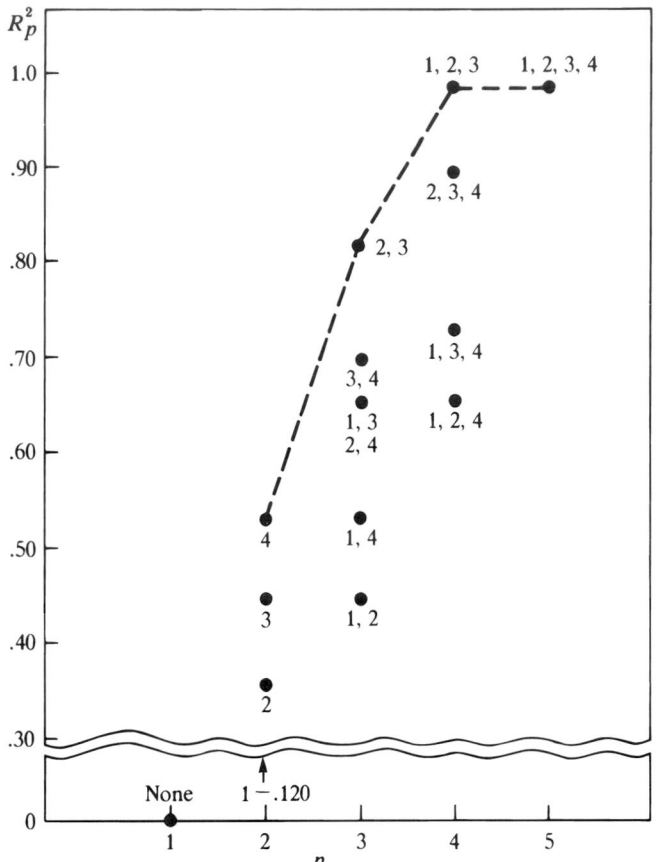

This coefficient takes the number of parameters in the regression model into account through the degrees of freedom. It can be seen from (8.4) that R_a^2 increases if and only if *MSE* decreases since $SSTO/(n - 1)$ is fixed for the given Y observations. Hence, R_a^2 and *MSE* provide equivalent information. We shall consider here the criterion MSE_p, again showing the number of parameters in the regression model as a subscript of the criterion. The smallest MSE_p for a given number of parameters in the model, $\min(MSE_p)$, can, indeed, increase as p increases. This occurs when the reduction in *SSE* becomes so small that it is not sufficient to offset the loss of an additional degree of freedom. Users of the MSE_p criterion seek to find a few subsets for which MSE_p is at the minimum or so close to the minimum that adding more variables is not worthwhile.

Example.   The MSE_p values for all possible regression models for the surgical unit example are shown in Table 8.2, column 5. For instance, we have for the regression model containing only X_4:

$$MSE_2 = \frac{SSE(X_4)}{n - 2} = \frac{1.8776}{52} = .0361$$

FIGURE 8.5 MSE_p **Plot for Surgical Unit Example.**

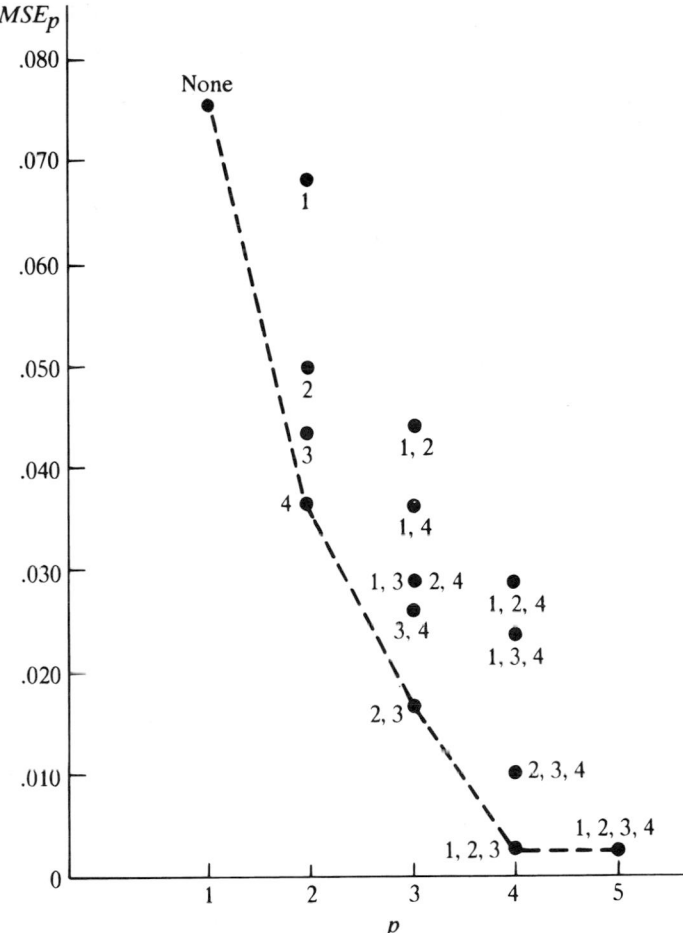

Figure 8.5 contains the MSE_p plot for the surgical unit example. We have again connected the $\min(MSE_p)$ values by dashed lines. The story told by the MSE_p plot in Figure 8.5 is very similar to that told by the R_p^2 plot in Figure 8.4. Consideration of the subsets (X_1, X_2, X_3) and (X_2, X_3, X_4) appears to be reasonable according to the MSE_p criterion. Indeed, the error mean square achieved with subset (X_1, X_2, X_3) is practically the same as that with the use of all potential X variables. The subset (X_2, X_3, X_4) involves a somewhat higher error mean square ($MSE_4 = .009$) than $MSE_4 = .002$ for subset (X_1, X_2, X_3).

C_p Criterion

This criterion is concerned with the *total mean squared error* of the n fitted values for each subset regression model. The mean squared error concept involves the total error in each fitted value:

(8.5)
$$\hat{Y}_i - \mu_i$$

where μ_i is the true mean response when the levels of the predictor variables X_k are those for the ith case. This total error is made up of a bias component and a random error component:

1. The bias component for the ith fitted value $\hat{Y}_i$, also called the model error component, is:

(8.5a)
$$E\{\hat{Y}_i\} - \mu_i$$

where $E\{\hat{Y}_i\}$ is the expectation of the ith fitted value for the given regression model. If the fitted model is not correct, $E\{\hat{Y}_i\}$ will differ from the true mean response μ_i and the difference represents bias of the fitted model.

2. The random error component for $\hat{Y}_i$ is:

(8.5b)
$$\hat{Y}_i - E\{\hat{Y}_i\}$$

This component represents the deviation of the fitted value $\hat{Y}_i$ for the given sample from the expected value when the ith fitted value is obtained by fitting the same regression model to all possible samples.

The mean squared error for $\hat{Y}_i$ is defined as the expected value of the square of the total error in (8.5) — in other words, the expected value of:

$$(\hat{Y}_i - \mu_i)^2 = [(E\{\hat{Y}_i\} - \mu_i) + (\hat{Y}_i - E\{\hat{Y}_i\})]^2$$

It can be shown that this expected value is:

(8.6)
$$E\{\hat{Y}_i - \mu_i\}^2 = (E\{\hat{Y}_i\} - \mu_i)^2 + \sigma^2\{\hat{Y}_i\}$$

where $\sigma^2\{\hat{Y}_i\}$ is the variance of the fitted value $\hat{Y}_i$. We see from (8.6) that the mean squared error for the fitted value $\hat{Y}_i$ is the sum of the squared bias and the variance of $\hat{Y}_i$.

The total mean squared error for all n fitted values $\hat{Y}_i$ is the sum of the n individual mean squared errors in (8.6):

(8.7)
$$\sum_{i=1}^{n}[(E\{\hat{Y}_i\} - \mu_i)^2 + \sigma^2\{\hat{Y}_i\}] = \sum_{i=1}^{n}(E\{\hat{Y}_i\} - \mu_i)^2 + \sum_{i=1}^{n}\sigma^2\{\hat{Y}_i\}$$

The criterion measure, denoted by Γ_p, is simply the total mean squared error in (8.7) divided by σ^2, the true error variance:

(8.8)
$$\Gamma_p = \frac{1}{\sigma^2}\left[\sum_{i=1}^{n}(E\{\hat{Y}_i\} - \mu_i)^2 + \sum_{i=1}^{n}\sigma^2\{\hat{Y}_i\}\right]$$

The model which includes all $P - 1$ potential X variables is assumed to have been carefully chosen so that $MSE(X_1, \ldots, X_{P-1})$ is an unbiased estimator of σ^2. It can then be shown that an estimator of Γ_p is C_p:

(8.9)
$$C_p = \frac{SSE_p}{MSE(X_1, \ldots, X_{P-1})} - (n - 2p)$$

where SSE_p is the error sum of squares for the fitted subset regression model with p parameters (i.e., with $p-1$ X variables).

When there is no bias in the regression model with $p-1$ X variables so that $E\{\hat{Y}_i\} \equiv \mu_i$, the expected value of C_p is approximately p:

(8.10) $$E\{C_p\} \simeq p \qquad \text{when } E\{\hat{Y}_i\} \equiv \mu_i$$

Thus, when the C_p values for all possible regression models are plotted against p, those models with little bias will tend to fall near the line $C_p = p$. Models with substantial bias will tend to fall considerably above this line. C_p values below the line $C_p = p$ are interpreted as showing no bias, being below the line due to sampling error. The C_p value for the regression model containing all $P-1$ X variables is, by definition, P. The C_p measure assumes that $MSE(X_1, \ldots, X_{P-1})$ is an unbiased estimator of σ^2, which is equivalent to assuming that this model contains no bias.

In using the C_p criterion, we seek to identify subsets of X variables for which (1) the C_p value is small and (2) the C_p value is near p. Subsets with small C_p values have a small total mean squared error, and when the C_p value is also near p, the bias of the regression model is small. It may sometimes occur that the regression model based on a subset of X variables with a small C_p value involves substantial bias. In that case, one may at times prefer a regression model based on a somewhat larger subset of X variables for which the C_p value is only slightly larger but which does not involve a substantial bias component. Reference 8.1 contains extended discussions of applications of the C_p criterion.

Example. Table 8.2, column 6, contains the C_p values for all possible regression models for the surgical unit example. For instance, when X_4 is the only X variable in the regression model, the C_p value is:

$$C_2 = \frac{SSE(X_4)}{MSE(X_1, X_2, X_3, X_4)} - [n - 2(2)]$$
$$= \frac{1.8776}{.00224} - (54 - 4) = 788.2$$

The C_p values for all possible regression models are plotted in Figure 8.6. We find that subset (X_1, X_2, X_3) has the smallest C_p value, with no indication of any bias in the regression model. The fact that the C_p measure for this model, $C_4 - 3.1$, is below $p = 4$ is, as stated earlier, considered to be the result of random variation in the C_p estimate.

Note that use of all potential X variables (X_1, X_2, X_3, X_4) results in a C_p value of exactly P, as expected; here, $C_5 = 5.00$. Also note that use of subset (X_2, X_3, X_4) with C_p value $C_4 = 161.7$ would be poor because of the substantial bias with this model. Thus, the C_p criterion suggests only one subset (X_1, X_2, X_3) for the surgical unit example.

Comments

1. Effective use of the C_p criterion requires careful development of the pool of $P-1$ potential X variables, with the predictor variables expressed in appropriate form (linear, quadratic, transformed), important interactions included, and useless variables excluded, so that $MSE(X_1, \ldots, X_{P-1})$ provides an unbiased estimate of the error variance σ^2.

2. The C_p criterion places major emphasis on the fit of the subset model for the n sample observations. At times, a modification of the C_p criterion that emphasizes new observations to be predicted may be preferable.

FIGURE 8.6 C_p **Plot for Surgical Unit Example.**

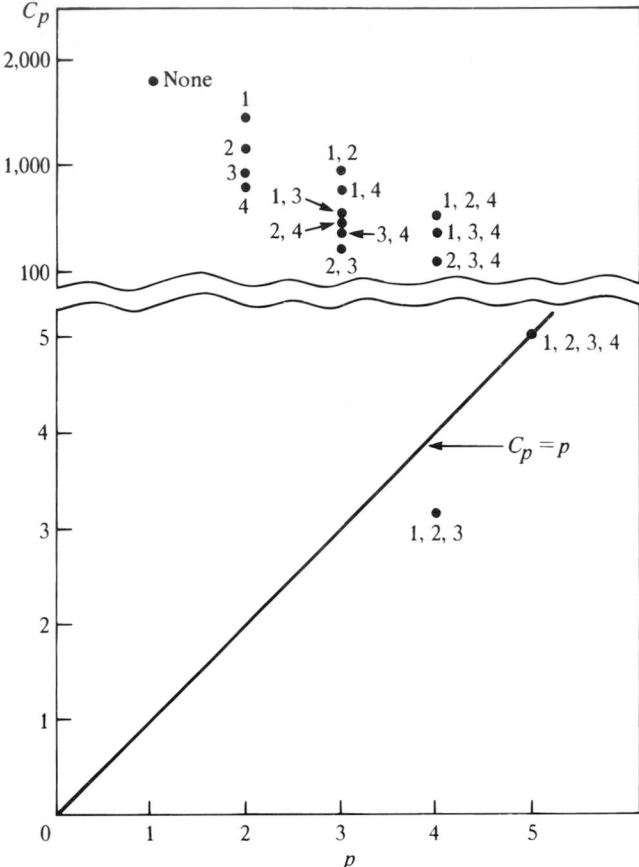

3.   To see why C_p as defined in (8.9) is an estimator of Γ_p, we need to utilize two results that we shall simply state. First, it can be shown that:

$$(8.11) \qquad \sum_{i=1}^{n} \sigma^2\{\hat{Y}_i\} = p\sigma^2$$

Thus, the total random error of the n fitted values $\hat{Y}_i$ increases as the number of variables in the regression model increases.

Further, it can be shown that:

$$(8.12) \qquad E\{SSE_p\} = \sum(E\{\hat{Y}_i\} - \mu_i)^2 + (n - p)\sigma^2$$

Hence, Γ_p in (8.8) can be expressed as follows:

$$(8.13) \qquad \Gamma_p = \frac{1}{\sigma^2}[E\{SSE_p\} - (n - p)\sigma^2 + p\sigma^2]$$

$$= \frac{E\{SSE_p\}}{\sigma^2} - (n - 2p)$$

Replacing $E\{SSE_p\}$ by the estimator SSE_p and using $MSE(X_1, \ldots, X_{P-1})$ as an estimator of σ^2 yields C_p in (8.9).

4. To show that the C_p value for the regression model containing all $P - 1$ X variables is P, we substitute in (8.9), as follows:

$$C_p = \frac{SSE(X_1, \ldots, X_{P-1})}{\dfrac{SSE(X_1, \ldots, X_{P-1})}{n - P}} - (n - 2P)$$

$$= (n - P) - (n - 2P)$$

$$= P \qquad \blacksquare$$

$PRESS_p$ Criterion

The $PRESS_p$ (prediction sum of squares) criterion is a measure of how well the use of the fitted values for a subset model can predict the observed responses Y_i. The error sum of squares, $SSE = \Sigma(Y_i - \hat{Y}_i)^2$, is also such a measure. The $PRESS$ measure differs from SSE in that each fitted value $\hat{Y}_i$ for the $PRESS$ criterion is obtained by deleting the ith case from the data set, estimating the regression function for the subset model from the remaining $n - 1$ cases, and then using the fitted regression function to obtain the predicted value $\hat{Y}_{i(i)}$ for the ith case. We use the notation $\hat{Y}_{i(i)}$ now for the fitted value to indicate, by the first subscript i, that it is a predicted value for the ith case and, by the second subscript (i), that the ith case was omitted when the regression function was fitted.

The $PRESS$ prediction error for the ith case then is:

$$(8.14) \qquad \qquad Y_i - \hat{Y}_{i(i)}$$

and the $PRESS_p$ criterion is the sum of the squared prediction errors over all n cases:

$$(8.15) \qquad \qquad PRESS_p = \sum_{i=1}^{n} (Y_i - \hat{Y}_{i(i)})^2$$

Models with small $PRESS_p$ values are considered good candidate models. The reason is that when the prediction errors $Y_i - \hat{Y}_{i(i)}$ are small, so are the squared prediction errors and the sum of the squared prediction errors. Thus, models with small $PRESS_p$ values fit well in the sense of having small prediction errors.

$PRESS_p$ values can be calculated without requiring n separate regression runs, each time deleting one of the n cases. The relationship in (9.21) and (9.21a), to be explained in the next chapter, enables one to calculate all $\hat{Y}_{i(i)}$ values from a single regression run.

Example.   Table 8.2, column 7, contains the $PRESS_p$ values for all possible regression models for the surgical unit example. The $PRESS_p$ values are plotted in Figure 8.7. We have connected the $\min(PRESS_p)$ values by dashed lines. The message which Figure 8.7 tells is very similar to that told by the other criteria. We find that subsets (X_1, X_2, X_3) and (X_2, X_3, X_4) have small $PRESS$ values; in fact, the set of all X variables (X_1, X_2, X_3, X_4) involves a slightly larger $PRESS$ value than subset (X_1, X_2, X_3). The subset (X_2, X_3, X_4) involves a $PRESS$ value of .5487, which is moderately larger than the $PRESS$ value of .1405 for subset (X_1, X_2, X_3).

FIGURE 8.7 $PRESS_p$ **Plot for Surgical Unit Example.**

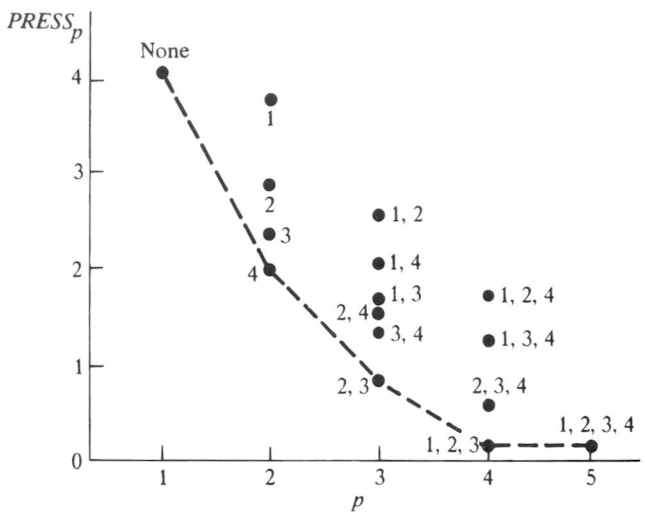

Note

PRESS values can also be useful for model validation, as will be explained in Chapter 10. ∎

"Best" Subsets Algorithms

Time-saving algorithms have been developed in which the "best" subsets according to a specified criterion are identified without requiring the fitting of all of the possible subset regression models. In fact, these algorithms require the calculation of only a small fraction of all possible regression models. For instance, if the C_p criterion is to be employed and the five "best" subsets according to this criterion are to be identified, these algorithms search for the five subsets of X variables with the smallest C_p values using much less computational effort than when all possible subsets are evaluated. These algorithms are called *"best" subsets algorithms*. Not only do these algorithms provide the best subsets according to the specified criterion, but they often also identify several "good" subsets for each possible number of X variables in the model to give the investigator additional helpful information in making the final selection of the subset of X variables to be employed in the regression model.

When the pool of potential X variables is very large, say greater than 40 to 60, even the "best" subsets algorithms may require excessive computer time. Under these conditions, one of the automatic selection procedures described in Section 8.4 may need to be employed to assist in the selection of X variables.

Example. Figure 8.8 contains for the surgical unit example the MINITAB output for its "best" subsets algorithm. Here, we specified that the best two subsets be identified. The MINITAB algorithm, unlike some others, also identifies the best two subsets for each number of variables in the regression model. The MINITAB algorithm uses the R_p^2 criterion, but also shows for each of the "best" subsets the R_a^2, C_p, and $\sqrt{MSE_p}$ (labeled s) values.

FIGURE 8.8   MINITAB Output for "Best" Two Subsets for Each Subset Size—Surgical Unit Example.

```
Best Subsets Regression of YPRIME

                     Adj.                      X X X X
     Vars   R-sq    R-sq    C-p       s        1 2 3 4

       1    52.7    51.8   788.1   0.19002            X
       1    44.2    43.2   938.9   0.20640        X
       2    81.3    80.6   283.7   0.12070      X X
       2    68.7    67.4   507.9   0.15626        X   X
       3    97.2    97.1     3.0   0.046874    X X X
       3    88.3    87.6   161.7   0.096458      X X X
       4    97.2    97.0     5.0   0.047331    X X X X
```

The right side of the tabulation shows the X variables in the subset. Note that the output in Figure 8.8 contains a portion of the results in Table 8.2 for one, two, three, and four X variables in the regression model. The slight differences in the results are due to rounding effects.

Some Final Comments

The all-possible-regressions procedure leads to the identification of a small number of subsets that are "good" according to a specified criterion. In the surgical unit example, three of the four criteria pointed to the same "best" subsets, while the fourth criterion ruled out one of these subsets. In other applications, the different criteria may lead to substantially different subset identifications. Consequently, one may wish at times to consider more than one criterion in evaluating possible subsets of X variables.

Once the investigator has identified a few "good" subsets for intensive examination, a final choice of the model variables must be made. This choice, as indicated by our model-building strategy in Figure 8.1, is aided by residual analyses, examination of influential observations, and other diagnostics for each of the competing models, and by the investigator's knowledge of the subject under study, and is finally confirmed by model validation. We shall take up some additional useful diagnostics in Chapter 9 and shall discuss validation of the selected regression model in Chapter 10.

8.4   Forward Stepwise Regression and Other Automatic Search Procedures for Variables Reduction

In those occasional cases when the pool of potential X variables contains 40 to 60 or even more variables, use of a "best" subsets algorithm may not be feasible. An automatic search procedure that develops the "best" subset of X variables sequentially may then be helpful. The forward stepwise regression procedure is probably the most widely used of the automatic search methods. It was developed to economize on computational efforts, as compared with the all-possible-regressions procedure. Essentially, this search method develops a sequence of regression models, at each step adding or deleting an X variable. The criterion for adding or deleting an X variable can be stated equivalently in terms of error sum of squares reduction, coefficient of partial correlation, t^* statistic, or F^* statistic.

An essential difference between automatic search procedures and the all-possible-regressions procedure is that the automatic search procedures end with the identification of a *single* regression model as "best." With the all-possible-regressions procedure, on the other hand, *several* regression models can be identified as "good" for final consideration. The identification of a single regression model as "best" by the automatic search procedures is a major weakness of these procedures. Experience has shown that each of the automatic search procedures can sometimes err by identifying a poor regression model as "best." In addition, the identification of a single regression model may hide the fact that several other regression models may also be "good." Finally, the "goodness" of a regression model can only be established by a thorough examination using a variety of diagnostics.

What then can we do on those occassions when the pool of potential X variables is very large and an automatic search procedure must be utilized? Basically, we should use the subset identified by the automatic search procedure as a starting point for searching for other "good" subsets. One possibility is to treat the number of X variables in the regression model identified by the automatic search procedure as being about the right subset size and then use the all-possible-regressions procedures for subsets of this and nearby sizes.

Forward Stepwise Regression

We shall describe the forward stepwise regression search algorithm in terms of the F^* statistic for the partial F test.

1. The stepwise regression routine first fits a simple linear regression model for each of the $P - 1$ potential X variables. For each simple linear regression model, the F^* statistic (2.60) for testing whether or not the slope is zero is obtained:

$$(8.16) \qquad F_k^* = \frac{MSR(X_k)}{MSE(X_k)}$$

Recall that $MSR(X_k) = SSR(X_k)$ measures the reduction in the total variation of Y associated with the use of variable X_k. The X variable with the largest F^* value is the candidate for first addition. If this F^* value exceeds a predetermined level, the X variable is added. Otherwise, the program terminates with no X variable considered sufficiently helpful to enter the regression model.

2. Assume X_7 is the variable entered at step 1. The stepwise regression routine now fits all regression models with two X variables, where X_7 is one of the pair. For each such regression model, the partial F test statistic (7.24):

$$(8.17) \qquad F_k^* = \frac{MSR(X_k|X_7)}{MSE(X_7, X_k)} = \left(\frac{b_k}{s\{b_k\}}\right)^2$$

is obtained. This is the statistic for testing whether or not $\beta_k = 0$ when X_7 and X_k are the variables in the model. The X variable with the largest F^* value is the candidate for addition at the second stage. If this F^* value exceeds a predetermined level, the second X variable is added. Otherwise, the program terminates.

3. Suppose X_3 is added at the second stage. Now the stepwise regression routine examines whether any of the other X variables already in the model should be dropped. For our illustration, there is at this stage only one other X variable in the model, X_7, so that

only one partial F test statistic is obtained:

$$(8.18) \qquad F_7^* = \frac{MSR(X_7|X_3)}{MSE(X_3, X_7)}$$

At later stages, there would be a number of these F^* statistics, for each of the variables in the model besides the one last added. The variable for which this F^* value is smallest is the candidate for deletion. If this F^* value falls below a predetermined limit, the variable is dropped from the model; otherwise, it is retained.

4. Suppose X_7 is retained so that both X_3 and X_7 are now in the model. The stepwise regression routine now examines which X variable is the next candidate for addition, then examines whether any of the variables already in the model should now be dropped, and so on until no further X variables can either be added or deleted, at which point the search terminates.

Note that the stepwise regression algorithm allows an X variable, brought into the model at an earlier stage, to be dropped subsequently if it is no longer helpful in conjunction with variables added at later stages.

Example.   Figure 8.9 shows the BMDP computer printout for the forward stepwise regression procedure for the surgical unit example. The minimum acceptable F limit for adding a variable and the maximum acceptable F limit for removing a variable were specified to be 4.0 and 3.9, respectively, as shown at the top right of Figure 8.9. Since the degrees of freedom associated with *MSE* vary, depending on the number of X variables in the model, and since repeated tests on the same data are undertaken, fixed F limits for adding or deleting a variable have no precise probabilistic meaning. Note, however, that $F(.95; 1, 50) = 4.03$, so that the specified F limits of 4.0 and 3.9 would correspond roughly to a level of significance of .05 for any single test based on approximately 50 degrees of freedom.

The minimum acceptable tolerance of .01 shown in the upper right of Figure 8.9 is a specification to guard against the entry of a variable that is highly correlated with the other X variables already in the model. The tolerance is defined as $1 - R_k^2$, where R_k^2 is the coefficient of multiple determination when X_k is regressed on the other X variables in the regression model. The tolerance specification of .01 in Figure 8.9 provides that no variable is to be added to the model when the coefficient of multiple determination for this variable regressed on the other X variables already in the model exceeds $1 - .01 = .99$ or when it would cause the R_k^2 for any variable in the model to exceed .99.

We now follow through the steps.

1. At step 0, no X variable is in the model so that the model to be fitted is $Y_i = \beta_0 + \varepsilon_i$. The residual or error sum of squares shown in the ANOVA table in Figure 8.9 for step 0 is therefore $\Sigma(Y_i - \bar{Y})^2 = SSTO = 3.9728$. For each potential X variable, the F^* statistic (8.16) is calculated. In Figure 8.9, these F_k^* values are shown under the heading VARIABLES NOT IN EQUATION and are called F TO ENTER values. We see that F_4^* is the largest one:

$$F_4^* = \frac{MSR(X_4)}{MSE(X_4)} = \frac{2.095140}{.03610831} = 58.02$$

Since this value exceeds the minimum acceptable F-to-enter value of 4.0, X_4 is added to the model.

The column headed LEVEL refers to a package option that permits the user to give different priorities to the various potential X variables. Note that in the present example all X variables have the same priority.

FIGURE 8.9 BMDP Forward Stepwise Regression Output—Surgical Unit Example.

```
STEPPING ALGORITHM. . . . . . . . . . . . . . .F          MINIMUM ACCEPTABLE F TO ENTER . . . . . . . . .    4.000,   4.000
MAXIMUM NUMBER OF STEPS . . . . . . . . . . .   10         MAXIMUM ACCEPTABLE F TO REMOVE. . . . . . . .     3.900,   3.900
DEPENDENT VARIABLE. . . . . . . . . . . . .    5 y         MINIMUM ACCEPTABLE TOLERANCE. . . . . . . . . . 0.01000
                                                           SUBSCRIPTS OF THE INDEPENDENT VARIABLES . . . .    1    2    3    4
STEP NO.     0
---------------

STD. ERROR OF EST.      0.2738                              ANALYSIS OF VARIANCE
                                                                            SUM OF SQUARES    DF    MEAN SQUARE
                                                             RESIDUAL        3.9727724        53   0.7495797E-01  ◄—SSTO/(n-1)
                             VARIABLES IN EQUATION FOR y          SSTO               VARIABLES NOT IN EQUATION

                      STD. ERROR STD REG           F                              PARTIAL                 F
        VARIABLE   COEFFICIENT OF COEFF  COEFF  TOLERANCE TO REMOVE LEVEL.  VARIABLE   CORR.   TOLERANCE  TO ENTER  LEVEL
(Y-INTERCEPT       2.20614 )                                         .  x1       1  0.34640  1.00000     7.09      1
                     ↑                                               .  x2       2  0.59289  1.00000    28.19      1
                     Y                                               .  x3       3  0.66512  1.00000    41.25      1
                                                                     .  x4       4  0.72621  1.00000    58.02      1
STEP NO.     1
---------------
VARIABLE ENTERED    4  x4  ◄—R          ANALYSIS OF VARIANCE     rYk            F*k    MSR(X4)

MULTIPLE R            0.7262  ◄—R           SSR(X4)              SUM OF SQUARES   DF   MEAN SQUARE     F RATIO
MULTIPLE R-SQUARE    0.5274  ◄—R²       REGRESSION   2.0951402       1    2.095140       58.02
ADJUSTED R-SQUARE    0.5183  ◄—R²a      RESIDUAL     1.8776320      52   0.3610831E-01
                                                                    F*
STD. ERROR OF EST.   0.1900  ◄—√MSE                   SSE(X4)           MSE(X4)
                             VARIABLES IN EQUATION FOR y               VARIABLES NOT IN EQUATION

                      STD. ERROR STD REG           F                              PARTIAL                 F
        VARIABLE   COEFFICIENT OF COEFF  COEFF  TOLERANCE TO REMOVE LEVEL.  VARIABLE   CORR.   TOLERANCE  TO ENTER  LEVEL
(Y-INTERCEPT       1.69639 )                                         .  x1       1  -0.03104  0.74758     0.05      1
x4          4        0.18575    0.0244   0.726  1.00000    58.02     1 .  x2       2   0.50849  0.86382    17.78      1
                                                                     .  x3       3   0.58031  0.82659    25.89      1
              bk      s{bk}     b'k              F*k                      rYk.4      1-r²4k     F*k
STEP NO.     2
---------------
VARIABLE ENTERED    3  x3                ANALYSIS OF VARIANCE     SUM OF SQUARES   DF   MEAN SQUARE     F RATIO
MULTIPLE R            0.8286                 REGRESSION   2.7274444       2    1.363722       55.85
MULTIPLE R-SQUARE    0.6865                 RESIDUAL     1.2453278      51   0.2441819E-01
ADJUSTED R-SQUARE    0.6742

STD. ERROR OF EST.   0.1563
                             VARIABLES IN EQUATION FOR y    .          VARIABLES NOT IN EQUATION

                      STD. ERROR STD REG           F                              PARTIAL                 F
        VARIABLE   COEFFICIENT OF COEFF  COEFF  TOLERANCE TO REMOVE LEVEL.  VARIABLE   CORR.   TOLERANCE  TO ENTER  LEVEL
(Y-INTERCEPT       1.38878 )                                         .  x1       1  0.32276  0.59179     5.81      1
x3          3        0.00565    0.0011   0.439  0.82659    25.89     1 .  x2       2  0.79148  0.82580    83.85      1
x4          4        0.13901    0.0221   0.543  0.82659    39.72     1 .
                                                                    1-R²k
STEP NO.     3
---------------
VARIABLE ENTERED    2  x2                ANALYSIS OF VARIANCE     SUM OF SQUARES   DF   MEAN SQUARE     F RATIO
MULTIPLE R            0.9396                 REGRESSION   3.5075624       3    1.169187      125.66
MULTIPLE R-SQUARE    0.8829                 RESIDUAL     0.46520978     50   0.9304196E-02
ADJUSTED R-SQUARE    0.8759

STD. ERROR OF EST.   0.0965
                             VARIABLES IN EQUATION FOR y    .          VARIABLES NOT IN EQUATION

                      STD. ERROR STD REG           F                              PARTIAL                 F
        VARIABLE   COEFFICIENT OF COEFF  COEFF  TOLERANCE TO REMOVE LEVEL.  VARIABLE   CORR.   TOLERANCE  TO ENTER  LEVEL
(Y-INTERCEPT       0.94226 )                                         .  x1       1  0.87409  0.55586    158.66      1
x2          2        0.78987E-02 0.8626E-03 0.488 0.82580  83.85     1 .
x3          3        0.69997E-02 0.7013E-03 0.543 0.79021  99.63     1 .
x4          4        0.08185    0.0150   0.320  0.68298    29.86     1 .

STEP NO.     4
---------------
VARIABLE ENTERED    1  x1                ANALYSIS OF VARIANCE     SUM OF SQUARES   DF   MEAN SQUARE     F RATIO
MULTIPLE R            0.9861                 REGRESSION   3.8630006       4    0.9657502      431.09
MULTIPLE R-SQUARE    0.9724                 RESIDUAL     0.10977174     49   0.2240240E-02
ADJUSTED R-SQUARE    0.9701

STD. ERROR OF EST.   0.0473
                             VARIABLES IN EQUATION FOR y    .          VARIABLES NOT IN EQUATION

                      STD. ERROR STD REG           F                              PARTIAL                 F
        VARIABLE   COEFFICIENT OF COEFF  COEFF  TOLERANCE TO REMOVE LEVEL.  VARIABLE   CORR.   TOLERANCE  TO ENTER  LEVEL
(Y-INTERCEPT       0.48876 )                                         .
x1          1        0.06852    0.0054   0.401  0.55586   158.66     1 .
x2          2        0.92541E-02 0.4367E-03 0.571 0.77567 448.98     1 .
x3          3        0.94745E-02 0.3963E-03 0.736 0.59594 571.70     1 .
x4          4        0.00193    0.0097   0.008  0.39134     0.04     1 .

STEP NO.     5
---------------
VARIABLE REMOVED    4  x4                ANALYSIS OF VARIANCE     SUM OF SQUARES   DF   MEAN SQUARE     F RATIO
MULTIPLE R            0.9861                 REGRESSION   3.8629124       3    1.287637      586.04
MULTIPLE R-SQUARE    0.9723                 RESIDUAL     0.10985984     50   0.2197197E-02
ADJUSTED R-SQUARE    0.9707

STD. ERROR OF EST.   0.0469
                             VARIABLES IN EQUATION FOR y    .          VARIABLES NOT IN EQUATION

                      STD. ERROR STD REG           F                              PARTIAL                 F
        VARIABLE   COEFFICIENT OF COEFF  COEFF  TOLERANCE TO REMOVE LEVEL.  VARIABLE   CORR.   TOLERANCE  TO ENTER  LEVEL
(Y-INTERCEPT       0.48362 )                                         .
x1          1        0.06923    0.0041   0.405  0.97011   288.16     1 .  x4       4  0.02832  0.39134     0.04      1
x2          2        0.92945E-02 0.3825E-03 0.574 0.99177 590.44     1 .
x3          3        0.95236E-02 0.3064E-03 0.739 0.97751 966.06     1 .

***** F LEVELS(  4.000,  3.900) OR TOLERANCE INSUFFICIENT FOR FURTHER STEPPING
```

2. At this stage, step 1 has been completed. The current regression model contains X_4, and the printout provides the estimated regression coefficients, the analysis of variance table, and selected other information about the current model.

Next, all regression models containing X_4 and another X variable are fitted, and the F^* statistics calculated. They are now:

$$F_k^* = \frac{MSR(X_k|X_4)}{MSE(X_4, X_k)}$$

These statistics are shown in step 1 under the heading VARIABLES NOT IN EQUATION. X_3 has the highest F^* value, which exceeds 4.0, so that X_3 now enters the model.

3. Step 2 in Figure 8.9 summarizes the situation at this point. X_3 and X_4 are now in the model, and information about this model is provided. Next, a test whether X_4 should be dropped is undertaken. The F^* statistic is shown under the heading VARIABLES IN EQUATION and is called F TO REMOVE:

$$F_4^* = \frac{MSR(X_4|X_3)}{MSE(X_3, X_4)} = 39.72$$

Since this F^* value exceeds the maximum acceptable F-to-remove value of 3.9, X_4 is not dropped.

4. Next, all regression models containing X_3, X_4, and one of the remaining potential X variables are fitted. The appropriate F^* statistics now are:

$$F_k^* = \frac{MSR(X_k|X_3, X_4)}{MSE(X_3, X_4, X_k)}$$

These statistics are shown in step 2 under the heading VARIABLES NOT IN EQUATION. X_2 has the highest F^* value, which exceeds 4.0, so that X_2 now enters the model.

5. Step 3 in Figure 8.9 summarizes the situation at this point. X_2, X_3, and X_4 are now in the model. Next, a test is undertaken whether X_3 or X_4 should be dropped. The F^* statistics to remove a variable are shown under the heading VARIABLES IN EQUATION in step 3. F_4^* is smallest:

$$F_4^* = \frac{MSR(X_4|X_2, X_3)}{MSE(X_2, X_3, X_4)} = 29.86$$

Since its value exceeds 3.9, X_4 is not dropped from the model.

6. At this point, only X_1 remains in the potential pool. Its F^* value to enter exceeds 4.0 (see VARIABLES NOT IN EQUATION under step 3), so X_1 is entered into the model.

7. Step 4 in Figure 8.9 summarizes the addition of variable X_1 into the model containing variables X_2, X_3, and X_4. Next, a test is undertaken to determine whether either X_2, X_3, or X_4 should be dropped. The F^* statistics are shown under the heading VARIABLES IN EQUATION in step 4. Note that:

$$F_4^* = \frac{MSR(X_4|X_1, X_2, X_3)}{MSE(X_1, X_2, X_3, X_4)} = .04$$

is smallest, and that its value is less than 3.9; hence, X_4 is deleted.

8. Step 5 summarizes the dropping of X_4 from the model. Since the only potential variable remaining is X_4, which has just been dropped, it cannot enter the regression now. The algorithm therefore next considers the F-to-remove values in step 5 which indicate that

F_1^* is smallest. However, since its value exceeds 3.9, X_1 is not dropped from the model and the search process is terminated.

Thus, the stepwise search algorithm identifies (X_1, X_2, X_3) as the "best" subset of X variables, a result that happens to be consistent with our previous analyses based on the all-possible-regressions procedure.

Comments

1. In the surgical unit example, the tolerance requirement was always met; hence, no variable was excluded from the model as a result of too high a correlation with the other X variables in the model.

2. Variations of the rules for entering and removing variables illustrated in the example are possible. For instance, different F-to-enter and F-to-remove values can be employed in accordance with the degrees of freedom associated with *MSE* in the F^* statistic. However, this refinement often is not utilized and fixed values are employed instead, since the repeated testing in the search procedure does not permit precise probabilistic interpretations.

3. The F limits for adding and deleting a variable need not be selected in terms of approximate significance levels, but may be determined descriptively in terms of error reduction. For instance, an F limit of 2.0 for adding a variable may be specified with the thought that the marginal error reduction associated with the added variable should be at least twice as great as the remaining error mean square once that variable has been added.

4. The choice of F-to-enter and F-to-remove values essentially represents a balancing of opposing tendencies. Simulation studies have shown that for large pools of uncorrelated predictor variables that have been generated to be uncorrelated with the response variable, use of small or moderately small F-to-enter values as the entry criterion results in a procedure that is too liberal; that is, it allows too many predictor variables into the model. On the other hand, models produced by an automatic selection procedure with large F-to-enter values are often underspecified, resulting in σ^2 being badly overestimated and the procedure being too conservative (see, for example, References 8.2 and 8.3).

5. The minimum acceptable F-to-enter value should never be smaller than the maximum acceptable F-to-remove value; otherwise, cycling is possible where a variable is continually entered and removed.

6. The order in which variables enter the regression model does not reflect their importance. In the surgical unit example, for instance, X_4 was the first variable to enter the model, yet it was eventually dropped because it could be predicted well from the other three predictor variables.

7. The BMDP stepwise regression routine prints out the partial correlation coefficients at each stage. These could be used equivalently to the F^* values for screening the X variables, and indeed some routines use the partial correlation coefficients for screening.   ∎

Other Automatic Search Procedures

Other automatic search procedures are available to find a "best" subset of predictor variables. We mention two of these.

Forward Selection.   The forward selection search procedure is a simplified version of forward stepwise regression, omitting the test whether a variable once entered into the model should be dropped.

Backward Elimination.   The backward elimination search procedure is the opposite of forward selection. It begins with the model containing all potential X variables and identifies the one with the smallest F^* value. For instance, the F^* value for X_1 is:

$$(8.19) \qquad F_1^* = \frac{MSR(X_1 | X_2, \ldots, X_{P-1})}{MSE(X_1, \ldots, X_{P-1})}$$

If the minimum F_k^* value is less than a predetermined limit, that X variable is dropped. The model with the remaining $P - 2$ X variables is then fitted, and the next candidate for dropping is identified. This process continues until no further X variables can be dropped. A stepwise modification can also be adapted that allows variables eliminated earlier to be added later; this modification is called the backward stepwise regression procedure.

Note

For small and moderate numbers of variables in the pool of potential X variables, some statisticians argue for backward stepwise search over forward stepwise search (see Reference 8.4). This argument is based primarily on situations where it is useful as a first step to look at each X variable in the regression function adjusted for all the other X variables in the pool.   ∎

Computer Options and Refinements

Our discussion of the major automatic selection procedures for identifying the "best" subset of X variables has focused on the main conceptual issues and not on options, variations, and refinements available with particular computer packages. It is essential that the specific features of the package employed be fully understood so that intelligent use of the package can be made. In some packages, there is an option for regression models through the origin. Some packages permit variables to be brought into the model and tested in pairs or other groupings instead of singly, to save computing time or for other reasons. Some packages, once a "best" regression model is identified, will fit all the possible regression models in the same number of variables and will develop information for each model so that a final choice can be made by the user. Some stepwise programs have options for forcing variables into the regression model; such variables are not removed even if their F^* values become too low.

The diversity of these options and special features serves to emphasize a point made earlier: there is no unique way of searching for "good" subsets of X variables, and subjective elements must play an important role in the search process.

8.5   Some Final Comments on Model Building for Exploratory Observational Studies

As the discussion of the all-possible-regressions procedure and the automatic search procedures has made clear, there is no easy way to build a regression model for an exploratory observational study involving a large number of intercorrelated explanatory variables. We have considered a number of important issues related to exploratory model building, but there are many others. (A good discussion of many of these issues may be found in Reference 8.5.) Most important for good model building is the recognition that no automatic search procedure will always find the "best" model, and that, indeed, there may exist several "good" regression models whose appropriateness for the purpose at hand needs to be investigated.

Judgment needs to play an important role in model building for exploratory studies. Some explanatory variables may be known to be more fundamental than others and therefore should be retained in the regression model if the primary purpose is to develop a good explanatory model. When a qualitative predictor variable is represented in the pool of potential X variables by a number of indicator variables (e.g., geographic region is represented by several indicator variables), it is often appropriate to keep these indicator variables together as a group to represent the qualitative variable, even if a subset containing only some of the indicator variables is "better" according to the criterion employed. Similarly, if second-order terms X_k^2 or interaction terms $X_k X_{k'}$ need to be present in a regression model, one would ordinarily wish to have the first-order terms in the model as representing the main effects.

An important issue in exploratory model building that we have not yet considered is the bias in estimated regression coefficients and in estimated mean responses, as well as in their estimated standard deviations, that may result when the coefficients and error mean square for the finally selected regression model are estimated from the same data that were used for selecting the model. Sometimes, these biases may be substantial (see, for example, References 8.5 and 8.6). We explain in Chapter 10 how one can examine whether the estimated regression coefficients and error mean square are biased to a substantial extent. One method of avoiding bias is not to use the entire data set for the model-building process. This can be done if the data set is large. A portion of the data set is then used for developing the regression model, and the remainder of the data set is used for estimating the regression coefficients for the selected model. Consider, for example, a study where the pool of potential X variables consists of six variables and 150 cases are available for building the regression model. Ninety cases selected at random might then be used to develop the regression model, and the remaining 60 cases would be used to fit the chosen model.

The selection of a subset regression model for exploratory observational studies has been the subject of much recent research. Reference 8.5 provides information about many of these studies. New methods of identifying the "best" subset have been proposed, including methods based on deleting one case at a time and on bootstrapping. With the first method, the criterion is evaluated for identified subsets n times, each time with one case omitted, in order to select the "best" subset. With bootstrapping, repeated samples of cases are selected with replacement from the data set (alternatively, repeated samples of residuals from the model fitted to all X variables are selected with replacement to obtain observed Y values), and the criterion is evaluated for identified subsets in order to select the "best" subset. Research by Breiman and Spector (Ref. 8.7) has evaluated these methods from the standpoint of the closeness of the selected model to the true model and has found the two methods promising, the bootstrap method requiring larger data sets.

As we have noted, the identification of one or several "good" regression models is not the end of the model-building process. These models must be evaluated by various diagnostic procedures (discussed in Chapter 9) before the final regression model is determined. This model then needs to be validated (discussed in Chapter 10) before it is considered to be satisfactory.

Cited References

8.1. Daniel, C., and F. S. Wood. *Fitting Equations to Data*. 2nd ed. New York: Wiley-Interscience, 1980.

8.2. Freedman, D. A. "A Note on Screening Regression Equations," *The American Statistician* 37 (1983), pp. 152–55.

8.3. Pope, P. T., and J. T. Webster. "The Use of an F-Statistic in Stepwise Regression," *Technometrics* 14 (1972), pp. 327–40.

8.4. Mantel, N. "Why Stepdown Procedures in Variable Selection," *Technometrics* 12 (1970), pp. 621–25.

8.5. Miller, A. J. *Subset Selection in Regression*. London: Chapman and Hall, 1990.

8.6. Faraway, J. J. "On the Cost of Data Analysis," *Journal of Computational and Graphical Statistics* 1 (1992), pp. 213–29.

8.7. Breiman, L., and P. Spector. "Submodel Selection and Evaluation in Regression. The X-Random Case," *International Statistical Review* 60 (1992), pp. 291–319.

Problems

8.1. A speaker stated: "In well-designed experiments involving quantitative explanatory variables, a procedure for reducing the number of explanatory variables after the data are obtained is not necessary." Discuss.

8.2. The dean of a graduate school wishes to predict the grade point average in graduate work for recent applicants. List a dozen variables that might be useful explanatory variables here.

8.3. Two researchers, investigating factors affecting summer attendance at privately operated beaches on Lake Ontario, collected information on attendance and 11 explanatory variables for 42 beaches. Two summers were studied, of relatively hot and relatively cool weather, respectively. A "best" subsets algorithm now is to be used to reduce the number of explanatory variables for the final regression model.

   a. Should the variables reduction be done for both summers combined, or should it be done separately for each summer? Explain the problems involved and how you might handle them.

   b. Will the "best" subsets selection procedure choose those explanatory variables that are most important in a causal sense for determining beach attendance?

8.4. In forward stepwise regression, what advantage is there in using a relatively large F-to-enter value for adding variables? What advantage is there in using a smaller F-to-enter value?

8.5. In forward stepwise regression, why should the F-to-remove value for deleting variables never exceed the F-to-enter value for adding variables?

8.6.   Prepare a flowchart of each of the following selection methods: (1) forward stepwise regression, (2) forward selection, (3) backward elimination.

8.7.   An engineer has stated: "Reduction of the number of explanatory variables should always be done using the objective forward stepwise regression procedure." Discuss.

√ 8.8.   Refer to **Patient satisfaction** Problem 6.15. The hospital administrator wishes to determine the best subset of predictor variables for predicting patient satisfaction.

a.   Indicate which subset of predictor variables you would recommend as best for predicting patient satisfaction according to each of the following criteria: (1) R_p^2, (2) MSE_p, (3) C_p, (4) $PRESS_p$. Support your recommendations with appropriate graphs.

b.   Do the four criteria in part (a) identify the same best subset? Does this always happen?

c.   Would forward stepwise regression have any advantages here as a screening procedure over the all-possible-regressions procedure?

√ 8.9.   **Roofing shingles**. Data on sales last year (Y, in thousand squares) in 26 sales districts are given below for a maker of asphalt roofing shingles. Shown also are promotional expenditures (X_1, in thousand dollars), number of active accounts (X_2), number of competing brands (X_3), and district potential (X_4, coded) for each of the districts.

District i	X_{i1}	X_{i2}	X_{i3}	X_{i4}	Y_i
1	5.5	31	10	8	79.3
2	2.5	55	8	6	200.1
3	8.0	67	12	9	163.2
...	...	...	...	...	...
24	4.2	26	8	3	93.5
25	4.5	75	8	19	259.0
26	5.6	71	4	9	331.2

a.   Prepare separate dot plots for each of the explanatory variables. Are there any noteworthy features in these plots? Comment.

b.   Obtain the scatter plot matrix. Also obtain the correlation matrix of the X variables. Do the relationships between the response variable Y and each of the explanatory variables appear to be linear or curvilinear? Are any serious multicollinearity problems evident? Explain.

c.   Fit the multiple regression model containing all four explanatory variables as first-order terms. Does it appear that all predictor variables should be retained?

√ 8.10.   Refer to **Roofing shingles** Problem 8.9.

a.   Using only first-order terms for the predictor variables, find the three best subset regression models according to the C_p criterion.

b.   Is there relatively little bias in each of these subset models?

8.11.   **Job proficiency**. A personnel officer in a governmental agency administered four newly developed aptitude tests to each of 25 applicants for entry-level clerical positions in the agency. For purpose of the study, all 25 applicants were accepted for positions irrespective of their test scores. After a probationary period, each applicant was rated for proficiency on the job. The scores on the four tests (X_1, X_2, X_3, X_4) and the job proficiency score (Y) for the 25 employees were as follows:

Subject	Test Score				Job Proficiency Score
i	X_{i1}	X_{i2}	X_{i3}	X_{i4}	Y_i
1	86	110	100	87	88
2	62	97	99	100	80
3	110	107	103	103	96
...	...	...	...	...	...
23	104	73	93	80	78
24	94	121	115	104	115
25	91	129	97	83	83

a. Prepare separate stem-and-leaf plots of the test scores for each of the four newly developed aptitude tests. Are there any noteworthy features in these plots? Comment.

b. Obtain the scatter plot matrix. Also obtain the correlation matrix of the X variables. What do the scatter plots suggest about the nature of the functional relationship between the response variable Y and each of the predictor variables? Are any serious multicollinearity problems evident? Explain.

c. Fit the multiple regression function containing all four predictor variables as first-order terms. Does it appear that all predictor variables should be retained?

8.12. Refer to **Job proficiency** Problem 8.11.

a. Using only first-order terms for the predictor variables in the pool of potential X variables, find the four best subset regression models according to the adjusted R^2 criterion.

b. Since there is relatively little difference in R_a^2 for the four best subset models, what other criteria would you use to help in the selection of the best model? Discuss.

8.13. **Lung pressure.** Increased arterial blood pressure in the lungs frequently leads to the development of heart failure in patients with chronic obstructive pulmonary disease (COPD). The standard method for determining arterial lung pressure is invasive, technically difficult, and involves some risk to the patient. Radionuclide imaging is a noninvasive, less risky method for estimating arterial pressure in the lungs. To investigate the predictive ability of this method, a cardiologist collected data on 19 mild-to-moderate COPD patients. The data that follow on page 358 include the invasive measure of systolic pulmonary arterial pressure (Y) and three potential noninvasive predictor variables. Two were obtained by using radionuclide imaging—emptying rate of blood into the pumping chamber of the heart (X_1) and ejection rate of blood pumped out of the heart into the lungs (X_2)—and the third predictor variable measures a blood gas (X_3).

a. Prepare separate dot plots for each of the three predictor variables. Are there any noteworthy features in these plots? Comment.

b. Obtain the scatter plot matrix. Also obtain the correlation matrix of the X variables. What do the scatter plots suggest about the nature of the functional relationship between Y and each of the predictor variables? Are any serious multicollinearity problems evident? Explain.

c. Fit the multiple regression function containing the three predictor variables as first-order terms. Does it appear that all predictor variables should be retained?

Subject

i	X_{i1}	X_{i2}	X_{i3}	Y_i
1	45	36	45	49
2	30	28	40	55
3	11	16	42	85
...	...	...	...	...
17	27	51	44	29
18	37	32	54	40
19	34	40	36	31

Adapted from A. T. Marmor et al., "Improved Radionuclide Method for Assessment of Pulmonary Artery Pressure in COPD," *Chest* 89 (1986), pp. 64–69.

8.14. Refer to **Lung pressure** Problem 8.13.

a. Using first-order and second-order terms for each of the three predictor variables
(centered around the mean) in the pool of potential X variables (including cross
products of the first-order terms), find the three best hierarchical subset regression
models according to the R_a^2 criterion.

b. Is there much difference in R_a^2 for the three best subset models?

8.15. **Kidney function**. Creatinine clearance (Y) is an important measure of kidney function,
but is difficult to obtain in a clinical office setting because it requires 24-hour urine
collection. To determine whether this measure can be predicted from some data that are
easily available, a kidney specialist obtained the data that follow for 33 male subjects. The
predictor variables are serum creatinine concentration (X_1), age (X_2), and weight (X_3).

Subject

i	X_{i1}	X_{i2}	X_{i3}	Y_i
1	.71	38	71	132
2	1.48	78	69	53
3	2.21	69	85	50
...	...	...	...	...
30	.82	62	107	120
31	1.53	70	75	52
32	1.58	63	62	73
33	1.37	68	52	57

Adapted from W. J. Shih and S. Weisberg, "Assessing
Influence in Multiple Linear Regression with Incomplete
Data," *Technometrics* 28 (1986), pp. 231–40.

a. Prepare separate dot plots for each of the three predictor variables. Are there any
noteworthy features in these plots? Comment.

b. Obtain the scatter plot matrix. Also obtain the correlation matrix of the X variables.
What do the scatter plots suggest about the nature of the functional relationship
between the response variable Y and each predictor variable? Discuss. Are any serious
multicollinearity problems evident? Explain.

c. Fit the multiple regression function containing the three predictor variables as first-order terms. Does it appear that all predictor variables should be retained?

8.16. Refer to **Kidney function** Problem 8.15.

a. Using first-order and second-order terms for each of the three predictor variables (centered around the mean) in the pool of potential X variables (including cross products of the first-order terms), find the three best hierarchical subset regression models according to the R_a^2 criterion.

b. Is there much difference in R_a^2 for the three best subset models?

√ 8.17. Refer to **Patient satisfaction** Problems 6.15 and 8.8. The hospital administrator was interested to learn how the forward stepwise selection procedure and some of its variations would perform here.

a. Determine the subset of variables that is selected as best by the forward stepwise regression procedure, using F limits of 3.0 and 2.9 to add or delete a variable, respectively. Show your steps.

b. To what level of significance in any individual test is the F limit of 3.0 for adding a variable approximately equivalent here?

c. Determine the subset of variables that is selected as best by the forward selection procedure, using an F limit of 3.0 to add a variable. Show your steps.

d. Determine the subset of variables that is selected as best by the backward elimination procedure, using an F limit of 2.9 to delete a variable. Show your steps.

e. Compare the results of the three selection procedures. How consistent are these results? How do the results compare with those for all possible regressions in Problem 8.8?

√ 8.18. Refer to **Roofing shingles** Problems 8.9 and 8.10.

a. Using forward stepwise regression, find the best subset of predictor variables to predict sales. Use F limits for adding or deleting a variable of 4.0 and 3.9, respectively.

b. How does the best subset according to forward stepwise regression compare with the best subset according to the C_p criterion obtained in Problem 8.10a?

c. Suppose that variable X_1, because of its causal importance, is to be forced into the best subset by entering it first and not removing it even if its F^* value is too low. Which subset of variables (including X_1) is now selected as best by the forward stepwise regression procedure if F limits of 4.0 and 3.9 are used to add or delete a variable, respectively? Did the forced inclusion of X_1 affect the selection of the other variables in the best subset? Will this always happen?

8.19. Refer to **Job proficiency** Problems 8.11 and 8.12.

a. Using forward stepwise regression, find the best subset of predictor variables to predict job proficiency. Use F limits of 4.0 and 3.9 for adding or deleting a variable, respectively.

b. How does the best subset according to forward stepwise regression compare with the best subset according to the adjusted R^2 criterion obtained in Problem 8.12a?

8.20. Refer to **Kidney function** Problems 8.15 and 8.16.

a. Using the same pool of potential X variables as in Problem 8.16a, find the best subset of variables according to forward stepwise regression with F limits of 4.0 and 3.9 to add or delete a variable, respectively.

b. How does the best subset according to forward stepwise regression compare with the best subset according to the R_a^2 criterion obtained in Problem 8.16a?

Exercises

8.21. The true quadratic regression function is $E\{Y\} = 15 + 20X + 3X^2$. The fitted linear regression function is $\hat{Y} = 13 + 40X$, for which $E\{b_0\} = 10$ and $E\{b_1\} = 45$. What are the bias and sampling error components of the mean squared error for $X_i = 10$ and for $X_i = 20$?

8.22. Refer to (8.17). Show that the same variable X_k that maximizes the test statistic F_k^* also maximizes the coefficient of partial determination $r_{Yk.7}^2$.

Projects

8.23. Refer to the **SENIC** data set. Length of stay (Y) is to be predicted, and the pool of potential predictor variables includes all other variables in the data set except medical school affiliation and region. It is believed that a model with $\log_{10} Y$ as the response variable and the predictor variables in first-order terms with no interaction terms will be appropriate. Consider cases 57–113 to constitute the model-building data set to be used for the following analyses.

    a. Prepare separate dot plots for each of the predictor variables. Are there any noteworthy features in these plots? Comment.

    b. Obtain the scatter plot matrix. Also obtain the correlation matrix of the X variables. Is there evidence of strong linear pairwise associations among the predictor variables here?

    c. Obtain the three best subsets according to the C_p criterion. Which of these subset models appears to have the smallest bias?

8.24. Refer to the **SMSA** data set. A public safety official wishes to predict the rate of serious crimes in an SMSA (Y, total number of serious crimes per 100,000 population). The pool of potential predictor variables includes all other variables in the data set except total population and region. It is believed that a model with predictor variables in first-order terms with no interaction terms will be appropriate. Consider the even-numbered cases to constitute the model-building data set to be used for the following analyses.

    a. Prepare separate stem-and-leaf plots for each of the predictor variables. Are there any noteworthy features in these plots? Comment.

    b. Obtain the scatter plot matrix. Also obtain the correlation matrix of the X variables. Is there evidence of strong linear pairwise associations among the predictor variables here?

    c. Using the C_p criterion, obtain the three best subsets. Which of these subset models appears to have the smallest bias?

CHAPTER 9

Building the Regression Model II: Diagnostics

In this chapter we take up a number of refined diagnostics for checking the adequacy of a regression model. These include methods for detecting improper functional form for a predictor variable, outliers, influential observations, and multicollinearity. We conclude the chapter by illustrating the use of these diagnostic procedures in the surgical unit example. In the following chapter, we take up some remedial measures that are useful when the diagnostic procedures indicate model inadequacies.

9.1 Model Adequacy for a Predictor Variable—Partial Regression Plots

We discussed in Chapters 3 and 6 how a plot of residuals against a predictor variable in the regression model can be used to check whether a curvature effect for that variable is required in the model. We also described the plotting of residuals against predictor variables not yet in the regression model to determine whether it would be helpful to add one or more of these variables to the model.

A limitation of these residual plots is that they may not properly show the nature of the marginal effect of a predictor variable, given the other predictor variables in the model. *Partial regression plots*, also called *added variable plots* and *adjusted variable plots*, are refined residual plots that are another aid for identifying the nature of the marginal relation for a predictor variable X_k in the regression model, given the other predictor variables already in the model. In addition, partial regression plots provide graphic information about the marginal importance of a predictor variable that is to be added to the regression model.

Partial regression plots need to be used with caution for identifying the nature of the marginal effect of a predictor variable. These plots may not show the proper form of the marginal effect of a predictor variable if the functional relations for some or all of the predictor variables already in the regression model are misspecified. For example, if X_2 and X_3 are related in a curvilinear fashion to the response variable but the regression model uses linear terms only, the partial regression plots for X_2 and X_3 may not show the proper relationships to the response variable, especially when the predictor variables are correlated. Since partial regression plots for the several predictor variables are all concerned with marginal effects only, they may therefore not be effective when the relations of the predictor variables to the response variable are complex. Also, partial regression plots may not detect interaction effects that are present. Finally, high multicollinearity among the predictor variables may cause the partial regression plots to show an improper functional relation for the marginal effect of a predictor variable.

Partial regression plots are *partial* in the sense that they consider the marginal role of a predictor variable X_k, given that the other predictor variables under consideration are already in the model. In a partial regression plot, both the response variable Y and the predictor variable X_k under consideration are regressed against the other predictor variables in the regression model and the residuals are obtained for each. These residuals reflect the part of each variable that is not linearly associated with the other predictor variables already in the regression model. The plot of these residuals against each other (1) provides information about the nature of the marginal regression relation for the predictor variable X_k under consideration for possible inclusion in the regression model and (2) shows the marginal importance of this variable in reducing the residual variability.

To make these ideas more specific, we consider a first-order multiple regression model with two predictor variables X_1 and X_2. The extension to more than two predictor variables is direct. Suppose we are concerned about the nature of the regression effect for X_1, given that X_2 is already in the model. We regress Y on X_2 and obtain the fitted values and residuals:

(9.1a)
$$\hat{Y}_i(X_2) = b_0 + b_2 X_{i2}$$

(9.1b)
$$e_i(Y|X_2) = Y_i - \hat{Y}_i(X_2)$$

The notation here indicates explicitly the response and predictor variables in the fitted model. We also regress X_1 on X_2 and obtain:

(9.2a)
$$\hat{X}_{i1}(X_2) = b_0^* + b_2^* X_{i2}$$

(9.2b)
$$e_i(X_1|X_2) = X_{i1} - \hat{X}_{i1}(X_2)$$

The partial regression plot for predictor variable X_1 consists of a plot of the Y residuals $e(Y|X_2)$ against the X_1 residuals $e(X_1|X_2)$.

Figure 9.1 contains several prototype partial regression plots for our example, where X_2 is already in the regression model and X_1 is under consideration to be added. Figure 9.1a shows a horizontal band, indicating that X_1 contains no additional information useful for predicting Y beyond that contained in X_2, so that it is not helpful to add X_1 to the regression model here.

Figure 9.1b shows a linear band with a nonzero slope. This plot indicates that a linear term in X_1 may be a helpful addition to the regression model already containing X_2. It can be shown that the slope of the least squares line through the origin fitted to the plotted residuals is b_1, the regression coefficient of X_1 if this variable were added to the regression model already containing X_2.

Figure 9.1c shows a curvilinear band, indicating that the addition of X_1 to the regression model may be helpful and suggesting the possible nature of the curvature effect by the pattern shown.

Partial regression plots, in addition to providing information about the possible nature of the marginal relationship for a predictor variable, given the other predictor variables already in the regression model, also provide information about the strength of this relationship. To see how this additional information is provided, consider Figure 9.2. Figure 9.2a illustrates a partial regression plot for X_1 when X_2 is already in the model, based on

FIGURE 9.1   **Prototype Partial Regression Plots.**

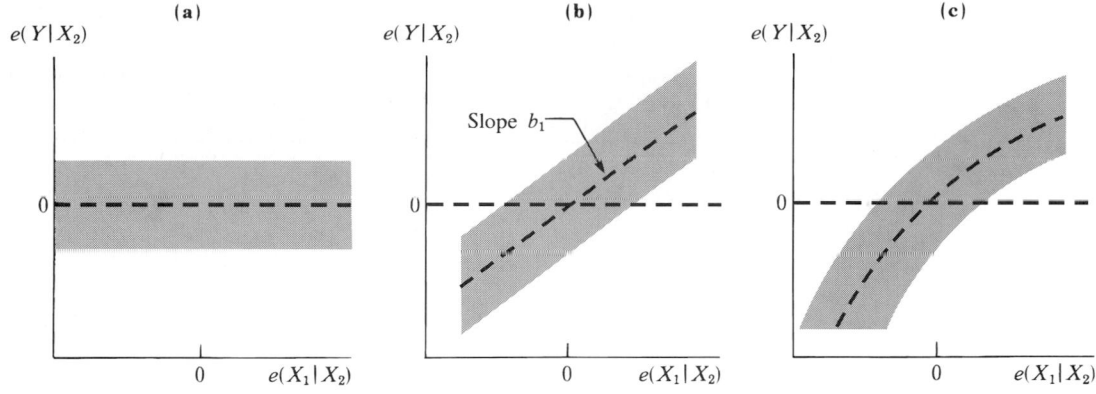

FIGURE 9.2   **Illustration of Deviations in a Partial Regression Plot.**

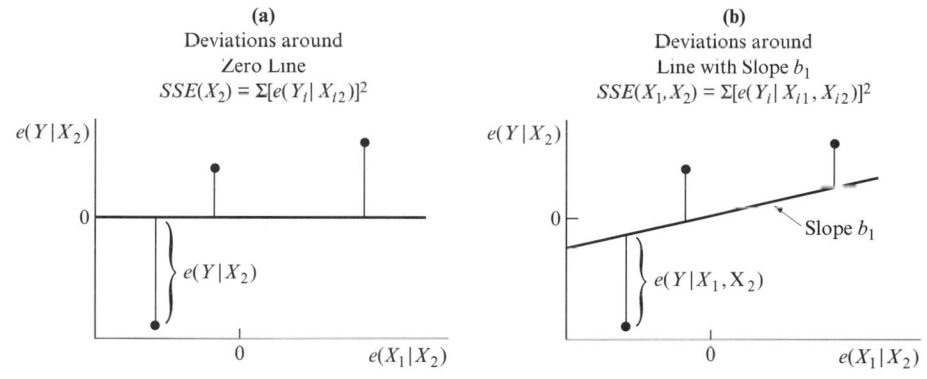

$n = 3$ cases. The vertical deviations of the plotted points around the horizontal line $e(Y|X_2) = 0$ shown in Figure 9.2a represent the Y residuals when X_2 alone is in the regression model. When these deviations are squared and summed, we obtain the error sum of squares $SSE(X_2)$. Figure 9.2b shows the same plotted points, but here the vertical deviations of these points are around the least squares line through the origin with slope b_1. These deviations are the residuals $e(Y|X_1, X_2)$ when both X_1 and X_2 are in the regression model. Hence, the sum of the squares of these deviations is the error sum of squares $SSE(X_1, X_2)$.

The difference between the two sums of squared deviations in Figures 9.2a and 9.2b according to (7.1a) is the extra sum of squares $SSR(X_1|X_2)$. Hence, the difference in the magnitudes of the two sets of deviations provides information about the marginal strength of the linear relation of X_1 to the response variable, given that X_2 is in the model. If the scatter of the points around the line through the origin with slope b_1 is much less than the scatter around the horizontal line, inclusion of the variable X_1 in the regression model will provide a substantial further reduction in the error sum of squares.

TABLE 9.1   **Basic Data—Life Insurance Example.**

Manager i	Average Annual Income (thousand dollars) X_{i1}	Risk Aversion Score X_{i2}	Amount of Life Insurance Carried (thousand dollars) Y_i
1	45.010	6	91
2	57.204	4	162
3	26.852	5	11
...	...	...	...
16	46.130	4	91
17	30.366	3	14
18	39.060	5	63

Partial regression plots are also useful for uncovering outlying data points that may have a strong influence in estimating the relationship of the predictor variable X_k to the response variable, given the other predictor variables already in the model.

Example 1

Table 9.1 shows a portion of the data on average annual income of managers during the past two years (X_1), a score measuring each manager's risk aversion (X_2), and the amount of life insurance carried (Y) for a sample of 18 managers in the 30–39 age group. Risk aversion was measured by a standard questionnaire administered to each manager: the higher the score, the greater the degree of risk aversion. Income and risk aversion are mildly correlated here, the coefficient of correlation being $r_{12} = .254$.

A fit of the first-order regression model yields:

$$(9.3) \qquad \hat{Y} = -205.72 + 6.2880X_1 + 4.738X_2$$

The residuals for this fitted model are plotted against X_1 in Figure 9.3a. This residual plot clearly suggests that a linear relation for X_1 is not appropriate in the model already containing X_2. To obtain more information about the nature of this relationship, we shall use a partial regression plot. We regress Y and X_1 each against X_2. When doing this, we obtain:

$$(9.4a) \qquad \hat{Y}(X_2) = 50.70 + 15.54X_2$$

$$(9.4b) \qquad \hat{X}_1(X_2) = 40.779 + 1.718X_2$$

The residuals from these two fitted models are plotted against each other in the partial regression plot in Figure 9.3b. This plot also contains the least squares line through the origin, which has slope $b_1 = 6.2880$. The partial regression plot suggests that the curvilinear relation between Y and X_1 when X_2 is already in the regression model is strongly positive, and that a slight concave upward shape may be present. The suggested concavity of the relationship is also evident from the vertical deviations around the line through the origin with slope b_1. These deviations are positive at the left, negative in the middle, and positive

FIGURE 9.3   **Residual Plot and Partial Regression Plot—Life Insurance Example.**

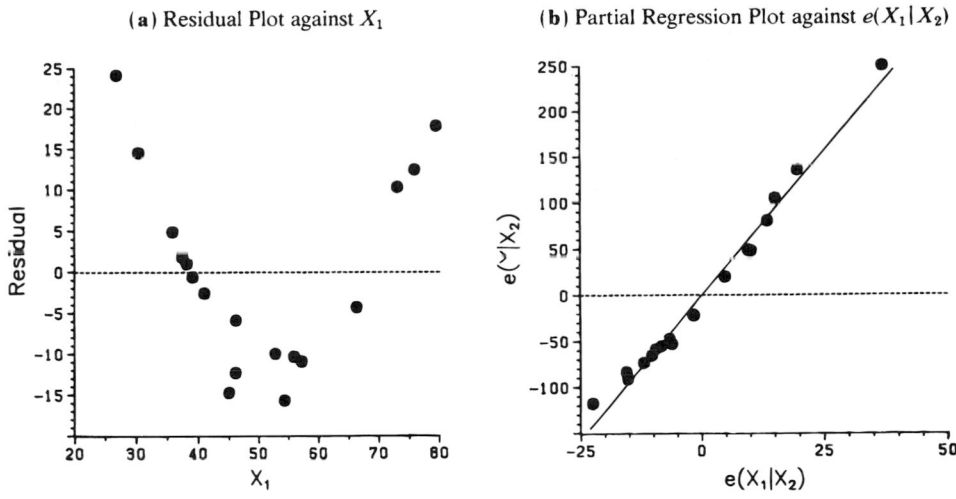

(**a**) Residual Plot against X_1

(**b**) Partial Regression Plot against $e(X_1|X_2)$

again at the right. Overall, the deviations from linearity appear to be modest in the range of the predictor variables.

Note also that the scatter of the points around the least squares line through the origin with slope $b_1 = 6.2880$ is much smaller than is the scatter around the horizontal line $e(Y|X_2) = 0$, indicating that adding X_1 to the regression model with a linear relation will substantially reduce the error sum of squares. In fact, the coefficient of partial determination for the linear effect of X_1 is $r_{Y1.2}^2 = .984$. Incorporating a curvilinear effect for X_1 will lead to only a modest further reduction in the error sum of squares since the plotted points are already quite close to the linear relation through the origin with slope b_1.

Finally, the partial regression plot in Figure 9.3b shows one outlying case, in the upper right corner. The influence of this case needs to be investigated by procedures to be explained later in this chapter.

Example 2

For the body fat example in Table 7.1 (page 261), we consider here the regression of body fat (Y) only on triceps skinfold thickness (X_1) and thigh circumference (X_2). We omit the third predictor variable (X_3, midarm circumference) to focus the discussion of partial regression plots on its essentials. Recall that X_1 and X_2 are highly correlated ($r_{12} = .92$). The fitted regression function was obtained in Table 7.2c (page 263):

$$\hat{Y} = -19.174 + .2224X_1 + .6594X_2$$

Figures 9.4a and 9.4c contain plots of the residuals against X_1 and X_2, respectively. These plots do not indicate any lack of fit for the linear terms in the regression model or the existence of unequal variances of the error terms.

Figures 9.4b and 9.4d contain the partial regression plots for X_1 and X_2, respectively, when the other predictor variable is already in the regression model. Both plots also show the line through the origin with slope equal to the regression coefficient for the predictor

FIGURE 9.4   Residual Plots and Partial Regression Plots—Body Fat Example with Two Predictor Variables.

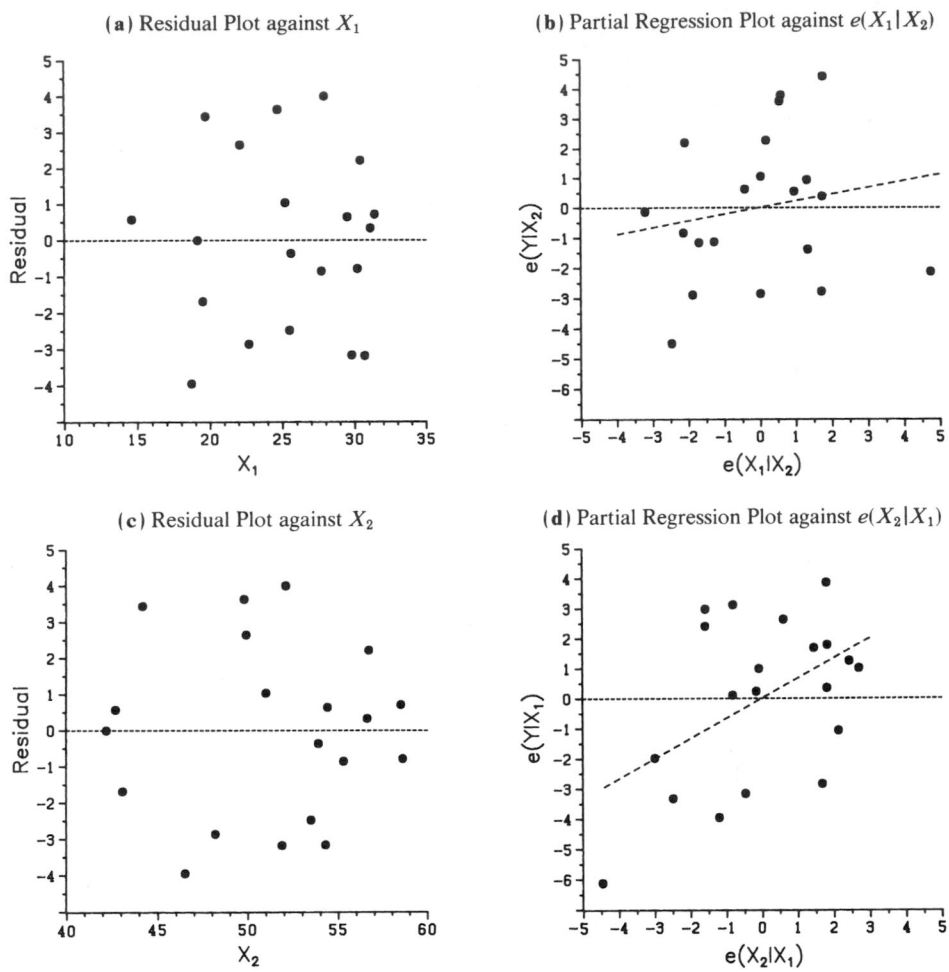

variable if it were added to the fitted model. These two plots provide some useful additional information. The scatter in Figure 9.4b follows the prototype in Figure 9.1a, suggesting that X_1 is of little additional help in the model when X_2 is already present. This information is not provided by the regular residual plot in Figure 9.4a. The fact that X_1 appears to be of little marginal help when X_2 is already in the regression model is in accord with earlier findings in Chapter 7. We saw there that the coefficient of partial determination is only $r_{Y1.2}^2 = .031$ and that the t^* statistic for b_1 is only .73.

The partial regression plot for X_2 in Figure 9.4d follows the prototype in Figure 9.1b, showing a linear scatter with positive slope. We also see in Figure 9.4d that there is somewhat less variability around the line with slope b_2 than around the horizontal line $e(Y|X_1) = 0$. This suggests that: (1) Variable X_2 may be helpful in the regression model even when X_1 is already in the model. (2) A linear term in X_2 appears to be adequate because no curvilinear relation is suggested by the scatter of points. Thus, the partial regression plot for X_2 in Figure 9.4d complements the regular residual plot in Figure 9.4c by indicating the potential usefulness of thigh circumference (X_2) in the regression model when triceps skinfold thickness (X_1) is already in the model. This information is consistent with the t^* statistic for b_2 of 2.26 in Table 7.2c and the moderate coefficient of partial determination of $r^2_{Y2.1} = .232$. Finally, the partial regression plot in Figure 9.4d reveals the presence of one potentially influential case (case 3) in the lower left corner. The influence of this case will be investigated in greater detail in Section 9.4.

Comments

1. A partial regression plot only suggests the nature of the functional relation in which a predictor variable should be added to the regression model but does not provide an analytic expression of the relation. Furthermore, the relation shown is for X_k adjusted for the other predictor variables in the regression model, not for X_k directly. Hence, a variety of transformations or curvature effect terms may need to be investigated and additional residual plots utilized to identify the best transformation or curvature effect terms.

2. When several partial regression plots are required for a set of predictor variables, it is not necessary to fit entirely new regression models each time. Computational procedures are available that economize on the calculations required; these are explained in specialized texts such as Reference 9.1.

3. Any fitted multiple regression function can be obtained from a sequence of fitted partial regressions. To illustrate this, consider again the life insurance example, where the fitted regression of Y on X_2 is given in (9.4a) and the fitted regression of X_1 on X_2 is given in (9.4b). If we now regress the residuals $e(Y|X_2) = Y - \hat{Y}(X_2)$ on the residuals $e(X_1|X_2) = X_1 - \hat{X}_1(X_2)$, using regression through the origin, we obtain (calculations not shown):

$$(9.5) \qquad \widehat{e(Y|X_2)} = 6.2880[e(X_1|X_2)]$$

By simple substitution, using (9.4a) and (9.4b), we obtain:

$$[Y - (50.70 + 15.54X_2)] = 6.2880[X_1 - (40.779 + 1.718X_2)]$$

or:

$$(9.6) \qquad \hat{Y} = \quad 205.72 + 6.2880X_1 + 4.737X_2$$

where the solution for Y is the fitted value $\hat{Y}$ when X_1 and X_2 are included in the regression model. Note that the fitted regression function in (9.6) is the same as when the regression model was fitted to X_1 and X_2 directly in (9.3), except for a minor difference due to rounding effects.

4. A residual plot closely related to the partial regression plot is the *partial residual plot*. This plot also is used as an aid for identifying the nature of the relationship for a predictor variable X_k under consideration for addition to the regression model. The partial residual plot takes as the starting point the usual residuals $e_i = Y_i - \hat{Y}_i$ when the model including X_k is fitted, to which the regression effect for X_k is added. Specifically, the partial residuals for examining the effect of predictor variable X_k, denoted by $p_i(X_k)$, are defined as follows:

$$(9.7) \qquad p_i(X_k) = e_i + b_k X_{ik}$$

Thus, for a partial residual, we add the effect of X_k, as reflected by the fitted model term $b_k X_{ik}$,

FIGURE 9.5   **Scatter Plot for Regression with One Predictor Variable Illustrating Outlying Cases.**

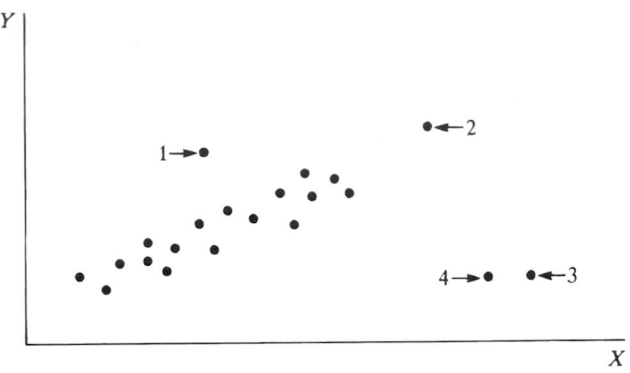

back onto the residual. A plot of these partial residuals against X_k is referred to as a partial residual plot. The reader is referred to References 9.2 and 9.3 for more details on partial residual plots.   ∎

9.2   Identifying Outlying Y Observations—Studentized Deleted Residuals

Outlying Cases

Frequently in regression analysis applications, the data set contains some cases that are outlying or extreme; that is, the observations for these cases are well separated from the remainder of the data. These outlying cases may involve large residuals and often have dramatic effects on the fitted least squares regression function. It is therefore important to study the outlying cases carefully and decide whether they should be retained or eliminated, and if retained, whether their influence should be reduced in the fitting process and/or the regression model should be revised.

A case may be outlying or extreme with respect to its Y value, its X value(s), or both. Figure 9.5 illustrates this for the case of regression with a single predictor variable. In the scatter plot in Figure 9.5, case 1 is outlying with respect to its Y value. Note that this point falls far outside the scatter, although its X value is near the middle of the range of observations on the predictor variable. Cases 2, 3, and 4 are outlying with respect to their X values since they have much larger X values than those for the other cases; cases 3 and 4 are also outlying with respect to their Y values.

Not all outlying cases have a strong influence on the fitted regression function. Case 1 in Figure 9.5 may not be too influential because a number of other cases have similar X values that will keep the fitted regression function from being displaced too far by the outlying case. Likewise, case 2 may not be too influential because its Y value is consistent with the regression relation displayed by the nonextreme cases. Cases 3 and 4, on the other hand, are likely to be very influential in affecting the fit of the regression function. They are outlying with regard to their X values, and their Y values are not consistent with the regression relation for the other cases.

A basic step in any regression analysis is to determine if the regression model under consideration is heavily influenced by one or a few cases in the data set. For regression with one or two predictor variables, it is relatively simple to identify outlying cases with respect to their X or Y values by means of box plots, stem-and-leaf plots, scatter plots, and residual plots, and to study whether they are influential in affecting the fitted regression function. When more than two predictor variables are included in the regression model, however, the identification of outlying cases by simple graphic means becomes difficult because single-variable or two-variable examinations do not necessarily help find outliers relative to a multivariable regression model. Some univariate outliers may not be extreme in a multiple regression model, and, conversely, some multivariable outliers may not be detectable in single-variable or two-variable analyses.

We now discuss the use of some refined measures for identifying cases with outlying Y observations. In the following section we take up the identification of cases that are multivariable outliers with respect to their X values.

Residuals and Semistudentized Residuals

The detection of outlying or extreme Y observations based on an examination of the residuals has been considered in earlier chapters. We utilized there either the residual e_i:

$$(9.8) \qquad\qquad e_i = Y_i - \hat{Y}_i$$

or the semistudentized residuals e_i^*:

$$(9.9) \qquad\qquad e_i^* = \frac{e_i}{\sqrt{MSE}}$$

We introduce now two refinements to make the analysis of residuals more effective for identifying outlying Y observations. These refinements require the use of the hat matrix, which we encountered in Chapters 5 and 6.

Hat Matrix

The hat matrix was defined in (6.30a):

$$(9.10) \qquad\qquad \underset{n \times n}{\mathbf{H}} = \mathbf{X}(\mathbf{X'X})^{-1}\mathbf{X'}$$

We noted in (6.30) that the fitted values $\hat{Y}_i$ can be expressed as linear combinations of the observations Y_i through the hat matrix:

$$(9.11) \qquad\qquad \hat{\mathbf{Y}} = \mathbf{HY}$$

and similarly we noted in (6.31) that the residuals e_i can also be expressed as linear combinations of the observations Y_i by means of the hat matrix:

$$(9.12) \qquad\qquad \mathbf{e} = (\mathbf{I} - \mathbf{H})\mathbf{Y}$$

Further, we noted in (6.32) that the variance-covariance matrix of the residuals involves the hat matrix:

$$\text{(9.13)} \qquad \boldsymbol{\sigma}^2\{\mathbf{e}\} = \sigma^2(\mathbf{I} - \mathbf{H})$$

Therefore, the variance of residual e_i, denoted by $\sigma^2\{e_i\}$, is:

$$\text{(9.14)} \qquad \sigma^2\{e_i\} = \sigma^2(1 - h_{ii})$$

where h_{ii} is the ith element on the main diagonal of the hat matrix, and the covariance between residuals e_i and e_j $(i \neq j)$ is:

$$\text{(9.15)} \qquad \sigma\{e_i, e_j\} = \sigma^2(0 - h_{ij}) = -h_{ij}\sigma^2 \qquad i \neq j$$

where h_{ij} is the element in the ith row and jth column of the hat matrix.

These variances and covariances are estimated by using *MSE* as the estimator of the error variance σ^2:

$$\text{(9.16a)} \qquad s^2\{e_i\} = MSE(1 - h_{ii})$$

$$\text{(9.16b)} \qquad s\{e_i, e_j\} = -h_{ij}(MSE) \qquad i \neq j$$

We shall illustrate these different roles of the hat matrix by an example.

Example.   A small data set based on $n = 4$ cases for examining the regression relation between a response variable Y and two predictor variables X_1 and X_2 is shown in Table 9.2a, columns 1–3. The fitted first-order model and the error mean square are:

$$\text{(9.17)} \qquad \hat{Y} = 80.93 - 5.84X_1 + 11.32X_2$$

$$MSE = 574.9$$

The fitted values and the residuals for the four cases are shown in columns 4 and 5 of Table 9.2a.

The hat matrix for these data is shown in Table 9.2b. It was obtained by means of (9.10), based on the $\mathbf{X}$ matrix:

$$\mathbf{X} = \begin{bmatrix} 1 & 14 & 25 \\ 1 & 19 & 32 \\ 1 & 12 & 22 \\ 1 & 11 & 15 \end{bmatrix}$$

Note from (9.10) that the hat matrix is solely a function of the predictor variable(s). Also note from Table 9.2b that the hat matrix is symmetric. The diagonal elements h_{ii} of the hat matrix are repeated in column 6 of Table 9.2a.

We illustrate that the fitted values are linear combinations of the Y values by calculating $\hat{Y}_1$ by means of (9.11):

$$\hat{Y}_1 = h_{11}Y_1 + h_{12}Y_2 + h_{13}Y_3 + h_{14}Y_4$$

$$= .3877(301) + .1727(327) + .4553(246) - .0157(187)$$

$$= 282.2$$

TABLE 9.2   Illustration of Hat Matrix.

(a) Data and Basic Results

i	(1) X_{i1}	(2) X_{i2}	(3) Y_i	(4) $\hat{Y}_i$	(5) e_i	(6) h_{ii}	(7) $s^2\{e_i\}$
1	14	25	301	282.2	18.8	.3877	352.0
2	19	32	327	332.3	−5.3	.9513	28.0
3	12	22	246	260.0	−14.0	.6614	194.6
4	11	15	187	186.5	.5	.9996	.2

(b) H

$$\begin{bmatrix} .3877 & .1727 & .4553 & -.0157 \\ .1727 & .9513 & -.1284 & .0044 \\ .4553 & -.1284 & .6614 & .0117 \\ -.0157 & .0044 & .0117 & .9996 \end{bmatrix}$$

(c) $s^2\{e\}$

$$\begin{bmatrix} 352.0 & -99.3 & -261.8 & 9.0 \\ -99.3 & 28.0 & 73.8 & -2.5 \\ -261.8 & 73.8 & 194.6 & -6.7 \\ 9.0 & -2.5 & -6.7 & .2 \end{bmatrix}$$

This is the same result, except for possible rounding effects, as obtained from the fitted regression function (9.17):

$$\hat{Y}_1 = 80.93 - 5.84(14) + 11.32(25) = 282.2$$

The estimated variance-covariance matrix of the residuals, $s^2\{e\} = MSE(\mathbf{I} - \mathbf{H})$, is shown in Table 9.2c. It was obtained by using $MSE = 574.9$. The estimated variances of the residuals are shown in the main diagonal of the variance-covariance matrix in Table 9.2c and are repeated in column 7 of Table 9.2a. We illustrate their direct calculation for case 1 by using (9.16a):

$$s^2\{e_1\} = 574.9(1 - .3877) = 352.0$$

We see from Table 9.2a, column 7, that the residuals do not have constant variance. In fact, the variances differ greatly here because the data set is so small. As we shall note in Section 9.3, residuals for cases that are outlying with respect to the X variables have smaller variances.

Note also that the covariances in the matrix in Table 9.2c are not zero; hence, pairs of residuals are correlated, some positively and some negatively. We noted this correlation in Chapter 3, but also pointed out there that the correlations become very small for larger data sets.

Note

The diagonal element h_{ii} of the hat matrix can be obtained directly from:

(9.18) $$h_{ii} = \mathbf{X}'_i(\mathbf{X}'\mathbf{X})^{-1}\mathbf{X}_i$$

where:

(9.18a)

$$\underset{p \times 1}{\mathbf{X}_i} = \begin{bmatrix} 1 \\ X_{i,1} \\ \vdots \\ X_{i,p-1} \end{bmatrix}$$

Note that $\mathbf{X}_i$ corresponds to the $\mathbf{X}_h$ vector in (6.53) except that $\mathbf{X}_i$ pertains to the ith case, and that $\mathbf{X}_i'$ is simply the ith row of the $\mathbf{X}$ matrix, pertaining to the ith case.   ∎

Studentized Residuals

The first refinement in making residuals more effective for detecting outlying Y observations involves recognition of the fact that the residuals e_i may have substantially different variances $\sigma^2\{e_i\}$. It is therefore appropriate to consider the magnitude of each e_i relative to its estimated standard deviation to give recognition to differences in the sampling errors of the residuals. We see from (9.16a) that an estimator of the standard deviation of e_i is:

(9.19)
$$s\{e_i\} = \sqrt{MSE(1 - h_{ii})}$$

The ratio of e_i to $s\{e_i\}$ is called the *studentized residual* and will be denoted by r_i:

(9.20)
$$r_i = \frac{e_i}{s\{e_i\}}$$

While the residuals e_i will have substantially different sampling variations if their standard deviations differ markedly, the studentized residuals r_i have constant variance (when the model is appropriate). Studentized residuals often are called *internally studentized residuals*.

Deleted Residuals

The second refinement to make residuals more effective for detecting outlying Y observations is to measure the ith residual $e_i = Y_i - \hat{Y}_i$ when the fitted regression is based on all of the cases except the ith one. The reason for this refinement is that if Y_i is far outlying, the fitted least squares regression function based on all cases including the ith one may be influenced to come close to Y_i, yielding a fitted value $\hat{Y}_i$ near Y_i. In that event, the residual e_i will be small and will not disclose that Y_i is outlying. On the other hand, if the ith case is excluded before the regression function is fitted, the least squares fitted value $\hat{Y}_i$ is not influenced by the outlying Y_i observation, and the residual for the ith case will then tend to be larger and therefore more likely to disclose the outlying Y observation.

The procedure then is to delete the ith case, fit the regression function to the remaining $n - 1$ cases, and obtain the point estimate of the expected value when the X levels are those of the ith case, to be denoted by $\hat{Y}_{i(i)}$. The difference between the actual observed value Y_i and the estimated expected value $\hat{Y}_{i(i)}$ will be denoted by d_i:

(9.21)
$$d_i = Y_i - \hat{Y}_{i(i)}$$

The difference d_i is called the *deleted residual* for the ith case. We encountered this same difference in (8.14), where it was called the *PRESS* prediction error for the ith case.

An algebraically equivalent expression for d_i that does not require a recomputation of the fitted regression function omitting the ith case is:

$$(9.21a) \qquad\qquad d_i = \frac{e_i}{1 - h_{ii}}$$

where e_i is the ordinary residual for the ith case and h_{ii} is the ith diagonal element in the hat matrix, as given in (9.18). Note that the larger is the value h_{ii}, the larger will be the deleted residual as compared to the ordinary residual.

Thus, deleted residuals will at times identify outlying Y observations when ordinary residuals would not identify these; at other times deleted residuals lead to the same identifications as ordinary residuals.

Note that a deleted residual also corresponds to the prediction error for a new observation in the numerator of (2.35). There, we are predicting a new $n + 1$ observation from the fitted regression function based on the earlier n cases. Modifying the earlier notation for the context of deleted residuals, where $n - 1$ cases are used for predicting the "new" nth case, we can restate the result in (6.63a) to obtain the estimated variance of d_i:

$$(9.22) \qquad\qquad s^2\{d_i\} = MSE_{(i)}(1 + \mathbf{X}_i'(\mathbf{X}_{(i)}'\mathbf{X}_{(i)})^{-1}\mathbf{X}_i)$$

where $\mathbf{X}_i$ is the X observations vector (9.18a) for the ith case, $MSE_{(i)}$ is the mean square error when the ith case is omitted in fitting the regression function, and $\mathbf{X}_{(i)}$ is the $\mathbf{X}$ matrix with the ith case deleted. An algebraically equivalent expression for $s^2\{d_i\}$ is:

$$(9.22a) \qquad\qquad s^2\{d_i\} = \frac{MSE_{(i)}}{1 - h_{ii}}$$

It follows from (6.63) that:

$$(9.23) \qquad\qquad \frac{d_i}{s\{d_i\}} \sim t(n - p - 1)$$

Remember that $n - 1$ cases are used here in predicting the ith observation; hence, the degrees of freedom are $(n - 1) - p = n - p - 1$.

Studentized Deleted Residuals

Combining the above two refinements, we utilize for diagnosis of outlying or extreme Y observations the deleted residual d_i in (9.21) and studentize it by dividing it by its estimated standard deviation given by (9.22). The *studentized deleted residual*, denoted by t_i, therefore is:

$$(9.24) \qquad\qquad t_i = \frac{d_i}{s\{d_i\}}$$

It follows from (9.21a) and (9.22a) that an algebraically equivalent expression for t_i is:

$$(9.24a) \qquad\qquad t_i = \frac{e_i}{\sqrt{MSE_{(i)}(1 - h_{ii})}}$$

The studentized deleted residual t_i in (9.24) is also called an *externally studentized residual*, in contrast to the internally studentized residual r_i in (9.20). We know from (9.23) that each studentized deleted residual t_i follows the t distribution with $n - p - 1$ degrees of freedom. The t_i, however, are not independent.

Fortunately, the studentized deleted residuals t_i in (9.24) can be calculated without having to fit new regression functions each time a different case is omitted. A simple relationship exists between MSE and $MSE_{(i)}$:

$$(9.25) \qquad (n - p)MSE = (n - p - 1)MSE_{(i)} + \frac{e_i^2}{1 - h_{ii}}$$

Using this relationship in (9.24a) yields the following equivalent expression for t_i:

$$(9.26) \qquad t_i = e_i \left[\frac{n - p - 1}{SSE(1 - h_{ii}) - e_i^2} \right]^{1/2}$$

Thus, the studentized deleted residuals t_i can be calculated from the residuals e_i, the error sum of squares SSE, and the hat matrix values h_{ii}, all for the fitted regression based on the n cases.

Test for Outliers.   We identify as outlying Y observations those cases whose studentized deleted residuals are large in absolute value. In addition, we can conduct a formal test by means of the Bonferroni test procedure of whether the case with the largest absolute studentized deleted residual is an outlier. Since we do not know in advance which case will have the largest absolute value $|t_i|$, we consider the family of tests to include n tests, one for each case. If the regression model is appropriate, so that no case is outlying because of a change in the model, then each studentized deleted residual will follow the t distribution with $n - p - 1$ degrees of freedom. The appropriate Bonferroni critical value therefore is $t(1 - \alpha/2n; n - p - 1)$. Note that the test is two-sided since we are not concerned with the direction of the residuals but only with their absolute values.

Example.   For the body fat example with two predictor variables (X_1, X_2), we wish to examine whether there are outlying Y observations. Table 9.3 presents the residuals e_i in column 1, the diagonal elements h_{ii} of the hat matrix in column 2, and the studentized deleted residuals t_i in column 3. We illustrate the calculation of the studentized deleted residual for the first case. The X values for this case, given in Table 7.1, are $X_{11} = 19.5$ and $X_{12} = 43.1$. Using the fitted regression function from Table 7.2c, we obtain:

$$\hat{Y}_1 = -19.174 + .2224(19.5) + .6594(43.1) = 13.583$$

Since $Y_1 = 11.9$, the residual for this case is $e_1 = 11.9 - 13.583 = -1.683$. We also know from Table 7.2c that $SSE = 109.95$ and from Table 9.3 that $h_{11} = .201$. Hence, by (9.26), we find:

$$t_1 = -1.683 \left[\frac{20 - 3 - 1}{109.95(1 - .201) - (-1.683)^2} \right]^{1/2} = -.730$$

Note from Table 9.3, column 3, that cases 3, 8, and 13 have the largest absolute studentized deleted residuals. Incidentally, consideration of the residuals e_i (shown in

TABLE 9.3   **Residuals, Diagonal Elements of the Hat Matrix, and Studentized Deleted Residuals—Body Fat Example with Two Predictor Variables.**

	(1)	(2)	(3)
i	e_i	h_{ii}	t_i
1	−1.683	.201	−.730
2	3.643	.059	1.534
3	−3.176	.372	−1.656
4	3.158	.111	−1.348
5	.000	.248	.000
6	−.361	.129	−.148
7	.716	.156	.298
8	4.015	.096	1.760
9	2.655	.115	1.117
10	−2.475	.110	−1.034
11	.336	.120	.137
12	2.226	.109	.923
13	−3.947	.178	−1.825
14	3.447	.148	1.524
15	.571	.333	.267
16	.642	.095	.258
17	−.851	.106	.344
18	−.783	.197	.335
19	−2.857	.067	−1.176
20	1.040	.050	.409

Table 9.3, column 1) here would have identified cases 2, 8, and 13 as the most outlying ones, but not case 3.

We would like to test whether case 13, which has the largest absolute studentized deleted residual, is an outlier resulting from a change in the model. We shall use the Bonferroni simultaneous test procedure with a family significance level of $\alpha = .10$. We therefore require:

$$t(1 − \alpha/2n; n − p − 1) = t(.9975; 16) = 3.252$$

Since $|t_{13}| = 1.825 \leq 3.252$, we conclude that case 13 is not an outlier. Still, we might wish to investigate whether case 13 and perhaps a few other outlying cases are influential in determining the fitted regression function because the Bonferroni test is very conservative before it classifies a case as an outlier.

9.3   Identifying Outlying X Observations—Hat Matrix Leverage Values

Use of Hat Matrix for Identifying Outlying X Observations

The hat matrix, as we saw, plays an important role in determining the magnitude of a studentized deleted residual and therefore in identifying outlying Y observations. The hat

FIGURE 9.6   **Illustration of Leverage Values as Distance Measures—Table 9.2 Example.**

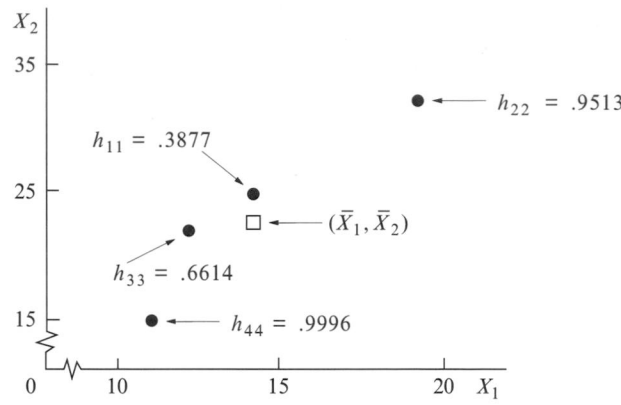

matrix also is helpful in directly identifying outlying X observations. In particular, the diagonal elements of the hat matrix are a useful indicator in a multivariable setting of whether or not a case is outlying with respect to its X values.

The diagonal elements h_{ii} of the hat matrix have some useful properties. In particular, their values are always between 0 and 1 and their sum is p:

$$(9.27) \qquad 0 \le h_{ii} \le 1 \qquad \sum_{i=1}^{n} h_{ii} = p$$

where p is the number of regression parameters in the regression function including the intercept term. In addition, it can be shown that h_{ii} is a measure of the distance between the X values for the ith case and the means of the X values for all n cases. Thus, a large value h_{ii} indicates that the ith case is distant from the center of all X observations. The diagonal element h_{ii} in this context is called the *leverage* (in terms of the X values) of the ith case.

Figure 9.6 illustrates the role of the leverage values h_{ii} as distance measures for our earlier example in Table 9.2. Figure 9.6 shows a scatter plot of X_2 against X_1 for the four cases, and the center of the four cases located at $(\bar{X}_1, \bar{X}_2)$. This center is called the *centroid*. Here, the centroid is $(\bar{X}_1 = 14.0, \bar{X}_2 = 23.5)$. In addition, Figure 9.6 shows the leverage value for each case. Note that cases 1 and 3, which are closest to the centroid, have the smallest leverage values, while cases 2 and 4, which are farthest from the center, have the largest leverage values. Note also that the four leverage values sum to $p = 3$.

If the ith case is outlying in terms of its X observations and therefore has a large leverage value h_{ii}, it exercises substantial leverage in determining the fitted value $\hat{Y}_i$. This is so for the following reasons:

1. The fitted value $\hat{Y}_i$ is a linear combination of the observed Y values, as shown by (9.11), and h_{ii} is the weight of observation Y_i in determining this fitted value. Thus, the larger is h_{ii}, the more important is Y_i in determining $\hat{Y}_i$. Remember that h_{ii} is a function only of the X values, so h_{ii} measures the role of the X values in determining how important Y_i is in affecting the fitted value $\hat{Y}_i$.

2. The larger is h_{ii}, the smaller is the variance of the residual e_i, as we noted earlier from (9.14). Hence, the larger is h_{ii}, the closer the fitted value $\hat{Y}_i$ will tend to be to the observed value Y_i. In the extreme case where $h_{ii} = 1$, the variance $\sigma^2\{e_i\}$ equals 0, so the fitted value $\hat{Y}_i$ is then forced to equal the observed value Y_i.

A leverage value h_{ii} is usually considered to be large if it is more than twice as large as the mean leverage value, denoted by $\bar{h}$, which according to (9.27) is:

$$(9.28) \qquad \bar{h} = \frac{\sum\limits_{i=1}^{n} h_{ii}}{n} = \frac{p}{n}$$

Hence, leverage values greater than $2p/n$ are considered by this rule to indicate outlying cases with regard to their X values. Another suggested guideline is that h_{ii} values exceeding .5 indicate very high leverage, whereas those between .2 and .5 indicate moderate leverage. Additional evidence of an outlying case is the existence of a gap between the leverage values for most of the cases and the unusually large leverage value(s).

The rules just mentioned for identifying cases that are outlying with respect to their X values are intended for data sets that are reasonably large, relative to the number of parameters in the regression function. They are not applicable, for instance, to the simple example in Table 9.2 where there are $n = 4$ cases and $p = 3$ parameters in the regression function. Here, the mean leverage value is $3/4 = .75$, and one cannot obtain a leverage value twice as large as the mean value since leverage values cannot exceed 1.0.

Example.   We continue with the body fat example of Table 7.1. We again use only the two predictor variables triceps skinfold thickness (X_1) and thigh circumference (X_2) so that the results using the hat matrix can be compared to simple graphic plots. Figure 9.7 contains a scatter plot of X_2 against X_1, where the data points are identified by their case number. We note from Figure 9.7 that cases 15 and 3 appear to be outlying ones with respect to the pattern of the X values. Case 15 is outlying for X_1 and at the low end of the range for X_2, whereas case 3 is outlying in terms of the pattern of multicollinearity, though it is not outlying for either of the predictor variables separately. Cases 1 and 5 also appear to be somewhat extreme.

Table 9.3, column 2, contains the leverage values h_{ii} for the body fat example. Note that the two largest leverage values are $h_{33} = .372$ and $h_{15,15} = .333$. Both exceed the criterion of twice the mean leverage value, $2p/n = 2(3)/20 = .30$, and both are separated by a substantial gap from the next largest leverage values, $h_{55} = .248$ and $h_{11} = .201$. Having identified cases 3 and 15 as outlying in terms of their X values, we shall need to ascertain how influential these cases are in the fitting of the regression function.

Use of Hat Matrix to Identify Hidden Extrapolation

We have seen that the hat matrix is useful in the model-building stage for identifying cases that are outlying with respect to their X values and that, therefore, may be influential in affecting the fitted model. The hat matrix is also useful after the model has been selected and fitted for determining whether an inference for a mean response or a new observation involves a substantial extrapolation beyond the range of the data. When there are only two predictor variables, it is easy to see from a scatter plot of X_2 against X_1 whether an inference for a particular (X_1, X_2) set of values is outlying beyond the range of the data,

FIGURE 9.7   **Scatter Plot of Thigh Circumference against Triceps Skinfold Thickness—Body Fat Example with Two Predictor Variables.**

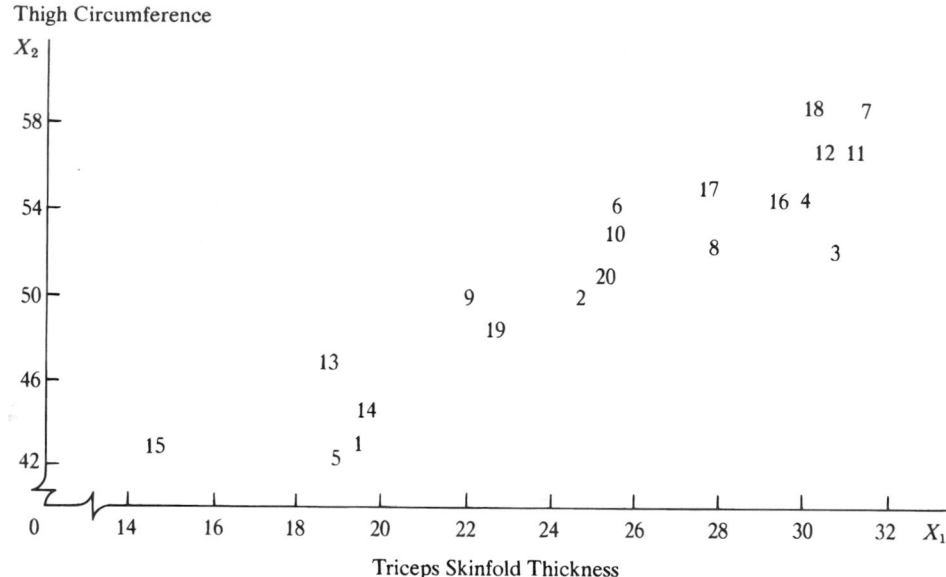

such as from Figure 9.7. This simple graphic analysis is no longer available with larger numbers of predictor variables, where extrapolations may be hidden.

To spot hidden extrapolations, we can utilize the direct leverage calculation in (9.18) for the new set of X values for which inferences are to be made:

$$(9.29) \qquad h_{\text{new,new}} = \mathbf{X}'_{\text{new}}(\mathbf{X}'\mathbf{X})^{-1}\mathbf{X}_{\text{new}}$$

where $\mathbf{X}_{\text{new}}$ is the vector containing the X values for which an inference about a mean response or a new observation is to be made, and the $\mathbf{X}$ matrix is the one based on the data set used for fitting the regression model. If $h_{\text{new,new}}$ is well within the range of leverage values h_{ii} for the cases in the data set, no extrapolation is involved. On the other hand, if $h_{\text{new,new}}$ is much larger than the leverage values for the cases in the data set, an extrapolation is indicated.

9.4   Identifying Influential Cases—*DFFITS*, Cook's Distance, and *DFBETAS* Measures

After identifying cases that are outlying with respect to their Y values and/or their X values, the next step is to ascertain whether or not these outlying cases are influential. We shall consider a case to be *influential* if its exclusion causes major changes in the fitted regression function. As noted in Figure 9.5, not all outlying cases need be influential. For example, case 1 in Figure 9.5 may not affect the fitted regression function to any substantial extent.

We take up three measures of influence that are widely used in practice, each based on the omission of a single case to measure its influence.

Influence on Single Fitted Value—DFFITS

A useful measure of the influence that case i has on the fitted value $\hat{Y}_i$ is given by:

$$(9.30) \qquad (DFFITS)_i = \frac{\hat{Y}_i - \hat{Y}_{i(i)}}{\sqrt{MSE_{(i)} h_{ii}}}$$

The letters DF stand for the difference between the fitted value $\hat{Y}_i$ for the ith case when all n cases are used in fitting the regression function and the predicted value $\hat{Y}_{i(i)}$ for the ith case obtained when the ith case is omitted in fitting the regression function. The denominator of (9.30) is the estimated standard deviation of $\hat{Y}_i$, but it uses the error mean square when the ith case is omitted in fitting the regression function for estimating the error variance σ^2. The denominator provides a standardization so that the value $(DFFITS)_i$ for the ith case represents the number of estimated standard deviations of $\hat{Y}_i$ that the fitted value $\hat{Y}_i$ increases or decreases with the inclusion of the ith case in fitting the regression model.

It can be shown that the $DFFITS$ values can be computed by using only the results from fitting the entire data set, as follows:

$$(9.30a) \qquad (DFFITS)_i = e_i \left[\frac{n - p - 1}{SSE(1 - h_{ii}) - e_i^2} \right]^{1/2} \left(\frac{h_{ii}}{1 - h_{ii}} \right)^{1/2} = t_i \left(\frac{h_{ii}}{1 - h_{ii}} \right)^{1/2}$$

Note from the last expression that the $DFFITS$ value for the ith case is a studentized deleted residual, as given in (9.26), increased or decreased by a factor that is a function of the leverage value for this case. If case i is an X outlier and has a high leverage value, this factor will be greater than 1 and $(DFFITS)_i$ will tend to be large absolutely.

As a guideline for identifying influential cases, we suggest considering a case influential if the absolute value of $DFFITS$ exceeds 1 for small to medium data sets and $2\sqrt{p/n}$ for large data sets.

Example.   Table 9.4, column 1, lists the $DFFITS$ values for the body fat example with two predictor variables. To illustrate the calculations, consider the $DFFITS$ value for case 3, which was identified as outlying with respect to its X values. From Table 9.3, we know that the studentized deleted residual for this case is $t_3 = -1.656$ and the leverage value is $h_{33} = .372$. Hence, using (9.30a) we obtain:

$$(DFFITS)_3 = -1.656 \left(\frac{.372}{1 - .372} \right)^{1/2} = -1.27$$

The only $DFFITS$ value in Table 9.4 that exceeds our guideline for a medium-size data set is for case 3, where $|(DFFITS)_3| = 1.273$. This value is somewhat larger than our guideline of 1. However, the value is close enough to 1 that the case may not be influential enough to require remedial action.

Note

The estimated variance of $\hat{Y}_i$ used in the denominator of (9.30) is developed from the relation $\hat{\mathbf{Y}} = \mathbf{HY}$ in (9.11). Using (5.46), we obtain:

$$\sigma^2\{\hat{\mathbf{Y}}\} = \mathbf{H}\sigma^2\{\mathbf{Y}\}\mathbf{H}' = \mathbf{H}(\sigma^2\mathbf{I})\mathbf{H}'$$

TABLE 9.4 *DFFITS*, Cook's Distances, and *DFBETAS*—Body Fat Example with Two Predictor Variables.

	(1)	(2)	(3)	(4) DFBETAS	(5)
i	$(DFFITS)_i$	D_i	b_0	b_1	b_2
1	−.366	.046	−.305	−.132	.232
2	.384	.046	.173	.115	−.143
3	−1.273	.490	−.847	−1.183	1.067
4	−.476	.072	−.102	−.294	.196
5	.000	.000	.000	.000	.000
6	−.057	.001	.040	.040	−.044
7	.128	.006	−.078	−.016	.054
8	.575	.098	.261	.391	−.333
9	.402	.053	−.151	−.295	.247
10	−.364	.044	.238	.245	−.269
11	.051	.001	−.009	.017	−.003
12	.323	.035	−.131	.023	.070
13	−.851	.212	.119	.592	−.390
14	.636	.125	.452	.113	−.298
15	.189	.013	−.003	−.125	.069
16	.084	.002	.009	.043	−.025
17	−.118	.005	.080	.055	−.076
18	−.166	.010	.132	.075	−.116
19	−.315	.032	−.130	−.004	.064
20	.094	.003	.010	.002	−.003

Since **H** is a symmetric matrix, so $\mathbf{H}' = \mathbf{H}$, and it is also idempotent, so $\mathbf{HH} = \mathbf{H}$, we obtain:

$$(9.31) \qquad \sigma^2\{\hat{\mathbf{Y}}\} = \sigma^2\mathbf{H}$$

Hence, the variance of $\hat{Y}_i$ is:

$$(9.32) \qquad \sigma^2\{\hat{Y}_i\} = \sigma^2 h_{ii}$$

where h_{ii} is the ith diagonal element of the hat matrix. The error term variance σ^2 is estimated in (9.30) by the error mean square $MSE_{(i)}$ obtained when the ith case is omitted in fitting the regression model. ∎

Influence on All Fitted Values—Cook's Distance

In contrast to the *DFFITS* measure in (9.30), which considers the influence of the ith case on the fitted value $\hat{Y}_i$ for this case, Cook's distance measure considers the influence of the ith case on all n fitted values. Cook's distance measure, denoted by D_i, is an aggregate influence measure, showing the effect of the ith case on all n fitted values:

$$(9.33) \qquad D_i = \frac{\sum\limits_{j=1}^{n} (\hat{Y}_j - \hat{Y}_{j(i)})^2}{pMSE}$$

Note that the numerator involves similar differences as in the *DFFITS* measure, but here each of the n fitted values $\hat{Y}_j$ is compared with the corresponding fitted value $\hat{Y}_{j(i)}$ when the ith case is deleted in fitting the regression model. These differences are then squared and summed, so that the aggregate influence of the ith case is measured without regard to the signs of the effects. Finally, the denominator serves as a standardizing measure. In matrix terms, Cook's distance measure can be expressed as follows:

(9.33a)
$$D_i = \frac{(\hat{\mathbf{Y}} - \hat{\mathbf{Y}}_{(i)})'(\hat{\mathbf{Y}} - \hat{\mathbf{Y}}_{(i)})}{p\,MSE}$$

Here, $\hat{\mathbf{Y}}$ as usual is the vector of the fitted values when all n cases are used for the regression fit and $\hat{\mathbf{Y}}_{(i)}$ is the vector of the fitted values when the ith case is deleted.

For interpreting Cook's distance measure, it has been found useful to relate D_i to the $F(p, n - p)$ distribution and ascertain the corresponding percentile value. If the percentile value is less than about 10 or 20 percent, the ith case has little apparent influence on the fitted values. If, on the other hand, the percentile value is near 50 percent or more, the fitted values obtained with and without the ith case should be considered to differ substantially, implying that the ith case has a major influence on the fit of the regression function.

Fortunately, Cook's distance measure D_i can be calculated without fitting a new regression function each time a different case is deleted. An algebraically equivalent expression is:

(9.33b)
$$D_i = \frac{e_i^2}{p\,MSE}\left[\frac{h_{ii}}{(1 - h_{ii})^2}\right]$$

Note from (9.33b) that D_i depends on two factors: (1) the size of the residual e_i and (2) the leverage value h_{ii}. The larger either e_i or h_{ii} is, the larger D_i is. Thus, the ith case can be influential: (1) by having a large residual e_i and only a moderate leverage value h_{ii}, or (2) by having a large leverage value h_{ii} with only a moderately sized residual e_i, or (3) by having both a large residual e_i and a large leverage value h_{ii}.

Example.   For the body fat example with two predictor variables, Table 9.4, column 2, presents the D_i values. To illustrate the calculations, we consider again case 3, which is outlying with regard to its X values. We know from Table 9.3 that $e_3 = -3.176$ and $h_{33} = .372$. Further, $MSE = 6.47$ according to Table 7.2c and $p = 3$ for the model with two predictor variables. Hence, we obtain:

$$D_3 = \frac{(-3.176)^2}{3(6.47)}\left[\frac{.372}{(1 - .372)^2}\right] = .490$$

We note from Table 9.4, column 2 that case 3 clearly has the largest D_i value, with the next largest distance measure $D_{13} = .212$ being substantially smaller. Figure 9.8 presents the information provided by Cook's distance measure about the influence of each case in two different plots. Shown in Figure 9.8a is a proportional influence plot of the residuals e_i against the corresponding fitted values $\hat{Y}_i$, the size of the plotted points being proportional to Cook's distance measure D_i. Figure 9.8b presents the information about the Cook's distance measures in the form of an index influence plot, where Cook's distance measure D_i is plotted against the corresponding case index i. Both plots in Figure 9.8 clearly show that one case stands out as most influential (case 3) and that all the other cases are much less

FIGURE 9.8   **Proportional Influence Plot (Points Porportional in Size to Cook's Distance Measure) and Index Influence Plot—Body Fat Example with Two Predictor Variables.**

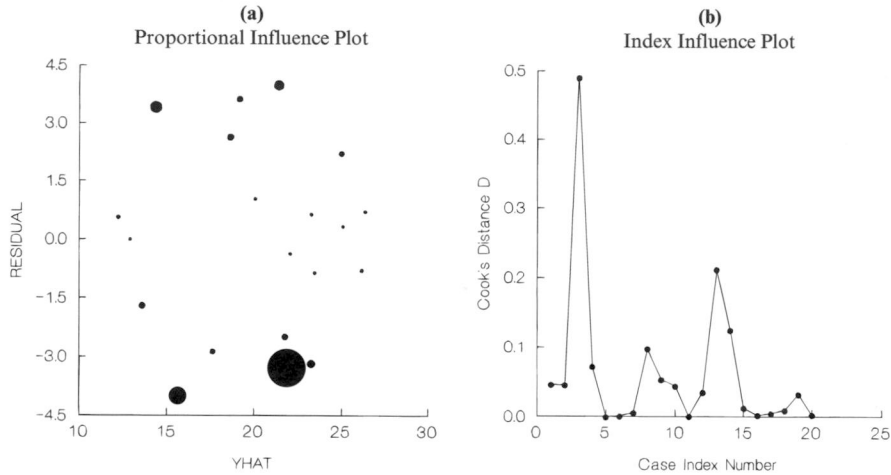

(a)
Proportional Influence Plot

(b)
Index Influence Plot

influential. The proportional influence plot in Figure 9.8a shows that the residual for the most influential case is large negative, but does not identify the case. The index influence plot in Figure 9.8b, on the other hand, identifies the most influential case as case 3 but does not provide any information about the magnitude of the residual for this case.

To assess the magnitude of the influence of case 3 ($D_3 = .490$), we refer to the corresponding F distribution, namely, $F(p, n - p) = F(3, 17)$. We find that .490 is the 30.6th percentile of this distribution. Hence, it appears that case 3 does influence the regression fit, but the extent of the influence may not be large enough to call for consideration of remedial measures.

Influence on the Regression Coefficients—DFBETAS

A measure of the influence of the ith case on each regression coefficient b_k ($k = 0, 1, \ldots, p - 1$) is the difference between the estimated regression coefficient b_k based on all n cases and the regression coefficient obtained when the ith case is omitted, to be denoted by $b_{k(i)}$. When this difference is divided by an estimate of the standard deviation of b_k, we obtain the measure *DFBETAS*:

$$(9.34) \qquad (DFBETAS)_{k(i)} = \frac{b_k - b_{k(i)}}{\sqrt{MSE_{(i)} c_{kk}}} \qquad k = 0, 1, \ldots, p - 1$$

where c_{kk} is the kth diagonal element of $(\mathbf{X'X})^{-1}$. Recall from (6.46) that the variance-covariance matrix of the regression coefficients is given by $\sigma^2\{\mathbf{b}\} = \sigma^2(\mathbf{X'X})^{-1}$. Hence the variance of b_k is:

$$(9.35) \qquad\qquad\qquad \sigma^2\{b_k\} = \sigma^2 c_{kk}$$

The error term variance σ^2 here is estimated by $MSE_{(i)}$, the error mean square obtained when the ith case is deleted in fitting the regression model.

The *DFBETAS* value by its sign indicates whether inclusion of a case leads to an increase or a decrease in the estimated regression coefficient, and its absolute magnitude shows the size of the difference relative to the estimated standard deviation of the regression coefficient. A large absolute value of $(DFBETAS)_{k(i)}$ is indicative of a large impact of the ith case on the kth regression coefficient. As a guideline for identifying influential cases, we recommend considering a case influential if the absolute value of *DFBETAS* exceeds 1 for small to medium data sets and $2/\sqrt{n}$ for large data sets.

Example. For the body fat example with two predictor variables, Table 9.4 lists the *DFBETAS* values in columns 3, 4, and 5. Note that case 3, which is outlying with respect to its X values, is the only case that exceeds our guideline of 1 for medium-size data sets for both b_1 and b_2. Thus, case 3 is again tagged as potentially influential. Again, however, the *DFBETAS* values do not exceed 1 by very much so that case 3 may not be so influential as to require remedial action.

Note

Cook's distance measure of the aggregate influence of a case on the n fitted values, which was defined in (9.33), is algebraically equivalent to a measure of the aggregate influence of a case on the p regression coefficients. In fact, Cook's distance measure was originally derived from the concept of a confidence region for all p regression coefficients β_k $(k = 0, 1, \ldots, p - 1)$ simultaneously. It can be shown that the boundary of this joint confidence region for the normal error multiple regression model (6.19) is given by:

$$(9.36) \qquad \frac{(\mathbf{b} - \boldsymbol{\beta})'\mathbf{X}'\mathbf{X}(\mathbf{b} - \boldsymbol{\beta})}{pMSE} = F(1 - \alpha; p, n - p)$$

Cook's distance measure D_i uses the same structure for measuring the combined impact of the ith case on the differences in the estimated regression coefficients:

$$(9.37) \qquad D_i = \frac{(\mathbf{b} - \mathbf{b}_{(i)})'\mathbf{X}'\mathbf{X}(\mathbf{b} - \mathbf{b}_{(i)})}{pMSE}$$

where $\mathbf{b}_{(i)}$ is the vector of the estimated regression coefficients obtained when the ith case is omitted and $\mathbf{b}$, as usual, is the vector when all n cases are used. The expressions for Cook's distance measure in (9.33a) and (9.37) are algebraically identical.   ∎

Influence on Inferences

To round out the determination of influential cases, it is usually a good idea to examine in a direct fashion the inferences from the fitted regression model that would be made with and without the case(s) of concern. If the inferences are not essentially changed, there is little need to think of remedial actions for the cases diagnosed as influential. On the other hand, serious changes in the inferences drawn from the fitted model when a case is omitted will require consideration of remedial measures.

Example. In the body fat example with two predictor variables, cases 3 and 15 were identified as outlying X observations and cases 8 and 13 as outlying Y observations. All three influence measures (*DFFITS*, Cook's distance, and *DFBETAS*) identified only case 3 as influential, and, indeed, suggested that its influence may be of marginal importance so that remedial measures might not be required.

The analyst in the body fat example was primarily interested in the fit of the regression model because the model was intended to be used for making predictions within the range of the observations on the predictor variables in the data set. Hence, the analyst considered the fitted regression functions with and without case 3:

$$\text{With case 3:} \quad \hat{Y} = -19.174 + .2224X_1 + .6594X_2$$

$$\text{Without case 3:} \quad \hat{Y} = -12.428 + .5641X_1 + .3635X_2$$

Because of the high multicollinearity between X_1 and X_2, the analyst was not surprised by the shifts in the magnitudes of b_1 and b_2 when case 3 is omitted. Remember that the estimated standard deviations of the coefficients, given in Table 7.2c, are very large and that a single case can change the estimated coefficients substantially when the predictor variables are highly correlated.

To examine the effect of case 3 on inferences to be made from the fitted regression function in the range of the X observations in a direct fashion, the analyst calculated for each of the 20 cases the relative difference between the fitted value $\hat{Y}_i$ based on all 20 cases and the fitted value $\hat{Y}_{i(3)}$ obtained when case 3 is omitted. The measure of interest was the average absolute percent difference:

$$\frac{\sum_{i=1}^{n} \left| \dfrac{\hat{Y}_{i(3)} - \hat{Y}_i}{\hat{Y}_i} \right| 100}{n}$$

This mean difference is 3.1 percent; further, 17 of the 20 differences are less than 5 percent (calculations not shown). On the basis of this direct evidence about the effect of case 3 on the inferences to be made, the analyst was satisfied that case 3 does not exercise undue influence so that no remedial action is required for handling this case.

Some Final Comments

Analysis of outlying and influential cases is a necessary component of good regression analysis. However, it is neither automatic nor foolproof and requires good judgment by the analyst. The methods described often work well, but at times are ineffective. For example, if two influential outlying cases are nearly coincident, as depicted in Figure 9.5 by cases 3 and 4, an analysis that deletes one case at a time and estimates the change in fit will result in virtually no change for these two outlying cases. The reason is that the retained outlying case will mask the effect of the deleted outlying case. Extensions of the single-case diagnostic procedures described here have been developed which involve deleting two or more cases at a time. However, the computational requirements for these extensions are much more demanding than for the single-case diagnostics. Reference 9.4 describes some of these extensions.

Remedial measures for outlying cases that are determined to be highly influential by the diagnostic procedures will be discussed in the next chapter.

9.5 Multicollinearity Diagnostics—Variance Inflation Factor

When we discussed multicollinearity in Chapter 7, we noted some key problems that typically arise when the predictor variables being considered for the regression model are highly correlated among themselves:

1. Adding or deleting a predictor variable changes the regression coefficients.

2. The extra sum of squares associated with a predictor variable varies, depending upon which other predictor variables are already included in the model.

3. The estimated standard deviations of the regression coefficients become large when the predictor variables in the regression model are highly correlated with each other.

4. The estimated regression coefficients individually may not be statistically significant even though a definite statistical relation exists between the response variable and the set of predictor variables.

These problems can also arise without substantial multicollinearity being present, but only under unusual circumstances not likely to be found in practice.

We first consider some informal diagnostics for multicollinearity and then a highly useful formal diagnostic, the variance inflation factor.

Informal Diagnostics

Indications of the presence of serious multicollinearity are given by the following informal diagnostics:

1. Large changes in the estimated regression coefficients when a predictor variable is added or deleted, or when an observation is altered or deleted.

2. Nonsignificant results in individual tests on the regression coefficients for important predictor variables.

3. Estimated regression coefficients with an algebraic sign that is the opposite of that expected from theoretical considerations or prior experience.

4. Large coefficients of simple correlation between pairs of predictor variables in the correlation matrix $\mathbf{r}_{XX}$.

5. Wide confidence intervals for the regression coefficients representing important predictor variables.

Example. We consider again the body fat example of Table 7.1, this time with all three predictor variables—triceps skinfold thickness (X_1), thigh circumference (X_2), and midarm circumference (X_3). We noted in Chapter 7 that the predictor variables triceps skinfold thickness and thigh circumference are highly correlated with each other. We also noted large changes in the estimated regression coefficients and their estimated standard deviations when a variable was added, nonsignificant results in individual tests on anticipated important variables, and an estimated negative coefficient when a positive coefficient was expected. These are all informal indications that suggest serious multicollinearity among the predictor variables.

Note

The informal methods just described have important limitations. They do not provide quantitative measurements of the impact of multicollinearity and they may not identify the nature of the multicollinearity. For instance, if predictor variables X_1, X_2, and X_3 have low pairwise correlations, then the examination of simple correlation coefficients may not disclose the existence of relations among groups of predictor variables, such as a high correlation between X_1 and a linear combination of X_2 and X_3.

Another limitation of the informal diagnostic methods is that sometimes the observed behavior may occur without multicollinearity being present.   ∎

Variance Inflation Factor

A formal method of detecting the presence of multicollinearity that is widely used is by means of variance inflation factors. These factors measure how much the variances of the estimated regression coefficients are inflated as compared to when the predictor variables are not linearly related.

To understand the significance of variance inflation factors, we begin with the precision of least squares estimated regression coefficients, which is measured by their variances. We know from (6.46) that the variance-covariance matrix of the estimated regression coefficients is:

$$(9.38) \qquad\qquad \boldsymbol{\sigma}^2\{\mathbf{b}\} = \sigma^2(\mathbf{X}'\mathbf{X})^{-1}$$

For purposes of measuring the impact of multicollinearity, it is useful to work with the standardized regression model (7.45), which is obtained by transforming the variables by means of the correlation transformation (7.44). When the standardized regression model is fitted, the estimated regression coefficients b_k' are standardized coefficients that are related to the estimated regression coefficients for the untransformed variables according to (7.53). The variance-covariance matrix of the estimated standardized regression coefficients is obtained from (9.38) by using the result in (7.50), which states that the $\mathbf{X}'\mathbf{X}$ matrix for the transformed variables is the correlation matrix of the X variables $\mathbf{r}_{XX}$. Hence, we obtain:

$$(9.39) \qquad\qquad \boldsymbol{\sigma}^2\{\mathbf{b}\} = (\sigma')^2 \mathbf{r}_{XX}^{-1}$$

where $\mathbf{r}_{XX}$ is the matrix of the pairwise simple correlation coefficients among the X variables, as defined in (7.47), and $(\sigma')^2$ is the error term variance for the transformed model.

Note from (9.39) that the variance of b_k' ($k = 1, \ldots, p-1$) is equal to the following, letting $(VIF)_k$ denote the kth diagonal element of the matrix $\mathbf{r}_{XX}^{-1}$:

$$(9.40) \qquad\qquad \sigma^2\{b_k'\} = (\sigma')^2 (VIF)_k$$

The diagonal element $(VIF)_k$ is called the *variance inflation factor* (*VIF*) for b_k'. It can be shown that this variance inflation factor is equal to:

$$(9.41) \qquad\qquad (VIF)_k = (1 - R_k^2)^{-1} \qquad k = 1, 2, \ldots, p-1$$

where R_k^2 is the coefficient of multiple determination when X_k is regressed on the $p - 2$ other X variables in the model. Hence, we have:

$$(9.42) \qquad \sigma^2\{b_k'\} = \frac{(\sigma')^2}{1 - R_k^2}$$

We presented in (7.65) the special results for $\sigma^2\{b_k'\}$ when $p - 1 = 2$, for which $R_k^2 = r_{12}^2$, the coefficient of simple determination between X_1 and X_2.

The variance inflation factor $(VIF)_k$ is equal to 1 when $R_k^2 = 0$, i.e., when X_k is not linearly related to the other X variables. When $R_k^2 \neq 0$, then $(VIF)_k$ is greater than 1, indicating an inflated variance for b_k' as a result of the intercorrelations among the X variables. When X_k has a perfect linear association with the other X variables in the model so that $R_k^2 = 1$, then $(VIF)_k$ and $\sigma^2\{b_k'\}$ are unbounded.

Diagnostic Uses. The largest *VIF* value among all X variables is often used as an indicator of the severity of multicollinearity. A maximum *VIF* value in excess of 10 is frequently taken as an indication that multicollinearity may be unduly influencing the least squares estimates.

The mean of the *VIF* values also provides information about the severity of the multicollinearity in terms of how far the estimated standardized regression coefficients b_k' are from the true values β_k'. It can be shown that the expected value of the sum of these squared errors $(b_k' - \beta_k')^2$ is given by:

$$(9.43) \qquad E\left\{ \sum_{k=1}^{p-1} (b_k' - \beta_k')^2 \right\} = (\sigma')^2 \sum_{k=1}^{p-1} (VIF)_k$$

Thus, large *VIF* values result, on the average, in larger differences between the estimated and true standardized regression coefficients.

When no X variable is linearly related to the others in the regression model, $R_k^2 \equiv 0$; hence, $(VIF)_k \equiv 1$, their sum is $p - 1$, and the expected value of the sum of the squared errors is:

$$(9.43a) \qquad E\left\{ \sum_{k=1}^{p-1} (b_k' - \beta_k')^2 \right\} = (\sigma')^2(p - 1) \qquad \text{when } (VIF)_k \equiv 1$$

A ratio of the results in (9.43) and (9.43a) provides useful information about the effect of multicollinearity on the sum of the squared errors:

$$\frac{(\sigma')^2 \Sigma(VIF)_k}{(\sigma')^2(p - 1)} = \frac{\Sigma(VIF)_k}{p - 1}$$

Note that this ratio is simply the mean of the *VIF* values, to be denoted by $(\overline{VIF})$:

$$(9.44) \qquad (\overline{VIF}) = \frac{\sum\limits_{k=1}^{p-1} (VIF)_k}{p - 1}$$

Mean *VIF* values considerably larger than 1 are indicative of serious multicollinearity problems.

TABLE 9.5   **Variance Inflation Factors for Body Fat Example with Three Predictor Variables.**

Variable	b'_k	$(VIF)_k$
X_1	4.2637	708.84
X_2	-2.9287	564.34
X_3	-1.5614	104.61

Maximum $(VIF)_k = 708.84$ $(\overline{VIF}) = 459.26$

Example.   Table 9.5 contains the estimated standardized regression coefficients and the *VIF* values for the body fat example with three predictor variables (calculations not shown). The maximum of the *VIF* values is 708.84 and their mean value is $(\overline{VIF}) = 459.26$. Thus, the expected sum of the squared errors in the least squares standardized regression coefficients is nearly 460 times as large as it would be if the *X* variables were uncorrelated. In addition, all three *VIF* values greatly exceed 10, which again indicates that serious multicollinearity problems exist.

It is interesting to note that $(VIF)_3 = 105$ despite the fact that both r_{13}^2 and r_{23}^2 (see Figure 7.3b) are not large. Here is an instance where X_3 is strongly related to X_1 and X_2 together ($R_3^2 = .990$), even though the pairwise coefficients of simple determination are not large. Examination of the pairwise correlations does not disclose this multicollinearity.

Comments

1. Some computer regression programs use the reciprocal of the variance inflation factor to detect instances where an *X* variable should not be allowed into the fitted regression model because of excessively high interdependence between this variable and the other *X* variables in the model. Tolerance limits for $1/(VIF)_k = 1 - R_k^2$ frequently used are .01, .001, or .0001, below which the variable is not entered into the model.

2. A limitation of variance inflation factors for detecting multicollinearities is that they cannot distinguish between several simultaneous multicollinearities.

3. A number of other formal methods for detecting multicollinearity have been proposed. These are more complex than variance inflation factors and are discussed in specialized texts such as References 9.5 and 9.6.   ∎

9.6   Surgical Unit Example—Continued

In Chapter 8 we began building a regression model for the surgical unit example (data in Table 8.1). Recall that all criteria for the selection of variables suggested that a model containing variables X_1, X_2, and X_3 is "good." We now proceed into the model refinement stage by focusing on further study of curvature and interaction effects, multicollinearity, and influential cases for the regression model containing X_1, X_2, and X_3, using residuals and other diagnostics.

To examine interaction effects further, a regression model containing first-order terms in X_1, X_2, and X_3 and all pairwise interaction terms was fitted and the residuals for this model were plotted against the three-variable interaction term $X_1 X_2 X_3$. This plot (not shown) did not suggest any need for a three-variable interaction term in the regression model.

Additional plots were prepared for residuals based on the first-order model. Plots of these residuals against each of the two-variable interaction terms did not suggest that any strong two-variable interactions are present and need to be included in the model. The absence of any strong interactions was also noted by fitting a regression model containing X_1, X_2, and X_3 in first-order terms and all two-variable interaction terms and the three-variable interaction term. Adding all of the interaction terms increased R^2 only to .979, as compared to an R^2 of .972 for the first-order model in the three predictor variables. Still, the P-value of the formal F test statistic (7.19) for dropping all of the interaction terms from the model containing both the first-order effects and the interaction effects is .01, indicating that some interaction effects are present. Here is an example of the capability of a moderately large data set to produce a statistically significant result even though the incremental effect on R^2 from .972 to .979 is not large. Based on these and earlier indications that any interaction effects present are not strong, it was decided not to include any interaction terms in the regression model.

Figure 9.9 contains some of the additional diagnostic plots that were generated to check on the adequacy of the first-order model:

(9.45)
$$Y'_i = \beta_0 + \beta_1 X_{i1} + \beta_2 X_{i2} + \beta_3 X_{i3} + \varepsilon_i$$

where $Y'_i = \log_{10} Y_i$. The following points are worth noting:

1. The residual plot against the fitted values in Figure 9.9a shows no evidence of serious departures from the model.

2. Figure 9.9b shows the plot of the residuals against X_4, the predictor variable not in the model. This plot shows no need to include liver function (X_4) in the model to predict survival time.

3. The partial regression plot in Figure 9.9c shows a possible curvature effect for X_1. This was investigated by adding the squared term X_1^2 to the model and also by using the logarithmic transformation of X_1. Neither of these remedial measures improved things appreciably.

4. The normal probability plot of the residuals in Figure 9.9d shows some departure from linearity. Also, the coefficient of correlation between the ordered residuals and their expected values under normality is .959, which is slightly below the critical value for significance level .01 in Table B.6, thus indicating some departure from normality.

However, the problem of nonnormality was not considered to be serious here. An examination of the residuals and of the normal probability plot (Figure 9.9d) suggests that the departure from normality is chiefly in the tails of the distribution. There are somewhat more outlying residuals than would be expected under normality. Still, there is only one studentized residual among the 54 whose absolute value exceeds 3, and all of the other outlying residuals are much smaller. In view of this indication that the outlying residuals are only moderately large and because the sample size of 54 cases is reasonably large, it was felt that the effect of a moderate departure from normality would not have any serious impact on inferences to be made from the regression model.

Multicollinearity was studied by calculating the variance inflation factors:

Variable	$(VIF)_k$
X_1	1.03
X_2	1.01
X_3	1.02

FIGURE 9.9   **Residual and Other Diagnostic Plots for Surgical Unit Example—Regression Model (9.45).**

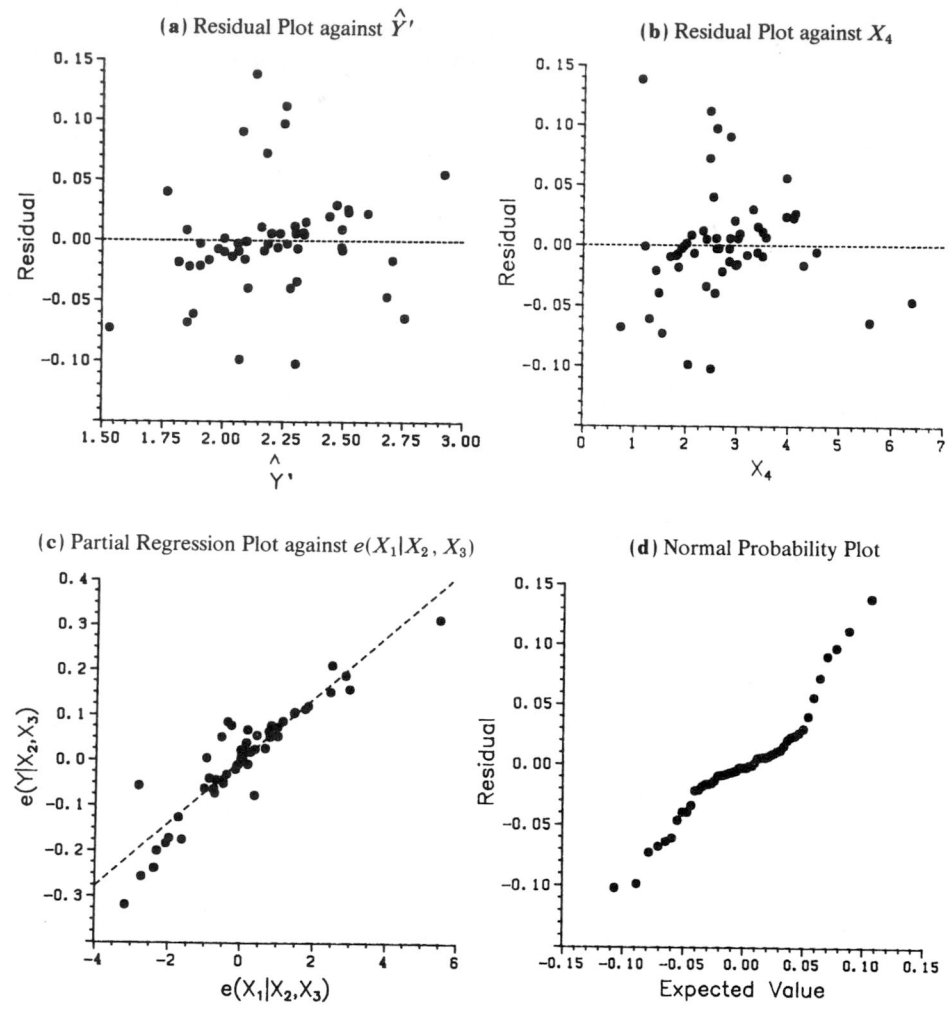

(a) Residual Plot against $\hat{Y}'$

(b) Residual Plot against X_4

(c) Partial Regression Plot against $e(X_1|X_2, X_3)$

(d) Normal Probability Plot

As may be seen from these results, multicollinearity among the three predictor variables is not a problem.

Table 9.6 contains the results of some diagnostic checks for cases found to be outlying. The measures presented in columns 1–5 are the residuals e_i in (9.8), the leverage values h_{ii} in (9.18), the studentized deleted residuals t_i in (9.24), the $(DFFITS)_i$ values in (9.30), and the Cook's distance measures D_i in (9.33). The following are noteworthy points about the diagnostics in Table 9.6:

1. Case 22 was identified as outlying with regard to its Y value according to its studentized deleted residual, outlying by more than three standard deviations. Case 27 was considered to be marginally outlying with regard to its Y value. We test formally whether case 22 is outlying by means of the Bonferroni test procedure. For a family significance

TABLE 9.6   **Various Diagnostics for Outlying Cases—Surgical Unit Example, Regression Model (9.45).**

Case Number i	(1) e_i	(2) h_{ii}	(3) t_i	(4) $(DFFITS)_i$	(5) D_i
13	.0560	.1495	1.3046	.5469	.0737
17	−.0162	.1499	−.3709	−.1558	.0062
22	.1383	.1274	3.4951	1.3353	.3641
27	.1118	.0311	2.5522	.4571	.0471
28	−.0636	.2619	−1.6027	−.9546	.2209
32	.0402	.2113	.9656	.4997	.0625
38	.0902	.2902	2.3903	1.5282	.5336

level of $\alpha = .05$ and sample size $n = 54$, we require $t(1 - \alpha/2n; n - p - 1) = t(.99954; 49) = 3.528$. Since $|t_{22}| = 3.4951 \leq 3.528$, the formal outlier test indicates that case 22 is not an outlier. Still, t_{22} is very close to the critical value, and although this case does not appear to be outlying to any substantial extent, we may wish to investigate the influence of case 22 to remove any doubts.

2. With $2p/n = 2(4)/54 = .148$ as a guide for identifying outlying X observations, cases 13, 17, 28, 32, and 38 were identified as outlying according to their leverage values. Incidentally, the univariate stem-and-leaf plots did not clearly identify case 13 as outlying. Here we see the value of multivariable outlier identification.

3. To determine the influence of cases 13, 17, 22, 27, 28, 32, and 38, we consider their *DFFITS* and Cook's distance values. According to each of these measures, case 38 is the most influential, with $(DFFITS)_{38} = 1.5282$ and Cook's distance $D_{38} = .5336$. Referring to the F distribution with 4 and 50 degrees of freedom, we note that the Cook's value corresponds to the 29th percentile. It thus appears that the influence of case 38 is not large enough to warrant remedial measures, and consequently the other outlying cases also do not appear to be overly influential.

A direct check of the influence of case 38 on the inferences of interest was also conducted. Here, the inferences of primary interest are in the fit of the regression model because the model is intended to be used for making predictions in the range of the X observations. Hence, each fitted value $\hat{Y}_i$ based on all 54 observations was compared with the fitted value $\hat{Y}_{i(38)}$ when case 38 is deleted in fitting the regression model. The average of the absolute percent differences:

$$\left| \frac{\hat{Y}_{i(38)} - \hat{Y}_i}{\hat{Y}_i} \right| 100$$

is only .2 percent, and the largest absolute percent difference (which is for case 38) is only 1.85 percent. Thus, case 38 does not have such a disproportionate influence on the fitted values that remedial action would be required.

4. In summary, the diagnostic analyses identified a number of potential problems, but none of these was considered to be serious enough to require further remedial action.

Consequently regression model (9.45) was selected from among the various competing models for final model validation. The estimated regression function for the selected model is:

(9.46) $$\hat{Y}' = .484 + .0692X_1 + .00929X_2 + .00952X_3$$

We shall complete the discussion of the surgical unit example in Chapter 10 when we consider the validation of the selected regression model.

Cited References

9.1.   Atkinson, A. C. *Plots, Transformations, and Regression.* Oxford: Clarendon Press, 1987.

9.2.   Mansfield, E. R., and M. D. Conerly. "Diagnostic Value of Residual and Partial Residual Plots," *The American Statistician* 41 (1987), pp. 107–16.

9.3.   Cook, R. D. "Exploring Partial Residual Plots," *Technometrics* 35 (1993), pp. 351–62.

9.4.   Rousseeuw, P. J., and A. M. Leroy. *Robust Regression and Outlier Detection.* New York: John Wiley & Sons, 1987.

9.5.   Belsley, D. A.; E. Kuh; and R. E. Welsch. *Regression Diagnostics: Identifying Influential Data and Sources of Collinearity.* New York: John Wiley & Sons, 1980.

9.6.   Belsley, D. A. *Conditioning Diagnostics: Collinearity and Weak Data in Regression.* New York: John Wiley & Sons, 1991.

Problems

9.1.   A student asked: "Why is it necessary to perform diagnostic checks of the fit when R^2 is large?" Comment.

9.2.   A researcher stated: "One good thing about partial regression plots is that they are extremely useful for identifying model adequacy even when the predictor variables are not properly specified in the regression model." Comment.

9.3.   A student suggested: "If extremely influential outlying cases are detected in a data set, simply discard these cases from the data set." Comment.

9.4.   Describe several informal methods that can be helpful in identifying multicollinearity among the X variables in a multiple regression model.

9.5.   Refer to **Brand preference** Problem 6.5b.
   a. Prepare a partial regression plot for each of the predictor variables.
   b. Do your plots in part (a) suggest that the regression relationships in the fitted regression function in Problem 6.5b are inappropriate for any of the predictor variables? Explain.
   c. Obtain the fitted regression function in Problem 6.5b by separately regressing both Y and X_2 on X_1, and then regressing the residuals in an appropriate fashion.

9.6. Refer to **Chemical shipment** Problem 6.10a.

    a. Prepare a partial regression plot for each of the predictor variables.

    b. Do your plots in part (a) suggest that the regression relationships in the fitted regression function in Problem 6.10a are inappropriate for any of the predictor variables? Explain.

    c. Obtain the fitted regression function in Problem 6.10a by separately regressing both Y and X_2 on X_1, and then regressing the residuals in an appropriate fashion.

9.7. Refer to **Patient satisfaction** Problem 6.15c.

    a. Prepare a partial regression plot for each of the predictor variables.

    b. Do your plots in part (a) suggest that the regression relationships in the fitted regression function in Problem 6.15c are inappropriate for any of the predictor variables? Explain.

9.8. Refer to **Mathematicians' salaries** Problem 6.18c.

    a. Prepare a partial regression plot for each of the predictor variables.

    b. Do your plots in part (a) suggest that the regression relationships in the fitted regression function in Problem 6.18c are inappropriate for any of the predictor variables? Explain.

9.9. Refer to **Brand preference** Problem 6.5. The diagonal elements of the hat matrix are provided in the data disk in the last column.

    a. Obtain the studentized deleted residuals and identify any outlying Y observations. Use the Bonferroni outlier test procedure with $\alpha = .10$. State the decision rule and conclusion.

    b. Explain the reason for the pattern in the diagonal elements of the hat matrix.

    c. Are any of the observations outlying with regard to their X values according to the rule of thumb stated in the chapter?

    d. Management wishes to estimate the mean degree of brand liking for moisture content $X_1 = 10$ and sweetness $X_2 = 3$. Construct a scatter plot of X_2 against X_1 and determine visually whether this prediction involves an extrapolation beyond the range of the data. Also, use (9.29) to determine whether an extrapolation is involved. Do your conclusions from the two methods agree?

    e. The largest absolute studentized deleted residual is for case 14. Obtain the *DFFITS*, *DFBETAS*, and Cook's distance values for this case to assess the influence of this case. What do you conclude?

    f. Calculate the average absolute percent difference in the fitted values with and without case 14. What does this measure indicate about the influence of case 14?

    g. Calculate Cook's distance D_i for each case and prepare an index plot. Are any cases influential according to this measure?

√ 9.10. Refer to **Chemical shipment** Problems 6.9 and 6.10. The diagonal elements of the hat matrix are provided in the data disk in the last column.

    a. Obtain the studentized deleted residuals and identify any outlying Y observations. Use the Bonferroni outlier test procedure with $\alpha = .05$. State the decision rule and conclusion.

    b. Identify any outlying X observations using the rule of thumb presented in the chapter.

    c. Management wishes to predict the number of minutes required to handle the next shipment containing $X_1 = 15$ drums whose total weight is $X_2 = 8$ (hundred pounds). Construct a scatter plot of X_2 against X_1 and determine visually whether this prediction involves an extrapolation beyond the range of the data. Also, use (9.29) to determine whether an extrapolation is involved. Do your conclusions from the two methods agree?

d. Case 7 appears to be an outlying X observation and case 12 an outlying Y observation. Obtain the *DFFITS*, *DFBETAS*, and Cook's distance values for each of these cases to assess their influence. What do you conclude?

e. Calculate the average absolute percent difference in the fitted values with and without case 7 and with and without case 12. What does this measure indicate about the influence of each of the two cases?

f. Calculate Cook's distance D_i for each case and prepare an index plot. Are any cases influential according to this measure?

√ 9.11. Refer to **Patient satisfaction** Problem 6.15. The diagonal elements of the hat matrix are provided in the data disk in the last column.

a. Obtain the studentized deleted residuals and identify any outlying Y observations. Use the Bonferroni outlier test procedure with $\alpha = .10$. State the decision rule and conclusion.

b. Identify any outlying X observations.

c. Hospital management wishes to estimate mean patient satisfaction for patients who are $X_1 = 30$ years old, whose index of illness severity is $X_2 = 58$, and whose index of anxiety level is $X_3 = 2.0$. Use (9.29) to determine whether this estimate will involve a hidden extrapolation.

d. The largest absolute studentized deleted residual is for case 14. Obtain the *DFFITS*, *DFBETAS*, and Cook's distance values for this case to assess its influence. What do you conclude?

e. Calculate the average absolute percent difference in the fitted values with and without case 14. What does this measure indicate about the influence of case 14?

f. Calculate Cook's distance D_i for each case and prepare an index plot. Are any cases influential according to this measure?

9.12. Refer to **Mathematicians' salaries** Problem 6.18. The diagonal elements of the hat matrix are provided in the data disk in the last column.

a. Obtain the studentized deleted residuals and identify any outlying Y observations. Use the Bonferroni outlier test procedure with $\alpha = .01$. State the decision rule and conclusion.

b. Identify any outlying X observations.

c. The researcher wishes to estimate the average salary of mathematicians whose index of work quality is $X_1 = 5$, whose number of years of experience is $X_2 = 15$, and whose index of publication success is $X_3 = 7.5$. Use (9.29) to determine whether this estimate will involve a hidden extrapolation.

d. Case 19 appears to be a borderline outlying Y observation. Obtain the *DFFITS*, *DFBETAS*, and Cook's distance values for this case to assess its influence. What do you conclude?

e. Calculate the average absolute percent difference in the fitted values with and without case 19. What does this measure indicate about the influence of case 19?

f. Calculate Cook's distance D_i for each case and prepare an index plot. Are any cases influential according to this measure?

9.13. **Cosmetics sales**. An assistant in the district sales office of a national cosmetics firm obtained data, shown below, on advertising expenditures and sales last year in the district's 14 territories. X_1 denotes expenditures for point-of-sale displays in beauty salons and department stores (in thousand dollars), and X_2 and X_3 represent the corresponding expenditures for local media advertising and prorated share of national media advertising, respectively. Y denotes sales (in thousand cases). The assistant was instructed to estimate the increase in expected sales when X_1 is increased by 1 thousand dollars and X_2 and X_3 are held constant, and was told to use an ordinary multiple regression model with linear terms for the predictor variables and with independent normal error terms.

i:	1	2	3	. . .	12	13	14
X_{i1}:	4.2	6.5	3.0	. . .	5.5	2.2	3.0
X_{i2}:	4.0	6.5	3.5	. . .	5.5	2.0	2.8
X_{i3}:	3.0	5.0	4.0	. . .	5.0	4.0	3.0
Y_i:	8.26	14.70	9.73	. . .	10.46	7.15	6.74

a. State the regression model to be employed and fit it to the data.

b. Test whether there is a regression relation between sales and the three predictor variables; use $\alpha = .05$. State the alternatives, decision rule, and conclusion.

c. Test for each of the regression coefficients β_k ($k = 1, 2, 3$) individually whether or not $\beta_k = 0$; use $\alpha = .05$ each time. Do the conclusions of these tests correspond to that obtained in part (b)?

d. Obtain the correlation matrix of the X variables.

e. What do the results in parts (b), (c), and (d) suggest about the suitability of the data for the research objective?

9.14. Refer to **Cosmetics sales** Problem 9.13.

a. Obtain the three variance inflation factors. What do these suggest about the effects of multicollinearity here?

b. The assistant eventually decided to drop variables X_2 and X_3 from the model "to clear up the picture." Fit the assistant's revised model. Is the assistant now in a better position to achieve the research objective?

c. Why would an experiment here be more effective in providing suitable data to meet the research objective? How would you design such an experiment? What regression model would you employ?

9.15. Refer to **Brand preference** Problem 6.5a.

a. What do the scatter plot matrix and the correlation matrix show about pairwise linear associations among the predictor variables?

b. Find the two variance inflation factors. Why are they both equal to 1?

√ 9.16. Refer to **Chemical shipment** Problem 6.9c.

a. What do the scatter plot matrix and the correlation matrix show about pairwise linear associations among the predictor variables?

b. Find the two variance inflation factors. Do they indicate that a serious multicollinearity problem exists here?

√ 9.17. Refer to **Patient satisfaction** Problem 6.15b.

    a. What do the scatter plot matrix and the correlation matrix show about pairwise linear associations among the predictor variables?

    b. Obtain the three variance inflation factors. What do these results suggest about the effects of multicollinearity here? Are these results more revealing than those in part (a)?

9.18. Refer to **Mathematicians' salaries** Problem 6.18b.

    a. What do the scatter plot matrix and the correlation matrix show about pairwise linear associations among the predictor variables?

    b. Obtain the three variance inflation factors. Do they indicate that a serious multicollinearity problem exists here?

√ 9.19. Refer to **Roofing shingles** Problems 8.9 and 8.10. The subset model containing only first-order terms in X_2 and X_3 is to be evaluated in detail.

    a. Obtain the residuals and plot them separately against $\hat{Y}$, each of the four predictor variables, and the cross-product term X_2X_3. On the basis of these plots, should any modifications of the regression model be investigated?

    b. Prepare separate partial regression plots against $e(X_2|X_3)$ and $e(X_3|X_2)$. Do these plots suggest that any modifications in the model form are warranted?

    c. Prepare a normal probability plot of the residuals. Also obtain the coefficient of correlation between the ordered residuals and their expected values under normality. Test the reasonableness of the normality assumption, using Table B.6 and $\alpha = .05$. What do you conclude?

    d. Obtain the studentized deleted residuals and identify any outlying Y observations. Use the Bonferroni outlier test procedure with $\alpha = .10$. State the decision rule and conclusion.

    e. Obtain the diagonal elements of the hat matrix. Using the rule of thumb in the text, identify any outlying X observations. Are the findings consistent with those in Problem 8.9a? Should they be? Discuss.

    f. Case 8 appears to be reasonably far outlying with respect to its Y value. Obtain the *DFFITS*, *DFBETAS*, and Cook's distance values for this case to assess its influence. What do you conclude?

    g. Obtain the variance inflation factors. Are there any indications of serious multicollinearity here?

9.20. Refer to **Job proficiency** Problems 8.11 and 8.12. The subset model containing only first-order terms in X_1 and X_3 is to be evaluated in detail.

    a. Obtain the residuals and plot them separately against $\hat{Y}$, each of the four predictor variables, and the cross-product term X_1X_3. On the basis of these plots, should any modifications in the regression model be investigated?

    b. Prepare separate partial regression plots against $e(X_1|X_3)$ and $e(X_3|X_1)$. Do these plots suggest that any modifications in the model form are warranted?

    c. Prepare a normal probability plot of the residuals. Also obtain the coefficient of correlation between the ordered residuals and their expected values under normality. Test the reasonableness of the normality assumptions, using Table B.6 and $\alpha = .01$. What do you conclude?

  d. Obtain the studentized deleted residuals and identify any outlying Y observations. Use the Bonferroni outlier test procedure with $\alpha = .05$. State the decision rule and conclusion.

  e. Obtain the diagonal elements of the hat matrix. Using the rule of thumb in the text, identify any outlying X observations. Are your findings consistent with those in Problem 8.11a? Should they be? Comment.

  f. Cases 7 and 18 appear to be moderately outlying with respect to their X values, and case 16 is reasonably far outlying with respect to its Y value. Obtain *DFFITS*, *DFBETAS*, and Cook's distance values for these cases to assess their influence. What do you conclude?

  g. Obtain the variance inflation factors. What do they indicate?

9.21. Refer to **Lung pressure** Problems 8.13 and 8.14. The subset regression model containing first-order terms for X_1 and X_2 and the cross-product term $X_1 X_2$ is to be evaluated in detail.

  a. Obtain the residuals and plot them separately against $\hat{Y}$ and each of the three predictor variables. On the basis of these plots, should any further modifications of the regression model be attempted?

  b. Prepare a normal probability plot of the residuals. Also obtain the coefficient of correlation between the ordered residuals and their expected values under normality. Does the normality assumption appear to be reasonable here?

  c. Obtain the variance inflation factors. Are there any indications that serious multicollinearity problems are present? Explain.

  d. Obtain the studentized deleted residuals and identify any outlying Y observations. Use the Bonferroni outlier test procedure with $\alpha = .05$. State the decision rule and conclusion.

  e. Obtain the diagonal elements of the hat matrix. Using the rule of thumb in the text, identify any outlying X observations. Are your findings consistent with those in Problem 8.13a? Should they be? Discuss.

  f. Cases 3, 8, and 15 are moderately far outlying with respect to their X values, and case 7 is relatively far outlying with respect to its Y value. Obtain *DFFITS*, *DFBETAS*, and Cook's distance values for these cases to assess their influence. What do you conclude?

√ 9.22. Refer to **Kidney function** Problem 8.15 and the regression model fitted in part (c).

  a. Obtain the variance inflation factors. Are there indications that serious multicollinearity problems exist here? Explain.

  b. Obtain the residuals and plot them separately against $\hat{Y}$ and each of the predictor variables. Also prepare a normal probability plot of the residuals.

  c. Prepare separate partial regression plots against $e(X_1|X_2, X_3)$, $e(X_2|X_1, X_3)$, and $e(X_3|X_1, X_2)$.

  d. Do the plots in parts (b) and (c) suggest that the regression model should be modified?

√ 9.23. Refer to **Kidney function** Problems 8.15 and 9.22. Theoretical arguments suggest use of the following regression function:

$$E\{\log_e Y\} = \beta_0 + \beta_1 \log_e X_1 + \beta_2 \log_e (140 - X_2) + \beta_3 \log_e X_3$$

  a. Fit the regression function based on theoretical considerations.

b. Obtain the residuals and plot them separately against $\hat{Y}$ and each predictor variable in the fitted model. Also prepare a normal probability plot of the residuals. Have the difficulties noted in Problem 9.22 now largely been eliminated?

c. Obtain the variance inflation factors. Are there indications that serious multicollinearity problems exist here? Explain.

d. Obtain the studentized deleted residuals and identify any outlying Y observations. Use the Bonferroni outlier test procedure with $\alpha = .10$. State the decision rule and conclusion.

e. Obtain the diagonal elements of the hat matrix. Using the rule of thumb in the text, identify any outlying X observations.

f. Cases 28 and 29 are relatively far outlying with respect to their Y values. Obtain *DFFITS*, *DFBETAS*, and Cook's distance values for these cases to assess their influence. What do you conclude?

Exercises

9.24. Show that (9.37) is algebraically equivalent to (9.33a).

9.25. If $n = p$ and the **X** matrix is invertible, use (5.34) and (5.37) to show that the hat matrix **H** is given by the $p \times p$ identity matrix. In this case, what are h_{ii} and $\hat{Y}_i$?

9.26. Show that (9.26) follows from (9.24a) and (9.25).

9.27. Prove (8.11), using (9.27) and Exercise 5.31.

Projects

9.28. Refer to the **SENIC** data set and Project 8.23. The regression model containing age, routine chest X-ray ratio, and average daily census in first-order terms is to be evaluated in detail based on the model-building data set.

a. Obtain the residuals and plot them separately against $\hat{Y}$, each of the predictor variables in the model, and each of the related cross-product terms. On the basis of these plots, should any modifications of the model be made?

b. Prepare a normal probability plot of the residuals. Also obtain the coefficient of correlation between the ordered residuals and their expected values under normality. Test the reasonableness of the normality assumption, using Table B.6 and $\alpha = .05$. What do you conclude?

c. Obtain the scatter plot matrix, the correlation matrix of the X variables, and the variance inflation factors. Are there any indications that serious multicollinearity problems are present? Explain.

d. Obtain the studentized deleted residuals and prepare a dot plot of these residuals. Are any outliers present? Use the Bonferroni outlier test procedure with $\alpha = .01$. State the decision rule and conclusion.

    e. Obtain the diagonal elements of the hat matrix. Using the rule of thumb in the text, identify any outlying X observations.

    f. Cases 62, 75, 106, and 112 are moderately outlying with respect to their X values, and case 87 is reasonably far outlying with respect to its Y value. Obtain *DFFITS*, *DFBETAS*, and Cook's distance values for these cases to assess their influence. What do you conclude?

9.29. Refer to the **SMSA** data set and Project 8.24. The regression model containing land area and percent high school graduates in first-order terms is to be evaluated in detail based on the model-building data set.

    a. Obtain the residuals and plot them separately against $\hat{Y}$, each predictor variable in the model, and the related cross-product term. On the basis of these plots, should any modifications in the model be made?

    b. Prepare a normal probability plot of the residuals. Also obtain the coefficient of correlation between the ordered residuals and their expected values under normality. Test the reasonableness of the normality assumption, using Table B.6 and $\alpha = .01$. What do you conclude?

    c. Obtain the scatter plot matrix, the correlation matrix of the X variables, and the variance inflation factors. Are there any indications that serious multicollinearity problems are present? Explain.

    d. Obtain the studentized deleted residuals and prepare a dot plot of these residuals. Are any outliers present? Use the Bonferroni outlier test procedure with $\alpha = .05$. State the decision rule and conclusion.

    e. Obtain the diagonal elements of the hat matrix. Using the rule of thumb in the text, identify any outlying X observations.

    f. Cases 42, 74, 92, 94, 124, and 138 are moderately outlying with respect to their X values, and cases 40 and 54 are reasonably far outlying with respect to their Y values. Obtain *DFFITS*, *DFBETAS*, and Cook's distance values for these cases to assess their influence. What do you conclude?

Building the Regression Model III: Remedial Measures and Validation

When the diagnostics indicate that a regression model is not appropriate or that one or several cases are very influential, remedial measures may need to be taken. In earlier chapters, we discussed some remedial measures, such as transformations to linearize the regression relation, to make the error distributions more nearly normal, or to make the variances of the error terms more nearly equal. In this chapter, we take up some additional remedial measures to deal with unequal error variances, high degree of multicollinearity, and influential observations. Since these remedial measures often involve relatively complex estimation procedures, we consider next a general approach, called bootstrapping, for evaluating the precision of these complex estimators. We then discuss the final stage of model building, which involves the validation of the regression model. We conclude the chapter by presenting a case that illustrates some of the issues that arise in model building. In Chapter 11, we present another case to further demonstrate how some of the issues that arise in model building may be handled.

10.1 Unequal Error Variances Remedial Measures—Weighted Least Squares

We explained in Chapters 3 and 6 how transformations of Y may be helpful in reducing or eliminating unequal variances of the error terms. A difficulty with transformations of Y is that they may create an inappropriate regression relationship. When an appropriate regression relationship has been found but the variances of the error terms are unequal, an alternative to transformations is weighted least squares, a procedure based on a generalization of multiple regression model (6.7). We shall now denote the variance of the error term ε_i by σ_i^2 to recognize that different error terms may have different variances. The generalized multiple regression model can then be expressed as follows:

(10.1)
$$Y_i = \beta_0 + \beta_1 X_{i1} + \cdots + \beta_{p-1} X_{i,p-1} + \varepsilon_i$$

where:

$\beta_0, \beta_1, \ldots, \beta_{p-1}$ are parameters

$X_{i1}, \ldots, X_{i,p-1}$ are known constants

ε_i are independent $N(0, \sigma_i^2)$

$i = 1, \ldots, n$

The variance-covariance matrix of the error terms for the generalized multiple regression model (10.1) is more complex than before:

$$(10.2) \qquad \underset{n \times n}{\boldsymbol{\sigma}^2\{\boldsymbol{\varepsilon}\}} = \begin{bmatrix} \sigma_1^2 & 0 & \cdots & 0 \\ 0 & \sigma_2^2 & \cdots & 0 \\ \vdots & \vdots & & \vdots \\ 0 & 0 & \cdots & \sigma_n^2 \end{bmatrix}$$

The estimation of the regression coefficients in generalized model (10.1) could be done by using the estimators in (6.25) for regression model (6.7) with equal error variances. These estimators are still unbiased and consistent for generalized regression model (10.1), but they no longer have minimum variance. To obtain unbiased estimators with minimum variance, we must take into account that the different Y observations for the n cases no longer have the same reliability. Observations with small variances provide more reliable information about the regression function than those with large variances. We shall first consider the estimation of the regression coefficients when the error variances σ_i^2 are known. This case is usually unrealistic, but it provides guidance as to how to proceed when the error variances are not known.

Error Variances Known

When the error variances σ_i^2 are known, we can use the method of maximum likelihood to obtain estimators of the regression coefficients in generalized regression model (10.1). The likelihood function in (6.26) for the case of equal error variances σ^2 is modified by replacing the σ^2 terms with the respective variances σ_i^2 and expressing the likelihood function in the first form of (1.26):

$$(10.3) \quad L(\boldsymbol{\beta}) = \prod_{i=1}^{n} \frac{1}{(2\pi\sigma_i^2)^{1/2}} \exp\left[-\frac{1}{2\sigma_i^2}(Y_i - \beta_0 - \beta_1 X_{i1} - \cdots - \beta_{p-1} X_{i,p-1})^2\right]$$

where $\boldsymbol{\beta}$ as usual denotes the vector of the regression coefficients. We define the reciprocal of the variance σ_i^2 as the *weight* w_i:

$$(10.4) \qquad\qquad w_i = \frac{1}{\sigma_i^2}$$

We can then express the likelihood function (10.3) as follows, after making some simplifications:

$$(10.5)$$
$$L(\boldsymbol{\beta}) = \left[\prod_{i=1}^{n}\left(\frac{w_i}{2\pi}\right)^{1/2}\right] \exp\left[-\frac{1}{2}\sum_{i=1}^{n} w_i(Y_i - \beta_0 - \beta_1 X_{i1} - \cdots - \beta_{p-1} X_{i,p-1})^2\right]$$

We find the maximum likelihood estimators of the regression coefficients by *maximizing* $L(\boldsymbol{\beta})$ in (10.5) with respect to $\beta_0, \beta_1, \ldots, \beta_{p-1}$. Since the error variances σ_i^2 and hence the weights w_i are assumed to be known, maximizing $L(\boldsymbol{\beta})$ with respect to the regression coefficients is equivalent to *minimizing* the exponential term:

$$(10.6) \qquad Q_w = \sum_{i=1}^{n} w_i (Y_i - \beta_0 - \beta_1 X_{i1} - \cdots - \beta_{p-1} X_{i,p-1})^2$$

This term to be minimized for obtaining the maximum likelihood estimators is also the *weighted least squares criterion*, denoted by Q_w. Thus, the methods of maximum likelihood and weighted least squares lead to the same estimators for the generalized multiple regression model (10.1), as is also the case for the ordinary multiple regression model (6.7).

Note how the weighted least squares criterion (10.6) generalizes the ordinary least squares criterion in (6.22) by replacing equal weights of 1 by w_i. Since the weight w_i is inversely related to the variance σ_i^2, it reflects the amount of information contained in the observation Y_i. Thus, an observation Y_i that has a large variance receives less weight than another observation that has a smaller variance. Intuitively, this is reasonable. The more precise is Y_i (i.e., the smaller is σ_i^2), the more information Y_i provides about $E\{Y_i\}$ and therefore the more weight it should receive in fitting the regression function.

It is easiest to express the maximum likelihood and weighted least squares estimators of the regression coefficients for model (10.1) in matrix terms. Let the matrix $\mathbf{W}$ be a diagonal matrix containing the weights w_i:

$$(10.7) \qquad \underset{n \times n}{\mathbf{W}} = \begin{bmatrix} w_1 & 0 & \cdots & 0 \\ 0 & w_2 & \cdots & 0 \\ \vdots & \vdots & & \vdots \\ 0 & 0 & \cdots & w_n \end{bmatrix}$$

The normal equations can then be expressed as follows:

$$(10.8) \qquad (\mathbf{X'WX})\mathbf{b}_w = \mathbf{X'WY}$$

and the weighted least squares and maximum likelihood estimators of the regression coefficients are:

$$(10.9) \qquad \underset{p \times 1}{\mathbf{b}_w} = (\mathbf{X'WX})^{-1}\mathbf{X'WY}$$

where $\mathbf{b}_w$ is the vector of the estimated regression coefficients obtained by weighted least squares. The variance-covariance matrix of the weighted least squares estimated regression coefficients is:

$$(10.10) \qquad \underset{p \times p}{\sigma^2\{\mathbf{b}_w\}} = (\mathbf{X'WX})^{-1}$$

Note that this variance-covariance matrix is known since the variances σ_i^2 are assumed to be known.

Many computer regression packages will provide the weighted least squares estimated regression coefficients. The user simply needs to provide the weights w_i.

Error Variances Known up to Proportionality Constant

We now relax the requirement that the variances σ_i^2 are known by considering the case where only the relative magnitudes of the variances are known. For instance, if we know that σ_2^2 is twice as large as σ_1^2, we might use the weights $w_1 = 1$, $w_2 = 1/2$. In that case, the relative weights w_i are a constant multiple of the unknown true weights $1/\sigma_i^2$:

$$(10.11) \qquad w_i = k\left(\frac{1}{\sigma_i^2}\right)$$

where k is the proportionality constant. It can be shown that the weighted least squares and maximum likelihood estimators are unaffected by the unknown proportionality constant k and are still given by (10.9). The reason is that the proportionality constant k appears on both sides of the normal equations (10.8) and cancels out. The variance-covariance matrix of the weighted least squares regression coefficients is now as follows:

$$(10.12) \qquad \underset{p \times p}{\sigma^2\{\mathbf{b}_w\}} = k(\mathbf{X'WX})^{-1}$$

This matrix is unknown because the proportionality constant k is not known. It can be estimated, however. The estimated variance-covariance matrix of the regression coefficients $\mathbf{b}_w$ is:

$$(10.13) \qquad \underset{p \times p}{s^2\{\mathbf{b}_w\}} = MSE_w(\mathbf{X'WX})^{-1}$$

where MSE_w is based on the weighted squared residuals:

$$(10.13a) \qquad MSE_w = \frac{\Sigma w_i(Y_i - \hat{Y}_i)^2}{n - p} = \frac{\Sigma w_i e_i^2}{n - p}$$

Thus, MSE_w here is an estimator of the proportionality constant k.

Error Variances Unknown

If the variances σ_i^2 were known, or even known up to a proportionality constant, the use of weighted least squares with weights w_i would be straightforward. Unfortunately, one rarely has knowledge of the variances σ_i^2. We are then forced to use estimates of the variances. These can be obtained in a variety of ways. We discuss two methods of obtaining estimates of the variances σ_i^2.

Estimation of Variance Function or Standard Deviation Function.   The first method of obtaining estimates of the error term variances σ_i^2 is based on empirical findings that the magnitudes of σ_i^2 and σ_i often vary in a regular fashion with one or several predictor variables X_k or with the mean response $E\{Y_i\}$. Figure 3.4c, for example, shows a typical "megaphone" prototype residual plot where σ_i^2 increases as the predictor variable X becomes larger. Such a relationship between σ_i^2 and one or several predictor variables can be estimated because the squared residual e_i^2 obtained from an ordinary least squares regression fit is an estimate of σ_i^2, provided that the regression function is appropriate. We know from (A.15a) that the variance of the error term ε_i, denoted by σ_i^2, can be expressed as follows:

$$(10.14) \qquad\qquad \sigma_i^2 = E\{\varepsilon_i^2\} - (E\{\varepsilon_i\})^2$$

Since $E\{\varepsilon_i\} = 0$ according to the regression model, we obtain:

$$(10.15) \qquad\qquad \sigma_i^2 = E\{\varepsilon_i^2\}$$

Hence, the squared residual e_i^2 is an estimator of σ_i^2. Furthermore, the absolute residual $|e_i|$ is an estimator of the standard deviation σ_i, since $\sigma_i = \left|\sqrt{\sigma_i^2}\right|$.

We can therefore estimate the variance function describing the relation of σ_i^2 to relevant predictor variables by first fitting the regression model using unweighted least squares and then regressing the squared residuals e_i^2 against the appropriate predictor variables. Alternatively, we can estimate the standard deviation function describing the relation of σ_i to relevant predictor variables by regressing the absolute residuals $|e_i|$ obtained from fitting the regression model using unweighted least squares against the appropriate predictor variables. If there are any outliers in the data, it is generally advisable to estimate the standard deviation function rather than the variance function, because regressing absolute residuals is less affected by outliers than regressing squared residuals. Reference 10.1 provides a detailed discussion of the issues encountered in estimating variance and standard deviation functions.

We illustrate the use of some possible variance and standard deviation functions:

1. A residual plot against X_1 exhibits a megaphone shape. Regress the absolute residuals against X_1.

2. A residual plot against $\hat{Y}$ exhibits a megaphone shape. Regress the absolute residuals against $\hat{Y}$.

3. A plot of the squared residuals against X_3 exhibits an upward tendency. Regress the squared residuals against X_3.

4. A plot of the residuals against X_2 suggests that the variance increases rapidly with increases in X_2 up to a point and then increases more slowly. Regress the absolute residuals against X_2 and X_2^2.

After the variance function or the standard deviation function is estimated, the fitted values from this function are used to obtain the estimated weights:

$$(10.16a) \quad w_i = \frac{1}{(\hat{s}_i)^2} \quad \text{where } \hat{s}_i \text{ is fitted value from standard deviation function}$$

$$(10.16b) \quad w_i = \frac{1}{\hat{v}_i} \quad \text{where } \hat{v}_i \text{ is fitted value from variance function}$$

The estimated weights are then placed in the weight matrix $\mathbf{W}$ in (10.7) and the estimated regression coefficients are obtained by (10.9), as follows:

$$(10.17) \qquad\qquad \mathbf{b}_w = (\mathbf{X}'\mathbf{W}\mathbf{X})^{-1}\mathbf{X}'\mathbf{W}\mathbf{Y}$$

The weighted error mean square MSE_w may be viewed here as an estimator of the proportionality constant k in (10.11). If the modeling of the variance or standard deviation function is done well, the proportionality constant will be near 1 and MSE_w should then be near 1.

We summarize the estimation process:

1. Fit the regression model by unweighted least squares and analyze the residuals.

2. Estimate the variance function or the standard deviation function by regressing either the squared residuals or the absolute residuals on the appropriate predictor(s).

3. Use the fitted values from the estimated variance or standard deviation function to obtain the weights w_i.

4. Estimate the regression coefficients using these weights.

If the estimated coefficients differ substantially from the estimated regression coefficients obtained by ordinary least squares, it is usually advisable to iterate the weighted least squares process by using the residuals from the weighted least squares fit to reestimate the variance or standard deviation function and then obtain revised weights. Often one or two iterations are sufficient to stabilize the estimated regression coefficients. This iteration process is often called *iteratively reweighted least squares*.

Use of Replicates or Near Replicates.   A second method of obtaining estimates of the error term variances σ_i^2 can be utilized in designed experiments where replicate observations are made at each combination of levels of the predictor variables. If the number of replications is large, the weights w_i may be obtained directly from the sample variances of the Y observations at each combination of levels of the X variables. Otherwise, the sample variances or sample standard deviations should first be regressed against appropriate predictor variables to estimate the variance or standard deviation function, from which the weights can then be obtained. Note that each case in a replicate group receives the same weight with this method.

In observational studies, replicate observations often are not present. Near replicates may then be used. For example, if the residual plot against X_1 shows a megaphone appearance, cases with similar X_1 values can be grouped together and the variance of the residuals in each group calculated. The reciprocals of these variances are then used as the weights w_i if the number of replications is large. Otherwise, a variance or standard deviation function may be estimated to obtain the weights. Again, all cases in a near-replicate group receive the same weight. If the estimated regression coefficients differ substantially from those obtained with ordinary least squares, the procedure may be iterated, as when using an estimated variance or standard deviation function.

Inference Procedures when Weights Are Estimated.   When the error variances σ_i^2 are unknown so that the weights w_i need to be estimated, which almost always is the case, the variance-covariance matrix of the estimated regression coefficients is usually estimated by means of (10.13), using the estimated weights, provided the sample size is not very small. Confidence intervals for regression coefficients are then obtained by means of (6.50), with the estimated standard deviation $s\{b_{wk}\}$ obtained from the matrix (10.13). Confidence intervals for mean responses are obtained by means of (6.59), using $s^2\{\mathbf{b}_w\}$ from (10.13) in (6.58). These inference procedures are now only approximate, however, because the estimation of the variances σ_i^2 introduces another source of variability. The approximation is often quite good when the sample size is not too small. One means of determining

FIGURE 10.1   **Diagnostic Plots Detecting Unequal Error Variances—Blood Pressure Example.**

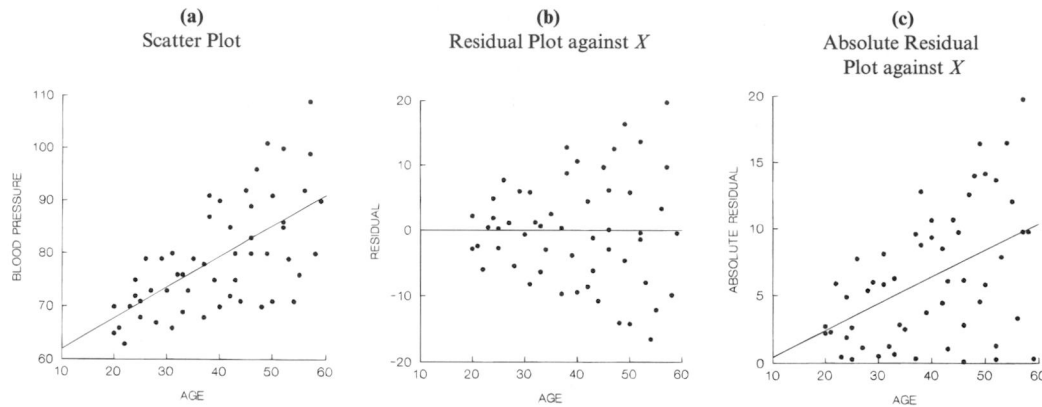

whether the approximation is good is to use bootstrapping, a statistical procedure that will be explained in Section 10.5.

Example

A health researcher, interested in studying the relationship between diastolic blood pressure and age among healthy adult women 20 to 60 years old, collected data on 54 subjects. A portion of the data is presented in Table 10.1, columns 1 and 2. The scatter plot of the data in Figure 10.1a strongly suggests a linear relationship between diastolic blood pressure and age but also indicates that the error term variance increases with age. The researcher fitted a linear regression function by unweighted least squares to conduct some preliminary analyses of the residuals. The fitted regression function and the estimated standard deviations of b_0 and b_1 are:

$$(10.18) \qquad \hat{Y} = 56.157 + .58003X$$
$$\phantom{(10.18) \qquad \hat{Y} = 56.157} (3.994) \quad (.09695)$$

The residuals are shown in Table 10.1, column 3, and the absolute residuals are presented in column 4. Figure 10.1a presents this estimated regression function. Figure 10.1b presents a plot of the residuals against X, which confirms the nonconstant error variance. A plot of the absolute residuals against X in Figure 10.1c suggests that a linear relation between the error standard deviation and X may be reasonable. The analyst therefore regressed the absolute residuals against X and obtained:

$$(10.19) \qquad \hat{s} = -1.54946 + .198172X$$

Here, $\hat{s}$ denotes the estimated expected standard deviation. The estimated standard deviation function in (10.19) is shown in Figure 10.1c.

To obtain the weights w_i, the analyst obtained the fitted values from the standard deviation function in (10.19). For example, for case 1, for which $X_1 = 27$, the fitted value is:

$$\hat{s}_1 = -1.54946 + .198172(27) = 3.801$$

TABLE 10.1   Weighted Least Squares—Blood Pressure Example.

Subject i	(1) Age X_i	(2) Diastolic Blood Pressure Y_i	(3) e_i	(4) $|e_i|$	(5) $\hat{s}_i$	(6) w_i
1	27	73	1.18	1.18	3.801	.06921
2	21	66	−2.34	2.34	2.612	.14656
3	22	63	−5.92	5.92	2.810	.12662
...	...	...	...	...	...	...
52	52	100	13.68	13.68	8.756	.01304
53	58	80	−9.80	9.80	9.944	.01011
54	57	109	19.78	19.78	9.746	.01053

The fitted values are shown in Table 10.1, column 5. The weights are then obtained by using (10.16a). For case 1, we obtain:

$$w_1 = \frac{1}{(\hat{s}_1)^2} = \frac{1}{(3.801)^2} = .0692$$

The weights w_i are shown in Table 10.1, column 6.

Using these weights in a regression program that has weighted least squares capability, the analyst obtained the following estimated regression function.

$$(10.20) \qquad\qquad \hat{Y} = 55.566 + .59634X$$

Note that the estimated regression coefficients are not much different from those in (10.18) obtained with unweighted least squares. Since the regression coefficients changed only a little, the analyst concluded that there was no need to reestimate the standard deviation function and the weights based on the residuals for the weighted regression in (10.20).

The analyst next obtained the estimated variance-covariance matrix of the estimated regression coefficients by means of (10.13) to find the approximate estimated standard deviation $s\{b_{w1}\} = .07924$. It is interesting to note that this standard deviation is somewhat smaller than the standard deviation of the estimate obtained by ordinary least squares in (10.18), .09695. The reduction of about 18 percent is the result of the recognition of unequal error variances when using weighted least squares.

To obtain an approximate 95 percent confidence interval for β_1, the analyst employed (6.50) and required $t(.975; 52) = 2.007$. The confidence limits then are .59634 ± 2.007(.07924) and the approximate 95 percent confidence interval is:

$$.437 \le \beta_1 \le .755$$

We shall consider the appropriateness of this inference approximation in Section 10.5.

Comments

1. The condition of the error variance not being constant over all cases is called *heteroscedasticity*, in contrast to the condition of equal error variances, called *homoscedasticity*.

2. Heteroscedasticity is inherent when the response in regression analysis follows a distribution in which the variance is functionally related to the mean. (Significant nonnormality in Y is encountered as well in most such cases.) Consider, in this connection, a regression analysis where X is the speed of a machine which puts a plastic coating on cable and Y is the number of blemishes in the coating per thousand feet of cable. If Y is Poisson distributed with a mean which increases as X increases, the distributions of Y cannot have constant variance at all levels of X since the variance of a Poisson variable equals the mean, which is increasing with X.

3. Estimation of the weights by means of an estimated variance or standard deviation function or by means of groups of replicates or near replicates can be very helpful when there are major differences in the variances of the error terms. When the differences are only small or modest, however, weighted least squares with these approximate methods will not be particularly helpful.

4. The weighted least squares output of some multiple regression software packages includes R^2, the coefficient of multiple determination. Users of these packages need to treat this measure with caution, because R^2 does not have a clear-cut meaning for weighted least squares.

5. The weighted least squares estimators of the regression coefficients in (10.9) for the case of known error variances σ_i^2 can be derived readily. The derivation also shows that weighted least squares may be viewed as ordinary least squares of transformed variables. The generalized multiple regression model in (10.1) may be expressed as follows in matrix form:

$$(10.21) \qquad \mathbf{Y} = \mathbf{X}\boldsymbol{\beta} + \boldsymbol{\varepsilon}$$

where:

$$\mathbf{E}\{\boldsymbol{\varepsilon}\} = \mathbf{0}$$

$$\boldsymbol{\sigma}^2\{\boldsymbol{\varepsilon}\} = \mathbf{W}^{-1}$$

The notation is the standard one. Note that the variance-covariance matrix of the error terms in (10.2) is the inverse of the weight matrix defined in (10.7).

We now define a diagonal matrix containing the square roots of the weights w_i and denote it by $\mathbf{W}^{1/2}$:

$$(10.22) \qquad \underset{n \times n}{\mathbf{W}^{1/2}} = \begin{bmatrix} \sqrt{w_1} & 0 & \cdots & 0 \\ 0 & \sqrt{w_2} & \cdots & 0 \\ \vdots & \vdots & & \vdots \\ 0 & 0 & \cdots & \sqrt{w_n} \end{bmatrix}$$

Note that $\mathbf{W}^{1/2}$ is symmetric and that $\mathbf{W}^{1/2}\mathbf{W}^{1/2} = \mathbf{W}$. The latter relation also holds for the corresponding inverse matrices: $\mathbf{W}^{-1/2}\mathbf{W}^{-1/2} = \mathbf{W}^{-1}$.

We premultiply the terms on both sides of regression model (10.21) by $\mathbf{W}^{1/2}$ and obtain:

$$(10.23) \qquad \mathbf{W}^{1/2}\mathbf{Y} = \mathbf{W}^{1/2}\mathbf{X}\boldsymbol{\beta} + \mathbf{W}^{1/2}\boldsymbol{\varepsilon}$$

which can be expressed as:

$$(10.23a) \qquad \mathbf{Y}_w = \mathbf{X}_w\boldsymbol{\beta} + \boldsymbol{\varepsilon}_w$$

where:

(10.23b)

$$\mathbf{Y}_w = \mathbf{W}^{1/2}\mathbf{Y}$$

$$\mathbf{X}_w = \mathbf{W}^{1/2}\mathbf{X}$$

$$\boldsymbol{\varepsilon}_w = \mathbf{W}^{1/2}\boldsymbol{\varepsilon}$$

By (5.45) and (5.46), we obtain:

(10.24a)
$$\mathbf{E}\{\boldsymbol{\varepsilon}_w\} = \mathbf{W}^{1/2}\mathbf{E}\{\boldsymbol{\varepsilon}\} = \mathbf{W}^{1/2}\mathbf{0} = \mathbf{0}$$

(10.24b)
$$\boldsymbol{\sigma}^2\{\boldsymbol{\varepsilon}_w\} = \mathbf{W}^{1/2}\boldsymbol{\sigma}^2\{\boldsymbol{\varepsilon}\}\mathbf{W}^{1/2} = \mathbf{W}^{1/2}\mathbf{W}^{-1}\mathbf{W}^{1/2}$$
$$= \mathbf{W}^{1/2}\mathbf{W}^{-1/2}\mathbf{W}^{-1/2}\mathbf{W}^{1/2} = \mathbf{I}$$

Thus, regression model (10.23a) involves independent error terms with mean zero and constant variance $\sigma_i^2 \equiv 1$. We can therefore apply standard regression procedures to this transformed regression model.

For example, the ordinary least squares estimators of the regression coefficients in (6.25) here become:

$$\mathbf{b}_w = (\mathbf{X}_w'\mathbf{X}_w)^{-1}\mathbf{X}_w'\mathbf{Y}_w$$

Using the definitions in (10.23b), we obtain the result for weighted least squares given in (10.9):

$$\mathbf{b}_w = \left[(\mathbf{W}^{1/2}\mathbf{X})'\mathbf{W}^{1/2}\mathbf{X}\right]^{-1}(\mathbf{W}^{1/2}\mathbf{X})'\mathbf{W}^{1/2}\mathbf{Y}$$
$$= (\mathbf{X}'\mathbf{W}^{1/2}\mathbf{W}^{1/2}\mathbf{X})^{-1}\mathbf{X}'\mathbf{W}^{1/2}\mathbf{W}^{1/2}\mathbf{Y}$$
$$= (\mathbf{X}'\mathbf{W}\mathbf{X})^{-1}\mathbf{X}'\mathbf{W}\mathbf{Y}$$

6. Weighted least squares is a special case of *generalized least squares* where the error terms not only may have different variances but pairs of error terms may also be correlated.

7. For simple linear regression, the weighted least squares normal equations in (10.8) become:

(10.25)
$$\sum w_i Y_i = b_{w0} \sum w_i + b_{w1} \sum w_i X_i$$
$$\sum w_i X_i Y_i = b_{w0} \sum w_i X_i + b_{w1} \sum w_i X_i^2$$

and the weighted least squares estimators b_{w0} and b_{w1} in (10.9) are:

(10.26a)
$$b_{w1} = \frac{\sum w_i X_i Y_i - \dfrac{\sum w_i X_i \sum w_i Y_i}{\sum w_i}}{\sum w_i X_i^2 - \dfrac{(\sum w_i X_i)^2}{\sum w_i}}$$

(10.26b)
$$b_{w0} = \frac{\sum w_i Y_i - b_1 \sum w_i X_i}{\sum w_i}$$

Note that if all weights are equal so w_i is identically equal to a constant, the normal equations (10.25) for weighted least squares reduce to the ones for unweighted least squares in (1.9) and the weighted least squares estimators (10.26) reduce to the ones for unweighted least squares in (1.10).   ∎

10.2 Multicollinearity Remedial Measures—Ridge Regression

We consider first some remedial measures for serious multicollinearity that can be implemented with ordinary least squares, and then take up ridge regression, a method of overcoming serious multicollinearity problems by modifying the method of least squares.

Some Remedial Measures

1. As we saw in Chapter 7, the presence of serious multicollinearity often does not affect the usefulness of the fitted model for estimating mean responses or making predictions, provided that the values of the predictor variables for which inferences are to be made follow the same multicollinearity pattern as the data on which the regression model is based. Hence, one remedial measure is to restrict the use of the fitted regression model to inferences for values of the predictor variables that follow the same pattern of multicollinearity.

2. In polynomial regression models, as we noted in Chapter 7, use of centered data for the predictor variable(s) serves to reduce the multicollinearity among the first-order, second-order, and higher-order terms for any given predictor variable.

3. One or several predictor variables may be dropped from the model in order to lessen the multicollinearity and thereby reduce the standard errors of the estimated regression coefficients of the predictor variables remaining in the model. This remedial measure has two important limitations. First, no direct information is obtained about the dropped predictor variables. Second, the magnitudes of the regression coefficients for the predictor variables remaining in the model are affected by the correlated predictor variables not included in the model.

4. Sometimes it is possible to add some cases that break the pattern of multicollinearity. Often, however, this option is not available. In business and economics, for instance, many predictor variables cannot be controlled, so that new cases will tend to show the same intercorrelation patterns as the earlier ones.

5. In some economic studies, it is possible to estimate the regression coefficients for different predictor variables from different sets of data and thereby avoid the problems of multicollinearity. Demand studies, for instance, may use both cross-section and time series data to this end. Suppose the predictor variables in a demand study are price and income, and the relation to be estimated is:

$$(10.27) \qquad Y_i = \beta_0 + \beta_1 X_{i1} + \beta_2 X_{i2} + \varepsilon_i$$

where Y is demand, X_1 is income, and X_2 is price. The income coefficient β_1 may then be estimated from cross-section data. The demand variable Y is thereupon adjusted:

$$(10.28) \qquad Y_i' = Y_i - b_1 X_{i1}$$

Finally, the price coefficient β_2 is estimated by regressing the adjusted demand variable Y' on X_2.

6. Another remedial measure for multicollinearity that can be used with ordinary least squares is to form one or several composite indexes based on the highly correlated predictor variables, an index being a linear combination of the correlated predictor variables. The methodology of *principal components* provides composite indexes that are uncorrelated. Often, a few of these composite indexes capture much of the information contained in the predictor variables. These few uncorrelated composite indexes are then used in the

FIGURE 10.2 **Biased Estimator with Small Variance May Be Preferable to Unbiased Estimator with Large Variance.**

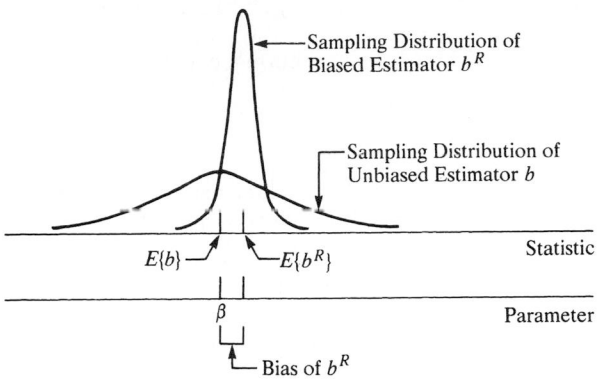

regression analysis as predictor variables instead of the original highly correlated predictor variables. A limitation of principal components regression, also called latent root regression, is that it may be difficult to attach concrete meanings to the indexes.

More information about these remedial approaches as well as about Bayesian regression, where prior information about the regression coefficients is incorporated into the estimation procedure, may be obtained from specialized works such as Reference 10.2.

Ridge Regression

Biased Estimation. Ridge regression is one of several methods that have been proposed to remedy multicollinearity problems by modifying the method of least squares to allow biased estimators of the regression coefficients. When an estimator has only a small bias and is substantially more precise than an unbiased estimator, it may well be the preferred estimator since it will have a larger probability of being close to the true parameter value. Figure 10.2 illustrates this situation. Estimator b is unbiased but imprecise, whereas estimator b^R is much more precise but has a small bias. The probability that b^R falls near the true value β is much greater than that for the unbiased estimator b.

A measure of the combined effect of bias and sampling variation is the mean squared error, a concept that we encountered in Chapter 8 in connection with Mallow's C_p criterion. Here, the mean squared error is the expected value of the squared deviation of the biased estimator b^R from the true parameter β. As before, this expected value is the sum of the variance of the estimator and the squared bias:

$$(10.29) \qquad E\{b^R - \beta\}^2 = \sigma^2\{b^R\} + (E\{b^R\} - \beta)^2$$

Note that if the estimator is unbiased, the mean squared error is identical to the variance of the estimator.

Ridge Estimators. For ordinary least squares, the normal equations are given by (6.24):

$$(10.30) \qquad (\mathbf{X'X})\mathbf{b} = \mathbf{X'Y}$$

When all variables are transformed by the correlation transformation (7.44), the transformed regression model is given by (7.45):

$$(10.31) \qquad Y_i' = \beta_1' X_{i1}' + \beta_2' X_{i2}' + \cdots + \beta_{p-1}' X_{i,p-1}' + \varepsilon_i'$$

and the least squares normal equations are given by (7.52a):

$$(10.32) \qquad \mathbf{r}_{XX}\mathbf{b} = \mathbf{r}_{YX}$$

where $\mathbf{r}_{XX}$ is the correlation matrix of the X variables defined in (7.47) and $\mathbf{r}_{YX}$ is the vector of coefficients of simple correlation between Y and each X variable defined in (7.48).

The ridge standardized regression estimators are obtained by introducing into the least squares normal equations (10.32) a biasing constant $c \geq 0$, in the following form:

$$(10.33) \qquad (\mathbf{r}_{XX} + c\mathbf{I})\mathbf{b}^R = \mathbf{r}_{YX}$$

where $\mathbf{b}^R$ is the vector of the standardized ridge regression coefficients b_k^R:

$$(10.33a) \qquad \underset{(p-1)\times 1}{\mathbf{b}^R} = \begin{bmatrix} b_1^R \\ b_2^R \\ \vdots \\ b_{p-1}^R \end{bmatrix}$$

and $\mathbf{I}$ is the $(p-1) \times (p-1)$ identity matrix. Solution of the normal equations (10.33) yields the ridge standardized regression coefficients:

$$(10.34) \qquad \mathbf{b}^R = (\mathbf{r}_{XX} + c\mathbf{I})^{-1}\mathbf{r}_{YX}$$

The constant c reflects the amount of bias in the estimators. When $c = 0$, (10.34) reduces to the ordinary least squares regression coefficients in standardized form, as given in (7.52b). When $c > 0$, the ridge regression coefficients are biased but tend to be more stable (i.e., less variable) than ordinary least squares estimators.

Choice of Biasing Constant c. It can be shown that the bias component of the total mean squared error of the ridge regression estimator $\mathbf{b}^R$ increases as c gets larger (with all b_k^R tending toward zero) while the variance component becomes smaller. It can further be shown that there always exists some value c for which the ridge regression estimator $\mathbf{b}^R$ has a smaller total mean squared error than the ordinary least squares estimator $\mathbf{b}$. The difficulty is that the optimum value of c varies from one application to another and is unknown.

A commonly used method of determining the biasing constant c is based on the *ridge trace* and the variance inflation factors $(VIF)_k$ in (9.41). The ridge trace is a simultaneous plot of the values of the $p - 1$ estimated ridge standardized regression coefficients for different values of c, usually between 0 and 1. Extensive experience has indicated that the estimated regression coefficients b_k^R may fluctuate widely as c is changed slightly from 0, and some may even change signs. Gradually, however, these wide fluctuations cease and the magnitudes of the regression coefficients tend to move slowly toward zero as c is increased further. At the same time, the values of $(VIF)_k$ tends to fall rapidly as c is changed from 0, and gradually the $(VIF)_k$ values also tend to change only moderately as c is increased

FIGURE 10.3 **Ridge Trace of Estimated Standardized Regression Coefficients —Body Fat Example with Three Predictor Variables.**

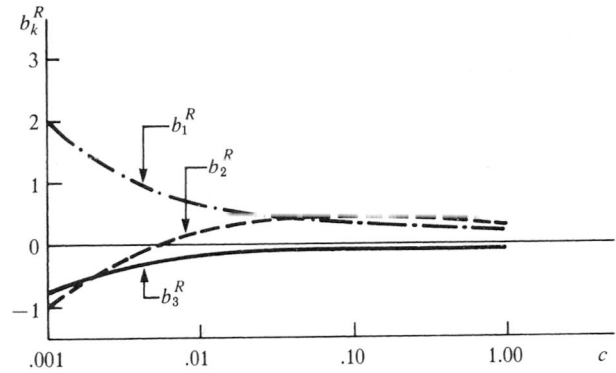

further. One therefore examines the ridge trace and the *VIF* values and chooses the smallest value of c where it is deemed that the regression coefficients first become stable in the ridge trace and the *VIF* values have become sufficiently small. The choice is thus a judgmental one.

Example. In the body fat example with three predictor variables in Table 7.1, we noted previously several informal indications of severe multicollinearity in the data. Indeed, in the fitted model with three predictor variables (Table 7.2d), the estimated regression coefficient b_2 is negative even though it was expected that amount of body fat is positively related to thigh circumference. Ridge regression calculations were made for the body fat example data in Table 7.1 (calculations not shown). The ridge standardized regression coefficients for selected values of c are presented in Table 10.2, and the variance inflation factors are given in Table 10.3. The coefficients of multiple determination R^2 are also shown in the latter table. Figure 10.3 presents the ridge trace of the estimated standardized regression coefficients based on calculations for many more values of c than those shown in Table 10.2. To facilitate the analysis, the horizontal c scale in Figure 10.3 is logarithmic.

Note the instability in Figure 10.3 of the regression coefficients for very small values of c. The estimated regression coefficient b_2^R, in fact, changes signs. Also note the rapid decrease in the *VIF* values in Table 10.3. It was decided to employ $c = .02$ here because for this value of the biasing constant the ridge regression coefficients have *VIF* values near 1 and the estimated regression coefficients appear to have become reasonably stable. The resulting fitted model for $c = .02$ is:

$$\hat{Y}' = .5463X_1' + .3774X_2' - .1369X_3'$$

Transforming back to the original variables by (7.53), we obtain:

$$\hat{Y} = -7.3978 + .5553X_1 + .3681X_2 - .1917X_3$$

where $\bar{Y} = 20.195$, $\bar{X}_1 = 25.305$, $\bar{X}_2 = 51.170$, $\bar{X}_3 = 27.620$, $s_Y = 5.106$, $s_1 = 5.023$, $s_2 = 5.235$, and $s_3 = 3.647$.

TABLE 10.2 **Ridge Estimated Standardized Regression Coefficients for Different Biasing Constants c—Body Fat Example with Three Predictor Variables.**

c	b_1^R	b_2^R	b_3^R
.000	4.264	−2.929	−1.561
.002	1.441	−.4113	−.4813
.004	1.006	−.0248	−.3149
.006	.8300	.1314	−.2472
.008	.7343	.2158	−.2103
.010	.6742	.2684	−.1870
.020	.5463	.3774	−.1369
.030	.5004	.4134	−.1181
.040	.4760	.4302	−.1076
.050	.4605	.4392	−.1005
.100	.4234	.4490	−.0812
.500	.3377	.3791	−.0295
1.000	.2798	.3101	−.0059

TABLE 10.3 *VIF Values for Regression Coefficients and R^2 for Different Biasing Constants c—Body Fat Example with Three Predictor Variables.*

c	$(VIF)_1$	$(VIF)_2$	$(VIF)_3$	R^2
.000	708.84	564.34	104.61	.8014
.002	50.56	40.45	8.28	.7901
.004	16.98	13.73	3.36	.7864
.006	8.50	6.98	2.19	.7847
.008	5.15	4.30	1.62	.7838
.010	3.49	2.98	1.38	.7832
.020	1.10	1.08	1.01	.7818
.030	.63	.70	.92	.7812
.040	.45	.56	.88	.7808
.050	.37	.49	.85	.7804
.100	.25	.37	.76	.7784
.500	.15	.21	.40	.7427
1.000	.11	.14	.23	.6818

The improper sign on the estimate for β_2 has now been eliminated, and the estimated regression coefficients are more in line with prior expectations. The sum of the squared residuals for the transformed variables, which increases with c, has only increased from .1986 at $c = 0$ to .2182 at $c = .02$ while R^2 decreased from .8014 to .7818. These changes are relatively modest. The estimated mean body fat when $X_{h1} = 25.0$, $X_{h2} = 50.0$, and $X_{h3} = 29.0$ is 19.33 for the ridge regression at $c = .02$ compared to 19.19 utilizing the ordinary least squares solution. Thus, the ridge solution at $c = .02$ appears to be quite satisfactory here and a reasonable alternative to the ordinary least squares solution.

Comments

1. The normal equations (10.33) for the ridge estimators are as follows:

(10.35)

$$
\begin{aligned}
(1+c)b_1^R + \quad r_{12}b_2^R + \cdots + r_{1,p-1}b_{p-1}^R &= r_{Y1} \\
r_{21}b_1^R + (1+c)b_2^R + \cdots + r_{2,p-1}b_{p-1}^R &= r_{Y2} \\
&\;\;\vdots \\
r_{p-1,1}b_1^R + \quad r_{p-1,2}b_2^R + \cdots + (1+c)b_{p-1}^R &= r_{Y,p-1}
\end{aligned}
$$

where r_{ij} is the coefficient of simple correlation between the ith and jth X variables and r_{Yj} is the coefficient of simple correlation between the response variable Y and the jth X variable.

2. *VIF* values for ridge regression coefficients b_k^R are defined analogously to those for ordinary least squares regression coefficients. Namely, the *VIF* value for b_k^R measures how large is the variance of b_k^R relative to what the variance would be if the predictor variables were uncorrelated. It can be shown that the *VIF* values for the ridge regression coefficients b_k^R are the diagonal elements of the following $(p-1) \times (p-1)$ matrix:

(10.36)
$$
(\mathbf{r}_{XX} + c\mathbf{I})^{-1}\mathbf{r}_{XX}(\mathbf{r}_{XX} + c\mathbf{I})^{-1}
$$

3. The coefficient of multiple determination R^2, which for ordinary least squares is given in (6.40):

(10.37)
$$
R^2 = 1 - \frac{SSE}{SSTO}
$$

can be defined analogously for ridge regression. A simplification occurs, however, because the total sum of squares for the correlation-transformed dependent variable Y' in (7.44a) is:

(10.38)
$$
SSTO_R = \sum(Y_i' - \bar{Y}')^2 = 1
$$

The fitted values with ridge regression are:

(10.39)
$$
\hat{Y}_i' = b_1^R X_{i1}' + \cdots + b_{p-1}^R X_{i,p-1}'
$$

where the X_{ik}' are the X variables transformed according to the correlation transformation (7.44b). The error sum of squares, as usual, is:

(10.40)
$$
SSE_R = \sum(Y_i' - \hat{Y}_i')^2
$$

where $\hat{Y}_i'$ is given in (10.39). R^2 for ridge regression then becomes:

(10.41)
$$
R_R^2 = 1 - SSE_R
$$

4. Ridge regression estimates tend to be stable in the sense that they are usually little affected by small changes in the data on which the fitted regression is based. In contrast, ordinary least squares estimates may be highly unstable under these conditions when the predictor variables are highly multicollinear. Predictions of new observations made from ridge estimated regression functions tend to be more precise than predictions made from ordinary least squares regression functions when the predictor variables are correlated and the new observations follow the same

multicollinearity pattern (see, for instance, Reference 10.3). The prediction precision advantage with ridge regression is especially great when the intercorrelations among the predictor variables are high.

5. Ridge estimated regression functions at times will provide good estimates of mean responses or predictions of new observations for levels of the predictor variables outside the region of the observations on which the regression function is based. In contrast, estimated regression functions based on ordinary least squares may perform quite poorly in such circumstances. Of course, any estimation or prediction well outside the region of the observations should always be made with great caution.

6. A major limitation of ridge regression is that ordinary inference procedures are not applicable and exact distributional properties are not known. Bootstrapping, a computer-intensive procedure to be discussed in Section 10.5, can be employed to evaluate the precision of ridge regression coefficients. Another limitation of ridge regression is that the choice of the biasing constant c is a judgmental one. Although a variety of formal methods have been developed for making this choice, these have their own limitations.

7. The ridge regression procedures have been generalized to allow for differing biasing constants for the different estimated regression coefficients; see, for instance, Reference 10.2.

8. Ridge regression can be used to help in reducing the number of potential predictor variables in exploratory observational studies by analyzing the ridge trace. Variables whose ridge trace is unstable, with the coefficient tending toward the value of zero, are dropped with this approach. Also, variables whose ridge trace is stable but at a very small value are dropped. Finally, variables with unstable ridge traces that do not tend toward zero are considered as candidates for dropping.   ∎

10.3 Remedial Measures for Influential Cases—Robust Regression

We noted in Chapter 9 that the hat matrix and studentized deleted residuals are valuable tools for identifying cases that are outlying with respect to the X and Y variables. In addition, we considered there how to measure the influence of these outlying cases on the fitted values and estimated regression coefficients by means of the *DFFITS*, Cook's distance, and *DFBETAS* measures. The reason for our concern with outlying cases is that the method of least squares is particularly susceptible to these cases, resulting sometimes in a seriously distorted fitted model for the remaining cases. A crucial question that arises now is how to handle highly influential cases.

A first step is to examine whether an outlying case is the result of a recording error, breakdown of a measurement instrument, or the like. For instance, in a study of the waiting time in a telephone reservation system, one waiting time was recorded as 1,000 rings. This observation was so extreme and unrealistic that it was clearly erroneous. If erroneous data can be corrected, this should be done. Often, however, erroneous data cannot be corrected later on and should be discarded. Many times, unfortunately, it is not possible after the data have been obtained to tell for certain whether the observations for an outlying case are erroneous. Such cases should usually not be discarded.

If an outlying influential case is not clearly erroneous, the next step should be to examine the adequacy of the model. Scientists frequently have primary interest in the outlying cases because they deviate from the currently accepted model. Examination of these outlying cases may provide important clues as to how the model needs to be modified. In a study of the yield of a process, a first-order model was fitted for the two important factors under consideration because previous studies had not found any interaction effects between these factors on the yield. One case in the current study was outlying and highly influential, with extremely high yield; it corresponded to unusually high levels of the two factors. The tentative conclusion drawn was that an interaction effect is present; this was subsequently confirmed in a follow-up study. The improved model, resulting from the outlying case, led to greatly improved process productivity.

Outlying cases may also lead to the finding of other types of model inadequacies, such as the omission of an important variable or the choice of an incorrect functional form (e.g., a quadratic function instead of an exponential function). The analysis of outlying influential cases can frequently lead to valuable insights for strengthening the model such that the outlying case is no longer an outlier but is accounted for by the model.

Discarding of outlying influential cases that are not clearly erroneous and that cannot be accounted for by model improvements should be done only rarely, such as when the model is not intended to cover the special circumstances related to the outlying cases. For example, a few cases in an industrial study were outlying and highly influential. These cases occurred early in the study, when the plant was in transition from one process to the new one under study. Discarding of these early cases was deemed to be reasonable since the model was intended for use after the new process had stabilized.

An alternative to discarding outlying cases that is less severe is to dampen the influence of these cases. That is the purpose of robust regression.

Robust Regression

Robust regression procedures dampen the influence of outlying cases, as compared to ordinary least squares estimation, in an effort to provide a better fit for the majority of cases. They are useful when a known, smooth regression function is to be fitted to data that are "noisy," with a number of outlying cases, so that the assumption of a normal distribution for the error terms is not appropriate. Robust regression procedures are also useful when automated regression analysis is required. For example, a complex measurement instrument used for internal medical examinations must be calibrated for each use. There is no time for a thorough identification of outlying cases and an analysis of their influence, nor for a careful consideration of remedial measures. Instead, an automated regression calibration must be used. Robust regression procedures will automatically guard against undue influence of outlying cases in this situation.

Numerous robust regression procedures have been developed. They are described in specialized texts, such as References 10.4 and 10.5. We mention briefly a few of these procedures and then describe in more detail one commonly used procedure based on iteratively reweighted least squares.

LAR Regression. Least absolute residuals (LAR) regression, also called *minimum L_1-norm regression*, is an early robust regression procedure. It is insensitive to both outlying data values and inadequacies of the model employed. The method of least absolute residuals estimates the regression coefficients by minimizing the sum of the absolute deviations of the Y observations from their means. The criterion to be minimized, denoted by L_1, is:

(10.42)
$$L_1 = \sum_{i=1}^{n} |Y_i - (\beta_0 + \beta_1 X_{i1} + \cdots + \beta_{p-1} X_{i, p-1})|$$

Since absolute deviations rather than squared ones are involved here, the LAR method places less emphasis on outlying observations than does the method of least squares.

The estimated LAR regression coefficients can be obtained by linear programming techniques. Details about computational aspects may be found in specialized texts, such as Reference 10.6. The LAR fitted regression model differs from the least squares fitted model in that the residuals ordinarily will not sum to zero. Also, the solution for the estimated regression coefficients with the method of least absolute residuals may not be unique.

IRLS Robust Regression.   Iteratively reweighted least squares (IRLS) robust regression uses the weighted least squares procedures discussed in Section 10.1 to dampen the influence of outlying observations. Instead of weights based on the error variances, IRLS robust regression uses weights based on how far outlying a case is, as measured by the residual for that case. The weights are revised with each iteration until a robust fit has been obtained. We shall discuss this procedure in more detail shortly.

LMS Regression.   Least median of squares (LMS) regression replaces the sum of squared deviations in ordinary least squares by the median of the squared deviations, which is a robust estimator of location. The criterion for this procedure is to minimize the median squared deviation:

$$(10.43) \qquad \text{median}\{[Y_i - (\beta_0 + \beta_1 X_{i1} + \cdots + \beta_{p-1} X_{i,p-1})]^2\}$$

with respect to the regression coefficients. Thus, this procedure leads to estimated regression coefficients $b_0, b_1, \ldots, b_{p-1}$ that minimize the median of the squared residuals.

Other Robust Regression Procedures.   There are many other robust regression procedures. Some involve trimming one or several of the extreme squared deviations before applying the least squares criterion; others are based on ranks. Many of the robust regression procedures require extensive computing.

IRLS Robust Regression

Iteratively reweighted least squares was encountered in Section 10.1 as a remedial measure for unequal error variances in connection with the obtaining of weights from an estimated variance or standard deviation function. For robust regression, weighted least squares is used to reduce the influence of outlying cases by employing weights that vary inversely with the size of the residual. Outlying cases that have large residuals are thereby given smaller weights. The weights are revised as each iteration yields new residuals until the estimation process stabilizes. A summary of the steps follows:

1. Choose a weight function for weighting the cases.

2. Obtain starting weights for all cases.

3. Use the starting weights in weighted least squares and obtain the residuals from the fitted regression function.

4. Use the residuals in step 3 to obtain revised weights.

5. Continue the iterations until convergence is obtained.

We now discuss each of the steps in IRLS robust regression.

FIGURE 10.4   Two Weight Functions Used in IRLS Robust Regression.

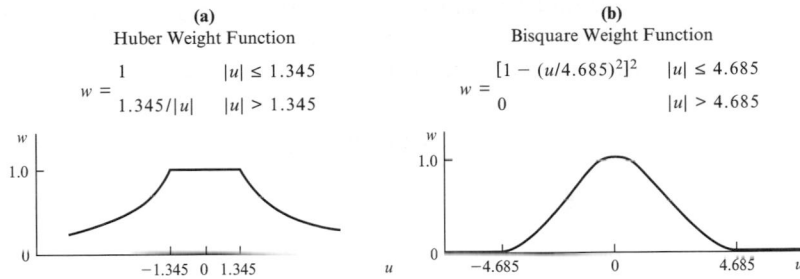

(a)
Huber Weight Function

$$w = \begin{array}{ll} 1 & |u| \le 1.345 \\ 1.345/|u| & |u| > 1.345 \end{array}$$

(b)
Bisquare Weight Function

$$w = \begin{array}{ll} [1 - (u/4.685)^2]^2 & |u| \le 4.685 \\ 0 & |u| > 4.685 \end{array}$$

Weight Function.   Many weight functions have been proposed for dampening the influence of outlying cases. Two widely used weight functions are the Huber and bisquare weight functions:

(10.44)   Huber: $w = \begin{cases} 1 & |u| \le 1.345 \\[2mm] \dfrac{1.345}{|u|} & |u| > 1.345 \end{cases}$

(10.45)   Bisquare: $w = \begin{cases} \left[1 - \left(\dfrac{u}{4.685} \right)^2 \right]^2 & |u| \le 4.685 \\[4mm] 0 & |u| > 4.685 \end{cases}$

As before, w denotes the weight, and u denotes the scaled residual to be defined shortly. The constant 1.345 in the Huber weight function and the constant 4.685 in the bisquare weight function are called *tuning constants*. They were chosen to make the IRLS robust procedure 95 percent efficient for data generated by the normal error regression model (6.7). Figure 10.4 shows graphs of the two weight functions. Note how the weight w according to each weight function declines as the absolute scaled residual gets larger, and that each weight function is symmetric around $u = 0$. Also note that the Huber weight function does not reduce the weight of a case from 1.0 until the absolute scaled residual exceeds 1.345, and that all cases receive some positive weight, no matter how large the absolute scaled residual. In contrast, the bisquare weight function reduces the weights of all cases from 1.0 (unless the residual is zero). In addition, the bisquare weight function gives weight 0 to all cases whose absolute scaled residual exceeds 4.685, thereby entirely excluding these extreme cases.

Starting Values.   Calculations with some of the weight functions are very sensitive to the starting values; with others, this is less of a problem. When the Huber weight function is employed, the initial residuals may be those obtained from an ordinary least squares fit. The bisquare function calculations, on the other hand, are more sensitive to the starting values. To obtain good starting values for the bisquare weight function, the Huber weight function is often used to obtain an initial robust regression fit, and the residuals for this fit are then employed as starting values for several iterations with the bisquare weight function. Alternatively, least absolute residuals regression in (10.42) may be used to obtain starting residuals when the bisquare weight function is used.

Scaled Residuals.   The weight functions (10.44) and (10.45) are each designed to be used with scaled residuals. The semistudentized residuals in (3.5) are scaled residuals and could be employed. However, in the presence of outlying observations, $\sqrt{MSE}$ is not a resistant estimator of the error term standard deviation σ; the magnitude of $\sqrt{MSE}$ can be greatly influenced by one or several outlying observations. Also, $\sqrt{MSE}$ is not a robust estimator of σ when the distribution of the error terms is far from normal. Instead, the resistant and robust median absolute deviation (MAD) estimator is often employed:

$$(10.46) \qquad\qquad MAD = \frac{1}{.6745} \, \text{median}\left\{ |e_i - \text{median}\{e_i\}| \right\}$$

The constant .6745 provides an unbiased estimate of σ for independent observations from a normal distribution. Here, it serves to provide an estimate that is approximately unbiased.

   The scaled residual u_i based on (10.46) then is:

$$(10.47) \qquad\qquad u_i = \frac{e_i}{MAD}$$

Number of Iterations.   The iterative process of obtaining a new fit, new residuals and thereby new weights, and then refitting with the new weights continues until the process converges. Convergence can be measured by observing whether the weights change relatively little, whether the residuals change relatively little, whether the estimated regression coefficients change relatively little, or whether the fitted values change relatively little.

Example

The example of robust regression using iteratively reweighted least squares to be presented involves only one predictor variable. In this way, simple plots can be used to present the data and the fitted regression function. The robust procedure for fitting a multiple regression model will be exactly the same.

   Table 10.4 contains a portion of the data from a study investigating the relation between the home environment and school performance for eighth-grade students (Ref. 10.7). Shown in column 1 are data on average mathematics proficiency of eighth-grade students obtained in the 1990 National Assessment of Educational Progress for 37 states, the District of Columbia, Guam, and the Virgin Islands. Column 2 of Table 10.4 presents the percentage of eighth-grade students who had available at home three or more types of reading materials (books, encyclopedias, magazines, and newspapers). Figure 10.5a presents a scatter plot of the data. The relationship between home reading resources and average mathematics proficiency appears to be fairly linear for the majority of states, but three points are clear outliers. The District of Columbia and the Virgin Islands are outliers with respect to mathematics proficiency (Y), and Guam appears to be an outlier primarily with respect to available reading resources (X). Figure 10.5b presents a plot against X of the residuals obtained when a linear regression function is fitted by ordinary least squares. This plot shows clearly the two outlying Y cases. Note also from the residual plot that there is a group of six states with low reading resources levels, between 68 and 73, whose average mathematics proficiency scores are all above the fitted regression line. A linear regression function, fitted robustly or otherwise, is not likely to fit these states well and at the same time fit the majority of the states well. A curvilinear response function may not be reasonable here for two reasons, however. Other factors likely account for the performance of the group of six states. In fact, when we consider additional predictor variables in Section 10.7, we find no evidence of curvilinearity in the regression relation between average mathematics proficiency and

TABLE 10.4   **Data for Mathematics Proficiency Example.**

i	State	(1) Average Mathematics Proficiency Y_i	(2) Percent of Students with Several Reading Materials X_i
1	Alabama	252	78
2	Arizona	259	73
3	Arkansas	256	77
4	California	256	68
...	...	...	...
8	D. of Columbia	231	76
...	...	...	...
11	Guam	231	64
...	...	...	...
36	Virgin Islands	218	76
37	Virginia	264	82
38	W. Virginia	256	80
39	Wisconsin	274	86
40	Wyoming	272	86

Source: ETS Policy Information Center, *America's Smallest School: The Family* (Princeton, New Jersey: Educational Testing Service, 1992), p. 44.

FIGURE 10.5   **Scatter Plot and Plot of Ordinary Least Squares Residuals against Predictor Variable—Mathematics Proficiency Example.**

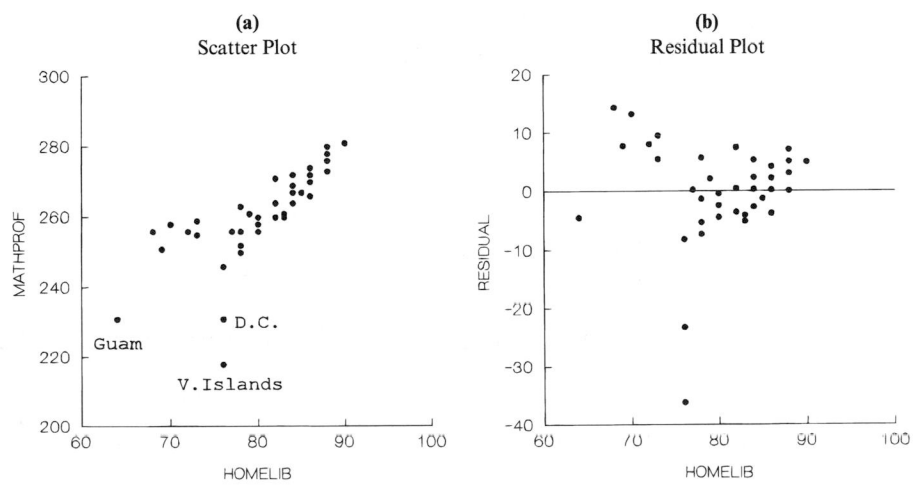

TABLE 10.5   **Iteratively Huber-Reweighted Least Squares Calculations—Mathematics Proficiency Example.**

	(1)	(2)	(3)	(4)	(5)	(6)
				Iteration		
	0		1		7	
i	e_i	u_i	w_i	e_i	w_i	e_i
1	−5.207	−.773	1.0	−6.177	1.0	−6.362
2	9.591	1.425	.944	8.345	1.0	8.036
3	.353	.052	1.0	−.673	1.0	−.883
4	14.389	2.137	.629	12.868	.705	12.434
...	...	...	...	...	...	...
8	−23.088	−3.429	.392	−24.168	.359	−24.403
...	...	...	...	...	...	...
11	−4.372	−.649	1.0	−6.114	1.0	−6.648
...	...	...	...	...	...	...
36	−36.088	−5.360	.251	−37.168	.234	−37.403
37	.555	.082	1.0	−.196	1.0	−.281
38	−4.326	−.643	1.0	−5.186	1.0	−5.321
39	4.316	.641	1.0	3.786	1.0	3.801
40	2.316	.344	1.0	1.786	1.0	1.801

home reading resources. A second reason why a curvilinear response function may not be reasonable here is that the pull of the group of six states toward curvilinearity is met with a counterpull from the two outlying Y cases.

In view of the outlying cases, we shall fit a linear regression function robustly, using iteratively reweighted least squares and the Huber weight function (10.44). We illustrate the calculations for case 1, Alabama. The regression model to be fitted is the first-order model:

$$(10.48) \qquad\qquad Y_i = \beta_0 + \beta_1 X_i + \varepsilon_i$$

An ordinary least squares fit of this model yields:

$$(10.49) \qquad\qquad \hat{Y} = 135.56 + 1.5596X$$

The residual for Alabama is $e_1 = -5.2069$. The residuals are shown in Column 1 of Table 10.5. The median of the 40 residuals is median$\{e_i\} = .39404$. Hence, $e_1 - $ median$\{e_i\} = -5.2069 - .39404 = -5.60094$, and the absolute deviation is $|e_1 - $ median$\{e_i\}| = 5.60094$. The median of the 40 absolute deviations is:

$$\text{median}\{|e_i - \text{median}\{e_i\}|\} = 4.5413$$

so that the *MAD* estimator (10.46) is:

$$MAD = \frac{4.5413}{.6745} = 6.7328$$

Hence, the scaled residual (10.47) for Alabama is:

$$u_1 = \frac{-5.2069}{6.7328} = -.77336$$

The scaled residuals are shown in Table 10.5, column 2. Since $|u_1| = .773 \leq 1.345$, the initial Huber weight for Alabama is $w_1 = 1.0$. The initial weights are shown in Table 10.5, column 3. To interpret these weights, remember that ordinary least squares may be viewed as a special case of weighted least squares with the weights for all cases being equal to 1. We note in column 3 that the initial weights for cases 8 and 36 (District of Columbia and Virgin Islands) are substantially reduced, and that the weights for some other states are reduced somewhat.

The first iteration of weighted least squares uses the initial weights in column 3, leading to the fitted regression model:

(10.50) $\hat{Y} = 140.82 + 1.5045X$

This fitted regression function differs somewhat from the ordinary least squares fit in (10.49), but not too greatly. This can also be seen by comparing the residuals from iteration 1, shown in column 4 of Table 10.5, with the residuals from the ordinary least squares fit in column 1. The residuals differ somewhat, but most differences are modest.

Iteration 2 uses the residuals in column 4 of Table 10.5, scales them, and obtains revised Huber weights, which are then used in iteration 2 of weighted least squares. The weights obtained for the eighth iteration differed relatively little from those for the seventh iteration; hence the iteration process was stopped with the seventh iteration. The final weights are shown in Table 10.5, column 5. Note that only minor changes in the weights occurred between iterations 1 and 7. Use of the weights in column 5 leads to the final fitted model:

(10.51) $\hat{Y} = 142.95 + 1.4796X$

The residuals for the final fit are shown in Table 10.5, column 6. Just as the weights changed only moderately between iterations 1 and 7, so the residuals changed only to a small extent after iteration 1. Figure 10.6a shows the scatter plot and the ordinary least squares fitted regression function, and Figure 10.6b shows the robust fitted regression function. The latter perhaps fits the majority of the states a little better, but the differences between the two fits are very small. Robust regression therefore has been valuable here in showing that the ordinary least squares fit of regression model (10.48) is not seriously distorted by the outlying cases.

We conclude from the ordinary least squares fit in Figure 10.6a that there is a clear positive association between availability of reading resources in the home and average mathematics proficiency at the state level; the coefficient of simple determination is $r^2 = .56$. This does not necessarily imply a causal relation, of course. The availability of reading resources may be positively correlated with other variables that are causally related to mathematics proficiency. We shall continue exploring this example in Section 10.7.

Comments

1. Robust regression requires knowledge of the regression function. When the appropriate regression function is not clear, nonparametric regression may be useful. Nonparametric regression is discussed in Section 10.4.

FIGURE 10.6   **Comparison of Ordinary Least Squares Fit with Robust Fit — Mathematics Proficiency Example.**

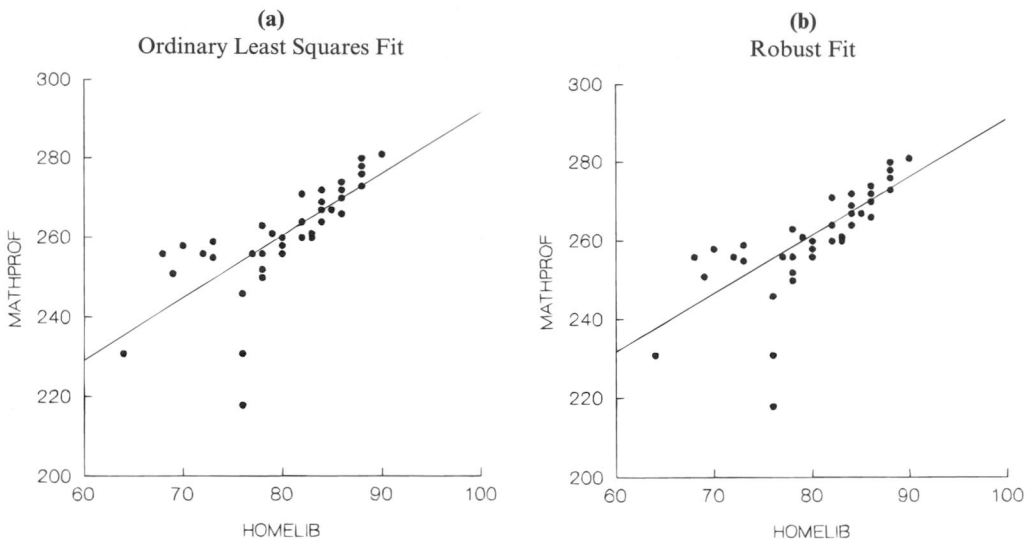

2. Robust regression can be employed to identify outliers in situations where there are multiple outliers whose presence is masked with diagnostic measures that delete one case at a time. Cases whose final weights are relatively small are outlying.

3. As illustrated by the mathematics proficiency example, robust regression is often useful for confirming the reasonableness of ordinary least squares results. When robust regression yields similar results as ordinary least squares (for example, the residuals are similar), one obtains some reassurance that ordinary least squares is not unduly influenced by outlying cases.

4. A limitation of robust regression is that the evaluation of the precision of the estimated regression coefficients is more complex than for ordinary least squares. Some large-sample results have been obtained (see, for example, Reference 10.4), but they may not perform well in the presence of outliers. Bootstrapping (to be discussed in Section 10.5) may also be used for evaluating the precision of robust regression results.

5. When the Huber, bisquare, and other weight functions are based on the scaled residuals in (10.47), they primarily reduce the influence of cases that are outlying with respect to their Y values. To make the robust regression fit more sensitive to cases that are outlying with respect to their X values, studentized residuals in (9.20) or studentized deleted residuals in (9.24) may be used instead of the scaled residuals in (10.47). Again, $\sqrt{MSE}$ may be replaced by MAD in (10.46) for better resistance and robustness when calculating the studentized or studentized deleted residuals.

In addition, the weights w_i obtained from the weight function may be modified to reduce directly the influence of cases with large X leverage. One suggestion is to multiply the weight function weight w_i by $\sqrt{1 - h_{ii}}$, where h_{ii} is the leverage value of the ith case defined in (9.18).

Methods that reduce the influence of cases that are outlying with respect to their X values are called *bounded influence regression* methods.   ∎

10.4 Remedial Measures for Unknown Response Function—Nonparametric Regression

We considered nonparametric regression in Chapter 3 when there is one predictor variable in the regression model. We noted there that nonparametric regression fits are useful for exploring the nature of the response function, to confirm the nature of a particular response function that has been fitted to the data, and to obtain estimates of mean responses without specifying the nature of the response function.

Nonparametric regression can be extended to multiple regression when there are two or more predictor variables. Additional complexities are encountered, however, when making this extension. With more than two predictor variables, it is not possible to show the fitted response surface graphically, so one cannot see its appearance. Unlike parametric regression, no analytic expression for the response surface is provided by nonparametric regression. Also, as the number of predictor variables increases, there may be fewer and fewer cases in a neighborhood, leading to erratic smoothing. This latter problem is less serious when the predictor variables are highly correlated and interest in the response surface is confined to the region of the X observations.

Numerous procedures have been developed for fitting a response surface when there are two or more predictor variables without specifying the nature of the response function. Reference 10.8 discusses a number of these procedures. These include locally weighted regressions (Ref. 10.9), regression trees (Ref. 10.10), projection pursuit (Ref. 10.11), and smoothing splines (Ref. 10.12). We discuss the loess method here, which we described briefly in Chapter 3 for regression with one predictor variable. We extend this method now to multiple regression and will be able to describe it in more detail because we have established the necessary foundation of weighted least squares in Section 10.1.

Loess Method

The loess method for multiple regression, developed by Cleveland and Devlin (Ref. 10.9), assumes that the predictor variables have already been selected, that the response function is smooth, and that appropriate transformations have been made or other remedial steps taken so that the error terms are approximately normally distributed with constant variance. For any combination of X levels, the loess method fits either a first-order model or a second-order model based on cases in the neighborhood, with more distant cases in the neighborhood receiving smaller weights. We shall explain the loess method for the case of two predictor variables when we wish to obtain the fitted value at (X_{h1}, X_{h2}).

Distance Measure.   We need a distance measure showing how far each case is from (X_{h1}, X_{h2}). Usually, a Euclidean distance measure is employed. For the ith case, this measure is denoted by d_i and is defined:

$$(10.52) \qquad d_i = \left[(X_{i1} - X_{h1})^2 + (X_{i2} - X_{h2})^2 \right]^{1/2}$$

When the predictor variables are measured on different scales, each should be scaled by dividing it by its standard deviation. The median absolute deviation estimator in (10.46) can be used in place of the standard deviation if outliers are present.

Weight Function.   The neighborhood about the point (X_{h1}, X_{h2}) is defined in terms of the proportion q of cases that are nearest to the point. Let d_q denote the Euclidean distance of the furthest case in the neighborhood. The weight function used in the loess method is the tricube weight function, which is defined as follows:

$$
(10.53) \qquad w_i = \begin{array}{ll} \left[1 - (d_i/d_q)^3\right]^3 & d_i < d_q \\ 0 & d_i \geq d_q \end{array}
$$

Thus, cases outside the neighborhood receive weight zero and cases within the neighborhood receive weights between 0 and 1, the weight decreasing with greater distance. In this way, the mean response at (X_{h1}, X_{h2}) is estimated locally.

The choice of the proportion q defining the neighborhood requires a balancing of two opposing tendencies. The larger is q, the smoother will be the fit but at the same time the greater may be the bias in the fitted value. A choice of q between .4 and .6 may often be appropriate.

Local Fitting.   Given the weights for the n cases based on (10.52) and (10.53), weighted least squares is then used to fit either the first-order model (6.1) or the second-order model (6.16). The second-order model is helpful when the response surface has substantial curvature; moderate curvilinearities can be detected by using the first-order model. After the regression model is fitted by weighted least squares, the fitted value $\hat{Y}_h$ at (X_{h1}, X_{h2}) then serves as the nonparametric estimate of the mean response at these X levels. By recalculating the weights for different (X_{h1}, X_{h2}) levels, fitting the response function repeatedly, and each time obtaining the fitted value $\hat{Y}_h$, we obtain information about the response surface without making any assumptions about the nature of the response function.

Example

We shall fit a nonparametric regression function for the life insurance example in Chapter 9. A portion of the data for a second group of 18 managers is given in Table 10.6, columns 1–3. The relation between amount of life insurance carried (Y) and income (X_1) and risk aversion (X_2) is to be investigated, the data pertaining to managers in the 30–39 age group. The local fitting will be done using the first-order model in (6.1) because the number of available cases is not too large. For the same reason, the proportion of cases defining the local neighborhoods is set at $q = .5$; in other words, each local neighborhood is to consist of half of the cases.

The exploration of the response surface begins at $X_{h1} = 30$, $X_{h2} = 3$. To obtain a locally fitted value at $X_{h1} = 30$, $X_{h2} = 3$, we need to obtain the Euclidean distances of each case from this point. We shall use the sample standard deviations of the two predictor variables to standardize the variables in obtaining the Euclidean distance since the two variables are measured on different scales. The sample standard deviations are $s_1 = 14.739$ and $s_2 = 2.3044$. For case 1, the Euclidean distance from $X_{h1} = 30$, $X_{h2} = 3$ is obtained as follows:

$$
d_1 = \left[\left(\frac{66.290 - 30}{14.739}\right)^2 + \left(\frac{7 - 3}{2.3044}\right)^2\right]^{1/2} = 3.013
$$

TABLE 10.6   **Loess Calculations for Nonparametric Regression Fit at $X_{h1} = 30$, $X_{h2} = 3$ — Life Insurance Example.**

	(1)	(2)	(3)	(4)	(5)
i	X_{i1}	X_{i2}	Y_i	d_i	w_i
1	66.290	7	240	3.013	0
2	40.964	5	73	1.143	.300
3	72.996	10	311	4.212	0
...	...	...	...	...	...
16	79.380	1	316	3.461	0
17	52.766	8	154	2.663	0
18	55.916	6	164	2.188	0

The Euclidean distances are shown in Table 10.6, column 4. The Euclidean distance of the furthest case in the neighborhood of $X_{h1} = 30$, $X_{h2} = 3$ for $q = .5$ is for the ninth case when these are ordered according to their Euclidean distance. It is $d_q = 1.653$. Since $d_1 = 3.013 > 1.653$, the weight assigned for case 1 is $w_1 = 0$. For case 2, the Euclidean distance is $d_2 = 1.143$. Since this is less than 1.653, the weight for case 2 is:

$$w_2 = \left[1 - (1.143/1.653)^3\right]^3 = .300$$

The weights are shown in Table 10.6, column 5.

The fitted first order regression function using these weights is:

$$\hat{Y} = -134.076 + 3.571X_1 + 10.532X_2$$

The fitted value for $X_{h1} = 30$, $X_{h2} = 3$ therefore is:

$$\hat{Y}_h = -134.076 + 3.571(30) + 10.532(3) = 4.65$$

In the same fashion, locally fitted values at other values of X_{h1} and X_{h2} are calculated. Figure 10.7a contains a contour plot of the fitted response surface. The surface clearly ascends as X_1 increases, but the effect of X_2 is more difficult to see from the contour plot. The effect of X_2 can be seen more easily by the conditional effects plots of Y against X_1 at low, middle, and high levels of X_2 in Figure 10.7b. The conditional effects plots in Figure 10.7b are also called *two-variable conditioning plots*. Note that the expected amount of life insurance carried increases with income (X_1) at all levels of risk aversion (X_2). The response functions for $X_2 = 3$ and $X_2 = 6$ appear to be approximately linear. The dip in the left part of the response function for $X_2 = 9$ may be the result of an interaction or of noisy data and inadequate smoothing. Note also from Figure 10.7b that the expected amount of life insurance carried at the higher income levels increases as the risk aversion becomes very high.

Comments

1. The fitted nonparametric response surface can be used, just as for simple regression, for examining the appropriateness of a fitted parametric regression model. If the fitted nonparametric

FIGURE 10.7   **Contour and Conditioning Plots for Loess Nonparametric Regression—Life Insurance Example.**

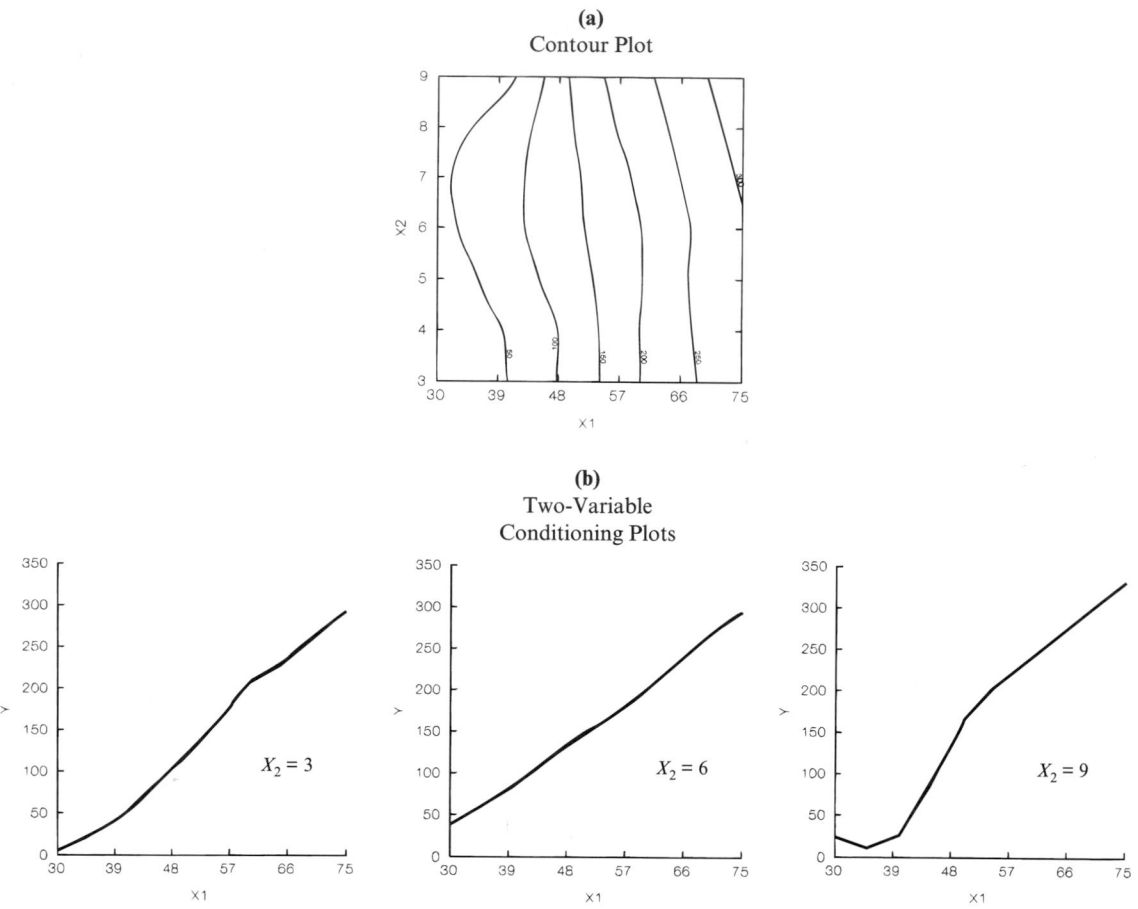

(a)
Contour Plot

(b)
Two-Variable
Conditioning Plots

response surface falls within the confidence band in (6.60) for the parametric regression function, the nonparametric fit supports the appropriateness of the parametric regression function.

2. Reference (10.9) discusses a procedure to assist in choosing the proportion q for defining a local neighborhood. It also describes how the precision of any fitted value $\hat{Y}_h$ obtained with loess nonparametric multiple regression can be approximated.

3. The assumptions of normality and constant variance of the error terms required by the loess nonparametric procedure can be checked in the usual fashion. The residuals are obtained by fitting the loess nonparametric regression function for each case and calculating $e_i = Y_i - \hat{Y}_i$ as usual. These residuals will not have the least squares property of summing to zero, but can be examined for normality and constancy of variance. The residuals can also serve to identify outliers that might not be disclosed by standard diagnostic procedures.

4. A discussion of some of the advantages of the loess smoothing procedure is presented in Reference 10.13.   ∎

10.5   Remedial Measures for Evaluating Precision in Nonstandard Situations—Bootstrapping

For standard fitted regression models, methods described in earlier chapters are available for evaluating the precision of estimated regression coefficients, fitted values, and predictions of new observations. However, in many nonstandard situations, such as when nonconstant error variances are estimated by iteratively reweighted least squares or when robust regression estimation is used, standard methods for evaluating the precision may not be available or may only be approximately applicable when the sample size is large. Bootstrapping was developed by Efron (Ref. 10.14) to provide estimates of the precision of sample estimates for these complex cases. A number of bootstrap methods have now been developed. The bootstrap method that we shall explain is simple in principle and nonparametric in nature. Like all bootstrap methods, it requires extensive computer calculations.

General Procedure

We shall explain the bootstrap method in terms of evaluating the precision of an estimated regression coefficient. The explanation applies identically to any other estimate, such as a fitted value. Suppose that we have fitted a regression model (simple or multiple) by some procedure and obtained the estimated regression coefficient b_1; we now wish to evaluate the precision of this estimate by the bootstrap method. In essence, the bootstrap method calls for the selection from the observed sample data of a random sample of size n with replacement. Sampling with replacement implies that the bootstrap sample may contain some duplicate data from the original sample and omit some other data in the original sample. Next, the bootstrap method calculates the estimated regression coefficient from the bootstrap sample, using the same fitting procedure as employed for the original fitting. This leads to the first bootstrap estimate b_1^*. This process is repeated a large number of times; each time a bootstrap sample of size n is selected with replacement from the original sample and the estimated regression coefficient is obtained for the bootstrap sample. The estimated standard deviation of all of the bootstrap estimates b_1^*, denoted by $s^*\{b_1^*\}$, is an estimate of the variability of the sampling distribution of b_1 and therefore is a measure of the precision of b_1.

Bootstrap Sampling

Bootstrap sampling for regression can be done in two basic ways. When the regression function being fitted is a good model for the data, the error terms have constant variance, and the predictor variable(s) can be regarded as fixed, *fixed X sampling* is appropriate. Here the residuals e_i from the original fitting are regarded as the sample data to be sampled with replacement. After a bootstrap sample of the residuals of size n has been obtained, denoted by $e_1^*, \ldots, e_n^*$, the bootstrap sample residuals are added to the fitted values from the original fitting to obtain new bootstrap Y values, denoted by $Y_1^*, \ldots, Y_n^*$:

(10.54)
$$Y_i^* = \hat{Y}_i + e_i^*$$

These bootstrap Y^* values are then regressed on the original X variable(s) by the same procedure used initially to obtain the bootstrap estimate b_1^*.

When there is some doubt about the adequacy of the regression function being fitted, the error variances are not constant, and/or the predictor variables cannot be regarded as fixed, *random X sampling* is appropriate. For simple regression, the pairs of X and Y data in the original sample are considered to be the data to be sampled with replacement. Thus, this second procedure samples cases with replacement n times, yielding a bootstrap sample of n pairs of (X^*, Y^*) values. This bootstrap sample is then used for obtaining the bootstrap estimate b_1^*, as with fixed X sampling.

The number of bootstrap samples to be selected for evaluating the precision of an estimate depends on the special circumstances of each application. Sometimes, as few as 50 bootstrap samples are sufficient. Often, 200–500 bootstrap samples are adequate. One can observe the variability of the bootstrap estimates by calculating $s^*\{b_1^*\}$ as the number of bootstrap samples is increased. When $s^*\{b_1^*\}$ stabilizes fairly reasonably, bootstrapping can be terminated.

Bootstrap Confidence Intervals

Bootstrapping can also be used to arrive at approximate confidence intervals. Much research is ongoing on different procedures for obtaining bootstrap confidence intervals (see, for example, References 10.15 and 10.16). A relatively simple procedure for setting up a $1 - \alpha$ confidence interval is the *reflection method*. This procedure often produces a reasonable approximation, but not always. The reflection method confidence interval for β_1 is based on the $(\alpha/2)100$ and $(1 - \alpha/2)100$ percentiles of the bootstrap distribution of b_1^*. These percentiles are denoted by $b_1^*(\alpha/2)$ and $b_1^*(1 - \alpha/2)$, respectively. The distances of these percentiles from b_1, the estimate of β_1 from the original sample, are denoted by d_1 and d_2:

(10.55a) $$d_1 = b_1 - b_1^*(\alpha/2)$$

(10.55b) $$d_2 = b_1^*(1 - \alpha/2) - b_1$$

The approximate $1 - \alpha$ confidence interval for β_1 then is:

(10.56) $$b_1 - d_2 \leq \beta_1 \leq b_1 + d_1$$

Bootstrap confidence intervals by the reflection method require a larger number of bootstrap samples than do bootstrap estimates of precision because tail percentiles are required. About 500 bootstrap samples may be a reasonable minimum number for reflection bootstrap confidence intervals.

Examples

We illustrate the bootstrap method by two examples. In the first one, standard analytical methods are available and bootstrapping is used simply to show that it produces similar results. In the second example, the estimation procedure is complex, and bootstrapping provides a means for assessing the precision of the estimate.

Example 1—Toluca Company.   We use the Toluca Company example of Table 1.1 to illustrate how the bootstrap method approximates standard analytical results. We found in Chapter 2 that the estimate of the slope β_1 is $b_1 = 3.5702$, that the estimated precision of this estimate is $s\{b_1\} = .3470$, and that the 95 percent confidence interval for β_1 is $2.85 \leq \beta_1 \leq 4.29$.

To evaluate the precision of the estimate $b_1 = 3.5702$ by the bootstrap method, we shall use fixed X sampling. Here, the simple linear regression function fits the data well, the error

TABLE 10.7 **Bootstrapping with Fixed X Sampling—Toluca Company Example.**

	(1)	(2)	(3)	(4)	(5)	(6)
		Original Sample			Bootstrap Sample 1	
i	X_i	Y_i	$\hat{Y}_i$	e_i	e_i^*	Y_i^*
1	80	399	347.98	51.02	−19.88	328.1
2	30	121	169.47	−48.47	10.72	180.2
3	50	221	240.88	−19.88	−6.68	234.2
...	...	...	...	...	...	...
23	40	244	205.17	38.83	4.02	209.2
24	80	342	347.98	−5.98	−45.17	3ʹ2.8
25	70	323	312.28	10.72	51.02	363.3

FIGURE 10.8 **Histogram of Bootstrap Estimates b_1^*—Toluca Company Example.**

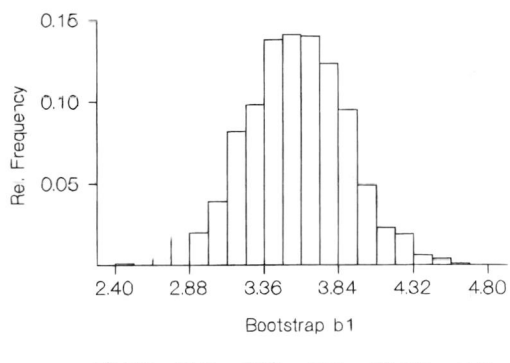

$b_1^*(.025) = 2.940$ $s^*\{b_1^*\} = .3251$ $b_1^*(.975) = 4.211$

variance appears to be constant, and it is reasonable to consider a repetition of the study with the same lot sizes. A portion of the data on lot size (X) and work hours (Y) is repeated in Table 10.7, columns 1 and 2. The fitted values and residuals obtained from the original sample are repeated from Table 1.2 in columns 3 and 4. Column 5 of Table 10.7 shows the first bootstrap sample of n residuals e_i^*, selected from column 4 with replacement. Finally, column 6 shows the first bootstrap sample Y_i^* observations. For example, by (10.54), we obtain $Y_1^* = \hat{Y}_1 + e_1^* = 347.98 - 19.88 = 328.1$.

When the Y_i^* values in column 6 are regressed against the X values in column 1, based on simple linear regression model (2.1), we obtain $b_1^* = 3.7564$. In the same way, 999 other bootstrap samples were selected and b_1^* obtained for each. Figure 10.8 contains a histogram of the 1,000 bootstrap b_1^* estimates. Note that this bootstrap sampling distribution is fairly symmetrical and appears to be close to a normal distribution. We also see in Figure 10.8 that the standard deviation of the 1,000 b_1^* estimates is $s^*\{b_1^*\} = .3251$, which is quite close to the analytical estimate $s\{b_1\} = .3470$.

To obtain an approximate 95 percent confidence interval for β_1 by the bootstrap reflection method, we note in Figure 10.8 that the 2.5th and 97.5th percentiles of the bootstrap sampling distribution are $b_1^*(.025) = 2.940$ and $b_1^*(.975) = 4.211$, respectively. Using (10.55), we obtain:

$$d_1 = 3.5702 - 2.940 = .630$$

$$d_2 = 4.211 - 3.5702 = .641$$

Finally, we use (10.56) to obtain the confidence limits $3.5702 + .630 = 4.20$ and $3.5702 - .641 = 2.93$ so that the approximate 95 percent confidence interval for β_1 is:

$$2.93 \leq \beta_1 \leq 4.20$$

Note that these limits are quite close to the confidence limits 2.85 and 4.29 obtained by analytical methods.

Example 2—Blood Pressure.   For the blood pressure example in Table 10.1, the analyst used weighted least squares in order to recognize the unequal error variances and fitted a standard deviation function to estimate the unknown weights. The standard inference procedures employed by the analyst for estimating the precision of the estimated regression coefficient $b_{w1} = .59634$ and for obtaining a confidence interval for β_1 are therefore only approximate. To examine whether the approximation is good here, we shall evaluate the precision of the estimated regression coefficient in a way that recognizes the impreciseness of the weights by using bootstrapping. The X variable (age) probably should be regarded as random and the error variance varies with the level of X, so we shall use random X sampling. Table 10.8 repeats from Table 10.1 the original data for age (X) and diastolic blood pressure (Y) in columns 1 and 2. Columns 3 and 4 contain the (X_i^*, Y_i^*) observations for the first bootstrap sample selected with replacement from columns 1 and 2. When we now regress Y^* on X^* by ordinary least squares, we obtain the fitted regression function:

$$\hat{Y}^* = 50.384 + .7432X^*$$

The residuals for this fitted function are shown in column 5. When the absolute values of these residuals are regressed on X^*, the fitted standard deviation function obtained is:

$$\hat{s}^* = -5.409 + .32745X^*$$

The fitted values $\hat{s}_i^*$ are shown in column 6. Finally, the weights $w_i^* = 1/(\hat{s}_i^*)^2$ are shown in column 7. For example, $w_1^* = 1/(10.64)^2 = .0088$. Finally, Y^* is regressed on X^* by using the weights in column 7, to yield the bootstrap estimate $b_1^* = .838$.

This process was repeated 1,000 times. The histogram of the 1,000 bootstrap values b_1^* is shown in Figure 10.9 and appears to approximate a normal distribution. The standard deviation of the 1,000 bootstrap values is shown in Figure 10.9; it is $s^*\{b_1^*\} = .0825$. When we compare this precision with that obtained by the approximate use of (10.13), .0825 versus .07924, we see that recognition of the use of estimated weights has led here only to a small increase in the estimated standard deviation. Hence, the variability in b_{w1} associated with the use of estimated variances in the weights is not substantial and the standard inference procedures therefore provide a good approximation here.

A 95 percent bootstrap confidence interval for β_1 can be obtained from (10.56) by using the percentiles $b_1^*(.025) = .4375$ and $b_1^*(.975) = .7583$ shown in Figure 10.9. The

TABLE 10.8   Bootstrapping with Random X Sampling—Blood Pressure Example.

	(1)	(2)	(3)	(4)	(5)	(6)	(7)
	Original Sample		Bootstrap Sample 1				
i	X_i	Y_i	X_i^*	Y_i^*	e_i^*	$\hat{s}_i^*$	w_i^*
1	27	73	49	101	14.20	10.64	.0088
2	21	66	34	73	−2.65	5.72	.0305
3	22	63	49	101	14.20	10.64	.0088
...	...	...	...	...	...	...	...
52	52	100	46	89	4.43	9.65	.0107
53	58	80	27	73	2.55	3.43	.0850
54	57	109	40	70	−10.11	7.69	.0169

FIGURE 10.9   Histogram of Bootstrap Estimates b_1^*—Blood Pressure Example.

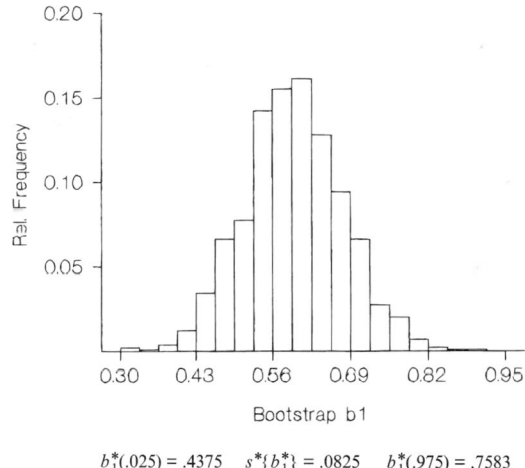

$$b_1^*(.025) = .4375 \qquad s^*\{b_1^*\} = .0825 \qquad b_1^*(.975) = .7583$$

approximate 95 percent confidence limits are [recall from (10.20) that $b_{w1} = .59634$]:

$$b_{w1} - d_2 = .59634 - (.7583 - .59634) = .4344$$

$$b_{w1} + d_1 = .59634 + (.59634 - .4375) = .7552$$

and the confidence interval for β_1 is:

$$.434 \le \beta_1 \le .755$$

Note that this confidence interval is almost the same as that obtained earlier by standard inference procedures ($.437 \le \beta_1 \le .755$). This again confirms that it is appropriate to use standard inference procedures here even though the weights were estimated.

Note

The reason why d_1 is associated with the upper confidence limit in (10.56) and d_2 with the lower limit is that the upper $(1 - \alpha/2)100$ percentile in the sampling distribution of b_1 identifies the lower confidence limit for β_1, whereas the lower $(\alpha/2)100$ percentile identifies the upper confidence limit. To see this, consider the sampling distribution for b_1, for which we can state with probability $1 - \alpha$ that b_1 will fall between:

(10.57)
$$b_1(\alpha/2) \le b_1 \le b_1(1 - \alpha/2)$$

where $b_1(\alpha/2)$ and $b_1(1-\alpha/2)$ denote the $(\alpha/2)100$ and $(1-\alpha/2)100$ percentiles of the sampling distribution of b_1. We now express these percentiles in terms of distances from the mean of the sampling distribution, $E\{b_1\} = \beta_1$:

(10.58)
$$D_1 = \beta_1 - b_1(\alpha/2)$$
$$D_2 = b_1(1 - \alpha/2) - \beta_1$$

and obtain:

(10.59)
$$b_1(\alpha/2) = \beta_1 - D_1$$
$$b_1(1 - \alpha/2) = \beta_1 + D_2$$

Substituting (10.59) into (10.57) and rearranging the inequalities so that β_1 is in the middle leads to the limits:

$$b_1 - D_2 \le \beta_1 \le b_1 + D_1$$

The confidence interval in (10.56) is obtained by replacing D_1 and D_2 by d_1 and d_2, which involves using the percentiles of the bootstrap sampling distribution as estimates of the corresponding percentiles of the sampling distribution of b_1 and using b_1 as the estimate of the mean β_1 of the sampling distribution.   ∎

10.6   Model Validation

After needed remedial measures have been taken and diagnostics analyzed to make sure that the remedial measures were successful, the final step in the model-building process is the validation of the selected regression model. Model validation usually involves checking the model against independent data. Three basic ways of validating a regression model are:

1. Collection of new data to check the model and its predictive ability.

2. Comparison of results with theoretical expectations, earlier empirical results, and simulation results.

3. Use of a holdout sample to check the model and its predictive ability.

When a regression model is used in a controlled experiment, a repetition of the experiment and its analysis serves to validate the findings in the initial study if similar results for the regression coefficients, predictive ability, and the like are obtained. Similarly, findings in confirmatory observational studies are validated by a repetition of the study with other data. As we noted in Chapter 8, there are generally no extensive problems in the selection of predictor variables in controlled experiments and confirmatory observational studies. In contrast, explanatory observational studies frequently involve large pools of explanatory variables and the selection of a subset of these for the final regression model. For these studies, validation of the regression model involves also the appropriateness of the variables selected, as well as the magnitudes of the regression coefficients, the predictive ability of the model, and the like. Our discussion of validation will focus primarily on issues that arise in validating regression models for exploratory observational studies. A good discussion of the need for replicating any study to establish the generalizability of the findings may be found in Reference 10.17. Reference 10.18 provides a helpful presentation of issues arising in the validation of regression models.

Collection of New Data to Check Model

The best means of model validation is through the collection of new data. The purpose of collecting new data is to be able to examine whether the regression model developed from the earlier data is still applicable for the new data. If so, one has assurance about the applicability of the model to data beyond those on which the model is based.

Methods of Checking Validity.   There are a variety of methods of examining the validity of the regression model against the new data. One validation method is to reestimate the model form chosen earlier using the new data. The estimated regression coefficients and various characteristics of the fitted model are then compared for consistency to those of the regression model based on the earlier data. If the results are consistent, they provide strong support that the chosen regression model is applicable under broader circumstances than those related to the original data.

Another validation method is to reestimate from the new data all of the "good" models that had originally been considered to see if the selected regression model is still the preferred model according to the new data. If so, one has assurance about the efficacy of the selected model under new conditions.

A third validation method is designed to calibrate the predictive capability of the selected regression model. When a regression model is developed from given data, it is inevitable that the selected model is chosen, at least in large part, because it fits well the data at hand. For a different set of random outcomes, one may likely have arrived at a different model in terms of the predictor variables selected and/or their functional forms and interaction terms present in the model. A result of this model development process is that the error mean square *MSE* will tend to understate the inherent variability in making future predictions from the selected model.

A means of measuring the actual predictive capability of the selected regression model is to use this model to predict each case in the new data set and then to calculate the mean of the squared prediction errors, to be denoted by *MSPR*, which stands for *mean squared prediction error*:

(10.60)
$$MSPR = \frac{\sum_{i=1}^{n^*}(Y_i - \hat{Y}_i)^2}{n^*}$$

where:

Y_i is the value of the response variable in the ith validation case

$\hat{Y}_i$ is the predicted value for the ith validation case based on the model-building data set

n^* is the number of cases in the validation data set

If the mean squared prediction error *MSPR* is fairly close to *MSE* based on the regression fit to the model-building data set, then the error mean square *MSE* for the selected regression model is not seriously biased and gives an appropriate indication of the predictive ability of the model. If the mean squared prediction error is much larger than *MSE*, one should rely on the mean squared prediction error as an indicator of how well the selected regression model will predict in the future.

Difficulties in Replicating a Study.   Difficulties often arise when new data are collected to validate a regression model, especially with observational studies. Even with controlled experiments, however, there may be difficulties in replicating an earlier study in identical fashion. For instance, the laboratory equipment for the new study to be conducted in a different laboratory may differ from that used in the initial study, resulting in somewhat different calibrations for the response measurements.

The difficulties in replicating a study are particularly acute in the social sciences where controlled experiments often are not feasible. Repetition of an observational study usually involves different conditions, the differences being related to changes in setting and/or time. For instance, a study investigating the relation between amount of delegation of authority by executives in a firm to the age of the executive was repeated in another firm which has a somewhat different management philosophy. As another example, a study relating consumer purchases of a product to special promotional incentives was repeated in another year when the business climate differed substantially from that during the initial study.

It may be thought that an inability to reproduce a study identically makes the replication study useless for validation purposes. This is not the case. No single study is fully useful until we know how much the results of the study can be generalized. If a replication study for which the conditions of the setting differ only slightly from those of the initial study yields substantially different regression results, then we learn that the results of the initial study cannot be readily generalized. On the other hand, if the conditions differ substantially and the regression results are still similar, we find that the regression results can be generalized to apply under substantially varying conditions. Still another possibility is that the regression results for the replication study differ substantially from those of the initial study, the differences being related to changes in the setting. This information may be useful for enriching the regression model by including new explanatory variables that make the model more widely applicable.

Note

When the new data are collected under controlled conditions in an experiment, it is desirable to include data points of major interest to check out the model predictions. If the model is to be used for making predictions over the entire range of the *X* observations, a possibility is to include data points that are uniformly distributed over the *X* space.   ∎

Comparison with Theory, Empirical Evidence, or Simulation Results

In some cases, theory, simulation results, or previous empirical results may be helpful in determining whether the selected model is reasonable. Comparisons of regression coefficients and predictions with theoretical expectations, previous empirical results, or simulation results should be made. Unfortunately, there is often little theory that can be used to validate regression models.

Data Splitting

By far the preferred method to validate a regression model is through the collection of new data. Often, however, this is neither practical nor feasible. An alternative when the data set is large enough is to split the data into two sets. The first set, called the *model-building set* or the *training sample*, is used to develop the model. The second data set, called the *validation* or *prediction set*, is used to evaluate the reasonableness and predictive ability of the selected model. This validation procedure is often called *cross-validation*. Data splitting in effect is an attempt to simulate replication of the study.

The validation data set is used for validation in the same way as when new data are collected. The regression coefficients can be reestimated for the selected model and then compared for consistency with the coefficients obtained from the model-building data set. Also, predictions can be made for the data in the validation data set from the regression model developed from the model-building data set to calibrate the predictive ability of this regression model for the new data. When the calibration data set is large enough, one can also study how the "good" models considered in the model selection phase fare with the new data.

Data sets are often split equally into model-building and validation data sets. It is important, however, that the model-building data set be sufficiently large so that a reliable model can be developed. Recall in this connection that the number of cases should be at least 6 to 10 times the number of variables in the pool of predictor variables. Thus, when 10 variables are in the pool, the model-building data set should contain at least 60 to 100 cases. If the entire data set is not large enough under these circumstances for making an equal split, the validation data set will need to be smaller than the model-building data set.

Splits of the data can be made at random. Another possibility is to match cases in pairs and place one of each pair into one of the two split data sets. When data are collected sequentially in time, it is often useful to pick a point in time to divide the data. Generally, the earlier data are selected for the model-building set and the later data for the validation set. When seasonal or cyclical effects are present in the data (e.g., sales data), the split should be made at a point where the cycles are balanced.

Use of time or some other characteristic of the data to split the data set provides the opportunity to test the generalizability of the model since conditions may differ for the two data sets. Data in the validation set may have been created under different causal conditions than those of the model-building set. In some cases, data in the validation set may represent extrapolations with respect to the data in the model-building set (e.g., sales data collected over time may contain a strong trend component). Such differential conditions may lead to a lack of validity of the model based on the model-building data set and indicate a need to broaden the regression model so that it is applicable under a broader scope of conditions.

A possible drawback of data splitting is that the variances of the estimated regression coefficients developed from the model-building data set will usually be larger than those that would have been obtained from the fit to the entire data set. If the model-building data set is reasonably large, however, these variances generally will not be that much larger than those for the entire data set. In any case, once the model has been validated, it is customary practice to use the entire data set for estimating the final regression model.

Example

In the surgical unit example, fitted regression model (9.46) was finally selected as the model to be checked for validity. The estimated regression coefficients, their estimated standard

TABLE 10.9   **Regression Results Based on Model-Building and Validation Data Sets for Surgical Unit Example—Regression Model (9.46).**

Statistic	(1) Model-Building Data Set	(2) Validation Data Set
b_0	.484	.501
$s\{b_0\}$	.043	.042
b_1	.0692	.0674
$s\{b_1\}$	.0041	.0050
b_2	.00929	.0101
$s\{b_2\}$	.00038	.00037
b_3	.00952	.00974
$s\{b_3\}$	.00031	.00030
SSE	.1099	.1056
PRESS	.1405	—
MSE	.0022	.0021
MSPR	—	.0072
R^2	.972	.978

deviations, and some other statistics pertaining to the fitted model are shown in Table 10.9, column 1.

Some evidence of the internal validity of this fitted model was mentioned earlier. We noted in Table 8.2 the closeness for this model of *PRESS* = .1405 and *SSE* = .1099. The *PRESS* value is always larger than *SSE* because the regression fit for the ith case when this case is deleted in fitting can never be as good as that when the ith case is included. A *PRESS* value reasonably close to *SSE*, as here, supports the validity of the fitted regression model and of *MSE* as an indicator of the predictive capability of this model.

To validate the selected regression model externally, 54 additional cases had been held out for a validation data set. A portion of the data for these cases is shown in Table 10.10. The correlation matrix for these new data (not shown) is quite similar to the one in Figure 8.3 for the model-building data set. The estimated regression coefficients, their estimated standard deviations, and some other statistics when regression model (9.45) is fitted to the validation data set are shown in Table 10.9, column 2. Note the good agreement between the two sets of estimated regression coefficients, and between the two *MSE* and R^2 values.

To calibrate the predictive ability of the regression model fitted from the model-building data set, the mean squared prediction error *MSPR* in (10.60) was calculated for the 54 cases in the validation data set in Table 10.10; it is *MSPR* = .0072. The mean squared prediction error generally will be larger than *MSE* based on the model-building data set because entirely new data are involved in the validation data set. The fact that *MSPR* here does not differ too greatly from *MSE* implies that the error mean square *MSE* based on the model-building data set is a reasonably valid indicator of the predictive ability of the fitted regression model.

These validation results support the appropriateness of the model selected.

Comments

1. Algorithms are available to split data so that the two data sets have similar statistical properties. The reader is referred to Reference 10.18 for a discussion of this and other issues associated with validation of regression models.

FIGURE 11.4   **Another Illustration of Regression Model (11.6) with Indicator Variable X_2 and Interaction Term—Insurance Innovation Example.**

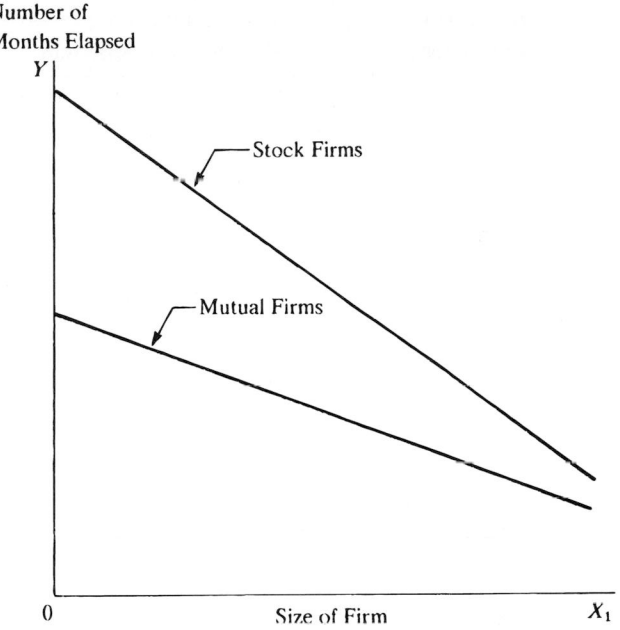

The values for the interaction term $X_1 X_2$ for the insurance innovation example are shown in Table 11.1, column 5. Note that this column contains 0 for mutual companies and X_{i1} for stock companies.

Again, the regression fit is routine. Basic results from a computer run regressing Y on X_1, X_2, and $X_1 X_2$ are shown in Table 11.3. To test for the presence of interaction effects:

$$H_0 \colon \beta_3 = 0$$

$$H_a \colon \beta_3 \neq 0$$

the economist used the t^* statistic from Table 11.3a:

$$t^* = \frac{b_3}{s\{b_3\}} = \frac{-.0004171}{.01833} = -.02$$

For level of significance .05, we require $t(.975; 16) = 2.120$. Since $|t^*| = .02 \leq 2.120$, we conclude H_0, that $\beta_3 = 0$. The conclusion of no interaction effects is supported by the two-sided P-value for the test, which is very high, namely, .98. It was because of this result that the economist adopted regression model (11.4) with no interaction term, which we discussed earlier.

TABLE 11.3   **Regression Results for Fit of Regression Model (11.6) with Interaction Term—Insurance Innovation Example.**

(a) Regression Coefficients

Regression Coefficient	Estimated Regression Coefficient	Estimated Standard Deviation	t^*
β_0	33.83837	2.44065	13.86
β_1	−.10153	.01305	−7.78
β_2	8.13125	3.65405	2.23
β_3	−.0004171	.01833	−.02

(b) Analysis of Variance

Source of Variation	SS	df	MS
Regression	1,504.42	3	501.47
Error	176.38	16	11.02
Total	1,680.80	19	

Note

Fitting regression model (11.6) yields the same response functions as would fitting separate regressions for stock firms and mutual firms. An advantage of using model (11.6) with an indicator variable is that one regression run will yield both fitted regressions.

Another advantage is that tests for comparing the regression functions for the different classes of the qualitative variable can be clearly seen to involve tests of regression coefficients in a general linear model. For instance, Figure 11.3 for the insurance innovation example shows that a test of whether the two regression functions have the same slope involves:

$$H_0: \ \beta_3 = 0$$

$$H_a: \ \beta_3 \neq 0$$

Similarly, Figure 11.3 shows that a test of whether the two regression functions are identical involves:

$$H_0: \ \beta_2 = \beta_3 = 0$$

$$H_a: \ \text{not both } \beta_2 = 0 \text{ and } \beta_3 = 0$$ ∎

11.3 More Complex Models

We now briefly consider more complex models involving qualitative predictor variables.

Qualitative Variable with More than Two Classes

If a qualitative predictor variable has more than two classes, we require additional indicator variables in the regression model. Consider the regression of tool wear (Y) on tool speed (X_1) and tool model, where the latter is a qualitative variable with four classes (M1, M2, M3, M4). We therefore require three indicator variables. Let us define them as follows:

(11.8)

$$X_2 = \begin{cases} 1 & \text{if tool model M1} \\ 0 & \text{otherwise} \end{cases}$$

$$X_3 = \begin{cases} 1 & \text{if tool model M2} \\ 0 & \text{otherwise} \end{cases}$$

$$X_4 = \begin{cases} 1 & \text{if tool model M3} \\ 0 & \text{otherwise} \end{cases}$$

First-Order Model.   A first-order regression model is:

(11.9)
$$Y_i = \beta_0 + \beta_1 X_{i1} + \beta_2 X_{i2} + \beta_3 X_{i3} + \beta_4 X_{i4} + \varepsilon_i$$

For this model, the data input for the X variables would be as follows:

Tool Model	X_1	X_2	X_3	X_4
M1	X_{i1}	1	0	0
M2	X_{i1}	0	1	0
M3	X_{i1}	0	0	1
M4	X_{i1}	0	0	0

The response function for regression model (11.9) is:

(11.10)
$$E\{Y\} = \beta_0 + \beta_1 X_1 + \beta_2 X_2 + \beta_3 X_3 + \beta_4 X_4$$

To understand the meaning of the regression coefficients, consider first what response function (11.10) becomes for tool models M4 for which $X_2 = 0$, $X_3 = 0$, and $X_4 = 0$:

(11.10a)
$$E\{Y\} = \beta_0 + \beta_1 X_1 \qquad \text{Tool models M4}$$

For tool models M1, $X_2 = 1$, $X_3 = 0$, and $X_4 = 0$, and response function (11.10) becomes:

(11.10b)
$$E\{Y\} = \beta_0 + \beta_1 X_1 + \beta_2 = (\beta_0 + \beta_2) + \beta_1 X_1 \qquad \text{Tool models M1}$$

Similarly, response functions (11.10) becomes for tool models M2 and M3:

(11.10c)
$$E\{Y\} = (\beta_0 + \beta_3) + \beta_1 X_1 \qquad \text{Tool models M2}$$

(11.10d)
$$E\{Y\} = (\beta_0 + \beta_4) + \beta_1 X_1 \qquad \text{Tool models M3}$$

Thus, response function (11.10) implies that the regression of tool wear on tool speed is linear, with the same slope for all four tool models. The coefficients β_2, β_3, and β_4 indicate, respectively, how much higher (lower) the response functions for tool models M1, M2, and M3 are than the one for tool models M4, for any given level of tool speed. Thus, β_2, β_3, and β_4 measure the differential effects of the qualitative variable classes on the height of the response function for any given level of X_1, always compared with the class for

FIGURE 11.5   **Illustration of Regression Model (11.9)—Tool Wear Example.**

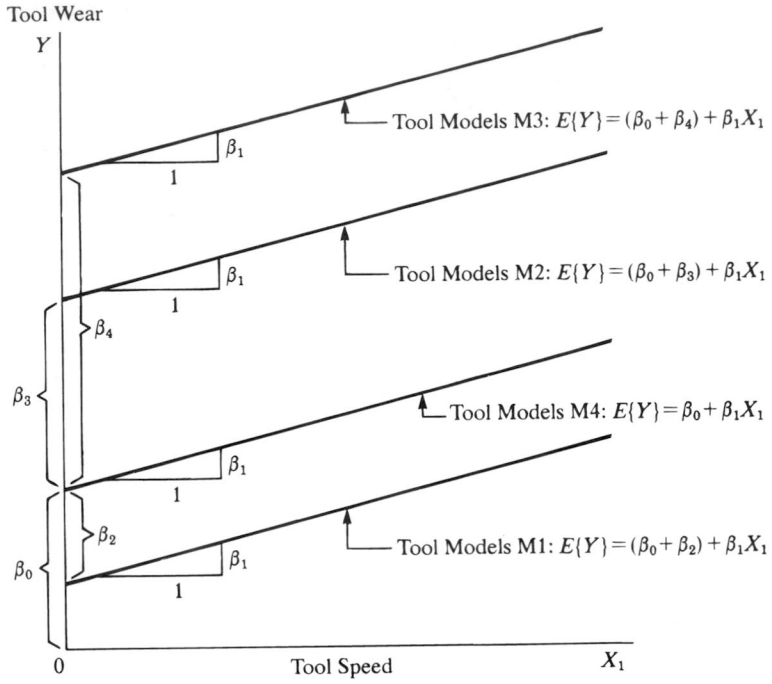

which $X_2 = X_3 = X_4 = 0$. Figure 11.5 illustrates a possible arrangement of the response functions.

When using regression model (11.9), we may wish to estimate differential effects other than against tool models M4. This can be done by estimating differences between regression coefficients. For instance, $\beta_4 - \beta_3$ measures how much higher (lower) the response function for tool models M3 is than the response function for tool models M2 for any given level of tool speed, as may be seen by comparing (11.10c) and (11.10d). The point estimator of this quantity is, of course, $b_4 - b_3$, and the estimated variance of this estimator is:

$$(11.11) \qquad s^2\{b_4 - b_3\} = s^2\{b_4\} + s^2\{b_3\} - 2s\{b_4, b_3\}$$

The needed variances and covariance can be readily obtained from the estimated variance-covariance matrix of the regression coefficients.

First-Order Model with Interactions Added.   If interaction effects between tool speed and tool model are present in our illustration, regression model (11.9) can be modified as follows:

$$(11.12)\quad Y_i = \beta_0 + \beta_1 X_{i1} + \beta_2 X_{i2} + \beta_3 X_{i3} + \beta_4 X_{i4} + \beta_5 X_{i1} X_{i2} + \beta_6 X_{i1} X_{i3} + \beta_7 X_{i1} X_{i4} + \varepsilon_i$$

The response function for tool models M4, for which $X_2 = 0$, $X_3 = 0$, and $X_4 = 0$, is as follows:

$$(11.13a) \qquad\qquad E\{Y\} = \beta_0 + \beta_1 X_1 \qquad\qquad \text{Tool models M4}$$

Similarly, we find for the other tool models:

(11.13b)
$$E\{Y\} = (\beta_0 + \beta_2) + (\beta_1 + \beta_5)X_1 \qquad \text{Tool models M1}$$

(11.13c)
$$E\{Y\} = (\beta_0 + \beta_3) + (\beta_1 + \beta_6)X_1 \qquad \text{Tool models M2}$$

(11.13d)
$$E\{Y\} = (\beta_0 + \beta_4) + (\beta_1 + \beta_7)X_1 \qquad \text{Tool models M3}$$

Thus, interaction regression model (11.12) implies that each tool model has its own regression line, with different intercepts and slopes for the different tool models.

More than One Qualitative Predictor Variable

Regression models can readily be constructed for cases where two or more of the predictor variables are qualitative. Consider the regression of advertising expenditures (Y) on sales (X_1), type of firm (incorporated, not incorporated), and quality of sales management (high, low). We may define:

(11.14)
$$X_2 = \begin{array}{ll} 1 & \text{if firm incorporated} \\ 0 & \text{otherwise} \end{array}$$

$$X_3 = \begin{array}{ll} 1 & \text{if quality of sales management high} \\ 0 & \text{otherwise} \end{array}$$

First-Order Model. A first-order regression model for the above example is:

(11.15)
$$Y_i = \beta_0 + \beta_1 X_{i1} + \beta_2 X_{i2} + \beta_3 X_{i3} + \varepsilon_i$$

This model implies that the response function of advertising expenditures on sales is linear, with the same slope for all "type of firm—quality of sales management" combinations, and β_2 and β_3 indicate the additive differential effects of type of firm and quality of sales management on the height of the regression line for any given levels of X_1 and the other predictor variable.

First-Order Model with Certain Interactions Added. A first-order regression model to which are added interaction effects between each pair of the predictor variables for the advertising example is:

(11.16) $\quad Y_i = \beta_0 + \beta_1 X_{i1} + \beta_2 X_{i2} + \beta_3 X_{i3} + \beta_4 X_{i1} X_{i2} + \beta_5 X_{i1} X_{i3} + \beta_6 X_{i2} X_{i3} + \varepsilon_i$

Note the implications of this model:

Type of Firm	Quality of Sales Management	Response Function
Incorp.	High	$E\{Y\} = (\beta_0 + \beta_2 + \beta_3 + \beta_6) + (\beta_1 + \beta_4 + \beta_5)X_1$
Not incorp.	High	$E\{Y\} = (\beta_0 + \beta_3) + (\beta_1 + \beta_5)X_1$
Incorp.	Low	$E\{Y\} = (\beta_0 + \beta_2) + (\beta_1 + \beta_4)X_1$
Not incorp.	Low	$E\{Y\} = \beta_0 + \beta_1 X_1$

Not only are all response functions different for the various "type of firm—quality of sales management" combinations, but the differential effects of one qualitative variable on the intercept depend on the particular class of the other qualitative variable. For instance, when we move from "not incorporated—low quality" to "incorporated—low quality," the intercept changes by β_2. But if we move from "not incorporated—high quality" to "incorporated—high quality," the intercept changes by $\beta_2 + \beta_6$.

Qualitative Predictor Variables Only

Regression models containing only qualitative predictor variables can also be constructed. With reference to our advertising example, we could regress advertising expenditures only on type of firm and quality of sales management. The first-order regression model then would be:

$$(11.17) \qquad Y_i = \beta_0 + \beta_2 X_{i2} + \beta_3 X_{i3} + \varepsilon_i$$

where X_{i2} and X_{i3} are defined in (11.14).

Comments

1. Models in which all explanatory variables are qualitative are called *analysis of variance models*.

2. Models containing some quantitative and some qualitative explanatory variables, where the chief explanatory variables of interest are qualitative and the quantitative variables are introduced primarily to reduce the variance of the error terms, are called *covariance models*. ∎

11.4 Comparison of Two or More Regression Functions

Frequently we encounter regressions for two or more populations and wish to study their similarities and differences. We present three examples.

1. A company operates two production lines for making soap bars. For each line, the relation between the speed of the line and the amount of scrap for the day was studied. A scatter plot of the data for the two production lines suggests that the regression relation between production line speed and amount of scrap is linear but not the same for the two production lines. The slopes appear to be about the same, but the heights of the regression lines seem to differ. A formal test is desired whether or not the two regression lines are identical. If it is found that the two regression lines are not the same, an investigation is to be made of why the difference in scrap yield exists.

2. An economist is studying the relation between amount of savings and level of income for middle-income families from urban and rural areas, based on independent samples from the two populations. Each of the two relations can be modeled by linear regression. The economist wishes to compare whether, at given income levels, urban and rural families tend to save the same amount—i.e., whether the two regression lines are the same. If they are not, the economist wishes to explore whether at least the amounts of savings out of an additional dollar of income are the same for the two groups—i.e., whether the slopes of the two regression lines are the same.

3. Two instruments were constructed for a company to identical specifications to measure pressure in an industrial process. A study was then made for each instrument of the relation between its gauge readings and actual pressures as determined by an almost exact but slow and costly method. If the two regression lines are the same, a single calibration

TABLE 11.4   **Data for Soap Production Lines Example (all data are coded).**

	Production Line 1				Production Line 2		
Case i	Amount of Scrap Y_i	Line Speed X_{i1}	X_{i2}	Case i	Amount of Scrap Y_i	Line Speed X_{i1}	X_{i2}
1	218	100	1	16	140	105	0
2	248	125	1	17	277	215	0
3	360	220	1	18	384	270	0
4	351	205	1	19	341	255	0
5	470	300	1	20	215	175	0
6	394	255	1	21	180	135	0
7	332	225	1	22	260	200	0
8	321	175	1	23	361	275	0
9	410	270	1	24	252	155	0
10	260	170	1	25	422	320	0
11	241	155	1	26	273	190	0
12	331	190	1	27	410	295	0
13	275	140	1				
14	425	290	1				
15	367	265	1				

schedule can be developed for the two instruments; otherwise, two different calibration schedules will be required.

When it is reasonable to assume that the error term variances in the regression models for the different populations are equal, we can use indicator variables to test the equality of the different regression functions. If the error variances are not equal, transformations of the response variable may equalize them at least approximately.

We have already seen how regression models with indicator variables that contain interaction terms permit testing of the equality of regression functions for the different classes of a qualitative variable. This methodology can be used directly for testing the equality of regression functions for different populations. We simply consider the different populations as classes of a predictor variable, define indicator variables for the different populations, and develop a regression model containing appropriate interaction terms. Since no new principles arise in the testing of the equality of regression functions for different populations, we immediately proceed with two of the earlier examples to illustrate the approach.

Soap Production Lines Example

The data on amount of scrap (Y) and line speed (X_1) for the soap production lines example are presented in Table 11.4. The variable X_2 is a code for the production line. A symbolic scatter plot of the data, using different symbols for the two production lines, is shown in Figure 11.6.

FIGURE 11.6   **Symbolic Scatter Plot for Soap Production Lines Example.**

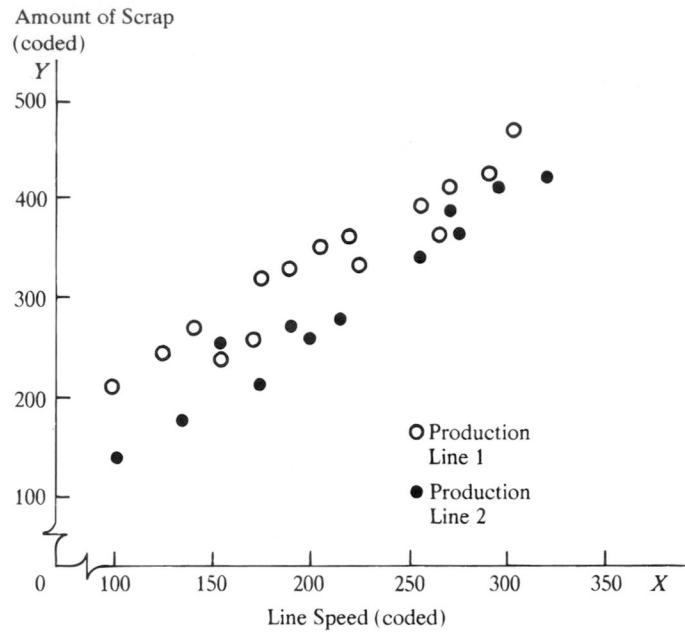

Tentative Model.   Based on the symbolic scatter plot in Figure 11.6, the analyst decided to tentatively fit regression model (11.6). This model assumes that the regression relation between amount of scrap and line speed is linear for both production lines and that the variances of the error terms are the same, but permits the two regression lines to have different slopes and intercepts:

$$(11.18) \qquad Y_i = \beta_0 + \beta_1 X_{i1} + \beta_2 X_{i2} + \beta_3 X_{i1} X_{i2} + \varepsilon_i$$

where:

$$X_{i1} = \text{line speed}$$

$$X_{i2} = \begin{matrix} 1 \\ 0 \end{matrix} \quad \begin{matrix} \text{if production line 1} \\ \text{if production line 2} \end{matrix}$$

$$i = 1, 2, \dots, 27$$

Note that for purposes of this model, the 15 cases for production line 1 and the 12 cases for production line 2 are combined into one group of 27 cases.

Diagnostics.   A fit of regression model (11.18) to the data in Table 11.4 led to the results presented in Table 11.5 and the following fitted regression function:

$$\hat{Y} = 7.57 + 1.322X_1 + 90.39X_2 - .1767X_1 X_2$$

Plots of the residuals against $\hat{Y}$ are shown in Figure 11.7 for each production line. Two plots are used in order to facilitate the diagnosis of possible differences between the

TABLE 11.5   Regression Results for Fit of Regression Model (11.18) — Soap Production Lines Example.

(a) Regression Coefficients

Regression Coefficient	Estimated Regression Coefficient	Estimated Standard Deviation	t^*
β_0	7.57	20.87	.36
β_1	1.322	.09262	14.27
β_2	90.39	28.35	3.19
β_3	−.1767	.1288	−1.37

(b) Analysis of Variance

Source of Variation	SS	df	MS
Regression	169,165	3	56,388
X_1	149,661	1	149,661
$X_2\|X_1$	18,694	1	18,694
$X_1X_2\|X_1, X_2$	810	1	810
Error	9,904	23	430.6
Total	179,069	26	

FIGURE 11.7   Residual Plots against $\hat{Y}$ for Soap Production Lines Example.

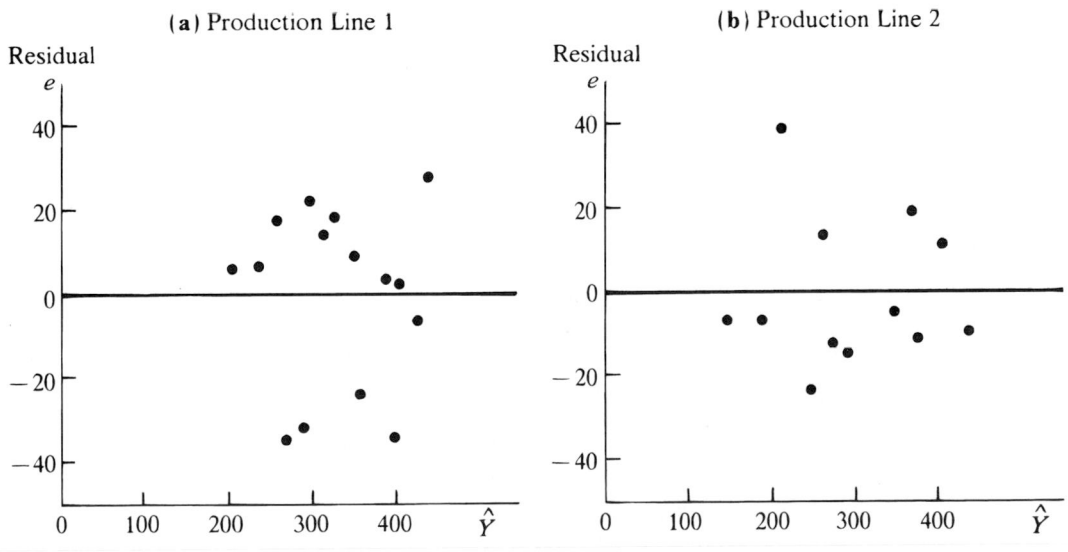

(a) Production Line 1

(b) Production Line 2

two production lines. Both plots in Figure 11.7 are reasonably consistent with regression model (11.18). The splits between positive and negative residuals of 10 to 5 for production line 1 and 4 to 8 for production line 2 can be accounted for by randomness of the outcomes. Plots of the residuals against X_2 and a normal probability plot of the residuals (not shown) also support the appropriateness of the fitted model. For the latter plot, the coefficient of correlation between the ordered residuals and their expected values under normality is .990. This is sufficiently high according to Table B.6 to support the assumption of normality of the error terms.

Finally, the analyst desired to make a formal test of the equality of the variances of the error terms for the two production lines, using the modified Levene test described in Section 3.6. Separate linear regression models were fitted to the data for the two production lines, the residuals were obtained, and the absolute deviations d_{i1} and d_{i2} in (3.8) of the residuals around the median residual for each group were obtained for each production line. The results were as follows:

Production Line 1	Production Line 2
$\hat{Y} = 97.965 + 1.145X_1$	$\hat{Y} = 7.574 + 1.322X_1$
$\bar{d}_1 = 16.132$	$\bar{d}_2 = 12.648$
$\Sigma(d_{i1} - \bar{d}_1)^2 = 2{,}952.20$	$\Sigma(d_{i2} - \bar{d}_2)^2 = 2{,}045.82$

The pooled variance s^2 in (3.9a) therefore is:

$$s^2 = \frac{2{,}952.20 + 2{,}045.82}{27 - 2} = 199.921$$

Hence, the pooled standard deviation is $s = 14.139$, and the test statistic in (3.9) is:

$$t_L^* = \frac{16.132 - 12.648}{14.139\sqrt{\frac{1}{15} + \frac{1}{12}}} = .636$$

For $\alpha = .05$, we require $t(.975; 25) = 2.060$. Since $|t_L^*| = .636 \le 2.060$, we conclude that the error term variances for the two production lines do not differ. The two-sided P-value for this test is .53.

At this point, the analyst was satisfied about the aptness of regression model (11.18) with normal error terms and was ready to proceed with comparing the regression relation between amount of scrap and line speed for the two production lines.

Inferences about Two Regression Lines.   Identity of the regression functions for the two production lines is tested by considering the alternatives:

(11.19)
$$H_0: \beta_2 = \beta_3 = 0$$
$$H_a: \text{not both } \beta_2 = 0 \text{ and } \beta_3 = 0$$

The appropriate test statistic is given by (7.27):

(11.19a)
$$F^* = \frac{SSR(X_2, X_1X_2|X_1)}{2} \div \frac{SSE(X_1, X_2, X_1X_2)}{n - 4}$$

where n represents the combined sample size for both populations. Using the regression results in Table 11.5, we find:

$$SSR(X_2, X_1X_2|X_1) = SSR(X_2|X_1) + SSR(X_1X_2|X_1, X_2)$$

$$= 18{,}694 + 810 = 19{,}504$$

$$F^* = \frac{19{,}504}{2} \div \frac{9{,}904}{23} = 22.65$$

To control α at level .01, we require $F(.99; 2, 23) = 5.67$. Since $F^* = 22.65 > 5.67$, we conclude H_a, that the regression functions for the two production lines are not identical.

Next, the analyst examined whether the slopes of the regression lines are the same. The alternatives here are:

(11.20)
$$H_0: \ \beta_3 = 0$$
$$H_a: \ \beta_3 \neq 0$$

and the appropriate test statistic is either the t^* statistic (7.25) or the partial F test statistic (7.24):

(11.20a)
$$F^* = \frac{SSR(X_1X_2|X_1, X_2)}{1} \div \frac{SSE(X_1, X_2, X_1X_2)}{n - 4}$$

Using the regression results in Table 11.5 and the partial F test statistic, we obtain:

$$F^* = \frac{810}{1} \div \frac{9{,}904}{23} = 1.88$$

For $\alpha = .01$, we require $F(.99; 1, 23) = 7.88$. Since $F^* = 1.88 \leq 7.88$, we conclude H_0, that the slopes of the regression functions for the two production lines are the same.

Using the Bonferroni inequality (4.2), the analyst can therefore conclude at family significance level .02 that a given increase in line speed leads to the same amount of increase in expected scrap in each of the two production lines, but that the expected amount of scrap for any given line speed differs by a constant amount for the two production lines.

We can estimate this constant difference in the regression lines by obtaining a confidence interval for β_2. For a 95 percent confidence interval, we require $t(.975; 23) = 2.069$. Using the results in Table 11.5, we obtain the confidence limits $90.39 \pm 2.069(28.35)$. Hence, the confidence interval for β_2 is:

$$31.7 \leq \beta_2 \leq 149.0$$

We thus conclude, with 95 percent confidence, that the mean amount of scrap for production line 1, at any given line speed, exceeds that for production line 2 by somewhere between 32 and 149.

Instrument Calibration Study Example

The engineer making the calibration study believed that the regression functions relating gauge reading (Y) to actual pressure (X_1) for both instruments are second-order polynomials:

$$E\{Y\} = \beta_0 + \beta_1 X_1 + \beta_2 X_1^2$$

but that they might differ for the two instruments. Hence, the model employed (using a centered variable for X_1 to reduce multicollinearity problems—see Section 7.7) was:

(11.21) $$Y_i = \beta_0 + \beta_1 x_{i1} + \beta_2 x_{i1}^2 + \beta_3 X_{i2} + \beta_4 x_{i1} X_{i2} + \beta_5 x_{i1}^2 X_{i2} + \varepsilon_i$$

where:

$x_{i1} = X_{i1} - \bar{X}_1 =$ centered actual pressure

$X_{i2} = \begin{matrix} 1 & \text{if instrument B} \\ 0 & \text{otherwise} \end{matrix}$

Note that for instrument A, where $X_2 = 0$, the response function is:

(11.22a) $$E\{Y\} = \beta_0 + \beta_1 x_1 + \beta_2 x_1^2 \qquad \text{Instrument A}$$

and for instrument B, where $X_2 = 1$, the response function is:

(11.22b) $$E\{Y\} = (\beta_0 + \beta_3) + (\beta_1 + \beta_4)x_1 + (\beta_2 + \beta_5)x_1^2 \qquad \text{Instrument B}$$

Hence, the test for equality of the two response functions involves the alternatives:

(11.23) $$H_0:\ \beta_3 = \beta_4 = \beta_5 = 0$$
$$H_a:\ \text{not all } \beta_k \text{ in } H_0 \text{ equal zero}$$

and the appropriate test statistic is (7.27):

(11.23a) $$F^* = \frac{SSR(X_2, x_1 X_2, x_1^2 X_2 | x_1, x_1^2)}{3} \div \frac{SSE(x_1, x_1^2, X_2, x_1 X_2, x_1^2 X_2)}{n-6}$$

where n represents the combined sample size for both populations.

Comments

1. The approach just described is completely general. If three or more populations are involved, additional indicator variables are simply added to the model.

2. The use of indicator variables for testing whether two or more regression functions are the same is equivalent to the general linear test approach where fitting the full model involves fitting separate regressions to the data from each population, and fitting the reduced model involves fitting one regression to the combined data.   ∎

11.5   Other Uses of Indicator Variables

Piecewise Linear Regressions

Sometimes the regression of Y on X follows a particular linear relation in some range of X, but follows a different linear relation elsewhere. For instance, unit cost (Y) regressed on lot size may follow a certain linear regression up to $X_p = 500$, at which point the slope changes because of some operating efficiencies only possible with lot sizes of more than

FIGURE 11.8   Illustration of Piecewise Linear Regression.

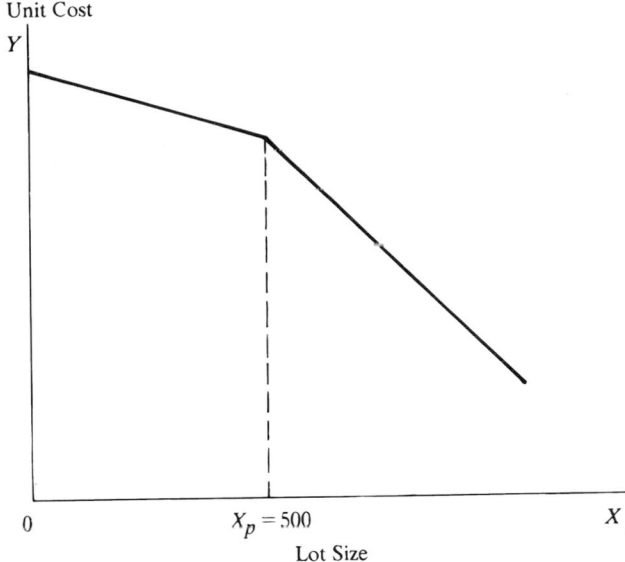

500. For example, there may be a break in the unit price when raw materials are purchased for lots greater than 500. Figure 11.8 illustrates this situation.

We consider now how indicator variables may be used to fit piecewise linear regressions consisting of two pieces. We take up the case where X_p, the point where the slope changes, is known.

We return to our lot size illustration, for which it is known that the slope changes at $X_p = 500$. The model for our illustration may be expressed as follows:

$$(11.24) \qquad Y_i = \beta_0 + \beta_1 X_{i1} + \beta_2 (X_{i1} - 500) X_{i2} + \varepsilon_i$$

where:

$$X_{i1} = \text{lot size}$$

$$X_{i2} = \begin{matrix} 1 & \text{if } X_{i1} > 500 \\ 0 & \text{otherwise} \end{matrix}$$

To check that regression model (11.24) does provide a two-piecewise linear regression, consider the response function for this model:

$$(11.25) \qquad E\{Y\} = \beta_0 + \beta_1 X_1 + \beta_2 (X_1 - 500) X_2$$

When $X_1 \le 500$, $X_2 = 0$ so that (11.25) becomes:

$$(11.25a) \qquad E\{Y\} = \beta_0 + \beta_1 X_1 \qquad X_1 \le 500$$

FIGURE 11.9 **Illustration of Meaning of Regression Coefficients of Piecewise Linear Response Function (11.25).**

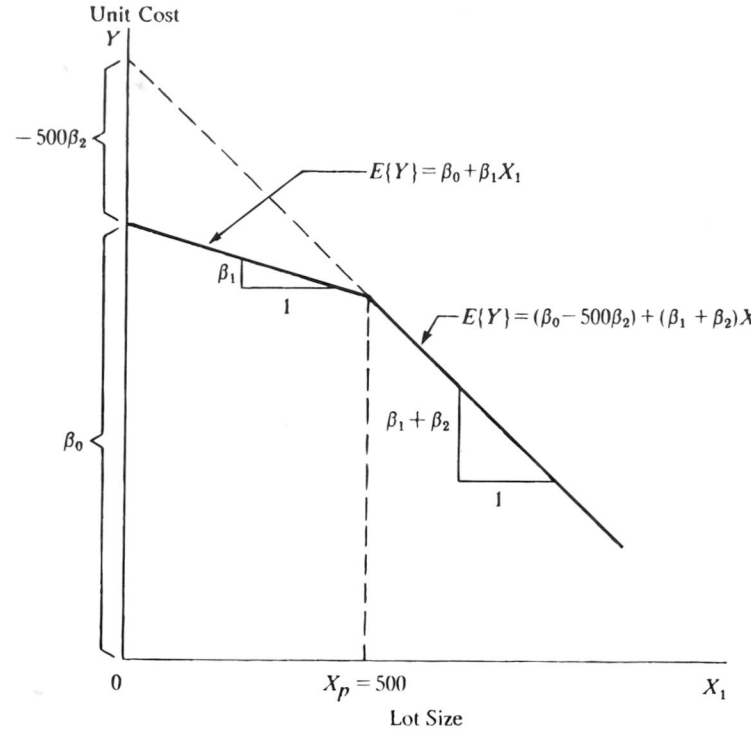

On the other hand, when $X_1 > 500$, $X_2 = 1$ and (11.25) becomes:

(11.25b) $$E\{Y\} = (\beta_0 - 500\beta_2) + (\beta_1 + \beta_2)X_1 \qquad X_1 > 500$$

Thus, β_1 and $\beta_1 + \beta_2$ are the slopes of the two regression lines, and β_0 and $\beta_0 - 500\beta_2$ are the two Y intercepts. These parameters are shown in Figure 11.9. The reason for subtracting $500\beta_2$ from β_0 to obtain the second intercept is that we are measuring the impact of the differential effect β_2 in the slope in the negative direction from $X_p = 500$ to zero.

Example. Table 11.6 contains data on unit cost and lot size for eight different lots in columns 1 and 2. It is known that the response function slope changes at $X_p = 500$ and that regression model (11.24) is appropriate. Column 3 in Table 11.6 contains $(X_{i1} - 500)X_{i2}$, which consists of 0s for all lot sizes up to 500, and of $X_{i1} - 500$ for all lot sizes above 500. The fitting of regression model (11.24) at this point becomes routine. The fitted response function when Y is regressed on X_1 and the coded variable $(X_1 - 500)X_2$ is:

$$\hat{Y} = 5.89545 - .00395X_1 - .00389(X_1 - 500)X_2$$

From this fitted regression function, we see that expected unit cost is estimated to decline by .00395 for a lot size increase of 1 when the lot size is less than 500 and by $.00395 + .00389 = .00784$ when the lot size is 500 or more.

TABLE 11.6   Data and Coded Variable for Piecewise Linear Regression—Lot Size Example.

Lot i	(1) Unit Cost (dollars) Y_i	(2) Lot Size X_{i1}	(3) $(X_{i1} - 500)X_{i2}$
1	2.57	650	150
2	4.40	340	0
3	4.52	400	0
4	1.39	800	300
5	4.75	300	0
6	3.55	570	70
7	2.49	720	220
8	3.77	480	0

Note

The extension of regression model (11.24) to more than two-piecewise regression lines is straightforward. For instance, if the slope of the regression line in the earlier lot size illustration actually changes at both $X = 500$ and $X = 800$, the model would be:

$$(11.26) \qquad Y_i = \beta_0 + \beta_1 X_{i1} + \beta_2 (X_{i1} - 500) X_{i2} + \beta_3 (X_{i1} - 800) X_{i3} + \varepsilon_i$$

where:

$$X_{i1} = \text{lot size}$$

$$X_{i2} = \begin{matrix} 1 & \text{if } X_{i1} > 500 \\ 0 & \text{otherwise} \end{matrix}$$

$$X_{i3} = \begin{matrix} 1 & \text{if } X_{i1} > 800 \\ 0 & \text{otherwise} \end{matrix}$$

∎

Discontinuity in Regression Function

Sometimes the linear regression function may not only change its slope at some value X_p but may also have a jump point there. Another indicator variable must then be introduced to take care of the jump. Figure 11.10 illustrates this case for an application where time required to solve a task successfully (Y) is to be regressed on complexity of task (X), when complexity of task is measured on a quantitative scale from 0 to 100. It is known that the slope of the response line changes at $X_p = 40$, and it is believed that the regression relation may be discontinuous there. We therefore set up the regression model:

$$(11.27) \qquad Y_i = \beta_0 + \beta_1 X_{i1} + \beta_2 (X_{i1} - 40) X_{i2} + \beta_3 X_{i3} + \varepsilon_i$$

FIGURE 11.10 **Illustration of Response Function (11.28) for Discontinuous Piecewise Linear Regression.**

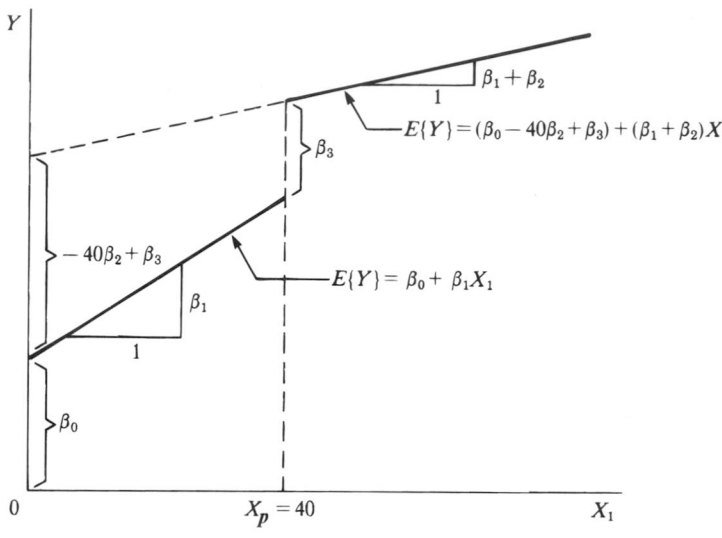

where:

$X_{i1} = $ complexity of task

$$X_{i2} = \begin{array}{ll} 1 & \text{if } X_{i1} > 40 \\ 0 & \text{otherwise} \end{array}$$

$$X_{i3} = \begin{array}{ll} 1 & \text{if } X_{i1} > 40 \\ 0 & \text{otherwise} \end{array}$$

The response function for regression model (11.27) is:

(11.28)
$$E\{Y\} = \beta_0 + \beta_1 X_1 + \beta_2(X_1 - 40)X_2 + \beta_3 X_3$$

When $X_1 \leq 40$, then $X_2 = 0$ and $X_3 = 0$, so response function (11.28) becomes:

(11.28a)
$$E\{Y\} = \beta_0 + \beta_1 X_1 \qquad X_1 \leq 40$$

Similarly, when $X_1 > 40$, then $X_2 = 1$ and $X_3 = 1$, so response function (11.28) becomes:

(11.28b)
$$E\{Y\} = (\beta_0 - 40\beta_2 + \beta_3) + (\beta_1 + \beta_2)X_1 \qquad X_1 > 40$$

These two response functions are shown in Figure 11.10, together with the parameters involved. Note that β_3 represents the difference in the mean responses for the two regression lines at $X_p = 40$ and β_2 represents the difference in the two slopes.

The estimation of the regression coefficients for model (11.27) presents no new problems. We may test whether or not $\beta_3 = 0$ in the usual manner. If it is concluded that $\beta_3 = 0$, the regression function is continuous at X_p so that the earlier piecewise linear regression model applies.

Time Series Applications

Economists and business analysts frequently use time series data in regression analysis. Indicator variables often are useful for time series regression models. For instance, savings (Y) may be regressed on income (X), where both the savings and income data are annual data for a number of years. The model employed might be:

$$(11.29) \qquad Y_t = \beta_0 + \beta_1 X_t + \varepsilon_t \qquad t = 1, \ldots, n$$

where Y_t and X_t are savings and income, respectively, for time period t. Suppose that the period covered includes both peacetime and wartime years, and that this factor should be recognized since savings in wartime years tend to be higher. The following model might then be appropriate:

$$(11.30) \qquad Y_t = \beta_0 + \beta_1 X_{t1} + \beta_2 X_{t2} + \varepsilon_t$$

where:

$$X_{t1} = \text{income}$$

$$X_{t2} = \begin{matrix} 1 & \text{if period } t \text{ peacetime} \\ 0 & \text{otherwise} \end{matrix}$$

Note that regression model (11.30) assumes that the marginal propensity to save (β_1) is constant in both peacetime and wartime years, and that only the height of the response function is affected by this qualitative variable.

Another use of indicator variables in time series applications occurs when monthly or quarterly data are used. Suppose that quarterly sales (Y) are regressed on quarterly advertising expenditures (X_1) and quarterly disposable personal income (X_2). If seasonal effects also have an influence on quarterly sales, a first-order regression model incorporating seasonal effects would be:

$$(11.31) \qquad Y_t = \beta_0 + \beta_1 X_{t1} + \beta_2 X_{t2} + \beta_3 X_{t3} + \beta_4 X_{t4} + \beta_5 X_{t5} + \varepsilon_t$$

where:

$$X_{t1} = \text{quarterly advertising expenditures}$$

$$X_{t2} = \text{quarterly disposable personal income}$$

$$X_{t3} = \begin{matrix} 1 & \text{if first quarter} \\ 0 & \text{otherwise} \end{matrix}$$

$$X_{t4} = \begin{matrix} 1 & \text{if second quarter} \\ 0 & \text{otherwise} \end{matrix}$$

$$X_{t5} = \begin{matrix} 1 & \text{if third quarter} \\ 0 & \text{otherwise} \end{matrix}$$

Regression models for time series data are susceptible to correlated error terms. It is particularly important in these cases to examine whether the modeling of the time series components of the data is adequate to make the error terms uncorrelated. We discuss in Chapter 12 a test for correlated error terms and a regression model that is often useful when the error terms are correlated.

11.6 Some Considerations in Using Indicator Variables

Indicator Variables versus Allocated Codes

An alternative to the use of indicator variables for a qualitative predictor variable is to employ *allocated codes*. Consider, for instance, the predictor variable "frequency of product use" which has three classes: frequent user, occasional user, nonuser. With the allocated codes approach, a single X variable is employed and values are assigned to the classes; for instance:

Class	X_1
Frequent user	3
Occasional user	2
Nonuser	1

The allocated codes are, of course, arbitrary and could be other sets of numbers. The first-order model with allocated codes for our example, assuming no other predictor variables, would be:

$$Y_i = \beta_0 + \beta_1 X_{i1} + \varepsilon_i \tag{11.32}$$

The basic difficulty with allocated codes is that they define a metric for the classes of the qualitative variable that may not be reasonable. To see this concretely, consider the mean responses with regression model (11.32) for the three classes of the qualitative variable:

Class	$E\{Y\}$
Frequent user	$E\{Y\} = \beta_0 + \beta_1(3) = \beta_0 + 3\beta_1$
Occasional user	$E\{Y\} = \beta_0 + \beta_1(2) = \beta_0 + 2\beta_1$
Nonuser	$E\{Y\} = \beta_0 + \beta_1(1) = \beta_0 + \beta_1$

Note the key implication:

$$E\{Y|\text{frequent user}\} - E\{Y|\text{occasional user}\} = E\{Y|\text{occasional user}\} - E\{Y|\text{nonuser}\} = \beta_1$$

Thus, the coding 1, 2, 3 implies that the mean response changes by the same amount when going from a nonuser to an occasional user as when going from an occasional user to a frequent user. This may not be in accord with reality and is the result of the coding 1, 2, 3, which assigns equal distances between the three user classes. Other allocated codes may, of course, imply different spacings of the classes of the qualitative variable, but these would ordinarily still be arbitrary.

Indicator variables, in contrast, make no assumptions about the spacing of the classes and rely on the data to show the differential effects that occur. If, for the same example, two indicator variables, say, X_1 and X_2, are employed to represent the qualitative variable, as follows:

Class	X_1	X_2
Frequent user	1	0
Occasional user	0	1
Nonuser	0	0

the first-order regression model would be:

$$(11.33) \qquad\qquad Y_i = \beta_0 + \beta_1 X_{i1} + \beta_2 X_{i2} + \varepsilon_i$$

Here, β_1 measures the differential effect:

$$E\{Y|\text{frequent user}\} - E\{Y|\text{nonuser}\}$$

and β_2 measures the differential effect:

$$E\{Y|\text{occasional user}\} - E\{Y|\text{nonuser}\}$$

Thus, β_2 measures the differential effect between occasional user and nonuser, and $\beta_1 - \beta_2$ measures the differential effect between frequent user and occasional user. Notice that there are no arbitrary restrictions to be satisfied by these two differential effects.

Indicator Variables versus Quantitative Variables

Indicator variables can be used even if the predictor variable is quantitative. For instance, the quantitative variable age may be transformed by grouping ages into classes such as under 21, 21–34, 35–49, etc. Indicator variables are then used for the classes of this new predictor variable. At first sight, this may seem to be a questionable approach because information about the actual ages is thrown away. Furthermore, additional parameters are placed into the model, which leads to a reduction of the degrees of freedom associated with *MSE*.

Nevertheless, there are occasions when replacement of a quantitative variable by indicator variables may be appropriate. Consider a large-scale survey in which the relation between liquid assets (Y) and age (X) of head of household is to be studied. Two thousand households were included in the study, so that the loss of 10 or 20 degrees of freedom is immaterial. The analyst is very much in doubt about the shape of the regression function, which could be highly complex, and hence may utilize the indicator variable approach in order to obtain information about the shape of the response function without making any assumptions about its functional form.

Another alternative utilizing indicator variables, piecewise linear regression, is available to the analyst for large-scale studies when the functional form of the regression relation is in doubt. This approach employs a large number of linear pieces. Again, degrees of freedom for estimating *MSE* are lost with this approach, but this is of no concern in large-scale studies. The benefit is that information about the shape of the regression function is obtained without making strong assumptions about its functional form.

Thus, for large data sets use of indicator variables can serve as an alternative to loess and other nonparametric fits of the response function.

Other Codings for Indicator Variables

As stated earlier, many different codings of indicator variables are possible. We now describe two alternatives to our 0, 1 coding for $c - 1$ indicator variables for a qualitative variable with c classes. We illustrate these alternative codings for the insurance innovation example, where Y is time to adopt an innovation, X_1 is size of insurance firm, and the second predictor variable is type of company (stock, mutual).

The first alternative coding is:

$$(11.34) \qquad X_2 = \begin{array}{ll} 1 & \text{if stock company} \\ -1 & \text{if mutual company} \end{array}$$

For this coding, the first-order linear regression model:

$$(11.35) \qquad Y_i = \beta_0 + \beta_1 X_{i1} + \beta_2 X_{i2} + \varepsilon_i$$

has the response function:

$$(11.36) \qquad E\{Y\} = \beta_0 + \beta_1 X_1 + \beta_2 X_2$$

This response function becomes for the two types of companies:

$$(11.36a) \qquad E\{Y\} = (\beta_0 + \beta_2) + \beta_1 X_1 \qquad \text{Stock firms}$$

$$(11.36b) \qquad E\{Y\} = (\beta_0 - \beta_2) + \beta_1 X_1 \qquad \text{Mutual firms}$$

Thus, β_0 here may be viewed as an "average" intercept of the regression line, from which the stock company and mutual company intercepts differ by β_2 in opposite directions. A test whether the regression lines are the same for both types of companies involves $H_0: \beta_2 = 0$, $H_a: \beta_2 \neq 0$.

A second alternative coding scheme is to use a 0, 1 indicator variable for each of the c classes of the qualitative variable and to drop the intercept term in the regression model. For the insurance innovation example, the model would be:

$$(11.37) \qquad Y_i = \beta_1 X_{i1} + \beta_2 X_{i2} + \beta_3 X_{i3} + \varepsilon_i$$

where:

$$X_{i1} = \text{size of firm}$$

$$X_{i2} = \begin{array}{ll} 1 & \text{if stock company} \\ 0 & \text{otherwise} \end{array}$$

$$X_{i3} = \begin{array}{ll} 1 & \text{if mutual company} \\ 0 & \text{otherwise} \end{array}$$

Here, the two response functions are:

$$(11.38a) \qquad E\{Y\} = \beta_2 + \beta_1 X_1 \qquad \text{Stock firms}$$

$$(11.38b) \qquad E\{Y\} = \beta_3 + \beta_1 X_1 \qquad \text{Mutual firms}$$

A test of whether or not the two regression lines are the same would involve the alternatives $H_0: \beta_2 = \beta_3$, $H_a: \beta_2 \neq \beta_3$. This type of test, discussed in Section 7.3, cannot be conducted using extra sums of squares and requires the fitting of both the full and reduced models.

11.7   Case Example—MNDOT Traffic Estimation

Traffic monitoring involves the collection of many types of data, such as traffic volume, traffic composition, vehicle speeds, and vehicle weights. These data provide information for highway planning, engineering design, and traffic control, as well as for legislative decisions concerning budget allocation, selection of state highway routes, and the setting of speed limits. One of the most important traffic monitoring variables is the average annual daily traffic (AADT) for a section of road or highway. AADT is defined as the average, over a year, of the number of vehicles that pass through a particular section of a road each day. Information on AADT is often collected by means of automatic traffic recorders (ATRs). Since it is not possible to install these recorders on all state road segments because of the expense involved, Cheng (Ref. 11.1) investigated the use of regression analysis for estimating AADT for road sections that are not monitored in the state of Minnesota.

The AADT Data Base

Seven potential predictors of traffic volume were chosen from the Minnesota Department of Transportation (MNDOT) road-log data base, including type of road section, population density in the vicinity of road section, number of lanes in road section, and road section's width. Four of the seven variables were qualitative, requiring 19 indicator variables. Preliminary regression analysis indicated that the large number of levels of two of the qualitative variables was not helpful. Consequently, judgment and statistical information about marginal reductions in the error sum of squares were used to collapse the categories, so only 10 instead of 19 indicator variables remained in the AADT data base.

The variables included in the initial analysis were as follows:

CTYPOP (X_1)—population of county in which road section is located (best proxy available for population density in immediate vicinity of road section)

LANES (X_2)—number of lanes in road section

WIDTH (X_3)—width of road section (in feet)

CONTROL (X_4)—two-category qualitative variable indicating whether or not there is control of access to road section (1 = access control; 2 = no access control)

CLASS (X_5, X_6, X_7)—four-category qualitative variable indicating road section function (1 = rural interstate; 2 = rural noninterstate; 3 = urban interstate, 4 = urban noninterstate)

TRUCK $(X_8, X_9, X_{10}, X_{11})$—five-category qualitative variable indicating availability status of road section to trucks (e.g., tonnage and time-of-year restrictions)

LOCALE (X_{12}, X_{13})—three-category qualitative variable indicating type of locale (1 = rural; 2 = urban, population $\leq 50,000$; 3 = urban, population $> 50,000$)

A portion of the data is shown in Table 11.7. Altogether, complete records for 121 ATRs were available. For conciseness, only the category is shown for a qualitative variable and not the coding of the indicator variables.

Model Development

A SYSTAT scatter plot matrix of the data set, with loess fits added, is presented in Figure 11.11. We see from the first row of the matrix that several of the predictor variables

TABLE 11.7   **Data for MNDOT Traffic Estimation Example.**

Road Section i	AADT Y_i	County Population X_{i1}	Lanes X_{i2}	Width X_{i3}	Access Control Category X_{i4}	Function Class Category (X_{i5} to X_{i7})	Truck Route Category (X_{i8} to $X_{i,11}$)	Locale Category ($X_{i,12}$, $X_{i,13}$)
1	1,616	13,404	2	52	2	2	5	1
2	1,329	52,314	2	60	2	2	5	1
3	3,933	30,982	2	57	2	4	5	2
4	3,786	25,207	2	64	2	4	5	2
...	...	...	...	...	...	...	...	...
119	14,905	459,784	4	68	2	4	5	2
120	15,408	459,784	2	40	2	4	5	3
121	1,266	43,784	2	44	2	4	5	2

Source: C. Cheng, "Optimal Sampling for Traffic Volume Estimation," unpublished Ph.D. dissertation, University of Minnesota, Carlson School of Management, 1992.

are related to AADT. The loess fits suggest a potentially curvilinear relationship between LANES and AADT. Although the loess fits of AADT to the qualitative categories designated 1, 2, 3, etc., are meaningless, they do highlight the average traffic volume for each category. For example, the loess fit of AADT to CLASS shows that average AADT for the third category of CLASS is higher than for the other three categories. The scatter plot matrix also suggests that the variability of AADT may be increasing with some predictor variables, for instance, with CTYPOP.

An initial regression fit of a first-order model with ordinary least squares, using all predictor variables, indicated that CTYPOP and LANES are important variables. Regression diagnostics for this initial fit suggested two potential problems. First, the residual plot against predicted values revealed that the error variance might not be constant. Also, the maximum variance inflation factor (9.41) was 24.55, suggesting a severe degree of multicollinearity. The maximum Cook's distance measure (9.33) was .2076, indicating that none of the individual cases is particularly influential. Since many of the variables appeared to be unimportant, we next considered the use of subset selection procedures to identify promising, initial models.

The SAS all-possible-regressions procedure, PROC RSQUARE, was used for subset selection. To reduce the volume of computation, CTYPOP and LANES were forced to be included. The SAS output is given in Figure 11.12 on page 486. The left column indicates the number of X variables in the model, i.e., $p - 1$. The names of the qualitative variables identify the predictor variable and the category for which the indicator variable is coded 1. For example, CLASS1 refers to the first indicator variable for the predictor variable CLASS, i.e., it refers to X_5, which is coded 1 for category 1 (rural interstate). Two simple models look particularly promising. The three-variable model consisting of X_1 (CTYPOP), X_2 (LANES), and X_7 (CLASS = 3) stands out as the best three-variable model, with $R^2 = .805$ and $C_p = 5.23$. Since $p = 4$ for this model, the C_p statistic suggests that this model contains little bias. The best four-variable model includes X_1 (CTYPOP), X_2 (LANES), X_4 (CONTROL = 1), and X_5 (CLASS = 1). With this model, some improvements in the selection criteria are realized: $R^2 = .812$ and $C_p = 2.65$. On the basis of these results, it was decided to investigate a model based on the five predictor variables included in these two models: X_1 (CTYPOP), X_2 (LANES), X_4 (CONTROL = 1), X_5 (CLASS = 1), and

FIGURE 11.11   **SYSTAT Scatter Plot Matrix—**
MNDOT Traffic Estimation Example.

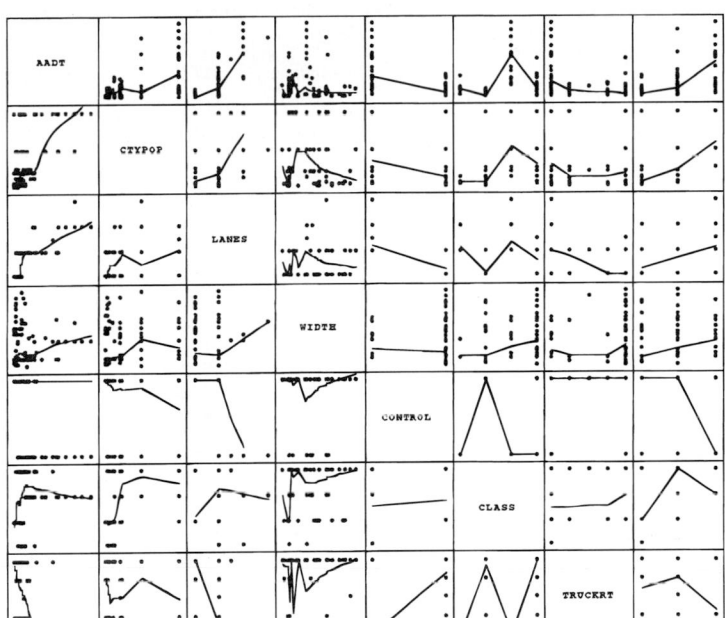

X_7 (CLASS = 3). Note that because X_6 (CLASS = 2) has been dropped from further consideration, the rural noninterstate (CLASS = 2) and urban noninterstate (CLASS = 4) categories of the CLASS variable have been collapsed into one category.

Figure 11.13a contains a plot of the studentized residuals against the fitted values for the five-variable model. The plot reveals two potential problems: (1) The residuals tend to be positive for small and large values of $\hat{Y}$ and negative for intermediate values, suggesting a curvilinearity in the response function. (2) The variability of the residuals tends to increase with increasing $\hat{Y}$, indicating nonconstancy of the error variance.

Curvilinearity was investigated next, together with possible interaction effects. A squared term for each of the two quantitative variables (CTYPOP and LANES) was added to the pool of potential X variables. To reduce potential multicollinearity problems, each of these variables was first centered. In addition, nine cross-product terms were added to the pool of potential X variables, consisting of the cross products of the X variables for the four predictor variables.

The SAS all possible-regressions procedure was run again for this enlarged pool of potential X variables (output not shown). Analysis of the results suggested a model with five X variables: CTYPOP, LANES, LANES², CONTROL1, and CTYPOP × CONTROL1. For this model, R^2 is .925, and all P-values for the regression coefficients are 0+. Although this model does not have the largest R^2 value among five-term models, it is desirable because it is

FIGURE 11.12   **SAS All-Possible-Regressions Output—MNDOT Traffic Estimation Example.**

```
N = 121      Regression Models for Dependent Variable: AADT


         R-square    C(p)  Variables in Model
   In

    2    0.694589  69.7231  CTYPOP LANES

NOTE: The above variables are included in all models to follow.

    ---------------------------------------------
    3    0.804522    5.2315  CLASS3
    3    0.751353   37.3903  CONTROL1
    3    0.725755   52.8725  TRUCK1
    3    0.704495   65.7318  LOCALE2
    3    0.704250   65.8798  CLASS1
    ---------------------------------
    4    0.812099    2.6490  CONTROL1 CLASS1
    4    0.810364    3.6986  CLASS3 LOCALE2
    4    0.808001    5.1275  CLASS3 LOCALE1
    4    0.807122    5.6590  CLASS2 CLASS3
    4    0.806300    6.1562  CLASS3 TRUCK4
    ---------------------------------------------
    5    0.816245    2.1414  CONTROL1 CLASS1 LOCALE2
    5    0.815842    2.3848  CONTROL1 CLASS1 LOCALE1
    5    0.814362    3.2803  CONTROL1 CLASS1 CLASS2
    5    0.813901    3.5589  CONTROL1 CLASS1 TRUCK4
    5    0.812788    4.2321  CONTROL1 CLASS1 TRUCK2
    ---------------------------------------------
    6    0.818304    2.8958  WIDTH CONTROL1 CLASS1 LOCALE1
    6    0.817992    3.0845  CONTROL1 CLASS1 TRUCK4 LOCALE2
    6    0.817915    3.1309  CONTROL1 CLASS1 TRUCK2 LOCALE2
    6    0.817741    3.2367  CONTROL1 CLASS1 TRUCK2 LOCALE1
    6    0.817738    3.2383  WIDTH CONTROL1 CLASS1 LOCALE2
    ---------------------------------------------
    7    0.820443    3.6023  WIDTH CONTROL1 CLASS1 TRUCK4 LOCALE1
    7    0.819942    3.9050  WIDTH CONTROL1 CLASS1 TRUCK4 LOCALE2
    7    0.819473    4.1891  WIDTH CONTROL1 CLASS1 TRUCK2 LOCALE1
    7    0.819180    4.3663  CONTROL1 CLASS1 TRUCK2 TRUCK4 LOCALE2
    7    0.819007    4.4705  WIDTH CONTROL1 CLASS1 CLASS2 LOCALE1
    ---------------------------------------------
```

easy to interpret and does not differ substantially from other models favorably identified by the C_p or R^2 criteria. A plot of the studentized residuals against $\hat{Y}$, shown in Figure 11.13b, indicates that curvilinearity is no longer present. Also, neither Cook's distance measure (maximum = .47) nor the variance inflation factors (maximum = 2.5) revealed serious problems at this stage. Nonconstancy of the error term variance has persisted, however, as confirmed by the Breusch-Pagan test.

Weighted Least Squares Estimation

To remedy the problem with nonconstancy of the error term variance, weighted least squares was implemented by developing a standard deviation function. Residual plots indicated that the absolute residuals vary with CTYPOP and LANES. A fit of a first-order model where the absolute residuals are regressed on CTYPOP and LANES yielded an estimated standard deviation function for which $R^2 = .386$ and the P-values for the regression coefficients for CTYPOP and LANES are .001 and 0+. Note that, as is often the case, the R^2 value for

FIGURE 11.13   **Plots of Studentized Residuals versus Fitted Values—MNDOT Traffic Estimation Example.**

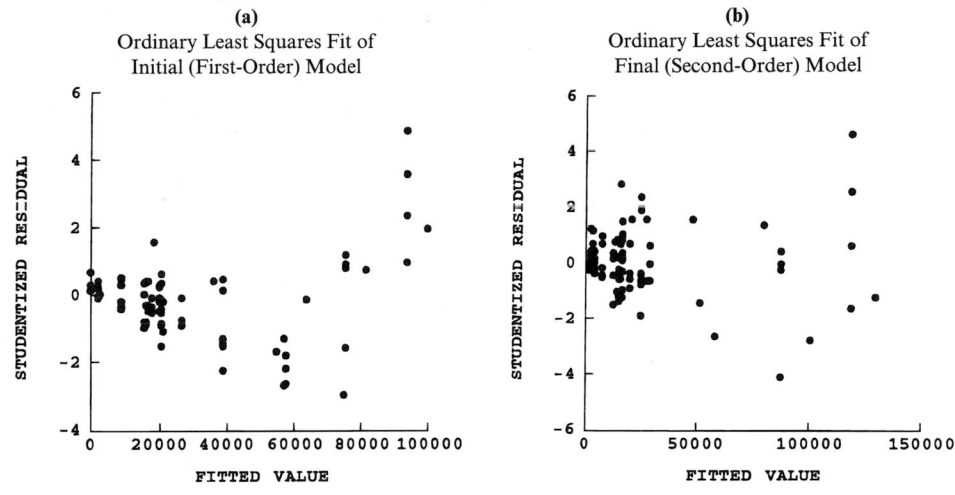

the estimated standard deviation function (.386) is substantially smaller than that for the estimated response function (.925).

Using the weights obtained from the standard deviation function, weighted least squares estimates of the regression coefficients were obtained. Since some of the estimated regression coefficients differed substantially from those obtained with unweighted least squares, the residuals from the weighted least squares fit were used to reestimate the standard deviation function, and revised weights were obtained. Two more iterations of this iteratively reweighted least squares process led to stable estimated coefficients.

MINITAB regression results for the weighted least squares fit based on the final weights are shown in Figure 11.14. Note that the signs of the regression coefficients are all positive, as might be expected:

CTYPOP: Traffic increases with local population density

LANES: Traffic increases with number of lanes

CONTROL1: Traffic is highest for road sections under access control

LANES^2: An upward-curving parabola is consistent with the shape of the loess fit of AADT to LANES in Figure 11.11

CTYPOP $\times$ CONTROL1: Traffic increase with access control is more pronounced for higher population density

Figure 11.15a contains a plot of the studentized residuals against the fitted values, and Figure 11.15b contains a normal probability plot of the studentized residuals. Notice that the variability of the studentized residuals is now approximately constant. While the normal probability plot in Figure 11.15b indicates some departure from normality (this was confirmed by the correlation test for normality), the departure does not appear to be serious, particularly in view of the large sample size.

FIGURE 11.14   **MINITAB Weighted Least Squares Regression Results —**
MNDOT Traffic Estimation Example.

```
The regression equation is
AADT = 9602 + 0.0146 CTYPOP + 6162 LANES + 16556 CONTROL1 + 2250 LANES2
       + 0.0637 POPXCTL1

Predictor      Coef       Stdev    t-ratio        p
Constant       9602        1432       6.71    0.000
CTYPOP      0.014567    0.003047       4.78    0.000
LANES        6161.8       933.9       6.60    0.000
CONTROL1      16556        2966       5.58    0.000
LANES2       2249.7       755.8       2.98    0.004
POPXCTL1    0.063696    0.008421       7.56    0.000

Analysis of Variance

SOURCE       DF          SS          MS        F         p
Regression    5      919.55      183.91    93.13    0.000
Error       115      227.10        1.97
Total       120     1146.65
```

FIGURE 11.15   **Residual Plots for Final Weighted Least Squares Regression Fit —**
MNDOT Traffic Estimation Example.

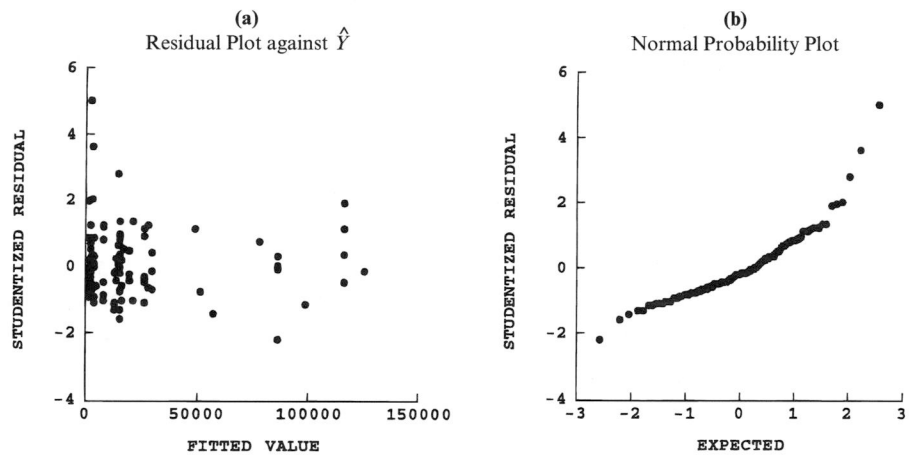

(a)
Residual Plot against $\hat{Y}$

(b)
Normal Probability Plot

To assess the usefulness of the model for estimating AADT, approximate 95 percent confidence intervals for mean traffic for typical rural, suburban, and urban road sections were constructed. The levels of the predictor variables for these road sections are given in Table 11.8, columns 1–3. The estimated mean traffic is given in column 4. The approximate estimated standard deviations of the estimated mean responses for each of these road sections, shown in column 5, were obtained by using $s^2\{\mathbf{b}_w\}$ from (10.13) in (6.58):

$$(11.39) \qquad s^2\{\hat{Y}_h\} = \mathbf{X}'_h s^2\{\mathbf{b}_w\}\mathbf{X}_h = MSE_w \mathbf{X}'_h (\mathbf{X}'\mathbf{W}\mathbf{X})^{-1}\mathbf{X}_h$$

where the vector $\mathbf{X}_h$ is defined in (6.53). Since the estimated standard deviations in column

TABLE 11.8   95 Percent Approximate Confidence Limits for Mean Responses—MNDOT Traffic Estimation Example.

| | (1) | (2) | (3) | (4) | (5) | (6) | (7) |
| | | | | | | Confidence Limits | |
Road Section	CTYPOP	LANES	CONTROL1	$\hat{Y}_h$	$s\{\hat{Y}_h\}$	Lower	Upper
Rural	113,571	2	0	3,365	354	2,663	4,066
Suburban	222,229	4	0	16,379	1,827	12,758	19,999
Urban	941,411	6	1	116,024	6,597	102,953	129,095

5 are only approximations because the least squares weights were estimated by means of a standard deviation function, bootstrapping with random X sampling was employed to assess the precision of the fitted values. The standard deviations of the bootstrap sampling distributions were close to the estimated standard deviations in column 5. The consistency of the results shows that the iterative estimation of the weights by means of the standard deviation function did not have any substantial effect here on the precision of the fitted values.

The approximate 95 percent confidence limits for $E\{Y_h\}$, computed using (6.59), are presented in columns 6 and 7 of Table 11.8. The precision of these estimates was considered to be sufficient for planning purposes. However, because the suburban and rural road estimates have the poorest relative precision, it was recommended that better records be developed for population density in the immediate vicinity of a road section, since county population does not always reflect local population density. The improved information could lead to a better regression model, with more precise estimates for road sections in rural and suburban settings.

The approach for developing the regression model described here is not, of course, the only approach that can lead to a useful regression model, nor is the analysis complete as described. For example, the residual plot in Figure 11.15a suggests the presence of at least one outlier ($r_{92} = 5.02$). Possible remedial measures for this case should be considered. In addition, the departure from normality might be remedied by a transformation of the response variable. This transformation might also stabilize the variance of the error terms sufficiently so that weighted least squares would not be needed. In fact, subsequent analysis using the Box-Cox transformation approach found that a cube root transformation of the response is very effective in this instance. A final choice between the model fit obtained by weighted least squares and a model fit developed by an alternative approach can be made on the basis of model validation studies.

Cited Reference

11.1.   Cheng, C. "Optimal Sampling for Traffic Volume Estimation," Unpublished Ph.D. dissertation, University of Minnesota, Carlson School of Management, 1992.

Problems

11.1.   A student who used a regression model that included indicator variables was upset when receiving only the following output on the multiple regression printout: XTRANSPOSE X SINGULAR. What is a likely source of the difficulty?

11.2.   Refer to regression model (11.4). Portray graphically the response curves for this model if $\beta_0 = 25.3$, $\beta_1 = .20$, and $\beta_2 = -12.1$.

11.3.   In a regression study of factors affecting learning time for a certain task (measured in minutes), gender of learner was included as a predictor variable (X_2) that was coded $X_2 = 1$ if male and 0 if female. It was found that $b_2 = 22.3$ and $s\{b_2\} = 3.8$. An observer questioned whether the coding scheme for gender is fair because it results in a positive coefficient, leading to longer learning times for males than females. Comment.

√ 11.4.   Refer to **Calculator maintenance** Problem 1.20. The users of the desk calculators are either training institutions that use a student model, or business firms that employ a commercial model. An analyst at Tri-City wishes to fit a regression model including both number of calculators serviced (X_1) and type of calculator (X_2) as predictor variables and estimate the effect of calculator model (S — student, C — commercial) on number of minutes spent on the service call. Records show that the models serviced in the 18 calls were:

i:	1	2	3	. . .	16	17	18
Model:	C	S	C	. . .	C	C	C

Assume that regression model (11.4) is appropriate, and let $X_2 = 1$ if student model and 0 if commercial model.

a.   Explain the meaning of all regression coefficients in the model.

b.   Fit the regression model and state the estimated regression function.

c.   Estimate the effect of calculator model on mean service time with a 95 percent confidence interval. Interpret your interval estimate.

d.   Why would the analyst wish to include X_1, number of calculators, in the regression model when interest is in estimating the effect of type of calculator model on service time?

e.   Obtain the residuals and plot them against $X_1 X_2$. Is there any indication that an interaction term in the regression model would be helpful?

11.5.   Refer to **Grade point average** Problem 1.19. An assistant to the director of admissions conjectures that the predictive power of the model could be improved by adding information on whether the student had chosen a major field of concentration at the time the application was submitted. Assume that regression model (11.4) is appropriate, where X_1 is entrance test score and $X_2 = 1$ if student had indicated a major field of concentration at the time of application and 0 if the major field was undecided. Students 3, 4, 5, 6, 9, and 17 had indicated a major field at the time of application.

a. Explain how each regression coefficient in model (11.4) is interpreted here.

b. Fit the regression model and state the estimated regression function.

c. Test whether the X_2 variable can be dropped from the regression model; use $\alpha = .01$. State the alternatives, decision rule, and conclusion.

d. Obtain the residuals for regression model (11.4) and plot them against $X_1 X_2$. Is there any evidence in your plot that it would be helpful to include an interaction term in the model?

11.6. Refer to regression models (11.4) and (11.6). Would the conclusion that $\beta_2 = 0$ have the same implication for each of these models? Explain.

11.7. Refer to regression model (11.6). Portray graphically the response curves for this model if $\beta_0 = 25$, $\beta_1 = .30$, $\beta_2 = -12.5$, and $\beta_3 = .05$. Describe the nature of the interaction effect.

√ 11.8. Refer to **Calculator maintenance** Problems 1.20 and 11.4.

a. Fit regression model (11.6) and state the estimated regression function.

b. Test whether the interaction term can be dropped from the model; control the α risk at .10. State the alternatives, decision rule, and conclusion. What is the P-value of the test? If the interaction term cannot be dropped from the model, describe the nature of the interaction effect.

11.9. Refer to **Grade point average** Problems 1.19 and 11.5.

a. Fit regression model (11.6) and state the estimated regression function.

b. Test whether the interaction term can be dropped from the model; use $\alpha = .05$. State the alternatives, decision rule, and conclusion. If the interaction term cannot be dropped from the model, describe the nature of the interaction effect.

11.10. In a regression analysis of on-the-job head injuries of warehouse laborers caused by falling objects, Y is a measure of severity of the injury, X_1 is an index reflecting both the weight of the object and the distance it fell, and X_2 and X_3 are indicator variables for nature of head protection worn at the time of the accident, coded as follows:

Type of Protection	X_2	X_3
Hard hat	1	0
Bump cap	0	1
None	0	0

The response function to be used in the study is $E\{Y\} = \beta_0 + \beta_1 X_1 + \beta_2 X_2 + \beta_3 X_3$.

a. Develop the response function for each type-of-protection category.

b. For each of the following questions, specify the alternatives H_0 and H_a for the appropriate test: (1) With X_1 fixed, does wearing a bump cap reduce the expected severity of injury as compared with wearing no protection? (2) With X_1 fixed, is the expected severity of injury the same when wearing a hard hat as when wearing a bump cap?

11.11. Refer to tool wear regression model (11.12). Suppose the indicator variables had been defined as follows: $X_2 = 1$ if tool model M2 and 0 otherwise, $X_3 = 1$ if tool model M3 and 0 otherwise, $X_4 = 1$ if tool model M4 and 0 otherwise. Indicate the meaning of each of the following: (1) β_3, (2) $\beta_4 - \beta_3$, (3) β_1, (4) β_7.

11.12. Refer to advertising expenditures regression model (11.16).

　　a. How is β_4 interpreted here? What is the meaning of $\beta_3 - \beta_2$ here?

　　b. State the alternatives for a test of whether the response functions are the same in incorporated and not-incorporated firms with high-quality sales management.

11.13. A marketing research trainee in the national office of a chain of shoe stores used the following response function to study seasonal (winter, spring, summer, fall) effects on sales of a certain line of shoes: $E\{Y\} = \beta_0 + \beta_1 X_1 + \beta_2 X_2 + \beta_3 X_3$. The Xs are indicator variables defined as follows: $X_1 = 1$ if winter and 0 otherwise, $X_2 = 1$ if spring and 0 otherwise, $X_3 = 1$ if fall and 0 otherwise. After fitting the model, the trainee tested the regression coefficients β_k ($k = 0, \ldots, 3$) and came to the following set of conclusions at an .05 family level of significance: $\beta_0 \neq 0$, $\beta_1 = 0$, $\beta_2 \neq 0$, $\beta_3 \neq 0$. In the report the trainee then wrote: "Results of regression analysis show that climatic and other seasonal factors have no influence in determining sales of this shoe line in the winter. Seasonal influences do exist in the other seasons." Do you agree with this interpretation of the test results? Discuss.

√ 11.14. **Assessed valuations**. A tax consultant studied the current relation between selling price and assessed valuation of one-family residential dwellings in a large tax district by obtaining data for a random sample of 9 recent "arm's-length" sales transactions of one-family dwellings located on corner lots and for a random sample of 14 recent sales of one-family dwellings not located on corner lots. In the data that follow, both selling price (Y) and assessed valuation (X_1) are expressed in thousand dollars. Assume that the error variances in the two populations are equal and that regression model (11.6) is appropriate.

Corner Lots

i:	1	2	3	. . .	7	8	9
X_{i1}:	17.5	12.5	20.0	. . .	17.5	12.3	11.5
Y_i:	56.2	42.5	68.6	. . .	56.9	34.0	39.0

Noncorner Lots

i:	1	2	3	. . .	12	13	14
X_{i1}:	10.0	13.8	15.0	. . .	17.0	10.8	15.0
Y_i:	31.2	36.9	41.0	. . .	46.1	30.0	42.0

　　a. Plot the sample data for the two populations as a symbolic scatter plot. Does the regression relation appear to be the same for the two populations?

　　b. Test for identity of the regression functions for dwellings on corner lots and dwellings in other locations; control the risk of Type I error at .10. State the alternatives, decision rule, and conclusion.

　　c. Plot the estimated regression functions for the two populations and describe the nature of the differences between them.

d. Estimate the difference in the slopes of the two regression functions using a 90 percent confidence interval.

e. Obtain the residuals and plot them separately against $\hat{Y}$ for each sample, using the same scales. Does the assumption of equal error variances appear to be reasonable here?

f. Conduct a formal F test for equality of the error variances for the two types of locations; use $\alpha = .05$. State the alternatives, decision rule, and conclusion. What is the P-value of the test?

g. Plot the residuals against X_1, X_2, and $X_1 X_2$ on separate graphs. Also prepare a normal probability plot of the residuals. Interpret your plots and summarize your findings.

11.15. **Tire testing**. A testing laboratory with equipment that simulates highway driving studied for two makes (A, B) of a certain type of truck tire the relation between operating cost per mile (Y) and cruising speed (X_1). The observations are shown below (all data are coded). An engineer now wishes to decide whether or not the regression of operating cost on cruising speed is the same for the two makes of tires. Assume that the error variances for the two makes of tires are the same and that regression model (11.6) is appropriate.

Make A

i:	1	2	3	4	5	6	7	8	9	10
X_{i1}:	10	20	20	30	40	40	50	60	60	70
Y_i:	9.8	12.5	14.2	14.9	19.0	16.5	20.9	22.4	24.1	25.8

Make B

i:	1	2	3	4	5	6	7	8	9	10
X_{i1}:	10	20	20	30	40	40	50	60	60	70
Y_i:	15.0	14.5	16.1	16.5	16.4	19.1	20.9	22.3	19.8	21.4

a. Plot the sample data for the two populations as a symbolic scatter plot. Does the relation between speed and cost appear to be the same for the two makes of tires?

b. Test whether or not the regression functions are the same for the two makes of tires. Control the risk of Type I error at .05. State the alternatives, decision rule, and conclusion.

c. Suppose the question of interest simply had been whether the two regression lines have equal slopes. Answer this question by setting up a 95 percent confidence interval for the difference between the two slopes. What do you find?

d. Obtain the residuals and plot them separately against $\hat{Y}$ for each make of tire, using the same scales. Does the assumption of equal error variances appear to be reasonable here?

e. Conduct a formal F test for equality of the error variances for the two makes of tires; use $\alpha = .01$. State the alternatives, decision rule, and conclusion. What is the P-value of the test?

f. Plot the residuals against X_1, X_2, and $X_1 X_2$ on separate graphs. Also prepare a normal probability plot of the residuals. Summarize the results of your analysis of these plots.

√ 11.16. Refer to **Muscle mass** Problem 1.27. The nutritionist conjectures that the regression of muscle mass on age follows a two-piece linear relation, with the slope changing at age 60 without discontinuity.

    a. State the regression model that applies if the nutritionist's conjecture is correct. What are the respective response functions when age is 60 or less and when age is over 60?

    b. Fit the regression model specified in part (a) and state the estimated regression function.

    c. Test whether a two-piece linear regression function is needed; use $\alpha = .01$. State the alternatives, decision rule, and conclusion. What is the P-value of the test?

11.17. **Shipment handling**. Global Electronics periodically imports shipments of a certain large part used as a component in several of its products. The size of the shipment varies depending upon production schedules. For handling and distribution to assembling plants, shipments of size 250 thousand parts or less are sent to warehouse A; larger shipments are sent to warehouse B since this warehouse has specialized equipment that provides greater economies of scale for large shipments. The data below were collected on the 10 most recent shipments; X is the size of the shipment (in thousand parts), and Y is the direct cost of handling the shipment in the warehouse (in thousand dollars).

i:	1	2	3	4	5	6	7	8	9	10
X_i:	225	350	150	200	175	180	325	290	400	125
Y_i:	11.95	14.13	8.93	10.98	10.03	10.13	13.75	13.30	15.00	7.97

A two-piece linear regression model with a possible discontinuity at $X = 250$ is to be fitted.

    a. Specify the regression model to be used.

    b. Fit this regression model. Plot the fitted response function and the data. Is there any indication that greater economies of scale are obtained in handling relatively large shipments than relatively small ones?

    c. Test whether or not both the two separate slopes and the discontinuity can be dropped from the model. Control the level of significance at .025. State the alternatives, decision rule, and conclusion.

    d. For relatively small shipments, what is the point estimate of the increase in expected handling cost for each increase of 1 thousand in the size of the shipment? What is the corresponding estimate for relatively large shipments?

11.18. In time series analysis, the X variable representing time usually is defined to take on values 1, 2, etc., for the successive time periods. Does this represent an allocated code when the time periods are actually 1989, 1990, etc.?

11.19. An analyst wishes to include number of older siblings in family as a predictor variable in a regression analysis of factors affecting maturation in eighth graders. The number of older siblings in the sample observations ranges from 0 to 4. Discuss whether this variable should be placed in the model as an ordinary quantitative variable or by means of four 0, 1 indicator variables.

11.20. Refer to regression model (11.2) for the insurance innovation study. Suppose β_0 were dropped from the model to eliminate the linear dependence in the **X** matrix so that the model becomes $Y_i = \beta_1 X_{i1} + \beta_2 X_{i2} + \beta_3 X_{i3} + \varepsilon_i$. What is the meaning here of each of the regression coefficients β_1, β_2, and β_3?

Exercises

11.21. Refer to the instrument calibration study example in Section 11.4. Suppose that three instruments (A, B, C) had been developed to identical specifications, that the regression functions relating gauge reading (Y) to actual pressure (X_1) are second-order polynomials for each instrument, that the error variances are the same, and that the polynomial coefficients may differ from one instrument to the next. Let X_3 denote a second indicator variable, where $X_3 = 1$ if instrument C and 0 otherwise.

   a. Expand regression model (11.21) to cover this situation.

   b. State the alternatives, define the test statistic, and give the decision rule for each of the following tests when the level of significance is .01: (1) test whether the second-order regression functions for the three instruments are identical, (2) test whether all three regression functions have the same intercept, (3) test whether both the linear and quadratic effects are the same in all three regression functions.

11.22. Refer to **Muscle mass** Problem 1.27. Specify the regression model for the case where the slope changes at age 40 and again at age 60 with no discontinuities.

11.23. In a regression study, three types of banks were involved, namely, commercial, mutual savings, and savings and loan. Consider the following system of indicator variables for type of bank:

Type of Bank	X_2	X_3
Commercial	1	0
Mutual savings	0	1
Savings and loan	−1	−1

   a. Develop a first-order linear regression model for relating last year's profit or loss (Y) to size of bank (X_1) and type of bank (X_2, X_3).

   b. State the response functions for the three types of banks.

   c. Interpret each of the following quantities: (1) β_2, (2) β_3, (3) $-\beta_2 - \beta_3$.

11.24. Refer to regression model (11.17) and exclude variable X_3.

   a. Obtain the $\mathbf{X'X}$ matrix for this special case of a single qualitative predictor variable, for $i = 1, \ldots, n$ when n_1 firms are not incorporated.

   b. Using (6.25), find $\mathbf{b}$.

   c. Using (6.35) and (6.36), find SSE and SSR.

Projects

11.25. Refer to the **SMSA** data set. The number of active physicians (Y) is to be regressed against total population (X_1), total personal income (X_2), and geographic region (X_3, X_4, X_5).

   a. Fit a first-order regression model. Let $X_3 = 1$ if NE and 0 otherwise, $X_4 = 1$ if NC and 0 otherwise, and $X_5 = 1$ if S and 0 otherwise.

b. Examine whether the effect for the northeastern region on number of active physicians differs from the effect for the north central region by constructing an appropriate 90 percent confidence interval. Interpret your interval estimate.

c. Test whether any geographic effects are present; use $\alpha = .10$. State the alternatives, decision rule, and conclusion. What is the P-value of the test?

11.26. Refer to the **SENIC** data set. Infection risk (Y) is to be regressed against length of stay (X_1), age (X_2), routine chest X-ray ratio (X_3), and medical school affiliation (X_4).

a. Fit a first-order regression model. Let $X_4 = 1$ if hospital has medical school affiliation and 0 if not.

b. Estimate the effect of medical school affiliation on infection risk using a 98 percent confidence interval. Interpret your interval estimate.

c. It has been suggested that the effect of medical school affiliation on infection risk may interact with the effects of age and routine chest X-ray ratio. Add appropriate interaction terms to the regression model, fit the revised regression model, and test whether the interaction terms are helpful; use $\alpha = .10$. State the alternatives, decision rule, and conclusion.

11.27. Refer to the **SENIC** data set. Length of stay (Y) is to be regressed on age (X_1), routine culturing ratio (X_2), average daily census (X_3), available facilities and services (X_4), and region (X_5, X_6, X_7).

a. Fit a first-order regression model. Let $X_5 = 1$ if NE and 0 otherwise, $X_6 = 1$ if NC and 0 otherwise, and $X_7 = 1$ if S and 0 otherwise.

b. Test whether the routine culturing ratio can be dropped from the model; use a level of significance of .05. State the alternatives, decision rule, and conclusion.

c. Examine whether the effect on length of stay for hospitals located in the western region differs from that for hospitals located in the other three regions by constructing an appropriate confidence interval for each pairwise comparison. Use the Bonferroni procedure with a 95 percent family confidence coefficient. Summarize your findings.

Autocorrelation in Time Series Data

The basic regression models considered so far have assumed that the random error terms ε_i are either uncorrelated random variables or independent normal random variables. In business and economics, many regression applications involve time series data. For such data, the assumption of uncorrelated or independent error terms is often not appropriate; rather, the error terms are frequently correlated positively over time. Error terms correlated over time are said to be *autocorrelated* or *serially correlated*.

A major cause of positively autocorrelated error terms in business and economic regression applications involving time series data is the omission of one or several key variables from the model. When time-ordered effects of such "missing" key variables are positively correlated, the error terms in the regression model will tend to be positively autocorrelated since the error terms include effects of missing variables. Consider, for example, the regression of annual sales of a product against average yearly price of the product over a period of 30 years. If population size has an important effect on sales, its omission from the model may lead to the error terms being positively autocorrelated because the effect of population size on sales likely is positively correlated over time.

Another cause of positively autocorrelated error terms in economic data is the presence of systematic coverage errors in the response variable time series, which errors often tend to be positively correlated over time.

12.1 Problems of Autocorrelation

When the error terms in the regression model are positively autocorrelated, the use of ordinary least squares procedures has a number of important consequences. We summarize these first, and then discuss them in more detail:

1. The estimated regression coefficients are still unbiased, but they no longer have the minimum variance property and may be quite inefficient.

2. *MSE* may seriously underestimate the variance of the error terms.

3. $s\{b_k\}$ calculated according to ordinary least squares procedures may seriously underestimate the true standard deviation of the estimated regression coefficient.

4. Confidence intervals and tests using the t and F distributions, discussed earlier, are no longer strictly applicable.

TABLE 12.1   Example of Positively Autocorrelated Error Terms.

t	(1) u_t	(2) $\varepsilon_{t-1} + u_t = \varepsilon_t$	(3) $Y_t = 2 + .5X_t + \varepsilon_t$
0	—	3.0	5.0
1	.5	$3.0 + .5 = 3.5$	6.0
2	−.7	$3.5 - .7 = 2.8$	5.8
3	.3	$2.8 + .3 = 3.1$	6.6
4	0	$3.1 + 0 = 3.1$	7.1
5	−2.3	$3.1 - 2.3 = .8$	5.3
6	−1.9	$.8 - 1.9 = -1.1$	3.9
7	.2	$-1.1 + .2 = -.9$	4.6
8	−.3	$-.9 - .3 = -1.2$	4.8
9	.2	$-1.2 + .2 = -1.0$	5.5
10	−.1	$-1.0 - .1 = -1.1$	5.9

To illustrate these problems intuitively, we consider the simple linear regression model with time series data:

$$Y_t = \beta_0 + \beta_1 X_t + \varepsilon_t$$

Here, Y_t and X_t are observations for period t. Let us assume that the error terms ε_t are positively autocorrelated as follows:

$$\varepsilon_t = \varepsilon_{t-1} + u_t$$

The u_t, called *disturbances*, are independent normal random variables. Thus, any error term ε_t is the sum of the previous error term ε_{t-1} and a new disturbance term u_t. We shall assume here that the u_t have mean 0 and variance 1.

In Table 12.1, column 1, we show 10 random observations on the normal variable u_t with mean 0 and variance 1, obtained from a standard normal random numbers generator. Suppose now that $\varepsilon_0 = 3.0$; we obtain then:

$$\varepsilon_1 = \varepsilon_0 + u_1 = 3.0 + .5 = 3.5$$

$$\varepsilon_2 = \varepsilon_1 + u_2 = 3.5 - .7 = 2.8$$

etc.

The error terms ε_t are shown in Table 12.1, column 2, and they are plotted in Figure 12.1. Note the systematic pattern in these error terms. Their positive relation over time is shown by the fact that adjacent error terms tend to be of the same magnitude.

Suppose that X_t in the regression model represents time, such that $X_1 = 1$, $X_2 = 2$, etc. Further, suppose we know that $\beta_0 = 2$ and $\beta_1 = .5$ so that the true regression function is $E\{Y\} = 2 + .5X$. The observed Y values based on the error terms in column 2 of Table 12.1 are shown in column 3. For example, $Y_0 = 2 + .5(0) + 3.0 = 5.0$, and $Y_1 = 2 + .5(1) + 3.5 = 6.0$. Figure 12.2a on page 500 contains the true regression line $E\{Y\} = 2 + .5X$ and the observed Y values shown in Table 12.1, column 3. Figure 12.2b contains the estimated regression line, fitted by ordinary least squares methods, and repeats the observed Y values.

FIGURE 12.1   **Example of Positively Autocorrelated Error Terms.**

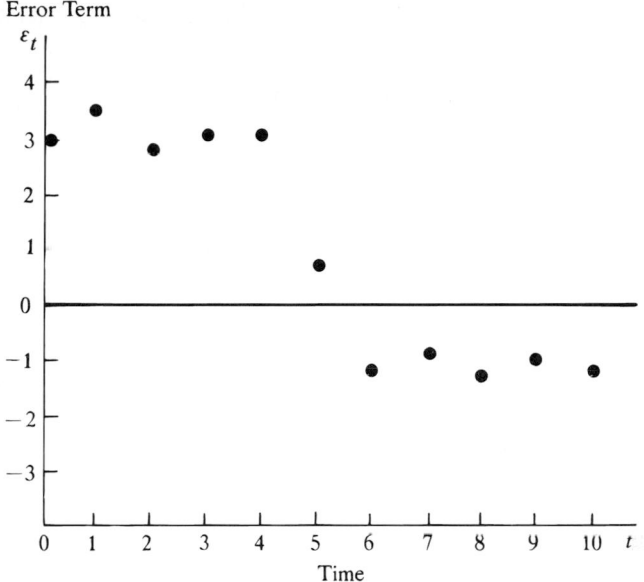

Notice that the fitted regression line differs sharply from the true regression line because the initial ε_0 value was large and the succeeding positively autocorrelated error terms tended to be large for some time. This persistency pattern in the positively autocorrelated error terms leads to a fitted regression line far from the true one. Had the initial ε_0 value been small, say, $\varepsilon_0 = -.2$, and the disturbances different, a sharply different fitted regression line might have been obtained because of the persistency pattern, as shown in Figure 12.2c. This variation from sample to sample in the fitted regression lines due to the positively autocorrelated error terms may be so substantial as to lead to large variances of the estimated regression coefficients when ordinary least squares methods are used.

Another key problem with applying ordinary least squares methods when the error terms are positively autocorrelated, as mentioned before, is that *MSE* may seriously underestimate the variance of the ε_t. Figure 12.2 makes this clear. Note that the variability of the Y values around the fitted regression line in Figure 12.2b is substantially smaller than the variability of the Y values around the true regression line in Figure 12.2a. This is one of the factors leading to an indication of greater precision of the regression coefficients than is actually the case when ordinary least squares methods are used in the presence of positively autocorrelated errors.

In view of the seriousness of the problems created by autocorrelated errors, it is important that their presence be detected. A plot of residuals against time is an effective, though subjective, means of detecting autocorrelated errors. Formal statistical tests have also been developed. A widely used test is based on the first-order autoregressive error model, which we take up next. This model is a simple one, yet experience suggests that it is frequently applicable in business and economics when the error terms are serially correlated.

FIGURE 12.2   Regression with Positively Autocorrelated Error Terms.

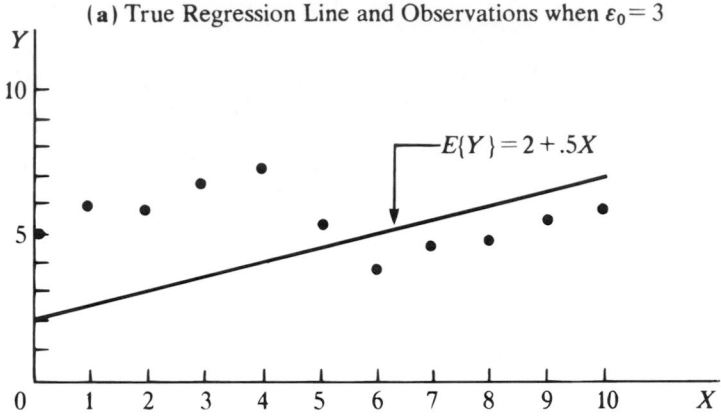

(**a**) True Regression Line and Observations when $\varepsilon_0 = 3$

$E\{Y\} = 2 + .5X$

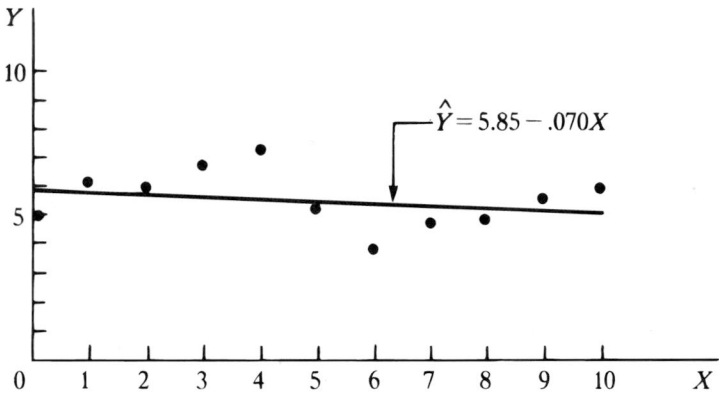

(**b**) Fitted Regression Line and Observations when $\varepsilon_0 = 3$

$\hat{Y} = 5.85 - .070X$

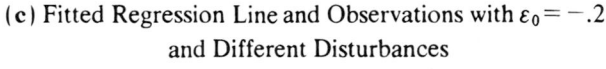

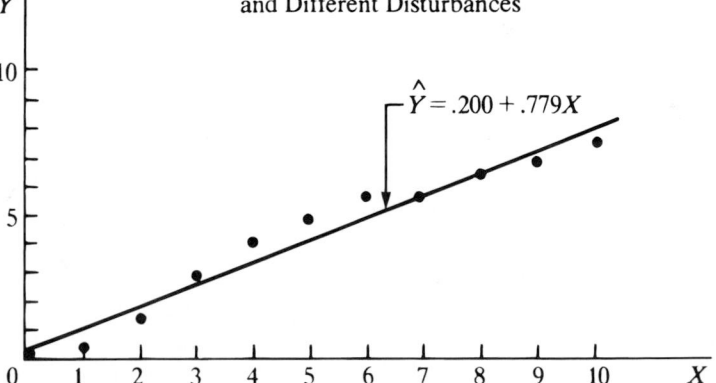

(**c**) Fitted Regression Line and Observations with $\varepsilon_0 = -.2$ and Different Disturbances

$\hat{Y} = .200 + .779X$

12.2   First-Order Autoregressive Error Model

Simple Linear Regression

The generalized simple linear regression model for one predictor variable when the random error terms follow a first-order autoregressive process is:

$$Y_t = \beta_0 + \beta_1 X_t + \varepsilon_t$$

(12.1)

$$\varepsilon_t = \rho \varepsilon_{t-1} + u_t$$

where:

    ρ is a parameter such that $|\rho| < 1$

    u_t are independent $N(0, \sigma^2)$

Note that generalized regression model (12.1) is identical to the simple linear regression model (2.1) except for the structure of the error terms. Each error term in model (12.1) consists of a fraction of the previous error term (when $\rho > 0$) plus a new disturbance term u_t. The parameter ρ is called the *autocorrelation parameter*.

Multiple Regression

The generalized multiple regression model when the random error terms follow a first-order autoregressive process is:

$$Y_t = \beta_0 + \beta_1 X_{t1} + \beta_2 X_{t2} + \cdots + \beta_{p-1} X_{t,p-1} + \varepsilon_t$$

(12.2)

$$\varepsilon_t = \rho \varepsilon_{t-1} + u_t$$

where:

    $|\rho| < 1$

    u_t are independent $N(0, \sigma^2)$

Thus, we see that generalized multiple regression model (12.2) is identical to the earlier multiple regression model (6.7) except for the structure of the error terms.

Properties of Error Terms

Regression models (12.1) and (12.2) are generalized regression models because the error terms ε_t in these models are correlated. However, the error terms still have mean zero and constant variance:

(12.3)

$$E\{\varepsilon_t\} = 0$$

(12.4)

$$\sigma^2\{\varepsilon_t\} = \frac{\sigma^2}{1 - \rho^2}$$

Note that the variance of the error terms here is a function of the autocorrelation parameter ρ.

The covariance between adjacent error terms ε_t and ε_{t-1} is:

$$(12.5) \qquad \sigma\{\varepsilon_t, \varepsilon_{t-1}\} = \rho\left(\frac{\sigma^2}{1 - \rho^2}\right)$$

The coefficient of correlation between ε_t and ε_{t-1}, denoted by $\rho\{\varepsilon_t, \varepsilon_{t-1}\}$, is defined as follows:

$$(12.6) \qquad \rho\{\varepsilon_t, \varepsilon_{t-1}\} = \frac{\sigma\{\varepsilon_t, \varepsilon_{t-1}\}}{\sigma\{\varepsilon_t\}\sigma\{\varepsilon_{t-1}\}}$$

Since the variance of each error term according to (12.4) is $\sigma^2/(1 - \rho^2)$, the coefficient of correlation using (12.5) is:

$$(12.6a) \qquad \rho\{\varepsilon_t, \varepsilon_{t-1}\} = \frac{\rho\left(\dfrac{\sigma^2}{1 - \rho^2}\right)}{\sqrt{\dfrac{\sigma^2}{1 - \rho^2}}\sqrt{\dfrac{\sigma^2}{1 - \rho^2}}} = \rho$$

Thus, the autocorrelation parameter ρ is the coefficient of correlation between adjacent error terms.

The covariance between error terms that are s periods apart can be shown to be:

$$(12.7) \qquad \sigma\{\varepsilon_t, \varepsilon_{t-s}\} = \rho^s\left(\frac{\sigma^2}{1 - \rho^2}\right) \qquad s \neq 0$$

and the coefficient of correlation between ε_t and ε_{t-s} therefore is:

$$(12.8) \qquad \rho\{\varepsilon_t, \varepsilon_{t-s}\} = \rho^s \qquad s \neq 0$$

Thus, when ρ is positive, all error terms are correlated, but the further apart they are, the less is the correlation between them. The only time the error terms for the autoregressive error models (12.1) and (12.2) are uncorrelated is when $\rho = 0$.

Based on the results for the variances and covariances of the error terms in (12.4) and (12.7), we can now state the variance-covariance matrix of the error terms for the first-order autoregressive generalized regression models (12.1) and (12.2):

$$(12.9) \qquad \underset{n \times n}{\sigma^2\{\varepsilon\}} = \begin{bmatrix} \kappa & \kappa\rho & \kappa\rho^2 & \cdots & \kappa\rho^{n-1} \\ \kappa\rho & \kappa & \kappa\rho & \cdots & \kappa\rho^{n-2} \\ \vdots & \vdots & \vdots & & \vdots \\ \kappa\rho^{n-1} & \kappa\rho^{n-2} & \kappa\rho^{n-3} & \cdots & \kappa \end{bmatrix}$$

where:

$$(12.9a) \qquad \kappa = \frac{\sigma^2}{1 - \rho^2}$$

Note again that the variance-covariance matrix (12.9) reflects the generalized nature of regression models (12.1) and (12.2) by containing nonzero covariance terms.

Comments

1. It is instructive to expand the definition of the first-order autoregressive error term ε_t:

$$\varepsilon_t = \rho\varepsilon_{t-1} + u_t$$

Since this definition holds for all t, we have $\varepsilon_{t-1} = \rho\varepsilon_{t-2} + u_{t-1}$. When we substitute this expression above, we obtain:

$$\varepsilon_t = \rho(\rho\varepsilon_{t-2} + u_{t-1}) + u_t = \rho^2\varepsilon_{t-2} + \rho u_{t-1} + u_t$$

Replacing now ε_{t-2} by $\rho\varepsilon_{t-3} + u_{t-2}$, we obtain:

$$\varepsilon_t = \rho^3\varepsilon_{t-3} + \rho^2 u_{t-2} + \rho u_{t-1} + u_t$$

Continuing in this fashion, we find:

(12.10)
$$\varepsilon_t = \sum_{s=0}^{\infty} \rho^s u_{t-s}$$

Thus, the error term ε_t in period t is a linear combination of the current and preceding disturbance terms. When $0 < \rho < 1$, (12.10) indicates that the further the period $t - s$ is in the past, the smaller is the weight of disturbance term u_{t-s} in determining ε_t.

2. The derivation of (12.3), that the error terms have expectation zero, follows directly from taking the expectation of ε_t in (12.10) and using the fact that $E\{u_t\} = 0$ for all t according to models (12.1) and (12.2).

3. To derive the variance of the error terms in (12.4), we utilize the assumption of models (12.1) and (12.2) that the u_t are independent with variance σ^2. It then follows from (12.10) that:

$$\sigma^2\{\varepsilon_t\} = \sum_{s=0}^{\infty} \rho^{2s}\sigma^2\{u_{t-s}\} = \sigma^2 \sum_{s=0}^{\infty} \rho^{2s}$$

Now for $|\rho| < 1$, it is known that:

$$\sum_{s=0}^{\infty} \rho^{2s} = \frac{1}{1 - \rho^2}$$

Hence, we have:

$$\sigma^2\{\varepsilon_t\} = \frac{\sigma^2}{1 - \rho^2}$$

4. To derive the covariance of ε_t and ε_{t-1} in (12.5), we need to recognize that:

$$\sigma^2\{\varepsilon_t\} = E\{\varepsilon_t^2\}$$

$$\sigma\{\varepsilon_t, \varepsilon_{t-1}\} = E\{\varepsilon_t \varepsilon_{t-1}\}$$

These results follow from theorems (A.15a) and (A.21a), respectively, since $E\{\varepsilon_t\} = 0$ by (12.3) for all t.

By (12.10), we have:

$$E\{\varepsilon_t \varepsilon_{t-1}\} = E\{(u_t + \rho u_{t-1} + \rho^2 u_{t-2} + \cdots)(u_{t-1} + \rho u_{t-2} + \rho^2 u_{t-3} + \cdots)\}$$

which can be rewritten:

$$E\{\varepsilon_t\varepsilon_{t-1}\} = E\{[u_t + \rho(u_{t-1} + \rho u_{t-2} + \cdots)][u_{t-1} + \rho u_{t-2} + \rho^2 u_{t-3} + \cdots]\}$$

$$= E\{u_t(u_{t-1} + \rho u_{t-2} + \rho^2 u_{t-3} + \cdots)\}$$

$$+ E\{\rho(u_{t-1} + \rho u_{t-2} + \rho^2 u_{t-3} + \cdots)^2\}$$

Since $E\{u_t u_{t-s}\} = 0$ for all $s \neq 0$ by the assumed independence of the u_t and the fact that $E\{u_t\} = 0$ for all t, the first term drops out and we obtain:

$$E\{\varepsilon_t\varepsilon_{t-1}\} = \rho E\{\varepsilon_{t-1}^2\} = \rho\sigma^2\{\varepsilon_{t-1}\}$$

Hence, by (12.4), which holds for all t, we have:

$$\sigma\{\varepsilon_t, \varepsilon_{t-1}\} = \rho\left(\frac{\sigma^2}{1-\rho^2}\right)$$

5. The first-order autoregressive error process in models (12.1) and (12.2) is the simplest kind. A second-order process would be:

(12.11)
$$\varepsilon_t = \rho_1\varepsilon_{t-1} + \rho_2\varepsilon_{t-2} + u_t$$

Still higher-order processes could be postulated. Specialized approaches have been developed for complex autoregressive error processes. These are discussed in treatments of time series procedures and forecasting, such as in Reference 12.1. ∎

12.3 Durbin-Watson Test for Autocorrelation

The Durbin-Watson test for autocorrelation assumes the first-order autoregressive error models (12.1) or (12.2), with the values of the predictor variable(s) fixed. The test consists of determining whether or not the autocorrelation parameter ρ in (12.1) or (12.2) is zero. Note that if $\rho = 0$, then $\varepsilon_t = u_t$. Hence, the error terms ε_t are independent when $\rho = 0$ since the disturbance terms u_t are independent.

Because correlated error terms in business and economic applications tend to show positive serial correlation, the usual test alternatives considered are:

(12.12)
$$H_0: \rho = 0$$
$$H_a: \rho > 0$$

The Durbin-Watson test statistic D is obtained by using ordinary least squares to fit the regression function, calculating the ordinary residuals:

(12.13)
$$e_t = Y_t - \hat{Y}_t$$

and then calculating the statistic:

(12.14)
$$D = \frac{\sum\limits_{t=2}^{n}(e_t - e_{t-1})^2}{\sum\limits_{t=1}^{n} e_t^2}$$

where n is the number of cases.

Exact critical values are difficult to obtain, but Durbin and Watson have obtained lower and upper bounds d_L and d_U such that a value of D outside these bounds leads to a definite decision. The decision rule for testing between the alternatives in (12.12) is:

(12.15)
$$\text{If } D > d_U, \text{ conclude } H_0$$
$$\text{If } D < d_L, \text{ conclude } H_a$$
$$\text{If } d_L \le D \le d_U, \text{ the test is inconclusive}$$

Small values of D lead to the conclusion that $\rho > 0$ because the adjacent error terms ε_t and ε_{t-1} tend to be of the same magnitude when they are positively autocorrelated. Hence, the differences in the residuals, $e_t - e_{t-1}$, would tend to be small when $\rho > 0$, leading to a small numerator in D and hence to a small test statistic D.

Table B.7 contains the bounds d_L and d_U for various sample sizes (n), for two levels of significance (.05 and .01), and for various numbers of X variables $(p-1)$ in the regression model.

Example

The Blaisdell Company wished to predict its sales by using industry sales as a predictor variable. (Accurate predictions of industry sales are available from the industry's trade association.) A portion of the seasonally adjusted quarterly data on company sales and industry sales for the period 1988–92 is shown in Table 12.2, columns 1 and 2. A scatter plot (not shown) suggested that a linear regression model is appropriate. The market research analyst was, however, concerned whether or not the error terms are positively autocorrelated.

The results of using ordinary least squares to fit a regression line to the data in Table 12.2 are shown at the bottom of Table 12.2. The residuals e_t are shown in column 3 of Table 12.2 and are plotted against time in Figure 12.3. Note how the residuals consistently are above or below the zero line for extended periods. Positive autocorrelation in the error terms is suggested by such a pattern when an appropriate regression function has been employed.

The analyst wished to confirm this graphic diagnosis by using the Durbin-Watson test for the alternatives:

$$H_0: \quad \rho = 0$$
$$H_a: \quad \rho > 0$$

Columns 4, 5, and 6 of Table 12.2 contain the necessary calculations for the test statistic D. The analyst then obtained:

$$D = \frac{\sum\limits_{t=2}^{20}(e_t - e_{t-1})^2}{\sum\limits_{t=1}^{20} e_t^2} = \frac{.09794}{.13330} = .735$$

TABLE 12.2   **Data for Blaisdell Company Example, Regression Results, and Durbin-Watson Test Calculations (company and industry sales data are seasonally adjusted).**

Year and Quarter	t	(1) Company Sales ($ millions) Y_t	(2) Industry Sales ($ millions) X_t	(3) Residual e_t	(4) $e_t - e_{t-1}$	(5) $(e_t - e_{t-1})^2$	(6) e_t^2
1988: 1	1	20.96	127.3	−.026052	—	—	.0006787
2	2	21.40	130.0	−.062015	−.035963	.0012933	.0038459
3	3	21.96	132.7	.022021	.084036	.0070620	.0004849
4	4	21.52	129.4	.163754	.141733	.0200882	.0268154
...	...	...	...	...	...	...	...
1992: 1	17	27.52	164.2	.029112	−.076990	.0059275	.0008475
2	18	27.78	165.6	.042316	.013204	.0001743	.0017906
3	19	28.24	168.7	−.044160	−.086476	.0074781	.0019501
4	20	28.78	171.7	−.033009	.011151	.0001243	.0010896
Total						.0979400	.1333018

$$\hat{Y} = -1.4548 + .17628X$$

$$s\{b_0\} = .21415 \qquad s\{b_1\} = .00144$$

$$MSE = .00741$$

FIGURE 12.3   **Residuals Plotted against Time—Blaisdell Company Example.**

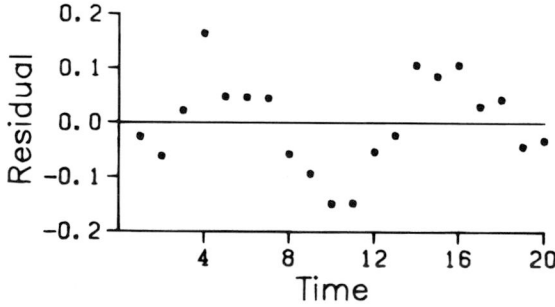

For level of significance of .01, we find in Table B.7 for $n = 20$ and $p - 1 = 1$:

$$d_L = .95 \qquad d_U = 1.15$$

Since $D = .735$ falls below $d_L = .95$, decision rule (12.15) indicates that the appropriate conclusion is H_a, namely, that the error terms are positively autocorrelated.

Comments

1. If a test for negative autocorrelation is required, the test statistic to be used is $4 - D$, where D is defined as above. The test is then conducted in the same manner described for testing for positive autocorrelation. That is, if the quantity $4 - D$ falls below d_L, we conclude $\rho < 0$, that negative autocorrelation exists, and so on.

2. A two-sided test for $H_0: \rho = 0$ versus $H_a: \rho \neq 0$ can be made by employing both one-sided tests separately. The Type I risk with the two-sided test is 2α, where α is the Type I risk for each one-sided test.

3. When the Durbin-Watson test employing the bounds d_L and d_U gives indeterminate results, in principle more cases are required. Of course, with time series data it may be impossible to obtain more cases, or additional cases may lie in the future and be obtainable only with great delay. Durbin and Watson (Ref. 12.2) do give an approximate test which may be used when the bounds test is indeterminate, but the degrees of freedom should be larger than about 40 before this approximate test will give more than a rough indication of whether autocorrelation exists.

A reasonable procedure is to treat indeterminate results as suggesting the presence of autocorrelated errors and employ one of the remedial actions to be discussed next. When remedial action does not lead to substantially different regression results as ordinary least squares, the assumption of uncorrelated error terms would appear to be satisfactory. When the remedial action does lead to substantially different regression results (such as larger estimated standard errors for the regression coefficients or the elimination of autocorrelated errors), the results obtained by means of the remedial action are probably the more useful ones.

4. The Durbin-Watson test is not robust against misspecifications of the model. For example, the Durbin-Watson test may not disclose the presence of autocorrelated errors that follow the second-order autoregressive pattern in (12.11).

5. The Durbin-Watson test is widely used; however, other tests for autocorrelation are available. One such test, due to Theil and Nagar, is found in Reference 12.3.   ∎

12.4   Remedial Measures for Autocorrelation

The two principal remedial measures when autocorrelated error terms are present are to add one or more predictor variables to the regression model or to use transformed variables.

Addition of Predictor Variables

As noted earlier, one major cause of autocorrelated error terms is the omission from the model of one or more key predictor variables that have time-ordered effects on the response variable. When autocorrelated error terms are found to be present, the first remedial action should always be to search for missing key predictor variables. In an earlier illustration, we mentioned population size as a missing variable in a regression of annual sales of a product on average yearly price of the product during a 30-year period.

When the long-term persistent effects in a response variable cannot be captured by one or several predictor variables, a trend component can be added to the regression model, such as a linear trend or an exponential trend. Use of indicator variables for seasonal effects can be helpful in eliminating or reducing autocorrelation in the error terms when the response variable is subject to seasonal effects (e.g., quarterly sales data).

Use of Transformed Variables

Only when use of additional predictor variables is not helpful in eliminating the problem of autocorrelated errors should a remedial action based on transformed variables be employed. A number of remedial procedures that rely on transformations of the variables have been developed. We shall explain three of these methods. Our explanation will be in terms of simple linear regression, but the extension to multiple regression is direct.

The three methods to be described are each based on an interesting property of the first-order autoregressive error term regression model (12.1). Consider the transformed dependent variable:

$$Y'_t = Y_t - \rho Y_{t-1}$$

Substituting in this expression for Y_t and Y_{t-1} according to regression model (12.1), we obtain:

$$Y'_t = (\beta_0 + \beta_1 X_t + \varepsilon_t) - \rho(\beta_0 + \beta_1 X_{t-1} + \varepsilon_{t-1})$$
$$= \beta_0(1 - \rho) + \beta_1(X_t - \rho X_{t-1}) + (\varepsilon_t - \rho \varepsilon_{t-1})$$

But, by (12.1), $\varepsilon_t - \rho \varepsilon_{t-1} = u_t$. Hence:

$$(12.16) \qquad \qquad Y'_t = \beta_0(1 - \rho) + \beta_1(X_t - \rho X_{t-1}) + u_t$$

where the u_t are the independent disturbance terms. Thus, when we use the transformed variable Y'_t, the regression model contains error terms that are independent. Further, model (12.16) is still a simple linear regression model with new X variable $X'_t = X_t - \rho X_{t-1}$, as may be seen by rewriting (12.16) as follows:

$$(12.17) \qquad \qquad Y'_t = \beta'_0 + \beta'_1 X'_t + u_t$$

where:

$$Y'_t = Y_t - \rho Y_{t-1}$$
$$X'_t = X_t - \rho X_{t-1}$$
$$\beta'_0 = \beta_0(1 - \rho)$$
$$\beta'_1 = \beta_1$$

Hence, by use of the transformed variables X'_t and Y'_t, we obtain a standard simple linear regression model with independent error terms. This means that ordinary least squares methods have their usual optimum properties with this model.

In order to be able to use the transformed model (12.17), one generally needs to estimate the autocorrelation parameter ρ since its value is usually unknown. The three methods to be described differ in how this is done. Often, however, the results obtained with the three methods are quite similar.

Once an estimate of ρ has been obtained, to be denoted by r, transformed variables are obtained using this estimate of ρ:

$$(12.18a) \qquad \qquad Y'_t = Y_t - r Y_{t-1}$$

$$(12.18b) \qquad \qquad X'_t = X_t - r X_{t-1}$$

Regression model (12.17) is then fitted to these transformed data, yielding an estimated regression function:

$$(12.19) \qquad \hat{Y}' = b_0' + b_1' X'$$

If this fitted regression function has eliminated the autocorrelation in the error terms, we can transform back to a fitted regression model in the original variables as follows:

$$(12.20) \qquad \hat{Y} = b_0 + b_1 X$$

where:

$$(12.20a) \qquad b_0 = \frac{b_0'}{1 - r}$$

$$(12.20b) \qquad b_1 = b_1'$$

The estimated standard deviations of the regression coefficients for the original variables can be obtained from those for the regression coefficients for the transformed variables as follows:

$$(12.21a) \qquad s\{b_0\} = \frac{s\{b_0'\}}{1 - r}$$

$$(12.21b) \qquad s\{b_1\} = s\{b_1'\}$$

Cochrane-Orcutt Procedure

The Cochrane-Orcutt procedure involves an iteration of three steps.

1. *Estimation of ρ.* This is accomplished by noting that the autoregressive error process assumed in model (12.1) can be viewed as a regression through the origin:

$$\varepsilon_t = \rho \varepsilon_{t-1} + u_t$$

where ε_t is the response variable, ε_{t-1} the predictor variable, u_t the error term, and ρ the slope of the line through the origin. Since the ε_t and ε_{t-1} are unknown, we use the residuals e_t and e_{t-1} obtained by ordinary least squares as the response and predictor variables, and estimate ρ by fitting a straight line through the origin. From our previous discussion of regression through the origin, we know by (4.14) that the estimate of the slope ρ, denoted by r, is:

$$(12.22) \qquad r = \frac{\sum\limits_{t=2}^{n} e_{t-1} e_t}{\sum\limits_{t=2}^{n} e_{t-1}^2}$$

2. *Fitting of transformed model (12.17).* Using the estimate r in (12.22), we next obtain the transformed variables Y_t' and X_t' in (12.18) and use ordinary least squares with these transformed variables to yield the fitted regression function (12.19).

3. *Test for need to iterate.* The Durbin-Watson test is then employed to test whether the error terms for the transformed model are uncorrelated. If the test indicates that they are

TABLE 12.3   **Calculations for Estimating ρ with the Cochrane-Orcutt Procedure—Blaisdell Company Example.**

t	(1) e_t	(2) e_{t-1}	(3) $e_{t-1}e_t$	(4) e_{t-1}^2
1	$-.026052$	—	—	—
2	$-.062015$	$-.026052$	.0016156	.0006787
3	.022021	$-.062015$	$-.0013656$	.0038459
4	.163754	.022021	.0036060	.0004849
...	...	...	...	...
17	.029112	.106102	.0030889	.0112576
18	.042316	.029112	.0012319	.0008475
19	$-.044160$	.042316	$-.0018687$	.0017906
20	$-.033009$	$-.044160$	.0014577	.0019501
Total			.0834478	.1322122

$$r = \frac{\Sigma e_{t-1}e_t}{\Sigma e_{t-1}^2} = \frac{.0834478}{.1322122} = .631166$$

uncorrelated, the procedure terminates. The fitted regression model in the original variables is then obtained by transforming the regression coefficients back according to (12.20).

If the Durbin-Watson test indicates that autocorrelation is still present after the first iteration, the parameter ρ is reestimated from the new residuals for the fitted regression model (12.20) with the original variables, which was derived from the fitted regression model (12.19) with the transformed variables. A new set of transformed variables is then obtained with the new r. This process may be continued for another iteration or two until the Durbin-Watson test suggests that the error terms in the transformed model are uncorrelated. If the process does not terminate after one or two iterations, a different procedure should be employed.

Example.   For the Blaisdell Company example, the necessary calculations for estimating the autocorrelation parameter ρ, based on the residuals obtained with ordinary least squares applied to the original variables, are illustrated in Table 12.3. Column 1 repeats the residuals from Table 12.2. Column 2 contains the residuals e_{t-1}, and columns 3 and 4 contain the necessary calculations. Hence, we estimate:

$$r = \frac{.0834478}{.1322122} = .631166$$

We now obtain the transformed variables Y_t' and X_t' in (12.18):

$$Y_t' = Y_t - .631166Y_{t-1}$$

$$X_t' = X_t - .631166X_{t-1}$$

These are found in Table 12.4. Columns 1 and 2 repeat the original variables Y_t and X_t, and columns 3 and 4 contain the transformed variables Y_t' and X_t'. Ordinary least squares

TABLE 12.4   **Transformed Variables and Regression Results for First Iteration with Cochrane-Orcutt Procedure—Blaisdell Company Example.**

	(1)	(2)	(3)	(4)
t	Y_t	X_t	$Y_t' = Y_t - .631166Y_{t-1}$	$X_t' = X_t - .631166X_{t-1}$
1	20.96	127.3	—	—
2	21.40	130.0	8.1708	49.653
3	21.96	132.7	8.4530	50.648
4	21.52	129.4	7.6596	45.644
...	...	...	...	
17	27.52	164.2	10.4911	62.772
18	27.78	165.6	10.4103	61.963
19	28.24	168.7	10.7062	64.179
20	28.78	171.7	10.9559	65.222

$$\hat{Y}' = -.3941 + .17376X'$$

$$s\{b_0'\} = .1672 \qquad s\{b_1'\} = .002957$$

$$MSE = .00451$$

fitting of linear regression is now used with these transformed variables based on the $n - 1$ cases remaining after the transformations. The fitted regression line and other regression results are shown at the bottom of Table 12.4. The fitted regression line in the transformed variables is:

(12.23) $$\hat{Y}' = -.3941 + .17376X'$$

where:

$$Y_t' = Y_t - .631166Y_{t-1}$$

$$X_t' = X_t - .631166X_{t-1}$$

Since the random term in the transformed regression model (12.17) is the disturbance term u_t, $MSE = .00451$ is an estimate of the variance of this disturbance term; recall that $\sigma^2\{u_t\} = \sigma^2$.

Based on the fitted regression function for the transformed variables in (12.23), residuals were obtained and the Durbin-Watson statistic calculated. The result was (calculations not shown) $D = 1.65$. From Table B.7, we find for $\alpha = .01$, $p - 1 = 1$, and $n = 19$:

$$d_L = .93 \qquad d_U = 1.13$$

Since $D = 1.65 > d_U = 1.13$, we conclude that the autocorrelation coefficient for the error terms in the model with the transformed variables is zero.

Having successfully handled the problem of autocorrelated error terms, we now transform the fitted model in (12.23) back to the original variables, using (12.20):

$$b_0 = \frac{b_0'}{1-r} = \frac{-.3941}{1-.631166} = -1.0685$$

$$b_1 = b_1' = .17376$$

leading to the fitted regression function in the original variables:

(12.24)
$$\hat{Y} = -1.0685 + .17376X$$

Finally, we obtain the estimated standard deviations of the regression coefficients for the original variables by using (12.21). Based on the results in Table 12.4, we find:

$$s\{b_0\} = \frac{s\{b_0'\}}{1-r} = \frac{.1672}{1-.631166} = .45332$$

$$s\{b_1\} = s\{b_1'\} = .002957$$

Comments

1. The Cochrane-Orcutt approach does not always work properly. A major reason is that when the error terms are positively autocorrelated, the estimate r in (12.22) tends to underestimate the autocorrelation parameter ρ. When this bias is serious, it can significantly reduce the effectiveness of the Cochrane-Orcutt approach.

2. There exists an approximate relation between the Durbin-Watson test statistic D in (12.14) and the estimated autocorrelation parameter r in (12.22):

(12.25)
$$D \simeq 2(1-r)$$

This relation indicates that the Durbin-Watson statistic ranges approximately between 0 and 4 since r takes on values between -1 and 1, and that D is approximately 2 when $r = 0$. Note that for the Blaisdell Company example ordinary least squares regression fit, $D = .735$, $r = .631$, and $2(1-r) = .738$.

3. Under certain circumstances, it may be helpful to construct pseudotransformed values for period 1 so that the regression for the transformed variables is based on n, rather than $n-1$, cases. Procedures for doing this are discussed in specialized texts such as Reference 12.4.

4. The least squares properties of the residuals, such as that the sum of the residuals is zero, apply to the residuals for the fitted regression function with the transformed variables, not to the residuals for the fitted regression function transformed back to the original variables.   ∎

Hildreth-Lu Procedure

The Hildreth-Lu procedure for estimating the autocorrelation parameter ρ for use in the transformations (12.18) is analogous to the Box-Cox procedure for estimating the parameter λ in the power transformation of Y to improve the appropriateness of the standard regression model. The value of ρ chosen with the Hildreth-Lu procedure is the one that minimizes the error sum of squares for the transformed regression model (12.17):

(12.26)
$$SSE = \sum(Y_t' - \hat{Y}_t')^2 = \sum(Y_t' - b_0' - b_1'X_t')^2$$

TABLE 12.5   **Hildreth-Lu Results for Blaisdell Company Example.**

ρ	SSE
.10	.1170
.30	.0938
.50	.0805
.70	.0758
.90	.0728
.92	.0723
.94	.0718
.95	.07171
.96	.07167
.97	.07175
.98	.07197

$$\text{For } \rho = .96: \quad \hat{Y}' = .07117 + .16045X'$$

$$s\{b_0'\} = .05798 \qquad s\{b_1'\} = .006840$$

$$MSE = .00422$$

Computer programs are available to find the value of ρ that minimizes *SSE*. Alternatively, one can do a numerical search, running repeated regressions with different values of ρ for identifying the approximate magnitude of ρ that minimizes *SSE*. In the region of ρ that leads to minimum *SSE*, a finer search can be conducted to obtain a more precise value of ρ.

Once the value of ρ that minimizes *SSE* is found, the fitted regression function corresponding to that value of ρ is examined to see if the transformation has successfully eliminated the autocorrelation. If so, the fitted regression function in the original variables can then be obtained by means of (12.20).

Example.   Table 12.5 contains the regression results for the Hildreth-Lu procedure when fitting the transformed regression model (12.17) to the Blaisdell Company data for different values of the autocorrelation parameter ρ. Note that *SSE* is minimized when ρ is near .96, so we shall let $r = .96$ be the estimate of ρ. The fitted regression function for the transformed variables corresponding to $r = .96$ and other regression results are given at the bottom of Table 12.5. The fitted regression function in the transformed variables is:

$$(12.27) \qquad \hat{Y}' = .07117 + .16\ )45X'$$

where:

$$Y_t' = Y_t - .96Y_{t-1}$$

$$X_t' = X_t - .96X_{t-1}$$

The Durbin-Watson test statistic for this fitted model is $D = 1.73$. Since for $n = 19$, $p - 1 = 1$, and $\alpha = .01$ the upper critical value is $d_U = 1.13$, we conclude that no autocorrelation remains in the transformed model.

Therefore, we shall transform regression function (12.27) back to the original variables. Using (12.20), we obtain:

(12.28) $$\hat{Y} = 1.7793 + .16045X$$

The estimated standard deviations of these regression coefficients are:

$$s\{b_0\} = 1.450 \qquad s\{b_1\} = .006840$$

Comments

1. The Hildreth-Lu procedure, unlike the Cochrane-Orcutt procedure, does not require any iterations once the estimate of the autocorrelation parameter ρ is obtained.

2. Note from Table 12.5 that *SSE* as a function of ρ is quite stable in a wide region around the minimum, as is often the case. It indicates that the numerical search for finding the best value of ρ need not be too fine unless there is particular interest in the intercept term β_0, since the estimate b_0 is sensitive to the value of r.   ∎

First Differences Procedure

Since the autocorrelation parameter ρ is frequently large and *SSE* as a function of ρ often is quite flat for large values of ρ up to 1.0, as in the Blaisdell Company example, some economists and statisticians have suggested use of $\rho = 1.0$ in the transformed model (12.17). If $\rho = 1$, $\beta'_0 = \beta_0(1 - \rho) = 0$, and the transformed model (12.17) becomes:

(12.29) $$Y'_t = \beta'_1 X'_t + u_t$$

where:

(12.29a) $$Y'_t = Y_t - Y_{t-1}$$

(12.29b) $$X'_t = X_t - X_{t-1}$$

Thus, again, the regression coefficient $\beta'_1 = \beta_1$ can be directly estimated by ordinary least squares methods, this time based on regression through the origin. Note that the transformed variables in (12.29a) and (12.29b) are ordinary first differences. It has been found that this first differences approach is effective in a variety of applications in reducing the autocorrelations of the error terms, and of course it is much simpler than the Cochrane-Orcutt and Hildreth-Lu procedures.

The fitted regression function in the transformed variables:

(12.30) $$\hat{Y}' = b'_1 X'$$

can be transformed back to the original variables as follows:

(12.31) $$\hat{Y} = b_0 + b_1 X$$

where:

(12.31a) $$b_0 = \bar{Y} - b'_1 \bar{X}$$

(12.31b) $$b_1 = b'_1$$

TABLE 12.6   **First Differences and Regression Results with First Differences Procedure—Blaisdell Company Example.**

t	(1) Y_t	(2) X_t	(3) $Y_t' = Y_t - Y_{t-1}$	(4) $X_t' = X_t - X_{t-1}$
1	20.96	127.3	—	—
2	21.40	130.0	.44	2.7
3	21.96	132.7	.56	2.7
4	21.52	129.4	−.44	−3.3
...	...	...	...	...
17	27.52	164.2	.54	3.5
18	27.78	165.6	.26	1.4
19	28.24	168.7	.46	3.1
20	28.78	171.7	.54	3.0

$$\hat{Y}' = .16849X'$$

$$s\{b_1'\} = .005096 \qquad MSE = .00482$$

Example.   Table 12.6 illustrates the transformed variables Y_t' and X_t', based on the first differences transformations in (12.29a, b) for the Blaisdell Company example. Application of ordinary least squares for estimating a linear regression through the origin leads to the results shown at the bottom of Table 12.6. The fitted regression function in the transformed variables is:

$$(12.32) \qquad\qquad \hat{Y}' = .16849X'$$

where:

$$Y_t' = Y_t - Y_{t-1}$$

$$X_t' = X_t - X_{t-1}$$

To examine whether the first differences procedure has removed the autocorrelations, we shall use the Durbin-Watson test. There are two points to note when using the Durbin-Watson test with the first differences procedure. Sometimes the first differences procedure can overcorrect, leading to negative autocorrelations in the error terms. Hence, it may be appropriate to use a two-sided Durbin-Watson test when testing for autocorrelation with first differences data. The second point is that the first differences model (12.29) has no intercept term, but the Durbin-Watson test requires a fitted regression with an intercept term. A valid test for autocorrelation in a no-intercept model can be carried out by fitting for this purpose a regression function with an intercept term. Of course, the fitted no-intercept model is still the model of basic interest.

In the Blaisdell Company example, the Durbin-Watson statistic for the fitted first differences regression model with an intercept term is $D = 1.75$. This indicates uncorrelated error terms for either a one-sided test (with $\alpha = .01$) or a two-sided test (with $\alpha = .02$).

With the first differences procedure successfully eliminating the autocorrelation, we return to a fitted model in the original variables by using (12.31):

$$(12.33) \qquad\qquad \hat{Y} = -.30349 + .16849X$$

TABLE 12.7   **Major Regression Results for Three Transformation Procedures—Blaisdell Company Example.**

Procedure	b_1	$s\{b_1\}$	r	Estimate of σ^2 (MSE)
Cochrane-Orcutt	.1738	.0030	.63	.0045
Hildreth-Lu	.1605	.0068	.96	.0042
First differences	.1685	.0051	1.0	.0048
Ordinary least squares	.1763	.0014	—	—

where:

$$b_0 = 24.569 - .16849(147.62) = -.30349$$

We know from Table 12.6 that the estimated standard deviation of b_1 is $s\{b_1\} = .005096$ since $b_1 = b_1'$.

Comparison of Three Methods

Table 12.7 contains some of the main regression results for the three transformation methods and also for the ordinary least squares regression fit to the original variables. A number of key points stand out.

3. All of the estimates of β_1 are quite close to each other.

4. The estimated standard deviations of b_1 based on Hildreth-Lu and first differences transformation methods are quite close to each other; that with the Cochrane-Orcutt procedure is somewhat smaller. The estimated standard deviation of b_1 based on ordinary least squares regression with the original variables is still smaller. This is as expected, since we noted earlier that the estimated standard deviations $s\{b_k\}$ calculated according to ordinary least squares may seriously underestimate the true standard deviations $\sigma\{b_k\}$ when positive autocorrelation is present.

5. All three transformation methods provide essentially the same estimate of σ^2, the variance of the disturbance terms u_t.

The three transformation methods do not always work equally well, as happens to be the case here for the Blaisdell Company example. The Cochrane-Orcutt procedure may fail to remove autocorrelation in one or two iterations, in which case the Hildreth-Lu or the first differences procedures may be preferable. When several of the transformation methods are effective in removing autocorrelation, then simplicity of calculations may be considered in choosing from among these procedures.

Note

Further discussions of the Cochrane-Orcutt, Hildreth-Lu, and first differences procedures, as well as of other remedial procedures for autocorrelated errors, may be found in specialized texts, such as Reference 12.4.   ■

12.5   Forecasting with Autocorrelated Error Terms

One important use of autoregressive error regression models is to make forecasts. With these models, information about the error term in the most recent period n can be incorporated into the forecast for period $n + 1$. This provides a more accurate forecast because, when autoregressive error regression models are appropriate, the error terms in successive periods are correlated. Thus, if sales in period n are above their expected value and successive error terms are positively correlated, it follows that sales in period $n + 1$ will likely be above their expected value also.

We shall explain the basic ideas underlying the development of forecasts using the presence of autocorrelated error terms by again employing the simple linear autoregressive error term regression model (12.1). The extension to multiple regression model (12.2) is direct. First, we consider forecasting when either the Cochrane-Orcutt or the Hildreth-Lu procedure has been utilized for estimating the regression parameters.

When we express regression model (12.1):

$$Y_t = \beta_0 + \beta_1 X_t + \varepsilon_t$$

by using the structure of the error terms:

$$\varepsilon_t = \rho \varepsilon_{t-1} + u_t$$

we obtain:

$$Y_t = \beta_0 + \beta_1 X_t + \rho \varepsilon_{t-1} + u_t$$

For period $n + 1$, we obtain:

$$(12.34) \qquad Y_{n+1} = \beta_0 + \beta_1 X_{n+1} + \rho \varepsilon_n + u_{n+1}$$

Thus, Y_{n+1} is made up of three components:

1. The expected value $\beta_0 + \beta_1 X_{n+1}$.

2. A multiple ρ of the preceding error term ε_n.

3. An independent, random disturbance term with $E\{u_{n+1}\} = 0$.

The forecast for next period $n + 1$, to be denoted by F_{n+1}, is constructed by dealing with each of the three components in (12.34):

1. Given X_{n+1}, we estimate the expected value $\beta_0 + \beta_1 X_{n+1}$ as usual from the fitted regression function:

$$\hat{Y}_{n+1} = b_0 + b_1 X_{n+1}$$

where b_0 and b_1 are the estimated regression coefficients for the original variables obtained from b_0' and b_1' for the transformed variables according to (12.20).

2. ρ is estimated by r in (12.22), and ε_n is estimated by the residual e_n:

$$e_n = Y_n - (b_0 + b_1 X_n) = Y_n - \hat{Y}_n$$

Thus, $\rho \varepsilon_n$ is estimated by $r e_n$.

3. The disturbance term u_{n+1} has expected value zero and is independent of earlier information. Hence, we use its expected value of zero in the forecast.

Thus, the forecast for period $n + 1$ is:

$$(12.35) \qquad F_{n+1} = \hat{Y}_{n+1} + r e_n$$

An approximate $1 - \alpha$ prediction interval for $Y_{n+1(\text{new})}$, the new observation on the response variable, may be obtained by employing the usual prediction limits for a new observation in (2.36), but based on the transformed observations. Thus, Y_i and X_i in formula (2.38a) for the estimated variance $s^2\{\text{pred}\}$ are replaced by Y'_t and X'_t as defined in (12.18).

The approximate $1 - \alpha$ prediction limits for $Y_{n+1(\text{new})}$ with simple linear regression therefore are:

$$(12.36) \qquad F_{n+1} \pm t(1 - \alpha/2; n - 3)s\{\text{pred}\}$$

where $s\{\text{pred}\}$, defined in (2.38a), is here based on the transformed observations. Note the use of $n - 3$ degrees of freedom for the t multiple, since there are only $n - 1$ transformed cases and two degrees of freedom are lost for estimating the two parameters in the simple linear regression function.

When forecasts are based on the first differences procedure, the forecast in (12.35) is still applicable, but $r = 1$ now. The estimated standard deviation $s\{\text{pred}\}$ now is calculated according to formula (4.20) in Table 4.1 for one predictor variable, using the transformed variables. Finally, the degrees of freedom for the t multiple in (12.36) will be $n - 2$, since only one parameter has to be estimated in the no-intercept regression model (12.29).

Example

For the Blaisdell Company example, the trade association has projected that deseasonalized industry sales in the first quarter of 1993 (i.e., quarter 21) will be $X_{21} = \$175.3$ million. To forecast Blaisdell Company sales for quarter 21, we shall use the Cochrane-Orcutt fitted regression function (12.24):

$$\hat{Y} = -1.0685 + .17376X$$

First, we need to obtain the residual e_{20}:

$$e_{20} = Y_{20} - \hat{Y}_{20} = 28.78 - [-1.0685 + .17376(171.7)] = .0139$$

The fitted value when $X_{21} = 175.3$ is:

$$\hat{Y}_{21} = -1.0685 + .17376(175.3) = 29.392$$

The forecast for period 21 then is:

$$F_{21} = \hat{Y}_{21} + r e_{20} = 29.392 + .631166(.0139) = 29.40$$

Note how the fact that company sales in quarter 20 were slightly above their estimated mean has a small positive influence on the forecast for company sales for quarter 21.

We wish to set up a 95 percent prediction interval for $Y_{21(\text{new})}$. Using the data for the transformed variables in Table 12.4, we calculate $s\{\text{pred}\}$ by (2.38) for:

$$X'_{n+1} = X_{n+1} - .631166 X_n = 175.3 - .631166(171.7) = 66.929$$

We obtain $s\{\text{pred}\} = .0757$ (calculations not shown). We require $t(.975; 17) = 2.110$. We therefore obtain the prediction limits $29.40 \pm 2.110(.0757)$ and the prediction interval:

$$29.24 \le Y_{21(\text{new})} \le 29.56$$

Given quarter 20 seasonally adjusted company sales of $28.78 million and other past sales, and given quarter 21 industry sales of $175.3 million, we predict with approximate 95 percent confidence that seasonally adjusted Blaisdell Company sales in quarter 21 will be between $29.24 and $29.56 million.

To obtain a forecast of actual sales including seasonal effects in quarter 21, the Blaisdell Company still needs to incorporate the first quarter seasonal effect into the forecast of seasonally adjusted sales.

The forecasts with the other transformation procedures are very similar to the one with the Cochrane-Orcutt procedure. With the first differences estimated regression function (12.33), the forecast for quarter 21 is:

$$F_{21} = [-.30349 + .16849(175.3)] + 1.0[28.78 + .30349 - .16849(171.70)]$$

$$= 29.39$$

The estimated standard deviation $s\{\text{pred}\}$ calculated according to (4.20) with the transformed data in Table 12.6 is $s\{\text{pred}\} = .0718$ (calculations not shown). For a 95 percent prediction interval, we require $t(.975; 18) = 2.101$. The prediction limits therefore are $29.39 \pm 2.101(.0718)$ and the approximate 95 percent prediction interval is:

$$29.24 \le Y_{21(\text{new})} \le 29.54$$

This forecast is practically the same as that with the Cochrane-Orcutt estimates.

The approximate 95 percent prediction interval with the estimated regression function (12.28) based on the Hildreth-Lu procedure is (calculations not shown):

$$29.24 \le Y_{21(\text{new})} \le 29.52$$

This forecast is practically the same as the other two.

Comments

1. Forecasts obtained with autoregressive error regression models (12.1) and (12.2) are conditional on the past observations Y_n, Y_{n-1}, etc. They are also conditional on X_{n+1}, which often has to be projected as in the Blaisdell Company example.

2. Forecasts for two or more periods ahead can also be developed, using the recursive relations of ε_t to earlier error terms developed in Section 12.2. For example, given X_{n+2} the forecast for period $n + 2$, based on either Cochrane-Orcutt or Hildreth-Lu estimates, is:

$$(12.37) \qquad\qquad F_{n+2} = \hat{Y}_{n+2} + r^2 e_n$$

For the first differences estimates, the forecast in (12.37) is calculated with $r = 1$.

3. The approximate prediction limits (12.36) assume that the value of r used in the transformations (12.18) is the true value of ρ; that is, $r = \rho$. If that is the case, the standard regression assumptions apply since we are then dealing with the transformed model (12.17). To see that the prediction limits obtained from the transformed model are applicable to the forecast F_{n+1}

in (12.35), recall that $\sigma^2\{\text{pred}\}$ in (2.37) is the variance of the difference $Y_{h(\text{new})} - \hat{Y}_h$. In terms of the situation here for the transformed variables, we have the following correspondences:

$$Y_{h(\text{new})} \text{ corresponds to } Y'_{n+1} = Y_{n+1} - rY_n$$

$$\hat{Y}_h \text{ corresponds to } \hat{Y}'_{n+1} = b'_0 + b'_1 X'_{n+1} = b_0(1-r) + b_1(X_{n+1} - rX_n)$$

The difference $Y'_{n+1} - \hat{Y}'_{n+1}$ is:

$$\begin{aligned}
Y'_{n+1} - \hat{Y}'_{n+1} &= (Y_{n+1} - rY_n) - b_0(1-r) - b_1(X_{n+1} - rX_n) \\
&= Y_{n+1} - (b_0 + b_1 X_{n+1}) - r(Y_n - b_0 - b_1 X_n) \\
&= Y_{n+1} - \hat{Y}_{n+1} - re_n \\
&= Y_{n+1} - F_{n+1}
\end{aligned}$$

Hence, Y_{n+1} plays the role of $Y_{h(\text{new})}$ and F_{n+1} plays the role of $\hat{Y}_h$ in (2.37). The prediction limits (12.36) are approximate because r is only an estimate of ρ.   ∎

Cited References

12.1.   Box, G. E. P., and G. M. Jenkins. *Time Series Analysis, Forecasting and Control.* Rev. ed. San Francisco: Holden-Day, 1976.

12.2.   Durbin, J., and G. S. Watson. "Testing for Serial Correlation in Least Squares Regression. II," *Biometrika* 38 (1951), pp. 159–78.

12.3.   Theil, H., and A. L. Nagar. "Testing the Independence of Regression Disturbances," *Journal of the American Statistical Association* 56 (1961), pp. 793–806.

12.4.   Pindyck, R. S., and D. L. Rubinfeld. *Econometric Models and Economic Forecasts.* 3rd ed. New York: McGraw-Hill, 1991.

Problems

12.1.   Refer to Table 12.1.

   a. Plot ε_t against ε_{t-1} for $t = 1, \ldots, 10$ on a graph. How is the positive first-order autocorrelation in the error terms shown by the plot?

   b. If you plotted u_t against ε_{t-1} for $t = 1, \ldots, 10$, what pattern would you expect?

12.2.   Refer to **Plastic hardness** Problem 1.22. If the same test item were measured at 12 different points in time, would the error terms in the regression model likely be autocorrelated? Discuss.

12.3.   A student stated that the first-order autoregressive error models (12.1) and (12.2) are too simple for business time series data because the error term in period t in such data is also influenced by random effects that occurred more than one period in the past. Comment.

12.4. A student writing a term paper used ordinary least squares in fitting a simple linear regression model to some time series data containing positively autocorrelated errors, and found that the 90 percent confidence interval for β_1 was too wide to be useful. The student then decided to employ regression model (12.1) to improve the precision of the estimate. Comment.

12.5. For each of the following tests concerning the autocorrelation parameter ρ in regression model (12.2) with three predictor variables, state the appropriate decision rule based on the Durbin-Watson test statistic for a sample of size 38: (1) $H_0: \rho = 0$, $H_a: \rho \neq 0$, $\alpha = .02$; (2) $H_0: \rho = 0$, $H_a: \rho < 0$, $\alpha = .05$; (3) $H_0: \rho = 0$, $H_a: \rho > 0$, $\alpha = .01$.

√ 12.6. Refer to **Calculator maintenance** Problem 1.20. The observations are listed in time order. Assume that regression model (12.1) is appropriate. Test whether or not positive autocorrelation is present; use $\alpha = .01$. State the alternatives, decision rule, and conclusion.

12.7. Refer to **Chemical shipment** Problem 6.9. The observations are listed in time order. Assume that regression model (12.2) is appropriate. Test whether or not positive autocorrelation is present; use $\alpha = .05$. State the alternatives, decision rule, and conclusion.

12.8. Refer to **Crop yield** Problem 7.36. The observations are listed in time order. Assume that regression model (12.2) with first- and second-order terms for the two predictor variables and no interaction term is appropriate. Test whether or not positive autocorrelation is present; use $\alpha = .01$. State the alternatives, decision rule, and conclusion.

√ 12.9. **Microcomputer components.** A staff analyst for a manufacturer of microcomputer components has compiled monthly data for the past 16 months on the value of industry production of processing units that use these components (X, in million dollars) and the value of the firm's components used (Y, in thousand dollars). The analyst believes that a simple linear regression relation is appropriate but anticipates positive autocorrelation. The data follow:

t:	1	2	3	. . .	14	15	16
X_t:	2.052	2.026	2.002	. . .	2.080	2.102	2.150
Y_t:	102.9	101.5	100.8	. . .	104.8	105.0	107.2

a. Fit a simple linear regression model by ordinary least squares and obtain the residuals. Also obtain $s\{b_0\}$ and $s\{b_1\}$.

b. Plot the residuals against time and explain whether you find any evidence of positive autocorrelation.

c. Conduct a formal test for positive autocorrelation using $\alpha = .05$. State the alternatives, decision rule, and conclusion. Is the residual analysis in part (b) in accord with the test result?

√ 12.10. Refer to **Microcomputer components** Problem 12.9. The analyst has decided to employ regression model (12.1) and use the Cochrane-Orcutt procedure to fit the model.

a. Obtain a point estimate of the autocorrelation parameter. How well does the approximate relationship (12.25) hold here between this point estimate and the Durbin-Watson test statistic?

b. Use one iteration to obtain the estimates b_0' and b_1' of the regression coefficients β_0' and β_1' in transformed model (12.17) and state the estimated regression function. Also obtain $s\{b_0'\}$ and $s\{b_1'\}$.

c. Test whether any positive autocorrelation remains after the first iteration using $\alpha = .05$. State the alternatives, decision rule, and conclusion.

d. Restate the estimated regression function obtained in part (b) in terms of the original variables. Also obtain $s\{b_0\}$ and $s\{b_1\}$. Compare the estimated regression coefficients obtained with the Cochrane-Orcutt procedure and their estimated standard deviations with those obtained with ordinary least squares in Problem 12.9a.

e. Based on the results in parts (c) and (d), does the Cochrane-Orcutt procedure appear to have been effective here?

f. The value of industry production in month 17 will be $2.210 million. Predict the value of the firm's components used in month 17; employ a 95 percent prediction interval. Interpret your interval.

g. Estimate β_1 with a 95 percent confidence interval. Interpret your interval.

√ 12.11. Refer to **Microcomputer components** Problem 12.9. Assume that regression model (12.1) is applicable.

a. Use the Hildreth-Lu procedure to obtain a point estimate of the autocorrelation parameter. Do a search at the values $\rho = .1, .2, \ldots, 1.0$ and select from these the value of ρ that minimizes *SSE*.

b. Based on your estimate in part (a), obtain an estimate of the transformed regression function (12.17). Also obtain $s\{b_0'\}$ and $s\{b_1'\}$.

c. Test whether any positive autocorrelation remains in the transformed regression model; use $\alpha = .05$. State the alternatives, decision rule, and conclusion.

d. Restate the estimated regression function obtained in part (b) in terms of the original variables. Also obtain $s\{b_0\}$ and $s\{b_1\}$. Compare the estimated regression coefficients obtained with the Hildreth-Lu procedure and their estimated standard deviations with those obtained with ordinary least squares in Problem 12.9a.

e. Based on the results in parts (c) and (d), has the Hildreth-Lu procedure been effective here?

f. The value of industry production in month 17 will be $2.210 million. Predict the value of the firm's components used in month 17; employ a 95 percent prediction interval. Interpret your interval.

g. Estimate β_1 with a 95 percent confidence interval. Interpret your interval.

√ 12.12. Refer to **Microcomputer components** Problem 12.9. Assume that regression model (12.1) is applicable and that the first differences procedure is to be employed.

a. Estimate the regression coefficient β_1' in the transformed regression model (12.29), and obtain the estimated standard deviation of this estimate. State the estimated regression function.

b. Test whether or not the error terms with the first differences procedure are autocorrelated, using a two-sided test and $\alpha = .10$. State the alternatives, decision rule, and conclusion. Why is a two-sided test meaningful here?

c. Restate the estimated regression function obtained in part (a) in terms of the original variables. Also obtain $s\{b_1\}$. Compare the estimated regression coefficients obtained with the first differences procedure and the estimated standard deviation $s\{b_1\}$ with the results obtained with ordinary least squares in Problem 12.9a.

d. Based on the results in parts (b) and (c), has the first differences procedure been effective here?

e. The value of industry production in month 17 will be $2.210 million. Predict the value of the firm's components used in month 17; employ a 95 percent prediction interval. Interpret your interval.

f. Estimate β_1 with a 95 percent confidence interval. Interpret your interval.

12.13. **Advertising agency**. The managing partner of an advertising agency is interested in the possibility of making accurate predictions of monthly billings. Monthly data on amount of billings (Y, in thousands of constant dollars) and on number of hours of staff time (X, in thousand hours) for the 20 most recent months follow. A simple linear regression model is believed to be appropriate, but positively autocorrelated error terms may be present.

t:	1	2	3	. . .	18	19	20
X_t:	2.521	2.171	2.234	. . .	3.117	3.623	3.618
Y_t:	220.4	203.9	207.2	. . .	252.4	278.6	278.5

a. Fit a simple linear regression model by ordinary least squares and obtain the residuals. Also obtain $s\{b_0\}$ and $s\{b_1\}$.

b. Plot the residuals against time and explain whether you find any evidence of positive autocorrelation.

c. Conduct a formal test for positive autocorrelation using $\alpha = .01$. State the alternatives, decision rule, and conclusion. Is the residual analysis in part (b) in accord with the test result?

12.14. Refer to **Advertising agency** Problem 12.13. Assume that regression model (12.1) is applicable and that the Cochrane-Orcutt procedure is to be employed.

a. Obtain a point estimate of the autocorrelation parameter. How well does the approximate relationship (12.25) hold here between the point estimate and the Durbin-Watson test statistic?

b. Use one iteration to obtain the estimates b_0' and b_1' of the regression coefficients β_0' and β_1' in transformed model (12.17) and state the estimated regression function. Also obtain $s\{b_0'\}$ and $s\{b_1'\}$.

c. Test whether any positive autocorrelation remains after the first iteration using $\alpha = .01$. State the alternatives, decision rule, and conclusion.

d. Restate the estimated regression function obtained in part (b) in terms of the original variables. Also obtain $s\{b_0\}$ and $s\{b_1\}$. Compare the estimated regression coefficients obtained with the Cochrane-Orcutt procedure and their estimated standard deviations with those obtained with ordinary least squares in Problem 12.13a.

e. Based on the results in parts (c) and (d), does the Cochrane-Orcutt procedure appear to have been effective here?

f. Staff time in month 21 is expected to be 3.625 thousand hours. Predict the amount of billings in constant dollars for month 21, using a 99 percent prediction interval. Interpret your interval.

g. Estimate β_1 with a 99 percent confidence interval. Interpret your interval.

12.15. Refer to **Advertising agency** Problem 12.13. Assume that regression model (12.1) is applicable.

a. Use the Hildreth-Lu procedure to obtain a point estimate of the autocorrelation parameter. Do a search at the values $\rho = .1, .2, \ldots, 1.0$ and select from these the value of ρ that minimizes SSE.

b. Based on your estimate in part (a), obtain an estimate of the transformed regression function (12.17). Also obtain $s\{b_0'\}$ and $s\{b_1'\}$.

c. Test whether any positive autocorrelation remains in the transformed regression model; use $\alpha = .01$. State the alternatives, decision rule, and conclusion.

d. Restate the estimated regression function obtained in part (b) in terms of the original variables. Also obtain $s\{b_0\}$ and $s\{b_1\}$. Compare the estimated regression coefficients obtained with the Hildreth-Lu procedure and their estimated standard deviations with those obtained with ordinary least squares in Problem 12.13a.

e. Based on the results in parts (c) and (d), has the Hildreth-Lu procedure been effective here?

f. Staff time in month 21 is expected to be 3.625 thousand hours. Predict the amount of billings in constant dollars for month 21, using a 99 percent prediction interval. Interpret your interval.

g. Estimate β_1 with a 99 percent confidence interval. Interpret your interval.

12.16. Refer to **Advertising agency** Problem 12.13. Assume that regression model (12.1) is applicable and that the first differences procedure is to be employed.

a. Estimate the regression coefficient β_1' in the transformed regression model (12.29) and obtain the estimated standard deviation of this estimate. State the estimated regression function.

b. Test whether or not the error terms with the first differences procedure are autocorrelated, using a two-sided test and $\alpha = .02$. State the alternatives, decision rule, and conclusion. Why is a two-sided test meaningful here?

c. Restate the estimated regression function obtained in part (a) in terms of the original variables. Also obtain $s\{b_1\}$. Compare the estimated regression coefficients obtained with the first differences procedure and the estimated standard deviation $s\{b_1\}$ with the results obtained with ordinary least squares in Problem 12.13a.

d. Based on the results in parts (b) and (c), has the first differences procedure been effective here?

e. Staff time in month 21 is expected to be 3.625 thousand hours. Predict the amount of billings in constant dollars for month 21, using a 99 percent prediction interval. Interpret your interval.

f. Estimate β_1 with a 99 percent confidence interval. Interpret your interval.

12.17. **McGill Company sales.** The data below show seasonally adjusted quarterly sales for the McGill Company (Y, in million dollars) and for the entire industry (X, in million dollars) for the most recent 20 quarters.

t:	1	2	3	. . .	18	19	20
X_t:	127.3	130.0	132.7	. . .	165.6	168.7	172.0
Y_t:	20.96	21.40	21.96	. . .	27.78	28.24	28.78

a. Would you expect the autocorrelation parameter ρ to be positive, negative, or zero here?

b. Fit a simple linear regression model by ordinary least squares and obtain the residuals. Also obtain $s\{b_0\}$ and $s\{b_1\}$.

c. Plot the residuals against time and explain whether you find any evidence of positive autocorrelation.

d. Conduct a formal test for positive autocorrelation using $\alpha = .01$. State the alternatives, decision rule, and conclusion. Is the residual analysis in part (c) in accord with the test result?

12.18. Refer to **McGill Company sales** Problem 12.17. Assume that regression model (12.1) is applicable and that the Cochrane-Orcutt procedure is to be employed.

    a. Obtain a point estimate of the autocorrelation parameter. How well does the approximate relationship (12.25) hold here between the point estimate and the Durbin-Watson test statistic?

    b. Use one iteration to obtain the estimates b_0' and b_1' of the regression coefficients β_0' and β_1' in transformed model (12.17) and state the estimated regression function. Also obtain $s\{b_0'\}$ and $s\{b_1'\}$.

    c. Test whether any positive autocorrelation remains after the first iteration; use $\alpha = .01$. State the alternatives, decision rule, and conclusion.

    d. Restate the estimated regression function obtained in part (b) in terms of the original variables. Also obtain $s\{b_0\}$ and $s\{b_1\}$. Compare the estimated regression coefficients obtained with the Cochrane-Orcutt procedure and their estimated standard deviations with those obtained with ordinary least squares in Problem 12.17b.

    e. Based on the results in parts (c) and (d), does the Cochrane-Orcutt procedure appear to have been effective here?

    f. Industry sales for quarter 21 are expected to be \$181.0 million. Predict the McGill Company sales for quarter 21, using a 90 percent prediction interval. Interpret your interval.

    g. Estimate β_1 with a 90 percent confidence interval. Interpret your interval.

12.19. Refer to **McGill Company sales** Problem 12.17. Assume that regression model (12.1) is applicable.

    a. Use the Hildreth-Lu procedure to obtain a point estimate of the autocorrelation parameter. Do a search at the values $\rho = .1, .2, \ldots, 1.0$ and select from these the value of ρ that minimizes SSE.

    b. Based on your estimate in part (a), obtain an estimate of the transformed regression function (12.17). Also obtain $s\{b_0'\}$ and $s\{b_1'\}$.

    c. Test whether any positive autocorrelation remains in the transformed regression model; use $\alpha = .01$. State the alternatives, decision rule, and conclusion.

    d. Restate the estimated regression function obtained in part (b) in terms of the original variables. Also obtain $s\{b_0\}$ and $s\{b_1\}$. Compare the estimated regression coefficients obtained with the Hildreth-Lu procedure and their estimated standard deviations with those obtained with ordinary least squares in Problem 12.17b.

    e. Based on the results in parts (c) and (d), has the Hildreth-Lu procedure been effective here?

    f. Industry sales for quarter 21 are expected to be \$181.0 million. Predict the McGill Company sales for quarter 21, using a 90 percent prediction interval. Interpret your interval.

    g. Estimate β_1 with a 90 percent confidence interval. Interpret your interval.

12.20. Refer to **McGill Company sales** Problem 12.17. Assume that regression model (12.1) is applicable and that the first differences procedure is to be employed.

a. Estimate the regression coefficient β_1' in the transformed regression model (12.29) and obtain the estimated standard deviation of this estimate. State the estimated regression function.

b. Test whether or not the error terms with the first differences procedure are positively autocorrelated using $\alpha = .01$. State the alternatives, decision rule, and conclusion.

c. Restate the estimated regression function obtained in part (a) in terms of the original variables. Also obtain $s\{b_1\}$. Compare the estimated regression coefficients obtained with the first differences procedure and the estimated standard deviation $s\{b_1\}$ with the results obtained with ordinary least squares in Problem 12.17b.

d. Based on the results in parts (b) and (c), has the first differences procedure been effective here?

e. Industry sales for quarter 21 are expected to be $181.0 million. Predict the McGill Company sales for quarter 21, using a 90 percent prediction interval. Interpret your interval.

f. Estimate β_1 with a 90 percent confidence interval. Interpret your interval.

12.21. A student applying the first differences transformations in (12.29a, b) found that several X_t' values equaled zero but that the corresponding Y_t' values were nonzero. Does this signify that the first differences transformations are not appropriate for the data?

Exercises

12.22. Derive (12.7) for $s = 2$.

12.23. Refer to first-order autoregressive error model (12.1). Suppose Y_t is company's percent share of the market, X_t is company's selling price as a percent of average competitive selling price, $\beta_0 = 100$, $\beta_1 = -.35$, $\rho = .6$, $\sigma^2 = 1$, and $\varepsilon_0 = 2.403$. Let X_t and u_t be as follows for $t = 1, \ldots, 10$:

t:	1	2	3	4	5	6	7	8	9	10
X_t:	100	115	120	90	85	75	70	95	105	110
u_t:	.764	.509	−.242	−1.808	−.485	.501	−.539	.434	−.299	.030

a. Plot the true regression line. Generate the observations Y_t ($t = 1, \ldots, 10$), and plot these on the same graph. Fit a least squares regression line to the generated observations Y_t and plot it also on the same graph. How does your fitted regression line relate to the true line?

b. Repeat the steps in part (a) but this time let $\rho = 0$. In which of the two cases does the fitted regression line come closer to the true line? Is this the expected outcome?

c. Generate the observations Y_t for $\rho = -.7$. For each of the cases $\rho = .6$, $\rho = 0$, and $\rho = -.7$, obtain the successive error term differences $\varepsilon_t - \varepsilon_{t-1}$ ($t = 1, \ldots, 10$).

d. For which of the three cases in part (c) is $\Sigma(\varepsilon_t - \varepsilon_{t-1})^2$ smallest? For which is it largest? What generalization does this suggest?

12.24. For multiple regression model (12.2) with $p - 1 = 2$, derive the transformed model in which the random terms are uncorrelated.

12.25. Suppose the autoregressive error process for the model $Y_t = \beta_0 + \beta_1 X_t + \varepsilon_t$ is that given by (12.11).

    a. What would be the transformed variables Y_t' and X_t' for which the random terms in the regression model are uncorrelated?

    b. How would you estimate the parameters ρ_1 and ρ_2 for use with the Cochrane-Orcutt procedure?

    c. How would you estimate the parameters ρ_1 and ρ_2 with the Hildreth-Lu procedure?

12.26. Derive the forecast F_{n+1} for a simple linear regression model with the second-order autoregressive error process (12.11).

Projects

12.27. The true regression model is $Y_t = 10 + 24X_t + \varepsilon_t$, where $\varepsilon_t = .8\varepsilon_{t-1} + u_t$ and u_t are independent $N(0, 25)$.

    a. Generate 11 independent random numbers from $N(0, 25)$. Use the first random number as ε_0, obtain the 10 error terms $\varepsilon_1, \ldots, \varepsilon_{10}$, and then calculate the 10 observations $Y_1, \ldots, Y_{10}$ corresponding to $X_1 = 1, X_2 = 2, \ldots, X_{10} = 10$. Fit a linear regression function by ordinary least squares and calculate *MSE*.

    b. Repeat part (a) 100 times, using new random numbers each time.

    c. Calculate the mean of the 100 estimates b_1. Does it appear that b_1 is an unbiased estimator of β_1 despite the presence of positive autocorrelation?

    d. Calculate the mean of the 100 estimates *MSE*. Does it appear that *MSE* is a biased estimator of σ^2? If so, does the magnitude of the bias appear to be small or large?

PART

III

Nonlinear Regression

Introduction to Nonlinear Regression

The linear regression models considered up to this point are generally satisfactory approximations for most regression applications. There are occasions, however, when an empirically indicated or a theoretically justified nonlinear regression model is more appropriate. We shall consider in this chapter and the next some nonlinear regression models, how to obtain estimates of the regression parameters in such models, and how to make inferences about these regression parameters.

In this chapter, we introduce exponential nonlinear regression models and present the basic methods of nonlinear regression. In Chapter 14, we present logistic nonlinear regression models and consider their uses when the response variable is qualitative.

13.1 Linear and Nonlinear Regression Models

Linear Regression Models

In previous chapters, we considered linear regression models, i.e., models that are linear in the parameters. Such models can be represented by the general linear regression model (6.7):

$$(13.1) \qquad Y_i = \beta_0 + \beta_1 X_{i1} + \beta_2 X_{i2} + \cdots + \beta_{p-1} X_{i,p-1} + \varepsilon_i$$

Linear regression models, as we have seen, include not only first-order models in $p-1$ predictor variables but also more complex models. For instance, a polynomial regression model in one or more predictor variables is linear in the parameters, such as the following model in two predictor variables with linear, quadratic, and interaction terms:

$$(13.2) \qquad Y_i = \beta_0 + \beta_1 X_{i1} + \beta_2 X_{i1}^2 + \beta_3 X_{i2} + \beta_4 X_{i2}^2 + \beta_5 X_{i1} X_{i2} + \varepsilon_i$$

Also, models with transformed variables that are linear in the parameters belong to the class of linear regression models, such as the following model:

$$(13.3) \qquad \log_{10} Y_i = \beta_0 + \beta_1 \sqrt{X_{i1}} + \beta_2 \exp(X_{i2}) + \varepsilon_i$$

In general, we can state a linear regression model in the form:

$$Y_i = f(\mathbf{X}_i, \boldsymbol{\beta}) + \varepsilon_i \tag{13.4}$$

where $\mathbf{X}_i$ is the vector of the observations on the predictor variables for the ith case:

$$\mathbf{X}_i = \begin{bmatrix} 1 \\ X_{i1} \\ \vdots \\ X_{i,p-1} \end{bmatrix} \tag{13.4a}$$

$\boldsymbol{\beta}$ is the vector of the regression coefficients in (6.18c), and $f(\mathbf{X}_i, \boldsymbol{\beta})$ represents the expected value $E\{Y_i\}$, which for linear regression models equals according to (6.54):

$$f(\mathbf{X}_i, \boldsymbol{\beta}) = \mathbf{X}_i'\boldsymbol{\beta} \tag{13.4b}$$

Nonlinear Regression Models

Nonlinear regression models are of the same basic form as that in (13.4) for linear regression models:

$$Y_i = f(\mathbf{X}_i, \boldsymbol{\gamma}) + \varepsilon_i \tag{13.5}$$

An observation Y_i is still the sum of a mean response $f(\mathbf{X}_i, \boldsymbol{\gamma})$ given by the nonlinear response function $f(\mathbf{X}, \boldsymbol{\gamma})$ and the error term ε_i. The error terms usually are assumed to have expectation zero, constant variance, and to be uncorrelated, just as for linear regression models. Often, a normal error model is utilized which assumes that the error terms are independent normal random variables with constant variance.

The parameter vector in the response function $f(\mathbf{X}, \boldsymbol{\gamma})$ is now denoted by $\boldsymbol{\gamma}$ rather than $\boldsymbol{\beta}$ as a reminder that the response function here is nonlinear in the parameters. We present now two examples of nonlinear regression models that are widely used in practice.

Exponential Regression Models.   One widely used nonlinear regression model is the exponential regression model. When there is only a single predictor variable, one form of this regression model with normal error terms is:

$$Y_i = \gamma_0 \exp(\gamma_1 X_i) + \varepsilon_i \tag{13.6}$$

where:

> γ_0 and γ_1 are parameters
> X_i are known constants
> ε_i are independent $N(0, \sigma^2)$

The response function for this model is:

$$f(\mathbf{X}, \boldsymbol{\gamma}) = \gamma_0 \exp(\gamma_1 X) \tag{13.7}$$

Note that this model is not linear in the parameters γ_0 and γ_1.

FIGURE 13.1   Plots of Exponential and Logistic Response Functions.

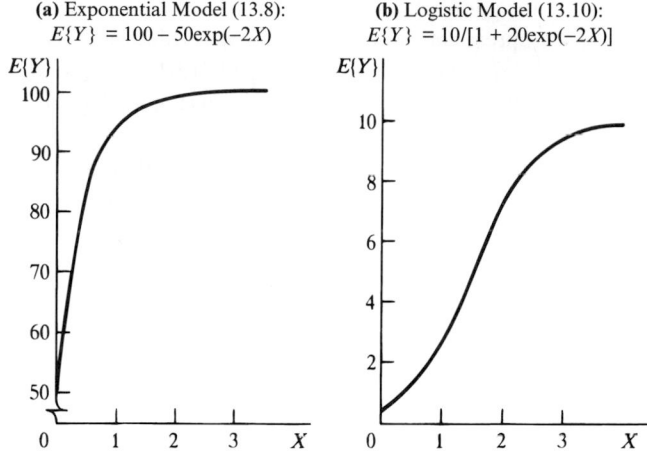

(a) Exponential Model (13.8):
$E\{Y\} = 100 - 50\exp(-2X)$

(b) Logistic Model (13.10):
$E\{Y\} = 10/[1 + 20\exp(-2X)]$

A more general nonlinear exponential regression model in one predictor variable with normal error terms is:

$$(13.8) \qquad Y_i = \gamma_0 + \gamma_1 \exp(\gamma_2 X_i) + \varepsilon_i$$

where the error terms are independent normal with constant variance σ^2. The response function for this regression model is:

$$(13.9) \qquad f(\mathbf{X}, \boldsymbol{\gamma}) = \gamma_0 + \gamma_1 \exp(\gamma_2 X)$$

Exponential regression model (13.8) is commonly used in growth studies where the rate of growth at a given time X is proportional to the amount of growth remaining as time increases, with γ_0 representing the maximum growth value. Another use of this regression model is to relate the concentration of a substance (Y) to elapsed time (X). Figure 13.1a shows the response function (13.9) for parameter values $\gamma_0 = 100$, $\gamma_1 = -50$, and $\gamma_2 = -2$. We shall discuss exponential regression models (13.6) and (13.8) in more detail later in this chapter.

Logistic Regression Models.   Another important nonlinear regression model is the *logistic regression model*. This model with one predictor variable and normal error terms is:

$$(13.10) \qquad Y_i = \frac{\gamma_0}{1 + \gamma_1 \exp(\gamma_2 X_i)} + \varepsilon_i$$

where the error terms ε_i are independent normal with constant variance σ^2. The response function here is:

$$(13.11) \qquad f(\mathbf{X}, \boldsymbol{\gamma}) = \frac{\gamma_0}{1 + \gamma_1 \exp(\gamma_2 X)}$$

Note again that this response function is not linear in the parameters γ_0, γ_1, and γ_2.

This logistic regression model has been used in population studies to relate, for instance, number of species (Y) to time (X). Figure 13.1b shows the logistic response function (13.11) for parameter values $\gamma_0 = 10$, $\gamma_1 = 20$, and $\gamma_2 = -2$. Note that the parameter $\gamma_0 = 10$ represents the maximum growth value here.

Logistic regression model (13.10) is also widely used when the response variable is qualitative. An example of this use of the logistic regression model is for predicting whether a household will purchase a new car this year (will, will not) based on the predictor variables age of presently owned car, household income, and size of household. In this use of logistic regression models, the response variable (will, will not purchase car, in our example) is qualitative and will be represented by a 0, 1 indicator variable. Consequently, the error terms are not normally distributed here with constant variance. Logistic regression models and their use when the response variable is qualitative will be discussed in detail in Chapter 14.

General Form of Nonlinear Regression Models. As we have seen from the two examples of nonlinear regression models, these models are similar in general form to linear regression models. Each Y_i observation is postulated to be the sum of a mean response $f(\mathbf{X}_i, \boldsymbol{\gamma})$ based on the given nonlinear response function and a random error term ε_i. Furthermore, the error terms ε_i are often assumed to be independent normal random variables with constant variance.

An important difference of nonlinear regression models is that the number of regression parameters is not necessarily directly related to the number of X variables in the model. In linear regression models, if there are $p - 1$ X variables in the model, then there are p regression coefficients in the model. For the exponential regression model in (13.8), there is one X variable but three regression coefficients. The same is found for logistic regression model (13.10). Hence, we now denote the number of X variables in the nonlinear regression model by q, but we continue to denote the number of regression parameters in the response function by p. In the exponential regression model (13.6), for instance, there are $p = 2$ regression parameters and $q = 1$ X variable.

Also, we shall define the vector $\mathbf{X}_i$ of the observations on the X variables without the initial element 1. The general form of a nonlinear regression model is therefore expressed as follows:

$$(13.12) \qquad\qquad Y_i = f(\mathbf{X}_i, \boldsymbol{\gamma}) + \varepsilon_i$$

where:

$$(13.12a) \qquad \underset{q \times 1}{\mathbf{X}_i} = \begin{bmatrix} X_{i1} \\ X_{i2} \\ \vdots \\ X_{iq} \end{bmatrix} \qquad \underset{p \times 1}{\boldsymbol{\gamma}} = \begin{bmatrix} \gamma_0 \\ \gamma_1 \\ \vdots \\ \gamma_{p-1} \end{bmatrix}$$

Note

Nonlinear response functions that can be linearized by a transformation are sometimes called *intrinsically linear* response functions. For example, the exponential response function:

$$f(\mathbf{X}, \boldsymbol{\gamma}) = \gamma_0[\exp(\gamma_1 X)]$$

is an intrinsically linear response function because it can be linearized by the logarithmic transformation:

$$\log_e f(\mathbf{X}, \boldsymbol{\gamma}) = \log_e \gamma_0 + \gamma_1 X$$

This tranformed response function can be represented in the linear model form:

$$g(\mathbf{X}, \boldsymbol{\gamma}) = \beta_0 + \beta_1 X$$

where $g(\mathbf{X}, \boldsymbol{\gamma}) = \log_e f(\mathbf{X}, \boldsymbol{\gamma})$, $\beta_0 = \log_e \gamma_0$, and $\beta_1 = \gamma_1$.

Just because a nonlinear response function is intrinsically linear does not necessarily imply that linear regression is appropriate. The reason is that the transformation to linearize the response function will affect the error term in the model. For example, suppose that the following exponential regression model with normal error terms that have constant variance is appropriate:

$$Y_i = \gamma_0 \exp(\gamma_1 X_i) + \varepsilon_i$$

A logarithmic transformation of Y to linearize the response function will affect the normal error term ε_i so that the error term in the linearized model will no longer be normal with constant variance. Hence, it is important to study any nonlinear regression model that has been linearized for appropriateness; it may turn out that the nonlinear regression model is preferable to the linearized version.   ∎

Estimation of Regression Parameters

Estimation of the parameters of a nonlinear regression model is usually carried out by the method of least squares or the method of maximum likelihood, just as for linear regression models. Also like linear regression, both of these methods of estimation yield the same parameter estimates when the error terms in nonlinear regression model (13.12) are independent normal with constant variance.

Unlike in linear regression, it is usually not possible to find analytical expressions for the least squares and maximum likelihood estimators for nonlinear regression models. Instead, numerical search procedures must be used with both of these estimation procedures, requiring intensive computations. The analysis of nonlinear regression models is therefore usually carried out by utilizing standard computer software programs.

13.2   Example

To illustrate the fitting and analysis of nonlinear regression models in a simple fashion, we shall use an example where the model has only two parameters and the sample size is reasonably small. In so doing, we shall be able to explain the concepts and procedures without overwhelming the reader with details.

A hospital administrator wished to develop a regression model for predicting the degree of long-term recovery after discharge from the hospital for severely injured patients. The predictor variable to be utilized is number of days of hospitalization (X), and the response variable is a prognostic index for long-term recovery (Y), with large values of the index reflecting a good prognosis. Data for 15 patients were studied and are presented in Table 13.1. A scatter plot of the data is shown in Figure 13.2. Related earlier studies reported in the literature found the relationship between the predictor variable and the response variable

TABLE 13.1   **Data for Severely Injured Patients Example.**

Patient i	Days Hospitalized X_i	Prognostic Index Y_i
1	2	54
2	5	50
3	7	45
4	10	37
5	14	35
6	19	25
7	26	20
8	31	16
9	34	18
10	38	13
11	45	8
12	52	11
13	53	8
14	60	4
15	65	6

to be exponential. Hence, it was decided to investigate the appropriateness of the two-parameter nonlinear exponential regression model (13.6):

$$(13.13) \qquad Y_i = \gamma_0 \exp(\gamma_1 X_i) + \varepsilon_i$$

where the ε_i are independent normal with constant variance. If this model is appropriate, it is desired to estimate the regression parameters γ_0 and γ_1.

13.3   Least Squares Estimation in Nonlinear Regression

We noted in Chapter 1 that the method of least squares for simple linear regression requires the minimization of the criterion Q in (1.8):

$$(13.14) \qquad Q = \sum_{i=1}^{n} [Y_i - (\beta_0 + \beta_1 X_i)]^2$$

Those values of β_0 and β_1 that minimize Q for the given sample observations (X_i, Y_i) are the least squares estimates and are denoted by b_0 and b_1.

We also noted in Chapter 1 that one method for finding the least squares estimates is by use of a numerical search procedure. With this approach, Q in (13.14) is evaluated for different values of β_0 and β_1, varying β_0 and β_1 systematically until the minimum value of Q is found. The values of β_0 and β_1 that minimize Q are the least squares estimates b_0 and b_1.

A second method for finding the least squares estimates is by means of the least squares normal equations. Here, the least squares normal equations are found analytically

FIGURE 13.2   **Scatter Plot and Fitted Nonlinear Regression Function—Severely Injured Patients Example.**

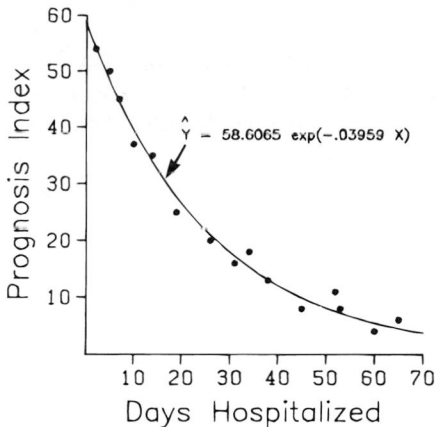

by differentiating Q with respect to β_0 and β_1 and setting the derivatives equal to zero. The solution of the normal equations yields the least squares estimates.

As we saw in Chapter 6, these procedures extend directly to multiple linear regression, for which the least squares criterion is given in (6.22). The concepts of least squares estimation for linear regression also extend directly to nonlinear regression models. The least squares criterion again is:

$$(13.15) \qquad Q = \sum_{i=1}^{n} [Y_i - f(\mathbf{X}_i, \boldsymbol{\gamma})]^2$$

where $f(\mathbf{X}_i, \boldsymbol{\gamma})$ is the mean response for the ith case according to the nonlinear response function $f(\mathbf{X}, \boldsymbol{\gamma})$. The least squares criterion Q in (13.15) must be minimized with respect to the nonlinear regression parameters $\gamma_0, \gamma_1, \ldots, \gamma_{p-1}$ to obtain the least squares estimates. The same two methods for finding the least squares estimates—numerical search and normal equations—may be used in nonlinear regression. A difference from linear regression is that the solution of the normal equations usually requires an iterative numerical search procedure because analytical solutions generally cannot be found.

Example

The response function in the severely injured patients example is seen from (13.13) to be:

$$f(\mathbf{X}, \boldsymbol{\gamma}) = \gamma_0 \exp(\gamma_1 X)$$

Hence, the least squares criterion Q here is:

$$Q = \sum_{i=1}^{n} [Y_i - \gamma_0 \exp(\gamma_1 X_i)]^2$$

We can see that the method of maximum likelihood leads to the same criterion here when the error terms ε_i are independent normal with constant variance by considering the likelihood function:

$$L(\boldsymbol{\gamma}, \sigma^2) = \frac{1}{(2\pi\sigma^2)^{n/2}} \exp\left[-\frac{1}{2\sigma^2} \sum_{i=1}^{n} [Y_i - \gamma_0 \exp(\gamma_1 X_i)]^2\right]$$

Just as for linear regression, maximizing this likelihood function with respect to the regression parameters γ_0 and γ_1 is equivalent to minimizing the sum in the exponent, so that the maximum likelihood estimates are the same here as the least squares estimates.

We now discuss how to obtain the least squares estimates, first by use of the normal equations and then by direct numerical search procedures.

Solution of Normal Equations

To obtain the normal equations for a nonlinear regression model:

$$Y_i = f(\mathbf{X}_i, \boldsymbol{\gamma}) + \varepsilon_i$$

we need to minimize the least squares criterion Q:

$$Q = \sum_{i=1}^{n} [Y_i - f(\mathbf{X}_i, \boldsymbol{\gamma})]^2$$

with respect to $\gamma_0, \gamma_1, \ldots, \gamma_{p-1}$. The partial derivative of Q with respect to γ_k is:

(13.16)
$$\frac{\partial Q}{\partial \gamma_k} = \sum_{i=1}^{n} -2[Y_i - f(\mathbf{X}_i, \boldsymbol{\gamma})]\left[\frac{\partial f(\mathbf{X}_i, \boldsymbol{\gamma})}{\partial \gamma_k}\right]$$

When the p partial derivatives are each set equal to 0 and the parameters γ_k are replaced by the least squares estimates g_k, we obtain after some simplification the p normal equations:

(13.17)
$$\sum_{i=1}^{n} Y_i \left[\frac{\partial f(\mathbf{X}_i, \boldsymbol{\gamma})}{\partial \gamma_k}\right]_{\boldsymbol{\gamma}=\mathbf{g}} - \sum_{i=1}^{n} f(\mathbf{X}_i, \mathbf{g}) \left[\frac{\partial f(\mathbf{X}_i, \boldsymbol{\gamma})}{\partial \gamma_k}\right]_{\boldsymbol{\gamma}=\mathbf{g}} = 0$$

$$k = 0, 1, \ldots, p-1$$

where $\mathbf{g}$ is the vector of the least squares estimates g_k:

(13.18)
$$\underset{p \times 1}{\mathbf{g}} = \begin{bmatrix} g_0 \\ g_1 \\ \vdots \\ g_{p-1} \end{bmatrix}$$

Note that the terms in brackets in (13.17) are the partial derivatives in (13.16) with the parameters γ_k replaced by the least squares estimates g_k.

The normal equations (13.17) for nonlinear regression models are nonlinear in the parameter estimates g_k and are usually difficult to solve, even in the simplest of cases. Hence, numerical search procedures are ordinarily required to obtain a solution of the normal equations iteratively. To make things still more difficult, multiple solutions may be possible.

Example.   In the severely injured patients example, the mean response for the ith case is:

(13.19)
$$f(\mathbf{X}_i, \boldsymbol{\gamma}) = \gamma_0 \exp(\gamma_1 X_i)$$

Hence, the partial derivatives of $f(\mathbf{X}_i, \boldsymbol{\gamma})$ are:

(13.20a)
$$\frac{\partial f(\mathbf{X}_i, \boldsymbol{\gamma})}{\partial \gamma_0} = \exp(\gamma_1 X_i)$$

(13.20b)
$$\frac{\partial f(\mathbf{X}_i, \boldsymbol{\gamma})}{\partial \gamma_1} = \gamma_0 X_i \exp(\gamma_1 X_i)$$

Replacing γ_0 and γ_1 in (13.19), (13.20a), and (13.20b) by the respective least squares estimates g_0 and g_1, the normal equations (13.17) therefore are:

$$\sum Y_i \exp(g_1 X_i) - \sum g_0 \exp(g_1 X_i) \exp(g_1 X_i) \quad = 0$$

$$\sum Y_i g_0 X_i \exp(g_1 X_i) - \sum g_0 \exp(g_1 X_i) g_0 X_i \exp(g_1 X_i) = 0$$

Upon simplification, the normal equations become:

$$\sum Y_i \exp(g_1 X_i) - g_0 \sum \exp(2 g_1 X_i) \quad = 0$$

$$\sum Y_i X_i \exp(g_1 X_i) \quad g_0 \sum X_i \exp(2 g_1 X_i) = 0$$

These normal equations are not linear in g_0 and g_1, and no closed-form solution exists. Thus, numerical methods will be required to find the solution for the least squares estimates iteratively.

Direct Numerical Search—Gauss-Newton Method

In many nonlinear regression problems, it is more practical to find the least squares estimates by direct numerical search procedures rather than by first obtaining the normal equations and then using numerical methods to find the solution for these equations iteratively. The major statistical computer packages employ one or more direct numerical search procedures for solving nonlinear regression problems. We now explain one of these direct numerical search methods.

The *Gauss-Newton method*, also called the *linearization method*, uses a Taylor series expansion to approximate the nonlinear regression model with linear terms and then employs ordinary least squares to estimate the parameters. Iteration of these steps generally leads to a solution to the nonlinear regression problem.

The Gauss-Newton method begins with initial or starting values for the regression parameters $\gamma_0, \gamma_1, \ldots, \gamma_{p-1}$. We denote these by $g_0^{(0)}, g_1^{(0)}, \ldots, g_{p-1}^{(0)}$, where the superscript in parentheses denotes the iteration number. The starting values $g_k^{(0)}$ may be obtained from previous or related studies, theoretical expectations, or a preliminary search for parameter values that lead to a comparatively low criterion value Q in (13.15). We shall later discuss in more detail the choice of the starting values.

Once the starting values for the parameters have been obtained, we approximate the mean responses $f(\mathbf{X}_i, \boldsymbol{\gamma})$ for the n cases by the linear terms in the Taylor series expansion around the starting values $g_k^{(0)}$. We obtain for the ith case:

$$(13.21) \qquad f(\mathbf{X}_i, \boldsymbol{\gamma}) \simeq f(\mathbf{X}_i, \mathbf{g}^{(0)}) + \sum_{k=0}^{p-1} \left[\frac{\partial f(\mathbf{X}_i, \boldsymbol{\gamma})}{\partial \gamma_k} \right]_{\boldsymbol{\gamma} = \mathbf{g}^{(0)}} (\gamma_k - g_k^{(0)})$$

where:

$$(13.21a) \qquad \underset{p \times 1}{\mathbf{g}^{(0)}} = \begin{bmatrix} g_0^{(0)} \\ g_1^{(0)} \\ \vdots \\ g_{p-1}^{(0)} \end{bmatrix}$$

Note that $\mathbf{g}^{(0)}$ is the vector of the parameter starting values. The terms in brackets in (13.21) are the same partial derivatives of the regression function we encountered earlier in the normal equations (13.17), but here they are evaluated at $\gamma_k = g_k^{(0)}$ for $k = 0, 1, \ldots, p-1$.

Let us now simplify the notation as follows:

$$(13.22a) \qquad f_i^{(0)} = f(\mathbf{X}_i, \mathbf{g}^{(0)})$$

$$(13.22b) \qquad \beta_k^{(0)} = \gamma_k - g_k^{(0)}$$

$$(13.22c) \qquad D_{ik}^{(0)} = \left[\frac{\partial f(\mathbf{X}_i, \boldsymbol{\gamma})}{\partial \gamma_k} \right]_{\boldsymbol{\gamma} = \mathbf{g}^{(0)}}$$

The Taylor approximation (13.21) for the mean response for the ith case then becomes in this notation:

$$f(\mathbf{X}_i, \boldsymbol{\gamma}) \simeq f_i^{(0)} + \sum_{k=0}^{p-1} D_{ik}^{(0)} \beta_k^{(0)}$$

and an approximation to the nonlinear regression model (13.12):

$$Y_i = f(\mathbf{X}_i, \boldsymbol{\gamma}) + \varepsilon_i$$

is:

$$(13.23) \qquad Y_i \simeq f_i^{(0)} + \sum_{k=0}^{p-1} D_{ik}^{(0)} \beta_k^{(0)} + \varepsilon_i$$

When we shift the $f_i^{(0)}$ term to the left and denote the difference $Y_i - f_i^{(0)}$ by $Y_i^{(0)}$, we obtain the following linear regression model approximation:

$$(13.24) \qquad Y_i^{(0)} \simeq \sum_{k=0}^{p-1} D_{ik}^{(0)} \beta_k^{(0)} + \varepsilon_i \qquad i = 1, \ldots, n$$

where:

$$(13.24a) \qquad Y_i^{(0)} = Y_i - f_i^{(0)}$$

Note that the linear regression model approximation (13.24) is of the form:

$$Y_i = \beta_0 X_{i0} + \beta_1 X_{i1} + \cdots + \beta_{p-1} X_{i,p-1} + \varepsilon_i$$

The responses $Y_i^{(0)}$ in (13.24) are residuals, namely, the deviations of the observations around the nonlinear regression function with the parameters replaced by the starting estimates. The X variables observations $D_{ik}^{(0)}$ are the partial derivatives of the mean response evaluated for each of the n cases with the parameters replaced by the starting estimates. Each regression coefficient $\beta_k^{(0)}$ represents the difference between the true regression parameter and the initial estimate of the parameter. Thus, the regression coefficients represent the adjustment amounts by which the initial regression coefficients must be corrected. The purpose of fitting the linear regression model approximation (13.24) is therefore to estimate the regression coefficients $\beta_k^{(0)}$ and use these estimates to adjust the initial starting estimates of the regression parameters. In fitting this linear regression approximation, note that there is no intercept term in the model. Use of a computer multiple regression package therefore requires a specification of no intercept.

We shall represent the linear regression model approximation (13.24) in matrix form as follows:

$$(13.25) \qquad \mathbf{Y}^{(0)} \simeq \mathbf{D}^{(0)}\boldsymbol{\beta}^{(0)} + \boldsymbol{\varepsilon}$$

where:

$$(13.25\text{a}) \qquad \underset{n \times 1}{\mathbf{Y}^{(0)}} = \begin{bmatrix} Y_1 - f_1^{(0)} \\ \vdots \\ Y_n - f_n^{(0)} \end{bmatrix} \qquad (13.25\text{b}) \qquad \underset{n \times p}{\mathbf{D}^{(0)}} = \begin{bmatrix} D_{10}^{(0)} & \cdots & D_{1,p-1}^{(0)} \\ \vdots & & \vdots \\ D_{n0}^{(0)} & \cdots & D_{n,p-1}^{(0)} \end{bmatrix}$$

$$(13.25\text{c}) \qquad \underset{p \times 1}{\boldsymbol{\beta}^{(0)}} = \begin{bmatrix} \beta_0^{(0)} \\ \vdots \\ \beta_{p-1}^{(0)} \end{bmatrix} \qquad (13.25\text{d}) \qquad \underset{n \times 1}{\boldsymbol{\varepsilon}} = \begin{bmatrix} \varepsilon_1 \\ \vdots \\ \varepsilon_n \end{bmatrix}$$

Note again that the approximation model (13.25) is precisely in the form of the general linear regression model (6.19), with the $\mathbf{D}$ matrix of partial derivatives now playing the role of the $\mathbf{X}$ matrix (but without a column of 1s for the intercept). We can therefore estimate the parameters $\boldsymbol{\beta}^{(0)}$ by ordinary least squares and obtain according to (6.25):

$$(13.26) \qquad \mathbf{b}^{(0)} = (\mathbf{D}^{(0)\prime}\mathbf{D}^{(0)})^{-1}\mathbf{D}^{(0)\prime}\mathbf{Y}^{(0)}$$

where $\mathbf{b}^{(0)}$ is the vector of the least squares estimated regression coefficients. As we noted earlier, an ordinary multiple regression computer program can be used to obtain the estimated regression coefficients $b_k^{(0)}$, with a specification of no intercept.

We then use these least squares estimates to obtain revised estimated regression coefficients $g_k^{(1)}$ by means of (13.22b):

$$g_k^{(1)} = g_k^{(0)} + b_k^{(0)}$$

where $g_k^{(1)}$ denotes the revised estimate of γ_k at the end of the first iteration. In matrix form, we represent the revision process as follows:

$$(13.27) \qquad \mathbf{g}^{(1)} = \mathbf{g}^{(0)} + \mathbf{b}^{(0)}$$

At this point, we can examine whether the revised regression coefficients represent adjustments in the proper direction. We shall denote the least squares criterion measure Q in (13.15) evaluated for the starting regression coefficients $\mathbf{g}^{(0)}$ by $SSE^{(0)}$; it is:

$$(13.28) \qquad SSE^{(0)} = \sum_{i=1}^{n} [Y_i - f(\mathbf{X}_i, \mathbf{g}^{(0)})]^2 = \sum_{i=1}^{n} (Y_i - f_i^{(0)})^2$$

At the end of the first iteration, the revised estimated regression coefficients are $\mathbf{g}^{(1)}$, and the least squares criterion measure evaluated at this stage, now denoted by $SSE^{(1)}$, is:

$$(13.29) \qquad SSE^{(1)} = \sum_{i=1}^{n} [Y_i - f(\mathbf{X}_i, \mathbf{g}^{(1)})]^2 = \sum_{i=1}^{n} (Y_i - f_i^{(1)})^2$$

If the Gauss-Newton method is working effectively in the first iteration, $SSE^{(1)}$ should be smaller than $SSE^{(0)}$ since the revised estimated regression coefficients $\mathbf{g}^{(1)}$ should be better estimates.

Note that the nonlinear regression functions $f(\mathbf{X}_i, \mathbf{g}^{(0)})$ and $f(\mathbf{X}_i, \mathbf{g}^{(1)})$ are used in calculating $SSE^{(0)}$ and $SSE^{(1)}$, and not the linear approximations from the Taylor series expansion.

The revised regression coefficients $\mathbf{g}^{(1)}$ are not, of course, the least squares estimates for the nonlinear regression problem because the fitted model (13.25) is only an approximation of the nonlinear model. The Gauss-Newton method therefore repeats the procedure just described, with $\mathbf{g}^{(1)}$ now used for the new starting values. This produces a new set of revised estimates, denoted by $\mathbf{g}^{(2)}$, and a new least squares criterion measure $SSE^{(2)}$. The iterative process is continued until the differences between successive coefficient estimates $\mathbf{g}^{(s+1)} - \mathbf{g}^{(s)}$ and/or the difference between successive least squares criterion measures $SSE^{(s+1)} - SSE^{(s)}$ become negligible. We shall denote the final estimates of the regression coefficients simply by $\mathbf{g}$ and the final least squares criterion measure, which is the error sum of squares, by SSE.

The Gauss-Newton method works effectively in many nonlinear regression applications. In some instances, however, the method may require numerous iterations before converging, and in a few cases it may not converge at all.

Example.   In the severely injured patients example, the initial values of the parameters γ_0 and γ_1 were obtained by noting that a logarithmic transformation of the response function linearizes it:

$$\log_e \gamma_0 [\exp(\gamma_1 X)] = \log_e \gamma_0 + \gamma_1 X$$

Hence, a linear regression model with a transformed Y variable was fitted as an initial approximation to the exponential model:

$$Y_i' = \beta_0 + \beta_1 X_i + \varepsilon_i$$

where:

$$Y_i' = \log_e Y_i$$
$$\beta_0 = \log_e \gamma_0$$
$$\beta_1 = \gamma_1$$

This linear regression model was fitted by ordinary least squares and yielded the estimated regression coefficients $b_0 = 4.0371$ and $b_1 = -.03797$ (calculations not shown). Hence, the initial starting values are $g_0^{(0)} = \exp(b_0) = \exp(4.0371) = 56.6646$ and $g_1^{(0)} = b_1 = -.03797$.

The least squares criterion measure at this stage requires evaluation of the nonlinear regression function (13.7) for each case, utilizing the starting parameter values $g_0^{(0)}$ and $g_1^{(0)}$. For instance, for the first case, for which $X_1 = 2$, we obtain:

$$f(\mathbf{X}_1, \mathbf{g}^{(0)}) = f_1^{(0)} = g_0^{(0)} \exp(g_1^{(0)} X_1)$$
$$= (56.6646) \exp[-.03797(2)]$$
$$= 52.5208$$

Since $Y_1 = 54$, the deviation from the mean response is:

$$Y_1^{(0)} = Y_1 - f_1^{(0)} = 54 - 52.5208 = 1.4792$$

Note again that the deviation $Y_1^{(0)}$ is the residual for case 1 at the initial fitting stage since $f_1^{(0)}$ is the estimated mean response when the initial estimates $\mathbf{g}^{(0)}$ of the parameters are employed. The stage 0 residuals for this and the other sample cases are presented in Table 13.2 and constitute the $\mathbf{Y}^{(0)}$ vector.

The least squares criterion measure at this initial stage then is simply the sum of the squared stage 0 residuals:

$$SSE^{(0)} = \sum (Y_i - f_i^{(0)})^2 = \sum (Y_i^{(0)})^2$$
$$= (1.4792)^2 + \cdots + (1.1977)^2 = 56.0869$$

To revise the initial estimates for the parameters, we require the $\mathbf{D}^{(0)}$ matrix and the $\mathbf{Y}^{(0)}$ vector. The latter was already obtained in the process of calculating the least squares criterion measure at stage 0. To obtain the $\mathbf{D}^{(0)}$ matrix, we need the partial derivatives of the regression function (13.19) evaluated at $\boldsymbol{\gamma} = \mathbf{g}^{(0)}$. The partial derivatives are given in (13.20). Table 13.2 shows the $\mathbf{D}^{(0)}$ matrix entries in symbolic form and also the numerical values. To illustrate the calculations for case 1, we know from Table 13.1 that $X_1 = 2$. Hence, evaluating the partial derivatives at $\mathbf{g}^{(0)}$, we find:

$$D_{10}^{(0)} = \left[\frac{\partial f(\mathbf{X}_1, \boldsymbol{\gamma})}{\partial \gamma_0} \right]_{\boldsymbol{\gamma} = \mathbf{g}^{(0)}} = \exp(g_1^{(0)} X_1)$$
$$= \exp[-.03797(2)] = .92687$$

$$D_{11}^{(0)} = \left[\frac{\partial f(\mathbf{X}_1, \boldsymbol{\gamma})}{\partial \gamma_1} \right]_{\boldsymbol{\gamma} = \mathbf{g}^{(0)}} = g_0^{(0)} X_1 \exp(g_1^{(0)} X_1)$$
$$= 56.6646(2) \exp[-.03797(2)] = 105.0416$$

TABLE 13.2 $\mathbf{Y}^{(0)}$ and $\mathbf{D}^{(0)}$ Matrices for Severely Injured Patients Example.

$$
\underset{15 \times 1}{\mathbf{Y}^{(0)}} =
\begin{bmatrix}
Y_1 - f_1^{(0)} \\
\\
\vdots \\
\\
Y_{15} - f_{15}^{(0)}
\end{bmatrix}
=
\begin{bmatrix}
Y_1 - g_0^{(0)} \exp(g_1^{(0)} X_1) \\
\\
\vdots \\
\\
Y_{15} - g_0^{(0)} \exp(g_1^{(0)} X_{15})
\end{bmatrix}
=
\begin{bmatrix}
1.4792 \\
3.1337 \\
1.5609 \\
-1.7624 \\
1.6996 \\
-2.5422 \\
-1.1139 \\
-1.4629 \\
2.4172 \\
-.3871 \\
-2.2625 \\
3.1327 \\
.4259 \\
-1.8063 \\
1.1977
\end{bmatrix}
$$

$$
\underset{15 \times 2}{\mathbf{D}^{(0)}} =
\begin{bmatrix}
\exp(g_1^{(0)} X_1) & g_0^{(0)} X_1 \exp(g_1^{(0)} X_1) \\
\\
\vdots & \vdots \\
\\
\exp(g_1^{(0)} X_{15}) & g_0^{(0)} X_{15} \exp(g_1^{(0)} X_{15})
\end{bmatrix}
=
\begin{bmatrix}
.92687 & 105.0416 \\
.82708 & 234.3317 \\
.76660 & 304.0736 \\
.68407 & 387.6236 \\
.58768 & 466.2057 \\
.48606 & 523.3020 \\
.37261 & 548.9603 \\
.30818 & 541.3505 \\
.27500 & 529.8162 \\
.23625 & 508.7088 \\
.18111 & 461.8140 \\
.13884 & 409.0975 \\
.13367 & 401.4294 \\
.10247 & 348.3801 \\
.08475 & 312.1510
\end{bmatrix}
$$

We are now ready to obtain the least squares estimates $\mathbf{b}^{(0)}$ by regressing the response variable $Y^{(0)}$ in Table 13.2 on the two X variables in $\mathbf{D}^{(0)}$ in Table 13.2, using regression with no intercept. A standard multiple regression computer program yielded $b_0^{(0)} = 1.8932$ and $b_1^{(0)} = -.001563$. Hence, the vector $\mathbf{b}^{(0)}$ of the estimated regression coefficients is:

$$
\mathbf{b}^{(0)} =
\begin{bmatrix}
1.8932 \\
-.001563
\end{bmatrix}
$$

TABLE 13.3   **Gauss-Newton Method Iterations and Final Nonlinear Least Squares Estimates—Severely Injured Patients Example.**

(a) Estimates of Parameters and Least Squares Criterion Measure

Iteration	g_0	g_1	SSE
0	56.6646	−.03797	56.0869
1	58.5578	−.03953	49.4638
2	58.6065	−.03959	49.4593
3	58.6065	−.03959	49.4593

(b) Final Least Squares Estimates

k	g_k	$s\{g_k\}$
0	58.6065	1.472
1	−.03959	.00171

$$MSE = \frac{49.4593}{13} = 3.80456$$

(c) Estimated Approximate Variance-Covariance Matrix of Estimated Regression Coefficients

$$s^2\{\mathbf{g}\} = MSE(\mathbf{D'D})^{-1} = 3.80456 \begin{bmatrix} 5.696E-1 & -4.682E-4 \\ -4.682E-4 & 7.697E-7 \end{bmatrix}$$

$$= \begin{bmatrix} 2.1672 & -1.781E-3 \\ -1.781E-3 & 2.928E-6 \end{bmatrix}$$

By (13.27), we now obtain the revised least squares estimates $\mathbf{g}^{(1)}$:

$$\mathbf{g}^{(1)} = \mathbf{g}^{(0)} + \mathbf{b}^{(0)} = \begin{bmatrix} 56.6646 \\ -.03797 \end{bmatrix} + \begin{bmatrix} 1.8932 \\ -.001563 \end{bmatrix}$$

$$= \begin{bmatrix} 58.5578 \\ -.03953 \end{bmatrix}$$

Hence, $g_0^{(1)} = 58.5578$ and $g_1^{(1)} = -.03953$ are the revised parameter estimates at the end of the first iteration. Note that the estimated regression coefficients have been revised moderately from the initial values, as can be seen from Table 13.3a, which presents the estimated regression coefficients and the least squares criterion measures for the starting values and the first iteration. Note also that the least squares criterion measure has been reduced in the first iteration.

Iteration 2 requires that we now revise the residuals from the exponential regression function and the first partial derivatives, based on the revised parameter estimates $g_0^{(1)} = 58.5578$ and $g_1^{(1)} = -.03953$. For case 1, for which $Y_1 = 54$ and $X_1 = 2$, we obtain:

$$Y_1^{(1)} = Y_1 - f_1^{(1)} = 54 - (58.5578) \exp[-.03953(2)] = -.1065$$

$$D_{10}^{(1)} = \exp(g_1^{(1)} X_1) = \exp[-.03953(2)] = .92398$$

$$D_{11}^{(1)} = g_0^{(1)} X_1 \exp(g_1^{(1)} X_1) = 58.5578(2) \exp[-.03953(2)] = 108.2130$$

By comparing these results with the comparable stage 0 results for case 1 in Table 13.2, we see that the absolute magnitude of the residual for case 1 is substantially reduced as a result of the stage 1 revised fit and that the two partial derivatives are changed to a moderate extent. After the revised residuals $Y_i^{(1)}$ and the partial derivatives $D_{i0}^{(1)}$ and $D_{i1}^{(1)}$ have been obtained for all cases, the revised residuals are regressed on the revised partial derivatives, using a no-intercept regression fit, and the estimated regression parameters are again revised according to (13.27).

This process was carried out for three iterations. Table 13.3a contains the estimated regression coefficients and the least squares criterion measure for each iteration. We see that while iteration 1 led to moderate revisions in the estimated regression coefficients and a substantially better fit according to the least squares criterion, iteration 2 resulted only in minor revisions of the estimated regression coefficients and little improvement in the fit. Iteration 3 led to no change in either the estimates of the coefficients or the least squares criterion measure.

Hence, the search procedure was terminated after three iterations. The final regression coefficient estimates therefore are $g_0 = 58.6065$ and $g_1 = -.03959$, and the fitted regression function is:

$$(13.30) \qquad \hat{Y} = (58.6065)\exp(-.03959X)$$

The error sum of squares for this fitted model is $SSE = 49.4593$. Figure 13.2 shows a plot of this estimated regression function, together with a scatter plot of the data. The fit appears to be a good one.

Comments

1. The choice of initial starting values is very important with the Gauss-Newton method because a poor choice may result in slow convergence, convergence to a local minimum, or even divergence. Good starting values will generally result in faster convergence, and if multiple minima exist, will lead to a solution that is the global minimum rather than a local minimum. Fast convergence, even if the initial estimates are far from the least squares solution, generally indicates that the linear approximation model (13.25) is a good approximation to the nonlinear regression model. Slow convergence, on the other hand, especially from initial estimates reasonably close to the least squares solution, usually indicates that the linear approximation model is not a good approximation to the nonlinear model.

2. A variety of methods are available for obtaining starting values for the regression parameters. Often, related earlier studies can be utilized to provide good starting values for the regression parameters. Another possibility is to select p representative observations, set the regression function $f(\mathbf{X}_i, \boldsymbol{\gamma})$ equal to Y_i for each of the p observations (thereby ignoring the random error), solve the p equations for the p parameters, and use the solutions as the starting values, provided they lead to reasonably good fits of the observed data. Still another possibility is to do a grid search in the parameter space by selecting in a grid fashion various trial choices of $\mathbf{g}$, evaluating the least squares criterion Q for each of these choices, and using as the starting values that $\mathbf{g}$ vector for which Q is smallest.

3. When using the Gauss-Newton or another direct search procedure, it is often desirable to try other sets of starting values after a solution has been obtained to make sure that the same solution will be found.

4. Some computer packages for nonlinear regression require that the user specify the starting values for the regression parameters. Others do a grid search to obtain starting values.

5. Most nonlinear computer programs have a library of commonly used regression functions. For nonlinear response functions not in the library and specified by the user, some computer programs using the Gauss-Newton method require the user to input also the partial derivatives of the regression function, while others numerically calculate estimated partial derivatives from the regression function.

6. The Gauss-Newton method may produce iterations which oscillate widely or result in increases in the error sum of squares. Sometimes, these aberrations are only temporary, but occasionally serious convergence problems exist. Various modifications of the Gauss-Newton method have been suggested to improve its performance, such as the Hartley modification (Ref. 13.1).

7. Some properties that exist for linear regression least squares do not hold for nonlinear regression least squares. For example, the residuals do not necessarily sum to zero for nonlinear least squares. Additionally, the error sum of squares *SSE* and the regression sum of squares *SSR* do not necessarily sum to the total sum of squares *SSTO*. Consequently, the coefficient of multiple determination $R^2 = SSR/SSTO$ is not a meaningful descriptive statistic for nonlinear regression.   ∎

Other Direct Search Procedures

Two other direct search procedures, besides the Gauss-Newton method, that are frequently used are the method of steepest descent and the Marquardt algorithm. The *method of steepest descent* searches for the minimum least squares criterion measure Q by iteratively determining the direction in which the regression coefficients **g** should be changed. The method of steepest descent is particularly effective when the starting values $\mathbf{g}^{(0)}$ are not good, being far from the final values **g**.

The *Marquardt algorithm* seeks to utilize the best features of the Gauss-Newton method and the method of steepest descent, and occupies a middle ground between these two methods.

Additional information about direct search procedures can be found in specialized sources, such as References 13.2 and 13.3.

13.4   Model Building and Diagnostics

The model-building process for nonlinear regression models often differs somewhat from that for linear regression models. The reason is that the functional form of many nonlinear models is less suitable for adding or deleting predictor variables and curvature and interaction effects in the direct fashion that is feasible for linear regression models. Some types of nonlinear regression models do lend themselves to adding and deleting predictor variables in a direct fashion. We shall take up two such nonlinear regression models in Chapter 14, where we consider the logistic and Poisson multiple regression models.

Validation of the selected nonlinear regression model can be performed in the same fashion as for linear regression models.

Use of diagnostic tools to examine the appropriateness of a fitted model plays an important role in the process of building a nonlinear regression model. The appropriateness of a regression model must always be considered, whether the model is linear or nonlinear. Nonlinear regression models may not be appropriate for the same reasons as linear regression models. For example, when nonlinear growth models are used for time series data, there is the possibility that the error terms may be correlated. Also, unequal error variances are often present when nonlinear growth models with asymptotes are fitted, such as exponential models (13.6) and (13.8). Typically, the error variances for cases in the neighborhood of the asymptote(s) differ from the error variances for cases elsewhere.

When replicate observations are available and the sample size is reasonably large, the appropriateness of a nonlinear regression function can be tested formally by means of the lack of fit test for linear regression models in (6.68). This test will be an approximate one for nonlinear regression models, but the actual level of significance will be close to the specified level when the sample size is reasonably large. Thus, we calculate the pure error sum of squares by (3.16), obtain the lack of fit sum of squares by (3.24), and calculate test statistic (6.68b) in the usual fashion when performing a formal lack of fit test for a nonlinear response function.

Plots of residuals against time, against the fitted values, and against each of the predictor variables can be helpful in diagnosing departures from the assumed model, just as for linear regression models. In interpreting residual plots for nonlinear regression, one needs to remember that the residuals for nonlinear regression do not necessarily sum to zero.

If unequal error variances are found to be present, weighted least squares can be used in fitting the nonlinear regression model. Alternatively, transformations of the response variable can be investigated that may stabilize the variance of the error terms and also permit use of a linear regression model.

Example

In the severely injured patients example, the residuals were obtained by use of the fitted nonlinear regression function (13.30):

$$e_i = Y_i - (58.6065) \exp(-.03959 X_i)$$

A plot of the residuals against the fitted values is shown in Figure 13.3a, and a normal probability plot of the residuals is shown in Figure 13.3b. These plots do not suggest any serious departures from the model assumptions. The residual plot against the fitted values in Figure 13.3a does raise the question whether the error variance may be somewhat larger for cases with small fitted values near the asymptote. The modified Levene test (3.9) was conducted. Its P-value is .64, indicating that the residuals are consistent with constancy of the error variance.

On the basis of these, as well as some other diagnostics, it was concluded that exponential regression model (13.13) is appropriate for the data.

13.5 Inferences about Nonlinear Regression Parameters

Exact inference procedures about the regression parameters are available for linear regression models with normal error terms for any sample size. Unfortunately, this is not the case for nonlinear regression models with normal error terms, where the least squares and maximum likelihood estimators for any given sample size are not normally distributed, are not unbiased, and do not have minimum variance.

Consequently, inferences about the regression parameters in nonlinear regression are usually based on large-sample theory. This theory tells us that the least squares and maximum likelihood estimators for nonlinear regression models with normal error terms, when the sample size is large, are approximately normally distributed and almost unbiased, and have

FIGURE 13.3   **Diagnostic Residual Plots—Severely Injured Patients Example.**

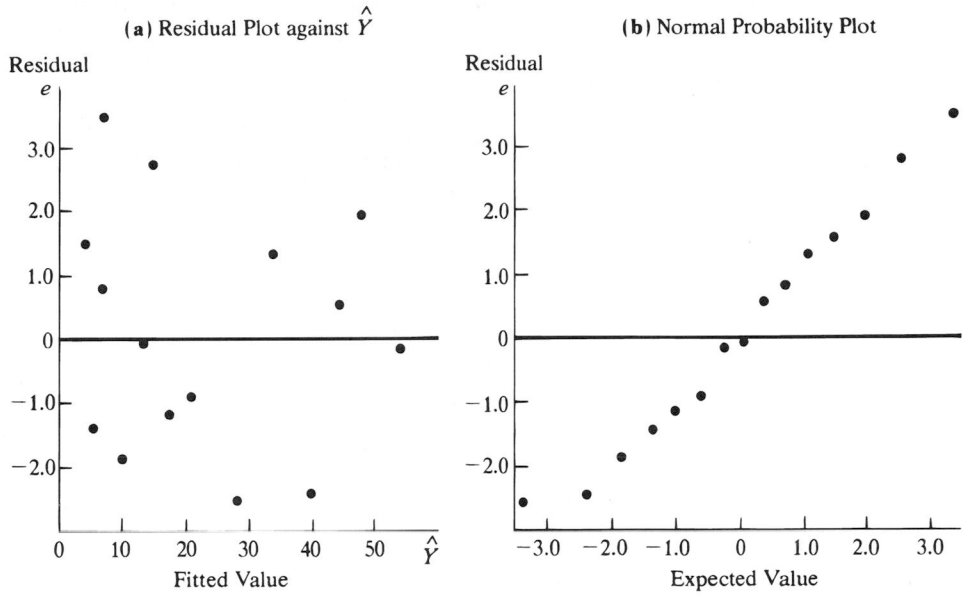

almost minimum variance. This large-sample theory also applies when the error terms are not normally distributed.

Before presenting details about large-sample inferences for nonlinear regression, we need to consider first how the error term variance σ^2 is estimated for nonlinear regression models.

Estimate of Error Term Variance

Inferences about nonlinear regression parameters require an estimate of the error term variance σ^2. This estimate is of the same form as for linear regression, the error sum of squares again being the sum of the squared residuals:

$$(13.31) \qquad MSE = \frac{SSE}{n-p} = \frac{\Sigma(Y_i - \hat{Y}_i)^2}{n-p} = \frac{\Sigma[Y_i - f(\mathbf{X}_i, \mathbf{g})]^2}{n-p}$$

Here $\mathbf{g}$ is the vector of the final parameter estimates, so that the residuals are the deviations around the fitted nonlinear regression function using the final estimated regression coefficients $\mathbf{g}$. For nonlinear regression, MSE is not an unbiased estimator of σ^2, but the bias is small when the sample size is large.

Large-Sample Theory

When the error terms are independent and normally distributed and the sample size is reasonably large, the following theorem provides the basis for inferences for nonlinear regression models:

(13.32)   When the error terms ε_i are independent $N(0, \sigma^2)$ and the sample size n is reasonably large, the sampling distribution of **g** is approximately normal. The expected value of the mean vector is approximately:

(13.32a) $$\mathbf{E\{g\}} \simeq \boldsymbol{\gamma}$$

The approximate variance-covariance matrix of the regression coefficients is estimated by:

(13.32b) $$\mathbf{s}^2\{\mathbf{g}\} = MSE(\mathbf{D}'\mathbf{D})^{-1}$$

Here **D** is the matrix of partial derivatives evaluated at the final least squares estimates **g**, just as $\mathbf{D}^{(0)}$ in (13.25b) is the matrix of partial derivatives evaluated at $\mathbf{g}^{(0)}$. Note that the estimated approximate variance-covariance matrix $\mathbf{s}^2\{\mathbf{g}\}$ is of exactly the same form as the one for linear regression in (6.48), with **D** again playing the role of the **X** matrix.

   Thus, when the sample size is large and the error terms are independent normal with constant variance, the least squares estimators in **g** for nonlinear regression are approximately normally distributed and almost unbiased. They also have near minimum variance, since the variance-covariance matrix in (13.32b) estimates the minimum variances. We should add that theorem (13.32) holds even if the error terms are not normally distributed.

   As a result of theorem (13.32), inferences for nonlinear regression parameters are carried out in the same fashion as for linear regression when the sample size is reasonably large. Thus, an interval estimate for a regression parameter is carried out by (6.50) and a test by (6.51). The needed estimated variance is obtained from the matrix $\mathbf{s}^2\{\mathbf{g}\}$ in (13.32b). These inference procedures when applied to nonlinear regression are only approximate, to be sure, but the approximation often is very good. For some nonlinear regression models, the sample size can be quite small for the large-sample approximation to be good. For other nonlinear regression models, however, the sample size may need to be quite large.

When Is Large-Sample Theory Applicable?

Ideally, we would like a rule that would tell us when the sample size in any given nonlinear regression application is large enough so that the large-sample inferences based on asymptotic theorem (13.32) are appropriate. Unfortunately, no simple rule exists that tells us when it is appropriate to use the large-sample inference methods and when it is not appropriate. However, a number of guidelines have been developed that are helpful in assessing the appropriateness of using the large-sample inference procedures in a given application.

   1. Quick convergence of the iterative procedure in finding the estimates of the nonlinear regression parameters is often an indication that the linear approximation in (13.25) to the nonlinear regression model is a good approximation and hence that the asymptotic properties of the regression estimates are applicable. Slow convergence suggests caution and consideration of other guidelines before large-sample inferences are employed.

   2. Several measures have been developed for providing guidance about the appropriateness of the use of large-sample inference procedures. Bates and Watts (Ref. 13.4) developed curvature measures of nonlinearity. These indicate the extent to which the nonlinear regression function fitted to the data can be reasonably approximated by the linear approximation in (13.25). Box (Ref. 13.5) obtained a formula for estimating the

bias of the estimated regression coefficients. A small bias supports the appropriateness of the large-sample inference procedures. Hougaard (Ref. 13.6) developed an estimate of the skewness of the sampling distributions of the estimated regression coefficients. An indication of little skewness supports the approximate normality of the sampling distributions and consequently the applicability of the large-sample inference procedures.

3. Bootstrap sampling described in Chapter 10 provides a direct means of examining whether the sampling distributions of the nonlinear regression parameter estimates are approximately normal, whether the variances of the sampling distributions are near the variances for the linear approximation model, and whether the bias in each of the parameter estimates is fairly small. If so, the sampling behavior of the nonlinear regression estimates is said to be *close-to-linear* and the large-sample inference procedures may appropriately be used. Nonlinear regression estimates whose sampling distributions are not close to normal, whose variances are much larger than the variances for the linear approximation model, and for which there is substantial bias are said to behave in a *far-from-linear* fashion and the large-sample inference procedures are then not appropriate.

Once many bootstrap samples have been obtained and the nonlinear regression parameter estimates calculated for each sample, the bootstrap sampling distribution for each parameter estimate can be examined to see if it is near normal. The variances of the bootstrap distributions of the estimated regression coefficients can be obtained next to see if they are close to the large-sample variance estimates obtained by (13.32b). Similarly, the bootstrap confidence intervals for the regression coefficients can be obtained and compared with the large-sample confidence intervals. Good agreement between these intervals again provides support for the appropriateness of the large-sample inference procedures. In addition, the difference between each final regression parameter estimate and the mean of its bootstrap sampling distribution is an estimate of the bias of the regression estimate. Small or negligible biases of the nonlinear regression estimates support the appropriateness of the large-sample inference procedures.

Remedial Measures.   When the diagnostics suggest that large-sample inference procedures are not appropriate in a particular instance, remedial measures should be explored. One possibility is to reparameterize the nonlinear regression model. For example, studies have shown that for the nonlinear model:

$$Y_i = \gamma_0 X_i / (\gamma_1 + X_i) + \varepsilon_i$$

the use of large-sample inference procedures is often not appropriate. However, the following reparameterization:

$$Y_i = X_i / (\theta_1 X_i + \theta_2) + \varepsilon_i$$

where $\theta_1 = 1/\gamma_0$ and $\theta_2 = \gamma_1/\gamma_0$, yields identical fits and generally involves no problems in using large-sample inference procedures for moderate sample sizes (see Ref. 13.7 for details).

Another remedial measure is to use the bootstrap estimates of precision and confidence intervals instead of the large-sample inferences. However, when the linear approximation in (13.25) is not a close approximation to the nonlinear regression model, convergence may be very slow and bootstrap estimates of precision and confidence intervals may be difficult to obtain. Still another remedial measure that is sometimes available is to increase the sample size.

Example.   For the severely injured patients example, we know from Table 13.3a that the final error sum of squares is $SSE = 49.4593$. Since $p = 2$ parameters are present in the nonlinear response function (13.19), we obtain:

$$MSE = \frac{SSE}{n - p} = \frac{49.4593}{15 - 2} = 3.80456$$

Table 13.3b presents this mean square, and Table 13.3c contains the large-sample estimated variance-covariance matrix of the estimated regression coefficients. The matrix $(\mathbf{D'D})^{-1}$ is based on the final regression coefficient estimates $\mathbf{g}$ and is shown without computational details.

We see from Table 13.3c that $s^2\{g_0\} = 2.1672$ and $s^2\{g_1\} = .000002928$. The estimated standard deviations of the regression coefficients are given in Table 13.3b.

To check on the appropriateness of the large-sample variances of the estimated regression coefficients and on the applicability of large-sample inferences in general, we have generated 1,000 bootstrap samples of size 15. The fixed X sampling procedure was used since the exponential model appears to fit the data well and the error term variance appears to be fairly constant. Histograms of the resulting bootstrap sampling distributions of g_0^* and g_1^* are shown in Figure 13.4, together with some characteristics of these distributions. We see that the g_0^* distribution is close to normal. The g_1^* distribution suggests that the sampling distribution may be slightly skewed to the left, but the departure from normality does not appear to be great. The means of the distribution, denoted by $\bar{g}_0^*$ and $\bar{g}_1^*$, are very close to the final least squares estimates, indicating that the bias in the estimates is negligible:

$$\bar{g}_0^* = 58.67 \qquad \bar{g}_1^* = -.03936$$

$$g_0 = 58.61 \qquad g_1 = -.03959$$

Furthermore, the standard deviations of the bootstrap sampling distributions are very close to the large-sample standard deviations in Table 13.3b:

$$s^*\{g_0^*\} = 1.423 \qquad s^*\{g_1^*\} = .00142$$

$$s\{g_0\} = 1.472 \qquad s\{g_1\} = .00171$$

These indications all point to the appropriateness of large-sample inferences here, even though the sample size ($n = 15$) is not very large.

Interval Estimation of a Single γ_k

Based on large-sample theorem (13.32), the following approximate result holds when the sample size is large and the error terms are normally distributed:

(13.33)
$$\frac{g_k - \gamma_k}{s\{g_k\}} \sim t(n - p) \qquad k = 0, 1, \ldots, p - 1$$

where $t(n - p)$ is a t variable with $n - p$ degrees of freedom. Hence, approximate $1 - \alpha$ confidence limits for any single γ_k are formed by means of (6.50):

(13.34)
$$g_k \pm t(1 - \alpha/2; n - p)s\{g_k\}$$

where $t(1 - \alpha/2; n - p)$ is the $(1 - \alpha/2)100$ percentile of the t distribution with $n - p$ degrees of freedom.

FIGURE 13.4   Bootstrap Sampling Distributions—Severely Injured Patients Example.

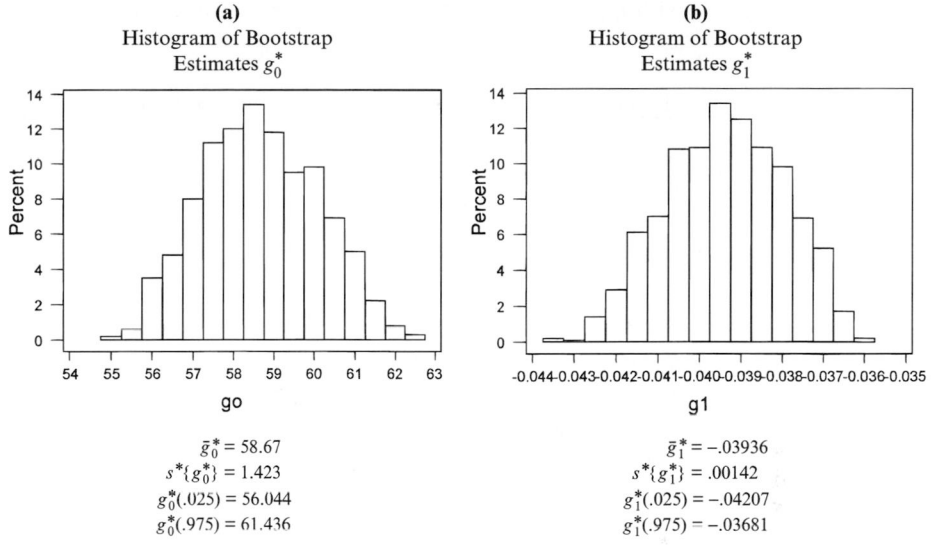

(a) Histogram of Bootstrap Estimates g_0^*	**(b)** Histogram of Bootstrap Estimates g_1^*
$\bar{g}_0^* = 58.67$	$\bar{g}_1^* = -.03936$
$s^*\{g_0^*\} = 1.423$	$s^*\{g_1^*\} = .00142$
$g_0^*(.025) = 56.044$	$g_1^*(.025) = -.04207$
$g_0^*(.975) = 61.436$	$g_1^*(.975) = -.03681$

Example.   For the severely injured patients example, it is desired to estimate γ_1 with a 95 percent confidence interval. We require $t(.975; 13) = 2.160$, and find from Table 13.3b that $g_1 = -.03959$ and $s\{g_1\} = .00171$. Hence, the confidence limits are $-.03959 \pm 2.160(.00171)$, and the approximate 95 percent confidence interval for γ_1 is:

$$-.0433 \leq \gamma_1 \leq -.0359$$

Thus, we can conclude with approximate 95 percent confidence that γ_1 is between $-.0433$ and $-.0359$. To confirm the appropriateness of this large-sample confidence interval, we shall obtain the 95 percent bootstrap confidence interval for γ_1. Using (10.55) and the results in Figure 13.4b, we obtain:

$$d_1 = g_1 - g_1^*(.025) = -.03959 + .04207 = .00248$$

$$d_2 = g_1^*(.975) - g_1 = -.03681 + .03959 = .00278$$

The reflection method confidence limits by (10.56) then are:

$$g_1 - d_2 = -.03959 - .00278 = -.04237$$

$$g_1 + d_1 = -.03959 + .00248 = -.03711$$

Hence, the 95 percent bootstrap confidence interval is $-.0424 \leq \gamma_1 \leq -.0371$. This confidence interval is very close to the large-sample confidence interval, again supporting the appropriateness of large-sample inference procedures here.

Simultaneous Interval Estimation of Several γ_k

Approximate joint confidence intervals for several regression parameters in nonlinear regression can be developed by the Bonferroni procedure. If m parameters are to be estimated with approximate family confidence coefficient $1 - \alpha$, the joint Bonferroni confidence limits are:

$$(13.35) \qquad\qquad g_k \pm Bs\{g_k\}$$

where:

$$(13.35a) \qquad\qquad B = t(1 - \alpha/2m; n - p)$$

Example.   In the severely injured patients example, it is desired to obtain simultaneous interval estimates for γ_0 and γ_1 with an approximate 90 percent family confidence coefficient. With the Bonferroni procedure we therefore require separate confidence intervals for the two parameters, each with a 95 percent statement confidence coefficient. We have already obtained a confidence interval for γ_1 with a 95 percent statement confidence coefficient. The approximate 95 percent statement confidence limits for γ_0, using the results in Table 13.3b, are $58.6065 \pm 2.160(1.472)$ and the confidence interval for γ_0 is:

$$55.43 \le \gamma_0 \le 61.79$$

Hence, the joint confidence intervals with approximate family confidence coefficient of 90 percent are:

$$55.43 \le \gamma_0 \le 61.79$$

$$-.0433 \le \gamma_1 \le -.0359$$

Test Concerning a Single γ_k

A large-sample test concerning a single γ_k is set up in the usual fashion. To test:

$$(13.36a) \qquad\qquad \begin{aligned} H_0&: \ \gamma_k = \gamma_{k0} \\ H_a&: \ \gamma_k \ne \gamma_{k0} \end{aligned}$$

where γ_{k0} is the specified value of γ_k, we may use the t^* test statistic based on (6.49) when n is reasonably large:

$$(13.36b) \qquad\qquad t^* = \frac{g_k - \gamma_{k0}}{s\{g_k\}}$$

The decision rule for controlling the risk of making a Type I error at approximately α then is:

$$(13.36c) \qquad\qquad \begin{aligned} &\text{If } |t^*| \le t(1 - \alpha/2; n - p), \ \text{conclude } H_0 \\ &\text{If } |t^*| > t(1 - \alpha/2; n - p), \ \text{conclude } H_a \end{aligned}$$

Example.   In the severely injured patients example, we wish to test:

$$H_0: \ \gamma_0 = 54$$

$$H_a: \ \gamma_0 \neq 54$$

The test statistic (13.36b) here is:

$$t^* = \frac{58.6065 - 54}{1.472} = 3.13$$

For $\alpha = .01$, we require $t(.995; 13) = 3.012$. Since $|t^*| = 3.13 > 3.012$, we conclude H_a, that $\gamma_0 \neq 54$. The approximate two-sided P-value of the test is .008.

Test Concerning Several γ_k

When a large-sample test concerning several γ_k simultaneously is desired, we use the same approach as for the general linear test, first fitting the full model and obtaining $SSE(F)$, then fitting the reduced model and obtaining $SSE(R)$, and finally calculating the same test statistic (2.70) as for linear regression:

$$(13.37) \qquad\qquad F^* = \frac{SSE(R) - SSE(F)}{df_R - df_F} \div MSE(F)$$

For large n, this test statistic is distributed approximately as $F(df_R - df_F, df_F)$ when H_0 holds.

13.6   Learning Curve Example

We now present a second example, to provide an additional illustration of the nonlinear regression concepts developed in this chapter. An electronics products manufacturer undertook the production of a new product in two locations (location A: coded $X_1 = 1$, location B: coded $X_1 = 0$). Location B has more modern facilities and hence was expected to be more efficient than location A, even after the initial learning period. An industrial engineer calculated the expected unit production cost for a modern facility after learning has occurred. Weekly unit production costs for each location were then expressed as a fraction of this expected cost. The reciprocal of this fraction is a measure of relative efficiency, and this relative efficiency measure was utilized as the response variable (Y) in the study.

It is well known that efficiency increases over time when a new product is produced, and that the improvements eventually slow down and the process stabilizes. Hence, it was decided to employ an exponential model with an upper asymptote for expressing the relation between relative efficiency (Y) and time (X_2), and to incorporate a constant effect for the difference in the two production locations. The model decided on was:

$$(13.38) \qquad\qquad Y_i = \gamma_0 + \gamma_1 X_{i1} + \gamma_3 \exp(\gamma_2 X_{i2}) + \varepsilon_i$$

When γ_2 and γ_3 are negative, γ_0 is the upper asymptote for location B as X_2 gets large, and $\gamma_0 + \gamma_1$ is the upper asymptote for location A. The parameters γ_2 and γ_3 reflect the speed of learning, which was expected to be the same in the two locations.

TABLE 13.4 **Data for Learning Curve Example.**

Observation i	Location X_{i1}	Week X_{i2}	Relative Efficiency Y_i
1	1	1	.483
2	1	2	.539
3	1	3	.618
. . .	. . .	. . .	. . .
13	1	70	.960
14	1	80	.967
15	1	90	.975
16	0	1	.517
17	0	2	.598
18	0	3	.635
. . .	. . .	. . .	. . .
28	0	70	1.028
29	0	80	1.017
30	0	90	1.023

FIGURE 13.5 **Scatter Plot and Fitted Nonlinear Regression Functions—Learning Curve Example.**

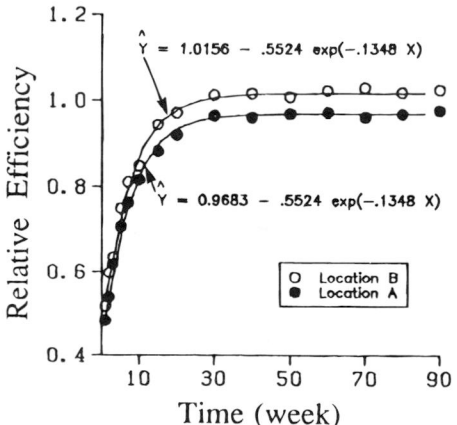

While weekly data on relative production efficiency for each location were available, we shall only use observations for selected weeks during the first 90 weeks of production to simplify the presentation. A portion of the data on location, week, and relative efficiency is presented in Table 13.4; a plot of the data is shown in Figure 13.5. Note that learning was relatively rapid in both locations, and that the relative efficiency in location B toward the end of the 90-week period even exceeded 1.0; i.e., the actual unit costs at this stage were lower than the industrial engineer's expected unit cost.

TABLE 13.5   **Nonlinear Least Squares Estimates and Standard Deviations and Bootstrap Results—Learning Curve Example.**

	(1)	(2)	(3)	(4)
	Nonlinear Least Squares		Bootstrap	
k	g_k	$s\{g_k\}$	$\bar{g}_k^*$	$s^*\{g_k^*\}$
0	1.0156	.003672	1.015605	.003374
1	−.04727	.004109	−.04724	.003702
2	−.5524	.008157	−.55283	.007275
3	−.1348	.004359	−.13495	.004102

Regression model (13.38) is nonlinear in the parameters γ_2 and γ_3. Hence, a direct numerical search estimation procedure was to be employed, for which starting values for the parameters are needed. These were developed partly from past experience, partly from analysis of the data. Previous studies indicated that γ_3 should be in the neighborhood of $-.5$, so $g_3^{(0)} = -.5$ was used as the starting value. Since the difference in the relative efficiencies between locations A and B for a given week tended to average $-.0459$ during the 90-week period, a starting value $g_1^{(0)} = -.0459$ was specified. The largest observed relative efficiency for location B was 1.028, so that a starting value $g_0^{(0)} = 1.025$ was felt to be reasonable. Only a starting value for γ_2 remains to be found. This was chosen by selecting a typical relative efficiency observation in the middle of the time period, $Y_{24} = 1.012$, and equating it to the response function with $X_{24,1} = 0$, $X_{24,2} = 30$, and the starting values for the other regression coefficients (thus ignoring the error term):

$$1.012 = 1.025 - (.5)\exp(30\gamma_2)$$

Solving this equation for γ_2, the starting value $g_2^{(0)} = -.122$ was obtained. Tests for several other representative observations yielded similar starting values, and $g_2^{(0)} = -.122$ was therefore considered to be a reasonable initial value.

With the four starting values $g_0^{(0)} = 1.025$, $g_1^{(0)} = -.0459$, $g_2^{(0)} = -.122$, and $g_3^{(0)} = -.5$, a computer package direct numerical search program was utilized to obtain the least squares estimates. The least squares regression coefficients stabilized after five iterations. The final estimates, together with the large-sample estimated standard deviations of their sampling distributions, are presented in Table 13.5, columns 1 and 2. The fitted regression function is:

(13.39) $$\hat{Y} = 1.0156 - .04727X_1 - (.5524)\exp(-.1348X_2)$$

The error sum of squares is $SSE = .00329$, with $30 - 4 = 26$ degrees of freedom. Figure 13.5 presents the fitted regression functions for the two locations, together with a plot of the data. The fit seems to be quite good, and residual plots (not shown) did not indicate any noticeable departures from the assumed model.

In order to explore the applicability of large-sample inference procedures here, bootstrap fixed X sampling was employed. One thousand bootstrap samples of size 30 were generated. The estimated bootstrap means and standard deviations for each of the sampling

FIGURE 13.6   **MINITAB Histograms of Bootstrap Sampling Distributions —**
Learning Curve Example.

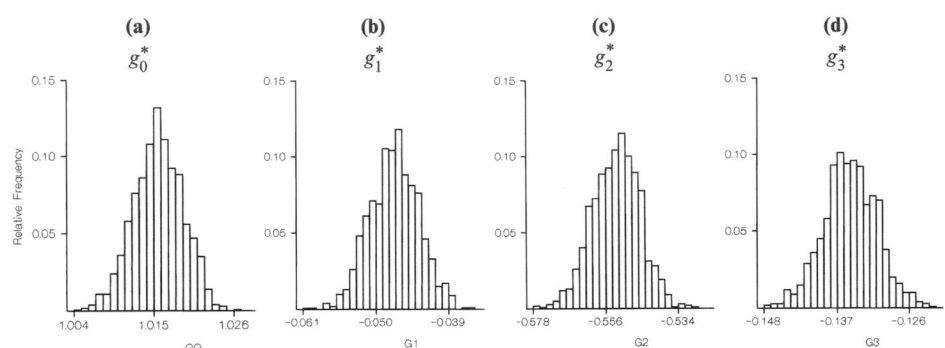

distributions are presented in Table 13.5, columns 3 and 4. Note first that each least squares estimate g_k in column 1 of Table 13.5 is very close to the mean $\bar{g}_k^*$ of its respective bootstrap sampling distribution in column 3, indicating that the estimates have very little bias. Note also that each large-sample standard deviation $s\{g_k\}$ in column 2 of Table 13.5 is fairly close to the respective bootstrap standard deviation $s^*\{g_k^*\}$ in column 4, again supporting the applicability of large-sample inference procedures here. Finally, we present in Figure 13.6 MINITAB plots of the histograms of the four bootstrap sampling distributions. They appear to be consistent with approximately normal sampling distributions. These results all indicate that the sampling behavior of the nonlinear regression estimates is close to linear and therefore support the use of large-sample inferences here.

There was special interest in the parameter γ_1, which reflects the effect of location. An approximate 95 percent confidence interval is to be constructed. We require $t(.975;26) = 2.056$. The estimated standard deviation from Table 13.5 is $s\{g_1\} = .004109$. Hence, the approximate 95 percent confidence limits for γ_1 are $-.04727 \pm 2.056(.004109)$, and the confidence interval for γ_1 is:

$$-.0557 \leq \gamma_1 \leq -.0388$$

An approximate 95 percent confidence interval for γ_1 by the bootstrap reflection method was also obtained for comparative purposes using (10.56). It is:

$$-.0547 \leq \gamma_1 \leq -.0400$$

This is very close to that obtained by large-sample inference procedures. Since γ_1 is seen to be negative, these confidence intervals confirm that location A with its less modern facilities tends to be less efficient.

Comments

1. When learning curve models are fitted to data constituting repeated observations on the same unit, such as efficiency data for the same production unit at different points in time, the error terms may be correlated. Hence, in these situations it is important to ascertain whether or not a model assuming uncorrelated error terms is reasonable. In the learning curve example, a

plot of the residuals against time order did not suggest any serious correlations among the error terms.

2. With learning curve models, it is not uncommon to find that the error variances are unequal. Again, therefore, it is important to check whether the assumption of constancy of error variance is reasonable. In the learning curve example, plots of the residuals against the fitted values and time did not suggest any serious heteroscedasticity problem. ■

Cited References

13.1. Hartley, H. O. "The Modified Gauss-Newton Method for the Fitting of Non-linear Regression Functions by Least Squares," *Technometrics* 3 (1961), pp. 269–80.

13.2. Gallant, A. R. *Nonlinear Statistical Models.* New York: John Wiley & Sons, 1987.

13.3. Kennedy, W. J., Jr., and J. E. Gentle. *Statistical Computing.* New York: Marcel Dekker, 1980.

13.4. Bates, D. M., and D. G. Watts. *Nonlinear Regression Analysis and Its Applications.* New York: John Wiley & Sons, 1988.

13.5. Box, M. J. "Bias in Nonlinear Estimation," *Journal of the Royal Statistical Society B* 33 (1971), pp. 171–201.

13.6. Hougaard, P. "The Appropriateness of the Asymptotic Distribution in a Nonlinear Regression Model in Relation to Curvature," *Journal of the Royal Statistical Society B* 47 (1985), pp. 103–14.

13.7. Ratkowsky, D. A. *Nonlinear Regression Modeling.* New York: Marcel Dekker, 1983.

Problems

√ 13.1. For each of the following response functions, indicate whether it is a linear response function, an intrinsically linear response function, or a nonlinear response function. In the case of an intrinsically linear response function, state how it can be linearized by a suitable transformation:

  a. $f(\mathbf{X}, \boldsymbol{\gamma}) = \exp(\gamma_0 + \gamma_1 X)$

  b. $f(\mathbf{X}, \boldsymbol{\gamma}) = \gamma_0 + \gamma_1(\gamma_2)^{X_1} - \gamma_3 X_2$

  c. $f(\mathbf{X}, \boldsymbol{\gamma}) = \gamma_0 + \dfrac{\gamma_1}{\gamma_0} X$

13.2. For each of the following response functions, indicate whether it is a linear response function, an intrinsically linear response function, or a nonlinear response function. In the case of an intrinsically linear response function, state how it can be linearized by a suitable transformation:

  a. $f(\mathbf{X}, \boldsymbol{\gamma}) = \exp(\gamma_0 + \gamma_1 \log_e X)$

  b. $f(\mathbf{X}, \boldsymbol{\gamma}) = \gamma_0(X_1)^{\gamma_1}(X_2)^{\gamma_2}$

  c. $f(\mathbf{X}, \boldsymbol{\gamma}) = \gamma_0 - \gamma_1(\gamma_2)^X$

√ 13.3. a. Plot the logistic response function:

$$f(\mathbf{X}, \boldsymbol{\gamma}) = \frac{300}{1 + (30)\exp(-1.5X)} \qquad X \geq 0$$

b. What is the asymptote of this response function? For what value of X does the response function reach 90 percent of its asymptote?

13.4. a. Plot the exponential response function:

$$f(\mathbf{X}, \boldsymbol{\gamma}) = 49 - (30)\exp(-1.1X) \qquad X \geq 0$$

b. What is the asymptote of this response function? For what value of X does the response function reach 95 percent of its asymptote?

√ 13.5. **Home computers.** A computer manufacturer hired a market research firm to investigate the relationship between the likelihood a family will purchase a home computer and the price of the home computer. The data that follow are based on replicate surveys done in two similar cities. One thousand heads of households in each city were randomly selected and asked if they would be likely to purchase a home computer at a given price. Ten prices (X, in hundred dollars) were studied, and 100 heads of households in each city were randomly assigned to a given price. The proportion likely to purchase at a given price is denoted by Y.

City A

i:	1	2	3	4	5	6	7	8	9	10
X_i:	1	2.5	5	10	20	30	40	50	75	100
Y_i:	.90	.80	.65	.46	.34	.26	.17	.15	.06	.04

City B

i:	11	12	13	14	15	16	17	18	19	20
X_i:	1	2.5	5	10	20	30	40	50	75	100
Y_i:	.93	.77	.63	.50	.30	.24	.19	.12	.08	.05

No location effect is expected and the data are to be treated as independent replicates at each of the 10 prices. The following exponential model with independent normal error terms is deemed to be appropriate:

$$Y_i = \gamma_0 + \gamma_2 \exp(-\gamma_1 X_i) + \varepsilon_i$$

a. To obtain initial estimates of γ_0, γ_1, and γ_2, note that $f(\mathbf{X}, \boldsymbol{\gamma})$ approaches a lower asymptote γ_0 as X increases without bound. Hence, let $g_0^{(0)} = 0$ and observe that when we ignore the error term, a logarithmic transformation then yields $Y_i' = \beta_0 + \beta_1 X_i$, where $Y_i' = \log_e Y_i$, $\beta_0 = \log_e \gamma_2$, and $\beta_1 = -\gamma_1$. Therefore, fit a linear regression function based on the transformed data and use as initial estimates $g_0^{(0)} = 0$, $g_1^{(0)} = -b_1$, and $g_2^{(0)} = \exp(b_0)$.

b. Using the starting values obtained in part (a), find the least squares estimates of the parameters γ_0, γ_1, and γ_2.

√ 13.6.   Refer to **Home computers** Problem 13.5.

   a.   Plot the estimated nonlinear regression function and the data. Does the fit appear to be adequate?

   b.   Obtain the residuals and plot them against the fitted values and against X on separate graphs. Also obtain a normal probability plot. Does the model appear to be adequate?

√ 13.7.   Refer to **Home computers** Problem 13.5. Assume that large-sample inferences are appropriate here. Conduct a formal approximate test for lack of fit of the nonlinear regression function; use $\alpha = .01$. State the alternatives, decision rule, and conclusion.

√ 13.8.   Refer to **Home computers** Problem 13.5. Assume that the fitted model is appropriate and that large-sample inferences can be employed. Obtain approximate joint confidence intervals for the parameters γ_0, γ_1, and γ_2, using the Bonferroni procedure and a 90 percent family confidence coefficient.

√ 13.9.   Refer to **Home computers** Problem 13.5. A question has been raised whether the two cities are similar enough so that the data can be considered to be replicates. Adding a location effect parameter analogous to (13.38) to the model proposed in Problem 13.5 yields the four-parameter nonlinear regression model:

$$Y_i = \gamma_0 + \gamma_3 X_{i2} + \gamma_2 \exp(-\gamma_1 X_{i1}) + \varepsilon_i$$

where:

$$X_2 = \begin{array}{l} 0 \quad \text{if city A} \\ 1 \quad \text{if city B} \end{array}$$

   a.   Using the same starting values as those obtained in Problem 13.5a and $g_3^{(0)} = 0$, find the least squares estimates of the parameters γ_0, γ_1, γ_2, and γ_3.

   b.   Assume that large-sample inferences can be employed reasonably here. Obtain an approximate 95 percent confidence interval for γ_3. What does this interval indicate about city differences? Is this result consistent with your conclusion in Problem 13.7? Does it have to be? Discuss.

13.10.   **Enzyme kinetics.** In an enzyme kinetics study the velocity of a reaction (Y) is expected to be related to the concentration (X) as follows:

$$Y_i = \frac{\gamma_0 X_i}{\gamma_1 + X_i} + \varepsilon_i$$

Eighteen concentrations have been studied and the results follow:

i:	1	2	3	. . .	16	17	18
X_i:	1	1.5	2	. . .	30	35	40
Y_i:	2.1	2.5	4.9	. . .	19.7	21.3	21.6

   a.   To obtain starting values for γ_0 and γ_1, observe that when the error term is ignored we have $Y_i' = \beta_0 + \beta_1 X_i'$, where $Y_i' = 1/Y_i$, $\beta_0 = 1/\gamma_0$, $\beta_1 = \gamma_1/\gamma_0$, and $X_i' = 1/X_i$. Therefore fit a linear regression function to the transformed data to obtain initial estimates $g_0^{(0)} = 1/b_0$ and $g_1^{(0)} = b_1/b_0$.

   b.   Using the starting values obtained in part (a), find the least squares estimates of the parameters γ_0 and γ_1.

13.11. Refer to **Enzyme kinetics** Problem 13.10.

   a. Plot the estimated nonlinear regression function and the data. Does the fit appear to be adequate?

   b. Obtain the residuals and plot them against the fitted values and against X on separate graphs. Also obtain a normal probability plot. What do your plots show?

   c. Can you conduct an approximate formal lack of fit test here? Explain.

   d. Given that only 18 trials can be made, what are some advantages and disadvantages of considering fewer concentration levels but with some replications, as compared to considering 18 different concentration levels as was done here?

13.12. Refer to **Enzyme kinetics** Problem 13.10. Assume that the fitted model is appropriate and that large-sample inferences can be employed here. (1) Obtain an approximate 95 percent confidence interval for γ_0. (2) Test whether or not $\gamma_1 = 20$; use $\alpha = .05$. State the alternatives, decision rule, and conclusion.

√ 13.13. **Drug responsiveness**. A pharmacologist modeled the responsiveness to a drug using the following nonlinear regression model:

$$Y_i = \gamma_0 - \frac{\gamma_0}{1 + \left(\dfrac{X_i}{\gamma_2}\right)^{\gamma_1}} + \varepsilon_i$$

X denotes the dose level, in coded form, and Y the responsiveness expressed as a percent of the maximum possible responsiveness. In the model, γ_0 is the expected response at saturation, γ_2 is the concentration that produces a half-maximal response, and γ_1 is related to the slope. The data for 19 cases at 13 dose levels follow:

i:	1	2	3	. . .	17	18	19
X_i:	1	2	3	. . .	7	8	9
Y_i:	.5	2.3	3.4	. . .	94.8	96.2	96.4

Obtain least squares estimates of the parameters γ_0, γ_1, and γ_2, using starting values $g_0^{(0)} = 100$, $g_1^{(0)} = 5$, and $g_2^{(0)} = 4.8$.

√ 13.14. Refer to **Drug responsiveness** Problem 13.13.

   a. Plot the estimated nonlinear regression function and the data. Does the fit appear to be adequate?

   b. Obtain the residuals and plot them against the fitted values and against X on separate graphs. Also obtain a normal probability plot. What do your plots show about the adequacy of the regression model?

√ 13.15. Refer to **Drug responsiveness** Problem 13.13. Assume that large-sample inferences are appropriate here. Conduct a formal approximate test for lack of fit of the nonlinear regression function; use $\alpha = .01$. State the alternatives, decision rule, and conclusion.

√ 13.16. Refer to **Drug responsiveness** Problem 13.13. Assume that the fitted model is appropriate and that large-sample inferences can be employed here. Obtain approximate joint confidence intervals for the parameters γ_0, γ_1, and γ_2 using the Bonferroni procedure with a 91 percent family confidence coefficient. Interpret your results.

13.17. **Process yield**. The yield (Y) of a chemical process depends on the temperature (X_1) and pressure (X_2). The following nonlinear regression model is expected to be applicable:

$$Y_i = \gamma_0 (X_{i1})^{\gamma_1} (X_{i2})^{\gamma_2} + \varepsilon_i$$

Prior to beginning full-scale production, 18 tests were undertaken to study the process yield for various temperature and pressure combinations. The results follow.

i:	1	2	3	. . .	16	17	18
X_{i1}:	1	10	100	. . .	1	10	100
X_{i2}:	1	1	1	. . .	100	100	100
Y_i:	12	32	103	. . .	43	128	398

a. To obtain starting values for γ_0, γ_1, and γ_2, note that when we ignore the random error term, a logarithmic transformation yields $Y_i' = \beta_0 + \beta_1 X_{i1}' + \beta_1 X_{i2}'$, where $Y_i' = \log_{10} Y_i$, $\beta_0 = \log_{10} \gamma_0$, $\beta_1 = \gamma_1$, $X_{i1}' = \log_{10} X_{i1}$, $\beta_2 = \gamma_2$, and $X_{i2}' = \log_{10} X_{i2}$. Fit a first-order multiple regression model to the transformed data, and use as starting values $g_0^{(0)} = \text{antilog}_{10} b_0$, $g_1^{(0)} = b_1$, and $g_2^{(0)} = b_2$.

b. Using the starting values obtained in part (a), find the least squares estimates of the parameters γ_0, γ_1, and γ_2.

13.18. Refer to **Process yield** Problem 13.17.

a. Plot the estimated nonlinear regression function and the data. Does the fit appear to be adequate?

b. Obtain the residuals and plot them against $\hat{Y}$, X_1, and X_2 on separate graphs. Also obtain a normal probability plot. What do your plots show about the adequacy of the model?

13.19. Refer to **Process yield** Problem 13.17. Assume that large-sample inferences are appropriate here. Conduct a formal approximate test for lack of fit of the nonlinear regression function; use $\alpha = .05$. State the alternatives, decision rule, and conclusion.

13.20. Refer to **Process yield** Problem 13.17. Assume that the fitted model is appropriate and that large-sample inferences are applicable here.

a. Test the hypotheses $H_0: \gamma_1 = \gamma_2$ against $H_a: \gamma_1 \neq \gamma_2$ using $\alpha = .05$. State the alternatives, decision rule, and conclusion.

b. Obtain approximate joint confidence intervals for the parameters γ_1 and γ_2, using the Bonferroni procedure and a 95 percent family confidence coefficient.

c. What do you conclude about the parameters γ_1 and γ_2 based on the results in parts (a) and (b)?

Exercises

13.21. (Calculus needed.) Refer to **Home computers** Problem 13.5.

a. Obtain the least squares normal equations and show that they are nonlinear in the estimated regression coefficients g_0, g_1, and g_2.

    b. State the likelihood function for the nonlinear regression model, assuming that the error terms are independent $N(0, \sigma^2)$.

13.22. (Calculus needed.) Refer to **Enzyme kinetics** Problem 13.10.

    a. Obtain the least squares normal equations and show that they are nonlinear in the estimated regression coefficients g_0 and g_1.

    b. State the likelihood function for the nonlinear regression model, assuming that the error terms are independent $N(0, \sigma^2)$.

13.23. (Calculus needed.) Refer to **Process yield** Problem 13.17.

    a. Obtain the least squares normal equations and show that they are nonlinear in the estimated regression coefficients g_0, g_1, and g_2.

    b. State the likelihood function for the nonlinear regression model, assuming that the error terms are independent $N(0, \sigma^2)$.

13.24. Refer to **Drug responsiveness** Problem 13.13.

    a. Assuming that $E\{\varepsilon_i\} = 0$, show that:

$$E\{Y\} = \gamma_0 \left(\frac{A}{1+A} \right)$$

where:

$$A = \exp[\gamma_1 (\log_e X - \log_e \gamma_2)] = \exp(\beta_0 + \beta_1 X')$$

and $\beta_0 = -\gamma_1 \log_e \gamma_2$, $\beta_1 = \gamma_1$, and $X' = \log_e X$.

    b. Assuming γ_0 is known, show that:

$$\frac{E\{Y'\}}{1 - E\{Y'\}} = \exp(\beta_0 + \beta_1 X')$$

where $Y' = Y/\gamma_0$.

    c. What transformation do these results suggest for obtaining a simple linear regression function in the transformed variables?

    d. How can starting values for finding the least squares estimates of the nonlinear regression parameters be obtained from the estimates of the linear regression coefficients?

Projects

13.25. Refer to **Enzyme kinetics** Problem 13.10. Starting values for finding the least squares estimates of the nonlinear regression model parameters are to be obtained by a grid search. The following bounds for the two parameters have been specified:

$$5 \le \gamma_0 \le 65$$

$$5 \le \gamma_1 \le 65$$

Obtain 49 grid points by using all possible combinations of the boundary values and five other equally spaced points for each parameter range. Evaluate the least squares criterion (13.15) for each grid point and identify the point providing the best fit. Does this point give reasonable starting values here?

13.26. Refer to **Process yield** Problem 13.17. Starting values for finding the least squares estimates of the nonlinear regression model parameters are to be obtained by a grid search. The following bounds for the parameters have been postulated:

$$1 \leq \gamma_0 \leq 21$$

$$.2 \leq \gamma_1 \leq .8$$

$$.1 \leq \gamma_2 \leq .7$$

Obtain 27 grid points by using all possible combinations of the boundary values and the midpoint for each of the parameter ranges. Evaluate the least squares criterion (13.15) for each grid point and identify the point providing the best fit. Does this point give reasonable starting values here?

13.27. Refer to **Home computers** Problem 13.5.

    a. To check on the appropriateness of large-sample inferences here, generate 1,000 bootstrap samples of size 20 using the fixed X sampling procedure. For each bootstrap sample, obtain the least squares estimates g_0^*, g_1^*, and g_2^*.

    b. Plot histograms of the bootstrap sampling distributions of g_0^*, g_1^*, and g_2^*. Do these distributions appear to be approximately normal?

    c. Compute the means and standard deviations of the bootstrap sampling distributions for g_0^*, g_1^*, and g_2^*. Are the bootstrap means and standard deviations close to the final least squares estimates?

    d. Obtain a confidence interval for γ_1 using the reflection method in (10.56) and confidence coefficient .9667. How does this interval compare with the one obtained in Problem 13.8 by the large-sample inference method?

    e. What are the implications of your findings in parts (b), (c), and (d) about the appropriateness of large-sample inferences here? Discuss.

13.28. Refer to **Enzyme kinetics** Problem 13.10.

    a. To check on the appropriateness of large-sample inferences here, generate 1,000 bootstrap samples of size 18 using the fixed X sampling procedure. For each bootstrap sample, obtain the least squares estimates g_0^* and g_1^*.

    b. Plot histograms of the bootstrap sampling distributions of g_0^* and g_1^*. Do these distributions appear to be approximately normal?

    c. Compute the means and standard deviations of the bootstrap sampling distributions for g_0^* and g_1^*. Are the bootstrap means and standard deviations close to the final least squares estimates?

    d. Obtain a confidence interval for γ_0 using the reflection method in (10.56) and confidence coefficient .95. How does this interval compare with the one obtained in Problem 13.12 by the large-sample inference method?

    e. What are the implications of your findings in parts (b), (c), and (d) about the appropriateness of large-sample inferences here? Discuss.

13.29. Refer to **Drug responsiveness** Problem 13.13.

   a. To check on the appropriateness of large-sample inferences here, generate 1,000 bootstrap samples of size 19 using the fixed X sampling procedure. For each bootstrap sample, obtain the least squares estimates g_0^*, g_1^*, and g_2^*.

   b. Plot histograms of the bootstrap sampling distributions of g_0^*, g_1^*, and g_2^*. Do these distributions appear to be approximately normal?

   c. Compute the means and standard deviations of the bootstrap sampling distributions for g_0^*, g_1^*, and g_2^*. Are the bootstrap means and standard deviations close to the final least squares estimates?

   d. Obtain a confidence interval for γ_2 using the reflection method in (10.56) and confidence coefficient .97. How does this interval compare with the one obtained in Problem 13.16 by the large-sample inference method?

   e. What are the implications of your findings in parts (b), (c), and (d) about the appropriateness of large-sample inferences here? Discuss.

13.30. Refer to **Process yield** Problem 13.17.

   a. To check on the appropriateness of large-sample inferences here, generate 1,000 bootstrap samples of size 18 using the fixed X sampling procedure. For each bootstrap sample, obtain the least squares estimates g_0^*, g_1^*, and g_2^*.

   b. Plot histograms of the bootstrap sampling distributions of g_0^*, g_1^*, and g_2^*. Do these distributions appear to be approximately normal?

   c. Compute the means and standard deviations of the bootstrap sampling distributions for g_0^*, g_1^*, and g_2^*. Are the bootstrap means and standard deviations close to the final least squares estimates?

   d. Obtain a confidence interval for γ_1 using the reflection method in (10.56) and confidence coefficient .975. How does this interval compare with the one obtained in Problem 13.20b by the large-sample inference method?

   e. What are the implications of your findings in parts (b), (c), and (d) about the appropriateness of large-sample inferences here? Discuss.

14 Logistic Regression, Poisson Regression, and Generalized Linear Models

In Chapter 13 we considered nonlinear regression models where the error terms are normally distributed. In this chapter, we take up nonlinear regression models for two important cases where the response outcomes are discrete and the error terms are not normally distributed. First, we consider the logistic nonlinear regression model for use when the response variable is qualitative with two possible outcomes, such as financial status of firm (sound status, headed toward insolvency) or blood pressure status (high blood pressure, not high blood pressure). This model can be extended when the qualitative variable has more than two possible outcomes; for instance, blood pressure status might be classified as high, normal or low.

Next we take up the Poisson regression model for use when the response variable is a count where large counts are a rare event, such as the number of tornadoes in an upper Midwest locality during a year. Finally, we explain that all of the nonlinear regression models discussed in Chapter 13 and in this chapter, as well as the normal error linear models discussed earlier, belong to a family of regression models called generalized linear models.

The nonlinear regression models presented in this chapter are appropriate for analyzing data arising from either observational studies or from experimental studies based on a completely randomized design.

14.1 Regression Models with Binary Response Variable

In a variety of regression applications, the response variable of interest has only two possible qualitative outcomes, and therefore can be represented by a binary indicator variable taking on values 0 and 1.

1. In an analysis of whether or not business firms have an industrial relations department, according to size of firm, the response variable was defined to have the two possible outcomes: firm has industrial relations department, firm does not have industrial relations department. These outcomes may be coded 1 and 0, respectively (or vice versa).

2. In a study of labor force participation of wives, as a function of age of wife, number of children, and husband's income, the response variable Y was defined to have the two possible outcomes: wife in labor force, wife not in labor force. Again, these outcomes may be coded 1 and 0, respectively.

3. In a study of liability insurance possession, according to age of head of household, amount of liquid assets, and type of occupation of head of household, the response variable Y was defined to have the two possible outcomes: household has liability insurance, household does not have liability insurance. These outcomes again may be coded 1 and 0, respectively.

4. In a longitudinal study of coronary heart disease as a function of age, gender, smoking history, cholesterol level, percent of ideal body weight, and blood pressure, the response variable Y was defined to have the two possible outcomes: person developed heart disease during the study, person did not develop heart disease during the study. These outcomes again may be coded 1 and 0, respectively.

These examples show the wide range of applications in which the response variable is binary and hence may be represented by an indicator variable. A binary response variable, taking on the values 0 and 1, is said to involve *binary responses* or *dichotomous responses*. We consider first the meaning of the response function when the outcome variable is binary, and then we take up some special problems that arise with this type of response variable.

Meaning of Response Function when Outcome Variable Is Binary

Consider the simple linear regression model:

$$(14.1) \qquad Y_i = \beta_0 + \beta_1 X_i + \varepsilon_i \qquad Y_i = 0, 1$$

where the outcome Y_i is binary taking on the value of either 0 or 1. The expected response $E\{Y_i\}$ has a special meaning in this case. Since $E\{\varepsilon_i\} = 0$ we have:

$$(14.2) \qquad E\{Y_i\} = \beta_0 + \beta_1 X_i$$

Consider Y_i to be a Bernoulli random variable for which we can state the probability distribution as follows:

Y_i	Probability
1	$P(Y_i = 1) = \pi_i$
0	$P(Y_i = 0) = 1 - \pi_i$

Thus, π_i is the probability that $Y_i = 1$, and $1 - \pi_i$ is the probability that $Y_i = 0$. By the definition of expected value of a random variable in (A.12), we obtain:

$$(14.3) \qquad E\{Y_i\} = 1(\pi_i) + 0(1 - \pi_i) = \pi_i$$

Equating (14.2) and (14.3), we thus find:

$$(14.4) \qquad E\{Y_i\} = \beta_0 + \beta_1 X_i = \pi_i$$

The mean response $E\{Y_i\} = \beta_0 + \beta_1 X_i$ as given by the response function is therefore simply the probability that $Y_i = 1$ when the level of the predictor variable is X_i. This interpretation of the mean response applies whether the response function is a simple linear one, as here, or a complex multiple regression one. The mean response, when the outcome variable is a 0, 1 indicator variable, always represents the probability that $Y = 1$ for the given levels of the predictor variables. Figure 14.1 illustrates a simple linear response function for an indicator outcome variable. Here, the indicator variable Y refers to whether or not a firm has an industrial relations department, and the predictor variable X is size of firm. The response

FIGURE 14.1   **Illustration of Response Function when Response Variable Is Binary—Industrial Relations Department Example.**

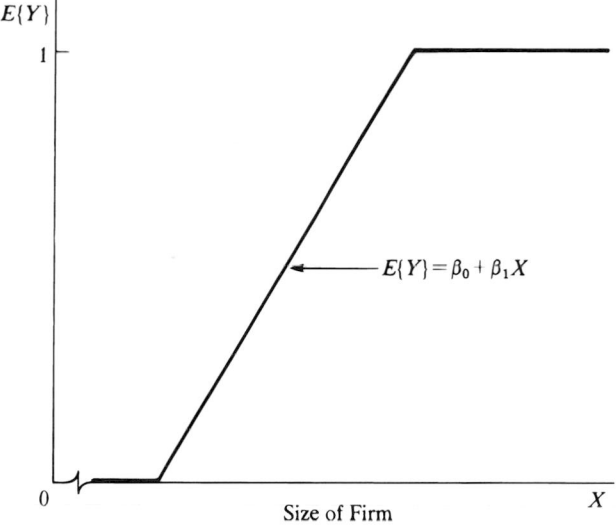

Probability That Firm Has
Industrial Relations Department

$E\{Y\}$

1

$E\{Y\} = \beta_0 + \beta_1 X$

0

Size of Firm

X

function in Figure 14.1 shows the probability that firms of given size have an industrial relations department.

Special Problems when Response Variable Is Binary

Special problems arise, unfortunately, when the response variable is an indicator variable. We consider three of these now, using a simple linear regression model as an illustration.

1. *Nonnormal Error Terms.* For a binary 0, 1 response variable, each error term $\varepsilon_i = Y_i - (\beta_0 + \beta_1 X_i)$ can take on only two values:

(14.5a)   When $Y_i = 1$: $\varepsilon_i = 1 - \beta_0 - \beta_1 X_i$

(14.5b)   When $Y_i = 0$: $\varepsilon_i = -\beta_0 - \beta_1 X_i$

Clearly, normal error regression model (2.1), which assumes that the ε_i are normally distributed, is not appropriate.

2. *Nonconstant Error Variance.* Another problem with the error terms ε_i is that they do not have equal variances when the response variable is an indicator variable. To see this, we shall obtain $\sigma^2\{Y_i\}$ for the simple linear regression model (14.1), utilizing (A.15):

$$\sigma^2\{Y_i\} = E\{(Y_i - E\{Y_i\})^2\} = (1 - \pi_i)^2 \pi_i + (0 - \pi_i)^2 (1 - \pi_i)$$

or:

(14.6) $$\sigma^2\{Y_i\} = \pi_i(1 - \pi_i) = (E\{Y_i\})(1 - E\{Y_i\})$$

The variance of ε_i is the same as that of Y_i because $\varepsilon_i = Y_i - \pi_i$ and π_i is a constant:

$$(14.7) \qquad \sigma^2\{\varepsilon_i\} = \pi_i(1 - \pi_i) = (E\{Y_i\})(1 - E\{Y_i\})$$

or:

$$(14.7a) \qquad \sigma^2\{\varepsilon_i\} = (\beta_0 + \beta_1 X_i)(1 - \beta_0 - \beta_1 X_i)$$

Note from (14.7a) that $\sigma^2\{\varepsilon_i\}$ depends on X_i. Hence, the error variances will differ at different levels of X, and ordinary least squares will no longer be optimal.

3. *Constraints on Response Function.* Since the response function represents probabilities when the outcome variable is a 0, 1 indicator variable, the mean responses should be constrained as follows:

$$(14.8) \qquad 0 \le E\{Y\} = \pi \le 1$$

Many response functions do not automatically possess this constraint. A linear response function, for instance, may fall outside the constraint limits within the range of the predictor variable in the scope of the model.

The difficulties created by the need for the restriction in (14.8) on the response function are the most serious. One could use weighted least squares to handle the problem of unequal error variances. In addition, with large sample sizes the method of least squares provides estimators that are asymptotically normal under quite general conditions, even if the distribution of the error terms is far from normal. However, the constraint on the mean responses to fall between 0 and 1 frequently will rule out a linear response function. In the industrial relations department example, for instance, use of a linear response function subject to the constraints on the mean response might require a probability of 0 for the mean response for all small firms and a probability of 1 for the mean response for all large firms, as illustrated in Figure 14.1. Such a model would often be considered unreasonable. Instead, a model where the probabilities 0 and 1 are reached asymptotically, as illustrated in Figure 14.2, would usually be more appropriate.

14.2 Simple Logistic Response Function

Both theoretical and empirical considerations suggest that when the response variable is binary, the shape of the response function will frequently be curvilinear. Figures 14.2a and 14.2b exhibit, for the case of a single predictor variable, two curvilinear response functions that have been found appropriate in many instances involving a binary response variable. Note that these response functions are shaped either as a tilted S or as a reverse tilted S, and that they are approximately linear except at the ends. These response functions are often referred to as *sigmoidal*. They have asymptotes at 0 and 1 and thus automatically meet the constraints on $E\{Y\}$ in (14.8).

The response functions plotted in Figures 14.2a and 14.2b are called *logistic response functions* and are of the form:

$$(14.9) \qquad E\{Y\} = \frac{\exp(\beta_0 + \beta_1 X)}{1 + \exp(\beta_0 + \beta_1 X)}$$

FIGURE 14.2   **Examples of Logistic Response Functions.**

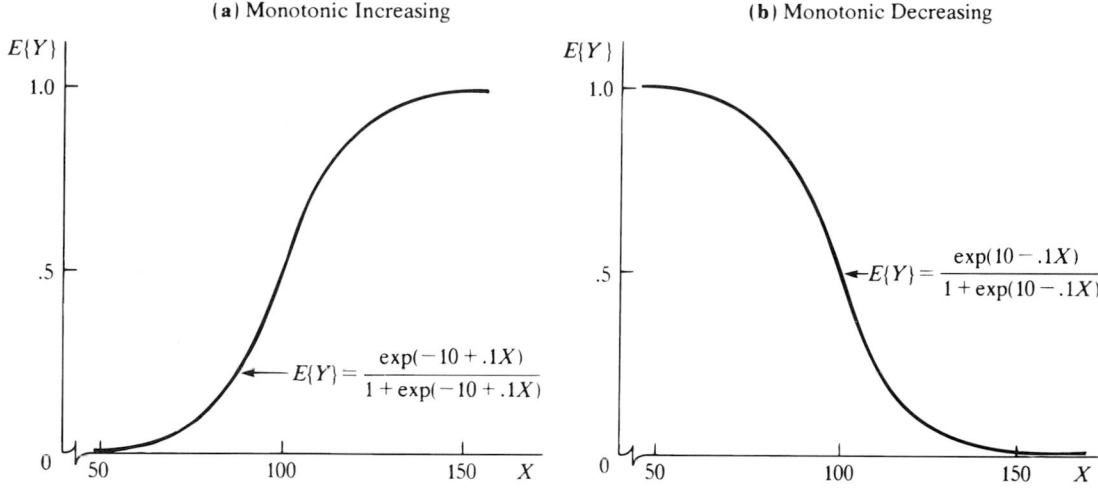

(a) Monotonic Increasing

(b) Monotonic Decreasing

$$E\{Y\} = \frac{\exp(-10+.1X)}{1+\exp(-10+.1X)}$$

$$E\{Y\} = \frac{\exp(10-.1X)}{1+\exp(10-.1X)}$$

An equivalent form of (14.9) is given by:

(14.9a)
$$E\{Y\} = [1 + \exp(-\beta_0 - \beta_1 X)]^{-1}$$

Properties of Logistic Response Function

As shown by Figure 14.2, a logistic response function is either monotonic increasing or monotonic decreasing, depending on the sign of β_1. Further, it is almost linear in the range where $E\{Y\}$ is between .2 and .8 and gradually approaches 0 and 1 at the two ends of the X range.

Another interesting property of a logistic response function is that it can be linearized easily. Let us denote $E\{Y\}$ by π, since the mean response is a probability when the response variable is a 0, 1 indicator variable. Then if we make the transformation:

(14.10)
$$\pi' = \log_e\left(\frac{\pi}{1-\pi}\right)$$

we obtain from (14.9):

(14.11)
$$\pi' = \beta_0 + \beta_1 X$$

The transformation (14.10) is called the *logit transformation* of the probability π. The ratio $\pi/(1-\pi)$ in the logit transformation is called the *odds*. The transformed response function (14.11) is referred to as the *logit response function*, and π' is called the *logit mean response*.

Note from (14.11) that the logit mean response π' has a range from $-\infty$ to ∞ as X ranges within $-\infty$ to ∞.

Uses of Logistic Response Function

Logistic response functions, like the other response functions that we have considered, are used for describing the nature of the relationship between the mean response (e.g., probability of heart disease) and one (or more) predictor variable(s). They are also used for making predictions, such as whether a person will purchase an automobile in the coming year, given the person's income; whether a person will develop heart disease, given the person's cholesterol level; and the like.

For both descriptive and prediction purposes, we first need to estimate the parameters of the logistic response function. We turn next to the fitting of the logistic response function in (14.9).

Comments

1. The logistic response function sometimes is motivated by threshold theory. Consider the breaking strength of concrete blocks, measured in pounds per square inch. Each block is assumed to have a threshold T_i, such that it will break if pressure equal to or greater than T_i is applied and it will not break if smaller pressure is applied. A block can be tested for only one pressure level, since some weakening of the block occurs with the first test. Thus, it is not possible to find the actual threshold of each block, but only whether or not the threshold level is above or below a particular pressure applied to the block. Of course, different pressures can be applied to different blocks in order to obtain information about the breaking strength thresholds of the blocks in the population.

Let $Y_i = 1$ if the block breaks when pressure X_i is applied, and $Y_i = 0$ if the block does not break. The earlier statement of threshold theory then implies:

$$(14.12) \qquad \begin{aligned} Y_i &= 1 \qquad \text{whenever } T_i \leq X_i \\ Y_i &= 0 \qquad \text{whenever } T_i > X_i \end{aligned}$$

It follows that for given pressure X_i applied to a block selected at random:

$$(14.13) \qquad \pi_i = P(Y_i = 1|X_i) = P(T_i \leq X_i)$$

Now $P(T \leq X)$ is the cumulative probability distribution of the thresholds of all blocks in the population. If this cumulative probability distribution of thresholds is logistic:

$$P(T \leq X) = \frac{\exp(\beta_0 + \beta_1 X)}{1 + \exp(\beta_0 + \beta_1 X)}$$

we arrive at the logistic response function (14.9).

2. A curvilinear response function of almost the same shape as logistic function (14.9) is obtained by transforming π by means of the cumulative normal distribution. This transformation is called the *probit transformation*. Reference 14.1 describes this transformation. The probit regression model is less flexible than the logistic regression model because it cannot be readily extended to more than one predictor variable. Also, formal inference procedures are more difficult to carry out with the probit regression model. In many instances the logistic and probit regression models agree closely except near the asymptotes.

The probit regression model can be obtained by the same threshold theory as explained in Comment 1 for the logistic regression model, except that the probability distribution of thresholds is now assumed to be normal.

3. Another curvilinear response function of almost the same shape as the logistic response function is the *complementary log-log transformation* of the probability π given by $\log_e[-\log_e(1-\pi)]$. This function transforms the probability π, whose range is 0 to 1, to a value from $-\infty$ to ∞. Unlike the logistic and probit transformations, this response function is not symmetric about $\pi = .5$. In many instances the complementary log-log transformation agrees quite closely with the logistic transformation. ∎

14.3 Simple Logistic Regression

We shall use the method of maximum likelihood to estimate the parameters of the logistic response function. This method is well suited to deal with the problems associated with the responses Y_i being binary. As explained in Section 1.8, we first need to develop the joint probability function of the sample observations. Instead of using the normal distribution for the Y observations as earlier in (1.26), we now need to utilize the Bernoulli distribution for a binary random variable.

Simple Logistic Regression Model

First, we require a formal statement of the simple logistic regression model. Recall that when the response variable is binary, taking on the values 1 and 0 with probabilities π and $1 - \pi$, respectively, Y is a Bernoulli random variable with parameter $E\{Y\} = \pi$. We could state the simple logistic regression model in the usual form:

$$Y_i = E\{Y_i\} + \varepsilon_i$$

Since the distribution of the error term ε_i depends on the Bernoulli distribution of the response Y_i, it is preferable to state the simple logistic regression model in the following fashion:

(14.14) Y_i are independent Bernoulli random variables with expected values $E\{Y_i\} = \pi_i$, where:

$$E\{Y_i\} = \pi_i = \frac{\exp(\beta_0 + \beta_1 X_i)}{1 + \exp(\beta_0 + \beta_1 X_i)}$$

The X observations are assumed to be known constants. Alternatively, if the X observations are random, $E\{Y_i\}$ is viewed as a conditional mean, given the value of X_i.

Likelihood Function

Since each Y_i observation is an ordinary Bernoulli random variable, where:

$$P(Y_i = 1) = \pi_i$$
$$P(Y_i = 0) = 1 - \pi_i$$

we can represent its probability distribution as follows:

(14.15) $f_i(Y_i) = \pi_i^{Y_i}(1 - \pi_i)^{1-Y_i} \qquad Y_i = 0, 1; \quad i = 1, \ldots, n$

Note that $f_i(1) = \pi_i$ and $f_i(0) = 1 - \pi_i$. Hence, $f_i(Y_i)$ simply represents the probability that $Y_i = 1$ or 0.

Since the Y_i observations are independent, their joint probability function is:

$$(14.16) \qquad g(Y_1, \ldots, Y_n) = \prod_{i=1}^{n} f_i(Y_i) = \prod_{i=1}^{n} \pi_i^{Y_i} (1 - \pi_i)^{1-Y_i}$$

Again, it will be easier to find the maximum likelihood estimates by working with the logarithm of the joint probability function:

$$(14.17) \qquad \log_e g(Y_1, \ldots, Y_n) = \log_e \prod_{i=1}^{n} \pi_i^{Y_i} (1 - \pi_i)^{1-Y_i}$$

$$= \sum_{i=1}^{n} \left[Y_i \log_e \left(\frac{\pi_i}{1 - \pi_i} \right) \right] + \sum_{i=1}^{n} \log_e (1 - \pi_i)$$

Since $E\{Y_i\} = \pi_i$ for a binary variable, it follows from (14.9a) that:

$$(14.18) \qquad 1 - \pi_i = [1 + \exp(\beta_0 + \beta_1 X_i)]^{-1}$$

Furthermore, from (14.10) and (14.11), we obtain:

$$(14.19) \qquad \log_e \left(\frac{\pi_i}{1 - \pi_i} \right) = \beta_0 + \beta_1 X_i$$

Hence, (14.17) can be expressed as follows:

$$(14.20) \qquad \log_e L(\beta_0, \beta_1) = \sum_{i=1}^{n} Y_i (\beta_0 + \beta_1 X_i) - \sum_{i=1}^{n} \log_e [1 + \exp(\beta_0 + \beta_1 X_i)]$$

where $L(\beta_0, \beta_1)$ replaces $g(Y_1, \ldots, Y_n)$ to show explicitly that we now view this function as the likelihood function of the parameters to be estimated, given the sample observations.

Maximum Likelihood Estimation

The maximum likelihood estimates of β_0 and β_1 in the simple logistic regression model are those values of β_0 and β_1 that maximize the log-likelihood function in (14.20). No closed-form solution exists for the values of β_0 and β_1 in (14.20) that maximize the log-likelihood function. Computer-intensive numerical search procedures are therefore required to find the maximum likelihood estimates b_0 and b_1. There are several widely used numerical search procedures; one of these employs iteratively reweighted least squares, which we shall explain in Section 14.4. Reference 14.2 provides a discussion of several numerical search procedures for finding maximum likelihood estimates. We shall rely on standard statistical software programs specifically designed for logistic regression to obtain the maximum likelihood estimates b_0 and b_1.

Once the maximum likelihood estimates b_0 and b_1 are found, we substitute these values into the response function in (14.14) to obtain the fitted response function. We shall use $\hat{\pi}_i$ to denote the fitted value for the ith case:

$$(14.21) \qquad \hat{\pi}_i = \frac{\exp(b_0 + b_1 X_i)}{1 + \exp(b_0 + b_1 X_i)}$$

The fitted logistic response function is as follows:

$$(14.22) \qquad \hat{\pi} = \frac{\exp(b_0 + b_1 X)}{1 + \exp(b_0 + b_1 X)}$$

If we utilize the logit transformation in (14.10), we can express the fitted response function in (14.22) as follows:

$$(14.23) \qquad \hat{\pi}' = b_0 + b_1 X$$

where:

$$(14.23a) \qquad \hat{\pi}' = \log_e \left(\frac{\hat{\pi}}{1 - \hat{\pi}} \right)$$

We call (14.23) the *fitted logit response function.*

Once the fitted logistic response function has been obtained, the usual next steps are to examine the appropriateness of the fitted response function and, if the fit is good, to make a variety of inferences and predictions. We shall postpone a discussion of how to examine the goodness of fit of a logistic response function and how to make inferences and predictions until we have considered the multiple logistic regression model with a number of predictor variables.

Example

A systems analyst studied the effect of computer programming experience on ability to complete within a specified time a complex programming task, including debugging. Twenty-five persons were selected for the study. They had varying amounts of programming experience (measured in months of experience), as shown in Table 14.1a, column 1. All persons were given the same programming task, and the results of their success in the task are shown in column 2. The results are coded in binary fashion: $Y = 1$ if the task was completed successfully in the allotted time, and $Y = 0$ if the task was not completed successfully. Figure 14.3 contains a scatter plot of the data. This plot is not too informative because of the nature of the response variable, other than to indicate that ability to complete the task successfully appears to increase with amount of experience. A loess nonparametric response curve was fitted to the data and is also shown in Figure 14.3. A sigmoidal S-shaped response function is clearly suggested by the nonparametric fit. It was therefore decided to fit the logistic regression model (14.14).

A standard logistic regression package was run on the data. The results are contained in Table 14.1b. Since $b_0 = -3.0597$ and $b_1 = .1615$, the estimated logistic regression function (14.22) is:

$$(14.24) \qquad \hat{\pi} = \frac{\exp(-3.0597 + .1615X)}{1 + \exp(-3.0597 + .1615X)}$$

The fitted values are given in Table 14.1a, column 3. For instance, the estimated mean response for $i = 1$, where $X_1 = 14$, is:

$$\hat{\pi}_1 = \frac{\exp[-3.0597 + .1615(14)]}{1 + \exp[-3.0597 + .1615(14)]} = .310$$

TABLE 14.1   **Data and Maximum Likelihood Estimates—Programming Task Example.**

(a) Data

Person i	(1) Months of Experience X_i	(2) Task Success Y_i	(3) Fitted Value $\hat{\pi}_i$	(4) Deviance Residual dev_i
1	14	0	.310	−.862
2	29	0	.835	−1.899
3	6	0	.110	−.483
4	25	1	.727	.799
. . .	. . .	. . .	. . .	. . .
23	28	1	.812	.646
24	22	1	.621	.976
25	8	1	.146	1.962

(b) Maximum Likelihood Estimates

Regression Coefficient	Estimated Regression Coefficient	Estimated Standard Deviation	Estimated Odds Ratio
β_0	−3.0597	1.259	—
β_1	.1615	.0650	1.175

FIGURE 14.3   **Scatter Plot and Loess Curve—Programming Task Example.**

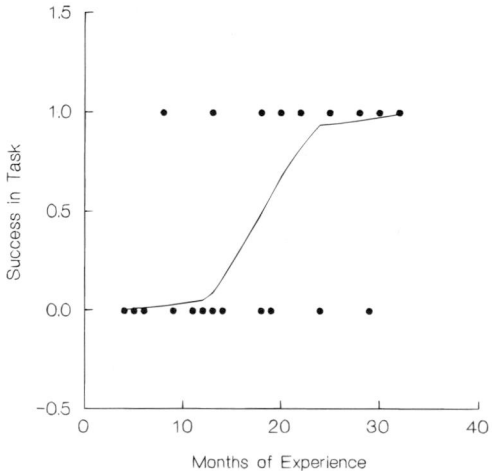

This fitted value is the estimated probability that a person with 14 months experience will successfully complete the programming task.

Interpretation of b_1

The interpretation of the estimated regression coefficient b_1 in the fitted logistic response function (14.22) is not the straightforward interpretation of the slope in a linear regression model. The reason is that the effect of a unit increase in X varies for the logistic regression model according to the location of the starting point on the X scale. An interpretation of b_1 is found in the property of the fitted logistic function that the estimated odds $\hat{\pi}/(1-\hat{\pi})$ are multiplied by $\exp(b_1)$ for any unit increase in X.

To see this, we consider the value of the fitted logit response function (14.23) at $X = X_j$:

$$\hat{\pi}'(X_j) = b_0 + b_1 X_j$$

The notation $\hat{\pi}'(X_j)$ indicates specifically the X level associated with the fitted value. We also consider the value of the fitted logit response function at $X = X_j + 1$:

$$\hat{\pi}'(X_j + 1) = b_0 + b_1(X_j + 1)$$

The difference between the two fitted values is simply:

$$\hat{\pi}'(X_j + 1) - \hat{\pi}'(X_j) = b_1$$

Now according to (14.23a), $\hat{\pi}'(X_j)$ is the logarithm of the estimated odds when $X = X_j$; we shall denote it by $\log_e(\text{odds}_1)$. Similarly, $\hat{\pi}'(X_j + 1)$ is the logarithm of the estimated odds when $X = X_j + 1$; we shall denote it by $\log_e(\text{odds}_2)$. Hence, the difference between the two fitted logit response values can be expressed as follows:

$$\log_e(\text{odds}_2) - \log_e(\text{odds}_1) = \log_e\left(\frac{\text{odds}_2}{\text{odds}_1}\right) = b_1$$

Taking antilogs of each side, we see that the estimated ratio of the odds, called the *odds ratio* and denoted by $\widehat{OR}$, equals $\exp(b_1)$.

$$(14.25) \qquad\qquad \widehat{OR} = \frac{\text{odds}_2}{\text{odds}_1} = \exp(b_1)$$

Example.   For the programming task example, we see from Figure 14.3 that the probability of success increases sharply with experience. Specifically, Table 14.1b shows that the odds ratio is $\widehat{OR} = \exp(b_1) = \exp(.1615) = 1.175$, so that the odds increase by 17.5 percent with each additional month of experience.

Since a unit increase of one month is quite small, the estimated odds ratio of 1.175 may not adequately show the change in odds for a longer difference in time. In general, the estimated odds ratio when there is a difference of c units of X is $\exp(cb_1)$. For example, should we wish to compare individuals with little experience to those with extensive experience, say 10 months versus 25 months so that $c = 15$, then the odds ratio would be estimated to be $\exp[15(.1615)] = 11.3$. This indicates that the odds of completing the task increase over 11-fold for experienced persons compared to relatively inexperienced persons.

Note

The odds ratio interpretation of the estimated regression coefficient b_1 makes the logistic regression model especially attractive for modeling and interpreting epidemiologic studies. ∎

Repeat Observations

In some cases, particularly for designed experiments, a number of repeat observations are obtained at several levels of the predictor variable X. For instance, a pricing experiment involved showing a new product to 1,000 consumers, providing information about it, and then asking each consumer whether he or she would buy the product at a given price. Five prices were studied, and 200 persons were exposed to each price. The response variable here is binary (would purchase, would not purchase); the predictor variable is price and has five levels.

When repeat observations are present, the log-likelihood function in (14.20) can be simplified. We shall denote the X levels at which repeat observations are obtained by $X_1, \ldots, X_c$. The number of observations at level X_j is denoted by n_j ($j = 1, \ldots, c$), and R_j denotes the number of 1s at level X_j. The proportion of 1s at level X_j is denoted by p_j:

(14.26)
$$p_j = \frac{R_j}{n_j}$$

The log-likelihood function in (14.20) then can be stated as follows:

(14.27)
$$\log_e L(\beta_0, \beta_1) = \sum_{j=1}^{c} \left\{ \log_e \binom{n_j}{R_j} + R_j(\beta_0 + \beta_1 X_j) - n_j \log_e[1 + \exp(\beta_0 + \beta_1 X_j)] \right\}$$

where:

$$\binom{n_j}{R_j} = \frac{n_j!}{R_j!(n_j - R_j)!}$$

The factorial notation $a!$ represents $a(a-1)(a-2)\cdots 1$.

Example.   In a study of the effectiveness of coupons offering a price reduction on a given product, 1,000 homes were selected and a coupon and advertising material for the product were mailed to each. The coupons offered different price reductions (5, 10, 15, 20, and 30 dollars), and 200 homes were assigned at random to each of the price reduction categories. The predictor variable X in this study is the amount of price reduction, and the response variable Y is a binary variable indicating whether or not the coupon was redeemed within a six-month period.

Table 14.2 contains the data for this study. X_j denotes the price reduction offered by a coupon, n_j the number of households that received a coupon with price reduction X_j, R_j the number of these households that redeemed the coupon, and p_j the proportion of households receiving a coupon with price reduction X_j that redeemed the coupon. The logistic regression model (14.14) was fitted by a regression package and the fitted response function was found to be:

(14.28)
$$\hat{\pi} = \frac{\exp(-2.04435 + .096834X)}{1 + \exp(-2.04435 + .096834X)}$$

TABLE 14.2   Data for Coupon Effectiveness Example.

Level j	(1) Price Reduction X_j	(2) Number of Households n_j	(3) Number of Coupons Redeemed R_j	(4) Proportion of Coupons Redeemed p_j
1	5	200	30	.150
2	10	200	55	.275
3	15	200	70	.350
4	20	200	100	.500
5	30	200	137	.685

FIGURE 14.4   Plot of Proportions of Coupons Redeemed and Fitted Logistic Response Function—Coupon Effectiveness Example.

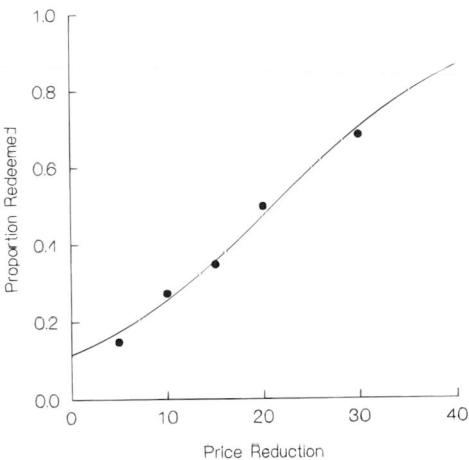

Figure 14.4 shows the fitted response function, as well as the proportions of coupons redeemed at each of the X_j levels. The logistic response function appears to provide a very good fit. The odds ratio here is:

$$\widehat{OR} = \exp(b_1) = \exp(.096834) = 1.102$$

Hence, the odds of a coupon being redeemed are estimated to increase by 10.2 percent with each one dollar increase in the coupon value, that is, with each one dollar reduction in price.

Note

The maximum likelihood estimates b_0 and b_1, when the number of replicate observations n_j at each X_j is large, can be obtained by iteratively reweighted least squares. It can be shown that the estimated variance of p'_j:

(14.29)
$$p'_j = \log_e\left(\frac{p_j}{1 - p_j}\right)$$

is approximately as follows when the sample sizes n_j are large:

(14.30)
$$s^2\{p'_j\} = \frac{1}{n_j p_j (1 - p_j)}$$

Hence, the weights to be used for weighted least squares in the initial regressing of p' on X for fitting the ordinary linear regression function $\pi' = \beta_0 + \beta_1 X$ are:

(14.31)
$$w_j = n_j p_j (1 - p_j)$$

The estimates b_0 and b_1 are then placed in the fitted logistic regression function to obtain the fitted values $\hat{\pi}_j$ in (14.21) for each of the X_j. These estimated probabilities are then used to revise the weights w_j in (14.31), and a new weighted least squares fit when regressing p' on X is obtained. The weights are then revised again, and a new weighted regression fit is obtained. This process continues until the values of b_0 and b_1 stabilize. ∎

14.4   Multiple Logistic Regression

Multiple Logistic Regression Model

The simple logistic regression model (14.14) is easily extended to more than one predictor variable. In fact, several predictor variables are usually required with logistic regression to obtain adequate description and useful predictions.

In extending the simple logistic regression model, we simply replace $\beta_0 + \beta_1 X$ in (14.14) by $\beta_0 + \beta_1 X_1 + \cdots + \beta_{p-1} X_{p-1}$. To simplify the formulas, we shall use matrix notation and the following three vectors:

(14.32)
$$\underset{p \times 1}{\boldsymbol{\beta}} = \begin{bmatrix} \beta_0 \\ \beta_1 \\ \vdots \\ \beta_{p-1} \end{bmatrix} \qquad \underset{p \times 1}{\mathbf{X}} = \begin{bmatrix} 1 \\ X_1 \\ X_2 \\ \vdots \\ X_{p-1} \end{bmatrix} \qquad \underset{p \times 1}{\mathbf{X}_i} = \begin{bmatrix} 1 \\ X_{i1} \\ X_{i2} \\ \vdots \\ X_{i,p-1} \end{bmatrix}$$

We then have:

(14.33a)
$$\boldsymbol{\beta}'\mathbf{X} = \beta_0 + \beta_1 X_1 + \cdots + \beta_{p-1} X_{p-1}$$

(14.33b)
$$\boldsymbol{\beta}'\mathbf{X}_i = \beta_0 + \beta_1 X_{i1} + \cdots + \beta_{p-1} X_{i,p-1}$$

With this notation, the simple logistic response function (14.9) extends to the multiple logistic response function as follows:

(14.34)
$$E\{Y\} = \frac{\exp(\boldsymbol{\beta}'\mathbf{X})}{1 + \exp(\boldsymbol{\beta}'\mathbf{X})}$$

and the equivalent simple logistic response form (14.9a) extends to:

(14.34a)
$$E\{Y\} = [1 + \exp(-\boldsymbol{\beta}'\mathbf{X})]^{-1}$$

Similarly, the logit transformation (14.10):

(14.35)
$$\pi' = \log_e\left(\frac{\pi}{1 - \pi}\right)$$

now leads to the logit response function:

(14.36)
$$\pi' = \boldsymbol{\beta}'\mathbf{X}$$

The multiple logistic regression model can therefore be stated as follows:

(14.37) Y_i are independent Bernoulli random variables with expected values $E\{Y_i\} = \pi_i$, where:

$$E\{Y_i\} = \pi_i = \frac{\exp(\boldsymbol{\beta}'\mathbf{X}_i)}{1 + \exp(\boldsymbol{\beta}'\mathbf{X}_i)}$$

Again, the X observations are considered to be known constants. Alternatively, if the X variables are random, $E\{Y_i\}$ is viewed as a conditional mean, given the values of $X_{i1}, \ldots, X_{i,p-1}$.

Like the simple logistic response function (14.9), the multiple logistic response function (14.34) is monotonic and sigmoidal in shape with respect to $\boldsymbol{\beta}'\mathbf{X}$ and is almost linear when π is between .2 and .8. The X variables may be different predictor variables, or some may represent curvature and/or interaction effects. Also, the predictor variables may be quantitative, or they may be qualitative and represented by indicator variables. This flexibility makes the multiple logistic regression model very attractive.

Note

When the logistic regression model contains only qualitative variables, it is often referred to as a log-linear model. The reader is referred to Reference 14.3 for an in-depth discussion of the analysis of log-linear models. ∎

Fitting of Model

Again, we shall utilize the method of maximum likelihood to estimate the parameters of the multiple logistic response function (14.34). The log-likelihood function for simple logistic regression in (14.20) extends directly for multiple logistic regression:

(14.38)
$$\log_e L(\boldsymbol{\beta}) = \sum_{i=1}^{n} Y_i(\boldsymbol{\beta}'\mathbf{X}_i) - \sum_{i=1}^{n} \log_e[1 + \exp(\boldsymbol{\beta}'\mathbf{X}_i)]$$

Numerical search procedures are used to find the values of $\beta_0, \beta_1, \ldots, \beta_{p-1}$ that maximize $\log_e L(\boldsymbol{\beta})$. These maximum likelihood estimates will be denoted by $b_0, b_1, \ldots, b_{p-1}$. Let

b denote the vector of the maximum likelihood estimates:

$$(14.39) \qquad \underset{p \times 1}{\mathbf{b}} = \begin{bmatrix} b_0 \\ b_1 \\ \vdots \\ b_{p-1} \end{bmatrix}$$

The fitted logistic response function and fitted values can then be expressed as follows:

$$(14.40a) \qquad \hat{\pi} = \frac{\exp(\mathbf{b}'\mathbf{X})}{1 + \exp(\mathbf{b}'\mathbf{X})} = [1 + \exp(-\mathbf{b}'\mathbf{X})]^{-1}$$

$$(14.40b) \qquad \hat{\pi}_i = \frac{\exp(\mathbf{b}'\mathbf{X}_i)}{1 + \exp(\mathbf{b}'\mathbf{X}_i)} = [1 + \exp(-\mathbf{b}'\mathbf{X}_i)]^{-1}$$

where:

$$(14.40c) \qquad \mathbf{b}'\mathbf{X} = b_0 + b_1 X_1 + \cdots + b_{p-1} X_{p-1}$$

$$(14.40d) \qquad \mathbf{b}'\mathbf{X}_i = b_0 + b_1 X_{i1} + \cdots + b_{p-1} X_{i,p-1}$$

We shall rely on standard statistical packages for logistic regression to conduct the numerical search procedures for obtaining the maximum likelihood estimates. We therefore proceed directly to an example to illustrate the fitting of a multiple logistic regression model.

Example. In a health study to investigate an epidemic outbreak of a disease that is spread by mosquitoes, individuals were randomly sampled within two sectors in a city to determine if the person had recently contracted the disease under study. This was ascertained by the interviewer, who asked pertinent questions to assess whether certain specific symptoms associated with the disease were present during the specified period. The response variable Y was coded 1 if this disease was determined to have been present, and 0 if not.

Three predictor variables were included in the study, representing known or potential risk factors. They are age, socioeconomic status of household, and sector within city. Age (X_1) is a quantitative variable. Socioeconomic status is a categorical variable with three levels. It is represented by two indicator variables $(X_2$ and $X_3)$, as follows:

Class	X_2	X_3
Upper	0	0
Middle	1	0
Lower	0	1

City sector is also a categorical variable. Since there were only two sectors in the study, one indicator variable (X_4) was used, defined so that $X_4 = 0$ for sector 1 and $X_4 = 1$ for sector 2.

The reason why the upper socioeconomic class was chosen as the reference class (i.e., the class for which the indicator variables X_2 and X_3 are coded 0) is that it was expected that this class would have the lowest disease rate among the socioeconomic classes. By making this class the reference class, the odds ratios associated with regression coefficients β_2 and β_3 would then be expected to be greater than 1, facilitating their interpretation. For

TABLE 14.3   Portion of Model-Building Data Set—Disease Outbreak Example.

	(1)	(2)	(3)	(4)	(5)	(6)
		Socioeconomic Status		City Sector	Disease Status	Fitted Value
Case	Age					
i	X_{i1}	X_{i2}	X_{i3}	X_{i4}	Y_i	$\hat{\pi}_i$
1	33	0	0	0	0	.209
2	35	0	0	0	0	.219
3	6	0	0	0	0	.106
4	60	0	0	0	0	.371
5	18	0	1	0	1	.111
6	26	0	1	0	0	.136
...	...	...	...	...	...	...
98	35	0	1	0	0	.171

the same reason, sector 1, where the epidemic was less severe, was chosen as the reference class for the sector indicator variable X_4.

The data for 196 individuals in the sample are given in the DISEASE data set in Appendix C.3. The first 98 cases were selected for fitting the model. The remaining 98 cases were saved to serve as a validation data set. Table 14.3 in columns 1–5 contains the data for a portion of the 98 cases used for fitting the model. Note the use of the indicator variables as just explained for the two categorical variables. The primary purpose of the study was to assess the strength of the association between each of the predictor variables and the probability of a person having contracted the disease.

A first-order multiple logistic regression model with the three predictor variables was considered a priori to be reasonable:

$$(14.41) \qquad E\{Y\} = [1 + \exp(-\boldsymbol{\beta}'\mathbf{X})]^{-1}$$

where:

$$(14.41a) \qquad \boldsymbol{\beta}'\mathbf{X} = \beta_0 + \beta_1 X_1 + \beta_2 X_2 + \beta_3 X_3 + \beta_4 X_4$$

This model was fitted by the method of maximum likelihood to the data for the 98 cases. The results are summarized in Table 14.4a. The estimated logistic response function is:

$$(14.42) \quad \hat{\pi} = [1 + \exp(2.3129 - .02975 X_1 - .4088 X_2 + .30525 X_3 - 1.5747 X_4]^{-1}$$

The interpretation of the estimated regression coefficients in the fitted first-order multiple logistic response function parallels that for the simple logistic response function: $\exp(b_k)$ is the estimated odds ratio for predictor variable X_k. The only difference in interpretation for multiple logistic regression is that the estimated odds ratio for predictor variable X_k assumes that all other predictor variables are held constant. The levels at which they are held constant does not matter in a first-order model. We see from Table 14.4a, for instance, that the odds of a person having contracted the disease increase by about 3.0 percent with each additional year of age (X_1), for given socioeconomic status and city sector location.

TABLE 14.4 **Maximum Likelihood Estimates of Logistic Regression Function (14.41)—Disease Outbreak Example.**

(a) Estimated Coefficients, Standard Deviations, and Odds Ratios

Regression Coefficient	Estimated Regression Coefficient	Estimated Standard Deviation	Estimated Odds Ratio
β_0	−2.3129	.6426	—
β_1	.02975	.01350	1.030
β_2	.4088	.5990	1.505
β_3	−.30525	.6041	.737
β_4	1.5747	.5016	4.829

(b) Estimated Approximate Variance-Covariance Matrix

$$
\mathbf{s}^2\{\mathbf{b}\} = \begin{array}{ccccc} b_0 & b_1 & b_2 & b_3 & b_4 \\ \begin{bmatrix} .4129 & -.0057 & -.1836 & -.2010 & -.1632 \\ -.0057 & .00018 & .00115 & .00073 & .00034 \\ -.1836 & .00115 & .3588 & .1482 & .0129 \\ -.2010 & .00073 & .1482 & .3650 & .0623 \\ -.1632 & .00034 & .0129 & .0623 & .2516 \end{bmatrix} \end{array}
$$

Also, the odds of a person in sector 2 (X_4) having contracted the disease are almost five times as great as for a person in sector 1, for given age and socioeconomic status. These are point estimates, to be sure, and we shall need to consider how precise these estimates are.

Table 14.3, column 6, contains the fitted values $\hat{\pi}_i$. These are calculated as usual. For instance, the estimated mean response for case $i = 1$, where $X_{11} = 33$, $X_{12} = 0$, $X_{13} = 0$, $X_{14} = 0$, is:

$$\hat{\pi}_1 = \{1 + \exp[2.3129 - .02975(33) - .4088(0) + .30525(0) - 1.5747(0)]\}^{-1} = .209$$

Comments

1. The maximum likelihood estimates of the parameters $\boldsymbol{\beta}$ for the logistic regression model can be obtained by iteratively reweighted least squares. The procedure is straightforward, although it involves intensive use of a computer.

a. Obtain starting values for the regression parameters, to be denoted by $\mathbf{b}(0)$. Often, reasonable starting values can be obtained by ordinary least squares regression of Y on the predictor variables $X_1, \ldots, X_{p-1}$, using a first-order linear model.

b. Using these starting values, obtain:

(14.43a)
$$\hat{\pi}'_i(0) = [\mathbf{b}(0)]'\mathbf{X}_i$$

(14.43b)
$$\hat{\pi}_i(0) = \frac{\exp[\hat{\pi}'_i(0)]}{1 + \exp[\hat{\pi}'_i(0)]}$$

c. Calculate the new response variable:

$$(14.44a) \qquad Y_i'(0) = \hat{\pi}_i'(0) + \frac{Y_i - \hat{\pi}_i(0)}{\hat{\pi}_i(0)[1 - \hat{\pi}_i(0)]}$$

and the weights:

$$(14.44b) \qquad w_i(0) = \hat{\pi}_i(0)[1 - \hat{\pi}_i(0)]$$

d. Regress $Y'(0)$ in (14.44a) on the predictor variables $X_1, \ldots, X_{p-1}$ using a first-order linear model with weights in (14.44b) to obtain revised estimated regression coefficients, denoted by $\mathbf{b}(1)$.

e. Repeat steps a through d, making revisions in (14.43) and (14.44) by using the latest revised estimated regression coefficients until there is little if any change in the estimated coefficients. Often three or four iterations are sufficient to obtain convergence.

2. When the multiple logistic regression model is not a first-order model and contains quadratic or higher-power terms for the predictor variables and/or cross-product terms for interaction effects, the estimated regression coefficients b_k no longer have a simple interpretation.

3. When the assumptions of a monotonic sigmoidal relation between π and $\boldsymbol{\beta}'\mathbf{X}$, required for the multiple logistic regression model, are not appropriate, an alternative is to convert all predictor variables to categorical variables and employ a log-linear model. In the disease outbreak example, for instance, age could be converted into a categorical variable with three classes 0–18, 19–50, and 51–75. Reference 14.3 describes the use of log-linear models for binary response variables when the predictor variables are categorical.

4. Convergence difficulties in the numerical search procedures for finding the maximum likelihood estimates of the multiple logistic regression function may be encountered when the predictor variables are highly correlated; also, when there is a large number of predictor variables. When convergence problems occur, it may be necessary to reduce the number of predictor variables in order to obtain convergence.   ■

14.5   Model Building: Selection of Predictor Variables

The discussion in Chapters 8, 9, and 10 on model building for linear multiple regression models generally applies to logistic regression models. We therefore take up only a few selected topics about model building of logistic regression models and illustrate the main points by means of examples. In this section, we consider the selection of predictor variables and validation of the logistic regression model. The use of diagnostics for building logistic regression models will be taken up in the next section.

Stepwise Model Building

When building logistic regression models, we can add or delete predictor variables and terms for curvature and interaction effects in direct fashion, just as for linear regression models. Use of the all-possible-regressions approach for logistic model building for exploratory observational studies often is not feasible, however, because of the extensive numerical search calculations required to find the maximum likelihood estimates for a logistic regression model. Consequently, stepwise selection procedures are frequently employed in logistic regression model building for exploratory observational studies. These procedures need to be used with great caution, as we noted earlier. Backward stepwise selection is often employed when there are only a few key predictor variables and a limited number of other potentially useful predictor variables. This situation is frequently encountered in epidemiologic studies. Nonautomatic backward stepwise regression can then be used to discard those predictor variables of secondary importance that do not impair the goodness of fit, while keeping the key predictor variables in the model.

Test Whether Several $\beta_k = 0$

Frequently in model building there is interest in determining whether a subset of the X variables in a multiple logistic regression model can be dropped, that is, in testing whether the associated regression coefficients β_k equal zero. The test procedure we shall employ is a general one for use with maximum likelihood estimation, just like the general linear test procedure for linear models. The test is called the *likelihood ratio test*. It requires a large sample size and is based on a statistic called the model deviance.

Model Deviance.   The deviance of a fitted model compares the log-likelihood of the fitted model to the log-likelihood of a model with n parameters that fits the n observations perfectly. Such a perfectly fitting model is called a *saturated model*. Consider again the log-likelihood function in (14.17) for n independent Bernoulli (0, 1) variables. If we let π_i be unconstrained so that each Y_i observation takes on the value 1 with a different probability π_i without restricting π_i in any way, then we will have n parameters for the n observations and can obtain a perfect fit (i.e., the residuals will all be zero). It can be shown that the log-likelihood function (14.17) is maximized if $\pi_i = Y_i$. Hence, the maximum likelihood estimator of π_i for the saturated model, denoted by $\hat{\pi}_{is}$, is $\hat{\pi}_{is} = Y_i$. It can be shown that the likelihood of the sample observations evaluated at $\hat{\pi}_{is} = Y_i$, denoted by $L(\hat{\pi}_{1s}, \ldots, \hat{\pi}_{ns})$, is equal to 1 so that the log-likelihood is equal to 0:

$$(14.45) \qquad \log_e L(\hat{\pi}_{1s}, \ldots, \hat{\pi}_{ns}) = \sum_{i=1}^{n} [Y_i \log_e(Y_i) + (1 - Y_i) \log_e(1 - Y_i)] = 0$$

This log-likelihood value for the saturated model will now be compared with the log-likelihood value for the fitted model. We therefore need to consider next the log-likelihood function for the logistic model, where $\pi_i' = \beta_0 + \beta_1 X_{i1} + \cdots + \beta_{p-1} X_{i,p-1}$. The log-likelihood function is given in (14.38), and the log-likelihood value for the sample observations when the maximum likelihood estimates are used in the log-likelihood function (the values that maximize the log-likelihood function for the fitted model) is as follows, now denoted by $\log_e L(b_0, b_1, \ldots, b_{p-1})$:

$$(14.46) \qquad \log_e L(b_0, b_1, \ldots, b_{p-1}) = \sum_{i=1}^{n} Y_i (\mathbf{b}'\mathbf{X}_i) - \sum_{i=1}^{n} \log_e[1 + \exp(\mathbf{b}'\mathbf{X}_i)]$$

The log-likelihood value for the fitted model can never be larger than the log-likelihood value for the saturated model because the fitted model has fewer parameters. The deviance is based on the difference between the two log-likelihood values. We denote the deviance for the fitted model by $DEV(X_0, X_1, \ldots, X_{p-1})$; $X_0 \equiv 1$ is the dummy variable associated with β_0. The deviance is defined as follows:

$$(14.47) \qquad DEV(X_0, X_1, \ldots, X_{p-1}) = 2 \log_e L(\hat{\pi}_{1s}, \ldots, \hat{\pi}_{ns})$$
$$-2 \log_e L(b_0, b_1, \ldots, b_{p-1})$$

For logistic regression model (14.37), the deviance can be expressed as follows:

$$(14.48) \qquad DEV(X_0, X_1, \ldots, X_{p-1}) = -2 \sum_{i=1}^{n} [Y_i \log_e(\hat{\pi}_i) + (1 - Y_i) \log_e(1 - \hat{\pi}_i)]$$

where $\hat{\pi}_i$ is the ith fitted value for the logistic regression model in (14.40b).

The smaller the difference in the two log-likelihood values, the smaller is the deviance and the closer is the fitted model to the saturated model. Hence, the model deviance can be used as a goodness of fit criterion. The larger the model deviance, the poorer is the fit.

Note

For the normal error linear regression model, the definition of the deviance in (14.47) is modified slightly, the right side being multiplied by σ^2. The deviance for the normal error linear regression model turns out to be simply $SSE = \Sigma(Y_i - \hat{Y}_i)^2$. ∎

Partial Deviance. For each fitted model, we can calculate its deviance. The difference between the deviances for two fitted models is called a *partial deviance* and enables us to test whether some predictor variables can be dropped from the model.

We begin with the full logistic model with response function:

$$(14.49) \qquad \pi = [1 + \exp(-\boldsymbol{\beta}'_F \mathbf{X})]^{-1} \qquad\qquad \text{Full model}$$

where:

$$(14.49a) \qquad \boldsymbol{\beta}'_F \mathbf{X} = \beta_0 + \beta_1 X_1 + \cdots + \beta_{p-1} X_{p-1}$$

Note that we now denote the vector of regression coefficients for the full model by $\boldsymbol{\beta}_F$. We then find the maximum likelihood estimates for the full model, now denoted by $\mathbf{b}_F$, and the deviance $DEV(X_0, X_1, \ldots, X_{p-1})$ for the full model.

The hypothesis we wish to test is:

$$(14.50)$$
$$H_0: \quad \beta_q = \beta_{q+1} = \cdots = \beta_{p-1} = 0$$
$$H_a: \quad \text{not all of the } \beta_k \text{ in } H_0 \text{ equal zero}$$

where, for convenience, we arrange the model so that the last $p - q$ coefficients are those tested. The reduced logistic model therefore has the response function:

$$(14.51) \qquad \pi = [1 + \exp(-\boldsymbol{\beta}'_R \mathbf{X})]^{-1} \qquad\qquad \text{Reduced model}$$

where:

$$(14.51a) \qquad \boldsymbol{\beta}'_R \mathbf{X} = \beta_0 + \beta_1 X_1 + \cdots + \beta_{q-1} X_{q-1}$$

Now we obtain the maximum likelihood estimates $\mathbf{b}_R$ for the reduced model and its deviance $DEV(X_0, X_1, \ldots, X_{q-1})$. If this deviance is not much larger than the deviance for the full model, then the reduced model with fewer parameters provides almost as close a fit so that we should conclude H_0, that $X_q, \ldots, X_{p-1}$ can be dropped from the logistic regression model. A large difference between the two deviances indicates that the predictor variables $X_q, \ldots, X_{p-1}$ should be retained because they improve the fit substantially. The difference between the two deviances is a partial deviance, denoted by $DEV(X_q, \ldots, X_{p-1}|X_0, X_1, \ldots, X_{q-1})$:

$$(14.52) \quad DEV(X_q, \ldots, X_{p-1}|X_0, X_1, \ldots, X_{q-1})$$
$$= DEV(X_0, X_1, \ldots, X_{q-1}) - DEV(X_0, X_1, \ldots, X_{p-1})$$

Notice the analogy to extra sums of squares for linear regression models, hence the corresponding notation. In fact, for the normal error linear regression model, the partial deviance in (14.52) simplifies to the corresponding extra sum of squares.

It can be shown that if H_0 holds and n is reasonably large, the partial deviance in (14.52) follows approximately a chi-square distribution with $p - q$ degrees of freedom. The degrees of freedom correspond to the difference in the degrees of freedom for error for the two fitted models: $(n - q) - (n - p) = p - q$. Large values of the partial deviance lead to conclusion H_a. Hence, the decision rule for testing the alternatives in (14.50) is:

$$(14.53)$$
$$\text{If } DEV(X_q, \ldots, X_{p-1}|X_0, X_1, \ldots, X_{q-1}) \leq \chi^2(1 - \alpha; p - q), \text{ conclude } H_0$$
$$\text{If } DEV(X_q, \ldots, X_{p-1}|X_0, X_1, \ldots, X_{q-1}) > \chi^2(1 - \alpha; p - q), \text{ conclude } H_a$$

Three illustrations of the use of partial deviance tests follow.

1. The logistic regression model containing X_1, X_2, and X_3 is fitted and the deviance $DEV(X_0, X_1, X_2, X_3)$ is obtained. To test $H_0: \beta_2 = \beta_3 = 0$, the logistic regression model containing only X_1 is fitted next and the deviance $DEV(X_0, X_1)$ is obtained. The partial deviance required is:

$$DEV(X_2, X_3|X_0, X_1) = DEV(X_0, X_1) - DEV(X_0, X_1, X_2, X_3)$$

The appropriate chi-square distribution is the one with $(n - 2) - (n - 4) = 2$ degrees of freedom.

2. In the same situation as in illustration 1, we wish to test $H_0: \beta_1 = \beta_2 = \beta_3 = 0$, that the entire set of predictor variables should be dropped. We now need to fit the logistic regression model with $\pi_i' = \beta_0$ for all i and obtain $DEV(X_0)$. The required partial deviance is:

$$DEV(X_1, X_2, X_3|X_0) = DEV(X_0) - DEV(X_0, X_1, X_2, X_3)$$

The appropriate chi-square distribution has $(n - 1) - (n - 4) = 3$ degrees of freedom.

3. In the same situation to test $H_0: \beta_1 = 0$, we require:

$$DEV(X_1|X_0, X_2, X_3) = DEV(X_0, X_2, X_3) - DEV(X_0, X_1, X_2, X_3)$$

The appropriate chi-square distribution has one degree of freedom.

Example. In the disease outbreak example, the model building began with the three predictor variables that were considered a priori to be key explanatory variables—age, socioeconomic status, and city sector. A logistic regression model was fitted containing these three predictor variables and the deviance for this model was obtained. Then tests were conducted to see whether a variable could be dropped from the model. First, X_1 was dropped from the logistic model and the deviance for this reduced model was obtained. The results were:

$$DEV(X_0, X_1, X_2, X_3, X_4) = 101.054 \qquad DEV(X_0, X_2, X_3, X_4) = 106.204$$

Hence the required partial deviance is:

$$DEV(X_1|X_0, X_2, X_3, X_4) - DEV(X_0, X_2, X_3, X_4) - DEV(X_0, X_1, X_2, X_3, X_4)$$
$$= 106.204 - 101.054 = 5.150$$

For $\alpha = .05$, we require $\chi^2(.95; 1) = 3.84$. Hence to test $H_0: \beta_1 = 0$, $H_a: \beta_1 \neq 0$, the appropriate decision rule is:

$$\text{If } DEV(X_1|X_0, X_2, X_3, X_4) \leq 3.84, \text{ conclude } H_0$$

$$\text{If } DEV(X_1|X_0, X_2, X_3, X_4) > 3.84, \text{ conclude } H_a$$

Since $DEV(X_1|X_0, X_2, X_3, X_4) = 5.15 \geq 3.84$, we conclude H_a, that X_1 should not be dropped from the model. The P-value of this test is .023.

Similar tests for socioeconomic status (X_2, X_3) and city sector (X_4) led to P-values of .55 and .001. The P-value for socioeconomic status suggests that it can be dropped from the model containing the other two predictor variables. However, since this variable was considered a priori to be important, additional analyses were conducted. When socioeconomic status is the only predictor in the logistic regression model, the P-value for the test whether this predictor variable is helpful at all is .16, suggesting marginal importance for this variable. In addition, the estimated regression coefficients for age and city sector and their estimated standard deviations are not appreciably affected by whether or not socioeconomic status is in the regression model. Hence, it was decided to keep socioeconomic status in the logistic regression model in view of its a priori importance.

The next question of concern was whether any two-factor interaction terms are required in the model. The full model now includes all possible two-factor interactions, in addition to the main effects, so that $\boldsymbol{\beta}_F'\mathbf{X}$ for this model is as follows:

$$\boldsymbol{\beta}_F'\mathbf{X} = \beta_0 + \beta_1 X_1 + \beta_2 X_2 + \beta_3 X_3 + \beta_4 X_4 + \beta_5 X_1 X_2 + \beta_6 X_1 X_3$$
$$+ \beta_7 X_1 X_4 + \beta_8 X_2 X_4 + \beta_9 X_3 X_4 \qquad \text{Full model}$$

We wish to test:

$$H_0: \ \beta_5 = \beta_6 = \beta_7 = \beta_8 - \beta_9 = 0$$

$$H_a: \ \text{not all } \beta_k \text{ in } H_0 \text{ equal zero}$$

so that $\boldsymbol{\beta}_R'\mathbf{X}$ for the reduced model is:

$$\boldsymbol{\beta}_R'\mathbf{X} = \beta_0 + \beta_1 X_1 + \beta_2 X_2 + \beta_3 X_3 + \beta_4 X_4 \qquad \text{Reduced model}$$

A computer run of a multiple logistic regression package yielded:

$$DEV(X_0, X_1, \ldots, X_3 X_4) = 93.996$$

$$DEV(X_0, X_1, \ldots, X_4) = 101.054$$

$$DEV(X_1 X_2, \ldots, X_3 X_4 | X_0, X_1, \ldots, X_4) = 7.058$$

If H_0 holds, the partial deviance follows approximately the chi-square distribution with five degrees of freedom. For $\alpha = .05$, we require $\chi^2(.95; 5) = 11.07$. Since the partial deviance 7.058 is less than 11.07, we conclude H_0, that the two-factor interactions are not needed in the logistic regression model. The P-value of this test is .22. We note again that a logistic regression model without interaction terms is desirable, because otherwise $\exp(\beta_k)$ no longer can be interpreted as the odds ratio.

Thus, the fitted logistic regression model (14.42) was accepted as the model to be checked diagnostically and, finally, to be validated.

Likelihood Ratio Test.   The partial deviance test in (14.53) is the same as the likelihood ratio test. With the general likelihood ratio test procedure, the alternatives in (14.50) are tested by first fitting the full model in (14.49), obtaining the maximum likelihood estimates $\mathbf{b}_F$, and evaluating the likelihood function at $\boldsymbol{\beta} = \mathbf{b}_F$. This likelihood value is denoted by $L(F)$:

$$L(F) = L(b_0, b_1, \ldots, b_{p-1})$$

Next the reduced model in (14.51) is fitted, the maximum likelihood estimates are obtained, and the likelihood function is evaluated at $\mathbf{b} = \mathbf{b}_R$. This likelihood value is denoted by $L(R)$:

$$L(R) = L(b_0, b_1, \ldots, b_{q-1})$$

The ratio of the two likelihoods is the likelihood ratio:

$$\frac{L(R)}{L(F)}$$

The actual test statistic for the likelihood ratio test, denoted by X^2, is:

$$(14.54) \qquad X^2 = -2 \log_e \left[\frac{L(R)}{L(F)} \right] = 2 \log_e L(F) - 2 \log_e L(R)$$

$$= 2 \log_e L(b_0, b_1, \ldots, b_{p-1}) - 2 \log_e L(b_0, b_1, \ldots, b_{q-1})$$

But this is exactly the partial deviance $DEV(X_q, \ldots, X_{p-1} | X_0, X_1, \ldots, X_{q-1})$ in (14.52). We see this by replacing the two deviances on the right side of (14.52) by their definitions in (14.47) and noting that the log-likelihood terms for the saturated model drop out.

Validation

Our discussion in Chapter 10 about validating a linear regression model applies in its entirety to logistic regression models. New data or a holdout sample should be used whenever possible to examine whether the same model would be developed from the new data set, whether the estimated regression coefficients and their estimated standard deviations are similar, and whether the same inference conclusions would be drawn.

14.6   Diagnostics

The appropriateness of the fitted logistic regression model needs to be examined before it is accepted for use, as is the case for all regression models. In particular, we need to examine whether the estimated response function for the data is monotonic and sigmoidal in shape, key properties of the logistic response function. Diagnosing whether the fitted logistic regression model is appropriate, detecting outliers, and identifying influential observations are much more difficult to carry out for binary response variables than for continuous response variables because each residual e_i can take on only one of two values. We present now some informal and formal goodness of fit procedures and discuss residual analysis for detecting outliers.

Informal Goodness of Fit Examination

The procedure consists of grouping into classes cases with similar fitted values $\hat{\pi}$, with approximately the same number of cases in each class, and obtaining for each class the estimated proportion of 1s, denoted by p_j. The grouping may be accomplished equivalently by using the fitted logit values $\hat{\pi}' = \mathbf{b}'\mathbf{X}$ since the logit values $\hat{\pi}'$ are monotonically related to the fitted mean responses $\hat{\pi}$. We shall do the grouping according to the fitted logit values $\hat{\pi}'$. The estimated proportions are then plotted against the midpoints of the $\hat{\pi}'$ intervals to check the appropriateness of monotonicity and sigmoidal shape.

Example 1.   In the programming task example of Table 14.1 with $n = 25$ cases, four groups with approximately the same number of cases in each were set up as follows:

Class j	$\hat{\pi}'$ Interval	Midpoint	n_j	p_j
1	−2.42—under −1.29	−1.86	7	.143
2	−1.29—under −.16	−.72	5	.200
3	−.16—under .97	.40	7	.571
4	.97—under 2.11	1.54	6	.833

A plot of the estimated proportions p_j against the midpoints is shown in Figure 14.5. The plot suggests that a monotonic, sigmoidal relationship is tenable. Note, however, that the number of cases within each interval is extremely small, even with the use of only four groups, and consequently the estimated proportions are not very precise.

Example 2.   In the disease outbreak example of Table 14.3 with $n = 98$ cases, five classes were used and the results were as follows:

Class j	$\hat{\pi}'$ Interval	Midpoint	n_j	p_j
1	−2.60—under −2.08	−2.34	20	.05
2	−2.08—under −1.43	−1.76	20	.15
3	−1.43—under −.70	−1.07	20	.30
4	−.70—under .16	−.27	19	.53
5	.16—under 1.70	.93	19	.58

A plot of the proportions p_j against the midpoints of the $\hat{\pi}'$ intervals is presented in Figure 14.6. The plot supports the appropriateness of a monotonic sigmoidal response function.

Chi-Square Goodness of Fit Test

The informal diagnostic procedure just presented can be extended into a formal chi-square goodness of fit test. The test assumes only that the Y_i observations are independent and that the sample size is reasonably large. The test can detect major departures from a logistic

FIGURE 14.5 **Diagnostic Plot of Estimated Proportions—Programming Task Example.**

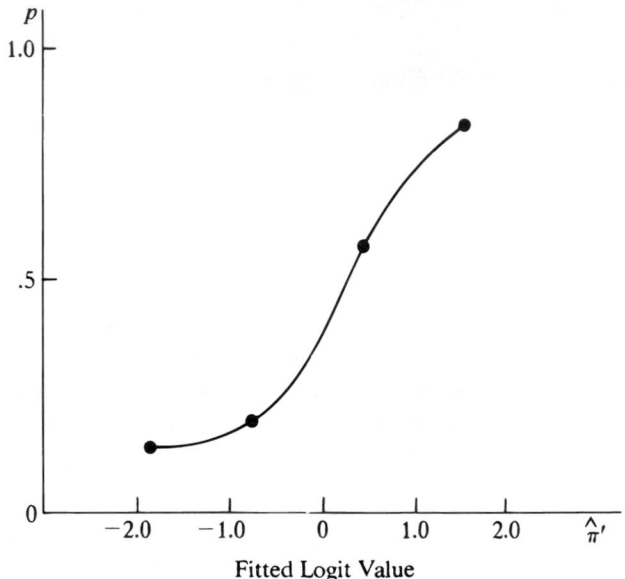

Fitted Logit Value

FIGURE 14.6 **Diagnostic Plot of Estimated Proportions—Disease Outbreak Example.**

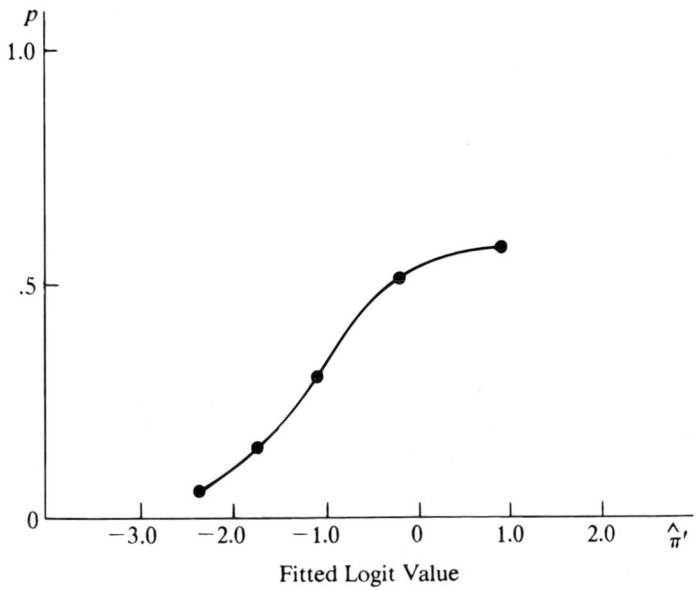

Fitted Logit Value

response function, but is not sensitive to small departures from a logistic response function. The alternatives of interest are:

(14.55)
$$H_0: E\{Y\} = [1 + \exp(-\boldsymbol{\beta}'\mathbf{X})]^{-1}$$
$$H_a: E\{Y\} \neq [1 + \exp(-\boldsymbol{\beta}'\mathbf{X})]^{-1}$$

As with the informal diagnostic procedure, the sample cases are grouped into classes, with approximately an equal number of cases in each class. Here again, we shall do the grouping according to the fitted logit values $\hat{\pi}'$, although grouping by the fitted mean responses $\hat{\pi}$ is equivalent. We shall denote the number of classes by c. Use of 5 to 10 classes is common. The number of cases in the jth class ($j = 1, \ldots, c$) will be denoted by n_j. It follows that:

(14.56)
$$\sum_{j=1}^{c} n_j = n$$

The number of cases in the jth class with outcome 1 will be denoted by O_{j1} and the number of cases in the jth class with outcome 0 will be denoted by O_{j0}. Because the response variable Y_i is a Bernoulli variable whose outcomes are 1 and 0, the number of cases O_{j1} and O_{j0} are given as follows:

(14.57a)
$$O_{j1} = \sum Y_i$$

(14.57b)
$$O_{j0} = \sum(1 - Y_i) = n_j - O_{j1}$$

where each summation is over the n_j cases in the jth class.

If the logistic response function is appropriate, the expected value of Y_i is given by:

(14.58)
$$E\{Y_i\} = \pi_i = [1 + \exp(-\boldsymbol{\beta}'\mathbf{X}_i)]^{-1}$$

and is estimated by the fitted value $\hat{\pi}_i$:

(14.59)
$$\hat{\pi}_i = [1 + \exp(-\mathbf{b}'\mathbf{X}_i)]^{-1}$$

Consequently, if the logistic response function is appropriate, the expected numbers of cases with $Y_i = 1$ and $Y_i = 0$ for the jth class are estimated to be:

(14.60a)
$$E_{j1} = \sum \hat{\pi}_i$$

(14.60b)
$$E_{j0} = \sum(1 - \hat{\pi}_i) = n_j - E_{j1}$$

where each summation is again over the n_j cases in the jth class, E_{j1} denotes the estimated expected number of cases with $Y_i = 1$ in the jth class, and E_{j0} denotes the estimated expected number of cases with $Y_i = 0$.

The test statistic is the usual chi-square goodness of fit test statistic:

(14.61)
$$X^2 = \sum_{j=1}^{c} \sum_{k=0}^{1} \frac{(O_{jk} - E_{jk})^2}{E_{jk}}$$

TABLE 14.5   **Goodness of Fit Test for Logistic Regression Function—Disease Outbreak Example.**

Class			Number of Persons without Disease		Number of Persons with Disease	
			Observed	Expected	Observed	Expected
j	$\hat{\pi}'$ Interval	n_j	O_{j0}	E_{j0}	O_{j1}	E_{j1}
1	−2.60—under −2.08	20	19	18.196	1	1.804
2	−2.08—under −1.43	20	17	17.093	3	2.907
3	−1.43—under −.70	20	14	14.707	6	5.293
4	−.70—under .16	19	9	10.887	10	8.113
5	.16—under 1.70	19	8	6.297	11	12.703
	Total	98	67	67.180	31	30.820

If the logistic response function is appropriate, X^2 follows approximately a χ^2 distribution with $c - 2$ degrees of freedom when n is large and $p < c$. (See Ref. 14.4 for a discussion of goodness of fit tests for logistic regression models.) As with other chi-square goodness of fit tests, it is advisable that most expected frequencies E_{jk} be moderately large, say 5 or greater, and none smaller than 1.

Large values of the test statistic X^2 indicate that the logistic response function is not appropriate. The decision rule for testing the alternatives in (14.55), when controlling the level of significance at α, therefore is:

$$(14.62) \qquad \begin{aligned} &\text{If } X^2 \leq \chi^2(1 - \alpha; c - 2), \text{ conclude } H_0 \\ &\text{If } X^2 > \chi^2(1 - \alpha; c - 2), \text{ conclude } H_a \end{aligned}$$

Example.   For the disease outbreak example, we shall use the same five classes as for the informal diagnostic procedure discussed earlier. Table 14.5 repeats the class intervals for the logit fitted values $\hat{\pi}'$ and the number of cases n_j in each class. It also gives O_{j0} and O_{j1}, the number of cases with $Y_i = 0$ and $Y_i = 1$ for each class. Finally, Table 14.5 contains the estimated expected frequencies E_{j0} and E_{j1} if the logistic regression model is appropriate (calculations not shown).

Test statistic (14.61) is calculated as follows:

$$X^2 = \frac{(19 - 18.196)^2}{18.196} + \frac{(1 - 1.804)^2}{1.804} + \cdots + \frac{(8 - 6.297)^2}{6.297} + \frac{(11 - 12.703)^2}{12.703}$$

$$= 1.98$$

Since the sample size $n = 98$ is large and only two expected frequencies are less than 5 and both are greater than 1, the chi-square test is appropriate here. For $\alpha = .05$ and $c - 2 = 3$, we require $\chi^2(.95; 3) = 7.81$. Since $X^2 = 1.98 \leq 7.81$, we conclude H_0, that the logistic response function is appropriate. The P-value of the test is $P\{\chi^2(3) > 1.98\} = .58$.

Deviance Goodness of Fit Test

Another formal test of the fit of the logistic response function can be based on the model deviance $DEV(X_0, X_1, \ldots, X_{p-1})$. If the logistic response function is the correct response function and the sample size n is large, then the deviance will follow approximately a chi-square distribution with about $n - p$ degrees of freedom. Large values of the deviance indicate that the fitted logistic model is not correct. Hence, to test the alternatives in (14.55), the appropriate decision rule is:

(14.63)
$$\text{If } DEV(X_0, X_1, \ldots, X_{p-1}) \le \chi^2(1 - \alpha; n - p), \text{ conclude } H_0$$
$$\text{If } DEV(X_0, X_1, \ldots, X_{p-1}) > \chi^2(1 - \alpha; n - p), \text{ conclude } H_a$$

Example.   In the disease outbreak example, the fitted logistic model adopted for diagnosis and validation was given in (14.42). The deviance for this fitted model is $DEV(X_0, X_1, X_2, X_3, X_4) = 101.054$. For $\alpha = .05$ and $n - p = 98 - 5 = 93$, we require $\chi^2(.95; 93) = 116.5$. Since $DEV(X_0, X_1, \ldots, X_4) = 101.054 \le 116.5$, we conclude H_0, that the logistic model is a satisfactory fit. The P-value of this test is approximately .27. Note that this P-value differs from the P-value for the chi-square goodness of fit test, which is .58. The reason is that these are two different tests. They both support the appropriateness of the logistic function here.

Deviance Residuals for Logistic Regression

Residual analysis for logistic regression is more difficult than for linear regression models because the responses Y_i take on only the values 0 and 1. Consequently, the residuals will not be normally distributed and, indeed, their distribution under the assumption that the fitted model is correct is unknown. Plots of residuals against fitted values or predictor variables will be uninformative.

A useful type of residual for logistic regression is the *deviance residual*. The deviance residual for case i, denoted by dev_i, is defined as the signed square root of the contribution of the ith case to the sum for the model deviance DEV in (14.48):

(14.64)
$$dev_i = \pm\{-2[Y_i \log_e(\hat{\pi}_i) + (1 - Y_i) \log_e(1 - \hat{\pi}_i)]\}^{1/2}$$

where the sign is positive when $Y_i \ge \hat{\pi}_i$ and negative when $Y_i < \hat{\pi}_i$.

An important property of the deviance residuals is that the sum of the squared deviance residuals equals the model deviance in (14.48):

(14.65)
$$\sum_{i=1}^{n} (dev_i)^2 = DEV(X_0, X_1, \ldots, X_{p-1})$$

This follows directly from the definitions of the model deviance in (14.48) and the deviance residuals in (14.64).

Example.   For the programming task example, Table 14.1 contains the deviance residuals in column 4. To illustrate their calculation, we have for case 1:

$$Y_1 = 0 \qquad \hat{\pi}_1 = .3103$$

for logistic regression can be obtained as follows:

$$(14.68) \qquad \mathbf{s}^2\{\mathbf{b}\} = [(-g_{ij})_{\boldsymbol{\beta}=\mathbf{b}}]^{-1}$$

The estimated approximate variances and covariances in (14.68) are routinely provided by most logistic regression computer packages.

Inferences about the regression coefficients for the simple logistic regression model (14.14) or the multiple logistic regression model (14.37) are based on the following approximate result when the sample size is large:

$$(14.69) \qquad \frac{b_k - \beta_k}{s\{b_k\}} \sim z \qquad k = 0, 1, \ldots, p-1$$

where z is a standard normal variable and $s\{b_k\}$ is the estimated approximate standard deviation of b_k obtained from (14.68).

Interval Estimation of a Single β_k

From (14.69), we obtain directly the approximate $1 - \alpha$ confidence limits for β_k:

$$(14.70) \qquad b_k \pm z(1 - \alpha/2)s\{b_k\}$$

where $z(1 - \alpha/2)$ is the $(1 - \alpha/2)100$ percentile of the standard normal distribution.

The corresponding confidence limits for the odds ratio $\exp(\beta_k)$ are:

$$(14.71) \qquad \exp[b_k \pm z(1 - \alpha/2)s\{b_k\}]$$

Example. For the programming task example, it is desired to estimate β_1 with an approximate 95 percent confidence interval. We require $z(.975) = 1.960$, as well as the estimates $b_1 = .1615$ and $s\{b_1\} = .0650$ which are given in Table 14.1b. Hence, the confidence limits are $.1615 \pm 1.960(.0650)$, and the approximate 95 percent confidence interval for β_1 is:

$$.0341 \leq \beta_1 \leq .2889$$

Thus, we can conclude with approximately 95 percent confidence that β_1 is between .0341 and .2889. The corresponding 95 percent confidence limits for the odds ratio are $\exp(.0341) = 1.03$ and $\exp(.2889) = 1.33$.

To examine whether the large-sample inference procedures are applicable here when $n = 25$, bootstrap sampling can be employed, as described in Chapter 13. Alternatively, estimation procedures have been developed for logistic regression that do not depend on any large-sample approximations. LogXact (Ref. 14.9) was run on the data and produced 95 percent confidence limits for β_1 of .041 and .296. The large-sample limits of .034 and .289 are reasonably close to the LogXact limits, confirming the applicability of large-sample theory here.

If we wish to consider the odds ratio for persons whose experience differs by, say, five months, the point estimate of this odds ratio would be $\exp(5b_1) = \exp[5(.1615)] = 2.242$, and the 95 percent confidence limits would be obtained from the confidence limits for b_1 as follows: $\exp[5(.0341)] = 1.186$ and $\exp[5(.2889)] = 4.240$. Thus, with 95 percent confidence we estimate that the odds of success increase by between 19 percent and 324 percent with an additional five months of experience.

Point Estimator

As usual, we denot[...]
by $\mathbf{X}_h$:

(14.74)

and the mean resp[...]

(14.75)

The point estim[...]

(14.76)

where $\mathbf{b}$ is the vect[...]

Interval Estimation

We obtain a confid[...]
for the logit mean r[...]
for the mean respo[...]

and restate the exp[...]

(14.77)

It is this relation in [...]
limits for π_h.
The point estim[...]
$\mathbf{X}_h'\mathbf{b}$ because it is a [...]
according to (5.46)[...]

(14.78)

where $s^2\{\mathbf{b}\}$ is the [...]
coefficients in (14.[...]
Approximate 1[...]
then obtained in th[...]

(14.79a)

(14.79b)

Comments

1. If the large-sample conditions for inferences are not met, the bootstrap procedure can be employed to obtain confidence limits for the regression coefficients. The bootstrap here requires generating Bernoulli random variables as discussed earlier for the construction of simulated envelopes.

2. We are using the z approximation here for large-sample inferences rather than the t approximation used in Chapter 13 for nonlinear regression. This choice is conventional for logistic regression. For large sample sizes, there is little difference between the t distribution and the standard normal distribution. ∎

Simultaneous Interval Estimation of Several β_k

Approximate joint confidence intervals for several logistic regression parameters can be developed by the Bonferroni procedure. If g parameters are to be estimated with family confidence coefficient of approximately $1 - \alpha$, the joint Bonferroni confidence limits are:

(14.72)
$$b_k \pm B s\{b_k\}$$

where:

(14.72a)
$$B = z(1 - \alpha/2g)$$

Example. In the programming task example, it is desired to obtain simultaneous interval estimates for β_0 and β_1 with an approximate 90 percent family confidence coefficient. We therefore require the confidence interval for each parameter to have a 95 percent statement confidence coefficient. We have already obtained a confidence interval for β_1 with a 95 percent statement confidence coefficient. To obtain a 95 percent statement confidence interval for β_0, we use the results in Table 14.1b. The confidence limits are $-3.0597 \pm 1.960(1.259)$ so that the 95 percent confidence interval for β_0 is:

$$-5.5273 \le \beta_0 \le -.5921$$

Hence, the joint confidence intervals for β_0 and β_1, with an approximate 90 percent family confidence coefficient, are:

$$-5.5273 \le \beta_0 \le -.5921$$
$$.0341 \le \beta_1 \le .2889$$

Test Concerning a Single β_k

We have already described a large-sample test for regression parameter β_k based on the partial deviance statistic in (14.52). An alternative large-sample test can be constructed based on (14.69). For the alternatives:

(14.73a)
$$H_0: \beta_k = 0$$
$$H_a: \beta_k \ne 0$$

the appropriate tes

(14.73b)

and the decision ru

(14.73c)

One-sided alternati

Example. In the
alternatives of inte

Test statistic (14.73

For $\alpha = .05$, we re

Since $z^* = 2.485 >$
P-value of this test

Note

The large-sample tes
in (14.52). The latte
also for one-sided tes
When testing H_0: β_k
conclusions.

14.8   Inferences about Me

Frequently, estimati
predictor variables i
interest in the proba
city sector 1 having

Here, L and U are, respectively, the lower and upper confidence limits for π'_h.

Finally, we use the monotonic relation between π_h and π'_h in (14.77) to convert the confidence limits L and U for π'_h into approximate $1 - \alpha$ confidence limits L^* and U^* for the mean response π_h:

(14.80a)
$$L^* = [1 + \exp(-L)]^{-1}$$

(14.80b)
$$U^* = [1 + \exp(-U)]^{-1}$$

Simultaneous Confidence Intervals for Several Mean Responses

When it is desired to estimate several mean responses π_h corresponding to different $\mathbf{X}_h$ vectors with family confidence coefficient $1 - \alpha$, Bonferroni simultaneous confidence intervals may be used. The procedure for g confidence intervals is the same as that for a single confidence interval except that $z(1 - \alpha/2)$ in (14.79) is replaced by $z(1 - \alpha/2g)$.

Example

In the disease outbreak example of Table 14.4, it is desired to find an approximate 95 percent confidence interval for the probability π_h that persons 10 years old who are of lower socioeconomic status and live in sector 1 have contracted the disease. The vector $\mathbf{X}_h$ in (14.74) here is:

$$\mathbf{X}_h = \begin{bmatrix} 1 \\ 10 \\ 0 \\ 1 \\ 0 \end{bmatrix}$$

Using the results in Table 14.4a, we obtain the point estimate of the logit mean response:

$$\hat{\pi}'_h = \mathbf{b}'\mathbf{X}_h = -2.3129(1) + .02975(10) + .4088(0) - .30525(1) + 1.5747(0)$$

$$= -2.32065$$

The estimated variance of $\hat{\pi}'_h$ is obtained by using (14.78) (calculations not shown):

$$s^2\{\hat{\pi}'_h\} = .2945$$

so that $s\{\hat{\pi}'_h\} = .54268$. For $1 - \alpha = .95$, we require $z(.975) = 1.960$. Hence, the confidence limits for the logit mean response π'_h are according to (14.79):

$$L = -2.32065 - 1.960(.54268) = -3.38430$$

$$U = -2.32065 + 1.960(.54268) = -1.25700$$

Finally, we use (14.80) to obtain the confidence limits for the mean response π_h:

$$L^* = [1 + \exp(3.38430)]^{-1} = .033$$

$$U^* = [1 + \exp(1.25700)]^{-1} = .22$$

Thus, the approximate 95 percent confidence interval for the mean response π_h is:

$$.033 \le \pi_h \le .22$$

We therefore find, with approximate 95 percent confidence, that the probability is between .033 and .22 that 10-year-old persons of lower socioeconomic status who live in sector 1 have contracted the disease. This confidence interval is useful for indicating that persons with the specified characteristics are not subject to a very high probability of having contracted the disease, but the confidence interval is quite wide and thus not precise.

Note

The confidence limits for π_h in (14.80) are not symmetric around the point estimate. In the disease outbreak example, for instance, the point estimate is:

$$\hat{\pi}_h = [1 + \exp(2.32065)]^{-1} = .089$$

while the confidence limits are .033 and .22. The reason for the asymmetry is that π_h is not a linear function of π_h'. ∎

14.9   Prediction of a New Observation

Multiple logistic regression is frequently employed for making predictions for new observations. In one application, for example, health personnel wished to predict whether a certain surgical procedure will ameliorate a new patient's condition, given the patient's age, gender, and various symptoms. In another application, marketing officials of a computer firm wished to predict whether a retail chain will purchase a new computer, based on the age of the company's current computer, the company's current workload, and other factors.

Choice of Prediction Rule

Forecasting a binary outcome for given levels $\mathbf{X}_h$ of the X variables is simple in the sense that the outcome 1 will be predicted if the estimated value $\hat{\pi}_h$ is large, and the outcome 0 will be predicted if $\hat{\pi}_h$ is small. The difficulty in making predictions of a binary outcome is in determining the cutoff point, below which the outcome 0 is predicted and above which the outcome 1 is predicted. A variety of approaches are possible to determine where this cutoff point is to be located. We consider three approaches.

1. *Use .5 as the cutoff.* With this approach, the prediction rule is:

If $\hat{\pi}_h$ exceeds .5, predict 1; otherwise predict 0.

This approach is reasonable when (a) it is equally likely in the population of interest that outcomes 0 and 1 will occur; and (b) the costs of incorrectly predicting 0 and 1 are approximately the same.

2. *Find the best cutoff for the data set on which the multiple logistic regression model is based.* This approach involves evaluating different cutoffs. For each cutoff, the rule is employed on the n cases in the model-building data set and the proportion of cases incorrectly predicted is ascertained. The cutoff for which the proportion of incorrect predictions is lowest is the one to be employed.

This approach is reasonable when (a) the data set is a random sample from the relevant population, and thus reflects the proper proportions of 0s and 1s in the population; and (b) the costs of incorrectly predicting 0 and 1 are approximately the same. The proportion of incorrect predictions observed for the optimal cutoff is likely to be an overstatement of the ability of the cutoff to correctly predict new observations, especially if the model-building data set is not large. The reason is that the cutoff is chosen with reference to the same data set from which the logistic model was fitted and thus is best for these data only. Consequently, as we explained in Chapter 10, it is important that a validation data set be employed to indicate whether the observed predictive ability for a fitted regression model is a valid indicator for predicting new observations.

3. *Use prior probabilities and costs of incorrect predictions in determining the cutoff.* When prior information is available about the likelihood of 1s and 0s in the population and the data set is not a random sample from the population, the prior information can be used in finding an optimal cutoff. In addition, when the cost of incorrectly predicting outcome 1 differs substantially from the cost of incorrectly predicting outcome 0, these costs of incorrect consequences can be incorporated into the determination of the cutoff so that the expected cost of incorrect predictions will be minimized. Specialized references, such as Reference 14.10, discuss the use of prior information and costs of incorrect predictions for determining the optimal cutoff.

Example

We shall use the disease outbreak example of Table 14.3 to illustrate how to obtain the cutoff point for predicting a new observation, even though the main purpose of that study was to determine whether age, socioeconomic status, and city sector are important risk factors. We assume that the cost of incorrectly predicting that a person has contracted the disease is about the same as the cost of incorrectly predicting that a person has not contracted the disease. The estimated logistic response function is given in (14.42).

Since a random sample of individuals was selected in the two city sectors, the 98 cases in the study constitute a cross section of the relevant population. Consequently, information is provided in the sample about the proportion of persons who have contracted the disease in the population. Of the 98 persons in the study, 31 had contracted the disease (see the DISEASE data set); hence the estimated proportion of persons who had contracted the disease is $31/98 = .316$. This proportion can be used as the starting point in the search for the best cutoff in the prediction rule.

Thus, the first rule investigated was:

(14.81)   Predict 1 if $\hat{\pi}_h \geq .316$; predict 0 if $\hat{\pi}_h < .316$

Note from Table 14.3, column 6, that $\hat{\pi}_1 = .209$ for case 1; hence prediction rule (14.81) calls for a prediction that the person has not contracted the disease. This would be a correct prediction. Similarly, prediction rule (14.81) would correctly predict cases 2 and 3 not to have contracted the disease. However, the prediction with rule (14.81) for case 4 (person has contracted the disease because $\hat{\pi}_4 = .371 \geq .316$) would be incorrect. Similarly, the prediction for case 5 (person has not contracted the disease because $\hat{\pi}_5 = .111 < .316$) would be incorrect. Altogether, 28 of the 98 predictions would be incorrect, so that the prediction error rate for rule (14.81) is $28/98 = .286$ or 28.6 percent. Of the 31 persons with the disease, eight would be incorrectly predicted with rule (14.81) not to have contracted the disease, or 25.8 percent. Of the 67 persons without the disease, 20 would be incorrectly predicted to have contracted the disease, or an error rate of 29.9 percent.

TABLE 14.7   **Prediction Error Rates with Fitted Logistic Regression Function (14.42) for Different Cutoffs—Disease Outbreak Example Model-Building Data Set (in percent).**

| | Disease Status | | |
Cutoff	With Disease	Without Disease	Total
.225	16.1	38.8	31.6
.242	16.1	37.3	30.6
.258	19.4	35.8	30.6
.275	22.6	34.3	30.6
.292	22.6	32.8	29.6
.308	25.8	29.9	28.6
.316	25.8	29.9	28.6
.325	29.0	25.4	26.5
.342	35.5	25.4	28.6
.358	35.5	23.9	27.6
.375	41.9	22.4	28.6
.392	45.2	20.9	28.6
.408	45.2	20.9	28.6

These error rates are entered in Table 14.7 in the line corresponding to the cutoff .316. Similar analyses were made for other cutoff points and the results are also shown in Table 14.7. It appears from this table that among the cutoffs considered, use of the following rule may be best:

$$(14.82) \qquad \text{Predict 1 if } \hat{\pi}_h \geq .325; \text{ predict 0 if } \hat{\pi}_h < .325$$

The prediction error rate for this rule is about 26.5 percent. Note also that for this rule, the error rates for persons with and without the disease are quite close to each other. Thus, the risks of incorrect predictions for the two groups are fairly balanced, which is often desirable. Note also that the error rates for persons with and without the disease are much less balanced as the cutoff is shifted further away from the optimal one in either direction

A validation study will now be required to determine whether the observed prediction error rate for the optimal cutoff properly indicates the risks of incorrect predictions for new observations, or whether it seriously understates them. In any case, it appears already that fitted logistic regression model (14.42) may not be too useful as a predictive model because of the relatively high risks of making incorrect predictions.

Note

An alternative to multiple logistic regression for predicting a binary response variable when the predictor variables are continuous is *discriminant analysis*. This approach assumes that the predictor variables follow a joint multivariate normal distribution. Discriminant analysis can also be used when this condition is not met, but the approach is not optimal then and logistic regression frequently is preferable. The reader is referred to Reference 14.11 for an in-depth discussion of discriminant analysis.   ∎

Validation of Prediction Error Rate

The reliability of the prediction error rate observed in the model-building data set is examined by applying the chosen prediction rule to a validation data set. If the new prediction error rate is about the same as that for the model-building data set, then the latter gives a reliable indication of the predictive ability of the fitted logistic regression model and the chosen prediction rule. If the new data lead to a considerably higher prediction error rate, then the fitted logistic regression model and the chosen prediction rule do not predict new observations as well as originally indicated.

Example.   In the disease outbreak example, the fitted logistic regression function (14.42) based on the model-building data set:

$$\hat{\pi} = [1 + \exp(2.3129 - .02975X_1 - .4088X_2 + .30525X_3 - 1.5747X_4)]^{-1}$$

was used to calculate estimated probabilities $\hat{\pi}_h$ for cases 99–196 in the DISEASE data set in Appendix C.3. These cases constitute the validation data set. The chosen prediction rule (14.82):

$$\text{Predict 1 if } \hat{\pi}_h \geq .325; \text{ predict 0 if } \hat{\pi}_h < .325$$

was then applied to these estimated probabilities. The percent prediction error rates were as follows:

Disease Status		
With Disease	Without Disease	Total
46.2	38.9	40.8

Note that the total prediction error rate of 40.8 percent is considerably higher than the 26.5 percent error rate based on the model-building data set. The latter therefore is not a reliable indicator of the predictive capability of the fitted logistic regression model and the chosen prediction rule.

We should mention again that making predictions was not the primary objective in the disease outbreak study. Rather, the main purpose was to identify key explanatory variables. Still, the prediction error rate for the validation data set shows that there must be other key explanatory variables affecting whether a person has contracted the disease that have not yet been identified for inclusion in the logistic regression model.

14.10   Polytomous Logistic Regression

Logistic regression is most frequently used to model the relationship between a dichotomous response variable and a set of predictor variables. On occasion, however, the response variable may have more than two levels. Logistic regression can still be employed, by means of a *polytomous* logistic regression model. Polytomous logistic regression models are used in many fields. In business, for instance, a researcher may wish to relate a firm's commitment of resources to total quality management (large, moderate, small) to size of firm, type of industry, and several other potential explanatory variables. As another example, the relation between severity of disease (mild, moderate, severe) and age of patient, gender of patient, and some other explanatory variables may be of interest.

Polytomous logistic regression is an extension of the logistic regression analysis discussed earlier where the response variable has two possible outcomes. Various complexities arise from the extension, but the basic ideas of modeling, the use of deviances, and making inferences discussed so far carry over. Reference 14.4 provides useful details about polytomous logistic regression.

An approximate way of carrying out polytomous logistic regression analysis is to fit several individual binary logistic regression models. For instance, if the response variable has three categories, the data with responses in categories 1 and 2 would be used to fit a binary logistic regression and the data with responses in categories 1 and 3 would be used to fit another binary logistic regression. The estimates of the logistic regression coefficients so obtained are consistent estimates of the polytomous logistic regression parameters and often involve only a moderate loss of efficiency (Ref. 14.12).

14.11   Poisson Regression

We consider now another nonlinear regression model where the response outcomes are discrete. Poisson regression is useful when the outcome is a count, with large outcomes being rare events. For instance, the number of times a household shops at a particular supermarket in a week is a count, with large numbers of shopping trips to the store during the week being rare events. A researcher may wish to study the relation between a family's number of shopping trips to the store during a particular week and the family's income, number of children, distance from the store, and some other explanatory variables. As another example, the relation between the number of hospitalizations of a member of a health maintenance organization during the past year and the member's age, income, and previous health status may be of interest.

Poisson Distribution

The Poisson distribution models outcomes that are counts ($Y_i = 0, 1, 2, \ldots$), with a large number of occurrences being a rare event. The Poisson probability distribution is as follows:

(14.83)
$$f(Y) = \frac{\mu^Y \exp(-\mu)}{Y!} \qquad Y = 0, 1, 2, \ldots$$

where $f(Y)$ denotes the probability that the outcome is Y and $Y! = Y(Y-1)\cdots 3 \cdot 2 \cdot 1$.

The mean and variance of the Poisson probability distribution are:

(14.84a)
$$E\{Y\} = \mu$$

(14.84b)
$$\sigma^2\{Y\} = \mu$$

Note that the variance is the same as the mean. Hence, if the number of store trips follows the Poisson distribution and the mean number of store trips for a family with three children is larger than the mean number of trips for a family with no children, the variances of the distributions of outcomes for the two families will also differ.

Note

At times, the count responses Y will pertain to different units of time or space. For instance, in a survey intended to obtain the total number of store trips during a particular month, some of the counts pertained only to the last week of the month. In such cases, let μ denote the mean response for Y for a unit of time or space (e.g., one month), and let t denote the number of units of time or space to which Y corresponds. For instance, $t = 7/30$ if Y is the number of store trips during one week where the unit time is one month; $t = 1$ if Y is the number of store trips during the month. The Poisson probability distribution is then expressed as follows:

$$(14.85) \qquad f(Y) = \frac{(t\mu)^Y \exp(-t\mu)}{Y!} \qquad Y = 0, 1, 2, \ldots$$

Our discussion throughout this section assumes that all responses Y_i pertain to the same unit of time or space.   ■

Poisson Regression Model

The Poisson regression model, like any nonlinear regression model, can be stated as follows:

$$Y_i = E\{Y_i\} + \varepsilon_i \qquad i = 1, 2, \ldots, n$$

The mean response for the ith case, to be denoted now by μ_i for simplicity, is assumed as always to be a function of the set of predictor variables, $X_1, \ldots, X_{p-1}$. We use the notation $\mu(\mathbf{X}_i, \boldsymbol{\beta})$ to denote the function that relates the mean response μ_i to $\mathbf{X}_i$, the values of the predictor variables for case i, and $\boldsymbol{\beta}$, the values of the regression coefficients. Some commonly used functions for Poisson regression are:

$$(14.86a) \qquad \mu_i = \mu(\mathbf{X}_i, \boldsymbol{\beta}) = \mathbf{X}_i'\boldsymbol{\beta}$$

$$(14.86b) \qquad \mu_i = \mu(\mathbf{X}_i, \boldsymbol{\beta}) = \exp(\mathbf{X}_i'\boldsymbol{\beta})$$

$$(14.86c) \qquad \mu_i = \mu(\mathbf{X}_i, \boldsymbol{\beta}) = \log_e(\mathbf{X}_i'\boldsymbol{\beta})$$

In all three cases, the mean responses μ_i must be nonnegative.

Since the distribution of the error terms ε_i for Poisson regression is a function of the distribution of the response Y_i, which is Poisson, it is easiest to state the Poisson regression model in the following form:

$$(14.87) \qquad Y_i \text{ are independent Poisson random variables with expected values } \mu_i, \text{ where:}$$

$$\mu_i = \mu(\mathbf{X}_i, \boldsymbol{\beta})$$

Maximum Likelihood Estimation

For Poisson regression model (14.87), the likelihood function is as follows:

$$(14.88) \qquad L(\boldsymbol{\beta}) = \prod_{i=1}^{n} f_i(Y_i) = \prod_{i=1}^{n} \frac{[\mu(\mathbf{X}_i, \boldsymbol{\beta})]^{Y_i} \exp[-\mu(\mathbf{X}_i, \boldsymbol{\beta})]}{Y_i!}$$

$$= \frac{\left\{ \prod_{i=1}^{n} [\mu(\mathbf{X}_i, \boldsymbol{\beta})]^{Y_i} \right\} \exp\left[-\sum_{i=1}^{n} \mu(\mathbf{X}_i, \boldsymbol{\beta}) \right]}{\prod_{i=1}^{n} Y_i!}$$

Once the functional form of $\mu(\mathbf{X}_i, \boldsymbol{\beta})$ is chosen, the maximization of (14.88) produces the maximum likelihood estimates of the regression coefficients $\boldsymbol{\beta}$. As before, it is easier to work with the logarithm of the likelihood function:

$$(14.89) \qquad \log_e L(\boldsymbol{\beta}) = \sum_{i=1}^{n} Y_i \log_e[\mu(\mathbf{X}_i, \boldsymbol{\beta})] - \sum_{i=1}^{n} \mu(\mathbf{X}_i, \boldsymbol{\beta}) - \sum_{i=1}^{n} \log_e(Y_i!)$$

Numerical search procedures are used to find the maximum likelihood estimates b_0, $b_1, \ldots, b_{p-1}$. Iteratively reweighted least squares can again be used to obtain these estimates. We shall rely on standard statistical software packages specifically designed to handle Poisson regression to obtain the maximum likelihood estimates.

After the maximum likelihood estimates have been found, we can obtain the fitted response function and the fitted values:

$$(14.90a) \qquad\qquad\qquad \hat{\mu} = \mu(\mathbf{X}, \mathbf{b})$$

$$(14.90b) \qquad\qquad\qquad \hat{\mu}_i = \mu(\mathbf{X}_i, \mathbf{b})$$

For the three functions in (14.86), the fitted response functions and fitted values are:

$$(14.90c) \qquad \mu = \mathbf{X}'\boldsymbol{\beta}: \qquad \hat{\mu} = \mathbf{X}'\mathbf{b} \qquad \hat{\mu}_i = \mathbf{X}_i'\mathbf{b}$$

$$(14.90d) \qquad \mu = \exp(\mathbf{X}'\boldsymbol{\beta}): \qquad \hat{\mu} = \exp(\mathbf{X}'\mathbf{b}) \qquad \hat{\mu}_i = \exp(\mathbf{X}_i'\mathbf{b})$$

$$(14.90e) \qquad \mu = \log_e(\mathbf{X}'\boldsymbol{\beta}): \qquad \hat{\mu} = \log_e(\mathbf{X}'\mathbf{b}) \qquad \hat{\mu}_i = \log_e(\mathbf{X}_i'\mathbf{b})$$

Model Development

Model development for a Poisson regression model is carried out in similar fashion as for logistic regression, using the deviances for different models and conducting tests based on partial deviances. For Poisson regression model (14.87), the model deviance is as follows:

$$(14.91) \qquad DEV(X_0, X_1, \ldots, X_{p-1}) = 2\left[\sum_{i=1}^{n} Y_i \log_e\left(\frac{Y_i}{\hat{\mu}_i}\right) - \sum_{i=1}^{n}(Y_i - \hat{\mu}_i) \right]$$

where $\hat{\mu}_i$ is the fitted value for the ith case according to (14.90b). The deviance residual for the ith case is:

$$(14.92) \qquad dev_i = \pm\left[2Y_i \log_e\left(\frac{Y_i}{\hat{\mu}_i}\right) - 2(Y_i - \hat{\mu}_i) \right]^{1/2}$$

The sign of the deviance residual is selected according to whether $Y_i - \hat{\mu}_i$ is positive or negative. Index plots of the deviance residuals and half-normal probability plots with simulated envelopes are useful for identifying outliers and checking the model fit.

Note

If $Y_i = 0$, the term $[Y_i \log_e(Y_i/\hat{\mu}_i)]$ in (14.91) and (14.92) equals 0.   ∎

Inferences

Inferences for a Poisson regression model are carried out in a similar fashion as for logistic regression. For instance, there is often interest in estimating the mean response for predictor variables $\mathbf{X}_h$. This estimate is obtained by substituting $\mathbf{X}_h$ into (14.90a).

In Poisson regression analysis, there is sometimes also interest in estimating probabilities of certain outcomes for given levels of the predictor variables, for instance, $P(Y = 0 \mid \mathbf{X}_h)$. Such an estimated probability can be obtained readily by substituting $\hat{\mu}_h$ into (14.83).

Interval estimation of individual regression coefficients can be carried out by use of the large-sample estimated standard deviations furnished by regression programs with Poisson regression capabilities.

Example

The Miller Lumber Company is a large retailer of lumber and paint, as well as of plumbing, electrical, and other household supplies. During a representative two-week period, in-store surveys were conducted and addresses of customers were obtained. The addresses were then used to identify the metropolitan area census tracts in which the customers reside. At the end of the survey period, the total number of customers who visited the store from each census tract within a 10-mile radius was determined and relevant demographic information for each tract (e.g., average income, number of housing units, etc.) was obtained. Several other variables expected to be related to customer counts were constructed from maps, including distance from census tract to nearest competitor and distance to store.

Initial screening of the potential predictor variables was conducted which led to the retention of five predictor variables:

X_1: Number of housing units

X_2: Average income, in dollars

X_3: Average housing unit age, in years

X_4: Distance to nearest competitor, in miles

X_5: Distance to store, in miles

Y_i: Number of customers who visited store from census tract

Data for a portion of the $n = 110$ census tracts are shown in Table 14.8.

Poisson regression model (14.87) with response function:

$$\mu(\mathbf{X}, \boldsymbol{\beta}) = \exp(\mathbf{X}'\boldsymbol{\beta})$$

was fitted to the data, using LISP-STAT (Ref. 14.13). Some principal results are presented in Table 14.9. Note that the deviance for this model is 114.985, with associated degrees of freedom $n - p = 110 - 6 = 104$. The P-value for the model deviance is .22, suggesting that the fitted model is a reasonably good fit.

Poisson regression models omitting one predictor variable at a time were fitted, their deviances obtained, and partial deviances were calculated. These partial deviances are shown in Table 14.9b, together with their associated P-values, each based on the chi-square

TABLE 14.8   **Data for Miller Lumber Company Example.**

Census Tract i	Housing Units X_1	Average Income X_2	Average Age X_3	Competitor Distance X_4	Store Distance X_5	Number of Customers Y
1	606	41,393	3	3.04	6.32	9
2	641	23,635	18	1.95	8.89	6
3	505	55,475	27	6.54	2.05	28
...	...	...	...	...	...	...
108	817	54,429	47	1.90	9.90	6
109	268	34,022	54	1.20	9.51	4
110	519	52,850	43	2.92	8.62	6

TABLE 14.9   **Fitted Poisson Response Function and Related Results—Miller Lumber Company Example.**

(a) Fitted Poisson Response Function

$$\hat{\mu} = \exp[2.942 + .000606X_1 - .0000117X_2 - .00373X_3 + .168X_4 - .129X_5]$$

$$DEV(X_0, X_1, X_2, X_3, X_4, X_5) = 114.985$$

(b) Estimated Coefficients, Standard Deviations, and Partial Deviances

Regression Coefficient	Estimated Regression Coefficient	Estimated Standard Deviation	Partial Deviance	P-value
β_0	2.9424	.207		
β_1	.0006058	.00014	18.21	.000
β_2	.00001169	.0000021	31.80	.000
β_3	−.003726	.0018	4.38	.036
β_4	.1684	.026	41.66	.000
β_5	−.1288	.016	67.50	.000

distribution with one degree of freedom. We note from the P-values that each predictor variable makes a marginal contribution to the fit of the regression model and consequently should be retained in the model.

A portion of the deviance residuals dev_i is shown in Table 14.10, together with the responses Y_i and the fitted values $\hat{\mu}_i$. Analysis of the deviance residuals did not disclose any major problems. Figure 14.9 contains an index plot of the deviance residuals. We note a few large negative deviance residuals; these are for census tracts where $Y = 0$; i.e., there were no customers from these areas. These may be difficult cases to fit with a Poisson

TABLE 14.10   **Responses, Fitted Values, and Deviance Residuals—Miller Lumber Company Example.**

Census Tract i	Y_i	$\hat{\mu}_i$	dev_i
1	9	12.3	−.999
2	6	8.8	−.992
3	28	28.1	−.024
. . .	. . .	. . .	. . .
108	6	5.3	.289
109	4	4.4	−.197
110	6	6.4	−.171

FIGURE 14.9   **Index Plot of Deviance Residuals—Miller Lumber Company Example.**

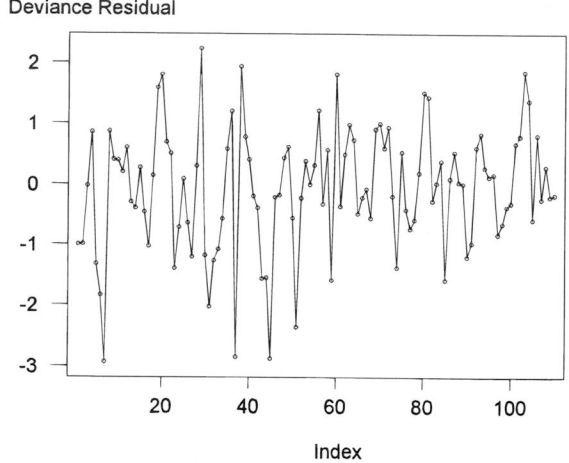

regression model. In view of the fact that the overall goodness of fit test based on the model deviance suggested that the fitted model is adequate, the model development process was concluded.

14.12   Generalized Linear Models

We conclude this chapter and the regression portion of this book by noting that all of the regression models considered, linear and nonlinear, belong to a family of models called *generalized linear models*. This family was first introduced by Nelder and Wedderburn (Ref. 14.14) and encompasses normal error linear regression models and the nonlinear exponential, logistic, and Poisson regression models, as well as many other models, such as log-linear models for categorical data.

The class of generalized linear models can be described as follows:

1. $Y_1, \ldots, Y_n$ are n independent responses that follow a probability distribution belonging to the *exponential family* of probability distributions, with expected value $E\{Y_i\} = \mu_i$.

2. A *linear predictor* based on the predictor variables $X_{i1}, \ldots, X_{i,p-1}$ is utilized, denoted by $\mathbf{X}_i'\boldsymbol{\beta}$:

$$\mathbf{X}_i'\boldsymbol{\beta} = \beta_0 + \beta_1 X_{i1} + \cdots + \beta_{p-1} X_{i,p-1}$$

3. The *link function g* relates the linear predictor to the mean response:

$$\mathbf{X}_i'\boldsymbol{\beta} = g(\mu_i)$$

Generalized linear models may have nonconstant variances σ_i^2 for the responses Y_i, but the variance σ_i^2 must be a function of the predictor variables through the mean response μ_i.

To illustrate the concept of the link function, consider first logistic regression model (14.37). There, the logit transformation in (14.19) serves to link the linear predictor $\mathbf{X}_i'\boldsymbol{\beta}$ to the mean response $\mu_i = \pi_i$:

$$g(\mu_i) = g(\pi_i) = \log_e\left(\frac{\pi_i}{1 - \pi_i}\right) = \mathbf{X}_i'\boldsymbol{\beta}$$

As a second example, consider Poisson regression model (14.87). There we considered several response functions in (14.86). For the response function $\mu_i = \exp(\mathbf{X}_i'\boldsymbol{\beta})$ in (14.86b), the linking relation is:

$$g(\mu_i) = \log_e(\mu_i) = \mathbf{X}_i'\boldsymbol{\beta}$$

We see from the Poisson regression models that there may be many different possible link functions that can be employed. They need only be monotonic and differentiable.

Finally, we consider the normal error regression model in (6.7). There the link function is simply:

$$g(\mu_i) = \mu_i$$

since the linking relation is:

$$\mathbf{X}_i'\boldsymbol{\beta} = \mu_i$$

The link function $g(\mu_i)$ for the normal error case is called the identity or unity link function.

Any regression model that belongs to the family of generalized linear models can be analyzed in a unified fashion. The maximum likelihood estimates of the regression parameters can be obtained by iteratively reweighted least squares [by ordinary least squares for normal error linear regression models (6.7)]. Tests for model development to determine whether some predictor variables may be dropped from the model can be conducted using partial deviances. A goodness of fit test can be conducted by means of the model deviance. Reference 14.15 provides further details about generalized linear models and their analysis.

Cited References

14.1. Finney, D. J. *Probit Analysis*. 3rd ed. Cambridge, England: Cambridge University Press, 1971.

14.2. Kennedy, W. J., Jr., and J. E. Gentle. *Statistical Computing*. New York: Marcel Dekker, 1980.

14.3. Agresti, A. *Categorical Data Analysis*. New York: John Wiley & Sons, 1990.

14.4. Hosmer, D. W., and S. Lemeshow. *Applied Logistic Regression*. New York: John Wiley & Sons, 1989.

14.5. Atkinson, A. C. "Two Graphical Displays for Outlying and Influential Observations in Regression," *Biometrika* 68 (1981), pp. 13–20.

14.6. Pregibon, D. "Logistic Regression Diagnostics," *Annals of Statistics* 9 (1981), pp. 705–24.

14.7. Landwehr, J. M., D. Pregibon, and A. C. Shoemaker. "Graphical Methods for Assessing Logistic Regression Models (with discussion)," *Journal of the American Statistical Association* 79 (1984), pp. 61–83.

14.8. Collett, D. *Modelling Binary Data*. London: Chapman and Hall, 1991.

14.9. *LogXact*. Cytel Software Corporation. Cambridge, Massachusetts, 1992.

14.10. Johnson, R. A., and D. W. Wichern. *Applied Multivariate Statistical Analysis*. 3rd ed. Englewood Cliffs, N. J.: Prentice Hall, 1992.

14.11. Lachenbruch, P. A. *Discriminant Analysis*. New York: Hafner Press, 1975.

14.12. Begg, C. B., and R. Gray. "Calculation of Polytomous Logistic Regression Parameters Using Individualized Regressions," *Biometrika* 71 (1984), pp. 11–18.

14.13. Tierney, L. *LISP-STAT: An Object-Oriented Environment for Statistical Computing and Dynamic Graphics*. New York: John Wiley & Sons, 1990.

14.14. Nelder, J. A., and R. W. M. Wedderburn. "Generalized Linear Models," *Journal of the Royal Statistical Society A* 135 (1972), pp. 370–84.

14.15. McCullagh, P., and J. A. Nelder. *Generalized Linear Models*. 2nd ed. London: Chapman and Hall, 1989.

Problems

14.1. A student stated: "I fail to see why the response function needs to be constrained between 0 and 1 when the response variable is binary and has a Bernoulli distribution. The fit to 0, 1 data will take care of this problem for any response function." Comment.

14.2. Since the logit transformation (14.10) linearizes the logistic response function, why can't this transformation be used on the individual responses Y_i and a linear response function then fitted? Explain.

14.3. If the true response function is J-shaped when the response variable is binary, would the use of the logistic response function be appropriate? Explain.

√ 14.4.   a. Plot the logistic response function (14.9) when $\beta_0 = -25$ and $\beta_1 = .2$.

b. For what value of X is the mean response equal to .5?

c. Find the odds when $X = 150$ and when $X = 151$. Is the odds ratio equal to $\exp(\beta_1)$ as it should be?

14.5.   a. Plot the logistic response function (14.9) when $\beta_0 = 20$ and $\beta_1 = -.2$.

b. For what value of X is the mean response equal to .5?

c. Find the odds when $X = 125$ and when $X = 126$. Is the odds ratio equal to $\exp(\beta_1)$ as it should be?

√ 14.6.   **Annual dues.** The board of directors of a professional association conducted a random sample survey of 30 members to assess the effects of several possible amounts of dues increase. The sample results follow. X denotes the dollar increase in annual dues posited in the survey interview, and $Y = 1$ if the interviewee indicated that the membership will not be renewed at that amount of dues increase and 0 if the membership will be renewed.

i:	1	2	3	. . .	28	29	30
X_i:	30	30	30	. . .	49	50	50
Y_i:	0	1	0	. . .	0	1	1

Logistic regression model (14.14) is assumed to be appropriate.

a. Find the maximum likelihood estimates of β_0 and β_1. State the fitted response function.

b. Obtain $\exp(b_1)$ and interpret this number.

c. What is the estimated probability that association members will not renew their membership if the dues are increased by $40?

d. Estimate the amount of dues increase for which 75 percent of the members are expected not to renew their association membership.

14.7.   **Performance ability.** A psychologist conducted a study to examine the nature of the relation, if any, between an employee's emotional stability (X) and the employee's ability to perform in a task group (Y). Emotional stability was measured by a written test for which the higher the score, the greater is the emotional stability. Ability to perform in a task group ($Y = 1$ if able, $Y = 0$ if unable) was evaluated by the supervisor. The results for 27 employees were:

i:	1	2	3	. . .	25	26	27
X_i:	474	432	453	. . .	562	506	600
Y_i:	0	0	0	. . .	1	0	1

Logistic regression model (14.14) is assumed to be appropriate.

a. Find the maximum likelihood estimates of β_0 and β_1. State the fitted response function.

b. Obtain $\exp(b_1)$ and interpret this number.

c. What is the estimated probability that employees with an emotional stability test score of 550 will be able to perform in a task group?

d. Estimate the emotional stability test score for which 70 percent of the employees with this test score are expected to be able to perform in a task group.

√ 14.8. **Bottle return**. A carefully controlled experiment was conducted to study the effect of the size of the deposit level on the likelihood that a returnable one-liter soft-drink bottle will be returned. A bottle return was scored 1, and no return was scored 0. The data to follow show the number of bottles that were returned (R_j) out of 500 sold (n_j) at each of six deposit levels (X_j, in cents):

j:	1	2	3	4	5	6
Deposit level X_j:	2	5	10	20	25	30
Number sold n_j:	500	500	500	500	500	500
Number returned R_j:	72	103	170	296	406	449

An analyst believes that logistic response function (14.9) is appropriate for studying the relation between size of deposit and the probability a bottle will be returned.

a. Plot the estimated proportions $p_j = R_j/n_j$ against X_j. Does the plot support the analyst's belief that the logistic response function is appropriate?

b. Find the maximum likelihood estimates of β_0 and β_1. State the fitted response function.

c. Obtain $\exp(b_1)$ and interpret this number.

d. What is the estimated probability that a bottle will be returned when the deposit is 15 cents?

e. Estimate the amount of deposit for which 75 percent of the bottles are expected to be returned.

14.9. **Toxicity experiment**. In an experiment testing the effect of a toxic substance, 1,500 experimental insects were divided at random into six groups of 250 each. The insects in each group were exposed to a fixed dose of the toxic substance. A day later, each insect was observed. Death from exposure was scored 1, and survival was scored 0. The results are shown below; X_j denotes the dose level (on a logarithmic scale) received by the insects in group j and R_j denotes the number of insects that died out of the 250 (n_j) in the group.

j:	1	2	3	4	5	6
X_j:	1	2	3	4	5	6
n_j:	250	250	250	250	250	250
R_j:	28	53	93	126	172	197

Logistic response function (14.9) is assumed to be appropriate.

a. Find the maximum likelihood estimates of β_0 and β_1. State the fitted response function.

b. Plot the fitted response function and the estimated proportions p_j on the same graph. Does the fit appear to be a good one?

c. Obtain $\exp(b_1)$ and interpret this number.

d. What is the estimated probability that an insect dies when the dose level is $X = 3.5$?

e. What is the estimated median lethal dose—that is, the dose for which 50 percent of the experimental insects are expected to die?

14.10. **Car purchase**. A marketing research firm was engaged by an automobile manufacturer to conduct a pilot study to examine the feasibility of using logistic regression for ascertaining the likelihood that a family will purchase a new car during the next year. A random sample of 33 suburban families was selected. Data on annual family income (X_1, in thousand dollars) and the current age of the oldest family automobile (X_2, in years) were obtained. A follow-up interview conducted 12 months later was used to determine whether the family actually purchased a new car ($Y = 1$) or did not purchase a new car ($Y = 0$) during the year.

i:	1	2	3	. . .	31	32	33
X_{i1}:	32	45	60	. . .	21	32	17
X_{i2}:	3	2	2	. . .	3	5	1
Y_i:	0	0	1	. . .	0	1	0

Multiple logistic regression model (14.37) with two predictor variables in first-order terms is assumed to be appropriate.

a. Find the maximum likelihood estimates of β_0, β_1, and β_2. State the fitted response function.

b. Obtain $\exp(b_1)$ and $\exp(b_2)$ and interpret these numbers.

c. What is the estimated probability that a family with annual income of $50 thousand and an oldest car of 3 years will purchase a new car next year?

√ 14.11. **Flu shots.** A local health clinic sent fliers to its clients to encourage everyone, but especially older persons at high risk of complications, to get a flu shot in time for protection against an expected flu epidemic. In a pilot follow-up study, 50 clients were randomly selected and asked whether they actually received a flu shot. In addition, data were collected on their age (X_1) and their health awareness. The latter data were combined into a health awareness index (X_2), for which higher values indicate greater awareness. A client who received a flu shot was coded $Y = 1$, and a client who did not receive a flu shot was coded $Y = 0$.

i:	1	2	3	. . .	48	49	50
X_{i1}:	38	52	41	. . .	56	45	33
X_{i2}:	40	60	36	. . .	46	35	45
Y_i:	0	1	0	. . .	0	0	0

Multiple logistic regression model (14.37) with two predictor variables in first-order terms and the interaction term $\beta_3 X_1 X_2$ is assumed to be appropriate.

a. Find the maximum likelihood estimates of β_0, β_1, β_2, and β_3. State the fitted response function.

b. Obtain $\exp(b_1)$. Does this number have a ready interpretation? Explain.

c. What is the estimated probability that clients aged 55 with a health awareness index of 60 will receive a flu shot?

√ 14.12. Refer to **Annual dues** Problem 14.6.

a. To assess the appropriateness of the logistic regression function, form three groups of 10 cases each according to their fitted logit values $\hat{\pi}'$. Plot the estimated proportions p_j against the midpoints of the $\hat{\pi}'$ intervals. Is the plot consistent with a response function of monotonic sigmoidal shape? Explain.

b. Obtain the model deviance and test the goodness of fit of logistic regression model (14.14); use $\alpha = .01$. State the alternatives, decision rule, and conclusion.

c. Obtain the deviance residuals and present them in an index plot. Do there appear to be any outlying cases?

    d. Construct a half-normal probability plot of the absolute deviance residuals. Do any cases here appear to be outlying?

14.13. Refer to **Performance ability** Problem 14.7.

    a. To assess the appropriateness of the logistic regression function, form three groups of nine cases each according to their fitted logit values $\hat{\pi}'$. Plot the estimated proportions p_j against the midpoints of the $\hat{\pi}'$ intervals. Is the plot consistent with a response function of monotonic sigmoidal shape? Explain.

    b. Obtain the model deviance and test the goodness of fit of logistic regression model (14.14); use $\alpha = .005$. State the alternatives, decision rule, and conclusion.

    c. Obtain the deviance residuals and present them in an index plot. Does this plot suggest any outlying cases?

    d. Construct a half-normal probability plot of the absolute deviance residuals. Do any cases here appear to be outlying?

√ 14.14. Refer to **Bottle return** Problem 14.8. Use the groups given there to conduct a chi-square goodness of fit test of the appropriateness of logistic response function (14.9). Control the risk of a Type I error at .005. State the alternatives, decision rule, and conclusion.

14.15. Refer to **Toxicity experiment** Problem 14.9. Use the groups given there to conduct a chi-square goodness of fit test of the appropriateness of logistic response function (14.9). Control the risk of a Type I error at .01. State the alternatives, decision rule, and conclusion.

14.16. Refer to **Car purchase** Problem 14.10.

    a. To assess the appropriateness of the logistic regression function, form three groups of 11 cases each according to their fitted logit values $\hat{\pi}'$. Plot the estimated proportions p_j against the midpoints of the $\hat{\pi}'$ intervals. Is the plot consistent with a response function of monotonic sigmoidal shape? Explain.

    b. Obtain the model deviance and test the goodness of fit of logistic regression model (14.37); use $\alpha = .01$. State the alternatives, decision rule, and conclusion.

    c. Obtain the deviance residuals and present them in an index plot. Do there appear to be any outlying cases?

    d. Construct a half-normal probability plot of the absolute deviance residuals. Do any cases here appear to be outlying?

√ 14.17. Refer to **Flu shots** Problem 14.11.

    a. To assess the appropriateness of the logistic regression function, form four groups of approximately 12 cases each according to their fitted logit values $\hat{\pi}'$. Plot the estimated proportions p_j against the midpoints of the $\hat{\pi}'$ intervals. Is the plot consistent with a response function of monotonic sigmoidal shape? Explain.

    b. Obtain the model deviance and test the goodness of fit of logistic regression model (14.37); use $\alpha = .005$. State the alternatives, decision rule, and conclusion.

    c. Obtain the deviance residuals and present them in an index plot. Do there appear to be any outlying cases?

    d. Construct a half-normal probability plot of the absolute deviance residuals. Do any cases here appear to be outlying?

√ 14.18. Refer to **Annual dues** Problem 14.6. Assume that the fitted model is appropriate and that large-sample inferences are applicable.

a. Obtain an approximate 90 percent confidence interval for $\exp(\beta_1)$. Interpret your interval.

b. Obtain an approximate 90 percent confidence interval for the mean response π_h for a dues increase of $X_h = \$40$.

14.19. Refer to **Performance ability** Problem 14.7. Assume that the fitted model is appropriate and that large-sample inferences are applicable.

a. Obtain an approximate 95 percent confidence interval for $\exp(\beta_1)$. Interpret your interval.

b. Obtain joint confidence intervals for the mean response π_h for persons with emotional stability test scores $X_h = 550$ and 625, respectively, with an approximate 90 percent family confidence coefficient. Interpret your intervals.

√ 14.20. Refer to **Bottle return** Problem 14.8. Assume that the fitted model is appropriate and that large-sample inferences are applicable.

a. Obtain an approximate 95 percent confidence interval for β_1. Convert this confidence interval into one for the odds ratio. Interpret this latter interval.

b. Obtain an approximate 95 percent confidence interval for the probability of a bottle return for deposit $X_h = 15$ cents. Interpret your interval.

14.21. Refer to **Toxicity experiment** Problem 14.9. Assume that the fitted model is appropriate and that large-sample inferences are applicable.

a. Obtain an approximate 99 percent confidence interval for β_1. Convert this confidence interval into one for the odds ratio. Interpret this latter interval.

b. Obtain joint confidence intervals for the mean response π_h for dose levels $X_h = 3.5$ and 5.0, with an approximate 90 percent family confidence coefficient. Interpret your intervals.

14.22. Refer to **Car purchase** Problem 14.10. Assume that the fitted model is appropriate and that large-sample inferences are applicable.

a. Obtain joint confidence intervals for the family income odds ratio $\exp(20\beta_1)$ for families whose incomes differ by 20 thousand dollars and for the age of the oldest family automobile odds ratio $\exp(2\beta_2)$ for families whose oldest automobiles differ in age by 2 years, with family confidence coefficient of approximately .80. Interpret your intervals.

b. Use the appropriate partial deviance to test whether X_2, age of oldest family automobile, can be dropped from the regression model; use $\alpha = .15$. State the alternatives, decision rule, and conclusion. What is the approximate P-value of the test?

c. Test whether the two-factor interaction effect between annual family income and age of oldest automobile should be added to the regression model containing family income and age of oldest automobile as first-order terms; use $\alpha = .05$. State the alternatives, full and reduced models, decision rule, and conclusion. What is the approximate P-value of the test?

√ 14.23. Refer to **Flu shots** Problem 14.11. Assume that the fitted model is appropriate and that large-sample inferences are applicable.

a. Obtain joint confidence intervals for the odds of flu shots for clients of age 45 with a health awareness index of 60 and for clients of age 55 with a health awareness index of 60, with family confidence coefficient of approximately 95 percent. Interpret your intervals.

    b. Obtain approximate 95 percent joint confidence intervals as in part (a) but for clients with a health awareness index of 30. What appears to be the effect of health awareness on the odds ratio for age? Discuss.

    c. Use the appropriate partial deviance to test whether the two-factor interaction effect between age and health awareness index can be dropped from the regression model; use $\alpha = .05$. State the alternatives, decision rule, and conclusion. What is the approximate P-value of the test?

√ 14.24. Refer to **Annual dues** Problem 14.6. A prediction rule is to be developed, based on the fitted regression function in Problem 14.6a.

    a. Based on the sample cases, find the total error rate, the error rate for renewers, and the error rate for nonrenewers for the following cutoffs: .40, .45, .50, .55, .60.

    b. Based on your results in part (a), which cutoff minimizes the total error rate? Are the error rates for renewers and nonrenewers fairly balanced at this cutoff?

    c. How can you establish whether the observed total error rate for the best cutoff in part (b) is a reliable indicator of the predictive ability of the fitted regression function and the chosen cutoff?

14.25. Refer to **Performance ability** Problem 14.7. A prediction rule is to be developed, based on the fitted regression function in Problem 14.7a.

    a. Based on the sample cases, find the total error rate, the error rate for employees able to perform in a task group, and the error rate for employees not able to perform for the following cutoffs: .325, .425, .525, .625.

    b. Based on your results in part (a), which cutoff minimizes the total error rate? Are the error rates for employees able to perform in a task group and for employees not able to perform fairly balanced at this cutoff?

    c. How can you establish whether the observed total error rate for the best cutoff in part (b) is a reliable indicator of the predictive ability of the fitted regression function and the chosen cutoff?

14.26. Refer to **Car purchase** Problem 14.10. A prediction rule is to be developed, based on the fitted regression function in Problem 14.10a.

    a. Based on the sample cases, find the total error rate, the error rate for purchasers, and the error rate for nonpurchasers for the following cutoffs: .350, .375, .400, .425, .450.

    b. Based on your results in part (a), which cutoff minimizes the total error rate? Are the error rates for purchasers and nonpurchasers fairly balanced at this cutoff?

    c. How can you establish whether the observed total error rate for the best cutoff in part (b) is a reliable indicator of the predictive ability of the fitted regression function and the chosen cutoff?

√ 14.27. Refer to **Flu shots** Problem 14.11. A prediction rule is to be developed, based on the fitted regression function in Problem 14.11a.

    a. Based on the sample cases, find the total error rate, the error rate for clients receiving the flu shot, and the error rate for clients not receiving the flu shot for the following cutoffs: .40, .50, .60, .70.

    b. Based on your results in part (a), which cutoff minimizes the total error rate? Are the error rates for clients receiving the flu shot and for clients not receiving the flu shot fairly balanced at this cutoff?

   c. How can you establish whether the observed total error rate for the best cutoff in part (b) is a reliable indicator of the predictive ability of the fitted regression function and the chosen cutoff?

√ 14.28. Refer to **Airfreight breakage** Problem 1.21.

   a. Fit the Poisson regression model (14.87) with the response function $\mu(\mathbf{X}, \boldsymbol{\beta}) = \exp(\beta_0 + \beta_1 X)$. State the estimated regression coefficients, their estimated standard deviations, and the estimated response function.

   b. Obtain the model deviance and test the goodness of fit of Poisson regression model (14.87); use $\alpha = .01$. State the alternatives, decision rule, and conclusion.

   c. Obtain the deviance residuals and present them in an index plot. Do there appear to be any outlying cases?

   d. Estimate the mean number of ampules broken when $X = 0$, 1, 2, 3. Compare these estimates with those obtained by means of the fitted linear regression function in Problem 1.21a.

   e. Plot the Poisson and linear regression functions, together with the data. Which regression function appears to be a better fit here? Discuss.

   f. Management wishes to estimate the probability that 10 or fewer ampules are broken when there is no transfer of the shipment. Use the fitted Poisson regression function to obtain this estimate.

   g. Obtain an approximate 95 percent confidence interval for β_1. Interpret your interval estimate.

14.29. **Geriatric study**. A researcher in geriatrics designed a prospective study to investigate the effects of two interventions on the frequency of falls. One hundred subjects were randomly assigned to one of the two interventions: education only ($X_1 = 0$) and education plus aerobic exercise training ($X_1 = 1$). Subjects were at least 65 years of age and in reasonably good health. Three variables considered to be important as control variables were gender (X_2: 0 =female; 1 = male), a balance index (X_3), and a strength index (X_4). The higher the balance index, the more stable is the subject; and the higher the strength index, the stronger is the subject. Each subject kept a diary recording the number of falls (Y) during the six months of the study. The data follow:

Subject i	Number of Falls Y_i	Intervention X_{i1}	Gender X_{i2}	Balance Index X_{i3}	Strength Index X_{i4}
1	1	1	0	45	70
2	1	1	0	62	66
3	2	1	1	43	64
...	...	...	...	...	...
98	4	0	0	69	48
99	4	0	1	50	52
100	2	0	0	37	56

   a. Fit the Poisson regression model (14.87) with the response function $\mu(\mathbf{X}, \boldsymbol{\beta}) = \exp(\beta_0 + \beta_1 X_1 + \beta_2 X_2 + \beta_3 X_3 + \beta_4 X_4)$. State the estimated regression coefficients, their estimated standard deviations, and the estimated response function.

   b. Obtain the model deviance and test the goodness of fit of Poisson regression model (14.87); use $\alpha = .005$. State the alternatives, decision rule, and conclusion.

c. Obtain the deviance residuals and present them in an index plot. Do there appear to be any outlying cases?

d. Assuming that the fitted model is appropriate, use the relevant partial deviance to test whether gender (X_2) can be dropped from the model; control α at .05. State the alternatives, decision rule, and conclusion.

e. For the fitted model containing only X_1, X_3, and X_4 in first-order terms, obtain an approximate 95 percent confidence interval for β_1. Interpret your confidence interval. Does aerobic exercise reduce the frequency of falls when controlling for balance and strength?

Exercises

14.30. Show the equivalence of (14.9) and (14.9a).

14.31. Derive (14.27) from (14.20).

14.32. Derive (14.48), using (14.45) and (14.46).

14.33. (Calculus needed.) Maximum likelihood estimation theory states that the estimated large-sample variance-covariance matrix for maximum likelihood estimators is given by the inverse of the information matrix, the elements of which are the negatives of the expected values of the second-order partial derivatives of the logarithm of the likelihood function evaluated at $\boldsymbol{\beta} = \mathbf{b}$:

$$\left[-E\left\{ \frac{\partial^2 \log_e L(\boldsymbol{\beta})}{\partial \beta_i \, \partial \beta_j} \right\}_{\boldsymbol{\beta}=\mathbf{b}} \right]^{-1}$$

Show that this matrix simplifies to (14.68) for logistic regression. Consider the case where $p - 1 = 1$.

14.34. (Calculus needed.) Estimate the approximate variance-covariance matrix of the estimated regression coefficients for the programming task example in Table 14.1a, using (14.68), and verify the estimated standard deviations in Table 14.1b.

14.35. Show that the logistic response function (13.10) reduces to the response function in (14.14) when the Y_i are independent Bernoulli random variables with $E\{Y_i\} = \pi_i$.

14.36. Consider the multiple logistic regression model with $\boldsymbol{\beta}'\mathbf{X} = \beta_0 + \beta_1 X_1 + \beta_2 X_2 + \beta_3 X_1 X_2$. Derive an expression for the odds ratio for X_1. Does $\exp(\beta_1)$ have the same meaning here as for a regression model containing no interaction term?

14.37. A Bernoulli response Y_i has expected value:

$$E\{Y_i\} = \pi_i = 1 - \exp\left[-\exp\left(\frac{X_i - \gamma_0}{\gamma_1} \right) \right]$$

Show that the link function here is the complementary log-log transformation of π_i, namely, $\log_e[-\log_e(1 - \pi_i)]$.

Projects

14.38. Refer to the **DISEASE** data set. Savings account status is the response variable and age, socioeconomic status, and city sector are the predictor variables. Cases 1–98 are to be utilized for developing the regression model.

   a. Fit logistic regression model (14.37) containing the predictor variables in first-order terms and interaction terms for all pairs of predictor variables. State the fitted response function.

   b. Test whether all interaction terms can be dropped from the regression model; use $\alpha = .01$. State the alternatives, full and reduced models, decision rule, and conclusion. What is the approximate P-value of the test?

   c. For logistic regression model (14.37) containing the predictor variables in first-order terms only, use backward elimination to decide which predictor variables can be dropped from the regression model. Control the α risk at .05 at each stage. Which variables should be retained in the regression model?

14.39. Refer to the **DISEASE** data set and Project 14.38. Logistic regression model (14.37) with predictor variables age and socioeconomic status in first-order terms is to be further evaluated.

   a. Conduct an approximate chi-square goodness of fit test for the appropriateness of the logistic regression function by forming five groups of approximately 20 cases each; use $\alpha = .05$. State the alternatives, decision rule, and conclusion. What is the approximate P-value of the test?

   b. Obtain the model deviance and use it to test the goodness of fit of the logistic regression model, with $\alpha = .05$. State the alternatives, decision rule, and conclusion. Is your conclusion the same as for the chi-square test in part (a)?

   c. Obtain the deviance residuals and present them in an index plot. Do there appear to be any outlying cases?

   d. Construct a half-normal probability plot of the absolute deviance residuals and super-impose a simulated envelope. Are any cases outlying? Does the logistic model appear to be a good fit? Discuss.

   e. To predict savings account status, you must identify the optimal cutoff. Based on the sample cases, find the total error rate, the error rate for persons with a savings account, and the error rate for persons with no savings account for the following cutoffs: .45, .50, .55, .60. Which of the cutoffs minimizes the total error rate? Are the two error rates for persons with and without savings accounts fairly balanced at this cutoff?

14.40. Refer to the **DISEASE** data set and Project 14.39. The regression model identified in Project 14.39 is to be validated using cases 99–196.

   a. Use the rule obtained in Project 14.39e to make a prediction for each of the holdout validation cases. What are the total and the two component prediction error rates for the validation data set? How do these error rates compare with those for the model-building data set in Project 14.39e?

   b. Combine the model-building and validation data sets and fit the model identified in Project 14.39 to the combined data. Are the estimated coefficients and their estimated standard deviations similar to those obtained for the model-building data set? Should they be? Comment.

c. Based on the fitted regression model in part (b), obtain joint 90 percent confidence intervals for the odds ratios for age and socioeconomic status. Interpret your intervals.

14.41. Refer to the **SENIC** data set. Medical school affiliation is the response variable, to be coded $Y = 1$ if medical school affiliation and $Y = 0$ if no medical school affiliation. The pool of potential predictor variables includes age, routine chest X-ray ratio, average daily census, and number of nurses. All 113 cases are to be used in developing the regression model.

   a. Fit logistic regression model (14.37) containing all predictor variables in the pool in first-order terms and interaction terms for all pairs of predictor variables. State the fitted response function.

   b. Test whether all interaction terms can be dropped from the regression model; use $\alpha = .05$. State the alternatives, full and reduced models, decision rule, and conclusion. What is the approximate P-value of the test?

   c. For logistic regression model (14.37) containing the predictor variables in first-order terms only, use backward elimination to decide which predictor variables can be dropped from the regression model. Control the α risk at .10 at each stage. Which variables should be retained in the regression model?

14.42. Refer to the **SENIC** data set and Project 14.41. Logistic regression model (14.37) with predictor variables age and average daily census in first-order terms is to be further evaluated.

   a. Conduct an approximate chi-square goodness of fit test for the appropriateness of the logistic regression function by forming five groups of approximately 23 cases each; use $\alpha = .05$. State the alternatives, decision rule, and conclusion. What is the approximate P-value of the test?

   b. Obtain the model deviance and use it to test the goodness of fit of the logistic regression model, with $\alpha = .05$. State the alternatives, decision rule, and conclusion. Is your conclusion the same as for the chi-square test in part (a)?

   c. Obtain the deviance residuals and present them in an index plot. Do there appear to be any outlying cases?

   d. Construct a half-normal probability plot of the absolute deviance residuals and super-impose a simulated envelope. Are any cases outlying? Does the logistic model appear to be a good fit? Discuss.

   e. To predict medical school affiliation, you must identify the optimal cutoff. Based on the sample cases, find the total error rate, the error rate for hospitals with medical school affiliation, and the error rate for hospitals without medical school affiliation for the following cutoffs: .30, .40, .50, .60. Which of the cutoffs minimizes the total error rate? Are the two error rates for hospitals with and without medical school affiliation fairly balanced at this cutoff?

   f. Estimate by means of an approximate 90 percent confidence interval the odds of a hospital having medical school affiliation for hospitals with average age of patients of 55 years and average daily census of 500 patients.

14.43. Refer to **Annual dues** Problems 14.6 and 14.12. Obtain a simulated envelope and super-impose it on the half-normal probability plot of the absolute deviance residuals obtained in Problem 14.12d. Are there any indications that the fitted model is not appropriate? Are there any outlying cases? Discuss.

14.44. Refer to **Annual dues** Problems 14.6 and 14.18. In order to assess the appropriateness of large-sample inferences here, employ the following parametric bootstrap procedure: For each of the 30 cases, generate a Bernoulli outcome $(0, 1)$, using the estimated probability $\hat{\pi}_i$ for the original X_i level according to the fitted model. Fit the logistic regression model to the bootstrap sample and obtain the bootstrap estimates b_0^* and b_1^*. Repeat this procedure 500 times. Compute the mean and standard deviation of the 500 bootstrap estimates b_0^*, and do the same for b_1^*. Plot separate histograms of the bootstrap distributions of b_0^* and b_1^*. Are these distributions approximately normal? Compare the point estimates b_0 and b_1 and their estimated standard deviations obtained in the original fit to the means and standard deviations of the bootstrap distributions. What do you conclude about the appropriateness of large-sample inferences here? Discuss.

14.45. Refer to **Car purchase** Problems 14.10 and 14.16. Obtain a simulated envelope and super-impose it on the half-normal probability plot of the absolute deviance residuals obtained in Problem 14.16d. Are there any indications that the fitted model is not appropriate? Are there any outlying cases? Discuss.

14.46. Refer to **Car purchase** Problems 14.10 and 14.22. In order to assess the appropriateness of large-sample inferences here, employ the following parametric bootstrapping procedure: For each of the 33 cases, generate a Bernoulli outcome $(0, 1)$, using the estimated probability $\hat{\pi}_i$ for the original levels of the predictor variables according to the fitted model. Fit the logistic regression model to the bootstrap sample. Repeat this procedure 500 times. Compute the mean and standard deviation of the 500 bootstrap estimates b_1^*, and do the same for b_2^*. Plot separate histograms of the bootstrap distributions of b_1^* and b_2^*. Are these distributions approximately normal? Compare the point estimates b_1 and b_2 and their estimated standard deviations obtained in the original fit to the means and standard deviations of the bootstrap distributions. What do you conclude about the appropriateness of large-sample inferences here? Discuss.

Correlation Analysis

Normal Correlation Models

The purpose of this chapter is to indicate the relation between regression models and their uses, discussed in Chapters 1–14, and normal correlation models. We first take up bivariate normal correlation models and then consider multivariate normal models.

15.1 Distinction between Regression and Correlation Models

The basic regression models taken up in this book assume that the predictor variables $X_1, \ldots, X_{p-1}$ are fixed constants, and primary interest exists in making inferences about the response variable Y on the basis of the predictor variables. We also saw in Chapter 2, for the case of a single predictor variable, that the regression analysis for a normal error regression model is applicable even when X is a random variable, provided that the conditional distributions of Y follow certain specifications and the marginal distribution of X does not involve the regression model parameters β_0, β_1, and σ^2. Thus, in the case where X is a random variable, only the conditional distributions of Y need be specified and a restriction placed on the marginal distribution of X. We do not, however, need to completely specify the joint distribution of X and Y. While the discussion in Chapter 2 dealt with only a single predictor variable, all of the points apply to multiple regression models containing a number of predictor variables that are random.

Correlation models, like regression models with random predictor variables, consist of variables all of which are random. Correlation models differ from regression models with random predictor variables in that they specify the joint distribution of the variables completely, not only the conditional distributions of Y. Furthermore, the variables in a correlation model play a symmetrical role, with no one variable automatically designated as the response variable. Correlation models are employed to study the nature of the relations between the variables; they also may be used for making inferences about any one of the variables on the basis of the others.

Thus, an analyst may use a correlation model for the two variables "height of person" and "weight of person" in a study of a sample of persons, each variable being taken as random. The analyst might wish to study the relation between the two variables or might be interested in making inferences about weight of a person on the basis of the person's height, in making inferences about height on the basis of weight, or in both.

Other examples where a correlation model may be appropriate are:

1. To study the relations between service station sales of gasoline, auxiliary products, and repair services.

2. To study the relation between company net income determined by generally accepted accounting principles and net income according to tax regulations.

3. To study the relations between a person's blood pressure, age, and weight.

The correlation model most widely employed is the normal correlation model. We discuss it first for the case of two variables.

15.2 Bivariate Normal Distribution

The normal correlation model for the case of two variables is based on the *bivariate normal distribution*. Let us denote the two variables as Y_1 and Y_2. (We do not use the notation X and Y in this chapter because both variables play a symmetrical role in correlation analysis.) We say that Y_1 and Y_2 are *jointly normally distributed* if the density function of their joint distribution is that of the bivariate normal distribution.

Density Function

The density function of the bivariate normal distribution is as follows:

$$(15.1) \quad f(Y_1, Y_2) = \frac{1}{2\pi\sigma_1\sigma_2\sqrt{1-\rho_{12}^2}} \exp\left\{ -\frac{1}{2(1-\rho_{12}^2)}\left[\left(\frac{Y_1-\mu_1}{\sigma_1}\right)^2 \right.\right.$$

$$\left.\left. -2\rho_{12}\left(\frac{Y_1-\mu_1}{\sigma_1}\right)\left(\frac{Y_2-\mu_2}{\sigma_2}\right) + \left(\frac{Y_2-\mu_2}{\sigma_2}\right)^2 \right] \right\}$$

Note that this density function involves five parameters: $\mu_1, \mu_2, \sigma_1, \sigma_2, \rho_{12}$. We shall explain the meaning of these parameters shortly. First, let us consider a graphic representation of the bivariate normal distribution.

Graphic Representation

Figure 15.1 contains a SYSTAT three-dimensional plot of a bivariate normal probability distribution. The probability distribution is a surface in three-dimensional space. For every pair of (Y_1, Y_2) values, the density $f(Y_1, Y_2)$ represents the height of the surface at that point. The surface is continuous, and probability corresponds to volume under the surface.

Marginal Distributions

If Y_1 and Y_2 are jointly normally distributed, it can be shown that their marginal distributions have the following characteristics:

(15.2a) The marginal distribution of Y_1 is normal with mean μ_1 and standard deviation σ_1:

FIGURE 15.1   Example of Bivariate Normal Distribution.

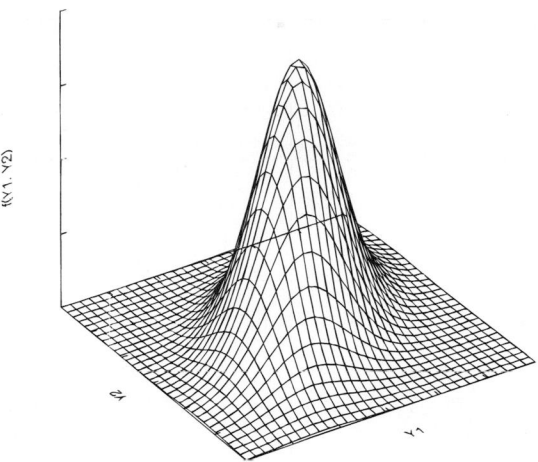

$$f_1(Y_1) = \frac{1}{\sqrt{2\pi}\,\sigma_1} \exp\left[-\frac{1}{2}\left(\frac{Y_1 - \mu_1}{\sigma_1}\right)^2\right]$$

(15.2b) The marginal distribution of Y_2 is normal with mean μ_2 and standard deviation σ_2:

$$f_2(Y_2) = \frac{1}{\sqrt{2\pi}\,\sigma_2} \exp\left[-\frac{1}{2}\left(\frac{Y_2 - \mu_2}{\sigma_2}\right)^2\right]$$

Thus, when Y_1 and Y_2 are jointly normally distributed, each of the two variables by itself is normally distributed. The converse, however, is not generally true; if Y_1 and Y_2 are each normally distributed, they need not be jointly normally distributed in accord with (15.1).

Meaning of Parameters

The five parameters of the bivariate normal density function (15.1) have the following meaning:

1. μ_1 and σ_1 are the mean and standard deviation of the marginal distribution of Y_1.
2. μ_2 and σ_2 are the mean and standard deviation of the marginal distribution of Y_2.
3. ρ_{12} is the *coefficient of correlation* between the random variables Y_1 and Y_2. This coefficient is denoted by $\rho\{Y_1, Y_2\}$ in Appendix A, using the correlation operator notation, and defined in (A.25a):

(15.3) $$\rho_{12} = \rho\{Y_1, Y_2\} = \frac{\sigma_{12}}{\sigma_1 \sigma_2}$$

FIGURE 15.2   **Contour Diagram for a Bivariate Normal Surface.**

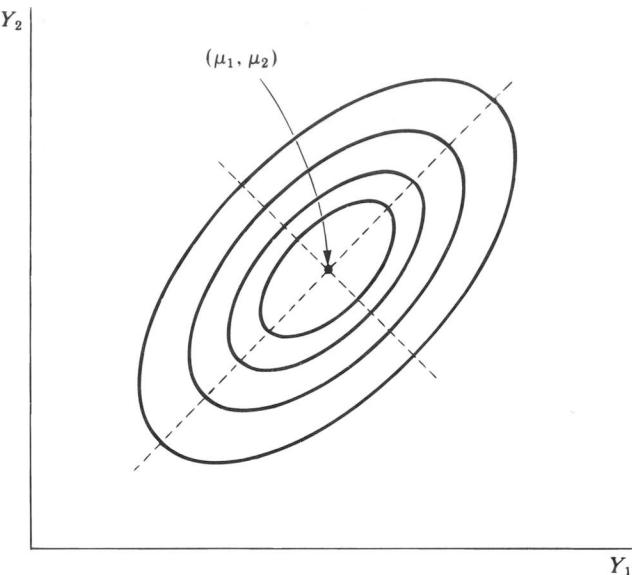

Here, σ_1 and σ_2, as just mentioned, denote the standard deviations of Y_1 and Y_2, and σ_{12} denotes the covariance $\sigma\{Y_1, Y_2\}$ between Y_1 and Y_2 as defined in (A.21):

$$(15.4) \qquad \sigma_{12} = \sigma\{Y_1, Y_2\} = E\{(Y_1 - \mu_1)(Y_2 - \mu_2)\}$$

If Y_1 and Y_2 are independent, $\sigma_{12} = 0$ according to (A.28) so that $\rho_{12} = 0$ then. If Y_1 and Y_2 are positively related—that is, Y_1 tends to be large when Y_2 is large, or small when Y_2 is small—σ_{12} is positive and so is ρ_{12}. On the other hand, if Y_1 and Y_2 are negatively related—that is, Y_1 tends to be large when Y_2 is small, or vice versa—σ_{12} is negative and so is ρ_{12}. The coefficient of correlation ρ_{12} can take on any value between -1 and 1 inclusive. It assumes 1 if the linear relation between Y_1 and Y_2 is perfectly positive (direct) and -1 if it is perfectly negative (inverse).

Contour Representation

Bivariate normal distributions frequently are portrayed in terms of a contour diagram. As discussed in Chapter 7, a contour curve on such a diagram is composed of all the points on the surface that are equidistant from the Y_1Y_2 plane. To put this another way, a contour curve is composed of all (Y_1, Y_2) outcomes that have constant density $f(Y_1, Y_2)$. Figure 15.2 presents a contour diagram for a bivariate normal distribution. It is a property of any bivariate normal distribution that all contour curves are ellipses, except when $\rho_{12} = 0$ and $\sigma_1 = \sigma_2$, in which case the contour curves are circles. Note that the ellipses have a common center at (μ_1, μ_2), and have common major and minor axes.

Figure 15.3 illustrates the effects of different parameter values on the location and shape of the bivariate normal surface. Note that when Y_1 and Y_2 are positively related so that $\rho_{12} > 0$, the principal axis has positive slope, implying that the surface tends to run

FIGURE 15.3 **Effects of Parameter Values on Location and Shape of Bivariate Normal Distribution.**

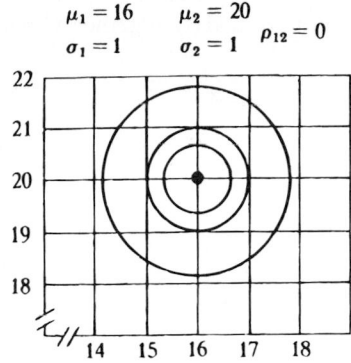

$\mu_1 = 16$ $\mu_2 = 20$ $\rho_{12} = 0$
$\sigma_1 = 1$ $\sigma_2 = 1$

$\mu_1 = 30$ $\mu_2 = 20$ $\rho_{12} = 0$
$\sigma_1 = 2$ $\sigma_2 = 1$

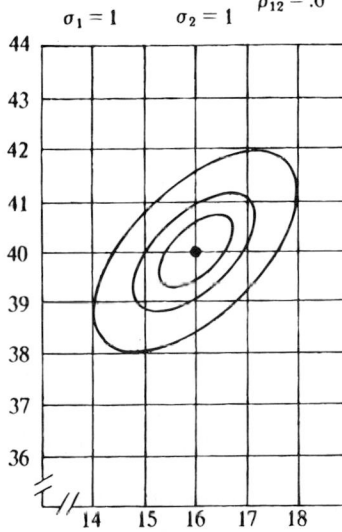

$\mu_1 = 16$ $\mu_2 = 40$ $\rho_{12} = .6$
$\sigma_1 = 1$ $\sigma_2 = 1$

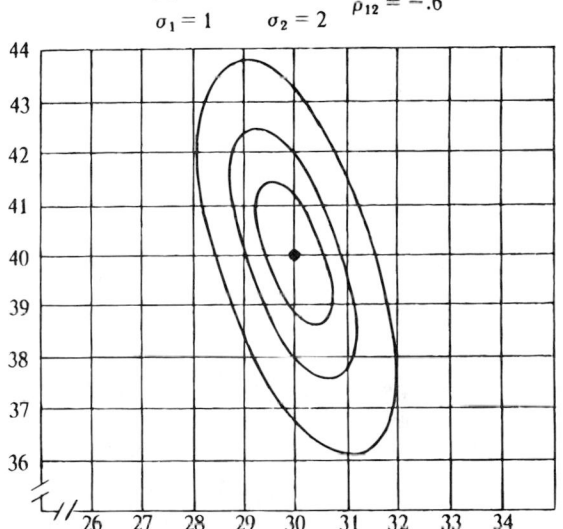

$\mu_1 = 30$ $\mu_2 = 40$ $\rho_{12} = -.6$
$\sigma_1 = 1$ $\sigma_2 = 2$

$\mu_1 = 16$ $\mu_2 = 15$ $\rho_{12} = .8$
$\sigma_1 = 1$ $\sigma_2 = 1$

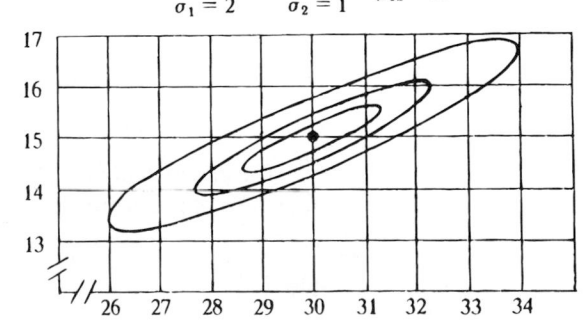

$\mu_1 = 30$ $\mu_2 = 15$ $\rho_{12} = .8$
$\sigma_1 = 2$ $\sigma_2 = 1$

along a line with positive slope. When Y_1 and Y_2 are negatively related so that $\rho_{12} < 0$, the principal axis has a negative slope, implying that the surface tends to run along a line with negative slope.

Figure 15.3 also demonstrates how the mean values μ_1 and μ_2 affect the location of the surface, and how the standard deviations σ_1 and σ_2, together with the correlation coefficient ρ_{12}, affect the shape of the surface.

15.3   Conditional Inferences

As noted, one principal use of bivariate correlation models is to make conditional inferences regarding one variable, given the other variable. Suppose Y_1 represents a service station's gasoline sales and Y_2 its sales of auxiliary products and services. We may then wish to predict a service station's sales of auxiliary products and services Y_2, given that its gasoline sales are $Y_1 = \$5,500$.

Such conditional inferences require the use of conditional probability distributions, which we discuss next.

Conditional Probability Distribution of Y_1

The density function of the conditional probability distribution of Y_1 for any given value of Y_2 is denoted by $f(Y_1|Y_2)$ and defined as follows:

$$(15.5) \qquad f(Y_1|Y_2) = \frac{f(Y_1, Y_2)}{f_2(Y_2)}$$

where $f(Y_1, Y_2)$ is the joint density function of Y_1 and Y_2, and $f_2(Y_2)$ is the marginal density function of Y_2. When Y_1 and Y_2 are jointly normally distributed according to (15.1) so that the marginal density function $f_2(Y_2)$ is given by (15.2b), it can be shown that:

(15.6)   The conditional probability distribution of Y_1 for any given value of Y_2 is normal with mean $\alpha_{1.2} + \beta_{12}Y_2$ and standard deviation $\sigma_{1.2}$ and its density function is:

$$f(Y_1|Y_2) = \frac{1}{\sqrt{2\pi}\sigma_{1.2}} \exp\left[-\frac{1}{2}\left(\frac{Y_1 - \alpha_{1.2} - \beta_{12}Y_2}{\sigma_{1.2}} \right)^2 \right]$$

The parameters $\alpha_{1.2}$, β_{12}, and $\sigma_{1.2}$ of the conditional probability distributions of Y_1 are functions of the parameters of the joint probability distribution (15.1), as follows:

$$(15.7a) \qquad \alpha_{1.2} = \mu_1 - \mu_2\rho_{12}\frac{\sigma_1}{\sigma_2}$$

$$(15.7b) \qquad \beta_{12} = \rho_{12}\frac{\sigma_1}{\sigma_2}$$

$$(15.7c) \qquad \sigma_{1.2}^2 = \sigma_1^2(1 - \rho_{12}^2)$$

FIGURE 15.4   **Cross Section of Bivariate Normal Distribution at Y_{h2}.**

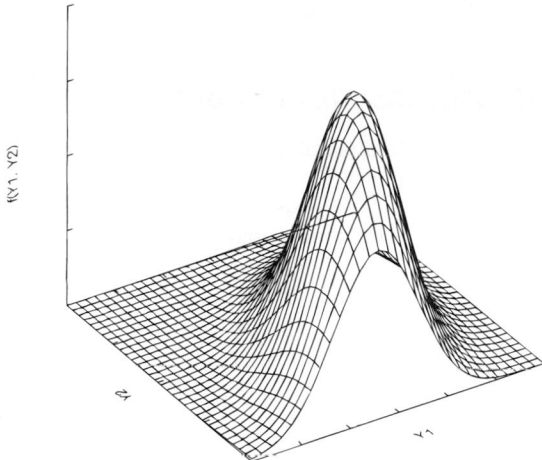

Important Characteristics of Conditional Distributions.   Three important characteristics of the conditional probability distributions of Y_1 are normality, linear regression, and constant variance. We take up each of these in turn.

1. The conditional probability distribution of Y_1 for any given value of Y_2 is normal. Imagine that we slice a bivariate normal distribution vertically at a given value of Y_2, say, at Y_{h2}. That is, we slice it parallel to the Y_1 axis. This slicing is shown in Figure 15.4. The exposed cross section has the shape of a normal distribution, and after being scaled so that its area is 1, it portrays the conditional probability distribution of Y_1, given that $Y_2 = Y_{h2}$.

This property of normality holds no matter what the value Y_{h2} is. Thus, whenever we slice the bivariate normal distribution parallel to the Y_1 axis, we obtain (after proper scaling) a normal conditional probability distribution.

2. The means of the conditional probability distributions of Y_1 fall on a straight line, and hence are a linear function of Y_2:

$$(15.8) \qquad\qquad E\{Y_1|Y_2\} = \alpha_{1.2} + \beta_{12}Y_2$$

Here, $\alpha_{1.2}$ is the intercept parameter and β_{12} the slope parameter. Thus, the relation between the conditional means and Y_2 is given by a linear regression function.

3. All conditional probability distributions of Y_1 have the same standard deviation $\sigma_{1.2}$. Thus, no matter where we slice the bivariate normal distribution parallel to the Y_1 axis, the resulting conditional probability distribution (after scaling to have an area of 1) has the same standard deviation. Hence, constant variances characterize the conditional probability distributions of Y_1.

Equivalence to Normal Error Regression Model.   Suppose that we select a random sample of observations (Y_1, Y_2) from a bivariate normal population and wish to make conditional inferences about Y_1, given Y_2. The preceding discussion makes it clear that the normal error regression model (1.24) is entirely applicable because:

1. The Y_1 observations are independent.

2. The Y_1 observations when Y_2 is considered given or fixed are normally distributed with mean $E\{Y_1|Y_2\} = \alpha_{1.2} + \beta_{12}Y_2$ and constant variance $\sigma_{1.2}^2$.

Conditional Probability Distributions of Y_2

The random variables Y_1 and Y_2 play symmetrical roles in the bivariate normal probability distribution (15.1). Hence, it follows:

(15.9)   The conditional probability distribution of Y_2 for any given value of Y_1 is normal with mean $\alpha_{2.1} + \beta_{21}Y_1$ and standard deviation $\sigma_{2.1}$ and its density function is:

$$f(Y_2|Y_1) = \frac{1}{\sqrt{2\pi}\sigma_{2.1}} \exp\left[-\frac{1}{2}\left(\frac{Y_2 - \alpha_{2.1} - \beta_{21}Y_1}{\sigma_{2.1}}\right)^2\right]$$

The parameters $\alpha_{2.1}$, β_{21}, and $\sigma_{2.1}$ of the conditional probability distributions of Y_2 are functions of the parameters of the joint probability distribution (15.1), as follows:

(15.10a)
$$\alpha_{2.1} = \mu_2 - \mu_1 \rho_{12}\frac{\sigma_2}{\sigma_1}$$

(15.10b)
$$\beta_{21} = \rho_{12}\frac{\sigma_2}{\sigma_1}$$

(15.10c)
$$\sigma_{2.1}^2 = \sigma_2^2(1 - \rho_{12}^2)$$

The parameter $\alpha_{2.1}$ is the intercept of the line of regression of Y_2 on Y_1, and the parameter β_{21} is the slope of this line.

Again, we find that the conditional correlation model of Y_2, given Y_1, is equivalent to the normal error regression model (1.24).

Comments

1. The notation for the parameters of the conditional correlation models departs somewhat from our previous notation for regression models. The symbol α is now used to denote the regression intercept. The subscript 1.2 to α indicates that Y_1 is regressed on Y_2. Similarly, the subscript 2.1 to α indicates that Y_2 is regressed on Y_1. The symbol β_{12} indicates that it is the slope in the regression of Y_1 on Y_2, while β_{21} is the slope in the regression of Y_2 on Y_1. Finally, $\sigma_{2.1}$ is the standard deviation of the conditional probability distributions of Y_2 for any given Y_1, while $\sigma_{1.2}$ is the standard deviation of the conditional probability distributions of Y_1 for any given Y_2. This notation can be extended straightforwardly for multivariate correlation models.

2. Two distinct regressions are involved in a bivariate normal model, that of Y_1 on Y_2 when Y_2 is fixed and that of Y_2 on Y_1 when Y_1 is fixed. In general, the two regression lines are not the same. For instance, the two slopes β_{12} and β_{21} are the same only if $\sigma_1 = \sigma_2$, as can be seen from (15.7b) and (15.10b).

Figure 15.5 illustrates the relation of the two different regression lines to the contour ellipses. Note that both regression lines go through the point (μ_1, μ_2). If $\rho_{12} = 0$, the two regression

FIGURE 15.5   Illustration of Relation between Two Lines of Regression and Contour Ellipses.

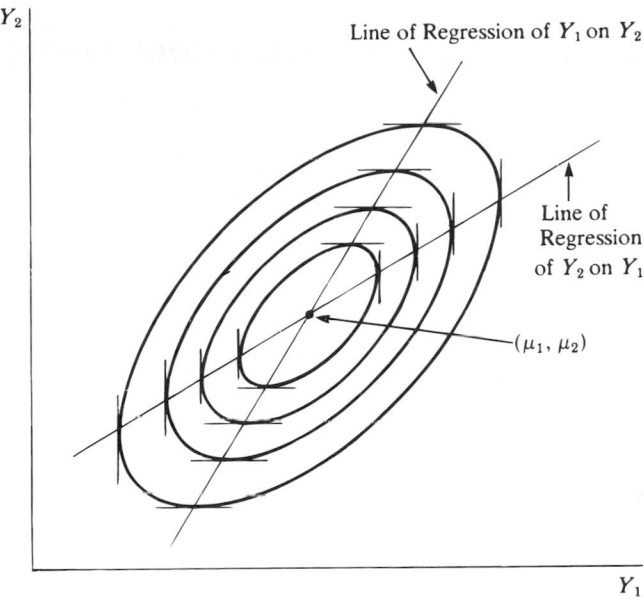

lines intersect at right angles. The larger absolutely is ρ_{12}, the smaller is the angle between the two regression lines.   ■

Use of Regression Analysis

In view of the equivalence of each of the conditional bivariate normal correlation models (15.6) and (15.9) with the normal error regression model (1.24), all conditional inferences with these correlation models can be made by means of the usual regression methods. For instance, if a researcher has data that can be appropriately described as having been generated from a bivariate normal distribution and wishes to make inferences about Y_2, given a particular value of Y_1, the ordinary regression techniques will be applicable. Thus, the regression function of Y_2 on Y_1 can be estimated by means of (1.12), the slope of the regression line can be estimated by means of the interval estimate (2.15), a new observation Y_2, given the value of Y_1, can be predicted by means of (2.36), and so on. Computer regression packages can be used in the usual manner. To avoid notational problems, it may be helpful to relabel the variables according to regression usage: $Y = Y_2$, $X = Y_1$. Of course, if conditional inferences on Y_1 for given values of Y_2 are desired, the notation correspondences would be: $Y = Y_1$, $X = Y_2$.

Note

When interval estimates for the conditional correlation models are obtained, the confidence coefficient refers to repeated samples where pairs of observations (Y_1, Y_2) are obtained from the bivariate normal population. We noted a similar point for regression models when the predictor variables are random.   ∎

15.4   Inferences on Correlation Coefficients

A principal use of correlation models is to study the relationships between the variables. In a bivariate normal model, the parameter ρ_{12} and its square, ρ_{12}^2, provide information about the degree of the linear relationship between the two variables Y_1 and Y_2. Of the two measures, ρ_{12}^2 is the more meaningful one.

Coefficient of Determination

The square of the coefficient of correlation ρ_{12} is called the *coefficient of determination*. We noted earlier in (15.7c) and (15.10c) that:

(15.11a)
$$\sigma_{1.2}^2 = \sigma_1^2(1 - \rho_{12}^2)$$

(15.11b)
$$\sigma_{2.1}^2 = \sigma_2^2(1 - \rho_{12}^2)$$

We can rewrite these expressions as follows:

(15.12a)
$$\rho_{12}^2 = \frac{\sigma_1^2 - \sigma_{1.2}^2}{\sigma_1^2}$$

(15.12b)
$$\rho_{12}^2 = \frac{\sigma_2^2 - \sigma_{2.1}^2}{\sigma_2^2}$$

The meaning of ρ_{12}^2 is now clear. Consider first (15.12a). ρ_{12}^2 measures how much smaller relatively is the variability in the conditional distributions of Y_1, for any given level of Y_2, than is the variability in the marginal distribution of Y_1. Thus, ρ_{12}^2 measures the relative reduction in the variability of Y_1 associated with the use of variable Y_2. Correspondingly, (15.12b) shows that ρ_{12}^2 also measures the relative reduction in the variability of Y_2 associated with the use of variable Y_1.

It can be shown that:

(15.13)
$$0 \le \rho_{12}^2 \le 1$$

The limiting value $\rho_{12}^2 = 0$ occurs when Y_1 and Y_2 are independent, so that the variances of each variable in the conditional probability distributions are then no smaller than the variance in the marginal distribution. The limiting value $\rho_{12}^2 = 1$ occurs when there is no variability in the conditional probability distributions for each variable, so perfect predictions of either variable can be made from the other.

Note

The interpretation of ρ_{12}^2 as measuring the relative reduction in the conditional variances as compared with the marginal variance is valid for the case of a bivariate normal population, but not for many other bivariate populations. Of course, the interpretation implies nothing in a causal sense.   ∎

Point Estimators of ρ_{12} and ρ_{12}^2

The maximum likelihood estimator of ρ_{12}, denoted by r_{12}, is given by:

$$(15.14) \qquad r_{12} = \frac{\Sigma(Y_{i1} - \bar{Y}_1)(Y_{i2} - \bar{Y}_2)}{\left[\Sigma(Y_{i1} - \bar{Y}_1)^2 \, \Sigma(Y_{i2} - \bar{Y}_2)^2\right]^{1/2}}$$

This estimator is often called the *Pearson product-moment correlation coefficient*. It is a biased estimator of ρ_{12} (unless $\rho_{12} = 0$ or 1), but the bias is small when n is large.

The coefficient of determination ρ_{12}^2 is estimated by the square of the sample coefficient of correlation, r_{12}^2.

Note

The maximum likelihood estimator (15.14) of the population correlation coefficient is the same as the descriptive coefficient of correlation in (2.76) for the regression model. With a correlation model, r_{12} is an estimator of a parameter. With a regression model, in contrast, r_{12} is only a descriptive measure. Specifically, r_{12}^2 for a regression model reflects the proportion of the total sum of squares that is partitioned into the regression sum of squares. Another difference is that in the standard regression case where the X_i are fixed, the magnitude of r_{12} can be arbitrarily affected by the spacing pattern chosen for the observations X_i. For the bivariate normal model, on the other hand, the magnitude of r_{12} cannot be so affected since neither variable is under the control of the investigator. ∎

Test Whether $\rho_{12} = 0$

When the population is bivariate normal, it is frequently desired to test whether the coefficient of correlation is zero:

$$(15.15) \qquad \begin{aligned} H_0&: \rho_{12} = 0 \\ H_a&: \rho_{12} \neq 0 \end{aligned}$$

The reason for interest in this test is that in the case where Y_1 and Y_2 are jointly normally distributed, $\rho_{12} = 0$ implies that Y_1 and Y_2 are independent.

We can use regression procedures for the test since (15.7b) implies that the following alternatives are equivalent to those in (15.15):

$$(15.15a) \qquad \begin{aligned} H_0&: \beta_{12} = 0 \\ H_a&: \beta_{12} \neq 0 \end{aligned}$$

and (15.10b) implies that the following alternatives are also equivalent to the ones in (15.15):

$$(15.15b) \qquad \begin{aligned} H_0&: \beta_{21} = 0 \\ H_a&: \beta_{21} \neq 0 \end{aligned}$$

It can be shown that the test statistics for testing either (15.15a) or (15.15b) are the same and can be expressed directly in terms of r_{12}:

(15.16)
$$t^* = \frac{r_{12}\sqrt{n-2}}{\sqrt{1-r_{12}^2}}$$

If H_0 holds, t^* follows the $t(n-2)$ distribution. The appropriate decision rule to control the Type I error at α is:

(15.17)
$$\text{If } |t^*| \leq t(1-\alpha/2; n-2), \quad \text{conclude } H_0$$
$$\text{If } |t^*| > t(1-\alpha/2; n-2), \quad \text{conclude } H_a$$

Test statistic (15.16) is identical to the regression t^* test statistic (2.17).

Interval Estimation of ρ_{12}

Because the sampling distribution of r_{12} is complicated when $\rho_{12} \neq 0$, interval estimation of ρ_{12} is usually carried out by means of an approximate procedure based on a transformation.

z' **Transformation.**   This transformation, known as the Fisher z transformation, is as follows:

(15.18)
$$z' = \frac{1}{2} \log_e \left(\frac{1+r_{12}}{1-r_{12}} \right)$$

When n is large (25 or more is a useful rule of thumb), the distribution of z' is approximately normal with approximate mean and variance:

(15.19)
$$E\{z'\} = \zeta = \frac{1}{2} \log_e \left(\frac{1+\rho_{12}}{1-\rho_{12}} \right)$$

(15.20)
$$\sigma^2\{z'\} = \frac{1}{n-3}$$

Note that the transformation from r_{12} to z' in (15.18) is the same as the relation in (15.19) between ρ_{12} and $E\{z'\} = \zeta$. Also note that the approximate variance of z' is a known constant, depending only on the sample size n.

Table B.8 gives paired values for the left and right sides of (15.18) and (15.19), thus eliminating the need for calculations. For instance, if r_{12} or ρ_{12} equals .25, Table B.8 indicates that z' or ζ equals .2554, and vice versa. The values on the two sides of the transformation always have the same sign. Thus, if r_{12} or ρ_{12} is negative, a minus sign is attached to the value in Table B.8. For instance, if $r_{12} = -.25$, $z' = -.2554$.

Interval Estimate.   When the sample size is large ($n \geq 25$), the standardized statistic:

(15.21)
$$\frac{z' - \zeta}{\sigma\{z'\}}$$

is approximately a standard normal variable. Therefore, approximate $1 - \alpha$ confidence limits for ζ are:

(15.22)
$$z' \pm z(1 - \alpha/2)\sigma\{z'\}$$

where $z(1 - \alpha/2)$ is the $(1 - \alpha/2)100$ percentile of the standard normal distribution. The $1 - \alpha$ confidence limits for ρ_{12} are then obtained by transforming the limits on ζ by means of (15.19).

Example.   An economist investigated food purchasing patterns by households in a midwestern city. Two hundred households with family incomes between \$15,000 and \$30,000 were selected to ascertain, among other things, the proportions of the food budget expended for beef and poultry, respectively. The economist expected these to be negatively related, and wished to estimate the coefficient of correlation with a 95 percent confidence interval. Some supporting evidence suggested that the joint distribution of the two variables does not depart markedly from a bivariate normal one.

The point estimate of ρ_{12} was $r_{12} = -.61$ (data and calculations not shown). To obtain an approximate 95 percent confidence interval estimate, we require:

$$z' = -.7089 \quad \text{when } r_{12} = -.61 \quad \text{(from Table B.8)}$$

$$\sigma\{z'\} = \frac{1}{\sqrt{200 - 3}} = .07125$$

$$z(.975) = 1.960$$

Hence, the confidence limits for ζ, by (15.22), are $-.7089 \pm 1.960(.07125)$, and the approximate 95 percent confidence interval is:

$$-.849 \leq \zeta \leq -.569$$

Using Table B.8 to transform back to ρ_{12}, we obtain:

$$-.69 \leq \rho_{12} \leq -.51$$

This confidence interval was sufficiently precise to be useful to the economist, confirming the negative relation and indicating that the degree of linear association is moderately high.

Comments

1. As usual, a confidence interval for ρ_{12} can be employed to test whether or not ρ_{12} has a specified value—say, .5—by noting whether or not the specified value falls within the confidence limits.

2. Confidence limits for ρ_{12}^2 can be obtained by squaring the respective confidence limits for ρ_{12}, provided the latter limits do not differ in sign.   ∎

Comparison of Two Correlation Coefficients

In Chapter 11 we presented methods for comparing the regression functions and their parameters for two populations, based on independent samples from the two populations. Analogously, we may be interested in whether two bivariate normal populations have the same coefficient of correlation, based on independent samples from the two populations.

Let us denote the two population coefficients of correlation between Y_1 and Y_2 by ρ_1 and ρ_2, respectively. Further, we denote the two sample sizes by n_1 and n_2 and the two sample correlation coefficients by r_1 and r_2.

The alternatives to be considered are:

$$(15.23) \qquad \begin{aligned} H_0: \ \rho_1 &= \rho_2 \\ H_a: \ \rho_1 &\neq \rho_2 \end{aligned}$$

The test statistic makes use of the Fisher z transformation in (15.18) for each of the two sample correlation coefficients. Let z_1' and z_2' denote the Fisher z values for r_1 and r_2. The test statistic then is:

$$(15.24) \qquad z^* = \frac{z_1' - z_2'}{\sqrt{\dfrac{1}{n_1 - 3} + \dfrac{1}{n_2 - 3}}}$$

The denominator is the approximate standard deviation of the difference $z_1' - z_2'$. When H_0 holds and n_1 and n_2 are each reasonably large (≥ 25), z^* is distributed approximately as a standard normal variable. Hence, the appropriate decision rule for testing the alternatives in (15.23) to control the risk of Type I error at α is:

$$(15.25) \qquad \begin{aligned} &\text{If } |z^*| \leq z(1 - \alpha/2), \ \text{ conclude } H_0 \\ &\text{If } |z^*| > z(1 - \alpha/2), \ \text{ conclude } H_a \end{aligned}$$

Example.   A hospital operations analyst wanted to know whether the correlations between response time to patients' calls and number of patients in the ward are the same for two wards. Sample data for the two wards are as follows:

$$\text{Ward 1:} \qquad n_1 = 52 \qquad r_1 = .62 \qquad z_1' = .7250$$

$$\text{Ward 2:} \qquad n_2 = 43 \qquad r_2 = .51 \qquad z_2' = .5627$$

The operations analyst believed it is reasonable to treat these data as the result of independent random sampling from two bivariate normal populations.

Test statistic (15.24) here is:

$$z^* = \frac{.7250 - .5627}{\sqrt{\dfrac{1}{49} + \dfrac{1}{40}}} = .762$$

For $\alpha = .01$, we require $z(.995) = 2.576$. Since $|z^*| = .762 \leq 2.576$, we conclude H_0, that the coefficient of correlation between response time and number of patients in the ward is the same for the two wards. The two-sided P-value of the test is .45.

Note

The test for the equality of the correlations in two bivariate normal populations can be extended to more than two populations. The reader is referred to Reference 15.1 for this extension.   ∎

Caution

Correlation models, like regression models, do not express any causal relations. Earlier cautions about drawing conclusions as to causality from regression findings apply equally to correlation studies. Correlation findings can be useful in analyzing causal relationships, but they do not by themselves establish causal patterns.

15.5   Multivariate Normal Distribution

Density Function

The normal correlation model for the case of p variables $Y_1, \ldots, Y_p$ is based on the *multivariate normal distribution*. This distribution is an extension of the bivariate normal distribution. The density function for the multivariate normal distribution is best given in matrix form. We first need to define some vectors and matrices. The observations vector $\mathbf{Y}$ containing an observation on each of the p Y variables is defined as usual:

$$(15.26) \qquad \underset{p \times 1}{\mathbf{Y}} = \begin{bmatrix} Y_1 \\ Y_2 \\ \vdots \\ Y_p \end{bmatrix}$$

The mean vector $E\{\mathbf{Y}\}$, denoted by $\boldsymbol{\mu}$, contains the expected values for each of the p Y variables:

$$(15.27) \qquad \underset{p \times 1}{\boldsymbol{\mu}} = \begin{bmatrix} \mu_1 \\ \mu_2 \\ \vdots \\ \mu_p \end{bmatrix}$$

Finally, the variance-covariance matrix $\boldsymbol{\sigma}^2\{\mathbf{Y}\}$ is denoted by $\boldsymbol{\Sigma}$ and contains as always the variances and covariances of the p Y variables:

$$(15.28) \qquad \underset{p \times p}{\boldsymbol{\Sigma}} = \begin{bmatrix} \sigma_1^2 & \sigma_{12} & \cdots & \sigma_{1p} \\ \sigma_{21} & \sigma_2^2 & \cdots & \sigma_{2p} \\ \vdots & \vdots & & \vdots \\ \sigma_{p1} & \sigma_{p2} & \cdots & \sigma_p^2 \end{bmatrix}$$

Here, σ_1^2 denotes the variance of Y_1, σ_{12} denotes the covariance of Y_1 and Y_2, and the like.

The density function of the multivariate normal distribution can now be stated as follows:

$$(15.29) \qquad f(\mathbf{Y}) = \frac{1}{(2\pi)^{p/2}|\mathbf{\Sigma}|^{1/2}} \exp\left[-\frac{1}{2}(\mathbf{Y} - \boldsymbol{\mu})'\mathbf{\Sigma}^{-1}(\mathbf{Y} - \boldsymbol{\mu})\right]$$

Here, $|\mathbf{\Sigma}|$ is the determinant of the variance-covariance matrix $\mathbf{\Sigma}$. When there are $p = 2$ variables, the multivariate normal density function (15.29) simplifies to the bivariate normal density function (15.1).

The multivariate normal density function has properties that correspond to the ones described for the bivariate normal distribution. For instance, if $Y_1, \ldots, Y_p$ are jointly normally distributed (i.e., they follow the multivariate normal distribution), the marginal probability distribution of each variable Y_k is normal, with mean μ_k and standard deviation σ_k.

Conditional Inferences

One major use of multivariate correlation models is to make conditional inferences on one variable when the other variables have given values. It can be shown in the case of the multivariate normal distribution that:

(15.30)   The conditional probability distribution of Y_k for any given set of values for the other variables is normal with mean given by a linear regression function and constant variance.

Suppose Y_1, Y_2, Y_3, and Y_4 are jointly normally distributed. The conditional probability distribution of, say, Y_3, when Y_1, Y_2, and Y_4 are fixed at any specified levels, has these characteristics:

1. It is normal.

2. It has a mean given by:

$$E\{Y_3|Y_1, Y_2, Y_4\} = \alpha_{3.124} + \beta_{31.24}Y_1 + \beta_{32.14}Y_2 + \beta_{34.12}Y_4$$

3. It has constant variance $\sigma^2_{3.124}$.

The notation is a straightforward extension of that for the bivariate correlation case. Thus, $\beta_{31.24}$ denotes the regression coefficient of Y_1 when Y_3 is regressed on Y_1, Y_2, and Y_4.

It is clear from the above that the conditional multivariate correlation models are equivalent to the normal error multiple regression model (6.7). Hence, in the case where the variables are jointly normally distributed, all inferences on one variable conditional on the other variables being fixed are carried out by the usual multiple regression techniques. For instance, an interval estimate of a conditional mean would be obtained by (6.59), or a prediction of a new observation on the variable of interest, given the values of the other variables, would be obtained by (6.63). To facilitate use of the regression formulas, it may be helpful to relabel the variable of interest Y and the other variables Xs. Computer multiple regression packages can be used in ordinary fashion.

Coefficients of Multiple Correlation and Determination

A major use of multivariate correlation models is to study the relationships between the variables. One set of measures useful to this end consists of the *coefficients of multiple determination* and the *coefficients of multiple correlation*.

Meaning of Coefficients. A coefficient of multiple determination is associated with each variable. Suppose that Y_1, Y_2, Y_3, and Y_4 are included in the correlation model. The coefficient of multiple determination associated with, say, Y_1 is denoted by $\rho^2_{1.234}$, and defined as follows:

$$(15.31) \qquad \rho^2_{1.234} = \frac{\sigma^2_1 - \sigma^2_{1.234}}{\sigma^2_1}$$

where $\sigma^2_{1.234}$ is the variance of the conditional distributions of Y_1 when the other variables are fixed. Thus, $\rho^2_{1.234}$ measures how much smaller, relatively, is the variability in the conditional distributions of Y_1, when the other variables are fixed at given values, than is the variability in the marginal distribution of Y_1. The other coefficients of multiple determination are defined and interpreted in similar fashion.

It can be shown that coefficients of multiple determination take on values between 0 and 1 inclusive. Thus:

$$(15.32) \qquad 0 \le \rho^2_{1.234} \le 1$$

The limiting value $\rho^2_{1.234} = 0$ occurs when no reduction in the variability of Y_1 takes place by considering the other variables. Equivalently, $\rho^2_{1.234} = 0$ in the case of the normal correlation model implies that Y_1 is independent of Y_2, Y_3, and Y_4 so that $\rho_{12} = \rho_{13} = \rho_{14} = 0$. The other limiting value, $\rho^2_{1.234} = 1$ occurs when the conditional distributions of Y_1, given Y_2, Y_3, and Y_4, have no variability so that perfect predictions can be made of Y_1 from knowledge of the other variables.

The positive square root of a coefficient of multiple determination is the coefficient of multiple correlation. Thus, for Y_1, we have in our example:

$$(15.33) \qquad \rho_{1.234} = \sqrt{\rho^2_{1.234}}$$

$\rho_{1.234}$ can also be viewed as a simple correlation coefficient, namely, between Y_1 and $\alpha_{1.234} + \beta_{12.34}Y_2 + \beta_{13.24}Y_3 + \beta_{14.23}Y_4$.

Estimation of Coefficients. Coefficients of multiple determination and correlation are estimated by (6.40) and (6.43), respectively, the descriptive coefficients in the regression case. For example, to estimate $\rho^2_{1.234}$, we need the total sum of squares for Y_1, denoted by $SSTO(Y_1)$. Then we require the regression sum of squares when Y_1 is regressed on Y_2, Y_3, and Y_4, denoted by $SSR(Y_2, Y_3, Y_4)$. The estimator, denoted by $R^2_{1.234}$, is:

$$(15.34) \qquad R^2_{1.234} = \frac{SSR(Y_2, Y_3, Y_4)}{SSTO(Y_1)}$$

The positive square root of $R^2_{1.234}$, denoted by $R_{1.234}$, is the estimated coefficient of multiple correlation for Y_1.

Testing of Coefficients. To test, say:

$$(15.35) \qquad \begin{aligned} H_0&: \rho_{1.234} = 0 \\ H_a&: \rho_{1.234} \ne 0 \end{aligned}$$

we can utilize the equivalent test on the regression coefficients:

(15.35a)
$$H_0: \beta_{12.34} = \beta_{13.24} = \beta_{14.23} = 0$$
$$H_a: \text{ not all } \beta s \text{ in } H_0 \text{ equal zero}$$

It turns out that the F^* statistic for this test, given in (6.39b), can be expressed directly in terms of $R^2_{1.234}$, as follows:

(15.36)
$$F^* = \left(\frac{R^2_{1.234}}{1 - R^2_{1.234}} \right) \left(\frac{n - 4}{3} \right)$$

In general, the factor on the right is $(n - q - 1)/q$ when there are q predictor variables.

If H_0 holds, F^* follows the $F(q, n - q - 1)$ distribution so that the decision rule to control the Type I error risk at α is set up in the usual fashion:

(15.37)
$$\text{If } F^* \leq F(1 - \alpha; q, n - q - 1), \text{ conclude } H_0$$
$$\text{If } F^* > F(1 - \alpha; q, n - q - 1), \text{ conclude } H_a$$

Coefficients of Partial Correlation and Determination

Meaning of Coefficients.   Suppose again that four variables $Y_1, Y_2, Y_3,$ and Y_4 are included in a multivariate normal correlation model. Consider now the correlation between Y_1 and Y_2 in the conditional joint distribution when each of the variables Y_3 and Y_4 is fixed at a given level. When all variables are jointly normally distributed, this correlation does not depend on the levels where Y_3 and Y_4 are fixed and is given by:

(15.38)
$$\rho_{12.34} = \frac{\sigma_{12.34}}{\sigma_{1.34}\sigma_{2.34}}$$

$\rho_{12.34}$ is called the *coefficient of partial correlation* between Y_1 and Y_2 when Y_3 and Y_4 are fixed. $\sigma_{12.34}$ denotes the covariance between Y_1 and Y_2 in the conditional joint distribution of Y_1 and Y_2 when Y_3 and Y_4 are fixed at given levels. $\sigma_{1.34}$ and $\sigma_{2.34}$ denote the standard deviations of the conditional distributions of Y_1 and Y_2, respectively, when Y_3 and Y_4 are fixed at given levels.

Note that the coefficient of partial correlation $\rho_{12.34}$ has the same sign as the covariance $\sigma_{12.34}$, and therefore indicates whether the linear statistical relation between Y_1 and Y_2 is positive or negative in the conditional joint distributions when Y_3 and Y_4 are fixed.

The square of $\rho_{12.34}$ is called the *coefficient of partial determination* and is denoted by $\rho^2_{12.34}$. The following relation holds:

(15.39)
$$\rho^2_{12.34} = \frac{\sigma^2_{1.34} - \sigma^2_{1.234}}{\sigma^2_{1.34}}$$

Thus, $\rho^2_{12.34}$ measures how much smaller, relatively, is the variability in the conditional distributions of Y_1, given $Y_2, Y_3,$ and Y_4, than it is in the conditional distributions of Y_1, given Y_3 and Y_4 only.

The other partial correlation coefficients are defined and interpreted in similar fashion. For instance, $\rho_{12.3}$ measures the correlation between Y_1 and Y_2 when only Y_3 is fixed.

A coefficient of partial correlation $\rho_{12.3}$ is called a *first-order coefficient*, a coefficient $\rho_{12.34}$ a *second-order coefficient*, and so on. All partial correlation coefficients measure the correlation between two variables; the order of the coefficient simply indicates how many other variables are fixed in the conditional bivariate distribution.

Point Estimation of Coefficients. Point estimators of the coefficients of partial determination and correlation are the descriptive regression measures encountered earlier; see, for instance, (7.35). Thus, to estimate $\rho_{12.3}^2$, we regress Y_1 on Y_3 and obtain the error sum of squares $SSE(Y_3)$. Next, we regress Y_1 on Y_2 and Y_3 and obtain the error sum of squares $SSE(Y_2, Y_3)$. The estimator of $\rho_{12.3}^2$ then is:

$$(15.40) \qquad r_{12.3}^2 = \frac{SSE(Y_3) - SSE(Y_2, Y_3)}{SSE(Y_3)} = \frac{SSR(Y_2 | Y_3)}{SSE(Y_3)}$$

Tests Concerning Coefficients. Researchers often wish to test whether two variables are correlated in the conditional probability distributions when other variables are fixed. For instance, when four variables Y_1, Y_2, Y_3, and Y_4 are being considered and the correlation of interest is between Y_1 and Y_2 when Y_3 and Y_4 are fixed, the following test may be desired to see if Y_1 and Y_2 are correlated in the conditional joint distributions:

$$(15.41) \qquad \begin{aligned} H_0 &: \rho_{12.34} = 0 \\ H_a &: \rho_{12.34} \neq 0 \end{aligned}$$

Such tests of partial correlation coefficients can be carried out via test statistic (15.16) for the bivariate case, with r_{12} replaced by the estimated partial correlation coefficient and n replaced by $n - q$, where q is the number of variables that are held fixed.

Interval Estimation of Coefficients. Interval estimates of partial correlation coefficients are obtained via the Fisher z transformation (15.18) in identical fashion to that for simple correlation coefficients. Only the approximate standard deviation $\sigma\{z'\}$ need be modified. It is, for q variables being held fixed:

$$(15.42) \qquad \sigma\{z'\} = \frac{1}{\sqrt{n - q - 3}}$$

Example

An operations analyst, wishing to study the relations between three types of test scores made by applicants for entry-level clerical positions in a large insurance company, drew a sample of 250 such applicants from recent records and ascertained their scores. The variables were:

Y_1 verbal aptitude test score

Y_2 reading aptitude test score

Y_3 personal interview score

The multivariate normal model was considered to be applicable for the study.

The analyst's initial interest was in the partial correlation coefficient $\rho_{23.1}$. Since the available computer program did not have an option for calculating partial correlation coefficients by a single command (many programs have such an option), the analyst ran two separate regressions—Y_2 on Y_1, and Y_2 on Y_1 and Y_3. The results were $SSE(Y_1) = 6{,}340$ and $SSE(Y_1, Y_3) = 6{,}086$. The point estimate of $\rho^2_{23.1}$ then was calculated corresponding to (15.40):

$$r^2_{23.1} = \frac{SSE(Y_1) - SSE(Y_1, Y_3)}{SSE(Y_1)} = \frac{6{,}340 - 6{,}086}{6{,}340} = .040$$

Hence $r_{23.1} = .20$. (The sign of $r_{23.1}$ here is positive because the regression coefficient for Y_3 when Y_2 is regressed on Y_1 and Y_3 is positive.) Desiring a confidence interval with an approximate 95 percent confidence coefficient, the analyst required:

$$z' = .2027 \qquad \text{when } r_{23.1} = .20$$

$$\sigma\{z'\} = \frac{1}{\sqrt{250 - 1 - 3}} = \frac{1}{\sqrt{246}} = .06376$$

$$z(.975) = 1.960$$

The confidence limits for ζ by (15.22) are $.2027 \pm 1.960(.06376)$ and the approximate 95 percent confidence interval is:

$$.0777 \leq \zeta \leq .3277$$

In transforming from ζ to ρ, the analyst obtained:

$$.08 \leq \rho_{23.1} \leq .32$$

Thus, the coefficient of partial correlation between reading aptitude score and interview score, with verbal aptitude score fixed, was at best relatively low and could, indeed, be close to zero.

Next the analyst ascertained from the computer printout that the coeffcient of simple correlation between Y_2 and Y_3 is $r_{23} = .83$. An approximate 95 percent confidence interval for ρ_{23} is:

$$.79 \leq \rho_{23} \leq .86$$

Thus, ρ_{23} turns out to be substantially larger than $\rho_{23.1}$.

The comparative magnitudes of $\rho_{23.1}$ and ρ_{23} suggested to the analyst (and further investigation verified) that in the company's interviewing procedure the interview scores (Y_3) depend in good part on verbal skills. Also, the reading aptitude scores (Y_2) obtained with the test used by the company tend to be heavily influenced by verbal aptitude. Thus, when verbal aptitude is not considered, the degree of relation between Y_2 and Y_3 is relatively high since applicants with relatively good (poor) verbal aptitude tend to score well (poorly) in both the reading aptitude test and the personal interview. Among applicants at any given level of verbal aptitude score, however, the degree of relationship between reading score and interview score tends to be low.

15.6   Spearman Rank Correlation Coefficient

At times the joint distribution of two random variables Y_1 and Y_2 differs considerably from the bivariate normal distribution (15.1). In those cases, transformations of the variables Y_1 and Y_2 may be sought to make the joint distribution of the transformed variables approximately bivariate normal and thus permit the use of the inference procedures about ρ_{12} described earlier.

When no appropriate transformations can be found, a nonparametric *rank correlation* procedure is useful for making inferences about the association between Y_1 and Y_2. The *Spearman rank correlation coefficient* is widely used for this purpose. First, the observations on Y_1 (i.e., $Y_{11}, \ldots, Y_{n1}$) are expressed in ranks from 1 to n. We denote the rank of Y_{i1} by R_{i1}. Similarly, the observations on Y_2 (i.e., $Y_{12}, \ldots, Y_{n2}$) are ranked, with the rank of Y_{i2} denoted by R_{i2}. The Spearman rank correlation coefficient, to be denoted by r_S, is then defined as the ordinary Pearson product-moment correlation coefficient in (15.14) based on the rank data:

$$(15.43) \qquad r_S = \frac{\Sigma(R_{i1} - \bar{R}_1)(R_{i2} - \bar{R}_2)}{\left[\Sigma(R_{i1} - \bar{R}_1)^2 \, \Sigma(R_{i2} - \bar{R}_2)^2 \right]^{1/2}}$$

Here $\bar{R}_1$ is the mean of the ranks R_{i1} and $\bar{R}_2$ is the mean of the ranks R_{i2}. Of course, since the ranks R_{i1} and R_{i2} are the integers $1, \ldots, n$, it follows that $\bar{R}_1 = \bar{R}_2 = (n+1)/2$.

Like an ordinary correlation coefficient, the Spearman rank correlation coefficient takes on values between -1 and 1 inclusive:

$$(15.44) \qquad 1 \leq r_S \leq 1$$

The coefficient r_S equals 1 when the ranks for Y_1 are identical to those for Y_2, that is, when the case with rank 1 for Y_1 also has rank 1 for Y_2, and so on. In that case, there is perfect association between the ranks for the two variables. The coefficient r_S equals -1 when the case with rank 1 for Y_1 has rank n for Y_2, the case with rank 2 for Y_1 has rank $n - 1$ for Y_2, and so on. In that event, there is perfect inverse association between the ranks for the two variables. When there is little, if any, association between the ranks of Y_1 and Y_2, the Spearman rank correlation coefficient tends to have a value near zero.

The Spearman rank correlation coefficient can be used to test the alternatives:

$$(15.45) \qquad \begin{aligned} &H_0: \text{ There is no association between } Y_1 \text{ and } Y_2 \\ &H_a: \text{ There is an association between } Y_1 \text{ and } Y_2 \end{aligned}$$

A two-sided test is conducted here since H_a includes either positive or negative association. When the alternative H_a is:

$$(15.46) \qquad H_a: \text{ There is positive (negative) association between } Y_1 \text{ and } Y_2$$

an upper-tail (lower-tail) one-sided test is conducted.

The probability distribution of r_S under H_0 is not difficult to obtain. It is based on the condition that, for any ranking of Y_1, all rankings of Y_2 are equally likely when there is no association between Y_1 and Y_2. Tables have been prepared and are presented in specialized texts such as Reference 15.2. Computer packages generally do not present the probability distribution of r_S under H_0 but only give the two-sided P-value. When the sample size n exceeds 10, the test can be carried out approximately by using test statistic (15.16):

$$(15.47) \qquad t^* = \frac{r_S \sqrt{n-2}}{\sqrt{1 - r_S^2}}$$

based on the t distribution with $n - 2$ degrees of freedom.

As mentioned in Chapter 3, one use of the Spearman rank correlation coefficient is to test whether the variance of the error terms in a regression model is constant. We shall illustrate this use in the second of the two examples to follow.

Example 1

A market researcher wished to examine whether an association exists between population size (Y_1) and per capita expenditures for a new food product (Y_2). The data for a random sample of 12 test markets are given in Table 15.1, columns 1 and 2. Because the distributions of the variables are not nearly normal, a nonparametric test of association is desired. The ranks for the variables are given in Table 15.1, columns 3 and 4. A computer package found that the coefficient of simple correlation between the ranked data in columns 3 and 4 is $r_S = .895$. The alternatives of interest are the two-sided ones in (15.45). Since n exceeds 10 here, we use test statistic (15.47):

$$t^* = \frac{.895\sqrt{12 - 2}}{\sqrt{1 - (.895)^2}} = 6.34$$

For $\alpha = .05$, we require $t(.975; 10) = 2.228$. Since $|t^*| = 6.34 > 2.228$, we conclude H_a, that there is an association between population size and per capita expenditures for the food product. The two-sided P-value of the test is .00008.

Example 2

The data for the Dwaine Studios example were given in Figure 6.5b, as were the residuals. These residuals were plotted against X_1 in Figure 6.7b to examine, among other things, whether the variance of the error terms varies in a systematic fashion with X_1. No evidence was found in this plot that the error variance is not constant.

We can conduct a nonparametric test for constancy of the error variance by means of the Spearman rank correlation coefficient here. The number of cases is large enough so that the residuals are almost uncorrelated and can be treated as if they were independent observations. To conduct a test of the constancy of the error variance, we shall examine whether the absolute size of the residuals is associated, either directly or inversely, with the level of X_1. Table 15.2 repeats a portion of the values of X_1 and the residuals in columns 1 and 2, respectively. Column 3 contains the absolute residuals, and columns 4 and 5 contain the ranks of X_{i1} and $|e_i|$, respectively. The Spearman rank correlation coefficient (15.43) is $r_S = .275$ (calculations not shown). The alternatives to be considered here are the two-sided ones in (15.45). Since $n = 21$ here, we can use test statistic (15.47):

$$t^* = \frac{.275\sqrt{21 - 2}}{\sqrt{1 - (.275)^2}} = 1.247$$

TABLE 15.1   **Data on Population and Expenditures and Their Ranks—Sales Marketing Example.**

Test Market i	(1) Population (in thousands) Y_{i1}	(2) Per Capita Expenditure (dollars) Y_{i2}	(3) R_{i1}	(4) R_{i2}
1	29	127	1	2
2	435	214	8	11
3	86	133	3	4
4	1,090	208	11	10
5	219	153	7	6
6	503	184	9	8
7	47	130	2	3
8	3,524	217	12	12
9	185	141	6	5
10	98	154	5	7
11	952	194	10	9
12	89	103	4	1

TABLE 15.2   **Rank Correlation Test for Constancy of Error Variance—Dwaine Studios Example.**

Case i	(1) X_{i1}	(2) e_i	(3) $|e_i|$	(4) R_{i1}	(5) R_{i2}
1	68.5	−12.7841	12.7841	14	17
2	45.2	10.1706	10.1706	4	14
3	91.3	9.8037	9.8037	21	13
...	...	...	...	...	...
19	89.6	1.6130	1.6130	20	5
20	82.7	−6.2160	6.2160	16	9
21	52.3	9.4356	9.4356	11	11

For $\alpha = .01$, we require $t(.995; 19) = 2.861$. Since $|t^*| = 1.247 \leq 2.861$, we conclude H_0, that there is no association between the size of the absolute residuals and the level of X_1. The two-sided P-value of the test is .23. Thus again, there is no evidence that the error variance systematically varies with the level of X_1.

Comments

1. In case of ties among some data values, each of the tied values is given the average of the ranks involved.

2. Another nonparametric rank procedure similar to Spearman's r_S is *Kendall's* τ. This statistic also measures how far the rankings of Y_1 and Y_2 differ from each other, but in a somewhat different way than the Spearman rank correlation coefficient. A discussion of Kendall's τ may be found in Reference 15.3.   ∎

Cited References

15.1.   Snedecor, G. W., and W. G. Cochran. *Statistical Methods*. 8th ed. Ames, Iowa: Iowa State University Press, 1989.

15.2.   Gibbons, J. D. *Nonparametric Methods for Quantitative Analysis*. 2nd ed. Columbus, Ohio: American Sciences Press, 1985.

15.3.   Kendall, M. G., and J. D. Gibbons. *Rank Correlation Methods*. 5th ed. London: Charles Griffin, 1990.

Problems

15.1.   A management trainee in a production department wished to study the relation between weight of rough casting and machining time to produce the finished block. The trainee selected castings so that the weights would be spaced equally apart in the sample and then observed the corresponding machining times. Would you recommend that a regression or a correlation model be used? Explain.

15.2.   A social scientist stated: "The conditions for the bivariate and multivariate normal distributions are so rarely met in my experience that I feel much safer using a regression model." Comment.

15.3.   A student was investigating from a large sample whether variables Y_1 and Y_2 follow a bivariate normal distribution. The student obtained the residuals when regressing Y_1 on Y_2, and also obtained the residuals when regressing Y_2 on Y_1, and then prepared a normal probability plot for each set of residuals. Do these two normal probability plots provide sufficient information for determining whether the two variables follow a bivariate normal distribution? Explain.

15.4.   Refer to Figures 15.1 and 15.3. Where in the $Y_1 Y_2$ plane is the height of the bivariate normal surface greatest? How can this point be ascertained from inspection of the density function (15.1)?

15.5.   Prepare a contour plot for the bivariate normal distribution with parameters $\mu_1 = 50$, $\mu_2 = 100$, $\sigma_1 = 3$, $\sigma_2 = 4$, and $\rho_{12} = .80$.

15.6.   Refer to Problem 15.5.

   a.   State the characteristics of the marginal distribution of Y_1.

   b.   State the characteristics of the conditional distribution of Y_2 when $Y_1 = 55$.

   c.   State the characteristics of the conditional distribution of Y_1 when $Y_2 = 95$.

15.7. Refer to Problem 15.5.

    a. Give the two regression lines for this model.

    b. Why are there two regression lines for a bivariate normal distribution and not just one? What is the meaning of each?

    c. Must β_{12} and β_{21} have the same sign?

15.8. Refer to Figure 15.5. For any specified value Y_{h2}, can you identify where the conditional density $f(Y_1|Y_{h2})$ is maximized? How can this result be ascertained also from inspection of the conditional density function (15.6)?

15.9.   a. Prepare a contour plot for the bivariate normal distribution with parameters $\mu_1 = 14$, $\mu_2 = 350$, $\sigma_1 = 2$, $\sigma_2 = 25$, and $\rho_{12} = .90$.

    b. Give the two regression lines for this model. Why are there two regression lines and not just one?

15.10. Refer to Figure 15.5. If the two regression lines were not labeled, could you determine by inspection which line pertains to the regression of Y_2 on Y_1 and which to the regression of Y_1 on Y_2? Explain.

15.11. Explain whether any of the following would be affected if the bivariate normal model (15.1) were employed instead of the normal error regression model (2.1) with fixed levels of the predictor variable: (1) point estimates of the regression coefficients, (2) confidence limits for the regression coefficients, (3) interpretation of the confidence coefficient.

15.12. Refer to **Plastic hardness** Problem 1.22. A student was analyzing these data and received the following standard query from the interactive regression and correlation computer package: CALCULATE CONFIDENCE INTERVAL FOR POPULATION CORRELA TION COEFFICIENT RHO? ANSWER Y OR N. Would a "yes" response lead to meaningful information here? Explain.

√ 15.13. **Property assessments**. The data that follow show assessed value for property tax purposes (Y_1, in thousand dollars) and sales price (Y_2, in thousand dollars) for a sample of 15 parcels of land for industrial development sold recently in "arm's length" transactions in a tax district. Assume that bivariate normal model (15.1) is appropriate here.

i:	1	2	3	. . .	13	14	15
Y_{i1}:	13.9	16.0	10.3	. . .	14.9	12.9	15.8
Y_{i2}:	28.6	34.7	21.0	. . .	35.1	30.0	36.2

    a. Plot the data in a scatter diagram. Does the bivariate normal model appear to be appropriate here? Discuss.

    b. Calculate r_{12}. What parameter is estimated by r_{12}? What is the interpretation of this parameter?

    c. Test whether or not Y_1 and Y_2 are statistically independent in the population, using test statistic (15.16) and level of significance .01. State the alternatives, decision rule, and conclusion.

    d. To test $\rho_{12} = .6$ versus $\rho_{12} \neq .6$, would it be appropriate to use test statistic (15.16)?

15.14. **Contract profitability**. A cost analyst for a drilling and blasting contractor examined 84 contracts handled in the last two years and found that the coefficient of correlation between value of contract (Y_1) and profit contribution generated by the contract (Y_2) is $r_{12} = .61$. Assume that bivariate normal model (15.1) applies.

a. Test whether or not Y_1 and Y_2 are statistically independent in the population; use $\alpha = .05$. State the alternatives, decision rule, and conclusion.

b. Estimate ρ_{12} with a 95 percent confidence interval.

c. Convert the confidence interval in part (b) to a 95 percent confidence interval for ρ_{12}^2. Interpret this interval estimate.

√ 15.15. **Bid preparation**. A building construction consultant studied the relationship between cost of bid preparation (Y_1) and amount of bid (Y_2) for the consulting firm's clients. In a sample of 103 bids prepared by clients, $r_{12} = .87$. Assume that bivariate normal model (15.1) applies.

a. Test whether or not $\rho_{12} = 0$; control the risk of Type I error at .10. State the alternatives, decision rule, and conclusion. What would be the implication if $\rho_{12} = 0$?

b. Obtain a 90 percent confidence interval for ρ_{12}. Interpret this interval estimate.

c. Convert the confidence interval in part (b) to a 90 percent confidence interval for ρ_{12}^2.

15.16. **Water flow**. An engineer, desiring to estimate the coefficient of correlation ρ_{12} between rate of water flow at point A in a stream (Y_1) and concurrent rate of flow at point B (Y_2), obtained $r_{12} = .83$ in a sample of 147 cases. Assume that bivariate normal model (15.1) is appropriate.

a. Obtain a 99 percent confidence interval for ρ_{12}.

b. Convert the confidence interval in part (a) to a 99 percent confidence interval for ρ_{12}^2.

15.17. Refer to **Contract profitability** Problem 15.14. An independent random sample of 100 contracts was selected during the following two years and the coefficient of correlation between value of contract and profit contribution for the 100 contracts was .85. Assume that bivariate normal model (15.1) also applies for the more recent period.

a. Test whether or not the population coefficient of correlation ρ_2 for the more recent period is the same as the coefficient ρ_1 for the earlier period; use $\alpha = .05$. State the alternatives, decision rule, and conclusion.

b. What is the P-value of the test?

√ 15.18. Refer to **Bid preparation** Problem 15.15. A year later the building construction consultant selected an independent random sample of 89 bids and found the coefficient of correlation between cost of bid preparation and amount of bid for the 89 bids to be .58. Assume that bivariate normal model (15.1) also applies for the more recent year.

a. Test whether or not the population coefficient of correlation ρ_2 for the more recent year is smaller than the coefficient ρ_1 for the previous year; use $\alpha = .10$. State the alternatives, decision rule, and conclusion.

b. What is the P-value of the test?

15.19. Refer to **Water flow** Problem 15.16. A year later, the engineer made 120 additional pairs of observations independent of those for the previous year. The coefficient of correlation between the rates of water flow at points A and B for the 120 new cases was .91. Assume that bivariate normal model (15.1) also applies for the more recent period.

a. Test whether or not the population coefficient of correlation ρ_2 for the more recent year is larger than the coefficient ρ_1 for the previous year; use $\alpha = .025$. State the alternatives, decision rule, and conclusion.

b. What is the P-value of the test?

15.20. **Pharmaceutical study**. A marketing research analyst in a pharmaceutical firm wishes to study the relation between the following quantified variables in the target population:

Y_1 socioeconomic status of homemaker

Y_2 magazine media exposure to homemaker

Y_3 homemaker's awareness of firm's new product

The analyst believes it is reasonable to assume that the variables follow multivariate normal distribution (15.29).

a. Explain what is measured by each of the following: (1) $\sigma^2_{3.12}$, (2) $\sigma_{31.2}$, (3) $\sigma^2_{1.3}$.

b. Explain the meaning of each of the following: (1) $\rho^2_{2.13}$, (2) $\rho^2_{2.3}$, (3) $\rho^2_{12.3}$.

15.21. **Household survey**. In a random sample of 250 households, the coefficient of multiple correlation between purchases of soft drinks (Y_1) and purchases of snack foods (Y_2) and purchases of dairy products (Y_3) was $R_{1.23} = .892$. The coefficient of partial correlation $r_{13.2}$ was found to be $-.413$.

a. Test whether or not $\rho_{1.23} = 0$; use $\alpha = .05$. State the alternatives, decision rule, and conclusion.

b. Test whether or not $\rho_{13.2} = 0$; use $\alpha = .05$. State the alternatives, decision rule, and conclusion.

c. Estimate $\rho_{13.2}$ with a 95 percent confidence interval. Convert this confidence interval into a 95 percent confidence interval for $\rho^2_{13.2}$. Interpret this latter interval estimate.

√ 15.22. **Microcomputer assembly**. A consultant studied the relation between visual acuity (Y_1), manual dexterity (Y_2), and tactile reflex (Y_3) in persons who had proven to be proficient as assemblers of microcomputer components. Observations on these variables were obtained for a random sample of 30 persons. Sums of squares for regressions run by the consultant follow. Assume that multivariate normal model (15.29) applies.

Sum of Squares	Regression				
	Y_1 on Y_2	Y_1 on Y_3	Y_1 on Y_2, Y_3	Y_2 on Y_1	Y_2 on Y_3
Regression	7,436	66	7,439	6,900	42
Error	392	7,762	389	363	7,221
Total	7,828	7,828	7,828	7,263	7,263

Sum of Squares	Regression			
	Y_2 on Y_1, Y_3	Y_3 on Y_1	Y_3 on Y_2	Y_3 on Y_1, Y_2
Regression	6,901	46	32	64
Error	362	5,327	5,341	5,309
Total	7,263	5,373	5,373	5,373

a. What does $\rho^2_{1.23}$ denote here? Estimate this parameter by a point estimate. What information is provided by this estimate?

b. Test whether or not $\rho_{1.23} = 0$, using $\alpha = .01$. State the alternatives, decision rule, and conclusion.

c. Test whether or not $\rho_{12.3} = 0$; use $\alpha = .01$. State the alternatives, decision rule, and conclusion.

d. Estimate $\rho_{12.3}$ with a 99 percent confidence interval. Interpret your interval estimate.

√ 15.23. Refer to **Microcomputer assembly** Problem 15.22. Obtain r_{12}, r_{13}, and r_{23}. Also obtain $r_{12.3}$, $r_{13.2}$, and $r_{23.1}$. Summarize the information provided by these coefficients.

15.24. Refer to **Grade point average** Problem 1.19.

a. Test by means of the Spearman rank correlation coefficient whether an association (direct or inverse) exists between the absolute residuals and the level of X; use $\alpha = .05$. State the alternatives, decision rule, and conclusion.

b. What is the P-value of the test?

c. What does your conclusion imply about the constancy of the error variance?

√ 15.25. Refer to **Calculator maintenance** Problem 1.20.

a. Test by means of the Spearman rank correlation coefficient whether an association (direct or inverse) exists between the absolute residuals and the level of X; use $\alpha = .01$. State the alternatives, decision rule, and conclusion.

b. What is the P-value of the test?

c. What does your conclusion imply about the constancy of the error variance?

15.26. Refer to **Plastic hardness** Problem 1.22.

a. Test by means of the Spearman rank correlation coefficient whether an association (direct or inverse) exists between the absolute residuals and the level of X; use $\alpha = .02$. State the alternatives, decision rule, and conclusion.

b. What is the P-value of the test?

c. What does your conclusion imply about the constancy of the error variance?

15.27. Refer to **Computer-assisted learning** Problem 10.6.

a. Test by means of the Spearman rank correlation coefficient whether an association (direct or inverse) exists between the absolute residuals and the level of X; use $\alpha = .01$. State the alternatives, decision rule, and conclusion.

b. What is the P-value of the test?

c. What does your conclusion imply about the constancy of the error variance?

√ 15.28. Refer to **Machine speed** Problem 10.7.

a. Test by means of the Spearman rank correlation coefficient whether an association (direct or inverse) exists between the absolute residuals and the level of X; use $\alpha = .05$. State the alternatives, decision rule, and conclusion.

b. What is the P-value of the test?

c. What does your conclusion imply about the constancy of the error variance?

Exercises

15.29. The random variables Y_1 and Y_2 follow the bivariate normal distribution in (15.1). Show that if $\rho_{12} = 0$, Y_1 and Y_2 are independent random variables.

15.30. (Calculus needed.)

    a. Obtain the maximum likelihood estimators of the parameters of the bivariate normal distribution in (15.1).

    b. Using the results in part (a), obtain the maximum likelihood estimators of the parameters of the conditional probability distribution of Y_1 for any value of Y_2 in (15.7).

    c. Show that the maximum likelihood estimators of $\alpha_{1.2}$ and β_{12} obtained in part (b) are the same as the least squares estimators (1.10) for the regression coefficients in the simple linear regression model.

15.31. Show that test statistics (2.17) and (15.16) are equivalent.

15.32. Show that test statistic (6.39b) for $p = 4$ is equivalent to test statistic (15.36).

15.33. Show that the ratio *SSR/SSTO* is the same whether Y_1 is regressed on Y_2 or Y_2 is regressed on Y_1. [*Hint*: Use (1.10a) and (2.51).]

15.34. Show that when there are $p = 2$ variables, the multivariate normal density function (15.29) simplifies to the bivariate normal density function (15.1).

Projects

15.35. Refer to **Pharmaceutical study** Problem 15.20. The following data were obtained in a pilot study involving a random sample of 42 homemakers:

Homemaker i	Y_{i1}	Y_{i2}	Y_{i3}
1	76	81	53
2	92	89	78
3	85	84	66
. . .	. . .	. . .	. . .
40	38	40	16
41	52	46	35
42	76	68	42

    a. The analyst first wished to test whether or not $\rho_{3.12} = 0$. Perform the test using a level of significance of .01. State the alternatives, decision rule, and conclusion. What is the implication for the analyst if $\rho_{3.12} = 0$?

    b. Estimate each coefficient of simple correlation and each coefficient of partial correlation with a separate 99 percent confidence interval. What is the family confidence coefficient for the entire set of estimates?

    c. Analyze the results obtained in part (b) and summarize your findings.

Analysis of Variance: I

16 Single-Factor ANOVA Model and Tests

Analysis of variance (ANOVA) models are versatile statistical tools for studying the relation between a response variable and one or more explanatory or predictor variables. These models do not require any assumptions about the nature of the statistical relation between the response and explanatory variables, nor do they require that the explanatory variables be quantitative.

In the present chapter, we consider first the relation between analysis of variance and regression. We then take up the basic elements of single-factor analysis of variance models, which involve one explanatory or predictor variable. In the remainder of Part V, we continue our discussion of single-factor analysis of variance. In Part VI, we take up multifactor analysis of variance models when two or more predictor variables are under investigation.

16.1 Relation between Regression and Analysis of Variance

Regression analysis, as we have seen, is concerned with the statistical relation between one or more predictor variables and a response variable. Both the predictor and response variables in ordinary regression models are quantitative. (We exclude from this discussion the use of indicator variables in regression models, discussed in Chapter 11.) The regression function describes the nature of the statistical relation between the mean response and the level(s) of the predictor variable(s).

We encountered the analysis of variance in our consideration of regression. It was used there for a variety of tests concerning the regression coefficients, the fit of the regression model, and the like. The analysis of variance is actually much more general than its use with regression models indicated. Analysis of variance models are a basic type of statistical model. They are concerned, like regression models, with the statistical relation between one or more predictor variables and a response variable. Like regression models, analysis of variance models are appropriate for both observational data and data based on formal experiments. Further, like the usual regression models, the response variable for analysis of variance models is a quantitative variable. Analysis of variance models differ from ordinary regression models in two key respects:

FIGURE 16.1   **Relation between Regression and Analysis of Variance Models.**

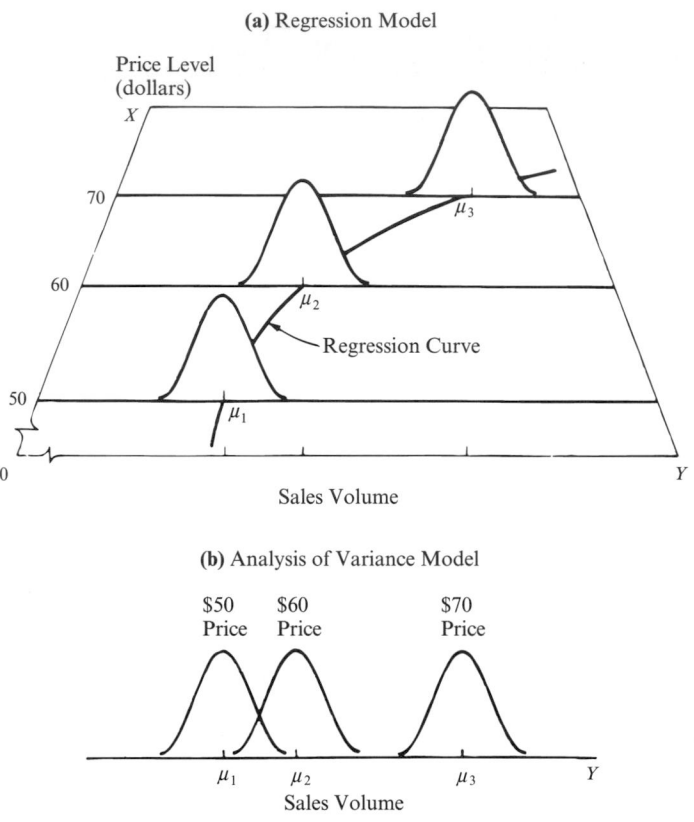

(a) Regression Model

(b) Analysis of Variance Model

1. The explanatory or predictor variables in analysis of variance models may be qualitative (gender, geographic location, plant shift, etc.).

2. If the predictor variables are quantitative, no assumption is made in analysis of variance models about the nature of the statistical relation between them and the response variable. Thus, the need to specify the nature of the regression function encountered in ordinary regression analysis does not arise in analysis of variance models.

Illustrations

Figure 16.1 illustrates the essential differences between regression and analysis of variance models for the case where the predictor variable is quantitative. Shown in Figure 16.1a is the regression model for a pricing study involving three different price levels, $X = \$50$, $\$60$, $\$70$. Note that the XY plane has been rotated from its usual position so that the Y axis faces the viewer. For each level of the predictor variable, there is a probability distribution of sales volumes. The means of these probability distributions fall on the regression curve, which describes the statistical relation between price and mean sales volume.

The analysis of variance model for the same study is illustrated in Figure 16.1b. The three price levels are treated as separate populations, each leading to a probability distribution of sales volumes. The quantitative differences in the three price levels and their

FIGURE 16.2   **Analysis of Variance Model Representation for Incentive Pay Example.**

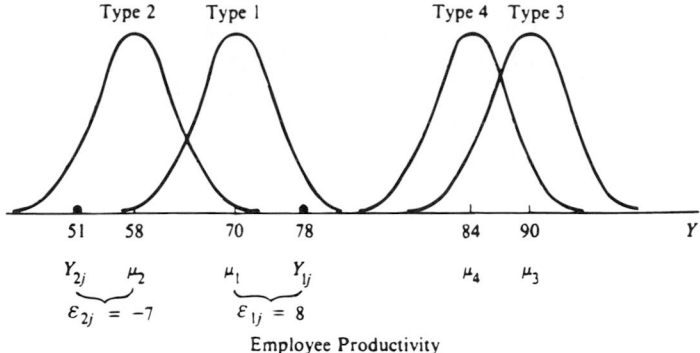

statistical relation to expected sales volume are not considered by the analysis of variance model.

Figure 16.2 illustrates the analysis of variance model for a study of the effects of four different types of incentive pay systems on employee productivity. Here, each type of incentive pay system corresponds to a different population, and there is associated with each a probability distribution of employee productivities (Y). Since type of incentive pay system is a qualitative variable, Figure 16.2 does not contain a corresponding regression model representation.

Choice between Two Types of Models

As we have seen in Chapter 11, regression analysis can handle qualitative predictor variables by means of indicator variables. When indicator variables are so used with regression models, the regression results will be identical to those obtained with analysis of variance models. The reason why analysis of variance exists as a distinct statistical methodology is that the structure of the predictor indicator variables permits computational simplifications that are explicitly recognized in the statistical procedures for the analysis of variance. Hence, there is no fundamental choice between regression and analysis of variance models when the predictor variables are qualitative.

On the other hand, there is a choice in modeling when the predictor variables are quantitative. One possibility is to recognize the quantitative nature of the predictor variables explicitly; this can only be done by a regression model. The other possibility is to set up classes for each quantitative variable and then employ either indicator variables in a regression model or an analysis of variance model. As we mentioned in Chapter 11, the strategy of setting up classes for quantitative variables is sometimes followed in large-scale studies as a means of obtaining a nonparametric regression fit when there is substantial doubt about the nature of the statistical relation. Here again, analysis of variance models and regression models with indicator variables will lead to identical results.

16.2 Experimental and Observational Studies, Factors, and Treatments

As noted before, analysis of variance models, like regression models, may be employed for experimental data and for observational data. Similarly, analysis of variance models are intended for applications where the effects of one or more predictor variables on the response variable are of interest. A different terminology is often employed, however, for analysis of variance models. For instance, the explanatory or predictor variables for analysis of variance models are called factors or treatments.

We shall now consider the role of experimental and observational studies in the analysis of variance, and the correspondence of factors and treatments in the analysis of variance to explanatory or predictor variables in regression.

Experimental and Observational Studies

Analysis of variance models are useful for data from both experimental and observational studies.

Example 1. The effects of four cooking temperatures on the fluffiness of omelets prepared from a mix was studied by randomly assigning five packages of mix to each of four cooking temperatures. This is an experimental study because the explanatory variable of interest (cooking temperature) is controlled by the experimenter. The experimental units here are the 20 packages of mix. The experimental design used is a completely randomized design, with each of the 20 packages of mix having an equal chance to be assigned to each of the four cooking temperatures.

Example 2. A study of the effects of education and type of experience of salespeople on the sales volumes of the salespeople was made by selecting a random sample of salespeople currently employed by the company and obtaining information on highest degree obtained, type of experience, and sales volume for each of the selected employees. This is an observational study because the data were obtained without controlling the predictor variables of interest (education and type of experience).

Factor

A *factor* is an explanatory or predictor variable to be studied in an investigation. For instance, in an investigation of the effect of price on sales of a luxury item, the factor being studied is price. Similarly, in a study comparing the appeal of four different television programs, the factor under investigation is television program. In the omelet fluffiness example, the factor under investigation is cooking temperature.

Factor Level

A *factor level* is a particular form of that factor. In the pricing study in Figure 16.1, three prices were used, namely, $50, $60, and $70. Each of these prices is a level of the factor under study, and we say that the price factor has three levels in this study. As another example, in a study of the effect of color of the paper of the mail questionnaire on response rate, color of paper is the factor under study, and each different color used is a level of that factor. In the omelet fluffiness example, each of the four cooking temperatures is a factor level.

Single-Factor and Multifactor Studies

Investigations differ as to the number of factors studied. Some are *single-factor studies*, where only one factor is of concern. For instance, the study of the appeal of four different television programs mentioned earlier is an example of a single-factor study. In *multifactor studies*, two or more factors are investigated simultaneously. An example of a multifactor investigation is a study of the effects of temperature and concentration of the solvent upon the yield of a chemical process. Here, two factors—temperature and concentration—are studied simultaneously to obtain information about their effects on the yield. Similarly, in the earlier sales volume example, two factors were studied simultaneously—education and type of experience. Multifactor investigations will be discussed in Part VI; we focus now on single-factor studies.

Experimental and Classification Factors

A factor may be categorized as to whether it is an experimental factor or a classification factor. In any investigation based on observational data, the factors under study are classification factors. A *classification factor* pertains to the characteristic of the units under study and is not under the control of the investigator. For instance, in the sales volume example, education and type of experience are classification factors because they refer to the characteristics of the salespeople in the study and were not manipulated experimentally. An *experimental factor* is one where the level of the factor is assigned at random to the experimental unit. An illustration is the factor cooking temperature in the omelet fluffiness example.

We have pointed out before that experimental data provide firmer foundations for conclusions than do observational data. If experimental factors were only to appear in experimental studies and classification factors only in observational studies, there would be no need to distinguish between these types of factors. However, classification factors can be found in experimental studies, and therefore it is important to recognize them as such, since the inferences pertaining to these factors will not be as clear as those for experimental factors.

Example. An appliance manufacturer operates three regional training centers in the United States for training mechanics to service the company's products. At each regional center, two different training programs were studied, with the trainees from the region assigned at random to one of the two training programs. One may view this as a two-factor study, the factors being training program (experimental factor) and training center (classification factor). If the same training program is superior to the other in all three centers, the evidence is quite clear as to the effects of the training programs since at each center the trainees from the region were assigned at random to the two programs.

Differences between the three training centers cannot be interpreted as clearly. Note that training center is a classification factor because each trainee was assigned to the center for the region in which the trainee is located. Consequently, one center may excel for any number of reasons, such as because its staff is doing a better training job, it has better facilities, or because trainees assigned to it come from a geographic region in which better education is provided. Evidence external to this study would be required as to whether or not the education of trainees at the three centers is the same, whether or not the facilities are equal, and the like, before a clear understanding of the reasons for differences between training centers could be obtained.

Qualitative and Quantitative Factors

Finally, we need to distinguish between qualitative and quantitative factors. A *qualitative factor* is one where the levels differ by some qualitative attribute. Examples are type of advertisement or brand of rust inhibitor. A *quantitative factor* is one where each level is described by a numerical quantity on a scale. Examples are temperature in degrees centigrade, age in years, or price in dollars.

Treatments

In single-factor studies, a treatment corresponds to a factor level. Thus, in a study of five advertisements, each advertisement is a treatment. In multifactor studies, a treatment corresponds to a combination of factor levels. For instance, in a study of the effects on sales volume of price ($.25, $.29) and package color (red, blue), each price-color combination, such as red package color—$.25 price, is a treatment. This particular study contains four treatments since there are four price-color combinations.

16.3   Design of Analysis of Variance Studies

We now briefly discuss a few important considerations in designing analysis of variance studies. Some of the considerations are particularly relevant to experimental studies, while others pertain to both observational and experimental studies.

Choice of Treatments

The choice of treatments to be included in an investigation is basically a matter to be decided by the investigator. In a scientific investigation, the treatments included should be able to provide some insights into the mechanism underlying the phenomenon under study. Initial studies should not attempt to examine this mechanism in full detail, but rather should seek to find the principal factors involved and obtain indications of the magnitudes of their effects. Subsequent studies can then be conducted to provide more detailed findings.

Even when the investigation is not of scientific but rather of practical interest, inclusion of treatments to provide some explanation of the results is often desirable. Consider a company that is planning to purchase a new type of tool machine from a new maker and wishes to compare this new type with the present machines by means of an experiment. Since the new machines are of a much larger size than the present ones, the company wishes to include a third type of machine in the experiment, namely, one corresponding in size to the present ones, but from the new maker. By doing so, the company will get information as to whether any differences that might be observed between the present machines and the new ones are connected with the maker, the size of the machine, or both.

Definition of Treatment.   The definition of a treatment can be a difficult problem. Consider an experiment to study whether C or PASCAL is a better programming language to teach in an introductory computing course. Some teachers will prefer C, others PASCAL. Should the treatments then be defined as the programming language taught by instructors who prefer that language? If so, differences in findings may be due to differences between the two groups of instructors. Should the definition of a treatment not include the instructor, and instructors be randomized, with some being forced to teach a language they do not prefer? Or should instructor preference be a second factor, with each instructor teaching both languages? Problems of this kind need careful resolution so that the results of the study will be useful.

Control Treatment.   A control treatment is needed in some experiments, but not in all. A control treatment consists of applying the identical procedures to experimental units that are used with the other treatments, except for the effects under investigation. In a study of food additives, for instance, a treatment may consist of a portion of a vegetable containing a particular additive that is served to a consumer in a particular experimental setting in the laboratory. A control treatment here would consist of a portion of the same vegetable served to a consumer in the identical experimental setting except that no food additive has been used.

A control treatment is required when the general effectiveness of the treatments under study is not known, or when the general effectiveness of the treatments is known but is not consistent under all conditions. In the food additives example, suppose it is known that food additive A is highly effective in enhancing the tastiness of vegetables and it is desired to see if additives B and C are equally effective or possibly even more effective. In that case, a standard of comparison is available and no control treatment is required. On the other hand, suppose there is no knowledge about the general effectiveness of the three additives, and the following results are obtained (ratings can range between 0 and 60):

Additive	Mean Rating
A	39
B	37
C	41

Assume that the sample sizes are large so that the mean ratings are very precise. In the absence of a standard of comparison, one would not know here whether each of the three additives is effective or whether none of the additives is effective.

It is crucial that the control treatment be conducted in the identical experimental setting as the other treatments. In the food additives example, for instance, a survey of consumers at home, in which persons are asked to rate the general tastiness of the vegetable (without any additive) on the same scale as in the experiment, would not qualify as a control treatment. Such a survey might yield a mean rating of 22, suggesting that the three additives substantially increase the tastiness of the vegetable. This conclusion, however, could be grossly misleading. If the control treatment actually were incorporated into the experiment so that consumers are given portions of the vegetable with no additive in the laboratory setting, the mean rating for the control treatment might be 40. This result would imply that none of the three additives is effective in enhancing the tastiness of the vegetable. The reason for the higher mean rating in the laboratory setting could be a "halo" effect connected with the experimental procedures. Possibly, foods served in the experimental setting taste better than at home, or perhaps consumers try to oblige by giving higher ratings when they participate in an experimental study. Thus, only a control treatment incorporated into the experiment can serve as the proper standard of comparison.

Basic Unit of Study

Another important issue in both experimental and observational studies is how to define the basic unit of the study. Consider, for instance, an experimental study of two incentive pay systems. Should the study unit be an individual employee, a shift, or a plant? Often, technical considerations dictate the choice of the size of the study unit. For instance, morale considerations might preclude the use of different incentive pay systems in the same plant.

A different aspect of defining the basic unit of study occurs in investigations of sales and similar phenomena. Suppose that we wish to measure the effectiveness of five different television commercials in terms of sales during a period of time subsequent to their showing. Should the length of time be one week, two weeks, one month, or some other time period? Clearly, the purposes of the study will need to govern the length of time which makes up the basic study unit here.

Representativeness of the study units is another important consideration in the design of analysis of variance studies. Consider a study of management behavior with different communications networks. A university investigator may be tempted to use students as subjects because of their ready availability. If, however, information is desired about the behavior of business people, the students may not be representative experimental units. It hardly needs to be stated that an investigator should make every effort to obtain representative study units. Conversely, one should be cautious in extending results of an investigation to groups for which the study units are not representative. Thus, if the communications network study cited above *did* use students, one should not automatically assume that the findings are relevant to business people.

16.4   Uses of Analysis of Variance Models

Analysis of variance models basically are used to analyze the effects of the explanatory variable(s) under study on the response variable. Specifically, single-factor studies are utilized to compare different factor level effects, to ascertain the "best" factor level, and the like. In multifactor studies, analysis of variance models are employed to determine whether the different factors interact, which factors are the key ones, which factor combinations are "best," and so on. We illustrate these points with three examples.

Example 1

A hospital was using a standard type of therapy to treat a medical problem. Recently two new types of therapy were proposed. The analysis of variance model was then utilized to determine whether either of the two new types of therapy is superior to the present type and, if so, which one is best.

Example 2

Four machines in a plant were studied with respect to the diameters of ball bearings they produced. The purpose of using the analysis of variance model in the study was to determine whether substantial differences between the machines existed. If so, the machines would need to be calibrated.

Example 3

In a study of a random sample of employees of an organization, the employees' absentee rates were analyzed according to length of service, gender, marital status, and type of job of the employee. The analysis of variance model for this multifactor investigation was utilized to determine whether the effects on the absentee rate of these explanatory variables interact in important ways and which one of these variables shows the strongest statistical relation to the response variable.

16.5   Use of Computers

For analysis of variance, as for regression analysis, packaged computer programs are readily available for handling calculations. We will assume, as in our regression analysis discussions, that computers or programmable calculators are used in handling analysis of variance calculations for all but the simplest data sets.

For regression analysis, a single "multiple regression" packaged program frequently suffices for a variety of applications such as simple linear regression, polynomial regression, and multiple regression. Packaged analysis of variance programs, on the other hand, are often keyed to specific analyses. Thus, a library may contain one program for single-factor analysis of variance and other programs for different types of multifactor analysis of variance. Formats for input of cases and output of results often differ substantially from one library to another, and may even differ somewhat among the different analysis of variance programs in a given library.

We noted, in discussing roundoff errors in regression analysis, that least squares results tend to be highly sensitive to roundoff effects and that different regression packages do not control such effects equally well. Similarly, different analysis of variance packages differ in quality, and it is a good idea to check a library program before using it for the first time. One procedure is to test the program on a complex data set for which accurate results are already known.

16.6   ANOVA Model I—Fixed Factor Levels

Distinction between ANOVA Models I and II

We shall consider two single-factor analysis of variance models. For brevity, we shall refer to these as ANOVA models I and II. ANOVA model I, to be taken up here, applies to such cases as a comparison of five different advertisements or a comparison of four different rust inhibitors, where the conclusions pertain to just those factor levels included in the study. ANOVA model II, to be discussed in Chapter 24, applies to a different type of situation, namely, where the conclusions extend to a population of factor levels of which the levels in the study are a sample. Consider, for instance, a company that owns several hundred retail stores throughout the country. Seven of these stores are selected at random, and a sample of employees from each store is then chosen and asked in a confidential interview for an evaluation of the management of the store. The seven stores in the study constitute the seven levels of the factor under study, namely, retail store. In this case, however, management is not just interested in the seven stores included in the study but wishes to generalize the study results to all of the retail stores it owns. Another example when ANOVA model II is applicable is when three machines out of 75 in a plant are selected at random and their daily output is studied for a period of 10 days. The three machines constitute the three factor levels in this study, but interest is not just in the three machines in the study but in all machines in the plant.

Thus, the essential difference between situations where ANOVA models I and II are applicable is that model I is the relevant one when the factor levels are chosen because of intrinsic interest in them (e.g., five different advertisements) and they are not considered to be a sample from a larger population. ANOVA model II is appropriate when the factor levels constitute a sample from a larger population (e.g., three machines out of 75) and interest is in this larger population.

Basic Ideas

The basic elements of ANOVA model I for a single-factor study are quite simple. Corresponding to each factor level, there is a probability distribution of responses. For example, in a study of the effects of four types of incentive pay on employee productivity, there is a probability distribution of employee productivities for each type of incentive pay. ANOVA model I assumes that:

1. Each probability distribution is normal.

2. Each probability distribution has the same variance.

3. The responses for each factor level are random selections from the corresponding probability distribution and are independent of the responses for any other factor level.

Figure 16.2 illustrates these conditions. Note the normality of the probability distributions and the constant variability. The probability distributions differ only with respect to their means. Differences in the means therefore reflect the essential factor level effects, and it is for this reason that the analysis of variance focuses on the mean responses for the different factor levels.

The analysis of the sample data from the factor level probability distributions usually proceeds in two steps:

1. Determine whether or not the factor level means are the same.

2. If the factor level means differ, examine how they differ and what the implications of the differences are.

In this chapter, we consider step 1, the testing procedure for determining whether or not the factor level means are the same. In the next chapter, we take up the analysis of the factor level effects when the means differ.

ANOVA Model I—Cell Means Model

Before stating ANOVA model I for single-factor studies, we need to develop some notation. We shall denote by r the number of levels of the factor under study (e.g., $r = 4$ types of incentive pay), and we shall denote any one of these levels by the index i ($i = 1, \ldots, r$). The number of cases for the ith factor level is denoted by n_i, and the total number of cases in the study is denoted by n_T, where:

(16.1)
$$n_T = \sum_{i=1}^{r} n_i$$

This notation differs from that used earlier for regression models, where the subscript i identifies the case or trial.

For analysis of variance models we shall always use the last subscript to represent the case or trial for a given factor level or treatment. Here, the index j will be used to identify the given case or trial for a particular factor level. We shall let Y_{ij} denote the value of the response variable in the jth trial for the ith factor level. For instance, Y_{ij} is the productivity of the jth employee in the ith incentive plan, or the sales volume of the jth store featuring the ith type of shelf display. Since the number of cases or trials for the ith factor level is denoted by n_i, we have $j = 1, \ldots, n_i$.

ANOVA model I can now be stated as follows:

$$(16.2) \qquad\qquad Y_{ij} = \mu_i + \varepsilon_{ij}$$

where:

Y_{ij} is the value of the response variable in the jth trial for the ith factor level or treatment

μ_i are parameters

ε_{ij} are independent $N(0, \sigma^2)$

$i = 1, \ldots, r; j - 1, \ldots, n_i$

This model is called the *cell means model* for reasons to be explained shortly. This model may be used for data from observational studies or for data from experimental studies based on a completely randomized design.

Important Features of Model

1. The observed value of Y in the jth trial for the ith factor level or treatment is the sum of two components: (a) a constant term μ_i and (b) a random error term ε_{ij}.

2. Since $E\{\varepsilon_{ij}\} = 0$, it follows that:

$$(16.3) \qquad\qquad E\{Y_{ij}\} - \mu_i$$

Thus, all responses or observations Y_{ij} for the ith factor level have the same expectation μ_i, and this parameter is the mean response for the ith factor level or treatment.

3. Since μ_i is a constant, it follows from (A.16a) that:

$$(16.4) \qquad\qquad \sigma^2\{Y_{ij}\} = \sigma^2\{\varepsilon_{ij}\} = \sigma^2$$

Thus, all observations have the same variance, regardless of factor level.

4. Since each ε_{ij} is normally distributed, so is each Y_{ij}. This follows from (A.36) because Y_{ij} is a linear function of ε_{ij}.

5. The error terms are assumed to be independent. Hence, the error term outcome on any one trial has no effect on the error term for the outcome of any other trial for the same factor level or for a different factor level. Since the ε_{ij} are independent, so are the responses Y_{ij}.

6. In view of these features, ANOVA model (16.2) can be restated as follows:

$$(16.5) \qquad\qquad Y_{ij} \text{ are independent } N(\mu_i, \sigma^2)$$

Example

Suppose that ANOVA model (16.2) is applicable to the earlier incentive pay study illustration and that the parameters are as follows:

$$\mu_1 = 70 \qquad \mu_2 = 58 \qquad \mu_3 = 90 \qquad \mu_4 = 84 \qquad \sigma = 4$$

Figure 16.2 contains a representation of this model. Note that employee productivities for incentive pay type 1 according to this model are normally distributed with mean $\mu_1 = 70$ and standard deviation $\sigma = 4$.

Suppose that in the jth trial of incentive pay type 1, the observed productivity is $Y_{1j} = 78$. In that case, the error term value is $\varepsilon_{1j} = 8$, for we have:

$$\varepsilon_{1j} = Y_{1j} - \mu_1 = 78 - 70 = 8$$

Figure 16.2 shows this observation Y_{1j}. Note that the deviation of Y_{1j} from the mean μ_1 represents the error term ε_{1j}. This figure also shows the observation $Y_{2j} = 51$, for which the error term value is $\varepsilon_{2j} = -7$.

ANOVA Model I Is Linear Model

ANOVA model (16.2) is a linear model because it can be expressed in matrix terms in the form (6.19), i.e., as $\mathbf{Y} = \mathbf{X}\boldsymbol{\beta} + \boldsymbol{\varepsilon}$. We illustrate this for a study involving $r = 3$ treatments, for each of which two observations are made; thus, $n_1 = n_2 = n_3 = 2$. $\mathbf{Y}$, $\mathbf{X}$, $\boldsymbol{\beta}$, and $\boldsymbol{\varepsilon}$ are then defined as follows here:

$$(16.6) \qquad \mathbf{Y} = \begin{bmatrix} Y_{11} \\ Y_{12} \\ Y_{21} \\ Y_{22} \\ Y_{31} \\ Y_{32} \end{bmatrix} \qquad \mathbf{X} = \begin{bmatrix} 1 & 0 & 0 \\ 1 & 0 & 0 \\ 0 & 1 & 0 \\ 0 & 1 & 0 \\ 0 & 0 & 1 \\ 0 & 0 & 1 \end{bmatrix} \qquad \boldsymbol{\beta} = \begin{bmatrix} \mu_1 \\ \mu_2 \\ \mu_3 \end{bmatrix} \qquad \boldsymbol{\varepsilon} = \begin{bmatrix} \varepsilon_{11} \\ \varepsilon_{12} \\ \varepsilon_{21} \\ \varepsilon_{22} \\ \varepsilon_{31} \\ \varepsilon_{32} \end{bmatrix}$$

Note the simple structure of the $\mathbf{X}$ matrix and that the $\boldsymbol{\beta}$ vector consists of the means μ_i.

To see that these matrices yield ANOVA model (16.2), recall from (6.20) that the vector of expected values $E\{Y_{ij}\}$ is given by $E\{\mathbf{Y}\} = \mathbf{X}\boldsymbol{\beta}$. We thus obtain:

$$(16.7) \qquad E\{\mathbf{Y}\} = \begin{bmatrix} E\{Y_{11}\} \\ E\{Y_{12}\} \\ E\{Y_{21}\} \\ E\{Y_{22}\} \\ E\{Y_{31}\} \\ E\{Y_{32}\} \end{bmatrix} = \mathbf{X}\boldsymbol{\beta} = \begin{bmatrix} 1 & 0 & 0 \\ 1 & 0 & 0 \\ 0 & 1 & 0 \\ 0 & 1 & 0 \\ 0 & 0 & 1 \\ 0 & 0 & 1 \end{bmatrix} \begin{bmatrix} \mu_1 \\ \mu_2 \\ \mu_3 \end{bmatrix} = \begin{bmatrix} \mu_1 \\ \mu_1 \\ \mu_2 \\ \mu_2 \\ \mu_3 \\ \mu_3 \end{bmatrix}$$

This indicates properly that $E\{Y_{ij}\} = \mu_i$. Hence, ANOVA model (16.2)—$Y_{ij} = \mu_i + \varepsilon_{ij}$—in matrix form is given by $\mathbf{Y} = \mathbf{X}\boldsymbol{\beta} + \boldsymbol{\varepsilon}$:

$$(16.8) \qquad \mathbf{Y} = \begin{bmatrix} Y_{11} \\ Y_{12} \\ Y_{21} \\ Y_{22} \\ Y_{31} \\ Y_{32} \end{bmatrix} = \mathbf{X}\boldsymbol{\beta} + \boldsymbol{\varepsilon} = \begin{bmatrix} \mu_1 \\ \mu_1 \\ \mu_2 \\ \mu_2 \\ \mu_3 \\ \mu_3 \end{bmatrix} + \begin{bmatrix} \varepsilon_{11} \\ \varepsilon_{12} \\ \varepsilon_{21} \\ \varepsilon_{22} \\ \varepsilon_{31} \\ \varepsilon_{32} \end{bmatrix}$$

Since the error terms for ANOVA model I have the same structure as those in general linear regression model (6.19)—namely, independence and constant variance, the variance-covariance matrix of the error terms in the ANOVA model is the same as in (6.19):

$$(16.9) \qquad \boldsymbol{\sigma}^2\{\boldsymbol{\varepsilon}\} = \begin{bmatrix} \sigma^2 & 0 & \cdots & 0 \\ 0 & \sigma^2 & \cdots & 0 \\ \vdots & \vdots & & \vdots \\ 0 & 0 & \cdots & \sigma^2 \end{bmatrix} = \sigma^2 \mathbf{I}$$

In addition, like for general linear regression model (6.19), the variance-covariance matrix of the Y responses is the same as that of the error terms:

$$(16.10) \qquad \boldsymbol{\sigma}^2\{\mathbf{Y}\} = \sigma^2 \mathbf{I}$$

When ANOVA model (16.2) is expressed as a linear model, as in (16.8), it can be seen why it is called the cell means model, because the $\boldsymbol{\beta}$ vector contains the means of the "cells"—here factor levels. In Section 16.10 we discuss an equivalent ANOVA model called the factor effects model, where the $\boldsymbol{\beta}$ vector contains components of the factor level means.

Interpretation of Factor Level Means

Observational Data. In an observational study, the factor level means μ_i correspond to the means for the different factor level populations. For instance, in a study of the productivity of employees in each of three shifts operated in a plant, the populations consist of the employee productivities for each of the three shifts. The population mean μ_1 is the mean productivity for employees in shift 1; and μ_2 and μ_3 are interpreted similarly. The variance σ^2 refers to the variability of employee productivities within a shift.

Experimental Data. In an experimental study, the factor level mean μ_i stands for the mean response that would be obtained if the ith treatment were applied to all units in the population of experimental units about which inferences are to be drawn. Similarly, the variance σ^2 refers to the variability of responses if any given experimental treatment were applied to the entire population of experimental units. For instance, in a completely randomized design to study the effects of three different training programs on employee productivity, in which 90 employees participate, a third of these employees is assigned at random to each of the three programs. The mean μ_1 here denotes the mean productivity if training program 1 were given to each employee in the population of experimental units; the means μ_2 and μ_3 are interpreted correspondingly. The variance σ^2 denotes the variability in productivities if any one training program were given to each employee in the population of experimental units.

Comments

1. ANOVA model I, like any other statistical model, is not likely to be met exactly by any real-world situation. However, it will be met approximately in many cases. As we shall note later, the statistical procedures based on ANOVA model I are quite robust so that even if the actual conditions differ substantially from those of ANOVA model I, the statistical analysis may still be an appropriate approximation.

2. At times, all treatments under study are given to each of the units in the study. For instance, a person may be asked to use toothpaste A for a week and then give it a rating, which is followed by a week's use of toothpastes B and C each. In this type of situation, ANOVA model I is usually not appropriate since the several responses by the same person for the different treatments under study are likely to be correlated. For instance, if a person prefers tooth powder to toothpaste, all of the ratings for the different toothpastes are likely to be low. In Chapter 29, we take up models for this situation.   ■

16.7   Fitting of ANOVA Model

The parameters of ANOVA model (16.2) are ordinarily unknown and must be estimated from sample data. As with normal error regression models, the method of least squares and the method of maximum likelihood lead to the same estimators of the model parameters μ_i in normal error ANOVA model (16.2). Before turning to these estimators, we shall describe an example to be used throughout the remainder of this chapter and shall develop needed additional notation.

Example

The Kenton Food Company wished to test four different package designs for a new breakfast cereal. Twenty stores, with approximately equal sales volumes, were selected as the experimental units. Each store was randomly assigned one of the package designs, with each package design assigned to five stores. A fire occurred in one store during the study period, so this store had to be dropped from the study. Hence, one of the designs was tested in only four stores. The stores were chosen to be comparable in location and sales volume. Other relevant conditions that could affect sales, such as price, amount and location of shelf space, and special promotional efforts, were kept the same for all of the stores in the experiment. Sales, in number of cases, were observed for the study period, and the results are recorded in Table 16.1.

Figure 16.3 contains aligned dot plots of the data. We readily see that designs 3 and 4 led to the largest sales, and that designs 1 and 2 led to smaller sales. We also see that the variability in store sales appears to be about the same for the four designs, consistent with ANOVA model (16.2). To make more formal inferences, we first need to develop some additional notation.

TABLE 16.1 **Number of Cases Sold by Stores for Each of Four Package Designs—Kenton Food Company Example.**

| Package Design i | Store (j) | | | | | Total $Y_{i\cdot}$ | Mean $\bar{Y}_{i\cdot}$ | Number of Stores n_i |
	1 Y_{i1}	2 Y_{i2}	3 Y_{i3}	4 Y_{i4}	5 Y_{i5}			
1	11	17	16	14	15	73	14.6	5
2	12	10	15	19	11	67	13.4	5
3	23	20	18	17		78	19.5	4
4	27	33	22	26	28	136	27.2	5
All designs						$Y_{\cdot\cdot} = 354$	$\bar{Y}_{\cdot\cdot} = 18.63$	19

FIGURE 16.3 **Dot Plots of Number of Cases Sold by Package Design —Kenton Food Company Example.**

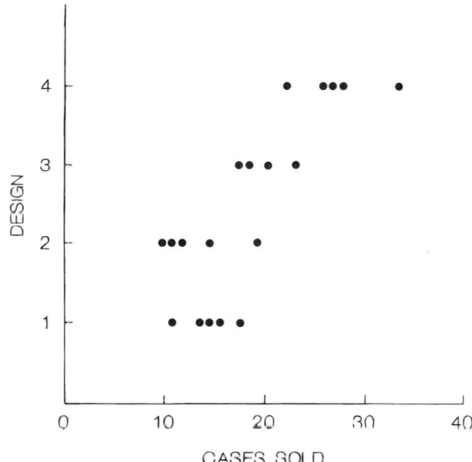

Notation

As explained earlier, Y_{ij} represents the observation or response for the jth sample unit for the ith factor level. For the Kenton Food Company example, Y_{ij} denotes the number of cases sold by the jth store assigned to the ith package design. For instance, Y_{11} represents the sales of the first store assigned package design 1. For our example, $Y_{11} = 11$ cases. Similarly, sales of the second store assigned package design 3 are $Y_{32} = 20$ cases.

The total of the observations for the ith factor level is denoted by $Y_{i\cdot}$:

(16.11)
$$Y_{i\cdot} = \sum_{j=1}^{n_i} Y_{ij}$$

Note that the dot in $Y_{i\cdot}$ indicates an aggregation over the j index; in our example, the aggregation is over all stores assigned to the ith package design. For instance, the total sales for all stores assigned package design 1 are, according to Table 16.1, $Y_1. = 73$ cases. Similarly, total sales for all stores assigned package design 4 are $Y_4. = 136$ cases.

The sample mean for the ith factor level is denoted by $\bar{Y}_{i.}$:

$$(16.12) \qquad \bar{Y}_{i.} = \frac{\sum_{j=1}^{n_i} Y_{ij}}{n_i} = \frac{Y_{i.}}{n_i}$$

In our example, the mean number of cases sold by stores assigned package design 1 is $\bar{Y}_1. = 73/5 = 14.6$. Note that the dot in the subscript $\bar{Y}_1.$ indicates that the averaging is done over j (stores).

The total of all observations in the study is denoted by $Y_{..}$:

$$(16.13) \qquad Y_{..} = \sum_{i=1}^{r} \sum_{j=1}^{n_i} Y_{ij}$$

where the two dots indicate aggregation over both the j and i indexes (in our example, over all stores for any one package design and then over all package designs). In our example, the total sales for all stores for all designs are $Y_{..} = 354$.

Finally, the overall mean for all responses is denoted by $\bar{Y}_{..}$:

$$(16.14) \qquad \bar{Y}_{..} = \frac{\sum_i \sum_j Y_{ij}}{n_T} = \frac{Y_{..}}{n_T}$$

The two dots here indicate that the averaging is done over both i and j. For our example, we have from Table 16.1 that $\bar{Y}_{..} = 354/19 = 18.63$.

Least Squares and Maximum Likelihood Estimators

According to the least squares criterion, the sum of the squared deviations of the observations around their expected values must be minimized with respect to the parameters. For ANOVA model (16.2), we know from (16.3) that the expected value of observation Y_{ij} is $E\{Y_{ij}\} = \mu_i$. Hence, the quantity to be minimized is:

$$(16.15) \qquad Q = \sum_i \sum_j (Y_{ij} - \mu_i)^2$$

Now (16.15) can be written as follows:

$$(16.15a) \qquad Q = \sum_j (Y_{1j} - \mu_1)^2 + \sum_j (Y_{2j} - \mu_2)^2 + \cdots + \sum_j (Y_{rj} - \mu_r)^2$$

Note that each of the parameters appears in only one of the component sums in (16.15a). Hence, Q can be minimized by minimizing each of the component sums separately. It is well known that the sample mean minimizes a sum of squared deviations. Hence, the least squares estimator of μ_i, denoted by $\hat{\mu}_i$, is:

$$(16.16) \qquad \hat{\mu}_i = \bar{Y}_{i.}$$

Thus, the *fitted value* for observation Y_{ij}, denoted as for regression models by $\hat{Y}_{ij}$, is simply the corresponding factor level sample mean here:

$$(16.17) \qquad \hat{Y}_{ij} = \bar{Y}_{i.}$$

The same estimators are obtained by the method of maximum likelihood. The likelihood function here corresponds to that in (1.26) for the normal error simple linear regression model, except that the regression model expected value $\beta_0 + \beta_1 X_i$ is replaced here by μ_i:

$$(16.18) \qquad L(\mu_1, \ldots, \mu_r, \sigma^2) = \frac{1}{(2\pi\sigma^2)^{n/2}} \exp\left[-\frac{1}{2\sigma^2} \sum_i \sum_j (Y_{ij} - \mu_i)^2\right]$$

Maximizing this likelihood function with respect to the parameters μ_i is equivalent to minimizing the sum $\Sigma\Sigma(Y_{ij} - \mu_i)^2$ in the exponent, which is the least squares criterion in (16.15).

Example.   For the Kenton Food Company example, the least squares and maximum likelihood estimates of the model parameters are as follows according to Table 16.1:

Parameter	Estimate
μ_1	$\hat{\mu}_1 = \bar{Y}_{1.} = 14.6$
μ_2	$\hat{\mu}_2 = \bar{Y}_{2.} = 13.4$
μ_3	$\hat{\mu}_3 = \bar{Y}_{3.} = 19.5$
μ_4	$\hat{\mu}_4 = \bar{Y}_{4.} = 27.2$

Thus, the mean sales per store with package design 1 are estimated to be 14.6 cases for the population of stores under study, and the fitted value for each of the observations for package design 1 is $\hat{Y}_{1j} = \bar{Y}_{1.} = 14.6$. Similarly, the mean sales for package design 2 are estimated to be 13.4 cases per store, and the fitted values for each response for this package design is $\hat{Y}_{2j} = \bar{Y}_{2.} = 13.4$.

Comments

1. The least squares and maximum likelihood estimators in (16.16) have all of the desirable properties mentioned in Chapter 1 for the regression estimators. For example, they are minimum variance unbiased estimators.

2. To derive the least squares estimator of μ_i, we need to minimize, with respect to μ_i, the ith component sum of squares in (16.15a):

$$(16.19) \qquad Q_i = \sum_j (Y_{ij} - \mu_i)^2$$

Differentiating with respect to μ_i, we obtain:

$$\frac{dQ_i}{d\mu_i} = \sum_j -2(Y_{ij} - \mu_i)$$

TABLE 16.2 **Residuals for Kenton Food Company Example.**

Package Design	Store (j)					Total
i	1	2	3	4	5	
1	−3.6	2.4	1.4	−.6	.4	0
2	−1.4	−3.4	1.6	5.6	−2.4	0
3	3.5	.5	−1.5	−2.5		0
4	−.2	5.8	−5.2	−1.2	.8	0
All designs						0

When we set this derivative equal to zero and replace the parameter μ_i by the least squares estimator $\hat{\mu}_i$, we obtain the result in (16.16):

$$-2 \sum_{j=1}^{n_i} (Y_{ij} - \hat{\mu}_i) = 0$$

$$\sum_j Y_{ij} = n_i \hat{\mu}_i$$

$$\hat{\mu}_i = \bar{Y}_{i\cdot}. \qquad \blacksquare$$

Residuals

Residuals are highly useful for examining the aptness of ANOVA models. The residual e_{ij} is again defined, as for regression models, as the difference between the observed and fitted values:

$$(16.20) \qquad e_{ij} = Y_{ij} - \hat{Y}_{ij} = Y_{ij} - \bar{Y}_{i\cdot}.$$

Thus, a residual here represents the deviation of an observation from its estimated factor level mean.

An important property of the residuals for ANOVA model (16.2) is that they sum to zero for each factor level i:

$$(16.21) \qquad \sum_j e_{ij} = 0 \qquad i = 1, \dots, r$$

As for regression analysis, residuals for ANOVA models are useful for examining the appropriateness of the ANOVA model. We shall discuss this use of residuals in Chapter 18.

Example. Table 16.2 contains the residuals for the Kenton Food Company example. For instance, from Table 16.1, we find:

$$e_{11} = Y_{11} - \bar{Y}_{1\cdot} = 11 - 14.6 = -3.6$$

$$e_{21} = Y_{21} - \bar{Y}_{2\cdot} = 12 - 13.4 = -1.4$$

Note from Table 16.2 that the residuals sum to zero for each factor level, as expected.

16.8   Analysis of Variance

Just as the analysis of variance for a regression model partitions the total sum of squares into the regression sum of squares and the error sum of squares, so a corresponding partitioning exists for ANOVA model (16.2).

Partitioning of SSTO

The total variability of the Y_{ij} observations, not using any information about factor levels, is measured in terms of the total deviation of each observation, i.e., the deviation of Y_{ij} around the overall mean $\bar{Y}_{..}$:

$$(16.22) \qquad\qquad Y_{ij} - \bar{Y}_{..}$$

When we utilize information about the factor levels, the deviations reflecting the uncertainty remaining in the data are those of each observation Y_{ij} around its respective estimated factor level mean $\bar{Y}_{i.}$:

$$(16.23) \qquad\qquad Y_{ij} - \bar{Y}_{i.}$$

The difference between the deviations (16.22) and (16.23) reflects the difference between the estimated factor level mean and the overall mean:

$$(16.24) \qquad\qquad (Y_{ij} - \bar{Y}_{..}) - (Y_{ij} - \bar{Y}_{i.}) = \bar{Y}_{i.} - \bar{Y}_{..}$$

Note from (16.24) that we can decompose the total deviation $Y_{ij} - \bar{Y}_{..}$ into two components:

$$(16.25) \qquad\qquad \underbrace{Y_{ij} - \bar{Y}_{..}}_{\substack{\text{Total} \\ \text{deviation}}} = \underbrace{\bar{Y}_{i.} - \bar{Y}_{..}}_{\substack{\text{Deviation of} \\ \text{estimated} \\ \text{factor level} \\ \text{mean around} \\ \text{overall mean}}} + \underbrace{Y_{ij} - \bar{Y}_{i.}}_{\substack{\text{Deviation} \\ \text{around} \\ \text{estimated} \\ \text{factor} \\ \text{level mean}}}$$

Thus, the total deviation $Y_{ij} - \bar{Y}_{..}$ can be viewed as the sum of two components:

1. The deviation of the estimated factor level mean around the overall mean.

2. The deviation of Y_{ij} around its estimated factor level mean, which is simply the residual e_{ij} according to (16.20).

Figure 16.4 illustrates this decomposition for the Kenton Food Company example for two of the observations, Y_{11} and Y_{45}.

When we square (16.25) and then sum, the cross products on the right drop out and we obtain:

$$(16.26) \qquad \sum_i \sum_j (Y_{ij} - \bar{Y}_{..})^2 = \sum_i n_i (\bar{Y}_{i.} - \bar{Y}_{..})^2 + \sum_i \sum_j (Y_{ij} - \bar{Y}_{i.})^2$$

FIGURE 16.4 **Illustration of Partitioning of Total Deviations $Y_{ij} - \bar{Y}_{..}$—Kenton Food Company Example (not presented to scale; only observations Y_{11} and Y_{45} are shown).**

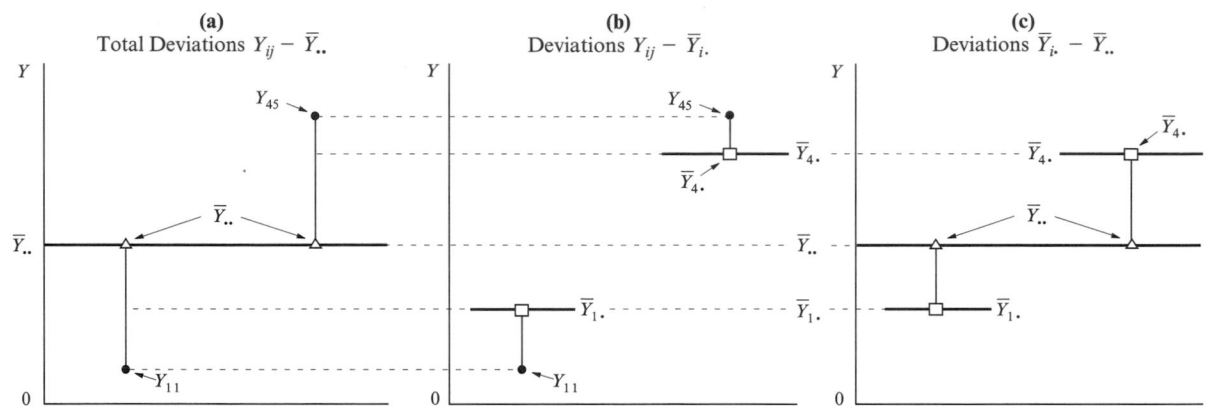

The term on the left measures the total variability of the Y_{ij} observations and is denoted, as for regression, by *SSTO* for *total sum of squares*:

$$(16.27) \qquad SSTO = \sum_i \sum_j (Y_{ij} - \bar{Y}_{..})^2$$

The first term on the right in (16.26) will be denoted by *SSTR*, standing for *treatment sum of squares*:

$$(16.28) \qquad SSTR = \sum_i n_i (\bar{Y}_{i.} - \bar{Y}_{..})^2$$

The second term on the right in (16.26) will be denoted by *SSE*, standing for *error sum of squares*:

$$(16.29) \qquad SSE = \sum_i \sum_j (Y_{ij} - \bar{Y}_{i.})^2 = \sum_i \sum_j e_{ij}^2$$

Thus, (16.26) can be written equivalently:

$$(16.30) \qquad SSTO = SSTR + SSE$$

The correspondence to the regression decomposition in (2.50) is readily apparent.

The total sum of squares for the analysis of variance model is therefore made up of these two components:

1. *SSE*: A measure of the random variation of the observations around the respective estimated factor level means. The less variation among the observations for each factor level, the smaller is *SSE*. If *SSE* = 0, the observations for any given factor level are all the same, and this holds for all factor levels. The more the observations for each factor level differ among themselves, the larger will be *SSE*.

2. *SSTR*: A measure of the extent of differences between the estimated factor level means, based on the deviations of the estimated factor level means $\bar{Y}_{i.}$ around the overall

mean $\bar{Y}_{..}$. If all estimated factor level means $\bar{Y}_{i.}$ are the same, then $SSTR = 0$. The more the estimated factor level means differ, the larger will be $SSTR$.

Example. The analysis of variance breakdown of the total sum of squares for the Kenton Food Company example in Table 16.1 is obtained as follows, using (16.27), (16.28) and (16.29):

$$SSTO = (11 - 18.63)^2 + (17 - 18.63)^2 + (16 - 18.63)^2 + \cdots + (28 - 18.63)^2$$

$$= 746.42$$

$$SSTR = 5(14.6 - 18.63)^2 + 5(13.4 - 18.63)^2 + 4(19.5 - 18.63)^2 + 5(27.2 - 18.63)^2$$

$$= 588.22$$

$$SSE = (11 - 14.6)^2 + (17 - 14.6)^2 + (16 - 14.6)^2 + \cdots + (28 - 27.2)^2$$

$$= 158.20$$

Thus, the decomposition of $SSTO$ is:

$$746.42 = 588.22 + 158.20$$

$$SSTO = SSTR + SSE$$

Note that much of the total variation in the observations is associated with variation between the estimated factor level means.

Comments

1. To prove (16.26), we begin by considering (16.25):

$$Y_{ij} - \bar{Y}_{..} = (\bar{Y}_{i.} - \bar{Y}_{..}) + (Y_{ij} - \bar{Y}_{i.})$$

Squaring both sides we obtain:

$$(Y_{ij} - \bar{Y}_{..})^2 = (\bar{Y}_{i.} - \bar{Y}_{..})^2 + (Y_{ij} - \bar{Y}_{i.})^2 + 2(\bar{Y}_{i.} - \bar{Y}_{..})(Y_{ij} - \bar{Y}_{i.})$$

When we sum over all sample observations in the study (i.e., over both i and j), we obtain:

$$(16.31) \quad \sum_i \sum_j (Y_{ij} - \bar{Y}_{..})^2 = \sum_i \sum_j (\bar{Y}_{i.} - \bar{Y}_{..})^2 + \sum_i \sum_j (Y_{ij} - \bar{Y}_{i.})^2 + \sum_i \sum_j 2(\bar{Y}_{i.} - \bar{Y}_{..})(Y_{ij} - \bar{Y}_{i.})$$

The first term on the right in (16.31) equals:

$$(16.32) \qquad \sum_i \sum_j (\bar{Y}_{i.} - \bar{Y}_{..})^2 = \sum_i n_i (\bar{Y}_{i.} - \bar{Y}_{..})^2$$

since $(\bar{Y}_{i.} - \bar{Y}_{..})^2$ is constant when summed over j; hence, n_i such terms are picked up for the summation over j.

The third term on the right in (16.31) equals zero:

$$(16.33) \qquad \sum_i \sum_j 2(\bar{Y}_{i.} - \bar{Y}_{..})(Y_{ij} - \bar{Y}_{i.}) = 2\sum_i (\bar{Y}_{i.} - \bar{Y}_{..}) \sum_j (Y_{ij} - \bar{Y}_{i.}) = 0$$

This follows because $\bar{Y}_{i.} - \bar{Y}_{..}$ is constant for the summation over j; hence, it can be brought in front of the summation sign over j. Further, $\sum_j (Y_{ij} - \bar{Y}_{i.}) = 0$ for all i, since the sum of the deviations around the arithmetic mean is always zero.

Thus, (16.31) reduces to (16.26).

2. The squared estimated factor level mean deviations $(\bar{Y}_{i.} - \bar{Y}_{..})^2$ in *SSTR* in (16.28) are weighted by the number of cases n_i for that factor level. The reason is that for each observation Y_{ij} at factor level i, the deviation component $\bar{Y}_{i.} - \bar{Y}_{..}$ is the same.   ∎

Breakdown of Degrees of Freedom

Corresponding to the decomposition of the total sum of squares, we can also obtain a breakdown of the associated degrees of freedom.

SSTO has $n_T - 1$ degrees of freedom associated with it. There are altogether n_T deviations $Y_{ij} - \bar{Y}_{..}$, but one degree of freedom is lost because the deviations are not independent in that they must sum to zero; i.e., $\sum\sum(Y_{ij} - \bar{Y}_{..}) = 0$.

SSTR has $r - 1$ degrees of freedom associated with it. There are r estimated factor level mean deviations $\bar{Y}_{i.} - \bar{Y}_{..}$, but one degree of freedom is lost because the deviations are not independent in that the weighted sum must equal zero; i.e., $\sum n_i(\bar{Y}_{i.} - \bar{Y}_{..}) = 0$.

SSE has $n_T - r$ degrees of freedom associated with it. This can be readily seen by considering the component of *SSE* for the ith factor level:

$$(16.34) \qquad \sum_{j=1}^{n_i} (Y_{ij} - \bar{Y}_{i.})^2$$

The expression in (16.34) is the equivalent of a total sum of squares considering only the ith factor level. Hence, there are $n_i - 1$ degrees of freedom associated with this sum of squares. Since *SSE* is a sum of component sums of squares such as the one in (16.34), the degrees of freedom associated with *SSE* are the sum of the component degrees of freedom:

$$(16.35) \qquad (n_1 - 1) + (n_2 - 1) + \cdots + (n_r - 1) = n_T - r$$

Example.   For the Kenton Food Company example, for which $n_T = 19$ and $r = 4$, the degrees of freedom associated with the three sums of squares are as follows:

SS	df
SSTO	$19 - 1 = 18$
SSTR	$4 - 1 = \ 3$
SSE	$19 - 4 = 15$

Note that degrees of freedom, like sums of squares, are additive:

$$18 = 3 + 15$$

Mean Squares

The mean squares, as usual, are obtained by dividing each sum of squares by its associated degrees of freedom. We therefore have:

$$(16.36a) \qquad MSTR = \frac{SSTR}{r - 1}$$

TABLE 16.3 **ANOVA Table for Single-Factor Study.**

Source of Variation	SS	df	MS	E{MS}
Between treatments	$SSTR = \Sigma n_i(\bar{Y}_{i.} - \bar{Y}_{..})^2$	$r - 1$	$MSTR = \dfrac{SSTR}{r - 1}$	$\sigma^2 + \dfrac{\Sigma n_i(\mu_i - \mu_.)^2}{r - 1}$
Error (within treatments)	$SSE = \Sigma\Sigma(Y_{ij} - \bar{Y}_{i.})^2$	$n_T - r$	$MSE = \dfrac{SSE}{n_T - r}$	σ^2
Total	$SSTO = \Sigma\Sigma(Y_{ij} - \bar{Y}_{..})^2$	$n_T - 1$		

$$(16.36b) \qquad MSE = \frac{SSE}{n_T - r}$$

Here, *MSTR* stands for *treatment mean square* and *MSE*, as before, stands for *error mean square*.

Example.   For the Kenton Food Company example, we obtain from earlier results:

$$MSTR = \frac{588.22}{3} = 196.07$$

$$MSE = \frac{158.20}{15} = 10.55$$

Note that the two mean squares do not add to $SSTO/(n_T - 1) = 746.42/18 = 41.47$. Thus, the mean squares here, as in regression, are not additive.

Analysis of Variance Table

The breakdowns of the total sum of squares and degrees of freedom, together with the resulting mean squares, are presented in an ANOVA table such as Table 16.3. The ANOVA table for the Kenton Food Company example is presented in Figure 16.5 which contains the BMDP output for single-factor analysis of variance. Note that the output contains the number of cases, the estimated factor level means $\bar{Y}_{i.}$, and the ANOVA table. In this table, the line for the treatments source of variation is labeled EQUALITY OF CELL MEANS. The results in the BMDP output are shown to more decimal places than we have shown, but are consistent with our calculations. Note also that the BMDP ANOVA table shows the degrees of freedom column before the sum of squares column.

Expected Mean Squares

The expected values of *MSE* and *MSTR* can be shown to be as follows:

$$(16.37a) \qquad E\{MSE\} = \sigma^2$$

$$(16.37b) \qquad E\{MSTR\} = \sigma^2 + \frac{\Sigma n_i(\mu_i - \mu_.)^2}{r - 1}$$

FIGURE 16.5 **Portion of BMDP Output for Single-Factor Analysis of Variance—Kenton Food Company Example.**

```
NUMBER OF CASES PER GROUP
-------------------------
*1          5.
*2          5.
*3          4.
*4          5.
TOTAL      19.
***************************************************************


ESTIMATES OF MEANS
------------------


              *1          *2          *3          *4         TOTAL
                 1           2           3           4           5

SOLD       2     14.6000     13.4000     19.5000     27.2000     18.6316




ANALYSIS OF VARIANCE TABLE
--------------------------
SOURCE OF VARIATION     D.F.   SUM OF SQ.   MEAN SQ.    F-VALUE    PROB(TAIL)
EQUALITY OF CELL MEANS     3    588.2211    196.0737    18.5911      0.0000
      ERROR               15    158.2000     10.5467
```

where:

$$(16.37c) \qquad\qquad \mu_. = \frac{\sum n_i \mu_i}{n_T}$$

These expected values are shown in the $E\{MS\}$ column of Table 16.3.

Two important features of the expected mean squares deserve attention:

1. *MSE* is an unbiased estimator of σ^2, the variance of the error terms ε_{ij}, whether or not the factor level means μ_i are equal. This is intuitively reasonable since the variability of the observations within each factor level is not affected by the magnitudes of the estimated factor level means for normal populations.

2. When all factor level means μ_i are equal and hence equal to the weighted mean $\mu_.$, then $E\{MSTR\} = \sigma^2$ since the second term on the right in (16.37b) becomes zero. Hence, *MSTR* and *MSE* both estimate the error variance σ^2 when all factor level means μ_i are equal. When, however, the factor level means are not equal, *MSTR* tends on the average to be larger than *MSE*, since the second term in (16.37b) will then be positive. This is intuitively reasonable, as illustrated in Figure 16.6 for four treatments. The situation portrayed there assumes that all sample sizes are equal, i.e., $n_i \equiv n$. When all μ_i are equal, then all $\bar{Y}_{i.}$ follow the same sampling distribution, with common mean μ_c and variance σ^2/n; this is portrayed in Figure 16.6a. When the μ_i are not equal, on the other hand, the $\bar{Y}_{i.}$ follow different sampling distributions, each with the same variability σ^2/n but centered on different means μ_i. One such possibility is shown in Figure 16.6b. Hence, the $\bar{Y}_{i.}$ will tend to differ more from each other when the μ_i differ than when the μ_i are equal, and

FIGURE 16.6   **Sampling Distributions of $\overline{Y}_i.$ for Four Treatments ($n_i \equiv n$).**

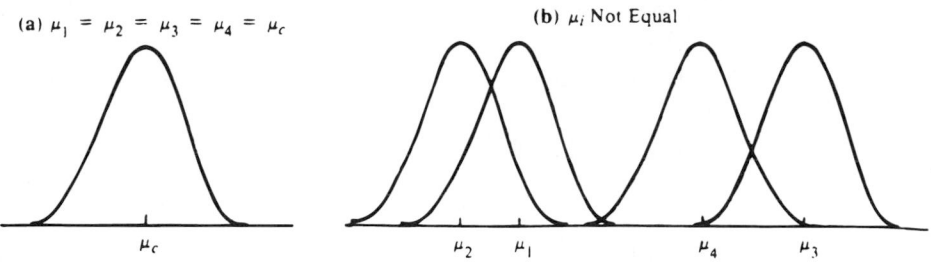

(a) $\mu_1 = \mu_2 = \mu_3 = \mu_4 = \mu_c$ (b) μ_i Not Equal

consequently *MSTR* will tend to be larger when the factor level means are not the same than when they are equal. This property of *MSTR* is utilized in constructing the statistical test discussed in the next section to determine whether or not the factor level means μ_i are the same. If *MSTR* and *MSE* are of the same order of magnitude, this is taken to suggest that the factor level means μ_i are equal. If *MSTR* is substantially larger than *MSE*, this is taken to suggest that the μ_i are not equal.

Comments

1. To find the expected value of *MSE*, we first note that *MSE* can be expressed as follows:

(16.38)
$$MSE = \frac{1}{n_T - r} \sum_i \sum_j (Y_{ij} - \overline{Y}_{i.})^2$$

$$= \frac{1}{n_T - r} \sum_i \left[(n_i - 1) \frac{\sum_j (Y_{ij} - \overline{Y}_{i.})^2}{n_i - 1} \right]$$

Now let us denote the ordinary sample variance of the observations for the ith factor level by s_i^2:

(16.39)
$$s_i^2 = \frac{\sum_j (Y_{ij} - \overline{Y}_{i.})^2}{n_i - 1}$$

Hence, (16.38) can be expressed as follows:

(16.40)
$$MSE = \frac{1}{n_T - r} \sum_i (n_i - 1)s_i^2$$

Since it is well known that the sample variance (16.39) is an unbiased estimator of the population variance, which in our case is σ^2 for all factor levels, we obtain:

$$E\{MSE\} = \frac{1}{n_T - r} \sum_i (n_i - 1)E\{s_i^2\}$$

$$= \frac{1}{n_T - r} \sum_i (n_i - 1)\sigma^2$$

$$= \sigma^2$$

2. We shall derive the expected value of *MSTR* for the special case when all sample sizes n_i are the same, namely, when $n_i \equiv n$. The general result in (16.37b) becomes for this special case:

$$(16.41) \qquad E\{MSTR\} = \sigma^2 + \frac{n \Sigma (\mu_i - \mu_.)^2}{r - 1} \qquad \text{when } n_i \equiv n$$

Further, when all factor level sample sizes are *n*, *MSTR* as defined in (16.28) and (16.36a) becomes:

$$(16.42) \qquad MSTR = \frac{n \Sigma (\bar{Y}_{i.} - \bar{Y}_{..})^2}{r - 1} \qquad \text{when } n_i \equiv n$$

To derive (16.41), consider the model formulation for Y_{ij} in (16.2):

$$Y_{ij} = \mu_i + \varepsilon_{ij}$$

Averaging the Y_{ij} for the *i*th factor level, we obtain:

$$(16.43) \qquad \bar{Y}_{i.} = \mu_i + \bar{\varepsilon}_{i.}$$

where $\bar{\varepsilon}_{i.}$ is the average of the ε_{ij} for the *i*th factor level:

$$(16.44) \qquad \bar{\varepsilon}_{i.} = \frac{\sum_j \varepsilon_{ij}}{n}$$

Averaging the Y_{ij} over all factor levels, we obtain:

$$(16.45) \qquad \bar{Y}_{..} = \mu_. + \bar{\varepsilon}_{..}$$

where $\mu_.$, which is defined in (16.37c), becomes for $n_i \equiv n$:

$$(16.46) \qquad \mu_. = \frac{n \Sigma \mu_i}{nr} = \frac{\Sigma \mu_i}{r} \qquad \text{when } n_i \equiv n$$

and $\bar{\varepsilon}_{..}$ is the average of all ε_{ij}:

$$(16.47) \qquad \bar{\varepsilon}_{..} = \frac{\Sigma\Sigma \varepsilon_{ij}}{nr}$$

Since the sample sizes are equal, we also have:

$$(16.48) \qquad \bar{Y}_{..} = \frac{\Sigma \bar{Y}_{i.}}{r} \qquad \bar{\varepsilon}_{..} = \frac{\Sigma \bar{\varepsilon}_{i.}}{r}$$

Using (16.43) and (16.45), we obtain:

$$(16.49) \qquad \bar{Y}_{i.} - \bar{Y}_{..} = (\mu_i + \bar{\varepsilon}_{i.}) - (\mu_. + \bar{\varepsilon}_{..}) = (\mu_i - \mu_.) + (\bar{\varepsilon}_{i.} - \bar{\varepsilon}_{..})$$

When we square $\bar{Y}_{i.} - \bar{Y}_{..}$ and sum over the factor levels, we obtain:

$$(16.50) \qquad \Sigma(\bar{Y}_{i.} - \bar{Y}_{..})^2 = \Sigma(\mu_i - \mu_.)^2 + \Sigma(\bar{\varepsilon}_{i.} - \bar{\varepsilon}_{..})^2 + 2\Sigma(\mu_i - \mu_.)(\bar{\varepsilon}_{i.} - \bar{\varepsilon}_{..})$$

We now wish to find $E\{\Sigma(\bar{Y}_{i.} - \bar{Y}_{..})^2\}$, and therefore need to find the expected value of each term on the right in (16.50):

a. Since $\Sigma(\mu_i - \mu_.)^2$ is a constant, its expectation is:

$$(16.51) \qquad E\left\{\sum(\mu_i - \mu_.)^2\right\} = \sum(\mu_i - \mu_.)^2$$

b. Before finding the expectation of the second term on the right, consider first the expression:

$$\frac{\Sigma(\bar{\varepsilon}_{i.} - \bar{\varepsilon}_{..})^2}{r - 1}$$

This is an ordinary sample variance, since $\bar{\varepsilon}_{..}$ is the sample mean of the r terms $\bar{\varepsilon}_{i.}$ per (16.48). We further know that the sample variance is an unbiased estimator of the variance of the variable, in this case the variable being $\bar{\varepsilon}_{i.}$. But $\bar{\varepsilon}_{i.}$ is just the mean of n independent error terms ε_{ij} by (16.44). Hence:

$$\sigma^2\{\bar{\varepsilon}_{i.}\} = \frac{\sigma^2\{\varepsilon_{ij}\}}{n} = \frac{\sigma^2}{n}$$

Therefore:

$$E\left\{\frac{\Sigma(\bar{\varepsilon}_{i.} - \bar{\varepsilon}_{..})^2}{r - 1}\right\} = \frac{\sigma^2}{n}$$

so that:

$$(16.52) \qquad E\left\{\sum(\bar{\varepsilon}_{i.} - \bar{\varepsilon}_{..})^2\right\} = \frac{(r - 1)\sigma^2}{n}$$

c. Since both $\bar{\varepsilon}_{i.}$ and $\bar{\varepsilon}_{..}$ are means of ε_{ij} terms, all of which have expectation 0, it follows that:

$$E\{\bar{\varepsilon}_{i.}\} = 0 \qquad E\{\bar{\varepsilon}_{..}\} = 0$$

Hence:

$$(16.53) \qquad E\left\{2\sum(\mu_i - \mu_.)(\bar{\varepsilon}_{i.} - \bar{\varepsilon}_{..})\right\} = 2\sum(\mu_i - \mu_.)E\{\bar{\varepsilon}_{i.} - \bar{\varepsilon}_{..}\} = 0$$

We have thus shown, by (16.51), (16.52), and (16.53), that:

$$E\left\{\sum(\bar{Y}_{i.} - \bar{Y}_{..})^2\right\} = \sum(\mu_i - \mu_.)^2 + \frac{(r - 1)\sigma^2}{n}$$

But then (16.41) follows at once:

$$E\{MSTR\} = E\left\{\frac{n\,\Sigma(\bar{Y}_{i.} - \bar{Y}_{..})^2}{r - 1}\right\} = \frac{n}{r - 1}\left[\sum(\mu_i - \mu_.)^2 + \frac{(r - 1)\sigma^2}{n}\right]$$

$$= \sigma^2 + \frac{n\,\Sigma(\mu_i - \mu_.)^2}{r - 1} \qquad \text{when } n_i \equiv n \qquad \blacksquare$$

16.9 F Test for Equality of Factor Level Means

It is customary to begin the analysis of a single-factor study by determining whether or not the factor level means μ_i are equal. If, for instance, the four package designs in the Kenton Food Company example lead to the same mean sales volumes, there is no need for further analysis, such as to determine which design is best or how two particular designs compare in stimulating sales.

Thus, the alternative conclusions we wish to consider are:

(16.54)
$$H_0: \mu_1 = \mu_2 = \cdots = \mu_r$$
$$H_a: \text{ not all } \mu_i \text{ are equal}$$

Test Statistic

The test statistic to be used for choosing between the alternatives in (16.54) is:

(16.55)
$$F^* = \frac{MSTR}{MSE}$$

Note that *MSTR* here plays the role corresponding to *MSR* for a regression model.

Large values of F^* support H_a, since *MSTR* will tend to exceed *MSE* when H_a holds, as we saw from (16.37). Values of F^* near 1 support H_0, since both *MSTR* and *MSE* have the same expected value when H_0 holds. Hence, the appropriate test is an upper-tail one.

Distribution of F^*

When all treatment means μ_i are equal, each response Y_{ij} has the same expected value. In view of the additivity of sums of squares and degrees of freedom, Cochran's theorem (2.61) then implies:

When H_0 holds, $\dfrac{SSE}{\sigma^2}$ and $\dfrac{SSTR}{\sigma^2}$ are independent χ^2 variables

It follows in the same fashion as for regression:

When H_0 holds, F^* is distributed as $F(r - 1, n_T - r)$

When H_a holds, that is, when the μ_i are not all equal, F^* does *not* follow the F distribution. Rather, it follows a complex distribution called the *noncentral F distribution*. We shall make use of the noncentral F distribution when we discuss the power of the F test in Chapter 26.

Note

SSTR and *SSE* are independent even if all μ_i are not equal. *SSTR* is solely based on the estimated factor level means $\bar{Y}_{i\cdot}$. On the other hand, *SSE* reflects the variability within the factor level samples, and this within-sample variability is not affected by the magnitudes of the estimated factor level means when the error terms are normally distributed.   ∎

Construction of Decision Rule

Usually, the risk of making a Type I error is controlled in constructing the decision rule. This provides protection against making further, more detailed, analyses of the factor effects when in fact there are no differences in the factor level means. The Type II error can also be controlled, as we shall see later, through sample size determination.

Since we know that F^* is distributed as $F(r-1, n_T - r)$ when H_0 holds and that large values of F^* lead to conclusion H_a, the appropriate decision rule to control the level of significance at α is:

(16.56)
$$\text{If } F^* \leq F(1-\alpha; r-1, n_T - r), \text{ conclude } H_0$$
$$\text{If } F^* > F(1-\alpha; r-1, n_T - r), \text{ conclude } H_a$$

where $F(1-\alpha; r-1, n_T - r)$ is the $(1-\alpha)100$ percentile of the appropriate F distribution.

Example

For the Kenton Food Company example, we wish to test whether or not mean sales are the same for the four package designs:

$$H_0: \ \mu_1 = \mu_2 = \mu_3 = \mu_4$$
$$H_a: \text{ not all } \mu_i \text{ are equal}$$

Management wishes to control the risk of making a Type I error at $\alpha = .05$. We therefore require $F(.95; 3, 15)$, where the degrees of freedom are those shown in Figure 16.5. From Table B.4 in the Appendix, we find $F(.95; 3, 15) = 3.29$. Hence, the decision rule is:

$$\text{If } F^* \leq 3.29, \text{ conclude } H_0$$
$$\text{If } F^* > 3.29, \text{ conclude } H_a$$

Using the data in the ANOVA table in Figure 16.5, we obtain the test statistic:

$$F^* = \frac{MSTR}{MSE} = \frac{196.07}{10.55} = 18.6$$

Since $F^* = 18.6 > 3.29$, we conclude H_a, that the factor level means μ_i are not equal, or that the four different package designs do not lead to the same mean sales volume. Thus, we conclude that there is a relation between package design and sales volume.

The P-value for the test statistic is the probability $P\{F(3, 15) > F^* = 18.6\}$, which is .00003. This P-value again indicates that the data from the experiment are not consistent with all designs having the same effect on sales volume.

The conclusion of a relation between package design and sales volume did not surprise the sales manager of the Kenton Food Company. The study was conducted in the first place because the sales manager expected the four package designs to have different effects on sales volume and was interested in finding out the nature of these differences. In the next chapter, we discuss the second stage of the analysis, namely, how to study the nature of the factor level effects when differences exist.

Comments

1. If there are only two factor levels so that $r = 2$, it can easily be shown that the test employing F^* in (16.55) is the equivalent of the two-population, two-sided t test in Table A.2a. The F test here has $(1, n_T - 2)$ degrees of freedom, and the t test has $n_1 + n_2 - 2$ or $n_T - 2$ degrees of freedom; thus both tests lead to equivalent critical regions. For comparing two population means, the t test generally is to be preferred since it can be used to conduct both two-sided and one-sided tests (Table A.2); the F test can be used only for two-sided tests.

2. Since the F test for testing the alternatives (16.54) is a test of a linear statistical model, it can be obtained by the general method explained in Section 2.8:

a. The full model is ANOVA model (16.2):

$$(16.57) \qquad\qquad Y_{ij} = \mu_i + \varepsilon_{ij} \qquad\qquad \text{Full model}$$

Fitting the full model by either the method of least squares or the method of maximum likelihood leads to the fitted values $\hat{Y}_{ij} = \bar{Y}_{i.}$, per (16.17), and to the resulting error sum of squares:

$$SSE(F) = \sum\sum(Y_{ij} - \hat{Y}_{ij})^2 = \sum\sum(Y_{ij} - \bar{Y}_{i.})^2$$

$SSE(F)$ has $df_F = n_T - r$ degrees of freedom associated with it because r parameter values $(\mu_1, \ldots, \mu_r)$ have to be estimated.

b. The reduced model under H_0 is:

$$(16.58) \qquad\qquad Y_{ij} = \mu_c + \varepsilon_{ij} \qquad\qquad \text{Reduced model}$$

where μ_c is the common mean for all factor levels. Fitting the reduced model leads to the estimator $\hat{\mu}_c = \bar{Y}_{..}$ so that all fitted values are $\hat{Y}_{ij} \equiv \bar{Y}_{..}$, and the resulting error sum of squares is:

$$SSE(R) = \sum\sum(Y_{ij} - \hat{Y}_{ij})^2 = \sum\sum(Y_{ij} - \bar{Y}_{..})^2$$

The degrees of freedom associated with $SSE(R)$ are $df_R = n_T - 1$ because one parameter (μ_c) had to be estimated.

c. Since, according to (16.27) and (16.29), respectively:

$$SSE(R) = SSTO$$

$$SSE(F) = SSE$$

and since by (16.30) $SSTO - SSE = SSTR$, the general linear test statistic (2.70) becomes here:

$$F^* = \frac{SSE(R) - SSE(F)}{df_R - df_F} \div \frac{SSE(F)}{df_F}$$

$$= \frac{SSTO - SSE}{(n_T - 1) - (n_T - r)} \div \frac{SSE}{n_T - r} = \frac{SSR}{r - 1} \div \frac{SSE}{n_T - r} = \frac{MSTR}{MSE} \qquad\blacksquare$$

16.10   Alternative Formulation of Model I

ANOVA Model I—Factor Effects Model

At times, an alternative but completely equivalent formulation of the single-factor ANOVA model I in (16.2) is used. This alternative formulation is called the *factor effects model*. With this alternative formulation, the treatment means μ_i are expressed in an equivalent fashion by means of the identity:

$$(16.59) \qquad\qquad \mu_i \equiv \mu_{.} + (\mu_i - \mu_{.})$$

where $\mu_{.}$ is a constant that can be defined to fit the purpose of the study. We shall denote the difference $\mu_i - \mu_{.}$ by τ_i:

$$(16.60) \qquad\qquad \tau_i = \mu_i - \mu_{.}$$

so that (16.59) can be expressed in equivalent fashion as:

$$(16.61) \qquad\qquad \mu_i \equiv \mu_{.} + \tau_i$$

The difference $\tau_i = \mu_i - \mu_{.}$ is called the *i th factor level effect* or the *i th treatment effect*.
ANOVA model I in (16.2) can now be stated equivalently as follows:

$$(16.62) \qquad\qquad Y_{ij} = \mu_{.} + \tau_i + \varepsilon_{ij}$$

where:

$\mu_{.}$ is a constant component common to all observations

τ_i is the effect of the ith factor level (a constant for each factor level)

ε_{ij} are independent $N(0, \sigma^2)$

$i = 1, \ldots, r;\ j = 1, \ldots, n_i$

ANOVA model (16.62) is called a factor effects model because it is expressed in terms of the factor effects τ_i, in distinction to the cell means model (16.2), which is expressed in terms of the cell (treatment) means μ_i.

Factor effects model (16.62) is a linear model, like the equivalent cell means model (16.2). We shall demonstrate this in the next section.

Definition of $\mu_{.}$

The splitting up of the factor level mean μ_i into two components, an overall constant $\mu_{.}$ and a factor level or treatment effect τ_i, depends on the definition of $\mu_{.}$, which can be defined in many ways. We now explain two basic ways to define $\mu_{.}$.

Unweighted Mean.   Often, a definition of $\mu_{\cdot}$ as the unweighted average of all factor level means μ_i is found to be useful:

$$(16.63) \qquad \mu_{\cdot} = \frac{\sum\limits_{i=1}^{r} \mu_i}{r}$$

This definition implies that:

$$(16.64) \qquad \sum_{i=1}^{r} \tau_i = 0$$

because by (16.60) we have:

$$\sum \tau_i = \sum (\mu_i - \mu_{\cdot}) = \sum \mu_i - r\mu_{\cdot}.$$

and by (16.63) we have:

$$\sum \mu_i = r\mu_{\cdot}.$$

Thus, the definition of the overall constant $\mu_{\cdot}$ in (16.63) implies a restriction on the τ_i, in this case that their sum must be zero.

Example.   For the earlier incentive pay example in Figure 16.2, we have $\mu_1 = 70$, $\mu_2 = 58$, $\mu_3 = 90$, and $\mu_4 = 84$. When $\mu_{\cdot}$ is defined according to (16.63), we obtain:

$$\mu_{\cdot} = \frac{70 + 58 + 90 + 84}{4} = 75.5$$

Hence:

$$\tau_1 = 70 - 75.5 = \quad -5.5$$
$$\tau_2 = 58 - 75.5 = -17.5$$
$$\tau_3 = 90 - 75.5 = \quad 14.5$$
$$\tau_4 = 84 - 75.5 = \quad 8.5$$

The first treatment effect $\tau_1 = -5.5$, for instance, indicates that the mean employee productivity for incentive pay type 1 is 5.5 units less than the average productivity for all four types of incentive pay. Figure 16.7 provides an illustration of these treatment effects.

Weighted Mean.   The constant $\mu_{\cdot}$ can also be defined as some weighted average of the factor level means μ_i:

$$(16.65) \qquad \mu_{\cdot} = \sum_{i=1}^{r} w_i \mu_i \qquad \text{where } \sum_{i=1}^{r} w_i = 1$$

Note that the w_i are weights defined so that their sum is 1. The restriction on the τ_i implied by definition (16.65) is:

$$(16.66) \qquad \sum_{i=1}^{r} w_i \tau_i = 0$$

This follows in the same fashion as (16.64).

FIGURE 16.7 **Illustration of Treatment Effects—Incentive Pay Example.**

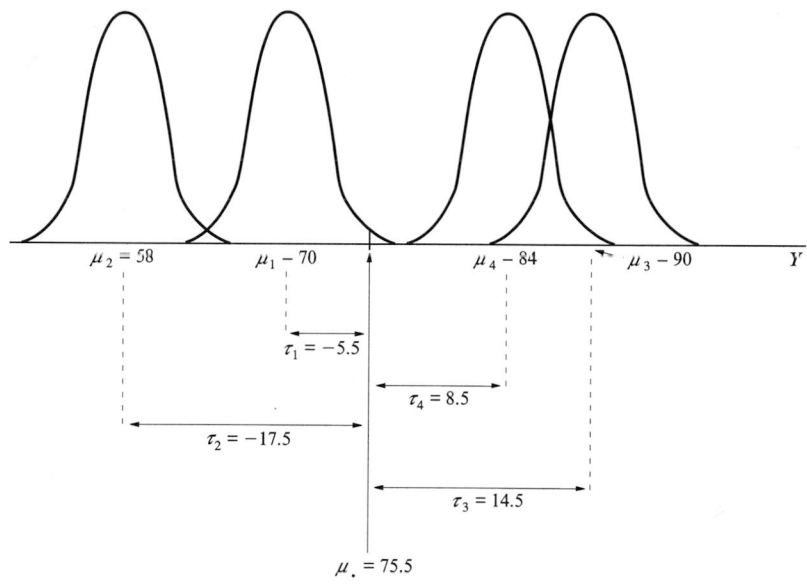

The choice of weights w_i should depend on the meaningfulness of the resulting measures of the factor level effects. We present now two examples where different weightings are appropriate: (1) weighting according to a known measure of importance and (2) weighting according to sample size.

Example 1. A car rental firm wanted to estimate the average fuel consumption (in miles per gallon) for its large fleet of cars which consists of 50 percent compacts, 30 percent sedans, and 20 percent station wagons. Here, a meaningful measure of $\mu.$ might be in terms of overall mean fuel consumption:

(16.67)
$$\mu. = .5\mu_1 + .3\mu_2 + .2\mu_3$$

where μ_1, μ_2, and μ_3 are the mean fuel consumptions for the three types of cars in the fleet. An estimate of $\mu.$ here is:

(16.68)
$$\hat{\mu}. = .5\bar{Y}_1. + .3\bar{Y}_2. + .2\bar{Y}_3.$$

Example 2. When exact weights are unknown, the subgroup sample sizes in a random sample may be useful as weights of relative importance. For instance, the proportions of households in a city with no children, one child, and more than one child are not known. A random sample of n_T households was selected, which contained n_1 households with no child, n_2 households with one child, and n_3 households with more than one child. For testing whether mean entertainment expenditures are the same for the three types of households, use of the proportions n_1/n_T, n_2/n_T, and n_3/n_T as weights might be meaningful. The resulting definition of the overall entertainment expenditures constant $\mu_\cdot$ would then be:

(16.69)
$$\mu_\cdot = \frac{n_1}{n_T}\mu_1 + \frac{n_2}{n_T}\mu_2 + \frac{n_3}{n_T}\mu_3$$

This quantity would be estimated by $\bar{Y}_{\cdot\cdot}$:

(16.70)
$$\hat{\mu}_\cdot = \frac{n_1}{n_T}\bar{Y}_{1\cdot} + \frac{n_2}{n_T}\bar{Y}_{2\cdot} + \frac{n_3}{n_T}\bar{Y}_{3\cdot} = \bar{Y}_{\cdot\cdot}$$

When all sample sizes are equal, $\mu_\cdot$ as defined in (16.69) reduces to the unweighted mean (16.63).

Test for Equality of Factor Level Means

Since the factor effects model (16.62) is equivalent to the cell means model (16.2), the test for equality of factor level means uses the same test statistic F^* in (16.55). The only difference is in the statement of the alternatives. For the cell means model (16.2), the alternatives are as specified in (16.54):

$$H_0:\ \mu_1 = \mu_2 = \cdots = \mu_r$$

$$H_a:\ \text{not all } \mu_i \text{ are equal}$$

For the factor effects model (16.62), these same alternatives in terms of the factor effects are:

(16.71)
$$H_0:\ \tau_1 = \tau_2 = \cdots = \tau_r = 0$$

$$H_a:\ \text{not all } \tau_i \text{ equal zero}$$

The equivalence of the two forms can be readily established. The equality of the factor level means $\mu_1 = \mu_2 = \cdots = \mu_r$ implies that all τ_i are equal. The equalities of the τ_i follow from (16.61) since the constant term $\mu_\cdot$ is common to all factor level effects τ_i. The equality of the factor level means in turn implies that all $\tau_i = 0$, whether the restriction on the τ_i is of the form in (16.64) or (16.66). In either case, the restriction can be satisfied in only one way given the equality of the τ_i, namely, that $\tau_i \equiv 0$. Thus, it is equivalent to state that all factor level means μ_i are equal or that all factor level effects τ_i equal zero.

16.11   Regression Approach to Single-Factor Analysis of Variance

We noted earlier that cell means model (16.2) is a linear model, and that we can obtain test statistic F^* for testing the equality of the factor level means μ_i by means of the general linear test (2.70). We shall now explain the regression approach to single-factor analysis of variance. For this purpose, it is convenient to utilize the equivalent factor effects model (16.62):

$$Y_{ij} = \mu_\cdot + \tau_i + \varepsilon_{ij}$$

We assume that equal weightings of the factor level means are appropriate for defining the overall constant $\mu_\cdot$.

To state ANOVA model (16.62) as a linear model, we need to represent the parameters $\mu_{.}, \tau_1, \ldots, \tau_r$ in the model. However, constraint (16.64) for the case of equal weightings:

$$\sum_{i=1}^{r} \tau_i = 0$$

implies that one of the r parameters τ_i is not needed since it can be expressed in terms of the other $r - 1$ parameters. We shall drop the parameter τ_r, which according to constraint (16.64) can be expressed in terms of the other $r - 1$ parameters τ_i as follows:

(16.72)
$$\tau_r = -\tau_1 - \tau_2 - \cdots - \tau_{r-1}$$

Thus, we shall use only the parameters $\mu_{.}, \tau_1, \ldots, \tau_{r-1}$ for the linear model.

To illustrate how a linear model is developed with this approach, consider a single-factor study with $r = 3$ factor levels when $n_1 = n_2 = n_3 = 2$. The $\mathbf{Y}, \mathbf{X}, \boldsymbol{\beta}$, and $\boldsymbol{\varepsilon}$ matrices for this case are as follows:

(16.73)
$$\mathbf{Y} = \begin{bmatrix} Y_{11} \\ Y_{12} \\ Y_{21} \\ Y_{22} \\ Y_{31} \\ Y_{32} \end{bmatrix} \qquad \mathbf{X} = \begin{bmatrix} 1 & 1 & 0 \\ 1 & 1 & 0 \\ 1 & 0 & 1 \\ 1 & 0 & 1 \\ 1 & -1 & -1 \\ 1 & -1 & -1 \end{bmatrix} \qquad \boldsymbol{\beta} = \begin{bmatrix} \mu_{.} \\ \tau_1 \\ \tau_2 \end{bmatrix} \qquad \boldsymbol{\varepsilon} = \begin{bmatrix} \varepsilon_{11} \\ \varepsilon_{12} \\ \varepsilon_{21} \\ \varepsilon_{22} \\ \varepsilon_{31} \\ \varepsilon_{32} \end{bmatrix}$$

Note that the vector of expected values, $\mathbf{E}\{\mathbf{Y}\} = \mathbf{X}\boldsymbol{\beta}$, yields the following:

(16.74)
$$\mathbf{E}\{\mathbf{Y}\} = \begin{bmatrix} E\{Y_{11}\} \\ E\{Y_{12}\} \\ E\{Y_{21}\} \\ E\{Y_{22}\} \\ E\{Y_{31}\} \\ E\{Y_{32}\} \end{bmatrix} = \mathbf{X}\boldsymbol{\beta} = \begin{bmatrix} 1 & 1 & 0 \\ 1 & 1 & 0 \\ 1 & 0 & 1 \\ 1 & 0 & 1 \\ 1 & -1 & -1 \\ 1 & -1 & -1 \end{bmatrix} \begin{bmatrix} \mu_{.} \\ \tau_1 \\ \tau_2 \end{bmatrix} = \begin{bmatrix} \mu_{.} + \tau_1 \\ \mu_{.} + \tau_1 \\ \mu_{.} + \tau_2 \\ \mu_{.} + \tau_2 \\ \mu_{.} - \tau_1 - \tau_2 \\ \mu_{.} - \tau_1 - \tau_2 \end{bmatrix}$$

Since $\tau_3 = -\tau_1 - \tau_2$ according to (16.72), we see that $E\{Y_{31}\} = E\{Y_{32}\} = \mu_{.} + \tau_3$. Thus, the above $\mathbf{X}$ matrix and $\boldsymbol{\beta}$ vector representation provides in all cases the appropriate expected values:

$$E\{Y_{ij}\} = \mu_{.} + \tau_i$$

The illustration in (16.73) indicates how we need to define in general the multiple regression model so that it is the equivalent of the single-factor ANOVA model (16.62). Note that we require indicator variables that take on values 0, 1, or -1. This coding was discussed in Section 11.6. While this coding is not as simple as a 0, 1 coding, it is desirable here because it leads to regression coefficients in the $\boldsymbol{\beta}$ vector that are the parameters in the factor effects ANOVA model, i.e., $\mu_{.}, \tau_1 \ldots, \tau_{r-1}$.

We shall let X_{ij1} denote the value of indicator variable X_1 for the jth case from the ith factor level, X_{ij2} the value of indicator variable X_2 for this same case, and so on, using altogether $r - 1$ indicator variables in the model. The multiple regression model then is as follows:

(16.75) $Y_{ij} = \mu_{.} + \tau_1 X_{ij1} + \tau_2 X_{ij2} + \cdots + \tau_{r-1} X_{ij,r-1} + \varepsilon_{ij}$ **Full model**

where:

$$X_{ij1} = \begin{array}{ll} 1 & \text{if case from factor level 1} \\ -1 & \text{if case from factor level } r \\ 0 & \text{otherwise} \end{array}$$

$$\vdots$$

$$X_{ij,r-1} = \begin{array}{ll} 1 & \text{if case from factor level } r-1 \\ -1 & \text{if case from factor level } r \\ 0 & \text{otherwise} \end{array}$$

Note how the ANOVA model parameters play the role of regression function parameters in (16.75); the intercept term is $\mu_.$, and the regression coefficients are $\tau_1, \tau_2, \ldots, \tau_{r-1}$.

To test the equality of the treatment means μ_i by means of the regression approach, we state the alternatives in the equivalent formulation (16.71), noting that τ_r must equal zero when $\tau_1 = \tau_2 = \cdots = \tau_{r-1} = 0$ according to (16.72):

(16.76)
$$H_0: \tau_1 = \tau_2 = \cdots = \tau_{r-1} = 0$$
$$H_a: \text{ not all } \tau_i \text{ equal zero}$$

Note that H_0 states that all regression coefficients in regression model (16.75) are zero. Thus, we employ the usual test statistic (6.39b) for testing whether or not there is a regression relation:

(16.77)
$$F^* = \frac{MSR}{MSE}$$

Example

To test the equality of mean sales for the four cereal package designs in the Kenton Food Company example by means of the regression approach, we shall employ the regression model:

(16.78)
$$Y_{ij} = \mu_. + \tau_1 X_{ij1} + \tau_2 X_{ij2} + \tau_3 X_{ij3} + \varepsilon_{ij}$$

where:

$$X_{ij1} = \begin{array}{ll} 1 & \text{if case from factor level 1} \\ -1 & \text{if case from factor level 4} \\ 0 & \text{otherwise} \end{array}$$

$$X_{ij2} = \begin{array}{ll} 1 & \text{if case from factor level 2} \\ -1 & \text{if case from factor level 4} \\ 0 & \text{otherwise} \end{array}$$

$$X_{ij3} = \begin{array}{ll} 1 & \text{if case from factor level 3} \\ -1 & \text{if case from factor level 4} \\ 0 & \text{otherwise} \end{array}$$

A portion of the data in Table 16.1 is repeated in Table 16.4a, together with the coding of the indicator variables X_1, X_2, and X_3. For observation Y_{11}, for instance, note that $X_1 = 1$,

TABLE 16.4   **Regression Approach to the Analysis of Variance—Kenton Food Company Example.**

(a) Data for Regression Model (16.78)

i	j	Y_{ij}	X_{ij1}	X_{ij2}	X_{ij3}
1	1	11	1	0	0
1	2	17	1	0	0
1	3	16	1	0	0
1	4	14	1	0	0
1	5	15	1	0	0
2	1	12	0	1	0
...	...	...	...	...	...
4	4	26	−1	−1	−1
4	5	28	−1	−1	−1

(b) Fitted Regression Function

$$\hat{Y} = 18.675 - 4.075X_1 - 5.275X_2 + .825X_3$$

(c) Regression Analysis of Variance Table

Source of Variation	SS	df	MS
Regression	$SSR = 588.22$	3	$MSR = 196.07$
Error	$SSE = 158.20$	15	$MSE = 10.55$
Total	$SSTO = 746.42$	18	

$X_2 = 0$, and $X_3 = 0$; hence, we obtain from (16.78):

$$E\{Y_{11}\} = \mu. + \tau_1$$

Similarly, for observation Y_{45} we have $X_1 = -1$, $X_2 = -1$, and $X_3 = -1$; hence:

$$E\{Y_{45}\} = \mu. - \tau_1 - \tau_2 - \tau_3 = \mu. + \tau_4$$

since $\tau_4 = -\tau_1 - \tau_2 - \tau_3$.

   Note that we employ the following codings in the indicator variables for cases from each of the four factor levels:

	Coding		
Factor Level	X_1	X_2	X_3
1	1	0	0
2	0	1	0
3	0	0	1
4	−1	−1	−1

A computer run of the multiple regression of Y on X_1, X_2, and X_3 yielded the fitted regression function and analysis of variance table presented in Tables 16.4b and 16.4c. Test statistic (16.77) therefore is:

$$F^* = \frac{MSR}{MSE} = \frac{196.07}{10.55} = 18.6$$

This is the same test statistic obtained earlier based on the analysis of variance calculations. Indeed, the analysis of variance table in Table 16.4c obtained with the regression approach is the same as the one in Figure 16.5 obtained with the analysis of variance approach except that the treatment sum of squares and mean square are called the regression sum of squares and mean square in Table 16.4c.

From this point on, the test procedure based on the regression approach parallels the analysis of variance test procedure explained earlier.

Comments

1. In the fitted regression function in Table 16.4b, the intercept term 18.675 is the unweighted average of the estimated factor level means $\bar{Y}_{i.}$ because $\mu_.$ was defined as the unweighted average of the factor level means μ_i. The regression coefficient $b_1 = -4.075$ is simply the difference between $\bar{Y}_{1.} = 14.6$ and the overall unweighted mean 18.675, and b_2 and b_3 represent similar differences between the estimated factor level mean and the overall unweighted mean.

2. The regression approach is not utilized generally for ordinary analysis of variance problems. The reason is that the **X** matrix for analysis of variance problems usually is of a very simple structure, as we have seen earlier. This simple structure permits computational simplifications that are explicitly recognized in the statistical procedures for analysis of variance. We take up the regression approach to analysis of variance here, and in later chapters, for two principal reasons. First, we see that analysis of variance models are encompassed by the general linear statistical model (6.19). Second, the regression approach is very useful for analyzing some multifactor studies when the structure of the **X** matrix is not simple.

3. When the analysis of variance test is to be conducted by means of the regression approach based on the cell means model (16.2):

$$Y_{ij} = \mu_i + \varepsilon_{ij}$$

the **β** vector is defined to contain all r treatment means μ_i:

(16.79)
$$\boldsymbol{\beta} = \begin{bmatrix} \mu_1 \\ \vdots \\ \mu_r \end{bmatrix}$$

and r indicator variables $X_1, X_2, \ldots, X_r$ are utilized, each defined as a 0, 1 variable as illustrated in Chapter 11:

$$X_1 = \begin{matrix} 1 & \text{if case from factor level 1} \\ 0 & \text{otherwise} \end{matrix}$$

(16.80)

$$\vdots$$

$$X_r = \begin{matrix} 1 & \text{if case from factor level } r \\ 0 & \text{otherwise} \end{matrix}$$

The regression model therefore is:

(16.81) $$Y_{ij} = \mu_1 X_{ij1} + \mu_2 X_{ij2} + \cdots + \mu_r X_{ijr} + \varepsilon_{ij} \qquad \text{Full model}$$

with the μ_i playing the role of regression coefficients.

The **X** matrix with this approach contains only 0 and 1 entries. For example, for $r = 3$ factor levels with $n_1 = n_2 = n_3 = 2$ cases, the **X** matrix (observations in order Y_{11}, Y_{12}, Y_{21}, etc.) and $\boldsymbol{\beta}$ vector would be as follows:

$$\mathbf{X} = \begin{bmatrix} 1 & 0 & 0 \\ 1 & 0 & 0 \\ 0 & 1 & 0 \\ 0 & 1 & 0 \\ 0 & 0 & 1 \\ 0 & 0 & 1 \end{bmatrix} \qquad \boldsymbol{\beta} = \begin{bmatrix} \mu_1 \\ \mu_2 \\ \mu_3 \end{bmatrix}$$

Note that regression model (16.81) has no intercept term. When a computer regression package is to be employed for this case, it is important that a fit with no intercept term be specified.

The test of whether the factor level means are equal, i.e., $\mu_1 = \mu_2 = \cdots = \mu_r$, asks only whether or not the regression coefficients in (16.81) are equal, not whether or not they equal zero. Hence, we need to fit the full model and then the reduced model to conduct this test. The reduced model when H_0: $\mu_1 = \cdots = \mu_r$ holds is:

(16.82) $$Y_{ij} = \mu_c + \varepsilon_{ij} \qquad \text{Reduced model}$$

where μ_c is the common value of all μ_i under H_0. The **X** matrix here consists simply of a column of 1s. The **X** matrix and $\boldsymbol{\beta}$ vector for the reduced model in our example would be:

$$\mathbf{X} = \begin{bmatrix} 1 \\ 1 \\ 1 \\ 1 \\ 1 \\ 1 \end{bmatrix} \qquad \boldsymbol{\beta} = [\mu_c]$$

After the full and reduced models are fitted and the error sums of squares are obtained for each fit, the usual general linear test statistic (2.70) is then calculated. ∎

Problems

16.1.   Refer to Figure 16.1a. Could you determine the mean sales level when the price level is 68 dollars if you knew the true regression function? Could you make this determination from Figure 16.1b if you only knew the values of the parameters μ_1, μ_2, and μ_3 of ANOVA model (16.2)? What distinction between regression models and ANOVA models is demonstrated by your answers?

16.2.   A market researcher, having collected data on breakfast cereal expenditures by families with 1, 2, 3, 4, and 5 children living at home, plans to use an ordinary regression model to estimate the mean expenditures at each of these five family size levels. However, the researcher is undecided between fitting a linear or a quadratic regression model, and the data do not give clear evidence in favor of one model or the other. A colleague suggests: "For your purposes you might simply use an ANOVA model." Is this a useful suggestion? Explain.

16.3.   Refer to the **SENIC** data set. An analyst has set up four age groupings for variable 3 (age) and wishes to apply ANOVA model (16.2) to determine whether the mean infection risk (variable 4) is the same in the four age groups.

   a.   What is the response variable here?

   b.   Identify the factor studied. What are the factor levels?

   c.   Is the factor quantitative or qualitative?

   d.   Is the factor an experimental or a classification factor?

16.4.   Thirty trainees are randomly divided into three groups of 10 and each group is given instruction in the use of a different word-processing system. At the end of the training period, each trainee is given the same "benchmark" word-processing project to complete and the time required for completion is recorded. ANOVA model (16.2) will be used to test whether or not the mean time is the same for the three systems.

   a.   What is the response variable here?

   b.   Identify the factor studied and the factor levels.

   c.   Is the factor an experimental or a classification factor? Would your answer differ if each trainee had been allowed to select the word-processing system of his or her choice?

16.5.   In a study of intentions to get flu-vaccine shots in an area threatened by an epidemic, 90 persons were classified into three groups of 30 according to the degree of risk of getting flu. Each group was together when the persons were asked about the likelihood of getting the shots, on a probability scale ranging from 0 to 1.0. Unavoidably, most persons overheard the answers of nearby respondents. An analyst wishes to test whether the mean intent scores are the same for the three risk groups. Consider each assumption for ANOVA model (16.2) and explain whether this assumption is likely to hold in the present situation.

16.6.   In a study of the effectiveness of subliminal advertising, subjects are brought to a studio and shown a film with one of three types of subliminal advertising for a product. Each subject's attitudes toward the product before and after the film viewing are measured.

   a.   In this type of situation, should a control treatment be employed?

   b.   Explain precisely what would be the nature of the control treatment for this study.

16.7. A company, studying the relation between job satisfaction and length of service of employees, classified employees into three length-of-service groups (less than 5 years, 5–10 years, more than 10 years). Suppose $\mu_1 = 65$, $\mu_2 = 80$, $\mu_3 = 95$, and $\sigma = 3$, and that ANOVA model (16.2) is applicable.

a. Draw a representation of this model in the format of Figure 16.2.

b. Find $E\{MSTR\}$ and $E\{MSE\}$ if 25 employees from each group are selected at random for intensive interviewing about job satisfaction. Is $E\{MSTR\}$ substantially larger than $E\{MSE\}$ here? What is the implication of this?

16.8. In a study of length of hospital stay (in number of days) of persons in four income groups, the parameters are as follows: $\mu_1 = 5.1$, $\mu_2 = 6.3$, $\mu_3 = 7.9$, $\mu_4 = 9.5$, $\sigma = 2.8$. Assume that ANOVA model (16.2) is appropriate.

a. Draw a representation of this model in the format of Figure 16.2.

b. Suppose 100 persons from each income group are randomly selected for the study. Find $E\{MSTR\}$ and $E\{MSE\}$. Is $E\{MSTR\}$ substantially larger than $E\{MSE\}$ here? What is the implication of this?

c. If $\mu_2 = 5.6$ and $\mu_3 = 9.0$, everything else remaining the same, what would $E\{MSTR\}$ be? Why is $E\{MSTR\}$ substantially larger here than in part (b) even though the range of the factor level means is the same?

16.9. A student asks: "Why is the F test for equality of factor level means not a two-tail test since any differences among the factor level means can occur in either direction?" Explain, utilizing the expressions for the expected mean squares in (16.37).

√ 16.10. **Productivity improvement**. An economist compiled data on productivity improvements last year for a sample of firms producing electronic computing equipment. The firms were classified according to the level of their average expenditures for research and development in the past three years (low, moderate, high). The results of the study follow (productivity improvement is measured on a scale from 0 to 100). Assume that ANOVA model (16.2) is appropriate.

							j					
i	1	2	3	4	5	6	7	8	9	10	11	12
1 Low	7.6	8.2	6.8	5.8	6.9	6.6	6.3	7.7	6.0			
2 Moderate	6.7	8.1	9.4	8.6	7.8	7.7	8.9	7.9	8.3	8.7	7.1	8.4
3 High	8.5	9.7	10.1	7.8	9.6	9.5						

a. Prepare aligned dot plots of the data. Do the factor level means appear to differ? Does the variability of the observations within each factor level appear to be approximately the same for all factor levels?

b. Obtain the fitted values.

c. Obtain the residuals. Do they sum to zero in accord with (16.21)?

d. Obtain the analysis of variance table.

e. Test whether or not the mean productivity improvement differs according to the level of research and development expenditures. Control the α risk at .05. State the alternatives, decision rule, and conclusion.

f. What is the P-value of the test in part (e)? How does it support the conclusion reached in part (e)?

g. What appears to be the nature of the relationship between research and development expenditures and productivity improvement?

16.11. **Questionnaire color**. In an experiment to investigate the effect of color of paper (blue, green, orange) on response rates for questionnaires distributed by the "windshield method" in supermarket parking lots, 15 representative supermarket parking lots were chosen in a metropolitan area and each color was assigned at random to five of the lots. The response rates (in percent) follow. Assume that ANOVA model (16.2) is appropriate.

				j		
i		1	2	3	4	5
1	Blue	28	26	31	27	35
2	Green	34	29	25	31	29
3	Orange	31	25	27	29	28

a. Prepare aligned dot plots of the data. Do the factor level means appear to differ? Does the variability of the observations within each factor level appear to be approximately the same for all factor levels?

b. Obtain the fitted values.

c. Obtain the residuals.

d. Obtain the analysis of variance table.

e. Conduct a test to determine whether or not the mean response rates for the three colors differ. Use level of significance $\alpha = .10$. State the alternatives, decision rule, and conclusion. What is the P-value of the test?

f. When informed of the findings, an executive said: "See? I was right all along. We might as well print the questionnaires on plain white paper, which is cheaper." Does this conclusion follow from the findings of the study? Discuss.

16.12. **Rehabilitation therapy**. A rehabilitation center researcher was interested in examining the relationship between physical fitness prior to surgery of persons undergoing corrective knee surgery and time required in physical therapy until successful rehabilitation. Patient records in the rehabilitation center were examined, and 24 male subjects ranging in age from 18 to 30 years who had undergone similar corrective knee surgery during the past year were selected for the study. The number of days required for successful completion of physical therapy and the prior physical fitness status (below average, average, above average) for each patient follow.

						j					
i		1	2	3	4	5	6	7	8	9	10
1	Below Average	29	42	38	40	43	40	30	42		
2	Average	30	35	39	28	31	31	29	35	29	33
3	High Average	26	32	21	20	23	22				

Assume that ANOVA model (16.2) is appropriate.

a. Prepare aligned dot plots of the data. Do the factor level means appear to differ? Does the variability of the observations within each factor level appear to be approximately the same for all factor levels?

b. Obtain the fitted values.

c. Obtain the residuals. Do they sum to zero in accord with (16.21)?

d. Obtain the analysis of variance table.

e. Test whether or not the mean number of days required for successful rehabilitation is the same for the three fitness groups. Control the α risk at .01. State the alternatives, decision rule, and conclusion.

f. Obtain the P-value for the test in part (e). Explain how the same conclusion reached in part (e) can be obtained by knowing the P-value.

g. What appears to be the nature of the relationship between physical fitness status and duration of required physical therapy?

√ 16.13. **Cash offers.** A consumer organization studied the effect of age of automobile owner on size of cash offer for a used car by utilizing 12 persons in each of three age groups (young, middle, elderly) who acted as the owner of a used car. A medium price, six-year-old car was selected for the experiment, and the "owners" solicited cash offers for this car from 36 dealers selected at random from the dealers in the region. Randomization was used in assigning the dealers to the "owners." The offers (in hundred dollars) follow. Assume that ANOVA model (16.2) is applicable.

| | | | | | | | | | | | | | | j |
i		1	2	3	4	5	6	7	8	9	10	11	12
1	Young	23	25	21	22	21	22	20	23	19	22	19	21
2	Middle	28	27	27	29	26	29	27	30	28	27	26	29
3	Elderly	23	20	25	21	22	23	21	20	19	20	22	21

a. Prepare aligned dot plots of the data. Do the factor level means appear to differ? Does the variability of the observations within each factor level appear to be approximately the same for all factor levels?

b. Obtain the fitted values.

c. Obtain the residuals.

d. Obtain the analysis of variance table.

e. Conduct the F test for equality of factor level means; use $\alpha = .01$. State the alternatives, decision rule, and conclusion. What is the P-value of the test?

f. What appears to be the nature of the relationship between age of owner and mean cash offer?

√ 16.14. **Filling machines.** A company uses six filling machines of the same make and model to place detergent into cartons that show a label weight of 32 ounces. The production manager has complained that the six machines do not place the same amount of fill into the cartons. A consultant requested that 20 filled cartons be selected randomly from each of the six machines and the content of each carton carefully weighed. The observations (stated for convenience as deviations from 32.00 ounces) follow. Assume that ANOVA model (16.2) is applicable.

			j				
i	1	2	3	. . .	18	19	20
1	−.14	.20	.07	. . .	.07	−.01	−.19
2	.46	.11	.12	. . .	.02	.11	.12
3	.21	.78	.32	. . .	.50	.20	.61
4	.49	.58	.52	. . .	.42	.45	.20
5	−.19	.27	.06	. . .	.14	.35	−.18
6	.05	−.05	.28	. . .	.35	−.09	.05

a. Prepare aligned box plots of the data. Do the factor level means appear to differ? Does the variability of the observations within each factor level appear to be approximately the same for all factor levels?

b. Obtain the fitted values.

c. Obtain the residuals. Do they sum to zero in accord with (16.21)?

d. Obtain the analysis of variance table.

e. Test whether or not the mean fill differs among the six machines; control the α risk at .05. State the alternatives, decision rule, and conclusion. Does your conclusion support the production manager's complaint?

f. What is the P-value of the test in part (e)? Is this value consistent with your conclusion in part (e)? Explain.

g. Based on the box plots obtained in part (a), does the variation between the mean fills for the six machines appear to be large relative to the variability in fills between cartons for any given machine? Explain.

16.15. **Premium distribution**. A soft-drink manufacturer uses five agents (1, 2, 3, 4, 5) to handle premium distributions for its various products. The marketing director desired to study the timeliness with which the premiums are distributed. Twenty transactions for each agent were selected at random, and the time lapse (in days) for handling each transaction was determined. The results follow. Assume that ANOVA model (16.2) is appropriate.

			j				
i	1	2	3	. . .	18	19	20
1	24	24	29	. . .	27	26	25
2	18	20	20	. . .	26	22	21
3	10	11	8	. . .	9	11	12
4	15	13	18	. . .	17	14	16
5	33	22	28	. . .	26	30	29

a. Prepare aligned box plots of the data. Do the factor level means appear to differ? Does the variability of the observations within each factor level appear to be approximately the same for all factor levels?

b. Obtain the fitted values.

c. Obtain the residuals. Do they sum to zero in accord with (16.21)?

d. Obtain the analysis of variance table.

e. Test whether or not the mean time lapse differs for the five agents; use $\alpha = .10$. State the alternatives, decision rule, and conclusion.

    f. What is the P-value of the test in part (e)? Explain how the same conclusion as in part (e) can be reached by knowing the P-value.

    g. Based on the box plots obtained in part (a), does there appear to be much variation in the mean time lapse for the five agents? Is this variation necessarily the result of differences in the efficiency of operations of the five agents? Discuss.

16.16. Four treatments are to be studied in a completely randomized design, and 16 experimental units are available. Each treatment is to be assigned to four experimental units selected at random. There are four observers; each is to be assigned at random to one experimental unit for each treatment. Make all appropriate randomizations.

16.17. Five treatments are to be studied in a completely randomized design, and 30 experimental units are available. Each treatment is to be assigned to six experimental units selected at random. The study is to be conducted over a period of six days, with each treatment included on each day. The order of the five treatments within each day is to be randomized. Make all appropriate randomizations.

16.18. Refer to **Questionnaire color** Problem 16.11. Explain how you would make the random assignments of supermarket parking lots to colors in this single-factor study. Make all appropriate randomizations.

16.19. Refer to **Cash offers** Problem 16.13. Explain how you would make the random assignments of dealers to "owners" in this single-factor study. Make all appropriate randomizations.

16.20. Refer to Problem 16.7. What are the values of τ_1, τ_2, and τ_3 if the ANOVA model is expressed in the factor effects formulation (16.62), and $\mu.$ is defined by (16.63)?

16.21. Refer to Problem 16.8. What are the values of τ_i if the ANOVA model is expressed in the factor effects formulation (16.62), and $\mu.$ is defined by (16.63)?

16.22. Refer to **Premium distribution** Problem 16.15. Suppose that 25 percent of all premium distributions are handled by agent 1, 20 percent by agent 2, 20 percent by agent 3, 20 percent by agent 4, and 15 percent by agent 5.

    a. Obtain a point estimate of $\mu.$ when the ANOVA model is expressed in the factor effects formulation (16.62) and $\mu.$ is defined by (16.65), with the weights being the proportions of premium distribution handled by each agent.

    b. State the alternatives for the test of equality of factor level means in terms of factor effects model (16.62) for the present case. Would this statement be affected if $\mu.$ were defined according to (16.63)? Explain.

√ 16.23. Refer to **Productivity improvement** Problem 16.10. Regression model (16.75) is to be employed for testing the equality of the factor level means.

    a. Set up the **Y**, **X**, and **β** matrices.

    b. Obtain **Xβ**. Develop equivalent expressions of the elements of this vector in terms of the cell means μ_i.

    c. Obtain the fitted regression function. What is estimated by the intercept term?

    d. Obtain the regression analysis of variance table.

    e. Conduct the test for equality of factor level means; use $\alpha = .05$. State the alternatives, decision rule, and conclusion.

16.24. Refer to **Questionnaire color** Problem 16.11. Regression model (16.75) is to be employed for testing the equality of the factor level means.

   a. Set up the **Y**, **X**, and **β** matrices.

   b. Obtain **Xβ**. Develop equivalent expressions of the elements of this vector in terms of the cell means μ_i.

   c. Obtain the fitted regression function. What is estimated by the intercept term?

   d. Obtain the regression analysis of variance table.

   e. Conduct the test for equality of factor level means; use $\alpha = .10$. State the alternatives, decision rule, and conclusion.

√ 16.25. Refer to **Cash offers** Problem 16.13.

   a. Fit regression model (16.75) to the data. What is estimated by the intercept term?

   b. Obtain the regression analysis of variance table and test whether or not the factor level means are equal; use $\alpha = .01$. State the alternatives, decision rule, and conclusion.

16.26. Refer to **Rehabilitation therapy** Problem 16.12.

   a. Fit the full regression model (16.81) to the data. Why would a fitted regression model containing an intercept term not be proper here?

   b. Fit the reduced model (16.82) to the data.

   c. Use test statistic (2.70) for testing the equality of the factor level means; employ level of significance $\alpha = .01$.

Exercises

16.27. (Calculus needed.) State the likelihood function for ANOVA model (16.2) when $r = 3$ and $n_i \equiv 2$ and obtain the maximum likelihood estimators.

16.28. Show that when test statistic t^* in Table A.2a is squared, it is equivalent to the F^* test statistic (16.55) for $r = 2$.

16.29. Derive the restriction in (16.66) when the constant $\mu_.$ is defined according to (16.65).

16.30. a. Obtain the least squares estimators of the regression coefficients in full regression model (16.81). What is $SSE(F)$ here?

   b. Obtain the least squares estimator of μ_c in reduced regression model (16.82). What is $SSE(R)$ here?

Projects

16.31. Refer to the **SENIC** data set. Test whether or not the mean infection risk (variable 4) is the same in the four geographic regions (variable 9); use $\alpha = .05$. Assume that ANOVA model (16.2) is applicable. State the alternatives, decision rule, and conclusion.

16.32. Refer to the **SENIC** data set. The effect of average age of patient (variable 3) on mean infection risk (variable 4) is to be studied. For purposes of this ANOVA study, average age is to be classified into four categories: Under 50.0, 50.0-54.9, 55.0-59.9, 60.0 and over. Assume that ANOVA model (16.2) is applicable. Test whether or not the mean infection risk differs for the four age groups. Control the α risk at .10. State the alternatives, decision rule, and conclusion.

16.33. Refer to the **SMSA** data set. The effect of geographic region (variable 12) on the crime rate (variable 11 ÷ variable 3) is to be studied. Assume that ANOVA model (16.2) is applicable. Test whether or not the mean crime rates for the four geographic regions differ; use $\alpha = .05$. State the alternatives, decision rule, and conclusion.

16.34. Consider a test involving H_0: $\mu_1 = \mu_2 = \mu_3$. Five observations are to be taken for each factor level, and level of significance $\alpha = .05$ is to be employed in the test.

   a. Generate five random normal observations when $\mu_1 = 100$ and $\sigma = 12$ to represent the observations for treatment 1. Repeat this for the other two treatments when $\mu_2 = \mu_3 = 100$ and $\sigma = 12$. Finally, calculate F^* test statistic (16.55).

   b. Repeat part (a) 100 times.

   c. Calculate the mean of the 100 F^* statistics.

   d. What proportion of the F^* statistics lead to conclusion H_0? Is this consistent with theoretical expectations?

   e. Repeat parts (a) and (b) when $\mu_1 = 80$, $\mu_2 = 60$, $\mu_3 = 160$, and $\sigma = 12$. Calculate the mean of the 100 F^* statistics. How does this mean compare with the mean obtained in part (c) when $\mu_1 = \mu_2 = \mu_3 = 100$? Is this result consistent with the expectation in (16.37b)?

   f. What proportion of the 100 test statistics obtained in part (e) lead to conclusion H_a? Does it appear that the test has satisfactory power when $\mu_1 = 80$, $\mu_2 = 60$, and $\mu_3 = 160$?

CHAPTER 17

Analysis of Factor Level Effects

17.1 Introduction

In Chapter 16, we discussed the F test for determining whether or not the factor level means μ_i differ. This is a preliminary test to establish whether detailed analysis of the factor level effects is warranted. When this test leads to the conclusion that the factor level means μ_i are equal, and ANOVA model (16.2) is appropriate, no relation between the factor and the response variable is present and no further analysis of factor effects is therefore indicated. On the other hand, when the F test leads to the z conclusion that the factor level means μ_i differ, a relation between the factor and the response variable is present. In this latter case, a thorough analysis of the nature of the factor level effects is usually undertaken. This is done in two principal ways:

1. Analysis of the factor level effects of interest using estimation techniques.

2. Statistical tests concerning the factor level effects of interest.

Often, the analysis of factor level effects combines the two approaches. For instance, a two-sided confidence interval may be constructed initially for an effect of interest. A test concerning this effect is then carried out either by determining whether or not the confidence interval contains the hypothesized value or by constructing the appropriate test statistic.

When many related comparisons are to be made, testing often precedes estimation. This occurs, for instance, when comparing each factor level effect with every other one and the number of factor levels is not small. Here, statistical tests are often performed first to determine the *active* or statistically significant set of comparisons. Estimation techniques are then used to construct confidence intervals for the active comparisons.

Special simultaneous estimation and testing procedures, called multiple comparison procedures, are required when a series of interval estimates or tests are performed. These multiple comparison procedures preserve the overall confidence coefficient $1 - \alpha$, or the overall significance level α, for the family of inferences.

We first discuss two simple graphical methods for displaying the factor level means. Much of the remainder of the chapter is devoted to a consideration of important multiple comparison procedures. The chapter concludes with a discussion of the analysis of factor effects when the factor is quantitative.

TABLE 17.1   **Summary of Results—Kenton Food Company Example.**

	Package Design (i)				
	1	2	3	4	Total
n_i	5	5	4	5	19
$Y_i.$	73	67	78	136	354
$\bar{Y}_i.$	14.6	13.4	19.5	27.2	18.63

Source of Variation	SS	df	MS
Between designs	588.22	3	196.07
Error	158.20	15	10.55
Total	746.42	18	

Package Design	Characteristics
1	3 colors, with cartoons
2	3 colors, without cartoons
3	5 colors, with cartoons
4	5 colors, without cartoons

Throughout this chapter, we continue to assume ANOVA model I. The cell means version of this model was given in (16.2):

$$(17.1) \qquad\qquad Y_{ij} = \mu_i + \varepsilon_{ij}$$

where:

μ_i are parameters

ε_{ij} are independent $N(0, \sigma^2)$

Our discussion of the analysis of factor effects will be illustrated by two examples. The first is the Kenton Food Company example, for which the data were given in Table 16.1 and the ANOVA table in Figure 16.5. For convenience, we repeat the main results in Table 17.1. The second example, the rust inhibitor example, follows.

Example

In a study of the effectiveness of different rust inhibitors, four brands (A, B, C, D) were tested. Altogether, 40 experimental units were randomly assigned to the four brands, with 10 units assigned to each brand. A portion of the results after exposing the experimental units to severe weather conditions is given in coded form in Table 17.2a. The higher the coded value, the more effective is the rust inhibitor. Note in Table 17.2a that the treatments are shown in columns because of layout considerations.

The analysis of variance is shown in Table 17.2b. For level of significance $\alpha = .05$ for testing whether or not the four rust inhibitors differ in effectiveness, we require

TABLE 17.2 **Data and Analysis of Variance Results—Rust Inhibitor Example (data are coded).**

(a) Data

Rust Inhibitor Brand

j	A $i = 1$	B $i = 2$	C $i = 3$	D $i = 4$
1	43.9	89.8	68.4	36.2
2	39.0	87.1	69.3	45.2
3	46.7	92.7	68.5	40.7
...	...	...	...	...
8	38.9	88.1	65.2	38.7
9	43.6	90.8	63.8	40.9
10	40.0	89.1	69.2	39.7
$\bar{Y}_{i.}$	43.14	89.44	67.95	40.47

$$\bar{Y}_{..} = 60.25$$

(b) Analysis of Variance

Source of Variation	SS	df	MS
Between brands	15,953.47	3	5,317.82
Error	221.03	36	6.140
Total	16,174.50	39	

$F(.95; 3, 36) = 2.87$. Using the mean squares from Table 17.2b, we obtain the test statistic:

$$F^* = \frac{MSTR}{MSE} = \frac{5,317.82}{6.140} = 866.1$$

Since $F^* = 866.1 > 2.87$, we conclude that the four rust inhibitors differ in effectiveness. The P-value of the test is 0+. We therefore wish to analyze the nature of the factor level effects, particularly whether one rust inhibitor is substantially more effective than the others.

17.2 Plots of Estimated Factor Level Means

Before undertaking formal analysis of the nature of the factor level effects, it is usually helpful to examine these factor effects informally from a plot of the estimated factor level means $\bar{Y}_{i.}$. We shall take up two types of plots: (1) a line plot, which is appropriate whether the sample sizes n_i are equal or not; and (2) a normal probability plot, which is appropriate when the sample sizes n_i are equal.

FIGURE 17.1   **Line Plot of Estimated Factor Level Means—Kenton Food Company Example.**

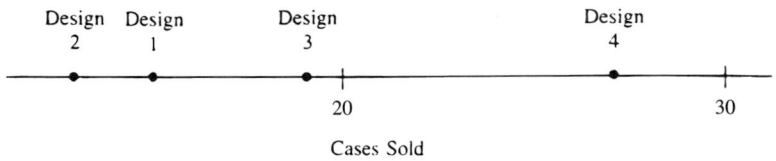

Line Plot

A line plot of the estimated factor level means simply shows the positions of the $\bar{Y}_{i\cdot}$ on a line scale. It is a very simple, but effective, device for indicating when one or several factor level means may differ substantially from the others.

Example.   In Figure 17.1 we present a line plot of the estimated factor level means $\bar{Y}_{i\cdot}$ for the Kenton Food Company example. It is clear from Figure 17.1 that design 4 led by far to the highest mean sales in the study, and that package designs 1 and 2 led to the smallest mean sales which did not differ much from each other. The purpose of the formal inference procedures to be taken up shortly is to determine whether the pattern noted here reflects underlying differences in the factor level means μ_i or is simply the result of random variation.

Normal Probability Plot

A normal probability plot of the estimated factor level means recognizes that the $\bar{Y}_{i\cdot}$ are subject to random variation and permits an assessment in an informal fashion whether the differences in the estimated means reflect real effects. The use of normal probability plots of the estimated factor level means requires that *all sample sizes be equal*, in other words, that $n_i \equiv n$.

We encountered normal probability plots in Chapter 3. In these plots, the regression residuals are positioned against their expected values under normality, as given in (3.6), to determine whether the error term distribution is normal. In normal probability plots of estimated factor level means, normality of the observations Y_{ij}, with constant variance σ^2, is assumed. The condition being tested is whether the factor level means μ_i are equal. If they are, the estimated means $\bar{Y}_{i\cdot}$ have the same expected value and the same variance (because of the constant variance of the Y_{ij} and the equal sample sizes). Hence, the estimated means $\bar{Y}_{i\cdot}$ when shown in a normal probability plot should behave like random observations from the same normal distribution if the factor level means are equal. A substantial departure from a linear pattern therefore indicates that the factor level means are not equal, and the nature of the plot may suggest which of the factor level means differ from the others.

The expected value of the kth ordered estimated factor level mean, if all factor level means are equal, is approximately as follows:

$$(17.2) \qquad \text{Expected value} = \bar{Y}_{\cdot\cdot} + z\left(\frac{k - .375}{r + .25}\right)\sqrt{\frac{MSE}{n}}$$

FIGURE 17.2   **Prototype Normal Probability Plots of Estimated Factor Level Means.**

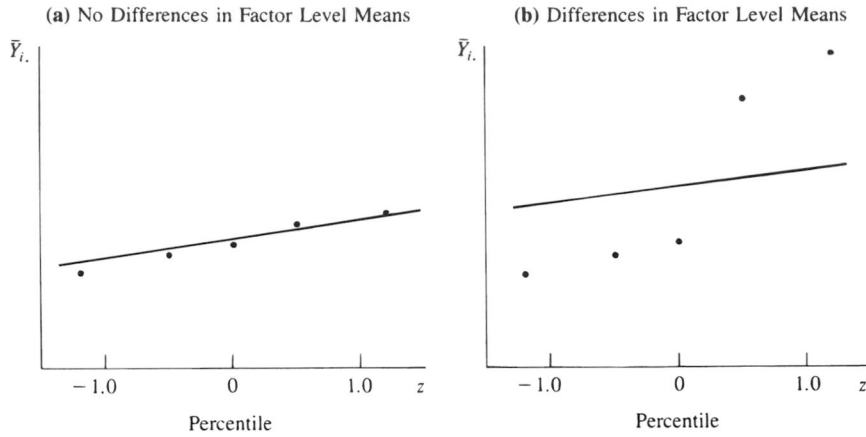

(a) No Differences in Factor Level Means   (b) Differences in Factor Level Means

where the square root term is the estimated standard deviation of the kth ordered estimated factor level mean $\bar{Y}_{i.}$, $k = 1, \ldots, r$, as will be explained shortly. Rather than plotting the estimated factor level means $\bar{Y}_{i.}$ against their expected values, as we did for residual plots, it will be more effective here to plot the $\bar{Y}_{i.}$ against the corresponding normal percentiles z. Since the expected values are a linear function of the percentiles z, a linear pattern of the points is preserved whether we plot against the percentiles or the expected values. We also plot the line:

$$y = \text{expected value}$$

on the same graph to serve as a reference line to assist in judging whether any estimated mean is far from its expected value.

Figure 17.2a shows a prototype pattern suggesting that all treatment means μ_i are equal. Each of the points is close to the reference line $y = $ expected value, and the pattern of the points therefore is reasonably linear.

Figure 17.2b shows a prototype pattern where the jump in the points suggests that the two largest factor level means differ from the other three factor level means. The fact that the points for the three smallest $\bar{Y}_{i.}$ follow a linear pattern approximately parallel to the reference line $y = $ expected value suggests that these factor level means do not differ from each other. The substantial deviations of these points from the reference line is the result of a major difference between the two groups of factor level means.

Example.   We found earlier in the rust inhibitor example that the four rust inhibitors differ in mean effectiveness. We shall now prepare both a line plot and a normal probability plot of the estimated factor level means to examine how the four rust inhibitors differ. Figure 17.3a contains a line plot of the estimated factor level means $\bar{Y}_{i.}$. This plot suggests that brands B and C perform much better, on the average, than the other two brands and that brand B may be the most effective.

In preparing a normal probability plot of the estimated factor level means, we first list them in treatment order in Table 17.3, column 1. Column 2 shows the ranks of the $\bar{Y}_{i.}$, column 3 shows the standard normal percentiles z, and column 4 shows the expected

FIGURE 17.3   Plots of Estimated Factor Level Means—Rust Inhibitor Example.

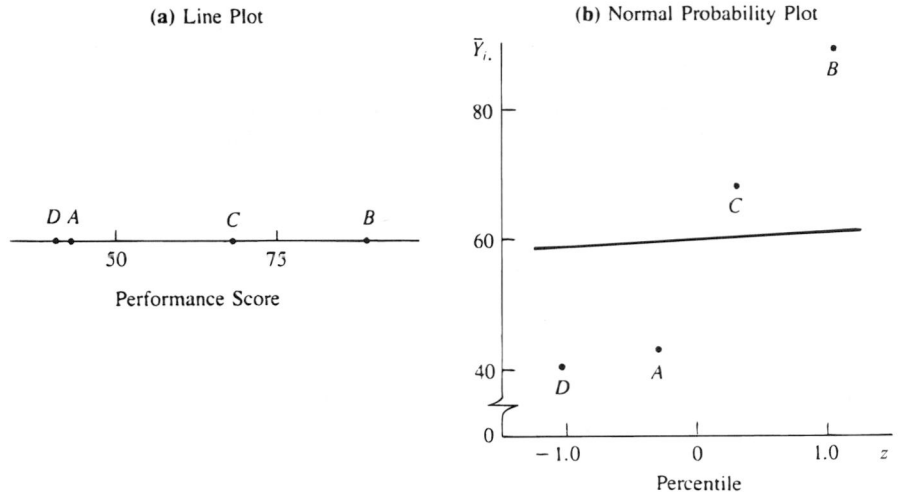

(a) Line Plot

(b) Normal Probability Plot

TABLE 17.3   Estimated Factor Level Means $\bar{Y}_{i.}$ and Expected Values Under Assumption of Equality of μ_i—Rust Inhibitor Example.

Treatment i	(1) $\bar{Y}_{i.}$	(2) Rank k	(3) $z\left(\dfrac{k-.375}{4+.25}\right)$	(4) Expected Value under Equality
1	43.1	2	−.299	60.0
2	89.4	4	1.049	61.1
3	68.0	3	.299	60.5
4	40.5	1	−1.049	59.4

$$\bar{Y}_{..} = 60.25$$

$$\sqrt{\frac{MSE}{n}} = \sqrt{\frac{6.140}{10}} = .784$$

---

values of the estimated means under the assumption that the factor level means are equal. We illustrate the calculations for the smallest estimated factor level mean, $\bar{Y}_{4.} = 40.5$, for which the rank is $k = 1$. The standard normal percentile required is:

$$z\left(\frac{k-.375}{r+.25}\right) = z\left(\frac{1-.375}{4+.25}\right) = z(.147) = -1.049$$

We know from Table 17.2 that $\bar{Y}_{..} = 60.25$ and $MSE = 6.140$. Hence, using (17.2) we obtain the approximate expected value:

$$60.25 + (-1.049)\sqrt{\frac{6.140}{10}} = 59.4$$

The expected values for the other estimated factor level means are obtained in similar fashion and are shown in Table 17.3, column 4.

Figure 17.3b contains the normal probability plot of the estimated factor level means in column 1 of Table 17.3 plotted against the percentiles in column 3. The plot suggests strongly, like the line plot in Figure 17.3a, that the four rust inhibitors differ in effectiveness because the points deviate substantially from the reference line. In addition, the normal probability plot suggests that rust inhibitors B and C performed better than rust inhibitors A and D. Further, the normal probability plot suggests that the mean performance for brands A and D may be the same since these two points form a line that is fairly parallel to the reference line. On the other hand, the mean performance for rust inhibitor B appears to be greater than that for rust inhibitor C because these two points form a line with a slope far greater than that of the reference line.

Formal inference procedures are now required to confirm the suggestions made by these plots.

Note

A normal probability plot of the estimated factor level means may also be prepared when the sample sizes n_i are unequal but do not differ very much. In that case, the plot is an approximation, but this approximation will be good if the sample sizes are close to each other. In substituting in formula (17.2) for the expected value, the average sample size or the most prevalent sample size may be used.   ∎

17.3   Estimation and Testing of Factor Level Effects

Inferences for factor level effects are generally concerned with one or more of the following:

1. A single factor level mean μ_i

2. A difference between two factor level means

3. A contrast among factor level means

4. A linear combination of factor level means

We discuss each of these types of inferences in turn.

Inferences for Single Factor Level Mean

Estimation.   An unbiased point estimator of the factor level mean μ_i is given in (16.16):

(17.3) $\hat{\mu}_i = \bar{Y}_i.$

This estimator has mean and variance:

(17.4a)
$$E\{\bar{Y}_{i\cdot}\} = \mu_i$$

(17.4b)
$$\sigma^2\{\bar{Y}_{i\cdot}\} = \frac{\sigma^2}{n_i}$$

The latter result follows because (16.43) indicates that $\bar{Y}_{i\cdot} = \mu_i + \bar{\varepsilon}_{i\cdot}$, the sum of a constant plus a mean of n_i independent ε_{ij} error terms, each of which has variance σ^2. Further, $\bar{Y}_{i\cdot}$ is normally distributed because the error terms ε_{ij} are independent normal random variables.

The estimated variance of $\bar{Y}_{i\cdot}$ is denoted by $s^2\{\bar{Y}_{i\cdot}\}$ and is obtained as usual by replacing σ^2 in (17.4b) by the unbiased point estimator *MSE*:

(17.5)
$$s^2\{\bar{Y}_{i\cdot}\} = \frac{MSE}{n_i}$$

The estimated standard deviation $s\{\bar{Y}_{i\cdot}\}$ is the positive square root of (17.5).

It can be shown that:

(17.6)
$$\frac{\bar{Y}_{i\cdot} - \mu_i}{s\{\bar{Y}_{i\cdot}\}} \text{ is distributed as } t(n_T - r) \text{ for ANOVA model (17.1)}$$

where the degrees of freedom are those associated with *MSE*. The result (17.6) follows from the definition of t in (A.44) since: (1) $\bar{Y}_{i\cdot}$ is normally distributed and (2) MSE/σ^2 is distributed independently of $\bar{Y}_{i\cdot}$ as $\chi^2(n_T - r)/(n_T - r)$ according to the following theorem:

(17.7)   For ANOVA model (17.1), SSE/σ^2 is distributed as χ^2 with $n_T - r$ degrees of freedom, and is independent of $\bar{Y}_{1\cdot}, \ldots, \bar{Y}_{r\cdot}$.

It follows directly from (17.6) that the $1 - \alpha$ confidence limits for μ_i are:

(17.8)
$$\bar{Y}_{i\cdot} \pm t(1 - \alpha/2; n_T - r)s\{\bar{Y}_{i\cdot}\}$$

Testing.   The confidence interval based on the limits in (17.8) can be used to test a hypothesis of the form:

(17.9)
$$H_0:\ \mu_i = c$$
$$H_a:\ \mu_i \neq c$$

where c is an appropriate constant. We conclude H_0, at level of significance α, when c is contained in the confidence interval, and we conclude H_a when the confidence interval does not contain c. Equivalently, one can compute the test statistic:

(17.10)
$$t^* = \frac{\bar{Y}_{i\cdot} - c}{s\{\bar{Y}_{i\cdot}\}}$$

Test statistic t^* follows a t distribution with $n_T - r$ degrees of freedom when H_0 is true, according to (17.6). Consequently, we conclude H_0 whenever $|t^*| \leq t(1 - \alpha/2; n_T - r)$; otherwise, we conclude H_a.

Example.   In the Kenton Food Company example, the sales manager wished to estimate mean sales for package design 1 with a 95 percent confidence interval. Using the results from Table 17.1, we have:

$$\bar{Y}_{1.} = 14.6 \qquad n_1 = 5 \qquad MSE = 10.55$$

We require $t(.975; 15) = 2.131$. Finally, we need $s\{\bar{Y}_{1.}\}$. We have:

$$s^2\{\bar{Y}_{1.}\} = \frac{MSE}{n_1} = \frac{10.55}{5} = 2.110$$

so that $s\{\bar{Y}_{1.}\} = 1.453$. Hence, we obtain the confidence limits $14.6 \pm 2.131(1.453)$ and the 95 percent confidence interval is:

$$11.5 \leq \mu_1 \leq 17.7$$

Thus, we estimate with confidence coefficient .95 that the mean sales per store for package design 1 are between 11.5 and 17.7 cases.

Inferences for Difference between Two Factor Level Means

Estimation.   Frequently two treatments or factor levels are to be compared by estimating the difference D between the two factor level means, say, μ_i and $\mu_{i'}$:

$$(17.11) \qquad\qquad D = \mu_i - \mu_{i'}$$

Such a difference between two factor level means is called a *pairwise comparison*. A point estimator of D in (17.11), denoted by $\hat{D}$, is:

$$(17.12) \qquad\qquad \hat{D} = \bar{Y}_{i.} - \bar{Y}_{i'.}$$

This point estimator is unbiased:

$$(17.13) \qquad\qquad E\{\hat{D}\} = \mu_i - \mu_{i'}$$

Since $\bar{Y}_{i.}$ and $\bar{Y}_{i'.}$ are independent, the variance of $\hat{D}$ follows from (A.31b):

$$(17.14) \qquad \sigma^2\{\hat{D}\} = \sigma^2\{\bar{Y}_{i.}\} + \sigma^2\{\bar{Y}_{i'.}\} = \sigma^2\left(\frac{1}{n_i} + \frac{1}{n_{i'}}\right)$$

The estimated variance of $\hat{D}$, denoted by $s^2\{\hat{D}\}$, is given by:

$$(17.15) \qquad\qquad s^2\{\hat{D}\} = MSE\left(\frac{1}{n_i} + \frac{1}{n_{i'}}\right)$$

Finally, $\hat{D}$ is normally distributed by (A.40) because $\hat{D}$ is a linear combination of independent normal variables.

It follows from these characteristics, theorem (17.7), and the definition of t in (A.44) that:

(17.16) $\qquad \dfrac{\hat{D} - D}{s\{\hat{D}\}}$ is distributed as $t(n_T - r)$ for ANOVA model (17.1)

Hence, the $1 - \alpha$ confidence limits for D are:

(17.17) $\qquad\qquad\qquad \hat{D} \pm t(1 - \alpha/2; n_T - r)s\{\hat{D}\}$

Testing. There is often interest in testing whether two factor level means are the same. The alternatives here are of the form:

(17.18)
$$H_0: \mu_i = \mu_{i'}$$
$$H_a: \mu_i \neq \mu_{i'}$$

The alternatives in (17.18) can be stated equivalently as follows:

(17.18a)
$$H_0: \mu_i - \mu_{i'} = 0$$
$$H_a: \mu_i - \mu_{i'} \neq 0$$

Conclusion H_0 is reached at the α level of significance if zero is contained within the confidence limits (17.17); otherwise, conclusion H_a is reached. An equivalent procedure is based on the test statistic:

(17.19)
$$t^* = \dfrac{\hat{D}}{s\{\hat{D}\}}$$

Conclusion H_0 is reached if $|t^*| \leq t(1 - \alpha/2; n_T - r)$; otherwise, H_a is concluded.

Example. For the Kenton Food Company example, package designs 1 and 2 used 3-color printing and designs 3 and 4 used 5-color printing, as shown in Table 17.1. We wish to estimate the difference in mean sales for 5-color designs 3 and 4 using a 95 percent confidence interval. That is, we wish to estimate $D = \mu_3 - \mu_4$. From Table 17.1, we have:

$$\bar{Y}_{3.} = 19.5 \qquad n_3 = 4 \qquad MSE = 10.55$$
$$\bar{Y}_{4.} = 27.2 \qquad n_4 = 5$$

Hence:

$$\hat{D} = \bar{Y}_{3.} - \bar{Y}_{4.} = 19.5 - 27.2 = -7.7$$

The estimated variance of $\hat{D}$ is:

$$s^2\{\hat{D}\} = MSE\left(\dfrac{1}{n_3} + \dfrac{1}{n_4}\right) = 10.55\left(\dfrac{1}{4} + \dfrac{1}{5}\right) = 4.748$$

so that the estimated standard deviation of $\hat{D}$ is $s\{\hat{D}\} = 2.179$. We require $t(.975; 15) = 2.131$. The confidence limits therefore are $-7.7 \pm 2.131(2.179)$, and the desired 95 percent confidence interval is:

$$-12.3 \leq \mu_3 - \mu_4 \leq -3.1$$

Thus, we estimate with confidence coefficient .95 that the mean sales for package design 3 fall short of those for package design 4 by somewhere between 3.1 and 12.3 cases per store.

Note from Table 17.1 that the only difference between package designs 3 and 4 is the presence of cartoons; both designs used 5-color printing. The sales manager may therefore wish to test whether the addition of cartoons affects sales for 5-color designs. The alternatives here are:

$$H_0: \mu_3 - \mu_4 = 0$$

$$H_a: \mu_3 - \mu_4 \neq 0$$

Since the hypothesized difference zero in H_0 is not contained between the 95 percent confidence limits -12.3 and -3.1, we conclude H_a, that the presence of cartoons has an effect. We could also obtain test statistic (17.19):

$$t^* = \frac{\hat{D}}{s\{\hat{D}\}} = \frac{-7.7}{2.179} = -3.53$$

Since $|t^*| = 3.53 > t(.975; 15) = 2.131$, we conclude H_a. The two-sided P-value for this test is .003.

Inferences for Contrast of Factor Level Means

A *contrast* is a comparison involving two or more factor level means and includes the previous case of a pairwise difference between two factor level means in (17.11). A contrast will be denoted by L, and is defined as a linear combination of the factor level means μ_i where the coefficients c_i sum to zero:

(17.20) $$L = \sum_{i=1}^{r} c_i \mu_i \qquad \text{where} \quad \sum_{i=1}^{r} c_i = 0$$

Illustrations of Contrasts. In the Kenton Food Company example, package designs 1 and 2 used 3-color printing and designs 3 and 4 used 5-color printing, as shown in Table 17.1. Also, package designs 1 and 3 utilized cartoons while no cartoons were utilized in designs 2 and 4. The following contrasts here may be of interest:

1. Comparison of the mean sales for the two 3-color designs:

$$L = \mu_1 - \mu_2$$

Here, $c_1 = 1$, $c_2 = -1$, $c_3 = 0$, $c_4 = 0$, and $\Sigma c_i = 0$.

2. Comparison of the mean sales for the 3-color and 5-color designs:

$$L = \frac{\mu_1 + \mu_2}{2} - \frac{\mu_3 + \mu_4}{2}$$

Here, $c_1 = 1/2$, $c_2 = 1/2$, $c_3 = -1/2$, $c_4 = -1/2$, and $\Sigma c_i = 0$.

3. Comparison of the mean sales for designs with and without cartoons:

$$L = \frac{\mu_1 + \mu_3}{2} - \frac{\mu_2 + \mu_4}{2}$$

Here, $c_1 = 1/2$, $c_2 = -1/2$, $c_3 = 1/2$, $c_4 = -1/2$, and $\Sigma c_i = 0$.

4. Comparison of the mean sales for design 1 with average sales for all four designs:

$$L = \mu_1 - \frac{\mu_1 + \mu_2 + \mu_3 + \mu_4}{4}$$

Here, $c_1 = 3/4$, $c_2 = -1/4$, $c_3 = -1/4$, $c_4 = -1/4$, and $\Sigma c_i = 0$.

Note that the first contrast is simply a pairwise comparison. In the second and third contrasts, averages of several factor level means are compared. The fourth contrast is the factor effect τ_1 defined by (16.60) and (16.63).

The averages used here are unweighted averages of the means μ_i; these are ordinarily the averages of interest. In special cases one might be interested in weighted averages of the μ_i to describe the mean response for a group of several factor levels. For example, if both 3-color and 5-color designs were to be employed, with 3-color printing used three times as often as 5-color printing, the comparison of the effect of cartoons versus no cartoons might be based on the contrast:

$$L = \frac{3\mu_1 + \mu_3}{4} - \frac{3\mu_2 + \mu_4}{4}$$

Here, $c_1 = 3/4$, $c_2 = -3/4$, $c_3 = 1/4$, $c_4 = -1/4$, and $\Sigma c_i = 0$.

Estimation.   An unbiased estimator of a contrast L is:

(17.21)
$$\hat{L} = \sum_{i=1}^{r} c_i \bar{Y}_{i\cdot}.$$

Since the $\bar{Y}_{i\cdot}$ are independent, the variance of $\hat{L}$ according to (A.31) is:

(17.22)
$$\sigma^2\{\hat{L}\} = \sum_{i=1}^{r} c_i^2 \sigma^2\{\bar{Y}_{i\cdot}\} = \sum_{i=1}^{r} c_i^2 \left(\frac{\sigma^2}{n_i}\right) = \sigma^2 \sum_{i=1}^{r} \frac{c_i^2}{n_i}$$

An unbiased estimator of this variance is:

(17.23)
$$s^2\{\hat{L}\} = MSE \sum_{i=1}^{r} \frac{c_i^2}{n_i}$$

$\hat{L}$ is normally distributed by (A.40) because it is a linear combination of independent normal random variables. It can be shown by theorem (17.7), the characteristics of $\hat{L}$ just mentioned, and the definition of t that:

(17.24)
$$\frac{\hat{L} - L}{s\{\hat{L}\}} \text{ is distributed as } t(n_T - r) \text{ for ANOVA model (17.1)}$$

Consequently, the $1 - \alpha$ confidence limits for L are:

(17.25)
$$\hat{L} \pm t(1 - \alpha/2; n_T - r)s\{\hat{L}\}$$

Testing. The confidence interval based on the limits in (17.25) can be used to test a hypothesis of the form:

$$H_0: \; L = 0$$

(17.26)

$$H_a: \; L \neq 0$$

H_0 is concluded at the α level of significance if zero is contained in the interval; otherwise H_a is concluded. An equivalent procedure is based on the test statistic:

(17.27)
$$t^* = \frac{\hat{L}}{s\{\hat{L}\}}$$

If $|t^*| \leq t(1 - \alpha/2; n_T - r)$, H_0 is concluded; otherwise, H_a is concluded.

Example.   In the Kenton Food Company example, the mean sales for the 3-color designs are to be compared to the mean sales for the 5-color designs with a 95 percent confidence interval. We wish to estimate:

$$L = \frac{\mu_1 + \mu_2}{2} - \frac{\mu_3 + \mu_4}{2}$$

The point estimate is (see data in Table 17.1):

$$\hat{L} = \frac{\bar{Y}_{1.} + \bar{Y}_{2.}}{2} - \frac{\bar{Y}_{3.} + \bar{Y}_{4.}}{2} = \frac{14.6 + 13.4}{2} - \frac{19.5 + 27.2}{2} = -9.35$$

Since $c_1 = 1/2$, $c_2 = 1/2$, $c_3 = -1/2$, and $c_4 = -1/2$, we obtain:

$$\sum \frac{c_i^2}{n_i} = \frac{(1/2)^2}{5} + \frac{(1/2)^2}{5} + \frac{(-1/2)^2}{4} + \frac{(-1/2)^2}{5} = .2125$$

and:

$$s^2\{\hat{L}\} = MSE \sum \frac{c_i^2}{n_i} = 10.55(.2125) = 2.242$$

so that $s\{\hat{L}\} = 1.50$.

For a 95 percent confidence interval, we require $t(.975; 15) = 2.131$. The confidence limits for L therefore are $-9.35 \pm 2.131(1.50)$, and the desired 95 percent confidence interval is:

$$-12.5 \leq L \leq -6.2$$

Therefore, we conclude with confidence coefficient .95 that mean sales for the 3-color designs fall below those for the 5-color designs by somewhere between 6.2 and 12.5 cases per store.

To test the hypothesis of no difference in mean sales for the 3-color and 5-color designs:

$$H_0: \; L = 0$$

$$H_a: \; L \neq 0$$

at the $\alpha = .05$ level of significance, we simply note that the hypothesized value zero is not contained in the 95 percent confidence interval. Hence, we conclude H_a, that the mean sales differ. To obtain a P-value of the test, test statistic (17.27) must be obtained. We find:

$$t^* = \frac{-9.35}{1.50} = -6.23$$

and the corresponding two-sided P-value is 0+.

Note

Many single-factor analysis of variance programs permit the user to specify a contrast of interest and then will furnish the t^* test statistic or the equivalent F^* test statistic.   ■

Inferences for Linear Combination of Factor Level Means

Occasionally, we are interested in a linear combination of the factor level means that is not a contrast. For example, suppose that the Kenton Food Company will use all four package designs, one in each of its four major marketing regions, and that these marketing regions account for 35, 28, 12, and 25 percent of sales, respectively. In that case, there might be interest in the overall mean sales per store for all regions:

$$L = .35\mu_1 + .28\mu_2 + .12\mu_3 + .25\mu_4$$

Note that this linear combination is of the form $L = \Sigma c_i \mu_i$ but that the coefficients c_i sum to 1.0, not to zero as they must for a contrast.

We define a *linear combination of the factor level means* μ_i as:

$$(17.28) \qquad\qquad L = \sum_{i=1}^{r} c_i \mu_i$$

with no restrictions on the coefficients c_i. Confidence limits and test statistics for a linear combination L are obtained in exactly the same way as those for a contrast by means of (17.25) and (17.27), respectively. Point estimator (17.21) and estimated variance (17.23) are still applicable when $\Sigma c_i \neq 0$.

Single Degree of Freedom Tests.   The alternatives for tests concerning a factor level mean in (17.9), a difference between two factor level means in (17.18a), and a contrast of factor level means in (17.26) are all special cases of a test concerning a linear combination of factor level means:

$$H_0: \ \sum c_i \mu_i = c$$
$$H_a: \ \sum c_i \mu_i \neq c$$

where the c_i and c are appropriate constants. Test statistics (17.10), (17.19), and (17.27) can each be converted to an equivalent F^* test statistic by means of the relation in (A.50a):

$$F^* = (t^*)^2$$

Test statistic F^* follows the $F(1, n_T - r)$ distribution when H_0 holds. Note that the numerator degrees of freedom are always one. Hence, these tests are often referred to as *single-degree-of-freedom tests*. The t^* version of the test statistic is more versatile because it can also be used for one-sided tests while the F^* version cannot.

17.4   Need for Simultaneous Inference Procedures

The procedures for estimating and testing factor level effects discussed up to this point have two important limitations:

1. The confidence coefficient $1-\alpha$ for the estimation procedures described is a statement confidence coefficient and applies only to a particular estimate, not to a series of estimates. Similarly, the specified Type I error rate, α, applies only to a particular test and not to a series of tests.

2. The confidence coefficient $1-\alpha$ and the specified significance level α are appropriate only if the estimate or test was not suggested by the data.

The first limitation is familiar from regression analysis. It is particularly serious for analysis of variance models because frequently many different comparisons are of interest here, and one needs to piece the different findings together. Consider the very simple case where three different advertisements are being compared for their effectiveness in stimulating sales. The following estimates of their comparative effectiveness have been obtained, each with a 95 percent statement confidence coefficient:

$$59 \leq \mu_2 - \mu_1 \leq 62$$

$$-2 \leq \mu_3 - \mu_1 \leq \;\; 3$$

$$58 \leq \mu_2 - \mu_3 \leq 64$$

It would be natural here to piece the different comparisons together and conclude that advertisement 2 leads to highest mean sales, while advertisements 1 and 3 are substantially less effective and do not differ much among themselves. One would therefore like a family confidence coefficient for this family of statements, to provide known assurance that the set of conclusions is correct.

The same concern for assurance of correct conclusions exists when the inferences involve tests. An analysis of factor effects by testing procedures usually involves several single degree of freedom tests to answer related questions. For instance, the sales manager of the Kenton Food Company might wish to know both whether the number of colors has an effect on mean sales and whether the use of cartoons has an effect. Whenever several tests are conducted, both the level of significance and the power, insofar as the family of tests is concerned, are affected. Consider, for example, three different t tests, each conducted with $\alpha = .05$. The probability that each of the tests will lead to conclusion H_0 when indeed H_0 is correct in each case, assuming independence of the tests, is $(.95)^3 = .857$. Thus, the level of significance that at least one of the three tests leads to conclusion H_a when H_0 holds in each case would be $1 - .857 = .143$, not .05. We see then that the level of significance and power for a *family* of tests is not the same as that for an *individual* test. Actually, the t^* statistics are dependent when they all are based on the same sample data and use the same *MSE* value. It is often therefore more difficult to determine the actual level of significance and power for a family of tests.

The second limitation of the procedures for estimating or testing factor level effects discussed so far, namely, that the estimate or test must not be suggested by the data, is an important one in exploratory investigations where many new questions are often suggested once the data are being analyzed. The process of studying effects suggested by the data is sometimes called *data snooping*. One form of data snooping is to investigate comparisons where the effect appears to be large from the sample data, for example, testing whether there is a difference between the two treatment means corresponding to the smallest and largest estimated factor level means $\bar{Y}_i$.. Choosing the test in this manner implies a larger significance level than the nominal level used in constructing the decision rule. For example, it can be shown for a study with six factor levels that if the analyst will always compare the smallest and largest estimated factor level means by using the confidence limits (17.17) with a 95 percent confidence coefficient, the interval estimate will not contain zero and therefore suggest a real effect 40 percent of the time when indeed there is no difference between any of the factor level means (Ref. 17.1). Hence, the α level for the test is .40, not .05. With a larger number of factor levels, the likelihood of an erroneous indication of a real effect, i.e., the actual α level, would be even greater. The reason for the higher actual level of significance here is that a family of tests is being conducted implicitly since the analyst does not know in advance which estimated factor level means will be the extreme ones. The situation here is analogous to that in Chapter 9 where the test to determine whether the largest absolute residual is an outlier considers the family of tests for each of the n residuals.

One solution to this problem of making comparisons that are suggested by initial analysis of the data is to use a multiple comparison procedure where the family of inferences includes all the possible inferences that can be anticipated to be of potential interest after the data are examined. For instance, in an investigation where five factor level means are being studied, it is decided in advance that principal interest is in three pairwise comparisons. However, it is also agreed that other pairwise comparisons that will appear interesting should be studied as well. In this case, the family of *all* pairwise comparisons can be used as the basis for obtaining an appropriate family confidence coefficient or significance level for the comparisons suggested by the data.

In the next four sections, we shall discuss four multiple comparison procedures for analysis of variance models that permit the family confidence coefficient and the family α risk to be controlled. Two of these procedures, the Tukey and Scheffé procedures, allow data snooping to be undertaken naturally without affecting the confidence coefficient or significance level. The other two procedures, the Bonferroni and Holm procedures, are applicable only when the effects to be investigated are identified in advance of the study.

17.5   Tukey Multiple Comparison Procedure

The Tukey multiple comparison procedure that we will consider here applies when:

The family of interest is the set of all pairwise comparisons of factor level means; in other words, the family consists of estimates of all pairs $D = \mu_i - \mu_{i'}$ or of all tests of the form:

$$H_0: \ \mu_i - \mu_{i'} = 0$$
$$H_a: \ \mu_i - \mu_{i'} \neq 0$$

When all sample sizes are equal, the family confidence coefficient for the Tukey method is exactly $1 - \alpha$ and the family significance level is exactly α. When the sample sizes are not equal, the family confidence coefficient is greater than $1 - \alpha$ and the family significance level is less than α. In other words, the Tukey procedure is conservative when the sample sizes are not equal.

Studentized Range Distribution

The Tukey procedure utilizes the *studentized range distribution*. Suppose that we have r independent observations $Y_1, \ldots, Y_r$ from a normal distribution with mean μ and variance σ^2. Let w be the range for this set of observations; thus:

$$(17.29) \qquad w = \max(Y_i) - \min(Y_i)$$

Suppose further that we have an estimate s^2 of the variance σ^2 which is based on ν degrees of freedom and is independent of the Y_i. Then, the ratio w/s is called the *studentized range*. It is denoted by:

$$(17.30) \qquad q(r, \nu) = \frac{w}{s}$$

where the arguments in parentheses remind us that the distribution of q depends on r and ν. The distribution of q has been tabulated, and selected percentiles are presented in Table B.9.

This table is simple to use. Suppose that $r = 5$ and $\nu = 10$. The 95th percentile is then $q(.95; 5, 10) = 4.65$, which means:

$$P\left\{\frac{w}{s} = q(5, 10) \leq 4.65\right\} = .95$$

Thus, with five normal Y observations, the probability is .95 that their range is not more than 4.65 times as great as an independent sample standard deviation based on 10 degrees of freedom.

Simultaneous Estimation

The Tukey multiple comparison confidence limits for all pairwise comparisons $D = \mu_i - \mu_{i'}$ with family confidence coefficient of at least $1 - \alpha$ are as follows:

$$(17.31) \qquad \hat{D} \pm Ts\{\hat{D}\}$$

where:

$$(17.31a) \qquad \hat{D} = \bar{Y}_{i.} - \bar{Y}_{i'.}$$

$$(17.31b) \qquad s^2\{\hat{D}\} = s^2\{\bar{Y}_{i.}\} + s^2\{\bar{Y}_{i'.}\} = MSE\left(\frac{1}{n_i} + \frac{1}{n_{i'}}\right)$$

$$(17.31c) \qquad T = \frac{1}{\sqrt{2}}q(1 - \alpha; r, n_T - r)$$

Note that the point estimator $\hat{D}$ in (17.31a) and the estimated variance in (17.31b) are the same as those in (17.12) and (17.15) for a single pairwise comparison. Thus, the only difference between the Tukey confidence limits (17.31) for simultaneous comparisons and those in (17.17) for a single comparison is the multiple of the estimated standard deviation.

The family confidence coefficient $1 - \alpha$ pertaining to the multiple pairwise comparisons refers to the proportion of correct families, each consisting of all pairwise comparisons, when repeated sets of samples are selected and all pairwise confidence intervals are calculated each time. A family of pairwise comparisons is considered to be correct if every pairwise comparison in the family is correct. Thus, a family confidence coefficient of $1 - \alpha$ indicates that all pairwise comparisons in the family will be correct in $(1 - \alpha)100$ percent of the repetitions.

Simultaneous Testing

When we wish to conduct a family of tests of the form:

(17.32)
$$H_0: \mu_i - \mu_{i'} = 0$$
$$H_a: \mu_i - \mu_{i'} \neq 0$$

for all pairwise comparisons, the family of confidence intervals based on (17.31) may be utilized for this purpose. We simply determine for each interval whether or not zero is contained in the interval. If zero is contained, conclusion H_0 is reached; otherwise, H_a is concluded. By following this procedure, the family level of significance will not exceed α.

Equivalently, the pairwise tests can be conducted directly by calculating for each pairwise comparison the test statistic:

(17.33)
$$q^* = \frac{\sqrt{2}\hat{D}}{s\{\hat{D}\}}$$

where $\hat{D}$ and $s^2\{\hat{D}\}$ are given in (17.31). Conclusion H_0 in (17.32) is reached if $|q^*| \leq q(1 - \alpha; r; n_T - r)$; otherwise, H_a is concluded.

A *paired comparison plot* provides still another means of conducting all pairwise tests with the Tukey procedure when all sample sizes are equal, i.e., when $n_i \equiv n$. This plot provides a graphic means of making all pairwise comparisons. Around each estimated treatment mean $\bar{Y}_{i\cdot}$ is plotted an interval whose limits are:

(17.34)
$$\bar{Y}_{i\cdot} \pm \frac{1}{2}Ts\{\hat{D}\}$$

Figure 17.4 provides an illustration of a paired comparison plot for the rust inhibitor example, which we shall discuss shortly. When the intervals overlap on this plot, the formal test leads to the conclusion that the treatment means do not differ. When the intervals do not overlap, the formal test leads to the conclusion that the two treatment means differ. In addition, the paired comparison plot shows the direction of the difference. For instance, there is no overlap in Figure 17.4 between the intervals for rust inhibitors B and C, indicating that the mean performances differ for these two rust inhibitors. Figure 17.4 in addition shows that rust inhibitor B is superior to C since its interval is higher than that for C, thus providing directional information about the difference in mean performance for the two rust inhibitors.

Example 1—Equal Sample Sizes

In the rust inhibitor example in Table 17.2, it was desired to estimate all pairwise comparisons by means of the Tukey procedure, using a family confidence coefficient of 95 percent. Since $r = 4$ and $n_T - r = 36$, we find the required percentile of the studentized range distribution from Table B.9 to be $q(.95; 4, 36) = 3.814$. Hence, by (17.31c), we obtain:

$$T = \frac{1}{\sqrt{2}}(3.814) = 2.70$$

FIGURE 17.4   Paired Comparison Plot—Rust Inhibitor Example.

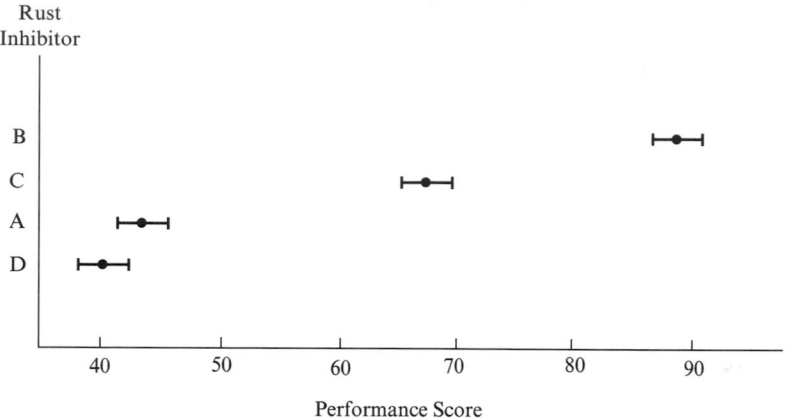

Further, we need $s\{\hat{D}\}$. Using (17.31b), we find for any pairwise comparison since equal sample sizes were employed:

$$s^2\{\hat{D}\} = MSE\left(\frac{1}{n_i} + \frac{1}{n_{i'}}\right) = 6.140\left(\frac{1}{10} + \frac{1}{10}\right) = 1.23$$

so that $s\{\hat{D}\} = 1.11$. Hence, we obtain for each pairwise comparison:

$$Ts\{\hat{D}\} = 2.70(1.11) = 3.0$$

To illustrate the calculation of the pairwise confidence limits, consider the estimation of the difference between the treatment means for rust inhibitors A and B, $\mu_2 - \mu_1$:

$$\hat{D} = \bar{Y}_{2.} - \bar{Y}_{1.} = 89.44 - 43.14 = 46.3$$

The confidence limits from (17.31) therefore are 46.3 ± 3.0 and the confidence interval is:

$$43.3 \leq \mu_2 - \mu_1 \leq 49.3$$

The complete family of pairwise confidence intervals is listed in the left column of Table 17.4. The pairwise comparisons indicate that all but one of the differences (D and A) are statistically significant (confidence interval does not cover zero).

We incorporate this information in a line plot of the estimated factor level means by underlining nonsignificant comparisons.

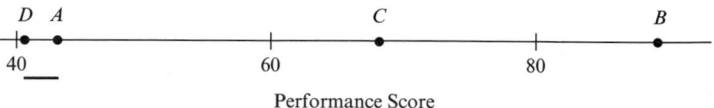

TABLE 17.4   **Simultaneous Confidence Intervals and Tests for Pairwise Differences Using the Tukey Procedure—Rust Inhibitor Example.**

Confidence Interval	H_0	Test H_a	q^*
$43.3 \leq \mu_2 - \mu_1 \leq 49.3$	$\mu_2 = \mu_1$	$\mu_2 \neq \mu_1$	58.99
$21.8 \leq \mu_3 - \mu_1 \leq 27.8$	$\mu_3 = \mu_1$	$\mu_3 \neq \mu_1$	31.61
$-.3 \leq \mu_1 - \mu_4 \leq 5.7$	$\mu_1 = \mu_4$	$\mu_1 \neq \mu_4$	3.40
$18.5 \leq \mu_2 - \mu_3 \leq 24.5$	$\mu_2 = \mu_3$	$\mu_2 \neq \mu_3$	27.37
$46.0 \leq \mu_2 - \mu_4 \leq 52.0$	$\mu_2 = \mu_4$	$\mu_2 \neq \mu_4$	62.39
$24.5 \leq \mu_3 - \mu_4 \leq 30.5$	$\mu_3 = \mu_4$	$\mu_3 \neq \mu_4$	35.01

The line between D and A indicates that there is no clear evidence whether D or A is the better rust inhibitor. The absence of a line signifies that a difference in performance has been found and the location of the points indicates the direction of the difference. Thus, the multiple comparison procedure permits us to infer with a 95 percent family confidence coefficient for the chain of conclusions that B is the best inhibitor (better by somewhere between 18.5 and 24.5 units than the second best), C is second best, and A and D follow substantially behind with little or no difference between them. Thus, the effects suggested by the normal probability plot in Figure 17.3b are confirmed by this analysis.

The same conclusions are obtained if we carry out all pairwise tests using the simultaneous testing procedure based on test statistic (17.33). For example, to test:

$$H_0: \mu_2 - \mu_1 = 0$$

$$H_a: \mu_2 - \mu_1 \neq 0$$

we require the test statistic:

$$q^* = \frac{\sqrt{2}(89.44 - 43.14)}{1.11} = 58.99$$

Because $|q^*| = 58.99 > q(.95, 4, 36) = 3.814$, we conclude H_a, that the two treatment means differ. The test statistics q^* for the family of all pairwise tests are listed in the right column of Table 17.4. The absolute values of all test statistics exceed 3.814 except for one, so that all differences are found to be statistically significant except for that involving μ_1 and μ_4 (A and D). For this case, $|q^*| = 3.40$ does not exceed the critical value 3.814.

Figure 17.4 presents a paired comparison plot for the rust inhibitor example. Here are plotted the estimated treatment means $\bar{Y}_{i \cdot}$ with the comparison intervals based on (17.34). For example, for rust inhibitor A, we have from earlier:

$$\bar{Y}_{1 \cdot} = 43.14 \qquad T = 2.70 \qquad s\{\hat{D}\} = 1.11$$

so that the comparison limits in (17.34) are:

$$43.14 \pm \frac{1}{2}(2.70)(1.11) \qquad \text{or} \qquad 41.64 \text{ and } 44.64$$

We readily see that only the intervals for A and D overlap, that rust inhibitor B is clearly best, that rust inhibitor C is second best, and that rust inhibitors A and D are the least effective.

Example 2—Unequal Sample Sizes

In the Kenton Food Company example in Table 17.1, the sales manager was interested in the comparative performance of the four package designs. The analyst developed all pairwise comparisons by means of the Tukey procedure with a family confidence coefficient of at least 90 percent. Since the sample sizes are not equal here, the estimated standard deviation $s\{\hat{D}\}$ must be recalculated for each pairwise comparison. To compare designs 1 and 2, for instance, we obtain:

$$\hat{D} = \bar{Y}_{1.} - \bar{Y}_{2.} = 14.6 - 13.4 = 1.2$$

$$s^2\{\hat{D}\} = MSE\left(\frac{1}{n_1} + \frac{1}{n_2}\right) = 10.55\left(\frac{1}{5} + \frac{1}{5}\right) = 4.22$$

$$s\{\hat{D}\} = 2.05$$

For a 90 percent family confidence coefficient, we require $q(.90; 4, 15) = 3.54$ so that we obtain:

$$T = \frac{1}{\sqrt{2}}(3.54) = 2.50$$

Hence, the confidence limits are $1.2 \pm 2.50(2.05)$ and the confidence interval for $\mu_1 - \mu_2$ is:

$$-3.9 \leq \mu_1 - \mu_2 \leq 6.3$$

In the same way, we obtain the other five confidence intervals:

$$-.6 = (19.5 - 14.6) - 2.50(2.18) \leq \mu_3 - \mu_1 \leq (19.5 - 14.6) + 2.50(2.18) = 10.4$$

$$7.5 = (27.2 - 14.6) - 2.50(2.05) \leq \mu_4 - \mu_1 \leq (27.2 - 14.6) + 2.50(2.05) = 17.7$$

$$.7 = (19.5 - 13.4) - 2.50(2.18) \leq \mu_3 - \mu_2 \leq (19.5 - 13.4) + 2.50(2.18) = 11.6$$

$$8.7 = (27.2 - 13.4) - 2.50(2.05) \leq \mu_4 - \mu_2 \leq (27.2 - 13.4) + 2.50(2.05) = 18.9$$

$$2.3 = (27.2 - 19.5) - 2.50(2.18) \leq \mu_4 - \mu_3 \leq (27.2 - 19.5) + 2.50(2.18) = 13.2$$

We summarize the comparative performance by a line plot, indicating each nonsignificant difference by a rule.

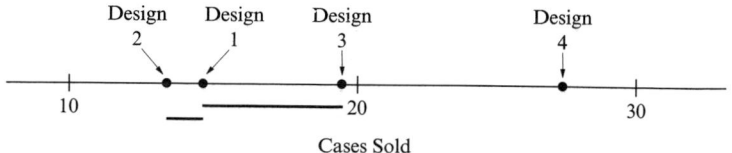

We can conclude with at least 90 percent family confidence that design 4 is clearly the most effective design. However, the small-scale study does not permit a complete ordering among the other three designs. Design 3 is more effective than design 2 but may not be more effective than design 1, which in turn may not be more effective than design 2.

Often, the results of the family of pairwise tests are summarized by setting up groups of factor levels whose means do not differ according to the single degree of freedom tests. For the Kenton Food Company example, there are three such groups:

Group 1		Group 2		Group 3	
Design 4	$\bar{Y}_{4.} = 27.2$	Design 3	$\bar{Y}_{3.} = 19.5$	Design 1	$\bar{Y}_{1.} = 14.6$
		Design 1	$\bar{Y}_{1.} = 14.6$	Design 2	$\bar{Y}_{2.} = 13.4$

Comments

1. When the Tukey procedure is used with unequal sample sizes, it is sometimes called the *Tukey-Kramer procedure*.

2. When not all pairwise comparisons are of interest, the confidence coefficient for the family of comparisons under consideration will be greater than the specification $1 - \alpha$ used in setting up the Tukey intervals. Similarly, the family significance level for simultaneous testing will be less than α.

3. The Tukey procedure can be used for data snooping as long as the effects to be studied on the basis of preliminary data analysis are pairwise comparisons.

4. The Tukey procedure can be modified to handle general contrasts of factor level means. We do not discuss this modification since the Scheffé method (to be discussed next) is to be preferred for this situation.

5. To derive the Tukey simultaneous confidence intervals for the case when all sample sizes are equal, i.e., when $n_i \equiv n$ so that $n_T = rn$, consider the deviations:

$$(17.35) \qquad (\bar{Y}_{1.} - \mu_1), \ldots, (\bar{Y}_{r.} - \mu_r)$$

and assume that ANOVA model (17.1) applies. The deviations in (17.35) are then independent variables (because the error terms are independent), they are normally distributed (because the error terms are independent normal variables), they have the same expectation zero (because μ_i is subtracted from $\bar{Y}_{i.}$), and they have the same variance σ^2/n. Further, MSE/n is an estimator of σ^2/n that is independent of the deviations $(\bar{Y}_{i.} - \mu_i)$ per theorem (17.7). Thus, it follows from the definition of the studentized range q in (17.30) that:

$$(17.36) \qquad \frac{\max(\bar{Y}_{i.} - \mu_i) - \min(\bar{Y}_{i.} - \mu_i)}{\sqrt{\dfrac{MSE}{n}}} \sim q(r, n_T - r)$$

where $n_T - r$ is the number of degrees of freedom associated with MSE, $\max(\bar{Y}_{i.} - \mu_i)$ is the largest deviation, and $\min(\bar{Y}_{i.} - \mu_i)$ is the smallest deviation.

In view of (17.36), we can write the following probability statement:

$$(17.37) \qquad P\left\{ \frac{\max(\bar{Y}_{i.} - \mu_i) - \min(\bar{Y}_{i.} - \mu_i)}{\sqrt{\dfrac{MSE}{n}}} \leq q(1 - \alpha; r, n_T - r) \right\} = 1 - \alpha$$

Note now that the following inequality holds for *all* pairs of factor levels i and i':

(17.38) $$|(\bar{Y}_{i\cdot} - \mu_i) - (\bar{Y}_{i'\cdot} - \mu_{i'})| \leq \max(\bar{Y}_{i\cdot} - \mu_i) - \min(\bar{Y}_{i\cdot} - \mu_i)$$

The absolute value at the left is needed since the factor levels i and i' are not ordered so that we may be subtracting the larger deviation from the smaller. To put this another way, we are merely concerned here with the difference between the two factor level deviations regardless of direction.

Since inequality (17.38) holds for all pairs of factor levels i and i', it follows from (17.37) that the probability:

(17.39) $$P\left\{\left|\frac{(\bar{Y}_{i\cdot} - \mu_i) - (\bar{Y}_{i'\cdot} - \mu_{i'})}{\sqrt{\dfrac{MSE}{n}}}\right| \leq q(1-\alpha; r, n_T - r)\right\} = 1 - \alpha$$

holds for all $r(r-1)/2$ pairwise comparisons among the r factor levels. By rearranging the inequality in (17.39), using the definitions of $s^2\{\hat{D}\}$ in (17.31b) and of T in (17.31c), and noting that for the equal sample size case $s^2\{\hat{D}\}$ becomes:

$$s^2\{\hat{D}\} = MSE\left(\frac{1}{n} + \frac{1}{n}\right) = \frac{2MSE}{n} \qquad \text{when } n_i \equiv n$$

we obtain the Tukey multiple comparison confidence limits in (17.31).

6. When the Tukey multiple comparison procedure is used for testing pairwise differences as in (17.32), the tests are sometimes called *honestly significant difference tests*.

7. The pairwise comparison plot can be used as an approximate plot when the sample sizes are not equal, provided that the sample sizes do not differ greatly. For this case, the comparison limits should be obtained as follows:

(17.40) $$\bar{Y}_{i\cdot} \pm \frac{1}{2}q(1-\alpha; r, n_T - r)s\{\bar{Y}_{i\cdot}\}$$

The limits in (17.40) are identical to those in (17.34) when the sample sizes are equal. ∎

17.6 Scheffé Multiple Comparison Procedure

The Scheffé multiple comparison procedure was encountered previously for regression models. It is also applicable for analysis of variance models. It applies for analysis of variance models when:

The family of interest is the set of all possible contrasts among the factor level means:

(17.41) $$L = \sum c_i \mu_i \qquad \text{where} \qquad \sum c_i = 0$$

In other words, the family consists of estimates of all possible contrasts L or of tests concerning all possible contrasts of the form:

$$H_0: \ L = 0$$

$$H_a: \ L \neq 0$$

Thus, infinitely many statements belong to this family. The family confidence level for the Scheffé procedure is exactly $1 - \alpha$, and the family significance level is exactly α, whether the factor level sample sizes are equal or unequal.

Simultaneous Estimation

We noted earlier that an unbiased estimator of L is:

$$(17.42) \qquad \hat{L} = \sum c_i \bar{Y}_i.$$

for which the estimated variance is:

$$(17.43) \qquad s^2\{\hat{L}\} = MSE \sum \frac{c_i^2}{n_i}$$

The Scheffé confidence intervals for the family of contrasts L are of the form:

$$(17.44) \qquad \hat{L} \pm Ss\{\hat{L}\}$$

where:

$$(17.44a) \qquad S^2 = (r - 1)F(1 - \alpha; r - 1, n_T - r)$$

and $\hat{L}$ and $s\{\hat{L}\}$ are given by (17.42) and (17.43), respectively. If we were to calculate the confidence intervals in (17.44) for all conceivable contrasts, then in $(1 - \alpha)100$ percent of repetitions of the experiment, the entire set of confidence intervals in the family would be correct.

Note that the simultaneous confidence limits in (17.44) differ from those for a single confidence limit in (17.25) only with respect to the multiple of the estimated standard deviation.

Simultaneous Testing

Tests involving contrasts of the form:

$$(17.45) \qquad \begin{array}{l} H_0: \ L = 0 \\ H_a: \ L \neq 0 \end{array}$$

can be carried out by examination of the corresponding Scheffé confidence intervals based on (17.44). H_0 is concluded at the α family level of significance if the confidence interval includes zero; otherwise H_a is concluded. An equivalent direct testing procedure for the alternatives in (17.45) uses the test statistic:

$$(17.46) \qquad\qquad F^* = \frac{\hat{L}^2}{(r-1)s^2\{\hat{L}\}}$$

Conclusion H_0 in (17.45) is reached at the α family significance level if $F^* \leq F(1 - \alpha; r - 1, n_T - r)$; otherwise, H_a is concluded.

Example

In the Kenton Food Company example, interest centered on estimating the following four contrasts with family confidence coefficient .90:

Comparison of 3-color and 5-color designs:

$$L_1 = \frac{\mu_1 + \mu_2}{2} - \frac{\mu_3 + \mu_4}{2}$$

Comparison of designs with and without cartoons:

$$L_2 = \frac{\mu_1 + \mu_3}{2} - \frac{\mu_2 + \mu_4}{2}$$

Comparison of the two 3-color designs:

$$L_3 = \mu_1 - \mu_2$$

Comparison of the two 5-color designs:

$$L_4 = \mu_3 - \mu_4$$

Consider first the estimation of L_1. Earlier, we found:

$$\hat{L}_1 = -9.35$$

$$s\{\hat{L}_1\} = 1.50$$

Since $r - 1 = 3$ and $n_T - r = 15$ (Table 17.1), we have:

$$S^2 = (r-1)F(1 - \alpha; r - 1, n_T - r) = 3F(.90; 3, 15) = 3(2.49) = 7.47$$

so that $S = 2.73$. Hence, the 90 percent confidence limits for L_1 by the Scheffé multiple comparison procedure are $-9.35 \pm 2.73(1.50)$ and the desired confidence interval is:

$$-13.4 \leq L_1 \leq -5.3$$

In similar fashion, we obtain the other desired confidence intervals, and the entire set is:

$$-13.4 \leq L_1 \leq -5.3$$

$$-7.3 \leq L_2 \leq .8$$

$$-4.4 \leq L_3 \leq 6.8$$

$$-13.7 \leq L_4 \leq -1.7$$

Note that the confidence interval for L_1 does not include zero. Hence, if we wished to test $H_0: L_1 = 0$ versus $H_a: L_1 \neq 0$, we would conclude H_a, that the mean sales for 3-color and 5-color designs differ. The confidence interval provides additional information, however; namely, that mean sales for 5-color designs exceed mean sales for 3-color designs, by somewhere between 5.3 and 13.4 cases per store.

Any chain of conclusions derived from the set of confidence intervals has associated with it family confidence coefficient .90. The principal conclusions drawn by the sales manager were as follows: 5-color designs lead to higher mean sales than 3-color designs, the increase being somewhere between 5 and 13 cases per store. No overall effect of cartoons in the package design is indicated, although the use of a cartoon in 5-color designs leads to lower mean sales than when no cartoon is used.

Comments

1. If in the Kenton Food Company example we had wished to estimate a single contrast with statement confidence coefficient .90, the required t value would have been $t(.95; 15) = 1.753$. This t value is smaller than the Scheffé multiple $S = 2.73$, so that the single confidence interval would be somewhat narrower. The increased width of the interval with the Scheffé procedure is the price paid for a known confidence coefficient for a family of statements and a chain of conclusions drawn from them, and for the possibility of making comparisons not specified in advance of the data analysis.

2. Since applications of the Scheffé procedure never involve all conceivable contrasts, the confidence coefficient for the finite family of statements actually considered will be greater than $1 - \alpha$ so that $1 - \alpha$ serves as a guaranteed lower bound. Similarly, the significance level for the finite family of tests considered will be less than α. For this reason, it has been suggested that lower confidence levels and higher significance levels be used with the Scheffé procedure than would ordinarily be employed. Confidence coefficients of 90 percent and 95 percent and significance levels of $\alpha = .10$ and $\alpha = .05$ with the Scheffé procedure are frequently mentioned.

3. The Scheffé procedure can be used for a wide variety of data snooping since the family of statements contains all possible contrasts. ■

Comparison of Scheffé and Tukey Procedures

1. If only pairwise comparisons are to be made, the Tukey procedure gives narrower confidence limits and is therefore the preferred method.

2. In the case of general contrasts, the Scheffé procedure tends to give narrower confidence limits and is therefore the preferred method.

3. The Scheffé procedure has the property that if the F test of factor level equality indicates that the factor level means μ_i are not equal, the corresponding Scheffé multiple comparison procedure will find at least one contrast (out of all possible contrasts) that differs

significantly from zero (the confidence interval does not cover zero). It may be, though, that this contrast is not one of those that has been estimated.

17.7 Bonferroni Multiple Comparison Procedure

The Bonferroni multiple comparison procedure was encountered earlier for regression models. It is also applicable for analysis of variance models when:

> The family of interest is a particular set of pairwise comparisons, contrasts, or linear combinations that is specified by the user in advance of the data analysis.

The Bonferroni procedure is applicable whether the factor level sample sizes are equal or unequal and whether inferences center on pairwise comparisons, contrasts, linear combinations, or a mixture of these.

Simultaneous Estimation

We shall denote the number of statements in the family by g and treat them all as linear combinations since pairwise comparisons and contrasts are special cases of linear combinations. The Bonferroni inequality (4.4) then implies that the confidence coefficient is at least $1 - \alpha$ that the following confidence limits for the g linear combinations L are all correct:

(17.47)
$$\hat{L} \pm Bs\{\hat{L}\}$$

where:

(17.47a)
$$B = t(1 - \alpha/2g; n_T - r)$$

Simultaneous Testing

When we wish to conduct a series of tests of the form:

$$H_0:\ L = 0$$
$$H_a:\ L \neq 0$$

we can use either the confidence intervals based on (17.47) or the test statistics:

(17.48)
$$t^* = \frac{\hat{L}}{s\{\hat{L}\}}$$

If $|t^*| \leq t(1 - \alpha/2g; n_T - r)$, we conclude H_0; otherwise, H_a is concluded.

Example

The sales manager of the Kenton Food Company is interested in estimating the following two contrasts with family confidence coefficient .975:

Comparison of 3-color and 5-color designs:

$$L_1 = \frac{\mu_1 + \mu_2}{2} - \frac{\mu_3 + \mu_4}{2}$$

Comparison of designs with and without cartoons:

$$L_2 = \frac{\mu_1 + \mu_3}{2} - \frac{\mu_2 + \mu_4}{2}$$

Earlier we found:

$$\hat{L}_1 = -9.35 \qquad s\{\hat{L}_1\} = 1.50$$

$$\hat{L}_2 = -3.25 \qquad s\{\hat{L}_2\} = 1.50$$

For a 97.5 percent family confidence coefficient with the Bonferroni method, we require:

$$B = t[1 - .025/2(2); 15] = t(.99375; 15) = 2.84$$

We can now complete the confidence intervals for the two contrasts. For L_1, we have confidence limits $-9.35 \pm 2.84(1.50)$, which lead to the confidence interval:

$$-13.6 \le L_1 \le -5.1$$

Similarly, we obtain the other confidence interval:

$$-7.5 \le L_2 \le 1.0$$

These confidence intervals have a guaranteed family confidence coefficient of 97.5 percent, which means that in at least 97.5 percent of repetitions of the experiment, both intervals will be correct.

Again, we would conclude from this family of estimates that mean sales for 5-color designs are higher than those for 3-color designs (by somewhere between 5 and 14 cases per store), and that no overall effect of cartoons in the package design is indicated.

The Scheffé multiple for a 97.5 percent family confidence coefficient in this case would have been:

$$S^2 = 3F(.975; 3, 15) = 3(4.15) = 12.45$$

or $S = 3.53$, as compared to the Bonferroni multiple $B = 2.84$. Thus, the Scheffé procedure here would have led to wider confidence intervals than the Bonferroni procedure.

Note

It is not necessary that all comparisons be estimated with statement confidence coefficients $1 - \alpha/g$ for the Bonferroni family confidence coefficient to be $1 - \alpha$. Different statement confidence coefficients may be used, depending upon the importance of each statement, provided that $\alpha_1 + \alpha_2 + \cdots + \alpha_g = \alpha$. ∎

Comparison of Bonferroni Procedure with Scheffé and Tukey Procedures

1. If all pairwise comparisons are of interest, the Tukey procedure is superior to the Bonferroni procedure, leading to narrower confidence intervals. If not all pairwise comparisons are to be considered, the Bonferroni procedure may be the better one at times.

2. The Bonferroni procedure will be better than the Scheffé procedure when the number of contrasts of interest is about the same as the number of factor levels, or less. Indeed, the number of contrasts of interest must exceed the number of factor levels by a considerable amount before the Scheffé procedure becomes better.

3. In any given problem, one may compute the Bonferroni multiple as well as the Scheffé multiple and, when appropriate, the Tukey multiple, and select the one that is smallest. This choice is proper since it does not depend on the observed data.

4. The Bonferroni multiple comparison procedure does not lend itself to data snooping unless one can specify in advance the family of inferences in which one may be interested and provided this family is not large. On the other hand, the Tukey and Scheffé procedures involve families of inferences that lend themselves naturally to data snooping.

Analysis of Means

One use of the Bonferroni simultaneous testing procedure is in the analysis of means (ANOM), introduced by Ott (Ref. 17.2). ANOM is an alternative to the standard F test for the equality of treatment means. It is conducted by testing $H_0: \tau_1 = 0$ versus $H_a: \tau_1 \neq 0$, $H_0: \tau_2 = 0$ versus $H_a: \tau_2 \neq 0$, and so on for all treatment effects τ_i. The statistics employed are the r estimated treatment effects:

$$(17.49) \qquad \hat{L}_i = \bar{Y}_{i.} - \hat{\mu}. \qquad i = 1, \ldots, r$$

where $\hat{\mu}.$ is the estimator of the unweighted overall average $\mu.$ defined in (16.63):

$$(17.49a) \qquad \hat{\mu}. = \frac{\Sigma \bar{Y}_{i.}}{r}$$

The estimated variance of $\hat{L}_i$ is obtained by (17.23) since $\hat{L}_i$ is a contrast of the estimated treatment means $\bar{Y}_{i.}$:

$$(17.50) \qquad s^2\{\hat{L}_i\} = \frac{MSE}{n_i}\left(\frac{r-1}{r}\right)^2 + \frac{MSE}{r^2} \sum_{h \neq i} \frac{1}{n_h}$$

Simultaneous testing by the Bonferroni procedure can be carried out by setting up for each treatment effect the confidence interval using (17.47) and noting whether or not the interval contains zero. If any confidence interval does not include zero, the conclusion is drawn that the treatment means are not all the same.

An advantage of the analysis of means is that, when the treatment means are not equal, this analysis also provides information about which treatments have the strongest effects. Various enhancements for the analysis of means have been provided, including those in References 17.3 and 17.4.

17.8   Holm Simultaneous Testing Procedure

The Holm simultaneous testing procedure (Ref. 17.5), is a refinement of the Bonferroni simultaneous testing procedure for conducting a family of tests. It is applicable under the same conditions as the Bonferroni procedure, namely, when:

> The family of interest is a particular set of pairwise comparisons, contrasts, or linear combinations that is specified by the user in advance of the data analysis.

The Holm procedure is applicable whether the factor level sample sizes are equal or unequal and whether inferences center on pairwise comparisons, contrasts, linear combinations, or a mixture of these. We shall consider a series of g tests of the form:

$$H_0: \ L = 0$$

$$H_a: \ L \neq 0$$

The standard Bonferroni procedure could be conducted here by comparing the value of each test statistic t^* in (17.48) with $t(1 - \alpha/2g; n_T - r)$. Equivalently, this procedure could be carried out by obtaining the two-sided P-value of each test statistic and comparing it with α/g. If the P-value equals or exceeds α/g, H_0 is concluded. If the P-value is less than α/g, H_a is concluded.

The Holm procedure is a refinement of this standard Bonferroni procedure. It carries out the simultaneous testing by obtaining the P-value for each test but then modifies the level against which the P-value is compared in order to improve the power of the test. Consequently, the Holm procedure may find significant effects when the Bonferroni procedure does not, for the same guaranteed α family significance level. The Holm procedure is slightly more complex computationally, because the two-sided P-value must be found for each test.

With the Holm procedure, the two-sided P-values for the set of tests are ranked, with rank 1 assigned to the smallest P-value. The P-value with rank 1 is then compared with α/g to determine whether H_0 or H_a is to be concluded, just as with the Bonferroni procedure. If H_0 is concluded, the testing is terminated and H_0 is concluded for all other tests, just as with the Bonferroni procedure. If H_a is concluded for the test with the smallest P-value, the Holm procedure considers next the test with the second-smallest P-value. This P-value is compared with $\alpha/(g - 1)$. If H_0 is concluded, testing is terminated and H_0 is concluded for all remaining tests. If H_a is concluded, the third-smallest P-value is compared with $\alpha/(g - 2)$, and so on. As soon as a test leads to conclusion H_0, testing is stopped and H_0 is concluded for all remaining tests.

To summarize, if testing has led to conclusion H_a for the test with the $k - 1$ smallest P-value, the next test is the one with the kth smallest P-value, and the test is done as follows:

$$
\text{If } P_k < \frac{\alpha}{g - k + 1}, \quad \text{conclude } H_a \text{ and proceed to testing the}
$$

(17.51)
$$
k + 1 \text{ smallest } P\text{-value}
$$

$$
\text{If } P_k \geq \frac{\alpha}{g - k + 1}, \quad \text{conclude } H_0 \text{ for this and all remaining tests}
$$

The Holm procedure, like the Bonferroni procedure, ensures that the family significance level does not exceed α. In other words, if no effects are present, the risk with the Holm procedure of concluding that one or more significant effects are present is guaranteed to be at most α. The Holm procedure will identify as significant all effects so identified by the Bonferroni procedure since the Holm criterion is never smaller than the Bonferroni criterion; i.e., $\alpha/(g - k + 1) \geq \alpha/g$. In addition, the Holm procedure may identify as significant some effects that are not so identified by the Bonferroni procedure. Thus, the Holm procedure is more powerful than the Bonferroni procedure.

A disadvantage of the Holm procedure is that, unlike for the Bonferroni procedure, the Holm tests do not have a corresponding set of confidence intervals to provide information about the directions and magnitudes of the effects. If the Holm procedure is carried out at family significance level α, one could set up the corresponding $1 - \alpha$ Bonferroni confidence intervals. However, these confidence intervals may show as nonsignificant some effects that the Holm procedure had identified as significant. One approach that may be taken is to construct Bonferroni confidence intervals for those effects found significant by the Holm procedure with a lower family confidence coefficient, based on the α level for the last Holm criterion before testing stopped. We illustrate this approach in the following example.

Example

In the Kenton Food Company example, the analyst wished to test whether the number of colors in the design has an effect and whether a cartoon in the design has an effect. Six tests were specified in advance of the data analysis and are to be conducted using the Holm procedure with family significance level $\alpha = .05$. The tests of interest are as follows:

Test 1: H_0: $L_1 = \dfrac{\mu_1 + \mu_2}{2} - \dfrac{\mu_3 + \mu_4}{2} = 0$

H_a: $L_1 = \dfrac{\mu_1 + \mu_2}{2} - \dfrac{\mu_3 + \mu_4}{2} \neq 0$

Test 2: H_0: $L_2 = \dfrac{\mu_1 + \mu_3}{2} - \dfrac{\mu_2 + \mu_4}{2} = 0$

H_a: $L_2 = \dfrac{\mu_1 + \mu_3}{2} - \dfrac{\mu_2 + \mu_4}{2} \neq 0$

Test 3: H_0: $L_3 = \mu_1 - \mu_2 = 0$

H_a: $L_3 = \mu_1 - \mu_2 \neq 0$

Test 4: H_0: $L_4 = \mu_1 - \mu_3 = 0$

H_a: $L_4 = \mu_1 - \mu_3 \neq 0$

Test 5: H_0: $L_5 = \mu_2 - \mu_4 = 0$

H_a: $L_5 = \mu_2 - \mu_4 \neq 0$

Test 6: H_0: $L_6 = \mu_3 - \mu_4 = 0$

H_a: $L_6 = \mu_3 - \mu_4 \neq 0$

Table 17.5a contains the basic test results. To illustrate the calculations, the overall comparison of 3-color and 5-color designs in test 1 involves the estimated contrast $\hat{L}_1 = -9.35$ and the estimated standard deviation $s\{\hat{L}_1\} = 1.50$, results which we had obtained earlier. The t^* test statistic therefore is $t_1^* = -9.35/1.50 = -6.23$. The two-sided P-value for this test statistic is:

$$2P\{t(15) < -6.23\} = 2(.000008) = .000016$$

These results for test 1 are shown in Table 17.5a, columns 1–4, together with the results for the other five tests. The P-values are ranked in ascending order in column 5.

Table 17.5b presents the P-values for the six tests in ascending order in column 3. The smallest P-value, for test 5, is compared with $\alpha/(g - 1 + 1) = .05/(6 - 1 + 1) = .0083$, shown in column 4. Since $.000007 < .0083$, we conclude H_a, indicating a significant effect for test 5. Similarly, the second smallest P-value ($.000016$) is smaller than the critical value $.05/(6 - 2 + 1) = .010$, indicating a significant effect for test 1. A significant effect is also found for test 6, which has the third smallest P-value. When we come to consider

TABLE 17.5 Holm Testing Procedure ($\alpha = .05$, $g = 6$)—Kenton Food Company Example.

(a) Test Results

Test i	(1) $\hat{L}_i$	(2) $s\{\hat{L}_i\}$	(3) t_i^*	(4) Two-Sided P-value	(5) Rank k
1	−9.35	1.50	−6.23	.000016	2
2	−3.25	1.50	−2.17	.0465	5
3	1.20	2.05	.585	.567	6
4	−4.90	2.18	−2.25	.0399	4
5	−13.8	2.05	−6.73	.000007	1
6	−7.70	2.18	−3.53	.00303	3

(b) Holm Testing

(1) Rank k	(2) Test i	(3) P_k	(4) $\dfrac{\alpha}{g-k+1}$	(5) Conclusion
1	5	.000007	.0083	H_a
2	1	.000016	.010	H_a
3	6	.00303	.0125	H_a
4	4	.0399	.0167	H_0
5	2	.0465		H_0
6	3	.567		H_0

$P_4 = .0399$, we find that it exceeds its critical value of .0167. Hence we conclude H_0 for this and all subsequent tests, indicating no significant effects. Based on the Holm procedure, we conclude therefore that color of the design affects mean sales overall (test 1), that the color effect is significant when no cartoons are present in the design (test 5) but not when cartoons are present (test 4), and that a cartoon in the design has a significant effect with the 5-color design (test 6) but not for both colors overall (test 2).

To examine the directions and magnitudes of the significant effects, we shall construct Bonferroni confidence intervals. The family confidence coefficient will be based on the α criterion for the last significant test. This α level was .0125, as may be seen from Table 17.5b, columns 4 and 5. Since this level corresponds to the α level for a single statement, the family confidence level for $g = 6$ statements in the family is $1 - 6(.0125) = .925$. The required Bonferroni multiple in (17.47a) therefore is $B = t(.99375; 15) = 2.84$. Using the results in Table 17.5a, columns 1 and 2, for $\hat{L}_i$ and $s\{\hat{L}_i\}$, we obtain the Bonferroni confidence intervals for the significant effects:

$$-13.6 \le L_1 \le -5.1$$

$$-19.6 \le L_5 \le -8.0$$

$$-13.9 \le L_6 \le -1.5$$

We now see the directions of the effects and can note that the magnitudes of some of the effects are substantial. For instance, 3-color designs overall lead to higher mean sales than 5-color designs by somewhere between 5 and 14 cases per store.

Comments

1. Both the Holm and Bonferroni procedures can be used for tests other than single degree of freedom tests.

2. The Holm procedure assumes that no test in the family is equivalent to two or more other tests in the family.

3. Various enhancements have been made to the Holm procedure that generally provide an increase in power at the cost of increased complexity or decreased generality; see, for example, References 17.6, 17.7, and 17.8.

4. There are still other methods of making multiple comparisons. Many of these are designed for special cases, such as for comparing experimental treatments with a control treatment. Good reference books on multiple comparisons are those by Miller (Ref. 17.9) and Hochberg and Tamhane (Ref. 17.10). ∎

17.9   Analysis of Factor Effects when Factor Quantitative

When the factor under investigation is quantitative, the analysis of factor effects can be carried beyond the point of multiple comparisons to include a study of the nature of the response function. Consider an experimental study undertaken to investigate the effect on sales of the price of a product. Five different price levels are investigated (78 cents, 79 cents, 85 cents, 88 cents, and 89 cents), and the experimental unit is a store. After a preliminary test whether mean sales differ for the five price levels studied, the analyst might use multiple comparisons to examine whether "odd pricing" at 79 cents actually leads to higher sales than "even pricing" at 78 cents, as well as other questions of interest. In addition, the analyst may wish to study whether mean sales are a specified function of price, in the range of prices studied in the experiment. Further, once the relation has been established, the analyst may wish to use it for estimating sales volumes at various price levels not studied.

The methods of regression analysis discussed earlier are, of course, appropriate for the analysis of the response function. Since the single-factor studies discussed in this chapter almost always involve replications at the different factor levels, the lack of fit of a specified response function can be tested. For this purpose, the analysis of variance error sum of squares in (16.29) serves as the pure error sum of squares in (3.16), the two being identical. We illustrate this relation in the following example.

Example

In a study to reduce raw material costs in a glass working firm, an operations analyst collected the experimental data in Table 17.6 on the number of acceptable units produced from equal amounts of raw material by 28 entry-level piecework employees who had received special training as part of the experiment. Four training levels were used (6, 8, 10, and 12 hours), with seven of the employees being assigned at random to each level. The higher the number of acceptable pieces, the more efficient is the employee in utilizing the raw material.

TABLE 17.6   Data for Piecework Trainees Example.

Treatment (hours of training) i		Employee (j)						
		1	2	3	4	5	6	7
1	6 hours	40	39	39	36	42	43	41
2	8 hours	53	48	49	50	51	50	48
3	10 hours	53	58	56	59	53	59	58
4	12 hours	63	62	59	61	62	62	61

Preliminary Analysis.   The analyst first tested whether or not the mean number of acceptable pieces is the same for the four training levels. ANOVA model (17.1) was employed:

(17.52) $$Y_{ij} = \mu_i + \varepsilon_{ij}$$

The alternative conclusions and appropriate test statistic are:

$$H_0: \mu_1 = \mu_2 = \mu_3 = \mu_4$$

$$H_a: \text{ not all } \mu_i \text{ are equal}$$

$$F^* = \frac{MSTR}{MSE}$$

The SPSS^X output for single factor ANOVA is shown in Figure 17.5. Residual analysis (to be discussed in Chapter 18) showed ANOVA model (17.52) to be apt. Therefore, the analyst proceeded with the test, using $\alpha = .05$. The decision rule is:

If $F^* \leq F(.95; 3, 24) = 3.01$, conclude H_0

If $F^* > 3.01$, conclude H_a

From Figure 17.5, we have:

$$F^* = \frac{MSTR}{MSE} = \frac{602.8926}{4.2619} = 141.5$$

Since $F^* = 141.5 > 3.01$, the analyst concluded H_a, that training level effects differed and that further analysis of them is warranted. The P-value for the test statistic is 0+, as shown in Figure 17.5.

Investigation of Treatment Effects.   The analyst's interest next centered on multiple comparisons of all pairs of treatment means. A Tukey multiple comparison option in the SPSS^X computer package was used. It gave the output shown in the lower portion of Figure 17.5. This output presents the results of single degree of freedom tests conducted by means of the Tukey multiple comparison procedure for all pairwise comparisons. (The confidence intervals for the pairwise comparisons are not shown in the output.) All factor levels for which the test concludes that the pairwise means are equal are placed in the same group. This form of summary of single degree of freedom tests was illustrated earlier for

FIGURE 17.5   **SPSS^X Computer Output for Piecework Trainees Example.**

| | | n_i | $\bar{Y}_{i.}$ | |
GROUP		COUNT	MEAN	STANDARD DEVIATION
Treatment →	GRP01	7	40 0000	2 3094
	GRP02	7	49 8571	1 7728
	GRP03	7	56 5714	2 6367
	GRP04	7	61 4286	1 2724
	TOTAL	28	51 9643	8 4129

ANALYSIS OF VARIANCE

SOURCE	D F	SUM OF SQUARES	MEAN SQUARES
BETWEEN GROUPS	3	SSTR → 1808 6778	602 8926 ← MSTR
WITHIN GROUPS	24	SSE → 102 2856	4 2619 ← MSE
TOTAL	27	SSTO → 1910 9634	

F RATIO   F PROB.

141.461   0.0000

F^* *One-sided P-value*

MULTIPLE RANGE TEST

TUKEY-HSD PROCEDURE
RANGES FOR THE 0.050 LEVEL -

3.90 ← **q(.95; 4, 24)**

HOMOGENEOUS SUBSETS

SUBSET 1		SUBSET 3	
GROUP	GRP01	GROUP	GRP03
MEAN	40.0000	MEAN	56.5714
- - - - - - - - -		- - - - - - - - -	

SUBSET 2		SUBSET 4	
GROUP	GRP02	GROUP	GRP04
MEAN	49.8571	MEAN	61.4286
- - - - - - - - -		- - - - - - - - -	

the Kenton Food Company example. When a group contains only one factor level, as is the case for all groups in the output of Figure 17.5, the implication is that all single degree of freedom tests involving this factor level and each of the other factor levels lead to conclusion H_a, that the two factor level means being compared are not equal.

Two points should be noted in particular from the results in Figure 17.5: (1) All pairwise factor level differences are statistically significant. (2) There is some indication that differences between the means for adjoining factor levels diminish as the number of hours of training increases; that is, diminishing returns appear to set in as the length of training is increased.

Estimation of Response Function.   These findings were in accord with the analyst's expectations that the treatment means μ_i would most likely follow a quadratic response function with respect to training level. The scatter plot in Figure 17.6 supports this ex-

FIGURE 17.6   **Scatter Plot and Fitted Quadratic Response Function—Piecework Trainees Example.**

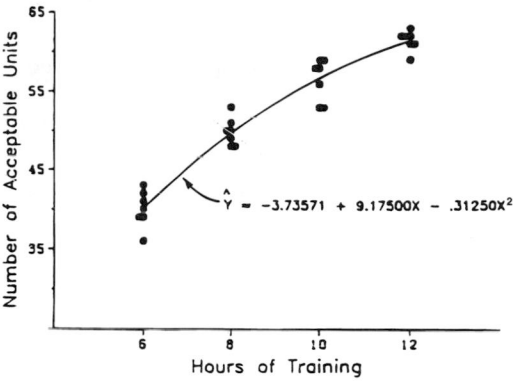

$$\hat{Y} = -3.73571 + 9.17500X - .31250X^2$$

TABLE 17.7   **Illustration of Data for Regression Analysis—Piecework Trainees Example.**

i	j	Y_{ij}	x_i	x_i^2
1	1	40	$6 - 9 = -3$	9
1	2	39	$6 - 9 = -3$	9
...	...	...	...	...
2	1	53	$8 - 9 = -1$	1
2	2	48	$8 - 9 = -1$	1
...	...	...	...	...
4	6	62	$12 - 9 = \ \ 3$	9
4	7	61	$12 - 9 = \ \ 3$	9

pectation. The analyst now wished to investigate this point further by fitting a quadratic regression model. The model to be fitted and tested is:

$$(17.53) \qquad Y_{ij} = \beta_0 + \beta_1 x_i + \beta_{11} x_i^2 + \varepsilon_{ij}$$

where Y_{ij} and ε_{ij} are defined as earlier, the βs are regression parameters, and x_i denotes the number of hours of training in the ith training level (X_i) centered around $\bar{X} = 9$, i.e., $x_i = X_i - 9$.

A portion of the data for the regression analysis is given in Table 17.7. Regressing Y on x and x^2 yielded the estimated regression function:

$$(17.54) \qquad \hat{Y} = 53.52679 + 3.55000x - .31250x^2$$

The analysis of variance for regression model (17.53) is shown in Table 17.8a. For completeness, we repeat in Table 17.8b the analysis of variance for ANOVA model (17.52).

Since the data contain replicates, the analyst could test regression model (17.53) for lack of fit, utilizing the fact that the ANOVA error sum of squares in (16.29) is identical to

---

TABLE 17.8   **Analyses of Variance for Piecework Trainees Example.**

(a) Regression Model (17.53)

Source of Variation	SS	df	MS
Regression	1,808.100	2	904.05
Error	102.864	25	4.11
Total	1,910.964	27	

(b) Analysis of Variance Model (17.52)

Source of Variation	SS	df	MS
Treatments	1,808.678	3	602.89
Error	102.286	24	4.26
Total	1,910.964	27	

(c) ANOVA for Lack of Fit Test

Source of Variation	SS	df	MS
Regression	1,808.100	2	904.05
Error	102.864	25	4.11
Lack of fit	.578	1	.58
Pure error	102.286	24	4.26
Total	1,910.964	27	

the regression pure error sum of squares in (3.16). Both measure variation around the mean of the Y observations at any given level of X (i.e., around the estimated treatment mean $\bar{Y}_{i.}$). Hence, the lack of fit sum of squares can be readily obtained from previous results:

$$(17.55) \quad SSLF = \underset{\text{(Table 17.8a)}}{SSE} - \underset{\text{(Table 17.8b)}}{SSPE} = 102.864 - 102.286 = .578$$

Since there are $c = r = 4$ levels of X here and $p = 3$ parameters in the regression model, *SSLF* has associated with it $c - p = 4 - 3 = 1$ degree of freedom. Hence, we obtain $MSLF = .578/1 = .578$. Table 17.8c contains the analysis of variance for the regression model, with the error sum of squares and degrees of freedom broken down into lack of fit and pure error components.

The alternative conclusions (6.68a) for the test of lack of fit here are:

$$H_0: \ E\{Y\} = \beta_0 + \beta_1 x + \beta_{11} x^2$$

$$H_a: \ E\{Y\} \neq \beta_0 + \beta_1 x + \beta_{11} x^2$$

and test statistic (6.68b) is:

$$F^* = \frac{MSLF}{MSPE}$$

For $\alpha = .05$, decision rule (6.68c) becomes:

If $F^* \leq F(.95; 1, 24) = 4.26$, conclude H_0

If $F^* > 4.26$, conclude H_a

We calculate the test statistic from Table 17.8c:

$$F^* = \frac{.58}{4.26} = .136$$

Since $F^* = .136 \leq 4.26$, the analyst concluded that the quadratic response function is a good fit. Consequently, the fitted regression function in (17.54) was used in further evaluation of the relation between mean number of acceptable pieces produced and level of training, after expressing the fitted response function in the original predictor variable X (number of hours of training):

$$\hat{Y} = -3.73571 + 9.17500X - .31250X^2$$

Figure 17.6 displays this fitted response function.

Cited References

17.1. Cochran, W. G., and G. M. Cox. *Experimental Designs*. 2nd ed. New York: John Wiley & Sons, 1957, p. 74.

17.2. Ott, E. R. "Analysis of Means—A Graphical Procedure," *Industrial Quality Control* 24 (1967), pp. 101–109.

17.3. Nelson, L. S. "Exact Critical Values for Use with the Analysis of Means," *Journal of Quality Technology* 15 (1983), pp. 40–44.

17.4. Nelson, P. R. "Additional Uses for the Analysis of Means and Extended Tables of Critical Values," *Technometrics* 35 (1993), pp. 61–71.

17.5. Holm, S. "A Simple Sequentially Rejective Multiple Test Procedure," *Scandinavian Journal of Statistics* 6 (1979), pp. 65–70.

17.6. Holland, B., and Copenhaven, M. D. "An Improved Sequentially Rejective Bonferroni Test Procedure," *Biometrics* 43 (1987), pp. 417–23.

17.7. Holland, B., and Copenhaven, M. D. "Improved Bonferroni-Type Multiple Testing Procedures," *Psychological Bulletin* 104 (1988), pp. 145–49.

17.8.   Shaffer, J. P. "Modified Sequentially Rejective Multiple Test Procedures," *Journal of the American Statistical Association* 81 (1986), pp. 826–31.

17.9.   Miller, R. G., Jr. *Simultaneous Statistical Inference*. New York: Springer-Verlag, 1991.

17.10. Hochberg, Y., and A. C. Tamhane. *Multiple Comparison Procedures*. New York: John Wiley & Sons, 1987.

Problems

17.1.   Refer to Figure 17.5 for the piecework trainees example. To estimate the treatment mean μ_1 by means of an interval estimate, would it be valid to use for the estimated variance of $\bar{Y}_1$.:

$$s^2\{\bar{Y}_1.\} = \frac{s_1^2}{n_1} = \frac{(2.3094)^2}{7}$$

instead of (17.5):

$$s^2\{\bar{Y}_1.\} = \frac{MSE}{n_1} = \frac{4.2619}{7}$$

What is the advantage of using (17.5)? What is a disadvantage?

17.2.   Refer to **Premium distribution** Problem 16.15. A student, asked to give a class demonstration of the use of a confidence interval for comparing two treatment means, proposed to construct a 99 percent confidence interval for the pairwise comparison $D = \mu_5 - \mu_3$. The student selected this particular comparison because the estimated treatment means $\bar{Y}_5$. and $\bar{Y}_3$. are the largest and smallest, respectively, and stated: "This confidence interval is particularly useful. If it does not straddle zero, it indicates, with significance level $\alpha = .01$, that the factor level means are not equal."

   a.   Explain why the student's assertion is not correct.

   b.   How should the confidence interval be constructed so that the assertion can be made with significance level $\alpha = .01$?

17.3.   A trainee examined a set of experimental data to find comparisons that "look promising" and calculated a family of Bonferroni confidence intervals for these comparisons with a 90 percent family confidence coefficient. Upon being informed that the Bonferroni procedure is not applicable in this case because the comparisons had been suggested by the data, the trainee stated: "This makes no difference. I would use the same formulas for the point estimates and the estimated standard errors even if the comparisons were not suggested by the data." Respond.

17.4.   Consider the following linear combinations of interest in a single-factor study involving four factor levels:

$$\text{(i)} \quad \mu_1 + 3\mu_2 - 4\mu_3$$

$$\text{(ii)} \quad .3\mu_1 + .5\mu_2 + .1\mu_3 + .1\mu_4$$

$$\text{(iii)} \quad \frac{\mu_1 + \mu_2 + \mu_3}{3} - \mu_4$$

a. Which of the linear combinations are contrasts? State the coefficients for each of the contrasts.

b. Give an unbiased estimator for each of the linear combinations. Also give the estimated variance of each estimator assuming that $n_i \equiv n$.

17.5. A single-factor ANOVA study consists of $r = 6$ treatments with sample sizes $n_i \equiv 10$.

a. Assuming that pairwise comparisons of the treatment means are to be made with a 90 percent family confidence coefficient, find the T, S, and B multiples for the following numbers of pairwise comparisons in the family: $g = 2, 5, 15$. What generalization is suggested by your results?

b. Assuming that contrasts of the treatment means are to be estimated with a 90 percent family confidence coefficient, find the S and B multiples for the following numbers of contrasts in the family: $g = 2, 5, 15$. What generalization is suggested by your results?

17.6. Consider a single-factor study with $r = 5$ treatments and sample sizes $n_i \equiv 5$.

a. Find the T, S, and B multiples if $g = 2, 5$, and 10 pairwise comparisons are to be made with a 95 percent family confidence coefficient. What generalization is suggested by your results?

b. What would be the T, S, and B multiples for sample sizes $n_i \equiv 20$? Does the generalization obtained in part (a) still hold?

17.7. In making multiple comparisons, why is it appropriate to use the multiple comparison procedure that leads to the tightest confidence intervals for the sample data obtained? Discuss.

17.8. For a single-factor study with $r = 2$ treatments and sample sizes $n_i = 10$, find the T, S, and B multiples for $g = 1$ pairwise comparison with a 99 percent family confidence coefficient. What generalization is suggested by your results?

√ 17.9. Refer to **Productivity improvement** Problem 16.10.

a. Prepare a line plot of the estimated factor level means $\overline{Y}_{i\cdot}$. What does this plot suggest regarding the effect of the level of research and development expenditures on mean productivity improvement?

b. Estimate the mean productivity improvement for firms with high research and development expenditures levels; use a 95 percent confidence interval.

c. Obtain a 95 percent confidence interval for $D = \mu_2 - \mu_1$. Interpret your interval estimate.

d. Obtain confidence intervals for all pairwise comparisons of the treatment means; use the Tukey procedure and a 90 percent family confidence coefficient. State your findings and prepare a graphic summary by underlining nonsignificant comparisons in your line plot in part (a).

e. Is the Tukey procedure employed in part (d) the most efficient one that could be used here? Explain.

17.10. Refer to **Questionnaire color** Problem 16.11.

a. Prepare a normal probability plot of the estimated factor level means $\overline{Y}_{i\cdot}$. What does this plot suggest about the effect of color on the response rate? Is your conclusion in accord with the test result in Problem 16.11e?

b. Estimate the mean response rate for blue questionnaires; use a 90 percent confidence interval.

c. Test whether or not $D = \mu_3 - \mu_2 = 0$; use $\alpha = .10$. State the alternatives, decision rule, and conclusion. In light of the result for the ANOVA test in Problem 16.11e, is your conclusion surprising? Explain.

17.11. Refer to **Rehabilitation therapy** Problem 16.12.

a. Prepare a line plot of the estimated factor level means $\bar{Y}_{i\cdot}$. What does this plot suggest about the effect of prior physical fitness on the mean time required in therapy?

b. Estimate with a 99 percent confidence interval the mean number of days required in therapy for persons of average physical fitness.

c. Obtain confidence intervals for $D_1 = \mu_2 - \mu_3$ and $D_2 = \mu_1 - \mu_2$; use the Bonferroni procedure with a 95 percent family confidence coefficient. Interpret your results.

d. Would the Tukey procedure have been more efficient to use in part (c)? Explain.

e. If the researcher also wished to estimate $D_3 = \mu_1 - \mu_3$, still with a 95 percent family confidence coefficient, would the B multiple in part (c) need to be modified? Would this also be the case if the Tukey procedure had been employed?

f. Test for all pairs of factor level means whether or not they differ; use the Tukey procedure with $\alpha = .05$. Set up groups of factor levels whose means do not differ.

√ 17.12. Refer to **Cash offers** Problem 16.13.

a. Prepare a normal probability plot of the estimated factor level means $\bar{Y}_{i\cdot}$. What does this plot suggest regarding the effect of the owner's age on the mean cash offer?

b. Estimate the mean cash offer for young owners; use a 99 percent confidence interval.

c. Construct a 99 percent confidence interval for $D = \mu_3 - \mu_1$. Interpret your interval estimate.

d. Test whether or not $\mu_2 - \mu_1 = \mu_3 - \mu_2$; control the α risk at .01. State the alternatives, decision rule, and conclusion.

e. Obtain confidence intervals for all pairwise comparisons between the treatment means; use the Tukey procedure and a 90 percent family confidence coefficient. Interpret your results and provide a graphic summary by preparing a paired comparison plot. Are your conclusions in accord with those in part (a)?

f. Would the Bonferroni procedure have been more efficient to use in part (e) than the Tukey procedure? Explain.

√ 17.13. Refer to **Filling machines** Problem 16.14.

a. Prepare a normal probability plot of the estimated factor level means $\bar{Y}_{i\cdot}$. What does this plot suggest regarding the variation in the mean fills for the six machines?

b. Construct a 95 percent confidence interval for the mean fill for machine 1.

c. Obtain a 95 percent confidence interval for $D = \mu_2 - \mu_1$. Interpret your interval estimate.

d. Prepare a paired comparison plot and interpret it.

e. The consultant is particularly interested in comparing the mean fills for machines 1, 4, and 5. Use the Bonferroni testing procedure for all pairwise comparisons among these three treatment means with family level of significance $\alpha = .10$. Interpret your results and provide a graphic summary by preparing a line plot of the estimated factor level means with nonsignificant differences underlined. Do your conclusions agree with those in part (a)?

f. Would the Tukey testing procedure have been more efficient to use in part (e) than the Bonferroni testing procedure? Explain.

g. Use the Holm testing procedure in part (e), with family level of significance $\alpha = .10$, to identify significant differences between the three machines. Is the Holm procedure refinement helpful here? Explain.

17.14. Refer to **Premium distribution** Problem 16.15.

a. Prepare a normal probability plot of the estimated factor level means $\bar{Y}_{i\cdot}$. What does this plot suggest about the variation in the mean time lapses for the five agents?

b. Test for all pairs of factor level means whether or not they differ; use the Tukey procedure with $\alpha = .10$. Set up groups of factor levels whose means do not differ. Use a paired comparison plot to summarize the results.

c. Construct a 90 percent confidence interval for the mean time lapse for agent 1.

d. Obtain a 90 percent confidence interval for $D = \mu_2 - \mu_1$. Interpret your interval estimate.

e. The marketing director wishes to compare the mean time lapses for agents 1, 3, and 5. Obtain confidence intervals for all pairwise comparisons among these three treatment means; use the Bonferroni procedure with a 90 percent family confidence coefficient. Interpret your results and present a graphic summary by preparing a line plot of the estimated factor level means with nonsignificant differences underlined. Do your conclusions agree with those in part (a)?

f. Would the Tukey procedure have been more efficient to use in part (e) than the Bonferroni procedure? Explain.

g. Use the Holm testing procedure in part (e), with family level of significance $\alpha = .10$, to identify significant differences between the three agents. Is the Holm procedure refinement helpful here? Explain.

√ 17.15. Refer to **Productivity improvement** Problem 16.10.

a. Estimate the difference in mean productivity improvement between firms with low or moderate research and development expenditures and firms with high expenditures; use a 95 percent confidence interval. Employ an unweighted mean for the low and moderate expenditures groups. Interpret your interval estimate.

b. The sample sizes for the three factor levels are proportional to the population sizes. The economist wishes to estimate the mean productivity gain last year for all firms in the population. Estimate this overall mean productivity improvement with a 95 percent confidence interval.

c. Using the Scheffé procedure, obtain confidence intervals for the following comparisons with 90 percent family confidence coefficient:

$$D_1 = \mu_3 - \mu_2 \qquad D_3 = \mu_2 - \mu_1$$

$$D_2 = \mu_3 - \mu_1 \qquad L_1 = \frac{\mu_1 + \mu_2}{2} - \mu_3$$

Interpret your results and describe your findings.

d. Use the Holm testing procedure in part (c), with family level of significance $\alpha = .10$, to identify significant effects. Is the Holm procedure helpful here? Explain.

17.16. Refer to **Rehabilitation therapy** Problem 16.12.

a. Estimate the contrast $L = (\mu_1 - \mu_2) - (\mu_2 - \mu_3)$ with a 99 percent confidence interval. Interpret your interval estimate.

b. Estimate the following comparisons using the Bonferroni procedure with a 95 percent family confidence coefficient:

$$D_1 = \mu_1 - \mu_2 \qquad D_3 = \mu_2 - \mu_3$$
$$D_2 = \mu_1 - \mu_3 \qquad L_1 = D_1 - D_3$$

Interpret your results and describe your findings.

c. Would the Scheffé procedure have been more efficient to use in part (b) than the Bonferroni procedure? Explain.

√ 17.17. Refer to **Cash offers** Problem 16.13.

a. Estimate the contrast $L = (\mu_3 - \mu_2) - (\mu_2 - \mu_1)$ with a 99 percent confidence interval. Interpret your interval estimate.

b. Estimate the following comparisons with a 90 percent family confidence coefficient; employ the most efficient multiple comparison procedure:

$$D_1 = \mu_2 - \mu_1 \qquad D_3 = \mu_3 - \mu_1$$
$$D_2 = \mu_3 - \mu_2 \qquad L_1 = D_2 - D_1$$

Interpret your results.

√ 17.18. Refer to **Filling machines** Problem 16.14. Machines 1 and 2 were bought new five years ago, machines 3 and 4 were bought in a reconditioned state five years ago, and machines 5 and 6 were bought new last year.

a. Estimate the contrast:
$$L = \frac{\mu_1 + \mu_2}{2} - \frac{\mu_3 + \mu_4}{2}$$

with a 95 percent confidence interval. Interpret your interval estimate.

b. Estimate the following comparisons with a 90 percent family confidence coefficient; use the most efficient multiple comparison procedure:

$$D_1 = \mu_1 - \mu_2 \qquad L_1 = \frac{\mu_1 + \mu_2}{2} - \frac{\mu_3 + \mu_4}{2}$$

$$D_2 = \mu_3 - \mu_4 \qquad L_2 = \frac{\mu_1 + \mu_2}{2} - \frac{\mu_5 + \mu_6}{2}$$

$$D_3 = \mu_5 - \mu_6 \qquad L_3 = \frac{\mu_1 + \mu_2 + \mu_5 + \mu_6}{4} - \frac{\mu_3 + \mu_4}{2}$$

$$L_4 = \frac{\mu_1 + \mu_2 + \mu_3 + \mu_4}{4} - \frac{\mu_5 + \mu_6}{2}$$

Interpret your results. What can the consultant learn from these results about the differences between the six filling machines?

c. Use the Holm testing procedure in part (b), with family level of significance .10, to identify significant effects. Is the Holm procedure refinement helpful here? Explain.

17.19. Refer to **Premium distribution** Problem 16.15. Agents 1 and 2 distribute merchandise only, agents 3 and 4 distribute cash-value coupons only, and agent 5 distributes both merchandise and coupons.

a. Estimate the contrast:

$$L = \frac{\mu_1 + \mu_2}{2} - \frac{\mu_3 + \mu_4}{2}$$

with a 90 percent confidence interval. Interpret your interval estimate.

b. Estimate the following comparisons with 90 percent family confidence coefficient; use the Scheffé procedure:

$$D_1 = \mu_1 - \mu_2 \qquad L_1 = \frac{\mu_1 + \mu_2}{2} - \mu_5$$

$$D_2 = \mu_3 - \mu_4 \qquad L_2 = \frac{\mu_3 + \mu_4}{2} - \mu_5$$

$$L_3 = \frac{\mu_1 + \mu_2}{2} - \frac{\mu_3 + \mu_4}{2}$$

Interpret your results.

c. Use the Holm testing procedure in part (b), with family level of significance $\alpha = .10$, to identify significant effects. Is the Holm procedure helpful here? Explain.

d. Of all premium distributions, 25 percent are handled by agent 1, 20 percent by agent 2, 20 percent by agent 3, 20 percent by agent 4, and 15 percent by agent 5. Estimate the overall mean time lapse for premium distributions with a 90 percent confidence interval.

√ 17.20. Refer to **Filling machines** Problem 16.14. Use the analysis of means procedure on page 738 to test for equality of treatment effects, with family significance level .05. Which treatments have the strongest effects?

17.21. Refer to **Premium distribution** Problem 16.15. Use the analysis of means procedure on page 738 to test for equality of treatment effects, with family significance level .10. Which treatments have the strongest effects?

17.22. Refer to **Solution concentration** Problem 3.15. Suppose the chemist initially wishes to employ ANOVA model (16.2) to determine whether or not the concentration of the solution is affected by the amount of time that has elapsed since preparation.

a. State the analysis of variance model.

b. Prepare a normal probability plot of the estimated factor level means $\bar{Y}_{i\cdot}$. What does this plot suggest about the relation between the solution concentration and time?

c. Obtain the analysis of variance table.

d. Test whether or not the factor level means are equal; use $\alpha = .025$. State the alternatives, decision rule, and conclusion.

e. Make pairwise comparisons of factor level means between all adjacent lengths of time; use the Bonferroni procedure with a 95 percent family confidence coefficient. Are your conclusions in accord with those in part (b)? Do your results suggest that the regression relation is not linear?

17.23. Refer to **Rehabilitation therapy** Problem 16.12. A biometrician has developed a scale for physical fitness status, as follows:

Physical Fitness Status	Scale Value
Below average	83
Average	100
Above average	121

a. Using this physical fitness status scale, fit first-order regression model (1.1) for regressing number of days required for therapy (Y) on physical fitness status (X).

b. Obtain the residuals and plot them against X. Does a linear regression model appear to fit the data?

c. Perform an F test to determine whether or not there is lack of fit of a linear regression function; use $\alpha = .05$. State the alternatives, decision rule, and conclusion.

d. Could you test for lack of fit of a quadratic regression function here? Explain.

√ 17.24. Refer to **Filling machines** Problem 16.14. A maintenance engineer has suggested that the differences in mean fills for the six machines are largely related to the length of time since a machine last received major servicing. Service records indicate these lengths of time to be as follows (in months):

Filling Machine	Number of Months	Filling Machine	Number of Months
1	.4	4	5.3
2	3.7	5	1.4
3	6.1	6	2.1

a. Fit second-order polynomial regression model (7.66a) for regressing amount of fill (Y) on number of months since major servicing (X).

b. Obtain the residuals and plot them against X. Does a quadratic regression function appear to fit the data?

c. Perform an F test to determine whether or not there is lack of fit of a quadratic regression function; use $\alpha = .01$. State the alternatives, decision rule, and conclusion.

d. Test whether or not the quadratic term in the response function can be dropped from the model; use $\alpha = .01$. State the alternatives, decision rule, and conclusion.

Exercises

17.25. Show that when $r = 2$ and $n_i \equiv n$, q defined in (17.36) is equivalent to $\sqrt{2}|t^*|$, where t^* is defined in (A.65) in Appendix A.

17.26. Starting with (17.39), complete the derivation of (17.31).

17.27. Show that when $r = 2$, S^2 defined in (17.44a) is equivalent to $[t(1 - \alpha/2; n_T - 2)]^2$.

17.28. Show that the estimated variance of $\hat{L}_i$ in (17.49) is given by (17.50).

Projects

17.29. Refer to the **SENIC** data set and Project 16.31. Obtain confidence intervals for all pairwise comparisons between the four regions; use the Tukey procedure and a 90 percent family confidence coefficient. Interpret your results and state your findings. Prepare a line plot of the estimated factor level means and underline all nonsignificant comparisons.

17.30. Refer to the **SMSA** data set and Project 16.33. Obtain confidence intervals for all pairwise comparisons between the four regions; use the Tukey procedure and a 90 percent family confidence coefficient. Interpret your results and state your findings. Prepare a line plot of the estimated factor level means and underline all nonsignificant comparisons.

17.31. Refer to Project 16.34e.

   a. For each replication, construct confidence intervals for all pairwise comparisons among the three treatment means; use the Tukey procedure with a 95 percent family confidence coefficient. Then determine whether all confidence intervals for the replication are correct, given that $\mu_1 = 80$, $\mu_2 = 60$, and $\mu_3 = 160$.

   b. For what proportion of the 100 replications are all confidence intervals correct? Is this proportion close to theoretical expectations? Discuss.

ANOVA Diagnostics and Remedial Measures

When discussing regression analysis, we emphasized the importance of examining the appropriateness of the regression model under consideration, and noted the effectiveness of residual plots and other diagnostics for spotting major departures from the tentative model. Examination of the appropriateness of analysis of variance models is no less important.

In this chapter, we take up the use of residual plots for diagnosing the appropriateness of analysis of variance models, as well as formal tests for the constancy of the error variance. We also discuss the use of transformations of the response variable as a remedial measure to improve the appropriateness of the analysis of variance model for estimation and test inferences.

For pedagogic reasons, as in regression analysis, we have discussed inference procedures before diagnostics and remedial measures. The actual sequence of developing and using any statistical model is, of course, the reverse:

1. Examine whether the proposed model is appropriate for the set of data at hand.

2. If the proposed model is not appropriate, consider remedial measures, such as transformation of the data or modification of the model.

3. After review of the appropriateness of the model and completion of any necessary remedial measures and an evaluation of their effectiveness, inferences based on the model can be undertaken.

It is not necessary, nor is it usually possible, that an ANOVA model fit the data perfectly. As will be noted later, ANOVA models are reasonably robust against certain types of departures from the model, such as the error terms not being exactly normally distributed. The major purpose of the examination of the appropriateness of the model is therefore to detect serious departures from the conditions assumed by the model.

18.1 Residual Analysis

Residual analysis for ANOVA models corresponds closely to that for regression models. We therefore discuss only briefly some key issues in the use of residual analysis for ANOVA models.

Residuals

The residuals e_{ij} for the ANOVA cell means model (16.2) were defined in (16.20):

$$(18.1) \qquad e_{ij} = Y_{ij} - \hat{Y}_{ij} = Y_{ij} - \bar{Y}_i.$$

As in regression, semistudentized residuals, studentized residuals, and studentized deleted residuals are often helpful for diagnosing ANOVA model departures. The definitions of these residuals for regression in Chapters 3 and 9 are still applicable for ANOVA models. However, in view of the simple nature of the $\mathbf{X}$ matrix for ANOVA models, the regression formulas often simplify here. The semistudentized residuals e_{ij}^* in (3.5) for regression remain unchanged:

$$(18.2) \qquad e_{ij}^* = \frac{e_{ij}}{\sqrt{MSE}}$$

The studentized residuals r_{ij} in (9.20) become here:

$$(18.3) \qquad r_{ij} = \frac{e_{ij}}{s\{e_{ij}\}}$$

where:

$$(18.3a) \qquad s\{e_{ij}\} = \sqrt{\frac{MSE(n_i - 1)}{n_i}}$$

Finally, the studentized deleted residuals t_{ij} in (9.26) become here:

$$(18.4) \qquad t_{ij} = e_{ij} \left[\frac{n_T - r - 1}{SSE\left(1 - \dfrac{1}{n_i}\right) - e_{ij}^2} \right]^{1/2}$$

Note

For ANOVA model (16.2), it can be shown that the leverage of Y_{ij}, defined in (9.18), is given by:

$$(18.5) \qquad h_{ij,ij} = \frac{1}{n_i}$$

Hence, the variance of the residual e_{ij} for ANOVA model (16.2) can be obtained by substituting (18.5) into (9.14):

$$(18.6) \qquad \sigma^2\{e_{ij}\} = \frac{\sigma^2(n_i - 1)}{n_i}$$

Replacing σ^2 by the unbiased estimator MSE and taking the square root leads to the estimated standard deviation $s\{e_{ij}\}$ in (18.3a).

sequence, a plot of the residuals against this ordering is helpful for ascertaining whether the error terms are serially correlated according to this ordering.

Outliers.   The detection of outliers is facilitated by various plots of the studentized deleted residuals. *Residual plots against fitted values, residual dot plots*, *box plots*, and *stem-and-leaf plots* are particularly helpful. These plots easily reveal outlying observations, that is, observations that differ from the fitted value by far more than do other observations. As noted in Chapter 3, it is wise practice to discard outlying observations only if they can be identified as being due to such specific causes as instrumentation malfunctioning, observer measurement blunder, or recording error.

The test for outliers in regression discussed in Chapter 9 is applicable to analysis of variance as well. The appropriate Bonferroni critical value here is $t(1-\alpha/2n_T; n_T -r-1)$. If the largest absolute studentized deleted residual exceeds this critical value, that case should be considered an outlier. Note that the implicit family of tests here consists of the tests on all n_T residuals for the study since we do not know in advance which case will have the largest absolute studentized deleted residual.

Occasionally, a test for an outlier is suggested in advance of the analysis, as when a substitute operator is used for one of the production runs in a manufacturing experiment. Concern about the validity of this response observation might lead to an outlier test. In this case, the Bonferroni critical value would be $t(1 - \alpha/2; n_T - r - 1)$.

Omission of Important Explanatory Variables.   Residual analysis may also be used to study whether or not the single-factor ANOVA model is an adequate model. In a learning experiment involving three motivational treatments, the residuals shown in Figure 18.5 were obtained. The residual plot against the fitted values in Figure 18.5 shows no unusual overall pattern. The experimenter wondered, however, whether the treatment effects differ according to the gender of the subject. In Figure 18.5 the residuals for male subjects are shown by a box, and those for females by dots. The results in Figure 18.5 suggest strongly that for each of the motivational treatments studied, the treatment effects do differ according to gender. Hence, a multifactor model recognizing both motivational treatment and gender of subject as explanatory variables might be more useful.

Note that residual analysis here does not invalidate the original single-factor model. Rather, the residual analysis points out that the original model overlooks differences in treatment effects that may be important to recognize. Since there are usually many explanatory variables that have some effect on the response, the analyst needs to identify for residual analysis those explanatory variables that most likely have an important effect on the response.

Nonnormality of Error Terms.   The normality of the error terms can be studied from *histograms, dot plots, box plots,* and *normal probability plots* of the residuals. In addition, comparisons can be made of observed frequencies with expected frequencies if normality holds, and formal chi-square goodness of fit or related tests can be utilized. The discussion in Chapter 3 about these methods for assessing the normality of the error terms for regression is entirely applicable to ANOVA models.

When the factor level sample sizes are large, the study of normality can be made separately for each treatment. When the factor level sample sizes are small, one can combine the residuals e_{ij} for all treatments into one group, provided that the evidence suggests that there are no major differences in the error variances for the treatments studied. This combining was done in the rust inhibitor example in Figure 18.1c. This figure does not indicate any serious departures from normality. The pattern of the points is reasonably linear

FIGURE 18.5   Residual Plot against Fitted Values Illustrating Omission of Important Explanatory Variable.

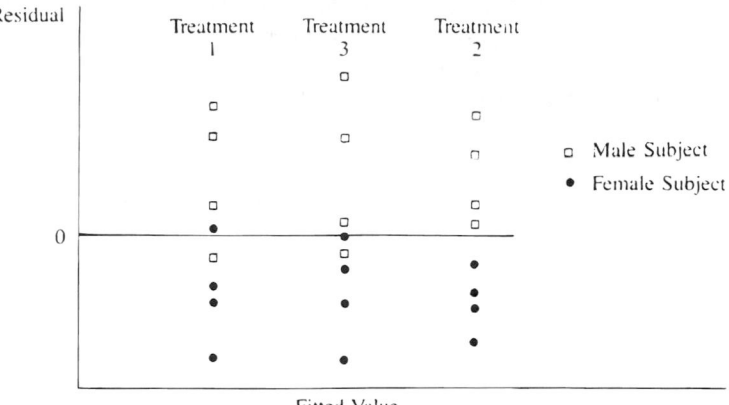

except possibly in the tails. The coefficient of correlation between the ordered residuals and their expected values under normality is .987, which also supports the reasonableness of the normality assumption.

When unequal variances of the error terms for the different factor levels are indicated and normality must be examined for the combined data, studentized residuals (18.3) should be used, with *MSE* replaced by the sample variance s_i^2 in (16.39) for observations from the ith treatment. If ordinary residuals were used, nonnormality might be indicated solely because of the failure of the error terms to have equal variances.

Note

As for regression models, the ANOVA residuals e_{ij} are not independent random variables. For ANOVA model (16.2), they are subject to the restrictions in (16.21). Consequently, statistical tests that require independent observations are not exactly appropriate for ANOVA residuals. If, however, the number of residuals for each factor level is not small, the effect of the correlations will only be modest. It has been noted that graphic plots of residuals are less subject to the effects of correlation than are statistical tests because graphic plots contain the individual residuals and not simply functions of them.   ■

18.2   Tests for Constancy of Error Variance

Several formal tests are available for studying the constancy of the error variance, as required by the ANOVA model. We shall consider two of these, the Hartley test and the modified Levene test. Both tests assume that independent random samples are obtained from each population. The Hartley test is simple to carry out, but is applicable only if the sample sizes are equal and if the error terms are normally distributed. The test is designed to be sensitive to substantial differences between the largest and the smallest factor level variances. The modified Levene test, discussed in Chapter 3, is slightly more difficult to compute but is more generally applicable. The test has been shown to be robust to departures from normality, and sample sizes need not be equal.

Both the Hartley test and the modified Levene test are often conducted at low α levels when used for testing the constancy of the error variance in the analysis of variance. The reason is that, as we note in Section 18.6, the F test for equality of factor level means is robust against nonconstancy of the error variance when the factor level sample sizes are approximately equal, as long as the differences in the variances are not extremely large. Hence, the purpose of using the Hartley or modified Levene tests in ANOVA is often to determine whether extremely large differences in the error variances exist. For this purpose, a low α level may be employed since only large differences in the error variances need to be detected.

Hartley Test

We shall describe the Hartley test in general terms. The test considers r normal populations; the variance of the ith population is denoted by σ_i^2. Independent samples of equal size are selected from the r populations; the sample variance for the ith population is denoted by s_i^2 and the common number of degrees of freedom associated with each sample variance is denoted by df. The alternatives to be tested are:

$$(18.7) \qquad \begin{aligned} H_0&: \ \sigma_1^2 = \sigma_2^2 = \cdots = \sigma_r^2 \\ H_a&: \ \text{not all} \ \sigma_i^2 \ \text{are equal} \end{aligned}$$

The Hartley test statistic, denoted by H, is based solely on the largest sample variance, denoted by $\max(s_i^2)$, and the smallest sample variance, denoted by $\min(s_i^2)$:

$$(18.8) \qquad H = \frac{\max(s_i^2)}{\min(s_i^2)}$$

Values of H near 1 support H_0, and large values of H support H_a. The distribution of H when H_0 holds has been tabulated, and selected percentiles are presented in Table B.10. The distribution of H depends on the number of populations r and the common number of degrees of freedom df.

The appropriate decision rule for controlling the risk of making a Type I error at α is:

$$(18.9) \qquad \begin{aligned} &\text{If} \ H \leq H(1 - \alpha; r, df), \ \text{conclude} \ H_0 \\ &\text{If} \ H > H(1 - \alpha; r, df), \ \text{conclude} \ H_a \end{aligned}$$

where $H(1 - \alpha; r, df)$ is the $(1 - \alpha)100$ percentile of the distribution of H when H_0 holds, for r populations and df degrees of freedom for each sample variance.

When the Hartley test is used for the single-factor ANOVA model (16.2) with equal sample sizes, $n_i \equiv n$, we have $df = n - 1$. The r normal populations are the normal probability distributions of the Y observations for the r factor levels. The sample variance s_i^2 is the variance of the n_i observations Y_{ij} for the ith factor level or equivalently the

TABLE 18.2   **Solder Joint Pull Strengths—ABT Electronics Example.**

Joint	Flux Type (i)				
j	$i = 1$	$i = 2$	$i = 3$	$i = 4$	$i = 5$
1	14.87	18.43	16.95	8.59	11.55
2	16.81	18.76	12.28	10.90	13.36
$\cdots$	$\cdots$	$\cdots$	$\cdots$	$\cdots$	$\cdots$
7	17.40	17.16	19.35	9.41	12.05
8	14.62	16.40	15.52	10.04	11.95
$\bar{Y}_{i\cdot}$	15.420	18.528	15.004	9.741	12.340
$\tilde{Y}_i$	15.170	18.595	15.255	10.010	12.105
s_i^2	1.531	1.570	6.183	.667	.592

variance of the n_i residuals e_{ij}, defined in (16.39); for $n_i \equiv n$, s_i^2 becomes:

$$(18.10) \qquad s_i^2 = \frac{\sum\limits_{j=1}^{n} (Y_{ij} - \bar{Y}_{i\cdot})^2}{n - 1} = \frac{\sum\limits_{j=1}^{n} e_{ij}^2}{n - 1} \qquad \text{when} \quad n_i \equiv n$$

Example.   The ABT Electronics Corporation performed an experiment to evaluate five types of flux for use in soldering printed wiring boards. A major concern of the firm's reliability engineers was the strength of the soldered joints. To test the five types of flux, 40 printed wiring boards were selected at random. Each of the five flux types was randomly assigned to 8 of the 40 circuit boards and an electronic switch was soldered to each board using the designated flux type. Following a four-week storage period, the 40 circuit boards were tested by an hydraulically operated testing machine which exerted increasing pulling force on each switch. The force (in pounds) required to break a joint, termed the pull strength, is the response of interest.

A portion of the observed pull strengths in the experiment is shown in Table 18.2, along with the estimated treatment means $\bar{Y}_{i\cdot}$ and sample variances s_i^2. A dot plot of these data is presented in Figure 18.6. Notice that the variability in pull strengths for the third solder type appears to be larger than for the others.

Since approximate normality is required by the Hartley test, normal probability plots of the residuals were first constructed for each treatment (not shown). The approximate normality of the residuals for each treatment was supported by the plots and by the correlation test (the correlations in the five plots are .982, .981, .977, .958 and .939; the critical value for $\alpha = .05$ from Table B.6 is .906).

The alternatives for the Hartley test here are:

$$H_0: \ \sigma_1^2 = \sigma_2^2 = \cdots = \sigma_5^2$$

$$H_a: \ \text{not all } \sigma_i^2 \text{ are equal}$$

For level of significance $\alpha = .05$, $r = 5$, and $df = 8 - 1 = 7$, we require

FIGURE 18.6   Dot Plots of Pull Strengths—ABT Electronics Example.

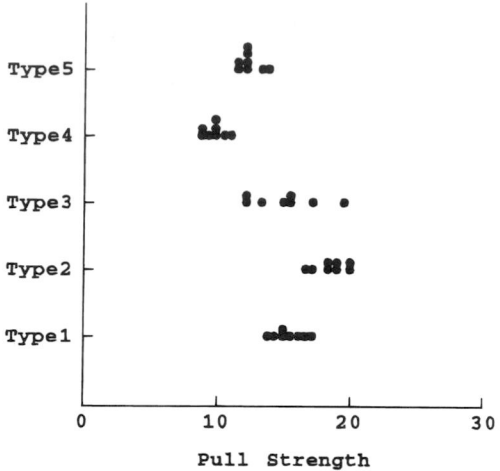

$H(.95; 5, 7) = 9.70$. Hence the appropriate decision rule is:

$$\text{If } H \leq 9.70, \text{ conclude } H_0$$

$$\text{If } H > 9.70, \text{ conclude } H_a$$

From Table 18.2 we see that $\max(s_i^2) = 6.183$ and $\min(s_i^2) = .592$. Hence the test statistic is:

$$H = \frac{6.183}{.592} = 10.44$$

Since $H = 10.44 > 9.70$, we conclude H_a, that the five treatment variances are not equal.

Comments

1. The Hartley test strictly requires equal sample sizes. If the sample sizes are unequal but do not differ greatly, the Hartley test may still be used as an approximate test. For this purpose, the average number of degrees of freedom would be used for entering Table B.10.

2. The Hartley test is quite sensitive to departures from the assumption of normal populations and should not be used when substantial departures from normality exist.   ∎

Modified Levene Test

The modified Levene test for constancy of the error variance in regression was discussed in Chapter 3. The test was originally developed for use in ANOVA applications and is more general than its use for regression described in Chapter 3. The Levene test, just like the Hartley test, can be used to study the equality of r population variances. Unlike the Hartley test, the Levene test is robust against departures from normality, which often occur together with unequal variances. Also, the Levene test does not require equal sample sizes.

To test the alternatives in (18.7) using the modified Levene test, we first compute the absolute deviations of the Y_{ij} observations about their respective factor level medians $\tilde{Y}_i$:

$$(18.11) \qquad d_{ij} = \left| Y_{ij} - \tilde{Y}_i \right|$$

The modified Levene test then determines whether or not the expected values of the absolute deviations for the r treatments are equal. If the r error variances σ_i^2 are equal, so will the expected values of the absolute deviations be equal. Unequal error variances imply differing expected values of the absolute deviations. The Levene test statistic is simply the ordinary F^* statistic in (16.55) for testing differences in the treatment means, but now based on the absolute deviations d_{ij} in (18.11):

$$(18.12) \qquad F_L^* = \frac{MSTR}{MSE}$$

where:

$$(18.12a) \qquad MSTR = \frac{\sum n_i (\bar{d}_{i.} - \bar{d}_{..})^2}{r - 1}$$

$$(18.12b) \qquad MSE = \frac{\sum\sum (d_{ij} - \bar{d}_{i.})^2}{n_T - r}$$

$$(18.12c) \qquad \bar{d}_{i.} = \frac{\sum\limits_j d_{ij}}{n_i}$$

$$(18.12d) \qquad \bar{d}_{..} = \frac{\sum\sum d_{ij}}{n_T}$$

If the error terms have constant variance and the factor level sample sizes are not extremely small, F_L^* follows approximately an F distribution with $r - 1$ and $n_T - r$ degrees of freedom. Large F_L^* values indicate that the error terms do not have constant variance.

Example.   Table 18.2 for the ABT Electronics Corporation example provides the sample medians $\tilde{Y}_i$ for the five treatments. The absolute deviations d_{ij} in (18.11) are shown in Table 18.3. We illustrate their calculation for d_{11}:

$$d_{11} = |Y_{11} - \tilde{Y}_1| = |14.87 - 15.170| = .300$$

The F_L^* test statistic (18.12) based on the absolute deviations is obtained in the usual manner; it is $F_L^* = 2.94$. For $\alpha = .05$, we require $F(.95; 4, 35) = 2.64$. Since $F_L^* = 2.94 > 2.64$, we conclude H_a, that the error terms do not have constant variance. The P-value for this test is .034.

TABLE 18.3   **Absolute Deviations of Responses from Treatment Medians —ABT Electronics Example.**

Joint	Flux Type (i)				
j	$i = 1$	$i = 2$	$i = 3$	$i = 4$	$i = 5$
1	.300	.165	1.695	1.420	.555
2	1.640	.165	2.975	.890	1.255
...	...	...	...	...	...
7	2.230	1.435	4.095	.600	.055
8	.550	2.195	.265	.030	.155

18.3   Overview of Remedial Measures

In the remainder of this chapter, we consider three remedial measures for two common departures from ANOVA model (16.2)—nonconstancy of the error variance and nonnormality of the distribution of the error terms.

1. If the error terms are normally distributed but the variance of the error terms is not constant, a standard remedial measure is to use weighted least squares. We have already considered weighted least squares for nonconstancy of the error variance in regression models. These weighted least squares procedures for regression carry over directly to analysis of variance models.

2. Often, nonconstancy of the error variance is accompanied by nonnormality of the error term distribution. A standard remedial measure here is to transform the response variable Y. We shall present two approaches to finding an appropriate transformation to make the error distribution more nearly normal and to help stabilize the variance of the error terms—some simple guides and the Box-Cox procedure. The latter was considered in Chapter 3 for regression models and is directly applicable to analysis of variance models.

3. When there are major departures from ANOVA model (16.2) and transformations are not successful in stabilizing the error variance and bringing the error distribution close to normal, a nonparametric test for the equality of the factor level means may be used instead of the standard F test. We shall consider a nonparametric test that is based on the ranks of the Y observations.

We begin our discussion of remedial measures with weighted least squares.

18.4   Weighted Least Squares

When the errors ϵ_{ij} are normally distributed but their variances are not the same for the different factor levels, cell means model (16.2) becomes:

(18.13) $$Y_{ij} = \mu_i + \varepsilon_{ij}$$

where:

ε_{ij} are independent $N(0, \sigma_i^2)$

Weighted least squares is a standard remedial measure here, just as for the comparable situation in regression. In fact, we shall use the regression approach to the analysis of variance for implementing weighted least squares. All of the earlier discussion on weighted least squares for regression is applicable to the analysis of variance.

Since the factor level variances σ_i^2 are usually unknown, they must be estimated. This is ordinarily done by means of the sample variances s_i^2 in (16.39), in which case the weight w_{ij} for the jth case of the ith factor level is:

$$(18.14) \qquad w_{ij} = \frac{1}{s_i^2}$$

The test for the equality of the factor level means in (16.54) is now conducted by the general linear test approach described in Chapter 2. The full model is fitted, using the weights in (18.14), and the error sum of squares is obtained, now denoted by $SSE_w(F)$. Next, the reduced model under H_0 is fitted and the error sum of squares $SSE_w(R)$ is obtained. Test statistic (2.70) is employed, as usual. We shall see that $df_F = n_T - r$ and $df_R = n_T - 1$. Hence, the general linear test statistic here is:

$$(18.15) \qquad F_w^\star = \frac{SSE_w(R) - SSE_w(F)}{r - 1} \div \frac{SSE_w(F)}{n_T - r}$$

Since the weights are based on the estimated variances s_i^2, the distribution of $F_w^\star$ under H_0 is only approximately an F distribution with $r - 1$ and $n_T - r$ degrees of freedom. When the factor level sample sizes are reasonably large, the approximation generally is satisfactory. As explained in Chapter 10, bootstrapping can be employed to examine the effect of using estimated weights.

Example

Recall in the ABT Electronics example that the normality assumption appears to be reasonably well supported by the data, but the error variance is not constant. Weighted least squares will now be used to test the alternatives:

$$(18.16) \qquad \begin{aligned} H_0 &: \ \mu_1 = \mu_2 = \cdots = \mu_5 \\ H_a &: \ \text{not all } \mu_i \text{ are equal} \end{aligned}$$

The weights will be based on the sample variances in Table 18.2:

$$ w_{1j} = \frac{1}{1.531} = .653 \qquad w_{2j} = \frac{1}{1.570} = .637 \qquad w_{3j} = \frac{1}{6.183} = .162 $$

$$ w_{4j} = \frac{1}{.667} = 1.499 \qquad w_{5j} = \frac{1}{.592} = 1.689 $$

We shall use regression model (16.81) to represent cell means model (18.13):

$$(18.17) \qquad Y_{ij} = \mu_1 X_{ij1} + \mu_2 X_{ij2} + \cdots + \mu_5 X_{ij5} + \varepsilon_{ij} \qquad\qquad \text{Full model}$$

TABLE 18.4   **Data for Weighted Least Squares Regression—ABT Electronics Example.**

		(1)	(2)	(3)	(4)	(5)	(6)	(7)	(8)
					Full Model			Weights	Reduced Model
i	j	Y_{ij}	X_{ij1}	X_{ij2}	X_{ij3}	X_{ij4}	X_{ij5}	w_{ij}	X_{ij}
1	1	14.87	1	0	0	0	0	.653	1
1	2	16.81	1	0	0	0	0	.653	1
...	...	...	...	...	...	...	...	...	...
1	7	17.40	1	0	0	0	0	.653	1
1	8	14.62	1	0	0	0	0	.653	1
2	1	18.43	0	1	0	0	0	.637	1
2	2	18.76	0	1	0	0	0	.637	1
...	...	...	...	...	...	...	...	...	...
5	7	12.05	0	0	0	0	1	1.689	1
5	8	11.95	0	0	0	0	1	1.689	1

where:

$$X_1 = \begin{matrix} 1 \\ 0 \end{matrix} \quad \begin{matrix} \text{if case from factor level 1} \\ \text{otherwise} \end{matrix}$$

$$\vdots$$

$$X_5 = \begin{matrix} 1 \\ 0 \end{matrix} \quad \begin{matrix} \text{if case from factor level 5} \\ \text{otherwise} \end{matrix}$$

Note that the factor level means μ_i play the role of regression coefficients and that the regression model has no intercept.

Table 18.4 repeats from Table 18.2 a portion of the experimental data in column 1 and contains the coding of the indicator variables in columns 2–6 and the weights in column 7. Note, for instance, that the coding for cases from the first treatment is $X_1 = 1$, $X_2 = 0$, $X_3 = 0$, $X_4 = 0$, and $X_5 = 0$, and similarly for cases from the other treatments.

Figure 18.7a contains the MINITAB output when Y in column 1 of Table 18.4 is regressed on X_1, X_2, X_3, X_4, and X_5 in columns 2–6, using the weights in column 7 and specifying no intercept. We see that $SSE_w(F) = 35.0$.

The reduced model under H_0 is given by (16.82):

$$(18.18) \qquad\qquad Y_{ij} = \mu_c + \varepsilon_{ij} \qquad\qquad \text{Reduced model}$$

where μ_c is the common mean response under H_0. The corresponding regression model is:

$$(18.19) \qquad\qquad Y_{ij} = \mu_c X_{ij} + \varepsilon_{ij}$$

FIGURE 18.7   MINITAB Weighted Regression Output for Full and Reduced Models—ABT Electronics Example.

(a) Full Model

```
The regression equation is
Y = 15.4 X1 + 18.5 X2 + 15.0 X3 + 9.74 X4 + 12.3 X5

Predictor        Coef        Stdev      t-ratio          p
Noconstant
X1            15.4200       0.4375       35.24       0.000
X2            18.5275       0.4430       41.82       0.000
X3            15.0037       0.8785       17.08       0.000
X4             9.7413       0.2888       33.73       0.000
X5            12.3400       0.2721       45.36       0.000

Analysis of Variance

SOURCE        DF          SS          MS          F          p
Regression     5       6478.7      1295.7     1295.56     0.000
Error         35         35.0         1.0
Total         40       6513.7
```

(b) Reduced Model

```
The regression equation is
Y = 12.9 X

Predictor        Coef        Stdev      t-ratio          p
Noconstant
X            12.8764       0.4981       25.85       0.000

Analysis of Variance

SOURCE        DF          SS          MS          F          p
Regression     1       6154.5      6154.5      668.28     0.000
Error         39        359.2         9.2
Total         40       6513.7
```

where:

$$X_{ij} \equiv 1$$

Note that regression model (18.19) has no intercept.

The new X variable is shown in Table 18.4, column 8. Regressing Y in column 1 on X in column 8, using the weights in column 7 and specifying no intercept, leads to the MINITAB output in Figure 18.7b. We see that $SSE_w(R) = 359.2$. We have $n_T - 1 = 40 - 1 = 39$ and $n_T - r = 40 - 5 = 35$. Hence, test statistic (18.15) is:

$$F_w^* = \frac{359.2 - 35.0}{39 - 35} \div \frac{35.0}{35} = 81.05$$

For $\alpha = .01$, we require $F(.99; 4, 35) = 3.908$. Since $F^* = 81.05 > 3.908$, the approximate F test leads to conclusion H_a, that the factor level means differ. The approximate P-value of the test is 0+.

Comments

1. The weighted least squares estimates of the factor level means μ_i are always the estimated factor level means $\bar{Y}_{i\cdot}$, as may be seen by comparing the estimated regression coefficients in

Figure 18.7a with the estimated factor level means in Table 18.2. Hence, for ANOVA model (18.13), the weighted and ordinary least squares estimates of the factor level means μ_i are the same.

2. When using the sample variances s_i^2 as weights, the error sum of squares for the fit of full model (18.17) will always be $SSE_w(F) = n_T - r$. Note that in our example $SSE_w(F) = 35.0$ and $n_T - r = 40 - 5 = 35$.

3. Some analysis of variance computer packages have an option for weighted least squares, with the user specifying the weights. ∎

18.5   Transformations of Response Variable

When both the model assumptions of constancy of the error variance and normality of the error distributions are violated, a transformation of the response variable is often useful. We describe now two approaches to finding a useful transformation—some simple guides and the Box-Cox procedure.

Simple Guides to Finding a Transformation

The following are four simple guides to finding a useful transformation. The guides were developed from theoretical considerations to stabilize the error variances, but these transformations often also are helpful in bringing the distribution of the error terms more closely to a normal distribution.

Variance Proportional to μ_i.   When the variance of the error terms for each factor level (denoted by σ_i^2) is proportional to the factor level mean μ_i, a square root transformation is helpful:

(18.20)   If σ_i^2 proportional to μ_i:

$$Y' = \sqrt{Y} \quad \text{or} \quad Y' = \sqrt{Y} + \sqrt{Y+1}$$

This type of situation is often found when the observed variable Y is a count, such as the number of attempts by a subject before the correct solution is found.

Standard Deviation Proportional to μ_i.   When the standard deviation of the error terms for each factor level is proportional to the factor level mean, a helpful transformation is the logarithmic transformation:

(18.21)   If σ_i proportional to μ_i: $Y' = \log Y$

Standard Deviation Proportional to μ_i^2.   When the error term standard deviation is proportional to the square of the factor level mean for the different factor levels, an appropriate transformation is the reciprocal transformation:

(18.22)   If σ_i proportional to μ_i^2: $Y' = \dfrac{1}{Y}$

Response Is a Proportion.   At times, the observed variable Y_{ij} is a proportion p_{ij}. For instance, the treatments may be different training procedures, the unit of observation is a company training class, and the observed variable Y_{ij} is the proportion of employees in the jth class for the ith training procedure who benefited substantially by the training. Note that n_i here refers to the number of classes receiving the ith training procedure, not to the number of students.

It is well known that in the binomial case the variance of the sample proportion depends on the true proportion. When the number of cases on which each sample proportion is based is the same, this variance is:

$$(18.23) \qquad \sigma^2\{p_{ij}\} = \frac{\pi_i(1 - \pi_i)}{m}$$

Here π_i denotes the population proportion for the ith treatment and m is the common number of cases on which each sample proportion is based. Since $\sigma^2\{p_{ij}\}$ depends on the treatment proportion π_i, the variances of the error terms will not be stable if the treatment proportions π_i differ. An appropriate transformation for this case is the arc sine transformation:

$$(18.24) \qquad \text{If response is a proportion:} \qquad Y' = 2 \arcsin \sqrt{Y}$$

When the proportions p_{ij} are based on different numbers of cases (for instance, in our earlier illustration there may be different numbers of employees in each training class), transformation (18.24) should be employed together with a weighted least squares analysis as described in Section 18.4.

Use of Simple Guides.   To examine whether one of the simple transformation guides is applicable, the statistics $s_i^2/\bar{Y}_{i\cdot}$, $s_i/\bar{Y}_{i\cdot}$, and $s_i/\bar{Y}_{i\cdot}^2$ should be calculated for each factor level, where s_i^2 is the sample variance of the Y observations for the ith factor level, defined in (16.39). Approximate constancy of one of the three statistics over all factor levels would suggest the corresponding transformation as useful for stabilizing the error variance and making the error distributions more nearly normal.

Example.   Servo-Data, Inc., operates mainframe computers at three different locations. The computers are identical as to make and model, but are subject to different degrees of voltage fluctuation in the power lines serving the respective installations. Table 18.5 contains the lengths of time between computer failures Y_{ij} for the three locations, for five failure intervals each. Even though the sample sizes are small, the data suggest highly skewed distributions having nonconstant error variance.

To study whether one of the simple guides is helpful here, we have calculated the following statistics based on the results in Table 18.5.

i	$\dfrac{s_i^2}{\bar{Y}_{i\cdot}}$	$\dfrac{s_i}{\bar{Y}_{i\cdot}}$	$\dfrac{s_i}{\bar{Y}_{i\cdot}^2}$
1	35.5	.84	.017
2	49.9	1.50	.068
3	133.4	1.05	.009

The relation $s_i/\bar{Y}_{i\cdot}$ is the most stable, hence the logarithmic transformation (18.21) may be helpful here. We shall continue this example after discussing the use of the Box-Cox procedure for finding an appropriate transformation in the analysis of variance.

3. The variance stabilizing transformations (18.20), (18.21), (18.22), and (18.24) are obtained by using a Taylor series expansion for the variance of Y. An explanation of the approach may be found in Reference 18.1. ∎

18.6 Effects of Departures from Model

In preceding sections, we considered how residual analysis and other diagnostic techniques can be helpful in assessing the appropriateness of the ANOVA model for the data at hand. We also discussed the use of transformations for both stabilizing the variance and obtaining an error distribution more nearly normal. The question now arises: what are the effects of any remaining departures from the model on the inferences made? A thorough review of the many studies investigating these effects has been made by Scheffé (Ref. 18.2). Here, we summarize the findings.

Nonnormality

For the fixed ANOVA model I, lack of normality is not an important matter, provided the departure from normality is not extreme. It may be noted in this connection that *kurtosis* of the error distribution (either more or less peaked than a normal distribution) is more important than skewness of the distribution in terms of the effects on inferences.

The point estimators of factor level means and contrasts are unbiased whether or not the populations are normal. The F test for the equality of factor level means is but little affected by lack of normality, either in terms of the level of significance or power of the test. Hence, the F test is a *robust* test against departures from normality. For instance, while the specified level of significance might be .05, the actual level for a nonnormal error distribution might be .04 or .065. Typically, the achieved level of significance in the presence of nonnormality is slightly higher than the specified one, and the achieved power of the test is slightly less than the calculated one. Single interval estimates of factor level means and contrasts and the Scheffé multiple comparison procedure also are not much affected by lack of normality, provided that the sample sizes are not extremely small.

For the random ANOVA model II (to be discussed in Chapter 24), lack of normality has more serious implications. The estimators of the variance components are still unbiased, but the actual confidence coefficient for interval estimates may be substantially different from the specified one.

Unequal Error Variances

When the error variances are unequal, the F test for the equality of means with the fixed ANOVA model is only slightly affected if all factor level sample sizes are equal or do not differ greatly. Specifically, unequal error variances then raise the actual level of significance slightly higher than the specified level. Similarly, the Scheffé multiple comparison procedure based on the F distribution is not affected to any substantial extent by unequal variances when the sample sizes are equal or are approximately the same. Thus, the F test and related analyses are robust against unequal variances when the sample sizes are approximately equal. Single comparisons between factor level means, on the other hand, can be substantially affected by unequal variances, so that the actual and specified confidence coefficients may differ markedly in these cases.

The use of equal sample sizes for all factor levels not only tends to minimize the effects of unequal variances on inferences with the F distribution but also simplifies calculational procedures. Thus, here at least, simplicity and robustness go hand in hand.

For the random ANOVA model, unequal error variances can have pronounced effects on inferences about the variance components, even with equal sample sizes.

Nonindependence of Error Terms

Lack of independence of the error terms can have serious effects on inferences in the analysis of variance, for both fixed and random ANOVA models. Since this defect is often difficult to correct, it is important to prevent it in the first place whenever feasible. The use of randomization in those stages of a study that are likely to lead to correlated error terms can be a most important insurance policy. In the case of observational data, however, randomization may not be possible. Here, in the presence of correlated error terms, it may be possible to modify the model. For instance, in the earlier discussion based on Figure 18.3, we noted that inclusion in the model of a linear term for the learning effect of the analyst might remove the correlation of the error terms.

Modification of the model because of correlated error terms may also be necessary in experimental studies. In one case, the experimenter asked each of 10 subjects to give ratings to four new flavors of a fruit syrup and to the standard flavor, on a scale from 0 to 100. When the single-factor analysis of variance model was applied, the experimenter found high degrees of correlation in the residuals for each subject. The experimenter thereupon modified the model to a repeated measures design model (Chapter 29). This latter type of model is intended for situations where the same subject is given each of the different treatments and differences between subjects are expected.

18.7   Nonparametric Rank F Test

When transformations are not successful in sufficiently stabilizing the error variance and bringing the distribution of the error terms close enough to normality to meet the robustness properties of the standard inference procedures, a nonparametric inference procedure can be useful. Nonparametric procedures do not depend on the distribution of the error terms; often the only requirement is that the distribution is continuous. The nonparametric procedure considered here is very simple. All n_T observations are ranked from 1 to n_T in ascending order. Then, the usual F^* test statistic in (16.55) is calculated, but now based on the ranks, and the F test is carried out in the ordinary manner.

Test Procedure

The Y_{ij} observations first need to be ranked in ascending order from 1 to n_T. We shall let R_{ij} denote the rank of Y_{ij}. In the case of ties among some observations, each of the tied observations is given the mean of the ranks involved. For instance, if two observations are tied for what would otherwise have been the third- and fourth-ranked positions, each would be given the mean value 3.5.

To test whether the treatment means are equal, the usual F^* test statistic is obtained based on the ranks R_{ij}. This test statistic is now denoted by F_R^*:

$$(18.25) \qquad F_R^* = \frac{MSTR}{MSE}$$

where:

$$(18.25a) \qquad MSTR = \frac{\sum n_i (\bar{R}_{i.} - \bar{R}_{..})^2}{r - 1}$$

$$(18.25b) \qquad MSE = \frac{\sum\sum (R_{ij} - \bar{R}_{i.})^2}{n_T - r}$$

$$(18.25c) \qquad \bar{R}_{i.} = \frac{\sum\limits_j R_{ij}}{n_i}$$

$$(18.25d) \qquad \bar{R}_{..} = \frac{\sum\sum R_{ij}}{n_T} = \frac{(n_T + 1)}{2}$$

Note that $\bar{R}_{..}$, the overall mean of the ranks, is a constant for any given total number of cases n_T.

When the treatment means are the same, test statistic F_R^* follows approximately the $F(r - 1, n_T - r)$ distribution provided that the sample sizes n_i are not very small. To test the alternatives:

$$(18.26a) \qquad \begin{array}{l} H_0:\ \mu_1 = \mu_2 = \cdots = \mu_r \\ H_a:\ \text{not all } \mu_i \text{ are equal} \end{array}$$

the appropriate decision rule to control the Type I error at α is:

$$(18.26b) \qquad \begin{array}{l} \text{If } F_R^* \le F(1 - \alpha; r - 1, n_T - r), \text{ conclude } H_0 \\ \text{If } F_R^* > F(1 - \alpha; r - 1, n_T - r), \text{ conclude } H_a \end{array}$$

Example.   In the Servo-Data example of Table 18.5, we noted earlier that the logarithmic transformation of Y improves considerably the appropriateness of the assumptions of normality and constancy of the error variance. If the search for a transformation of Y had not been successful, or as an alternative to the transformation approach, we could use the nonparametric rank F test. To use this test, we first rank the data in Table 18.5 from 1 to 15. The ranks are shown in Table 18.5. Note, incidentally, from Table 18.5 that the rank transformation has helped to stabilize the variances of the transformed observations (i.e., the ranks) for the three treatments. We now calculate $SSTR$ and SSE as follows:

$$SSTR = 5[(8.4 - 8.0)^2 + (4.8 - 8.0)^2 + (10.8 - 8.0)^2] = 91.20$$
$$SSE = (2 - 8.4)^2 + (13 - 8.4)^2 + \cdots + (8 - 10.8)^2 = 188.80$$

Note that the overall mean $\bar{R}_{..}$ here is $(n_T + 1)/2 = (15 + 1)/2 = 8.0$. The F_R^* test statistic is therefore:

$$F_R^* = \frac{91.20}{3 - 1} \div \frac{188.8}{15 - 3} = 2.90$$

For $\alpha = .10$, we require $F(.90; 2, 12) = 2.81$. Since $F_R^* = 2.90 > 2.81$, we conclude H_a. The P-value of the test is .094.

If we had conducted the standard F test based on the logarithmic transformation of Y, which was suggested both by the simple guides and the Box-Cox procedure, we would find that it leads to the same conclusion here; its P-value is .053. Thus, both tests show that the mean time between computer failures differs for the three locations.

Note

The *Kruskal-Wallis test*, a widely used nonparametric test for testing the equality of treatment means, is based on a test statistic that is equivalent to the rank F test statistic. The Kruskal-Wallis test statistic, denoted by X_{KW}^2, is also based on the ranks R_{ij} from 1 to n_T and is defined as follows:

$$(18.27) \qquad X_{KW}^2 = \frac{SSTR}{\dfrac{SSTO}{n_T - 1}}$$

where:

$$(18.27a) \qquad SSTO = \sum\sum (R_{ij} - \bar{R}_{..})^2$$

Instead of using the F distribution approximation, the Kruskal-Wallis test uses a chi-square distribution approximation. If the n_i are reasonably large (five or more is the usual advice), X_{KW}^2 is approximately a χ^2 random variable with $r - 1$ degrees of freedom when all treatment means are equal. The decision rule therefore is:

$$(18.28) \qquad \begin{aligned} &\text{If } X_{KW}^2 \leq \chi^2(1 - \alpha; r - 1), \text{ conclude } H_0 \\ &\text{If } X_{KW}^2 > \chi^2(1 - \alpha; r - 1), \text{ conclude } H_a \end{aligned}$$

The F_R^* and X_{KW}^2 test statistics are equivalent, being related as follows.

$$(18.29) \qquad F_R^* = \frac{(n_T - r)X_{KW}^2}{(r - 1)(n_T - 1 - X_{KW}^2)} \qquad\blacksquare$$

Multiple Pairwise Testing Procedure

If the rank F test (or the Kruskal-Wallis test) leads to the conclusion that the factor level means μ_i are not equal, it is frequently desired to obtain information about the comparative magnitudes of these means based on the rank data. A large-sample testing analogue of the Bonferroni pairwise comparison procedure discussed in Section 17.7 based on the ranks of the observations may be employed for this purpose, provided that the sample sizes are not too small. Testing limits for all $g = r(r - 1)/2$ pairwise tests using the mean ranks $\bar{R}_{i.}$ are set up as follows for family level of significance α :

$$(18.30) \qquad (\bar{R}_{i.} - \bar{R}_{i'.}) \pm B \left[\frac{n_T(n_T + 1)}{12} \left(\frac{1}{n_i} + \frac{1}{n_{i'}} \right) \right]^{1/2}$$

where:

$$(18.30a) \qquad B = z(1 - \alpha/2g)$$

$$(18.30b) \qquad g = \frac{r(r - 1)}{2}$$

If the testing limits include zero, we conclude that the corresponding treatment means μ_i and $\mu_{i'}$ do not differ. If the testing limits do not include zero, we conclude that the two corresponding treatment means differ. Based on all pairwise tests, we then set up groups of treatment means whose members do not differ according to the simultaneous testing procedure. In this way, we obtain information about the comparative magnitudes of the treatment means μ_i.

Example.   For the Servo-Data example in Table 18.5, we wish to ascertain, if possible, which location has the longest mean time between computer failures based on the rank data. For a family significance level of $\alpha = .10$ and $g = r(r-1)/2 = 3(2)/2 = 3$ pairwise tests, we require $B = z(.9833) = 2.13$. Since all treatment sample sizes are equal, we need calculate the right term in (18.30) only once:

$$B\left[\frac{n_T(n_T+1)}{12}\left(\frac{1}{n_i}+\frac{1}{n_{i'}}\right)\right]^{1/2} = 2.13\left[\frac{15(16)}{12}\left(\frac{1}{5}+\frac{1}{5}\right)\right]^{1/2} = 6.02$$

Hence, the testing limits for the three pairwise tests are:

Locations 1 and 2:	$(8.4 - 4.8) \pm 6.02$	or	-2.4 and 9.6
Locations 3 and 2:	$(10.8 - 4.8) \pm 6.02$	or	$-.02$ and 12.0
Locations 3 and 1:	$(10.8 - 8.4) \pm 6.02$	or	-3.6 and 8.4

Since no test shows a significant difference, we obtain only one grouping:

Group 1
―――――――
Location 1
Location 2
Location 3

Thus, no conclusion about the comparative magnitudes of the means is possible from this rank data analysis.

18.8   Case Example—Heart Transplant

In heart transplants, the similarity of the donor's tissue type and that of the recipient is of importance because large differences may increase the probability that the transplanted heart is rejected. Table 18.7 shows a portion of the survival times (in days) for 39 patients following heart transplant surgery. The data are grouped into three categories, according to the degree of mismatch between the donor tissue and the recipient tissue. Investigators would like to determine if the mean survival time changes with the degree of mismatch. The alternatives of interest are:

$$H_0: \ \mu_1 = \mu_2 = \mu_3$$
$$H_a: \ \text{not all } \mu_i \text{ are equal}$$

A SYSTAT dot plot of the data by mismatch category is provided in Figure 18.9a. The plot suggests that average survival time may decrease with higher degree of mismatch. An

TABLE 18.7 **Survival Times of Patients Following Heart Transplant Surgery—Heart Transplant Example.**

| Case | Degree of Tissue Mismatch (i) | | |
| | Low | Medium | Low |
j	$i = 1$	$i = 2$	$i = 3$
1	44	15	3
2	551	280	136
3	127	1,024	65
...	...	...	...
12	47	836	48
13	994	51	
14	26		

Source: M. L. Puri and P. K. Sen, *Nonparametric Methods in General Linear Models* (New York: John Wiley & Sons, 1985).

FIGURE 18.9 **SYSTAT Diagnostic Plots—Heart Transplant Example.**

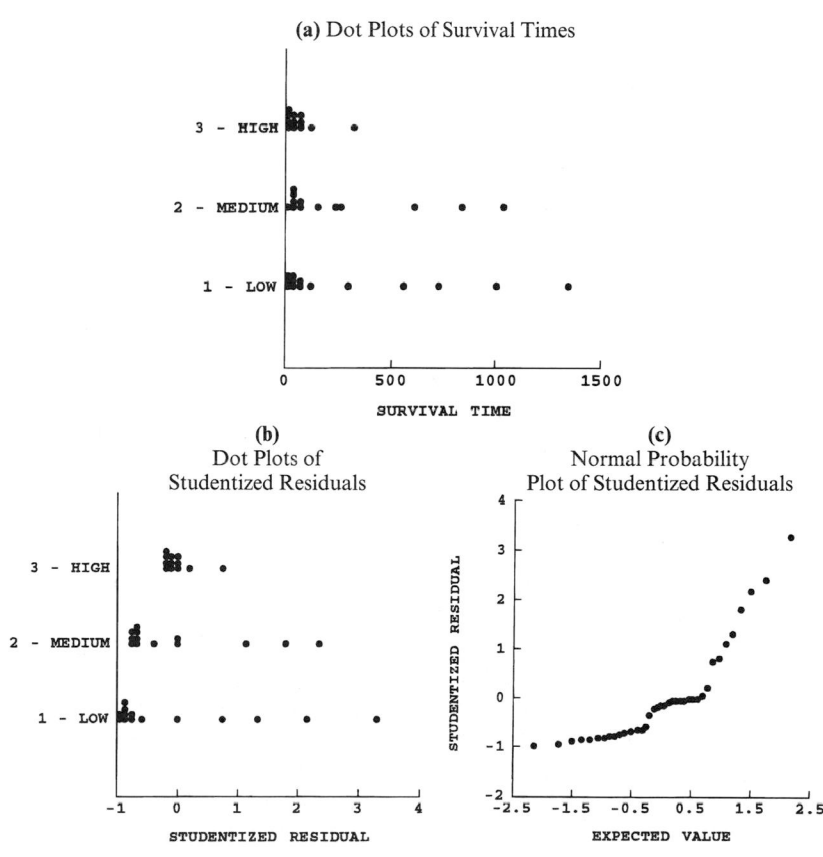

(a) Dot Plots of Survival Times

(b) Dot Plots of Studentized Residuals

(c) Normal Probability Plot of Studentized Residuals

FIGURE 18.10   **Diagnostic Plots and ANOVA Table for Transformed Data—Heart Transplant Example.**

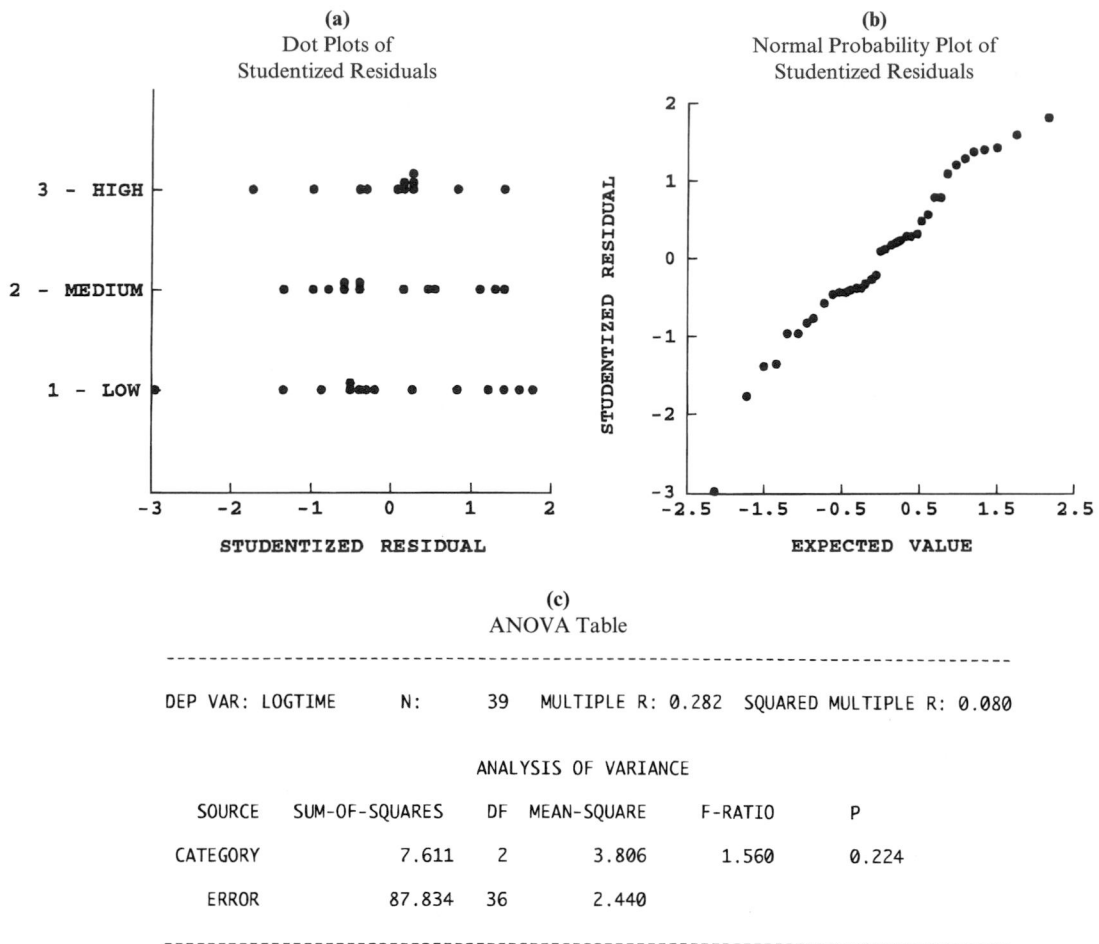

(a)
Dot Plots of
Studentized Residuals

(b)
Normal Probability Plot of
Studentized Residuals

(c)
ANOVA Table

```
--------------------------------------------------------------------------

DEP VAR: LOGTIME      N:     39   MULTIPLE R: 0.282  SQUARED MULTIPLE R: 0.080


                          ANALYSIS OF VARIANCE

     SOURCE   SUM-OF-SQUARES   DF   MEAN-SQUARE   F-RATIO      P

    CATEGORY           7.611    2         3.806     1.560    0.224

     ERROR            87.834   36         2.440

--------------------------------------------------------------------------
```

initial fit of analysis of variance model (16.2) was made and the studentized residuals were obtained for diagnostic purposes. Two residual plots are presented in Figures 18.9b and 18.9c. The dot plot of the studentized residuals in Figure 18.9b shows that the distribution of the residuals is positively skewed. It also suggests that the error variance may be smaller in the high mismatch group. The modified Levene test in (18.12) was conducted to examine the constancy of the error variance. The Levene test statistic is $F_L^* = 1.91$ and the P-value is .163, supporting constancy of the error variance. On the other hand, the positive skewness of the residuals is confirmed by the upward-curving shape of the normal probability plot in Figure 18.9c and the correlation test for normality ($r = .895$; for $\alpha = .05$, the interpolated critical value in Table B.6 is .971).

A transformation of the response variable was therefore investigated. The Box-Cox procedure led to the maximum likelihood estimate $\hat{\lambda} = .06$, which suggested the logarithmic transformation ($\lambda = 0$). The new response variable $Y' = \log_e Y$ was therefore obtained and ANOVA model (16.2) was fitted to this transformed variable. Two plots of studentized residuals are shown in Figure 18.10. A dot plot of the studentized residuals is presented in

Figure 18.10a. Notice that the distribution of the residuals now appears to be symmetric, with constant variance. The normality of the distribution of the error terms is supported by the normal probability plot in Figure 18.10b and the correlation test for normality ($r = .982 > .971$).

The residual dot plot in Figure 18.10a shows the possible presence of an outlier in the low tissue mismatch category (studentized residual = -2.99). For this case the studentized deleted residual is -3.40. The Bonferroni critical value for the outlier test is $t(1 - .05/2(39); 36) = t(.999359; 36) = 3.49$. Since $|-3.40| = 3.40 \leq 3.49$, we conclude that this case is not an outlier.

It therefore appears that the logarithmic transformation was successful so that ANOVA model (16.2) is appropriate for the transformed survival times. The ANOVA table for the transformed data is shown in Figure 18.10c. We see that $F^* = 1.56$ and that the P-value for the test is .224. For $\alpha = .10$, we therefore conclude H_0, that the mean survival time for heart transplant patients with the characteristics of those included in the study does not depend on the degree of tissue mismatch.

Cited References

18.1.   Snedecor, G. W., and W. G. Cochran. *Statistical Methods.* 8th ed. Ames, Iowa: Iowa State University Press, 1989.

18.2.   Scheffé, H. *The Analysis of Variance.* New York: John Wiley & Sons, 1959.

Problems

18.1.   Refer to Figures 18.3 and 18.4. What feature of the residual sequence plots enables you to diagnose that in one case the error variance changes over time whereas in the other case the effect is of a different nature? Could you make a diagnosis about time effects from a residual dot plot?

18.2.   A student proposed in class that deviations of the observations Y_{ij} around the estimated overall mean $\overline{Y}_{..}$ be plotted to assist in evaluating the appropriateness of ANOVA model (16.2). Would these deviations be helpful in studying the independence of the error terms? The constancy of the variance of the error terms? The normality of the error terms? Discuss.

18.3.   A consultant discussing ANOVA applications in a seminar stated: "Sometimes I find that treatment effects in an experiment do not show up through differences in the treatment means. Hence, it is important to compare the residual plots for the treatments." A member of the audience asked: "I don't think I understood your point regarding differences in treatment means being explored using residual plots." Discuss.

√ 18.4.   Refer to **Productivity improvement** Problem 16.10.

   a. Prepare aligned residual dot plots by factor level. What departures from ANOVA model (16.2) can be studied from these plots? What are your findings?

b. Prepare a normal probability plot of the residuals. Also obtain the coefficient of correlation between the ordered residuals and their expected values under normality. Does the normality assumption appear to be reasonable here?

c. Obtain the studentized deleted residuals and conduct the Bonferroni outlier test; use $\alpha = .01$. State the alternatives, decision rule, and conclusion.

d. The economist wishes to investigate whether location of the firm's home office is related to productivity improvement. The home office locations are as follows (U: U.S.; E: Europe):

							j					
i	1	2	3	4	5	6	7	8	9	10	11	12
1	U	E	E	E	E	U	U	U	U			
2	E	E	E	E	U	U	U	U	U	E	E	E
3	E	U	E	U	U	E						

Prepare aligned residual dot plots by factor level in which the location of the home office is identified. Does it appear that ANOVA model (16.2) could be improved by adding location of home office as a second factor? Explain.

18.5. Refer to **Questionnaire color** Problem 16.11.

a. Prepare aligned residual dot plots by color. What departures from ANOVA model (16.2) can be studied from these plots? What are your findings?

b. Prepare a normal probability plot of the residuals. Also obtain the coefficient of correlation between the ordered residuals and their expected values under normality. Does the normality assumption appear to be reasonable here?

c. The observations within each factor level are in geographic sequence. Prepare residual sequence plots. What can be studied from these plots? What are your findings?

d. Obtain the studentized deleted residuals and conduct the Bonferroni outlier test; use $\alpha = .025$. State the alternatives, decision rule, and conclusion.

18.6. Refer to **Rehabilitation therapy** Problem 16.12.

a. Obtain the residuals and prepare aligned residual dot plots by factor level. What departures from ANOVA model (16.2) can be studied from these plots? What are your findings?

b. Prepare a normal probability plot of the residuals. Also obtain the coefficient of correlation between the ordered residuals and their expected values under normality. Does the normality assumption appear to be reasonable here?

c. The observations within each factor level are in time order. Prepare residual sequence plots and analyze them. What are your findings?

d. Obtain the studentized deleted residuals and conduct the Bonferroni outlier test; use $\alpha = .01$. State the alternatives, decision rule, and conclusion.

√ 18.7. Refer to **Cash offers** Problem 16.13.

a. Obtain the residuals and prepare aligned residual dot plots by factor level. What departures from ANOVA model (16.2) can be studied from these plots? What are your findings?

b. Prepare a normal probability plot of the residuals. Also obtain the coefficient of correlation between the ordered residuals and their expected values under normality. Does the normality assumption appear to be reasonable here?

c. The observations within each factor level are in time order. Prepare residual sequence plots and interpret them. What are your findings?

d. Obtain the studentized deleted residuals and conduct the Bonferroni outlier test; use $\alpha = .025$. State the alternatives, decision rule, and conclusion.

e. An executive in the consumer organization has been told that used-car dealers in the region tend to make lower cash offers during weekends (Friday evening through Sunday) than at other times. The times when offers were obtained are as follows (W: weekend; O: other time):

i	1	2	3	4	5	6	7	8	9	10	11	12
1	O	O	W	O	W	O	W	O	W	O	W	W
2	O	W	W	O	W	O	W	O	O	W	W	O
3	O	W	O	W	O	O	O	W	W	W	O	W

j

Prepare aligned residual dot plots by factor level in which the time of the offer is identified. Does it appear that ANOVA model (16.2) could be improved by adding time of offer as a second factor? Explain.

√ 18.8. Refer to **Filling machines** Problem 16.14.

a. Obtain the residuals and prepare aligned residual dot plots by machine. What departures from ANOVA model (16.2) can be studied from these plots? What are your findings?

b. Prepare a normal probability plot of the residuals. Also obtain the coefficient of correlation between the ordered residuals and their expected values under normality. Does the normality assumption appear to be reasonable here?

c. The observations within each factor level are in time order. Prepare residual sequence plots and interpret them. What are your findings?

d. Obtain the studentized deleted residuals and conduct the Bonferroni outlier test; use $\alpha = .01$. State the alternatives, decision rule, and conclusion.

18.9. Refer to **Premium distribution** Problem 16.15.

a. Obtain the residuals and prepare aligned residual dot plots by agent. What departures from ANOVA model (16.2) can be studied from these plots? What are your findings?

b. Prepare a normal probability plot of the residuals. Also obtain the coefficient of correlation between the ordered residuals and their expected values under normality. Does the normality assumption appear to be reasonable here?

c. The observations within each factor level are in time order. Prepare residual sequence plots and interpret them. What are your findings?

d. Obtain the studentized deleted residuals and conduct the Bonferroni outlier test; use $\alpha = .025$. State the alternatives, decision rule, and conclusion.

18.10. **Computerized game.** Four teams competed in 20 trials of a computerized business game. Each trial involved a new game, the objective for each team being to maximize profits in the given trial. A researcher fitted ANOVA model (16.2) to determine whether or not the mean profits for the four teams are the same and obtained the following residuals:

				j			
i	1	2	3	$\cdots$	18	19	20
1	.10	.28	.10	$\cdots$	.10	.28	.28
2	−1.44	−1.44	−1.12	$\cdots$	1.02	1.18	1.51
3	−.93	−.70	−.81	$\cdots$	.54	.43	.65
4	−.15	.11	.25	$\cdots$	.11	.25	.38

The residuals for each team are given in time order. Construct appropriate residual plots to study whether the error terms are independent from trial to trial for each team. What are your findings?

√ 18.11. Refer to **Productivity improvement** Problem 16.10. Examine by means of the modified Levene test whether or not the treatment error variances are equal; use $\alpha = .05$. State the alternatives, decision rule, and conclusion. What is the P-value of the test?

18.12. Refer to **Rehabilitation therapy** Problem 16.12. Examine by means of the modified Levene test whether or not the treatment error variances are equal; use $\alpha = .10$. State the alternatives, decision rule, and conclusion. What is the P-value of the test?

√ 18.13. Refer to **Cash offers** Problem 16.13. Assume that the error terms are approximately normally distributed.

    a. Examine by means of the Hartley test whether or not the treatment error variances are equal; use $\alpha = .01$. State the alternatives, decision rule, and conclusion. What is the P-value of the test?

    b. Would you reach the same conclusion as in part (a) with the modified Levene test?

18.14. Refer to **Filling machines** Problem 16.14. Assume that the error terms are approximately normally distributed.

    a. Examine by means of the Hartley test whether or not the treatment error variances are equal; use $\alpha = .01$. State the alternatives, decision rule, and conclusion. What is the P-value of the test?

    b. Would you reach the same conclusion as in part (a) with the modified Levene test statistic?

18.15. **Helicopter service**. An operations analyst in a sheriff's department studied how frequently their emergency helicopter was used during a recent 20-day period, by time of day (shift 1: 2 A.M.–8 A.M.; shift 2: 8 A.M.–2 P.M.; shift 3: 2 P.M.–8 P.M.; shift 4: 8 P.M.–2 A.M.). The data follow (in time order):

				j			
i	1	2	3	$\cdots$	18	19	20
1	4	3	5	$\cdots$	4	1	6
2	0	2	0	$\cdots$	2	2	0
3	2	1	0	$\cdots$	0	2	4
4	5	2	4	$\cdots$	5	2	3

Since the data are counts, the analyst was concerned about the normality and equal variances assumptions of ANOVA model (16.2).

a. Obtain the fitted values and residuals for ANOVA model (16.2).

b. Prepare suitable residual plots to study whether or not the error variances are equal for the four shifts. What are your findings?

c. Test by means of the modified Levene test whether or not the treatment error variances are equal; use $\alpha = .10$. What is the P-value of the test? Are your results consistent with the diagnosis in part (b)?

d. For each shift, calculate $\bar{Y}_{i.}$ and s_i. Examine the three relations found in the table on page 773 and determine the transformation that is most appropriate here. What do you conclude?

e. Use the Box-Cox procedure to find an appropriate power transformation of Y, first adding the constant 1 to each Y observation. Evaluate SSE for the values of λ given in Table 18.6. Does $\lambda = .5$, a square-root transformation, appear to be reasonable, based on the Box-Cox procedure?

18.16. Refer to **Helicopter service** Problem 18.15. The analyst decided to apply the square root transformation $Y' = \sqrt{Y}$ and examine its effectiveness.

a. Obtain the transformed response data, fit ANOVA model (16.2), and obtain the residuals.

b. Prepare suitable plots of the residuals to study the equality of the error variances of the transformed response variable for the four shifts. Also obtain a normal probability plot and the coefficient of correlation between the ordered residuals and their expected values under normality. What are your findings? Does the transformation appear to have been effective?

c. Test by means of the modified Levene test whether or not the treatment error variances for the transformed response variable are equal; use $\alpha = .10$. State the alternatives, decision rule, and conclusion. Are your findings in part (b) consistent with your conclusion here?

√ 18.17. **Winding speeds.** In an experiment to study the effect of the speed of winding thread (1: slow; 2: normal; 3: fast; 4: maximum) onto 75-yard spools, 16 runs of 10,000 spools each were made at each of the four winding speeds. The response variable is the number of thread breaks during the production run. The results (in time order) are as follows:

	j						
i	1	2	3	...	14	15	16
1	4	3	2	...	2	3	4
2	7	6	4	...	4	7	6
3	12	6	14	...	13	10	14
4	17	15	7	...	19	9	23

Since the responses are counts, the researcher was concerned about the normality and equal variances assumptions of ANOVA model (16.2).

a. Obtain the fitted values and residuals for ANOVA model (16.2).

b. Prepare suitable residual plots to study whether or not the error variances are equal for the four winding speeds. What are your findings?

c. Test by means of the modified Levene test whether or not the treatment error variances are equal; use $\alpha = .05$. What is the P-value of the test? Are your results consistent with the diagnosis in part (b)?

d. For each winding speed, calculate $\bar{Y}_{i\cdot}$ and s_i. Examine the three relations found in the table on page 773 and determine the transformation that is most appropriate here. What do you conclude?

e. Use the Box-Cox procedure to find an appropriate power transformation of Y. Evaluate SSE for the values of λ given in Table 18.6. Does $\lambda = 0$, a logarithmic transformation, appear to be reasonable, based on the Box-Cox procedure?

$\sqrt{}$ 18.18. Refer to **Winding speeds** Problem 18.17. The researcher decided to apply the logarithmic transformation $Y' = \log_{10} Y$ and investigate its effectiveness.

a. Obtain the transformed response data, fit ANOVA model (16.2), and obtain the residuals.

b. Prepare suitable plots of the residuals to study the equality of the error variances of the transformed response variable for the four winding speeds. Also obtain a normal probability plot and the coefficient of correlation between the ordered residuals and their expected values under normality. What are your findings about the effectiveness of the transformation?

c. Test by means of the modified Levene test whether or not the treatment error variances for the transformed response variable are equal; use $\alpha = .05$. State the alternatives, decision rule, and conclusion. Are your findings in part (b) consistent with your conclusion here?

18.19. Refer to **Helicopter service** Problem 18.15. Assume that ANOVA model (18.13) is appropriate. Use weighted least squares with the untransformed data to test for the equality of the shift means; control the α risk at .05. State the alternatives, full and reduced regression models, decision rule, and conclusion.

$\sqrt{}$ 18.20. Refer to **Winding speeds** Problem 18.17. Assume that ANOVA model (18.13) is appropriate. Use weighted least squares with the untransformed data to test for the equality of the winding thread speed means; use $\alpha = .01$. State the alternatives, full and reduced regression models, decision rule, and conclusion.

18.21. Why is the nonparametric rank F test a nonparametric test?

18.22. Explain why the limits in (18.30) are testing limits and not confidence limits.

$\sqrt{}$ 18.23. Refer to **Productivity improvement** Problem 16.10.

a. Conduct the nonparametric rank F test; use $\alpha = .05$. State the alternatives, decision rule, and conclusion.

b. What is the P-value of the test in part (a)?

c. Does the conclusion in part (a) differ from the one in Problem 16.10e?

d. Do the data suggest that a nonparametric test is needed here?

e. Conduct multiple pairwise tests based on the ranked data to group the three types of firms according to mean productivity improvement. Use family level of significance $\alpha = .10$. Describe your findings.

18.24. Refer to **Cash offers** Problem 16.13.

a. Conduct the nonparametric rank F test; use $\alpha = .01$. State the alternatives, decision rule, and conclusion.

b. What is the P-value of the test in part (a)?

c. Does the conclusion in part (a) differ from the one in Problem 16.13e?

d. Do the data suggest that a nonparametric test is needed here?

e. Conduct multiple pairwise tests based on the ranked data to group the three age categories according to mean cash offer. Use family level of significance $\alpha = .10$. Describe your findings.

18.25. **Telephone communications**. A management consultant was engaged by a firm to improve the cost effectiveness of its communications. As part of the study, the consultant selected 10 home-office executives at random from each of the (1) sales, (2) production, and (3) research and development divisions, and studied the communications of these executives during the past 10 weeks in great detail. Among other data, the consultant obtained the following information on weekly dollar costs of long-distance telephone calls to branch offices by the executives:

					j					
i	1	2	3	4	5	6	7	8	9	10
1	666	920	495	602	1,499	960	796	343	894	813
2	488	362	156	546	216	542	345	291	516	126
3	391	450	609	910	705	472	645	496	763	1,309

The consultant decided to employ a nonparametric approach to test whether or not the mean telephone expenses for the three divisions are equal.

a. What feature of the data may have suggested the use of a nonparametric test?

b. Conduct the nonparametric rank F test, controlling the risk of Type I error at $\alpha = .05$. State the alternatives, decision rule, and conclusion. What is the P-value of the test?

c. Conduct multiple pairwise tests based on the ranked data to group the three divisions according to mean telephone expenditures; use family level of significance $\alpha = .05$. Describe your findings.

Exercises

18.26. Refer to Figure 18.3. Modify ANOVA model (16.2) to include a linear trend term for the time effect. Is this modified model still an ANOVA model? A linear model?

18.27. Show that $n_T(n_T + 1)/12$ in (18.30) is the sample variance of the consecutive integers 1 to n_T.

18.28. Show that test statistics (18.25) and (18.27) are related according to (18.29).

Projects

18.29. Refer to the **SENIC** data set and Project 16.31.

a. Obtain the residuals and prepare aligned residual dot plots by region. Are any serious departures from ANOVA model (16.2) suggested by your plots?

b. Obtain a normal probability plot of the residuals and calculate the coefficient of correlation between the ordered residuals and their expected values under normality. Is the normality assumption reasonable here?

c. Examine by means of the modified Levene test whether or not the geographic region error variances are equal; use $\alpha = .05$. State the alternatives, decision rule, and conclusion. What is the P-value of the test?

18.30. Refer to the **SENIC** data set. A test of whether or not mean length of stay (variable 2) is the same in the four geographic regions (variable 9) is desired, but concern exists about the normality and equal variances assumptions of ANOVA model (16.2).

a. Obtain the residuals and plot them against the fitted values to study whether or not the error variances are equal for the four geographic regions. What are your findings?

b. For each geographic region, calculate $\bar{Y}_{i.}$ and s_i. Examine the three relations found in the table on page 773 and determine the transformation that is the most appropriate one here. What do you conclude?

c. Use the Box-Cox procedure to find an appropriate power transformation of Y. Evaluate SSE for the values of λ given in Table 18.6. Does $\lambda = -1$, a reciprocal transformation, appear to be reasonable, based on the Box-Cox procedure?

d. Use the reciprocal transformation $Y' = 1/Y$ to obtain transformed response data.

e. Fit ANOVA model (16.2) to the transformed data and obtain the residuals. Plot these residuals against the fitted values to study the equality of the error variances of the transformed response variable for the four regions. Also obtain a normal probability plot of the residuals and the coefficient of correlation between the ordered residuals and their expected values under normality. What are your findings?

f. Examine by means of the modified Levene test whether or not the geographic region variances for the transformed response variable are equal; use $\alpha = .01$. State the alternatives, decision rule, and conclusion. What is the P-value of the test?

g. Assume that ANOVA model (16.2) is appropriate for the transformed response variable. Test whether or not the mean length of stay in the transformed units is the same in the four geographic regions. Control the α risk at .01. State the alternatives, decision rule, and conclusion. What is the P-value of the test?

18.31. Refer to the **SMSA** data set and Project 16.33.

a. Obtain the residuals and prepare aligned residual dot plots by region. Are any serious departures from ANOVA model (16.2) suggested by your plots?

b. Obtain a normal probability plot of the residuals and calculate the coefficient of correlation between the ordered residuals and their expected values under normality. Is the normality assumption reasonable here?

c. Examine by means of the modified Levene test whether or not the geographic region error variances are equal; use $\alpha = .01$. State the alternatives, decision rule, and conclusion. What is the P-value of the test?

18.32. Refer to the **SENIC** data set and Project 16.31.

    a. Use the nonparametric rank F test to determine whether or not the mean infection risk is the same in the four regions; control the level of significance at $\alpha = .05$. State the alternatives, decision rule, and conclusion. What is the P-value of the test?

    b. Is your conclusion in part (a) the same as that obtained in Project 16.31? Is the nonparametric test more reasonable here?

    c. Use the multiple pairwise testing procedure (18.30) to group the regions; employ family significance level $\alpha = .10$. What are your findings?

18.33. Refer to the **SMSA** data set and Project 16.33.

    a. Use the nonparametric rank F test to determine whether or not the mean crime rate is the same in the four regions; control the level of significance at $\alpha = .05$. State the alternatives, decision rule, and conclusion. What is the P-value of the test?

    b. Is your conclusion in part (a) the same as that obtained in Project 16.33? Is the nonparametric test more reasonable here?

    c. Use the multiple pairwise testing procedure (18.30) to group the regions; employ family significance level $\alpha = .05$. What are your findings?

18.34. Obtain the exact sampling distribution of the nonparametric rank F_R^* test statistic in (18.25) when H_0 holds, for the case $r = 2$ and $n_i \equiv 2$. [*Hint*: What does the equality of the treatment means imply about the arrangement of the ranks 1, 2, 3, 4?]

18.35. Three populations are being studied; each is uniform between 300 and 800.

    a. Generate 10 random observations from each of the three uniform populations and calculate the F_R^* test statistic (18.25).

    b. Repeat part (a) 500 times.

    c. Calculate the mean and standard deviation of the 500 test statistics. How do these values compare with the characteristics of the relevant F distribution?

    d. What proportion of the 500 test statistics obtained in part (b) is less than $F(.90; 2, 27)$? What proportion is less than $F(.99; 2, 27)$? How do these proportions agree with theoretical expectations?

Analysis of Variance: II

PART VI

Analysis of Variance II

Two-Factor Analysis of Variance—Equal Sample Sizes

In Part V, we considered analysis of variance studies in which the effects of one factor are investigated. Now we are concerned with investigations of the simultaneous effects of two or more factors. In this chapter, we take up the analysis of variance for two-factor studies when all sample sizes are equal. In Chapters 20, 21, and 22, we continue the discussion of two-factor studies by taking up the analysis of factor effects, the analysis of variance when the sample sizes are unequal, and a number of other topics. In Chapter 23, we extend the analysis of variance to studies with three or more factors. Random and mixed effects models are the subjects of Chapter 24, and, finally in Chapter 25, we take up the analysis of covariance for factorial studies.

19.1 Multifactor Studies

Before focusing specifically on two-factor studies, we shall first make some general remarks about multifactor studies, which encompass investigations of two or more factors. Multifactor studies, like single-factor studies, can be based on experimental or observational data.

Examples of Two-Factor Studies

Example 1. A company investigated the effects of selling price and type of promotional campaign on sales of one of its products. Three selling prices (59 cents, 60 cents, 64 cents) were studied, as were two types of promotional campaigns (radio advertising, newspaper advertising). Let us consider selling price to be factor A and promotional campaign to be factor B. Factor A here was studied at three price levels; in general, we use the symbol a to denote the number of levels of factor A investigated. Factor B was here studied at two levels; we use the symbol b to denote the number of levels of factor B investigated. Each combination of price and promotional campaign was studied, as shown in the table at the top of the next page.

Treatment	Description
1	59¢ price, radio advertising
2	60¢ price, radio advertising
3	64¢ price, radio advertising
4	59¢ price, newspaper advertising
5	60¢ price, newspaper advertising
6	64¢ price, newspaper advertising

Each combination of a factor level of A and a factor level of B is a *treatment*. Thus, there are $3 \times 2 = 6$ treatments here altogether. In general, the total number of possible treatments in a two-factor study is ab.

Twelve communities throughout the United States, of approximately equal size and similar socioeconomic characteristics, were selected and the treatments were assigned to them at random, such that each treatment was given to two experimental units. As before, we use n for the number of units receiving a given treatment when all treatment sample sizes are the same. In the two communities that were assigned treatment 1, for instance, the product price was fixed at 59 cents and radio advertising was employed, and so on for the other communities in the study.

This is an experimental study because control was exercised in assigning the factor A and factor B levels to the experimental units by means of random assignments of the treatments to the communities. The design used was a completely randomized design.

Example 2.   A steel company studied the effects of carbon content and tempering temperature on the strength of steel. Carbon content was investigated at a high level and at a low level (the precise definitions of these levels are not important here). Tempering temperature was also studied at a high level and at a low level. Altogether, $2 \times 2 = 4$ treatments were defined for this study.

Treatment	Description
1	High carbon level, high tempering temperature
2	High carbon level, low tempering temperature
3	Low carbon level, high tempering temperature
4	Low carbon level, low tempering temperature

These four treatments were then assigned to 12 production batches in randomized fashion, with each treatment assigned to three batches.

This again is an experimental study because control was exercised over carbon content and tempering temperature by means of the random assignment of treatments to the production batches. The design used again was a completely randomized design.

Example 3.   An analyst studied the effects of family income (under $15,000, $15,000–$29,999, $30,000–$49,999, $50,000 and more) and stage in the life cycle of the family (stages 1, 2, 3, 4) on appliance purchases. Here, $4 \times 4 = 16$ treatments are defined. These are in part:

Treatment	Description
1	Under $15,000 income, stage 1
2	Under $15,000 income, stage 2
⋮	⋮
16	$50,000 and more income, stage 4

The analyst selected 20 families with the required income and life-cycle characteristics for each of the "treatment" classes for this study, yielding 320 families for the entire study.

This study is an observational one because the data were obtained without assigning income and life-cycle stage to the families. Rather, the families were selected because they had the specified characteristics.

Comments

1. When we considered single-factor studies, we did not place any restrictions on the nature of the r factor levels under study. Formally, the ab treatments in a two-factor investigation could be considered as the r factor levels in a single-factor investigation and analyzed according to the methods discussed in Part V. The reason why new methods of analysis are required is that we wish to analyze the ab treatments in special ways that recognize two factors are involved and enable us to obtain information about the main effects of each of the two factors as well as about any special joint effects.

2. When a completely randomized design is used in a multifactor study, the random assignments of treatments to the experimental units are made in the same manner as for a single-factor study. No new problems are encountered once the treatments are defined in terms of the factor levels of the various factors under study.   ∎

Complete and Fractional Factorial Studies

The three examples cited above are *complete factorial studies* because all possible combinations of factor levels for the different factors were included. At times, it is not feasible or desirable to include all possible combinations of factor levels for the different factors. For instance, suppose the steel company mentioned in Example 2 wished to study six tempering temperatures, five levels of carbon content, and four methods of cooling the steel. A complete factorial study would then involve $6 \times 5 \times 4 = 120$ treatments. Such a study might be extremely costly and time-consuming. Under these conditions, it may be possible to design a *fractional factorial study* containing only a fraction of the 120 factor level combinations, which will still provide information about the main effects of each of the three factors as well as about any important special joint effects of these factors. Fractional factorial designs are discussed in Chapters 30 and 31.

The discussion of multifactor investigations in Part VI deals solely with complete factorial studies.

Advantages of Multifactor Studies

Efficiency.   Multifactor studies are more efficient than the traditional experimental approach of manipulating only one factor at a time and keeping all other conditions constant. With reference to Example 1, the traditional approach to studying the effect of promotional campaign would be to keep price constant at a given level and vary only the promotional campaign. An important problem with this approach is the choice of the price level to be held constant. This choice is especially difficult when one is not sure whether the promotional effects are the same at different price levels. Even though the traditional approach devotes all resources to studying the effect of only one factor, it does not yield any more precise information about that factor than a multifactor experiment of the same size. With reference to Example 1 again, suppose that 12 communities were to be utilized in a traditional study, six assigned to radio advertising and the other six to newspaper advertising, and that the price would be kept constant at 59 cents. For this traditional study, the comparison between the two types of promotional campaigns would be based on two samples of six communities each. The same is true for the two-factor study in Example 1, since each promotional campaign occurs there in three treatments and each treatment has two communities assigned to it.

Amount of Information.   A traditional study provides less information than a two-factor study. Specifically in our previous illustration, it does not provide any information about the effects of price, nor about any special joint effects of price and promotional campaign. Information about price effects would require an additional traditional experiment for which promotional campaign would be kept constant at a given level and price varied. Thus, the traditional approach would require a larger sample to provide information about both price and promotional campaign effects, and unless the traditional study were yet further enlarged, it would still not provide full information about any special joint effects of the two factors. Such special joint effects are called *interactions*, just as in regression. We will discuss interactions in the context of analysis of variance models in the next section. Here it suffices to point out that interaction effects may be very important. For instance, it might be that the price effects are not large when the promotional campaign is in newspapers but are large with radio advertising. Such interaction effects can be readily investigated from factorial studies.

Validity of Findings.   In addition to being more efficient and readily providing information about interaction effects, multifactor studies also can strengthen the validity of the findings. Suppose that in Example 1, management was principally interested in investigating the effects of price on sales. If the promotional campaign used in the price study had been newspaper advertising, doubts might exist as to whether or not the price effects differ for other promotional vehicles. By including type of promotional campaign as another factor in the study, management can get information about the persistence of the price effects with different promotional vehicles, without increasing the number of experimental units in the study. Thus, multifactor studies can include some factors of secondary importance to permit inferences about the primary factors with a greater range of validity.

Comments

1. Multifactor analysis permits a ready evaluation of interaction effects for observational data and economizes on the number of cases required for the analysis, just as for experimental studies.

2. The advantages of multifactor experiments just described should not lead one to think that the more factors are included in the study, the better. Experiments involving many factors, each at numerous levels, become complex, costly, and time-consuming. It is often a better research strategy to begin with fewer factors and/or fewer levels for each factor, and then extend the investigation in accordance with the results obtained to date. In this way, resources can be devoted principally to the most promising avenues of investigation, and a better understanding of the working of the factors can be obtained.   ∎

TABLE 19.1   **Age Effect but No Gender Effect, with No Interactions—Learning Example.**

(a) Mean Learning Times (in minutes)

	Factor B—Age			
Factor A—Gender	$j = 1$ Young	$j = 2$ Middle	$j = 3$ Old	Row Average
$i = 1$ Male	9 (μ_{11})	11 (μ_{12})	16 (μ_{13})	12 $(\mu_{1.})$
$i = 2$ Female	9 (μ_{21})	11 (μ_{22})	16 (μ_{23})	12 $(\mu_{2.})$
Column average	9 $(\mu_{.1})$	11 $(\mu_{.2})$	16 $(\mu_{.3})$	12 $(\mu_{..})$

(b) Main Gender Effects (in minutes)

$$\alpha_1 = \mu_{1.} - \mu_{..} = 12 - 12 = 0$$
$$\alpha_2 = \mu_{2.} - \mu_{..} = 12 - 12 = 0$$

(c) Main Age Effects (in minutes)

$$\beta_1 = \mu_{.1} - \mu_{..} = 9 - 12 = -3$$
$$\beta_2 = \mu_{.2} - \mu_{..} = 11 - 12 = -1$$
$$\beta_3 = \mu_{.3} - \mu_{..} = 16 - 12 = 4$$

19.2   Meaning of ANOVA Model Elements

Before presenting a formal statement of the analysis of variance model for two-factor studies, we shall develop the model elements and discuss their meaning. This will not only be helpful in understanding the ANOVA model but will also provide insights into how the analysis of two-factor studies should proceed. *Throughout this section, we assume that all population means are known and are of equal importance when averages of these means are required.*

Illustration

To illustrate the meaning of the ANOVA model elements, we consider a simple two-factor study in which the effects of gender and age on learning of a task are of interest. For simplicity, the age factor has been defined in terms of only three factor levels (young, middle, old), as shown in Table 19.1a.

Treatment Means

The mean response for a given treatment in a two-factor study is denoted by μ_{ij}, where i refers to the level of factor A $(i = 1, \ldots, a)$ and j refers to the level of factor B $(j = 1, \ldots, b)$. Table 19.1a contains the true treatment means μ_{ij} for the learning example. Note, for instance, that $\mu_{11} = 9$, which indicates that the mean learning time for young males is 9 minutes. Similarly, we see that $\mu_{22} = 11$, so that the mean learning time for middle-aged females is 11 minutes.

Note

The interpretation of a treatment mean μ_{ij} depends on whether the study is an observational or an experimental one. In an observational study, the treatment mean μ_{ij} corresponds to the population mean for the elements having the characteristics of the ith level of factor A and the jth level of factor B. For instance, in the learning example, the treatment mean μ_{11} is the mean learning time for the population of young males.

In an experimental study, the treatment mean μ_{ij} stands for the mean response that would be obtained if the treatment consisting of the ith level of factor A and the jth level of factor B were applied to all units in the population of experimental units about which inferences are to be drawn. For instance, in a study where factor A is type of training program (highly structured, partially structured, unstructured) and factor B is time of training (during work, after work), $6n$ employees are selected and n are assigned at random to each of the six treatments. The mean μ_{ij} here represents the mean response, say, mean gain in productivity, if the ith training program administered during the jth time were given to all employees in the population of experimental units.

∎

Factor Level Means

The treatment means in Table 19.1a for the learning example indicate that the mean learning times for men and women are the same for each age group. On the other hand, the mean learning time increases with age for each gender. Thus, gender has no effect on mean learning time, but age does. This can also be seen quickly from the row averages and column averages shown in Table 19.1a, which in this case tell the complete story. The row averages are the gender *factor level means*, and the column averages are the age factor level means. We denote the column average for the first column by $\mu_{\cdot1}$, which is the average of μ_{11} and μ_{21}. In general, the column average for the jth column is denoted by $\mu_{\cdot j}$:

$$(19.1) \qquad \mu_{\cdot j} = \frac{\sum\limits_{i=1}^{a} \mu_{ij}}{a}$$

and the row average for the ith row is denoted by $\mu_{i\cdot}$:

$$(19.2) \qquad \mu_{i\cdot} = \frac{\sum\limits_{j=1}^{b} \mu_{ij}}{b}$$

The overall mean learning time for all ages and both genders is denoted by $\mu_{\cdot\cdot}$, and is defined in the following equivalent fashions:

$$(19.3a) \qquad \mu_{\cdot\cdot} = \frac{\sum\limits_{i}\sum\limits_{j} \mu_{ij}}{ab}$$

$$(19.3b) \qquad \mu_{\cdot\cdot} = \frac{\sum\limits_{i} \mu_{i\cdot}}{a}$$

$$(19.3c) \qquad \mu_{\cdot\cdot} = \frac{\sum\limits_{j} \mu_{\cdot j}}{b}$$

In Table 19.1a, the gender factor level means are $\mu_{1.} = \mu_{2.} = 12$ for the two genders, the age factor level means are $\mu_{.1} = 9$, $\mu_{.2} = 11$, and $\mu_{.3} = 16$ for the three age groups, and the overall mean learning time is $\mu_{..} = 12$ minutes.

Main Effects

Main Age Effects.   To summarize the main age effects, we shall consider the differences between each factor level mean and the overall mean. These differences are called main age effects. For instance, the main effect for young persons in Table 19.1a is the difference between $\mu_{.1}$, the mean learning time for young persons, and $\mu_{..}$, the overall mean. This difference is denoted by β_1:

$$\beta_1 = \mu_{.1} - \mu_{..} = 9 - 12 = -3$$

β_1 is called the *main effect* for factor B at the first level. This and the other main effects for factor B are shown in Table 19.1c.

Main Gender Effects.   The main gender effects are defined in corresponding fashion, and denoted by α_i. For instance, we have:

$$\alpha_1 = \mu_{1.} - \mu_{..} = 12 - 12 = 0$$

α_1 is called the main effect for factor A at the first level. The main effects for factor A are shown in Table 19.1b. They are both zero, indicating that gender does not affect mean learning time.

General Definitions.   In general, we define the main effect of factor A at the ith level as follows:

$$(19.4) \qquad\qquad\qquad\qquad \alpha_i = \mu_{i.} - \mu_{..}$$

Similarly, the main effect of the jth level of factor B is defined:

$$(19.5) \qquad\qquad\qquad\qquad \beta_j = \mu_{.j} - \mu_{..}$$

It follows from (19.3b) and (19.3c) that:

$$(19.6) \qquad\qquad\qquad \sum_i \alpha_i = 0 \qquad \sum_j \beta_j = 0$$

Thus, the sum of the main effects for each factor is zero.

Note again that a main effect indicates how much the factor level mean deviates from the overall mean. The greater the main effect, the more the factor level mean differs from the overall mean response averaged over the factor levels for both factors.

Additive Factor Effects

The factor effects in Table 19.1 have an interesting property. Each mean response μ_{ij} can be obtained by adding the respective gender and age main effects to the overall mean $\mu_{..}$. For instance, we have:

$$\mu_{11} = \mu_{..} + \alpha_1 + \beta_1 = 12 + 0 + (-3) = 9$$
$$\mu_{23} = \mu_{..} + \alpha_2 + \beta_3 = 12 + 0 + 4 = 16$$

In general, we have for Table 19.1a:

(19.7) $$\mu_{ij} = \mu_{..} + \alpha_i + \beta_j \qquad \text{Additive factor effects}$$

which can be expressed equivalently, using the definitions of α_i in (19.4) and of β_j in (19.5), as:

(19.7a) $$\mu_{ij} = \mu_{i.} + \mu_{.j} - \mu_{..} \qquad \text{Additive factor effects}$$

It can also be shown that each treatment mean μ_{ij} in Table 19.1a can be expressed in terms of three other treatment means:

(19.7b) $$\mu_{ij} = \mu_{ij'} + \mu_{i'j} - \mu_{i'j'} \qquad \text{Additive factor effects}$$
$$i \neq i', j \neq j'$$

For instance, we have:

$$\mu_{11} = \mu_{12} + \mu_{21} - \mu_{22} = 11 + 9 - 11 = 9$$

or:

$$\mu_{11} = \mu_{13} + \mu_{21} - \mu_{23} = 16 + 9 - 16 = 9$$

When all treatment means can be expressed in the form of (19.7), (19.7a), or (19.7b), we say that the *factors do not interact*, or that *no factor interactions are present*, or that the *factor effects are additive*. The significance of no factor interactions is that the effect of either factor does not depend on the level of the other factor. Consequently, the effects of the two factors can be described separately merely by analyzing the factor level means or the factor main effects. For instance, in the learning example in Table 19.1a, the two gender means signify that gender has no influence regardless of age, and the three age means portray the influence of age regardless of gender. The analysis of factor effects is therefore quite simple when there are no factor interactions.

Graphic Presentation. Figure 19.1 presents the mean learning times of Table 19.1a in the form of a *treatment means plot*. The X axis contains the gender factor levels (denoted by A_1 and A_2), and the Y axis contains learning time. Separate curves are drawn for each of the age factor levels (denoted by B_1, B_2, and B_3). The zero slope of each curve indicates that gender has no effect. The differences in the heights of the three curves show the age effects on learning time.

The points on each curve are conventionally connected by straight lines even though the variable on the X axis (gender, in our example) is not a continuous variable. When the variable on the X axis is qualitative, the slopes of the curves have no meaning, except when

FIGURE 19.1   Age Effect but No Gender Effect, with No Interactions —Learning Example.

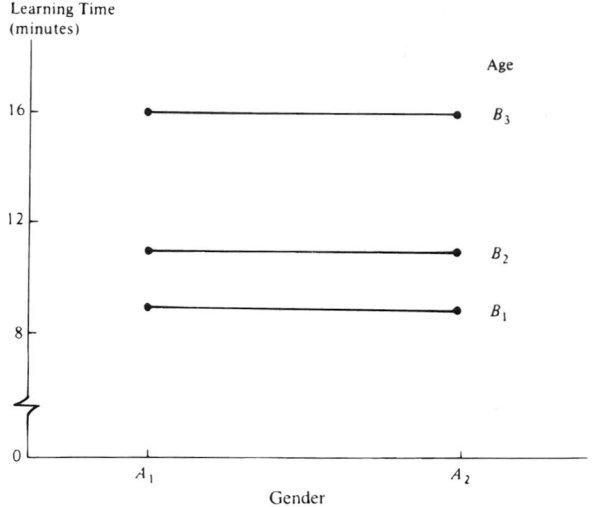

the slope is zero, which implies there are no factor level effects. If one of the two factors is a quantitative variable, it is ordinarily advisable to place that factor on the X scale.

Note that the treatment means plot in Figure 19.1 corresponds to a conditional effects plot in regression, such as the ones shown in Figure 7.10. In each case, the effect of one variable is shown at different levels of the other variable.

A Second Example with Additive Factor Effects.   Table 19.2a contains another illustration of factor effects that do not interact, for the same gender-age learning example as before. The situation here differs from that of Table 19.1a in that not only age but also gender affects the learning time. This is evident from the fact that the mean learning times for men and women are not the same for any age group.

In Table 19.2a, as in Table 19.1a, every mean response can be decomposed according to (19.7):

$$\mu_{ij} = \mu_{..} + \alpha_i + \beta_j$$

For instance:

$$\mu_{11} = \mu_{..} + \alpha_1 + \beta_1 = 12 + 2 + (-3) = 11$$

Hence, the two factors do not interact, and the factor effects can be analyzed separately by examining the factor level means $\mu_{i.}$ and $\mu_{.j}$, respectively.

Figure 19.2 presents the data from Table 19.2a in the form of a treatment means plot. This time we have placed age on the X axis and used different curves for each gender. Note that the difference in the heights of the two curves reflects the gender difference and the departure from horizontal for each of the curves reflects the age effect.

Equivalent Statements of Additive Factor Effects.   We have said that two factors do not interact if *all* treatment means μ_{ij} can be expressed according to (19.7), (19.7a), or (19.7b).

TABLE 19.2   **Age and Gender Effects, with No Interactions—Learning Example.**

(a) Mean Learning Times (in minutes)

Factor A—Gender	Factor B—Age			Row Average
	$j = 1$ Young	$j = 2$ Middle	$j = 3$ Old	
$i = 1$ Male	11 (μ_{11})	13 (μ_{12})	18 (μ_{13})	14 ($\mu_{1.}$)
$i = 2$ Female	7 (μ_{21})	9 (μ_{22})	14 (μ_{23})	10 ($\mu_{2.}$)
Column average	9 ($\mu_{.1}$)	11 ($\mu_{.2}$)	16 ($\mu_{.3}$)	12 ($\mu_{..}$)

(b) Main Gender Effects (in minutes)

$$\alpha_1 = \mu_{1.} - \mu_{..} = 14 - 12 = 2$$
$$\alpha_2 = \mu_{2.} - \mu_{..} = 10 - 12 = -2$$

(c) Main Age Effects (in minutes)

$$\beta_1 = \mu_{.1} - \mu_{..} = 9 - 12 = -3$$
$$\beta_2 = \mu_{.2} - \mu_{..} = 11 - 12 = -1$$
$$\beta_3 = \mu_{.3} - \mu_{..} = 16 - 12 = 4$$

FIGURE 19.2   **Age and Gender Effects, with No Interactions—Learning Example.**

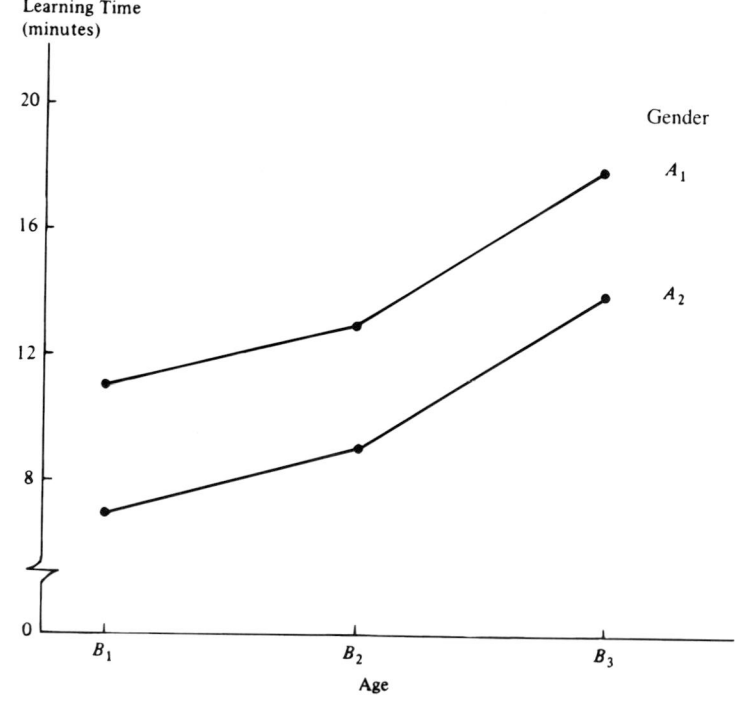

TABLE 19.3   Age and Gender Effects, with Interactions—Learning Example.

(a) Mean Learning Times (in minutes)

Factor A—Gender	Factor B—Age $j = 1$ Young	$j = 2$ Middle	$j = 3$ Old	Row Average	Main Gender Effect
$i = 1$ Male	9 (μ_{11})	12 (μ_{12})	18 (μ_{13})	13 $(\mu_{1.})$	1 (α_1)
$i = 2$ Female	9 (μ_{21})	10 (μ_{22})	14 (μ_{23})	11 $(\mu_{2.})$	-1 (α_2)
Column average	9 $(\mu_{.1})$	11 $(\mu_{.2})$	16 $(\mu_{.3})$	12 $(\mu_{..})$	
Main age effect	-3 (β_1)	-1 (β_2)	4 (β_3)		

(b) Interactions (in minutes)

	$j = 1$	$j = 2$	$j = 3$	Row Average
$i = 1$	-1	0	1	0
$i = 2$	1	0	-1	0
Column average	0	0	0	0

There are a number of other, equivalent, methods of recognizing when two factors do not interact. These are:

1. The difference between the mean responses for any two levels of factor B is the same for all levels of factor A. (For instance, in Table 19.2a, going from young to middle age leads to an increase of two minutes for both males and females, and going from middle age to old leads to an increase of five minutes for both males and females.) Note that it is *not* required that the changes, say, between levels 1 and 2 and between levels 2 and 3 of factor B are the same. These, of course, may differ depending upon the nature of the factor B effect.

2. The difference between the mean responses for any two levels of factor A is the same for all levels of factor B. (For instance, in Table 19.2a, going from male to female leads to a decrease of four minutes for all three age groups.)

3. The curves of the mean responses for the different levels of a factor are all parallel (such as the two gender curves in Figure 19.2).

All of these conditions are equivalent, implying that the two factors do not interact.

Interacting Factor Effects

Table 19.3a contains an illustration for the learning example where the factor effects do interact. The mean learning times for the different gender-age combinations in Table 19.3a indicate that gender has no effect on learning time for young persons but has a substantial effect for old persons. This differential influence of gender, which depends on the age of the person, implies that the age and gender factors interact in their effect on learning time.

Definition of Interaction.   We can study the existence of interacting factor effects formally by examining whether or not all treatment means μ_{ij} can be expressed according to (19.7):

$$\mu_{ij} = \mu_{..} + \alpha_i + \beta_j$$

If they can, the factor effects are additive; otherwise, the factor effects are interacting.

For the learning example in Table 19.3a, the main factor effects α_i and β_j are shown in the margins of the table. It is clear that the factors interact. For instance, $\mu_{11} = 9$ while:

$$\mu_{..} + \alpha_1 + \beta_1 = 12 + 1 + (-3) = 10$$

If the two factors were additive, these would be the same.

The difference between the treatment mean μ_{ij} and the value $\mu_{..} + \alpha_i + \beta_j$ that would be expected if the two factors were additive is called the *interaction effect*, or more simply the *interaction*, of the ith level of factor A with the jth level of factor B, and is denoted by $(\alpha\beta)_{ij}$. Thus, we define $(\alpha\beta)_{ij}$ as follows:

(19.8) $$(\alpha\beta)_{ij} = \mu_{ij} - (\mu_{..} + \alpha_i + \beta_j)$$

Replacing α_i and β_j by their definitions in (19.4) and (19.5), respectively, we obtain an alternative definition:

(19.8a) $$(\alpha\beta)_{ij} = \mu_{ij} - \mu_{i.} - \mu_{.j} + \mu_{..}$$

To repeat, the interaction of the ith level of A with the jth level of B, denoted by $(\alpha\beta)_{ij}$, is simply the difference between the treatment mean μ_{ij} and the value that would be expected if the factors were additive. If in fact the two factors are additive, all interactions equal zero; i.e., $(\alpha\beta)_{ij} \equiv 0$.

The interactions for the learning example in Table 19.3a are shown in Table 19.3b. We have, for instance:

$$(\alpha\beta)_{13} = \mu_{13} - (\mu_{..} + \alpha_1 + \beta_3)$$
$$= 18 - (12 + 1 + 4)$$
$$= 1$$

Recognition of Interactions.   We may recognize whether or not interactions are present in one of the following equivalent fashions:

1. By examining whether all μ_{ij} can be expressed as the sums $\mu_{..} + \alpha_i + \beta_j$.

2. By examining whether the difference between the mean responses for any two levels of factor B is the same for all levels of factor A. (For instance, note in Table 19.3a that the mean learning time increases when going from young to middle-aged persons by three minutes for men but only by one minute for women.)

3. By examining whether the difference between the mean responses for any two levels of factor A is the same for all levels of factor B. (For instance, note in Table 19.3a that there is no difference between genders for young persons, but there is a difference of four minutes for old persons.)

4. By examining whether the treatment means curves for the different factor levels in a treatment means plot are parallel. (Figure 19.3 presents a plot of the treatment means in Table 19.3a, with age on the X axis. Note that the treatment means curves for the two genders are not parallel.)

FIGURE 19.3   **Age and Gender Effects, with Important Interactions —Learning Example.**

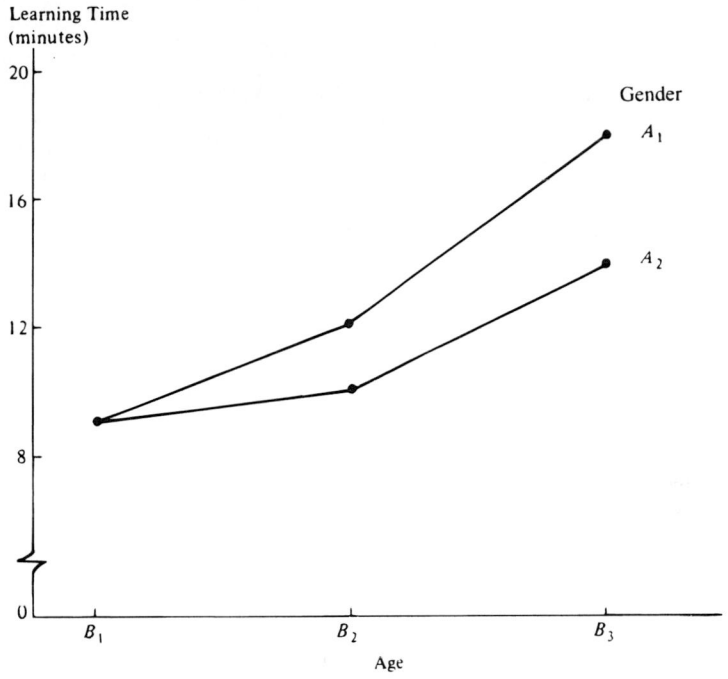

Comments

1. Note from Table 19.3b that some interactions are zero even though the two factors are interacting. *All* interactions must equal zero in order for the two factors to be additive.

2. Table 19.3b illustrates that interactions sum to zero when added over either rows or columns:

$$(19.9a) \qquad \sum_i (\alpha\beta)_{ij} = 0 \qquad j = 1, \ldots, b$$

$$(19.9b) \qquad \sum_j (\alpha\beta)_{ij} = 0 \qquad i = 1, \ldots, a$$

Consequently, the sum of all interactions is also zero:

$$(19.9c) \qquad \sum_i \sum_j (\alpha\beta)_{ij} = 0$$

We show this for (19.9a):

$$\sum_i (\alpha\beta)_{ij} = \sum_{i=1}^{a} (\mu_{ij} - \mu_{..} - \alpha_i - \beta_j)$$

$$= \sum_i \mu_{ij} - a\mu_{..} - \sum_i \alpha_i - a\beta_j$$

TABLE 19.4 **Age and Gender Effects, with Unimportant Interactions—Learning Example.**

| Factor A—Gender | Factor B—Age | | | Row Average |
	$j = 1$ Young	$j = 2$ Middle	$j = 3$ Old	
$i = 1$ Male	9.75	12.00	17.25	13.00
$i = 2$ Female	8.25	10.00	14.75	11.00
Column average	9.00	11.00	16.00	12.00

Now $\sum_i \mu_{ij} = a\mu_{.j}$ by (19.1) and $\sum \alpha_i = 0$ by (19.6). Finally, $\beta_j = \mu_{.j} - \mu_{..}$ by (19.5). Hence, we obtain:

$$\sum_i (\alpha\beta)_{ij} = a\mu_{.j} - a\mu_{..} - a(\mu_{.j} - \mu_{..}) = 0 \qquad \blacksquare$$

Important and Unimportant Interactions

When two factors interact, the question arises whether the factor level means are still meaningful measures. In Table 19.3a, for instance, it may well be argued that the gender factor level means 13 and 11 are misleading measures. They indicate that some difference exists in learning time for men and women, but that this difference is not too great. These factor level means hide the fact that there is no difference in mean learning time between genders for young persons, but there is a relatively large difference for old persons. The interactions in Table 19.3a would therefore be considered *important interactions*, implying that one should not ordinarily examine the effects of each factor separately in terms of the factor levels means. A treatment means plot, such as in Figure 19.3, presents effectively a description of the nature of the interacting effects of the two factors.

Sometimes when two factors interact, the interaction effects are so small that they are considered to be *unimportant interactions*. Table 19.4 and Figure 19.4 present such a case. Note from Figure 19.4 that the curves are *almost* parallel. For practical purposes, one may say that the mean learning time for women is two minutes less than that for men, and this statement is approximately true for all age groups. Similarly, statements based on average learning time for different age groups will hold approximately for both genders.

Thus, in the case of unimportant interactions, the analysis of factor effects can proceed as for the case of no interactions. Each factor can be studied separately, based on the factor level means $\mu_{i.}$ and $\mu_{.j}$, respectively. This separate analysis of factor effects is, of course, much simpler than a joint analysis for the two factors based on the treatment means μ_{ij}, which is required when the interactions are important.

Comments

1. The determination of whether interactions are important or unimportant is admittedly sometimes difficult because it depends on the context of the application, just as the determination of whether an effect in a single-factor study is important. The subject area specialist (researcher) needs to play a prominent role in deciding whether an interaction is important or unimportant. The advantage of unimportant (or no) interactions, namely, that one is then able to analyze the factor effects separately, is especially great when the study contains more than two factors.

FIGURE 19.4 **Age and Gender Effects, with Unimportant Interactions (curves almost parallel)—Learning Example.**

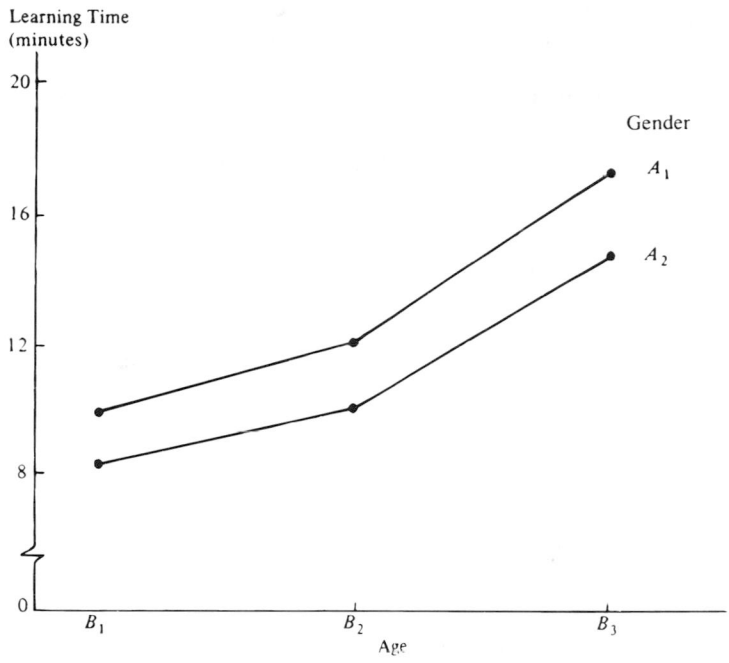

2. Occasionally, it is meaningful to consider the effects of each factor in terms of the factor level means even when important interactions are present. For example, two methods of teaching college mathematics (abstract and standard) were used in teaching students of excellent, good, and moderate quantitative ability. Important interactions between teaching method and student's quantitative ability were found to be present. Students with excellent quantitative ability tended to perform equally well with the two teaching methods, whereas students of moderate or good quantitative ability tended to perform better when taught by the standard method. If equal numbers of students with moderate, good, and excellent quantitative ability are to be taught by one of the two teaching methods, then the method that produces the best average result for all students might be of interest even in the presence of important interactions. A comparison of the teaching method factor level means would then be relevant, even though important interactions are present. ∎

Transformable and Nontransformable Interactions

When important interactions exist, they are sometimes the result of the scale on which the response variable is measured. Consider, for instance, factor effects that act multiplicatively, rather than additively as in (19.7):

$$(19.10) \qquad \mu_{ij} = \mu_{..}\alpha_i\beta_j \qquad \text{Multiplicative factor effects}$$

If we were to assume here that the factor effects are additive, we would find that condition (19.7) does not hold and therefore that interactions are present. These interactions can be removed, however, by applying a logarithmic transformation to (19.10):

$$(19.11) \qquad \log \mu_{ij} = \log \mu_{..} + \log \alpha_i + \log \beta_j$$

This result can be restated equivalently as follows:

$$(19.11a) \qquad \mu'_{ij} = \mu'_{..} + \alpha'_i + \beta'_j$$

where:

$$\mu'_{ij} = \log \mu_{ij}$$

$$\mu'_{..} = \log \mu_{..}$$

$$\alpha'_i = \log \alpha_i$$

$$\beta'_j = \log \beta_j$$

The result in (19.11a) suggests that the original measurement scale for the response variable Y may not be the most appropriate one in the sense of leading to easily understood results. Rather, use of $Y' = \log Y$ for the response variable may be better, making the additive model (19.7) then more appropriate.

We say that the interactions present when the factor effects are actually multiplicative are *transformable interactions* because a simple transformation of Y will remove most of these interaction effects and thus make them unimportant.

Another instance of transformable interactions occurs when each interaction effect equals the product of functions of the main effects, for example:

$$(19.12) \qquad \mu_{ij} = \alpha_i + \beta_j + 2\sqrt{\alpha_i}\sqrt{\beta_j} \qquad \text{Multiplicative interactions}$$

An equivalent form of (19.12) is:

$$(19.12a) \qquad \mu_{ij} = \left(\sqrt{\alpha_i} + \sqrt{\beta_j}\right)^2$$

If we now apply the square root transformation, we obtain an additive effects model:

$$(19.13) \qquad \mu'_{ij} = \alpha'_i + \beta'_j$$

where:

$$\mu'_{ij} = \sqrt{\mu_{ij}}$$

$$\alpha'_i = \sqrt{\alpha_i}$$

$$\beta'_j = \sqrt{\beta_j}$$

Some simple transformations that may be helpful in making important interactions unimportant are the square, square root, logarithmic, and reciprocal transformations. When interactions cannot be largely removed by a transformation, they are called *nontransformable interactions*.

Table 19.5a contains an example of important interactions that are transformable. When a square root transformation is applied to these means, the resulting treatment means in Table

TABLE 19.5   Illustration of a Transformable Interaction.

(a) Treatment Means— Original Scale			(b) Treatment Means after Square Root Transformation		
	Factor *B*			Factor *B*	
Factor *A*	*j* = 1	*j* = 2	Factor *A*	*j* = 1	*j* = 2
i = 1	16	64	*i* = 1	4	8
i = 2	49	121	*i* = 2	7	11
i = 3	64	144	*i* = 3	8	12

19.5b show no interacting effects. Ordinarily, of course, one cannot hope that a simple transformation of scale removes all interactions as in Table 19.5, but only that interactions become unimportant after the transformation.

Interpretation of Interactions

The interpretation of interactions can be quite difficult when the interacting effects are complex. There are many occasions, however, when the interactions have a simple structure, such as in Table 19.3a, so that the joint factor effects can be described in a straightforward manner. Table 19.6 provides several additional illustrations. The corresponding treatment means plots are shown in Figure 19.5.

In Table 19.6a and Figure 19.5a, we have a situation where either raising the pay or increasing the authority of low-paid executives with small authority leads to increased productivity. However, combining both higher pay and greater authority does not lead to any substantial further improvement in productivity than increasing either one alone. Table 19.6b and Figure 19.5b represent a case where both higher pay and greater authority are required before any substantial increase in productivity takes place. Table 19.6c and Figure 19.5c portray a situation where size of crew and personality of crew chief interact in a complex fashion. Productivity with an extrovert crew chief and a crew of four is substantially larger than with an introvert crew chief. The advantage becomes small with crews of six and eight, and with a crew of 10 an introvert crew chief leads to a slightly larger productivity.

Comments

1. It is possible that two factors interact, yet the main effects for one (or both) factors are zero. This would be the result of interactions in opposite directions that balance out over one (or both) factors. Thus, there would be definite factor effects, but these would not be disclosed by the factor level means. The case of interacting factors with no main effects for one (or both) factors fortunately is unusual. Typically, interaction effects are smaller than main effects.

2. The terminology of reinforcement and interference interactions described in Chapter 7 for regression models where both predictor variables are quantitative is applicable to analysis of variance models if the two factors are quantitative or can be ordered on a measurement scale. In Figures 19.5a and 19.5b, pay level and authority both can be ordered on a scale. Hence, the interaction in Figure 19.5a can be described as an interference interaction (the slope decreases

TABLE 19.6   **Examples of Different Types of Interactions.**

(a) Productivity of Executives

Factor *A*—Pay	Factor *B*—Authority	
	Small	Great
Low	50	72
High	74	75

(b) Productivity of Executives

Factor *A*—Pay	Factor *B*—Authority	
	Small	Great
Low	50	52
High	53	75

(c) Productivity per Person in Crew

Factor *A*—Crew Size	Factor *B*—Personality of Crew Chief	
	Extrovert	Introvert
4 persons	28	20
6 persons	22	20
8 persons	20	19
10 persons	17	18

for higher levels of factor *B*), while that in Figure 19.5b can be described as a reinforcement interaction (the slope increases for higher levels of factor *B*).

Similarly, the terminology of ordinal and disordinal interactions described in Chapter 11 for regression models where one predictor variable is quantitative and the other qualitative is applicable to analysis of variance models if one factor is quantitative or can be ordered on a measurement scale and the other factor is qualitative. In Figure 19.5c, crew size is a quantitative factor and personality is a qualitative factor. Therefore, the interaction in Figure 19.5c can be described as disordinal because the treatment means curves intersect.   ■

19.3   Model I (Fixed Factor Levels) for Two-Factor Studies

Having explained the model elements, we are now ready to develop ANOVA model I with fixed factor levels for two-factor studies *when all treatment sample sizes are equal and all treatment means are of equal importance.* This ANOVA model is applicable to observational studies and to experimental studies based on a completely randomized design. In Part VII we shall consider ANOVA models for some other experimental designs.

FIGURE 19.5   Treatment Means Plots for Examples in Table 19.6.

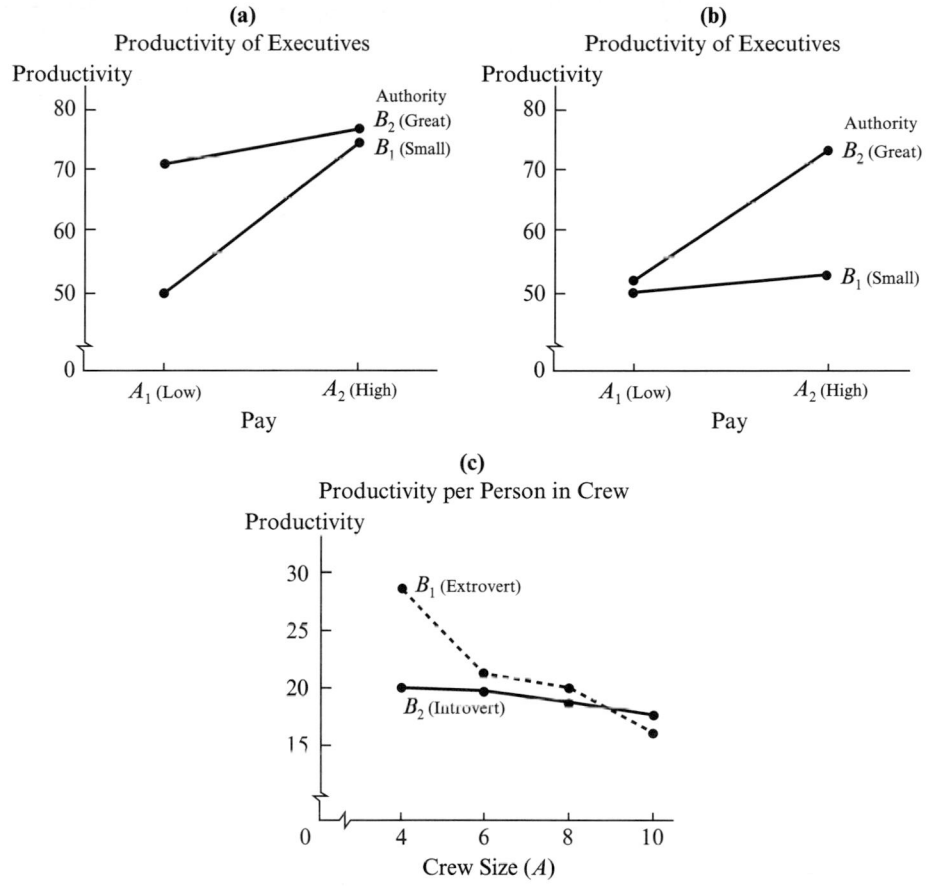

The basic situation is as follows: Factor A is studied at a levels, and these are of intrinsic interest in themselves; in other words, the a levels are not considered to be a sample from a larger population of factor A levels. Similarly, factor B is studied at b levels that are of intrinsic interest in themselves. All ab factor level combinations are included in the study. The number of cases for each of the ab treatments is the same, denoted by n, and it is required that $n > 1$. Thus, the total number of cases for the study is:

$$(19.14) \qquad\qquad n_T = abn$$

The kth observation ($k = 1, \ldots, n$) for the treatment where A is at the ith level and B at the jth level is denoted by Y_{ijk} ($i = 1, \ldots, a; j = 1, \ldots, b$). Table 19.7 on page 818 illustrates this notation for an example where A is at three levels, B is at two levels, and two replications have been made for each treatment.

We shall state the fixed ANOVA model for two-factor studies in two equivalent versions—the cell means version and the factor effects version—and later will use one or the other as convenience dictates.

Cell Means Model

Model Formulation.   When we regard the ab treatments without explicitly considering the factorial structure of the study, we express the analysis of variance model in terms of the cell (treatment) means μ_{ij} :

$$(19.15) \qquad Y_{ijk} = \mu_{ij} + \varepsilon_{ijk}$$

where:

μ_{ij} are parameters

ε_{ijk} are independent $N(0, \sigma^2)$

$i = 1, \ldots, a; \ j = 1 \ldots, b; \ k = 1, \ldots, n$

Important Features of Model.   Some important features of the cell means model are:

1. The parameter μ_{ij} is the mean response for the treatment in which factor A is at the ith level and factor B is at the jth level. This follows because $E\{\varepsilon_{ijk}\} = 0$:

$$(19.16) \qquad E\{Y_{ijk}\} = \mu_{ij}$$

2. Since μ_{ij} is a constant, the variance of Y_{ijk} is:

$$(19.17) \qquad \sigma^2\{Y_{ijk}\} = \sigma^2\{\varepsilon_{ijk}\} = \sigma^2$$

3. Since the error terms ε_{ijk} are independent and normally distributed, so are the observations Y_{ijk}. Hence, we can state ANOVA model (19.15) also as follows:

$$(19.18) \qquad Y_{ijk} \text{ are independent } N(\mu_{ij}, \sigma^2)$$

4. ANOVA model (19.15) is a linear model because it can be expressed in the form $\mathbf{Y} = \mathbf{X}\boldsymbol{\beta} + \boldsymbol{\varepsilon}$. Consider a two-factor study with each factor having two levels (i.e., $a = b = 2$) and two trials for each treatment (i.e., $n = 2$). Then $\mathbf{Y}, \mathbf{X}, \boldsymbol{\beta}$, and $\boldsymbol{\varepsilon}$ are defined as follows:

$$(19.19) \quad \mathbf{Y} = \begin{bmatrix} Y_{111} \\ Y_{112} \\ Y_{121} \\ Y_{122} \\ Y_{211} \\ Y_{212} \\ Y_{221} \\ Y_{222} \end{bmatrix} \quad \mathbf{X} = \begin{bmatrix} 1 & 0 & 0 & 0 \\ 1 & 0 & 0 & 0 \\ 0 & 1 & 0 & 0 \\ 0 & 1 & 0 & 0 \\ 0 & 0 & 1 & 0 \\ 0 & 0 & 1 & 0 \\ 0 & 0 & 0 & 1 \\ 0 & 0 & 0 & 1 \end{bmatrix} \quad \boldsymbol{\beta} = \begin{bmatrix} \mu_{11} \\ \mu_{12} \\ \mu_{21} \\ \mu_{22} \end{bmatrix} \quad \boldsymbol{\varepsilon} = \begin{bmatrix} \varepsilon_{111} \\ \varepsilon_{112} \\ \varepsilon_{121} \\ \varepsilon_{122} \\ \varepsilon_{211} \\ \varepsilon_{212} \\ \varepsilon_{221} \\ \varepsilon_{222} \end{bmatrix}$$

Recall that the $E\{\mathbf{Y}\}$ vector, which consists of the elements $E\{Y_{ijk}\}$, equals $\mathbf{X}\boldsymbol{\beta}$ according to (6.20). This vector here is:

$$(19.20) \qquad E\{\mathbf{Y}\} = \mathbf{X}\boldsymbol{\beta} = \begin{bmatrix} 1 & 0 & 0 & 0 \\ 1 & 0 & 0 & 0 \\ 0 & 1 & 0 & 0 \\ 0 & 1 & 0 & 0 \\ 0 & 0 & 1 & 0 \\ 0 & 0 & 1 & 0 \\ 0 & 0 & 0 & 1 \\ 0 & 0 & 0 & 1 \end{bmatrix} \begin{bmatrix} \mu_{11} \\ \mu_{12} \\ \mu_{21} \\ \mu_{22} \end{bmatrix} = \begin{bmatrix} \mu_{11} \\ \mu_{11} \\ \mu_{12} \\ \mu_{12} \\ \mu_{21} \\ \mu_{21} \\ \mu_{22} \\ \mu_{22} \end{bmatrix}$$

Thus, $E\{Y_{ijk}\} = \mu_{ij}$, as it must according to (19.16), and we have the proper matrix representation for the two-factor ANOVA model (19.15):

$$(19.21) \qquad \mathbf{Y} = \begin{bmatrix} Y_{111} \\ Y_{112} \\ Y_{121} \\ Y_{122} \\ Y_{211} \\ Y_{212} \\ Y_{221} \\ Y_{222} \end{bmatrix} = \mathbf{X}\boldsymbol{\beta} + \boldsymbol{\varepsilon} = \begin{bmatrix} \mu_{11} \\ \mu_{11} \\ \mu_{12} \\ \mu_{12} \\ \mu_{21} \\ \mu_{21} \\ \mu_{22} \\ \mu_{22} \end{bmatrix} + \begin{bmatrix} \varepsilon_{111} \\ \varepsilon_{112} \\ \varepsilon_{121} \\ \varepsilon_{122} \\ \varepsilon_{211} \\ \varepsilon_{212} \\ \varepsilon_{221} \\ \varepsilon_{222} \end{bmatrix}$$

In view of the error terms being independent with constant variance σ^2, the variance-covariance matrix of the error terms is $\boldsymbol{\sigma}^2\{\boldsymbol{\varepsilon}\} = \sigma^2\mathbf{I}$, as in (16.9) for the single-factor ANOVA model. Also as before, we have $\boldsymbol{\sigma}^2\{\mathbf{Y}\} = \boldsymbol{\sigma}^2\{\boldsymbol{\varepsilon}\}$ for two-factor ANOVA model (19.15).

5. ANOVA model (19.15) is therefore similar to the single-factor ANOVA model (16.2), except for the two subscripts now needed to identify the treatment. Normality, independent error terms, and constant variances for the error terms are properties of the ANOVA models for both single-factor and two-factor studies.

Factor Effects Model

Model Formulation.   An equivalent version of cell means model (19.15) can be obtained by replacing each treatment mean μ_{ij} with an identical expression in terms of factor effects based on the definition of an interaction in (19.8):

$$(\alpha\beta)_{ij} = \mu_{ij} - (\mu_{..} + \alpha_i + \beta_j)$$

Rearranging terms, we obtain the identity:

$$(19.22) \qquad \mu_{ij} = \mu_{..} + \alpha_i + \beta_j + (\alpha\beta)_{ij}$$

where:

$$\mu_{..} = \frac{\sum_i \sum_j \mu_{ij}}{ab}$$

$$\alpha_i = \mu_{i.} - \mu_{..}$$

$$\beta_j = \mu_{.j} - \mu_{..}$$

$$(\alpha\beta)_{ij} = \mu_{ij} - \mu_{i.} - \mu_{.j} + \mu_{..}$$

This formulation indicates that each cell mean μ_{ij} can be viewed as the sum of four component factor effects. Specifically, (19.22) states that the mean response for the treatment where factor A is at the ith level and factor B is at the jth level is the sum of:

1. An overall constant $\mu_{..}$.

2. The main effect α_i for factor A at the ith level.

3. The main effect β_j for factor B at the jth level.

4. The interaction effect $(\alpha\beta)_{ij}$ when factor A is at the ith level and factor B is at the jth level.

Replacing μ_{ij} in ANOVA model (19.15) by the expression in (19.22), we obtain an equivalent factor effects ANOVA model for two-factor studies:

$$(19.23) \qquad Y_{ijk} = \mu_{..} + \alpha_i + \beta_j + (\alpha\beta)_{ij} + \varepsilon_{ijk}$$

where:

$\mu_{..}$ is a constant

α_i are constants subject to the restriction $\sum \alpha_i = 0$

β_j are constants subject to the restriction $\sum \beta_j = 0$

$(\alpha\beta)_{ij}$ are constants subject to the restrictions:

$$\sum_i (\alpha\beta)_{ij} = 0 \qquad j = 1 \ldots, b$$

$$\sum_j (\alpha\beta)_{ij} = 0 \qquad i = 1 \ldots, a$$

ε_{ijk} are independent $N(0, \sigma^2)$

$i = 1 \ldots, a; \; j = 1, \ldots, b; k = 1, \ldots, n$

Important Features of Model.   Some important features of the factor effects model are:

1. ANOVA model (19.23) corresponds to the fixed factor effects ANOVA model (16.62) for a single-factor study except that the single-factor treatment effect is here replaced by the sum of a factor A effect, a factor B effect, and an interaction effect.

2. The properties of the observations Y_{ijk} for factor effects model (19.23) are the same as those for the equivalent cell means model (19.15). Since $E\{\varepsilon_{ijk}\} = 0$, we have:

$$(19.24) \qquad E\{Y_{ijk}\} = \mu_{..} + \alpha_i + \beta_j + (\alpha\beta)_{ij} = \mu_{ij}$$

The second equality follows from identity (19.22). Further, we have:

$$(19.25) \qquad \sigma^2\{Y_{ijk}\} = \sigma^2$$

because the error term ε_{ijk} is the only random term on the right-hand side in (19.23) and $\sigma^2\{\varepsilon_{ijk}\} = \sigma^2$. Finally, the Y_{ijk} are independent normal random variables because the error terms are independent normal random variables. Hence, we can also state ANOVA model (19.23) as follows:

$$(19.26) \qquad Y_{ijk} \text{ are independent } N[\mu_{..} + \alpha_i + \beta_j + (\alpha\beta)_{ij}, \ \sigma^2]$$

3. ANOVA model (19.23) is a linear model because it can be stated in the form $\mathbf{Y} = \mathbf{X}\boldsymbol{\beta} + \boldsymbol{\varepsilon}$. We shall show this explicitly in Section 19.7.

19.4   Analysis of Variance

Illustration

Table 19.7 contains an illustration that we shall employ in this chapter and the next. The Castle Bakery Company supplies wrapped Italian bread to a large number of supermarkets in a metropolitan area. An experimental study was made of the effects of height of the shelf display (factor A: bottom, middle, top) and the width of the shelf display (factor B: regular, wide) on sales of this bakery's bread during the experimental period (Y, measured in cases). Twelve supermarkets, similar in terms of sales volume and clientele, were utilized in the study. The six treatments were assigned at random to two stores each according to a completely randomized design, and the display of the bread in each store followed the treatment specifications for that store. Sales of the bread were recorded, and these results are presented in Table 19.7.

Notation

Table 19.7 illustrates the notation we shall use for two-factor studies. It is a straightforward extension of the notation for single-factor studies. An observation is denoted by Y_{ijk}. The subscripts i and j specify the levels of factors A and B, respectively, and the subscript k refers to the given case or trial for a particular treatment (i.e., factor level combination).

A dot in the subscript indicates aggregation or averaging over the variable represented by the index. For instance, the sum of the observations for the treatment corresponding to the ith level of factor A and the jth level of factor B is:

$$(19.27a) \qquad Y_{ij.} = \sum_{k=1}^{n} Y_{ijk}$$

The corresponding mean is:

$$(19.27b) \qquad \bar{Y}_{ij.} = \frac{Y_{ij.}}{n}$$

The total of all observations for the ith factor level of A is:

$$(19.27c) \qquad Y_{i..} = \sum_{j}^{b} \sum_{k}^{n} Y_{ijk}$$

TABLE 19.7   **Sample Data and Notation for Two-Factor Study—Castle Bakery Example (sales in cases).**

Factor A (display height) i	Factor B (display width) j		Row Total	Display Height Average
	B_1 (regular)	B_2 (wide)		
A_1 (bottom)	47 (Y_{111})	46 (Y_{121})		
	43 (Y_{112})	40 (Y_{122})		
Total	90 ($Y_{11.}$)	86 ($Y_{12.}$)	176 ($Y_{1..}$)	
Average	45 ($\bar{Y}_{11.}$)	43 ($\bar{Y}_{12.}$)		44 ($\bar{Y}_{1..}$)
A_2 (middle)	62 (Y_{211})	67 (Y_{221})		
	68 (Y_{212})	71 (Y_{222})		
Total	130 ($Y_{21.}$)	138 ($Y_{22.}$)	268 ($Y_{2..}$)	
Average	65 ($\bar{Y}_{21.}$)	69 ($\bar{Y}_{22.}$)		67 ($\bar{Y}_{2..}$)
A_3 (top)	41 (Y_{311})	42 (Y_{321})		
	39 (Y_{312})	46 (Y_{322})		
Total	80 ($Y_{31.}$)	88 ($Y_{32.}$)	168 ($Y_{3..}$)	
Average	40 ($\bar{Y}_{31.}$)	44 ($\bar{Y}_{32.}$)		42 ($\bar{Y}_{3..}$)
Column total	300 ($Y_{.1.}$)	312 ($Y_{.2.}$)	612 ($Y_{...}$)	
Display width average	50 ($\bar{Y}_{.1.}$)	52 ($\bar{Y}_{.2.}$)		51 ($\bar{Y}_{...}$)

and the corresponding mean is:

$$(19.27d) \qquad \bar{Y}_{i..} = \frac{Y_{i..}}{bn}$$

Similarly, for the jth factor level of B the sum of all observations and their mean are denoted by:

$$(19.27e) \qquad Y_{.j.} = \sum_i^a \sum_k^n Y_{ijk}$$

$$(19.27f) \qquad \bar{Y}_{.j.} = \frac{Y_{.j.}}{an}$$

Finally, the sum of all observations in the study is:

$$(19.27g) \qquad Y_{...} = \sum_i^a \sum_j^b \sum_k^n Y_{ijk}$$

and the overall mean is:

$$(19.27h) \qquad \bar{Y}_{...} = \frac{Y_{...}}{nab}$$

Fitting of ANOVA Model

Cell Means Model (19.15). Fitting the two-factor cell means model (19.15) to the sample data by either the method of least squares or the method of maximum likelihood leads to minimizing the criterion:

$$(19.28) \qquad Q = \sum_i \sum_j \sum_k (Y_{ijk} - \mu_{ij})^2$$

When we perform the minimization of Q, we obtain the least squares and maximum likelihood estimators:

$$(19.29) \qquad \hat{\mu}_{ij} = \bar{Y}_{ij\cdot}$$

Thus, the *fitted values* are the estimated treatment means:

$$(19.30) \qquad \hat{Y}_{ijk} = \bar{Y}_{ij\cdot}$$

The *residuals*, as usual, are defined as the difference between the observed and fitted values:

$$(19.31) \qquad e_{ijk} = Y_{ijk} - \hat{Y}_{ijk} = Y_{ijk} - \bar{Y}_{ij\cdot}$$

Residuals are highly useful for assessing the appropriateness of two-factor ANOVA model (19.15), as they also are for the statistical models considered earlier.

Factor Effects Model (19.23). For the equivalent factor effects model (19.23), the least squares and maximum likelihood methods both lead to minimizing the criterion:

$$(19.32) \qquad Q = \sum_i \sum_j \sum_k [Y_{ijk} - \mu_{\cdot\cdot} - \alpha_i - \beta_j - (\alpha\beta)_{ij}]^2$$

subject to the restrictions:

$$\sum_i \alpha_i = 0 \qquad \sum_j \beta_j = 0 \qquad \sum_i (\alpha\beta)_{ij} = 0 \qquad \sum_j (\alpha\beta)_{ij} = 0$$

When we perform this minimization, we obtain the following least squares and maximum likelihood estimators of the parameters:

	Parameter	Estimator
(19.33a)	$\mu_{\cdot\cdot}$	$\hat{\mu}_{\cdot\cdot} = \bar{Y}_{\cdot\cdot\cdot}$
(19.33b)	$\alpha_i = \mu_{i\cdot} - \mu_{\cdot\cdot}$	$\hat{\alpha}_i = \bar{Y}_{i\cdot\cdot} - \bar{Y}_{\cdot\cdot\cdot}$
(19.33c)	$\beta_j = \mu_{\cdot j} - \mu_{\cdot\cdot}$	$\hat{\beta}_j = \bar{Y}_{\cdot j\cdot} - \bar{Y}_{\cdot\cdot\cdot}$
(19.33d)	$(\alpha\beta)_{ij} = \mu_{ij} - \mu_{i\cdot} - \mu_{\cdot j} + \mu_{\cdot\cdot}$	$\widehat{(\alpha\beta)}_{ij} = \bar{Y}_{ij\cdot} - \bar{Y}_{i\cdot\cdot} - \bar{Y}_{\cdot j\cdot} + \bar{Y}_{\cdot\cdot\cdot}$

The correspondences of these estimators to the definitions of the parameters are readily apparent.

FIGURE 19.6   Estimated Treatment Means Plot—Castle Bakery Example.

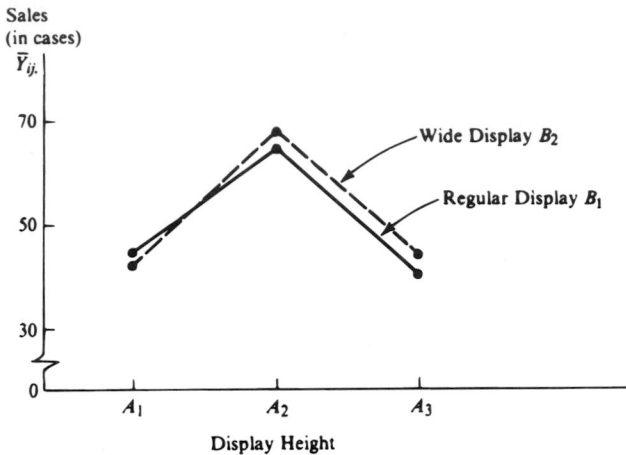

The fitted values and residuals for factor effects model (19.23) are exactly the same as those for cell means model (19.15). Specifically, the fitted values for ANOVA model (19.23) are:

$$(19.34) \qquad \hat{Y}_{ijk} = \bar{Y}_{...} + (\bar{Y}_{i..} - \bar{Y}_{...}) + (\bar{Y}_{.j.} - \bar{Y}_{...}) + (\bar{Y}_{ij.} - \bar{Y}_{i..} - \bar{Y}_{.j.} + \bar{Y}_{...}) = \bar{Y}_{ij.}$$

so that the residuals are again:

$$(19.35) \qquad\qquad\qquad e_{ijk} = Y_{ijk} - \bar{Y}_{ij.}$$

Example.   For the Castle Bakery example, the fitted values, i.e., the estimated treatment means $\bar{Y}_{ij.}$, are shown in Table 19.7. A plot of these estimated treatment means is presented in Figure 19.6. We see from this estimated treatment means plot that, for both display widths, mean sales for the middle display height are substantially larger than those for the other two display heights. The effect of display width does not appear to be large. Indeed, there may be no effect of display width; the variations between the estimated treatment means for any given display height may be solely of a random nature. In that event, there would be no interactions between display height and display width in their effects on sales.

Figure 19.6 differs from the earlier treatment means plots because the earlier figures presented the true treatment means μ_{ij}, while Figure 19.6 presents sample estimates. We therefore need to test whether or not the effects shown in Figure 19.6 are real effects or represent only random variations. To conduct these tests, we require a partitioning of the total sum of squares, to be discussed next.

Partitioning of Total Sum of Squares

Partitioning of Total Deviation.   We shall partition the total deviation of an observation Y_{ijk} from the overall mean $\bar{Y}_{...}$ in two stages. First, we shall obtain a decomposition of the total deviation $Y_{ijk} - \bar{Y}_{...}$ by viewing the study as consisting of ab treatments:

(19.36)
$$\underbrace{Y_{ijk} - \bar{Y}_{...}}_{\substack{\text{Total} \\ \text{deviation}}} = \underbrace{\bar{Y}_{ij.} - \bar{Y}_{...}}_{\substack{\text{Deviation of estimated} \\ \text{treatment mean around} \\ \text{overall mean}}} + \underbrace{Y_{ijk} - \bar{Y}_{ij.}}_{\substack{\text{Deviation} \\ \text{around estimated} \\ \text{treatment mean}}}$$

Note that the deviation around the estimated treatment mean is simply the residual e_{ijk} in (19.35):

$$e_{ijk} = Y_{ijk} - \bar{Y}_{ij.}$$

Treatment and Error Sums of Squares. When we square (19.36) and sum over all cases, the cross-product term drops out and we obtain:

(19.37)
$$SSTO = SSTR + SSE$$

where:

(19.37a)
$$SSTO = \sum_i \sum_j \sum_k (Y_{ijk} - \bar{Y}_{...})^2$$

(19.37b)
$$SSTR = n \sum_i \sum_j (\bar{Y}_{ij.} - \bar{Y}_{...})^2$$

(19.37c)
$$SSE = \sum_i \sum_j \sum_k (Y_{ijk} - \bar{Y}_{ij.})^2 = \sum_i \sum_j \sum_k e_{ijk}^2$$

SSTR reflects the variability between the ab estimated treatment means and is the ordinary *treatment sum of squares*, and *SSE* reflects the variability within treatments and is the usual *error sum of squares*. The only difference between these formulas and those for the single-factor case is the use of the two subscripts i and j to designate a treatment.

Example. For the Castle Bakery example, the decomposition of the total sum of squares in (19.37) is obtained as follows, using the data in Table 19.7:

$$SSTO = (47 - 51)^2 + (43 - 51)^2 + (46 - 51)^2 + \cdots + (46 - 51)^2 = 1{,}642$$

$$SSTR = 2[(45 - 51)^2 + (43 - 51)^2 + (65 - 51)^2 + \cdots + (44 - 51)^2] = 1{,}580$$

$$SSE = (47 - 45)^2 + (43 - 45)^2 + (46 - 43)^2 + \cdots + (46 - 44)^2 = 62$$

Partitioning of Treatment Sum of Squares. Next, we shall decompose the estimated treatment mean deviation $\bar{Y}_{ij.} - \bar{Y}_{...}$ in terms of components reflecting the factor A main effect, the factor B main effect, and the AB interaction effect:

(19.38)
$$\underbrace{\bar{Y}_{ij.} - \bar{Y}_{...}}_{\substack{\text{Deviation of} \\ \text{estimated treatment} \\ \text{mean around} \\ \text{overall mean}}} = \underbrace{\bar{Y}_{i..} - \bar{Y}_{...}}_{\substack{A \text{ main} \\ \text{effect}}} + \underbrace{\bar{Y}_{.j.} - \bar{Y}_{...}}_{\substack{B \text{ main} \\ \text{effect}}} + \underbrace{\bar{Y}_{ij.} - \bar{Y}_{i..} - \bar{Y}_{.j.} + \bar{Y}_{...}}_{\substack{AB \text{ interaction} \\ \text{effect}}}$$

When we square (19.38) and sum over all treatments and over the n cases associated with each estimated treatment mean $\bar{Y}_{ij.}$, all cross-product terms drop out and we obtain:

(19.39)
$$SSTR = SSA + SSB + SSAB$$

where:

(19.39a)
$$SSA = nb \sum_i (\bar{Y}_{i..} - \bar{Y}_{...})^2$$

(19.39b)
$$SSB = na \sum_j (\bar{Y}_{.j.} - \bar{Y}_{...})^2$$

(19.39c)
$$SSAB = n \sum_i \sum_j (\bar{Y}_{ij.} - \bar{Y}_{i..} - \bar{Y}_{.j.} + \bar{Y}_{...})^2$$

The interaction sum of squares can also be obtained as a remainder:

(19.39d)
$$SSAB = SSTO - SSE - SSA - SSB$$

or from:

(19.39e)
$$SSAB = SSTR - SSA - SSB$$

where *SSTO* and *SSTR* are given in (19.37a) and (19.37b), respectively.

SSA, called the *factor A sum of squares*, measures the variability of the estimated factor A level means $\bar{Y}_{i..}$. The more variable they are, the bigger will be *SSA*. Similarly, *SSB*, called the *factor B sum of squares*, measures the variability of the estimated factor B level means $\bar{Y}_{.j.}$. Finally, *SSAB*, called the *AB interaction sum of squares*, measures the variability of the estimated interactions $\bar{Y}_{ij.} - \bar{Y}_{i..} - \bar{Y}_{.j.} + \bar{Y}_{...}$ for the ab treatments. Since the mean of all estimated interactions is zero, the deviations of the estimated interactions around their mean is not explicitly shown, as it was in *SSA* and *SSB*. The larger absolutely are the estimated interactions, the larger will be *SSAB*.

The partitioning of *SSTR* into the components *SSA*, *SSB*, and *SSAB* is called an *orthogonal decomposition*. An orthogonal decomposition is one where the component sums of squares add to the total sum of squares (*SSTR* here), and likewise for the degrees of freedom. Thus, the decompositions of *SSTO* into *SSTR* and *SSE* for single-factor and two-factor studies are also orthogonal decompositions. While many different orthogonal decompositions of *SSTR* are possible here, the one into the *SSA*, *SSB*, and *SSAB* components is of interest because these three components provide information about the factor A main effects, the factor B main effects, and the AB interactions, respectively, as will be seen shortly.

Example.   For the Castle Bakery example, we obtain the following decomposition of *SSTR*, using the data in Table 19.7 and the formulas in (19.39):

$$SSA = 2(2)[(44 - 51)^2 + (67 - 51)^2 + (42 - 51)^2] = 1{,}544$$

$$SSB = 2(3)[(50 - 51)^2 + (52 - 51)^2] = 12$$

$$SSAB = 1{,}580 - 1{,}544 - 12 = 24$$

Hence, we have:

$$1{,}580 = 1{,}544 + 12 + 24$$

$$SSTR = SSA + SSB + SSAB$$

Combined Partitioning. Combining the decompositions in (19.37) and (19.39), we have established that:

(19.40) $$SSTO = SSA + SSB + SSAB + SSE$$

where the component sums of squares are defined in (19.37) and (19.39).

Example. For the Castle Bakery example, we have found:

$$1{,}642 = 1{,}544 + 12 + 24 + 62$$

$$SSTO = SSA + SSB + SSAB + SSE$$

Thus, much of the total variability in this instance is associated with the factor A (display height) effects.

Partitioning of Degrees of Freedom

We are familiar from single-factor analysis of variance as to how the degrees of freedom are divided between the treatment and error components. For two-factor studies with n cases for each treatment, there are a total of $n_T = nab$ cases and $r = ab$ treatments; hence, the degrees of freedom associated with $SSTO$, $SSTR$, and SSE are $nab - 1$, $ab - 1$, and $nab - ab = (n - 1)ab$, respectively. These degrees of freedom for the Castle Bakery example are $2(3)(2) - 1 = 11$, $3(2) - 1 = 5$, and $(2 - 1)(3)(2) = 6$, respectively.

Corresponding to the further partitioning of the treatment sum of squares in (19.39), we can also obtain a breakdown of the associated $ab - 1$ degrees of freedom. SSA has $a - 1$ degrees of freedom associated with it. There are a factor level deviations $\bar{Y}_{i..} - \bar{Y}_{...}$, but one degree of freedom is lost because the deviations are subject to one restriction, i.e., $\Sigma(\bar{Y}_{i..} - \bar{Y}_{...}) = 0$. Similarly, SSB has $b - 1$ degrees of freedom associated with it. The degrees of freedom associated with $SSAB$, the interaction sum of squares, is the remainder:

$$(ab - 1) - (a - 1) - (b - 1) = (a - 1)(b - 1)$$

The degrees of freedom associated with $SSAB$ may be understood as follows: There are ab interaction terms. These are subject to b restrictions since:

$$\sum_i (\bar{Y}_{ij.} - \bar{Y}_{i..} - \bar{Y}_{.j.} + \bar{Y}_{...}) = 0 \qquad j = 1, \ldots, b$$

There are a additional restrictions since:

$$\sum_j (\bar{Y}_{ij.} - \bar{Y}_{i..} - \bar{Y}_{.j.} + \bar{Y}_{...}) = 0 \qquad i = 1, \ldots, a$$

However, only $a - 1$ of these latter restrictions are independent since the last one is implied by the previous b restrictions. Altogether, therefore, there are $b + (a - 1)$ independent restrictions. Hence, the degrees of freedom are:

$$ab - (b + a - 1) = (a - 1)(b - 1)$$

Example.   For the Castle Bakery example, SSA has $3 - 1 = 2$ degrees of freedom associated with it, SSB has $2 - 1 = 1$ degree of freedom, and $SSAB$ has $(3 - 1)(2 - 1) = 2$ degrees of freedom.

Mean Squares

Mean squares are obtained in the usual way by dividing the sums of squares by their associated degrees of freedom. We thus obtain:

(19.41a)
$$MSA = \frac{SSA}{a - 1}$$

(19.41b)
$$MSB = \frac{SSB}{b - 1}$$

(19.41c)
$$MSAB = \frac{SSAB}{(a - 1)(b - 1)}$$

Example.   For the Castle Bakery example, these mean squares are:

$$MSA = \frac{1{,}544}{2} = 772$$

$$MSB = \frac{12}{1} = 12$$

$$MSAB = \frac{24}{2} = 12$$

Expected Mean Squares

It can be shown, along the same lines used for single-factor ANOVA, that the mean squares for two-factor ANOVA model (19.23) have the following expectations:

(19.42a) $$E\{MSE\} = \sigma^2$$

(19.42b) $$E\{MSA\} = \sigma^2 + nb\frac{\Sigma\alpha_i^2}{a - 1} = \sigma^2 + nb\frac{\Sigma(\mu_{i\cdot} - \mu_{\cdot\cdot})^2}{a - 1}$$

(19.42c) $$E\{MSB\} = \sigma^2 + na\frac{\Sigma\beta_j^2}{b - 1} = \sigma^2 + na\frac{\Sigma(\mu_{\cdot j} - \mu_{\cdot\cdot})^2}{b - 1}$$

(19.42d) $$E\{MSAB\} = \sigma^2 + n\frac{\Sigma\Sigma(\alpha\beta)_{ij}^2}{(a - 1)(b - 1)}$$

$$= \sigma^2 + n\frac{\Sigma\Sigma(\mu_{ij} - \mu_{i\cdot} - \mu_{\cdot j} + \mu_{\cdot\cdot})^2}{(a - 1)(b - 1)}$$

These expectations show that if there are no factor A main effects (i.e., if all $\mu_{i.}$ are equal, or all $\alpha_i = 0$), MSA and MSE have the same expectation; otherwise MSA tends to be larger than MSE. Similarly, if there are no factor B main effects, MSB and MSE have the same expectation; otherwise MSB tends to be larger than MSE. Finally, if there are no interactions [i.e., if all $(\alpha\beta)_{ij} = 0$] so that the factor effects are additive, $MSAB$ has the same expectation as MSE; otherwise, $MSAB$ tends to be larger than MSE. This suggests that F^* test statistics based on the ratios MSA/MSE, MSB/MSE, and $MSAB/MSE$ will provide information about the main effects and interactions of the two factors, with large values of the test statistics indicating the presence of factor effects. We shall see shortly that tests based on these statistics are regular F tests.

Analysis of Variance Table

The decomposition of the total sum of squares in (19.40) into the several factor and error components is shown in Table 19.8. Also shown there are the associated degrees of freedom, the mean squares, and the expected mean squares. Table 19.9 contains the two-factor analysis of variance for the Castle Bakery example.

Figure 19.7 presents a portion of the BMDP output for the Castle Bakery example. The first output block shows ANOVA results similar to those presented in Table 19.9, except that a source of variation attributable to the mean is given. This line in the ANOVA table can be used to test whether $\mu_{..} = 0$ and usually is not of interest (see Table 2.3 for an analogous ANOVA table in regression). The correction for mean sum of squares here is $n_T \bar{Y}_{...}^2$, which has one degree of freedom associated with it. For the Castle Bakery example, we have $n_T \bar{Y}_{...}^2 = 12(51)^2 = 31{,}212$.

The second block presents various estimated means. The final block shows point estimates of the effects (labeled cell deviations) α_i, β_j, and $(\alpha\beta)_{ij}$. The respective estimated effects are given in (19.33); they are $\bar{Y}_{i..} - \bar{Y}_{...}$, $\bar{Y}_{.j.} - \bar{Y}_{...}$, and $\bar{Y}_{ij.} - \bar{Y}_{i..} - \bar{Y}_{.j.} + \bar{Y}_{...}$.

19.5   Evaluation of Appropriateness of ANOVA Model

Before undertaking formal inference procedures, we need to evaluate the appropriateness of two-factor ANOVA model (19.23). No new problems arise here. The residuals in (19.35):

$$e_{ijk} = Y_{ijk} - \bar{Y}_{ij.}$$

are examined for normality, constancy of error variance, and independence of error terms in the same fashion as for a single-factor study.

Weighted least squares is a standard remedial measure when the error terms are normally distributed but do not have constant variance. When both the assumptions of normality and constancy of the error variance are violated, a transformation of the response variable may be sought to stabilize the error variance and to bring the distribution of the error terms closer to a normal distribution. Our discussion of these topics in Chapter 18 for single-factor ANOVA applies completely to two-factor ANOVA.

Our earlier discussion on the effects of departures from the single-factor ANOVA model applies fully to two-factor ANOVA. In particular, the employment of equal sample sizes for each treatment minimizes the effect of unequal error variances.

TABLE 19.8   ANOVA Table for Two-Factor Study with Fixed Factor Levels.

Source of Variation	SS	df	MS	E{MS}
Factor A	$SSA = nb\sum(\bar{Y}_{i..} - \bar{Y}_{...})^2$	$a-1$	$MSA = \dfrac{SSA}{a-1}$	$\sigma^2 + bn\dfrac{\sum(\mu_{i.} - \mu_{..})^2}{a-1}$
Factor B	$SSB = na\sum(\bar{Y}_{.j.} - \bar{Y}_{...})^2$	$b-1$	$MSB = \dfrac{SSB}{b-1}$	$\sigma^2 + an\dfrac{\sum(\mu_{.j} - \mu_{..})^2}{b-1}$
AB interactions	$SSAB = n\sum\sum(\bar{Y}_{ij.} - \bar{Y}_{i..} - \bar{Y}_{.j.} + \bar{Y}_{...})^2$	$(a-1)(b-1)$	$MSAB = \dfrac{SSAB}{(a-1)(b-1)}$	$\sigma^2 + n\dfrac{\sum\sum(\mu_{ij} - \mu_{i.} - \mu_{.j} + \mu_{..})^2}{(a-1)(b-1)}$
Error	$SSE = \sum\sum\sum(Y_{ijk} - \bar{Y}_{ij.})^2$	$ab(n-1)$	$MSE = \dfrac{SSE}{ab(n-1)}$	σ^2
Total	$SSTO = \sum\sum\sum(Y_{ijk} - \bar{Y}_{...})^2$	$nab-1$		

TABLE 19.9 ANOVA Table for Two-Factor Study—Castle Bakery Example.

Source of Variation	SS	df	MS
Factor A (display height)	1,544	2	772
Factor B (display width)	12	1	12
AB interactions	24	2	12
Error	62	6	10.3
Total	1,642	11	

FIGURE 19.7 Segment of BMDP Computer Output for Two-Factor Analysis of Variance—Castle Bakery Example.

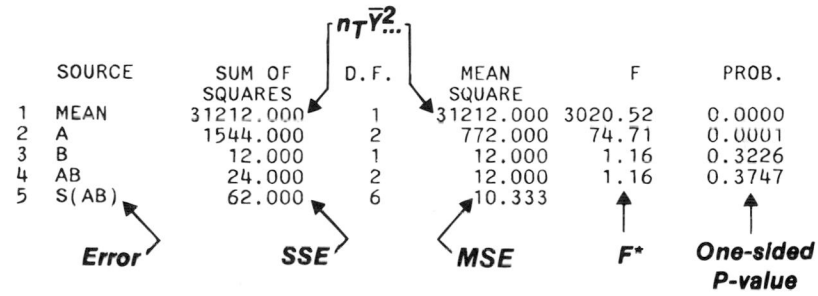

```
                            ┌nₜȲ²...┐
        SOURCE      SUM OF    D.F.     MEAN         F       PROB.
                    SQUARES          SQUARE
    1   MEAN       31212.000    1    31212.000   3020.52    0.0000
    2   A           1544.000    2      772.000     74.71    0.0001
    3   B             12.000    1       12.000      1.16    0.3226
    4   AB            24.000    2       12.000      1.16    0.3747
    5   S(AB)         62.000    6       10.333
```

        Error   **SSE**   **MSE**   **F***   **One-sided P-value**

```
        GRAND MEAN        51.00000  ⟵ Ȳ...

        CELL AND MARGINAL MEANS

            A =       1          2          3
                   44.00000   67.00000   42.00000  ⟵ Ȳᵢ..

            B =       1          2
                   50.00000   52.00000  ⟵ Ȳ.ⱼ

            B =       1          2
        A = 1     45.00000   43.00000
            2     65.00000   69.00000  ⟵ Ȳᵢⱼ
            3     40.00000   44.00000


        CELL DEVIATIONS


            A =       1          2          3
                   -7.00000   16.00000   -9.00000  ⟵ Ȳᵢ.. - Ȳ...


            B =       1          2
                   -1.00000    1.00000  ⟵ Ȳ.ⱼ - Ȳ...


            B =       1          2
        A = 1      2.00000   -2.00000
            2     -1.00000    1.00000  ⟵ Ȳᵢⱼ - Ȳᵢ.. - Ȳ.ⱼ + Ȳ...
            3     -1.00000    1.00000
```

FIGURE 19.8   Diagnostic Residual Plots—Castle Bakery Example.

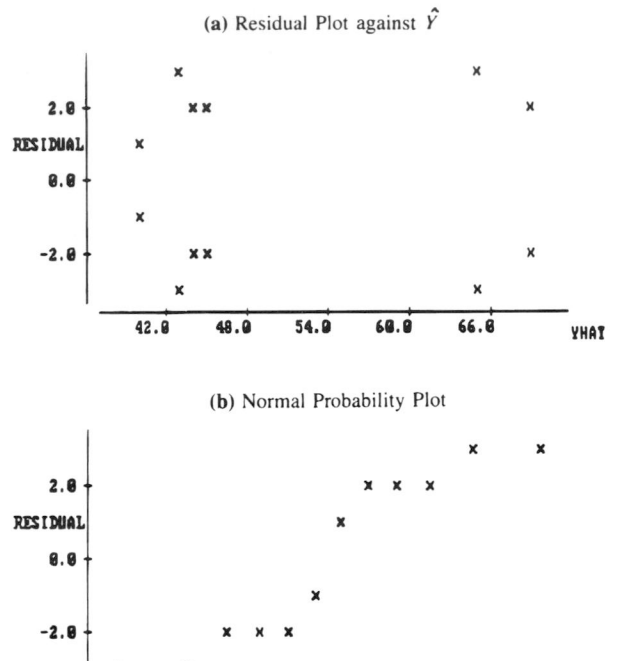

(a) Residual Plot against $\hat{Y}$

(b) Normal Probability Plot

Example

In the Castle Bakery example, there are only two replications for each treatment. Also, the data are rounded to keep the illustrative computations simple. As a result, the analysis of residuals will only be of limited value here. The residuals are obtained according to (19.35). Using the data in Table 19.7, we have, for instance:

$$e_{111} = 47 - 45 = 2$$
$$e_{121} = 46 - 43 = 3$$

A plot of the residuals against the fitted values $\hat{Y}_{ijk} = \bar{Y}_{ij.}$ is presented in Figure 19.8a. There is no strong evidence of unequal error variances for the different treatments here. A normal probability plot of the residuals is presented in Figure 19.8b. The plot is moderately linear; the flat steps are due to the rounded nature of the data. The coefficient of correlation between the ordered residuals and their expected values under normality is .940, which tends to support the reasonableness of approximate normality.

On the basis of these diagnostics and since the inference procedures for ANOVA model (19.23) are robust, it appears to be reasonable to proceed with tests for factor effects and other inference procedures.

19.6 F Tests

In view of the additivity of sums of squares and degrees of freedom, Cochran's theorem (2.61) applies when no factor effects are present. Hence, the F^* test statistics based on the appropriate mean squares then follow the F distribution, leading to the usual type of F tests for factor effects.

Test for Interactions

Ordinarily, the analysis of a two-factor study begins with a test to determine whether or not the two factors interact:

(19.43)
$$H_0: \mu_{ij} - \mu_{i.} - \mu_{.j} + \mu_{..} = 0 \qquad \text{for all } i, j$$
$$H_a: \mu_{ij} - \mu_{i.} - \mu_{.j} + \mu_{..} \neq 0 \qquad \text{for some } i, j$$

or equivalently:

(19.43a)
$$H_0: \text{ all } (\alpha\beta)_{ij} = 0$$
$$H_a: \text{ not all } (\alpha\beta)_{ij} \text{ equal zero}$$

As we noted from an examination of the expected mean squares in Table 19.8, the appropriate test statistic is:

(19.44)
$$F^* = \frac{MSAB}{MSE}$$

Large values of F^* indicate the existence of interactions. When H_0 holds, F^* is distributed as $F[(a-1)(b-1), (n-1)ab]$. Hence, the appropriate decision rule to control the Type I error at α is:

(19.45)
$$\text{If } F^* \leq F[1 - \alpha; (a-1)(b-1), (n-1)ab], \text{ conclude } H_0$$
$$\text{If } F^* > F[1 - \alpha; (a-1)(b-1), (n-1)ab], \text{ conclude } H_a$$

where $F[1 - \alpha; (a-1)(b-1), (n-1)ab]$ is the $(1 - \alpha)100$ percentile of the appropriate F distribution.

Test for Factor A Main Effects

Tests for factor A main effects and for factor B main effects ordinarily follow the test for interactions when no important interactions exist. To test whether or not A main effects are present:

(19.46)
$$H_0: \mu_{1.} = \mu_{2.} = \cdots = \mu_{a.}$$
$$H_a: \text{ not all } \mu_{i.} \text{ are equal}$$

or equivalently:

$$(19.46a) \qquad \begin{aligned} H_0 &: \alpha_1 = \alpha_2 = \cdots = \alpha_a = 0 \\ H_a &: \text{ not all } \alpha_i \text{ equal zero} \end{aligned}$$

we use the test statistic:

$$(19.47) \qquad F^* = \frac{MSA}{MSE}$$

Again, large values of F^* indicate the existence of factor A main effects. Since F^* is distributed as $F[a-1, (n-1)ab]$ when H_0 holds, the appropriate decision rule for controlling the risk of making a Type I error at α is:

$$(19.48) \qquad \begin{aligned} &\text{If } F^* \leq F[1-\alpha; a-1, (n-1)ab], \text{ conclude } H_0 \\ &\text{If } F^* > F[1-\alpha; a-1, (n-1)ab], \text{ conclude } H_a \end{aligned}$$

Test for Factor B Main Effects

This test is similar to the one for factor A main effects. The alternatives are:

$$(19.49) \qquad \begin{aligned} H_0 &: \mu_{.1} = \mu_{.2} = \cdots = \mu_{.b} \\ H_a &: \text{ not all } \mu_{.j} \text{ are equal} \end{aligned}$$

or equivalently:

$$(19.49a) \qquad \begin{aligned} H_0 &: \beta_1 = \beta_2 = \cdots = \beta_b = 0 \\ H_a &: \text{ not all } \beta_j \text{ equal zero} \end{aligned}$$

The test statistic is:

$$(19.50) \qquad F^* = \frac{MSB}{MSE}$$

and the appropriate decision rule for controlling the risk of a Type I error at α is:

$$(19.51) \qquad \begin{aligned} &\text{If } F^* \leq F[1-\alpha; b-1, (n-1)ab], \text{ conclude } H_0 \\ &\text{If } F^* > F[1-\alpha; b-1, (n-1)ab], \text{ conclude } H_a \end{aligned}$$

Example

We shall investigate in the Castle Bakery example the presence of display height and display width effects, using a level of significance of $\alpha = .05$ for each test. First, we begin by testing whether or not interaction effects are present:

$$\begin{aligned} H_0 &: \text{ all } (\alpha\beta)_{ij} = 0 \\ H_a &: \text{ not all } (\alpha\beta)_{ij} \text{ equal zero} \end{aligned}$$

Using the ANOVA results from Table 19.9 in test statistic (19.44), we obtain:

$$F^* = \frac{12}{10.3} = 1.17$$

For $\alpha = .05$, we require $F(.95; 2, 6) = 5.14$, so that the decision rule is:

$$\text{If } F^* \leq 5.14, \text{ conclude } H_0$$

$$\text{If } F^* > 5.14, \text{ conclude } H_a$$

Since $F^* = 1.17 \leq 5.14$, we conclude H_0, that display height and display width do not interact in their effects on sales. The *P*-value of this test is $P\{F(2, 6) > 1.17\} = .37$.

Since the two factors do not interact, we turn to test for display height (factor *A*) main effects; the alternative conclusions are given in (19.46). Test statistic (19.47) for our example becomes:

$$F^* = \frac{772}{10.3} = 75.0$$

For $\alpha = .05$, we require $F(.95; 2, 6) = 5.14$. Since $F^* = 75.0 > 5.14$, we conclude H_a, that the factor *A* level means $\mu_{i.}$ are not equal, or that some definite effects associated with height of display level exist. The *P*-value of this test is $P\{F(2, 6) > 75.0\} = .0001$.

Next, we test for display width (factor *B*) main effects; the alternative conclusions are given in (19.49). Test statistic (19.50) becomes for our example:

$$F^* = \frac{12}{10.3} = 1.17$$

For $\alpha = .05$, we require $F(.95; 1, 6) = 5.99$. Since $F^* = 1.17 \leq 5.99$, we conclude H_0, that all $\mu_{.j}$ are equal, or that display width has no effect on sales. The *P*-value of this test is $P\{F(1, 6) > 1.17\} = .32$.

Thus, the analysis of variance tests confirm the impressions from the estimated treatment means plot in Figure 19.6 — that only display height has an effect on sales for the treatments studied. At this point, it is clearly desirable to conduct further analyses of the nature of the display height effects. We shall discuss analyses of the nature of the factor effects in Chapter 20.

Comments

1. If the test for interactions is conducted with level of significance α_1, that for factor *A* main effects with level of significance α_2, and that for factor *B* main effects with level of significance α_3, the level of significance α for the *family* of three tests is greater than the individual levels of significance. From the Bonferroni inequality in (4.4), we can derive the inequality:

(19.52)
$$\alpha \leq \alpha_1 + \alpha_2 + \alpha_3$$

For the case considered here, a somewhat tighter inequality can be used, the *Kimball inequality*, which utilizes the fact that the numerators of the three test statistics are independent and the denominator is the same in each case. This inequality states:

(19.53)
$$\alpha \leq 1 - (1 - \alpha_1)(1 - \alpha_2)(1 - \alpha_3)$$

For the Castle Bakery example, where $\alpha_1 = \alpha_2 = \alpha_3 = .05$, the Bonferroni inequality yields as the bound for the family level of significance:

$$\alpha \leq .05 + .05 + .05 = .15$$

while the Kimball inequality yields the bound:

$$\alpha \leq 1 - (.95)(.95)(.95) = .143$$

This illustration makes it clear that the level of significance for the family of three tests may be substantially higher than the levels of significance for the individual tests.

2. The F^* test statistics in (19.44), (19.47), and (19.50) can be obtained by the general linear test approach explained in Chapter 2. For example, in testing for the presence of interaction effects, the alternatives are those given in (19.43) and the full model is ANOVA model (19.23):

$$(19.54) \qquad Y_{ijk} = \mu_{..} + \alpha_i + \beta_j + (\alpha\beta)_{ij} + \varepsilon_{ijk} \qquad \text{Full model}$$

Fitting this full model leads to the fitted values $\hat{Y}_{ijk} = \bar{Y}_{ij}$ and the error sum of squares:

$$(19.55) \qquad SSE(F) = \sum\sum\sum(Y_{ijk} - \hat{Y}_{ijk})^2 = \sum\sum\sum(Y_{ijk} - \bar{Y}_{ij.})^2 = SSE$$

which is the usual ANOVA error sum of squares in (19.37c). This error sum of squares has $ab(n-1)$ degrees of freedom associated with it.

The reduced model under H_0: $(\alpha\beta)_{ij} \equiv 0$ is:

$$(19.56) \qquad Y_{ijk} = \mu_{..} + \alpha_i + \beta_j + \varepsilon_{ijk} \qquad \text{Reduced model}$$

It can be shown that the fitted values for the reduced model are $\hat{Y}_{ijk} = \bar{Y}_{i..} + \bar{Y}_{.j.} - \bar{Y}_{...}$, so that the error sum of squares for the reduced model is:

$$(19.57) \qquad SSE(R) = \sum\sum\sum(Y_{ijk} - \hat{Y}_{ijk})^2 = \sum\sum\sum(Y_{ijk} - \bar{Y}_{i..} - \bar{Y}_{.j.} + \bar{Y}_{...})^2$$

This error sum of squares can be shown to have $nab - a - b + 1$ degrees of freedom associated with it. Test statistic (2.70) then simplifies to $F^* = MSAB/MSE$ in (19.44). ∎

19.7   Regression Approach to Two-Factor Analysis of Variance

We shall explain the regression approach to two-factor analysis of variance in terms of the factor effects model (19.23):

$$(19.58) \qquad Y_{ijk} = \mu_{..} + \alpha_i + \beta_j + (\alpha\beta)_{ij} + \varepsilon_{ijk}$$

As we know from (19.24), the mean responses for this model are given by:

$$(19.59) \qquad E\{Y_{ijk}\} = \mu_{..} + \alpha_i + \beta_j + (\alpha\beta)_{ij}$$

To represent this model in matrix terms, we proceed in the same fashion as in the regression approach to single-factor ANOVA. Since $\sum\alpha_i = 0$, we need only $a-1$ parameters α_i in the regression model, and we represent the parameter α_a as follows:

$$(19.60) \qquad \alpha_a = -\alpha_1 - \alpha_2 - \cdots - \alpha_{a-1}$$

Hence, we utilize $a - 1$ indicator variables that can take on values $1, -1$, or 0 for the α_i parameters, as in the single-factor ANOVA representation. Similarly, we need only $b - 1$ parameters β_j in the regression model, and we represent the parameter β_b as follows:

$$(19.61) \qquad \beta_b = -\beta_1 - \beta_2 - \cdots - \beta_{b-1}$$

Hence, we utilize $b - 1$ indicator variables that can take on values $1, -1$, or 0 for the β_j parameters.

For the interaction parameters, we need to recognize that:

$$(19.62) \qquad \begin{aligned} \sum_i (\alpha\beta)_{ij} &= 0 \qquad j = 1, \ldots, b \\[1em] \sum_j (\alpha\beta)_{ij} &= 0 \qquad i = 1, \ldots, a \end{aligned}$$

Therefore, we represent the parameters $(\alpha\beta)_{ib}$ and $(\alpha\beta)_{aj}$ as follows:

$$(19.63) \qquad (\alpha\beta)_{ib} = -(\alpha\beta)_{i1} - (\alpha\beta)_{i2} \quad \cdots - (\alpha\beta)_{l,b-1}$$

$$(19.64) \qquad (\alpha\beta)_{aj} = -(\alpha\beta)_{1j} - (\alpha\beta)_{2j} - \cdots - (\alpha\beta)_{a-1,j}$$

Indeed, because of the interrelations in the constraints in (19.62), only $(a - 1)(b - 1)$ terms $(\alpha\beta)_{ij}$ are needed in the regression model. These are the terms associated with the cross products between the indicator variables for the factor A and factor B main effects, as we will now demonstrate.

Example

We develop the regression model for the Castle Bakery example that is equivalent to the factor effects ANOVA model (19.23) by first defining the $1, -1, 0$ indicator variables for the factor A and factor B main effects, as follows:

$$X_1 = \begin{array}{ll} 1 & \text{if case from level 1 for factor } A \\ -1 & \text{if case from level 3 for factor } A \\ 0 & \text{otherwise} \end{array}$$

$$(19.65) \qquad X_2 = \begin{array}{ll} 1 & \text{if case from level 2 for factor } A \\ -1 & \text{if case from level 3 for factor } A \\ 0 & \text{otherwise} \end{array}$$

$$X_3 = \begin{array}{ll} 1 & \text{if case from level 1 for factor } B \\ -1 & \text{if case from level 2 for factor } B \end{array}$$

Since $X_1 = 1$ for level 1 of factor A, we know from our discussion in Chapter 16 for single-factor ANOVA that the regression coefficient associated with X_1 is α_1. Similarly, α_2 is the regression coefficient associated with X_2, and β_1 is the regression coefficient associated with X_3. There will need to be two cross-product terms in the regression model for interaction effects between factors A and B, namely, $X_1 X_3$ and $X_2 X_3$. Since the term $X_1 X_3$ corresponds to factor A at level 1 ($i = 1$) and factor B at level 1 ($j = 1$), the corresponding regression coefficient is $(\alpha\beta)_{11}$, the interaction effect when factor A is at level 1 and factor B is at level 1. Similarly, $(\alpha\beta)_{21}$ is the interaction effect associated with the cross-product term $X_2 X_3$.

The multiple regression model that is the equivalent of the two-factor ANOVA model for the Castle Bakery example therefore is:

$$(19.66) \qquad Y_{ijk} = \mu_{..} + \underbrace{\alpha_1 X_{ijk1} + \alpha_2 X_{ijk2}}_{A \text{ main effect}} + \underbrace{\beta_1 X_{ijk3}}_{B \text{ main effect}}$$

$$+ \underbrace{(\alpha\beta)_{11} X_{ijk1} X_{ijk3} + (\alpha\beta)_{21} X_{ijk2} X_{ijk3}}_{AB \text{ interaction effect}} + \varepsilon_{ijk} \qquad \text{Full model}$$

$$i = 1, 2, 3; \quad j = 1, 2; \quad k = 1, 2$$

where:

X_1, X_2, X_3 are indicator variables defined in (19.65)

Here X_{ijk1} denotes the value of indicator variable X_1 for the kth case from the treatment for which factor A is at the ith level and factor B is at the jth level, and X_{ijk2} and X_{ijk3} have corresponding meanings. Note that the intercept term in the regression model, $\mu_{..}$, is the overall constant in ANOVA model (19.23).

To verify that regression model (19.66) yields the proper expected values, we shall consider a few examples. Note first that the definitions of the X variables in (19.65) imply the following codings for observations from each of the six treatments:

Treatment

i	j	X_1	X_2	X_3	$X_1 X_3$	$X_2 X_3$
1	1	1	0	1	1	0
2	1	0	1	1	0	1
3	1	−1	−1	1	−1	−1
1	2	1	0	−1	−1	0
2	2	0	1	−1	0	−1
3	2	−1	−1	−1	1	1
Regression coefficient:		α_1	α_2	β_1	$(\alpha\beta)_{11}$	$(\alpha\beta)_{21}$

First, we shall consider $E\{Y_{111}\}$ for which $X_1 = 1$, $X_2 = 0$, $X_3 = 1$, $X_1 X_3 = 1$, $X_2 X_3 = 0$:

$$E\{Y_{111}\} = \mu_{..} + \alpha_1 + \beta_1 + (\alpha\beta)_{11}$$

As another example, consider $E\{Y_{121}\}$, for which $X_1 = 1$, $X_2 = 0$, $X_3 = -1$, $X_1 X_3 = -1$, $X_2 X_3 = 0$:

$$E\{Y_{121}\} = \mu_{..} + \alpha_1 - \beta_1 - (\alpha\beta)_{11}$$

$$= \mu_{..} + \alpha_1 + \beta_2 + (\alpha\beta)_{12}$$

since $\beta_2 = -\beta_1$ by (19.61) and $(\alpha\beta)_{12} = -(\alpha\beta)_{11}$ by (19.63).

Finally, we shall consider $E\{Y_{322}\}$, for which $X_1 = -1$, $X_2 = -1$, $X_3 = -1$, $X_1 X_3 = 1$, $X_2 X_3 = 1$:

$$E\{Y_{322}\} = \mu_{..} - \alpha_1 - \alpha_2 - \beta_1 + (\alpha\beta)_{11} + (\alpha\beta)_{21}$$
$$= \mu_{..} + \alpha_3 + \beta_2 + (\alpha\beta)_{32}$$

since:

$$\alpha_3 = -\alpha_1 - \alpha_2 \qquad \text{by (19.60)}$$
$$\beta_2 = -\beta_1 \qquad \text{by (19.61)}$$

$$-(\alpha\beta)_{12} = (\alpha\beta)_{11} \quad \text{and} \quad -(\alpha\beta)_{22} = (\alpha\beta)_{21} \qquad \text{by (19.63)}$$
$$-(\alpha\beta)_{12} - (\alpha\beta)_{22} = (\alpha\beta)_{32} \qquad \text{by (19.64)}$$

Thus, the regression model representation in (19.66) yields the proper mean response for each observation.

The tests for interaction effects, factor A main effects, and factor B main effects for the Castle Bakery example involve testing whether certain of the regression coefficients in regression model (19.66) equal zero, as follows:

Test for interaction effects

(19.67)
$$H_0: (\alpha\beta)_{11} = (\alpha\beta)_{21} = 0$$
$$H_a: \text{ not both } (\alpha\beta)_{11} \text{ and } (\alpha\beta)_{21} \text{ equal zero}$$

Test for factor A main effects

(19.68)
$$H_0: \alpha_1 = \alpha_2 = 0$$
$$H_a: \text{ not both } \alpha_1 \text{ and } \alpha_2 \text{ equal zero}$$

Test for factor B main effects

(19.69)
$$H_0: \beta_1 = 0$$
$$H_a: \beta_1 \neq 0$$

Thus, the test statistic in each case is the F^* statistic in (7.27), and only the appropriate extra sum of squares and numerator degrees of freedom vary for the three tests.

To conduct the analysis of variance tests for the Castle Bakery example by means of the regression approach, we assemble the data as shown in Table 19.10a for a portion of the cases. The response data in column 1 are repeated from Table 19.7. Note that the coding of the X variables follows the definitions in (19.65). Regressing Y in column 1 of Table 19.10a on the X variables in columns 2–6 yields the fitted regression function shown in Table 19.10b and the ANOVA table in Table 19.10c, including the extra sums of squares for each X variable in the order of the X variables in the regression model.

It can be shown that when all treatment sample sizes are equal, as they are for the Castle Bakery example, the total of the extra sums of squares for the factor A regression terms equals SSA. Similarly, the totals of the extra sums of squares for the factor B regression terms and the interaction regression terms equal, respectively, SSB and $SSAB$. Because of the balance in the $\mathbf{X}$ matrix when all treatment sample sizes are equal, these totals of the

---

TABLE 19.10   **Regression Approach to Two-Factor Analysis of Variance —Castle Bakery Example.**

(a) Data For Regression Model (19.66)

			(1)	(2)	(3)	(4)	(5)	(6)
i	j	k	Y	X_1	X_2	X_3	$X_1 X_3$	$X_2 X_3$
1	1	1	47	1	0	1	1	0
1	1	2	43	1	0	1	1	0
1	2	1	46	1	0	-1	-1	0
			$\cdots$	$\cdots$	$\cdots$	$\cdots$	$\cdots$	$\cdots$
3	1	2	39	-1	-1	1	-1	-1
3	2	1	42	-1	-1	-1	1	1
3	2	2	46	-1	-1	-1	1	1

(b) Fitted Regression Function

$$\hat{Y} = 51.0 - 7.0X_1 + 16.0X_2 - 1.0X_3 + 2.0X_1 X_3 - 1.0X_2 X_3$$

(c) ANOVA Table

Source of Variation	SS		df		MS
Regression	1,580		5		$MSTR = 316$
X_1	8		1		
$X_2\|X_1$	1,536 $\Big\}$ $SSA = 1,544$		1 $\Big\}$ 2		$MSA = 772$
$X_3\|X_1, X_2$	12 $\big\}$ $SSB = 12$		1 $\big\}$ 1		$MSB = 12$
$X_1 X_3\|X_1, X_2, X_3$	18		1		
$X_2 X_3\|X_1, X_2, X_3, X_1 X_3$	6 $\Big\}$ $SSAB = 24$		1 $\Big\}$ 2		$MSAB = 12$
Error	62		6		$MSE = 10.3$
Total	1,642		11		

extra sums of squares are the same regardless of the order of the factor A, factor B, and interaction extra sums of squares.

We see from Table 19.10c that the totals SSA, SSB, and $SSAB$ and also the error sum of squares SSE obtained with the regression approach are the same as in Table 19.9 where they were calculated by means of the ANOVA formulas.

From this point on, the test procedures based on the regression approach are identical to the analysis of variance tests explained earlier.

19.8   Pooling Sums of Squares in Two-Factor Analysis of Variance

The testing approach presented in this chapter assumes that ANOVA model (19.23) is the full model for all tests of factor effects, regardless of the conclusions reached in any of these tests. The rationale for this approach is that ANOVA model (19.23) is based on the identity (19.22) for the treatment means μ_{ij}. Once the analysis of residuals and other diagnostics demonstrate that this model is appropriate, it is used for all tests.

Some statisticians take the view that ANOVA model (19.23) should be revised when the test for interaction effects leads to the conclusion that no interactions are present. With this approach, the full model considered in testing for factor A and factor B main effects when the test for interaction effects leads to the conclusion that no interactions are present is the revised model:

$$(19.70) \qquad\qquad Y_{ijk} = \mu_{..} + \alpha_i + \beta_j + \varepsilon_{ijk} \qquad\qquad \text{Revised full model}$$

As we just noted with the regression approach for the Castle Bakery example, the extra sums of squares for factor A and factor B main effects do not depend on the order of the extra sums of squares for factor effects when all treatment sample sizes are equal. Hence, the numerator sums of squares SSA and SSB of the test statistic F^* are not affected by this revision in the full model when the treatment sample sizes are equal. The denominator sum of squares of the F^* test statistic is affected, however, leading to the following error sum of squares for the full model:

$$(19.71) \qquad\qquad SSE(F) = SSE + SSAB$$

Thus, the error sum of squares for the full model with this approach involves the *pooling* of the interaction and error sums of squares. Likewise, the degrees of freedom are pooled; the degrees of freedom associated with $SSE(F)$ are:

$$df_F = (a - 1)(b - 1) + (n - 1)ab = nab - a - b + 1$$

For the Castle Bakery example, the pooled error sum of squares for testing factor A and factor B main effects would be (Table 19.9):

$$SSE(F) = 62 + 24 = 86$$

and the pooled degrees of freedom would be:

$$df_F = 6 + 2 = 8$$

Hence, the error mean square for testing factor A or factor B main effects with the model revision approach here would be $86/8 = 10.75$.

This pooling procedure affects both the level of significance and the power of the tests for factor A and factor B main effects, in ways not yet fully understood. It has been suggested therefore by some statisticians that pooling should not be considered unless: (1) the degrees of freedom associated with MSE are small, perhaps 5 or less, and (2) the test statistic $MSAB/MSE$ falls substantially below the action limit of the decision rule, perhaps when $MSAB/MSE < 2$ for $\alpha = .05$. Part (1) of this rule is designed to limit pooling to cases where the gains may be substantial, while part (2) is designed to give reasonable assurance that there are indeed no interactions.

Problems

19.1. Refer to the **SENIC** data set. An analyst wishes to investigate the effects of medical school affiliation (factor A) and geographic region (factor B) on infection risk. All factor level combinations will be included in the study.

   a. How many treatments are being studied?

   b. What is the response variable here?

19.2. A student in a class discussion stated: "A treatment is a treatment, whether the study involves a single factor or multiple factors. The number of factors has little effect on the interpretation of the results." Discuss.

19.3. Verify the interactions in Table 19.3b.

√ 19.4. In a two-factor study, the treatment means μ_{ij} are as follows:

	Factor B		
Factor A	B_1	B_2	B_3
A_1	34	23	36
A_2	40	29	42

   a. Obtain the factor A level means.

   b. Obtain the main effects of factor A.

   c. Does the fact that $\mu_{12} - \mu_{11} = -11$ while $\mu_{13} - \mu_{12} = 13$ imply that factors A and B interact? Explain.

   d. Prepare a treatment means plot and determine whether the two factors interact. What do you find?

19.5. In a two-factor study, the treatment means μ_{ij} are as follows:

	Factor B			
Factor A	B_1	B_2	B_3	B_4
A_1	250	265	268	269
A_2	288	273	270	269

   a. Obtain the factor B main effects. What do your results imply about factor B?

   b. Prepare a treatment means plot and determine whether the two factors interact. How can you tell that interactions are present? Are the interactions important or unimportant?

   c. Make a logarithmic transformation of the μ_{ij} and plot the transformed values to explore whether this transformation is helpful in reducing the interactions. What are your findings?

19.6. Three sets of treatment means μ_{ij} for students' grades in a course follow, where factor A is student's major (A_1: computer science; A_2: mathematics) and factor B is student's class affiliation (B_1: junior; B_2: senior; B_3: graduate).

	Set 1				Set 2				Set 3		
	B_1	B_2	B_3		B_1	B_2	B_3		B_1	B_2	B_3
A_1	80	80	80	A_1	75	80	90	A_1	75	80	85
A_2	90	90	90	A_2	80	86	97	A_2	75	85	100

Prepare a treatment means plot for each set of μ_{ij} to study interaction effects. Interpret each plot and state your findings. If interactions are present, describe their nature and indicate whether they are important or unimportant.

√ 19.7. Refer to Problem 19.4. Assume that $\sigma = 1.4$ and $n = 10$.

   a. Obtain $E\{MSE\}$ and $E\{MSA\}$.

   b. Is $E\{MSA\}$ substantially larger than $E\{MSE\}$? What is the implication of this?

19.8. Refer to Problem 19.5. Assume that $\sigma = 4$ and $n = 6$.

   a. Obtain $E\{MSE\}$ and $E\{MSAB\}$.

   b. Is $E\{MSAB\}$ substantially larger than $E\{MSE\}$? What is the implication of this?

19.9. A psychologist stated: "I feel uncomfortable about deciding in a research study whether the interactions are important or unimportant. I would rather have the statistician make that decision." Comment.

√ 19.10. Refer to **Cash offers** Problem 16.13. Six male and six female volunteers were used in each age group. The observations (in hundred dollars), classified by age (factor A) and gender of owner (factor B), follow.

	Factor B (gender of owner)	
Factor A (age)	$j = 1$ Male	$j = 2$ Female
$i = 1$ Young	21	21
	23	22
	...	...
	23	25
$i = 2$ Middle	30	26
	29	29
	...	...
	27	29
$i = 3$ Elderly	25	23
	22	19
	...	...
	21	20

   a. Obtain the fitted values for ANOVA model (19.23).

   b. Obtain the residuals. Do they sum to zero for each treatment?

   c. Prepare aligned residual dot plots for the treatments. What departures from ANOVA model (19.23) can be studied from these plots? What are your findings?

d. Prepare a normal probability plot of the residuals. Also obtain the coefficient of correlation between the ordered residuals and their expected values under normality. Does the normality assumption appear to be reasonable here?

e. The observations for each treatment were obtained in the order shown. Prepare residual sequence plots and interpret them. What are your findings?

√ 19.11. Refer to **Cash offers** Problems 16.13 and 19.10. Assume that ANOVA model (19.23) is applicable.

a. Prepare an estimated treatment means plot. Does it appear that any factor effects are present? Explain.

b. Set up the analysis of variance table. Does any one source account for most of the total variability in cash offers in the study? Explain.

c. Test whether or not interaction effects are present; use $\alpha = .05$. State the alternatives, decision rule, and conclusion. What is the P-value of the test?

d. Test whether or not age and gender main effects are present. In each case, use $\alpha = .05$ and state the alternatives, decision rule, and conclusion. What is the P-value of the test? Is it meaningful here to test for main factor effects? Explain.

e. Obtain an upper bound on the family level of significance for the tests in parts (c) and (d); use the Kimball inequality.

f. Do the results in parts (c) and (d) confirm your graphic analysis in part (a)?

g. What are the relations between the sums of squares in the two-factor analysis of variance in part (b) and the sums of squares in the single-factor analysis of variance in Problem 16.13d? Do the same relations hold for the degrees of freedom?

19.12. **Eye contact effect**. In a study of the effect of applicant's eye contact (factor A) and personnel officer's gender (factor B) on the personnel officer's assessment of likely job success of applicant, 10 male and 10 female personnel officers were shown a front view photograph of an applicant's face and were asked to give the person in the photograph a success rating on a scale of 0 (total failure) to 20 (outstanding success). Half of the officers in each gender group were chosen at random to receive a version of the photograph in which the applicant made eye contact with the camera lens. The other half received a version in which there was no eye contact. The success ratings follow.

	Factor B (gender of officer)	
Factor A (eye contact)	$j = 1$ Male	$j = 2$ Female
$i = 1$ Present	11	15
	7	12
	...	...
	10	16
$i = 2$ Absent	12	14
	16	17
	...	...
	14	18

a. Obtain the fitted values for ANOVA model (19.23).

b. Obtain the residuals. Do they sum to zero for each treatment?

c. Prepare aligned residual dot plots for the treatments. What departures from ANOVA model (19.23) can be studied from these plots? What are your findings?

d. Prepare a normal probability plot of the residuals. Also obtain the coefficient of correlation between the ordered residuals and their expected values under normality. Does the normality assumption appear to be reasonable here?

e. The observations for each treatment were obtained in the order shown. Prepare residual sequence plots and interpret them. What are your findings?

19.13. Refer to **Eye contact effect** Problem 19.12. Assume that ANOVA model (19.23) is applicable.

a. Prepare an estimated treatment means plot. Does it appear that any factor effects are present? Explain.

b. Set up the analysis of variance table. Does any one source account for most of the total variability in the success ratings in the study? Explain.

c. Test whether or not interaction effects are present; use $\alpha = .01$. State the alternatives, decision rule, and conclusion. What is the P-value of the test?

d. Test whether or not eye contact and gender main effects are present. In each case, use $\alpha = .01$ and state the alternatives, decision rule, and conclusion. What is the P-value of each test? Is it meaningful here to test for main factor effects? Explain.

e. Obtain an upper bound on the family level of significance for the tests in parts (c) and (d); use the Kimball inequality.

f. Do the results in parts (c) and (d) confirm your graphic analysis in part (a)?

√ 19.14. **Hay fever relief**. A research laboratory was developing a new compound for the relief of severe cases of hay fever. In an experiment with 36 volunteers, the amounts of the two active ingredients (factors A and B) in the compound were varied at three levels each. Randomization was used in assigning four volunteers to each of the nine treatments. The data on hours of relief follow.

Factor A (ingredient 1)	Factor B (ingredient 2)		
	$j = 1$ Low	$j = 2$ Medium	$j = 3$ High
$i = 1$ Low	2.4	4.6	4.8
	. . .	. . .	. . .
	2.5	4.7	4.6
$i = 2$ Medium	5.8	8.9	9.1
	. . .	. . .	. . .
	5.3	9.0	9.4
$i = 3$ High	6.1	9.9	13.5
	. . .	. . .	. . .
	6.2	10.1	13.2

a. Obtain the fitted values for ANOVA model (19.23).

b. Obtain the residuals.

c. Plot the residuals against the fitted values. What departures from ANOVA model (19.23) can be studied from this plot? What are your findings?

d. Prepare a normal probability plot of the residuals. Also obtain the coefficient of correlation between the ordered residuals and their expected values under normality. Does the normality assumption appear to be reasonable here?

√ 19.15. Refer to **Hay fever relief** Problem 19.14. Assume that ANOVA model (19.23) is applicable.

a. Prepare an estimated treatment means plot. Does your graph suggest that any factor effects are present? Explain.

b. Obtain the analysis of variance table. Does any one source account for most of the total variability in hours of relief in the study? Explain.

c. Test whether or not the two factors interact; use $\alpha = .05$. State the alternatives, decision rule, and conclusion. What is the P-value of the test?

d. Test whether or not main effects for the two ingredients are present. Use $\alpha = .05$ in each case and state the alternatives, decision rule, and conclusion. What is the P-value of each test? Is it meaningful here to test for main factor effects? Explain.

e. Obtain an upper bound on the family level of significance for the tests in parts (c) and (d); use the Kimball inequality.

f. Do the results in parts (c) and (d) confirm your graphic analysis in part (a)?

19.16. **Disk drive service.** The staff of a service center for electronic equipment includes three technicians who specialize in repairing three widely used makes of disk drives for desktop computers. It was desired to study the effects of technician (factor A) and make of disk drive (factor B) on the service time. The data that follow show the number of minutes required to complete the repair job in a study where each technician was randomly assigned to five jobs on each make of disk drive.

Factor A (technician)	Factor B (make of drive)		
	$j = 1$ Make 1	$j = 2$ Make 2	$j = 3$ Make 3
$i = 1$ Technician 1	62	57	59
	48	45	53
	. . .	. . .	. . .
	69	44	47
$i = 2$ Technician 2	51	61	55
	57	58	58
	. . .	. . .	. . .
	39	51	49
$i = 3$ Technician 3	59	58	47
	65	63	56
	. . .	. . .	. . .
	70	60	50

a. Obtain the fitted values for ANOVA model (19.23).

b. Obtain the residuals.

c. Plot the residuals against the fitted values. What departures from ANOVA model (19.23) can be studied from this plot? What are your findings?

d. Prepare a normal probability plot of the residuals. Also obtain the coefficient of correlation between the ordered residuals and their expected values under normality. Does the normality assumption appear to be reasonable here?

e. The observations for each treatment were obtained in the order shown. Prepare residual sequence plots and analyze them. What are your findings?

19.17. Refer to **Disk drive service** Problem 19.16. Assume that ANOVA model (19.23) is applicable.

a. Prepare an estimated treatment means plot. Does your graph suggest that any factor effects are present? Explain.

b. Obtain the analysis of variance table. Does any one source account for most of the total variability? Explain.

c. Test whether or not the two factors interact; use $\alpha = .01$. State the alternatives, decision rule, and conclusion. What is the P-value of the test?

d. Test whether or not main effects for technician and make of drive are present. Use $\alpha = .01$ in each case and state the alternatives, decision rule, and conclusion. What is the P-value of each test? Is it meaningful here to test for main factor effects? Explain.

e. Obtain an upper bound on the family level of significance for the tests in parts (c) and (d); use the Kimball inequality.

f. Do the results in parts (c) and (d) confirm your graphic analysis in part (a)?

19.18. **Kidney failure hospitalization**. Kidney failure patients are commonly treated on dialysis machines that filter toxic substances from the blood. The appropriate "dose" for effective treatment depends, among other things, on duration of treatment and weight gain between treatments as a result of fluid buildup. To study the effects of these two factors on the number of days hospitalized (attributable to the disease) during a year, a random sample of 10 patients per group who had undergone treatment at a large dialysis facility was obtained. Treatment duration (factor A) was categorized into two groups: short duration (average dialysis time for the year under four hours) and long duration (average dialysis time for the year equal to or greater than four hours). Average weight gain between treatments (factor B) during the year was categorized into three groups: slight, moderate, and severe. The data on number of days hospitalized follow.

Factor A (duration)	Factor B (weight gain)					
	$j = 1$ Mild		$j = 2$ Moderate		$j = 3$ Severe	
$i = 1$ Short	0	2	2	4	15	16
	2	0	4	3	10	7
	. . .	. . .	. . .	. . .	. . .	. . .
	0	8	15	20	25	27
$i = 2$ Long	0	2	5	1	10	15
	1	7	3	3	8	4
	. . .	. . .	. . .	. . .	. . .	. . .
	4	3	1	9	7	1

The transformed data $Y' = \log_{10}(Y + 1)$ are to be used for the analysis.

a. Obtain the fitted values and residuals for ANOVA model (19.23) for the transformed data.

b. Prepare aligned residual dot plots for the treatments. What departures from ANOVA model (19.23) can be studied from these plots? What are your findings?

c. Prepare a normal probability plot of the residuals. Also obtain the coefficient of correlation between the ordered residuals and their expected values under normality. Does the normality assumption appear to be reasonable here?

19.19. Refer to **Kidney failure hospitalization** Problem 19.18. Assume that ANOVA model (19.23) is appropriate for the transformed response variable.

a. Prepare an estimated treatment means plot. Does your graph suggest that any factor effects are present? Explain.

b. Obtain the analysis of variance table. Does any one source account for most of the total variability? Explain.

c. Test whether or not the two factors interact; use $\alpha = .05$. State the alternatives, decision rule, and conclusion. What is the P-value of the test?

d. Test whether or not main effects for duration and weight gain are present. Use $\alpha = .05$ in each case and state the alternatives, decision rule, and conclusion. What is the P-value of each test? Is it meaningful here to test for main factor effects? Explain.

e. Obtain an upper bound on the family level of significance for the tests in parts (c) and (d); use the Kimball inequality.

f. Do the results in parts (c) and (d) confirm your graphic analysis in part (a)?

√ 19.20. **Programmer requirements.** A computer software firm was encountering difficulties in forecasting the programmer requirements for large-scale programming projects. As part of a study to remedy the difficulties, 24 programmers, classified into equal groups by type of experience (factor A) and amount of experience (factor B), were asked to predict the number of programmer-days required to complete a large project about to be initiated. After this project was completed, the prediction errors (actual minus predicted programmer-days) were determined. The data on prediction errors follow.

Factor A (type of experience)	Factor B (years of experience)		
	$j = 1$ Under 5	$j = 2$ 5–under 10	$j = 3$ 10 or more
$i = 1$ Small	240	110	56
systems only	206	118	60
	217	103	68
	225	95	58
$i = 2$ Small and	71	47	37
large systems	53	52	33
	68	31	40
	57	49	45

a. Obtain the fitted values for ANOVA model (19.23).

b. Obtain the residuals.

   c. Prepare aligned residual dot plots for the treatments. What departures from ANOVA model (19.23) can be studied from these plots? What are your findings?

   d. Prepare a normal probability plot of the residuals. Also obtain the coefficient of correlation between the ordered residuals and their expected values under normality. Does the normality assumption appear to be reasonable here?

$\sqrt{}$ 19.21. Refer to **Programmer requirements** Problem 19.20. Assume that ANOVA model (19.23) is applicable.

   a. Prepare an estimated treatment means plot. Does your graph suggest that any factor effects are present? Explain.

   b. Obtain the analysis of variance table. Does any one source account for most of the total variability? Explain.

   c. Test whether or not the two factors interact; use $\alpha = .01$. State the alternatives, decision rule, and conclusion. What is the P-value of the test?

   d. Test whether or not main effects for type of experience and years of experience are present. Use $\alpha = .01$ in each case and state the alternatives, decision rule, and conclusion. What is the P-value of each test? Is it meaningful here to test for main factor effects? Explain.

   e. Obtain an upper bound on the family level of significance for the tests in parts (c) and (d); use the Kimball inequality.

   f. Do the results in parts (c) and (d) confirm your graphic analysis in part (a)?

19.22. How does the randomization of treatment assignments in a two-factor study differ when both factors are experimental factors and when only one factor is an experimental factor?

19.23. Refer to **Eye contact effect** Problem 19.12.

   a. Explain how you would make the assignments of personnel officers to treatments in this two-factor study. Make all appropriate randomizations.

   b. Did you randomize the officers to the factor levels of each factor?

19.24. Refer to **Hay fever relief** Problem 19.14.

   a. Explain how you would make the assignments of volunteers to treatments in this study. Make all appropriate randomizations.

   b. Did you randomize the volunteers to the factor levels of each factor?

19.25. Refer to **Disk drive service** Problem 19.16.

   a. Is any randomization of treatment assignments called for in this study? Is any randomization utilized? Explain.

   b. Would you consider this study to be experimental in nature? Discuss.

19.26. Refer to **Eye contact effect** Problem 19.12.

   a. Modify regression model (19.66) to apply to this two-factor study with $a = 2$ and $b = 2$.

   b. Set up the $\mathbf{Y}$, $\mathbf{X}$, and $\boldsymbol{\beta}$ matrices for the regression model in part (a).

   c. Obtain $\mathbf{X}\boldsymbol{\beta}$. Verify the correctness of the expected values.

   d. Obtain the fitted regression function. What is estimated by the intercept term?

   e. Obtain the regression analysis of variance table based on appropriate extra sums of squares.

    f. Test separately for interaction effects, factor A main effects, and factor B main effects. Use $\alpha = .01$ for each test and state the alternatives, decision rule, and conclusion.

√ 19.27. Refer to **Hay fever relief** Problem 19.14.

    a. Modify regression model (19.66) to apply to this two-factor study with $a = 3$ and $b = 3$.

    b. Set up the **Y**, **X**, and **β** matrices for the regression model in part (a).

    c. Obtain **Xβ**. Verify the correctness of the expected values.

    d. Obtain the fitted regression function. What is estimated by $\hat{\alpha}_1$?

    e. Obtain the regression analysis of variance table based on appropriate extra sums of squares.

    f. Test separately for interaction effects, factor A main effects, and factor B main effects. Use $\alpha = .05$ for each test and state the alternatives, decision rule, and conclusion.

19.28. Refer to **Disk drive service** Problem 19.16.

    a. Modify regression model (19.66) to apply to this two-factor study with $a = 3$ and $b = 3$.

    b. Obtain the fitted regression function. What is estimated by $\hat{\beta}_1$?

    c. Obtain the regression analysis of variance table based on appropriate extra sums of squares.

    d. Test separately for interaction effects, factor A main effects, and factor B main effects. Use $\alpha = .01$ for each test and state the alternatives, decision rule, and conclusion.

Exercises

19.29. Derive (19.7a) from (19.7).

19.30. Prove the result in (19.9b).

19.31. (Calculus needed.) State the likelihood function for ANOVA model (19.15) when $a = 2$, $b = 2$, and $n = 2$. Find the maximum likelihood estimators.

19.32. (Calculus needed.) Derive (19.29).

19.33. Derive (19.39) from (19.38).

Projects

19.34. Refer to the **SENIC** data set. The following hospitals are to be considered in a study of the effects of region (factor A: variable 9) and average age of patients (factor B: variable 3) on the mean length of hospital stay of patients (variable 2):

1–44	46	48	51	53	57	58	60	63	66	74
76	79	80	83	84	88	94	101	103	111	

For purposes of this ANOVA study, average age is to be classified into two categories: less than or equal to 53.9 years, 54.0 years or more.

   a. Assemble the required data and obtain the fitted values for ANOVA model (19.23).

   b. Obtain the residuals.

   c. Plot the residuals against the fitted values. What departures from ANOVA model (19.23) can be studied from this plot? What are your findings?

   d. Prepare a normal probability plot of the residuals. Also obtain the coefficient of correlation between the ordered residuals and their expected values under normality. Does the normality assumption appear to be reasonable here?

19.35. Refer to the **SENIC** data set and Project 19.34. Assume that ANOVA model (19.23) is applicable.

   a. Prepare an estimated treatment means plot. Does it appear that any factor effects are present? Explain.

   b. Obtain the analysis of variance table. Does any one source account for most of the total variability in the study? Explain.

   c. Test whether or not interaction effects are present; use $\alpha = .05$. State the alternatives, decision rule, and conclusion. What is the P-value of the test?

   d. Test whether or not region and age main effects are present. In each case, use $\alpha = .05$ and state the alternatives, decision rule, and conclusion. What is the P-value of each test? Is it meaningful here to test for main factor effects? Explain.

   e. Obtain an upper bound on the family level of significance for the tests in parts (c) and (d); use the Kimball inequality.

   f. Do the results in parts (c) and (d) confirm your graphic analysis in part (a)?

19.36. Refer to the **SMSA** data set. The following metropolitan areas are to be considered in a study of the effects of region (factor A: variable 12) and percent of population in central cities (factor B: variable 4) on the crime rate (variable 11 $\div$ variable 3):

1–36	38	39	45	46	49	53	62	71	73	101	123	130

For purposes of this ANOVA study, percent of population in central cities is to be classified into two categories: less than or equal to 38.9 percent, 39.0 percent or more.

   a. Assemble the required data and obtain the fitted values for ANOVA model (19.23).

   b. Obtain the residuals.

   c. Prepare aligned residual dot plots for the treatments. What departures from ANOVA model (19.23) can be studied from these plots? What are your findings?

   d. Prepare a normal probability plot of the residuals. Also obtain the coefficient of correlation between the ordered residuals and their expected values under normality. Does the normality assumption appear to be reasonable here?

19.37. Refer to the **SMSA** data set and Project 19.36. Assume that ANOVA model (19.23) is applicable.

   a. Prepare an estimated treatment means plot. Does it appear that any factor effects are present? Explain.

   b. Set up the analysis of variance table. Does any one source account for most of the total variability in the study? Explain.

c. Test whether or not interaction effects are present; use $\alpha = .01$. State the alternatives, decision rule, and conclusion. What is the P-value of the test?

d. Test whether or not region and percent of population in central cities main effects are present. In each case, use $\alpha = .01$ and state the alternatives, decision rule, and conclusion. What is the P-value of each test? Is it meaningful here to test for main factor effects? Explain.

e. Obtain an upper bound on the family level of significance for the tests in parts (c) and (d); use the Kimball inequality.

f. Do the results in parts (c) and (d) confirm your graphic analysis in part (a)?

Analysis of Factor Effects in Two-Factor Studies—Equal Sample Sizes

When the analysis of variance tests described in Chapter 19 indicate the presence of factor effects in two-factor studies, the next step is to analyze the nature of the factor effects. In this chapter, we discuss how to conduct such analyses. We continue to consider the two-factor ANOVA model (19.23), *when there are n observations for each treatment and all treatment means are deemed to be of equal importance*. We first discuss the analysis of factor effects when both factors are qualitative and then the analysis of factor effects when one or both factors are quantitative.

20.1 Strategy for Analysis

Scientific inquiry is often guided by the principle that the simplest explanations of observed phenomena tend to be the most effective. Data analysis is guided by this principle, seeking to obtain a simple, clear explanation of the data. In the context of ANOVA studies, additive effects provide a much simpler explanation of factor effects than do interacting effects. The presence of interacting effects complicates the explanation of the factor effects because they must then be described in terms of the *combined* effects of the two factors. Of course, some phenomena are complex so that the factor effects cannot be described simply by additive effects. The desire for a simple, parsimonious explanation, when possible, suggests the following basic strategy for analyzing factor effects in two-factor studies:

1. Examine whether the two factors interact.

2. If they do not interact, examine whether the main effects for factors A and B are important. For important A or B main effects, describe the nature of these effects in terms of the factor level means $\mu_{i\cdot}$ or $\mu_{\cdot j}$, respectively. In some special cases, there may also be interest in the treatment means μ_{ij}.

3. If the factors do interact, examine if the interactions are important or unimportant.

4. If the interactions are unimportant, proceed as in step 2.

5. If the interactions are important, consider whether they can be made unimportant by a meaningful simple transformation of scale. If so, make the transformation and proceed as in step 2.

849

FIGURE 20.1   **Strategy for Analysis of Two-Factor Studies.**

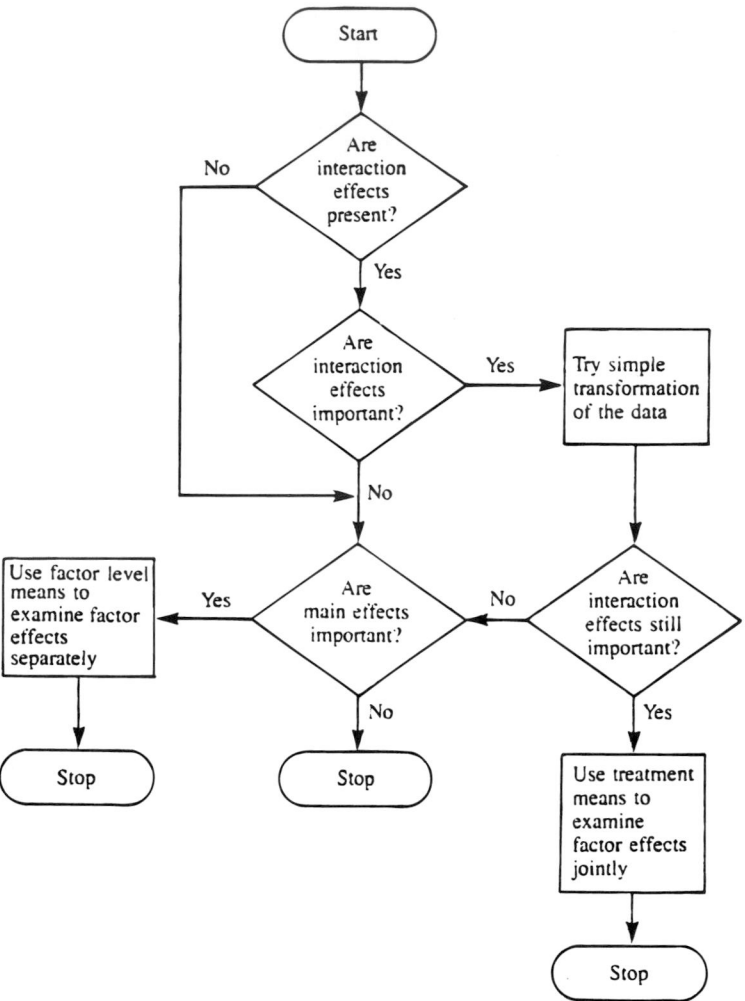

---

6. For important interactions that cannot be made unimportant by a simple transformation, analyze the two factor effects jointly in terms of the treatment means μ_{ij}. In some special cases, there may also be interest in the factor level means $\mu_{i.}$ and $\mu_{.j}$.

A flowchart of this strategy is presented in Figure 20.1.

Step 1 of this strategy, testing for interaction effects, was discussed in Chapter 19. Also discussed there was step 5, the possible diminution of important interactions by a meaningful simple transformation, as well as how to test for the presence of factor main effects. Now we turn to steps 2 and 6 of the strategy for analysis, namely, how to compare factor level means $\mu_{i.}$ or $\mu_{.j}$ when there are no interactions or only unimportant ones, and how to compare treatment means μ_{ij} when there are important interactions. We begin with a discussion of the analysis of factor effects when the factors do not interact or interact only in an unimportant fashion.

20.2   Analysis of Factor Effects when Factors Do Not Interact

As just noted, the analysis of factor effects usually only involves the factor level means μ_i. and $\mu_{.j}$ when the two factors do not interact, or when they interact only in an unimportant fashion. Before proceeding with formal estimation procedures, it is often useful to plot the estimated factor level means in a normal probability plot, as explained in Section 17.2 for single-factor studies.

Estimation of Factor Level Mean

Unbiased point estimators of μ_i. and $\mu_{.j}$ are:

$$(20.1a) \qquad\qquad \hat{\mu}_{i.} = \bar{Y}_{i..}$$

$$(20.1b) \qquad\qquad \hat{\mu}_{.j} = \bar{Y}_{.j.}$$

where $\bar{Y}_{i..}$ and $\bar{Y}_{.j.}$ are defined in (19.27d) and (19.27f), respectively. The variance of $\bar{Y}_{i..}$ is:

$$(20.2a) \qquad\qquad \sigma^2\{\bar{Y}_{i..}\} = \frac{\sigma^2}{bn}$$

since $\bar{Y}_{i..}$ contains bn independent observations, each with variance σ^2. Similarly, we have:

$$(20.2b) \qquad\qquad \sigma^2\{\bar{Y}_{.j.}\} = \frac{\sigma^2}{an}$$

Unbiased estimators of these variances are obtained by replacing σ^2 with *MSE*:

$$(20.3a) \qquad\qquad s^2\{\bar{Y}_{i..}\} = \frac{MSE}{bn}$$

$$(20.3b) \qquad\qquad s^2\{\bar{Y}_{.j.}\} = \frac{MSE}{an}$$

Confidence limits for μ_i. and $\mu_{.j}$ utilize, as usual, the t distribution:

$$(20.4a) \qquad\qquad \bar{Y}_{i..} \pm t[1 - \alpha/2; (n-1)ab]s\{\bar{Y}_{i..}\}$$

$$(20.4b) \qquad\qquad \bar{Y}_{.j.} \pm t[1 - \alpha/2; (n-1)ab]s\{\bar{Y}_{.j.}\}$$

The degrees of freedom $(n-1)ab$ are those associated with *MSE*.

Estimation of Contrast of Factor Level Means

A contrast among the factor level means μ_i.:

$$(20.5) \qquad\qquad L = \sum c_i \mu_{i.} \qquad \text{where } \sum c_i = 0$$

is estimated unbiasedly by:

$$(20.6) \qquad \hat{L} = \sum c_i \bar{Y}_{i..}$$

Because of the independence of the $\bar{Y}_{i..}$, the variance of this estimator is:

$$(20.7) \qquad \sigma^2\{\hat{L}\} = \sum c_i^2 \sigma^2\{\bar{Y}_{i..}\} = \frac{\sigma^2}{bn} \sum c_i^2$$

An unbiased estimator of this variance is:

$$(20.8) \qquad s^2\{\hat{L}\} = \frac{MSE}{bn} \sum c_i^2$$

Finally, the appropriate $1 - \alpha$ confidence limits for L are:

$$(20.9) \qquad \hat{L} \pm t[1 - \alpha/2; (n-1)ab]s\{\hat{L}\}$$

To estimate a contrast among the factor level means $\mu_{.j}$:

$$(20.10) \qquad L = \sum c_j \mu_{.j} \qquad \text{where } \sum c_j = 0$$

we use the estimator:

$$(20.11) \qquad \hat{L} = \sum c_j \bar{Y}_{.j.}$$

whose estimated variance is:

$$(20.12) \qquad s^2\{\hat{L}\} = \frac{MSE}{an} \sum c_j^2$$

The $1 - \alpha$ confidence limits for L in (20.9) are still appropriate, with $\hat{L}$ and $s\{\hat{L}\}$ now defined in (20.11) and (20.12), respectively.

Estimation of Linear Combination of Factor Level Means

A linear combination of the factor level means $\mu_{i.}$:

$$(20.13) \qquad L = \sum c_i \mu_{i.}$$

is estimated unbiasedly by $\hat{L}$ in (20.6). The variance of this estimator is given in (20.7), and an unbiased estimator of this variance is given in (20.8). The appropriate $1 - \alpha$ confidence limits for L are given in (20.9).

Analogous results follow for a linear combination of the factor level means $\mu_{.j}$:

$$(20.14) \qquad L = \sum c_j \mu_{.j}$$

Multiple Pairwise Comparisons of Factor Level Means

Usually, more than one pairwise comparison is of interest, and the multiple comparison procedures discussed in Chapter 17 for single-factor ANOVA studies can be employed with only minor modifications for two-factor studies. If all or a large number of pairwise comparisons among the factor level means $\mu_{i.}$ or $\mu_{.j}$ are to be made, the Tukey procedure of Section 17.5 is appropriate. When only a few pairwise comparisons are to be made that are specified in advance of the analysis, the Bonferroni procedure of Section 17.7 may be best. Often, tests for differences between pairs of factor level means precede the construction of interval estimates so that the analysis of the interval estimates can be confined to active comparisons. When the Bonferroni procedure is used for initial simultaneous testing, it can be refined by means of the Holm procedure, described in Section 17.8 for single-factor studies, to achieve greater discriminating power.

Tukey Procedure. The Tukey multiple comparison confidence limits for all pairwise comparisons:

$$(20.15) \qquad\qquad D = \mu_{i.} - \mu_{i'.}$$

with family confidence coefficient of at least $1 - \alpha$ are:

$$(20.16) \qquad\qquad \hat{D} \pm T s\{\hat{D}\}$$

where:

$$(20.16a) \qquad\qquad \hat{D} = \bar{Y}_{i..} - \bar{Y}_{i'..}$$

$$(20.16b) \qquad\qquad s^2\{\hat{D}\} = \frac{2MSE}{bn}$$

$$(20.16c) \qquad\qquad T = \frac{1}{\sqrt{2}} q[1 - \alpha; a, (n-1)ab]$$

To use the Tukey procedure to conduct all simultaneous tests of the form:

$$(20.17) \qquad\qquad \begin{aligned} H_0: & \ D = \mu_{i.} - \mu_{i'.} = 0 \\ H_a: & \ D = \mu_{i.} - \mu_{i'.} \neq 0 \end{aligned}$$

the test statistic and decision rule are:

$$(20.17a) \qquad q^* = \frac{\sqrt{2}\hat{D}}{s\{\hat{D}\}}; \quad \text{If } |q^*| > q[1 - \alpha; a, (n-1)ab], \text{ conclude } H_a$$

For conciseness in this chapter, we state only the portion of the decision rule leading to conclusion H_a. As for single-factor ANOVA, the family level of significance for all pairwise tests here is $1 - \alpha$; in other words, the probability of concluding that there exist any pairwise differences when there are none is α.

For pairwise comparisons of the factor level means $\mu_{.j}$, the only changes are:

$$(20.18) \qquad D = \mu_{.j} - \mu_{.j'}$$

$$(20.19) \qquad \hat{D} = \bar{Y}_{.j.} - \bar{Y}_{.j'.}$$

$$(20.20) \qquad s^2\{\hat{D}\} = \frac{2MSE}{an}$$

$$(20.21) \qquad T = \frac{1}{\sqrt{2}}q[1 - \alpha; b, (n - 1)ab]$$

$$(20.22) \qquad q^* = \frac{\sqrt{2}\hat{D}}{s\{\hat{D}\}}; \quad \text{If } |q^*| > q[1 - \alpha; b, (n - 1)ab], \text{ conclude } H_a$$

Bonferroni Procedure. When only a few pairwise comparisons specified in advance are to be made, the Bonferroni method may be best. The simultaneous estimation formulas above still apply, with the Tukey multiple T replaced by the Bonferroni multiple B:

$$(20.23) \qquad B = t[1 - \alpha/2g; (n - 1)ab]$$

where g is the number of statements in the family.

To simultaneously test each of g pairwise differences with the Bonferroni procedure, the test statistic and decision rule are:

$$(20.24) \qquad t^* = \frac{\hat{D}}{s\{\hat{D}\}}; \quad \text{If } |t^*| > t[1 - \alpha/2g; (n - 1)ab], \text{ conclude } H_a$$

Combined Factor A and Factor B Family. When important factor A and factor B effects both are present, it is often desired to have a family confidence coefficient $1 - \alpha$, or family significance level α, for the joint set of pairwise comparisons involving *both* factor A and factor B means. The Bonferroni method can be used directly for this purpose, with g representing the total number of statements in the joint set.

Alternatively, the Bonferroni method can be used in conjunction with the Tukey method. To illustrate this use, if the pairwise comparisons for factor A are made with the Tukey procedure with a family confidence coefficient of .95, and likewise for the pairwise comparisons for factor B, the Bonferroni inequality then assures us that the family confidence coefficient for the joint set of comparisons for both factors is at least .90.

Multiple Contrasts of Factor Level Means

Scheffé Procedure. When a large number of contrasts among the factor level mean $\mu_{i.}$ or $\mu_{.j}$ are of interest, the Scheffé method should be used. If the contrasts involve the $\mu_{i.}$ as in (20.5), the Scheffé confidence limits are:

$$(20.25) \qquad \hat{L} \pm Ss\{\hat{L}\}$$

where:

(20.25a) $$S^2 = (a-1)F[1-\alpha; a-1, (n-1)ab]$$

and $\hat{L}$ is given by (20.6) and $s^2\{\hat{L}\}$ is given by (20.8). The probability is then $1 - \alpha$ that every confidence interval (20.25) in the family of all possible contrasts is correct. If the contrasts involve the $\mu_{.j}$ as in (20.10), $\hat{L}$ is given by (20.11), $s^2\{\hat{L}\}$ is given by (20.12), and the Scheffé multiple in (20.25) is:

(20.25b) $$S^2 = (b-1)F[1-\alpha; b-1, (n-1)ab]$$

When the Scheffé procedure is employed to conduct simultaneous tests of the form:

(20.26)
$$H_0: \ L = 0$$
$$H_a: \ L \neq 0$$

for contrasts involving the factor level means $\mu_{i.}$, the test statistic and decision rule are:

(20.26a) $$F^* = \frac{\hat{L}^2}{(a-1)s^2\{\hat{L}\}}; \quad \text{If } F^* > F[1-\alpha; a-1, (n-1)ab], \text{ conclude } H_a$$

When the contrasts involve the factor level means $\mu_{.j}$, the test statistic and decision rule are:

(20.26b) $$F^* = \frac{\hat{L}^2}{(b-1)s^2\{\hat{L}\}}; \quad \text{If } F^* > F[1-\alpha, b-1, (n-1)ab], \text{ conclude } H_a$$

Bonferroni Procedure.   When the number of contrasts of interest is small and has been specified in advance, the Bonferroni procedure may be best. Confidence limits (20.25) are modified by replacing the Scheffé multiple S with the Bonferroni multiple B:

(20.27) $$B = t[1 - \alpha/2g; (n-1)ab]$$

where g is the number of statements in the family.

Simultaneous testing of g tests with the Bonferroni procedure is based on the following test statistic and decision rule:

(20.28) $$t^* = \frac{\hat{L}}{s\{\hat{L}\}}; \quad \text{If } |t^*| > t[1 - \alpha/2g; (n-1)ab], \text{ conclude } H_a$$

Combined Factor A and Factor B Family.   When important factor A and factor B effects are present and contrasts for each of the two factors are of interest, it is often desired that the inference procedure provide assurance for the combined family of factor A and factor B contrasts. Several possibilities exist to accomplish this:

1. The Bonferroni method may be used directly, with g representing the total number of statements in the joint set.

2. The Bonferroni method can be used to join the two sets of Scheffé multiple comparison families in the same way explained earlier for joining two Tukey sets.

3. The Scheffé confidence limits (20.25) can be modified to use the S multiple defined by:

$$(20.29) \qquad S^2 = (a + b - 2)F[1 - \alpha; a + b - 2, (n - 1)ab]$$

For simultaneous testing, the test statistics and decision rules in (20.26a) and (20.26b) can be replaced by:

$$(20.30) \qquad F^* = \frac{\hat{L}^2}{(a + b - 2)s^2\{\hat{L}\}};$$

$$\text{If } F^* > F[1 - \alpha; a + b - 2, (n - 1)ab], \text{ conclude } H_a$$

Estimates Based on Treatment Means

Occasionally in analyzing the factor effects in a two-factor study when no interactions are present, there is interest in particular treatment means μ_{ij}. For example, in a two-factor study of the effects of price and type of advertisement on sales, interest may exist in estimating the mean sales for two different price levels when a particular advertisement is used. In such cases, the methods of analysis for single-factor studies discussed in Chapter 17 are appropriate. The number of treatments now is simply $r = ab$, the degrees of freedom associated with MSE are $n_T - r = nab - ab = (n - 1)ab$, and the estimated treatment means are $\bar{Y}_{ij.}$, based on n observations each.

Example 1—Pairwise Comparisons of Factor Level Means

In the Castle Bakery example of Chapter 19, the estimated treatment means plot in Figure 19.6 suggested that no interaction effects are present and that display width may not have any effect. The formal analysis of variance based on Table 19.9 supported both of these conclusions. Our interest now is in examining the nature of the display height effects in more detail.

First, we shall obtain a preliminary view of the display height effects by plotting the estimated factor level means in Table 19.7 in a normal probability plot. Figure 20.2a contains a normal probability plot of the estimated factor A level means $\bar{Y}_{i..}$. For comparison, we show in Figure 20.2b a similar plot for the estimated factor B level means $\bar{Y}_{.j.}$. These plots are prepared in the same fashion as the one in Figure 17.3b for a single-factor study. Again, we show in each plot the line $y = $ expected value, representing the expected values if all factor level means are equal. The expected values are obtained as follows:

$$\text{Factor } A: \qquad \bar{Y}_{...} + z\left(\frac{k - .375}{a + .25}\right)\sqrt{\frac{MSE}{bn}}$$

$$\text{Factor } B: \qquad \bar{Y}_{...} + z\left(\frac{k - .375}{b + .25}\right)\sqrt{\frac{MSE}{an}}$$

Figure 20.2a suggests that level 2 of factor A (middle shelf height) leads to significantly larger sales than the other two factor levels. In addition, Figure 20.2a suggests that the effects of shelf height levels 1 and 3 may not differ significantly because the slope of the

FIGURE 20.2   **Normal Probability Plots of Estimated Factor Level Means —Castle Bakery Example.**

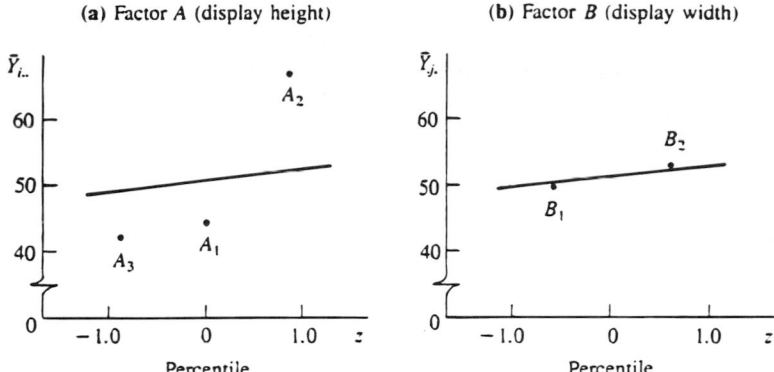

(a) Factor *A* (display height)

(b) Factor *B* (display width)

line connecting these two points is nearly parallel to the line of expected values. As expected because there are no factor *B* main effects, Figure 20.2b follows the prototype pattern in Figure 17.2a, indicating no factor level effects for display width.

Turning now to formal inference procedures, we shall first test simultaneously all pairwise differences among the shelf height means, using the Tukey multiple comparison procedure with family significance level $\alpha = .05$. The alternatives to be tested for the comparisons of display height means ($i = 1$—bottom, 2—middle, 3—top) are shown in Table 20.1, column 1. From Tables 19.7 and 19.9 we obtain the following information:

$$\hat{D}_1 = \bar{Y}_{2..} - \bar{Y}_{1..} = 67 - 44 = 23 \qquad MSE = 10.3$$
$$\qquad\qquad\qquad\qquad\qquad\qquad\qquad a = 3$$
$$\hat{D}_2 = \bar{Y}_{1..} - \bar{Y}_{3..} = 44 - 42 = 2 \qquad b = 2$$
$$\qquad\qquad\qquad\qquad\qquad\qquad\qquad n = 2$$
$$\hat{D}_3 = \bar{Y}_{2..} - \bar{Y}_{3..} = 67 - 42 = 25 \qquad (n-1)ab = 6$$

Hence, by (20.16b) we obtain:

$$s^2\{\hat{D}_1\} = s^2\{\hat{D}_2\} = s^2\{\hat{D}_3\} = \frac{2(10.3)}{2(2)} = 5.15$$

so that $s\{\hat{D}_1\} = s\{\hat{D}_2\} = s\{\hat{D}_3\} = 2.27$. The test statistics and decision rules based on (20.17a) are given in Table 20.1, columns 2 and 3, and the conclusions from the tests are shown in column 4.

It can be concluded from the tests in Table 20.1 with family significance level $\alpha = .05$ that for the product studied and the types of stores in the experiment, the middle shelf height is far better than either the bottom or the top heights, and that the latter two do not differ significantly in sales effectiveness. All of these conclusions are covered by the family significance level of .05.

Next, we wish to estimate how much greater are mean sales at the middle shelf height than at either of the other two shelf heights. We shall continue to use the Tukey multiple comparison procedure because the two pairwise comparisons now of interest are the result

TABLE 20.1 **Pairwise Testing of Factor A Level Means—Castle Bakery Example.**

(1) Alternatives	(2) Test Statistic (20.17a)	(3) Decision Rule Conclude H_a if $|q^*| >$	(4) Conclusion
$H_0: D_1 = \mu_{2.} - \mu_{1.} = 0$ $H_a: D_1 = \mu_{2.} - \mu_{1.} \neq 0$	$q^* = \dfrac{\sqrt{2}(23)}{2.27} = 14.33$	$q(.95; 3, 6) = 4.34$	H_a
$H_0: D_2 = \mu_{1.} - \mu_{3.} = 0$ $H_a: D_2 = \mu_{1.} - \mu_{3.} \neq 0$	$q^* = \dfrac{\sqrt{2}(2)}{2.27} = 1.25$	$q(.95; 3, 6) = 4.34$	H_0
$H_0: D_3 = \mu_{2.} - \mu_{3.} = 0$ $H_a: D_3 = \mu_{2.} - \mu_{3.} \neq 0$	$q^* = \dfrac{\sqrt{2}(25)}{2.27} = 15.58$	$q(.95; 3, 6) = 4.34$	H_a

of the earlier testing of all pairwise comparisons. From our previous work, we have:

$$\hat{D}_1 = \bar{Y}_{2..} - \bar{Y}_{1..} = 23 \qquad \hat{D}_3 = \bar{Y}_{2..} - \bar{Y}_{3..} = 25 \qquad s\{\hat{D}_1\} = s\{\hat{D}_3\} = 2.27$$

We also require, based on (20.16):

$$q(.95; 3, 6) = 4.34$$

$$T = \frac{4.34}{\sqrt{2}} = 3.07$$

$$Ts\{\hat{D}_1\} = Ts\{\hat{D}_3\} = 3.07(2.27) = 7.0$$

We therefore find the following confidence intervals for the two pairwise comparisons of the shelf height factor level means:

$$16 = 23 - 7.0 \leq \mu_{2.} - \mu_{1.} \leq 23 + 7.0 = 30$$

$$18 = 25 - 7.0 \leq \mu_{2.} - \mu_{3.} \leq 25 + 7.0 = 32$$

With family confidence coefficient of .95, we conclude that mean sales for the middle shelf height exceed those for the bottom shelf height by between 16 and 30 cases and those for the top shelf height by between 18 and 32 cases.

We can summarize the effects of shelf height on mean sales by the following line plot:

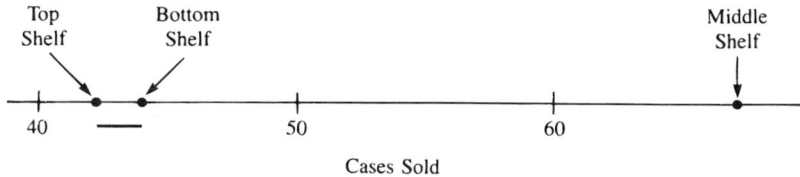

Example 2—Estimation of Treatment Means

The manager of a supermarket that has sales volume and clientele similar to the supermarkets included in the Castle Bakery study has room only for the regular shelf display width, and wishes to obtain estimates of mean sales for the middle and top shelf heights. We shall now obtain interval estimates with a 90 percent family confidence coefficient using the Bonferroni procedure.

From Tables 19.7 and 19.9, we have:

$$\bar{Y}_{21.} = 65 \qquad \bar{Y}_{31.} = 40 \qquad MSE = 10.3$$

Hence, we obtain:

$$s^2\{\bar{Y}_{21.}\} = s^2\{\bar{Y}_{31.}\} = \frac{MSE}{n} = \frac{10.3}{2} = 5.15$$
$$s\{\bar{Y}_{21.}\} = s\{\bar{Y}_{31.}\} = 2.27$$

For $g = 2$, we require $B = t[1 - \alpha/2g; (n-1)ab] = t(.975; 6) = 2.447$. Thus, we obtain the confidence limits:

$$65 \pm 2.447(2.27) \qquad 40 \pm 2.447(2.27)$$

and the desired confidence intervals are:

$$59.4 \leq \mu_{21} \leq 70.6 \qquad 34.4 \leq \mu_{31} \leq 45.6$$

20.3   Analysis of Factor Effects when Interactions Are Important

When important interactions exist that cannot be made unimportant by a simple transformation, the analysis of factor effects generally must be based on the treatment means μ_{ij}. Typically, this analysis will involve estimation of multiple comparisons of treatment means or single degree of freedom tests.

Multiple Pairwise Comparisons of Treatment Means

If pairs of treatment means μ_{ij} are to be compared, either the Tukey or the Bonferroni multiple comparison procedure may be used, depending on which is more advantageous. In effect, the analysis is equivalent to that for single-factor ANOVA, with the total number of treatments here equal to $r = ab$, the degrees of freedom associated with MSE here equal to $n_T - r = (n-1)ab$, and each estimated treatment mean, now denoted by $\bar{Y}_{ij.}$, based on n cases. For simultaneous testing, the Bonferonni procedure may be refined by means of the Holm procedure, discussed in Section 17.8, to achieve greater power.

Tukey Procedure.   The Tukey $1 - \alpha$ multiple comparison confidence limits for all pairwise comparisons:

(20.31) $$D = \mu_{ij} - \mu_{i'j'} \qquad i, j \neq i', j'$$

are:

(20.32)
$$\hat{D} \pm T s\{\hat{D}\}$$

where:

(20.32a)
$$\hat{D} = \bar{Y}_{ij \cdot} - \bar{Y}_{i'j' \cdot}$$

(20.32b)
$$s^2\{\hat{D}\} = \frac{2MSE}{n}$$

(20.32c)
$$T = \frac{1}{\sqrt{2}} q[1 - \alpha; ab, (n - 1)ab]$$

The test statistic and decision rule for all simultaneous Tukey tests of the form:

(20.33)
$$H_0: \ D = 0$$
$$H_a: \ D \neq 0$$

are as follows when the family significance level is controlled at α:

(20.33a)
$$q^* = \frac{\sqrt{2}\hat{D}}{s\{\hat{D}\}}; \quad \text{If } |q^*| > q[1 - \alpha; ab, (n - 1)ab], \text{ conclude } H_a$$

Bonferroni Procedure.   If the Bonferroni method is employed for a family of g comparisons, the multiple T in confidence interval (20.32) is replaced by:

(20.34)
$$B = t[1 - \alpha/2g; (n - 1)ab]$$

and the test statistic and decision rule in (20.33a) become:

(20.35)
$$t^* = \frac{\hat{D}}{s\{\hat{D}\}}; \quad \text{If } |t^*| > t[1 - \alpha/2g; (n - 1)ab], \text{ conclude } H_a$$

Multiple Contrasts of Treatment Means

Scheffé Procedure.   The Scheffé multiple comparison procedure for single-factor studies is directly applicable to the estimation of contrasts involving the treatment means μ_{ij}. The joint confidence limits for contrasts of the form:

(20.36)
$$L = \sum \sum c_{ij} \mu_{ij} \qquad \text{where} \quad \sum \sum c_{ij} = 0$$

are:

(20.37)
$$\hat{L} \pm S s\{\hat{L}\}$$

where:

(20.37a)
$$\hat{L} = \sum\sum c_{ij}\bar{Y}_{ij\cdot}$$

(20.37b)
$$s^2\{\hat{L}\} = \frac{MSE}{n}\sum\sum c_{ij}^2$$

(20.37c)
$$S^2 = (ab-1)F[1-\alpha; ab-1, (n-1)ab]$$

The test statistic and associated decision rule for all simultaneous Scheffé tests of the form:

(20.38)
$$H_0: \ L = 0$$
$$H_a: \ L \neq 0$$

are as follows when the family significance level is controlled at α:

(20.38a) $\quad F^* = \dfrac{\hat{L}^2}{(ab-1)s^2\{\hat{L}\}}$; $\quad$ If $F^* > F[1-\alpha; ab-1, (n-1)ab]$, conclude H_a

Bonferroni Procedure. When the number of contrasts is small, the Bonferroni procedure may be preferable. The confidence intervals (20.37) are simply modified by replacing S with B as defined in (20.34). The test statistic and decision rule in (20.38a) are replaced by:

(20.39) $\qquad t^* = \dfrac{\hat{L}}{s\{\hat{L}\}}$; $\quad$ If $|t^*| > t[1-\alpha/2g; (n-1)ab]$, conclude H_a

Example 1—Pairwise Comparisons of Treatment Means

A junior college system studied the effects of teaching method (factor A) and student's quantitative ability (factor B) on learning of college mathematics. Two teaching methods were studied—the standard method of teaching (to be called the standard method) and a method that emphasizes teaching of concepts in the abstract before going into drill routines (to be called the abstract method). The quantitative ability of a student was determined by a standard aptitude test, on the basis of which the student was classified as having excellent, good, or moderate quantitative ability. Thus, factor A (teaching method) has $a = 2$ levels, and factor B (student's quantitative ability) has $b = 3$ levels.

For each quantitative ability group, 42 students were selected and randomly placed into classes according to the designated teaching method, with each class containing equal numbers of students of each quantitative ability level. For simplicity, it is assumed that any effects associated with the classes are negligible.

The response variable of interest is the amount of learning of college mathematics, as measured by a standard mathematics achievement test. The results of the study are summarized in Table 20.2 (the original data are not shown). The estimated treatment means are shown in Table 20.2a, and the analysis of variance table is presented in Table 20.2b.

Figure 20.3 contains two plots of the estimated treatment means $\bar{Y}_{ij\cdot}$. In Figure 20.3a, the two curves represent the different factor A levels, and in Figure 20.3b, the three curves represent the different factor B levels. The clear lack of parallelism of the curves suggests the

TABLE 20.2   **Results of Study on Mathematics Learning.**

(a) Mean Learning Scores ($n = 21$)

Teaching Method i	Quantitative Ability (j)		
	Excellent	Good	Moderate
Abstract	92 ($\bar{Y}_{11.}$)	81 ($\bar{Y}_{12.}$)	73 ($\bar{Y}_{13.}$)
Standard	90 ($\bar{Y}_{21.}$)	86 ($\bar{Y}_{22.}$)	82 ($\bar{Y}_{23.}$)

(b) ANOVA Table

Source of Variation	SS	df	MS
Factor A (teaching methods)	504	1	504
Factor B (quantitative ability)	3,843	2	1,921.5
AB interactions	651	2	325.5
Error	3,360	120	28
Total	8,358	125	

presence of interaction effects between teaching method and student's quantitative ability on amount of mathematics learning. A formal test for interactions confirms this. From Table 20.2b, we have $F^* = MSAB/MSE = 325.5/28 = 11.625$. For $\alpha = .01$ we require $F(.99; 2, 120) = 4.79$. Since $F^* = 11.625 > 4.79$, we conclude that interaction effects are present. The P-value of this test is 0+.

Figure 20.3 suggests that the interactions are important: students with excellent quantitative ability are but little affected by teaching method (perhaps doing slightly better with the abstract method); students with good or moderate abilities learn much better with the standard teaching method. Hence, we shall first investigate whether some simple transformation can make the interactions unimportant. We do this in an approximate fashion by considering some transformations of $\bar{Y}_{ij.}$. In Figure 20.4a we present the teaching method curves for $\bar{Y}'_{ij.} = \sqrt{\bar{Y}_{ij.}}$, and in Figure 20.4b we present the teaching method curves for $\bar{Y}'_{ij.} = \log_{10} \bar{Y}_{ij.}$. In neither case have the interactions become unimportant, so it appears that the interactions here may be nontransformable.

We now wish to investigate the nature of the interaction effects in Figure 20.3. We shall do this by estimating separately for students with excellent, good, and moderate quantitative abilities how large is the difference in mean learning for the two teaching methods. Thus, we wish to estimate:

$$D_1 = \mu_{11} - \mu_{21}$$

$$D_2 = \mu_{12} - \mu_{22}$$

$$D_3 = \mu_{13} - \mu_{23}$$

FIGURE 20.3   **Plots of Estimated Treatment Means—Mathematics Learning Example.**

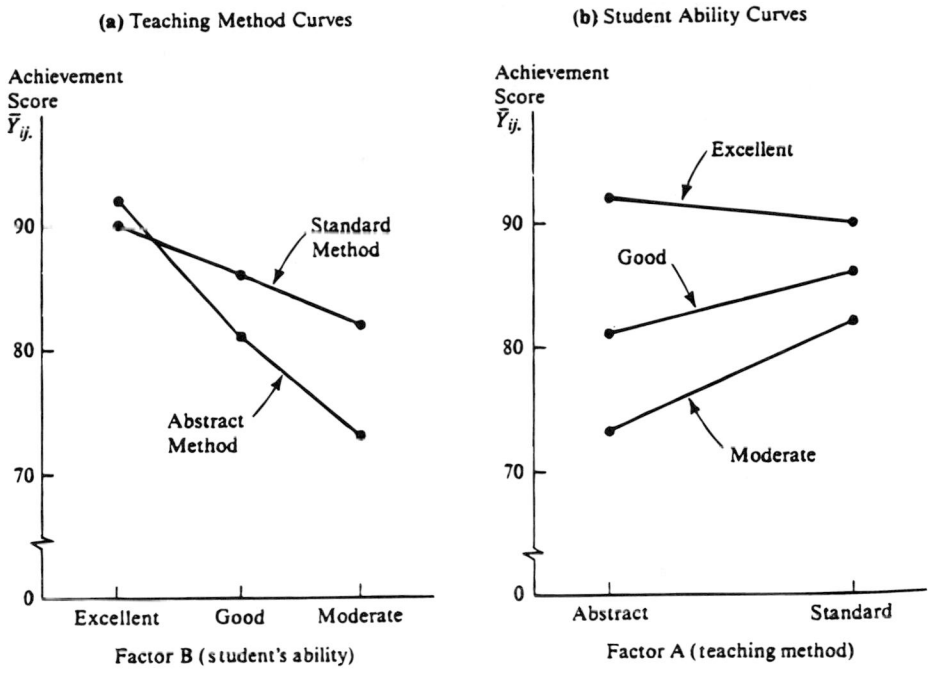

(a) Teaching Method Curves   **(b) Student Ability Curves**

FIGURE 20.4   **Plots of Teaching Method Curves with Transformed Estimated Means—Mathematics Learning Example.**

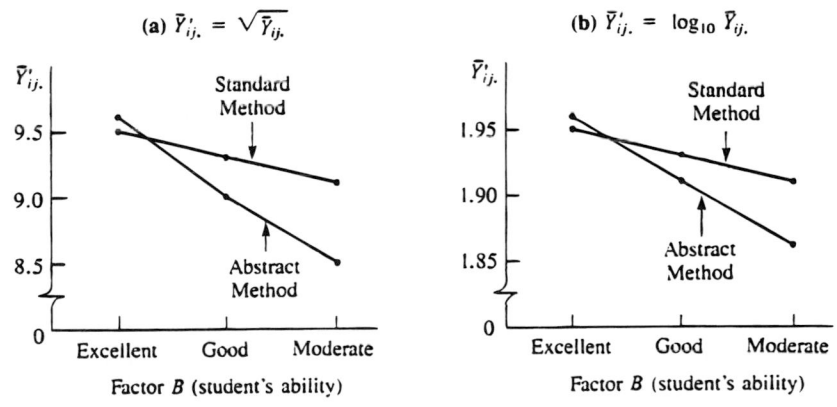

(a) $\bar{Y}'_{ij.} = \sqrt{\bar{Y}_{ij.}}$ (b) $\bar{Y}'_{ij.} = \log_{10} \bar{Y}_{ij.}$

We shall employ the Bonferroni multiple comparison procedure with family confidence coefficient .95. (Since only three pairwise comparisons are of interest, the Bonferroni method yields more precise estimates here than the Tukey method.)

Using the data in Table 20.2a, the point estimates of the pairwise comparisons are:

$$\hat{D}_1 = 92 - 90 = 2$$

$$\hat{D}_2 = 81 - 86 = -5$$

$$\hat{D}_3 = 73 - 82 = -9$$

We find the estimated variances of these estimates by (20.32b), for $n = 21$:

$$s^2\{\hat{D}_1\} = s^2\{\hat{D}_2\} = s^2\{\hat{D}_3\} = \frac{2(28)}{21} = 2.667$$

so that:

$$s\{\hat{D}_1\} = s\{\hat{D}_2\} = s\{\hat{D}_3\} = 1.633$$

Finally, for family confidence coefficient $1 - \alpha = .95$ and $g = 3$, we require $B = t[1 - .05/2(3); 120] = t(.99167; 120) = 2.428$. Hence, the confidence limits are by (20.32) and (20.34):

$$2 \pm 2.428(1.633) \qquad -5 \pm 2.428(1.633) \qquad -9 \pm 2.428(1.633)$$

and the 95 percent confidence intervals for the family of comparisons are:

$$-1.96 \leq \mu_{11} - \mu_{21} \leq 5.96$$

$$-8.96 \leq \mu_{12} - \mu_{22} \leq -1.04$$

$$-12.96 \leq \mu_{13} - \mu_{23} \leq -5.04$$

For this family of confidence intervals, the following conclusions may be drawn with family confidence coefficient of 95 percent: (1) For students with excellent quantitative ability, the mean learning scores with the two teaching methods do not differ. (2) For students with either good or moderate quantitative abilities, the mean learning score with the abstract teaching method is lower than that with the standard method. The superiority of the standard teaching method may be particularly strong for students with moderate quantitative ability.

Example 2—Contrasts of Treatment Means

In the mathematics learning example, a school administrator also wished to know whether the amount of learning gain with the standard teaching method over the abstract method is greater for students with moderate quantitative ability than for students with good quantitative ability. This question had been raised before the study began. We shall estimate the single contrast:

$$L = (\mu_{23} - \mu_{13}) - (\mu_{22} - \mu_{12})$$

by means of a one-sided lower confidence interval. Utilizing the results in Table 20.2a, the point estimate of L is $\hat{L} = (82 - 73) - (86 - 81) = 4$. The estimated variance by (20.37b) is:

$$s^2\{\hat{L}\} = \frac{28}{21}[(1)^2 + (-1)^2 + (-1)^2 + (1)^2] = 5.333$$

so that the estimated standard deviation is $s\{\hat{L}\} = 2.309$. For a 95 percent confidence coefficient, we require $t(.05; 120) = -1.658$. Hence, the lower confidence limit is $4 - 1.658(2.309)$ and the desired confidence interval is:

$$L \geq .17$$

We conclude, therefore, with 95 percent confidence coefficient that the gain in learning with the standard teaching method over the abstract method is greater for students with moderate quantitative ability than for students with good quantitative ability, the difference in the mean gain being at least .17 point.

20.4   Analysis when One or Both Factors Are Quantitative

When one or both of the factors in a two-factor study are quantitative, the analysis of factor effects can be carried beyond the point of multiple comparisons to include a study of the nature of the response function. Since the familiar methods of regression analysis then come into use, we shall only briefly discuss this extension of the analysis. The initial study of factor effects by multiple comparison techniques can be very helpful in choosing an appropriate functional form for the regression relation.

Analysis of Response Function when One Factor Is Quantitative

Consider an experiment in which the effect of type of cake mix (factor A) and baking temperature (factor B) on the lightness of the cake texture, suitably measured, is to be investigated. Two kinds of cake mixes (G, H) and four baking temperatures ($300°$, $315°$, $330°$, $345°$) are studied. The analyst in this case might be interested in extending the investigation of factor effects into the nature of the response function relating cake texture to baking temperature. Since factor A is qualitative, indicator variables will be used to represent it in the response function. If type of cake mix and baking temperature do not interact, a first-order model might be appropriate:

(20.40) $$Y_{ijk} = \beta_0 + \beta_1 X_{ijk1} + \beta_2 X_{ijk2} + \varepsilon_{ijk}$$

where:

$$X_1 = \begin{cases} 1 & \text{if case from first level of factor } A \\ 0 & \text{otherwise} \end{cases}$$

$X_2 =$ baking temperature for the case

The βs denote regression parameters here, and X_{ijk1} and X_{ijk2} are the respective values of X_1 and X_2 for the kth case or trial for the treatment corresponding to the ith level of factor A and the jth level of factor B.

We know from Chapter 11 that regression model (20.40) implies a linear relation between cake texture and baking temperature that has constant slope for both kinds of cake mixes but at different heights. Figure 11.1 provides an illustration of this model.

If cake mix and baking temperature interact, an appropriate model might be:

(20.41) $$Y_{ijk} = \beta_0 + \beta_1 X_{ijk1} + \beta_2 X_{ijk2} + \beta_3 X_{ijk1} X_{ijk2} + \varepsilon_{ijk}$$

From Chapter 11, we know that this model implies a linear relation between cake texture and baking temperature with different slopes and intercepts for the two kinds of cake mixes. Figure 11.3 provides an illustration of this model.

If the regression relation is quadratic and no interactions between the two factors exist, a suitable model would be:

$$(20.42) \qquad Y_{ijk} = \beta_0 + \beta_1 X_{ijk1} + \beta_2 x_{ijk2} + \beta_3 x_{ijk2}^2 + \varepsilon_{ijk}$$

where:

$$x_{ijk2} = X_{ijk2} - \bar{X}_2$$

Analysis of Response Function when Both Factors Are Quantitative

When both factors are quantitative, the analysis of the nature of the response function involves standard multiple regression. We shall denote the two factor variables as X_1 and X_2. A first-order model would then be:

$$(20.43) \qquad Y_{ijk} = \beta_0 + \beta_1 X_{ijk1} + \beta_2 X_{ijk2} + \varepsilon_{ijk}$$

where X_{ijk1} and X_{ijk2} are the respective values of X_1 and X_2 for the kth case or trial for the treatment corresponding to the ith level of factor A and the jth level of factor B. A second-order model, including linear-by-linear interactions between the two factors, would be:

$$(20.44) \quad Y_{ijk} = \beta_0 + \beta_1 x_{ijk1} + \beta_2 x_{ijk2} + \beta_3 x_{ijk1}^2 + \beta_4 x_{ijk2}^2 + \beta_5 x_{ijk1} x_{ijk2} + \varepsilon_{ijk}$$

where:

$$x_{ijk1} = X_{ijk1} - \bar{X}_1$$
$$x_{ijk2} = X_{ijk2} - \bar{X}_2$$

The discussion of polynomial and interaction regression models in Chapter 7 is completely applicable here.

Example.   (adapted from Ref. 20.1) A study was conducted to improve the efficiency of a burr remover in a wool textile carding machine. The rollers in the burr remover are adjustable as to speed and spacing. Four spacings and three speeds, as shown in Table 20.3, were used in the study. Four replications were made for each treatment, but only the estimated treatment means are presented in Table 20.3. The observed variable is a measure of the efficiency of the carding. Plots of the estimated treatment means are presented in Figure 20.5.

An analysis of variance was conducted for this two-factor study. The results are summarized in Table 20.4a on page 868. The test for interactions utilizes the test statistic:

$$F^* = \frac{MSAB}{MSE} = \frac{4.92}{1.32} = 3.73$$

For level of significance $\alpha = .05$, we require $F(.95; 6, 36) = 2.36$. Since $F^* = 3.73 > 2.36$, it was concluded that spacing and speed interact. The P-value of the test is .0055.

TABLE 20.3   **Estimated Treatment Means in Two-Factor Burr Remover Study with Both Factors Quantitative ($n = 4$).**

Spacing (units)	Speed (rpm) 300	Speed (rpm) 400	Speed (rpm) 500
1.0	21.6	22.3	22.9
1.2	18.7	19.1	21.6
1.4	15.8	17.9	19.4
1.6	13.2	16.7	19.5

Reprinted, with permission, from D. R. Cox, *Planning of Experiments* (New York: John Wiley & Sons, 1958), p. 124.

FIGURE 20.5   **Plots of Estimated Treatment Means—Burr Remover Example.**

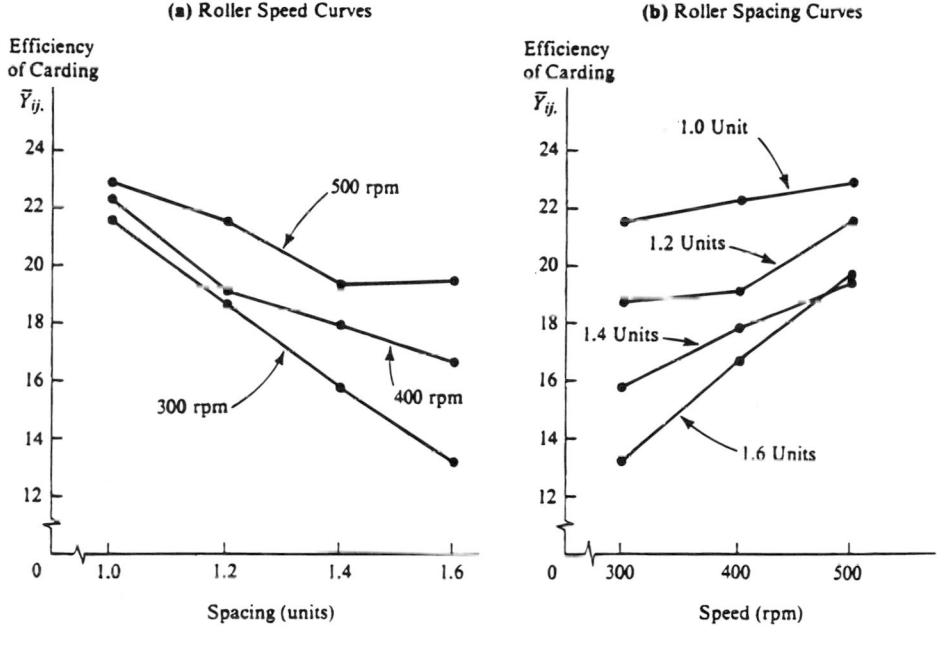

where X_1 represents spacing and X_2 speed. This model was fitted by a multiple regression computer package, and the results are summarized in Table 20.4b.

Since replications were used in the study, a test of the appropriateness of the response function can be conducted. The lack of fit sum of squares is readily obtainable because *SSE*

Figure 20.5, along with further analysis, suggested that a first-order model with interaction effects added might be appropriate. The response function for this model is:

$$(20.45) \qquad E\{Y\} = \beta_0 + \beta_1 X_1 + \beta_2 X_2 + \beta_3 X_1 X_2$$

TABLE 20.4 **Analysis of Variance Tables for Burr Remover Study.**

(a) Analysis of Variance Model

Source of Variation	SS	df	MS
Spacing (A)	232.86	3	77.62
Speed (B)	99.49	2	49.74
AB interactions	29.53	6	4.92
Error	47.61	36	1.32
Total	409.49	47	

(b) Regression Model

$$\hat{Y} = 45.09333 - 25.45000X_1 - .03340X_2 + .03925X_1X_2$$

Source of Variation	SS	df	MS
Regression	352.20	3	117.40
Error	57.29	44	1.30
Total	409.49	47	

(c) ANOVA for Lack of Fit Test

Source of Variation	SS	df	MS
Regression	352.20	3	117.40
Error	57.29	44	1.30
Lack of fit	9.68	8	1.21
Pure error	47.61	36	1.32
Total	409.49	47	

for the ANOVA model is the same as *SSPE* for the regression model. Hence, we find:

$$SSLF = \underset{\text{(Table 20.4b)}}{SSE} - \underset{\text{(Table 20.4a)}}{SSPE} = 57.29 - 47.61 = 9.68$$

Table 20.4c contains the decomposition needed for testing lack of fit. The appropriate test statistic is:

$$F^* = \frac{MSLF}{MSE} = \frac{1.21}{1.32} = .92$$

For level of significance $\alpha = .05$, we require $F(.95; 8, 36) = 2.21$. Since $F^* = .92 \leq 2.21$, we conclude that response function (20.45) is appropriate. The *P*-value of this test is .51.

Let us take a closer look at the estimated response function:

$$\hat{Y} = 45.09333 - 25.45000X_1 - .03340X_2 + .03925X_1X_2$$

Note that b_3 is positive. It implies here, as a glance at Figure 20.5 will confirm, that efficiency declines with increased spacing for all speeds (e.g., if $X_2 = 300$, $\hat{Y} = 35.073 - 13.675X_1$), but the decline is smaller for high speeds. Correspondingly, efficiency increases with speed for all spacings (e.g., if $X_1 = 1.0$, $\hat{Y} = 19.643 + .00585X_2$), but the increase is larger for large spacings.

Cited Reference

20.1. Cox, D. R. *Planning of Experiments*. New York: John Wiley & Sons, 1958.

Problems

20.1. Why is it suggested in the flowchart in Figure 20.1 that a test for interactions should be conducted before tests for main factor effects? Explain.

√ 20.2. A two-factor study was conducted with $a = 5$, $b = 5$, and $n = 4$. No interactions between factors A and B were noted, and the analyst now wishes to estimate all pairwise comparisons among the factor A level means and all pairwise comparisons among the factor B level means. The family confidence coefficient for the joint set of interval estimates is to be 90 percent.

    a. Is it more efficient to use the Bonferroni procedure for the entire family or to use the Tukey procedure for each family of factor level mean comparisons and then to join the two families by means of the Bonferroni procedure?

    b. Would your answer differ if each factor had three levels, everything else remaining the same?

20.3. A two-factor study was conducted with $a = 6$, $b = 6$, and $n = 10$. No interactions between factors A and B were found, and it is now desired to estimate five contrasts of factor A level means and four contrasts of factor B level means. The family confidence coefficient for the joint set of estimates is to be 95 percent. Which of the three procedures on pages 855 and 856 will be most efficient here?

20.4. Refer to the Castle Bakery example on page 856, where two pairwise comparison estimates were made by means of the Tukey procedure. Why would it not be appropriate to use the Bonferroni procedure here? Discuss.

√ 20.5. Refer to **Cash offers** Problems 19.10 and 19.11.

    a. Estimate μ_{11} with a 95 percent confidence interval. Interpret your interval estimate.

    b. Prepare a normal probability of the estimated factor B level means. What does this plot suggest about the equality of the factor B level means?

c. Estimate $D = \mu_{.1} - \mu_{.2}$ by means of a 95 percent confidence interval. Is your confidence interval consistent with the test result in Problem 19.11d? Is your confidence interval consistent with your finding in part (b)? Explain.

d. Prepare a normal probability plot of the estimated factor A level means. What does this plot suggest about the factor A main effects?

e. Obtain all pairwise comparisons among the factor A level means; use the Tukey procedure with a 90 percent family confidence coefficient. Present your findings graphically and summarize your results. Are your conclusions consistent with those in part (d)?

f. Is the Tukey procedure used in part (e) the most efficient one that could be used here? Explain.

g. Estimate the contrast:

$$L = \frac{\mu_{1.} + \mu_{3.}}{2} - \mu_{.2.}$$

with a 95 percent confidence interval. Interpret your interval estimate.

h. Suppose that in the population of female owners, 30 percent are young, 60 percent are middle-aged, and 10 percent are elderly. Obtain a 95 percent confidence interval for the mean cash offer in the population of female owners.

20.6. Refer to **Eye contact effect** Problems 19.12 and 19.13.

a. Estimate μ_{21} with a 99 percent confidence interval. Interpret your interval estimate.

b. Estimate $\mu_{1.}$ with a 99 percent confidence interval. Interpret your interval estimate.

c. Prepare a normal probability plot of the estimated factor B level means. What does this plot suggest about the factor B main effects?

d. Obtain confidence intervals for $\mu_{.1}$ and $\mu_{.2}$, each with a 99 percent confidence coefficient. Interpret your interval estimates. What is the family confidence coefficient for the set of two estimates?

e. Prepare a normal probability plot of the estimated factor A level means. What does this plot suggest about the factor A main effects?

f. Obtain confidence intervals for $D_1 = \mu_{2.} - \mu_{1.}$ and $D_2 = \mu_{.2} - \mu_{.1}$; use the Bonferroni procedure and a 95 percent family confidence coefficient. Summarize your findings. Are your findings consistent with those in parts (c) and (e)?

g. Is the Bonferroni procedure used in part (f) the most efficient one that could be used here? Explain.

√ 20.7. Refer to **Hay fever relief** Problems 19.14 and 19.15.

a. Estimate μ_{23} with a 95 percent confidence interval. Interpret your interval estimate.

b. Estimate $D = \mu_{12} - \mu_{11}$ with a 95 percent confidence interval. Interpret your interval estimate.

c. The analyst decided to study the nature of the interacting factor effects by means of the following contrasts:

$$L_1 = \frac{\mu_{12} + \mu_{13}}{2} - \mu_{11} \qquad L_4 = L_2 - L_1$$

$$L_2 = \frac{\mu_{22} + \mu_{23}}{2} - \mu_{21} \qquad L_5 = L_3 - L_1$$

$$L_3 = \frac{\mu_{32} + \mu_{33}}{2} - \mu_{31} \qquad L_6 = L_3 - L_2$$

Obtain confidence intervals for these contrasts; use the Scheffé multiple comparison procedure with a 90 percent family confidence coefficient. Interpret your findings.

d. The analyst also wished to identify the treatment(s) yielding the longest mean relief. Using the Tukey testing procedure with family significance level $\alpha = .10$, identify the treatment(s) providing the longest mean relief.

e. To examine whether a transformation of the data would make the interactions unimportant, plot separately the transformed estimated treatment means for the reciprocal and square root transformations in the format of Figure 20.4. Would either of these transformations have made the interaction effects unimportant? Explain.

20.8. Refer to **Disk drive service** Problems 19.16 and 19.17.

a. Estimate μ_{11} with a 99 percent confidence interval. Interpret your interval estimate.

b. Estimate $D = \mu_{22} - \mu_{21}$ with a 99 percent confidence interval. Interpret your interval estimate.

c. The nature of the interaction effects is to be studied by making, for each technician, all three pairwise comparisons among the disk drive makes in order to identify, if possible, the make of disk drive for which the technician's mean service time is lowest. The family confidence coefficient for each set of three pairwise comparisons is to be 95 percent. Use the Bonferroni procedure to make all required pairwise comparisons. Summarize your findings.

d. The service center currently services 30 disk drives of each of the three makes per week, with each technician servicing 10 machines of each make. Estimate the expected total amount of service time required per week to service the 90 disk drives; use a 99 percent confidence interval.

e. How much time could be saved per week, on the average, if technician 1 services only make 2, technician 2 services only make 1, and technician 3 services only make 3? Use a 99 percent confidence interval.

f. To examine whether a transformation of the data would make the interactions unimportant, plot separately the transformed estimated treatment means for the reciprocal and logarithmic transformations in the format of Figure 20.4. Would either of these transformations have made the interaction effects unimportant? Explain.

20.9. Refer to **Kidney failure hospitalization** Problems 19.18 and 19.19. Continue to work with the transformed observations $Y' = \log_{10}(Y + 1)$.

a. Estimate μ_{22} with a 95 percent confidence interval. Interpret your interval estimate.

b. Estimate $D = \mu_{23} - \mu_{21}$ with a 95 percent confidence interval. Interpret your interval estimate.

c. Prepare separate normal probability plots of the estimated factor A and factor B level means. What do these plots suggest about the factor main effects?

d. The researcher wishes to study the main effects of each of the two factors by making all pairwise comparisons of factor level means with a 90 percent family confidence coefficient for the entire set of comparisons. Which multiple comparison procedure is most efficient here?

e. Using the Bonferroni procedure, make all pairwise comparisons called for in part (d). State your findings and prepare a graphic summary. Are your findings consistent with those in part (c)?

f. It is known from past experience that 30 percent of patients have mild weight gains, 40 percent have moderate weight gains, and 30 percent have severe weight gains, and that these proportions are the same for the two duration groups. Estimate the mean number of days hospitalized (in transformed units) in the entire population with a 95 percent confidence interval. Convert your confidence limits to the original units. Does it appear that the mean number of days is less than 7?

√ 20.10. Refer to **Programmer requirements** Problems 19.20 and 19.21.

   a. Estimate μ_{23} with a 99 percent confidence interval. Interpret your interval estimate.

   b. Estimate $D = \mu_{12} - \mu_{13}$ with a 99 percent confidence interval. Interpret your interval estimate.

   c. The nature of the interaction effects is to be studied by comparing the effect of type of experience for each years-of-experience group. Specifically, the following comparisons are to be estimated:

$$D_1 = \mu_{11} - \mu_{21} \qquad L_1 = D_1 - D_2$$
$$D_2 = \mu_{12} - \mu_{22} \qquad L_2 = D_1 - D_3$$
$$D_3 = \mu_{13} - \mu_{23} \qquad L_3 = D_2 - D_3$$

   The family confidence coefficient is to be 95 percent. Which multiple comparison procedure is most efficient here?

   d. Use the most efficient procedure to estimate the comparisons specified in part (c). State your findings.

   e. Use the Tukey testing procedure with family significance level $\alpha = .05$ to identify the type of experience-years of experience group(s) with the smallest mean prediction errors.

   f. For each group identified in part (e), obtain a confidence interval for the mean prediction error. Use the Bonferroni procedure with a 95 percent family confidence coefficient. Does any group have a mean prediction error that could be zero? Explain.

   g. To examine whether a transformation of the data would make the interactions unimportant, plot separately the transformed estimated treatment means for the reciprocal and logarithmic transformations in the format of Figure 20.4. Would either of these transformations have made the interaction effects unimportant? Explain.

20.11. Refer to **Brand preference** Problem 6.5. Suppose the market researcher first wished to employ analysis of variance model (19.23) to determine whether or not moisture content (factor A) and sweetness (factor B) affect the degree of brand liking.

   a. State the analysis of variance model for this case.

   b. Obtain the analysis of variance table.

   c. Test whether or not the two factors interact; use $\alpha = .01$. State the alternatives, decision rule, and conclusion.

   d. Study possible curvilinearity of the moisture content effect by estimating the following contrast:

$$L = (\mu_{4.} - \mu_{3.}) - (\mu_{2.} - \mu_{1.})$$

   Use a 95 percent confidence interval. What do you conclude?

   e. Test whether or not sweetness affects brand liking; use $\alpha = .01$. State the alternatives, decision rule, and conclusion.

√ 20.12. Refer to **Cash offers** Problem 19.10. The mean ages of the "owners" in the three age classes were:

Young: 24.8
Middle: 45.3
Elderly: 66.7

Since the actual ages of the "owners" in each age group for both genders were close to the mean age, each mean age can be used to represent the ages (X_1) of the "owners" in that group.

a. Fit the regression model:

$$Y_{ijk} = \beta_0 + \beta_1 x_{ijk1} + \beta_2 x_{ijk1}^2 + \beta_3 X_{ijk2} + \varepsilon_{ijk}$$

where $x_{ijk1} = X_{ijk1} - \bar{X}_1$ and $X_{ijk2} = 1$ if owner is male and 0 if female.

b. Obtain the residuals and plot them against the fitted values. What does your plot show?

c. Conduct a formal test for lack of fit using level of significance $\alpha = .01$. State the alternatives, decision rule, and conclusion.

d. Test whether or not the quadratic term in the regression model in part (a) can be dropped; use $\alpha = .01$. State the alternatives, decision rule, and conclusion.

20.13. Refer to **Hay fever relief** Problem 19.14. The researcher now wishes to study the nature of the relationship between the amounts of the two active ingredients and the duration of relief. The amounts of the ingredients used in the study were as follows:

Factor Level	Quantity (in milligrams)	
	X_1 (ingredient 1)	X_2 (ingredient 2)
Low	5.0	7.5
Medium	10.0	10.0
High	15.0	12.5

a. Fit regression model (20.44).

b. Estimate the mean duration of relief when $X_1 = 7.50$ and $X_2 = 8.75$; use a 95 percent confidence interval. Could this estimate have been obtained from the ANOVA model? Explain.

c. Obtain the residuals and plot them against the fitted values. What does your plot show?

d. Conduct a formal test for lack of fit; use $\alpha = .005$. State the alternatives, decision rule, and conclusion.

e. Test whether or not the interaction term can be dropped from the model; use $\alpha = .05$. State the alternatives, decision rule, and conclusion.

Exercises

20.14. Show that the point estimator (20.11) is unbiased. Find the variance of this estimator.

20.15. Find the variance of the estimator (20.37a).

20.16. Consider a two-factor study with $a = 2$ and $b = 2$. Show that the interactions $(\alpha\beta)_{12}$ and $(\alpha\beta)_{21}$ are equal.

Projects

20.17. Refer to the **SENIC** data set and Projects 19.34 and 19.35.
   a. Prepare a normal probability plot of the estimated factor level means $\bar{Y}_{i..}$. What does this plot suggest regarding the region main effects?
   b. Analyze the effects of region on mean length of hospital stay by making all pairwise comparisons between regions; use the Tukey procedure and a 90 percent family confidence coefficient. State your findings and present a graphic summary. Are your findings consistent with those in part (a)?

20.18. Refer to the **SMSA** data set and Projects 19.36 and 19.37.
   a. Prepare a normal probability plot of the estimated factor level means $\bar{Y}_{i..}$. What does this plot suggest regarding the region main effects?
   b. Analyze the effects of region on crime rate by making all pairwise comparisons between regions; use the Tukey procedure and a 95 percent family confidence coefficient. State your findings and present a graphic summary. Are your findings consistent with those in part (a)?

Two-Factor Studies— One Case Per Treatment

In many experimental investigations, constraints on cost, time, and materials severely limit the number of observations that can be obtained. For example, a process engineer in a manufacturing company may have only a limited time to experiment with the production line. If the line is available for one day and only eight batches of product can be produced in a day, the experiment may have to be limited to eight observations. If the study involves one factor at four levels and a second factor at two levels so that there are eight factor level combinations, only one replication of the experiment is then possible for each treatment.

Another reason why some experimental studies contain only one case per treatment is that the response of interest is a single aggregate measure of performance. For example, in a marketing research study of alternative package designs, evaluation of each alternative may require a separate market test. The response of interest is the observed market share, and this results in a single response for each treatment combination.

A modification of the ANOVA model is required for the analysis of two-factor studies containing only one replication per treatment because no degrees of freedom are available for estimation of the experimental error with the standard two-factor ANOVA model (19.23). In this chapter, we describe a modification of the ANOVA model that permits the two-factor analysis of variance to be conducted with only one case per treatment. This modification requires the assumption that the two factors do not interact. We then discuss inference procedures with this additive model. We conclude the chapter by considering a test for examining the reasonableness of the assumption of additivity of the two factors—the Tukey test. This test is important not only when there is just a single case for each treatment in a two-factor study, but it is also useful for a variety of experimental designs to be discussed in later chapters.

21.1 No-Interaction Model

When there is only one case for each treatment, we no longer can work with two-factor ANOVA model (19.23) because no estimate of the error variance σ^2 will be available. Recall from (19.37c) that SSE is a sum of squares made up of components measuring the variability within each treatment, $\sum_k (Y_{ijk} - \bar{Y}_{ij.})^2$. With only one case per treatment, there is no variability within a treatment, and SSE will then always be zero.

A way out of this difficulty is to change the model. Formula (19.42d) indicates that if the two factors do not interact so that $(\alpha\beta)_{ij} \equiv 0$, the interaction mean square $MSAB$ has expectation σ^2. Thus, if it is possible to assume that the two factors do not interact, we may use $MSAB$ as the estimator of the error variance σ^2 and proceed with the analysis of factor effects as usual. If it is unreasonable to assume that the two factors do not interact, transformations may be tried to remove the interaction effects. We shall say more about this in the next section.

Model

The two-factor ANOVA model with fixed factor levels in (19.23), when all interactions are zero so that $(\alpha\beta)_{ij} \equiv 0$, becomes for $n = 1$, the case considered here:

$$(21.1) \qquad\qquad Y_{ij} = \mu_{..} + \alpha_i + \beta_j + \varepsilon_{ij}$$

Note that the third subscript has been dropped from the Y and ε terms because there is now only one case per treatment.

Analysis of Variance

The factor effects sums of squares SSA and SSB are calculated as before from (19.39a) and (19.39b), respectively, with $n = 1$. The interaction sum of squares in (19.39c) with $n = 1$ now is expressed as follows:

$$(21.2) \qquad\qquad SSAB = \sum_i \sum_j (Y_{ij} - \bar{Y}_{i.} - \bar{Y}_{.j} + \bar{Y}_{..})^2 \qquad n = 1$$

Note that $SSAB$ in (21.2) is identical to $SSAB$ in (19.39c) with $n = 1$; the third subscript has been dropped because there is only one case per treatment, and the mean $\bar{Y}_{ij.}$ is replaced by the observation Y_{ij} for the same reason. The number of degrees of freedom associated with $SSAB$ in (21.2) is the same as before, namely, $(a-1)(b-1)$. The analysis of variance table for the case $n = 1$ for no-interaction model (21.1) is shown in Table 21.1.

Inference Procedures

No new problems arise in the tests for factor A and factor B main effects, nor in estimating these effects. Since the expected value of $MSAB$ is σ^2 for no-interaction model (21.1), as shown in the last column of Table 21.1, the F^* test statistics for testing factor A and factor B main effects will now utilize $MSAB$ in the denominator, instead of MSE as before:

$$(21.3a) \qquad\qquad \text{Factor } A \text{ main effects:} \qquad F^* = \frac{MSA}{MSAB}$$

$$(21.3b) \qquad\qquad \text{Factor } B \text{ main effects:} \qquad F^* = \frac{MSB}{MSAB}$$

TABLE 21.1   ANOVA Table for No-Interaction Two-Factor Model (21.1) with Fixed Factor Levels, $n = 1$.

Source of Variation	SS	df	MS	$E\{MS\}$
Factor A	$SSA = b\sum(\bar{Y}_{i\cdot} - \bar{Y}_{\cdot\cdot})^2$	$a - 1$	$MSA = \dfrac{SSA}{a - 1}$	$\sigma^2 + b\dfrac{\sum(\mu_{i\cdot} - \mu_{\cdot\cdot})^2}{a - 1}$
Factor B	$SSB = a\sum(\bar{Y}_{\cdot j} - \bar{Y}_{\cdot\cdot})^2$	$b - 1$	$MSB = \dfrac{SSB}{b - 1}$	$\sigma^2 + a\dfrac{\sum(\mu_{\cdot j} - \mu_{\cdot\cdot})^2}{b - 1}$
Error	$SSAB = \sum\sum(Y_{ij} - \bar{Y}_{i\cdot} - \bar{Y}_{\cdot j} + \bar{Y}_{\cdot\cdot})^2$	$(a - 1)(b - 1)$	$MSAB = \dfrac{SSAB}{(a - 1)(b - 1)}$	σ^2
Total	$SSTO = \sum\sum(Y_{ij} - \bar{Y}_{\cdot\cdot})^2$	$ab - 1$		

TABLE 21.2   **Two-Factor Study with $n = 1$—Insurance Premium Example.**

(a) Premiums for Automobile Insurance Policy (in dollars)

Size of City (factor A)	Region (factor B) East ($j = 1$)	West ($j = 2$)	Average
Small ($i = 1$)	140	100	120
Medium ($i = 2$)	210	180	195
Large ($i = 3$)	220	200	210
Average	190	160	175

(b) ANOVA Table

Source of Variation	SS	df	MS
Size of city (A)	9,300	2	4,650
Region (B)	1,350	1	1,350
Error	100	2	50
Total	10,750	5	

Similarly, for estimating comparisons of factor A and factor B level means, we simply replace *MSE* in all of the earlier results with *MSAB* as the estimator of the error variance σ^2 and modify the degrees of freedom accordingly.

A special problem exists in estimating treatment means. We shall explain how to handle this problem after presenting an example.

Example

An analyst in an insurance commissioner's office studied the premiums for automobile insurance charged by an insurance company in six cities. The six cities were selected to represent different regions of the state and different sizes of cities. Table 21.2a shows the amounts of three-month premiums charged by the automobile insurance firm for a specific type and amount of coverage in a given risk category for each of the six cities, classified by size of city (factor A) and geographic region (factor B). Note there is only one observation per cell, namely, the amount of the premium charged in the city for each factor level combination. The analyst wished to evaluate the effects of city size and geographic region on the amount of the premium.

Figure 21.1 contains a plot of the observations Y_{ij}. Note since $n = 1$ here that the observations Y_{ij} constitute estimates of the treatment means μ_{ij}. It appears from Figure 21.1 that there could be a slight interaction between region and size of city in their effects on the premium. However, since there is only one observation per treatment, the moderate lack of parallelism in the response lines could simply be the result of random effects within each treatment cell. The analyst conducted the Tukey test for interactions (to be discussed

FIGURE 21.1   **Plot of Observations Y_{ij}—Insurance Premium Example.**

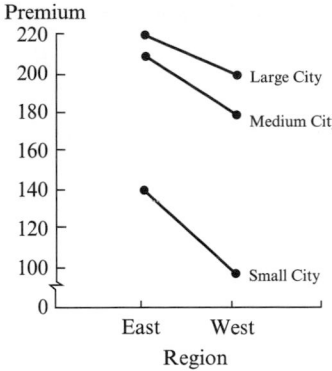

in Section 21.2), which indicated that no interaction effects are present. Hence, the analyst adopted the no-interaction model (21.1).

The analyst obtained the required sums of squares as follows, using (19.37a) and (19.39) for $n = 1$:

$$SSA = 2[(120 - 175)^2 + (195 - 175)^2 + (210 - 175)^2] = 9,300$$

$$SSB = 3[(190 - 175)^2 + (160 - 175)^2] = 1,350$$

$$SSAB = (140 - 120 - 190 + 175)^2 + \cdots + (200 - 210 - 160 + 175)^2 = 100$$

$$SSTO = (140 - 175)^2 + \cdots + (200 - 175)^2 = 10,750$$

The ANOVA table is given in Table 21.2b. For the test of city size (factor A) effects, the alternative conclusions are:

$$H_0: \alpha_1 = \alpha_2 = \alpha_3 = 0$$

$$H_a: \text{ not all } \alpha_i \text{ equal zero}$$

The F^* test statistic is given by (21.3a):

$$F^* = \frac{MSA}{MSAB} = \frac{4,650}{50} = 93$$

and the decision rule for $\alpha = .05$ is [remember that the denominator of F^* here involves $(a - 1)(b - 1)$ degrees of freedom]:

If $F^* \leq F[1 - \alpha; a - 1, (a - 1)(b - 1)] = F(.95; 2, 2) = 19.0$, conclude H_0

If $F^* > F[1 - \alpha; a - 1, (a - 1)(b - 1)] = F(.95; 2, 2) = 19.0$, conclude H_a

Since $F^* = 93 > 19.0$, we conclude H_a, that city size effects are present. The P-value of the test is .011.

The test for geographic region (factor B) effects proceeds similarly, the alternative conclusions being:

$$H_0: \beta_1 = \beta_2 = 0$$

$$H_a: \text{ not all } \beta_j \text{ equal zero}$$

For $\alpha = .05$ the decision rule is:

If $F^* \leq F(.95; 1, 2) = 18.5$, conclude H_0

If $F^* > F(.95; 1, 2) = 18.5$, conclude H_a

Test statistic (21.3b) here is:

$$F^* = \frac{MSB}{MSAB} = \frac{1,350}{50} = 27$$

Since $F^* = 27 > 18.5$, we conclude H_a, that geographic region effects are present. The P-value of this test is .035.

The analysis of the magnitudes of the geographic region and city size main effects involves no new problems. The analyst employed three pairwise comparisons of the factor level means $\mu_{i.}$ for city size effects and a pairwise comparison of the geographic region factor level means $\mu_{.j}$. The methods described in Section 20.2 are entirely applicable here; the error variance σ^2 is now estimated by $MSAB$, and the degrees of freedom associated with the estimate of the error variance now are $(a-1)(b-1)$. Since no new issues are involved in the analysis, we do not present further details.

Estimation of Treatment Mean

Occasionally when no-interaction model (21.1) is employed with $n = 1$, there is interest in estimating a treatment mean μ_{ij}. We could estimate treatment mean μ_{ij} in the usual fashion with the sample mean $\bar{Y}_{ij.}$, here simply the single observation Y_{ij}. However, we can obtain an improved estimate by making use of the model assumption of no interactions. We know from (19.7a) that when the factor effects are additive, the treatment mean μ_{ij} can be expressed as follows:

(21.4) $$\mu_{ij} = \mu_{i.} + \mu_{.j} - \mu_{..}$$

Hence, we can estimate μ_{ij} for additive model (21.1) by substituting the estimated values $\hat{\mu}_{i.} = \bar{Y}_{i.}, \hat{\mu}_{.j} = \bar{Y}_{.j}$, and $\hat{\mu}_{..} = \bar{Y}_{..}$ into (21.4):

(21.5) $$\hat{\mu}_{ij} = \bar{Y}_{i.} + \bar{Y}_{.j} - \bar{Y}_{..}$$

The estimator of the treatment mean μ_{ij} in (21.5) is an improved estimator because it has minimum variance in the class of unbiased linear estimators according to an extension of the Gauss-Markov theorem (1.11).

Example.   For the insurance premium example in Table 21.2a, we shall use (21.5) to obtain improved estimates of the treatment means μ_{ij}. We obtain, for instance:

$$\hat{\mu}_{11} = 120 + 190 - 175 = 135$$
$$\hat{\mu}_{12} = 120 + 160 - 175 = 105$$

The other treatment mean estimates are:

$$\hat{\mu}_{21} = 210 \qquad \hat{\mu}_{22} = 180 \qquad \hat{\mu}_{31} = 225 \qquad \hat{\mu}_{32} = 195$$

Note that these improved estimates differ only slightly from the simpler estimates Y_{ij} in Table 21.2a.

Precision of Estimated Treatment Mean.   To set up a confidence interval for a treatment mean μ_{ij}, we require the estimated variance of $\hat{\mu}_{ij}$ in (21.5). One simple method of estimating this variance is by means of the regression model equivalent to ANOVA model (21.1). For the insurance premium example, this equivalent regression model is:

$$Y_{ij} = \mu_{..} + \alpha_1 X_{ij1} + \alpha_2 X_{ij2} + \beta_1 X_{ij3} + \varepsilon_{ij}$$

where:

$$X_1 = \begin{array}{ll} 1 & \text{if small city} \\ -1 & \text{if large city} \\ 0 & \text{if medium city} \end{array}$$

$$X_2 = \begin{array}{ll} 1 & \text{if medium city} \\ -1 & \text{if large city} \\ 0 & \text{if small city} \end{array}$$

$$X_3 = \begin{array}{ll} 1 & \text{if region East} \\ -1 & \text{if region West} \end{array}$$

Note that the fitted value for observation Y_{ij} will be:

$$\hat{Y}_{ij} = \bar{Y}_{..} + \hat{\alpha}_i + \hat{\beta}_j$$

which is identical to $\hat{\mu}_{ij}$ in (21.5):

$$\hat{Y}_{ij} = \bar{Y}_{..} + (\bar{Y}_{i.} - \bar{Y}_{..}) + (\bar{Y}_{.j} - \bar{Y}_{..}) = \bar{Y}_{i.} + \bar{Y}_{.j} - \bar{Y}_{..} = \hat{\mu}_{ij}$$

Hence, the estimated variance of $\hat{Y}_{ij}$ is also the estimated variance of $\hat{\mu}_{ij}$. The estimated variance $s^2\{\hat{Y}_{ij}\}$ is furnished by most computer regression packages or can be calculated by means of (6.58).

Comments

1. The analysis of two-factor studies with $n = 1$ just outlined depends on the assumption that the two factors do not interact. If this analysis is used when in fact interactions are present, the result is that the actual level of significance for testing factor A and factor B main effects is below the specified level and the actual power of the tests is lower than the expected power. Correspondingly, confidence intervals for contrasts of factor level means will tend to be too wide. This means that when interactions are present, the analysis is more likely to fail to disclose real effects than anticipated. However, when the analysis based on the no-interaction model does indicate the presence of factor A or factor B main effects, they may be taken as real effects even though interactions are actually present.

2. Sometimes, the case $n = 1$ is encountered when the observations Y_{ij} are proportions. For instance, the data may consist of the proportion of employees in a plant absent during the past week, with the plants classified by size and geographic area. As noted earlier, the arc sine transformation can be used for such data to stabilize the error variance. The transformed data then can be analyzed using no-interaction model (21.1), provided that each proportion is based on roughly the same number of cases. If the number of cases differs greatly, weighted least squares should be utilized. ∎

21.2 Tukey Test for Additivity

We describe now the Tukey test that may be used for examining, when $n = 1$, whether or not the two factors in a two-factor study interact. This test is also useful for a variety of experimental designs to be discussed in later chapters.

Development of Test Statistic

As noted in Section 21.1, we considered no-interaction model (21.1) when $n = 1$ to enable us to obtain an estimate of the error variance in this case. It would have been possible, however, to impose less severe restrictions on the interaction effects $(\alpha\beta)_{ij}$ and include the restricted interaction effects in the ANOVA model. Suppose we assume that:

$$(21.6) \qquad (\alpha\beta)_{ij} = D\alpha_i\beta_j$$

where D is some constant. One motivation for this restriction is that if $(\alpha\beta)_{ij}$ is any second-degree polynomial function of α_i and β_j, then it must be of the form (21.6) because of the restrictions on the α_i, β_j, and $(\alpha\beta)_{ij}$ in (19.23) that the sums over each subscript be zero.

Using (21.6) in a regular two-factor ANOVA model with interactions for the case $n = 1$, we obtain:

$$(21.7) \qquad Y_{ij} = \mu_{..} + \alpha_i + \beta_j + D\alpha_i\beta_j + \varepsilon_{ij}$$

where each term has the usual meaning. Remember there is no third subscript here because $n = 1$. The interaction sum of squares $\Sigma\Sigma D^2\alpha_i^2\beta_j^2$ now needs to be obtained. Assuming the other parameters are known, the least squares and maximum likelihood estimator of D turns out to be:

$$(21.8) \qquad \hat{D} = \frac{\sum_i \sum_j \alpha_i \beta_j Y_{ij}}{\sum_i \alpha_i^2 \sum_j \beta_j^2}$$

The usual estimator of α_i is $\bar{Y}_{i.} - \bar{Y}_{..}$ and that of β_j is $\bar{Y}_{.j} - \bar{Y}_{..}$. Replacing the parameters in $\hat{D}$ by these estimators, we obtain:

$$(21.8a) \qquad \hat{D} = \frac{\sum_i \sum_j (\bar{Y}_{i.} - \bar{Y}_{..})(\bar{Y}_{.j} - \bar{Y}_{..}) Y_{ij}}{\sum_i (\bar{Y}_{i.} - \bar{Y}_{..})^2 \sum_j (\bar{Y}_{.j} - \bar{Y}_{..})^2}$$

The sample counterpart of the interaction sum of squares $\sum\sum D^2 \alpha_i^2 \beta_j^2$ will be denoted by $SSAB^*$ to remind us that this interaction sum of squares is for the special form of interaction in model (21.7). Substituting the sample estimates into $\sum\sum D^2 \alpha_i^2 \beta_j^2$, we obtain the interaction sum of squares:

$$(21.9) \qquad SSAB^* = \sum_i \sum_j \hat{D}^2 (\bar{Y}_{i.} - \bar{Y}_{..})^2 (\bar{Y}_{.j} - \bar{Y}_{..})^2$$

$$= \frac{\left[\sum_i \sum_j (\bar{Y}_{i.} - \bar{Y}_{..})(\bar{Y}_{.j} - \bar{Y}_{..}) Y_{ij} \right]^2}{\sum_i (\bar{Y}_{i.} - \bar{Y}_{..})^2 \sum_j (\bar{Y}_{.j} - \bar{Y}_{..})^2}$$

The analysis of variance decomposition for the special interaction model (21.7) therefore is:

$$(21.10) \qquad SSTO = SSA + SSB + SSAB^* + SSRem^*$$

where $SSRem^*$ is the *remainder sum of squares*:

$$(21.10a) \qquad SSRem^* = SSTO - SSA - SSB - SSAB^*$$

It can be shown that if $D = 0$—that is, if no interactions of the type $D\alpha_i\beta_j$ exist—$SSAB^*$ and $SSRem^*$ are independently distributed as chi-square random variables with 1 and $ab - a - b$ degrees of freedom, respectively. Hence, if $D = 0$, the test statistic:

$$(21.11) \qquad F^* = \frac{SSAB^*}{1} \div \frac{SSRem^*}{ab - a - b}$$

is distributed as $F(1, ab - a - b)$.

Thus, for testing:

$$(21.12a) \qquad \begin{aligned} H_0&: D = 0 \quad \text{(no interactions present)} \\ H_a&: D \neq 0 \quad \text{(interactions } D\alpha_i\beta_j \text{ present)} \end{aligned}$$

we use test statistic F^* defined in (21.11). Large values of F^* lead to conclusion H_a. The appropriate decision rule for controlling the risk of a Type I error at α is:

$$(21.12b) \qquad \begin{aligned} &\text{If } F^* \leq F(1 - \alpha; 1, ab - a - b), \text{ conclude } H_0 \\ &\text{If } F^* > F(1 - \alpha; 1, ab - a - b), \text{ conclude } H_a \end{aligned}$$

The power of this test has been studied, and it appears that if interactions of approximately the type postulated in (21.6) are present and the factor A and factor B main effects are large, the test is effective in detecting the interactions. The test is usually called the *Tukey one degree of freedom test*. This test also may be used for testing for the presence of general interactions.

Example

We shall conduct the Tukey test for the insurance premium example. The data are presented in Table 21.2a. First, we obtain the elements of $SSAB^*$:

$$\sum\sum(\bar{Y}_{i.} - \bar{Y}_{..})(\bar{Y}_{.j} - \bar{Y}_{..})Y_{ij} = (120 - 175)(190 - 175)(140) + \cdots$$

$$+ (210 - 175)(160 - 175)(200) = -13,500$$

$$\sum(\bar{Y}_{i.} - \bar{Y}_{..})^2 = \frac{SSA}{2} = \frac{9,300}{2} = 4,650$$

$$\sum(\bar{Y}_{.j} - \bar{Y}_{..})^2 = \frac{SSB}{3} = \frac{1,350}{3} = 450$$

Hence, the special interaction sum of squares is:

$$SSAB^* = \frac{(-13,500)^2}{4,650(450)} = 87.1$$

Using the ANOVA sums of squares in Table 21.2b, we have by (21.10a):

$$SSRem^* = 10,750 - 9,300 - 1,350 - 87.1 = 12.9$$

Finally, we obtain the test statistic by (21.11):

$$F^* = \frac{87.1}{1} \div \frac{12.9}{3(2) - 3 - 2} = 6.8$$

For $\alpha = .10$, we require $F(.90; 1, 1) = 39.9$. Since $F^* = 6.8 \leq 39.9$, we conclude that region and size of city do not interact. The P-value of this test is .23. Use of the no-interaction model for the data in Table 21.2a therefore appears to be reasonable.

Remedial Actions if Interaction Effects Are Present

When the Tukey test indicates the presence of interaction effects in an analysis of variance application where $n = 1$, efforts should be made to remove the interactions so that the analysis described in Section 21.1 can be utilized. As we described in Chapter 19, transformations of the data can often be used to remove interaction effects or to make them unimportant.

One possibility is to try simple transformations of the response variable, such as a square root or a logarithmic transformation. Another possibility is to search in the family of power transformations on Y described in Chapter 3 in connection with the Box-Cox transformations. The procedure is to make transformations on Y according to (3.36) for selected values of λ. For each value of λ, the Tukey test statistic (21.11) is then obtained. If a λ value leads to a nonsignificant F^* test statistic, a transformation will then have been found that removes the interaction effect. Frequently, a range of λ values will yield nonsignificant test statistics, in which case a simple λ value in this range, such as $\lambda = .5$, may be chosen.

If no transformation can be found to make the interactions unimportant, an approximate method of analysis can be employed; see, for instance, Reference 21.1.

Note

If one or both factors are quantitative, a test for interactions effects can be obtained by regression methods. For example, consider a study in which both factors are quantitative, each has three levels, and $n = 1$ so that $n_T = 9$. Let X_{ij1} denote the value of the first factor for the treatment for which factor A is at the ith level and factor B is at the jth level. X_{ij2} is defined similarly for the second factor. Second-order regression model (20.44), with the replication index k dropped, may then be used:

$$ Y_{ij} = \beta_0 + \beta_1 x_{ij1} + \beta_2 x_{ij2} + \beta_3 x_{ij1}^2 + \beta_4 x_{ij2}^2 + \beta_5 x_{ij1} x_{ij2} + \varepsilon_{ij} $$

where:

$$ x_{ij1} = X_{ij1} - \bar{X}_1 $$
$$ x_{ij2} = X_{ij2} - \bar{X}_2 $$

With this model, there would be $n_T - p = 9 - 6 = 3$ degrees of freedom for estimating the error variance σ^2, and the test for the presence of an interaction effect would be the usual test in (6.51) for testing whether $\beta_5 = 0$.

Still other tests for interactions could be conducted since additional cross-product terms could be incorporated into the regression model. However, this would not be desirable here since the number of degrees of freedom available for estimating the error variance σ^2 is already very small. ∎

Cited Reference

21.1. Johnson, D. E., and F. A. Graybill. "Estimation of σ^2 in a Two-Way Classification Model with Interaction," *Journal of the American Statistical Association* 67 (1972), pp. 388–94.

Problems

21.1. Suppose that two-factor analysis of variance model (19.23) were to be employed with $n = 1$ for each factor level combination. How many degrees of freedom would be associated with SSE in (19.37c)? What does this imply?

√ 21.2. **Coin-operated terminals.** A university computer service conducted an experiment in which one coin-operated computer graphics terminal was placed at each of four different locations on the campus last semester during the midterm week and again during the final week of classes. The data that follow show the number of hours each terminal was *not* in use during the week at the four locations (factor A) and for the two different weeks (factor B).

| Factor A | Factor B (week) | |
(location)	$j = 1$ Midterm	$j = 2$ Final
$i = 1$	16.5	21.4
$i = 2$	11.8	17.3
$i = 3$	12.3	16.9
$i = 4$	16.6	21.0

Assume that no-interaction ANOVA model (21.1) is appropriate.

a. Plot the data in the format of Figure 19.6. Does it appear that interaction effects are present? Does it appear that factor A and factor B main effects are present? Discuss.

b. Conduct separate tests for location and week main effects. In each test, use level of significance $\alpha = .05$ and state the alternatives, decision rule, and conclusion. Give an upper bound for the family level of significance; use the Kimball inequality. What is the P-value for each test?

c. Make all pairwise comparisons among location means and estimate the difference between the means for the two weeks; use the Bonferroni procedure with a 90 percent family confidence coefficient. State your findings.

√ 21.3. Refer to **Coin-operated terminals** Problem 21.2. It is desired to estimate μ_{32}.

a. Obtain a point estimate of μ_{32} using (21.5).

b. Obtain the estimated variance of $\hat{\mu}_{32}$ by fitting the equivalent regression model.

c. Construct a 95 percent confidence interval for μ_{32}. Interpret your interval estimate. Is your interval estimate applicable if next year two graphics terminals will be placed at location 3? Explain.

√ 21.4. Refer to **Coin-operated terminals** Problem 21.2. Conduct the Tukey test for additivity; use $\alpha = .025$. State the alternatives, decision rule, and conclusion. If the additive model is not appropriate, what might you do?

21.5. **Brainstorming**. A researcher investigated whether brainstorming is more effective for larger groups than for smaller ones by setting up four groups of agribusiness executives, the group sizes being two, three, four, and five, respectively. He also set up four groups of agribusiness scientists, the group sizes being the same as for the agribusiness executives. The researcher gave each group the same problem: "How can Canada increase the value of its agricultural exports?" Each group was allowed 30 minutes to generate ideas. The variable of interest was the number of different ideas proposed by the group. The results, classified by type of group (factor A) and size of group (factor B), were:

| Factor A | Factor B (size of group) | | | |
(type of group)	$j = 1$ Two	$j = 2$ Three	$j = 3$ Four	$j = 4$ Five
$i = 1$ Agribusiness executives	18	22	31	32
$i = 2$ Agribusiness scientists	15	23	29	33

Assume that no-interaction ANOVA model (21.1) is appropriate.

a. Plot the data in the format of Figure 19.6. Does it appear that interaction effects are present? Does it appear that factor A and factor B main effects are present? Discuss.

b. Conduct separate tests for type of group and size of group main effects. In each test, use level of significance $\alpha = .01$ and state the alternatives, decision rule, and conclusion. Give an upper bound for the family level of significance; use the Kimball inequality. What is the P-value for each test?

c. Obtain confidence intervals for $D_1 = \mu_{.2} - \mu_{.1}$, $D_2 = \mu_{.3} - \mu_{.2}$, and $D_3 = \mu_{.4} - \mu_{.3}$; use the Bonferroni procedure with a 95 percent family confidence coefficient. State your findings.

d. Is the Bonferroni procedure used in part (c) the most efficient one here? Explain.

21.6. Refer to **Brainstorming** Problem 21.5. It is desired to estimate μ_{14}.

a. Obtain a point estimate of μ_{14} using (21.5).

b. Obtain the estimated variance of $\hat{\mu}_{14}$ by fitting the equivalent regression model.

c. Construct a 99 percent confidence interval for μ_{14}. Interpret your interval estimate. Is your interval estimate applicable if the two factors interact?

21.7. Refer to **Brainstorming** Problem 21.5. Conduct the Tukey test for additivity; use $\alpha = .01$. State the alternatives, decision rule, and conclusion. If the additive model is not appropriate, what might you do?

21.8. **Soybean sausage**. A food technologist, testing storage capabilities for a newly developed type of imitation sausage made from soybeans, conducted an experiment to test the effects of humidity level (factor A) and temperature level (factor B) in the freezer compartment on color change in the sausage. Three humidity levels and four temperature levels were considered. Five hundred sausages were stored at each of the 12 humidity-temperature combinations for 90 days. At the end of the storage period, the researcher determined the proportion of sausages for each humidity-temperature combination that exhibited color changes. The researcher transformed the data by means of the arc sine transformation (18.24) to stabilize the variances. The transformed data $Y' = 2 \arcsin \sqrt{Y}$ follow.

Factor A (humidity level)	Factor B (temperature level)			
	$j = 1$	$j = 2$	$j = 3$	$j = 4$
$i = 1$	13.9	14.2	20.5	24.8
$i = 2$	15.7	16.3	21.7	23.6
$i = 3$	15.1	15.4	19.9	26.1

Assume that no-interaction ANOVA model (21.1) is appropriate.

a. Plot the data in the format of Figure 19.6. Does it appear that interaction effects are present? Does it appear that factor A and factor B main effects are present? Discuss.

b. Conduct separate tests for humidity and temperature main effects. In each test, use level of significance $\alpha = .025$ and state the alternatives, decision rule, and conclusion. What is the P-value for each test?

c. Obtain confidence intervals for $D_1 = \mu_{.2} - \mu_{.1}$, $D_2 = \mu_{.3} - \mu_{.2}$, and $D_3 = \mu_{.4} - \mu_{.3}$; use the Bonferroni procedure with a 95 percent family confidence coefficient. State your findings.

d. Is the Bonferroni procedure used in part (c) the most efficient one here? Explain.

21.9.   Refer to **Soybean sausage** Problem 21.8. It is desired to estimate μ_{23}.

   a. Obtain a point estimate of μ_{23} using (21.5).

   b. Obtain the estimated variance of $\hat{\mu}_{23}$ by fitting the equivalent regression model.

   c. Construct a 98 percent confidence interval for μ_{23} and transform it back to the original units. Interpret your interval estimate. Is your interval estimate applicable if the two factors interact?

21.10. Refer to **Soybean sausage** Problem 21.8. Conduct the Tukey test for additivity; use $\alpha = .005$. State the alternatives, decision rule, and conclusion. If the additive model is not appropriate, what might you do?

Exercises

21.11. Modify formulas (19.39a) and (19.39b) to apply to ANOVA model (21.1), where $n = 1$.

21.12. Show that (21.6) is the only second-degree polynomial function of α_i and β_j such that $\sum_i (\alpha\beta)_{ij} = \sum_j (\alpha\beta)_{ij} = 0$.

Two-Factor Studies—Unequal Sample Sizes and Unequal Treatment Importance

Up to this point in our discussion of two-factor studies we have restricted ourselves to equal treatment sample sizes for the two-factor ANOVA model (19.23) and to equal importance of all treatment means. Often, however, two-factor studies involve unequal treatment sample sizes. The resulting imbalance destroys the orthogonality of the ANOVA decomposition. Consequently, the general linear test approach is required for ANOVA tests. In Sections 22.1 through 22.4 we shall take up procedures for handling two-factor studies with unequal treatment sample sizes. We continue to assume that all treatment means are of equal importance in these sections.

In occasional ANOVA studies, the treatment means are not of equal importance. This also makes the standard ANOVA decomposition inappropriate, and the general linear test approach consequently is required. We consider in Section 22.5 procedures for conducting the analysis of variance when the treatment means have unequal importance. We conclude this chapter by discussing briefly the use of statistical computing packages in the presence of unequal treatment sample sizes or unequal importance of treatment means.

22.1 Unequal Sample Sizes

Two-factor studies frequently involve unequal treatment or cell sample sizes for a variety of reasons. In observational studies, the investigator often has little or no control over the cell sample sizes. For example, in a comparative study of U.S. manufacturing practices, researchers examined the performance of manufacturing plants as a function of size of plant (factor A: small, medium, large) and ownership (factor B: Japan, United States). In this two-factor study, cell sample sizes for the six treatments were not under the complete control of the researchers. First, the number of plants available for study in each size-ownership category varied. Second, many plants were unable or unwilling to participate in the study.

Unequal treatment sample sizes are also encountered in experimental studies. For instance, an experimenter may seek to have the same number of cases for each treatment, but for a variety of reasons (e.g., illness of subject, incomplete records, technical problems) ends up with unequal cell sample sizes.

Another reason for unequal treatment sample sizes is that investigators in both observational and experimental studies may use larger sample sizes for treatments for which the cost is lower. In still other instances, unequal treatment sample sizes may be desired to enable certain treatment means or certain linear combinations of treatment means to be estimated with greater precision. For example, a packaged foods manufacturer wished to measure the impact on consumer product ratings of a change from corn syrup to a low-calorie sweetener (factor A) in one of its breakfast cereals. Three categories of consumers, (factor B: children, female adults, and male adults) were considered to be important. It was known that about 60 percent of the consumers are children, 20 percent are adult males, and 20 percent are adult females. It was therefore considered to be reasonable to require that 60 percent of the subjects be children, 20 percent be adult males, and 20 percent be adult females to provide greater precision for the most important consumer group.

The fact that treatment sample sizes are unequal often does not affect the importance of the treatment means. As we just noted, sample sizes frequently are unequal for reasons that have nothing to do with the importance of treatment means. In our discussion of unequal treatment sample sizes in Sections 22.2–22.4, we shall continue to assume that all treatment means have the same importance. Procedures for handling ANOVA inferences when treatments have unequal importance are considered in Section 22.5.

Throughout Sections 22.1–22.3, we assume that there is at least one case for each treatment. Techniques for the analysis of studies with one or more cells empty are discussed in Section 22.4.

Notation

Our notation remains the same as before, except that the sample size for the treatment consisting of the ith level of factor A and the jth level of factor B will now be denoted by n_{ij}. The total number of cases for the ith level of factor A will be denoted by:

$$(22.1a) \qquad n_{i.} = \sum_j n_{ij}$$

the total number of cases for the jth level of factor B by:

$$(22.1b) \qquad n_{.j} = \sum_i n_{ij}$$

and the total number of cases for the entire study by:

$$(22.1c) \qquad n_T = \sum_i \sum_j n_{ij}$$

The estimated treatment mean when factor A is at the ith level and factor B is at the jth level is defined as usual:

$$(22.2) \qquad \bar{Y}_{ij.} = \frac{Y_{ij.}}{n_{ij}}$$

where:

$$(22.2a) \qquad Y_{ij.} = \sum_{k=1}^{n_{ij}} Y_{ijk}$$

22.2   Use of Regression Approach for Testing Factor Effects when Sample Sizes Are Unequal

When the treatment sample sizes are unequal, the analysis of variance for two-factor studies becomes more complex. The least squares equations are no longer of a simple structure, yielding direct and easy solutions, and the regular analysis of variance formulas in (19.37) and (19.39) are now inappropriate. Furthermore, the factor effect component sums of squares are no longer orthogonal; that is, they do not sum to *SSTR*.

Hence, the general linear test approach described in Section 2.8 must be utilized when the treatment sample sizes are unequal. An easy way to obtain the proper error sums of squares for testing factor interactions and main effects by the general linear test approach is through the regression formulation of the ANOVA model described in Section 19.7. The only difference when cell sample sizes are unequal is that a reduced regression model needs to be fitted explicitly for each test of factor interactions and main effects because of the lack of orthogonality. Since no new principles are involved, we turn directly to an example to illustrate how ANOVA tests are conducted by means of the regression approach when the treatment sample sizes are unequal.

Example

Synthetic growth hormone was administered at a clinical research center to growth hormone deficient, short children who had not yet reached puberty. The investigator was interested in the effects of a child's gender (factor *A*) and bone development (factor *B*) on the rate of growth induced by hormone administration. A child's bone development was classified into one of three categories: severely depressed, moderately depressed, mildly depressed. Three children were randomly selected for each gender-bone development group. The response variable (*Y*) of interest was the difference between the growth rate during growth hormone treatment and the normal growth rate prior to the treatment, expressed in centimeters per month. Four of the 18 children were unable to complete the year-long study, thus creating unequal treatment sample sizes.

Table 22.1 presents the study data. A plot of the estimated treatment means is shown in Figure 22.1. It is clearly suggested there that a child's bone development has a major impact on the change in growth rate. The plot also raises the questions whether some interaction effects are present and whether the gender of a child affects the growth rate.

To test formally whether or not these factor effects are present, we utilize the general linear test approach and the equivalent regression model formulation because of the unequal sample sizes.

Development of Regression Model.   The two-factor ANOVA model (19.23) here is:

$$(22.3) \qquad Y_{ijk} = \mu_{..} + \alpha_i + \beta_j + (\alpha\beta)_{ij} + \varepsilon_{ijk} \qquad i = 1, 2; \quad j = 1, 2, 3$$

To express this model in regression terms, we utilize indicator variables that take on the values 1, -1, or 0, as explained in Section 19.7. Specifically, we need $a - 1 = 2 - 1 = 1$ indicator variable for the factor *A* main effects and $b - 1 = 3 - 1 = 2$ indicator variables for the factor *B* main effects. The interaction terms correspond to the cross products of the indicator variables for factor *A* and factor *B* main effects. Specifically, the regression model

TABLE 22.1 **Sample Data and Notation for Growth Hormone Example (growth rate difference in centimeters per month).**

Gender (factor A) i	Bone Development (factor B) j		
	Severely Depressed (B_1)	Moderately Depressed (B_2)	Mildly Depressed (B_3)
Male (A_1)	1.4 (Y_{111}) 2.4 (Y_{112}) 2.2 (Y_{113})	2.1 (Y_{121}) 1.7 (Y_{122})	.7 (Y_{131}) 1.1 (Y_{132})
Mean	2.0 ($\bar{Y}_{11.}$)	1.9 ($\bar{Y}_{12.}$)	.9 ($\bar{Y}_{13.}$)
Female (A_2)	2.4 (Y_{211})	2.5 (Y_{221}) 1.8 (Y_{222}) 2.0 (Y_{223})	.5 (Y_{231}) .9 (Y_{232}) 1.3 (Y_{233})
Mean	2.4 ($\bar{Y}_{21.}$)	2.1 ($\bar{Y}_{22.}$)	.9 ($\bar{Y}_{23.}$)

FIGURE 22.1 **Estimated Treatment Means Plot—Growth Hormone Example.**

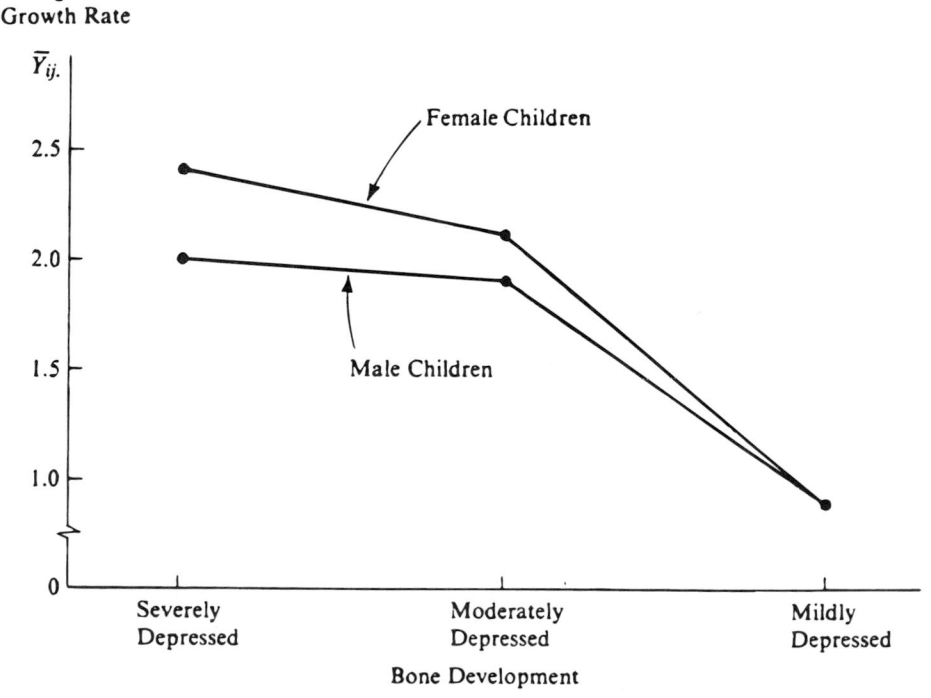

equivalent to ANOVA model (22.3) is:

$$(22.4) \qquad Y_{ijk} = \mu_{..} + \underbrace{\alpha_1 X_{ijk1}}_{A \text{ main effect}} + \underbrace{\beta_1 X_{ijk2} + \beta_2 X_{ijk3}}_{B \text{ main effect}}$$

$$+ \underbrace{(\alpha\beta)_{11} X_{ijk1} X_{ijk2} + (\alpha\beta)_{12} X_{ijk1} X_{ijk3}}_{AB \text{ interaction effect}} + \varepsilon_{ijk} \qquad \text{Full model}$$

where:

$$X_1 = \begin{array}{ll} 1 & \text{if case from level 1 for factor } A \\ -1 & \text{if case from level 2 for factor } A \end{array}$$

$$X_2 = \begin{array}{ll} 1 & \text{if case from level 1 for factor } B \\ -1 & \text{if case from level 3 for factor } B \\ 0 & \text{otherwise} \end{array}$$

$$X_3 = \begin{array}{ll} 1 & \text{if case from level 2 for factor } B \\ -1 & \text{if case from level 3 for factor } B \\ 0 & \text{otherwise} \end{array}$$

The regression coefficients in (22.4) are the ANOVA model parameters:

$$\mu_{..}$$

$$\alpha_1 = \mu_{1.} - \mu_{..}$$

$$(22.5) \qquad \beta_1 = \mu_{.1} - \mu_{..}$$

$$\beta_2 = \mu_{.2} - \mu_{..}$$

$$(\alpha\beta)_{11} = \mu_{11} - \mu_{1.} - \mu_{.1} + \mu_{..}$$

$$(\alpha\beta)_{12} = \mu_{12} - \mu_{1.} - \mu_{.2} + \mu_{..}$$

The remaining ANOVA model parameters are not required in the regression model because of the constraints in (19.23). Thus, for instance:

$$\alpha_2 = -\alpha_1$$

$$\beta_3 = -\beta_1 - \beta_2$$

$$(22.6) \qquad (\alpha\beta)_{13} = -(\alpha\beta)_{11} - (\alpha\beta)_{12}$$

$$(\alpha\beta)_{21} = -(\alpha\beta)_{11}$$

Table 22.2 repeats in column 1 a portion of the response data from Table 22.1. The codings of the indicator variables and the interaction terms are shown in columns 2–6. Note, for instance, that the codings for the first male child whose bone development is severely depressed ($i = 1, j = 1, k = 1$) are $X_1 = 1$, $X_2 = 1$, and $X_3 = 0$, so that $X_1 X_2 = 1$ and $X_1 X_3 = 0$. Table 22.3a presents the fitted regression function and regression ANOVA table when the full regression model (22.4) is fitted to the data; i.e., when Y in column 1 of Table 22.2 is regressed on the X variables in columns 2–6. Note that the fitted values for the full

TABLE 22.2 Data for Regression Fits—Growth Hormone Example.

i	j	k	(1) Y	(2) X_1	(3) X_2	(4) X_3	(5) $X_1 X_2$	(6) $X_1 X_3$
1	1	1	1.4	1	1	0	1	0
1	1	2	2.4	1	1	0	1	0
...			...	...	...	...	...	...
1	2	2	1.7	1	0	1	0	1
1	3	1	.7	1	−1	−1	−1	−1
...			...	...	...	...	...	...
2	3	2	.9	−1	−1	−1	1	1
2	3	3	1.3	−1	−1	−1	1	1

model are the estimated treatment means $\bar{Y}_{ij.}$, just as when all treatment sample sizes are equal. For instance, we have for the first case ($k = 1$) from treatment $i = 1$, $j = 1$:

$$\hat{Y}_{111} = 1.7 - .1(1) + .5(1) + .3(0) - .1(1) - 0(0) = 2.0 = \bar{Y}_{11.}$$

and for the last case ($k = 3$) from treatment $i = 2$, $j = 3$:

$$\hat{Y}_{233} = 1.7 - .1(-1) + .5(-1) + .3(-1) - .1(1) - 0(1) = .9 = \bar{Y}_{23.}$$

Test for Interaction Effects. To test whether or not interaction effects are present, the ANOVA model alternatives:

(22.7)
$$H_0: \text{ all } (\alpha\beta)_{ij} = 0$$
$$H_a: \text{ not all } (\alpha\beta)_{ij} \text{ equal zero}$$

become for regression model (22.4):

(22.7a)
$$H_0: (\alpha\beta)_{11} = (\alpha\beta)_{12} = 0$$
$$H_a: \text{ not both } (\alpha\beta)_{11} \text{ and } (\alpha\beta)_{12} \text{ equal zero}$$

Thus, we are simply testing whether or not two regression coefficients equal zero. The reduced regression model therefore is:

(22.8)
$$Y_{ijk} = \mu_{..} + \alpha_1 X_{ijk1} + \beta_1 X_{ijk2} + \beta_2 X_{ijk3} + \varepsilon_{ijk} \qquad \text{Reduced model}$$

When this reduced model is fitted by regressing Y in column 1 of Table 22.2 on X_1, X_2, and X_3 in columns 2–4, the results presented in Table 22.3b are obtained. The general linear test statistic (2.70) therefore is:

$$F^* = \frac{SSE(R) - SSE(F)}{df_R - df_F} \div \frac{SSE(F)}{df_F}$$

$$= \frac{1.3754 - 1.3000}{10 - 8} \div \frac{1.3000}{8} = \frac{.0377}{.1625} = .23$$

TABLE 22.3   Fits of Full and Reduced Regression Models—Growth Hormone Example.

(a) Full Model (22.4)

Source of Variation	SS	df
Regression	4.4743	5
Error	1.3000	8
Total	5.7743	13

$$\hat{Y} = 1.7 - .1X_1 + .5X_2 + .3X_3 - .1X_1X_2 - 0.0X_1X_3$$

(b) Reduced Model (22.8)

Source of Variation	SS	df
Regression	4.3989	3
Error	1.3754	10
Total	5.7743	13

$$\hat{Y} = 1.68 - .0857X_1 + .467X_2 + .327X_3$$

$$SSE(R) - SSE(F) = 1.3754 - 1.3000 = .0754$$

(c) Reduced Model (22.10)

Source of Variation	SS	df
Regression	4.3543	4
Error	1.4200	9
Total	5.7743	13

$$\hat{Y} = 1.69 + .444X_2 + .328X_3 - .0667X_1X_2 - .0167X_1X_3$$

$$SSE(R) - SSE(F) = 1.4200 - 1.3000 = .1200$$

(d) Reduced Model (22.11)

Source of Variation	SS	df
Regression	.2846	3
Error	5.4897	10
Total	5.7743	13

$$\hat{Y} = 1.63 + .0190X_1 + .0667X_1X_2 - .193X_1X_3$$

$$SSE(R) - SSE(F) = 5.4897 - 1.3000 = 4.1897$$

To control the risk of making a Type I error at $\alpha = .05$, we require $F(.95; 2, 8) = 4.46$. Since $F^* = .23 \le 4.46$, we conclude H_0, that no interaction effects are present. The *P*-value for this test statistic is .80.

Tests for Factor Main Effects.   We now proceed to test whether or not factor *A* and factor *B* main effects are present. The ANOVA model alternatives:

(22.9)
$$H_0: \alpha_1 = \alpha_2 = 0 \qquad\qquad H_0: \beta_1 = \beta_2 = \beta_3 = 0$$
$$H_a: \text{not both } \alpha_i \text{ equal zero} \qquad H_a: \text{not all } \beta_j \text{ equal zero}$$

become for regression model (22.4):

$$(22.9a) \qquad \begin{array}{ll} H_0: \alpha_1 = 0 & H_0: \beta_1 = \beta_2 = 0 \\ H_a: \alpha_1 \neq 0 & H_a: \text{not both } \beta_j \text{ equal zero} \end{array}$$

The reduced regression models for testing for factor A main effects and factor B main effects therefore are:

Test for factor A main effects

$$(22.10) \quad Y_{ijk} = \mu_{..} + \beta_1 X_{ijk2} + \beta_2 X_{ijk3} + (\alpha\beta)_{11} X_{ijk1} X_{ijk2} + (\alpha\beta)_{12} X_{ijk1} X_{ijk3} + \varepsilon_{ijk}$$

Reduced model

Test for factor B main effects

$$(22.11) \qquad Y_{ijk} = \mu_{..} + \alpha_1 X_{ijk1} + (\alpha\beta)_{11} X_{ijk1} X_{ijk2} + (\alpha\beta)_{12} X_{ijk1} X_{ijk3} + \varepsilon_{ijk}$$

Reduced model

Table 22.3c presents the results of fitting reduced model (22.10), where Y in column 1 of Table 22.2 is regressed on X_2, X_3, $X_1 X_2$, and $X_1 X_3$ in columns 3–6. Finally, Table 22.3d contains the results of fitting reduced model (22.11), where Y in column 1 of Table 22.2 is regressed on X_1, $X_1 X_2$, and $X_1 X_3$ in columns 2, 5, and 6. The two test statistics therefore are:

$$F_1^* = \frac{1.4200 - 1.3000}{9 - 8} \div \frac{1.3000}{8} = \frac{.1200}{.1625} = .74$$

$$F_2^* = \frac{5.4897 - 1.3000}{10 - 8} \div \frac{1.3000}{8} = \frac{2.0949}{.1625} = 12.89$$

For $\alpha = .05$, we require $F(.95; 1, 8) = 5.32$ and $F(.95; 2, 8) = 4.46$ for the two tests. Since $F_1^* = .74 \leq 5.32$ and $F_2^* = 12.89 > 4.46$, we conclude that there are no factor A main effects but that factor B main effects are present. The respective P-values for these two test statistics are .41 and .003.

Thus, these tests support the indications obtained previously from the estimated treatment means plot in Figure 22.1, that a child's bone development affects the change in growth rate during growth hormone treatment and that there are no gender and interaction effects. The family level of significance for the set of three tests just conducted, according to the Bonferroni inequality (4.4), is .15.

At this point, the next step in the analysis of the study results is to examine the nature of the bone development effects. We shall discuss this analysis in the next section.

TABLE 22.4 **Consolidated ANOVA Table—Growth Hormone Example.**

Source of Variation	SS ·	df	MS	F^*
Gender (A)	.1200	1	.1200	.74
Bone development (B)	4.1897	2	2.0949	12.89
AB interactions	.0754	2	.0377	.23
Error	1.3000	8	.1625	

Table 22.4 contains a consolidated ANOVA table presenting the results from fitting the four regression models in Table 22.3. The sum of squares for a factor effect in each instance is the difference between the error sums of squares for the reduced and full models shown in Table 22.3, and the associated degrees of freedom are the difference between the respective degrees of freedom for these error sums of squares. Note that a total sum of squares is not shown in Table 22.4 because the sums of squares for the three factor effects and for error do not add to *SSTO* when the treatment sample sizes are unequal.

Note

In the event that pooling of sums of squares is desired for testing factor main effects when the test for interactions leads to the conclusion that there are none, as discussed in Section 19.8, the full regression model for testing factor A and factor B main effects needs to be revised. Specifically with reference to the growth hormone example, the full regression model in (22.4) would need to be revised by excluding the interaction effects and would be as follows:

$$(22.12) \qquad Y_{ijk} = \mu_{..} + \alpha_1 X_{ijk1} + \beta_1 X_{ijk2} + \beta_2 X_{ijk3} + \varepsilon_{ijk} \qquad \text{Revised full model}$$

■

22.3 Inferences about Factor Effects when Sample Sizes Are Unequal

The estimation of factor effects when the treatment sample sizes are unequal is completely analogous to when the sample sizes are equal. The nature of the analysis depends on whether or not strong interactions are present. When no important interactions are present, the analysis generally is concerned with the factor level means $\mu_{i.}$ and $\mu_{.j}$. On the other hand, when important interactions are present, the analysis usually focuses on the treatment means μ_{ij}.

The estimators and estimated variances presented in Chapter 20 for equal sample sizes must, of course, be modified to recognize the unequal treatment sample sizes. For instance, if interest is in estimating the factor level means $\mu_{i.}$ as defined in (19.2) when all treatment means are of equal importance:

$$\mu_{i.} = \frac{\sum\limits_{j} \mu_{ij}}{b}$$

TABLE 22.5 **Point Estimators and Estimated Variances for Two-Factor Analyses when Sample Sizes Are Unequal.**

(a) Factor Level Mean

$$\mu_{i.} = \frac{\sum_j \mu_{ij}}{b} \qquad\qquad \mu_{.j} = \frac{\sum_i \mu_{ij}}{a}$$

(22.13)
$$\hat{\mu}_{i.} = \frac{\sum_j \bar{Y}_{ij.}}{b} \qquad\qquad \hat{\mu}_{.j} = \frac{\sum_i \bar{Y}_{ij.}}{a}$$

$$s^2\{\hat{\mu}_{i.}\} = \frac{MSE}{b^2} \sum_j \frac{1}{n_{ij}} \qquad\qquad s^2\{\hat{\mu}_{.j}\} = \frac{MSE}{a^2} \sum_i \frac{1}{n_{ij}}$$

(b) Pairwise Comparison of Factor Level Means

$$D = \mu_{i.} - \mu_{i'.} \qquad\qquad D = \mu_{.j} - \mu_{.j'}$$

(22.14)
$$\hat{D} = \hat{\mu}_{i.} - \hat{\mu}_{i'.} \qquad\qquad \hat{D} = \hat{\mu}_{.j} - \hat{\mu}_{.j'}$$

$$s^2\{\hat{D}\} = \frac{MSE}{b^2} \sum_j \left(\frac{1}{n_{ij}} + \frac{1}{n_{i'j}} \right) \qquad\qquad s^2\{\hat{D}\} = \frac{MSE}{a^2} \sum_i \left(\frac{1}{n_{ij}} + \frac{1}{n_{ij'}} \right)$$

(c) Contrast or Linear Combination of Factor Level Means

$$L = \sum_i c_i \mu_{i.} \qquad\qquad L = \sum_j c_j \mu_{.j}$$

(22.15)
$$\hat{L} = \sum_i c_i \hat{\mu}_{i.} \qquad\qquad \hat{L} = \sum_j c_j \hat{\mu}_{.j}$$

$$s^2\{\hat{L}\} = \frac{MSE}{b^2} \sum_i c_i^2 \sum_j \frac{1}{n_{ij}} \qquad\qquad s^2\{\hat{L}\} = \frac{MSE}{a^2} \sum_j c_j^2 \sum_i \frac{1}{n_{ij}}$$

(d) Confidence Interval Multiple

Single Estimate

$$t(1 - \alpha/2; n_T - ab) \qquad\qquad t(1 - \alpha/2; n_T - ab)$$

Multiple Comparisons

(22.16)
$$B = t(1 - \alpha/2g; n_T - ab) \qquad\qquad B = t(1 - \alpha/2g; n_T - ab)$$

$$T = \frac{1}{\sqrt{2}} q(1 - \alpha; a, n_T - ab) \qquad\qquad T = \frac{1}{\sqrt{2}} q(1 - \alpha; b, n_T - ab)$$

$$S^2 = (a - 1)F(1 - \alpha; a - 1, n_T - ab) \qquad\qquad S^2 = (b - 1)F(1 - \alpha; b - 1, n_T - ab)$$

TABLE 22.5   **Point Estimators and Estimated Variances for Two-Factor Analyses when Sample Sizes Are Unequal (concluded).**

(e) Treatment Mean

$$\mu_{ij}$$

(22.17)

$$\hat{\mu}_{ij} = \bar{Y}_{ij\cdot}$$

$$s^2\{\hat{\mu}_{ij}\} = \frac{MSE}{n_{ij}}$$

(f) Pairwise Comparison of Treatment Means

$$D = \mu_{ij} - \mu_{i'j'}$$

(22.18)

$$\hat{D} = \bar{Y}_{ij\cdot} - \bar{Y}_{i'j'\cdot}$$

$$s^2\{\hat{D}\} = MSE\left(\frac{1}{n_{ij}} + \frac{1}{n_{i'j'}}\right)$$

(g) Contrast or Linear Combination of Treatment Means

$$L = \Sigma\Sigma c_{ij}\mu_{ij}$$

(22.19)

$$\hat{L} = \Sigma\Sigma c_{ij}\bar{Y}_{ij\cdot}$$

$$s^2\{\hat{L}\} = MSE\,\Sigma\Sigma\,\frac{c_{ij}^2}{n_{ij}}$$

(h) Confidence Interval Multiple

Single Estimate

$$t(1 - \alpha/2; n_T - ab)$$

Multiple Comparisons

(22.20)

$$B = t(1 - \alpha/2g; n_T - ab)$$

$$T = \frac{1}{\sqrt{2}}q(1 - \alpha; ab, n_T - ab)$$

$$S^2 = (ab - 1)F(1 - \alpha; ab - 1, n_T - ab)$$

the appropriate estimator is simply the unweighted average of the estimated treatment means $\bar{Y}_{ij\cdot}$:

$$\hat{\mu}_{i\cdot} = \frac{\sum\limits_{j} \bar{Y}_{ij\cdot}}{b}$$

Since the $\bar{Y}_{ij\cdot}$ are independent, the variance of this estimator is:

$$\sigma^2\{\hat{\mu}_{i\cdot}\} = \frac{1}{b^2} \sum_j \sigma^2\{\bar{Y}_{ij\cdot}\} = \frac{1}{b^2} \sum_j \frac{\sigma^2}{n_{ij}} = \frac{\sigma^2}{b^2} \sum_j \frac{1}{n_{ij}}$$

and the estimated variance is:

$$s^2\{\hat{\mu}_{i\cdot}\} = \frac{MSE}{b^2} \sum_j \frac{1}{n_{ij}}$$

Table 22.5 presents the formulas for the point estimator and estimated variance when estimating factor level means, pairwise comparisons of factor level means, and contrasts or linear combinations of factor level means, when the sample sizes are unequal. The corresponding formulas for treatment means, pairwise comparisons of treatment means, and contrasts or linear combinations of treatment means are also presented in this table.

All multiple comparison procedures applicable for equal sample sizes are appropriate when the treatment sample sizes are unequal. The Tukey pairwise comparison procedure then is conservative. The degrees of freedom associated with MSE are $n_T - ab$, as before. [Recall for equal sample sizes that $n_T = nab$; hence, $n_T - ab = (n-1)ab$.] Table 22.5 also presents the appropriate simultaneous comparison multiples for making inferences about factor level means or treatment means.

Test statistics and decision rules for simultaneous tests based on the Bonferroni, Tukey, and Scheffé procedures are easily adapted from the formulas in Chapter 20. The form of a test statistic does not change, but the degrees of freedom associated with MSE in each decision rule must now be expressed as $n_T - ab$.

Since no new issues are involved in estimating factor effects when the sample sizes are unequal, we proceed directly to two examples.

Example 1—Pairwise Comparisons of Factor Level Means

We continue with the growth hormone example. We found earlier that a child's gender and bone development do not interact in their effects on the change in the growth rate when growth hormone is administered. We further found no main gender (factor A) effects, but concluded that a child's bone development (factor B) does affect the change in growth rate. We shall now analyze the nature of the bone development effects by means of pairwise comparisons among the three bone development groups. The Tukey multiple comparison procedure will be used. This procedure is conservative when sample sizes are unequal, and use of the Bonferroni procedure would lead to wider confidence intervals here. The family confidence coefficient has been specified to be .90.

We use formulas (22.14) in Table 22.5 for the point estimates and estimated variances. The estimated treatment means are given in Table 22.1, and MSE is found in Table 22.4. For the pairwise comparisons of the bone development factor level means ($j = 1$: severely depressed; $j = 2$: moderately depressed; $j = 3$: mildly depressed), we obtain:

$$\hat{\mu}_{\cdot 1} = \frac{\bar{Y}_{11\cdot} + \bar{Y}_{21\cdot}}{2} = \frac{2.0 + 2.4}{2} = 2.2$$

$$\hat{\mu}_{\cdot 2} = \frac{\bar{Y}_{12\cdot} + \bar{Y}_{22\cdot}}{2} = \frac{1.9 + 2.1}{2} = 2.0$$

$$\hat{\mu}_{\cdot 3} = \frac{\bar{Y}_{13\cdot} + \bar{Y}_{23\cdot}}{2} = \frac{.9 + .9}{2} = .9$$

$$\hat{D}_1 = \hat{\mu}_{\cdot 1} - \hat{\mu}_{\cdot 2} = 2.2 - 2.0 = .2$$

$$\hat{D}_2 = \hat{\mu}_{\cdot 1} - \hat{\mu}_{\cdot 3} = 2.2 - .9 = 1.3$$

$$\hat{D}_3 = \hat{\mu}_{\cdot 2} - \hat{\mu}_{\cdot 3} = 2.0 - .9 = 1.1$$

$$s^2\{\hat{D}_1\} = \frac{.1625}{(2)^2}\left(\frac{1}{3} + \frac{1}{2} + \frac{1}{1} + \frac{1}{3}\right) = .0880 \qquad s\{\hat{D}_1\} = .297$$

$$s^2\{\hat{D}_2\} = \frac{.1625}{(2)^2}\left(\frac{1}{3} + \frac{1}{2} + \frac{1}{1} + \frac{1}{3}\right) = .0880 \qquad s\{\hat{D}_2\} = .297$$

$$s^2\{\hat{D}_3\} = \frac{.1625}{(2)^2}\left(\frac{1}{2} + \frac{1}{2} + \frac{1}{3} + \frac{1}{3}\right) = .0677 \qquad s\{\hat{D}_3\} = .260$$

For a 90 percent family confidence coefficient, we require:

$$T = \frac{1}{\sqrt{2}}q(.90; 3, 8) = \frac{1}{\sqrt{2}}(3.37) = 2.38$$

Hence, we obtain the following confidence intervals:

$$-.51 = .2 - 2.38(.297) \leq \mu_{\cdot 1} - \mu_{\cdot 2} \leq .2 + 2.38(.297) = .91$$

$$.59 = 1.3 - 2.38(.297) \leq \mu_{\cdot 1} - \mu_{\cdot 3} \leq 1.3 + 2.38(.297) = 2.01$$

$$.48 = 1.1 - 2.38(.260) \leq \mu_{\cdot 2} - \mu_{\cdot 3} \leq 1.1 + 2.38(.260) = 1.72$$

We conclude from these confidence intervals with 90 percent family confidence coefficient that growth–hormone–deficient short children with mildly depressed bone development on the average have a substantially smaller increase in the growth rate than children with either moderately depressed or severely depressed bone development. Further, the latter two groups of children do not show significantly different mean changes in the growth rate. We summarize these findings in the following line plot of the estimated factor level means:

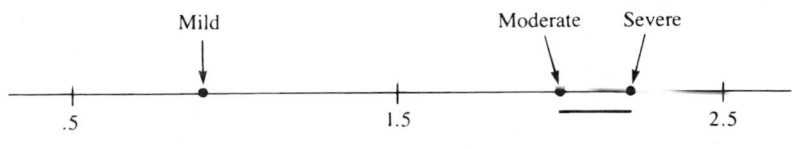

Change in Growth Rate

Example 2—Single Degree of Freedom Test

In the growth hormone example, a researcher wanted to know whether children with only mildly depressed bone development obtain, on the average, any increase in the growth rate with administration of growth hormone. Thus, the alternatives to be considered are those for a one-sided test:

$$H_0: \mu_{.3} \leq 0$$

$$H_a: \mu_{.3} > 0$$

The level of significance is to be controlled at $\alpha = .05$.

The test statistic to be employed is:

$$t^* = \frac{\hat{\mu}_{.3}}{s\{\hat{\mu}_{.3}\}}$$

We found earlier that $\hat{\mu}_{.3} = .9$ and $MSE = .1625$. Using (22.13), we obtain:

$$s^2\{\hat{\mu}_{.3}\} = \frac{.1625}{(2)^2}\left(\frac{1}{2} + \frac{1}{3}\right) = .0339 \qquad s\{\hat{\mu}_{.3}\} = .184$$

Hence, the test statistic is:

$$t^* = \frac{.9}{.184} = 4.89$$

For $\alpha = .05$, we require $t(.95; 8) = 1.860$. Therefore the one-sided decision rule is:

$$\text{If } t^* \leq 1.860, \text{ conclude } H_0$$

$$\text{If } t^* > 1.860, \text{ conclude } H_a$$

Since $t^* = 4.89 > 1.860$, we conclude H_a, that the mean change in the growth rate for children with mildly depressed bone development is greater than zero. The one-sided P-value for this test statistic is .0006.

22.4 Empty Cells in Two-Factor Studies

Occasionally after a two-factor study has been completed, it turns out that there are no cases in one or several treatment cells. Not only are the treatment sample sizes unequal then, but there is no sample information about the treatment means for the empty cells. Consider again Table 22.1 for the growth hormone study. Note that two female children with severely depressed bone condition dropped out of the study before its completion so that only one case ($n_{21} = 1$) is present for that treatment. We can imagine easily that all three of these children could have dropped out of the study. Then we would have had $n_{21} = 0$, and no sample information would have been available about the treatment mean μ_{21}.

FIGURE 22.2 **Schematic Representation of Growth Hormone Study with Empty Cell—Growth Hormone Example ($n_{21} = 0$).**

Gender	Bone Development		
	Severely Depressed B_1	Moderately Depressed B_2	Mildly Depressed B_3

(a) Empty Cell

Male (A_1)	μ_{11}	μ_{12}	μ_{13}
Female (A_2)	Empty cell	μ_{22}	μ_{23}

(b) Partial Study of Interactions

Male (A_1)		μ_{12}	μ_{13}
Female (A_2)		μ_{22}	μ_{23}

(c) Partial Study of Factor A and Factor B Main Effects

Male (A_1)		μ_{12}	μ_{13}
Female (A_2)		μ_{22}	μ_{23}

(d) Partial Study of Factor B Main Effects

Male (A_1)	μ_{11}	μ_{12}	μ_{13}
Female (A_2)			

Partial Analysis of Factor Effects

When one or several treatment cells are empty, the analysis of variance for unequal sample sizes by means of the equivalent regression model, as explained earlier, cannot be conducted. This does not mean, however, that the entire two-factor study has become useless. A variety of partial analyses usually can be conducted that will provide at least some information about the nature of the factor effects. The analyses that can be undertaken depend on the particular cells for which no sample information is available. We illustrate by means of an example how partial information can be obtained from two-factor studies with empty cells.

Example. In the growth hormone example, suppose that there are no observations for female children with severely depressed bone development; i.e., $n_{21} = 0$. In that case no sample information is available about the treatment mean μ_{21}. We represent this situation in Figure 22.2a.

Partial information about interactions can still be obtained by restricting attention to children with moderately depressed and mildly depressed bone development, as represented in Figure 22.2b. For these children, interactions are present if the differences between the treatment means for the two genders are not the same for the two bone development groups. The two differences are:

$$\mu_{12} - \mu_{22} \qquad \mu_{13} - \mu_{23}$$

Thus, we consider the following contrast among the treatment means:

$$L = \mu_{12} - \mu_{22} - \mu_{13} + \mu_{23}$$

We can either estimate L by means of a confidence interval and note whether or not the interval includes zero, or we can conduct a single degree of freedom test to establish whether or not interactions are present. With either approach, we use MSE based on all sample observations so that the associated degrees of freedom for MSE would be $n_T - (ab - 1) = 13 - 5 = 8$ (remember that $n_{21} = 0$ now).

If the partial analysis of interactions were to suggest that no interactions are present, the effect of gender can be studied by comparing the factor level means excluding children with severely depressed bone development, as represented in Figure 22.2c:

$$\mu_{1.} = \frac{\mu_{12} + \mu_{13}}{2} \qquad \mu_{2.} = \frac{\mu_{22} + \mu_{23}}{2}$$

In addition, the effect of bone development can be studied for male children by comparing the treatment means μ_{11}, μ_{12}, and μ_{13}, as represented in Figure 22.2d, or it can be studied for children of both genders by excluding those with severely depressed bone development, as represented in Figure 22.2c:

$$\mu_{.2} = \frac{\mu_{12} + \mu_{22}}{2} \qquad \mu_{.3} = \frac{\mu_{13} + \mu_{23}}{2}$$

Analysis if Model with No Interactions Can Be Employed

Occasionally, information is available from previous studies that the two factors in a two-factor study do not interact. In that case, a model with no interaction effects can be employed. Such a model was introduced in (21.1) for the case $n = 1$. When there are n_{ij} observations for the treatment consisting of the ith level of factor A and the jth level of factor B, the no-interaction model is:

$$(22.21) \qquad\qquad Y_{ijk} = \mu_{..} + \alpha_i + \beta_j + \varepsilon_{ijk} \qquad\qquad \text{No-interaction model}$$

When no-interaction model (22.21) is appropriate, the analysis of variance and the analysis of factor main effects can be conducted by means of the equivalent regression model even when one or several cells are empty, as long as relevant other cells are not empty. [The relevant other cells are ones that satisfy the relations in (19.7b).]

The reason why the usual analysis of variance by means of the equivalent regression model can be conducted for ANOVA model (22.21), even though one or more cells are empty, is that the assumption of no interactions permits us in effect to estimate the empty cell means. Conceptually, estimation of an empty cell mean, say μ_{21}, requires two steps. First, we need to estimate the treatment means for the nonempty cells. These estimates are more complicated than simply using the estimated treatment means because the model assumption of no interactions needs to be utilized. We encountered such estimates for a no-interaction model in Chapter 21 when we considered studies where $n = 1$ for each cell. Once we have estimates of the treatment means μ_{ij} for the nonempty cells, the second step in estimating the empty cell mean μ_{21} is to utilize the relation in (19.7b) for the no-interaction case, whereby we can express μ_{21} in terms of three other treatment means. For instance, μ_{21} can be estimated from $\hat{\mu}_{21} = \hat{\mu}_{22} + \hat{\mu}_{11} - \hat{\mu}_{12}$.

Example.   In the growth hormone example, suppose that the cell for female children with severely depressed bone development is empty. From past knowledge, the researcher is able to assume that there are no interactions between gender and bone development. In that case, regression model (22.4) reduces to:

$$(22.22) \qquad Y_{ijk} = \mu_{..} + \alpha_1 X_{ijk1} + \beta_1 X_{ijk2} + \beta_2 X_{ijk3} + \varepsilon_{ijk} \qquad \text{Full model}$$

To test for, say, gender main effects, we first fit this full model and obtain $SSE(F)$. The alternatives to be tested are:

$$H_0: \alpha_1 = 0$$

$$H_a: \alpha_1 \neq 0$$

Hence, the reduced model is:

$$(22.23) \qquad Y_{ijk} = \mu_{..} + \beta_1 X_{ijk2} + \beta_2 X_{ijk3} + \varepsilon_{ijk} \qquad \text{Reduced model}$$

We then fit this reduced model, obtain $SSE(R)$, and calculate the general linear test statistic (2.70) in the usual fashion. A test for bone development effects is carried out similarly.

Comments

1. We need to caution that it is not appropriate in the presence of empty cells to use a no-interaction model as the full model when no prior information about the absence of interactions is available. Only partial analyses of factor effects should then be undertaken, as explained earlier.

2. We have considered one cause of empty cells, when cases are missing or lost at random in an experimental study or when the sample in an observational study fails to include any cases for a particular cell. In these situations, the cell mean for the empty cell exists even though no cases are available for that cell. In contrast, a *structural empty cell* occurs when it is known a priori that it is impossible to obtain data for that cell. In this latter situation, the factorial structure is partially destroyed since the cell mean for the empty cell does not exist, and it is therefore meaningless to estimate the mean for such a structural empty cell based on the other cases.   ∎

22.5   ANOVA Inferences when Treatment Means Are of Unequal Importance

On occasion, the treatment means μ_{ij} in a two-factor study are not of equal importance so that the unweighted factor level means $\mu_{.j}$ and $\mu_{i.}$ defined in (19.1) and (19.2) are not relevant. Recall in the breakfast cereal study mentioned earlier that 60 percent of the consumers of this product were children, 20 percent male adults, and 20 percent female adults. In this study, factor A was type of sweetener ($i = 1$: corn syrup, $i = 2$: low-calorie sweetener) and factor B was consumer category ($j = 1$: child, $j = 2$: male adult, $j = 3$: female adult). The company wishes to determine if a change to a low-calorie sweetener will change the mean rating of its product in the *population of consumers*. Here, the treatment means μ_{ij} have unequal importance and the company therefore wishes to compare the two weighted means:

$$\text{Corn syrup:} \quad .6\mu_{11} + .2\mu_{12} + .2\mu_{13}$$

$$\text{Low-calorie sweetener:} \quad .6\mu_{21} + .2\mu_{22} + .2\mu_{23}$$

This can be done by estimating the contrast:

$$L = (.6\mu_{11} + .2\mu_{12} + .2\mu_{13}) - (.6\mu_{21} + .2\mu_{22} + .2\mu_{23})$$

or by testing the alternatives:

$$H_0: \ L = 0$$

$$H_a: \ L \neq 0$$

Note the use of the weights .6, .2, and .2 to reflect the unequal importance of the treatment means μ_{ij}.

Estimation of Treatment Means and Factor Effects

Estimation of treatment means and factor effects when the treatment means have unequal importance does not lead to any additional complexities. The general formulas in Section 22.3 for estimating treatment means μ_{ij} and for contrasts of treatment means still apply. We illustrate the analysis of factor effects when the treatment means are of unequal importance by returning to the mathematics learning example in Table 20.2.

Example.   A school administrator in the mathematics learning example had requested information about which teaching method leads to better learning of college mathematics when 20 percent of the students in the class have excellent quantitative ability, 50 percent have good ability, and 30 percent have moderate ability. The mean learning scores for such a class mix with the two teaching methods are the following linear combinations of the treatment means:

$$\text{Abstract method:} \quad L_1 = .2\mu_{11} + .5\mu_{12} + .3\mu_{13}$$

$$\text{Standard method:} \quad L_2 = .2\mu_{21} + .5\mu_{22} + .3\mu_{23}$$

We assume here that the mean learning scores for students with different quantitative abilities will not be affected by a class mix that is somewhat different from the one in the experimental study.

Point estimates of the mean scores are (data in Table 20.2a):

$$\hat{L}_1 = .2(92) + .5(81) + .3(73) = 80.8$$

$$\hat{L}_2 = .2(90) + .5(86) + .3(82) = 85.6$$

The difference between the two mean scores is a contrast:

$$L = L_1 - L_2$$

This contrast is estimated to be:

$$\hat{L} = \hat{L}_1 - \hat{L}_2 = 80.8 \quad 85.6 - -4.8$$

We can obtain the estimated variance of $\hat{L}$ by (20.37b) since there are equal sample sizes here:

$$s^2\{\hat{L}\} = \frac{28}{21}[(.2)^2 + (.5)^2 + (.3)^2 + (-.2)^2 + (-.5)^2 + (-.3)^2] = 1.013$$

so that the estimated standard deviation is $s\{\hat{L}\} = 1.006$. For a 95 percent confidence coefficient, we require $t(.975; 120) = 1.980$. Hence, the confidence limits are $-4.8 \pm 1.980(1.006)$ and the desired confidence interval is:

$$-6.79 \leq L \leq -2.81$$

With 95 percent confidence we conclude that the standard teaching method is better for the specified class mix, leading to a mean learning score that is at least 2.8 points greater than that for the abstract teaching method and may be as much as 6.8 points greater.

Test for Interactions

The test for interactions also is not affected by unequal importance of treatment means since this test is concerned with the parallelism, or lack of it, of the treatment mean curves. This was illustrated in Figures 19.1, 19.2, and 19.3. The treatment mean curves are based solely on the individual treatment means μ_{ij} and hence do not involve averages of the treatment means. Thus, the test for interactions is conducted as explained in Section 19.6 when the sample sizes are equal and as explained in Section 22.2 when the sample sizes are unequal, whether the treatment means are of equal or unequal importance.

Tests for Factor Main Effects by Use of Equivalent Regression Models

Tests for factor main effects when the treatment means are of unequal importance are carried out by the general linear test approach of Chapter 2. First, we shall explain how to implement factor tests with the general linear test approach by use of equivalent regression models; we then shall explain implementation by means of matrix formulation.

When the treatment means are of unequal importance, the use of equivalent regression models to carry out the general linear test approach is easiest when cell means model (19.15) is employed. Since no new principles with the regression approach are involved, we turn to an example to illustrate the tests for main effects.

Example. In the growth hormone example in Table 22.1, it is known that twice as many male as female children undergo growth hormone treatment therapy, and that this ratio is the same for children who have severe, moderate, and mild depression in bone development. Inferences are desired about the target population of children undergoing therapy. Specifically, we wish to test whether or not the state of bone development affects the change in growth rate in the target population. The alternatives therefore are:

$$H_0: \frac{2\mu_{11} + \mu_{21}}{3} = \frac{2\mu_{12} + \mu_{22}}{3} = \frac{2\mu_{13} + \mu_{23}}{3}$$

(22.24)

$$H_a: \text{ not all equalities hold}$$

We restate the alternative H_0 in the following equivalent fashion:

$$(22.24a) \qquad H_0: \begin{array}{c} \dfrac{2\mu_{11} + \mu_{21}}{3} - \dfrac{2\mu_{12} + \mu_{22}}{3} = 0 \\[3mm] \dfrac{2\mu_{11} + \mu_{21}}{3} - \dfrac{2\mu_{13} + \mu_{23}}{3} = 0 \end{array}$$

Implementation of the general linear test (2.70) requires that we fit the full model and then fit the reduced model under H_0. The full ANOVA model is cell means model (19.15):

$$Y_{ijk} = \mu_{ij} + \varepsilon_{ijk}$$

Following the example in (16.81), we obtain the equivalent full regression model:

$$(22.25) \quad Y_{ijk} = \mu_{11}X_{ijk1} + \mu_{12}X_{ijk2} + \mu_{13}X_{ijk3} + \mu_{21}X_{ijk4} + \mu_{22}X_{ijk5} + \mu_{23}X_{ijk6} + \varepsilon_{ijk}$$

Full model

where:

$$X_1 = \begin{array}{ll} 1 & \text{if case from level 1 of factor } A \text{ and level 1 of factor } B \\ 0 & \text{otherwise} \end{array}$$

$$X_2 = \begin{array}{ll} 1 & \text{if case from level 1 of factor } A \text{ and level 2 of factor } B \\ 0 & \text{otherwise} \end{array}$$

$$\vdots$$

$$X_6 = \begin{array}{ll} 1 & \text{if case from level 2 of factor } A \text{ and level 3 of factor } B \\ 0 & \text{otherwise} \end{array}$$

Table 22.6 repeats in column 1 a portion of the data on the Y observations from Table 22.1 and presents in columns 2–7 the codings of the X variables for the full model. Note, for instance, that the codings of the X variables for observation Y_{111} are $X_1 = 1$, $X_2 = X_3 = X_4 = X_5 = X_6 = 0$.

When Y in column 1 of Table 22.6 is regressed on the X variables in columns 2–7 for a no-intercept regression model, we obtain $SSE(F) = 1.3000$, associated with $df_F = 14 - 6 = 8$ degrees of freedom. These results, of course, are the same as in Table 22.3a when the equivalent regression model in the factor effects form was used.

To obtain the reduced regression model under H_0, we need to incorporate the conditions in (22.24a) into the full model. We shall do this by solving the system of two equations in (22.24a) for any two of the parameters and replacing these two parameters in the full model by the resulting expressions. Arbitrarily choosing μ_{21} and μ_{23}, we find in solving the two equations in (22.24a):

$$(22.26) \qquad \begin{array}{l} \mu_{21} = 2\mu_{12} + \mu_{22} - 2\mu_{11} \\[2mm] \mu_{23} = 2\mu_{12} - 2\mu_{13} + \mu_{22} \end{array}$$

Replacing μ_{21} and μ_{23} in full model (22.25) by the expressions in (22.26), we obtain the reduced model:

$$Y_{ijk} = \mu_{11}X_{ijk1} + \mu_{12}X_{ijk2} + \mu_{13}X_{ijk3} + (2\mu_{12} + \mu_{22} - 2\mu_{11})X_{ijk4}$$
$$+ \mu_{22}X_{ijk5} + (2\mu_{12} - 2\mu_{13} + \mu_{22})X_{ijk6} + \varepsilon_{ijk}$$

TABLE 22.6 **Data for Regression Fits when Treatment Means of Unequal Importance—Growth Hormone Example.**

			(1)	(2)	(3)	(4)	(5)	(6)	(7)	(8)	(9)	(10)	(11)
						Full Model					Reduced Model		
i	j	k	Y	X_1	X_2	X_3	X_4	X_5	X_6	Z_1	Z_2	Z_3	Z_4
1	1	1	1.4	1	0	0	0	0	0	1	0	0	0
1	1	2	2.4	1	0	0	0	0	0	1	0	0	0
...			...	...	...	...	...	...	...	...	...	...	...
1	2	2	1.7	0	1	0	0	0	0	0	1	0	0
1	3	1	.7	0	0	1	0	0	0	0	0	1	0
...			...	...	...	...	...	...	...	...	...	...	...
2	3	2	.9	0	0	0	0	0	1	0	2	-2	1
2	3	3	1.3	0	0	0	0	0	1	0	2	-2	1

This model can be simplified algebraically, as follows:

$$(22.27) \qquad Y_{ijk} = \mu_{11}Z_{ijk1} + \mu_{12}Z_{ijk2} + \mu_{13}Z_{ijk3} + \mu_{22}Z_{ijk4} + \varepsilon_{ijk} \qquad \text{Reduced model}$$

where:

$$Z_{ijk1} = X_{ijk1} - 2X_{ijk4}$$
$$Z_{ijk2} = X_{ijk2} + 2X_{ijk4} + 2X_{ijk6}$$
$$Z_{ijk3} = X_{ijk3} - 2X_{ijk6}$$
$$Z_{ijk4} = X_{ijk4} + X_{ijk5} + X_{ijk6}$$

Table 22.6 shows the codings of the new Z variables in columns 8–11. For instance, the codings for the new Z variables associated with Y_{111} are obtained as follows:

$$X_1 = 1 \qquad X_2 = 0 \qquad X_3 = 0 \qquad X_4 = 0 \qquad X_5 = 0 \qquad X_6 = 0$$

$$Z_1 = 1 - 2(0) = 1$$
$$Z_2 = 0 + 2(0) + 2(0) = 0$$
$$Z_3 = 0 - 2(0) = 0$$
$$Z_4 = 0 + 0 + 0 = 0$$

When Y in column 1 of Table 22.6 is regressed on the Z variables in columns 8–11 with a no-intercept regression model, we obtain $SSE(R) = 4.754$ and $df_R = 14 - 4 = 10$. Hence, the general linear test statistic (2.70) is:

$$F^* = \frac{SSE(R) - SSE(F)}{df_R - df_F} \div \frac{SSE(F)}{df_F}$$
$$= \frac{4.754 - 1.3000}{10 - 8} \div \frac{1.3000}{8} = 10.63$$

If H_0 holds, F^* follows the F distribution with 2 and 8 degrees of freedom. To control the level of significance at $\alpha = .05$, we require $F(.95; 2, 8) = 4.46$. Since $F^* = 10.63 > 4.46$, we conclude H_a, that the weighted mean change in the growth rate is not the same for the three bone development groups. The P-value of this test is .006.

Tests for Factor Main Effects by Use of Matrix Formulation

We saw in the growth hormone example when using the equivalent regression models to implement the general linear test approach that it was necessary to solve a system of two equations in six unknown parameters in terms of any two of the parameters. As the number of equations in H_0 increases, the algebra can become quite tedious. Under these circumstances, it may be easier to carry out the F test when the treatment means are of unequal importance by means of formulating the general linear test in matrix terms.

The full model, as before in (22.25), is represented by:

$$(22.28) \qquad \underset{n \times 1}{\mathbf{Y}} = \underset{n \times p}{\mathbf{X}} \underset{p \times 1}{\boldsymbol{\beta}} + \underset{n \times 1}{\boldsymbol{\varepsilon}}$$

For the growth hormone example, the $\mathbf{X}$ matrix is a 14×6 matrix consisting of the columns for X_1–X_6 in Table 22.6, and the $\boldsymbol{\beta}$ vector is:

$$\underset{6 \times 1}{\boldsymbol{\beta}} = \begin{bmatrix} \mu_{11} \\ \mu_{12} \\ \mu_{13} \\ \mu_{21} \\ \mu_{22} \\ \mu_{23} \end{bmatrix}$$

The least squares and maximum likelihood estimators of the parameters in the full normal error model (22.28) will now be denoted by $\mathbf{b}_F$ and are, as before, given by (6.25):

$$(22.29) \qquad \mathbf{b}_F = (\mathbf{X}'\mathbf{X})^{-1}\mathbf{X}'\mathbf{Y}$$

Also, the error sum of squares is given by (6.35):

$$(22.30) \qquad SSE(F) = (\mathbf{Y} - \mathbf{X}\mathbf{b}_F)'(\mathbf{Y} - \mathbf{X}\mathbf{b}_F) = \mathbf{Y}'\mathbf{Y} - \mathbf{b}_F'\mathbf{X}'\mathbf{Y}$$

A linear test hypothesis H_0 is represented in matrix form as follows:

$$(22.31) \qquad H_0: \underset{s \times p}{\mathbf{C}} \underset{p \times 1}{\boldsymbol{\beta}} = \underset{s \times 1}{\mathbf{h}}$$

where $\mathbf{C}$ is a specified $s \times p$ matrix of rank s and $\mathbf{h}$ is a specified $s \times 1$ vector. For the growth hormone example, the hypothesis H_0 in (22.24a) can be stated in the form (22.31) with the following matrices:

$$\underset{2 \times 6}{\mathbf{C}} = \begin{bmatrix} \frac{2}{3} & -\frac{2}{3} & 0 & \frac{1}{3} & -\frac{1}{3} & 0 \\ \frac{2}{3} & 0 & -\frac{2}{3} & \frac{1}{3} & 0 & -\frac{1}{3} \end{bmatrix}$$

$$\boldsymbol{\beta}_{6\times1} = \begin{bmatrix} \mu_{11} \\ \mu_{12} \\ \mu_{13} \\ \mu_{21} \\ \mu_{22} \\ \mu_{23} \end{bmatrix} \qquad \mathbf{h}_{2\times1} = \begin{bmatrix} 0 \\ 0 \end{bmatrix}$$

Note that this formulation yields (22.24a):

$$\mathbf{C}\boldsymbol{\beta}_{2\times1} = \begin{bmatrix} \frac{2}{3}\mu_{11} - \frac{2}{3}\mu_{12} + \frac{1}{3}\mu_{21} - \frac{1}{3}\mu_{22} \\ \frac{2}{3}\mu_{11} - \frac{2}{3}\mu_{13} + \frac{1}{3}\mu_{21} - \frac{1}{3}\mu_{23} \end{bmatrix} = \begin{bmatrix} 0 \\ 0 \end{bmatrix} = \mathbf{h}$$

The reduced model then is:

$$(22.32) \qquad\qquad \mathbf{Y} = \mathbf{X}\boldsymbol{\beta} + \boldsymbol{\varepsilon} \qquad \text{where} \qquad \mathbf{C}\boldsymbol{\beta} = \mathbf{h}$$

It can be shown that the least squares and maximum likelihood estimators under the reduced model, to be denoted by $\mathbf{b}_R$, are:

$$(22.33) \qquad\qquad \mathbf{b}_R = \mathbf{b}_F - (\mathbf{X}'\mathbf{X})^{-1}\mathbf{C}'(\mathbf{C}(\mathbf{X}'\mathbf{X})^{-1}\mathbf{C}')^{-1}(\mathbf{C}\mathbf{b}_F - \mathbf{h})$$

and the error sum of squares is:

$$(22.34) \qquad\qquad SSE(R) = (\mathbf{Y} - \mathbf{X}\mathbf{b}_R)'(\mathbf{Y} - \mathbf{X}\mathbf{b}_R)$$

which has associated with it $df_R = n - (p - s)$ degrees of freedom. It can be shown also that the difference $SSE(R) - SSE(F)$ can be expressed as follows:

$$(22.35) \qquad\qquad SSE(R) - SSE(F) = (\mathbf{C}\mathbf{b}_F - \mathbf{h})'(\mathbf{C}(\mathbf{X}'\mathbf{X})^{-1}\mathbf{C}')^{-1}(\mathbf{C}\mathbf{b}_F - \mathbf{h})$$

which has associated with it $df_R - df_F = (n - p + s) - (n - p) = s$ degrees of freedom. Hence, the general linear test statistic (2.70) here is:

$$(22.36) \qquad\qquad F^* = \frac{SSE(R) - SSE(F)}{s} \div \frac{SSE(F)}{n - p}$$

where $SSE(R) - SSE(F)$ is given by (22.35) and $SSE(F)$ is given by (22.30). Note for the growth hormone example that the numerator degrees of freedom are $s = 2$ and the denominator degrees of freedom are $n - p = 14 - 6 = 8$, which agree with the degrees of freedom obtained when using the equivalent regression models.

Comments

1. Many of the major statistical packages require only that the user furnish H_0 in the matrix form (22.31) and will then conduct the general linear test.

2. The least squares estimators $\mathbf{b}_R$ in (22.33) under the reduced model can be derived by minimizing the least squares criterion $Q = (\mathbf{Y} - \mathbf{X}\boldsymbol{\beta})'(\mathbf{Y} - \mathbf{X}\boldsymbol{\beta})$ subject to the constraint $\mathbf{C}\boldsymbol{\beta} - \mathbf{h} = \mathbf{0}$, using Lagrange multipliers.

3. The test for the alternatives (22.24a) in the growth hormone example can also be conducted by estimating the two contrasts:

$$L_1 = \frac{2\mu_{11} + \mu_{21}}{3} - \frac{2\mu_{12} + \mu_{22}}{3} \qquad L_2 = \frac{2\mu_{11} + \mu_{21}}{3} - \frac{2\mu_{13} + \mu_{23}}{3}$$

with a multiple comparison procedure (e.g., the Bonferroni procedure) and noting whether or not both confidence intervals include zero. ∎

Tests for Factor Main Effects when Weights Are Proportional to Sample Sizes

Simplifications in determining the term $SSE(R) - SSE(F)$ in the general linear test statistic for testing factor A and factor B main effects occur when the weights for the treatment means μ_{ij} are proportional to the treatment sample sizes n_{ij}. Such weights are appropriate in some circumstances but not in many others.

Consider a study of retail stores. The effects on shoplifting losses of size of store (factor A) and location of store within the city (factor B) are to be studied. Inferences about all retail stores in the population of interest are to be made. A random sample of n_T retail stores is selected from the population of all stores, and the selected stores are then classified by size and location. We denote the resulting cell sample sizes as usual by n_{ij}. If the proportions of stores in the different size-location groups in the population were known, these known proportions would serve as the appropriate weights in making inferences about size and location main effects, and the general linear test procedures just discussed would be employed. Often, however, these proportions are not known. Under these conditions, the cell sample sizes n_{ij} may be used to estimate the unknown proportions and therefore may serve as reasonable weights.

To illustrate this, suppose that $a = 2$ store sizes and $b = 3$ locations are employed in the study of retail stores, and that a random sample of $n_T = 60$ stores resulted in the following cell sample sizes n_{ij}:

Store Size	Location (j)			
i	$j = 1$	$j = 2$	$j = 3$	Total
$i = 1$	20	5	4	29
$i = 2$	10	15	6	31
Total	30	20	10	60

Thus $n_{11} = 20$, $n_{21} = 10$, and so on. Further, denoting by $n_{i\cdot}$ and $n_{\cdot j}$ the total factor A and factor B level sample sizes as defined in (22.1a) and (22.1b), respectively, we have $n_{1\cdot} = 29$, $n_{\cdot 1} = 30$, and so on.

The test for factor A main effects, when the sample sizes n_{ij} reflect the importance of the treatment means, would then involve a comparison of the weighted mean for factor A level $i = 1$:

$$\frac{20\mu_{11} + 5\mu_{12} + 4\mu_{13}}{29}$$

and the weighted mean for factor A level $i = 2$:

$$\frac{10\mu_{21} + 15\mu_{22} + 6\mu_{23}}{31}$$

Expressed in symbolic notation, the alternatives would be:

$$H_0: \left(\frac{n_{11}}{n_{1\cdot}}\right)\mu_{11} + \left(\frac{n_{12}}{n_{1\cdot}}\right)\mu_{12} + \left(\frac{n_{13}}{n_{1\cdot}}\right)\mu_{13} = \left(\frac{n_{21}}{n_{2\cdot}}\right)\mu_{21} + \left(\frac{n_{22}}{n_{2\cdot}}\right)\mu_{22} + \left(\frac{n_{23}}{n_{2\cdot}}\right)\mu_{23}$$

H_a: equality does not hold

Similarly, the alternatives for testing factor B main effects would be as follows when the sample sizes reflect the importance of the treatment means:

$$H_0: \left(\frac{n_{11}}{n_{\cdot1}}\right)\mu_{11} + \left(\frac{n_{21}}{n_{\cdot1}}\right)\mu_{21} = \left(\frac{n_{12}}{n_{\cdot2}}\right)\mu_{12} + \left(\frac{n_{22}}{n_{\cdot2}}\right)\mu_{22} = \left(\frac{n_{13}}{n_{\cdot3}}\right)\mu_{13} + \left(\frac{n_{23}}{n_{\cdot3}}\right)\mu_{23}$$

H_a: not all equalities hold

We must caution that sample sizes often do not reflect appropriate importance. Sample sizes may have been chosen arbitrarily or they may reflect unequal attrition losses in a study. Sample sizes may reflect cost considerations; for instance, larger sample sizes may be used by a market researcher for children than for adults because selection costs are lower. In all of these instances, use of weights based on sample sizes may lead to misleading inferences.

When sample sizes do constitute appropriate weights, the alternatives for testing for factor A main effects can be stated in general as follows:

(22.37)
$$H_0: \sum_j \left(\frac{n_{1j}}{n_{1\cdot}}\right)\mu_{1j} = \cdots = \sum_j \left(\frac{n_{aj}}{n_{a\cdot}}\right)\mu_{aj}$$

H_a: not all equalities hold

and the alternatives for testing for factor B main effects are:

(22.38)
$$H_0: \sum_i \left(\frac{n_{i1}}{n_{\cdot1}}\right)\mu_{i1} = \cdots = \sum_i \left(\frac{n_{ib}}{n_{\cdot b}}\right)\mu_{ib}$$

H_a: not all equalities hold

It can be shown that the term $SSE(R) - SSE(F)$ for testing factor A main effects involving the alternatives in (22.37) simplifies to the ordinary single-factor treatment sum of squares in (16.28), with the factor A levels considered to be the treatments:

(22.39)
$$SSA = \sum_i n_{i\cdot}(\bar{Y}_{i\cdot\cdot} - \bar{Y}_{\cdots})^2$$

where:

(22.39a)
$$\bar{Y}_{i\cdot\cdot} = \frac{Y_{i\cdot\cdot}}{n_{i\cdot}}$$

(22.39b)
$$\bar{Y}_{\cdots} = \frac{Y_{\cdots}}{n_T}$$

(22.39c)
$$Y_{i\cdot\cdot} = \sum_{j=1}^{b}\sum_{k=1}^{n_{ij}} Y_{ijk}$$

(22.39d)
$$Y_{\ldots} = \sum_{i=1}^{a} \sum_{j=1}^{b} \sum_{k=1}^{n_{ij}} Y_{ijk}$$

Similarly, the term $SSE(R) - SSE(F)$ for testing factor B main effects involving the alternatives in (22.38) simplifies to the single-factor treatment sum of squares in (16.28), with the factor B levels considered to be the treatments:

(22.40)
$$SSB = \sum_{j} n_{.j} (\bar{Y}_{.j.} - \bar{Y}_{\ldots})^2$$

where:

(22.40a)
$$\bar{Y}_{.j.} = \frac{Y_{.j.}}{n_{.j}}$$

(22.40b)
$$Y_{.j.} = \sum_{i=1}^{a} \sum_{k=1}^{n_{ij}} Y_{ijk}$$

Example.   In the growth hormone example of Table 22.1, suppose that the treatment sample sizes n_{ij} reflect the relative importance of the treatment means. We saw in Section 22.2 that gender (factor A) and bone development (factor B) do not interact. We now wish to test whether gender affects the weighted mean change in the growth rate. The alternatives (22.37) here are:

$$H_0: \frac{3}{7}\mu_{11} + \frac{2}{7}\mu_{12} + \frac{2}{7}\mu_{13} = \frac{1}{7}\mu_{21} + \frac{3}{7}\mu_{22} + \frac{3}{7}\mu_{23}$$
$$H_a: \text{ equality does not hold}$$

To calculate SSA in (22.39), we require from Table 22.1:

$Y_{1..} = 11.6$	$n_{1.} = 7$	$\bar{Y}_{1..} = 1.65714$
$Y_{2..} = 11.4$	$n_{2.} = 7$	$\bar{Y}_{2..} = 1.62857$
$Y_{\ldots} = 23.0$	$n_T = 14$	$\bar{Y}_{\ldots} = 1.64286$

We then obtain:

$$SSA = 7(1.65714 - 1.64286)^2 + 7(1.62857 - 1.64286)^2 = .002857$$

The number of degrees of freedom associated with SSA is $a - 1 = 2 - 1 = 1$.

We found earlier in Table 22.3a that the error sum of squares for the full model is $SSE(F) = 1.3000$, with 8 degrees of freedom associated with it. Hence, the general linear test statistic here is:

$$F^* = \frac{SSE(R) - SSE(F)}{df_R - df_F} \div \frac{SSE(F)}{df_F} = \frac{SSA}{1} \div MSE(F)$$
$$= \frac{.002857}{1} \div \frac{1.3000}{8} = .018$$

For $\alpha = .05$, we require $F(.95; 1, 8) = 5.32$. Since $F^* = .018 \leq 5.32$, we conclude H_0, that the weighted mean change in the growth rate is the same for male and female children. The P-value of the test is .897.

The test for factor B main effects would be carried out in similar fashion.

Note

The cell sample sizes in alternatives (22.37) and (22.38) are considered to be fixed, not random variables. Thus, the relevance of the alternatives depends on the reasonableness of the actual cell sample sizes as indicators of the importance of the treatment means.   ∎

22.6   Statistical Computing Packages

Extreme care must be exercised when using packaged analysis of variance programs with unequal sample sizes because the default option of the package may not necessarily assign proper importance to each treatment mean. The user should read the package documentation carefully and make sure that the package generates the appropriate sums of squares for the tests of interest.

For the BMDP, MINITAB, SAS, SPSS, and SYSTAT statistical packages, the outputs that are the equivalents of the regression results obtained in Sections 22.1–22.3 for the case of treatment means with equal importance and no empty cells are obtained as follows at the time of this writing:

> BMDP2V—Default option
>
> MINITAB—GLM
>
> SAS PROC GLM—Type III or Type IV sums of squares
>
> SPSS ANOVA—Option 9
>
> SYSTAT—Default option

Extreme caution should also be used with ANOVA computer packages that provide results when some treatment cells are empty. The package may make assumptions about interactions that the researcher is unwilling to make. In the absence of a clear description of how the package handles empty cells, it is preferable that appropriate analyses be conducted without the assistance of the package other than for obtaining the estimated treatment means and *MSE*.

When weights assigned to the treatment means are proportional to the sample sizes, numerator sums of squares *SSA* and *SSB* given in (22.39) and (22.40) may be obtained using SAS PROC GLM—Type I sum of squares, SPSS ANOVA—Option 10, and SYSTAT—Option Weighted Means Model. BMDP 2V and MINITAB do not provide these results directly, although they can be obtained by running a separate, single-factor analysis of variance on each factor.

A simple option in using computer packages when the cell sample sizes are unequal, cell means have unequal importance, and/or some cells are empty is to use a single-factor ANOVA package that permits specification of contrasts to be estimated. The user can then specify the various contrasts of interest.

Problems

22.1.   A market research intern selected a random sample of 400 communities and classified them according to population size (four levels) and geographic region (five levels) to study the effects of these factors on sales of the company's products. When the intern found that the treatment sample sizes were unequal, the smallest cell frequency being four, the intern generated random numbers to reduce the number of communities in each cell to four and then proceeded to analyze the effects of population size and region on the basis of the 80 communities remaining.

   a.   Does the method of randomly discarding cases lead to any biases? Explain.

   b.   Was it wise for the intern to discard 320 cases randomly in order to obtain equal treatment sample sizes?

22.2.   A student asked: "If two-factor studies with unequal sample sizes must be analyzed by a regression approach, why bother with the two-factor analysis of variance model at all?" Comment.

√ 22.3.   Refer to **Cash offers** Problem 19.10. Suppose that observations $Y_{214} = 28$ and $Y_{323} = 20$ are missing because the offer received in each of these cases was a trade-in offer, not a cash offer.

   a.   State the ANOVA model for this case. Also state the equivalent regression model; use $1, -1, 0$ indicator variables.

   b.   Present the **X** and **β** matrices for the regression model in part (a).

   c.   Obtain **Xβ** and show that the proper treatment means are obtained by your model.

   d.   What is the reduced regression model for testing for interaction effects?

   e.   Test whether or not interaction effects are present by fitting the full and reduced regression models; use $\alpha = .05$. State the alternatives, decision rule, and conclusion. What is the P-value of the test?

   f.   State the reduced regression models for testing for age and gender main effects, respectively, and conduct each of the tests. Use $\alpha = .05$ each time and state the alternatives, decision rule, and conclusion. What is the P-value of each test?

   g.   To study the nature of the age main effects, estimate the following pairwise comparisons:

$$D_1 = \mu_1. - \mu_2. \qquad D_2 = \mu_1. - \mu_3. \qquad D_3 = \mu_2. - \mu_3.$$

   Use the most efficient multiple comparison procedure with a 90 percent family confidence coefficient.

   h.   In the population of female owners, 30 percent are young, 60 percent are middle-aged, and 10 percent are elderly. Estimate the mean cash offer for this population with a 95 percent confidence interval.

√ 22.4.   Refer to **Hay fever relief** Problem 19.14. Suppose that observations $Y_{113} = 2.3$, $Y_{221} = 8.9$, and $Y_{224} = 9.0$ are missing because the subjects did not immediately record the time when they began to suffer again from hay fever.

   a.   State the ANOVA model for this case. Also state the equivalent regression model; use $1, -1, 0$ indicator variables.

   b.   Present the **X** and **β** matrices for the regression model in part (a).

c. Obtain **Xβ** and show that the proper treatment means are obtained by your model.

d. What is the reduced regression model for testing for interaction effects?

e. Test whether or not interaction effects are present by fitting the full and reduced regression models; use $\alpha = .05$. State the alternatives, decision rule, and conclusion. What is the P-value of the test?

f. The nature of the interaction effects is to be studied by means of the following contrasts:

$$L_1 = \frac{\mu_{12} + \mu_{13}}{2} - \mu_{11} \qquad L_4 = L_2 - L_1$$

$$L_2 = \frac{\mu_{22} + \mu_{23}}{2} - \mu_{21} \qquad L_5 = L_3 - L_1$$

$$L_3 = \frac{\mu_{32} + \mu_{33}}{2} - \mu_{31} \qquad L_6 = L_3 - L_2$$

Obtain confidence intervals for these contrasts; use the Scheffé multiple comparison procedure with a 90 percent family confidence coefficient. Interpret your findings.

22.5. Refer to **Kidney failure hospitalization** Problem 19.18. Suppose that observations $Y_{124} = 12$, $Y_{216} = 2$, and $Y_{238} = 9$ are missing because the hospitalization records for these patients were not complete. Continue to work with the transformed data $Y' = \log_{10}(Y+1)$.

a. State the ANOVA model for this case. Also state the equivalent regression model; use $1, -1, 0$ indicator variables.

b. Present the **X** and **β** matrices for the regression model in part (a).

c. Obtain **Xβ** and show that the proper treatment means are obtained by your model.

d. What is the reduced regression model for testing for interaction effects?

e. Test whether or not interaction effects are present by fitting the full and reduced regression models; use $\alpha = .05$. State the alternatives, decision rule, and conclusion. What is the P-value of the test?

f. State the reduced regression models for testing for treatment duration and weight gain main effects, respectively. Conduct each of the tests. Use $\alpha = .05$ each time and state the alternatives, decision rule, and conclusion. What is the P-value of each test?

g. Use the single degree of freedom t^* statistic for testing whether or not the mean number of days hospitalized (in transformed units) for persons with mild weight gains exceeds .5; use $\alpha = .05$. State the alternatives, decision rule, and conclusion. What is the P-value of the test?

h. To analyze the nature of the factor main effects, estimate the following pairwise comparisons:

$$D_1 = \mu_{1.} - \mu_{2.} \qquad D_3 = \mu_{.3} - \mu_{.1}$$

$$D_2 = \mu_{.2} - \mu_{.1} \qquad D_4 = \mu_{.3} - \mu_{.2}$$

Use the Bonferroni procedure with a 90 percent family confidence coefficient. State your findings.

22.6. **Adjunct professors.** A sociologist selected a random sample of 45 adjunct professors who teach in the evening division of a large metropolitan university for a study of special problems associated with teaching in the evening division. The data collected include the amount of payment received by the faculty member for teaching a course during the past semester. The sociologist classified the faculty members by subject matter of course (factor A) and highest degree earned (factor B). The earnings per course (in thousand dollars) follow.

Factor A (subject matter)	Factor B (highest degree)		
	$j = 1$ Bachelor's	$j = 2$ Master's	$j = 3$ Doctorate
$i = 1$ Humanities	1.7	1.8	2.5
	1.9	2.1	2.7
			$\cdots$
			2.9
$i = 2$ Social sciences	2.5	2.7	3.5
	2.3	2.4	3.3
	$\cdots$	$\cdots$	$\cdots$
	2.4	2.5	3.4
$i = 3$ Engineering	2.7	2.9	3.7
	2.8	3.0	3.6
		$\cdots$	$\cdots$
		2.7	3.9
$i = 4$ Management	2.5	2.3	3.3
	2.6	2.8	3.4
			$\cdots$
			3.6

a. State the ANOVA model for this case. Also state the equivalent regression model; use $1, -1, 0$ indicator variables.

b. Present the $\mathbf{X}$ and $\boldsymbol{\beta}$ matrices for the regression model in part (a).

c. Obtain $\mathbf{X}\boldsymbol{\beta}$ and show that the proper treatment means are obtained by your model.

d. Fit the equivalent regression model and obtain the residuals. Prepare aligned residual dot plots for the treatments. What are your findings?

e. Prepare a normal probability plot of the residuals. Also obtain the coefficient of correlation between the ordered residuals and their expected values under normality. Does the normality assumption appear to be reasonable here?

22.7. Refer to **Adjunct professors** Problem 22.6. Assume that ANOVA model (19.23), is appropriate, except that now $k = 1, \ldots, n_{ij}$.

a. Plot the estimated treatment means $\overline{Y}_{ij\cdot}$ in the format of Figure 22.1. Does it appear that any factor effects are present? Explain.

b. What is the reduced regression model for testing for interaction effects?

c. Test whether or not interaction effects are present by fitting the full and reduced regression models; use $\alpha = .01$. State the alternatives, decision rule, and conclusion. What is the P-value of the test?

d. State the reduced regression models for testing for subject matter and highest degree main effects, respectively, and conduct each of the tests. Use $\alpha = .01$ each time and state the alternatives, decision rule, and conclusion. What is the P-value of each test?

e. Make all pairwise comparisons between the subject matter means; use the Tukey procedure with a 95 percent family confidence coefficient. State your findings and present a graphic summary.

f. Make all pairwise comparisons between the highest degree means; use the Tukey procedure with a 95 percent family confidence coefficient. State your findings and present a graphic summary.

22.8. Refer to **Adjunct professors** Problem 22.6. Suppose that the sociologist had prior information indicating that the two factors do not interact and that no-interaction model (22.21) is therefore appropriate.

   a. State the equivalent full regression model for this case. Also state the reduced regression models for testing for factor A and factor B main effects. Use $1, -1, 0$ indicator variables.

   b. Fit the full and reduced regression models and test for factor A and factor B main effects; use $\alpha = .05$ for each test. State the alternatives, decision rule, and conclusion for each test. What is the P-value of each test?

√ 22.9. Refer to **Hay fever relief** Problem 19.14. Suppose that the data for the treatment when each of the two active ingredients is at the medium level were lost and immediate analyses of the available data are required; i.e., assume that $n_T = 32$ and $n_{22} = 0$.

   a. To study whether or not interaction effects are present, estimate the following comparisons:

$$D_1 = \mu_{13} - \mu_{11} \qquad L_1 = D_1 - D_2$$

$$D_2 = \mu_{23} - \mu_{21} \qquad L_2 = D_1 - D_3$$

$$D_3 = \mu_{33} - \mu_{31}$$

   Use the Bonferroni procedure with a 90 percent family confidence coefficient. State your findings.

   b. To further explore the nature of possible interaction effects, conduct separate single degree of freedom tests of whether $\mu_{12} = \mu_{13}$ and whether $\mu_{32} = \mu_{33}$. Use $\alpha = .02$ for each test and state the alternatives, decision rule, and conclusion. What is the family level of significance, using the Bonferroni inequality?

22.10. Refer to **Kidney failure hospitalization** Problem 19.18. Suppose that there were no patients who received the dialysis treatment for long duration and had mild weight gains; i.e., assume that $n_T = 50$ and $n_{21} = 0$. Continue to work with the transformed data $Y' = \log_{10}(Y + 1)$.

   Based on related research, the analyst believes it is reasonable to assume that the two factors do not interact and that no-interaction model (22.21) is appropriate.

   a. State the equivalent full regression model for this case. Also state the reduced regression models for testing for factor A and factor B main effects. Use $1, -1, 0$ indicator variables in the regression model.

   b. Fit the full and reduced regression models. Test for factor A and factor B main effects; use $\alpha = .05$ for each test. State the alternatives, decision rule, and conclusion for each test. What is the P-value of each test?

√ 22.11. Refer to **Programmer requirements** Problem 19.20. Suppose that there were no programmers with experience on both small and large systems who had less than five years' experience; i.e., assume that $n_T = 20$ and $n_{21} = 0$.

a. To study whether or not interaction effects are present, estimate the following comparisons:

$$D_1 = \mu_{12} - \mu_{13} \qquad L_1 = D_1 - D_2$$
$$D_2 = \mu_{22} - \mu_{23}$$

Use the Bonferroni procedure with a 95 percent family confidence coefficient. State your findings.

b. To study further the nature of possible interaction effects, test whether or not μ_{22} exceeds μ_{23}; use $\alpha = .05$. State the alternatives, decision rule, and conclusion. What is the P-value of the test?

22.12. Refer to **Adjunct professors** Problem 22.6. Suppose that there were no professors teaching humanities courses who had only a bachelor's degree, so that the study consists of $n_T = 43$ adjunct professors and $n_{11} = 0$. On the basis of previous research, the sociologist believes it is reasonable to assume that the two factors do not interact and that no-interaction model (22.21) is appropriate here.

a. State the equivalent full regression model for this case. Also state the reduced regression models for testing for factor A and factor B main effects. Use 1, −1, 0 indicator variables in the regression model.

b. Fit the full and reduced regression models and test for factor A and factor B main effects. Use $\alpha = .01$ for each test and state the alternatives, decision rule, and conclusion. What is the P-value of each test?

√ 22.13. Refer to **Cash offers** Problem 19.10. It is known that in both populations of male and female owners, 30 percent are young, 60 percent are middle-aged, and 10 percent are elderly. Test by means of the single degree of freedom t^* test statistic whether or not the mean cash offers for male and female owners are equal; use $\alpha = .05$. State the alternatives, decision rule, and conclusion. What is the P-value of the test?

22.14. Refer to **Kidney failure hospitalization** Problem 19.18. Continue to work with the transformed data $Y' = \log_{10}(Y + 1)$. It is known that 75 percent of patients in each weight gain group receive the short duration treatment. Inferences are desired about the target population of patients at the dialysis facility.

a. Use cell means model (19.15) to express the two alternatives for testing whether or not factor B main effects are present in the form of (22.24a).

b. State the regression model equivalent to ANOVA model (19.15), using 1, 0 indicator variables.

c. State the reduced regression model for testing for factor B main effects; express μ_{11} and μ_{13} in terms of the other cell means.

d. Fit the full and reduced regression models and test for factor B main effects; use $\alpha = .05$. State the decision rule and conclusion. What is the P-value of the test?

e. Compare the mean number of days of hospitalization (in transformed units) for patients with severe and mild weight gains; use a 95 percent confidence interval.

22.15. Refer to **Adjunct professors** Problem 22.6. It is known that 10 percent of professors in each subject matter area have a bachelor's degree, 20 percent have a master's degree, and 70 percent have a doctorate. Inferences are desired about the target population of adjunct professors.

a. Use cell means model (19.15) to express the two alternatives for testing whether or not factor A main effects are present in the form of (22.24a).

b. Define the **X** matrix and $\boldsymbol{\beta}$ vector for expressing full model (19.15) in matrix form for this case.

c. Express the two alternatives in part (a) in matrix form (22.31).

d. Use (22.35) to calculate $SSE(R) - SSE(F)$.

e. Test whether or not factor A main effects are present; use $\alpha = .01$. State the decision rule and conclusion. What is the P-value of the test?

f. Compare the mean amounts of payment received by faculty members teaching humanities and engineering courses; use a 99 percent confidence interval. Interpret your interval estimate.

√ 22.16. Refer to **Programmer requirements** Problem 19.20. Suppose that the observations $Y_{133} = 68$, $Y_{134} = 58$, and $Y_{234} = 45$ did not exist and that the sample sizes reflect the importance of the treatment means. Test whether or not type of experience main effects are present; control the level of significance at $\alpha = .01$. State the alternatives, decision rule, and conclusion. What is the P-value of the test?

22.17. Refer to **Adjunct professors** Problem 22.6. Assume that the sample sizes reflect the importance of the treatment means. Test whether or not subject matter main effects are present; control the level of significance at $\alpha = .05$. State the alternatives, decision rule, and conclusion. What is the P-value of the test?

Exercises

22.18. Derive $\sigma^2\{\hat{L}\}$ for the estimated contrast involving μ_i. in (22.13).

22.19. Show that $s^2\{\hat{L}\}$ in (22.19) is an unbiased estimator of $\sigma^2\{\hat{L}\}$.

22.20. Consider a two-factor study where $a = 2$, $b = 2$, $n_{11} = n_{12} = n_{21} = 2$, $n_{22} = 1$, and no-interaction model (22.21) applies. Use the matrix methods in Section 22.5 to obtain the estimator of μ_{22}. [*Hint*: Begin with interaction model (22.3) as the full model, express the assumption of no interactions in the form of (22.31), and use (22.33) to obtain the estimator of μ_{22} for the no-interaction model.]

22.21. Refer to **Kidney failure hospitalization** Problem 22.10. Suppose that you are going to use the matrix approach in Section 22.5, rather than the regression approach, to test for factor A main effects.

a. State the **X** and $\boldsymbol{\beta}$ matrices to be used in the full model.

b. State the test hypothesis in matrix form (22.31).

Projects

22.22. Refer to the **SENIC** data set. The effects of region (factor A: variable 9) and average age of patients (factor B: variable 3) on mean length of hospital stay (variable 2) are to be studied. For purposes of this ANOVA study, average age is to be classified into three categories: under 52.0 years, 52.0–under 55.0 years, 55.0 years or more.

    a. State the ANOVA model for this case. Also state the equivalent regression model; use $1, -1, 0$ indicator variables.

    b. Fit the regression model, obtain the residuals, and prepare aligned residual dot plots for the treatments. What are your findings?

    c. Prepare a normal probability plot of the residuals. Also obtain the coefficient of correlation between the ordered residuals and their expected values under normality. Does the normality assumption appear to be reasonable here?

22.23. Refer to the **SENIC** data set and Project 22.22. Assume that ANOVA model (19.23), with $k = 1, \ldots, n_{ij}$, is appropriate.

    a. Plot the estimated treatment means $\bar{Y}_{ij}$. in the format of Figure 22.1. Does it appear that any factor effects are present? Explain.

    b. State the reduced regression model for testing for interaction effects.

    c. Fit the reduced regression model and test whether or not interaction effects are present; use $\alpha = .01$. State the alternatives, decision rule, and conclusion. What is the P-value of the test?

    d. State the reduced regression model for testing for factor A main effects. Conduct this test using $\alpha = .01$. State the alternatives, decision rule, and conclusion. What is the P-value of the test?

    e. State the reduced regression model for testing for factor B main effects. Conduct this test using $\alpha = .01$. State the alternatives, decision rule, and conclusion. What is the P-value of the test?

    f. Make all pairwise comparisons between regions; use the Tukey procedure and a 95 percent family confidence coefficient. State your findings and present a graphic summary.

22.24. Refer to the **SMSA** data set. The effects of region (factor A: variable 12) and percent of population in central cities (factor B: variable 4) on the crime rate (variable $11 \div$ variable 3) are to be studied. For purposes of this ANOVA study, percent of population in central cities is to be classified into three categories: under 30.0 percent, 30.0–under 50.0 percent, 50.0 percent or more.

    a. State the ANOVA model for this case. Also state the equivalent regression model; use $1, -1, 0$ indicator variables.

    b. Fit the regression model, obtain the residuals, and prepare aligned residual dot plots for the treatments. What are your findings?

    c. Prepare a normal probability plot of the residuals. Also obtain the coefficient of correlation between the ordered residuals and their expected values under normality. Does the normality assumption appear to be reasonable here?

22.25. Refer to the **SMSA** data set and Project 22.24. Assume that ANOVA model (19.23), with $k = 1, \ldots, n_{ij}$, is appropriate.

    a. Plot the estimated treatment means $\bar{Y}_{ij\cdot}$ in the format of Figure 22.1. Does it appear that any factor effects are present? Explain.

    b. State the reduced regression model for testing for interaction effects.

    c. Fit the reduced regression model and test whether or not interaction effects are present; use $\alpha = .005$. State the alternatives, decision rule, and conclusion. What is the P-value of the test?

    d. State the reduced regression model for testing for factor A main effects. Conduct this test using $\alpha = .005$. State the alternatives, decision rule, and conclusion. What is the P-value of the test?

    e. State the reduced regression model for testing for factor B main effects. Conduct this test using $\alpha = .005$. State the alternatives, decision rule, and conclusion. What is the P-value of the test?

    f. Make all pairwise comparisons between regions; use the Tukey procedure and a 95 percent family confidence coefficient. State your findings and present a graphic summary.

22.26. Refer to the **SENIC** data set and Projects 22.22 and 22.23. Assume that the sample sizes reflect the importance of the treatment means.

    a. Test for region (factor A) main effects; use $\alpha = .01$. State the alternatives, decision rule, and conclusion. What is the P-value of the test?

    b. Test for average age of patients (factor B) main effects; use $\alpha = .01$. State the alternatives, decision rule, and conclusion. What is the P-value of the test?

22.27. Refer to the **SMSA** data set and Projects 22.24 and 22.25. Assume that the sample sizes reflect the importance of the treatment means.

    a. Test for region (factor A) main effects; use $\alpha = .005$. State the alternatives, decision rule, and conclusion. What is the P-value of the test?

    b. Test for percent of population in central cities (factor B) main effects; use $\alpha = .005$. State the alternatives, decision rule, and conclusion. What is the P-value of the test?

Multifactor Studies

When three or more factors are studied simultaneously, the model and analysis employed are straightforward extensions of the two-factor case. We shall illustrate the nature of the extensions with reference to three-factor studies. Ordinarily, computer ANOVA packages will be utilized for performing the needed calculations for multifactor studies involving three or more factors. For completeness, however, we shall present the necessary definitional formulas for three-factor studies. ANOVA model I with fixed factor levels *when all treatment sample sizes are equal and all treatment means are of equal importance* is considered in Sections 23.1–23.5. The analysis of variance with unequal sample sizes is discussed in Section 23.6.

23.1 ANOVA Model I for Three-Factor Studies

We now turn to the development of ANOVA model I with fixed factor levels for three-factor studies. This ANOVA model will be applicable to observational studies and to experimental studies based on a completely randomized design.

Notation

Three factors, A, B, and C, are investigated at a, b, and c levels, respectively. The mean response for the treatment when factor A is at the ith level ($i = 1, \ldots, a$), factor B is at the jth level ($j = 1, \ldots, b$), and factor C is at the kth level ($k = 1, \ldots, c$) is denoted by μ_{ijk}. The number of cases for each treatment is assumed to be constant, denoted by n. We assume $n \geq 2$. The mean response when A is at the ith level and B is at the jth level is denoted by $\mu_{ij\cdot}$, and similar notation is used for other pairs of factor levels. Since all treatment means are assumed to have equal importance, we define:

(23.1a) $$\mu_{ij\cdot} = \frac{\sum_k \mu_{ijk}}{c}$$

(23.1b) $$\mu_{i\cdot k} = \frac{\sum_j \mu_{ijk}}{b}$$

TABLE 23.1   **Mean Learning Times according to Gender, Age, and Intelligence (in minutes)—Learning Example.**

Factor A— Gender	Intelligence (factor C) and Age (factor B)											
	$k = 1$ High IQ				$k = 2$ Normal IQ				Average			
	$j = 1$ Young	$j = 2$ Middle	$j = 3$ Old	Average	$j = 1$ Young	$j = 2$ Middle	$j = 3$ Old	Average	$j = 1$ Young	$j = 2$ Middle	$j = 3$ Old	Average
$i = 1$ Male	9 (μ_{111})	12 (μ_{121})	18 (μ_{131})	13 $(\mu_{1\cdot1})$	19 (μ_{112})	20 (μ_{122})	21 (μ_{132})	20 $(\mu_{1\cdot2})$	14 $(\mu_{11\cdot})$	16 $(\mu_{12\cdot})$	19.5 $(\mu_{13\cdot})$	16.5 $(\mu_{1\cdot\cdot})$
$i = 2$ Female	9 (μ_{211})	10 (μ_{221})	14 (μ_{231})	11 $(\mu_{2\cdot1})$	19 (μ_{212})	20 (μ_{222})	21 (μ_{232})	20 $(\mu_{2\cdot2})$	14 $(\mu_{21\cdot})$	15 $(\mu_{22\cdot})$	17.5 $(\mu_{23\cdot})$	15.5 $(\mu_{2\cdot\cdot})$
Average	9 $(\mu_{\cdot11})$	11 $(\mu_{\cdot21})$	16 $(\mu_{\cdot31})$	12 $(\mu_{\cdot\cdot1})$	19 $(\mu_{\cdot12})$	20 $(\mu_{\cdot22})$	21 $(\mu_{\cdot32})$	20 $(\mu_{\cdot\cdot2})$	14 $(\mu_{\cdot1\cdot})$	15.5 $(\mu_{\cdot2\cdot})$	18.5 $(\mu_{\cdot3\cdot})$	16 $(\mu_{\cdots})$

$$(23.1c) \qquad \mu_{\cdot jk} = \frac{\sum\limits_{i} \mu_{ijk}}{a}$$

The mean response when A is at the ith level is denoted by $\mu_{i\cdot\cdot}$, and similar notation is used for the other factor level means. We define:

$$(23.2a) \qquad \mu_{i\cdot\cdot} = \frac{\sum\limits_{j}\sum\limits_{k} \mu_{ijk}}{bc}$$

$$(23.2b) \qquad \mu_{\cdot j\cdot} = \frac{\sum\limits_{i}\sum\limits_{k} \mu_{ijk}}{ac}$$

$$(23.2c) \qquad \mu_{\cdot\cdot k} = \frac{\sum\limits_{i}\sum\limits_{j} \mu_{ijk}}{ab}$$

Finally, the overall mean response is denoted by $\mu_{\cdots}$ and is defined:

$$(23.3) \qquad \mu_{\cdots} = \frac{\sum\limits_{i}\sum\limits_{j}\sum\limits_{k} \mu_{ijk}}{abc}$$

Illustration

To illustrate the meaning of the model terms for a three-factor analysis of variance model, we consider a study of the effects of gender, age, and intelligence level of college graduates on learning of a complex task. Gender is factor A and has $a = 2$ levels (male, female). Age is factor B and is defined in terms of $b = 3$ levels (young, middle, old). Finally, intelligence is factor C and is defined in terms of $c = 2$ levels (high IQ, normal IQ). Table 23.1 shows the treatment means μ_{ijk} for all factor level combinations, as well as the notational representation for each. Also shown in Table 23.1 are the various means of the μ_{ijk}. We shall refer repeatedly to this learning example as we explain the model terms for a three-factor study.

Main Effects

The main effects in a three-factor study are defined analogously to those for a two-factor study. Thus, the *main effect* of the ith level of factor A is defined:

(23.4a)
$$\alpha_i = \mu_{i..} - \mu_{...}$$

For the learning example in Table 23.1, we have, for instance:

$$\alpha_1 = \mu_{1..} - \mu_{...} = 16.5 - 16 = .5$$

Similarly, we define the main effect of the jth level of factor B:

(23.4b)
$$\beta_j = \mu_{.j.} - \mu_{...}$$

and the main effect of the kth level of factor C:

(23.4c)
$$\gamma_k = \mu_{..k} - \mu_{...}$$

It follows from these definitions that the sums of the main effects are zero:

(23.5)
$$\sum_i \alpha_i = \sum_j \beta_j = \sum_k \gamma_k = 0$$

Two-Factor Interactions

The two-factor interaction effects in a three-factor study are defined in the same fashion as for a two-factor study, except that all means are averaged over the third factor. Thus, following (19.8a) we define the two-factor interaction between factor A at the ith level and factor B at the jth level, denoted as before by $(\alpha\beta)_{ij}$, as follows:

(23.6a)
$$(\alpha\beta)_{ij} = \mu_{ij.} - \mu_{i..} - \mu_{.j.} + \mu_{...}$$

For the learning example in Table 23.1, we have for instance:

$$(\alpha\beta)_{11} = 14 - 16.5 - 14 + 16 = -.5$$

In corresponding fashion, we define the AC and BC two-factor interactions:

(23.6b)
$$(\alpha\gamma)_{ik} = \mu_{i.k} - \mu_{i..} - \mu_{..k} + \mu_{...}$$

(23.6c)
$$(\beta\gamma)_{jk} = \mu_{.jk} - \mu_{.j.} - \mu_{..k} + \mu_{...}$$

The two-factor interactions $(\alpha\beta)_{ij}$, $(\alpha\gamma)_{ik}$, and $(\beta\gamma)_{jk}$ are often called *first-order interactions*. It can readily be shown that the sums of the first-order interactions over each subscript are zero:

(23.7a)
$$\sum_i (\alpha\beta)_{ij} = 0 \quad \text{for all } j \qquad \sum_j (\alpha\beta)_{ij} = 0 \quad \text{for all } i$$

(23.7b)
$$\sum_i (\alpha\gamma)_{ik} = 0 \quad \text{for all } k \qquad \sum_k (\alpha\gamma)_{ik} = 0 \quad \text{for all } i$$

(23.7c)
$$\sum_j (\beta\gamma)_{jk} = 0 \quad \text{for all } k \qquad \sum_k (\beta\gamma)_{jk} = 0 \quad \text{for all } j$$

Three-Factor Interactions

Just as in a two-factor study, where the interaction between the ith level of factor A and the jth level of factor B is defined as the difference between the treatment mean μ_{ij} and the value that would be expected if the factor effects were additive, so in a three-factor study the three-factor interaction $(\alpha\beta\gamma)_{ijk}$ is defined as the difference between the treatment mean μ_{ijk} and the value that would be expected if main effects and first-order interactions were sufficient to account for all factor effects. The value that would be expected from main effects and first-order interactions when A is at the ith level, B at the jth level, and C at the kth level is:

$$(23.8) \qquad \mu_{...} + \alpha_i + \beta_j + \gamma_k + (\alpha\beta)_{ij} + (\alpha\gamma)_{ik} + (\beta\gamma)_{jk}$$

Hence, the *three-factor interaction* $(\alpha\beta\gamma)_{ijk}$, also called the *second-order interaction*, is defined as:

$$(23.9a) \qquad (\alpha\beta\gamma)_{ijk} = \mu_{ijk} - [\mu_{...} + \alpha_i + \beta_j + \gamma_k + (\alpha\beta)_{ij} + (\alpha\gamma)_{ik} + (\beta\gamma)_{jk}]$$

or equivalently:

$$(23.9b) \qquad (\alpha\beta\gamma)_{ijk} = \mu_{ijk} - \mu_{ij.} - \mu_{i.k} - \mu_{.jk} + \mu_{i..} + \mu_{.j.} + \mu_{..k} - \mu_{...}$$

From the definition of the three-factor interactions, it follows that they sum to zero when added over any index:

$$(23.10) \qquad \sum_i (\alpha\beta\gamma)_{ijk} = 0 \qquad \sum_j (\alpha\beta\gamma)_{ijk} = 0 \qquad \sum_k (\alpha\beta\gamma)_{ijk} = 0$$
$$\text{for all } j, k \qquad\qquad \text{for all } i, k \qquad\qquad \text{for all } i, j$$

If *all* three-factor interactions $(\alpha\beta\gamma)_{ijk}$ are zero, we say that there are no three-factor interactions among factors A, B, and C. If some $(\alpha\beta\gamma)_{ijk}$ are not zero, we say that three-factor interactions are present.

Let us find the three-factor interaction $(\alpha\beta\gamma)_{111}$ for the learning example in Table 23.1. We require the following terms:

$$\mu_{111} = 9 \qquad\qquad\qquad \gamma_1 = 12 - 16 = -4$$
$$\mu_{...} = 16 \qquad\qquad\qquad (\alpha\beta)_{11} = 14 - 16.5 - 14 + 16 = -.5$$
$$\alpha_1 = 16.5 - 16 = .5 \qquad\qquad (\alpha\gamma)_{11} = 13 - 16.5 - 12 + 16 = .5$$
$$\beta_1 = 14 - 16 = -2 \qquad\qquad (\beta\gamma)_{11} = 9 - 14 - 12 + 16 = -1$$

Hence, we have:

$$(\alpha\beta\gamma)_{111} = 9 - (16 + .5 - 2 - 4 - .5 + .5 - 1) = -.5$$

Since $(\alpha\beta\gamma)_{111}$ is not zero, we know at once that three-factor interactions are present in this example.

Interpretation of Interactions in Three-Factor Studies

To shed light on the nature of interactions in three-factor studies, we shall examine some examples by means of tables and graphs, beginning with very simple factor effects and building up to complex three-factor interaction effects. In each example, we present the true treatment means μ_{ijk}.

FIGURE 23.1   *A, B,* and *C* **Main Effects and No Interactions.**

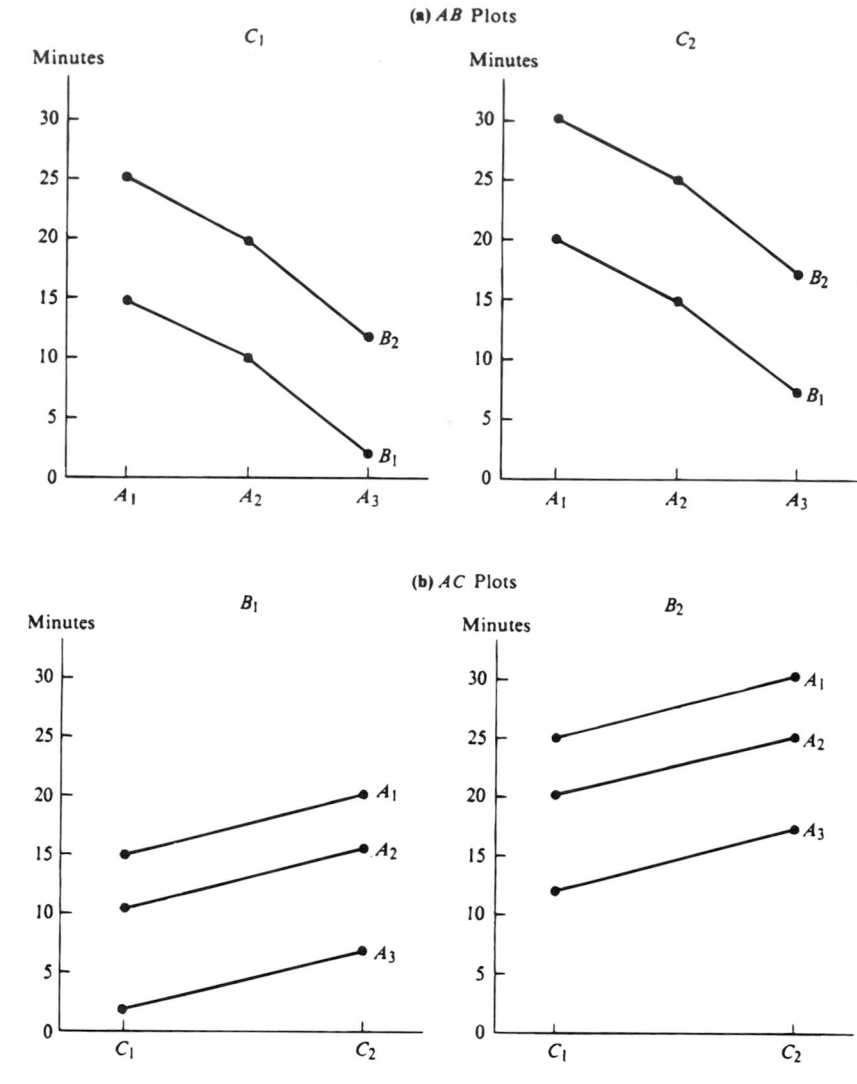

(a) *AB* **Plots**

(b) *AC* **Plots**

Example 1—Main Effects Only.   Figure 23.1 illustrates a situation where there are *A,* *B,* and *C* main effects but no interactions of any kind. The *AB* treatment means curves in Figure 23.1a are plots of the treatment means μ_{ijk} against *C*. Here, the main *A* effects are reflected by the slopes of the *AB* curves not being zero. The main *B* effects are reflected by the differences in the heights of the two *AB* curves within each panel, and the main *C* effects are reflected by the corresponding curves in the two panels being at different heights.

The absence of *AB* interactions is shown by the parallel treatment means curves in each panel. We know from our discussion of two-factor analysis that parallel curves imply absence of interactions. Here, the parallel curves within each panel imply:

1. The *AB* interactions $(\alpha\beta)_{ij}$ equal zero.

FIGURE 23.2   *A*, *B*, and *C* **Main Effects and** *AB* **Interactions.**

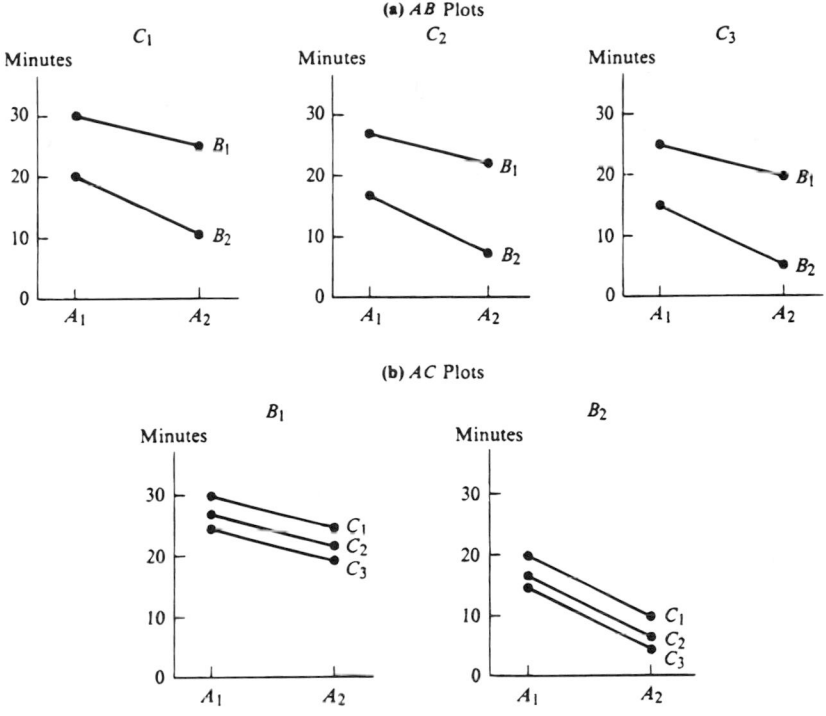

2. The *ABC* interactions $(\alpha\beta\gamma)_{ijk}$ equal zero.

The absences of *BC* and *AC* interactions in this example become evident when the *BC* and *AC* treatment means curves are plotted against *A* and *B*, respectively. For example, in Figure 23.1b, the same treatment means μ_{ijk} are shown with *AC* curves plotted against *B*. Note that these curves are parallel in each panel, implying that the *AC* interactions are zero.

Example 2—Main Effects and *AB* Interactions.   Figure 23.2 illustrates a situation where there are *A*, *B*, and *C* main effects and *AB* interactions but no other interactions. Note that the two *AB* treatment means curves in each panel of Figure 23.2a are no longer parallel, reflecting the presence of *AB* interactions. However, the upper curves in the three panels are parallel, as are the lower curves. This implies that when the *AC* curves are plotted against *B*, the *AC* treatment means curves within each panel will be parallel. This is shown in Figure 23.2b, which contains the *AC* curves plotted against *B* for the same treatment means as in Figure 23.2a. The parallelism of the *AC* curves within each panel in Figure 23.2b in turn implies that there are no *AC* interactions, as well as no *ABC* interactions, that is, all $(\alpha\gamma)_{ik} = 0$ and all $(\alpha\beta\gamma)_{ijk} = 0$.

Thus, if the *AB* (*AC*, *BC*) treatment means curves corresponding to any given level of factor *C* (*B*, *A*) are parallel for all levels of factor *C* (*B*, *A*), as in Figure 23.2a, even though the response curves within a panel are not parallel, it follows that there are no three-factor interactions.

FIGURE 23.3   *A*, *B*, and *C* **Main Effects and** *AB* **and** *AC* **Interactions —AB Plots.**

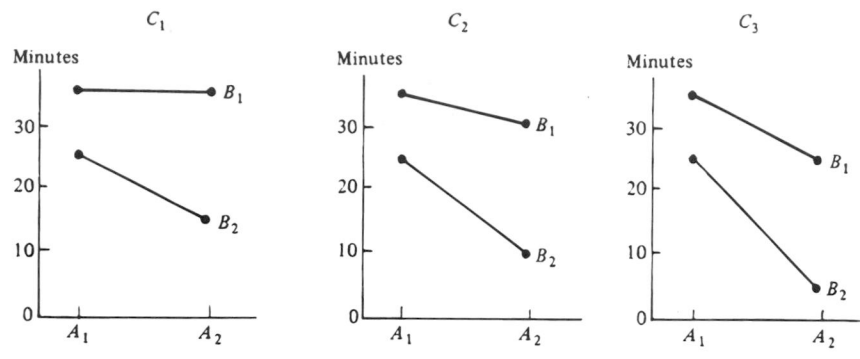

Example 3—Main Effects and *AB* and *AC* Interactions.   It does not follow, however, that lack of parallelism either within or between panels implies the presence of three-factor interactions. Figure 23.3 portrays a situation where main *A*, *B*, and *C* effects and *AB* and *AC* two-factor interactions are present but no three-factor interactions exist. Yet there are no parallel treatment means curves either within or between panels. The fact that the *AB* curves when factor *B* is at level B_1 are not parallel for the three levels of factor *C* reflects the presence of *AC* interactions. The lack of parallelism of the *AB* curves within each panel reflects the presence of *AB* interactions. Note, however, that the differences $\mu_{11k} - \mu_{12k}$ are the same for all levels of factor *C*, as are the differences $\mu_{21k} - \mu_{22k}$. Hence, no three-factor interactions are present.

Example 4—Main Effects and *AB*, *AC*, *BC*, and *ABC* Interactions.   Figure 23.4 shows the *AB* treatment means plots for the different levels of factor *C* for the learning example in Table 23.1. Recall that the learning example considers the effects of gender (factor *A*), age (factor *B*), and intelligence (factor *C*) on learning time. The plots of the treatment means in Figure 23.4 reflect, as we have seen earlier, the presence of main effects and first-order and second-order interactions. Specifically, Figure 23.4 shows that for persons with normal IQ, gender has no effect on mean learning time, and age has only a small effect leading to slightly longer learning times for older persons. For persons with high IQ, on the other hand, females tend to learn more quickly than males for older persons but not for young persons, and older persons tend to require substantially longer learning times than young persons.

Note

If three-factor interactions are difficult to understand, higher-order interactions such as four-factor interactions are yet more abstruse. Fortunately, it is often found in practice that these higher-order interactions are quite small or nonexistent. When this is the case, they can be disregarded in the analysis of factor effects.   ∎

FIGURE 23.4   *A*, *B*, and *C* **Main Effects and** *AB*, *AC*, *BC*, **and** *ABC*
Interactions—Table 23.1 Learning Example.

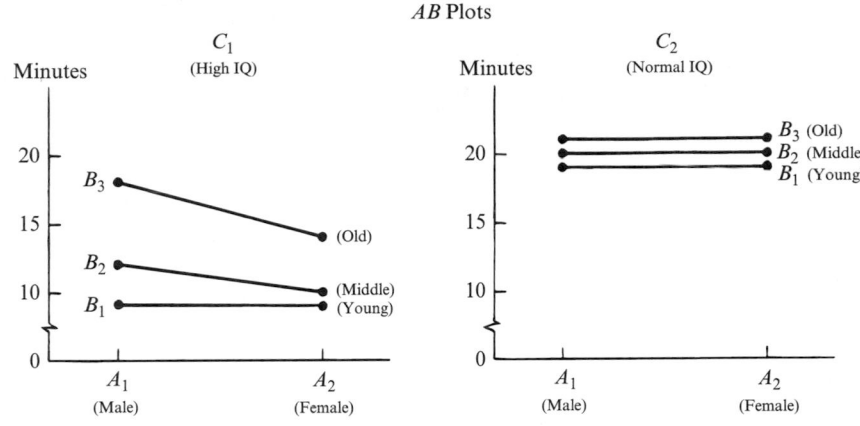

Cell Means Model

Let Y_{ijkm} denote the observation for the mth case or trial ($m = 1, \ldots, n$) for the treatment consisting of the ith level of A ($i = 1, \ldots, a$), the jth level of B ($j = 1, \ldots, b$), and the kth level of C ($k = 1, \ldots, c$). Thus, the total number of cases in the study is:

$$(23.11) \qquad\qquad n_T = nabc$$

The ANOVA model for a three-factor study in terms of the cell (treatment) means μ_{ijk} with fixed factor levels is:

$$(23.12) \qquad\qquad Y_{ijkm} = \mu_{ijk} + \varepsilon_{ijkm}$$

where:

μ_{ijk} are parameters

ε_{ijkm} are independent $N(0, \sigma^2)$

$i = 1, \ldots, a; j = 1, \ldots, b; k = 1, \ldots, c; m = 1, \ldots, n$

Factor Effects Model

An equivalent factor effects model can be developed that incorporates the factorial structure by expressing each treatment mean μ_{ijk} in terms of the various factor effects. From the three-factor interaction definition (23.9a), we have the identity:

$$(23.13) \qquad \mu_{ijk} \equiv \mu_{\ldots} + \alpha_i + \beta_j + \gamma_k + (\alpha\beta)_{ij} + (\alpha\gamma)_{ik} + (\beta\gamma)_{jk} + (\alpha\beta\gamma)_{ijk}$$

where:

$$\mu_{...} = \frac{\sum\sum\sum \mu_{ijk}}{abc}$$

$$\alpha_i = \mu_{i..} - \mu_{...}$$

$$\beta_j = \mu_{.j.} - \mu_{...}$$

$$\gamma_k = \mu_{..k} - \mu_{...}$$

$$(\alpha\beta)_{ij} = \mu_{ij.} - \mu_{i..} - \mu_{.j.} + \mu_{...}$$

$$(\alpha\gamma)_{ik} = \mu_{i.k} - \mu_{i..} - \mu_{..k} + \mu_{...}$$

$$(\beta\gamma)_{jk} = \mu_{.jk} - \mu_{.j.} - \mu_{..k} + \mu_{...}$$

$$(\alpha\beta\gamma)_{ijk} = \mu_{ijk} - \mu_{ij.} - \mu_{i.k} - \mu_{.jk} + \mu_{i..} + \mu_{.j.} + \mu_{..k} - \mu_{...}$$

Hence, the equivalent factor effects ANOVA model for a three-factor study is:

(23.14) $\quad Y_{ijkm} = \mu_{...} + \alpha_i + \beta_j + \gamma_k + (\alpha\beta)_{ij} + (\alpha\gamma)_{ik} + (\beta\gamma)_{jk} + (\alpha\beta\gamma)_{ijk} + \varepsilon_{ijkm}$

where:

ε_{ijkm} are independent $N(0, \sigma^2)$

$\alpha_i, \beta_j, \gamma_k, (\alpha\beta)_{ij}, (\alpha\gamma)_{ik}, (\beta\gamma)_{jk}, (\alpha\beta\gamma)_{ijk}$ are constants subject to the restrictions:

$$\sum_i \alpha_i = \sum_j \beta_j = \sum_k \gamma_k = 0$$

$$\sum_i (\alpha\beta)_{ij} = \sum_j (\alpha\beta)_{ij} = \sum_i (\alpha\gamma)_{ik} = 0$$

$$\sum_k (\alpha\gamma)_{ik} = \sum_j (\beta\gamma)_{jk} = \sum_k (\beta\gamma)_{jk} = 0$$

$$\sum_i (\alpha\beta\gamma)_{ijk} = \sum_j (\alpha\beta\gamma)_{ijk} = \sum_k (\alpha\beta\gamma)_{ijk} = 0$$

Both the cell means model (23.12) and the equivalent factor effects model (23.14) are linear models, just as in the two-factor case. We shall illustrate this for an example later in the chapter.

23.2 Analysis of Variance

Notation

The notation for sample totals and means is a straightforward extension of that for two-factor studies. As usual, a dot in the subscript indicates aggregation or averaging over the index represented by the dot. We have:

(23.15a) $\qquad Y_{ijk.} = \sum_m Y_{ijkm} \qquad\qquad \bar{Y}_{ijk.} = \dfrac{Y_{ijk.}}{n}$

(23.15b) $\qquad Y_{ij..} = \sum_k \sum_m Y_{ijkm} \qquad\qquad \bar{Y}_{ij..} = \dfrac{Y_{ij..}}{cn}$

$$(23.15c) \qquad Y_{i \cdot k \cdot} = \sum_j \sum_m Y_{ijkm} \qquad\qquad \bar{Y}_{i \cdot k \cdot} = \frac{Y_{i \cdot k \cdot}}{bn}$$

$$(23.15d) \qquad Y_{\cdot jk \cdot} = \sum_i \sum_m Y_{ijkm} \qquad\qquad \bar{Y}_{\cdot jk \cdot} = \frac{Y_{\cdot jk \cdot}}{an}$$

$$(23.15e) \qquad Y_{i \cdots} = \sum_j \sum_k \sum_m Y_{ijkm} \qquad\qquad \bar{Y}_{i \cdots} = \frac{Y_{i \cdots}}{bcn}$$

$$(23.15f) \qquad Y_{\cdot j \cdot \cdot} = \sum_i \sum_k \sum_m Y_{ijkm} \qquad\qquad \bar{Y}_{\cdot j \cdot \cdot} = \frac{Y_{\cdot j \cdot \cdot}}{acn}$$

$$(23.15g) \qquad Y_{\cdot \cdot k \cdot} = \sum_i \sum_j \sum_m Y_{ijkm} \qquad\qquad \bar{Y}_{\cdot \cdot k \cdot} = \frac{Y_{\cdot \cdot k \cdot}}{abn}$$

$$(23.15h) \qquad Y_{\cdots} = \sum_i \sum_j \sum_k \sum_m Y_{ijkm} \qquad\qquad \bar{Y}_{\cdots} = \frac{Y_{\cdots}}{abcn}$$

Table 23.4 (p. 943) illustrates this notation for a study of the effects of gender, body fat, and smoking history on exercise tolerance in stress testing. Each of the three factors has two levels, and there are three replications for each treatment. Tables 23.4a and b show, respectively, the data and estimated means, together with the corresponding notation.

Fitting of ANOVA Model

When the normal error cell means model (23.12) is fitted by the method of least squares or the method of maximum likelihood, the estimators as usual turn out to be the estimated treatment means:

$$(23.16) \qquad \hat{\mu}_{ijk} = \bar{Y}_{ijk \cdot}$$

Thus, the *fitted values* for the observations are the estimated treatment means:

$$(23.17) \qquad \hat{Y}_{ijkm} = \bar{Y}_{ijk \cdot}$$

and the *residuals* are the deviations of the observed values from the estimated treatment means:

$$(23.18) \qquad e_{ijkm} = Y_{ijkm} - \hat{Y}_{ijkm} = Y_{ijkm} - \bar{Y}_{ijk \cdot}$$

For the equivalent factor effects model (23.14), the least squares and maximum likelihood estimators of the parameters are as follows:

	Parameter	Estimator
(23.19a)	$\mu_{\cdots}$	$\hat{\mu}_{\cdots} = \bar{Y}_{\cdots}$
(23.19b)	α_i	$\hat{\alpha}_i = \bar{Y}_{i \cdots} - \bar{Y}_{\cdots}$
(23.19c)	β_j	$\hat{\beta}_j = \bar{Y}_{\cdot j \cdot \cdot} - \bar{Y}_{\cdots}$
(23.19d)	γ_k	$\hat{\gamma}_k = \bar{Y}_{\cdot \cdot k \cdot} - \bar{Y}_{\cdots}$
(23.19e)	$(\alpha\beta)_{ij}$	$\widehat{(\alpha\beta)}_{ij} = \bar{Y}_{ij \cdot \cdot} - \bar{Y}_{i \cdots} - \bar{Y}_{\cdot j \cdot \cdot} + \bar{Y}_{\cdots}$

	Parameter	Estimator
(23.19f)	$(\alpha\gamma)_{ik}$	$\widehat{(\alpha\gamma)}_{ik} = \bar{Y}_{i\cdot k\cdot} - \bar{Y}_{i\cdots} - \bar{Y}_{\cdot\cdot k\cdot} + \bar{Y}_{\cdots\cdot}$
(23.19g)	$(\beta\gamma)_{jk}$	$\widehat{(\beta\gamma)}_{jk} = \bar{Y}_{\cdot jk\cdot} - \bar{Y}_{\cdot j\cdot\cdot} - \bar{Y}_{\cdot\cdot k\cdot} + \bar{Y}_{\cdots\cdot}$
(23.19h)	$(\alpha\beta\gamma)_{ijk}$	$\widehat{(\alpha\beta\gamma)}_{ijk} = \bar{Y}_{ijk\cdot} - \bar{Y}_{ij\cdot\cdot} - \bar{Y}_{i\cdot k\cdot} - \bar{Y}_{\cdot jk\cdot}$

$$+ \bar{Y}_{i\cdots} + \bar{Y}_{\cdot j\cdot\cdot} + \bar{Y}_{\cdot\cdot k\cdot} - \bar{Y}_{\cdots\cdot}$$

The fitted values and residuals for factor effects model (23.14) are the same as those in (23.17) and (23.18) for cell means model (23.12), as was the case for two-factor studies.

Partitioning of Total Sum of Squares

Neglecting the factorial structure of the three-factor study and simply considering it to contain *abc* treatments, we obtain the usual breakdown of the total sum of squares:

$$(23.20) \qquad\qquad SSTO = SSTR + SSE$$

where:

$$(23.20a) \qquad SSTO = \sum_i \sum_j \sum_k \sum_m (Y_{ijkm} - \bar{Y}_{\cdots\cdot})^2$$

$$(23.20b) \qquad SSTR = n \sum_i \sum_j \sum_k (\bar{Y}_{ijk\cdot} - \bar{Y}_{\cdots\cdot})^2$$

$$(23.20c) \qquad SSE = \sum_i \sum_j \sum_k \sum_m (Y_{ijkm} - \bar{Y}_{ijk\cdot})^2 = \sum_i \sum_j \sum_k \sum_m e_{ijkm}^2$$

Consider now the estimated treatment mean deviation $\bar{Y}_{ijk\cdot} - \bar{Y}_{\cdots\cdot}$, which appears in *SSTR*. This can be decomposed in terms of the estimators in (23.19) of the main effects, two-factor interactions, and three-factor interaction:

$$\underbrace{\bar{Y}_{ijk\cdot} - \bar{Y}_{\cdots\cdot}}_{\substack{\text{Estimated} \\ \text{treatment} \\ \text{mean deviation}}} = \underbrace{\bar{Y}_{i\cdots} - \bar{Y}_{\cdots\cdot}}_{A\text{ main effect}} + \underbrace{\bar{Y}_{\cdot j\cdot\cdot} - \bar{Y}_{\cdots\cdot}}_{B\text{ main effect}} + \underbrace{\bar{Y}_{\cdot\cdot k\cdot} - \bar{Y}_{\cdots\cdot}}_{C\text{ main effect}}$$

$$+ \underbrace{\bar{Y}_{ij\cdot\cdot} - \bar{Y}_{i\cdots} - \bar{Y}_{\cdot j\cdot\cdot} + \bar{Y}_{\cdots\cdot}}_{AB\text{ interaction effect}} + \underbrace{\bar{Y}_{i\cdot k\cdot} - \bar{Y}_{i\cdots} - \bar{Y}_{\cdot\cdot k\cdot} + \bar{Y}_{\cdots\cdot}}_{AC\text{ interaction effect}}$$

$$+ \underbrace{\bar{Y}_{\cdot jk\cdot} - \bar{Y}_{\cdot j\cdot\cdot} - \bar{Y}_{\cdot\cdot k\cdot} + \bar{Y}_{\cdots\cdot}}_{BC\text{ interaction effect}}$$

$$+ \underbrace{\bar{Y}_{ijk\cdot} - \bar{Y}_{ij\cdot\cdot} - \bar{Y}_{i\cdot k\cdot} - \bar{Y}_{\cdot jk\cdot} + \bar{Y}_{i\cdots} + \bar{Y}_{\cdot j\cdot\cdot} + \bar{Y}_{\cdot\cdot k\cdot} - \bar{Y}_{\cdots\cdot}}_{ABC\text{ interaction effect}}$$

When we square each side and sum over i, j, k, and m, all cross-product terms drop out and we obtain:

$$(23.21) \qquad SSTR = SSA + SSB + SSC + SSAB + SSAC + SSBC + SSABC$$

where:

$$(23.21a) \qquad SSA = nbc \sum_i (\bar{Y}_{i\cdots} - \bar{Y}_{\cdots})^2$$

$$(23.21b) \qquad SSB = nac \sum_j (\bar{Y}_{\cdot j\cdot\cdot} - \bar{Y}_{\cdots})^2$$

$$(23.21c) \qquad SSC = nab \sum_k (\bar{Y}_{\cdot\cdot k\cdot} - \bar{Y}_{\cdots})^2$$

$$(23.21d) \qquad SSAB = nc \sum_i \sum_j (\bar{Y}_{ij\cdot\cdot} - \bar{Y}_{i\cdots} - \bar{Y}_{\cdot j\cdot\cdot} + \bar{Y}_{\cdots})^2$$

$$(23.21e) \qquad SSAC = nb \sum_i \sum_k (\bar{Y}_{i\cdot k\cdot} - \bar{Y}_{i\cdots} - \bar{Y}_{\cdot\cdot k\cdot} + \bar{Y}_{\cdots})^2$$

$$(23.21f) \qquad SSBC = na \sum_j \sum_k (\bar{Y}_{\cdot jk\cdot} - \bar{Y}_{\cdot j\cdot\cdot} - \bar{Y}_{\cdot\cdot k\cdot} + \bar{Y}_{\cdots})^2$$

$$(23.21g) \qquad SSABC = n \sum_i \sum_j \sum_k (\bar{Y}_{ijk\cdot} - \bar{Y}_{ij\cdot\cdot} - \bar{Y}_{i\cdot k\cdot} - \bar{Y}_{\cdot jk\cdot} + \bar{Y}_{i\cdots}$$
$$+ \bar{Y}_{\cdot j\cdot\cdot} + \bar{Y}_{\cdot\cdot k\cdot} - \bar{Y}_{\cdots})^2$$

Combining (23.20) and (23.21), we have thus established the orthogonal decomposition:

$$(23.22) \qquad SSTO = SSA + SSB + SSC + SSAB + SSAC + SSBC + SSABC + SSE$$

SSA, *SSB*, and *SSC* are the usual main effects sums of squares. For instance, the larger (absolutely) are the estimated main *B* effects $\bar{Y}_{\cdot j\cdot\cdot} - \bar{Y}_{\cdots}$, the larger will be *SSB*.

SSAB, *SSAC*, and *SSBC* are the usual two-factor interactions sums of squares. For instance, the larger (absolutely) are the estimated *AB* interactions $\bar{Y}_{ij\cdot\cdot} - \bar{Y}_{i\cdots} - \bar{Y}_{\cdot j\cdot\cdot} + \bar{Y}_{\cdots}$, the larger will be *SSAB*.

Finally, *SSABC* is the three-factor interactions sum of squares. The larger (absolutely) are these estimated three-factor interactions, the larger will be *SSABC*.

Degrees of Freedom and Mean Squares

Table 23.2 contains the general ANOVA table for three-factor ANOVA model (23.14). The degrees of freedom for main effects and two-factor interactions sums of squares correspond to those for two-factor studies. The number of degrees of freedom associated with *SSABC* is obtained by subtraction and corresponds to the number of independent linear relations among all the interaction terms $(\alpha\beta\gamma)_{ijk}$.

The expected mean squares are also given in Table 23.2. Note that *MSA*, *MSB*, *MSC*, *MSAB*, *MSAC*, *MSBC*, and *MSABC* all have expectations equal to σ^2 if there are no factor effects of the type reflected by the mean square. If such effects are present, each mean square has an expectation exceeding σ^2. As usual, $E\{MSE\} = \sigma^2$ always. Hence, the tests

TABLE 23.2 **General ANOVA Table for Three-Factor Study with Fixed Factor Levels.**

Source of Variation	SS	df	MS	E{MS}
Factor A	SSA	$a - 1$	MSA	$\sigma^2 + bcn\dfrac{\Sigma \alpha_i^2}{a - 1}$
Factor B	SSB	$b - 1$	MSB	$\sigma^2 + acn\dfrac{\Sigma \beta_j^2}{b - 1}$
Factor C	SSC	$c - 1$	MSC	$\sigma^2 + abn\dfrac{\Sigma \gamma_k^2}{c - 1}$
AB interactions	$SSAB$	$(a - 1)(b - 1)$	$MSAB$	$\sigma^2 + cn\dfrac{\Sigma\Sigma(\alpha\beta)_{ij}^2}{(a - 1)(b - 1)}$
AC interactions	$SSAC$	$(a - 1)(c - 1)$	$MSAC$	$\sigma^2 + bn\dfrac{\Sigma\Sigma(\alpha\gamma)_{ik}^2}{(a - 1)(c - 1)}$
BC interactions	$SSBC$	$(b - 1)(c - 1)$	$MSBC$	$\sigma^2 + an\dfrac{\Sigma\Sigma(\beta\gamma)_{jk}^2}{(b - 1)(c - 1)}$
ABC interactions	$SSABC$	$(a - 1)(b - 1)(c - 1)$	$MSABC$	$\sigma^2 + n\dfrac{\Sigma\Sigma\Sigma(\alpha\beta\gamma)_{ijk}^2}{(a - 1)(b - 1)(c - 1)}$
Error	SSE	$abc(n - 1)$	MSE	σ^2
Total	$SSTO$	$abcn - 1$		

Note: $\mu..., \alpha_i, \beta_j, \gamma_k, (\alpha\beta)_{ij}, (\alpha\gamma)_{ik}, (\beta\gamma)_{jk}$, and $(\alpha\beta\gamma)_{ijk}$ are defined in (23.13).

for factor effects consist of comparing the appropriate mean square against MSE by means of an F^* test statistic, with large values of F^* indicating the presence of factor effects.

Tests for Factor Effects

The various tests for factor effects all follow the same pattern; we illustrate them with the test for three-factor interactions. The alternatives are:

(23.23a)
$$H_0: \text{all } (\alpha\beta\gamma)_{ijk} = 0$$
$$H_a: \text{not all } (\alpha\beta\gamma)_{ijk} \text{ equal zero}$$

The appropriate test statistic is:

(23.23b)
$$F^* = \frac{MSABC}{MSE}$$

If H_0 holds, F^* follows the F distribution with $(a-1)(b-1)(c-1)$ degrees of freedom for the numerator and $abc(n - 1)$ degrees of freedom for the denominator. Hence, the decision rule to control the Type I error at α is:

TABLE 23.3   **Test Statistics for Three-Factor Study with Fixed Factor Levels.**

Alternatives	Test Statistic	Percentile
H_0: all $\alpha_i = 0$ H_a: not all $\alpha_i = 0$	$F^* = \dfrac{MSA}{MSE}$	$F[1-\alpha; a-1, (n-1)abc]$
H_0: all $\beta_j = 0$ H_a: not all $\beta_j = 0$	$F^* = \dfrac{MSB}{MSE}$	$F[1-\alpha; b-1, (n-1)abc]$
H_0: all $\gamma_k = 0$ H_a: not all $\gamma_k = 0$	$F^* = \dfrac{MSC}{MSE}$	$F[1-\alpha; c-1, (n-1)abc]$
H_0: all $(\alpha\beta)_{ij} = 0$ H_a: not all $(\alpha\beta)_{ij} = 0$	$F^* = \dfrac{MSAB}{MSE}$	$F[1-\alpha; (a-1)(b-1), (n-1)abc]$
H_0: all $(\alpha\gamma)_{ik} = 0$ H_a: not all $(\alpha\gamma)_{ik} = 0$	$F^* = \dfrac{MSAC}{MSE}$	$F[1-\alpha; (a-1)(c-1), (n-1)abc]$
H_0: all $(\beta\gamma)_{jk} = 0$ H_a: not all $(\beta\gamma)_{jk} = 0$	$F^* = \dfrac{MSBC}{MSE}$	$F[1-\alpha; (b-1)(c-1), (n-1)abc]$
H_0: all $(\alpha\beta\gamma)_{ijk} = 0$ H_a: not all $(\alpha\beta\gamma)_{ijk} = 0$	$F^* = \dfrac{MSABC}{MSE}$	$F[1-\alpha; (a-1)(b-1)(c-1), (n-1)abc]$

(23.23c) If $F^* \le F[1-\alpha; (a-1)(b-1)(c-1), (n-1)abc]$, conclude H_0
         If $F^* > F[1-\alpha; (a-1)(b-1)(c-1), (n-1)abc]$, conclude H_a

Table 23.3 contains the test statistics and percentiles of the F distribution for the various tests in a three-factor study.

Comments

1. The Kimball inequality for the family level of significance α in a three-factor study when the family consists of the combined set of seven tests, including three on main effects, three on two-factor interactions, and one on three-factor interactions, is:

(23.24) $$\alpha < 1 - (1-\alpha_1)(1-\alpha_2)\cdots(1-\alpha_7)$$

where α_i is the level of significance for the ith test.

2. If the three-factor interactions (and also perhaps some sets of two-factor interactions) equal zero, the question sometimes arises whether the corresponding sums of squares should be pooled with the error sum of squares. Our earlier discussion on revising the ANOVA model in Section 19.8 is applicable here also.

3. If there is only one case per treatment in a three-factor study with fixed factor levels, analysis of variance tests can only be conducted if it is possible to assume that some interactions

equal zero. Usually, the interactions most likely to equal zero are the three-factor interactions. If it is possible to assume that all three-factor interactions equal zero, *MSABC* has expectation σ^2 and plays the role of the error mean square *MSE*. All mean squares are calculated in the usual manner, except that $n = 1$.

4. The F^* test statistics in Table 23.3 can be obtained by the general linear test approach explained in Chapter 2. For example, for testing whether all three-factor interactions are zero, the full model is that in (23.14), the alternatives are those in (23.23a), and the reduced model under H_0: $(\alpha\beta\gamma)_{ijk} \equiv 0$ is:

$$(23.25) \qquad Y_{ijkm} = \mu_{...} + \alpha_i + \beta_j + \gamma_k + (\alpha\beta)_{ij} + (\alpha\gamma)_{ik} + (\beta\gamma)_{jk} + \varepsilon_{ijkm}$$

Reduced model   ■

23.3   Evaluation of Appropriateness of ANOVA Model

No new problems arise in examining the appropriateness of the three-factor analysis of variance model. The residuals (23.18):

$$(23.26) \qquad\qquad e_{ijkm} = Y_{ijkm} - \bar{Y}_{ijk.}$$

may be examined for normality, constancy of error variance, and independence of error terms in the same fashion as for single-factor and two-factor studies.

Weighted least squares as usual is a standard remedial measure when the error variance is not constant but the distribution of the error terms is normal. A transformation of the response variable may be helpful to stabilize the error variance, to make the error distributions more normal, and/or to make important interactions unimportant. Our earlier discussions of these topics apply completely to the three-factor case.

Finally, our earlier discussion on the effects of departures from the ANOVA model applies fully to the three-factor case. In particular, the employment of equal sample sizes for all treatments minimizes the effect of unequal variances.

23.4   Analysis of Factor Effects

No new problems are encountered in the analysis of factor effects for three-factor studies with fixed factor levels. As for two-factor studies, the focus of the analysis is usually on factor level means when no important interactions are present, and on treatment means when there are important interactions. We now present some selected results for estimating factor effects. Other analyses follow the same pattern.

Analysis of Factor Effects when Factors Do Not Interact

Estimation of Factor Level Mean.   The factor A level mean $\mu_{i..}$ is estimated by:

$$(23.27) \qquad\qquad \hat{\mu}_{i..} = \bar{Y}_{i...}$$

The estimated variance of this estimator is:

$$(23.28) \qquad\qquad s^2\{\bar{Y}_{i...}\} = \frac{MSE}{nbc}$$

Confidence limits for $\mu_{i..}$ are obtained by means of the t distribution with $(n-1)abc$ degrees of freedom:

$$(23.29) \qquad \bar{Y}_{i...} \pm t[1-\alpha/2; (n-1)abc]s\{\bar{Y}_{i...}\}$$

Estimation of factor level means for factors B or C is done in similar fashion.

Inferences for Contrast of Factor Level Means. Inference procedures for a contrast involving the factor A level means $\mu_{i..}$:

$$(23.30) \qquad L = \sum c_i \mu_{i..} \qquad \text{where} \qquad \sum c_i = 0$$

are easily developed. The $1-\alpha$ confidence limits for L are:

$$(23.31) \qquad \hat{L} \pm t[1-\alpha/2; (n-1)abc]s\{\hat{L}\}$$

where L is estimated unbiasedly by:

$$(23.31a) \qquad \hat{L} = \sum c_i \bar{Y}_{i...}$$

and the estimated variance of $\hat{L}$ is:

$$(23.31b) \qquad s^2\{\hat{L}\} = \frac{MSE}{nbc} \sum c_i^2$$

Contrasts of factor level means for factors B or C are estimated in similar fashion.

The test statistic and decision rule for the following alternatives concerning a contrast L in (23.30):

$$(23.32) \qquad \begin{array}{c} H_0: \ L = 0 \\ H_a: \ L \neq 0 \end{array}$$

are:

$$(23.33) \qquad t^* = \frac{\hat{L}}{s\{\hat{L}\}}; \quad \text{If } |t^*| > t[1-\alpha/2; (n-1)abc], \text{ conclude } H_a$$

where $\hat{L}$ and $s\{\hat{L}\}$ are given by (23.31). Again for conciseness, we present only the portion of the decision rule leading to conclusion H_a.

Multiple Contrasts of Factor Level Means. When inferences are to be made concerning a number of contrasts of factor A level means $\mu_{i..}$, the Tukey, Scheffé, and Bonferroni procedures are easily adapted. As before, the Tukey procedure applies to the set of all pairwise comparisons of the form $D = \mu_{i..} - \mu_{i'..}$.

To obtain simultaneous confidence interval estimates, the t multiple in (23.31) is replaced by the T, S, or B multiple defined as follows:

	Procedure	Multiple
(23.34a)	Tukey	$T = \frac{1}{\sqrt{2}}q[1-\alpha; a, (n-1)abc]$
(23.34b)	Scheffé	$S^2 = (a-1)F[1-\alpha; a-1, (n-1)abc]$
(23.34c)	Bonferroni	$B = t[1-\alpha/2g; (n-1)abc]$

Test statistics and decision rules for simultaneous testing of a number of contrasts of the form (23.30) for the alternatives H_0: $L = 0$, H_a: $L \neq 0$ are:

Procedure	Test Statistic and Decision Rule
(23.35a) Tukey	$q^* = \dfrac{\sqrt{2}\hat{D}}{s\{\hat{D}\}}$
	If $\|q^*\| > q[1 - \alpha; a, (n-1)abc]$, conclude H_a
(23.35b) Scheffé	$F^* = \dfrac{\hat{L}^2}{(a-1)s^2\{\hat{L}\}}$
	If $F^* > F[1 - \alpha; a-1, (n-1)abc]$, conclude H_a
(23.35c) Bonferroni	$t^* = \dfrac{\hat{L}}{s\{\hat{L}\}}$
	If $\|t^*\| > t[1 - \alpha/2g; (n-1)abc]$, conclude H_a

Inferences concerning multiple contrasts based on the factor level means $\mu_{.j.}$ or $\mu_{..k}$ are made in corresponding fashion.

Analysis of Factor Effects when Interactions Important

As explained earlier for two-factor studies, a simple transformation of the data is usually first attempted to make important interactions unimportant. If that effort is not successful, the important interactions are then typically analyzed in terms of the treatment means μ_{ijk}.

Estimation of Treatment Mean.   The treatment mean μ_{ijk} is estimated by:

$$(23.36) \qquad \hat{\mu}_{ijk} = \bar{Y}_{ijk.}$$

The estimated variance of $\bar{Y}_{ijk.}$ is:

$$(23.37) \qquad s^2\{\bar{Y}_{ijk.}\} = \frac{MSE}{n}$$

Confidence limits for μ_{ijk} are:

$$(23.38) \qquad \bar{Y}_{ijk.} \pm t[1 - \alpha/2; (n-1)abc]s\{\bar{Y}_{ijk.}\}$$

Inferences for Contrast of Treatment Means.   When important interactions are present, contrasts among the treatment means μ_{ijk} are ordinarily desired. Let, as usual, L denote such a contrast:

$$(23.39) \qquad L = \sum\sum\sum c_{ijk}\mu_{ijk} \qquad \text{where} \qquad \sum\sum\sum c_{ijk} = 0$$

Confidence limits for L are:

$$(23.40) \qquad \hat{L} \pm t[1 - \alpha/2; (n-1)abc]s\{\hat{L}\}$$

where:

(23.40a)
$$\hat{L} = \sum \sum \sum c_{ijk} \bar{Y}_{ijk}.$$

(23.40b)
$$s^2\{\hat{L}\} = \frac{MSE}{n} \sum \sum \sum c_{ijk}^2$$

The test statistic and decision rule for alternatives $H_0: L = 0$, $H_a: L \neq 0$ are:

(23.41)
$$t^* = \frac{\hat{L}}{s\{\hat{L}\}}; \quad \text{If } |t^*| > t[1 - \alpha/2; (n-1)abc], \text{ conclude } H_a$$

At times, not all types of interaction effects are present. In such a case, the desired contrasts may involve means of the μ_{ijk} taken over one of the factors. For example, when the only interactions present are the BC interactions, there may be interest in contrasts of the means $\mu_{\cdot jk}$:

(23.42)
$$L = \sum \sum c_{jk} \mu_{\cdot jk} \quad \text{where} \quad \sum \sum c_{jk} = 0$$

Such contrasts are, of course, special cases of contrasts of the treatment means μ_{ijk} in (23.39). The estimator of the contrast in (23.42) can be obtained from (23.40a) and the estimated variance from (23.40b); they are:

(23.43)
$$\hat{L} = \sum \sum c_{jk} \bar{Y}_{\cdot jk}.$$

(23.44)
$$s^2\{\hat{L}\} = \frac{MSE}{na} \sum \sum c_{jk}^2$$

Multiple Contrasts of Treatment Means. For simultaneous interval estimates of contrasts of treatment means μ_{ijk}, the t multiple in (23.40) is replaced by the T, S, or B multiple defined as follows:

	Procedure	Multiple
(23.45a)	Tukey	$T = \frac{1}{\sqrt{2}} q[1 - \alpha; abc, (n-1)abc]$
(23.45b)	Scheffé	$S^2 = (abc - 1)F[1 - \alpha; abc - 1, (n-1)abc]$
(23.45c)	Bonferroni	$B = t[1 - \alpha/2g; (n-1)abc]$

Simultaneous testing of a number of alternatives of the form $H_0: L = 0$, $H_a: L \neq 0$ using the Tukey, Scheffé, and Bonferroni procedures can be accomplished with the following test statistics and decision rules:

	Procedure	Test Statistic and Decision Rule
(23.46a)	Tukey	$q^* = \frac{\sqrt{2}\hat{D}}{s\{\hat{D}\}}$

If $|q^*| > q[1 - \alpha; abc, (n-1)abc]$, conclude H_a

FIGURE 23.5   **Cube Plot of Estimated Treatment Means—Stress Test Example.**

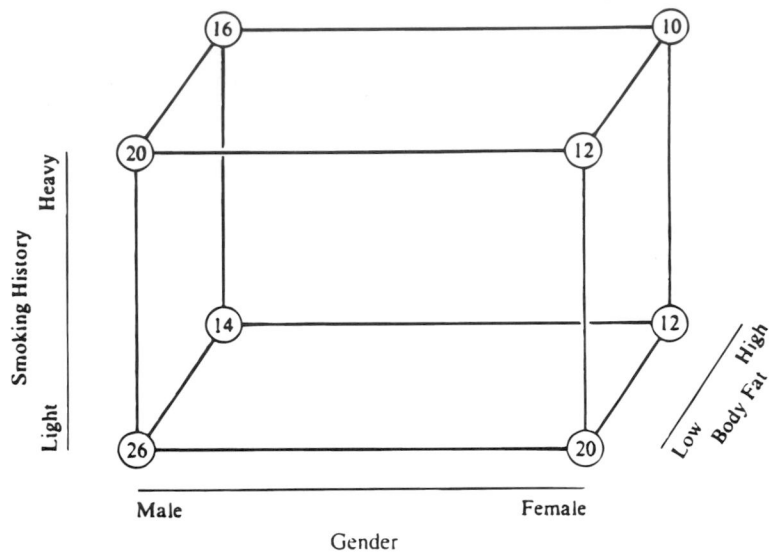

Procedure	Test Statistic and Decision Rule

(23.46b)   Scheffé $$F^* = \frac{\hat{L}^2}{(abc-1)s^2\{\hat{L}\}}$$

If $F^* > F[1-\alpha; abc-1, (n-1)abc]$, conclude H_a

(23.46c)   Bonferroni $$t^* = \frac{\hat{L}}{s\{\hat{L}\}}$$

If $|t^*| > t[1-\alpha/2g; (n-1)abc]$, conclude H_a

As before, the Tukey procedure concerns only pairwise comparisons.

23.5   Example of Three-Factor Study

The effects of gender of subject (factor A), body fat of subject (measured in percent, factor B), and smoking history of subject (factor C) on exercise tolerance (Y) were studied in a small-scale investigation of persons 25 to 35 years old. Exercise tolerance was measured in minutes until fatigue occurs while the subject is performing on a bicycle apparatus. Three subjects for each gender-body fat-smoking history group were given the exercise tolerance stress test. The results are recorded in Table 23.4a. Note that each factor has two levels ($a = b = c = 2$) and that there are three replications ($n = 3$) for each treatment.

The estimated treatment and factor level means are presented in Table 23.4b. Figure 23.5 presents the estimated treatment means $\overline{Y}_{ijk}$. in a simple, geometric format known as a *cube plot*. Figure 23.6 on page 944 contains the usual estimated treatment means plot. It appears from both of these figures that some factors may interact in their effect on exercise tolerance and that gender, in particular, may affect the endurance in stress testing. The researcher now wishes to analyze the nature of the factor effects in detail.

TABLE 23.4   **Sample Data and Estimated Treatment and Factor Level Means for Three-Factor Study—Stress Test Example.**

(a) Data

	Smoking History	
	$k = 1$ Light	$k = 2$ Heavy
$j = 1$ Low fat:		
$\quad i = 1$ Male	24.1 (Y_{1111}) 29.2 (Y_{1112}) 24.6 (Y_{1113})	17.6 (Y_{1121}) 18.8 (Y_{1122}) 23.2 (Y_{1123})
$\quad i = 2$ Female	20.0 (Y_{2111}) 21.9 (Y_{2112}) 17.6 (Y_{2113})	14.8 (Y_{2121}) 10.3 (Y_{2122}) 11.3 (Y_{2123})
$j = 2$ High fat:		
$\quad i = 1$ Male	14.6 (Y_{1211}) 15.3 (Y_{1212}) 12.3 (Y_{1213})	14.9 (Y_{1221}) 20.4 (Y_{1222}) 12.8 (Y_{1223})
$\quad i = 2$ Female	16.1 (Y_{2211}) 9.3 (Y_{2212}) 10.8 (Y_{2213})	10.1 (Y_{2221}) 14.4 (Y_{2222}) 6.1 (Y_{2223})

(b) Estimated Means

	$k = 1$	$k = 2$	All k
$j = 1$:			
$\quad i = 1$	25.97 $(\bar{Y}_{111.})$	19.87 $(\bar{Y}_{112.})$	22.92 $(\bar{Y}_{11..})$
$\quad i = 2$	19.83 $(\bar{Y}_{211.})$	12.13 $(\bar{Y}_{212.})$	15.98 $(\bar{Y}_{21..})$
$\quad$ All i	22.90 $(\bar{Y}_{11.})$	16.00 $(\bar{Y}_{12.})$	19.45 $(\bar{Y}_{1..})$
$j = 2$:			
$\quad i = 1$	14.07 $(\bar{Y}_{121.})$	16.03 $(\bar{Y}_{122.})$	15.05 $(\bar{Y}_{12..})$
$\quad i = 2$	12.07 $(\bar{Y}_{221.})$	10.20 $(\bar{Y}_{222.})$	11.13 $(\bar{Y}_{22..})$
$\quad$ All i	13.07 $(\bar{Y}_{21.})$	13.12 $(\bar{Y}_{22.})$	13.09 $(\bar{Y}_{2..})$
All j :			
$\quad i = 1$	20.02 $(\bar{Y}_{1.1.})$	17.95 $(\bar{Y}_{1.2.})$	18.98 $(\bar{Y}_{1...})$
$\quad i = 2$	15.95 $(\bar{Y}_{2.1.})$	11.17 $(\bar{Y}_{2.2.})$	13.56 $(\bar{Y}_{2...})$
$\quad$ All i	17.98 $(\bar{Y}_{.1.})$	14.56 $(\bar{Y}_{.2.})$	16.27 $(\bar{Y}_{...})$

FIGURE 23.6   **Plots of Estimated Treatment Means—Stress Test Example.**

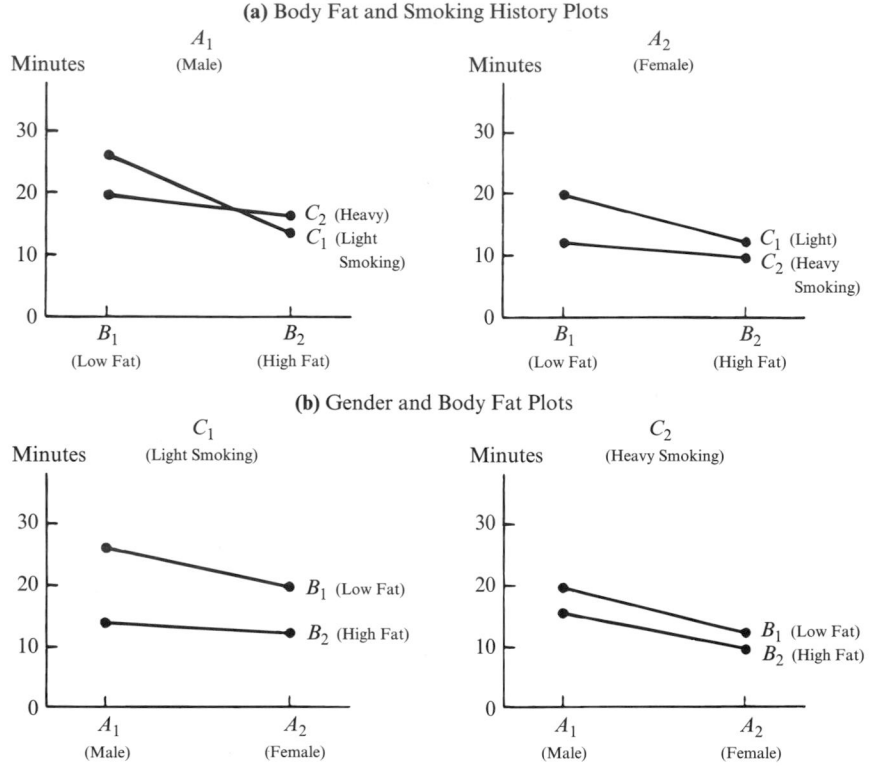

(a) Body Fat and Smoking History Plots

(b) Gender and Body Fat Plots

Residual Analysis

The researcher first prepared aligned residual dot plots for the eight treatments. These plots (not shown), though based on only three observations for each treatment, did not suggest any gross differences in the error variances for the eight treatments. The researcher also obtained a normal probability plot of the residuals, shown in Figure 23.7. The points in this plot form a moderately linear pattern. Normality of the error terms is supported by the high coefficient of correlation between the ordered residuals and their expected values under normality, namely, .969. The researcher was therefore satisfied that three-factor ANOVA model (23.14) is applicable here.

Tests for Factor Effects

The researcher first wished to test for the various factor effects. Figure 23.8 contains a portion of the SYSTAT ANOVA output. The researcher desired to conduct the seven potential tests with a family level of significance of $\alpha = .10$. This will ensure that if in fact no factor effects are present, there will be only one chance in 10 for one or more of the seven tests to lead to the conclusion of the presence of factor effects. Using the Kimball inequality (23.24), the researcher solved the equation:

$$\alpha = .10 = 1 - (1 - \alpha_i)^7$$

FIGURE 23.7   **Normal Probability Plot of Residuals—Stress Test Example.**

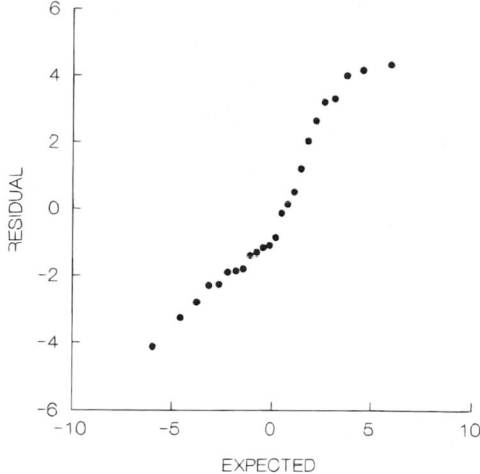

FIGURE 23.8   **SYSTAT ANOVA Output—Stress Test Example.**

ANALYSIS OF VARIANCE

SOURCE	SUM-OF-SQUARES	DF	MEAN-SQUARE	F-RATIO	P
GENDER	176.584	1	176.584	18.915	0.000
FAT	242.570	1	242.570	25.984	0.000
SMOKING	70.384	1	70.384	7.539	0.014
GENDER*FAT	13.650	1	13.650	1.462	0.244
GENDER *SMOKING	11.070	1	11.070	1.186	0.292
FAT*SMOKING	72.454	1	72.454	7.761	0.013
GENDER*FAT *SMOKING	1.870	1	1.870	0.200	0.660
ERROR	149.367	16	9.335		

and found $\alpha_i = .015$. Thus, use of significance level $\alpha_i = .015$ for each test ensures that the family level of significance will not exceed .10.

The ANOVA table in Figure 23.8 shows the seven test statistics and their *P*-values. Each test statistic has in the numerator the appropriate factor effect mean square, and the denominator of each test statistic is *MSE*.

Test for Three-Factor Interactions.   The first test was conducted for three-factor interactions. The alternatives are:

$$H_0: \text{ all } (\alpha\beta\gamma)_{ijk} = 0$$

$$H_a: \text{ not all } (\alpha\beta\gamma)_{ijk} \text{ equal zero}$$

The decision rule is:

$$\text{If } F^* \le F(.985; 1, 16) = 7.42, \text{ conclude } H_0$$

$$\text{If } F^* > F(.985; 1, 16) = 7.42, \text{ conclude } H_a$$

The F^* test statistic obtained from Figure 23.8 is:

$$F^* = \frac{MSABC}{MSE} = \frac{1.870}{9.335} = .20$$

Since $F^* = .20 \le 7.42$, the researcher concluded that no ABC interactions are present. The P-value of this test is .66.

Tests for Two-Factor Interactions. The researcher next tested for two-factor interactions. In the test for AB interactions, the decision rule is (the alternatives are given in Table 23.3):

$$\text{If } F^* \le F(.985; 1, 16) = 7.42, \text{ conclude } H_0$$

$$\text{If } F^* > F(.985; 1, 16) = 7.42, \text{ conclude } H_a$$

and the test statistic is:

$$F^* = \frac{MSAB}{MSE} = \frac{13.650}{9.335} = 1.46$$

Since $F^* = 1.46 \le 7.42$, the researcher concluded that no AB interactions are present. The P-value of this test is .24.

The tests for AC and BC interactions proceeded similarly. We obtain:

1. $F^* = \dfrac{MSAC}{MSE} = \dfrac{11.070}{9.335} = 1.19 \le F(.985; 1, 16) = 7.42 \qquad P\text{-value} = .29$

   Conclusion: No AC interactions are present.

2. $F^* = \dfrac{MSBC}{MSE} = \dfrac{72.454}{9.335} = 7.76 > F(.985; 1, 16) = 7.42 \qquad P\text{-value} = .01$

   Conclusion: Some BC interactions are present.

At this point, the researcher considered several simple transformations of the data to see if the BC interactions could be removed. However, this effort was not successful.

Tests for Main Effects. Since factor A (gender) did not interact with the other two factors, attention next turned to testing for factor A main effects. In testing for factor A main effects, the decision rule is (the alternatives are given in Table 23.3):

$$\text{If } F^* \le F(.985; 1, 16) = 7.42, \text{ conclude } H_0$$

$$\text{If } F^* > F(.985; 1, 16) = 7.42, \text{ conclude } H_a$$

The test statistic is:

$$F^* = \frac{MSA}{MSE} = \frac{176.584}{9.335} = 18.92$$

Since $F^* = 18.92 > 7.42$, the conclusion was reached that factor A main effects are present. The P-value of this test is 0+.

The factor B and factor C main effects were not tested at this point because BC interactions were found to be present. The researcher first wished to study the nature of the BC interaction effects before determining whether the factor B and factor C main effects are of any practical interest under the circumstances.

Family of Conclusions.   The five separate F tests for factor effects led the researcher to conclude (with family level of significance $\leq .10$):

1. There are no three-factor interactions.

2. There are no two-factor interactions between gender (factor A) and either of the other two factors—body fat (factor B) and smoking history (factor C). Body fat and smoking history interactions do exist, however.

3. Main effects for gender (factor A) are present.

This set of test results was most useful to the researcher. The next step in the analysis was to examine the nature of the BC interaction effects and of the factor A main effects.

Estimation of Contrasts of Treatment Means

To study the nature of the BC interaction effects, the researcher wished to estimate separately, for persons with high and low body fat, the difference in mean fatigue time for light smokers and heavy smokers. The desired contrasts are:

$$L_1 = \mu_{.11} - \mu_{.12}$$

$$L_2 = \mu_{.21} - \mu_{.22}$$

In addition, a single comparison between the factor level means for factor A is sufficient to analyze the factor A main effects since factor A has only two levels. The contrast of interest (here a pairwise comparison of factor level means) is:

$$L_3 = \mu_{1..} - \mu_{2..}$$

These three contrasts are estimated as follows, using the results in Table 23.4b:

$$\hat{L}_1 = \bar{Y}_{11.} - \bar{Y}_{12.} = 22.90 - 16.00 = 6.90$$

$$\hat{L}_2 = \bar{Y}_{21.} - \bar{Y}_{22.} = 13.07 - 13.12 = -.05$$

$$\hat{L}_3 = \bar{Y}_{1...} - \bar{Y}_{2...} = 18.98 - 13.56 = 5.42$$

The researcher obtained the estimated variances by using (23.44) and (23.31b) and the Bonferroni multiple for a 95 percent family confidence coefficient:

$$s^2\{\hat{L}_1\} = s^2\{\hat{L}_2\} = \frac{MSE}{na}[(1)^2 + (-1)^2] = \frac{9.335}{6}(2) = 3.112$$

$$s^2\{\hat{L}_3\} = \frac{MSE}{nbc}[(1)^2 + (-1)^2] = \frac{9.335}{12}(2) = 1.556$$

$$s\{\hat{L}_1\} = s\{\hat{L}_2\} = 1.764 \qquad s\{\hat{L}_3\} = 1.247$$

$$B = t(1 - .05/6; 16) = 2.673$$

The desired confidence intervals using (23.40) therefore are:

$$2.2 = 6.90 - 2.673(1.764) \leq \mu_{.11} - \mu_{.12} \leq 6.90 + 2.673(1.764) = 11.6$$

$$-4.8 = -.05 - 2.673(1.764) \leq \mu_{.21} - \mu_{.22} \leq -.05 + 2.673(1.764) = 4.7$$

$$2.1 = 5.42 - 2.673(1.247) \leq \mu_{1..} - \mu_{2..} \leq 5.42 + 2.673(1.247) = 8.8$$

The researcher therefore concluded with family confidence coefficient .95: (1) Among people with low body fat, those who have a light smoking history have a mean stress test endurance that is 2.2 to 11.6 minutes longer than the mean endurance for people with a heavy smoking history. (2) People with high body fat do not differ in mean stress test endurance whether they have a light or a heavy smoking history. (3) The mean stress test endurance for men is 2.1 to 8.8 minutes longer than the mean endurance for women.

In view of the important interaction effects between body fat and smoking history on stress test endurance noted in the study findings, the researcher concluded that factor B and factor C main effects are of no interest, and therefore terminated the analysis at this point. The principal findings are presented graphically in Figure 23.9. Figure 23.9a shows the magnitude of the effect of gender on stress test endurance, and Figure 23.9b shows the nature of the interaction effects between body fat and smoking history on stress test endurance.

23.6   Unequal Sample Sizes in Multifactor Studies

When the treatment sample sizes in a multifactor study are not equal, the procedures explained in Sections 22.1–22.3 for two-factor studies with unequal treatment sample sizes should be followed with routine modifications. We continue to assume that *all treatment means are of equal importance and that there are no empty cells.*

Tests for Factor Effects

Tests for factor effects in multifactor studies with unequal sample sizes can be conducted by means of the regression approach. Indicator variables taking on the values 1, −1, 0, are designated for each factor, the number of such variables for each factor being one less than the number of factor levels. Interaction effects are represented by cross-product terms, as

FIGURE 23.9   Key Findings from Stress Test Endurance Study.

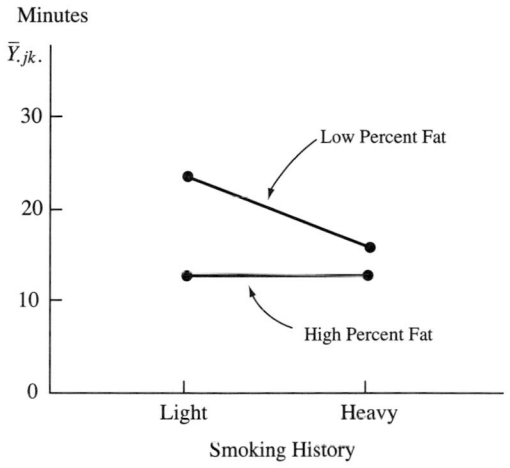

(a) Effect of Gender

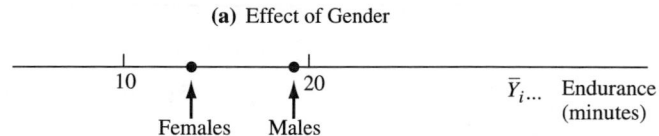

(b) Effects of Body Fat and Smoking History

usual. Since the sums of squares are no longer orthogonal when the treatment sample sizes are unequal, different reduced models need to be fitted for the tests of interest.

Example.   Suppose that in the stress test example of Table 23.4, observations Y_{1113} and Y_{2212} were missing. To develop a regression model for this example, we note that each of the three factors is at two levels. Hence, one indicator variable is required for each factor. The full regression model therefore is:

$$(23.47) \quad Y_{ijkm} = \mu_{...} + \alpha_1 X_{ijkm1} + \beta_1 X_{ijkm2} + \gamma_1 X_{ijkm3} + (\alpha\beta)_{11} X_{ijkm1} X_{ijkm2}$$
$$+ (\alpha\gamma)_{11} X_{ijkm1} X_{ijkm3} + (\beta\gamma)_{11} X_{ijkm2} X_{ijkm3}$$
$$+ (\alpha\beta\gamma)_{111} X_{ijkm1} X_{ijkm2} X_{ijkm3} + \varepsilon_{ijkm} \qquad \text{Full model}$$

where:

TABLE 23.5   **Data for Regression Model (23.47)—Stress Test Example with Y_{1113} and Y_{2212} Missing.**

				(1)	(2)	(3)	(4)	(5)	(6)	(7)	(8)
i	j	k	m	Y	X_1	X_2	X_3	$X_1 X_2$	$X_1 X_3$	$X_2 X_3$	$X_1 X_2 X_3$
1	1	1	1	24.1	1	1	1	1	1	1	1
1	1	1	2	29.2	1	1	1	1	1	1	1
1	1	2	1	17.6	1	1	−1	1	−1	−1	−1
$\cdots$				$\cdots$	$\cdots$	$\cdots$	$\cdots$	$\cdots$	$\cdots$	$\cdots$	$\cdots$
2	2	1	1	16.1	−1	−1	1	1	−1	−1	1
2	2	1	3	10.8	−1	−1	1	1	−1	−1	1
2	2	2	1	10.1	−1	−1	−1	1	1	1	−1
2	2	2	2	14.4	−1	−1	−1	1	1	1	−1
2	2	2	3	6.1	−1	−1	−1	1	1	1	−1

$$X_1 = \begin{matrix} 1 & \text{if case from level 1 for factor } A \\ -1 & \text{if case from level 2 for factor } A \end{matrix}$$

$$X_2 = \begin{matrix} 1 & \text{if case from level 1 for factor } B \\ -1 & \text{if case from level 2 for factor } B \end{matrix}$$

$$X_3 = \begin{matrix} 1 & \text{if case from level 1 for factor } C \\ -1 & \text{if case from level 2 for factor } C \end{matrix}$$

The regression parameters in model (23.47) are the ANOVA model parameters as defined in (23.13).

Table 23.5 repeats in column 1 a portion of the Y observations for the stress test example in Table 23.4 with observations Y_{1113} and Y_{2212} missing. The coded indicator variables X_1, X_2, and X_3 are shown in columns 2–4 and the cross-product interaction terms are shown in columns 5–8. The full model in (23.47) is fitted by regressing Y in column 1 of Table 23.5 on the X variables in columns 2–8. To test a particular factor effect, the reduced model is obtained by dropping the appropriate X variable(s). For instance, to test for factor A main effects, X_1 would be dropped to obtain the reduced model and Y would be regressed on the X variables in columns 3–8.

Note

The discussion in Section 22.6 on the use of statistical packages for analysis of variance with unequal sample sizes and/or empty cells is applicable in its entirety for multifactor studies.   ∎

Inferences for Contrasts of Factor Level Means

Estimation and testing of contrasts of factor level means in multifactor studies with unequal sample sizes are conducted in similar fashion as for two-factor studies. The formulas in

Table 22.5 for the development of interval estimates need simply be extended to three or more factors. Testing procedures may be devised from these extensions in the usual fashion.

To illustrate such an extension, consider pairwise comparisons of factor A level means in a three-factor study with unequal samples sizes. Extending formula (22.14), we obtain for the comparison, its estimator, and the estimated variance:

$$(23.48a) \qquad D = \mu_{i..} - \mu_{i'..}$$

$$(23.48b) \qquad \hat{D} = \hat{\mu}_{i..} - \hat{\mu}_{i'..} \qquad \text{where} \qquad \hat{\mu}_{i..} = \frac{\sum_j \sum_k \bar{Y}_{ijk.}}{bc}$$

$$(23.48c) \qquad s^2\{\hat{D}\} = \frac{MSE}{b^2 c^2} \sum_j \sum_k \left(\frac{1}{n_{ijk}} + \frac{1}{n_{i'jk}} \right)$$

The appropriate degrees of freedom associated with MSE are $n_T - abc$.

Problems

23.1. Refer to Table 23.1 containing the mean responses μ_{ijk} for a three-factor study.

   a. Find the main effects of age.

   b. Find the interaction effect of young age and normal IQ.

   c. Find the interaction effect of young age, normal IQ, and female gender.

23.2. Prepare AC plots of the mean responses μ_{ijk} in Table 23.1 in the format of Figure 23.2b. Do your plots convey the same information as Figure 23.4? Discuss.

23.3. Prepare BC plots of the mean responses μ_{ijk} in Figure 23.3. Do your plots bring out any information on main effects and interactions not readily seen from Figure 23.3? Discuss.

23.4. In a three-factor study, the mean responses μ_{ijk} are as follows:

	$k = 1$		$k = 2$	
	$j = 1$	$j = 2$	$j = 1$	$j = 2$
$i = 1$	130	138	140	144
$i = 2$	126	130	134	136
$i = 3$	122	125	122	131

   a. Find α_1, α_2, and α_3.

   b. Find β_2 and γ_1.

   c. Find $(\alpha\beta)_{12}$, $(\alpha\gamma)_{21}$, and $(\beta\gamma)_{12}$.

   d. Find $(\alpha\beta\gamma)_{111}$ and $(\alpha\beta\gamma)_{322}$.

23.5. Refer to Problem 23.4. Prepare AB plots of the mean responses μ_{ijk} in the format of Figure 23.3. What do these plots show about factor main effects and interactions?

√ 23.6.   **Case hardening**. An experiment involving the case hardening of lightweight shafts machined from bars of an alloy was run to study the effects of the amount of a chemical agent added to the alloy in a molten state (factor A), the temperature of the hardening process (factor B), and the time duration of the hardening process (factor C) on the outside hardness of the shaft. All factors were at two levels (1: low, 2: high), and the number of rods tested for each treatment was $n = 3$. The data on hardness (in Brinell units) follow.

	$k = 1$		$k = 2$	
	$j = 1$	$j = 2$	$j = 1$	$j = 2$
$i = 1$	39.9	53.5	56.0	70.9
	32.2	50.7	56.9	73.3
	36.3	52.8	56.6	71.6
$i = 2$	45.2	63.3	69.4	82.9
	48.0	65.5	66.6	85.2
	47.5	63.6	68.8	82.3

a. Obtain the residuals for ANOVA model (23.14) and prepare aligned residual dot plots for each level of factor A. Do the same for each of the other two factors. What information do these plots provide about the appropriateness of ANOVA model (23.14)?

b. Prepare a normal probability plot of the residuals. Also obtain the coefficient of correlation between the ordered residuals and their expected values under normality. Does the normality assumption appear to be reasonable here?

√ 23.7.   Refer to **Case hardening** Problem 23.6. Assume that fixed ANOVA model (23.14) is appropriate.

a. Prepare AB plots of the estimated treatment means $\overline{Y}_{ijk}$. in the format of Figure 23.6b. Does it appear that any interactions are present? Any main effects?

b. Obtain the analysis of variance table.

c. Test for three-factor interactions; use $\alpha = .025$. State the alternatives, decision rule, and conclusion. What is the P-value of the test?

d. Test for AB, AC, and BC interactions. For each test, use $\alpha = .025$ and state the alternatives, decision rule, and conclusion. What is the P-value of each test?

e. Test for A, B, and C main effects. For each test, use $\alpha = .025$ and state the alternatives, decision rule, and conclusion. What is the P-value of each test?

f. State the set of conclusions that can be reached from the tests in parts (c), (d), and (e). Obtain an upper bound for the family level of significance for the set of tests; use the Kimball inequality.

g. Do the results in part (f) confirm your graphic analysis in part (a)?

√ 23.8.   Refer to **Case hardening** Problems 23.6 and 23.7.

a. To study the nature of the main factor effects, estimate the following pairwise comparisons:

$$D_1 = \mu_{2..} - \mu_{1..} \qquad D_2 = \mu_{.2.} - \mu_{.1.} \qquad D_3 = \mu_{..2} - \mu_{..1}$$

Use the Bonferroni procedure with a 95 percent family confidence coefficient. State your findings.

    b. Estimate μ_{222} with a 95 percent confidence interval.

23.9. **Marketing research contractors.** A marketing research consultant evaluated the effects of fee schedule (factor A), scope of work (factor B), and type of supervisory control (factor C) on the quality of work performed under contract by independent marketing research agencies. The factor levels in the study were as follows:

Factor	Factor Levels
A Fee level	$i = 1$: High $i = 2$: Average $i = 3$: Low
B Scope	$j = 1$: All contract work performed in house $j = 2$: Some work subcontracted out
C Supervision	$k = 1$: Local supervisors $k = 2$: Traveling supervisors only

The quality of work performed was measured by an index taking into account several characteristics of quality. Four agencies were chosen for each factor level combination and the quality of their work evaluated. The data on quality follow.

	$k = 1$		$k = 2$	
	$j = 1$	$j = 2$	$j = 1$	$j = 2$
$i = 1$	124.3	115.1	112.7	88.2
	$\cdots$	$\cdots$	$\cdots$	$\cdots$
	122.6	117.3	108.6	90.1
$i = 2$	119.3	117.2	113.6	92.7
	$\cdots$	$\cdots$	$\cdots$	$\cdots$
	121.4	120.0	112.3	87.9
$i = 3$	90.9	89.9	78.6	58.6
	$\cdots$	$\cdots$	$\cdots$	$\cdots$
	92.0	82.7	77.1	62.3

    a. Obtain the residuals for ANOVA model (23.14) and plot them against the fitted values. What does your plot suggest about the appropriateness of ANOVA model (23.14)?

    b. Prepare a normal probability plot of the residuals. Also obtain the coefficient of correlation between the ordered residuals and their expected values under normality. Does the normality assumption appear to be reasonable here?

23.10. Refer to **Marketing research contractors** Problem 23.9. Assume that fixed ANOVA model (23.14) is appropriate.

    a. Prepare AB plots of the estimated treatment means $\bar{Y}_{ijk}$ in the format of Figure 23.6b. Does it appear that any interactions are present? Any main effects?

    b. Prepare a normal probability plot of the estimated factor A level means. What does this plot suggest about the nature of the factor A main effects?

    c. Obtain the analysis of variance table.

    d. Test for three-factor interactions; use $\alpha = .01$. State the alternatives, decision rule, and conclusion. What is the P-value of the test?

e. Test for AB, AC, and BC interactions. For each test, use $\alpha = .01$ and state the alternatives, decision rule, and conclusion. What is the P-value of each test?

f. Test for factor A main effects; use $\alpha = .01$. State the alternatives, decision rule, and conclusion. What is the P-value of the test?

g. State the set of conclusions that can be reached from the tests in parts (d), (e), and (f). Obtain an upper bound for the family level of significance for the set of tests; use the Kimball inequality.

h. Do the results in part (g) confirm your graphic analysis in parts (a) and (b)?

23.11. Refer to **Marketing research contractors** Problems 23.9 and 23.10.

a. To study the nature of the factor A main effects and the BC interactions, it is desired to estimate the following comparisons:

$$D_1 = \mu_{1..} - \mu_{2..} \qquad D_4 = \mu_{.11} - \mu_{.12}$$

$$D_2 = \mu_{2..} - \mu_{3..} \qquad D_5 = \mu_{.21} - \mu_{.22}$$

$$D_3 = \mu_{1..} - \mu_{3..} \qquad L_1 = D_4 - D_5$$

Use the Bonferroni procedure with a 90 percent family confidence coefficient to make the desired comparisons. State your findings.

b. Estimate $D = \mu_{121} - \mu_{221}$ with a 95 percent confidence interval.

c. The consultant wishes to identify the type(s) of independent marketing research agencies that provide the highest quality of work. Use the Tukey testing procedure with family level of significance $\alpha = .10$ to make the desired identifications.

23.12. **Electronics assembly.** Assemblers in an electronics firm will attach 12 components to a newly developed "board" that will be used in automatic-control equipment in manufacturing plants. An operations analyst conducted an experiment to study the effects of three factors on the mean time to assemble a board. Factor A was the gender of the assembler ($i = 1$: male; $i = 2$: female), factor B was the sequence of assembling the components ($j = 1, 2, 3$), and factor C was the amount of experience by the assembler ($k = 1$: under 18 months; $k = 2$: 18 months or more). Randomization was used to assign 15 assemblers of each gender with a given amount of experience to each of the three assembly sequences, with each sequence assigned to five assemblers. After a learning period, the total time (in minutes) to assemble 50 boards was observed. The data follow.

	$k = 1$			$k = 2$		
	$j = 1$	$j = 2$	$j = 3$	$j = 1$	$j = 2$	$j = 3$
$i = 1$	1,250	1,319	1,217	1,021	1,119	1,033
	1,175	1,251	1,190	1,099	1,110	1,067
	$\cdots$	$\cdots$	$\cdots$	$\cdots$	$\cdots$	$\cdots$
	1,193	1,265	1,251	1,070	1,163	1,022
$i = 2$	1,066	1,105	1,021	864	927	841
	1,076	1,043	1,020	848	944	865
	$\cdots$	$\cdots$	$\cdots$	$\cdots$	$\cdots$	$\cdots$
	1,034	1,060	1,026	868	933	868

    a. Obtain the residuals for ANOVA model (23.14) and plot them against the fitted values. What does your plot suggest about the appropriateness of ANOVA model (23.14)?

    b. Prepare a normal probability plot of the residuals. Also obtain the coefficient of correlation between the ordered residuals and their expected values under normality. Does the normality assumption appear to be reasonable here?

23.13. Refer to **Electronics assembly** Problem 23.12. Assume that fixed ANOVA model (23.14) is appropriate.

    a. Prepare AB plots of the estimated treatment means $\bar{Y}_{ijk\cdot}$ in the format of Figure 23.6b. Does it appear that any interactions are present? Any main effects?

    b. For each factor, prepare a normal probability plot of the estimated factor level means. What do these plots suggest about the nature of the factor effects?

    c. Obtain the analysis of variance table.

    d. Test for three-factor interactions; use $\alpha = .05$. State the alternatives, decision rule, and conclusion. What is the P-value of the test?

    e. Test for AB, AC, and BC interactions. For each test, use $\alpha = .05$ and state the alternatives, decision rule, and conclusion. What is the P-value of each test?

    f. Test for A, B, and C main effects. For each test, use $\alpha = .05$ and state the alternatives, decision rule, and conclusion. What is the P-value of each test?

    g. State the set of conclusions that can be reached from the tests in parts (d), (e), and (f). Obtain an upper bound for the family level of significance for the set of tests; use the Kimball inequality.

    h. Do the results in part (g) confirm your graphic analysis in parts (a) and (b)?

23.14. Refer to **Electronics assembly** Problems 23.12 and 23.13.

    a. To study the nature of the factor main effects, estimate the following pairwise comparisons:

$$D_1 = \mu_{1\cdot\cdot} - \mu_{2\cdot\cdot} \qquad D_4 = \mu_{\cdot2\cdot} - \mu_{\cdot3\cdot}$$

$$D_2 = \mu_{\cdot1\cdot} - \mu_{\cdot2\cdot} \qquad D_5 = \mu_{\cdot\cdot1} - \mu_{\cdot\cdot2}$$

$$D_3 = \mu_{\cdot1\cdot} - \mu_{\cdot3\cdot}$$

    Use the Bonferroni procedure with a 90 percent family confidence coefficient. State your findings.

    b. Estimate μ_{231} with a 95 percent confidence interval.

√ 23.15. Refer to **Case hardening** Problem 23.6. Suppose that observations $Y_{1211} = 53.5$ and $Y_{1212} = 50.7$ are missing.

    a. State the full regression model equivalent to ANOVA model (23.14); use 1, −1, 0 indicator variables.

    b. What is the reduced regression model for testing for factor A main effects?

    c. Test whether or not factor A main effects are present by fitting the full and reduced regression models; use $\alpha = .025$. State the alternatives, decision rule, and conclusion. What is the P-value of the test?

    d. Estimate $D = \mu_{2\cdot\cdot} - \mu_{1\cdot\cdot}$ with a 95 percent confidence interval.

23.16. Refer to **Electronics assembly** Problem 23.12. Suppose that observations $Y_{1224} = 1,097$, $Y_{2213} = 1,051$, and $Y_{2125} = 868$ are missing.

a. State the full regression model equivalent to ANOVA model (23.14); use 1, −1, 0 indicator variables.

b. What is the reduced regression model for testing for factor C main effects?

c. Test whether or not factor C main effects are present by fitting the full and reduced regression models; use $\alpha = .05$. State the alternatives, decision rule, and conclusion. What is the P-value of the test?

d. Estimate $D = \mu_{..1} - \mu_{..2}$ with a 95 percent confidence interval.

Exercises

23.17. For fixed ANOVA model (23.14), show that $\sum_i (\alpha\beta\gamma)_{ijk} = 0$.

23.18. State the fixed ANOVA model for a three-factor study with $n = 1$ when all three-factor interactions are zero. Show the ANOVA table for this case.

23.19. For fixed ANOVA model (23.14), derive the variance of the estimated contrast $\hat{L} = \Sigma\Sigma c_{ij}\bar{Y}_{ij..}$

Projects

23.20. Refer to the **SENIC** data set. The following hospitals are to be considered in a study of the effects of average age of patients (factor A: variable 3), available facilities and services (factor B: variable 12), and region (factor C: variable 9) on the mean length of hospital stay of patients (variable 2):

1–14	16–28	31	32	34	35	37–39	41	44	46	50
52	53	57	58	63	66	76	77	83	111	

For purposes of this ANOVA study, average age is to be classified into two categories (less than 53.0 years, 53.0 years or more) and available facilities and services are to be classified into two categories (less than 40.2 percent, 40.2 percent or more).

a. Assemble the required data and obtain the residuals for ANOVA model (23.14).

b. Plot the residuals against the fitted values. What does your plot suggest about the appropriateness of ANOVA model (23.14)?

c. Prepare a normal probability plot of the residuals. Also obtain the coefficient of correlation between the ordered residuals and their expected values under normality. Does the normality assumption appear reasonable here?

23.21. Refer to the **SENIC** data set and Project 23.20. Assume that fixed ANOVA model (23.14) is appropriate.

a. Plot the estimated treatment means $\bar{Y}_{ijk.}$ in the format of Figure 23.6a. Does it appear that any factor effects are present? Explain.

b. Prepare a separate normal probability plot of the estimated factor level means for each factor. What do these plots suggest about the nature of the factor main effects?

   c. Obtain the analysis of variance table. Does any one source account for most of the total variability in the study? Explain.

   d. Test for three-factor interactions; use $\alpha = .01$. State the alternatives, decision rule, and conclusion. What is the P-value of the test?

   e. Test for AB, AC, and BC interactions. For each test, use $\alpha = .01$ and state the alternatives, decision rule, and conclusion. What is the P-value of each test?

   f. Test for A, B, and C main effects. For each test, use $\alpha = .01$ and state the alternatives, decision rule, and conclusion. What is the P-value of each test?

   g. To study the nature of the available facilities and region main effects, make all pairwise comparisons for each of these two factors. Use the Bonferroni procedure with a 90 percent family confidence coefficient. State your findings.

23.22. Refer to the **SMSA** data set. The effects of region (factor A: variable 12), percent of population in central cities (factor B: variable 4), and percent of population 65 or older (factor C: variable 5) on the crime rate (variable 11 ÷ variable 3) are to be studied. For purposes of this ANOVA study, percent of population in central cities is to be classified into two categories (40.0 percent or less, 40.1 percent or more) and percent of population 65 or older is to be classified into two categories (9.9 percent or less, 10.0 percent or more).

   a. Assemble the required data and obtain the residuals for ANOVA model (23.14) with $m = 1, \ldots, n_{ijk}$.

   b. Plot the residuals against the fitted values. What does your plot suggest about the appropriateness of ANOVA model (23.14)?

   c. Prepare a normal probability plot of the residuals. Also obtain the coefficient of correlation between the ordered residuals and their expected values under normality. Does the normality assumption appear reasonable here?

23.23. Refer to the **SMSA** data set and Project 23.22. Assume that fixed ANOVA model (23.14) with $m = 1, \ldots, n_{ijk}$ is appropriate.

   a. Plot the estimated treatment means $\bar{Y}_{ijk.}$ in the format of Figure 23.6b. Does it appear that any factor effects are present?

   b. State the equivalent regression model for this case; use $1, -1, 0$ indicator variables, and fit this full model.

   c. Test for three-factor interactions and for AB, AC, and BC interactions. For each test, use $\alpha = .025$ and state the alternatives, reduced regression model, decision rule, and conclusion. What is the P-value of each test?

   d. Test for A, B, and C main effects. For each test, use $\alpha = .025$ and state the alternatives, reduced regression model, decision rule, and conclusion. What is the P-value of each test?

   e. To study the nature of the region main effects, make all pairwise comparisons between the region means. Use the Tukey procedure with a 95 percent family confidence coefficient. State your findings.

24 Random and Mixed Effects Models

Until now, we have been concerned exclusively with ANOVA model I in which the factor levels are considered fixed. This model is applicable for studies where our interest centers on the effects of the specific factor levels chosen. There are still other studies where the factor levels are a sample from a larger population of potential factor levels and inferences are desired about the populations of factor levels. For example, in Section 16.6 we described a single-factor study by a company that owns several hundred retail stores. Seven of these stores were selected at random, and a sample of employees in each store was asked to evaluate the management of the store. The seven stores chosen for the study constitute the seven levels of the random factor, retail stores. In this case, management was not just interested in the management of the seven stores chosen; it wanted to generalize the results to the entire population of stores. Because the retail stores were selected at random, the factor retail stores in this example is considered a random factor. Random factors may also be present in two-factor and multifactor studies; either all of the factors may be random or some may be random and some fixed. For instance, suppose in the previous example that eight employees were selected at random from each of the five departments in each of the stores. Interest now is in the employee evaluations of management by department and store. Here, stores would be a random factor because the seven selected stores are a sample of all stores. On the other hand, departments would be a fixed factor because there are only five departments in each store and interest is in these five departments.

Analysis of variance models for studies in which all factors are random are called ANOVA models II and those for studies in which some factors are random and some fixed are called ANOVA models III. In this chapter, we consider ANOVA model II for single-factor studies and ANOVA models II and III for two-factor and three-factor studies. Throughout Sections 24.1 to 24.5, we assume that all treatment sample sizes are equal. In Section 24.6 we consider studies where the treatment sample sizes are unequal. We begin our discussion with random ANOVA model II for single-factor studies.

24.1 Single-Factor Studies—ANOVA Model II

As we noted earlier, there are occasions when the factor levels or treatments in a single-factor study are not of intrinsic interest in themselves but constitute a sample from a larger population of factor levels. ANOVA model II is designed for this type of situation. Consider, for instance, Apex Enterprises, a company that builds roadside restaurants carrying one of several promoted trade names, leases franchises to individuals to operate the restaurants, and provides management services. This company employs a large number of personnel officers who interview applicants for jobs in the restaurants. At the end of an interview, the personnel officer assigns a rating between 0 and 100 to indicate the applicant's potential value on the job. Five personnel officers were selected at random, and each was assigned four candidates at random. In this case, the company did not wish to make inferences concerning the five personnel officers who happened to be selected but rather about the population of all personnel officers. Questions of interest included: How great is the variation in ratings among all personnel officers? What is the mean rating by all personnel officers?

The distinction between this situation, for which ANOVA model II is designed, and one where fixed ANOVA model I is appropriate can be seen readily by modifying our example slightly. If a smaller company had only five personnel officers who were all included in the study and interest is limited to these five officers, ANOVA model I would be relevant since the factor levels (the five personnel officers) would then not be considered a sample from a larger population. A repetition of the experiment for the smaller company would involve the same five personnel officers, but in the case of Apex Enterprises a repetition would involve a new random sample of five personnel officers which would probably consist of different officers.

Random Cell Means Model

The cell means version of ANOVA model II for single-factor studies is as follows when all factor level sample sizes are equal, i.e., when $n_i \equiv n$:

$$(24.1) \qquad\qquad Y_{ij} = \mu_i + \varepsilon_{ij}$$

where:

> μ_i are independent $N(\mu_., \sigma_\mu^2)$
>
> ε_{ij} are independent $N(0, \sigma^2)$
>
> μ_i and ε_{ij} are independent random variables
>
> $i = 1, \ldots, r; j = 1, \ldots, n$

ANOVA model (24.1) is similar in appearance to fixed ANOVA model (16.2). The main distinction is that the factor level means μ_i are constants for ANOVA model I but are random variables for ANOVA model II. Hence, ANOVA model II is often called a *random ANOVA model*.

Meaning of Model Terms.   We shall explain the meaning of the model terms with reference to the personnel officers in the Apex Enterprises example. The term μ_i corresponds to the mean of all ratings by the ith personnel officer if the officer interviewed all prospective employees. The expected value of μ_i is $\mu_.$. Thus, $\mu_.$ represents here the mean rating for all prospective employees by all personnel officers. The variability of the personnel officers' mean ratings μ_i is measured by the variance σ_μ^2. The more the different personnel officers vary in their mean ratings (for instance, some may rate consistently higher than others), the greater will be σ_μ^2. If all personnel officers rate at the same mean level, all μ_i will be equal to $\mu_.$ and then $\sigma_\mu^2 = 0$.

The term ε_{ij} represents the variation associated with the different potential values as assessed by the ith personnel officer for the different prospective employees. Note that ANOVA model (24.1) assumes that all ε_{ij} have the same variance σ^2. This means that the

FIGURE 24.1   **Representation of ANOVA Model II.**

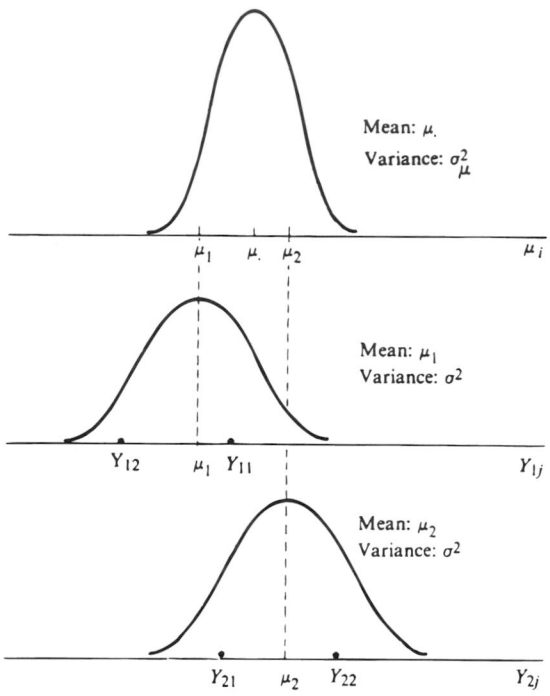

distributions of ratings for prospective employees by the different personnel officers are assumed to have the same variability. The distributions for the different personnel officers may differ with respect to their means but not with respect to their variability according to ANOVA model (24.1).

Figure 24.1 illustrates ANOVA model II. On the top is shown the distribution of the personnel officers' mean ratings μ_i, which is normal. Several μ_i (two personnel officers' mean ratings in the illustration) are selected at random from this distribution. Each in turn leads to a distribution of the potential values of prospective employees as evaluated by the ith personnel officer, $Y_{ij} = \mu_i + \varepsilon_{ij}$, which are all normal distributions with the same variance. Several Y_{ij} responses are then selected from each of these distributions (two responses for each personnel officer in the illustration).

Important Features of Model.

1. The expected value of a response Y_{ij} is:

(24.2a) $$E\{Y_{ij}\} = \mu.$$

because we have by (24.1):

$$E\{Y_{ij}\} = E\{\mu_i\} + E\{\varepsilon_{ij}\}$$
$$= \mu. + 0$$
$$= \mu.$$

Note that this expectation averages over the selections of both μ_i and ε_{ij}.

2. The variance of Y_{ij}, to be denoted by σ_Y^2, is:

$$(24.2b) \qquad \sigma^2\{Y_{ij}\} = \sigma_Y^2 = \sigma_\mu^2 + \sigma^2$$

Thus, all observations Y_{ij} have the same variance. The result in (24.2b) follows because ANOVA model II assumes that μ_i and ε_{ij} are independent random variables, and $\sigma^2\{\mu_i\} = \sigma_\mu^2$ and $\sigma^2\{\varepsilon_{ij}\} = \sigma^2$ according to ANOVA model (24.1). Because the variance of Y in this model is the sum of two components, σ_μ^2 and σ^2, this model is sometimes called a *components of variance model* and σ_Y^2 is referred to as the *total variance*. (Reference 24.1 provides detailed discussions of variance components models.)

3. The Y_{ij} are normally distributed because they are linear combinations of the independent normal variables μ_i and ε_{ij}.

4. Unlike for fixed ANOVA model I where all observations Y_{ij} are independent, the Y_{ij} for random ANOVA model II are only independent if they pertain to different factor levels. The covariance of any two observations with random ANOVA model (24.1) can be shown to be:

$$(24.2c) \qquad \sigma\{Y_{ij}, Y_{ij'}\} = \sigma_\mu^2 \qquad j \neq j'$$

$$(24.2d) \qquad \sigma\{Y_{ij}, Y_{i'j'}\} = 0 \qquad i \neq i'$$

Thus, random ANOVA model (24.1) assumes that the covariance between any two responses for the same factor level is constant for all factor levels.

We illustrate the nature of the variance-covariance matrix of the responses Y_{ij} for random ANOVA model (24.1) for a simple illustration where there are $r = 2$ factor levels and $n = 2$ cases for each level. The observations vector is:

$$\mathbf{Y} = \begin{bmatrix} Y_{11} \\ Y_{12} \\ Y_{21} \\ Y_{22} \end{bmatrix}$$

and the variance-covariance matrix of the Y observations is:

$$\boldsymbol{\sigma}^2\{\mathbf{Y}\} = \begin{bmatrix} \sigma_Y^2 & \sigma_\mu^2 & 0 & 0 \\ \sigma_\mu^2 & \sigma_Y^2 & 0 & 0 \\ 0 & 0 & \sigma_Y^2 & \sigma_\mu^2 \\ 0 & 0 & \sigma_\mu^2 & \sigma_Y^2 \end{bmatrix}$$

Note that all observations have the same variance σ_Y^2, as indicated by (24.2b), any two observations from the same factor level have covariance σ_μ^2 as indicated by (24.2c), and any two observations from different factor levels are uncorrelated as indicated by (24.2d).

The reason why any two responses from the same factor level are correlated is that, in advance of the random trials, the responses are expected to be similar because they will both have the same random component μ_i and will differ only because of the error terms ε_{ij}.

Once the factor levels have been selected, however, random ANOVA model (24.1) assumes that any two responses from the same factor level are independent because the factor level mean μ_i is then fixed and the two observations differ only because of the error terms ε_{ij} which are assumed to be independent. Thus, in the Apex Enterprises example, once the personnel officers have been selected, random ANOVA model (24.1) assumes that the different ratings Y_{ij} by a given personnel officer are independent.

Note

At times, the population of the μ_i may be relatively small and should be treated as a finite population. This can be done, but we do not discuss this case here. If the population of the μ_i is finite but large, little is lost in treating it as an infinite population. We did this, in fact, in our Apex Enterprises illustration. The number of personnel officers employed by Apex Enterprises is finite, but since there are many we treated the population of the μ_i as an infinite one. Thus, there are two basic situations when the population of the μ_i is treated as infinite—when the population is finite but large, and when interest centers in the underlying *process* generating the μ_i. ∎

Questions of Interest

When ANOVA model II is appropriate, there is usually no interest in inferences about the particular μ_i included in the study, such as which is the largest or smallest, but rather in inferences about the entire population of the μ_i. Specifically, interest often centers on $\mu_.$, the mean of the μ_i, and on σ_μ^2, the variability of the μ_i. In the Apex Enterprises example, for instance, management would not ordinarily be as interested in the mean ratings of the five personnel officers who happened to be included in the study as in the mean rating by all personnel officers and in the variability of mean ratings among all personnel officers.

While σ_μ^2 is a direct measure of the variability of the μ_i, the effect of this variability is often measured more meaningfully relative to the total variability σ_Y^2 in (24.2b):

$$(24.3) \qquad \frac{\sigma_\mu^2}{\sigma_Y^2} = \frac{\sigma_\mu^2}{\sigma_\mu^2 + \sigma^2}$$

Note that this ratio measures the proportion of the total variability of the Y_{ij} that is accounted for by the variability of the μ_i. It takes on the value 0 when $\sigma_\mu^2 = 0$ and values near 1 when σ_μ^2 is large relative to σ^2.

With reference to the Apex Enterprises example, the ratio measures the proportion of the total variability of ratings for all candidates by all personnel officers that is accounted for by differences in the mean ratings among the personnel officers. If the ratio is near zero, differences in the mean ratings among personnel officers are relatively insignificant. On the other hand, if the ratio is large, say, .8 or more, then much of the total variability is accounted for by differences between personnel officers, and management may wish to study the advisability of giving the personnel officers more training to obtain improved consistency of ratings between officers.

Note

It can be shown that the coefficient of correlation between any two responses from the same factor level with random ANOVA model (24.1) is:

$$(24.4) \qquad \rho\{Y_{ij}, Y_{ij'}\} = \frac{\sigma_\mu^2}{\sigma_Y^2} = \frac{\sigma_\mu^2}{\sigma_\mu^2 + \sigma^2} \qquad j \neq j'$$

Thus, the measure in (24.3), which indicates the proportion of the total variability of the Y_{ij} that is accounted for by the variability of the μ_i, is actually the coefficient of correlation between any two observations from the same factor level. It is called the *intraclass correlation coefficient*.

The result in (24.4) follows from the definition of the coefficient of correlation in (A.25a):

$$\rho\{Y_{ij}, Y_{ij'}\} = \frac{\sigma\{Y_{ij}, Y_{ij'}\}}{\sigma\{Y_{ij}\}\sigma\{Y_{ij'}\}}$$

The covariance in the numerator is given in (24.2c), and $\sigma\{Y_{ij}\} = \sigma\{Y_{ij'}\} = \sigma_Y$ according to (24.2b). ∎

Test Whether $\sigma_\mu^2 = 0$

We first consider how to test whether all μ_i are equal:

(24.5)
$$H_0: \sigma_\mu^2 = 0$$
$$H_a: \sigma_\mu^2 > 0$$

H_0 implies that all μ_i are equal; that is, $\mu_i \equiv \mu_{\cdot}$. H_a implies that the μ_i differ. For the personnel officers example, H_0 implies that the mean ratings for all personnel officers are the same, while H_a implies that they differ.

Despite the fact that ANOVA model II differs from ANOVA model I, the analysis of variance for a single-factor study is conducted in identical fashion. (This is not always the case in more complex situations.) The difference between the two models appears in the expected mean squares. It can be shown, in a manner similar to that employed in our derivation for ANOVA model I, that the expected mean squares for ANOVA model II when all treatment sample sizes equal n are as follows:

(24.6)
$$E\{MSE\} = \sigma^2$$

(24.7)
$$E\{MSTR\} = \sigma^2 + n\sigma_\mu^2$$

It follows from (24.6) and (24.7) that if $\sigma_\mu^2 = 0$, *MSE* and *MSTR* have the same expectation σ^2. Otherwise, $E\{MSTR\} > E\{MSE\}$ since $n > 0$ always. Hence, large values of the test statistic:

(24.8)
$$F^* = \frac{MSTR}{MSE}$$

will lead to conclusion H_a in (24.5). Since F^* again follows the F distribution when H_0 holds, the decision rule for controlling the risk of making a Type I error at α is the same as the one for ANOVA model I:

(24.9)
$$\text{If } F^* \leq F[1 - \alpha; r - 1, r(n - 1)], \text{ conclude } H_0$$
$$\text{If } F^* > F[1 - \alpha; r - 1, r(n - 1)], \text{ conclude } H_a$$

Note that the degrees of freedom associated with *MSE* here are $n_T - r = r(n - 1)$ since $n_T = rn$ when all factor level sample sizes are equal.

TABLE 24.1 Ratings by Five Personnel Officers—Apex Enterprises Example.

Officer	Candidate (j)				
i	1	2	3	4	Mean
A	76	65	85	74	$\bar{Y}_{1.} = 75.0$
B	59	75	81	67	$\bar{Y}_{2.} = 70.5$
C	49	63	61	46	$\bar{Y}_{3.} = 54.75$
D	74	71	85	89	$\bar{Y}_{4.} = 79.75$
E	66	84	80	79	$\bar{Y}_{5.} = 77.25$
Mean					$\bar{Y}_{..} = 71.45$

FIGURE 24.2 Dot Plots of Ratings by Five Personnel Officers—
Apex Enterprises Example.

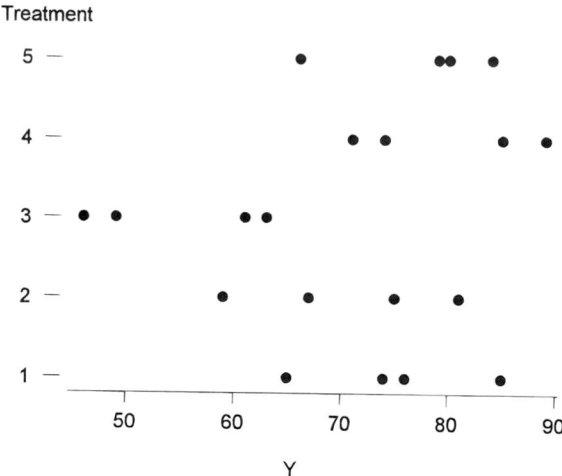

Example. Table 24.1 contains the results of the study by Apex Enterprises on the evaluation ratings of potential employees by its personnel officers. Five personnel officers were selected at random, and four prospective employees were assigned at random to each selected officer. Figure 24.2 contains dot plots of the ratings for each of the five personnel officers. It appears that the locations of the rating distributions for the personnel officers differ, that the variability within each of the five distributions is approximately the same, and that the variability within each of the rating distributions may be almost as large as the variability between the personnel officers.

The ANOVA calculations are routine and are shown in Table 24.2, which also shows the expected mean squares in general and for the Apex Enterprises example. Using the results from Table 24.2, the appropriate test statistic for determining whether $\sigma_\mu^2 = 0$ is:

$$F^* = \frac{394.9}{73.3} = 5.39$$

TABLE 24.2   ANOVA Table for Single-Factor ANOVA Model II—Apex Enterprises Example.

Source of Variation	SS	df	MS	E{MS} General	Example
Between personnel officers	$SSTR = 1{,}579.7$	4	$MSTR = 394.9$	$\sigma^2 + n\sigma_\mu^2$	$\sigma^2 + 4\sigma_\mu^2$
Error (within personnel officers)	$SSE = 1{,}099.3$	15	$MSE = 73.3$	σ^2	σ^2
Total	$SSTO = 2{,}678.9$	19			

To control the risk of making a Type I error at $\alpha = .05$, we require $F(.95; 4, 15) = 3.06$. Hence, the decision rule is:

$$\text{If } F^* \le 3.06, \text{ conclude } H_0$$

$$\text{If } F^* > 3.06, \text{ conclude } H_a$$

Since $F^* = 5.39 > 3.06$, we conclude H_a, that $\sigma_\mu^2 > 0$ or that the mean ratings of the personnel officers differ. The P-value of the test is .01.

Comments

1. We illustrate the derivation of an expected mean square for ANOVA model II by sketching the development for deriving $E\{MSTR\}$ in (24.7) when $n_i = n$. The proof parallels that for ANOVA model I. According to ANOVA model (24.1), we can write:

$$\bar{Y}_{i.} = \mu_i + \bar{\varepsilon}_{i.}$$

$$\bar{Y}_{..} = \bar{\mu}_{.} + \bar{\varepsilon}_{..}$$

where $\bar{\varepsilon}_{i.}$ and $\bar{\varepsilon}_{..}$ are defined in (16.44) and (16.47), respectively, and:

$$\bar{\mu}_{.} = \frac{\sum\limits_{i=1}^{r} \mu_i}{r}$$

(Note the use of a different notation for the mean of the μ_i here than for ANOVA model I to emphasize the random nature of the mean of the r values μ_i for ANOVA model II.) Corresponding to (16.49), we obtain:

$$\bar{Y}_{i.} - \bar{Y}_{..} = (\mu_i - \bar{\mu}_{.}) + (\bar{\varepsilon}_{i.} - \bar{\varepsilon}_{..})$$

so that:

$$\sum(\bar{Y}_{i.} - \bar{Y}_{..})^2 = \sum(\mu_i - \bar{\mu}_{.})^2 + \sum(\bar{\varepsilon}_{i.} - \bar{\varepsilon}_{..})^2 + 2\sum(\mu_i - \bar{\mu}_{.})(\bar{\varepsilon}_{i.} - \bar{\varepsilon}_{..})$$

When we take the expectation, the cross-product term drops out because of the independence of the μ_i and the ε_{ij} and because the deviations $\mu_i - \bar{\mu}_{.}$ and $\bar{\varepsilon}_{i.} - \bar{\varepsilon}_{..}$ all have expectations zero.

From (16.52) we know that:

$$E\left\{\sum(\bar{\varepsilon}_{i\cdot} - \bar{\varepsilon}_{\cdot\cdot})^2\right\} = \frac{(r-1)\sigma^2}{n}$$

Lastly, since $\Sigma(\mu_i - \bar{\mu}_\cdot)^2$ is the numerator of an ordinary sample variance for r independent μ_i values, it follows from the unbiasedness of the sample variance that:

$$E\left\{\sum(\mu_i - \bar{\mu}_\cdot)^2\right\} = (r-1)\sigma_\mu^2$$

Hence, we obtain:

$$E\left\{\frac{n}{r-1}\sum(\bar{Y}_{i\cdot} - \bar{Y}_{\cdot\cdot})^2\right\} = \frac{n}{r-1}\left[(r-1)\sigma_\mu^2 + \frac{r-1}{n}\sigma^2\right] = n\sigma_\mu^2 + \sigma^2$$

which is the result in (24.7).

2. The F^* test statistic in (24.8) and the decision rule in (24.9) is also appropriate when the factor level sample sizes are not equal. The degrees of freedom associated with *MSE* are then denoted, as usual, by $n_T - r$, where $n_T = \Sigma n_i$. The expected value of *MSTR* becomes:

(24.10)
$$E\{MSTR\} = \sigma^2 + n'\sigma_\mu^2$$

where:

(24.10a)
$$n' = \frac{1}{r-1}\left[\left(\sum n_i\right) - \frac{\Sigma n_i^2}{\Sigma n_i}\right]$$

∎

Estimation of $\mu_\cdot$

When ANOVA model II is applicable, there is frequent interest in estimating the overall mean $\mu_\cdot$. We now develop an interval estimate for $\mu_\cdot$ when all factor level sample sizes are equal. We know from (24.2a) that:

$$E\{Y_{ij}\} = \mu_\cdot$$

Hence, an unbiased estimator of $\mu_\cdot$ is:

(24.11)
$$\hat{\mu}_\cdot = \bar{Y}_{\cdot\cdot}$$

It can be shown that the variance of this estimator is:

(24.12)
$$\sigma^2\{\bar{Y}_{\cdot\cdot}\} = \frac{\sigma_\mu^2}{r} + \frac{\sigma^2}{rn} = \frac{n\sigma_\mu^2 + \sigma^2}{rn}$$

Formula (24.12) shows that the variance of $\bar{Y}_{\cdot\cdot}$ is made up of two components. The first corresponds to the variance of a sample mean based on r values when sampling from the population of the μ_i, and it reflects the contribution due to sampling the factor levels. The second component corresponds to the variance of a sample mean based on rn observations when sampling from the populations of the Y_{ij}, given the μ_i, and it reflects the contribution due to variation within factor levels.

An unbiased estimator of $\sigma^2\{\bar{Y}_{..}\}$ is:

$$(24.13) \qquad\qquad s^2\{\bar{Y}_{..}\} = \frac{MSTR}{rn}$$

This estimator is unbiased because we know from (24.7) that $E\{MSTR\} = n\sigma_\mu^2 + \sigma^2$. Dividing the result in (24.7) by rn yields (24.12).

It can be shown that:

$$(24.14) \qquad\qquad \frac{\bar{Y}_{..} - \mu_.}{s\{\bar{Y}_{..}\}} \text{ is distributed as } t(r-1) \text{ for ANOVA model (24.1)}$$

Hence, we obtain in usual fashion the confidence limits for $\mu_.$:

$$(24.15) \qquad\qquad \bar{Y}_{..} \pm t(1 - \alpha/2; r - 1)s\{\bar{Y}_{..}\}$$

Example. Management of Apex Enterprises wishes to estimate the mean rating for all prospective employees by all personnel officers with a 90 percent confidence interval. We have from Tables 24.1 and 24.2:

$$\bar{Y}_{..} = 71.45 \qquad MSTR = 394.9 \qquad rn = 20$$

We require $t(.95; 4) = 2.132$ and:

$$s^2\{\bar{Y}_{..}\} = \frac{394.9}{20} = 19.75$$

Hence, $s\{\bar{Y}_{..}\} = 4.44$, the confidence limits are $71.45 \pm 2.132(4.44)$, and the desired 90 percent confidence interval is:

$$62 \leq \mu_. \leq 81$$

Thus, with a 90 percent confidence coefficient, we conclude that the mean rating assigned by all personnel officers to all prospective employees is between 62 and 81. The interval estimate is not very precise because of the relatively small samples of personnel officers and potential employees.

Note

The variance of $\bar{Y}_{..}$ in (24.12) can be derived readily. First, we consider:

$$\bar{Y}_{i.} = \mu_i + \bar{\varepsilon}_{i.}$$

where $\bar{\varepsilon}_{i.}$ is defined in (16.44). Because of the independence of μ_i and the ε_{ij}, we have:

$$\sigma^2\{\bar{Y}_{i.}\} = \sigma_\mu^2 + \frac{\sigma^2}{n}$$

Remember that $\bar{\varepsilon}_{i.}$ is just an ordinary mean of n independent ε_{ij} values.

For the case $n_i \equiv n$ that we are considering here, we have:

$$\bar{Y}_{..} = \frac{\sum\limits_{i=1}^{r} \bar{Y}_{i.}}{r}$$

In view of the independence of the μ_i and the ε_{ij} among themselves and between each other, it follows that the $\bar{Y}_{i.}$ are independent so that:

$$\sigma^2\{\bar{Y}_{..}\} = \frac{\sigma^2\{\bar{Y}_{i.}\}}{r} = \frac{\sigma_\mu^2}{r} + \frac{\sigma^2}{rn} = \frac{n\sigma_\mu^2 + \sigma^2}{rn} \qquad \blacksquare$$

Estimation of $\sigma_\mu^2/(\sigma_\mu^2 + \sigma^2)$

As noted earlier, the ratio $\sigma_\mu^2/(\sigma_\mu^2 + \sigma^2)$ reveals meaningfully the effect of the extent of variation between the μ_i. We shall develop an interval estimate for this ratio by first obtaining confidence limits for the ratio σ_μ^2/σ^2. It can be shown that *MSTR* and *MSE* are independent random variables for ANOVA model II, just as for ANOVA model I. When $n_i \equiv n$, the case considered here, it can be shown further that:

$$(24.16) \qquad \frac{MSTR}{n\sigma_\mu^2 + \sigma^2} \div \frac{MSE}{\sigma^2} \sim F[r - 1, r(n - 1)]$$

Hence, we can write the probability statement:

$$(24.17) \qquad P\left\{ F[\alpha/2; r - 1, r(n - 1)] \leq \frac{MSTR}{n\sigma_\mu^2 + \sigma^2} \div \frac{MSE}{\sigma^2} \right.$$
$$\left. \leq F[1 - \alpha/2; r - 1, r(n - 1)] \right\} = 1 - \alpha$$

Rearranging the inequalities, we obtain the following confidence limits L and U for σ_μ^2/σ^2:

$$(24.18a) \qquad L = \frac{1}{n}\left[\frac{MSTR}{MSE}\left(\frac{1}{F[1 - \alpha/2; r - 1, r(n - 1)]} \right) - 1 \right]$$

$$(24.18b) \qquad U = \frac{1}{n}\left[\frac{MSTR}{MSE}\left(\frac{1}{F[\alpha/2; r - 1, r(n - 1)]} \right) - 1 \right]$$

where L is the lower confidence limit and U the upper.

The confidence limits L^* and U^* for $\sigma_\mu^2/(\sigma_\mu^2 + \sigma^2)$ can now be obtained and are as follows:

$$(24.19) \qquad L^* = \frac{L}{1 + L} \qquad U^* = \frac{U}{1 + U}$$

Example.   Management of Apex Enterprises wishes to obtain a 90 percent confidence interval for $\sigma_\mu^2/(\sigma_\mu^2 + \sigma^2)$. From previous work, we have:

$$MSTR = 394.9 \qquad MSE = 73.3 \qquad n = 4 \qquad r = 5$$

For a 90 percent confidence interval, we require:

$$F(.05; 4, 15) = .170 \qquad F(.95; 4, 15) = 3.06$$

Hence, the 90 percent confidence limits for σ_μ^2/σ^2 are by (24.18):

$$L = \frac{1}{4}\left[\frac{394.9}{73.3}\left(\frac{1}{3.06}\right) - 1\right] = .19 \qquad U = \frac{1}{4}\left[\frac{394.9}{73.3}\left(\frac{1}{.170}\right) - 1\right] = 7.7$$

and the confidence interval for σ_μ^2/σ^2 is:

$$.19 \leq \frac{\sigma_\mu^2}{\sigma^2} \leq 7.7$$

Finally, the confidence limits for $\sigma_\mu^2/(\sigma_\mu^2 + \sigma^2)$ are obtained by (24.19); they are $L^* = .19/1.19 = .16$ and $U^* = 7.7/8.7 = .89$. Hence, the 90 percent confidence interval is:

$$.16 \leq \frac{\sigma_\mu^2}{\sigma_\mu^2 + \sigma^2} \leq .89$$

With confidence coefficient .90, we conclude that the variability of the mean ratings for the different personnel officers accounts for somewhere between 16 and 89 percent of the total variability of the ratings. Note that this interval estimate is not precise, partly the result of relatively small sample sizes and partly because variance components are much more difficult to estimate precisely than means. The confidence interval does indicate, though, that the variability among personnel officers is not negligible since it accounts for at least 16 percent of the total variability.

Comments

1. It may happen occasionally that the lower limit of the confidence interval for σ_μ^2/σ^2 is negative. Since this ratio cannot be negative, the usual practice is to consider the lower limit L in (24.18a) to be zero in that case.

2. If one-sided or two-sided tests concerning the relative magnitudes of σ_μ^2 and σ^2 are desired, such as the following (where c is a specified constant):

$$H_0: \sigma_\mu^2 \leq c\sigma^2 \qquad H_0: \sigma_\mu^2 = c\sigma^2$$
$$H_a: \sigma_\mu^2 > c\sigma^2 \qquad H_a: \sigma_\mu^2 \neq c\sigma^2$$

a decision rule can be constructed by utilizing (24.16). Alternatively, one-sided or two-sided confidence intervals can be used to draw the appropriate conclusion.

3. The ratio σ_μ^2/σ^2 is of relevance when planning investigations. In the Apex Enterprises example dealing with the personnel officers, suppose that the mean rating $\mu.$ is to be estimated, and that the costs of including in the study a personnel officer and a candidate are c_1 and c_2, respectively. For a given total budget C, the ratio σ_μ^2/σ^2 is the determining variable for finding the optimum balance between the number of personnel officers and the number of candidates to include in the study so as to minimize the variance of the estimator. If the populations are not large, the model will need to take account of their finite nature. ∎

Estimation of σ^2

At times, it is desired to estimate σ^2 and σ_μ^2 separately. According to (24.6), an unbiased estimator of σ^2 is *MSE*. An interval estimate for σ^2 is easily constructed. We make use of the fact that $[r(n-1)MSE]/\sigma^2$ is distributed as a χ^2 random variable with $r(n-1)$ degrees of freedom:

$$(24.20) \qquad \frac{r(n-1)MSE}{\sigma^2} \sim \chi^2[r(n-1)]$$

It follows that a $1 - \alpha$ confidence interval for σ^2 is:

$$(24.21) \qquad \frac{r(n-1)MSE}{\chi^2[1-\alpha/2; r(n-1)]} \leq \sigma^2 \leq \frac{r(n-1)MSE}{\chi^2[\alpha/2; r(n-1)]}$$

Example.   To construct a 90 percent confidence interval for σ^2 for the Apex Enterprises example, we require:

$$MSE = 73.3 \qquad \chi^2(.05; 15) = 7.26 \qquad \chi^2(95; 15) = 25.0$$

The desired confidence interval by (24.21) then is:

$$44.0 = \frac{15(73.3)}{25.0} \leq \sigma^2 \leq \frac{15(73.3)}{7.26} = 151.4$$

An approximate 90 percent confidence interval for σ is obtained by taking the square roots of the confidence limits for σ^2:

$$6.6 \leq \sigma \leq 12.3$$

With 90 percent confidence, we conclude that the standard deviation of the ratings of prospective employees for each personnel officer is between 6.6 and 12.3 points.

Note

Confidence interval (24.21) is also appropriate when the factor level sample sizes are not equal. The degrees of freedom associated with *MSE* are then denoted by $n_T - r$.   ∎

Point Estimation of σ_μ^2

An unbiased estimator of σ_μ^2 is available by noting that we have from (24.6) and (24.7):

$$E\{MSE\} = \sigma^2$$

$$E\{MSTR\} = \sigma^2 + n\sigma_\mu^2$$

It follows that:

$$(24.22) \qquad \sigma_\mu^2 = \frac{E\{MSTR\} - E\{MSE\}}{n}$$

An unbiased estimator of σ_μ^2 is obtained by substituting the observed mean squares for the corresponding expected mean squares:

$$(24.23) \qquad\qquad s_\mu^2 = \frac{MSTR - MSE}{n}$$

Occasionally, this point estimator will turn out to be negative. Since a variance cannot be negative, the usual practice is to consider the estimator to be zero in that event.

Note

An unbiased estimator of σ_μ^2 when the factor level sample sizes are not equal can be obtained by slightly modifying the expression in (24.23). The denominator n is simply replaced by n' as defined in (24.10a). ∎

Interval Estimation of σ_μ^2

It is not possible to construct exact confidence intervals for σ_μ^2. However, several approximate confidence intervals have been developed. We shall now describe two approximate confidence intervals for σ_μ^2, assuming as before that the study is balanced; that is, $n_i \equiv n$. Procedures for constructing confidence intervals for σ_μ^2 when the factor level sample sizes are not equal are presented in Section 24.6 and in Reference 24.2.

Satterthwaite Procedure.   The Satterthwaite procedure (Ref. 24.3) is a general procedure for constructing approximate confidence intervals for linear combinations of expected mean squares. Note that σ_μ^2 is such a linear combination since we can express (24.22) as follows:

$$(24.24) \qquad\qquad \sigma_\mu^2 = \left(\frac{1}{n}\right) E\{MSTR\} + \left(-\frac{1}{n}\right) E\{MSE\}$$

In general, we shall state a linear combination of expected mean squares as follows:

$$(24.25) \qquad\qquad L = c_1 E\{MS_1\} + \cdots + c_h E\{MS_h\}$$

where the c_i are coefficients.

An unbiased estimator of L is:

$$(24.26) \qquad\qquad \hat{L} = c_1 MS_1 + \cdots + c_h MS_h$$

Let df_i denote the degrees of freedom associated with mean square MS_i. Satterthwaite has suggested that the distribution of the statistic:

$$(24.27) \qquad\qquad \frac{(df)\hat{L}}{L}$$

can be approximated by a χ^2 distribution whose degrees of freedom, denoted by df, are given by:

$$(24.28) \qquad\qquad df = \frac{(c_1 MS_1 + \cdots + c_h MS_h)^2}{\dfrac{(c_1 MS_1)^2}{df_1} + \cdots + \dfrac{(c_h MS_h)^2}{df_h}}$$

An approximate $1 - \alpha$ confidence interval for L therefore is:

$$(24.29) \qquad \frac{(df)\hat{L}}{\chi^2(1 - \alpha/2; df)} \leq L \leq \frac{(df)\hat{L}}{\chi^2(\alpha/2; df)}$$

where df is given by (24.28).

For the single-factor random ANOVA model (24.1) for a balanced study ($n_i \equiv n$), we have the following correspondences:

$$MS_1 = MSTR \qquad\qquad MS_2 = MSE$$

$$df_1 = r - 1 \qquad\qquad df_2 = n_T - r = r(n - 1)$$

$$(24.30) \qquad c_1 = \frac{1}{n} \qquad\qquad c_2 = -\frac{1}{n}$$

$$L = \sigma_\mu^2 = \left(\frac{1}{n}\right) E\{MSTR\} + \left(-\frac{1}{n}\right) E\{MSE\}$$

$$\hat{L} = s_\mu^2 = \left(\frac{1}{n}\right) MSTR + \left(-\frac{1}{n}\right) MSE$$

Hence, an approximate $1 - \alpha$ confidence interval for σ_μ^2 by the Satterthwaite procedure (24.29) is:

$$(24.31) \qquad \frac{(df)s_\mu^2}{\chi^2(1 - \alpha/2; df)} \leq \sigma_\mu^2 \leq \frac{(df)s_\mu^2}{\chi^2(\alpha/2; df)}$$

where:

$$(24.31a) \qquad df = \frac{(ns_\mu^2)^2}{\dfrac{(MSTR)^2}{r - 1} + \dfrac{(MSE)^2}{r(n - 1)}}$$

Usually, the degrees of freedom will not turn out to be an integer. Interpolation in the χ^2 table or rounding to the nearest integer may then be used.

While the Satterthwaite procedure is general and easy to carry out, the accuracy of the approximation can be quite limited when some of the coefficients c_i are negative and some are positive. Note that this is the case here in (24.30), since $c_1 = 1/n$ and $c_2 = -1/n$. More detailed guidelines as to when the Satterthwaite approximation is appropriate are given in Reference 24.4.

Example.   For the Apex Enterprises example, we shall first obtain a point estimate of σ_μ^2 by means of (24.23). We require:

$$MSE = 73.3 \qquad MSTR = 394.9 \qquad n = 4$$

Hence we find:

$$s_\mu^2 = \frac{394.9 - 73.3}{4} = 80.4$$

and the estimated standard deviation of the mean ratings of all personnel officers is $\sqrt{80.4} = 9.0$ points.

Next, we obtain a 90 percent confidence interval for σ_μ^2 by the Satterthwaite procedure. Using the earlier results:

$$s_\mu^2 = 80.4 \qquad MSTR = 394.9 \qquad MSE = 73.3 \qquad n = 4 \qquad r = 5$$

we obtain the degrees of freedom df by means of (24.31a):

$$df = \frac{[4(80.4)]^2}{\dfrac{(394.9)^2}{5-1} + \dfrac{(73.3)^2}{5(4-1)}} = 2.63$$

which we shall round up to 3.0. Confidence limits (24.31) also require:

$$\chi^2(.05; 3) = .352 \qquad \chi^2(.95; 3) = 7.81$$

so that the Satterthwaite approximate 90 percent confidence interval for σ_μ^2 is:

$$30.9 = \frac{3(80.4)}{7.81} \leq \sigma_\mu^2 \leq \frac{3(80.4)}{.352} = 685.2$$

By taking square roots of the two limits, we obtain an approximate confidence interval for σ_μ:

$$5.6 \leq \sigma_\mu \leq 26.2$$

Hence, with approximate 90 percent confidence coefficient, we conclude that the standard deviation of the mean ratings of all of the personnel officers is between 5.6 and 26.2 points.

MLS Procedure. An improved procedure for obtaining an approximate confidence interval for σ_μ^2 is based on the modified large sample (*MLS*) procedure (Ref. 24.5). It involves somewhat greater computational complexity than the Satterthwaite procedure, and is designed to estimate a linear combination of two expected mean squares for balanced studies of the form:

$$(24.32) \qquad L = c_1 E\{MS_1\} + c_2 E\{MS_2\} \qquad c_1 > 0, \quad c_2 < 0$$

where c_1 is positive and c_2 is negative. An unbiased estimator of L is:

$$(24.33) \qquad \hat{L} = c_1 MS_1 + c_2 MS_2 \qquad c_1 > 0, \quad c_2 < 0$$

If $(df_1)MS_1/E\{MS_1\}$ and $(df_2)MS_2/E\{MS_2\}$ are independent χ^2 random variables with df_1 and df_2 degrees of freedom, respectively, an approximate $1 - \alpha$ confidence interval for L is given by:

$$(24.34) \qquad \hat{L} - H_L \leq L \leq \hat{L} + H_U$$

where $\hat{L}$ is defined in (24.33) and H_L and H_U are defined by the equations in Table 24.3.

To obtain an approximate $1 - \alpha$ confidence interval for σ_μ^2 with the *MLS* procedure, we simply observe that the correspondences in (24.30) for the Satterthwaite procedure apply here also and confidence interval (24.34) becomes:

$$(24.35) \qquad s_\mu^2 - H_L \leq \sigma_\mu^2 \leq s_\mu^2 + H_U$$

TABLE 24.3 Computational Formulas for MLS Approximate $1 - \alpha$ Confidence Limits in (24.34).

(24.34a) $\qquad\qquad F_1 = F(1 - \alpha/2; df_1, \infty)$

(24.34b) $\qquad\qquad F_2 = F(1 - \alpha/2; df_2, \infty)$

(24.34c) $\qquad\qquad F_3 = F(1 - \alpha/2; \infty, df_1)$

(24.34d) $\qquad\qquad F_4 = F(1 - \alpha/2; \infty, df_2)$

(24.34e) $\qquad\qquad F_5 = F(1 - \alpha/2; df_1, df_2)$

(24.34f) $\qquad\qquad F_6 = F(1 - \alpha/2, df_2, df_1)$

(24.34g) $\qquad\qquad G_1 = 1 - \dfrac{1}{F_1}$

(24.34h) $\qquad\qquad G_2 = 1 - \dfrac{1}{F_2}$

(24.34i) $\qquad\qquad G_3 = \dfrac{(F_5 - 1)^2 - (G_1 F_5)^2 - (F_4 - 1)^2}{F_5}$

(24.34j) $\qquad\qquad G_4 = F_6 \left[\left(\dfrac{F_6 - 1}{F_6}\right)^2 - \left(\dfrac{F_3 - 1}{F_6}\right)^2 - G_2^2 \right]$

(24.34k) $\qquad\qquad H_L = \{[G_1 c_1 MS_1]^2 + [(F_4 - 1)c_2 MS_2]^2 - G_3 c_1 c_2 MS_1 MS_2\}^{1/2}$

(24.34l) $\qquad\qquad H_U = \{[(F_3 - 1)c_1 MS_1]^2 + (G_2 c_2 MS_2)^2 - G_4 c_1 c_2 MS_1 MS_2\}^{1/2}$

Example. For the Apex Enterprises example, we shall obtain a 90 percent confidence interval for σ_μ^2 by means of the *MLS* procedure. From earlier, we have:

$$c_1 = 1/n = 1/4 = .25 \qquad MS_1 = MSTR = 394.9 \qquad df_1 = r - 1 = 4$$

$$c_2 = -1/n = -1/4 = -.25 \qquad MS_2 = MSE = 73.3 \qquad df_2 = r(n - 1) = 15$$

$$\hat{L} = s_\mu^2 = 80.4$$

We first determine the six percentiles (24.34a) to (24.34f):

$$F_1 = F(.95; 4, \infty) = 2.37 \qquad F_2 = F(.95; 15, \infty) = 1.67$$

$$F_3 = F(.95; \infty, 4) = 5.63 \qquad F_4 = F(.95; \infty, 15) = 2.07$$

$$F_5 = F(.95; 4, 15) = 3.06 \qquad F_6 = F(.95; 15, 4) = 5.86$$

Intermediate calculations required are:

$$G_1 - 1 - \frac{1}{2.37} = .5781$$

$$G_2 = 1 - \frac{1}{1.67} = .4012$$

$$G_3 = \frac{(3.06 - 1)^2 - [(.5781)3.06]^2 - (2.07 - 1)^2}{3.06} = -.0100$$

$$G_4 = 5.86 \left[\left(\frac{5.86 - 1}{5.86} \right)^2 - \left(\frac{5.63 - 1}{5.86} \right)^2 - (.4012)^2 \right] = -.5708$$

H_L and H_U are then computed as follows:

$$H_L = \{[(.5781)(.25)394.9]^2 + [(2.07 - 1)(-.25)73.3]^2$$

$$- (-.0100)(.25)(-.25)(394.9)73.3\}^{1/2}$$

$$= 60.2$$

$$H_U = \{[(5.63 - 1)(.25)394.9]^2 + [(.4012)(-.25)73.3]^2$$

$$- (-.5708)(.25)(-.25)(394.9)73.3\}^{1/2}$$

$$= 456.0$$

The approximate 90 percent percent confidence interval for σ_μ^2 therefore is:

$$20.2 = 80.4 - 60.2 \leq \sigma_\mu^2 \leq 80.4 + 456.0 = 536.4$$

Taking the square roots of the confidence limits, we obtain an approximate confidence interval for σ_μ :

$$4.5 \leq \sigma_\mu \leq 23.2$$

Notice that in this instance the confidence limits obtained by the Satterthwaite procedure (5.6 and 26.2) are quite similar to the ones just obtained by the more accurate *MLS* procedure. Note also the impreciseness of the *MLS* confidence interval here, a result of the small sample sizes and the difficulty in estimating variance components precisely.

Random Factor Effects Model

We can express the single-factor random cell means model (24.1) in an equivalent random factor effects fashion, just as we did for fixed factor levels in Chapter 16. We do this by expressing each factor level mean μ_i as a deviation from its expected value, $E\{\mu_i\} = \mu.$, as follows:

(24.36) $$\tau_i = \mu_i - \mu.$$

Then we simply replace μ_i in ANOVA model (24.1) by its equivalent expression from (24.36):

(24.37) $$\mu_i = \mu. + \tau_i$$

The random factor effects model therefore is expressed as follows:

(24.38)
$$Y_{ij} = \mu. + \tau_i + \varepsilon_{ij}$$

where:

$\mu.$ is a constant component common to all observations

τ_i are independent $N(0, \sigma_\mu^2)$

ε_{ij} are independent $N(0, \sigma^2)$

τ_i and ε_{ij} are independent

$i = 1, \ldots, r; j = 1, \ldots, n$

Note that the τ_i are random variables in ANOVA model (24.38). With reference to the personnel officers in the Apex Enterprises example, τ_i represents the effect of the ith personnel officer who is selected at random. Specifically, τ_i measures by how much the mean rating of all potential employees by the ith personnel officer differs from the overall mean rating by all personnel officers.

24.2   Two-Factor Studies—ANOVA Models II and III

ANOVA Model II—Random Factor Effects

Consider an investigation of the effects of machine operators (factor A) and machines (factor B) on the number of pieces produced in a day. Five operators and three machines are used in the study. Yet the inferences are not to be confined to the particular five operators and three machines participating in the study, but rather they are to pertain to all operators and all machines available to the company. Here a random ANOVA model (model II) would be appropriate for the two-factor study, since each of the two sets of factor levels may be considered the result of sampling a population (all operators, all machines) about which inferences are to be drawn.

In the random factor effects version of ANOVA model II for a two-factor study, we assume analogously to a single-factor study that both the factor A main effects α_i and the factor B main effects β_j are independent random variables. Further, we assume that the interaction effects $(\alpha\beta)_{ij}$ are independent random variables. Thus, the random factor level effects version of ANOVA model II for a two-factor study with equal sample sizes n is:

(24.39)
$$Y_{ijk} = \mu.. + \alpha_i + \beta_j + (\alpha\beta)_{ij} + \varepsilon_{ijk}$$

where:

$\mu..$ is a constant

α_i, β_j, $(\alpha\beta)_{ij}$ are independent normal random variables with expectations zero and respective variances $\sigma_\alpha^2, \sigma_\beta^2, \sigma_{\alpha\beta}^2$

ε_{ijk} are independent $N(0, \sigma^2)$

α_i, β_j, $(\alpha\beta)_{ij}$, and ε_{ijk} are pairwise independent

$i = 1, \ldots, a; j = 1, \ldots, b; k = 1, \ldots, n$

Meaning of Model Terms.   We shall explain the meaning of the terms in random ANOVA model (24.39) with reference to the production example involving the two factors machine operators and machines. The main effect of operator i in the study (selected at random from the population of operators) is α_i. Similarly, the main effect of machine j in the study (selected at random from the population of machines) is β_j. Further, the interaction effect between operator i and machine j on the number of pieces produced per day is $(\alpha\beta)_{ij}$. ANOVA model (24.39) assumes that the main effects of operators on output per day are normally distributed with zero mean and variance σ_α^2. Similarly, the main effects of machines are normally distributed with zero mean and variance σ_β^2. Finally, the operator-machine interaction effects are normally distributed with mean zero and variance $\sigma_{\alpha\beta}^2$. Since random ANOVA model (24.39) assumes these three effects to be independent random variables, the mean output for operator i–machine j, namely, $\mu_{ij} = \mu_{..} + \alpha_i + \beta_j + (\alpha\beta)_{ij}$, may be viewed as the sum of independent selections of α_i, β_j, and $(\alpha\beta)_{ij}$ from three different normal distributions.

Note

We caution that random ANOVA model (24.39) should only be used if the factor levels of the two factors do indeed represent random samples from populations of interest. Also, when a study involves only a few levels of each random factor, precise estimation of the factor variance components will usually be very difficult because of the small number of factor levels sampled.   ■

Important Features of Model.

   1. For ANOVA model (24.39), the expected value of response Y_{ijk} is:

(24.40a)
$$E\{Y_{ijk}\} = \mu_{..}$$

   2. The variance of Y_{ijk}, denoted by σ_Y^2, is:

(24.40b)
$$\sigma^2\{Y_{ijk}\} = \sigma_Y^2 = \sigma_\alpha^2 + \sigma_\beta^2 + \sigma_{\alpha\beta}^2 + \sigma^2$$

The Y_{ijk} thus have constant variance. They are normally distributed because they are linear combinations of independent normal random variables.

   3. In advance of the random trials, different responses Y_{ijk} are independent except for responses from the same factor A level and/or from the same factor B level, which are correlated because they contain some common random terms. The covariances are as follows:

(24.41a) $\sigma\{Y_{ijk}, Y_{ij'k'}\} = \sigma_\alpha^2$ $j \neq j'$

(24.41b) $\sigma\{Y_{ijk}, Y_{i'jk'}\} = \sigma_\beta^2$ $i \neq i'$

(24.41c) $\sigma\{Y_{ijk}, Y_{ijk'}\} = \sigma_\alpha^2 + \sigma_\beta^2 + \sigma_{\alpha\beta}^2$ $k \neq k'$

(24.41d) $\sigma\{Y_{ijk}, Y_{i'j'k'}\} = 0$ $i \neq i', j \neq j'$

ANOVA Model III—Mixed Factor Effects

When one of the two factors has fixed factor levels while the other has random factor levels, a mixed ANOVA model (model III) is applicable. An instance where this model may be appropriate is an investigation of the effects of four different training methods (factor A) and five instructors (factor B) upon learning in a company training program. The four levels for training methods may be considered fixed, since interest centers in these particular training methods. In contrast, the levels for instructors may be viewed as random, since inferences are to be made about a population of instructors of which the five used in the study are viewed as a sample.

Two mixed ANOVA models are widely used. They are related to each other and are called the *restricted* and *unrestricted* mixed models. The restricted model is somewhat more general, and will be the mixed model that we shall present. When factor A has fixed factor levels and factor B has random factor levels, the α_i effects are constants and the β_j effects are random variables. The interaction effects $(\alpha\beta)_{ij}$ are also random variables because the factor B levels are random. As for the fixed effects ANOVA model for two-factor studies, the fixed effects α_i in the restricted mixed model will be subject to the restriction that their sum is zero; i.e., $\Sigma\alpha_i = 0$. Similarly, the interaction terms $(\alpha\beta)_{ij}$ will be subject to a restriction related to the fact that all fixed factor A levels are included in the study; the restriction is that $\sum_i(\alpha\beta)_{ij} = 0$ for each level j of random factor B. Any two interaction terms will be independent, as in the random effects model (24.39), except if they come from the same level of random factor B in which case they will be correlated. The correlation is related to the restriction that $\sum_i(\alpha\beta)_{ij} = 0$ for each level j of random factor B.

The restricted mixed ANOVA model for two-factor studies, where factor A is fixed and factor B is random, can now be stated as follows:

$$(24.42) \qquad Y_{ijk} = \mu_{..} + \alpha_i + \beta_j + (\alpha\beta)_{ij} + \varepsilon_{ijk}$$

where:

$\mu_{..}$ is a constant

α_i are constants subject to the restriction $\Sigma\alpha_i = 0$

β_j are independent $N(0, \sigma_\beta^2)$

$(\alpha\beta)_{ij}$ are $N(0, \dfrac{a-1}{a}\sigma_{\alpha\beta}^2)$, subject to the restrictions:

$\qquad \sum_i(\alpha\beta)_{ij} = 0 \qquad$ for all j

$\qquad \sigma\{(\alpha\beta)_{ij}, (\alpha\beta)_{i'j}\} = -\dfrac{1}{a}\sigma_{\alpha\beta}^2 \qquad i \neq i'$

ε_{ijk} are independent $N(0, \sigma^2)$

$\beta_j, (\alpha\beta)_{ij},$ and ε_{ijk} are pairwise independent

$i = 1, \ldots, a; \; j = 1, \ldots, b; \; k = 1, \ldots, n$

Comments

1. Note that $\sigma_{\alpha\beta}^2$ is not the variance of the interaction terms in model (24.42) but is proportional to their variance, the proportionality constant being $(a-1)/a$. The reason why the variance of the interaction terms in ANOVA model (24.42) is expressed as $(a-1)\sigma_{\alpha\beta}^2/a$ rather than simply as $\sigma_{\alpha\beta}^2$ is so that the expected mean squares will be relatively simple expressions.

This facilitates the making of inferences for this model. Some texts denote the variance of $(\alpha\beta)_{ij}$ by $\sigma^2_{\alpha\beta}$.

2. The unrestricted mixed ANOVA model for two-factor studies is quite similar to the restricted model in (24.42). In the unrestricted model, there are no restrictions on the interaction effects $(\alpha\beta)_{ij}$ and they are pairwise independent. Denote the unrestricted random effects by β_j^* and $(\alpha\beta)_{ij}^*$. Also let $(\overline{\alpha\beta})_{\cdot j}^*$ denote the mean of the unrestricted interaction terms $(\alpha\beta)_{1j}^*$, $(\alpha\beta)_{2j}^*, \ldots, (\alpha\beta)_{aj}^*$ for the fixed factor A levels for any factor level j of random factor B. Then the terms β_j and $(\alpha\beta)_{ij}$ in restricted model (24.42) are related to the unrestricted terms as follows:

$$(24.43) \qquad \beta_j = \beta_j^* + (\overline{\alpha\beta})_{\cdot j}^* \qquad (\alpha\beta)_{ij} = (\alpha\beta)_{ij}^* - (\overline{\alpha\beta})_{\cdot j}^*$$

The restrictions on the $(\alpha\beta)_{ij}$ in model (24.42) follow from the relation in (24.43). References 24.6 and 24.7 contain detailed discussions of the restricted and unrestricted mixed ANOVA models. ∎

Important Features of Model. The expected value of response Y_{ijk} for mixed ANOVA model (24.42) is:

$$(24.44) \qquad E\{Y_{ijk}\} = \mu_{..} + \alpha_i$$

The variance of Y_{ijk} follows directly from the pairwise independence of α_i, β_j, and $(\alpha\beta)_{ij}$:

$$(24.45) \qquad \sigma^2\{Y_{ijk}\} = \sigma_Y^2 = \sigma_\beta^2 + \frac{a-1}{a}\sigma_{\alpha\beta}^2 + \sigma^2$$

Notice that the Y_{ijk} have constant variance. Further, they are normally distributed because each is a linear combination of independent normal random variables.

In advance of the random trials, different responses Y_{ijk} are independent if they are not from the same random factor B level. Responses from the same random factor B level are correlated; their covariances are as follows:

$$(24.46a) \qquad \sigma\{Y_{ijk}, Y_{ijk'}\} = \sigma_\beta^2 + \frac{a-1}{a}\sigma_{\alpha\beta}^2 \qquad k \neq k'$$

$$(24.46b) \qquad \sigma\{Y_{ijk}, Y_{i'jk'}\} = \sigma_\beta^2 - \frac{1}{a}\sigma_{\alpha\beta}^2 \qquad i \neq i'$$

$$(24.46c) \qquad \sigma\{Y_{ijk}, Y_{i'j'k'}\} = 0 \qquad j \neq j'$$

Covariance Structure of Observations. We shall illustrate the form of the variance-covariance matrix of the responses Y_{ijk} for mixed ANOVA model (24.42) for a simple example. Here, A is a fixed factor with $a = 2$ levels, B is a random factor with $b = 2$ levels, and $n = 2$ responses are obtained for each of the six treatments. The variance of response Y_{ijk} is according to (24.45) for $a = 2$:

$$\sigma^2\{Y_{ijk}\} = \sigma_Y^2 = \sigma_\beta^2 + \sigma_{\alpha\beta}^2/2 + \sigma^2$$

TABLE 24.4 **Illustration of Variance-Covariance Matrix for Mixed Model (24.42)—$a = 2$, $b = 2$, $n = 2$.**

(a) Observations Vector

$$\mathbf{Y} = \begin{bmatrix} Y_{111} \\ Y_{112} \\ Y_{211} \\ Y_{212} \\ Y_{121} \\ Y_{122} \\ Y_{221} \\ Y_{222} \end{bmatrix}$$

(b) Variance-Covariance Matrix in Block Form

$$\underset{8 \times 8}{\boldsymbol{\sigma}^2\{\mathbf{Y}\}} = \begin{bmatrix} \underset{4 \times 4}{\boldsymbol{\Sigma}_b} & \underset{4 \times 4}{\mathbf{0}} \\ \underset{4 \times 4}{\mathbf{0}} & \underset{4 \times 4}{\boldsymbol{\Sigma}_b} \end{bmatrix}$$

where:

$\mathbf{0} = 4 \times 4$ matrix containing all 0s

$$\boldsymbol{\Sigma}_b = \begin{bmatrix} \sigma_Y^2 & \sigma_{kk'} & \sigma_{ii'} & \sigma_{ii'} \\ \sigma_{kk'} & \sigma_Y^2 & \sigma_{ii'} & \sigma_{ii'} \\ \sigma_{ii'} & \sigma_{ii'} & \sigma_Y^2 & \sigma_{kk'} \\ \sigma_{ii'} & \sigma_{ii'} & \sigma_{kk'} & \sigma_Y^2 \end{bmatrix}$$

$$\sigma_Y^2 = \sigma_\beta^2 + \sigma_{\alpha\beta}^2/2 + \sigma^2$$

$$\sigma_{kk'} = \sigma_\beta^2 + \sigma_{\alpha\beta}^2/2$$

$$\sigma_{ii'} = \sigma_\beta^2 - \sigma_{\alpha\beta}^2/2$$

The covariance in (24.46a) will be denoted by $\sigma_{kk'}$ to indicate that the two Y_{ijk} observations only differ for the replication. Similarly, the covariance in (24.46b) will be denoted by $\sigma_{ii'}$ to indicate that the two observations come from different factor A levels but not from different factor B levels. Using this notation, the two pairwise covariances are for $a = 2$:

$$\sigma_{kk'} = \sigma_\beta^2 + \sigma_{\alpha\beta}^2/2$$

$$\sigma_{ii'} = \sigma_\beta^2 - \sigma_{\alpha\beta}^2/2$$

The response vector $\mathbf{Y}$ for this example is shown in Table 24.4a. Note that the observations are listed in the vector with i varying within j. This permits a simple block structure presentation of the variance-covariance matrix in Table 24.4b. In this presentation, four rows and four columns are represented by a block matrix. Because of the symmetry of the blocks, only two different block matrices are required. These are shown in Table 24.4b. Note the correlations between pairs of observations on the block main diagonal and the uncorrelatedness elsewhere.

Note

The reason why the restricted mixed model in (24.42) is somewhat more general than the unrestricted model is that two observations from the same random factor B level can be positively or negatively related for the restricted model according to (24.46b) but cannot be negatively related for the unrestricted model. ∎

TABLE 24.5   **Expected Mean Squares for Balanced Two-Factor ANOVA Models.**

Mean Square	df	Fixed ANOVA Model (A and B fixed)	Random ANOVA Model (A and B random)	Mixed ANOVA Model (A fixed, B random)
MSA	$a - 1$	$\sigma^2 + nb\dfrac{\Sigma \alpha_i^2}{a - 1}$	$\sigma^2 + nb\sigma_\alpha^2 + n\sigma_{\alpha\beta}^2$	$\sigma^2 + nb\dfrac{\Sigma \alpha_i^2}{a - 1} + n\sigma_{\alpha\beta}^2$
MSB	$b - 1$	$\sigma^2 + na\dfrac{\Sigma \beta_j^2}{b - 1}$	$\sigma^2 + na\sigma_\beta^2 + n\sigma_{\alpha\beta}^2$	$\sigma^2 + na\sigma_\beta^2$
MSAB	$(a - 1)(b - 1)$	$\sigma^2 + n\dfrac{\Sigma\Sigma(\alpha\beta)_{ij}^2}{(a - 1)(b - 1)}$	$\sigma^2 + n\sigma_{\alpha\beta}^2$	$\sigma^2 + n\sigma_{\alpha\beta}^2$
MSE	$(n - 1)ab$	σ^2	σ^2	σ^2

24.3   Two-Factor Studies—ANOVA Tests for Models II and III

For both the mixed and random ANOVA models for two-factor studies, the analysis of variance calculations for sums of squares are identical to those for the fixed ANOVA model. Thus, formulas (19.37) and (19.39) are entirely applicable for two-factor ANOVA models II and III. Similarly, the degrees of freedom and mean squares are exactly the same as those shown in Table 19.8 for the fixed two-factor ANOVA model. The random and mixed ANOVA models depart from the fixed ANOVA model only in the expected mean squares and the consequent choice of the appropriate test statistic.

Expected Mean Squares

The expected mean squares for the random and mixed ANOVA models for balanced two-factor studies can be worked out by utilizing the properties of the model and applying the usual expectation theorems. They are shown in Table 24.5, together with those for the fixed ANOVA model. The derivations are tedious, but simple rules have been developed for finding the expected mean squares. These rules are described in Appendix D.

Construction of Test Statistics

As usual, each statistic for testing factor effects is constructed by comparing two mean squares that have the properties:

1. Under H_0, both mean squares have the same expectation.

2. Under H_a, the numerator mean square has a larger expectation than the denominator mean square.

It can be shown that such a test statistic follows the F distribution if H_0 holds. The decision rule is constructed in the ordinary fashion, with large values of the test statistic leading to H_a.

TABLE 24.6   **Test Statistics for Balanced Two-Factor ANOVA Models.**

Test for Presence of Effects of	Fixed ANOVA Model (A and B fixed)	Random ANOVA Model (A and B random)	Mixed ANOVA Model (A fixed, B random)
Factor A	*MSA/MSE*	*MSA/MSAB*	*MSA/MSAB*
Factor B	*MSB/MSE*	*MSB/MSAB*	*MSB/MSE*
AB interactions	*MSAB/MSE*	*MSAB/MSE*	*MSAB/MSE*

For instance, to test for the presence of factor A main effects in random ANOVA model (24.39), namely:

$$(24.47) \qquad \begin{aligned} H_0: \ & \sigma_\alpha^2 = 0 \\ H_a: \ & \sigma_\alpha^2 > 0 \end{aligned}$$

we see from Table 24.5 that *MSA* and *MSAB* both have the same expectation if $\sigma_\alpha^2 = 0$, that is, if factor A has no main effects. If $\sigma_\alpha^2 > 0$, $E\{MSA\}$ is greater than $E\{MSAB\}$. Hence, the appropriate test statistic is:

$$(24.48) \qquad F^* = \frac{MSA}{MSAB}$$

and the decision rule for controlling the Type I error at α is:

$$(24.49) \qquad \begin{aligned} &\text{If } F^* \le F[1 - \alpha; a - 1, (a - 1)(b - 1)], \text{ conclude } H_0 \\ &\text{If } F^* > F[1 - \alpha; a - 1, (a - 1)(b - 1)], \text{ conclude } H_a \end{aligned}$$

Note that the denominator for testing for factor A main effects in the random ANOVA model is *MSAB*, whereas it is *MSE* in the fixed ANOVA model.

We summarize the appropriate test statistics for mixed and random ANOVA models in Table 24.6. For comparison purposes, we also present the test statistics for the fixed ANOVA model there. As may be seen from Table 24.6, the denominator of the test statistic for mixed and random ANOVA models in a number of instances differs from that for the fixed ANOVA model. Hence, it is important that the expected mean squares be known when random or mixed models are utilized so that the appropriate test statistics can be determined.

Example

We return to our earlier mixed ANOVA model example of four different training methods (factor A, fixed) and five instructors (factor B, random). Four classes were assigned to each training method–instructor combination. The response variable of interest was the mean improvement per student in the class at the end of the training program. The data are not shown, but the ANOVA table is presented in Table 24.7. To test whether or not training methods and instructors interact:

$$H_0: \ \sigma_{\alpha\beta}^2 = 0$$
$$H_a: \ \sigma_{\alpha\beta}^2 > 0$$

TABLE 24.7 **ANOVA Table for Mixed ANOVA Model—Training Example (A fixed, B Random, $a = 4$, $b = 5$, $n = 4$).**

Source of Variation	SS	df	MS	F^*
Factor A (training methods, fixed)	42.1	3	14.0	$14.0/3.9 = 3.59$
Factor B (instructors, random)	53.9	4	13.5	$13.5/2.1 = 6.43$
AB interactions	46.7	12	3.9	$3.9/2.1 = 1.86$
Error	126.4	60	2.1	
Total	269.1	79		

$$F(.95; 3, 12) = 3.49 \quad F(.95; 4, 60) = 2.53$$
$$F(.95; 12, 60) = 1.92$$

we utilize according to Table 24.6 the test statistic:

$$F^* = \frac{MSAB}{MSE}$$

Using the results from Table 24.7, we obtain:

$$F^* = \frac{3.9}{2.1} = 1.86$$

For level of significance $\alpha = .05$, we require $F(.95; 12, 60) = 1.92$. Since $F^* = 1.86 \leq 1.92$, we conclude that training methods and instructors do not interact. The P-value of this test is .06.

The test statistics for testing training method main effects and instructor main effects are shown in Table 24.7. By comparing the test statistics with the appropriate percentiles of the F distribution shown at the bottom of Table 24.7 for level of significance $\alpha = .05$ each, we find that both training methods and instructors differ in effectiveness.

Note

When there is only one case per treatment ($n = 1$) with the fixed two-factor ANOVA model, we know from Section 21.1 that no exact tests are possible unless the model can be modified. The reason is that $MSE = 0$ always in that case so that no estimate of σ^2 can be obtained. In contrast, Table 24.5 indicates that exact tests for both factor A and factor B main effects are possible with the random two-factor ANOVA model when $n = 1$ without any restrictive assumptions about the interactions. This is because $MSAB$ is the appropriate denominator of the test statistic here, and $MSAB$ can be determined regardless of sample size. With the mixed ANOVA model where factor A is the fixed factor, the presence of factor A main effects can also be tested when $n = 1$ without the need for restrictive assumptions about the interactions. However, an exact test for factor B main effects would require the assumption that all interactions are zero or some other modification of the ANOVA model. ∎

24.4   Two-Factor Studies—Estimation of Factor Effects for Models II and III

Estimation of Variance Components

When a random factor has significant main effects, we often wish to estimate the magnitude of the variance component. Unbiased estimators can readily be derived from appropriate linear combinations of the expected mean squares in Table 24.5. For instance, the variance component σ_β^2 in mixed ANOVA model (24.42) can be estimated by noting that:

$$E\{MSB\} - E\{MSE\} = \sigma^2 + na\sigma_\beta^2 - \sigma^2 = na\sigma_\beta^2$$

Hence, we have:

(24.50)
$$\sigma_\beta^2 = \frac{E\{MSB\} - E\{MSE\}}{na}$$

and an unbiased estimator of σ_β^2 is:

(24.50a)
$$s_\beta^2 = \frac{MSB - MSE}{na}$$

Approximate confidence intervals for the variance components in balanced two-factor studies can be obtained by either the Satterthwaite procedure in (24.29) or the *MLS* procedure in (24.34). For example, the *MLS* procedure can be used to estimate the variance component σ_β^2 in mixed ANOVA model (24.42) by noting from (24.50a) that s_β^2 can be expressed in the form (24.33):

$$\hat{L} = s_\beta^2 = \left(\frac{1}{na}\right) MSB + \left(-\frac{1}{na}\right) MSE$$

The correspondences are $MS_1 = MSB$, $MS_2 = MSE$, $c_1 = 1/na$, and $c_2 = -1/na$. The approximate $1 - \alpha$ *MLS* confidence limits therefore are:

(24.51)
$$s_\beta^2 - H_L \le \sigma_\beta^2 \le s_\beta^2 + H_U$$

where H_L and H_U are determined using the formulas in Table 24.3, with $df_1 = b - 1$ and $df_2 = (n - 1)ab$.

Example.   In the training example of Table 24.7 with one fixed and one random factor, random factor B (instructors) had significant effects. To estimate σ_β^2, we utilize the estimator in (24.50a). Substituting, we obtain:

$$s_\beta^2 = \frac{13.5 - 2.1}{16} = .71$$

To construct an approximate 95 percent confidence interval for σ_β^2 by the *MLS* procedure, we first note that the correspondences to the form in (24.33) are:

$$c_1 = \frac{1}{na} = \frac{1}{4(4)} = .0625 \qquad\qquad MS_1 = MSB = 13.5$$

$$c_2 = -\frac{1}{na} = -\frac{1}{4(4)} = -.0625 \qquad\qquad MS_2 = MSE = 2.1$$

$$df_1 = b - 1 = 4 \qquad\qquad\qquad df_2 = (n-1)ab = 60$$

Carrying out the calculations indicated in Table 24.3, we first obtain the percentiles:

$$F_1 = F(.975; 4, \infty) = 2.79 \qquad\qquad F_2 = (.975; 60, \infty) = 1.39$$

$$F_3 = F(.975; \infty, 4) = 8.26 \qquad\qquad F_4 = (.975; \infty, 60) = 1.48$$

$$F_5 = F(.975; 4, 60) = 3.01 \qquad\qquad F_6 = F(.975; 60, 4) = 8.36$$

and then:

$$G_1 = .6416 \qquad\qquad G_4 = -.4834$$

$$G_2 = .2806 \qquad\qquad H_L = .55$$

$$G_3 = .0266 \qquad\qquad H_U = 6.12$$

The desired confidence interval is obtained from (24.51):

$$.16 = .71 - .55 \le \sigma_\beta^2 \le .71 + 6.12 = 6.83$$

Hence, an approximate 95 percent confidence interval for σ_β, the standard deviation measuring the variability among instructors, is:

$$.4 \le \sigma_\beta \le 2.6$$

Estimation of Fixed Effects in Mixed Model

Point Estimators.   We now consider point and interval estimation of fixed effect parameters for balanced mixed model (24.42), where factor A is fixed and factor B is random. The situation is more complicated than for fixed ANOVA model I because certain pairs of observations are correlated for the mixed model, as we have seen in (24.46). When the responses Y are correlated, the method of generalized least squares must be used to obtain minimum variance unbiased estimators. Weighted least squares, discussed in Chapter 10, is a special case of generalized least squares. It turns out, however, that the generalized least squares estimators of the fixed effects α_i for the balanced case are the same as the ones obtained by the method of ordinary least squares:

$$(24.52) \qquad\qquad \hat{\alpha}_i = \bar{Y}_{i..} - \bar{Y}_{...}$$

Frequently, the marginal mean $\mu_{i.}$ is also of interest. Since $\mu_{i.} = \mu_{..} + \alpha_i$, it follows from (24.52) that a best linear unbiased estimator of $\mu_{i.}$ for balanced studies is:

$$(24.53) \qquad\qquad \hat{\mu}_{i.} = \bar{Y}_{...} + (\bar{Y}_{i..} - \bar{Y}_{...}) = \bar{Y}_{i..}$$

Often a contrast of the fixed effects α_i is also of interest:

(24.54)
$$L = \sum c_i \alpha_i \qquad \text{where} \quad \sum c_i = 0$$

An unbiased estimator of L is:

(24.55)
$$\hat{L} = \sum c_i \hat{\alpha}_i = \sum c_i (\bar{Y}_{i..} - \bar{Y}_{...}) = \sum c_i \bar{Y}_{i..}$$

Variances of Estimators. For mixed ANOVA model (24.42) for balanced studies, it can be shown that the variance of $\hat{\alpha}_i$ is as follows:

(24.56)
$$\sigma^2\{\hat{\alpha}_i\} = \frac{\sigma^2 + n\sigma^2_{\alpha\beta}}{bn} = \frac{E\{MSAB\}}{bn}$$

It can also be shown that the variance of a contrast $\hat{L}$ of the estimated fixed factor A effects $\hat{\alpha}_i$, defined in (24.55), is as follows:

(24.57)
$$\sigma^2\{\hat{L}\} = \sum c_i^2 \sigma^2\{\hat{\alpha}_i\}$$

where $\sigma^2\{\hat{\alpha}_i\}$ is given in (24.56).

Since $\sigma^2\{\hat{\alpha}_i\}$ is a constant multiple of an expected mean square, it can be estimated unbiasedly and exact confidence intervals for α_i and for contrasts of the α_i can be obtained. An unbiased estimator of the variance of $\hat{\alpha}_i$ is:

(24.58)
$$s^2\{\hat{\alpha}_i\} = \frac{MSAB}{bn}$$

and of a contrast of the $\hat{\alpha}_i$ is:

(24.59)
$$s^2\{\hat{L}\} = \frac{MSAB}{bn} \sum c_i^2$$

Note

The variances in (24.56) and (24.57) are obtained by recognizing that $\hat{\alpha}_i$ and $\hat{L}$ are linear combinations of the responses Y_{ijk}. For instance, consider an experiment with $a = b = n = 2$. Then $\hat{\alpha}_1$ in (24.52) is as follows:

$$\hat{\alpha}_1 = \bar{Y}_{1..} - \bar{Y}_{...} = \frac{1}{4}(Y_{111} + Y_{112} + Y_{121} + Y_{122}) - \frac{1}{8}(Y_{111} + \cdots + Y_{222})$$

$$= \left(\frac{1}{8}\right)Y_{111} + \left(\frac{1}{8}\right)Y_{112} + \left(\frac{1}{8}\right)Y_{121} + \left(\frac{1}{8}\right)Y_{122} + \left(-\frac{1}{8}\right)Y_{211}$$

$$+ \left(-\frac{1}{8}\right)Y_{212} + \left(-\frac{1}{8}\right)Y_{221} + \left(-\frac{1}{8}\right)Y_{222}$$

Let the coefficients of the responses Y be denoted by c and define the row vector of the coefficients as follows:

$$\mathbf{c}' = (c_1 \quad c_2 \quad \cdots \quad c_{n_T})$$

and let **Y** as always denote the vector of the responses. We can then represent the estimator $(\hat{\alpha}_i$ or $\hat{L})$ as $\mathbf{c}'\mathbf{Y}$.

We know the variances and covariances of the responses Y_{ijk} from (24.45) and (24.46). Let $\boldsymbol{\sigma}^2\{\mathbf{Y}\}$, as usual, denote the variance-covariance matrix containing these variances and covariances. We then utilize (5.46) to obtain the variance of the estimator, namely $\mathbf{c}'\boldsymbol{\sigma}^2\{\mathbf{Y}\}\mathbf{c}$. The resulting variance will be expressed in terms of the variance components σ^2, σ_β^2, and $\sigma_{\alpha\beta}^2$. We then use the expected mean squares in Table 24.5 for the mixed model to express the variance, if possible, in terms of expected mean squares.   ∎

Confidence Intervals for Fixed Effects Contrasts.   It is not always possible to obtain exact confidence intervals for the fixed effects in mixed models. Exact confidence intervals are available only when the variance of the estimated parameter or contrast of interest is proportional to an expected mean square from the analysis of variance table. In cases where the variance is not directly proportional to an expected mean square, Satterthwaite's method can sometimes be used to construct approximate confidence intervals. For mixed ANOVA model (24.42), it is possible to obtain exact confidence intervals for contrasts of the fixed effects α_i because $\sigma^2\{\hat{\alpha}_i\}$ in (24.56) is a constant multiple of $E\{MSAB\}$. It can be shown that:

(24.60)
$$\frac{\hat{L} - L}{s\{\hat{L}\}} \text{ is distributed as } t[(a-1)(b-1)]$$

As a result, the $1 - \alpha$ confidence limits for L are:

(24.61)
$$\hat{L} \pm t[1 - \alpha/2; (a-1)(b-1)]s\{\hat{L}\}$$

where $\hat{L}$ is given by (24.55) and $s^2\{\hat{L}\}$ is given by (24.59).

Notice that confidence limits (24.61) are identical to those in (20.9) for the fixed ANOVA model, except that:

1. *MSAB* replaces *MSE* in the estimated variance of the contrast.

2. The degrees of freedom now are $(a-1)(b-1)$ instead of $(n-1)ab$ since a different mean square is utilized.

Example.   In the training example of Table 24.7, no interaction effects were found to be present. We now wish to estimate the difference $L = \alpha_1 - \alpha_2$ in the mean improvements between training methods 1 and 2, using a 95 percent confidence interval. The relevant sample results are:

$$\bar{Y}_{1..} = 43.1 \qquad \bar{Y}_{2..} = 40.8$$

Hence, our point estimate of $L = \alpha_1 - \alpha_2 = \mu_{1.} - \mu_{2.}$ is:

$$\hat{L} = \bar{Y}_{1..} - \bar{Y}_{2..} = 43.1 - 40.8 = 2.3$$

Using (24.59), the estimated variance is:

$$s^2\{\hat{L}\} = \frac{MSAB}{bn}(1+1) = \frac{2(3.9)}{20} = .39$$

or $s\{\hat{L}\} = .62$. There are 12 degrees of freedom associated with $MSAB$; hence, we require $t(.975; 12) = 2.179$. The confidence limits (24.61) therefore are $2.3 \pm 2.179(.62)$ and the desired confidence interval is:

$$.9 \leq \mu_1. - \mu_2. \leq 3.7$$

Thus, we conclude with confidence coefficient .95 that training method 1 is more effective than training method 2, its mean improvement being somewhere between .9 and 3.7 units larger.

Multiple Comparison Procedures.   Multiple comparison procedures can be utilized for the main effects of the fixed factor in a mixed two-factor ANOVA model in the same way as for the fixed ANOVA model. For example, suppose we wish to obtain all pairwise comparisons between the different training methods in the training example in Table 24.7 by means of the Tukey procedure. We would calculate $s^2\{\hat{L}\}$ as in the previous example. The t multiple in (24.61) now would be:

(24.62) $$T = \frac{1}{\sqrt{2}}q[1 - \alpha; a, (a - 1)(b - 1)]$$

With specific reference to the training example in Table 24.7, we would require for constructing 95 percent family confidence coefficient intervals for all pairwise comparisons between training methods:

$$q(.95; 4, 12) = 4.20 \qquad T = \frac{1}{\sqrt{2}}(4.20) = 2.97$$

Confidence Intervals for Marginal Means.   An exact confidence interval for a marginal mean $\mu_i.$ in mixed ANOVA model (24.42) cannot be obtained because the variance of the marginal mean $\hat{\mu}_i.$ in (24.53) is not a multiple of a single expected mean square. Rather, the variance is a linear combination of two expected mean squares, as follows:

(24.63) $$\sigma^2\{\hat{\mu}_i.\} = c_1 E\{MSAB\} + c_2 E\{MSB\}$$

where:

(24.63a) $$c_1 = \frac{a - 1}{nab}$$

(24.63b) $$c_2 = \frac{1}{nab}$$

An unbiased estimator of $\sigma^2\{\hat{\mu}_i.\}$ is:

(24.64) $$s^2\{\hat{\mu}_i.\} = c_1 MSAB + c_2 MSB$$

Since the form of the variance of estimated marginal mean $\hat{\mu}_i.$ is that in (24.25), the Satterthwaite approximation can be employed, where the degrees of freedom associated with the estimated variance $s^2\{\hat{\mu}_{i.}\}$ are according to (24.28):

$$(24.65) \qquad df = \frac{\left(\dfrac{a-1}{nab}MSAB + \dfrac{1}{nab}MSB\right)^2}{\dfrac{\left(\dfrac{a-1}{nab}MSAB\right)^2}{(a-1)(b-1)} + \dfrac{\left(\dfrac{1}{nab}MSB\right)^2}{b-1}}$$

Approximate $1 - \alpha$ confidence limits for $\mu_{i.}$ therefore are:

$$(24.66) \qquad \hat{\mu}_{i.} \pm t(1 - \alpha/2; df)s\{\hat{\mu}_{i.}\}$$

where $s^2\{\hat{\mu}_{i.}\}$ is given in (24.64) and df is given in (24.65).

Example. Referring again to the training example of Table 24.7, a 95 percent confidence interval for $\mu_{1.}$ is desired. As noted previously, the estimated mean improvement for training method 1 is:

$$\hat{\mu}_{1.} = \bar{Y}_{1..} = 43.1$$

Using (24.64) and noting that $nab = 4(4)5 = 80$, we obtain:

$$s^2\{\hat{\mu}_{1.}\} = \frac{3}{80}(3.9) + \frac{1}{80}(13.5) = .315$$

or $s\{\hat{\mu}_{1.}\} = .561$. From (24.65) we find:

$$df = \frac{\left[\dfrac{3}{80}(3.9) + \dfrac{1}{80}(13.5)\right]^2}{\dfrac{\left[\dfrac{3}{80}(3.9)\right]^2}{3(4)} + \dfrac{\left[\dfrac{1}{80}(13.5)\right]^2}{4}} = 11.1$$

Using $df = 11$, the required t percentile is $t(.975; 11) = 2.201$. The confidence limits are therefore $43.1 \pm 2.201(.561)$ and the desired confidence interval is:

$$41.9 \le \mu_{1.} \le 44.3$$

We conclude with approximate confidence coefficient .95 that the mean improvement for training method 1 averaged over all instructors is between 41.9 and 44.3.

24.5 Three-Factor Studies—ANOVA Models II and III

Just as for single-factor and two-factor studies, the analysis of variance sums of squares and degrees of freedom for random and mixed multifactor models are the same as those for the corresponding fixed ANOVA model. The principal issue with random and mixed multifactor models, as we saw for two-factor models, is the determination of the expected mean squares. Once these are known, the proper test statistics and confidence intervals can be constructed. Rules for finding expected mean squares for random and mixed models

TABLE 24.8 Expected Mean Squares for Balanced Random Three-Factor ANOVA Model (24.67).

Mean Square	df	Expected Mean Square
MSA	$a-1$	$\sigma^2 + nbc\sigma_\alpha^2 + nc\sigma_{\alpha\beta}^2 + nb\sigma_{\alpha\gamma}^2 + n\sigma_{\alpha\beta\gamma}^2$
MSB	$b-1$	$\sigma^2 + nac\sigma_\beta^2 + nc\sigma_{\alpha\beta}^2 + na\sigma_{\beta\gamma}^2 + n\sigma_{\alpha\beta\gamma}^2$
MSC	$c-1$	$\sigma^2 + nab\sigma_\gamma^2 + nb\sigma_{\alpha\gamma}^2 + na\sigma_{\beta\gamma}^2 + n\sigma_{\alpha\beta\gamma}^2$
MSAB	$(a-1)(b-1)$	$\sigma^2 + nc\sigma_{\alpha\beta}^2 + n\sigma_{\alpha\beta\gamma}^2$
MSAC	$(a-1)(c-1)$	$\sigma^2 + nb\sigma_{\alpha\gamma}^2 + n\sigma_{\alpha\beta\gamma}^2$
MSBC	$(b-1)(c-1)$	$\sigma^2 + na\sigma_{\beta\gamma}^2 + n\sigma_{\alpha\beta\gamma}^2$
MSABC	$(a-1)(b-1)(c-1)$	$\sigma^2 + n\sigma_{\alpha\beta\gamma}^2$
MSE	$(n-1)abc$	σ^2

are given in Appendix D for balanced studies with any number of factors. We now present model II (random factor levels) and model III (mixed factor levels) for three-factor studies and show how appropriate tests are conducted. We consider again the balanced case where all treatment sample sizes are equal.

ANOVA Model II—Random Factor Effects

In a study of the effects of operators, machines, and batches of raw material on daily output, all three factors may be considered to have random factor levels. The random ANOVA model for such a three-factor study is:

$$(24.67) \quad Y_{ijkm} = \mu_{...} + \alpha_i + \beta_j + \gamma_k + (\alpha\beta)_{ij} + (\alpha\gamma)_{ik} + (\beta\gamma)_{jk} + (\alpha\beta\gamma)_{ijk} + \varepsilon_{ijkm}$$

where:

$\mu_{...}$ is a constant

α_i, β_j, γ_k, $(\alpha\beta)_{ij}$, $(\alpha\gamma)_{ik}$, $(\beta\gamma)_{jk}$, $(\alpha\beta\gamma)_{ijk}$, ε_{ijkm} are independent normal random variables with expectations zero and respective variances σ_α^2, σ_β^2, σ_γ^2, $\sigma_{\alpha\beta}^2$, $\sigma_{\alpha\gamma}^2$, $\sigma_{\beta\gamma}^2$, $\sigma_{\alpha\beta\gamma}^2$, σ^2

$i = 1, \ldots, a; \ j = 1, \ldots, b; \ k = 1, \ldots, c; \ m = 1, \ldots, n$

Just as for two-factor random ANOVA model (24.39), the responses Y_{ijkm} for three-factor random ANOVA model (24.67) are normally distributed with constant variance. The expected value and variance of response Y_{ijkm} are:

$$(24.68a) \quad E\{Y_{ijkm}\} = \mu_{...}$$

$$(24.68b) \quad \sigma^2\{Y_{ijkm}\} = \sigma_Y^2 = \sigma_\alpha^2 + \sigma_\beta^2 + \sigma_\gamma^2 + \sigma_{\alpha\beta}^2 + \sigma_{\alpha\gamma}^2 + \sigma_{\beta\gamma}^2 + \sigma_{\alpha\beta\gamma}^2 + \sigma^2$$

Any two responses are independent except when they have one or more common factor levels; these latter are correlated because they contain some common random terms.

Table 24.8 contains the degrees of freedom and the expected mean squares for all components of the ANOVA table for random ANOVA model (24.67).

ANOVA Model III—Mixed Factor Effects

Consider a three-factor study where factors B and C have random factor levels while factor A has fixed factor levels. The restricted mixed ANOVA model for such a three-factor balanced study is:

$$(24.69) \quad Y_{ijkm} = \mu_{...} + \alpha_i + \beta_j + \gamma_k + (\alpha\beta)_{ij} + (\alpha\gamma)_{ik} + (\beta\gamma)_{jk} + (\alpha\beta\gamma)_{ijk} + \varepsilon_{ijkm}$$

where:

$\mu_{...}$ is a constant

α_i are constants

β_j, γ_k, $(\alpha\beta)_{ij}$, $(\alpha\gamma)_{ik}$, $(\beta\gamma)_{jk}$, $(\alpha\beta\gamma)_{ijk}$ are pairwise independent normal random variables with expectations zero and constant variances

ε_{ijkm} are independent $N(0, \sigma^2)$, and are independent of the other random components

$\sum_i \alpha_i = \sum_i (\alpha\beta)_{ij} = \sum_i (\alpha\gamma)_{ik} = \sum_i (\alpha\beta\gamma)_{ijk} = 0$

$i = 1, \ldots, a; j = 1, \ldots, b; k = 1, \ldots, c; m = 1, \ldots, n$

Note that all interaction terms in this model are random, since at least one of the factors contained in each has random factor levels. Note also that all sums of effects over the fixed factor levels are zero. Various correlations exist between the random effects terms, which we shall not detail.

The responses Y_{ijkm} for three-factor mixed ANOVA model (24.69) are normally distributed with constant variance. The expected value of observation Y_{ijkm} is:

$$(24.70) \quad E\{Y_{ijkm}\} = \mu_{...} + \alpha_i$$

In advance of the random trials, any two responses are independent except for those that contain common and/or correlated random effects terms; these observations are correlated.

Table 24.9 contains all the expected mean squares for mixed ANOVA model (24.69).

Other mixed ANOVA models can be developed in similar fashion. The expected mean squares for these mixed models can be found by employing the rules presented in Appendix D.

Appropriate Test Statistics

From the expected mean squares, we seek to determine the appropriate F^* statistic for a given test. An exact test statistic can often be found for random and mixed multifactor models, but not always.

Exact F Test. Suppose we wish to determine whether or not BC interactions are present in random ANOVA model (24.67). We see from Table 24.8 that the appropriate test statistic is $MSBC/MSABC$. If we wish to study the same question for mixed ANOVA model (24.69), we see from Table 24.9 that an appropriate test statistic is available, but this time it is $MSBC/MSE$. We thus note that the two test statistics are not the same, even though the same factor effects are being studied, because of the differences between the two models.

It is not always possible to find an exact F test for mixed and random multifactor ANOVA models. For instance, we cannot directly test for the presence of factor A main effects in random ANOVA model (24.67). Note from Table 24.8 that there is no expected mean square that consists of the components of $E\{MSA\}$ except for the $nbc\sigma_\alpha^2$ term.

TABLE 24.9 Expected Mean Squares for Balanced Mixed Three-Factor ANOVA Model (24.69) (*A* fixed, *B* and *C* random).

Mean Square	df	Expected Mean Square
MSA	$a - 1$	$\sigma^2 + nbc\dfrac{\sum \alpha_i^2}{a-1} + nc\sigma_{\alpha\beta}^2 + nb\sigma_{\alpha\gamma}^2 + n\sigma_{\alpha\beta\gamma}^2$
MSB	$b - 1$	$\sigma^2 + nac\sigma_\beta^2 + na\sigma_{\beta\gamma}^2$
MSC	$c - 1$	$\sigma^2 + nab\sigma_\gamma^2 + na\sigma_{\beta\gamma}^2$
MSAB	$(a-1)(b-1)$	$\sigma^2 + nc\sigma_{\alpha\beta}^2 + n\sigma_{\alpha\beta\gamma}^2$
MSAC	$(a-1)(c-1)$	$\sigma^2 + nb\sigma_{\alpha\gamma}^2 + n\sigma_{\alpha\beta\gamma}^2$
MSBC	$(b-1)(c-1)$	$\sigma^2 + na\sigma_{\beta\gamma}^2$
MSABC	$(a-1)(b-1)(c-1)$	$\sigma^2 + n\sigma_{\alpha\beta\gamma}^2$
MSE	$(n-1)abc$	σ^2

Sometimes it is possible to assume that certain interactions are zero, and then proceed in the usual way with an exact F test. For example, to test for factor A main effects in random ANOVA model (24.67) (see Table 24.8), it may be possible to assume that $\sigma_{\alpha\gamma}^2 = 0$ (indeed, this can be tested with $MSAC/MSABC$). If this assumption is appropriate, we can use the test statistic $MSA/MSAB$ to test for factor A main effects.

Satterthwaite Approximate F Test. Often, it is not known whether certain interactions are zero. In that case, an approximate F test may be employed which utilizes a *pseudo F* or *quasi F* test statistic. This approximate test, called the *Satterthwaite test*, involves developing a linear combination of mean squares that has the same expectation when H_0 holds as the factor effects mean square. As noted in our discussion of the Satterthwaite procedure for constructing approximate confidence limits for variance components, this linear combination is expressed in the form:

$$\hat{L} = c_1 MS_1 + \cdots + c_h MS_h$$

where the c_i are constants. The approximate number of degrees of freedom associated with this linear combination of mean squares is given by (24.28). The test statistic is then set up in the usual way and follows approximately the F distribution when H_0 holds.

We illustrate this procedure for testing factor A main effects in random ANOVA model (24.67):

(24.71)
$$H_0: \sigma_\alpha^2 = 0$$
$$H_a: \sigma_\alpha^2 > 0$$

Note from Table 24.8 that:

(24.72) $\quad E\{MSAB\} + E\{MSAC\} - E\{MSABC\} = \sigma^2 + nc\sigma_{\alpha\beta}^2 + nb\sigma_{\alpha\gamma}^2 + n\sigma_{\alpha\beta\gamma}^2$

TABLE 24.10 **ANOVA Table for Random Three-Factor Study** $(a = 3, b = 2, c = 5, n = 3)$.

Source of Variation	SS	df	MS
Factor A (operators)	17.3	2	8.65
Factor B (machines)	4.2	1	4.20
Factor C (batches)	24.8	4	6.20
AB interactions	4.8	2	2.40
AC interactions	31.7	8	3.96
BC interactions	12.5	4	3.13
ABC interactions	11.9	8	1.49
Error	137.7	60	2.30
Total	244.9	89	

This equals precisely $E\{MSA\}$ when $\sigma_\alpha^2 = 0$. Hence, the suggested test statistic is:

$$(24.73) \qquad F^{**} = \frac{MSA}{MSAB + MSAC - MSABC}$$

where we denote the test statistic as F^{**} as a reminder that a pseudo F test is involved.

Example. Table 24.10 contains the analysis of variance for a study of the effects of operators, machines, and batches on the daily output of a highly automated process. Each factor is assumed to be a random factor. To test whether operators (factor A) have a main effect on output, we use test statistic (24.73):

$$F^{**} = \frac{8.65}{2.40 + 3.96 - 1.49} = \frac{8.65}{4.87} = 1.78$$

The approximate number of degrees of freedom associated with the denominator is:

$$df = \frac{(4.87)^2}{\frac{(2.40)^2}{2} + \frac{(3.96)^2}{8} + \frac{(-1.49)^2}{8}} = 4.63$$

which we round to 5. For level of significance $\alpha = .05$, we require $F(.95; 2, 5) = 5.79$. Since $F^{**} = 1.78 \le 5.79$, we conclude H_0, that operators do not have a main effect on daily output.

Note

Since the Satterthwaite pseudo F test is an approximate one, it must be employed with caution. Some alternative procedures are provided in References 24.2 and 24.8. ∎

Estimation of Effects

No new problems arise in the estimation of variance components for random factors or in the estimation of contrasts for fixed factors in mixed models, when three or more factors are studied at one time. Confidence limits for contrasts of the factor level means of a fixed factor are obtained by using the mean square utilized in the denominator of the test statistic for examining the presence of main effects for that factor. The degrees of freedom are those associated with the mean square utilized.

24.6   ANOVA Models II and III with Unequal Sample Sizes

We noted in Chapter 22 for the fixed two-factor ANOVA model that unequal treatment sample sizes make the analysis of variance more complicated because the sums of squares no longer are orthogonal. Tests of hypotheses must then be based on the general linear test approach. When sample sizes are unequal for studies involving random effects, the level of complexity increases in a similar fashion. Most of the methods described thus far for two-factor and multifactor ANOVA models II and III do not apply to unbalanced studies. For example, in unbalanced studies typically neither exact nor Satterthwaite approximate *F* tests exist.

A number of alternative approaches have been developed for making inferences for ANOVA models II and III in the presence of unequal sample sizes. We shall discuss an approach based on the method of maximum likelihood. This approach has the advantage of conceptual simplicity and is a general procedure that possesses a number of optimality properties. Detailed discussions of this and alternative approaches can be found in References 24.2, 24.7, and 24.9.

We shall illustrate the maximum likelihood approach using an example involving a two-factor experiment where one factor has fixed factor levels and the second factor has random factor levels.

Example

The Sheffield Foods Company markets a variety of dairy products, including milk, ice cream, and yogurt. Recently, the company received a complaint from a government agency that the actual levels of milkfat in its yogurt exceeded the labeled amount. Company personnel were concerned that the government's laboratory method for measuring fat content in yogurt might be unreliable because it is primarily designed for use with milk and ice cream. To study the reliability of Sheffield's and the government's laboratory methods, a small interlaboratory study was carried out. Four testing laboratories were randomly selected from the population of laboratories in the United States. Each laboratory was sent 12 samples of yogurt, with instructions to evaluate six of the samples using the government's method and six by the company's method. The yogurt had been mixed under carefully controlled conditions and the fat content of each sample was known to be 3.0 percent.

In this study, measurement method is a fixed factor with $a = 2$ levels ($i = 1$: Government method; $i = 2$: Sheffield method) and laboratories is a random factor with $b = 4$ levels. Due to technical difficulties with the Government method, none of the laboratories was able to obtain fat content determinations for all of the six samples assigned to that method in the time available. The results of the study are given in Table 24.11. Figure 24.3 contains dot plots of the data. The variability of the sample fat

TABLE 24.11   **Laboratory Fat Content Determinations—Sheffield Foods Company Example.**

Measurement Method	k	Laboratory			
		$j = 1$	$j = 2$	$j = 3$	$j = 4$
$i = 1$	1	5.19	4.09	4.62	3.71
Government	2	5.09	3.99	4.32	3.86
	3		3.75	4.35	3.79
	4		4.04	4.59	3.63
	5		4.06		
$i = 2$	1	3.26	3.02	3.08	2.98
Sheffield	2	3.48	3.32	2.95	2.89
	3	3.24	2.83	2.98	2.75
	4	3.41	2.96	2.74	3.04
	5	3.35	3.23	3.07	2.88
	6	3.04	3.07	2.70	3.20

FIGURE 24.3   **Dot Plots of Fat Content Determinations by Laboratory and Measurement Method—Sheffield Foods Company Example.**

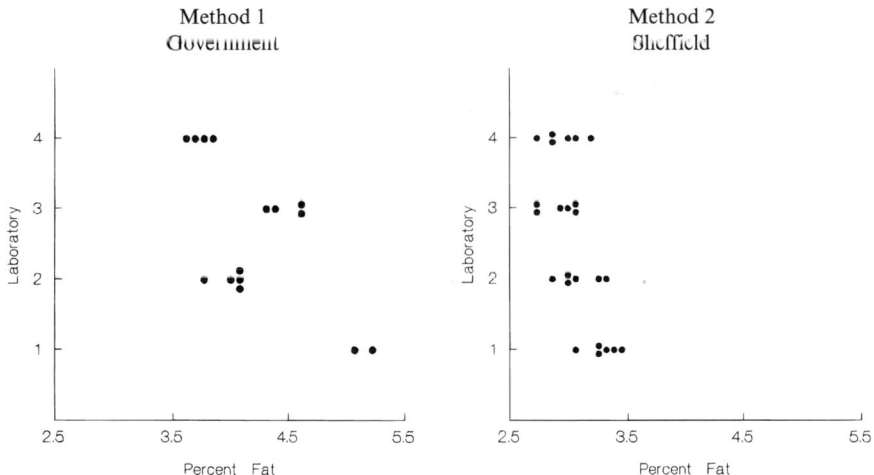

determinations appears to be reasonably constant for all measurement method–laboratory combinations. Figure 24.4 contains a MINITAB estimated treatment means plot. For the four laboratories included in the study, no major interaction effects between laboratory and measurement method on fat content determination appear to be present. The plot suggests a definite measurement method effect and possibly also some differences between laboratories. We shall now analyze the data formally by means of the maximum likelihood approach.

FIGURE 24.4 **MINITAB Estimated Treatment Means Plot—Sheffield Foods Company Example.**

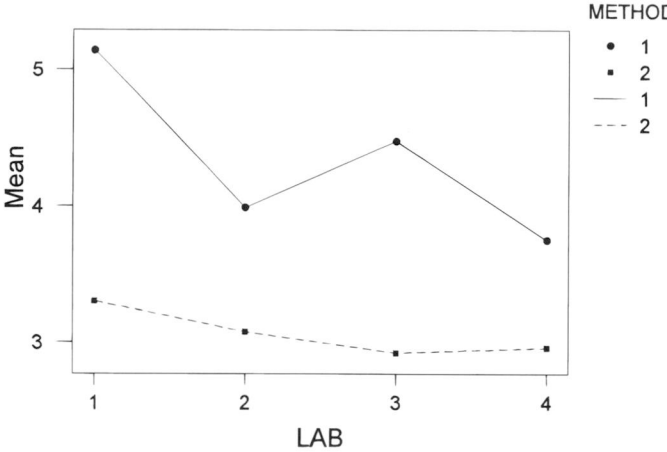

Interaction Plot - Means for PCTFAT

Maximum Likelihood Approach

The maximum likelihood approach which we shall utilize for the Sheffield Foods Company example makes somewhat stronger assumptions than mixed ANOVA model (24.42), which we would use if the study were balanced. We first review mixed ANOVA model (24.42) as it applies to the Sheffield Foods Company example.

Mixed ANOVA Model (24.42). This model for the Sheffield Foods Company example is as follows:

$$(24.74) \qquad Y_{ijk} = \mu_{..} + \alpha_i + \beta_j + (\alpha\beta)_{ij} + \varepsilon_{ijk}$$

$$\sigma^2\{\beta_j\} = \sigma_\beta^2$$

$$\sigma^2\{(\alpha\beta)_{ij}\} = \frac{2-1}{2}\sigma_{\alpha\beta}^2 = \frac{\sigma_{\alpha\beta}^2}{2}$$

$$\sigma^2\{\varepsilon_{ijk}\} = \sigma^2$$

$$i = 1, 2; \; j = 1, \ldots, 4; \; k = 1, \ldots, n_{ij}$$

For this model, the expected value and variance of Y_{ijk} are according to (24.44) and (24.45):

$$(24.75) \qquad E\{Y_{ijk}\} = \mu_{..} + \alpha_i$$

$$(24.76) \qquad \sigma^2\{Y_{ijk}\} = \sigma_Y^2 = \sigma_\beta^2 + \frac{\sigma_{\alpha\beta}^2}{2} + \sigma^2$$

TABLE 24.12 Matrix Formulation for Sheffield Foods Company Example.

$$\mathbf{Y} = \begin{bmatrix} Y_{111} \\ Y_{112} \\ Y_{121} \\ Y_{122} \\ \vdots \\ Y_{144} \\ Y_{211} \\ Y_{212} \\ Y_{213} \\ Y_{214} \\ \vdots \\ Y_{246} \end{bmatrix} = \begin{bmatrix} 5.19 \\ 5.09 \\ 4.09 \\ 3.99 \\ \vdots \\ 3.63 \\ 3.26 \\ 3.48 \\ 3.24 \\ 3.41 \\ \vdots \\ 3.20 \end{bmatrix} \qquad \mathbf{X} = \begin{bmatrix} 1 & 1 \\ 1 & 1 \\ 1 & 1 \\ 1 & 1 \\ \vdots & \vdots \\ 1 & 1 \\ 1 & -1 \\ 1 & -1 \\ 1 & -1 \\ 1 & -1 \\ \vdots & \vdots \\ 1 & -1 \end{bmatrix} \qquad \boldsymbol{\beta} = \begin{bmatrix} \mu_{..} \\ \alpha_1 \end{bmatrix}$$

Also, the responses Y_{ijk} are correlated as follows according to (24.46):

(24.77a)
$$\sigma\{Y_{ijk}, Y_{ijk'}\} = \sigma_\beta^2 + \frac{\sigma_{\alpha\beta}^2}{2} \qquad k \neq k'$$

(24.77b)
$$\sigma\{Y_{ijk}, Y_{i'jk'}\} = \sigma_\beta^2 - \frac{\sigma_{\alpha\beta}^2}{2} \qquad i \neq i'$$

(24.77c)
$$\sigma\{Y_{ijk}, Y_{i'j'k'}\} = 0 \qquad j \neq j'$$

We also know that the responses Y_{ijk} for mixed ANOVA model (24.42) are normally distributed.

Since the expected value of Y_{ijk} depends only on the fixed effects $\mu_{..}$ and α_i (the random effects have expectations zero), we can represent the vector of expected values, $\mathbf{E}\{\mathbf{Y}\}$, in the matrix form $\mathbf{X}\boldsymbol{\beta}$. We illustrate this in Table 24.12 for the Sheffield Foods Company example. This table contains the vector of responses $\mathbf{Y}$, the vector of parameters $\boldsymbol{\beta}$, and the $\mathbf{X}$ matrix containing the usual column of 1s associated with $\mu_{..}$ and an indicator variable taking on the values 1 and -1 associated with α_1. Recall that $\alpha_2 = -\alpha_1$ since $\Sigma\alpha_i = 0$.

The variance-covariance matrix of the responses Y_{ijk}, $\boldsymbol{\sigma}^2\{\mathbf{Y}\}$, has on the main diagonal the constant variance from (24.76) and off the main diagonal the covariances from (24.77). We illustrated such a variance-covariance matrix in Table 24.4 for a study in which $a = b = n = 2$.

Density Function. To employ the method of maximum likelihood, we make a somewhat stronger assumption than with ANOVA model (24.42). We assume all of the properties of model (24.42) and in addition assume that the Y_{ijk} are jointly normally distributed. The density function of the multivariate normal distribution is given in (15.29). The mean vector $\boldsymbol{\mu}$ in (15.29) corresponds here to $\mathbf{X}\boldsymbol{\beta}$, and the variance-covariance matrix $\boldsymbol{\Sigma}$ in (15.29) corresponds to $\boldsymbol{\sigma}^2\{\mathbf{Y}\}$. We shall continue to use $\boldsymbol{\Sigma}$ to represent the variance-covariance matrix of the responses Y_{ijk}. The number of Y variables p in (15.29) corresponds here to

n_T. We can then express the joint density function of the responses Y_{ijk} as follows:

$$(24.78) \qquad f(\mathbf{Y}) = \frac{1}{(2\pi)^{n_T/2}|\mathbf{\Sigma}|^{1/2}} \exp\left[-\frac{1}{2}(\mathbf{Y} - \mathbf{X}\boldsymbol{\beta})'\mathbf{\Sigma}^{-1}(\mathbf{Y} - \mathbf{X}\boldsymbol{\beta})\right]$$

Viewing the joint density as a function of the unknown parameters (for the Sheffield Foods Company example, $\mu_{..}$ and α_1 in $\boldsymbol{\beta}$ and σ^2, σ^2_β, and $\sigma^2_{\alpha\beta}$ in $\mathbf{\Sigma}$), given the observations Y_{ijk}, the function in (24.78) is called the likelihood function and denoted by L.

Maximum Likelihood Estimates. To obtain the maximum likelihood estimates of the unknown parameters, it is easiest to work with the logarithm of the likelihood function:

$$(24.79) \qquad \log_e L = -\frac{n_T}{2}\log_e(2\pi) - \frac{1}{2}\log_e|\mathbf{\Sigma}| - \frac{1}{2}(\mathbf{Y} - \mathbf{X}\boldsymbol{\beta})'\mathbf{\Sigma}^{-1}(\mathbf{Y} - \mathbf{X}\boldsymbol{\beta})$$

The maximum likelihood estimates of $\mu_{..}$, α_1, σ^2, σ^2_β, and $\sigma^2_{\alpha\beta}$ for the Sheffield Foods Company example are those values of these parameters that maximize the log-likelihood function in (24.79), subject to the constraints that the variance components are nonnegative. For unbalanced studies, numerical search procedures are generally required to obtain the maximum likelihood estimates. We shall rely on standard statistical software programs to carry out the numerical search procedures.

Inference Procedures. Inference procedures are analogous to those explained in Chapter 14 for maximum likelihood estimation of the regression parameters in logistic regression. The estimated approximate variance-covariance matrix of the estimated parameters is obtained through the Hessian matrix in (14.67), which contains the second-order partial derivatives of the logarithm of the likelihood function with respect to the parameters. This estimated variance-covariance matrix is usually provided by a statistical package in conjunction with the numerical search for maximum likelihood estimates.

Large-sample inference procedures are described in Chapter 14. In the Sheffield Foods Company example, for instance, the following approximate result for estimating the fixed laboratory method effect α_1 is obtained from (14.69):

$$(24.80) \qquad \frac{\hat{\alpha}_1 - \alpha_1}{s\{\hat{\alpha}_1\}} \sim z$$

An approximate confidence interval for α_1 or a test concerning α_1 can then be developed readily. Simultaneous estimation of several parameters can be done as usual by means of the Bonferroni procedure. Tests whether several parameters equal zero (e.g., $\sigma^2_\beta = \sigma^2_{\alpha\beta} = 0$) are carried out by fitting the full and reduced models and obtaining the likelihood ratio test statistic (14.54). This test should not be used if any of the estimated variance components equals zero.

Often, there is interest in a linear combination of the parameters. For instance, the marginal mean $\mu_{1.}$ may be of interest in the Sheffield Foods Company example. Since $\mu_{1.} = \mu_{..} + \alpha_1$, the maximum likelihood estimator of this quantity is the following linear combination of the estimated parameters:

$$(24.81) \qquad \hat{\mu}_{1.} = \hat{\mu}_{..} + \hat{\alpha}_1 = (1 \quad 1 \quad 0 \quad 0 \quad 0) \begin{bmatrix} \hat{\mu}_{..} \\ \hat{\alpha}_1 \\ \hat{\sigma}^2 \\ \hat{\sigma}_\beta^2 \\ \hat{\sigma}_{\alpha\beta}^2 \end{bmatrix}$$

Denoting the row vector of coefficients by $\mathbf{c}'$, we use (5.46) to obtain the estimated variance of $\hat{\mu}_{1.}$:

$$(24.82) \qquad s^2\{\hat{\mu}_{1.}\} = \mathbf{c}'s^2\{\mathbf{b}\}\mathbf{c}$$

where $s^2\{\mathbf{b}\}$ is the estimated approximate variance-covariance matrix of the parameter estimates. Large-sample inferences are then conducted in the usual manner, utilizing the standard normal distribution.

We caution again that the inference procedures discussed here require large sample sizes. In studies with random factor levels, the number of factor levels frequently is not large. For instance, in the Sheffield Foods Company example only four laboratories were employed in the study. Use of a much larger number of laboratories would have been much too costly. An estimate of interlaboratory variability based on four randomly selected laboratories is likely not to be precise and use of a large-sample approximation for obtaining an interval estimate may not be appropriate.

Bootstrapping, as explained in Chapter 10, may be used to examine the appropriateness of large-sample inference procedures for maximum likelihood estimates in unbalanced studies. However, in some cases bootstrapping for variance components may not perform properly, which could be an indication that large-sample inference procedures are not appropriate.

Example. In the Sheffield Foods Company example, the investigators were primarily interested in determining whether the two different measurement methods yield systematic differences in the determination of fat content. The BMDP3V computer package was used, together with transformations (24.43) to go from the unrestricted to the restricted model, to obtain the maximum likelihood estimates of the parameters in the log-likelihood function (24.79) for the mixed ANOVA model. Table 24.13a contains the maximum likelihood estimates of the parameters and the estimated approximate standard deviations of these estimates. Table 24.13b contains the estimated approximate variance-covariance matrix of the maximum likelihood estimates obtained through the Hessian matrix in (14.67).

Since the sample sizes are not large here, bootstrapping was employed to examine whether the large-sample inference procedures for maximum likelihood estimates described in Chapter 14 are appropriate. Five hundred bootstrap samples were generated, the maximum likelihood estimates were obtained for each using SAS PROC MIXED, and a bootstrap distribution of the parameter estimates was created for each parameter. Table 24.14 contains the means and standard deviations of these bootstrap distributions, together with the maximum likelihood estimates and the approximate standard deviations repeated from Table 24.13a.

Before examining whether the two measurement methods differ in their fat content determinations, we need to consider whether measurement method-laboratory interactions

TABLE 24.13 Maximum Likelihood Estimates and Estimated Variance-Covariance Matrix—Sheffield Foods Company Example.

(a) Estimated Parameters and Standard Deviations

Parameter	Estimated Parameter	Estimated Standard Deviation
$\mu_{..}$	3.694	.158
α_1	.633	.107
σ^2	.023	.006
σ_β^2	.097	.071
$\sigma_{\alpha\beta}^2$	.086	.064

(b) Estimated Approximate Variance-Covariance Matrix

$$
\mathbf{s}^2\{\mathbf{b}\} = \begin{array}{c} \hat{\mu}_{..} \\ \hat{\alpha}_1 \\ \hat{\sigma}^2 \\ \hat{\sigma}_\beta^2 \\ \hat{\sigma}_{\alpha\beta}^2 \end{array}
\begin{bmatrix}
\overset{\hat{\mu}_{..}}{.0250} & \overset{\hat{\alpha}_1}{.0002} & \overset{\hat{\sigma}^2}{.0000} & \overset{\hat{\sigma}_\beta^2}{.0000} & \overset{\hat{\sigma}_{\alpha\beta}^2}{.0000} \\
.0002 & .0114 & .0000 & .0000 & .0000 \\
.0000 & .0000 & .0000 & .0000 & -.0000 \\
.0000 & .0000 & .0000 & .0050 & -.0001 \\
.0000 & .0000 & -.0000 & -.0001 & .0041
\end{bmatrix}
$$

TABLE 24.14 Means and Standard Deviations of Bootstrap Distributions and Maximum Likelihood Estimates—Sheffield Foods Company Example.

Parameter	Bootstrap Mean	Maximum Likelihood Estimate	Standard Deviation Bootstrap	Maximum Likelihood
$\mu_{..}$	3.69	3.69	.157	.158
α_1	.637	.633	.110	.107
σ_β^2	.092	.097	.128	.071
$\sigma_{\alpha\beta}^2$	.078	.086	.190	.064
σ^2	.023	.023	.006	.006

FIGURE 24.5   **Bootstrap Distribution for $\hat{\alpha}_1$—Sheffield Foods Company Example.**

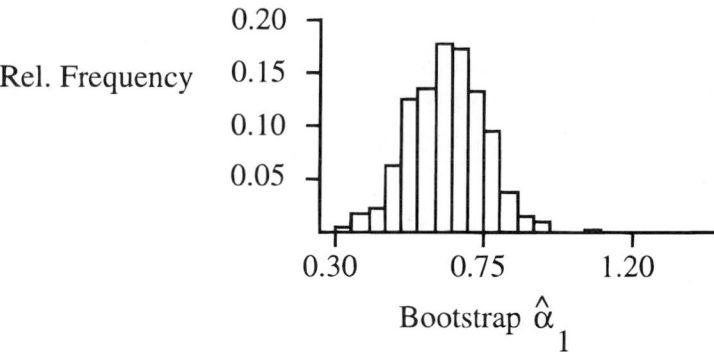

are present. The large-sample test statistic (14.69) for testing H_0: $\sigma^2_{\alpha\beta} = 0$ is, using the results in Table 24.13a, $z^* = .086/.064 = 1.34$. This small value of the test statistic supports H_0, that there are no interaction effects. However, the bootstrap distribution of $\hat{\sigma}^2_{\alpha\beta}$ is highly skewed, with a large concentration at zero. Furthermore, the bootstrap standard deviation according to Table 24.14, $s^*\{\hat{\sigma}^2_{\alpha\beta}\} = .190$, is much larger than the large-sample estimate. Thus, use of large-sample inference procedures may not be appropriate here. Nevertheless, the bootstrap results are consistent with the large-sample results, suggesting even more strongly that there are no interaction effects between measurement methods and laboratories.

We therefore examine next the measurement method main effects. The bootstrap distribution for $\hat{\alpha}_1$ is shown in Figure 24.5. It is approximately normal. Also, Table 24.14 shows that the bootstrap standard deviation for $\hat{\alpha}_1$ and the large-sample standard deviation are very similar. These findings support the use of large-sample inference procedures for α_1. Hence, we use the large-sample confidence interval in (14.70) to estimate $\alpha_1 - \alpha_2 = 2\alpha_1$. For a 95 percent confidence interval, we require:

$$z(.975) = 1.960 \qquad\qquad 2\hat{\alpha}_1 = 2(.633) = 1.266$$

$$2s\{\hat{\alpha}_1\} = 2(.107) = .214$$

The confidence limits therefore are $1.266 \pm 1.960(.214)$ and the approximate 95 percent confidence interval is:

$$.85 \le \alpha_1 - \alpha_2 \le 1.69$$

We conclude, with approximate confidence coefficient .95, that the mean government method fat determination is between .85 and 1.69 percent points higher than that for the Sheffield method. Since the true fat content in the samples was three percent, Figure 24.4 indicates that the government method is biased upward and that the Sheffield method is more accurate.

Cited References

24.1. Searle, S. R., G. Casella, and C. E. McCulloch. *Variance Components*. New York: John Wiley & Sons, 1992.

24.2. Burdick, R. K., and F. A. Graybill. *Confidence Intervals on Variance Components*. New York: Marcel Dekker, Inc., 1992.

24.3. Satterthwaite, F. E. "An Approximate Distribution of Estimates of Variance Components," *Biometrics Bulletin* 2 (1946), pp. 110–14.

24.4. Gaylor, D. W., and F. N. Hopper. "Estimating the Degrees of Freedom for Linear Combinations of Mean Squares by Satterthwaite's Formula," *Technometrics* 11 (1969), pp. 691–706.

24.5. Ting, N., R. K. Burdick, F. A. Graybill, S. Jeyaratnam, and T. F. C. Lu. "Confidence Intervals on Linear Combinations of Variance Components That Are Unrestricted in Sign," *Journal of Statistical Computation and Simulation* 35 (1990), pp. 135–43.

24.6. Schwarz, C. J. "The Mixed-Model ANOVA: The Truth, the Computer Packages, the Books. Part I: Balanced Data." *The American Statistician* 47 (1993), pp. 48–59.

24.7. Hocking, R. R. *The Analysis of Linear Models*. Monterey, Calif.: Brooks/Cole, 1985.

24.8. Burdick, R. K. "Using Confidence Intervals to Test Variance Components." *Journal of Quality Technology* 26 (1994), pp. 30–38.

24.9. Searle, S. R. *Linear Models for Unbalanced Data*. New York: John Wiley & Sons, 1987.

Problems

24.1. A student asks why ε_{ij} is shown as a separate term in random effects model (24.1) in view of μ_i being a random variable in this model. Respond.

24.2. Refer to Figure 24.1. Here, the situation portrayed is one where the variance σ^2 is larger than the variance σ_μ^2. Is this always the case? Explain.

24.3. In each of the following cases, indicate whether ANOVA model I or model II is more appropriate and state your reasons:

(1) In a study of absenteeism at a plant, the treatments are the three 8-hour shifts.

(2) In a study of employee productivity, the treatments are 10 production employees selected at random from all production employees in a large company.

(3) In a study of anticipated annual income at retirement, the treatments are the four types of retirement plans available to employees.

(4) In a study of tire wear in 18-wheel trucks, the treatments are four tire locations selected at random.

24.4. Refer to the Apex Enterprises personnel officers example on page 964. Explain with reference to this example over what the expectation in (24.2a) is taken. Over what is the variance in (24.2b) taken? Over what is the covariance in (24.2c) taken?

√ 24.5. Refer to **Filling machines** Problem 16.14. Suppose that the company uses a large number of filling machines and the six machines studied were selected randomly. Assume that ANOVA model (24.1) is applicable.

   a. Interpret the following with reference to this example:

   (1) $\mu.$, (2) σ_μ^2, (3) σ^2, (4) $\sigma^2\{Y_{ij}\}$.

   b. Test whether or not all machines in the population have the same mean fill; use $\alpha = .05$. State the alternatives, decision rule, and conclusion. What is the P-value of the test?

   c. Estimate the mean fill for all machines in the population with a 95 percent confidence interval.

√ 24.6. Refer to **Filling machines** Problems 16.14 and 24.5.

   a. Estimate the proportion of the total variability in carton fills that reflects the differences in mean fills between machines; use a 95 percent confidence interval.

   b. Estimate σ^2 with a 95 percent confidence interval. Interpret your interval estimate.

   c. Obtain a point estimate of σ_μ^2 .

   d. Obtain separate approximate 95 percent confidence intervals for σ_μ^2 using the Satterthwaite procedure and the *MLS* procedure. Are these intervals similar? Comment.

24.7. **Sodium content**. A researcher studied the sodium content in lager beer by selecting at random six brands from the large number of brands of U.S. and Canadian beers sold in a metropolitan area. The researcher then chose eight 12-ounce cans or bottles of each selected brand at random from retail outlets in the area and measured the sodium content (in milligrams) of each can or bottle. The observations follow.

				j				
i	1	2	3	4	5	6	7	8
1	24.4	22.6	23.8	22.0	24.5	22.3	25.0	24.5
2	10.2	12.1	10.3	10.2	9.9	11.2	12.0	9.5
...	...	...	...	...	...	...	...	...
6	21.3	20.2	20.7	20.8	20.1	18.8	21.1	20.3

Assume that ANOVA model (24.1) is applicable.

   a. Test whether or not the mean sodium content is the same in all brands sold in the metropolitan area; use $\alpha = .01$. State the alternatives, decision rule, and conclusion. What is the P-value of the test?

   b. Estimate the mean sodium content for all brands; use a 99 percent confidence interval.

24.8. Refer to **Sodium content** Problem 24.7.

   a. Estimate $\sigma_\mu^2/(\sigma_\mu^2 + \sigma^2)$ with a 99 percent confidence interval. Interpret your interval estimate.

   b. Obtain point estimates of σ^2 and σ_μ^2.

   c. Estimate σ^2 with a 99 percent confidence interval.

   d. It has been conjectured that the variance of sodium content between brands is more than twice as great as that within brands. Conduct an appropriate test using $\alpha = .01$. State the alternatives, decision rule, and conclusion.

   e. Obtain an approximate 99 percent confidence interval for σ_μ^2 using the *MLS* procedure. Interpret your confidence interval.

24.9. **Coil winding machines**. A plant contains a large number of coil winding machines. A production analyst studied a certain characteristic of the wound coils produced by these machines by selecting four machines at random and then choosing 10 coils at random from the day's output of each selected machine. The results follow.

						j				
i	1	2	3	4	5	6	7	8	9	10
1	205	204	207	202	208	206	209	205	207	206
2	201	204	198	203	209	207	199	206	205	204
3	198	204	196	201	199	203	202	198	202	197
4	210	209	214	215	211	208	210	209	211	210

Assume that ANOVA model (24.1) is appropriate.

a. Test whether or not the mean coil characteristic is the same for all machines in the plant; use $\alpha = .10$. State the alternatives, decision rule, and conclusion. What is the P-value of the test?

b. Estimate the mean coil characteristic for all coil winding machines in the plant; use a 90 percent confidence interval.

24.10. Refer to **Coil winding machines** Problem 24.9.

a. Estimate $\sigma_\mu^2/(\sigma_\mu^2 + \sigma^2)$ with a 90 percent confidence interval. Interpret your interval estimate.

b. Test whether or not σ_μ^2 and σ^2 are equal; use $\alpha = .10$. State the alternatives, decision rule, and conclusion.

c. Estimate σ^2 with a 90 percent confidence interval. Interpret your interval estimate.

d. Obtain a point estimate of σ_μ^2.

e. Obtain separate approximate 90 percent confidence intervals for σ_μ^2 using the Satterthwaite procedure and the *MLS* procedure. Are these intervals similar? Comment.

24.11. For mixed effects model (24.42), why is $\sum_i (\alpha\beta)_{ij} = 0$ while usually $\sum_j (\alpha\beta)_{ij} \neq 0$?

24.12. A marketing consultant is designing several experiments involving a newly developed low-cost food processor. The initial experiment has the objectives (1) to compare the effects on unit sales of three possible prices recommended by the sales department ($23.99, $25.49, $25.95) and (2) to determine whether the color scheme used for the appliance affects unit sales. A great many color schemes are feasible; three (white, green, pink) have been selected for the initial experiment to represent the range of possible colors. If the experiment suggests that color scheme does have an effect, this aspect of the product design will be investigated in detail in a follow-up study. Which ANOVA model would you employ for analyzing the initial experiment? Discuss.

24.13. In a two-factor ANOVA study with $a = 3$, $b = 2$, and $n = 5$, the two factor effects are both random with $\sigma^2 = 5.0$, $\sigma_\alpha^2 = 8.0$, $\sigma_\beta^2 = 10.0$, and $\sigma_{\alpha\beta}^2 = 6.0$. Assume that ANOVA model (24.39) is applicable.

a. Obtain $E\{MSA\}$, $E\{MSB\}$, and $E\{MSAB\}$.

b. What would be the expected mean squares if $\sigma_{\alpha\beta}^2 = 0$, all other parameters remaining the same?

24.14. A survey statistician has commented: "I am rather suspicious of uses of random effects and mixed effects ANOVA models. Seldom are the factor levels chosen by a random mechanism from a known population." Discuss.

24.15. **Miles per gallon**. An automobile manufacturer wished to study the effects of differences between drivers (factor A) and differences between cars (factor B) on gasoline consumption. Four drivers were selected at random; also five cars of the same model with manual transmission were randomly selected from the assembly line. Each driver drove each car twice over a 40-mile test course and the miles per gallon were recorded. The data follow.

Factor A	Factor B (car)				
(driver)	$j = 1$	$j = 2$	$j = 3$	$j = 4$	$j = 5$
$i = 1$	25.3	28.9	24.8	28.4	27.1
	25.2	30.0	25.1	27.9	26.6
$i = 2$	33.6	36.7	31.7	35.6	33.7
	32.9	36.5	31.9	35.0	33.9
$i = 3$	27.7	30.7	26.9	29.7	29.2
	28.5	30.4	26.3	30.2	28.9
$i = 4$	29.2	32.4	27.7	31.8	30.3
	29.3	32.4	28.9	30.7	29.9

Assume that random ANOVA model (24.39) is applicable.

a. Test whether or not the two factors interact; use $\alpha = .05$. State the alternatives, decision rule, and conclusion. What is the P value of the test?

b. Test separately whether or not factor A and factor B main effects are present. For each test, use $\alpha = .05$ and state the alternatives, decision rule, and conclusion. What is the P-value for each test?

c. Obtain point estimates of σ_α^2 and σ_β^2. Which factor appears to have the greater effect on gasoline consumption?

d. Use the *MLS* procedure to obtain an approximate 95 percent confidence interval for σ_α^2. Interpret your interval estimate.

e. Use the Satterthwaite procedure to obtain an approximate 95 percent confidence interval for σ_β^2. Is your interval estimate reasonably precise? Comment.

√ 24.16. Refer to **Disk drive service** Problem 19.16. Suppose that the service center employs a large number of technicians and that the three included in the study were selected at random. Assume that the conditions of mixed ANOVA model (24.42) are applicable, except that here factor A effects are random and factor B effects are fixed. Under current conditions, all technicians service each of the three makes with approximately equal frequency.

a. Test whether or not the two factors interact; use $\alpha = .01$. State the alternatives, decision rule, and conclusion. What is the P-value of the test?

b. Obtain a point estimate of $\sigma_{\alpha\beta}^2$. Does $\sigma_{\alpha\beta}^2$ appear to be large relative to σ^2? Explain.

c. Test whether or not factor A main effects are present; use $\alpha = .01$. State the alternatives, decision rule, and conclusion. Why is it meaningful here to test for factor A main effects?

d. Test whether or not factor B main effects are present; use $\alpha = .01$. State the alternatives, decision rule, and conclusion. Why is it meaningful here to test for factor B main effects?

e. It is desired to obtain all pairwise comparisons between the means for the three disk drive makes. Use the Tukey procedure and a 95 percent family confidence coefficient to make these comparisons. State your findings.

f. Use the Satterthwaite procedure to obtain an approximate 99 percent confidence interval for $\mu_{.1}$. Interpret your interval estimate.

g. Obtain an approximate 99 percent confidence interval for σ_α^2 using the *MLS* procedure. Does the variability between technicians appear to be large? Explain.

24.17. **Imitation pearls**. Preliminary research on the production of imitation pearls entailed studying the effect of the number of coats of a special lacquer (factor A) applied to an opalescent plastic bead used as the base of the pearl on the market value of the pearl. Four batches of 12 beads (factor B) were used in the study, and it is desired to also consider their effect on the market value. The three levels of factor A (6, 8, and 10 coats) were fixed in advance, while the four batches can be regarded as a random sample of batches from the bead production process. The market value of each pearl was determined by a panel of experts. The market value data (coded) follow.

Factor A (number of coats)		Factor B (batch)			
		$j = 1$	$j = 2$	$j = 3$	$j = 4$
$i = 1$	6	72.0	72.1	75.2	70.4
		...	...	...	...
		72.8	73.3	77.8	72.4
$i = 2$	8	76.9	80.3	80.2	74.3
		...	...	...	...
		74.2	77.2	79.9	72.9
$i = 3$	10	76.3	80.9	79.2	71.6
		...	...	...	...
		75.0	80.2	81.2	74.4

Assume that mixed ANOVA model (24.42) is applicable.

a. Test for interaction effects; use $\alpha = .05$. State the alternatives, decision rule, and conclusion. What is the P-value of the test?

b. Test for factor A and factor B main effects. For each test, use $\alpha = .05$ and state the alternatives, decision rule, and conclusion. What is the P-value for each test?

c. Estimate $D_1 = \mu_{2.} - \mu_{1.}$ and $D_2 = \mu_{3.} - \mu_{2.}$ by means of the Bonferroni procedure with a 90 percent family confidence coefficient. State your findings.

d. Use the Satterthwaite procedure to obtain an approximate 95 percent confidence interval for $\mu_{2.}$. Interpret your confidence interval.

e. Use the *MLS* procedure to obtain an approximate 90 percent confidence interval for σ_β^2. Does σ_β^2 appear to be large compared to σ^2?

24.18. Refer to **Coin-operated terminals** Problem 21.2. Suppose that the weeks (factor B) had been selected intentionally but the locations (factor A) had been selected at random from a large number of possible locations. Assume that the conditions of mixed ANOVA model

(24.42) are appropriate, except that here factor A effects are random and factor B effects are fixed.

   a. Test for factor B main effects; use $\alpha = .05$. State the alternatives, decision rule, and conclusion. What is the P-value of the test?

   b. Why can you not test for factor A main effects here?

√ 24.19. Refer to Table 24.10. All three factors in this study have random effects.

   a. Test whether or not AB interactions are present. Use significance level $\alpha = .01$. State the alternatives, decision rule, and conclusion.

   b. Test whether machines (factor B) have main effects. Use significance level $\alpha = .01$. State the alternatives, decision rule, and conclusion.

   c. Use the Satterthwaite procedure to obtain an approximate 95 percent confidence interval for σ_α^2. Interpret your interval estimate.

24.20. Refer to **Electronics assembly** Problem 23.12. Suppose that the number of feasible sequences in which the components can be attached to the board is very large and that the three sequences studied were selected randomly from the set of operationally feasible sequences. Assume that a normal error ANOVA model is applicable where factors A and C have fixed effects and factor B has random effects. Some relevant expected mean squares for this model are:

$$E\{MSA\} = \sigma^2 + bcn\frac{\Sigma\alpha_i^2}{a-1} + cn\sigma_{\alpha\beta}^2 \qquad E\{MSABC\} = \sigma^2 + n\sigma_{\alpha\beta\gamma}^2$$

$$E\{MSB\} = \sigma^2 + acn\sigma_\beta^2 \qquad\qquad E\{MSE\} = \sigma^2$$

$$E\{MSAC\} = \sigma^2 + bn\frac{\Sigma\Sigma(\alpha\gamma)_{ik}^2}{(a-1)(c-1)} + n\sigma_{\alpha\beta\gamma}^2$$

   a. What is the appropriate test statistic for testing for AC interactions? For testing for factor B main effects?

   b. Test whether or not AC interactions are present; use $\alpha = .05$. State the alternatives, decision rule, and conclusion.

   c. Test whether or not factor B main effects are present; use $\alpha = .05$. State the alternatives, decision rule, and conclusion.

   d. Estimate σ_β^2 using the *MLS* procedure with a 95 percent confidence coefficient. Interpret your interval estimate.

24.21. Consider mixed ANOVA model (24.69) where factor A has fixed effects and the other two factors have random effects. Find the Satterthwaite test statistic F^{**} for testing for factor A main effects. What is the approximate number of degrees of freedom associated with the denominator of this test statistic?

√ 24.22. Refer to **Disk drive service** Problems 19.16 and 24.16. Suppose that observations $Y_{114} = 57$, $Y_{221} = 61$, and $Y_{224} = 66$ are missing because the time recording instrument malfunctioned. Assume that the conditions of mixed ANOVA model (24.42) are applicable (except that here factor A effects are random, factor B effects are fixed, and unequal sample sizes exist) and that the observations Y_{ijk} are jointly normally distributed. Use the maximum likelihood approach to answer the following.

   a. Obtain maximum likelihood estimates of all unknown parameters. Are any of the estimated variances of the random effects equal to zero? If so, what would this imply about the applicability of the likelihood ratio statistic (14.54)?

b. Revise the model by dropping the main factor A effect and obtain maximum likelihood estimates of the unknown parameters in the revised model. Do these estimates differ from the ones obtained in part (a)?

c. Use the z^* test statistic to test whether or not the two factors interact; use $\alpha = .01$. State the alternatives, decision rule, and conclusion. What is the P-value of the test?

d. Use the likelihood ratio test statistic (14.54) to test whether or not factor B main effects are present; control the risk of Type I error at $\alpha = .01$. State the alternatives, decision rule, and conclusion.

e. Obtain an approximate 99 percent confidence interval for $\sigma_{\alpha\beta}^2$. Interpret your confidence interval.

24.23. Refer to **Imitation pearls** Problem 24.17. Suppose that observations $Y_{113} = 67.4$ and $Y_{322} = 73.7$ are missing because of flaws in the beads. Assume that the conditions of mixed ANOVA model (24.42) are applicable (except that unequal sample sizes are present here) and that the observations Y_{ijk} are jointly normally distributed. Use the maximum likelihood approach to answer the following.

a. Obtain maximum likelihood estimates of all unknown parameters. Are any of the estimated variances of the random effects equal to zero? If so, what would this imply about the applicability of the likelihood ratio statistic (14.54)?

b. Revise the model by dropping the interaction term and obtain maximum likelihood estimates of the unknown parameters in the revised model. Do these estimates differ from the ones obtained in part (a)?

c. Use the likelihood ratio test statistic (14.54) to test for factor B main effects; use $\alpha = .05$. State the alternatives, decision rule, and conclusion. What is the P-value of the test?

d. Use the likelihood ratio test statistic (14.54) to test whether factor A main effects are present; control the risk of Type I error at $\alpha = .05$. State the alternatives, decision rule, and conclusion. What is the P-value of the test?

e. Obtain an approximate 95 percent confidence interval for σ_β^2. Interpret your interval estimate.

Exercises

24.24. Show that n' defined in (24.10a) equals n when $n_i \equiv n$.

24.25. What are the values r and n that minimize $\sigma^2\{\bar{Y}_{..}\}$ in (24.12) for a given total sample size n_T?

24.26. Derive the confidence limits in (24.19) from those in (24.18).

24.27. For random ANOVA model (24.39), derive $\sigma^2\{\bar{Y}_{i..}\}$.

24.28. For random ANOVA model (24.67), find the variance of the estimated mean $\bar{Y}_{i...}$.

Projects

24.29. Consider a two-factor study with $a = 3$, $b = 2$, and $n = 5$. Random ANOVA model (24.39) is applicable with $\mu_{..} = 92$, $\sigma_\alpha^2 = 24$, $\sigma_\beta^2 = 11$, $\sigma_{\alpha\beta}^2 = .1$, and $\sigma^2 = 8$.

   a. Using a normal random number generator, obtain a value for each of the main effects α_i $(i = 1, 2, 3)$ and β_j $(j = 1, 2)$ and for each interaction effect $(\alpha\beta)_{ij}$.

   b. Generate five error terms for each treatment.

   c. Combine the parameter values obtained in part (a), the error terms obtained in part (b), and $\mu_{..} = 92$ to yield five observations Y_{ijk} for each treatment.

   d. Based on the observations obtained in part (c), calculate the F^* test statistic for testing whether or not factor A main effects are present. What is your conclusion using $\alpha = .05$?

   e. Repeat the steps in parts (a)–(d) 100 times. Calculate the mean of the 100 numerator mean squares and the mean of the 100 denominator mean squares. Are these means close to theoretical expectations?

   f. In what proportion of the 100 trials did the test lead to the conclusion of the presence of factor A main effects? Does the test have good power for the case considered here?

24.30. Refer to **Miles per gallon** Problem 24.15. Suppose that observation $Y_{232} = 31.9$ is missing because the record was lost for this experimental trial. Assume that random ANOVA model (24.39) is applicable (except that the sample sizes are unequal here) and that the oberservations Y_{ijk} are jointly normally distributed.

   a. Use the method of maximum likelihood to estimate $\mu_{..}$ and the variance components σ_α^2, σ_β^2, $\sigma_{\alpha\beta}^2$, and σ^2. Which variance component appears to be largest? Also obtain the estimated standard deviation for each of the estimated variance components.

   b. Obtain a bootstrap sample by using a normal random number generator to provide normal values with means zero and variances equal to the estimates of the variance components in part (a) for (1) the α_i $(i = 1, \ldots, 4)$, (2) the β_j $(j = 1, \ldots, 5)$, (3) the $(\alpha\beta)_{ij}$, and (4) the n_{ij} error terms ε_{ijk} for each treatment. Combine these with $\hat{\mu}_{..}$ obtained in part (a) to create the n_{ij} bootstrap outcomes Y_{ijk} for each treatment.

   c. Use the method of maximum likelihood to estimate σ_α^2, σ_β^2, and $\sigma_{\alpha\beta}^2$ for the bootstrap sample obtained in part (b).

   d. Repeat parts (b) and (c) 250 times.

   e. Obtain histograms of the bootstrap distributions for the 250 bootstrap estimates of σ_α^2, σ_β^2, and $\sigma_{\alpha\beta}^2$. Also obtain the mean and standard deviation for each of the bootstrap distributions. Based on these results and the results in part (a), does it appear that large-sample inference procedures are appropriate here? Explain.

CHAPTER
25

Analysis of Covariance

Analysis of covariance (ANCOVA) is a technique that combines features of analysis of variance and regression. It can be used for either observational studies or designed experiments. The basic idea is to augment the analysis of variance model containing the factor effects with one or more additional quantitative variables that are related to the response variable. This augmentation is intended to reduce the variance of the error terms in the model, i.e., to make the analysis more precise. We considered covariance models briefly in Chapter 11, and noted there that they are linear models containing both qualitative and quantitative predictor variables. Thus, covariance models are just a special type of regression model.

In this chapter, we shall first consider how a covariance model can be more effective than an ordinary ANOVA model. Then we shall discuss how to use a single-factor covariance model for making inferences. We conclude by taking up analysis of covariance models for multifactor studies and some additional considerations for the use of covariance analysis.

25.1 Basic Ideas

How Covariance Analysis Reduces Error Variability

Covariance analysis may be helpful in reducing large error term variances that sometimes are present in analysis of variance models. Consider a study in which the effects of three different films promoting travel in a state are studied. A subject receives an initial questionnaire to elicit information about the subject's attitudes toward the state. The subject is then shown one of the three five-minute films, and immediately afterwards is questioned about the film, about desire to travel in the state, and so on.

In this type of situation, covariance analysis can be utilized. To see why it might be highly effective, consider Figure 25.1a. Here are plotted the desire-to-travel scores, obtained after each of the three promotional films was shown to a different group of five subjects. Three different symbols are used to distinguish the different treatments. It is evident from Figure 25.1a that the error terms, as shown by the scatter around the treatment means μ_i, are fairly large, indicating a large error term variance.

Suppose now that we were to utilize also the subjects' initial attitude scores. We plot in Figure 25.1b the desire-to-travel score (obtained after exposure to the film) against the initial

FIGURE 25.1   Illustration of Error Variability Reduction by Covariance Analysis.

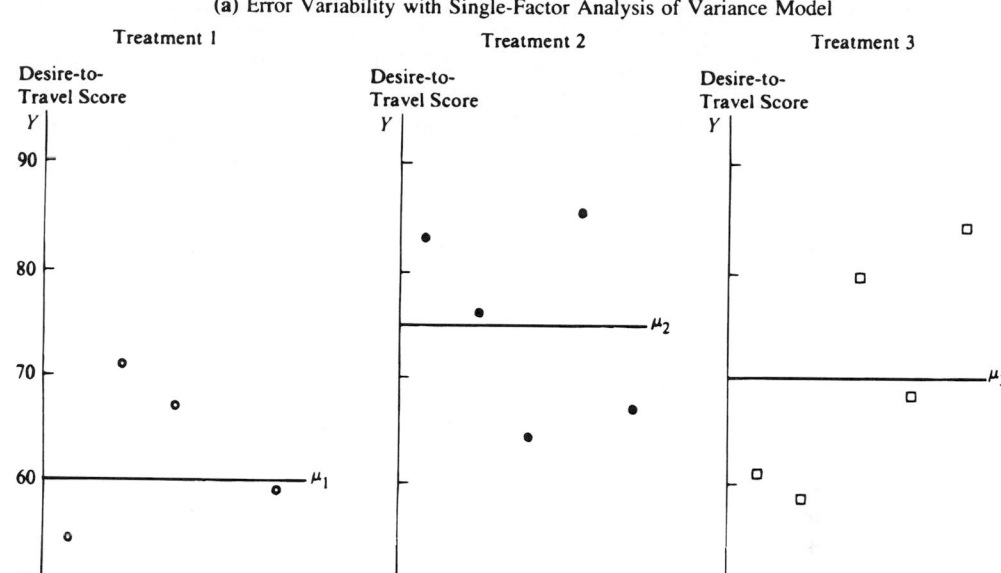

(a) Error Variability with Single-Factor Analysis of Variance Model

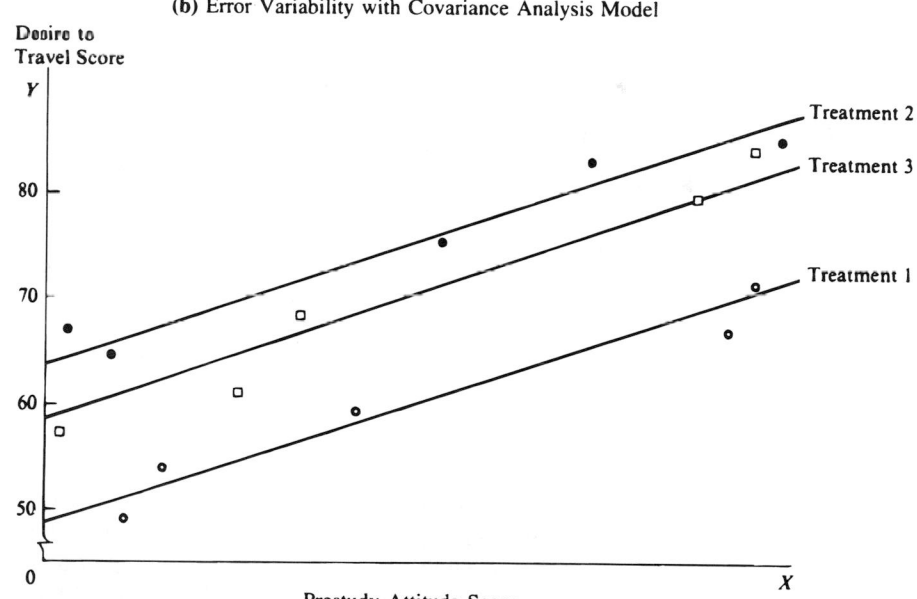

(b) Error Variability with Covariance Analysis Model

attitude score for each of the 15 subjects. Note that the three treatment regression relations happen to be linear (this need not be so). Also note that the scatter around the treatment regression lines is much less than the scatter in Figure 25.1a around the treatment means μ_i, as a result of the desire-to-travel scores being highly linearly related to the initial attitude scores. The relatively large scatter in Figure 25.1a reflects the large error term variability that would be encountered with an analysis of variance model for this single-factor study. The smaller scatter in Figure 25.1b reflects the smaller error term variability that would be involved in an analysis of covariance model.

Covariance analysis, it is thus seen, utilizes the relationship between the response variable (desire-to-travel score, in our example) and one or more quantitative variables for which observations are available (prestudy attitude score, in our example) in order to reduce the error term variability and make the study a more powerful one for comparing treatment effects.

Concomitant Variables

In covariance analysis terminology, each quantitative variable added to the ANOVA model is called a *concomitant variable*. We already encountered concomitant variables in Chapter 8, though not by that name. We mentioned in Chapter 8 that *supplemental* or *uncontrolled* variables are sometimes used in regression models for controlled experiments to reduce the variance of the experimental error terms. We also noted in that chapter that *control* variables may be added to the regression model in confirmatory observational studies to reflect the effects of previously identified explanatory variables as the effects of the new, primary explanatory variables on the response variable are being tested. Both the supplemental or uncontrolled variables in a controlled experiment and the control variables in a confirmatory observational study are concomitant variables that are added to the model primarily to reduce the variance of the error terms. Concomitant variables are sometimes also called *covariates*.

Choice of Concomitant Variables.   The choice of concomitant variables is an important one. If such variables have no relation to the response variable, nothing is to be gained by covariance analysis, and one might as well use a simpler analysis of variance model. Concomitant variables frequently used with human subjects include prestudy attitudes, age, socioeconomic status, and aptitude. When retail stores are used as study units, concomitant variables might be last period's sales or number of employees.

Concomitant Variables Unaffected by Treatments.   For a clear interpretation of the results, a concomitant variable should be observed before the study; or if observed during the study, it should not be influenced by the treatments in any way. A prestudy attitude score meets this requirement. Also, if a subject's age is ascertained during the study, it would be reasonable in many instances to expect that the information about age provided by the subject will not be affected by the treatment. The reason for this requirement can readily be seen from the following example. A company was conducting a training school for engineers to teach them accounting and budgeting principles. Two teaching methods were used, and engineers were assigned at random to one of the two. At the end of the program, a score was obtained for each engineer reflecting the amount of learning. The analyst decided to use as a concomitant variable in covariance analysis the amount of time devoted to study (which the engineers were required to record). After conducting the analysis of covariance, the analyst found that training method had virtually no effect. The analyst was baffled by this finding until it was pointed out that the amount of study time probably was also affected by the treatments, and analysis indeed confirmed this. One of the training methods involved

FIGURE 25.2   **Illustration of Treatments Affecting the Concomitant Variable—Engineer Training Example.**

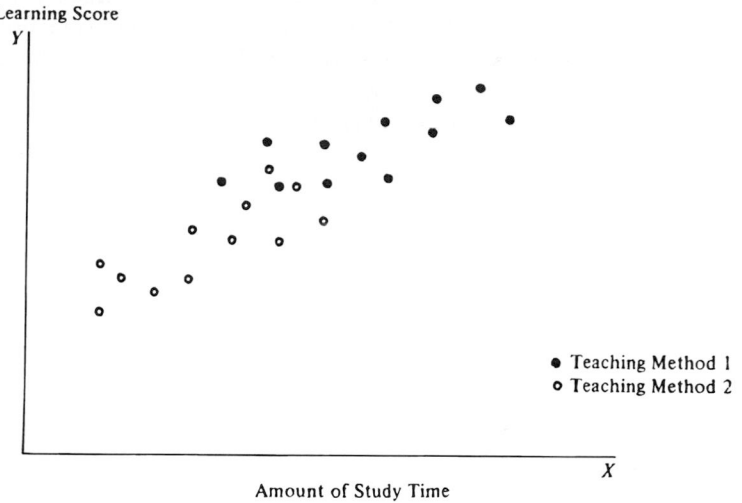

computer-assisted learning which appealed to the engineers so that they spent more time studying and also learned more. In other words, both the learning score and the amount of study time were influenced by the treatment in this case. As a result of the high correlation between the amount of study time and the learning score, the marginal treatment effect of the teaching methods on amount of learning was small and the test for treatment effects showed no significant difference between the two teaching methods.

Whenever a concomitant variable is affected by the treatments, covariance analysis will fail to show some (or much) of the effects that the treatments had on the response variable, so that an uncritical analysis may be badly misleading.

A symbolic scatter plot can provide evidence as to whether the concomitant variable is affected by the treatments. Figure 25.2 shows a scatter plot of learning score and amount of study time for the engineer training example. Treatment 1 is the one using computer-assisted learning. Note that most persons with this treatment devoted large amounts of time to study. On the other hand, persons receiving treatment 2 tended to devote smaller amounts of time to study. As a result, the observations for the two treatments tend to be concentrated over different intervals on the X scale.

Contrast this situation with the one seen in Figure 25.1b for the study on promotional films. Figure 25.1b illustrates how the concomitant variable observations should be scattered in a randomized experiment if the treatments have no effect on the concomitant variable. Here, the distribution of subjects along the X scale by prestudy attitude scores is roughly similar for all treatments, subject only to chance variation.

Note

Covariance analysis is concerned with quantitative concomitant variables. When qualitative concomitant variables need to be added (e.g., gender, geographic region), the model remains an analysis of variance model where some of the factors are of primary interest and the others represent concomitant variables that are included for the purpose of error variance reduction. ∎

25.2 Single-Factor Covariance Model

The covariance models to be presented in this chapter are applicable to observational studies and to experimental studies based on a completely randomized design. In the earlier engineer training example, the 24 engineers participating in the study were randomly assigned to the two teaching methods, with 12 engineers assigned to each teaching method. Thus, this experimental study was based on a completely randomized design.

The covariance models to be taken up in this chapter are also applicable to observational studies, such as an investigation of the salary increases of a company's employees in the accounting department by gender, where age is utilized as a concomitant variable.

Notation

We shall employ the notation for single-factor analysis of variance. The number of cases for the ith factor level is denoted by n_i, the total number of cases by $n_T = \Sigma n_i$, and the jth observation on the response variable for the ith factor level is denoted by Y_{ij}. We shall initially consider a single-factor covariance model with only one concomitant variable. Later we shall take up models with more than one concomitant variable. We shall denote the value of the concomitant variable associated with the jth case for the ith factor level by X_{ij}.

Development of Covariance Model

The single-factor ANOVA model in terms of fixed factor effects was given in (16.62):

$$(25.1) \qquad Y_{ij} = \mu. + \tau_i + \varepsilon_{ij}$$

The covariance model starts with this ANOVA model and adds another term (or several), reflecting the relationship between the response variable and the concomitant variable. Usually, a linear relation is utilized as a first approximation:

$$(25.2) \qquad Y_{ij} = \mu. + \tau_i + \gamma X_{ij} + \varepsilon_{ij}$$

Here γ is a regression coefficient for the relation between Y and X. The constant $\mu.$ now is no longer an overall mean. We can, however, make this constant an overall mean, and incidentally simplify some computations, if we center the concomitant variable around the overall mean $\overline{X}_{..}$. The resulting model is the usual covariance model for a single-factor study with fixed factor levels:

$$(25.3) \qquad Y_{ij} = \mu. + \tau_i + \gamma(X_{ij} - \overline{X}_{..}) + \varepsilon_{ij}$$

where:

> $\mu.$ is an overall mean
> τ_i are the fixed treatment effects subject to the restriction $\Sigma \tau_i = 0$
> γ is a regression coefficient for the relation between Y and X
> X_{ij} are constants
> ε_{ij} are independent $N(0, \sigma^2)$
> $i = 1, \ldots, r; \; j = 1, \ldots, n_i$

Covariance model (25.3) corresponds to ANOVA model (25.1) except for the term $\gamma(X_{ij} - \bar{X}..)$, which is added to reflect the relationship between Y and X. Note that the concomitant observations X_{ij} are assumed to be constants. Since ε_{ij} is the only random variable on the right side of (25.3), it follows at once that:

(25.4a)
$$E\{Y_{ij}\} = \mu. + \tau_i + \gamma(X_{ij} - \bar{X}..)$$

(25.4b)
$$\sigma^2\{Y_{ij}\} = \sigma^2$$

In view of the independence of the ε_{ij}, the Y_{ij} are also independent. Hence, an alternative statement of covariance model (25.3) is:

(25.5)
$$Y_{ij} \text{ are independent } N(\mu_{ij}, \sigma^2)$$

where:

$$\mu_{ij} = \mu. + \tau_i + \gamma(X_{ij} - \bar{X}..)$$

$$\sum \tau_i = 0$$

Properties of Covariance Model

Some of the properties of covariance model (25.3) are identical to those of ANOVA model (25.1). For instance, the error terms ε_{ij} are independent and have constant variance. There are also some new properties, and we discuss these now.

Comparisons of Treatment Effects.   With the analysis of variance model, all observations for the ith treatment have the same mean response; i.e., $E\{Y_{ij}\} = \mu_i$ for all j. This is not so with the covariance model, since the mean response $E\{Y_{ij}\}$ here depends not only on the treatment but also on the value of the concomitant variable X_{ij} for the study unit. Thus, the expected response for the ith treatment with covariance model (25.3) is given by a regression line:

(25.6)
$$\mu_{ij} = \mu. + \tau_i + \gamma(X_{ij} - \bar{X}..)$$

This regression line indicates, for any value of X, the mean response with treatment i. Figure 25.3 illustrates for a study with three treatments how these treatment regression lines might appear. Note that $\mu. + \tau_i$ is the ordinate of the line for the ith treatment when $X - \bar{X}.. = 0$, that is, when $X = \bar{X}..$, and that γ is the slope of each line. Since all treatment regression lines have the same slope, they are parallel.

While we no longer can speak of *the* mean response with the ith treatment since it varies with X, we can still measure the effect of any treatment compared with any other by a single number. In Figure 25.3, for instance, treatment 1 leads to a higher mean response than treatment 2 by an amount that is the same no matter what is the value of X. The difference between the two mean responses is the same for all values of X because the slopes of the regression lines are equal. Hence, we can measure the difference at any convenient X, say, at $X = \bar{X}..$:

(25.7)
$$\mu. + \tau_1 - (\mu. + \tau_2) = \tau_1 - \tau_2$$

FIGURE 25.3 **Example of Treatment Regression Lines with Covariance Model (25.3).**

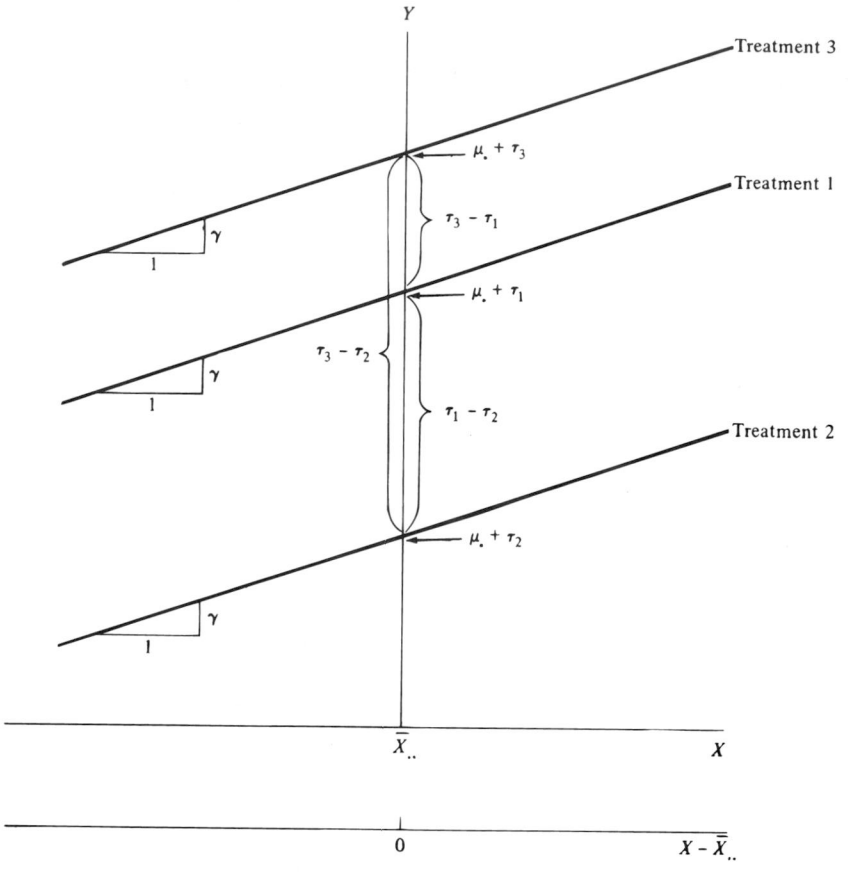

Thus, $\tau_1 - \tau_2$ measures how much higher the mean response is with treatment 1 than with treatment 2 for any value of X. We can compare any other two treatments similarly. It follows directly from this discussion that when all treatments have the same mean responses for any X (i.e., the treatments have no differential effects), the treatment regression lines must be identical; and hence, $\tau_1 - \tau_2 = 0$, $\tau_1 - \tau_3 = 0$, etc. Indeed, all τ_i equal zero in that case.

Constancy of Slopes. The assumption in covariance model (25.3) that all treatment regression lines have the same slope is a crucial one. Without it, the difference between the effects of two treatments cannot be summarized by a single number based on the main effects, such as $\tau_2 - \tau_1$. Figure 25.4 illustrates the case of nonparallel slopes for two treatments. Here, treatment 1 leads to higher mean responses than treatment 2 for smaller values of X, and the reverse holds for larger values of X. When the treatments interact with the concomitant variable X, resulting in nonparallel slopes, covariance analysis is not appropriate. Instead, separate treatment regression lines need to be estimated and then compared.

FIGURE 25.4   **Example of Nonparallel Treatment Regression Lines.**

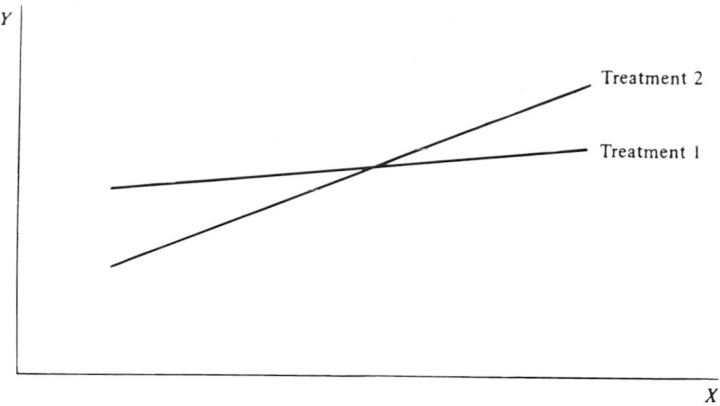

Generalizations of Covariance Model

Covariance model (25.3) for single-factor studies can be generalized in several respects. We mention briefly three ways in which this model can be generalized.

Nonconstant Xs.   Covariance model (25.3) assumes that the observations X_{ij} on the concomitant variable are constants. At times, it might be more reasonable to consider the concomitant observations as random variables. In that case, if covariance model (25.3) can be interpreted as a conditional one, applying for any X values that might be observed, the covariance analysis to be presented is still appropriate.

Nonlinearity of Relation.   The linear relation between Y and X assumed in covariance model (25.3) is not essential to covariance analysis. Any other relation could be used. For instance, the model for a quadratic relation is as follows:

$$(25.8) \qquad Y_{ij} = \mu_. + \tau_i + \gamma_1(X_{ij} - \overline{X}_{..}) + \gamma_2(X_{ij} - \overline{X}_{..})^2 + \varepsilon_{ij}$$

Linearity of the relation leads to simpler analysis and is often a sufficiently good approximation to provide meaningful results. If a linear relation is not a good approximation, however, a more adequate description of the relation should be utilized in the covariance model. Covariance analysis does require, however, that the treatment response functions be parallel; in other words, there must not be any interaction effects between the treatment and concomitant variables.

Several Concomitant Variables.   Covariance model (25.3) uses a single concomitant variable. This is often sufficient to reduce the error variability substantially. However, the model can be extended in a straightforward fashion to include two or more concomitant variables. The single-factor covariance model for two concomitant variables, X_1 and X_2, to the first order is as follows:

$$(25.9) \qquad Y_{ij} = \mu_. + \tau_i + \gamma_1(X_{ij1} - \overline{X}_{..1}) + \gamma_2(X_{ij2} - \overline{X}_{..2}) + \varepsilon_{ij}$$

Regression Formulation of Covariance Model

An easy way to estimate the parameters of covariance model (25.3) and make inferences is through the regression approach. Computational formulas for manual calculation were developed before the advent of computers, making use of the special structure of the $\mathbf{X}$ matrix for covariance models. Today, however, covariance calculations can be carried out readily by means of standard regression packages.

As for the regression formulation of analysis of variance models, we shall employ $r - 1$ indicator variables taking on the values 1, -1, or 0 to represent the r treatments in a covariance analysis model:

$$
I_1 = \begin{array}{cl} 1 & \text{if case from treatment 1} \\ -1 & \text{if case from treatment } r \\ 0 & \text{otherwise} \end{array}
$$

(25.10)

$$
\vdots
$$

$$
I_{r-1} = \begin{array}{cl} 1 & \text{if case from treatment } r - 1 \\ -1 & \text{if case from treatment } r \\ 0 & \text{otherwise} \end{array}
$$

Note that we now denote the indicator variables by the symbol I to clearly distinguish the treatment effects from the concomitant variable X.

In expressing covariance model (25.3) in regression form, we shall, as in the regression chapters, denote the centered observations $X_{ij} - \bar{X}_{..}$ by x_{ij}. Covariance model (25.3) can then be expressed as follows:

(25.11) $$Y_{ij} = \mu_. + \tau_1 I_{ij1} + \cdots + \tau_{r-1} I_{ij,r-1} + \gamma x_{ij} + \varepsilon_{ij}$$

where:

$$x_{ij} = X_{ij} - \bar{X}_{..}$$

Here, I_{ij1} is the value of indicator variable I_1 for the jth case from treatment i, and similarly for the other indicator variables. Note that the treatment effects $\tau_1, \ldots, \tau_{r-1}$ are the regression coefficients for the indicator variables.

Now that we have formulated covariance model (25.3) as a regression model, our discussion of regression analysis in previous chapters applies. We therefore consider only briefly how to examine the appropriateness of the covariance model and how to make relevant inferences before turning to an example to illustrate the procedures.

Appropriateness of Covariance Model

Some of the key issues concerning the appropriateness of covariance model (25.3) and the equivalent regression model (25.11) deal with:

1. Normality of error terms

2. Equality of error variances for different treatments

3. Equality of slopes of the different treatment regression lines

4. Linearity of regression relation with concomitant variable

5. Uncorrelatedness of error terms

The third issue, concerning the equality of the slopes of the different treatment regression lines, is particularly important in evaluating the appropriateness of covariance model (25.3). The test in Section 11.4 to compare several regression lines is applicable for determining whether the condition of equal slopes in the covariance model is met. We shall illustrate this test in the example in Section 25.3.

Inferences of Interest

The key statistical inferences of interest in covariance analysis are the same as with analysis of variance models, namely, whether the treatments have any effects, and if so what these effects are. Testing for fixed treatment effects involves the same alternatives as for analysis of variance models:

$$(25.12) \qquad \begin{aligned} H_0&: \ \tau_1 = \tau_2 = \cdots = \tau_r = 0 \\ H_a&: \ \text{not all } \tau_i \text{ equal zero} \end{aligned}$$

As we can see by referring to the equivalent regression model (25.11), this test involves testing whether several regression coefficients equal zero. The appropriate test statistic therefore is (7.27).

If the treatment effects are found to differ, the next step usually is to investigate the nature of these effects. Pairwise comparisons of treatment effects $\tau_i - \tau_{i'}$ (the vertical distance between the two treatment regression lines) may be of interest, or more general contrasts of the τ_i may be relevant. In either case, linear combinations of the regression coefficients $\tau_1, \ldots, \tau_{r-1}$ are to be estimated.

Occasionally, the nature of the regression relationship between Y and X is of interest, but usually the concomitant variable X is only employed in ANCOVA models to help reduce the error variability.

Note

In covariance analysis there is usually no concern with whether the regression coefficient γ is zero, that is, whether there is indeed a regression relation between Y and X. If there is no relation, no bias results in the covariance analysis. The error mean square would simply be the same as for the analysis of variance model (allowing for sampling variation), and one degree of freedom would be lost for the error mean square.   ∎

25.3   Example of Single-Factor Covariance Analysis

A company studied the effects of three different types of promotions on sales of its crackers:

Treatment 1—Sampling of product by customers in store and regular shelf space

Treatment 2—Additional shelf space in regular location

Treatment 3—Special display shelves at ends of aisle in addition to regular shelf space

Fifteen stores were selected for the study, and a completely randomized experimental design was utilized. Each store was randomly assigned one of the promotion types, with five stores

TABLE 25.1   **Data for Cracker Promotion Example (number of cases sold).**

Treatment i	Store (j)									
	1		2		3		4		5	
	Y_{i1}	X_{i1}	Y_{i2}	X_{i2}	Y_{i3}	X_{i3}	Y_{i4}	X_{i4}	Y_{i5}	X_{i5}
1	38	21	39	26	36	22	45	28	33	19
2	43	34	38	26	38	29	27	18	34	25
3	24	23	32	29	31	30	21	16	28	29

assigned to each type of promotion. Other relevant conditions under the control of the company, such as price and advertising, were kept the same for all stores in the study. Data on the number of cases of the product sold during the promotional period, denoted by Y, are presented in Table 25.1, as are also data on the sales of the product in the preceding period, denoted by X. Sales in the preceding period are to be used as the concomitant variable.

Development of Model

Figure 25.5 presents the data of Table 25.1 in the form of a symbolic scatter plot. Linear regression and parallel slopes for the treatment regression lines appear to be reasonable. Therefore, the following regression model was tentatively selected:

$$(25.13) \qquad Y_{ij} = \mu_. + \tau_1 I_{ij1} + \tau_2 I_{ij2} + \gamma x_{ij} + \varepsilon_{ij} \qquad \text{Full model}$$

where:

$$I_1 = \begin{array}{ll} 1 & \text{if store received treatment 1} \\ -1 & \text{if store received treatment 3} \\ 0 & \text{otherwise} \end{array}$$

$$I_2 = \begin{array}{ll} 1 & \text{if store received treatment 2} \\ -1 & \text{if store received treatment 3} \\ 0 & \text{otherwise} \end{array}$$

$$x_{ij} = X_{ij} - \bar{X}_{..}$$

Table 25.2 repeats a portion of the data on the responses Y and the concomitant variable X in columns 1 and 2. The centered concomitant variable x is presented in column 3 and the indicator variables for the treatments in columns 4 and 5. Note that the centering of the concomitant variable is around the overall mean $\bar{X}_{..} = 25$. Regressing Y in column 1 of Table 25.2 on x, I_1, and I_2 in columns 3–5 by a computer package led to the results summarized in Table 25.3.

Various residual plots were obtained to examine the appropriateness of regression model (25.13). Figure 25.6 contains two of these. Figure 25.6a contains aligned residual dot plots for the three treatments. These do not suggest any major differences in the variances of the error terms. Figure 25.6b contains a normal probability plot of the residuals, which shows some modest departure from linearity. However, the coefficient of correlation between the

FIGURE 25.5 **Symbolic Scatter Plot of Cracker Sales—Cracker Promotion Example.**

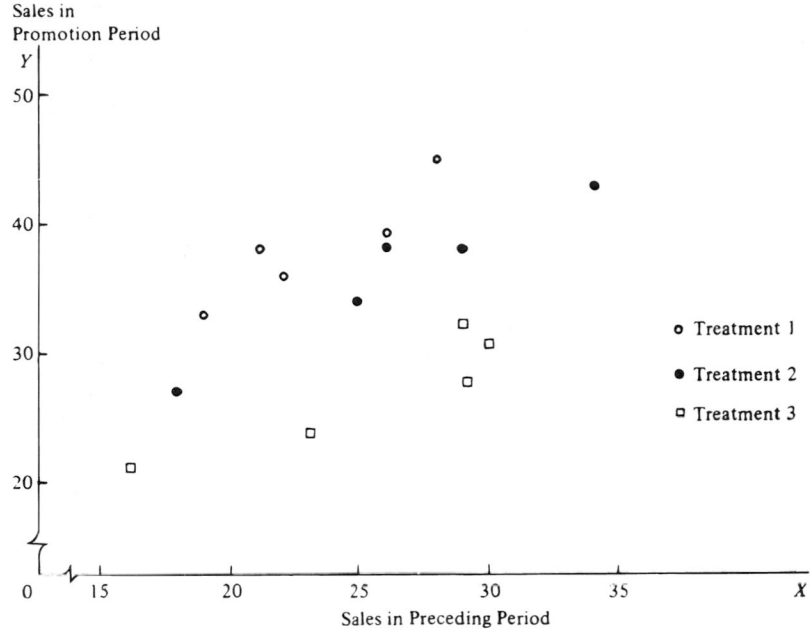

TABLE 25.2 **Regression Variables for Single-Factor Covariance Analysis —Cracker Promotion Example.**

		(1)	(2)	(3)	(4)	(5)	(6)	(7)
i	j	Y	X	x	I_1	I_2	$I_1 x$	$I_2 x$
1	1	38	21	−4	1	0	−4	0
1	2	39	26	1	1	0	1	0
	...	...	...	...	...	...	...	...
2	1	43	34	9	0	1	0	9
2	2	38	26	1	0	1	0	1
	...	...	...	...	...	...	...	...
3	4	21	16	−9	−1	−1	9	9
3	5	28	29	4	−1	−1	−4	−4

$$\overline{X}_{..} = 25$$

ordered residuals and their expected values under normality is .958, for which Table B.6 does not suggest any significant departure from normality. The analyst also conducted a test to confirm the equality of the slopes of the three treatment regression lines. This test will be described shortly. On the basis of these analyses, the analyst concluded that regression model (25.13) is appropriate here.

TABLE 25.3 Computer Output for Covariance Model (25.13)—Cracker Promotion Example.

(a) Regression Coefficients

$$\hat{\mu}_. = 33.800 \qquad \hat{\tau}_2 = .942$$
$$\hat{\tau}_1 = 6.017 \qquad \hat{\gamma} = .899$$

(b) Analysis of Variance

Source of Variation	SS	df	MS
Regression	$SSR = 607.829$	3	$MSR = 202.610$
Error	$SSE = 38.571$	11	$MSE = 3.506$
Total	$SSTO = 646.400$	14	

(c) Estimated Variance-Covariance Matrix of Regression Coefficients

$$
\begin{array}{c}
\hat{\mu}_. \\
\hat{\tau}_1 \\
\hat{\tau}_2 \\
\hat{\gamma}
\end{array}
\begin{array}{cccc}
\hat{\mu}_. & \hat{\tau}_1 & \hat{\tau}_2 & \hat{\gamma} \\
\left[\begin{array}{cccc}
.2338 & & & \\
0 & .5016 & & \\
0 & -.2603 & .4882 & \\
0 & .0189 & -.0147 & .0105
\end{array}\right]
\end{array}
$$

Test for Treatment Effects

To test whether or not the three cracker promotions differ in effectiveness, we can either follow the general linear test approach of fitting full and reduced models and using test statistic (2.70) or use extra sums of squares and test statistic (7.27). In either case, the alternatives are:

(25.14)
$$H_0: \ \tau_1 = \tau_2 = 0$$
$$H_a: \ \text{not both } \tau_1 \text{ and } \tau_2 \text{ equal zero}$$

Note that $\tau_3 = -\tau_1 - \tau_2$ must equal zero when $\tau_1 = \tau_2 = 0$.

We shall conduct the test by means of the general linear test approach. First, we develop the reduced model under H_0:

(25.15)
$$Y_{ij} = \mu_. + \gamma x_{ij} + \varepsilon_{ij} \qquad \text{Reduced model}$$

FIGURE 25.6   **Diagnostic Residual Plots—Cracker Promotion Example.**

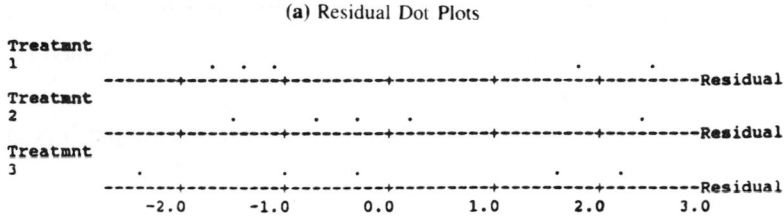

(a) Residual Dot Plots

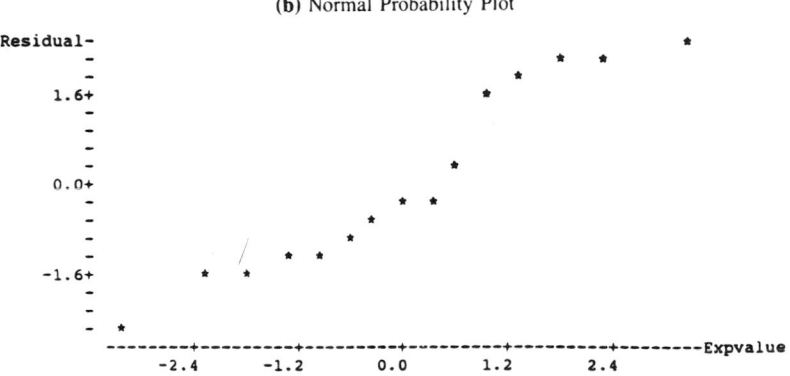

(b) Normal Probability Plot

TABLE 25.4   **Regression ANOVA Results for Reduced Model (25.15)—Cracker Promotion Example.**

Source of Variation	SS	df
Regression	$SSR = 190.678$	1
Error	$SSE = 455.722$	13
Total	$SSTO = 646.400$	14

Model (25.15) is just a simple linear regression model where none of the parameters vary for the different treatments. When regressing Y in column 1 of Table 25.2 on x in column 3, we obtain the analysis of variance results in Table 25.4.

We see from Table 25.4 that $SSE(R) = 455.722$ and from Table 25.3b that $SSE(F) = 38.571$. Hence, test statistic (2.70) here is:

$$F^* = \frac{SSE(R) - SSE(F)}{(n_T - 2) - [n_T - (r + 1)]} \div \frac{SSE(F)}{n_T - (r + 1)}$$

$$= \frac{455.722 - 38.571}{13 - 11} \div \frac{38.571}{11} = 59.5$$

The level of significance is to be controlled at $\alpha = .05$; hence, we need to obtain

$F(.95; 2, 11) = 3.98$. The decision rule therefore is:

$$\text{If } F^* \leq 3.98, \text{ conclude } H_0$$

$$\text{If } F^* > 3.98, \text{ conclude } H_a$$

Since $F^* = 59.5 > 3.98$, we conclude H_a, that the three cracker promotions differ in sales effectiveness. The P-value of the test is 0+.

Note

Occasionally, a test whether or not $\gamma = 0$ is of interest. This is simply the ordinary test whether or not a single regression coefficient equals zero. It can be conducted by means of the t^* test statistic (7.25) or by means of the F^* test statistic (7.24). ■

Estimation of Treatment Effects

Since treatment effects were found to be present in the cracker promotion study, the analyst next wished to investigate the nature of these effects. We noted earlier that a comparison of two treatments involves $\tau_i - \tau_{i'}$, the vertical distance between the two treatment regression lines. Using the fact that $\tau_3 = -\tau_1 - \tau_2$ and theorem (A.30b) for the variance of a linear combination of two random variables, we see that the estimators of all pairwise comparisons and their variances are as follows:

	Comparison	Estimator	Variance
	$\tau_1 - \tau_2$	$\hat{\tau}_1 - \hat{\tau}_2$	$\sigma^2\{\hat{\tau}_1\} + \sigma^2\{\hat{\tau}_2\} - 2\sigma\{\hat{\tau}_1, \hat{\tau}_2\}$
(25.16)	$\tau_1 - \tau_3 = 2\tau_1 + \tau_2$	$2\hat{\tau}_1 + \hat{\tau}_2$	$4\sigma^2\{\hat{\tau}_1\} + \sigma^2\{\hat{\tau}_2\} + 4\sigma\{\hat{\tau}_1, \hat{\tau}_2\}$
	$\tau_2 - \tau_3 = \tau_1 + 2\tau_2$	$\hat{\tau}_1 + 2\hat{\tau}_2$	$\sigma^2\{\hat{\tau}_1\} + 4\sigma^2\{\hat{\tau}_2\} + 4\sigma\{\hat{\tau}_1, \hat{\tau}_2\}$

Table 25.3a furnishes the needed estimated regression coefficients, and Table 25.3c provides their estimated variances and covariances. We obtain from there:

	Comparison	Estimate	Variance
	$\tau_1 - \tau_2$	$6.017 - .942$ $= 5.075$	$.5016 + .4882 - 2(-.2603)$ $= 1.5104$
(25.16a)	$\tau_1 - \tau_3$	$2(6.017) + .942$ $= 12.976$	$4(.5016) + .4882 + 4(-.2603)$ $= 1.4534$
	$\tau_2 - \tau_3$	$6.017 + 2(.942)$ $= 7.901$	$.5016 + 4(.4882) + 4(-2.2603)$ $= 1.4132$

When a single interval estimate is to be constructed, the t distribution with $n_T - r - 1$ degrees of freedom is used. (The degrees of freedom are those associated with MSE in the full covariance model.) Usually, however, a family of interval estimates is desired. In that case, the Scheffé multiple comparison procedure may be employed with the S multiple defined by:

$$(25.17) \qquad S^2 = (r - 1)F(1 - \alpha; r - 1, n_T - r - 1)$$

or the Bonferroni method may be employed with the B multiple:

$$(25.18) \qquad B = t(1 - \alpha/2g; n_T - r - 1)$$

where g is the number of statements in the family. The Tukey method is not appropriate for covariance analysis.

In the case at hand, the analyst wished to obtain all pairwise comparisons with a 95 percent family confidence coefficient. The analyst used the Scheffé procedure in anticipation that some additional estimates of contrasts might be desired. We require therefore:

$$S^2 = (3 - 1)F(.95; 2, 11) = 2(3.98) = 7.96 \qquad S = 2.82$$

Using the results in (25.16a), the confidence intervals for all pairwise treatment comparisons with a 95 percent family confidence coefficient then are:

$$1.61 = 5.075 - 2.82\sqrt{1.5104} \leq \tau_1 - \tau_2 \leq 5.075 + 2.82\sqrt{1.5104} = 8.54$$

$$9.58 = 12.976 - 2.82\sqrt{1.4534} \leq \tau_1 - \tau_3 \leq 12.976 + 2.82\sqrt{1.4534} = 16.38$$

$$4.55 = 7.901 - 2.82\sqrt{1.4132} \leq \tau_2 - \tau_3 \leq 7.901 + 2.82\sqrt{1.4132} = 11.25$$

These results indicate clearly that sampling in the store (treatment 1) is significantly better for stimulating cracker sales than either of the two shelf promotions, and that increasing the regular shelf space (treatment 2) is superior to additional displays at the end of the aisle (treatment 3).

Comments

1. Occasionally, more general contrasts among treatment effects than pairwise comparisons are desired. No new problems arise either in the use of the t distribution for a single contrast or in the use of the Scheffé or Bonferroni procedures for multiple comparisons. For instance, if the analyst desired in the cracker promotion example to compare the treatment effect for sampling in the store (treatment 1) with the two treatments involving shelf displays (treatments 2 and 3), the following contrast would be of interest:

$$(25.19) \qquad L = \tau_1 - \frac{\tau_2 + \tau_3}{2}$$

The appropriate estimator is:

$$(25.20) \qquad \hat{L} = \hat{\tau}_1 - \frac{\hat{\tau}_2 + (-\hat{\tau}_1 - \hat{\tau}_2)}{2} = \frac{3}{2}\hat{\tau}_1$$

The variance of this estimator is by (A.16b):

$$(25.21) \qquad \sigma^2\{\hat{L}\} = \frac{9}{4}\sigma^2\{\hat{\tau}_1\}$$

2. Sometimes there is interest in estimating the mean response with the ith treatment for a "typical" value of X. Frequently $X = \bar{X}_{..}$ is considered to be a "typical" value. We know from Figure 25.3 that at $X = \bar{X}_{..}$, the mean response for the ith treatment is the intercept of the treatment regression line, $\mu_{.} + \tau_i$. An estimator of $\mu_{.} + \tau_i$ can be readily developed. For the cracker promotion example, we obtain the following estimators and their variances:

Mean Response at $X = \bar{X}_{..}$	Estimator	Variance
$\mu_{.} + \tau_1$	$\hat{\mu}_{.} + \hat{\tau}_1$	$\sigma^2\{\hat{\mu}_{.}\} + \sigma^2\{\hat{\tau}_1\} + 2\sigma\{\hat{\mu}_{.}, \hat{\tau}_1\}$
$\mu_{.} + \tau_2$	$\hat{\mu}_{.} + \hat{\tau}_2$	$\sigma^2\{\hat{\mu}_{.}\} + \sigma^2\{\hat{\tau}_2\} + 2\sigma\{\hat{\mu}_{.}, \hat{\tau}_2\}$
$\mu_{.} + \tau_3$	$\hat{\mu}_{.} - \hat{\tau}_1 - \hat{\tau}_2$	$\sigma^2\{\hat{\mu}_{.}\} + \sigma^2\{\hat{\tau}_1\} + \sigma^2\{\hat{\tau}_2\}$

(25.22)

$$-2\sigma\{\hat{\mu}_{.}, \hat{\tau}_1\} - 2\sigma\{\hat{\mu}_{.}, \hat{\tau}_2\}$$

$$+2\sigma\{\hat{\tau}_1, \hat{\tau}_2\}$$

Use of the results in Table 25.3 leads to the following estimates:

Treatment	Estimated Mean Response at $\bar{X}_{..}$	Estimated Variance
1	$33.800 + 6.017 = 39.817$	$.2338 + .5016 + 2(0) = .7354$
2	$33.800 + .942 = 34.742$	$.2338 + .4882 + 2(0) = .7220$
3	$33.800 - 6.017 - .942$	$.2338 + .5016 + .4882 - 2(0) - 2(0)$
	$= 26.841$	$+ 2(-.2603) = .7030$

The estimated mean response for treatment i at $X = \bar{X}_{..}$ is often called the *adjusted estimated treatment mean*. It is said to be "adjusted" because it takes into account the effect of the concomitant variable. A comparison of the adjusted treatment means leads, of course, to the same pairwise comparisons of treatment effects as before; for instance, $39.817 - 34.742 = 5.075 = \hat{\tau}_1 - \hat{\tau}_2$. ∎

Test for Parallel Slopes

An important assumption in covariance analysis is that all treatment regression lines have the same slope γ. The analyst who conducted the cracker promotion study, indeed, tested this assumption before proceeding with the analysis discussed earlier. We know from Chapter 11 that regression model (25.13) can be generalized to allow for different slopes for the treatments by introducing cross-product interaction terms. Specifically, interaction variables $I_1 x$ and $I_2 x$ will be required here. We shall denote the corresponding regression coefficients by β_1 and β_2. Thus, the generalized model is:

(25.23)
$$Y_{ij} = \mu_{.} + \tau_1 I_{ij1} + \tau_2 I_{ij2} + \gamma x_{ij} + \beta_1 I_{ij1} x_{ij} + \beta_2 I_{ij2} x_{ij} + \varepsilon_{ij}$$

Generalized model

Table 25.2 contains in columns 6 and 7 the interaction variables for this model for the cracker promotion example. Regressing the response variable Y in column 1 of Table 25.2 on $x, I_1, I_2, I_1 x, I_2 x$ in columns 3–7 by means of a computer multiple regression package

TABLE 25.5 **Regression ANOVA Results for Generalized Model (25.23)—Cracker Promotion Example.**

Source of Variation	SS	df
Regression	$SSR = 614.879$	5
Error	$SSE = 31.521$	9
Total	$SSTO = 646.400$	14

yielded the ANOVA results in Table 25.5. The error sum of squares SSE obtained by fitting generalized model (25.23) is the equivalent of fitting separate regression lines for each treatment and summing these error sums of squares.

The test for parallel slopes is equivalent to testing for no interactions in generalized model (25.23):

$$(25.24) \qquad \begin{aligned} &H_0: \ \beta_1 = \beta_2 = 0 \\ &H_a: \ \text{not both } \beta_1 \text{ and } \beta_2 \text{ equal zero} \end{aligned}$$

We need to recognize that generalized model (25.23) now is the "full" model and covariance model (25.13) is the "reduced" model. Hence, we have from Tables 25.3b and 25.5:

$$SSE(F) = 31.521 \qquad SSE(R) = 38.571$$

Thus, test statistic (2.70) becomes here:

$$F^* = \frac{38.571 - 31.521}{11 - 9} \div \frac{31.521}{9} = 1.01$$

For level of significance $\alpha = .05$, we require $F(.95; 2, 9) = 4.26$. Since $F^* = 1.01 \leq 4.26$, we conclude H_0, that the three treatment regression lines have the same slope. The P-value of the test is .40. Hence, the requirement of equal treatment slopes in analysis of covariance model (25.13) is met in the cracker promotion example.

Comments

1. An indication of the effectiveness of the analysis of covariance in reducing error variability can be obtained by comparing MSE for covariance analysis with MSE for regular analysis of variance. For the cracker promotion example, we know from Table 25.3 that MSE for the covariance analysis is 3.51. It can be shown that the error mean square for regular analysis of variance would have been 25.63. Hence, in this case covariance analysis was able to reduce the residual variance by about 86 percent, a substantial reduction.

2. Covariance analysis and analysis of variance need not lead to the same conclusions about the treatment effects. For instance, analysis of variance might not indicate any treatment effects, whereas covariance analysis with a smaller error variance could show significant treatment effects. Ordinarily, of course, one should decide in advance which of the two analyses is to be used. ∎

25.4 Multifactor Covariance Analysis

We have until now considered covariance analysis for single-factor studies with r treatments. Covariance analysis can also be employed with two-factor and multifactor studies. We illustrate now the use of covariance analysis for two-factor studies with one concomitant variable. For notational simplicity, we consider the case where the treatment sample size is the same for all treatments. However, the regression approach to covariance analysis is general and applies directly when the study is unbalanced, with unequal treatment sample sizes.

Covariance Model for Two-Factor Studies

The fixed effects ANOVA model for a two-factor balanced study was given in (19.23):

$$(25.25) \qquad Y_{ijk} = \mu_{..} + \alpha_i + \beta_j + (\alpha\beta)_{ij} + \varepsilon_{ijk}$$

$$i = 1, \ldots, a; \, j = 1, \ldots, b; \, k = 1, \ldots, n$$

where α_i is the main effect of factor A at the ith level, β_j is the main effect of factor B at the jth level, and $(\alpha\beta)_{ij}$ is the interaction effect when factor A is at the ith level and factor B is at the jth level. The covariance model for a two-factor study with a single concomitant variable, assuming the relation between Y and the concomitant variable X is linear, is:

$$(25.26) \qquad Y_{ijk} = \mu_{..} + \alpha_i + \beta_j + (\alpha\beta)_{ij} + \gamma(X_{ijk} - \bar{X}_{...}) + \varepsilon_{ijk}$$

$$i = 1, \ldots, a; \, j = 1, \ldots, b; \, k = 1, \ldots, n$$

Regression Approach

We illustrate the regression approach to covariance analysis for a balanced two-factor study with one concomitant variable when both factors A and B are at two levels, i.e., when $a = b = 2$. The regression model counterpart to covariance model (25.26) then is:

$$(25.27) \qquad Y_{ijk} = \mu_{..} + \alpha_1 I_{ijk1} + \beta_1 I_{ijk2} + (\alpha\beta)_{11} I_{ijk1} I_{ijk2} + \gamma x_{ijk} + \varepsilon_{ijk}$$

where:

$$I_1 = \begin{array}{ll} 1 & \text{if case from level 1 for factor } A \\ -1 & \text{if case from level 2 for factor } A \end{array}$$

$$I_2 = \begin{array}{ll} 1 & \text{if case from level 1 for factor } B \\ -1 & \text{if case from level 2 for factor } B \end{array}$$

$$x_{ijk} = X_{ijk} - \bar{X}_{...}$$

Note that the regression coefficients in (25.27) are the analysis of variance factor effects α_1, β_1, and $(\alpha\beta)_{11}$ and the concomitant variable coefficient γ.

Testing for factor A main effects requires that $\alpha_1 = 0$ in the reduced model. Correspondingly, $\beta_1 = 0$ is required in the reduced model when testing for factor B main effects, and $(\alpha\beta)_{11} = 0$ is required in the reduced model when testing for AB interactions.

TABLE 25.6 **Data for Salable Flowers Example.**

Factor A (flower variety) i	Factor B (moisture level) j			
	B_1 (low)		B_2 (high)	
	Y_{i1k}	X_{i1k}	Y_{i2k}	X_{i2k}
A_1 (variety LP)	98	15	71	10
	60	4	80	12
	...	...	...	...
	64	5	55	3
A_2 (variety WB)	55	4	76	11
	60	5	68	10
	...	...	...	...
	78	11	70	9

Estimation of factor A and factor B main effects can easily be done in terms of comparisons among the regression coefficients. The use of the Scheffé and Bonferroni multiple comparison procedures presents no new issues. For instance, the S multiple for multiple comparisons among the factor A level means is defined as follows:

(25.28) $$S^2 = (a-1)F(1-\alpha; a-1, nab-ab-1)$$

and the B multiple is the same as in (25.18), with $n_T = nab$ and $r = ab$.

Example

A horticulturist conducted an experiment to study the effects of flower variety (factor A: varieties LP, WB) and moisture level (factor B: low, high) on yield of salable flowers (Y). Because the plots were not of the same size, the horticulturist wished to use plot size (X) as the concomitant variable. Six replications were made for each treatment. A portion of the data are presented in Table 25.6. Figure 25.7 contains a symbolic scatter plot of the data. The model assumptions of linear relations between Y and the concomitant variable X, as well as of parallel slopes for the four treatments, appear to be reasonable here.

A fit of regression model (25.27) to the data by a computer regression package yielded the fitted regression function in Table 25.7a. The analyst plotted the data together with the fitted regression lines and made a variety of residual plots and tests (not shown). On the basis of these diagnostics, the analyst was satisfied that regression model (25.27), which assumes parallel linear regression functions and constant error variances, is suitable here.

To examine the nature of the factor effects, we show in Figure 25.8 the estimated treatment means plot for the two moisture levels B_1 and B_2. These estimated means all correspond to plot size $X = \bar{X}_{...} = 8.25$ or $x = 0$. Any other plot size would yield exactly the same relationships as those in Figure 25.8. It appears from Figure 25.8 that there are no important interactions between flower variety and moisture level, and that there may be main effects for both factors, particularly for moisture level.

FIGURE 25.7   **Symbolic Scatter Plot of Salable Flowers and Size of Plot—Salable Flowers Example.**

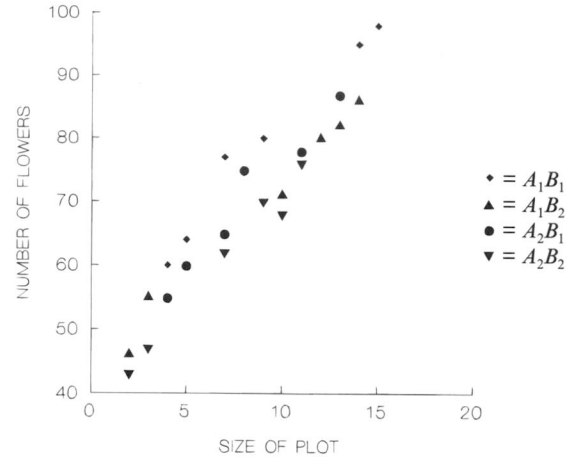

TABLE 25.7   **Computer Output for Fit of Regression Model (25.27)—Salable Flowers Example.**

(a) Fitted Regression Function

$$\hat{Y} = 70.0 + 2.04234I_1 + 3.68078I_2 + .81922I_1I_2 + 3.27688x$$

Regression Coefficient	Estimated Regression Coefficient	Estimated Standard Deviation
α_1	2.04234	.52108
β_1	3.68078	.51291
$(\alpha\beta)_{11}$	.81922	.51291
γ	3.27688	.13002

(b) Extra Sums of Squares

Effect	Source of Variation	SS	df	MS
Concomitant variable	$x \mid I_1, I_2, I_1I_2$	3,994.52	1	3,994.52
A	$I_1 \mid x, I_2, I_1I_2$	96.60	1	96.60
B	$I_2 \mid x, I_1, I_1I_2$	323.85	1	323.85
AB	$I_1I_2 \mid x, I_1, I_2$	16.04	1	16.04
	Error	119.48	19	6.2884

To study formally the factor effects, reduced models were formed by deleting from regression model (25.27) one predictor variable at a time (recall that both factors have only two levels), and the reduced models were then fitted. The extra sums of squares so obtained, as well as the error sum of squares for the full model, are presented in Table 25.7b, together

FIGURE 25.8 **Estimated Treatment Means Plot—Salable Flowers Example.**

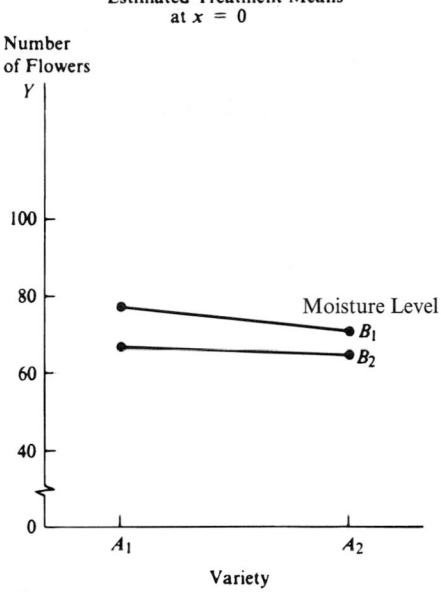

with the degrees of freedom and mean squares. No total sum of squares is shown because the factor effect components are not orthogonal.

We test first for the presence of interactions by means of the usual general linear test statistic F^*, using the results in Table 25.7b:

$$F^* = \frac{SSR(I_1 I_2 | x, I_1, I_2)}{1} \div MSE = \frac{16.04}{6.2884} = 2.55$$

For $\alpha = .01$, we require $F(.99; 1, 19) = 8.18$. Since $F^* = 2.55 \le 8.18$, we conclude that no interactions are present. The P-value of the test is .13.

We now wish to compare both the factor A main effects and the factor B main effects by means of confidence intervals, with a 95 percent family confidence coefficient. Since $\alpha_2 = -\alpha_1$, we have for our example:

$$L_1 = \alpha_1 - \alpha_2 = \alpha_1 - (-\alpha_1) = 2\alpha_1$$

Similarly, we obtain for the comparison of factor B main effects:

$$L_2 = 2\beta_1$$

Point estimates are readily obtained from the results in Table 25.7a:

$$\hat{L}_1 = 2\hat{\alpha}_1 = 2(2.04234) = 4.08$$

$$\hat{L}_2 = 2\hat{\beta}_1 = 2(3.68078) = 7.36$$

The estimated standard deviations also follow easily, using (A.16b):

$$s\{\hat{L}_1\} = 2s\{\hat{\alpha}_1\} = 2(.52108) = 1.042$$

$$s\{\hat{L}_2\} = 2s\{\hat{\beta}_1\} = 2(.51291) = 1.026$$

We utilize the Bonferroni simultaneous estimation procedure for $g = 2$ comparisons. For a 95 percent family confidence coefficient, we require $t[1 - .05/2(2); 19] = t(.9875; 19) = 2.433$. The two desired confidence intervals therefore are:

$$1.5 = 4.08 - 2.433(1.042) \le \alpha_1 - \alpha_2 \le 4.08 + 2.433(1.042) = 6.6$$

$$4.9 = 7.36 - 2.433(1.026) \le \beta_1 - \beta_2 \le 7.36 + 2.433(1.026) = 9.9$$

With family confidence coefficient .95, we conclude that variety LP yields, on the average, between 1.5 and 6.6 more salable flowers for any given plot size than variety WB. Also, for any given plot size, the mean number of salable flowers is between 4.9 and 9.9 flowers greater for the low moisture level than for the high one, thus indicating a substantial effect of moisture level on yield.

If interactions had been present, we could have studied the nature of the interaction effects by, for instance, comparing the effect of the moisture level for each of the two flower varieties. It can be shown that this comparison is given by $(\alpha\beta)_{12} = -(\alpha\beta)_{11}$. Hence, we could estimate the desired interaction effect by using the estimated regression coefficient $\widehat{(\alpha\beta)}_{11}$ and its estimated standard deviation in Table 25.7a.

Note

Some computer packages for covariance analysis produce analyses that are only valid when all treatment sample sizes in multifactor studies are equal. Computer packages should therefore be used with great care when the treatment sample sizes in multifactor studies are unequal, to make sure that the package conducts the tests of interest.   ■

25.5 Additional Considerations for the Use of Covariance Analysis

Use of Differences

In a variety of studies, a prestudy observation X and a poststudy observation Y on the same variable are available for each unit. For instance, X may be the score for a subject's attitude toward a company prior to reading its annual report, and Y may be the score after reading the report. In this situation, an obvious alternative to covariance analysis is to do an analysis of variance on the differences $Y - X$. Sometimes, $Y - X$ is called an *index of response* because it makes one observation out of two.

If the slope of the treatment regression lines is $\gamma = 1$, analysis of covariance and analysis of variance on $Y - X$ are essentially equivalent. When $\gamma = 1$, covariance model (25.2) becomes:

$$(25.29) \qquad\qquad Y_{ij} = \mu_{\cdot} + \tau_i + X_{ij} + \varepsilon_{ij}$$

which can be written as a regular analysis of variance model:

(25.29a) $$Y_{ij} - X_{ij} = \mu_{.} + \iota_i + \varepsilon_{ij}$$

Thus, if a unit change in X leads to about the same change in Y, it makes sense to perform an analysis of variance on $Y - X$ rather than to use covariance analysis, because the analysis of variance model is a simpler model. If the regression slope is not near 1, however, covariance analysis may be substantially more effective than use of the differences $Y - X$.

In the earlier cracker promotion example, use of $Y - X$ would have been effective. It would have yielded the error mean square $MSE = 3.500$, which is practically the same as the error mean square for covariance analysis, $MSE = 3.506$ (see Table 25.3b). Recall that the regression slope in our example is close to 1 ($\hat{\gamma} = .899$); hence, the approximate equivalence of the two procedures.

Correction for Bias

The suggestion is sometimes made that analysis of covariance can be helpful in correcting for bias with observational data. With such data, the groups under study may differ substantially with respect to a concomitant variable, and this may bias the comparisons of the groups. Consider, for instance, a study in which attitudes toward no-fault automobile insurance were compared for persons who are risk averse and persons who are risk seeking. It was found that many persons in the risk-averse group tended to be older (50 to 70 years old), while many persons in the risk-seeking group tended to be younger (20 to 40 years old). In this type of situation, some researchers would advise that covariance analysis, with age as the concomitant variable, be employed to help remove any bias in the analysis of the observational data on attitudes toward no-fault insurance because the two age groups differ so much.

Even though there is great appeal in the idea of removing bias in observational data, covariance analysis should be used with caution for this purpose. In the first place, comparisons of means at a common value of X may require substantial extrapolation of the regression lines to a region where there are no or only few data points (in our example, to near 45 years). It may well be that the regression relationship used in the covariance analysis is not appropriate for substantial extrapolation. In the second place, the treatment variable may depend on the concomitant variable (or vice versa), which could affect the proper conclusions to be drawn.

Interest in Nature of Treatment Effects

Covariance analysis is sometimes employed for the principal purpose of shedding more light on the nature of the treatment effects, rather than merely for increasing the precision of the analysis. For instance, a market researcher in a study of the effects of three different advertisements on the maximum price consumers are willing to pay for a new type of home siding may use covariance analysis, with value of the consumer's home as the concomitant variable. The reason is because the researcher is truly interested in the relation for each advertisement between home value and maximum price. Reduction of error variance in this instance may be a secondary consideration.

As in all regression analyses, care must be used in drawing inferences about the causal nature of the relation between the concomitant variable and the response. In the advertising example, it might well be that value of a consumer's home is largely influenced by income. If this were so, the relation between value of the consumer's home and maximum price the consumer is willing to pay may actually be largely a reflection of the underlying relation between income and maximum price.

Problems

25.1.   A student's reaction to the instructor's statement that covariance analysis is inappropriate when the treatment regression lines do not have the same slope was as follows: "It seems to me that this is ducking a real-world problem. If the treatment slopes are different, just use a covariance model that allows for different treatment slopes." Evaluate this reaction.

25.2.   A survey analyst remarked: "When covariance analysis is used with survey data, there is a danger that the treatments may be related to the concomitant variable." What is the nature of the problem? Does this same problem exist when the treatments are randomly assigned to the experimental units?

25.3.   Portray, analogous to the format of Figure 1.6 on page 12 for a regression model, the nature of covariance model (25.3) when there are three treatments and the parameter values are: $\mu_. = 150$, $\tau_1 = 15$, $\tau_2 = -5$, $\tau_3 = -10$, $\gamma = 6$, $\bar{X}_{..} = 70$, $\sigma = 5$. Show several distributions of Y for each treatment.

25.4.   Refer to the cracker promotion example on page 1019. A student stated, in discussing this case: "Strictly speaking, you cannot conclude anything about whether the three promotions differ in effectiveness because there was no control. The preceding period does not qualify as a control because it might have differed from the promotion period due to seasonal factors or other unique circumstances." Comment.

25.5.   Refer to the cracker promotion example on page 1025, where three pairwise comparisons of treatment effects were made by the Scheffé procedure.

   a.   What would be the value of the Bonferroni multiple here for estimating the three comparisons?

   b.   Did the analyst obtain substantially less precise interval estimates using the Scheffé procedure, which permits making additional estimates without modifying the present ones?

25.6.   State the analysis of covariance model for a single-factor study with four treatments when there are two concomitant variables, each with linear and quadratic terms in the model.

√ 25.7.   Refer to **Productivity improvement** Problem 16.10. The economist also has information on annual productivity improvement in the prior year and wishes to use this information as a concomitant variable. The data on the prior year's productivity improvement (X_{ij}) follow.

												j	
i	1	2	3	4	5	6	7	8	9	10	11	12
1	8.2	7.9	7.0	5.7	7.2	7.0	6.5	7.9	6.3			
2	8.8	10.0	10.7	10.0	9.7	9.4	10.6	9.8	10.0	10.3	8.9	10.0
3	11.5	12.2	12.8	11.0	12.3	12.1						

   a.   Obtain the residuals for covariance model (25.3).

b. For each treatment, plot the residuals against the fitted values. Also prepare a normal probability plot of the residuals and calculate the coefficient of correlation between the ordered residuals and their expected values under normality. What do you conclude from your analysis?

c. State the generalized regression model to be employed for testing whether or not the treatment regression lines have the same slope. Conduct this test using $\alpha = .01$. State the alternatives, decision rule, and conclusion. What is the *P*-value of the test?

d. Could you conduct a formal test here as to whether the regression functions are linear? If so, how many degrees of freedom are there for the denominator mean square in the test statistic?

√ 25.8. Refer to **Productivity improvement** Problems 16.10 and 25.7. Assume that covariance model (25.3) is appropriate.

a. Prepare a symbolic scatter plot of the data. Does it appear that there are effects of the level of research and development expenditures on mean productivity improvement? Discuss.

b. State the regression model equivalent to covariance model (25.3) for this case; use 1,−1, 0 indicator variables. Also state the reduced regression model for testing for treatment effects.

c. Fit the full and reduced regression models and test for treatment effects; use $\alpha = .05$. State the alternatives, decision rule, and conclusion. What is the *P*-value of the test?

d. Is $MSE(F)$ for the covariance model substantially smaller than MSE for the analysis of variance model in Problem 16.10d? Does this affect the conclusion reached about treatment effects? Does it affect the *P*-value?

e. Estimate the mean productivity improvement for firms with moderate research and development expenditures who had a prior productivity improvement of $X = 9.0$; use a 95 percent confidence interval.

f. Make all pairwise comparisons between the treatment effects; use either the Bonferroni or the Scheffé procedure with a 90 percent family confidence coefficient, whichever is more efficient. State your findings.

25.9. Refer to **Questionnaire color** Problem 16.11. It has been suggested to the investigator that size of parking lot might be a useful concomitant variable. The number of spaces (X_{ij}) in each parking lot utilized in the study follow.

			j		
i	1	2	3	4	5
1	300	381	226	350	100
2	153	334	473	264	325
3	144	359	296	243	252

a. Obtain the residuals for covariance model (25.3).

b. For each treatment, plot the residuals against the fitted values. Also prepare a normal probability plot of the residuals and calculate the coefficient of correlation between the ordered residuals and their expected values under normality. What do you conclude from your analysis?

c. State the generalized regression model to be employed for testing whether or not the treatment regression lines have the same slope. Conduct this test using $\alpha = .005$. State the alternatives, decision rule, and conclusion. What is the P-value of the test?

d. Could you conduct a formal test here as to whether the regression functions are linear? Explain.

25.10. Refer to **Questionnaire color** Problems 16.11 and 25.9. Assume that covariance model (25.3) is applicable.

a. Prepare a symbolic scatter plot of the data. Does it appear that there are color effects on the mean response rate? Discuss.

b. State the regression model equivalent to covariance model (25.3) for this case; use $1, -1, 0$ indicator variables. Also state the reduced regression model for testing for treatment effects.

c. Fit the full and reduced regression models and test for treatment effects; use $\alpha = .10$. State the alternatives, decision rule, and conclusion. What is the P-value of the test?

d. Is $MSE(F)$ for the covariance model substantially smaller than MSE for the analysis of variance model in Problem 16.11d? How does this affect the conclusion reached about treatment effects?

e. Estimate the mean response rate for blue questionnaires in parking lots of size $X = 280$; use a 90 percent confidence interval.

f. Make all pairwise comparisons between the treatment effects; use either the Bonferroni or the Scheffé procedure with a 90 percent family confidence coefficient, whichever is more efficient. State your findings.

25.11. Refer to **Rehabilitation therapy** Problem 16.12. The rehabilitation researcher wishes to use age of patient as a concomitant variable. The ages (X_{ij}) of patients in the study follow.

					j					
i	1	2	3	4	5	6	7	8	9	10
1	18.3	30.0	26.5	28.1	29.7	27.8	19.8	29.3		
2	20.8	25.2	29.2	20.0	21.5	22.1	19.7	24.7	20.2	22.9
3	22.7	28.7	18.9	18.0	21.7	20.0				

a. Obtain the residuals for covariance model (25.3).

b. For each treatment, plot the residuals against the fitted values. Also prepare a normal probability plot of the residuals and calculate the coefficient of correlation between the ordered residuals and their expected values under normality. What do you conclude from your analysis?

c. State the generalized regression model to be employed for testing whether or not the treatment regression lines have the same slope. Conduct this test using $\alpha = .05$. State the alternatives, decision rule, and conclusion. What is the P-value of the test?

d. Could you conduct a formal test here as to whether the regression functions are linear? Explain.

25.12. Refer to **Rehabilitation therapy** Problems 16.12 and 25.11. Assume that covariance model (25.3) is applicable.

a. Prepare a symbolic scatter plot of the data. Does it appear that there are effects of physical fitness status on the mean number of days required for therapy? Discuss.

b. State the regression model equivalent to covariance model (25.3) for this case; use 1, −1, 0 indicator variables. Also state the reduced regression model for testing for treatment effects.

c. Fit the full and reduced regression models and test for treatment effects; use $\alpha = .01$. State the alternatives, decision rule, and conclusion. What is the P-value of the test?

d. Is $MSE(F)$ for the covariance model substantially smaller than MSE for the analysis of variance model in Problem 16.12d? Does this affect the conclusion reached about treatment effects? Does it affect the P-value?

e. Estimate the mean number of days required for therapy for patients of average physical fitness and age 24 years; use a 99 percent confidence interval.

f. Make all pairwise comparisons between the treatment effects; use either the Bonferroni or the Scheffé procedure with a 95 percent family confidence coefficient, whichever is more efficient. State your findings.

25.13. **Product display.** A manufacturer of felt-tip markers investigated by an experiment whether a proposed new display, featuring a picture of a physician, is more effective in drugstores than the present counter display, featuring a picture of an athlete and designed to be located in the stationery area. Fifteen drugstores of similar characteristics were chosen for the study. They were assigned at random in equal numbers to one of the following three treatments: (1) present counter display in stationery area, (2) new display in stationery area, (3) new display in checkout area. Sales with the present display (X_{ij}) were recorded in all 15 stores for a three-week period. Then the new display was set up in the 10 stores receiving it, and sales for the next three-week period (Y_{ij}) were recorded in all 15 stores. The data on sales (in dollars) follow.

			j		
i	1	2	3	4	5
Treatment 1					
First 3 weeks	92	68	74	52	65
Second 3 weeks	69	44	58	38	54
Treatment 2					
First 3 weeks	77	80	70	73	79
Second 3 weeks	74	75	73	78	82
Treatment 3					
First 3 weeks	64	43	81	68	71
Second 3 weeks	66	49	84	75	77

The analyst wishes to analyze the effects of the three different display treatments by means of covariance analysis.

a. Obtain the residuals for covariance model (25.3).

b. For each treatment, plot the residuals against the fitted values. Also prepare a normal probability plot of the residuals and calculate the coefficient of correlation between the ordered residuals and their expected values under normality. What do you conclude from your analysis?

   c. State the generalized regression model to be employed for testing whether or not the treatment regression lines have the same slope. Conduct this test using $\alpha = .05$. State the alternatives, decision rule, and conclusion. What is the P-value of the test?

   d. Could you conduct a formal test here as to whether the regression functions are linear? Explain.

25.14. Refer to **Product display** Problem 25.13. Assume that covariance model (25.3) is applicable.

   a. Prepare a symbolic scatter plot of the data. Does it appear that there are display effects on mean sales? Discuss.

   b. State the regression model equivalent to covariance model (25.3) for this case; use $1, -1, 0$ indicator variables. Also state the reduced regression model for testing for treatment effects.

   c. Fit the full and reduced regression models and test for treatment effects; use $\alpha = .05$. State the alternatives, decision rule, and conclusion. What is the P-value of the test?

   d. Is $MSE(F)$ for the covariance model substantially smaller than the mean square error if analysis of variance model (16.2) had been employed?

   e. Estimate the mean sales with display treatment 2 for stores whose sales in the preceding three-week period were $75; use a 95 percent confidence interval.

   f. Make all pairwise comparisons between the treatment effects; use either the Bonferroni or the Scheffé procedure with a 90 percent family confidence coefficient, whichever is more efficient. State your findings.

$\sqrt{}$ 25.15. Refer to **Cash offers** Problem 19.10. An analyst wishes to use each dealer's sales volume as a concomitant variable. The sales data (X_{ijk}, in hundred thousand dollars) follow.

	$i = 1$		$i = 2$		$i = 3$	
	$j = 1$	$j = 2$	$j = 1$	$j = 2$	$j = 1$	$j = 2$
	3.0	3.5	6.5	2.2	5.0	4.0
	5.1	4.2	4.1	5.4	3.1	.8
	$\cdots$	$\cdots$	$\cdots$	$\cdots$	$\cdots$	$\cdots$
	4.9	6.6	3.0	5.0	2.9	1.9

   a. Obtain the residuals for covariance model (25.26).

   b. For each treatment, plot the residuals against the fitted values. Also prepare a normal probability plot of the residuals and calculate the coefficient of correlation between the ordered residuals and their expected values under normality. What do you conclude from your analysis?

   c. State the generalized regression model to be employed for testing whether or not the treatment regression lines have the same slope. Conduct this test using $\alpha = .01$. State the alternatives, decision rule, and conclusion. What is the P-value of the test?

$\sqrt{}$ 25.16. Refer to **Cash offers** Problems 19.10 and 25.15. Assume that covariance model (25.26) is applicable.

   a. State the regression model equivalent to covariance model (25.26) for this case; use $1, -1, 0$ indicator variables. Fit this full model.

   b. State the reduced regression models for testing for interaction and factor A and factor B main effects, respectively. Fit these reduced regression models.

c. Test for interaction effects; use $\alpha = .05$. State the alternatives, decision rule, and conclusion. What is the P-value of the test?

d. Test for factor A main effects; use $\alpha = .05$. State the alternatives, decision rule, and conclusion. What is the P-value of the test?

e. Test for factor B main effects; use $\alpha = .05$. State the alternatives, decision rule, and conclusion. What is the P-value of the test?

f. For each factor, make all pairwise comparisons between the factor level main effects. Use the Bonferroni procedure with a 90 percent family confidence coefficient. State your findings.

25.17. Refer to **Eye contact effect** Problem 19.12. Age of personnel officer is to be used as a concomitant variable. The ages (X_{ijk}) of the personnel officers follow.

	$i = 1$		$i = 2$	
$j = 1$	$j = 2$	$j = 1$	$j = 2$
42	51	43	42
30	35	53	47
...	...	...	...
35	49	49	56

a. Obtain the residuals for covariance model (25.26).

b. For each treatment, plot the residuals against the fitted values. Also prepare a normal probability plot of the residuals and calculate the coefficient of correlation between the ordered residuals and their expected values under normality. What do you conclude from your analysis?

c. State the generalized regression model to be employed for testing whether or not the treatment regression lines have the same slope. Conduct this test using $\alpha = .005$. State the alternatives, decision rule, and conclusion. What is the P-value of the test?

25.18. Refer to **Eye contact effect** Problems 19.12 and 25.17. Assume that covariance model (25.26) is applicable.

a. State the regression model equivalent to covariance model (25.26) for this case; use $1, -1, 0$ indicator variables. Fit this full model.

b. State the reduced regression models for testing for interaction and factor A and factor B main effects, respectively. Fit these reduced regression models.

c. Test for interaction effects; use $\alpha = .01$. State the alternatives, decision rule, and conclusion. What is the P-value of the test?

d. Test for factor A main effects; use $\alpha = .01$. State the alternatives, decision rule, and conclusion. What is the P-value of the test?

e. Test for factor B main effects; use $\alpha = .01$. State the alternatives, decision rule, and conclusion. What is the P-value of the test?

f. Compare the gender main effects by means of a 99 percent confidence interval. Interpret your interval estimate.

g. Estimate the mean success rating by female personnel officers aged 40 when eye contact is present; use a 99 percent confidence interval.

√ 25.19. Refer to **Productivity improvement** Problems 25.7 and 25.8. The analyst is considering the use of the difference between the productivity improvements in the two years $(Y_{ij} - X_{ij})$ as the response variable with the regular analysis of variance model (25.29a).

a. Obtain the analysis of variance table.

b. How effective here is the use of differences with the regular ANOVA model compared to the use of covariance model (25.3)? Discuss.

25.20. Refer to **Product display** Problems 25.13 and 25.14. The analyst is considering the use of the difference in sales between the two periods $(Y_{ij} - X_{ij})$ as the response variable with the regular analysis of variance model (25.29a).

a. Obtain the analysis of variance table.

b. How effective here is the use of differences with the regular ANOVA model compared to the use of covariance model (25.3)? Discuss.

Exercise

25.21. (Calculus needed.) Denote $\mu_\cdot + \tau_i$ in covariance model (25.3) by Δ_i. Derive the least squares estimators for Δ_i and γ in covariance model (25.3).

Projects

25.22. Refer to the **SENIC** data set. The following hospitals are to be considered in a study of the effects of region (variable 9) on the mean length of hospital stay of patients (variable 2), with available facilities and services (variable 12) as a concomitant variable:

> 1–52   54   55   57   58   63   76   83   84   94   101   103   111

a. Obtain the residuals for covariance model (25.3).

b. For each region, plot the residuals against the fitted values. Also prepare a normal probability plot of the residuals and calculate the coefficient of correlation between the ordered residuals and their expected values under normality. What do you conclude from your analysis?

c. State the generalized regression model to be employed for testing whether or not the treatment regression lines have the same slope. Conduct this test using $\alpha = .005$. State the alternatives, decision rule, and conclusion. What is the P-value of the test?

25.23. Refer to the **SENIC** data set and Project 25.22. Assume that covariance model (25.3) is applicable.

a. Prepare a symbolic scatter plot of the data. Does it appear that there are region effects on the mean length of hospital stay? Discuss.

b. State the regression model equivalent to covariance model (25.3) for this case; use $1, -1, 0$ indicator variables. Also state the reduced regression model for testing for treatment effects.

c. Fit the full and reduced regression models and test for treatment effects; use $\alpha = .05$. State the alternatives, decision rule, and conclusion. What is the P-value of the test?

d. Make all pairwise comparisons between the region effects; use either the Bonferroni or the Scheffé procedure with a 90 percent family confidence coefficient, whichever is more efficient. State your findings.

25.24. Refer to the **SMSA** data set. The following metropolitan areas are to be considered in a study of the effects of region (factor A: variable 12) and percent of population in central cities (factor B: variable 4) on crime rate (variable 11 $\div$ variable 3), with percent of population 65 or older (variable 5) as a concomitant variable:

1–45	49	51–54	58	60–62	64	66	71
73	80	92	101	123	130	131	

For purposes of this analysis of covariance study, percent of population in central cities is to be classified into two categories: 37.0 percent or less, 37.1 percent or more.

a. Obtain the residuals for covariance model (25.26).

b. For each treatment, plot the residuals against the fitted values. Also prepare a normal probability plot of the residuals and calculate the coefficient of correlation between the ordered residuals and their expected values under normality. What do you conclude from your analysis?

c. State the generalized regression model to be employed for testing whether or not the treatment regression lines have the same slope. Conduct this test using $\alpha = .001$. State the alternatives, decision rule, and conclusion. What is the P-value of the test?

25.25. Refer to the **SMSA** data set and Project 25.24. Assume that covariance model (25.26) is applicable.

a. State the regression model equivalent to covariance model (25.26) for this case; use $1, -1, 0$ indicator variables. Fit this full model.

b. State the reduced regression models for testing for interaction and factor A and factor B main effects, respectively. Fit these reduced regression models.

c. Test for interaction effects; use $\alpha = .01$. State the alternatives, decision rule, and conclusion. What is the P-value of the test?

d. Test for factor A main effects; use $\alpha = .01$. State the alternatives, decision rule, and conclusion. What is the P-value of the test?

e. Test for factor B main effects; use $\alpha = .01$. State the alternatives, decision rule, and conclusion. What is the P-value of the test?

f. Make all pairwise comparisons between the region main effects; use either the Bonferroni or the Scheffé procedure with a 95 percent family confidence coefficient, whichever is more efficient. State your findings.

PART VII Study Designs

Design of Experiments, Randomization, and Sample Size Planning

Formal experimentation is widely employed in the biological and social sciences. It has come of age more recently in business, engineering, and economics. One example is an experiment conducted to investigate the best level of aggregation of company data furnished to middle management by a management information system. Another is an experiment on the effect of a guaranteed annual income on the consumption behavior of families. The latter experiment was designed by dividing designated low-income families at random into two groups; the families in the first group received income supplements up to a guaranteed annual income while the families in the second group received no supplements. The consumption behavior of the families in each group was then observed.

There are many types of experimental designs that are widely used. Up to this point we have considered only the analysis of experimental data from studies based on a completely randomized design. We shall examine in this part some important other experimental designs.

We begin this chapter by considering the major elements of any experimental design and the statistical contributions to effective experimental designs. We then take up three methods for planning sample sizes in ANOVA studies. In succeeding chapters, we shall discuss randomized block designs and other widely used experimental designs.

26.1 Design of Experiments

The *design of an experiment* refers to the structure of the experiment, with particular reference to:

1. The set of treatments included in the study.

2. The set of experimental units included in the study.

3. The rules and procedures by which the treatments are assigned to the experimental units (or vice versa).

4. The measurements that are made on the experimental units after the treatments have been applied.

Statistical designs for experiments are concerned with the third element—the rules and procedures whereby treatments are assigned to the experimental units. Statistical methodology also makes contributions to the other elements of experimental design, but we shall dwell chiefly on how to assign the treatments to experimental units so that efficient use is made of the experimental units.

Use of improper rules and procedures in assigning the treatments to experimental units can lead to serious difficulties. For instance, in a medical study designed to compare a standard treatment to a potentially risky new treatment, the group of patients undergoing the new treatment consisted of volunteers. These volunteers were less healthy at the beginning of the study than the patients receiving the standard treatment. Despite the fact that both the standard and new treatments were equally effective, the analysis of the health conditions of the patients at the end of the study showed a significant difference between the two groups, namely, that the new treatment group was in poorer health. A conclusion that the new treatment is therefore less effective would be biased. The source of bias here is called *selection bias* because the experimental units for the two treatment groups were not similar. Selection bias can be minimized by randomization. The use of randomization tends to balance the experimental units in each treatment group with regard to factors, other than the treatment, that affect the outcome.

The measurement process is another important element of experimental designs. Ideally, the measurement process should produce measurements that are unbiased and precise. *Measurement bias* can cause serious difficulties in the analysis of a study. An important source of measurement bias is due to unrecognized differences in the evaluation process. For example, a group of plants randomly assigned to a new fungicide treatment might unintentionally be evaluated by the investigators to be responding better to the treatment than actually is the case because of a desire to show the new treatment to be effective. When the experimental unit is a person, knowledge of the treatment by the person may also influence the measurement obtained. For instance, a person who knows that the food additive is salt may respond differently in the evaluation of the tastiness of a vegetable than if the additive were unknown. This source of measurement bias can be minimized by concealing the treatment assignment to both the experimental subject and the evaluator. A study using this kind of concealment is called a *double-blind study*. When knowledge of the assignment is withheld only from the experimental subject or the evaluator, the study is called a *single-blind study*.

26.2 Contributions of Statistics to Experimentation

Statistics has made a number of important contributions to experimentation. We consider briefly four major ones.

Factorial Experiments

This contribution was considered in Chapter 19. There we noted that multifactor investigations permit the analysis of a number of factors with the same precision as if the entire experiment had been devoted to the study of only one factor. In addition, one factorial experiment provides information on interaction effects while the classical one-factor-at-a-time approach requires a series of experiments for doing so.

Replication

Replication refers to the repetition of an experiment. Consider an experiment consisting of three treatments. The assignment of three experimental units at random, one to each treatment, constitutes one replication of the experiment. The assignment of an additional three experimental units at random to the three treatments constitutes a second replication, and so on.

Not all repetitions are replications. Suppose that two incentive pay plans are being investigated and that two plants are used in the study, with one plant assigned to each incentive plan. Assume now that 10 employees in each plant are selected and their productivity measured. For purposes of comparing the incentive pay plans, the plants are the experimental units so that there is only one replication (one plant for each plan), not 10 (the number of employees studied in each plant). Indeed, with only one replication here, plant effects and incentive pay plan effects cannot be disentangled and are said to be confounded. Selecting additional employees will not permit a disentangling of the incentive pay plan effects from the plant effects; only repetition of the experiment in additional plants (i.e., replicating the experiment) will permit this.

Replication makes it possible to assess the error mean square, which is required for testing the presence of treatment effects or for establishing confidence interval estimates of these effects, as we have seen in earlier chapters. Replication also plays a second role; namely, it permits control over the precision of the estimates or the power of the tests through manipulation of the replication (sample) size. We shall discuss this use in later sections of this chapter.

Randomization

Randomization in experiments is a relatively recent idea, first introduced by the famous British statistician Sir R. A. Fisher. In the past, treatments had been assigned to experimental units either on a systematic or on a subjective basis. We noted earlier how serious biases can arise when self-selection is employed to assign experimental units to the treatments. The same dangers exist with systematic and subjective selection. For instance, consider an experiment using 10 employees and two treatments, where the first five employees on the payroll listing are assigned treatment 1 and the next five treatment 2. Suppose that the payroll listing is by seniority, and that experience is related to productivity, the phenomenon under study. A comparison of treatments 1 and 2 then will reflect not only differences between the two treatments but also differences in the amount of experience between the two groups of employees. This potential bias may be so transparent that no good experimenter would use the type of systematic assignment just described. Nevertheless, there may be many other sources of bias in systematic selection that are not so apparent.

Subjective assignments of treatments to experimental units can also lead to selection bias, as when an experimenter subconsciously tends to assign one treatment to highly extrovert subjects and the other treatment to less extrovert subjects.

With randomization, the treatments are assigned to experimental units at random. Randomization tends to average out between the treatments whatever systematic effects may be present, apparent or hidden, so that comparisons between treatments measure only the pure treatment effects. Thus, randomization tends to eliminate the influence of extraneous factors not under the direct control of the experimenter and thereby precludes the presence of selection bias. Cochran and Cox (Ref. 26.1, p. 8) have likened randomization to an insurance policy in that it is a precaution against biases that may or may not occur.

Randomization is appropriate not only for the assignment of treatments to experimental units but also for any other phases of the experiment where systematic effects not under the control of the experimenter may be present. For instance, consider an experiment in which five treatments (alternative methods of measuring subjective probability) are studied and 20 subjects are used. Only one subject can be run per day; thus, four weeks are required to complete the experiment. In this type of situation, it usually is highly desirable to determine the order of the treatments randomly since a variety of systematic time effects could be present. The experimenter may with time improve the explanation of the methods of measuring subjective probability, there may be a streak of extremely hot weather during a week, and the like. With these possible time effects, a systematic assignment of one treatment per week could lead to seriously biased results. Randomization, on the other hand, will tend to average out whatever systematic effects are present, whether anticipated or not.

Advice on when randomization is needed in addition to the assignment of treatments to experimental units can only be general. Certainly, randomization should be employed whenever the consequences of systematic effects could be serious. In our illustration of a study on methods of measuring subjective probability, suppose that two observers conduct the experiment. Randomization of observers to treatment-experimental unit combinations would then be highly desirable, since large differences between observers are known to occur in this kind of situation. If the seriousness of the consequences is not known, the safe course is to randomize when it is feasible and not too costly. If randomization cannot be carried out easily and no serious consequences of systematic effects are anticipated, the experimenter may be willing to forgo randomization. The experimenter must then realize, however, that the validity of the treatment comparisons depends on the absence of serious systematic effects.

Randomization also can provide the basis for making inferences without requiring assumptions about the distribution of the error terms. We shall discuss this use of randomization in Section 26.3.

Comments

1. The implications of randomization may be viewed in a somewhat different fashion than that presented so far. The random errors of experimental units that are adjacent in time or space are often correlated, not independent, as a result of various systematic effects over time or space. Randomization does not erase this correlation pattern but, by making it equally likely that any two treatments are adjacent, tends to eliminate the correlations between treatments with increasing replications. Thus, randomization makes it reasonable to analyze the data as though the model random error terms are independent, an assumption that has been made in almost all models discussed so far.

2. Occasionally, randomization may provide a pattern that makes the experimenter uneasy. For instance, randomization of the time sequence in which four experimental units are exposed to treatment 1 and four exposed to treatment 2 may result in a randomized sequence where the four experimental units for treatment 1 are exposed first and then the four experimental units for treatment 2 are exposed. This is not a likely occurrence, but one that can take place. Some solutions have been suggested for this problem, but none provides a final answer. In practice, the experimenter typically will discard a randomization sequence that has apparent dangers of systematic effects for the particular experiment and select another randomization. ∎

Local Control

The fourth contribution of statistics to experimental design is the concept of local control, which often is considered statistical design proper. Local control is intended to reduce experimental errors and make the experiment more powerful by suitable restrictions on the randomization of treatments to experimental units. Consider again the study of five methods of measuring subjective probability, which is to be conducted over a period of four weeks. The thought may have occurred in our earlier discussion that complete randomization might not provide full balance of all treatments within the four-week period. Would it not be better if we required that each week contain each of the five treatments once? If a substantial time effect is likely, it would indeed be desirable to use this form of restricted randomization, called *blocking*. Thus, we would randomize the order of treatments subject to the restriction that each treatment occur once in each week. It will be seen in Chapter 27 that if a time effect is present, blocking by time will lead to more precise results than complete randomization.

Let us consider this same example from a slightly different point of view. With unrestricted randomization, the five observations in a single replication of the experiment will differ among themselves because of treatment effects, because of time effects (since the treatments may end up in any of the four weeks), and so on. If we require that each of the five treatments be conducted in each week, then a week's observations constitute a replication. Within such a replication, the observations will differ again because of treatment effects and a variety of other causes, but not because of any time effects from one week to another. The only effect of time that is left is that within a week, and that may be anticipated to be substantially smaller than the effect between weeks. Thus, blocking by week will reduce the experimental error variability when a time effect is present, and in this way will make the experiment more powerful.

Another benefit of blocking is that it can increase the range of validity for the conclusions from the experiment. In general, experimental errors can be made smaller (i.e., the variance of the random component ε can be made smaller) by using homogeneous experimental units, leading to more precise experimental results. For instance, in a learning experiment, the use of persons of the same age, intelligence, and economic and social background will tend to lead to smaller experimental errors than if a more heterogeneous group of subjects were used. However, the more homogeneous the experimental units, the smaller is the range for which the experimental results are valid. For instance, findings for persons in one age group may not be valid for persons in other age groups. Thus, to make the conclusions broadly valid, the characteristics of experimental units should vary, but the cost of this variability is less precision in the experimental results. Blocking of experimental units according to their characteristics (e.g., by age) can be employed to have one's cake and eat it too, namely, to have sufficient variability between experimental units for a wide range of validity and yet achieve high precision due to small experimental errors.

Blocking by characteristics of the experimental units can be particularly helpful in business, economics, and the life sciences. The experimental units utilized in these areas are frequently highly heterogeneous—for example, persons, families, towns, metropolitan areas. Blocking people by age or income or blocking towns by population size may be highly effective in reducing the experimental error variability.

In large-scale experimental studies, local control is often obtained by means of *stratification* of the experimental units. For instance, in a large clinical trial of three treatments, where age and gender may affect the outcome of interest, the persons available for the study may be randomly assigned to the treatments so that they are balanced according to age and gender. In this way, the three treatment samples are stratified to achieve local control.

26.3 Randomization Tests

As we mentioned earlier, randomization can provide the basis for making inferences without requiring assumptions about the distribution of the error terms ε. Consider factor effects model (16.62) for a single-factor study:

$$Y_{ij} = \mu. + \tau_i + \varepsilon_{ij}$$

Rather than assuming that the ε_{ij} are independent normal random variables with mean zero and constant variance σ^2, we shall now consider each ε_{ij} to be a fixed effect associated with the experimental unit. In this framework, we view the n_T experimental units to be a finite population, and associated with each unit is the unit-specific effect ε_{ij}. When randomization assigns this experimental unit to treatment i, the observed response will be $Y_{ij} = \mu. + \tau_i + \varepsilon_{ij}$. The response Y_{ij} is still a random variable, but under the randomization view the randomness arises because the treatment effect τ_i is the result of a random assignment of the experimental unit to treatment i.

If there are no treatment effects, that is, if all $\tau_i = 0$, then the response $Y_{ij} = \mu. + \varepsilon_{ij}$ depends only on the experimental unit. Since with randomization the experimental unit is equally likely to be assigned to any treatment, the observed response Y_{ij}, if there are no treatment effects, could with equal likelihood have been observed for any of the treatments. Thus, when there are no treatment effects, randomization will lead to an assignment of the finite population of n_T observations Y_{ij} to the treatments such that all treatment combinations of observations are equally likely. This, in turn, leads to an exact sampling distribution of the test statistic under H_0: $\tau_i \equiv 0$, sometimes termed the *randomization distribution* of the test statistic. Percentiles of the randomization distribution can then be used to test for the presence of factor effects. This use of the randomization distribution provides the basis of a nonparametric test for treatment effects.

To illustrate the concept of a randomization distribution, consider a single-factor experiment consisting of two treatments and two replications. In this experiment, the alternatives of interest are:

$$H_0: \tau_1 = \tau_2 = 0$$

$$H_a: \text{ not both } \tau_1 \text{ and } \tau_2 \text{ equal zero}$$

Test statistic F^* in (16.55) will be used to conduct the test. The sample results are:

Treatment 1 Y_{1j}	Treatment 2 Y_{2j}
3	8
7	10

For these data, $F^* = 3.20$.

Since the treatments are assigned to experimental units at random, it would have been just as likely, if there are no treatment effects, to have observed 3 and 8 for treatment 1 and 7 and 10 for treatment 2. In that event, the test statistic would have been $F^* = 1.06$. In fact, any division of the four observations into two groups of size two is equally likely with randomization if there are no treatment effects. Because this experiment is small, we can easily list all $4!/(2!2!) = 6$ possible outcomes of the experiment, assuming no treatment effects are present:

Randomization	Treatment 1	Treatment 2	F^*	Probability
1	3, 7	8, 10	3.20	1/6
2	3, 8	7, 10	1.06	1/6
3	3, 10	8, 7	.08	1/6
4	8, 7	3, 10	.08	1/6
5	7, 10	3, 8	1.06	1/6
6	8, 10	3, 7	3.20	1/6

The last two columns give the randomization distribution of test statistic F^* under H_0. Randomization assures us that, when H_0 is true, each possible value of the test statistic has probability 1/6. From the randomization distribution, we see that the P-value for the test is the probability:

$$P\{F^* \geq 3.20\} = \frac{2}{6} = .33$$

This P-value is somewhat different than the usual (normal theory) P-value:

$$P\{F(1, 2) \geq 3.20\} = .22$$

In this instance, because the sample sizes are very small, the F distribution does not provide a particularly good approximation to the exact sampling distribution of F^* under H_0. However, both empirical and theoretical studies have shown that the F distribution is a good approximation to the exact randomization distribution when the sample sizes are not small. Thus, randomization alone can justify the F test as a good approximate test, without requiring any assumption of independent, normal error terms. We shall next demonstrate the use of the randomization test in a more realistic setting.

Note

Because of the discreteness of the randomization distribution, it is conservative to define the P-value as the probability of equaling or exceeding the observed value of the test statistic when H_0 holds. For continuous sampling distributions, it does not matter whether the P-value is defined as the probability of exceeding the observed value of the test statistic or as the probability of equaling or exceeding it. For instance, $P\{F(1, 2) > 3.20\} = P\{F(1, 2) \geq 3.20\}$. ∎

Example

A manufacturer of children's plastic toys considered the introduction of statistical process control (SPC) and engineering process control (EPC) in order to reduce the volume of scrap and rework at each of its nine manufacturing plants. To assess the effects of these quality practices, a single-factor experiment was conducted for a six-month period. The treatments were:

Treatment i	Quality Practice
1	None (control group)
2	SPC
3	Both SPC and EPC

The three treatments were each randomly assigned to three of the nine available plants. The response of interest was the reduction in the defect rate at the end of the six-month trial period. The results are given in the first row (randomization 1) in Table 26.1. Management

TABLE 26.1 **Randomization Samples and Test Statistics—Quality Control Example.**

Randomi- zation	Treatment 1			Treatment 2			Treatment 3			F^*	Proba- bility
1	1.1,	.5,	−2.1	4.2,	3.7,	.8	3.2,	2.8,	6.3	4.39	1/1,680
2	1.1,	.5,	−2.1	4.2,	3.7,	3.2	.8,	2.8,	6.3	3.74	1/1,680
3	1.1,	.5,	−2.1	4.2,	3.7,	2.8	3.2,	.8,	6.3	3.67	1/1,680
. . .	. . .			. . .			. . .			. . .	. . .
1,680	3.2,	2.8,	6.3	4.2,	3.7,	.8	1.1,	.5,	−2.1	4.39	1/1,680

wishes to test whether or not the mean reduction in the defect rate is the same for the three treatments:

$$H_0: \tau_1 = \tau_2 = \tau_3 = 0$$

$$H_a: \text{not all } \tau_i \text{ equal zero}$$

The risk of a Type I error is to be controlled at $\alpha = .10$. We shall now conduct this test by obtaining the exact randomization distribution.

In this experimental study, there are $9!/(3!3!3!) = 1,680$ possible combinations of assigning the nine experimental units to the three treatments. A computer program was utilized to enumerate these 1,680 combinations and to calculate the F^* statistic for each. A partial listing of results is presented in Table 26.1.

Of the 1,680 possible values of the test statistic F^*, 126 were equal to or greater than the observed value 4.39. Thus, from the randomization distribution we find:

$$P\text{-value} = P\{F^* \geq 4.39\} = \frac{126}{1,680} = .075$$

Since $.075 < \alpha = .10$, we conclude that the mean reduction in the defect rate is not the same for the three treatments.

Even though the sample sizes are not very large here, the exact randomization distribution is well approximated by the F distribution. Figure 26.1 shows both the randomization distribution in the form of a histogram and the density function for the corresponding F distribution, $F(2, 6)$. Note how well the F distribution approximates the randomization distribution. The P-value according to the F distribution is $P\{F(2, 6) \geq 4.39\} = .067$. This is very close to the randomization P-value of .075.

26.4 Planning of Sample Sizes with Power Approach

For analysis of variance studies, as for other statistical studies, it is important to plan the sample sizes so that needed protection against both Type I and Type II errors can be obtained, or so that the estimates of interest have sufficient precision to be useful. This planning is necessary for both observational and experimental ANOVA studies to ensure that the sample sizes are large enough to detect important differences with high probability. At the same time, the sample sizes should not be so large that the cost of the study becomes excessive and that unimportant differences become statistically significant with high probability. Planning of sample sizes is therefore an integral part of the design of an analysis of variance study.

FIGURE 26.1 **Randomization Distribution of F^* and Corresponding F Distribution—Quality Control Example.**

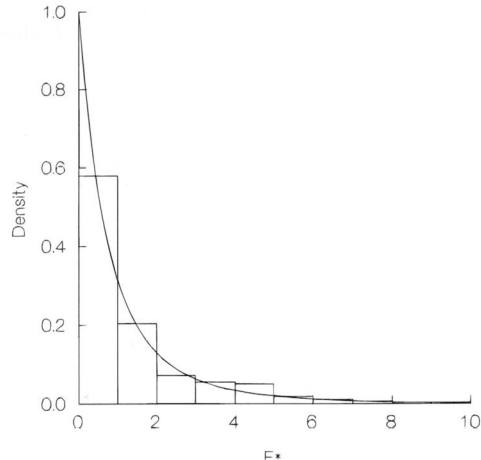

We shall generally assume in our discussion of planning sample sizes that all treatments are to have equal sample sizes, reflecting that they are about equally important. Indeed, when major interest lies in pairwise comparisons of all treatment means, it can be shown that equal sample sizes maximize the precision of the comparisons. Another reason for equal sample sizes is that certain departures from the assumed ANOVA model are less troublesome if all factor levels have the same sample size, as noted earlier.

There will be times, however, when unequal sample sizes are appropriate. For instance, when four experimental treatments are each to be compared to a control, it may be reasonable to make the sample size for the control larger. We shall comment later on the planning of sample sizes for such a case.

Planning of sample sizes can be approached in terms of (1) controlling the risks of making Type I and Type II errors, (2) controlling the widths of desired confidence intervals, or (3) a combination of these two. The procedures for planning sample sizes that we shall discuss here are applicable to both observational studies and to experimental studies based on a completely randomized design. In later chapters, we shall consider the planning of sample sizes for other experimental designs. In this section, we consider planning of sample sizes with the power approach, which permits controlling the risks of making Type I and Type II errors. In Section 26.5, we take up planning of sample sizes to control the precision of estimates of important effects. Finally, in Section 26.6 we discuss planning of sample sizes when the best treatment is to be identified.

Before we can discuss planning of sample sizes with the power approach, we need to consider the power of the F test.

Power of F Test

Single-Factor Studies. By the power of the F test for a single-factor study, we refer to the probability that the decision rule will lead to conclusion H_a, that the treatment means differ, when in fact H_a holds. Specifically, the power is given by the following expression for fixed cell means model (16.2):

(26.1) $$\text{Power} = P\{F^* > F(1 - \alpha; r - 1, n_T - r) | \phi\}$$

where ϕ is the *noncentrality parameter*, that is, a measure of how unequal the treatment means μ_i are:

(26.1a) $$\phi = \frac{1}{\sigma} \sqrt{\frac{\sum n_i (\mu_i - \mu.)^2}{r}}$$

and:

(26.1b) $$\mu. = \frac{\sum n_i \mu_i}{n_T}$$

When all factor level samples are of equal size n, the parameter ϕ becomes:

(26.2) $$\phi = \frac{1}{\sigma} \sqrt{\frac{n}{r} \sum (\mu_i - \mu.)^2} \qquad \text{when} \quad n_i \equiv n$$

where:

(26.2a) $$\mu. = \frac{\sum \mu_i}{r}$$

Power probabilities are determined by utilizing the noncentral F distribution since this is the sampling distribution of F^* when H_a holds. The resulting calculations are quite complex. We present a series of tables in Appendix Table B.11 that can be used readily to look up power probabilities directly. The proper table to use depends on the number of factor levels and the level of significance employed in the decision rule. Specifically, Table B.11 is used as follows:

1. Each page refers to a different v_1, the number of degrees of freedom for the numerator of F^*. For ANOVA model (16.2), $v_1 = r - 1$, or the number of factor levels minus one. Table B.11 contains power tables for $v_1 = 2, 3, 4, 5,$ and 6, as shown at the top of each page.

2. Two levels of significance, denoted by α, are presented in Table B.11, namely, $\alpha = .05$ and $\alpha = .01$. The upper table on each page refers to $\alpha = .05$ and the lower table to $\alpha = .01$.

3. Within each table, the rows refer to different values of v_2, the degrees of freedom for the denominator of F^*. The columns refer to different values of ϕ, the noncentrality parameter defined in (26.1a). For ANOVA model (16.2), $v_2 = n_T - r$.

Examples.

1. Consider the case where $v_1 = 2$, $v_2 = 10$, $\phi = 3$, and $\alpha = .05$. We then find from Table B.11 (p. 1356) that the power is $1 - \beta = .98$.

2. Suppose that for the Kenton Food Company example in Chapter 16, the analyst wishes to determine the power of the decision rule on page 691 when there are substantial differences between the factor level means. Specifically, the analyst wishes to consider the

case when $\mu_1 = 12.5$, $\mu_2 = 13$, $\mu_3 = 18$, and $\mu_4 = 21$. The weighted mean in (26.1b) therefore is:

$$\mu. = \frac{5(12.5) + 5(13) + 4(18) + 5(21)}{19} - 16.03$$

Thus, the specified value of ϕ is:

$$\phi = \frac{1}{\sigma} \left[\frac{5(-3.53)^2 + 5(-3.03)^2 + 4(1.97)^2 + 5(4.97)^2}{4} \right]^{1/2}$$

$$= \frac{1}{\sigma}(7.86)$$

Note that we still need to know σ, the standard deviation of the error terms ε_{ij} in the model. Suppose that from past experience it is known that $\sigma = 2.5$ cases approximately. Then we have:

$$\phi = \frac{1}{2.5}(7.86) = 3.14$$

Further, we have for this example:

$$\nu_1 = r - 1 = 3 \qquad \nu_2 = n_T - r = 15 \qquad \alpha = .05$$

The table on page 1357 indicates that the power is $1 - \beta = 1.00$. In other words, there are 100 chances in 100 that the decision rule, based on the sample sizes employed, will lead to the detection of differences in the mean sales volumes for the four package designs when the differences are the ones specified earlier.

Comments

1. Any given value of ϕ encompasses many different combinations of factor level means μ_i. Thus, in the Kenton Food Company example, the means $\mu_1 = 12.5$, $\mu_2 = 13$, $\mu_3 = 18$, $\mu_4 = 21$ and the means $\mu_1 = 21$, $\mu_2 = 12.5$, $\mu_3 = 18$, $\mu_4 = 13$ lead to the same value of $\phi = 3.14$ and hence to the same power.

2. The larger ϕ—that is, the larger the differences between the factor level means—the greater the power and hence the smaller the probability of making a Type II error for a given risk α of making a Type I error. Also, the smaller the specified α risk, the smaller is the power for any given ϕ, and hence the larger the risk of a Type II error.

3. Since many single-factor studies are undertaken because of the expectation that the factor level means differ and it is desired to investigate these differences, the α risk used in constructing the decision rule for determining whether or not the factor level means are equal is often set relatively high (e.g., .05 or .10 instead of .01) so as to increase the power of the test.

4. The power table for $\nu_1 = 1$ is not reproduced in Table B.11 since this case corresponds to the comparison of two population means. As noted previously, the F test is the equivalent of the two-sided t test for this case, and the power tables for the two-sided t test presented in Table B.5 can then be used, with noncentrality parameter:

(26.3)
$$\delta = \frac{|\mu_1 - \mu_2|}{\sigma\sqrt{\dfrac{1}{n_1} + \dfrac{1}{n_2}}}$$

and degrees of freedom $n_1 + n_2 - 2$. ∎

Multifactor Studies. Table B.11 can be used for determining the power of tests for multifactor studies in the same fashion as for single-factor studies. The only differences arise in the definition of the noncentrality parameter and the degrees of freedom. For two-factor fixed effects ANOVA model (19.23) with equal treatment sample sizes, the noncentrality parameter ϕ and the degrees of freedom ν_1 and ν_2 for testing for interaction effects, factor A main effects, and factor B main effects are as follows:

(26.4a)   Test for interactions:

$$\phi = \frac{1}{\sigma} \sqrt{\frac{n \, \Sigma \Sigma (\alpha\beta)_{ij}^2}{(a-1)(b-1)+1}} = \frac{1}{\sigma} \sqrt{\frac{n \, \Sigma \Sigma (\mu_{ij} - \mu_{i.} - \mu_{.j} + \mu_{..})^2}{(a-1)(b-1)+1}}$$

$$\nu_1 = (a-1)(b-1) \qquad \nu_2 = ab(n-1)$$

(26.4b)   Test for A main effects:

$$\phi = \frac{1}{\sigma} \sqrt{\frac{nb \, \Sigma \alpha_i^2}{a}} = \frac{1}{\sigma} \sqrt{\frac{nb \, \Sigma (\mu_{i.} - \mu_{..})^2}{a}}$$

$$\nu_1 = a-1 \qquad \nu_2 = ab(n-1)$$

(26.4c)   Test for B main effects:

$$\phi = \frac{1}{\sigma} \sqrt{\frac{na \, \Sigma \beta_j^2}{b}} = \frac{1}{\sigma} \sqrt{\frac{na \, \Sigma (\mu_{.j} - \mu_{..})^2}{b}}$$

$$\nu_1 = b-1 \qquad \nu_2 = ab(n-1)$$

For three-factor fixed effects ANOVA model (23.14) with equal treatment sample sizes, the noncentrality parameter ϕ for a given test is defined as follows:

(26.5) $$\phi = \frac{1}{\sigma} \left[\frac{\text{numerator of second term in } E\{MS\} \text{ in Table 23.2}}{\text{denominator of second term in } E\{MS\} \text{ plus } 1} \right]^{1/2}$$

For example, for testing for three-factor interactions, we have:

$$\phi = \frac{1}{\sigma} \left[\frac{n \, \Sigma \Sigma \Sigma (\alpha\beta\gamma)_{ijk}^2}{(a-1)(b-1)(c-1)+1} \right]^{1/2}$$

Example.   For the test of A main effects (display height) in the Castle Bakery two-factor example of Chapter 19, we wish to find the power of the test when $\mu_1. = 50, \mu_2. = 55$, and $\mu_3. = 45$ or, equivalently, when $\alpha_1 = 0, \alpha_2 = 5$, and $\alpha_3 = -5$. Assume that we know from past experience that $\sigma = 3$ cases. We have for this test from Table 19.7:

$$n = 2 \qquad a = 3 \qquad b = 2 \qquad \alpha = .05$$

Using (26.4b), we obtain:

$$\phi = \frac{1}{3} \sqrt{\frac{2(2)[(0)^2 + (5)^2 + (-5)^2]}{3}} = 2.7$$

$$\nu_1 = 3 - 1 = 2 \qquad \nu_2 = 3(2)(2 - 1) = 6$$

For $\nu_1 = 2, \nu_2 = 6, \alpha = .05$, and $\phi = 2.7$, we find from Table B.11 that the (interpolated) power is about .89. Thus, if $\mu_1. = 50, \mu_2. = 55$, and $\mu_3. = 45$ (and $\sigma = 3$), the probability is about .89 that the F test will detect the differences in the display height means.

Use of Table B.12 for Single-Factor Studies

The power approach in planning sample sizes can be implemented by use of the power tables for F tests presented in Table B.11. A trial-and-error process is required, however, with these tables. Instead, we shall use other tables that furnish the appropriate sample sizes directly. Table B.12 presents sample size determinations that are applicable when all treatments are to have equal sample sizes and all effects are fixed.

The planning of sample sizes for single-factor studies with fixed factor levels using Table B.12 is done in terms of the noncentrality parameter (26.2) for equal sample sizes. However, instead of requiring a direct specification of the levels of μ_i for which it is important to control the risk of making a Type II error, Table B.12 only requires a specification of the minimum range of factor level means for which it is important to detect differences between the μ_i with high probability. This minimum range is denoted by Δ:

(26.6) $$\Delta = \max(\mu_i) - \min(\mu_i)$$

The following three specifications need to be made in using Table B.12:

1. The level α at which the risk of making a Type I error is to be controlled.
2. The magnitude of the minimum range Δ of the μ_i which it is important to detect with high probability. The magnitude of σ, the standard deviation of the probability distributions of Y, must also be specified since entry into Table B.12 is in terms of the ratio:

(26.7) $$\frac{\Delta}{\sigma}$$

3. The level β at which the risk of making a Type II error is to be controlled for the specification given in 2. Entry into Table B.12 is in terms of the power $1 - \beta$.

When using Table B.12, four α levels are available at which the risk of making a Type I error can be controlled ($\alpha = .2, .1, .05, .01$). The Type II error risk can be controlled at one of four β levels ($\beta = .3, .2, .1, .05$) through the specification of the power $1 - \beta$. Table B.12 provides necessary sample sizes for studies consisting of $r = 2, \ldots, 10$ factor levels or treatments.

Example.   A company owning a large fleet of trucks wishes to determine whether or not four different brands of snow tires have the same mean tread life (in thousands of miles). It is important to conclude that the four brands of snow tires have different mean tread lives when the difference between the means of the best and worst brands is 3 (thousand miles) or more. Thus, the minimum range specification is $\Delta = 3$. It is known from past experience that the standard deviation of the tread lives of these tires is $\sigma = 2$ (thousand miles), approximately. Management would like to control the risks of making incorrect decisions at the following levels:

$$\alpha = .05$$

$$\beta = .10 \quad \text{or} \quad \text{Power} = 1 - \beta = .90$$

Entering Table B.12 for $\Delta/\sigma = 3/2 = 1.5$, $\alpha = .05$, $1 - \beta = .90$, and $r = 4$, we find $n = 14$. Hence, 14 snow tires of each brand need to be tested in order to control the risks of making incorrect decisions at the desired levels.

Specification of Δ/σ Directly.   Table B.12 can also be used when the minimum range is specified directly in units of the standard deviation σ. Let the specification of Δ in this case be $k\sigma$ so that we have by (26.7):

$$\frac{\Delta}{\sigma} = \frac{k\sigma}{\sigma} = k$$

Hence, Table B.12 is entered directly for the specified value k with this approach.

Example.   Suppose it is specified in the snow tires example that it is important to detect differences between the mean tread lives if the range of the mean tread lives is $k = 2$ standard deviations or more. Suppose also that the other specifications are:

$$\alpha = .10$$

$$\beta = .05 \quad \text{or} \quad \text{Power} = 1 - \beta = .95$$

From Table B.12, we find for $k = 2$ and $r = 4$ that $n = 9$ tires will need to be tested for each brand in order that the specified risk protection will be achieved.

Note

While specifying Δ/σ directly does not require an advance planning value of the standard deviation σ, this is not of as much advantage as it might seem because a meaningful specification of Δ in units of σ will frequently require knowledge of the approximate magnitude of the standard deviation. ∎

Some Further Comments on Use of Table B.12.

1. The exact specification of Δ/σ has great effect on the sample sizes n when Δ/σ is small, but it has much less effect when Δ/σ is large. For instance, when $r = 3$, $\alpha = .05$, and $\beta = .10$, we have from Table B.12:

Δ/σ	n
1.0	27
1.5	13
2.0	8
2.5	6

Thus, unless Δ/σ is quite small, one need not be too concerned about some imprecision in specifying Δ/σ.

2. Reducing either the specified α or β risks or both increases the required sample sizes. For instance, when $r = 4$, $\alpha = .10$, and $\Delta/\sigma = 1.25$, we have:

β	$1 - \beta$	n
.20	.80	13
.10	.90	16
.05	.95	20

3. A moderate error in the advance planning value of σ can cause a substantial miscalculation of required sample sizes. For instance, when $r = 5$, $\alpha = .05$, $\beta = .10$, and $\Delta = 3$, we have:

σ	Δ/σ	n
1	3.0	5
2	1.5	15
3	1.0	32

In view of the usual approximate nature of the advance planning value of σ, it is generally desirable to investigate the needed sample sizes for a range of likely values of σ before deciding on the sample sizes to be employed.

4. Table B.12 is based on the noncentrality parameter ϕ in (26.2) even though no specification is made of the individual factor level means μ_i for which it is important to conclude that the factor level means differ. To see how Table B.12 utilizes the noncentrality parameter ϕ, consider again the snow tires example where $r = 4$ brands are to be tested and a minimum range of $\Delta = 3$ (thousand miles) of the four mean tread lives μ_i is to be detected with high probability. The following are some possible sets of values of the μ_i, each of which has range $\Delta = 3$:

Case	μ_1	μ_2	μ_3	μ_4	$\Sigma(\mu_i - \mu.)^2$
1	24	27	25	26	5.00
2	25	25	26	23	4.75
3	25	25	25	28	6.75
4	25	25	26.5	23.5	4.50

The term $\Sigma(\mu_i - \mu.)^2$ of the noncentrality parameter ϕ in (26.2) differs for each of these four possibilities and hence the power differs, even though the range is the same in all cases. Note that the term $\Sigma(\mu_i - \mu.)^2$ is smallest for case 4, where two factor level means are at $\mu.$ and the other two are equally spaced around $\mu.$. It can be shown that for a given range Δ, the term $\Sigma(\mu_i - \mu.)^2$ is minimized when all but two factor level means are at $\mu.$ and the two remaining factor level means are equally spaced around $\mu.$. Thus, we have:

$$(26.8) \qquad \min \sum_{i=1}^{r} (\mu_i - \mu.)^2 = \left(\frac{\Delta}{2}\right)^2 + \left(-\frac{\Delta}{2}\right)^2 + 0 + \cdots + 0 = \frac{\Delta^2}{2}$$

Since the power of the test varies directly with $\Sigma(\mu_i - \mu.)^2$, use of (26.8) in calculating Table B.12 ensures that the power is at least $1 - \beta$ for any combination of μ_i values with range Δ.   ∎

Use of Table B.12 for Multifactor Studies

When planning sample sizes for two-factor studies with the power approach, one is concerned typically with both the power of detecting factor A main effects and the power of detecting factor B main effects. One can first specify the minimum range of factor A level means for which it is important to detect factor A main effects, and obtain the needed sample sizes from Table B.12, with $r = a$. The resulting sample size is bn, from which n can be obtained readily. The use of Table B.12 for this purpose is appropriate provided the resulting sample size is not small, specifically provided $a(bn - 1) \geq 20$. If this condition is not met, the ANOVA power tables in Table B.11 should be used. These tables, as noted earlier, require an iterative approach for determining needed sample sizes.

In the same way, the minimum range of factor B level means can then be specified for which it is important to detect factor B main effects, and the needed sample sizes found. If the sample sizes obtained from the factor A and factor B power specifications differ substantially, a judgment will need to be made as to the final sample sizes.

When planning sample sizes for three-factor studies with the power approach, one is typically concerned with the power of detecting factor A main effects, the power of detecting factor B main effects, and the power of detecting factor C main effects. One can first specify the minimum range of factor A level means for which it is important to detect factor A main effects and obtain the needed sample sizes from Table B.12, with $r = a$. The resulting sample size is bcn, from which n can be obtained readily. The use of Table B.12 for this purpose is appropriate provided the resulting sample sizes are not small, specifically provided $a(bcn - 1) \geq 20$. If this condition is not met, the ANOVA power tables in Table B.11 should be used with an iterative approach.

In the same way, the values for the minimum range of factor level means for factors B and C can be specified for which it is important to detect the factor main effects, and the needed sample sizes found. If the sample sizes obtained from the factor A, factor B, and factor C power specifications differ substantially, a judgment will need to be made as to the final sample sizes.

26.5   Planning of Sample Sizes with Estimation Approach

The estimation approach to planning sample sizes may be used either in conjunction with the control of Type I and Type II errors or by itself. The essence of the approach is to specify the major comparisons of interest and to determine the expected widths of the confidence intervals for various sample sizes, given an advance planning value for the standard deviation σ. The approach is iterative, starting with an initial judgment of needed sample sizes. This initial judgment may be based on the needed sample sizes to control the risks of Type I and Type II errors when these have been obtained previously. If the anticipated widths of the confidence intervals based on the initial sample sizes are satisfactory, the iteration process is terminated. If one or more widths are too great, larger sample sizes need to be tried next. If the widths are narrower than they need be, smaller sample sizes should be tried next. This process is continued until those sample sizes are found that yield satisfactory anticipated widths for the important confidence intervals. We proceed to illustrate the estimation approach to planning sample sizes with three examples.

Example 1—Single-Factor Study

We are to plan sample sizes for the snow tires example by means of the estimation approach; the sample sizes for each tire brand are to be equal, that is, $n_i \equiv n$. Management wishes three types of estimates:

1. A comparison of the mean tread lives for each pair of brands:

$$\mu_i - \mu_{i'}$$

2. A comparison of the mean tread lives for the two high-priced brands (1 and 4) and the two low-priced brands (2 and 3):

$$\frac{\mu_1 + \mu_4}{2} - \frac{\mu_2 + \mu_3}{2}$$

3. A comparison of the mean tread lives for the national brands (1, 2, and 4) and the local brand (3):

$$\frac{\mu_1 + \mu_2 + \mu_4}{3} - \mu_3$$

Management further has indicated that it wishes a family confidence coefficient of .95 for the entire set of comparisons.

We first need a planning value for the standard deviation of the tread lives of tires. Suppose that from past experience we judge the standard deviation to be approximately $\sigma = 2$ (thousand miles). Next, we require an initial judgment of needed sample sizes and shall consider $n = 10$ as a starting point.

We know from (17.22) that the variance of an estimated contrast $\hat{L}$ when $n_i \equiv n$ is:

$$\sigma^2\{\hat{L}\} = \frac{\sigma^2}{n} \sum c_i^2 \qquad \text{when} \quad n_i \equiv n$$

Hence, given $\sigma = 2$ and $n = 10$, the anticipated values of the standard deviations of the required estimators are:

Contrast	Anticipated Variance	Anticipated Standard Deviation
Pairwise comparisons	$\frac{(2)^2}{10}[(1)^2 + (-1)^2] = .80$	.89
High- and low-priced brands	$\frac{(2)^2}{10}\left[\left(\frac{1}{2}\right)^2 + \left(\frac{1}{2}\right)^2 + \left(-\frac{1}{2}\right)^2 + \left(-\frac{1}{2}\right)^2\right] = .40$	.63
National and local brands	$\frac{(2)^2}{10}\left[\left(\frac{1}{3}\right)^2 + \left(\frac{1}{3}\right)^2 + \left(\frac{1}{3}\right)^2 + (-1)^2\right] = .53$	.73

We shall employ the Scheffé multiple comparison procedure and therefore require the Scheffé multiple S in (17.44a) for $r = 4$, $n_T = 10(4) = 40$, and $1 - \alpha = .95$:

$$S^2 = (r - 1)F(1 - \alpha; r - 1, n_T - r) = 3F(.95; 3, 36) = 3(2.87) = 8.61$$

or $S = 2.93$. Hence, the anticipated widths of the confidence intervals are:

Contrast	Anticipated Width of Confidence Interval $= \pm S\sigma\{\hat{L}\}$
Pairwise comparisons	$\pm 2.93(.89) = \pm 2.61$ (thousand miles)
High- and low-priced brands	$\pm 2.93(.63) = \pm 1.85$ (thousand miles)
National and local brands	$\pm 2.93(.73) = \pm 2.14$ (thousand miles)

Management was satisfied with these anticipated widths. However, it was decided to increase the sample sizes from 10 to 15 in case the actual standard deviation of the tread lives of tires is somewhat greater than the anticipated value $\sigma = 2$ (thousand miles).

Example 2—Unequal Sample Sizes

In the snow tires example, suppose that tire brand 4 is the snow tire presently used and is to serve as the basis of comparison for the other brands. The comparisons of interest therefore are $\mu_1 - \mu_4$, $\mu_2 - \mu_4$, and $\mu_3 - \mu_4$. The sample size for brand 4 is to be twice as large as for the other brands in order to improve the precision of the three pairwise comparisons. The desired precision, with a family confidence coefficient of .90, is to be ± 1 (thousand miles). The Bonferroni procedure will be used to provide assurance as to the family confidence level.

We know from (17.14) that the variance of an estimated difference $\hat{L}_i = \bar{Y}_{i.} - \bar{Y}_{4.}$ (the difference is now denoted more generally by $\hat{L}$) is for $i = 1, 2, 3$:

$$\sigma^2\{\hat{L}_i\} = \sigma^2 \left(\frac{1}{n_i} + \frac{1}{n_4} \right)$$

We shall denote the sample sizes for brands 1, 2, and 3 by n and for brand 4 by $2n$. Hence, the variance of $\hat{L}_i$ becomes:

$$\sigma^2\{\hat{L}_i\} = \sigma^2 \left(\frac{1}{n} + \frac{1}{2n} \right) = \frac{3\sigma^2}{2n}$$

Using again the planning value $\sigma = 2$ and an initial sample size $n = 10$, we find $\sigma^2\{\hat{L}_i\} = .60$ and $\sigma\{\hat{L}_i\} = .77$. For $\alpha = .10$ and $g = 3$ comparisons, the Bonferroni multiple is $B = t(.9833; 46) = 2.19$. Note that $n_T = 3(10) + 20 = 50$ for the first iteration; hence $n_T - r = 50 - 4 = 46$. The anticipated width of the confidence intervals therefore is $2.19(.77) = \pm 1.69$. This is larger than the specified width ± 1.0, so a larger sample size needs to be tried next.

We shall try $n = 30$ next. We find that $\sigma\{\hat{L}_i\} = .45$ now, and the Bonferroni multiple will be $B = t(.9833; 146) = 2.15$. Hence, the anticipated width of the confidence intervals for $n = 30$ is $2.15(.45) = \pm .97$. This is slightly smaller than the specified width ± 1.0. However, since the planning value for σ may not be entirely accurate, management may decide to use 30 tires for each of the new brands and 60 tires for brand 4, the presently used snow tires.

Example 3—Two-Factor Study

In a two-factor study, factor A has $a = 3$ levels and factor B has $b = 2$ levels. No interaction effects are anticipated, and all pairwise comparisons of factor level means are to be made for each of the two factors. A family confidence coefficient of .90 is specified for the $3 + 1 = 4$ pairwise comparisons. Equal treatment sample sizes of n experimental units are to be used. The width of each confidence interval is to be ± 30. A reasonable planning value for the standard deviation of the error terms is $\sigma = 50$.

We know from (20.7) that the variance of a comparison of factor A level means, $\hat{L} = \bar{Y}_{i..} - \bar{Y}_{i'..}$, is:

$$\sigma^2\{\hat{L}\} = \frac{\sigma^2}{bn} \sum c_i^2 = \frac{2\sigma^2}{bn} \qquad \text{Factor } A \text{ comparisons}$$

Similarly, the variance of the comparison of the two factor B level means, $\hat{L} = \bar{Y}_{.1.} - \bar{Y}_{.2.}$, is:

$$\sigma^2\{\hat{L}\} = \frac{2\sigma^2}{an} \qquad \text{Factor } B \text{ comparison}$$

Since equal precision is specified for all pairwise comparisons and since $a = 3$ and $b = 2$, the variance for the factor A comparisons will be larger for any given treatment sample size n and hence will be the critical consideration.

Suppose that we begin the iterative process with $n = 30$. We then find for the factor A comparisons that $\sigma^2\{\hat{L}\} = 2(50)^2/2(30) = 83.33$ or $\sigma\{\hat{L}\} = 9.13$. For $n_T = 6(30) = 180$, $\alpha = .10$, and $g = 4$ comparisons, the Bonferroni multiple is $B = t(.9875; 174) = 2.26$. Hence, the anticipated width of the confidence intervals is $2.26(9.13) = \pm 20.6$. This anticipated width is somewhat tighter than the specified width ± 30, and a smaller treatment sample size should be tried in the next iteration.

Note

Since one cannot usually be certain that the planning value for the standard deviation is correct, it is advisable to study a range of values for the standard deviation before making a final decision on sample size. ∎

26.6   Planning of Sample Sizes to Find "Best" Treatment

There are occasions when the chief purpose of the study is to ascertain the treatment with the highest or lowest mean. In the snow tires example, for instance, it may be desired to determine which of the four brands has the longest mean tread life.

Table B.13, developed by Bechhofer, enables us to determine the necessary sample sizes so that with probability $1 - \alpha$ the highest (lowest) estimated treatment mean is from the treatment with the highest (lowest) population mean. We need to specify the probability $1 - \alpha$, the standard deviation σ, and the smallest difference λ between the highest (lowest) and second highest (second lowest) treatment means that it is important to recognize. Table B.13 assumes that equal sample sizes are to be used for all r treatments. The table is applicable for single-factor studies, as well as for multifactor studies where the objective is to identify the best factor level combination. For multifactor studies, r is defined as the number of factor level combinations in the experiment. For example, in a three-factor study, $r = abc$.

Example—Single-Factor Study

Suppose that in the snow tires example, the chief objective is to identify the brand with the longest mean tread life. There are $r = 4$ brands. We anticipate, as before, that $\sigma = 2$ (thousand miles). Further, we are informed that a difference $\lambda = 1$ (thousand miles) between the highest and second highest brand means is important to recognize, and that the probability is to be $1 - \alpha = .90$ or greater that we identify correctly the brand with the highest mean tread life when $\lambda \geq 1$.

The entry in Table B.13 is $\lambda \sqrt{n}/\sigma$. For $r = 4$ and probability $1 - \alpha = .90$, we find from Table B.13 that $\lambda \sqrt{n}/\sigma = 2.4516$. Hence, since the λ specification is $\lambda = 1$, we obtain:

$$\frac{(1)\sqrt{n}}{2} = 2.4516$$
$$\sqrt{n} = 4.9032 \quad \text{or} \quad n = 25$$

Thus, when the mean tread life for the best brand exceeds that of the second best by at least 1 (thousand miles) and when $\sigma = 2$ (thousand miles), sample sizes of 25 tires for each brand provide an assurance of at least .90 that the brand with the highest estimated mean $\bar{Y}_{i.}$ is the brand with the highest population mean.

Note

If the planning value for the standard deviation is not accurate, the probability of identifying the population with the highest (lowest) mean correctly is, of course, affected. This is no different from the other approaches, where a misjudgment of the standard deviation affects the risks of making a Type II error or the widths of the confidence intervals actually obtained.   ■

Cited Reference

26.1.   Cochran, W. G., and G. M. Cox. *Experimental Designs*. 2nd ed. New York: John Wiley & Sons, 1957.

Problems

26.1.   Give an example of an experimental study where a repetition is not a replication.

26.2.   In an experiment to study the effect of the location of a product display in drugstores of a chain, the manager of one of the drugstores rearranged the displays of other products so as to increase the traffic flow at the experimental display. Does this action potentially lead to either selection bias or measurement bias? Discuss.

26.3.   In a study of the effect of size of team on the volume of communications within the team, can a double-blind procedure be utilized? A single-blind procedure? Discuss.

26.4.   Refer to Example 1 on page 1054. Find the power of the test if $\alpha = .01$, everything else remaining unchanged. How does this power compare with that in Example 1?

26.5. Refer to Example 2 on page 1054. The analyst is also interested in the power of the test when $\mu_1 = \mu_2 = 13$ and $\mu_3 = \mu_4 = 18$. Assume that $\sigma = 2.5$.

a. Obtain the power of the test if $\alpha = .05$.

b. What would be the power of the test if $\alpha = .01$?

√ 26.6. Refer to **Productivity improvement** Problem 16.10. Obtain the power of the test in Problem 16.10e if $\mu_1 = 7.0$, $\mu_2 = 8.0$, and $\mu_3 = 9.0$. Assume that $\sigma = .9$.

26.7. Refer to **Rehabilitation therapy** Problem 16.12. Obtain the power of the test in Problem 16.12e if $\mu_1 = 37$, $\mu_2 = 35$, and $\mu_3 = 28$. Assume that $\sigma = 4.5$.

√ 26.8. Refer to **Cash offers** Problem 16.13. Obtain the power of the test in Problem 16.13e if the mean cash offers are $\mu_1 = 22$, $\mu_2 = 28$, and $\mu_3 = 22$. Assume that $\sigma = 1.6$.

26.9. In a two-factor study, factor A has four levels, factor B has three levels, and $n = 6$. Separate tests were conducted for factor A and factor B main effects, each with significance level $\alpha = .05$. The researcher now wishes to investigate the power of the two tests. Assume that $\sigma = 20$.

a. What is the power of the test for factor A main effects when $\alpha_1 = -10$, $\alpha_2 = 7$, $\alpha_3 = 3$, and $\alpha_4 = 0$?

b. What is the power of the test for factor B main effects when $\beta_1 = -4$, $\beta_2 = 8$, and $\beta_3 = -4$?

√ 26.10. Refer to **Cash offers** Problems 19.10 and 19.11. Assume that $\sigma = 2.0$.

a. What is the power of the test for interaction effects in Problem 19.11c if $(\alpha\beta)_{11} = -.2$, $(\alpha\beta)_{12} = .2$, $(\alpha\beta)_{21} = -.8$, $(\alpha\beta)_{22} = .8$, $(\alpha\beta)_{31} = 1.0$, and $(\alpha\beta)_{32} = -1.0$?

b. What is the power of the test for factor A main effects in Problem 19.11d if $\mu_{1.} = 23$, $\mu_{2.} = 25$, and $\mu_{3.} = 21$?

c. What is the power of the test for factor B main effects in Problem 19.11d if $\mu_{.1} = 24$ and $\mu_{.2} = 20$? (*Hint*: Use Table B.5.)

√ 26.11. Refer to **Hay fever relief** Problems 19.14 and 19.15. Assume that $\sigma = .28$.

a. What is the power of the test for factor A main effects in Problem 19.15d if $\mu_{1.} = 6.6$, $\mu_{2.} = 7.0$, and $\mu_{3.} = 7.4$?

b. How is the power of the test in part (a) affected if $\mu_{2.} = 7.3$, everything else remaining the same?

c. What is the power of the test for factor B main effects in Problem 19.15d if $\beta_1 = -.25$, $\beta_2 = -.25$, and $\beta_3 = .50$?

26.12. Refer to **Programmer requirements** Problems 19.20 and 19.21. Obtain the power of the test for factor B main effects in Problem 19.21d if $\beta_1 = 15$, $\beta_2 = -5$, and $\beta_3 = -10$. Assume that $\sigma = 9.0$.

26.13. For three-factor fixed ANOVA model (23.14), what is the noncentrality parameter ϕ for testing for factor A main effects? For testing for AB interactions?

√ 26.14. Refer to **Marketing research contractors** Problem 23.9 and 23.10. Assume that $\sigma = 3.0$. What is the power of the test for factor A main effects in Problem 23.10f if $\mu_{1..} = 97$, $\mu_{2..} = 95$, and $\mu_{3..} = 90$?

26.15. Refer to **Electronics assembly** Problems 23.12 and 23.13. Assume that $\sigma = 29$. What is the power of the test for factor B main effects in Problem 23.13f if $\mu_{.1.} = 1,050$, $\mu_{.2.} = 1,100$, and $\mu_{.3.} = 1,060$?

26.16. A market researcher stated in a seminar: "The power approach to determining sample sizes for analysis of variance problems is not meaningful; only the estimation approach should be used. We never conduct a study where all treatment means are expected to be equal, so we are always interested in a variety of estimates." Discuss.

26.17. Why do you think that the approach to planning sample sizes to find the best treatment by means of Table B.13 does not consider the risk of an incorrect identification when the best two treatment means are the same or practically the same?

√ 26.18. Consider a single-factor study where $r = 5$, $\alpha = .01$, $\beta = .05$, and $\sigma = 10$, and equal treatment sample sizes are desired by means of the approach in Table B.12.

  a. What are the required sample sizes if $\Delta = 10, 15, 20, 30$? What generalization is suggested by your results?

  b. What are the required sample sizes for the same values of Δ as in part (a) if $\alpha = .05$, all other specifications remaining the same? How do these sample sizes compare with those in part (a)?

26.19. Consider a single-factor study where $r = 6$, $\alpha = .05$, $\beta = .10$, and $\Delta = 50$, and equal treatment sample sizes are desired by means of the approach in Table B.12.

  a. What are the required sample sizes if $\sigma = 50, 25, 20$? What generalization is suggested by your results?

  b. What are the required sample sizes for the same values of σ as in part (a) if $r = 4$, all other specifications remaining the same? How do these sample sizes compare with those in part (a)?

26.20. Consider a single-factor study where $r = 5$, $1 - \alpha = .95$, and $\sigma = 20$, and equal sample sizes are desired by means of the approach in Table B.13.

  a. What are the required sample sizes if $\lambda = 20, 10, 5$? What generalization is suggested by your results?

  b. What are the required sample sizes for the same values of λ as in part (a) if $\sigma = 30$, all other specifications remaining the same? How do these sample sizes compare with those in part (a)?

√ 26.21. Refer to **Questionnaire color** Problem 16.11. Suppose that the sample sizes have not yet been determined but it has been decided to sample the same number of supermarket parking lots for each questionnaire color. A reasonable planning value for the error standard deviation is $\sigma = 3.0$.

  a. What would be the required sample sizes if: (1) differences in the response rates are to be detected with probability .90 or more when the range of the treatment means is 4.5, and (2) the α risk is to be controlled at .05?

  b. If the sample sizes determined in part (a) were employed, what would be the minimum power of the test for treatment mean differences (using $\alpha = .05$) when the range of the treatment means is 6.0?

  c. Suppose estimates of all pairwise comparisons are of primary importance. What would be the required sample sizes if the precision of all pairwise comparisons is to be ±3.0, using the Tukey procedure with a 95 percent family confidence coefficient?

  d. Suppose the chief objective is to identify the color with the highest mean response rate. The probability should be at least .99 that the best color is recognized correctly when the difference between the response rates for the best and second best colors is 1.5 percent points or more. What are the required sample sizes?

26.22. Refer to **Rehabilitation therapy** Problem 16.12. Suppose that the sample sizes have not yet been determined but it has been decided to use the same number of patients for each physical fitness group. Assume that a reasonable planning value for the error standard deviation is $\sigma = 4.5$ days.

a. What would be the required sample sizes if: (1) differences in the mean times for the three physical fitness categories are to be detected with probability .80 or more when the range of the treatment means is 5.63 days, and (2) the α risk is to be controlled at .01?

b. If the sample sizes determined in part (a) were employed, what would be the power of the test for treatment mean differences when $\mu_1 = 37$, $\mu_2 = 32$, and $\mu_3 = 28$?

c. Suppose primary interest is in estimating the two pairwise comparisons:

$$L_1 = \mu_1 - \mu_2 \qquad L_2 = \mu_3 - \mu_2$$

What would be the required sample sizes if the precision of each comparison is to be ± 3.0 days, using the most efficient multiple comparison procedure with a 95 percent family confidence coefficient?

d. Suppose the chief objective is to identify the physical fitness group with the smallest mean required time for therapy. The probability should be at least .90 that the correct group is identified when the mean required time for the second best group differs by 2.0 days or more. What are the required sample sizes?

√ 26.23. Refer to **Filling machines** Problem 16.14. Suppose that the sample sizes have not yet been determined but it has been decided to sample the same number of cartons for each filling machine. Assume that a reasonable planning value for the error standard deviation is $\sigma - .15$ ounce.

a. What would be the required sample sizes if: (1) differences in the mean amount of fill for the six filling machines are to be detected with probability .70 or more when the range of the treatment means is .15 ounce, and (2) the α risk is to be controlled at .05?

b. For the sample sizes determined in part (a), what would be the power of the test if $\mu_1 = .09$, $\mu_2 = .18$, $\mu_3 = .30$, $\mu_4 = .20$, $\mu_5 = .10$, and $\mu_6 = .20$?

c. Suppose primary interest is in estimating the following comparisons:

$$L_1 = \mu_1 - \mu_2 \qquad L_3 = \frac{\mu_1 + \mu_2}{2} - \frac{\mu_3 + \mu_4}{2}$$

$$L_2 = \mu_3 - \mu_4 \qquad L_4 = \frac{\mu_1 + \mu_2 + \mu_3 + \mu_4}{4} - \frac{\mu_5 + \mu_6}{2}$$

What would be the required sample sizes if the precision of each of these comparisons is not to exceed $\pm.08$ ounce, using the best multiple comparison procedure with a 95 percent family confidence coefficient?

d. Suppose the chief objective is to identify the filling machine with the smallest mean fill. The probability should be at least .95 that the filling machine with the smallest mean fill is recognized correctly when the filling machine with the next smallest mean fill differs by .10 ounce or more. What are the required sample sizes?

26.24. Refer to **Premium distribution** Problem 16.15. Suppose that the sample sizes have not yet been determined but it has been decided to sample the same number of premium distributions for each agent. Assume that a reasonable planning value for the error standard deviation is $\sigma = 3.0$ days.

a. What would be the required sample sizes if: (1) differences in the mean time lapse for the five agents are to be detected with probability .95 or more when the range of the treatment means is 3.75 days, and (2) the α risk is to be controlled at .10?

b. Suppose primary interest is in estimating the following comparisons:

$$L_1 = \mu_1 - \mu_2 \qquad L_3 = \frac{\mu_1 + \mu_2}{2} - \mu_5$$

$$L_2 = \mu_3 - \mu_4 \qquad L_4 = \frac{\mu_1 + \mu_2}{2} - \frac{\mu_3 + \mu_4}{2}$$

What would be the required sample sizes if the precision of each of the estimated comparisons is not to exceed ± 1.0 day, using the most efficient multiple comparison procedure with a 90 percent family confidence coefficient?

c. Suppose the chief objective is to identify the best agent, i.e., the one with the smallest mean time lapse. The probability should be at least .90 that the best agent is recognized correctly when the mean time lapse for the second best agent differs by 1.0 day or more. What are the required sample sizes?

26.25. Refer to **Rehabilitation therapy** Problem 16.12. Suppose that primary interest is in comparing the below-average and above-average physical fitness groups, respectively, with the average physical fitness group. Thus, two comparisons are of interest:

$$L_1 = \mu_1 - \mu_2 \qquad L_2 = \mu_3 - \mu_2$$

Assume that a reasonable planning value for the error standard deviation is $\sigma = 4.5$ days.

a. It has been decided to use equal sample sizes (n) for the below-average and above-average groups. If twice this sample size ($2n$) were to be used for the average physical fitness group, what would be the required sample sizes if the precision of each pairwise comparison is to be ± 2.5 days, using the Bonferroni procedure and a 90 percent family confidence coefficient?

b. Repeat the calculations in part (a) if the sample size for the average physical fitness group is to be: (1) n and (2) $3n$, all other specifications remaining the same.

c. Compare your results in parts (a) and (b). Which design leads to the smallest total sample size here?

26.26. A market research manager is planning to study the effects of duration of advertising (factor A) and price level (factor B) on sales. Each factor has three levels. No important interactions are expected, and the primary analysis is to consist of pairwise comparisons of factor level means for each factor. Equal sample sizes are to be used for each treatment. The precision of each comparison is to be ± 3 thousand dollars. The family confidence coefficient for the joint set of comparisons is to be 90 percent, the Tukey procedure is to be used in making the comparisons for each factor, and the Bonferroni procedure is then to be used to join the two sets of comparisons. Assume that $\sigma = 7$ thousand dollars is a reasonable planning value for the error standard deviation. What sample sizes do you recommend?

√ 26.27. Refer to **Cash offers** Problem 19.10. Suppose that the sample sizes have not yet been determined but it has been decided to use the same number of "owners" in each age-gender group. What are the required sample sizes if: (1) differences in the age factor level means are to be detected with probability .90 or more when the range of the factor level means is 3 (hundred dollars), and (2) the α risk is to be controlled at .05? Assume that a reasonable planning value for the error standard deviation is $\sigma = 1.5$ (hundred dollars).

26.28. Refer to **Eye contact effect** Problem 19.12. Suppose that the sample sizes have not yet been determined but it has been decided to use equal sample sizes for each treatment. Primary interest is in the two comparisons $L_1 = \mu_{1.} - \mu_{2.}$ and $L_2 = \mu_{.1} - \mu_{.2}$. What are the required sample sizes if each of these comparisons is to be estimated with precision not to exceed ± 1.2 with a 95 percent family confidence coefficient, using the most efficient multiple comparison procedure? Assume that a reasonable planning value for the error standard deviation is $\sigma = 2.4$.

√ 26.29. Refer to **Hay fever relief** Problem 19.14. Suppose that the sample sizes have not yet been determined but it has been decided to use equal sample sizes for each treatment. The chief objective is to identify the dosage combination that yields the longest mean relief. The probability should be at least .99 that the correct dosage combination is identified when the mean relief duration for the second best combination differs by .5 hour or more. What are the required sample sizes? Assume that a reasonable planning value for the error standard deviation is $\sigma = .29$ hour.

26.30. Refer to **Kidney failure hospitalization** Problem 19.18. Suppose that the sample sizes have not yet been determined but it has been decided to use equal sample sizes for each treatment. The chief objective is to estimate the pairwise comparisons:

$$L_1 = \mu_{1.} - \mu_{2.} \qquad L_3 = \mu_{.1} - \mu_{.3}$$
$$L_2 = \mu_{.1} - \mu_{.2} \qquad L_4 = \mu_{.2} - \mu_{.3}$$

What are the required sample sizes if the precision of each of the estimates should not exceed $\pm .20$ (in transformed units), using the Bonferroni procedure with a family confidence coefficient of 90 percent for the joint set of comparisons? A reasonable planning value for the error standard deviation is $\sigma = .32$ (in transformed units).

√ 26.31. Refer to **Programmer requirements** Problem 19.20. Suppose that the sample sizes have not yet been determined but it has been decided to use equal sample sizes for each treatment. Primary interest is in identifying the type of experience-years of experience combination for which the mean prediction error is smallest. The probability should be at least .95 that the correct combination is identified when the mean prediction error for the second best combination differs by 8.0 programmer-days or more. Assume that a reasonable planning value for the error standard deviation is $\sigma = 9.1$ days. What are the required sample sizes?

√ 26.32. Refer to **Case hardening** Problem 23.6. Suppose that the sample sizes have not yet been determined but it has been decided to use equal sample sizes for all treatments. The chief objective is to identify the treatment that leads to the highest mean hardness. The probability should be at least .99 that the correct treatment is identified when the mean hardness for the second best treatment differs by 2.0 or more Brinell units. Assume that a reasonable planning value for the error standard deviation is $\sigma = 1.8$. What are the required sample sizes?

26.33. Refer to **Electronics assembly** Problem 23.12. Suppose that the sample sizes have not yet been determined but it has been decided to use equal sample sizes for all treatments.

The chief objective is to estimate the following pairwise comparisons:

$$L_1 = \mu_{1..} - \mu_{2..} \qquad L_4 = \mu_{.2.} - \mu_{.3.}$$

$$L_2 = \mu_{.1.} - \mu_{.2.} \qquad L_5 = \mu_{..1} - \mu_{..2}$$

$$L_3 = \mu_{.1.} - \mu_{.3.}$$

What are the required sample sizes if the precision of each of the estimates should not exceed ± 20, using the Bonferroni procedure with a 90 percent family confidence coefficient for the joint set of comparisons? A reasonable planning value for the error standard deviation is $\sigma = 29$.

Exercises

26.34. A completely randomized experiment is to be conducted involving $r = 3$ treatments, with $n = 2$ experimental trials for each treatment. Because the normality of the error terms is strongly in doubt, the test for treatment effects based on the F^* test statistic in (16.55) is to be carried out by means of the randomization distribution.

   a. Determine the number of ways that the six experimental units can be divided into three groups of size two. How many unique F^* statistics are possible?

   b. Using the results in part (a), what is the smallest P-value that is possible with the randomization test? What does this suggest about the adequacy of the planned sample size?

26.35. (Calculus needed.) Given $\mu_1 = 0$, $\mu_3 = 1$, and $0 \le \mu_2 \le 1$, show that $\Sigma(\mu_i - \mu_.)^2$ is minimized when $\mu_2 = .5$, where $\mu_. = (\mu_1 + \mu_2 + \mu_3)/3$.

26.36. (Calculus needed.) Refer to **Rehabilitation therapy** Problem 16.12. The sample sizes for the below-average, average, and above-average physical fitness groups are to be n, kn, and n, respectively. Assuming that ANOVA model (16.2) is appropriate, find the optimal value of k to minimize the variances of $\hat{L}_1 = \bar{Y}_{1.} - \bar{Y}_{2.}$ and $\hat{L}_2 = \bar{Y}_{3.} - \bar{Y}_{2.}$ for a given total sample size n_T.

Projects

26.37. A completely randomized experiment involving $r = 2$ treatments was carried out, based on $n = 3$ experimental trials for each treatment. The test for equality of the treatment means is to be carried out by means of the randomization distribution of the F^* test statistic (16.55).

   a. Determine the number of ways that the six experimental units can be divided into two groups of size three each. How many unique F^* statistics are possible?

b. For the sample results:

j:	1	2	3
Y_{1j}:	23	34	78
Y_{2j}:	17	29	23

obtain the randomization distribution of the test statistic F^* and the P-value of the randomization test.

c. Obtain the P-value of the normal-theory F^* statistic for the sample results in part (b). How does this P-value compare with the one from the randomization test in part (b)? What does this suggest about the appropriateness of the F distribution here if the error terms are far from normally distributed?

26.38. A completely randomized psychological reinforcement experiment was conducted in which a standard treatment and an experimental treatment were each applied to four subjects. The sample results are:

j:	1	2	3	4
Y_{1j} (standard treatment):	16	14	18	16
Y_{2j} (experimental treatment):	12	15	13	12

The test for equality of treatment means is to be carried out by means of the randomization distribution of the F^* test statistic (16.55), with $\alpha = .10$.

a. Obtain the randomization distribution of the test statistic F^* and carry out the indicated test. State the alternatives, decision rule, and conclusion. What is the P-value of the randomization test?

b. For the randomization distribution in part (a), determine the proportion of F^* values that exceed $F(.90; 1, 6)$, the proportion of F^* values that exceed $F(.95; 1, 6)$, and the proportion that exceed $F(.99; 1, 6)$.

c. How do the proportions obtained in part (b) compare with the probabilities for the normal error model? Discuss.

Randomized Block Designs

In the preceding chapter, we introduced the concept of blocking. We noted there that when the available experimental units are not homogeneous, grouping the experimental units into blocks of homogeneous units will reduce the experimental error variance and also increase the range of validity for inferences about the treatment effects.

In this chapter, we shall take up the design and analysis of randomized block experiments in detail. We discuss when and how to conduct a randomized block design, the analysis of a randomized block design, and planning of sample sizes for blocked experiments. We shall also consider the regression approach to the analysis of randomized block designs and the analysis of experiments where the block effects are considered to be random.

Our discussion in this chapter will focus on the use of complete block designs. In such designs, each block consists of one complete replication of the set of treatments. When the number of experimental units available in a block is less than the number of treatments, incomplete block designs may at times be useful. We shall consider incomplete block designs in Chapters 30 and 31.

27.1 Elements of Randomized Block Designs

Description of Designs

A randomized block design is a restricted randomization design in which the experimental units are first sorted into homogeneous groups, called *blocks*, and the treatments are then assigned at random within the blocks. We illustrate randomized block designs by considering three examples.

1. In an experiment on the effects of four levels of newspaper advertising saturation on sales volume, the experimental unit is a city, and 16 cities are available for the study. Size of city usually is highly correlated with the response variable, sales volume. Hence, it is desirable to block the 16 cities into four groups of four cities each, according to population size. Thus, the four largest cities will constitute block 1, and so on. Within each block, the four treatments are then assigned at random to the four cities, and the assignments from one block to another are made independently.

2. In an experiment on the effects of three different incentive pay schemes on employee productivity of electronic assemblies, the experimental unit is an employee, and

30 employees are available for the study. Since productivity here is highly correlated with manual dexterity, it is desirable to block the 30 employees into 10 groups of three according to their manual dexterity. Thus, the three employees with the highest manual dexterity ratings are grouped into one block, and so on for the other employees. Within each block, the three incentive pay schemes are then assigned randomly to the three employees.

3. A chemist is studying the reaction rate of five chemical agents. Only five agents can be analyzed effectively per day. Since day-to-day differences may affect the reaction rate, each day is used as a block, and all five chemical agents are tested each day in independently randomized orders.

As these examples imply, the key objective in blocking the experimental units is to make them as homogeneous as possible within blocks with respect to the response variable under study, and to make the different blocks as heterogeneous as possible with respect to the response variable. The design in which each treatment is included once in each block is called a *randomized complete block design*. Often, we shall drop the term "complete" because the context makes it clear that all treatments are included in each block.

Comments

1. In a complete block design, each block constitutes a replication of the experiment. For that reason, it is highly desirable that the experimental units within a block be processed together whenever this will help to reduce experimental error variability. As an example, an experimenter may tend to make changes in experimental techniques over time (e.g., in the administration of the experiment to subjects) without being aware of it. Consecutive processing of the experimental units block by block will tend to exclude such sources of variation from the within-blocks analysis and thereby make the experimental results more precise.

2. In factorial experiments, some of the factors of interest may be characteristics of the experimental units, such as gender, age, and amount of experience on the job. Even though these factors are not introduced to reduce experimental error variability but rather are included for their intrinsic interest, we shall nevertheless consider such experiments to be randomized block designs because the randomization of the experimental factors to the experimental units is restricted by the nature of the classification factors considered. ∎

Criteria for Blocking

As noted earlier, the purpose of blocking is to sort experimental units into groups within each of which the elements are homogeneous with respect to the response variable, such that the differences between groups are as great as possible. To help recognize some of the characteristics of experimental units that are fruitful criteria for blocking, we need a precise definition of an experimental unit. All elements of the experimental situation that are not included in the definition of a treatment need to be assigned to the definition of an experimental unit. Suppose the treatment in an experiment consists of a portion of a vegetable containing a particular additive served in the laboratory. The experimental unit might then be defined as a homemaker of a given age, processed by a given observer on a specified day during a particular part of the day, and served food from a given batch of cooked vegetable. Still other elements of the experimental setting might be included in the definition of the experimental unit, and should be if they could be the cause of material variability in the responses.

A full definition of the experimental unit such as the one just given suggests two types of blocking criteria:

1. Characteristics associated with the unit—for persons: gender, age, income, intelligence, education, job experience, attitudes, etc.; for geographic areas: population size, average income, etc.

2. Characteristics associated with the experimental setting—observer, time of processing, machine, batch of material, measuring instrument, etc.

Use of time as a blocking variable frequently captures a number of different sources of variability, such as learning by observer, changes in equipment, and drifts in environmental conditions (e.g., weather). Blocking by observers often eliminates a substantial amount of interobserver variability; similarly, blocking by batches of material frequently is very effective.

There is no need to use only a single blocking criterion; several may be employed if the experimental error can be reduced substantially thereby. We shall consider in Section 27.14 the use of more than one blocking criterion, such as when a block consists of subjects in a given age group processed by a particular observer.

The design of effective randomized block experiments requires the ability to select blocking variables that will reduce the experimental error variability. Often, past experience in the subject matter field enables the experimenter to select good blocking variables. If some experiments have been run in the past in which blocking has been employed, these results can be analyzed to determine the effectiveness of the blocking variables. We shall discuss an appropriate method of analysis for doing this in Section 27.7. In the absence of any information on the effectiveness of potential blocking variables, uniformity trials can be run where all experimental units are assigned the same treatment. From these trials, information can be obtained on the effectiveness of different blocking variables.

Note

There is another blocking variable often used in social science research that has not been mentioned yet, namely, the subject. With the subject as a complete block, all treatments are given to every subject. Such designs are often called *repeated measures designs*. Since they involve some special problems, we will discuss them separately in Chapter 29.   ∎

Advantages and Disadvantages

The advantages of a randomized complete block design are:

1. It can, with effective grouping, provide substantially more precise results than a completely randomized design of comparable size.

2. It can accommodate any number of treatments and replications.

3. Different treatments need not have equal sample sizes. For instance, if the control is to have twice as large a sample size as each of three treatments, blocks of size five would be used; three units in a block are then assigned at random to the three treatments and two to the control.

4. The statistical analysis is relatively simple.

5. If an entire treatment or a block needs to be dropped from the analysis for some reason, such as spoiled results, the analysis is not complicated thereby.

6. Variability in experimental units can be deliberately introduced to widen the range of validity of the experimental results without sacrificing the precision of the results.

Disadvantages include:

1. Missing observations within a block require more complex analysis.

2. The degrees of freedom for experimental error are not as large as with a completely randomized design. One degree of freedom is lost for each block after the first.

3. More assumptions are required for the model (e.g., no interactions between treatments and blocks, constant variance from block to block) than for a completely randomized design model.

How to Randomize

The randomization procedure for a randomized block design is straightforward. Within each block a random permutation is used to assign treatments to experimental units, just as in a completely randomized design. Independent permutations are selected for the several blocks.

Illustration

In an experiment on decision making, executives were exposed to one of three methods of quantifying the maximum risk premium they would be willing to pay to avoid uncertainty in a business decision. The three methods are the utility method, the worry method, and the comparison method. After using the assigned method, the subjects were asked to state their degree of confidence in the method of quantifying the risk premium on a scale from 0 (no confidence) to 20 (highest confidence).

Fifteen subjects were used in the study. They were grouped into five blocks of three executives, according to age. Block 1 contained the three oldest executives, and so on. The design layout, after five independent random permutations of three were employed, is shown in Figure 27.1. Table 27.1 contains the results of the experiment, and Figure 27.2 presents graphically the confidence ratings for each method by block. It appears from Figure 27.2 that there is much variation between blocks, but that in all blocks the comparison method has the highest confidence rating and the utility method the lowest. It also appears that there are no important interaction effects between blocks and treatments on the responses; the response curves do not seem to deviate too much from being parallel. We discuss next a widely used model for randomized block designs and the analysis of variance for this model before undertaking a formal analysis of the results in our example.

27.2 Model for Randomized Block Designs

Table 27.1 is similar in appearance to Table 21.2a, which shows the data for a two-factor study with one observation in each cell. In fact, a randomized complete block design may be viewed as corresponding to a two-factor study (blocks and treatments are the factors), with one observation in each cell. As we noted in Section 21.1, the assumption of no interactions between the two factors permits an analysis of factor effects when there is only one observation in each cell and the factors have fixed effects.

FIGURE 27.1 **Layout for Randomized Block Design—Risk Premium Example.**

	Experimental Unit		
	1	2	3
Block 1 (oldest executives)	C	W	U
2	C	U	W
3	U	W	C
4	W	U	C
5 (youngest executives)	W	C	U

C: Comparison method
W: Worry method
U: Utility method

TABLE 27.1 **Data on Confidence Ratings (ratings on scale from 0 to 20)—Risk Premium Example.**

Block i	Method (j)			Average
	Utility	Worry	Comparison	
1 (oldest)	1	5	8	4.7
2	2	8	14	8.0
3	7	9	16	10.7
4	6	13	18	12.3
5 (youngest)	12	14	17	14.3
Average	5.6	9.8	14.6	10.0

The model for a randomized complete block design containing the assumption of no interaction effects, when both the block and treatment effects are fixed and there are n blocks (replications) and r treatments, is as follows:

$$(27.1) \qquad Y_{ij} = \mu_{..} + \rho_i + \tau_j + \varepsilon_{ij}$$

where:

$\mu_{..}$ is a constant

ρ_i are constants for the block (row) effects, subject to the restriction $\Sigma \rho_i = 0$

τ_j are constants for the treatment effects, subject to the restriction $\Sigma \tau_j = 0$

ε_{ij} are independent $N(0, \sigma^2)$

$i = 1, \ldots, n; j = 1, \ldots, r$

FIGURE 27.2 **Plot of Confidence Ratings by Blocks—Risk Premium Example.**

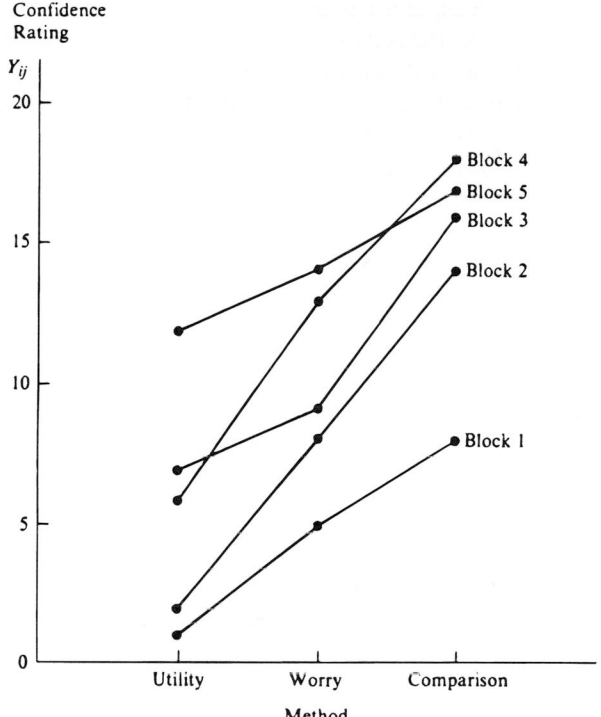

The responses Y_{ij} with randomized block model (27.1) are independent and normally distributed, with mean:

$$(27.2a) \qquad\qquad E\{Y_{ij}\} = \mu_{..} + \rho_i + \tau_j$$

and constant variance:

$$(27.2b) \qquad\qquad \sigma^2\{Y_{ij}\} = \sigma^2$$

Randomized block model (27.1) is identical to the two-factor, no-interaction model (21.1), except that we now use ρ_i for the block effect, τ_j for the treatment effect, and n to designate the total number of blocks. Note that Y_{ij} here stands for the response for the jth treatment in the ith block.

Comments

1. When the experimental units are grouped according to specified categories, such as into particular age groups, income groups, and order of processing groups, the block effects ρ_i are usually considered to be fixed. Sometimes the block effects are viewed as random. For instance, when observers or subjects are used as blocks, the particular observers or subjects in the study may be considered to be a sample from a population of observers or subjects. The case of random block effects will be taken up in Section 27.12.

2. If the treatment effects are random, the only changes in model (27.1) are that the τ_j now represent independent normal variables with expectation zero and variance σ_τ^2, and that the τ_j are independent of the ε_{ij}.

3. The additive model (27.1) implies that the expected values of observations in different blocks for the same treatment may differ (e.g., older executives may tend to have lower confidence ratings for any of the methods of quantifying the risk premium than younger executives), but the treatment effects (e.g., how much higher the confidence rating for one method is over that for another) are the same for all blocks. We shall consider the possibility of interactions between blocks and treatments later in this chapter. ∎

27.3 Analysis of Variance and Tests

Fitting of Randomized Block Model

The least squares and maximum likelihood estimators of the parameters in randomized block model (27.1) are obtained in the customary fashion and again are the same. Employing our usual notation, they are:

	Parameter	Estimator
(27.3a)	$\mu_{..}$	$\hat{\mu}_{..} = \bar{Y}_{..}$
(27.3b)	ρ_i	$\hat{\rho}_i = \bar{Y}_{i.} - \bar{Y}_{..}$
(27.3c)	τ_j	$\hat{\tau}_j = \bar{Y}_{.j} - \bar{Y}_{..}$

The fitted values therefore are:

$$(27.4) \qquad \hat{Y}_{ij} = \bar{Y}_{..} + (\bar{Y}_{i.} - \bar{Y}_{..}) + (\bar{Y}_{.j} - \bar{Y}_{..}) = \bar{Y}_{i.} + \bar{Y}_{.j} - \bar{Y}_{..}$$

and the residuals are:

$$(27.5) \qquad e_{ij} = Y_{ij} - \hat{Y}_{ij} = Y_{ij} - \bar{Y}_{i.} - \bar{Y}_{.j} + \bar{Y}_{..}$$

Analysis of Variance

The analysis of variance for a randomized complete block design is identical to that for a two-factor, no-interaction model with one observation per cell, as described in Section 21.1:

$$(27.6a) \qquad SSBL = r \sum_i (\bar{Y}_{i.} - \bar{Y}_{..})^2$$

$$(27.6b) \qquad SSTR = n \sum_j (\bar{Y}_{.j} - \bar{Y}_{..})^2$$

$$(27.6c) \qquad SSBL.TR = \sum_i \sum_j (Y_{ij} - \bar{Y}_{i.} - \bar{Y}_{.j} + \bar{Y}_{..})^2 = \sum_i \sum_j e_{ij}^2$$

Here, *SSBL* denotes the *sum of squares for blocks*, *SSTR* denotes, as usual, the treatment sum of squares, and *SSBL.TR* denotes the *interaction sum of squares between blocks and*

TABLE 27.2   **ANOVA Table for Randomized Complete Block Design, Block Effects Fixed.**

Source of Variation	SS	df	MS	$E\{MS\}$ Treatments Fixed	Treatments Random
Blocks	SSBL	$n-1$	MSBL	$\sigma^2 + r\dfrac{\Sigma \rho_i^2}{n-1}$	$\sigma^2 + r\dfrac{\Sigma \rho_i^2}{n-1}$
Treatments	SSTR	$r-1$	MSTR	$\sigma^2 + n\dfrac{\Sigma \tau_j^2}{r-1}$	$\sigma^2 + n\sigma_\tau^2$
Error	SSBL.TR	$(n-1)(r-1)$	MSBL.TR	σ^2	σ^2
Total	SSTO	$nr-1$			

treatments (note from (27.5) that this sum of squares here is the same as the sum of the squared residuals); rn is the total number of experimental units in the study.

A summary of the analysis of variance, including the expected mean squares for both fixed and random treatment effects, is given in Table 27.2. Note that since there are no interaction terms in the model, the expected mean squares contain only σ^2 and, as appropriate, the treatment or block main effects term. Also note from the $E\{MS\}$ columns in Table 27.2 that the appropriate denominator in the F^* test statistic for testing treatment effects is the interaction mean square, here denoted by *MSBL.TR*, whether the treatment effects are fixed or random. This is the same as in Section 21.1 for the two factor no interaction model with $n = 1$. Hence, to test for treatment effects:

	Fixed Treatment Effects	Random Treatment Effects
(27.7a)	H_0: all $\tau_j = 0$	H_0: $\sigma_\tau^2 = 0$
	H_a: not all τ_j equal zero	H_a: $\sigma_\tau^2 > 0$

we use the same test statistic whether the treatment effects are fixed or random:

$$(27.7b) \qquad F^* = \frac{MSTR}{MSBL.TR}$$

and the decision rule for controlling the Type I error at α is:

(27.7c)   If $F^* \leq F[1 - \alpha; r - 1, (n - 1)(r - 1)]$, conclude H_0

If $F^* > F[1 - \alpha; r - 1, (n - 1)(r - 1)]$, conclude H_a

Example

Table 27.3 contains the analysis of variance for the risk premium example in Table 27.1. The calculations are straightforward and were carried out by a computer package. To test

TABLE 27.3 ANOVA Table for Randomized Complete Block Design—Risk Premium Example of Table 27.1.

Source of Variation	SS	df	MS
Blocks	171.3	4	42.8
Methods for risk premium specification	202.8	2	101.4
Error	23.9	8	2.99
Total	398.0	14	

for treatment effects:

$$H_0: \tau_1 = \tau_2 = \tau_3 = 0$$

$$H_a: \text{not all } \tau_j \text{ equal zero}$$

we use the results in Table 27.3:

$$F^* = \frac{MSTR}{MSBL.TR} = \frac{101.4}{2.99} = 33.9$$

For level of significance $\alpha = .01$, we require $F(.99; 2, 8) = 8.65$. Since $F^* = 33.9 > 8.65$, we conclude H_a, that the mean confidence ratings for the three methods differ. The P-value of the test is .0001.

Comments

1. Sometimes one may also wish to conduct a test for block effects:

(27.8a)
$$H_0: \text{all } \rho_i = 0$$
$$H_a: \text{not all } \rho_i \text{ equal zero}$$

Usually, however, the treatments are of primary interest, and blocks are chiefly the means for reducing the experimental error variability. Table 27.2 indicates that the test for fixed block effects uses the test statistic:

(27.8b)
$$F^* = \frac{MSBL}{MSBL.TR}$$

For the risk premium example, this test statistic is:

$$F^* = \frac{42.8}{2.99} = 14.3$$

For level of significance $\alpha = .01$, we require $F(.99; 4, 8) = 7.01$. Since $F^* = 14.3 > 7.01$, we conclude that the mean confidence ratings (averaged over treatments) differ for the various blocks.

Since blocks correspond to a classification factor, care needs to be used in interpreting the implications of block effects. In our risk premium example, for instance, the block effects might not be due to age, even though age was the grouping variable. Education could be the pivotal explanatory variable, the effect by age appearing if older executives have less formal education than younger ones.

2. If only two treatments are investigated in a randomized complete block design, it can be shown that the F test for treatment effects based on test statistic (27.7b) is equivalent to the two-sided t test for paired observations based on test statistic (A.69).   ∎

27.4   Evaluation of Appropriateness of Randomized Block Model

The importance of examining the appropriateness of a statistical model for a given set of data has been mentioned many times. Since the techniques of examination are similar, we shall make only a few points of special relevance to randomized block designs here.

Diagnostic Plots

Some of the chief ways in which the data may not fit randomized block model (27.1) are:

1. Unequal error variability by blocks

2. Unequal error variability by treatments

3. Time effects

4. Block-treatment interactions

Use of residual plots in connection with points 2 and 3 has been considered in Section 18.1 with reference to a completely randomized design. The discussion there applies also to the residuals of a randomized block design, given in (27.5):

$$e_{ij} = Y_{ij} - \bar{Y}_{i.} - \bar{Y}_{.j} + \bar{Y}_{..}$$

We simply add here that if treatments do have unequal error variability in a randomized complete block design, the differences between any two treatments can always be estimated by working with the differences between the paired observations, $Y_{ij} - Y_{ij'}$, which are unaffected by any unequal treatment variances.

Unequal error variability by blocks can be studied by aligned residual dot plots for each block, as shown in Figure 27.3 for a randomized block study with 10 treatments run in three blocks. The residual dot plots in Figure 27.3 are suggestive of increasing error variability with increasing block number. If, for instance, the blocks were processed in block number order, some modifications in procedures may have taken place leading to larger experimental error variability over time. Tests concerning the equality of variances, such as those described in Section 18.2, may be employed for a more formal determination, provided that the sample sizes are reasonably large so that the residuals can be treated as if they were independent.

Interactions between treatments and blocks are somewhat more difficult to detect from residual plots. Figure 27.4 contains the residuals for an experiment with two treatments run in four blocks. The reversal in pattern of the residuals is suggestive of an interaction effect. There are, however, many other possible types of interaction patterns that would appear very much different from that in Figure 27.4.

Another diagnostic plot that may be helpful to detect interaction effects is a plot of the residuals e_{ij} against the fitted values $\hat{Y}_{ij}$. A curvilinear pattern of the residuals in such a plot often suggests the presence of interaction effects between blocks and treatments. This plot also provides information about the constancy of the error variance.

FIGURE 27.3   **Residual Dot Plots Suggesting Unequal Error Variances by Blocks.**

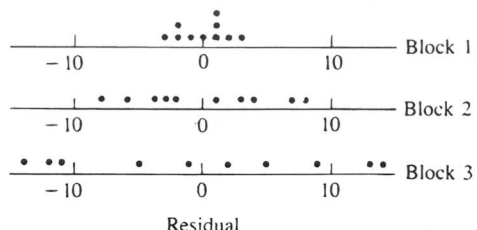

FIGURE 27.4   **Residual Dot Plots Suggesting Block-Treatment Interactions.**

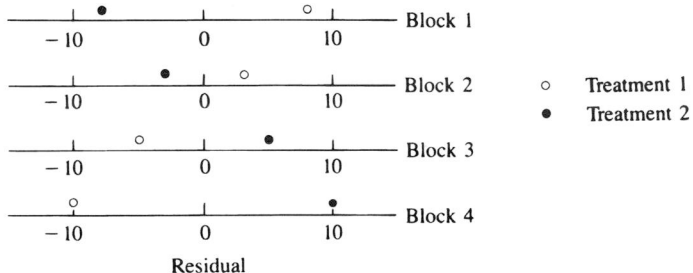

Still another diagnostic plot for interactions, which is often more effective than a residual plot, is a plot of the responses Y_{ij} by blocks. Figure 27.2 illustrates this type of plot. A severe lack of parallelism in such a plot is a strong indication that blocks and treatments interact in their effects on the response.

Example.   We already noted that the plot of responses by block in Figure 27.2 for the risk premium example does not exhibit a severe lack of parallelism, thus suggesting that blocks and treatments do not interact in any major fashion. Figure 27.5a, which presents a plot of the residuals against the fitted values, leads to a similar conclusion. There is no strong evidence of a curvilinear pattern here. In addition, Figure 27.5a does not indicate the existence of substantially unequal error variances.

Figure 27.5b contains a normal probability plot of the residuals. This plot does not suggest any strong departures from a normal error distribution. The coefficient of correlation between the ordered residuals and their expected values under normality is .959 and supports this conclusion. Residual dot plots for each treatment and for each block were also prepared (they are not shown here). They suggested that the error variances did not differ substantially between treatments and between blocks. These results, in addition to a formal test that found no interactions between block and treatment effects (to be discussed next), led the analyst to conclude that randomized block model (27.1) is appropriate for the data.

FIGURE 27.5   **Diagnostic Residual Plots—Risk Premium Example.**

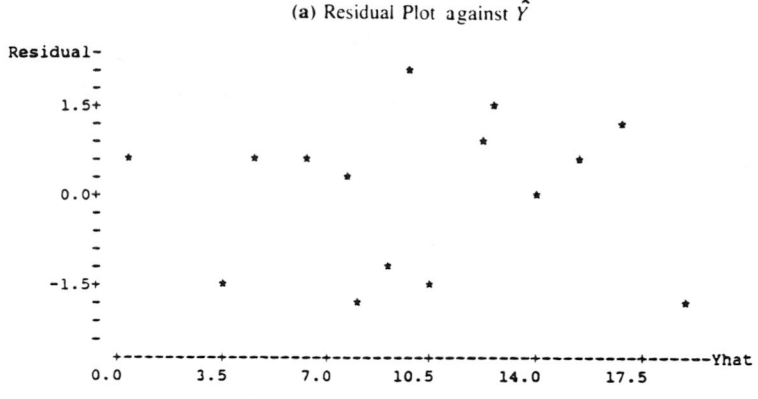

(a) Residual Plot against $\hat{Y}$

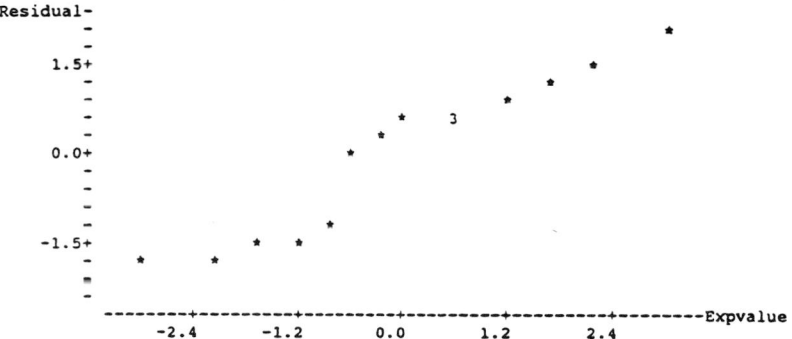

(b) Normal Probability Plot

Tukey Test for Additivity

The Tukey test for additivity, discussed in Section 21.2, may be employed for a formal test of interaction effects between blocks and treatments for a randomized block design. The special interaction sum of squares in (21.9) will be denoted here by $SSBL.TR^*$.

Example.   To test for interaction effects between blocks and treatments in the risk premium example, we calculate the special interaction sum of squares in (21.9) as follows, using the data in Tables 27.1 and 27.3:

$$\sum\sum(\bar{Y}_{i\cdot} - \bar{Y}_{\cdot\cdot})(\bar{Y}_{\cdot j} - \bar{Y}_{\cdot\cdot})Y_{ij} = 24.80$$

$$\sum(\bar{Y}_{i\cdot} - \bar{Y}_{\cdot\cdot})^2 = \frac{SSBL}{r} = \frac{171.3}{3} = 57.10$$

$$\sum(\bar{Y}_{\cdot j} - \bar{Y}_{\cdot\cdot})^2 = \frac{SSTR}{n} = \frac{202.8}{5} = 40.56$$

Hence:

$$SSBL.TR^* = \frac{(24.80)^2}{57.10(40.56)} = .27$$

Using the results from Table 27.3, we can now obtain the remainder sum of squares (21.10a) for the special interaction model (21.7):

$$SSRem^* = SSTO - SSBL - SSTR - SSBL.TR^*$$

$$= 398.0 - 171.3 - 202.8 - .27$$

$$= 23.63$$

Hence, test statistic (21.11) is:

$$F^* = \frac{SSBL.TR^*}{1} \div \frac{SSRem^*}{rn - r - n}$$

$$= \frac{.27}{1} \div \frac{23.63}{7} = .08$$

For level of significance $\alpha = .05$, we need $F(.95; 1, 7) = 5.59$. Since $F^* = .08 \le 5.59$, we conclude that no block-treatment interaction effects are present. The P-value of this test is .79.

Note

When interaction effects are present, transformations of the data should be attempted to remove at least the important interaction effects. The discussion in Section 21.2 is relevant to this point. ∎

27.5 Analysis of Treatment Effects

Once the existence of fixed treatment effects has been established through the analysis of variance, the analysis of these effects proceeds as described in Chapter 17 for single-factor studies. Often, a useful preliminary view of the treatment effects can be obtained from a normal probability plot of the estimated treatment means $\bar{Y}_{.j}$. The formal analysis of the treatment effects usually involves estimation of one or more contrasts of the treatment means $\mu_{.j}$, where $\mu_{.j}$ is the mean response for treatment j averaged over all blocks. The formulas in Chapter 17 for estimating contrasts of the treatment means apply here, with the treatment means now denoted by $\mu_{.j}$ and the estimated treatment means by $\bar{Y}_{.j}$. The appropriate mean square term to be used in the estimated variance of the contrast is $MSBL.TR$, obtained from (27.6c), since it is the denominator of the F^* statistic for testing fixed treatment effects. The multiples for the estimated standard deviation of the contrast are now as follows:

(27.9a)	Single comparison	$t[1 - \alpha/2; (n - 1)(r - 1)]$
(27.9b)	Tukey procedure (for pairwise comparisons)	$T = \frac{1}{\sqrt{2}} q[1 - \alpha; r, (n - 1)(r - 1)]$
(27.9c)	Scheffé procedure	$S^2 = (r - 1)F[1 - \alpha; r - 1, (n - 1)(r - 1)]$
(27.9d)	Bonferroni procedure	$B = t[1 - \alpha/2g; (n - 1)(r - 1)]$

FIGURE 27.6   **Normal Probability Plot of Estimated Treatment Means—Risk Premium Example.**

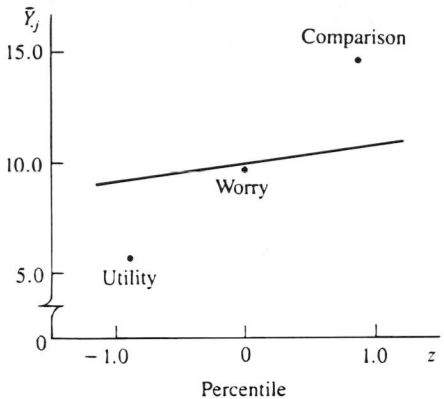

Example

The researcher who conducted the risk premium study was satisfied, on the basis of the residual analyses and tests, that randomized block model (27.1) is appropriate for the experiment. The researcher therefore began the analysis of the treatment effects by preparing a normal probability plot of the estimated treatment means $\bar{Y}_{.j}$. This plot is shown in Figure 27.6. The reference line shown in Figure 27.6 is $y =$ expected value, where the expected value is given in (17.2) and here is for the kth ordered estimated factor level mean:

$$\text{Expected value} = \bar{Y}_{..} + z\left(\frac{k - .375}{r + .25}\right) \sqrt{\frac{MSBL.TR}{n}} = 10.0 + z\left(\frac{k - .375}{3.25}\right) \sqrt{\frac{2.99}{5}}$$

where $\bar{Y}_{..} = 10.0$ (Table 27.1), $MSBL.TR = 2.99$ (Table 27.3), and $n = 5$ because each treatment occurred once in each of five blocks.

The plot in Figure 27.6 clearly shows that treatment effects are present. It also suggests, by the fact that the slopes connecting each pair of treatments differ so substantially from that of the reference line, that significant differences are present between each pair of methods of quantifying the maximum risk premium.

To analyze the treatment effects formally, the researcher wished to obtain all pairwise comparisons with a 95 percent family confidence coefficient, utilizing the Tukey procedure. Using (17.31b), with *MSE* replaced by *MSBL.TR* and the results in Table 27.3, we obtain:

$$s^2\{\hat{L}\} = MSBL.TR\left(\frac{1}{n} + \frac{1}{n}\right) = \frac{2MSBL.TR}{n} = \frac{2(2.99)}{5} = 1.20$$

Remember that each estimated treatment mean $\bar{Y}_{.j}$ consists of n observations (one from each of n blocks). Using (27.9b), we find for a 95 percent family confidence coefficient:

$$T = \frac{1}{\sqrt{2}}q(.95; 3, 8) = \frac{1}{\sqrt{2}}(4.04) = 2.86$$

Hence:

$$Ts\{\hat{L}\} = 2.86\sqrt{1.20} = 3.1$$

We now obtain for the pairwise comparisons using (17.31) and Table 27.1 for the $\bar{Y}_{\cdot j}$:

$$1.7 = (14.6 - 9.8) - 3.1 \le \mu_{\cdot 3} - \mu_{\cdot 2} \le (14.6 - 9.8) + 3.1 = 7.9$$

$$5.9 = (14.6 - 5.6) - 3.1 \le \mu_{\cdot 3} - \mu_{\cdot 1} \le (14.6 - 5.6) + 3.1 = 12.1$$

$$1.1 = (9.8 - 5.6) - 3.1 \le \mu_{\cdot 2} - \mu_{\cdot 1} \le (9.8 - 5.6) + 3.1 = 7.3$$

Here $\mu_{\cdot 1}$ is the mean confidence rating, averaged over all blocks, for the utility method, and $\mu_{\cdot 2}$ and $\mu_{\cdot 3}$ are the mean confidence ratings for the worry and comparison methods, respectively.

We conclude, just as Figure 27.6 had suggested, that the comparison method has a higher mean confidence rating than the worry method, which in turn has a higher mean confidence rating than the utility method. The family confidence coefficient of .95 applies to this entire set of comparisons. A line plot of the estimated treatment means summarizes the results:

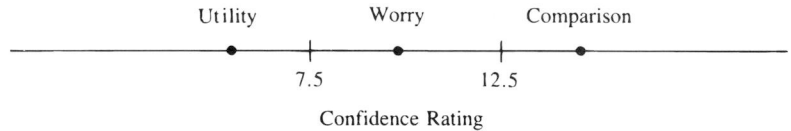

27.6 Factorial Treatments

When the treatments in a randomized block design are combinations of different factor levels, the ANOVA model can be modified by showing the component factor effects in place of the treatment effect. For a two-factor study, we have:

$$(27.10) \qquad Y_{ijk} = \mu_{\cdots} + \rho_i + \alpha_j + \beta_k + (\alpha\beta)_{jk} + \varepsilon_{ijk}$$

where the terms in the model have the usual meaning and (j, k) identifies the treatment.

In the analysis of variance, we proceed as always by decomposing the treatment sum of squares *SSTR* into sums of squares for the factor main effects and interactions. This is shown in Table 27.4 for a two-factor study, the factors having a and b levels, respectively. Thus, the total number of treatments here is $r = ab$. The decomposition is done in the usual fashion, as explained in Section 19.4, utilizing the relation in (19.39):

$$SSTR = SSA + SSB + SSAB$$

Formulas (19.39a, b, c) are still appropriate for calculating the component sums of squares, remembering that (i, j) subscripts are there used to identify the treatments in terms of the factor level combinations. Tests for factor effects are conducted as usual, and no new problems are encountered in the estimation of fixed factor effects.

TABLE 27.4 ANOVA Table for a Two-Factor Study in a Randomized Complete Block Design—Randomized Block Model (27.10).

Source of Variation	SS	df	MS
Blocks	SSBL	$n - 1$	MSBL
Treatments	SSTR	$r - 1$	MSTR
Factor A	SSA	$a - 1$	MSA
Factor B	SSB	$b - 1$	MSB
AB interactions	SSAB	$(a - 1)(b - 1)$	MSAB
Error	SSBL.TR	$(n - 1)(r - 1)$	MSBL.TR
Total	SSTO	$nr - 1$	

Note: $r = ab$

FIGURE 27.7 Layout for a Two-Factor Study in a Randomized Complete Block Design.

	A_1		A_2	
	B_1	B_2	B_1	B_2
Block 1	Y_{111}	Y_{112}	Y_{121}	Y_{122}
2	Y_{211}	Y_{212}	Y_{221}	Y_{222}
3	Y_{311}	Y_{312}	Y_{321}	Y_{322}

Note

Randomized block model (27.10) assumes no interactions between treatments and blocks. Specifically, it implies that all block-factor A interactions (denoted by *BL.A*) equal zero, and similarly that all *BL.B* and *BL.AB* interactions equal zero. A less restrictive model can be formulated by assuming only that the *BL.AB* interactions equal zero. To see this, consider the layout for a two-factor study with $a = 2$, $b = 2$ in $n = 3$ blocks, as shown in Figure 27.7. Here Y_{ijk} denotes the observation in the ith block for the (j, k) factor level combination. Note that this layout corresponds to the three-factor layout in Table 23.4a but with only one observation per cell. Table 23.2 contains the general analysis of variance for a three-factor study. It can be seen from there that if all *BL.AB* interactions (*BL.AB* corresponds to *ABC* in Table 23.2) equal zero, the *BL.AB* interaction mean square is an unbiased estimator of σ^2, the experimental error variance, and is the appropriate denominator mean square in the F^* test statistic for testing all factor effects. Hence, we can conduct all tests and make all desired estimates with a factorial experiment in a complete block design by only assuming that the *BL.AB* interactions are zero. The price of the less restrictive assumptions is fewer degrees of freedom for the experimental error mean square.

The ANOVA model for this less restrictive case is:

$$(27.11) \qquad Y_{ijk} = \mu_{...} + \rho_i + \alpha_j + \beta_k + (\alpha\beta)_{jk} + (\rho\alpha)_{ij} + (\rho\beta)_{ik} + \varepsilon_{ijk}$$

where the model terms have the usual meaning. The sums of squares may be calculated using formulas (23.21a–g), remembering that n in these formulas (number of observations per cell) now is 1, and that the number of levels for blocks (corresponding to factor C) is n. ■

27.7 Planning Randomized Block Experiments

The planning of sample sizes for a randomized complete block design is very similar to that for a completely randomized design. The needed number of blocks n may be determined either by specifying protection needed against making Type I and Type II errors or by specifying precision required for key contrasts of the treatment means. With either approach, it is necessary to assess in advance the magnitude of the experimental error variance σ^2.

Power Approach

Power of F Test. The power of the F test for treatment effects for a randomized complete block design involves the same noncentrality parameter as for a completely randomized design. Formula (26.2) gives the appropriate measure. Despite the same form of the noncentrality parameter, the two designs generally lead to different power levels even when based on the same sample sizes, for two reasons. First, the experimental error variance σ^2 will differ for the two designs. Second, the degrees of freedom associated with the denominator of the F^* statistic differ for the two designs.

Use of Table B.12. As when planning the sample sizes for a completely randomized design, an easy way to implement the power approach for planning the sample sizes for a randomized block design is to use Table B.12. This table may be used for planning randomized block designs provided that the number of treatments and blocks are not very small, specifically provided that $r(n - 1) \geq 20$. If this condition is not met, Table B.11 must be used iteratively to implement the power approach.

Example. In the risk premium example, suppose that the number of blocks had not yet been determined and the experimenter desired the following risk protections:

1. Type I error is to be controlled at $\alpha = .05$.

2. If any two treatment means differ by three or more rating points, i.e., if the minimum range of the treatment means is $\Delta = 3$, the risk of concluding that there are no treatment effects should not exceed $\beta = .20$.

The experimenter anticipates that the experimental error standard deviation when executives are grouped by age will be approximately $\sigma = 2$. Thus, the specifications can be summarized as follows:

$$r = 3 \qquad \alpha = .05 \qquad \Delta = 3$$
$$\beta = .20 \text{ or Power } = .80 \qquad \sigma = 2$$

Using (26.7) we find:

$$\frac{\Delta}{\sigma} = \frac{3}{2} = 1.5$$

Entering Table B.12 for $1 - \beta = .80$, $r = 3$, $\Delta/\sigma = 1.5$, and $\alpha = .05$, we find $n = 10$. Thus, the experimenter requires approximately 10 blocks of three executives each in order to obtain the desired protection against incorrect decisions.

Estimation Approach

For planning the number of blocks n by means of the estimation approach, we evaluate the anticipated standard deviations of key contrasts for different sample sizes until the desired precision is attained. Often, a multiple comparison procedure will be used for encompassing the different estimates under a family confidence coefficient.

Example.   For the risk premium example, all pairwise comparisons are of interest. The desired width of the confidence intervals is ± 1.5. The Tukey procedure is to be used with a 95 percent family confidence coefficient. A planning value of $\sigma = 2$ is reasonable. Using $n = 10$ as a starting point, the anticipated variance of any pairwise difference is:

$$\sigma^2\{\hat{L}\} = \sigma^2\left(\frac{1}{n} + \frac{1}{n}\right) = (2)^2\left(\frac{1}{10} + \frac{1}{10}\right) = .8$$

or $\sigma\{\hat{L}\} = .89$. Further:

$$T = \frac{1}{\sqrt{2}}q[.95; r, (n-1)(r-1)] = \frac{1}{\sqrt{2}}q(.95; 3, 18) = \frac{1}{\sqrt{2}}(3.61) = 2.55$$

Thus, the anticipated half-width of the confidence interval is $T\sigma\{\hat{L}\} = 2.55(.89) = 2.3$. Since this precision is not adequate, a larger number of blocks should be tried next. Continuing this iterative process, we find that $n = 21$ blocks are anticipated to meet the precision specification.

Efficiency of Blocking Variable

Once a randomized complete block experiment has been run, we often wish to estimate the efficiency of the blocking variable for guidance in future experimentation. This can be done readily. Let σ_b^2 stand for the experimental error variance for the randomized block design. Up to this point, we have used σ^2 for this error variance, but now that we will compare two designs we need to be more specific. Let σ_r^2 denote the experimental error variance for a completely randomized design. The relative efficiency of blocking, compared to a completely randomized design, is then defined as follows:

$$(27.12) \qquad\qquad E = \frac{\sigma_r^2}{\sigma_b^2}$$

The measure E indicates how much larger the replications need be with a completely randomized design as compared to a randomized block design in order that the variance of any estimated treatment contrast be the same for the two designs.

We know that for the randomized block design, *MSBL.TR* is an unbiased estimator of σ_b^2. The question is how to estimate σ_r^2 from the data for the randomized block design.

Since the same experimental units are involved in either case and there are assumed to be no interactions between treatments and blocks, it can be shown that an unbiased estimator of σ_r^2 is:

$$(27.13) \qquad s_r^2 = \frac{(n-1)MSBL + n(r-1)MSBL.TR}{nr - 1}$$

Hence, we estimate E as follows:

$$(27.14) \qquad \hat{E} = \frac{s_r^2}{MSBL.TR} = \frac{(n-1)MSBL + n(r-1)MSBL.TR}{(nr-1)MSBL.TR}$$

Since the number of degrees of freedom for experimental error for a randomized block design is not as great as for a completely randomized design, E overstates the efficiency a little because it considers only the error variances. Several modified measures of efficiency have been suggested to take this overstatement into account. Unless the degrees of freedom for experimental error with both designs are very small, these modifications have little effect. One frequently used modification, applicable for assessing any design relative to another, is:

$$(27.15) \qquad \hat{E}' = \frac{(df_2 + 1)(df_1 + 3)}{(df_2 + 3)(df_1 + 1)}\hat{E}$$

where df_1 denotes the degrees of freedom for the experimental error in the base design (completely randomized design, in our case) and df_2 denotes the degrees of freedom for the experimental error in the design whose efficiency is being assessed (randomized block design, in our case).

Example.   We shall evaluate the efficiency of blocking by age of executives in the risk premium example. Placing the appropriate results from Table 27.3 in efficiency measure (27.14), we obtain:

$$\hat{E} = \frac{4(42.8) + 5(2)(2.99)}{14(2.99)} = 4.8$$

Thus, we would have required almost five times as many replications per treatment with a completely randomized design to achieve the same variance of any estimated contrast as is obtained with blocking by age. Clearly, blocking by age was highly effective here.

If we had used modified efficiency measure (27.15), we would have found:

$$\hat{E}' = \frac{(8+1)(12+3)}{(8+3)(12+1)}(4.8) = 4.5$$

This result does not differ greatly from that obtained by using (27.14).

Note

The efficiency measure $\hat{E}$ in (27.14) equals 1 if $MSBL = MSBL.TR$; it is greater than 1 if $MSBL > MSBL.TR$; and it is less than 1 if $MSBL < MSBL.TR$. Since the test statistic for block effects in (27.8b) is $F^* = MSBL/MSBL.TR$, it follows that good blocking is achieved when this F^* value exceeds 1 by a considerable margin.   ■

Covariance Analysis as Alternative to Blocking

At times, a choice exists between: (1) a completely randomized design, with covariance analysis used to reduce the experimental errors; and (2) a randomized block design, with the blocks formed by means of the concomitant variable. Generally, the latter alternative is to be preferred. There are several reasons for this:

1. If the regression between the response variable and the concomitant (blocking) variable is linear, a randomized block design and covariance analysis are about equally efficient. If the regression is not linear but covariance analysis with a linear relationship is utilized, covariance analysis with a completely randomized design will tend to be not as effective as a randomized block design.

2. Computations with randomized block designs are simpler than those with covariance analysis.

3. Randomized block designs are essentially free of assumptions about the nature of the relationship between the blocking variable and the response variable, while covariance analysis assumes a definite form of relationship.

A drawback of randomized block designs is that somewhat fewer degrees of freedom are available for experimental error than with covariance analysis for a completely randomized design. However, in all but small scale experiments, this difference in degrees of freedom has little effect on the precision of the estimates.

27.8   Regression Approach to Randomized Block Designs

Randomized block design model (27.1) is a linear model and hence can be stated equivalently as a regression model. The regression approach to randomized block designs is especially useful when some observations are missing, thereby destroying the balance of the design. ANOVA model (27.1) for a randomized block design with both block and treatment effects fixed:

$$(27.16) \qquad Y_{ij} = \mu_{..} + \rho_i + \tau_j + \varepsilon_{ij}$$

$$i = 1, \ldots, n; \; j = 1, \ldots, r$$

can be expressed in straightforward fashion in the form of a regression model with indicator variables taking on values 1, −1, or 0. For instance, the regression model for the risk premium example in Table 27.1, with $r = 3$ treatments and $n = 5$ blocks, can be written as follows:

$$(27.17) \quad Y_{ij} = \mu_{..} + \underbrace{\rho_1 X_{ij1} + \rho_2 X_{ij2} + \rho_3 X_{ij3} + \rho_4 X_{ij4}}_{\text{Block effect}} + \underbrace{\tau_1 X_{ij5} + \tau_2 X_{ij6}}_{\text{Treatment effect}} + \varepsilon_{ij}$$

where:

$$X_1 = \begin{matrix} 1 \\ -1 \\ 0 \end{matrix} \quad \begin{matrix} \text{if experimental unit from block 1} \\ \text{if experimental unit from block 5} \\ \text{otherwise} \end{matrix}$$

X_2, X_3, X_4 are defined similarly

TABLE 27.5 Data for Regression Fits—Risk Premium Example in Table 27.1.

		(1)	(2)	(3)	(4)	(5)	(6)	(7)
i	j	Y	X_1	X_2	X_3	X_4	X_5	X_6
1	1	1	1	0	0	0	1	0
1	2	5	1	0	0	0	0	1
1	3	8	1	0	0	0	−1	−1
2	1	2	0	1	0	0	1	0
...	...	...	...	...	...	...	...	...
5	2	14	−1	−1	−1	−1	0	1
5	3	17	−1	−1	−1	−1	−1	−1

$$
X_5 = \begin{array}{ll} 1 & \text{if experimental unit received treatment 1} \\ -1 & \text{if experimental unit received treatment 3} \\ 0 & \text{otherwise} \end{array}
$$

$$
X_6 = \begin{array}{ll} 1 & \text{if experimental unit received treatment 2} \\ -1 & \text{if experimental unit received treatment 3} \\ 0 & \text{otherwise} \end{array}
$$

Table 27.5 repeats in column 1 a portion of the Y observations for the risk premium example. The six indicator variables are shown in columns 2–7. Note that these indicator variables provide the correct expectations. For instance, the indicator variables for observation Y_{13} have the values:

$$ X_1 = 1 \qquad X_2 = 0 \qquad X_3 = 0 \qquad X_4 = 0 \qquad X_5 = -1 \qquad X_6 = -1 $$

Hence:

$$ E\{Y_{13}\} = \mu_{..} + \rho_1 - \tau_1 - \tau_2 $$
$$ = \mu_{..} + \rho_1 + \tau_3 $$

because $\tau_3 = -\tau_1 - \tau_2$.

The test for treatment effects is carried out as usual, either by the general linear test approach or by use of extra sums of squares. For the general linear test approach, we first regress Y in column 1 of Table 27.5 on the six indicator variables in columns 2–7 and obtain $SSE(F)$. We then regress Y on the X variables for the reduced model $(X_1, \ldots, X_4)$ in columns 2–5 and obtain $SSE(R)$. The test statistic as always is that in (2.70). Estimation of treatment effects with the regression approach follows readily and will not be discussed further here.

27.9 Covariance Analysis for Randomized Block Designs

Covariance analysis can be employed to further reduce the experimental error variability in a randomized block design. The extension is a straightforward one from covariance analysis for a completely randomized design.

Covariance Model

The usual randomized block design model was given in (27.1). The covariance model for a randomized block design with one concomitant variable is obtained by simply adding a term (or several terms) for the relation between the response variable Y and the concomitant variable X. Assuming this relation can be described by a linear function, we obtain:

$$(27.18) \qquad Y_{ij} = \mu_{..} + \rho_i + \tau_j + \gamma(X_{ij} - \bar{X}_{..}) + \varepsilon_{ij}$$

$$i = 1, \ldots, n; \, j = 1, \ldots, r$$

Regression Approach

The regression approach to covariance model (27.18) involves no new principles. As in Chapter 25, we shall denote the centered variable $X_{ij} - \bar{X}_{..}$ in covariance model (27.18) by x_{ij}. Further, we shall again use $1, -1, 0$ indicator variables for the block and treatment effects. To illustrate an equivalent regression model, consider a randomized complete block design study with $n = 4$ blocks and $r = 3$ treatments. The regression model counterpart to covariance model (27.18) then is:

$$(27.19) \qquad Y_{ij} = \mu_{..} + \rho_1 I_{ij1} + \rho_2 I_{ij2} + \rho_3 I_{ij3} + \tau_1 I_{ij4}$$

$$+ \tau_2 I_{ij5} + \gamma x_{ij} + \varepsilon_{ij} \qquad \text{Full model}$$

where:

$$I_1 = \begin{matrix} 1 \\ -1 \\ 0 \end{matrix} \quad \begin{matrix} \text{if experimental unit from block 1} \\ \text{if experimental unit from block 4} \\ \text{otherwise} \end{matrix}$$

I_2, I_3 are defined similarly

$$I_4 = \begin{matrix} 1 \\ -1 \\ 0 \end{matrix} \quad \begin{matrix} \text{if experimental unit received treatment 1} \\ \text{if experimental unit received treatment 3} \\ \text{otherwise} \end{matrix}$$

$$I_5 = \begin{matrix} 1 \\ -1 \\ 0 \end{matrix} \quad \begin{matrix} \text{if experimental unit received treatment 2} \\ \text{if experimental unit received treatment 3} \\ \text{otherwise} \end{matrix}$$

$$x_{ij} = X_{ij} - \bar{X}_{..}$$

To test for treatment effects:

$$(27.20) \qquad \begin{matrix} H_0: \; \tau_1 = \tau_2 = \tau_3 = 0 \\ H_a: \; \text{not all} \; \tau_j \; \text{equal zero} \end{matrix}$$

we would either need to fit the reduced model under H_0:

$$(27.21) \qquad Y_{ij} = \mu_{..} + \rho_1 I_{ij1} + \rho_2 I_{ij2} + \rho_3 I_{ij3} + \gamma x_{ij} + \varepsilon_{ij} \qquad \text{Reduced model}$$

or else use the appropriate extra sum of squares. The test for treatment effects is then conducted in the usual way.

Comparisons of two treatment effects by the regression approach are straightforward. For estimating $\tau_1 - \tau_2$, for instance, we use the unbiased estimator $\hat{\tau}_1 - \hat{\tau}_2$ based on the estimated regression coefficients obtained when fitting the full model (27.19). The estimated variance of this estimator is:

$$(27.22) \qquad s^2\{\hat{\tau}_1 - \hat{\tau}_2\} = s^2\{\hat{\tau}_1\} + s^2\{\hat{\tau}_2\} - 2s\{\hat{\tau}_1, \hat{\tau}_2\}$$

The estimated variance-covariance matrix of the regression coefficients, available in many regression package printouts, can then be used to obtain the required estimated variances and covariances.

27.10   Nonparametric Rank F Test

When the responses Y_{ij} in a randomized complete block design are far from normally distributed with constant variance, and transformations of the data are not successful to meet the robustness properties of the standard inference procedures, a nonparametric test of treatment effects may be useful. This test is similar to the nonparametric rank F test introduced in Section 18.7 for single-factor studies. The r observations in each block are ranked from 1 to r in ascending order and the usual F^* test in (27.7b) for testing treatment effects in a randomized block design is carried out, but now based on the ranked data.

Test Procedure

The observations Y_{ij} for each block need to be ranked first in ascending order. Let R_{ij} denote the rank of Y_{ij} when the observations in the ith block are ranked from 1 to r. In the case of ties among observations, each of the tied observations is given the mean of the ranks involved. The usual F^* test statistic based on the ranks now is denoted by F_R^*:

$$(27.23) \qquad F_R^* = \frac{MSTR}{MSBL.TR}$$

where:

$$(27.23a) \qquad MSTR = \frac{n\,\Sigma(\bar{R}_{\cdot j} - \bar{R}_{\cdot\cdot})^2}{r - 1}$$

$$(27.23b) \qquad MSBL.TR = \frac{\Sigma\Sigma(R_{ij} - \bar{R}_{\cdot j})^2}{(n - 1)(r - 1)}$$

$$(27.23c) \qquad \bar{R}_{\cdot j} = \frac{\underset{i}{\Sigma} R_{ij}}{n}$$

$$(27.23d) \qquad \bar{R}_{\cdot\cdot} = \bar{R}_{i\cdot} = \frac{r + 1}{2}$$

If there are no treatment differences, all ranking permutations for a block are assumed to be equally likely and the statistic F_R^* will be distributed approximately as F with $r - 1$ and $(n - 1)(r - 1)$ degrees of freedom, provided the number of blocks is not too small. Large values of the test statistic lead to the conclusion that the treatments have unequal effects.

TABLE 27.6   Sales Data and Ranks—Produce Layout Example.

	(a) Sales ($ thousands)				(b) Ranks		
Block	Layout (j)			Block	Layout (j)		
i	1	2	3	i	1	2	3
1	75.3	69.8	87.7	1	2	1	3
2	64.3	70.0	71.1	2	1	2	3
3	59.0	45.4	71.8	3	2	1	3
4	44.2	35.1	61.0	4	2	1	3
5	21.7	59.9	25.3	5	1	3	2
				$R_{\cdot j}$	8	8	14
				$\bar{R}_{\cdot j}$	1.6	1.6	2.8

Example.   Table 27.6a contains sales data for a randomized complete block design experiment in which 15 stores were grouped into five blocks according to size of store, and three different layouts of the produce section were assigned at random to the three stores in each block. The data in Table 27.6a are produce sales (in thousands of dollars) for each of the 15 stores. Because these sales data appear to depart substantially from normality, it was decided to use the rank F test to examine whether mean sales differ for the three layouts. The ranks of the sales data in Table 27.6a are shown in Table 27.6b. Conducting the usual analysis of variance for a randomized block design on the rank data in Table 27.6b, we obtain:

$$MSTR = 2.4$$

$$MSBL.TR = .65$$

Hence, from (27.23) we find:

$$F^* = \frac{MSTR}{MSBL.TR} = \frac{2.4}{.65} = 3.69$$

To test the alternatives:

$$H_0: \mu_{\cdot 1} = \mu_{\cdot 2} = \mu_{\cdot 3}$$

$$H_a: \text{ not all } \mu_{\cdot j} \text{ are equal}$$

where $\mu_{\cdot j}$ is the mean for treatment j averaged over all blocks, we use the decision rule:

$$\text{If } F_R^* \leq F[1 - \alpha; r - 1, (n - 1)(r - 1)], \text{ conclude } H_0$$

$$\text{If } F_R^* > F[1 - \alpha; r - 1, (n - 1)(r - 1)], \text{ conclude } H_a$$

For level of significance $\alpha = .10$, we need $F(.90; 2, 8) = 3.11$. Since $F_R^* = 3.69 > 3.11$, we conclude H_a, that the mean sales for the three layouts are not equal. The P-value of this test is .07.

Comments

1. Test statistic (27.23) should not be used if there are many tied ranks.

2. The rank F test statistic is equivalent to the statistic for the *Friedman test*, a widely used nonparametric rank procedure for testing the equality of treatment means in randomized complete block designs. The Friedman test is also based on the within-block ranks R_{ij} of the data. The Friedman test statistic is:

$$(27.24a) \qquad X_F^2 = SSTR \div \frac{SSTR + SSBL.TR}{n(r-1)}$$

which can be reduced to (when no ties are present):

$$(27.24b) \qquad X_F^2 = \left[\frac{12}{nr(r+1)} \sum_j R_{.j}^2 \right] - 3n(r+1)$$

Instead of using the F distribution, the Friedman test approximates the distribution of X_F^2 when H_0 holds by the chi-square distribution with $r-1$ degrees of freedom, provided that the number of blocks is not too small. The decision rule is therefore:

$$(27.25) \qquad \begin{array}{l} \text{If } X_F^2 \le \chi^2(1-\alpha; r-1), \text{ conclude } H_0 \\ \text{If } X_F^2 > \chi^2(1-\alpha; r-1), \text{ conclude } H_a \end{array}$$

The F_R^* and X_F^2 statistics are related as follows:

$$(27.26) \qquad F_R^* = \frac{(n-1)X_F^2}{n(r-1) - X_F^2} \qquad \blacksquare$$

Multiple Pairwise Testing Procedure

Just like in the case of the rank F test for single-factor studies (Section 18.7), we can use a large-sample testing analog of the Bonferroni pairwise comparison procedure to obtain information about the comparative magnitudes of the treatment means for randomized block designs when the rank F test (or the Friedman test) indicates that the treatment means differ. Testing limits for all $g = r(r-1)/2$ pairwise comparisons using the mean ranks $\bar{R}_{.j}$ are set up as follows for family level of significance α:

$$(27.27) \qquad \bar{R}_{.j} - \bar{R}_{.j'} \pm B \left[\frac{r(r+1)}{6n} \right]^{1/2}$$

where:

$$(27.27a) \qquad B = z(1 - \alpha/2g)$$

$$(27.27b) \qquad g = \frac{r(r-1)}{2}$$

If the testing limits include zero, we conclude that the corresponding treatment means $\mu_{.j}$ and $\mu_{.j'}$ do not differ. If the testing limits do not include zero, we conclude that the two corresponding treatment means differ. We can then set up groups of treatments whose means do not differ according to this simultaneous testing procedure.

Example.   For the produce layout example of Table 27.6, we wish to make all pairwise tests with family level of significance $\alpha = .20$. The mean ranks $\bar{R}_{\cdot j}$ are presented in Table 27.6b. For $r = 3$, we have $g = 3(2)/2 = 3$. Also, for $\alpha = .20$ we require $B = z[1 - .20/2(3)] = z(.9667) = 1.834$. Thus, the right term in (27.27) is:

$$B\left[\frac{r(r+1)}{6n}\right]^{1/2} = 1.834\left[\frac{3(4)}{6(5)}\right]^{1/2} = 1.16$$

We note from Table 27.6b that the differences between the mean ranks for layout 3 and each of the other two layouts exceed 1.16 and are therefore significant, and that the difference between layouts 1 and 2 is less than 1.16. Hence, we can set up two groups, within which the treatment means do not differ:

	Group 1			Group 2	
Layout 1	$\bar{R}_{\cdot 1} = 1.6$		Layout 3	$\bar{R}_{\cdot 3} = 2.8$	
Layout 2	$\bar{R}_{\cdot 2} = 1.6$				

Thus, we can conclude with family level of significance .20 that layout 3 leads to larger mean sales than do layouts 1 and 2, and that the mean sales for the latter two do not differ.

27.11   Missing Observations

There are occasions when one or several observations in a randomized complete block design are "missing"—a subject may have been sick, a record may have been mislaid, a treatment may have been applied incorrectly in one instance. Such missing responses destroy the balance (orthogonality) of the complete block design and make the usual ANOVA calculations inappropriate. However, the regression approach to the analysis of randomized block designs, discussed in Section 27.8, is ordinarily still appropriate when there are missing responses. The reason is that the no-interaction randomized block design model (27.1) enables us, in effect, to estimate the mean response for a missing cell. We explained earlier how this is done for a two-factor no-interaction model (Section 21.1), and the same reasoning applies here.

Since no new principles are involved, we turn to an example to illustrate the use of the regression approach when observations are missing in a randomized block design experiment.

Example

Table 27.7a contains the data for a simple randomized block design experiment with $r = 3$ treatments and $n = 3$ blocks, where observation Y_{11} is missing. We set up the regression model equivalent to randomized block design model (27.1) as follows:

$$(27.28) \qquad Y_{ij} = \mu_{\cdot\cdot} + \underbrace{\rho_1 X_{ij1} + \rho_2 X_{ij2}}_{\text{Block effect}} + \underbrace{\tau_1 X_{ij3} + \tau_2 X_{ij4}}_{\text{Treatment effect}} + \varepsilon_{ij} \qquad \text{Full model}$$

TABLE 27.7   **Example of Missing Observation in Randomized Block Design** $(r = 3, n = 3)$.

(a) Response Data

Block	Treatment (j)		
i	1	2	3
1	Missing	10	9
2	11	10	7
3	6	4	3

(b) Regression Variables

		(1)	(2)	(3)	(4)	(5)
i	j	Y	X_1	X_2	X_3	X_4
1	2	10	1	0	0	1
1	3	9	1	0	-1	-1
2	1	11	0	1	1	0
2	2	10	0	1	0	1
2	3	7	0	1	-1	-1
3	1	6	-1	-1	1	0
3	2	4	-1	-1	0	1
3	3	3	-1	-1	-1	-1

where:

$$X_1 = \begin{matrix} 1 \\ -1 \\ 0 \end{matrix} \quad \begin{matrix} \text{if experimental unit from block 1} \\ \text{if experimental unit from block 3} \\ \text{otherwise} \end{matrix}$$

$$X_2 = \begin{matrix} 1 \\ -1 \\ 0 \end{matrix} \quad \begin{matrix} \text{if experimental unit from block 2} \\ \text{if experimental unit from block 3} \\ \text{otherwise} \end{matrix}$$

$$X_3 = \begin{matrix} 1 \\ -1 \\ 0 \end{matrix} \quad \begin{matrix} \text{if experimental unit received treatment 1} \\ \text{if experimental unit received treatment 3} \\ \text{otherwise} \end{matrix}$$

$$X_4 = \begin{matrix} 1 \\ -1 \\ 0 \end{matrix} \quad \begin{matrix} \text{if experimental unit received treatment 2} \\ \text{if experimental unit received treatment 3} \\ \text{otherwise} \end{matrix}$$

Table 27.7b repeats the Y observations in column 1 and presents the four indicator variables in columns 2–5.

The analysis of variance for testing treatment effects and block effects is carried out in the usual manner by first fitting the full model (27.28) and then fitting each of the following reduced models:

Test for Block Effects

$$(27.29) \qquad Y_{ij} = \mu_{..} + \tau_1 X_{ij3} + \tau_2 X_{ij4} + \varepsilon_{ij} \qquad \text{Reduced model}$$

Test for Treatment Effects

$$(27.30) \qquad Y_{ij} = \mu_{..} + \rho_1 X_{ij1} + \rho_2 X_{ij2} + \varepsilon_{ij} \qquad \text{Reduced model}$$

The extra sums of squares $SSR(X_1, X_2 | X_3, X_4)$ for blocks and $SSR(X_3, X_4 | X_1, X_2)$ for treatments are then calculated in the usual manner. Table 27.8a presents these extra sums of squares for our example obtained from fitting the full and reduced models, as well as the error sum of squares for the full model. No total sum of squares is shown because of lack of orthogonality as a result of the missing observation.

The test for treatment effects is conducted as usual. From Table 27.8a we find:

$$F^* = \frac{MSR(X_3, X_4 | X_1, X_2)}{MSE} = \frac{6.25}{.44} = 14.2$$

For $\alpha = .05$, we need $F(.95; 2, 3) = 9.55$. Since $F^* = 14.2 > 9.55$, we conclude that differential treatment effects are present. The P-value of this test is .03. The test for block effects can be carried out along similar lines when it is of interest.

No new problems are encountered with the regression approach in analyzing fixed treatment effects when there are missing observations. For instance, to estimate the pairwise comparison $L = \mu_{.1} - \mu_{.3} = \tau_1 - \tau_3$, we utilize the fact that $\tau_3 = -\tau_1 - \tau_2$ so that we have:

$$(27.31) \qquad L = \mu_{.1} - \mu_{.3} = \tau_1 - \tau_3 = \tau_1 - (-\tau_1 - \tau_2) = 2\tau_1 + \tau_2$$

An unbiased estimator of (27.31) is:

$$(27.32) \qquad \hat{L} = 2\hat{\tau}_1 + \hat{\tau}_2$$

whose estimated variance is, using (A.30b):

$$(27.33) \qquad s^2\{\hat{L}\} = 4s^2\{\hat{\tau}_1\} + s^2\{\hat{\tau}_2\} + 4s\{\hat{\tau}_1, \hat{\tau}_2\}$$

Table 27.8b contains the estimated regression coefficients for the full model, and Table 27.8c contains the estimated variance-covariance matrix of the regression coefficients. We therefore obtain the following estimates:

$$\hat{L} = 2(1.667) + 0.0 = 3.334$$

$$s^2\{\hat{L}\} = 4(.14815) + .11111 + 4(-.07407) = .4074$$

so that the estimated standard deviation is $s\{\hat{L}\} = .638$. A 95 percent confidence interval for L requires $t(.975; 3) = 3.182$, yielding the confidence limits $3.334 \pm 3.182(.638)$ and the confidence interval:

$$1.3 \le \mu_{.1} - \mu_{.3} \le 5.4$$

TABLE 27.8 **ANOVA Table and Other Regression Output for Missing Data Example of Table 27.7.**

(a) ANOVA Table

Source of Variation	SS	df	MS
Blocks	53.83	2	26.92
Treatments	12.50	2	6.25
Error	1.33	3	.44

(b) Estimated Regression Coefficients for Full Model (27.28)

Regression Coefficient	Estimated Regression Coefficient
$\mu_{..}$	$\hat{\mu}_{..} = 8.000$
ρ_1	$\hat{\rho}_1 = 2.333$
ρ_2	$\hat{\rho}_2 = 1.333$
τ_1	$\hat{\tau}_1 = 1.667$
τ_2	$\hat{\tau}_2 = 0.0$

(c) Estimated Variance-Covariance Matrix of Regression Coefficients

	$\hat{\mu}_{..}$	$\hat{\rho}_1$	$\hat{\rho}_2$	$\hat{\tau}_1$	$\hat{\tau}_2$
$\hat{\mu}_{..}$	.06173				
$\hat{\rho}_1$	.02469	.14815			
$\hat{\rho}_2$	−.01235	−.07407	.11111		
$\hat{\tau}_1$	.02469	.04938	−.02469	.14815	
$\hat{\tau}_2$	−.01235	−.02469	.01235	−.07407	.11111

27.12 Random Block Effects

Sometimes the blocks can be considered a random sample from a population so that the block effects in the randomized block model should be considered to be random variables, as in the following two examples.

1. A researcher investigated the improvement in learning in third-grade classes by augmenting the teacher with one or two teaching assistants. Ten schools were selected at random, and three third-grade classes in each school were utilized in the study. In each school, one class was randomly chosen to have no teaching assistant, one class was

randomly chosen to have one teaching assistant, and the third class was assigned two teaching assistants. The amount of learning by the class at the end of the school year, suitably measured, was the response variable. Here the blocks are schools, which may be viewed as a random sample from the population of all schools eligible for the study.

2. In a study of the effectiveness of four different dosages of a drug, 20 litters of mice, each consisting of four mice, were utilized. The 20 litters (blocks) here may be viewed as a random sample from the population of all litters that could have been used for the study.

When blocks can be considered to be a random sample from a population of blocks, either an additive (i.e., no-interaction) or a nonadditive (i.e., interaction) model can be employed. The choice can be assisted by the diagnostics discussed in Section 27.4. In particular, plots of the responses Y_{ij} for each block, such as in Figure 27.2, can be helpful in examining whether blocks and treatments interact. A severe lack of parallelism in such a plot would be a clear indication that the interaction model may be preferable. The Tukey test statistic for interactions in (21.11) may also be utilized, with the interpretation here that the test applies to the given blocks that have been selected. Finally, the nature of the correlations between the experimental units within a block may be examined because, as we shall see, the two models make different assumptions about these correlations.

When the primary emphasis of the analysis is on testing and estimating treatment effects, which is the usual case, the choice between the two models actually is not critical because the inference procedures for fixed treatment effects, as we shall see, are exactly the same for the two models.

We first explain the additive, no-interaction model for randomized block designs with random block effects, and then we will take up the interaction model. Both of these models are special cases of two-factor mixed model (24.42). We shall repeat the principal results here because the notation for randomized block designs is slightly different.

Note

A special case of random blocks occurs when the blocks are experimental units such as persons, stores, or cities, where each receives all of the treatments over time or where the effect of a given treatment (e.g., advertising) is evaluated at different points of time. These repeated measures designs are discussed in Chapter 29.   ∎

Additive Model

The additive model for random block effects and fixed treatment effects is a special case of mixed two-factor model (24.42), with $n = 1$, the interaction term dropped, and fixed factor A effects now being the treatment effects denoted by τ_j and random factor B effects now being the block effects denoted by ρ_i:

(27.34)
$$Y_{ij} = \mu_{..} + \rho_i + \tau_j + \varepsilon_{ij}$$

where:

$\mu_{..}$ is a constant

ρ_i are independent $N(0, \sigma_\rho^2)$

τ_j are constants subject to the restriction $\Sigma \tau_j = 0$

ε_{ij} are independent $N(0, \sigma^2)$, and independent of the ρ_i

$i = 1, \ldots, n; \ j = 1, \ldots, r$

Properties of Model.   The important properties of mixed two-factor model (24.42) were given in (24.44)–(24.46). These properties for randomized block design model (27.34) are:

(27.35a)
$$E\{Y_{ij}\} = \mu_{..} + \tau_j$$

(27.35b)
$$\sigma^2\{Y_{ij}\} = \sigma_Y^2 = \sigma_\rho^2 + \sigma^2$$

(27.35c)
$$\sigma\{Y_{ij}, Y_{ij'}\} = \sigma_\rho^2 \qquad j \neq j'$$

(27.35d)
$$\sigma\{Y_{ij}, Y_{i'j'}\} = 0 \qquad i \neq i'$$

Thus, the variance of Y_{ij}, again denoted by σ_Y^2, is a constant for all observations; any two observations from different blocks are independent; and any two observations from the same block are correlated for this model. Note that the covariance for any two observations from the same block must be positive in advance of the random trials and that the covariance is the same for all blocks. A positive covariance is reasonable for many applications. For example, class learning in different classes in the same school will tend to be more similar than for classes in different schools because of similar facilities, similar quality of teachers, and the like.

The coefficient of correlation between any two observations from the same block for model (27.34) is constant for all blocks and will be denoted by ω:

(27.36)
$$\omega = \frac{\sigma_\rho^2}{\sigma_Y \sigma_Y} = \frac{\sigma_\rho^2}{\sigma_Y^2}$$

This follows from the definition of a coefficient of correlation in (15.3) and the fact that $\sigma\{Y_{ij}\} = \sigma\{Y_{ij'}\} = \sigma_Y$. Note also that the covariance in (27.35c) can be expressed as follows, using (27.36):

(27.37)
$$\sigma\{Y_{ij}, Y_{ij'}\} = \omega \sigma_Y^2 \qquad j \neq j'$$

Covariance Structure of Observations.   Since any two Y_{ij} observations within a given block in advance of the random trials are correlated in the same fashion, the variance-covariance matrix of the observations in a given block is of a particular form. We illustrate this variance-covariance matrix for the observations in a block for a randomized block study with $r = 3$ treatments, using the covariance expression in (27.37):

(27.38)
$$\boldsymbol{\sigma}^2\{\mathbf{Y}\} = \begin{bmatrix} \sigma_Y^2 & \omega\sigma_Y^2 & \omega\sigma_Y^2 \\ \omega\sigma_Y^2 & \sigma_Y^2 & \omega\sigma_Y^2 \\ \omega\sigma_Y^2 & \omega\sigma_Y^2 & \sigma_Y^2 \end{bmatrix} = \sigma_Y^2 \begin{bmatrix} 1 & \omega & \omega \\ \omega & 1 & \omega \\ \omega & \omega & 1 \end{bmatrix}$$

where:

$$\mathbf{Y} = \begin{bmatrix} Y_{i1} \\ Y_{i2} \\ Y_{i3} \end{bmatrix}$$

Note that the main diagonal of the matrix contains the constant variance of the Y_{ij}, σ_Y^2, and the entries off the main diagonal are the constant covariances, $\omega\sigma_Y^2$. The particular pattern of the variance-covariance matrix in (27.38) is called *compound symmetry*.

While any two observations in a given block are correlated in advance of the random trials, once a block has been selected, additive model (27.34) assumes that the observations in that block are independent. The only remaining random variation in an observation Y_{ij} then is the error term ε_{ij}, and additive model (27.34) assumes that these are independent. Thus, in the teacher assistant study, model (27.34) assumes that once the schools have been selected, any one class performance is independent of that of another class in each selected school, given all of the common conditions for the classes in that school as reflected in the block effect ρ_i.

Comments

1. The variance of Y_{ij} in (27.35b) can be expressed as follows using (27.36):

$$\sigma_Y^2 = \omega \sigma_Y^2 + \sigma^2$$

Hence, we obtain:

(27.39) $$\sigma_Y^2 = \frac{\sigma^2}{1 - \omega}$$

2. The assumption of compound symmetry in additive model (27.34) is restrictive. While this assumption is sufficient so that the F^* statistic for testing treatment effects will follow the F distribution when H_0 holds (i.e., when no treatment effects are present), the assumption is not necessary. For this purpose, it suffices that the condition of *sphericity* be met. This condition requires that the variance of the difference between any two estimated treatment means be constant; that is:

(27.40) $$\sigma^2\{\bar{Y}_{\cdot j} - \bar{Y}_{\cdot j'}\} = \text{constant} \qquad j \neq j'$$

This condition can be met without the compound symmetry requirement. For example, consider the following variance-covariance matrix for the Y_{ij} observations in any block for a randomized complete block study with $r = 3$ treatments:

$$\sigma^2\{\mathbf{Y}\} = \begin{bmatrix} 2 & 1 & 2 \\ 1 & 4 & 3 \\ 2 & 3 & 6 \end{bmatrix}$$

This matrix does not exhibit compound symmetry. Yet the requirement for sphericity in (27.40) is met because $\sigma^2\{\bar{Y}_{\cdot j} - \bar{Y}_{\cdot j'}\} = 4/n$ always. For example, we have:

$$\sigma^2\{\bar{Y}_{\cdot 1} - \bar{Y}_{\cdot 3}\} = \frac{2}{n} + \frac{6}{n} - 2\left(\frac{2}{n}\right) = \frac{4}{n} \qquad \blacksquare$$

Analysis of Variance.   Table 27.9 contains the analysis of variance for additive model (27.34). The sums of squares are the same as in (27.6) for the fixed effects model. Table 27.9 also contains the expected mean squares for model (27.34). The expected mean squares correspond to those in Table 24.5 for the mixed two-factor model, with $n = 1$, no interaction effects, and change of notation associated with fixed factor A being treatments and random factor B being blocks. The statistic for testing for treatment effects is $F^* = MSTR/MSBL.TR$, as may be seen from the $E\{MS\}$ column in Table 27.9. Thus, the

TABLE 27.9   **ANOVA for Randomized Complete Block Design—Block Effects Random, Treatment Effects Fixed.**

Source of Variation	SS	df	MS	E{MS} Additive Model (27.34)	E{MS} Interaction Model (27.41)
Blocks	SSBL	$n-1$	MSBL	$\sigma^2 + r\sigma_\rho^2$	$\sigma^2 + r\sigma_\rho^2$
Treatments	SSTR	$r-1$	MSTR	$\sigma^2 + n\dfrac{\Sigma \tau_j^2}{r-1}$	$\sigma^2 + \sigma_{\rho\tau}^2 + n\dfrac{\Sigma \tau_j^2}{r-1}$
Error	SSBL.TR	$(n-1)(r-1)$	MSBL.TR	σ^2	$\sigma^2 + \sigma_{\rho\tau}^2$
Total	SSTO	$nr-1$			

test statistic is the same as when block effects are fixed. Confidence intervals for treatment contrasts also present no new issues. Again, *MSBL.TR* will be used as the mean square in the estimated variance of the contrast.

Interaction Model

When blocks are a random sample from a population of blocks, the presence of interactions between blocks and treatments can be accommodated by a model including these interaction effects:

$$(27.41) \qquad Y_{ij} = \mu_{..} + \rho_i + \tau_j + (\rho\tau)_{ij} + \varepsilon_{ij}$$

where:

$\mu_{..}$ is a constant

ρ_i are independent $N(0, \sigma_\rho^2)$

τ_j are constants subject to the restriction $\Sigma \tau_j = 0$

$(\rho\tau)_{ij}$ are $N\left(0, \dfrac{r-1}{r}\sigma_{\rho\tau}^2\right)$, subject to the restrictions:

$\quad \underset{j}{\Sigma}(\rho\tau)_{ij} = 0 \qquad$ for all i

$\quad \sigma\{(\rho\tau)_{ij}, (\rho\tau)_{ij'}\} = -\dfrac{1}{r}\sigma_{\rho\tau}^2 \qquad$ for $j \neq j'$

$(\rho\tau)_{ij}$ are independent of the ρ_i

ε_{ij} are independent $N(0, \sigma^2)$ and independent of the ρ_i and of the $(\rho\tau)_{ij}$

$i = 1, \ldots, n; \ j = 1, \ldots, r$

This model is a special case of mixed two-factor model (24.42), with $n = 1$ and with some changes in notation to recognize that fixed factor A now is treatments and random factor B now is blocks.

Properties of Model.   The properties of interaction model (27.41) are obtained directly from those in (24.44)–(24.46) for the mixed two-factor model:

(27.42a)
$$E\{Y_{ij}\} = \mu_{..} + \tau_j$$

(27.42b)
$$\sigma^2\{Y_{ij}\} = \sigma_Y^2 = \sigma_\rho^2 + \frac{r-1}{r}\sigma_{\rho\tau}^2 + \sigma^2$$

(27.42c)
$$\sigma\{Y_{ij}, Y_{ij'}\} = \sigma_\rho^2 - \frac{1}{r}\sigma_{\rho\tau}^2 \qquad j \neq j'$$

(27.42d)
$$\sigma\{Y_{ij}, Y_{i'j'}\} = 0 \qquad i \neq i'$$

Note again that the Y_{ij} have constant variance, that observations from different blocks are assumed to be independent, and that any two observations Y_{ij} and $Y_{ij'}$ from the same block are correlated, the covariance being the same for all blocks. Unlike for additive model (27.34), the covariance between any two observations from the same block can be negative or positive for interaction model (27.41).

The coefficient of correlation between any two observations in the same block, denoted by ω^*, is:

(27.43)
$$\omega^* = \frac{\sigma_\rho^2 - \frac{1}{r}\sigma_{\rho\tau}^2}{\sigma_Y^2}$$

Interaction model (27.41) assumes, just like additive model (27.34), that, once the blocks have been selected, any two observations from a given block are uncorrelated.

Analysis of Variance.   The sums of squares and degrees of freedom for interaction model (27.41) are the same as those for additive model (27.34). The principal difference in the use of the two models occurs because of the difference in the expected mean squares, as shown in Table 27.9. No exact test for block effects is possible with the interaction model, whereas an exact test is possible with the additive model. This distinction is unimportant whenever blocks are used primarily to reduce the experimental error variability and are not of intrinsic interest themselves.

The F^* test statistic for treatment effects is the same for the two models, namely $F^* = MSTR/MSBL.TR$, which is exactly the same as test statistic (27.7b) for randomized block model (27.1) with fixed block effects. Similarly, estimation of fixed treatment effects for both models with random block effects is carried out in the manner described in Section 27.3 for fixed block effects.

Some Final Comments

1. Table 27.9 indicates that when the block effects are random, *MSBL.TR* estimates σ^2 for additive model (27.34). For interaction model (27.41), however, *MSBL.TR* estimates the sum of the error term variance σ^2 and the interaction variance $\sigma_{\rho\tau}^2$. Separate estimation of these two components is not possible for this latter model, and the two components are said to be confounded.

2. When the assumption of compound symmetry, which underlies both additive model (27.34) and interaction model (27.41), and the less restrictive requirement of sphericity is

not met, the usual F test becomes biased. Some computer packages provide the user with the option of formally testing for compound symmetry or sphericity.

When these conditions are violated, an approximate conservative test procedure is as follows:

    a. Conduct the usual F test; if it leads to conclusion H_0, accept this conclusion.

    b. If the usual F test leads to conclusion H_a, replace $F[1 - \alpha; r - 1, (n - 1)(r - 1)]$ in decision rule (27.7c) by $F(1 - \alpha; 1, n - 1)$. If this modified decision rule leads to H_a, accept this conclusion.

    c. If the modified decision rule leads to H_0, revise the degrees of freedom in the modified decision rule by one of the *epsilon adjustment procedures*, as described in References 27.1 and 27.2.

Alternatively, multivariate analysis of variance techniques may be employed provided that $n > r$. See Reference 27.3 for further discussions of these issues.

3. Mixed models based on less restrictive assumptions regarding the variance-covariance matrix and the parameters in the ANOVA model have also been proposed. See Reference 27.4 for a discussion of these models.

      ■

27.13   Generalized Randomized Block Designs

When block effects are fixed, use of an additive model in the presence of interactions between blocks and treatments has the effect of reducing the power of the test and increasing the width of interval estimates of treatment effects, thus making the experiment less sensitive. In addition, there are occasions when the nature of the interactions between blocks and treatments is of interest. It is possible to use a design that permits an interaction term in the model even when the block effects are fixed, and that allows the nature of the interaction effects to be investigated. This design is called a *generalized randomized block design*. It is the same as a randomized block design except that d experimental units are assigned to each treatment within a block. This generalized design increases the size of a block from r units for a randomized block design to dr units. The increase in block size will often have the effect of increasing experimental error variability when the total number of experimental units is fixed. In the social sciences, however, increasing the size of the block moderately may cause little loss in efficiency. For instance, having one block of 10 persons aged 20–29 instead of two blocks of five persons of ages 20–24 and 25–29, respectively, will for many types of experiments involve little loss of efficiency.

As we shall demonstrate by an example, a generalized randomized block design is analyzed like an ordinary multifactor study where blocks are one factor. Hence, no new problems are encountered with a generalized randomized block design in testing for treatment effects or in estimating them. In particular, we can now calculate *MSE* and use it as an estimator of the error variance σ^2.

Example

Table 27.10 contains the data for a two-factor experiment in which the effects of motivation (factor A: high level, low level) and distraction (factor B: high level, low level) on the time required to complete a task were studied, using eight men and eight women. Two men were assigned at random to each of the $ab = 4$ treatments, and independently two women were assigned at random to each treatment. Here gender is the blocking variable. Each block

TABLE 27.10   **Two-Factor Study in Generalized Randomized Block Design with** $d = 2$ **(observations are times for task completion).**

	Block (gender)	
	Male	Female
High motivation:		
High distraction	12	3
	8	9
Low distraction	7	5
	5	9
Low motivation:		
High distraction	14	11
	16	9
Low distraction	15	10
	13	14

contains eight persons, with two randomly assigned to each treatment within the block. The layout in Table 27.10 corresponds to the layout in Table 23.4a for a three-factor study; to stress the correspondence, we have placed the blocks in columns rather than in rows as usual. Since blocks, motivation levels, and distraction levels are considered to be fixed, we utilize the fixed effects three-factor model (23.14), with notation modified to fit the present context:

$$(27.44) \quad Y_{ijkm} = \mu_{...} + \rho_i + \alpha_j + \beta_k + (\rho\alpha)_{ij} + (\rho\beta)_{ik} + (\alpha\beta)_{jk} + (\rho\alpha\beta)_{ijk} + \varepsilon_{ijkm}$$

where:

$\mu_{...}$ is a constant

ρ_i, α_j, and β_k are constants subject to the restrictions $\Sigma \rho_i = \Sigma \alpha_j = \Sigma \beta_k = 0$

$(\rho\alpha)_{ij}, (\rho\beta)_{ik}, (\alpha\beta)_{jk}, (\rho\alpha\beta)_{ijk}$ are constants subject to the restrictions that the sums over any subscript are zero

ε_{ijkm} are independent $N(0, \sigma^2)$

$i = 1, \ldots, n; j = 1, \ldots, a; k = 1, \ldots, b; m = 1, \ldots, d$

The analysis of variance for generalized randomized block model (27.44) is the ordinary three-factor ANOVA of Table 23.2, with slight modifications in notation. A computer package was employed to obtain the analysis of variance for the data in Table 27.10, and the results are shown in Table 27.11. We know from Table 23.2 that all test statistics use MSE in the denominator. These F^* statistics are shown in Table 27.11. For $\alpha = .01$, we require $F(.99; 1, 8) = 11.3$ for each of the tests. It is evident from the results in Table 27.11 (see also the P-values given there) that blocks do not interact with the factorial treatments and that among the two factors, only motivation affects the time required to complete the task. At this point, further analysis of the motivation effects would be indicated.

TABLE 27.11 **Analysis of Variance for Task Completion Example of Table 27.10**
($n = 2, a = 2, b = 2, d = 2$).

Source of Variation	SS	df	MS	F^*	P-value
Blocks (gender)	$SSBL =$ 25.00	$n - 1 = 1$	$MSBL =$ 25.00	4.00	.08
Factor A (motivation)	$SSA =$ 121.00	$a - 1 = 1$	$MSA =$ 121.00	19.36	.002
Factor B (distraction)	$SSB =$ 1.00	$b - 1 = 1$	$MSB =$ 1.00	.16	.70
$BL.A$ interactions	$SSBL.A =$ 4.00	$(n - 1)(a - 1) = 1$	$MSBL.A =$ 4.00	.64	.45
$BL.B$ interactions	$SSBL.B =$ 16.00	$(n - 1)(b - 1) = 1$	$MSBL.B =$ 16.00	2.56	.15
AB interactions	$SSAB =$ 4.00	$(a - 1)(b - 1) = 1$	$MSAB =$ 4.00	.64	.45
$BL.AB$ interactions	$SSBL.AB =$ 1.00	$(n - 1)(a - 1)(b - 1) = 1$	$MSBL.AB =$ 1.00	.16	.70
Error	$SSE =$ 50.00	$(d - 1)nab = 8$	$MSE =$ 6.25		
Total	$SSTO = 222.00$	$dnab - 1 = 15$			

$F(.99; 1, 8) = 11.3$

27.14 Use of More Than One Blocking Variable

Sometimes, a substantial reduction in the experimental error variability can only be obtained by utilizing more than one variable for determining blocks. For instance, both age and gender might be needed for designating blocks:

Block	Characteristics of Experimental Units	
1	Male,	aged 20–29
2	Female,	aged 20–29
3	Male,	aged 30–39
etc.	etc.	

As another example, both observer and day of treatment application may be helpful as blocking variables:

Block	Characteristics of Experimental Units
1	Observer 1, day 1
2	Observer 2, day 1
3	Observer 1, day 2
etc.	etc.

Unless the separate effects of each of the blocking variables need to be studied, no new problems arise when the blocks are defined by two or more variables. The n blocks are simply treated as ordinary blocks, and the usual block sum of squares is calculated.

When the effect of each of the blocking variables is to be isolated and the blocks are defined in a complete factorial fashion (e.g., nine blocks are used when three observers and three days are employed for blocking), the analysis simply treats each of the blocking variables as a factor and utilizes the methods developed in Chapter 23.

A problem that sometimes arises when two or more blocking variables are to be used is the large number of blocks called for. Suppose an experiment is to be conducted where the experimental units are stores. In order to reduce the experimental error variability to a reasonable level, it would be desirable to group the stores into six sales volume classes and also into six location classes (suburban shopping center, suburban other, etc.). Thirty-six blocks result from combining these two blocking variables. If six treatments are to be studied, 216 stores would be required for the experiment. Often, use of this many stores would be much too costly. Latin square designs, to be discussed in Chapter 30, permit in this type of study the use of a much smaller number of experimental units while still preserving the full benefits of error variance reduction by using both blocking variables in six classes each.

Cited References

27.1. Greenhouse, S. W., and S. Geisser. "On Methods in the Analysis of Profile Data," *Psychometrika* 24 (1959), pp. 95–112.

27.2. Huynh, H., and L. Feldt. "Estimation of the Box Correction for Degrees of Freedom from Sample Data in the Randomized Block and Split-Plot Designs," *Journal of Educational Statistics* 1 (1976), pp. 69–82.

27.3. Winer, B. J., D. R. Brown, and K. M. Michels. *Statistical Principles in Experimental Design*. 3rd ed. New York: McGraw-Hill, 1991.

27.4. Hocking, R. R. *The Analysis of Linear Models*. Monterey, Calif.: Brooks/Cole, 1985.

Problems

27.1. A student commented in a discussion group: "Random permutations are used to assign treatments to experimental units with a randomized block design just as with a completely randomized design. Hence, there is no basic difference between these two designs." Comment.

27.2. a. What might be some useful blocking variables for an experiment about the effects of different price levels on sales of a product, using stores as experimental units?

   b. What might be some useful blocking variables for an experiment about the effects of different flight crew schedules on the morale of crews, using flight crews as experimental units?

   c. What might be some useful blocking variables for an experiment about the effects of different drugs on the speed of a response to a stimulus, using laboratory animals as experimental units?

27.3. Five treatments are studied in an experiment with a randomized complete block design using four blocks. Obtain randomized assignments of treatments to experimental units.

27.4. Two treatments and a control are studied in an experiment with a randomized block design. Five blocks are employed, each containing four experimental units. In each block, each treatment is to be assigned to one experimental unit, and the control is to be assigned to two experimental units. Obtain randomized assignments of treatments to experimental units.

√ 27.5. **Auditor training.** An accounting firm, prior to introducing in the firm widespread training in statistical sampling for auditing, tested three training methods: (1) study at home with programmed training materials, (2) training sessions at local offices conducted by local staff, and (3) training session in Chicago conducted by national staff. Thirty auditors were grouped into 10 blocks of three, according to time elapsed since college graduation, and the auditors in each block were randomly assigned to the three training methods. At the end of the training, each auditor was asked to analyze a complex case involving statistical applications; a proficiency measure based on this analysis was obtained for each auditor. The results were (block 1 consists of auditors graduated most recently, block 10 consists of those graduated most distantly):

Block	Training Method (j)			Block	Training Method (j)		
i	1	2	3	i	1	2	3
1	73	81	92	6	73	75	86
2	76	78	89	7	68	72	88
3	75	76	87	8	64	74	82
4	74	77	90	9	65	73	81
5	76	71	88	10	62	69	78

a. Why do you think the blocking variable "time elapsed since college graduation" was employed?

b. Obtain the residuals for randomized block model (27.1) and plot them against the fitted values. Also prepare a normal probability plot of the residuals. What are your findings?

c. Plot the responses Y_{ij} by blocks in the format of Figure 27.2. What does this plot suggest about the appropriateness of the no-interaction assumption here?

d. Conduct the Tukey test for additivity of block and treatment effects; use $\alpha = .01$. State the alternatives, decision rule, and conclusion. What is the P-value of the test?

√ 27.6. Refer to **Auditor training** Problem 27.5. Assume that randomized block model (27.1) is appropriate.

a. Obtain the analysis of variance table.

b. Prepare a normal probability plot of the estimated treatment means. Does it appear that the treatment means differ substantially here?

c. Test whether or not the mean proficiency is the same for the three training methods. Use level of significance $\alpha = .05$. State the alternatives, decision rule, and conclusion. What is the P-value of the test?

d. Make all pairwise comparisons between the training method means; use the Tukey procedure with a 90 percent family confidence coefficient. State your findings.

e. Test whether or not blocking effects are present; use $\alpha = .05$. State the alternatives, decision rule, and conclusion. What is the P-value of the test?

27.7. **Fat in diets**. A researcher studied the effects of three experimental diets with varying fat contents on the total lipid (fat) level in plasma. Total lipid level is a widely used predictor of coronary heart disease. Fifteen male subjects who were within 20 percent of their ideal body weight were grouped into five blocks according to age. Within each block, the three experimental diets were randomly assigned to the three subjects. Data on reduction in lipid level (in grams per liter) after the subjects were on the diet for a fixed period of time follow.

Block		Fat Content of Diet		
		$j = 1$	$j = 2$	$j = 3$
	i	Extremely Low	Fairly Low	Moderately Low
1	Ages 15-24	.73	.67	.15
2	Ages 25-34	.86	.75	.21
3	Ages 35-44	.94	.81	.26
4	Ages 45-54	1.40	1.32	.75
5	Ages 55-64	1.62	1.41	.78

a. Why do you think that age of subject was used as a blocking variable?

b. Obtain the residuals for randomized block model (27.1) and plot them against the fitted values. Also prepare a normal probability plot of the residuals. What are your findings?

c. Plot the responses Y_{ij} by blocks in the format of Figure 27.2. What does this plot suggest about the appropriateness of the no-interaction assumption here?

d. Conduct the Tukey test for additivity of block and treatment effects; use $\alpha = .01$. State the alternatives, decision rule, and conclusion. What is the P-value of the test?

27.8. Refer to **Fat in diets** Problem 27.7. Assume that randomized block model (27.1) is appropriate.

a. Obtain the analysis of variance table.

b. Prepare a normal probability plot of the estimated treatment means. Does it appear that the treatment means differ substantially here?

c. Test whether or not the mean reductions in lipid level differ for the three diets; use $\alpha = .05$. State the alternatives, decision rule, and conclusion. What is the P-value of the test?

d. Estimate $L_1 = \mu_{.1} - \mu_{.2}$ and $L_2 = \mu_{.2} - \mu_{.3}$ using the Bonferroni procedure with a 95 percent family confidence coefficient. State your findings.

e. Test whether or not blocking effects are present; use $\alpha = .05$. State the alternatives, decision rule, and conclusion. What is the P-value of the test?

f. A standard diet was not used in this experiment as a control. What justification do you think the experimenters might give for not having a control treatment here for comparative purposes?

27.9. **Dental pain**. An anesthesiologist made a comparative study of the effects of acupuncture and codeine on postoperative dental pain in male subjects. The four treatments were: (1) placebo treatment—a sugar capsule and two inactive acupuncture points $(A_1 B_1)$, (2) codeine treatment only—a codeine capsule and two inactive acupuncture points $(A_2 B_1)$, (3) acupuncture treatment only—a sugar capsule and two active acupuncture points $(A_1 B_2)$, and (4) codeine and acupuncture treatment—a codeine capsule and two active acupuncture points ($A_2 B_2$). Thirty-two subjects were grouped into eight blocks of four according to an initial evaluation of their level of pain tolerance. The subjects in each block were then randomly assigned to the four treatments. Pain relief scores were obtained for all subjects two hours after dental treatment. Data were collected on a double-blind basis. The data on pain relief scores follow (the higher the pain relief score, the more effective the treatment).

Block		Treatment (j, k)			
i		$A_1 B_1$	$A_2 B_1$	$A_1 B_2$	$A_2 B_2$
1	(Lowest)	0.0	.5	.6	1.2
2		.3	.6	.7	1.3
...		...	...	...	...
7		1.0	1.8	1.7	2.1
8	(Highest)	1.2	1.7	1.6	2.4

a. Why do you think that pain tolerance of the subjects was used as a blocking variable?

b. Which of the assumptions involved in randomized block model (27.10) are you most concerned with here?

c. Obtain the residuals for randomized block model (27.10) and plot them against the fitted values. Also prepare a normal probability plot of the residuals. What are your findings?

d. Plot the responses Y_{ijk} by blocks in the format of Figure 27.2, ignoring the factorial structure of the treatments. What does this plot suggest about the appropriateness of the no-interaction assumption here?

e. Conduct the Tukey test for additivity of block and treatment effects, ignoring the factorial structure of the treatments; use $\alpha = .01$. State the alternatives, decision rule, and conclusion. What is the P-value of the test?

27.10. Refer to **Dental pain** Problem 27.9. Assume that randomized block model (27.10) is appropriate.

a. Obtain the analysis of variance table.

b. Test whether or not the two factors interact; use $\alpha = .01$. State the alternatives, decision rule, and conclusion. What is the P-value of the test?

c. Prepare separate normal probability plots for each set of estimated factor level means. Does it appear that substantial main effects are present here?

d. Test separately whether main effects are present for each of the factors; use $\alpha = .01$ for each test. State the alternatives, decision rule, and conclusion for each test. What is the P-value of each test?

e. Estimate:

$$L_1 = \mu_{.1.} - \mu_{.2.} = \alpha_1 - \alpha_2$$

$$L_2 = \mu_{..1} - \mu_{..2} = \beta_1 - \beta_2$$

Use the Bonferroni procedure with a 95 percent family confidence coefficient. State your findings.

f. Test whether or not blocking effects are present; use $\alpha = .01$. State the alternatives, decision rule, and conclusion. What is the P-value of the test?

27.11. Refer to **Dental pain** Problem 27.9. Assume that randomized block model (27.11) with fixed effects is to be employed.

  a. Obtain the analysis of variance table.

  b. Test whether or not the two factors interact; use $\alpha = .01$. State the alternatives, decision rule, and conclusion. What is the P-value of the test?

  c. Test separately whether or not blocks interact with each of the factors. For each test, use $\alpha = .01$ and state the alternatives, decision rule, and conclusion. What is the P-value for each test? What do your conclusions imply about the choice between randomized block models (27.10) and (27.11)? Discuss.

  d. Test separately whether main effects are present for each of the factors; use $\alpha = .01$. State the alternatives, decision rule, and conclusion for each test. What is the P-value of each test? Did the choice of models affect your conclusions here?

√ 27.12. Refer to **Auditor training** Problems 27.5 and 27.6. Assume that $\sigma = 2.5$. What is the power of the test for training method effects in Problem 27.6c if $\mu_{.1} = 70$, $\mu_{.2} = 73$, and $\mu_{.3} = 76$?

27.13. Refer to **Fat in diets** Problems 27.7 and 27.8. Assume that $\sigma = .04$. What is the power of the test for diet effects in Problem 27.8c if $\mu_{.1} = 1.1$, $\mu_{.2} = 1.0$, and $\mu_{.3} = .9$?

√ 27.14. Refer to **Auditor training** Problem 27.5. Another accounting firm wishes to conduct the same experiment with some of its auditors, using the same design and model. How many blocks would you recommend that this firm employ if it wishes to make all pairwise treatment comparisons with precision ± 1.5 with a 99 percent family confidence coefficient? Assume that a reasonable planning value for the error standard deviation in model (27.1) is $\sigma = 2.5$.

27.15. Refer to **Fat in diets** Problem 27.7. Suppose that the number of blocks to be used in the study, to consist of male subjects of similar ages, has not yet been determined. Assume that a reasonable planning value for the error standard deviation in model (27.1) is $\sigma = .04$.

  a. What would be the required number of blocks if it is desired to make all pairwise diet comparisons with precision $\pm .03$ with a 95 percent family confidence coefficient?

  b. What would be the required number of blocks if: (1) differences in lipid level reduction means for the three diets are to be detected with probability .95 or more when the range of the treatment means is .12, and (2) the α risk is to be controlled at .01?

√ 27.16. Refer to **Auditor training** Problems 27.5 and 27.6. Based on the estimated efficiency measure (27.14), how effective was the use of the blocking variable as compared to a completely randomized design?

27.17. Refer to **Fat in diets** Problems 27.7 and 27.8. Based on the estimated efficiency measure (27.15), how effective was the use of the blocking variable as compared to a completely randomized design?

27.18. Refer to **Dental pain** Problems 27.9 and 27.10. Based on the estimated efficiency measure (27.14), how effective was the use of the blocking variable as compared to a completely randomized design?

√ 27.19. Refer to **Auditor training** Problem 27.5.

    a. State the regression model equivalent to randomized block model (27.1); use $1, -1, 0$ indicator variables.

    b. Fit the regression model to the data.

    c. Obtain the regression analysis of variance table based on appropriate extra sums of squares.

    d. Test for treatment main effects; use $\alpha = .05$. State the alternatives, decision rule, and conclusion.

27.20. Refer to **Fat in diets** Problem 27.7.

    a. State the regression model equivalent to randomized block model (27.1); use $1, -1, 0$ indicator variables.

    b. Fit the regression model to the data.

    c. Obtain the regression analysis of variance table based on appropriate extra sums of squares.

    d. Test for treatment main effects; use $\alpha = .05$. State the alternatives, decision rule, and conclusion.

√ 27.21. Refer to **Auditor training** Problem 27.5. The analyst wishes to examine whether use of pretraining statistical proficiency scores as a concomitant variable would help to reduce the experimental error variability significantly. The pretraining statistical proficiency scores for the auditors are as follows:

Block i	Training Method (j) 1	2	3	Block i	Training Method (j) 1	2	3
1	93	98	91	6	75	74	78
2	94	93	94	7	79	76	72
3	89	91	92	8	71	69	64
4	86	84	90	9	74	71	70
5	78	76	84	10	63	68	64

    a. Would you expect the auditor's age to have been a better concomitant variable here than the pretraining statistical proficiency score? Discuss.

    b. State the regression model equivalent to covariance model (27.18); use $1, -1, 0$ indicator variables.

    c. Fit the full regression model.

    d. State the reduced regression model for testing treatment effects. Fit the reduced model.

    e. Test whether or not the training methods differ in mean effectiveness; use $\alpha = .05$. State the alternatives, decision rule, and conclusion. What is the P-value of the test?

    f. Obtain a 95 percent confidence interval for $L = \tau_1 - \tau_2$. Interpret your interval estimate.

    g. Has the error variance been reduced substantially by adding the concomitant variable? Explain.

27.22. Refer to **Fat in diets** Problem 27.7. The researcher wishes to examine whether each subject's body weight expressed as a percent of the ideal weight for that person would be a useful concomitant variable. The body weights as percents of the ideal weights for the 15 subjects are as follows:

Block	Fat Content of Diet		
i	$j = 1$	$j = 2$	$j = 3$
1	94	96	101
2	97	102	99
3	105	100	106
4	108	107	112
5	118	115	107

a. State the regression model equivalent to covariance model (27.18); use 1, −1, 0 indicator variables.

b. Fit the full regression model.

c. State the reduced regression model for testing treatment effects. Fit the reduced model.

d. Test whether or not the mean reductions in lipid level differ for the three diets; use $\alpha = .05$. State the alternatives, decision rule, and conclusion. What is the P-value of the test?

e. Obtain confidence intervals for $L_1 = \tau_1 - \tau_2$ and $L_2 = \tau_2 - \tau_3$, using the Bonferroni procedure with a 95 percent family confidence coefficient. Interpret your interval estimates.

f Has the error variance been reduced substantially by adding the concomitant variable? Explain.

√ 27.23. Refer to **Auditor training** Problems 27.5 and 27.6. It has been suggested that the nonparametric rank F test should be used here.

a. Rank the data within each block and perform the rank F test; use $\alpha = .05$. State the alternatives, decision rule, and conclusion. What is the P-value of the test? Is your conclusion the same as that obtained in Problem 27.6c?

b. Use the multiple pairwise testing procedure (27.27) to group the three training methods according to mean proficiency; employ a family significance level of $\alpha = .10$. Summarize your findings.

27.24. Refer to **Dental pain** Problem 27.9; ignore the factorial treatment structure. A consultant, concerned about the validity of the model assumptions, suggested that the study be analyzed by means of the rank F test.

a. Rank the data within each block and perform the rank F test; use $\alpha = .025$. State the alternatives, decision rule, and conclusion. What is the P-value of the test?

b. Use the multiple pairwise testing procedure (27.27) to group the four treatments according to mean pain relief; employ a family significance level of $\alpha = .05$. State your findings.

√ 27.25. Refer to **Auditor training** Problem 27.5. Assume that observation $Y_{23} = 89$ is missing because the auditor became ill and dropped out from the study.

a. State the ANOVA model for this case. Also state the equivalent regression model; use 1, −1, 0 indicator variables.

b. State the reduced regression model for testing for differences in the mean proficiency scores for the three training methods.

c. Test whether or not the mean proficiency scores for the three training methods differ by fitting the full and reduced models; use $\alpha = .05$. State the alternatives, decision rule, and conclusion.

d. Compare the mean proficiency scores for training methods 2 and 3 by means of the regression approach; use a 95 percent confidence interval.

27.26. Refer to **Fat in diets** Problem 27.7. Assume that observations $Y_{13} = .15$ and $Y_{51} = 1.62$ are missing because the subjects did not stay on the prescribed diet.

a. State the ANOVA model for this case. Also state the equivalent regression model; use $1, -1, 0$ indicator variables.

b. State the reduced regression model for testing for differences in the mean reductions in lipid level for the three diets.

c. Test whether or not the mean reductions in lipid level differ for the three diets by fitting the full and reduced models; use $\alpha = .05$. State the alternatives, decision rule, and conclusion.

d. Compare the mean reductions in lipid level for diets 1 and 3 by means of the regression approach; use a 98 percent confidence interval.

√ 27.27. **Road paint wear.** A state highway department studied the wear characteristics of five different paints at eight locations in the state. The standard, currently used paint (paint 1) and four experimental paints (paints 2, 3, 4, 5) were included in the study. The eight locations were randomly selected, thus reflecting variations in traffic densities throughout the state. At each location, a random ordering of the paints to the chosen road surface was employed. After a suitable period of exposure to weather and traffic, a combined measure of wear, considering both durability and visibility, was obtained. The data on wear follow (the higher the score, the better the wearing characteristics).

Location	Paint (j)					Location	Paint (j)				
i	1	2	3	4	5	i	1	2	3	4	5
1	11	13	10	18	15	5	14	16	13	22	16
2	20	28	15	30	18	6	25	27	26	33	25
3	8	10	8	16	12	7	43	46	41	55	42
4	30	35	27	41	28	8	13	14	12	20	13

a. Obtain the residuals for additive randomized block model (27.34) and plot them against the fitted values. Also prepare a normal probability plot of the residuals. Summarize your findings about the appropriateness of model (27.34).

b. Plot the responses by location in the format of Figure 27.2. What does this plot suggest about the appropriateness of the no-interaction assumption here?

c. Conduct the Tukey test for additivity of location and treatment effects, conditional on the locations selected; use $\alpha = .005$. State the alternatives, decision rule, and conclusion.

√ 27.28. Refer to **Road paint wear** Problem 27.27. Assume that additive randomized block model (27.34) is appropriate.

    a. Obtain the analysis of variance table.

    b. Test whether or not the mean wear differs for the five paints; use $\alpha = .05$. State the alternatives, decision rule, and conclusion. What is the P-value of the test?

    c. Compare the mean wear of each experimental paint against that of the standard paint; use the most efficient multiple comparison procedure with a 90 percent family confidence coefficient. Summarize your findings.

    d. Paints 1, 3, and 5 are white, whereas paints 2 and 4 are yellow. Estimate the difference in the mean wear for the two groups of paints with a 95 percent confidence interval. Interpret your findings.

27.29. **Muscle tissue**. A physiologist studied the effects of three reagents on muscle tissue in dogs. Ten litters of three dogs each were randomly selected and the three reagents were randomly assigned to the three dogs in each litter. The data on the effects of the reagents follow (the higher the value, the higher the activity level):

Litter	Reagent (j)			Litter	Reagent (j)		
i	1	2	3	i	1	2	3
1	10	15	14	6	7	9	10
2	8	12	13	7	24	30	27
3	21	27	25	8	16	18	20
4	14	17	17	9	23	29	32
5	12	18	16	10	18	22	21

    a. Obtain the residuals for additive randomized block model (27.34) and plot them against the fitted values. Also prepare a normal probability plot of the residuals. Summarize your findings.

    b. Plot the responses by litter in the format of Figure 27.2. What does this plot suggest about the appropriateness of the no-interaction assumption here?

    c. Conduct the Tukey test for additivity of litter and reagent effects, conditional on the litters selected; use $\alpha = .025$. State the alternatives, decision rule, and conclusion.

    d. Based on parts (b) and (c), would interaction randomized block model (27.41) be more appropriate here? What practical differences exist in using models (27.34) and (27.41)?

27.30. Refer to **Muscle tissue** Problem 27.29. Assume that additive randomized block model (27.34) is applicable.

    a. Obtain the analysis of variance table.

    b. Test whether or not the mean activity level differs for the three reagents; use significance level $\alpha = .025$. State the alternatives, decision rule, and conclusion. What is the P-value of the test?

    c. Reagents 2 and 3 were expected to be similar to each other but to differ from reagent 1. Use the most efficient multiple comparison procedure with a 95 percent family confidence coefficient to estimate:

$$L_1 = \mu_{.2} - \mu_{.3}$$

$$L_2 = \frac{\mu_{.2} + \mu_{.3}}{2} - \mu_{.1}$$

Summarize your findings.

d. Test whether or not σ_ρ^2 equals zero; use $\alpha = .025$. State the alternatives, decision rule, and conclusion. What is the P-value of the test?

27.31. A social scientist, after learning about generalized randomized block designs, asked: "Why would anyone use a randomized complete block design that requires the assumption that block and treatment effects do not interact when this assumption can be avoided with a generalized randomized block design?" Comment.

√ 27.32. Refer to the task completion example in Table 27.10.

a. Verify the analysis of variance in Table 27.11.

b. Estimate the difference in mean effects for the two motivation levels using a 99 percent confidence interval.

27.33. Refer to **Auditor training** Problem 27.5. The accounting firm repeated the experiment with another group of 30 auditors, but this time grouped them into five blocks of six each. In each block, each treatment was randomly assigned to two auditors. The results were:

Block	Training Method (j)			Block	Training Method (j)		
i	1	2	3	i	1	2	3
1	74	84	91	4	65	73	84
	71	78	95		70	78	87
2	73	75	93	5	64	71	81
	69	83	98		61	74	74
3	75	81	89				
	67	74	86				

Assume that generalized randomized block model (27.44), modified for a single-factor study, is appropriate.

a. State the generalized randomized block model for this application.

b. Obtain the analysis of variance table.

c. Test whether or not the mean proficiency scores for the three training methods differ; use $\alpha = .01$. State the alternatives, decision rule, and conclusion. What is the P-value of the test?

d. Make all pairwise comparisons between the three training methods; use the Tukey procedure with a 95 percent family confidence coefficient. Summarize your findings.

e. Obtain the residuals and plot them against the fitted values. Also prepare a normal probability plot of the residuals. State your findings.

f. Test whether or not blocks interact with treatments; use $\alpha = .01$. State the alternatives, decision rule, and conclusion. What is the P-value of the test?

Exercises

27.34. Consider randomized block model (27.1), but with random treatment effects. Derive $\sigma^2\{Y_{ij}\}$ and $\sigma^2\{\bar{Y}_j\}$.

27.35. (Calculus needed.) State the likelihood function for the randomized block fixed effects model (27.1) when $n = 3$ and $r = 2$. Find the maximum likelihood estimators of the parameters.

27.36. For randomized block fixed effects model (27.1), derive $E\{MSTR\}$.

27.37. Show that when two treatments are studied in a randomized complete block design, the F^* test statistic (27.7b) for treatment effects is equivalent to the square of the two-sided t test statistic for paired observations based on (A.69).

27.38. Refer to regression model (27.17), the equivalent to ANOVA model (27.16) when $n = 5$ and $r = 3$. Suppose that the indicator variables in model (27.17) were coded as follows:

$$X_1 = \begin{matrix} 1 & \text{if experimental unit from block 1} \\ 0 & \text{otherwise} \end{matrix}$$

X_2, X_3, X_4 are defined similarly

$$X_5 = \begin{matrix} 1 & \text{if experimental unit received treatment 1} \\ 0 & \text{otherwise} \end{matrix}$$

$$X_6 = \begin{matrix} 1 & \text{if experimental unit received treatment 2} \\ 0 & \text{otherwise} \end{matrix}$$

and that the regression coefficients are denoted by $\beta_0, \beta_1, \beta_2, \beta_3, \beta_4, \beta_5$, and β_6.

a. Exhibit the **X** matrix for this regression model.

b. Find the correspondences between the regression coefficients $\beta_0, \beta_1, \ldots, \beta_6$ and the parameters in ANOVA model (27.16).

c. Discuss the advantages and disadvantages of using $1, 0$ indicator variables and $1, -1, 0$ indicator variables here.

27.39. Derive (27.24b) from (27.24a) when no ties are present.

27.40. Show that relation (27.26) follows from (27.23) and (27.24a).

27.41. Refer to **Dental pain** Problem 27.9. Suppose that the subjects in the study had been randomly selected from eight towns (blocks), and that the towns were randomly selected from a population of towns. Assume that additive randomized block model (27.34) is applicable, except that the factorial structure of the fixed treatment effects needs to be recognized.

a. State the randomized block model for this case.

b. What is the appropriate test statistic for testing whether or not the two factors interact? What are the appropriate test statistics for testing for main effects? [*Hint*: Consider the test for treatment effects in model (27.34).]

27.42. Derive (27.35c).

Projects

27.43. Refer to **Road paint wear** Problem 27.27.

    a. Estimate the variance-covariance matrix of the treatment observations in a block; use (29.8) to obtain the entries in the matrix.

    b. Does the compound symmetry property of (27.38) appear to be reasonable here? Explain.

    c. Does the sphericity property of (27.40) appear to be reasonable here? Explain.

27.44. Refer to **Muscle tissue** Problem 27.29.

    a. Estimate the variance-covariance matrix of the treatment observations in a block; use (29.8) to obtain the entries in the matrix.

    b. Does the compound symmetry property of (27.38) appear to be reasonable here? Explain.

    c. Does the sphericity property of (27.40) appear to be reasonable here? Explain.

Nested Designs, Subsampling, and Partially Nested Designs

In this chapter, we take up the basic elements of nested designs, including the use of subsampling. We begin by considering the general concept of nested designs and describe how these designs differ from crossed designs. We then take up in detail two-factor nested designs and their analysis. We conclude by considering subsampling designs and partially nested designs.

28.1 Distinction between Nested and Crossed Factors

In the factorial studies considered so far, where every level of one factor appears with each level of every other factor, the factors are said to be crossed. A different situation occurs when factors are nested. The distinction between nested and crossed factors will now be illustrated by some examples involving two-factor studies.

Example 1

A large manufacturing company operates three regional training schools for mechanics, one in each of its operating districts. The schools have two instructors each, who teach classes of about 15 mechanics in three-week sessions. The company was concerned about the effect of school (factor A) and instructor (factor B) on the learning achieved. To investigate these effects, classes in each district were formed in the usual way and then randomly assigned to one of the two instructors in the school. This was done for two sessions, and at the end of each session a suitable summary measure of learning for the class was obtained. The results are presented in Table 28.1.

The layout of Table 28.1 appears identical to an ordinary two-factor investigation, with two observations per cell (see, e.g., Table 19.7). In fact, however, the study is not an ordinary two-factor study. The reason is that the instructors in the Atlanta school did not also teach in the other two schools, and similarly for the other instructors. Thus, six different instructors were involved. An ordinary two-factor investigation with six different instructors would have consisted of 18 treatments, as shown in Figure 28.1a. In the training school example, however, only six treatments were included, as shown in Figure 28.1b, where the crossed-out cells represent treatments not studied. Figure 28.2 contains an alternative graphic representation of the nested design for the training school example, including the two replications of the study.

TABLE 28.1 Sample Data for Nested Two-Factor Study—Training School Example (class learning scores, coded).

Factor A (school) i	Factor B (instructor) j: 1	2	Average
Atlanta	25	14	
	29	11	
Average	$\bar{Y}_{11\cdot} = 27$	$\bar{Y}_{12\cdot} = 12.5$	$\bar{Y}_{1\cdot\cdot} = 19.75$
Chicago	11	22	
	6	18	
Average	$\bar{Y}_{21\cdot} = 8.5$	$\bar{Y}_{22\cdot} = 20$	$\bar{Y}_{2\cdot\cdot} = 14.25$
San Francisco	17	5	
	20	2	
Average	$\bar{Y}_{31\cdot} = 18.5$	$\bar{Y}_{32\cdot} = 3.5$	$\bar{Y}_{3\cdot\cdot} = 11.00$
		Average	$\bar{Y}_{\cdot\cdot\cdot} = 15$

FIGURE 28.1 Illustration of Crossed and Nested Factors—Training School Example.

(a) Crossed Factors

School (factor A)	*Instructor (factor B)* 1	2	3	4	5	6
Atlanta						
Chicago						
San Francisco						

(b) Nested Factors

School (factor A)	*Instructor (factor B)* 1	2	3	4	5	6
Atlanta			X	X	X	X
Chicago	X	X			X	X
San Francisco	X	X	X	X		

FIGURE 28.2   **Graphic Representation of Two-Factor Nested Design—Training School Example.**

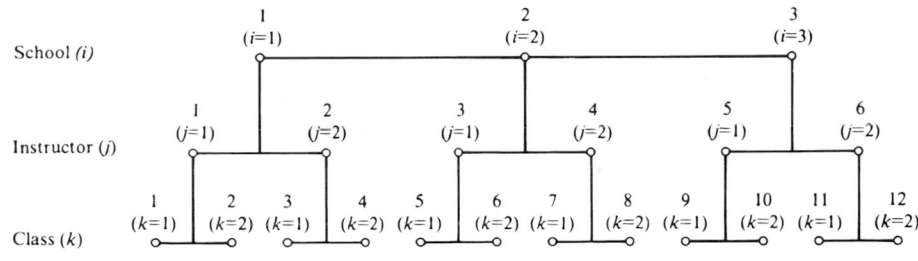

It is clear from Figure 28.1b that the experimental design for the training school example involves an incomplete factorial arrangement of a special type, where each level of factor B (instructor) occurs with only one level of factor A (school). Specifically here, each instructor teaches in only one school. Factor B is therefore said to be *nested* within factor A. As noted earlier, in an ordinary factorial study where every factor level of A appears with every factor level of B, factors A and B are said to be *crossed*.

There is another way to look at the distinction between nested and crossed designs. Let μ_{ij} denote the mean response when factor A is at the ith level and factor B is at the jth level. If the factors are crossed, the jth level of B is the same for all levels of A. If, on the other hand, factor B is nested within factor A, the jth level of B when A is at level 1 has nothing in common with the jth level of B when A is at level 2, and so on. For instance, in a crossed factorial study of the effects of price ($\$1.99$, $\$2.49$) and advertising level (high, low), a particular advertising level is the same no matter with which price it appears, and similarly for the price levels. On the other hand, in the nested design for the training school example, the first instructor in school 1 is not the same as the first instructor in school 2, and so on.

Example 2

An analyst was interested in the effects of community (factor A) and neighborhood (factor B) on the spread of information about new products. Information was obtained from samples of families in various neighborhoods within selected communities. Since the neighborhood designated 1 in a given community is not the same as the neighborhoods designated 1 in the other communities, and similarly for the other neighborhoods, neighborhoods here are nested within communities.

Comments

1. The distinction between crossed and nested factors is often a fine one. In Example 2, if the neighborhoods of each community represented specified average income levels so that, say, the first neighborhoods in each community had an average income of $\$5,000$–$\$9,999$, the second neighborhoods an average income of $\$10,000$–$\$19,999$, and so on for the other neighborhoods, one could view the design as a crossed one. The factors would be community and economic level of neighborhood, and these would be crossed since a given economic level is the same for all communities, and vice versa.

2. Nested factors are frequently encountered in observational studies where the researcher cannot manipulate the factors under study, or in experiments where only some factors can be manipulated. Factors that cannot be manipulated, it will be recalled, are designated classification factors, in distinction to experimental factors that can be assigned at will to the experimental units. Example 2 is an observational study where both community and neighborhood are classification factors since families (the study units) were not randomly assigned to either community or neighborhood. In Example 1, school is a classification factor because the classes of a school (the experimental units) are made up of mechanics from the district in which the school is located. Instructors in this example are an experimental factor since they are assigned randomly to a class, but a nested design results because the randomization of instructors is restricted to within a school.   ∎

28.2 Two-Factor Nested Designs

We now consider nested designs involving two factors, one of which is nested inside the other. For consistency, we always consider the case where factor B is nested within factor A. We initially assume that both factor effects are fixed, but later we also consider the case of random effects. We assume throughout that *all treatment means are of equal importance*.

Development of Model Elements

We shall use the customary notation for a two-factor study, and let μ_{ij} denote the mean response when factor A is at the ith level ($i = 1, \ldots, a$) and factor B is at the jth level ($j = 1, \ldots, b$). As usual, when all mean responses are of equal importance we define:

$$(28.1) \qquad \mu_{i.} = \frac{\sum_j \mu_{ij}}{b}$$

For the training school example of Table 28.1, $\mu_{1.}$ represents the mean learning score for the Atlanta school, averaged over the instructors of that school, and $\mu_{2.}$ and $\mu_{3.}$ are interpreted similarly. Note once more that the $\mu_{i.}$ here represent mean learning scores that have been averaged over *different* instructors.

We define the main effect of the ith level of factor A as usual:

$$(28.2) \qquad \alpha_i = \mu_{i.} - \mu_{..}$$

where:

$$(28.2a) \qquad \mu_{..} = \frac{\sum_i \sum_j \mu_{ij}}{ab} = \frac{\sum_i \mu_{i.}}{a}$$

is the overall mean response. It follows from (28.2a) that:

$$(28.3) \qquad \sum_i \alpha_i = 0$$

In a nested design, it is not meaningful to employ a model component for the main effect of the jth level of factor B. To see why, consider again the training school example. Since each school employs different instructors and the jth instructors in the various schools are not the same, it would be meaningless to consider the effect of the jth instructor, averaged over all schools. Instead, the individual effects of each instructor in each school need to be considered. We denote these individual effects by $\beta_{j(i)}$, where the subscript $j(i)$ indicates that the jth factor level of B is nested within the ith factor level of A. $\beta_{j(i)}$ is defined as follows:

$$(28.4) \qquad \beta_{j(i)} = \mu_{ij} - \mu_i.$$

which can be rewritten, utilizing (28.2):

$$(28.4a) \qquad \beta_{j(i)} = \mu_{ij} - \alpha_i - \mu_{..}$$

It follows from (28.4) and (28.1) that:

$$(28.5) \qquad \sum_j \beta_{j(i)} = 0 \qquad i = 1, \ldots, a$$

The meaning of $\beta_{j(i)}$ can be seen most clearly from (28.4). With reference to the training school example, $\beta_{j(i)}$ is simply the difference in the mean learning score for the jth instructor of school i and the average of the mean learning scores for all instructors in that school. Thus, the effect of the jth instructor in the ith school is measured with respect to the overall mean learning score for the school in which the instructor teaches. We shall call $\beta_{j(i)}$ the *specific effect* of the jth level of factor B nested within the ith level of factor A.

We have now expressed the mean response μ_{ij} in terms of the overall mean, the main effect of the ith level of factor A, and the specific effect of the jth level of factor B nested within the ith level of factor A, as can be seen from (28.4a):

$$(28.6) \qquad \mu_{ij} \equiv \mu_{..} + \alpha_i + \beta_{j(i)} \equiv \mu_{..} + (\mu_{i.} - \mu_{..}) + (\mu_{ij} - \mu_{i.})$$

For the training school example, the mean learning score for the jth instructor in school i has been expressed in terms of the overall mean, the main effect of school i, and the specific effect of instructor j within school i.

To complete the model, we need only add a random error term ε_{ijk}.

Nested Design Model

Let Y_{ijk} denote the response for the kth trial when factor A is at the ith level and factor B is at the jth level. We assume that there are n replications for each factor level combination, i.e., $k = 1, \ldots, n$, and that $i = 1, \ldots, a$ and $j = 1, \ldots, b$. Such a study is said to be *balanced* because the same number of factor B levels is nested within each factor A level and the number of replications is the same throughout.

When both factors A and B have fixed effects, an appropriate nested design model is:

$$(28.7) \qquad Y_{ijk} = \mu_{..} + \alpha_i + \beta_{j(i)} + \varepsilon_{ijk}$$

where:

$\mu_{..}$ is a constant

α_i are constants subject to the restriction $\Sigma \alpha_i = 0$

$\beta_{j(i)}$ are constants subject to the restrictions $\sum_j \beta_{j(i)} = 0$ for all i

ε_{ijk} are independent $N(0, \sigma^2)$

$i = 1, \ldots, a; j = 1, \ldots, b; k = 1, \ldots, n$

The expected value and variance of observation Y_{ijk} for nested design model (28.7) with fixed factor effects are:

(28.8a) $$E\{Y_{ijk}\} = \mu_{..} + \alpha_i + \beta_{j(i)}$$

(28.8b) $$\sigma^2\{Y_{ijk}\} = \sigma^2$$

Thus, all observations have a constant variance. Further, the observations Y_{ijk} are independent and normally distributed for this model.

Comments

1. It is not necessary, as in model (28.7), that the study be balanced; that is, that the number of replications be equal for all factor combinations and that the number of levels of nested factor B (number of instructors in the training school example) be the same for each level of factor A (school in this example). We shall discuss the removal of some of these restrictions in Section 28.6. We only point out now that the computations become more complex when the study is unbalanced.

2. There is no interaction term in nested design model (28.7). There is no need for it since factor B is nested within factor A, not crossed with it. To put this somewhat differently, with reference to the training school example, it is not possible to estimate a school-instructor interaction when each instructor teaches in only one school. The teacher effect $\beta_{j(i)}$, since it is specific to a given school i, in a sense incorporates the interaction effect between the particular teacher j (in the ith school) and the ith school, but it is not possible in a nested design to disentangle this interaction effect.

3. The factor level means $\mu_{i.}$ in a nested design are not generally the same as the corresponding means in a crossed design. Remember that in a nested design, the $\mu_{i.}$ are obtained by averaging over only some of the distinctive levels of factor B. With reference to the training school example, the $\mu_{i.}$ are obtained by averaging over only those teachers who instruct in the ith school. In a crossed design, on the other hand, the $\mu_{i.}$ would be obtained by averaging over all instructors included in the study. ∎

Random Factor Effects

If both factors A and B have random factor levels, nested design model (28.7) is modified with α_i, $\beta_{j(i)}$, and ε_{ijk} being independent normal random variables with expectations 0 and variances σ_α^2, σ_β^2, and σ^2, respectively. Thus, it is assumed that all $\beta_{j(i)}$ have the same variance σ_β^2. The assumption that all $\beta_{j(i)}$ have the same variance also is made if only factor B is random. It is important to check whether this assumption is appropriate, since it may well be that the mean responses $\mu_{i1}, \mu_{i2}, \ldots,$ in one factor A level (plant, school, city, etc.) differ in variability from those in other factor A levels (other plants, schools, cities, etc.). Tests for equality of variances are discussed in Section 18.2.

28.3   Analysis of Variance for Two-Factor Nested Designs

Fitting of Model

The least squares and maximum likelihood estimators of the parameters in nested design model (28.7) are obtained in the usual fashion. Employing our customary notation for sample data in factorial studies, the estimators are:

	Parameter	Estimator
(28.9a)	$\mu_{..}$	$\hat{\mu}_{..} = \bar{Y}_{...}$
(28.9b)	α_i	$\hat{\alpha}_i = \bar{Y}_{i..} - \bar{Y}_{...}$
(28.9c)	$\beta_{j(i)}$	$\hat{\beta}_{j(i)} = \bar{Y}_{ij.} - \bar{Y}_{i..}$

The fitted values therefore are:

$$(28.10) \qquad \hat{Y}_{ijk} = \bar{Y}_{...} + (\bar{Y}_{i..} - \bar{Y}_{...}) + (\bar{Y}_{ij.} - \bar{Y}_{i..}) = \bar{Y}_{ij.}$$

and the residuals are:

$$(28.11) \qquad e_{ijk} = Y_{ijk} - \hat{Y}_{ijk} = Y_{ijk} - \bar{Y}_{ij.}$$

Sums of Squares

The analysis of variance for nested design model (28.7) is obtained by decomposing the total deviation $Y_{ijk} - \bar{Y}_{...}$ as follows:

$$(28.12) \qquad \underbrace{Y_{ijk} - \bar{Y}_{...}}_{\text{Total deviation}} = \underbrace{\bar{Y}_{i..} - \bar{Y}_{...}}_{\substack{A \text{ main effect}}} + \underbrace{\bar{Y}_{ij.} - \bar{Y}_{i..}}_{\substack{\text{Specific } B \\ \text{effect when } A \\ \text{at } i\text{th level}}} + \underbrace{Y_{ijk} - \bar{Y}_{ij.}}_{\text{Residual}}$$

When we square (28.12) and sum over all cases, all cross-product terms drop out and we obtain:

$$(28.13) \qquad SSTO = SSA + SSB(A) + SSE$$

where:

$$(28.13a) \qquad SSTO = \sum_i \sum_j \sum_k (Y_{ijk} - \bar{Y}_{...})^2$$

$$(28.13b) \qquad SSA = bn \sum_i (\bar{Y}_{i..} - \bar{Y}_{...})^2$$

$$(28.13c) \qquad SSB(A) = n \sum_i \sum_j (\bar{Y}_{ij.} - \bar{Y}_{i..})^2$$

$$(28.13d) \qquad SSE = \sum_i \sum_j \sum_k (Y_{ijk} - \bar{Y}_{ij.})^2 = \sum_i \sum_j \sum_k e_{ijk}^2$$

TABLE 28.2   **Relation between Nested Two-Factor ANOVA and Single-Factor ANOVAs—Training School Example.**

| Source of Variation | Single-Factor ANOVAs | | | | | | Nested Two-Factor ANOVA | |
| | School 1 | | School 2 | | School 3 | | | |
	SS	df	SS	df	SS	df	SS	df
Between instructors (within schools)	$SSB(A_1)$	$2-1$ +	$SSB(A_2)$	$2-1$ +	$SSB(A_3)$	$2-1$ =	$SSB(A)$	$3(2-1)$
Error	$SSE(A_1)$	$2(2-1)$ +	$SSE(A_2)$	$2(2-1)$ +	$SSE(A_3)$	$2(2-1)$ =	SSE	$3(2)(2-1)$
Total within schools	$SSTO(A_1)$	$2(2)-1$	$SSTO(A_2)$	$2(2)-1$	$SSTO(A_3)$	$2(2)-1$		
Between schools							SSA	$3-1$
Total							$SSTO$	$3(2)(2)-1$

$SSTO$ is the usual total sum of squares, and SSA is the ordinary factor A sum of squares, reflecting the variability of the estimated factor level means $\bar{Y}_{i..}$.

$SSB(A)$ is the factor B sum of squares, with the notation reflecting that factor B is nested within factor A. $SSB(A)$ is made up of terms such as:

$$(28.14) \qquad n\sum_j (\bar{Y}_{ij.} - \bar{Y}_{i..})^2$$

The term in (28.14) is simply the ordinary factor B sum of squares when factor A is at level i. These terms are then summed over all levels of factor A.

Finally, the error sum of squares SSE is, as usual, the sum of the squared residuals and reflects the variability of each observation Y_{ijk} around the corresponding estimated treatment mean $\bar{Y}_{ij.}$. Alternatively, we can view SSE as being made up of terms such as:

$$(28.15) \qquad \sum_j \sum_k (Y_{ijk} - \bar{Y}_{ij.})^2$$

The term in (28.15) is simply the ordinary error sum of squares within the ith level of factor A. These terms are then summed over all levels of factor A.

Thus, a nested two-factor design can be viewed as a series of single-factor investigations at the successive levels of the other factor. In terms of the training school example, a study of the effects of instructors (B) within any given school (A_i) leads to the usual sums of squares for instructors and errors in a single-factor analysis of variance within school A_i, denoted by $SSB(A_i)$ and $SSE(A_i)$:

$$SSB(A_i) = n\sum_j (\bar{Y}_{ij.} - \bar{Y}_{i..})^2 \qquad SSE(A_i) = \sum_j \sum_k (Y_{ijk} - \bar{Y}_{ij.})^2$$

These are then aggregated to yield $SSB(A)$ and SSE, respectively. It is only the between-schools sum of squares SSA that introduces explicitly the other factor. Table 28.2 demonstrates this relation between the single-factor analyses of variance for each school and the two-factor analysis of variance for the nested design.

TABLE 28.3   **ANOVA Table for Nested Balanced Two-Factor Fixed Effects Model (28.7) (B nested within A).**

Source of Variation	SS	df	MS	E{MS}
Factor A	$SSA = bn \Sigma(\bar{Y}_{i..} - \bar{Y}_{...})^2$	$a - 1$	MSA	$\sigma^2 + bn\dfrac{\Sigma \alpha_i^2}{a - 1}$
Factor B (within A)	$SSB(A) = n \Sigma\Sigma(\bar{Y}_{ij.} - \bar{Y}_{i..})^2$	$a(b - 1)$	$MSB(A)$	$\sigma^2 + n\dfrac{\Sigma\Sigma \beta_{j(i)}^2}{a(b - 1)}$
Error	$SSE = \Sigma\Sigma\Sigma(Y_{ijk} - \bar{Y}_{ij.})^2$	$ab(n - 1)$	MSE	σ^2
Total	$SSTO = \Sigma\Sigma\Sigma(Y_{ijk} - \bar{Y}_{...})^2$	$abn - 1$		

Degrees of Freedom

The degrees of freedom associated with the various sums of squares can be deduced directly from the known relationships already studied. Since there is a total of abn cases, the degrees of freedom associated with $SSTO$ are $abn - 1$. For any level of factor A, there are $b(n - 1)$ degrees of freedom associated with the error sum of squares. Aggregating over all levels of factor A, there are $ab(n - 1)$ degrees of freedom associated with SSE. Similarly, for any level of factor A, there are $b - 1$ degrees of freedom associated with the factor B sum of squares. Hence, by aggregating over all levels of factor A, we find that there are $a(b - 1)$ degrees of freedom associated with $SSB(A)$. Finally, since there are a levels of factor A, there are $a - 1$ degrees of freedom associated with SSA.

Table 28.2 shows this aggregation of the degrees of freedom for the training school example, and Table 28.3 presents the general analysis of variance table for two-factor nested design model (28.7) where factor B is nested within factor A.

Example

In the training school example of Table 28.1, both schools and instructors were regarded as fixed factors; hence, model (28.7) was deemed appropriate. Figure 28.3 presents aligned dot plots of the class learning scores Y_{ijk} for each school. Note that different symbols are used for the two instructors within each school. Figure 28.3 suggests strongly that differences between instructors within a school are present and that there may be differences in the mean learning for the three schools. Note also from the dot plots that the variability of the class learning scores for the two classes taught by each of the six instructors appears to be reasonably constant, as required by model (28.7).

To analyze the instructor and school effects formally, we begin by obtaining the analysis of variance. The sums of squares were obtained as follows using formulas (28.13):

$$SSTO = (25 - 15)^2 + (29 - 15)^2 + \cdots + (2 - 15)^2 = 766$$

$$SSA = 2(2)[(19.75 - 15)^2 + (14.25 - 15)^2 + (11.00 - 15)^2] = 156.5$$

$$SSB(A) = 2[(27 - 19.75)^2 + (12.5 - 19.75)^2 + \cdots + (3.5 - 11.00)^2] = 567.5$$

$$SSE = (25 - 27)^2 + (29 - 27)^2 + \cdots + (2 - 3.5)^2 = 42$$

FIGURE 28.3   Dot Plots of Class Learning Scores—Training School Example.

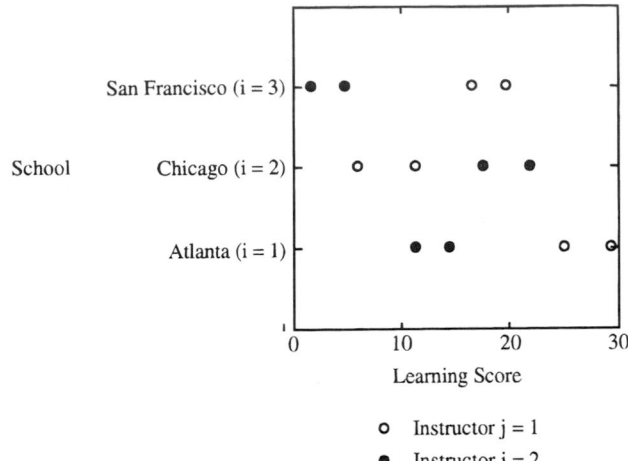

TABLE 28.4   ANOVA for Two-Factor Nested Design—Training School Example.

(a) ANOVA Table

Source of Variation	SS	df	MS
Schools (A)	$SSA = 156.5$	2	78.25
Instructors, within schools [$B(A)$]	$SSB(A) = 567.5$	3	189.17
Error (E)	$SSE =$ 42.0	6	7.00
Total	$SSTO = 766.0$	11	

(b) Decomposition of $SSB(A)$

Source of Variation	$SSB(A_i)$	df	$MSB(A_i)$
Instructors, Atlanta	210.25	1	210.25
Instructors, Chicago	132.25	1	132.25
Instructors, San Francisco	225.00	1	225.00
Total	567.5	3	

Table 28.4a contains the analysis of variance.

Note

Most analysis of variance computer packages provide an option for obtaining the ANOVA for nested designs. Should this option be unavailable, the ordinary ANOVA for crossed factors can be used with only slight inconvenience when the nested study is balanced. *SSTO, SSA,* and *SSE* with the crossed-factor analysis will be the same, and $SSB(A)$ is obtained from the relation:

$$(28.16) \qquad \underbrace{SSB(A)}_{\text{Nested}} = \underbrace{SSB + SSAB}_{\text{Crossed}}$$

The same relation holds for the associated degrees of freedom. ∎

Tests for Factor Effects

Tests for factor effects in a nested two-factor study are straightforward. The appropriate test statistics are determined, as for a crossed two-factor study, by comparing the expected values of the ANOVA mean squares. The expected mean squares for nested fixed effects model (28.7) are shown in Table 28.3. They can be obtained by somewhat tedious derivations. We do not illustrate these derivations because Appendix D describes a relatively simple method of finding expected mean squares for any balanced nested design. Also, many computer packages provide the expected mean squares for nested models.

The $E\{MS\}$ column in Table 28.3 indicates that for fixed effects model (28.7), the test for factor A main effects:

$$(28.17a) \qquad \begin{aligned} H_0&: \text{ all } \alpha_i = 0 \\ H_a&: \text{ not all } \alpha_i \text{ equal zero} \end{aligned}$$

is based on the test statistic:

$$(28.17b) \qquad F^* = \frac{MSA}{MSE}$$

and the decision rule to control the level of significance at α is:

$$(28.17c) \qquad \begin{aligned} &\text{If } F^* \le F[1 - \alpha; a - 1, (n - 1)ab], \text{ conclude } H_0 \\ &\text{If } F^* > F[1 - \alpha; a - 1, (n - 1)ab], \text{ conclude } H_a \end{aligned}$$

Similarly, to test for factor B specific effects:

$$(28.18a) \qquad \begin{aligned} H_0&: \text{ all } \beta_{j(i)} = 0 \\ H_a&: \text{ not all } \beta_{j(i)} \text{ equal zero} \end{aligned}$$

the appropriate test statistic is:

$$(28.18b) \qquad F^* = \frac{MSB(A)}{MSE}$$

and the appropriate decision rule is:

$$(28.18c) \qquad \begin{aligned} &\text{If } F^* \le F[1 - \alpha; a(b - 1), (n - 1)ab], \text{ conclude } H_0 \\ &\text{If } F^* > F[1 - \alpha; a(b - 1), (n - 1)ab], \text{ conclude } H_a \end{aligned}$$

Example. Based on the analysis of variance in Table 28.4a for the training school example, we conduct the first test to determine whether or not main school effects exist. The alternatives are given in (28.17a), and test statistic (28.17b) here is:

$$F^* = \frac{78.25}{7.00} = 11.2$$

For level of significance $\alpha = .05$, we require $F(.95; 2, 6) = 5.14$. Since $F^* = 11.2 > 5.14$, we conclude that the three schools differ in mean learning effects. The P-value of the test is .0094.

Next is a test for differences in mean learning effects between instructors within each school. The alternatives are given in (28.18a), and test statistic (28.18b) here is:

$$F^* = \frac{189.17}{7.00} = 27.0$$

For $\alpha = .05$, we require $F(.95; 3, 6) = 4.76$. Since $F^* = 27.0 > 4.76$, we conclude that instructors within at least one school differ in terms of mean learning effects. The P-value of this test is .0007.

Comments

1. The alternative H_0 in (28.18a) can also be expressed in terms of the treatment means μ_{ij}:

(28.19) $H_0: \mu_{11} = \mu_{12} = \cdots = \mu_{1b}; \mu_{21} = \mu_{22} = \cdots = \mu_{2b}; \cdots$

In terms of the training school example, H_0 states that the mean learning scores for all instructors in Atlanta are the same, and similarly for the other schools. It does *not* state that the mean learning scores for all instructors in the different schools are the same.

2. If it is concluded that factor B effects are present, it is often desired to ascertain whether they are present in all levels of factor A or only in some. (In some cases, indeed, one may wish to proceed immediately to this analysis.) With reference to the training school example, the question would be whether the instructor effects differ in all schools or only in some schools. As noted earlier, $SSB(A)$ in Table 28.4a is made up of the instructor sums of squares within the individual schools. These component sums of squares can be used for testing instructor effects within each school. Table 28.4b contains the relevant component sums of squares. To test for instructor differences within the Atlanta school, for instance, we use test statistic $F^* = MSB(A_1)/MSE = 210.25/7.00 = 30.0$. For level of significance $\alpha = .05$, we need $F(.95; 1, 6) = 5.99$. Since $F^* = 30.0 > 5.99$, we conclude that the two instructors in Atlanta have different mean learning effects. Using the same level of significance each time, similar conclusions are reached for the other two schools. The family level of significance for the three tests according to the Bonferroni inequality is at most .15.

3. If the assumption of constant error variance were violated in the training school example through unequal variances for the different schools, it would still be possible to study instructor effects within each school by separate analyses of variance for each school.

4. The power of the tests for fixed factor A and factor B effects can be ascertained by using (26.5) together with the expected mean squares in Table 28.3.   ∎

TABLE 28.5 Expected Mean Squares for Nested Balanced Two-Factor Designs with Random Factor Effects (B nested within A).

	Expected Mean Square	
Mean Square	A Fixed, B Random	A Random, B Random
MSA	$\sigma^2 + bn\dfrac{\Sigma \alpha_i^2}{a-1} + n\sigma_\beta^2$	$\sigma^2 + bn\sigma_\alpha^2 + n\sigma_\beta^2$
$MSB(A)$	$\sigma^2 + n\sigma_\beta^2$	$\sigma^2 + n\sigma_\beta^2$
MSE	σ^2	σ^2

	Appropriate Test Statistic	
Test for	A Fixed, B Random	A Random, B Random
Factor A	$MSA/MSB(A)$	$MSA/MSB(A)$
Factor $B(A)$	$MSB(A)/MSE$	$MSB(A)/MSE$

Random Factor Effects

Test statistic (28.17b) for factor A main effects is not appropriate if either or both factor effects are random. Table 28.5 gives the expected mean squares for these cases and also the appropriate test statistics.

28.4 Evaluation of Appropriateness of Nested Design Model

The diagnostic procedures described earlier are entirely applicable for examining whether nested design model (28.7) is appropriate. The residuals in (28.11):

$$(28.20) \qquad e_{ijk} = Y_{ijk} - \bar{Y}_{ij}.$$

may be examined as usual for normality, constancy of the error variance, and independence of the error terms. In particular, aligned dot plots of the residuals for each factor A level may be helpful in examining whether the variance of the error terms is constant for the different factor A levels within which factor B is nested.

Example

Figure 28.4a contains MINITAB aligned dot plots of the residuals for each school for the training school example. These plots are affected by the rounded nature of the data, but they support the appropriateness of the assumption of constancy of the error variance. Figure 28.4b presents a normal probability plot of the residuals. This plot is also affected by the rounded nature of the observations, but does not indicate any gross departure from normality. This conclusion is supported by the coefficient of correlation between the ordered residuals and their expected values under normality, which is .927. These and other diagnostics (not shown here) support the appropriateness of nested design model (28.7) for the training school example.

FIGURE 28.4 MINITAB Diagnostic Residual Plots—Training School Example.

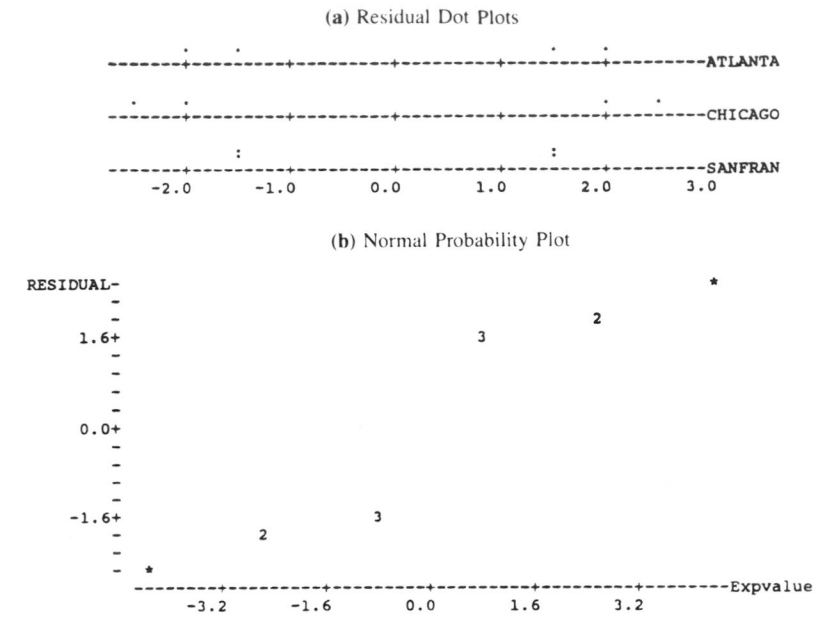

(a) Residual Dot Plots

(b) Normal Probability Plot

Note

Since there are numerous ties among the residuals in the training school example, the normal probability plot in Figure 28.4b is obtained by plotting each of the tied residuals against the expected value for the mean of the tied order positions and showing the number of tied residuals at that position. ∎

28.5 Analysis of Factor Effects in Two-Factor Nested Designs

When factor effects are present in a nested design, estimates and/or comparisons of these effects are usually desired.

Estimation of Factor Level Means $\mu_{i.}$

When factor A (fixed effects factor) has significant main effects, there is frequent interest in estimating the factor level means $\mu_{i.}$. The estimated factor level mean $\bar{Y}_{i..}$ is an unbiased estimator of $\mu_{i.}$. As usual for a fixed effects factor, the estimated variance of $\bar{Y}_{i..}$ is based on the mean square in the denominator of the statistic used for testing for factor A main effects, and on the number of cases on which $\bar{Y}_{i..}$ is based. Confidence limits for $\mu_{i.}$ are of the customary form:

$$(28.21) \qquad \bar{Y}_{i..} \pm t(1 - \alpha/2; df)s\{\bar{Y}_{i..}\}$$

where:

$$(28.21a) \qquad s^2\{\bar{Y}_{i..}\} = \frac{MSE}{bn} \qquad df = ab(n-1) \qquad A \text{ and } B \text{ fixed}$$

$$(28.21b) \qquad s^2\{\bar{Y}_{i..}\} = \frac{MSB(A)}{bn} \qquad df = a(b-1) \qquad A \text{ fixed}, B \text{ random}$$

Confidence limits for contrasts $L = \Sigma c_i \mu_{i.}$, where $\Sigma c_i = 0$, are set up in the usual way, utilizing the estimator $\hat{L} = \Sigma c_i \bar{Y}_{i..}$ and the t distribution with degrees of freedom those associated with the appropriate mean square:

$$(28.22) \qquad \hat{L} \pm t(1 - \alpha/2; df) s\{\hat{L}\}$$

where:

$$(28.22a) \qquad s^2\{\hat{L}\} = \sum c_i^2 s^2\{\bar{Y}_{i..}\} \qquad \text{as given by (28.21a) or (28.21b)}$$

The Tukey and Bonferroni simultaneous comparison procedures can be utilized in the usual way for making pairwise comparisons with family confidence coefficient $1 - \alpha$, and the Scheffé and Bonferroni simultaneous comparison procedures can be employed for a family of contrasts.

Example. For the training school example in Table 28.1, it was desired to estimate the mean learning score for the Atlanta school with a 95 percent confidence coefficient. Using our earlier results in Tables 28.1 and 28.4a, we obtain for the fixed effects model:

$$\bar{Y}_{1..} = 19.75$$

$$s^2\{\bar{Y}_{1..}\} = \frac{MSE}{bn} = \frac{7.00}{4} = 1.75$$

$$s\{\bar{Y}_{1..}\} = 1.32$$

$$t(.975; 6) = 2.447$$

$$16.5 = 19.75 - 2.447(1.32) \le \mu_{1.} \le 19.75 + 2.447(1.32) = 23.0$$

In addition, pairwise comparisons of the three schools were to be made with family confidence coefficient .90. We shall utilize the Tukey procedure and require:

$$T = \frac{1}{\sqrt{2}} q[1 - \alpha; a, ab(n-1)] = \frac{1}{\sqrt{2}} q(.90; 3, 6) = \frac{1}{\sqrt{2}}(3.56) = 2.52$$

The estimated variance is the same for all pairwise comparisons:

$$s^2\{\hat{L}\} = \frac{MSE}{bn} + \frac{MSE}{bn} = \frac{2(7.00)}{4} = 3.5$$

so that the estimated standard deviation is $s\{\hat{L}\} = 1.87$ and $Ts\{\hat{L}\} = 2.52(1.87) = 4.71$.
Using the results in Table 28.1, we have:

$$\bar{Y}_{1..} = 19.75 \qquad \bar{Y}_{2..} = 14.25 \qquad \bar{Y}_{3..} = 11.00$$

Hence, the 90 percent family of confidence intervals is:

$$.8 = (19.75 - 14.25) - 4.71 \leq \mu_{1.} - \mu_{2.} \leq (19.75 - 14.25) + 4.71 = 10.2$$

$$4.0 = (19.75 - 11.00) - 4.71 \leq \mu_{1.} - \mu_{3.} \leq (19.75 - 11.00) + 4.71 = 13.5$$

$$-1.5 = (14.25 - 11.00) - 4.71 \leq \mu_{2.} - \mu_{3.} \leq (14.25 - 11.00) + 4.71 = 8.0$$

We conclude with 90 percent family confidence coefficient that the mean learning score is highest in Atlanta and that the difference in the observed mean scores for Chicago and San Francisco is not statistically significant. We summarize these results by the following line plot:

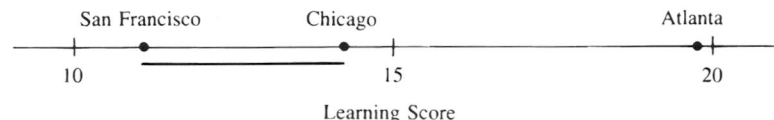

Estimation of Treatment Means μ_{ij}

Confidence limits for μ_{ij} are set up in the usual fashion using the t distribution when both factors A and B have fixed effects:

$$(28.23) \qquad \bar{Y}_{ij.} \pm t[1 - \alpha/2; (n-1)ab]s\{\bar{Y}_{ij.}\}$$

where:

$$(28.23a) \qquad s^2\{\bar{Y}_{ij.}\} = \frac{MSE}{n}$$

To make a comparison within any factor A level, we estimate the contrast $L = \Sigma c_j \mu_{ij}$, where $\Sigma c_j = 0$, with the estimator $\hat{L} = \Sigma c_j \bar{Y}_{ij.}$ and employ the confidence limits:

$$(28.24) \qquad \hat{L} \pm t[1 - \alpha/2; (n-1)ab]s\{\hat{L}\}$$

where:

$$(28.24a) \qquad s^2\{\hat{L}\} = \frac{MSE}{n} \Sigma c_j^2$$

The Bonferroni procedure may be used when several comparisons are to be made and the family confidence level is to be controlled. The Tukey procedure is also applicable for paired comparisons and the Scheffé procedure for contrasts, but these procedures often will not be efficient since ordinarily only comparisons within each factor level are of interest, whereas the Tukey and Scheffé families are based on comparisons among all ab treatments.

Example. In the training school example, we are to compare the mean scores for the two instructors in each school, using the Bonferroni procedure with a 90 percent family confidence coefficient. For $g = 3$ comparisons, we require $B = t[1 - .10/2(3); 6] = t(.983; 6) = 2.748$. The estimated variance in each case is:

$$s^2\{\hat{L}\} = \frac{7.00}{2}(2) = 7.0$$

Hence, $Bs\{\hat{L}\} = 2.748\sqrt{7.0} = 7.27$. Obtaining the estimated treatment means $\bar{Y}_{ij}$ from Table 28.1, we find:

$$7.2 = (27 - 12.5) - 7.27 \leq \mu_{11} - \mu_{12} \leq (27 - 12.5) + 7.27 = 21.8$$
$$-18.8 = (8.5 - 20) - 7.27 \leq \mu_{21} - \mu_{22} \leq (8.5 - 20) + 7.27 = -4.2$$
$$7.7 = (18.5 - 3.5) - 7.27 \leq \mu_{31} - \mu_{32} \leq (18.5 - 3.5) + 7.27 = 22.3$$

It is evident that substantial differences between the two instructors exist at each school.

Estimation of Overall Mean $\mu_{..}$

Sometimes there is interest in estimating the overall mean $\mu_{..}$. For the training school example, $\mu_{..}$ is the overall mean learning score for all training schools and all instructors in these schools. The point estimator is $\bar{Y}_{...}$. The confidence limits are constructed utilizing the t distribution as follows:

$$(28.25) \qquad \bar{Y}_{...} \pm t(1 - \alpha/2; df)s\{\bar{Y}_{...}\}$$

where:

$$(28.25a) \qquad s^2\{\bar{Y}_{...}\} = \frac{MSE}{abn} \qquad df = ab(n - 1) \qquad A \text{ and } B \text{ fixed}$$

$$(28.25b) \qquad s^2\{\bar{Y}_{...}\} = \frac{MSA}{abn} \qquad df = a - 1 \qquad A \text{ and } B \text{ random}$$

$$(28.25c) \qquad s^2\{\bar{Y}_{...}\} = \frac{MSB(A)}{abn} \qquad df = a(b - 1) \qquad A \text{ fixed, } B \text{ random}$$

Example. For the training school example, we wish to estimate the overall mean $\mu_{..}$ with a 95 percent confidence interval. The estimated variance (28.25a) is appropriate here since the model involves fixed factor effects. Hence, we obtain:

$$s^2\{\bar{Y}_{...}\} = \frac{7.00}{12} = .583 \qquad s\{\bar{Y}_{...}\} = .764$$

For confidence coefficient .95, we require $t(.975; 6) = 2.447$. From Table 28.1, we find $\bar{Y}_{...} = 15$. The desired confidence interval therefore is:

$$13.1 = 15 - 2.447(.764) \leq \mu_{..} \leq 15 + 2.447(.764) = 16.9$$

Estimation of Variance Components

With random factor effects, estimates of the variance components may be of interest. No new problems arise for balanced nested designs. For instance, we see from Table 28.5 that when both factors A and B are random factors, the variance component σ_α^2 can be expressed as follows:

$$(28.26) \qquad \sigma_\alpha^2 = \frac{E\{MSA\} - E\{MSB(A)\}}{bn}$$

Hence, an unbiased estimator of σ_α^2 is:

$$(28.27) \qquad s_\alpha^2 = \frac{MSA - MSB(A)}{bn}$$

Approximate confidence intervals for variance components σ_α^2 or σ_β^2 can be obtained using the MLS interval (24.34). For example, to estimate σ_α^2 when both A and B are random factors, we see from (28.26) that the correspondences to (24.32) are:

$$c_1 = \frac{1}{bn} \qquad MS_1 = MSA$$

$$c_2 = -\frac{1}{bn} \qquad MS_2 = MSB(A)$$

Hence, the MLS confidence interval for σ_α^2 is:

$$(28.28) \qquad s_\alpha^2 - H_L \le \sigma_\alpha^2 \le s_\alpha^2 + H_U$$

where H_L and H_U are given by the formulas in Table 24.3, $df_1 = a - 1$, $df_2 = a(b - 1)$, and s_α^2 is given by (28.27).

28.6   Unbalanced Nested Two-Factor Designs

Up to this point, we have assumed that the nested study is balanced; that is, the same number of levels of factor B is nested within each of the levels of factor A, and the same number of replications is made for each factor level combination. There are occasions, however, when a study is unbalanced. For instance, in our earlier example dealing with the effects of school (factor A) and instructor (factor B) on the learning achieved by classes of mechanics, there might have been b_i instructors in the ith school and n_{ij} classes taught by the jth instructor in school i.

The ANOVA sums of squares formulas given earlier are not appropriate for unbalanced studies. Ordinarily, it is best to use the regression approach for unbalanced studies when the factor effects are fixed. Since no new principles are involved, we proceed directly to an example.

Example

The manufacturing company that conducted the training school study subsequently made a follow-up study involving only Atlanta and Chicago. At that time, three instructors were used in Atlanta and two in Chicago. All instructors were to train two classes, but one class

TABLE 28.6   **Nested Unbalanced Two-Factor Study—Follow-up Training School Study.**

(a) Data

Replication	Atlanta (A_1)			Chicago (A_2)	
k	B_1	B_2	B_3	B_1	B_2
1	20	8	9	4	16
2	22		13	8	20

(b) Y and X Variables for Regression Approach

			(1)	(2)	(3)	(4)	(5)
i	j	k	Y	X_1	X_2	X_3	X_4
1	1	1	20	1	1	0	0
1	1	2	22	1	1	0	0
1	2	1	8	1	0	1	0
1	3	1	9	1	−1	−1	0
1	3	2	13	1	−1	−1	0
2	1	1	4	−1	0	0	1
2	1	2	8	−1	0	0	1
2	2	1	16	−1	0	0	−1
2	2	2	20	−1	0	0	−1

for one of the instructors in Atlanta had to be canceled. The data for this follow-up study are presented in Table 28.6a. We shall again assume that a fixed effects nested design model is appropriate:

$$(28.29) \qquad Y_{ijk} = \mu_{..} + \alpha_i + \beta_{j(i)} + \varepsilon_{ijk}$$

$$i = 1, 2; \; j = 1, \ldots, b_i; \; k = 1, \ldots, n_{ij}$$

$$b_1 = 3, \quad b_2 = 2 \quad n_{11} = n_{13} = 2, \quad n_{12} = 1, \quad n_{21} = n_{22} = 2$$

$$\sum_{i=1}^{2} \alpha_i = 0 \qquad \sum_{j=1}^{3} \beta_{j(1)} = 0 \qquad \sum_{j=1}^{2} \beta_{j(2)} = 0$$

Proceeding as usual, we shall incorporate the parameters α_1, $\beta_{1(1)}$, $\beta_{2(1)}$, and $\beta_{1(2)}$ into the regression model. The other parameters are not required since according to the constraints in (28.29) we have:

$$(28.30) \qquad \alpha_2 = -\alpha_1 \qquad \beta_{3(1)} = -\beta_{1(1)} - \beta_{2(1)} \qquad \beta_{2(2)} = -\beta_{1(2)}$$

Thus, we require four indicator variables for our example, each taking on values 1, −1, or 0.

The equivalent regression model therefore is:

$$(28.31) \quad Y_{ijk} = \mu_{..} + \underbrace{\alpha_1 X_{ijk1}}_{\substack{\text{School main} \\ \text{effect}}} + \underbrace{\beta_{1(1)} X_{ijk2} + \beta_{2(1)} X_{ijk3} + \beta_{1(2)} X_{ijk4}}_{\substack{\text{Specific instructor within} \\ \text{school effect}}} + \varepsilon_{ijk} \quad \text{Full model}$$

where:

$$X_1 = \begin{array}{ll} 1 & \text{if class from school 1} \\ -1 & \text{if class from school 2} \end{array}$$

$$X_2 = \begin{array}{ll} 1 & \text{if class for instructor 1 in school 1} \\ -1 & \text{if class for instructor 3 in school 1} \\ 0 & \text{otherwise} \end{array}$$

$$X_3 = \begin{array}{ll} 1 & \text{if class for instructor 2 in school 1} \\ -1 & \text{if class for instructor 3 in school 1} \\ 0 & \text{otherwise} \end{array}$$

$$X_4 = \begin{array}{ll} 1 & \text{if class for instructor 1 in school 2} \\ -1 & \text{if class for instructor 2 in school 2} \\ 0 & \text{otherwise} \end{array}$$

The Y observations and X indicator variables for this example are shown in Table 28.6b.

To test for school main effects, we first fit full model (28.31) by regressing Y in Table 28.6b, column 1, on X_1, X_2, X_3, X_4 in columns 2–5, and obtain $SSE(F)$. We then fit the reduced model for H_0: $\alpha_1 = 0$:

$$(28.32) \quad Y_{ijk} = \mu_{..} + \beta_{1(1)} X_{ijk2} + \beta_{2(1)} X_{ijk3} + \beta_{1(2)} X_{ijk4} + \varepsilon_{ijk} \quad \text{Reduced model}$$

by regressing Y in column 1 on X_2, X_3, X_4 in columns 3–5, and obtain $SSE(R)$. The difference $SSE(R) - SSE(F)$ equals SSA. Test statistic (2.70) is then obtained in the usual fashion.

To test for specific instructor effects, we employ the reduced model for H_0: $\beta_{1(1)} = \beta_{2(1)} = \beta_{1(2)} = 0$:

$$(28.33) \quad Y_{ijk} = \mu_{..} + \alpha_1 X_{ijk1} + \varepsilon_{ijk} \quad \text{Reduced model}$$

We therefore regress Y in column 1 on X_1 in column 2, and obtain $SSE(R)$. The difference $SSE(R) - SSE(F)$ equals $SSB(A)$.

Table 28.7 contains the ANOVA table for the follow-up training school study. No total sum of squares is shown because the component sums of squares are not orthogonal.

The tests for school and instructor effects are carried out as before. Estimation of factor effects is done by means of the regression parameters. For instance, a comparison of the mean scores for the two schools involves:

$$\mu_{1.} - \mu_{2.} = \alpha_1 - \alpha_2$$

Since $\alpha_2 = -\alpha_1$ by (28.30), we need to estimate:

$$\mu_{1.} - \mu_{2.} = \alpha_1 - (-\alpha_1) = 2\alpha_1$$

An unbiased estimator is $2\hat{\alpha}_1$. Other desired estimates are obtained in a similar fashion.

TABLE 28.7   **ANOVA Table for Nested Unbalanced Two-Factor Study—Follow-up Training School Study.**

Source of Variation	SS	df	MS	F*
Schools (A)	3.76	1	3.76	3.76/6.5 = .58
Instructors [$B(A)$]	295.20	3	98.4	98.4/6.5 = 15.1
Error (E)	26.00	4	6.5	

28.7   Subsampling in Single-Factor Study with Completely Randomized Design

Up to this point in our discussion of experimental designs, we have considered only designs in which one observation of the response variable is made on an experimental unit. There are occasions, however, when more than one observation is desirable. Consider an experiment to study the effect of oven temperature on crustiness of bread. Three temperatures were utilized, and two experimental units (batches of flour mix) were randomly assigned to each treatment. It was not economical to use the entire batch to bake breads, nor was it technically feasible to use a batch as a block. Hence, three subsamples were selected from each batch to make three loaves, which were baked at a given temperature. Here, then, three observations (subsamples) were made on each experimental unit (batch).

Another instance of several observations on the response variable being made for each experimental unit occurred in an experiment on the effectiveness of three different training methods. The experimental units here were persons, and the experiment sought to measure the length of time required to perform a certain engine assembly operation after the given training program was completed. Ten consecutive assemblies were timed, and these constituted the subsamples of the experimental unit (person).

Formally, subsampling (i.e., repeated observations on the same experimental unit) is completely analogous to nested factors. We shall demonstrate this for a completely randomized design.

Model

Consider again the experiment to study the effect of oven temperature on the crustiness of bread. The model for this study can be written as follows:

$$(28.34) \qquad Y_{ijk} = \mu_{..} + \tau_i + \varepsilon_{j(i)} + \eta_{ijk}$$

The meaning of the symbols is as follows:

1. $\mu_{..}$ is an overall constant.

2. τ_i is the temperature (i.e., treatment) effect (fixed effect, here).

3. $\varepsilon_{j(i)}$ is the experimental error associated with the particular batch (random effect, here). The experimental error is nested within the treatment, since the jth batch for treatment i was not used with any other treatment.

4. η_{ijk} is the error associated with the kth subsample or observation on the jth experimental unit for the ith treatment (random effect, here).

Note that subsampling model (28.34) appears the same as nested design model (28.7) for a nested two-factor design, except for changes in notation to reflect the fact that subsampling model (28.34) is a single-factor model and contains both experimental and observation errors. Specifically, the treatment effect τ_i here corresponds to α_i in the nested two-factor model, the batch effect $\varepsilon_{j(i)}$ corresponds to $\beta_{j(i)}$, and the observation error term η_{ijk} corresponds to ε_{ijk}. Consequently, the analysis of variance for the case of subsampling in a single-factor study with a completely randomized design parallels that for a nested two-factor study.

In general, the model for subsampling in a balanced single-factor study with a completely randomized design where the treatment effects are fixed is:

$$(28.35) \qquad Y_{ijk} = \mu_{..} + \tau_i + \varepsilon_{j(i)} + \eta_{ijk}$$

where:

$\mu_{..}$ is a constant

τ_i are constants subject to the restriction $\Sigma \tau_i = 0$

$\varepsilon_{j(i)}$ are independent $N(0, \sigma^2)$

η_{ijk} are independent $N(0, \sigma_\eta^2)$

$\varepsilon_{j(i)}$ and η_{ijk} are independent

$i = 1, \ldots, r; j = 1, \ldots, n; k = 1, \ldots, m$

The mean and variance of observation Y_{ijk} for this model are:

$$(28.36a) \qquad E\{Y_{ijk}\} = \mu_{..} + \tau_i$$

$$(28.36b) \qquad \sigma^2\{Y_{ijk}\} = \sigma_Y^2 = \sigma^2 + \sigma_\eta^2$$

Further, the observations Y_{ijk} are normally distributed for this model. Observations from different replications (i.e., from different subsamples) are independent, but any two observations from the same replication are correlated in advance of the random trials because they contain the same random term $\varepsilon_{j(i)}$:

$$(28.36c) \qquad \sigma\{Y_{ijk}, Y_{ijk'}\} = \sigma^2 \qquad k \neq k'$$

$$(28.36d) \qquad \sigma\{Y_{ijk}, Y_{i'j'k'}\} = 0 \qquad i \neq i' \text{ and/or } j \neq j'$$

Analysis of Variance and Tests of Effects

The appropriate sums of squares for the analysis of variance for balanced subsampling model (28.35) are as follows:

$$(28.37a) \qquad SSTO = \sum_i \sum_j \sum_k (Y_{ijk} - \bar{Y}_{...})^2$$

$$(28.37b) \qquad SSTR = nm \sum_i (\bar{Y}_{i..} - \bar{Y}_{...})^2$$

TABLE 28.8   **ANOVA for Single-Factor Completely Randomized Balanced Experiment with Subsampling.**

Source of Variation	SS	df	MS	$E\{MS\}$	
				τ_i Fixed	τ_i Random
Treatments	SSTR	$r-1$	MSTR	$\sigma_\eta^2 + m\sigma^2 + nm\dfrac{\Sigma\tau_i^2}{r-1}$	$\sigma_\eta^2 + m\sigma^2 + nm\sigma_\tau^2$
Experimental error	SSEE	$r(n-1)$	MSEE	$\sigma_\eta^2 + m\sigma^2$	$\sigma_\eta^2 + m\sigma^2$
Observation error	SSOE	$rn(m-1)$	MSOE	σ_η^2	σ_η^2
Total	SSTO	$rnm-1$			

$$(28.37c) \qquad SSEE = m \sum_i \sum_j (\bar{Y}_{ij.} - \bar{Y}_{i..})^2$$

$$(28.37d) \qquad SSOE = \sum_i \sum_j \sum_k (Y_{ijk} - \bar{Y}_{ij.})^2$$

Here, *SSEE* stands for the *experimental error sum of squares*, and *SSOE* stands for the *observation error sum of squares*. Note the correspondence of formulas (28.37) to formulas (28.13) for nested two-factor designs. The only difference is that we now have $i = 1, \ldots, r$, $j = 1, \ldots, n$, and $k = 1, \ldots, m$, whereas before i, j, and k ran to a, b, and n, respectively.

Table 28.8 contains the ANOVA for a single-factor completely randomized balanced experiment with subsampling. Also shown there are the expected mean squares for both fixed and random treatment effects. Note that regardless of whether treatment effects are fixed or random, the appropriate statistic for testing treatment effects is:

$$(28.38a) \qquad F^* = \frac{MSTR}{MSEE}$$

A test for the presence of experimental error effects, i.e., H_0: $\sigma^2 = 0$, H_a: $\sigma^2 > 0$, also uses the same test statistic for both fixed and random treatment effects:

$$(28.38b) \qquad F^* = \frac{MSEE}{MSOE}$$

Example.   The data for the study of the effects of baking temperature on the crustiness of bread are contained in Table 28.9. The data are scores on a scale from 1 to 20. Figure 28.5 presents SYSTAT aligned dot plots of the data. These plots suggest the presence of temperature effects and possibly also batch effects. Note that crustiness increases steadily with the level of temperature.

The appropriate analysis of variance was obtained from a computer run and is presented in Table 28.10. To test for temperature effects:

$$H_0: \ \tau_1 = \tau_2 = \tau_3 = 0$$

$$H_a: \ \text{not all } \tau_i \text{ equal zero}$$

TABLE 28.9   Data for Single-Factor Completely Randomized Balanced Experiment with Subsampling—Bread Crustiness Example.

Observation Unit k	Temperature					
	Low ($i = 1$)		Medium ($i = 2$)		High ($i = 3$)	
	Batch 1 $j = 1$	Batch 2 $j = 2$	Batch 3 $j = 1$	Batch 4 $j = 2$	Batch 5 $j = 1$	Batch 6 $j = 2$
1	4	12	14	9	14	16
2	7	8	13	10	17	19
3	5	10	11	12	15	18

FIGURE 28.5   SYSTAT Dot Plots for Subsampling Experiment— Bread Crustiness Example.

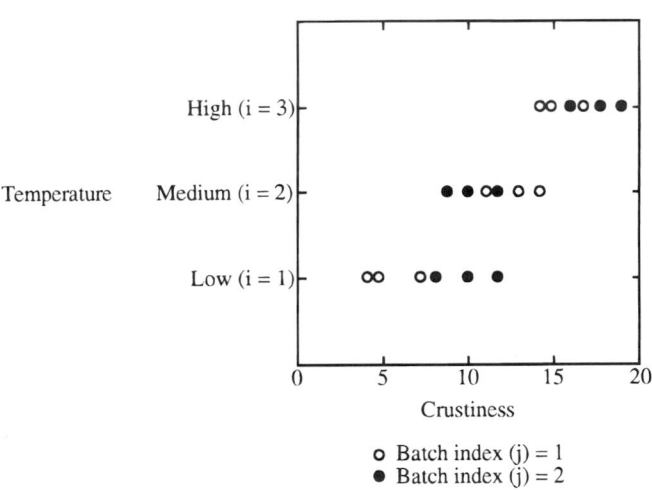

we use test statistic (28.38a):

$$F^* = \frac{117.72}{16.33} = 7.21$$

For level of significance $\alpha = .10$, we need $F(.90; 2, 3) = 5.46$. Since $F^* = 7.21 > 5.46$, we conclude H_a, that baking temperature does have an effect on the crustiness of the bread. The P-value of the test is .07.

To test for batch differences:

$$H_0: \sigma^2 = 0$$

$$H_a: \sigma^2 > 0$$

we employ test statistic (28.38b):

$$F^* = \frac{16.33}{2.61} = 6.26$$

TABLE 28.10   ANOVA for Bread Crustiness Example.

Source of Variation	SS	df	MS
Temperatures (*TR*)	235.44	2	117.72
Mix batches (*EE*)	49.00	3	16.33
Observation units (*OE*)	31.33	12	2.61
Total	315.78	17	

For level of significance $\alpha = .10$, we need $F(.90; 3, 12) = 2.61$. Since $F^* = 6.26 > 2.61$, we conclude H_a, that there are batch effects on the crustiness of bread. The P-value of this test is .01. Thus, both the particular batch of flour mix and the temperature at which the bread is baked affect the crustiness of the loaf.

Estimation of Treatment Effects

When the treatment effects are fixed, there is usually interest in obtaining confidence intervals for treatment means $\mu_{i.} = \mu_{..} + \tau_i$ and for pairwise comparisons and contrasts of the treatment means. These can be obtained in the usual manner, using *MSEE* as the error variance since this is the quantity in the denominator of the test statistic for fixed treatment effects. The degrees of freedom are those associated with *MSEE*, namely, $(n - 1)r$. For instance, the confidence limits for treatment mean $\mu_{i.}$ are:

(28.39) $$\bar{Y}_{i..} \pm t[1 - \alpha/2; (n-1)r]s\{\bar{Y}_{i..}\}$$

where:

(28.39a) $$s^2\{\bar{Y}_{i..}\} = \frac{MSEE}{nm}$$

Similarly, confidence limits for a contrast of treatment means, $L = \sum c_i \mu_{i.}$, where $\sum c_i = 0$, are obtained as follows:

(28.40) $$\hat{L} \pm t[1 - \alpha/2; (n-1)r]s\{\hat{L}\}$$

where:

(28.40a) $$\hat{L} = \sum c_i \bar{Y}_{i..}$$

(28.40b) $$s^2\{\hat{L}\} = \frac{MSEE}{nm} \sum c_i^2$$

The Bonferroni, Tukey, and Scheffé simultaneous inference procedures can be utilized in the usual manner.

Example.   In the bread crustiness example, we wish to estimate the mean crustiness of bread baked at a low temperature with a 95 percent confidence coefficient. We require, using the results in Tables 28.9 and 28.10:

$$\bar{Y}_{1..} = 7.67$$

$$s^2\{\bar{Y}_{1..}\} = \frac{16.33}{6} = 2.722 \qquad s\{\bar{Y}_{1..}\} = 1.65$$

$$t(.975; 3) = 3.182$$

Hence, the 95 percent confidence interval is:

$$2.4 = 7.67 - 3.182(1.65) \le \mu_1. \le 7.67 + 3.182(1.65) = 12.9$$

It was also desired to estimate the difference in mean crustiness of bread baked at high and low temperatures with a 95 percent confidence interval. Utilizing (28.40) and the results in Tables 28.9 and 28.10, we obtain:

$$\bar{Y}_{1..} = 7.67 \qquad \bar{Y}_{3..} = 16.5$$

$$\hat{L} = \bar{Y}_{3..} - \bar{Y}_{1..} = 16.5 - 7.67 = 8.83$$

$$s^2\{\hat{L}\} = \frac{2(16.33)}{6} = 5.443 \qquad s\{\hat{L}\} = 2.33$$

Hence, the desired confidence interval is:

$$1.4 = 8.83 - 3.182(2.33) \le \mu_3. - \mu_1. \le 8.83 + 3.182(2.33) = 16.2$$

Estimation of Variances

At times, there is interest in estimating σ^2, the experimental error variance, and σ_η^2, the observation error variance. It is evident from either of the $E\{MS\}$ columns in Table 28.8 that the following are unbiased estimators:

	Parameter	Unbiased Estimator
(28.41a)	σ^2	$s^2 = \dfrac{MSEE - MSOE}{m}$
(28.41b)	σ_η^2	$s_\eta^2 = MSOE$

An approximate confidence interval for the experimental error variance σ^2 is easily obtained by the modified large sample procedure in (24.34). From Table 28.8, we have:

$$\sigma^2 = \frac{E\{MSEE\} - E\{MSOE\}}{m}$$

Thus σ^2 takes the form (24.32) with correspondences:

$$c_1 = \frac{1}{m} \qquad MS_1 = MSEE$$

$$c_2 = -\frac{1}{m} \qquad MS_2 = MSOE$$

The MLS approximate $1 - \alpha$ confidence interval for σ^2 is therefore:

(28.42)
$$s^2 - H_L \leq \sigma^2 \leq s^2 + H_U$$

where H_L and H_U are given by the formulas in Table 24.3, $df_1 = r(n - 1)$ and $df_2 = rn(m - 1)$, and s^2 is given in (28.41a).

An exact confidence interval for the observation error variance σ_η^2 can be obtained by (24.21), with *MSOE* now being the mean square and $rn(m - 1)$ now being the degrees of freedom.

Example.   For the bread crustiness example, we wish to estimate σ^2, the variability between batches, with a 95 percent confidence interval. From Table 28.10, we obtain the point estimate:

$$s^2 = \frac{16.33 - 2.61}{3} = 4.57$$

To obtain an approximate 95 percent confidence interval for σ^2 using (28.42), we need the following calculational results for the formulas in Table 24.3:

$$F_1 = 3.12 \quad F_2 = 1.95 \quad F_3 = 13.92 \quad F_4 = 2.73 \quad F_5 = 4.47 \quad F_6 = 14.34$$

$$G_1 = .6795 \quad G_2 = .4872 \quad G_3 = -.0397 \quad G_4 = -2.6347$$

$$H_L = 3.97 \quad H_U = 70.24$$

The desired confidence interval for σ^2 is therefore:

$$.60 = 4.57 - 3.97 \leq \sigma^2 \leq 4.57 + 70.24 = 74.81$$

and for σ, the experimental error standard deviation, the confidence interval is:

$$.77 \leq \sigma \leq 8.65$$

Comments

1. Frequently, the units for subsampling are called *observation units*, to distinguish them from the *experimental units*. For instance, in the bread crustiness example, the batches of flour mix are the experimental units and the portions selected from a batch for making loaves of bread are the observation units.

2. Observation units may be different physical entities, as in the bread crustiness example where they are portions of a batch of flour mix. Observation units also may refer to repeated observations on the entire experimental unit. An example of the latter is the earlier illustration where an employee is timed for 10 consecutive assembly operations after receiving a given type of training.

3. Note that subsampling model (28.35) contains no interaction terms. This is because the experimental error terms $\varepsilon_{j(i)}$ are nested within treatments. When one variable is nested within another, we saw earlier that interaction terms are inapplicable.

4. We have considered only the balanced case for subsampling, where an equal number of experimental units (n) are applied to each treatment and a constant number of observations (m) are made on each experimental unit. Serious complications are encountered in the unbalanced case, and no exact test for treatment effects can be made. See an advanced text, such as Reference 28.1, for a discussion.   ∎

28.8   Pure Subsampling in Three Stages

Sometimes an investigation does not involve a comparison of treatments, but only sub-sampling at several levels. Consider, for instance, a quality control engineer who wishes to investigate a certain quality characteristic of a computer assembly. These assemblies are produced in lots of 2,000. The engineer will select a random sample of r lots; from each lot n assemblies will be selected, and m observations will be made on the quality characteristic for each assembly.

Model

Assuming that all random variables are normally distributed and that equal sample sizes are employed at each stage, the model for subsampling in three stages is:

$$(28.43) \qquad Y_{ijk} = \mu_{..} + \tau_i + \varepsilon_{j(i)} + \eta_{ijk}$$

where:

> $\mu_{..}$ is a constant
>
> τ_i, $\varepsilon_{j(i)}$, and η_{ijk} are independent normal random variables with expectations 0 and variances σ_τ^2, σ^2, and σ_η^2, respectively
>
> $i = 1, \ldots, r; j = 1, \ldots, n; k = 1, \ldots, m$

For our quality control illustration, τ_i represents the lot effect, $\varepsilon_{j(i)}$ represents the assembly effect that is nested within the lot, and η_{ijk} represents the observation effect.

The observations Y_{ijk} for subsampling model (28.43) are normally distributed, with mean and variance:

$$(28.44a) \qquad E\{Y_{ijk}\} = \mu_{..}$$

$$(28.44b) \qquad \sigma^2\{Y_{ijk}\} = \sigma_Y^2 = \sigma_\tau^2 + \sigma^2 + \sigma_\eta^2$$

Various correlations exist between two observations from the same lot.

Subsampling model (28.43) corresponds to subsampling model (28.35) for a single-factor study except that we assume here that the τ_i are independent $N(0, \sigma_\tau^2)$ and are independent of the $\varepsilon_{j(i)}$ and η_{ijk}. Formally, then, the only difference between models (28.35) and (28.43) is that the τ_i are fixed in one case and random in the other. Subsampling model (28.43) also corresponds to nested model (28.7) with both factor A and factor B effects random.

Analysis of Variance

The analysis of variance for pure subsampling model (28.43) uses the same sums of squares as before, namely, those in (28.37). The ANOVA table is the same as that in Table 28.8. The applicable expected mean squares are those for random τ_i effects.

Estimation of $\mu_{..}$

In the case of pure subsampling, there is often interest in estimating the overall mean $\mu_{..}$ (the process mean for the computer assembly quality characteristic in our earlier quality control example). A point estimator of $\mu_{..}$ in model (28.43) is $\bar{Y}_{...}$, and it can be shown that its variance is:

$$(28.45) \qquad \sigma^2\{\bar{Y}_{...}\} = \frac{\sigma_\tau^2}{r} + \frac{\sigma^2}{rn} + \frac{\sigma_\eta^2}{rnm} = \frac{nm\sigma_\tau^2 + m\sigma^2 + \sigma_\eta^2}{rnm}$$

An unbiased estimator of this variance is:

$$(28.46) \qquad s^2\{\bar{Y}_{...}\} = \frac{MSTR}{rnm}$$

and the $1 - \alpha$ confidence limits for $\mu_{..}$ are:

$$(28.47) \qquad \bar{Y}_{...} \pm t(1 - \alpha/2; r - 1)s\{\bar{Y}_{...}\}$$

28.9   Three-Factor Partially Nested Designs

Our discussion of nested designs and subsampling so far has been confined to hierarchical designs where no factors are crossed. In this section, we consider three-factor experiments where some but not all of the factors are nested. Such designs are called *partially nested*, *partially hierarchical*, or *cross-nested designs*. We shall utilize the following example to explain three-factor partially nested designs.

Example

The effect of cultural background on group decision making was studied by an experiment. Sixteen teams of students were formed and assigned a task. One of the response variables was the number of group interactions prior to the final group decision. Eight teams consisted of foreign students, eight of U.S. students. Half of the teams consisted of eight members, the other half of four members. Two foreign observers were used for the foreign teams, and two U.S. observers for the U.S. teams. Thus, the design may be represented as follows:

	U.S. Teams (A_1)		Foreign Teams (A_2)	
	Observer 1 (C_1)	Observer 2 (C_2)	Observer 3 (C_1)	Observer 4 (C_2)
Small team (B_1)	Replication 1 Replication 2	Replication 1 Replication 2	Replication 1 Replication 2	Replication 1 Replication 2
Large team (B_2)	Replication 1 Replication 2	Replication 1 Replication 2	Replication 1 Replication 2	Replication 1 Replication 2

Note that there are two replications (teams) in each cell.

Development of Model

Let nationality of team be factor A, size of team factor B, and observer factor C. Note that factor C is nested within factor A since the two observers for the U.S. teams were different from the two observers for the foreign teams. Also note that factors A and B are crossed, since each level of factor A appears with every level of factor B, and vice versa. Similarly, factors B and C are crossed. Factors A (nationality) and B (team size) were considered to have fixed effects, while the factor C (observer) effects were considered to be random.

In order to develop an appropriate model, we need to recognize that factor C is nested within factor A; hence the factor C effect is denoted by $\gamma_{k(i)}$. We also need to recognize that the AC and ABC interactions are to be excluded because factor C is nested within factor A. Finally, the BC interaction is nested within factor A since factor C is nested within factor A; thus, the BC interaction is denoted by $(\beta\gamma)_{jk(i)}$. Hence, the appropriate model is:

$$(28.48) \qquad Y_{ijkm} = \mu_{...} + \alpha_i + \beta_j + \gamma_{k(i)} + (\alpha\beta)_{ij} + (\beta\gamma)_{jk(i)} + \varepsilon_{ijkm}$$

where:

$\mu_{...}$ is an overall constant

α_i are the fixed nationality effects

β_j are the fixed team size effects

$\gamma_{k(i)}$ are the random observer (within nationality) effects

$(\alpha\beta)_{ij}$ are the fixed nationality–team size interaction effects

$(\beta\gamma)_{jk(i)}$ are the random team size–observer interaction (within nationality) effects

ε_{ijkm} are random error terms

$\underset{i}{\Sigma}\alpha_i = 0 \qquad \underset{j}{\Sigma}\beta_j = 0 \qquad \underset{i}{\Sigma}(\alpha\beta)_{ij} = 0 \quad$ for all j

$\underset{j}{\Sigma}(\alpha\beta)_{ij} = 0 \quad$ for all $i \qquad \underset{j}{\Sigma}(\beta\gamma)_{jk(i)} = 0 \quad$ for all $k(i)$

$i = 1, \ldots, a; \, j = 1, \ldots, b; \, k = 1, \ldots, c; \, m = 1, \ldots, n$

Appendix D contains a simple rule for constructing ANOVA models for complex designs, such as the one here.

We assume as usual that $\gamma_{k(i)}$, $(\beta\gamma)_{jk(i)}$, and ε_{ijkm} are normally distributed with expectations zero and with constant variances σ_γ^2, $\sigma_{\beta\gamma}^2$, and σ^2, respectively, and that the three groups of random variables are pairwise independent. The interaction effects $(\beta\gamma)_{jk(i)}$ for any given observer are correlated as a result of the restrictions in model (28.48).

Analysis of Variance

Table 28.11 contains the ANOVA table for model (28.48). The sums of squares, degrees of freedom, and expected mean squares shown in this table can be developed by using the rules in Appendix D. The expected mean squares also can be obtained from some computer packages with analysis of variance capabilities. The expected mean squares column in Table 28.11 indicates directly how to form test statistics for a variety of tests.

TABLE 28.11   ANOVA Table for Crossed-Nested Model (28.48).

Source of Variation	SS	df	MS	Expected Mean Squares
A	$SSA = bcn \sum (\bar{Y}_{i...} - \bar{Y}_{....})^2$	$a - 1$	MSA	$bcn \dfrac{\sum \alpha_i^2}{a - 1} + bn\sigma_\gamma^2 + \sigma^2$
B	$SSB = acn \sum (\bar{Y}_{.j..} - \bar{Y}_{....})^2$	$b - 1$	MSB	$acn \dfrac{\sum \beta_j^2}{b - 1} + n\sigma_{\beta\gamma}^2 + \sigma^2$
C(A)	$SSC(A) = bn \sum\sum (\bar{Y}_{i \cdot k \cdot} - \bar{Y}_{i...})^2$	$a(c - 1)$	MSC(A)	$bn\sigma_\gamma^2 + \sigma^2$
AB	$SSAB = cn \sum\sum (\bar{Y}_{ij..} - \bar{Y}_{i...} - \bar{Y}_{.j..} + \bar{Y}_{....})^2$	$(a - 1)(b - 1)$	MSAB	$cn \dfrac{\sum\sum (\alpha\beta)_{ij}^2}{(a - 1)(b - 1)} + n\sigma_{\beta\gamma}^2 + \sigma^2$
BC(A)	$SSBC(A) = n \sum\sum\sum (\bar{Y}_{ijk\cdot} - \bar{Y}_{ij..} - \bar{Y}_{i \cdot k \cdot} + \bar{Y}_{i...})^2$	$a(b - 1)(c - 1)$	MSBC(A)	$n\sigma_{\beta\gamma}^2 + \sigma^2$
Error	$SSE = \sum\sum\sum\sum (Y_{ijkm} - \bar{Y}_{ijk\cdot})^2$	$abc(n - 1)$	MSE	σ^2
Total	$SSTO = \sum\sum\sum\sum (Y_{ijkm} - \bar{Y}_{....})^2$	$abcn - 1$		

TABLE 28.12 Data for Crossed-Nested Three-Factor Study—Group Decision-Making Example.

	U.S. Teams ($i = 1$)		Foreign Teams ($i = 2$)	
Size of Team	Observer 1 ($k = 1$)	Observer 2 ($k = 2$)	Observer 3 ($k = 1$)	Observer 4 ($k = 2$)
4 members	16	14	7	4
($j = 1$)	20	19	5	9
8 members	21	28	11	12
($j = 2$)	25	19	17	15

FIGURE 28.6 SYSTAT Dot Plots for Crossed-Nested Design Experiment—Group Decision-Making Example.

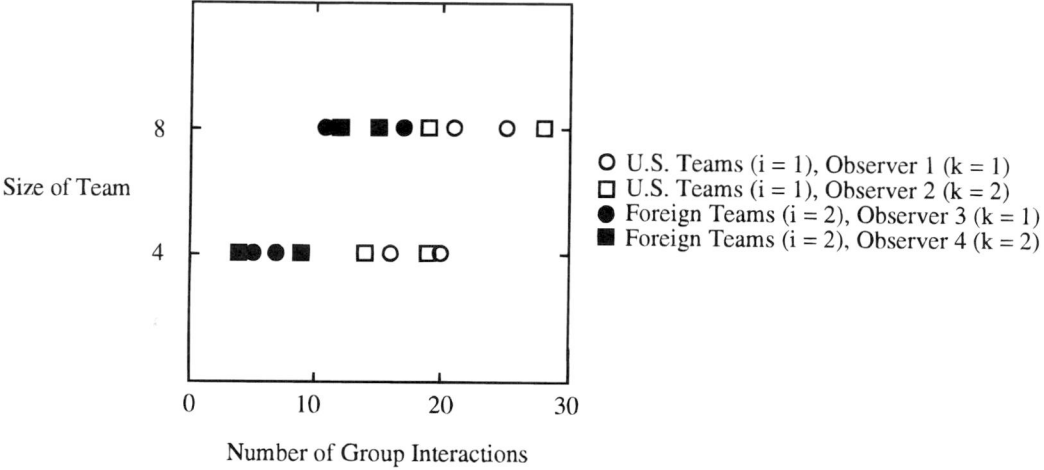

Example

Table 28.12 contains the results of the group decision-making experiment described earlier, and Figure 28.6 presents SYSTAT aligned dot plots of the data. The dot plots suggest a strong effect of nationality on the number of group interactions before the group decision is reached. Figure 28.7 contains the MINITAB printout of the ANOVA results, including the expected mean squares and the appropriate F tests. The correspondences between the symbols used in MINITAB in its expected mean square column and the model terms in Table 28.11 are as follows: Each term in an expected mean square is represented in the MINITAB output by (1) the numeric code, in parentheses, for the variance of the model term, and (2) the preceding number which is the numerical multiple. When the model effect is fixed, the letter Q is used in the printout to show that the variance of the model term is

FIGURE 28.7   MINITAB Output for Crossed-Nested Design Experiment—Group Decision-Making Example.

```
Analysis of Variance

Source      DF        SS        MS       F      P
A            1    420.25    420.25 1681.00  0.001
B            1    182.25    182.25  145.80  0.007
C(A)         2      0.50      0.25    0.02  0.981
A*B          1      2.25      2.25    1.80  0.312
B*C(A)       2      2.50      1.25    0.09  0.911
Error        8    106.00     13.25
Total       15    713.75

Source      Variance Error Expected Mean Square
            component term (using restricted model)
  1 A                   3   (6) + 4(3) + 8Q[1]
  2 B                   5   (6) + 2(5) + 8Q[2]
  3 C(A)      -3.250    6   (6) + 4(3)
  4 A*B                 5   (6) + 2(5) + 4Q[4]
  5 B*C(A)    -6.000    6   (6) + 2(5)
  6 Error     13.250        (6)
```

replaced by the sum of squared effects divided by degrees of freedom. For example:

$$E\{MSA\} = (6) + 4(3) + 8Q[1] = \sigma^2 + 4\sigma_\gamma^2 + 8\frac{\Sigma\alpha_i^2}{2-1}$$

$$E\{MSBC(A)\} = (6) + 2(5) = \sigma^2 + 2\sigma_{\beta\gamma}^2$$

To test for nationality effects, the alternatives are:

(28.49a)
$$H_0: \ \alpha_1 = \alpha_2 = 0$$
$$H_a: \ \text{not both} \ \alpha_i \ \text{equal zero}$$

Table 28.11 indicates that the appropriate test statistic is:

(28.49b)
$$F^* = \frac{MSA}{MSC(A)}$$

We have for our example, using the results in Figure 28.7:

$$F^* = \frac{420.25}{.25} = 1{,}681$$

For level of significance $\alpha = .05$, we require $F(.95; 1, 2) = 18.5$. Since $F^* = 1{,}681 > 18.5$, we conclude H_a, that nationality has an effect on the group behavior. The P-value of the test is .001. Other tests are conducted in a similar fashion. Results are summarized in Figure 28.7.

Next, we wish to estimate the difference between U.S. and foreign teams in the mean number of group interactions prior to a decision. Confidence intervals for contrasts of main factor effects are set up in the usual way when the factor effects are fixed. Hence, we require $MSC(A)$, as this is the mean square used in the denominator of the test statistic for examining nationality effects. Specifically, the confidence limits for $L = \mu_{1..} - \mu_{2..}$ are:

$$(28.50) \qquad\qquad \hat{L} \pm t[1 - \alpha/2; (c - 1)a]s\{\hat{L}\}$$

where:

$$(28.50a) \qquad\qquad s^2\{\hat{L}\} = \frac{2MSC(A)}{nbc}$$

For our example, we obtain from Table 28.12 and Figure 28.7:

$$\bar{Y}_{1...} = 20.25 \qquad \bar{Y}_{2...} = 10.00 \qquad \hat{L} = 20.25 - 10.00 = 10.25$$

$$s^2\{\hat{L}\} = \frac{2(.25)}{8} = .063 \qquad s\{\hat{L}\} = .25$$

For confidence coefficient .95, we require $t(.975; 2) = 4.303$. The confidence limits then are $10.25 \pm 4.303(.25)$, and the desired 95 percent confidence interval is:

$$9.2 \leq \mu_{1..} - \mu_{2..} \leq 11.3$$

With confidence coefficient .95, we conclude that U.S. teams engage in 9.2 to 11.3 more interactions, on average, than foreign teams before a group decision is reached.

Comments

1. The sums of squares *SSA*, *SSB*, and *SSAB* in Table 28.11 for the analysis of the crossed-nested experimental design are the usual sums of squares for factor *A* main effects, factor *B* main effects, and *AB* interactions. *SSC(A)* simply measures the variability of the factor *C* level estimated means for any given level of factor *A*, and then aggregates these sums of squares over factor *A*. Similarly, *SSBC(A)* contains the usual *BC* interaction sum of squares for a given level of factor *A*, and then aggregates these sums of squares over factor *A*.

2. If important *AB* interactions are present, analysis should usually focus on the means $\mu_{ij.}$ when the factors have fixed effects, rather than on the factor level means $\mu_{i..}$ and $\mu_{.j..}$. It can be shown that the estimated variance for comparing the two team sizes for any given nationality is:

$$(28.51) \qquad\qquad s^2\{\bar{Y}_{i1..} - \bar{Y}_{i2..}\} = \frac{2MSBC(A)}{cn}$$

This variance has associated with it $a(b - 1)(c - 1)$ degrees of freedom, as is evident from Table 28.11.

No exact confidence interval exists for comparing the two nationalities for any given team size. An unbiased variance estimator that can be utilized is:

$$(28.52) \qquad s^2\{\bar{Y}_{1j..} - \bar{Y}_{2j..}\} = \frac{2}{cn}\left[MSBC(A) + \frac{MSC(A) - MSE}{b}\right]$$

The approximate number of degrees of freedom associated with this variance is obtained from (24.28).

The reason for the different variances in (28.51) and (28.52) is that the observers are the same when the two team sizes for a given nationality are compared, while the observers differ when the two nationalities for a given team size are compared. ∎

Cited Reference

28.1. Searle, S. R. *Linear Models for Unbalanced Data*. New York: John Wiley & Sons, 1987.

Problems

28.1. A student asked: "Since the mean squares in the analysis of variance table for a two-factor nested design are the same whether the factor effects are assumed to be random or fixed, what difference does it make whether we assume the factors to have fixed effects or random effects?" Comment.

28.2. A researcher declared: "I prefer analyzing a nested two-factor study as a study with crossed factors because I can isolate more sources of variation." Comment on the researcher's strategy.

28.3. Consider a three-factor study where factor C is nested within factor B, and factor B in turn is nested within factor A, and $a = b = c = 2$. Illustrate in the format of Figure 28.1 the distinction between this nested design and the corresponding crossed design.

28.4. **Bottling plant production**. A production engineer studied the effects of machine model (factor A) and operator (factor B) on the output in a bottling plant. Three bottling machines were used, each a different model. Twelve operators were employed. Four operators were assigned to a machine and worked six-hour shifts each. Data on the number of cases produced by each machine and operator were collected for a week. The data that follow represent the number of cases produced per hour for each day during the week.

Machine i:	1				2				3			
Operator j:	1	2	3	4	1	2	3	4	1	2	3	4
Day $k = 1$:	65	68	56	45	74	69	52	73	69	63	81	67
$k = 2$:	58	62	65	56	81	76	56	78	83	70	72	79
$k = 3$:	63	75	58	54	76	80	62	83	74	72	73	73
$k = 4$:	57	64	70	48	80	78	58	75	78	68	76	77
$k = 5$:	66	70	64	60	68	73	51	76	80	75	70	71

a. Obtain the residuals for nested design model (28.7) with fixed factor effects and plot them against the fitted values. Also prepare a normal probability plot of the residuals. What are your findings about the appropriateness of model (28.7)?

b. Prepare aligned residual dot plots by machine. Do these plots support the assumption of constancy of the error variance? Discuss.

28.5. Refer to **Bottling plant production** Problem 28.4. Assume that nested design model (28.7) with fixed factor effects is appropriate.

a. Can the operator effects be distinguished from the effects of shifts in this study? Discuss.

b. Plot the data in the format of Figure 28.3. Does it appear that any factor effects are present?

c. Obtain the analysis of variance table.

d. Test whether or not the mean outputs differ for the three machine models; use $\alpha = .01$. State the alternatives, decision rule, and conclusion. What is the P-value of the test?

e. Test whether or not the mean outputs differ for the operators assigned to each machine; use $\alpha = .01$. State the alternatives, decision rule, and conclusion. What is the P-value of the test? What does your conclusion imply about the mean outputs for the four operators assigned to machine 3? Explain.

f. Test for each machine separately whether or not the mean outputs for the four operators differ. For each test, use $\alpha = .01$ and state the alternatives, decision rule, and conclusion.

g. What is the family level of significance for the combined tests in parts (d), (e), and (f) using the Bonferroni inequality? Summarize the set of conclusions reached in your tests.

28.6. Refer to **Bottling plant production** Problems 28.4 and 28.5.

a. Make all pairwise comparisons among the mean outputs for the three machines. Use the Tukey procedure with a 95 percent family confidence coefficient. State your findings.

b. Make all pairwise comparisons among the mean outputs for the four operators assigned to machine 1. Use the Bonferroni procedure with a 95 percent family confidence coefficient. State your findings.

c. Operator 4 assigned to machine 1 has relatively little experience compared to the other three operators. Estimate the contrast:

$$L = \frac{\mu_{11} + \mu_{12} + \mu_{13}}{3} - \mu_{14}$$

using a 99 percent confidence interval. Interpret your interval estimate.

28.7. Refer to **Bottling plant production** Problem 28.4. Assume that the four operators assigned to each machine were selected at random from a large number of operators.

a. How is nested design model (28.7) modified to fit this case?

b. Obtain a point estimate of the operator variance σ_β^2.

c. Test whether or not σ_β^2 equals zero; use $\alpha = .10$. State the alternatives, decision rule, and conclusion. What is the P-value of the test?

d. Use the MLS procedure to obtain an approximate 90 percent confidence interval for σ_β^2. Interpret your confidence interval.

e. Test whether or not the mean outputs differ for the three machine models; use $\alpha = .10$. State the alternatives, decision rule, and conclusion. What is the P-value of the test?

f. Make all pairwise comparisons among the mean outputs for the three machines. Use the Tukey procedure with a 90 percent family confidence coefficient. State your findings.

g. Test the assumption that the $\beta_{j(i)}$ for all machines have the same variance σ_β^2. Use the modified Levene test (Section 18.2) with $\alpha = .01$. State the alternatives, decision rule, and conclusion.

28.8. Refer to **Bottling plant production** Problem 28.4. Assume that the four operators assigned to each machine were selected at random from a large number of operators and that the three machines were chosen at random from a large number of machines.

a. How is nested design model (28.7) modified to fit this case?

b. Obtain point estimates of the operator and machine variances σ_β^2 and σ_α^2, respectively.

c. Test whether or not σ_α^2 equals zero; use $\alpha = .05$. State the alternatives, decision rule, and conclusion. What is the P-value of the test?

d. Use the MLS procedure to obtain an approximate 95 percent confidence interval for σ_β^2. Interpret your confidence interval.

e. The production engineer is interested in estimating the overall mean $\mu_{..}$ with a 95 percent confidence interval. Obtain the desired confidence interval and interpret your interval estimate.

√ 28.9. **Health awareness**. Three states (factor A) participated in a health awareness study. Each state independently devised a health awareness program. Three cities (factor B) within each state were selected for participation and five households within each city were randomly selected to evaluate the effectiveness of the program. All members of the selected households were interviewed before and after participation in the program and a composite index was formed for each household measuring the impact of the health awareness program. The data on health awareness follow (the larger the index, the greater the awareness).

State i:	1			2			3		
City j:	1	2	3	1	2	3	1	2	3
Household $k = 1$:	42	26	34	47	56	68	19	18	16
$k = 2$:	56	38	51	58	43	51	36	40	28
$k = 3$:	35	42	60	39	65	49	24	27	45
$k = 4$:	40	33	29	62	70	71	12	31	30
$k = 5$:	28	53	44	65	59	57	33	23	21

a. Obtain the residuals for nested design model (28.7) with fixed factor effects and plot them against the fitted values. Also prepare a normal probability plot of the residuals. What are your findings about the appropriateness of model (28.7)?

b. Prepare aligned residual dot plots by state. Do these plots support the assumption of constancy of the error variance? Discuss.

c. Plot the data in the format of Figure 28.3. Does it appear that any factor effects are present?

√ 28.10. Refer to **Health awareness** Problem 28.9. Assume that nested design model (28.7) with fixed factor effects is appropriate.

a. Obtain the analysis of variance table.

b. Test whether or not the mean awareness differs for the three states; use $\alpha = .05$. State the alternatives, decision rule, and conclusion. What is the P-value of the test?

c. Test whether or not the mean awareness differs for the three cities within each state; use $\alpha = .05$. State the alternatives, decision rule, and conclusion. What is the P-value of the test? What does your conclusion imply about the awareness means for the three cities in state 1? Explain.

d. What is the family level of significance for the combined tests in parts (b) and (c) using the Bonferroni inequality? Summarize the set of conclusions reached in your tests.

√ 28.11. Refer to **Health awareness** Problem 28.9 and 28.10.

    a. Estimate μ_{11} with a 95 percent confidence interval. Interpret your interval estimate.

    b. Obtain separate confidence intervals for $\mu_{1.}$, $\mu_{2.}$, and $\mu_{3.}$, each with a 99 percent confidence coefficient. Interpret your interval estimates.

    c. Obtain confidence intervals for all pairwise comparisons between the state means. Use the Tukey procedure and a 90 percent family confidence coefficient. Summarize your findings.

    d. It is desired to obtain a 95 percent confidence interval for $L = \mu_{11} - \mu_{32}$, since these two cities are of comparable size. Interpret your interval estimate.

√ 28.12. Refer to **Health awareness** Problem 28.9. Assume that the three cities in each state were chosen at random from all the cities in the state.

    a. How is nested design model (28.7) modified to fit this case?

    b. Obtain a point estimate of the city variance σ_β^2. Is there anything peculiar about the estimate here?

    c. Test whether or not σ_β^2 equals zero; use $\alpha = .10$. State the alternatives, decision rule, and conclusion. What is the P-value of the test?

    d. Test whether or not the mean awareness differs for the three states; use $\alpha = .10$. State the alternatives, decision rule, and conclusion. What is the P-value of the test?

    e. Obtain confidence intervals for all pairwise comparisons between the state means. Use the Tukey procedure and a 90 percent family confidence coefficient. Summarize your findings.

    f. Test the assumption that the $\beta_{j(i)}$ for all states have the same variance σ_β^2. Use the Hartley test (Section 18.2) with significance level $\alpha = .05$. State the alternatives, decision rule, and conclusion.

√ 28.13. Refer to **Health awareness** Problem 28.9. Assume that the three cities within each state and the three states were selected at random.

    a. How is nested design model (28.7) modified to fit this case?

    b. Obtain point estimates of the city and state variances σ_β^2 and σ_α^2, respectively.

    c. Test whether or not σ_α^2 equals zero; use $\alpha = .01$. State the alternatives, decision rule, and conclusion. What is the P-value of the test?

    d. Use the MLS procedure to obtain an approximate 99 percent confidence interval for σ_α^2. Interpret your confidence interval.

    e. Estimate the overall mean health awareness index $\mu_{..}$ using a 99 percent confidence interval. Interpret your interval estimate.

28.14. **Internal control**. A large retailer operates three regional accounting centers (factor A). Center 1 employs three audit teams, while the other two centers employ two audit teams each. One function of each center is to review whether a certain internal control operates properly in the processing of payroll. Data on the percent of transactions where the internal control was found to be operating properly were requested for each team in each region for the previous two months. Three months' data were received in one case, and data for only one month in another. The arc sine transformation $Y' = 2 \arcsin \sqrt{p}$ was employed to stabilize the error variances. The transformed data follow.

Region i:		1			2		3	
Team j:	1	2	3	1	2	1	2
Month $k = 1$:	151.6	143.2	131.4	163.8	151.6	157.0	160.0
$k = 2$:	141.2	139.4	136.0	154.2		147.2	151.6
$k = 3$:	149.4						

a. Set up the full regression model for this case, analogous to the illustrative full model (28.31), using 1, -1, 0 indicator variables.

b. Fit this model and obtain the residuals. Plot the residuals against the fitted values. Also prepare a normal probability plot of the residuals. What are your findings about the appropriateness of the model?

28.15. Refer to **Internal control** Problem 28.14. Assume that nested design model (28.7) with fixed factor effects, modified for unequal nestings and replications, is appropriate.

a. Test for region main effects using test statistic (7.27) and significance level $\alpha = .025$. State the alternatives, reduced model, decision rule, and conclusion. What is the P-value of the test?

b. Test for effects of audit teams within region using test statistic (7.27) and significance level $\alpha = .025$. State the alternatives, reduced model, decision rule, and conclusion.

c. Estimate $L = \mu_{1.} - \mu_{2.}$ (in transformed units) with a 98 percent confidence interval.

28.16. A student asked in class why all experiments do not make use of repeated observations since all measurement procedures are inexact to some degree. Comment.

28.17. Refer to **Questionnaire color** Problem 16.11. Suppose that the experiment was conducted by distributing the fliers to the assigned parking lots in two different weeks and noting the response rates for each week. The complete data on response rates follow.

Color i:	1 (Blue)					2 (Green)					3 (Orange)				
Lot j:	1	2	3	4	5	1	2	3	4	5	1	2	3	4	5
Week $k = 1$:	28	26	31	27	35	34	29	25	31	29	31	25	27	29	28
$k = 2$:	32	23	29	24	37	33	27	22	34	25	35	28	25	25	31

a. Obtain the residuals for subsampling model (28.35) with fixed treatment effects and plot them against the fitted values. Also prepare a normal probability plot of the residuals. What are your findings about the appropriateness of model (28.35)?

b. Test the assumption that the $\varepsilon_{j(i)}$ have the same variance σ^2 for all colors. Use the modified Levene test (Section 18.2) with significance level $\alpha = .01$. State the alternatives, decision rule, and conclusion.

28.18. Refer to **Questionnaire color** Problem 28.17. Assume that subsampling model (28.35) with fixed treatment effects is appropriate.

a. Obtain the analysis of variance table.

b. Test whether or not questionnaire color effects are present; use $\alpha = .05$. State the alternatives, decision rule, and conclusion. What is the P-value of the test?

c. Test whether or not lot differences within colors are present; use $\alpha = .05$. State the alternatives, decision rule, and conclusion. What is the P-value of the test?

    d. Estimate the mean response rate for blue questionnaires with a 95 percent confidence interval.

    e. Obtain point estimates of σ^2 and σ_η^2. Which variance appears to be larger here?

    f. Use the MLS procedure to obtain an approximate 95 percent confidence interval for σ^2. Also obtain a 95 percent confidence interval for σ_η^2. Interpret your interval estimates.

√ 28.19. **Plant acid levels**. Four plants of the same variety were randomly selected in an experiment to investigate the concentration of a particular acid. Three leaves per plant were randomly selected and three separate determinations of the acid concentration were obtained per leaf. The data follow.

Plant i:	1			2			3			4		
Leaf j:	1	2	3	1	2	3	1	2	3	1	2	3
Determination												
$k = 1$:	11.2	16.5	18.3	14.1	19.0	11.9	15.3	19.5	16.5	7.3	8.9	11.3
$k = 2$:	11.6	16.8	18.7	13.8	18.5	12.4	15.9	20.1	17.2	7.8	9.4	10.9
$k = 3$:	12.0	16.1	19.0	14.2	18.2	12.0	16.0	19.3	16.9	7.0	9.3	10.5

    Obtain the residuals for three-stage subsampling model (28.43) and plot them against the fitted values. Also prepare a normal probability plot of the residuals. What are your findings about the appropriateness of model (28.43)?

√ 28.20. Refer to **Plant acid levels** Problem 28.19. Assume that three-stage subsampling model (28.43) is appropriate.

    a. Obtain the analysis of variance table.

    b. Test whether or not there are variations in mean concentration levels between plants; use $\alpha = .05$. State the alternatives, decision rule, and conclusion. What is the P-value of the test?

    c. Test whether or not there are variations in mean concentration levels between leaves of the same plant; use $\alpha = .05$. State the alternatives, decision rule, and conclusion. What is the P-value of the test?

    d. Estimate the overall mean concentration in all plants of the variety; use a 95 percent confidence interval.

    e. Obtain point estimates of σ_τ^2, σ^2, and σ_η^2. Which component of variance appears to be most important in the total variance σ_Y^2?

    f. Use the MLS procedure to obtain an approximate 90 percent confidence interval for σ_τ^2. Does the experiment provide a precise estimate of this variance component?

28.21. **Chemical consistency**. A chemical company wished to study the consistency of the strength of one of its liquid chemical products. The product is made in batches in large vats and then is barreled. The barrels are subsequently stored for a period of time in a warehouse. To examine the consistency of the strength of the chemical, an analyst randomly selected five different batches of the product from the warehouse and then selected four barrels per batch at random. Three determinations per barrel were made. The data on strength follow.

Batch i:		1				2			...		5		
Barrel j:	1	2	3	4	1	2	3	4	...	1	2	3	4
Determination													
$k = 1$:	2.3	2.5	2.6	2.4	2.8	2.7	2.6	2.4	...	3.6	3.8	3.7	3.9
$k = 2$:	2.1	2.3	2.4	2.6	2.9	2.5	2.6	2.8	...	3.7	3.8	3.5	3.5
$k = 3$:	2.0	2.5	2.7	2.3	2.6	2.8	2.8	2.6	...	3.4	3.5	3.5	3.7

a. Obtain the residuals for three-stage subsampling model (28.43) and plot them against the fitted values. Also prepare a normal probability plot of the residuals. What are your findings about the appropriateness of model (28.43)?

b. Test the assumption that the $\varepsilon_{j(i)}$ have the same variance σ^2 for all batches. Use the Hartley test (Section 18.2) with significance level $\alpha = .01$. State the alternatives, decision rule, and conclusion.

28.22. Refer to **Chemical consistency** Problem 28.21. Assume that three-stage subsampling model (28.43) is appropriate.

a. Obtain the analysis of variance table.

b. Test whether or not there are variations in mean strength between batches; use $\alpha = .01$. State the alternatives, decision rule, and conclusion. What is the P-value of the test?

c. Test whether or not there are variations in mean strength between barrels within batches; use $\alpha = .01$. State the alternatives, decision rule, and conclusion. What is the P-value of the test?

d. Estimate the overall mean strength of the chemical using a 99 percent confidence interval

e. Obtain point estimates of σ_τ^2, σ^2, and σ_η^2. Which component of variance appears to be most important in the total variance σ_Y^2?

f. Use the MLS procedure to obtain an approximate 95 percent confidence interval for σ_τ^2. Does the experiment provide a precise estimate of this variance component?

Exercises

28.23. Derive (28.13) by squaring (28.12) and summing over all observations.

28.24. Derive (28.16) for a balanced nested two-factor design.

28.25. Consider a balanced nested two-factor design with factor A having fixed effects and factor B (nested within factor A) having random effects.

a. Derive $\sigma^2\{\bar{Y}_{i..}\}$ and $\sigma^2\{\bar{Y}_{...}\}$.

b. Find an unbiased point estimator of σ_β^2.

28.26. Show that $\sigma^2\{\bar{Y}_{i..}\} = (\sigma_\eta^2 + m\sigma^2)/nm$ for subsampling model (28.35) with fixed treatment effects.

28.27. Derive variance (28.45) for three-stage subsampling model (28.43). Using the expected mean squares in Table 28.8, show that the estimated variance (28.46) is an unbiased estimator of variance (28.45).

28.28. Use (28.52) and the fact that this estimated variance is unbiased to find $\sigma^2\{\bar{Y}_{1j..} - \bar{Y}_{2j..}\}$ for ANOVA model (28.48). What is the approximate number of degrees of freedom associated with the estimated variance?

Projects

28.29. Refer to the **Drug effect experiment** data set. Consider only Part I of the study and dosage level 4; i.e., include only observations for which variable 2 equals 1 and variable 5 equals 4. Assume that initial lever press rate (factor A) has fixed effects and that rats are a second factor (factor D) with random effects.

   a. State the appropriate model for this nested two-factor study.

   b. Obtain the residuals and plot them against the fitted values. Also prepare a normal probability plot of the residuals. What are your findings about the appropriateness of your model?

28.30. Refer to the **Drug effect experiment** data set and Project 28.29. Assume that nested design model (28.7), with $\beta_{j(i)}$ and ε_{ijk} random, is appropriate.

   a. Obtain the analysis of variance table.

   b. Test whether or not the mean lever press rate differs for the three initial rate groups; use $\alpha = .05$. State the alternatives, decision rule, and conclusion. What is the P-value of the test?

   c. Test whether or not the mean lever press rate differs for the rats within the initial rate groups; use $\alpha = .05$. State the alternatives, decision rule, and conclusion. What is the P-value of the test? What does your conclusion imply about the four rats in the slow initial rate group?

   d. Make all pairwise comparisons between the mean lever press rates for the three initial rate groups. Use the Tukey procedure with a 90 percent family confidence coefficient.

   e. Obtain an approximate 90 percent confidence interval for the between-rats variance, using the MLS procedure. Interpret your interval estimate.

28.31. Refer to the **Drug effect experiment** data set. Consider only Part II of the study and dosage level 3; i.e., include only observations for which variable 2 equals 2 and variable 5 equals 3. Assume that the initial lever press rate groups are the treatments with fixed effects, and that the rats are the experimental units with two observations for each experimental unit.

   a. State the appropriate model for this single-factor study with subsampling.

   b. Obtain the residuals and plot them against the fitted values. Also prepare a normal probability plot of the residuals. What are your findings about the appropriateness of your model?

   c. Test the assumption that the $\varepsilon_{j(i)}$ have the same variance σ^2 for all lever press rates. Use the modified Levene test (Section 18.2) with $\alpha = .01$. State the alternatives, decision rule, and conclusion.

28.32. Refer to the **Drug effect experiment** data set and Project 28.31. Assume that single-factor subsampling model (28.35) with fixed treatment effects is appropriate.

   a. Obtain the analysis of variance table.

   b. Test whether or not the mean lever press rate differs for the three initial rate groups; use $\alpha = .01$. State the alternatives, decision rule, and conclusion. What is the P-value of the test?

   c. Test whether or not differences in the mean lever press rate between rats are present; use $\alpha = .01$. State the alternatives, decision rule, and conclusion. What is the P-value of the test?

   d. Make all pairwise comparisons between the mean lever press rates for the three initial rate groups. Use the Tukey procedure with a 95 percent family confidence coefficient. Summarize your findings.

   e. Obtain interval estimates for σ^2 and σ_η^2, with confidence coefficient .90 for each. Interpret your confidence intervals. Which variance component appears to be larger?

Repeated Measures and Related Designs

In this chapter we take up repeated measures designs—designs that are widely used in the behavioral and life sciences. We begin by considering some basic elements of repeated measures designs. We then take up single-factor repeated measures designs, after which we consider two-factor experiments with repeated measures on both factors and on only one factor. We conclude this chapter with an introduction to split-plot designs, which include two-factor repeated measures designs with repeated measures on one factor.

29.1 Elements of Repeated Measures Designs

Description of Designs

Repeated measures designs utilize the same subject (person, store, plant, test market, etc.) for each of the treatments under study. The subject therefore serves as a block, and the experimental units within a block may be viewed as the different occasions when a treatment is applied to the subject. A repeated measures study may involve several treatments or only a single treatment that is evaluated at different points in time. Subjects used in repeated measures studies in the behavioral and life sciences include persons, households, observers, and experimental animals. At other times the subjects in repeated measures designs are stores, test markets, cities, and plants. We shall refer to all of these study units used in repeated measures designs as *subjects*.

Three examples of repeated measures designs follow.

1. Fifteen test markets are to be used to study each of two different advertising campaigns. In each test market, the order of the two campaigns will be randomized, with a sufficient time lapse between the two campaigns so that the effects of the initial campaign will not carry over into the second campaign. The subjects in this study are the test markets.

2. Two hundred persons who have persistent migraine headaches are each to be given two different drugs and a placebo, for two weeks each, with the order of the drugs randomized for each person. The subjects in the study are the persons with migraine headaches.

3. In a weight loss study, 100 overweight persons are to be given the same diet and their weights measured at the end of each week for 12 weeks to assess the weight loss over time. Here the subjects are the overweight persons, who are observed repeatedly to provide information about the effects of a single treatment over time.

Each of these studies involves a *repeated measures design* because the same subject is measured repeatedly. This key characteristic distinguishes this type of design from the designs considered earlier.

Advantages and Disadvantages

A principal advantage of repeated measures designs is that they provide good precision for comparing treatments because all sources of variability between subjects are excluded from the experimental error. Only variation within subjects enters the experimental error, since any two treatments can be compared directly for each subject. Thus, one may view the subjects as serving as their own controls. Another advantage of a repeated measures design is that it economizes on subjects. This is particularly important when only a few subjects (e.g., stores, plants, test markets) can be utilized for the experiment. Also, when interest is in the effects of a treatment over time, as when the shape of the learning curve for a new process operation is to be studied, it is usually desirable to observe the same subject at different points in time rather than observing different subjects at the specified points in time.

Repeated measures designs have a serious potential disadvantage, however, namely, that there may be several types of interference. One type of interference is an *order effect*, which is connected with the position in the treatment order. For instance, in evaluating five different advertisements, subjects may tend to give higher (or lower) ratings for advertisements shown toward the end of the sequence than at the beginning. Another type of interference is connected with the preceding treatment or treatments. For instance, in evaluating five different soup recipes, a bland recipe may get a higher (or lower) rating when preceded by a highly spiced recipe than when preceded by a blander recipe. This type of interference is called a *carryover effect*.

Various steps can be taken to minimize the danger of interference effects. Randomization of the treatment orders for each subject independently will make it more reasonable to analyze the data as if the error terms are independent. Allowing sufficient time between treatments is often an effective means of reducing carryover effects. It may be desirable at times to balance the order of treatment presentations and sometimes even the number of times each treatment is preceded by any other treatment. Latin square designs and crossover designs (discussed in Chapter 30) are helpful to this end.

How to Randomize

The randomization of the order of the treatments assigned to a subject is straightforward. For each subject, a random permutation is used to define the treatment order, and independent permutations are selected for the different subjects.

Note

Designs with repeated measures, discussed here, need to be distinguished from designs with repeated observations, discussed in Section 28.7. In repeated measures designs, several or all of the treatments are applied to the same subject. Designs with repeated observations, on the other hand, are designs where several observations on the response variable are made for a given treatment applied to an experimental unit. It is possible to develop a repeated measures design with repeated observations, as when a given subject is exposed to each of the treatments under study and a number of observations are made at the end of each treatment application.   ∎

FIGURE 29.1   **Layout for Single-Factor Repeated Measures Design ($n = 5, r = 4$).**

	Treatment Order			
	1	2	3	4
Subject 1	T_4	T_3	T_2	T_1
2	T_3	T_4	T_1	T_2
3	T_4	T_3	T_1	T_2
4	T_2	T_1	T_4	T_3
5	T_1	T_2	T_4	T_3

29.2   Single-Factor Experiments with Repeated Measures on All Treatments

We first consider repeated measures designs where the treatments are based on a single factor, as in the examples in Section 29.1. Almost always, the subjects in repeated measures designs (persons, stores, test markets, experimental animals) are viewed as a random sample from a population. Hence, *in all of the models for repeated measures designs to be presented in this chapter, the effects of subjects will be viewed as random.*

Figure 29.1 contains the layout for a single-factor experiment with repeated measures on all treatments. Here, there are five subjects and four treatments, with the order of treatments independently randomized for each subject. Notice that this layout corresponds to the one in Figure 27.1 for a randomized block design. Indeed, as we shall see next, the models for single-factor repeated measures designs are formally the same as the ones for randomized block designs, with blocks now considered to be subjects.

Model

When treatment effects are fixed, a model often appropriate for a single-factor repeated measures design is the following additive model:

$$(29.1) \qquad\qquad Y_{ij} = \mu_{..} + \rho_i + \tau_j + \varepsilon_{ij}$$

where:

> $\mu_{..}$ is a constant
>
> ρ_i are independent $N(0, \sigma_\rho^2)$
>
> τ_j are constants subject to $\Sigma \tau_j = 0$
>
> ε_{ij} are independent $N(0, \sigma^2)$
>
> ρ_i and ε_{ij} are independent
>
> $i = 1, \ldots, n; j = 1, \ldots, r$

Note that repeated measures model (29.1) is identical to randomized block model (27.34) with random block effects.

Hence, we know from Section 27.12 that repeated measures model (29.1) assumes the following about the observations Y_{ij}:

$$(29.2a) \qquad\qquad E\{Y_{ij}\} = \mu_{..} + \tau_j$$

$$(29.2b) \qquad\qquad \sigma^2\{Y_{ij}\} = \sigma_Y^2 = \sigma_\rho^2 + \sigma^2$$

$$(29.2c) \qquad\qquad \sigma\{Y_{ij}, Y_{ij'}\} = \sigma_\rho^2 = \omega\sigma_Y^2 \qquad j \neq j'$$

$$(29.2d) \qquad\qquad \sigma\{Y_{ij}, Y_{i'j'}\} = 0 \qquad\qquad i \neq i'$$

where ω is the coefficient of correlation between any two observations for the same subject:

$$(29.2e) \qquad\qquad \omega = \frac{\sigma_\rho^2}{\sigma_Y^2}$$

Thus, repeated measures model (29.1) assumes that in advance of the random trials, any two treatment observations Y_{ij} and $Y_{ij'}$ for a given subject are correlated in the same fashion for all subjects. This key assumption implies, as we saw in (27.38), that the variance-covariance matrix of the observations Y_{ij} for any given subject has compound symmetry. Any two observations from different subjects in advance of the random trials are independent according to model (29.1).

Equally important, we know from Chapter 27 that repeated measures model (29.1) assumes that, once the subjects have been selected, any two observations for a given subject are independent. Thus, model (29.1) assumes that there are no interference effects in the repeated measures study, such as order effects or carryover effects from one treatment to the next.

Note

If interaction effects between subjects and treatments are present, interaction model (27.41) can be employed. As we noted in Chapter 27, both the additive and interaction models lead to the same procedures for making inferences about the treatment effects. ∎

Analysis of Variance and Tests

Since repeated measures model (29.1) is the same as randomized block model (27.34), the analysis of variance and the test for treatment effects will be the same as before.

Analysis of Variance.   The ANOVA sums of squares for repeated measures model (29.1) are the same as in (27.6), but the names of two of the sums of squares are usually changed for repeated measures applications. The sum of squares for blocks in (27.6a) will now be called the *sum of squares for subjects*, and the interaction sum of squares between blocks and treatments in (27.6c) will now be called the *interaction sum of squares between treatments and subjects*. These two sums of squares will be denoted, respectively, by *SSS* and *SSTR.S*. Thus, the analysis of variance decomposition for single-factor repeated measures model (29.1) is:

$$(29.3) \qquad\qquad SSTO = SSS + SSTR + SSTR.S$$

TABLE 29.1   **ANOVA Table for Single-Factor Repeated Measures Design—ANOVA Model (29.1) with Subject Effects Random and Treatment Effects Fixed.**

Source of Variation	SS	df	MS	E{MS}
Subjects	SSS	$n - 1$	MSS	$\sigma^2 + r\sigma_\rho^2$
Treatments	SSTR	$r - 1$	MSTR	$\sigma^2 + n\dfrac{\Sigma \tau_j^2}{r - 1}$
Error	SSTR.S	$(r - 1)(n - 1)$	MSTR.S	σ^2
Total	SSTO	$nr - 1$		

where:

(29.3a)
$$SSTO = \sum_i \sum_j (Y_{ij} - \bar{Y}_{..})^2$$

(29.3b)
$$SSS = r \sum_i (\bar{Y}_{i.} - \bar{Y}_{..})^2$$

(29.3c)
$$SSTR = n \sum_j (\bar{Y}_{.j} - \bar{Y}_{..})^2$$

(29.3d)
$$SSTR.S = \sum_i \sum_j (Y_{ij} - \bar{Y}_{i.} - \bar{Y}_{.j} + \bar{Y}_{..})^2$$

Note that no error sum of squares is present because there are no replications here.

Table 29.1 contains the analysis of variance table for repeated measures model (29.1). It is the same as the ANOVA table in Table 27.9 for additive randomized block model (27.34), except for the change in notation. Note again that in the absence of interactions between treatments and subjects, the interaction mean square *MSTR.S* is an unbiased estimator of the error variance σ^2.

Note

In repeated measures studies, *SSTR* and *SSTR.S* are sometimes combined into a *within-subjects sum of squares SSW*:

(29.4)
$$SSW = SSTR + SSTR.S$$

which can be shown to equal:

(29.4a)
$$SSW = \sum_i \sum_j (Y_{ij} - \bar{Y}_{i.})^2$$

Hence, the ANOVA decomposition in (29.3) can also be expressed as follows:

(29.5)
$$SSTO = \underbrace{SSS}_{\substack{\text{between-}\\\text{subjects}\\\text{variability}}} + \underbrace{SSW}_{\substack{\text{within-}\\\text{subjects}\\\text{variability}}}$$

■

TABLE 29.2   **Data for Wine-Judging Example (ratings on a scale of 0 to 40).**

Judge i	Wine (j)				
	1	2	3	4	$\bar{Y}_{i\cdot}$
1	20	24	28	28	25
2	15	18	23	24	20
3	18	19	24	23	21
4	26	26	30	30	28
5	22	24	28	26	25
6	19	21	27	25	23
$\bar{Y}_{\cdot j}$	20.00	22.00	26.67	26.00	$23.67 = \bar{Y}_{\cdot\cdot}$

Test for Treatment Effects.   As the $E\{MS\}$ column in Table 29.1 indicates, the appropriate statistic for the test on treatment effects:

(29.6a)
$$H_0: \text{ all } \tau_j = 0$$
$$H_a: \text{ not all } \tau_j \text{ equal zero}$$

is:

(29.6b)
$$F^* = \frac{MSTR}{MSTR.S}$$

When H_0 holds, F^* follows the F distribution, and the decision rule for controlling the Type I error at α is:

(29.6c)
$$\text{If } F^* \leq F[1 - \alpha; r - 1, (r - 1)(n - 1)], \text{ conclude } H_0$$
$$\text{If } F^* > F[1 - \alpha; r - 1, (r - 1)(n - 1)], \text{ conclude } H_a$$

Example.   In a wine-judging competition, four Chardonnay wines of the same vintage were judged by six experienced judges. Each judge tasted the wines in a blind fashion, i.e., without knowing their identities. The order of the wine presentation was randomized independently for each judge. To reduce carryover and other interference effects, the judges did not drink the wines and rinsed their mouths thoroughly between tastings. Each wine was scored on a 40-point scale; the higher the score, the greater is the excellence of the wine. The data for this competition are presented in Table 29.2. A plot of the wine scores for each judge is shown in Figure 29.2. We see that there are some distinct differences in ratings between judges but that the ratings for wines 3 and 4 are consistently best and for wine 1 generally worst. We also see that the rating curves for the judges do not appear to exhibit substantial departures from being parallel. Hence, an additive model appears to be appropriate.

The six judges are considered to be a random sample from the population of possible judges, while the four wines tasted are of interest in themselves. Hence, single-factor repeated measures model (29.1) was expected to be appropriate, with the effects of subjects (judges) considered random and the effects of treatments (wines) considered fixed. As we

FIGURE 29.2   **Plot of Wine Scores for Each Judge—Wine-Judging Example.**

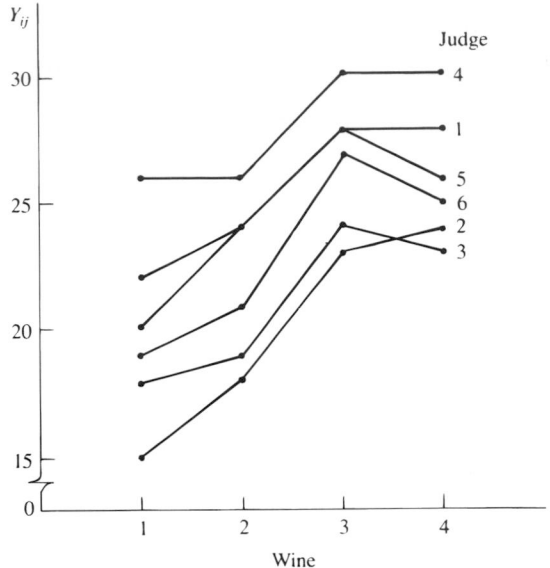

shall see later, additional diagnostic analysis supports the appropriateness of ANOVA model
(29.1).

Table 29.3 contains the analysis of variance table for the wine-judging data in Table
29.2. The calculations are straightforward and were carried out by a computer package. To
test for treatment effects:

$$H_0: \ \tau_1 = \tau_2 = \tau_3 = \tau_4 = 0$$

$$H_a: \ \text{not all} \ \tau_j \ \text{equal zero}$$

we use the results of Table 29.3:

$$F^* = \frac{MSTR}{MSTR.S} = \frac{61.333}{1.067} = 57.5$$

For level of significance $\alpha = .01$, we require $F(.99; 3, 15) = 5.42$. Since $F^* = 57.5 >$
5.42, we conclude H_a, that the mean wine ratings for the four wines differ. The P-value
for this test is 0+.

Comments

1. As we noted in Chapter 27 (in Comment 2 on p. 1105), a conservative test for treatment
effects should be used if the assumptions of compound symmetry in repeated measures model
(29.1) are not met (i.e., if either the variances of the observations for different treatments for a
given subject are not the same for all subjects or if the correlations between any two treatment
observations for a given subject are not the same for all treatment pairs and for all subjects). In
repeated measures studies, the compound symmetry assumption will be violated, for instance,
if repeated responses over time are more highly correlated for observations closer together than
for observations further apart in time.

TABLE 29.3 **ANOVA Table for Single-Factor Repeated Measures Design—Wine-Judging Example.**

Source of Variation	SS	df	MS
Judges	173.333	5	34.667
Wines	184.000	3	61.333
Error	16.000	15	1.067
Total	373.333	23	

2. When the treatment effects are random, test statistic (29.6b) and decision rule (29.6c) are still appropriate for testing treatment effects.

3. The efficiency of the repeated measures design in the wine-judging example, relative to a completely randomized design where each judge is used to assess a single wine, can be measured by means of (27.14). Using the results in Table 29.3, we obtain:

$$\hat{E} = \frac{(n-1)MSS + n(r-1)MSTR.S}{(nr-1)MSTR.S} = \frac{5(34.667) + 6(3)(1.067)}{23(1.067)} = 7.85$$

Thus, almost eight times as many replications per treatment would have been required with a completely randomized design in which each judge rates a single wine as in the repeated measures design to achieve the same precision for any estimated contrast.

4. When a single-factor repeated measures design involves $r = 2$ treatments, the F^* statistic in (29.6b) is equivalent to the two-sided t test for paired observations based on test statistic (A.69).

5. Occasionally, a formal test for subject effects is desired:

$$H_0: \sigma_\rho^2 = 0$$
$$H_a: \sigma_\rho^2 > 0$$

Table 29.1 indicates that the appropriate test statistic for repeated measures model (29.1) is $F^* = MSS/MSTR.S$. ∎

Evaluation of Appropriateness of Repeated Measures Model

Since repeated measures model (29.1) is equivalent to randomized block model (27.34), the earlier discussion on diagnostics for randomized block models is entirely applicable here. In particular, a plot of the responses Y_{ij} by subject, as in Figure 29.2, can be examined for indications of serious lack of parallelism, which would suggest that additive model (29.1) may not be appropriate.

Residual sequence plots by subject can be helpful for studying constancy of the error variance and presence of interference effects. The residuals for repeated measures models (29.1) are the same as in (27.5):

(29.7) $$e_{ij} = Y_{ij} - \bar{Y}_{i.} - \bar{Y}_{.j} + \bar{Y}_{..}$$

A normal probability plot of the estimated subject main effects $\bar{Y}_{i.} - \bar{Y}_{..}$ can be helpful for evaluating whether the subject main effects ρ_i are normally distributed with constant variance.

In addition to these graphic diagnostics, the estimated within-subjects variance-covariance and correlation matrices for the treatment observations Y_{ij} can be examined for appropriateness of the repeated measures model. A typical entry in the variance-covariance matrix is the estimated within-subjects covariance between observations for treatments j and j':

$$(29.8) \qquad \frac{\sum\limits_{i=1}^{n} (Y_{ij} - \bar{Y}_{.j})(Y_{ij'} - \bar{Y}_{.j'})}{n - 1}$$

The estimated within-subjects variance-covariance matrix should show variances of the same order of magnitude, and all of the covariances should be of similar magnitude. Of course, estimated variances and covariances tend to be subject to large sampling errors unless the sample sizes are very large. Hence, moderate differences in variances and covariances should be viewed as likely to be the result of sampling errors.

The estimated correlation matrix should show approximately similar coefficients of correlation between pairs of treatment observations within a subject.

Finally, the Tukey test described in Section 21.2 can be conducted to examine the appropriateness of the additive model. This test will need to be interpreted here as conditional on the subjects actually used in the repeated measures study.

Example.   For the wine-judging example, the residuals were obtained from (29.7), and are presented in Figure 29.3a in SAS/GRAPH aligned dot plots by wine. These plots support the assumption of constant error variance. Figure 29.3b presents residual sequence plots for each judge, where the residuals are plotted in the order in which the wines were tasted by the judge. These plots do not indicate any correlations of the error terms within a judge, and thus suggest that no interference effects are present. Finally, a normal probability plot of the residuals is presented in Figure 29.3c. This plot shows evidence of the effects of the rounded nature of the data, but does not suggest any major departure from normality. The correlation between the ordered residuals and their expected values under normality is .993, which also suggests that lack of normality is not a problem here.

Table 29.4 on page 1173 presents the estimated within-subjects variance-covariance matrix for the treatment observations. The differences found there could easily arise from sampling errors.

As we noted earlier, the plot of the responses by subject in Figure 29.2 also supports the appropriateness of model (29.1), since the plots for the judges are reasonably parallel. Thus, there is no indication of interactions between subjects and treatments.

Based on these and other diagnostics, it was concluded that repeated measures model (29.1) is reasonably appropriate for the data in the wine-judging example.

Analysis of Treatment Effects

The analysis of treatment effects for single-factor repeated measures model (29.1) proceeds in exactly the same fashion as described in Section 27.5 for randomized block designs with fixed treatment effects. The multiples in (27.9) for setting up confidence intervals are applicable here as they stand. The mean square used in estimating the variance of the

FIGURE 29.3   SAS/GRAPH Diagnostic Residual Plots—Wine-Judging Example.

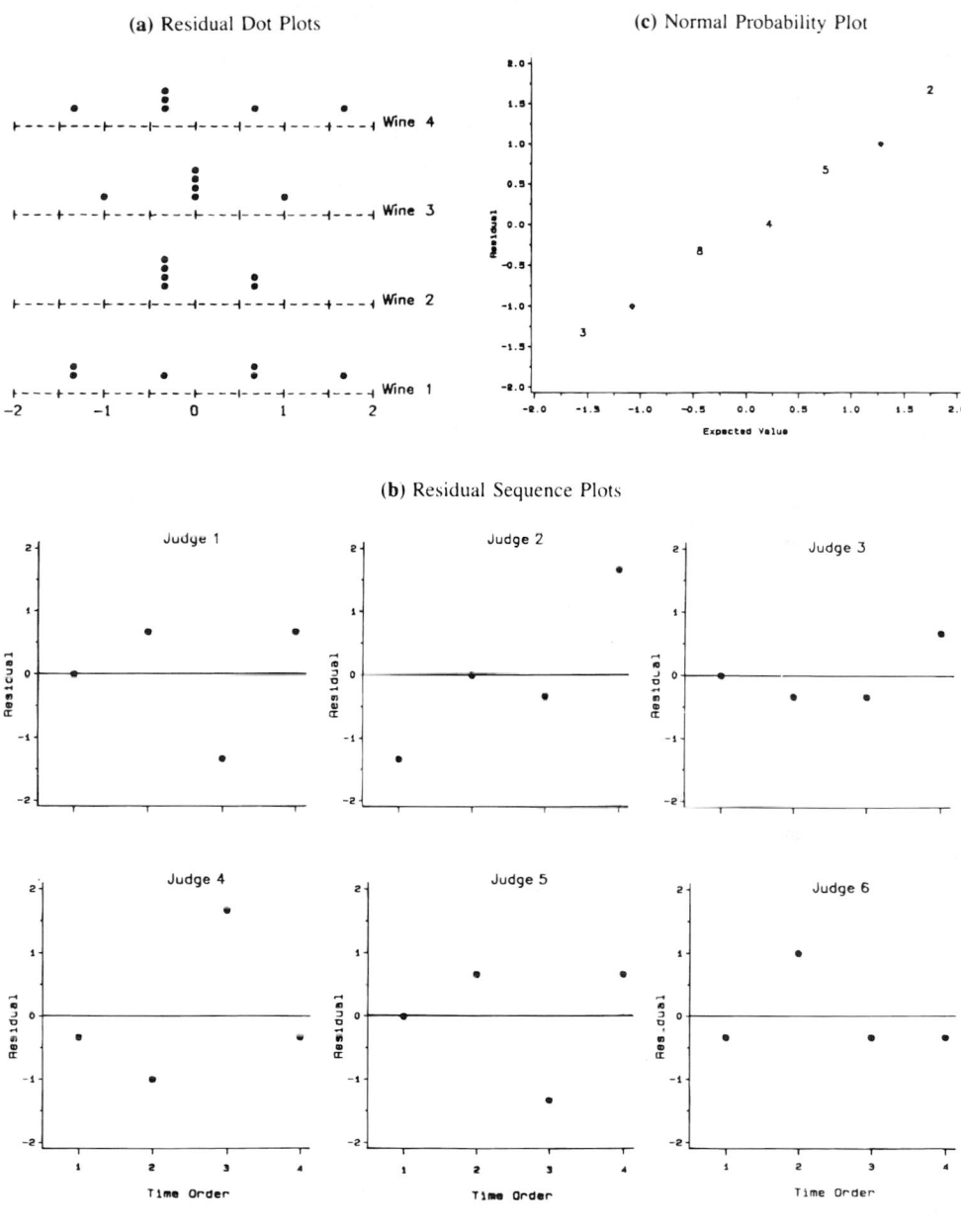

(a) Residual Dot Plots

(c) Normal Probability Plot

(b) Residual Sequence Plots

estimated contrast is still the interaction mean square, which is now denoted by *MSTR.S*. We shall illustrate the estimation procedures by an example.

Example.   In the wine-judging example, it was desired to compare all treatment means $\mu_{.j}$ pairwise, with a 95 percent family confidence coefficient. Here $\mu_{.j}$ is the mean rating of wine j averaged over judges. The Tukey procedure was utilized for this purpose. Using (17.31) with *MSE* replaced by *MSTR.S* and the estimated pairwise difference denoted by

TABLE 29.4   **Estimated Within-Subjects Variance-Covariance Matrix between Treatment Observations—Wine-Judging Example.**

$$
\begin{array}{c}
\\
j'\\
\begin{array}{cccc}
1 & 2 & 3 & 4
\end{array}\\
j\;
\begin{array}{c}
1\\2\\3\\4
\end{array}
\left[
\begin{array}{cccc}
14.000 & 11.000 & 9.200 & 8.200\\
       & 10.000 & 8.200 & 7.600\\
       &   & 7.067 & 6.200\\
       &   &   & 6.800
\end{array}
\right]
\end{array}
$$

$\hat{L}$, we obtain using the results in Table 29.3:

$$
s^2\{\hat{L}\} = MSTR.S\left(\frac{1}{n} + \frac{1}{n}\right) = 1.067\left(\frac{2}{6}\right) = .3557
$$

Using (27.9b), we find for a 95 percent family confidence coefficient:

$$
T = \frac{1}{\sqrt{2}}q(.95; 4, 15) = \frac{1}{\sqrt{2}}(4.08) = 2.885
$$

Hence:

$$
Ts\{\hat{L}\} = 2.885\sqrt{.3557} = 1.72
$$

Thus we obtain for the pairwise comparisons (see Table 29.2 for the $\overline{Y}_j$):

$$
-2.39 = (26.00 - 26.67) - 1.72 \le \mu_{.4} - \mu_{.3} \le (26.00 - 26.67) + 1.72 = 1.05
$$

$$
2.28 = (26.00 - 22.00) - 1.72 \le \mu_{.4} - \mu_{.2} \le (26.00 - 22.00) + 1.72 = 5.72
$$

$$
4.28 = (26.00 - 20.00) - 1.72 \le \mu_{.4} - \mu_{.1} \le (26.00 - 20.00) + 1.72 = 7.72
$$

$$
2.95 = (26.67 - 22.00) - 1.72 \le \mu_{.3} - \mu_{.2} \le (26.67 - 22.00) + 1.72 = 6.39
$$

$$
4.95 = (26.67 - 20.00) - 1.72 \le \mu_{.3} - \mu_{.1} \le (26.67 - 20.00) + 1.72 = 8.39
$$

$$
.28 = (22.00 - 20.00) - 1.72 \le \mu_{.2} - \mu_{.1} \le (22.00 - 20.00) + 1.72 = 3.72
$$

We display these results graphically as follows:

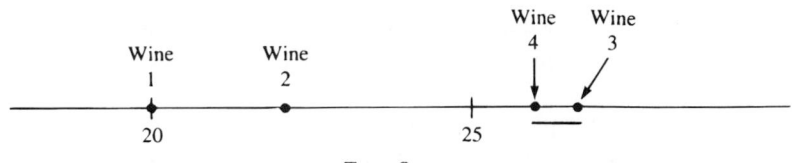

TABLE 29.5   **Ranked Data for Coffee Sweeteners in a Repeated Measures Design—Coffee Sweeteners Example.**

| Subject | Sweetener (j) | | | | |
i	A	B	C	D	E
1	5	1	2	4	3
2	4	2	1	5	3
3	3	2	1	4	5
4	5	2	3	4	1
5	4	1	2	3	5
6	4	1	3	5	2
$\bar{R}_{\cdot j}$	4.17	1.50	2.00	4.17	3.17

We conclude from these pairwise comparisons that wines 3 and 4 are judged best, and do not differ significantly from each other. Wines 1 and 2 are judged to be inferior to wines 3 and 4, with wine 1 receiving a mean rating significantly lower than that for wine 2. The family confidence coefficient of .95 applies to the entire set of comparisons.

Note

When the treatments are time order positions, as when process rework is observed for a new manufacturing process at periodic intervals, the nature of the time effect may be analyzed by developing an appropriate regression model.   ∎

Ranked Data

In repeated measures studies, the observations are frequently ranks, as when a number of tasters are each asked to rank recipes or when several university admissions officers are each asked to rank applicants for admission. When the data in a repeated measures study are ranks, the nonparametric rank F test described in Section 27.10 may be used for testing whether the treatment means are equal. No new principles are involved, so we shall proceed directly to an example.

Example.   Six subjects were each asked to rank five coffee sweeteners according to their taste preferences, with rank 5 assigned to the most preferred sweetener. The data are presented in Table 29.5 and suggest that a sweetener effect may be present. For example, no judge ranked sweetener B higher than 2 (not preferred).

Test statistic (27.23) here is:

$$F_R^* = \frac{9.00}{1.20} = 7.5$$

For level of significance $\alpha = .05$, we need $F(.95; 4, 20) = 2.87$. Since $F_R^* = 7.5 > 2.87$, we conclude that the five sweeteners are not equally liked. The P-value of the test is .0007.

We now wish to make all pairwise tests by means of (27.27) with family level of significance $\alpha = .20$. For $r = 5$, we have $g = 5(4)/2 = 10$ and obtain:

$$B = z[1 - .20/2(10)] = z(.99) = 2.326$$

Thus, the right term in (27.27) for $n = 6$ and $r = 5$ is:

$$B\left[\frac{r(r+1)}{6n}\right]^{1/2} = 2.326\left[\frac{5(6)}{6(6)}\right]^{1/2} = 2.12$$

We note from Table 29.5 that the pairs of mean ranks whose difference does not exceed 2.12 are (B, C), (B, E), (C, E), (A, E), (D, E), and (A, D). Hence, we can set up two groups, within which the treatment means do not differ:

Group 1		Group 2	
Sweetener B	$\bar{R}_{.2} = 1.50$	Sweetener E	$\bar{R}_{.5} = 3.17$
Sweetener C	$\bar{R}_{.3} = 2.00$	Sweetener A	$\bar{R}_{.1} = 4.17$
Sweetener E	$\bar{R}_{.5} = 3.17$	Sweetener D	$\bar{R}_{.4} = 4.17$

Thus, we conclude with family level of significance of .20 that sweeteners A and D are preferred to sweeteners B and C, and that it is not clear whether sweetener E belongs in the preferred group or in the other group.

Comments

1. The rank F test can also be used for repeated measures designs where the observations are not ranked, in case the distribution of the error terms departs far from normality. Ranks of the observations Y_{ij} are then assigned within each subject, and the rank F test is carried out in the usual manner.

2. The test statistic F_R^* is related to Kendall's coefficient of concordance W in the following way:

$$(29.9) \qquad W = \frac{F_R^*}{F_R^* + n - 1}$$

The coefficient of concordance W is a measure of the agreement of the rankings of the n subjects. It equals 1 if there is perfect agreement, and equals 0 if there is no agreement, that is, if all treatments receive the same mean ranking. For the coffee sweeteners example in Table 29.5, the coefficient of concordance W is:

$$W = \frac{7.5}{7.5 + 6 - 1} = .60$$

This measure indicates that a fair amount of agreement exists between the subjects.   ∎

29.3   Two-Factor Experiments with Repeated Measures on Both Factors

In the preceding section we considered single-factor repeated measures studies. The model for these designs can be extended easily when the treatments actually follow a factorial structure. For example, consider a study where four treatments are employed that represent two levels of each of two factors. Figure 29.4 depicts the layout for such a design when four subjects are utilized in the study. Note that the order of the treatments is randomized within each subject. When the treatments represent a factorial structure, we can explore as usual interaction effects as well as the main effects for the two factors. The design in Figure

FIGURE 29.4   **Layout for Two-Factor Repeated Measures Design with Repeated Measures on Both Factors ($n = 4$, $a = 2$, $b = 2$).**

	Treatment Order			
	1	2	3	4
Subject 1	$A_1 B_2$	$A_2 B_2$	$A_1 B_1$	$A_2 B_1$
2	$A_2 B_1$	$A_1 B_2$	$A_2 B_2$	$A_1 B_1$
3	$A_2 B_2$	$A_1 B_1$	$A_2 B_1$	$A_1 B_2$
4	$A_1 B_1$	$A_2 B_1$	$A_1 B_2$	$A_2 B_2$

29.4 is said to represent *repeated measures on both factors* because each subject receives all treatments defined by the factorial structure.

Model

When both factor effects are fixed, the subjects constitute a random sample, and there are repeated measures on both factors, a model frequently appropriate is an additive model that assumes, like model (29.1), that treatments and subjects do not interact:

$$(29.10) \qquad Y_{ijk} = \mu_{...} + \rho_i + \alpha_j + \beta_k + (\alpha\beta)_{jk} + \varepsilon_{ijk}$$

where:

$\mu_{...}$ is a constant

ρ_i are independent $N(0, \sigma_\rho^2)$

α_j are constants subject to $\Sigma \alpha_j = 0$

β_k are constants subject to $\Sigma \beta_k = 0$

$(\alpha\beta)_{jk}$ are constants subject to $\sum_j (\alpha\beta)_{jk} = 0$ for all k and $\sum_k (\alpha\beta)_{jk} = 0$ for all j

ε_{ijk} are independent $N(0, \sigma^2)$

ρ_i and ε_{ijk} are independent

$i = 1, \ldots, n; \ j = 1, \ldots, a; \ k = 1, \ldots, b$

The observations Y_{ijk} for repeated measures model (29.10) have the following properties:

$$(29.11a) \qquad E\{Y_{ijk}\} = \mu_{...} + \alpha_j + \beta_k + (\alpha\beta)_{jk}$$

$$(29.11b) \qquad \sigma^2\{Y_{ijk}\} = \sigma_Y^2 = \sigma_\rho^2 + \sigma^2$$

$$(29.11c) \qquad \sigma\{Y_{ijk}, Y_{ij'k'}\} = \sigma_\rho^2 \qquad j \neq j' \text{ and/or } k \neq k'$$

$$(29.11d) \qquad \sigma\{Y_{ijk}, Y_{i'j'k'}\} = 0 \qquad i \neq i'$$

Thus, repeated measures model (29.10) assumes that the observations Y_{ijk} have constant variance, and that any two treatment observations for the same subject in advance of the random trials have constant covariance. Any two observations from different subjects in advance of the random trials are independent according to model (29.10). Finally, all observations are assumed to be normally distributed.

Model (29.10) is a direct extension of the single-factor repeated measures model (29.1), where the treatment effect τ_j is now decomposed into factor A and factor B main effects and an AB interaction effect.

Once the subjects have been selected, repeated measures model (29.10), like the earlier repeated measures model (29.1), assumes that all of the treatment observations for a given subject are independent—that is, that there are no interference effects.

Analysis of Variance and Tests

Analysis of Variance.   The ANOVA sums of squares for model (29.10) and the expected mean squares can be obtained readily by following the rules in Appendix D. The sum of squares for estimating the error variance turns out to be the interaction sum of squares *SSTR.S*, reflecting interactions between treatments and subjects. Table 29.6 presents the ANOVA decomposition, degrees of freedom, and expected mean squares for two-factor repeated measures model (29.10).

Tests for Factor Effects.   It is clear from the expected mean squares column in Table 29.6a that the test for AB interaction effects:

(29.12a)
$$H_0: \text{ all } (\alpha\beta)_{jk} = 0$$
$$H_a: \text{ not all } (\alpha\beta)_{jk} \text{ equal zero}$$

uses the test statistic:

(29.12b)
$$F^* = \frac{MSAB}{MSTR.S}$$

and the decision rule for controlling the Type I error at α is:

(29.12c)
$$\text{If } F^* \leq F[1 - \alpha; (a-1)(b-1), (n-1)(ab-1)], \text{ conclude } H_0$$
$$\text{If } F^* > F[1 - \alpha; (a-1)(b-1), (n-1)(ab-1)], \text{ conclude } H_a$$

The test for factor A main effects:

(29.13a)
$$H_0: \text{ all } \alpha_j = 0$$
$$H_a: \text{ not all } \alpha_j \text{ equal zero}$$

uses the test statistic:

(29.13b)
$$F^* = \frac{MSA}{MSTR.S}$$

and the decision rule for controlling the Type I error at α is:

(29.13c)
$$\text{If } F^* \leq F[1 - \alpha; a - 1, (n-1)(ab-1)], \text{ conclude } H_0$$
$$\text{If } F^* > F[1 - \alpha; a - 1, (n-1)(ab-1)], \text{ conclude } H_a$$

TABLE 29.6   ANOVA Table and Sums of Squares for Two-Factor Repeated Measures Design with Repeated Measures on Both Factors—Subjects Random, Factors A and B Fixed.

(a) ANOVA Table

Source of Variation	SS	df	MS	$E\{MS\}$
Subjects	SSS	$n - 1$	MSS	$\sigma^2 + ab\sigma_\rho^2$
Factor A	SSA	$a - 1$	MSA	$\sigma^2 + nb\dfrac{\Sigma\alpha_j^2}{a - 1}$
Factor B	SSB	$b - 1$	MSB	$\sigma^2 + na\dfrac{\Sigma\beta_k^2}{b - 1}$
AB interactions	SSAB	$(a - 1)(b - 1)$	MSAB	$\sigma^2 + n\dfrac{\Sigma\Sigma(\alpha\beta)_{jk}^2}{(a - 1)(b - 1)}$
Error	SSTR.S	$(n - 1)(ab - 1)$	MSTR.S	σ^2
Total	SSTO	$abn - 1$		

(b) Sums of Squares

$$SSS = ab \sum_i (\bar{Y}_{i..} - \bar{Y}_{...})^2$$

$$SSA = nb \sum_j (\bar{Y}_{.j.} - \bar{Y}_{...})^2$$

$$SSB = na \sum_k (\bar{Y}_{..k} - \bar{Y}_{...})^2$$

$$SSAB = n \sum_j \sum_k (\bar{Y}_{.jk} - \bar{Y}_{.j.} - \bar{Y}_{..k} + \bar{Y}_{...})^2$$

$$SSTR.S = \sum_i \sum_j \sum_k (Y_{ijk} - \bar{Y}_{i..} - \bar{Y}_{.jk} + \bar{Y}_{...})^2$$

Similarly, the test for factor B main effects:

(29.14a)
$$H_0: \text{ all } \beta_k = 0$$
$$H_a: \text{ not all } \beta_k \text{ equal zero}$$

uses the test statistic:

(29.14b)
$$F^* = \frac{MSB}{MSTR.S}$$

and the decision rule for controlling the Type I error at α is:

(29.14c)
$$\text{If } F^* \leq F[1 - \alpha; b - 1, (n - 1)(ab - 1)], \text{ conclude } H_0$$
$$\text{If } F^* > F[1 - \alpha; b - 1, (n - 1)(ab - 1)], \text{ conclude } H_a$$

Comments

1. When the effects of either factor A or factor B are random, the expected mean squares can be found by employing the rules in Appendix D. In turn, these expected mean squares will identify the appropriate test statistics.

2. The conservative F test described in Section 27.12 should be used when the assumption of compound symmetry in repeated measures model (29.10) is not met.

3. Repeated measures model (29.10) assumes that treatments and subjects do not interact. This assumption can be relaxed because the treatment-subject interaction sum of squares here is made up of three components:

$$SSTR.S = SSAS + SSBS + SSABS$$

where $SSAS$ is the interaction sum of squares between factor A and subjects and the other terms are defined similarly. Thus, it is possible to include the first-order interactions in the model (the factor A–subject interactions and the factor B–subject interactions) and only assume that the second-order interactions (the factor A–factor B–subject interactions) equal zero. When the repeated measures model allows for some interactions between treatments and subjects, the analysis of factor effects becomes somewhat more complex.   ∎

Evaluation of Appropriateness of Repeated Measures Model

Our earlier discussion on the evaluation of the appropriateness of repeated measures model (29.1) applies here as well. In particular, residual sequence plots by subject should be constructed to examine whether interference effects are present and whether the error variance is constant. Plots of the observations by subject should be utilized to see whether the assumption of no treatment-subject interactions is appropriate.

Analysis of Factor Effects

If factors A and B do not interact or interact only in unimportant fashion, the analysis of factor A and factor B main effects proceeds as usual. For the analysis of either factor A or factor B main effects, $MSTR.S$ will be used in the estimated variance of the estimated contrast since this mean square is the denominator of the F^* test statistic for testing factor A or factor B main effects.

The multiples for the estimated standard deviation of an estimated contrast of factor A or factor B level means are as follows:

	Main A Effect	Main B Effect
	Single comparison	
(29.15a)	$t[1 - \alpha/2; (n-1)(ab-1)]$	$t[1 - \alpha/2; (n-1)(ab-1)]$
	Tukey procedure (for pairwise comparisons)	
(29.15b)	$T = \dfrac{1}{\sqrt{2}} q[1 - \alpha; a, (n-1)(ab-1)]$	$T = \dfrac{1}{\sqrt{2}} q[1 - \alpha; b, (n-1)(ab-1)]$
	Scheffé procedure	
(29.15c)	$S^2 = (a-1)F[1 - \alpha; a-1, (n-1)(ab-1)]$	
		$S^2 = (b-1)F[1 - \alpha; b-1, (n-1)(ab-1)]$
	Bonferroni procedure	
(25.15d)	$B = t[1 - \alpha/2g; (n-1)(ab-1)]$	$B = t[1 - \alpha/2g; (n-1)(ab-1)]$

TABLE 29.7   Data for Blood Flow Example.

Subject i	Treatment			
	$A_1 B_1$	$A_1 B_2$	$A_2 B_1$	$A_2 B_2$
1	2	10	9	25
2	−1	8	6	21
3	0	11	8	24
. . .	. . .	. . .	. . .	. . .
10	−2	10	10	28
11	2	8	10	25
12	−1	8	6	23

If strong interactions between factors A and B exist that cannot be made unimportant by some simple transformation, the analysis of the factor effects should be performed in terms of the treatment means $\mu_{.jk}$, which are averaged over subjects. This analysis is similar to that in Section 29.2 for a single-factor study, with $\mu_{.jk}$ corresponding there to a treatment mean $\mu_{.j}$. The mean square $MSTR.S$ will again be used in estimating the variance of any estimated contrast of the treatment means.

Example

A clinician studied the effects of two drugs used either alone or together on the blood flow in human subjects. Twelve healthy middle-aged males participated in the study and they are viewed as a random sample from a relevant population of middle-aged males. The four treatments used in the study are defined as follows:

$A_1 B_1$ placebo (neither drug)

$A_1 B_2$ drug B alone

$A_2 B_1$ drug A alone

$A_2 B_2$ both drugs A and B

The 12 subjects received each of the four treatments in independently randomized orders. The response variable is the increase in blood flow from before to shortly after the administration of the treatment. The treatments were administered on successive days. This prevented any carryover effects because the effect of each drug is short-lived. The experiment was conducted in a double-blind fashion so that neither the physician nor the subject knew which treatment was administered when the change in blood flow was measured.

Table 29.7 contains the data for this study. A negative entry denotes a decrease in blood flow. Figure 29.5 contains the MINITAB output for the fit of repeated measures model (29.10). Included in the output are the expected mean squares for the specified ANOVA model. As explained in Chapter 28, each term in an expected mean square is represented in the MINITAB output by (1) the numeric code, in parentheses, for the variance of the model term, and (2) the preceding number which is the numerical multiple. When the model term is fixed, the letter Q is used in the printout to show that the variance is replaced by the sum

---

FIGURE 29.5 **MINITAB Output for ANOVA—Blood Flow Example.**

Factor	Type	Levels				Values			
S	random	12	1	2	3	4	5	6	7	8
						9	10	11	12
A	fixed	2	1	2					
B	fixed	2	1	2					

Analysis of Variance for Y

Source	DF	SS	MS	F	P
S	11	258.50	23.50	10.01	0.000
A	1	1587.00	1587.00	675.75	0.000
B	1	2028.00	2028.00	863.54	0.000
A*B	1	147.00	147.00	62.59	0.000
Error	33	77.50	2.35		
Total	47	4098.00	87.19		

Source	Variance component	Error term	Expected Mean Square (using restricted model)
1 S	5.288	5	(5) + 4(1)
2 A		5	(5) + 24Q[2]
3 B		5	(5) + 24Q[3]
4 A*B		5	(5) + 12Q[4]
5 Error	2.348		(5)

MEANS

A	B	N	Y
1	1	12	0.500
1	2	12	10.000
2	1	12	8.500
2	2	12	25.000

---

of squared effects divided by degrees of freedom. For example, the expected value of *MSA* as shown in Figure 29.5 is:

$$(5) + 24Q[2] = \sigma^2 + 24\frac{\Sigma \alpha_j^2}{2-1}$$

which corresponds, of course, to the expected mean square shown in Table 29.6a.

Various diagnostics were utilized to see if repeated measures model (29.10) is appropriate for the data in Table 29.7. The results (not shown here) supported the appropriateness of this model. The clinician expected the two drugs to interact in increasing the blood flow. To test for interaction effects:

$$H_0: \text{ all } (\alpha\beta)_{jk} = 0$$

$$H_a: \text{ not all } (\alpha\beta)_{jk} \text{ equal zero}$$

we use test statistic (29.12b) and the results from Figure 29.5:

$$F^* = \frac{MSAB}{MSTR.S} = \frac{147.000}{2.35} = 62.6$$

For level of significance $\alpha = .01$, we require $F(.99; 1, 33) = 7.47$. Since $F^* = 62.6 > 7.47$, we conclude H_a, that interaction effects exist. The *P*-value for this test is 0+.

FIGURE 29.6   Interaction Plot with Responses Superimposed—Blood Flow Example.

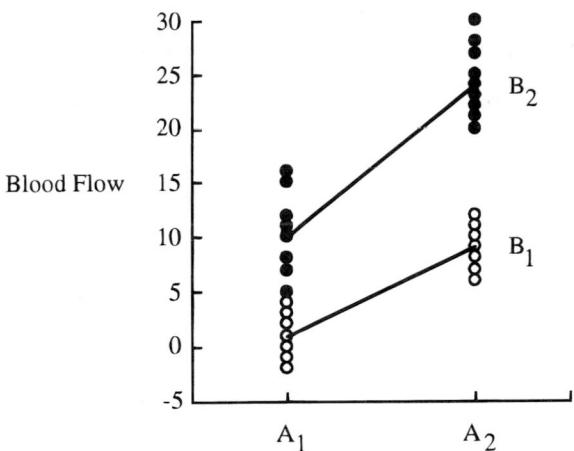

Figure 29.6 contains an interaction plot of the estimated treatment means, with the responses superimposed. Substantial interaction effects are evident. To study the nature of the interaction effects, the clinician wished to compare the joint use of the two drugs with the use of each drug alone, drug A with drug B, and each drug with no drug. Thus, the following pairwise comparisons are to be made:

$$L_1 = \mu_{.22} - \mu_{.21} \qquad L_4 = \mu_{.21} - \mu_{.11}$$
$$L_2 = \mu_{.22} - \mu_{.12} \qquad L_5 = \mu_{.12} - \mu_{.11}$$
$$L_3 = \mu_{.21} - \mu_{.12}$$

Point estimates of these pairwise comparisons are ($\overline{Y}_{jk}$ values are in Figure 29.5):

$$\hat{L}_1 = 25.0 - 8.5 = 16.5 \qquad \hat{L}_4 = 8.5 - .5 = 8.0$$
$$\hat{L}_2 = 25.0 - 10.0 = 15.0 \qquad \hat{L}_5 = 10.0 - .5 = 9.5$$
$$\hat{L}_3 = 8.5 - 10.0 = -1.5$$

The estimated variance of each estimate $\hat{L}$ is given in (17.15), with the relevant mean square here being $MSTR.S$. Hence, we have:

$$s^2\{\hat{L}\} = MSTR.S\left(\frac{1}{n} + \frac{1}{n}\right) = 2.348\left(\frac{2}{12}\right) = .3913$$

and $s\{\hat{L}\} = .626$. Using the Bonferroni procedure with a 95 percent family confidence coefficient, we require $B = t[1 - (.05)/2(5); 33] = t(.995; 33) = 2.733$. Hence, $t(.995; 33)s\{\hat{L}\} = 2.733(.626) = 1.71$ and the desired confidence intervals with a 95 percent family confidence coefficient are:

$$14.8 \leq \mu_{.22} - \mu_{.21} \leq 18.2 \qquad 6.3 \leq \mu_{.21} - \mu_{.11} \leq 9.7$$

$$13.3 \leq \mu_{.22} - \mu_{.12} \leq 16.7 \qquad 7.8 \leq \mu_{.12} - \mu_{.11} \leq 11.2$$

$$-3.2 \leq \mu_{.21} - \mu_{.12} \leq .2$$

It is clear from these results that either drug A alone or drug B alone tends to lead to an increase in blood flow, and that the combination of the two drugs leads to a substantial additional increase in blood flow as compared to when either drug is used alone. Finally, no significant difference exists in the mean effects of the two drugs used alone.

29.4   Two-Factor Experiments with Repeated Measures on One Factor

Description of Design

In many two-factor studies, repeated measures can only be made on one of the two factors. Consider, for instance, an experimenter who wished to study the effects of two types of incentives (factor A) on a person's ability to solve problems. The researcher also wanted to study two types of problems (factor B)—abstract and concrete problems. Each experimental subject could be asked to do each type of problem, but could not be exposed to more than one type of incentive stimulus because of potential interference effects. Thus, the design the experimenter utilized may be represented schematically as shown in Figure 29.7.

In a two-factor experiment with repeated measures on one factor, two randomizations generally need to be employed. First, the level of the nonrepeated factor (A, in Figure 29.7) needs to be randomly assigned to the subjects. Second, the order of the levels of the repeated factor (B, in Figure 29.7) needs to be randomized independently for all subjects.

Since n subjects are randomly assigned incentive stimulus A_1 and n subjects are randomly assigned incentive stimulus A_2, as far as factor A is concerned the experiment is a completely randomized one. On the other hand, as far as factor B (type of problem) is concerned, each subject is a block. Thus, for factor B, the experiment is a randomized block design, with block effects random. We call this experimental design a *two-factor experiment with repeated measures on factor B*.

In the experiment depicted in Figure 29.7, comparisons between factor A level means involve differences between groups of subjects as well as differences associated with the two factor A levels. On the other hand, comparisons between factor B level means at the same level of factor A are based on the same subject, and hence only involve differences associated with the two factor B levels. Thus, for these latter comparisons, each subject serves as its own control. The main effects of factor A are therefore said to be confounded with differences between groups of subjects, whereas the main effects of factor B are free of such confounding. It is for this reason that tests on factor B main effects will generally be more sensitive than tests on the main effects for factor A.

FIGURE 29.7 Layout for Two-Factor Design with Random Assignments of Factor A Level to Subjects and Repeated Measures on Factor B.

Incentive Stimulus	Subject	Treatment Order 1	Treatment Order 2
		1	**2**
	1	$A_1 B_1$	$A_1 B_2$
A_1	.	.	.
	.	.	.
	.	.	.
	n	$A_1 B_1$	$A_1 B_2$
	$n + 1$	$A_2 B_2$	$A_2 B_1$
A_2	.	.	.
	.	.	.
	.	.	.
	$2n$	$A_2 B_1$	$A_2 B_2$

Comments

1. A two-factor experiment with repeated measures on one factor may be viewed as an incomplete block design. With reference to the repeated measures design in Figure 29.7, there are four treatments ($A_1 B_1$, $A_1 B_2$, $A_2 B_1$, and $A_2 B_2$) and one-half of the blocks (subjects) contain treatments $A_1 B_1$ and $A_1 B_2$ while the other half of the blocks contain treatments $A_2 B_1$ and $A_2 B_2$.

2. When the factor on which repeated measures are taken is time, no randomization of the levels of the repeated factor is required. Consider, for instance, a study of two different advertising campaigns in which the effect on sales is to be measured in 10 test markets during four consecutive months. Here, the only randomization required is for assigning the advertising campaigns to the test markets. Similarly, when the nonrepeated factor is a characteristic of the subjects, such as age of subject, no randomization is involved for that factor. ∎

Model

The development of a model for a two-factor experiment with repeated measures on one factor is only a little more complex than for earlier cases. As before, we shall develop the model for random subject effects and fixed factor A and factor B effects. Let, as usual, α_j and β_k denote the factor A and factor B main effects, respectively, $(\alpha\beta)_{jk}$ the AB interaction effect, and ρ the subject (block) main effect. We do need to recognize, however, that the subject effect in this design is nested within factor A. Therefore, we will denote this effect by $\rho_{i(j)}$. As before, we assume that there are no interactions between treatments and subjects, although this condition is not essential here. A model that incorporates the above specifications is as follows for a balanced study, where the number of subjects receiving each level of factor A is the same:

$$(29.16) \qquad Y_{ijk} = \mu_{...} + \rho_{i(j)} + \alpha_j + \beta_k + (\alpha\beta)_{jk} + \varepsilon_{ijk}$$

where:

> $\mu_{...}$ is a constant
>
> $\rho_{i(j)}$ are independent $N(0, \sigma_\rho^2)$
>
> α_j are constants subject to $\Sigma \alpha_j = 0$
>
> β_k are constants subject to $\Sigma \beta_k = 0$
>
> $(\alpha\beta)_{jk}$ are constants subject to $\underset{j}{\Sigma}(\alpha\beta)_{jk} = 0$ for all k and $\underset{k}{\Sigma}(\alpha\beta)_{jk} = 0$ for all j
>
> ε_{ijk} are independent $N(0, \sigma^2)$
>
> $\rho_{i(j)}$ and ε_{ijk} are independent
>
> $i = 1, \ldots, n; \ j = 1, \ldots, a; \ k = 1, \ldots, b$

The observations Y_{ijk} for repeated measures model (29.16) have the following properties:

$$(29.17\text{a}) \qquad E\{Y_{ijk}\} = \mu_{...} + \alpha_j + \beta_k + (\alpha\beta)_{jk}$$

$$(29.17\text{b}) \qquad \sigma^2\{Y_{ijk}\} = \sigma_Y^2 = \sigma_\rho^2 + \sigma^2$$

$$(29.17\text{c}) \qquad \sigma\{Y_{ijk}, Y_{ijk'}\} = \sigma_\rho^2 \qquad k \neq k'$$

$$(29.17\text{d}) \qquad \sigma\{Y_{ijk}, Y_{i'j'k'}\} = 0 \qquad i \neq i' \text{ and/or } j \neq j'$$

Note that the observations Y_{ijk} have constant variance. In addition, in advance of the random trials any two observations for different levels of factor B for the same subject have constant covariance, for all subjects, while observations for different subjects are independent. Also, all observations are assumed to be normally distributed.

Once the subjects have been selected, repeated measures model (29.16) assumes that any two observations for the same subject are independent, that is, that there are no interference effects.

Analysis of Variance and Tests

Analysis of Variance.   The ANOVA sums of squares for repeated measures model (29.16) can be obtained by means of the rules in Appendix D. The sum of squares that is used for estimating the error variance turns out to be the interaction sum of squares $SSB.S(A)$. The ANOVA sums of squares are shown in Table 29.8. Also shown there are the degrees of freedom for each sum of squares.

Tests for Factor Effects.   The expected mean squares for the analysis of variance in Table 29.8 are given in Table 29.9. These expected mean squares can be obtained by means of the rules in Appendix D.

TABLE 29.8 Analysis of Variance for Two-Factor Experiment with Repeated Measures on Factor B—Model (29.16).

Source of Variation	SS	df
Factor A	$SSA = bn \sum_j (\bar{Y}_{.j.} - \bar{Y}_{...})^2$	$a - 1$
Factor B	$SSB = an \sum_k (\bar{Y}_{..k} - \bar{Y}_{...})^2$	$b - 1$
AB interactions	$SSAB = n \sum_j \sum_k (\bar{Y}_{.jk} - \bar{Y}_{.j.} - \bar{Y}_{..k} + \bar{Y}_{...})^2$	$(a-1)(b-1)$
Subjects (within factor A)	$SSS(A) = b \sum_i \sum_j (\bar{Y}_{ij.} - \bar{Y}_{.j.})^2$	$a(n-1)$
Error	$SSB.S(A) = \sum_i \sum_j \sum_k (Y_{ijk} - \bar{Y}_{.jk} - \bar{Y}_{ij.} + \bar{Y}_{.j.})^2$	$a(n-1)(b-1)$
Total	$SSTO = \sum_i \sum_j \sum_k (Y_{ijk} - \bar{Y}_{...})^2$	$abn - 1$

TABLE 29.9 Expected Mean Squares for Two-Factor Experiment with Repeated Measures on Factor B—Model (29.16) (A, B fixed, subjects random).

Source of Variation	MS	E{MS}
Factor A	MSA	$\sigma^2 + b\sigma_\rho^2 + bn \frac{\sum \alpha_j^2}{a-1}$
Factor B	MSB	$\sigma^2 + an \frac{\sum \beta_k^2}{b-1}$
AB interactions	$MSAB$	$\sigma^2 + n \frac{\sum\sum(\alpha\beta)_{jk}^2}{(a-1)(b-1)}$
Subjects (within factor A)	$MSS(A)$	$\sigma^2 + b\sigma_\rho^2$
Error	$MSB.S(A)$	σ^2

It is clear from the expected mean squares in Table 29.9 that the test for AB interaction effects:

$$H_0: \text{all } (\alpha\beta)_{jk} = 0$$
$$H_a: \text{not all } (\alpha\beta)_{jk} \text{ equal zero}$$

(29.18a)

uses the test statistic:

$$(29.18\text{b}) \qquad\qquad F^* = \frac{MSAB}{MSB.S(A)}$$

and the decision rule for controlling the Type I error at α is:

(29.18c)
> If $F^* \le F[1 - \alpha; (a - 1)(b - 1), a(n - 1)(b - 1)]$, conclude H_0
> If $F^* > F[1 - \alpha; (a - 1)(b - 1), a(n - 1)(b - 1)]$, conclude H_a

The test for factor A main effects:

(29.19a)
$$H_0: \text{ all } \alpha_j = 0$$
$$H_a: \text{ not all } \alpha_j \text{ equal zero}$$

uses the test statistic:

$$(29.19\text{b}) \qquad\qquad F^* = \frac{MSA}{MSS(A)}$$

and the decision rule for controlling the Type I error at α is:

(29.19c)
> If $F^* \le F[1 - \alpha; a - 1, a(n - 1)]$, conclude H_0
> If $F^* > F[1 - \alpha; a - 1, a(n - 1)]$, conclude H_a

Finally, the test for factor B main effects:

(29.20a)
$$H_0: \text{ all } \beta_k = 0$$
$$H_a: \text{ not all } \beta_k \text{ equal zero}$$

uses the test statistic:

$$(29.20\text{b}) \qquad\qquad F^* = \frac{MSB}{MSB.S(A)}$$

and the decision rule for controlling the Type I error at α is:

(29.20c)
> If $F^* \le F[1 - \alpha; b - 1, a(n - 1)(b - 1)]$, conclude H_0
> If $F^* > F[1 - \alpha; b - 1, a(n - 1)(b - 1)]$, conclude H_a

Comments

1. When the assumption of compound symmetry in repeated measures model (29.16) is not met, the conservative test discussed in Section 27.12 should be employed.

2. When the study is not balanced (i.e., when the number of subjects within each level of factor A is not the same), the tests described here are no longer appropriate. Instead, the methods for unbalanced mixed and random effects models discussed in Section 24.6 can be employed. ∎

Evaluation of Appropriateness of Repeated Measures Model

Our earlier discussion on evaluating the appropriateness of a repeated measures model applies here also. The residuals for repeated measures model (29.16) are:

$$(29.21) \qquad\qquad e_{ijk} = Y_{ijk} - \bar{Y}_{jk} - \bar{Y}_{ij.} + \bar{Y}_{.j.}$$

A special feature of repeated measures model (29.16) also warrants attention. This model requires that the variance between subjects, σ_ρ^2, be constant for all levels of factor A. This assumption can be examined by dot plots of the estimated subject effects $\bar{Y}_{ij.} - \bar{Y}_{.j.}$ for each level of factor A.

We can also conduct a formal test of the equality of the between-subjects variances by noting that the variation between subjects within factor A, $SSS(A)$, can be decomposed into components for each factor A level:

$$(29.22) \qquad SSS(A) = SSS(A_1) + SSS(A_2) + \cdots + SSS(A_a)$$

where:

$$(29.22a) \qquad SSS(A_j) = b \sum_i (\bar{Y}_{ij.} - \bar{Y}_{.j.})^2$$

Each component sum of squares has $n - 1$ degrees of freedom associated with it. We can therefore make a test of the equality of the between-subjects variances by means of the Hartley test statistic (18.8) or the modified Levene test statistic (18.12). For the latter test, d_{ij} in (18.11) is defined as the absolute difference between the estimated mean, $\bar{Y}_{ij.}$, and the median of the estimated means $\bar{Y}_{1j.}, \ldots, \bar{Y}_{nj.}$.

Similarly, the error variation, $SSB.S(A)$, can be decomposed into components for each factor A level:

$$(29.23) \qquad SSB.S(A) = SSB.S(A_1) + SSB.S(A_2) + \cdots + SSB.S(A_a)$$

where:

$$(29.23a) \qquad SSB.S(A_j) = \sum_i \sum_k (Y_{ijk} - \bar{Y}_{jk} - \bar{Y}_{ij.} + \bar{Y}_{.j.})^2$$

Each component has $(n - 1)(b - 1)$ degrees of freedom associated with it. The Hartley and modified Levene tests can be conducted here also, this time to test for the equality of the error variance σ^2 for the different factor A levels.

The Hartley test assumes normality and is sensitive to this assumption. Hence, the appropriateness of the normality assumption should be established first before the Hartley test is employed. Unlike the Hartley test, the modified Levene test is robust and relatively insensitive to departures from normality.

Analysis of Factor Effects

When the two factors do not interact or the interactions are not important, the main effects may be analyzed in a straightforward fashion. The relevant mean square to be used in the estimated variance of an estimated contrast of factor A level means for repeated measures model (29.16) is $MSS(A)$ because this mean square is the denominator of the appropriate

TABLE 29.10   **Data for Athletic Shoes Sales Example.**

Advertising Campaign	Test Market	Time Period		
		$k = 1$	$k = 2$	$k = 3$
	$i = 1$	958	1,047	933
	$i = 2$	1,005	1,122	986
$j = 1$	$i = 3$	351	436	339
	$i = 4$	549	632	512
	$i = 5$	730	784	707
	$i = 1$	780	897	718
	$i = 2$	229	275	202
$j = 2$	$i = 3$	883	964	817
	$i = 4$	624	695	599
	$i = 5$	375	436	351

F^* statistic for testing factor A main effects. Similarly, the mean square for estimating contrasts of factor B level means is $MSB.S(A)$.

The multiples in (29.15) need to be modified only for the degrees of freedom associated with the mean square used; $a(n-1)$ for the analysis of factor A effects and $a(n-1)(b-1)$ for the analysis of factor B effects.

Note from Table 29.9 that the analysis of factor B effects can be carried out more precisely than that for factor A effects. The reason is that comparisons among factor A levels utilize $MSS(A)$, which involves the variability among the subjects as well as the experimental error, while comparisons among factor B levels utilize $MSB.S(A)$, which involves only experimental error.

When interactions exist between the two factors, the analysis of factor effects becomes considerably more complex; see, for example, Reference 29.1 for a discussion of this case.

Example

A national retail chain wanted to study the effects of two advertising campaigns (factor A) on the volume of sales of athletic shoes over time (factor B). Ten similar test markets (subjects, S) were chosen at random to participate in this study. The two advertising campaigns (A_1 and A_2) were similar in all respects except that a different national sports personality was used in each. Sales data were collected for three two-week periods (B_1: two weeks prior to campaign; B_2: two weeks during which campaign occurred; B_3: two weeks after campaign was concluded.) The experiment was conducted during a six-week period when sales of athletic shoes are usually quite stable.

The data on sales (coded) are presented in Table 29.10, and are plotted in Figure 29.8 by test market for each advertising campaign. There is no evidence in Figure 29.8 of any interactions between the test markets and the treatments. In general, sales tended to increase during each advertising campaign, and then tended to decline to previous or lower levels than just before the campaign.

Based on Figure 29.8 and other diagnostic analyses (not shown), it was concluded that repeated measures model (29.16) is appropriate here. Figure 29.9 on page 1192 contains the MINITAB output for the fit of this model.

FIGURE 29.8 Plots of Sales Data by Test Market and Campaign—Athletic Shoes Sales Example.

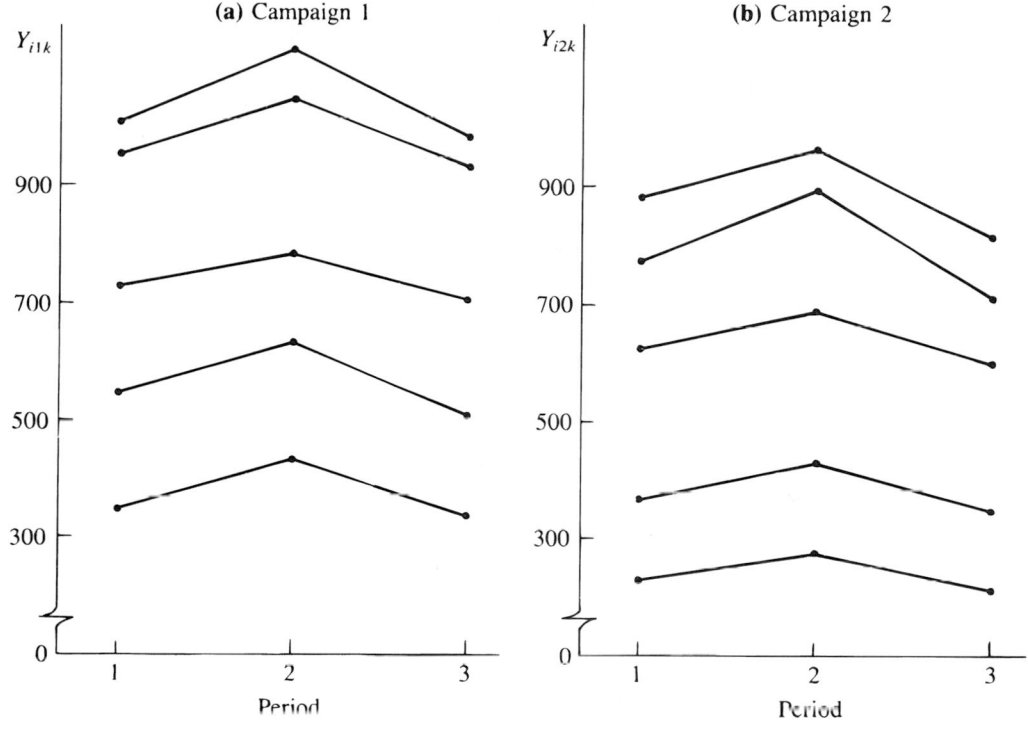

First we wish to test for campaign-time interaction effects:

$$H_0: \text{ all } (\alpha\beta)_{jk} = 0$$

$$H_a: \text{ not all } (\alpha\beta)_{jk} \text{ equal zero}$$

We use the results from Figure 29.9 in test statistic (29.18b):

$$F^* = \frac{MSAB}{MSB.S(A)} = \frac{196}{358} = .55$$

For level of significance $\alpha = .05$, we require $F(.95; 2, 16) = 3.63$. Since $F^* = .55 \leq 3.63$, we conclude H_0, that no significant interaction effects are present. The P-value for the test is .59.

Next we wish to test for advertising campaign main effects:

$$H_0: \text{ all } \alpha_j = 0$$

$$H_a: \text{ not all } \alpha_j \text{ equal zero}$$

FIGURE 29.9   MINITAB Output for ANOVA—Athletic Shoes Sales Example.

```
Factor    Type     Levels              Values
A         fixed      2        1    2
S(A)      random     5        1    2    3    4    5
B         fixed      3        1    2    3


Analysis of Variance for Y

Source    DF        SS          MS        F      P
A          1      168151      168151     0.73   0.417
S(A)       8     1833681      229210   640.31   0.000
B          2       67073       33537    93.69   0.000
A*B        2         391         196     0.55   0.589
Error     16        5727         358
Total     29     2075023       71553


Source      Variance    Error    Expected Mean Square
            component    term     (using restricted model)
 1 A                      2       (5) + 3(2) + 15Q[1]
 2 S(A)      76284.0      5       (5) + 3(2)
 3 B                      5       (5) + 10Q[3]
 4 A*B                    5       (5) + 5Q[4]
 5 Error       358.0              (5)


      MEANS

A     N          Y
1    15      739.40
2    15      589.67

B     N          Y
1    10      648.40
2    10      728.80
3    10      616.40
```

We use the results from Figure 29.9 in test statistic (29.19b):

$$F^* = \frac{MSA}{MSS(A)} = \frac{168,151}{229,210} = .73$$

For level of significance $\alpha = .05$, we require $F(.95; 1, 8) = 5.32$. Since $F^* = .73 \leq 5.32$, we conclude H_0, that no advertising campaign main effects exist. The P-value for the test is .42. Thus, either of the two national sports personalities is equally effective in the advertising campaign.

Finally, we wish to test for time period effects:

$$H_0: \text{ all } \beta_k = 0$$

$$H_a: \text{ not all } \beta_k \text{ equal zero}$$

Using the results from Figure 29.9 in test statistic (29.20b), we obtain:

$$F^* = \frac{MSB}{MSB.S(A)} = \frac{33,537}{358} = 93.7$$

For level of significance $\alpha = .05$, we require $F(.95; 2, 16) = 3.63$. Since $F^* = 93.7 > 3.63$, we conclude H_a, that period main effects exist. The P-value for the test is 0+.

To examine the nature of the time period effects, we shall conduct pairwise comparisons of mean sales for the three time periods:

$$L = \mu_{..k} - \mu_{..k'}$$

The Tukey procedure will be employed, with a 99 percent family confidence coefficient. We require:

$$T = \frac{1}{\sqrt{2}} q(.99; 3, 16) = \frac{1}{\sqrt{2}} (4.78) = 3.38$$

$$s^2\{\hat{L}\} = \frac{2MSB.S(A)}{an} = \frac{2(358)}{2(5)} = 71.60$$

Hence, $T s\{\hat{L}\} = 3.38\sqrt{71.60} = 28.6$.

The point estimates of the changes in mean sales, based on the estimated factor B level means $\bar{Y}_{..k}$ in Figure 29.9, are:

$$\hat{L}_1 = \bar{Y}_{..2} - \bar{Y}_{..1} = 728.8 - 648.4 = 80.4$$

$$\hat{L}_2 = \bar{Y}_{..3} - \bar{Y}_{..1} = 616.4 - 648.4 = -32.0$$

$$\hat{L}_3 = \bar{Y}_{..3} - \bar{Y}_{..2} = 616.4 - 728.8 = -112.4$$

and the desired confidence intervals therefore are:

$$52 \le \mu_{..2} - \mu_{..1} \le 109$$

$$-61 \le \mu_{..3} - \mu_{..1} \le -3$$

$$-141 \le \mu_{..3} - \mu_{..2} \le -84$$

We conclude with family confidence coefficient .99 that the two advertising campaigns lead to an immediate increase in mean sales of between 52 and 109 (8 to 17 percent), but that mean sales in the following period fall below those for the period preceding the campaign by somewhere between 3 and 61 (.5 to 9 percent).

Blocking of Subjects

As already noted, comparisons among factor B effects can usually be carried out with greater precision than those for factor A effects because the latter involve between-subject variability as well as experimental error. To improve the precision when analyzing factor A effects, it is often helpful to block the subjects by some appropriate characteristic(s) so that the subjects within a block are homogeneous. Figure 29.10 illustrates the blocking of subjects in connection with the repeated measures design of Figure 29.7. Altogether, n blocks are used, each consisting of two similar subjects. One subject in each block is assigned at random to factor level A_1, the other is assigned to factor level A_2. In the second stage of randomization, each subject is randomly assigned the order of the two problems. Thus, the only difference between the repeated measures designs in Figures 29.10 and 29.7 is the blocking of the subjects for purposes of studying factor A effects more precisely.

When there is a choice between which of the two factors should be the one on which repeated measures are taken (factor B), it should be the one for which more precise estimates are required. The reason is that even with blocking, the variability between subjects within a block will usually be greater than the variability within a subject.

FIGURE 29.10 Layout for Blocked Repeated Measures Design with Random Assignments of Factor A Level to Subjects and Repeated Measures on Factor B.

		Treatment Order	
		1	2
Block 1	Subject 1	$A_2 B_1$	$A_2 B_2$
	Subject 2	$A_1 B_2$	$A_1 B_1$
Block 2	Subject 3	$A_1 B_2$	$A_1 B_1$
	Subject 4	$A_2 B_2$	$A_2 B_1$
	$\vdots$	$\vdots$	$\vdots$
Block n	Subject $2n-1$	$A_1 B_1$	$A_1 B_2$
	Subject $2n$	$A_2 B_2$	$A_2 B_1$

29.5 Regression Approach to Repeated Measures Designs

When the repeated measures study is balanced and the treatment effects are fixed, the analysis of variance model can be expressed in the form of a regression model with indicator variables for purposes of obtaining the various sums of squares and conducting tests for treatment effects. Repeated measures models (29.1) and (29.10) can be stated in the form of a regression model as explained in Section 27.8. Repeated measures model (29.16), which also involves nested effects, can be expressed in the form of a regression model by including suitable indicator variables as explained in Section 28.6.

When the repeated measures study is not balanced, as, for instance, when there are missing observations, the tests based on the expected mean squares in Tables 29.1, 29.6, and 29.9 are no longer appropriate. Methods for analyzing unbalanced mixed and random effects models are discussed in Section 24.6.

29.6 Split-Plot Designs

Split-plot designs are frequently used in field, laboratory, industrial, and social science experiments. The repeated measures design in Figure 29.7 for a study with repeated measures on one factor is a type of split-plot design. We shall discuss split-plot designs only for two-factor studies, but these designs can be extended to apply when three or more factors are under investigation.

Split-plot designs were originally developed for agricultural experiments. Consider an investigation to study the effects of two irrigation methods (factor A) and two fertilizers (factor B) on yield of a crop, using four available fields as experimental units. In a completely

FIGURE 29.11   **Layout for Two-Factor Split-Plot Experiment—Agricultural Experiment Example (factor A is whole-plot treatment and factor B is split-plot treatment).**

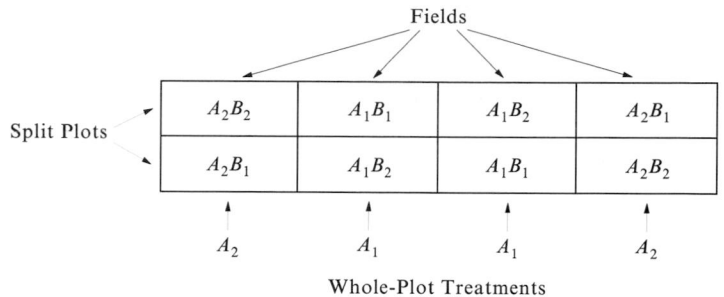

randomized design, four treatments $(A_1B_1, A_1B_2, A_2B_1, A_2B_2)$ would then be assigned at random to the four fields. Since there are four treatments and just four experimental units, there will be no degrees of freedom for estimation of error, as shown in the following abbreviated ANOVA table, listing source of variation and degrees of freedom only:

Source of Variation	Degrees of Freedom
Factor A (irrigation methods)	1
Factor B (fertilizer types)	1
AB interactions	1
Error	0
Total	3

If the fields could be subdivided into smaller experimental units, replicates of each factor-level combination could be obtained and the error variance could then be estimated. Unfortunately, in this investigation it is not possible to apply different irrigation methods (factor A) in areas smaller than a field, although different fertilizer types (factor B) could be applied in relatively small areas. A split-plot design can accommodate this situation.

In a split-plot design, each of the two irrigation methods is randomly assigned to two of the four fields, which are usually called *whole plots*. In turn, each whole plot is then subdivided into two or more smaller areas called *split plots*, and the two fertilizers are then randomly assigned to the split plots within each whole plot. The key feature of split-plot designs is the use of two (or more) distinct levels of randomization. At the first level of randomization, the whole-plot treatments are randomly assigned to whole plots; at the second level, the split-plot treatments are randomly assigned to split plots.

The layout for the agricultural experiment example is shown in Figure 29.11. Note that this layout is conceptually identical to the layout for the two-factor repeated measures design in Figure 29.7. The fields in Figure 29.11 correspond to the subjects in Figure 29.7, and the split plots correspond to the occasions on which treatments can be applied to a subject. Consequently, the split-plot model here is the same as in (29.16):

(29.24)
$$Y_{ijk} = \mu_{...} + \rho_{i(j)} + \alpha_j + \beta_k + (\alpha\beta)_{jk} + \varepsilon_{ijk}$$

TABLE 29.11   ANOVA Table for Two-Factor Split-Plot Experiment.

Source of Variation	SS	df	MS
Whole plots			
Factor A	SSA	$a-1$	MSA
Whole-plot error	$SSW(A)$	$a(n-1)$	$MSW(A)$
Split plots			
Factor B	SSB	$b-1$	MSB
AB interactions	$SSAB$	$(a-1)(b-1)$	$MSAB$
Split-plot error	$SSB.W(A)$	$a(n-1)(b-1)$	$MSB.W(A)$
Total	$SSTO$	$abn-1$	

For the split-plot agricultural experiment example, α_j denotes the main effect of the jth irrigation method (jth whole-plot treatment) and β_k denotes the main effect of the kth fertilizer type (kth split-plot treatment). Also, $\rho_{i(j)}$ denotes the effect of the ith whole plot, nested within the jth level of factor A (irrigation method).

Some computer packages produce special ANOVA tables that list the whole-plot effects and split-plot effects separately. Table 29.11 illustrates such a table. These tables serve as a reminder that the denominator of the F test for the whole-plot treatments is given by the error mean square for whole plots and that the denominator of the F test for the split-plot treatments and for the interactions between the whole-plot and split-plot treatments is given by the split-plot error mean square, as shown in Table 29.11. Note that this table is simply a rearrangement of the ANOVA table in Table 29.8 for a two-factor study with repeated measures on one factor. $SSS(A)$ is now denoted by $SSW(A)$ and $SSB.S(A)$ is now denoted by $SSB.W(A)$. The expected mean squares are the same as in Table 29.9.

Comments

1. Whenever subjects can receive all treatments in a two-factor study without interference effects, a repeated measures design with repeated measures on both factors is preferable, because the factor effects for both factors can then usually be estimated more precisely than in a split-plot design.

2. Split-plot designs are useful in industrial experiments when one factor requires larger experimental units than another. Consider, for instance, a study of the effects of two additives (factor A) and two different containers (factor B) for prolonging the shelf life of a milk product. Here, it is easier to make larger batches of the milk product with a given additive, whereas the different containers can be used with smaller batches.

3. Split-plot designs may be viewed as a type of incomplete block design where the whole plots are considered to be the blocks, with each whole plot being given only some of the full set of treatments.

4. A wide variety of split-plot designs has been developed. For instance, split-plot designs can involve more than two stages of randomization. In a split-split-plot experiment, three stages of randomization are generally involved. Whole plots are divided into split plots and split plots are further divided into split split plots. Three treatments are then assigned to the various levels of experimental units, using three distinct stages of randomization. References 29.2 and 29.3 provide further information about these designs.   ∎

Cited References

29.1. Winer, B. J., D. R. Brown, and K. M. Michels. *Statistical Principles in Experimental Design.* 3rd ed. New York: McGraw-Hill Book Co., 1991.

29.2. Steel, R. G. D., and J. H. Torrie. *Principles and Procedures of Statistics.* 2nd ed. New York: McGraw-Hill Book Co., 1980.

29.3. Koch, G. G., J. D. Elashoff, and I. A. Amara. "Repeated Measurements—Design and Analysis," in *Encyclopedia of Statistical Sciences*, vol. 8, eds. S. Kotz and N. L. Johnson. New York: John Wiley & Sons, 1988, pp. 46–73.

Problems

29.1. A serious potential problem with repeated measures designs is associated with carryover effects. Describe some steps that can be taken to minimize this problem.

29.2. In designing a two-factor repeated measures study with repeated measures on one factor, does it matter which of the two factors is included as the repeated measures factor? Explain fully.

29.3. **Blood pressure.** The relationship between the dose of a drug that increases blood pressure and the actual amount of increase in mean diastolic blood pressure was investigated in a laboratory experiment. Twelve rabbits received in random order six different dose levels of the drug, with a suitable interval between each drug administration. The increase in blood pressure was used as the response variable. The data on blood pressure increase follow.

Rabbit	Dose (j)						Rabbit	Dose (j)					
i	.1	.3	.5	1.0	1.5	3.0	i	.1	.3	.5	1.0	1.5	3.0
1	21	21	23	35	36	48	7	9	12	17	22	33	40
2	19	24	27	36	36	46	8	20	20	30	30	38	41
3	12	25	27	26	33	40	9	18	18	27	31	42	49
4	9	17	18	27	34	39	10	8	12	11	24	26	31
5	7	10	19	25	31	38	11	18	22	25	32	38	38
6	18	26	26	29	39	44	12	17	23	26	28	34	35

a. Obtain the residuals for repeated measures model (29.1) and plot them against the fitted values. Also prepare a normal probability plot of the residuals. What do you conclude about the appropriateness of model (29.1)?

b. Prepare aligned residual dot plots by dose level. Do these plots support the assumption of constancy of the error variance? Discuss.

c. Plot the observations Y_{ij} for each rabbit in the format of Figure 29.2. Does the assumption of no interactions between subjects (rabbits) and treatments appear to be reasonable here?

d. Conduct the Tukey test for additivity, conditional on the rabbits actually selected; use $\alpha = .005$. State the alternatives, decision rule, and conclusion. What is the P-value of the test?

29.4.   Refer to **Blood pressure** Problem 29.3. Assume that repeated measures model (29.1) is appropriate.

a. Obtain the analysis of variance table.

b. Test whether or not the mean increase in blood pressure differs for the various dose levels; use $\alpha = .01$. State the alternatives, decision rule, and conclusion. What is the P-value of the test?

c. Analyze the effects of the six dose levels by comparing the means for successive dose levels using the Bonferroni procedure with a 95 percent family confidence coefficient. State your findings and summarize them by a suitable line plot.

d. Based on the estimated efficiency measure (27.14), how effective was the repeated measures design here as compared to a completely randomized design?

29.5.   Refer to **Blood pressure** Problems 29.3 and 29.4.

a. Develop a regression model in which the subject effects are represented by $1, -1, 0$ indicator variables and the dose effect is represented by linear, quadratic, and cubic terms in $x = X - \bar{X}$, where X is the dose level. For instance, the x value for the first dose level ($X = .1$) is $x = .1 - 1.07 = -.97$.

b. Fit the regression model to the data.

c. Obtain the residuals and plot them against the fitted values. Does the model utilized appear to provide a reasonable fit?

d. Test whether or not the cubic effect is required in the model; use $\alpha = .05$. State the alternatives, decision rule, and conclusion. What is the P-value of the test?

$\sqrt{}$ 29.6.   **Grapefruit sales.** A supermarket chain studied the relationship between grapefruit sales and the price at which grapefruits are offered. Three price levels were studied: (1) the chief competitor's price, (2) a price slightly higher than the chief competitor's price, and (3) a price moderately higher than the chief competitor's price. Eight stores of comparable size were randomly selected for the study. Sales data were collected for three one-week periods, with the order of the three price levels randomly assigned for each store. The experiment was conducted during a time period when sales of grapefruits are usually quite stable, and no carryover effects were anticipated for this product. Data on store sales of grapefruits during the study period follow (data coded).

Store	Price level (j)		
i	1	2	3
1	62.1	61.3	60.8
2	58.2	57.9	55.1
$\cdots$	$\cdots$	$\cdots$	$\cdots$
7	46.8	43.2	41.5
8	51.2	49.8	47.9

a. Obtain the residuals for repeated measures model (29.1) and plot them against the fitted values. Also prepare a normal probability plot of the residuals. What do you conclude about the appropriateness of model (29.1)?

b. Prepare aligned residual dot plots by price level. Do these plots support the assumption of constancy of the error variance? Discuss.

c. Plot the observations Y_{ij} for each store in the format of Figure 29.2. Does the assumption of no interactions between subjects (stores) and treatments appear to be reasonable here?

d. Conduct the Tukey test for additivity, conditional on the stores actually selected; use $\alpha = .01$. State the alternatives, decision rule, and conclusion. What is the P-value of the test?

√ 29.7. Refer to **Grapefruit sales** Problem 29.6. Assume that repeated measures model (29.1) is appropriate.

a. Obtain the analysis of variance table.

b. Test whether or not the mean sales of grapefruits differ for the three price levels; use $\alpha = .05$. State the alternatives, decision rule, and conclusion. What is the P-value of the test?

c. Analyze the effects of the three price levels by estimating all pairwise comparisons of the price level means. Use the most efficient multiple comparison procedure with a 95 percent family confidence coefficient. State your findings and summarize them by a suitable line plot.

d. Based on the estimated efficiency measure (27.14), how effective was the repeated measures design compared to a completely randomized design?

29.8. Refer to **Blood pressure** Problem 29.3. A consultant is concerned about the validity of the model assumptions and suggests that the study should be analyzed by means of the nonparametric rank F test. Rank the data within each rabbit and perform the rank F test; use $\alpha = .01$. State the alternatives, decision rule, and conclusion. Comment on the consultant's concern here.

√ 29.9. Refer to **Grapefruit sales** Problem 29.6. It has been suggested that the nonparametric rank F test should be used here. Rank the data within each store and perform the rank F test; use $\alpha = .05$. State the alternatives, decision rule, and conclusion. Is your conclusion the same as that obtained in Problem 29.7b?

29.10. **Truth in advertising**. A consumer research organization showed five different advertisements to 10 subjects and asked each to rank them in order of truthfulness. A rank of 1 denotes the most truthful. The results were:

Subject	Advertisement (j)					Subject	Advertisement (j)				
i	A	B	C	D	E	i	A	B	C	D	E
1	3	1	2	5	4	6	4	2	1	3	5
2	4	2	1	3	5	7	4	1	2	3	5
3	4	2	3	1	5	8	5	1	3	2	4
4	3	1	2	5	4	9	4	2	3	1	5
5	4	1	2	5	3	10	5	1	2	3	4

a. Do the subjects perceive the five advertisements as having equal truthfulness? Conduct the nonparametric rank F test using level of significance $\alpha = .05$. State the alternatives, decision rule, and conclusion. What is the P-value of the test?

b. Use the multiple pairwise testing procedure (27.27) to group the five different advertisements according to mean perceived truthfulness; employ family significance level $\alpha = .10$. Summarize your findings.

c. Obtain the coefficient of concordance (29.9) and interpret this measure.

29.11. **Calculator efficiency.** To test the efficiency of its new programmable calculator, a computer company selected at random six engineers who were proficient in the use of both this calculator and an earlier model and asked them to work out two problems on both calculators. One of the problems was statistical in nature, the other was an engineering problem. The order of the four calculations was randomized independently for each engineer. The length of time (in minutes) required to solve each problem was observed. The results follow (type of problem is factor A and calculator model is factor B):

		$j = 1$ Statistical Problem		$j = 2$ Engineering Problem	
		---	---	---	---
		$k = 1$	$k = 2$	$k = 1$	$k = 2$
Engineer		New	Earlier	New	Earlier
i		Model	Model	Model	Model
1	Jones	3.1	7.5	2.5	5.1
2	Williams	3.8	8.1	2.8	5.3
3	Adams	3.0	7.6	2.0	4.9
4	Dixon	3.4	7.8	2.7	5.5
5	Erickson	3.3	6.9	2.5	5.4
6	Maynes	3.6	7.8	2.4	4.8

a. Obtain the residuals for repeated measures model (29.10) and plot them against the fitted values. Also prepare a normal probability plot of the residuals. What do you conclude about the appropriateness of model (29.10)?

b. Prepare aligned residual dot plots by treatment. Do these plots support the assumption of constancy of the error variance? Discuss.

c. Plot the observations Y_{ijk} for each engineer in the format of Figure 29.2, ignoring the factorial nature of the treatments. Does the assumption of no interactions between subjects (engineers) and treatments appear to be reasonable here?

d. Conduct the Tukey test for additivity, conditional on the engineers actually selected; use $\alpha = .01$. State the alternatives, decision rule, and conclusion. What is the P-value of the test?

29.12. Refer to **Calculator efficiency** Problem 29.11. Assume that repeated measures model (29.10) is appropriate.

a. Obtain the analysis of variance table.

b. Plot the data and the estimated treatment means in the format of Figure 29.6. Does it appear that interaction effects are present?

c. Test whether or not the two factors interact; use $\alpha = .01$. State the alternatives, decision rule, and conclusion. What is the P-value of the test?

d. It is desired to study the nature of the interaction effects by considering the three comparisons:

$$L_1 = \mu_{.12} - \mu_{.11} \qquad L_3 = L_2 - L_1$$

$$L_2 = \mu_{.22} - \mu_{.21}$$

Obtain confidence intervals for these comparisons; use the Bonferroni procedure with a 95 percent family confidence coefficient. State your findings.

e. Test whether or not subject effects are present; use $\alpha = .01$. State the alternatives, decision rule, and conclusion. What is the P-value of the test?

√ 29.13. **Migraine headaches**. Two experimental pain killer drugs for relief of migraine headaches were studied at a major medical center. Ten persistent migraine sufferers were randomly selected for a pilot study and received in random order each of the four treatment combinations, with a suitable interval between drug administrations. The decrease in pain intensity was used as the response variable. The four treatments used in the study are defined as follows: $A_1 B_1$ = low dose of both drugs; $A_1 B_2$ = low dose of drug A, high dose of drug B; $A_2 B_1$ = high dose of drug A, low dose of drug B; $A_2 B_2$ = high dose of both drugs. The data on reduction in pain intensity follow (the higher the score, the greater the reduction in pain).

Person	A_1 $(j = 1)$		A_2 $(j = 2)$	
i	B_1 $(k = 1)$	B_2 $(k = 2)$	B_1 $(k = 1)$	B_2 $(k = 2)$
1	1.6	3.4	2.7	4.3
2	2.3	5.1	4.2	6.5
3	4.2	5.3	4.6	6.0
...	...	...	...	...
8	6.0	7.2	6.3	7.3
9	1.2	1.4	1.3	1.7
10	2.7	3.0	3.0	3.1

a. Obtain the residuals for repeated measures model (29.10) and plot them against the fitted values. Also prepare a normal probability plot of the residuals. What do you conclude about the appropriateness of model (29.10)?

b. Prepare aligned residual dot plots by treatment. Do these plots support the assumption of constancy of the error variance? Discuss.

c. Plot the observations Y_{ijk} for each person in the format of Figure 29.2, ignoring the factorial nature of the treatments. Does the assumption of no interactions between subjects (persons) and treatments appear to be reasonable here?

d. Conduct the Tukey test for additivity, conditional on the subjects actually selected; use $\alpha = .005$. State the alternatives, decision rule, and conclusion. What is the P-value of the test?

√ 29.14. Refer to **Migraine headaches** Problem 29.13. Assume that repeated measures model (29.10) is appropriate.

a. Obtain the analysis of variance table.

b. Plot the data and the estimated treatment means in the format of Figure 29.6. Does it appear that interaction effects are present? That main effects are present?

c. Test whether or not the two factors interact; use $\alpha = .005$. State the alternatives, decision rule, and conclusion. What is the P-value of the test?

d. Test separately whether or not factor A and factor B main effects are present; use $\alpha = .005$ for each test. State the alternatives, decision rule, and conclusion for each test. What is the P-value for each test?

e. Estimate the following comparisons by means of confidence intervals:

$$L_1 = \mu_{\cdot 21} - \mu_{\cdot 11} \qquad L_3 = \mu_{\cdot 21} - \mu_{\cdot 12}$$

$$L_2 = \mu_{\cdot 12} - \mu_{\cdot 11} \qquad L_4 = \mu_{\cdot 22} - \mu_{\cdot 11}$$

Use the Bonferroni procedure and family confidence coefficient .95. Summarize your findings.

29.15. **Incentive stimulus.** Refer to the example in Section 29.4 about the effects of two types of incentives (factor A) on a person's ability to solve two types of problems (factor B); the repeated measures design is illustrated in Figure 29.7. Twelve persons were randomly selected and assigned in equal numbers to the two incentive groups. The order of the two types of problems was then randomized independently for each person. The problem-solving ability scores follow (the higher the score, the greater the ability to solve problems).

Incentive Stimulus	Subject	Problem Type	
		Abstract $(k = 1)$	Concrete $(k = 2)$
	$i = 1$	10	18
	$i = 2$	14	19
$j = 1$	$i = 3$	17	18
	$i = 4$	8	12
	$i = 5$	12	14
	$i = 6$	15	20
	$i = 1$	16	25
	$i = 2$	19	22
$j = 2$	$i = 3$	22	27
	$i = 4$	20	23
	$i = 5$	24	29
	$i = 6$	21	22

a. Obtain the residuals for repeated measures model (29.16) and plot them against the fitted values. Also prepare a normal probability plot of the residuals. What do you conclude about the appropriateness of model (29.16)?

b. Plot the problem-solving ability scores by incentive stimulus and problem type, in the format of Figure 29.8. What do you conclude about the appropriateness of model (29.16)? Discuss.

29.16. Refer to **Incentive stimulus** Problem 29.15. Assume that repeated measures model (29.16) is appropriate.

a. Obtain the analysis of variance table.

b. Plot the data and the estimated treatment means in the format of Figure 29.6. Does it appear that interaction effects are present? That main effects are present?

c. Test whether or not the two factors interact; use $\alpha = .05$. State the alternatives, decision rule, and conclusion. What is the P-value of the test?

d. Test separately whether or not factor A and factor B main effects are present; use $\alpha = .05$ for each test. State the alternatives, decision rule, and conclusion for each test. What is the P-value for each test?

e. The following comparisons are of interest:

$$L_1 = \mu_{.2.} - \mu_{.1.} \qquad L_2 = \mu_{..2} - \mu_{..1}$$

Estimate these comparisons by means of confidence intervals. Use the Bonferroni procedure with a 90 percent family confidence coefficient. State your findings.

√ 29.17. **Store displays**. An experimental study was conducted to examine the effects of two different store displays for a household product (factor A) on sales in four successive time periods (factor B). Eight stores were randomly selected, and four were assigned at random to each display. The sales data (coded) follow.

Type of Display	Store	Time Period			
		$k = 1$	$k = 2$	$k = 3$	$k = 4$
	$i = 1$	956	953	938	1,049
$j = 1$	$i = 2$	1,008	1,032	1,025	1,123
	$i = 3$	350	352	338	438
	$i = 4$	412	449	385	532
	$i = 1$	769	766	739	859
$j = 2$	$i = 2$	880	875	860	915
	$i = 3$	176	185	168	280
	$i = 4$	209	223	217	301

a. Obtain the residuals for repeated measures model (29.16) and plot them against the fitted values. Also prepare a normal probability plot of the residuals. What do you conclude about the appropriateness of model (29.16)?

b. Plot the sales data by type of display and time period, in the format of Figure 29.8. What do you conclude about the appropriateness of model (29.16)? Discuss.

√ 29.18. Refer to **Store displays** Problem 29.17. The experimenter wished to explore further the appropriateness of repeated measures model (29.16).

a. Conduct a formal test of the constancy of the between-subjects variance σ_ρ^2. Use (29.22) and perform the Hartley test, with $\alpha = .01$. State the alternatives, decision rule, and conclusion.

b. Decompose the error variation $SSB.S(A)$ into components using (29.23), and perform the Hartley test for the constancy of the error variance σ^2 for the different factor A levels; use $\alpha = .01$. State the alternatives, decision rule, and conclusion.

√ 29.19. Refer to **Store displays** Problem 29.17. Assume that repeated measures model (29.16) is appropriate.

a. Obtain the analysis of variance table.

b. Plot the data and the estimated treatment means in the format of Figure 29.6. Does it appear that interaction effects are present? That main effects are present?

c. Test whether or not the two factors interact; use $\alpha = .025$. State the alternatives, decision rule, and conclusion. What is the P-value for the test?

d. Test separately whether or not display and time main effects are present; use $\alpha = .025$ for each test. State the alternatives, decision rule, and conclusion for each test. What is the P-value for each test?

e. To study the nature of the factor A and factor B main effects, estimate the following pairwise comparisons:

$$L_1 = \mu_{.1.} - \mu_{.2.} \qquad L_3 = \mu_{..2} - \mu_{..3}$$

$$L_2 = \mu_{..1} - \mu_{..2} \qquad L_4 = \mu_{..3} - \mu_{..4}$$

Use the Bonferroni procedure with a 90 percent family confidence coefficient. State your findings.

29.20. **Wheat yield**. Refer to the split-plot agricultural experiment of Section 29.6, for which the layout is shown in Figure 29.11. The results of this experiment to investigate the effects of two irrigation methods (factor A) and two fertilizers (factor B) on wheat yield follow for the 10 fields used in the study.

Irrigation Method j:		1					2			
Field i:	1	2	3	4	5	1	2	3	4	5
Fertilizer $k = 1$:	43	40	31	27	36	63	52	45	47	54
$k = 2$:	48	43	36	30	39	70	53	48	51	57

a. Obtain the residuals for split-plot model (29.24) and plot them against the fitted values. Also prepare a normal probability plot of the residuals. What do you conclude about the appropriateness of model (29.24)?

b. Plot the wheat yield data by irrigation method and type of fertilizer in the format of Figure 29.8. What do you conclude about the appropriateness of model (29.24)? Discuss.

29.21. Refer to **Wheat yield** Problem 29.20. Assume that split-plot model (29.24) is appropriate.

a. Obtain the analysis of variance table.

b. Plot the data and the estimated treatment means in the format of Figure 29.6. Does it appear that interaction effects are present? That main effects are present?

c. Test whether or not the two factors interact; use $\alpha = .05$. State the alternatives, decision rule, and conclusion. What is the P-value for the test?

d. Test separately whether or not factor A and factor B main effects are present; use $\alpha = .05$. State the alternatives, decision rule, and conclusion for each test. What is the P-value for each test?

e. To study the nature of the factor A and factor B main effects, estimate the following pairwise comparisons:

$$L_1 = \mu_{.1.} - \mu_{.2.} \qquad L_2 = \mu_{..1} - \mu_{..2}$$

Use the Bonferroni procedure with a 90 percent family confidence coefficient. State your findings.

Exercise

29.22. Derive the total sum of squares breakdown in (29.5).

Projects

29.23. Refer to **Blood pressure** Problem 29.3. Obtain the estimated within-subjects variance-covariance matrix using (29.8). Are the estimated variances and covariances of the same orders of magnitude? Is the compound symmetry assumption reasonable here?

29.24. Refer to **Grapefruit sales** Problem 29.6. Obtain the estimated within-subjects variance-covariance matrix using (29.8). Are the variances and covariances roughly of the same order of magnitude? Is the compound symmetry assumption reasonably satisfied here?

29.25. Refer to the **Drug effect experiment** data set. Consider only Part I of the study and observation unit 1 for each drug dosage level; i.e., include only observations for which variable 2 equals 1 and variable 6 equals 1. Treat the 12 rats as subjects and ignore the classification of the rats into the three initial lever press rate groups. Assume that the subjects (rats) have random effects and that the treatments (dosage levels) have fixed effects.

   a. State the additive repeated measures model for this study.

   b. Obtain the residuals and plot them against the fitted values. Also prepare a normal probability plot of the residuals. What do you conclude about the appropriateness of the model employed?

   c. Plot the responses for each rat in the format of Figure 29.2. Does the assumption of no interactions between subjects (rats) and treatments appear to be appropriate?

29.26. Refer to the **Drug effect experiment** data set and Project 29.25.

   a. Obtain the analysis of variance table.

   b. Test whether or not the drug dosage level affects the mean lever press rate; use $\alpha = .05$. State the alternatives, decision rule, and conclusion. What is the P-value of the test?

   c. Analyze the effects of the four dosage levels by comparing the mean responses for each pair of successive dosage levels; use the Bonferroni procedure with a 90 percent family confidence coefficient. State your findings.

   d. Fit a regression model in which the subject effects are represented by 1, -1, 0 indicator variables and the dosage effect is represented by linear and quadratic terms in $x = X - \bar{X}$, where X is the dosage level. Assume that there are no interactions between subjects and treatments.

   e. Obtain the residuals and plot them against the fitted values. Does the regression model appear to provide a good fit? Discuss.

   f. Test whether or not the quadratic term can be dropped from the regression model; use $\alpha = .01$. State the alternatives, decision rule, and conclusion.

29.27. Refer to the **Drug effect experiment** data set. Consider the combined study. Assume that subjects (rats) and observation units have random effects, and that factor A (initial lever press rate), factor B (dosage level), and factor C (reinforcement schedule) have fixed effects. Also assume that there are no interactions between subjects and treatments.

   a. Use rules (D.1) and (D.6) in Appendix D to develop the model for this experiment.

   b. Fit the model in part (a), obtain the residuals, and plot them against the fitted values. Also prepare a normal probability plot of the residuals. What do you conclude about the appropriateness of your model?

29.28. Refer to the **Drug effect experiment** data set and Project 29.27. Assume that the model in Project 29.27a is appropriate.

   a. Use an appropriate statistical package to obtain the analysis of variance table and the expected mean squares.

   b. Test whether or not ABC interactions are present; use $\alpha = .01$. State the alternatives, decision rule, and conclusion. What is the P-value of the test?

   c. For each reinforcement schedule, plot the estimated treatment means against dosage level with different curves for the three initial lever press rate groups, in the format of Figure 23.6. Examine your plots for the nature of the interaction effects and report your findings.

29.29. Consider a repeated measures design study with $n = 3$ and $r = 3$, where each subject ranks all treatments (with no ties allowed).

   a. Develop the exact sampling distribution of F_R^* when H_0 holds. [*Hint*: All ranking permutations for a subject are equally likely under H_0 and all subjects are assumed to act independently.]

   b. How does the 90th percentile of the exact sampling distribution obtained in part (a) compare with $F(.90; 2, 4)$? What is the implication of this?

30 Latin Square and Related Designs

In this chapter we consider latin square designs. These are designs that employ two blocking variables to reduce experimental errors while requiring only a small number of experimental trials.

30.1 Basic Elements

Complete and Incomplete Block Designs

We saw in Section 27.14 that two blocking variables can be used simultaneously in randomized complete block designs to eliminate from experimental error the variation associated with each of the blocking variables. For instance, the blocking variables might be age and income of subject, with a block containing subjects in a given age and income group.

However, the full use of two blocking variables in a complete block design often requires too many experimental units. For instance, if the age and income variables in the illustration have six classes each, 36 blocks would be required. If six treatments were to be studied, 216 subjects would be needed for the experiment. Cost considerations may not permit the use of this many experimental units, yet precision and range of validity considerations may require the simultaneous use of two blocking variables, each with six classes, in order to reduce the experimental error variance sufficiently and to have a reasonable variety of experimental subjects.

In this type of situation, an *incomplete block design* may be helpful. In such a design, all 36 blocks in our example would still be used, but now each block would not contain all six treatments. Latin square designs are a special type of incomplete block design. (A general discussion of incomplete block designs can be found in Ref. 30.1.)

Latin Square Designs

Taking incomplete block designs to the extreme in our example, given the employment of 36 blocks, the number of experimental units is minimized if only one treatment is run

1207

TABLE 30.1   Complete and Incomplete Block Designs.

Block Description	(1) Complete Block Design	(2) Incomplete Block Design (three treatments per block)	(3) Incomplete Block Design (one treatment per block)
Age under 25, income under $10,000	$T_1, T_2, T_3,$ T_4, T_5, T_6	T_1, T_3, T_5	T_2
Age under 25, income $10,000–$19,999	$T_1, T_2, T_3,$ T_4, T_5, T_6	T_2, T_4, T_6	T_5
...	...	...	...
Age 25–34, income under $10,000	$T_1, T_2, T_3,$ T_4, T_5, T_6	T_2, T_4, T_5	T_3
...	...	...	...
Age 35–44, income under $10,000	$T_1, T_2, T_3,$ T_4, T_5, T_6	T_3, T_4, T_6	T_2
etc.	etc.	etc.	etc.

in each block. This extreme case, where each block contains only one treatment, is the type of situation for which a latin square design is appropriate. Table 30.1 provides an illustration of the difference between complete and incomplete block designs for the example considered. Column 1 shows the complete block design for this case, while columns 2 and 3 illustrate incomplete block designs, with three treatments and one treatment in each block, respectively.

There is another reason, besides economy, why a latin square design with only one treatment per block is used, namely, that blocks sometimes cannot contain more than one treatment. Consider the repeated measures design discussed in Section 29.2 where each subject receives every treatment. The repeated measures model in (29.1) assumes that no interference effects due to order position are present. If, indeed, such effects are possible, it may be desirable to use the order position as another blocking variable. Thus, "subject" would be one blocking variable and "order position of treatment" a second blocking variable. Blocks would then be defined as follows for a study involving six treatments:

> Block 1:   Subject 1, position 1
>
> Block 2:   Subject 1, position 2
>
> ...   ...
>
> Block 6:   Subject 1, position 6
>
> Block 7:   Subject 2, position 1
>
> etc.   etc.

Notice that the blocks so defined can contain only one treatment, since the order position refers to the place of a single treatment in the sequence of treatments for a subject.

Description of Latin Square Designs

Let A, B, C represent three treatments; it is conventional with latin square designs to use Latin letters for the treatments. Suppose that day of week (Monday, Tuesday, Wednesday) and operator (1, 2, 3) are to be used as blocking variables. A latin square design might then be shown as follows:

	Operator		
Day	1	2	3
Monday	B	A	C
Tuesday	A	C	B
Wednesday	C	B	A

Operator 1 would run treatment B on Monday, treatment A on Tuesday, and treatment C on Wednesday, and so on for the other operators. Note that each operator runs each treatment, and that all treatments are run on each day.

A latin square design thus has the following features:

1. There are r treatments.

2. There are two blocking variables, each containing r classes.

3. Each row and each column in the design square contains all treatments; that is, each class of each blocking variable constitutes a replication.

Advantages and Disadvantages of Latin Square Designs

Advantages of a latin square design include:

1. The use of two blocking variables often permits greater reductions in the variability of experimental errors than can be obtained with either blocking variable alone.

2. Treatment effects can be studied from a small-scale experiment. This is particularly helpful in preliminary or pilot studies.

3. It is often helpful in repeated measures experiments to take into account the order position effect of treatments by means of a latin square design.

Disadvantages of a latin square design are:

1. The number of classes of each blocking variable must equal the number of treatments. This restriction is often difficult to meet in practice.

2. The assumptions of the model are restrictive (e.g., that there are no interactions between either blocking variable and treatments, and also none between the two blocking variables).

3. The use of a latin square design will lead to a very small number of degrees of freedom for experimental error when only a few treatments are studied. On the other hand, when many treatments are studied, the degrees of freedom for experimental error may be larger than necessary.

4. The randomization required is somewhat more complex than that for earlier designs considered.

Because of the limitations on the degrees of freedom for experimental error just described, latin squares are rarely used when more than eight treatments are being investigated. For the same reason, when there are only a few treatments, say, four or less, additional replications are usually required when a latin square design is employed.

Randomization of Latin Square Design

There exist many latin squares for a given number of treatments. For example, for $r = 3$, there are altogether 12 different possible arrangements. Four of the 12 possible arrangements are (we omit the row and column blocking variable labels):

1			2			3			4		
A	B	C	A	C	B	B	A	C	C	B	A
B	C	A	B	A	C	C	B	A	A	C	B
C	A	B	C	B	A	A	C	B	B	A	C

The number of possible latin square designs increases rapidly as the number of treatments gets larger; for $r = 5$, there are 161,280 possible arrangements.

The objective of randomization is to select one of all possible latin squares for the given number of treatments r, such that each square has an equal probability of being selected. Clearly, it is not generally feasible to list all possible latin squares so that one can be selected at random. Instead, we utilize *standard latin squares*, which are latin squares in which the elements of the first row and the first column are arranged alphabetically. The earlier latin square 1 is a standard latin square. Table B.14 contains all the standard squares for $r = 3$ and 4, and a single selected standard square for $r = 5, 6, 7, 8,$ and 9.

The randomization procedure usually employed with Table B.14 is as follows:

1. For $r = 3$, independently arrange the rows and columns of the standard square at random.

2. For $r = 4$, select one of the standard squares at random. Then, independently arrange its rows and columns at random.

3. For $r = 5$ and higher, independently arrange the rows, columns, and treatments of the given standard square at random.

It can be shown that this procedure selects one latin square at random from all possible squares for $r = 3$ and 4. For $r = 5$ or higher, the randomization procedure is not based on all possible latin squares, but rather on very large and suitable subsets thereof.

Example

An experiment was conducted to study the effects of different types of background music on the productivity of bank tellers. The treatments were defined as various combinations of tempo music (slow, medium, fast) and style of music (instrumental and vocal, instrumental only). The treatments and Latin letter designations were as follows:

TABLE 30.2   **Latin Square Design and Experimental Results—Background Music Example (productivity of crew—data coded).**

Week	M	T	W	Th	F	Mean
			Day			
1	18 (D)	17 (C)	14 (A)	21 (B)	17 (E)	$\bar{Y}_{1..} = 17.4$
2	13 (C)	34 (B)	21 (E)	16 (A)	15 (D)	$\bar{Y}_{2..} = 19.8$
3	7 (A)	29 (D)	32 (B)	27 (E)	13 (C)	$\bar{Y}_{3..} = 21.6$
4	17 (E)	13 (A)	24 (C)	31 (D)	25 (B)	$\bar{Y}_{4..} = 22.0$
5	21 (B)	26 (E)	26 (D)	31 (C)	7 (A)	$\bar{Y}_{5..} = 22.2$
Mean	$\bar{Y}_{.1.} = 15.2$	$\bar{Y}_{.2.} = 23.8$	$\bar{Y}_{.3.} = 23.4$	$\bar{Y}_{.4.} = 25.2$	$\bar{Y}_{.5.} = 15.4$	$\bar{Y}_{...} = 20.6$

$$\bar{Y}_{..1} = 11.4 \qquad \bar{Y}_{..4} = 23.8$$

$$\bar{Y}_{..2} = 26.6 \qquad \bar{Y}_{..5} = 21.6$$

$$\bar{Y}_{..3} = 19.6$$

Treatment	Latin Letter Designation	Tempo and Style of Music
1	A	Slow, instrumental and vocal
2	B	Medium, instrumental and vocal
3	C	Fast, instrumental and vocal
4	D	Medium, instrumental only
5	E	Fast, instrumental only

Table 30.2 contains the results of this experiment. The treatment in each cell is shown in parentheses. The experimental unit in this study is a working day for the crew of bank tellers; the productivity data pertain to the performance of the entire crew. Let Y_{ijk} denote the observation in the cell defined by the ith class of the row blocking variable and the jth class of the column blocking variable. The subscript k indicates the treatment assigned to this cell by the particular latin square design employed. For instance, $Y_{123} = 17$ is the productivity on Tuesday of the first week, and Table 30.2 indicates that the type of music on that day was C.

The subscript k in Y_{ijk} is actually redundant for a latin square design because the row and cell designation (i, j) determines the treatment for the particular latin square employed. However, we continue to use all three subscripts for ease of identification.

We shall analyze the results of this study in Section 30.3.

30.2   Latin Square Model

A latin square design model involves the main effect of the row blocking variable, denoted by ρ_i, the main effect of the column blocking variable, denoted by κ_j, and the treatment main effect, denoted by τ_k. It is assumed that no interactions exist between these three variables. Thus, the model employed is an additive one. For the case of fixed treatment and block effects, the model is:

$$(30.1) \qquad Y_{ijk} = \mu_{...} + \rho_i + \kappa_j + \tau_k + \varepsilon_{ijk}$$

where:

$\mu_{...}$ is a constant

ρ_i, κ_j, τ_k are constants subject to the restrictions $\Sigma \rho_i = \Sigma \kappa_j = \Sigma \tau_k = 0$

ε_{ijk} are independent $N(0, \sigma^2)$

$i = 1, \dots, r;\ j = 1, \dots, r;\ k = 1, \dots, r$

Note again that the number of classes for each of the two blocking variables is the same as the number of treatments, and that the total number of experimental trials is r^2.

Note

If the treatment effects are random, the only change in model (30.1) is that the τ_k now are independent $N(0, \sigma_\tau^2)$ and are independent of the ε_{ijk}.   ∎

30.3   Analysis of Latin Square Experiments

Notation

We shall employ the usual notation for row, column, and treatment totals and means:

$$(30.2a) \qquad Y_{i..} = \sum_j Y_{ijk} \qquad \bar{Y}_{i..} = \frac{Y_{i..}}{r}$$

$$(30.2b) \qquad Y_{.j.} = \sum_i Y_{ijk} \qquad \bar{Y}_{.j.} = \frac{Y_{.j.}}{r}$$

$$(30.2c) \qquad Y_{..k} = \sum_{i,j} Y_{ijk} \qquad \bar{Y}_{..k} = \frac{Y_{..k}}{r}$$

The overall total and mean are denoted as usual by:

$$(30.2d) \qquad Y_{...} = \sum_i \sum_j Y_{ijk} \qquad \bar{Y}_{...} = \frac{Y_{...}}{r^2}$$

Note the redundancy of any one of the three subscripts, arising from the fact that the treatment is uniquely determined by the row and column specifications for the latin square utilized. The various means for the background music example are shown in Table 30.2. The estimated treatment means are calculated by first collecting the data for each treatment and then averaging these values. For instance, we have:

$$\bar{Y}_{..1} = \frac{7 + 13 + 14 + 16 + 7}{5} = 11.4$$

TABLE 30.3   ANOVA Table for Latin Square Design Model (30.1) with Fixed Effects.

Source of Variation	SS	df	MS	E{MS}
Row blocking variable	SSROW	$r-1$	$MSROW = \dfrac{SSROW}{r-1}$	$\sigma^2 + r\dfrac{\Sigma \rho_i^2}{r-1}$
Column blocking variable	SSCOL	$r-1$	$MSCOL = \dfrac{SSCOL}{r-1}$	$\sigma^2 + r\dfrac{\Sigma \kappa_j^2}{r-1}$
Treatments	SSTR	$r-1$	$MSTR = \dfrac{SSTR}{r-1}$	$\sigma^2 + r\dfrac{\Sigma \tau_k^2}{r-1}$
Error	SSRem	$(r-1)(r-2)$	$MSRem = \dfrac{SSRem}{(r-1)(r-2)}$	σ^2
Total	SSTO	$r^2 - 1$		

Fitting of Model

The least squares and maximum likelihood estimators of the parameters in latin square model (30.1) are:

	Parameter	Estimator
(30.3a)	$\mu_{...}$	$\hat{\mu}_{...} = \bar{Y}_{...}$
(30.3b)	ρ_i	$\hat{\rho}_i = \bar{Y}_{i..} - \bar{Y}_{...}$
(30.3c)	κ_j	$\hat{\kappa}_j = \bar{Y}_{.j.} - \bar{Y}_{...}$
(30.3d)	τ_k	$\hat{\tau}_k = \bar{Y}_{..k} - \bar{Y}_{...}$

The fitted values therefore are:

$$(30.4) \qquad \hat{Y}_{ijk} = \bar{Y}_{i..} + \bar{Y}_{.j.} + \bar{Y}_{..k} - 2\bar{Y}_{...}$$

and the residuals are:

$$(30.5) \qquad e_{ijk} = Y_{ijk} - \hat{Y}_{ijk} = Y_{ijk} - \bar{Y}_{i..} - \bar{Y}_{.j.} - \bar{Y}_{..k} + 2\bar{Y}_{...}$$

Analysis of Variance

Table 30.3 presents the ANOVA table for latin square model (30.1). The sums of squares can be obtained by the rules in Appendix D, remembering that one subscript is redundant. The definitional forms of the sums of squares are as follows:

$$(30.6a) \qquad SSTO = \sum_i \sum_j (Y_{ijk} - \bar{Y}_{...})^2$$

$$(30.6b) \qquad SSROW = r \sum_i (\bar{Y}_{i..} - \bar{Y}_{...})^2$$

(30.6c)
$$SSCOL = r \sum_j (\bar{Y}_{\cdot j \cdot} - \bar{Y}_{\cdot \cdot \cdot})^2$$

(30.6d)
$$SSTR = r \sum_k (\bar{Y}_{\cdot \cdot k} - \bar{Y}_{\cdot \cdot \cdot})^2$$

(30.6e)
$$SSRem = \sum_i \sum_j (Y_{ijk} - \bar{Y}_{i \cdot \cdot} - \bar{Y}_{\cdot j \cdot} - \bar{Y}_{\cdot \cdot k} + 2\bar{Y}_{\cdot \cdot \cdot})^2$$

SSROW is the *row sum of squares*. The more the row means $\bar{Y}_{i \cdot \cdot}$ differ, the larger is *SSROW*. Similarly, *SSCOL* is the *column sum of squares* and measures the variability of the column means $\bar{Y}_{\cdot j \cdot}$. *SSTR* denotes, as usual, the treatment sum of squares. Finally, *SSRem* stands for the remainder sum of squares reflecting the error variability. We use this notation here since this sum of squares is made up of several different interaction components.

The degrees of freedom in Table 30.3 can be understood as follows. There are r^2 observations, and hence *SSTO* has $r^2 - 1$ degrees of freedom associated with it. Since there are r classes for the row and column blocking variables each, and also r treatments, each of the corresponding sums of squares has $r - 1$ degrees of freedom associated with it. The number of degrees of freedom associated with *SSRem* is the remainder, namely, $(r^2 - 1) - 3(r - 1) = (r - 1)(r - 2)$. Note that the addition of a second blocking variable has reduced the number of degrees of freedom for the error sum of squares from $(r - 1)^2$ for a randomized complete block design based on r blocks and r treatments to $(r - 1)(r - 2)$, a reduction of $r - 1$ degrees of freedom.

The $E\{MS\}$ column in Table 30.3 for latin square model (30.1) can be obtained by using the rules in Appendix D, remembering that one subscript is redundant, or by a computer package that provides expected mean squares.

Test for Treatment Effects

To test for treatment effects in latin square model (30.1) with fixed effects:

(30.7a)
$$H_0: \text{ all } \tau_k = 0$$
$$H_a: \text{ not all } \tau_k \text{ equal zero}$$

we see from the $E\{MS\}$ column in Table 30.3 that the appropriate test statistic is:

(30.7b)
$$F^* = \frac{MSTR}{MSRem}$$

The appropriate decision rule to control the risk of a Type I error at α is:

(30.7c)
$$\text{If } F^* \leq F[1 - \alpha; r - 1, (r - 1)(r - 2)], \text{ conclude } H_0$$
$$\text{If } F^* > F[1 - \alpha; r - 1, (r - 1)(r - 2)], \text{ conclude } H_a$$

Comments

1. If the presence of blocking variable effects is to be tested, we see from the $E\{MS\}$ column in Table 30.3 that the appropriate test statistics are:

$$(30.8a) \qquad F^* = \frac{MSROW}{MSRem}$$

$$(30.8b) \qquad F^* = \frac{MSCOL}{MSRem}$$

2. If the treatment effects are random, the alternatives to be considered are:

$$(30.9) \qquad \begin{aligned} H_0&: \sigma_\tau^2 = 0 \\ H_a&: \sigma_\tau^2 > 0 \end{aligned}$$

but the test statistic and decision rule are the same as in (30.7) for the fixed treatment effects case. ∎

Analysis of Treatment Effects

When differential treatment effects are found by the analysis of variance and the treatments have fixed effects, estimates of contrasts involving the treatment effects are usually desired, often utilizing multiple comparison procedures. The appropriate mean square to be used in the estimated variance of the contrast is *MSRem* obtained from (30.6e), and the multiples for the estimated standard deviation of the contrast are as follows:

(30.10a)   Single comparison $t[1 - \alpha/2; (r-1)(r-2)]$

(30.10b)   Tukey procedure (for pairwise comparisons) $T = \frac{1}{\sqrt{2}} q[1 - \alpha; r, (r-1)(r-2)]$

(30.10c)   Scheffé procedure $S^2 = (r-1)F[1 - \alpha; r-1, (r-1)(r-2)]$

(30.10d)   Bonferroni procedure (g comparisons) $B = t[1 - \alpha/2g; (r-1)(r-2)]$

Residual Analysis

The use of the residuals in (30.5) for examining the aptness of a latin square model presents no new issues; the basic points made earlier for other designs apply also to latin square designs. The Tukey test for additivity in a randomized complete block design, discussed in Section 27.4, can be extended to latin square designs. Reference 30.2 describes the extension.

Example

The analysis of variance calculations for the background music data in Table 30.2 were made by using a computer package and the results are shown in Table 30.4. The residuals were also obtained and analyzed. Figure 30.1a contains a plot of the residuals against the

TABLE 30.4   **ANOVA Table for Background Music Example.**

Source of Variation	SS	df	MS
Weeks	82.0	4	20.5
Days within week	477.2	4	119.3
Type of music	664.4	4	166.1
Error	188.4	12	15.7
Total	1,412.0	24	

FIGURE 30.1   **Diagnostic Residual Plots—Background Music Example.**

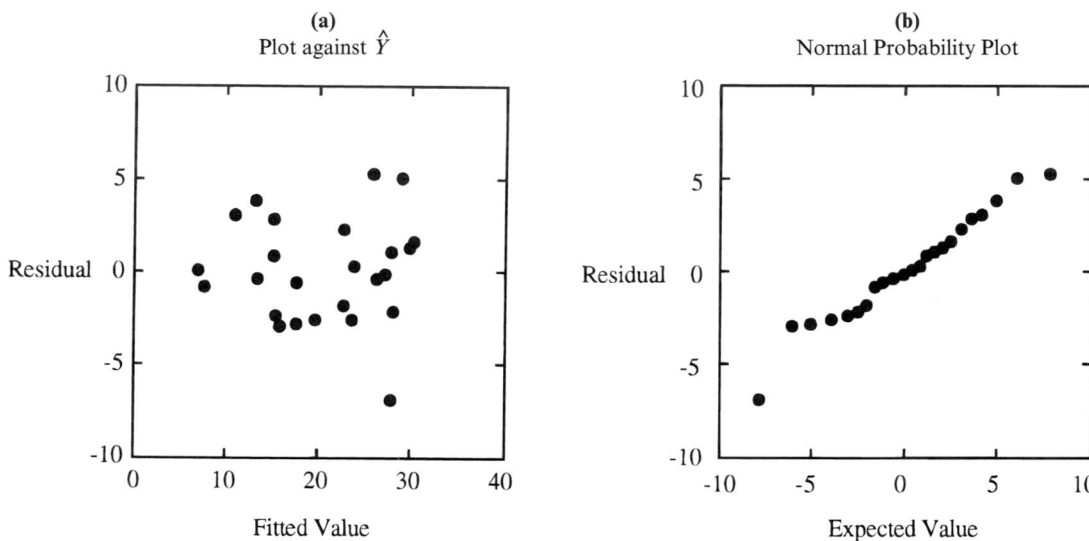

fitted values, and Figure 30.1b contains a normal probability plot of the residuals. These plots do not reveal any serious departures from the model assumptions, though they show one case that appears to be outlying. The Bonferroni outlier test, explained in Section 9.2, was employed to test whether this case is an outlier but did not identify it as such. Based on these and other diagnostics, including the Tukey test for additivity, it was concluded that model (30.1) is appropriate for the data.

To test for treatment effects:

$$H_0:\ \tau_1 = \tau_2 = \tau_3 = \tau_4 = \tau_5 = 0$$

$$H_a:\ \text{not all } \tau_k \text{ equal zero}$$

we find from Table 30.4:

$$F^* = \frac{MSTR}{MSRem} = \frac{166.1}{15.7} = 10.6$$

To control the risk of making a Type I error at $\alpha = .01$, we require $F(.99; 4, 12) = 5.41$. Since $F^* = 10.6 > 5.41$, we conclude H_a, that the various types of background music have differential effects on the productivity of the bank tellers. The P-value of this test is .0007.

Pairwise comparisons between the different kinds of music were desired with a family confidence coefficient of .90, using the Tukey procedure. Substituting into (17.15) with $n_i = n_{i'} = r$ and using *MSRem* from Table 30.4 as the mean square, we obtain:

$$s^2\{\hat{L}\} = \frac{2MSRem}{r} = \frac{2(15.7)}{5} = 6.28 \qquad s\{\hat{L}\} = 2.51$$

Remember that each estimated treatment mean $\bar{Y}_{..k}$ is based on five observations here. Next, we require the T multiple in (30.10b):

$$T = \frac{1}{\sqrt{2}}q(.90; 5, 12) = \frac{1}{\sqrt{2}}(3.92) = 2.77$$

so that:

$$Ts\{\hat{L}\} = 2.77(2.51) = 6.95$$

Conducting pairwise tests based on the confidence intervals, the treatments can be placed into three groups:

Group 1		Group 2		Group 3	
Music 2	$\bar{Y}_{.2} = 26.6$	Music 4	$\bar{Y}_{.4} = 23.8$	Music 1	$\bar{Y}_{.1} = 11.4$
Music 4	$\bar{Y}_{.4} = 23.8$	Music 5	$\bar{Y}_{.5} = 21.6$		
Music 5	$\bar{Y}_{.5} = 21.6$	Music 3	$\bar{Y}_{.3} = 19.6$		

The most promising treatment appears to be mixed instrumental-vocal music in medium tempo ($k = 2$). There is clear evidence that it is better than instrumental-vocal music in slow tempo ($k = 1$) or instrumental-vocal music in fast tempo ($k = 3$). The point estimates suggest it also is better than solely instrumental music in medium ($k = 4$) or fast ($k = 5$) tempo, but the experimental evidence on these latter two comparisons is inconclusive.

Factorial Treatments

If the treatments in a latin square design are factorial in nature, the treatment sum of squares *SSTR* is decomposed in the usual manner. For a two-factor experiment involving factors A and B, we have:

$$(30.11) \qquad\qquad SSTR = SSA + SSB + SSAB$$

Estimates of fixed factor effects can be made readily since they are simply contrasts of the treatment means.

Random Blocking Variable Effects

If the row and/or column blocking variable(s) in a latin square design have classes that should be viewed as random selections from a population, the fixed effects latin square model (30.1) needs to be modified in the usual fashion. The analysis of variance is the same as for the fixed blocking variable effects model and all tests and estimates of treatment effects are conducted as for fixed blocking variable effects.

30.4   Planning Latin Square Experiments

Power of *F* Test

The power of the *F* test for treatment effects in latin square model (30.1) involves the noncentrality parameter:

$$(30.12) \qquad \phi = \frac{1}{\sigma}\sqrt{\Sigma \tau_k^2}$$

with degrees of freedom $r - 1$ for the numerator and $(r - 1)(r - 2)$ for the denominator. Other than these modifications, no new issues are encountered in obtaining the power of the test for treatment effects in a latin square design.

Necessary Number of Replications

A latin square design provides r replications for each treatment. Power and/or estimation considerations similar to those for randomized complete block designs may indicate that r replications are too few, particularly when r is small, say, 3, 4, or 5. Two methods of increasing the number of replications with a latin square design are discussed in Section 30.6. With either method, it is necessary to assess in advance the magnitude of the experimental error variance σ^2 in order to plan the necessary number of replications.

Efficiency of Blocking Variables

The efficiency of a latin square design can be assessed relative to a completely randomized design or relative to a randomized complete block design. The efficiency relative to a completely randomized design is defined by:

$$(30.13a) \qquad E_1 = \frac{\sigma_r^2}{\sigma_L^2}$$

where σ_r^2 and σ_L^2 are the experimental error variances with a completely randomized design and a latin square design, respectively. The efficiency relative to a randomized complete block design can be measured in two ways, depending on whether the row or the column blocking variable is used in the randomized block design:

$$(30.13b) \qquad E_2 = \frac{\sigma_{br}^2}{\sigma_L^2}$$

$$(30.13c) \qquad E_3 = \frac{\sigma_{bc}^2}{\sigma_L^2}$$

where σ_{br}^2 and σ_{bc}^2 are the experimental error variances with a randomized block design if the row blocking variable or the column blocking variable is utilized, respectively.

We can estimate σ_r^2, σ_{br}^2, and σ_{bc}^2 from the results for a latin square design as follows:

(30.14a)
$$s_r^2 = \frac{MSROW + MSCOL + (r-1)MSRem}{r+1}$$

(30.14b)
$$s_{br}^2 = \frac{MSCOL + (r-1)MSRem}{r}$$

(30.14c)
$$s_{bc}^2 = \frac{MSROW + (r-1)MSRem}{r}$$

Thus, the estimated measures of efficiency are:

(30.15a)
$$\hat{E}_1 = \frac{MSROW + MSCOL + (r-1)MSRem}{(r+1)MSRem}$$

(30.15b)
$$\hat{E}_2 = \frac{MSCOL + (r-1)MSRem}{rMSRem}$$

(30.15c)
$$\hat{E}_3 = \frac{MSROW + (r-1)MSRem}{rMSRem}$$

When r is small, the efficiency measures may be modified by means of (27.15) to account for differences in the number of degrees of freedom associated with the mean squares used for estimating the experimental error variances for the two designs being compared.

Example.   For the background music example, we obtain the following efficiency measures from the results in Table 30.4:

$$\hat{E}_1 = \frac{20.5 + 119.3 + 4(15.7)}{6(15.7)} = 2.2$$

$$\hat{E}_2 = \frac{119.3 + 4(15.7)}{5(15.7)} = 2.3$$

$$\hat{E}_3 = \frac{20.5 + 4(15.7)}{5(15.7)} = 1.1$$

We see that the latin square design was efficient relative to a completely randomized design. The latter would have required over twice as many replications for each treatment as the latin square design so that the variance for any specified estimated treatment contrast would be the same with both designs. Most of this efficiency was gained by the column blocking variable (days within week), because the efficiency of the latin square design relative to a complete block design with the column blocking variable is poor, being close to 1. Hence, little was achieved by also blocking by the row blocking variable (week).

30.5   Regression Approach to Latin Square Designs

Regression Formulation

Model (30.1) for a latin square design with fixed blocking and treatment effects:

$$(30.16) \qquad Y_{ijk} = \mu_{...} + \rho_i + \kappa_j + \tau_k + \varepsilon_{ijk}$$

$$i = 1, \dots, r; \; j = 1, \dots, r; \; k = 1, \dots, r$$

can be expressed easily in the form of a regression model with indicator variables. As before, we shall use $1, -1, 0$ indicator variables. The regression model for the background music example of Table 30.2, with $r = 5$, can be expressed as follows:

$$(30.17) \qquad Y_{ijk} = \mu_{...} + \underbrace{\rho_1 X_{ijk1} + \rho_2 X_{ijk2} + \rho_3 X_{ijk3} + \rho_4 X_{ijk4}}_{\text{Row blocking effect}}$$

$$+ \underbrace{\kappa_1 X_{ijk5} + \kappa_2 X_{ijk6} + \kappa_3 X_{ijk7} + \kappa_4 X_{ijk8}}_{\text{Column blocking effect}}$$

$$+ \underbrace{\tau_1 X_{ijk9} + \tau_2 X_{ijk10} + \tau_3 X_{ijk11} + \tau_4 X_{ijk12}}_{\text{Treatment effect}}$$

$$+ \varepsilon_{ijk}$$

where:

$$X_1 = \begin{matrix} 1 \\ -1 \\ 0 \end{matrix} \quad \begin{matrix} \text{if experimental unit from row blocking class 1} \\ \text{if experimental unit from row blocking class 5} \\ \text{otherwise} \end{matrix}$$

X_2, X_3, X_4 are defined similarly

$$X_5 = \begin{matrix} 1 \\ -1 \\ 0 \end{matrix} \quad \begin{matrix} \text{if experimental unit from column blocking class 1} \\ \text{if experimental unit from column blocking class 5} \\ \text{otherwise} \end{matrix}$$

X_6, X_7, X_8 are defined similarly

$$X_9 = \begin{matrix} 1 \\ -1 \\ 0 \end{matrix} \quad \begin{matrix} \text{if experimental unit received treatment 1} \\ \text{if experimental unit received treatment 5} \\ \text{otherwise} \end{matrix}$$

X_{10}, X_{11}, X_{12} are defined similarly

A portion of the Y observations and X indicator variables for the background music example of Table 30.2 are shown in Table 30.5. Note, for instance, that for observation Y_{534}, $X_1 = X_2 = X_3 = X_4 = -1$, $X_7 = X_{12} = 1$, and all other Xs equal zero. Hence, we have:

$$E\{Y_{534}\} = \mu_{...} - \rho_1 - \rho_2 - \rho_3 - \rho_4 + \kappa_3 + \tau_4$$

$$= \mu_{...} + \rho_5 + \kappa_3 + \tau_4$$

TABLE 30.5   **Regression Variables for Regression Model (30.17)—Background Music Example of Table 30.2.**

i	j	k	Y	X_1	X_2	X_3	X_4	X_5	X_6	X_7	X_8	X_9	X_{10}	X_{11}	X_{12}
1	1	4	18	1	0	0	0	1	0	0	0	0	0	0	1
1	2	3	17	1	0	0	0	0	1	0	0	0	0	1	0
1	3	1	14	1	0	0	0	0	0	1	0	1	0	0	0
...	...	...	...	...	...	...	...	...	...	...	...	...	...	...	...
5	3	4	26	−1	−1	−1	−1	0	0	1	0	0	0	0	1
5	4	3	31	−1	−1	−1	−1	0	0	0	1	0	0	1	0
5	5	1	7	−1	−1	−1	−1	−1	−1	−1	−1	1	0	0	0

which is the appropriate expected value of Y_{534} according to ANOVA model (30.16) for the particular latin square used in the example.

Tests and estimation of fixed treatment effects with the regression approach are conducted in the usual fashion.

Missing Observations

While missing observations destroy the symmetry (orthogonality) of the latin square design and make the usual ANOVA calculations inappropriate, the regression approach ordinarily remains appropriate when observations in a latin square design are missing. We just set up the regression model for the available observations and then fit the model to the data. The procedure is analogous to that discussed in Section 27.11 for complete block designs. Tests are conducted by fitting the full and appropriate reduced regression models. Estimation of fixed treatment effects is done in terms of the regression coefficients for the full model in the usual manner.

30.6   Additional Replications with Latin Square Designs

A latin square design, as noted earlier, provides r replications for each treatment. If power and/or estimation considerations indicate that these are too few replications, two basic methods are available for increasing the number of replications—replications within cells and additional latin squares. We consider each in turn.

Replications within Cells

This method of increasing the replications per treatment is feasible when two or more experimental units can be obtained for each cell defined by the row and column blocking variables. Consider, for instance, an experiment in which IQ (low, normal, high) and age (young, middle, old) are the blocking variables. In this type of situation, it is possible to obtain two or more experimental subjects for each cell, and each of the subjects in a cell will then receive the treatment assigned to that cell by the latin square employed.

Let n denote the number of experimental units available for each cell, and let Y_{ijkm} denote the observation for the mth unit ($m = 1, \ldots, n$) in the (i, j) cell for which the assigned treatment is k. The additive fixed effects model (30.1) is modified for the n

replications in each cell as follows:

$$(30.18) \qquad Y_{ijkm} = \mu_{...} + \rho_i + \kappa_j + \tau_k + \varepsilon_{ijkm}$$

where:

> $\mu_{...}$ is a constant
>
> ρ_i, κ_j, τ_k are constants subject to the restrictions $\Sigma \rho_i = \Sigma \kappa_j = \Sigma \tau_k = 0$
>
> ε_{ijkm} are independent $N(0, \sigma^2)$
>
> $i = 1, \ldots, r; \, j = 1, \ldots, r; \, k = 1, \ldots, r; \, m = 1, \ldots, n$

The ANOVA sums of squares and degrees of freedom for model (30.18) can be obtained by the rules in Appendix D, remembering that one subscript is redundant. The treatment, row, and column sums of squares are, respectively:

$$(30.19a) \qquad SSTR = rn \sum_k (\bar{Y}_{..k.} - \bar{Y}_{....})^2$$

$$(30.19b) \qquad SSROW = rn \sum_i (\bar{Y}_{i...} - \bar{Y}_{....})^2$$

$$(30.19c) \qquad SSCOL = rn \sum_j (\bar{Y}_{.j..} - \bar{Y}_{....})^2$$

The total sum of squares as usual is:

$$(30.19d) \qquad SSTO = \sum_i \sum_j \sum_m (Y_{ijkm} - \bar{Y}_{....})^2$$

while *SSRem* is obtained as a remainder:

$$(30.19e) \qquad SSRem = SSTO - SSROW - SSCOL - SSTR$$

The degrees of freedom for row, column, and treatment sums of squares are unchanged, while those associated with *SSRem* are increased from $(r-1)(r-2)$ to $nr^2 - 3r + 2$, an increase of $(n-1)r^2$ degrees of freedom.

The analysis of variance is shown in Table 30.6. The expected mean squares can be obtained by the rules in Appendix D, remembering that one subscript is redundant, or from a suitable computer package. The test statistic for testing treatment effects is again $F^* = MSTR/MSRem$.

When n replications are present within a cell for a latin square, it is possible to obtain a pure error measure and conduct a test for lack of fit of model (30.18) in the usual manner.

Example.   A state university, while developing a retraining program to teach general computer repair skills to persons displaced from their previous occupations, conducted an experiment to evaluate the effects of three different incentive methods on achievement during the program. The blocking variables were IQ and age of subject. Two replications per cell were utilized. Table 30.7a contains the achievement scores for the participants in the experiment, while Table 30.7b contains the analysis of variable table obtained from a computer package.

TABLE 30.6   **ANOVA Table for Latin Square Design Model (30.18) with n Replications per Cell.**

Source of Variation	SS	df	MS
Row blocking variable	SSROW	$r - 1$	MSROW
Column blocking variable	SSCOL	$r - 1$	MSCOL
Treatments	SSTR	$r - 1$	MSTR
Error	SSRem	$nr^2 - 3r + 2$	MSRem
Total	SSTO	$nr^2 - 1$	

TABLE 30.7   **Example of Latin Square Design with Two Replications per Cell—Retraining Program Experiment.**

(a) Data

IQ i	Age (j)		
	Young	Middle	Old
High	(B) 19 16	(A) 20 24	(C) 25 21
Normal	(C) 24 22	(B) 14 15	(A) 14 14
Low	(A) 10 14	(C) 12 13	(B) 7 4

(b) Analysis of Variance

Source of Variation	SS	df	MS
IQ	364.3	2	182.2
Age	34.3	2	17.2
Treatments	147.0	2	73.5
Error	52.4	11	4.76
Lack of fit	16.4	2	8.2
Pure error	36.0	9	4.0
Total	598.0	17	

TABLE 30.8 Two-Latin-Squares Design—Background Music Example of Table 30.2.

				Day		
Square	Week	M	T	W	Th	F
	1	D	C	A	B	E
	2	C	B	E	A	D
1	3	A	D	B	E	C
	4	E	A	C	D	B
	5	B	E	D	C	A
	6	E	D	C	A	B
	7	B	A	E	D	C
2	8	D	C	A	B	E
	9	A	E	B	C	D
	10	C	B	D	E	A

To test the appropriateness of additive model (30.18), we use the usual test statistic for lack of fit:

$$F^* = \frac{MSLF}{MSPE} = \frac{8.2}{4.0} = 2.05$$

For level of significance $\alpha = .05$, we need $F(.95; 2, 9) = 4.26$. Since $F^* = 2.05 \leq 4.26$, we conclude that additive model (30.18) is appropriate here. The P-value of the test is .18. The comparison of the three incentive methods was then carried out in the usual fashion.

Additional Latin Squares

At times, it is not possible to obtain additional experimental units within a cell. This is the case, for instance, in the background music example of Table 30.2, where only one type of music can be played in one day in a bank. When it is not possible to replicate within cells, additional replications for each treatment frequently can be obtained by adding one or more latin squares to one of the blocking variables. In the background music example of Table 30.2, for instance, the experiment could be run for another five weeks. In an experiment using plant crews as experimental units and employing as blocking variables plant shift (morning, afternoon, evening) and production department (1, 2, 3), additional replications can be obtained by running the experiment in other production departments.

The layout for the background music example of Table 30.2, when run over another five weeks, is shown in Table 30.8. The second latin square, and additional ones when required, is selected independently of the first.

Frequently, the additional squares may be viewed as classes of a third blocking variable. For instance, in the background music example of Table 30.8, the two latin squares may be considered to be two levels of the blocking variable "time period." The first five weeks may be viewed as time period 1, and the second five weeks as time period 2. As another example, in the experiment with plant crews mentioned previously, the production departments for the first latin square may be on an hourly rate, while the departments for the second latin square may be on incentive pay. Thus, with additional latin squares, one can, in effect, introduce a third blocking variable. As a consequence, the variation associated with the third blocking variable can be removed from the experimental error variability. In addition, the interactions between the third blocking variable and the other variables can be studied.

30.7 Replications in Repeated Measures Studies

We noted earlier that a latin square design is highly suitable for repeated measures studies when there are r treatments and r subjects. If additional replications are needed, however, replications within cells cannot be used since a cell pertains to an individual subject. Instead, latin square crossover designs or independent latin squares may be used.

Latin Square Crossover Designs

These designs, also called *latin square changeover designs*, are often useful when a latin square is to be used in a repeated measures study to balance the order positions of treatments, yet more subjects are required than called for by a single latin square. With this type of design, the subjects are randomly assigned to the different treatment order patterns given by a latin square (several latin squares may be used at times). Consider an experiment in which treatments A, B, and C are to be administered to each subject, and the three treatment order patterns are given by the latin square:

	Order Position		
Pattern	1	2	3
1	A	B	C
2	B	C	A
3	C	A	B

Suppose that $3n$ subjects are available for the study. Then n subjects will be assigned at random to each of the three order patterns in a latin square crossover design. Note that this design is a mixture of repeated measures (within subjects) and latin square (order patterns form a latin square).

Assuming that all effects are additive and fixed except that the effects for subjects are random, a relatively simple model for latin square crossover designs can be developed for r treatments and n subjects per order pattern. In the following model, ρ_i denotes the effect of the ith treatment order pattern, κ_j denotes the effect of the jth order position, τ_k denotes the effect of the kth treatment, and $\eta_{m(i)}$ denotes the effect of subject m which is nested within the ith treatment order pattern:

$$(30.20) \qquad Y_{ijkm} = \mu_{...} + \rho_i + \kappa_j + \tau_k + \eta_{m(i)} + \varepsilon_{ijkm}$$

where:

$\mu_{...}$ is a constant

ρ_i, κ_j, τ_k are constants subject to the restrictions $\Sigma \rho_i = \Sigma \kappa_j = \Sigma \tau_k = 0$

$\eta_{m(i)}$ are independent $N(0, \sigma_\eta^2)$

ε_{ijkm} are independent $N(0, \sigma^2)$ and independent of the $\eta_{m(i)}$

$i = 1, \ldots, r; j = 1, \ldots, r; k = 1, \ldots, r; m = 1, \ldots, n$

TABLE 30.9 ANOVA Table for Latin Square Crossover Design Model (30.20).

Source of Variation	SS	df	MS	E{MS}
Patterns (P)	SSP	$r-1$	MSP	$\sigma^2 + r\sigma_\eta^2 + nr\dfrac{\Sigma \rho_i^2}{r-1}$
Order positions (O)	SSO	$r-1$	MSO	$\sigma^2 + nr\dfrac{\Sigma \kappa_j^2}{r-1}$
Treatments (TR)	SSTR	$r-1$	MSTR	$\sigma^2 + nr\dfrac{\Sigma \tau_k^2}{r-1}$
Subjects (S) (within patterns)	SSS	$r(n-1)$	MSS	$\sigma^2 + r\sigma_\eta^2$
Error	SSRem	$(r-1)(nr-2)$	MSRem	σ^2
Total	SSTO	$nr^2 - 1$		

The analysis of variance sums of squares, degrees of freedom, and expected mean squares for this model can be obtained by the rules in Appendix D, remembering that one subscript is redundant. The formulas for the sums of squares follow the usual pattern:

$$(30.21a) \qquad SSTO = \sum_i \sum_j \sum_m (Y_{ijkm} - \bar{Y}_{....})^2$$

$$(30.21b) \qquad SSP = nr \sum_i (\bar{Y}_{i...} - \bar{Y}_{....})^2$$

$$(30.21c) \qquad SSO = nr \sum_j (\bar{Y}_{.j..} - \bar{Y}_{....})^2$$

$$(30.21d) \qquad SSTR = nr \sum_k (\bar{Y}_{..k.} - \bar{Y}_{....})^2$$

$$(30.21e) \qquad SSS = r \sum_i \sum_m (\bar{Y}_{i..m} - \bar{Y}_{i...})^2$$

$$(30.21f) \qquad SSRem = SSTO - SSP - SSO - SSTR - SSS$$

Here, *SSP* is the (treatment) *pattern sum of squares*, *SSO* is the *order position sum of squares*, *SSS* is the *subject sum of squares*, and the other sums of squares have their usual meanings. Table 30.9 contains the ANOVA table.

Example. Table 30.10a contains data for a study of the effects of three different displays on the sale of apples, using a latin square crossover design. Six stores were used, with two assigned at random to each of the three treatment order patterns shown. Each display was kept for two weeks, and the observed variable was sales per 100 customers. Table 30.10b contains the analysis of variance. The sums of squares were obtained from a computer run.

TABLE 30.10   Latin Square Crossover Design—Apple Sales Example.

(a) Data (coded)

Pattern i	Store	Two-Week Period (j)		
		1	2	3
1	$m = 1$	9 (B)	12 (C)	15 (A)
1	$m = 2$	4 (B)	12 (C)	9 (A)
2	$m = 1$	12 (A)	14 (B)	3 (C)
2	$m = 2$	13 (A)	14 (B)	3 (C)
3	$m = 1$	7 (C)	18 (A)	6 (B)
3	$m = 2$	5 (C)	20 (A)	4 (B)

(b) Analysis of Variance

Source of Variation	SS	df	MS
Patterns	.33	2	.17
Order positions	233.33	2	116.67
Displays	189.00	2	94.50
Stores (within patterns)	21.00	3	7.00
Error	20.33	8	2.54
Total	464.0	17	

To test for treatment effects, we use:

$$F^* = \frac{MSTR}{MSRem} = \frac{94.5}{2.54} = 37.2$$

For $\alpha = .05$, we require $F(.95; 2, 8) = 4.46$. Since $F^* = 37.2 > 4.46$, we conclude that there are differential sales effects for the three displays. The P-value of the test is 0+. Tests for pattern effects, order position effects, and store effects were also carried out. They indicated that order position effects were present, but no pattern or store effects. Order position effects here are associated with the three time periods in which the displays were studied, and may reflect seasonal effects as well as the results of special events, such as unusually hot weather in one period.

Use of Independent Latin Squares

If the order position effects are not approximately constant for all subjects (stores, etc.), a crossover design is not fully effective. It may then be preferable to place the subjects into homogeneous groups with respect to the order position effects and use independent latin squares for each group. Suppose that four treatments are to be administered to eight subjects each, four males and four females, and that the experimenter expects the fatigue effect to

TABLE 30.11   **Illustration of a Latin Square Double Crossover Design.**

		Two-Week Period		
Square	Store	1	2	3
	1	A	B	C
1	2	B	C	A
	3	C	A	B
	4	A	C	B
2	5	B	A	C
	6	C	B	A

be stronger for females than for males. The use of two independent latin squares, one for male subjects and the other for female subjects, may then be advisable.

Carryover Effects

If carryover effects from one treatment to another are anticipated, that is, if not only the order position but also the preceding treatment has an effect, these carryover effects may be balanced out by choosing a latin square in which every treatment follows every other treatment an equal number of times. For $r = 4$, an example of such a latin square is:

	Period			
Subject	1	2	3	4
1	A	B	D	C
2	B	C	A	D
3	C	D	B	A
4	D	A	C	B

Note that treatment *A* follows each of the other treatments once, and similarly for the other treatments. This design is appropriate when the carryover effects do not persist for more than one period.

When *r* is odd, the sequence balance can be obtained by using a pair of latin squares with the property that the treatment sequences in one square are reversed in the other square. Indeed, even when *r* is even, it is usually desirable to use a pair of such squares so that the degrees of freedom associated with *MSRem* are reasonably large. Such a design is sometimes called a *latin square double crossover design*. This type of design retains the advantages of employing two blocking variables in a latin square, while enabling the experimenter also to balance and measure the carryover effects.

For the earlier apple display illustration in which three displays were studied in six stores, the two latin squares might be as shown in Table 30.11. The stores should first be placed into two homogeneous groups and these should then be assigned to the two latin squares.

Cited References

30.1. Cochran, W. G., and G. M. Cox. *Experimental Designs*. 2nd ed. New York: John Wiley & Sons, 1957.

30.2. Snedecor, G. W., and W. G. Cochran. *Statistical Methods*. 8th ed. Ames, Iowa: The Iowa State University Press, 1989.

Problems

30.1. A behavioral scientist explained why latin square designs are used so frequently: "Many times in behavioral science, we require the use of repeated measures designs because variability between human subjects is so great. Since an order effect may be present in this situation, we employ latin square designs to eliminate any bias due to order effects." Comment.

30.2. a. Using random permutations, select randomly a 3 by 3 latin square. Show all steps.

b. Using random permutations, select randomly a 6 by 6 latin square. Show all steps.

√ 30.3. **Hardware sales**. A manufacturer conducted a small pilot study of the effect of the price of one of its products on sales of this product in hardware stores. Since it might be confusing to customers if prices were switched repeatedly within a store, only one price was used for any one store during the six-month study period. Sixteen stores were employed in the study. To reduce experimental error variability, stores were chosen so that there would be one store for each sales volume-geographic location class. The four price levels (A: $1.79; B: $1.69; C: $1.59; D: $1.49) were assigned to the stores according to the latin square design shown below. Data on sales during the six-month period (in thousand dollars) follow.

Sales Volume Class	Geographic Location Class (j)			
i	Northeast	Northwest	Southeast	Southwest
1 (smallest)	1.2 (B)	1.5 (C)	1.0 (A)	1.7 (D)
2	1.4 (A)	1.9 (D)	1.6 (B)	1.5 (C)
3	2.8 (C)	2.1 (B)	2.7 (D)	2.0 (A)
4 (largest)	3.4 (D)	2.5 (A)	2.9 (C)	2.7 (B)

Obtain the residuals for latin square model (30.1) and plot them against the fitted values. Also prepare a normal probability plot of the residuals and calculate the coefficient of correlation between the ordered residuals and their expected values under normality. Summarize your findings about the appropriateness of model (30.1) here.

√ 30.4. Refer to **Hardware sales** Problem 30.3. Assume that latin square model (30.1) is appropriate.

a. Prepare a normal probability plot of the estimated treatment means. What does the plot suggest about the effects of the four price levels on sales?

b. Test whether or not price level affects mean sales; use $\alpha = .05$. State the alternatives, decision rule, and conclusion. What is the P-value of the test?

c. Analyze the nature of the price effect on sales by making all pairwise comparisons among the treatment means. Use the Tukey procedure and a 90 percent family confidence coefficient. Summarize your findings.

d. Does there appear to be a linear relationship between price level and mean sales? Could you formally test for linearity? Explain.

√ 30.5. Refer to **Hardware sales** Problems 30.3 and 30.4.

a. Calculate the three estimated efficiency measures in (30.15).

b. Would a randomized block design have been adequate here? If so, which blocking variable would have been best?

30.6. **Summary reports**. A management information systems consultant conducted a small-scale study of five different daily summary reports (A: greatest amount of detail; B; C; D; E: least amount of detail). Five sales executives were used in the study. Each was given one type of daily report for a month and then was asked to rate its helpfulness on a 25-point scale (0: no help; 25: extremely helpful). Over a five-month period, each executive received each type of report for one month according to the latin square design shown below. The helpfulness ratings follow.

Executive	Month (j)				
i	March	April	May	June	July
Harrison	21 (D)	8 (A)	17 (C)	9 (B)	16 (E)
Smith	5 (A)	10 (E)	3 (B)	12 (C)	15 (D)
Carmichael	20 (C)	10 (B)	15 (E)	22 (D)	12 (A)
Loeb	4 (B)	17 (D)	3 (A)	9 (E)	10 (C)
Munch	17 (E)	16 (C)	20 (D)	7 (A)	11 (B)

Obtain the residuals for latin square model (30.1) and plot them against the fitted values. Also prepare a normal probability plot of the residuals and calculate the coefficient of correlation between the ordered residuals and their expected values under normality. Summarize your findings about the appropriateness of model (30.1) here.

30.7. Refer to **Summary reports** Problem 30.6. Assume that latin square model (30.1) is appropriate.

a. Prepare a normal probability plot of the estimated treatment means. What does the plot suggest about the effects of the five types of reports?

b. Test whether or not the five types of reports differ in mean helpfulness; use significance level $\alpha = .01$. State the alternatives, decision rule, and conclusion. What is the P-value of the test?

c. Analyze the effectiveness of the five types of reports by making all pairwise comparisons among the treatment means. Use the Tukey procedure and a 95 percent family confidence coefficient. Summarize your findings.

30.8. Refer to **Summary reports** Problems 30.6 and 30.7.

a. Calculate the three estimated efficiency measures in (30.15).

b. How effective was the use of the latin square design here?

√ 30.9. Refer to **Hardware sales** Problems 30.3 and 30.4. Assume that $\sigma = .15$. What is the power of the test for treatment effects in Problem 30.4b if $\tau_1 = -.4$, $\tau_2 = 0$, $\tau_3 = .1$, and $\tau_4 = .3$?

30.10. Refer to **Summary reports** Problems 30.6 and 30.7. Assume that $\sigma = 1.4$. What is the power of the test for treatment effects in Problem 30.7b if $\tau_1 = -2$, $\tau_2 = -1$, $\tau_3 = 0$, $\tau_4 = 1.5$, $\tau_5 = 1.5$?

30.11. **Drugs interaction**. A pilot study was undertaken on the interaction effects of two drugs to stimulate growth in girls who are of short stature because of a particular syndrome. Each drug was known to be modestly effective singly, but the combination of the two drugs had never been investigated. Blocking by both subject and time period was desired whereby repeated measures for different treatments applied to the same subject are obtained. A 4 by 4 latin square design, shown below, was utilized for four subjects, four time periods, and four treatments. The four time periods consisted of one month each, separated by an intervening month during which no treatment was given. The four treatments were *A*: no treatment (placebo); *B*: drug X alone; *C*: drug Y alone; *D*: both drugs X and Y. The response variable was the difference in the growth rates (in centimeters per month) during the treatment period and the base period before the experiment began. The results of the study follow.

Subject	Period (j)			
i	1	2	3	4
1	.02 (*A*)	.15 (*B*)	.45 (*D*)	.18 (*C*)
2	.27 (*B*)	.24 (*C*)	−.01 (*A*)	.58 (*D*)
3	.11 (*C*)	.35 (*D*)	.14 (*B*)	−.03 (*A*)
4	.48 (*D*)	.04 (*A*)	.18 (*C*)	.22 (*B*)

Obtain the residuals in (30.5) for latin square model (30.1) and plot them against the fitted values. Also prepare a normal probability plot of the residuals and calculate the coefficient of correlation between the ordered residuals and their expected values under normality. Summarize your findings.

30.12. Refer to **Drugs interaction** Problem 30.11. Assume that an appropriate model is latin square model (30.1), modified so that subjects have random effects and a factorial structure for the treatments is incorporated (factor *A*: drug X; factor *B*: drug Y).

a. State the model to be employed.

b. Test for interaction effects between the two drugs; use $\alpha = .10$. State the alternatives, decision rule, and conclusion. What is the *P*-value of the test?

c. Estimate the interaction contrast:

$$L = \left(\frac{\mu_{..2} + \mu_{..3}}{2} - \mu_{..1} \right) - \left(\mu_{..4} - \frac{\mu_{..2} + \mu_{..3}}{2} \right) = \mu_{..2} - \mu_{..1} - \mu_{..4} + \mu_{..3}$$

using a 90 percent confidence interval. Interpret your result.

√ 30.13. Refer to **Hardware sales** Problem 30.3.

a. Set up the regression model equivalent to latin square model (30.1) using 1, −1, 0 indicator variables.

    b. Test by means of the regression approach whether or not price level affects mean sales; use $\alpha = .05$. State the alternatives, decision rule, and conclusion.

    c. Obtain a 95 percent confidence interval by the regression approach for $L = \tau_3 - \tau_4$. Interpret your interval estimate.

    d. Suppose that observation $Y_{232} = 1.6$ were missing.

       (i) Use the regression approach to test whether price level affects mean sales; control the α risk at .05. State the alternatives, decision rule, and conclusion.

       (ii) Use the regression approach to estimate $L = \tau_1 - \tau_2$ by means of a 95 percent confidence interval.

30.14. Refer to **Summary reports** Problem 30.6. Suppose that observations $Y_{114} = 21$ and $Y_{453} = 10$ were missing.

    a. Use the regression approach to test whether the five types of reports differ in mean effectiveness; employ significance level $\alpha = .01$. State the alternatives, decision rule, and conclusion.

    b. Use the regression approach to estimate $L = \tau_4 - \tau_1$ by means of a 99 percent confidence interval.

30.15. **TV commercials**. A study was undertaken to determine whether the volume of sound of a television commercial affects recall and whether this effect varies by product. Thirty-two subjects were chosen, two each for 16 groups defined according to age (class 1: youngest; 2; 3; 4: oldest) and amount of education (class 1: lowest education level; 2; 3; 4: highest education level). Each subject was exposed to one of four television commercial showings (*A*: high volume, product X; *B*: low volume, product X; *C*: high volume, product Y; *D*: low volume, product Y) according to the latin square design shown below. Two different commercials were involved, one for each product. During the following week, the subjects were asked to mention everything they could remember about the advertisement. Scores were based on the number of learning points mentioned, suitably standardized. The results follow.

Age Class i:	1	2	3	4
Education Level				
$j = 1$:	83 86 (*D*)	70 76 (*B*)	67 74 (*C*)	56 60 (*A*)
$j = 2$:	64 69 (*A*)	81 75 (*C*)	67 61 (*B*)	72 67 (*D*)
$j = 3$:	78 75 (*C*)	64 60 (*A*)	76 81 (*D*)	63 67 (*B*)
$j = 4$:	76 74 (*B*)	87 81 (*D*)	64 57 (*A*)	64 66 (*C*)

Obtain the residuals for latin square model (30.18) and plot them against the fitted values. Also prepare a normal probability plot of the residuals and calculate the coefficient of correlation between the ordered residuals and their expected values under normality. Summarize your findings about the appropriateness of the model utilized here.

30.16. Refer to **TV commercials** Problem 30.15. Assume that latin square model (30.18), modified to allow for factorial treatments (factor *A*: volume; factor *B*: product), is appropriate.

    a. State the model to be employed.

    b. Test for volume-product interaction effects; use $\alpha = .01$. State the alternatives, decision rule, and conclusion. What is the P-value of the test?

    c. Test for volume main effects and product main effects. For each test, use $\alpha = .01$ and state the alternatives, decision rule, and conclusion. What is the P-value of each test?

d. To study the nature of the volume and product main effects, estimate the difference between the two factor level means for each factor. Use the Bonferroni procedure and a 95 percent family confidence coefficient. State your findings.

30.17. **Recall decay**. In an experiment to study recall decay with three different questionnaires (A, B, C), nine subjects were questioned at three different times three months apart about the number of trips to a shopping center during the preceding three months. Each time a different questionnaire was used. The latin square design shown below was used to determine the questionnaire order for each subject, with three subjects assigned randomly to each of the three treatment order patterns. The data on number of shopping trips reported follow.

Pattern i	Subject	Time Period (j) 1	2	3
	$m = 1$	40 (C)	18 (A)	30 (B)
1	$m = 2$	35 (C)	25 (A)	37 (B)
	$m = 3$	31 (C)	22 (A)	28 (B)
	$m = 1$	10 (B)	43 (C)	33 (A)
2	$m = 2$	18 (B)	49 (C)	37 (A)
	$m = 3$	15 (B)	48 (C)	29 (A)
	$m = 1$	7 (A)	19 (B)	59 (C)
3	$m = 2$	11 (A)	24 (B)	51 (C)
	$m = 3$	19 (A)	21 (B)	62 (C)

Obtain the residuals for latin square crossover model (30.20) and plot them against the fitted values. Also prepare a normal probability plot of the residuals and calculate the coefficient of correlation between the ordered residuals and their expected values under normality. Summarize your findings about the appropriateness of model (30.20) here.

30.18. Refer to **Recall decay** Problem 30.17. Assume that latin square crossover model (30.20) is appropriate.

a. Test for the presence of treatment order pattern, time period, and questionnaire effects. For each test, use level of significance $\alpha = .05$ and state the alternatives, decision rule, and conclusion. What is the P-value of each test?

b. Analyze the questionnaire main effects by estimating all pairwise comparisons of treatment means. Use the Tukey procedure and a 90 percent family confidence coefficient. Summarize your findings.

CHAPTER
31

Exploratory Experiments– Two-Level Factorial and Fractional Factorial Designs

Up to this point, much of our discussion of the design of experiments has focused on the planning of *confirmatory* experiments. Generally, confirmatory experiments employ a relatively small number of explanatory factors. The factors under investigation usually are suggested by existing theory or by previous experimental findings. *Exploratory* experimental studies are typically encountered during the early stages of a new research study, when little is known about the set of important or *active* explanatory factors. At this stage of the investigation, the experimenter often needs to consider a large number of factors in order to identify the factors with the most important effects. One means of including a large number of factors in an experiment while keeping the total number of treatment combinations at a manageable level is to study each factor at only two levels. For example, in a four-factor experiment, one replication of a two-level factorial experiment consists of just $2^4 = 16$ treatment trials. In contrast, if each factor were studied at three levels, a single replication would require $3^4 = 81$ treatment trials—over five times that required by the two-level experiment.

Even when only two levels are employed for each factor, the size of the experiment can still become prohibitively large when a large number of factors is to be studied. In such cases, a carefully selected subset, or *fraction*, of the treatments can be used with little or no loss of information about the main effects and key low-order interactions. *Fractional factorial designs* permit the study of a large number of factors with relatively few experimental trials.

Another means of keeping the number of trials small in exploratory experiments is to use a single replication or to employ replications for only one or a few of the treatments.

In this chapter, we first discuss the use of two-level factorial experiments and then consider two-level experiments with only one replication. We then take up fractional factorial designs and their analysis, including designs for screening a large number of factors. We conclude the chapter by discussing briefly the use of blocking in two-level experiments. Unless explicitly stated otherwise, we assume throughout the chapter that *all treatment sample sizes are equal and all factor effects are fixed*.

31.1   Two-Level Full Factorial Experiments

Design of Two-Level Studies

Experimental studies involving k factors, each at two levels, are often referred to as 2^k factorial studies. The choice of the two levels for each factor in a two-level factorial experiment at times is automatic. Some factors exist naturally at two levels. For instance, in a marketing research study of the effects of including or excluding special features, such as antilock brakes and automatic headlight dimmers in an automobile, the factors automatically have two levels. At other times, a deliberate choice of the two levels must be made. For instance, in a study of a rubber extrusion process, curing time was one of the factors of interest. Economic and engineering considerations dictated that curing time be at least 30 minutes and not longer than 45 minutes. The two levels selected here were 30 and 45 minutes to provide information at the limits of the range of the factor.

An example of a two-level factorial study involving three factors with three replications is the stress test study in Table 23.4. There, the gender levels were male and female, and subjects were classified as having low or high body fat and being light or heavy smokers.

Since two-level factorial studies are a special case of the factorial studies discussed in earlier chapters, we already know how to analyze such studies. For our purposes here, however, we need to modify our earlier notation because it becomes awkward when there are many factors. Also, we shall see that some simplifications arise in the calculational formulas when all factors have two levels.

Notation

Consider our usual formulation of the regression version of a three-factor ANOVA model for a balanced study where each factor has two levels:

$$
(31.1) \quad \begin{aligned}
Y_{ijkm} = {}& \mu_{...} + \alpha_1 X_{ijkm1} + \beta_1 X_{ijkm2} + \gamma_1 X_{ijkm3} \\
& + (\alpha\beta)_{11} X_{ijkm1} X_{ijkm2} + (\alpha\gamma)_{11} X_{ijkm1} X_{ijkm3} \\
& + (\beta\gamma)_{11} X_{ijkm2} X_{ijkm3} + (\alpha\beta\gamma)_{111} X_{ijkm1} X_{ijkm2} X_{ijkm3} \\
& + \varepsilon_{ijkm}
\end{aligned}
$$

where X_1, X_2, X_3 take on the values 1 and -1 for the two factor levels. Even though in a two-level factorial study there is only one main effect term for each factor, one two-factor interaction for each pair of factors, and so on, it is evident that with more factors the notation used in model (31.1) will become very cumbersome.

We therefore will change the notation as follows, using the conventions for polynomial regression in Section 7.7:

1. The main effects will be represented by β_1, β_2, etc. The overall constant will be represented by β_0.

2. The two-factor interaction effects will be represented by β_{12}, β_{13}, etc.

3. Three-factor and higher-order interaction effects will be represented correspondingly; for instance, by β_{123} and β_{1234}.

4. The index i will be used to denote the observation number, running from 1 to n_T.

5. Cross-product terms will be represented by a single X. For instance, $X_1 X_2$ will be represented by X_{12}; $X_1 X_2 X_3$ will be represented by X_{123}; and so on. The value of $X_1 X_2$ for the ith observation will be represented by X_{i12}.

6. When the factor is quantitative, the low level will be the first level and will be coded -1, and the high level will be the second level and will be coded 1. This coding for quantitative factors is equivalent to standardizing the levels by subtracting the mean and dividing by half of the range. For a qualitative factor, the first level correspondingly will be coded -1 and the second level coded 1. Note that the -1, 1 coding here is the opposite of the convention followed earlier.

With these conventions, model (31.1) is now stated as follows, using $X_0 \equiv 1$ as the dummy variable associated with β_0:

$$(31.2) \quad Y_i = \beta_0 X_{i0} + \beta_1 X_{i1} + \beta_2 X_{i2} + \beta_3 X_{i3} + \beta_{12} X_{i12} + \beta_{13} X_{i13} + \beta_{23} X_{i23} \\ + \beta_{123} X_{i123} + \varepsilon_i$$

where:

ε_i are independent $N(0, \sigma^2)$

$X_0 \equiv 1$

$$X_1 = \begin{array}{ll} -1 & \text{if case from first level of factor 1} \\ 1 & \text{if case from second level of factor 1} \end{array}$$

$$X_2 = \begin{array}{ll} -1 & \text{if case from first level of factor 2} \\ 1 & \text{if case from second level of factor 2} \end{array}$$

$$X_3 = \begin{array}{ll} -1 & \text{if case from first level of factor 3} \\ 1 & \text{if case from second level of factor 3} \end{array}$$

β_0 in model (31.2) corresponds to $\mu_{...}$ in model (31.1). Because the codes -1, 1 are now reversed from our earlier convention, β_1 corresponds to $-\alpha_1 = \alpha_2$. Similarly, β_2 corresponds to $-\beta_1 = \beta_2$, and β_3 corresponds to $-\gamma_1 = \gamma_2$. The parameter β_{12} corresponds to $(\alpha\beta)_{11} = (\alpha\beta)_{22}$ because of two reversals in the signs of the indicator variables.

For k factors, model (31.2) is extended as follows:

$$(31.2a) \quad Y_i = \beta_0 X_{i0} + \beta_1 X_{i1} + \cdots + \beta_k X_{ik} + \beta_{12} X_{i12} + \cdots + \beta_{12\cdots k} X_{i12\cdots k} + \varepsilon_i$$

where:

$$X_{ij} = \begin{array}{ll} -1 & \text{if case } i \text{ from first level of factor } j \\ 1 & \text{if case } i \text{ from second level of factor } j \end{array}$$

and X_0 and ε_i are defined as in (31.2).

It is often helpful to list the treatments in a two-level factorial experiment in a standard order. We shall use as the *standard order* a listing of the treatments such that the level of factor 1, X_1, changes most frequently, the level of factor 2, X_2, changes with second greatest frequency, and so on. In a three-factor study, for instance, the standard order of the treatments is obtained by listing factor levels in the following sequence:

Treatment	X_1	X_2	X_3
1	−1	−1	−1
2	1	−1	−1
3	−1	1	−1
4	1	1	−1
5	−1	−1	1
6	1	−1	1
7	−1	1	1
8	1	1	1

Note that treatment 1 consists of all three factors at their first levels, treatment 2 consists of factor A at its second level and factors B and C at their first levels, and so on. The matrix consisting of the X_1, X_2, and X_3 columns is called the *design matrix* because it identifies the treatments in the experimental study.

A standard order for treatments is simply a convention for listing treatments in two-level factorial experiments; the actual ordering of the treatment trials in the experiment and the assignment of the treatments to experimental units are determined by randomization.

Estimation of Factor Effects

When a balanced factorial experiment is carried out at two levels for each factor and a −1, 1 coding is employed, the $\mathbf{X}'\mathbf{X}$ matrix is greatly simplified. Consider a two-factor study with $n = 1$ replication. The $\mathbf{X}$ matrix, using the coding in (31.2), is as follows (treatments are in standard order):

$$
\mathbf{X} = \begin{array}{cccc} X_0 & X_1 & X_2 & X_{12} \\ \begin{bmatrix} 1 & -1 & -1 & 1 \\ 1 & 1 & -1 & -1 \\ 1 & -1 & 1 & -1 \\ 1 & 1 & 1 & 1 \end{bmatrix} \end{array}
$$

The simplifications in the $\mathbf{X}'\mathbf{X}$ matrix arise because:

1. Any two columns of the $\mathbf{X}$ matrix are orthogonal; that is, $\mathbf{X}'_q\mathbf{X}_{q'} = 0$. In our simple example, for instance:

$$
\mathbf{X}'_1\mathbf{X}_2 = \begin{bmatrix} -1 & 1 & -1 & 1 \end{bmatrix} \begin{bmatrix} -1 \\ -1 \\ 1 \\ 1 \end{bmatrix} = 0
$$

2. The sum of squares of the elements in each column, $\mathbf{X}'_q\mathbf{X}_q$, is always n_T. In our simple example, for instance:

$$
\mathbf{X}'_1\mathbf{X}_1 = \begin{bmatrix} -1 & 1 & -1 & 1 \end{bmatrix} \begin{bmatrix} -1 \\ 1 \\ -1 \\ 1 \end{bmatrix} = 4
$$

TABLE 31.1   **Y and X Data Matrices in Standard Order—Stress Test Example of Table 23.4.**

$$
\mathbf{Y} = \begin{bmatrix} Y_{1111} \\ Y_{1112} \\ Y_{1113} \\ Y_{2111} \\ Y_{2112} \\ Y_{2113} \\ Y_{1211} \\ \vdots \\ Y_{2221} \\ Y_{2222} \\ Y_{2223} \end{bmatrix} = \begin{bmatrix} Y_{1} \\ Y_{2} \\ Y_{3} \\ Y_{4} \\ Y_{5} \\ Y_{6} \\ Y_{7} \\ \vdots \\ Y_{22} \\ Y_{23} \\ Y_{24} \end{bmatrix} = \begin{bmatrix} 24.1 \\ 29.2 \\ 24.6 \\ 20.0 \\ 21.9 \\ 17.6 \\ 14.6 \\ \vdots \\ 10.1 \\ 14.4 \\ 6.1 \end{bmatrix}
$$

	X_0	X_1	X_2	X_3	X_{12}	X_{13}	X_{23}	X_{123}
	1	−1	−1	−1	1	1	1	−1
	1	−1	−1	−1	1	1	1	−1
	1	−1	−1	−1	1	1	1	−1
$\mathbf{X} =$	1	1	−1	−1	−1	−1	1	1
	1	1	−1	−1	−1	−1	1	1
	1	1	−1	−1	−1	−1	1	1
	1	−1	1	−1	−1	1	−1	1
	$\vdots$							
	1	1	1	1	1	1	1	1
	1	1	1	1	1	1	1	1
	1	1	1	1	1	1	1	1

Consequently, the elements on the main diagonal of the $\mathbf{X'X}$ matrix are all n_T and the elements off the main diagonal are all zero so that $\mathbf{X'X}$ is a diagonal matrix:

$$(31.3) \qquad\qquad \mathbf{X'X} = n_T \mathbf{I}$$

The inverse of $\mathbf{X'X}$ therefore is a diagonal matrix with the diagonal elements being the reciprocals of the elements in (31.3):

$$(31.4) \qquad\qquad (\mathbf{X'X})^{-1} = \frac{1}{n_T} \mathbf{I}$$

The least squares and maximum likelihood estimators in (6.25) therefore become simple in form:

$$(31.5) \qquad\qquad \mathbf{b} = (\mathbf{X'X})^{-1}\mathbf{X'Y} = \frac{1}{n_T}\mathbf{X'Y}$$

Letting $\mathbf{X}_q$ denote the column vector containing the qth column of the $\mathbf{X}$ matrix, the estimated regression coefficient b_q therefore is:

$$(31.6) \qquad\qquad b_q = \frac{1}{n_T}\mathbf{X}_q'\mathbf{Y}$$

Since each column vector $\mathbf{X}_q$ contains only 1s and −1s, the estimated coefficients b_q are very simple linear combinations of the observations.

We illustrate this in Table 31.1, which contains the $\mathbf{Y}$ vector and the $\mathbf{X}$ matrix for the stress test example of Table 23.4, with the observations listed in standard order. The Y observations are shown both in the earlier notation and the current notation to facilitate recognition of the treatments involved. (Note that the coding of the factor levels in the $\mathbf{X}$ matrix is the opposite of that in Table 23.5 and that the ordering of the observations also differs.) We see that the estimated coefficient b_{12}, for instance, is simply:

$$(31.7) \qquad b_{12} = \frac{1}{n_T} \mathbf{X}'_{12} \mathbf{Y} = \frac{1}{24} [1 \quad 1 \quad 1 \quad -1 \quad \cdots \quad 1] \begin{bmatrix} 24.1 \\ 29.2 \\ 24.6 \\ 20.0 \\ \vdots \\ 6.1 \end{bmatrix} = .754$$

The variance-covariance matrix of $\mathbf{b}$ in (6.46) is also greatly simplified:

$$(31.8) \qquad \sigma^2\{\mathbf{b}\} = \sigma^2 (\mathbf{X}'\mathbf{X})^{-1} = \frac{\sigma^2}{n_T} \mathbf{I}$$

Note from this matrix that the estimated regression coefficients here are uncorrelated and have constant variance:

$$(31.9) \qquad \sigma^2\{b_q\} = \frac{\sigma^2}{n_T}$$

The estimated variance-covariance matrix in (6.48) becomes:

$$(31.10) \qquad s^2\{\mathbf{b}\} = \frac{MSE}{n_T} \mathbf{I}$$

so that the estimated variance of b_q is simply:

$$(31.11) \qquad s^2\{b_q\} = \frac{MSE}{n_T}$$

Comments

1. Some texts and software packages define the effect of a factor as an observed difference between responses when that factor changes from its first level to its second level. For example, the estimated main effect of factor 1 (factor A) is defined as:

$$(31.12) \qquad A = \left(\begin{array}{c} \text{Average response for all} \\ \text{trials in which } X_1 = 1 \end{array} \right) - \left(\begin{array}{c} \text{Average response for all} \\ \text{trials in which } X_1 = -1 \end{array} \right)$$

A is an estimate of $\alpha_2 - \alpha_1 = 2\alpha_2$; recall that $\alpha_1 = -\alpha_2$ when the factors are at two levels. Consequently, the relation between A and our estimate b_1 (which now estimates $\alpha_2 = -\alpha_1$) is:

$$(31.13) \qquad A = 2b_1$$

The relations for the other main effects and interaction effects are similar.

2. The $-1, 1$ coding used for the predictor variables in (31.2) is sometimes referred to as an *orthogonal coding* because it leads for balanced two-level factorial designs to a diagonal $\mathbf{X}'\mathbf{X}$ matrix.   ∎

FIGURE 31.1   MINITAB FFactorial Output—Stress Test Example of Table 23.4.

```
Estimated Effects and Coefficients for TOLERNCE

Term                        Effect      Coef  Std Coef  t-value      P
Constant                              16.271    0.6237    26.09  0.000
GENDER                      -5.425    -2.713    0.6237    -4.35  0.000
BODYFAT                     -6.358    -3.179    0.6237    -5.10  0.000
SMOKING                     -3.425    -1.713    0.6237    -2.75  0.014
GENDER*BODYFAT               1.508     0.754    0.6237     1.21  0.244
GENDER*SMOKING              -1.358    -0.679    0.6237    -1.09  0.292
BODYFAT*SMOKING              3.475     1.737    0.6237     2.79  0.013
GENDER*BODYFAT*SMOKING      -0.558    -0.279    0.6237    -0.45  0.660

Analysis of Variance for TOLERNCE

Source               DF     Seq SS     Adj SS     Adj MS      F      P
Main Effects          3    489.538    489.538    163.179  17.48  0.000
2-Way Interactions    3     97.175     97.175     32.392   3.47  0.041
3-Way Interactions    1      1.870      1.870      1.870   0.20  0.660
Residual Error       16    149.367    149.367      9.335
  Pure Error         16    149.367    149.367      9.335
Total                23    737.950
```

Inferences about Factor Effects

As noted earlier, a main objective in two-level exploratory studies is usually the identification of active effects. An effect is considered active if the corresponding factor effect coefficient is nonzero. Since all estimated factor effects have the same variance for balanced studies, as noted in (31.9), a normal probability plot can be made of all estimated main and interaction effects to identify those that appear to be active. We shall illustrate this plot shortly.

Formal tests for a regression coefficient, with the alternatives $H_0: \beta_q = 0$, $H_a: \beta_q \neq 0$, are carried out in the usual manner, based on either the t^* statistic in (7.25) or the F^* statistic in (7.24). In many instances, the testing procedure will be used for each of the factor effects. The family level of significance then can be controlled at α by either the Bonferroni inequality (4.4) or the Kimball inequality (19.53).

Example.   Figure 31.1 contains the MINITAB FFactorial output for the stress test example of Table 23.4. In this study, the effects of gender of subject (factor A), body fat of subject (factor B), and smoking history of subject (factor C) on exercise tolerance were studied. The MINITAB ANOVA output is based on the coding of the factor levels in Table 31.1. The estimated factor effect coefficients b_q are shown in the column marked "Coef." The column marked "Effect" contains the alternative definition of effects in (31.12). Notice that when each entry in this column is divided by 2, as shown in (31.13), the estimated coefficients b_q are obtained. Also note that the estimated standard deviations in the column labeled "Std Coef" are all the same, as required by (31.11):

$$s\{b_q\} = \left(\frac{MSE}{n_T}\right)^{1/2} = \left(\frac{9.335}{24}\right)^{1/2} = .6237$$

Using a significance level of .015 for each of the seven tests on the estimated factor effect coefficients so as to assure a family level of significance of .10 by the Kimball inequality, we see from the P-values in Figure 31.1 that the set of active factor effects consists of the gender, body fat, and smoking main effects, and the body fat–smoking interaction.

31.2 Analysis of Unreplicated Two-Level Studies

In many applications of two-level factorial experiments, particularly when many factors are included, only a single replication can be run because of time, budgetary, or other resource limitations. As discussed in Chapter 21, no degrees of freedom are available for obtaining an estimate of the error variance σ^2 when only one replication is employed. Special procedures instead must be used for statistical analysis.

We shall now describe three approaches for analyzing unreplicated experiments:

1. The pooling of higher-order interactions to obtain an estimate of the variance.

2. The use of graphical procedures for identifying active effects.

3. The use of replications at the center point to obtain a pure error estimate of the error variance σ^2.

First, however, we shall describe an unreplicated 2^4 factorial experiment that will be used as an illustration.

Example

The Pecos Foods Corporation initiated an experimental study to characterize the effects of process temperature (factor 1 or A), an antimicrobial agent or preservative (factor 2 or B), moisture level (factor 3 or C), and acidity (factor 4 or D) on the microbial growth in a fruit bar. Microbial growth is measured by counting microbes in a sample of the product following three months in storage. The four factors were studied at the following low and high levels:

Factor	Low Level	High Level
Process temperature	152	178
Preservative	0.0	.1
Moisture	.65	.85
Acidity	4.8	6.8

One replication of a 2^4 factorial experiment was run. The $\mathbf{X}$ matrix for the standard 2^4 factorial ANOVA model and the response vector are shown in Table 31.2, in standard order. Note that the columns X_1, X_2, X_3, and X_4 constitute the design matrix, identifying each of the treatments. The response, denoted for simplicity by Y, is the natural logarithm of the microbial count. This transformation was chosen partly because the actual counts ranged from 87 to 104,410 over several orders of magnitude. In addition, the Box-Cox procedure (3.36) supported the use of the logarithmic transformation.

The regression model version of the four-factor ANOVA model was fitted, using the X variables in Table 31.2. The MINITAB regression results for the full ANOVA model ($p = n_T = 16$) are presented in Figure 31.2. Because there are no degrees of freedom available for error, no estimate of the error variance and no t statistics and P-values for the estimated regression coefficients are shown. Note that three estimated factor effect coefficients, $b_2 = -1.25$, $b_3 = 1.40$, and $b_{23} = -1.40$ are substantially larger in absolute value than the next largest coefficient, $b_{134} = -.24$. Consequently, the preservative and moisture factors (2 and 3) may be active. We shall now consider the use of pooling, Pareto plots, dot plots, and normal probability plots in an effort to identify more definitively the set of active effects.

TABLE 31.2   Y Vector and X Matrix—Pecos Foods Corporation Example.

Treatment	Y	X_0	X_1	X_2	X_3	X_4	X_{12}	X_{13}	X_{14}	X_{23}	X_{24}	X_{34}	X_{123}	X_{124}	X_{134}	X_{234}	X_{1234}
1	5.55	1	−1	−1	−1	−1	1	1	1	1	1	1	−1	−1	−1	−1	1
2	4.47	1	1	−1	−1	−1	−1	−1	−1	1	1	1	1	1	1	−1	−1
3	5.19	1	−1	1	−1	−1	−1	1	1	−1	−1	1	1	1	−1	1	−1
4	5.32	1	1	1	−1	−1	1	−1	−1	−1	−1	1	−1	−1	1	1	1
5	10.54	1	−1	−1	1	−1	1	−1	1	−1	1	−1	1	−1	1	1	−1
6	11.56	1	1	−1	1	−1	−1	1	−1	−1	1	−1	−1	1	−1	1	1
7	5.08	1	−1	1	1	−1	−1	−1	1	1	−1	−1	−1	1	1	−1	1
8	5.45	1	1	1	1	−1	1	1	−1	1	−1	−1	1	−1	−1	−1	−1
9	5.12	1	−1	−1	−1	1	1	1	−1	1	−1	−1	−1	1	1	1	−1
10	5.63	1	1	−1	−1	1	−1	−1	1	1	−1	−1	1	−1	−1	1	1
11	6.18	1	−1	1	−1	1	−1	1	−1	−1	1	−1	1	−1	1	−1	1
12	5.24	1	1	1	−1	1	1	−1	1	−1	1	−1	−1	1	−1	−1	−1
13	10.73	1	−1	−1	1	1	1	−1	−1	−1	−1	1	1	1	−1	−1	1
14	10.33	1	1	−1	1	1	−1	1	1	−1	−1	1	−1	−1	1	−1	−1
15	6.53	1	−1	1	1	1	−1	−1	−1	1	1	1	−1	−1	−1	1	−1
16	4.93	1	1	1	1	1	1	1	1	1	1	1	1	1	1	1	1

Pooling of Interactions

A common approach to analyzing unreplicated experiments is to assume that some higher-order interactions are inactive. The extra sums of squares corresponding to these interaction terms are then used to form an estimate of the error variance σ^2. For example, in a 2^4 factorial experiment, it may be reasonable to assume that all three-factor and four-factor interactions are small or negligible in relation to main effects and two-factor interactions. This implies that $\beta_{123} = \beta_{124} = \beta_{134} = \beta_{234} = \beta_{1234} = 0$. By dropping the corresponding terms from the model, five degrees of freedom will be available for an estimate of σ^2. For balanced two-level experiments, it can be shown that the extra sum of squares for X_q is:

$$(31.14) \qquad\qquad SSR(X_q) = n_T b_q^2$$

Since for balanced two-level factorial studies, the columns of the **X** matrix are orthogonal, any extra sum of squares does not depend on the order of the variables and the extra sums of squares are additive. Hence, the pooled estimator of σ^2 is as follows:

$$(31.15) \qquad MSE = n_T \left(\frac{\Sigma b_q^2 \text{ for pooled estimated coefficients}}{\text{Number of pooled coefficients}} \right)$$

Inferences can then be made in customary fashion.

Example.   In the Pecos Foods Corporation example, it was decided that all three-factor and four-factor interactions are unimportant. Using (31.15) and the results in Figure 31.2,

FIGURE 31.2   MINITAB Regression Results for Full ANOVA Model—Pecos Foods Corporation Example.

```
The regression equation is
lnmicrob = 6.74 - 0.124 x1 - 1.25 x2 + 1.40 x3 + 0.0956 x4 - 0.131 x12
              + 0.0481 x13 - 0.179 x14 - 1.40 x23 + 0.134 x24 - 0.109 x34
              - 0.101 x123 - 0.201 x124 - 0.244 x134 + 0.112 x234 + 0.132 x1234

Predictor        Coef        Stdev      t-ratio           p
Constant      6.74062      0.00000         *             *
x1           -0.124375     0.000000        *             *
x2           -1.25063      0.00000         *             *
x3            1.40313      0.00000         *             *
x4            0.0956249    0.0000000       *             *
x12          -0.130625     0.000000        *             *
x13           0.0481250    0.0000000       *             *
x14          -0.179375     0.000000        *             *
x23          -1.39562      0.00000         *             *
x24           0.134375     0.000000        *             *
x34          -0.109375     0.000000        *             *
x123         -0.100625     0.000000        *             *
x124         -0.200625     0.000000        *             *
x134         -0.244375     0.000000        *             *
x234          0.111875     0.000000        *             *
x1234         0.131875     0.000000        *             *


s = *
Analysis of Variance

SOURCE        DF           SS           MS         F           p
Regression    15      91.62849      6.10857        *           *
Error          0          *             *
Total         15      91.62849
```

an estimate of the error variance based on five degrees of freedom is:

$$
MSE = n_T \left(\frac{b_{123}^2 + b_{124}^2 + b_{134}^2 + b_{234}^2 + b_{1234}^2}{5} \right)
$$

$$
= 16 \left[\frac{(-.101)^2 + (-.201)^2 + (-.244)^2 + (.112)^2 + (.132)^2}{5} \right] = .448
$$

MINITAB regression results for the model based on main effects and two-factor interactions are presented in Figure 31.3. Notice that $MSE = .448$, as just calculated. Residual analysis (not shown) did not reveal any violations in assumptions.

The P-values in Figure 31.3 indicate that the main effects for preservative and moisture (factors 2 and 3) and the preservative-moisture interaction effect are statistically significant; each of the associated P-values is .001 or less. The active factors in the Pecos Foods Corporation example are therefore preservative and moisture. Figure 31.4 presents a MINITAB interactions plot of the estimated means $\bar{Y}_{.jk}$ for the two active factors. We see that increasing preservative at high levels of moisture decreases microbial growth. At low moisture levels, however, preservative has little effect. Correspondingly, at low preservative levels, decreasing moisture decreases microbial growth while at high preservative levels, changing the moisture level has little effect on microbial growth.

FIGURE 31.3   **MINITAB Regression Results for ANOVA Model without Higher-Order Interactions—Pecos Foods Corporation Example.**

```
The regression equation is
lnmicrob = 6.74 - 0.124 x1 - 1.25 x2 + 1.40 x3 + 0.096 x4 - 0.131 x12
           + 0.048 x13 - 0.179 x14 - 1.40 x23 + 0.134 x24 - 0.109 x34

Predictor       Coef       Stdev      t-ratio          p
Constant      6.7406      0.1673       40.28      0.000
x1           -0.1244      0.1673       -0.74      0.491
x2           -1.2506      0.1673       -7.47      0.001
x3            1.4031      0.1673        8.39      0.000
x4            0.0956      0.1673        0.57      0.592
x12          -0.1306      0.1673       -0.78      0.470
x13           0.0481      0.1673        0.29      0.785
x14          -0.1794      0.1673       -1.07      0.333
x23          -1.3956      0.1673       -8.34      0.000
x24           0.1344      0.1673        0.80      0.458
x34          -0.1094      0.1673       -0.65      0.542

s = 0.6693      R-sq = 97.6%      R-sq(adj) = 92.7%

Analysis of Variance

SOURCE      DF         SS          MS          F          p
Regression  10    89.3885      8.9388      19.95      0.002
Error        5     2.2400      0.4480
Total       15    91.6285
```

FIGURE 31.4   **MINITAB Interactions Plot—Pecos Foods Corporation Example.**

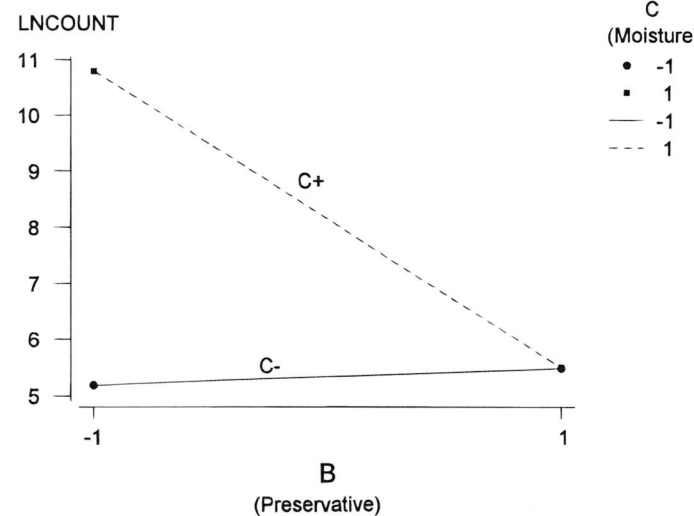

Pareto Plot

The Pareto plot is a qualitative tool for visually identifying important effects in unreplicated two-level studies. It shows the percentage of the total sum of squares *SSTO* that is associated with each estimated effect in the full factorial model. (Remember that for an unreplicated

FIGURE 31.5   JMP Pareto Plot—Pecos Foods Corporation Example.

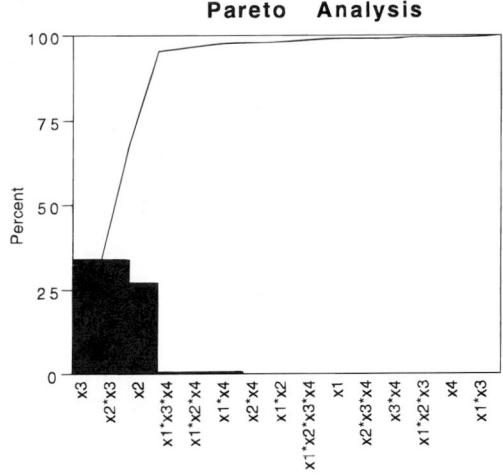

full factorial model, $SSTO = SSR$.) Based on (31.14), this percentage is:

$$(31.16) \qquad \frac{n_T b_q^2}{SSTO}(100)$$

Large percentage contributions correspond to large (absolute) estimated coefficients, and therefore to active factor effects. Pareto plots present the percent contributions to $SSTO$ in decreasing order, either as a bar plot, a cumulative line plot, or both.

Example.   To calculate the percent contribution to the total sum of squares for each factor effect in the Pecos Foods Corporation example, we use (31.16) and the regression results in Figure 31.2 for the full factorial model. For example, the percent contribution associated with X_3 is:

$$\frac{n_T b_3^2}{SSTO}(100) = \frac{16(1.40)^2}{91.63}(100) = 34.2\%$$

A JMP Pareto plot shown in Figure 31.5 contains both a bar plot and a cumulative line plot. Notice that the effects X_2, X_3. and X_2X_3 account for nearly all of the total variation in the data. Thus, the Pareto plot identifies the same factor effects as active as does pooling of higher-order interactions.

Comments

1. Other forms of Pareto plots are also used. For example, some statistics packages provide a Pareto plot of estimated effects. In these plots, the bars correspond to the absolute magnitudes of the estimated effect coefficients. Such plots are sometimes referred to as *scree* plots.

2. While Pareto plots are useful for identifying active effects, they can be misused. For example, a Pareto plot is sometimes used to identify the smallest effects for pooling to estimate σ^2. This approach often will lead to an estimate of the error variance that is too small, making the Type I error rates for tests for active effects larger than desired. ∎

FIGURE 31.6   **Dot Plot of Estimated Factor Effect Coefficients—Pecos Foods Corporation Example.**

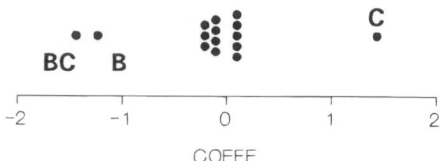

Dot Plot

Another graphic plot often used in the analysis of unreplicated factorial studies to help identify active effects is a simple dot plot of estimated factor effect coefficients. This plot will show whether any estimated coefficients are far outlying. We know from (31.9) that the variances for all estimated effect coefficients are the same for unreplicated 2^k factorial studies so that the estimated effect coefficients will follow the same normal distribution if no effects are present. Inactive factors will tend to be clustered in the middle of the distribution. A large departure from the middle of the distribution suggests that the factor may be active.

Example.   A dot plot of the estimated factor effect coefficients for the Pecos Foods Corporation example is presented in Figure 31.6. Note that most factor effects fall near zero; these presumably are the inactive factor effects. The three outlying coefficients, for factors B and C, correspond to the three factor effects identified already by the other techniques as the active effects.

Normal Probability Plot

A normal probability plot of the estimated factor effect coefficients in an unreplicated 2^k factorial study can be constructed in the same fashion as those in Figure 20.2 for a replicated study. Unlike the normal probability plot in Figure 20.2, a normal probability plot for an unreplicated 2^k factorial study includes all main effects and interaction effects because the standard deviations of all estimated coefficients are the same. If no effects are present, all estimated coefficients follow the same normal distribution $N(0, \sigma^2/n_T)$ and should fall along a straight line in the plot. Strong deviations from a straight line are indicative of active effects, in which case all estimated coefficients do not come from the same normal distribution. Typically, the middle points represent inactive effects and fall along a straight line. If they do not, it may be an indication that the error terms are not normally distributed.

Example.   Figure 31.7 shows a normal probability plot of the estimated effect coefficients for the Pecos Foods Corporation example. A line has been fitted judgmentally to the center points that appear to represent inactive effects. Notice that the estimated effect coefficients for the factor B and factor C main effects and for the BC interaction effect fall away from the line fitted to the inactive effects.

FIGURE 31.7   **Normal Probability Plot of Estimated Effect Coefficients—Pecos Foods Corporation Example.**

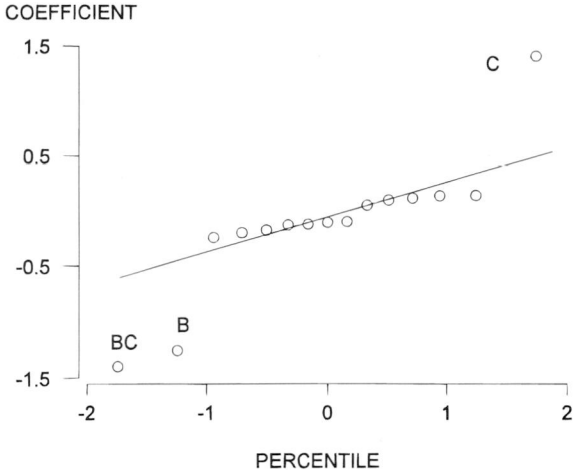

Comments

1. When many factor effects are active and only a few are inactive, it may be difficult to fit a line to the few inactive effects at the center. Consequently, a normal probability plot with many active factor effects is often difficult to interpret.

2. Half-normal probability plots, as described in Section 14.6, are often used in place of (full) normal probability plots discussed here. One advantage of half-normal probability plots is that identification of active effects is sometimes facilitated. This is because the active effects in a half-normal plot all fall at the right upper end of the plot whereas in a (full) normal plot active effects may be at both ends of the plot.

3. A normal probability plot containing all factor effects is also appropriate for 2^k factorial experiments with replications provided that there are equal numbers of replications for each treatment.   ∎

Center Point Replications

When all factors are quantitative, two-level experiments can be augmented by replications at the *center point*. A center point is a new treatment in which each of the factors is set at the midpoint of its range. For example, in the Pecos Foods Corporation example, the center point treatment levels are:

$$\text{Temperature} = \frac{152 + 178}{2} = 165$$

$$\text{Preservative} = \frac{0 + .1}{2} = .05$$

$$\text{Moisture} = \frac{.65 + .85}{2} = .75$$

$$\text{Acidity} = \frac{4.8 + 6.8}{2} = 5.8$$

We shall use n_0 to denote the number of center point replicates. Two important advantages stem from the inclusion of two or more such replicates:

1. A pure error estimate of σ^2 based on $n_0 - 1$ degrees of freedom can be obtained, avoiding any bias that otherwise might be associated with inferential procedures based on the pooling of what appear to be small higher-order effects.

2. With replications at the center point, it is possible to test whether or not the model is a good fit.

Pure Error Estimate of σ^2.   Let Y_{0i} denote the response associated with the ith replicate at the center point, and let $\bar{Y}_{0.}$ denote the mean of the n_0 responses at the center point. A pure error estimate of σ^2 is given by the sample variance of the center point replicates:

$$(31.17) \qquad MSPE = \frac{\Sigma(Y_{0i} - \bar{Y}_{0.})^2}{n_0 - 1}$$

Test for Lack of Fit.   Once a pure error mean square has been obtained, the test for lack of fit in (6.68) proceeds as usual. For a two-level factorial study with no replications that is augmented by n_0 observations at the center point, one degree of freedom is associated with $SSLF$ and $n_0 - 1$ degrees of freedom with $SSPE$.

A conclusion of lack of fit indicates that curvature is present in one or more of the factor effects, but it is not possible to attribute the curvature effect to a specific factor without further experimentation. Methods for augmenting two-level factorial experiments for assessment of curvature effects are discussed in Chapter 32.

Example.   Suppose that four center point replicates had been included in the Pecos Foods Corporation study and that these responses are:

$$Y_{01} = 7.23 \qquad Y_{02} = 7.89 \qquad Y_{03} = 7.80 \qquad Y_{04} = 7.39$$

We then find $\bar{Y}_{0.} = 7.578$, $SSPE = .303$, and $MSPE = .101$. From the regression analysis of the augmented data set (output not shown), we find that $SSE = 2.544$. Hence, using (3.24), we obtain:

$$SSLF = SSE - SSPE = 2.544 - .303 = 2.241$$

Hence, test statistic (6.68b) here is:

$$F^* = \frac{2.241}{1} \div \frac{.303}{3} = 22.2$$

For $\alpha = .05$, we require $F(.95; 1, 3) = 10.1$. Since $F^* = 22.2 > 10.1$ we conclude H_a, that curvature is present. The P-value of the test is .018.

We can obtain some information about the nature of the curvature by comparing the average of the responses at the center point, $\bar{Y}_{0.} = 7.578$, with the average of the responses at the corner points, which is 6.74. Since the mean response is higher at the center point than would be expected from a linear interpolation of the corner points, a mound-shaped surface may be required to model the response adequately in the interior of the experimental region.

Note

When a lack of fit test is conducted after the ANOVA model has been revised by dropping effects that appear to be unimportant, a conclusion of lack of fit does not necessarily imply the presence of curvature effects. Lack of fit could then also be due, for instance, to the absence of important interaction effects.   ∎

31.3   Two-Level Fractional Factorial Designs

Even when each factor is studied at only two levels, the number of treatments grows rapidly with the number of factors, as the following table demonstrates:

Number of Factors	Number of Treatments
2	4
4	16
6	64
8	256
10	1,024

The use of 1,024 experimental trials for just one replication to study 10 factors will be prohibitive in most instances. In this situation, a subset of all factorial treatments can often be used with little loss of information. The use of fractional factorial designs is the subject of this section.

A basic notion that underlies the use of fractional factorial designs is the *sparsity of effects* principle. This principle states that in most systems, responses are driven largely by a limited number of main effects and lower-order interactions, and that higher-order interactions usually are relatively unimportant. For example, information concerning three-factor and higher-order interactions is often not important compared to main effects and two-factor interactions. Under these conditions, a full factorial design can be very wasteful when many factors are of interest. For instance, in the analysis of a full six-factor, two-level factorial experiment, the degrees of freedom associated with the various factor effects are as follows:

Model Terms	Degrees of Freedom
Intercept term	1
Main effect coefficients	6
Two-factor interaction coefficients	15
Three-factor interaction coefficients	20
Four-factor interaction coefficients	15
Five-factor interaction coefficients	6
Six-factor interaction coefficients	1

Note that 42 degrees of freedom will be devoted to the study of three-factor and higher-order interactions. Thus, about 2/3 (42/64) of the degrees of freedom for the study of factor effects in this experiment will be used to estimate factor effects that are ordinarily of little interest. In contrast, in a fractional factorial design, a subset of the treatments is

TABLE 31.3 X Matrices for Two Half-Fraction Designs of the 2^4 Full Factorial Design in Table 31.2—Pecos Foods Corporation Example.

(a) Treatments 2, 3, 6, 7, 10, 11, 14, 15 deleted

Treatment	X_0	X_1	X_2	X_3	X_4	X_{12}	X_{13}	X_{14}	X_{23}	X_{24}	X_{34}	X_{123}	X_{124}	X_{134}	X_{234}	X_{1234}
1	1	-1	-1	-1	-1	1	1	1	1	1	1	-1	-1	-1	-1	1
4	1	1	1	-1	-1	1	-1	-1	-1	-1	1	-1	-1	1	1	1
5	1	-1	-1	1	-1	1	-1	1	-1	1	-1	1	-1	1	1	-1
8	1	1	1	1	-1	1	1	-1	1	-1	-1	1	-1	-1	-1	-1
9	1	-1	-1	-1	1	1	1	-1	1	-1	-1	-1	1	1	1	-1
12	1	1	1	-1	1	1	-1	1	-1	1	-1	-1	1	-1	-1	-1
13	1	-1	-1	1	1	1	-1	-1	-1	-1	1	1	1	-1	-1	1
16	1	1	1	1	1	1	1	1	1	1	1	1	1	1	1	1

(b) Treatments 2, 3, 5, 8, 9, 12, 14, 15 deleted

Treatment	X_0	X_1	X_2	X_3	X_4	X_{12}	X_{13}	X_{14}	X_{23}	X_{24}	X_{34}	X_{123}	X_{124}	X_{134}	X_{234}	X_{1234}
1	1	-1	-1	-1	-1	1	1	1	1	1	1	-1	-1	-1	-1	1
4	1	1	1	-1	-1	1	-1	-1	-1	-1	1	-1	-1	1	1	1
6	1	1	-1	1	-1	-1	1	-1	-1	1	-1	-1	1	-1	1	1
7	1	-1	1	1	-1	-1	-1	1	1	-1	-1	-1	1	1	-1	1
10	1	1	-1	-1	1	-1	-1	1	1	-1	-1	1	-1	-1	1	1
11	1	-1	1	-1	1	-1	1	-1	-1	1	-1	1	-1	1	-1	1
13	1	-1	-1	1	1	1	-1	-1	-1	-1	1	1	1	-1	-1	1
16	1	1	1	1	1	1	1	1	1	1	1	1	1	1	1	1

selected in such a way that most of the degrees of freedom for the study of factor effects are devoted to main effects and low-order interactions, with only some loss of information about higher-order interactions.

Confounding

A fractional factorial design achieves the efficiency of providing full information about main effects and low-order interactions with fewer experimental trials by confounding these effects with unimportant higher-order interactions. To understand the concept of confounding, consider again the **X** matrix of the Pecos Foods Corporation example in Table 31.2. A single replication of a 2^4 full factorial design was employed here, requiring 16 experimental trials. Suppose that in advance of the experiment, it had been determined that only half of the 16 treatments could be used due to budgetary constraints. Which eight of the 16 treatments should be eliminated? Suppose that the experimenter considered dropping treatments 2, 3, 6, 7, 10, 11, 14, 15. The **X** matrix for the remaining eight treatments is given in Table 31.3a.

This choice of treatments to be dropped involves a number of potentially serious problems. Notice first that column vectors X_1 and X_2 are identical in the eight-run design of Table 31.3a; i.e., $\mathbf{X}_1 = \mathbf{X}_2$. Because the columns of this $\mathbf{X}$ matrix are linearly dependent, the matrix $\mathbf{X}'\mathbf{X}$ is singular and does not have an inverse. To be able to obtain least squares and maximum likelihood estimates, we must remove the redundancy resulting from the equality of the $\mathbf{X}_1$ and $\mathbf{X}_2$ column vectors. We do this by retaining only one of the two column vectors. Suppose that we drop the $\mathbf{X}_2$ column vector. In our original model, the main effects for factors 1 and 2 were represented by:

(31.18)
$$\beta_1 X_1 + \beta_2 X_2$$

When $X_1 = X_2$, the model terms become:

(31.18a)
$$\beta_1 X_1 + \beta_2 X_1 = (\beta_1 + \beta_2) X_1 \qquad \text{when} \quad X_1 = X_2$$

Thus, with the experimental design in Table 31.3a, we will not be able to estimate the factor 1 and factor 2 main effects separately but only their combined main effects. If the experimental results indicate that the effect associated with X_1 is active, we will not know whether the result is due to the effect of factor 1, the effect of factor 2, or to a combination of the effects of these two factors. Factors 1 and 2 are said to be *confounded* or *aliased* in this experiment.

Upon further inspection of Table 31.3a, we find seven more pairs of identical columns, resulting in the following correspondences among the columns of $\mathbf{X}$:

(31.19)
$$\mathbf{X}_1 = \mathbf{X}_2 \qquad \mathbf{X}_3 = \mathbf{X}_{123} \qquad \mathbf{X}_4 = \mathbf{X}_{124} \qquad \mathbf{X}_{13} = \mathbf{X}_{23}$$
$$\mathbf{X}_{14} = \mathbf{X}_{24} \qquad \mathbf{X}_{234} = \mathbf{X}_{134} \qquad \mathbf{X}_{1234} = \mathbf{X}_{34} \qquad \mathbf{X}_{12} = \mathbf{X}_0$$

Consequently, the following effects will be confounded:

(31.20)
$$\beta_1 + \beta_2 \qquad \beta_3 + \beta_{123} \qquad \beta_4 + \beta_{124} \qquad \beta_{13} + \beta_{23}$$
$$\beta_{14} + \beta_{24} \qquad \beta_{234} + \beta_{134} \qquad \beta_{1234} + \beta_{34} \qquad \beta_{12} + \beta_0$$

Since β_{12} is confounded with β_0, the overall mean, β_{12} is sometimes said to be *unmeasurable*.

The relations in either (31.19) or (31.20) define the complete *confounding scheme* for this fractional factorial design. We shall generally describe a confounding scheme in the form of (31.19) and, for simplicity, shall show the column correspondences by means of the subscripts of the column vectors. For our example in Table 31.3a, the confounding scheme is represented in this fashion as follows:

$$1 = 2 \qquad 3 = 123 \qquad 4 = 124 \qquad 13 = 23$$
$$14 = 24 \qquad 234 = 134 \qquad 1234 = 34 \qquad 12 = 0$$

The subscript numbers are now shown in italics as a reminder that the equality sign applies not to the numbers shown but to the column vectors for which the numbers are the subscripts.

The proposed eight-treatment design in Table 31.3a is clearly undesirable since main effects are confounded with each other. Suppose instead that the investigator chose to eliminate treatments 2, 3, 5, 8, 9, 12, 14, 15. The resulting $\mathbf{X}$ matrix is given in Table 31.3b. Notice that the correspondences among the columns of the $\mathbf{X}$ matrix now are:

(31.21)
$$1 = 234 \qquad 2 = 134 \qquad 3 = 124 \qquad 4 = 123$$
$$12 = 34 \qquad 13 = 24 \qquad 14 = 23 \qquad 0 = 1234$$

TABLE 31.4   **Abbreviated ANOVA Table for Fractional Factorial Design in Table 31.3b.**

Source of Variation	df
$X_0 = X_{1234}$	1
$X_1 = X_{234}$	1
$X_2 = X_{134}$	1
$X_3 = X_{124}$	1
$X_4 = X_{123}$	1
$X_{12} = X_{34}$	1
$X_{13} = X_{24}$	1
$X_{14} = X_{23}$	1
Error	0
Total	8

We see that main effects are now confounded only with three-factor interactions and that two-factor interactions are confounded with other two-factor interactions, while the four-factor interaction is confounded with the overall mean. If three-factor and four-factor interactions are negligible, this design could be quite useful. In that case, if $\beta_1 + \beta_{234}$ were found to be statistically significant, we could safely conclude that the observed effect is due to factor 1 and not to the three-factor interaction among factors 2, 3, and 4.

A potential drawback of the design in Table 31.3b is that the two-factor interactions are confounded with other two-factor interactions. If any effects associated with two-factor interactions turn out to be active, additional experimental trials will be required to separate these effects.

An abbreviated ANOVA table for the fractional factorial design in Table 31.3b showing only source of variation and degrees of freedom is given in Table 31.4. Notice that only eight factor effect coefficients can be estimated, corresponding to the eight confounded pairs of effects. Since no degrees of freedom are available for estimation of σ^2, the tools described in Section 31.2 for the analysis of unreplicated factorial studies need to be employed for the analysis of factor effects.

Defining Relation

In our explanation of confounding, we began with a full factorial design, arbitrarily dropped some treatments from the experiment, and then examined whether the choice of the dropped treatments was a good one by considering the confounding scheme of the resulting fractional factorial design. Finding an appropriate fractional factorial design is actually done in reverse order by first specifying an acceptable confounding scheme. In order to proceed from this specification to find the corresponding fractional factorial design, we need to utilize the defining relation of the confounding scheme.

Consider again the fractional factorial design in Table 31.3b. The defining relation for this design is the correspondence in (31.21) involving the X_0 column:

$$(31.22) \qquad\qquad 0 = 1234$$

Recall that (31.22) is a shorthand stating that the X_0 column equals the X_{1234} column. Hence, $X_{i0} = X_{i1234}$ for all column entries. The confounding scheme for the design can be determined from this defining relation by multiplying the column on each side of the defining relation by successive columns of the **X** matrix, the multiplication being carried out term by term.

Since all column entries for a two-level factorial design are either 1 or -1, some general column multiplication results are useful.

1. When multiplying the X_0 column by the X_0 column (the resulting column entries being $X_{i0}X_{i0}$), all entries remain 1 since $X_{i0} \equiv 1$ and $(1)^2 = 1$. We state this in the following fashion:

(31.23)
$$0 \times 0 = 0^2 = 0$$

2. Multiplying any column X_q by X_0 (the resulting column entries being $X_{i0}X_{iq}$) leaves the column entries unchanged because $X_{i0} \equiv 1$:

(31.24)
$$0 \times q = q$$

3. Multiplying any column by itself (the resulting column entries being $X_{iq}X_{iq}$) yields the X_0 column since $(1)^2 = (-1)^2 = 1$:

(31.25)
$$q \times q = q^2 = 0$$

Returning now to the defining relation in (31.22), let us multiply the columns on both sides of the defining relation by the X_1 column. On the left side we obtain by (31.24):

(31.26)
$$1 \times 0 = 1$$

and on the right side we find:

(31.27)
$$1 \times 1234 = 1^2 234 = 0234 = 234$$

The result in (31.27) follows because we obtain for each column entry:

$$X_{i1}X_{i1234} = X_{i1}(X_{i1}X_{i2}X_{i3}X_{i4}) = X_{i1}^2 X_{i2}X_{i3}X_{i4} = X_{i2}X_{i3}X_{i4}$$

Combining the results in (31.26) and (31.27), we have found:

(31.28a)
$$1 \times 0 = 1 = 1 \times 1234 = 234 \qquad (1 = 234)$$

Continuing the process of multiplying both sides of (31.22) by successive columns of the **X** matrix we find:

(31.28b)
$$
\begin{aligned}
2 \times 0 &= 2 \times 1234 = 12^2 34 = 134 & (2 &= 134)\\
3 \times 0 &= 3 \times 1234 = 123^2 4 = 124 & (3 &= 124)\\
4 \times 0 &= 4 \times 1234 = 1234^2 = 123 & (4 &= 123)\\
12 \times 0 &= 12 \times 1234 = 1^2 2^2 34 = 34 & (12 &= 34)\\
13 \times 0 &= 13 \times 1234 = 1^2 23^2 4 = 24 & (13 &= 24)\\
14 \times 0 &= 14 \times 1234 = 1^2 234^2 = 23 & (14 &= 23)
\end{aligned}
$$

We stop at this point because multiplication by succeeding columns will yield no new confounding relations.

Notice that the operations in (31.28a) and (31.28b) have reproduced the complete confounding scheme in (31.21). The relation on which these operations were based, $0 = 1234$, is called the *defining relation*. The defining relation is always the one that shows the equality with the X_0 column.

Half-Fraction Designs

Once the desired defining relation (and hence, the confounding scheme) is specified, the fractional factorial design corresponding to the desired confounding scheme can be constructed in the following manner:

Step 1.   Construct the **X** matrix for the full factorial design.

Step 2.   Choose those rows (treatments) for which the defining relation holds.

To illustrate the use of this procedure, consider again the Pecos Foods Corporation example in Table 31.2. The desired defining relation is that in (31.22), namely, $0 = 1234$. Hence, we need to select those treatments for which $X_{i1234} = X_{i0}$. We see from Table 31.2 that $X_{i1234} = 1$ for treatments 1, 4, 6, 7, 10, 11, 13, 16. This is the design in Table 31.3b. It is called a 2^{4-1} fractional factorial design. As noted before, the 4 in the exponent refers to the number of factors. The 1 indicates the level of fractionation; here the full factorial design was fractionated one time. In general, we shall refer to a 2^{k-f} fractional factorial design, where k denotes the number of factors and f the fraction.

An equally useful half-fraction design can be constructed from the eight treatments that were omitted (2, 3, 5, 8, 9, 12, 14, 15). Notice from Table 31.2 that $X_{i0} = -X_{i1234}$ for these treatments. The defining relation for this alternate half-fraction design is therefore:

$$(31.29) \qquad\qquad 0 = -1234$$

It is easy to verify that the complete confounding scheme for this design is:

$$(31.30) \quad \begin{array}{cccc} 1 = -234 & 2 = -134 & 3 = -124 & 4 = -123 \\ 12 = -34 & 13 = -24 & 14 = -23 & 0 = -1234 \end{array}$$

We see that confounding scheme (31.30) for the omitted treatments is the same as that of the retained treatments in (31.28) except that the sign of the second term has changed. Statistically, both of these half-fractions provide similar information, and either one can be used. The choice is sometimes based on the investigator's desire to include one or more specific treatments in the experiment. For example, when the treatment consisting of all runs at the first level (-1) is the control treatment, the investigator who wishes to include this treatment would select the half-fraction corresponding to the defining relation $0 = 1234$.

Note

The identification of the treatments to be included in a 2^{k-f} fractional factorial design can be carried out without first constructing the **X** matrix for the full 2^k factorial study. The use of *design generators* permits the construction of a 2^{k-f} fractional factorial design by constructing the **X** matrix for a full factorial study in only $k - f$ factors and then augmenting this matrix. Details are provided in Reference 31.1.   ∎

TABLE 31.5   **Quarter-Fraction Design of 2^4 Full Factorial Design in Table 31.2, Based on Defining Relation: *0 = 1234 = 12 = 34*—Pecos Foods Corporation Example.**

Treat-ment	X_0	X_1	X_2	X_3	X_4	X_{12}	X_{13}	X_{14}	X_{23}	X_{24}	X_{34}	X_{123}	X_{124}	X_{134}	X_{234}	X_{1234}
1	1	−1	−1	−1	−1	1	1	1	1	1	1	−1	−1	−1	−1	1
4	1	1	1	−1	−1	1	−1	−1	−1	−1	1	−1	−1	1	1	1
13	1	−1	−1	1	1	1	−1	−1	−1	−1	1	1	1	−1	−1	1
16	1	1	1	1	1	1	1	1	1	1	1	1	1	1	1	1

Quarter-Fraction and Smaller-Fraction Designs

When the number of factors is large, the number of treatments in even a one-half fraction design may still be prohibitively large. In such cases, smaller fractions may be obtained by continuing the process of fractionation. For example, in the Pecos Foods Corporation example, a single replication of a full factorial study involves $2^4 = 16$ experimental trials and a half-fraction design involves $2^{4-1} = 8$ trials. A single replication of a quarter-fraction design will involve only $2^{4-2} = 4$ trials and an eighth-fraction design will consist of $2^{4-3} = 2$ trials. We shall now describe the construction and analysis of 2^{k-f} fractional factorial designs. The number of treatments in such a design is 2^{k-f}.

We shall illustrate how to obtain the confounding scheme for a quarter-fraction design by returning to the Pecos Foods Corporation example in Table 31.3b, where the half-fraction design is based on the defining relation *0 = 1234*. Let us fractionate this design in half by using the defining relation *0 = 12*. From Table 31.3b, we see that $X_{i12} = X_{i0} = 1$ for treatments 1, 4, 13, 16. The **X** matrix for this new quarter-fraction design is given in Table 31.5. Notice that the confounding of effects has become quite severe. From an inspection of the columns of the **X** matrix, we find that the complete confounding scheme is:

$$0 = 1234 = 12 = 34 \qquad \text{(defining relation)}$$

$$1 = 234 = 2 = 134$$

$$3 = 124 = 123 = 4$$

$$13 = 24 = 23 = 14$$

Since main effects are confounded with each other (1 with 2, and 3 with 4) this design is clearly undesirable.

As in the case of a half-fraction design, the confounding scheme for a quarter-fraction design can be determined directly without constructing the **X** matrix. We begin with the half-fraction defining relation:

(31.31a) $$0 = 1234$$

We then augment this with the defining relation for the second fractionation:

(31.31b) $$0 = 1234 = 12$$

Finally, we need to add a term to recognize that the X_{34} column is also equal to the X_{1234} and X_{12} columns:

(31.31c) $$0 = 1234 = 12 = 34$$

34 is called the *generalized interaction*. It can be automatically identified by multiplying the two interaction columns X_{1234} and X_{12} in the augmented defining relation in (31.31b):

$$1234 \times 12 = 1^2 2^2 34 = 34$$

In general, for a 2^{k-f} fractional factorial design, there are 2^f terms in the defining relation. These consist of:

1. The constant term, *0*.

2. The f interaction terms used to define the f successive fractionations.

3. The $2^f - f - 1$ generalized interactions, constructed from the cross products involving pairs, triples, and so on, of the f interaction terms used to define the f successive fractionations. Since there are 2^f terms in the defining relation for a 2^{k-f} fractional factorial design, we see that each factor effect is confounded with $2^f - 1$ other factor effects.

Once the defining relation has been obtained for a 2^{k-f} design, the complete confounding scheme can be found by multiplying all terms in the defining relation successively by the main effect and interaction columns in the **X** matrix.

Example.   A two-level, five-factor experiment is to be fractionated, first on the basis of the relation:

(31.32a) $$0 = 124$$

and a second time using:

(31.32b) $$0 = -135$$

We shall now determine the complete confounding scheme for the experiment. Combining (31.32a) and (31.32b), we obtain:

$$0 = 124 = -135$$

The generalized interaction is therefore:

$$124 \times -135 = -1^2 2345 = -2345$$

The defining relation consequently is:

(31.33) $$0 = 124 = -135 = -2345$$

The complete confounding scheme is determined by multiplying the terms in (31.33) successively by each of the $2^5 - 1 = 31$ main effect and interaction columns. For example:

$$1 \times 0 = 1 \times 124 = 1 \times -135 = 1 \times -2345 \quad \text{or} \quad 1 = 24 = -35 = -12345$$

In summary we find (omitting any redundant entries):

$$0 = 124 = -135 = -2345$$
$$1 = 24 = -35 = -12345$$
$$2 = 14 = -1235 = -345$$
$$3 = 1234 = -15 = -245$$
$$4 = 12 = -1345 = -235$$
$$5 = 1245 = -13 = -234$$
$$23 = 134 = -125 = -45$$
$$34 = 123 = -145 = -25$$

The eight treatments to be included in this fractional factorial design are those for which $X_{i124} = 1$, $X_{i135} = -1$, and $X_{i2345} = -1$ simultaneously.

Resolution

The resolution of a two-level fractional factorial design, denoted by R, is the number of factors involved in the lowest-order effect in the defining relation, excluding the constant term (0). This is a critical characteristic of a design because it indicates the severity of the confounding scheme. For instance, recall that the defining relation of the 2^{4-1} fractional factorial design of Table 31.3b is:

$$0 = 1234$$

The resolution of this half-fraction design is $R = 4$ because there are four factors involved in the term *1234*. The resolution $R = 4$ tells us that the most severe cases of confounding will involve:

1. A main effect and a three-factor interaction (e.g., $1 = 234$)

2. A two-factor interaction and another two-factor interaction (e.g., $12 = 34$)

Roman numerals are commonly used to denote the resolution to avoid confusion with the number of factors. We characterize the design in Table 31.3b as a 2^{4-1}_{IV} fractional factorial design to indicate that it has resolution $R = IV$.

In general, the higher is the resolution of a design, the less severe is the degree of confounding. The resolution should never be less than III. In a resolution II design, at least one pair of main effects will be confounded together. For example, consider the 2^{5-2}_{II} quarter-fraction design with defining relation:

(31.34)
$$0 = 123 = 45 = 12345$$

Since the lowest order effect in this defining relation is *45*, the design has resolution II. Here the factor 4 main effect is confounded with the factor 5 main effect ($4 = 5$), which is clearly most undesirable. Fractional factorial designs of resolution III, IV, and V are most commonly used. The relationship between resolution and degree of confounding for these three classes of designs can be summarized as follows:

Design Resolution	Worst-Case Degree of Confounding
III	Some main effects are confounded with two-factor interactions.
IV	Some main effects are confounded with three-factor interactions. Some two-factor interactions are confounded with other two-factor interactions.
V	Some main effects are confounded with four-factor interactions. Some two-factor interactions are confounded with three-factor interactions.

Projection Property.   A useful property of fractional factorial designs is that any design of resolution R contains complete factorial designs in any subset of $R-1$ factors. For example, consider the resolution IV half-fraction design in Table 31.3b. Note that if we were to drop the fourth factor, for instance, a full factorial eight-run design would result for the first three factors. This has important design implications. Suppose that an experimenter expects that at most three of the five factors in a study will turn out to be active. By choosing a fractional design with resolution IV, the experimenter will be assured that once the inactive factors are identified and dropped from the analysis, the experimental design for the remaining active factors will be a full factorial design with no confounding.

Selecting a Fraction of Highest Resolution

Clearly, it is desirable that a defining relation be chosen so that the resolution of the design is as large as possible. For half-fraction designs, this is easy: equate the highest-order interaction column with the X_0 column. For example, to provide the maximum resolution (V) in a five-factor study, set the defining relation as follows:

$$0 = 12345$$

In general, the resulting resolution is equal to the number of factors in the study.

For quarter replicates, eighth replicates, and so on, identifying the defining relation that yields the maximum resolution is not so simple. For example, consider the choice of a defining relation for a 2^{6-2} design. If we fractionate first on the basis of:

$$0 = 123456$$

the highest resolution possible will be III:

$$0 = 123456 = 123 = 456$$

However, an alternative defining relation leads to a resolution IV design:

$$0 = 1235 = 2346 = 1456$$

This is, in fact, the highest possible resolution in a 2^{6-2} fractional factorial design.

The 2^{k-f} fractional factorial designs that have highest resolution have been identified and catalogued for choices of k and f that are of general interest (Ref. 31.1). Table 31.6 lists the defining relations for these designs for $3 \leq k \leq 9$; the generalized interactions

TABLE 31.6   Two-Level Fractional Factorial Designs with Maximum Resolution for Three to Nine Factors.

Number of Factors	Fraction	Number of Runs	Defining Relation (omitting generalized interactions)
3	2_{III}^{3-1}	4	$0 = 123$
4	2_{IV}^{4-1}	8	$0 = 1234$
5	2_{V}^{5-1}	16	$0 = 12345$
	2_{III}^{5-2}	8	$0 = 124 = 135$
6	2_{VI}^{6-1}	32	$0 = 123456$
	2_{IV}^{6-2}	16	$0 = 1235 = 2346$
	2_{III}^{6-3}	8	$0 = 124 = 135 = 236$
7	2_{VII}^{7-1}	64	$0 = 1234567$
	2_{IV}^{7-2}	32	$0 = 12346 = 12457$
	2_{IV}^{7-3}	16	$0 = 1235 = 2346 = 1347$
	2_{III}^{7-4}	8	$0 = 124 = 135 = 236 = 1237$
8	2_{V}^{8-2}	64	$0 = 12347 = 12568$
	2_{IV}^{8-3}	32	$0 = 1236 = 1247 = 23458$
	2_{IV}^{8-4}	16	$0 = 2345 = 1346 = 1237 = 1248$
9	2_{VI}^{9-2}	128	$0 = 134678 = 235679$
	2_{IV}^{9-3}	64	$0 = 12347 = 13568 = 34569$
	2_{IV}^{9-4}	32	$0 = 23456 = 13457 = 12458 = 12359$
	2_{III}^{9-5}	16	$0 = 1235 = 2346 = 1347 = 1248 = 12349$

have been omitted in this listing for the sake of brevity. A number of software packages also will construct fractional factorial designs with highest possible resolution for specified numbers of factors and experimental trials. Most of these packages construct fractional factorial designs employing the defining relations in Table 31.6.

Example

The Iowa Aluminum Corporation manufactures sheet aluminum from recycled aluminum beverage containers. The manufacturing process first casts molten aluminum onto a conveyor belt in a continuous strip. The strip is then sprayed with a coolant comprised of a mixture of water and oil as it enters each of three mills. After the processing in the third mill, the strip is automatically coiled and packaged for shipping. The surface of the aluminum sheets must be sufficiently clean and free of defects or the product will not be shipped. Historically, the rejection rate was about 25 percent.

FIGURE 31.8 **MINITAB Fractional Factorial Design Summary—Iowa Aluminum Corporation Example.**

```
Fractional Factorial Design

Factors:   6    Design:      6, 16    Resolution: IV
Runs:      16   Replicates:     1     Fraction: 1/4
Blocks: none    Center points:  0

Design Generators:  E = ABC   F = BCD

Alias Structure

I + ABCE + ADEF + BCDF

A + BCE + DEF + ABCDF
B + ACE + CDF + ABDEF
C + ABE + BDF + ACDEF
D + AEF + BCF + ABCDE
E + ABC + ADF + BCDEF
F + ADE + BCD + ABCEF
AB + CE + ACDF + BDEF
AC + BE + ABDF + CDEF
AD + EF + ABCF + BCDE
AE + BC + DF + ABCDEF
AF + DE + ABCD + BCEF
BD + CF + ABEF + ACDE
BF + CD + ABDE + ACEF
ABD + ACF + BEF + CDE
ABF + ACD + BDE + CEF
```

In an effort to reduce the percentage of rejected coils, an experimental study was undertaken. Management committed two days of production to the experiment, which permitted about 20 experimental trials. Six factors that might affect the quality of the aluminum were identified: (1) temperature of the coolant; (2) percentage of oil in coolant; (3, 4, 5) volume of coolant applied to the strip at each of the three mills (as a percentage of full volume); and (6) strip speed. Low and high limits for each of the factors were identified for the two-level six-factor experiment. Since a 2^6 experiment involves 64 factor level combinations or treatments and since only about 20 experimental trials were feasible, a one-quarter fractional factorial design was needed.

Figure 31.8 contains a summary of the one-quarter fraction design for the two-level six-factor experiment provided by the MINITAB Fractional Factorial procedure. We see that a resolution IV design is the highest-resolution design that can be attained in a 16-run, six-factor fractional factorial study. For this resolution, we know that all main effects are clear of other main effects and two-factor interactions and that some main effects will be confounded with three-factor interactions. Also, some two-factor interactions will be confounded with other two-factor interactions. The complete confounding scheme is shown in Figure 31.8, where the factors are denoted A through F (instead of *1* through *6*) and the symbol I is used (instead of *0*) to denote the constant term. Also, MINITAB uses the format in (31.20) to represent the confounding scheme. For example, the defining relation is listed by MINITAB as:

$$I + ABCE + ADEF + BCDF$$

In our representation, the defining relation is expressed as follows:

$$0 = 1235 = 1456 = 2346$$

TABLE 31.7   **Experimental Design Matrix and Y Observations—Iowa Aluminum Corporation Example.**

	Design Matrix						
Treatment	Coolant Temperature X_1	Oil Percentage X_2	Coolant Volume 1 X_3	Coolant Volume 2 X_4	Coolant Volume 3 X_5	Strip Speed X_6	Impurity Score Y
1	−1	−1	−1	−1	−1	−1	4
2	1	−1	−1	−1	1	−1	6
3	−1	1	−1	−1	1	1	7
4	1	1	−1	−1	−1	1	2
5	−1	−1	1	−1	1	1	3
6	1	−1	1	−1	−1	1	1
7	−1	1	1	−1	−1	−1	5
8	1	1	1	−1	1	−1	9
9	−1	−1	−1	1	−1	1	3
10	1	−1	−1	1	1	1	2
11	−1	1	−1	1	1	−1	8
12	1	1	−1	1	−1	−1	5
13	−1	−1	1	1	1	−1	4
14	1	−1	1	1	−1	−1	4
15	−1	1	1	1	−1	1	4
16	1	1	1	1	1	1	6
17	0	0	0	0	0	0	3
18	0	0	0	0	0	0	5
19	0	0	0	0	0	0	4
20	0	0	0	0	0	0	6

Management was willing to assume that all three-factor interactions would be quite small in relation to main effects and two-factor interactions. It also recognized that if important two-factor interactions are found to be present, it may be necessary to conduct additional experimental trials to separate confounded interaction effects. Management therefore decided to use the fractional factorial design in Figure 31.8, with four replications added at the center point to provide a rough estimate of the error variance and a test of the fit of the model.

Table 31.7 contains the design matrix for the MINITAB fractional factorial design augmented by four replications at the center point. In the right column are shown the results of the experiment. The response of interest is the surface impurity score, where surface impurities are rated on a 0–10 scale (0 = no impurity, 10 = high impurity). The MINITAB output for an initial factorial ANOVA fit is shown in Figure 31.9. Because four replications at the center point were made, an estimate of σ^2 is available. From an initial inspection of the absolute size of the factor effect coefficients and their associated P-values, it appears that the active effects are main effects for oil percentage, coolant volume 3, and strip speed, and the two-factor interaction between coolant temperature and coolant volume 1 (which is confounded with the two-factor interaction between oil percentage and coolant volume 3).

Since this study was exploratory in nature, a new model was developed in which only the factor effects identified as active (X_2, X_5, X_6, $X_{13} = X_{25}$) are retained. An ANOVA model

FIGURE 31.9   MINITAB Fractional Factorial Output for Initial Model—Iowa Aluminum Corporation Example.

```
Estimated Effects and Coefficients for Defects

Term                         Effect     Coef  Std Coef t-value      P
Constant                               4.550    0.2503   18.18  0.000
Cooltemp                     -0.375   -0.187    0.2799   -0.67  0.540
Oilpct                        2.375    1.187    0.2799    4.24  0.013
Coolvol1                     -0.125   -0.062    0.2799   -0.22  0.834
Coolvol2                     -0.125   -0.062    0.2799   -0.22  0.834
Coolvol3                      2.125    1.062    0.2799    3.80  0.019
Stripspd                     -2.125   -1.062    0.2799   -3.80  0.019
Cooltemp*Oilpct              -0.125   -0.062    0.2799   -0.22  0.834
Cooltemp*Coolvol1             1.375    0.687    0.2799    2.46  0.070
Cooltemp*Coolvol2            -0.125   -0.062    0.2799   -0.22  0.834
Cooltemp*Coolvol3             0.625    0.312    0.2799    1.12  0.327
Cooltemp*Stripspd            -1.125   -0.563    0.2799   -2.01  0.115
Oilpct*Coolvol2               0.125    0.062    0.2799    0.22  0.834
Oilpct*Stripspd               0.125    0.062    0.2799    0.22  0.834
Cooltemp*Oilpct*Coolvol2      0.125    0.062    0.2799    0.22  0.834
Cooltemp*Oilpct*Stripspd      0.125    0.062    0.2799    0.22  0.834


Analysis of Variance for Defects

Source               DF    Seq SS    Adj SS    Adj MS      F      P
Main Effects          6   59.3750   59.3750   9.89583   7.90  0.033
2-Way Interactions    7   14.4375   14.4375   2.06250   1.65  0.330
3-Way Interactions    2    0.1250    0.1250   0.06250   0.05  0.952
Residual Error        4    5.0125    5.0125   1.25312
  Curvature           1    0.0125    0.0125   0.01250   0.01  0.936
  Pure Error          3    5.0000    5.0000   1.66667
Total                19   78.9500
```

containing the three main effects and one interaction effect was fitted. Residual analysis (not shown) did not reveal any serious departures from the model assumptions. Figure 31.10 contains the MINITAB output for a regression fit of the revised ANOVA model. Note that the lack of fit statistic is shown, $F^* = MSLF/MSPE = .04$, for which the P-value is .9958. Hence, the fit of the revised model appears to be good. We see from the ANOVA output that the statistical significance of the estimated factor effect coefficients b_2, b_5, b_6, and $b_{13} + b_{25}$ is confirmed.

We turn now to the interpretation of the experimental results. Because the 13 and 25 interaction terms are confounded, the source of this effect cannot be determined on the basis of the experimental results. Notice, however, that both the factor 2 and factor 5 main effects were identified as active and that neither the factor 1 nor the factor 3 main effects were statistically significant. These results suggest (but do not prove) that the observed effect is likely due to the 25 interaction. To investigate this further, a small follow-up 2×2 factorial experiment was run involving only factors 1 and 3. No 13 interaction effect was found, and it was therefore concluded that the $\beta_{13} + \beta_{25}$ confounded interaction effect in the original experiment is due to the β_{25} interaction effect.

The results of the experiment are summarized in Figure 31.11 by a main effects plot for factor 6 (strip speed) and an interactions plot for factors 2 (oil percentage) and 5 (coolant volume 3). The results can be qualitatively summarized as follows:

1. Figure 31.11a shows that increasing strip speed decreases observed surface impurities. Strip speed should therefore be set at its high level ($X_6 = 1$).

2. Figure 31.11b shows that when oil percentage is at its high level, increasing coolant volume 3 increases surface impurities. When oil percentage is at its low level, increasing

FIGURE 31.10   MINITAB Fractional Factorial Regression Output for Revised Model—Iowa Aluminum Corporation Example.

```
The regression equation is
Defects = 4.55 + 1.19 Oilpct + 1.06 Coolvol3 - 1.06 Stripspd + 0.687 Tmp*vol1

Predictor        Coef      Stdev     t-ratio       p
Constant       4.5500     0.2058       22.11    0.000
Oilpct         1.1875     0.2300        5.16    0.000
Coolvol3       1.0625     0.2300        4.62    0.000
Stripspd      -1.0625     0.2300       -4.62    0.000
Tmp*vol1       0.6875     0.2300        2.99    0.009

s = 0.9201      R-sq = 83.9%    R-sq(adj) = 79.6%

Analysis of Variance

SOURCE         DF         SS          MS        F        p
Regression      4     66.250      16.562    19.56    0.000
Error          15     12.700       0.847
Total          19     78.950

SOURCE         DF     SEQ SS
Oilpct          1     22.562
Coolvol3        1     18.062
Stripspd        1     18.062
Tmp*vol1        1      7.563


     Fit   Stdev.Fit      95.0% C.I.          95.0% P.I.
   1.925       0.504   (  0.851,   2.999)  ( -0.312,   4.162)


Pure error test - F = 0.04  P = 0.9958  DF(pure error) = 11
```

FIGURE 31.11   Main Effect and Interactions Plots—Iowa Aluminum Corporation Example.

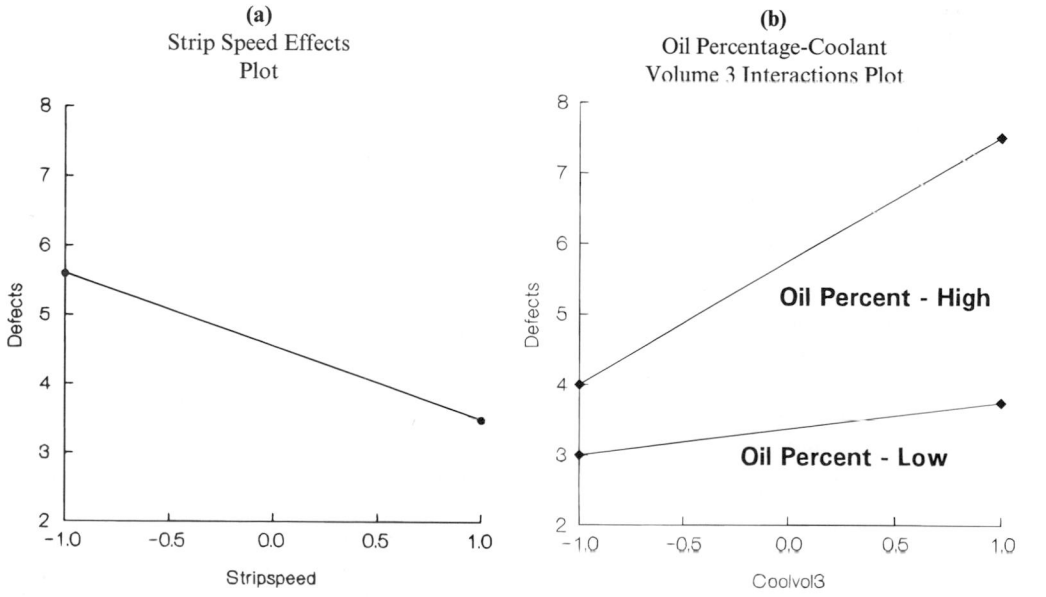

coolant volume 3 has relatively little effect on surface impurities. We also see that increasing the oil percentage increases surface impurities; the effect is particularly strong when coolant volume 3 is at its high level. Thus, both oil percentage and coolant volume 3 should be set at their low levels ($X_2 = -1$ and $X_5 = -1$).

We can predict the mean impurity level produced by the process at the optimum (coded) settings of the control variables:

$$X_2 = \text{Oil percentage } = -1$$
(31.35)
$$X_5 = \text{Coolant volume 3} = -1$$
$$X_6 = \text{Strip speed } = 1$$

by using the fitted regression model equivalent to the final ANOVA model in Figure 31.10:

(31.36) $$\hat{Y} = 4.5500 + 1.1875X_2 + 1.0625X_5 - 1.0625X_6 + .6875X_{25}$$

The estimated impurity response for process setting (31.35) is:

$$\hat{Y}_h = 4.5500 + 1.1875(-1) + 1.0625(-1) - 1.0625(1) + .6875(-1)(-1) = 1.925$$

A confirmation run at the optimum setting can be carried out to assess the validity of the estimated regression function. The validity is supported if the new response falls inside the $1 - \alpha$ prediction limits (6.63). The 95 percent limits turn out to be (see Figure 31.10):

$$-.312 \leq Y_{h(\text{new})} \leq 4.162$$

Since the impurity response cannot be negative, the prediction limits should be modified as follows:

$$0 \leq Y_{h(\text{new})} \leq 4.162$$

A new response at the optimum levels less than 4.162 will be consistent with the model's prediction.

31.4   Screening Experiments

In the early stages of an investigation, it is not uncommon for investigators to identify a large number of potential explanatory variables. Unfortunately, the number of model terms required for a large number of factors becomes enormous. For example, in a manufacturing process optimization study, a brainstorming session involving manufacturing engineers, product development scientists, and line operators resulted in the identification of 28 potentially important factors. In addition to 28 parameters for main effects, there would be $28(27)/2 = 378$ parameters for two-factor interactions, $28(27)(26)/2(3) = 3{,}276$ parameters for three-factor interactions, and there would be many additional parameters for higher-order interactions. Even an investigation of just the main effects and two-factor interactions for 28 factors by use of a resolution IV or a resolution V fractional factorial design would be impossible here.

For these circumstances, screening designs are useful. With these designs, the objective is simply to identify the set of active factors. No information about interactions or curvature is typically obtained. In this section, we shall discuss the use of resolution III fractional factorial designs and Plackett-Burman designs for the purpose of screening large numbers of factors.

2_{III}^{k-f} *Fractional Factorial Designs*

Recall that in a resolution III fractional factorial design, main effects are confounded with two-factor interactions. If it can be assumed that first-order interactions are small relative to the main effects, then a resolution III design can be used to identify the active factors.

As a simple example, consider a study of three factors, each at two levels, to be conducted with four experimental trials. A half-fraction of highest resolution is obtained by fractionating the 2^3 factorial on the basis of the defining relation:

$$0 = 123$$

The confounding scheme is therefore:

$$1 = 23$$
$$2 = 13$$
$$3 = 12$$

If it can be safely assumed that the two-factor interactions 12, 13, and 23 are small in relation to the main effects 1, 2, and 3, then this half-fraction design can be used for identifying the set of active factors.

The use of resolution III designs for initial screening is typically followed by one or more experiments involving those factors that are identified as important. For example, a 10-factor, resolution III experiment (2_{III}^{10-6}) involving 16 experimental trials was used to study the effects of six process variables and four ingredient variables on the extent of crystallization in ice cream. Three factors were identified as important. The interactions among these three factors were then studied in a follow-up 2^3 factorial experiment.

Note

Any resolution III fractional factorial design can be augmented by a second fraction of the same size to yield a new design of resolution IV or higher. The design matrix for the second fraction is obtained from that for the first fraction by simply reversing all signs. This process is sometimes called *folding over* the first fraction, and the resulting, combined design is sometimes referred to as a *foldover* design. ∎

Plackett-Burman Designs

One limitation of resolution III fractional factorial designs is the requirement that the number of treatment combinations be a power of 2. The total experimental trials must therefore be 4, 8, 16, 32, 64, and so on. Plackett-Burman designs are two-level, resolution III designs that can be used for studying up to $n_T - 1$ factors in n_T experimental trials, where n_T is a multiple of 4. Valid run sizes for Plackett-Burman designs are therefore 4, 8, 12, 16, 20, and so on. Plackett-Burman designs for $n_T \leq 100$ are given (with the exception $n_T = 92$) in Reference 31.2. When n_T is a power of 2, the Plackett-Burman designs correspond to the resolution III fractional factorial designs already discussed. When n_T is not a power of 2, the confounding structure of the Plackett-Burman designs is very complicated. Plackett-Burman designs are available in many statistical software packages that provide capabilities for the design of experiments.

The analysis of Plackett-Burman designs is carried out in the same manner as for fractional factorial designs. Since these designs are usually run in a single replication, the various graphical procedures discussed in Section 31.2 can be used to identify active effects. Center point replications can also be added to provide an estimate of the error variance σ^2 and a test for lack of fit.

31.5   Incomplete Block Designs for Two-Level Factorial Experiments

When we considered randomized complete block designs in Chapter 27, we noted that each block consists of one or more complete replications of the experiment. Blocks are chosen so that the experimental units within a block are homogeneous while they differ from block to block. When the number of treatments is large, it may be difficult to find blocks of sufficient size that still contain homogeneous units. For example, if a block is a mold of four plastic parts, an experiment with eight treatments cannot be run using a mold as a complete block. However, an incomplete block design can be used here, with one-half of the treatments placed in one mold and the other four treatments in a second mold. Incomplete block designs are frequently required in factorial studies with a large number of factors. In this section, we discuss the use incomplete block designs in two-level factorial experiments. The only restriction is that the incomplete block size must be a power of 2. We shall start with an example for purposes of illustration.

Example

Steichen Bakeries was developing a partially baked french bread for national distribution. A study was undertaken to investigate the effects of proofing time, proofing temperature, baking time, and baking temperature on the volume and texture of the final product. A two-level, four-factor experiment was under consideration, involving 16 treatments. The production facility could produce from 8 to 10 batches of bread in a given day. Since ambient temperature and humidity in the plant can change significantly from day to day, blocking by day was considered to be important. Hence, an incomplete block design was required such that the 16 treatments are placed into two blocks of size eight. We will now consider how to place the 16 treatments into two blocks.

Assignment of Treatments to Blocks

The design matrix for the 2^4 full factorial study in the Steichen Bakeries example is shown in Table 31.8a. Suppose that the treatments are allocated to blocks in accordance with the level of the 1234 interaction column (X_{1234}). That is, all treatments for which $X_{1234} = -1$ are allocated to block 1 (day 1), and all treatments for which $X_{1234} = 1$ are assigned to block 2 (day 2). With this arrangement, it can be seen that the block effect (i.e., the day effect) will be completely confounded with the four-factor interaction effect. We thus forfeit the ability to obtain an estimate of the four-factor interaction effect β_{1234} that is free of block (day) effects. However, estimates of all main effects, two-factor interactions, and three-factor interactions will be independent of the block effect.

The blocking arrangement chosen by confounding the block effect with the 1234 interaction effect is displayed in Table 31.8a. Notice that each of the four factors appears four times at its low level and four times at its high level within each block. Thus, if ambient temperature is exceptionally high on day 1, causing the loaves of bread baked on that day to have volumes that are larger than usual, this effect will not bias the estimates of any of the

TABLE 31.8   Blocking Arrangements—Steichen Bakeries Example.

(a) 2^4 Experiment in Two Blocks

Block (Day)	Treatment	Proofing Time X_1	Proofing Temperature X_2	Baking Time X_3	Baking Temperature X_4
1	1	1	−1	−1	−1
1	2	−1	1	−1	−1
1	3	−1	−1	1	−1
1	4	1	1	1	−1
1	5	−1	−1	−1	1
1	6	1	1	−1	1
1	7	1	−1	1	1
1	8	−1	1	1	1
2	9	−1	−1	−1	−1
2	10	1	1	−1	−1
2	11	1	−1	1	−1
2	12	−1	1	1	−1
2	13	1	−1	−1	1
2	14	−1	1	−1	1
2	15	−1	−1	1	1
2	16	1	1	1	1

(b) 2^4 Experiment in Four Blocks

Block (Day)	Treatment	Proofing Time X_1	Proofing Temperature X_2	Baking Time X_3	Baking Temperature X_4
1	1	1	1	−1	−1
1	2	−1	−1	1	−1
1	3	−1	1	−1	1
1	4	1	−1	1	1
2	5	−1	−1	−1	−1
2	6	1	1	1	−1
2	7	1	−1	−1	1
2	8	−1	1	1	1
3	9	−1	1	−1	−1
3	10	1	−1	1	−1
3	11	1	1	−1	1
3	12	−1	−1	1	1
4	13	1	−1	−1	−1
4	14	−1	1	1	−1
4	15	−1	−1	−1	1
4	16	1	1	1	1

main effects. It can be verified that the same balance of high and low levels (1s and -1s) within each block is also present for all interaction columns except for the X_{1234} column.

The analysis of the experiment is identical to that of a full 2^4 factorial study. The only difference concerns the interpretation of results, where it must be remembered that the four-factor interaction effect is confounded with the block (day) effect.

In general, blocking of factorial and fractional factorial designs is accomplished by confounding block effects with carefully chosen, high-order interaction effects. The division of treatments into blocks is performed in three steps:

Step 1.   Identify the high-order interaction effects to be confounded with the block effects. If the number of desired blocks is $b = 2^v$, v interaction effects need to be identified.

Step 2.   Construct the v columns of the X matrix that correspond to the interaction effects chosen. The patterns of 1s and -1s in these columns are used to identify the blocks.

Step 3.   The v interaction effects chosen, along with their generalized interactions, are confounded with the block effects. In all, $b - 1$ effects are so confounded.

In effect, this procedure fractionates the chosen design v times, and the 2^v resulting fractions define the divisions of treatments into blocks. This will result in 2^v blocks of size 2^{k-v}, in the case of a full factorial study, or 2^v blocks of size 2^{k-f-v} in the case of a 2^{k-f} fractional factorial study.

As when constructing fractional factorial designs, the v interactions selected to define the blocks must be carefully chosen so that, to the greatest extent possible, low-order effects remain clear of block effects. Useful blocking arrangements have been catalogued (Ref. 31.1). They are also usually provided by statistical software packages that have capabilities for the design of experiments.

Example.   In the Steichen Bakeries example, the investigator wished to run the 2^4 factorial study in four blocks. Here, the number of blocks is $b = 4 = 2^v$, so that $v = 2$. Thus, two higher-order interaction effects that are to be confounded with block effects need to be chosen for identifying the treatments assigned to the blocks. The investigator chose interactions 23 and 124. The treatments were then assigned to blocks in the following fashion:

Value of X_{23}	Value of X_{124}	Treatment Assigned to
-1	-1	Block 1
1	-1	Block 2
-1	1	Block 3
1	1	Block 4

Since there are $b = 4$ blocks, $b - 1 = 3$ factor effects are confounded with block effects. These are the 23 interaction, the 124 interaction, and their generalized interaction:

$$23 \times 124 = 12^2 34 = 134$$

The resulting design is shown in Table 31.8b. Notice again the balance of levels within each block: each factor appears twice at its high level and twice at its low level. This will also be true for all interaction columns except X_{23}, X_{124}, and X_{134}; these columns will be constant within each block. An abbreviated ANOVA table is shown in Table 31.9. Note

TABLE 31.9   Abbreviated ANOVA Table—Steichen Bakeries Example.

Source of Variation	df
X_0	1
X_1	1
X_2	1
X_3	1
X_4	1
X_{12}	1
X_{13}	1
X_{14}	1
X_{24}	1
X_{34}	1
X_{123}	1
X_{234}	1
X_{1234}	1
Blocks (confounded with X_{23}, X_{124}, X_{134})	3
Error	0
Total	16

that this table shows the confounding of the three interaction effects, 23, 124, and 134, with blocks.

Use of Center Point Replications

We noted earlier that two or more replications are often added at the center point when the factors are quantitative to provide an estimate of the error variance σ^2 and a test for lack of fit. When blocking is used, center point replications must be placed within the same block to obtain a valid measure of pure error. Otherwise, differences in responses will be due to both experimental error and block-to-block differences. Use of an equal number of center point replications in each block leads to all estimated factor (and block) effect coefficients being uncorrelated.

Cited References

31.1.   Box, G. E. P., W. G. Hunter, and J. S. Hunter, *Statistics for Experimenters*. New York: John Wiley & Sons, 1978.

31.2.   Plackett, R. L., and J. P. Burman. "The Design of Optimum Multifactorial Experiments," *Biometrika* 33 (1946), pp. 305–25.

Problems

31.1.   A plant manager used a 2^4 factorial design with two replicates for each treatment to study the effects of four process variables $(X_1, \ldots, X_4)$ on product quality (Y). State the response model in the form of (31.2a). How many two-factor interaction terms are there? How many three-factor interaction terms? How many four-factor interaction terms?

31.2.   A scientist observed: "Two-level factorial designs are useful if the number of factors is small. But I am concerned when there are 10 or more factors; the number of trials required for a 2^{10} experiment is simply too large." Discuss.

√ 31.3.   **Reaction yield.** A chemical engineer decided to employ a single replicate of a 2^6 factorial design to study the effects of the process variables on the yield of a chemical reaction.

    a.   How may factors are involved? How many levels are there for each factor? How many experimental trials will be required for the single replicate of the experiment?

    b.   Can a test for lack of fit be obtained here?

31.4.   A biologist considered studying the effects of various environmental pollutants on the health of mice by using a 2^{7-4} fractional factorial design.

    a.   How many factors are involved? How many levels are there for each factor? How many trials will be required for a single replicate of the experiment? Can a test for lack of fit be obtained?

    b.   The biologist decided to augment the design with six center-point replicates. Can a test for lack of fit now be obtained? If so, can the biologist determine which factors caused a curvature effect?

31.5.   State the **X** matrix (including all main effects and interaction columns) for a single replicate of a 2^3 factorial design, with the rows listed in standard order. Show numerically that (31.3) holds for your **X** matrix.

31.6.   Refer to **Reaction yield** Problem 31.3. Past experience indicates that the standard deviation of reaction yield is $\sigma = 5$.

    a.   Find the variance of the estimated main effect coefficient b_1. Is the variance of the interaction effect coefficient b_{12} the same? Should it be?

    b.   How many replicates of the experiment are required in order to estimate factor effect coefficent b_1 within $\pm$ .5 with 95 percent confidence?

√ 31.7.   **Pilot training**. An unreplicated 2^5 full factorial design was used to investigate the effects of five factors on the learning rates of flight trainees when using flight simulators. The factors were display type ($X_1 = -1$: symbolic; $X_1 = 1$: pictorial), display orientation ($X_2 = -1$: outside in; $X_2 = 1$: inside out), crosswind ($X_3 = -1$: no wind present; $X_3 = 1$: crosswind present), command guidance ($X_4 = -1$: constant guidance; $X_4 = 1$: guidance only when trainee strays far from best flight path), and flight path prediction ($X_5 = -1$: no prediction; $X_5 = 1$: constant prediction). The response Y is the average squared distance from the optimal flight path for 12 landing attempts by the trainee. The smaller is Y, the better is the trainee's performance. Thirty-two subjects (trainees) were selected at random from a large group of trainees with no prior flying experience. The design matrix for the experiment and the observed trainee flight scores (Y) follow.

Y	X_1	X_2	X_3	X_4	X_5
8.69	−1	−1	−1	−1	−1
7.71	1	−1	−1	−1	−1
9.03	−1	1	−1	−1	−1
...	...	...	...	...	...
6.67	1	−1	1	1	1
2.78	−1	1	1	1	1
7.45	1	1	1	1	1

Adapted in part from L. Lintern et al., "Display Principles, Control Dynamics, and Environmental Factors in Pilot Training and Transfer," *Human Factors* 32 (1990), pp. 64–69.

a. State the regression model in the form (31.2a). Fit this model and obtain the estimated factor effect coefficients. Does it appear from the magnitudes of the estimated coefficients that some factors may be active here?

b. Prepare a dot plot of the estimated factor effect coefficients. Which effects appear to be active?

c. Obtain a normal probability plot of the estimated factor effect coefficients. Which effects appear to be active? Do the estimated factor effects appear to be normally distributed? How do your results compare with those in parts (a) and (b)?

√ 31.8. Refer to **Pilot Training** Problem 31.7. The regression model was revised by dropping all three-factor and higher-order interactions.

a. State the revised regression model. Fit the revised regression model and prepare a plot of the residuals against the fitted values. Do the standard regression assumptions appear to be satisfied?

b. Obtain a normal probability plot of the residuals. Also conduct the correlation test for normality; use $\alpha = .05$. Does the assumption of normality appear to be reasonable here?

c. Using the P-values for the estimated factor effect coefficients, test for the significance of each factor effect. Control the family level of significance at $\alpha = .05$ using the Kimball inequality. Which effects appear to be active?

d. Summarize the results of the experiment with an appropriate set of plots of main effects and interactions. Interpret the results.

31.9. **Computer monitors**. A single replicate of a 2^4 full factorial design, augmented by three replicates at the center point, was used to determine the most reliable design of a computer monitor base. Factors of interest were clearance under the base (X_1), interface board height (X_2), side vent size (X_3), and interface board angle (X_4). All factors are quantitative and are coded with $X_i = -1$ for the low level of the factor and $X_i = 1$ for the high level. The response (Y) is the failure rate of the interface board, with lower failure rates representing higher product quality. The design matrix for the experiment and the observed design failure rates (Y) follow.

Y	X_1	X_2	X_3	X_4
3.88	−1	−1	−1	−1
3.17	1	−1	−1	−1
4.07	−1	1	−1	−1
. . .	. . .	. . .	. . .	. . .
3.80	0	0	0	0
3.99	0	0	0	0
4.16	0	0	0	0

a. State the regression model in the form (31.2a). Fit this model and obtain the estimated factor effect coefficients. Does it appear from the magnitudes of the estimated coefficients that some factors may be active here?

b. Prepare a dot plot of the estimated factor effect coefficients. Which effects appear to be active?

c. Obtain a normal probability plot of the estimated factor effect coefficients. Which effects appear to be active? Do the estimated factor effects appear to be normally distributed? How do your results compare with those in parts (a) and (b)?

d. Obtain *MSPE* using the three center-point replicates and (31.17). Use this estimate to determine the *P*-value for each estimated factor effect coefficient. Determine which effects are active; use $\alpha = .05$ for each test.

31.10. Refer to **Computer monitors** Problem 31.9. The regression model was revised by including only the main effects of factors 1, 3, and 4 and the 34 interaction.

a. Fit the revised model and prepare a plot of the residuals against the fitted values. Do the standard regression assumptions appear to be satisfied?

b. Obtain a normal probability plot of the residuals. Also conduct the correlation test for normality; use $\alpha = .05$. Does the assumption of normality appear to be a reasonable one here?

c. Using the *P*-values for the estimated factor effect coefficients, test for the significance of each effect; use $\alpha = .01$ for each test. Which effects are active?

d. Conduct a test for lack of fit; use $\alpha = .05$. State the decision rule and conclusion.

e. Summarize the results of the experiment with an appropriate set of plots of main effects and interactions. Interpret the results. How should the monitor base be designed to achieve a minimum failure rate?

31.11. Refer to the **X** matrix for a 2^4 full factorial design in Table 31.2.

a. Identify the defining relation for the fractional design obtained by dropping treatments 3 to 6, 9, 10, 15, and 16. What is the resolution of the fractional design so obtained?

b. Give the complete confounding scheme for the fractional design obtained in part (a).

31.12. a. Construct a design for four two-level factors with eight experimental trials that has the highest possible resolution. What is the resolution of this design?

b. Verify the projection property for the design constructed in part (a)—that any subset of three (or fewer) factors yields a full factorial design in those factors.

31.13. Is it possible to construct a resolution III design for four two-level factors with four experimental trials? If so, construct such a design. If not, indicate why this is not possible.

31.14. Construct a 2^{4-1}_{III} design using the defining relation $0 = 123$. Is there an alternative eight-run design of higher resolution?

√ 31.15. Obtain the complete defining relation and the confounding scheme for the eight-run, five-factor design that is fractionated on the basis of the relation $0 = 123 = 245$. What is the resolution of this design? Is there an alternative design with higher resolution?

31.16. The following design matrix was used in an eight-run, five-factor experiment:

X_1	X_2	X_3	X_4	X_5
-1	-1	-1	-1	-1
1	-1	-1	-1	1
-1	1	-1	1	1
1	1	-1	1	-1
-1	-1	1	1	1
1	-1	1	1	-1
-1	1	1	-1	-1
1	1	1	-1	1

Obtain the defining relation and the complete confounding scheme for this design. What is the resolution of this design? Can an alternative five-factor, eight-run design with higher resolution be constructed?

31.17. Construct a 2^{6-3} fractional factorial design of highest resolution using Table 31.6. What is the defining relation for this design? What is its resolution?

√ 31.18. **Peanut solids** A food scientist conducted a single replicate of a 2^{7-3} fractional factorial design in an effort to identify factors that affect the extraction of food solids from peanuts using water. Factors of interest were the pH level of the water ($X_1 = -1$: 6.95; $X_1 = 1$: 8.00), water temperature ($X_2 = -1$: 20°C; $X_2 = 1$: 60°C), extraction time ($X_3 = -1$: 15 minutes; $X_3 = 1$: 40 minutes), water-to-peanuts ratio ($X_4 = -1$: 5; $X_4 = 1$: 9), agitation speed ($X_5 = -1$: 5,000 rpm; $X_5 = 1$: 10,000 rpm), hydrolysis ($X_6 = -1$: unhydrolyzed; $X_6 = 1$: hydrolyzed), and presoaking level ($X_7 = -1$: dry; $X_7 = 1$: soaked). The experimental units were 16 randomly selected batches of peanuts. The response (Y) is the percentage of the total solids removed from each batch. The defining relation used to construct the 2^{7-3} fractional design (excluding generalized interactions) is $0 = 1235 = 2346 = 1247$. The design matrix for the experiment and the observed percentage extractions (Y) follow.

Y	X_1	X_2	X_3	X_4	X_5	X_6	X_7
10.82	-1	-1	-1	-1	-1	-1	-1
10.59	1	-1	-1	-1	1	-1	1
8.19	-1	1	-1	-1	1	1	1
...	...	...	...	...	...	...	...
5.12	1	-1	1	1	-1	-1	-1
5.60	-1	1	1	1	-1	1	-1
5.73	1	1	1	1	1	1	1

Adapted from I. Y. S. Rustom et al., "A Study of Factors Affecting Extraction of Peanut (*Arachis hypogaea* L.) Solids with Water," *Food Chemistry* 42 (1991), pp. 153–65.

   a. Obtain the generalized interactions and the complete defining relation. What is the resolution of the design? Could a design of higher resolution have been used here?

   b. Using the defining relation in part (a), determine the confounding pattern for all main effects and two-factor interactions.

   c. State the regression model in the form (31.2a). Remember that confounded effects must not be included in your model. Fit this model and obtain the estimated factor effect coefficients. Prepare a dot plot of the estimated factor effect coefficients. Which effects appear to be active?

   d. Obtain a normal probability plot of the estimated factor effect coefficients. Which effects appear to be active? Do the estimated effects appear to be normally distributed? How do your results compare with those in part (c)?

   e. Test whether all two-factor interaction effects can be dropped from the model; use $\alpha = .01$. State the alternatives, decision rule, and conclusion.

$\sqrt{}$ 31.19. Refer to **Peanut Solids** Problem 31.18. The regression model was revised by dropping all interaction effects.

   a. Fit the revised model and prepare a plot of the residuals against the fitted values. Do the standard regression assumptions appear to be satisfied?

   b. Cases 3 and 14 have fairly large absolute residuals. Conduct the Bonferroni outlier test for each of these cases; use $\alpha = .05$ for each test. What do you conclude?

   c. Obtain a normal probability plot of the residuals. Also conduct the correlation test for normality; use $\alpha = .025$. Does the assumption of normality appear to be reasonable here?

   d. Using the P-values of the estimated factor effect coefficients, test for the significance of each effect; use $\alpha = .02$ for each test. Which effects are active?

   e. Summarize the results of the experiment with an appropriate set of plots of main effects. Interpret the results. How should maximum food solids extraction be achieved?

31.20. **Fiber optics**. A chemist conducted a screening experiment to identify factors that affect the viscosity of a gel used in the manufacture of fiber optic cabling. To minimize the loss of telephone signal, the inner glass fibers must be allowed to move freely within the cabling for a range of temperatures. A lubricant (gel) is used to promote this movement. The viscosity of the gel must be sufficiently low to allow such movement; yet it must not be so low as to lead to dripping (leakage) from the ends. A single replicate of a 2^{9-5} fractional factorial design was conducted. The factors of interest were silica particle size ($X_1 = -1$: 380; $X_1 = 1$: 200), silica weight ($X_2 = -1$: low; $X_2 = 1$: high), oil ratio ($X_3 = -1$: low; $X_3 = 1$: high), oil temperature ($X_4 = -1$: low; $X_4 = 1$: high), stabilizer level ($X_5 = -1$: low; $X_5 = 1$: high), premix time ($X_6 = -1$: short; $X_6 = 1$: long), postmix time ($X_7 = -1$: short; $X_7 = 1$: long), postmix vacuum ($X_8 = -1$: no; $X_8 = 1$: yes), and filter mesh size ($X_9 = -1$: small; $X_9 = 1$: large). The response of interest is gel viscosity (Y); management feels that an optimal (target) gel viscosity is 74.5. The design matrix for the experiment and the observed viscosities (Y) follow.

Y	X_1	X_2	X_3	X_4	X_5	X_6	X_7	X_8	X_9
101.2	1	1	1	1	−1	1	−1	−1	1
92.9	−1	−1	−1	−1	−1	−1	−1	−1	1
129.9	1	1	1	1	1	−1	−1	−1	−1
...	...	...	...	...	...	...	...	...	...
73.4	−1	−1	−1	−1	1	1	−1	−1	−1
31.6	1	1	−1	−1	−1	−1	1	−1	−1
121.6	1	−1	1	−1	1	−1	−1	1	1

Adapted from T. L. Reed, "Quality Improvement of Silica-Based Polysiloxane Gel Used in Fiber Optic Cabling by Process Optimization via Taguchi Methods," *Fifth Symposium on Taguchi Methods*, Detroit: ASI Press (1987), pp. 555–71.

a. State the regression model containing only factor main effects in the form (31.2a). Fit this model and obtain the estimated factor effect coefficients. Does it appear from the magnitudes of the estimated coefficients that some factors may be active here?

b. Prepare a Pareto plot of the estimated factor effect coefficients. Which effects appear to be active?

c. Obtain a normal probability plot of the estimated factor effect coefficients. Which effects appear to be active? Do the estimated factor effects appear to be normally distributed? How do your results compare with those in part (b)?

d. Using the P-values of the estimated factor effect coefficients, test for the significance of each effect term; use $\alpha = .10$ for each test. Which effects are active?

31.21. Refer to **Fiber optics** Problem 31.20. The regression model was revised to include only the main effects for factors 1, 5, and 7.

a. Fit the revised regression model and prepare a plot of the residuals against the fitted values. Do the standard regression assumptions appear to be satisfied?

b. Obtain a normal probability plot of the residuals. Also conduct the correlation test for normality; use $\alpha = .05$. Does the assumption of normality appear to be reasonable here?

c. Conduct a lack of fit test for the revised regression model; use $\alpha = .05$. State the alternatives, decision rule, and conclusion. What does your conclusion suggest about the possible presence of interactions?

31.22. Refer to **Fiber optics** Problems 31.20 and 31.21. Since the experimental design consists of two complete replicates of a 2^3 factorial in the three active factors 1, 5, and 7, consider now a revised model containing the main effects of factors 1, 5, and 7 and all interactions among these three factors.

a. State the revised regression model and fit it. Using the P-values of the estimated factor effect coefficients, test for the signficance of each factor effect; use $\alpha = .01$ for each test. Which effects are active?

b. Obtain a normal probability plot of the residuals. Compare this plot to that obtained in Problem 31.21b. What do you conclude?

c. Summarize the experimental results with an appropriate set of plots of the main effects and interactions. Interpret the results.

d. How might you proceed to determine the levels of factors 1, 5, and 7 so that the expected viscosity of the resulting gel would be on target at 74.5?

31.23. **Windshield molding manufacture**. An experimental study was undertaken in an effort to reduce the occurence of dents in a windshield molding manufacturing process. The dents are caused by pieces of metal or plastic that are carried into the dies during stamping and forming operations. Four factors were identified for use in an eight-run experiment: poly-film thickness—used to protect the metal strip during manufacturing to reduce surface blemishes ($X_1 = -1$: .00175; $X_1 = 1$: .0025), oil mixture ratio for surface lubrication ($X_2 = -1$: .05; $X_2 = 1$: .10), operator glove type ($X_3 = -1$: cotton; $X_3 = 1$: nylon), underside oil coating ($X_4 = -1$: no coating; $X_4 = 1$: coating). During each run of the experiment, 1,000 moldings were fabricated; the response (Y) is the number of defect-free moldings produced. The design matrix for the experiment and the observed numbers of defect-free moldings produced (Y) follow.

Y	X_1	X_2	X_3	X_4
338	1	−1	−1	−1
826	1	−1	1	1
350	1	1	−1	−1
647	1	1	1	1
917	−1	−1	−1	1
977	−1	−1	1	−1
953	−1	1	−1	1
972	−1	1	1	−1

Adapted from G. Adel, "Minimize Slugging by Optimizing Controllable Factors on Topaz Windshield Molding," *Fifth Symposium on Taguchi Methods*, Detroit: ASI Press (1987), pp. 519–26.

a. Determine the defining relation and the complete confounding scheme used in the experiment. Could a design of higher resolution have been used?

b. State the regression model in the form (31.2a). Remember that confounded factor effects must not be included in your model. Fit this model and obtain the estimated factor effect coefficients.

c. Prepare a dot plot of the estimated factor effect coefficients. Which effects appear to be active?

d. Obtain a normal probability plot of the estimated factor effect coefficients. Which effects appear to be active? How do your results compare with those in part (c)? Do the estimated factor effects appear to be normally distributed?

31.24. Refer to **Windshield molding manufacture** Problem 31.23. The regression model was revised to include only the main effects for the four factors.

a. Fit the revised regression model. Using the P-values for the estimated factor effect coefficients, test for the significance of each effect; use $\alpha = .05$ in each case. Which effects are active?

b. Summarize the results of the experiment with an appropriate set of plots of main effects. Interpret the results. Identify the settings of the experimental factors within the operating range that lead to the maximum number of defect-free moldings.

31.25. Construct a 2_{III}^{5-2} design in two blocks of size four such that main effects are not confounded with the block effect.

√ 31.26. **Team effectiveness**. A researcher employed a single replicate of a 2^6 full factorial design, with eight blocks containing eight treatments each, to study the effects of team member's ability level and motivation level on the performance of three-person military teams consisting of an operator, a loader, and a mover. The factors studied were operator's ability (X_1), operator's motivation (X_2), loader's ability (X_3), loader's motivation (X_4), mover's ability (X_5), and mover's motivation (X_6). All factors are quantitative and are coded with $X_i = -1$ referring to the low level of the factor and $X_i = 1$ referring to its high level. The 64 teams were formed by assigning persons to teams in accordance with the 2^6 full factorial design.

The team ratings (Y) were assigned by unit commanders following two months of military activity. Because unit commanders could observe at most 10 teams, and because it was expected that some scoring biases might result, the teams were assigned to commanders in blocks of size eight. Levels of the interaction terms X_{135}, X_{146}, and X_{245} were used to determine the blocks. The observed team ratings, the design matrix, and the blocking arrangement follow.

Y	Block	X_1	X_2	X_3	X_4	X_5	X_6
43	1	−1	−1	−1	−1	−1	−1
61	1	1	1	1	1	1	−1
60	1	−1	1	1	−1	1	−1
...	...	...	...	...	...	...	...
66	8	1	−1	−1	1	−1	1
64	8	−1	−1	−1	−1	1	1
91	8	1	1	1	1	1	1

Adapted in part from A.E. Tziner, "Effects of Team Composition on Ranked Team Effectiveness," *Small Group Behavior* 19 (1988), pp. 363–78.

a. Obtain a scatter plot of team ratings against block number. Does it appear that blocking was effective here?

b. Identify the complete confounding scheme for blocks. Are any main effects confounded with blocks? Any two-factor interactions?

c. State the regression model in the form (31.2a). Fit this model and obtain the estimated factor effect coefficients. Prepare a dot plot of the estimated factor effect coefficients. Which effects appear to be active?

d. Obtain a normal probability plot of the estimated factor effect coefficients. Which effects appear to be active? How do your findings compare with those in part (c)? Do the estimated factor effects appear to be normally distributed?

√ 31.27. Refer to **Team effectiveness** Problem 31.26. The regression model was revised to include only the factor main effects, two-factor interactions, and block main effects.

a. Fit the revised model and prepare a plot of the residuals against the fitted values. Do the standard regression assumptions appear to be satisfied?

b. Obtain a normal probability plot of the residuals. Also conduct the correlation test for normality; use $\alpha = .05$. Does the assumption of normality appear to be reasonable here?

c. Using the P-values for the estimated factor effect coefficients, test for the significance of each factor effect; use $\alpha = .01$ for each test. Which effects are active?

√ 31.28. Refer to **Team effectiveness** Problems 31.26 and 31.27. The finally revised regression model consists of all block main effects and all factor main effects only.

a. Fit the finally revised regression model.

b. Summarize the results of the experiment with an appropriate set of plots of the factor main effects. Interpret the results. How is maximum team effectiveness achieved?

c. Obtain a 95 percent prediction interval for the team performance for a single new team formed as described in part (b); assume that the rater (block) effect is zero in making your prediction.

31.29. **Whipped topping**. Food scientists had developed a prototype soybean-based whipped topping, but the product suffered in that the volume of the whipped product did not meet expectations. In an effort to maximize the topping volume, a 2^{5-1} fractional factorial design of highest resolution was used in an experiment in two blocks of size eight each, with three center-point replicates in each block. The design confounded the block effect with the 45 interaction. The factors studied were soybean solids level (X_1), fat level (X_2), emulsifier level (X_3), and the levels of two stabilizers: methocel (X_4), and avicel (X_5). All factors are quantitative and are coded with $X_i = -1$ referring to the low level of the factor and $X_i = 1$ referring to its high level. The response (Y) is the percent increase in volume of the product due to whipping; large increases are desirable. The observed responses, the design matrix, and the blocking arrangement follow.

Y	Block	X_1	X_2	X_3	X_4	X_5
124	1	−1	−1	−1	−1	1
144	1	1	1	−1	−1	1
144	1	1	−1	1	−1	1
. . .	. . .	. . .	. . .	. . .	. . .	
121	2	0	0	0	0	0
127	2	0	0	0	0	0
115	2	0	0	0	0	0

a. What is the defining relation for this design? What is the resolution, ignoring blocks?

b. State the regression model in the form (31.2a). Remember that confounded factor effects must not be included in your model. Fit this regression model and obtain the estimated factor effect coefficients. Prepare a dot plot of the estimated factor effect coefficients. Which effects appear to be active?

c. Obtain a normal probability plot of the estimated factor effect coefficients. Which effects appear to be active? How do your results compare with those in part (b)? Do the estimated factor effects appear to be normally distributed?

d. Test for the presence of block effects; use $\alpha = .05$. State the alternatives, decision rule, and conclusion.

e. Fit a revised regression model, omitting the block effect term. Obtain a pure error estimate of the error variance using the six center-point replicates and (31.17) and conduct a test for lack of fit; use $\alpha = .05$. State the decision rule and conclusion. Does your test indicate the presence of curvature?

f. Using the P-values for the estimated factor effect coefficients obtained in part (e) based on the pure error estimate $MSPE$, test for the significance of the factor effects; use $\alpha = .025$ for each test. Which factors are active?

31.30. Refer to **Whipped topping** Problem 31.29. The model has been finally revised to include only the main effects for factors 1, 2, and 5 and the 12 interaction term.

a. Fit the revised model and prepare a plot of the residuals against the fitted values. Do the standard regression assumptions appear to be satisfied?

b. Obtain a normal probability plot of the residuals. Also conduct the correlation test for normality; use $\alpha = .05$. Does the assumption of normality appear to be reasonable here?

c. Summarize the results of the experiment with an appropriate set of plots of the main effects and interactions. Interpret the results. How is maximum whippability achieved?

d. Obtain a 95 percent confidence interval for the expected percent volume increase for the whipped topping product when formulated as recommended in part (c).

Exercises

31.31. Show that (31.14) holds for balanced two-level experiments; use (2.51) and the additivity of the extra sums of squares in this situation.

31.32. Suppose that the true (full) regression model in matrix form is:

$$\mathbf{Y} = \mathbf{X}_1\boldsymbol{\beta}_1 + \mathbf{X}_2\boldsymbol{\beta}_2 + \boldsymbol{\varepsilon}$$

However, the analyst assumes that the (reduced) model:

$$\mathbf{Y} = \mathbf{X}_1\boldsymbol{\beta}_1 + \boldsymbol{\varepsilon}$$

is correct and uses it for purposes of estimation. For example, the $\mathbf{X}$ matrix for the reduced model ($\mathbf{X}_1$) might include only an intercept column and columns for first-order terms, while the true model involves first-order terms ($\mathbf{X}_1$) and some two-factor interaction terms ($\mathbf{X}_2$).

a. Show that:

$$E\{\hat{\boldsymbol{\beta}}_1\} = \boldsymbol{\beta}_1 + \mathbf{A}\boldsymbol{\beta}_2$$

where $\mathbf{A} = (\mathbf{X}_1'\mathbf{X}_1)^{-1}\mathbf{X}_1'\mathbf{X}_2$ is called the alias matrix.

b. Let $\mathbf{X}_1$ be the $\mathbf{X}$ matrix (based on the intercept and first-order terms only) for the 2_{III}^{3-1} design constructed from the defining relation $0 = 123$. Let $\mathbf{X}_2$ consist of the columns X_{12}, X_{13}, and X_{23}, corresponding to the omitted two-factor interaction effects β_{12}, β_{13}, and β_{23}. Use the result in part (a) and $\mathbf{b} = (\mathbf{X}_1'\mathbf{X}_1)^{-1}\mathbf{X}_1'\mathbf{Y} = \mathbf{X}_1'\mathbf{Y}/8$ to show that $E\{b_1\} = \beta_1 + \beta_{23}$, $E\{b_2\} = \beta_2 + \beta_{13}$, and $E\{b_3\} = \beta_3 + \beta_{12}$. Thus, for this design we have: $1 = 23$, $2 = 13$, and $3 = 12$.

Response Surface Methodology

Chapter 31 was devoted to a discussion of the design of two-level factorial experiments. With these designs, main effects and two-factor interactions can often be studied with relatively few experimental trials. One limitation of two-level designs for factorial studies where the factors are quantitative is that they cannot identify curvatures in the response surface. Modeling curvature effects can be very important when the objective of the experiment is to identify the combination of levels of the quantitative factors that leads to an optimum response. Response surface experiments can be used for this purpose. In this chapter, we discuss the design and analysis of response surface experiments for studies where the factors are quantitative. Response surface designs are generally used in the latter stages of an investigation, when five or fewer factors are under investigation.

32.1   Response Surface Experiments

When a factorial study involves quantitative factors and the shape of the response surface is of interest, the response surface is usually approximated by a second-order regression model. The rationale is that the main effects and second-order effects will generally capture the essence of the response function since third-order and higher effects are usually unimportant.

The second-order response function for three quantitative factors was given in (7.74). We shall generalize it now for k quantitative factors. We continue to use the special coding employed in Chapter 31 for the level X_j of the jth quantitative factor:

$$(32.1) \quad E\{Y\} = \beta_0 + \beta_1 X_1 + \cdots + \beta_k X_k + \beta_{11} X_1^2 + \cdots + \beta_{kk} X_k^2$$
$$+ \beta_{12} X_1 X_2 + \cdots + \beta_{k-1,k} X_{k-1} X_k$$

where the level X_j of the jth factor is coded as follows:

$$(32.2) \qquad X_j = \frac{\text{Actual Level} - \dfrac{\text{High Level} + \text{Low Level}}{2}}{\dfrac{\text{High Level} - \text{Low Level}}{2}}$$

This coding scheme results in a coded value of -1 for the low level of factor j, a coded value of 1 for the high level, a coded value of 0 for the mid-level, and so on. For instance, if the temperature levels of factor j in a study range from $75°$ to $85°$, the following coded values X_j will be used:

Temperature Level	Coded Value X_j
75	-1
78	$-.4$
80	0
85	1

Occasionally, the experimental design will be supplemented with treatments consisting of factor levels outside the original range. This will result in coded values below -1 or above 1. For instance, if a supplemental treatment in our example involves factor j at temperature level $70°$, the coded value will be $X_j = (70 - 80)/5 = -2$.

As before, the coefficients $\beta_1, \ldots, \beta_k$ in regression model (32.1) are the linear main effect coefficients, the coefficients $\beta_{11}, \ldots, \beta_{kk}$ are the quadratic main effect coefficients, and the coefficients $\beta_{12}, \beta_{13}, \ldots, \beta_{k-1,k}$ are the interaction effect coefficients. Notice that model (32.1) involves $p = 1+k+k+k(k-1)/2 = (k+1)(k+2)/2$ regression parameters.

When designing a response surface study, a minimal requirement is that the design must be capable of providing estimates of the $p = (k+1)(k+2)/2$ parameters in model (32.1). Any design of resolution V or higher for a two-level factorial study will provide estimates of linear main effects and all two-factor interaction effects that are confounded only with higher-order effects. However, at least three levels of each factor must be present to obtain estimates of the k quadratic main effects.

One type of design that provides estimates of all parameters in regression model (32.1) is the full factorial design with each factor at three levels. Full factorial designs with each factor at three levels are referred to as 3^k designs, where k denotes the number of factors in the study. A number of practical limitations are associated with 3^k designs. The first is expense. The number of treatments required by a 3^k design grows rapidly with the number of factors. For four factors, for instance, a three-level full factorial design consists of $3^4 = 81$ treatments. A second disadvantage is that each factor appears at exactly three levels so that it will not be possible to test for the presence of cubic or higher-order main effects.

In Sections 32.2 and 32.3, we shall discuss a variety of response surface designs that have been developed for estimation of response surfaces based on second-order model (32.1) that overcome the limitations of 3^k designs. Central composite designs, discussed in the next section, are general purpose designs that are widely used in practice. Optimal response surface designs, discussed in Section 32.3, are designs that meet an optimality criterion specified by the experimenter.

32.2   Central Composite Response Surface Designs

Structure of Central Composite Designs

Central composite designs are two-level full or fractional factorial designs that have been augmented with a small number of carefully chosen treatments to permit estimation of the second-order response surface model (32.1). Consider first the 2^2 factorial design pictured in terms of its coded factor levels in Figure 32.1a. If we add a single center point and four

FIGURE 32.1   **Two Central Composite Designs for Two Factors.**

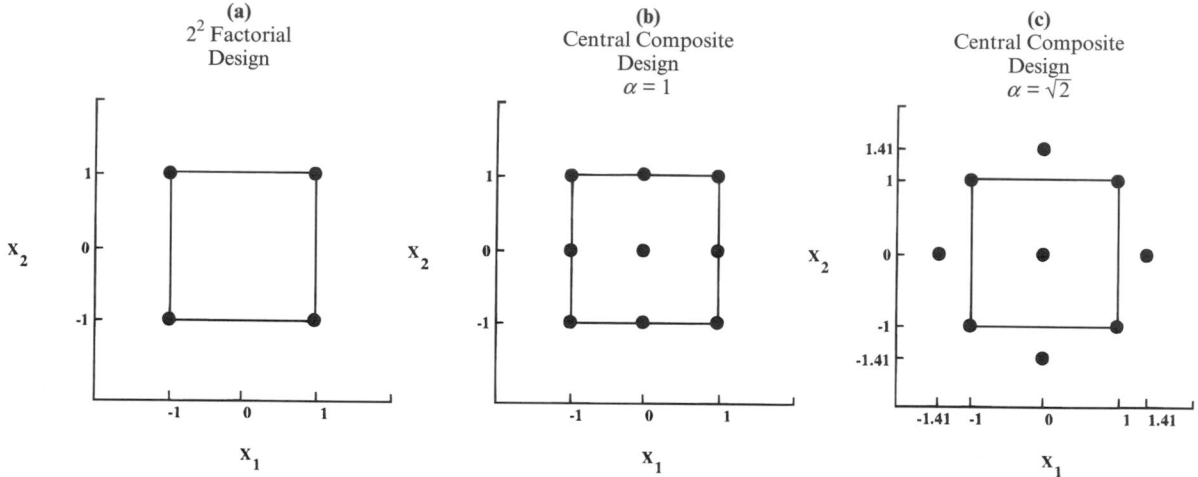

star points (also called *axial* points), as shown in Figure 32.1b, the resulting design is a central composite design. A star point is one in which all factors but one are set at their mid-levels. In terms of the coded values, the coordinates of the four star points in Figure 32.1b are $(-1, 0)$, $(1, 0)$, $(0, -1)$, and $(0, 1)$. As shown in Figure 32.1b, the four star points are located at the centers of each of the four edges of the experimental region. Notice that the central composite design in Figure 32.1b is in fact a 3^2 factorial design, where both factors are at three levels and all factor level combinations are included.

The distance from a star point to the center point in coded units is typically denoted by α. In Figure 32.1b, the star points are one coded unit from the center; hence for this design $\alpha = 1$. It is sometimes possible to place the star points beyond the experimental region defined by the original upper and lower limits of the factors. Figure 32.1c presents a central composite design where the star points are located at a distance $\alpha = \sqrt{2} = 1.414$ from the center. As may be seen from Figure 32.1c, each factor is run at five distinct levels when α is larger than 1.0, whereas use of $\alpha = 1.0$ yields just three distinct levels for each factor, as shown in Figure 32.1b. One advantage of setting α greater than 1.0, therefore, is that tests for cubic and quartic curvature effects can then be conducted.

To summarize, central composite designs consist of three components:

1. 2^{k-f} *corner points*. At the base of any central composite design is a two-level full factorial design or a fractional factorial design of resolution V or higher. This component provides for the estimation of linear main effects and all two-factor interaction effects. Corner points have coded coordinates of the form $(\pm 1, \pm 1, \ldots, \pm 1)$.

2. $2k$ *star points*. These factor level combinations permit the estimation of all quadratic main effects. In addition, when $\alpha > 1.0$, significance tests for higher-order curvature effects can be conducted. Star points have coordinates $(\pm\alpha, 0, \ldots, 0)$, $(0, \pm\alpha, 0, \ldots, 0)$, etc.

3. n_0 *center points*. If $n_0 > 1$, a pure error estimate of σ^2 is available and a lack of fit test is possible. The coded coordinates of the center point replicates are $(0, 0, \ldots, 0)$.

Table 32.1 presents the coded factor level settings for central composite designs for three factors, with $n_0 = 4$ replications at the center point.

TABLE 32.1   **Three-Factor Central Composite Designs with $n_0 = 4$ Replications at Center Point.**

Experimental Trial	Factor Level Settings		
	X_1	X_2	X_3
1	-1	-1	-1
2	1	-1	-1
3	-1	1	-1
4	1	1	-1
5	-1	-1	1
6	1	-1	1
7	-1	1	1
8	1	1	1
9	$-\alpha$	0	0
10	α	0	0
11	0	$-\alpha$	0
12	0	α	0
13	0	0	$-\alpha$
14	0	0	α
15	0	0	0
16	0	0	0
17	0	0	0
18	0	0	0

Commonly Used Central Composite Designs

As we have seen, the term "central composite design" refers to a family of experimental designs. Within that family, numerous designs exist, depending on the choice of the base corner points, α, and the extent of replications. Not only may there be n_0 replications at the center point but there may also be replications at the corner and star points. We shall let n_c and n_s denote, respectively, the number of replications at each corner point and star point. The number of experimental trials at the corner points then is:

$$(32.3a) \qquad\qquad 2^{k-f} n_c$$

where k is the number of factors and f is the level of fractionation in the two-level factorial design selected. Similarly, the number of replications at the star points is:

$$(32.3b) \qquad\qquad 2kn_s$$

Thus, the total number of experimental trials planned, denoted by n_T as usual, is:

$$(32.3c) \qquad\qquad n_T = 2^{k-f} n_c + 2kn_s + n_0$$

The characteristics of any particular central composite design therefore depend on the choices of k, f, α, n_0, n_s, and n_c.

A list of widely used central composite designs is given in Table 32.2 for studies involving two to eight factors. (The meaning of the term "rotatability" in Table 32.2 will

TABLE 32.2 **Some Useful Central Composite Designs.**

Design Characteristic	Number of Factors						
	2	3	4	5	6	7	8
Base factorial design	2^2	2^3	2^4	2_V^{5-1}	2_V^{6-1}	2_V^{7-1}	2_V^{8-2}
Star points	4	6	8	10	12	14	16
Center point	1	1	1	1	1	1	1
α for rotatability ($n_c = n_s = 1$)	1.4142	1.6818	2.0000	2.0000	2.3784	2.8284	3.3636
Total number of trials ($n_c = n_s = 1, n_0 = 4$)	12	18	28	30	48	82	84

be explained shortly.) The base fractional factorial designs for five to eight factors are the smallest such designs that will provide resolution $R = V$. Table 32.2 also shows the total number of experimental trials required when a single replication at the corner and star points of the design (i.e., $n_c = n_s = 1$) and $n_0 = 4$ replications at the center point are sufficient. When the error variance σ^2 is large relative to the factor effects, larger numbers of replications at each treatment will be needed.

Rotatable Central Composite Designs

When choosing a particular central composite design, a criterion that is often considered is that of rotatability. The rotatability criterion is concerned with the precision of the estimator $\hat{Y}_h$ since a main purpose of response surface designs is to estimate the response surface, i.e., to estimate the mean response $E\{Y_h\}$ in (32.1) at different locations $\mathbf{X}_h$, the vector of the given levels of the k factors. Rotatable designs have the property that the variance of the fitted value at $\mathbf{X}_h$, $\sigma^2\{\hat{Y}_h\}$, is the same for any point $\mathbf{X}_h$ that is a given distance from the center point, regardless of the direction. The property of equal precision at any given distance from the center point is desirable because it is not usually known in advance which direction from the center point will be of later interest. A rotatable design provides assurance that the precision of the fitted values is not affected by the direction, only by the distance from the center point.

We can examine whether a central composite design is rotatable by considering the variance of $\hat{Y}_h$ as a function of $\mathbf{X}_h$. The variance was given in (6.57):

$$(32.4) \qquad \sigma^2\{\hat{Y}_h\} = \sigma^2 \mathbf{X}_h'(\mathbf{X}'\mathbf{X})^{-1}\mathbf{X}_h = \sigma^2 V_h$$

where:

$$(32.4a) \qquad V_h = \mathbf{X}_h'(\mathbf{X}'\mathbf{X})^{-1}\mathbf{X}_h$$

V_h is sometimes called the *variance function*. Note that V_h is a function solely of the coded values of the factor levels for the treatments in the design and of the point $\mathbf{X}_h$ where the mean response is to be estimated. Also note that the variance of $\hat{Y}_h$ is a constant multiple of V_h, the constant being the error variance σ^2. Hence, the variance function provides

FIGURE 32.2   Contours of Variance Functions for Two-Factor Central Composite Designs.

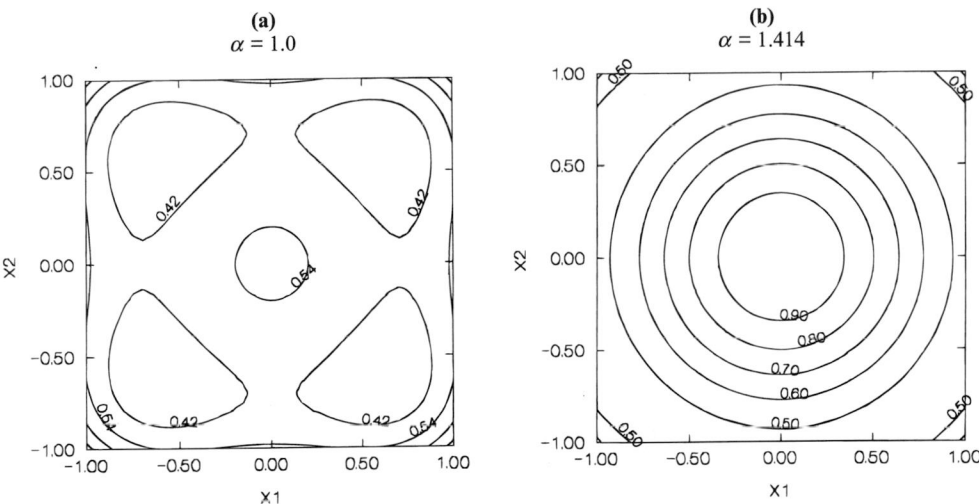

complete information of how the variance $\sigma^2\{\hat{Y}_h\}$ behaves for different points $\mathbf{X}_h$. Figure 32.2 presents contour plots of the variance functions for the two central composite designs in Figure 32.1. For both of these designs, $n_c = n_s = n_0 = 1$, and both use a 2^2 factorial design as the base design. They differ only with respect to α. Notice in Figure 32.2b that the contours of the variance function for the central composite design with $\alpha = \sqrt{2}$ are circular, indicating equal precision at a given distance from the center point. Hence, this is a rotatable design. On the other hand, the contours of the variance function in Figure 32.2a are not circular, indicating that the design with $\alpha = 1$ is not rotatable.

It can be shown that a central composite design is rotatable if:

$$(32.5) \qquad \alpha = \left[\frac{2^{k-f}(n_c)}{n_s}\right]^{1/4}$$

For the example in Figure 32.2b, we have $n_c = n_s = 1$, $k = 2$, and $f = 0$. Hence, the choice of:

$$\alpha = \left[\frac{2^{2-0}(1)}{1}\right]^{1/4} = \sqrt{2}$$

leads to a rotatable design. Values of α that lead to rotatable designs when $n_c = n_s = 1$ are provided in Table 32.2.

While rotatability is a desirable property of a central composite design, it should not be the sole basis for making the choice of α. For example, in many instances, it may be physically difficult or impossible to extend the star points beyond the experimental region defined by the upper and lower limits of each factor. In such cases, α must not exceed 1.0. Also, a design with $\alpha = 1$ is sometimes easy to implement because only three levels are involved for each factor. In these cases, the resulting lack of rotatability may not be considered a serious disadvantage.

Example.   The levels of four ingredients of a prototype solid chocolate bar developed by food scientists at Fisher Company were to be fine-tuned prior to national distribution. The factors and associated ranges were as follows:

Factor	Low Level	High Level
Cocoa butter	8.0	10.0
Added milk solids	2.0	3.0
Flavoring	2.5	3.5
Sugar	12.5	18.5

The response of interest was the overall consumer acceptability as measured on a 10-point scale. The objective of the experiment was to determine the levels of cocoa butter, added milk solids, flavoring, and sugar that lead to highest acceptability. To carry out the experiment, chocolate bars were to be made with different factor level combinations for the ingredients, and each type of chocolate bar was then to be subjected to a small consumer test. The firm's marketing research department determined that each consumer test would cost about $2,500. Because the total cost of the study was not to exceed $75,000, 30 or fewer consumer tests could be performed. From Table 32.2, we see that the total number of trials for a central composite four-factor design with $n_0 = 4$ replications at the center point is 28, and that this design is rotatable when $\alpha = 2$. The selected design in coded units is shown in Table 32.3.

Comments

1. A central composite design with $\alpha = 1$ is often called a *face-centered design*. For $k = 3$ factors, for instance, this design locates the star points at the center of each of the six faces of the base design cube.

2. When it is not possible to extend the star points beyond the factorial region defined by the original ranges of the factors, a *rotatable inscribed central composite design* can often be used. In such an inscribed design, the coded factor level settings are rescaled by the factor $1/\alpha$ so that all coded factor levels fall between -1 and 1. To illustrate the rescaling, we know from Table 32.2 that a two-factor central composite rotatable design requires the choice of $\alpha = 1.414$ when $n_c = n_s = 1$. To obtain an inscribed two-factor, rotatable central composite design, each coded factor level is multiplied by $1/1.414$. The original rotatable design, with $n_0 = n_c = n_s = 1$, and the corresponding inscribed design are shown in Table 32.4 on page 1288. The inscribed design has the appropriate value of α (1.0), and no factor levels are outside the original ranges for each factor. Note that the actual factor levels now need to be rescaled as well. Consequently, the corner points of the design will no longer be at the limits of the ranges for the factor levels. When this is undesirable, an inscribed design will not be appropriate.   ∎

Other Criteria for Choosing a Central Composite Design

Other criteria for the choice of a central composite response surface design, besides rotatability, have been proposed. Two of these are *orthogonality* and *uniform precision*. An unblocked central composite design is orthogonal if the estimated factor effect coefficients are all uncorrelated. A proper choice of n_0, the number of center point replicates, will lead to an orthogonal central composite design. For example, some orthogonal central composite designs for two to five factors are as follows for $n_s = n_c = 1$ replicate at each star and corner point:

TABLE 32.3   **Three-Factor Central Composite Design with $\alpha = 2.0$
—Fisher Company Example.**

Experimental Trial	Factor Level Settings			
	X_1	X_2	X_3	X_4
1	−1	−1	−1	−1
2	1	−1	−1	−1
3	−1	1	−1	−1
4	1	1	−1	−1
5	−1	−1	1	−1
6	1	−1	1	−1
7	−1	1	1	−1
8	1	1	1	−1
9	−1	−1	−1	1
10	1	−1	−1	1
11	−1	1	−1	1
12	1	1	−1	1
13	−1	−1	1	1
14	1	−1	1	1
15	−1	1	1	1
16	1	1	1	1
17	−2.0	0	0	0
18	2.0	0	0	0
19	0	−2.0	0	0
20	0	2.0	0	0
21	0	0	−2.0	0
22	0	0	2.0	0
23	0	0	0	−2.0
24	0	0	0	2.0
25	0	0	0	0
26	0	0	0	0
27	0	0	0	0
28	0	0	0	0

Design Characteristic	Number of Factors			
	2	3	4	5
Base factorial design	2^2	2^3	2^4	2^5
n_0	8	9	12	17

Notice that for each of these designs, the required number of replications at the center point is quite large. While orthogonality is desirable because it simplifies the analysis of the results, at times it will be difficult to justify large expenditures for replications at the center point. Lack of orthogonality is not a serious disadvantage in practice today because the analysis of the experimental results is easily handled by using a computer regression package.

TABLE 32.4   **Two-Factor Inscribed Central Composite Design with**
$n_0 = n_c = n_s = 1, \alpha = 1.414$.

Experimental Trial	Central Composite Design		Inscribed Central Composite Design	
	X_1	X_2	X_1	X_2
1	−1	−1	−.707	−.707
2	1	−1	.707	−.707
3	−1	1	−.707	.707
4	1	1	.707	.707
5	−1.414	0	−1	0
6	1.414	0	1	0
7	0	−1.414	0	−1
8	0	1.414	0	1
9	0	0	0	0

A uniform precision central composite design is a rotatable design for which the precision of the estimated mean response is the same at the center point as it is one unit from the center point (in any direction). Uniform precision designs are obtained by appropriate choices of α and n_0. The following are the required values of α and n_0 for studies with two to five factors:

Design Characteristic	Number of Factors			
	2	3	4	5
Base factorial design	2^2	2^3	2^4	2^5
α for rotatability	1.414	1.682	2.000	2.378
n_0	5	6	7	10

Like for the orthogonal designs above, the number of center point replications required for uniform precision may be too large. Uniform precision is therefore often used only as a secondary criterion for determining the number of replications at the center point.

Blocking Central Composite Designs

One useful characteristic of central composite response surface designs is that they can be blocked easily. The corner points of the central composite design, which constitute a 2^{k-f} factorial design, can be blocked by the methods described in Section 31.5. As noted there, one or more center point replications can be allocated to each of these blocks. Any remaining center point replications and all star points will constitute a final, separate block. Thus, if the base 2^{k-f} factorial design is run in b blocks, the central composite design is run in $b + 1$ blocks. The resulting blocking arrangement is then as follows:

(32.6)

Blocks 1 to b: 2^{k-f} base factorial design in b blocks, with n_0^* center point replications in each block

Block $b + 1$: $2k$ star points, with $n_0 - bn_0^*$ center point replications added

Augmenting Two-Level Studies.   The blocking arrangement just described can also be used to facilitate the implementation of a central composite design in two stages, which is often desirable. In the first stage, a two-level study with some center point replications is conducted in one or more blocks. If the test for lack of fit suggests the presence of curvature, or if a better approximation of the response surface is desired, the initial two-level study is augmented with star points and additional center point replications. These additional experimental trials constitute an additional block.

Note

Blocking arrangement (32.6) ensures that estimated block effects will be uncorrelated with estimated linear main effects and two-factor interactions, but the estimated block effects may be correlated with the estimated quadratic main effects. A central composite design that is *orthogonally blocked* will also provide that the estimated block effects are uncorrelated with the estimated quadratic main effects. It is not always possible to achieve both rotatability and orthogonal blocking. Often, however, orthogonal blocking and approximate rotatability can be achieved by suitable choices of the locations of the star points and by the allocation of the center point replications to the blocks. Reference 32.1 provides further information on orthogonally blocked central composite designs.   ∎

Additional General-Purpose Response Surface Designs

While central composite designs are the most widely used general-purpose response surface designs, other general-purpose designs are available. One important class of alternative designs is the Box-Behnken family of designs. Box-Behnken designs differ from central composite designs in two ways. First, only three levels for each factor are employed. Second, Box-Behnken designs have no corner points. Box-Behnken designs are sometimes preferred to central composite designs when physical or economic constraints prevent the use of the corner points—where all factor levels are at an extreme. A listing of Box-Behnken designs and their blocking arrangements is provided in Reference 32.2.

32.3   Optimal Response Surface Designs

Purpose of Optimal Designs

Central composite response surface designs have been developed for fairly standard experimental situations where the response surface of interest can be reasonably approximated by the second-order polynomial response function (32.1) and the experimental region is defined by the upper and lower limits of the factor levels. Also, since central composite designs are general purpose designs, they are not oriented to provide either optimum precision of the regression parameters or optimum precision for estimating mean responses for particular circumstances.

Optimal designs are useful when optimization of the precision is of key importance and/or when nonstandard experimental situations are encountered. We consider now three main types of nonstandard experimental conditions where central composite designs may not be feasible—irregular experimental regions, nonstandard models, and nonstandard sample sizes.

FIGURE 32.3   **Operating Region and Three Alternative Designs with $n_T = 11$—Rutgers Experimental Station Example.**

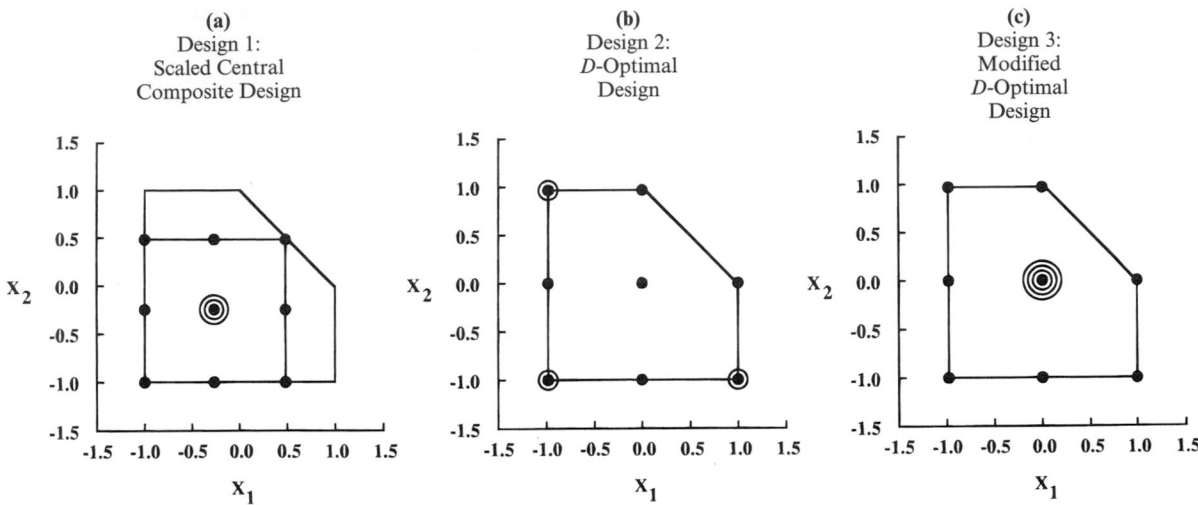

Irregular Experimental Regions.   Irregular experimental regions are quite common in industrial studies. One simple example, described in Reference 32.3, involved the application of two fertilizers at the Rutgers Experimental Station to determine the levels of the fertilizers that would optimize the yield of a particular crop. It was known in advance of the experiment that a toxic level of the chemicals would result if both of the fertilizers were applied simultaneously at their high levels. The investigators determined that the sum of the two fertilizers (in coded units) should not exceed 1.0:

$$(32.7) \qquad\qquad X_1 + X_2 \leq 1.0$$

This constraint leads to the irregular experimental region shown in Figure 32.3a. Also shown in Figure 32.3a is a face-centered central composite design with three replications at the center point. Notice that the ranges of the two factors must be considerably reduced to accommodate the standard central composite design here. Figure 32.3 also contains two other designs for this experimental study that we shall discuss shortly.

Nonstandard Models.   Nonstandard models can arise for a variety of reasons. For example, the investigator may know that the response function for a two-factor study is approximately linear in X_1 for constant X_2 and approximately quadratic in X_2. An appropriate regression function then would be:

$$E\{Y\} = \beta_0 + \beta_1 X_1 + \beta_2 X_2 + \beta_{12} X_1 X_2 + \beta_{22} X_2^2$$

Nonstandard models also arise in response surface experiments when both qualitative and quantitative factors are present. In the above example, if the first factor were a qualitative factor with two levels, a response function of the following form would be appropriate:

$$E\{Y\} = \beta_0 + \beta_1 I_1 + \beta_2 X_2 + \beta_{12} I_1 X_2 + \beta_{22} X_2^2$$

where:

$$I_1 = \begin{array}{ll} -1 & \text{if factor 1 at level 1} \\ 1 & \text{if factor 1 at level 2} \end{array}$$

Nonstandard Sample Sizes.   In the chocolate bar optimization study of Section 32.2, budgetary considerations required that the number of runs in the experiment not exceed 30. From Table 32.2, we found that a four-factor central composite design with four replications at the center point was feasible since it would require $n_T = 28$ experimental trials. Suppose now that the budget for the experiment were only $50,000. At $2,500 per market test, the maximum number of trials now would be 20, and the selected central composite design would no longer be feasible, even with no replications at the center point.

It is possible, nonetheless, to construct experimental designs that will provide estimates of all of the parameters in the full second-order response function (32.1) in fewer than 20 runs since there are only 15 parameters in this model when $k = 4$. Optimal design techniques can be used here to construct a potentially useful second-order design for any feasible experimental size between 15 and 20 trials.

Optimal Design Approach

In order to construct an optimal experimental design, the investigator must first specify the following:

1. The number of experimental trials, n_T.

2. The response function of interest.

3. A *candidate list*, C, of feasible treatments.

4. A statistical *design criterion* for the selection of the treatments from the candidate list C and for the allocation of the n_T trials to the selected treatments.

Once these specifications have been made, numerical computer search procedures are usually employed to find the experimental design that meets optimally the design criterion.

Example.   To illustrate the optimal design approach, consider again the Rutgers Experimental Station example. The feasible experimental region is shown in Figure 32.4a. Suppose that no more than $n_T = 11$ experimental trials can be made, and that the response function is the second-order one in (32.1):

$$(32.8) \qquad E\{Y\} = \beta_0 + \beta_1 X_1 + \beta_2 X_2 + \beta_{11} X_1^2 + \beta_{22} X_2^2 + \beta_{12} X_1 X_2$$

To obtain an optimal design, it is still necessary to specify a candidate list of treatments and a criterion for design selection. Often, the candidate list of treatments is obtained from a grid of regularly spaced points in the feasible experimental region. Figure 32.4a shows a 5×5 grid of treatment points over the unconstrained region. Of the 25 grid points, three fall in the infeasible region because the sum $X_1 + X_2$ for these points exceeds the constraint in (32.7). These three infeasible grid points therefore need to be deleted, resulting in the 22-point candidate set shown in Figure 32.4b.

Finally, a statistical criterion for the selection of the experimental design with n_T trials must be provided. We shall now discuss two such criteria that are widely employed.

FIGURE 32.4 **Candidate Set of Treatments—Rutgers Experimental Station Example.**

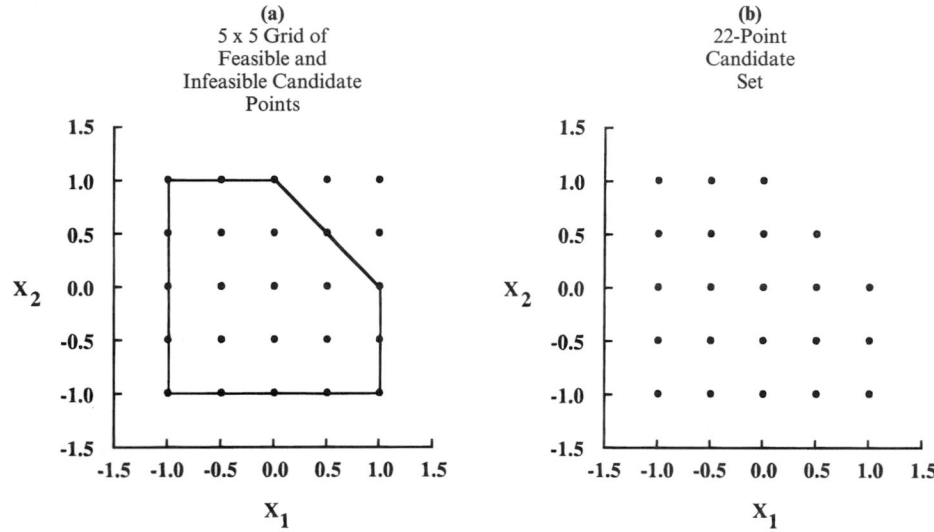

Design Criteria for Optimal Design Selection

D **Criterion.** When precise estimation of model parameters is of primary interest, the *D* (determinant) criterion provides a useful measure of the precision of an experiment. This criterion is based on the joint confidence region for the parameters in the normal error regression model. This joint confidence region is given by the set of coefficient vectors $\boldsymbol{\beta}$ that satisfy the inequality:

$$(32.9) \qquad \frac{(\mathbf{b} - \boldsymbol{\beta})'\mathbf{X}'\mathbf{X}(\mathbf{b} - \boldsymbol{\beta})}{pMSE} \leq F(1 - \alpha; p, n - p)$$

For simple linear regression, where the unknown parameters are β_0 and β_1, the boundary of this region is an ellipse. For models with three or more parameters, the boundary of the confidence region is an ellipsoid. One measure of the precision of the parameter estimates is the area or volume (for three or more parameters) of the confidence region. A small confidence region area or volume implies high precision. When the objective of the experiment is to estimate the vector $\boldsymbol{\beta}$ precisely, the confidence ellipse or ellipsoid for $\boldsymbol{\beta}$ should therefore be small. It can be shown that minimizing the volume of the confidence region (32.9) is equivalent to minimizing:

$$(32.10) \qquad D = |(\mathbf{X}'\mathbf{X})^{-1}|$$

where $|(\mathbf{X}'\mathbf{X})^{-1}|$ denotes the determinant of $(\mathbf{X}'\mathbf{X})^{-1}$. Hence, the smaller is the determinant $|(\mathbf{X}'\mathbf{X})^{-1}|$, the smaller is the volume of the confidence region. A design that minimizes $|(\mathbf{X}'\mathbf{X})^{-1}|$ is said to be *D-optimal*.

Example.   We illustrate the use of the D criterion for the Rutgers Experimental Station example by considering the three experimental designs in Figure 32.3. The design in Figure 32.3a, as we noted earlier, is a scaled central composite design with three replications at the center point, requiring $n_T = 11$ trials. The designs in Figures 32.3b and 32.3c also require $n_T = 11$ trials but involve a different set of treatments than the scaled central composite design. The designs in Figures 32.3b and 32.3c utilize the same set of treatments but differ as to which treatments receive more than one replication. Calculation of the determinant $|(\mathbf{X}'\mathbf{X})^{-1}|$ will be done ordinarily by use of a computer or a programmable calculator. We find that the values of the determinant criterion for the three designs under consideration are:

$$\text{Design 1:}\quad D = |(\mathbf{X}'\mathbf{X})^{-1}| = .009117$$

$$\text{Design 2:}\quad D = |(\mathbf{X}'\mathbf{X})^{-1}| = .000161$$

$$\text{Design 3:}\quad D = |(\mathbf{X}'\mathbf{X})^{-1}| = .000347$$

Since design 2 yields the smallest value of D among the three proposed designs, design 2 is preferred to designs 1 and 3 on the basis of the determinant criterion.

Relative Efficiency of Two Designs.   A measure of the relative efficiency of design 1 relative to design 2 according to the D criterion is the following, where $\mathbf{X}_1$ and $\mathbf{X}_2$ are the $\mathbf{X}$ matrices for the two designs:

$$(32.11) \qquad\qquad E_D = \left(\frac{|(\mathbf{X}_2'\mathbf{X}_2)^{-1}|}{|(\mathbf{X}_1'\mathbf{X}_1)^{-1}|} \right)^{1/p}$$

For the Rutgers Experimental Station example, the relative efficiency of design 1 compared to design 2 is:

$$E_D = \left(\frac{.000161}{.009117} \right)^{1/6} = .51$$

The relative efficiency measure states that design 1 is only 51 percent as efficient as design 2. This means that design 1 would need to be replicated $1/.51 = 1.96$ times in order to achieve as small a confidence region for the regression parameters as design 2.

V Criterion.   The objective of response surface experiments often is the estimation of the mean response $E\{Y_h\}$ at different combinations of factor level settings, denoted by $\mathbf{X}_h$. The estimation of these mean responses often is used to identify the factor settings $\mathbf{X}_h$ for which the mean response $E\{Y_h\}$ is either maximized or minimized. The V criterion considers the variances $\sigma^2\{\hat{Y}_h\}$ at factor level combinations $\mathbf{X}_h$ of interest and employs the average of these variances as the criterion. Let P denote the set of n_P factor level combinations ($\mathbf{X}_h$ vectors) at which the experimenter wishes to estimate the mean response. Often, the estimation set P is the same as the candidate set C. At other times, the two sets do not coincide, as when P contains points outside of the experimental region because the investigator anticipates the need for estimating mean responses in a region where experimentation is costly. Using (32.4) to express the variance $\sigma^2\{\hat{Y}_h\}$ in terms of the variance function V_h, we can state the average of the variances of $\hat{Y}_h$ for the estimation set P as follows:

$$(32.12) \qquad\qquad \frac{\Sigma\sigma^2\{\hat{Y}_h\}}{n_P} = \frac{\Sigma\sigma^2 V_h}{n_P} = \sigma^2 \overline{V}$$

FIGURE 32.5   **Design 2 Variance Function V_h Evaluated at Points in Estimation Set—Rutgers Experimental Station Example.**

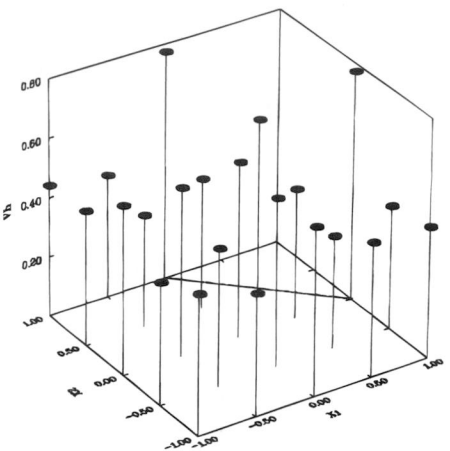

where:

(32.12a)
$$\overline{V} = \frac{\Sigma V_h}{n_P}$$

A design that minimizes $\overline{V}$ in (32.12a) is called a *V-optimal design*.

Example.   In the Rutgers Experimental Station example, the estimation set P is to consist of the 22 candidate treatments in Figure 32.4b. The variance function V_h was evaluated first for design 2 for the 22 treatments in the estimation set. The results are shown in Figure 32.5. Note that the treatments at (1, 0) and (0, 1), the two vertices of the operating region with no replications, have large V_h values. Consequently, with design 2 the mean responses for these two treatments will not be estimated as precisely as for the other treatments. The mean of the 22 V_h values for design 2 is $\overline{V} = .500$. In the same fashion, we find $\overline{V}$ for the other two designs. The comparative results for the three designs are:

Design	$\overline{V}$
1	1.192
2	.500
3	.486

Hence, according to the V criterion design 3 is slightly preferred over design 2, and both of these designs are substantially better than design 1.

Relative Efficiency of Two Designs.   A measure of the relative efficiency of design 1 relative to design 2 according to the V criterion is the following, where $\overline{V}_1$ and $\overline{V}_2$ denote the averages of the V_h values for the two designs:

(32.13)
$$E_V = \frac{\overline{V}_2}{\overline{V}_1}$$

For the Rutgers Experimental Station example, the relative efficiency of design 1 relative to design 3 is:

$$E_V = \frac{.486}{1.192} = .408$$

Design 1 is only 41 percent as efficient as design 3 according to the V criterion, implying that it would require $1/.408 = 2.45$ replications of design 1 to achieve the same average precision as with design 3.

Note

Other criteria that have been proposed for identifying a design as optimal involve minimizing the average variance of the estimated regression coefficients (A-optimality) and minimizing the maximum variance of $\hat{Y}_h$ over the estimation set (G-optimality when the estimation set P is the same as the candidate set C). ∎

Construction of Optimal Response Surface Designs

On occasion, the optimal design for a given criterion is known or can be found analytically. Usually, however, a computer search is required to find the optimal design. Many statistical software packages provide capabilities for finding optimal designs. To reduce the amount of computing required, these packages do not evaluate all possible designs. Instead, fast, special-purpose computer search procedures, called *exchange algorithms*, are used to find designs that are either optimal or nearly optimal. These algorithms begin the search with a starting design, sometimes randomly chosen. They then alternately add new points to the design and subtract points from the design in ways that lead to improvements in the design criterion. Since these algorithms do not evaluate every possible design, they cannot guarantee that an optimal design has been found. To increase the likelihood that a best or near-best design is found, some software packages provide capabilities for repeated attempts, beginning the search from different, randomly selected starting designs. A discussion of these search procedures is given in Reference 32.4

Example.   IC Technologies is a manufacturer of dashboard displays used in the automotive industry. An important component of the manufacturing process involves the bonding of a computer chip to a glass surface with adhesive. Management wished to determine which of two types of adhesive, provided by two different suppliers, was superior. Identification of the optimum processing temperature was also of interest. The response of interest was bonding strength—the amount of force required to break the chip free of the surface. The factors and associated levels were as follows:

Factors	Levels		
Adhesive	Type 1	Type 2	
Process temperature	210	240	270

Notice that adhesive is a qualitative factor that can assume only two levels. Process temperature is a quantitative factor that has a range from 210 to 270. The process engineers wished to limit the number of temperature levels to the limits of the range (210, 270) and to the middle (240). The candidate set of treatments is therefore given by the six factor level combinations shown in Figure 32.6a.

FIGURE 32.6   **SAS Optimal Design Construction—IC Technologies Example.**

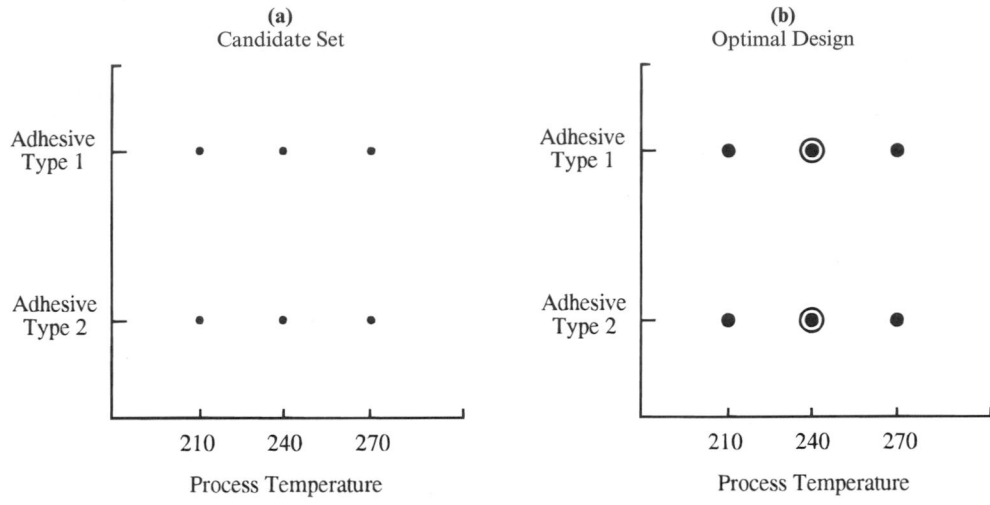

Since adhesive type is a qualitative factor with two levels and a quadratic (second-order) temperature effect was expected, the response function chosen was the following:

$$E\{Y\} = \beta_0 + \beta_1 I_1 + \beta_2 X_2 + \beta_{22} X_2^2 + \beta_{12} I_1 X_2$$

where:

$$I_1 = \begin{array}{ll} -1 & \text{if adhesive is type 1} \\ 1 & \text{if adhesive is type 2} \end{array}$$

$X_2 =$ coded temperature

Management determined that at most eight experimental trials could be handled and specified that the V criterion be employed. The estimation set of interest consisted of 21 equally spaced points spanning the process temperature range for each of the two types of adhesive. Note that the 42-point estimation set P here is not the same as the candidate set C. The SAS PROC OPTEX program was used to obtain the V-optimal design for $n_T = 8$ shown in Figure 32.6b. Notice that the medium level of temperature (240) is replicated twice for each adhesive type. Thus, two degrees of freedom will be available for a pure error estimate of the error variance and a lack of fit test will be possible.

Some Final Cautions

Caution in using optimal designs is important because these designs are best for particular choices of sample size, design space, response function, and design criterion. For example, designs that are optimal according to one criterion may be far from optimal according to another criterion. Also, optimal designs are highly sensitive to the choice of response function. A design that is optimal for a second-order response function is generally not optimal if a first-order response function is the true function. Consequently, the experimenter needs to consider whether the optimal design will be far from being optimal if the assumed response function is incorrect, and whether the optimal design will provide sufficient information about the true response function if the assumed one is incorrect.

Another reason for caution when choosing optimal designs is that they are constructed on the basis of a single design criterion. Frequently, an experimenter has a number of potentially conflicting objectives. It is therefore important that any candidate design be evaluated for its ability to satisfy each of these goals. Small modifications to computer-generated designs—such as the addition of replications at the center point—can be useful for increasing the overall utility of a design even if it is then no longer an optimal design according to a given criterion. It is often useful to construct optimal designs for a range of sample sizes and a variety of response functions and criteria. A final design can then be chosen on the basis of its ability to reasonably meet the different objectives over the range of response functions and criteria.

A thorough discussion of optimal designs is presented in Reference 32.5.

32.4   Analysis of Response Surface Experiments

The analysis of second-order response surface designs frequently involves three phases:

1. Estimation of response function

2. Model interpretation and visualization

3. Identification of optimum operating conditions

In phase 1, standard regression tools are used to estimate the response function and obtain a good regression fit. The fitted surface is then explored graphically in phase 2. Finally, in phase 3, factor level combinations that lead to an optimum response are identified. Fitting of polynomial regression models was already discussed in Chapter 7. Here, we shall focus on the visualization of the fitted model and the identification of optimum operating conditions.

Model Interpretation and Visualization

Three-dimensional plots of the response surface, contour plots, and conditional effects plots are the primary visual tools for interpreting and communicating the results of response surface experiments. Generally, three kinds of fitted surfaces arise in practice.

1. A mound-shaped surface, which is characterized by contours that are ellipses or circles. Figure 32.7 presents a three-dimensional response surface plot and a contour plot of the fitted response function:

$$\hat{Y} = 65 + 3X_1 + 4X_2 - 10X_1^2 - 15X_2^2 + 15X_1X_2$$

The contour plot in Figure 32.7b shows that the estimated mean response increases from a minimum of $\hat{Y} = 34$ in the lower right corner ($X_1 = 1$, $X_2 = -1$) to a maximum in the center of the region bounded by the $\hat{Y} = 66$ contour.

2. A bowl-shaped surface, which also has elliptical or circular contours; however, the response function decreases in the direction of the smallest ellipse. Figure 32.8 presents the response surface and a contour plot of the fitted response function:

$$\hat{Y} = 6.5 + 6X_1 + 2X_2 + 9X_1^2 + 4X_2^2 + X_1X_2$$

FIGURE 32.7   **Two-Factor Response Surface and Contour Plot—Mound-Shaped Surface.**

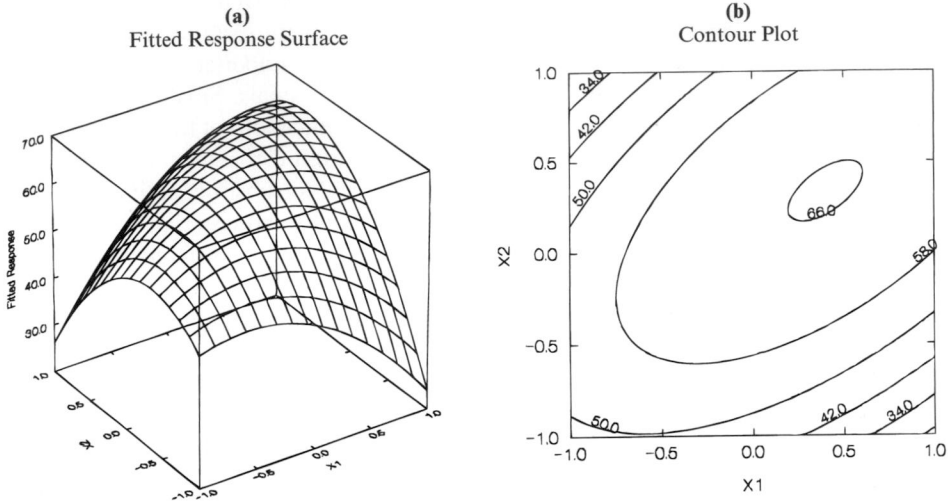

(a)
Fitted Response Surface

(b)
Contour Plot

FIGURE 32.8   **Two-Factor Response Surface and Contour Plot—Bowl-Shaped Surface.**

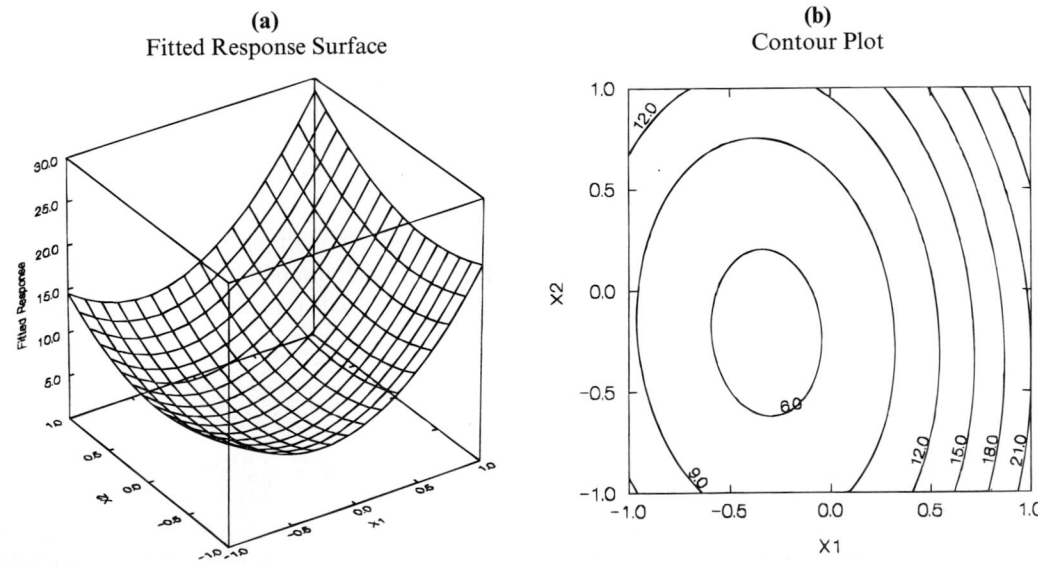

(a)
Fitted Response Surface

(b)
Contour Plot

From the contour plot in Figure 32.8b, we see that the surface decreases from a maximum in the upper right corner ($X_1 = 1$, $X_2 = 1$) to a minimum in the center of the region bounded by the $\hat{Y} = 6$ contour.

FIGURE 32.9 **Two-Factor Response Surface and Contour Plot—Saddle-Shaped Surface.**

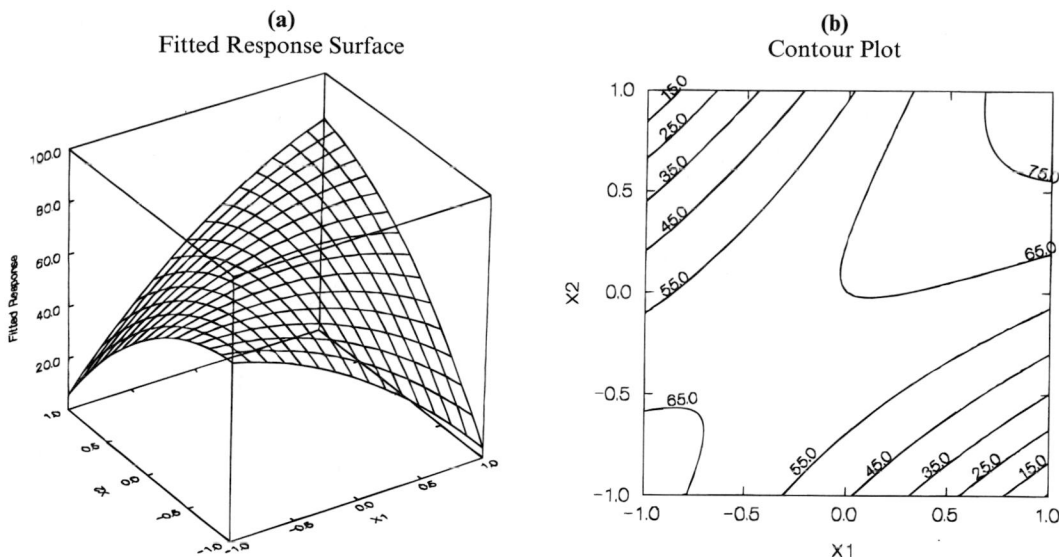

(a)
Fitted Response Surface

(b)
Contour Plot

3. A response surface with a *saddle* or a *minimax*. Figure 32.9 presents the response surface and a contour plot of the fitted response function:

$$\hat{Y} = 65 + 3X_1 + 4X_2 - 10X_1^2 - 15X_2^2 + 35X_1X_2$$

From the contour plot in Figure 32.9b, notice that the mean response increases from the upper left corner to a maximum in the center of the region and then decreases as we approach the lower right corner. The opposite occurs when moving from the upper right corner to the lower left corner.

Conditional effects plots, or interactions plots, can also provide useful insights. Figure 32.10 presents a conditional effects plot for the saddle-shaped surface in Figure 32.9 at $X_2 = -1, 0, 1$:

$$X_2 = -1: \quad \hat{Y} = 46 - 32X_1 - 10X_1^2$$

$$X_2 = \quad 0: \quad \hat{Y} = 65 + 3X_1 - 10X_1^2$$

$$X_2 = \quad 1: \quad \hat{Y} = 54 + 38X_1 - 10X_1^2$$

Notice that at low X_2 the mean response is decreasing in X_1, whereas at high X_2 the mean response is increasing in X_1. Thus, the presence of interaction effects is clearly indicated by the plot. Absence of interaction effects would be indicated, as usual, by parallel curves.

Response Surface Optimum Conditions

Response surfaces are frequently fitted for the purpose of finding the combination of factor levels that leads to an optimum response. Usually, either a maximum response (e.g., maximum yield) or a minimum response (e.g., minimum waste) is sought. Mound-shaped

FIGURE 32.10   Conditional Effects Plots for Saddle-Shaped Surface in Figure 32.9.

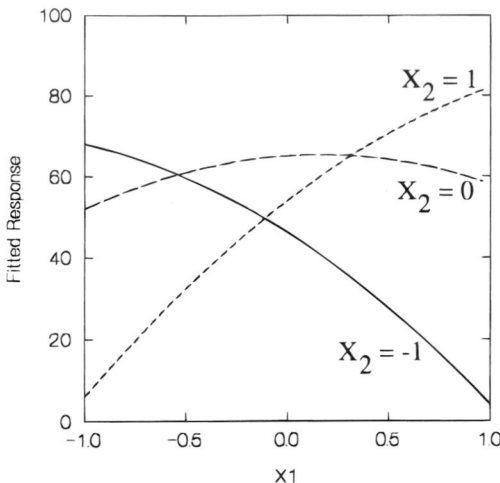

response surfaces, such as in Figure 32.7, have a unique maximum, while bowl-shaped response surfaces, such as in Figure 32.8, have a unique minimum. Occasionally, more complex response surfaces are encountered that have saddle points, such as in Figure 32.9, or a number of local maximum or minimum points.

For a second-order fitted response surface, the point where a maximum, a minimum, or a saddle point occurs, denoted by the vector $\mathbf{X}_s$, is:

$$(32.14) \qquad \mathbf{X}_s = -\frac{1}{2}\mathbf{B}^{-1}\mathbf{b}^*$$

where:

$$(32.14a) \qquad \underset{k \times k}{\mathbf{B}} = \begin{bmatrix} b_{11} & b_{12}/2 & \cdots & b_{1k}/2 \\ b_{12}/2 & b_{22} & \cdots & b_{2k}/2 \\ \vdots & \vdots & & \vdots \\ b_{1k}/2 & b_{2k}/2 & \cdots & b_{kk} \end{bmatrix} \qquad \mathbf{b}^* = \begin{bmatrix} b_1 \\ b_2 \\ \vdots \\ b_k \end{bmatrix}$$

To determine whether the point $\mathbf{X}_s$ corresponds to a maximum, a minimum, or a saddle-point, the nature of the response surface must be known. If a contour plotting capability is available and there are just two or three factors, the nature of the surface can usually be determined by examining the contours in the vicinity of $\mathbf{X}_s$. Otherwise, characteristics of the matrix $\mathbf{B}$ called *eigenvalues* can be used to determine whether the point at $\mathbf{X}_s$ is a maximum, a minimum, or a saddle point. Many computer packages for response surface analysis provide these eigenvalues. If the eigenvalues are all positive, the point is a minimum. If the eigenvalues are all negative, the point is a maximum. Finally, if some eigenvalues are positive and some negative, the point is a saddle point.

Example. Consider again the mound-shaped response surface in Figure 32.7:

$$\hat{Y} = 65 + 3X_1 + 4X_2 - 10X_1^2 - 15X_2^2 + 15X_1X_2$$

We know that this surface has a maximum and wish to locate it. We require the matrix **B** and the vector **b***. Using (32.14a), we obtain:

$$\mathbf{B} = \begin{bmatrix} -10 & 15/2 \\ 15/2 & -15 \end{bmatrix} \qquad \mathbf{b}^* = \begin{bmatrix} 3 \\ 4 \end{bmatrix}$$

Using (32.14), we find the point where the response surface is at the maximum:

$$\mathbf{X}_s = -\frac{1}{2}\begin{bmatrix} -10 & 15/2 \\ 15/2 & -15 \end{bmatrix}^{-1}\begin{bmatrix} 3 \\ 4 \end{bmatrix}$$

$$= -\frac{1}{2}\begin{bmatrix} -.1600 & -.0800 \\ -.0800 & -.1067 \end{bmatrix}\begin{bmatrix} 3 \\ 4 \end{bmatrix} = \begin{bmatrix} .40 \\ .25 \end{bmatrix}$$

The maximum response on the fitted surface, at $X_1 = .40$ and $X_2 = .25$, is:

$$\hat{Y} = 65 + 3(.40) + 4(.25) - 10(.40)^2 - 15(.25)^2 + 15(.40)(.25) = 66.16$$

Comments

1. When the maximum or minimum point for the response surface falls well outside the operating region, it may not be feasible to operate at this point and the investigator must then search for the factor level combination that optimizes the mean response within the operating region. For problems involving just two or three predictors, this point can usually be pinpointed using contour plots and conditional effects plots. For problems involving four or more factors, constrained nonlinear programming methods can be used to identify the optimum factor level combination. Many statistical software packages that provide capabilities for the design of experiments include this feature. Alternatively, a grid of points (such as those used to identify candidate points for optimal design construction) can be constructed and the estimated mean response for each gridpoint is then obtained. If the grid is sufficiently dense, the gridpoint that leads to the maximum (minimum) estimated mean response will closely approximate the optimum point.

When it is feasible to operate outside the experimental region and the optimum point falls well outside this region, it is often necessary to extend the experiment because of uncertainty about the shape of the response surface outside the region of experimentation.

2. In most experiments, more than a single response variable is of interest. For example, in food processing experiments, response variables such as taste, texture, aftertaste, mouthfeel, shelf life, and cost are all frequently of interest. Another variable of interest in many studies is the variance of the response variable. In the IC Technologies example, for instance, the manufacturer is concerned not only that the mean bonding strength be adequately high but also that the process variability be small so that almost all components will be bonded with sufficient strength. To analyze experiments with multiple responses, a response surface must be fitted to each response variable. Unfortunately, it is rare that a single factor level combination can be found that simultaneously optimizes all fitted response surfaces. In fact, often the conditions that lead to an optimum value of one response variable (such as texture) lead to a poor response for another variable (such as taste). The investigator must then search for conditions that lead to acceptable responses for all response variables. ∎

Example

Dorle Exterior Trim manufactures polyurethane bumpers for automobiles and light trucks. During the initial production stages of a new model, blemishes appeared on the surface of the bumpers. These blemishes, resulting from a high degree of surface porosity, were so extensive that none of the bumpers could be shipped. A response surface experiment was quickly conducted to investigate the effects of three key process variables on porosity and to identify the optimum operating levels for the active process variables. The three factors were chemical temperature, mold temperature, and curing time. The operating ranges for these factors were:

Factor	Low Level	High Level
Chemical temperature	405	425
Mold temperature	100	240
Curing time	20	40

A three-factor central composite response surface design with $\alpha = 1$ and $n_0 = 3$ replications at the center point was chosen. Porosity counts were obtained from visual inspections of the surface of the bumpers.

The analyst first obtained an initial fit of the three-factor second-order response function (32.1). Residual analysis did not reveal any departures from the standard regression assumptions. The fit suggested that the third factor, curing time, was unrelated to porosity. All P-values for terms involving curing time were greater than or equal to .600. A test of $H_0: \beta_3 = \beta_{33} = \beta_{13} = \beta_{23} = 0$ by the general linear test statistic (2.70) resulted in the test statistic $F^* = .179$ and the P-value .943. The analyst therefore concluded H_0, that curing time is unrelated to porosity.

The SAS PROC RSREG output for the fit of the second-order response surface model with only chemical temperature and mold temperature as the explanatory variables is shown in Figure 32.11. The fitted response surface is:

$$\hat{Y} = 16.30 - 22.30X_1 + 3.20X_2 + 12.44X_1^2 + 11.94X_2^2 + 3.75X_1X_2$$

Notice that the P-values for all estimated coefficients are less than .1, and that R^2 is .957. A lack of fit test was conducted with $\alpha = .01$. The results ($F^* = 3.10$; P-value $= .089$) supported the appropriateness of the model fitted.

A response surface plot and a contour plot for the fitted response function are shown in Figure 32.12 on page 1304. The X_1 scale has been reversed in these plots to provide a better view of the response surface. Notice that the surface is bowl-shaped. Since a main objective of the experiment was to find the levels of the process variables that minimize the porosity on the bumper surface, the analyst next determined the optimum levels of X_1 and X_2 by means of (32.14). Substituting into this formula, the analyst obtained:

$$\mathbf{X}_s = -\frac{1}{2}\mathbf{B}^{-1}\mathbf{b}^* = -\frac{1}{2}\begin{bmatrix} 12.44 & 1.875 \\ 1.875 & 11.94 \end{bmatrix}^{-1}\begin{bmatrix} -22.30 \\ 3.20 \end{bmatrix} = \begin{bmatrix} .94 \\ -.28 \end{bmatrix}$$

The estimated mean response at $X_1 = .94$ and $X_2 = -.28$ is $\hat{Y} = 5.4$. To find the optimal process settings in the original units, the analyst employed (32.2) and found that the optimal process setting for chemical temperature is $415 + .94(10) = 424.4$ and for mold temperature the optimal setting is $170 - .28(70) = 150.4$.

These results are confirmed by the SAS output in Figure 32.11. Note the agreement for the optimum coded values of X_1 and X_2 and for $\hat{Y}$ at the minimum point. Also note that the

FIGURE 32.11   SAS PROC RSREG Regression Output—Dorle Exterior Trim Example.

Regression	Degrees of Freedom	Type I Sum of Squares	R-Square	F-Ratio	Prob > F
Linear	2	5075.300000	0.6894	87.308	0.0000
Quadratic	2	1854.363485	0.2519	31.900	0.0000
Crossproduct	1	112.500000	0.0153	3.871	0.0749
Total Regress	5	7042.163485	0.9566	48.457	0.0000

Residual	Degrees of Freedom	Sum of Squares	Mean Square
Total Error	11	319.718868	29.065352

Parameter	Degrees of Freedom	Parameter Estimate	Standard Error	T for H0: Parameter=0	Prob > |T|
INTERCEPT	1	16.301887	2.221627	7.338	0.0000
X1	1	-22.300000	1.704856	-13.080	0.0000
X2	1	3.200000	1.704856	1.877	0.0873
X1*X1	1	12.443396	3.097911	4.017	0.0020
X2*X1	1	3.750000	1.906087	1.967	0.0749
X2*X2	1	11.943396	3.097911	3.855	0.0027

	Critical Value	
Factor	Coded	Uncoded
X1	0.938443	0.938443
X2	-0.281292	-0.281292

Predicted value at stationary point   5.388176

	Eigenvectors	
Eigenvalues	X1	X2
14.084989	0.752384	0.658725
10.301803	-0.658725	0.752384

two eigenvalues are positive, indicating that the response surface is bowl-shaped so that a minimum point has been identified.

32.5   Sequential Search for Optimum Conditions—Method of Steepest Ascent

Often the researcher does not know in advance the region in which the optimum response exists. In that event, a sequential strategy is usually employed. First, a screening design is run in a region thought to contain the optimum response. On the basis of this initial experiment, an estimate of the direction in which the optimum response is located can be obtained. This direction is called the *path of steepest ascent (descent)*. Some additional, sequential experimental runs are then made along this path to identify more clearly the region that contains the optimum response. A new experiment is then conducted in the revised region, and the search process is iterated until the optimum region is identified with sufficient precision.

FIGURE 32.12   Fitted Response Surface and Contour Plot—Dorle Exterior Trim Example.

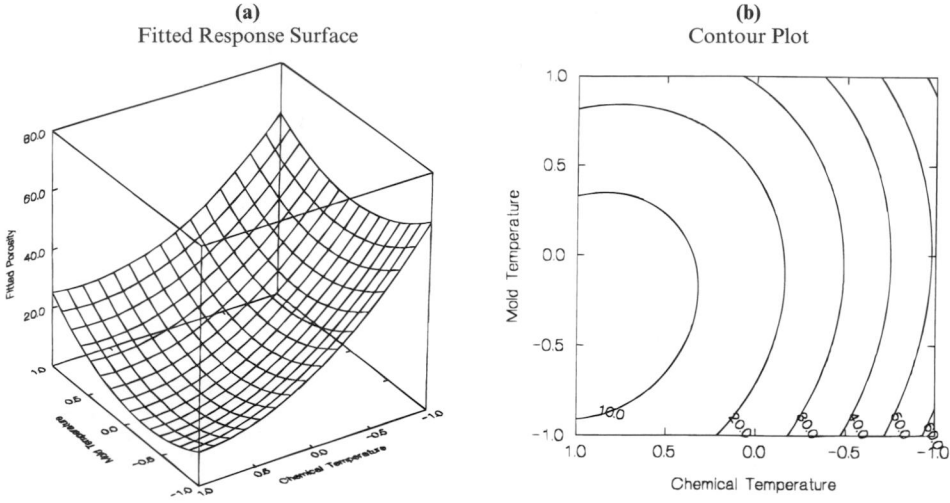

(a)
Fitted Response Surface

(b)
Contour Plot

Example

In the power cells example of Table 7.9 (p. 303), a researcher studied the effects of charge rate and temperature on the life of a new type of power cell. A 3^2 factorial design with three replications at the center point was used. The analysis of the experiment led to the conclusion that a first-order model is sufficient. In terms of the coded predictor variables, the final estimated response function was given in (7.82) (we now use X_1 and X_2 to denote the coded variables):

(32.15)
$$\hat{Y} = 172.00 - 55.83X_1 + 75.50X_2$$

Figure 32.13 contains the design points of the initial study and contour lines of the fitted response plane.

To search for the conditions maximizing the expected life of the power cells, we need to study the responses along the path of steepest ascent. This path is perpendicular to the contour lines. If a step of length t from the center point is taken along the path of steepest ascent (descent), the coordinates of the test point will be:

(32.16)
$$\mathbf{X}_h = \frac{t}{s}\mathbf{b}^*$$

where:

(32.16a)
$$\mathbf{b}^* = \begin{bmatrix} b_1 \\ \vdots \\ b_k \end{bmatrix} \qquad s = \sqrt{b_1^2 + \cdots + b_k^2}$$

and t is positive for ascending direction and negative for descending direction.

FIGURE 32.13   **Response Contours and Line of Steepest Ascent for Fitted Response Function (32.15)—Power Cells Example.**

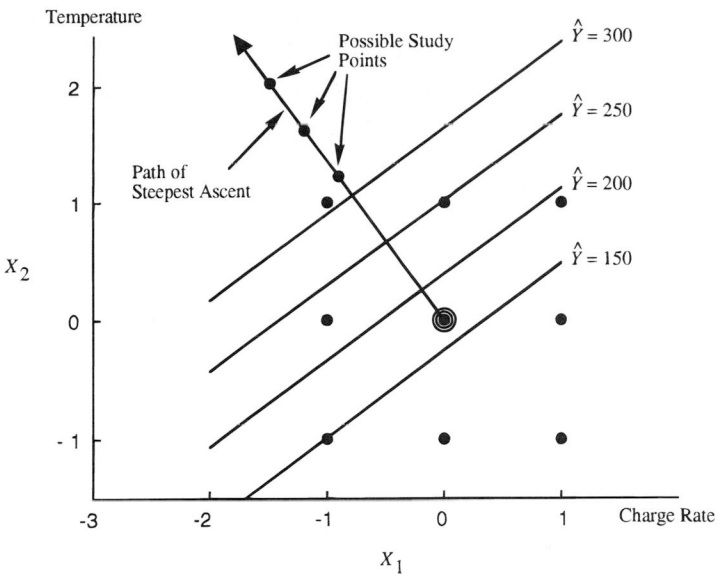

Suppose that three new test points are to be obtained at distances of 1.5, 2.0, and 2.5 coded units from the center point along the path of steepest ascent. We have, using (32.16a):

$$\mathbf{b}^* = \begin{bmatrix} -55.83 \\ 75.50 \end{bmatrix} \qquad s = \sqrt{(-55.83)^2 + (75.50)^2} = 93.90$$

Using (32.16), the coded coordinates of the test points are:

$$t = 1.5: \quad \mathbf{X}_h = \frac{1.5}{93.90} \begin{bmatrix} -55.83 \\ 75.50 \end{bmatrix} = \begin{bmatrix} -.89 \\ 1.21 \end{bmatrix}$$

$$t = 2.0: \quad \mathbf{X}_h = \frac{2.0}{93.90} \begin{bmatrix} -55.83 \\ 75.50 \end{bmatrix} = \begin{bmatrix} -1.19 \\ 1.61 \end{bmatrix}$$

$$t = 2.5: \quad \mathbf{X}_h = \frac{2.5}{93.90} \begin{bmatrix} -55.83 \\ 75.50 \end{bmatrix} = \begin{bmatrix} -1.49 \\ 2.01 \end{bmatrix}$$

These three study points are identified in Figure 32.13.

After exploration along the line of steepest ascent, another experimental design is then conducted in the region that the additional study points have identified as being nearer the optimum conditions. It may well be that a second-order model may then be required to describe adequately the response function in that region. This process is repeated as necessary until the region of optimum response conditions has been precisely identified.

Cited References

32.1.   Montgomery, D. C. *Design and Analysis of Experiments*. 3rd ed. New York: John Wiley & Sons, 1991.

32.2.   Box, G. E. P., and N. R. Draper. *Empirical Model-Building and Response Surfaces*. New York: John Wiley & Sons, 1987.

32.3.   Snee, R. D. "Computer-Aided Design of Experiments—Some Practical Experiences," *Journal of Quality Technology* 17 (1985), pp. 222–36.

32.4.   Meyer, R. K., and C. J. Nachtsheim. "The Coordinate Exchange Algorithm for Constructing Exact Optimal Experimental Designs," *Technometrics* 37 (1995), 60–69.

32.5.   Atkinson, A. C., and A. N. Donev. *Optimum Experimental Designs*. Oxford: Clarendon Press, 1992.

Problems

32.1.   What information do response surface experiments provide that two-level factorial experiments do not? In what ways do the analyses differ?

32.2.   A four-factor two-level full factorial design with $n_0 = 3$ replicates at the center point was run. The design is now to be augmented in a second block so that the combined design is a rotatable central composite design. Identify the treatments to be included in the second block.

32.3.   An attendee at a workshop on the design of experiments remarked: "Central composite response surface designs should almost always be preferred to two-level factorial designs since nearly all real-world response functions are nonlinear." Comment.

32.4.   A student asked: "If I have the capability to construct an optimal response surface design, why should I ever consider the use of a central composite design—unless it is also optimal?" Discuss.

32.5.   Optimal designs require that the response surface model be identified in advance of the experiment. In what sense is this also true of two-level full factorial and 2^{k-f} fractional factorial designs?

32.6.   Describe three different situations where the use of optimal response surface designs might be desirable.

32.7.   A five-factor response surface experiment is to be carried out and the second-order response function (32.1) is to be estimated.

    a.   Find the number of regression coefficients in the response function.

    b.   How many linear main effect terms are there? How many quadratic main effect terms? How many two-factor interactions?

    c.   What is the minimum number of distinct design points required to estimate all regression coefficients? How many distinct design points are there in the five-factor central composite design that is based on a 2_V^{5-1} fractional factorial design?

32.8. List the design matrix for a rotatable central composite response surface design that is based on a 2_V^{5-1} fractional factorial design with defining relation $0 = -12345$. Assume that $n_0 = 3$ and that $n_c = n_s = 1$.

32.9. A consultant has suggested that a rotatable central composite design be constructed for $k = 5$ factors with $f = 2$, $n_c = n_s = 1$, and $n_0 = 4$. Will all factor effect terms in the response function (32.1) be unconfounded? Explain.

32.10. A computer simulation experiment of a truck assembly operation is being planned by plant management. A rotatable central composite design is desired for $k = 9$ factors with $f = 3$, $n_0 = 10$, and $n_s = n_c = 1$. Determine α.

√ 32.11. **Television commercial recall**. A three-factor, face-centered central composite design was carried out to study the effects of length of commercial, frequency of viewing, and length of recall on the ability of subjects to recall an advertised product. Subjects were shown a video containing a number of programs with advertisements for three products. The factors of interest are all quantitative: commercial length ($X_1 = -1$: 10 seconds; $X_1 = 0$: 20 seconds; $X_1 = 1$: 30 seconds), number of repetitions of commercial ($X_2 = -1$: 1 viewing; $X_2 = 0$: 2 viewings; $X_2 = 1$: 3 viewings), delay between time of viewing and time of recall ($X_3 = -1$: 1 week; $X_3 = 0$: 3 weeks, $X_3 = 1$: 5 weeks). Each of the 15 treatments in the central composite design was assigned at random to 20 subjects. The response of interest (Y) is the average number of products recalled (out of three) by the 20 subjects that received a particular treatment. The observed responses and the design matrix follow.

Y	X_1	X_2	X_3
1.80	−1	−1	−1
2.00	1	−1	−1
2.10	−1	1	−1
...	...	...	...
2.10	0	0	−1
1.80	0	0	1
1.65	0	0	0

Adapted from S. Singh et al., "Recognition versus Recall as Measures of Television Commercial Forgetting," *Journal of Marketing Research*, 25 (1988) pp. 72–80.

a. Judging from the nature of the response variable, is normality of the error terms a reasonable assumption here? Is a constant error variance a reasonable assumption? Discuss.

b. Fit the second-order response function (32.1) and obtain the estimated factor effect coefficients. Which effects appear to be active?

c. Plot the residuals against the fitted values. Do any of the standard regression assumptions appear to be violated?

d. Using the P-values of the estimated factor effect coefficients, test for the significance of each of the factor effects; use $\alpha = .05$ for each test. Which factors are active?

√ 32.12. Refer to **Television commercial recall** Problem 32.11. The response surface model was revised to include only the three linear main effects, the 12 interaction effect, and the factor 1 quadratic main effect.

a. Fit the revised model and prepare a plot of the residuals against the fitted values. Do the standard regression assumptions appear to be satisfied?

b. Obtain a normal probability plot of the residuals. Also conduct the correlation test for normality; use $\alpha = .05$. Does the assumption of normality appear to be reasonable here?

c. Summarize the results of the experiment with an appropriate set of plots. Interpret the results.

32.13. Refer to **Whipped topping** Problem 31.29. A follow-up response surface study was conducted to explore the effects of soybean solids (X_1) and fat level (X_2) in more detail. The third factor found to be important in the earlier study, avicel (X_5), was to be fixed at its optimum level, the highest possible level. A two-factor, rotatable central composite design was employed, with four replications at the center point. The coded factor levels and the observed volume responses (Y) for the second experiment follow.

Y	X_1	X_2
144	-1	-1
192	1	-1
112	-1	1
...	...	...
191	0	0
177	0	0
195	0	0

a. Fit the second-order response function (32.1) and obtain the estimated factor effect coefficients. Which effects appear to be active for a hierarchical model?

b. Plot the residuals against the fitted values. Do any of the standard regression assumptions appear to be violated?

c. Conduct a lack of fit test; use $\alpha = .01$. State the alternatives, decision rule, and conclusion. Has an adequate fit been obtained?

d. Summarize the results of the experiment with a three-dimensional response surface plot and a contour plot. Judging from your contour plot, what coded values of the experimental factors maximize whipped topping volume?

e. Use (32.14) to determine the coded values of soybean solids and fat level that lead to a maximum on the fitted response surface.

f. Obtain a 95 percent confidence interval for the mean response at the point where the fitted response surface is maximized. Is the interval estimate reasonably precise? Discuss.

32.14. A two-factor inscribed rotatable orthogonal central composite design is to be utilized in a response surface experiment with $n_c = n_s = 1$.

a. List the design matrix. What are the coordinates of the corner points?

b. Calculate $(\mathbf{X'X})^{-1}$ and use your result to verify that the regression coefficients (excluding the intercept) are pairwise uncorrelated.

32.15. A two-factor rotatable central composite design having uniform precision is to be utilized in a response surface experiment.

a. List the design matrix. How many replications at the center point are required for uniform precision here?

b. Obtain a contour plot of the variance function. How does it confirm that the design is rotatable and of uniform precision?

√ 32.16. Refer to **Peanut solids** Problems 31.18 and 31.19. Consider the response function containing only the linear main effects for factors 4 and 5 obtained in Problem 31.19a.

    a. For the path of steepest ascent, identify the components in (32.16a). How can (32.16) be used to determine the operating ranges for the factors in a follow-up experiment?

    b. Identify the coded factor levels along the path of steepest ascent for steps of length $t = 1.5$, $t = 2.5$, and $t = 3.5$.

32.17. Refer to **Fiber optics** Problem 31.20 and 31.21. Consider the response function containing only the linear main effects for factors 1, 5, and 7 obtained in Problem 31.21a. Management is interested in minimizing the gel viscosity.

    a. For the path of steepest descent, identify the components in (32.16a). How can (32.16) be used to determine the operating ranges for the factors in a follow-up experiment?

    b. Identify the coded factor levels along the path of steepest descent for steps of length $t = -1$, $t = -2$, and $t = -3$.

Projects

32.18. **Blood sugar calibration**. A new, quick method for measuring low concentrations of galactose (sugar) in blood is to be evaluated. Twelve samples containing known concentrations (X) are to be employed. The researchers expect that the second-order response function $E\{Y\} = \beta_0 + \beta_1 X + \beta_{11} X^2$ will be appropriate for modeling the measured concentration (Y) as a function of the known concentration (X). In advance of the experiment, three alternative layouts are under discussion. In design 1, three samples at $X = 1, 4, 7, 10$ are employed. In design 2, four samples at $X = 1, 5.5, 10$ are employed. In design 3, three samples at $X = 1, 10$, and six samples at $X = 5.5$ are employed.

    a. Plot the variance functions for the three designs on the same graph, for $1 \leq X \leq 10$. Which of the three designs appears to provide minimum average variance?

    b. For each of the three designs, calculate the average variance of the estimated mean response for the estimation set $P = \{1.0, 1.5, 2.0, 2.5, \ldots, 10.0\}$. Which design is preferred according to the V criterion?

    c. Determine the V-efficiency of design 1 relative to design 2, of design 1 relative to design 3, and of design 2 relative to design 3. How many times must design 1 be replicated in order to achieve the precision of design 3 according to the V criterion?

    d. For each of the three designs, calculate $|(\mathbf{X}'\mathbf{X})^{-1}|$. Which design is preferred according to the D criterion?

    e. Determine the D-efficiency of design 1 relative to design 2, of design 1 relative to design 3, and of design 2 relative to design 3. How many times must design 1 be replicated in order to achieve the precision of design 2 according to the D criterion?

32.19. Refer to **Blood sugar calibration** Problem 32.18. Assume that the candidate set C is the same as the estimation set P in Problem 32.18b.

    a. Use a computer optimal design package to find the D-optimal design. Does the D-optimal design coincide with any of the designs considered in Problem 32.18?

    b. Use a computer optimal design package to find the V-optimal design. Does the V-optimal design coincide with any of the designs considered in Problem 32.18?

c. Which of the two optimal designs is better suited to the calibration problem under study? Discuss.

32.20. **Weatherstrip extrusion.** In an effort to improve the sealing properties of a rubber weatherstrip produced by an automotive supplier, chemical engineers plan to conduct a small response surface study. Two factors, extrusion temperature (X_1) and line speed (X_2), are of interest. The feasible experimental region (in terms of the coded factors) is given by the set of treatments satisfying (1) $-1 \leq X_1 \leq 1$, (2) $-1 \leq X_2 \leq 1$, (3) $X_2 \leq 1 + 2X_1$, and (4) $X_2 \geq (-1 + 4X_1)/3$. Two alternative designs, each based on nine experimental trials, have been proposed:

	Design 1		Design 2	
Trial	X_1	X_2	X_1	X_2
1	-1	-1	-1	-1
2	$-.75$	-1	$-.5$	-1
3	$-.5$	-1	$-.5$	0
4	$-.5$	0	0	0
5	0	0	0	0
6	.25	0	0	0
7	0	1	.25	0
8	.5	1	0	1
9	1	1	1	1

a. Plot the design space. Is it a regular or an irregular design space?

b. Superimpose each of the proposed designs on the design space in part (a). Does one design appear to be preferable to the other? Explain.

c. For each of the two designs, calculate the average variance of the estimated mean response for the estimation set P given by the feasible points obtained from a 9×9 grid of regularly spaced points over the unconstrained region. Which design is preferred according to the V criterion?

d. Determine the V-efficiency of design 1 relative to design 2. According to the V criterion, how many times must design 1 be replicated in order to achieve the precision of design 2?

e. Calculate $|(\mathbf{X'X})^{-1}|$ for each of the two designs. Which design is preferred according to the D criterion?

f. Determine the D-efficiency of design 2 relative to design 1. According to the D criterion, how many times must design 2 be replicated in order to achieve the precision of design 1?

32.21. Refer to **Weatherstrip extrusion** Problem 32.20. Assume that the candidate set C is the same as the estimation set P in Problem 32.20c.

a. Use a computer optimal design package to find the D-optimal design. Does the D-optimal design coincide with either of the two designs considered in Problem 32.20?

b. Use a computer optimal design package to find the V-optimal design. Does the V-optimal design coincide with either of the two designs considered in Problem 32.20?

c. Which of the two optimal designs is better suited to the response surface study here? Discuss.

Appendices

Appendices

Some Basic Results in Probability and Statistics

This appendix contains some basic results in probability and statistics. It is intended as a reference to which you may refer as you read the book.

A.1 Summation and Product Operators

Summation Operator

The summation operator Σ is defined as follows:

$$(A.1) \qquad \sum_{i=1}^{n} Y_i = Y_1 + Y_2 + \cdots + Y_n$$

Some important properties of this operator are:

$$(A.2a) \qquad \sum_{i=1}^{n} k = nk \qquad \text{where } k \text{ is a constant}$$

$$(A.2b) \qquad \sum_{i=1}^{n} (Y_i + Z_i) = \sum_{i=1}^{n} Y_i + \sum_{i=1}^{n} Z_i$$

$$(A.2c) \qquad \sum_{i=1}^{n} (a + cY_i) = na + c \sum_{i=1}^{n} Y_i \qquad \text{where } a \text{ and } c \text{ are constants}$$

The double summation operator $\Sigma\Sigma$ is defined as follows:

$$(A.3) \qquad \sum_{i=1}^{n} \sum_{j=1}^{m} Y_{ij} = \sum_{i=1}^{n} (Y_{i1} + \cdots + Y_{im})$$
$$= Y_{11} + \cdots + Y_{1m} + Y_{21} + \cdots + Y_{2m} + \cdots + Y_{nm}$$

An important property of the double summation operator is:

$$(A.4) \qquad \sum_{i=1}^{n} \sum_{j=1}^{m} Y_{ij} = \sum_{j=1}^{m} \sum_{i=1}^{n} Y_{ij}$$

Product Operator

The product operator $\prod$ is defined as follows:

$$(A.5) \qquad \prod_{i=1}^{n} Y_i = Y_1 \cdot Y_2 \cdot Y_3 \cdots Y_n$$

A.2 Probability

Addition Theorem

Let A_i and A_j be two events defined on a sample space. Then:

$$(A.6) \qquad P(A_i \cup A_j) = P(A_i) + P(A_j) - P(A_i \cap A_j)$$

where $P(A_i \cup A_j)$ denotes the probability of either A_i or A_j or both occurring; $P(A_i)$ and $P(A_j)$ denote, respectively, the probability of A_i and the probability of A_j; and $P(A_i \cap A_j)$ denotes the probability of both A_i and A_j occurring.

Multiplication Theorem

Let $P(A_i|A_j)$ denote the conditional probability of A_i occurring, given that A_j has occurred, and let $P(A_j|A_i)$ denote the conditional probability of A_j occurring, given that A_i has occurred. These conditional probabilities are defined as follows:

$$(A.7a) \qquad P(A_i|A_j) = \frac{P(A_i \cap A_j)}{P(A_j)} \qquad P(A_j) \neq 0$$

$$(A.7b) \qquad P(A_j|A_i) = \frac{P(A_i \cap A_j)}{P(A_i)} \qquad P(A_i) \neq 0$$

The multiplication theorem states:

$$(A.8) \qquad P(A_i \cap A_j) = P(A_i)P(A_j|A_i) = P(A_j)P(A_i|A_j)$$

Complementary Events

The complementary event of A_i is denoted by $\bar{A}_i$. The following results for complementary events are useful:

$$(A.9) \qquad P(\bar{A}_i) = 1 - P(A_i)$$

$$(A.10) \qquad P(\overline{A_i \cup A_j}) = P(\bar{A}_i \cap \bar{A}_j)$$

A.3   Random Variables

Throughout this section, except as noted, we assume that the random variable Y assumes a finite number of outcomes.

Expected Value

Let the random variable Y assume the outcomes $Y_1, \ldots, Y_k$ with probabilities given by the probability function:

$$(A.11) \qquad f(Y_s) = P(Y = Y_s) \qquad s = 1, \ldots, k$$

The expected value of Y, denoted by $E\{Y\}$, is defined by:

$$(A.12) \qquad E\{Y\} = \sum_{s=1}^{k} Y_s f(Y_s)$$

$E\{\ \}$ is called the *expectation operator*.

An important property of the expectation operator is:

$$(A.13) \qquad E\{a + cY\} = a + cE\{Y\} \qquad \text{where } a \text{ and } c \text{ are constants}$$

Special cases of this are:

$$(A.13a) \qquad E\{a\} = a$$

$$(A.13b) \qquad E\{cY\} = cE\{Y\}$$

$$(A.13c) \qquad E\{a + Y\} = a + E\{Y\}$$

Note

If the random variable Y is continuous, with density function $f(Y)$, $E\{Y\}$ is defined as follows:

$$(A.14) \qquad E\{Y\} = \int_{-\infty}^{\infty} Yf(Y)dY \qquad\qquad \blacksquare$$

Variance

The variance of the random variable Y is denoted by $\sigma^2\{Y\}$ and is defined as follows:

$$(A.15) \qquad \sigma^2\{Y\} = E\{(Y - E\{Y\})^2\}$$

An equivalent expression is:

$$(A.15a) \qquad \sigma^2\{Y\} = E\{Y^2\} - (E\{Y\})^2$$

$\sigma^2\{\ \}$ is called the *variance operator*.

The variance of a linear function of Y is frequently encountered. We denote the variance of $a + cY$ by $\sigma^2\{a + cY\}$ and have:

$$(A.16) \qquad \sigma^2\{a + cY\} = c^2\sigma^2\{Y\} \qquad \text{where } a \text{ and } c \text{ are constants}$$

Special cases of this result are:

(A.16a)
$$\sigma^2\{a + Y\} = \sigma^2\{Y\}$$

(A.16b)
$$\sigma^2\{cY\} = c^2\sigma^2\{Y\}$$

Note

If Y is continuous, $\sigma^2\{Y\}$ is defined as follows:

(A.17)
$$\sigma^2\{Y\} = \int_{-\infty}^{\infty} (Y - E\{Y\})^2 f(Y) dY$$ ■

Joint, Marginal, and Conditional Probability Distributions

Let the joint probability function for the two random variables Y and Z be denoted by $g(Y, Z)$:

(A.18)
$$g(Y_s, Z_t) = P(Y = Y_s \cap Z = Z_t) \qquad s = 1, \ldots, k; t = 1, \ldots, m$$

The marginal probability function of Y, denoted by $f(Y)$, is:

(A.19a)
$$f(Y_s) = \sum_{t=1}^{m} g(Y_s, Z_t) \qquad s = 1, \ldots, k$$

and the marginal probability function of Z, denoted by $h(Z)$, is:

(A.19b)
$$h(Z_t) = \sum_{s=1}^{k} g(Y_s, Z_t) \qquad t = 1, \ldots, m$$

The conditional probability function of Y, given $Z = Z_t$, is:

(A.20a)
$$f(Y_s|Z_t) = \frac{g(Y_s, Z_t)}{h(Z_t)} \qquad h(Z_t) \neq 0; s = 1, \ldots, k$$

and the conditional probability function of Z, given $Y = Y_s$, is:

(A.20b)
$$h(Z_t|Y_s) = \frac{g(Y_s, Z_t)}{f(Y_s)} \qquad f(Y_s) \neq 0; t = 1, \ldots, m$$

Covariance

The covariance of Y and Z is denoted by $\sigma\{Y, Z\}$ and is defined by:

(A.21)
$$\sigma\{Y, Z\} = E\{(Y - E\{Y\})(Z - E\{Z\})\}$$

An equivalent expression is:

(A.21a)
$$\sigma\{Y, Z\} = E\{YZ\} - (E\{Y\})(E\{Z\})$$

$\sigma\{\ ,\ \}$ is called the *covariance operator*.

The covariance of $a_1 + c_1 Y$ and $a_2 + c_2 Z$ is denoted by $\sigma\{a_1 + c_1 Y, a_2 + c_2 Z\}$, and we have:

$$(A.22) \quad \sigma\{a_1 + c_1 Y, a_2 + c_2 Z\} = c_1 c_2 \sigma\{Y, Z\} \qquad \text{where } a_1, a_2, c_1, c_2 \text{ are constants}$$

Special cases of this are:

$$(A.22a) \qquad\qquad \sigma\{c_1 Y, c_2 Z\} = c_1 c_2 \sigma\{Y, Z\}$$

$$(A.22b) \qquad\qquad \sigma\{a_1 + Y, a_2 + Z\} = \sigma\{Y, Z\}$$

By definition, we have:

$$(A.23) \qquad\qquad \sigma\{Y, Y\} = \sigma^2\{Y\}$$

where $\sigma^2\{Y\}$ is the variance of Y.

Coefficient of Correlation

The standardized form of a random variable Y, whose mean and variance are $E\{Y\}$ and $\sigma^2\{Y\}$, respectively, is as follows:

$$(A.24) \qquad\qquad Y' = \frac{Y - E\{Y\}}{\sigma\{Y\}}$$

where Y' denotes the *standardized random variable* form of random variable Y.

The coefficient of correlation between random variables Y and Z, denoted by $\rho\{Y, Z\}$, is the covariance between the standardized variables Y' and Z':

$$(A.25) \qquad\qquad \rho\{Y, Z\} = \sigma\{Y', Z'\}$$

Equivalently, the coefficient of correlation can be expressed as follows:

$$(A.25a) \qquad\qquad \rho\{Y, Z\} = \frac{\sigma\{Y, Z\}}{\sigma\{Y\}\sigma\{Z\}}$$

$\rho\{\ ,\ \}$ is called the *correlation operator*.

The coefficient of correlation can take on values between -1 and 1:

$$(A.26) \qquad\qquad -1 \leq \rho\{Y, Z\} \leq 1$$

When $\sigma\{Y, Z\} = 0$, it follows from (A.25a) that $\rho\{Y, Z\} = 0$ and Y and Z are said to be uncorrelated.

Independent Random Variables

The independence of two discrete random variables is defined as follows:

(A.27)   Random variables Y and Z are independent if and only if:

$$g(Y_s, Z_t) = f(Y_s)h(Z_t) \qquad s = 1, \ldots, k; t = 1, \ldots, m$$

If Y and Z are independent random variables:

(A.28) $\sigma\{Y, Z\} = 0$ and $\rho\{Y, Z\} = 0$ when Y and Z are independent

(In the special case where Y and Z are jointly normally distributed, $\sigma\{Y, Z\} = 0$ implies that Y and Z are independent.)

Functions of Random Variables

Let $Y_1, \ldots, Y_n$ be n random variables. Consider the function $\Sigma a_i Y_i$, where the a_i are constants. We then have:

(A.29a) $E\left\{\sum_{i=1}^{n} a_i Y_i\right\} = \sum_{i=1}^{n} a_i E\{Y_i\}$ where the a_i are constants

(A.29b) $\sigma^2\left\{\sum_{i=1}^{n} a_i Y_i\right\} = \sum_{i=1}^{n}\sum_{j=1}^{n} a_i a_j \sigma\{Y_i, Y_j\}$ where the a_i are constants

Specifically, we have for $n = 2$:

(A.30a) $E\{a_1 Y_1 + a_2 Y_2\} = a_1 E\{Y_1\} + a_2 E\{Y_2\}$

(A.30b) $\sigma^2\{a_1 Y_1 + a_2 Y_2\} = a_1^2 \sigma^2\{Y_1\} + a_2^2 \sigma^2\{Y_2\} + 2a_1 a_2 \sigma\{Y_1, Y_2\}$

If the random variables Y_i are independent, we have:

(A.31) $\sigma^2\left\{\sum_{i=1}^{n} a_i Y_i\right\} = \sum_{i=1}^{n} a_i^2 \sigma^2\{Y_i\}$ when the Y_i are independent

Special cases of this are:

(A.31a) $\sigma^2\{Y_1 + Y_2\} = \sigma^2\{Y_1\} + \sigma^2\{Y_2\}$ when Y_1 and Y_2 are independent

(A.31b) $\sigma^2\{Y_1 - Y_2\} = \sigma^2\{Y_1\} + \sigma^2\{Y_2\}$ when Y_1 and Y_2 are independent

When the Y_i are independent random variables, the covariance of two linear functions $\Sigma a_i Y_i$ and $\Sigma c_i Y_i$ is:

(A.32) $\sigma\left\{\sum_{i=1}^{n} a_i Y_i, \sum_{i=1}^{n} c_i Y_i\right\} = \sum_{i=1}^{n} a_i c_i \sigma^2\{Y_i\}$ when the Y_i are independent

Central Limit Theorem

The central limit theorem is basic for much of statistical inference.

(A.33) If $Y_1, \ldots, Y_n$ are independent random observations from a population with probability function $f(Y)$ for which $\sigma^2\{Y\}$ is finite, the sample mean $\bar{Y}$:

$$\bar{Y} = \frac{\sum\limits_{i=1}^{n} Y_i}{n}$$

is approximately normally distributed when the sample size n is reasonably large, with mean $E\{Y\}$ and variance $\sigma^2\{Y\}/n$.

A.4 Normal Probability Distribution and Related Distributions

Normal Probability Distribution

The density function for a normal random variable Y is:

(A.34) $$f(Y) = \frac{1}{\sqrt{2\pi}\sigma} \exp\left[-\frac{1}{2}\left(\frac{Y - \mu}{\sigma}\right)^2 \right] \qquad -\infty < Y < \infty$$

where μ and σ are the two parameters of the normal distribution and $\exp(a)$ denotes e^a.

The mean and variance of a normal random variable Y are:

(A.35a) $$E\{Y\} = \mu$$

(A.35b) $$\sigma^2\{Y\} = \sigma^2$$

Linear Function of Normal Random Variable.   A linear function of a normal random variable Y has the following property:

(A.36) If Y is a normal random variable, the transformed variable $Y' = a + cY$ (a and c are constants) is normally distributed, with mean $a + cE\{Y\}$ and variance $c^2\sigma^2\{Y\}$.

Standard Normal Random Variable.   The standard normal random variable z:

(A.37) $$z = \frac{Y - \mu}{\sigma} \qquad \text{where } Y \text{ is a normal random variable}$$

is normally distributed, with mean 0 and variance 1. We denote this as follows:

$$z \text{ is } N(0, 1)$$

Mean   Variance

Table B.1 in Appendix B contains the cumulative probabilities A for percentiles $z(A)$ where:

(A.39) $$P\{z \leq z(A)\} = A$$

For instance, when $z(A) = 2.00$, $A = .9772$. Because the normal distribution is symmetrical about 0, when $z(A) = -2.00$, $A = 1 - .9772 = .0228$.

Linear Combination of Independent Normal Random Variables.   Let $Y_1, \ldots, Y_n$ be independent normal random variables. We then have:

(A.40)   When $Y_1, \ldots, Y_n$ are independent normal random variables, the linear combination $a_1 Y_1 + a_2 Y_2 + \cdots + a_n Y_n$ is normally distributed, with mean $\Sigma a_i E\{Y_i\}$ and variance $\Sigma a_i^2 \sigma^2 \{Y_i\}$.

χ^2 Distribution

Let $z_1, \ldots, z_\nu$ be ν independent standard normal random variables. We then define a chi-square random variable as follows:

(A.41) $\chi^2(\nu) = z_1^2 + z_2^2 + \cdots + z_\nu^2$ where the z_i are independent

The χ^2 distribution has one parameter, ν, which is called the *degrees of freedom (df)*. The mean of the χ^2 distribution with ν degrees of freedom is:

(A.42) $$E\{\chi^2(\nu)\} = \nu$$

Table B.3 in Appendix B contains percentiles of various χ^2 distributions. We define $\chi^2(A; \nu)$ as follows:

(A.43) $$P\{\chi^2(\nu) \leq \chi^2(A; \nu)\} = A$$

Suppose $\nu = 5$. The 90th percentile of the χ^2 distribution with 5 degrees of freedom is $\chi^2(.90; 5) = 9.24$.

t Distribution

Let z and $\chi^2(\nu)$ be independent random variables (standard normal and χ^2, respectively). We then define a t random variable as follows:

(A.44) $$t(\nu) = \frac{z}{\left[\dfrac{\chi^2(\nu)}{\nu}\right]^{1/2}}$$ where z and $\chi^2(\nu)$ are independent

The t distribution has one parameter, the *degrees of freedom* ν. The mean of the t distribution with ν degrees of freedom is:

(A.45) $$E\{t(\nu)\} = 0$$

Table B.2 in Appendix B contains percentiles of various t distributions. We define $t(A; \nu)$ as follows:

(A.46) $$P\{t(\nu) \leq t(A; \nu)\} = A$$

Suppose $\nu = 10$. The 90th percentile of the t distribution with 10 degrees of freedom is $t(.90; 10) = 1.372$. Because the t distribution is symmetrical about 0, we have $t(.10; 10) = -1.372$.

F *Distribution*

Let $\chi^2(v_1)$ and $\chi^2(v_2)$ be two independent χ^2 random variables. We then define an F random variable as follows:

$$(A.47)\quad F(v_1, v_2) = \frac{\chi^2(v_1)}{v_1} \div \frac{\chi^2(v_2)}{v_2} \qquad \text{where } \chi^2(v_1) \text{ and } \chi^2(v_2) \text{ are independent}$$

Numerator   Denominator
df   df

The F distribution has two parameters, the *numerator degrees of freedom* and the *denominator degrees of freedom*, here v_1 and v_2, respectively.

Table B.4 in Appendix B contains percentiles of various F distributions. We define $F(A; v_1, v_2)$ as follows:

$$(A.48)\qquad P\{F(v_1, v_2) \le F(A; v_1, v_2)\} = A$$

Suppose $v_1 = 2$, $v_2 = 3$. The 90th percentile of the F distribution with 2 and 3 degrees of freedom, respectively, in the numerator and denominator is $F(.90; 2, 3) = 5.46$.

Percentiles below 50 percent can be obtained by utilizing the relation:

$$(A.49)\qquad F(A; v_1, v_2) = \frac{1}{F(1 - A; v_2, v_1)}$$

Thus, $F(.10; 3, 2) = 1/F(.90; 2, 3) = 1/5.46 = .183$.

The following relation exists between the t and F random variables:

$$(A.50a)\qquad |t(v)|^2 = F(1, v)$$

and the percentiles of the t and F distributions are related as follows:

$$(A.50b)\qquad [t(.5 + A/2; v)]^2 = F(A; 1, v)$$

Note

Throughout this text, we consider $z(A), \chi^2(A; v), t(A; v)$, and $F(A; v_1, v_2)$ as $A(100)$ percentiles. Equivalently, they can be considered as A fractiles.   ∎

A.5   Statistical Estimation

Properties of Estimators

Four important properties of estimators are as follows:

(A.51)   An estimator $\hat{\theta}$ of the parameter θ is *unbiased* if:

$$E\{\hat{\theta}\} = \theta$$

(A.52)   An estimator $\hat{\theta}$ is a *consistent estimator* of θ if:

$$\lim_{n \to \infty} P(|\hat{\theta} - \theta| \ge \varepsilon) = 0 \qquad \text{for any } \varepsilon > 0$$

(A.53)   An estimator $\hat{\theta}$ is a *sufficient estimator* of θ if the conditional joint probability function of the sample observations, given $\hat{\theta}$, does not depend on the parameter θ.

(A.54)   An estimator $\hat{\theta}$ is a *minimum variance estimator* of θ if for any other estimator $\hat{\theta}^*$:

$$\sigma^2\{\hat{\theta}\} \leq \sigma^2\{\hat{\theta}^*\} \text{ for all } \hat{\theta}^*$$

Maximum Likelihood Estimators

The method of maximum likelihood is a general method of finding estimators. Suppose we are sampling a population whose probability function $f(Y; \theta)$ involves one parameter, θ. Given independent observations $Y_1, \ldots, Y_n$, the joint probability function of the sample observations is:

(A.55a)
$$g(Y_1, \ldots, Y_n) = \prod_{i=1}^{n} f(Y_i; \theta)$$

When this joint probability function is viewed as a function of θ, with the observations given, it is called the *likelihood function $L(\theta)$*:

(A.55b)
$$L(\theta) = \prod_{i=1}^{n} f(Y_i; \theta)$$

Maximizing $L(\theta)$ with respect to θ yields the maximum likelihood estimator of θ. Under quite general conditions, maximum likelihood estimators are consistent and sufficient.

Least Squares Estimators

The method of least squares is another general method of finding estimators. The sample observations are assumed to be of the form (for the case of a single parameter θ):

(A.56)
$$Y_i = f_i(\theta) + \varepsilon_i \qquad i = 1, \ldots, n$$

where $f_i(\theta)$ is a known function of the parameter θ and the ε_i are random variables, usually assumed to have expectation $E\{\varepsilon_i\} = 0$.

With the method of least squares, for the given sample observations, the sum of squares:

(A.57)
$$Q = \sum_{i=1}^{n} [Y_i - f_i(\theta)]^2$$

is considered as a function of θ. The least squares estimator of θ is obtained by minimizing Q with respect to θ. In many instances, least squares estimators are unbiased and consistent.

A.6   Inferences about Population Mean—Normal Population

We have a random sample of n observations $Y_1, \ldots, Y_n$ from a normal population with mean μ and standard deviation σ. The sample mean and sample standard deviation are:

(A.58a)
$$\bar{Y} = \frac{\sum_i Y_i}{n}$$

(A.58b)
$$s = \left[\frac{\sum_i (Y_i - \bar{Y})^2}{n-1} \right]^{1/2}$$

and the estimated standard deviation of the sampling distribution of $\bar{Y}$, denoted by $s\{\bar{Y}\}$, is:

(A.58c)
$$s\{\bar{Y}\} = \frac{s}{\sqrt{n}}$$

We then have:

(A.59) $\dfrac{\bar{Y} - \mu}{s\{\bar{Y}\}}$ is distributed as t with $n - 1$ degrees of freedom when the random sample is from a normal population.

Interval Estimation

The confidence limits for μ with confidence coefficient $1 - \alpha$ are obtained by means of (A.59):

(A.60)
$$\bar{Y} \pm t(1 - \alpha/2; n - 1)s\{\bar{Y}\}$$

Example 1.   Obtain a 95 percent confidence interval for μ when:
$$n = 10 \qquad \bar{Y} = 20 \qquad s = 4$$

We require:
$$s\{\bar{Y}\} = \frac{4}{\sqrt{10}} = 1.265 \qquad t(.975; 9) = 2.262$$

The 95 percent confidence limits therefore are $20 \pm 2.262(1.265)$ and the 95 percent confidence interval for μ is:
$$17.1 \leq \mu \leq 22.9$$

Tests

One-sided and two-sided tests concerning the population mean μ are constructed by means of (A.59), based on the test statistic:

(A.61)
$$t^* = \frac{\bar{Y} - \mu_0}{s\{\bar{Y}\}}$$

Table A.1 contains the decision rules for three possible cases, with the risk of making a Type I error controlled at α.

TABLE A.1 **Decision Rules for Tests Concerning Mean μ of Normal Population.**

Alternatives	Decision Rule
	(a)
H_0: $\mu = \mu_0$	If $|t^*| \leq t(1 - \alpha/2; n - 1)$, conclude H_0
H_a: $\mu \neq \mu_0$	If $|t^*| > t(1 - \alpha/2; n - 1)$, conclude H_a

where:
$$t^* = \frac{\bar{Y} - \mu_0}{s\{\bar{Y}\}}$$

Alternatives	Decision Rule
	(b)
H_0: $\mu \geq \mu_0$	If $t^* \geq t(\alpha; n - 1)$, conclude H_0
H_a: $\mu < \mu_0$	If $t^* < t(\alpha; n - 1)$, conclude H_a
	(c)
H_0: $\mu \leq \mu_0$	If $t^* \leq t(1 - \alpha; n - 1)$, conclude H_0
H_a: $\mu > \mu_0$	If $t^* > t(1 - \alpha; n - 1)$, conclude H_a

Example 2. Choose between the alternatives:

$$H_0: \mu \leq 20$$
$$H_a: \mu > 20$$

when α is to be controlled at .05 and:

$$n = 15 \qquad \bar{Y} = 24 \qquad s = 6$$

We require:

$$s\{\bar{Y}\} = \frac{6}{\sqrt{15}} = 1.549$$

$$t(.95; 14) = 1.761$$

The decision rule is:

If $t^* \leq 1.761$, conclude H_0

If $t^* > 1.761$, conclude H_a

Since $t^* = (24 - 20)/1.549 = 2.58 > 1.761$, we conclude H_a.

Example 3. Choose between the alternatives:

$$H_0: \mu = 10$$
$$H_a: \mu \neq 10$$

when α is to be controlled at .02 and:

$$n = 25 \qquad \bar{Y} = 5.7 \qquad s = 8$$

We require:

$$s\{\bar{Y}\} = \frac{8}{\sqrt{25}} = 1.6$$

$$t(.99; 24) = 2.492$$

The decision rule is:

$$\text{If } |t^*| \leq 2.492, \text{ conclude } H_0$$

$$\text{If } |t^*| > 2.492, \text{ conclude } H_a$$

where the symbol $|\quad|$ stands for the absolute value. Since $|t^*| = |(5.7 - 10)/1.6| = |-2.69| = 2.69 > 2.492$, we conclude H_a.

P-Value for Sample Outcome.   The P-value for a sample outcome is the probability that the sample outcome could have been more extreme than the observed one when $\mu = \mu_0$. Large P-values support H_0 while small P-values support H_a. A test can be carried out by comparing the P-value with the specified α risk. If the P-value equals or is greater than the specified α, H_0 is concluded. If the P-value is less than α, H_a is concluded.

Example 4.   In Example 2, $t^* = 2.58$. The P-value for this sample outcome is the probability $P\{t(14) > 2.58\}$. From Table B.2, we find $t(.985; 14) = 2.415$ and $t(.990; 14) = 2.624$. Hence, the P-value is between .010 and .015. The exact P-value can be found from many statistical calculators or statistical computer packages; it is .0109. Thus, for $\alpha = .05$, H_a is concluded.

Example 5.   In Example 3, $t^* = -2.69$. We find from Table B.2 that the one-sided P-value, $P\{t(24) < -2.69\}$, is between .005 and .0075. The exact one-sided P-value is .0064. Because the test is two-sided and the t distribution is symmetrical, the two-sided P-value is twice the one-sided value, or $2(.0064) = .013$. Hence, for $\alpha = .02$, we conclude H_a.

Relation between Tests and Confidence Intervals.   There is a direct relation between tests and confidence intervals. For example, the two-sided confidence limits (A.60) can be used for testing:

$$H_0: \mu = \mu_0$$

$$H_a: \mu \neq \mu_0$$

If μ_0 is contained within the $1 - \alpha$ confidence interval, then the two-sided decision rule in Table A.1a, with level of significance α, will lead to conclusion H_0, and vice versa. If μ_0 is not contained within the confidence interval, the decision rule will lead to H_a, and vice versa.

There are similar correspondences between one-sided confidence intervals and one-sided decision rules.

A.7 Comparisons of Two Population Means—Normal Populations

Independent Samples

There are two normal populations, with means μ_1 and μ_2, respectively, and with the same standard deviation σ. The means μ_1 and μ_2 are to be compared on the basis of independent samples for each of the two populations:

$$\text{Sample 1: } Y_1, \ldots, Y_{n_1}$$

$$\text{Sample 2: } Z_1, \ldots, Z_{n_2}$$

Estimators of the two population means are the sample means:

$$(A.62a) \qquad \bar{Y} = \frac{\sum_i Y_i}{n_1}$$

$$(A.62b) \qquad \bar{Z} = \frac{\sum_i Z_i}{n_2}$$

and an estimator of $\mu_1 - \mu_2$ is $\bar{Y} - \bar{Z}$.

An estimator of the common variance σ^2 is:

$$(A.63) \qquad s^2 = \frac{\sum_i (Y_i - \bar{Y})^2 + \sum_i (Z_i - \bar{Z})^2}{n_1 + n_2 - 2}$$

and an estimator of $\sigma^2\{\bar{Y} - \bar{Z}\}$, the variance of the sampling distribution of $\bar{Y} - \bar{Z}$, is:

$$(A.64) \qquad s^2\{\bar{Y} - \bar{Z}\} = s^2 \left(\frac{1}{n_1} + \frac{1}{n_2} \right)$$

We have:

$(A.65) \quad \dfrac{(\bar{Y} - \bar{Z}) - (\mu_1 - \mu_2)}{s\{\bar{Y} - \bar{Z}\}}$ is distributed as t with $n_1 + n_2 - 2$ degrees of freedom when the two independent samples come from normal populations with the same standard deviation.

Interval Estimation.   The confidence limits for $\mu_1 - \mu_2$ with confidence coefficient $1 - \alpha$ are obtained by means of (A.65):

$$(A.66) \qquad (\bar{Y} - \bar{Z}) \pm t(1 - \alpha/2; n_1 + n_2 - 2)s\{\bar{Y} - \bar{Z}\}$$

TABLE A.2 **Decision Rules for Tests Concerning Means μ_1 and μ_2 of Two Normal Populations ($\sigma_1 = \sigma_2 = \sigma$) — Independent Samples.**

Alternatives	Decision Rule
	(a)
$H_0: \ \mu_1 = \mu_2$	If $|t^*| \leq t(1 - \alpha/2; n_1 + n_2 - 2)$, conclude H_0
$H_a: \ \mu_1 \neq \mu_2$	If $|t^*| > t(1 - \alpha/2; n_1 + n_2 - 2)$, conclude H_a

where:
$$t^* = \frac{\bar{Y} - \bar{Z}}{s\{\bar{Y} - \bar{Z}\}}$$

	(b)
$H_0: \ \mu_1 \geq \mu_2$	If $t^* \geq t(\alpha; n_1 + n_2 - 2)$, conclude H_0
$H_a: \ \mu_1 < \mu_2$	If $t^* < t(\alpha; n_1 + n_2 - 2)$, conclude H_a

	(c)
$H_0: \ \mu_1 \leq \mu_2$	If $t^* \leq t(1 - \alpha; n_1 + n_2 - 2)$, conclude H_0
$H_a: \ \mu_1 > \mu_2$	If $t^* > t(1 - \alpha; n_1 + n_2 - 2)$, conclude H_a

Example 6. Obtain a 95 percent confidence interval for $\mu_1 - \mu_2$ when:

$$n_1 = 10 \qquad \bar{Y} = 14 \qquad \sum(Y_i - \bar{Y})^2 = 105$$

$$n_2 = 20 \qquad \bar{Z} = 8 \qquad \sum(Z_i - \bar{Z})^2 = 224$$

We require:

$$s^2 = \frac{105 + 224}{10 + 20 - 2} = 11.75$$

$$s^2\{\bar{Y} - \bar{Z}\} = 11.75\left(\frac{1}{10} + \frac{1}{20}\right) = 1.7625$$

$$s\{\bar{Y} - \bar{Z}\} = 1.328$$

$$t(.975; 28) = 2.048$$

Hence, the 95 percent confidence interval for $\mu_1 - \mu_2$ is:

$$3.3 = (14 - 8) - 2.048(1.328) \leq \mu_1 - \mu_2 \leq (14 - 8) + 2.048(1.328) = 8.7$$

Tests. One-sided and two-sided tests concerning $\mu_1 - \mu_2$ are constructed by means of (A.65). Table A.2 contains the decision rules for three possible cases, based on the test statistic:

(A.67)
$$t^* = \frac{\bar{Y} - \bar{Z}}{s\{\bar{Y} - \bar{Z}\}}$$

with the risk of making a Type I error controlled at α.

Example 7.   Choose between the alternatives:

$$H_0: \; \mu_1 = \mu_2$$

$$H_a: \; \mu_1 \neq \mu_2$$

when α is to be controlled at .10 and the data are those of Example 6. We require $t(.95; 28) = 1.701$, so that the decision rule is:

$$\text{If } |t^*| \leq 1.701, \text{ conclude } H_0$$

$$\text{If } |t^*| > 1.701, \text{ conclude } H_a$$

Since $|t^*| = |(14 - 8)/1.328| = |4.52| = 4.52 > 1.701$, we conclude H_a.

The one-sided P-value here is the probability $P\{t(28) > 4.52\}$. We see from Table B.2 that this P-value is less than .0005; the exact one-sided P-value is .00005. Hence, the two-sided P-value is .0001. For $\alpha = .10$, the appropriate conclusion therefore is H_a.

Paired Observations

When the observations in the two samples are paired (e.g., attitude scores Y_i and Z_i for the ith sample employee before and after a year's experience on the job), we use the differences:

$$(A.68) \qquad W_i = Y_i - Z_i \qquad i = 1, \ldots, n$$

in the fashion of a sample from a single population. Thus, when the W_i can be treated as observations from a normal population, we have:

$(A.69)$ $\dfrac{\overline{W} - (\mu_1 - \mu_2)}{s\{\overline{W}\}}$ is distributed as t with $n - 1$ degrees of freedom when the differences W_i can be considered to be observations from a normal population and:

$$\overline{W} = \frac{\sum\limits_i W_i}{n}$$

$$s^2\{\overline{W}\} = \left(\frac{\sum\limits_i (W_i - \overline{W})^2}{n - 1} \right) \div n$$

A.8   Inferences about Population Variance—Normal Population

When sampling from a normal population, the following holds for the sample variance s^2, where s is defined in (A.58b):

$(A.70)$ $\dfrac{(n - 1)s^2}{\sigma^2}$ is distributed as χ^2 with $n - 1$ degrees of freedom when the random sample is from a normal population.

TABLE A.3   **Decision Rules for Tests Concerning Variance σ^2 of Normal Populations.**

Alternatives	Decision Rule

(a)

H_0: $\sigma^2 = \sigma_0^2$ If $\chi^2(\alpha/2; n-1) \leq \dfrac{(n-1)s^2}{\sigma_0^2} \leq \chi^2(1 - \alpha/2; n-1)$,

H_a: $\sigma^2 \neq \sigma_0^2$ conclude H_0

               Otherwise conclude H_a

(b)

H_0: $\sigma^2 \geq \sigma_0^2$ If $\dfrac{(n-1)s^2}{\sigma_0^2} \geq \chi^2(\alpha; n-1)$, conclude H_0

H_a: $\sigma^2 < \sigma_0^2$ If $\dfrac{(n-1)s^2}{\sigma_0^2} < \chi^2(\alpha; n-1)$, conclude H_a

(c)

H_0: $\sigma^2 \leq \sigma_0^2$ If $\dfrac{(n-1)s^2}{\sigma_0^2} \leq \chi^2(1 - \alpha; n-1)$, conclude H_0

H_a: $\sigma^2 > \sigma_0^2$ If $\dfrac{(n-1)s^2}{\sigma_0^2} > \chi^2(1 - \alpha; n-1)$, conclude H_a

Interval Estimation

The lower confidence limit L and the upper confidence limit U in a confidence interval for the population variance σ^2 with confidence coefficient $1 - \alpha$ are obtained by means of (A.70):

$$(A.71) \qquad L = \frac{(n-1)s^2}{\chi^2(1 - \alpha/2; n-1)} \qquad U = \frac{(n-1)s^2}{\chi^2(\alpha/2; n-1)}$$

Example 8.   Obtain a 98 percent confidence interval for σ^2, using the data of Example 1 ($n = 10$, $s = 4$).

We require:

$$s^2 = 16 \qquad \chi^2(.01; 9) = 2.09 \qquad \chi^2(.99; 9) = 21.67$$

The 98 percent confidence interval for σ^2 therefore is:

$$6.6 = \frac{9(16)}{21.67} \leq \sigma^2 \leq \frac{9(16)}{2.09} = 68.9$$

Tests

One-sided and two-sided tests concerning the population variance σ^2 are constructed by means of (A.70). Table A.3 contains the decision rules for three possible cases, with the risk of making a Type I error controlled at α.

Note

The inference procedures about the population variance described here are very sensitive to the assumption of a normal population, and the procedures are not robust to departures from normality. ∎

A.9 Comparisons of Two Population Variances—Normal Populations

Independent samples are selected from two normal populations, with means and variances μ_1 and σ_1^2 and μ_2 and σ_2^2, respectively. Using the notation of Section A.7, the two sample variances are:

(A.72a)
$$s_1^2 = \frac{\sum_i (Y_i - \bar{Y})^2}{n_1 - 1}$$

(A.72b)
$$s_2^2 = \frac{\sum_i (Z_i - \bar{Z})^2}{n_2 - 1}$$

We have:

(A.73) $\dfrac{s_1^2}{\sigma_1^2} \div \dfrac{s_2^2}{\sigma_2^2}$ is distributed as $F(n_1 - 1, n_2 - 1)$ when the two independent samples come from normal populations.

Interval Estimation

The lower and upper confidence limits L and U for σ_1^2/σ_2^2 with confidence coefficient $1 - \alpha$ are obtained by means of (A.73):

(A.74)
$$L = \frac{s_1^2}{s_2^2} \left[\frac{1}{F(1 - \alpha/2; n_1 - 1, n_2 - 1)} \right]$$

$$U = \frac{s_1^2}{s_2^2} \left[\frac{1}{F(\alpha/2; n_1 - 1, n_2 - 1)} \right]$$

Example 9.   Obtain a 90 percent confidence interval for σ_1^2/σ_2^2 when the data are:

$$n_1 = 16 \qquad n_2 = 21$$

$$s_1^2 = 54.2 \qquad s_2^2 = 17.8$$

We require:

$$F(.05; 15, 20) = 1/F(.95; 20, 15) = 1/2.33 = .429$$

$$F(.95; 15, 20) = 2.20$$

TABLE A.4   **Decision Rules for Tests Concerning Variances σ_1^2 and σ_2^2 of Two Normal Populations—Independent Samples.**

Alternatives	Decision Rule
	(a)
H_0: $\sigma_1^2 = \sigma_2^2$	If $F(\alpha/2; n_1 - 1, n_2 - 1) \leq \dfrac{s_1^2}{s_2^2}$
H_a: $\sigma_1^2 \neq \sigma_2^2$	$\leq F(1 - \alpha/2; n_1 - 1, n_2 - 1)$, conclude H_0
	Otherwise conclude H_a
	(b)
H_0: $\sigma_1^2 \geq \sigma_2^2$	If $\dfrac{s_1^2}{s_2^2} \geq F(\alpha; n_1 - 1, n_2 - 1)$, conclude H_0
H_a: $\sigma_1^2 < \sigma_2^2$	If $\dfrac{s_1^2}{s_2^2} < F(\alpha; n_1 - 1, n_2 - 1)$, conclude H_a
	(c)
H_0: $\sigma_1^2 \leq \sigma_2^2$	If $\dfrac{s_1^2}{s_2^2} \leq F(1 - \alpha; n_1 - 1, n_2 - 1)$, conclude H_0
H_a: $\sigma_1^2 > \sigma_2^2$	If $\dfrac{s_1^2}{s_2^2} > F(1 - \alpha; n_1 - 1, n_2 - 1)$, conclude H_a

The 90 percent confidence interval for σ_1^2/σ_2^2 therefore is:

$$1.4 = \frac{54.2}{17.8}\left(\frac{1}{2.20}\right) \leq \frac{\sigma_1^2}{\sigma_2^2} \leq \frac{54.2}{17.8}\left(\frac{1}{.429}\right) = 7.1$$

Tests

One-sided and two-sided tests concerning σ_1^2/σ_2^2 are constructed by means of (A.73). Table A.4 contains the decision rules for three possible cases, with the risk of making a Type 1 error controlled at α.

Example 10.   Choose between the alternatives:

$$H_0: \sigma_1^2 = \sigma_2^2$$

$$H_a: \sigma_1^2 \neq \sigma_2^2$$

when α is to be controlled at .02 and the data are those of Example 9.

We require:

$$F(.01; 15, 20) = 1/F(.99; 20, 15) = 1/3.37 = .297$$

$$F(.99; 15, 20) = 3.09$$

The decision rule is:

$$\text{If } .297 \leq \frac{s_1^2}{s_2^2} \leq 3.09, \text{ conclude } H_0$$

Otherwise conclude H_a

Since $s_1^2/s_2^2 = 54.2/17.8 = 3.04$, we conclude H_0.

Note

The inference procedures about the ratio of two population variances described here are very sensitive to the assumption of normal populations, and the procedures are not robust to departures from normality. ∎

APPENDIX B Tables

TABLE B.1   **Cumulative Probabilities of the Standard Normal Distribution.**

Entry is area A under the standard normal curve from $-\infty$ to $z(A)$

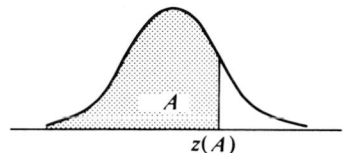

z	.00	.01	.02	.03	.04	.05	.06	.07	.08	.09
.0	.5000	.5040	.5080	.5120	.5160	.5199	.5239	.5279	.5319	.5359
.1	.5398	.5438	.5478	.5517	.5557	.5596	.5636	.5675	.5714	.5753
.2	.5793	.5832	.5871	.5910	.5948	.5987	.6026	.6064	.6103	.6141
.3	.6179	.6217	.6255	.6293	.6331	.6368	.6406	.6443	.6480	.6517
.4	.6554	.6591	.6628	.6664	.6700	.6736	.6772	.6808	.6844	.6879
.5	.6915	.6950	.6985	.7019	.7054	.7088	.7123	.7157	.7190	.7224
.6	.7257	.7291	.7324	.7357	.7389	.7422	.7454	.7486	.7517	.7549
.7	.7580	.7611	.7642	.7673	.7704	.7734	.7764	.7794	.7823	.7852
.8	.7881	.7910	.7939	.7967	.7995	.8023	.8051	.8078	.8106	.8133
.9	.8159	.8186	.8212	.8238	.8264	.8289	.8315	.8340	.8365	.8389
1.0	.8413	.8438	.8461	.8485	.8508	.8531	.8554	.8577	.8599	.8621
1.1	.8643	.8665	.8686	.8708	.8729	.8749	.8770	.8790	.8810	.8830
1.2	.8849	.8869	.8888	.8907	.8925	.8944	.8962	.8980	.8997	.9015
1.3	.9032	.9049	.9066	.9082	.9099	.9115	.9131	.9147	.9162	.9177
1.4	.9192	.9207	.9222	.9236	.9251	.9265	.9279	.9292	.9306	.9319
1.5	.9332	.9345	.9357	.9370	.9382	.9394	.9406	.9418	.9429	.9441
1.6	.9452	.9463	.9474	.9484	.9495	.9505	.9515	.9525	.9535	.9545
1.7	.9554	.9564	.9573	.9582	.9591	.9599	.9608	.9616	.9625	.9633
1.8	.9641	.9649	.9656	.9664	.9671	.9678	.9686	.9693	.9699	.9706
1.9	.9713	.9719	.9726	.9732	.9738	.9744	.9750	.9756	.9761	.9767
2.0	.9772	.9778	.9783	.9788	.9793	.9798	.9803	.9808	.9812	.9817
2.1	.9821	.9826	.9830	.9834	.9838	.9842	.9846	.9850	.9854	.9857
2.2	.9861	.9864	.9868	.9871	.9875	.9878	.9881	.9884	.9887	.9890
2.3	.9893	.9896	.9898	.9901	.9904	.9906	.9909	.9911	.9913	.9916
2.4	.9918	.9920	.9922	.9925	.9927	.9929	.9931	.9932	.9934	.9936
2.5	.9938	.9940	.9941	.9943	.9945	.9946	.9948	.9949	.9951	.9952
2.6	.9953	.9955	.9956	.9957	.9959	.9960	.9961	.9962	.9963	.9964
2.7	.9965	.9966	.9967	.9968	.9969	.9970	.9971	.9972	.9973	.9974
2.8	.9974	.9975	.9976	.9977	.9977	.9978	.9979	.9979	.9980	.9981
2.9	.9981	.9982	.9982	.9983	.9984	.9984	.9985	.9985	.9986	.9986
3.0	.9987	.9987	.9987	.9988	.9988	.9989	.9989	.9989	.9990	.9990
3.1	.9990	.9991	.9991	.9991	.9992	.9992	.9992	.9992	.9993	.9993
3.2	.9993	.9993	.9994	.9994	.9994	.9994	.9994	.9995	.9995	.9995
3.3	.9995	.9995	.9995	.9996	.9996	.9996	.9996	.9996	.9996	.9997
3.4	.9997	.9997	.9997	.9997	.9997	.9997	.9997	.9997	.9997	.9998

Selected Percentiles

Cumulative probability A:	.90	.95	.975	.98	.99	.995	.999
$z(A)$:	1.282	1.645	1.960	2.054	2.326	2.576	3.090

TABLE B.2   Percentiles of the *t* Distribution.

Entry is $t(A; \nu)$ where $P\{t(\nu) \leq t(A; \nu)\} = A$

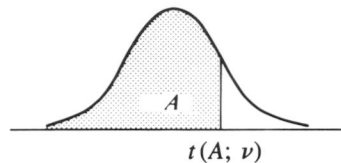

$t(A; \nu)$

	A						
ν	.60	.70	.80	.85	.90	.95	.975
1	0.325	0.727	1.376	1.963	3.078	6.314	12.706
2	0.289	0.617	1.061	1.386	1.886	2.920	4.303
3	0.277	0.584	0.978	1.250	1.638	2.353	3.182
4	0.271	0.569	0.941	1.190	1.533	2.132	2.776
5	0.267	0.559	0.920	1.156	1.476	2.015	2.571
6	0.265	0.553	0.906	1.134	1.440	1.943	2.447
7	0.263	0.549	0.896	1.119	1.415	1.895	2.365
8	0.262	0.546	0.889	1.108	1.397	1.860	2.306
9	0.261	0.543	0.883	1.100	1.383	1.833	2.262
10	0.260	0.542	0.879	1.093	1.372	1.812	2.228
11	0.260	0.540	0.876	1.088	1.363	1.796	2.201
12	0.259	0.539	0.873	1.083	1.356	1.782	2.179
13	0.259	0.537	0.870	1.079	1.350	1.771	2.160
14	0.258	0.537	0.868	1.076	1.345	1.761	2.145
15	0.258	0.536	0.866	1.074	1.341	1.753	2.131
16	0.258	0.535	0.865	1.071	1.337	1.746	2.120
17	0.257	0.534	0.863	1.069	1.333	1.740	2.110
18	0.257	0.534	0.862	1.067	1.330	1.734	2.101
19	0.257	0.533	0.861	1.066	1.328	1.729	2.093
20	0.257	0.533	0.860	1.064	1.325	1.725	2.086
21	0.257	0.532	0.859	1.063	1.323	1.721	2.080
22	0.256	0.532	0.858	1.061	1.321	1.717	2.074
23	0.256	0.532	0.858	1.060	1.319	1.714	2.069
24	0.256	0.531	0.857	1.059	1.318	1.711	2.064
25	0.256	0.531	0.856	1.058	1.316	1.708	2.060
26	0.256	0.531	0.856	1.058	1.315	1.706	2.056
27	0.256	0.531	0.855	1.057	1.314	1.703	2.052
28	0.256	0.530	0.855	1.056	1.313	1.701	2.048
29	0.256	0.530	0.854	1.055	1.311	1.699	2.045
30	0.256	0.530	0.854	1.055	1.310	1.697	2.042
40	0.255	0.529	0.851	1.050	1.303	1.684	2.021
60	0.254	0.527	0.848	1.045	1.296	1.671	2.000
120	0.254	0.526	0.845	1.041	1.289	1.658	1.980
∞	0.253	0.524	0.842	1.036	1.282	1.645	1.960

TABLE B.2 *(concluded)*   **Percentiles of the *t* Distribution.**

ν	A						
	.98	.985	.99	.9925	.995	.9975	.9995
1	15.895	21.205	31.821	42.434	63.657	127.322	636.590
2	4.849	5.643	6.965	8.073	9.925	14.089	31.598
3	3.482	3.896	4.541	5.047	5.841	7.453	12.924
4	2.999	3.298	3.747	4.088	4.604	5.598	8.610
5	2.757	3.003	3.365	3.634	4.032	4.773	6.869
6	2.612	2.829	3.143	3.372	3.707	4.317	5.959
7	2.517	2.715	2.998	3.203	3.499	4.029	5.408
8	2.449	2.634	2.896	3.085	3.355	3.833	5.041
9	2.398	2.574	2.821	2.998	3.250	3.690	4.781
10	2.359	2.527	2.764	2.932	3.169	3.581	4.587
11	2.328	2.491	2.718	2.879	3.106	3.497	4.437
12	2.303	2.461	2.681	2.836	3.055	3.428	4.318
13	2.282	2.436	2.650	2.801	3.012	3.372	4.221
14	2.264	2.415	2.624	2.771	2.977	3.326	4.140
15	2.249	2.397	2.602	2.746	2.947	3.286	4.073
16	2.235	2.382	2.583	2.724	2.921	3.252	4.015
17	2.224	2.368	2.567	2.706	2.898	3.222	3.965
18	2.214	2.356	2.552	2.689	2.878	3.197	3.922
19	2.205	2.346	2.539	2.674	2.861	3.174	3.883
20	2.197	2.336	2.528	2.661	2.845	3.153	3.849
21	2.189	2.328	2.518	2.649	2.831	3.135	3.819
22	2.183	2.320	2.508	2.639	2.819	3.119	3.792
23	2.177	2.313	2.500	2.629	2.807	3.104	3.768
24	2.172	2.307	2.492	2.620	2.797	3.091	3.745
25	2.167	2.301	2.485	2.612	2.787	3.078	3.725
26	2.162	2.296	2.479	2.605	2.779	3.067	3.707
27	2.158	2.291	2.473	2.598	2.771	3.057	3.690
28	2.154	2.286	2.467	2.592	2.763	3.047	3.674
29	2.150	2.282	2.462	2.586	2.756	3.038	3.659
30	2.147	2.278	2.457	2.581	2.750	3.030	3.646
40	2.123	2.250	2.423	2.542	2.704	2.971	3.551
60	2.099	2.223	2.390	2.504	2.660	2.915	3.460
120	2.076	2.196	2.358	2.468	2.617	2.860	3.373
∞	2.054	2.170	2.326	2.432	2.576	2.807	3.291

TABLE B.3   Percentiles of the χ^2 Distribution.

Entry is $\chi^2(A; \nu)$ where $P\{\chi^2(\nu) \leq \chi^2(A; \nu)\} = A$

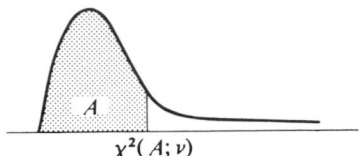

$\chi^2(A; \nu)$

ν	.005	.010	.025	.050	.100	.900	.950	.975	.990	.995
1	0.0^4393	0.0^3157	0.0^3982	0.0^2393	0.0158	2.71	3.84	5.02	6.63	7.88
2	0.0100	0.0201	0.0506	0.103	0.211	4.61	5.99	7.38	9.21	10.60
3	0.072	0.115	0.216	0.352	0.584	6.25	7.81	9.35	11.34	12.84
4	0.207	0.297	0.484	0.711	1.064	7.78	9.49	11.14	13.28	14.86
5	0.412	0.554	0.831	1.145	1.61	9.24	11.07	12.83	15.09	16.75
6	0.676	0.872	1.24	1.64	2.20	10.64	12.59	14.45	16.81	18.55
7	0.989	1.24	1.69	2.17	2.83	12.02	14.07	16.01	18.48	20.28
8	1.34	1.65	2.18	2.73	3.49	13.36	15.51	17.53	20.09	21.96
9	1.73	2.09	2.70	3.33	4.17	14.68	16.92	19.02	21.67	23.59
10	2.16	2.56	3.25	3.94	4.87	15.99	18.31	20.48	23.21	25.19
11	2.60	3.05	3.82	4.57	5.58	17.28	19.68	21.92	24.73	26.76
12	3.07	3.57	4.40	5.23	6.30	18.55	21.03	23.34	26.22	28.30
13	3.57	4.11	5.01	5.89	7.04	19.81	22.36	24.74	27.69	29.82
14	4.07	4.66	5.63	6.57	7.79	21.06	23.68	26.12	29.14	31.32
15	4.60	5.23	6.26	7.26	8.55	22.31	25.00	27.49	30.58	32.80
16	5.14	5.81	6.91	7.96	9.31	23.54	26.30	28.85	32.00	34.27
17	5.70	6.41	7.56	8.67	10.09	24.77	27.59	30.19	33.41	35.72
18	6.26	7.01	8.23	9.39	10.86	25.99	28.87	31.53	34.81	37.16
19	6.84	7.63	8.91	10.12	11.65	27.20	30.14	32.85	36.19	38.58
20	7.43	8.26	9.59	10.85	12.44	28.41	31.41	34.17	37.57	40.00
21	8.03	8.90	10.28	11.59	13.24	29.62	32.67	35.48	38.93	41.40
22	8.64	9.54	10.98	12.34	14.04	30.81	33.92	36.78	40.29	42.80
23	9.26	10.20	11.69	13.09	14.85	32.01	35.17	38.08	41.64	44.18
24	9.89	10.86	12.40	13.85	15.66	33.20	36.42	39.36	42.98	45.56
25	10.52	11.52	13.12	14.61	16.47	34.38	37.65	40.65	44.31	46.93
26	11.16	12.20	13.84	15.38	17.29	35.56	38.89	41.92	45.64	48.29
27	11.81	12.88	14.57	16.15	18.11	36.74	40.11	43.19	46.96	49.64
28	12.46	13.56	15.31	16.93	18.94	37.92	41.34	44.46	48.28	50.99
29	13.12	14.26	16.05	17.71	19.77	39.09	42.56	45.72	49.59	52.34
30	13.79	14.95	16.79	18.49	20.60	40.26	43.77	46.98	50.89	53.67
40	20.71	22.16	24.43	26.51	29.05	51.81	55.76	59.34	63.69	66.77
50	27.99	29.71	32.36	34.76	37.69	63.17	67.50	71.42	76.15	79.49
60	35.53	37.48	40.48	43.19	46.46	74.40	79.08	83.30	88.38	91.95
70	43.28	45.44	48.76	51.74	55.33	85.53	90.53	95.02	100.4	104.2
80	51.17	53.54	57.15	60.39	64.28	96.58	101.9	106.6	112.3	116.3
90	59.20	61.75	65.65	69.13	73.29	107.6	113.1	118.1	124.1	128.3
100	67.33	70.06	74.22	77.93	82.36	118.5	124.3	129.6	135.8	140.2

Source: Reprinted, with permission, from C. M. Thompson, "Table of Percentage Points of the Chi-Square Distribution," *Biometrika* 32 (1941), pp. 188–89.

TABLE B.4   **Percentiles of the *F* Distribution.**

Entry is $F(A; \nu_1, \nu_2)$ where $P\{F(\nu_1, \nu_2) \le F(A; \nu_1, \nu_2)\} = A$

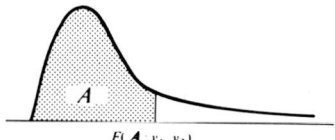

$$F(A; \nu_1, \nu_2) = \frac{1}{F(1 - A; \nu_2, \nu_1)}$$

TABLE B.4 *(continued)*   **Percentiles of the *F* Distribution.**

Den. df	A	\multicolumn{9}{c}{Numerator df}
		1	2	3	4	5	6	7	8	9
1	.50	1.00	1.50	1.71	1.82	1.89	1.94	1.98	2.00	2.03
	.90	39.9	49.5	53.6	55.8	57.2	58.2	58.9	59.4	59.9
	.95	161	200	216	225	230	234	237	239	241
	.975	648	800	864	900	922	937	948	957	963
	.99	4,052	5,000	5,403	5,625	5,764	5,859	5,928	5,981	6,022
	.995	16,211	20,000	21,615	22,500	23,056	23,437	23,715	23,925	24,091
	.999	405,280	500,000	540,380	562,500	576,400	585,940	592,870	598,140	602,280
2	.50	0.667	1.00	1.13	1.21	1.25	1.28	1.30	1.32	1.33
	.90	8.53	9.00	9.16	9.24	9.29	9.33	9.35	9.37	9.38
	.95	18.5	19.0	19.2	19.2	19.3	19.3	19.4	19.4	19.4
	.975	38.5	39.0	39.2	39.2	39.3	39.3	39.4	39.4	39.4
	.99	98.5	99.0	99.2	99.2	99.3	99.3	99.4	99.4	99.4
	.995	199	199	199	199	199	199	199	199	199
	.999	998.5	999.0	999.2	999.2	999.3	999.3	999.4	999.4	999.4
3	.50	0.585	0.881	1.00	1.06	1.10	1.13	1.15	1.16	1.17
	.90	5.54	5.46	5.39	5.34	5.31	5.28	5.27	5.25	5.24
	.95	10.1	9.55	9.28	9.12	9.01	8.94	8.89	8.85	8.81
	.975	17.4	16.0	15.4	15.1	14.9	14.7	14.6	14.5	14.5
	.99	34.1	30.8	29.5	28.7	28.2	27.9	27.7	27.5	27.3
	.995	55.6	49.8	47.5	46.2	45.4	44.8	44.4	44.1	43.9
	.999	167.0	148.5	141.1	137.1	134.6	132.8	131.6	130.6	129.9
4	.50	0.549	0.828	0.941	1.00	1.04	1.06	1.08	1.09	1.10
	.90	4.54	4.32	4.19	4.11	4.05	4.01	3.98	3.95	3.94
	.95	7.71	6.94	6.59	6.39	6.26	6.16	6.09	6.04	6.00
	.975	12.2	10.6	9.98	9.60	9.36	9.20	9.07	8.98	8.90
	.99	21.2	18.0	16.7	16.0	15.5	15.2	15.0	14.8	14.7
	.995	31.3	26.3	24.3	23.2	22.5	22.0	21.6	21.4	21.1
	.999	74.1	61.2	56.2	53.4	51.7	50.5	49.7	49.0	48.5
5	.50	0.528	0.799	0.907	0.965	1.00	1.02	1.04	1.05	1.06
	.90	4.06	3.78	3.62	3.52	3.45	3.40	3.37	3.34	3.32
	.95	6.61	5.79	5.41	5.19	5.05	4.95	4.88	4.82	4.77
	.975	10.0	8.43	7.76	7.39	7.15	6.98	6.85	6.76	6.68
	.99	16.3	13.3	12.1	11.4	11.0	10.7	10.5	10.3	10.2
	.995	22.8	18.3	16.5	15.6	14.9	14.5	14.2	14.0	13.8
	.999	47.2	37.1	33.2	31.1	29.8	28.8	28.2	27.6	27.2
6	.50	0.515	0.780	0.886	0.942	0.977	1.00	1.02	1.03	1.04
	.90	3.78	3.46	3.29	3.18	3.11	3.05	3.01	2.98	2.96
	.95	5.99	5.14	4.76	4.53	4.39	4.28	4.21	4.15	4.10
	.975	8.81	7.26	6.60	6.23	5.99	5.82	5.70	5.60	5.52
	.99	13.7	10.9	9.78	9.15	8.75	8.47	8.26	8.10	7.98
	.995	18.6	14.5	12.9	12.0	11.5	11.1	10.8	10.6	10.4
	.999	35.5	27.0	23.7	21.9	20.8	20.0	19.5	19.0	18.7
7	.50	0.506	0.767	0.871	0.926	0.960	0.983	1.00	1.01	1.02
	.90	3.59	3.26	3.07	2.96	2.88	2.83	2.78	2.75	2.72
	.95	5.59	4.74	4.35	4.12	3.97	3.87	3.79	3.73	3.68
	.975	8.07	6.54	5.89	5.52	5.29	5.12	4.99	4.90	4.82
	.99	12.2	9.55	8.45	7.85	7.46	7.19	6.99	6.84	6.72
	.995	16.2	12.4	10.9	10.1	9.52	9.16	8.89	8.68	8.51
	.999	29.2	21.7	18.8	17.2	16.2	15.5	15.0	14.6	14.3

TABLE B.4 *(continued)* **Percentiles of the *F* Distribution.**

Den. df	A	Numerator df 10	12	15	20	24	30	60	120	∞
1	.50	2.04	2.07	2.09	2.12	2.13	2.15	2.17	2.18	2.20
	.90	60.2	60.7	61.2	61.7	62.0	62.3	62.8	63.1	63.3
	.95	242	244	246	248	249	250	252	253	254
	.975	969	977	985	993	997	1,001	1,010	1,014	1,018
	.99	6,056	6,106	6,157	6,209	6,235	6,261	6,313	6,339	6,366
	.995	24,224	24,426	24,630	24,836	24,940	25,044	25,253	25,359	25,464
	.999	605,620	610,670	615,760	620,910	623,500	626,100	631,340	633,970	636,620
2	.50	1.34	1.36	1.38	1.39	1.40	1.41	1.43	1.43	1.44
	.90	9.39	9.41	9.42	9.44	9.45	9.46	9.47	9.48	9.49
	.95	19.4	19.4	19.4	19.4	19.5	19.5	19.5	19.5	19.5
	.975	39.4	39.4	39.4	39.4	39.5	39.5	39.5	39.5	39.5
	.99	99.4	99.4	99.4	99.4	99.5	99.5	99.5	99.5	99.5
	.995	199	199	199	199	199	199	199	199	200
	.999	999.4	999.4	999.4	999.4	999.5	999.5	999.5	999.5	999.5
3	.50	1.18	1.20	1.21	1.23	1.23	1.24	1.25	1.26	1.27
	.90	5.23	5.22	5.20	5.18	5.18	5.17	5.15	5.14	5.13
	.95	8.79	8.74	8.70	8.66	8.64	8.62	8.57	8.55	8.53
	.975	14.4	14.3	14.3	14.2	14.1	14.1	14.0	13.9	13.9
	.99	27.2	27.1	26.9	26.7	26.6	26.5	26.3	26.2	26.1
	.995	43.7	43.4	43.1	42.8	42.6	42.5	42.1	42.0	41.8
	.999	129.2	128.3	127.4	126.4	125.9	125.4	124.5	124.0	123.5
4	.50	1.11	1.13	1.14	1.15	1.16	1.16	1.18	1.18	1.19
	.90	3.92	3.90	3.87	3.84	3.83	3.82	3.79	3.78	3.76
	.95	5.96	5.91	5.86	5.80	5.77	5.75	5.69	5.66	5.63
	.975	8.84	8.75	8.66	8.56	8.51	8.46	8.36	8.31	8.26
	.99	14.5	14.4	14.2	14.0	13.9	13.8	13.7	13.6	13.5
	.995	21.0	20.7	20.4	20.2	20.0	19.9	19.6	19.5	19.3
	.999	48.1	47.4	46.8	46.1	45.8	45.4	44.7	44.4	44.1
5	.50	1.07	1.09	1.10	1.11	1.12	1.12	1.14	1.14	1.15
	.90	3.30	3.27	3.24	3.21	3.19	3.17	3.14	3.12	3.11
	.95	4.74	4.68	4.62	4.56	4.53	4.50	4.43	4.40	4.37
	.975	6.62	6.52	6.43	6.33	6.28	6.23	6.12	6.07	6.02
	.99	10.1	9.89	9.72	9.55	9.47	9.38	9.20	9.11	9.02
	.995	13.6	13.4	13.1	12.9	12.8	12.7	12.4	12.3	12.1
	.999	26.9	26.4	25.9	25.4	25.1	24.9	24.3	24.1	23.8
6	.50	1.05	1.06	1.07	1.08	1.09	1.10	1.11	1.12	1.12
	.90	2.94	2.90	2.87	2.84	2.82	2.80	2.76	2.74	2.72
	.95	4.06	4.00	3.94	3.87	3.84	3.81	3.74	3.70	3.67
	.975	5.46	5.37	5.27	5.17	5.12	5.07	4.96	4.90	4.85
	.99	7.87	7.72	7.56	7.40	7.31	7.23	7.06	6.97	6.88
	.995	10.2	10.0	9.81	9.59	9.47	9.36	9.12	9.00	8.88
	.999	18.4	18.0	17.6	17.1	16.9	16.7	16.2	16.0	15.7
7	.50	1.03	1.04	1.05	1.07	1.07	1.08	1.09	1.10	1.10
	.90	2.70	2.67	2.63	2.59	2.58	2.56	2.51	2.49	2.47
	.95	3.64	3.57	3.51	3.44	3.41	3.38	3.30	3.27	3.23
	.975	4.76	4.67	4.57	4.47	4.42	4.36	4.25	4.20	4.14
	.99	6.62	6.47	6.31	6.16	6.07	5.99	5.82	5.74	5.65
	.995	8.38	8.18	7.97	7.75	7.65	7.53	7.31	7.19	7.08
	.999	14.1	13.7	13.3	12.9	12.7	12.5	12.1	11.9	11.7

TABLE B.4 *(continued)*   **Percentiles of the *F* Distribution.**

Den. df	α	1	2	3	4	5	6	7	8	9
						Numerator df				
8	.50	0.499	0.757	0.860	0.915	0.948	0.971	0.988	1.00	1.01
	.90	3.46	3.11	2.92	2.81	2.73	2.67	2.62	2.59	2.56
	.95	5.32	4.46	4.07	3.84	3.69	3.58	3.50	3.44	3.39
	.975	7.57	6.06	5.42	5.05	4.82	4.65	4.53	4.43	4.36
	.99	11.3	8.65	7.59	7.01	6.63	6.37	6.18	6.03	5.91
	.995	14.7	11.0	9.60	8.81	8.30	7.95	7.69	7.50	7.34
	.999	25.4	18.5	15.8	14.4	13.5	12.9	12.4	12.0	11.8
9	.50	0.494	0.749	0.852	0.906	0.939	0.962	0.978	0.990	1.00
	.90	3.36	3.01	2.81	2.69	2.61	2.55	2.51	2.47	2.44
	.95	5.12	4.26	3.86	3.63	3.48	3.37	3.29	3.23	3.18
	.975	7.21	5.71	5.08	4.72	4.48	4.32	4.20	4.10	4.03
	.99	10.6	8.02	6.99	6.42	6.06	5.80	5.61	5.47	5.35
	.995	13.6	10.1	8.72	7.96	7.47	7.13	6.88	6.69	6.54
	.999	22.9	16.4	13.9	12.6	11.7	11.1	10.7	10.4	10.1
10	.50	0.490	0.743	0.845	0.899	0.932	0.954	0.971	0.983	0.992
	.90	3.29	2.92	2.73	2.61	2.52	2.46	2.41	2.38	2.35
	.95	4.96	4.10	3.71	3.48	3.33	3.22	3.14	3.07	3.02
	.975	6.94	5.46	4.83	4.47	4.24	4.07	3.95	3.85	3.78
	.99	10.0	7.56	6.55	5.99	5.64	5.39	5.20	5.06	4.94
	.995	12.8	9.43	8.08	7.34	6.87	6.54	6.30	6.12	5.97
	.999	21.0	14.9	12.6	11.3	10.5	9.93	9.52	9.20	8.96
12	.50	0.484	0.735	0.835	0.888	0.921	0.943	0.959	0.972	0.981
	.90	3.18	2.81	2.61	2.48	2.39	2.33	2.28	2.24	2.21
	.95	4.75	3.89	3.49	3.26	3.11	3.00	2.91	2.85	2.80
	.975	6.55	5.10	4.47	4.12	3.89	3.73	3.61	3.51	3.44
	.99	9.33	6.93	5.95	5.41	5.06	4.82	4.64	4.50	4.39
	.995	11.8	8.51	7.23	6.52	6.07	5.76	5.52	5.35	5.20
	.999	18.6	13.0	10.8	9.63	8.89	8.38	8.00	7.71	7.48
15	.50	0.478	0.726	0.826	0.878	0.911	0.933	0.949	0.960	0.970
	.90	3.07	2.70	2.49	2.36	2.27	2.21	2.16	2.12	2.09
	.95	4.54	3.68	3.29	3.06	2.90	2.79	2.71	2.64	2.59
	.975	6.20	4.77	4.15	3.80	3.58	3.41	3.29	3.20	3.12
	.99	8.68	6.36	5.42	4.89	4.56	4.32	4.14	4.00	3.89
	.995	10.8	7.70	6.48	5.80	5.37	5.07	4.85	4.67	4.54
	.999	16.6	11.3	9.34	8.25	7.57	7.09	6.74	6.47	6.26
20	.50	0.472	0.718	0.816	0.868	0.900	0.922	0.938	0.950	0.959
	.90	2.97	2.59	2.38	2.25	2.16	2.09	2.04	2.00	1.96
	.95	4.35	3.49	3.10	2.87	2.71	2.60	2.51	2.45	2.39
	.975	5.87	4.46	3.86	3.51	3.29	3.13	3.01	2.91	2.84
	.99	8.10	5.85	4.94	4.43	4.10	3.87	3.70	3.56	3.46
	.995	9.94	6.99	5.82	5.17	4.76	4.47	4.26	4.09	3.96
	.999	14.8	9.95	8.10	7.10	6.46	6.02	5.69	5.44	5.24
24	.50	0.469	0.714	0.812	0.863	0.895	0.917	0.932	0.944	0.953
	.90	2.93	2.54	2.33	2.19	2.10	2.04	1.98	1.94	1.91
	.95	4.26	3.40	3.01	2.78	2.62	2.51	2.42	2.36	2.30
	.975	5.72	4.32	3.72	3.38	3.15	2.99	2.87	2.78	2.70
	.99	7.82	5.61	4.72	4.22	3.90	3.67	3.50	3.36	3.26
	.995	9.55	6.66	5.52	4.89	4.49	4.20	3.99	3.83	3.69
	.999	14.0	9.34	7.55	6.59	5.98	5.55	5.23	4.99	4.80

TABLE B.4 *(continued)*   **Percentiles of the *F* Distribution.**

Den. df	A	Numerator df 10	12	15	20	24	30	60	120	∞
8	.50	1.02	1.03	1.04	1.05	1.06	1.07	1.08	1.08	1.09
	.90	2.54	2.50	2.46	2.42	2.40	2.38	2.34	2.32	2.29
	.95	3.35	3.28	3.22	3.15	3.12	3.08	3.01	2.97	2.93
	.975	4.30	4.20	4.10	4.00	3.95	3.89	3.78	3.73	3.67
	.99	5.81	5.67	5.52	5.36	5.28	5.20	5.03	4.95	4.86
	.995	7.21	7.01	6.81	6.61	6.50	6.40	6.18	6.06	5.95
	.999	11.5	11.2	10.8	10.5	10.3	10.1	9.73	9.53	9.33
9	.50	1.01	1.02	1.03	1.04	1.05	1.05	1.07	1.07	1.08
	.90	2.42	2.38	2.34	2.30	2.28	2.25	2.21	2.18	2.16
	.95	3.14	3.07	3.01	2.94	2.90	2.86	2.79	2.75	2.71
	.975	3.96	3.87	3.77	3.67	3.61	3.56	3.45	3.39	3.33
	.99	5.26	5.11	4.96	4.81	4.73	4.65	4.48	4.40	4.31
	.995	6.42	6.23	6.03	5.83	5.73	5.62	5.41	5.30	5.19
	.999	9.89	9.57	9.24	8.90	8.72	8.55	8.19	8.00	7.81
10	.50	1.00	1.01	1.02	1.03	1.04	1.05	1.06	1.06	1.07
	.90	2.32	2.28	2.24	2.20	2.18	2.16	2.11	2.08	2.06
	.95	2.98	2.91	2.84	2.77	2.74	2.70	2.62	2.58	2.54
	.975	3.72	3.62	3.52	3.42	3.37	3.31	3.20	3.14	3.08
	.99	4.85	4.71	4.56	4.41	4.33	4.25	4.08	4.00	3.91
	.995	5.85	5.66	5.47	5.27	5.17	5.07	4.86	4.75	4.64
	.999	8.75	8.45	8.13	7.80	7.64	7.47	7.12	6.94	6.76
12	.50	0.989	1.00	1.01	1.02	1.03	1.03	1.05	1.05	1.06
	.90	2.19	2.15	2.10	2.06	2.04	2.01	1.96	1.93	1.90
	.95	2.75	2.69	2.62	2.54	2.51	2.47	2.38	2.34	2.30
	.975	3.37	3.28	3.18	3.07	3.02	2.96	2.85	2.79	2.72
	.99	4.30	4.16	4.01	3.86	3.78	3.70	3.54	3.45	3.36
	.995	5.09	4.91	4.72	4.53	4.43	4.33	4.12	4.01	3.90
	.999	7.29	7.00	6.71	6.40	6.25	6.09	5.76	5.59	5.42
15	.50	0.977	0.989	1.00	1.01	1.02	1.02	1.03	1.04	1.05
	.90	2.06	2.02	1.97	1.92	1.90	1.87	1.82	1.79	1.76
	.95	2.54	2.48	2.40	2.33	2.29	2.25	2.16	2.11	2.07
	.975	3.06	2.96	2.86	2.76	2.70	2.64	2.52	2.46	2.40
	.99	3.80	3.67	3.52	3.37	3.29	3.21	3.05	2.96	2.87
	.995	4.42	4.25	4.07	3.88	3.79	3.69	3.48	3.37	3.26
	.999	6.08	5.81	5.54	5.25	5.10	4.95	4.64	4.48	4.31
20	.50	0.966	0.977	0.989	1.00	1.01	1.01	1.02	1.03	1.03
	.90	1.94	1.89	1.84	1.79	1.77	1.74	1.68	1.64	1.61
	.95	2.35	2.28	2.20	2.12	2.08	2.04	1.95	1.90	1.84
	.975	2.77	2.68	2.57	2.46	2.41	2.35	2.22	2.16	2.09
	.99	3.37	3.23	3.09	2.94	2.86	2.78	2.61	2.52	2.42
	.995	3.85	3.68	3.50	3.32	3.22	3.12	2.92	2.81	2.69
	.999	5.08	4.82	4.56	4.29	4.15	4.00	3.70	3.54	3.38
24	.50	0.961	0.972	0.983	0.994	1.00	1.01	1.02	1.02	1.03
	.90	1.88	1.83	1.78	1.73	1.70	1.67	1.61	1.57	1.53
	.95	2.25	2.18	2.11	2.03	1.98	1.94	1.84	1.79	1.73
	.975	2.64	2.54	2.44	2.33	2.27	2.21	2.08	2.01	1.94
	.99	3.17	3.03	2.89	2.74	2.66	2.58	2.40	2.31	2.21
	.995	3.59	3.42	3.25	3.06	2.97	2.87	2.66	2.55	2.43
	.999	4.64	4.39	4.14	3.87	3.74	3.59	3.29	3.14	2.97

TABLE B.4 *(continued)*   **Percentiles of the *F* Distribution.**

Den. df	*A*	\multicolumn{9}{c}{Numerator df}
		1	2	3	4	5	6	7	8	9
30	.50	0.466	0.709	0.807	0.858	0.890	0.912	0.927	0.939	0.948
	.90	2.88	2.49	2.28	2.14	2.05	1.98	1.93	1.88	1.85
	.95	4.17	3.32	2.92	2.69	2.53	2.42	2.33	2.27	2.21
	.975	5.57	4.18	3.59	3.25	3.03	2.87	2.75	2.65	2.57
	.99	7.56	5.39	4.51	4.02	3.70	3.47	3.30	3.17	3.07
	.995	9.18	6.35	5.24	4.62	4.23	3.95	3.74	3.58	3.45
	.999	13.3	8.77	7.05	6.12	5.53	5.12	4.82	4.58	4.39
60	.50	0.461	0.701	0.798	0.849	0.880	0.901	0.917	0.928	0.937
	.90	2.79	2.39	2.18	2.04	1.95	1.87	1.82	1.77	1.74
	.95	4.00	3.15	2.76	2.53	2.37	2.25	2.17	2.10	2.04
	.975	5.29	3.93	3.34	3.01	2.79	2.63	2.51	2.41	2.33
	.99	7.08	4.98	4.13	3.65	3.34	3.12	2.95	2.82	2.72
	.995	8.49	5.80	4.73	4.14	3.76	3.49	3.29	3.13	3.01
	.999	12.0	7.77	6.17	5.31	4.76	4.37	4.09	3.86	3.69
120	.50	0.458	0.697	0.793	0.844	0.875	0.896	0.912	0.923	0.932
	.90	2.75	2.35	2.13	1.99	1.90	1.82	1.77	1.72	1.68
	.95	3.92	3.07	2.68	2.45	2.29	2.18	2.09	2.02	1.96
	.975	5.15	3.80	3.23	2.89	2.67	2.52	2.39	2.30	2.22
	.99	6.85	4.79	3.95	3.48	3.17	2.96	2.79	2.66	2.56
	.995	8.18	5.54	4.50	3.92	3.55	3.28	3.09	2.93	2.81
	.999	11.4	7.32	5.78	4.95	4.42	4.04	3.77	3.55	3.38
∞	.50	0.455	0.693	0.789	0.839	0.870	0.891	0.907	0.918	0.927
	.90	2.71	2.30	2.08	1.94	1.85	1.77	1.72	1.67	1.63
	.95	3.84	3.00	2.60	2.37	2.21	2.10	2.01	1.94	1.88
	.975	5.02	3.69	3.12	2.79	2.57	2.41	2.29	2.19	2.11
	.99	6.63	4.61	3.78	3.32	3.02	2.80	2.64	2.51	2.41
	.995	7.88	5.30	4.28	3.72	3.35	3.09	2.90	2.74	2.62
	.999	10.8	6.91	5.42	4.62	4.10	3.74	3.47	3.27	3.10

TABLE B.4 *(concluded)*   **Percentiles of the *F* Distribution.**

Den. df	A	\multicolumn{9}{c}{Numerator df}
		10	12	15	20	24	30	60	120	∞
30	.50	0.955	0.966	0.978	0.989	0.994	1.00	1.01	1.02	1.02
	.90	1.82	1.77	1.72	1.67	1.64	1.61	1.54	1.50	1.46
	.95	2.16	2.09	2.01	1.93	1.89	1.84	1.74	1.68	1.62
	.975	2.51	2.41	2.31	2.20	2.14	2.07	1.94	1.87	1.79
	.99	2.98	2.84	2.70	2.55	2.47	2.39	2.21	2.11	2.01
	.995	3.34	3.18	3.01	2.82	2.73	2.63	2.42	2.30	2.18
	.999	4.24	4.00	3.75	3.49	3.36	3.22	2.92	2.76	2.59
60	.50	0.945	0.956	0.967	0.978	0.983	0.989	1.00	1.01	1.01
	.90	1.71	1.66	1.60	1.54	1.51	1.48	1.40	1.35	1.29
	.95	1.99	1.92	1.84	1.75	1.70	1.65	1.53	1.47	1.39
	.975	2.27	2.17	2.06	1.94	1.88	1.82	1.67	1.58	1.48
	.99	2.63	2.50	2.35	2.20	2.12	2.03	1.84	1.73	1.60
	.995	2.90	2.74	2.57	2.39	2.29	2.19	1.96	1.83	1.69
	.999	3.54	3.32	3.08	2.83	2.69	2.55	2.25	2.08	1.89
120	.50	0.939	0.950	0.961	0.972	0.978	0.983	0.994	1.00	1.01
	.90	1.65	1.60	1.55	1.48	1.45	1.41	1.32	1.26	1.19
	.95	1.91	1.83	1.75	1.66	1.61	1.55	1.43	1.35	1.25
	.975	2.16	2.05	1.95	1.82	1.76	1.69	1.53	1.43	1.31
	.99	2.47	2.34	2.19	2.03	1.95	1.86	1.66	1.53	1.38
	.995	2.71	2.54	2.37	2.19	2.09	1.98	1.75	1.61	1.43
	.999	3.24	3.02	2.78	2.53	2.40	2.26	1.95	1.77	1.54
∞	.50	0.934	0.945	0.956	0.967	0.972	0.978	0.989	0.994	1.00
	.90	1.60	1.55	1.49	1.42	1.38	1.34	1.24	1.17	1.00
	.95	1.83	1.75	1.67	1.57	1.52	1.46	1.32	1.22	1.00
	.975	2.05	1.94	1.83	1.71	1.64	1.57	1.39	1.27	1.00
	.99	2.32	2.18	2.04	1.88	1.79	1.70	1.47	1.32	1.00
	.995	2.52	2.36	2.19	2.00	1.90	1.79	1.53	1.36	1.00
	.999	2.96	2.74	2.51	2.27	2.13	1.99	1.66	1.45	1.00

Source: Reprinted from Table 5 of Pearson and Hartley, *Biometrika Tables for Statisticians,* Volume 2, 1972, published by the Cambridge University Press, on behalf of The Biometrika Society, by permission of the authors and publishers.

TABLE B.5   **Power Values for Two-Sided *t* Test.**

$\alpha = .05$

	δ								
df	1.0	2.0	3.0	4.0	5.0	6.0	7.0	8.0	9.0
1	.07	.13	.19	.25	.31	.36	.42	.47	.52
2	.10	.22	.39	.56	.72	.84	.91	.96	.98
3	.11	.29	.53	.75	.90	.97	.99	1.00	1.00
4	.12	.34	.62	.84	.95	.99	1.00	1.00	1.00
5	.13	.37	.67	.89	.98	1.00	1.00	1.00	1.00
6	.14	.39	.71	.91	.98	1.00	1.00	1.00	1.00
7	.14	.41	.73	.93	.99	1.00	1.00	1.00	1.00
8	.14	.42	.75	.94	.99	1.00	1.00	1.00	1.00
9	.15	.43	.76	.94	.99	1.00	1.00	1.00	1.00
10	.15	.44	.77	.95	.99	1.00	1.00	1.00	1.00
11	.15	.45	.78	.95	.99	1.00	1.00	1.00	1.00
12	.15	.45	.79	.96	1.00	1.00	1.00	1.00	1.00
13	.15	.46	.79	.96	1.00	1.00	1.00	1.00	1.00
14	.15	.46	.80	.96	1.00	1.00	1.00	1.00	1.00
15	.16	.46	.80	.96	1.00	1.00	1.00	1.00	1.00
16	.16	.47	.80	.96	1.00	1.00	1.00	1.00	1.00
17	.16	.47	.81	.96	1.00	1.00	1.00	1.00	1.00
18	.16	.47	.81	.97	1.00	1.00	1.00	1.00	1.00
19	.16	.48	.81	.97	1.00	1.00	1.00	1.00	1.00
20	.16	.48	.81	.97	1.00	1.00	1.00	1.00	1.00
21	.16	.48	.82	.97	1.00	1.00	1.00	1.00	1.00
22	.16	.48	.82	.97	1.00	1.00	1.00	1.00	1.00
23	.16	.48	.82	.97	1.00	1.00	1.00	1.00	1.00
24	.16	.48	.82	.97	1.00	1.00	1.00	1.00	1.00
25	.16	.49	.82	.97	1.00	1.00	1.00	1.00	1.00
26	.16	.49	.82	.97	1.00	1.00	1.00	1.00	1.00
27	.16	.49	.82	.97	1.00	1.00	1.00	1.00	1.00
28	.16	.49	.83	.97	1.00	1.00	1.00	1.00	1.00
29	.16	.49	.83	.97	1.00	1.00	1.00	1.00	1.00
30	.16	.49	.83	.97	1.00	1.00	1.00	1.00	1.00
40	.16	.50	.83	.97	1.00	1.00	1.00	1.00	1.00
50	.17	.50	.84	.98	1.00	1.00	1.00	1.00	1.00
60	.17	.50	.84	.98	1.00	1.00	1.00	1.00	1.00
100	.17	.51	.84	.98	1.00	1.00	1.00	1.00	1.00
120	.17	.51	.85	.98	1.00	1.00	1.00	1.00	1.00
∞	.17	.52	.85	.98	1.00	1.00	1.00	1.00	1.00

TABLE B.5 *(concluded)*   **Power Values for Two-Sided *t* Test.**

$\alpha = .01$

	δ								
df	1.0	2.0	3.0	4.0	5.0	6.0	7.0	8.0	9.0
1	.01	.03	.04	.05	.06	.08	.09	.10	.11
2	.02	.05	.09	.16	.23	.31	.39	.48	.56
3	.02	.08	.17	.31	.47	.62	.75	.85	.92
4	.03	.10	.25	.45	.65	.82	.92	.97	.99
5	.03	.12	.31	.55	.77	.91	.97	.99	1.00
6	.04	.14	.36	.63	.84	.95	.99	1.00	1.00
7	.04	.16	.40	.68	.88	.97	1.00	1.00	1.00
8	.04	.17	.43	.72	.91	.98	1.00	1.00	1.00
9	.04	.18	.45	.75	.93	.99	1.00	1.00	1.00
10	.04	.19	.47	.77	.94	.99	1.00	1.00	1.00
11	.04	.19	.49	.79	.95	.99	1.00	1.00	1.00
12	.04	.20	.50	.80	.96	.99	1.00	1.00	1.00
13	.05	.21	.52	.82	.96	1.00	1.00	1.00	1.00
14	.05	.21	.53	.83	.96	1.00	1.00	1.00	1.00
15	.05	.21	.54	.83	.97	1.00	1.00	1.00	1.00
16	.05	.22	.55	.84	.97	1.00	1.00	1.00	1.00
17	.05	.22	.55	.85	.97	1.00	1.00	1.00	1.00
18	.05	.22	.56	.85	.97	1.00	1.00	1.00	1.00
19	.05	.23	.56	.86	.98	1.00	1.00	1.00	1.00
20	.05	.23	.57	.86	.98	1.00	1.00	1.00	1.00
21	.05	.23	.57	.86	.98	1.00	1.00	1.00	1.00
22	.05	.23	.58	.87	.98	1.00	1.00	1.00	1.00
23	.05	.24	.58	.87	.98	1.00	1.00	1.00	1.00
24	.05	.24	.59	.87	.98	1.00	1.00	1.00	1.00
25	.05	.24	.59	.88	.98	1.00	1.00	1.00	1.00
26	.05	.24	.59	.88	.98	1.00	1.00	1.00	1.00
27	.05	.24	.59	.88	.98	1.00	1.00	1.00	1.00
28	.05	.24	.60	.88	.98	1.00	1.00	1.00	1.00
29	.05	.25	.60	.88	.98	1.00	1.00	1.00	1.00
30	.05	.25	.60	.88	.98	1.00	1.00	1.00	1.00
40	.05	.26	.62	.90	.99	1.00	1.00	1.00	1.00
50	.05	.26	.63	.90	.99	1.00	1.00	1.00	1.00
60	.05	.26	.63	.91	.99	1.00	1.00	1.00	1.00
100	.06	.27	.65	.91	.99	1.00	1.00	1.00	1.00
120	.06	.27	.65	.91	.99	1.00	1.00	1.00	1.00
∞	.06	.28	.66	.92	.99	1.00	1.00	1.00	1.00

TABLE B.6   **Critical Values for Coefficient of Correlation between Ordered Residuals and Expected Values under Normality when Distribution of Error Terms Is Normal.**

	Level of Significance α				
n	.10	.05	.025	.01	.005
5	.903	.880	.865	.826	.807
6	.910	.888	.866	.838	.820
7	.918	.898	.877	.850	.828
8	.924	.906	.887	.861	.840
9	.930	.912	.894	.871	.854
10	.934	.918	.901	.879	.862
12	.942	.928	.912	.892	.876
14	.948	.935	.923	.905	.890
16	.953	.941	.929	.913	.899
18	.957	.946	.935	.920	.908
20	.960	.951	.940	.926	.916
22	.963	.954	.945	.933	.923
24	.965	.957	.949	.937	.927
26	.967	.960	.952	.941	.932
28	.969	.962	.955	.944	.936
30	.971	.964	.957	.947	.939
40	.977	.972	.966	.959	.953
50	.981	.977	.972	.966	.961
60	.984	.980	.976	.971	.967
70	.986	.983	.979	.975	.971
80	.987	.985	.982	.978	.975
90	.988	.986	.984	.980	.977
100	.989	.987	.985	.982	.979

Source: Reprinted, with permission, from S.W. Looney and T.R. Gulledge, Jr. "Use of the Correlation Coefficient with Normal Probability Plots," *The American Statistician* 39 (1985), pp. 75–79.

TABLE B.7   Durbin-Watson Test Bounds.

Level of Significance $\alpha = .05$

n	$p-1=1$ d_L	d_U	$p-1=2$ d_L	d_U	$p-1=3$ d_L	d_U	$p-1=4$ d_L	d_U	$p-1=5$ d_L	d_U
15	1.08	1.36	0.95	1.54	0.82	1.75	0.69	1.97	0.56	2.21
16	1.10	1.37	0.98	1.54	0.86	1.73	0.74	1.93	0.62	2.15
17	1.13	1.38	1.02	1.54	0.90	1.71	0.78	1.90	0.67	2.10
18	1.16	1.39	1.05	1.53	0.93	1.69	0.82	1.87	0.71	2.06
19	1.18	1.40	1.08	1.53	0.97	1.68	0.86	1.85	0.75	2.02
20	1.20	1.41	1.10	1.54	1.00	1.68	0.90	1.83	0.79	1.99
21	1.22	1.42	1.13	1.54	1.03	1.67	0.93	1.81	0.83	1.96
22	1.24	1.43	1.15	1.54	1.05	1.66	0.96	1.80	0.86	1.94
23	1.26	1.44	1.17	1.54	1.08	1.66	0.99	1.79	0.90	1.92
24	1.27	1.45	1.19	1.55	1.10	1.66	1.01	1.78	0.93	1.90
25	1.29	1.45	1.21	1.55	1.12	1.66	1.04	1.77	0.95	1.89
26	1.30	1.46	1.22	1.55	1.14	1.65	1.06	1.76	0.98	1.88
27	1.32	1.47	1.24	1.56	1.16	1.65	1.08	1.76	1.01	1.86
28	1.33	1.48	1.26	1.56	1.18	1.65	1.10	1.75	1.03	1.85
29	1.34	1.48	1.27	1.56	1.20	1.65	1.12	1.74	1.05	1.84
30	1.35	1.49	1.28	1.57	1.21	1.65	1.14	1.74	1.07	1.83
31	1.36	1.50	1.30	1.57	1.23	1.65	1.16	1.74	1.09	1.83
32	1.37	1.50	1.31	1.57	1.24	1.65	1.18	1.73	1.11	1.82
33	1.38	1.51	1.32	1.58	1.26	1.65	1.19	1.73	1.13	1.81
34	1.39	1.51	1.33	1.58	1.27	1.65	1.21	1.73	1.15	1.81
35	1.40	1.52	1.34	1.58	1.28	1.65	1.22	1.73	1.16	1.80
36	1.41	1.52	1.35	1.59	1.29	1.65	1.24	1.73	1.18	1.80
37	1.42	1.53	1.36	1.59	1.31	1.66	1.25	1.72	1.19	1.80
38	1.43	1.54	1.37	1.59	1.32	1.66	1.26	1.72	1.21	1.79
39	1.43	1.54	1.38	1.60	1.33	1.66	1.27	1.72	1.22	1.79
40	1.44	1.54	1.39	1.60	1.34	1.66	1.29	1.72	1.23	1.79
45	1.48	1.57	1.43	1.62	1.38	1.67	1.34	1.72	1.29	1.78
50	1.50	1.59	1.46	1.63	1.42	1.67	1.38	1.72	1.34	1.77
55	1.53	1.60	1.49	1.64	1.45	1.68	1.41	1.72	1.38	1.77
60	1.55	1.62	1.51	1.65	1.48	1.69	1.44	1.73	1.41	1.77
65	1.57	1.63	1.54	1.66	1.50	1.70	1.47	1.73	1.44	1.77
70	1.58	1.64	1.55	1.67	1.52	1.70	1.49	1.74	1.46	1.77
75	1.60	1.65	1.57	1.68	1.54	1.71	1.51	1.74	1.49	1.77
80	1.61	1.66	1.59	1.69	1.56	1.72	1.53	1.74	1.51	1.77
85	1.62	1.67	1.60	1.70	1.57	1.72	1.55	1.75	1.52	1.77
90	1.63	1.68	1.61	1.70	1.59	1.73	1.57	1.75	1.54	1.78
95	1.64	1.69	1.62	1.71	1.60	1.73	1.58	1.75	1.56	1.78
100	1.65	1.69	1.63	1.72	1.61	1.74	1.59	1.76	1.57	1.78

TABLE B.7 *(concluded)*   **Durbin-Watson Test Bounds.**

Level of Significance $\alpha = .01$

n	$p-1=1$ d_L	d_U	$p-1=2$ d_L	d_U	$p-1=3$ d_L	d_U	$p-1=4$ d_L	d_U	$p-1=5$ d_L	d_U
15	0.81	1.07	0.70	1.25	0.59	1.46	0.49	1.70	0.39	1.96
16	0.84	1.09	0.74	1.25	0.63	1.44	0.53	1.66	0.44	1.90
17	0.87	1.10	0.77	1.25	0.67	1.43	0.57	1.63	0.48	1.85
18	0.90	1.12	0.80	1.26	0.71	1.42	0.61	1.60	0.52	1.80
19	0.93	1.13	0.83	1.26	0.74	1.41	0.65	1.58	0.56	1.77
20	0.95	1.15	0.86	1.27	0.77	1.41	0.68	1.57	0.60	1.74
21	0.97	1.16	0.89	1.27	0.80	1.41	0.72	1.55	0.63	1.71
22	1.00	1.17	0.91	1.28	0.83	1.40	0.75	1.54	0.66	1.69
23	1.02	1.19	0.94	1.29	0.86	1.40	0.77	1.53	0.70	1.67
24	1.04	1.20	0.96	1.30	0.88	1.41	0.80	1.53	0.72	1.66
25	1.05	1.21	0.98	1.30	0.90	1.41	0.83	1.52	0.75	1.65
26	1.07	1.22	1.00	1.31	0.93	1.41	0.85	1.52	0.78	1.64
27	1.09	1.23	1.02	1.32	0.95	1.41	0.88	1.51	0.81	1.63
28	1.10	1.24	1.04	1.32	0.97	1.41	0.90	1.51	0.83	1.62
29	1.12	1.25	1.05	1.33	0.99	1.42	0.92	1.51	0.85	1.61
30	1.13	1.26	1.07	1.34	1.01	1.42	0.94	1.51	0.88	1.61
31	1.15	1.27	1.08	1.34	1.02	1.42	0.96	1.51	0.90	1.60
32	1.16	1.28	1.10	1.35	1.04	1.43	0.98	1.51	0.92	1.60
33	1.17	1.29	1.11	1.36	1.05	1.43	1.00	1.51	0.94	1.59
34	1.18	1.30	1.13	1.36	1.07	1.43	1.01	1.51	0.95	1.59
35	1.19	1.31	1.14	1.37	1.08	1.44	1.03	1.51	0.97	1.59
36	1.21	1.32	1.15	1.38	1.10	1.44	1.04	1.51	0.99	1.59
37	1.22	1.32	1.16	1.38	1.11	1.45	1.06	1.51	1.00	1.59
38	1.23	1.33	1.18	1.39	1.12	1.45	1.07	1.52	1.02	1.58
39	1.24	1.34	1.19	1.39	1.14	1.45	1.09	1.52	1.03	1.58
40	1.25	1.34	1.20	1.40	1.15	1.46	1.10	1.52	1.05	1.58
45	1.29	1.38	1.24	1.42	1.20	1.48	1.16	1.53	1.11	1.58
50	1.32	1.40	1.28	1.45	1.24	1.49	1.20	1.54	1.16	1.59
55	1.36	1.43	1.32	1.47	1.28	1.51	1.25	1.55	1.21	1.59
60	1.38	1.45	1.35	1.48	1.32	1.52	1.28	1.56	1.25	1.60
65	1.41	1.47	1.38	1.50	1.35	1.53	1.31	1.57	1.28	1.61
70	1.43	1.49	1.40	1.52	1.37	1.55	1.34	1.58	1.31	1.61
75	1.45	1.50	1.42	1.53	1.39	1.56	1.37	1.59	1.34	1.62
80	1.47	1.52	1.44	1.54	1.42	1.57	1.39	1.60	1.36	1.62
85	1.48	1.53	1.46	1.55	1.43	1.58	1.41	1.60	1.39	1.63
90	1.50	1.54	1.47	1.56	1.45	1.59	1.43	1.61	1.41	1.64
95	1.51	1.55	1.49	1.57	1.47	1.60	1.45	1.62	1.42	1.64
100	1.52	1.56	1.50	1.58	1.48	1.60	1.46	1.63	1.44	1.65

Source: Reprinted, with permission, from J. Durbin and G. S. Watson, "Testing for Serial Correlation in Least Squares Regression. II," *Biometrika* 38 (1951), pp. 159–78.

TABLE B.8   Table of z' Transformation of Correlation Coefficient.

r ρ	z' ζ	r ρ	z' ζ	r ρ	z' ζ	r ρ	z' ζ
.00	.0000	.25	.2554	.50	.5493	.75	.973
.01	.0100	.26	.2661	.51	.5627	.76	.996
.02	.0200	.27	.2769	.52	.5763	.77	1.020
.03	.0300	.28	.2877	.53	.5901	.78	1.045
.04	.0400	.29	.2986	.54	.6042	.79	1.071
.05	.0500	.30	.3095	.55	.6184	.80	1.099
.06	.0601	.31	.3205	.56	.6328	.81	1.127
.07	.0701	.32	.3316	.57	.6475	.82	1.157
.08	.0802	.33	.3428	.58	.6625	.83	1.188
.09	.0902	.34	.3541	.59	.6777	.84	1.221
.10	.1003	.35	.3654	.60	.6931	.85	1.256
.11	.1104	.36	.3769	.61	.7089	.86	1.293
.12	.1206	.37	.3884	.62	.7250	.87	1.333
.13	.1307	.38	.4001	.63	.7414	.88	1.376
.14	.1409	.39	.4118	.64	.7582	.89	1.422
.15	.1511	.40	.4236	.65	.7753	.90	1.472
.16	.1614	.41	.4356	.66	.7928	.91	1.528
.17	.1717	.42	.4477	.67	.8107	.92	1.589
.18	.1820	.43	.4599	.68	.8291	.93	1.658
.19	.1923	.44	.4722	.69	.8480	.94	1.738
.20	.2027	.45	.4847	.70	.8673	.95	1.832
.21	.2132	.46	.4973	.71	.8872	.96	1.946
.22	.2237	.47	.5101	.72	.9076	.97	2.092
.23	.2342	.48	.5230	.73	.9287	.98	2.298
.24	.2448	.49	.5361	.74	.9505	.99	2.647

Source: Abridged from Table 14 of Pearson and Hartley, *Biometrika Tables for Statisticians*, Volume 1, 1966, published by the Cambridge University Press, on behalf of The Biometrika Society, by permission of the authors and publishers.

TABLE B.9   Percentiles of the Studentized Range Distribution.

Entry is $q(1-\alpha; r, \nu)$ where $P\{q(r, \nu) \le q(1-\alpha; r, \nu)\} = 1 - \alpha$

$$1 - \alpha = .90$$

ν	2	3	4	5	6	7	8	9	10	11	12	13	14	15	16	17	18	19	20
1	8.93	13.4	16.4	18.5	20.2	21.5	22.6	23.6	24.5	25.2	25.9	26.5	27.1	27.6	28.1	28.5	29.0	29.3	29.7
2	4.13	5.73	6.77	7.54	8.14	8.63	9.05	9.41	9.72	10.0	10.3	10.5	10.7	10.9	11.1	11.2	11.4	11.5	11.7
3	3.33	4.47	5.20	5.74	6.16	6.51	6.81	7.06	7.29	7.49	7.67	7.83	7.98	8.12	8.25	8.37	8.48	8.58	8.68
4	3.01	3.98	4.59	5.03	5.39	5.68	5.93	6.14	6.33	6.49	6.65	6.78	6.91	7.02	7.13	7.23	7.33	7.41	7.50
5	2.85	3.72	4.26	4.66	4.98	5.24	5.46	5.65	5.82	5.97	6.10	6.22	6.34	6.44	6.54	6.63	6.71	6.79	6.86
6	2.75	3.56	4.07	4.44	4.73	4.97	5.17	5.34	5.50	5.64	5.76	5.87	5.98	6.07	6.16	6.25	6.32	6.40	6.47
7	2.68	3.45	3.93	4.28	4.55	4.78	4.97	5.14	5.28	5.41	5.53	5.64	5.74	5.83	5.91	5.99	6.06	6.13	6.19
8	2.63	3.37	3.83	4.17	4.43	4.65	4.83	4.99	5.13	5.25	5.36	5.46	5.56	5.64	5.72	5.80	5.87	5.93	6.00
9	2.59	3.32	3.76	4.08	4.34	4.54	4.72	4.87	5.01	5.13	5.23	5.33	5.42	5.51	5.58	5.66	5.72	5.79	5.85
10	2.56	3.27	3.70	4.02	4.26	4.47	4.64	4.78	4.91	5.03	5.13	5.23	5.32	5.40	5.47	5.54	5.61	5.67	5.73
11	2.54	3.23	3.66	3.96	4.20	4.40	4.57	4.71	4.84	4.95	5.05	5.15	5.23	5.31	5.38	5.45	5.51	5.57	5.63
12	2.52	3.20	3.62	3.92	4.16	4.35	4.51	4.65	4.78	4.89	4.99	5.08	5.16	5.24	5.31	5.37	5.44	5.49	5.55
13	2.50	3.18	3.59	3.88	4.12	4.30	4.46	4.60	4.72	4.83	4.93	5.02	5.10	5.18	5.25	5.31	5.37	5.43	5.48
14	2.49	3.16	3.56	3.85	4.08	4.27	4.42	4.56	4.68	4.79	4.88	4.97	5.05	5.12	5.19	5.26	5.32	5.37	5.43
15	2.48	3.14	3.54	3.83	4.05	4.23	4.39	4.52	4.64	4.75	4.84	4.93	5.01	5.08	5.15	5.21	5.27	5.32	5.38
16	2.47	3.12	3.52	3.80	4.03	4.21	4.36	4.49	4.61	4.71	4.81	4.89	4.97	5.04	5.11	5.17	5.23	5.28	5.33
17	2.46	3.11	3.50	3.78	4.00	4.18	4.33	4.46	4.58	4.68	4.77	4.86	4.93	5.01	5.07	5.13	5.19	5.24	5.30
18	2.45	3.10	3.49	3.77	3.98	4.16	4.31	4.44	4.55	4.65	4.75	4.83	4.90	4.98	5.04	5.10	5.16	5.21	5.26
19	2.45	3.09	3.47	3.75	3.97	4.14	4.29	4.42	4.53	4.63	4.72	4.80	4.88	4.95	5.01	5.07	5.13	5.18	5.23
20	2.44	3.08	3.46	3.74	3.95	4.12	4.27	4.40	4.51	4.61	4.70	4.78	4.85	4.92	4.99	5.05	5.10	5.16	5.20
24	2.42	3.05	3.42	3.69	3.90	4.07	4.21	4.34	4.44	4.54	4.63	4.71	4.78	4.85	4.91	4.97	5.02	5.07	5.12
30	2.40	3.02	3.39	3.65	3.85	4.02	4.16	4.28	4.38	4.47	4.56	4.64	4.71	4.77	4.83	4.89	4.94	4.99	5.03
40	2.38	2.99	3.35	3.60	3.80	3.96	4.10	4.21	4.32	4.41	4.49	4.56	4.63	4.69	4.75	4.81	4.86	4.90	4.95
60	2.36	2.96	3.31	3.56	3.75	3.91	4.04	4.16	4.25	4.34	4.42	4.49	4.56	4.62	4.67	4.73	4.78	4.82	4.86
120	2.34	2.93	3.28	3.52	3.71	3.86	3.99	4.10	4.19	4.28	4.35	4.42	4.48	4.54	4.60	4.65	4.69	4.74	4.78
∞	2.33	2.90	3.24	3.48	3.66	3.81	3.93	4.04	4.13	4.21	4.28	4.35	4.41	4.47	4.52	4.57	4.61	4.65	4.69

TABLE B.9 *(continued)*   **Percentiles of the Studentized Range Distribution.**

$1 - \alpha = .95$

r

ν	2	3	4	5	6	7	8	9	10	11	12	13	14	15	16	17	18	19	20
1	18.0	27.0	32.8	37.1	40.4	43.1	45.4	47.4	49.1	50.6	52.0	53.2	54.3	55.4	56.3	57.2	58.0	58.8	59.6
2	6.08	8.33	9.80	10.9	11.7	12.4	13.0	13.5	14.0	14.4	14.7	15.1	15.4	15.7	15.9	16.1	16.4	16.6	16.8
3	4.50	5.91	6.82	7.50	8.04	8.48	8.85	9.18	9.46	9.72	9.95	10.2	10.3	10.5	10.7	10.8	11.0	11.1	11.2
4	3.93	5.04	5.76	6.29	6.71	7.05	7.35	7.60	7.83	8.03	8.21	8.37	8.52	8.66	8.79	8.91	9.03	9.13	9.23
5	3.64	4.60	5.22	5.67	6.03	6.33	6.58	6.80	6.99	7.17	7.32	7.47	7.60	7.72	7.83	7.93	8.03	8.12	8.21
6	3.46	4.34	4.90	5.30	5.63	5.90	6.12	6.32	6.49	6.65	6.79	6.92	7.03	7.14	7.24	7.34	7.43	7.51	7.59
7	3.34	4.16	4.68	5.06	5.36	5.61	5.82	6.00	6.16	6.30	6.43	6.55	6.66	6.76	6.85	6.94	7.02	7.10	7.17
8	3.26	4.04	4.53	4.89	5.17	5.40	5.60	5.77	5.92	6.05	6.18	6.29	6.39	6.48	6.57	6.65	6.73	6.80	6.87
9	3.20	3.95	4.41	4.76	5.02	5.24	5.43	5.59	5.74	5.87	5.98	6.09	6.19	6.28	6.36	6.44	6.51	6.58	6.64
10	3.15	3.88	4.33	4.65	4.91	5.12	5.30	5.46	5.60	5.72	5.83	5.93	6.03	6.11	6.19	6.27	6.34	6.40	6.47
11	3.11	3.82	4.26	4.57	4.82	5.03	5.20	5.35	5.49	5.61	5.71	5.81	5.90	5.98	6.06	6.13	6.20	6.27	6.33
12	3.08	3.77	4.20	4.51	4.75	4.95	5.12	5.27	5.39	5.51	5.61	5.71	5.80	5.88	5.95	6.02	6.09	6.15	6.21
13	3.06	3.73	4.15	4.45	4.69	4.88	5.05	5.19	5.32	5.43	5.53	5.63	5.71	5.79	5.86	5.93	5.99	6.05	6.11
14	3.03	3.70	4.11	4.41	4.64	4.83	4.99	5.13	5.25	5.36	5.46	5.55	5.64	5.71	5.79	5.85	5.91	5.97	6.03
15	3.01	3.67	4.08	4.37	4.59	4.78	4.94	5.08	5.20	5.31	5.40	5.49	5.57	5.65	5.72	5.78	5.85	5.90	5.96
16	3.00	3.65	4.05	4.33	4.56	4.74	4.90	5.03	5.15	5.26	5.35	5.44	5.52	5.59	5.66	5.73	5.79	5.84	5.90
17	2.98	3.63	4.02	4.30	4.52	4.70	4.86	4.99	5.11	5.21	5.31	5.39	5.47	5.54	5.61	5.67	5.73	5.79	5.84
18	2.97	3.61	4.00	4.28	4.49	4.67	4.82	4.96	5.07	5.17	5.27	5.35	5.43	5.50	5.57	5.63	5.69	5.74	5.79
19	2.96	3.59	3.98	4.25	4.47	4.65	4.79	4.92	5.04	5.14	5.23	5.31	5.39	5.46	5.53	5.59	5.65	5.70	5.75
20	2.95	3.58	3.96	4.23	4.45	4.62	4.77	4.90	5.01	5.11	5.20	5.28	5.36	5.43	5.49	5.55	5.61	5.66	5.71
24	2.92	3.53	3.90	4.17	4.37	4.54	4.68	4.81	4.92	5.01	5.10	5.18	5.25	5.32	5.38	5.44	5.49	5.55	5.59
30	2.89	3.49	3.85	4.10	4.30	4.46	4.60	4.72	4.82	4.92	5.00	5.08	5.15	5.21	5.27	5.33	5.38	5.43	5.47
40	2.86	3.44	3.79	4.04	4.23	4.39	4.52	4.63	4.73	4.82	4.90	4.98	5.04	5.11	5.16	5.22	5.27	5.31	5.36
60	2.83	3.40	3.74	3.98	4.16	4.31	4.44	4.55	4.65	4.73	4.81	4.88	4.94	5.00	5.06	5.11	5.15	5.20	5.24
120	2.80	3.36	3.68	3.92	4.10	4.24	4.36	4.47	4.56	4.64	4.71	4.78	4.84	4.90	4.95	5.00	5.04	5.09	5.13
∞	2.77	3.31	3.63	3.86	4.03	4.17	4.29	4.39	4.47	4.55	4.62	4.68	4.74	4.80	4.85	4.89	4.93	4.97	5.01

TABLE B.9 *(concluded)* **Percentiles of the Studentized Range Distribution.**

$1 - \alpha = .99$

v	2	3	4	5	6	7	8	9	10	11	12	13	14	15	16	17	18	19	20
1	90.0	135	164	186	202	216	227	237	246	253	260	266	272	277	282	286	290	294	298
2	14.0	19.0	22.3	24.7	26.6	28.2	29.5	30.7	31.7	32.6	33.4	34.1	34.8	35.4	36.0	36.5	37.0	37.5	37.9
3	8.26	10.6	12.2	13.3	14.2	15.0	15.6	16.2	16.7	17.1	17.5	17.9	18.2	18.5	18.8	19.1	19.3	19.5	19.8
4	6.51	8.12	9.17	9.96	10.6	11.1	11.5	11.9	12.3	12.6	12.8	13.1	13.3	13.5	13.7	13.9	14.1	14.2	14.4
5	5.70	6.97	7.80	8.42	8.91	9.32	9.67	9.97	10.2	10.5	10.7	10.9	11.1	11.2	11.4	11.6	11.7	11.8	11.9
6	5.24	6.33	7.03	7.56	7.97	8.32	8.61	8.87	9.10	9.30	9.49	9.65	9.81	9.95	10.1	10.2	10.3	10.4	10.5
7	4.95	5.92	6.54	7.01	7.37	7.68	7.94	8.17	8.37	8.55	8.71	8.86	9.00	9.12	9.24	9.35	9.46	9.55	9.65
8	4.74	5.63	6.20	6.63	6.96	7.24	7.47	7.68	7.87	8.03	8.18	8.31	8.44	8.55	8.66	8.76	8.85	8.94	9.03
9	4.60	5.43	5.96	6.35	6.66	6.91	7.13	7.32	7.49	7.65	7.78	7.91	8.03	8.13	8.23	8.32	8.41	8.49	8.57
10	4.48	5.27	5.77	6.14	6.43	6.67	6.87	7.05	7.21	7.36	7.48	7.60	7.71	7.81	7.91	7.99	8.07	8.15	8.22
11	4.39	5.14	5.62	5.97	6.25	6.48	6.67	6.84	6.99	7.13	7.25	7.36	7.46	7.56	7.65	7.73	7.81	7.88	7.95
12	4.32	5.04	5.50	5.84	6.10	6.32	6.51	6.67	6.81	6.94	7.06	7.17	7.26	7.36	7.44	7.52	7.59	7.66	7.73
13	4.26	4.96	5.40	5.73	5.98	6.19	6.37	6.53	6.67	6.79	6.90	7.01	7.10	7.19	7.27	7.34	7.42	7.48	7.55
14	4.21	4.89	5.32	5.63	5.88	6.08	6.26	6.41	6.54	6.66	6.77	6.87	6.96	7.05	7.12	7.20	7.27	7.33	7.39
15	4.17	4.83	5.25	5.56	5.80	5.99	6.16	6.31	6.44	6.55	6.66	6.76	6.84	6.93	7.00	7.07	7.14	7.20	7.26
16	4.13	4.78	5.19	5.49	5.72	5.92	6.08	6.22	6.35	6.46	6.56	6.66	6.74	6.82	6.90	6.97	7.03	7.09	7.15
17	4.10	4.74	5.14	5.43	5.66	5.85	6.01	6.15	6.27	6.38	6.48	6.57	6.66	6.73	6.80	6.87	6.94	7.00	7.05
18	4.07	4.70	5.09	5.38	5.60	5.79	5.94	6.08	6.20	6.31	6.41	6.50	6.58	6.65	6.72	6.79	6.85	6.91	6.96
19	4.05	4.67	5.05	5.33	5.55	5.73	5.89	6.02	6.14	6.25	6.34	6.43	6.51	6.58	6.65	6.72	6.78	6.84	6.89
20	4.02	4.64	5.02	5.29	5.51	5.69	5.84	5.97	6.09	6.19	6.29	6.37	6.45	6.52	6.59	6.65	6.71	6.76	6.82
24	3.96	4.54	4.91	5.17	5.37	5.54	5.69	5.81	5.92	6.02	6.11	6.19	6.26	6.33	6.39	6.45	6.51	6.56	6.61
30	3.89	4.45	4.80	5.05	5.24	5.40	5.54	5.65	5.76	5.85	5.93	6.01	6.08	6.14	6.20	6.26	6.31	6.36	6.41
40	3.82	4.37	4.70	4.93	5.11	5.27	5.39	5.50	5.60	5.69	5.77	5.84	5.90	5.96	6.02	6.07	6.12	6.17	6.21
60	3.76	4.28	4.60	4.82	4.99	5.13	5.25	5.36	5.45	5.53	5.60	5.67	5.73	5.79	5.84	5.89	5.93	5.98	6.02
120	3.70	4.20	4.50	4.71	4.87	5.01	5.12	5.21	5.30	5.38	5.44	5.51	5.56	5.61	5.66	5.71	5.75	5.79	5.83
∞	3.64	4.12	4.40	4.60	4.76	4.88	4.99	5.08	5.16	5.23	5.29	5.35	5.40	5.45	5.49	5.54	5.57	5.61	5.65

Source: Reprinted, with permission, from Henry Scheffé, *The Analysis of Variance* (New York: John Wiley & Sons, 1959), pp. 434–36.

TABLE B.10   Percentiles of H Statistic Distribution.

Entry is $H(1 - \alpha; r, df)$ where $P\{H \leq H(1 - \alpha; r, df)\} = 1 - \alpha$

$$1 - \alpha = .95$$

df	2	3	4	5	6	7	8	9	10	11	12
2	39.0	87.5	142	202	266	333	403	475	550	626	704
3	15.4	27.8	39.2	50.7	62.0	72.9	83.5	93.9	104	114	124
4	9.60	15.5	20.6	25.2	29.5	33.6	37.5	41.1	44.6	48.0	51.4
5	7.15	10.8	13.7	16.3	18.7	20.8	22.9	24.7	26.5	28.2	29.9
6	5.82	8.38	10.4	12.1	13.7	15.0	16.3	17.5	18.6	19.7	20.7
7	4.99	6.94	8.44	9.70	10.8	11.8	12.7	13.5	14.3	15.1	15.8
8	4.43	6.00	7.18	8.12	9.03	9.78	10.5	11.1	11.7	12.2	12.7
9	4.03	5.34	6.31	7.11	7.80	8.41	8.95	9.45	9.91	10.3	10.7
10	3.72	4.85	5.67	6.34	6.92	7.42	7.87	8.28	8.66	9.01	9.34
12	3.28	4.16	4.79	5.30	5.72	6.09	6.42	6.72	7.00	7.25	7.48
15	2.86	3.54	4.01	4.37	4.68	4.95	5.19	5.40	5.59	5.77	5.93
20	2.46	2.95	3.29	3.54	3.76	3.94	4.10	4.24	4.37	4.49	4.59
30	2.07	2.40	2.61	2.78	2.91	3.02	3.12	3.21	3.29	3.36	3.39
60	1.67	1.85	1.96	2.04	2.11	2.17	2.22	2.26	2.30	2.33	2.36
∞	1.00	1.00	1.00	1.00	1.00	1.00	1.00	1.00	1.00	1.00	1.00

$$1 - \alpha = .99$$

df	2	3	4	5	6	7	8	9	10	11	12
2	199	448	729	1,036	1,362	1,705	2,063	2,432	2,813	3,204	3,605
3	47.5	85	120	151	184	216	249	281	310	337	361
4	23.2	37	49	59	69	79	89	97	106	113	120
5	14.9	22	28	33	38	42	46	50	54	57	60
6	11.1	15.5	19.1	22	25	27	30	32	34	36	37
7	8.89	12.1	14.5	16.5	18.4	20	22	23	24	26	27
8	7.50	9.9	11.7	13.2	14.5	15.8	16.9	17.9	18.9	19.8	21
9	6.54	8.5	9.9	11.1	12.1	13.1	13.9	14.7	15.3	16.0	16.6
10	5.85	7.4	8.6	9.6	10.4	11.1	11.8	12.4	12.9	13.4	13.9
12	4.91	6.1	6.9	7.6	8.2	8.7	9.1	9.5	9.9	10.2	10.6
15	4.07	4.9	5.5	6.0	6.4	6.7	7.1	7.3	7.5	7.8	8.0
20	3.32	3.8	4.3	4.6	4.9	5.1	5.3	5.5	5.6	5.8	5.9
30	2.63	3.0	3.3	3.4	3.6	3.7	3.8	3.9	4.0	4.1	4.2
60	1.96	2.2	2.3	2.4	2.4	2.5	2.5	2.6	2.6	2.7	2.7
∞	1.00	1.0	1.0	1.0	1.0	1.0	1.0	1.0	1.0	1.0	1.0

Source: Reprinted, with permission, from H. A. David, "Upper 5 and 1% Points of the Maximum *F*-Ratio," *Biometrika* 39 (1952), pp. 422–24.

TABLE **B.11**   **Power Values for Analysis of Variance (fixed effects).**

$v_1 = 2$ and $\alpha = .05$

					ϕ				
v_2	1.0	1.5	2.0	2.5	3.0	3.5	4.0	4.5	5.0
1	.08	.11	.14	.18	.21	.24	.27	.31	.34
2	.12	.20	.30	.41	.52	.62	.71	.79	.85
3	.15	.28	.44	.60	.75	.86	.93	.97	.99
4	.18	.34	.54	.73	.86	.94	.98	.99	1.00
5	.20	.39	.61	.80	.92	.97	.99	1.00	1.00
6	.21	.42	.66	.85	.95	.99	1.00	1.00	1.00
7	.22	.45	.70	.88	.96	.99	1.00	1.00	1.00
8	.23	.47	.72	.90	.97	1.00	1.00	1.00	1.00
9	.24	.49	.74	.91	.98	1.00	1.00	1.00	1.00
10	.25	.50	.76	.92	.98	1.00	1.00	1.00	1.00
12	.26	.53	.78	.93	.99	1.00	1.00	1.00	1.00
14	.27	.54	.80	.94	.99	1.00	1.00	1.00	1.00
16	.27	.55	.81	.95	.99	1.00	1.00	1.00	1.00
18	.28	.56	.82	.95	.99	1.00	1.00	1.00	1.00
20	.28	.57	.83	.96	.99	1.00	1.00	1.00	1.00
22	.29	.58	.83	.96	.99	1.00	1.00	1.00	1.00
24	.29	.58	.84	.96	.99	1.00	1.00	1.00	1.00
26	.29	.59	.84	.96	.99	1.00	1.00	1.00	1.00
28	.29	.59	.85	.96	1.00	1.00	1.00	1.00	1.00
30	.29	.60	.85	.97	1.00	1.00	1.00	1.00	1.00
60	.31	.62	.87	.97	1.00	1.00	1.00	1.00	1.00
120	.31	.63	.88	.98	1.00	1.00	1.00	1.00	1.00
∞	.32	.64	.88	.98	1.00	1.00	1.00	1.00	1.00

$v_1 = 2$ and $\alpha = .01$

					ϕ				
v_2	1.0	1.5	2.0	2.5	3.0	3.5	4.0	4.5	5.0
1	.02	.02	.03	.04	.04	.05	.06	.06	.07
2	.02	.04	.07	.10	.14	.18	.22	.27	.32
3	.03	.07	.13	.20	.29	.40	.50	.60	.69
4	.04	.10	.19	.31	.46	.61	.73	.83	.91
5	.05	.13	.25	.42	.60	.75	.87	.94	.97
6	.06	.15	.30	.50	.69	.84	.93	.98	.99
7	.07	.17	.35	.57	.76	.90	.96	.99	1.00
8	.07	.19	.39	.62	.81	.93	.98	1.00	1.00
9	.08	.21	.42	.66	.85	.95	.99	1.00	1.00
10	.08	.22	.45	.69	.87	.96	.99	1.00	1.00
12	.09	.24	.49	.74	.91	.98	1.00	1.00	1.00
14	.09	.26	.52	.78	.93	.98	1.00	1.00	1.00
16	.10	.28	.55	.80	.94	.99	1.00	1.00	1.00
18	.10	.29	.57	.82	.95	.99	1.00	1.00	1.00
20	.10	.30	.58	.83	.95	.99	1.00	1.00	1.00
22	.11	.31	.60	.84	.96	.99	1.00	1.00	1.00
24	.11	.31	.61	.85	.96	.99	1.00	1.00	1.00
26	.11	.32	.62	.86	.97	1.00	1.00	1.00	1.00
28	.11	.32	.63	.86	.97	1.00	1.00	1.00	1.00
30	.11	.33	.63	.87	.97	1.00	1.00	1.00	1.00
60	.13	.36	.68	.90	.98	1.00	1.00	1.00	1.00
120	.13	.38	.70	.91	.98	1.00	1.00	1.00	1.00
∞	.14	.40	.72	.92	.99	1.00	1.00	1.00	1.00

TABLE B.11 *(continued)*   Power Values for Analysis of Variance (fixed effects).

$v_1 = 3$ and $\alpha = .05$

					ϕ				
v_2	1.0	1.5	2.0	2.5	3.0	3.5	4.0	4.5	5.0
1	.08	.10	.13	.16	.19	.22	.25	.28	.31
2	.11	.18	.27	.38	.48	.58	.68	.76	.82
3	.14	.26	.42	.58	.73	.84	.92	.96	.98
4	.17	.33	.53	.72	.86	.94	.98	.99	1.00
5	.19	.38	.61	.81	.93	.98	.99	1.00	1.00
6	.21	.43	.67	.86	.96	.99	1.00	1.00	1.00
7	.22	.46	.72	.89	.97	1.00	1.00	1.00	1.00
8	.24	.49	.75	.92	.98	1.00	1.00	1.00	1.00
9	.25	.51	.77	.93	.99	1.00	1.00	1.00	1.00
10	.25	.53	.79	.94	.99	1.00	1.00	1.00	1.00
12	.27	.56	.82	.96	.99	1.00	1.00	1.00	1.00
14	.28	.58	.84	.97	1.00	1.00	1.00	1.00	1.00
16	.29	.60	.86	.97	1.00	1.00	1.00	1.00	1.00
18	.29	.61	.87	.97	1.00	1.00	1.00	1.00	1.00
20	.30	.62	.87	.98	1.00	1.00	1.00	1.00	1.00
22	.31	.63	.88	.98	1.00	1.00	1.00	1.00	1.00
24	.31	.63	.89	.98	1.00	1.00	1.00	1.00	1.00
26	.31	.64	.89	.98	1.00	1.00	1.00	1.00	1.00
28	.32	.65	.89	.98	1.00	1.00	1.00	1.00	1.00
30	.32	.65	.90	.98	1.00	1.00	1.00	1.00	1.00
60	.34	.68	.92	.99	1.00	1.00	1.00	1.00	1.00
120	.35	.70	.93	.99	1.00	1.00	1.00	1.00	1.00
∞	.36	.71	.93	.99	1.00	1.00	1.00	1.00	1.00

$v_1 = 3$ and $\alpha = .01$

					ϕ				
v_2	1.0	1.5	2.0	2.5	3.0	3.5	4.0	4.5	5.0
1	.02	.02	.03	.03	.04	.04	.05	.06	.06
2	.02	.04	.06	.09	.12	.16	.20	.24	.29
3	.03	.06	.12	.19	.27	.37	.47	.58	.67
4	.04	.09	.18	.30	.45	.59	.72	.83	.90
5	.05	.12	.25	.42	.60	.76	.87	.94	.98
6	.06	.15	.31	.51	.71	.86	.94	.98	.99
7	.06	.17	.36	.59	.79	.91	.97	.99	1.00
8	.07	.20	.41	.65	.84	.95	.99	1.00	1.00
9	.08	.22	.45	.70	.88	.97	.99	1.00	1.00
10	.08	.23	.48	.74	.91	.98	1.00	1.00	1.00
12	.09	.26	.54	.79	.94	.99	1.00	1.00	1.00
14	.10	.29	.58	.83	.96	.99	1.00	1.00	1.00
16	.10	.31	.61	.86	.97	1.00	1.00	1.00	1.00
18	.11	.32	.63	.87	.97	1.00	1.00	1.00	1.00
20	.11	.34	.65	.89	.98	1.00	1.00	1.00	1.00
22	.12	.35	.67	.90	.98	1.00	1.00	1.00	1.00
24	.12	.36	.68	.91	.98	1.00	1.00	1.00	1.00
26	.12	.37	.69	.91	.99	1.00	1.00	1.00	1.00
28	.12	.37	.70	.92	.99	1.00	1.00	1.00	1.00
30	.13	.38	.71	.92	.99	1.00	1.00	1.00	1.00
60	.14	.43	.77	.95	.99	1.00	1.00	1.00	1.00
120	.15	.46	.80	.96	1.00	1.00	1.00	1.00	1.00
∞	.16	.48	.82	.97	1.00	1.00	1.00	1.00	1.00

TABLE B.11 *(continued)*   **Power Values for Analysis of Variance (fixed effects).**

$v_1 = 4$ and $\alpha = .05$

					ϕ				
v_2	1.0	1.5	2.0	2.5	3.0	3.5	4.0	4.5	5.0
1	.08	.10	.13	.15	.18	.21	.24	.27	.29
2	.11	.18	.26	.36	.46	.56	.66	.74	.80
3	.14	.26	.41	.57	.72	.83	.91	.96	.98
4	.17	.33	.53	.72	.86	.94	.98	.99	1.00
5	.19	.39	.62	.81	.93	.98	1.00	1.00	1.00
6	.21	.43	.69	.87	.96	.99	1.00	1.00	1.00
7	.23	.47	.73	.91	.98	1.00	1.00	1.00	1.00
8	.24	.50	.77	.93	.99	1.00	1.00	1.00	1.00
9	.25	.53	.80	.95	.99	1.00	1.00	1.00	1.00
10	.26	.55	.82	.96	.99	1.00	1.00	1.00	1.00
12	.28	.59	.85	.97	1.00	1.00	1.00	1.00	1.00
14	.29	.61	.87	.98	1.00	1.00	1.00	1.00	1.00
16	.30	.63	.89	.98	1.00	1.00	1.00	1.00	1.00
18	.31	.65	.90	.99	1.00	1.00	1.00	1.00	1.00
20	.32	.66	.91	.99	1.00	1.00	1.00	1.00	1.00
22	.33	.67	.91	.99	1.00	1.00	1.00	1.00	1.00
24	.33	.68	.92	.99	1.00	1.00	1.00	1.00	1.00
26	.33	.69	.92	.99	1.00	1.00	1.00	1.00	1.00
28	.34	.69	.93	.99	1.00	1.00	1.00	1.00	1.00
30	.34	.70	.93	.99	1.00	1.00	1.00	1.00	1.00
60	.37	.74	.95	1.00	1.00	1.00	1.00	1.00	1.00
120	.38	.76	.96	1.00	1.00	1.00	1.00	1.00	1.00
∞	.39	.77	.96	1.00	1.00	1.00	1.00	1.00	1.00

$v_1 = 4$ and $\alpha = .01$

					ϕ				
v_2	1.0	1.5	2.0	2.5	3.0	3.5	4.0	4.5	5.0
1	.02	.02	.03	.03	.04	.04	.05	.05	.06
2	.02	.04	.06	.08	.12	.15	.19	.23	.28
3	.03	.06	.11	.18	.26	.36	.46	.56	.65
4	.04	.09	.18	.30	.44	.59	.72	.82	.90
5	.05	.12	.25	.42	.60	.76	.88	.94	.98
6	.06	.15	.32	.52	.72	.87	.95	.98	1.00
7	.06	.18	.38	.61	.81	.93	.98	.99	1.00
8	.07	.20	.43	.68	.86	.96	.99	1.00	1.00
9	.08	.23	.47	.73	.90	.97	1.00	1.00	1.00
10	.08	.25	.51	.77	.93	.98	1.00	1.00	1.00
12	.09	.28	.58	.83	.96	.99	1.00	1.00	1.00
14	.10	.31	.62	.87	.97	1.00	1.00	1.00	1.00
16	.11	.34	.66	.89	.98	1.00	1.00	1.00	1.00
18	.12	.36	.69	.91	.99	1.00	1.00	1.00	1.00
20	.12	.37	.71	.92	.99	1.00	1.00	1.00	1.00
22	.13	.39	.73	.93	.99	1.00	1.00	1.00	1.00
24	.13	.40	.74	.94	.99	1.00	1.00	1.00	1.00
26	.13	.41	.76	.95	.99	1.00	1.00	1.00	1.00
28	.14	.42	.77	.95	1.00	1.00	1.00	1.00	1.00
30	.14	.43	.78	.96	1.00	1.00	1.00	1.00	1.00
60	.16	.49	.84	.98	1.00	1.00	1.00	1.00	1.00
120	.17	.53	.86	.98	1.00	1.00	1.00	1.00	1.00
∞	.19	.56	.88	.99	1.00	1.00	1.00	1.00	1.00

TABLE B.11 *(continued)* **Power Values for Analysis of Variance (fixed effects).**

$v_1 = 5$ and $\alpha = .05$

					ϕ				
v_2	1.0	1.5	2.0	2.5	3.0	3.5	4.0	4.5	5.0
1	.08	.10	.12	.15	.18	.20	.23	.26	.29
2	.11	.17	.26	.35	.45	.55	.64	.72	.79
3	.14	.25	.40	.56	.71	.83	.91	.95	.98
4	.17	.32	.53	.72	.86	.94	.98	.99	1.00
5	.19	.39	.62	.82	.93	.98	1.00	1.00	1.00
6	.21	.44	.70	.88	.97	.99	1.00	1.00	1.00
7	.23	.48	.75	.92	.98	1.00	1.00	1.00	1.00
8	.24	.52	.79	.94	.99	1.00	1.00	1.00	1.00
9	.26	.55	.82	.96	.99	1.00	1.00	1.00	1.00
10	.27	.57	.84	.97	1.00	1.00	1.00	1.00	1.00
12	.29	.61	.88	.98	1.00	1.00	1.00	1.00	1.00
14	.30	.64	.90	.99	1.00	1.00	1.00	1.00	1.00
16	.32	.66	.91	.99	1.00	1.00	1.00	1.00	1.00
18	.33	.68	.92	.99	1.00	1.00	1.00	1.00	1.00
20	.34	.70	.93	.99	1.00	1.00	1.00	1.00	1.00
22	.34	.71	.94	.99	1.00	1.00	1.00	1.00	1.00
24	.35	.72	.94	1.00	1.00	1.00	1.00	1.00	1.00
26	.36	.73	.95	1.00	1.00	1.00	1.00	1.00	1.00
28	.36	.73	.95	1.00	1.00	1.00	1.00	1.00	1.00
30	.36	.74	.95	1.00	1.00	1.00	1.00	1.00	1.00
60	.40	.78	.97	1.00	1.00	1.00	1.00	1.00	1.00
120	.41	.80	.97	1.00	1.00	1.00	1.00	1.00	1.00
∞	.43	.82	.98	1.00	1.00	1.00	1.00	1.00	1.00

$v_1 = 5$ and $\alpha = .01$

					ϕ				
v_2	1.0	1.5	2.0	2.5	3.0	3.5	4.0	4.5	5.0
1	.02	.02	.02	.03	.04	.04	.05	.05	.06
2	.02	.04	.06	.08	.11	.15	.18	.22	.27
3	.03	.06	.11	.18	.26	.35	.45	.55	.64
4	.04	.09	.18	.30	.44	.59	.72	.82	.90
5	.05	.12	.25	.42	.61	.77	.88	.95	.98
6	.06	.15	.32	.53	.73	.88	.95	.99	1.00
7	.06	.18	.39	.63	.82	.93	.98	1.00	1.00
8	.07	.21	.44	.70	.88	.97	.99	1.00	1.00
9	.08	.24	.49	.75	.92	.98	1.00	1.00	1.00
10	.09	.26	.54	.80	.94	.99	1.00	1.00	1.00
12	.10	.30	.61	.86	.97	1.00	1.00	1.00	1.00
14	.11	.34	.66	.90	.98	1.00	1.00	1.00	1.00
16	.12	.36	.70	.92	.99	1.00	1.00	1.00	1.00
18	.12	.39	.73	.94	.99	1.00	1.00	1.00	1.00
20	.13	.41	.76	.95	.99	1.00	1.00	1.00	1.00
22	.14	.43	.78	.96	1.00	1.00	1.00	1.00	1.00
24	.14	.44	.79	.96	1.00	1.00	1.00	1.00	1.00
26	.14	.45	.80	.97	1.00	1.00	1.00	1.00	1.00
28	.15	.46	.82	.97	1.00	1.00	1.00	1.00	1.00
30	.15	.47	.82	.97	1.00	1.00	1.00	1.00	1.00
60	.18	.55	.88	.99	1.00	1.00	1.00	1.00	1.00
120	.20	.59	.91	.99	1.00	1.00	1.00	1.00	1.00
∞	.21	.62	.93	1.00	1.00	1.00	1.00	1.00	1.00

TABLE **B.11** *(concluded)*   **Power Values for Analysis of Variance (fixed effects).**

$v_1 = 6$ and $\alpha = .05$

	ϕ								
v_2	1.0	1.5	2.0	2.5	3.0	3.5	4.0	4.5	5.0
1	.07	.10	.12	.15	.17	.20	.23	.25	.28
2	.10	.17	.25	.34	.44	.54	.63	.71	.78
3	.14	.25	.40	.56	.71	.82	.90	.95	.98
4	.16	.32	.53	.72	.86	.94	.98	.99	1.00
5	.19	.39	.63	.82	.94	.98	1.00	1.00	1.00
6	.21	.44	.70	.89	.97	.99	1.00	1.00	1.00
7	.23	.49	.76	.93	.98	1.00	1.00	1.00	1.00
8	.25	.53	.80	.95	.99	1.00	1.00	1.00	1.00
9	.26	.56	.83	.96	1.00	1.00	1.00	1.00	1.00
10	.28	.59	.86	.97	1.00	1.00	1.00	1.00	1.00
12	.30	.63	.89	.98	1.00	1.00	1.00	1.00	1.00
14	.32	.66	.91	.99	1.00	1.00	1.00	1.00	1.00
16	.33	.69	.93	.99	1.00	1.00	1.00	1.00	1.00
18	.34	.71	.94	.99	1.00	1.00	1.00	1.00	1.00
20	.35	.73	.95	1.00	1.00	1.00	1.00	1.00	1.00
22	.36	.74	.95	1.00	1.00	1.00	1.00	1.00	1.00
24	.37	.75	.96	1.00	1.00	1.00	1.00	1.00	1.00
26	.37	.76	.96	1.00	1.00	1.00	1.00	1.00	1.00
28	.38	.77	.96	1.00	1.00	1.00	1.00	1.00	1.00
30	.39	.77	.97	1.00	1.00	1.00	1.00	1.00	1.00
60	.42	.82	.98	1.00	1.00	1.00	1.00	1.00	1.00
120	.45	.84	.99	1.00	1.00	1.00	1.00	1.00	1.00
∞	.47	.86	.99	1.00	1.00	1.00	1.00	1.00	1.00

$v_1 = 6$ and $\alpha = .01$

	ϕ								
v_2	1.0	1.5	2.0	2.5	3.0	3.5	4.0	4.5	5.0
1	.01	.02	.02	.03	.04	.04	.05	.05	.06
2	.02	.04	.06	.08	.11	.14	.18	.22	.26
3	.03	.06	.11	.17	.25	.35	.45	.55	.64
4	.04	.09	.18	.30	.44	.59	.72	.82	.90
5	.05	.12	.25	.43	.61	.77	.88	.95	.98
6	.06	.15	.33	.54	.74	.88	.96	.99	1.00
7	.07	.19	.39	.64	.83	.94	.98	1.00	1.00
8	.07	.22	.46	.71	.89	.97	.99	1.00	1.00
9	.08	.24	.51	.77	.93	.98	1.00	1.00	1.00
10	.09	.27	.56	.82	.95	.99	1.00	1.00	1.00
12	.10	.32	.64	.88	.98	1.00	1.00	1.00	1.00
14	.11	.36	.69	.92	.99	1.00	1.00	1.00	1.00
16	.12	.39	.73	.94	.99	1.00	1.00	1.00	1.00
18	.13	.42	.77	.95	1.00	1.00	1.00	1.00	1.00
20	.14	.44	.79	.96	1.00	1.00	1.00	1.00	1.00
22	.14	.46	.81	.97	1.00	1.00	1.00	1.00	1.00
24	.15	.48	.83	.98	1.00	1.00	1.00	1.00	1.00
26	.16	.49	.84	.98	1.00	1.00	1.00	1.00	1.00
28	.16	.50	.85	.98	1.00	1.00	1.00	1.00	1.00
30	.16	.51	.86	.98	1.00	1.00	1.00	1.00	1.00
60	.20	.60	.92	.99	1.00	1.00	1.00	1.00	1.00
120	.22	.65	.94	1.00	1.00	1.00	1.00	1.00	1.00
∞	.24	.69	.96	1.00	1.00	1.00	1.00	1.00	1.00

TABLE B.12   Table for Determining Sample Size for Analysis of Variance (fixed factor levels model).

Power $1 - \beta = .70$

| | $\Delta/\sigma = 1.0$ | | | | $\Delta/\sigma = 1.25$ | | | | $\Delta/\sigma = 1.50$ | | | | $\Delta/\sigma = 1.75$ | | | | $\Delta/\sigma = 2.0$ | | | | $\Delta/\sigma = 2.5$ | | | | $\Delta/\sigma = 3.0$ | | | |
| | α | | | | α | | | | α | | | | α | | | | α | | | | α | | | | α | | | |
r	.2	.1	.05	.01	.2	.1	.05	.01	.2	.1	.05	.01	.2	.1	.05	.01	.2	.1	.05	.01	.2	.1	.05	.01	.2	.1	.05	.01
2	7	11	14	21	5	7	9	15	4	6	7	11	3	4	6	9	3	4	5	7	2	3	4	5	2	3	3	5
3	9	13	17	25	6	9	11	17	5	7	8	12	4	5	7	10	3	4	5	8	2	3	4	5	2	3	3	5
4	11	15	19	28	7	10	13	19	5	7	9	13	4	6	7	10	4	5	6	8	3	4	4	6	3	3	4	5
5	12	17	21	30	8	11	14	20	6	8	10	14	5	6	8	11	4	5	6	9	3	4	5	6	3	3	4	6
6	13	18	22	32	9	12	15	21	6	9	11	15	5	7	8	12	4	5	7	9	3	4	5	7	3	3	4	6
7	14	19	24	34	9	13	16	22	7	9	11	16	5	7	9	12	4	6	7	10	3	4	5	7	3	3	4	6
8	15	20	25	35	10	13	16	23	7	10	12	17	6	7	9	13	5	6	7	10	3	4	5	7	3	3	4	6
9	15	21	26	37	10	14	17	24	7	10	12	17	6	8	9	13	5	6	8	10	3	4	5	7	3	4	4	6
10	16	22	27	38	11	14	18	25	8	10	13	18	6	8	10	14	5	6	8	11	4	5	6	7	3	4	4	6

Power $1 - \beta = .80$

| | $\Delta/\sigma = 1.0$ | | | | $\Delta/\sigma = 1.25$ | | | | $\Delta/\sigma = 1.50$ | | | | $\Delta/\sigma = 1.75$ | | | | $\Delta/\sigma = 2.0$ | | | | $\Delta/\sigma = 2.5$ | | | | $\Delta/\sigma = 3.0$ | | | |
| | α | | | | α | | | | α | | | | α | | | | α | | | | α | | | | α | | | |
r	.2	.1	.05	.01	.2	.1	.05	.01	.2	.1	.05	.01	.2	.1	.05	.01	.2	.1	.05	.01	.2	.1	.05	.01	.2	.1	.05	.01
2	10	14	17	26	7	9	12	17	5	7	9	13	4	5	7	10	3	4	6	8	3	3	4	6	2	3	4	5
3	12	17	21	30	8	11	14	20	6	8	10	14	5	6	8	11	4	5	6	9	3	3	4	7	3	3	4	5
4	14	19	23	33	9	13	15	22	7	9	11	16	5	7	8	12	4	6	7	10	3	4	5	7	3	3	4	5
5	16	21	25	35	10	14	17	23	8	10	12	17	6	8	9	13	5	6	7	10	4	4	5	7	3	4	4	6
6	17	22	27	38	11	15	18	25	8	11	13	18	6	8	10	13	5	7	8	11	4	5	6	8	3	4	4	6
7	18	24	29	39	12	16	19	26	9	11	14	18	7	9	10	14	5	7	8	11	4	5	6	8	3	4	5	6
8	19	25	30	41	12	16	20	27	9	12	14	19	7	9	11	15	6	7	9	12	4	5	6	8	3	4	5	6
9	20	26	31	43	13	17	21	28	9	12	15	20	7	9	11	15	6	7	9	12	4	5	6	8	3	4	5	6
10	21	27	33	44	14	18	21	29	10	13	15	21	8	10	12	16	6	8	9	12	4	5	6	8	3	4	5	6

TABLE B.12 *(concluded)* **Table for Determining Sample Size for Analysis of Variance (fixed factor levels model).**

Power $1 - \beta = .90$

r	Δ/σ = 1.0 .2	.1	.05	.01	Δ/σ = 1.25 .2	.1	.05	.01	Δ/σ = 1.50 .2	.1	.05	.01	Δ/σ = 1.75 .2	.1	.05	.01	Δ/σ = 2.0 .2	.1	.05	.01	Δ/σ = 2.5 .2	.1	.05	.01	Δ/σ = 3.0 .2	.1	.05	.01
2	14	18	23	32	9	12	15	21	7	9	11	15	5	7	8	12	4	6	7	10	3	4	5	7	3	3	4	6
3	17	22	27	37	11	15	18	24	8	11	13	18	6	8	10	13	5	7	8	11	4	5	6	8	3	4	5	6
4	20	25	30	40	13	16	20	27	9	12	14	19	7	9	11	15	6	7	9	12	4	5	6	8	3	4	5	6
5	21	27	32	43	14	18	21	28	10	13	15	20	8	10	12	15	6	8	9	12	4	5	6	9	4	4	5	7
6	22	29	34	46	15	19	23	30	11	14	16	21	8	10	12	16	7	8	10	13	5	6	7	9	4	4	5	7
7	24	31	36	48	16	20	24	31	11	14	17	22	9	11	13	17	7	9	10	13	5	6	7	9	4	5	5	7
8	26	32	38	50	17	21	25	33	12	15	18	23	9	11	13	17	7	9	11	14	5	6	7	9	4	5	5	7
9	27	33	40	52	17	22	26	34	13	16	18	24	9	12	14	18	8	9	11	14	5	6	8	10	4	5	6	7
10	28	35	41	54	18	23	27	35	13	16	19	25	10	12	14	19	8	10	11	15	5	7	8	10	4	5	6	7

Power $1 - \beta = .95$

r	Δ/σ = 1.0 .2	.1	.05	.01	Δ/σ = 1.25 .2	.1	.05	.01	Δ/σ = 1.50 .2	.1	.05	.01	Δ/σ = 1.75 .2	.1	.05	.01	Δ/σ = 2.0 .2	.1	.05	.01	Δ/σ = 2.5 .2	.1	.05	.01	Δ/σ = 3.0 .2	.1	.05	.01
2	18	23	27	38	12	15	18	25	9	11	13	18	7	8	10	14	5	7	8	11	4	5	6	8	3	4	5	6
3	22	27	32	43	14	18	21	29	10	13	15	20	8	10	12	16	6	8	9	12	5	6	7	9	4	4	5	7
4	25	30	36	47	16	20	23	31	12	14	17	22	9	11	13	17	7	9	10	13	5	6	7	9	4	5	5	7
5	27	33	39	51	18	23	25	33	13	15	18	24	10	12	14	18	8	9	11	14	5	6	7	10	4	5	6	7
6	29	35	41	53	19	23	27	35	13	16	19	25	10	12	14	19	8	10	11	15	6	7	8	10	4	5	6	8
7	30	37	43	56	20	24	28	36	14	17	20	26	11	13	15	19	8	11	12	15	6	7	8	10	4	5	6	8
8	32	39	45	58	21	25	29	38	15	18	21	27	11	14	16	20	9	11	12	16	6	7	9	11	5	5	6	8
9	33	40	47	60	22	26	30	39	15	19	22	28	12	14	16	21	9	11	13	16	6	8	9	11	5	6	6	8
10	34	42	48	62	22	27	31	40	16	19	22	29	12	15	17	21	9	11	13	17	6	8	9	11	5	6	7	8

Source: Reprinted, with permission, from T. L. Bratcher, M. A. Moran, and W. J. Zimmer, "Tables of Sample Sizes in the Analysis of Variance," *Journal of Quality Technology* 2 (1970), pp. 156–64. Copyright American Society for Quality Control, Inc.

TABLE B.13   Table of $\lambda\sqrt{n}/\sigma$ for Determining Sample Size to Find "Best" of r Population Means.

Number of Populations (r)	Probability of Correct Identification $(1 - \alpha)$		
	.90	.95	.99
2	1.8124	2.3262	3.2900
3	2.2302	2.7101	3.6173
4	2.4516	2.9162	3.7970
5	2.5997	3.0552	3.9196
6	2.7100	3.1591	4.0121
7	2.7972	3.2417	4.0861
8	2.8691	3.3099	4.1475
9	2.9301	3.3679	4.1999
10	2.9829	3.4182	4.2456

Source: Reprinted, with permission, from R. E. Bechhofer, "A Single-Sample Multiple Decision Procedure for Ranking Means of Normal Populations with Known Variances," *The Annals of Mathematical Statistics* 25 (1954), pp. 16–39.

TABLE B.14   Selected Standard Latin Squares.

3 × 3

```
A  B  C
B  C  A
C  A  B
```

4 × 4

1	2	3	4

```
    1              2              3              4
A  B  C  D    A  B  C  D    A  B  C  D    A  B  C  D
B  A  D  C    B  C  D  A    B  D  A  C    B  A  D  C
C  D  B  A    C  D  A  B    C  A  D  B    C  D  A  B
D  C  A  B    D  A  B  C    D  C  B  A    D  C  B  A
```

5 × 5

```
A  B  C  D  E
B  A  E  C  D
C  D  A  E  B
D  E  B  A  C
E  C  D  B  A
```

6 × 6

```
A  B  C  D  E  F
B  F  D  C  A  E
C  D  E  F  B  A
D  A  F  E  C  B
E  C  A  B  F  D
F  E  B  A  D  C
```

7 × 7

```
A  B  C  D  E  F  G
B  C  D  E  F  G  A
C  D  E  F  G  A  B
D  E  F  G  A  B  C
E  F  G  A  B  C  D
F  G  A  B  C  D  E
G  A  B  C  D  E  F
```

8 × 8

```
A  B  C  D  E  F  G  H
B  C  D  E  F  G  H  A
C  D  E  F  G  H  A  B
D  E  F  G  H  A  B  C
E  F  G  H  A  B  C  D
F  G  H  A  B  C  D  E
G  H  A  B  C  D  E  F
H  A  B  C  D  E  F  G
```

9 × 9

```
A  B  C  D  E  F  G  H  I
B  C  D  E  F  G  H  I  A
C  D  E  F  G  H  I  A  B
D  E  F  G  H  I  A  B  C
E  F  G  H  I  A  B  C  D
F  G  H  I  A  B  C  D  E
G  H  I  A  B  C  D  E  F
H  I  A  B  C  D  E  F  G
I  A  B  C  D  E  F  G  H
```

Data Sets

Data Set C.1   SENIC

The primary objective of the Study on the Efficacy of Nosocomial Infection Control (**SENIC** Project) was to determine whether infection surveillance and control programs have reduced the rates of nosocomial (hospital-acquired) infection in United States hospitals. This data set consists of a random sample of 113 hospitals selected from the original 338 hospitals surveyed.

Each line of the data set has an identification number and provides information on 11 other variables for a single hospital. The data presented here are for the 1975-76 study period. The 12 variables are:

Variable Number	Variable Name	Description
1	Identification number	1-113
2	Length of stay	Average length of stay of all patients in hospital (in days)
3	Age	Average age of patients (in years)
4	Infection risk	Average estimated probability of acquiring infection in hospital (in percent)
5	Routine culturing ratio	Ratio of number of cultures performed to number of patients without signs or symptoms of hospital-acquired infection, times 100

Variable Number	Variable Name	Description
6	Routine chest X-ray ratio	Ratio of number of X-rays performed to number of patients without signs or symptoms of pneumonia, times 100
7	Number of beds	Average number of beds in hospital during study period
8	Medical school affiliation	1 = Yes, 2 = No
9	Region	Geographic region, where: 1 = NE, 2 = NC, 3 = S, 4 = W
10	Average daily census	Average number of patients in hospital per day during study period
11	Number of nurses	Average number of full-time equivalent registered and licensed practical nurses during study period (number full time plus one half the number part time)
12	Available facilities and services	Percent of 35 potential facilities and services that are provided by the hospital

Reference: Special Issue, "The SENIC Project," *American Journal of Epidemiology* 111 (1980), pp. 465-653.
Data obtained from Robert W. Haley, M.D., Hospital Infections Program, Center for Infectious Diseases, Centers for Disease Control, Atlanta, Georgia 30333.

1	2	3	4	5	6	7	8	9	10	11	12
1	7.13	55.7	4.1	9.0	39.6	279	2	4	207	241	60.0
2	8.82	58.2	1.6	3.8	51.7	80	2	2	51	52	40.0
3	8.34	56.9	2.7	8.1	74.0	107	2	3	82	54	20.0
...	...	...	...	...	...	...	...	...	...	...	...
111	7.70	56.9	4.4	12.2	67.9	129	2	4	85	136	62.9
112	17.94	56.2	5.9	26.4	91.8	835	1	1	791	407	62.9
113	9.41	59.5	3.1	20.6	91.7	29	2	3	20	22	22.9

Data Set C.2   SMSA

This data set provides information for 141 large Standard Metropolitan Statistical Areas (**SMSA**s) in the United States. A standard metropolitan statistical area includes a city (or cities) of specified population size which constitutes the central city and the county (or counties) in which it is located, as well as contiguous counties when the economic and social relationships between the central and contiguous counties meet specified criteria of metropolitan character and integration. An SMSA may have up to three central cities and may cross state lines.

Each line of the data set has an identification number and provides information on 11 other variables for a single SMSA. The information generally pertains to the years 1976 and 1977. The 12 variables are:

Variable Number	Variable Name	Description
1	Identification number	1-141
2	Land area	In square miles
3	Total population	Estimated 1977 population (in thousands)
4	Percent of population in central cities	Percent of 1976 SMSA population in central city or cities
5	Percent of population 65 or older	Percent of 1976 SMSA population 65 years old or older
6	Number of active physicians	Number of professionally active nonfederal physicians as of December 31, 1977
7	Number of hospital beds	Total number of beds, cribs, and bassinets during 1977
8	Percent high school graduates	Percent of adult population (persons 25 years old or older) who completed 12 or more years of school, according to the 1970 Census of the Population
9	Civilian labor force	Total number of persons in civilian labor force (persons 16 years old or older classified as employed or unemployed) in 1977 (in thousands)

Variable Number	Variable Name	Description
10	Total personal income	Total current income received in 1976 by residents of the SMSA from all sources, before deduction of income and other personal taxes but after deduction of personal contributiors to social security and other social insurance programs (in millions of dollars)
11	Total serious crimes	Total number of serious crimes in 1977, including murder, rape, robbery, aggravated assault, burglary, larceny-theft, and motor vehicle theft, as reported by law enforcement agencies
12	Geographic region	Geographic region classification is that used by the U.S. Bureau of the Census, where: 1 = NE, 2 = NC, 3 = S, 4 = W

Data obtained from U.S. Bureau of the Census, *State and Metropolitan Area Data Book, 1979* (a Statistical Abstract Supplement).

1	2	3	4	5	6	7	8	9	10	11	12
1	1384	9387	78.1	12.3	25627	69678	50.1	4083.9	72100	709234	1
2	4069	7031	44.0	10.0	15389	39699	62.0	3353.6	52737	499813	4
3	3719	7017	43.9	9.4	13326	43292	53.9	3305.9	54542	393162	2
...	...	...	...	...	...	...	...	...	...	...	...
139	1011	233	37.8	10.5	264	964	70.7	93.2	1337	14018	3
140	813	232	13.4	10.9	371	4355	58.0	97.0	1589	8428	1
141	654	231	28.8	3.9	140	1296	55.1	66.9	1148	15884	3

SMSA Identifications

1	NEW YORK, NY	48	NASHVILLE, TN	95	NEWPORT NEWS, VA
2	LOS ANGELES, CA	49	HONOLULU, HI	96	PEORIA, IL
3	CHICAGO, IL	50	JACKSONVILLE, FL	97	SHREVEPORT, LA
4	PHILADELPHIA, PA	51	AKRON, OH	98	YORK, PA
5	DETROIT, MI	52	SYRACUSE, NY	99	LANCASTER, PA
6	SAN FRANCISCO, CA	53	GARY, IN	100	DES MOINES, IA
7	WASHINGTON, DC	54	NORTHEAST, PA	101	UTICA, NY
8	NASSAU, NY	55	ALLENTOWN, PA	102	TRENTON, NJ
9	DALLAS, TX	56	TULSA, OK	103	SPOKANE, WA
10	HOUSTON, TX	57	CHARLOTTE, NC	104	MADISON, WI
11	ST. LOUIS, MO	58	ORLANDO, FL	105	STOCKTON, CA
12	PITTSBURG, PA	59	NEW BRUNSWICK, NJ	106	BINGHAMPTON, NY
13	BALTIMORE, MD	60	OMAHA, NE	107	READING, PA
14	MINNEAPOLIS, MN	61	GRAND RAPIDS, MI	108	CORPUS CHRISTI, TX
15	NEWARK, NJ	62	JERSEY CITY, NJ	109	HUNTINGTON, WV
16	CLEVELAND, OH	63	YOUNGSTOWN, OH	110	JACKSON, MS
17	ATLANTA, GA	64	GREENVILLE, SC	111	LEXINGTON, KY
18	ANAHEIM, CA	65	FLINT, MI	112	VALLEJO, CA
19	SAN DIEGO, CA	66	WILMINGTON, DE	113	COLORADO SPRINGS, CO
20	DENVER, CO	67	LONG BRANCH, NJ	114	EVANSVILLE, IN
21	MIAMI, FL	68	RALEIGH, NC	115	HUNTSVILLE, AL
22	SEATTLE, WA	69	W. PALM BEACH, FL	116	APPLETON, WI
23	MILWAUKEE, WI	70	AUSTIN, TX	117	SANTA BARBARA, CA
24	TAMPA, FL	71	FRESNO, CA	118	AUGUSTA, GA
25	CINCINNATI, OH	72	OXNARD, CA	119	SOUTH BEND, IN
26	BUFFALO, NY	73	PATERSON, NJ	120	LAKELAND, FL
27	RIVERSIDE, CA	74	TUCSON, AZ	121	SALINAS, CA
28	KANSAS CITY, MO	75	LANSING, MI	122	PENSACOLA, FL
29	PHOENIX, AZ	76	KNOXVILLE, TN	123	ERIE, PA
30	SAN JOSE, CA	77	BATON ROUGE, LA	124	DULUTH, MN
31	INDIANAPOLIS, IN	78	EL PASO, TX	125	KALAMAZOO, MI
32	NEW ORLEANS, LA	79	HARRISBURG, PA	126	ROCKFORD, IL
33	PORTLAND, OR	80	TACOMA, WA	127	JOHNSTOWN, PA
34	COLUMBUS, OH	81	MOBILE, AL	128	LORAIN, OH
35	SAN ANTONIO, TX	82	JOHNSON CITY, TN	129	CHARLESTON, WV
36	ROCHESTER, NY	83	ALBUQUERQUE, NM	130	SPRINGFIELD, MA
37	SACRAMENTO, CA	84	CANTON, OH	131	WORCESTER, MA
38	LOUISVILLE, KY	85	CHATANOOGA, TN	132	MONTGOMERY, AL
39	MEMPHIS, TN	86	WICHITA, KS	133	ANN ARBOR, MI
40	FT. LAUDERDALE, FL	87	CHARLESTON, SC	134	HAMILTON, OH
41	DAYTON, OH	88	COLUMBIA, SC	135	EUGENE, OR
42	SALT LAKE CITY, UT	89	DAVENPORT, IA	136	MACON, GA
43	BIRMINGHAM, AL	90	FORT WAYNE, IN	137	MODESTO, CA
44	ALBANY, NY	91	LITTLE ROCK, AR	138	MCALLEN, TX
45	TOLEDO, OH	92	BAKERSFIELD, CA	139	MELBOURNE, FL
46	GREENSBORO, NC	93	BEAUMONT, TX	140	POUGHKEEPSIE, NY
47	OKLAHOMA CITY, OK	94	LAS VEGAS, NV	141	FAYETTEVILLE, NC

Data Set C.3   DISEASE

This data set provides information from a study based on 196 persons selected in a probability sample within two sectors in a city. Each line of the data set has an identification number and provides information on five other variables for a single person. The six variables are:

Variable Number	Variable Name	Description
1	Identification number	1–196
2	Age	Age of person (in years)
3	Socioeconomic status	1 = upper, 2 = middle, 3 = lower
4	Sector	Sector within city, where: 1 = sector 1, 2 = sector 2
5	Disease status	1 = with disease, 0 = without disease
6	Savings account status	1 = has savings account, 0 = does not have savings account

Adapted in part from H. G. Dantes, J. S. Koopman, C. L. Addy, et al., "Dengue Epidemics on the Pacific Coast of Mexico," *International Journal of Epidemiology* 17 (1988), pp. 178-86.

1	2	3	4	5	6
1	33	1	1	0	1
2	35	1	1	0	1
3	6	1	1	0	0
. . .	. . .	. . .	. . .	. . .	. . .
194	31	3	1	0	0
195	85	3	1	0	1
196	24	2	1	0	0

Data Set C.4   Drug Effect Experiment

This data set provides results adapted from an experiment in which the effects of a drug on the behavior of rats were studied. The behavior under consideration was the rate at which a rat deprived of water presses a lever to obtain water. The experiment was carried out in two parts. Variable 2 identifies the two parts of the study (1, 2).

In Part I of the study, 12 male albino rats of the same strain and approximately the same weight were utilized. Variable 3 identifies each rat (1, . . . , 12). Prior to the experiment, each rat was trained to press a lever for water until a stable rate of pressing was reached. Two factors were studied in this experiment—initial lever press rate (factor *A*) and dosage of the drug (factor *B*). The 12 rats were classified into one of three groups according to their initial lever press rate. Variable 4 identifies the level of the initial lever press rate (1, 2, 3). Level 1 is a slow rate, level 2 a moderate rate, and level 3 a fast rate. The levels were defined such that one third of the rats were classified into each of the three levels.

Four dosage levels of the drug were studied, including a zero level consisting of a saline solution. Variable 5 identifies the drug dosage (1, . . . , 4). All dosage levels were specified in terms of milligrams of drug per kilogram of weight of the rat.

One hour after a drug dosage injection was administered, an experimental session began during which the rat received water each time after the second lever press. This reinforcement schedule will be denoted by FR-2. Each rat received all four drug dosage levels in a random order. Each of the four drug dosages was administered twice, thus providing two observation units for each treatment. Variable 6 identifies the observation unit (1, 2).

The response variable was defined as the total number of lever presses divided by the elapsed time (in seconds) during a session for the given treatment. Variable 7 is the response variable.

In Part II of the study, another 12 albino male rats of the same strain and approximately the same weight as the rats used in Part I were used. Variable 2 identifies this part of the study, and variable 3 identifies the 12 additional rats (13, . . . , 24). The experimental design for Part II of the study was exactly the same as for Part I, except that each rat received water each time after the fifth lever press. This reinforcement schedule will be denoted by FR-5. Variable 2 identifies the reinforcement schedule since Part I of the study used schedule FR-2 while Part II of the study used schedule FR-5. The reinforcement schedule thus is another factor (factor *C*) that was studied in the combined experiment.

To summarize, the variables for this experimental design are:

Variable Number	Variable Name	Description
1	Identification number	1–192
2	Part of study (factor *C*: reinforcement schedule)	1: Part I (FR-2) 2: Part II (FR-5)
3	Rat identification	1–24
4	Initial lever press rate (factor *A*)	1: Slow 2: Moderate 3: Fast

Variable Number	Variable Name	Description
5	Dosage level (mg/kg) (factor *B*)	1: 0 (saline solution) 2: .5 3: 1.0 4: 1.8
6	Observation unit	1, 2
7	Response variable—lever press rate	Total number of lever presses divided by elapsed time in seconds

Reference: T. G. Heffner, R. B. Drawbaugh, and M. J. Zigmond, "Amphetamine and Operant Behavior in Rats: Relationship between Drug Effect and Control Response Rate," *Journal of Comparative and Physiological Psychology* 86 (1974), pp. 1031–43.

1	2	3	4	5	6	7
1	1	1	1	1	1	.81
2	1	1	1	2	1	.80
3	1	1	1	3	1	.82
...	...	...	...	...	...	...
190	2	24	3	2	2	2.98
191	2	24	3	3	2	2.47
192	2	24	3	4	2	1.51

Rules for Developing ANOVA Models and Tables for Balanced Designs

In this appendix, we present and illustrate rules for developing models for nested and/or crossed factor designs, for finding the appropriate sums of squares and degrees of freedom for the needed mean squares, and for finding the expected values of the mean squares. The rules in Sections D.1–D.3 apply to all balanced designs with two or more replications and with no interactions assumed to equal zero. The rule modifications in Section D.4 show how these rules need to be modified to make them applicable to balanced designs with no replications and/or with some interaction terms assumed to equal zero.

As noted earlier, a design is *balanced* in the nested case when (1) the number of factor levels of a nested factor is the same for each level of the factor in which the nesting takes place, and (2) the number of replications is constant for the different factor level combinations. In the crossed case, a design is balanced whenever the number of replications is constant for all factor level combinations. In a subsampling design, balance requires that the subsample sizes at each stage of sampling be constant.

D.1 Rule for Model Development

We begin by presenting a rule for the development of a nested and/or crossed factor design model. *This rule is applicable when no interactions are assumed to equal zero.* We shall utilize as an illustration the training school example of Table 28.1, where the effects of three schools (factor A) and two instructors within each school (factor B) were studied and two replications were made in each instance.

Rule (D.1)

Step 1. *Include an overall constant and a main effect term for each factor, taking into account when one factor is nested within another.*

Example. For the training school example, we include:

$$\mu_{..} \qquad \alpha_i \qquad \beta_{j(i)}$$

Note that factor B is nested within factor A.

Step 2.   *Include all interaction terms except those containing both a nested factor and the factor within which it is nested.*

Example.   Since factor B is nested within factor A, the AB interaction term (the only possible interaction term here) is not included.

Step 3.   *Interactions between a nested factor and another factor with which the nested factor is crossed are always themselves nested.*

Example.   For the training school example, this situation does not arise.

Step 4.   *Include the error term, which is nested within all factors.*

Since the model formulation will be used for developing the needed ANOVA sums of squares, degrees of freedom, and expected mean squares, we now need to recognize that the error term ε is nested within a factor level combination. That is, the kth experimental unit when factor A is at level 1 and factor B is at level 1 is not the same unit as the kth experimental unit for another factor level combination.

Example.   For the training school example the error term is $\varepsilon_{k(ij)}$, and the appropriate model therefore is:

$$(D.2) \qquad\qquad Y_{ijk} = \mu_{..} + \alpha_i + \beta_{j(i)} + \varepsilon_{k(ij)}$$

$$i = 1, 2, 3; \quad j = 1, 2; \quad k = 1, 2$$

D.2   Rule for Finding Sums of Squares and Degrees of Freedom

This rule is applicable to all balanced designs with two or more replications and with no interaction terms assumed to equal zero. We shall continue to consider the training school example where factor B is nested within factor A. It does not matter for this rule whether the factor effects are fixed or random.

Rule (D.3) for Definitional Forms of Sums of Squares and Degrees of Freedom

Step 1.   *Write the model equation.*

Example.   The model equation for the training school example was given earlier. We show this model now in its general form, where factor A has a levels, factor B has b levels, and there are n replications:

$$(D.2a) \qquad\qquad Y_{ijk} = \mu_{..} + \alpha_i + \beta_{j(i)} + \varepsilon_{k(ij)}$$

$$i = 1, \ldots, a; \quad j = 1, \ldots, b; \quad k = 1, \ldots, n$$

Step 2.   *For each model term other than the overall constant, write the associated SS notation.*

Example.   We do this for the training school example in columns 1 and 2 of Table D.1 for α_i, $\beta_{j(i)}$, and $\varepsilon_{k(ij)}$. The line for Total will not be completed until step 9.

Step 3.   *Each sum of squares will have as coefficient the product of the limits of the subscripts not appearing in the model term. The coefficient is taken to be 1 if all subscripts appear in the model term.*

TABLE D.1 Derivation of Sums of Squares Formulas for Nested Two-Factor Experiment (B nested within A).

(1) Model Term	(2) SS	(3) Coefficient	(4) Σ	(5) Symbolic Product	(6) Term to Be Squared	(7) Sum of Squares	(8) Degrees of Freedom
α_i	SSA	bn	$\sum_i$	$i - 1$	$\bar{Y}_{i..} - \bar{Y}_{...}$	$bn\sum_i(\bar{Y}_{i..} - \bar{Y}_{...})^2$	$a-1$
$\beta_{j(i)}$	SSB(A)	n	$\sum_i\sum_j$	$i(j-i) = ij - i$	$\bar{Y}_{ij.} - \bar{Y}_{i..}$	$n\sum_i\sum_j(\bar{Y}_{ij.} - \bar{Y}_{i..})^2$	$a(b-1)$
$\varepsilon_{k(ij)}$	SSE	1	$\sum_i\sum_j\sum_k$	$(k-1)ij = ijk - ij$	$Y_{ijk} - \bar{Y}_{ij.}$	$\sum_i\sum_j\sum_k(Y_{ijk} - \bar{Y}_{ij.})^2$	$ab(n-1)$
Total	SSTO				$Y_{ijk} - \bar{Y}_{...}$	$\sum_i\sum_j\sum_k(Y_{ijk} - \bar{Y}_{...})^2$	$abn-1$

Example. The coefficients for our example are shown in column 3 of Table D.1. For instance, α_i does not contain j and k. These subscripts have limits of b and n, respectively. The coefficient for the *SSA* term is therefore bn. Since the model term $\varepsilon_{k(ij)}$ contains all subscripts, the coefficient is taken to be 1 here.

Step 4. *Each sum of squares is summed over all of the subscripts of the model term, whether in parentheses or not.*

Example. The summations for our example are shown in column 4. For instance, the sum of squares term corresponding to α_i is summed over i, the only subscript in that model term. Similarly, the sum of squares term corresponding to $\varepsilon_{k(ij)}$ is summed over i, j, and k since all of these appear in the model term.

Step 5. *Form a symbolic product from the subscripts of the model term, using the subscript if it is in parentheses, and the subscript minus 1 if it is not in parentheses. Expand the product.*

Example. The symbolic products for our example are shown in column 5. For instance, for α_i the symbolic product is $i - 1$. For $\beta_{j(i)}$, the symbolic product is $i(j - 1) = ij - i$. For $\varepsilon_{k(ij)}$, the symbolic product is $(k - 1)ij = ijk - ij$.

Step 6. *The typical term to be squared consists of means of the observations with the subscripts consisting of the symbolic product term and dots elsewhere. The sign of each mean is that of the symbolic product. A 1 refers to the overall mean.*

Example. The terms to be squared for our example are shown in column 6. Note that for α_i, the symbolic product is $i - 1$, and the typical term to be squared therefore is:

$$\bar{Y}_{i..} - \bar{Y}_{...}$$

For $\beta_{j(i)}$ the symbolic product is $ij - i$, and hence the typical term to be squared is:

$$\bar{Y}_{ij.} - \bar{Y}_{i..}$$

Similarly, for $\varepsilon_{k(ij)}$, the symbolic product is $ijk - ij$. Hence the typical term to be squared is:

$$Y_{ijk} - \bar{Y}_{ij.}$$

Note that we write the first term as Y_{ijk} since it is not averaged over any subscript.

Step 7. *Combining the steps of squaring, summing, and multiplying by the coefficient yields the appropriate sums of squares.*

Example. The sums of squares for our example are shown in column 7.

Step 8. *The degrees of freedom are obtained by replacing in each symbolic product the subscript variable by its limit.*

Example. For our example, the degrees of freedom are shown in column 8. For instance, for α_i the symbolic product is $i - 1$; hence $df = a - 1$. Similarly for $\varepsilon_{k(ij)}$, the symbolic product is $ijk - ij$; hence $df = abn - ab = ab(n - 1)$.

Step 9. *The total sum of squares is always defined as the sum, over all observations, of the squared deviations of the observations from the overall mean. The total degrees of freedom are always defined as one less than the total number of observations.*

D.3 Rule for Finding Expected Mean Squares

The rule for finding expected mean squares that we shall now present enables us to avoid tedious derivations. The rule applies to both nested factors and crossed factors. *The rule is applicable to all balanced designs with two or more replications and with no interaction terms assumed to equal zero.* We continue to use the training school example of Table 28.1 as our illustration. Here factor A (school) and factor B (instructor) are both fixed factors, factor B is nested within factor A, factor B has b levels within each level of factor A, factor A has a levels, and there are n replications.

Rule (D.4)

The rule for finding expected mean squares to be presented may appear to be a bit complex on first reading. However, with a little practice the desired expected mean squares can be obtained very quickly and easily.

Step 1. *List the model equation.*

   Example. The model equation is that of (D.2a):

$$Y_{ijk} = \mu_{..} + \alpha_i + \beta_{j(i)} + \varepsilon_{k(ij)}$$

Step 2. *For each term other than the overall constant, write the associated random effects variance term.*

   Example.

$$\begin{array}{ccc} \alpha_i & \beta_{j(i)} & \varepsilon_{k(ij)} \\ \sigma_\alpha^2 & \sigma_\beta^2 & \sigma^2 \end{array}$$

If factors have fixed effects, as in this example, we shall at the end replace these variance terms by sums of squared effects divided by degrees of freedom. For instance, in the training school example the term σ_α^2 later will be replaced by $\sum \alpha_i^2/(a-1)$, and likewise σ_β^2 will be replaced by $\sum\sum \beta_{j(i)}^2/a(b-1)$. In the meantime, however, it is easier to write the variance term rather than a sum of squared effects divided by degrees of freedom.

Step 3. *Set up a table, with the rows consisting of the model elements other than the overall constant.*

   Example.

α_i

$\beta_{j(i)}$

$\varepsilon_{k(ij)}$

Step 4.   *The column headings for the table are the subscripts in the model. Under each heading, write F if the factor indexed by the subscript is fixed, and write R if it is random. Also write the number of levels for that factor.*

   Example.

	i	j	k
	F	F	R
	a	b	n
α_i			
$\beta_{j(i)}$			
$\varepsilon_{k(ij)}$			

   For instance, i refers to school, a fixed factor that occurs at a levels. Note that the subscript k refers to replication, which is a random "factor" and occurs at n levels.

Step 5.   *In each row where one or more subscripts are in parentheses, enter a 1 in the column(s) corresponding to the subscript(s) in parentheses.*

   Example.

	i	j	k
	F	F	R
	a	b	n
α_i			
$\beta_{j(i)}$	1		
$\varepsilon_{k(ij)}$	1	1	

   Thus, in the $\beta_{j(i)}$ row, we enter a 1 in the i column, and so on.

Step 6.   *In each row where one or more subscripts are not in parentheses, enter in the column(s) corresponding to the subscript(s) not in parentheses a 1 if the subscript refers to a random factor, and a 0 if the factor is fixed.*

   Example.

	i	j	k
	F	F	R
	a	b	n
α_i	0		
$\beta_{j(i)}$	1	0	
$\varepsilon_{k(ij)}$	1	1	1

   Thus, for the $\beta_{j(i)}$ row, the subscript not in parentheses is j, which refers to factor B, a fixed factor. Hence, a 0 is entered in the j column.

Step 7.   *Fill in all remaining empty cells with the number of levels appearing in the column heading.*

Example.

	i	j	k
	F	F	R
	a	b	n
α_i	0	b	n
$\beta_{j(i)}$	1	0	n
$\varepsilon_{k(ij)}$	1	1	1

Each $E\{MS\}$ will consist of a linear combination of the variance terms enumerated in step 2, with the coefficients obtained by taking additional steps in the table just completed. Some of the coefficients may be zero, which means that the corresponding variance term is not present in the $E\{MS\}$.

Step 8.   *Adjoin on the right of the table just completed the variance term associated with the effect in that row. In addition, adjoin a column for each expected mean square to be found. Under each expected mean square, indicate all of the subscripts (including any parentheses) associated with the corresponding model term.*

Example.

	i	j	k	Variance	$E\{MSA\}$ i	$E\{MSB(A)\}$ $(i)j$	$E\{MSE\}$ $(ij)k$
	F	F	R				
	a	b	n				
α_i	0	b	n	σ_α^2			
$\beta_{j(i)}$	1	0	n	σ_β^2			
$\varepsilon_{k(ij)}$	1	1	1	σ^2			

Note that all of the subscripts of the associated model term, whether in parentheses or not, are shown under the expected mean square. For example, $E\{MSB(A)\}$ has associated with it the model term $\beta_{j(i)}$, so that the subscripts shown are (i) and j. Similarly, $E\{MSE\}$ has associated with it the model term $\varepsilon_{k(ij)}$, so that (ij) and k are shown.

Step 9.   *For each expected mean square column, the coefficient of any variance term is zero if the subscript(s) of the model term in that row (whether in parentheses or not) do not include all of the subscript(s) in the heading of that $E\{MS\}$ column (whether in parentheses or not).*

Example.

	i	j	k	Variance	$E\{MSA\}$ i	$E\{MSB(A)\}$ $(i)j$	$E\{MSE\}$ $(ij)k$
	F	F	R				
	a	b	n				
α_i	0	b	n	σ_α^2		0	0
$\beta_{j(i)}$	1	0	n	σ_β^2			0
$\varepsilon_{k(ij)}$	1	1	1	σ^2			

For the $E\{MSA\}$ column, it will be noted that the model terms in all rows contain the subscript i. Hence, none of the variances receives a zero coefficient as a result of this step.

For the $E\{MSB(A)\}$ column, note that the first row has a model term not containing both i and j. Hence, σ_α^2 receives a zero coefficient in the $E\{MSB(A)\}$ column.

Finally, for the $E\{MSE\}$ column, the first and second rows have model terms that do not contain the three subscripts i, j, and k. Hence, both σ_α^2 and σ_β^2 receive zero coefficients in the $E\{MSE\}$ column.

Step 10. *The coefficients of the variance terms that have not been assigned a zero coefficient as a result of step 9 are found as follows:*

    a. *For each expected mean square column, delete (e.g., mask or cover) the column(s) on the left corresponding to the subscripts not in parentheses in the heading of the $E\{MS\}$ column.*

    b. *Multiply the entries in the remaining columns for each row being considered.*

Step 11. *The expected mean square equals the sum of the products of each coefficient times the associated variance term, with the variance terms for fixed effects replaced by sums of squared effects divided by degrees of freedom.*

    Example.

	i	j	k		$E\{MSA\}$	$E\{MSB(A)\}$	$E\{MSE\}$
	F	F	R		i	$(i)j$	$(ij)k$
	a	b	n	Variance			
α_i	0	b	n	σ_α^2	bn	0 (step 9)	0 (step 9)
$\beta_{j(i)}$	1	0	n	σ_β^2	0	n	0 (step 9)
$\varepsilon_{k(ij)}$	1	1	1	σ^2	1	1	1

To find the coefficients for the $E\{MSA\}$ column, for example, we noted earlier that no zero coefficient is assigned as a result of step 9. Step 10a calls for column i on the left to be deleted. Hence, we obtain by multiplying the terms in the j and k columns:

	j	k		$E\{MSA\}$
	F	R		i
	b	n	Variance	
α_i	b	n	σ_α^2	bn
$\beta_{j(i)}$	0	n	σ_β^2	0
$\varepsilon_{k(ij)}$	1	1	σ^2	1

Thus:

$$E\{MSA\} = bn\sigma_\alpha^2 + (0)\sigma_\beta^2 + (1)\sigma^2 = bn\sigma_\alpha^2 + \sigma^2$$

Since factor A has fixed effects, we finally obtain:

$$E\{MSA\} = bn\frac{\Sigma\alpha_i^2}{a-1} + \sigma^2$$

We find the remaining coefficients for $E\{MSB(A)\}$ in similar fashion. We delete column j on the left, the subscript not in parentheses, and obtain:

	i	k		
	F	R		$E\{MSB(A)\}$
	a	n	Variance	$(i)\,j$
α_i	0	n	σ_α^2	0 (step 9)
$\beta_{j(i)}$	1	n	σ_β^2	n
$\varepsilon_{k(ij)}$	1	1	σ^2	1

Thus:

$$E\{MSB(A)\} = (0)\sigma_\alpha^2 + n\sigma_\beta^2 + (1)\sigma^2 = n\sigma_\beta^2 + \sigma^2$$

Since factor B has fixed effects, we finally obtain:

$$E\{MSB(A)\} = n\frac{\sum\sum \beta_{j(i)}^2}{a(b-1)} + \sigma^2$$

To find the remaining coefficient in the $E\{MSE\}$ column, we delete column k, and the product on the σ^2 line is $1 \cdot 1 = 1$. Thus:

$$E\{MSE\} = (0)\sigma_\alpha^2 + (0)\sigma_\beta^2 + (1)\sigma^2 = \sigma^2$$

Assembling our results, we have:

(D.5a)
$$E\{MSA\} = bn\frac{\sum \alpha_i^2}{a-1} + \sigma^2$$

(D.5b)
$$E\{MSB(A)\} = n\frac{\sum\sum \beta_{j(i)}^2}{a(b-1)} + \sigma^2$$

(D.5c)
$$E\{MSE\} = \sigma^2$$

Note

Some computer packages provide the expected mean squares for any balanced ANOVA study. An example is shown in Figure 28.7.   ∎

D.4   No Replications and/or Some Interactions Equal Zero

Modification of Rules

When a balanced design includes no replications and/or some interactions are assumed to equal zero—as, for instance, in a randomized complete block design with fixed block effects—rules (D.1) and (D.3) need to be modified slightly. Rule (D.4) requires no modification.

The modification of rule (D.1) is very slight. Step 2 now becomes:

(D.6)   *Rule (D.1) modification*: Step 2. *Include all interaction terms except those assumed to equal zero and those containing both a nested factor and the factor within which it is nested.*

The modification of rule (D.3) is also a simple one:

(D.7)   *Rule (D.3) modification*: Steps 2 through 8 do not apply to the model error term ε. Instead, the sum of squares associated with the model error term ε is obtained as a remainder from the total sum of squares. Likewise, the degrees of freedom associated with this remainder sum of squares are obtained as a remainder from the total degrees of freedom.

The sum of squares associated with the model error term ε in balanced designs where there are no replications and/or where some interaction terms are assumed to equal zero will be denoted by *SSRem*, which stands for the *remainder sum of squares*. Frequently, the remainder sum of squares will turn out to be an interaction sum of squares for the interaction terms in the model that are assumed to equal zero. The *remainder mean square* will be denoted by *MSRem*.

Additional Modification for Latin Squares Designs

For latin square design model (30.1), one of the subscripts in Y_{ijk} is redundant since the row and column indices define the treatment for a given latin square design. Hence, when using the rules presented in the case of a latin square design, one of the subscripts must be treated as redundant, i.e., it needs to be ignored.

D.5   Additional Examples of Use of Rules

Crossed Two-Factor Study – Mixed Factor Effects

Consider a two-factor experiment in a completely randomized design, where factors A and B are crossed, factor A has fixed effects and factor B has random effects, and n replications are obtained for each factor combination. The model equation is that of (24.42):

$$Y_{ijk} = \mu_{..} + \alpha_i + \beta_j + (\alpha\beta)_{ij} + \varepsilon_{k(ij)}$$

where we now recognize the nesting of the error term ε.

Table D.2 contains the derivation of the sums of squares. Table D.3a contains the preliminary tabulations for finding the expected mean squares, while Table D.3b presents the results of steps 9 and 10 of rule (D.4). The random effects variance terms corresponding to the model terms are:

α_i	β_j	$(\alpha\beta)_{ij}$	$\varepsilon_{k(ij)}$
σ_α^2	σ_β^2	$\sigma_{\alpha\beta}^2$	σ^2

Here, only the α_i are fixed effects, so at the end σ_α^2 will need to be replaced by a sum of squared effects divided by degrees of freedom. Note in Table D.3b that for finding $E\{MSA\}$, σ_β^2 receives a zero coefficient as a result of step 9 since the subscript in the β_j model term does not contain the subscript i in the $E\{MSA\}$ column. Column i is deleted for step 10 for

TABLE D.2 Derivation of Sums of Squares Formulas for Crossed Two-Factor Experiment in Completely Randomized Design.

(1) Model Term	(2) SS	(3) Coefficient Σ	(4) Σ	(5) Symbolic Product	(6) Term to Be Squared	(7) Sum of Squares	(8) Degrees of Freedom
α_i	SSA	bn	$\sum_i$	$i-1$	$\bar{Y}_{i\cdot\cdot} - \bar{Y}_{\cdots}$	$bn\sum_i(\bar{Y}_{i\cdot\cdot} - \bar{Y}_{\cdots})^2$	$a-1$
β_j	SSB	an	$\sum_j$	$j-1$	$\bar{Y}_{\cdot j\cdot} - \bar{Y}_{\cdots}$	$an\sum_j(\bar{Y}_{\cdot j\cdot} - \bar{Y}_{\cdots})^2$	$b-1$
$(\alpha\beta)_{ij}$	SSAB	n	$\sum_i\sum_j$	$(i-1)(j-1)=ij-i-j+1$	$\bar{Y}_{ij\cdot} - \bar{Y}_{i\cdot\cdot} - \bar{Y}_{\cdot j\cdot} + \bar{Y}_{\cdots}$	$n\sum_i\sum_j(\bar{Y}_{ij\cdot} - \bar{Y}_{i\cdot\cdot} - \bar{Y}_{\cdot j\cdot} + \bar{Y}_{\cdots})^2$	$(a-1)(b-1)$
$\varepsilon_{k(ij)}$	SSE	1	$\sum_i\sum_j\sum_k$	$(k-1)ij=ijk-ij$	$Y_{ijk} - \bar{Y}_{ij\cdot}$	$\sum_i\sum_j\sum_k(Y_{ijk} - \bar{Y}_{ij\cdot})^2$	$ab(n-1)$
Total	SSTO				$Y_{ijk} - \bar{Y}_{\cdots}$	$\sum_i\sum_j\sum_k(Y_{ijk} - \bar{Y}_{\cdots})^2$	$abn-1$

TABLE D.3 $E\{MS\}$ **Derivations for Crossed Two-Factor Experiment (A fixed, B random).**

(a) Table

	i	j	k
	F	R	R
	a	b	n
α_i	0	b	n
β_j	a	1	n
$(\alpha\beta)_{ij}$	0	1	n
$\varepsilon_{k(ij)}$	1	1	1

(b) Coefficients

Variance	$E\{MSA\}$ i	$E\{MSB\}$ j	$E\{MSAB\}$ ij	$E\{MSE\}$ $(ij)k$
σ_α^2	$b \cdot n$	0 (step 9)	0 (step 9)	0 (step 9)
σ_β^2	0 (step 9)	$a \cdot n$	0 (step 9)	0 (step 9)
$\sigma_{\alpha\beta}^2$	$1 \cdot n$	$0 \cdot n$	n	0 (step 9)
σ^2	$1 \cdot 1$	$1 \cdot 1$	1	$1 \cdot 1$
	(i col. deleted)	(j col. deleted)	(i, j cols. deleted)	(k col. deleted)

(c) $E\{MS\}$

$$E\{MSA\} = bn\frac{\Sigma \alpha_i^2}{a-1} + n\sigma_{\alpha\beta}^2 + \sigma^2$$

$$E\{MSB\} = an\sigma_\beta^2 + \sigma^2$$

$$E\{MSAB\} = n\sigma_{\alpha\beta}^2 + \sigma^2$$

$$E\{MSE\} = \sigma^2$$

finding the coefficients in the $E\{MSA\}$ column since it is the only subscript in the column heading and is not in parentheses. The other expected mean squares coefficients are found in similar fashion. Table D.3b indicates for each expected mean square whether the zero coefficients are obtained from step 9, and also which columns are deleted. The final expected mean squares, presented in Table D.3c, are identical to those shown in Table 24.5.

Subsampling in Randomized Block Design

The model usually employed for a randomized block design when only a single observation is made on an experimental unit is ANOVA model (27.1) in the case of fixed treatment and block effects:

$$(\text{D.8}) \qquad\qquad Y_{ij} = \mu_{..} + \rho_i + \tau_j + \varepsilon_{ij}$$

We shall now consider a slightly more complex case, namely when subsampling is used in a randomized block design–that is, when more than one observation is made on each experimental unit. Consider, for instance, an experiment to study how three different motivational stimuli affect the length of time a person requires to perform a task. The persons in the experiment are blocked into groups of three, according to age, and each person is assigned at random one of the three motivational stimuli. Three observations are then made on the time required to complete the task; that is, the subject is asked to perform the same task three times.

In this type of situation, we simply add a random observation error component to ANOVA model (D.8). Assuming that the treatment and block effects (motivational stimuli and age groups in our example) are fixed, an appropriate model is:

$$(\text{D.9}) \qquad\qquad Y_{ijk} = \mu_{..} + \rho_i + \tau_j + \varepsilon_{(ij)} + \eta_{k(ij)}$$

where:

$\quad\Sigma \rho_i = 0 \qquad \Sigma \tau_j = 0$

$\quad\varepsilon_{(ij)}$ and $\eta_{k(ij)}$ are independent normal random variables with expectations 0 and variances σ^2 and σ_η^2, respectively

$\quad i = 1, \ldots, n; \quad j = 1, \ldots, r; \quad k = 1, \ldots, m$

Here ρ_i is the block effect, τ_j the treatment effect, $\varepsilon_{(ij)}$ the random effect associated with the experimental unit, and $\eta_{k(ij)}$ the random effect associated with the kth observation on the experimental unit. Note that the experimental error ε is nested within the (ij) block treatment combination; there is no additional subscript since only one experimental unit is assigned to a treatment within a block. Thus, there are no replications for experimental units. Also note that the observation error η is nested within the (ij) block-treatment combination.

Since there are no replications present and the block-treatment interactions are assumed to equal zero, we need to use the modified rules, as explained in Section D.4. Table D.4 contains the derivation of the sums of squares for ANOVA model (D.9), and Table D.5 contains the derivation of the expected mean squares. Note that the sum of squares for experimental units is obtained as a remainder in Table D.4 because there is only one experimental unit assigned to a treatment within a block. As expected, *SSRem* turns out to be the block-treatment interaction sum of squares, as for a randomized block design without subsampling.

Table D.5b indicates that for ANOVA model (D.9) with fixed treatment and block effects, the test statistic for examining the presence of treatment effects is $F^* = MSTR/MSRem$, as is also the case when no subsampling occurs in a randomized complete block design–see (27.7b). Remember that *MSRem* denotes simply the interaction mean square *MSBL.TR* here.

TABLE D.4 **Derivation of Sums of Squares Formulas for Randomized Block Design with Subsampling–ANOVA Model (D.9).**

Model Term	Symbolic Product	Sum of Squares	Degrees of Freedom
ρ_i	$i - 1$	$SSBL = rm \, \Sigma(\bar{Y}_{i..} - \bar{Y}_{...})^2$	$n - 1$
τ_j	$j - 1$	$SSTR = nm \, \Sigma(\bar{Y}_{.j.} - \bar{Y}_{...})^2$	$r - 1$
$\varepsilon_{(ij)}$		$SSRem = SSBL.TR$ $= m \, \Sigma\Sigma(\bar{Y}_{ij.} - \bar{Y}_{i..} - \bar{Y}_{.j.} + \bar{Y}_{...})^2$	Remainder $= (n-1)(r-1)$
$\eta_{k(ij)}$	$(k-1)ij$ $= ijk - ij$	$SSOE = \Sigma\Sigma\Sigma(Y_{ijk} - \bar{Y}_{ij.})^2.$	$nr(m-1)$
Total		$SSTO = \Sigma\Sigma\Sigma(Y_{ijk} - \bar{Y}_{...})^2$	$nrm - 1$

TABLE D.5 **Derivation of Expected Mean Squares for Randomized Block Design with Subsampling—ANOVA Model (D.9).**

(a) Table

	i	j	k	Variance	Expected Mean Square of BL	TR	Rem	OE
	F	F	R		i	j	(ij)	$(ij)k$
	n	r	m					
ρ_i	0	r	m	σ_ρ^2	rm	0	0	0
τ_j	n	0	m	σ_τ^2	0	nm	0	0
$\varepsilon_{(ij)}$	1	1	m	σ^2	m	m	m	0
$\eta_{k(ij)}$	1	1	1	σ_η^2	1	1	1	1

(b) Expected Mean Squares

$$E\{MSBL\} = rm\frac{\Sigma \rho_i^2}{n-1} + m\sigma^2 + \sigma_\eta^2$$

$$E\{MSTR\} = nm\frac{\Sigma \tau_j^2}{r-1} + m\sigma^2 + \sigma_\eta^2$$

$$E\{MSRem\} = m\sigma^2 + \sigma_\eta^2$$

$$E\{MSOE\} = \sigma_\eta^2$$

Problems

D.1. Refer to ANOVA model (24.39). Use rule (D.4) to obtain the expected mean squares in Table 24.5 for this model.

D.2. Refer to ANOVA model (24.67).

    a. Use rule (D.3) to obtain the sums of squares formulas in (23.21) and the associated degrees of freedom.

    b. Use rule (D.4) to obtain the expected mean squares in Table 24.8.

D.3. Refer to ANOVA model (24.69).

    a. Use rule (D.3) to obtain the sums of squares formulas in (23.21) and the associated degrees of freedom.

    b. Use rule (D.4) to obtain the expected mean squares in Table 24.9.

D.4. Refer to nested design model (28.7), but assume that factor A is nested within factor B, factor A effects are random, and factor B effects are fixed. (See also "Random factor effects" on page 1126.)

    a. Use rule (D.3) to obtain the sums of squares formulas and the associated degrees of freedom.

    b. Use rule (D.4) to obtain the expected mean squares.

    c. What is the appropriate mean square to be used in constructing a confidence interval for $\mu_{.j}$?

D.5. Refer to randomized block model (27.1).

    a. Use rule (D.3) and modification (D.7) to obtain the sums of squares formulas in (27.6) and the associated degrees of freedom.

    b. Use rule (D.4) to obtain the expected mean squares in Table 27.2 for this model.

D.6. Refer to randomized block model (27.1), but assume that treatment effects are random. (See also Comment 2 on page 1078.)

    a. Use rule (D.3) and modification (D.7) to obtain the sums of squares formulas in (27.6) and the associated degrees of freedom.

    b. Use rule (D.4) to obtain the expected mean squares in Table 27.2 for this model.

D.7. Refer to randomized block model (27.34).

    a. Use rule (D.3) and modification (D.7) to obtain the sums of squares formulas in (27.6) and the associated degrees of freedom.

    b. Use rule (D.4) to obtain the expected mean squares in Table 27.9 for this model.

D.8. Refer to randomized block model (D.9), but assume that block effects are random.

    a. Use rule (D.3) and modification (D.7) to obtain the sums of squares formulas and the associated degrees of freedom.

    b. Use rule (D.4) to obtain the expected mean squares.

D.9. In a balanced three-factor study, factors A and C are crossed and factor B is nested within factor C. Factor A has fixed effects, and factors B and C have random effects. There are n replications for each treatment.

a. Use rule (D.3) to obtain the sums of squares formulas and the associated degrees of freedom.

b. Use rule (D.4) to obtain the expected mean squares.

c. What is the appropriate denominator mean square for testing for factor A main effects?

D.10. **Swimmer motivation**. A large metropolitan swim club for youths studied the effects of three motivational stimuli on performance. The three motivational stimuli were: (1) presentation of merit award, (2) granting of team leadership privileges, and (3) publicity in the club newsletter. Since age is known to be related to performance, the nine female swimmers included in the study were grouped according to age into three blocks of three each. Within each age block, the three swimmers were randomly assigned to one of the motivation treatments. After a suitable amount of training, each swimmer was timed on three separate occasions while swimming a fixed distance. The coded data on the time for each of the three trials follow.

		Motivation Treatment		
Block	Obser-vation	$j = 1$ Merit Award	$j = 2$ Leadership	$j = 3$ Publicity
$i = 1$	$k = 1$:	28	26	27
(7–8 years)	$k = 2$:	32	24	29
	$k = 3$:	31	27	30
$i = 2$	$k = 1$:	24	22	20
(9–10 years)	$k = 2$:	26	19	21
	$k = 3$:	23	18	22
$i = 3$	$k = 1$:	18	13	17
(11–12 years)	$k = 2$:	21	16	19
	$k = 3$:	20	15	19

Obtain the residuals for randomized block model (D.9) and plot them against the fitted values. Also prepare a normal probability plot of the residuals. What are your findings about the appropriateness of model (D.9)?

D.11. Refer to **Swimmer motivation** Problem D.10. Assume that randomized block model (D.9) with fixed block and treatment effects is appropriate.

a. Obtain the analysis of variance table.

b. Test whether or not the mean times are the same for the three motivational stimuli; use $\alpha = .05$. State the alternatives, decision rule, and conclusion. What is the P-value of the test?

c. Make all pairwise comparisons among the three treatment means; use the Tukey procedure with a 90 percent family confidence coefficient. State your findings.

d. Obtain point estimates of σ^2 and σ_η^2. Does one variance appear to be much larger than the other? Discuss.

D.12. Refer to repeated measures model (29.10).

a. Use rule (D.3) and modification (D.7) to obtain the sums of squares formulas in Table 29.6b and the associated degrees of freedom in Table 29.6a.

b. Use rule (D.4) to obtain the expected mean squares in Table 29.6a.

D.13. Refer to repeated measures model (29.16).

a. Use rule (D.3) and modification (D.7) to obtain the sums of squares formulas and the associated degrees of freedom in Table 29.8.

b. Use rule (D.4) to obtain the expected mean squares in Table 29.9.

D.14. Refer to the **Drug effect experiment** data set. Consider the combined study. Assume that subjects (rats) and observation units have random effects, and that factor A (initial lever press rate), factor B (dosage level), and factor C (reinforcement schedule) have fixed effects. Also assume that there are no interactions between subjects and treatments.

a. Use rule (D.1) and modification (D.6) to develop the model for this experiment.

b. Use rule (D.3) and modification (D.7) to obtain the sums of squares formulas and the associated degrees of freedom.

c. Use rule (D.4) to obtain the expected mean squares.

D.15. Derive the expected mean squares in Table 30.3 for latin square model (30.1) by using rule (D.4). (See also "Additional Modification for Latin Square Designs" on page 1382.)

D.16. Derive the expected mean squares for latin square model (30.18) with n replications by using rule (D.4). (See also "Additional Modification for Latin Square Designs" on page 1382.)

D.17. Derive the expected mean squares in Table 30.9 for latin square cross-over model (30.20) with n subjects for each treatment order pattern by using rule (D.4). (See also "Additional Modification for Latin Square Designs" on page 1382.)

Selected Bibliography

The selected references are grouped into the following categories:

1. General regression books

2. General linear models books

3. Diagnostics and model building

4. Statistical computing

5. Nonlinear regression

6. Miscellaneous regression topics

7. General experimental design and analysis of variance books

8. Miscellaneous experimental design and analysis of variance topics

1. General Regression Books

Bowerman, B. L.; R. T. O'Connell; and D. A. Dickey. *Linear Statistical Models: An Applied Approach*. 2nd. ed. Boston: Duxbury Press, 1990.

Chatterjee, S., and B. Price. *Regression Analysis by Example*. 2nd. ed. New York: John Wiley & Sons, 1991.

Cohen, J., and P. Cohen. *Applied Multiple Regression/Correlation Analysis for the Behavioral Sciences*. 2nd ed. Hillsdale, N. J.: Lawrence Erlbaum Associates, 1983.

Daniel, C., and F. S. Wood. *Fitting Equations to Data*. 2nd ed. New York: Wiley-Interscience, 1980.

Draper, N. R., and H. Smith. *Applied Regression Analysis*. 2nd ed. New York: John Wiley & Sons, 1981.

Dunn, O. J., and V. A. Clark. *Applied Statistics: Analysis of Variance and Regression*. 2nd ed. New York: John Wiley & Sons, 1987.

Edwards, A. L. *Multiple Regression and the Analysis of Variance and Covariance*. 2nd ed. New York: W. H. Freeman & Co., 1985.

Graybill, F. A., and H. Iyer. *Regression Analysis: Concepts and Applications*. Belmont, Calif.: Wadsworth, 1994.

Gunst, R. F., and R. L. Mason. *Regression Analysis and Its Application*. New York: Marcel Dekker, 1980.

Hamilton, L. C. *Regression with Graphics*. Pacific Grove, Calif.: Brooks/Cole Publishing, 1992.

Kleinbaum, D. G.; L. L. Kupper; and K. E. Muller. *Applied Regression Analysis and Other Multivariate Methods*. 2nd ed. Boston: PWS-Kent Publishing Co., 1988.

Mendenhall, W., and T. Sincich. *A Second Course in Business Statistics: Regression Analysis*. 4th ed. San Francisco: Dellen Publishing Co., 1992.

Montgomery, D. C., and E. A. Peck. *Introduction to Linear Regression Analysis*. 2nd. ed. New York: John Wiley & Sons, 1992.

Myers, R. H. *Classical and Modern Regression with Applications*. 2nd. ed. Boston: Duxbury Press, 1990.

Pedhazur, E. J. *Multiple Regression in Behavioral Research*. 2nd ed. New York: Holt, Rinehart & Winston, 1982.

Rawlings, J. O. *Applied Regression Analysis: A Research Tool*. Belmont, Calif.: Wadsworth, 1988.

Seber, G. A. F. *Linear Regression Analysis*. New York: John Wiley & Sons, 1977.

Sen, A., and M. Srivastava. *Regression Analysis: Theory, Methods, and Applications*. New York: Springer-Verlag, 1993.

Weisberg, S. *Applied Linear Regression*. 2nd ed. New York: John Wiley & Sons, 1985.

2. General Linear Models Books

Graybill, F. A. *Theory and Application of the Linear Model*. Boston: Duxbury Press, 1976.

Hocking, R. R. *The Analysis of Linear Models*. Monterey, Calif.: Brooks/Cole Publishing, 1985.

McCullagh, P., and J. A. Nelder. *Generalized Linear Models*. 2nd. ed. London: Chapman & Hall, 1989.

Searle, S. R. *Linear Models for Unbalanced Data*. New York: John Wiley & Sons, 1987.

3. Diagnostics and Model Building

Allen, D. M. "Mean Square Error of Prediction as a Criterion for Selecting Variables." *Technometrics* 13 (1971), pp. 469–75.

Anscombe, F. J., and J. W. Tukey. "The Examination and Analysis of Residuals." *Technometrics* 5 (1963), pp. 141–60.

Atkinson, A. C. "Two Graphical Displays for Outlying and Influential Observations in Regression." *Biometrika* 68 (1981), pp. 13–20.

Atkinson, A. C. *Plots, Transformations, and Regression*. Oxford: Clarendon Press, 1987.

Barnett, V., and T. Lewis. *Outliers in Statistical Data*. 3rd ed. New York: John Wiley & Sons, 1994.

Belsley, D. A. *Conditioning Diagnostics: Collinearity and Weak Data in Regression*. New York: John Wiley & Sons, 1991.

Belsley, D. A.; E. Kuh; and R. E. Welsch. *Regression Diagnostics: Identifying Influential Data and Sources of Collinearity*. New York: John Wiley & Sons, 1980.

Box, G. E. P., and D. R. Cox. "An Analysis of Transformations." *Journal of the Royal Statistical Society B* 26 (1964), pp. 211–43.

Box, G. E. P., and N. R. Draper. *Empirical Model-Building and Response Surfaces*. New York: John Wiley & Sons, 1987.

Box, G. E. P., and P. W. Tidwell. "Transformations of the Independent Variables." *Technometrics* 4 (1962), pp. 531–50.

Breiman, L., and P. Spector. "Submodel Selection and Evaluation in Regression. The *X*-Random Case." *International Statistical Review* 60 (1992), pp. 291–319.

Breusch, T. S., and A. R. Pagan. "A Simple Test for Heteroscedasticity and Random Coefficient Variation." *Econometrica* 47 (1979), pp. 1287–94.

Carroll, R. J., and D. Ruppert. *Transformation and Weighting in Regression*. New York: Chapman and Hall, 1988.

Chatterjee, S., and A. S. Hadi. *Sensitivity Analysis in Linear Regression*. New York: John Wiley & Sons, 1988.

Conover, W. J.; M. E. Johnson; and M. M. Johnson. "A Comparative Study of Tests for Homogeneity of Variances, with Applications to the Outer Continental Shelf Bidding Data." *Technometrics* 23 (1981), pp. 351–61.

Cook, R. D. "Exploring Partial Residual Plots." *Technometrics* 35 (1993), pp. 351–62.

Cook, R. D., and S. Weisberg. *Residuals and Influence in Regression*. London: Chapman & Hall, 1982.

Cook, R. D., and S. Weisberg. "Diagnostics for Heteroscedasticity in Regression." *Biometrika* 70 (1983), pp. 1–10.

Cook, R. D., and S. Weisberg. *An Introduction to Regression Graphics*. New York: John Wiley & Sons, 1994.

Cox, D. R. *Planning of Experiments*. New York: John Wiley & Sons, 1958.

Davidian, M., and R. J. Carroll. "Variance Function Estimation." *Journal of the American Statistical Association* 82 (1987), pp. 1079–91.

Durbin, J., and G. S. Watson. "Testing for Serial Correlation in Least Squares Regression. II." *Biometrika* 38 (1951), pp. 159–78.

Faraway, J. J. "On the Cost of Data Analysis." *Journal of Computational and Graphical Statistics* 1 (1992), pp. 213–29.

Flack, V. F., and P. C. Chang. "Frequency of Selecting Noise Variables in Subset-Regression Analysis: A Simulation Study." *The American Statistician* 41 (1987), pp. 84–86.

Freedman, D. A. "A Note on Screening Regression Equations." *The American Statistician* 37 (1983), pp. 152–55.

Hoaglin, D. C.; F. Mosteller; and J. W. Tukey. *Exploring Data Tables, Trends, and Shapes*. New York: John Wiley & Sons, 1985.

Hoaglin, D. C., and R. Welsch. "The Hat Matrix in Regression and ANOVA." *The American Statistician* 32 (1978), pp. 17–22.

Hocking, R. R. "The Analysis and Selection of Variables in Linear Regression." *Biometrics* 32 (1976), pp. 1–49.

Hoerl, A. E., and R. W. Kennard. "Ridge Regression: Applications to Nonorthogonal Problems." *Technometrics* 12 (1970), pp. 69–82.

Joglekar, G.; J. H. Schuenemeyer; and V. LaRiccia. "Lack-of-Fit Testing When Replicates Are Not Available." *The American Statistician* 43 (1989), pp. 135–43.

Levene, H. "Robust Tests for Equality of Variances," in *Contributions to Probability and Statistics*, ed. I. Olkin. Palo Alto, Calif.: Stanford University Press, 1960, pp. 278–92.

Lindsay, R. M., and A. S. C. Ehrenberg. "The Design of Replicated Studies." *The American Statistician* 47 (1993), pp. 217–28.

Looney, S. W., and T. R. Gulledge, Jr. "Use of the Correlation Coefficient with Normal Probability Plots." *The American Statistician* 39 (1985), pp. 75–79.

Mallows, C. L. "Some Comments on C_p." *Technometrics* 15 (1973), pp. 661–75.

Mansfield, E. R., and M. D. Conerly. "Diagnostic Value of Residual and Partial Residual Plots." *The American Statistician* 41 (1987), pp. 107–16.

Mantel, N. "Why Stepdown Procedures in Variable Selection." *Technometrics* 12 (1970), pp. 621–25.

Miller, A. J. *Subset Selection in Regression*. London: Chapman & Hall, 1990.

Pope, P. T., and J. T. Webster. "The Use of an F-Statistic in Stepwise Regression Procedures." *Technometrics* 14 (1972), pp. 327–40.

Rousseeuw, P. J., and A. M. Leroy. *Robust Regression and Outlier Detection*. New York: John Wiley & Sons, 1987.

Shapiro, S. S., and M. B. Wilk. "An Analysis of Variance Test for Normality (Complete Samples)." *Biometrika* 52 (1965), pp. 591–611.

Snee, R. D. "Validation of Regression Models: Methods and Examples." *Technometrics* 19 (1977), pp. 415–28.

Stone, M. "Cross-Validatory Choice and Assessment of Statistical Prediction." *Journal of the Royal Statistical Society B* 36 (1974), pp. 111–47.

Velleman, P. F., and D. C. Hoaglin. *Applications, Basics, and Computing of Exploratory Data Analysis*. Boston: Duxbury Press, 1981.

4. Statistical Computing

Dixon, W. J., chief editor. *BMDP Statistical Software Manual*. Revised edition. Berkeley, Calif.: University of California Press, 1992.

IMSL, Inc. *STAT/LIBRARY User's Manual, Version 1.1*. Houston: IMSL, 1989.

JMP IN User's Guide. Cary, N.C.: SAS Institute, Inc. 1993.

Kennedy, W. J., Jr., and J. E. Gentle. *Statistical Computing*. New York: Marcel Dekker, 1980.

LogXact. Cytel Software Corporation. Cambridge, Massachusetts, 1992.

MINITAB Reference Manual. PC version, Release 10. State College, Pa.: Minitab Inc., 1994.

NAG, The Generalized Linear Interactive Modelling (GLIM) System, Release 3.77. Downers Grove, Ill.: Numerical Algorithms Group, Inc., 1986.

SAS/GRAPH User's Guide. Release 6.03 edition. Cary, N.C.: SAS Institute, Inc., 1988.

SAS/STAT User's Guide. Release 6.03 edition. Cary, N.C.: SAS Institute, Inc., 1988.

SPSS-X User's Guide. 3rd ed. Chicago: SPSS Inc., 1987.

SYSTAT for Windows: Graphics. Version 5 edition. Evanston, Ill.: SYSTAT, Inc., 1992.

SYSTAT for Windows: Statistics. Version 5 edition. Evanston, Ill.: SYSTAT, Inc., 1992.

Tierney, L. *LISP-STAT: An Object-Oriented Environment for Statistical Computing and Dynamic Graphics*. New York: John Wiley & Sons, 1990.

5. Nonlinear Regression

Bates, D. M., and D. G. Watts. *Nonlinear Regression Analysis and Its Applications*. New York: John Wiley & Sons, 1988.

Begg, C. B., and R. Gray. "Calculation of Polytomous Logistic Regression Parameters Using Individualized Regressions." *Biometrika* 71 (1984), pp. 11–18.

Box, M. J. "Bias in Nonlinear Estimation." *Journal of the Royal Statistical Society B* 33 (1971), pp. 171–201.

Gallant, A. R. "Nonlinear Regression," *The American Statistician* 29 (1975), pp. 73–81.

Gallant, A. R. *Nonlinear Statistical Models*. New York: John Wiley & Sons, 1987.

Halperin, M.; W. C. Blackwelder; and J. I. Verter. "Estimation of the Multivariate Logistic Risk Function: A Comparison of Discriminant Function and Maximum Likelihood Approaches." *Journal of Chronic Diseases* 24 (1971), pp. 125–58.

Hartley, H. O. "The Modified Gauss-Newton Method for the Fitting of Non-linear Regression Functions by Least Squares." *Technometrics* 3 (1961), pp. 269–80.

Hosmer, D. W., and S. Lemeshow. "Goodness of Fit Tests for the Multiple Logistic Regression Model." *Communications in Statistics A* 9 (1980), pp. 1043–69.

Hosmer, D. W., and S. Lemeshow. *Applied Logistic Regression*. New York: John Wiley & Sons, 1989.

Hougaard, P. "The Appropriateness of the Asymptotic Distribution in a Nonlinear Regression Model in Relation to Curvature." *Journal of the Royal Statistical Society B* 47 (1985), pp. 103–14.

Kleinbaum, D. G.; L. L. Kupper; and L. E. Chambless. "Logistic Regression Analysis of Epidemiologic Data: Theory and Practice." *Communications in Statistics A* 11 (1982), pp. 485–547.

Landwehr, J. M.; D. Pregibon; and A. C. Shoemaker. "Graphical Methods for Assessing Logistic Regression Models (with discussion)." *Journal of the American Statistical Association* 79 (1984), pp. 61–83.

Marquardt, D. W. "An Algorithm for Least Squares Estimation of Non-linear Parameters." *Journal of the Society of Industrial and Applied Mathematics* 11 (1963), pp. 431–41.

Pregibon, D. "Logistic Regression Diagnostics." *Annals of Statistics* 9 (1981), pp. 705–24.

Prentice, R. L. "Use of the Logistic Model in Retrospective Studies." *Biometrics* 32 (1976), pp. 599–606.

Ratkowsky, D. A. *Nonlinear Regression Modeling*. New York: Marcel Dekker, 1983.

Ross, G. J. *Non–Linear Estimation*. New York: Springer-Verlag, 1990.

Seber, G. A. F., and C. J. Wild. *Nonlinear Regression*. New York: John Wiley & Sons, 1989.

Truett, J.; J. Cornfield; and W. Kannel. "A Multivariate Analysis of the Risk of Coronary Heart Disease in Framingham." *Journal of Chronic Diseases* 20 (1967), pp. 511–24.

6. Miscellaneous Regression Topics

Agresti, A. *Categorical Data Analysis*. New York: John Wiley & Sons, 1990.

Altman, N. S. "An Introduction to Kernel and Nearest-Neighbor Nonparametric Regression." *The American Statistician* 46 (1992), pp. 175–85.

Berkson, J. "Are There Two Regressions?" *Journal of the American Statistical Association* 45 (1950), pp. 164–80.

Birkes, D., and Y. Dodge. *Alternative Methods of Regression*. New York: John Wiley & Sons, 1993.

Bishop, Y. M. M.; S. E. Fienberg; and P. W. Holland. *Discrete Multivariate Analysis: Theory and Practice*. Cambridge, Mass.: MIT Press, 1975.

Box, G. E. P. "Use and Abuse of Regression." *Technometrics* 8 (1966), pp. 625–29.

Box, G. E. P., and G. M. Jenkins. *Time Series Analysis, Forecasting and Control*. Rev. ed. San Francisco: Holden-Day, 1976.

Breiman, L.; J. H. Friedman; R. A. Olshen; and C. J. Stone. *Classification and Regression Trees*. Belmont, Calif.: Wadsworth, 1984.

Cleveland, W. S. "Robust Locally Weighted Regression and Smoothing Scatterplots." *Journal of the American Statistical Association* 74 (1979), pp. 829–36.

Cleveland, W. S., and S. J. Devlin. "Locally Weighted Regression: An Approach to Regression Analysis by Local Fitting." *Journal of the American Statistical Association* 83 (1988), pp. 596–610.

Collett, D. *Modelling Binary Data*. London: Chapman & Hall, 1991.

Cox, D. R. "Notes on Some Aspects of Regression Analysis." *Journal of the Royal Statistical Society A* 131 (1968), pp. 265–79.

Cox, D. R. *The Analysis of Binary Data*. 2nd. ed. London: Chapman & Hall, 1989.

Efron, B. *The Jackknife, The Bootstrap, and Other Resampling Plans*. Philadelphia, Pennsylvania: Society for Industrial and Applied Mathematics, 1982.

Efron, B. "Better Bootstrap Confidence Intervals" (with discussion). *Journal of the American Statistical Association* 82 (1987), pp. 171–200.

Efron, B., and R. Tibshirani. "Bootstrap Methods for Standard Errors, Confidence Intervals, and Other Measures of Statistical Accuracy." *Statistical Science* 1 (1986), pp. 54–77.

Efron, B., and R. J. Tibshirani. *An Introduction to the Bootstrap*. New York: Chapman & Hall, 1993.

Eubank, R. L. *Spline Smoothing and Nonparametric Regression*. New York: Marcel Dekker, 1988.

Finney, D. J. *Probit Analysis*. 3rd ed. Cambridge, England: Cambridge University Press, 1971.

Frank, I. E., and J. H. Friedman. "A Statistical View of Some Chemometrics Regression Tools." *Technometrics* 35 (1993), pp. 109–35.

Friedman, J. H., and W. Stuetzle. "Projection Pursuit Regression." *Journal of the American Statistical Association* 76 (1981), pp. 817–23.

Fuller, W. A. *Measurement Error Models*. New York: John Wiley & Sons, 1987.

Gibbons, J. D. *Nonparametric Methods for Quantitative Analysis*. 2nd ed. Columbus, Ohio: American Sciences Press, 1985.

Graybill, F. A. *Matrices with Applications in Statistics*. 2nd ed. Belmont, Calif.: Wadsworth, 1982.

Haerdle, W. *Applied Nonparametric Regression*. Cambridge: Cambridge University Press, 1990.

Hastie, T., and C. Loader. "Local Regression: Automatic Kernel Carpentry" (with discussion). *Statistical Science* 8 (1993), pp. 120–43.

Hastie, T. J., and R. J. Tibshirani. *Generalized Additive Models*. New York: Chapman & Hall, 1990.

Hochberg, Y., and A. C. Tamhane. *Multiple Comparison Procedures*. John Wiley and Sons, 1987.

Hogg, R. V. "Statistical Robustness: One View of Its Use in Applications Today." *The American Statistician* 33 (1979), pp. 108–15.

Johnson, R. A., and D. W. Wichern. *Applied Multivariate Statistical Analysis*. 3rd ed. Englewood Cliffs, N. J.: Prentice-Hall, 1992.

Kendall, M. G., and J. D. Gibbons. *Rank Correlation Methods*. 5th ed. London: Charles Griffin, 1990.

Lachenbruch, P. A. *Discriminant Analysis*. New York: Hafner Press, 1975.

Miller, R. G., Jr. *Simultaneous Statistical Inference*. New York: Springer-Verlag, 1991.

Nelder, J. A., and R. W. M. Wedderburn. "Generalized Linear Models." *Journal of the Royal Statistical Society A* 135 (1972), pp. 370–84.

Pindyck, R. S., and D. L. Rubinfeld. *Econometric Models and Economic Forecasts*. 3rd ed. New York: McGraw-Hill, 1991.

Satterthwaite, F. E. "An Approximate Distribution of Estimates of Variance Components." *Biometrics Bulletin* 2 (1946), pp. 110–14.

Searle, S. R. *Matrix Algebra Useful for Statistics*. New York: John Wiley & Sons, 1982.

Snedecor, G. W., and W. G. Cochran. *Statistical Methods*. 8th ed. Ames, Iowa: Iowa State University Press, 1989.

Theil, H., and A. L. Nagar. "Testing the Independence of Regression Disturbances." *Journal of the American Statistical Association* 56 (1961), pp. 793–806.

7. *General Experimental Design and Analysis of Variance Books*

Atkinson, A. C., and A. N. Donev. *Optimum Experimental Designs*. Oxford: Clarendon Press, 1992.

Box, G. E. P., and N. R. Draper. *Empirical Model-Building and Response Surfaces*. New York: John Wiley & Sons, 1987.

Box, G. E. P.; W. G. Hunter; and J. S. Hunter. *Statistics for Experimenters*. New York: John Wiley & Sons, 1978.

Cochran, W. G., and G. M. Cox. *Experimental Designs*. 2nd ed. New York: John Wiley & Sons, 1957.

Cox, D. R. *Planning of Experiments*. New York: John Wiley & Sons, 1958.

Fisher, R. A. *The Design of Experiments*. 8th ed. New York: Hafner Publishing Co., 1966.

Hicks, C. R. *Fundamental Concepts in the Design of Experiments*. 3rd ed. New York: Holt, Rinehart and Winston, 1983.

Hinkelmann, K., and O. Kempthorne. *Design and Analysis of Experiments: Introduction to Experimental Design*. Vol. 1. New York: John Wiley & Sons, 1994.

Hoaglin, D. C.; F. Mosteller; and J. W. Tukey. *Fundamentals of Exploratory Analysis of Variance*. New York: John Wiley & Sons, 1991.

Kempthorne, O. *The Design and Analysis of Experiments*. New York: John Wiley & Sons, 1952.

Kirk, R. E. *Experimental Design: Procedures for the Behavioral Sciences*. 3rd. ed. Monterey Calif.: Brooks/Cole Publishing, 1995.

Krishnaiah, P. R. *Analysis of Variance*. New York: Elsevier, 1981.

Lorenzen, T. J., and V. L. Anderson. *Design of Experiments: A No-Name Approach*. New York: Marcel Dekker, 1993.

Mason, R. L.; R. F. Gunst; and J. L. Hess. *Statistical Design and Analysis of Experiments with Applications to Engineering and Science*. New York: John Wiley & Sons, 1989.

Maxwell, S. E. and H. D. Delaney. *Designing Experiments and Analyzing Data*. Pacific Grove, Calif.: Brooks/Cole Publishing, 1990.

Montgomery, D. C. *Design and Analysis of Experiments*. 3rd ed. New York: John Wiley & Sons, 1991.

Scheffé, H. *The Analysis of Variance*. New York: John Wiley & Sons, 1959.

Steel, R. G. D., and J. H. Torrie. *Principles and Procedures of Statistics*. 2nd ed. New York: McGraw-Hill, 1980.

Winer, B. J.; D. R. Brown; and K. M. Michels. *Statistical Principles in Experimental Design*. 3rd ed. New York: McGraw-Hill, 1991.

8. *Miscellaneous Experimental Design and Analysis of Variance Topics*

Burdick, R. K. "Using Confidence Intervals to Test Variance Components." *Journal of Quality Technology* 26 (1994), pp. 30–38.

Burdick, R. K., and F. A. Graybill. *Confidence Intervals on Variance Components*. New York: Marcel Dekker, 1992.

Gaylor, D. W., and F. N. Hopper. "Estimating the Degrees of Freedom for Linear Combinations of Mean Squares by Satterthwaite's Formula." *Technometrics* 11 (1969), pp. 691–706.

Greenhouse, S. W., and S. Geisser. "On Methods in the Analysis of Profile Data." *Psychometrika* 24 (1959), pp. 95–112.

Hocking, R. R. "A Discussion of the Two-Way Mixed Model." *The American Statistician* 27 (1973), pp. 148–52.

Holland, B., and Copenhaven, M. D. "An Improved Sequentially Rejective Bonferroni Test Procedure." *Biometrics* 43 (1987), pp. 417–23.

Holland, B., and Copenhaven, M. D. "Improved Bonferroni-Type Multiple Testing Procedures." *Psychological Bulletin* 104 (1988), pp. 145–49.

Holm, S. "A Simple Sequentially Rejective Multiple Test Procedure." *Scandinavian Journal of Statistics* 6 (1979), pp. 65–70.

Huynh, H., and L. Feldt. "Estimation of the Box Correction for Degrees of Freedom from Sample Data in the Randomized Block and Split-Plot Designs." *Journal of Educational Statistics* 1 (1976), pp. 69–82.

Johnson, D. E., and F. A. Graybill. "Estimation of σ^2 in a Two-Way Classification Model with Interaction." *Journal of the American Statistical Association* 67 (1972), pp. 388–94.

Koch, G. G.; J. D. Elashoff; and I. A. Amara. "Repeated Measurements–Design and Analysis." *In Encyclopedia of Statistical Sciences*, vol. 8, ed. S. Kotz and N. L. Johnson. New York: John Wiley & Sons, 1988, pp. 46–73.

Meyer, R. K., and C. J. Nachtsheim. "The Coordinate Exchange Algorithm for Constructing Exact Optimal Experimental Designs." *Technometrics* 37 (1995), pp. 60–69.

Nelson, L. S. "Exact Critical Values for Use With the Analysis of Means." *Journal of Quality Technology* 15 (1983) pp. 40–44.

Nelson, P. R. "Additional Uses for the Analysis of Means and Extended Tables of Critical Values." *Technometrics* 35 (1993), pp. 61–71.

Ott, E. R. "Analysis of Means—A Graphical Procedure." *Industrial Quality Control* 24 (1967), pp. 101–109.

Plackett, R. L., and J. P. Burman. "The Design of Optimum Multifactorial Experiments." *Biometrika* 33 (1946), pp. 305–25.

Puri, M. L., and P. K. Sen. *Nonparametric Methods in General Linear Models*. New York: John Wiley & Sons, 1985

Satterthwaite, F. E. "An Approximate Distribution of Estimates of Variance Components." *Biometrics Bulletin* 2 (1946), pp. 110–14.

Schwarz, C. J. "The Mixed-Model ANOVA: The Truth, the Computer Packages, the Books. Part I: Balanced Data." *The American Statistician* 47 (1993), pp. 48–59.

Searle, S. R.; G. Casella; and C. E. McCulloch. *Variance Components*. New York: John Wiley & Sons, 1992.

Shaffer, J. P. "Modified Sequentially Rejective Multiple Test Procedures." *Journal of the American Statistical Association* 81 (1986), pp. 826–31.

Snee, R. D. "Computer-Aided Design of Experiments—Some Practical Experiences." *Journal of Quality Technology* 17 (1985), pp. 222–36.

Ting, N.; R. K. Burdick; F. A. Graybill; S. Jeyaratnam; and T. F. C. Lu. "Confidence Intervals on Linear Combinations of Variance Components that are Unrestricted in Sign." *Journal of Statistical Computation and Simulation* 35 (1990), pp. 135–43.

Index

ABT Electronics Corporation, 765
Active explanatory factors, 1234
Addition theorem, 1314
Additive effects, 219
Additive factor effects, 802–905
Additive model for random block effects, 1101–1104
Addy, C. L., 1370
Adjusted coefficient of multiple determination, 230–231
Adjusted estimated treatment mean, 1026
Algorithms, 346–347
Aliased, 1251
Aligned dot plots, 758
Allocated codes, 480–471
All-possible regression selection procedure, 336–347
America's Smallest School: The Family, 439
Analysis of covariance, 1010–1013
  alternative to blocking, 1091
  correction for bias, 1033
  estimation of effects, 1024–1026, 1033–1034
  F tests, 1020–1024
  models
    appropriateness, 1018–1019
    multifactor, 1028–1032
    single-factor, 1014–1018
    two-factor, 1028–1029
  parallel slopes test, 1026–1027
  randomized block design, 1092–1094
  regression approach
    multifactor, 1028–1029
    single-factor, 1018
  uses of differences, 1032–1033
Analysis of means, 738
Analysis of variance, 663–665, 817–825, 932–938
  coefficient of multiple correlation, 231
  coefficient of multiple determination, 230–231
  computer programs, 671

Analysis of variance—*Cont.*
  concomitant variables, 1012–1013
  degrees of freedom, 72–73
  design of studies, 668–670
  empty cells, 902–905
  estimation of effects
    latin square design, 1215
    nested design, 1134–1138
    repeated measures design, 1172–1175, 1180–1181, 1189–1190
    single-factor, 716–742, 742–747
    three-factor, 938–942, 994
    two-factor, 852–869, 897–902, 905–915, 984–989
    two-level factorial design, 1237–1240
  expected mean squares, 74–76
  F tests, 76–78
    latin square design, 1214–1215
    nested design, 1131–1133
    power value charts, 1356–1360
    randomized block design, 1078–1081, 1094–1097, 1094–1097
    for regression relation, 229–230
    repeated measures design, 1167–1171, 1175–1176, 1178–1180, 1186–1188
    single-factor, 690–692, 696, 723, 777–781, 1053–1057
    three-factor, 935–937, 991–993
    two-factor, 827–832, 981–983
    two-level factorial design, 1240
  mean squares, 73, 228–229
  no replications and/or some interactions equal zero, 1381–1382
  partitioning
    latin square design, 1213–1214
    nested design, 1127–1133
    randomized block design, 1078–1079, 1078–1081, 1086–1088
    repeated measures design, 1167–1171, 1175–1176, 1178–1180, 1186–1188

Analysis of variance—*Cont.*
  partitioning—*Cont.*
    single-factor, 681–685
    three-factor, 934–935
    two-factor, 820–824
  partition of sum of squares, 70–72
  planning of sample size
    estimation approach, 1060–1063
    to find "best" treatment, 1063–1064
    latin square design, 1218–1219
    multifactor studies, 1056–1057, 1060
    power approach, 1052–1060
    randomized block design, 1088–1091
    single-factor, 1053–1055, 1061–1062, 1064
    tables, 1261–1363
    two-factor, 1063
  regression approach
    latin square design, 1220–1221
    randomized block design, 1091–1092, 1097–1100
    repeated measures design, 1194
    single-factor, 696–701
    three-factor, 948–950
    two-factor, 832–836, 891–897
  rule for finding expected mean squares, 1377–1381
  rule for finding sums of squares and degrees of freedom, 1374–1376
  statistical computing packages, 915
  sums of squares, 205–207, 228–229
  unequal sample sizes, 889–902, 948–951, 994–1001, 1062
  unequal treatment importance, 905–915
Analysis of variance models, 468, 663–665
  diagnosis of departures from, 759–763
  effects of departures from model, 776–777
  fitting of, 676–680
  meaning of model elements, 799–812
  no-interaction model, 875–882
  randomized block design, 1101–1105
  residual analysis, 942

Analysis of variance models—*Cont.*
  rule for model development, 1373–1374
  single-factor
    model I, 671–676, 683–696, 693–696
    model II, 958–962, 975–976
    repeated measures design, 1166–1176
    residual analysis for aptness, 756–763
    subsampling, 1141–1148
    weighted least squares, 768–772
  tests for constancy of error variance, 763–768
  three-factor, 942–948
    fitting of model, 933–934
    model I, 924–932
    model II, 990
    model III, 991
    partially nested design, 1149–1155
    residual analysis for appropriateness, 938
  transformations of response variables, 772–776
  treatment means comparisons, 859–865
  two-factor
    crossed, 1382–1384
    estimation of effects, 851–869
    fitting of model, 818–820
    model I, 812–917
    model II, 976–977
    model III, 978–980
    pooling sums of squares, 837
    repeated measures design, 1176–1194
    residual analysis, 825–827
    strategy for analysis, 849–850
    Tukey test for additivity, 882–885
  two-level factorial design, 1235–1237
  two-level fractional factorial design, 1249–1264
  unbalanced nested design, 1138–1141
  unequal sample sizes, 889–902
  uses of, 670–671
Analysis of variance table, 73–74, 116–117, 121–124, 229, 266–267, 685, 825
ANOVA; *see* Analysis of variance
ANOVA table; *see* Analysis of variance table
Antagonistic interaction effect, 311
A-optimality, 1295
Apex Enterprises, 958–962
Arc sine transformation, 773
Asymptotic normality, 55
Autocorrelation, 497–500
  Durbin-Watson test, 504–507
  parameters, 501
  remedial measures, 507–516
Autoregressive error model; *see* First-order autoregressive error model
Axial points, 1282

Backward elimination selection procedure, 353
Backward stepwise selection procedure, 585–586
Balanced nested design, 1121–1124
Bates, D. M., 550
Bechhofer procedure, 1063
Berkson, J., 166, 171
Berkson model, 166

Bernoulli random variables, 573
"Best" subsets algorithms, 346–347
"Best" treatment, 1063–1064
Bias correction, 1033
Biased estimation, 354, 411
Bilinear interaction term, 309
Binary response variable, 567–570
Binary variables, 457; *see also* Indicator variables
Bisquare weight function, 419
Bivariate normal distribution, 632–626
Blocking, 1049
  covariance analysis alternative, 1091
  criteria for, 1073–1074
Blocks, 1072
BMDP, 685–686, 825, 828, 915
BMDP3V, 999
Bonferroni inequality, 153–154, 1240
Bonferroni joint estimation procedure, 294, 374
  analysis of covariance, 1025, 1029
  confidence coefficient, 153–155
  latin square design, 1215
  logistic regression, 601
  mean responses, 157–158, 234
  multiple pairwise testing, 1096–1097
  nested design, 1135, 1136–1137
  nonlinear regression, 554
  prediction of new observations, 158–159, 235
  randomized block design, 1084
  regression coefficients, 233
  repeated measures design, 1180
  single-factor analysis of variance, 736–738
  three-factor analysis of variance, 939, 940, 942, 998
  two-factor analysis of variance, 854, 855, 860
Bootstrapping, 429–434, 551, 999–1001
Bounded influence regression methods, 424
Box, G. E. P., 241
Box, M. J., 551
Box-Behnken designs, 1289
Box-Cox transformation, 132–134, 141, 240–241, 774–775
Box plots, 96, 103, 106, 762
Breiman, L., 354
Breusch-Pagan test, 110, 115, 141–142, 239
Brushing, 238

Calibration problem, 169
Candidate list, 1291
Carryover effect, 1165, 1228
Case, 5
Castle Bakery Company, 817–823
Causality, 9–10
Cell means model, 672–673, 696, 814–815, 818, 930–931
Centering, 278
Center point, 1247, 1282
Center point replications, 1247–1249
Central composite designs, 1281–1289
Central limit theorem, 1319
Centroid, 376
Changeover design, 1225
Cheng, C., 483

Chi-square goodness of fit test, 592–594
Classification factors, 667–668
Cleveland, W. S., 136, 143, 425
Close-to-linear nonlinear regression estimates, 551
Cochran, W. G., 1047
Cochrane-Orcutt procedure, 509–512
Cochran's theorem, 76–77, 690, 829
Coefficient of determination, 81, 640
Coefficient of multiple correlation, 231
Coefficient of multiple determination, 230–231
Coefficient of partial correlation, 276, 648–650
Coefficient of partial determination, 274–276
Coefficient of simple correlation, 231
Coefficient of multiple correlation, 646–647
Coefficient of multiple determination, 646–647
Column sum of squares, 1213
Column vector, 178
Complementary events, 1314
Complementary log-log transformation, 573
Complete block design, 1207
Complete factorial study, 797
Completely randomized design, 15
Components of variance model, 961
Compound symmetry, 1102–1103
Concomitant variables, 1012–1013
Conditional effects plot, 310, 1299
Conditional probability distributions, 636–639
Confidence band, for regression line, 67–69
Confidence coefficient, 50, 54, 59–60, 724
  Bonferroni procedure, 153–155
  family, 152–153
  and risk of errors, 55
Confidence intervals, bootstrap, 430
Confirmatory experiments, 1234
Confounding, 1250–1252
  worst-case degree of, 1258
Confounding scheme, 1251
Consistent estimator, 1321
Constancy of error variance, tests for, 110, 112–115, 239
Constrained regression model, 315–316
Contour diagram, 634–636, 1297–1299
Contrast, 720–721
Controlled experiments, 329, 331
Control treatment, 669
Control variables, 329, 1012
Cook's distance measure, 360–382, 383
Corner points, 1282
Correlation coefficient, 633, 1317
  inferences, 640–645
  misunderstandings, 82–83
  table of critical values, 1348
  table of z' transformation, 1351
Correlation matrix of transformed variables, 279–280
Correlation models
  bivariate normal distribution, 632–636
  compared to regression models, 631–632
  conditional probability distributions, 636–639
  multivariate normal distribution, 645–650
  regression analysis, 639–640
Correlation operator, 1317
Correlation test for normality, 111, 238–239
Correlation transformation, 277, 278–279

Covariance, 1316–1317; *see also* Variance-covariance matrix

Covariance analysis, *see* Analysis of covariance

Covariance models, 468; *see also* Analysis of covariance

Covariance operator, 1316

Covariates, 1012

Cox, D. R., 170, 171, 867

Cox, G. M., 1047

C_p criterion, 341–345

Crossed factor, 1121–1124

Crossed two-factor study, 1382–1384

Crossed-nested design, 1149

Crossover designs, 1225–1227

Cross-validation, 437

Cube plot, 942

Curvilinear relationship, 4

Cutoff point, 605–606

Dantes, H. G., 1370

Data collection, 327–330, 435–436

Data sets, 1365–1372

Data snooping, 724–725

Data splitting, 437

Decision rule, 77

Defining relation, 1252–1265

Degree of linear association, 80–84

Degrees of freedom, 72–73, 684, 823–824, 935, 1129, 1320–1321

rule for finding, 1374–1376

Deleted residuals, 372–373

Density function, 997–998

of normal random variable, 1319

Dependent variables, 3, 4–5

Design criterion, 1291

Design generators, 1254

Design matrix, 1237

Design of experiments, 1045–1049

Design resolution, 1257–1258

Determinant criterion, 1292–1293

Determinant of matrix, 191

Deviance goodness of fit test, 595

Deviance residual, 595–597

Devlin, S. J., 525

DFBETAS, 382–383

DFFITS, 379–380

Diagnostic plots, 1081–1083

for predictor variables, 95–96

for residuals, 98–110

Diagonal matrix, 186–187

Dichotomous response; *see* Binary response variable

Direct numerical search, 539–546

Discriminant analysis, 607

DISEASE data set, 1370

Disordinal interaction, 462

Disturbances, 498

Dixon, W. J., 35

D-optimal design, 1292

Dorle Exterior Trim, 1302

Dot plots, 95–96, 103, 106, 758, 762

Dot plots of residuals, 760

Double-blind study, 1046

Double crossover design, 1228

Double cross-validation procedure, 439

Drawbaugh, R. B., 1372

Drug effect experiment data set, 1371–1372

Dummy variables, 13, 457; *see also* Indicator variables

Durbin, J., 505

Durbin-Watson test, 110, 504–507, 509–510

table of test bounds, 1349–1350

Educational Testing Service, 439

Efron, B., 429

Eigenvalues, 1300

Empty cells, 902–905

Error mean square, 73, 123

Error sum of squares, 28, 71, 123, 682, 821

in general linear test, 79

Error terms, 10–14, 761–762, 777

autocorrelated, 497–500

constancy of variance tests, 112–115

nonindependence of, 104–105, 125

nonnormality, 106–108, 126

Error terms variance, 27–29, 549

Error variability reduction, 1010–1012

Error variance, 400–409, 760, 776–777

nonconstancy, 102–103, 125

Estimates; *see* Tests

Estimation, 716–717

Estimation approach to sample size planning, 1060–1063

Estimators, 1321–1322

Exact F test, 991–992

Exchange algorithms, 1295

Expectation operator, 1315

Expected mean squares, 685–689, 824–825, 981–982

rule for finding, 1377–1381

Expected value, of random variable, 1315

Experimental data, 15

factor level means, 675–676

Experimental designs, 666

blocking, 1049

completely randomized design, 15

crossover, 1225–1227

double crossover, 1228

exploratory, 1234

factorial experiment, 1046

latin square, 1207–1210

local control, 1049

nested, 1121–1124

randomization, 1047–1048

randomization tests, 1050–1052

randomized block, 1072–1075

repeated measures, 1164–1166

replication, 1047

response surface methodology, 1280–1281

screening designs, 1264–1266

sequential search for optimal conditions, 1303–1305

split-plot design, 1194–1196

and statistics, 1046–1049

two-level factorial design, 1235–1237

two-level fractional factorial design, 1249–1250

Experimental error sums of squares, 1143

Experimental factors, 667–668

Experimental units, 15, 1073–1074, 1148

Explanatory variables, 4–5, 331–333

omission of, 762

Exponential family of probability distributions, 615

Exponential regression function, 125

Exponential regression model, 532–533

Externally studentized residuals, 374

Extra sums of squares, 260–267

effects of multicollinearity, 291–292

Face-centered design, 1286

Factor, 666

Factor A main effects, 829–830

Factor A sum of squares, 822

Factor B main effects, 830

Factor B sum of squares, 822

Factor effects model, 693–696, 815–817, 819–820, 931–932

Factorial experiments, 1046

Factor level, 666–667

Factor level means, 675–676, 690–692, 696, 800–801

estimation, 851–856

estimation and testing, 716–742

plots of, 712–716

weighted least squares estimation, 768–772

Factors; *see also* Control variables

classification, 667–668

experimental, 667–668

qualitative, 668

quantitative, 668

Family

of conclusions, 947

of estimates, 152–153

of tests, 724, 831, 937

Family confidence coefficient, 152–153

Far-from-linear nonlinear regression estimates, 551

F distribution, 1321

Scheffé procedure, 158–159

table of percentiles, 1339–1345

First differences procedure, 514–516

First-order autoregressive error model, 501–504

Cochrane-Orcutt procedure, 509–512

Durbin-Watson test, 504–507

first differences procedure, 514–516

forecasting with, 517–520

Hildreth-Lu procedure, 512–514

First-order coefficient, 649

First-order interactions, 926

First-order regression model, 10, 218–221, 465–468; *see also* Regression models

Fisher, R. A. 1047

Fisher Company, 1286

Fisher z transformation, 642, 644

Fitted logit response function, 575

Fitted values, 202–203, 227–228, 293–294, 379–382, 679, 818, 933

total mean square error, 341–342

Fitting, 300–301

Fixed effects contrasts, 987–988

Fixed X sampling, 429

Folding over, 1265

Foldover design, 1265

Forecasting with autoregressive error model, 517–520

Forward selection procedure, 352

Forward stepwise regression, 347–352

Fraction, 1234
Fractional factorial designs, 797, 1234
Friedman test, 1096
F test
    for analysis of variance, 76–78
    equivalence of *t* test, 78
    for lack of fit, 115–124, 239–240
    nonparametric rank, 777–781
    for regression relation, 229–230
Full model, 78–79, 118–119, 692, 701
Functional relation, 3–4

Galton, Francis, 6
Gauss-Markov theorem, 20, 47, 880
Gauss-Newton method, 539–546
Generalized interaction, 1256
Generalized least squares, 409
Generalized randomized block design,
    1106–1108
General linear regression models, 221–225,
    531–532, 614–615
General linear test, 78–80
    approach, 907–910
    for lack of fit, 118–124
Goodness of fit tests, 591–595
G-optimality, 1295
Gulledge, T. R., Jr., 111, 143, 1348

Half-fraction design, 1254
Half-normal probability plot, 596–598, 1247
Hartley test, 764–766, 1189
Hat matrix, 203, 369–372
    leverage values, 375–378
Heffner, T. G., 1372
Hessian matrix, 599–600, 998
Heteroscedasticity, 407–408
Hierarchical fitting, 300–301
Hildreth-Lu procedure, 512–514
Histograms, 106, 760, 762
Hochberg, Y., 742
Holm simultaneous testing procedure, 739–742,
    853
Homoscedasticity, 407
Honestly significant difference tests, 732
Hougaard, P., 551
H statistic, 764
    table of percentiles, 1355
Huber weight function, 419
Hyperplane, 220

IC Technologies, 1295–1296
Idempotent matrix, 203
Identity matrix, 186–187
Important interactions, 808–809, 940–941
Incomplete block design, 1207
    two-level factorial, 1266–1269
Independent random variables, 1318
Independent samples, 1326–1328
Independent variables, 3, 4–5
Index of response, 1032
Index plot, 596
Indicator variables, 455–457
    versus allocated codes, 480–481
    alternative codings, 481–482

Indicator variables—*Cont.*
    in analysis of variance, 665
    for comparing regression functions,
        468–474
    interaction effects, 461–464
    in piecewise linear regressions, 474–478
    versus quantitative variables, 481
    time series applications, 479
Individual outcome, 61–62
Individual test, 724
Instrumental variables, 165, 165
Interaction effect coefficient, 299
Interaction effects, 461–464
    with indicator variables, 461–464
    interference/antagonistic, 311
    reinforcement type, 311
Interaction model for random block effects,
    1104–1105
Interaction regression models, 308–315
Interactions, 798, 806
    in analysis of variance, 805–812
    generalized, 1256
    tests for, 827–829
    three-factor, 926–930, 940–941
    two-factor, 859–865
    two-level factorial design, 1242–1244
Interaction sum of squares, 822
Interaction sum of squares between blocks and
    treatments, 1078–1079
Interaction sum of squares between treatments
    and subjects, 1167
Intercorrelation; *see* Multicollinearity
Interference interaction effect, 311
Internally studentized residuals, 372
Intraclass correlation coefficient, 963
Intrinsically linear response functions, 534–535
Inverse of matrix, 189–193
Inverse predictions, 167–169, 167–169
Inverse regression, 169, 169
Iowa Aluminum Corporation, 1259–1264
IRLS robust regression, 418–420
Irregular experimental regions, 1290
Iteratively reweighted least squares, 405

Joint density function, 997–998
Joint estimation
    Bonferroni joint confidence intervals,
        153–155
    need for, 152–153
Joint probability function, 1316

Kendall's coefficient of concordance, 1176
Kendall's *τ*, 654
Kenton Food Company, 676–677
Kimball inequality, 831–832, 937, 942, 1240
Kolmogorov-Smirnov test, 111
Koopman, J. S., 1370
Kruskal-Wallis rank test, 779
Kurtosis, 776

Lack of fit mean square, 120
Lack of fit test, 115–124, 239–240, 745–747,
    1247–1249

LAR (least absolute residuals) regression,
    417–418
Large-sample theory, 549–552
Latent explanatory variables, 332
Latin square changeover design, 1225
Latin square design, 1207–1210
    ANOVA partitioning, 1213–1214
    crossover design, 1225–1227
    double crossover design, 1228
    efficiency, 1218–1219
    estimation of effects, 1215
    factorial treatment, 1217
    fitting of model, 1213
    F test, 1214–1215
    missing observations, 1221
    model, 1211–1213
    notation, 1212
    planning of sample sizes, 1218–1219
    random blocking effects, 1217
    randomization, 1210
    regression approach, 1220–1221
    repeated measures, 1225–1228
    replications, 1218
    replications within cells, 1221–1224
    residual analysis, 1215
    rule modification, 1382
    sums of squares, 1214–1215
    table, 1364
    Tukey test for additivity, 1216–1217
    use of independent squares, 1227–1228
    use of several squares, 1224–1225
Learning curve models, 555–559
Least squares estimation, 160, 1322; *see also*
    Weighted least squares
    criterion, 17, 21
    generalized, 409
    and maximum likelihood estimation, 34–35
    multiple regression, 227
    randomized block design, 1078
    simple linear regression, 200–202
    single-factor analysis of variance, 678–680
    standardized regression coefficients,
        281–284
    three-factor analysis of variance, 933–934
    two-factor analysis of variance, 818–820,
        910–911
Levene test; *see* Modified Levene test
Leverage, 376
Likelihood function, 32–35, 1322
    logistic regression, 573–574
Likelihood ratio test, 586, 590
Likelihood value, 31
Lilliefors test, 111
Linear-by-linear interaction term, 309
Linear combination of factor level means, 723
Linear dependence, 188–189
Linear effect coefficient, 297
Linear function of normal random variable,
    1319
Linearity, test for, 115–124
Linearization method; *see* Gauss-Newton
    method
Linear model, 224
    ANOVA model I, 674–675
Linear predictor, 615
Linear regression functions, 8
Line plot of estimated factor level means, 713

Link function, 615
LMS (least median of squares) regression, 418
Local control, 1049
Locally weighted regression scatter plot smoothing, 136–137
Loess method, 136–137, 425–426
Logistic regression, polytomous, 608–609
Logistic regression models, 533–534; *see also* Regression models
Logistic response functions, 572–573
Logit mean response, 571
Logit response function, 571
Logit transformation, 571
Looney, S. W., 111, 143, 1348

Main effects, 801, 946–947
Marginal probability function, 1316
Marquardt algorithm, 547
Matrix
  addition, 180–182
  with all elements unity, 187–188
  basic theorems, 194
  definition, 176–178
  determinant, 191
  diagonal, 186–187
  dimension, 176
  elements, 176–177
  equality of two, 179–180
  hat, 203, 369–372, 375–378
  Hessian, 599–600
  idempotent, 203
  identity, 186–187
  inverse, 189–193
  linear dependence, 188–189
  multiplication by matrix, 183–185
  multiplication by scalar, 182
  nonsingular, 190
  of quadratic form, 206–207
  random, 194–197
  rank, 189
  scalar, 187
  scatter plot, 236–238
  simple linear regression model, 198–199
  singular, 190
  square, 178
  subtraction, 180–182
  symmetric, 186
  transpose, 178–179
  vector, 178
  zero vector, 188
Maximum likelihood estimation, 1322
  logistic regression, 574–577
  mixed ANOVA models, 996–1001
  Poisson regression model, 610–611
  of regression parameters, 30–35
  single-factor analysis of variance, 678–680
Mean
  prediction of, 66–67
  of residuals, 97
Mean absolute deviation, 420
Mean of the distribution, 61–62
Mean response
  interval estimation, 56–57
  logistic regression
    interval estimation, 603–604
    point estimation, 602–605

Mean response—*Cont.*
  multiple regression estimation, 233–235
  point estimation, 23–25
  simple linear interval estimation, 209–210
  simultaneous estimation, 155–158
Mean squared error
  regression models, 411
  total, of n fitted values, 341–342
Mean square prediction error, 435–436
Mean squares, 27, 73, 685–685, 824, 935
  analysis of variance, 228–229
  expected, 74
Measurement bias, 1046
Measurement errors in observation, 164–166
Method of steepest descent, 547
Miller, R. G., Jr., 742
Minimax, 1299
Minimum L_1-norm regression, 417–418
Minimum variance estimator, 1322
MINITAB, 22–23, 50–51, 52, 54, 96, 98–99, 758, 915, 1151
MINITAB Fractional Factorial procedure, 1260–1263
Minnesota Department of Transportation, 483–489
Mixed factor effects model, 978–980
MLS procedure, 973–975
Model-building set, 437
Modified large sample procedure; *see* MLS procedure
Modified Levene test, 110, 112–114, 239, 766–767, 1189
Moving average method, 135
Multicollinearity, 285–295
  detection of, 385–388
  remedial measures, 410–416
  ridge regression, 411–416
Multifactor covariance analysis, 1028–1032
Multifactor studies, 667, 795–797
  advantages of, 797–799
  planning of sample sizes, 1056–1057, 1060
  unequal sample sizes, 948–951
Multiple comparison procedures, 725–738, 988
Multiple logistic regression, prediction of new observation, 605–608
Multiple pairwise comparisons, 779–780, 853–854, 859–865
Multiple regression; *see* Mean response, Prediction of new observation, Regression coefficients, Regression function, *and* Regression models
Multiplication theorem, 1314
Multivariate normal distribution, 645–650

Nested design, 1121–1124
  balanced, 1121–1124
  residual analysis, 1133–1134
  rule for model development, 1124–1125
  subsampling, 1141–1149
  three-factor partially nested, 1149–1155
  two-factor
    ANOVA partitioning, 1127–1133
    estimation of effects, 1134–1138
    fitting of model, 1127
    F test, 1131–1133

Nested design—*Cont.*
  two-factor—*Cont.*
    model, 1124–1126
    residual analysis, 1133–1134
    unbalanced, 1138–1141
Nested factor, 1121–1124
Noncentral F distribution, 690
Noncentrality parameter, 56, 1054
Nonconstant error variance, 569–570, 760
Nonindependence of error terms, 761–762, 777
Nonindependent residuals, 97
No-interaction model, 875–882
Nonlinear regression, transformations for, 126–129
Nonlinear regression models, 532–536; *see also* Regression models
Nonnormal error terms, 569
Nonnormality, 776
  transformations for, 129–132
Nonnormality of error terms, 762–763
Nonparametric rank F test, 777–781, 1094–1097
Nonparametric regression, 425–428
Nonparametric regression curves, 135
Nonsingular matrix, 190
Nonstandard models, 1290–1291
Nonstandard sample sizes, 1291
Nontransformable interactions, 809–811
Normal equations, 19–20
  nonlinear regression, 538–539
Normal equations calculations, 277
Normal error regression model, 29–35, 637–638
  confidence band for regression line, 67–69
  inferences concerning β_0, 53–56
  sampling distribution of b_1, 45–50
  X random, 85–86
Normality
  assessing, 108
  correlation test for, 111
  tests for, 111
Normal population
  one population mean, 1323–1325
  population variance, 1328–1330
  two population means, 1326–1328
  two population variances, 1330–1332
Normal probability distribution, 1319–1321
Normal probability plot, 106–108, 762, 1246
  of estimated factor level means, 713–716
  of residuals, 759
Numerator degrees of freedom, 1321

Observational data, 14–15
Observational studies, 329–330, 331–333, 353–354, 666
  factor level means, 675
Observation units, 1148
Observed value, 23
Odds ratio, 577
One-sided test, 52–53
Optimal response surface design, 1289–1297
Optimum conditions, 1303–1305
Order effect, 1165
Order position sum of squares, 1226
Ordinal interaction, 462
Orthogonal coding, 1239
Orthogonal decomposition, 822

Orthogonality, 1286–1287
Orthogonally blocked design, 1289
Orthogonal polynomials, 308
Ott, E. R., 738
Outliers, 103–104, 126
  detection of, 762
  tests for, 110–111, 374–375
Outlying cases, 368–369, 416–417
Overall F test, 269, 271–272

Paircd comparison plot, 727
Paired observations, 1328
Pairwise comparison, 718, 725, 779–780,
    853–854, 859–865, 900–901
Pareto plot, 1244–1245
Partial deviance test, 587
Partial F test, 269, 272–273
Partially hierarchical nested design, 1149
Partially nested design, 1149
Partial regression coefficients, 219
Partial regression plots, 361–368
Path of steepest ascent/descent, 1303
Pattern sum of squares, 1226
Pearson product-moment correlation
    cocfficient, 641, 651
Pecos Foods Corporation, 1241–1247
Piecewise linear regression, 474–478
Plackett-Burman designs, 1265–1266
Plots of estimated factor level means, 712–716
Plots of residuals against fitted values, 760
Plutonium measurement, 138–143
Point clouds, 238
Point estimators, 19, 23–25, 27–29, 603,
    985 986
Poisson regression model, 609–614
Polynomial regression model, 223, 296–308
Polytomous logistic regression, 608–609
Pooling sums of squares, 837
Population of consumers, 906
Power approach to sample planning, 1052–
    1060
Power of tests
  latin square design, 1218
  planning of sample size, 1053–1054
  randomized block design, 1088–1089
Prediction error rate, 608
Prediction interval, 63–66
Prediction of mean, 66–67
Prediction of new observation
  logistic regression, 605–608
  multiple regression, 235–236
  simple linear regression, 61–67, 210
Prediction set, 437
Predictor variables, 7–8
  in analysis of variance, 663–665
  diagnostics, 95–96
  measurement errors, 164–166
  multicollinearity, 285–295
  multiple regression, 217–221, 241–251
  omission of important, 108–110, 126
  partial regression plots, 361–368
  polynomial regression, 296–300
  qualitative, 222–223, 455–460
$PRESS_p$ criterion, 345–346
Primary variables, 329
Principal components regression, 410–411

Probability distribution
  departures from normality, 54–55
  in single-factor study, 672
  of Y, 56–57
Probability theorems, 1314
Probit transformation, 572
Product operator, 1314
Projection property, 1258
Proportionality constant, 403
Pseudo F test statistic, 992–993
Pure error estimate, 1248
Pure error mean square, 120
Pure error sum of squares, 118–119
Puri, M. L., 780

Quadratic effect coefficient, 297
Quadratic forms, 206–207
Quadratic linear regression model, 224
Quadratic regression function, 8, 125
Quadratic response function, 297, 308, 744–747
Qualitative factor, 668
Qualitative predictor variables, 222–223,
    455–460, 465–468
  in analysis of variance, 664–665
Quantitative factor, 668, 742–747
Quantitative predictor variables, in analysis of
    variance, 664–665
Quantitative variables, 481
Quarter-fraction design, 1255–1257
Quasi F test statistic, 992–993

R_a^2 criterion, 339–341
R_p^2 criterion, 338–339
Random ANOVA model, 959
Random cell means model, 959–962
Random factor effects model, 975
Randomization, 1047–1048, 1075, 1165–1166
  latin square design, 1210
Randomization distribution, 1050–1051
Randomization tests, 1050–1052
Randomized block design, 1072–1075
  analysis of covariance, 1092–1094
  ANOVA partitioning, 1078–1079,
    1078–1081, 1086–1088
  appropriateness of model, 1081–1084
  diagnostic plots, 1081–1083
  estimation of effects, 1084–1086
  factorial treatments, 1086–1088
  fitting of model, 1078
  F test, 1079–1081, 1094–1097
  generalized design, 1106–1108
  missing observations, 1097–1100
  models, 1075–1078, 1101–1105
  nonparametric rank F test, 1094–1097
  planning of sample sizes, 1088–1091
  random block effects, 1100–1106
  rank data, 1094–1097
  regression approach, 1091–1092,
    1093–1094, 1097–1100
  residual analysis, 1081–1083
  subsampling, 1384–1386
  Tukey test for additivity, 1083–1084
  use of more than one blocking variable,
    1108–1109
Randomized complete block design, 1073

Random matrix, 194–197
Randomness tests, 110
Random variables, 1315–1319
Random vector, 194–197
Random X sampling, 430
Rank correlation procedure, 651
Rank of matrix, 189
Reduced model, 79, 692, 701
Reflection method, 430
Regression, 6
  and causality, 9–10
Regression analysis, 3
  analysis of variance approach, 69–78
  approach to analysis of variance models,
    single-factor, 696–701
  compared to analysis of variance, 663–665
  completely randomized design, 15
  computer calculations, 10
  considerations in applying, 84–85
  in correlation models, 629–640
  experimental data, 15
  inferences concerning β_1, 44–53
  observational data, 14–15
  overview of steps, 13–17
  transformations of variables, 126–134
  uses, 9
Regression approach
  to analysis of covariance, 1018, 1028–1029
  to analysis of variance models
    three-factor, 948–950
    two-factor, 832–836, 891–897
  to latin square design, 1220–1221
  to randomized block design, 1091–1092,
    1093–1094, 1097–1100
  to repeated measures design, 1194
Regression coefficients, 382–383
  bootstrapping, 429–433
  constrained regression, 315–316
  effects of multicollinearity, 291
  interaction regression, 309–311
  interpretation for indicator variables, 457,
    461–462
  lack of comparability, 277–278
  multiple regression, 218–220
    interval estimation, 232, 233–234
    joint inferences, 233
    lcast squarcs cstimation, 227
    tests concerning, 232, 268–274
    variance-covariance matrix of, 231–233
  partial, 219
  simple linear regression, 12–13
    interval estimation, 50–51, 54, 56–61,
      59–60
    least squares estimation, 200–202
    tests for, 51–53, 55–56, 76–78
    variance-covariance matrix of, 208–
      209
  standardized, 281–284
Regression curve, 7
Regression function, 7
  constraints, 570
  discontinuity in, 478
  estimation, 17–27
  exploration of shape, 135–143
  exponential, 125
  hyperplane, 220
  indicator variables for comparing, 468–474

Regression function—*Cont.*
  interaction models, 311–312
  intrinsically linear, 534–535
  nonlinearity, 99–102, 125
  through origin, 159–163
  outlying cases, 368–369
  polynomial regression, 301
  quadratic, 125
  simple logistic, 570–573
  test for fit, 239–240
  test for lack of fit, 115–124
  test for regression relation, 229–230
Regression line, confidence band, 67–69
Regression mean square, 73
Regression models
  autocorrelation problems, 497–500
  basic concepts, 6–8
  with binary response variable, 567–570
  bootstrapping, 429–434
  building, 327–336, 353–354
  building process diagnostics, 361–392
  choice of levels, 169–170
  coefficient of correlation, 82
  coefficient of determination, 81
  compared to correlation models, 631–632
  constrained regression, 315–316
  construction of, 8–9
  degree of linear association, 80–84
  effect of measurement errors, 164–166
  estimation of error terms, 27–29
  first-order autoregressive, 501–504
  general linear, 118–124, 221–226, 531–532,
    614–615
  interaction, 308–315
  inverse predictions, 167–169
  logistic regression
    building, 585–590
    mean response, 602–605
    multiple, 580–585
    parameters, 599–602
    polytomous, 608–609
    simple, 573–580
    tests for, 590–599
  multiple regression, 217–225
    ANOVA table, 229
    diagnostics, 236–240
    extra sum of squares, 260–266
    general model, 221–225
    interaction effects, 224
    loess method, 425–426
    in matrix terms, 225–226
    multicollinearity effects, 285–295
    remedial measures, 240–241
    standardized, 277–285
    two predictor variables, 241–251
  nonlinear regression
    building, 547–548
    Gauss-Newton method, 539–546
    learning curve, 555–559
    least squares estimation, 536–547
    logistic, 573–609
    parameters, 548–555
    Poisson, 609–614
  normal error, X random, 85–86
  normal error terms, 29–35
  origin, 6
  overview of remedial measures, 124–126

Regression models—*Cont.*
  Poisson regression, 609–614
  polynomial, 223, 296–308
  with qualitative predictor variables, 455–489
  residual analysis, 97–111
  scope of, 8–9
  selection of predictor variables
    all-possible regression, 336–347
    backward estimation, 353
    forward selection, 352
    forward stepwise regression, 347–352
  simple linear
    ANOVA table, 73–74
    diagnostics for predictor variables,
      95–96
    error term distribution unspecified,
      10–14
    general test approach, 78–90
    interval estimation, 56–61
    joint estimation procedures, 152–159,
      152–159
    in matrix terms, 198–199
    normal error terms, 29–35
    through origin, 159–163
    prediction of new observation, 61–67
    regression coefficients, 12–13
    residual analysis, 97–111
    tests for coefficients, 51–52
  smoothing methods, 135–138
  third order, 298
  transformed variables, 223
  validation of, 334, 434–439, 590
Regression relation, functional form, 8
Regression sum of squares, 71
Regression surface, 218
  confidence region, 234
Regression through origin, 159–163
Reinforcement interaction effect, 311
Remainder sum of squares, 1382
Repeated measures design, 1074, 1164–1166
  estimation of effects, 1172–1175,
    1180–1181, 1189–1190
  F test, 1167–1171, 1175–1176, 1178–1180,
    1186–1188
  latin square crossover design, 1225–1227
  ranked data, 1175–1176
  regression approach, 1194
  repeated measures on both factors,
    1176–1186
  repeated measures on one factor,
    1184–1194
  residual analysis, 1171–1172, 1180, 1189
  single-factor, 1166–1176
  split-plot design, 1194–1196
Replicates, 116
Replication, 116, 405, 1047
Residual analysis
  analysis of variance, 756–763, 825–827, 938
  latin square design, 1215
  for logistic regression, 595–597
  nested design, 1133–1134
  randomized block design, 1081–1083
  regression models, 97–111
  repeated measures design, 1171–1172, 1180,
    1189
  three-factor analysis of variance, 942
Residual dot plots, 762

Residual plots, 99–110, 238
  partial regression, 361–368
Residual plots against fitted values, 758–759,
  762
Residuals, 203–205, 227–228, 680, 818, 933
  analysis of variance, 757–758
  deleted, 372–373
  departures from simple linear regression, 98
  and omitted predictor variables, 108–110
  outliers, 103–104
  overview of tests, 110–111
  properties, 97
  in regression models, 25–27
  scaled, 420
  semistudentized, 98, 369
  studentized, 372
  studentized deleted, 373–375
  variance-covariance matrix of, 204–205
Residual sequence plot, 761
Residual sum of squares, 28
Response function, 744; *see also* Regression
  function
  analysis, 865–869
Response surface, 218
Response surface design, 1280–1281
  blocking central composite design,
    1288–1289
  central composite design, 1281–1289
  design criteria, 1292–1295
  model interpretation and visualization,
    1297–1299
  optimal, 1289–1297
  optimal conditions, 1299–1301
  rotatable central composite design,
    1284–1286
Response variable, 4–5
  measurement errors, 164
  transformations, 772–776
Restricted mixed factor effects model, 978
Ridge regression, 411–416
Ridge trace, 412–413, 416
Robust regression, 416–424
Robust test, 776
Rotatable central composite design, 1284–286
Rotatable inscribed central composite design,
  1286
Roundoff errors, 277
Row sum of squares, 1213
Running medians method, 135
Rutgers Experimental Station, 1290–1295

Saddle point, 1299
Sample size planning for analysis of variance
  estimation approach, 1060–1063
  to find "best" treatment, 1063–1064
  latin square design, 1218–1219
  power approach, 1052–1060
  random block design, 1088–1091
  tables, 1361–1363
Sampling distribution
  of β_1, 49–50
  of β_0, 53–54
  of F^*, 76–77
  of $\hat{Y}_h$, 57–59
SAS PROC GLM, 915
SAS PROC MIXED, 999

SAS PROC OPTEX, 1296
Satterthwaite approximate *F* test, 992–993
Satterthwaite procedure, 971–973
Saturated model, 586
Scalar, 182
Scalar matrix, 186, 187
Scaled residuals, 420
Scaling, 278
Scatter diagram/plot, 5, 21–22, 99–100
Scatter plot matrix, 236–238
Scheffé, Henry, 776
Scheffé joint estimation procedure
    analysis of covariance, 1024–1025, 1029
    latin square design, 1215
    nested design, 1135, 1136
    prediction of new observation, 158–159, 235
    randomized block design, 1084
    repeated measures design, 1180
    single-factor analysis of variance, 1062
    three-factor analysis of variance, 939, 940, 941
    two-factor analysis of variance, 854–855, 860–861
Scheffé multiple comparison procedure, 776
    single-factor analysis of variance, 732–736
Screening designs, 1264–1266
Second-order coefficient, 649
Second-order interaction, 927
Second order regression model, 296–297, 299–300, 866, 885
Selection bias, 1046
Semistudentized residuals, 98, 369, 757–758
Sen, P. K., 780
SENIC data set, 1365–1366
Sequence plot, 96
    of the residuals, 104–105
Sequential experimental runs, 1303–1305
Servo-Data, Inc., 773
Shapiro-Wilk test, 111
Sheffield Foods Company, 994–1001
Sigmoidal response functions, 570
Simple linear regression model, 10–14; *see also* Regression models
Simple logistic response function, 570–573
Simulated envelope, 597–598
Simultaneous estimation, 726–727
Simultaneous testing, 727
Single-blind study, 1046
Single comparison procedure, 1084
Single degree of freedom test, 723, 902
Single-factor study, 667
    analysis of covariance, 1014–1027
    ANOVA partitioning, 681–685
    estimation of effects, 716–742, 742–747, 1024–1026
    expected mean squares, 685–689
    factor effects model, 693–696
    fitting of model, 676–680
    F tests, 690–692, 696, 723, 777–781, 1022–1024, 1053–1057
    least squares estimation, 678–680
    maximum likelihood estimation, 678–680
    model I, 671–676, 693–696
    model II, 958–962, 975–976

Single-factor study—*Cont.*
    planning of sample sizes, 1053–1055, 1053–1055, 1057–1060, 1061–1062, 1064
    regression approach, 690–701
    repeated measures design, 1166–1176
    residual analysis, 756–763
    subsampling, 1141–1148
Singular matrix, 190
Smoothing methods, 135–138
SMSA data set, 1367–1369
Sparsity of effects principle, 1249
Spearman rank correlation coefficient, 651–654
Spector, P., 354
Split-plot designs, 1194–1196
SPSS ANOVA, 915
SPSS^x, 743
Square matrix, 178
SSE; see Error sum of squares
SSTO; see Total sum of squares
SSTR; see Treatment sum of squares
Standard deviation, studentized statistic, 49
Standardized multiple regression model, 279
Standardized random variable, 1317
Standardized regression coefficients, 281–284
Standard latin squares, 1210
Standard normal distribution, table of cumulative probabilities, 1335
Standard normal random variable, 1319–1320
Standard order, 1236
Star points, 1282
Statement confidence coefficient, 152
Statistical computing packages, 915
Statistical estimation, 1321–1322
Statistical relation, 3, 4–6
Statistics, and experiments, 1046–1049
Steichen Bakeries, 1266–1269
Stem-and-leaf models, 96
Stem-and-leaf plots, 103, 106, 762
Stepwise regression selection procedure, 348–352, 585–586
Stratification, 1049
Structural empty cell, 905
Studentized deleted residuals, 373–375, 757–758
Studentized range, 726
Studentized range distribution, tables of percentiles, 1352–1354
Studentized residuals, 372, 757–758
Studentized statistic, 49, 64
Subjects, 1164
    blocking, 1193–1194
Subsampling
    randomized block design, 1384–1386
    single-factor study, 1141–1148
    in three stages, 1148–1149
Sufficient estimator, 1322
Summation operator, 1313
Sum of squares, 27–28, 228–229
    in matrix notation, 205–206
    nested design, 1127–1128
    partitioning, 70–72
    quadratic forms, 206–207
    rule for finding, 1374–1376
Sum of squares for blocks, 1078–1079

Sum of squares for subjects, 1167
Supplemental variables, 329, 331, 1012
Suppressor variable, 292
SYGRAPH, 96, 98–99
Symmetric matrix, 186
Synergistic interaction type, 311
SYSTAT, 915

Tamhane, A. C., 742
Taylor series expansion, 539–540
t distribution, 1320
    Bonferroni procedure, 158–159
    table of percentiles, 1336–1337
Testing, 717
Tests
    for constancy of error variance, 112–115, 763–768
    for constancy of variance, 110
    factor level means, 696
    family of, 152–153
    for lack of fit, 115–124
    for normality, 111
    for outliers, 110–111
    for randomness, 110
Third-order regression model, 298
Three-dimensional plots, 1297–1299
Three-dimensional scatter plots, 238
Three-factor interactions, 927, 944
Three-factor study
    ANOVA partitioning, 934–935
    estimation of effects, 938–942, 994
    evaluation of appropriateness, 938
    example, 942–948
    expected mean squares, 935, 936
    fitting of model, 933–934
    F tests, 935–937, 991–993
    model I, 924–932
    model II, 990
    model III, 991
    nested design, 1149–1155
    regression approach, 948–950
    residual analysis, 938, 942
    unequal sample sizes, 948–951, 994–1001
Tidwell, P. W., 241
Time series data, 479
Total mean squared error, 341–342
Total sum of squares, 70–72, 681–684
    partitioning, 820–823, 934–935
Total uncorrected sum of squares, 73
Total variance, 961
Training sample, 437
Transformable interactions, 809–811
Transformations of variables, 126–134, 223, 240, 508–509, 642–643, 651, 772–776
Transpose of matrix, 178–179
Treatment, 15, 668–669
Treatment effects
    analysis of covariance, 1015–1016, 1022–1024, 1033–1034
Treatment means, 743–744, 799–800, 856, 947–948
    of equal importance, 1124
    estimation, 880–882
    multiple comparisons, 859–865
    of unequal importance, 905–915
Treatment means plot, 802–803

Treatment mean square, 685
Treatment pattern sum of squares, 1226
Treatment sum of squares, 682, 821–822
Trial, 5
t test, 294
  equivalence of *F* test, 78
  power of, 55–56
  power value charts, 1346–1347
Tukey joint estimation procedure
  latin square design, 1215
  nested design, 1135, 1136
  randomized block design, 1084
  repeated measures design, 1180, 1193
  three-factor analysis of variance, 939, 940, 941
  two-factor analysis of variance, 853–854, 859–860
Tukey-Kramer procedure, 731
Tukey multiple comparison procedure, single-factor analysis of variance, 725–732
Tukey one degree of freedom test, 884
Tukey test for additivity
  latin square design, 1216–1217
  randomized block design, 1083–1084
  two-factor analysis of variance, 882–885
Tuning constants, 419
Two-factor interactions, 806, 926, 944–946
Two-factor study
  analysis of covariance, 1028–1029
  ANOVA partitioning, 820–824
  crossed, 1382–1384
  empty cells, 902–905
  estimation of effects, 851–869, 897–902, 905–915, 984–989
  example, 795–797
  expected mean squares, 824–825, 981–982
  fitting of model, 818–820
  F tests, 827–832, 981–983
  general linear test approach, 891, 907–910
  mean squares, 824
  model I, 812–817
  model II, 976–977
  model III, 978–980
  nested design, 1124–1126
  no-interaction model, 875–882
  partitioning, 820–824
  pooling sums of squares, 837
  regression approach, 832–836, 891–897
  repeated measures design, 1176–1194
  residual analysis, 825–827
  strategy for analysis, 849–850

Two-factor study—*Cont.*
  Tukey test for additivity, 882–885
  unequal sample sizes, 889–902
Two-level factorial design, 1235–1237
  center point replications, 1247–1249, 1269
  estimation of effects, 1237–1240
  F test, 1240
  incomplete block designs, 1266–1269
  normal probability plot, 1247–1247
  Pareto plot, 1244–1245
  pooling of interactions, 1242–1244
  unreplicated, 1241–1249
Two-level fractional factorial design, 1249–1250
  confounding, 1250–1252
  defining relation, 1252–1254
  half-fraction, 1254
  projection property, 1258
  quarter-fraction, 1255–1257
  resolution, 1257–1258
  setting a fraction of highest resolution, 1258–1264
  smaller-fraction design, 1255–1257
Two-sided test, 51–52, 56
Two-variable conditioning plots, 427

Unbalanced nested design, 1138–1141
Unbiased estimator, 1321
Uncontrolled variables, 1012; *see also* Supplemental variables
Unequal error variances, transformations, 129–132
Unequal sample sizes in analysis of variance, 889–902
  estimation of effects, 897–902, 905–915, 950–951
  testing of effects, 891–897, 948–950
  three-factor studies, 994–1001
Unequal treatment importance, 905–915
Uniform precision central composite design, 1286, 1288
Unimportant interactions, 808–809
Unmeasurable mean, 1251
Unrestricted mixed factor effects model, 978, 979
Unweighted mean, 694

Validation of regression model, 334, 434–439
Validation set, 437

Variables
  relations between, 3–6
  transformations, 126–134
Variance, 57–59
  of error terms, 10, 27–29, 30–31, 47–48
  of prediction error, 63–64
  of random variable, 1315–1316
  of residuals, 97
  tests for constancy of error variance, 110, 112–115, 239, 763–768
Variance analysis; *see* Analysis of variance
Variance components, 984–985
Variance-covariance matrix
  of random vector, 195–197
  of regression coefficients, 231–233
  of residuals, 204–205
Variance function, 1284–1285
Variance inflation factor, 385–388, 412–415
Variance operator, 1315
V criterion, 1293–1295
Vector, 178
  with all elements unity, 187–188
  random, 194–197
  zero, 188

Watson, G. S., 505
Watts, D. G., 550
Weighted least squares estimation, 125, 400–409
  ANOVA models, 768–772
Weighted mean, 694–695
Weight function, 419–420
Whole plots, 1195
Within-subjects sum of squares, 1168
Working-Hotelling joint estimation of mean responses
  confidence band, 67–68
  simple linear regression, 156–157
Working-Hotelling joint estimation of multiple responses, multiple regression, 234

χ^2 distribution, 1320
  table of percentiles, 1338
X levels, 169–170
X values, random, 85–86
z' transformation, 652
Zero vector, 188
Zigmond, M. J., 1372

Description of Data Files

This IBM compatible diskette contains 216 data set files in ASCII format for the two text books:

Applied Linear Regression Models, 3/E by Neter, Kutner, Nachtsheim, and Wasserman, Richard D. Irwin, Burr Ridge, Illinois, 1996.

and

Applied Linear Statistical Models, 4/E by Neter, Kutner, Nachtsheim, and Wasserman, Richard D. Irwin, Burr Ridge, Illinois, 1996.

This diskette includes the data set files for all text examples, the data sets for the problems, exercises, and projects at the end of chapters, and the data sets in the Appendices C and D. The data in a data set are arranged in columns that are separated by spaces. The ordering of the columns (variables) can be readily ascertained from the tabular display of the data set in the text since the text always provides the data for at least the initial and final cases.

Data sets have names in one of the following formats, depending on whether the data pertain to a problem, a table, a figure, or an appendix (xx or x denotes the number):

CHxxPRxx   For data sets from end-of-chapter problems, exercises, and projects.
            Example: CH04PR12 denotes the data set for Problem 4.12 in Chapter 4.

CHxxTAxx   For data sets from text tables.
            Example: CH17TA02 denotes the data set for Table 17.2 in Chapter 17.

CHxxFIxx   For data sets from text figures.
            Example: CH32FI11 denotes the data set for Figure 32.11 in Chapter 32.

APCx   For data sets from Appendix C.
            Example: APC1 denotes the data set in Appendix C.1

APDPRxx   For data sets from problems in Appendix D.
            Example: APDPR10 denotes the data set for Problem D.10 in Appendix D.

All file names are followed by the extension .DAT to identify that the file contains data.